THE WORLD IN LITERATURE

VOLUME ONE: *Backgrounds of the Modern World*

THE WORLD

IN LITERATURE

REVISED EDITION

GEORGE K. ANDERSON   *Brown University*

ROBERT WARNOCK   *Yale University*

Bibliography prepared by WERNER W. BEYER *Butler University*

SCOTT, FORESMAN AND COMPANY

The authors wish to express their deep appreciation to the following friends for
their valuable suggestions in the preparation of the first edition:
for China, Professor Shau Wing Chan;
for India, Dr. Horace Poleman;
for the Hebrews, Rabbi Maurice Zigmond;
for Greece, Professor James Notopoulos;
and for Rome, Dr. Annarie Cazel.
The authors wish also to acknowledge the courtesy of the publishers
who have granted permission to reprint selections in copyright.
Specific acknowledgment of these publishers is given on the pages
where the selections appear.

CONTENTS

The selections listed in the table are complete except where superior letters appear: ^A indicates very long works of necessity abridged (with a preservation of the scope and continuity of the whole); ^S indicates representative selection. A few negligible deletions are indicated in the text.

BOOK ONE

The Ancient Foundations

CHAPTER THREE

The West under Roman Sway

300 B.C. *to* 300 A.D

CHAPTER FIVE

Rebirth
and
Discovery

1350 *to* 1650

(The Table of Contents carries the translators' names for those longer works
where the translation used is of particular significance. Footnotes within the text
furnish a complete list of translators.)

$$\approx\!\!\!\!\approx\!\!\!\!\approx$$ *List of Illustrations*

THE ANCIENT FOUNDATIONS

ON *the general approach of this book*

and its beginning with

THE

ANCIENT EAST

LITERATURE is in part an abiding source of beauty and entertainment for all civilized men, and in part a record of the ideas and customs, the special visions and feelings, of the people who have created it. We realize this especially when we turn from writers of our own time to the great books of the past, produced in cultures very different from our own. In reading them, we soon discover that we must learn about the nations and times that gave us those books if we are to respond to their appeal and grasp their full significance. Great art is timeless in the sense that it speaks to men of all times, but it is of its own time too and speaks to us fully only if we know something of the age that shaped it. It tells us about our past as it tells us about ourselves, and through a poem or an essay we live vicariously the life of another era as well as the life of another man. Art is not produced in a vacuum, but in the minds and souls of men in close touch with the ideas and habits of their day. In so far as they felt love and anger, religious sentiment and patriotic fervor, they were human beings like ourselves, speaking a universal tongue. But conflict springs from changing issues; divinity may be envisioned and worshiped in numerous ways; and love has taken many forms in different lands and eras. Only through knowing the background of a great book can we translate the emotions and ideas embodied in it into terms close to our own. Only then can it give us the full measure of that enjoyment for which the author wrote it in the first place.

So knowing and understanding the great books of all time will lead us in several directions at once— to pleasure in the experiences of minds more creative than our own, to an awareness of the objectives and forms of literary art that we can apply to other books to come, to a knowledge of the evolution of human culture as great writers have unconsciously chronicled it, to a contact with ideas of long standing that will be new to us and will help us to gain a better comprehension of ourselves and the world in which we live. Such contact will free us from provincialism in the realm of ideas and give us a sympathy and respect for points of view that are no less worthy for seeming at first foreign and strange. It will also help us to discover unexpected likenesses in ages far apart and give us a warm sense of the kinship of the whole human race.

Our point of view in THE WORLD IN LITERATURE is international. It breaks through the barriers of language by means of translation—an imperfect medium, it is true, but the only avenue for the average reader to literature in many tongues. Our point of view is eclectic. It seeks an unprejudiced acquaintance with the contributions of many lands and epochs to the complete picture of human culture. It might concentrate entirely on the *periods* of world literature— the total of social, intellectual, and aesthetic traits that give each age its special character. Or it might emphasize the literary *movements* in world history —the "isms" that have allied groups of writers with each other and sometimes set them apart in warring camps. It might see literature in terms of the *nations* that have produced it and the special qualities of each national culture. Or it might present the great books in terms of the great *men* whose minds created them—a parade of titans from Homer to the present day. Each of these four approaches forms part of our eclectic point of view.

More importantly, we set out with two complementary convictions in mind: Through the ages each great nation and each era has had its special role to play and has stamped its special contributions with its own idiosyncrasies. But no one nation and no one age is chiefly responsible for human culture as we know it today.

Since we begin with the most distant past and the nations most remote from us, the problem of understanding may seem very complex at the start. Yet our century has gone far to reduce the distance between the East and West. The airplane links us in a matter of hours. Modern wars have brought conflicts and alliances between the nations of Asia and the Occident; political differences between East and West fade as monarchy, democracy, and communism exist side by side in both areas. But the intellectual gulf is still wide, and the manners and customs of the East often seem bizarre to us. Oriental literature has exotic qualities that will startle the new reader but should challenge him to search out its wisdom and charm.

Civilization in the East was already old when the first Europeans rose out of barbarism. Sumeria around 4500 B.C., Egypt five hundred years later,

Babylonia and Assyria about 2100 B.C.—all reached cultural maturity centuries before the Greeks appeared as the first great civilized nation in the West. Their contributions were to converge on the rising Greeks and to become the solid foundation from which Western culture evolved. But all of those ancient nations had lost their power by the time of Christ and, except for the Egyptians, had been assimilated in later peoples.

Three other great nations of the ancient East—the Chinese, the Hindus, and the Hebrews—escaped that fate and have survived to our day with national and religious ideals substantially unchanged for twenty-five centuries. All three are now engaged in a desperate struggle for survival and adjustment to a modern age. They are the patriarchs among us, as they are also the newest children in the political family of nations.

The experiences of the Chinese and the Hindus have marked similarities, but the tragic experience of the Hebrews is unique. China and India have each known an almost changeless civilization during two thousand years, securely based on a national religion and an ethical code that reflect a people's soul at peace with itself. Even the challenge of foreign religions—Buddhism in China and Mohammedanism in India—has not upset the basic pattern. Both nations have lived self-contained lives with little curiosity about the lands beyond their borders, except in commerce, but both have been exploited for the past four hundred years by more aggressive peoples from the West. Both hold immense lands which are nevertheless too small to support their vast populations. As a result both face bewildering problems of adjustment in the twentieth century.

Yet there are differences too. The Hindu is an extreme mystic, the Chinese an intensely practical thinker. The Hindu's caste system has long supported the aristocratic principle in Indian society, whereas the democratic tradition has always been strong in China, even through centuries of monarchy. Of all peoples the Hindus are most lacking in a sense of time, so that even the major events in Indian history are sometimes difficult to date. The Chinese, on the other hand, have a meticulous interest in chronology and consider history the most honorable form of literature. The greatest Indian poetry is narrative, especially epic; the Chinese poets have best expressed themselves in lyrics.

Hebrew history, too, is oriented by a national religion. It has been the one sure rock in the tempestuous chronicle of the Jews' struggle for survival. Through centuries of wandering and persecution, the Jews have clung to their faith for its golden promise of a better day. As their faith has served a different purpose in their national life, so it is different from the religions of China and India.

Whereas Confucianism and Hinduism at their loftiest development are as much philosophy as religion in their metaphysics, ethical systems, and social and political theories, Judaism is more narrowly a religion, dedicated to the worship of one God and to ordering the lives of His people with laws and prescriptions. While Confucianism and Hinduism remain essentially Eastern philosophies, the close spiritual ties between Judaism and Christianity place the Hebrews within the Western tradition. Indeed, the Hebraic tradition underlies the religion of the West, specifically in its holy books, more profoundly in its ethical outlook. The whole Biblical history of the Hebrews was grafted onto the Christian canon, to give background to the new religion and to amplify the personality of God, in his diverse moods of wrath and of love. From the Hebrews came monotheism as we know it in the West. Unlike the Chinese and the Hindus, the Jews have lived in close, indeed enforced, contact with other peoples and have been influenced by alien cultures to such an extent that today they are divided from each other by the barriers of language and custom in the many lands where they have settled. Their literature cuts into

A jade carving of Shou Lao, Chinese God of Longevity, symbolic of the antiquity of the civilization of the East. Ming dynasty sculpture.

the literary history of these many lands, and, except where it is anchored in the national religion, it is diverse and cosmopolitan.

Yet all three of these nations are dynamic forces in the world of our day; all three seem on the verge of a new life and a new influence in the world of the future. This chapter will try to show the ideals that have preserved their culture through so many centuries of the past and the literary art with which their great masters expressed those ideals.

CHINA

FOR more than two centuries we in the West have been gradually discovering the great culture and literature of China. Translation has come slowly, and her religious teachers and philosophers have reached us well before her poets. Only in our own century have the beauty and charm of her literature been revealed in English. To those who meet them for the first time, Li Po and Tu Fu in their poetry open a new world of enjoyment—a delicate, fragile world of bamboo and jade, yet inhabited by intensely human fellows and rollicking companions. As Confucius points to a sensible way of life, the two poets show us how to enjoy it with gusto. No others could represent the Chinese to us so well as these three master spirits.

The placid, cultured Chinese have inhabited for more than five thousand years a large area in eastern Asia roughly half the size of the United States. A kind of civilization flourished there at least fifteen hundred years before the Christian era, and reliable Chinese history extends back to 2200 B.C., many centuries before Europe emerged from barbarism. The great antiquity of Chinese culture, then, places it close to the very ancient civilizations of the Egyptians and Sumerians.

From early times the huge population of China, now nearly four times our own, has been divided into two rather distinct groups by the great Yangtze River, which flows from the rugged mountains of Tibet in the west through a fertile central plain into the East China Sea. The people to the north of the Yangtze, molded by a temperate climate, are tall, healthy children of the soil, robust in physique and mental outlook. From these hardy folk have come all the native dynasties of Chinese emperors. The people of the south, on the contrary, are physically small and soft, disposed by their warm, relaxing climate to enjoy easy comforts and artistic luxuries. Peaceful and even timid by nature, they have submitted for centuries to the rule of their northern brothers, but have excelled in their turn as shrewd merchants and traders. However, both north and south have contributed their share to the national philosophy, literature, and art, so that we are more impressed today by the homogeneity of Chinese culture in a population so vast than by the sectional differences in language and temperament.

Even more striking than this national uniformity is the remarkable stability of Chinese culture for the past two thousand years. Not only has there been no break in cultural tradition comparable to our Dark Ages, but actually no important change—no permanent revolutions in government from democracy to despotism, no great shift in social organization, no change in general philosophy from religious mysticism to scientific materialism, no wars between opposed schools of art. Struggle and change, for good or ill, are at the core of our Western tradition, but the complacent, conservative Chinese, satisfied with his pattern of life, has gone his accustomed way since the time of Confucius in the fifth century B.C. down to the Communist revolution of our day.

Of course, there have been periodic civil wars and invasions. In the third century B.C. the notorious Ch'in dynasty tried to submerge the Chinese democratic tradition in a unified state under despotic control, but after the Ch'in emperor had built the Great Wall to keep out Mongolian enemies from the north and burned the books of China to destroy intellectual enemies from within, he was paid for his ruthless efficiency by the destruction of his dynasty shortly after his death. The placid sanity of old China reasserted itself and digested this upstart as it has absorbed many a would-be conqueror in its long history. Only in our own century has the invasion of foreign ideas and political systems brought great changes in Chinese life, at first a pale imitation of Western democracy, now an Oriental version of communism. But in the long run it seems likely that the Chinese will assimilate these ideas also without losing their essential point of view.

The Chinese measure their long history by imperial dynasties, of which there were twenty-two between 2205 B.C., the dawn of authentic history, and 1911 A.D., the year in which China became a republic. For the outsider seeking to understand Chinese character and literature, two of these dynasties have a special interest. The Chou dynasty (1122–249 B.C.), the period of feudalism, saw the first flowering of Chinese culture, which reached its peak in the sixth and fifth centuries B.C., when China's two great philosophers, Lao-Tzŭ and Confucius, were establishing her rival religions. To the T'ang dynasty (618–906 A.D.), on the other hand,

"Lao-Tzǔ Delivering the Tao Teh Ching," a rare example of the work of the Sung dynasty painter, Li Lung-Mien (1070–1106). The silk scroll on which it is painted also contains the whole Tao Teh Ching, copied by a famous calligrapher of the Sung period. Courtesy of Mrs. Agnes E. Meyer.

belong China's greatest poets, Tu Fu and Li Po, and they are only the best-known names in this Golden Age. These two dynasties and these two groups of writers provide our key to the Chinese mind.

CHINESE PHILOSOPHY AND CHARAC- TER. The antagonism of China's two great religions, Taoism and Confucianism, is supposed to date from a meeting of their rival founders, Lao-Tzǔ and Confucius, toward the end of the sixth century B.C. According to tradition, Lao-Tzǔ rebuked Confucius for devoting himself to the mere forms and ceremonies of social life instead of concentrating on the higher meaning of the universe. False though the story may be, it suggests the essential difference between the two great schools of thought in China. Taoism represents Chinese mysticism, the search for a unifying principle in the universe beyond the diverse activities of practical life. Confucianism concentrates on everyday reality and instead of speculating about the infinite and eternal, sets as its goal a moral, well-regulated society on earth.

The holy Book of Tao (Tao Teh Ching), which was long ascribed to Lao-Tzǔ himself, teaches that man is part of a unified and harmonious universe governed by one eternal principle (or Tao). Caught up in the infinite flow of this great unity, man should not strive for position and power in the world of affairs. His happiness lies in the simple life, close to fundamental things. His behavior should be guided by the policy of *inaction*. "Do nothing, and all things will be done," said Lao-Tzǔ; and his great disciple,

Chuang-Tzǔ, added: "Pay no attention to time, nor to right and wrong. Move into the absolute Tao, and find your peace there." He was indifferent to right and wrong because in the great Tao there is no difference between them. There are not two poles, positive and negative, but only one pole, the Tao—the origin and end of everything. Like a true mystic, Lao-Tzǔ scorned the idea of defining his unifying principle. "Those who know do not tell," he said, "and those who tell do not know." Since it is the one reality, it cannot by its very nature be defined in practical terms. The meaning of the great Tao has to be accepted on faith and understood only as it is felt.

Although the typical Chinese is far from a mystic at heart, he has shown in his daily life and general outlook the strong influence of Taoism. He has believed in the passive way of life and been amazed by the restless activity of the Westerner. He is still a farmer by occupation, leading a simple life close to the soil. Until very recently he has been skeptical of the machine age and its promise of a superior standard of living. He was content with what he had and more interested in being happy than in getting ahead. Whether or not he was at one with the great Tao, the Chinese has been at peace with himself, and when oppressed by tyranny and injustice, he submitted with patience. The modern leaders of China have found this ancient lethargy one of their most baffling problems in arousing the people to national defense, material development, and social change.

Confucius, too, taught a passive philosophy in his negative version of the Golden Rule: "Do not do unto others what you would not have them do unto you." But unlike Lao-Tzŭ, he prescribed it as a code for living in society, not apart from it. Confucius had only contempt for a philosophy that turned its back on everyday reality and devoted itself to contemplating the infinite. Although he did not disbelieve in the world of spirits, he considered it beyond man's knowledge and concentrated on establishing a moral order in human society.

The Taoists believed in the immortality of man's spirit within the great Tao. Confucius taught a more tangible immortality on earth. One lives, he argued, so long as one's memory lives in the minds of men. And since the average man cannot be widely remembered as is a great emperor or philosopher or poet, it is the responsibility of his family to keep his spirit alive. For Confucius, the family was the foundation of society, and it consisted not only of its living members but also of their ancestors. This belief perpetuated the ancient ancestor worship of the Chinese, so that the Confucian temple represents neither God nor angels nor saints on its walls, but rather the names of long-departed ancestors who still care for their clans but who need in turn the endless homage of each descendant. For them he performs elaborate rituals prescribed by Confucius. The death of a relative demanded an established period of mourning —three years for a parent, one for a paternal uncle, nine months for a cousin. Many a young Chinese poet had his career interrupted by the untimely death of a father or mother.

This ritual of Confucius was as much social as religious, and Confucianism itself is more a code of social ethics than a religion. As a historian, Confucius had developed a deep respect for China's ancient feudal system. As an intensely rational thinker, he wished to reëstablish such an orderly social system, which should be held together and constantly linked to the past by an elaborate ritual of courtesy and good manners, of piety and devotion to ancestors. To this code of ritual and rational morality he gave the name *Li*. He argued that if the rulers and officials of China would live and govern by this strict ethical code, their example would inspire the common people and produce a genuinely healthy, moral society.

In his charming *Analects*, a collection of the Master's sayings reverently remembered by his disciples, Confucius defined this social code in detail, explaining the behavior of the true gentleman, whose life is governed by reason and morality. The Confucian gentleman is bound down by duty and convention; he seems old before his time, and, unlike the ambitious American, he aspires to be inconspicuous and a dutiful member of his family. Aristotle in Greece,

Horace in Rome, and the thinkers of eighteenth-century France and England who preached the Golden Mean as their way of life, would have understood the rational ethic of Confucius. And many a thoughtful American, critical of his own system, will admire the quiet good sense and clear-eyed realism of the Confucian, and envy him the peace of mind that his rigid social code can bring.

Mencius, the brilliant disciple of Confucius, extended his master's teachings to a democratic scheme of government, founded upon the belief of Confucius that all men are born equal. Although the Chinese state was a semifeudal empire from its known beginnings until 1911 A.D., the sovereign, or Son of Heaven, was supposed to reign on his Dragon Throne only so long as his rule brought peace and prosperity to the people. Parliaments were unthinkable, because they would suggest a conflict between the sovereign and the people, as if he were not devoted to their good. But if he should prove untrue to his mission, it was the duty of the people to rebel in order to reëstablish the rational order. Chinese history is punctuated by such periodic rebellions, not against the system, but against effete regimes. It becomes easy to see how the Chinese could readily throw over their decadent empire in our century and accept a democratic system without dislocating their national life. We have still to see whether the same may not be true of the Communist order.

The teachings of Confucius were long the basis of Chinese character. The family rather than the state was the center of national life, and the Chinese gained his gentleness and quiet conservatism from submitting to the veneration of his ancestors. His sense of social order and courtesy sprang from the formal ritual of Confucianism. Essentially unreligious by nature, he was always more interested in the relationship of men to each other than to God. Like the ancient Greek, he is rather indifferent to a life in heaven and concentrates on enjoying a well-ordered life on this earth. Only when his experiences are unfortunate or he fears misfortune does he take refuge in Taoist mysticism. In the words of Lin Yutang, "all Chinese are Confucianists when successful, and Taoists when they are failures."

POETRY IN CHINESE LIFE. Although the Chinese are not fundamentally religious, they are certainly poets to the core. And in a sense, their poetry, by expressing their wonderment at the beauty and immensity of the natural world, has fulfilled their need of religion. The quantity of Chinese poetry is staggering, for it had been seriously composed for centuries even before Confucius compiled *The Book of Songs* in the fifth century B.C. Other types of imaginative literature were long frowned on by the Chinese and hence developed comparatively late— the drama in the eleventh century A.D. and the novel in the fourteenth century. The drama was considered the vulgar amusement of the common people and the novel the secret entertainment of one's private hours, but poetry was the pastime of all men of culture. Gentlemen customarily met together to drink wine and compete in writing verses. And every government official had to be a professional poet to gain his office.

To maintain his rational social order, Confucius had taught the duty of public service for all gentlemen. Eventually the bureaucratic system which evolved was implemented by a system of examinations, the earliest known civil service tests, by which a candidate could qualify for four official grades, poetically named Flowering Talent, Promoted Man, Entered Scholar, and member of the Forest of Pens (the Imperial Academy). These examinations were entirely literary and required a knowledge of the ancient classics and the technique of writing poetry. So the very government of China was founded on respect for poetic skill.

After the poet had passed his examinations, he was forbidden to take office in his own province, because of the danger of political corruption, and he was usually sent to a remote post for a long term of public service. Since poets all aspired to the gay, stimulating life of the court, they looked upon this enforced exile as a great hardship and wrote melancholy poems of dejection and farewell to their friends as they obeyed the call of duty.

Hence the typical poet's career had three stages, each with its cluster of poetic themes. First, he is the carefree youth reveling in the life of the capital. He spends his time drinking wine, writing poetry, and enjoying the company of his male friends. Except in the very ancient period, love poetry from a man to a woman is almost never found. Women had generally a restricted and inferior status in Chinese society, and marriages were arranged by the elders of two families. Consequently, Chinese poets pose in their poems, not as romantic lovers, but as devoted friends whose greatest happiness lies in an intellectual camaraderie in which women play no part. Friendship, not love, is the great theme of this first stage, with the joys of wine as a convivial accompaniment.

The second stage finds the poet exiled at a provincial post, far from his friends at the capital. Economic need has forced him to accept his new office, and his poems now bemoan his isolation from the mental stimulation, good fellowship, and joys of the city. The themes of farewell and eventual loneliness dominate this stage. After years of provincial service the poet finally saves enough money to retire from office, but it is now useless to return to the capital, where new coteries dominate the intellectual life. Instead he settles down on a small estate with his family and perhaps a friend or two to share his quiet happiness. By now he is resigned to his fate, and his themes in this last stage are the delights of middle age and the memories of his happy youth.

CHARACTERISTICS OF CHINESE POETRY. Although narrative verse is not unknown in China, the great poetry is lyric; but the art of the Chinese lyric is considerably different from our own. The Western lyric, from the ancient Greeks and the medieval troubadours to modern times, has been identified with music and the intense emotion conveyed by music. Hence it has tended to express the poet's state of mind directly, and to describe natural objects around him indirectly through figures of speech. Chinese poetry, on the contrary, is more closely linked to the art of painting. Working with visual rather than with abstract material, the Chinese poet restrains the expression of his emotion and lets the concrete things that he describes reflect his state of mind. The Chinese looks directly at his object—a cloud, a bird, a rainstorm, a rich gown—and describes it matter-of-factly with little poetic metaphor. But, like a painter, he chooses the appropriate objects to fit his mood and subtly implies a parallel between the state of nature and the state of his mind.

Perhaps this pictorial expression springs from the nature of the Chinese language, which is still a picture language without an alphabet. The original pictograph characters have been modified into "ideographs," but to this day a Chinese poem makes as great an appeal to the eye as to the ear. Subtle differences in the appearance of the characters suggest shades of thought that bewilder the translator. But the reader need not explore these technical problems to appreciate the delicate imagery and evocative power of Chinese poetry in translation.

INDIA

To a Western reader Indian literature is the embodiment of a philosophy and a way of life complementary to our own, with an appeal that has captured the fancy of a host of Americans and Englishmen. Hindu mysticism first became known to the West around 1800, when translations of India's dramas and holy books profoundly influenced the German Romantic poets Herder and Goethe and the German philosophers Schelling and Schopenhauer. Emerson was fascinated by the message of

Vedanta in nineteenth-century America, and today a group of English writers—Christopher Isherwood, Aldous Huxley, John van Druten—have carried it to its widest public in the West. Ancient India may seem very remote from modern America, and yet many among us during this age of atomic science have sought peace of mind in its sweeping explanation of life.

Indian culture rivals Chinese in its antiquity. A primitive civilization flourished in the Indus Valley of northwestern India at least three thousand years before Christ. But modern Indian culture descends, not from the people of that civilization, but from warlike tribes which poured through the mountains to the northwest sometime between 2000 and 900 B.C., overran the Ganges Valley to the northeast, and finally conquered all of central and southern India except the extreme south. These invaders spoke the oldest known language in the so-called Aryan, or Indo-European, family, to which belong also most of the languages of Europe and America. The term Aryan has fallen into disrepute because Adolf Hitler and his followers, ignoring the mongrel composition of all modern peoples, notoriously misapplied the term to a nonexistent race, or family of races, which were mistakenly supposed to correspond to the kindred languages they spoke. This Indo-European language of India indicates, however, that the ancient invaders of the land had a common cultural origin with the other Aryan groups: Persian, Greek, Latin, Germanic, Slavic, and Celtic.

Actually India has never been a nation, but an amalgamation of many races held together by a common cultural tradition. The triangular peninsula in south-central Asia which they occupy has about the area of Europe (excluding Russia) and about half the area of the United States. On this subcontinent live about four hundred fifty million people (more than twice the population of the United States), to whom as many as fifty million more may

Symbolic of the influence of the Himalayas on Indian religious art is this Hindu structure, Kailasa Temple at Ellora. A monolith carved from solid rock, it was dedicated to the Himalayan paradise of the god Siva. According to the Mahâbhârata *the Vedas were taught here first. Construction of the temple was begun in the middle of the eighth century* A.D.

now be added each decade. This mass of people has long been administratively organized into numerous provinces and states, each with its own government. Unlike China, then, India has never been a political unit, and the antagonism of these separate states has made her an easy prey to conquerors, from Alexander the Great to the Britisher, Robert Clive. With the withdrawal of the British in 1948 after two centuries of rule, India became two distinct countries divided by hostile religious faiths—Hindu India with three quarters of the population and Moslem Pakistan with less than a quarter of the population spread over two separate states in east and west.

The original invaders of India developed their Indo-European tongue into a highly complex language called Sanskrit, which was spoken only by the learned Brahman class that was descended from the conquerors. Sanskrit was softened into a new tongue, Pali, during the Buddhist era (fifth century B.C.—fifth century A.D.) and eventually was split into many dialects, of which Hindustani and Bengali are today the most important. The Mohammedan population uses its own language, Urdu, which is largely Hindustani written in Persian script, and the Indians of the extreme south still speak their own non-Indo-European tongues, which remind us of their aboriginal ancestors. But Sanskrit remains the most important language for the foreign student of Indian culture, because it has continued as the special language of the Brahman caste, the priests and professional men. It came to have the same kind of status that Church Latin has in Catholic countries today. Most of the great literature of India is in a form of the Sanskrit language.

THE CASTE SYSTEM. When the invading tribes conquered the aborigines of India, they developed there a social system of caste which was to solidify as the characteristic pattern of Indian society to the present day. Instead of exterminating the conquered people, as many ancient invaders did, they devised a scheme of segregating them forever as a social class forbidden to intermarry or even fraternize with other classes of society. Originally this system recognized four castes, which were fancifully linked to four parts of the body of the creator god, Brahma: the priest (or Brahman) caste, associated with the head; the warrior caste, associated with the arms; the farmer-merchant caste, associated with the body; and the laborer-servant caste (for the aborigines), associated with the feet. Through the ages these four castes have been subdivided into hundreds of subcastes for weavers, barbers, blacksmiths, and other trades, but the Brahman caste has remained at the top. This social system of India, with its religious foundation, is called *Hinduism*.

The many castes correspond somewhat to the guilds of our Middle Ages, but the rigidity and exclusiveness of the Hindu system is unique in history. Each Hindu is born into his caste and can never change his predetermined trade and social status. A member of one caste may not marry into another, nor even eat with members of other castes. For each caste there is a prescribed *dharma*, or rule of conduct for each period and circumstance in life, originally codified in the so-called Code of Manu, dating from about the first century A.D. Following this code scrupulously constitutes the good or religious life. This the hero Arjuna learns in our selection from the *Bhagavad-Gita* when he asks the god Krishna whether it is right for a warrior to kill. At the bottom of the social scale for centuries were the Untouchables, whose very touch (or even shadow) brought pollution to a Brahman. These tragic people, who constitute one fifth of India's population, were doomed by an accident of birth to live apart from decent society and to perform the menial tasks of life as sweepers and scavengers. Until very recent times they were forbidden to own land or even to enter a temple. But the new government of India has finally outlawed the stigma of untouchability.

HINDU RELIGION. The caste system merely applies to society the religious principles of Hinduism, more properly called the philosophy of Vedanta. In placing the Brahman priest at the top of the scale, it recognized religion as the supreme reality, for Hinduism is man's whole way of life. India is of all countries the most religious. No other nation has ever approached her in subordinating every activity in life to the operation of the spirit. Confucianism places man and his society at the center of the universe. Hinduism mystically reduces man to a fragment of spirit at the mercy of nature and the great Spirit behind it.

The incentive to such a view of life came from nature itself. When the ancient Aryans arrived in India, they were confronted by the grandest and most terrifying forces of nature on earth. The world's highest mountains, the Himalayas, loomed to impassable heights in the north. The great plains below them were often devastated by the floods of long, unpredictable rivers; yet for over half the year the earth was parched by drought. In central India they found impenetrable jungles, from which wild beasts still slink forth at night to attack and kill the people. Frequent earthquakes would flatten their villages and destroy their crops in an instant, and pestilences might kill many thousands in a season. They found every extreme of climate from month-long snowfall in the north to moist tropical heat in the south. Nature in India has always been fierce and tyrannical. Hence the Aryans developed a religion of nature worship to personify these deadly, irrational forces and placate them through hymn and sacrifice. This primitive religion was polytheistic, with a god for each natural force, and closely resembled the religion of the Greeks.

The earliest Indian literature consists of four collections of hymns and prayers, called Vedas, which were composed between 2000 and 800 B.C. to honor these gods of nature. Later they were thought to be divine revelations, *seen* by the holy men rather than composed by them. The most important of the four, the *Rig-Veda* (meaning Verse-Knowledge), contains 1028 religious poems to Indra, the wielder of the thunderbolt; Agni, the god of fire; Yama, the king of the underworld; and many others. The tone of these ancient hymns is vigorous, positive, and optimistic, but this bright confidence in life was soon to disappear in the deepest pessimism that a nation ever developed. Perhaps because the Hindus despaired of ever finding a way to appease the malignant, destructive forces of nature, they came to turn their backs on human effort and material reality.

Like the later Greeks and the Romans, the Brahman Hindus grew dissatisfied with their naïve polytheism and sought a unifying force of divinity to supplant the earlier congress of gods. Gradually there emerged a single Over-Spirit, called Brahma, which was the source of gods, men, and all living things on earth. According to this view, which is still the foundation of Hindu faith, this one spirit eventually gave off the individual spirits of men, animals, insects, and plants, who were arranged in an order or rank from the Brahman caste down to the simplest plant. Men, as fragments of the Over-Spirit, are thus doomed to a sojourn in this material world, but they carry with them a longing for reabsorption in the Over-Spirit. This world through which they pass is nothing but *Maya*, or illusion, in comparison with the reality of the Over-Spirit. Man's life in this world of illusion is a kind of trial by which he is judged worthy or unworthy to move closer to final release. The worthy life is one lived in complete indifference to this material world, with complete lack of ambition and desire. The worthiest life of all is spent in ascetic meditation and inaction, free from worldly possessions and concerns.

Each individual spirit must go through a series of incarnations in *Maya*, in each of which his actions, or *karma*, will influence his next rebirth. If he performs his *dharma*, or appropriate duty, in one life, he will be reborn higher on the caste scale. If he does not and pursues selfish desire in this life, he may be born next time as a pig or a vegetable. The Brahman at the top of the caste scale is the holiest of living things, for if he performs his dharma he will be reabsorbed at death into the Over-Spirit. This final obliteration of the individual soul in the peace of the Over-Spirit is usually called by the Buddhist term, *Nirvana*. Only Nirvana can end the dismal round of reincarnations in this world of illusion.

So the Hindu ascetic lives his life in a studied contempt for life. His greatest objective is to subdue self and annihilate all human desire within himself. To be sure, this abstract philosophy of the Brahman had to be translated into concrete terms for the simpler-minded masses. The older polytheism has persevered, especially in the cults of Brahma, Vishnu, and Siva, who represent Creation, Preservation, and Destruction, the three stages in the career of an individual soul. But the Brahman sees in the stone and wooden idols of the masses only the endless representations of the Over-Spirit. Hence from the sixth century B.C. to the present there has been a cleavage in religious thought, or at least in interpretation, between the intellectual Brahman and the other castes. The religion of the masses still honors the many gods of the old Vedic hymns. The Brahman looks beyond them to the *Upanishads,* the later abstract interpretations of the Vedas.

BUDDHISM. According to Indian belief, the old religion is revitalized from time to time by a great religious teacher, or *buddha*, who might be compared with a Hebrew prophet in the Old Testament. The greatest of the *buddhas* was the Buddha Gautama (c.483–c.403 B.C.), who unintentionally founded a rival religion in attempting to rid popular Hinduism of its superstition and empty ritual. Born the son of a king, he renounced a life of luxury at twenty-nine and after six years of meditation received enlightenment under the Bo-tree at Gaya. After establishing a monastery to perpetuate his gospel, he spent the rest of his eighty years wandering in northern India and preaching to the populace. Years later he was deified by the Hindus as an incarnation of the god Vishnu.

Although Buddha left no writings of his own, his doctrine is preserved and broadly interpreted in volumes of Buddhist scripture composed long after his time. Apparently he accepted the tenets of Hinduism, that only through renouncing this world is man's spirit freed from the chain of painful reincarnation. But he emphasized the moral life for both gods and men and devised a system of rules for man's behavior that ignored the caste system. The Buddhist Five Commandments have a familiar sound: Kill no living thing. Do not take what is not given to you. Do not speak falsely. Drink no intoxicating drink. Do not be unchaste. For his monks, who had completely renounced the world, Buddha ordained five further commandments.

The cult of Buddha grew gradually after the deification of its founder and accumulated new ritual of the very kind that he had decried. Between 300

This statue of Buddha in Mathura, India, dates from c. 130–140 A.D. and shows the influence of Hellenistic art on India. The protuberance on the top of his head is one of the characteristic signs of Buddha.

B.C. and 500 A.D. it challenged orthodox Hinduism as the leading religion of India and eventually spread to Ceylon, China, Burma, Japan, and Siam. But in India it later declined and in the sixth century was permanently destroyed by a revival of Hinduism in its modern form. Today India's great religious teacher is honored chiefly outside his native land, from the island of Ceylon across eastern Asia to Japan.

SECULAR LITERATURE. The history of India and her literature is immeasurably confused by Hindu mysticism. In denying the reality of this world the Hindu disavowed any interest in its his-

tory and decided that time as we know it has no meaning in comparison with the timelessness of the Over-Spirit. Authentic records of Indian history are very few and the most important events can seldom be dated even by centuries. Our most reliable information about India appears in foreign records— Greek and Roman in antiquity, Mohammedan in the Middle Ages, Portuguese, French, and British in modern times. Since these records do not mention the two great ages of secular literature, we can date them only very inexactly.

During the later period of "Aryan" invasion (c. 1400–c.800 B.C.), a magnificent epic literature developed. As in many European lands, warriors were inspired by long tales of heroes who conquered great enemies against great odds. In India the ancient epics came to embody not only the national ideals and primitive culture but also the Hindu philosophy and laws of life. These poems are of great length and include many irrelevant episodes and moral precepts that have been added to them in centuries of retelling and re-editing. The greatest of them, the *Mahâbhârata,* tells in 100,000 couplets of a war of succession between two families of the Bhârata (or Kuru) kingdom, but upon this central story is hung a host of old legends and myths. The other well-known epic, the *Râmâyana,* relates in 24,-000 couplets how King Rama recovered his wife Sita from her evil abductor, the giant Râvana, again with numerous digressions into folklore and animal fables. Impossibly tedious in their entirety, these epics reveal much fine narrative poetry when read in the condensations worked out and translated by Romesh Dutt.

During the centuries of Buddhist supremacy secular literature languished, but at the end of the era came a second great school of poetry. This school is associated with the court of a noble king, Vikramáditya, who established a powerful empire, replaced Buddhism with Hinduism, and patronized the arts and sciences. But whether he ascended the throne in 375 A.D. or in the sixth century or whether he existed at all is now not definitely known. Attached to his court there are said to have been nine writers and scholars, styled "The Nine Gems," of whom Kalidasa, India's greatest poet, was the brightest luminary. His fanciful play, *Shakuntala,* inspired other playwrights: Bâna, author of the *Ratnâvalî,* in the seventh century and Bhavabhuti, author of two plays based on the *Râmâyana.* To this Golden Age belongs also the anonymous play, *The Little Clay Cart,* which has been successfully staged in Europe and America. Narrative poetry and the novel also flourished through these centuries, but in the ninth century Sanskrit literature entered a Dark Age, from which it has never really recovered. Of modern Indian writers only the mystical poet, Rabindranath

Tagore (1861–1941), who wrote in English as well as in Bengali, has been widely read in the West.

SANSKRIT DRAMA. The play *Shakuntala* takes us into a magical world of transcendent beauty, enveloped in Hindu thought and stylized according to the most rigid rules. Over five hundred Sanskrit plays survive to reveal the scope of the old drama and the conventions of its theater, but only about twenty-five of these are from the Golden Age. Written in the language of the aristocratic and learned classes, they were designed for a highly restricted and refined audience. They were presented in the palaces of the nobility without scenery and with stylized action far from the realism of today. Their appeal was to the sentiment and the intellect of their audience, and hence they are devoid of melodrama and vulgar theatricalism. But their very exclusiveness, their elevated style and atmosphere of religious serenity, deny them the vigor of a truly national drama such as that of the ancient Greeks or the Spanish and English during the Renaissance.

The supernatural honeycombs the plots of these plays and contributes to their dreamlike atmosphere. Human characters seem dwarfed by it and are often conventionalized into delicate phantoms. Their metaphorical speech, combined with musical background, further reflects the ideal realm they inhabit, where nature is rich and ever smiling and unhappiness is not for long. Violence was generally outlawed, as were even the physical aspects of everyday life, such as eating, biting, scratching, and kissing. Tragedy was forbidden, but there is abundant pathos in the separation and reunion of lovers and members of families. The humor is similarly restrained, and is embodied especially in the clown, who was still a Brahman despite his undignified role. As in Shakespeare, he is often the wisest character in the play.

THE HEBREWS

LESS ancient than the Chinese and Hindu cultures, yet older than any in the West, the culture of the Hebrews has followed a unique and unbroken tradition for over three thousand years. In 1500 B.C., when China, India, and Egypt had long enjoyed an advanced civilization, the Hebrews were still a small tribe of barbaric nomads tending their flocks in the Arabian desert. Their language allied them to a third family of nations with kindred tongues, the Semites, and they were cousins of their enemy neighbors, the Ammonites, Moabites, and Edomites, as well as of larger and more powerful Semitic peoples, the Phoenicians, Babylonians, Assyrians, and Carthaginians. All of these other Semitic tribes have since disappeared or been absorbed by later nations. But the Hebrews have managed to preserve their cultural integrity, if not their racial purity or their homeland, through centuries of unspeakable hardship and persecution.

THE PROMISED LAND OF ISRAEL. The ancient Hebrews endured a hard existence in the desert, plagued by the scorching sun and drought and the freezing winter wind. They grew up with a fear of nature that peopled their world with angry spirits. In their persistent trials they may have heard from their traditional patriarchs, Abraham, Isaac, and Jacob, of a fruitful land flowing with milk and honey—the Promised Land of Canaan (now Palestine), which was the western end of a Fertile Crescent extending eastward to the Persian Gulf. In time some Hebrew clans migrated to this land and battled with the Canaanites to settle there. Others wandered westward into Egypt, where they were overwhelmed and enslaved for the building of the pyramids.

Eventually, when the Egyptians were harassed by foreign enemies, a great leader, Moses, rose among the Hebrews and led his people through forty years of wandering in the desert to the verge of the Promised Land. It was Moses who replaced the primitive worship of the Hebrews with the new religion of Judaism, embodied in the Old Testament. According to legend, he compiled the first five books of the Bible (the so-called *Torah* of the Jews or *Pentateuch* of the Christians): *Genesis*,* containing the ancient myths of the Creation, the Flood, and the patriarchs Abraham, Isaac, Jacob, and Joseph; *Exodus*, relating the wanderings of the tribes from Egypt to Canaan under Moses; *Leviticus*, the ceremonial laws; *Numbers*, the census and further history of the Hebrew tribes; and *Deuteronomy*, the final pronouncements of Moses. Actually they were written by later scribes through many years and reveal the gradual evolution of the religion of the Israelites.

Judaism began as it has remained: a religion of one god; but in its first form the god, Yahveh (mistakenly called Jehovah), was the tribal god of the Hebrews, not the one God of all mankind. Originally thought to be the spirit of a mountain called Sinai, Yahveh had been worshiped by another tribe before Moses led his people to the foot of this mountain and made a Holy Covenant with Yahveh which dedicated the Israelites to him in return for his favor

* The books of the Old Testament are italicized in this introduction to suggest their chronology and place in Jewish history.

in their struggle for survival. Hence Yahveh began as one god among many tribal gods such as Moloch and Baal of the Canaanites, but was the one god worshiped by the Israelites. The Yahveh of Moses was a stern deity born out of the hard life of the persecuted Israelites, a god to be feared rather than loved. To implement the worship of Yahveh, Moses brought to his people from the top of Sinai the Ten Commandments engraved on tablets of stone. These symbols of the agreement were kept thereafter in an oblong chest called the Ark of the Covenant, which the Israelites carried with them everywhere.

It was *Joshua*, the fiery successor of Moses, who actually led the Israelites into the Promised Land in the twelfth century B.C. and began the conquest that was to carve out separate states for the twelve tribes. After his death, Israel was ruled by tribal priests, or *Judges*, until the greatest of them, *Samuel*, converted Israel into a kingdom and consecrated two successive kings, Saul and David. King David, famed in his youth as a singer, is traditionally supposed to have been the author of the *Psalms*, the Jewish hymnbook, but he was more certainly the warrior king who won for Israel a small empire. His son, King Solomon, whose forty-year reign in the tenth century B.C. is described in the first book of *Kings*, was renowned for his wisdom and was later credited with writing three books of the Bible: *Proverbs*, a treasure house of practical wisdom, *Ecclesiastes*, a philosophical inquiry into doubt, and *The Song of Songs*, a collection of love poems. He built a great temple for the worship of Yahveh which contained the Ark of the Covenant, but with his pomp and extravagance paved the way for a civil war in the reign of his selfish son, Rehoboam. As a result, the ten tribes of Israel in the north seceded in 931 B.C. under a new king, Jeroboam, while the two tribes of Judah in the south retained Rehoboam as king in their capital of Jerusalem. These two small kingdoms, never again united, wasted each other for two hundred years with constant warfare.

It was because of the laxity of the Israelites in their living and worship after the settlement in Canaan that the great line of Prophets arose to scourge kings, priests, and populace alike for their crimes against religion and Yahveh. Coming from all classes of society but especially from the country people in the wilderness, they sprang up like an invincible conscience out of the desert past to drive the nation back to righteousness. At a time when the Israelites were in danger of losing their national identity and were forsaking Yahveh for Moloch and Baal, the Prophets promised that a return to the rigorous traditions of their ancestors would bring a great future for Yahveh's people. Although often imprisoned and martyred, they persisted and in the end became the ethical spokesmen of the nation, who helped to maintain the Jews through the centuries as a distinct people, singular and aloof. In the recurrent periods of trial and persecution the Prophets have remained pillars of hope for eventual salvation.

The earliest Prophets flourished under the monarchy and are described in the Books of *Samuel* and *Kings*: Nathan, who denounced King David; Ahijah, who agitated for revolution against King Solomon; and Elijah, who attacked the worship of Baal in the northern kingdom of Israel. *Amos*, the first of the "literary Prophets," was a simple shepherd fired with the urge to reform a people lost in luxury. He lashed out against the emptiness of their religious ritual and insisted that righteous living was the only way for them to avoid the wrath of Yahveh. *Hosea*, who had suffered a personal tragedy because of a faithless wife, saw a similar disloyalty to Yahveh in the wanton living of Israel, yet preached for the first time the mercy and forgiveness of the god toward his erring people. Shortly after, in 722 B.C., the direst prophecies of Amos seemed to be justified. The great armies of Assyria conquered the northern kingdom of Israel and deported the ten tribes into an oblivion from which they have never returned.

The two tribes of Judah in the south continued another 135 years of independent existence and were to preserve the national identity of the Jewish people into the modern world. Again it was the Prophets—this time *Isaiah* and *Micah*—whose preaching purified the Jews of vice and assured them of their great future as the people of Yahveh. But the little kingdom of Judah was now squeezed between two powerful neighbors, Babylonia and Egypt. In 605 B.C. Nebuchadnezzar, the great king of Babylonia, began to absorb the militant little nation and in 587 B.C. destroyed the Temple of Solomon in Jerusalem and forced exile on the Jews.

Most of the Prophets down to this time had been vigorous nationalists who preached righteousness as the fulfillment of the Covenant between a tribal god and his people. Now there arose a new kind of prophet, *Jeremiah*, who was to broaden Judaism into a religion for all the world. To his own people he seemed a traitor because he sided with the Babylonians against the Egyptians and even remained in Jerusalem after the exile to act as liaison officer between the Babylonian governor and the remaining Jews. When the enraged Jews killed the governor, they took Jeremiah with them into Egypt, where he was eventually martyred.

Jeremiah was a man of peace, who was grieved by the brutality of his day and, as the "weeping prophet," is traditionally credited with the book of *Lamentations*. He reasoned that if Yahveh supported the Jews in their righteousness and abandoned them in their sin, He must help the enemies

The Hebrew Homelands

S. Fleishman

The larger map shows the areas of the Near East covered by the Hebrews in their wanderings. At the right Palestine is shown in more detail.

of the Jews when the Jews were unworthy of help. Hence He was not alone the one god of the Jews but rather the one God of all mankind. With Jeremiah and his international vision, Yahveh became God and Judaism became a true monotheism. Religion ceased to be for Jeremiah a national matter, and in becoming international it became really the individual and personal matter that it is for Christians and Jews today. Hence in the truest sense Jeremiah paved the way for Jesus Christ and linked the dogma of Judaism with Christianity.

EXILE AND THE PROMISED MESSIAH. Yet later Prophets reasoned from Jeremiah's internationalism an even greater future for the Jews. If Yahveh was the one God of all men, then His people must be the Chosen People of mankind. *Ezekiel*, the "priest-prophet," projected a revival of nationalism upon the rebuilding of the Temple, while the anonymous prophet of the *Second Book of Isaiah* preached that the destiny of the Jews was to be the "suffering servant" of God, chosen to bring moral enlightenment to all mankind.

The immediate events seemed to bear out these new hopes. The hero *Daniel* had allegedly foretold to Nebuchadnezzar the imminent end of the Babylonian Empire, and in 538 B.C. the Persians under Cyrus captured Babylon and freed the Jews. Many returned to what was left of the Promised Land and under the promptings of the prophets *Haggai* and *Zechariah* rebuilt Jerusalem and the Temple of Solomon. Two stern reformers, *Nehemiah* and *Ezra*, established a new, puritanical code of laws to insure the strict integrity and separateness of the Chosen People, but the gentle humanity of two anonymous books of this period, *Ruth* and *Jonah*, assures us that the tolerant internationalism of Jeremiah was by no means dead. Although Judea (as their tiny land was now called) remained a part of the Persian Empire, it flourished for a time, and according to a Biblical tradition, a Jewess named *Esther* even became the wife of a Persian emperor named Ahasuerus.

But the Jews chafed under the yoke of Persia and grew restless for the fulfillment of their destiny. The last of the Prophets, *Malachi*, had repeated the promise that a great Messiah would someday appear to lead the Jews out of their misery and establish the rule of right throughout the world. This promise from Yahveh sustained them—the most loyal of them—through the last centuries of the ancient era, and they dreamed of the day when their nation, their leader, and their God would rule the earth.

But years passed, and the Messiah did not come. The great line of Prophets and the writing of the Old Testament ceased, and Judaism passed largely into the hands of the priests, who crushed the power of the laymen and lived in luxury and corruption. Many disillusioned Jews left the homeland and set-

tled in Babylon, or Athens during the Golden Age, or Alexandria in Egypt, or Rome with the rise of the great new empire in the West. Judaism and Jewish culture sprang up in tiny colonies throughout the civilized world. But wherever they might be, the expatriate Jews always looked back to Jerusalem as their capital and the center of their spiritual life.

Judea itself passed from one conqueror to another—the Persians, the Macedonians under Alexander, the Egyptians under Ptolemy, the Syrians, the Egyptians again, then the Syrians once more. At last a great Jewish leader, Judas Maccabeus, rose up against the Syrian vandals, purified the temple of Jerusalem in 165 B.C., and established a dynasty that ruled Judea for a century. But the growth of the Roman Empire eventually cost the Maccabees their throne, and a depraved tyrant named Herod succeeded them under the favor of the Roman Emperor, Augustus.

Then during Herod's reign was born Jesus (or Joshua) of Nazareth, who was hailed at first as the long-awaited Messiah of the Jews. His doctrine of universal love exalted the downtrodden simple folk of Judea above their learned but worldly priests, and when after three years of preaching in the northern province of Galilee he made his triumphant entry into Jerusalem, a delirious crowd greeted him as the new King of the Jews. But both the Jewish priests and the Roman authorities feared his power over the people and had him hastily tried and then turned him over to the Roman governor, Pontius Pilate, for execution. The people were disillusioned by his death, and when his Jewish disciple Paul (or Saul) proclaimed in Christianity a world religion, the Jews shrank back within their walls and awaited once more their own Messiah.

DIASPORA. But instead of deliverance came the greatest tragedy of their history. Cruel Roman governors despoiled Judea in the first century A.D. during constant conflict with the adamant Jewish nation. Finally in 66 A.D. open rebellion broke out, and the Emperor Vespasian sent his son Titus to annihilate the Jews. For months the siege of Jerusalem dragged on, and when the Roman legions finally battered down the city, they killed a million of its people and dragged off thousands more as slaves. But many managed to escape in the great *Diaspora*, or Scattering, and eventually settled in every part of the known world from Spain to India and China. One of the greatest Jewish scholars, Johanan ben Zakkai, was allowed to establish a school at Jabneh nearby, which continued the study of the traditional lore for later generations. Titus imagined that he had finally destroyed the troublesome little nation, but a people that had thrived on hardship for centuries was to maintain its national identity through nineteen centuries more of wandering in hostile lands.

The crisis of the Diaspora forced a change in the government of the Jews. The reign of the corrupt priests ended with the destruction of their temple, and their power passed to the stern party of Pharisees, led by the *rabbis,* who developed the great tradition of Jewish learning and ritual which was to preserve the separateness of their people against all the forces of assimilation. Elaborating the prescriptions of the *Torah,* or Law of Moses, they built mountains of precise instructions for the conduct of daily life, which had the effect of keeping their people forever apart from the feared Gentiles. In the second century the Rabbi Judah compiled a six-volume text of rabbinical law called the *Mishna.* To this was added before the sixth century a huge, disjointed commentary in sixty-three sections, full of lore and law. The *Mishna* and this elaboration are called the *Talmud.* The special pattern of Jewish religious and community life is embodied in the *Torah* and *Talmud.*

The later history of the Jews is concerned with individuals and schools, which were often as significant for their adopted countries as for the submerged nation to which they belonged by blood and religion. The rabbinical schools were moved to Babylonia in the third century, and with the triumph of Mohammedanism over the Near East in the seventh they enjoyed three centuries of toleration and prosperity culminating in the work of the great scholar, Saadya (892–942). A brutal revival of persecution in Babylonia shifted the center of Jewish life to Spain around 1000 A.D., where for over two centuries they flourished in close cooperation with Mohammedan rulers. This new freedom gave confidence to the people to relax their strict attention to ritual and law and explore the world outside in new terms. Poetry flourished, especially in Judah Halevi (1085–1140), and Jewish scientists were renowned throughout the Mediterranean world for their skill in medicine, mathematics, astronomy, and chemistry.

But outside Spain the Jews of Europe endured unspeakable persecution, especially during the Crusades, when the Christian knights put many Jews to the sword in preparation for their massacre of Mohammedans in the Holy Land. In 1215 the Church in Rome proclaimed the "Jew-badge" law, forbidding all Jews under penalty of death to appear outside their homes without a certain badge sewn on their clothes, which should act as a brand at all times. Denied ownership of land, they took refuge in business and finance and became the moneylenders of Europe, since the Church would not sanction Christian usurers. Eventually even this segregation of the Jews would not satisfy their overlords, and one after another the rulers of Europe expelled all Jews—from England in 1290, France in 1394, Spain in 1492, Portugal in 1497.

Some remained in Germany and Italy to be shut up in special areas of the cities known as *ghettos,* but more wandered back to the East. The Jews from Spain settled in Turkey, which was periodically hospitable, yet they continued to speak a dialect of Spanish written in Hebrew characters, which is still called *Ladino.* The Jews of Germany went to Poland and Russia, but retained their dialect of German in Hebrew characters known as Yiddish (after *Jüdisch,* the German word for Jewish). Hebrew had practically ceased to exist as a spoken language around the time of Jesus.

Only with the coming of the democratic spirit in the seventeenth century did the condition of the Jew in the West begin to improve. Roger Williams invited Jews to settle in Rhode Island after 1636, and Cromwell readmitted them to England in 1655. The liberal spirit of Holland fostered a new center of Jewish culture in Amsterdam, made memorable by the great Jewish philosopher, Spinoza. A German Jew of the eighteenth century, Moses Mendelssohn, immortalized by his friend Lessing in the play *Nathan the Wise,* campaigned successfully for a more generous treatment of Jews in Germany, and the revolutions in America and France gave them equal rights with Christians in two new democratic lands. In the nineteenth century one country in western Europe after another guaranteed religious and political equality to the Jewish people, and they soon began to figure prominently in Western cultural life—Heine, Auerbach, Pinero, Bret Harte, Brandes in literature; Mendelssohn, Meyerbeer, Offenbach, Goldmark, Mahler in music; Rosa Bonheur, Pissarro, and Modigliani in art; Disraeli in politics; Marx and Bergson in philosophy; Freud in psychology; Einstein in science. But in Russian Poland under the czars and throughout eastern Europe persecution continued in the *pogroms,* systematic massacre and pillage encouraged by the government.

In our own day the one hideous instance of Jewish persecution has been the program of cold-blooded extermination carried on by the German government under Adolf Hitler with cynical success before and during World War II. Suddenly faced with annihilation in Europe, frightened Jewish refugees resumed the weary wandering that has dogged their ancestors since the Diaspora. Filled with the same urge for security and national fulfillment that drove the original tribes under Moses to the Promised Land, many banded together in the Zionist movement to establish a permanent and politically independent homeland in Palestine. Although the Arab dwellers in the Holy Land raised strong opposition to this revival of Jewish nationalism, a militant Jewish army succeeded in establishing the democratic state of Israel in 1948. At last after a gap of twenty centuries a Jewish commonwealth has been reborn among the nations.

Confucius

551–479 B.C.

Confucius was a social historian and political adviser who taught his disciples a way of life, but who had no intention of founding a religion or claiming divinity for himself. Since he died with the conviction that his teachings had been futile, he would be amazed to know that he has been venerated throughout China since his death and is known as the Divine Sage, whose pronouncements embody infallible truth.

The life of Confucius is associated with eastern China north of the Yangtze River, where he was born in the feudal state of Lu, now part of Shantung province. His impoverished father was over seventy at the time of his son's birth. Perhaps because his elder brother was a cripple, Confucius, who was precocious and old before his time, early assumed the headship of the family. His natural seriousness was emphasized by the death of his mother when he was twenty-three and his retirement in mourning for the conventional period of three years. He had just begun his career as a scholar and as a teacher of gentlemen's sons, but he accepted this interruption of his work with pious submission because he believed conservatively that a sound social order depended on keeping alive the ancient ceremonies and the memory of one's ancestors. During his three years of retirement and meditation Confucius worked out the foundations of his philosophy, to the teaching of which he was to devote the rest of his life.

Confucius once summarized his intellectual development in the following words: "At fifteen I set my mind to learning. At thirty I had formed my character. At forty I was free from doubts. At fifty I understood the will of heaven. At sixty nothing that I heard disturbed me. At seventy I could follow my own desires without violating moral law." Thus he achieved his rational ideal of life, a balanced way of thinking founded upon the Golden Mean. Believing that this *Li*, or way of life, had once been the code of China's feudal rulers, he preached the need to return to it and optimistically proclaimed that, if he were in control of a state, he could establish this moral order in government in three years. For years Confucius traveled from state to state, preaching his doctrine of the *Li* and seeking a ruler who would let him try it out in government. But at last he sadly returned to his native state of Lu, to submerge in a life of reflection his disappointment with a corrupt and cynical world.

In his role of scholar Confucius wrote little, but devoted himself to editing the so-called Five Classics, the ancient records of China which supported his insistence on historical continuity. "I transmit," he once said; "I do not create." It was his great knowledge of Chinese history, not his philosophical teachings, that attracted three thousand pupils to him, for of this number only seventy-two became his special disciples in following the *Li*. One of the Five Classics, a historical chronicle called *Spring and Autumn*, he wrote himself, but the other four he merely edited, or "transmitted": *The Book of History, The Book of Changes, The Book of Ritual*, and *The Book of Songs*. The last, a collection of 305 folk songs and sacred anthems, which Confucius interpreted allegorically to illustrate his teachings, is generally innocent of any religious purpose. In their remarkable variety the songs concern young people in love, old wives forsaken by their husbands, gentlemen at the hunt, soldiers at the wars, and the common people protesting the luxury of the rich. Although some of these charming songs are nearly four thousand years old, they have an astonishing freshness still.

The *Analects* of Confucius (so named by their first translator, James Legge) are a collection of the sayings of the Master, as they were remembered and eventually recorded by his disciples after his death. As with the *Little Flowers of Saint Francis*, the authenticity of these aphorisms has been questioned, but there can be no doubt that, taken as a whole, they represent accurately the sensible, humorous, but sometimes pontifical personality of the quiet Sage. Many of these conservative pronouncements suggest England's Dr. Johnson. Arranged in a haphazard way in the original, they do not read consecutively, but serve to illustrate the various precepts of Confucius.

Analects

CONFUCIUS THE MAN

DUKE Yeh asked Tselu about Confucius, and Tselu did not make a reply. Confucius said, "Why didn't you tell him that I am a person who forgets to eat when he is enthusiastic about something, forgets all his worries when he is happy, and is not aware that old age is coming on?"

Confucius said, "There is pleasure in lying pillowed against a bent arm after a meal of simple vegetables with a drink of water. On the other hand, to enjoy wealth and power without coming by it through the right means is to me like so many floating clouds." 10

Confucius said, "There are three things about the superior man that I have not been able to attain. The true man has no worries; the wise man has no perplexities; and the brave man has no fear." Tsekung said, "But, Master, you are exactly describing yourself."

Confucius said, "As to being a Sage and a true man, I am not so presumptuous. I will admit, however, that I have unceasingly tried to do my best and to teach other people." 20

"The things that trouble or concern me are the following: lest I should neglect to improve my charac-

Analects.[3] Translated by Lin Yutang. From *Wisdom of China and India* by Lin Yutang. Copyright, 1942, by Random House, Inc. Reprinted by permission of Random House, Inc.

ter, lest I should neglect my studies, and lest I should fail to move forward when I see the right course, or fail to correct myself when I see my mistake."

Confucius said, "I won't teach a man who is not anxious to learn, and will not explain to one who is not trying to make things clear to himself. And if I explain one-fourth and the man doesn't go back and reflect and think out the implications in the remaining three-fourths for himself, I won't bother to teach him again."

Confucius did not talk about monsters, physical exploits, unruly conduct, and the heavenly spirits.

Confucius was gentle but dignified, austere yet not harsh, polite and completely at ease.

When Confucius offered sacrifice to his ancestors, he felt as if his ancestors were present bodily, and when he offered sacrifice to the other gods, he felt as if the gods were present bodily. Confucius said, "If I don't offer sacrifice by being personally present, it is as if I didn't sacrifice at all."

Tsekung wanted to do away with the ceremony of sacrificing the lamb in winter. Confucius said, "Ah Sze, you love the lamb, but I love the institution."

Confucius said, "Wake yourself up with poetry, establish your character in li and complete your education in music."

For him rice could never be white enough and mince meat could never be chopped fine enough. When the food was mushy or the flavor had deteriorated, or when the fish had become bad or the meat was tainted, he would not eat. When its color had changed he would not eat. When the smell was bad, he would not eat. When it was not cooked right, he would not eat. When food was not in season, he would not eat. When the meat was not cut properly, he would not eat. When a food was not served with its proper sauce, he would not eat. Although there was a lot of meat on the table, he would not take it out of proportion with his rice; as for wine, he drank without any set limit, but would stop before getting drunk. Wine or shredded meat bought from the shops he would not eat. A meal without ginger on the table he would not eat. He did not overeat.

Tselu, Tseng Hsi, Jan Ch'iu, and Kunghsi Hua were sitting together one day, and Confucius said, "Do not think that I am a little bit older than you and therefore am assuming airs. You often say among yourselves that people don't know you. Suppose someone should know you, I should like to know how you would appear to that person." Tselu immediately replied, "I should like to rule over a country with a thousand carriages, situated between two powerful neighbors, involved in war and suffering from famine. I should like to take charge of such a country, and in three years the nation will become strong and orderly." Confucius smiled at this remark and said, "How about you, Ah Ch'iu?" Jan Ch'iu re-

plied, "Let me have a country sixty or seventy li square or perhaps only fifty or sixty li square. Put it in my charge, and in three years the people will have enough to eat, but as for teaching them moral order and music, I shall leave it to the superior man." (Turning to Kunghsi Hua) Confucius said, "How about you, Ah Ch'ih?" Kunghsi Hua replied, "Not that I say I can do it, but I'm willing to learn this. At the ceremonies of religious worship and at the conference of the princes, I should like to wear the ceremonial cap and gown and be a minor official assisting at the ceremony." "How about you, Ah Tien?" The latter (Tseng Hsi) was just playing on the seh, and with a bang he left the instrument and arose to speak. "My ambition is different from theirs." "It doesn't matter," said Confucius; "we are just trying to find out what each would like to do." Then he replied, "In late spring, when the new spring dress is made, I would like to go with five or six grownups and six or seven children to bathe in the River Yi, and after the bath go to enjoy the breeze in the Wuyu woods, and then sing on our way home." Confucius heaved a deep sigh and said, "You are the man after my own heart."

HIS CONVERSATION

Confucius said, "I have sometimes talked with Huei for a whole day, and he just sits there like a fool. But then he goes into his own room and thinks about what I have said and is able to think out some ideas of his own. He is not a fool."

Tsekung asked Confucius, "What kind of person do you think can be properly called a scholar?" Confucius replied, "A person who shows a sense of honor in his personal conduct and who can be relied upon to carry out a diplomatic mission in a foreign country with competence and dignity can be properly called a scholar." "What kind of person would come next?" "One who is known to be a good son in his family and has a reputation for humility and respect in a village." "What kind of person would come next after that?" "A person who is extremely careful of his conduct and speech and always keeps his word. That is a priggish, inferior type of person, but still he can rank below the above two types." "What do you think of the officials today?" "Oh!" said Confucius, "those rice-bags! They don't count at all."

Yuan Jang (who was reputed to sing at his mother's death) squatted in Confucius' presence and Confucius said, "As a child, you were impudent; after you are grown up, you have absolutely done nothing; and now in your old age you refuse to die! You blackguard!" And Confucius struck him in the shin with a cane.

58. *li,* here a unit of measure, roughly equal to one third of a mile.
70. *seh,* an ancient musical instrument of twenty-five strings, which is still in use in China.

Baron K'ang Chi was worried about thieves and burglars in the country and consulted Confucius about it. Confucius replied, "If you yourself don't love money the people will not steal, even though you reward the thieves."

Confucius said, "To know what you know and know what you don't know is the characteristic of one who knows."

Confucius said, "A man who has committed a mistake and doesn't correct it is committing another mistake."

Baron Wen Chi said that he always thought three times before he acted. When Confucius heard this, he remarked, "To think twice is quite enough."

Confucius said, "A man who has a beautiful soul always has some beautiful things to say, but a man who says beautiful things does not necessarily have a beautiful soul. A true man (or truly great man) will always be found to have courage, but a courageous man will not always be found to have true manhood."

Tsekung asked Confucius, "What would you say if all the people of the village like a person?" "That is not enough," replied Confucius. "What would you say if all the people of a village dislike a person?" "That is not enough," said Confucius. "It is better when the good people of the village like him, and the bad people of the village dislike him."

Confucius said, "It is easy to be rich and not haughty; it is difficult to be poor and not grumble."

Confucius said, "Can you ever imagine a petty soul serving as a minister of the state? Before he gets his post, he is anxious to get it, and after he has got it, he is anxious about losing it, and if he begins to be anxious about losing it, then there is nothing that he will not do."

Confucius said, "Do not worry about people not knowing you, but strive so that you may be worth knowing."

Confucius said, "A gentleman blames himself, while a common man blames others."

Someone said, "What do you think of repaying evil with kindness?" Confucius replied, "Then what are you going to repay kindness with? Repay kindness with kindness, but repay evil with justice (or severity)."

Confucius said, "Men are born pretty much alike, but through their habits they gradually grow further and further apart from each other."

Confucius said, "When you see a good man, try to emulate his example, and when you see a bad man, search yourself for his faults."

HIS PHILOSOPHY

Confucius said, "It is man that makes truth great, and not truth that makes man great."

Tselu asked about the worship of the celestial and earthly spirits. Confucius said, "We don't know yet how to serve men, how can we know about serving the spirits?" "What about death?" was the next question, and Confucius said, "We don't know yet about life, how can we know about death?"

Tsekung asked, "Is there one single word that can serve as a principle of conduct for life?" Confucius replied, "Perhaps the word 'reciprocity' (shu) will do. Do not do unto others what you do not want others to do unto you."

Yen Huei asked about true manhood, and Confucius said, "True manhood consists in realizing your true self and restoring the moral order or discipline (li). If a man can for just one day realize his true self, and restore complete moral discipline, the world will follow him. To be a true man depends on oneself. What has it got to do with others?"

Confucius said, "Humility is near to moral discipline (li); simplicity of character is near to true manhood; and loyalty is near to sincerity of heart. If a man will carefully cultivate these things in his conduct, he may still err a little, but he won't be far from the standard of true manhood. For with humility or a pious attitude, a man seldom commits errors; with sincerity of heart, a man is generally reliable; and with simplicity of character, he is usually generous. You seldom make a mistake when you start off from these points."

Confucius said, "The superior man loves his soul; the inferior man loves his property. The superior man always remembers how he was punished for his mistakes; the inferior man always remembers what presents he got."

Stages in the development of modern Chinese ideograph symbols from early pictographs.

Confucius said, "The superior man is liberal toward others' opinions, but does not completely agree with them; the inferior man completely agrees with others' opinions, but is not liberal toward them."

Confucius and his followers had to go for days without food in Ch'en, and some of his followers felt ill and were confined to bed. Tselu came to see Confucius in low spirits and asked, "Does the superior man also land in difficulties?" Confucius said, "Yes, the superior man also sometimes finds himself in difficulties, but when an inferior man finds himself in difficulties, he is likely to do anything."

Confucius said, "A gentleman is ashamed that his words are better than his deeds."

Confucius said, "A gentleman is careful about three things: In his youth, when his blood is strong, he is careful about sex. When he is grown up, and his blood is full, he is careful about getting into a fight (or struggle in general). When he is old, and his blood is getting thinner, he is careful about money." (A young man loves women; a middle-aged man loves struggle; and an old man loves money.)

Confucius said, "When a man has more solid worth than polish, he appears uncouth, and when a man has more polish than solid worth, he appears urbane. The proper combination of solid worth and polish alone makes a gentleman."

Confucius said, "I hate things that resemble the real things but are not the real things. I hate cockles because they get mixed up with the corn. I hate the ingratiating fellows, because they get mixed up with the good men. I hate the glib talkers, because they confuse us with honest people. I hate the music of Cheng, because it brings confusion into classical music. I hate the purple color, because it confuses us with the red color. I hate the goody-goodies, because they confuse us with the virtuous people." (Mencius)

Confucius said, "Women and the inferior people are most difficult to deal with. When you are familiar with them, they become cheeky, and when you ignore them, they resent it."

Confucius said, "Guide the people with governmental measures and control or regulate them by the threat of punishment, and the people will try to keep out of jail, but will have no sense of honor or shame. Guide the people by virtue and control or regulate them by *li*, and the people will have a sense of honor and respect."

Confucius said, "In presiding over lawsuits, I'm as good as any man. The thing is to aim so that there should be no lawsuits."

Baron K'ang Ch'i asked Confucius concerning government, and Confucius replied, "Government is merely setting things right. When you yourself lead them by the right example, who dares to go astray?"

Confucius said, "When the ruler himself does what is right, he will have influence over the people without giving commands, and when the ruler himself does not do what is right, all his commands will be of no avail."

Lin Fang asked concerning the foundation of *li*, and Confucius replied, "You are asking an important question! In this matter of rituals or ceremony, rather than be extravagant, be simple. In funeral ceremonies, rather than be expertly familiar, it is more important to have the real sentiment of sorrow."

Confucius said, "That type of scholarship which is bent on remembering things in order to answer people's questions does not qualify one to be a teacher."

Confucius said, "Ah Yu, have you heard of the six sayings about the six shortcomings?" "No," said Tselu. "Sit down, then, and I will tell you. If a man loves kindness, but doesn't love study, his shortcoming will be ignorance. If a man loves wisdom but does not love study, his shortcoming will be having fanciful or unsound ideas. If a man loves honesty and does not love study, his shortcoming will be a tendency to spoil or upset things. If a man loves simplicity but does not love study, his shortcoming will be sheer following of routine. If a man loves courage and does not love study, his shortcoming will be unruliness or violence. If a man loves decision of character and does not love study, his shortcoming will be self-will or headstrong belief in himself."

Confucius said, "Those who are born wise are the highest type of people; those who become wise through learning come next; those who learn by sheer diligence and industry, but with difficulty, come after that. Those who are slow to learn, but still won't learn, are the lowest type of people."

The Book of Songs

I

Written in B.C. 718. It is the Chinese rendering of "the world well lost."

THE gourd has still its bitter leaves,
And deep the crossing at the ford.
   I wait my lord.

The ford is brimming to its banks;
The pheasant cries upon her mate.
   My lord is late.

The boatman still keeps beckoning,
And others reach their journey's end.
   I wait my friend.

*The Book of Songs.*⁸ Translated by Helen Waddell (after James Legge). From *Lyrics from the Chinese* by Helen Waddell. Reprinted by permission of Constable and Company Ltd. and Henry Holt and Company, Inc.

II

Written in the twelfth century before Christ. It is possibly the oldest drinking song in the world.

The dew is heavy on the grass,
　At last the sun is set.
Fill up, fill up the cups of jade,
　The night's before us yet!

All night the dew will heavy lie　　　　5
　Upon the grass and clover.
Too soon, too soon, the dew will dry,
　Too soon the night be over!

III

Written in the twelfth century before Christ, c. 1121.

The morning glory climbs above my head,
Pale flowers of white and purple, blue and red.
　I am disquieted.

Down in the withered grasses something stirred;
I thought it was his footfall that I heard.　　5
　Then a grasshopper chirred.

I climbed the hill just as the new moon showed,
I saw him coming on the southern road.
　My heart lays down its load.

IV

Written b.c. 680. The 'Little Preface': 'A man's praise of his Poor Wife.'

I went out at the Eastern Gate,
　I saw the girls in clouds,
Like clouds they were, and soft and bright,
　But in the crowds
I thought on the maid who is my light,　　5
Down-drooping, soft as the grey twilight;
　She is my mate.

I went out by the Tower on the Wall,
　I saw the girls in flower,
Like flowering rushes they swayed and bent,　　10
　But in that hour
I thought on the maid who is my saint,
In her thin white robe and her coloring faint;
　She is my all.

V

Written 718 b.c. from the harem of the Palace of Wei.

The wind blows from the North.
　He looks and his eyes are cold.
He looks and smiles and then goes forth,
　My grief grows old.

The wind blows and the dust.　　　　5
　To-morrow he swears he will come.
His words are kind, but he breaks his trust,
　My heart is numb.

All day the wind blew strong,
　The sun was buried deep.　　　　10
I have thought of him so long, so long,
　I cannot sleep.

VI

Written b.c. 769 by a divorced woman.

Yellow's the robe for honor,
　And green is for disgrace.
I wear the green and not the gold,
　And turn away my face.

I wear the green of scorning,　　　　5
　Who wore the gold so long.
I think upon the Sages,
　Lest I should do them wrong.

It is for her he shames me.
　I sit and think apart.　　　　10
I wonder if the Sages knew
　A woman's heart.

VII

Written b.c. 718.

The K'e still ripples to its banks,
　The moorfowl cry.
My hair was gathered in a knot,
　And you came by.

Selling of silk you were, a lad　　　　5
　Not of our kin;
You passed at sunset on the road
　From far-off Ts'in.

The frogs were croaking in the dusk;
　The grass was wet.　　　　10
We talked together, and I laughed;
　I hear it yet.

I thought that I would be your wife;
　I had your word.
And so I took the road with you,　　　　15
　And crossed the ford.

I do not know when first it was
　Your eyes looked cold.
But all this was three years ago,
　And I am old

VIII

Written 675 B.C. "Is there anything whereof it may be said, 'See, this is new? it hath been already of old time, which was before us.'"

I would have gone to my lord in his need,
  Have galloped there all the way,
But this is a matter concerns the State,
  And I, being a woman, must stay.

I watched them leaving the palace yard,   5
  In carriage and robe of state.
I would have gone by the hills and the fords;
  I know they will come too late.

I may walk in the garden and gather
  Lilies of mother-of-pearl.   10
I had a plan would have saved the State.
  —But mine are the thoughts of a girl.

The Elder Statesmen sit on the mats,
  And wrangle through half the day;
A hundred plans they have drafted and dropped, 15
  And mine was the only way.

Li Po

701–762

The Chinese call Li Po affectionately "the Banished Angel," an immortal sent back to earth to do penance for a sin in Paradise. In reading his exuberant and exquisite poems on wine, friendship, and nature we can readily imagine in him the sublime beauty of the angels as well as the pagan's thirst for physical pleasure. His picturesque life is a series of anecdotes that all point to the romantic vagabond, steeped in wine and good fellowship, contemptuous of serious work or an official career, devoted to the open road and poetry.

The poet's mother named him Po (the White One) because on the night of his birth she dreamed of the Great White Star (Venus). But he was more aptly called by his later nickname, the Old Wine Genius, for his poetic gift and his taste for wine both appeared very early. Although he had mastered the Confucian Classics at ten, he was indifferent to study and postponed for years the examinations essential to an official career. The first of his four wives finally left him, taking their two children when he persisted in wasting his days with five cronies who formed with him the Six Idlers of the Bamboo Valley. In 738 he began his lifelong friendship with Tu Fu, his young rival, who revered him as a poet and yet shook his serious head at the romantic recklessness of Li Po.

At forty he went to Chang-An, the brilliant capital, and soon came to the attention of the Emperor through his wit and verses. Rewarded with a sinecure, he was a favorite alike at the tables of the great and the taverns of the poor. As one of the Eight Immortals of the Wine Cup, he caroused constantly, and once, when summoned by the Emperor, he was so drunk that his head had to be soused in water before he could entertain the court with poetry. Eventually he offended the Emperor's favorite, who jealously undermined his standing with the Emperor.

Li Po resumed his wanderings, visiting old friends who had been dispersed to provincial posts. Once he tried the official's life in the service of a prince, but the prince was deposed in a revolt and Li Po narrowly escaped hanging. This confirmed him in his career of idle pleasure, and, according to an old legend, he was drunk at the time of his death. It was said that he drowned one night when he fell out of a canoe while trying to kiss the reflection of the moon in the Yellow River.

Li Po represents for China the spirit of romance. The love of solitude and the mountains was as strong in him as the need for wine and convivial companions. He enjoyed life with a flourish, and part of his pleasure was a mystical communion with the great soul of nature. He never took to the conservative Confucian teaching of his childhood but was fascinated by Taoist mysticism and the simple, natural life. His poems to the lotus flower and the north wind are as typical of him as his drinking songs and his witty praise of women. In all of his many facets Li Po is always the romantic rebel.

Drinking Alone in the Moonlight

I

A POT of wine among flowers.
  I alone, drinking, without a companion.
I lift the cup and invite the bright moon.
My shadow opposite certainly makes us three.
But the moon cannot drink,   5
And my shadow follows the motions of my body in
  vain.
For the briefest time are the moon and my shadow
  my companions.
Oh, be joyful! One must make the most of Spring.
I sing—the moon walks forward rhythmically;
I dance, and my shadow shatters and becomes con-
  fused.   10
In my waking moments, we are happily blended.
When I am drunk, we are divided from one another
  and scattered.
For a long time I shall be obliged to wander without
  intention;
But we will keep our appointment by the far-off
  Cloudy River.

II

If Heaven did not love wine,   15
There would be no Wine Star in Heaven.

Drinking Alone. . . . Translated by Florence Ayscough and Amy Lowell. From *Fir Flower Tablets* by Florence Ayscough and Amy Lowell. Reprinted by permission of Houghton Mifflin Company.

The poet Li Po, by Liang K'ai, a Chinese artist of the 13th century.

If Earth did not love wine,
There should be no Wine Springs on Earth.
Why then be ashamed before Heaven to love wine.
I have heard that clear wine is like the Sages;   20
Again it is said that thick wine is like the Virtuous
        Worthies.
Wherefore it appears that we have swallowed both
        Sages and Worthies.
Why should we strive to be Gods and Immortals?
Three cups, and one can perfectly understand the
        Great Tao;

A gallon, and one is in accord with all nature.   25
Only those in the midst of it can fully comprehend
        the joys of wine;
I do not proclaim them to the sober.

A Summer Day

Naked I lie in the green forest of summer. . . .
        Too lazy to wave my white feathered fan.
I hang my cap on a crag,
And bare my head to the wind that comes
Blowing through the pine trees.   5

The Ching-ting Mountain

Flocks of birds have flown high and away;
        A solitary drift of cloud, too, has gone, wander-
        ing on.
And I sit alone with the Ching-ting Peak, towering
        beyond.
We never grow tired of each other, the mountain
        and I.   4

Parting at a Wine-Shop in Nan-king

A wind, bringing willow-cotton, sweetens the
        shop,
And a girl from Wu, pouring wine, urges me to
        share it
With my comrades of the city who are here to see
        me off;
And as each of them drains his cup, I say to him in
        parting,
Oh, go and ask this river running to the east   5
If I can travel farther than a friend's love!

Down Chung-nan Mountain to the Kind Pillow and Bowl of Hu Ssü

Down the blue mountain in the evening,
        Moonlight was my homeward escort.
Looking back, I saw my path
Lie in levels of deep shadow . . .
I was passing the farm-house of a friend,   5
When his children called from a gate of thorn
And led me twining through jade bamboos

A Summer Day; The Ching-ting Mountain. Translated by Shigeyoshi Obata. Taken from *The Works of Li Po* by Shigeyoshi Obata, published and copyrighted by E. P. Dutton & Co., Inc., New York. 1922.
Parting at a Wine-Shop; Down Chung-nan Mountain. From *The Jade Mountain*, by Witter Bynner. Copyright 1929 by Alfred A. Knopf, Inc. and renewed 1957. Reprinted by permission.

Where green vines caught and held my clothes.
And I was glad of a chance to rest   9
And glad of a chance to drink with my friend. . . .
We sang to the tune of the wind in the pines;
And we finished our songs as the stars went down,
When, I being drunk and my friend more than
    happy,
Between us we forgot the world.

In the Quiet Night

So bright a gleam on the foot of my bed—
    Could there have been a frost already?
Lifting myself to look, I found that it was moonlight.
Sinking back again, I thought suddenly of home.   4

Endless Yearning

I AM endlessly yearning
    To be in Ch'ang-an.
. . . Insects hum of autumn by the gold brim of the
    well;
A thin frost glistens like little mirrors on my cold
    mat;
The high lantern flickers; and deeper grows my
    longing.   5
I lift the shade and, with many a sigh, gaze upon
    the moon,
Single as a flower, centred from the clouds.
Above, I see the blueness and deepness of sky.
Below, I see the greenness and the restlessness of
    water . . .
Heaven is high, earth wide; bitter between them
    flies my sorrow.   10
Can I dream through the gateway, over the moun-
    tain?
Endless longing
Breaks my heart."

The Hard Road

PURE wine costs, for the golden cup, ten thousand
    coppers a flagon,
And a jade plate of dainty food calls for a million
    coins.
I fling aside my food-sticks and cup, I cannot eat nor
    drink . . .
I pull out my dagger, I peer four ways in vain.
I would cross the Yellow River, but ice chokes the
    ferry;   5

*In the Quiet Night; Endless Yearning; The Hard Road; A Song of
Ch'ang-kan.* From *The Jade Mountain*, by Witter Bynner. Copyright
1929 by Alfred A. Knopf, Inc. and renewed 1957. Reprinted by
permission.

I would climb the T'ai-hang Mountains, but the sky
    is blind with snow . . .
I would sit and poise a fishing-pole, lazy by a brook—
But I suddenly dream of riding a boat, sailing for
    the sun . . .
Journeying is hard,
Journeying is hard.   10
There are many turnings—
Which am I to follow? . . .
I will mount a long wind some day and break the
    heavy waves
And set my cloudy sail straight and bridge the deep,
    deep sea.

A Song
of Ch'ang-kan

MY hair had hardly covered my forehead.
    I was picking flowers, playing by my door.
When you, my lover, on a bamboo horse,
Came trotting in circles and throwing green plums.
We lived near together on a lane in Ch'ang-kan,   5
Both of us young and happy-hearted.
. . . At fourteen I became your wife,
So bashful that I dared not smile,
And I lowered my head toward a dark corner
And would not turn to your thousand calls;   10
But at fifteen I straightened my brows and laughed,
Learning that no dust could ever seal our love,
That even unto death I would await you by my post
And would never lose heart in the tower of silent
    watching.
. . . Then when I was sixteen, you left on a long
    journey   15
Through the Gorges of Ch'ŭ-t'ang, of rock and whirl-
    ing water.
And then came the Fifth-month, more than I could
    bear,
And I tried to hear the monkeys in your lofty far off
    sky.
Your footprints by our door, where I had watched
    you go,   19
Were hidden, every one of them, under green moss,
Hidden under moss too deep to sweep away.
And the first autumn wind added fallen leaves.
And now, in the Eighth-month, yellowing butterflies
Hover, two by two, in our west-garden grasses. . . .
And, because of all this, my heart is breaking   25
And I fear for my bright cheeks, lest they fade.
. . . Oh, at last, when you return through the three
        Pa districts,
Send me a message home ahead!
And I will come and meet you and will never mind
    the distance,
All the way to Chang-fêng Sha.

Addressed Humorously to Tu Fu

Here! is this you on the top of Fan-ko Mountain,
Wearing a huge hat in the noon-day sun?
How thin, how wretchedly thin, you have grown!
You must have been suffering from poetry again.   4

Tu Fu

713–770

Chinese scholars consider Tu Fu their greatest poet. Certainly he is the finest in the classical tradition, though foreign readers and the commoners of China have preferred Li Po, his close friend. Beside the reckless high spirits and romantic imagination of Li Po, Tu Fu seems sedate and precise, yet more admirable for his fine, sensitive character and carefully perfected style.

In contrast to the gay, dissipated life of Li Po, the career of Tu Fu is a record of endless misfortune and weary wandering. Born into a poor but respectable family, he was so precocious that at fifteen he had already a local following for his verse and essays. But when he first went to the capital to take the official examination, he was denied a degree because of some unorthodox opinions of his and so was forced to wander through the provinces in search of a place. Sixteen years later the old Emperor relented and gave the poet a post in a great library. But his prosperity was short-lived. A revolution turned him out, and he was captured by bandits and all but starved to death.

When he was eventually restored to favor, Tu Fu in his new post of Censor soon offended the new Emperor with attacks on his policy and was banished to a remote provincial post. Refusing to accept this dismal fate, he resigned from government service and lived the rest of his life with his family in abject poverty and hardship. At last on one of his many journeys he was caught by a flood in a ruined temple. When he was finally rescued and honored with a banquet, he died from overeating.

Despite his endless misfortunes, Tu Fu remained true to himself and the exacting standards of his craft. His themes, naturally enough, are serious and even melancholy, but are characterized by patient resignation, never revolt. The beauty of his sentiments is the sad beauty of the moon, and what humor appears is always quiet and restrained into irony. His simple pictorial style reminds us that he was a painter as well as a poet, but its subtlety has discouraged much English translation of his work.

Addressed Humorously. . . . Translated by Shigeyoshi Obata. Taken from *The Works of Li Po* by Shigeyoshi Obata, published and copyrighted by E. P. Dutton & Co., Inc., New York. 1922.

A Visit to Fan with Li Po

My honored friend, Li, writes excellent verses,
That ring at times like Ying-Kao's masterly lines.
I, too, a sojourner of Tung Meng,
Love him as a younger brother loves the elder.
Drunk, we sleep both under one cover at night;   5
And in daytime we go together hand in hand.
Now longing for a place of quiet company,
We come to visit you on the city's northside.
Your little boy waits on us so handsomely,
Joy leaps in our hearts as we enter your gate.   10
What solitude! We hear only the chilly mallets,
And see the clouds bivouac before the old city wall.
Having always sung the ode of the sweet citron,
Who cares to seek for the soup of the water-herbs?
You desire not the debasement of official life,   15
But remain untrammeled like the blue, boundless sea.

Sent to Li Po as a Gift

Autumn comes,
We meet each other.
You still whirl about as a thistledown in the wind.
Your Elixir of Immortality is not yet perfected
And, remembering Ko Hung, you are ashamed.   5
You drink a great deal,
You sing wild songs,
Your days pass in emptiness.
Your nature is a spreading fire,
It is swift and strenuous.   10
But what does all this bravery amount to?

The Thatched House Unroofed by an Autumn Gale

It is the Eighth Month, the very height of autumn.
The wind rages and roars.
It tears off three layers of my grass-roof.
The thatch flies—it crosses the river—it is scattered about in the open spaces by the river.

A Visit to Fan. . . . Translated by Shigeyoshi Obata. Taken from *The Works of Li Po* by Shigeyoshi Obata, published and copyrighted by E. P. Dutton & Co., Inc., New York. 1922.
A Visit to Fan. 3. **Tung Meng,** a district in Shantung province where Li Po and Tu Fu lived during the early period of their friendship.
Sent to Li Po . . . ; *The Thatched House.* . . . Translated by Florence Ayscough and Amy Lowell. From *Fir Flower Tablets* by Florence Ayscough and Amy Lowell. Reprinted by permission of Houghton Mifflin Company.
Sent to Li Po . . . 5. **Ko Hung,** a Chinese official who spent his last years trying to compound the Elixir of Immortality.

High-flying, it hangs, tangled and floating, from the
tops of the forest trees;   5
Low-flying, it whirls—turns—and sinks into the hollows of the marsh.
The swarm of small boys from the South Village
laugh at me because I am old and feeble.
How dare they act like thieves and robbers before
my face,
Openly seizing my thatch and running into my bamboo grove?
My lips are scorched, my mouth dry, I scream at
them, but to no purpose.   10
I return, leaning on my staff. I sigh and breathe
heavily.

Presently, of a sudden, the wind ceases. The clouds
are the color of ink.
The autumn sky is endless—endless—stretching to-
ward dusk and night.
My old cotton quilt is as cold as iron;
My restless son sleeps a troubled sleep, his moving
foot tears the quilt.   15
Over the head of the bed is a leak. Not a place is dry.
The rain streams and stands like hemp—there is no
break in its falling.
Since this misery and confusion, I have scarcely slept
or dozed.
All the long night, I am soaking wet. When will the
light begin to sift in?
If one could have a great house of one thousand, ten
thousand rooms—   20
A great shelter where all the Empire's shivering
scholars could have happy faces—
Not moved by wind or rain, solid as a mountain—
Alas! When shall I see that house standing before
my eyes?
Then, although my own hut were destroyed, although I might freeze and die, I should be
satisfied.

A Night Abroad

A LONG wind is rippling at the grassy shore. . . .
Through the night, to my motionless tall
mast,
The stars lean down from open space,
And the moon comes running up the river.
. . . If only my art might bring me fame   5
And free my sick old age from office!—
Flitting, flitting, what am I like
But a sand-snipe in the wide-wide world!

To My Retired Friend Wêi

I T is almost as hard for friends to meet
As for the morning and evening stars.
Tonight then is a rare event,

Joining, in the candlelight,
Two men who were young not long ago   5
But now are turning grey at the temples.
. . . To find that half our friends are dead
Shocks us, burns our hearts with grief.
We little guessed it would be twenty years
Before I could visit you again.   10
When I went away, you were still unmarried;
But now these boys and girls in a row
Are very kind to their father's old friend.
They ask me where I have been on my journey;
And then, when we have talked awhile,   15
They bring and show me wines and dishes,
Spring chives cut in the night-rain
And brown rice cooked freshly a special way.
. . . My host proclaims it a festival,
He urges me to drink ten cups—   20
But what ten cups could make me as drunk
As I always am with your love in my heart?
. . . Tomorrow the mountains will separate us;
After tomorrow—who can say?

The Excursion

A NUMBER of young gentlemen of rank, accompanied by singing-girls, go out to enjoy the
cool of the evening. They encounter a shower of
rain.

I

How delightful, at sunset, to loosen the boat!
A light wind is slow to raise waves.
Deep in the bamboo grove, the guests linger;
The lotus-flowers are pure and bright in the cool
evening air.
The young nobles stir the ice-water;   5
The Beautiful Ones wash the lotus-roots, whose
fibres are like silk threads.
A layer of clouds above our heads is black.
It will certainly rain, which impels me to write this
poem.

II

The rain comes, soaking the mats upon which we
are sitting.
A hurrying wind strikes the bow of the boat.   10
The rose-red rouge of the ladies from Yŭeh is wet;
The Yen beauties are anxious about their kingfisher-
eyebrows.
We throw out a rope and draw in to the sloping bank.

A Night Abroad; To My Retired Friend Wêi. From *The Jade Moun-
tain,* by Witter Bynner. Copyright 1929 by Alfred A. Knopf, Inc.
and renewed 1957. Reprinted by permission.
The Excursion. Translated by Florence Ayscough and Amy Lowell.
From *Fir Flower Tablets* by Florence Ayscough and Amy Lowell.
Reprinted by permission of Houghton Mifflin Company.

We tie the boat to the willow-trees.
We roll up the curtains and watch the floating wave-
 flowers.   15
Our return is different from our setting out. The wind
 whistles and blows in great gusts.
By the time we reach the shore, it seems as though
 the Fifth Month were Autumn.

Alone
in Her Beauty

WHO is lovelier than she?
 Yet she lives alone in an empty valley.
She tells me she came from a good family
Which is humbled now into the dust.
. . . When trouble arose in the Kuan district,   5
Her brothers and close kin were killed.
What use was their high offices,
Not even shielding their own lives?—
The world has but scorn for adversity;
Hope goes out, like the light of a candle.   10
Her husband, with a vagrant heart,
Seeks a new face like a new piece of jade;
And when morning-glories furl at night
And mandarin-ducks lie side by side,
All he can see is the smile of the new love,   15
While the old love weeps unheard.
The brook was pure in its mountain source,
But away from the mountain its waters darken.
. . . Waiting for her maid to come from selling
 pearls
For straw to cover the roof again,   20
She picks a few flowers, no longer for her hair,
And lets pine-needles fall through her fingers,
And, forgetting her thin silk sleeve and the cold,
She leans in the sunset by a tall bamboo.

Vedic Hymns

The ancient hymns and prayers of the Vedas,
composed by anonymous holy men between
2000 and 800 B.C., are the foundation of both the Hindu
and the Buddhist religions and are the oldest writings in
any Indo-European tongue. They remain the ultimate
source of Vedanta and hence are sacred to hundreds of
millions even today. Of the four great collections the *Rig-
veda* (Verse-Knowledge) is the oldest and is the source
of the other three. Compiled in stages over a long period,
it contains both primitive hymns to the folk gods of nature, such as Varuna (sky) and Agni (fire), and later
hymns to abstract concepts such as *The Origin of All
Things,* which lead into the philosophical discussions of
the *Upanishads.* The language of these religious lyrics
antedates classical Sanskrit, and their meter is based on
an alternation of long and short syllables in lines of eight,
eleven, or twelve syllables organized in quatrains. The
best of them project an exalted sympathy with nature
through noble imagery, vivid descriptions, simple, concrete diction, and a fine reverent tone.

Agni,
God of Fire

(RIG-VEDA V, 28)

LIGHTED Agni flames forth high,
 Flings a radiance on the sky,
And his lustre red and bright
Mingles with the morning light;
Facing east, with gifts and lays   5
Viswavara sings his praise.

First immortal of the skies,
Minister of our sacrifice,
Unto him thy gifts prolong
Who uplifts thy sacred songs,   10
Unto him thy blessings come
On whose altar is thy home!

Radiant on the altar shine,
Strength and lustre bright be thine;
Spread our riches with thy flame,   15
Quell our foeman's power and fame,
Bless our dwellings from above,
Men and women link in love!

Radiant on the altar shine,
Strength and lustre bright be thine;   20
Viswavara humbly bending
Chants thy glories never ending;
Form of splendor bright is thine,
On her altar ever shine.

Pious hands awake thy flame,   25
Pious lips repeat thy name;
Bear unto our sacrifice
Bright Immortals from the skies,
Bear unto the Gods in Heaven
Sacred offerings to thee given!   30

Pious lips the chant uplift,
Pious hands provide the gift,
Priest of Gods, Immortal bright,
Thine is morning's sacred rite,
Messenger of Gods in heaven,   35
Take these offerings humbly given.

The Origin
of All Things

(RIG-VEDA X, 129)

THERE then was neither Naught nor Aught,
        No air, nor sky beyond.
What covered all? Where rested all?
        In watery gulf profound?

Nor death was then, nor deathlessness,   5
        Nor change of night and day.
That One breathed calmly, self-sustained;
        Naught else beyond It lay.

Gloom, hid in gloom, existed first,—
        One sea excluding view.   10
That One, a void in chaos wrapped,
        By inward fervor grew.

Within It first arose desire,
        The primal germ of mind,
Which nothing with existence links,   15
        As sages searching find.

The kindling ray that shot across
        The dark and drear abyss,—
Was it beneath? or high aloft?
        What bard can answer this?   20

There fecundating powers were found,
        And mighty forces strove,—
A self-supporting mass beneath,
        And energy above.

Who knows, who ever told, from whence   25
        This great creation rose?
No gods had then been born,—then who
        Can e'er the truth disclose?

Whence sprang this world, and whether framed
        By hand divine or no,—   30
Its lord in heaven alone can tell,—
        If even He can show.

The Origin of All Things. Translated by J. Muir.
1. **Naught nor Aught;** that is, neither the Non-Existent nor the Existent.

The Kena–Upanishad

In later periods a large literature of commentary on the Vedic hymns and prayers was developed by learned priests. In the *Brahmanas* these explanations concern myths and points of ritual, but in the magnificent *Upanishads* they take the more general form of philosophical speculation and embody the Brahman mysticism that is the climax of Hindu thought. They were intended to guide the meditations of the Hindu hermits on the meaning of the Over-Spirit and the way to final reunion with it.

The term *Upanishad* means "sitting close," as their wisdom was traditionally thought to be communicated by a teacher to a pious student who sat close beside him. Though the names of many teachers are associated with the *Upanishads,* nothing is definitely known about their authors. The most vigorous and original of the nearly 250 surviving belong to the eighth through sixth centuries B.C.

The *Talavakâra-Upanishad,* better known as the *Kena-Upanishad* from its first word, is one of the thirteen principal *Upanishads.* In it the teacher explains to the inquiring student in typically negative terms the indefinable nature of the great Spirit, "living in all that lives." Through mystical revelation man achieves union with the Spirit and "the conquest of death." But if man does not "find Truth," his spirit "sinks among fouler shapes" in degenerate incarnations and his illusory life is really a series of deaths. Communion with Spirit is attained through renouncing desire and embracing "austerity, self-control, and meditation" on the Vedas. In this fine specimen of the *Upanishads,* given here in its entirety, mystical speculation about the universe is characteristically presented in the metaphorical language of poetry.

At Whose Command?

(THE KENA-UPANISHAD)

I

SPEECH, eyes, ears, limbs, life, energy, come to my help. These books have Spirit for theme. I shall never deny Spirit, nor Spirit deny me. Let me be in union, communion with Spirit. When I am one with Spirit, may the laws these books proclaim live in me, may the laws live.

The enquirer asked: 'What has called my mind to the hunt? What has made my life begin? What wags in my tongue? What God has opened eye and ear?'

The teacher answered: 'It lives in all that lives,

At Whose Command? From *The Ten Principal Upanishads,* translated by Shree Purohit Swami and William Butler Yeats. By permission of The Macmillan Company, publishers.

hearing through the ear, thinking through the mind, speaking through the tongue, seeing through the eye. The wise man clings neither to this nor that, rises out of sense, attains immortal life.

'Eye, tongue, cannot approach it nor mind know; not knowing, we cannot satisfy enquiry. It lies beyond the known, beyond the unknown. We know through those who have preached it, have learnt it from tradition.

'That which makes the tongue speak, but needs no tongue to explain, that alone is Spirit; not what sets the world by the ears.

'That which makes the mind think, but needs no mind to think, that alone is Spirit; not what sets the world by the ears.

'That which makes the eye see, but needs no eye to see, that alone is Spirit; not what sets the world by the ears.

'That which makes the ear hear, but needs no ear to hear, that alone is Spirit; not what sets the world by the ears.

'That which makes life live, but needs no life to live, that alone is Spirit; not what sets the world by the ears.'

2

'If you think that you know much, you know little. If you think that you know It from study of your own mind or of nature, study again.'

The enquirer said: 'I do not think that I know much, I neither say that I know, nor say that I do not.'

The teacher answered: 'The man who claims that he knows, knows nothing; but he who claims nothing, knows.

'Who says that Spirit is not known, knows; who claims that he knows, knows nothing. The ignorant think that Spirit lies within knowledge, the wise man knows It beyond knowledge.

'Spirit is known through revelation. It leads to freedom. It leads to power. Revelation is the conquest of death.

'The living man who finds Spirit, finds Truth. But if he fail, he sinks among fouler shapes. The man who can see the same Spirit in every creature, clings neither to this nor that, attains immortal life.'

3

Once upon a time, Spirit planned that the gods might win a great victory. The gods grew boastful; though Spirit had planned their victory, they thought they had done it all.

Spirit saw their vanity and appeared. They could not understand; they said: 'Who is that mysterious Person?'

They said to Fire: 'Fire! Find out who is that mysterious Person.'

Fire ran to Spirit. Spirit asked what it was. Fire said: 'I am Fire; known to all.'

Spirit asked: 'What can you do?' Fire said: 'I can burn anything and everything in this world.'

'Burn it,' said Spirit, putting a straw on the ground. Fire threw itself upon the straw, but could not burn it. Then Fire ran to the gods in a hurry and confessed it could not find out who was that mysterious Person.

Then the gods asked Wind to find out who was that mysterious Person.

Wind ran to Spirit and Spirit asked what it was. Wind said: 'I am Wind; I am the King of the Air.'

Spirit asked: 'What can you do?' and Wind said: 'I can blow away anything and everything in this world.'

'Blow it away,' said Spirit, putting a straw on the ground. Wind threw itself upon the straw, but could not move it. Then Wind ran to the gods in a hurry and confessed it could not find out who was that mysterious Person.

Then the gods went to Light and asked it to find out who was that mysterious Person. Light ran towards Spirit, but Spirit disappeared upon the instant.

There appeared in the sky that pretty girl, the Goddess of Wisdom, snowy Himalaya's daughter. Light went to her and asked who was that mysterious Person.

4

The Goddess said: 'Spirit, through Spirit you attained your greatness. Praise the greatness of Spirit.' Then Light knew that the mysterious Person was none but Spirit.

That is how these gods—Fire, Wind, and Light—attained supremacy; they came nearest to Spirit and were the first to call that Person Spirit.

Light stands above Fire and Wind; because closer than they, it was the first to call that Person Spirit.

This is the moral of the tale. In the lightning, in the light of an eye, the light belongs to Spirit.

The power of the mind when it remembers and desires, when it thinks again and again, belongs to Spirit. Therefore let Mind meditate on Spirit.

Spirit is the good in all. It should be worshipped as the Good. He that knows it as the Good is esteemed by all.

You asked me about spiritual knowledge, I have explained it.

Austerity, self-control, meditation are the foundation of this knowledge; the Vedas are its house, truth its shrine.

He who knows this shall prevail against all evil, enjoy the Kingdom of Heaven, yes, for ever enjoy the blessed Kingdom of Heaven.

The Mahâbhârata

Dating from perhaps 1000 B.C., India's greatest folk epic, the *Mahâbhârata*, has been frequently edited and enlarged by later Brahman scholars, until it is now the longest poem in the world. Its 100,000 couplets abound in loosely connected stories and essays, such as the charming tale of Savitri, whose love for her husband was stronger than death. The central plot of the epic concerns a great struggle between two families of royal cousins for succession to the Kuru (or Bhârata) throne. Upon the death of old King Pandu his brother succeeded him, and the five sons of Pandu were driven into exile by the hundred sons of the new king. The third of Pandu's sons, Arjuna, became their leader (and the hero of the epic). When by a feat of marksmanship he won as his wife a beautiful princess, Draupadi, all five brothers married her.* After thirteen more years of banishment they returned to do battle with their usurping cousins and slew them with the aid of the god Krishna, the incarnation of Vishnu. The poem ends with their retirement into the forest as devout Hindus and their rise to heaven. Modern scholars believe that, like the Trojan War of the Greeks, this mythical struggle has some foundation in a protracted war between two rival kingdoms.

The most famous section of the *Mahâbhârata* is a philosophical dialogue between Arjuna and the god Krishna, his charioteer, which is often printed separately as 'The Bhagavad-Gita,'' or simply "The Gita" (The Song of the Holy One). The subject of this poetic essay is the Hindu reconciliation of work and necessary activity in this world with the idea that the world is a mere illusion to be ignored. With his forces arrayed for battle, Arjuna hesitates to begin the slaughter and wonders how he can escape the stigma of worldly desire if he goes through with it. Krishna reassures him with a long discourse in eighteen cantos in which he explains that a disinterested performance of duty in this world involves no desire and hence no sin. The *dharma* of a warrior requires that he fight and kill. Only this subtle interpretation of actions in terms of attitude and intention has made the Hindu able to carry on even essential business in the material world.

The Gita

THEN beholding [the two armies,] drawn up on the battlefield, ready to begin the fight. . . . Arjuna noticed fathers, grandfathers, uncles, cousins, sons, grandsons, teachers, friends;

Fathers-in-law and benefactors, arrayed on both sides. Arjuna then gazed at all those kinsmen before him.

And his heart melted with pity and sadly he spoke: 'O my Lord! When I see all these, my own people, thirsting for battle, 10

'My limbs fail me and my throat is parched, my body trembles and my hair stands on end.

'The bow Gāndeeva slips from my hand, and my skin burns. I cannot keep quiet, for my mind is in a tumult.

'The omens are adverse; what good can come from the slaughter of my people on this battlefield?

'Ah, my Lord! I crave not for victory, nor for kingdom, nor for any pleasure. What were a kingdom or happiness or life to me, 20

'When those for whose sake I desire these things stand here about to sacrifice their property and their lives. . . .

'Although these men, blinded by greed, see no guilt in destroying their kin, or fighting against their friends,

'Should not we, whose eyes are open, who consider it to be wrong to annihilate our house, turn away from so great a crime? . . .

'If, on the contrary, [my enemies,] with weapons 30 in their hands, should slay me, unarmed and unresisting, surely that would be better for my welfare!' . . .

Thereupon the Lord, with a gracious smile, addressed him who was so much depressed in the midst between the two armies.

Lord Shri Krishna said: 'Why grieve for those for whom no grief is due, and yet profess wisdom. The wise grieve neither for the dead nor for the living.

'There was never a time when I was not, nor thou, 40 nor these princes were not; there will never be a time when we shall cease to be.

'As the soul experiences in this body, infancy, youth and old age, so finally it passes into another. The wise have no delusion about this.

'Those external relations which bring cold and heat, pain and happiness, they come and go; they are not permanent. Endure them bravely, O Prince!

'The hero whose soul is unmoved by circumstance, who accepts pleasure and pain with equanimity, 50 only he is fit for immortality.

'That which is not, shall never be; that which is, shall never cease to be. . . .

'He who knows the Spirit as Indestructible, Immortal, Unborn, Always-the-Same, how should he kill or cause to be killed?

'As a man discards his threadbare robes and puts on new, so the Spirit throws off Its worn-out bodies and takes fresh ones. . . .

'Even if thou thinkest of It as constantly being 60 born, constantly dying; even then, O Mighty Man! thou still hast no cause to grieve.

---

* Unlike polygamy, polyandry was uncommon among the ancient Hindus, but is vigorously defended in this case by the author of the epic.

The Gita.⁸ From *The Geeta*, translated by Shree Purohit Swami. Reprinted by permission of Faber and Faber Ltd.

'For death is as sure for that which is born, as birth is for that which is dead. Therefore grieve not for what is inevitable.

'The end and beginning of beings are unknown. We see only the intervening formations. Then what cause is there for grief? . . .

'Thou must look at thy duty. Nothing can be more welcome to a soldier than a righteous war. Therefore to waver in thy resolve is unworthy, O Arjuna!

10 'Blessed are the soldiers who find their opportunity. This opportunity has opened. for thee the gates of heaven. . . .

'If killed, thou shalt attain Heaven; if victorious, enjoy the kingdom of earth. Therefore arise, and fight.

'Look upon pleasure and pain, victory and defeat, with an equal eye. Make ready for the combat, and thou shalt commit no sin.

'I have told thee the philosophy of Knowledge. Now listen! and I will explain the philosophy of Ac-
20 tion, by means of which, O Arjuna thou shalt break through the bondage of all action . . .

'Thou hast only the right to work; but none to the fruit thereof. Let not then the fruit of thy action be thy motive; nor yet be thou enamored of inaction.

'Perform all thy actions with mind concentrated on the Divine, renouncing attachment and looking upon success and failure with an equal eye. . . .

'Physical action is far inferior to an intellect concentrated on the Divine. Have recourse then to the
30 Pure Intelligence. It is only the petty-minded who work for reward.

'When a man attains to Pure Reason, he renounces in this world the results of good and evil alike. Cling thou to Right Action. Spirituality is the real art of living.

'The sages guided by Pure Intellect renounce the fruit of action; and, freed from the chains of rebirth, they reach the highest bliss. . . .

'No man can attain freedom from activity by re-
40 fraining from action; nor can he reach perfection by merely refusing to act. . . .

'Do thy duty as prescribed; for action for duty's sake is superior to inaction. Even the maintenance of the body would be impossible if man remained inactive.

'In this world people are fettered by action, unless it is performed as a sacrifice. Therefore, O Arjuna! let thy acts be done without attachment, as sacrifice only. . . .

50 'There is nothing in this universe, O Arjuna! that I am compelled to do; nor anything for Me to attain; yet I am persistently active.

'For were I not to act without ceasing, O Prince! people would be glad to do likewise.

'And if I were to refrain from action, the human race would be ruined; I should lead the world to chaos, and destruction would follow. . . .

'The four divisions of society (the wise, the soldier, the merchant, the laborer) were created by Me, according to the natural distribution of Qualities and
60 instincts. I am the author of them. . . .

'In the light of this wisdom, our ancestors, who sought deliverance, performed their acts. Act thou also, as did our fathers of old. . . .

'What is action and what is inaction? . . .

'He who can see inaction in action, and action in inaction, is the wisest among men. . . .

'Having surrendered all claim to the results of his actions, always contented and independent, in reality he does nothing, even though he is apparently
70 acting.

'Expecting nothing, his mind and personality controlled, without greed, doing bodily actions only; though he acts, yet he remains untainted.

'Content with what comes to him without effort of his own, mounting above the pairs of opposites, free from envy, his mind balanced both in success and in failure, though he act, yet the consequences do not bind him.

'He who is without attachment, free, his mind cen-
80 tered in wisdom, his actions, being done as a sacrifice, leave no trace behind. . . .

'He who knows and lives in the Absolute remains unmoved and unperturbed; he is not elated by pleasure, or depressed by pain.

'He finds happiness in his own Self, and enjoys eternal bliss, whose heart does not yearn for the contacts of earth, and whose Self is one with the Everlasting.

'He who is happy within his Self, and has found
90 Its peace, and in whom the inner light shines, that sage attains Eternal Bliss and becomes the Spirit Itself. . . .

'Therefore, surrendering thy actions unto Me, thy thoughts concentrated on the Absolute, free from selfishness and without anticipation of reward, with mind devoid of excitement, begin thou to fight.'

The Tale of Savitri

IN the country of fair Madra lived a king in days of old,
Faithful to the holy Brahma, pure in heart and righteous-souled,

He was loved in town and country, in the court and hermit's den,
Sacrificer to the bright gods, helper to his brother men,

The Tale of Savitri. From *The Ramayana and the Mahabharata* translated by Romesh Dutt. (Everyman's Lib. Ed., E. P. Dutton & Co., Inc.) Reprinted by permission of A. C. Dutt, executor.

But the monarch, Aswapati, son or daughter had he
    none,   5
Old in years and sunk in anguish, and his days were
    almost done!

Vows he took and holy penance, and with pious
    rules conformed,
Spare in diet as *brahmachari* many sacred rites per-
    formed,

Sang the sacred hymn, *savitri*, to the gods oblations
    gave,
Through the lifelong day he fasted, uncomplaining,
    meek and brave!   10

Year by year he gathered virtue, rose in merit and
    in might,
Till the goddess of *savitri* smiled upon his sacred rite,

From the fire upon the altar which a holy radiance
    flung,
In the form of beauteous maiden, goddess of *savitri*
    sprung!

And she spake in gentle accents, blessed the monarch
    good and brave,   15
Blessed his rites and holy penance and a boon unto
    him gave:

"Penance and thy sacrifices can the Powers Immortal
    move,
And the pureness of thy conduct doth thy heart's
    affection prove,

Ask thy boon, king Aswapati, from creation's Ancient
    Sire,
True to virtue's sacred mandate speak thy inmost
    heart's desire."   20

"For an offspring brave and kingly," so the saintly
    king replied,
"Holy rites and sacrifices and this penance I have
    tried,

If these rites and sacrifices move thy favour and thy
    grace,
Grant me offspring, Prayer-Maiden, worthy of my
    noble race."

"Have thy object," spake the maiden, "Madra's pious-
    hearted king,   25
From Swaymbhu, Self-created, blessings unto thee
    I bring,

For He lists to mortal's prayer springing from a heart
    like thine,

8. *brahmachari*, those who have taken holy vows.

And He wills,—a noble daughter grace thy famed
    and royal line,

Aswapati, glad and grateful, take the blessing which
    I bring,
Part in joy and part in silence, bow unto Creation's
    King!"   30

Vanished then the Prayer-Maiden, and the king of
    noble fame,
Aswapati, Lord of coursers, to his royal city came,

Days of hope and nights of gladness Madra's happy
    monarch passed,
Till his queen of noble offspring gladsome promise
    gave at last!

As the moon each night increaseth chasing darksome
    nightly gloom,   35
Grew the unborn babe in splendour in its happy
    mother's womb,

And in fulness of the season came a girl with lotus-
    eye,
Father's hope and joy of mother, gift of kindly gods
    on high!

And the king performed its birth-rites with a glad
    and grateful mind,
And the people blessed the dear one with their wishes
    good and kind,   40

As *Savitri*, Prayer-Maiden, had the beauteous off-
    spring given,
Brahmans named the child *Savitri*, holy gift of boun-
    teous Heaven!

Grew the child in brighter beauty like a goddess from
    above,
And each passing season added fresher sweetness,
    deeper love,

Came with youth its lovelier graces, as the buds their
    leaves unfold,   45
Slender waist and rounded bosom, image as of bur-
    nished gold,

Deva-Kanya! born a goddess, so they said in all the
    land,
Princely suitors struck with splendour ventured not
    to seek her hand.

Once upon a time it happened on a bright and festive
    day,
Fresh from bath the beauteous maiden to the altar
    came to pray,   50

And with cakes and pure libations duly fed the
Sacred Flame,
Then like Sri in heavenly radiance to her royal father
came.

And she bowed to him in silence, sacred flowers beside him laid,
And her hands she folded meekly, sweetly her obeisance made,

With a father's pride, upon her gazed the ruler of the
land,   55
But a strain of sadness lingered, for no suitor claimed
her hand.

"Daughter," whispered Aswapati, "now, methinks,
the time is come,
Thou shouldst choose a princely suitor, grace a royal
husband's home,

Choose thyself a noble husband worthy of thy noble
hand,
Choose a true and upright monarch, pride and glory
of his land,   60

As thou choosest, gentle daughter, in thy loving
heart's desire,
Blessing and his free permission will bestow thy
happy sire.

For our sacred *sastras* sanction, holy Brahmans oft
relate,
That the duty-loving father sees his girl in wedded
state,

That the duty-loving husband watches o'er his consort's ways,   65
That the duty-loving offspring tends his mother's
widowed days,

Therefore choose a loving husband, daughter of my
house and love,
So thy father earn no censure or from men or gods
above."

Fair Savitri bowed unto him and for parting blessings prayed,
Then she left her father's palace and in distant regions strayed,   70

With her guard and aged courtiers whom her watchful father sent,
Mounted on her golden chariot unto sylvan woodlands went.

Far in pleasant woods and jungle wandered she from
day to day,
Unto *asrams,* hermitages, pious-hearted held her
way,

Oft she stayed in holy *tirthas* washed by sacred
limpid streams,   75
Food she gave unto the hungry, wealth beyond their
fondest dreams.

Many days and months are over, and it once did so
befall,
When the king and *rishi* Narad sat within the royal
hall,

From her journeys near and distant and from places
known to fame,
Fair Savitri with the courtiers to her father's palace
came,   80

Came and saw her royal father, *rishi* Narad by his
seat,
Bent her head in salutation, bowed unto their holy
feet.

II. THE FATED BRIDEGROOM

"Whence comes she," so Narad questioned, "whither
was Savitri led,
Wherefore to a happy husband hath Savitri not been
wed?"

"Nay, to choose her lord and husband," so the virtuous monarch said,   85
"Fair Savitri long hath wandered and in holy *tirthas*
stayed,

Maiden! speak unto the *rishi,* and thy choice and
secret tell,"
Then a blush suffused her forehead, soft and slow her
accents fell!

"Listen, father! Salwa's monarch was of old a king of
might,
Righteous-hearted Dyumat-sena, feeble now and
void of sight,   90

Foemen robbed him of his kingdom when in age he
lost his sight,
And from town and spacious empire was the monarch forced to flight,

With his queen and with his infant did the feeble
monarch stray,
And the jungle was his palace, darksome was his
weary way,

52. Sri, goddess of beauty and wealth.   63. *sastras,* scriptures.

75. *tirthas,* shrines.   78. *rishi,* holy man.

This Hindu-style painting of the 18th century now in the British Museum is called "Girl Walking in a Starry Night."

Holy vows assumed the monarch and in penance
    passed his life,   95
In the wild woods nursed his infant and with wild
    fruits fed his wife,

Years have gone in rigid penance, and that child is
    now a youth,
Him I choose my lord and husband, Satyavan, the
    Soul of Truth!"

Thoughtful was the *rishi* Narad, doleful were the
    words he said:
"Sad disaster waits Savitri if this royal youth she
    wed,   100

Truth-beloving is' her father, truthful is the royal
    dame,
Truth and virtue rule his actions, Satyavan his sacred
    name,

Steeds he loved in days of boyhood and to paint them
    was his joy,

Hence they called him young Chitraswa, art-belov-
    ing gallant boy,

But O pious-hearted monarch! fair Savitri hath in
    sooth   105
Courted Fate and sad disaster in that noble gallant
    youth!"

"Tell me," questioned Aswapati, "for I may not guess
    thy thought,
Wherefore is my daughter's action with a sad disaster
    fraught,

Is the youth of noble lustre, gifted in the gifts of art,
Blest with wisdom and with prowess, patient in his
    dauntless heart?"   110

"Surya's lustre in his shineth," so the *rishi* Narad said,
"Brihaspati's wisdom dwelleth in the youthful
    prince's head,

Like Mahendra in his prowess, and in patience like
    the Earth,
Yet O king! sad disaster marks the gentle youth from
    birth!"

"Tell me, *rishi*, then thy reason," so anxious monarch
    cried,   115
"Why to youth so great and gifted may this maid be
    not allied,

Is he princely in his bounty, gentle-hearted in his
    grace,
Duly versed in sacred knowledge, fair in mind and
    fair in face?"

"Free in gifts like Rantideva," so the holy *rishi* said,
"Versed in lore like monarch Sivi who all ancient
    monarchs led,   120

Like Yayati open-hearted and like Chandra in his
    grace,
Like the handsome heavenly Asvins fair and radiant
    in his face,

Meek and graced with patient virtue he controls his
    noble mind,
Modest in his kindly actions, true to friends and ever
    kind,

And the hermits of the forest praise him for his right-
    eous truth,   125
Nathless, king, thy daughter may not wed this noble-
    hearted youth!"

"Tell me, *rishi*," said the monarch, "for thy sense
    from me is hid,

Has this prince some fatal blemish, wherefore is this
    match forbid?"

"Fatal fault!" exclaimed the *rishi,* "fault that wipeth
    all his grace,
Fault that human power nor effort, rite nor penance
    can efface,   130

Fatal fault or destined sorrow! for it is decreed on
    high,
On this day, a twelve-month later, this ill-fated
    prince will die!"

Shook the startled king in terror and in fear and
    trembling cried:
"Unto short-lived, fated bridegroom ne'er my child
    shall be allied,

Come, Savitri, dear-loved maiden, choose another
    happier lord,   135
Rishi Narad speaketh wisdom, list unto his holy
    word!

Every grace and every virtue is effaced by cruel
    Fate,
On this day, a twelve-month later, leaves the prince
    his mortal state!"

"Father!" answered thus the maiden, soft and sad her
    accents fell,
"I have heard thy honoured mandate, holy Narad
    counsels well,   140

Pardon witless maiden's fancy, but beneath the eye
    of Heaven,
Only once a maiden chooseth, twice her troth may
    not be given,

Long his life or be it narrow, and his virtues great or
    none,
Satyavan is still my husband, he my heart and troth
    hath won,

What a maiden's heart hath chosen that a maiden's
    lips confess,   145
True to him thy poor Savitri goes into the wilder-
    ness!"

"Monarch!" uttered then the *rishi,* "fixed is she in
    mind and heart,
From her troth the true Savitri never, never will de-
    part,

More than mortal's share of virtue unto Satyavan is
    given,
Let the true maid wed her chosen, leave the rest to
    gracious Heaven!"   150

"*Rishi* and preceptor holy!" so the weeping monarch
    prayed,
"Heaven avert all future evils, and thy mandate is
    obeyed!"

Narad wished him joy and gladness, blessed the lov-
    ing youth and maid,
Forest hermits on their wedding every fervent bless-
    ing laid.

III. OVERTAKEN BY FATE

Twelve-month in the darksome forest by her true and
    chosen lord,   155
Sweet Savitri served his parents by her thought and
    deed and word,

Bark of tree supplied her garments draped upon her
    bosom fair,
Or the red cloth as in *asrams* holy women love to
    wear.

And the aged queen she tended with a fond and filial
    pride,
Served the old and sightless monarch like a daughter
    by his side,   160

And with love and gentle sweetness pleased her
    husband and her lord,
But in secret, night and morning, pondered still on
    Narad's word!

Nearer came the fatal morning by the holy Narad
    told,
Fair Savitri reckoned daily and her heart was still
    and cold,

Three short days remaining only! and she took a vow
    severe   165
Of *triratra,* three nights' penance, holy fasts and vigils
    drear.

Of Savitri's rigid penance heard the king with anxious
    woe,
Spake to her in loving accents, so the vow she might
    forgo:

"Hard the penance, gentle daughter, and thy wom-
    an's limbs are frail,
After three nights' fasts and vigils sure thy tender
    health may fail,"   170

"Be not anxious, loving father," meekly this Savitri
    prayed,
"Penance I have undertaken, will unto the gods be
    made."

Much misdoubting then the monarch gave his sad
    and slow assent,

Pale with fast and unseen tear-drops, lonesome nights
    Savitri spent.

Nearer came the fatal morning, and to-morrow he
    shall die,   175
Dark, lone hours of nightly silence! Tearless, sleepless
    is her eye!

"Dawns that dread and fated morning!" said Savitri,
    bloodless, brave,
Prayed her fervent prayers in silence, to the Fire
    oblations gave,

Bowed unto the forest Brahmans, to the parents kind
    and good,
Joined her hands in salutation and in reverent silence
    stood.   180

With the usual morning blessing, "Widow may'st
    thou never be,"
Anchorites and aged Brahmans blessed Savitri fer-
    vently,

O! that blessing fell upon her like the rain on thirsty
    air,
Struggling hope inspired her bosom as she drank
    those accents fair,

But returned the dark remembrance of the *rishi* Na-
    rad's word,   185
Pale she watched the creeping sunbeams, mused
    upon her fated lord!

"Daughter, now thy fast is over," so the loving par-
    ents said,
"Take thy diet after penance, for thy morning prayers
    are prayed,"

"Pardon, father," said Savitri, "let this other day be
    done,"
Unshed tear-drops filled her eyelids, glistened in the
    morning sun!   190

Satyavan, sedate and stately, ponderous axe on
    shoulder hung,
For the distant darksome jungle issued forth serene
    and strong,

But unto him came Savitri and in sweetest accents
    prayed,
As upon his manly bosom gently she her forehead
    laid:

"Long I wished to see the jungle where steals not
    the solar ray,   195
Take me to the darksome forest, husband, let me go
    to-day!"

"Come not, love," he sweetly answered with a loving
    husband's care,
"Thou art all unused to labour, forest paths thou
    may'st not dare,

And with recent fasts and vigils pale and bloodless
    is thy face,
And thy steps are weak and feeble, jungle paths thou
    may'st not trace."   200

"Fasts and vigils make me stronger," said the wife
    with wifely pride,
"Toil I shall not feel nor languor when my lord is by
    my side,

For I feel a woman's longing with my lord to trace
    the way,
Grant me, husband ever gracious, with thee let me go
    to-day!"

Answered then the loving husband, as his hands in
    hers he wove,   205
"Ask permission from my parents in the trackless
    woods to rove,"

Then Savitri to the monarch urged her longing
    strange request,
After duteous salutation thus her humble prayer ad-
    drest.

"To the jungle goes my husband, fuel and the fruit
    to seek,
I would follow if my mother and my loving father
    speak,   210

Twelve-month from this narrow *asram* hath Savitri
    stepped nor strayed,
In this cottage true and faithful ever hath Savitri
    stayed,

For the sacrificial fuel wends my lord his lonesome
    way,
Please my kind and loving parents, I would follow
    him to-day."

"Never since her wedding morning," so the loving
    king replied,   215
"Wish or thought Savitri whispered, for a boon or
    object sighed,

Daughter, thy request is granted, safely in the forest
    roam,
Safely with thy lord and husband seek again thy
    cottage home."

Bowing to her loving parents did the fair Savitri
    part,

Smile upon her pallid features, anguish in her inmost
    heart,   220

Round her sylvan greenwoods blossomed 'neath a
    cloudless Indian sky,
Flocks of pea-fowls gorgeous plumaged flew before
    her wondering eye,

Woodland rills and crystal nullahs gently roll'd o'er
    rocky bed,
Flower-decked hills in dewy brightness towering glit-
    tered overhead,

Birds of song and beauteous feather trilled a note in
    every grove,   225
Sweeter accents fell upon her, from her husband's
    lips of love!

Still with thoughtful eye Savitri watched her dear
    and fated lord,
Flail of grief was in her bosom but her pale lips
    shaped no word,

And she listened to her husband still on anxious
    thought intent,
Cleft in two her throbbing bosom as in silence still
    she went!   230

Gaily with the gathered wild-fruits did the prince his
    basket fill,
Hewed the interlacéd branches with his might and
    practised skill,

Till the drops stood on his forehead, weary was his
    aching head,
Faint he came unto Savitri and in faltering accents
    said:

"Cruel ache is on my forehead, fond and ever faith-
    ful wife,   235
And I feel a hundred needles pierce me and torment
    my life,

And my feeble footsteps falter and my senses seem
    to reel,
Fain would I beside thee linger for a sleep doth o'er
    me steal."

With a wild and speechless terror pale Savitri held
    her lord,
On her lap his head she rested as she laid him on the
    sward,   240

Narad's fatal words remembered as she watched her
    husband's head,
Burning lip and pallid forehead and the dark and
    creeping shade,

Clasped him in her beating bosom, kissed his lips
    with panting breath,
Darker grew the lonesome forest, and he slept the
    sleep of death!

IV. TRIUMPH OVER FATE

In the bosom of the shadows rose a Vision dark and
    dread,   245
Shape of gloom in inky garment and a crown was on
    his head,

Gleaming Form of sable splendour, blood-red was
    his sparkling eye,
And a fatal noose he carried, grim and godlike, dark
    and high!

And he stood in solemn silence, looked in silence on
    the dead,
And Savitri on the greensward gently placed her hus-
    band's head,   250

And a tremor shook Savitri, but a woman's love is
    strong,
With her hands upon her bosom thus she spake with
    quivering tongue:

"More than mortal is thy glory! If a radiant god thou
    be,
Tell me what bright name thou bearest, what thy
    message unto me."

"Know me," thus responded Yama, "mighty monarch
    of the dead,   255
Mortals leaving earthly mansion to my darksome
    realms are led,

Since with woman's full affection thou hast loved thy
    husband dear,
Hence before thee, faithful woman, Yama doth in
    form appear,

But his days and loves are ended, and he leaves his
    faithful wife,
In this noose I bind and carry spark of his immortal
    life,   260

Virtue graced his life and action, spotless was his
    princely heart,
Hence for him I came in person, princess, let thy
    husband part."

Yama from the prince's body, pale and bloodless,
    cold and dumb,
Drew the vital spark, *purusha*, smaller than the hu-
    man thumb,

In his noose the spark he fastened, silent went his
    darksome way,   265

Left the body shorn of lustre to its rigid cold decay,

Southward went the dark-hued Yama with the
youth's immortal life,
And, for woman's love abideth, followed still the
faithful wife.

"Turn, Savitri," outspake Yama, "for thy husband
loved and lost,
Do the rites due unto mortals by their Fate predestined crost,   270

For thy wifely duty ceases, follow not in fruitless
woe,
And no farther living creature may with monarch
Yama go!"

"But I may not choose but follow where thou takest
my husband's life,
For Eternal Law divides not loving man and faithful
wife,

For a woman's true affection, for a woman's sacred
woe,   275
Grant me in thy godlike mercy farther still with him
I go!

Fourfold are our human duties: first to study holy
lore,
Then to live as good householders, feed the hungry
at our door,

Then to pass our days in penance, last to fix our
thoughts above,
But the final goal of virtue, it is Truth and deathless
Love!"   280

"True and holy are thy precepts," listening Yama
made reply,
"And they fill my heart with gladness and with pious
purpose high,

I would bless thee, fair Savitri, but the dead come
not to life,
Ask for other boon and blessing, faithful, true and
virtuous wife!"

"Since you so permit me, Yama," so the good Savitri
said,   285
"For my husband's banished father let my dearest
suit be made,

Sightless in the darksome forest dwells the monarch
faint and weak,
Grant him sight and grant him vigour, Yama, in thy
mercy speak!"

"Duteous daughter," Yama answered, "be thy pious
wishes given,
And his eyes shall be restoréd to the cheerful light
of heaven,   290

Turn, Savitri, faint and weary, follow not in fruitless
woe,
And no farther living creature may with monarch
Yama go!"

"Faint nor weary is Savitri," so the noble princess
said,
"Since she waits upon her husband, gracious Monarch of the dead,

What befalls the wedded husband still befalls the
faithful wife,   295
Where he leads she ever follows, be it death or be it
life!

And our sacred writ ordaineth and our pious *rishis*
sing,
Transient meeting with the holy doth its countless
blessings bring,

Longer friendship with the holy purifies the mortal
birth,
Lasting union with the holy is the bright sky on the
earth,   300

Union with the pure and holy is immortal heavenly
life,
For Eternal Law divides not loving man and faithful wife!"

"Blessed are thy words," said Yama, "blessed is thy
pious thought,
With a higher purer wisdom are thy holy lessons
fraught,

I would bless thee, fair Savitri, but the dead come
not to life,   305
Ask for other boon and blessing, faithful, true and
virtuous wife!"

"Since you so permit me, Yama," so the good Savitri
said,
"Once more for my husband's father be my supplication made,

Lost his kingdom, in the forest dwells the monarch
faint and weak,
Grant him back his wealth and kingdom, Yama, in
thy mercy speak!"   310

"Loving daughter," Yama answered, "wealth and
kingdom I bestow,

Turn, Savitri, living mortal may not with King Yama
    go!"

Still Savitri, meek and faithful, followed her de-
    parted lord,
Yama still with higher wisdom listened to her saintly
    word,

And the Sable King was vanquished, and he turned
    on her again,   315
And his words fell on Savitri like the cooling summer
    rain,

"Noble woman, speak thy wishes, name thy boon
    and purpose high,
What the pious mortal asketh gods in heaven may not
    deny!"

"Thou hast," so Savitri answered, "granted father's
    realm and might,
To his vain and sightless eyeballs hast restored their
    blesséd sight,   320

Grant him that the line of monarchs may not all un-
    timely end,
Satyavan may see his kingdom to his royal sons de-
    scend!"

"Have thy object," answered Yama, "and thy lord
    shall live again,
He shall live to be a father, and his children too shall
    reign,

For a woman's troth abideth longer than the fleeting
    breath,   325
And a woman's love abideth higher than the doom
    of Death!"

V. RETURN HOME

Vanished then the Sable Monarch, and Savitri held
    her way
Where in dense and darksome forest still her husband
    lifeless lay,

And she sat upon the greensward by the cold un-
    conscious dead,
On her lap with deeper kindness placed her consort's
    lifeless head,   330

And that touch of true affection thrilled him back to
    waking life,
As returned from distant regions gazed the prince
    upon his wife,

"Have I lain too long and slumbered, sweet Savitri,
    faithful spouse,
But I dreamt a Sable Person took me in a fatal
    noose!"

A Rajput Indian painting of two lovers on a terrace.

"Pillowed on this lap," she answered, "long upon the
    earth you lay,   335
And the Sable Person, husband, he hath come and
    passed away,

Rise and leave this darksome forest if thou feelest
    light and strong,
For the night is on the jungle and our way is dark
    and long."

Rising as from happy slumber looked the young
    prince on all around,
Saw the wide-extending jungle mantling all the dark-
    some ground,   340

"Yes," he said, "I now remember, ever loving faithful
    dame,
We in search of fruit and fuel to this lonesome forest
    came,

As I hewed the gnarléd branches, cruel anguish filled
    my brain,

And I laid me on the greensward with a throbbing
    piercing pain,

Pillowed on thy gentle bosom, solaced by thy gentle
    love,   345
I was soothed, and drowsy slumber fell on me from
    skies above.

All was dark and then I witnessed, was it but a fleet-
    ing dream,
God or Vision, dark and dreadful, in the deepening
    shadows gleam,

Was this dream my fair Savitri, dost thou of this
    Vision know,
Tell me, for before my eyesight still the Vision seems
    to glow!"   350

"Darkness thickens," said Savitri, "and the evening
    waxeth late,
When the morrow's light returneth I shall all these
    scenes narrate,

Now arise, for darkness gathers, deeper grows the
    gloomy night,
And thy loving anxious parents trembling wait thy
    welcome sight,

Hark the rangers of the forest! how their voices strike
    the ear,   355
Prowlers of the darksome jungle! how they fill my
    breast with fear!

Forest-fire is raging yonder, for I see a distant gleam,
And the rising evening breezes help the red and
    radiant beam,

Let me fetch a burning faggot and prepare a friendly
    light,
With these fallen withered branches chase the shad-
    ows of the night,   360

And if feeble still thy footsteps,—long and weary is
    our way,—
By the fire repose, my husband, and return by light
    of day."

"For my parents, fondly anxious," Satyavan thus
    made reply,
"Pains my heart and yearns my bosom, let us to
    their cottage hie,   364

When I tarried in the jungle or by day or dewy eve,
Searching in the hermitages often did my parents
    grieve,

And with father's soft reproaches and with mother's
    loving fears,

Chid me for my tardy footsteps, dewed me with their
    gentle tears,

Think then of my father's sorrow, of my mother's
    woeful plight,
If afar in wood and jungle pass we now the livelong
    night,   370

Wife beloved, I may not fathom what mishap or load
    of care,
Unknown dangers, unseen sorrows, even now my
    parents share!"

Gentle drops of filial sorrow trickled down his manly
    eye,
Fond Savitri sweetly speaking softly wiped the tear-
    drops dry:

"Trust me, husband, if Savitri hath been faithful in
    her love,   375
If she hath with pious offerings served the righteous
    gods above,

If she hath a sister's kindness unto brother men per-
    formed,
If she hath in speech and action unto holy truth con-
    formed,

Unknown blessings, mighty gladness, trust thy ever
    faithful wife,
And not sorrows or disasters wait this eve our parents'
    life!"   380

Then she rose and tied her tresses, gently helped her
    lord to rise,
Walked with him the pathless jungle, looked with
    love into his eyes,

On her neck his clasping left arm sweetly winds in
    soft embrace,
Round his waist Savitri's right arm doth as sweetly
    interlace,

Thus they walked the darksome jungle, silent stars
    looked from above,   385
And the hushed and throbbing midnight watched
    Savitri's deathless love.

Kalidasa

Flourished fifth or sixth century A.D.

The work of Kalidasa reminds us that all the pessimism and asceticism in the Hindu's view of life could not stifle his natural longing for worldly beauty and human love. India's greatest poet wrote persistently of the happiness of love and marriage. As a devout Hindu, he chose his themes from ancient religious stories and wove into them the orthodox Brahman views. But we remember from his plays and epics especially the sympathetic pictures of women in love, the tender portraits of children, the revealing descriptions of nature in its countless phases.

The life of Kalidasa is lost in legend. A picturesque tradition makes him the orphaned son of a Brahman, who was reared as a humble ox-driver. When a certain intellectual princess rejected all her suitors as unequal to herself in learning, they sought revenge by representing the intelligent ox-driver as a great scholar. The princess, discovering the deception after their marriage, was angered, but the gods miraculously gave Kalidasa both erudition and poetic skill, and he became one of "The Nine Gems" at the court of King Vikramáditya in Ujjain. Later, because of a curse, he was murdered by a woman who was jealous of his fame. But the truth is that we know nothing for sure about Kalidasa except what his work suggests, and cannot even date his life within a century.

Kalidasa, as the greatest playwright of the Orient, has often been called "the Hindu Shakespeare"; and the parallel goes far. Like Shakespeare he was equally at home in narrative, lyric, and dramatic poetry. Two of his poems, *The Dynasty of Raghu* and *The Birth of the War-God*, are long epics of art based on ancient myths from the *Râmâyana* and other sources. *The Seasons* is a cycle of six lyrics describing the sentiments aroused in two lovers by each of nature's seasons. Of his three extant plays, the earliest, *Malavika and Agnimitra*, is a light comedy of court intrigue, *Urvashi* is a poetic spectacle play, and *Shakuntala* is a romantic love story. Kalidasa did not write tragedies, because tragedy was forbidden in the Hindu theater. To the Hindu, defeat and death in this world could have no tragic meaning. In the plan of his dramas, too, Kalidasa reminds us of Shakespeare, in his combination of serious and comic elements within the same play, especially in his use of clowns, and in his frequent interpolation of lyric verse in the midst of dramatic scenes.

Since its first English translation in 1789, *Shakuntala* has been for most Westerners the door to Indian literature. Its fantastic love theme attracted the German poet Goethe, who borrowed from the play for his *Faust*. The Concord school of American writers read it along with more philosophical Hindu literature. And Goldmark's overture to *Shakuntala* has long been a standard concert selection. Western acclaim of the play supports the Hindu critics, who consider it their greatest drama.

Since the plot of *Shakuntala* was taken from the *Mahâbhârata* and was familiar to Kalidasa's audience, he disposes of a good deal of it through a series of prologues, in which minor characters prepare us, a little clumsily, for the big scenes. In thus minimizing the plot he makes the central situation of a husband's failure to recognize his wife seem less absurd to us. The situation is made more credible, too, by Kalidasa's invention of the curse of Durvasas, which freed the husband from his moral responsibility in the original tale. To the simple story from the epic, Kalidasa adds a message of his own: the physical desire in the first meeting of the lovers must be trans-

formed through separation into the higher union of souls. The purifying agent is the child, who brings his parents together in a new-found happiness on a plane of lofty detachment, symbolized by the beautiful hill of Hemakûta. The whole play is enveloped in a magical unreality which makes the air chariot in the last act seem quite plausible. The characters are romantic types of dashing prince and faithful wife, and the exquisite verse of the original stamps it as a sophisticated rendering of a folk story.

Shakuntala

DRAMATIS PERSONÆ

KING DUSHYANTA.
BHARATA, *nicknamed* All-tamer, *his son.*
MADHAVYA, *a clown, his companion.*
His charioteer.
RAIVATAKA, *a door-keeper.*
BHADRASENA, *a general.*
KARABHAKA, *a servant.*
PARVATAYANA, *a chamberlain.*
SOMARATA, *a chaplain.*

KANVA, *hermit-father*
SHARNGARAVA ⎫
SHARADVATA ⎬ *his pupils.*
HARITA ⎭
DURVASAS, *an irascible sage.*

The chief of police.
SUCHAKA ⎫
⎬ *policemen.*
JANUKA ⎭
A fisherman.

SHAKUNTALA, *foster-child of Kanva.*
ANUSUYA ⎫
⎬ *her friends.*
PRIYAMVADA ⎭
GAUTAMI, *hermit-mother.*

KASHYAPA, *father of the gods.*
ADITI, *mother of the gods.*
MATALI, *charioteer of heaven's king.*
GALAVA, *a pupil in heaven.*
MISHRAKESHI, *a heavenly nymph.*

Stage-director and actress (in the prologue), hermits and hermit-women, two court poets, palace attendants, invisible fairies.

The first four acts pass in Kanva's forest hermitage; acts five and six in the king's palace; act

Shakuntala. Taken from *Shakuntala: A Play; and Other Works,* by Kalidasa, translated by Professor A. W. Ryder, published by E. P. Dutton & Co., Inc. (Everyman's Library), New York. Reprinted by permission of E. P. Dutton & Co. and J. M. Dent and Sons, Ltd.

seven on a heavenly mountain. The time is perhaps seven years.

ACT I

The Hunt

(Enter, in a chariot, pursuing a deer, KING DU-SHYANTA, bow and arrow in hand; and a charioteer.)

CHARIOTEER.

Your Majesty,
    I see you hunt the spotted deer
      With shafts to end his race,
    As though God Shiva should appear
      In his immortal chase.

KING. Charioteer, the deer has led us a long chase. And even now

    His neck in beauty bends
    As backward looks he sends
10   At my pursuing car
    That threatens death from far.
    Fear shrinks to half the body small;
    See how he fears the arrow's fall!

    The path he takes is strewed
    With blades of grass half-chewed
    From jaws wide with the stress
    Of fevered weariness.
    He leaps so often and so high,
    He does not seem to run, but fly.

20 Pursue as I may, I can hardly keep him in sight.
CHARIOTEER. Your Majesty, I have been holding the horses back because the ground was rough. This checked us and gave the deer a lead. Now we are on level ground, and you will easily overtake him.
KING. Then let the reins hang loose.
CHARIOTEER. Yes, your Majesty. Look, your Majesty!

    The lines hang loose; the steeds unreined
      Dart forward with a will.
30   Their ears are pricked; their necks are strained
      Their plumes lie straight and still.
    They leave the rising dust behind;
    They seem to float upon the wind.

KING *(joyfully)*. See! The horses are gaining on the deer.

    As onward and onward the chariot flies,
    The small flashes large to my dizzy eyes.
    What is cleft in twain, seems to blur and mate;
    What is crooked in nature, seems to be straight.

40   Things at my side in an instant appear
    Distant, and things in the distance, near.

A VOICE BEHIND THE SCENES. O King, this deer belongs to the hermitage, and must not be killed.
CHARIOTEER *(listening and looking)*. Your Majesty, here are two hermits, come to save the deer at the moment when your arrow was about to fall.
KING *(hastily)*. Stop the chariot.
CHARIOTEER. Yes, your Majesty. *(He does so. Enter a hermit with his pupil.)*
HERMIT *(lifting his hand)*. O King, this deer belongs to the hermitage.

50   Why should his tender form expire,
    As blossoms perish in the fire?
    How could that gentle life endure
    The deadly arrow, sharp and sure?

    Restore your arrow to the quiver;
      To you were weapons lent
    The broken-hearted to deliver,
      Not strike the innocent.

KING *(bowing low)*. It is done. *(He does so.)*
HERMIT *(joyfully)*. A deed worthy of you, scion of Puru's race, and shining example of kings. May you beget a son to rule earth and heaven.
KING *(bowing low)*. I am thankful for a Brahman's blessing.
THE TWO HERMITS. O King, we are on our way to gather firewood. Here, along the bank of the Malini, you may see the hermitage of Father Kanva, over which Shakuntala presides, so to speak, as guardian deity. Unless other deities prevent, pray enter here and receive a welcome. Besides,

70   Beholding pious hermit-rites
      Preserved from fearful harm,
    Perceive the profit of the scars
      On your protecting arm.

KING. Is the hermit father there?
THE TWO HERMITS. No, he has left his daughter to welcome guests, and has just gone to Somatirtha, to avert an evil fate that threatens her.
KING. Well, I will see her. She shall feel my devotion, and report it to the sage.
80 THE TWO HERMITS. Then we will go on our way. *(Exit hermit with pupil.)*
KING. Charioteer, drive on. A sight of the pious hermitage will purify us.
CHARIOTEER. Yes, your Majesty. *(He counterfeits motion again.)*
KING *(looking about)*. One would know, without being told, that this is the precinct of a pious grove.
CHARIOTEER. How so?
KING. Do you not see? Why, here

---

4. **God Shiva**, third deity of the Hindu triad, a five-headed god of destruction sometimes shown armed with a bow.

73–74. **Perceive . . . arm.** The king received the scars from his bow, bent in protection of the hermits' rites.

Are rice-grains, dropped from bills of parrot chicks
Beneath the trees; and pounding-stones where sticks
A little almond-oil; and trustful deer
That do not run away as we draw near;
And river-paths that are besprinkled yet
From trickling hermit-garments, clean and wet.

Besides,

The roots of trees are washed by many a stream
That breezes ruffle; and the flowers' red gleam
10 Is dimmed by pious smoke; and fearless fawns
Move softly on the close-cropped forest lawns.

CHARIOTEER. It is all true.
KING (*after a little*). We must not disturb the hermitage. Stop here while I dismount.
CHARIOTEER. I am holding the reins. Dismount, your Majesty.
KING (*dismounts and looks at himself*). One should wear modest garments on entering a hermitage. Take these jewels and the bow. (*He gives*
20 *them to the charioteer.*) Before I return from my visit to the hermits, have the horses' backs wet down.
CHARIOTEER. Yes, your Majesty. (*Exit.*)
KING (*walking and looking about*). The hermitage! Well, I will enter. (*As he does so, he feels a throbbing in his arm.*)

A tranquil spot! Why should I thrill?
 Love cannot enter there—
Yet to inevitable things
 Doors open everywhere.

30 A VOICE BEHIND THE SCENES. This way, girls!
KING (*listening*). I think I hear some one to the right of the grove. I must find out. (*He walks and looks about.*) Ah, here are hermit-girls, with watering-pots just big enough for them to handle. They are coming in this direction to water the young trees. They are charming!

The city maids, for all their pains,
 Seem not so sweet and good;
Our garden blossoms yield to these
40 Flower-children of the wood.

I will draw back into the shade and wait for them. (*He stands, gazing toward them. Enter* SHAKUNTALA, *and her two friends.*)
FIRST FRIEND. It seems to me, dear, that Father Kanva cares more for the hermitage trees than he does for you. You are delicate as a jasmine blossom, yet he tells you to fill the trenches about the trees.
SHAKUNTALA. Oh, it isn't Father's bidding so much. I feel like a real sister to them. (*She waters the trees.*)
PRIYAMVADA. Shakuntala, we have watered the trees that blossom in the summer-time. Now let's
50 sprinkle those whose flowering-time is past. That

will be a better deed, because we shall not be working for a reward.
SHAKUNTALA. What a pretty idea! (*She does so.*)
KING (*to himself*). And this is Kanva's daughter, Shakuntala. (*In surprise.*) The good Father does wrong to make her wear the hermit's dress of bark.

The sage who yokes her artless charm
 With pious pain and grief,
Would try to cut the toughest vine
 With a soft, blue lotus-leaf.   60

Well, I will step behind a tree and see how she acts with her friends. (*He conceals himself.*)
SHAKUNTALA. Oh, Anusuya! Priyamvada has fastened this bark dress so tight that it hurts. Please loosen it. (ANUSUYA *does so.*)
PRIYAMVADA (*laughing*). You had better blame your own budding charms for that.
KING. She is quite right.

Beneath the barken dress
 Upon the shoulder tied,   70
In maiden loveliness
 Her young breast seems to hide,

As when a flower amid
 The leaves by autumn tossed—
Pale, withered leaves—lies hid,
 And half its grace is lost.

Yet in truth the bark dress is not an enemy to her beauty. It serves as an added ornament. For

The meanest vesture glows
 On beauty that enchants: 80
The lotus lovelier shows
 Amid dull water-plants;

The moon in added splendour
 Shines for its spot of dark;
Yet more the maiden slender
 Charms in her dress of bark.

SHAKUNTALA (*looking ahead*). Oh, girls, that mango-tree is trying to tell me something with his branches that move in the wind like fingers. I must go and see him. (*She does so.*)   90
PRIYAMVADA. There, Shakuntala, stand right where you are a minute.
SHAKUNTALA. Why?
PRIYAMVADA. When I see you there, it looks as if a vine were clinging to the mango-tree.
SHAKUNTALA. I see why they call you the flatterer.
KING. But the flattery is true.

Her arms are tender shoots; her lips
 Are blossoms red and warm;
Bewitching youth begins to flower   100
 In beauty on her form.

ANUSUYA. Oh, Shakuntala! Here is the jasmine-vine that you named Light of the Grove. She has chosen the mango-tree as her husband.

SHAKUNTALA (*approaches and looks at it, joyfully*). What a pretty pair they make. The jasmine shows her youth in her fresh flowers, and the mango-tree shows his strength in his ripening fruit. (*She stands gazing at them.*)

PRIYAMVADA (*smiling*). Anusuya, do you know why Shakuntala looks so hard at the Light of the Grove?

10 ANUSUYA. No. Why?

PRIYAMVADA. She is thinking how the Light of the Grove has found a good tree, and hoping that she will meet a fine lover.

SHAKUNTALA. That's what you want for yourself. (*She tips her watering-pot.*)

ANUSUYA. Look, Shakuntala! Here is the spring-creeper that Father Kanva tended with his own hands—just as he did you. You are forgetting her.

SHAKUNTALA. I'd forget myself sooner. (*She goes*
20 *to the creeper and looks at it, joyfully.*) Wonderful! Wonderful! Priyamvada, I have something pleasant to tell you.

PRIYAMVADA. What is it, dear?

SHAKUNTALA. It is out of season, but the spring-creeper is covered with buds down to the very root.

THE TWO FRIENDS (*running up*). Really?

SHAKUNTALA. Of course. Can't you see?

PRIYAMVADA (*looking at it joyfully*). And I have something pleasant to tell *you*. You are to be married
30 soon.

SHAKUNTALA (*snappishly*). You know that's just what you want for yourself.

PRIYAMVADA. I'm not teasing. I really heard Father Kanva say that this flowering vine was to be a symbol of your coming happiness.

ANUSUYA. Priyamvada, that is why Shakuntala waters the spring-creeper so lovingly.

SHAKUNTALA. She is my sister. Why shouldn't I give her water? (*She tips her watering-pot.*)

40 KING. May I hope that she is the hermit's daughter by a mother of a different caste? But it *must* be so.

Surely, she may become a warrior's bride;
    Else, why these longings in an honest mind?
The motions of a blameless heart decide
    Of right and wrong, when reason leaves us blind.

Yet I will learn the whole truth.

SHAKUNTALA (*excitedly*). Oh, oh! A bee has left the jasmine-vine and is flying into my face. (*She shows herself annoyed by the bee.*)

40–41. **May . . . caste;** otherwise she could not marry into the warrior caste, to which the king belongs.

KING (*ardently*).

As the bee about her flies,   50
Swiftly her bewitching eyes
    Turn to watch his flight.
She is practising to-day
Coquetry and glances' play
    Not from love, but fright.

Eager bee, you lightly skim
O'er the eyelid's trembling rim
    Toward the cheek aquiver.
Gently buzzing round her cheek,
Whispering in her ear, you seek   60
    Secrets to deliver.

While her hands that way and this
Strike at you, you steal a kiss,
    Love's all, honeymaker.
I know nothing but her name,
Not her caste, nor whence she came—
    You, my rival, take her.

SHAKUNTALA. Oh, girls! Save me from this dreadful bee!

THE TWO FRIENDS (*smiling*). Who are we, that   70
we should save you? Call upon Dushyanta. For pious groves are in the protection of the king.

KING. A good opportunity to present myself. Have no—(*He checks himself. Aside.*) No, they would see that I am the king. I prefer to appear as a guest.

SHAKUNTALA. He doesn't leave me alone! I am going to run away. (*She takes a step and looks about.*) Oh, dear! Oh, dear! He is following me. Please save me.

KING (*hastening forward*). Ah!   80

A king of Puru's mighty line
    Chastises shameless churls;
What insolent is he who baits
    These artless hermit-girls?

ANUSUYA. It is nothing very dreadful, sir. But our friend (*indicating* SHAKUNTALA) was teased and frightened by a bee.

KING (*to* SHAKUNTALA). I hope these pious days are happy ones. (SHAKUNTALA's *eyes drop in embarrassment.*)

ANUSUYA. Yes, now that we receive such a dis-   90
tinguished guest.

PRIYAMVADA. Welcome, sir. Go to the cottage, Shakuntala, and bring fruit. This water will do to wash the feet.

KING. Your courteous words are enough to make me feel at home.

ANUSUYA. Then, sir, pray sit down and rest on this shady bench.

KING. You, too, are surely wearied by your pious task. Pray be seated a moment.

PRIYAMVADA (*aside to* SHAKUNTALA). My dear, we must be polite to our guest. Shall we sit down? (*The three girls sit.*)

SHAKUNTALA (*to herself*). Oh, why do I have such feelings when I see this man? They seem wrong in a hermitage.

KING. It is delightful to see your friendship. For you are all young and beautiful.

PRIYAMVADA (*aside to* ANUSUYA). Who is he, dear? With his mystery, and his dignity, and his 10 courtesy? He acts like a king and a gentleman.

ANUSUYA. I am curious too. I am going to ask him. (*Aloud.*) Sir, you are so very courteous that I make bold to ask you something. What royal family do you adorn, sir? What country is grieving at your absence? Why does a gentleman so delicately bred submit to the weary journey into our pious grove?

SHAKUNTALA (*aside*). Be brave, my heart. Anusuya speaks your very thoughts.

20 KING (*aside*). Shall I tell at once who I am, or conceal it? (*He reflects.*) This will do. (*Aloud.*) I am a student of Scripture. It is my duty to see justice done in the cities of the king. And I have come to this hermitage on a tour of inspection.

ANUSUYA. Then we of the hermitage have some one to take care of us. (SHAKUNTALA *shows embarrassment.*)

THE TWO FRIENDS (*observing the demeanour of the pair. Aside to* SHAKUNTALA). Oh, Shakuntala! If only Father were here to-day.

SHAKUNTALA. What would he do?

30 THE TWO FRIENDS. He would make our distinguished guest happy, if it took his most precious treasure.

SHAKUNTALA. Go away! You mean something. I'll not listen to you.

KING. I too would like to ask a question about your friend.

THE TWO FRIENDS. Sir, your request is a favour to us.

KING. Father Kanva lives a lifelong hermit. Yet 40 you say that your friend is his daughter. How can that be?

ANUSUYA. Listen, sir. There is a majestic royal sage named Kaushika—

KING. Ah, yes. The famous Kaushika.

ANUSUYA. Know, then, that he is the source of our friend's being. But Father Kanva is her real father, because he took care of her when she was abandoned.

KING. You waken my curiosity with the word 50 "abandoned." May I hear the whole story?

ANUSUYA. Listen, sir. Many years ago, that royal sage was leading a life of stern austerities, and the gods, becoming strangely jealous, sent the nymph Menaka to disturb his devotions.

KING. Yes, the gods feel this jealousy toward the austerities of others. And then—

ANUSUYA. Then in the lovely spring-time he saw her intoxicating beauty— (*She stops in embarrassment.*)

KING. The rest is plain. Surely, she is the daughter of the nymph. 60

ANUSUYA. Yes.

KING. It is as it should be.

> To beauty such as this
>   No woman could give birth;
> The quivering lightning flash
>   Is not a child of earth.

(*To himself*). Ah, my wishes become hopes.

PRIYAMVADA (*looking with a smile at* SHAKUNTALA). Sir, it seems as if you had more to say.

KING. You are right. Your pious life interests me, and I have another question. 70

PRIYAMVADA. Do not hesitate. We hermit people stand ready to answer all demands.

KING. My question is this:

> Does she, till marriage only, keep her vow
>   As hermit-maid, that shames the ways of love?
> Or must her soft eyes ever see, as now,
>   Soft eyes of friendly deer in peaceful grove?

PRIYAMVADA. Sir, we are under bonds to lead a life of virtue. But it is her father's wish to give her to a suitable lover. 80

KING (*joyfully to himself*).

> O heart, your wish is won!
>   All doubt at last is done;
> The thing you feared as fire,
>   Is the jewel of your desire.

SHAKUNTALA (*pettishly*). Anusuya, I'm going.

ANUSUYA. What for?

SHAKUNTALA. I am going to tell Mother Gautami that Priyamvada is talking nonsense. (*She rises.*)

ANUSUYA. My dear, we hermit people cannot neglect to entertain a distinguished guest, and go wan- 90 dering about.

KING (*aside*). She is going! (*He starts up as if to detain her, then checks his desires.*) A thought is as vivid as an act, to a lover.

> Though nurture, conquering nature, holds
>   Me back, it seems
> As had I started and returned
>   In waking dreams.

PRIYAMVADA (*approaching* SHAKUNTALA). You dear, peevish girl! You mustn't go. 100

SHAKUNTALA (*turns with a frown*). Why not?

87. **Mother Gautami,** the Mother Superior of the women's part of the hermitage.

PRIYAMVADA. You owe me the watering of two trees. You can go when you have paid your debt. (*She forces her to come back.*)

KING. It is plain that she is already wearied by watering the trees. See!

> Her shoulders droop; her palms are reddened yet;
>> Quick breaths are struggling in her bosom fair;
> The blossom o'er her ear hangs limply wet;
>> One hand restrains the loose, dishevelled hair.

I therefore remit her debt. (*He gives the two friends a ring. They take it, read the name engraved on it, and look at each other.*)

KING. Make no mistake. This is a present—from the king.

PRIYAMVADA. Then, sir, you ought not to part with it. Your word is enough to remit the debt.

ANUSUYA. Well, Shakuntala, you are set free by this kind gentleman—or rather, by the king himself. Where are you going now?

SHAKUNTALA (*to herself*). I would never leave him if I could help myself.

PRIYAMVADA. Why don't you go now?

SHAKUNTALA. I am not *your* servant any longer. I will go when I like.

KING (*looking at* SHAKUNTALA. *To himself*). Does she feel toward me as I do toward her? At least, there is ground for hope.

> Although she does not speak to me,
>> She listens while I speak;
> Her eyes turn not to see my face,
>> But nothing else they seek.

A VOICE BEHIND THE SCENES. Hermits! Hermits! Prepare to defend the creatures in our pious grove. King Dushyanta is hunting in the neighborhood.

> The dust his horses' hoofs have raised,
>> Red as the evening sky,
> Falls like a locust-swarm on boughs
>> Where hanging garments dry.

KING (*aside*). Alas! My soldiers are disturbing the pious grove in their search for me.

THE VOICE BEHIND THE SCENES. Hermits! Hermits! Here is an elephant who is terrifying old men, women, and children.

> One tusk is splintered by a cruel blow
> Against a blocking tree; his gait is slow,
> For countless fettering vines impede and cling;
> He puts the deer to flight; some evil thing
> He seems, that comes our peaceful life to mar,
> Fleeing in terror from the royal car.

(*The girls listen and rise anxiously.*)

KING. I have offended sadly against the hermits. I must go back.

THE TWO FRIENDS. Your Honour, we are frightened by this alarm of the elephant. Permit us to return to the cottage.

ANUSUYA (*to* SHAKUNTALA). Shakuntala dear, Mother Gautami will be anxious. We must hurry and find her.

SHAKUNTALA (*feigning lameness*). Oh, oh! I can hardly walk.

KING. You must go very slowly. And I will take pains that the hermitage is not disturbed.

THE TWO FRIENDS. Your honour, we feel as if we knew you very well. Pray pardon our shortcomings as hostesses. May we ask you to seek better entertainment from us another time?

KING. You are too modest. I feel honoured by the mere sight of you.

SHAKUNTALA. Anusuya, my foot is cut on a sharp blade of grass, and my dress is caught on an amaranth twig. Wait for me while I loosen it. (*She goes out with her two friends.*)

KING (*sighing*). They are gone. And I must go. The sight of Shakuntala has made me dread the return to the city. I will make my men camp at a distance from the pious grove. But I cannot turn my own thoughts from Shakuntala.

> It is my body leaves my love, not I;
>> My body moves away, but not my mind;
> For back to her my struggling fancies fly
>> Like silken banners borne against the wind.
>> (*Exit.*)

ACT II

THE SECRET

(*Enter the clown.*)

CLOWN (*sighing*). Damn! Damn! Damn! I'm tired of being friends with this sporting king. "There's a deer!" he shouts, "There's a boar!" And off he chases on a summer noon through woods where shade is few and far between. We drink hot, stinking water from the mountain streams, flavoured with leaves—nasty! At odd times we get a little tepid meat to eat. And the horses and the elephants make such a noise that I can't even be comfortable at night. Then the hunters and the bird-chasers—damn 'em—wake me up bright and early. They do make an ear-splitting rumpus when they start for the woods. But even that isn't the whole misery. There's a new pimple growing on the old boil. He left us behind and went hunting a deer. And there in a hermitage they say he found—oh, dear! oh, dear! he found a hermit-girl named Shakuntala. Since then he hasn't a thought of going back to town. I lay awake all night, thinking about it. What can I do? Well, I'll see my friend when he is dressed and beautified. (*He walks and looks about.*) Hello! Here he comes, with his bow in his hand, and his girl in his heart. He is wearing a wreath of wild flowers! I'll pretend to be all knocked up. Perhaps I can get a rest that way. (*He stands, leaning on his staff. Enter the king, as described.*)

KING (*to himself*).

Although my darling is not lightly won,
  She seemed to love me, and my hopes are bright;
Though love be balked ere joy be well begun,
  A common longing is itself delight.

(*Smiling.*) Thus does a lover deceive himself. He judges his love's feelings by his own desires.

10   Her glance was loving—but 'twas not for me;
  Her step was slow—'twas grace, not coquetry;
Her speech was short—to her detaining friend.
  In things like these love reads a selfish end!

CLOWN (*standing as before*). Well, king, I can't move my hand. I can only greet you with my voice.

KING (*looking and smiling*). What makes you lame?

CLOWN. Good! You hit a man in the eye, and then ask him why the tears come.

KING. I do not understand you. Speak plainly.

20 CLOWN. When a reed bends over like a hunch-back, do you blame the reed or the river-current?

KING. The river-current, of course.

CLOWN. And you are to blame for my troubles.

KING. How so?

CLOWN. It's a fine thing for you to neglect your royal duties and such a sure job—to live in the woods! What's the good of talking? Here I am, a Brahman, and my joints are all shaken up by this eternal running after wild animals, so that I can't 30 move. Please be good to me. Let us have a rest for just one day.

KING (*to himself*). He says this. And I too, when I remember Kanva's daughter, have little desire for the chase. For

  The bow is strung, its arrow near;
    And yet I cannot bend
  That bow against the fawns who share
    Soft glances with their friend.

CLOWN. He means more than he says. I might as 40 well weep in the woods.

KING (*smiling*). What more could I mean? I have been thinking that I ought to take my friend's advice.

CLOWN (*cheerfully*). Long life to you, then.

KING. Wait. Hear me out.

CLOWN. Well, sir?

KING. When you are rested, you must be my companion in another task—an easy one.

CLOWN. Crushing a few sweetmeats?

50 KING. I will tell you presently.

CLOWN. Pray command my leisure.

KING. Who stands without? (*Enter the door-keeper.*)

DOOR-KEEPER. I await your Majesty's commands.

KING. Raivataka, summon the general.

DOOR-KEEPER. Yes, your Majesty. (*He goes out, then returns with the general.*) Follow me, sir. There is his Majesty, listening to our conversation. Draw near, sir.

GENERAL (*to himself*). Hunting is declared to be a sin, yet it brings nothing but good to the king. See! 60

  He does not heed the cruel sting
  Of his recoiling, twanging string;
  The mid-day sun, the dripping sweat
  Affect him not, nor make him fret;
  His form, though sinewy and spare,
  Is most symmetrically fair;
  No mountain-elephant could be
  More filled with vital strength than he.

(*He approaches.*) Victory to your Majesty! The forest is full of deer-tracks, and beasts of prey cannot 70 be far off. What better occupation could we have?

KING. Bhadrasena, my enthusiasm is broken. Madhavya has been preaching against hunting.

GENERAL (*aside to the clown*). Stick to it, friend Madhavya. I will humour the king a moment. (*Aloud.*) Your Majesty, he is a chattering idiot. Your Majesty may judge by his own case whether hunting is an evil. Consider:

  The hunter's form grows sinewy, strong, and light;
  He learns, from beasts of prey, how wrath and fright 80
  Affect the mind; his skill he loves to measure
  With moving targets. 'Tis life's chiefest pleasure.

CLOWN (*angrily*). Get out! Get out with your strenuous life! The king has come to his senses. But you, you son of a slave-wench, can go chasing from forest to forest, till you fall into the jaws of some old bear that is looking for a deer or a jackal.

KING. Bhadrasena, I cannot take your advice, because I am in the vicinity of a hermitage. So for today 90

  The hornèd buffalo may shake
  The turbid water of the lake;
  Shade-seeking deer may chew the cud,
  Boars trample swamp-grass in the mud;
  The bow I bend in hunting, may
  Enjoy a listless holiday.

GENERAL. Yes, your Majesty.

KING. Send back the archers who have gone ahead. And forbid the soldiers to vex the hermitage, or even to approach it. Remember: 100

  There lurks a hidden fire in each
    Religious hermit-bower;
  Cool sun-stones kindle if assailed
    By any foreign power.

GENERAL. Yes, your Majesty.

CLOWN. Now will you get out with your strenuous life? (*Exit general.*)

KING (*to his attendants*). Lay aside your hunting dress. And you, Raivataka, return to your post of duty.

RAIVATAKA. Yes, your Majesty. (*Exit.*)

CLOWN. You have got rid of the vermin. Now be seated on this flat stone, over which the trees spread their canopy of shade. I can't sit down till you do.

KING. Lead the way.

CLOWN. Follow me. (*They sit down.*)

KING. Friend Madhavya, you do not know what vision is. You have not seen the fairest of all objects.

CLOWN. I see you, right in front of me.

KING. Yes, every one thinks himself beautiful. But I was speaking of Shakuntala, the ornament of the hermitage.

CLOWN (*to himself*). I mustn't add fuel to the flame. (*Aloud.*) But you can't have her because she is a hermit-girl. What is the use of seeing her?

KING. Fool!

> And is it selfish longing then,
>   That draws our souls on high
> Through eyes that have forgot to wink,
>   As the new moon climbs the sky?

Besides, Dushyanta's thoughts dwell on no forbidden object.

CLOWN. Well, tell me about her.

KING.
> Sprung from a nymph of heaven
>   Wanton and gay,
> Who spurned the blessing given,
>   Going her way;
>
> By the stern hermit taken
>   In her most need:
> So fell the blossom shaken,
>   Flower on a weed.

CLOWN (*laughing*). You are like a man who gets tired of good dates and longs for sour tamarind. All the pearls of the palace are yours, and you want this girl!

KING. My friend, you have not seen her, or you could not talk so.

CLOWN. She must be charming if she surprises *you.*

KING. Oh, my friend, she needs not many words.

> She is God's vision, of pure thought
>   Composed in His creative mind;
> His reveries of beauty wrought
>   The peerless pearl of womankind.
> So plays my fancy when I see
> How great is God, how lovely she.

CLOWN. How the women must hate her!

KING. This too is in my thought.

> She seems a flower whose fragrance none has tasted,
>   A gem uncut by workman's tool,
> A branch no desecrating hands have wasted,
>   Fresh honey, beautifully cool.
>
> No man on earth deserves to taste her beauty,
>   Her blameless loveliness and worth,
> Unless he has fulfilled man's perfect duty—
>   And is there such a one on earth?

CLOWN. Marry her quick, then, before the poor girl falls into the hands of some oily-headed hermit.

KING. She is dependent on her father, and he is not here.

CLOWN. But how does she feel toward you?

KING. My friend, hermit-girls are by their very nature timid. And yet

> When I was near, she could not look at me;
>   She smiled—but not to me—and half denied it;
> She would not show her love for modesty,
>   Yet did not try so very hard to hide it.

CLOWN. Did you want her to climb into your lap the first time she saw you?

KING. But when she went away with her friends, she almost showed that she loved me.

> When she had hardly left my side,
> "I cannot walk," the maiden cried,
> And turned her face, and feigned to free
> The dress not caught upon the tree.

CLOWN. She has given you some memories to chew on. I suppose that is why you are so in love with the pious grove.

KING. My friend, think of some pretext under which we may return to the hermitage.

CLOWN. What pretext do you need? Aren't you the king?

KING. What of that?

CLOWN. Collect the taxes on the hermit's rice.

KING. Fool! It is a very different tax which these hermits pay—one that outweighs heaps of gems.

> The wealth we take from common men,
>   Wastes while we cherish;
> These share with us such holiness
>   As ne'er can perish.

VOICES BEHIND THE SCENES. Ah, we have found him.

KING (*listening*). The voices are grave and tranquil. These must be hermits. (*Enter the door-keeper.*)

DOOR-KEEPER. Victory, O King. There are two hermit-youths at the gate.

90. **Collect . . . rice.** Since the rice eaten by the hermits was wild rather than cultivated, it was not subject to the king's tax.

KING. Bid them enter at once.

DOOR-KEEPER. Yes, your Majesty. (*He goes out, then returns with the youths.*) Follow me.

FIRST YOUTH (*looking at the king*). A majestic presence, yet it inspires confidence. Nor is this wonderful in a king who is half a saint. For to him

> The splendid palace serves as hermitage;
> His royal government, courageous, sage,
> Adds daily to his merit; it is given
> To him to win applause from choirs of heaven
> Whose anthems to his glory rise and swell,
> Proclaiming him a king, and saint as well.

SECOND YOUTH. My friend, is this Dushyanta, friend of Indra?

FIRST YOUTH. It is.

SECOND YOUTH.

> Nor is it wonderful that one whose arm
> Might bolt a city gate, should keep from harm
> The whole broad earth dark-belted by the sea;
> For when the gods in heaven with demons fight,
> Dushyanta's bow and Indra's weapon bright
> Are their reliance for the victory.

THE TWO YOUTHS (*approaching*). Victory, O King!

KING (*rising*). I salute you.

THE TWO YOUTHS. All hail! (*They offer fruit.*)

KING (*receiving it and bowing low*). May I know the reason of your coming?

THE TWO YOUTHS. The hermits have learned that you are here, and they request—

KING. They command rather.

THE TWO YOUTHS. The powers of evil disturb our pious life in the absence of the hermit-father. We therefore ask that you will remain a few nights with your charioteer to protect the hermitage.

KING. I shall be most happy to do so.

CLOWN (*to the king*). You rather seem to like being collared this way.

KING. Raivataka, tell my charioteer to drive up, and to bring the bow and arrows.

RAIVATAKA. Yes, your Majesty. (*Exit.*)

THE TWO YOUTHS.

> Thou art a worthy scion of
> The kings who ruled our nation
> And found, defending those in need,
> Their truest consecration.

KING. Pray go before. And I will follow straightway.

THE TWO YOUTHS. Victory, O King! (*Exeunt.*)

KING. Madhavya, have you no curiosity to see Shakuntala?

CLOWN. I *did* have an unending curiosity, but this talk about the powers of evil has put an end to it.

KING. Do not fear. You will be with me.

CLOWN. I'll stick close to your chariot-wheel. (*Enter the door-keeper.*)

DOOR-KEEPER. Your Majesty, the chariot is ready, and awaits your departure to victory. But one Karabhaka has come from the city, a messenger from the queen-mother.

KING (*respectfully*). Sent by my mother?

DOOR-KEEPER. Yes.

KING. Let him enter.

DOOR-KEEPER (*goes out and returns with* KARABHAKA). Karabhaka, here is his Majesty. You may draw near.

KARABHAKA (*approaching and bowing low*). Victory to your Majesty. The queen-mother sends her commands—

KING. What are her commands?

KARABHAKA. She plans to end a fasting ceremony on the fourth day from to-day. And on that occasion her dear son must not fail to wait upon her.

KING. On the one side is my duty to the hermits, on the other my mother's command. Neither may be disregarded. What is to be done?

CLOWN (*laughing*). Stay half-way between, like Trishanku.

KING. In truth, I am perplexed.

> Two inconsistent duties sever
> My mind with cruel shock,
> As when the current of a river
> Is split upon a rock.

(*He reflects.*) My friend, the queen-mother has always felt toward you as toward a son. Do you return, tell her what duty keeps me here, and yourself perform the offices of a son.

CLOWN. You don't think I am afraid of the devils?

KING (*smiling*). O mighty Brahman, who could suspect it?

CLOWN. But I want to travel like a prince.

KING. I will send all the soldiers with you, for the pious grove must not be disturbed.

CLOWN (*strutting*). Aha! Look at the heir-apparent!

KING (*to himself*). The fellow is a chatterbox. He might betray my longing to the ladies of the palace. Good, then! (*He takes the clown by the hand. Aloud.*) Friend Madhavya, my reverence for the hermits draws me to the hermitage. Do not think that I am really in love with the hermit-girl. Just think:

> A king, and a girl of the calm hermit-grove,
> Bred with the fawns, and a stranger to love!
> Then do not imagine a serious quest;
> The light words I uttered were spoken in jest.

74. Trishanku, a king in the *Ramáyana* who was hung between heaven and earth because a sage ordered him to heaven and the gods ordered him back to earth.

CLOWN. Oh, I understand that well enough.

(*Exeunt ambo.*)

ACT III

THE LOVE-MAKING

(*Enter a pupil, with sacred grass for the sacrifice.*)

PUPIL (*with meditative astonishment*). How great is the power of King Dushyanta! Since his arrival our rites have been undisturbed.

> He does not need to bend the bow;
> For every evil thing,
> Awaiting not the arrow, flees
> From the twanging of the string.

Well, I will take this sacred grass to the priests, to
10 strew the altar. (*He walks and looks about, then speaks to some one not visible.*) Priyamvada, for whom are you carrying this cuscus-salve and the fibrous lotus-leaves? (*He listens.*) What do you say? That Shakuntala has become seriously ill from the heat, and that these things are to relieve her suffering? Give her the best of care, Priyamvada. She is the very life of the hermit-father. And I will give Gautami the holy water for her. (*Exit. Enter the lovelorn king.*)

KING (*with a meditative sigh*).

> I know that stern religion's power
20 > Keeps guardian watch my maiden o'er;
> Yet all my heart flows straight to her
> Like water to the valley-floor.

Oh, mighty Love, thine arrows are made of flowers. How can they be so sharp? (*He recalls something.*) Ah, I understand.

> Shiva's devouring wrath still burns in thee,
> As burns the eternal fire beneath the sea;
> Else how couldst thou, thyself long since consumed,
30 > Kindle the fire that flames so ruthlessly?

Indeed, the moon and thou inspire confidence, only to deceive the host of lovers.

> Thy shafts are blossoms; coolness streams
> From moon-rays: thus the poets sing;
> But to the lovelorn, falsehood seems
> To lurk in such imagining;
> The moon darts fire from frosty beams;
> Thy flowery arrows cut and sting.

And yet

40 > If Love will trouble her
> Whose great eyes madden me,

23. **Oh . . . flowers.** Each of the five arrows of Káma, god of love, was tipped with a flower and was directed at one of the five senses.

> I greet him unafraid,
> Though wounded ceaselessly.

O mighty god, wilt thou not show me mercy after such reproaches?

> With tenderness unending
> I cherished thee when small,
> In vain—thy bow is bending;
> On me thine arrows fall.
> My care for thee to such a plight   50
> Has brought me; and it serves me right.

I have driven off the powers of evil, and the hermits have dismissed me. Where shall I go now to rest from my weariness? There is no rest for me except in seeing her whom I love. She usually spends these hours of midday heat with her friends on the vine-wreathed banks of the Malini. I will go there. (*He walks and looks about.*) I believe the slender maiden has just passed through this corridor of young trees.
For   60

> The stems from which she gathered flowers
> Are still unhealed;
> The sap where twigs were broken off
> Is uncongealed.

This is a pleasant spot, with the wind among the trees.

> Limbs that love's fever seizes,
> Their fervent welcome pay
> To lotus-fragrant breezes
> That bear the river-spray.   70

Ah, Shakuntala must be in this reedy bower. For

> In white sand at the door
> Fresh footprints appear,
> The toe lightly outlined,
> The heel deep and clear.

I will hide among the branches, and see what happens. Ah, my eyes have found their heaven. Here is the darling of my thoughts, lying upon a flower-strewn bench of stone, and attended by her two friends. I will hear what they say to each other.   80
(*Enter* SHAKUNTALA *with her two friends.*)

THE TWO FRIENDS (*fanning her*). Do you feel better, dear, when we fan you with these lotus-leaves?

SHAKUNTALA (*wearily*). Oh, are you fanning me, my dear girls? (*The two friends look sorrowfully at each other.*)

KING. She is seriously ill. (*Doubtfully.*) Is it the heat, or is it as I hope? (*Decidedly.*) It *must* be so.

> With salve upon her breast,
> With loosened lotus-chain,
> My darling, sore oppressed,   90
> Is lovely in her pain.

Though love and summer heat
  May work an equal woe,
No maiden seems so sweet
  When summer lays her low.

PRIYAMVADA (*aside to* ANUSUYA). Anusuya, since she first saw the good king, she has been greatly troubled. I do not believe her fever has any other cause.

ANUSUYA. I suspect you are right. I am going to ask her. My dear, I must ask you something. You are in a high fever.

KING. It is too true.

Her lotus-chains that were as white
  As moonbeams shining in the night,
Betray the fever's awful pain,
  And fading, show a darker stain.

SHAKUNTALA. Well, say whatever you like.

ANUSUYA. Shakuntala dear, you have not told us what is going on in your mind. But I have heard old, romantic stories, and I can't help thinking that you are in a state like that of a lady in love. Please tell us what hurts you. We have to understand the disease before we can even try to cure it.

KING. Anusuya expresses my own thoughts.

SHAKUNTALA. It hurts me terribly. I can't tell you all at once.

PRIYAMVADA. Anusuya is right, dear. Why do you hide your trouble? You are wasting away every day. You are nothing but a beautiful shadow.

KING. Priyamvada is right. See!

Her cheeks grow thin; her breast and shoulders fail;
Her waist is weary and her face is pale:
She fades for love; oh, pitifully sweet!
As vine-leaves wither in the scorching heat.

SHAKUNTALA. I could not tell any one else. But I shall be a burden to you.

THE TWO FRIENDS. That is why we insist on knowing, dear. Grief must be shared to be endured.

KING. To friends who share her joy and grief
    She tells what sorrow laid her here;
  She turned to look her love again
    When first I saw her—yet I fear!

SHAKUNTALA. Ever since I saw the good king who protects the pious grove—

THE TWO FRIENDS. Go on, dear.

SHAKUNTALA. I love him, and it makes me feel like this.

THE TWO FRIENDS. Good, good! You have found a lover worthy of your devotion. But of course, a great river always runs into the sea.

KING (*joyfully*). I have heard what I longed to hear.

'Twas love that caused the burning pain;
'Tis love that eases it again;

As when, upon a sultry day,
Rain breaks, and washes grief away.

SHAKUNTALA. Then, if you think best, make the good king take pity upon me. If not, remember that I was.

KING. Her words end all doubt.

PRIYAMVADA (*aside to* ANUSUYA). Anusuya, she is far gone in love and cannot endure any delay.

ANUSUYA. Priyamvada, can you think of any scheme by which we could carry out her wishes quickly and secretly?

PRIYAMVADA. We must plan about the "secretly." The "quickly" is not hard.

ANUSUYA. How so?

PRIYAMVADA. Why, the good king shows his love for her in his tender glances, and he has been wasting away, as if he were losing sleep.

KING. It is quite true.

The hot tears, flowing down my cheek
  All night on my supporting arm
And on its golden bracelet, seek
  To stain the gems and do them harm.

The bracelet slipping o'er the scars
  Upon the wasted arm, that show
My deeds in hunting and in wars,
  All night is moving to and fro.

PRIYAMVADA. Well, she must write him a love-letter. And I will hide it in a bunch of flowers and see that it gets into the king's hand as if it were a relic of the sacrifice.

ANUSUYA. It is a pretty plan, dear, and it pleases me. What does Shakuntala say?

SHAKUNTALA. I suppose I must obey orders.

PRIYAMVADA. Then compose a pretty little love-song, with a hint of yourself in it.

SHAKUNTALA. I'll try. But my heart trembles, for fear he will despise me.

KING.

Here stands the eager lover, and you pale
  For fear lest he disdain a love so kind:
The seeker may find fortune, or may fail;
  But how could fortune, seeking, fail to find?

And again:

The ardent lover comes, and yet you fear
  Lest he disdain love's tribute, were it brought,
The hope of which has led his footsteps here—
  Pearls need not seek, for they themselves are sought.

THE TWO FRIENDS. You are too modest about your own charms. Would anybody put up a parasol to keep off the soothing autumn moonlight?

84. **relic of the sacrifice.** Consecrated flowers left over from a sacrifice might be given to friends.

A Rajput Indian painting now in the British Museum.

SHAKUNTALA (*smiling*). I suppose I shall have to obey orders.

KING. It is only natural that I should forget to wink when I see my darling. For

> One clinging eyebrow lifted,
>   As fitting words she seeks,
> Her face reveals her passion
>   For me in glowing cheeks.

10 SHAKUNTALA. Well, I have thought out a little song. But I haven't anything to write with.

PRIYAMVADA. Here is a lotus-leaf, glossy as a parrot's breast. You can cut the letters in it with your nails.

SHAKUNTALA. Now listen, and tell me whether it makes sense.

THE TWO FRIENDS. Please.

SHAKUNTALA (*reads*).

> I know not if I read your heart aright;
>   Why, pitiless, do you distress me so?
> I only know that longing day and night
> 20   Tosses my restless body to and fro,
>   That yearns for you, the source of all its woe.

KING (*advancing*).

> Though Love torments you, slender maid,
>   Yet he consumes me quite,
> As daylight shuts night-blooming flowers
>   And slays the moon outright.

THE TWO FRIENDS (*perceive the king and rise joyfully*). Welcome to the wish that is fulfilled without delay. (SHAKUNTALA *tries to rise.*)

KING. Do not try to rise, beautiful Shakuntala.

> Your limbs from which the strength is fled,
> That crush the blossoms of your bed
> And bruise the lotus-leaves, may be
> Pardoned a breach of courtesy.   30

SHAKUNTALA (*sadly to herself*). Oh, my heart, you were so impatient, and now you find no answer to make.

ANUSUYA. Your Majesty, pray do this stone bench the honour of sitting upon it. (SHAKUNTALA *edges away.*)

KING (*seating himself*). Priyamvada, I trust your friend's illness is not dangerous.

PRIYAMVADA (*smiling*). A remedy is being applied   40 and it will soon be better. It is plain, sir, that you and she love each other. But I love her too, and I must say something over again.

KING. Pray do not hesitate. It always causes pain in the end, to leave unsaid what one longs to say.

PRIYAMVADA. Then listen, sir.

KING. I am all attention.

PRIYAMVADA. It is the king's duty to save hermit-folk from all suffering. Is not that good Scripture?

KING. There is no text more urgent.   50

PRIYAMVADA. Well, our friend has been brought to this sad state by her love for you. Will you not take pity on her and save her life?

KING. We cherish the same desire. I feel it a great honour.

SHAKUNTALA (*with a jealous smile*). Oh, don't detain the good king. He is separated from the court ladies, and he is anxious to go back to them.

KING.

> Bewitching eyes that found my heart,
>   You surely see   60
> It could no longer live apart,
>   Nor faithless be.
> I bear Love's arrows as I can;
> Wound not with doubt a wounded man.

ANUSUYA. But, your Majesty, we hear that kings have many favourites. You must act in such a way that our friend may not become a cause of grief to her family.

KING. What more can I say?

> Though many queens divide my court,   70
>   But two support the throne;
> Your friend will find a rival in
>   The sea-girt earth alone.

THE TWO FRIENDS. We are content.

PRIYAMVADA (*aside to* ANUSUYA). Look, Anusuya! See how the dear girl's life is coming back moment by moment—just like a peahen in summer when the first rainy breezes come.

SHAKUNTALA. You must please ask the king's pardon for the rude things we said when we were talk-   80 ing together.

THE TWO FRIENDS (*smiling*). Anybody who says it was rude, may ask his pardon. Nobody else feels guilty.

SHAKUNTALA. Your Majesty, pray forgive what we said when we did not know that you were present. I am afraid that we say a great many things behind a person's back.

KING (*smiling*).

> Your fault is pardoned if I may
> Relieve my weariness
> By sitting on the flower-strewn couch
> Your fevered members press.

PRIYAMVADA. But that will not be enough to satisfy him.

SHAKUNTALA (*feigning anger*). Stop! You are a rude girl. You make fun of me when I am in this condition.

ANUSUYA. Priyamvada, there is a little fawn, looking all about him. He has probably lost his mother and is trying to find her. I am going to help him.

PRIYAMVADA. He is a frisky little fellow. You can't catch him alone. I'll go with you. (*They start to go.*)

SHAKUNTALA. I will not let you go and leave me alone.

THE TWO FRIENDS (*smiling*). You alone, when the king of the world is with you! (*Exeunt.*)

SHAKUNTALA. Are my friends gone?

KING. Do not be anxious, beautiful Shakuntala. Have you not a humble servant here, to take the place of your friends? Then tell me:

> Shall I employ the moistened lotus-leaf
> To fan away your weariness and grief?
> Or take your lily feet upon my knee
> And rub them till you rest more easily?

SHAKUNTALA. I will not offend against those to whom I owe honour. (*She rises weakly and starts to walk away.*)

KING (*detaining her*). The day is still hot, beautiful Shakuntala, and you are feverish.

> Leave not the blossom-dotted couch
> To wander in the midday heat,
> With lotus-petals on your breast,
> With fevered limbs and stumbling feet.
> > (*He lays his hand upon her.*)

SHAKUNTALA. Oh, don't! Don't! For I am not mistress of myself. Yet what can I do now? I had no one to help me but my friends.

KING. I am rebuked.

SHAKUNTALA. I was not thinking of your Majesty. I was accusing fate.

KING. Why accuse a fate that brings what you desire?

SHAKUNTALA. Why not accuse a fate that robs me of self-control and tempts me with the virtues of another?

KING (*to himself*).

> Though deeply longing, maids are coy
> And bid their wooers wait;
> Though eager for united joy
> In love, they hesitate.

> Love cannot torture them, nor move
> Their hearts to sudden mating;
> Perhaps they even torture love
> By their procrastinating.
> > (SHAKUNTALA *moves away.*)

KING. Why should I not have my way? (*He approaches and seizes her dress.*)

SHAKUNTALA. Oh, sir! Be a gentleman. There are hermits wandering about.

KING. Do not fear your family, beautiful Shakuntala. Father Kanva knows the holy law. He will not regret it.

> For many a hermit maiden who
> By simple, voluntary rite
> Dispensed with priest and witness, yet
> Found favour in her father's sight.

Ah, I have come into the open air.

SHAKUNTALA. O King, I cannot do as you would have me. You hardly know me after this short talk. But oh, do not forget me.

KING.

> When evening comes, the shadows of the tree
> Is cast far forward, yet does not depart;
> Even so, belovèd, wheresoe'er you be,
> The thought of you can never leave my heart.

SHAKUNTALA (*to herself*). Oh, oh! When I hear him speak so, my feet will not move away. I will hide in this amaranth hedge and see how long his love lasts. (*She hides and waits.*)

KING. Oh, my belovèd, my love for you is my whole life, yet you leave me and go away without a thought.

> Your body, soft as siris-flowers,
> Engages passion's utmost powers;
> How comes it that your heart is hard
> As stalks that siris-blossoms guard?

SHAKUNTALA. When I hear this, I have no power to go.

KING. What have I to do here, where she is not? Ah, I cannot go.

> The perfumed lotus-chain
> That once was worn by her
> Fetters and keeps my heart
> A hopeless prisoner.

> > (*He lifts it reverently.*)

SHAKUNTALA (*looking at her arm*). Why, I was so

weak and ill that when the lotus-bracelet fell off, I
did not even notice it.

KING (*laying the lotus-bracelet on his heart*). Ah!

> Once, dear, on your sweet arm it lay,
> And on my heart shall ever stay;
> Though you disdain to give me joy,
> I find it in a lifeless toy.

SHAKUNTALA. I cannot hold back after that. I will
use the bracelet as an excuse for my coming. (*She
approaches.*)

10 KING (*seeing her*). The queen of my life! As soon
as I complained, fate proved kind to me.

> No sooner did the thirsty bird
> With parching throat complain,
> Than forming clouds in heaven stirred
> And sent the streaming rain.

SHAKUNTALA (*standing before the king*). When
I was going away, sir, I remembered that this lotus-
bracelet had fallen from my arm, and I have come
back for it. My heart seemed to tell me that you had
20 taken it. Please give it back, or you will betray me,
and yourself too, to the hermits.

KING. I will restore it on one condition.

SHAKUNTALA. What condition?

KING. That I may myself place it where it belongs.

SHAKUNTALA (*to herself*). What can I do?

KING. Let us sit on this stone bench. (*They walk
to the bench and sit down.*)

KING (*taking* SHAKUNTALA's *hand*). Ah!

> When Shiva's anger burned the tree
> Of love in quenchless fire,
30 > Did heavenly fate preserve a shoot
> To deck my heart's desire?

SHAKUNTALA. Hasten, my dear, hasten.

KING (*to himself*). Now I am content. She speaks
as a wife to her husband. (*Aloud.*) Beautiful Shakuntala, the clasp of the bracelet is not very firm. May I
fasten it in another way?

SHAKUNTALA (*smiling*). If you like.

KING. See, my beautiful girl!

> The lotus-chain is dazzling white
40 > As is the slender moon at night.
> Perhaps it was the moon on high
> That joined her horns and left the sky,
> Believing that your lovely arm
> Would, more than heaven, enhance her charm.

SHAKUNTALA. I cannot see it. The pollen from the
lotus over my ear has blown into my eye.

KING. Will you permit me to blow it away?

SHAKUNTALA. I should not like to be an object of
pity. But why should I not trust you?

50 KING. Do not have such thoughts. A new servant
does not transgress orders.

SHAKUNTALA. It is this exaggerated courtesy that
frightens me.

KING (*to himself*). I shall not break the bonds of
this sweet servitude. (*He starts to raise her face to
his.* SHAKUNTALA *resists a little, then is passive.*)

KING. Oh, my bewitching girl, have no fear of me.
(*Aside.*)

> Her sweetly trembling lip
> With virgin invitation
> Provokes my soul to sip
> Delighted fascination. 60

SHAKUNTALA. You seem slow, dear, in fulfilling
your promise.

KING. The lotus over your ear is so near your eye,
and so like it, that I was confused. (*He gently blows
her eye.*)

SHAKUNTALA. Thank you. I can see quite well now.
But I am ashamed not to make any return for your
kindness.

KING. What more could I ask?

> It ought to be enough for me
> To hover round your fragrant face; 70
> Is not the lotus-haunting bee
> Content with perfume and with grace?

SHAKUNTALA. But what does he do if he is not
content?

KING. This! This! (*He draws her face to his.*)

A VOICE BEHIND THE SCENES. O sheldrake bride,
bid your mate farewell. The night is come.

SHAKUNTALA (*listening excitedly*). Oh, my dear,
this is Mother Gautami, come to inquire about me.
Please hide among the branches. (*The king conceals* 80
himself. Enter GAUTAMI, *with a bowl in her hand.*)

GAUTAMI. Here is the holy water, my child. (*She
helps her to rise.*) So ill, and all alone here with the
gods?

SHAKUNTALA. It was just a moment ago that Priyamvada and Anusuya went down to the river.

GAUTAMI (*sprinkling* SHAKUNTALA *with the holy
water*). May you live long and happy, my child.
Has the fever gone down?

SHAKUNTALA. There is a difference, mother.

GAUTAMI. The sun is setting. Come, let us go to
the cottage. 90

SHAKUNTALA (*to herself*). Oh, my heart, you delayed when your desire came of itself. Now see what
you have done. (*Aloud.*) O bower that took away
my pain, I bid you farewell until another blissful
hour. (*Exeunt* SHAKUNTALA *and* GAUTAMI.)

KING (*advancing with a sigh.*) The path to happiness is strewn with obstacles.

> Her face, adorned with soft eye-lashes,
> Adorable with trembling flashes

76. **sheldrake,** a species of wild duck; here the Indian love-birds
doomed by a curse to part from each other with the coming of night.

Of half-denial, in memory lingers;
The sweet lips guarded by her fingers,
The head that drooped upon her shoulder—
Why was I not a little bolder?

Where shall I go now? Let me stay a moment in this bower where my belovèd lay.

The flower-strewn bed whereon her body tossed;
The bracelet, fallen from her arm and lost;
The dear love-missive, in the lotus-leaf
10 Cut by her nails: assuage my absent grief
And occupy my eyes—I have no power,
Though she is gone, to leave the reedy bower.

(*He reflects.*) Alas! I did wrong to delay when I had found my love. So now

If she will grant me but one other meeting,
I'll not delay; for happiness is fleeting;
So plans my foolish, self-defeated heart;
But when she comes, I play the coward's part.

A VOICE BEHIND THE SCENES. O King!

20 The flames rise heavenward from the evening altar;
And round the sacrifices, blazing high,
Flesh-eating demons stalk, like red cloud-masses,
And cast colossal shadows on the sky.

KING. Have no fear, hermits. I am here.

(*Exit.*)

ACT IV

SHAKUNTALA'S DEPARTURE

SCENE I

(*Enter the two friends, gathering flowers.*)

ANUSUYA. Priyamvada, dear Shakuntala has been properly married by the voluntary ceremony and she has a husband worthy of her. And yet I am not quite satisfied.

PRIYAMVADA. Why not?

30 ANUSUYA. The sacrifice is over and the good king was dismissed to-day by the hermits. He has gone back to the city and there he is surrounded by hundreds of court ladies. I wonder whether he will remember poor Shakuntala or not.

PRIYAMVADA. You need not be anxious about that. Such handsome men are sure to be good. But there is something else to think about. I don't know what Father will have to say when he comes back from his pilgrimage and hears about it.

40 ANUSUYA. I believe that he will be pleased.

PRIYAMVADA. Why?

ANUSUYA. Why not? You know he wanted to give his daughter to a lover worthy of her. If fate brings this about of itself, why shouldn't Father be happy?

25-26. has been . . . ceremony; that is, without the usual ceremony but by the Gandharva ceremony, named after the musician-nymphs of Indra's heaven, who practiced it.

PRIYAMVADA. I suppose you are right. (*She looks at her flower-basket.*) My dear, we have gathered flowers enough for the sacrifice.

ANUSUYA. But we must make an offering to the gods that watch over Shakuntala's marriage. We had better gather more.

50 PRIYAMVADA. Very well.

A VOICE BEHIND THE SCENES. Who will bid me welcome?

ANUSUYA (*listening*). My dear, it sounds like a guest announcing himself.

PRIYAMVADA. Well, Shakuntala is near the cottage. (*Reflecting.*) Ah, but to-day her heart is far away. Come, we must do with the flowers we have. (*They start to walk away.*)

THE VOICE. Do you dare despise a guest like me?

Because your heart, by loving fancies blinded, 60
Has scorned a guest in pious life grown old,
Your lover shall forget you though reminded,
Or think of you as of a story told.

PRIYAMVADA. Oh, dear! The very thing has happened. The dear, absent-minded girl has offended some worthy man.

ANUSUYA (*looking ahead*). My dear, this is no ordinary somebody. It is the great sage Durvasas, the irascible. See how he strides away!

70 PRIYAMVADA. Nothing burns like fire. Run, fall at his feet, bring him back, while I am getting water to wash his feet.

ANUSUYA. I will. (*Exit.*)

PRIYAMVADA (*stumbling*). There! I stumbled in my excitement, and the flower-basket fell out of my hand. (*She collects the scattered flowers.* ANUSUYA *returns.*)

ANUSUYA. My dear, he is anger incarnate. Who could appease him? But I softened him a little.

PRIYAMVADA. Even that is a good deal for him. 80
Tell me about it.

ANUSUYA. When he would not turn back, I fell at his feet and prayed to him. "Holy sir," I said, "remember her former devotion and pardon this offence. Your daughter did not recognise your great and holy power to-day."

PRIYAMVADA. And then——

ANUSUYA. Then he said: "My words must be fulfilled. But the curse shall be lifted when her lover sees a gem which he has given her for a token." And so he vanished. 90

PRIYAMVADA. We can breathe again. When the good king went away, he put a ring, engraved with his own name, on Shakuntala's finger to remember him by. That will save her.

ANUSUYA. Come, we must finish the sacrifice for her. (*They walk about.*)

PRIYAMVADA. Just look, Anusuya! There is the dear girl, with her cheek resting on her left hand.

She looks like a painted picture. She is thinking about him. How could she notice a guest when she has forgotten herself?

ANUSUYA. Priyamvada, we two must keep this thing to ourselves. We must be careful of the dear girl. You know how delicate she is.

PRIYAMVADA. Would any one sprinkle a jasmine-vine with scalding water? (*Exeunt ambo.*)

SCENE II. *Early Morning*

(*Enter a pupil of* KANVA, *just risen from sleep.*)

10 PUPIL. Father Kanva has returned from his pilgrimage, and has bidden me find out what time it is. I will go into the open air and see how much of the night remains. (*He walks and looks about.*) See! The dawn is breaking. For already

The moon behind the western mount is sinking;
The eastern sun is heralded by dawn;
From heaven's twin lights, their fall and glory linking,
Brave lessons of submission may be drawn.

And again:

20 Night-blooming lilies, when the moon is hidden,
Have naught but memories of beauty left.
Hard, hard to bear! Her lot whom heaven has bidden
To live alone, of love and lover reft. . . .

And yet again:

The moon that topped the loftiest mountain ranges,
That slew the darkness in the midmost sky,
Is fallen from heaven, and all her glory changes:
30 So high to rise, so low at last to lie!

ANUSUYA (*entering hurriedly. To herself*). That is just what happens to the innocent. Shakuntala has been treated shamefully by the king.

PUPIL. I will tell Father Kanva that the hour of morning sacrifice is come. (*Exit.*)

ANUSUYA. The dawn is breaking. I am awake bright and early. But what shall I do now that I am awake? My hands refuse to attend to the ordinary morning tasks. Well, let love take its course. For the 40 dear, pure-minded girl trusted him—the traitor! Perhaps it is not the good king's fault. It must be the curse of Durvasas. Otherwise, how could the good king say such beautiful things, and then let all this time pass without even sending a message? (*She reflects.*) Yes, we must send him the ring he left as a token. But whom shall we ask to take it? The hermits are unsympathetic because they have never suffered. It seemed as if her friends were to blame and so, try as we might, we could not tell Father 50 Kanva that Shakuntala was married to Dushyanta and was expecting a baby. Oh, what shall we do?

(*Enter* PRIYAMVADA.)

PRIYAMVADA. Hurry, Anusuya, hurry! We are getting Shakuntala ready for her journey.

ANUSUYA (*astonished.*) What do you mean, my dear?

PRIYAMVADA. Listen. I just went to Shakuntala, to ask if she had slept well.

ANUSUYA. And then——

PRIYAMVADA. I found her hiding her face for 60 shame, and Father Kanva was embracing her and encouraging her. "My child," he said, "I bring you joy. The offering fell straight in the sacred fire, and auspicious smoke rose toward the sacrificer. My pains for you have proved like instruction given to a good student; they have brought me no regret. This very day I shall give you an escort of hermits and send you to your husband."

ANUSUYA. But, my dear, who told Father Kanva about it?

PRIYAMVADA. A voice from heaven that recited a 70 verse when he had entered the fire-sanctuary.

ANUSUYA. What did it say?

PRIYAMVADA. Listen.

Know, Brahman, that your child,
Like the fire-pregnant tree,
Bears kingly seed that shall be born
For earth's prosperity.

ANUSUYA. I am so glad, dear. But my joy is half sorrow when I think that Shakuntala is going to be taken away this very day. 80

PRIYAMVADA. We must hide our sorrow as best we can. The poor girl must be made happy to-day.

ANUSUYA. Well, here is a cocoa-nut casket, hanging on a branch of the mango-tree. I put flower-pollen in it for this very purpose. It keeps fresh, you know. Now you wrap it in a lotus-leaf, and I will get yellow pigment and earth from a sacred spot and blades of panic grass for the happy ceremony. (PRIYAMVADA *does so. Exit* ANUSUYA.)

A VOICE BEHIND THE SCENES. Gautami, bid the worthy Sharngarava and Sharadvata make ready to 90 escort my daughter Shakuntala.

PRIYAMVADA. Hurry, Anusuya, hurry! They are calling the hermits who are going to Hastinapura. (*Enter* ANUSUYA, *with materials for the ceremony.*)

ANUSUYA. Come, dear, let us go. (*They walk about.*)

PRIYAMVADA (*looking ahead*). There is Shakuntala. She took the ceremonial bath at sunrise, and now the hermit-women are giving her rice-cakes and wishing her happiness. Let's go to her. (*They do so. Enter* SHAKUNTALA *with attendants as described, and* GAUTAMI.)

SHAKUNTALA. Holy women, I salute you.

GAUTAMI. My child, may you receive the happy

93. **Hastinapura,** the residence of the king, now Delhi.

title "queen," showing that your husband honours you.

HERMIT-WOMEN. My dear, may you become the mother of a hero. (*Exeunt all but* GAUTAMI.)

THE TWO FRIENDS. Did you have a good bath, dear?

SHAKUNTALA. Good morning, girls. Sit here.

THE TWO FRIENDS (*seating themselves*). Now stand straight, while we go through the happy cere-mony.

SHAKUNTALA. It has happened often enough, but I ought to be very grateful to-day. Shall I ever be adorned by my friends again? (*She weeps.*)

THE TWO FRIENDS. You ought not to weep, dear, at this happy time.

PRIYAMVADA. You are so beautiful, you ought to have the finest gems. It seems like an insult to give you these hermitage things. (*Enter* HARITA, *a hermit-youth, with ornaments.*)

HARITA. Here are ornaments for our lady. (*The women look at them in astonishment.*)

GAUTAMI. Harita, my son, whence come these things?

HARITA. From the holy power of Father Kanva.

GAUTAMI. A creation of his mind?

HARITA. Not quite. Listen. Father Kanva sent us to gather blossoms from the trees for Shakuntala, and then

> One tree bore fruit, a silken marriage dress
> That shamed the moon in its white loveliness;
> Another gave us lac-dye for the feet;
> From others, fairy hands extended, sweet
> Like flowering twigs, as far as to the wrist,
> And gave us gems, to adorn her as we list.

PRIYAMVADA (*looking at* SHAKUNTALA). A bee may be born in a hole in a tree, but she likes the honey of the lotus.

GAUTAMI. This gracious favour is a token of the queenly happiness which you are to enjoy in your husband's palace. (SHAKUNTALA *shows embarrass-ment.*)

HARITA. Father Kanva has gone to the bank of the Malini, to perform his ablutions. I will tell him of the favour shown us by the trees. (*Exit.*)

ANUSUYA. My dear, we poor girls never saw such ornaments. How shall we adorn you? But we have seen pictures. Perhaps we can arrange them right.

SHAKUNTALA. I know how clever you are. (*The two friends adorn her. Enter* KANVA, *returning after his ablutions.*)

KANVA.

> Shakuntala must go to-day;
> I miss her now at heart;
> I dare not speak a loving word
> Or choking tears will start.

> My eyes are dim with anxious thought;
> Love strikes me to the life:
> And yet I strove for pious peace—
> I have no child, no wife.

> What must a father feel, when come
> The pangs of parting from his child at home?

THE TWO FRIENDS. There, Shakuntala, we have ar-ranged your ornaments. Now put on this beautiful silk dress. (SHAKUNTALA *rises and does so.*)

GAUTAMI. My child, here is your father. The eyes with which he seems to embrace you are overflow-ing with tears of joy. You must greet him properly. (SHAKUNTALA *makes a shamefaced reverence.*)

KANVA. My child,

> Like Sharmishtha, Yayati's wife,
> Win favour measured by your worth;
> And may you bear a kingly son
> Like Puru, who shall rule the earth.

GAUTAMI. My child, this is not a prayer, but a benediction.

KANVA. My daughter, walk from left to right about the fires in which the offering has just been thrown.

> The holy fires around the altar kindle,
> And at their margins sacred grass is piled;
> Beneath their sacrificial odours dwindle
> Misfortunes. May the fires protect you, child!

KANVA. Now you may start, my daughter. Where are Sharngarava and Sharadvata? (*Enter the two pupils.*)

THE TWO PUPILS. We are here, Father.

KANVA. Sharngarava, my son, lead the way for your sister.

SHARNGARAVA. Follow me.

KANVA. O trees of the pious grove, in which the fairies dwell,

> She would not drink till she had wet
> Your roots, a sister's duty,
> Nor pluck your flowers; she loves you yet
> Far more than selfish beauty.

> 'Twas festival in her pure life
> When budding blossoms showed;
> And now she leaves you as a wife—
> Oh, speed her on her road!

SHARNGARAVA. Father,

> The trees are answering your prayer
> In cooing cuckoo-song,
> Bidding Shakuntala farewell,
> Their sister for so long.

63. **Like Sharmishtha, Yayati's wife.** Sharmishtha and Yayati were parents of Puru, hence ancestors of King Dushyanta.

INVISIBLE BEINGS.

May lily-dotted lakes delight your eye;
　　May shade-trees bid the heat of noonday
　　　　cease;
May soft winds blow the lotus-pollen nigh;
　　May all your path be pleasantness and peace.

GAUTAMI. My child, the fairies of the pious grove bid you farewell. For they love the household. Pay reverence to the holy ones.

SHAKUNTALA (*Aside to* PRIYAMVADA). Priyamvada, I long to see my husband, and yet my feet will hardly move. It is hard, hard to leave the hermitage.

PRIYAMVADA. You are not the only one to feel sad at this farewell. See how the whole grove feels at parting from you.

　　The grass drops from the feeding doe;
　　　　The peahen stops her dance;
　　Pale, trembling leaves are falling slow,
　　　　The tears of clinging plants.

SHAKUNTALA. Father, I must say good-bye to the spring-creeper, my sister among the vines.

KANVA. I know your love for her. See! Here she is at your right hand.

SHAKUNTALA. Vine sister, embrace me too with your arms, these branches. I shall be far away from you after to-day. Father, you must care for her as you did for me.

KANVA. My child, you found the lover who
　　　　Had long been sought by me;
　　No longer need I watch for you;
　　　　I'll give the vine a lover true,
　　　　This handsome mango-tree.

And now start on your journey.

SHAKUNTALA (*going to the two friends*). Dear girls, I leave her in your care too.

THE TWO FRIENDS. But who will care for poor us? (*They shed tears.*)

KANVA. Anusuya! Priyamvada! Do not weep. It is you who should cheer Shakuntala.

SHAKUNTALA. Father, there is the pregnant doe, wandering about near the cottage. When she becomes a happy mother, you must send some one to bring me the good news. Do not forget.

KANVA. I shall not forget, my child.

SHAKUNTALA (*stumbling*). Oh, oh! Who is it that keeps pulling at my dress, as if to hinder me? (*She turns round to see.*)

KANVA. It is the fawn whose lip, when torn
　　　　By kusha-grass, you soothed with oil;
　　The fawn who gladly nibbled corn
　　　　Held in your hand; with loving toil
　　You have adopted him, and he
　　　　Would never leave you willingly.

SHAKUNTALA. My dear, why should you follow me when I am going away from home? Your mother died when you were born and I brought you up. Now I am leaving you, and Father Kanva will take care of you. Go back, dear! Go back! (*She walks away, weeping.*)

KANVA. Do not weep, my child. Be brave. Look at the path before you.

　　Be brave, and check the rising tears
　　　　That dim your lovely eyes;
　　Your feet are stumbling on the path
　　　　That so uneven lies.

SHARNGARAVA. Holy Father, the Scripture declares that one should accompany a departing loved one only to the first water. Pray give us your commands on the bank of this pond, and then return.

KANVA. Then let us rest in the shade of this fig-tree. (*All do so.*) What commands would it be fitting for me to lay on King Dushyanta?

ANUSUYA. My dear, there is not a living thing in the whole hermitage that is not grieving to-day at saying good-bye to you. Look!

　　The sheldrake does not heed his mate
　　　　Who calls behind the lotus-leaf;
　　He drops the lily from his bill
　　　　And turns on you a glance of grief.

KANVA. Son Sharngarava, when you present Shakuntala to the king, give him this message from me.

　　Remembering my religious worth,
　　Your own high race, the love poured forth
　　By her, forgetful of her friends,
　　Pay her what honour custom lends
　　To all your wives. And what fate gives
　　Beyond, will please her relatives.

SHARNGARAVA. I will not forget your message, Father.

KANVA (*turning to* SHAKUNTALA). My child, I must now give you my counsel. Though I live in the forest, I have some knowledge of the world.

SHARNGARAVA. True wisdom, Father, gives insight into everything.

KANVA. My child, when you have entered your husband's home,

　　Obey your elders; and be very kind
　　To rivals; never be perversely blind
　　And angry with your husband, even though he
　　Should prove less faithful than a man might be;
　　Be as courteous to servants as you may,
　　Not puffed with pride in this your happy day:
　　Thus does a maiden grow into a wife;
　　But self-willed women are the curse of life.

But what does Gautami say?

GAUTAMI. This is advice sufficient for a bride. You will not forget, my child.

KANVA. Come, my daughter, embrace me and your friends.

SHAKUNTALA. Oh, Father! Must my friends turn back too?

KANVA. My daughter, they too must some day be given in marriage. Therefore they may not go to court. Gautami will go with you.

SHAKUNTALA (*throwing her arms about her father*). I am torn from my father's breast like a vine stripped from a sandal-tree on the Malabar hills. How can I live in another soil?

KANVA. My daughter, why distress yourself so?

A noble husband's honourable wife,
You are to spend a busy, useful life
In the world's eye; and soon, as eastern skies
Bring forth the sun, from you there shall arise
A child, a blessing and a comfort strong—
You will not miss me, dearest daughter, long.

SHAKUNTALA. Farewell, Father.

KANVA. My daughter, may all that come to you which I desire for you.

SHAKUNTALA (*going to her two friends*). Come, girls! Embrace me, both of you together.

THE TWO FRIENDS. Dear, if the good king should perhaps be slow to recognise you, show him the ring with his own name engraved on it.

SHAKUNTALA. Your doubts make my heart beat faster.

THE TWO FRIENDS. Do not be afraid, dear. Love is timid.

SHARNGARAVA. Father, the sun is in mid-heaven. She must hasten.

SHAKUNTALA. Father, when shall I see the pious grove again?

KANVA. My daughter,

When you have shared for many years
The king's thoughts with the earth,
When to a son who knows no fears
You shall have given birth,

When, trusted to the son you love,
Your royal labours cease,
Come with your husband to the grove
And end your days in peace.

GAUTAMI. My child, the hour of your departure is slipping by. Bid your father turn back. No, she would never do that. Pray turn back, sir.

KANVA. Child, you interrupt my duties in the pious grove.

SHAKUNTALA. Yes, Father. You will be busy in the grove. You will not miss me. But oh! I miss you.

8–9. **Therefore . . . court;** that is, they may not go to a public place.

KANVA. How can you think me so indifferent?

My lonely sorrow will not go,
For seeds you scattered here
Before the cottage door, will grow;
And I shall see them, dear.

Go. And peace go with you. (*Exit* SHAKUNTALA, *with* GAUTAMI, SHARNGARAVA, *and* SHARADVATA.)

THE TWO FRIENDS (*gazing long after her*). Oh, oh! Shakuntala is lost among the trees.

KANVA. Anusuya! Priyamvada! Your companion is gone. Choke down your grief and follow me.

THE TWO FRIENDS. Father, the grove seems empty without Shakuntala.

KANVA. So love interprets. Ah! I have sent Shakuntala away, and now I am myself again. For

A girl is held in trust, another's treasure;
To arms of love my child to-day is given;
And now I feel a calm and sacred pleasure;
I have restored the pledge that came from heaven.

(*Exeunt omnes.*)

ACT V
SHAKUNTALA'S REJECTION

(*Enter the king and his retinue.*)

CHAMBERLAIN (*approaching*). Victory to your Majesty. Here are hermits who dwell in the forest at the foot of the Himalayas. They bring women with them, and they carry a message from Kanva. What is your pleasure with regard to them?

KING (*astonished*). Hermits? Accompanied by women? From Kanva?

CHAMBERLAIN. Yes.

KING. Request my chaplain Somarata in my name to receive these hermits in the manner prescribed by Scripture, and to conduct them himself before me. I will await them in a place fit for their reception.

CHAMBERLAIN. Yes, your Majesty. (*Exit.*)

KING (*rising*). Vetravati, conduct me to the fire-sanctuary.

PORTRESS. Follow me, your Majesty. (*She walks about.*) Your Majesty, here is the terrace of the fire-sanctuary. It is beautiful, for it has just been swept, and near at hand is the cow that yields the milk of sacrifice. Pray ascend it.

KING (*ascends and stands leaning on the shoulder of an attendant.*) Vetravati, with what purpose does Father Kanva send these hermits to me?

Do leaguèd powers of sin conspire
To balk religion's pure desire?
Has wrong been done to beasts that roam
Contented round the hermits' home?
Do plants no longer bud and flower,

To warn me of abuse of power?
These doubts and more assail my mind,
But leave me puzzled, lost, and blind.

PORTRESS. How could these things be in a hermitage that rests in the fame of the king's arm? No, I imagine they have come to pay homage to their king, and to congratulate him on his pious rule.

(*Enter the chaplain and the chamberlain, conducting the two pupils of* KANVA, *with* GAUTAMI *and* SHAKUNTALA.)

CHAMBERLAIN. Follow me, if you please.

SHARNGARAVA. Friend Sharadvata,

10 The king is noble and to virtue true;
None dwelling here commit the deed of shame;
Yet we ascetics view the worldly crew
As in a house all lapped about with flame.

SHARADVATA. Sharngarava, your emotion on entering the city is quite just. As for me,

Free from the world and all its ways,
I see them spending worldly days
As clean men view men smeared with oil,
As pure men, those whom passions soil,
20 As waking men view men asleep,
As free men, those in bondage deep.

CHAPLAIN. That is why men like you are great.

SHAKUNTALA (*observing an evil omen*). Oh, why does my right eye throb?

GAUTAMI. Heaven avert the omen, my child. May happiness wait upon you. (*They walk about.*)

CHAPLAIN. O hermits, here is he who protects those of every station and of every age. He has already risen, and awaits you. Behold him.

30 SHARNGARAVA. Yes, it is admirable, but not surprising. For

Fruit-laden trees bend down to earth;
The water-pregnant clouds hang low;
Good men are not puffed up by power—
The unselfish are by nature so.

PORTRESS. Your Majesty, the hermits seem to be happy. They give you gracious looks.

KING (*observing* SHAKUNTALA). Ah!

Who is she, shrouded in the veil
40 That dims her beauty's lustre,
Among the hermits like a flower
Round which the dead leaves cluster?

PORTRESS. Your Majesty, she is well worth looking at.

KING. Enough! I must not gaze upon another's wife.

SHAKUNTALA (*Aside*). Oh, my heart, why tremble so? Remember his constant love and be brave.

CHAPLAIN (*advancing*). Hail, your Majesty. The
50 hermits have been received as Scripture enjoins.

They have a message from their teacher. May you be pleased to hear it.

KING. I am all attention.

THE TWO PUPILS (*raising their right hands*). Victory, O King.

KING (*bowing low*). I salute you all.

THE TWO PUPILS. All hail.

KING. Does your pious life proceed without disturbance?

THE TWO PUPILS.

How could the pious duties fail   60
While you defend the right?
Or how could darkness' power prevail
O'er sunbeams shining bright?

KING (*to himself*). Indeed, my royal title is no empty one. (*Aloud.*) Is holy Kanva in health?

SHARNGARAVA. O King, those who have religious power can command health. He asks after your welfare and sends this message.

KING. What are his commands?

SHARNGARAVA. He says: "Since you have met this   70
my daughter and have married her, I give you my glad consent. For

You are the best of worthy men, they say;
And she, I know, Good Works personified;
The Creator wrought for ever and a day,
In wedding such a virtuous groom and bride.

She is with child. Take her and live with her in virtue."

GAUTAMI. Bless you, sir. I should like to say that no one invites me to speak.   80

KING. Speak, mother.

GAUTAMI.

Did she with father speak or mother?
Did you engage her friends in speech?
Your faith was plighted each to other;
Let each be faithful now to each.

SHAKUNTALA. What will my husband say?

KING (*listening with anxious suspicion*). What is this insinuation?

SHAKUNTALA (*to herself*). Oh, oh! So haughty and so slanderous!   90

SHARNGARAVA. "What is this insinuation?" What is your question? Surely you know the world's ways well enough.

Because the world suspects a wife
Who does not share her husband's lot,
Her kinsmen wish her to abide
With him, although he love her not.

KING. You cannot mean that this young woman is my wife.

SHAKUNTALA (*sadly to herself*). Oh, my heart,   100
you feared it, and now it has come.

SHARNGARAVA. O King,

A king, and shrink when love is done,
Turn coward's back on truth, and flee!

KING. What means this dreadful accusation?

SHARNGARAVA (*furiously*).

O drunk with power! We might have known
That you were steeped in treachery.

KING. A stinging rebuke!

GAUTAMI (*to* SHAKUNTALA). Forget your shame,
my child. I will remove your veil. Then your hus-
10 band will recognise you. (*She does so.*)

KING (*observing* SHAKUNTALA. *To himself*).

As my heart ponders whether I could ever
Have wed this woman that has come to me
In tortured loveliness, as I endeavour
To bring it back to mind, then like a bee

That hovers round a jasmine flower at dawn,
While frosty dews of morning still o'erweave it,
And hesitates to sip ere they be gone,
I cannot taste the sweet, and cannot leave it.

PORTRESS (*to herself*). What a virtuous king he is!
20 Would any other man hesitate when he saw such a
pearl of a woman coming of her own accord?

SHARNGARAVA. Have you nothing to say, O King?

KING. Hermit, I have taken thought. I cannot believe that this woman is my wife. She is plainly
with child. How can I take her, confessing myself
an adulterer?

SHAKUNTALA (*to herself*). Oh, oh, oh! He even
casts doubt on our marriage. The vine of my hope
climbed high, but it is broken now.

30 SHARNGARAVA. Not so.

You scorn the sage who rendered whole
His child befouled, and choked his grief,
Who freely gave you what you stole
And added honour to a thief!

SHARADVATA. Enough, Sharngarava. Shakuntala,
we have said what we were sent to say. You hear
his words. Answer him.

SHAKUNTALA (*to herself*). He loved me so. He is
so changed. Why remind him? Ah, but I must clear
40 my own character. Well, I will try. (*Aloud.*) My
dear husband— (*She stops.*) No, he doubts my
right to call him that. Your Majesty, it was pure
love that opened my poor heart to you in the hermitage. Then you were kind to me and gave me
your promise. Is it right for you to speak so now,
and to reject me?

KING (*stopping his ears*). Peace, peace!

A stream that eats away the bank,
Grows foul, and undermines the tree.
50 So you would stain your honour, while
You plunge me into misery.

SHAKUNTALA. Very well. If you have acted so because you really fear to touch another man's wife, I
will remove your doubts with a token you gave me.

KING. An excellent idea!

SHAKUNTALA (*touching her finger*). Oh, oh! The
ring is lost. (*She looks sadly at* GAUTAMI.)

GAUTAMI. My child, you worshipped the holy
Ganges at the spot where Indra descended. The
ring must have fallen there. 60

KING. Ready wit, ready wit!

SHAKUNTALA. Fate is too strong for me there. I
will tell you something else.

KING. Let me hear what you have to say.

SHAKUNTALA. One day, in the bower of reeds,
you were holding a lotus-leaf cup full of water.

KING. I hear you.

SHAKUNTALA. At that moment the fawn came up,
my adopted son. Then you took pity on him and
coaxed him. "Let him drink first," you said. But he 70
did not know you, and he would not come to drink
water from your hand. But he liked it afterwards,
when I held the very same water. Then you smiled
and said: "It is true. Every one trusts his own sort.
You both belong to the forest."

KING. It is just such women, selfish, sweet, false,
that entice fools.

GAUTAMI. You have no right to say that. She grew
up in the pious grove. She does not know how to
deceive. 80

KING. Old hermit woman,

The female's untaught cunning may be seen
In beasts, far more in women selfish-wise;
The cuckoo's eggs are left to hatch and rear
By foster-parents, and away she flies.

SHAKUNTALA (*angrily*). Wretch! You judge all
this by your own false heart. Would any other man
do what you have done? To hide behind virtue,
like a yawning well covered over with grass!

KING (*to himself*). But her anger is free from 90
coquetry, because she has lived in the forest. See!

Her glance is straight; her eyes are flashing red;
Her speech is harsh, not drawlingly well-bred;
Her whole lip quivers, seems to shake with cold;
Her frown has straightened eyebrows arching bold.

No, she saw that I was doubtful, and her anger was
feigned. Thus

When I refused but now
Hard-heartedly, to know
Of love or secret vow, 100
Her eyes grew red; and so,
Bending her arching brow,
She fiercely snapped Love's bow.

(*Aloud.*) My good girl, Dushyanta's conduct is
known to the whole kingdom, but not this action.

SHAKUNTALA. Well, well. I had my way. I trusted a king, and put myself in his hands. He had a honey face and a heart of stone. (*She covers her face with her dress and weeps.*)

SHARNGARAVA. Thus does unbridled levity burn.

> Be slow to love, but yet more slow
>   With secret mate;
> With those whose hearts we do not know,
>   Love turns to hate.

KING. Why do you trust this girl, and accuse me
10 of an imaginary crime?

SHARNGARAVA (*disdainfully*). You have learned your wisdom upside down.

> It would be monstrous to believe
>   A girl who never lies;
> Trust those who study to deceive
>   And think it very wise.

KING. Aha, my candid friend! Suppose I were to admit that I am such a man. What would happen if I deceived the girl?

20 SHARNGARAVA. Ruin.

KING. It is unthinkable that ruin should fall on Puru's line.

SHARNGARAVA. Why bandy words? We have fulfilled our Father's bidding. We are ready to return.

> Leave her or take her, as you will;
>   She is your wife;
> Husbands have power for good or ill
>   O'er woman's life.

Gautami, lead the way. (*They start to go.*)

30 SHAKUNTALA. He has deceived me shamelessly. And will you leave me too? (*She starts to follow.*)

GAUTAMI (*turns around and sees her*). Sharngarava, my son, Shakuntala is following us, lamenting piteously. What can the poor child do with a husband base enough to reject her?

SHARNGARAVA (*turns angrily*). You self-willed girl! Do you dare show independence? (SHAKUNTALA *shrinks in fear.*) Listen.

> If you deserve such scorn and blame,
40 >   What will your father with your shame?
> But if you know your vows are pure,
>   Obey your husband and endure.

Remain. We must go.

KING. Hermit, why deceive this woman? Remember:

> Night-blossoms open to the moon,
>   Day-blossoms to the sun;
> A man of honour ever strives
>   Another's wife to shun.

18–19. **What . . . girl.** The king is not asking for information; he knows the answer to his question. This is simply his way of emphasizing the impossibility of his lying.

SHARNGARAVA. O King, suppose you had forgotten
50 your former actions in the midst of distractions. Should you now desert your wife—you who fear to fail in virtue?

KING. I ask *you* which is the heavier sin:

> Not knowing whether I be mad
>   Or falsehood be in her,
> Shall I desert a faithful wife
>   Or turn adulterer?

CHAPLAIN (*considering*). Now if this were
60 done——

KING. Instruct me, my teacher.

CHAPLAIN. Let the woman remain in my house until her child is born.

KING. Why this?

CHAPLAIN. The chief astrologers have told you that your first child was destined to be an emperor. If the son of the hermit's daughter is born with the imperial birthmarks, then welcome her and introduce her into the palace. Otherwise, she must re-
70 turn to her father.

KING. It is good advice, my teacher.

CHAPLAIN (*rising*). Follow me, my daughter.

SHAKUNTALA. O mother earth, give me a grave! (*Exit weeping, with the chaplain, the hermits, and* GAUTAMI. *The king, his memory clouded by the curse, ponders on* SHAKUNTALA.)

VOICES BEHIND THE SCENES. A miracle! A miracle!

KING (*listening*). What does this mean? (*Enter the chaplain.*)

CHAPLAIN (*in amazement*). Your Majesty, a wonderful thing has happened.

KING. What?

CHAPLAIN. When Kanva's pupils had departed,

> She tossed her arms, bemoaned her plight,   80
>   Accused her crushing fate—

KING. What then?

CHAPLAIN.

> Before our eyes a heavenly light
> In woman's form, but shining bright,
>   Seized her and vanished straight.

(*All betray astonishment.*)

KING. My teacher, we have already settled the matter. Why speculate in vain? Let us seek repose.

CHAPLAIN. Victory to your Majesty. (*Exit.*)

KING. Vetravati, I am bewildered. Conduct me to my apartment.   90

PORTRESS. Follow me, your Majesty.

KING (*walks about. To himself*).

> With a hermit-wife I had no part,
>   All memories evade me;
> And yet my sad and stricken heart
>   Would more than half persuade me.

(*Exeunt omnes.*)

ACT VI

SEPARATION FROM SHAKUNTALA

SCENE I. *In the street before the Palace*

(*Enter the chief of police, two policemen, and a man with his hands bound behind his back.*)

THE TWO POLICEMEN (*striking the man*). Now, pickpocket, tell us where you found this ring. It is the king's ring, with letters engraved on it, and it has a magnificent great gem.

FISHERMAN (*showing fright*). Be merciful, kind gentlemen. I am not guilty of such a crime.

FIRST POLICEMAN. No, I suppose the king thought you were a pious Brahman, and made you a present of it.

FISHERMAN. Listen, please. I am a fisherman, and I live on the Ganges, at the spot where Indra came down.

SECOND POLICEMAN. You thief, we didn't ask for your address or your social position.

CHIEF. Let him tell a straight story, Suchaka. Don't interrupt.

THE TWO POLICEMEN. Yes, chief. Talk, man, talk.

FISHERMAN. I support my family with things you catch fish with—nets, you know, and hooks, and things.

CHIEF (*laughing*). You have a sweet trade.

FISHERMAN. Don't say that, master.

> You can't give up a lowdown trade
> That your ancestors began;
> A butcher butchers things, and yet
> He's the tenderest-hearted man.

CHIEF. Go on. Go on.

FISHERMAN. Well, one day I was cutting up a carp. In its maw I see this ring with the magnificent great gem. And then I was just trying to sell it here when you kind gentlemen grabbed me. That is the only way I got it. Now kill me, or find fault with me.

CHIEF (*smelling the ring*). There is no doubt about it, Januka. It has been in a fish's maw. It has the real perfume of raw meat. Now we have to find out how he got it. We must go to the palace.

THE TWO POLICEMEN (*to the fisherman*). Move on, you cutpurse, move on. (*They walk about.*)

CHIEF. Suchaka, wait here at the big gate until I come out of the palace. And don't get careless.

THE TWO POLICEMEN. Go in, chief. I hope the king will be nice to you.

CHIEF. Good-bye. (*Exit.*)

SUCHAKA. Januka, the chief is taking his time.

JANUKA. You can't just drop in on a king.

SUCHAKA. Januka, my fingers are itching (*indicating the fisherman*) to kill this cutpurse.

FISHERMAN. Don't kill a man without any reason, master.

JANUKA (*looking ahead*). There is the chief, with a written order from the king. (*To the fisherman.*) Now you will see your family, or else you will feed the crows and jackals. (*Enter the chief.*)

CHIEF. Quick! Quick!

FISHERMAN. Oh, oh! I'm a dead man.

CHIEF. Release him, you. Release the fishnet fellow. It is all right, his getting the ring. Our king told me so himself.

SUCHAKA. All right, chief. He is a dead man come back to life. (*He releases the fisherman.*)

FISHERMAN (*bowing low to the chief*). Master, I owe you my life. (*He falls at his feet.*)

CHIEF. Get up, get up! Here is a reward that the king was kind enough to give you. It is worth as much as the ring. Take it. (*He hands the fisherman a bracelet.*)

FISHERMAN (*joyfully taking it*). Much obliged.

JANUKA. He *is* much obliged to the king. Just as if he had been taken from the stake and put on an elephant's back.

SUCHAKA. Chief, the reward shows that the king thought a lot of the ring. The gem must be worth something.

CHIEF. No, it wasn't the fine gem that pleased the king. It was this way.

THE TWO POLICEMEN. Well?

CHIEF. I think, when the king saw it, he remembered somebody he loves. You know how dignified he is usually. But as soon as he saw it, he broke down for a moment.

SUCHAKA. You have done the king a good turn, chief.

JANUKA. All for the sake of this fish-killer, it seems to me. (*He looks enviously at the fisherman.*)

FISHERMAN. Take half of it, masters, to pay for something to drink.

JANUKA. Fisherman, you are the biggest and best friend I've got. The first thing we want, is all the brandy we can hold. Let's go where they keep it. (*Exeunt omnes.*)

SCENE II. *In the Palace Gardens*

(*Enter* MISHRAKESHI, *flying through the air.*)

MISHRAKESHI. I have taken my turn in waiting upon the nymphs. And now I will see what this good king is doing. Shakuntala is like a second self to me, because she is the daughter of Menaka. And it was she who asked me to do this. (*She looks about.*) It is the day of the spring festival. But I see no preparations for a celebration at court. I might learn the reason by my power of divination. But I must do as my friend asked me. Good! I will make myself invisible and stand near these girls who take care of the garden. I shall find out that way. (*She descends to earth. Enter a maid, gazing at a mango branch, and behind her, a second.*)

92. **Menaka,** a close friend of Mishrakeshi among the nymphs.

FIRST MAID.

> First mango-twig, so pink, so green,
> First living breath of spring,
> You are sacrificed as soon as seen,
> A festival offering.

SECOND MAID. What are you chirping about to yourself, little cuckoo?

FIRST MAID. Why, little bee, you know that the cuckoo goes crazy with delight when she sees the mango-blossom.

SECOND MAID. Oh, has the spring really come?

FIRST MAID. Yes, little bee. And this is the time when you too buzz about in crazy joy.

SECOND MAID. Hold me, dear, while I stand on tiptoe and offer this blossom to Love, the divine.

FIRST MAID. If I do, you must give me half the reward of the offering.

SECOND MAID. That goes without saying, dear. We two are one. (*She leans on her friend and takes the mango-blossom.*) Oh, see! The mango-blossom hasn't opened, but it has broken the sheath, so it is fragrant. (*She brings her hands together.*) I worship mighty Love.

> O mango-twig I give to Love
> As arrow for his bow,
> Most sovereign of his arrows five,
> Strike maiden-targets low.

(*She throws the twig. Enter the chamberlain.*)

CHAMBERLAIN (*angrily*). Stop, silly girl. The king has strictly forbidden the spring festival. Do you dare pluck the mango-blossoms?

THE TWO MAIDS (*frightened*). Forgive us, sir. We did not know.

CHAMBERLAIN. What! You have not heard the king's command, which is obeyed even by the trees of spring and the creatures that dwell in them. See!

> The mango branches are in bloom,
> Yet pollen does not form;
> The cuckoo's song sticks in his throat,
> Although the days are warm;
>
> The amaranth-bud is formed, and yet
> Its power of growth is gone;
> The love-god timidly puts by
> The arrow he has drawn.

MISHRAKESHI. There is no doubt of it. This good king has wonderful power.

FIRST MAID. A few days ago, sir, we were sent to his Majesty by his brother-in-law Mitravasu to decorate the garden. That is why we have heard nothing of this affair.

CHAMBERLAIN. You must not do so again.

THE TWO MAIDS. But we are curious. If we girls may know about it, pray tell us, sir. Why did his Majesty forbid the spring festival?

MISHRAKESHI. Kings are fond of celebrations. There must be some good reason.

CHAMBERLAIN (*to himself*). It is in everybody's mouth. Why should I not tell it? (*Aloud.*) Have you heard the gossip concerning Shakuntala's rejection?

THE TWO MAIDS. Yes, sir. The king's brother-in-law told us, up to the point where the ring was recovered.

CHAMBERLAIN. There is little more to tell. When his Majesty saw the ring, he remembered that he had indeed contracted a secret marriage with Shakuntala, and had rejected her under a delusion. And then he fell a prey to remorse.

> He hates the things he loved; he intermits
> The daily audience, nor in judgment sits;
> Spends sleepless nights in tossing on his bed;
> At times, when he by courtesy is led
> To address a lady, speaks another name,
> Then stands for minutes, sunk in helpless shame.

MISHRAKESHI. I am glad to hear it.

CHAMBERLAIN. His Majesty's sorrow has forbidden the festival.

THE TWO MAIDS. It is only right.

A VOICE BEHIND THE SCENES. Follow me.

CHAMBERLAIN. Ah, his Majesty approaches. Go, and attend to your duties. (*Exeunt the two maids. Enter the king, wearing a dress indicative of remorse; the clown, and the portress.*)

CHAMBERLAIN. A beautiful figure charms in whatever state. Thus, his Majesty is pleasing even in his sorrow. For

> All ornament is laid aside; he wears
> One golden bracelet on his wasted arm;
> His lip is scorched by sighs; and sleepless cares
> Redden his eyes. Yet all can work no harm
> On that magnificent beauty, wasting, but
> Gaining in brilliance, like a diamond cut.

MISHRAKESHI (*observing the king*). No wonder Shakuntala pines for him, even though he dishonoured her by his rejection of her.

KING (*walks about slowly, sunk in thought*).

> Alas! My smitten heart, that once lay sleeping,
> Heard in its dreams my fawn-eyed love's laments,
> And wakened now, awakens but to weeping,
> To bitter grief, and tears of penitence.

MISHRAKESHI. That is the poor girl's fate.

CLOWN (*to himself*). He has got his Shakuntala-sickness again. I wish I knew how to cure him.

CHAMBERLAIN (*advancing*). Victory to your Majesty. I have examined the garden. Your Majesty may visit its retreats.

KING. Vetravati, tell the minister Pishuna in my name that a sleepless night prevents me from mounting the throne of judgment. He is to investigate the citizens' business and send me a memorandum.

PORTRESS. Yes, your Majesty. (*Exit.*)

KING. And you, Parvatayana, return to your post of duty.

CHAMBERLAIN. Yes, your Majesty. (*Exit.*)

CLOWN. You have got rid of the vermin. Now amuse yourself in this garden. It is delightful with the passing of the cold weather.

10 KING (*sighing*). My friend, the proverb makes no mistake. Misfortune finds the weak spot. See!

No sooner did the darkness lift
That clouded memory's power,
Than the god of love prepared his bow
And shot the mango-flower.

No sooner did the ring recall
My banished maiden dear,
No sooner do I vainly weep
For her, than spring is here.

20 CLOWN. Wait a minute, man. I will destroy Love's arrow with my stick. (*He raises his stick and strikes at the mango branch.*)

KING (*smiling*). Enough! I see your pious power. My friend, where shall I sit now to comfort my eyes with the vines? They remind me somehow of her.

CLOWN. Well, you told one of the maids, the clever painter, that you would spend this hour in the bower of spring-creepers. And you asked her to bring you there the picture of the lady Shakuntala which you painted on a tablet.

30 KING. It is my only consolation. Lead the way to the bower of spring-creepers.

CLOWN. Follow me. (*They walk about.* MISHRAKE-SHI *follows.*) Here is the bower of spring-creepers, with its jewelled benches. Its loneliness seems to bid you a silent welcome. Let us go in and sit down. (*They do so.*)

MISHRAKESHI. I will hide among the vines and see the dear girl's picture. Then I shall be able to tell her how deep her husband's love is. (*She hides.*)

KING (*sighing*). I remember it all now, my friend.
40 I told you how I first met Shakuntala. It is true, you were not with me when I rejected her. But I had told you of her at the first. Had you forgotten, as I did?

MISHRAKESHI. This shows that a king should not be separated a single moment from some intimate friend.

CLOWN. No, I didn't forget. But when you had told the whole story, you said it was a joke and there was nothing in it. And I was fool enough to believe
50 you. No, this is the work of fate.

MISHRAKESHI. It must be.

KING (*after meditating a moment*). Help me, my friend. . . .

CLOWN. Don't talk that way. Why, the ring shows that incredible meetings do happen.

KING (*looking at the ring*). This ring deserves pity. It has fallen from a heaven hard to earn.

Your virtue, ring, like mine,
Is proved to be but small;
Her pink-nailed finger sweet   60
You clasped. How could you fall?

MISHRAKESHI. If it were worn on any other hand, it would deserve pity. My dear girl, you are far away. I am the only one to hear these delightful words.

CLOWN. Tell me how you put the ring on her finger.

MISHRAKESHI. He speaks as if prompted by my curiosity.

KING. Listen, my friend. When I left the pious   70
grove for the city, my darling wept and said: "But how long will you remember us, dear?"

CLOWN. And then you said——

KING. Then I put this engraved ring on her finger, and said to her——

CLOWN. Well, what?

KING. Count every day one letter of my name;
Before you reach the end, dear,
Will come to lead you to my palace halls
A guide whom I shall send, dear.   80

Then, through my madness, it fell out cruelly.

MISHRAKESHI. It was too charming an agreement to be frustrated by fate.

CLOWN. But how did it get into a carp's mouth, as if it had been a fish-hook?

KING. While she was worshipping the Ganges at Shachitirtha, it fell.

CLOWN. I see.

MISHRAKESHI. That is why the virtuous king doubted his marriage with poor Shakuntala. Yet   90
such love does not ask for a token. How could it have been?

KING. Well, I can only reproach this ring. . . .

CLOWN. But that is no reason why I should starve to death. . . . If you get out of the trap alive, call for me at the Cloud Balcony. (*Exit on the run.*) . . .

MISHRAKESHI. Shall I make him happy now? No, I heard the mother of the gods consoling Shakuntala. She said that the gods, impatient for the sacrifice, would soon cause him to welcome his true wife. I   100
must delay no longer. I will comfort dear Shakuntala with my tidings. (*Exit through the air.*)

A VOICE BEHIND THE SCENES. Help, help!

KING (*comes to himself and listens*). It sounds as if Madhavya were in distress. . . .

CHAMBERLAIN. Save your friend, O King!

KING. From what?

CHAMBERLAIN. From great danger.

KING. Speak plainly, man.

CHAMBERLAIN. On the Cloud Balcony, open to the four winds of heaven——
KING. What has happened there?
CHAMBERLAIN.

> While he was resting on its height,
> Which palace peacocks in their flight
> Can hardly reach, he seemed to be
> Snatched up—by what, we could not see.

KING (*rising quickly*). My very palace is invaded by evil creatures. To be a king, is to be a disappointed man.

> The moral stumblings of mine own,
> The daily slips, are scarcely known;
> Who then that rules a kingdom, can
> Guide every deed of every man?

THE VOICE. Hurry, hurry!
KING (*hears the voice and quickens his steps*). Have no fear, my friend.
THE VOICE. Have no fear! When something has got me by the back of the neck, and is trying to break my bones like a piece of sugar-cane!
KING (*looks about*). A bow! a bow! (*Enter a Greek woman with a bow.*)
GREEK WOMAN. A bow and arrows, your Majesty. And here are the finger-guards. (*The king takes the bow and arrows.*)
ANOTHER VOICE BEHIND THE SCENES.

> Writhe, while I drink the red blood flowing clear
> And kill you, as a tiger kills a deer;
> Let King Dushyanta grasp his bow; but how
> Can all his kingly valour save you now?

KING (*angrily*). He scorns me, too! In one moment, miserable demon, you shall die. (*Stringing his bow.*) Where is the stairway, Parvatayana?
CHAMBERLAIN. Here, your Majesty. (*All make haste.*)
KING (*looking about*). There is no one here.
THE CLOWN'S VOICE. Save me, save me! I see you, if you can't see me. I am a mouse in the claws of the cat. I am done for.
KING. You are proud of your invisibility. But shall not my arrow see you? Stand still. Do not hope to escape by clinging to my friend.

> My arrow, flying when the bow is bent,
> Shall slay the wretch and spare the innocent;
> When milk is mixed with water in a cup,
> Swans leave the water, and the milk drink up.

(*He takes aim. Enter MATALI and the clown.*)
MATALI. O King, as Indra, king of the gods, commands,

> Seek foes among the evil powers alone;
> For them your bow should bend;

> Not cruel shafts, but glances soft and kind
> Should fall upon a friend.

KING (*hastily withdrawing the arrow*). It is Matali. Welcome to the charioteer of heaven's king.
CLOWN. Well! He came within an inch of butchering me. And you welcome him.
MATALI (*smiling*). Hear, O King, for what purpose Indra sends me to you.
KING. I am all attention.
MATALI. There is a host of demons who call themselves Invincible—the brood of Kalanemi.
KING. So Narada has told me.
MATALI.

> Heaven's king is powerless; you shall smite
> His foes in battle soon;
> Darkness that overcomes the day,
> Is scattered by the moon.

Take your bow at once, enter my heavenly chariot, and set forth for victory.
KING. I am grateful! for the honour which Indra shows me. But why did you act thus toward Madhavya?
MATALI. I will tell you. I saw that you were overpowered by some inner sorrow, and acted thus to rouse you. For

> The spurnèd snake will swell his hood;
> Fire blazes when 'tis stirred;
> Brave men are roused to fighting mood
> By some insulting word.

KING. Friend Madhavya, I must obey the bidding of heaven's king. Go, acquaint the minister Pishuna with the matter, and add these words of mine:

> Your wisdom only shall control
> The kingdom for a time;
> My bow is strung; a distant goal
> Calls me, and tasks sublime.

CLOWN. Very well. (*Exit.*)
MATALI. Enter the chariot. (*The king does so. Exeunt omnes.*)

ACT VII

(*Enter, in a chariot that flies through the air, the king and* MATALI.)

KING. Matali, though I have done what Indra commanded, I think myself an unprofitable servant, when I remember his most gracious welcome.
MATALI. O King, know that each considers himself the other's debtor. For

> You count the service given
> Small by the welcome paid,
> Which to the king of heaven
> Seems mean for such brave aid.

KING. Ah, no! For the honour given me at parting went far beyond imagination. Before the gods, he seated me beside him on his throne. And then

He smiled, because his son Jayanta's heart
Beat quicker, by the self-same wish oppressed,
And placed about my neck the heavenly wreath
Still fragrant from the sandal on his breast.

MATALI. But what do you not deserve from heaven's king? Remember:

Twice, from peace-loving Indra's sway
The demon-thorn was plucked away:
First, by Man-lion's crooked claws;
Again, by your smooth shafts to-day.

KING. This merely proves Indra's majesty. Remember:

All servants owe success in enterprise
To honour paid before the great deed's done;
Could dawn defeat the darkness otherwise
Than resting on the chariot of the sun?

MATALI. The feeling becomes you. (*After a little.*) See, O King! Your glory has the happiness of being published abroad in heaven.

With colours used by nymphs of heaven
To make their beauty shine,
Gods write upon the surface given
Of many a magic vine,
As worth their song, the simple story
Of those brave deeds that made your glory.

KING. Matali, when I passed before, I was intent on fighting the demons, and did not observe this region. Tell me. In which path of the winds are we?
MATALI.

It is the windpath sanctified
By holy Vishnu's second stride;
Which, freed from dust of passion, ever
Upholds the threefold heavenly river;
And, driving them with reins of light,
Guides the stars in wheeling flight.

KING. That is why serenity pervades me, body and soul. (*He observes the path taken by the chariot.*) It seems that we have descended into the region of the clouds.
MATALI. How do you perceive it?
KING.

Plovers that fly from mountain-caves,
Steeds that quick-flashing lightning laves,
And chariot-wheels that drip with spray—
A path o'er pregnant clouds betray.

33. **Vishnu's second stride.** The god conquered the earth in three great steps or strides. 35. **the threefold heavenly river,** the sacred Ganges of heaven, earth, and underworld.

MATALI. You are right. And in a moment you will be in the world over which you bear rule.
KING (*looking down*). Matali, our quick descent gives the world of men a mysterious look. For

The plains appear to melt and fall
From mountain peaks that grow more tall;
The trunks of trees no longer hide
Nor in their leafy nests abide;
The river network now is clear,
For smaller streams at last appear:
It seems as if some being threw
The world to me, for clearer view.

MATALI. You are a good observer, O King. There is a noble loveliness in the earth.
KING. Matali, what mountain is this, its flanks sinking into the eastern and into the western sea? It drips liquid gold like a cloud at sunset.
MATALI. O King, this is Gold Peak, the mountain of the fairy centaurs. Here it is that ascetics most fully attain to magic powers. See!

The ancient sage, Marichi's son,
Child of the Uncreated One,
Father of superhuman life,
Dwells here austerely with his wife.

KING. I must not neglect the happy chance. I cannot go farther until I have walked humbly about the holy one.
MATALI. It is a worthy thought, O King. (*The chariot descends.*) We have come down to earth.
KING (*astonished*). Matali,

The wheels are mute on whirling rim;
Unstirred, the dust is lying there;
We do not bump the earth, but skim:
Still, still we seem to fly through air.

MATALI. Such is the glory of the chariot which obeys you and Indra.
KING. In which direction lies the hermitage of Marichi's son?
MATALI (*pointing*). See!

Where stands the hermit, horridly austere,
Whom clinging vines are choking, tough and sere;
Half-buried in an ant-hill that has grown
About him, standing post-like and alone;
Sun-staring with dim eyes that know no rest,
The dead skin of a serpent on his breast:
So long he stood unmoved, insensate there
That birds build nests within his mat of hair.

64. **Gold Peak, the mountain of the fairy centaurs,** a holy mountain of the Himalayas beside the paradise of Kubera, the god of riches. 67–70. **The ancient sage . . . life.** The ancient saga Kashyapa, the father of Vishnu, Indra, and many other gods, was the son of Marichi, who was in turn the son of Brahma, the Creator. Also, Kashyapa's wife, Aditi, was a granddaughter of Brahmā. The god Brahmā was created by Brahma the First Cause.

KING. All honour to one who mortifies the flesh so terribly.

MATALI. We have entered the hermitage of the ancient sage, whose wife Aditi tends the coral-trees.

KING. Here is deeper contentment than in heaven. I seem plunged in a pool of nectar.

MATALI (*stopping the chariot*). Descend, O King.

KING (*descending*). But how will you fare?

MATALI. The chariot obeys the word of command.
10 I too will descend. (*He does so.*) Before you, O King, are the groves where the holiest hermits lead their self-denying life.

KING. I look with amazement both at their simplicity and at what they might enjoy.

> Their appetites are fed with air
> Where grows whatever is most fair;
> They bathe religiously in pools
> Which golden lily-pollen cools;
> They pray within a jewelled home,
20 Are chaste where nymphs of heaven roam:
> They mortify desire and sin
> With things that others fast to win.

MATALI. The desires of the great aspire high. (*He walks about and speaks to some one not visible.*) Ancient Shakalya, how is Marichi's holy son occupied? (*He listens.*) What do you say? That he is explaining to Aditi, in answer to her question, the duties of a faithful wife? My matter must await a fitter time. (*He turns to the king.*) Wait here, O
30 King, in the shade of the ashoka tree, till I have announced your coming to the sire of Indra.

KING. Very well. (*Exit* MATALI. *The king's arm throbs, a happy omen.*)

> I dare not hope for what I pray;
> Why thrill—in vain?
> For heavenly bliss once thrown away
> Turns into pain.

A VOICE BEHIND THE SCENES. Don't! You mustn't be so foolhardy. Oh, you are always the same.

KING. No naughtiness could feel at home in this spot. Who draws such a rebuke upon himself? (*He
40 looks towards the sound. In surprise.*) It is a child, but no child in strength. And two hermit-women are trying to control him.

> He drags a struggling lion cub,
> The lioness' milk half-sucked, half-missed,
> Towzles his mane, and tries to drub
> Him tame with small, imperious fist.

(*Enter a small boy, as described, and two hermit-women.*)

BOY. Open your mouth, cub. I want to count your teeth.

FIRST WOMAN. Naughty boy, why do you torment
50 our pets? They are like children to us. Your energy seems to take the form of striking something. No wonder the hermits call you All-tamer.

KING. Why should my heart go out to this boy as if he were my own son? No doubt my childless state makes me sentimental.

SECOND WOMAN. The lioness will spring at you if you don't let her baby go.

BOY (*smiling*). Oh, I'm dreadfully scared. (*He bites his lip.*)

KING (*in surprise*).

> The boy is seed of fire
> Which, when its grows, will burn;   60
> A tiny spark that soon
> To awful flame may turn.

FIRST WOMAN. Let the little lion go, dear. I will give you another plaything.

BOY. Where is it? Give it to me. (*He stretches out his hand.*)

KING (*looking at the hand.*) He has one of the imperial birthmarks! For

> Between the eager fingers grow
> The close-knit webs together drawn,
> Like some lone lily opening slow   70
> To meet the kindling blush of dawn.

SECOND WOMAN. Suvrata, we can't make him stop by talking. Go. In my cottage you will find a painted clay peacock that belongs to the hermit-boy Mankanaka. Bring him that.

FIRST WOMAN. I will. (*Exit.*)

BOY. Meanwhile I'll play with this one.

HERMIT-WOMAN (*looks and laughs*). Let him go.

KING. My heart goes out to this wilful child.

> They show their little buds of teeth   80
> In peals of causeless laughter;
> They hide their trustful heads beneath
> Your heart. And stumbling after
> Come sweet, unmeaning sounds that sing
> To you. The father warms
> And loves the very dirt they bring
> Upon their little forms.

HERMIT-WOMAN (*shaking her finger*). Won't you mind me? (*She looks about.*) Which one of the hermit-boys is here? (*She sees the king.*) Oh, sir,   90
please come here and free this lion cub. The little rascal is tormenting him, and I can't make him let go.

KING. Very well. (*He approaches, smiling.*) O little son of a great sage!

> Your conduct in this place apart,
> Is most unfit;
> 'Twould grieve your father's pious heart
> And trouble it.

> To animals he is as good   100
> As good can be;

You spoil it, like a black snake's brood
In sandal tree.

HERMIT-WOMAN. But, sir, he is not the son of a hermit.

KING. So it would seem, both from his looks and his actions. But in this spot, I had no suspicion of anything else. (*He loosens the boy's hold on the cub, and touching him, says to himself.*)

It makes me thrill to touch the boy,
The stranger's son, to me unknown;
What measureless content must fill
The man who calls the child his own!

HERMIT-WOMAN (*looking at the two*). Wonderful! wonderful!

KING. Why do you say that, mother?

HERMIT-WOMAN. I am astonished to see how much the boy looks like you, sir. You are not related. Besides, he is a perverse little creature and he does not know you. Yet he takes no dislike to you.

KING (*caressing the boy*). Mother, if he is not the son of a hermit, what is his family?

HERMIT-WOMAN. The family of Puru.

KING (*to himself*). He is of one family with me! Then could my thought be true? (*Aloud.*) But this is the custom of Puru's line:

In glittering palaces they dwell
While men, and rule the country well;
Then make the grove their home in age,
And die in austere hermitage.

But how could human beings, of their own mere motion, attain this spot?

HERMIT-WOMAN. You are quite right, sir. But the boy's mother was related to a nymph, and she bore her son in the pious grove of the father of the gods.

KING (*to himself*). Ah, a second ground for hope. (*Aloud.*) What was the name of the good king whose wife she was?

HERMIT-WOMAN. Who would speak his name? He rejected his true wife.

KING (*to himself*). This story points at me. Suppose I ask the boy for his mother's name. (*He reflects.*) No, it is wrong to concern myself with one who may be another's wife. (*Enter the first woman, with the clay peacock.*)

FIRST WOMAN. Look, All-tamer. Here is the bird, the *shakunta*. Isn't the *shakunta* lovely?

BOY (*looks about*). Where is my mamma? (*The two women burst out laughing.*)

FIRST WOMAN. It sounded like her name, and deceived him. He loves his mother.

SECOND WOMAN. She said: "See how pretty the peacock is." That is all.

KING (*to himself*). His mother's name is Shakuntala! But names are alike. I trust this hope may not prove a disappointment in the end, like a mirage.

BOY. I like this little peacock, sister. Can it fly? (*He seizes the toy.*)

FIRST WOMAN (*looks at the boy. Anxiously*). Oh, the amulet is not on his wrist.

KING. Do not be anxious, mother. It fell while he was struggling with the lion cub. (*He starts to pick it up.*)

THE TWO WOMEN. Oh, don't, don't! (*They look at him.*) He has touched it! (*Astonished, they lay their hands on their bosoms, and look at each other.*)

KING. Why did you try to prevent me?

FIRST WOMAN. Listen, your Majesty. This is a divine and most potent charm, called the Invincible. Marichi's holy son gave it to the baby when the birth-ceremony was performed. If it falls on the ground, no one may touch it except the boy's parents or the boy himself.

KING. And if another touch it?

FIRST WOMAN. It becomes a serpent and stings him.

KING. Did you ever see this happen to any one else?

BOTH WOMEN. More than once.

KING (*joyfully*). Then why may I not welcome my hopes fulfilled at last? (*He embraces the boy.*)

SECOND WOMAN. Come, Suvrata. Shakuntala is busy with her religious duties. We must go and tell her what has happened. (*Exeunt ambo.*)

BOY. Let me go. I want to see my mother.

KING. My son, you shall go with me to greet your mother.

BOY. Dushyanta is my father, not you.

KING (*smiling*). You show I am right by contradicting me. (*Enter SHAKUNTALA, wearing her hair in a single braid.*)

SHAKUNTALA (*doubtfully*). I have heard that Alltamer's amulet did not change when it should have done so. But I do not trust my own happiness. Yet perhaps it is as Mishrakeshi told me. (*She walks about.*)

KING (*looking at SHAKUNTALA. With plaintive joy*). It is she. It is Shakuntala.

The pale, worn face, the careless dress,
The single braid,
Show her still true, me pitiless,
The long vow paid.

SHAKUNTALA (*seeing the king pale with remorse. Doubtfully*). It is not my husband. Who is the man that soils my boy with his caresses? The amulet should protect him.

BOY (*running to his mother*). Mother, he is a man that belongs to other people. And he calls me his son.

KING. My darling, the cruelty I showed you has turned to happiness. Will you not recognise me?

SHAKUNTALA (*to herself*). Oh, my heart, believe

it. Fate struck hard, but its envy is gone and pity takes its place. It is my husband.

KING.

> Black madness flies;
> Comes memory;
> Before my eyes
> My love I see.
>
> Eclipse flees far;
> Light follows soon;
> The loving star
> Draws to the moon.

SHAKUNTALA. Victory, victo—— (*Tears choke her utterance.*)

KING.

> The tears would choke you, sweet, in vain;
> My soul with victory is fed,
> Because I see your face again—
> No jewels, but the lips are red.

BOY. Who is he, mother?

SHAKUNTALA. Ask fate, my child. (*She weeps.*)

KING.

> Dear, graceful wife, forget;
> Let the sin vanish;
> Strangely did madness strive
> Reason to banish.
>
> Thus blindness works in men,
> Love's joy to shake;
> Spurning a garland, lest
> It prove a snake. (*He falls at her feet.*)

SHAKUNTALA. Rise, my dear husband. Surely, it was some old sin of mine that broke my happiness— though it has turned again to happiness. Otherwise, how could you, dear, have acted so? You are so kind. (*The king rises.*) But what brought back the memory of your suffering wife?

KING. I will tell you when I have plucked out the dart of sorrow.

> 'Twas madness, sweet, that could let slip
> A tear to burden your dear lip;
> On graceful lashes seen to-day,
> I wipe it, and our grief, away. (*He does so.*)

SHAKUNTALA (*sees more clearly and discovers the ring*). My husband, it is the ring!

KING. Yes. And when a miracle recovered it, my memory returned.

SHAKUNTALA. That was why it was impossible for me to win your confidence.

KING. Then let the vine receive her flower, as earnest of her union with spring.

SHAKUNTALA. I do not trust it. I would rather you wore it. (*Enter* MATALI.)

MATALI. I congratulate you, O King, on reunion with your wife and on seeing the face of your son.

KING. My desires bear sweeter fruit because fulfilled through a friend. Matali, was not this matter known to Indra?

MATALI. What is hidden from the gods? Come. Marichi's holy son, Kashyapa, wishes to see you.

KING. My dear wife, bring our son. I could not appear without you before the holy one.

SHAKUNTALA. I am ashamed to go before such parents with my husband.

KING. It is the custom in times of festival. Come. (*They walk about.* KASHYAPA *appears seated, with* ADITI.)

KASHYAPA (*looking at the king*). Aditi,

> 'Tis King Dushyanta, he who goes before
> Your son in battle, and who rules the earth,
> Whose bow makes Indra's weapon seem no more
> Than a fine plaything, lacking sterner worth.

ADITI. His valour might be inferred from his appearance.

MATALI. O King, the parents of the gods look upon you with a glance that betrays parental fondness. Approach them.

KING. Matali,

> Sprung from the Creator's children, do I see
> Great Kashyapa and Mother Aditi? . . .

MATALI. It is indeed they.

KING (*falling before them*). Dushyanta, servant of Indra, does reverence to you both.

KASHYAPA. My son, rule the earth long.

ADITI. And be invincible. (SHAKUNTALA *and her son fall at their feet.*)

KASHYAPA. My daughter,

> Your husband equals Indra, king
> Of gods; your son is like his son;
> No further blessing need I bring:
> Win bliss such as his wife has won.

ADITI. My child, keep the favour of your husband. And may this fine boy be an honour to the families of both parents. Come, let us be seated. (*All seat themselves.*)

KASHYAPA.

> Faithful Shakuntala, the boy,
> And you, O King, I see
> A trinity to bless the world—
> Faith, Treasure, Piety.

KING. Holy one, your favour shown to us is without parallel. You granted the fulfillment of our wishes before you called us to your presence. For, holy one,

> The flower comes first, and then the fruit;
> The clouds appear before the rain;

Effect comes after cause; but you
First helped, then made your favour plain.

MATALI. O King, such is the favour shown by the parents of the world.

KING. Holy one, I married this your maid-servant by the voluntary ceremony. When after a time her relatives brought her to me, my memory failed and I rejected her. In so doing, I sinned against Kanva, who is kin to you. But afterwards, when I saw the ring, I perceived that I had married her. And this seems very wonderful to me.

Like one who doubts an elephant,
Though seeing him stride by,
And yet believes when he has seen
The footprints left; so I.

KASHYAPA. My son, do not accuse yourself of sin. Your infatuation was inevitable. Listen.

KING. I am all attention.

KASHYAPA. When the nymph Menaka descended to earth and received Shakuntala, afflicted at her rejection, she came to Aditi. Then I perceived the matter by my divine insight. I saw that the unfortunate girl had been rejected by her rightful husband because of Durvasas' curse. And that the curse would end when the ring came to light.

KING (to himself). Then I am free from blame.

SHAKUNTALA (to herself). Thank heaven! My husband did not reject me of his own accord. He really did not remember me. I suppose I did not hear the curse in my absent-minded state, for my friends warned me most earnestly to show my husband the ring.

KASHYAPA. My daughter, you know the truth. Do not now give way to anger against your rightful husband. Remember:

The curse it was that brought defeat and pain;
The darkness flies; you are his queen again.
Reflections are not seen in dusty glass,
Which, cleaned, will mirror all the things that pass.

KING. It is most true, holy one.

KASHYAPA. My son, I hope you have greeted as he deserves the son whom Shakuntala has borne you, for whom I myself have performed the birth-rite and the other ceremonies.

KING. Holy one, the hope of my race centres in him.

KASHYAPA. Know then that his courage will make him emperor.

Journeying over every sea,
His car will travel easily;
The seven islands of the earth
Will bow before his matchless worth;
Because wild beasts to him were tame,
All-tamer was his common name;

As Bharata he shall be known,
For he will bear the world alone.

KING. I anticipate everything from him, since you have performed the rites for him.

ADITI. Kanva also should be informed that his daughter's wishes are fulfilled. But Menaka is waiting upon me here and cannot be spared.

SHAKUNTALA (to herself). The holy one has expressed my own desire.

KASHYAPA. Kanva knows the whole matter through his divine insight. (He reflects.) Yet he should hear from us the pleasant tidings, how his daughter and her son have been received by her husband. Who waits without? (Enter a pupil.)

PUPIL. I am here, holy one.

KASHYAPA. Galava, fly through the air at once, carrying pleasant tidings from me to holy Kanva. Tell him how Durvasas' curse has come to an end, how Dushyanta recovered his memory, and has taken Shakuntala with her child to himself.

PUPIL. Yes, holy one. (Exit.)

KASHYAPA (to the king). My son, enter with child and wife the chariot of your friend Indra, and set out for your capital.

KING. Yes, holy one.

KASHYAPA. For now

May Indra send abundant rain,
Repaid by sacrificial gain;
With aid long mutually given,
Rule you on earth, and he in heaven.

KING. Holy one, I will do my best.

KASHYAPA. What more, my son, shall I do for you?

KING. Can there be more than this? Yet may this prayer be fulfilled.

May kingship benefit the land,
And wisdom grow in scholars' band;
May Shiva see my faith on earth
And make me free of all rebirth.
(Exeunt omnes.)

The Hebrew Bible

The Jews have a long literary tradition, dating from before the time of King David, in Hebrew, Aramaic, Yiddish, and other languages, and one of their books has a unique place in world culture. The Hebrew Bible, called simply "The Sacred Writings" by the Jews, was written in sections by many individuals between the tenth and fifth centuries B.C. By 400 B.C. the first five books, or Torah, had come to have a peculiar sacredness as the Word of God, but as late as 90 A.D. the rabbis were still debating whether some later sections, Esther, Ecclesiastes, and The Song of Songs, should have a place in the canon. Two other world religions, Christianity and Mohammedanism, eventually grafted their religious dogma onto the ancient writ, and the holy book of the Hebrews became sacred to half the world. It was a Christian divine, John Chrysostom, bishop of Constantinople in the fourth century A.D., who gave the name "Biblia," meaning "Books," to these holy books of the Jews.*

The name was well chosen, because the Hebrew Bible is not one book, but a library covering a wide variety of literary forms and subject matter. The thirty-nine books are divided by Jewish tradition into three sections: the *Law*, five books of folklore, national history, and religious code; the *Prophets,* consisting of twenty-one books of sermons, rhapsodies, and later history; and the *Writings*, a miscellaneous collection of thirteen books of hymns (Psalms), epigrams and adages (Proverbs), drama (Job), love poetry (The Song of Songs), short stories (Ruth, Esther, Daniel), and essays (Ecclesiastes). This arrangement emphasizes the literary classification of the books much better than the Christian arrangement.

Works of such diverse character served a variety of purposes in Hebrew national life. The *Law* was the basis of education in history and metaphysics; it was the source of authority in regulating the lives of men and punishing those who offended the code. Ezra originated the custom of public readings from the *Torah* on market days and on the Sabbath, when the reader would comment on the passages in the manner of a religious preacher in our day. Much of the *Prophets* obviously originated as sermons, delivered more often in the market place than in the temple. The Proverbs floated in the public memory and speech as ready rules of conduct. The Psalms were the group prayers of the temple and later of the synagogue, and were sometimes sung as hymns are sung in Christian churches. Thus all the major books sprang in one way or another from the core of Hebrew national life.

The Bible reflects several stages in the social development of the Hebrews. The tales of the patriarchs in Genesis picture simple shepherds living in tents and moving frequently to new grazing lands. But with the settlement in Canaan the tents gave way to huts and eventually to houses in villages as the Hebrews became largely an agricultural people. Since Moses recognized the cultivation

of the land as man's principal occupation, every family had its own estate, and the sons and daughters and their slaves went daily to tend the fields and the herds.

From the time of David, Jerusalem rose as the urban center of the Hebrew world, and commerce and craftsmanship gradually challenged sheepherding and farming as the chief occupations of the people. But the domestic life portrayed in the Bible remains essentially simple and earthy. The principal figures of speech are still those of the commoner's life and physical person, and the land, the plants, and the animals he knew. God is the good shepherd and we His sheep. "Keep me as the apple of the eye, hide me under the shadow of thy wings." (Psalm 17:8) "Speak to the earth, and it shall teach thee." (Job 12:8) "Flee as a bird to your mountain." (Psalm 11:1) "My days are swifter than a weaver's shuttle." (Job 7:6) "His heart is . . . as hard as a piece of the nether millstone." (Job 41:24)

Hardship made the Hebrew sober and earnest, little given to the public games and diversions so characteristic of the Greeks. Yet the love of music was strong in his nature and is reflected in the musical quality of language in the Psalms, The Song of Songs, and some of the prophetic writings. Stringed, wind, and percussion instruments are mentioned in the Bible, but it was the voice that gave utterance to the Hebrew's profound religious fervor. David directed a chorus of four thousand voices in the temple, singing the praises of the Lord, and under later kings music reached even greater heights. The tie between music and poetry was strong among the Hebrews as among the ancient Greeks.

Only in recent years has it become fashionable to see in the Bible a masterpiece of literary art. Yet its poetic power and beauty have been recognized by English authors for three centuries, and the distinctive phrasing of the King James Version has long been one of the fundamental styles in our language. Its primitive simplicity and nobility suggest Homer, although Hebrew poetry is innocent of the set accents and meters of classical verse. It depends for its effect on a few simple devices: repetition of phrase in refrain (Ecclesiastes 3:1–8), repetition of the same idea in different words (Psalm 19:7–9), contrast (Psalm 1), and abundant metaphor (The Song of Songs 2:2–3).

The prophetic books show a clear evolution in style. The early ones are close to primitive speech, with brief, loosely connected sentences and with the heightened rhythm of a chant. Later prophets show more polish, but are still highly direct and concrete in their imagery. Their message was to the people, and they shunned abstractions and literary decoration. Their chief device was parallel structure: "And he shall judge among the nations, and shall rebuke many people: and they shall beat their swords into ploughshares, and their spears into pruning hooks." (Isaiah 2:4) With simple literary devices such as these, the authors of the Hebrew Bible, largely anonymous, converted their religious and national fervor into glowing song and story.

The Psalms are the Hebrews' hymns of praise, the most important book in their third division of the Bible. Al-

---

* The oldest Hebrew text of the Bible dates from 916 A.D., but of equal importance in Biblical scholarship is a Greek translation called the *Septuagint*, made for the Alexandrian world in the third century B.C. and preserved in a manuscript of the eighth century. The Roman Catholic canon adds to the Hebrew Bible the fourteen books of the *Apocrypha*, but the Protestant canon follows the Jewish in outlawing these. Although the first complete translation of the Bible into English dates from the fourteenth century and John Wycliffe, the standard English version is the one authorized by King James I in 1604 and completed by a corps of forty-seven scholars in 1611. The simple dignity of this version has helped to make it a great English classic. The Catholic translation of comparable influence is popularly called the Douai Bible, after the University of Douai in northern France (originally Flanders), where exiled English Catholic scholars prepared it in its first form in the late sixteenth century. The several modern versions of the Douay Bible have been much revised.

though 73 of the 150 lyrics are ascribed to King David, nearly all of them are much later, dating from the periods immediately preceding and following the fifty-year exile of the Jews in Babylon. Some may be as late as the bloody reign of the Maccabees. In this supreme collection of hymns we find ecstatic avowals of the majesty of God (Psalm 97) and the universe that He created (Psalms 8 and 19) beside the humility of His worshipers (Psalms 23 and 90). The range of ideas is tremendous. All of nature finds its place in this impassioned tribute to God's power in the life of man.

Proverbs is a miscellaneous compilation of wise and witty epigrams, which, taken together, provide a practical code of living. Although devotion to God lies behind this sane advice, the emphasis is upon the earthly fruits of a sensible, virtuous life. Of the thirty-one chapters, 10 through 22 would seem to be the ancient core of the collection, traditionally attributed to wise King Solomon.

The ecstatic outcries of devotion found in Psalms and the *Prophets* meet a skeptical answer in the grim pessimism of Ecclesiastes. The ancient capacity of the Jew to bear suffering and even to enjoy it appears in the bitter conclusion that virtue does not lead to success in our world of chance. "The race is not to the swift, nor the battle to the strong." All is vanity in this soulless place, where men and beasts lead similar lives and come to the same end. What joy life holds lies not in the delusion of divine justice but in our enjoyment of work and simple, immediate pleasures. Later editors doctored this gloomy essay to read that worldly things are vain only in comparison with devotion to God.

If this melancholy appraisal of human aspiration had a hard time establishing itself in the holy canon, how can we account for the presence there of a collection of sensuous Oriental love lyrics called The Song of Songs? A series of wedding songs, ascribed alternately to bride and groom, have been arranged as a little dramatic dialogue, not unlike the idylls of the Greek Theocritus, with connecting refrains and speeches that suggest a chorus of bridesmaids. We need not speculate about the structure of this little play to enjoy the passionate tribute to nuptial love. Although the descriptions of love and the beloved seem earthly enough today, early religious commentaries interpreted them as a symbolic statement of the mutual love of God and Israel and hence admitted The Song of Songs to the Bible as a holy book.

The book of Jonah is more fable than prophecy, although its hero is ranked among the *Prophets*. The fine message of this enlightened tale has been popularly lost in the sensational incident of the "whale." Behind the frustrated career of a narrow-minded prophet lies the loftiest interpretation of Yahveh among the thirty-nine books. After being punished and forgiven for his foolish effort to escape his duty to God by running beyond His reach, Jonah must learn a second lesson: that God's mercy, as well as His authority, extends beyond His Chosen People to all others who deserve it. In saving the repentant sinners of Nineveh, God is seen to be universal in His power and His mercy.

Most charming of all the books is Ruth, the simple tale of a Moabite maiden who chose through love to follow her Jewish mother-in-law, Naomi, with her people and their god, and became the ancestor of King David himself. Behind its idyllic innocence lie a plea for the toleration of foreign marriages and an attack, as in the book of Jonah, on narrow nationalism.

Psalms

PSALM I

BLESSED is the man that walketh not in the counsel of the ungodly, nor standeth in the way of sinners, nor sitteth in the seat of the scornful.

But his delight is in the law of the Lord; and in his law doth he meditate day and night.

And he shall be like a tree planted by the rivers of water, that bringeth forth his fruit in his season; his leaf also shall not wither; and whatsoever he doeth shall prosper.

The ungodly are not so: but are like the chaff   10
which the wind driveth away.

Therefore the ungodly shall not stand in the judgment, nor sinners in the congregation of the righteous.

For the Lord knoweth the way of the righteous: but the way of the ungodly shall perish.

PSALM VIII

O Lord our Lord, how excellent is thy name in all the earth! who hast set thy glory above the heavens.

Out of the mouth of babes and sucklings hast thou ordained strength because of thine enemies, that   20
thou mightest still the enemy and the avenger.

When I consider thy heavens, the work of thy fingers, the moon and the stars, which thou hast ordained;

What is man, that thou art mindful of him? and the son of man, that thou visitest him?

For thou hast made him a little lower than the angels, and hast crowned him with glory and honour.

Thou madest him to have dominion over the works of thy hands; thou hast put all things under his feet: 30

All sheep and oxen, yea, and the beasts of the field;

The fowl of the air, and the fish of the sea, and whatsoever passeth through the paths of the seas.

O Lord our Lord, how excellent is thy name in all the earth!

PSALM XIX

The heavens declare the glory of God; and the firmament sheweth his handywork.

Day unto day uttereth speech, and night unto night sheweth knowledge.

There is no speech nor language, where their voice   40
is not heard.

Their line is gone out through all the earth, and their words to the end of the world. In them hath he set a tabernacle for the sun,

Which is as a bridegroom coming out of his chamber, and rejoiceth as a strong man to run a race.

His going forth is from the end of the heaven, and his circuit unto the ends of it: and there is nothing hid from the heat thereof.

The law of the Lord is perfect, converting the soul:
10 the testimony of the Lord is sure, making wise the simple.

The statutes of the Lord are right, rejoicing the heart: the commandment of the Lord is pure, enlightening the eyes.

The fear of the Lord is clean, enduring for ever: the judgments of the Lord are true and righteous altogether.

More to be desired are they than gold, yea, than much fine gold: sweeter also than honey and the
20 honeycomb.

Moreover by them is thy servant warned: and in keeping of them there is great reward.

Who can understand his errors? cleanse thou me from secret faults.

Keep back thy servant also from presumptuous sins; let them not have dominion over me: then shall I be upright, and I shall be innocent from the great transgression.

Let the words of my mouth, and the meditation
30 of my heart, be acceptable in thy sight, O Lord, my strength, and my redeemer.

PSALM XXIII

The Lord is my shepherd; I shall not want.

He maketh me to lie down in green pastures: he leadeth me beside the still waters.

He restoreth my soul: he leadeth me in the paths of righteousness for his name's sake.

Yea, though I walk through the valley of the shadow of death, I will fear no evil: for thou art with me; thy rod and thy staff they comfort me.

40 Thou preparest a table before me in the presence of mine enemies: thou anointest my head with oil; my cup runneth over.

Surely goodness and mercy shall follow me all the days of my life: and I will dwell in the house of the Lord for ever.

PSALM XC

Lord, thou hast been our dwelling place in all generations.

Before the mountains were brought forth, or ever thou hadst formed the earth and the world, even
50 from everlasting to everlasting, thou art God.

Thou turnest man to destruction; and sayest, Return, ye children of men.

For a thousand years in thy sight are but as yesterday when it is past, and as a watch in the night.

Thou carriest them away as with a flood; they are as a sleep: in the morning they are like grass which groweth up.

In the morning it flourisheth, and groweth up; in the evening it is cut down, and withereth.

For we are consumed by thine anger, and by thy 60 wrath are we troubled.

Thou hast set our iniquities before thee, our secret sins in the light of thy countenance.

For all our days are passed away in thy wrath: we spend our years as a tale that is told.

The days of our years are threescore years and ten; and if by reason of strength they be fourscore years; yet is their strength labor and sorrow; for it is soon cut off, and we fly away.

Who knoweth the power of thine anger? even ac- 70 cording to thy fear, so is thy wrath.

So teach us to number our days, that we may apply our hearts unto wisdom.

Return, O Lord, how long? and let it repent thee concerning thy servants.

O satisfy us early with thy mercy; that we may rejoice and be glad all our days.

Make us glad according to the days wherein thou hast afflicted us, and the years wherein we have seen evil. 80

Let thy work appear unto thy servants, and thy glory unto their children.

And let the beauty of the Lord our God be upon us: and establish thou the work of our hands upon us; yea, the work of our hands establish thou it.

Proverbs

WISDOM crieth without; she uttereth her voice in the streets. (i)

Wisdom is the principal thing; therefore get wisdom; and with all thy getting, get understanding. (iv) 90

Go to the ant, thou sluggard; consider her ways, and be wise: which having no chief, overseer or ruler, provideth her meat in the summer, and gathereth her food in the harvest. How long wilt thou sleep, O sluggard? When wilt thou arise out of thy sleep? Yet a little sleep, a little slumber, a little folding of the hands to sleep: so shall thy poverty come as one that travelleth, and thy want as an armed man. (vi)

A soft answer turneth away wrath, but grievous words stir up anger. (xv) 100

A merry heart maketh a cheerful countenance, but by sorrow of the heart the spirit is broken. (xv)

Better is a dinner of herbs where love is, than a stalled ox and hatred therewith. (xv)

Pride goeth before destruction, and an haughty spirit before a fall. (XVI)

He that is slow to anger is better than the mighty; and he that ruleth his spirit than he that taketh a city. (XVI)

A merry heart doeth good like a medicine. (XVII)

It is better to dwell in a corner of the housetop, than with a brawling woman in a wide house. (XXI)

10 A good name is rather to be chosen than great riches. (XXII)

Train up a child in the way he should go: and when he is old he will not depart from it. (XXII)

Look not thou upon the wine when it is red, when it giveth its color in the cup, when it goeth down smoothly; at the last it biteth like a serpent, and stingeth like an adder. (XXIII)

He that maketh haste to be rich shall not be innocent. (XXVIII)

There be three things that are too wonderful for 20 me, yea, four which I know not: the way of an eagle in the air; the way of a serpent upon a rock; the way of a ship in the midst of the sea; and the way of a man with a maid. (XXX)

Ecclesiastes

PROLOGUE

Vanity of vanities, saith the Preacher, vanity of vanities; all is vanity.

What profit hath a man of all his labour which he taketh under the sun?

One generation passeth away, and another generation cometh: but the earth abideth for ever.

30 The sun also ariseth, and the sun goeth down, and hasteth to his place where he arose.

The wind goeth toward the south, and turneth about unto the north; it whirleth about continually, and the wind returneth again according to his circuits.

All the rivers run into the sea; yet the sea is not full; unto the place from whence the rivers come, thither they return again.

All things are full of labour; man cannot utter it: 40 the eye is not satisfied with seeing, nor the ear filled with hearing.

The thing that hath been, it is that which shall be; and that which is done is that which shall be done: and there is no new thing under the sun.

Is there any thing whereof it may be said, See, this is new? it hath been already of old time, which was before us.

There is no remembrance of former things; neither shall there be any remembrance of things that are 50 to come with those that shall come after.

SOLOMON'S SEARCH FOR WISDOM

I the Preacher was king over Israel in Jerusalem.

And I gave my heart to seek and search out by wisdom concerning all things that are done under heaven: this sore travail hath God given to the sons of man to be exercised therewith.

I have seen all the works that are done under the sun; and, behold, all is vanity and vexation of spirit.

That which is crooked cannot be made straight: and that which is wanting cannot be numbered. 60

I communed with mine own heart, saying, Lo, I am come to great estate, and have gotten more wisdom than all they that have been before me in Jerusalem: yea, my heart had great experience of wisdom and knowledge.

And I gave my heart to know wisdom, and to know madness and folly: I perceived that this also is vexation of spirit.

For in much wisdom is much grief: and he that increaseth knowledge increaseth sorrow. 70

I said in mine heart, Go to now, I will prove thee with mirth, therefore enjoy pleasure: and, behold, this also is vanity.

I said of laughter, It is mad: and of mirth, What doeth it?

I sought in mine heart to give myself unto wine, yet acquainting mine heart with wisdom; and to lay hold on folly, till I might see what was that good for the sons of men, which they should do under the heaven all the days of their life. 80

I made me great works; I builded me houses; I planted me vineyards:

I made me gardens and orchards, and I planted trees in them of all kind of fruits:

I made me pools of water, to water therewith the wood that bringeth forth trees:

I got me servants and maidens and had servants born in my house; also I had great possessions of great and small cattle above all that were in Jerusalem before me: 90

I gathered me also silver and gold, and the peculiar treasure of kings and of the provinces: I gat me men singers and women singers, and the delights of the sons of men, as musical instruments, and that of all sorts.

So I was great, and increased more than all that were before me in Jerusalem: also my wisdom remained with me.

And whatsoever mine eyes desired I kept not from them, I withheld not my heart from any joy; for my 100 heart rejoiced in all my labour: and this was my portion of all my labour.

Then I looked on all the works that my hands had wrought, and on the labour that I had laboured to do: and, behold, all was vanity and vexation of spirit, and there was no profit under the sun.

And I turned myself to behold wisdom, and madness, and folly: for what can the man do that cometh after the king? even that which hath been already done.

Then I saw that wisdom excelleth folly, as far as light excelleth darkness.

The wise man's eyes are in his head; but the fool walketh in darkness: and I myself perceived also that one event happeneth to them all.

Then said I in my heart, As it happeneth to the fool, so it happeneth even to me; and why was I then more wise? Then I said in my heart, that this also is vanity.

For there is no remembrance of the wise more than of the fool for ever; seeing that which now is in the days to come shall all be forgotten. And how dieth the wise man? as the fool.

Therefore I hated life; because the work that is wrought under the sun is grievous unto me: for all is vanity and vexation of spirit.

Yea, I hated all my labour which I had taken under the sun: because I should leave it unto the man that shall be after me.

And who knoweth whether he shall be a wise man or a fool? yet shall he have rule over all my labour wherein I have laboured, and wherein I have shewed myself wise under the sun. This is also vanity.

Therefore I went about to cause my heart to despair of all the labour which I took under the sun.

For there is a man whose labour is in wisdom, and in knowledge, and in equity; yet to a man that hath not laboured therein shall he leave it for his portion. This also is vanity and a great evil.

For what hath man of all his labour, and of the vexation of his heart, wherein he hath laboured under the sun?

For all his days are sorrows, and his travail grief; yea, his heart taketh not rest in the night. This is also vanity. . . .

A TIME FOR EVERYTHING

To every thing there is a season, and a time to every purpose under the heaven:

A time to be born, and a time to die; a time to plant, and a time to pluck up that which is planted;

A time to kill, and a time to heal; a time to break down, and a time to build up;

A time to weep, and a time to laugh; a time to mourn, and a time to dance;

A time to cast away stones, and a time to gather stones together; a time to embrace, and a time to refrain from embracing;

A time to get, and a time to lose; a time to keep, and a time to cast away;

A time to rend, and a time to sew; a time to keep silence, and a time to speak;

A time to love, and a time to hate; a time of war, and a time of peace.

What profit hath he that worketh in that wherein he laboureth?

I have seen the travail, which God hath given to the sons of men to be exercised in it. . . .

And moreover I saw under the sun the place of judgment, that wickedness was there; and the place of righteousness, that iniquity was there.

I said in mine heart, God shall judge the righteous and the wicked: for there is a time there for every purpose and for every work.

I said in mine heart concerning the estate of the sons of men, that God might manifest them, and that they might see that they themselves are beasts.

For that which befalleth the sons of men befalleth beasts; even one thing befalleth them: as the one dieth, so dieth the other; yea, they have all one breath; so that a man hath no preeminence above a beast: for all is vanity.

All go unto one place; all are of the dust, and all turn to dust again.

Who knoweth the spirit of man that goeth upward, and the spirit of the beast that goeth downward to the earth?

Wherefore I perceive that there is nothing better, than that a man should rejoice in his own works; for that is his portion: for who shall bring him to see what shall be after him?

So I returned, and considered all the oppressions that are done under the sun: and behold the tears of such as were oppressed, and they had no comforter; and on the side of their oppressors there was power; but they had no comforter.

Wherefore I praised the dead which are already dead more than the living which are yet alive.

Yea, better is he than both they, which hath not yet been, who hath not seen the evil work that is done under the sun.

Again, I considered all travail, and every right work, that for this a man is envied of his neighbour. This is also vanity and vexation of spirit.

The fool foldeth his hands together, and eateth his own flesh.

Better is an handful with quietness, than both the hands full with travail and vexation of spirit.

Then I returned, and I saw vanity under the sun.

There is one alone, and there is not a second; yea, he hath neither child nor brother: yet is there no end of all his labour; neither is his eye satisfied with riches; neither saith he, For whom do I labour, and bereave my soul of good? This is also vanity, yea, it is a sore travail. . . .

THE VANITY OF HUMAN WISHES

He that loveth silver shall not be satisfied with silver; nor he that loveth abundance with increase: this is also vanity.

When goods increase, they are increased that eat them: and what good is there to the owners thereof, saving the beholding of them with their eyes?

The sleep of a labouring man is sweet, whether he eat little or much: but the abundance of the rich will not suffer him to sleep.

There is a sore evil which I have seen under the sun, namely, riches kept for the owners thereof to their hurt.

But those riches perish by evil travail: and he begetteth a son, and there is nothing in his hand.

As he came forth of his mother's womb, naked shall he return to go as he came, and shall take nothing of his labour, which he may carry away in his hand.

And this also is a sore evil, that in all points as he came, so shall he go: and what profit hath he that hath laboured for the wind?

All his days also he eateth in darkness, and he hath much sorrow and wrath with his sickness. . . .

There is an evil which I have seen under the sun, and it is common among men:

A man to whom God hath given riches, wealth, and honour, so that he wanteth nothing for his soul of all that he desireth, yet God giveth him not power to eat thereof, but a stranger eateth it: this is vanity, and it is an evil disease.

If a man beget an hundred children, and live many years, so that the days of his years be many, and his soul be not filled with good, and also that he have no burial; I say, that an untimely birth is better than he.

For he cometh in with vanity, and departeth in darkness, and his name shall be covered with darkness.

Moreover he hath not seen the sun, nor known any thing: this hath more rest than the other.

Yea, though he live a thousand years twice told, yet hath he seen no good: do not all go to one place?

All the labour of man is for his mouth, and yet the appetite is not filled.

For what hath the wise more than the fool? what hath the poor, that knoweth to walk before the living?

Better is the sight of the eyes than the wandering of the desire: this is also vanity and vexation of spirit.

That which hath been is named already, and it is known that it is man: neither may he contend with him that is mightier than he.

Seeing there be many things that increase vanity, what is man the better?

For who knoweth what is good for man in this life, all the days of his vain life which he spendeth as a shadow? for who can tell a man what shall be after him under the sun? . . .

Because to every purpose there is time and judg-ment, therefore the misery of man is great upon him.

For he knoweth not that which shall be: for who can tell him when it shall be?

There is no man that hath power over the spirit to retain the spirit; neither hath he power in the day of death: and there is no discharge in that war; neither shall wickedness deliver those that are given to it.

All this have I seen, and applied my heart unto every work that is done under the sun: there is a time wherein one man ruleth over another to his own hurt.

And so I saw the wicked buried, who had come and gone from the place of the holy, and they were forgotten in the city where they had so done: this is also vanity.

Because sentence against an evil work is not exe-cuted speedily, therefore the heart of the sons of men is fully set in them to do evil. . . .

There is a vanity which is done upon the earth; that there be just men, unto whom it happeneth according to the work of the wicked; again, there be wicked men, to whom it happeneth according to the work of the righteous: I said that this also is van-ity. . . .

All things come alike to all: there is one event to the righteous, and to the wicked; to the good and to the clean, and to the unclean; to him that sac-rificeth, and to him that sacrificeth not: as is the good, so is the sinner; and he that sweareth, as he that feareth an oath.

An early representation of the signs of the zodiac, com-mon in medieval Jewish art. This mosaic is from Beth Alpha Synagogue, Palestine, built fifth century A.D.

This is an evil among all things that are done under the sun, that there is one event unto all: yea, also the heart of the sons of men is full of evil, and madness is in their heart while they live, and after that they go to the dead.

For to him that is joined to all the living there is hope: for a living dog is better than a dead lion.

For the living know that they shall die: but the dead know not any thing, neither have they any more a reward; for the memory of them is forgotten.

Also their love, and their hatred, and their envy, is now perished; neither have they any more a portion for ever in any thing that is done under the sun.

THE WAY OF LIFE

Go thy way, eat thy bread with joy, and drink thy wine with a merry heart; for God now accepteth thy works.

Let thy garments be always white; and let thy head lack no ointment.

Live joyfully with the wife whom thou lovest all the days of the life of thy vanity, which he hath given thee under the sun, all the days of thy vanity: for that is thy portion in this life, and in thy labour which thou takest under the sun.

Whatsoever thy hand findeth to do, do it with thy might; for there is no work, nor device, nor knowledge, nor wisdom, in the grave, whither thou goest.

I returned, and saw under the sun, that the race is not to the swift, nor the battle to the strong, neither yet bread to the wise, nor yet riches to men of understanding, nor yet favour to men of skill; but time and chance happeneth to them all.

For man also knoweth not his time: as the fishes that are taken in an evil net, and as the birds that are caught in the snare; so are the sons of men snared in an evil time, when it falleth suddenly upon them.

This wisdom have I seen also under the sun, and it seemed great unto me:

There was a little city, and few men within it; and there came a great king against it, and besieged it, and built great bulwarks against it:

Now there was found in it a poor wise man, and he by his wisdom delivered the city; yet no man remembered that same poor man.

Then said I, Wisdom is better than strength: nevertheless the poor man's wisdom is despised, and his words are not heard.

Truly the light is sweet, and a pleasant thing it is for the eyes to behold the sun:

But if a man live many years, and rejoice in them all; yet let him remember the days of darkness; for they shall be many. All that cometh is vanity.

Rejoice, O young man, in thy youth; and let thy heart cheer thee in the days of thy youth, and walk in the ways of thine heart, and in the sight of thine eyes: but know thou, that for all these things God will bring thee into judgment.

Therefore remove sorrow from thy heart, and put away evil from thy flesh: for childhood and youth are vanity.

Remember now thy Creator in the days of thy youth, while the evil days come not, nor the years draw nigh, when thou shalt say, I have no pleasure in them;

While the sun, or the light, or the moon, or the stars, be not darkened, nor the clouds return after the rain:

In the day when the keepers of the house shall tremble, and the strong men shall bow themselves, and the grinders cease because they are few, and those that look out of the windows be darkened,

And the doors shall be shut in the streets, when the sound of the grinding is low, and he shall rise up at the voice of the bird, and all the daughters of musick shall be brought low;

Also when they shall be afraid of that which is high, and fears shall be in the way, and the almond tree shall flourish, and the grasshopper shall be a burden, and desire shall fail: because man goeth to his long home, and the mourners go about the streets:

Or ever the silver cord be loosed, or the golden bowl be broken, or the pitcher be broken at the fountain, or the wheel broken at the cistern.

Then shall the dust return to the earth as it was: and the spirit shall return unto God who gave it.

EPILOGUE

Vanity of vanities, saith the preacher; all is vanity.

And moreover, because the preacher was wise, he still taught the people knowledge; yea, he gave good heed, and sought out, and set in order many proverbs.

The preacher sought to find out acceptable words: and that which was written was upright, even words of truth.

The words of the wise are as goads, and as nails fastened by the masters of assemblies, which are given from one shepherd.

And further, by these, my son, be admonished: of making many books there is no end; and much study is a weariness of the flesh.

The Song of Songs

CH. II

I AM the rose of Sharon, and the lily of the valleys.

As the lily among thorns, so is my love among the daughters.

As the apple tree among the trees of the wood,

so is my beloved among the sons. I sat down under his shadow with great delight, and his fruit was sweet to my taste.

He brought me to the banqueting house, and his banner over me was love.

Stay me with flagons, comfort me with apples: for I am sick of love.

His left hand is under my head, and his right hand doth embrace me.

10 I charge you, O ye daughters of Jerusalem, by the roes, and by the hinds of the field, that ye stir not up, nor awake my love, till he please.

The voice of my beloved! behold, he cometh leaping upon the mountains, skipping upon the hills.

My beloved is like a roe or a young hart: behold, he standeth behind our wall, he looketh forth at the windows, shewing himself through the lattice.

My beloved spake, and said unto me, Rise up, my love, my fair one, and come away.

20 For, lo, the winter is past, the rain is over and gone;

The flowers appear on the earth; the time of the singing of birds is come, and the voice of the turtle is heard in our land;

The fig tree putteth forth her green figs, and the vines with the tender grape give a good smell. Arise, my love, my fair one, and come away.

O my dove, that art in the clefts of the rock, in the secret places of the stairs, let me see thy counte-
30 nance, let me hear thy voice; for sweet is thy voice, and thy countenance is comely.

Take us the foxes, the little foxes, that spoil the vines: for our vines have tender grapes.

My beloved is mine, and I am his: he feedeth among the lilies.

Until the day break, and the shadows flee away, turn, my beloved, and be thou like a roe or a young hart upon the mountains of Bether.

CH. III

By night on my bed I sought him whom my soul
40 loveth: I sought him, but I found him not.

I will rise now, and go about the city in the streets, and in the broad ways I will seek him whom my soul loveth: I sought him, but I found him not.

The watchmen that go about the city found me: to whom I said, Saw ye him whom my soul loveth?

It was but a little that I passed from them, but I found him whom my soul loveth: I held him, and would not let him go, until I had brought him into my mother's house, and into the chamber of her
50 that conceived me.

I charge you, O ye daughters of Jerusalem, by the roes, and by the hinds of the field, that ye stir not up, nor awake my love, till he please. . . .

CH. IV *Bridegroom's desc. of bride*

Behold, thou art fair, my love; behold, thou art fair; thou hast doves' eyes within thy locks: thy hair is as a flock of goats, that appear from mount Gilead.

Thy teeth are like a flock of sheep that are even shorn, which came up from the washing; whereof every one bear twins, and none is barren among them.
60

Thy lips are like a thread of scarlet, and thy speech is comely: thy temples are like a piece of a pomegranate within thy locks.

Thy neck is like the tower of David builded for an armoury, whereon there hang a thousand bucklers, all shields of mighty men.

Thy two breasts are like two young roes that are twins, which feed among the lilies.

Until the day break, and the shadows flee away, I will get me to the mountain of myrrh, and to the
70 hill of frankincense.

Thou art all fair, my love; there is no spot in thee. . . .

CH. V

. . . I sleep, but my heart waketh: it is the voice of my beloved that knocketh, saying, Open to me, my sister, my love, my dove, my undefiled: for my head is filled with dew, and my locks with the drops of the night.

I have put off my coat; how shall I put it on? I have washed my feet; how shall I defile them?
80

My beloved put in his hand by the hole of the door, and my bowels were moved for him.

I rose up to open to my beloved; and my hands dropped with myrrh, and my fingers with sweet smelling myrrh, upon the handles of the lock.

I opened to my beloved; but my beloved had withdrawn himself, and was gone: my soul failed when he spake: I sought him, but I could not find him; I called him, but he gave me no answer.

The watchmen that went about the city found me,
90 they smote me, they wounded me; the keepers of the walls took away my vail from me.

I charge you, O daughters of Jerusalem, if ye find my beloved, that ye tell him, that I am sick of love. . . .

What is thy beloved more than another beloved, O thou fairest among women? what is thy beloved more than another beloved, that thou dost so charge us?

My beloved is white and ruddy, the chiefest among
100 ten thousand.

His head is as the most fine gold, his locks are bushy, and black as a raven.

His eyes are as the eyes of doves by the rivers of waters, washed with milk, and fitly set.

His cheeks are as a bed of spices, as sweet flowers: his lips like lilies, dropping sweet smelling myrrh.

His hands are as gold rings set with the beryl: his belly is as bright ivory overlaid with sapphires.

His legs are as pillars of marble, set upon sockets of fine gold: his countenance is as Lebanon, excellent as the cedars.

His mouth is most sweet: yea, he is altogether lovely. This is my beloved, and this is my friend, O daughters of Jerusalem.

CH. VI

Whither is thy beloved gone, O thou fairest among women? whither is thy beloved turned aside? that we may seek him with thee.

My beloved is gone down into his garden, to the beds of spices, to feed in the gardens, and to gather lilies.

I am my beloved's, and my beloved is mine: he feedeth among the lilies. . . .

CH. VII

. . . I am my beloved's, and his desire is toward me.

Come, my beloved, let us go forth into the field; let us lodge in the villages.

Let us get up early to the vineyards; let us see if the vine flourish, whether the tender grape appear, and the pomegranates bud forth: there will I give thee my loves.

The mandrakes give a smell, and at our gates are all manner of pleasant fruits, new and old, which I have laid up for thee, O my beloved.

CH. VIII

O that thou wert as my brother, that sucked the breasts of my mother! when I should find thee without, I would kiss thee; yea, I should not be despised.

I would lead thee, and bring thee into my mother's house, who would instruct me: I would cause thee to drink of spiced wine of the juice of my pomegranate.

His left hand should be under my head, and his right hand should embrace me.

I charge you, O daughters of Jerusalem, that ye stir not up, nor awake my love, until he please. . . .

Set me as a seal upon thine heart, as a seal upon thine arm: for love is strong as death; jealousy is cruel as the grave: the coals thereof are coals of fire, which hath a most vehement flame.

Many waters cannot quench love, neither can the floods drown it: if a man would give all the substance of his house for love, it would utterly be contemned. . . .

Thou that dwellest in the gardens, the companions hearken to thy voice: cause me to hear it.

Make haste, my beloved, and be thou like to a roe or to a young hart upon the mountains of spices.

Jonah

Now the word of the Lord came unto Jonah the son of Amittai, saying,

Arise, go to Nineveh, that great city, and cry against it; for their wickedness is come up before me.

But Jonah rose up to flee unto Tarshish from the presence of the Lord, and went down to Joppa; and he found a ship going to Tarshish: so he paid the fare thereof, and went down into it, to go with them unto Tarshish from the presence of the Lord.

But the Lord sent out a great wind into the sea, and there was a mighty tempest in the sea, so that the ship was like to be broken.

Then the mariners were afraid, and cried every man unto his god, and cast forth the wares that were in the ship into the sea, to lighten it of them. But Jonah was gone down into the sides of the ship; and he lay, and was fast asleep.

So the shipmaster came to him, and said unto him, What meanest thou, O sleeper? arise, call upon thy God, if so be that God will think upon us, that we perish not.

And they said every one to his fellow, Come, and let us cast lots, that we may know for whose cause this evil is upon us. So they cast lots, and the lot fell upon Jonah.

Then said they unto him, Tell us, we pray thee, for whose cause this evil is upon us; What is thine occupation? and whence comest thou? what is thy country? and of what people art thou?

And he said unto them, I am an Hebrew; and I fear the Lord, the God of heaven, which hath made the sea and the dry land.

Then were the men exceedingly afraid, and said unto him, Why hast thou done this? For the men knew that he fled from the presence of the Lord, because he had told them.

Then said they unto him, What shall we do unto thee, that the sea may be calm unto us? for the sea wrought, and was tempestuous.

And he said unto them, Take me up, and cast me forth into the sea; so shall the sea be calm unto you: for I know that for my sake this great tempest is upon you.

Nevertheless the men rowed hard to bring it to the land; but they could not: for the sea wrought, and was tempestuous against them.

Wherefore they cried unto the Lord, and said, We beseech thee, O Lord, we beseech thee, let us not perish for this man's life, and lay not upon us innocent blood: for thou, O Lord, hast done as it pleased thee.

So they took up Jonah, and cast him forth into the sea: and the sea ceased from her raging.

Then the men feared the Lord exceedingly, and offered a sacrifice unto the Lord, and made vows.

Now the Lord had prepared a great fish to swallow up Jonah. And Jonah was in the belly of the fish three days and three nights.

Then Jonah prayed unto the Lord his God out of the fish's belly,

And said, I cried by reason of mine affliction unto the Lord, and he heard me; out of the belly of hell cried I, and thou heardest my voice.

10 For thou hadst cast me into the deep, in the midst of the seas; and the floods compassed me about: all thy billows and thy waves passed over me.

Then I said, I am cast out of thy sight; yet I will look again toward thy holy temple.

The waters compassed me about, even to the soul: the depth closed me round about, the weeds were wrapped about my head.

I went down to the bottoms of the mountains; the 20 earth with her bars was about me for ever: yet hast thou brought up my life from corruption, O Lord my God.

When my soul fainted within me I remembered the Lord: and my prayer came in unto thee, into thine holy temple.

They that observe lying vanities forsake their own mercy.

But I will sacrifice unto thee with the voice of thanksgiving; I will pay that that I have vowed. 30 Salvation is of the Lord.

And the Lord spake unto the fish, and it vomited out Jonah upon the dry land.

And the word of the Lord came unto Jonah the second time, saying,

Arise, go unto Nineveh, that great city, and preach unto it the preaching that I bid thee.

So Jonah arose, and went unto Nineveh, according to the word of the Lord. Now Nineveh was an exceeding great city of three days' journey.

40 And Jonah began to enter into the city a day's journey, and he cried, and said, Yet forty days, and Nineveh shall be overthrown.

So the people of Nineveh believed God, and proclaimed a fast and put on sackcloth, from the greatest of them even to the least of them.

For word came unto the king of Nineveh, and he arose from his throne, and he laid his robe from him, and covered him with sackcloth, and sat in ashes.

And he caused it to be proclaimed and published 50 through Nineveh by the decree of the king and his nobles, saying, Let neither man nor beast, herd nor flock, taste any thing: let them not feed, nor drink water:

But let man and beast be covered with sackcloth, and cry mightily unto God: yea, let them turn every

A tenth-century Byzantine miniature painting which gives the full story of Jonah. Below, Jonah is being swallowed by the monster and cast up; above, he gives thanks and preaches to the Ninevites.

one from his evil way, and from the violence that is in their hands.

Who can tell if God will turn and repent, and turn away from his fierce anger, that we perish not?

And God saw their works, that they turned from 60 their evil way; and God repented of the evil, that he had said that he would do unto them; and he did it not.

But it displeased Jonah exceedingly, and he was very angry. And he prayed unto the Lord, and said, I pray thee, O Lord, was not this my saying, when I was yet in my country? Therefore I fled before unto Tarshish: for I knew that thou art a gracious God, and merciful, slow to anger, and of great kindness, and repentest thee of the evil. 70

Therefore now, O Lord, take, I beseech thee, my life from me; for it is better for me to die than to live.

Then said the Lord, Doest thou well to be angry?

So Jonah went out of the city, and sat on the east side of the city, and there made him a booth, and sat under it in the shadow, till he might see what would become of the city.

And the Lord God prepared a gourd, and made it to come up over Jonah, that it might be a shadow over his head, to deliver him from his grief. So Jonah was exceeding glad of the gourd.

But God prepared a worm when the morning rose the next day, and it smote the gourd that it withered.

And it came to pass, when the sun did arise, that God prepared a vehement east wind; and the sun beat upon the head of Jonah, that he fainted, and wished in himself to die, and said, It is better for me to die than to live.

10 And God said to Jonah, Doest thou well to be angry for the gourd? And he said, I do well to be angry, even unto death.

Then said the Lord, Thou hast had pity on the gourd, for the which thou hast not laboured, neither madest it grow; which came up in a night, and perished in a night:

And should not I spare Nineveh, that great city, wherein are more than sixscore thousand persons that cannot discern between their right hand and their 20 left hand; and also much cattle?

Ruth

Now it came to pass in the days when the judges ruled, that there was a famine in the land. And a certain man of Bethlehem-judah went to sojourn in the country of Moab, he, and his wife, and his two sons.

And the name of the man was Elimelech, and the name of his wife Naomi, and the name of his two sons Mahlon and Chilion, Ephrathites of Bethlehem-judah. And they came into the country of Moab, and 30 continued there.

And Elimelech Naomi's husband died; and she was left, and her two sons.

And they took them wives of the women of Moab; the name of the one was Orpah, and the name of the other Ruth: and they dwelled there about ten years.

And Mahlon and Chilion died also both of them; and the woman was left of her two sons and her husband.

Then she arose with her daughters-in-law, that she 40 might return from the country of Moab: for she had heard in the country of Moab how that the Lord had visited his people in giving them bread.

Wherefore she went forth out of the place where she was, and her two daughters-in-law with her; and they went on the way to return unto the land of Judah.

And Naomi said unto her two daughters-in-law, Go, return each to her mother's house: the Lord deal kindly with you, as ye have dealt with the dead, and 50 with me.

The Lord grant you that ye may find rest, each of you in the house of her husband. Then she kissed them; and they lifted up their voice, and wept.

And they said unto her, Surely we will return with thee unto thy people.

And Naomi said, Turn again, my daughters: why will ye go with me? are there yet any more sons in my womb, that they may be your husbands?

Turn again, my daughters, go your way; for I am too old to have an husband. If I should say, I have 60 hope, if I should have an husband also to night, and should also bear sons;

Would ye tarry for them till they were grown? would ye stay for them from having husbands? nay, my daughters; for it grieveth me much for your sakes that the hand of the Lord is gone out against me.

And they lifted up their voice, and wept again: and Orpah kissed her mother-in-law; but Ruth clave unto her.

And she said, Behold, thy sister-in-law is gone 70 back unto her people, and unto her gods: return thou after thy sister-in-law.

And Ruth said, Intreat me not to leave thee, or to return from following after thee: for whither thou goest, I will go; and where thou lodgest, I will lodge: thy people shall be my people, and thy God my God:

Where thou diest, will I die, and there will I be buried: the Lord do so to me, and more also, if ought but death part thee and me.

When she saw that she was stedfastly minded to 80 go with her, then she left speaking unto her.

So they two went until they came to Bethlehem. And it came to pass, when they were come to Bethlehem, that all the city was moved about them, and they said, Is this Naomi?

And she said unto them, Call me not Naomi, call me Mara: for the Almighty hath dealt very bitterly with me.

I went out full, and the Lord hath brought me home again empty: why then call ye me Naomi, see- 90 ing the Lord hath testified against me, and the Almighty hath afflicted me?

So Naomi returned, and Ruth the Moabitess, her daughter-in-law, with her, which returned out of the country of Moab: and they came to Bethlehem in the beginning of barley harvest.

And Naomi had a kinsman of her husband's, a mighty man of wealth, of the family of Elimelech; and his name was Boaz.

And Ruth the Moabitess said unto Naomi, Let me 100 now go to the field, and glean ears of corn after him in whose sight I shall find grace. And she said unto her, Go, my daughter.

And she went, and came, and gleaned in the field after the reapers: and her hap was to light on a part of the field belonging unto Boaz, who was of the kindred of Elimelech.

And, behold, Boaz came from Bethlehem, and said unto the reapers, The Lord be with you. And they answered him, The Lord bless thee.

Then said Boaz unto his servant that was set over the reapers, Whose damsel is this?

And the servant that was set over the reapers answered and said, It is the Moabitish damsel that came back with Naomi out of the country of Moab:

And she said, I pray you, let me glean and gather after the reapers among the sheaves: so she came, and hath continued even from the morning until now, that she tarried a little in the house.

Then said Boaz unto Ruth, Hearest thou not, my daughter? Go not to glean in another field, neither go from hence, but abide here fast by my maidens:

Let thine eyes be on the field that they do reap, and go thou after them: have I not charged the young men that they shall not touch thee? and when thou art athirst, go unto the vessels, and drink of that which the young men have drawn.

Then she fell on her face, and bowed herself to the ground, and said unto him, Why have I found grace in thine eyes, that thou shouldest take knowledge of me, seeing I am a stranger?

And Boaz answered and said unto her, It hath fully been shewed me, all that thou hast done unto thy mother-in-law since the death of thine husband: and how thou hast left thy father and thy mother, and the land of thy nativity, and art come unto a people which thou knewest not heretofore.

The Lord recompense thy work, and a full reward be given thee of the Lord God of Israel, under whose wings thou art come to trust.

Then she said, Let me find favour in thy sight, my lord; for that thou hast comforted me, and for that thou hast spoken friendly unto thine handmaid, though I be not like unto one of thine handmaidens.

And Boaz said unto her, At mealtime come thou hither, and eat of the bread, and dip thy morsel in the vinegar. And she sat beside the reapers: and he reached her parched corn, and she did eat, and was sufficed, and left.

And when she was risen up to glean, Boaz commanded his young men, saying, Let her glean even among the sheaves, and reproach her not:

And let fall also some of the handfuls of purpose for her, and leave them, that she may glean them, and rebuke her not.

So she gleaned in the field until even, and beat out that she had gleaned: and it was about an ephah of barley.

And she took it up, and went into the city: and her mother-in-law saw what she had gleaned: and she brought forth, and gave to her that she had reserved after she was sufficed.

And her mother-in-law said unto her, Where hast thou gleaned to day? and where wroughtest thou?

blessed be he that did take knowledge of thee. And she shewed her mother-in-law with whom she had wrought, and said, The man's name with whom I wrought to day is Boaz.

And Naomi said unto her daughter-in-law, Blessed be he of the Lord, who hath not left off his kindness to the living and to the dead. And Naomi said unto her, The man is near of kin unto us, one of our next kinsmen.

And Ruth the Moabitess said, He said unto me also, Thou shalt keep fast by my young men, until they have ended all my harvest.

And Naomi said unto Ruth her daughter-in-law, It is good, my daughter, that thou go out with his maidens, that they meet thee not in any other field.

So she kept fast by the maidens of Boaz to glean unto the end of barley harvest and of wheat harvest; and dwelt with her mother-in-law.

Then Naomi her mother-in-law said unto her, My daughter, shall I not seek rest for thee, that it may be well with thee?

And now is not Boaz of our kindred, with whose maidens thou wast? Behold, he winnoweth barley to night in the threshingfloor.

Wash thyself therefore, and anoint thee, and put thy raiment upon thee, and get thee down to the floor: but make not thyself known unto the man, until he shall have done eating and drinking.

And it shall be, when he lieth down, that thou shalt mark the place where he shall lie, and thou shalt go in, and uncover his feet, and lay thee down; and he will tell thee what thou shalt do.

And she said unto her, All that thou sayest unto me I will do.

And she went down unto the floor, and did according to all that her mother-in-law bade her.

And when Boaz had eaten and drunk, and his heart was merry, he went to lie down at the end of the heap of corn: and she came softly, and uncovered his feet, and laid her down.

And it came to pass at midnight, that the man was afraid, and turned himself: and, behold, a woman lay at his feet.

And he said, Who art thou? And she answered, I am Ruth thine handmaid: spread therefore thy skirt over thine handmaid; for thou art a near kinsman.

And he said, Blessed be thou of the Lord, my daughter: for thou hast shewed more kindness in the latter end than at the beginning, inasmuch as thou followedst not young men, whether poor or rich.

And now, my daughter, fear not; I will do to thee all that thou requirest: for all the city of my people doth know that thou art a virtuous woman.

And now it is true that I am thy near kinsman: howbeit there is a kinsman nearer than I.

Tarry this night, and it shall be in the morning,

that if he will perform unto thee the part of a kinsman, well; let him do the kinsman's part: but if he will not do the part of a kinsman to thee, then will I do the part of a kinsman to thee, as the Lord liveth: lie down until the morning.

And she lay at his feet until the morning: and she rose up before one could know another. And he said, Let it not be known that a woman came into the floor.

10 Also he said, Bring the vail that thou hast upon thee, and hold it. And when she held it, he measured six measures of barley, and laid it on her: and she went into the city.

And when she came to her mother-in-law, she said, Who art thou, my daughter? And she told her all that the man had done to her.

And she said, These six measures of barley gave he me; for he said to me, Go not empty unto thy mother-in-law.

20 Then said she, Sit still, my daughter, until thou know how the matter will fall: for the man will not be in rest, until he have finished the thing this day.

Then went Boaz up to the gate, and sat him down there: and, behold, the kinsman of whom Boaz spake came by; unto whom he said, Ho, such a one! turn aside, sit down here. And he turned aside, and sat down.

And he took ten men of the elders of the city, and said, Sit ye down here. And they sat down.

30 And he said unto the kinsman, Naomi, that is come again out of the country of Moab, selleth a parcel of land, which was our brother Elimelech's:

And I thought to advertise thee, saying, Buy it before the inhabitants, and before the elders of my people. If thou wilt redeem it, redeem it: but if thou wilt not redeem it, then tell me, that I may know: for there is none to redeem it beside thee; and I am after thee. And he said, I will redeem it.

Then said Boaz, What day thou buyest the field 40 of the hand of Naomi, thou must buy it also of Ruth the Moabitess, the wife of the dead, to raise up the name of the dead upon his inheritance.

And the kinsman said, I cannot redeem it for myself, lest I mar mine own inheritance: redeem thou my right to thyself; for I cannot redeem it.

Now this was the manner in former time in Israel concerning redeeming and concerning changing, for to confirm all things; a man plucked off his shoe, and gave it to his neighbour: and this was a testimony in Israel. 50

Therefore the kinsman said unto Boaz, Buy it for thee. So he drew off his shoe.

And Boaz said unto the elders, and unto all the people, Ye are witnesses this day, that I have bought all that was Elimelech's, and all that was Chilion's and Mahlon's, of the hand of Naomi.

Moreover Ruth the Moabitess, the wife of Mahlon, have I purchased to be my wife, to raise up the name of the dead upon his inheritance, that the name of the dead be not cut off from among his brethren, 60 and from the gate of his place: ye are witnesses this day.

And all the people that were in the gate, and the elders, said, We are witnesses. The Lord make the woman that is come into thine house like Rachel and like Leah, which two did build the house of Israel: and do thou worthily in Ephratah, and be famous in Bethlehem:

And let thy house be like the house of Pharez, whom Tamar bare unto Judah, of the seed which the 70 Lord shall give thee of this young woman.

So Boaz took Ruth, and she was his wife: and when he went in unto her, the Lord gave her conception, and she bare a son.

And the women said unto Naomi, Blessed be the Lord, which hath not left thee this day without a kinsman, that his name may be famous in Israel.

And he shall be unto thee a restorer of thy life, and a nourisher of thine old age: for thy daughter-in-law, which loveth thee, which is better to thee than seven 80 sons, hath born him.

And Naomi took the child, and laid it in her bosom, and became nurse unto it.

And the women her neighbours gave it a name, saying, There is a son born to Naomi; and they called his name Obed: he is the father of Jesse, the father of David.

GREECE
AND THE BIRTH
OF THE WEST

800 B.C. TO 300 B.C.

A stone replica of a mask of comedy, from a Greek theater of the fourth century B.C.

WESTERN civilization was born with the Greeks. These are the people to whom chance gave the opportunity to found our culture and establish our basic institutions. Democracy and civil liberties, philosophy and an elemental science, drama and every kind of poetry, architecture and sculpture in the classic style—these things that we take for granted were evolved by them as they met the challenge of human problems that still confront us today.

Greek culture has about it the hardy recklessness of youth. With almost no past authority to guide or restrict them, the Greeks speculated and experimented through a sudden awareness of the world in which they lived. Like most enthusiastic pioneers they made many mistakes, which seem naïve and obvious in the light of our greater experience; but we learn as much from their failures as from their success. Beset by the complexity of our own situation, we profit from their approach to problems as varied and immediate as our own, yet outlined on a smaller scale with the issues more clearly defined. In about three hundred years their rich experience raised most of the problems of civilized living, and their solutions come very close to ours. The final decline of Greek culture, the absorption of the Greeks and their traditions in the more pragmatic empires of Macedonia and Rome point an ominous lesson that we may still have to learn.

The achievements of the Greeks seem even more remarkable when we consider how few these people were and how small a land they occupied. Although the Greek world in its heyday spread far beyond Greece proper, its center was always that mountainous little peninsula jutting into the eastern

Mediterranean, which was a mere 250 miles long and 45,000 square miles in area—roughly the size of New York State. In fact, the greatest cultural achievements of the Greeks were centered in a single city, Athens, which had in its Golden Age perhaps 200,000 inhabitants, of whom about a fifth were adult male citizens. A handful of great men living in close, free contact with each other made Athens the perennial ideal of Western culture.

Four fifths of Greece is covered with rugged mountains that only occasionally rise to peaks such as the sacred Olympus, Helicon, Parnassus, and Olympia. Since there are few passes through them, these mountains shut off the Greeks in self-contained communities and encouraged the clannish government of independent city-states rather than national unity and empire. Access to the sea was often simpler than contact with neighboring cities, and the settlement of colonies on the many islands surrounding the peninsula inspired a close bond between colonies and mother-states and a jealous suspicion of rival cities.

The bleak plateaus and barren mountains provided abundant marble for buildings and statues, rich veins of silver and copper, but little pasture land and even less soil for cultivation. Although their country was not so barren then as now after centuries of reckless deforestation and erosion, the Greeks were forced to till every precious foot of arable land for their meager crops of wheat, barley, flax, olives, and grapes. Inevitably they looked to the sea for sustenance from colonies, foreign trade, and even warfare. This was especially true of Athens, the great seafaring, trading city of the peninsula, be-

cause her state of Attica was the least fertile of the lot. Her chief rival, Sparta, shut off in a fruitful valley, developed a more agrarian and provincial culture. It is not hard to discern one reason why, in politics and social institutions, Sparta stood for conservative discipline, while Athens symbolized the progressive spirit of free inquiry.

The ruggedness of the cliffs of the west coast first caused the Greeks to turn their eyes eastward to their ports on the Aegean Sea and the beautiful islands that provided colonial stepping stones for trade with Asia Minor. Across this hospitable sea the early Greeks went to plunder Troy, and over this sea and around it came the lumbering armies of Persia in a later age to fight a second great war of East and West. It was the sea, not the land, that formed the unifying force in the Greek world; the

sea was the symbol of freedom to explore and exploit the world at will.

The Mediterranean climate of Greece was then more temperate than it is today. The lowlands enjoyed warm weather the year round, and Athens could boast of three hundred sunny days a year. The long dry season drained the few rivers, but the rainy winter brought back brief torrents to the parched river beds. Lacking rainfall and trees, Greece seemed as it does even today a land ablaze with light and open to the sky and the sea air. In such a land men lived constantly in the open, with less food, clothing, and shelter than northerners need. Life was natural, simple, and direct, and men living together out of doors enjoyed a free exchange of ideas and more leisure to create beautiful things.

THE COMING OF THE GREEKS

CIVILIZATION in the East was already old when the Greeks first settled Greece. Not simply China and India but the fertile valleys of the Euphrates and the Nile had produced great cultures as early as 3500 B.C. But Sumer and Egypt were long in decay when the hardy invaders whom we call Greeks battled their way with iron swords from the northeast into the rocky peninsula that was to become their home. Where they came from we do not know, but they brought with them an Indo-European language that links them in some way with the people of India and with others who spoke Indo-European tongues. They found an older people, the Aegeans, firmly settled in Greece, where for two thousand years they had been quietly evolving a remarkable culture. Although this prehistoric culture had important centers in Mycenae and Tiryns on the mainland, its greatest glory was in more ancient Cnossus on the island of Crete, where a legendary king Minos is supposed to have built the astounding palaces recently unearthed by archaeologists.* In his honor this whole precocious culture is now called Minoan.

The invading Greeks, who poured into the peninsula in successive waves after 2000 B.C., felt no awe of this superior Minoan culture. Cnossus was destroyed about 1400 B.C., perhaps by the Greeks, and Mycenae and Tiryns fell to them two centuries later. A dark period settled over the peninsula as the Greeks were assimilating the vanquished and absorbing the vestiges of their civilization. In some areas the Aegeans were annihilated or driven out; in others they apparently intermarried with the

Greeks to form one race. In Sparta, however, the Aegeans (and even some of the early Greek settlers) were subjected to perpetual slavery by the Dorians, the last group of the Greek conquerors, so that throughout Spartan history no more than ten thousand (eventually only seven hundred) free citizens ruled at least twenty times as many slaves, or *helots*. Herein lies another explanation of the difference between democratic Athens and aristocratic Sparta.

The invasions continued for five centuries and eventually spread the Greeks over the countless islands of the Aegean and along the coast of Asia Minor. The Greeks were actually many tribes and did not think of themselves as one people. To the end of their ancient history they remained a group of distinct and self-conscious city-states, jealous of their separate traditions, often at war with each other, yet bound together informally by a common religion and cultural heritage.

Although they are conveniently called "Greeks," they cannot be properly called that until they settled Greece. That name for them actually originated in Italy a thousand years later, and was used to identify those who spoke the common language of Greek. Homer in the eighth century B.C. referred to his race with old sectional names—the *Achaians,* the *Argives,* the *Danaians*—to identify various Greek peoples temporarily bound together in war. Eventually the Greeks developed the name *Hellenes* (after *Hellas,* a Greek name for the Greek world) to distinguish themselves from all non-Greeks, contemptuously called "barbarians." The culture of Greece at its height is often called "Hellenic," and the later culture which it was to inspire after the loss of Greek independence is called "Hellenistic."

* The Greeks associated the Palace of Cnossus with the labyrinth of Crete, in which the hero Theseus killed the Minotaur.

The spread of the Hellenes beyond Greece was carried out by sea, for the sea was the natural road for the Greeks. Despite the small area of Greece, its coastline is as long as the eastern coast of America from Maine to Florida. The rugged shoreline notches the land with endless bays and harbors. And from these harbors sailed the Greeks, bent on war, trade, colonization; thus Hellenic culture was disseminated.

GREEK CULTURAL TIES: LANGUAGE AND RELIGION

DESPITE tribal differences, there were common cultural bonds that set all the Greeks apart from their "barbarian" neighbors. The most obvious of these was their *language*, destined to develop into perhaps the most beautiful of all the Aryan, or Indo-European, tongues. The Aegeans had had a language of their own and even a "Minoan" script (still undeciphered), but the Greeks submerged this tongue and later borrowed an alphabet from another source when their civilization developed a need for writing. The source of the Greek alphabet (and, through Latin, of all European alphabets) was a Semitic people, the Phoenicians, whose trading activities led them from their native Syria in the Near East throughout the Mediterranean. They founded cities in Sicily, Sardinia, and Spain, and in northern Africa built Carthage, later to become the great rival of Rome. The Greeks adapted the Phoenician script to their own spoken language, shifting some consonant symbols to vowels, for which Semitic languages have no symbols, and reversing the Oriental method of writing from right to left. But not until the fourth century B.C. was the Greek alphabet standardized for the whole Hellenic world. Local dialects of spoken Greek persisted, for language is a dynamic instrument; but the political and intellectual ascendancy of Athens in the fifth century gradually established Attic Greek as the norm.

An equally important bond among the Greeks was their common *religion*, which varied somewhat because of local deities and yet preserved a common core. It was as restless as their language and enjoyed a gradual evolution. As invaders, they brought with them a primitive polytheism, which expressed the awe of all primitive peoples for natural powers greater than themselves, powers that were their source of food and very existence, and yet made life insecure because of their unpredictable ability to bring flood, drought, failure, and death. Fear of the unknown had led the Greeks to invent personalities like themselves to represent these forces, gods in human form with whom they could deal through worship and ritual. To these gods they sang prayers before an altar, offered libations of milk or wine, and sacrificed animals as burnt offerings.

THE GODS OF THE GREEKS. Our earliest formal picture of Greek belief comes from Hesiod, the eighth-century poet who lived in a time when poets were still considered seers of the tribe. In the beginning, he tells us, there was Chaos, out of which came Earth and Heaven with Love as the ruling principle of creation. Love shaped matter into Titans, male and female, with an instinctive affinity and the power of further creation. These unruly Titans, predecessors of the gods, seem to personify the mighty convulsions of the physical world as it took shape. Kronos, the greatest of these, ruled Heaven and Earth with Rhea, his sister-queen, and had three daughters and three sons. The last of these children, Zeus (Jupiter *), eventually overthrew Kronos, imprisoned all of the Titans under the earth except his friend Prometheus, and began with his brothers and sisters the rule of the gods from their throne on Mount Olympus in northern Thessaly.

As leader of the victorious gods, Zeus became ruler of the earth. To his brother Poseidon (Neptune) he assigned the sea, and to Hades (Pluto) the underworld of departed spirits. Of his three sisters, Hestia (Vesta) became the goddess of the hearth, Demeter (Ceres), the goddess of agriculture, and Hera (Juno), the goddess of womanhood. Zeus married Hera and had by her the children Ares (Mars), god of war, and Hephaestos (Vulcan), the god of fire. But the affairs of Zeus with other ladies were notorious in the halls of Olympus and won him not simply the wrath of shrewish Hera, but also a considerable family: the twins Apollo (Apollo), eventually god of the sun and the arts, and Artemis (Diana), virgin goddess of the moon, the hunt, and maidenhood; Aphrodite (Venus), capricious goddess of love and beauty; Hermes (Mercury), the wily messenger of the gods; and Dionysus (Bacchus), the youthful god of wine and physical joy. To these was added Athena (Minerva), goddess of wisdom, who sprang fully grown from the brain of Zeus.

These were the chief gods of heaven, earth, the sea, and the underworld; but in the course of time a galaxy of lesser deities was invented: Eros (Cupid), the mischievous son of Venus; Pan, the piper-god of woods and fields; the nine Muses presiding over arts and sciences from their haunts on Mount Helicon and Mount Olympus; the four Winds; the nymphs and satyrs of the woods; the punishing Furies of the underworld; and the graceful water

* The names of the Roman deities that were later identified with the Greek are given in parentheses.

nymphs. Around these personalities grew up a host of charming myths that reveal the rich resources of Greek imagination and have inspired Western poets from their day to ours. They are as much a part of our culture as the Bible stories or the folk tales of England and France.

HESIOD'S FIVE AGES OF MAN. Hesiod divided the history of the world into five ages, which, though fanciful, are convenient for showing the relation of Greek religion to the history of Greece. In the first, the Age of Gold, Kronos ruled the world and Prometheus, the most humane of the Titans, created man in the image of the gods and brought him the gift of fire as the symbol of civilization. So the life of early man was golden, free from toil and misery. In the Age of Silver, Zeus and the gods established their rule over the Titans and divided the year into seasons, which plagued man with extreme heat and cold. As man turned more brutish and neglected the gods, Zeus considered annihilating the race and actually deprived men of the use of fire. But Prome-

theus, the champion of mankind, regained it and thereby won the terrible wrath of Zeus, his former friend, as Aeschylus tells us in *Prometheus Bound*. The Age of Bronze that followed may be conveniently linked with the Minoan culture, which actually evolved in what anthropologists know today as the Bronze Age. The men of this day were strong warriors, such as Perseus, Heracles, Theseus, and Jason, who destroyed their race by their violence. Or did the invasion of the Greeks actually destroy them to establish the Age of Heroes? In the fourth age the Greek world was supposed to have been ruled by heroic men—Agamemnon, Menelaus, Achilles, Nestor, and Ajax—who proved their worth in the war with Troy in the twelfth century B.C. and went in spirit from the battlefield or the hearth to a separate abode in the underworld of Hades. Alas, says Hesiod, the deterioration is now complete, for he lived (as we do) in the Age of Iron, when men never cease from toil and sorrow by day, nor from perishing by night.

HOMER AND THE AGE OF HEROES

IT is the Heroic Age of gods and men that Homer presents in the *Iliad* and the *Odyssey*, the two great monuments of the first period of Greek literature. These works alone give us a living picture of the Heroic Age, even though they were certainly produced at least three centuries after the events they relate and hence distort the picture with the perspective of a later time. The Heroic Age was one of incessant movement, frequent wars, and exciting personal adventure.

The hardy Greek invaders who had destroyed the rich Minoan civilization were not unlike the Teutonic barbarians who later overran a moribund Roman empire. Their "kings" were warrior-leaders who depended in crisis on personal followers, the free males within the tribe who were also called "kings," but of a lesser grade. All the kings were descended from Zeus and inherited their power to rule from him. A "king of kings," such as Agamemnon, sought advice from his lesser kings or family heads within the tribe and held his supreme authority only so long as he could enforce it on the others. Without written laws, the clan was governed by custom as the elders remembered and interpreted it. Crimes were avenged by families, and the revenge was stark and bloody.

The institutions of this aristocratic society were feudalistic even to the fortified towns and castles (which were to develop into city-states). Freemen who owed loyalty to the kings, or heroes, were assigned lands to cultivate, but much of the work was

done by serfs or slaves. The heroes followed the road of adventure, where they challenged each other in sport and song and sought battle to prove their strength and courage, their cunning and their valor. Their weapons were bronze, and their treasures were rich jewels and armor which they could carry with them. Unlike the later Greeks, they had no temples but worshiped their gods at improvised altars out of doors. They cremated their dead, and no man might deny burial even to his enemy, since this sacred rite was essential to the peace of the soul in Hades.

These lusty heroes lived a simple, physical life close to the soil. The tall, powerful men were not ashamed of work in the fields. King Odysseus boasted that he had no peer in reaping and mowing and could make chairs and beds for his house, boots and saddles for his riding. The beautiful women too had nimble hands. Queen Penelope wove cloth in her palace, Helen was proud of her needlework, and Nausicaä, a princess, washed the royal linen.

These men of action had little time for moralizing and no thought of international law. Hospitality was generous but unpredictable. When a town was captured, its riches were plundered, its buildings destroyed, its men killed or sold into slavery, its women made concubines or slaves. Treachery for a practical end was not only condoned but praised, and Odysseus was everywhere admired for his ingenious mendacity. Like all the Greeks of this uncertain, disordered age, he had only himself to rely on, and in the incessant struggle of his day he was supposed to use whatever craft and skill and strength he could muster.

THE WAR WITH TROY. The early Greeks fought many "wars," if we may dignify their pillaging expeditions with the name, but their destruction of Cnossus, Mycenae, and Tiryns was not chronicled as the siege of Troy was immortalized by Homer. Actually, the *Iliad* has no more trustworthy connection with this war than does *The Song of Roland* with the Moorish campaigns of Charlemagne. But Homer's idealized account of the heroic struggle has some basis in fact. Since the first enthusiastic excavations of Heinrich Schliemann, the German archaeologist, seventy-five years ago, we have learned that nine cities were successively built in ancient times on the traditional site of Troy in Asia Minor and that the sixth of these cities was probably the one destroyed by the Greeks around the traditional date, 1184 B.C.

The cause of this war is romantically ascribed by Homer to the rape of Helen, wife of the Greek king Menelaus, by the Trojan prince, Paris. Today we know that the war was merely one incident in the general extermination of the older kingdoms. Troy, strategically located at the entrance to the Hellespont, was a special target because it commanded the trade route between the Aegean and the Propontis (Sea of Marmora) and probably exacted an insufferable toll from Greek ships passing by. The annihilation of Troy assured Greek domination of the Aegean Sea. But it brought as well a dark period to the whole area as the barbaric invaders settled down to develop slowly a culture of their own, eventually more glorious than the one they had destroyed. These Dark Ages of Greece are usually dated from the last of the invasions (c. 1104 B.C.), which brought the coarse, warlike Dorian Greeks into the Peloponnese and founded the military caste of Sparta. The four centuries that followed are the cloudiest in Greek history, though they did produce Homer in the eighth century and Hesiod in the seventh. This was the hazy period when the Aegean world was gradually becoming Greek.

THE NATIONS OF HELLAS. Before the sixth century B.C., this process was complete. Hellenic culture as we know it was born, and the various branches of the new nation had settled, not simply their own peninsula, but the islands of the Aegean and the coast of Macedonia, Thrace, the Black Sea region, Asia Minor, Sicily, and southern Italy. All of this was Hellas, the Greek world.

Three chief branches of the Greek people can be distinguished in Hellas, stretched in horizontal bands across the Aegean Sea. In their contrasting political and social systems, in their differing literary forms, in their trade rivalry and eventual war is written

The effect of blindness is conveyed by this imaginary portrait of Homer from the Hellenistic period, 340–146 B.C.

the history of Greece in its Golden Age. Spread across the north from Thessaly and Boeotia to the island of Lesbos and the nearby Asiatic mainland, the *Aeolians* had founded the cities of Thebes, Delphi, Plataea, and Mitylene, and later formed in Asia Minor the Aeolian League of twelve cities. This fiery branch of the Greeks was to produce in the sixth century B.C., a school of passionate lyric poets of whom Sappho and Alcaeus are the best known.

In the south were the *Dorians,* with their great mainland cities of Sparta and Corinth and their colonies on the islands of Melos and Rhodes and at Cnidus on the Asiatic coast. Descendants of the last and most ruthless Greek invaders, the Dorians had preserved their military tradition and a rigidly aristocratic social and political system carried over from their enslavement of the original inhabitants of the land. Blessed with a reasonably fertile soil, they became farmers and sheep-herding mountaineers. In the arts they were sluggish, at least in the Golden Age; their chief poetry was the public ode, which expressed the staunch patriotism of a simple, stalwart people.

Wedged into the center of Hellas was the third branch of the Greeks, the bright-eyed *Ionians,* who settled the islands of Andros, Naxos, and Samos and maintained on Asia Minor the Ionian Confederacy of twelve cities, notably Ephesus and Miletus. Akin to them were the Attic Greeks of Athens, who seemed to blend Aeolian fire and imagination with Spartan stamina and seriousness. These contrasting strains were harmonized in the Attic temperament to produce the great leaders of Hellas in war, trade, the arts, philosophy, and political enlightenment.

With poor soil but many harbors, the Athenians took to the sea and explored the physical world as boldly as they were to explore the world of ideas. Athens in her Golden Age * of the fifth century was to become the cosmopolitan spokesman for a free democracy, as Sparta, her Dorian rival, was the champion of military autocracy founded on caste and intense nationalism.

GOVERNMENT IN CITY-STATES

By 800 B.C. most of the Greeks had forsaken the open road and settled down in towns, many of which became the centers of the city-states in the Greek political system. These small units were a natural development of the feudal fortresses built by the tribes of the Heroic Age. Originally ruled by kings in the older tradition of Agamemnon and Menelaus, they gradually curtailed the monarch's power, until by 600 B.C. most of them were independent republics. The degree of actual democracy varied from state to state, but generally the system was oligarchic, with the state in the hands of the noble families, who alone could claim to be "citizens." This military aristocracy ruled the rural area of the state from its city stronghold and reduced the unarmed peasants to a humble position.

Such a repressive system flourished in Sparta, with its military caste and conservative provincialism. But in a mercantile city like Athens the rise of a powerful middle class brought a challenge to the old families and eventually produced rival political parties within a republic much closer to our understanding of the term. This did not happen immediately, because the biased law codes of the aristocratic governments did not provide for a widening of the governing class. Leaders of the upstart bourgeoisie, often renegade aristocrats eager for power, staged sudden revolutions and forced concessions from the nobles. Ruling as tyrants, they still depended upon the lower classes for continued

power, and engineered land reforms for the peasantry and political reforms for the mercantile classes. In their public works programs and their patronage of the arts these tyrants of the sixth century, especially Pisistratus of Athens, paved the way for the Golden Age of art, philosophy, and political freedom that Athens, at least, was to enjoy in the fifth.

By 500 B.C. such tyrannies had been displaced in most city-states by some form of popular government with a party system based on the conflicting interests of the aristocracy and the democratic classes. Whatever form it might take in individual states, such a republic generally provided the citizen with a voice in the government and the legal protection of the state as he pursued his work.

The demands of traders for some interstate (or "international") law and order eventually led to commercial treaties which granted outsiders legal representation in the courts and other privileges. The old piracy of the Heroic Age gave way to more civilized methods of trade, and even international arbitration of disputes was provided for and sometimes invoked. Unfortunately, the age-old rivalries among the cities kept them from moving further toward political union, and the tradition of violence bequeathed by the tyrants made intercity wrangling and warfare all too common. Only in the face of overwhelming danger from outside would the several states of the Greeks forget their differences and unite in a common cause.

THE PERSIAN WARS AND THE WARS OF THE CITY-STATES

Such a threat confronted them early in the fifth century, after five hundred years of relative peace with their neighbors. Around 550 B.C. the eastern kingdom of Lydia, resenting the Greek cities of Asia Minor which blocked her access to the Aegean, assumed control of them one by one. When soon afterwards Lydia was absorbed in turn by the greater kingdom of Persia, these Greek cities came under Persian rule for fifty years. This formidable neighbor

of Hellas to the east was an Oriental despotism which developed at about this time a remarkable dynasty of kings—among them Cambyses, Darius I, and Xerxes I—who rapidly extended their rule over the Near Eastern empires, including Egypt.

Persian rule of Asia Minor was comparatively benign, but in 499 B.C. the Ionian cities there,

* Not to be confused with Hesiod's Age of Gold, the first of his five ages of man previously discussed.

chafing under the unenlightened governorship of barbarians, dismissed the Persian satraps and proclaimed their independence. Athens sent them aid, but the revolt failed. Aroused by the impertinence of the Athenians, Darius resolved to conquer the Greek mainland in revenge. A naval expedition in 492 B.C. was wrecked before it could reach Athens, but Darius dispatched a second fleet in the following year. The arrival of an army of 200,000 men on the Euboean coast threw the Greeks into panic. But Athens sent a brave little band of 9000 men into the field, assisted by 1000 Plataeans, who came to their aid by forced marches. At Marathon the Greeks were outnumbered ten to one, but their courage and discipline carried the day. The lumbering Persian forces were utterly routed and pursued to their ships in one of the major battles in world history.

Darius died in 485 B.C., but his son Xerxes renewed the attack. For four years he slowly collected materials from all parts of the Persian empire and a mammoth polyglot army that Herodotus, the Greek historian of this war, numbered at two million. With a fleet of 1200 large ships and many smaller ones, this unwieldy host crossed the Hellespont in seven days and nights over two bridges of ships lashed together to provide a veritable road over the sea. Warned of the approach of this colossus, the Greek cities in the north surrendered without a fight, but Athens and Sparta, united by a common danger, made hasty and seemingly pathetic preparations for battle. As the Persians approached Athens, they found the narrow and treacherous pass of Thermopylae defended by 300 Spartans, under Leonidas, and several thousand allies. Xerxes lost thousands of his troops in a vain effort to overpower their defense, and succeeded only after a Greek traitor showed him an indirect route to the rear of the Greeks. The 300 Spartans allowed their allies to leave and held out with 700 Thespians until they were almost completely annihilated. Their noble defense inspired the most famous epitaph in the *Greek Anthology:*

"Go tell the Spartans, thou that passeth by,
   That here, obedient to their laws, we lie."

Themistocles, the commander of Athens, now ordered his people to flee for their lives, so that when Xerxes reached the city he found only a small garrison. These men he killed, and laid waste the city. But Themistocles had placed all his hope in a naval battle, where the seagoing Athenians might be a more even match for the Persians. The two fleets met in a narrow strait north of the Saronic Gulf, which gave Xerxes no space to maneuver his countless ships. From his seat on the Attic shore the Persian king watched his vast armada worsted in the decisive battle named Salamis after an island across the strait. With confusion and disease in the ranks of his army, he made a hasty retreat. A remnant of 300,000 men was left in Thessaly, but this last threat to Greek independence was defeated the next year in the battle of Plataea. In withstanding the Persian hordes the Greeks preserved their Western civilization from being engulfed by the ancient East and prepared the way for their Golden Age that followed.

The leadership of Athens in the Persian Wars gave her hegemony in Hellas through the remainder of the fifth century. She strengthened her position by forming the so-called Delian Confederacy, an arrangement whereby the Greek cities of Asia and the Aegean contributed a fixed sum of money to a common treasury at Delos (later moved to Athens) for defense against Persia. Her naval supremacy in the league converted it into a veritable Athenian empire and inevitably excited the envy and dissatisfaction of the other states. The brilliant but unscrupulous Themistocles was eventually succeeded as Athenian leader by the noble Pericles (c. 495–429 B.C.), who guided the democratic party to power, reformed the laws of the state in favor of the lower classes, and encouraged the flowering of Athenian art and philosophy. The greatest period of Greek culture is often called the Age of Pericles.

The political gulf between Athens and Sparta grew wider after the Persian enemy retired, as the power of Athens increased, and her democratic government threatened to affect the aristocratic states to the south. A rival confederacy to the Ionic had been organized by Sparta, and eventually led the Greek cities into new and shameful wars among themselves which were to destroy the vitality of Greek culture and lay Hellas open to conquest from without.

The so-called Peloponnesian War began in 431 B.C. when Sparta marched on Athens because of a protest from the Doric city of Corinth. During the siege of Athens, Pericles and many others died in a plague, but the demagogue Cleon persuaded the city to hold out, despite the satiric protests of the playwright Aristophanes. A technical defeat induced Sparta to offer peace, but the indecisive Peace of Nicias proved only the fruitlessness of these wars of the city-states. Soon afterwards Sparta was at odds with her former ally, Corinth, and Athens under the brilliant profligate Alcibiades dispatched a fleet against the Doric city of Syracuse in Sicily. But Alcibiades was deprived of his command on suspicion of sacrilege, so he turned traitor and engineered a crippling blow by the Spartans against his native city. The war between Athens and Sparta dragged on for several years, until with the loss of her fleet Athens fell to a siege in 404 B.C.

So the hegemony of Athens gave way to the hegemony of Sparta. The aristocratic Spartans promptly deposed the democratic party in Athens and established the atrocious rule of the Thirty Tyrants for a year. Overbearing methods soon roused enemies against Sparta in the other states just as Athenian rule had done. The intense individualism of the Greeks that made them withstand the threat of the Persian barbarian made them oppose as well any tyranny among themselves. It was Thebes that led the rebellion against Spartan hegemony, which did not end until 371 B.C., with the fall of Sparta. But the hegemony of Thebes, established in that year, was no more successful than the others, and dwindled to purely nominal leadership before the Sacred War (355–346 B.C.) and the Locrian War (339–338 B.C.) made the Greek cities an easy prey for a foreign conqueror, Philip of Macedonia.

The period of the interstate wars is a sad one to record. Deep-seated differences between Dorians and Athenians gave them opposed political systems and prevented their thinking as one nation. The love of freedom that emancipated the Greeks intellectually led them to waste their vitality and resources in internecine strife. Intense individualism created Greek culture and destroyed it as well, for the Greeks carried it to an extreme.

THE GREEK POINT OF VIEW

HEREIN lies one key to the Greek spirit in the great age of Pericles. The Greek point of view was founded upon freedom, freedom *from* certain things and freedom *to do* certain things. Paramount was the freedom of man to explore himself and his world without the sanction of any authority, past or present, to restrict him. He demanded the right to do so because he felt an inner compulsion to do so. Freedom to act required freedom to think; and, excited by the challenge of worlds to investigate, he focused a clear and unprejudiced eye on things around him, to explain them and enjoy them in their own terms.

Like the Chinese, the Greek mind was unusually free from mysticism, while it lacked the Chinese enslavement to convention or tradition. Nowhere do we see this practical realism of the Greeks more clearly than in their religion. The ancient pantheon of the Greeks was devised over a period of centuries while they were still illiterate and yet were seeking a plausible explanation of natural phenomena. It was a naïve and primitive theology, as thoughtful Greeks of the fourth century came to realize, and yet it was eminently clear and sensible.

Unlike Taoism, Hinduism, or Christianity, it was a concrete representation of their experience of nature, largely free from abstract concepts of morality. As the prehistoric Greeks invented one god after another to personify the natural forces with which they had to deal, they gave these deities minds like their own, operating by purely human motives. The gods were superior to men, not in their ethical standards or conduct, but in the concrete qualities of power, beauty, and immortality. The sacrifices of animals and other food that the Greeks burned to these deities implied a hard-headed bargain; through a concrete gift they expected a concrete return in the form of good weather for their crops; freedom from natural disasters; or success in war, athletic competition, or even love. This legalistic view of the relations between god and man may be implied in the prayers and penances of other religious peoples, but nowhere is it more frankly confessed than in Greek ritual. It reflected the purely external nature of the Greek's relation with his gods and the sanctity of his mind from even their prying eyes. Zeus could watch him act, but he could not watch him think. The god could see him commit a crime when other men might not; but he could not see him meditate a crime. Since the Greek felt no spiritual contact with his gods, he had no sense of sin, which is an abstract and spiritual concept. Instead he had a severe notion of crime, which is a concrete and external act. Hence the Greek lacked the Christian conception of conscience, which is founded upon a sense of sin.

If evil meant for the concrete-minded Greeks evildoing, or crime, the punishment of evil must be equally concrete. If the evil lay, not in meditating crime, but in doing it, the punishment must take place, not in the mind or "conscience" of the evildoer, but upon his physical person. Murder called for revenge in kind, and the murdered man's kin were duty-bound to carry out the punishment, as Orestes knew when he killed his mother Clytemnestra for the murder of his father (this story is told in Aeschylus' play, *The Libation-Bearers*). Thus a chain of family crimes extending through generations in the manner of a feud was sanctioned, as in Aeschylus' account of the House of Atreus. If no kinsman remained to avenge a crime, a thoughtful transgressor who recognized his crime might punish himself, as Oedipus did in plucking out his own eyes. Otherwise the gods might send against him the dreaded Erinyes (Furies), snaky-haired women who pursued criminals guilty of offenses such as family murder. In Aeschylus' play, *The Eumenides*, we see them harrying Orestes after his murder of his mother. Although these grisly deities may be a primitive approach to the concept of conscience, the

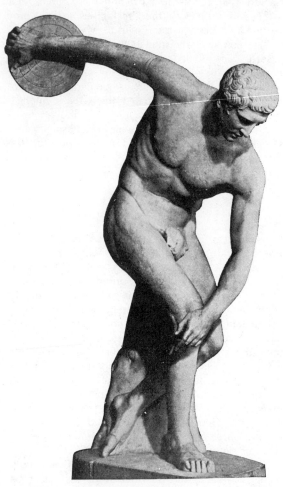

The Discus-Thrower by the Greek sculptor Myron remains the embodiment of the Greek ideal of physical beauty.

in the religious tolerance that generally prevailed among the cities. The Greeks had no bible to provide a canon of orthodox belief (though Homer was their bible in the cultural sense, their first of books, to be studied and even memorized by every schoolboy). Except at a few shrines, they had no sacerdotal class to codify holy tradition and preserve it without change, because the Greek view of the citizen demanded that every man should have open to him the experience of officiating at religious ceremonies. The laws of the states outlawed technical atheism, as we recall from the trial of Socrates, and public opinion, or simply good taste, protected the gods from such desecration as Alcibiades was once accused of perpetrating against the statues of Hermes. But otherwise free discussion of religious matters was widely tolerated, and resulted in frequent modification of general belief and gradual changes in practice. Soothsayers and the oracles at Delphi, Dodona, and elsewhere, who supposedly had the power to communicate with certain gods and foretell the future, were revered in earlier times, but in fifth-century Athens the seers had been discredited and the ambiguous pronouncements of the oracles already inspired skepticism. Euripides frequently casts aspersions on the seers.

The Greek citizen enjoyed another freedom less admirable in our eyes: freedom from menial work. From earliest times slavery had been accepted in the aristocratic society of the Greeks, as by all ancient nations from the Chinese to the Hebrews and Egyptians. Slaves were obtained especially by conquest of "barbarian" states, since the capture of a city usually sent a good share of the population into perpetual servitude. They did most of the menial tasks in Greek cities and enjoyed in return no legal rights. The master held a life-and-death power over them, though this was exercised more frequently in an aristocratic city like Sparta than in a democratic one like Athens, where slaves often held places of esteem in the family circle. A few advanced thinkers such as Euripides made guarded attacks on the institution, but the majority of citizens, including Plato and Aristotle, accepted slavery as the natural fate of more than half the population.

Lest we be too quick to condemn the Greeks for their institution of slavery, we should remember that slavery was continuously tolerated in Christian Europe for a thousand years after the decay of the Roman empire. Not until the thirteenth century A.D. did the practice of slavery decline. In comparison with the Orientals and the Romans, the Greek citizens were humane in their treatment of slaves, and accepted their freedom from toil, not as an invitation to idleness and vice, but as an opportunity to realize in themselves an ideal of human perfection.

concreteness of their personalities and their punishment suggests that they were bogey-women designed to discourage the committing of crime.

Freedom of the soul meant for the Greek freedom to explore and enjoy this world rather than freedom to choose his place in a world to come. He did believe in an after-place called Hades, and even the Elysian fields of the blessed spirits, but these gave him little comfort or satisfaction. Hades was a dark and static place which inspired the spirit of Achilles to tell Odysseus in the *Odyssey:* "I would rather be a slave on earth to a landless man without a fortune than be the king of the dead in the realm of the shadows." The Greek loved the challenge of life too much to look forward to "black Death." Happiness came, if at all, in this life; the hereafter, even though it carried no punishment, certainly entailed no reward.

The Greek love of intellectual freedom is reflected

'Know thyself" was the favorite motto of the Greeks, inscribed over the temple of Apollo at Delphi. Such a rule of life invited speculation, but not introspection in the limited sense, because the healthy-minded Greek believed that self-knowledge comes from experience in the world rather than retirement from it. To know oneself meant to the concrete-minded Greek the realization of all his powers—physical, intellectual, moral, and aesthetic—through developing and refining them to the highest possible degree. The Greek ideal of the individual was in no way limited: it demanded a rounded realization of the full personality of the citizen. As such, it has remained the cherished ideal of the humanistic thinker throughout the centuries, and was to inspire such men as Leonardo and Michelangelo of the Renaissance to unparalleled versatility.

The simple conditions of Greek life made it possible to achieve this ideal of human perfection, whereas the complexities of modern civilization work against it. Freed from manual labor, the Greek citizen still lived close enough to the earth to exult in physical living. His physical energies were devoted to athletics rather than toil, and their objective was the strengthening and beautifying of the body as a fit temple for the mind and spirit. The health and physical vigor of the Greek people is reflected in the advanced ages to which their great men lived and produced with no evidence of senility: Solon to seventy-nine, Pindar to eighty, Aeschylus to eighty-one, Euripides to seventy-four, Sophocles to eighty-nine, Plato to eighty-one, Isocrates to ninety-eight.

Yet health was no more important an objective of Greek athletics than was physical beauty. With their interpretation of the world in concrete terms, the Greeks saw physical perfection as a major phase of human goodness. "A sound mind in a sound body" is the conventional translation of a Greek motto that meant something closer to "a healthy mind in a beautiful body." The culture of the mind and the culture of the body were inseparable phases of the education of the individual toward a single ideal of goodness and beauty. Greek athletics had a moral purpose associated with the great public games which brought together the best citizen-athletes of all the Greek city-states for a religious festival of athletic competition on the templed slopes of Parnassus at Delphi or Olympia in the Peloponnese, two of the most sacred spots in Hellas. The display of physical beauty, strength, swiftness, and skill by the naked athletes confirmed their inner harmony of spirit, and when Pindar's chorus sang the praises of the victor at the evening celebration, they said as much of his mental qualities as of his physical prowess. This linking of physical goodness with mental goodness, of bodily beauty with spiritual beauty, is hard to grasp in a specialized age like ours that opposes the man of muscle to the man of brain.

The Greek citizen saw another facet of perfection in an active public life. The Greek system of government through a multiplicity of small city-states, rather than a centralized tyranny, gave each citizen a direct and intimate contact with all state decisions. The citizens were the state and must all take an active part in its civil and military functions. Each citizen served as soldier, as legislator, and potentially as judge and hierophant at religious ceremonies. Since he must attend the assembly personally to speak, decide, and vote on all public questions, political units were necessarily confined to the small city-state. The idea of representative government, by which one man could speak for a hundred or a thousand, is an abstract concept that seldom occurred to the concrete-minded Greeks.

Such a society tended to produce robust and vigorous extroverts who lived constantly in the market place, the gymnasium, and the Assembly rather than in the seclusion of their private homes. An introvert like Euripides felt out of place in such an open-air environment and suffered from the misunderstanding and taunts of his hardy associates. In a literal sense the Greek citizen knew no privacy; in Sparta he was actually taken from his mother's care at the age of seven or so, was reared under public guardians, and never again retreated into purely domestic life. The state allegiance took complete precedence over family ties, and marriage itself was thought to serve the good of the state rather than the private needs of the individual. Marriage was a means of producing children, and only healthy children were supposed to be reared at all. The sickly ones were commonly exposed within ten days after birth, to death or possible adoption—a practice that accounts for the ubiquitous character of the long-lost son or daughter who provides a happy ending for so many later Greek comedies and novels.

Since marriages were usually arranged by the children's fathers with no concern whatever for the young people's preference, romantic love as we know it was not idealized by the Greeks or even commonly thought to exist in the Golden Age. Domestic arrangements after marriage involved a strict division of labor: the wife managed the home and the husband took care of his public responsibilities. It goes without saying that woman's position in such a society was appallingly inferior to man's. It had not been so in the Heroic Age, when the Greeks fought a war for a woman and Homer exalted the conjugal devotion of Hector and Andromache in the *Iliad* and of Odysseus and Penelope in the *Odyssey*. But by the fifth century woman's position had de-

This Athenian red-figured provision jar shows Greek women c. 450 B.C. and typifies Greek vase painting of the Golden Age.

generated to that of childbearing servant to her husband and the state. A radical thinker like Euripides might offer a mild protest in *Alcestis* or *Medea*, but Pericles the statesman and Aristotle the social philosopher alike upheld the inferiority of woman as a natural and inevitable thing. This explains why literature of the Golden Age completely lacks the theme of romantic love so dominant in the fiction and poetry of our day. It is true that Plato in his *Symposium* gives an exalted tribute to Love as an inspiration of noble conduct, but what he has in mind is a passionate friendship between two men, the so-called "Greek love," which was generally accepted in his day but is peculiarly repugnant to our way of thinking.

These blemishes in the Greek view of life point up

its radical differences from our own, but they should not obscure the general perfection of the Greek objective as the most exalted view of individual development in history. The facets of the ideal which we have sketched thus far were understood in all Greek cities; only in Athens, however, did the culminating objectives of artistic and intellectual development approach perfection. Athens, the most democratic of all the city-states and the leader of Greece in the fifth century, epitomizes the freedom for individual thinking and expression that lay behind the finest achievements of Greek culture. The same urge that shaped her free political life produced the bold and beautiful pronouncements of her poets and the unbiased inquiry of her historians and philosophers.

Artistic expression was natural to the Greeks, because every aspect of their lives exalted beauty, the outer and inner harmony of man, as the great objective of his development. Greek art is a reflection of Greek life; in its Golden Age it was the imaginative expression for every citizen of the harmonious ideal toward which he was striving. The "art for art's sake" doctrine of a specialized and materialistic culture like our own had no meaning for the Greeks. The artistic outlook, the thirst for beauty and harmony, enriched every phase of the citizen's life, and was in turn enriched by its close contact with this broad reality. The good life was in the highest sense the beautiful life, reflected in the inner harmony of all phases of the individual—physical, moral, and intellectual. A work of art was beautiful in part because it exalted the moral ideals of the race and beautified the everyday life that men knew.

The close tie between the aesthetic ideal and Greek religion is reflected in all the arts. Greek architecture developed in terms of temples rather than palaces. Greek sculpture gave concrete personalities to the gods, who were represented as types of physical perfection and inner serenity. The Greek epic reflected the lives of the gods as well as heroes, and Greek drama originated in the chorus of religious ritual. The oneness of the aesthetic and ethical ideals explains why the cultivation of the arts was so fundamental to the Greek view of the citizen.

As the culture of the Greeks matured and their primitive polytheism came to seem a naïve and inadequate explanation of their environment, the more thoughtful citizens began to focus rational curiosity on the world around them. Philosophy, at first suspiciously received by the conservatives, became eventually the core of Greek education. The youth of Athens sat at the feet of the Sophists, and the political leaders of Hellas went for training to her philosophers—Pericles to Anaxagoras, Alcibiades to Socrates, Dionysius to Plato, and Alexander the Great to Aristotle. In this broadest expansion of their horizon, we see the Greek view of life as an eager awareness of the world in which they lived and an enthusiastic urge to explore every phase of its perfection.

The atmosphere and attitude of freedom were essential to the Greek achievement, but just as essential, finally, was their peculiar capacity for self-restraint. It was this that directed their creative energy and prevented it from wasting itself in extravagance. "Know thyself" said the favorite Greek motto, but beside it on the temple at Delphi was inscribed a further rule of life, "Nothing to excess," to guide the free expression of the self. Herodotus saw this rational control as obedience to a superior principle: "Though free, they are not absolutely free, for they have a master over them, the law." To explore oneself was to become aware at last of one's limitations and of the value of self-restraint. The gods dislike a proud man who puffs himself up with self-importance until he excites their envy and invites their wrath. Both Aeschylus in *The Persians* and Herodotus in his *History* present Xerxes the Oriental potentate as the awful type of unrestrained mortal whom the gods delight to cut down. Not servile acceptance of tradition but a lofty self-restraint that imposes a natural check on eccentricity appealed to the Greeks and guided their creative energies into a considered perfection. This is the last great key to the Greek spirit.

THE PERIODS OF GREEK LITERATURE

THE great age of Greece fell between the defeat of Persia at Salamis (480 B.C.) and the Macedonian defeat of the Greeks at Chaeronea (338 B.C.). It began with a magnificent burst of national energy in a triumphant defense of the Western homeland against the East; it continued through a century of pathfinding and building in many directions; it ended in a shocking defeat that came close to national suicide. The general tendency of its achievements was from an imaginative interpretation of the world through the arts to a rational inquiry into the facts of the universe through philosophy and science: the fifth century was the great century of literature, architecture, and law; the fourth, the great century of philosophy; and only in the decadent third century did science come into its own among the Greeks.

Greek literature was born almost with the birth of the Greek nation, and the four periods of Greek literature bear a close and illuminating relationship to the periods of Greek history. The Epic period of Homer and Hesiod (down to 700 B.C.) portrays the ideals of the Heroic Age of invasion and colonization. The Lyric period (700–480 B.C.), associated with poets from islands in the Aegean, expresses the maturing of Hellenic culture. The Golden period (480–338 B.C.) belongs to Athens in her eighty-year hegemony of the city-states, to the Athenian playwrights Aeschylus, Sophocles, Euripides, and Aristophanes and the Athenian historians Herodotus and Thucydides. The Hellenistic period (338–146 B.C.) of Menander and Theocritus takes us from Athens to Alexandria in Egypt and reflects the sophistication and dissemination of Greek culture.

The epic tradition disappeared in Greece with the end of the Heroic Age. The epic is everywhere the song of a hero who is usually supposed to have founded a nation or at least to illustrate in his warlike deeds its ideals and ethical standards. But in the maturing of a people the simple problems of primitive life give way to the more complex concerns of civilization, and the folk epic becomes a treasured heritage from an era that survives only in memory. The Heroic Age was already past when the Homeric epics received their final form in the eighth century B.C. Hesiod (fl. c. 700 B.C.), who followed Homer, shows the new interests of a population that had forsaken wandering and piracy and settled down to till the soil and develop a more stable civilization. His *Works and Days* is a long tribute to the dignity of the farmer's life, directed to 'his miscreant brother who has cheated him of his inheritance in order to enjoy a life of luxury. Whereas Homer exalted the Achaean aristocracy, Hesiod praises the common man with his simple virtues and, in describing the plowing, planting, and reaping of the fields, gives a homely treatise on practical husbandry. His crude verse and humorless complaints about his lot make Hesiod dull reading, but he invented in this didactic poem of farm life a type called the "georgic" that Virgil, over seven centuries later, was to perfect into an elegant masterpiece.

After another obscure century, Greek poetry had a sudden revival that was to carry it without a break through the Hellenistic Age. The poetic form this time was lyric, and its masters belong especially to the Aeolian branch of Greeks and to the islands of the Aegean Sea. The new poetry was written to be sung and was identified with the lyre. Since the musical settings of all the famous lyrics of Greece have been lost, we have today only an imperfect impression of the original effect of the poems.

During the sixth century B.C., when the cities of the Aegean, such as Mitylene, Miletus, and Ephesus, were the most brilliant in Hellas, the passionate Aeolian Greeks produced a magnificent school of lyricists, whose works today survive only in tantalizing fragments. Fiery individualists as they were, they developed the lyric of personal emotion, sung by a single voice and expressing the poet's feelings of love, of grief, or of convivial joy. The greatest of these lyric poets, Alcaeus and the woman Sappho, are both associated with the Aegean island of Lesbos, where music and poetry flourished in this period; but the Aeolians eventually inspired an Ionian school of lyric poets on the mainland of Greece. Symbolically, Anacreon (fl. 525 B.C.) moved from the city of Teos in Asia Minor to Thrace and eventually to Athens, but wherever he went he took with him his gay spirits and his delight in wine and love.

Of quite a different kind are the choral odes of Pindar (522–442 B.C.), the leader of the Dorian school, who was born in Thebes but became the patriotic spokesman for all of Greece. The conservative nationalism of the Dorian people, best exemplified in the military tradition of Sparta, produced the Pindaric ode, a formal lyric sung by a chorus of many voices and expressing the emotion of a group audience on an occasion that inspired national pride. Written to honor an athletic hero at the national games, the ode took his victory as a text to praise the state from which he came and a virtue which his career displayed. The personal feelings of the Dorian poet were submerged in the intricate structure of his ode. Pindar himself preserved a masterful balance between the poetic and musical elements, but his successors, Pratinas and Philoxenus, emphasized the music, and lyric verse fell into decay.

GREEK DRAMA

THE decline of the lyric made way for the rise of dramatic poetry in the Golden Age and the climax of Greek literature in the masterpieces of tragedy. Drama in the West was invented by the Greeks as a natural development of their religious rituals, and throughout the great period it retained a religious meaning that shaped its special character. Although the early plays of Aeschylus show some similarity to the Pindaric odes, drama had an independent evolution in the religious festival that is strikingly paralleled by the origin of modern drama in medieval church services.

Although religious ceremonies honored many gods in different seasons and different sections of Hellas,

it was the festival of Dionysus, youthful god of wine and physical joy, that produced drama in sixth-century Athens. The exact steps by which choral songs praising the god became full-scale tragedies and comedies have been conjecturally reconstructed, but they remain obscure. We are reasonably sure that the *dithyramb* sung by the chorus in honor of Dionysus included a myth of the god (later of other gods) which provided the narrative ingredient for drama. It is easy and convenient to believe that, in order to increase the effect of this tribute to the god, the chorus eventually dressed up as satyrs, mythical companions of Dionysus, half-human, half-animal, with snub noses, pointed ears, and goats' tails. By

The technique of playing the lyre and the youth's pleasure in it are evident in this relief from the "Ludovisi throne."

thus honoring the god through representing themselves as his followers, they may have contributed the fundamental ingredient of drama, impersonation, and incidentally originated the term *tragedy* (from τράγος, *a he-goat,* and τραγῳός, *a goatsinger*). Or it may have been the leader of the chorus who dressed up as a satyr or even as Dionysus himself. In any case, some such representation of satyrs lay behind the satyr play, one of the three types of drama recognized by the Greeks.

Dialogue, the literary ingredient of drama, was probably introduced by Thespis (fl. 534 B.C.) and at first took place between the leader of the chorus and the chorus itself; eventually a special member of the chorus, called the "answerer," emerged in the plays of Aeschylus as a second actor. But the chorus remained an integral part of Greek drama throughout the Golden Age. Serving in Aeschylus to point out the ethical significance of the action, to warn the characters bent on crime, and to express the emotions of the audience, the chorus provided the playwright with a means for direct comment on his action and a voice for normal and right thinking against which to evaluate the eccentric actions of the characters. With the emergence of the second and third actors the protagonists of the play gradually submerged the chorus, until in the plays of Euripides and Aristophanes the choral passages are mere musical interludes, though still a medium for exalted lyric verse.

As with the lyric, the script of a Greek drama conveys only part of the impression intended by the author. To it must be added all the features of staging that contributed to a single composite art: music, declamation, costumes, dancing, and the ecstatic atmosphere of the religious occasion. The performance took place in a great open-air amphitheater, of which the familiar ruins of the fourth-century Theater of Dionysus in Athens carved out of the south cliff of the Acropolis or the Theater of Epidaurus shown on page 100 give us a clear impression. New tragedies were produced only once a year, at the March festival of the god, and comedies usually at the festival in January. Both festivals were under the protection of the state, like all religious celebrations, and one of the archons, or chief magistrates, of Athens administered them. The plays were presented through a three-day competition, in which one day was reserved for each of three competitors, who entered not one play alone but three tragedies (called a trilogy if they told one connected story) and a satyr play—all to be presented on the same day. One complete trilogy, the *Oresteia* of Aeschylus, has come down to us.

A playwright who wished to compete submitted his plays first to the archon, who, if he gave them preliminary approval, assigned the poet a wealthy patron to bear the expense of production and a chorus of twelve or fifteen men to sing his lines. The playwright himself might rehearse the chorus and even play a leading part in his plays. The central stage of the Greek theater consisted of a circular "dancing place" (Greek, *orchestra*) where the chorus grouped themselves in rows three deep and sang their lines in unison, to the accompaniment of a flute, while engaged in a simple religious dance. The actors of the dialogue eventually appeared on a raised platform behind the orchestra with a *skene,* or scene building, behind them, to which *paraskenia,* or wings, were added around 410 B.C. Scenery in the form of painted backdrops was common, as were a few properties; but the general staging of a Greek drama was much simpler than ours. There were no lighting effects to represent day and night and no curtain to bar the audience before the play. The actors recited their lines with great feeling but little or no action in the modern sense. The religious solemnity of the tragic occasion demanded of them a stately deportment. Their rich raiment was cut to give an ideally graceful and full effect, and their stature was increased by *buskins,* stout boots with thick soles to make them look big and impressive in their roles of gods and heroes. Since large masks were worn to make their roles clear to the far-flung audience and also to represent the grandeur of godly physiognomy, actors had to rely on resonant voices and dignified gestures for their effects. The masks of comedy were usually grotesque, and the

The Greeks made use of natural outdoor amphitheaters for the staging of their dramas. This large theater was built by the architect Polyclitus the Younger at Epidaurus in the fourth century B.C. Constructed of limestone, it has a radius of 210 feet, and is so arranged that a good view of the actors and chorus could be obtained from almost any seat.

buskin was here replaced by the low-heeled *sock*. Men or boys played women's parts, as later in the Elizabethan theater.

The effect of a Greek play was consequently quite different from ours. The religious character of the occasion dictated a stylized, rather than realistic, production. The absence because of convention of any extensive movement or violent action (such as murder) on the sacred stage resulted in brief, simple plays that concentrated on a few characters in a single situation. Aristotle's insistence on unity of action, or a single plot, was a natural outgrowth of the special conditions of the Greek theater. Although he did not require also unity of time (a twenty-four-hour period) and unity of place (a single locality), as is often supposed, it is clear that the physical limitations of the Greek stage, as well as artistic concentration, recommended something of the sort. Yet once we have accepted the conventions of Greek drama, the emotional impact of a Greek tragedy in an adequate production, or even in the library, is uniquely powerful. Consider the excitement and exaltation that it must have aroused in the Greeks themselves, as they saw the gods and heroes of their race brought to life in their most sacred adventures.

Although we know the names of many Greek playwrights of the Golden Age, only four of them —three tragic and one comic—have survived in complete works. Their forty-two extant plays were produced within almost exactly a century (c. 490–388 B.C.) and are tightly related within a continuous flow of artistic development and even a mesh of personal associations. The earliest play of Aeschylus (c. 525–456 B.C.), *The Suppliant Women*, reflects the transition from choral lyric to full-scale drama. The chorus in this work still dominates the play with its singing and dancing, and the two players for the three speaking parts are allowed very limited action. As a result, little seems to happen in the play, and we can only regret the loss of the remaining parts of the trilogy that would have carried the careers of the fifty women doomed to marry their fifty hated cousins to its logical conclusion in their wholesale murder of their husbands. *Prometheus Bound* brings greater emphasis on the central character, and in the *Oresteia* trilogy Aeschylus reaches at last a perfect balance between actors and chorus.

As the earliest of the dramatists, he is the most conservative in his approach to the religious stories that formed the plot material of Greek tragedy. With his interest in theological problems he made the *Oresteia* an embodiment of the traditional Greek ethic. A chain of crimes within a family illustrates the inheritance of criminal taint as each generation acts as an instrument of divine punishment. Driving

them on in the background is the transcendent force of Moira, or Fate, an inescapable power above gods and men alike which had emerged as an impersonal law to unify the conglomeration of Greek gods and cults. Yet Aeschylus was concerned with mundane problems also. Speaking as a masterful general in the recent Persian Wars, he gave in his play, *The Persians,* the moral lesson that a tyrannical conqueror must inevitably fall before a free and modest people. And in his picture of the persecuted yet fighting individualist, Prometheus, he reminded the Athenians that they too had only recently won their freedom from tyranny.

But Aeschylus lived to see a development in public taste away from the traditional theology and pan-Hellenic patriotism for which he had stood. In the work of the noble Sophocles (c. 495–406 B.C.), only thirty years his junior, religious problems were gradually subordinated to the human drama, and the actors on the stage began to loom larger than the chorus below. Though the devout public of Aeschylus frowned on the appearance of more than two speaking actors at a time, Sophocles unhesitatingly experimented with three and four and thus enlarged the scope of his play considerably. Disliking the accepted trilogy form, he made each of his plays a self-contained and more ambitious unit. As a result, they come closer to our understanding of drama and are the only Greek tragedies commonly performed today. His *Oedipus the King* and *Antigone* are generally considered the high points of the ancient theater.

The tendencies of Sophocles were carried much further by Euripides (c. 480–407 B.C.), the most radical of the playwrights. Though Sophocles had shifted his dramatic emphasis from the heavens to humanity, he was no less a believer in the traditional religion than Aeschylus had been. Euripides, fifteen years younger than he, belonged to a new generation grown skeptical of the ancient cults. While he was still required to treat the traditional stories in his plays, he saw their problems in terms of a new philosophy rather than the pious theology supported by the state. In reducing the chorus to the status of musical interlude, he could concentrate on the characters in his drama and treat them all, gods and men alike, as human beings to be scrutinized and even criticized. In *Alcestis* he slyly condemns the Greek citizen's cavalier superiority to woman by his unsympathetic interpretation of a legendary hero who lets his wife die for him. In *Iphigenia at Aulis*, Agamemnon and Menelaus, the Homeric heroes, are represented as quarreling politicians. Euripides is the psychologist among the tragedians, though his approach is still ethical rather than scientific. By interpreting realistically the motives of the hallowed heroes, he reduces them to ordinary people, often quite inadmirable and some-times downright foolish. His objective view of traditional material makes Euripides seem the most readable of all the playwrights today.

Naturally his radical outlook excited alarm and criticism among the conservatives, who still formed the backbone of the Athenian public. Aristophanes (c. 446–c. 386 B.C.), the biting comedian of the Greek theater, was spokesman for the conservatives and used all the freedom that the comic tradition allowed him to discredit Euripides.

So-called Old Comedy (from κῶμος, revel, and κωμῳδός, reveler) is quite unlike comedy as we know it. The competition in comedy was originally held at the January festival to Dionysus,* when the god of wine was honored through heavy drinking and a resulting freedom from social restraints and personal inhibitions. The occasion acted as a social safety valve when everyone, citizen and slave, was liberated from conventional decorum, prisoners were freed from their cells for the duration, and carefree lovemaking was the order of the day. Old Comedy reflects this bacchanalian spirit in its grossly vulgar language and the broad satire in which it could traditionally indulge with impunity. It becomes a satiric reflection of many phases of the life of Ath-ens, full of topical allusions and brutally funny attacks on parties and individuals of the day. The political and intellectual leaders feared and condemned the shockingly personal abuse in Old Comedy and eventually succeeded in transforming it into the milder Middle Comedy; but the best-known plays of Aristophanes are of the brazen older style.

As a conservative troubled by the decline of the old spirit of Athens at Marathon and Salamis, Aristophanes tried to laugh the new spirit of skepticism and state jingoism out of fashion. In The Acharnians and The Knights he attacked the demagogue Cleon and the suicidal Peloponnesian War that Cleon supported. In The Clouds he turned on the philosopher Socrates and the cynical reasoning of the Sophists. In the Thesmophoriazusae and The Frogs it was Euripides who was condemned as an atheist and bad artist. Today we can see that Aristophanes fears were well founded, for no major tragedian followed Euripides; the health of Athenian society declined with the decline of its religious faith, and the interstate wars destroyed the morale and independence of the Greeks. But national evolution is, for good or ill, a dynamic thing, and all the efforts of an Aristophanes, however valiant, could not hold it back.

THE HISTORIANS AND PHILOSOPHERS

ANOTHER sign of the growing sophistication of Athenian society in the Golden Age was the rise of history as a critical record of the nation's past. As myth gave way to more accurate chronicling and prose replaced verse as the medium for preserving fact, the fifth-century Greeks came closer to the scientific spirit of free inquiry in modern times. In fact, the term history comes from the Greek word ἱστορίη, meaning inquiry, and originally encompassed geography and science as well.

Although we know that he had his predecessors, Herodotus (c. 485–c. 425 B.C.) is usually called the Father of Prose and the Father of History on the strength of his History of Persia and the Persian Wars with Greece, the earliest historical work to be preserved. Renowned for his incessant travels through the Mediterranean and Near East, he epitomized the urge to observe and to know that inspired Greek philosophy and science. He accumulated a vast store of notes in the manner of a modern scholar. Herodotus is often criticized for recording fantastic stories that are patently untrue, but these too he could set down in the objective spirit of the chronicler. A tribute to his aloofness is the fairness with which he presents the point of view and customs of the Persians. That stems in part from his deliberate desire to be accurate, in part from his natural kindliness, which beams out at us from every page of his charming work.

But it was the great Thucydides (c. 460–c. 400 B.C.) who brought Greek history to maturity in his History of the Peloponnesian War, which is our definitive account of the first twenty years of the tragic conflict. Dealing with more immediate and verifiable material than Herodotus, Thucydides is more scientific than his predecessor was in a position to be. He set for himself an ideal of absolute accuracy and recorded only what he was convinced was true. Yet he is not a routine chronicler of events. His magnificent art makes the facts and personalities live, as he reconstructs speeches, shows insight in selecting significant details, and crowds ideas into his compact and simple style. Not until Gibbon in our eighteenth century was the world to see again the equal of this master of historical method. In the century that followed Thucydides, Xenophon (c. 430–c. 359 B.C.) continued his history of the city-states in the Hellenica and wrote a popular account of an expedition of Greek mercenary troops in Asia

* The so-called Lenaea festival, although it was produced also at the city Dionysia in March. Comedy was officially sanctioned in 486 B.C.

The partially reconstructed Parthenon at Athens photographed from the Propylea.

Minor called the *Anabasis*, in which he himself figures very prominently. But the mediocrity of his mind and style is glaring after Thucydides.

Greek philosophy was born among the Ionians of Asia Minor in the sixth century B.C., where the broad religious freedom provided by the state invited a group of thinkers to explore the astronomical and mathematical science of the Near East. These earliest philosophers, Thales and Anaximander of Miletus, speculated on the physical composition of the universe in conflict with the naïve explanations of Hesiod. Shortly after, a competing school in southern Italy, including Pythagoras and Empedocles, gave rival explanations. But we know of these and other early philosophical writers largely through the comments of later writers, such as Plato, Xenophon, Aristotle, and Diogenes Laertius. The pioneers are remembered primarily because they established the Greek tradition of free inquiry that was to produce the great philosophers and scientists of a later day.

In a time when knowledge was not yet advanced or departmentalized, the field of philosophy was not so clearly limited as it is today. We think of philosophy now as covering all areas where the absence of exact information makes speculation necessary. But in any age before scientific method is exactly understood, these areas are very broad indeed and cover data as well as conclusions from them. Our Greek word *philosophy* means simply "the love of wisdom." Only late in the fifth century was the field restricted to religion, ethics, political philosophy, and metaphysics, and Aristotle in the fourth century included logic, aesthetics, and "natural philosophy" (physics, biology, and psychology) in his areas of investigation.

When Greek philosophy came of age in Socrates and Plato, the emphasis shifted from the metaphysics of the pioneers, with their inquiries into the origin and composition of things, to problems of ethics and religion. Socrates (470–399 B.C.) abandoned his interest in what he called "physics" for matters of right and wrong, the ethical issues of justice and injustice that seriously troubled democratic Athens in the fifth century B.C. Unlike the Sophists, those professional philosophers who charged fees for their highly practical lectures on how to win success and happiness, Socrates prided himself on being merely the great "gadfly" of Athens, who lounged in the market place or the homes of his friends to pose questions and force his hearers to define the terms and concepts that they used as carelessly as had their parents who taught them. His real business was to make people think and to jog them out of smugness and prejudice. Like Confucius he insisted not on the approximate but on the exact definition of terms such as virtue, courage, love, temperance, and friendship, because he believed that behind them lay absolute ideas, and the knowledge of this absolute and ultimate reality transcending material things was the key to right living. No one, he thought, is knowingly wicked; hence ignorance is the bane of the state.

In his discussions he pretended to know nothing himself but to follow the "Socratic method" of questioning others and drawing knowledge from them through subtle direction. In this pretense he was of course insincere, and the irony behind his questions made him a large number of enemies among the rival thinkers whom he sought to discredit by his ingenious questions. His scolding wife Xantippe thought her idle husband a wastrel, and the democratic statesmen of Athens came to consider his eternal questions dangerous to the tranquillity of the state. At last they condemned the seventy-year-old philosopher to death for atheism and corruption of youth, and, although he could easily have escaped, he chose to drink the hemlock and died a serene death among his friends.

Since Socrates left no writings, we know him today through the works of his disciple, Plato (c. 427–348 B.C.).° Plato was over forty years younger than his master and studied with him only during the last ten years of Socrates' life. Yet after the older man's death he dedicated himself to recording his philosophy and even his conversation in an idealized form. To suit the questioning method of Socrates he perfected the Platonic dialogue, a semidramatic form representing a concentrated discussion of an issue or idea by a group of men (including Socrates and a disciple or rival). At its best, as in the *Symposium*, the dialogue served to draw out a variety of opinions on a problem. Plato does not appear as a character in any of the dialogues, but he became himself such an independent thinker that he must have put many of his own opinions into the mouth of his teacher. The long dialogue, the *Republic*, is the crowning statement of his own philosophy. Plato's famous Academy, which he established in a grove of olive trees near Athens as a center for his teaching, continued until 529 A.D. and had Aristotle among its famous pupils.

Aristotle (384–322 B.C.) entered Plato's Academy at seventeen and studied there until Plato's death twenty years later. Thereafter he was the tutor of young Alexander of Macedonia and director of the Lyceum, a rival school to the Academy, which he founded around 336 B.C. The interests of Aristotle were broader than Plato's and centered in natural science rather than ethics. Yet in addition to his treatises on biology, physics, astronomy, and mathematics, we have the *Poetics*, the *Politics*, and the *Nicomachean Ethics* to remind us of the breadth

* As well as the *Memorabilia* of Xenophon.

of his inquiries. He was the great encyclopedist of human knowledge in his day and the last who dared presume to universal understanding. Although his science is primitive and often more speculation than exact knowledge, he paved the way for the more accurate science of the Hellenistic era which was to follow. In our own Dark Ages, when superstition choked off further investigation for a time, the great

Aristotle was gradually elevated to a canon of natural knowledge as he was read in the Latin translations of Boethius and others; and the medieval philosophers, Albertus Magnus and Thomas Aquinas, made him the foundation of their orthodox systems. The broad achievements of the man and his place in the evolution of human thought can hardly be overestimated.

THE MACEDONIAN CONQUEST

THE century of interstate wars in Greece invited foreign invasion and conquest. Persia was quick to exploit the disunity of the states by playing one off against another and eventually regained all the Greek cities on the coast of Asia Minor by the disgraceful peace of Antalcidas (387 B.C.). But Persia was now too weak to renew the war for the Greek mainland. It remained for another power, younger and more vigorous than either Hellas or Persia, to add them both to a great new empire.

Macedonia to the north of Greece was a country of fighting mountaineers, related to the Greeks by race and language, yet beyond the reach of Hellenic culture. Still devoted to their clannish chieftains as the primitive Greeks had been, the Macedonians offered a ready and loyal instrument to any conqueror who might rise among them. Such a king arrived in 356 B.C., when Philip ascended the throne, a masterful spirit fired with an ambition for conquest. As he trained his armies in the phalanx system that he had learned as a student in Thebes, Philip had his eye on the decadent kingdom of Persia and thought of the Greek states as mere stepping stones to a larger objective. It was his skill in diplomacy as much as his

ability as a soldier that made him take advantage of the disunity of the states to conquer them one by one. He interfered modestly at first in such typically Greek squabbles as the Sacred War and the Locrian War, so that when his designs on all of Greece at last became clear, the disorganized forces of Athens and Thebes were easily conquered at Chaeronea (338 B.C.). Philip's admiration for Greek character and art and his larger designs upon Persia made him deal mildly with the conquered states, as he posed simply as the commander in chief of their own Amphictyonic League of nations. Yet Greece actually lost her independence in that year and did not regain it for any appreciable period down to modern times.

As Philip was about to begin his conquest of Persia, he was assassinated by one of his officers. But his dashing son, Alexander, was to carry through Philip's plan with lightning speed. In the spring of 334 B.C. he crossed the Hellespont, leaving Antipater behind as governor of Macedonia and Greece, and began thirteen years of incessant campaigns that were to take him and his devoted armies eastward across the whole Persian empire into far-dis-

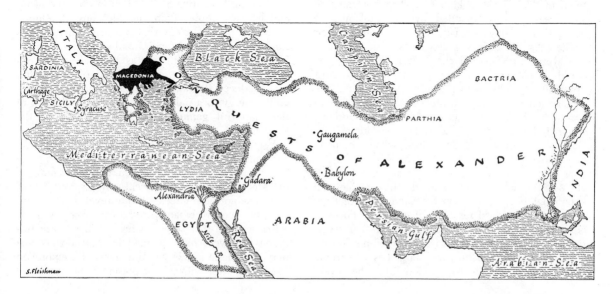

tant India. With the defeat of the Persian King Darius III at Gaugamela, Alexander set himself up in his stead as an Oriental potentate ruling one of the greatest empires in the history of the world. When he died suddenly of a fever at Babylon in 323 B.C., this thirty-three-year-old emperor had barely had time to organize his vast domain into a collection of kingdoms, which were to be ruled thereafter as separate units by his generals.

So Greece found unity at last, but in the humiliating role of vassal state to her Macedonian neighbor. Only a tiny unit in the vast empire of Alexander, she later formed part of the monarchy of Mace-

donia. But wherever Alexander went, he had carried with him a love of Greek culture, imbibed from his Greek tutor, Aristotle. Remote eastern states of the old Persian empire, such as Parthia and Bactria, were Hellenized for a time, and even northwestern India received a veneer of Greek civilization. In losing the freedom of her own development Hellas had the lesser satisfaction of seeing her cultural influence spread over a vast area to which she could never have carried it herself. Alexander's successors, the Seleucids in Asia and the Ptolemies in Egypt, continued the Hellenizing process until the coming of the Roman empire in the time of Christ.

HELLENISTIC CULTURE: THE LAST CHAPTER

THE smallest but most vigorous kingdom to be carved out of Alexander's empire was Egypt, which fell to his ablest general, Ptolemy. Here at one of the many mouths of the Nile, Alexander had projected a great new capital to be called Alexandria, the prototype of other Alexandrias that he established throughout his eastern realm. After Alexander's death Ptolemy loyally carried out his plan and made his capital the greatest city of the western world, a thriving commercial center at the juncture of several trade routes from East to West. His cultured son, Ptolemy II, invited the finest poets, philosophers, scholars, and artists of the Hellenistic world to settle in this pseudo-Greek metropolis. There resulted the curious phenomenon that the real center of Greek culture in the third century was not in Greece but in the deliberately planned Graeco-Macedonian city of Alexandria in northern Egypt.

The focal point of this activity was the great Museum of Alexandria, a kind of college for research and creative work founded by the Ptolemies to house their distinguished guests and facilitate their studies. As its name suggests, it was dedicated to the Muses and boasted the largest library in the world, a collection of half a million manuscripts (possibly 100,000 books in the modern sense). The literary scholars who gravitated to the Museum prepared our definitive texts of older Greek authors, eliminated the writers whom they considered unworthy, and generally determined what we today may know of the older literature of Greece.

Science and mathematics also made great strides at Alexandria. Euclid codified the geometrical knowledge of the Greeks in his *Elements,* which remained the standard textbook of geometry down to our own century. Archimedes (c. 287–212 B.C.), the greatest of ancient scientists, founded mechanics, statics, and dynamics, to which branches of learning no further knowledge was added until the seven-

teenth century. Eratosthenes (c. 276–c. 195 B.C.) first measured the circumference of the earth, assembled a source book for geography, and devised a system of historical chronology. Aristarchus of Samos in his third-century treatise *On the Sizes and Distances of the Sun and the Moon* evolved an astronomy close to our own which placed the sun, not the earth, at the center of our universe. But Hipparchus and Claudius Ptolemy, who followed him in the next century, revived the geocentric astronomy that was to be accepted by Christian theologians till Copernicus and the sixteenth century. We will find it in Dante's view of the universe.

The men of letters at Alexandria invented only one literary form, the pastoral or idyll, but it was to have a hardy development through Virgil, Spenser, Sidney, and Milton to Pope and Gay in the eighteenth century. Theocritus (third century B.C.) conceived the type as a charming picture of shepherd life in his native Sicily, often in dialogue form; and his two pupils, Bion and Moschus, developed it into the pastoral elegy that was to inspire Milton's *Lycidas,* Shelley's *Adonais,* and Arnold's *Thyrsis* The idylls of Theocritus are as artificial as the self-conscious and sophisticated society of Alexandria that produced them. The Hellenistic civilization, for all its energy, is a pale and stereotyped reflection of the masterful genius of Hellenic culture in the Golden Age.

For nearly a hundred years, between 330 B.C. and 243 B.C., Greece made no attempt to regain her independence. Then the weakening of the Macedonian kingdom eventually inspired Sparta and some northern Greek cities to revolt in the latter year, but the two emancipated areas promptly quarreled between themselves in the familiar Greek tradition and were overwhelmed by Macedonia once more at Sellasia in 221 B.C. But Macedonia embroiled itself soon after with a new power in the West, the

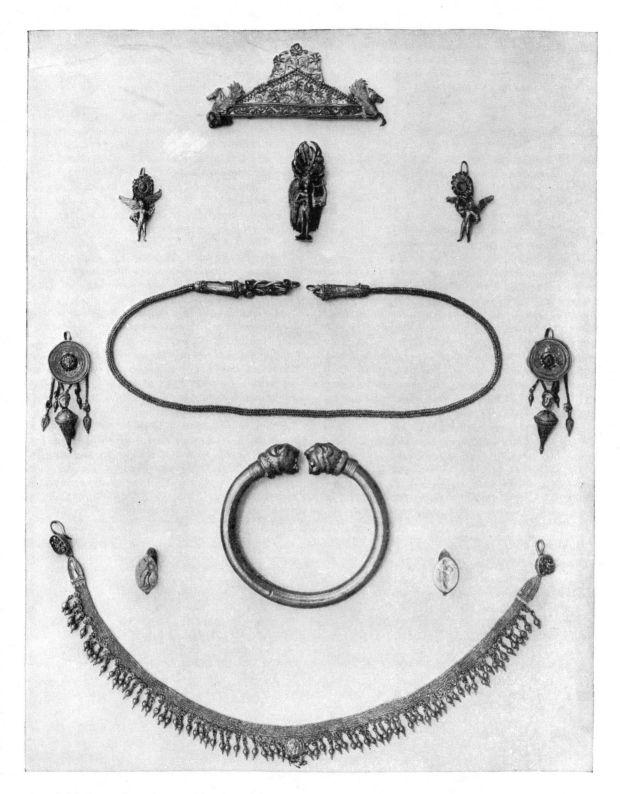

Remarkably fine workmanship in gold is displayed in this Greek jewelry of the fifth century B.C.

rising republic of Rome, by assisting the Carthaginian Hannibal in his ill-fated war with the Romans. To punish Macedonia, Rome technically freed the Greek states from her rule, but the Greeks soon found that they had merely exchanged one master for another. For a time the Romans preserved the fiction of Greek independence, but when the cities of the Achaean League openly resisted the indirect control of Rome, the Roman armies marched through them, destroyed Corinth in 146 B.C., and finally converted Greece into one province in the growing empire. This spelled the formal end of Greek independence.

Yet the prestige of Greek culture continued undimmed, as the practical Romans self-consciously borrowed the art and philosophy of Greece in its Golden and Silver Ages. Athens remained the traditional fountainhead of learning, and Plato's Academy continued to attract pupils down to the days of the emperor Justinian. Direct borrowing from Greek literature was the accepted thing in Rome, as Virgil imitated Theocritus, Hesiod, and Homer; Catullus imitated Sappho; Plautus and Terence took their plots and characters from the later comedians, Menander and Apollodorus; and Seneca borrowed from Euripides. Even the Greek language held its own as a medium of literature throughout the Roman period and especially during the so-called Greek Renaissance of the second century A.D., which was inspired by the Roman emperor Hadrian and distinguished by the Greek satires of Lucian.

But the "glory that was Greece" really died with Greek independence in the fourth century B.C. What Greece had to tell the world was complete with the last Athenian dramatists, Euripides and Aristophanes, and the last great Athenian philosophers, Plato and Aristotle. Those who followed were the scholars and the imitators, who had superior perspective but lacked the creative fire. So it is to the fifth century and the fourth that we return perennially for inspiration and wisdom. Across the centuries, those years in Athens seem more modern to us than any intervening century before the eighteenth. Her civilization, like our own, was based on experience and knowledge and the right of the individual to explore himself and his world, free from political or religious oppression. It exalted intelligence and curiosity rather than moral discipline because it believed that the ascendancy of reason over instinct could be trusted to lead to at least a pragmatic morality. The self-discipline of the Greeks had a practical end and the human perfection for which they strove had the practical goal of making man completely at home in his environment.

The success of their conquest is attested by what they handed on to Rome and even to the Asia that they Hellenized. We see it in what the Romans have handed down to us as the core of Western civilization. We should not be surprised that the Greeks did not achieve a continuing perfection or that their tragic defects—their inability to work together, their senseless wars, their subjection of women and slaves, their misuse of liberty in moral corruption and irresponsibility—eventually destroyed them altogether. No single civilization in the West has endured for long, but through the rise and decay of them all runs the enduring stream which had its source in ancient Greece.

Homer

Eighth century B.C.

The Homeric epics are the only survivals from a great school of Ionian poetry which flourished in the Greek states of Asia Minor in the eighth century B.C. The Greeks of the Golden Age knew as little about the poet Homer as we do, and many later critics have argued that "Homer" was really a group of minstrels in several generations who composed and reworked various sections of the *Iliad* and the *Odyssey*. Clearly a long oral tradition preceded these finished products, and in the *Odyssey* in particular we can see how many older stories have been grafted onto the central tale as adventures of Odysseus. But, however diverse their origin, each of the final poems must have been shaped into a consummate work of art by a single masterful hand. Perhaps both had the same arranger; perhaps both were finally composed by the traditional poet, Homer.

The century when the epic poet lived has been variously placed between the twelfth and the seventh B.C. by those who accept his existence, but the consensus of opinion links him now to the eighth. The dialect of the poems places him in Asia Minor, though whether his birthplace was Smyrna or one of the many other cities that claimed him, we cannot be sure. Tradition makes him a blind old minstrel (a favorite type in folk literature), wandering among the Ionian cities of Asia Minor.*

These speculations about the origins of the Homeric epics pale before the majesty of the works themselves. Later Greeks accepted the *Iliad* and the *Odyssey* as history, and we have seen (page 90) that the poems were probably inspired by a prehistoric war between the early invaders of Greece and the inhabitants of a strategic Aegean city in Asia Minor which Schliemann unearthed on the traditional site of Troy. The Trojan War was apparently one episode in the early Greeks' general destruction of the Minoan culture that preceded them. But to the later Greeks it took on the character of a holy war out of their Heroic Age in which the gods of Olympus fought each other in the human battles before Troy.

The war began in a contest among three goddesses, Hera, Athena, and Aphrodite, for a golden apple to be awarded to the most beautiful. Since Zeus was the husband of Hera and the father of both Athena and Aphrodite, he discreetly forced the decision on a handsome Trojan prince named Paris (or Alexandros), who was tending his flocks on Mount Ida. Hera tried to bribe Paris with the gift of an empire, and Athena with the gift of victorious war; but Aphrodite promised him the most beautiful woman in the world to be his wife, and he promptly awarded her the apple, gaining thereby the implacable hate of the other goddesses for himself and his native

Troy. Unfortunately, his prize, the paragon of loveliness, Queen Helen, was already married to Menelaus, the Greek king of Sparta, but Paris had no difficulty in carrying her away during Menelaus' absence, since Aphrodite had bewitched her with the spell of love.

Now before her marriage to Menelaus, Helen had been wooed by the principal kings of Greece, and they, to prevent bloodshed, had sworn to accept her choice and defend her husband. After the loss of Helen, Menelaus reminded the princes of their oath. All (even the reluctant Odysseus of Ithaca and Achilles, the great hero of the war) eventually joined their forces in a great Greek army to sail to Troy and recover Helen. Agamemnon of Mycenae, brother to Menelaus, who was chosen leader, was forced to sacrifice his innocent daughter, Iphigenia, at Aulis before the gods would send the Greek ships a fair wind for Troy.† When they reached Troy, the Trojans disputed their landing and shut themselves within the walls of their city, where for ten years they withstood incessant siege. Periodically King Priam of Troy would send out his armies to do battle under Hector, the mightiest of his fifty sons. Many a hero, both Greek and Trojan, fell in the fighting, but still the war dragged on.

Although the title "Iliad" is derived from *Ilios,* a Greek name for Troy, the poem does not tell the story of the whole war but rather one incident in the ninth year of the siege. Homer begins "in medias res" and leaves the reader to supply the background, which was well known to the Greek audience. The story of the *Iliad* is of the quarrel of Achilles and Agamemnon over a girl, Briseis; and of the wrath of Achilles that makes him sulk in his tent and refuse to fight, until the death of his friend Patroclus rouses him to kill his slayer, the noble Hector. The war is still in progress at the end of the *Iliad,* but we know that the Greeks won it the following year by the ruse of the Wooden Horse.

At the opening of the *Odyssey* all of the Greek princes have returned home except crafty Odysseus (Ulysses) of Ithaca. He had been doomed by the god Poseidon to wander through the Mediterranean for ten years as a punishment for blinding the god's son Polyphemus, a one-eyed Cyclops. He has already been nearly ten years on his journey when we first meet him, a forlorn fugitive bereft of his followers. The poem covers the last six weeks of his trials and shows how Odysseus is finally restored to his wife Penelope and son Telemachus and rules once more in Ithaca.

Achilles and Odysseus are the two great heroes of the Greeks, vastly different from each other, and both far removed from the Christian ideal of chivalry. In the sometimes shocking actions of these leaders we sense the realistic Greek mind at work, with its eye on the objective and its strong sense of immediate justice. Achilles is the great warrior, mighty in battle but fierce and implacable in his wrath. When Agamemnon offends him, he loses all sense of loyalty to his comrades and their cause and retires to brood over a personal grievance. His hysterical

---

* The Homeric epics were arranged in their present form in Athens around the years 537–527 B.C. The division of each epic into twenty-four books was probably made by Aristarchus, the Alexandrian scholar, in 156 B.C.

† However, the goddess Artemis substituted a deer for Iphigenia and made her a priestess in the land of the Tauri, according to the plays of Euripides.

grief for his friend Patroclus impresses us today as neu-rotic, and we find difficulty in rejoicing at his ferocious victory over Hector, the noble Trojan hero, so honorable in dealing even with his enemies, so devoted to his wife and little son. As Achilles in a delirium of triumph drags Hector's body at his chariot wheels, we are shocked that he should carry revenge beyond the grave.

Odysseus is the symbol of craft and guile, who fights through to victory only when he has paved the way with clever deceptions. As the princes were being rounded up for the Trojan War, he tried to escape the draft through pretending insanity. When Palamades discovered his ruse, he avenged himself by hiding gold in the tent of Palamades and falsely denouncing him as a traitor who had received a bribe of gold from Troy. It was Odysseus who led the Greek warriors in the trick of the Wooden Horse and saved his comrades from the terrible Cyclops by a series of ingenious stratagems. But the realistic Greeks justified both their heroes as resourceful men con-tending with a hostile world. Achilles was the pillar of strength and glorious action, Odysseus the tower of intel-ligence and cunning, who was wise to use his powers however he felt he had to.

Nearly as important in the epics as the human warriors are the gods above, who work out their personal griev-ances in the conflict of men. Aphrodite, the capricious goddess of love, intermittently supported the Trojans out of gratitude to Paris. Apollo, too, assisted the Ori-entals in their struggle with the Greeks from the west. But Athena, goddess of wisdom, and Hera, goddess of power, still chafing from Paris' slight to their beauty, fought a much more consistent battle on Olympus for the Greeks. Zeus, vacillating between the rival camps in his family, eventually gave in to his shrewish wife and his most terrifying daughter.

Although Homer accepted the traditional theology for poetic purposes, he represents the gods in a shocking way. Their petty squabbles and meanness, their total lack of moral principles suggest a veiled skepticism or comic in-tention hard to explain in so early a poet. Although the gods appear as highly concrete personalities, it is clear that he thought of them often as elaborate metaphors to represent prosaic happenings in poetic terms. Nearly every turn of the plot is initiated by a god through a human character. If we took these explanations literally, we should decide that the human actors had no power of choice whatever, that all their actions and destinies were determined by the gods and a Fate above even the gods. Actually the gods are largely convenient and poetic de-vices to which to attribute the inscrutable shifts of human fortune. Though the shadowy force of Fate, which grants the heroes an overwhelming foreknowledge of their own deaths, may represent an attempt to give a higher unity to the Greek pantheon, Homer usually invokes it to ex-plain past events. The Greeks acted as we act—with at least the illusion of free will—but when their plans went conspicuously awry or conspicuously well, they set it down to Fate, just as we often do today. Later generations of Greeks took the epics as a religious textbook, but Homer was innocent of any such purpose. The frivolous

bickerings of the gods provide a refreshing foil to the deadly serious exploits of men on earth.

In the most famous essay ever written about Homer, Matthew Arnold defined his poetic qualities as rapidity, plainness and directness of diction and syntax, plainness in thought, and nobility. Although many translators of Homer have rendered some of these qualities, none (thought Arnold) has combined them all. Homer's is the "grand style," which arises "when a noble nature, poetically gifted, treats with simplicity or with severity a serious subject." And the grand style does not flourish in modern times when nobility itself is out of fashion. Sev-eral English-speaking poets—Chapman, Pope, Bryant—have tried to reproduce the majestic sweep of Homer's hexameters, but the translation of verse into verse is at best a tour de force, occasionally very successful in ren-dering a brief lyric but almost certain to grow pedestrian or too free in a longer work. Although a prose version, such as the Butcher-Lang *Odyssey*, loses the stately mu-sic of Homer's verse, it may actually communicate more faithfully the poetic qualities that Arnold found in it.

Certainly a prose version is more likely to carry the simplicity of the narrative, and Homer is to be read first as a master storyteller and creator of characters. Writing at the very dawn of literature, he tells his tale with a frank delight in action but with a primitive grandeur that makes us believe in an age of heroes and miracles. The wonderful realism in his attention to details (as in the meticulously staged meeting of Odysseus and Nausicaä), the surprisingly subtle character portrayal (as in the complex study of Agamemnon, the vacillating leader who takes refuge in the power of his office) make Homer seem more modern (or more timeless) than many a titan who followed him. Of course, "Homer nods" occasionally, as Horace first remarked in his *Art of Poetry*. We weary of the catalogue of the ships (*Iliad*, Book II), but even such passages had a special interest for his Greek audience. We quickly forget the dull stretches in the beauty and excitement of the great scenes—Hector's farewell to An-dromache, Priam's visit to Achilles, Odysseus' slaughter of the suitors. The varying moods of these scenes—tender, sympathetic, and savage—suggest the great range of Homer. He is the one universal classic in Western lit-erature.*

---

* The great national epics are classified according to the circum-stances of their composition. The true folk epics, which evolved without known authorship, include the *Mahâbhârata* and *Râmâyana* (India), the *Iliad* and *Odyssey* (Greece), the *Nibelungenlied* (Ger-many), the *Saga of the Volsungs* (Scandinavia), *Beowulf* (England), *The Song of Roland* (France), the *Poem of the Cid* (Spain), and in a sense the *Kalevala* (Finland). The epics of art, sophisticated literary productions in imitation of folk epics (especially Homer), include the *Shahnama* of Firdousi (Persia), the *Aeneid* of Virgil (ancient Rome), and the *Lusiads* of Camoëns (Portugal). In addition to the true national epics, there are several special types: purely literary epics, such as the *Argonautica* of Apollonius of Rhodes, *Orlando Furioso* of Ariosto, *Jerusalem Delivered* of Tasso, and Spenser's *Faerie Queene;* religious epics, such as Dante's *Commedia*, Milton's *Paradise Lost*, and Klopstock's *Messias;* mock-epics, such as the ancient Greek burlesque of Homer, *The Battle of the Frogs and Mice*, Butler's *Hudibras*, Boileau's *Lutrin*, and Pope's *Dunciad;* and even beast epics, such as the medieval *Reynard the Fox*.

stock epithet

The Iliad

BOOK I

An angry man—there is my story: the bitter rancour of Achillês, prince of the house of Peleus, which brought a thousand troubles upon the Achaian host. Many a strong soul it sent down to Hadês, and left the heroes themselves a prey to dogs and carrion birds, while the will of God moved on to fulfillment.

It began first of all with a quarrel between my Lord King Agamemnon of Atreus' line and the Prince Achillês.

What god, then, made the feud between them? Apollo, son of Leto and Zeus. The King had offended him: so he sent a dire pestilence on the camp and the people perished. Agamemnon had affronted his priest Chrysês, when the priest came to the Achaian fleet, bringing a rich treasure to ransom his daughter. He held in his hand a golden staff, twined about with the sacred wreaths of Apollo Shootafar, and made his petition to the Achaian people in general but chiefly to the two royal princes of Atreus' line:

"My lords, and you their subjects, for you I pray that the gods who dwell in Olympos may grant you to sack Priam's city, and to have a happy return home! but my dear daughter—set her free, I beseech you, and accept this ransom, and respect Apollo Shootafar the son of Zeus!"

Then all the people said good words, and bade them respect the priest and accept the ransom; but my lord King Agamemnon was not well pleased. He told the priest to be off, and in harsh words too:

"Don't let me find you here any more, you; don't stay now and don't come again, or else your staff and sacred wreaths may not protect you. The woman I will not release! She shall live to old age in our house, far away in Argos, working the loom and lying in my bed. Begone now! don't provoke me, or it will be the worse for you."

The old man was afraid, and did as he was told. Silent he passed along the shore of the murmuring sea; and when he came home, he prayed earnestly to Apollo:

"Hear me, Silverbow! thou who dost bestride Chrysê and holy Cilla, thou who art the mighty lord of Tenedos, O Smintheus! If I have ever built a temple to thy pleasure, if I have ever burnt for thee fat slices of bulls or of goats, bestow on me this boon: may the Danaäns pay for my tears under thy shafts!"

Phoibos Apollo heard his prayer. Down from Olympos he strode, angry at heart, carrying bow and quiver: the arrows rattled upon his shoulders as the angry god moved on, looking black as night. He sank upon his heel not far from the ships, and let fly a shaft; terrible was the twang of the silver bow. First he attacked the mules and dogs, then he shot his keen arrows at the men, and each hit the mark: pyres of the dead began to burn up everywhere and never ceased.

Nine days the god's arrows fell on the camp; on the tenth day Achillês summoned all to a conference. The goddess Hera put this in his mind, for she was distressed to see the Danaäns dying. And when they were all gathered together, Achillês rose up and spoke.

"My lord King," he said, "I think we shall seem just foiled adventurers when we get home—if indeed we get off with our lives, now you see war and pestilence allied to beat us. Come then, let us inquire of some prophet or priest, or even a diviner of dreams—for God, it seems, doth send our dreams—and let him tell us what has made Phoibos Apollo so angry. Does he find fault with us for prayer or for sacrifice? Does he desire the savour of sheep or goats without blemish, that he may spare us this pestilence?"

He said his say, and sat down. Then up rose Calchas o' Thestor, most excellent diviner of dreams, who knew what is and what will be, and what has been in ancient days; he had guided the fleet to Ilios by the divination which Phoibos Apollo had taught him. He spoke to them from an honest heart, and said:

"Prince Achillês, whom Zeus delights to honour! you bid me explain the wrath of Lord Apollo Shootafar: therefore I will speak. Mark what I say, and swear me an oath that you will defend me with all your might in word and deed. For I think I shall provoke a man who rules all our people, one whom all the people obey. A king when angry always can be stronger than a common man; even if he smothers his anger for the day, yet indeed he keeps a grudge long in his heart until he can pay it off. Consider then if you will hold me safe."

Achillês answered:

"Fear nothing, but speak the word of God which you know. For I swear by Apollo, whom Zeus delights to honour, to whom you pray, Calchas, when you declare God's word to the nation: no man while I live and see the light shall lay heavy hands on you in this fleet, none of all the nation, not even if you name Agamemnon, who now claims to be first and best of us all."

Then the seer took courage and spoke out:

The Iliad. Abridged from *The Iliad*, translated by W. H. D. Rouse. First published by Thomas Nelson and Sons, Ltd., April 1938, and used with their permission.
4. **Achaian.** Homer calls the Greeks Achaians, Argives, or Danaäns. 16. **daughter.** Chrysês' daughter was Chryseïs, now the concubine of Agamemnon. 44. **Smintheus,** another name for Apollo.

"He finds no fault with us then, for prayer or sacrifice, but for his priest, whom Agamemnon affronted, when he would not accept a ransom and set his daughter free. For his sake Shootafar has sent us trouble, and will send. Nor will he stay the noisome pestilence among our people, until the King gives back to the father his lovely girl, unbought, unransomed, and sends a solemn sacrifice to Chrysê: then we may trust that the god will be appeased."

No sooner had he sat down, than up rose my lord King Agamemnon in his majesty. He was displeased, the dark places in his heart were full of resentment, his eyes were like flashing fire; and he began by rating Calchas:

"Prophet of evil, you have never had a decent word for me! It is always your delight to prophesy evil, but good you have never said and never done! And now you get up and harangue the people with your oracles. So *that* is the reason why Shootafar sends trouble! because of that girl Chryseïs! because I would not accept the ransom—but I want to keep her myself, and take her home! Why, I like her better than my own wife Clytaimnestra, she is just as good in face or figure, brains or fingers. Never mind, I will give her back if that is better. I would rather have the people alive than dead. Only get a prize ready for me at once, or else I shall be the only man in the army without a prize. That is not right! Just look here, all of you, my prize is going away somewhere else!"

Then Achillês answered:

"Your Majesty, gettings are keepings with you, there's no doubt about that. Pray how will our brave men give you a prize? I do not know of any common store anywhere. What we got from the towns we have taken, has been divided, and you cannot expect people to collect it all again in a heap. For the present, then, give the girl up to the god; and we will pay you threefold or fourfold, if Zeus ever allows us to sack the proud city of Troy."

King Agamemnon answered:

"None of that; you may be a great man, Achillês, you may be more than a man, but do not try cheating—you neither cajole me nor persuade me. Do you want to keep your own prize, and tell me to give up mine and just sit forlorn without any? If our brave men will give me a prize, and satisfy me that I get as much as I give, well and good; but if they will not give, then I will take—I'll come to you, or to Aias, for a prize, or Odysseus, and away I'll go with my gettings! Then it will be his turn to be angry. But we will see about that later. For the time being, let us launch a good ship and find a special crew and put Chryseïs on board; and let one of the princes from our council be in charge, Aias or Idomeneus or Prince Odysseus, or yourself, my young friend, you terror of the world, *you* shall pacify Shootafar by making sacrifice."

Achillês scowled at him, and said:

"Ha! greedyheart, shamelessness in royal dress! How could any man be willing to obey you, whether on some errand or in the battlefield? I cared nothing about the Trojans when I came here to fight; they had done nothing to me, never lifted my cattle or horses either, never destroyed my fruit or my harvest in Phthia—too many hills and forests between us, and roaring seas. No, it was you I came for, shameless man! to give you pleasure, to revenge Menelaos, and you too, dogface! for the Trojans' wrong. You don't trouble about that, you care nothing for that! And now you threaten to rob me of my prize, which I worked hard to get, which the army gave me. I never get a prize equal to yours if our men capture some town; but most of the hard fighting is done by my hands. Only when sharing-time comes, you get most of the good things, and I have a scrap to comfort me—not much, but all I can get!—as I come back tired out with fighting. Now I will just go home to Phthia, since it is much better to take ship and go, and I don't think I shall fill my hold with riches if I stay here despised."

King Agamemnon answered:

"Do go, if that's what you want, go by all means—I do not sink on my knees and beg you to stay for my sake. I have others in plenty who will honour me, first and foremost Zeus Allwise. I hate you more than any prince on earth, for you are always quarrelling and fighting. If you are such a mighty man, God gave you that, I suppose. Go home with your ships and your men and lord it over your Myrmidons, but I care nothing for you. I don't mind if you *are* in a rage. Now I give you fair warning: since Apollo robs me of Chryseïs, I will send her home with my own ship and crew; but I will take your beautiful Briseïs, and I will come for her myself to your quarters—for your prize! to show you how much stronger I am than you are. Then others will take care not to stand up to me and say they are as good as I am!"

This pierced Achillês to the heart; and he was of two minds, whether he should draw sword from thigh, to push through the crowd and strike down King Agamemnon, or whether he should calm his temper and keep himself in check. As these thoughts went through his mind, and he began to draw the great sword from the sheath, Athena came down from heaven: Queen Hera sent her, loving and anxious at once. She stood behind him, and held him back by his long red hair. No other man saw her, but Achillês alone. Achillês turned round startled—at once he knew Pallas Athenaia. His eyes flashed

---

91. **Myrmidons,** the people led by Achillês. 95. **Briseïs,** the concubine of Achillês.

wildly and he spoke words that winged like arrows to the mark:

"Why have you come again, daughter of Zeus Invincible? To see the insult of my lord King Agamemnon? I'll tell you what, and I will do it too: his own highhandedness one day may be his death!"

Athena replied, with her bright eyes glinting:

"I came to check your passion, if you will listen; and I was sent from heaven by Queen Hera, loving and anxious at once. Come, come, drop the quarrel, don't pull out that sword. Just give him a sound rating and tell him what to expect. For I declare to you that this is what will happen: a time will come when you shall have a magnificent offer, with three times as much offered to make up for this insult. Hold back now, and do what I say."

Achillês answered:

"I must observe the bidding of you both, goddess, angry though I am indeed. It is better so. What the gods command you, do, then the gods will listen to *you*."

So he stayed his heavy hand on the silver hilt, and drove back the sword into the sheath, in obedience to Athena; and she returned to Olympos, where Zeus Invincible dwells with the company of heaven.

But Achillês was angry still. Once more he addressed the King in violent words:

"You drunkard, with eyes like a bitch and heart like a fawn! You never arm yourself with your men for battle, you never go out on a raid with the fighting men—no pluck in you for that! You think that certain death! It is much better, isn't it, to stay in camp and rob any one who tells the truth to your face! The king feeds on his people, for they are a worthless lot—or else, my lord, this would be your last outrage. But one thing I will tell you, and take my solemn oath: as truly as this staff will never grow again, never again will put forth leaves and twigs, after it has been cut from the stump in the mountain forest, and the axe has scraped off leaves and bark, but now it is held in men's hands, men of judgment who guard the statutes of Zeus—hear my solemn oath to you: so truly a time shall come when Achillês will be missed by the nation one and all; then you shall not be able to help them for all your grief, while many are falling and dying before bloodthirsty Hector. Then you shall tear your temper to tatters that you would not respect the best man of all."

As he spoke, Achillês dashed down on the ground the gold-studded staff, and took his seat again; while King Agamemnon opposite fumed with rage. But Nestor rose: a famous orator he was, gracious in speech, whose voice ran off his tongue sweeter than honey. He had seen already in Pylos two generations of men grow up before him and pass away, and he was king still over the third. He now spoke with an honest heart and said:

Apollo playing his lyre, standing between his mother, Leto, and his sister, Artemis. From a Greek amphora or jar.

"For shame, sirs! Here is a great trouble for the Achaian land! How glad Priam would be, and Priam's sons, how all Troy would be in jubilation, if they could only hear you two quarrelling—you, the leaders in wisdom and leaders in war! Now listen to me. You are both younger than I am. Nay more, I have met even better men than you, and they never disregarded me. For never have I seen, and never shall I see, such men as Peirithoös, and that great ruler Dryas, Caineus and Exadios and the noble Prince Polyphemos. I tell you, those were the mightiest men ever born upon earth, mightiest I say and fought against mightiest foes, the monsters of the mountains, whom they horribly destroyed. Yes, those men I knew well; I travelled all the way from distant Pylos to visit them at their own request. And I fought by their side as a volunteer. Those were men whom no mortal now living on earth could fight! And they heard my advice and took it too. Listen to me then, you also, and take my advice, and you will find it better. You, sir, do not rob this man of the girl, although you are strong; leave her alone, as the army gave her to him at first for his especial prize. And you, Achillês, do not provoke your king, force against force; for greater honour belongs to a sceptred king, when Zeus has given him dignity. If you *are* a mighty man, if your mother *is* divine, yet he is above you for his dominion is greater. Your Grace, forget your bitterness: and I beseech Achillês to let his anger pass, for he is the strong tower of our nation against the horrors of war."

King Agamemnon answered:

"Indeed, sir, all that you say is fair and right. But this man wishes to be above all, to rule every one, to

68. **Polyphemos,** not the cannibal monster of the Odyssey.—Translator's note. 70. **monsters,** centaurs.—Translator's note.

be King over every one, to order every one about—and there is some one who will not obey, I think! If the gods everlasting have set him up as a warrior, does it follow that they have set him on to call ugly names?"

Achillês interposed, and said:

"Yes, for I should be called coward and outcast, if I yield to you in everything you choose to say. Lay your commands on others, don't order me about, for I do not think I shall obey you any more. I tell you one thing, and you will do well to remember it. I will never use my hands to fight for a girl, either with you or with any one—those who gave, may take away; but you shall never carry off anything else of what I have against my will. Just try and see, that these also may know: very soon there will be red blood on the spear-point!"

They finished their bout of hard words, and dismissed the assembly. Achillês with Patroclos and his friends returned to his quarters. Agamemnon launched a good ship, and put on board twenty men with the sacrifice, and brought Chryseïs; Odysseus took charge, and they set sail. Then Agamemnon ordered the people to purify themselves; they cast their peace-offerings into the sea, and slew bulls and goats on the shore to make full sacrifice to Apollo, and the savour went up to heaven through the wreathing smoke.

While all this business was going on, Agamemnon did not forget his quarrel with Achillês and the threats he had made. He called his two trusty servants, the heralds, Talthybios and Eurybatês, and gave them his orders:

"Go to the quarters of Prince Achillês, take Briseïs by the hand and bring her here. If he will not give her up, I will come with a larger party and take her myself, which will be more unpleasant for him."

So he sent his envoys with strict orders. They did not like their errand, but they went along the shore to the place where the Myrmidons had their ships. They found Achillês sitting before his hut, and he was not pleased to see them. They indeed were both afraid and ashamed before the young prince. They only stood, and said nothing to him, and asked nothing; but he understood what they wanted, and spoke:

"Heralds, I greet you, for the envoy is held sacred by gods and men. Come near, I find no fault in you, but in Agamemnon, who has sent you for the girl Briseïs. Here, Patroclos my friend, bring out the girl and let them take her away. Let them both be witnesses before the blessed gods and mortal men, and before this hard-hearted king, if ever the people shall need me to stand between them and dire destruction! Indeed, he is mad with fury and cannot look both before and behind, so that his army may live to fight before our camp."

Patroclos heard him, and brought out the beautiful Briseïs, and handed her over to the envoys. Then they returned to their ships, and the woman followed them unwillingly. But Achillês burst into tears, and went apart from his friends; he threw himself down by the grey salt sea, and gazing over the waters stretched out his hands, calling loudly to his mother:

"O my mother! I was born to die young, it is true, but honour I was to have from Zeus Olympian, Thunderer on high! And now he has not given me one little bit! Yes, my lord King Agamemnon has insulted me! He has taken my prize and keeps it, he has robbed me himself!" . . .

Then Thetis answered, as the tears ran down her cheeks:

"O my poor child, why did I ever bring you up for such a dreadful fate? Why could you not have stayed behind? Why could you not have been spared tears and tribulation, since your life is but a minute, no long day indeed! But now you have both a speedy doom and sorrow beyond all men! Indeed it was a cruel fate you were born for.

"Very well, I will tell your story to Zeus Thunderer—I will go myself to snowy Olympos and see if I can persuade him. Be sure now to stay beside your ships, and be as angry as you like but keep clear of battle altogether. For Zeus went yesterday to the Ocean stream on a visit to the pious Ethiopians, for a feast, and all the other gods with him; but he will be back in twelve days, and then I will go at once to the brazen halls, and make my prayer. I think I can persuade him."

And there she left him, brooding over the loss of his beautiful Briseïs, whom they had torn from him against his will.

But Odysseus came safely to Chrysê with his holy offerings. They entered the deep harbour and furled the sails, and stowed them below; quickly they lowered the mast into the crutch, and rowed the ship to her moorings, where they dropt the anchor stones and made fast the hawsers. Then they landed, and carried out the offerings for Apollo Shootafar. Chryseïs landed also, and Odysseus led her to the altar and gave her into her father's arms with these words:

"Chrysês, my lord Agamemnon has sent me to bring your daughter back, with a holy offering for Phoibos on behalf of the Danaäns; that we may propitiate the Lord who has lately sent mourning and trouble upon the people."

He gave her into her father's arms, and he received his daughter with joy. The men quickly set the holy offerings around the altar, then washed their hands and took up the barley-grains. Chrysês lifted up his hands, and prayed aloud:

"Hear me, Silverbow! thou who dost bestride Chrysê and holy Cilla, thou who art the mighty Lord of Tenedos! Verily thou hast heard my prayer, and done me honour, and smitten hard the Achaian people: grant me now again this boon, even now save the Danaäns from this dire pestilence!" . . .

When the sun set and darkness came they lay down to rest beside their moorings; but as soon as Dawn showed her rosy fingers through the mist, at once they rose and sailed for their own camp. Apollo Farworker sent them a following breeze. They lifted the mast, and spread the white sails; the wind filled the great sail, the purple wave swished and poppled against the stem, the ship ran free on her way over the waters. At last they arrived at their camp, and drew the ship ashore high on the sands, and set up the long line of dogshores; then all scattered among the huts and the ships.

But Achillês brooded still over his anger, and did not move from his vessels. He never went to the meeting-place, never to the battlefield, but wore out his heart where he was, although he longed for war and battle.

When the twelfth day dawned, the gods returned to Olympos in a body, led by Zeus.

Thetis did not forget her son's request; but she came out of the sea, and early in the morning she climbed to Olympos in the highest heavens. She found Allseeing Cronidês sitting apart from the rest on the topmost peak of craggy Olympos. There she knelt before him, and threw her left arm about his knees, catching his chin with the right hand as she made her prayer:

"O Father Zeus! If ever I have served you by word or deed, grant me this boon: give honour to my son! He of all others is to die an early death, but now see how my Lord Agamemnon has insulted him. He has taken his prize and keeps it, he has robbed my son himself! Satisfy my son, Zeus Olympian most wise! Let the Trojans prevail, until the Achaian nation shall satisfy my son and magnify him with honour!" . . .

Zeus answered in great vexation:

"Bother it all! You'll set me curry-worrying with Hera and make her scold me again! She is always at me as it is before them all, and says I help the Trojans to win. You just go away again now, and don't let Hera see: I will manage to do what you want. Look here, I will bow my head to you that you may believe me. That is my sure and certain sign here among us; when I bow my head, my word can never be recalled, and never deceive, and never fail."

As he spoke, Cronion bowed his black brows; the Lord's ambrosial locks swung forward from his immortal head, and high Olympos quaked.

So they had their talk and parted; Thetis dived from radiant Olympos into the deep sea, and Zeus entered his own hall. All the gods rose up from their seats to receive their father: not one of them dared to sit still, but all rose up to greet him. So he took his seat upon his throne.

But Hera had seen; she knew there had been a confabulation, and a visit from Silverfoot Thetis, the daughter of the Old Man of the Sea. She lost no time in scolding at Zeus Cronion:

"Who is it this time?" she began "who has been confabulating with you now, you deceiver? . . . I am dreadfully afraid this time. I can't put it out of my mind that you may be cajoled by Silverfoot Thetis, that daughter of the Old Man of the Sea. Early this morning she was kneeling and clasping your knees. I suppose you bowed your head and promised faithfully to honour Achillês and kill crowds on the battlefield."

Zeus Cloudgatherer answered:

"You are a strange creature: always supposing, always watching me. But you shall gain nothing by it. You will only make me dislike you more, and that will only be more unpleasant for you. If this is as you say, it must be my pleasure. Silence please, and sit down, and do what I tell you. All the gods in Olympos will not help you if I come near and lay my heavy hands upon you."

This frightened the Queen; she sat down in silence and took herself in hand. But the other gods were disturbed, and Hephaistos the master-craftsman was the first to speak. He took his mother's side, and said:

"Bother it all! It is really too bad, if you two quarrel like this about mortals, and make a brawl among the gods. What's the pleasure in good fare with bad manners everywhere? My advice to my mother is this, and she knows it is good; give way to dear Father Zeus, and don't let father scold any more and spoil our breakfast. . . . Be patient, mother dear, bear it patiently although it hurts! I love you, and I don't want to see you beaten before my eyes. . . ."

Queen Hera smiled at this, and smiling received the cup from her son's hand. Then he drew sweet nectar from the bowl, and carried it to all the gods, moving round rightways. Laughter unquenchable rose among the blessed gods when they saw Hephaistos butler puffing about the hall.

So they feasted all day until sunset, and there was no lack; plenty to eat and drink, a splendid harp with Apollo to play it, and the Muses singing turn by turn in their lovely voices. But when the bright light of the sun sank down they went each to his room for sleep; for the famous Crookshank Hephaistos had built them each a chamber by his clever skill. And Zeus Olympian Flashlightning went to his own bed, where he used to sleep sound when slumber came upon him; into that bed he climbed and slept, with Queen Hera by his side.

98. **rightways.** As the sun goes, as the clock goes, "through the button-hole": keeping the company on the right hand.—Translator's note

BOOK II

. . . By this time Dawn had come to high Olympos, proclaiming to Zeus and the gods that it was light. . . .

Agamemnon made no delay; he sent out the criers at once to sound the call for battle, and the army was soon assembled. He and his staff of princes were everywhere, arranging the men in their sections. With them went Athena, holding her goatskin-tippet, precious, unfading, incorruptible, with a hundred dangling tassels of solid gold, neatly braided, worth each a hundred oxen. Through the host she passed, dazzling them with the vision, and filling each heart with courage to wage war implacable and unceasing. In a moment war became sweeter to them than to sail back safely to their own native land.

As a ravening fire blazes over a vast forest on the mountains, and its light is seen afar, so while they marched the sheen from their forest of bronze went up dazzling into high heaven. . . .

But a messenger came to the Trojans, stormfoot Iris, with a lamentable message from Zeus Almighty. They were in conclave by the city gates, all assembled together, both young and old. Iris came near and spoke to Priam with the voice of his son Politês, who was the Trojan scout. He used to post himself on the barrow of old Aisyetês, to watch when the enemy was coming out, and then ran back at full speed. Iris made her voice like his, and said to Priam:

"Sir, you go on talking for ever, as if we were still at peace! But here is war upon us, overwhelming war! Indeed I have been in many battles already, but such a host, and so many men I never did see! Like the leaves of the forest, or the sands of the seashore, they are coming over the plain to attack our city. Hector, you are the man I want, and this is what you must do. We have many allies about the walls, from all parts of the country, and each has his own language. Let each man take charge of his countrymen, and tell them where to go."

Hector at once dismissed the assembly, and they hurried to arms. All the gates were opened, the men poured out, horse and foot; there was a great uproar. . . .

BOOK III

And now the two armies advanced, each under its own leaders.

The Trojans raised a loud din and clamour, like a huge flock of birds. So you may hear cranes honking out of the sky before a storm of rain, as they fly with a great noise towards the Ocean stream, bringing death and destruction to the Pygmy men; and in the early morning they open their fight. But the Achaians marched in silence, breathing fury, shoulder to shoulder, with grim determination. The dust rose in clouds under their feet as they marched apace over the plain, as thick as the mist which a south wind spreads over the mountains. Shepherds hate it, the robber likes it better than night; a man can see a stone's throw and no farther.

No sooner had the two armies come near than a champion stept out of the Trojan ranks, the noble prince Alexandros. A leopard-skin hung over his shoulders with bow and sword; he shook his two sharp spears, and challenged all comers to fight him man to man. So he strode out with long steps. Menelaos saw him with joy, as a lion spies a victim, when he is hungry and finds a horned stag or a wild goat: greedily he devours his prey, even if dogs and lusty lads set upon him. So Menelaos was glad when he set eyes on Alexandros, for he thought he was sure to punish the traitor; at once he leapt down from his chariot in his armour.

But as soon as Alexandros saw him come out in front, his heart sank and he slunk back into the ranks to save himself. He might have been some one walking through the woods who suddenly sees a snake, and jumps back all of a tremble pale with fear. So Alexandros jumped back, and so he slunk into safety.

Then Hector rated him with scorn:

"Damn you, Paris, you handsome woman-hunter, you seducer! I wish you had never been born, I wish you had died unwedded! Yes, I wish that! and it would have been much better than to be a public pest, a thing of contempt. What guffaws there must be over there! They thought you a prime champion because you are good-looking. But there's no pluck in you, no fight!

"Were you like this when you got your fine company and set sail over the sea, and travelled in foreign lands, and brought home a handsome woman? She was to marry into a warlike nation, she was to be the ruin of your father and all his people, a joy to your enemies, a disgrace to yourself! So you would not stand up to Menelaos? You ought to find out what sort of fellow he is whose wife you are keeping. There would be little use then for your harp and the gifts of Aphroditê, your fine hair and good looks, when you lie in the dust. Well, the Trojans are all cowards, or you would have had a coat of stone long ago for the evil you have done!"

Alexandros replied:

"That is true enough, Hector, that is true enough. Your heart is always as hard as steel. Like a shipwright's axe, when he slices off a spar from a tree with all the strength of a man! A hard heart indeed! Don't taunt me with Aphroditê's adorable gifts. You can't throw away a god's gifts, offered unasked, which none could win by wishing.

---

61. **Alexandros,** Paris, who had carried off Helen. 98. **coat of stone,** stoned to death.—Translator's note.

"Very well now, if you want me to fight, make both armies sit down on the ground, and put me between them with Menelaos to fight for Helen and all her wealth. Whichever proves the better man, let him take both wealth and woman home with him. Then let both sides swear friendship and peace: you to stay in Troy, they to go back to Argos, where there are plenty of fine women!"

. . . Then Hector spoke out between the armies.

"Hear me, Trojans, and you men of Achaia, while I give you a message from Alexandros, who was the cause of our war. He asks that both Trojans and Achaians lay down their arms on the ground, and let Menelaos and himself fight a duel for Helen and all her wealth. Whichever proves the better man shall take both wealth and woman home with him: then let both sides swear friendship and peace."

All heard this in silence; then Menelaos cried out:

"Hear me also! This touches me most nearly, but my mind is, that Achaians and Trojans should now be reconciled. You have suffered enough for this quarrel of mine which Alexandros began. Whichever of us is fated to die, let him die, and let the others make friends forthwith. . . ."

Achaians and Trojans were all glad that there was some hope to end that lamentable war. They arranged their chariots in order; the men got out and put off their armour, laying it all upon the ground close together, and leaving a small space between the armies. . . .

Meanwhile Iris had her own errand to Helen. She took the likeness of her goodsister, Laodicê, the most beautiful of Priam's daughters, the wife of Helicaon Antenor's son. Iris found Helen in her room. She was weaving a great web of purple stuff, double size; and embroidering in it pictures of the battles of that war which two armies were waging for her sake. Iris came up to Helen, and said:

"Come along, my love, and see a wonderful sight! They were all fighting in the plain like fury, and now all of a sudden they are sitting down, not a sound to be heard, no more battle, all leaning upon their shields, and their spears stuck in the ground! But Alexandros and Menelaos are going to fight for you! and you are to be the wife of the winner!"

These words pierced Helen to the heart. She longed for her husband of the old days, for home and family. At once she threw a white veil over her, and left the house quickly with tears running down her cheeks. Two maids were in attendance. . . . They made their way to the Scaian Gate.

Priam was sitting over the gatehouse in a group of the city elders, Panthoös and Thymoites, Lampos and Clytios, Hicetaon once well known in the field, and

two men of tried wisdom, Ucalegon and Antenor. These were old men long past their fighting days, but excellent speakers. There they all sat on the tower, chirruping in their thin old voices like so many crickets on a tree. As they saw Helen coming up, they whispered to one another in plain words:

"No wonder Achaians and Trojans have been fighting all these years for such a woman! I do declare she is like some divine creature come down from heaven. Well, all the same, I wish she would sail away, and not stay here to be the ruin of us and our children."

But Priam called Helen to his side:

"Come here, my dear child, and sit by me, to see your husband that was, and your family and friends. I don't blame you, my dear, I blame only the gods, for sending that host of enemies to bring tears to our eyes. Tell me the name of that prodigious man yonder? Who is he, that big handsome man? Others there are a head taller, that is true, but so fine a man I never did see, or so royal. He is every inch a king."

Helen answered: "You do me honour, my dear goodfather! How I wish I had died before I followed your son here, and left my bridal chamber and my family, my beloved daughter and all my young friends! But that was not to be; and so I pine away in sorrow. But I must answer your question. That is the great King Agamemnon of the house of Atreus, a good king and a strong spearman, both. He was my own goodbrother, to my shame, as sure as ever he was born." . . .

Next the old man asked about Odysseus.

"Tell me again, dear child, who is that—a head shorter than my lord King Agamemnon but broader in shoulders and chest? His arms lie on the ground, and he is patrolling the ranks of men like a tame wether; indeed, he looks very like a thick-fleeced ram marching through a flock of white ewes."

Helen answered, "That is Odysseus Laertês' son, the man who is never at a loss. He was bred in Ithaca, a rugged rocky land: there is no device or invention which he does not know." . . .

Then the old man saw Aias, and asked again:

"Who is that other big handsome man among the Achaians, standing head and broad shoulders above the rest?"

Helen answered: "That giant of a man is Aias, a real tower of strength. And opposite him is Idomeneus, standing among his Cretan captains like a god. Menelaos often entertained him in our house, when he used to over come from Crete. And now I can see all the others that I know. . . ."

Then . . . Alexandros armed himself. First he put on his fine greaves with silver anklets. Next a corselet across his chest, his brother Lycaon's which fitted him. Over his shoulders he slung the sword with silver knobs, then a strong broad shield, and upon his

32. **goodsister.** The traditional English names for the group of relations-in-law are goodfather, goodbrother, etc.—Translator's note.

head a fine helmet with horsehair plume that shook fit to frighten a man! Last he caught up a spear that suited his grip. Menelaos also armed himself in the same way.

Now the two strode out into the middle, with grim looks that struck awe into all beholders. They came to a stand in the measured space, shaking their spears at each other in defiance. Alexandros first cast his spear; Menelaos caught it neatly upon the shield. The spear did not break through the metal, but the point was bent.

Menelaos had the second shot, and before he cast he made his prayer to Father Zeus:

"O Lord Zeus, grant vengeance upon Alexandros, who has wronged me unprovoked! Bring him low by my hand, that many a man may shudder in long generations to come, at the thought of wronging a friend who shows him hospitality!"

He balanced the spear, and cast it, and struck the shield of Alexandros. Right through the shield ran the stout spear, tore right through his corselet, and cut through the tunic along his side; but he swerved away from his death. Then Atreidês drew his sword, and stretching over struck the horn of the helmet; but the blade broke upon it in three or four splinters and fell from his hand. Atreidês groaned, and looked up to heaven crying:

"O Father Zeus, such an unkind god as you there never was! You do spoil everything! I did think I had paid out that scoundrel, and here is my sword broken in my hand, and my spear missed and never touched him!"

He made one leap and caught hold of the horse-hair plume, turned and dragged Alexandros towards his own ranks; the helmet-strap choked him, pulled tight under his chin. And Menelaos almost got him— a glorious victory it would have been! But Aphroditê saw it and broke the strap, so all he got was the empty helmet. He threw it over with a swing to his friends, and leapt back to kill his enemy with the spear; but Aphroditê carried him off in a thick mist, as a god can easily do, and put him down in Helen's sweet-scented chamber.

Now she took the shape of an old woman who used to comb wool for Helen in her old home before she left Lacedaimon, one whom she dearly loved. In this shape she went in search of Helen. She found her on the battlements with a crowd of women, and plucked her by the skirt. "Come here!" she said, "thi man wants tha at home. He is in thi room, on the bed, all finery and shinery! That'st never think he's fresh from fighten a man! More like just come from a dance, or just goen maybe!" . . .

Helen . . . followed her in silence, wrapping her robe close about her; the other women saw nothing. When they reached the house, her attendants turned to their work and she went up to her room. Aphroditê

all smiles, put a chair for her in front of Alexandros; and there Helen sat down. But she turned her eyes away, and said with contempt:

"You have come back from the battle. I wish you had died there, and a strong man had killed you—he that was my husband before you! It was your boast once that you were the better man in fair fight. Then go and challenge Menelaos to fight again!—But no, I advise you not to try. Fight no duel with Menelaos; leave him alone, don't be a fool, or perhaps you may go down before his spear."

Paris answered:

"You need not scold me, my dear. This time Menelaos has won because Athena helped him. Next time it will be my turn; for I have my gods too. Let us love and be happy! I was never so much in love before, not even when I carried you off in my ship from Lacedaimon, and we shared our first love in that island. I am more in love with you now than ever, and I want you more!"

So saying, he lay down on the bed, and she came to him.

While they lay there together, Menelaos was striding up and down like a wild beast, looking everywhere for Alexandros. But no one could show him a glimpse of Alexandros among the Trojans or their allies. . . .

BOOK VI

So the great conflict was left to the Trojans and Achaians. This way and that way the battle moved over the plain between Simoeis and the estuary, as the two armies fought and struggled together. . . .

Into the space between the armies came out Glaucos, the son of Hippolochos and Diomedês Tydeus' son, hot for a fight. But as soon as they were close enough, Diomedês spoke first:

"Who are you, noble sir, of all men in the world? I have never seen you before in the battlefield, but now here you are in front of the whole host, bold enough to face my long spear! Unhappy are they whose sons will face my anger. But if you are some god come down from heaven, I had rather not fight against the gods of heaven. . . . But if you are a mortal and one of those who eat the fruits of the field, come here, and you shall soon be caught in the bonds of destruction!"

Glaucos answered undismayed:

"Proud son of Tydeus, why do you ask my name and generation? The generations of men are like the leaves of the forest. Leaves fall when the breezes blow, in the springtime others grow; as they go and come again so upon the earth do men. But if it is your

89-90. **Glaucos,** leader of the Lycians, allies of Troy. 90. **Diomedês,** a Greek hero.

pleasure to learn such a thing as that, and to know the generations of our house, which indeed many men know—there is a city Ephyra, in a nook of Argos the land of horses; and there lived Sisyphos the cleverest man ever born, Sisyphos Aiolidês. He had a son Glaucos, and Glaucos was father of the incomparable Bellerophontês. The gifts of the gods to him were handsome looks and noble manhood. But Proitos plotted mischief against him, and drove him from the land of Argos; for he was the stronger and Zeus had subdued the land under his sceptre.

". . . Kill the man he would not, for he thought that an impious thing; but he sent him to Lycia with a dangerous token. He gave him a folded tablet with a message scratched on it in deadly signs, and bade him show it to his goodfather, that he might be put to death.

"He travelled to Lycia, then, with the gods to guide him; and in Lycia, by Xanthos river, the king of that broad realm entertained him generously for nine days and killed nine oxen. Not until the tenth day dawned did he question him and ask to see any token that he brought from Proitos.

"When he received the fatal token, . . . he chose the best fellows out of all the country and set them in ambush. But not one of them ever returned home, for Bellerophontês killed them all.

"So the King saw at last that he was a true son of the godhead. Accordingly he kept him there, and gave him his own daughter, and half of all his royal honour. The Lycian people allotted him the finest estate in the land, orchards and farms for his use. His wife bore him three children, Isandros and Hippolochos and Laodameia. . . . Hippolochos was my father, and I am his son. He sent me to Troy, and commanded me strictly always to be first and foremost in the field, and not to disgrace my fathers who were first and best, both in Ephyra and in broad Lycia. There you have my lineage, and the blood which is my boast."

Diomedês was delighted with this speech. He planted his spear in the ground, and said in a friendly tone:

"I declare you are my family friend from a long way back! Oineus once entertained the incomparable Bellerophontês in his house, and kept him there for twenty days. When they parted, they exchanged gifts of friendship; Oineus gave a girdle bright with crimson, Bellerophontês a double cup of gold—it was there in my house when I came away! But Tydeus I do not remember, for I was only a little tot when he left me, at the time when the Achaian army perished before Thebes. So I am your friend and host in Argos, and you are mine when I go to Lycia! Let us avoid each other if we happen to meet. There are

9. **Proitos**, king of Argos. 45. **Oineus**, grandfather of Diomedês.

plenty of Trojans and Trojan allies for me to kill, if God grants me to catch them, and plenty of Achaians for you to spoil if you can. Let us exchange armour, and show the world that we are family friends!"

They both dismounted and clasped hands, and swore friendship. . . .

When Hector got to the oak tree at the Scaian Gate, the women ran crowding round, asking news of husbands and brothers, sons and friends. He exhorted them each and all to make their prayer to heaven; but sorrows hung over many.

. . . Meanwhile Hector had made his way to the mansion of Alexandros, a fine place built by the best workmen in the land. . . . He entered, holding his great spear eleven cubits long, with a bright blade of bronze made fast with a golden ferrule. He found Alexandros in his wife's room, handling his shield and corselet and fingering his bow. Helen was sitting there with her women and seeing about their work. Hector said to him reproachfully:

"My good man, you should not be sulking here. Men are falling in the fight outside our walls, war and battle is blazing round the city for your sake! You would be the first to attack any one else you might see shirking his part. Up, man! or soon fire will warm up the place!"

Paris answered:

"You are right to reproach me, Hector, quite right indeed! But let me tell you this: I give you my word that I was not sulking. It is not bad temper keeps me here, but simply a bitter heart. Just now my wife has been trying to persuade me with gentle words, and driving me back to the battle. I think it will be better so myself. Victory chops and changes. Just wait a bit, and I will put on my armour.—Or go on, and I will follow; I think I shall catch you up."

Hector answered nothing, but Helen said warmly:

"Brother dear, I am ashamed; I shudder at myself! I can do nothing but evil! I wish a whirlwind had carried me off to the mountains on the day that I was born, or thrown me into the roaring sea—I wish the waves had swept me away before all this was done! But since the gods ordained it so, I wish I had been mated with a better man, one who could feel the contempt and indignation of the world! But this man is unstable, and ever shall be; some day I think this fault will find him out. But do come in now, brother, come in and sit down; I know your heart is most heavy with this world of trouble about us—all for my shame and his infatuation. Indeed, Zeus has laid a cruel fate upon us, to be a byword for generations to come!"

Hector answered:

"Don't ask me to sit, Helen: I thank you all the same, my dear, but I must not stay. They miss me outside, and I must go and do my part. Just keep this man up to the mark; let him make haste himself and catch me up before I go out of the gates, for I am going home first for one look at my wife and my little boy. I don't know if I shall ever see them again. It may be God's will to lay me low by the enemy's hand."

So he took his leave and went on to his own house. But he did not find Andromachê there, for she was already upon the battlements with her boy and a servant, weeping in her sorrow. Hector, when he found she was not within, stood at the door, and said to the maids:

"Be so good as to tell me where your mistress has gone. To one of my sisters or to my goodsisters, or to Athena's temple where the women are making supplication?"

The housekeeper said:

"No, sir, not to any of the family, nor to Athena's where the women are all gone to offer their supplication. To tell the truth, she has gone up on the walls, because she heard that our people were in danger and the enemy were getting the best of it. She has just gone off in a great hurry like one distracted, and the nurse carrying the boy."

So Hector went back by the same way along the street till he reached the Scaian gates, by which he meant to go out into the plain; and there his precious wife came running to meet him. . . . and the nurse followed with the boy in her bosom: quite a little child, cheerful and merry—their little Hector, the tiny champion of Troy, like a shining star, whom they dearly loved. . . .

The father smiled quietly as he looked at his boy. But Andromachê stood by his side with tears running down her cheeks, and caught his hand fast while she said:

"My dearest, how can you do it? Your courage will be your death! Have you no pity for your baby boy, or your unhappy wife, who will soon be your widow! Soon they will all rush upon you and kill you! And I —if I lose you, it would be better for me to go down into my grave. There will be no more comfort for me if you are taken, but only sorrow.

"I have no father and no mother now. . . . My seven brothers all went down to Hadês in one day, for that terrible Achillês killed them all amid their cattle and sheep. . . .

"So you are my father and my mother, Hector, you are my brother, you are my loving husband! Then pity me and stay here behind the walls; do not make your boy an orphan and your wife a widow! But post your men by the fig-tree, where the wall may be scaled most easily, where the wall is open to assault. . . ."

Hector answered:

"I have not forgotten all that, my wife, but I could not show my face before the men or the women of Troy if I skulk like a coward out of the way. And I will not do it, for I have learnt how to bear myself bravely in the front of the battle, and to win credit for my father and myself. One thing I know indeed in my heart and soul: a day shall come when sacred Troy shall perish, and Priam and the people of Priam; but my sorrow is not so much for what will happen to the people, or Queen Hecabê herself, or King Priam or my brothers, when all those good men and true shall fall in the dust before their enemies—as for you, when some armed man shall drive you away weeping, and take from you the day of freedom. To think that you should live in a foreign land, and ply the loom at the orders of another woman: that you should carry water from strange fountains, crushed under stern necessity—a hateful task! that some one should see you shedding tears, and say, 'There is Hector's wife, and he was the first and best of the brave Trojans when there was that war about Troy'—and he will make your pain ever fresh, while there is no such man to save you from the day of slavery. May I be dead and buried deep in the earth before I hear your cries and see you dragged away!"

As he spoke, Hector held out his arms for his boy, but the boy shrank back into the nurse's bosom, crying, and scared at the sight of his father; for he was afraid of the gleaming metal and the horsehair crest, when he saw that dreadful thing nodding from the top of the helmet. Father and mother laughed aloud, and Hector took off the helmet and set it down on the ground shining and flashing. Then he kissed his son and dandled him in his hands, and prayed aloud to heaven:

"O Zeus and all ye heavenly gods! Grant that this my son may be as notable among our people as I am, and let him be strong, and let him rule Ilios in his strength! When he goes to war let them say, This man is much better than his father! May he kill his enemy and bring home the blood-stained spoils, and give joy to his mother's heart!"

Then he gave his boy back into the mother's arms, and she pressed him to her sweet-scented breast, laughing through the tears. Her husband was moved with pity as he saw this; he stroked her with his hand, and said:

"My dearest, do not grieve too much. No man will send me to my grave unless it be so ordained. But destiny is a thing which no man can escape, neither coward nor brave man, from the day he is born. Go home now, and see to your own household work, the loom and the distaff, and keep your servants to their tasks. War shall be men's business, and mine especially of all those who are in Ilios."

Then Hector took up the helmet with its nodding crest; but his wife went on her way home, turning again and again to look, as the tears flowed thick and fast. And when she got to her own house, all the women fell a-weeping too; they mourned for Hector in his own house while he still lived, for they never thought he would escape his enemies and return from the battle again.

Paris made no delay either. As soon as his armour was on, he hurried through the city at the top of his speed. He was like a stallion after a good feed at the manger, who breaks his halter and runs whinnying over the plain to his usual bath in the river; he bears himself proudly, arches his neck, the mane shakes over his shoulders, he knows his own fine looks as he gallops along to the place where the mares graze. Such was Paris Priamidês, as he marched down from Pergamon in armour shining like the sun, chuckling with glee as his quick feet ran.

He caught up his brother just as he was leaving the place where the two loving hearts had spoken. Paris at once said:

"Well, your worship, you see what a drag I am on you when you are in a hurry; I'm late, and I did not come along fair and square as you told me!"

Hector said:

"My good fellow, no fair-minded man could despise your work in battle, for you fight well. But you do not really want to fight, and you are glad to hang back. What I regret is that I hear people speak ill of you, when all their hardships are borne for your sake. But let us go on. We will satisfy them by and by, if Zeus ever grant us to set up a bowl of deliverance in our hall, in gratitude to the deathless gods of heaven, when we have driven the enemy host away from Troy."

BOOK VIII

Dawn was spreading her saffron robe over the world, when Thunderbolt Zeus called an assembly of the gods on high Olympos. He addressed them in these words:

"Listen to me, gods and goddesses all, and let me tell you what is in my mind. Not one of you, either male or female, shall try to chop and change my words; you must assent, one and all, that I may lose no time in bringing my will to pass.

"If I see any god going to help either Trojans or Danaäns on his own account, he shall get a thunder-stroke and go home very uncomfortable. Or I'll catch him and throw him down into Tartaros! A black hole that! A long way down! A bottomless pit under the earth! Iron gates and brazen threshold! As far below Hadês as heaven is above the earth! He shall discover how much stronger I am than all the rest of you.

"Come on now, have a try, my good gods, the whole lot of you, and I'll show you! Hang a gold chain from heaven, gods all and goddesses all, a long pull and a strong pull and a pull all together! You will not pull down most high Zeus to the ground, pull as hard as you like. But if I give one real good pull, up

you will come with the earth and sea besides. Then I will tie the chain round a peak of Olympos, and there in the air you will dangle! Gods or men, I am stronger than them all!" . . .

Then he had the horses harnessed to his chariot, that swift brazen-foot pair with flowing manes of gold. He clad himself in gold, and took his golden whip, and mounted the car. Then he touched them up, and they flew with a will between earth and sky, until they reached Ida with her mountain springs, Ida the mother of wild beasts; where stood an altar of his in a holy precinct. There he loosed the horses and hid them in a cloud. He sat on the hilltop by himself in great contentment, watching the city and the Achaian ships. . . .

While it was morning and the day was growing, the blows came thick and the people fell; but when the sun stood in the middle of the sky, the Father laid out his golden scales. In them he placed two fates of dolorous death, one for Trojans and one for Achaians; he took the balance by the middle, and lifted it up: down sank the day of death for the Achaians, and the lot of the Trojans rose high. Then Zeus thundered loud from Ida and cast a blazing light among the Achaians. They saw it with amazement, and grew pale with fear.

. . . The Olympian put courage into the Trojans, and they drove the Achaians back to their moat, Hector triumphant at their head. He hung on to the Achaians, ever striking down the rearmost. He was

Zeus pursuing a woman. From a painting on an Attic red-figured vase.

like a coursing hound which bites at a wild boar or a lion from behind, flank and buttock, watching his twists and dodges. At last the fugitives got over the moat and stakes, many falling by the way, and halted hemmed in beside the ships. How they prayed aloud to all the gods in heaven, and called to one another holding up their hands! And Hector wheeled his horses round and about, glaring like Gorgon or the bloodthirsty god of war.

10 . . . Then the sun's bright light fell in the Ocean, drawing black night over the fruitful earth. Unwilling indeed the Trojans were to see the light go; but for the Achaians welcome, thrice prayed-for, came the darkness of night.

Now Hector withdrew his men to an open space near the river, where the ground was clear of the dead; and there he called an assembly. All dismounted from their chariots, and came to hear his speech. Hector held the pole of his spear, eighteen feet in 20 length, with its gleaming blade of bronze held by a golden ring; and leaning upon this, he spoke:

"Trojans, Dardanians, allies! I thought but now to destroy those ships and all the Achaians with them, before we returned to Ilios. But darkness came on first, and this chiefly has saved them and their ships upon the seashore. So then we must yield now to the night. We will take some food, and unloose the horses and give them a feed. Bring out oxen and sheep, and wine to comfort us, and bread from the 30 stores, and collect plenty of firewood. We must keep the fires alight everywhere blazing high all night long until daylight comes again, or the enemy may try to get away during the night.

"Now then, you must not let them embark at their pleasure without a blow. Take care that some of them have a shot to digest when they get home—an arrow, or a spear-prod, as he jumps aboard. That may teach other people not to bring war to this country! Send criers through the city to cry, 'All young lads and 40 greyheads man the walls!' Every woman is to keep a big fire alight in the house. Keep strict watch that no enemy troop shall get in while the men are away.

"Those are my orders for the night, my brave boys, and see they are carried out; to-morrow I shall have wholesome orders for the day. Full of hope, I pray to Zeus and all the gods of heaven to drive out from this place in rout these mongrels whom the fates are now driving upon their ships!

"This night then we will guard ourselves well; to-50 morrow at dawn we will arm and assault the enemy ships. I will see whether Diomedês Tydeidês will be strong enough to throw me back upon our walls, or if I shall strike him down and carry off his blood-stained spoils! To-morrow he shall find out what he is worth, if he stands to face my spear. But I think he will fall among the first before me, and many of his companions around him, as the sun rises upon the morrow. I wish I were as surely an immortal God and worshipt like Athenaia and Apollo, as the coming day will surely bring ruin for the Argives!" 60

Hector's speech was loudly applauded. Then they loosed the sweating horses from the yoke, and tethered each by its car. They brought out from the city cattle and sheep in haste, and wine to comfort their hearts, and bread from the stores, and gathered plenty of firewood: the wind carried the savour of meat up to heaven.

Proud and hearty they spent that night on the battlefield, with watch-fires burning all round; fires as many between the ships and the river Scamandros, as 70 the stars in heaven that shine conspicuous round the shining moon, when no wind blows, and all the peaks and headlands and mountain glades are clear to view; a strip is peeled away down through the mists of the infinite heaven, and all stars are seen, so that the shepherd is glad at heart. So ten thousand fires burnt upon the plain, and beside each sat fifty men in the light of the blazing fire. The horses stood by their cars, champing white barley and gram, and waiting for Dawn upon her glorious throne. 80

BOOK IX

So the Trojans kept their watch; but the Achaians were possessed by Panic, the freezing handmaid of Rout, and their strongest were pierced with grief intolerable. Their spirit was torn in pieces, like the sea lashed by those two fierce winds from Thrace, Boreas from the north parts and Zephyros from the west, when they come in a sudden gale, and roll up the dark water into crests, and sweep the seaweed in heaps along the shore. . . .

But Atreidês led all the elder men to his quarters, 90 and gave them a good repast. When they had finished, Nestor was the first to speak, that grand old man whose counsel was always thought the best. He spoke with honesty and good courage, setting out his thoughts neat and clear, like a weaver weaving a pattern upon his loom. This is what he said:

"My lord King Agamemnon, I will begin with your gracious majesty, and I will end with you; for you are lord of many nations, and Zeus has placed in your hands the sceptre and the law, that you may take 100 counsel on their behalf. Therefore it is your duty above all both to speak and to listen, and to act for any other who may have something to say for the common good: another may begin, but the rest depends upon you. Then I will declare what seems best to me. For no one will think of a better plan than this which I have had in mind ever since that day when your Grace took away the girl Briseïs from Achillês, and he was angry. That was not what we wished, not at all. You know I spoke strongly to 110 dissuade you; but you gave way to your proud temper, and insulted a great man whom the gods delighted to honour, for you took and you still keep his prize. But even at this late hour let us consider how we can appease him, and win him with gentle words and kindly gifts."

The King answered:

"Sir, you speak only the truth about my blind madness. I was blind, I do not deny it. Worth more than many thousands is the man whom Zeus loves and honours, as he now has honoured this man and humiliated the Achaian nation. Then since I was blinded and gave way to my wretched passion, it is my wish to appease him and to offer anything in redress.

"Before you all I will proclaim what I have to offer: seven tripods untouched by the fire, ten ingots of gold, twenty bright cauldrons, twelve horses, grand creatures which have won prizes in the race. No man who owned all that my racers have won, could ever be called penniless or pinched for a bit of gold! And I will give seven women skilful in women's work, Lesbians whom I chose when he captured Lesbos himself, the most beautiful women in the world. . . ."

Gerenian Nestor replied:

"May it please your Grace, my lord King Agamemnon! Such gifts as you offer now to Achillês no one could despise. Then let us choose envoys to send at once—or rather let me look around and choose them. Phoinix first, let him lead the way; then big Aias and Odysseus; heralds—let Odios and Eurybatês go with them. Here, water for our hands if you please, and call a solemn silence, that we may pray to Zeus Cronidês and crave his mercy."

This was approved by all. At once heralds brought the hand-wash, boys filled the mixing bowls to the brim, wine was served all round with the usual solemnity, they poured their drops and drank. Then they separated; and Gerenian Nestor with many a nod and wink told the envoys exactly what to say, especially Odysseus, if they wished to persuade the redoubtable Achillês.

Phoinix had gone on, and the two others paced after him by the sounding sea, with many an earnest prayer to Poseidon Earthholder Earthshaker that they might successfully persuade that strong will. When they came to the lines of the Myrmidons, they found Achillês amusing himself with his harp; a beautiful thing it was, made by an artist, with a silver bridge and a clear lovely tone, part of the spoils of Thebê. Achillês was playing upon his harp and singing the glorious feats of heroes. Patroclos sat opposite by

29. **Phoinix,** tutor of Achillês. 49. **Thebê.** This touch will show how intricate the associations are in the story. Thebê in Mysia was sacked by Achillês, and the King and his seven sons were killed. His daughter was Hector's wife, Andromachê. And Chryseïs, the centre of the whole story, was there at the time, and taken with the spoil.—Translator's note.

himself, waiting until his friend should finish. The two envoys came forward, Odysseus first, and stood still.

Achillês jumped up from his seat in surprise, still holding the harp, and Patroclos got up too when he saw visitors. Achillês greeted them, and said:

"Welcome! I am glad to see friends. Just what I wanted! and you are my very best friends, though I am an angry man."

He led them indoors, and found them a comfortable seat with a fine purple rug; then he said to Patroclos by his side:

"A larger bowl, my dear fellow, if you please! stronger wine, and a cup apiece, for very good friends of mine are under my roof."

Patroclos was busy at once. He set a meat-block by the fire, and put on it a shoulder of mutton with another of goat, and the chine of a fine fat hog. Automedon held the meat and Achillês carved. When this was cut up and spitted Patroclos made a good fire, and when the flame had died down, he scattered the ashes, and laid the spits over them on the firedogs, sprinkling the grill with salt. Soon all was done brown and set out on platters; Patroclos handed round baskets of bread, and Achillês served the meat.

He sat down himself opposite Odysseus against the other wall, and told Patroclos to do grace to the gods, as he cast the firstlings into the fire.

When they had all had enough, Aias nodded to Phoinix; but Odysseus saw this, and filling his cup with wine he greeted Achillês himself:

"Your health, Achillês! We do not lack good fare and plenty, either at the board of King Agamemnon, or here and now. Indeed you have given us a regular feast.

"But feasting is not our business, bless it! An awful disaster is what we see, my prince, and we are afraid. Life or death is in question for our whole fleet, unless you put on your armour of might. Close beside our ships and wall is the bivouac of the Trojans, with their allies gathered from the wide world, all full of pride. There are the countless watch-fires of their host, and they believe we shall not hold out but be driven back upon our ships. Zeus Cronidês gives them favourable signs with his lightning; Hector in triumphant pride is like a raging madman—he trusts in Zeus, and cares for nothing in heaven or earth while that strong frenzy possesses him. He prays that dawn may soon appear, and vows he will chop the ensigns from our ships and burn them with ravening fire, that he will smother us in the smoke and destroy us beside them.

"This is what terribly affrights me. I fear the gods may fulfil his threats, and it may be our fate to perish in the land of Troy, far from home and Argos. Up, then! if now at last you have a mind to save our people in their extremity. You will be sorry yourself when it is too late, but when mischief is done there is no cure. Think first while you can how to save our people from the evil day.

". . . Agamemnon offers you ample atonement if you will relent. . . . And along with these he will give back Briseïs, the one whom he took away that time. And he will swear a solemn oath that she has never lain in his bed, and he has never touched her in the way of a man with a woman.

10 "That is what he offers now. Then if the gods grant later that we sack the city of Priam, you shall be there when we are dividing the spoil, and you shall load your ship with piles of gold and bronze, and choose for yourself twenty Trojan women, the most beautiful after Helen. . . . All this he will do if you will only relent.

"But if you hate and loathe Atreidês too much, him and his gifts, at least pity all the nations of Achaia in their extremity! They will honour you as if you were 20 a god, and a great name you will get among them. For now you may kill Hector! He will come close enough in that furious madness—for now he says there's not a match for himself among all the Danaäns who came to Troy."

Achillês answered:

"Prince Odysseus Laërtiadês, I must speak out without undue respect to you. I must tell you how I feel and how I am resolved, that you two may not sit cooing at me on both sides. I hate that man like the 30 gates of hell who says one thing and hides another thing in his heart! But I will tell you exactly what I have decided. I am not going to be persuaded by my lord King Agamemnon, or by any one else, because it seems one gets no thanks by fighting in battle for ever and for aye. Stay at home, or fight all day, you get only equal pay. Be a coward, or be brave, equal honour you will have. Death is coming if you shirk, death is coming if you work! I get no profit from suffering pain and risking my life for ever in battle. I 40 am like a bird that gives the callow chicks every morsel she can get, and comes off badly herself.

"Just so I have spent many sleepless nights, I have fought through many long bloody days, all for a man to win back his dainty dear! Twelve cities I have destroyed with my ships, eleven fighting on land. Out of all these I have taken treasures rich and rare, and always brought all to my lord King Agamemnon; this Lagamemnon lags behind and takes it, distributes a few trifles and keeps the rest! Some things he gave as 50 prizes to the princes and great men; the others keep theirs safe enough—I am the only one he has robbed! He has a wife of his own, let him sleep by her side and enjoy her.

"Why must Achaians make war on Trojans? Why did my lord King gather an army and bring it here? Was it not for lovely Helen? Are there only two men in the wide world who love their wives, my lord King

and his royal brother? Why, every man who is honest and faithful loves his own, as I loved mine in my heart although my spear had won her. But now he 60 has taken my prize from my hands and deceived me, let him not tempt me: I know him too well, he shall never move me. . . . I will not help him with advice or with action, for he has wholly deceived and beguiled me. Never again shall he deceive me with his words; he has done it once too often. Leave him alone to go to the devil, for Zeus has taken away his sense. I loathe his gifts, I value them not one splinter! Not if he offered me ten times as much, or twenty times, or any amount more, all that goes into Orcho- 70 menos, all that goes into Egyptian Thebes, the world's greatest treasure-house,—Thebes with its hundred gates, where two hundred men issue forth from each gate with horses and chariots, not if he gave me as much as the sands on the seashore and the dust on the earth, not even then would Agamemnon move me until he shall pay in full for the insult which torments my heart! . . .

"My mother Thetis Silverfoot says, that two different fates are carrying me on the road to death. 80 If I stay here and fight before the city of Troy, there will be no home-coming for me but my fame shall never die; if I go home to my native land, there will be no great fame for me, but I shall live long and not die an early death.

"Indeed, I would advise the others to sail away for home, since you will never make an end of Ilios. Clearly Zeus Allseeing has lifted a protecting hand over her, and the people have grown bold.

"But you return now and give your message to the 90 princes openly, your privilege as counsellors; then let them contrive some better plan than this, if they wish to save the ships and the army. For this plan which they thought of is not for them while I am angry. . . . However, go now and deliver your message. For I will not think of battle until prince Hector comes as far as the ships and camp of the Myrmidons in his career, and sets our ships in a blaze. Here, I say, beside my own hut and my ship, I think Hector will be held, and his fury stayed." 100

The envoys took cup in hand, and each poured the sacred drops; then Odysseus led the way back. . . .

BOOK XI

Now dawn arose from beside her lord Tithonos, to bring light for gods and men; and Zeus sent Discord towards the Achaian ships, carrying in her dreadful hands a portent of war.

She came to a stand beside the huge black hull of Odysseus' ship, which lay in the middle, from which a voice could reach to Aias Telamoniadês and to

70-71. **Orchomenos,** a wealthy city of Boeotia.

Achillês at the two farthest ends. There she stood, and uttered a loud and dreadful warcry, which put strength into the heart of every man in that host for battle and war unceasing. In a moment, battle seemed to them sweeter than a happy voyage to their native land.

Atreidês shouted orders to arm, and he armed himself.

First he buckled on his fine greaves with silver anklets. Next he donned the corselet which Cinyrês had given him as a guest-gift; for the great rumour had come to Cyprus that the fleet was about to sail for Troy, and therefore he gave him this gift to please him. There were ten stripes of dark blue enamel upon it, twelve of gold, and twenty of tin; blue dragons reached up toward the neck, three on each side, like the rainbow which Cronion sets in the cloud to be a portent for mortal men.

Over his shoulders he threw the sword, with shining knobs of solid gold, and a silver sheath with golden slings.

He caught up a brave shield of fine workmanship, covering the body on both sides. Ten circles of bronze ran round it, and it had twenty bosses of white tin with one of blue enamel in the middle. Upon this boss was the grim-faced Gorgon glaring horribly, and on either side Terror and Panic. The shield-strap was of silver, and a blue dragon was twining upon it, with three heads twisted together and growing from one neck.

Upon his head he put a helmet with two horns and four bosses and a horsehair plume. How terrible was that nodding plume!

He took a pair of sharp spears with blades of bronze, which sent their glittering gleam high into the air.

Then Athenaia and Hera thundered in honour to the King of rich Mycenê.

Now each man ordered his driver to keep back the horses in due order near the moat; the fighting men fully armed moved forward, and unquenchable rose the warcry to meet the morning. They were in place long before 'the chariots, which came and stood behind at a little distance.

Then Cronidês made a dreadful noise on them, and let fall a shower of bloody drops from the sky, since he was about to send to Hadês many a mighty head.

The Trojans were over against them upon the rising of the plain, ranged about Hector their great leader, and Polydamas the immaculate, Aineias whom the people honoured as more than man, and Antenor's three sons, Polybos and noble Agenor and young Acamas, glorious heroes all.

Hector was to be seen holding his round shield, now in front, now behind, giving his orders like a shining star of doom, which flashes out of a cloud and then dives again into the darkness: the metal of his armour gleamed like the lightning of Zeus Almighty.

The hosts were like two opposite lines of reapers driving their swathes in the wheat or barley of a great farm, while thick the handfuls fall. So Trojans and Achaians leapt at each other, and neither side thought of giving way: two equal ranks of heads, they were like raging wolves.

Discord Manymoan was joyful at the sight. She alone was present out of all the gods; the others remained quietly in their own abodes on high Olympos. They all blamed Cronion Thundercloud, because it seemed that he meant to give triumph to the Trojans. But the Father cared nothing about them, as it seemed. He sat apart by himself in great satisfaction, as he watched the Trojan city, and the Achaian ships, and the flashing arms, men slaying and men slain. . . .

BOOK XIV

. . . The voice of Lord Earthshaker sounded from his chest as loud as the noise of nine or ten thousand men shouting in hot battle; and every man of the Achaian host as he heard felt the strength increase within him to fight on and never yield.

But Queen Hera stood on a peak of Olympos, watching. She knew him at once, her own brother and her husband's, and glad she was to see him so busy in the battle. She saw Zeus also seated on Ida among the mountain brooks, and a hateful sight she thought him. She began at once to scheme how she might beguile him; and this seemed the best plan. She would prink herself out for a visit to Mount Ida, and entice him to lie by her side in love, so that quiet and balmy sleep might drown his eyes and mind.

So she went to her chamber—which her own son Hephaistos had built for her, with doors closed by a secret lock which no other god could open. She closed the doors, and first she washed every speck and stain from her lovely body with a bath of ambrosia. She anointed her body with oil, ambrosial, soft, scented with perfumes—do but stir it, and the fragrance fills the whole palace of Zeus with its brazen floor, heaven above and earth beneath! She combed her shining hair, and plaited long ambrosial braids to hang from her immortal head. About her she draped an ambrosial robe, which Athena had made so smooth and embroidered with beautiful patterns; she fastened this with golden pins at the breast. She put a girdle round her waist with a hundred dangling tassels, and hung in her dainty ears earrings with three mulberry-drops, delicate and graceful. She spread over her head a new and beautiful veil, white as the sunlight, and upon her feet she laced her shapely shoes.

When all was done, she issued from her chamber, and called Aphroditê apart to tell her a secret:

"Will you do something for me, dear child, if I ask you? Or are you too angry with me for favoring the Danaäns, and will you say no?"

Aphroditê replied:

"Say what you want, my gracious Queen! I will do it with all my heart, if I can do it, and if it is doable."

The artful Queen answered:

"Give me now your charm of love and desire, with which you subdue both mortal men and immortal gods. I am about to visit the ends of the earth, to see Oceanos the father of the gods, and Tethys their mother. You know they took me from Rheia's hands, and brought me up and cared for me in their own house, at the time when Zeus Allseeing thrust Cronos down below the earth and unvintaged sea. I want to see them and make up their old standing quarrel. They have been at odds for a long time, separate in bed and board, because of some grudge or other. If I can persuade them and bring them together again as loving as before, they will love me and make much of me for ever."

Aphroditê said with a smile:

"I could not say no to that, and I ought not, for you sleep in the arms of almighty Zeus."

So saying, she took out of her bosom the broidered strap with all the charms worked in it: there is love, there is desire, there is lovers' tender prattle, the cajolery which deceives the mind of the wisest. She dropt it into Hera's hands and said:

"Here you are, tuck this into your bosom, this embroidered strap in which everything is worked. I do not think you will fail in winning your heart's desire."

Queen Hera smiled with her lips and her limpid eyes, and smiling she laid it in her bosom.

Aphroditê returned into the house, and Hera sprang from the heights of Olympos. One step to Pieria, one step to Emathia, she sped over the snowy mountains of the Thracian horsemasters, stepping on the topmost peaks, for her feet did not touch the level ground; from Athos she stept over the sea to Lemnos, the realm of princely Thoas.

There she met Sleep, Death's brother, and grasped him by the hand as she said:

"My dear Sleep, you are lord of all gods and all mankind! This is not the first time you have done something for me—listen to me once more! and I will be grateful to you all my days. Lull me the bright eyes of Zeus under his brows as soon as I shall have lain by his side in love. I will reward you with a fine throne, incorruptible, made of solid gold; my son Crookshank Hephaistos shall make it with all his best craftsmanship, and a footstool underneath to rest your soft feet upon while you drink your wine."

Sleep answered:

"My most gracious and honoured Queen! Any other of the immortal gods I could easily put to sleep, even the stream of Oceanos who is father of all—but Zeus Cronion I would not dare to come near, nor could I put him to sleep unless he should himself command me. . . ."

Queen Hera said again, with a look from her limpid eyes:

"My dear Sleep, why do you worry about all that? . . . Look here, I will give you one of the young Graces, you shall woo her and wed her! You shall have Pasithea, whom you have always wanted!"

Sleep was delighted, and said:

"Very well, swear me an oath by the inviolate water of Styx, touching mother earth with one hand and the glittering sea with the other; call to witness the gods below with Cronos; and swear on your honour that you will give me one of the young Graces, Pasithea to wit, whom I have wanted all my days!"

Hera swore the oath as he asked, and called to witness all the gods under Tartaros who are called the Titans. . . .

Hera walked quickly up to Gargaros on the top of Mount Ida, and Zeus Cloudgatherer saw her come. When he saw her, what love filled his heart! He felt then as he did when first they mingled in love, that time when they had gone to bed and their parents knew nothing about it.

He rose and stood before her, saying:

"Why, Hera, whither away so fast? What brings you here? I don't see the chariot and horses!"

His artful queen answered:

"I am going to visit the ends of the earth. I want to see Oceanos, the father of all the gods, and their mother Tethys, who brought me up and cherished me in their own house. I want to reconcile their old quarrel; for they have been at odds this long time, and keep apart in bed and board for some grudge or other. My horses are down at the foot of the mountain, ready to carry me over moist and dry. You are the reason why I came here. I was afraid you might be angry with me afterwards if I go to the house of Oceanos without telling you."

Zeus Cloudgatherer answered:

"My dear, you can go there by and by, but now let us to bed and take our joy! Indeed, no love of goddess or woman has ever come over me like this in a flood and possessed my heart—not when I was in love with Ixion's wife who brought me the wise Peirithoös; not when I was in love with beautiful Danaë Acrisios' daughter, who brought me the glorious Perseus; not when I was in love with the daughter of famous Phoinix, who brought me Minos and Rhadamanthys; not when I loved Semelê or Alcmenê in Thebes, and one brought me mighty Heraclês, one Dionysos the darling of the world; not when I loved glorious Leto, nor indeed yourself—never was I in love so deeply as I love you now and sweet desire holds me captive!"

His artful queen said:

"You dreadful creature! What a thing to say! You want to make love on the top of a mountain where any one can see! What if one of us gods should see us asleep and go and tell tales to the whole family? I couldn't get up from this bed and go straight home, I should be ashamed. If it is really your wish, if you are bent upon it, there's my room for you, built by Hephaistos with good strong doors. Let us go and lie there, since you are pleased to desire bed."

Zeus Cloudgatherer answered:

"My dear, you need not be afraid that god or man will see. I will gather about us such a golden cloud that Helios himself could not see through, and his sunlight is the strongest light there is."

As he spoke, he took his wife in his arms: and under them the earth divine made a bed of fresh new grass to grow, with dewy clover and crocus and hyacinth soft and thick, which raised them high above the ground. There they lay, and a beautiful golden cloud spread over them, from which fell drops of sparkling dew.

While the Father lay motionless on the top of Gargaros, mastered by love and sleep, with his wife in his arms, Sleep ran quickly to the Achaian ships with news for Poseidon Earthshaker. As soon as he came near enough he blurted out:

"Have your way now, Poseidon! Help the Danaäns, give them victory just for a little, while Zeus is still asleep! I have drowned him in soft slumber myself—Hera has enticed him to bed with her!"

. . . When all [the Danaäns] were properly arranged, they marched forward. Poseidon Earthshaker led them like a thunderbolt of war, holding a terrible sword long and sharp. No man may meddle with him in the deadly combat, but fear holds them back.

On the other side Hector marshalled his forces. Then came the most dreadful tug of war between Seabluehair Poseidon and Hector the brilliant hero, the Trojans behind one, the Argives behind the other. The sea rolled up to the Argive camp and ships, and the armies met with deafening warcries. Not so loud are the waves of the sea booming against the land, when it rolls in from the deep before the blusterous northeaster; not so loud is the roar in the glens of a blazing mountain, when fire leaps upon the forest; not so loud is the shrieking wind in the treetops, the angriest wind that roars, as the terrible noise of Trojans and Achaians shouting and yelling while they leapt to their struggle for life and death.

Hector first cast a spear at Aias, who was turned full towards him. That cast was no miss—he struck his chest in the place where the shield-strap and sword-strap crossed. They saved his body from a wound; Hector was angry that his cast had no effect, and stept back into safety. As he retired, Aias picked up a large stone—there were many such knocking about under the feet of the men, mooring-stones for the ships—one of these Aias lifted high and threw it at Hector. The stone went over the shield-rim, and striking his chest near the neck sent him spinning like a top with the blow—round and round he went all over the place, and fell flat in the dust. . . .

The Argives assaulted more furiously than ever when they saw Hector retire. . . .

Now the battle had turned, and many of the Achaians lifted the blood-spoils of their enemies. Telamonian Aias stabbed Hyrtios Gyrtiadês the Mysian captain; Antilochos despoiled Phalcês and Mermeros; Merionês killed Morys and Hippotion; Teucros brought down Prothoön and Periphetês. Then Atreidês stabbed prince Hyperenor in the side and let out his bowels; his soul flew quickly out of the wound, and darkness covered his eyes. But Aias Oïliadês killed more than any other; for he was a quick runner, and no man was like him for running down those who ran away when Zeus put fear into their hearts.

BOOK XV

Thus the Trojans were driven over the moat and stakes, and many had fallen; now they halted beside their chariots, pale with fear, terror-stricken.

But Zeus awoke on Mount Ida by the side of Hera his consort. He sprang up and stood, looking at the battlefield. There were the Trojans in rout, there were the Achaians pelting in pursuit with Lord Poseidon among them; there was Hector lying on the plain, and his companions sitting around him—and he dazed, breathing heavily, vomiting blood, for no weak hand had dealt that blow.

The Father of gods and men was moved with pity to see the man, and he said to Hera with an angry frown:

"This is another of your evil schemes, you unmanageable creature! Your trick has driven him from the battle and routed his people. I should not be surprised if you were sorry by-and-by for your wicked web-spinning, when you get the first taste of the fruit, and a good thrashing from me. Don't you remember how I hung you up with two great stones tied to your feet and a golden chain round your wrists, too strong for any one to break? There you dangled in the clouds! The gods were indignant, but they could not go and set you free. . . . I'll give you cause to remember all this and stop your deceits. You shall soon find out if you get any good by your loving and your bedding and by coming all this way to deceive me!"

Hera shivered at these words, and protested:

*From a Greek
vase painting.*

"I call on Earth to witness, and the broad Heavens above, and the force of Styx, which is the most solemn oath for the blessed gods, and your sacred head, and our own marriage bed which I would never lightly name, it is not my doing that Poseidon Earthshaker plagues Hector and the Trojans and helps the other side! I suppose his own temper moves him, and pity for the Achaians hard pressed beside their own ships. Why, if he would take my advice, he would follow wherever you lead, Thundercloud!"

The Father of gods and men smiled and answered, very much to the point:

"Ah yes, my dear lady, if only *you* could have one mind with me as you sit in our family circle, Poseidon would soon change his mind to suit yours and mine, however much he might want something else.—But if you are really speaking the truth, go home and tell Iris and Archer Apollo to come here.

"I want to send Iris to tell Poseidon that he must stop meddling in the war and go home; and I want Apollo to breathe courage into Hector again, and make him forget the pain that torments him, and send him back to the battle. The Achaians are to be turned again in headlong flight, and to fall back on the ships of Achillês; he is to put up his friend Patroclos; and Hector is to kill Patroclos under the walls of Ilios, after he has killed many other fine fellows, and among them Sarpedon my own son. Then Achillês in revenge for Patroclos is to kill Hector.

"After that I will make the Achaians sweep the Trojans away from their camp completely, and they shall take the city according to Athena's plans. But meanwhile I will not relent, and I will not allow any other of the immortals to help the Danaäns here, until I fulfil the desire of Peleidês, as I promised to do and bowed my head to confirm it, on that day when Thetis embraced my knees and prayed to me to give renown to Achillês." . . .

The Argives stood in a mass to meet them, and a piercing war-cry arose from both sides. Arrows leapt from the bowstring, spears shot from steady hands— some to pierce the bodies of strong young men, many to fall between ere they could taste the white flesh, and to stick in the ground greedy for a taste.

So long as Apollo held the aegis-cape unmoving, the volleys hit their mark on both sides and the people fell. But when he looked the Danaäns full in the face and shook it, with a loud and terrible shout, he melted their hearts within them and they forgot their courage. Then like a herd of cattle or a great flock of sheep chased by a couple of wild beasts in the murk of night, with a sudden attack when the keeper is away, so fled the Achaians in panic; for Apollo put fear into them and gave victory to Hector and his Trojans. . . .

But the Trojans attacked still more furiously when they heard the thunder of Zeus Almighty. As a great billow from the open sea rolls over the bulwarks of a ship, when a strong wind piles it up as the winds do pile the waves, so the Trojans with a mighty noise came rolling over the wall; and driving their horses to the ships they fought with spears hand to hand—they from their chariots, the others from the ships where they had climbed, using the long jointed poles shod with bronze which were there at hand.

All this while, as long as the battle was outside the walls and far from the ships, Patroclos had been in the hut of gentle Eurypylos, amusing him with talk, and soothing the pain of his wound with plasters of his healing herbs. But when the Trojans came pouring in and when he heard the noise of the Danaäns in rout, he groaned and slapt his thighs, saying in distress to his friend:

"I can't stay here any longer, Eurypylos, although you need somebody with you, but just listen to this battle going on! Your man shall attend to you—I must hasten to Achillês and try to make him fight. Who knows whether I may not persuade him, with good luck? The persuasion of a friend often brings a happy end!" . . .

BOOK XVI

While this battle was going on round the ships, Patroclos appeared before Achillês with tears pouring down his cheeks—a veritable fountain, a mountain brook running over the rocks! Achillês was deeply grieved, and spoke to him plainly:

"My dear Patroclos, why are you crying like a baby? You might be some little girl running to her mother, and pulling at her apron, and keeping her from her work, and blubbering and looking up and saying, Nurse me mammy dear! That's what you look like, my dear man, crying like that. . . ."

Patroclos answered with a groan:

"Don't be angry, Achillês my prince, our strong deliverer! Such misfortune has come on our people! There they are, all who used to be best in the field, lying wounded, shot or stabbed, somewhere among the ships! Diomedês Tydeidês is wounded, Odysseus is wounded, Agamemnon is wounded, Eurypylos is wounded too—shot in the thigh with an arrow. They have the surgeons busy about them with all their medicines curing the wounds—but there's no curing you, Achillês! I pray I may never have such a grudge in my heart as you have. Curse your courage! What good will you be to any one from now to the end of the world, if you will not save the nation from destruction? Cruel man! your father was not Peleus nor your mother Thetis—you are a son of the green sea and the stony rock, with that hard heart!

"If there is some prophecy you are afraid of which your mother told you from the lips of Zeus, let *me* go at least and take out our Myrmidons, to see if there is any hope in that way! Put your armour upon my shoulders, and perhaps the Trojans may think it is you, and give a little rest to our tormented people. Little time to take your breath face to face with sudden death! And it will be easy for us coming into the battle fresh, to drive weary men from our camp away to their city!"

So he prayed, poor fool! for his prayer was destined to bring death and destruction for himself. Achillês replied in hot anger:

"Ah, what have you said, Patroclos, my dear friend! I care for no prophecy, if I do know any; my mother has told me none from the lips of Zeus. But I feel bitter grief in my heart, when here is a man who will rob his equal and take back his prize because he is the stronger. This is a terrible grief to me, and this has been my torment. . . .

"But we will let bygones be bygones. I see it was impossible to bear resentment for ever and ever. I did think I should not forget my resentment until fire and battle came to my own ships.—You go then; put on my armour and lead our brave men into the field, now that the enemy have swallowed up the Achaian ships like a great cloud, now that our people have their backs to the sea and only a small space is left them to hold, now that all Troy is here confident—for they see not the face of my helmet shining near them!—that would soon rout them and fill the gullies with their dead, if my lord King Agamemnon were kind to me!

"But now they are fighting round our camp! There is no spear in the hands of Diomedês Tydeidês, furiously raging to defend the Danaäns from ruin. I have not heard yet the voice of my lord King shouting out of his hateful head! But Hector's words of command are breaking upon me all round, his Trojans cover the whole plain with their clamour—they vanquish the Achaians in fair fight!

"Never mind—fall on them and beat them, Patroclos! Save our ships, or they will burn them and we shall never see home again. But listen carefully while I tell you exactly what to do, that you may win honour and glory for me from the whole nation, and they may send back that lovely girl and handsome gifts besides.

"When you have cleared them away from the ships, come straight back. If after that the loud-thundering lord of Hera gives you a chance of triumph, never think of fighting on your own account without me, you will steal my honours in that way. Don't be excited by fighting and victory so as to lead our men as far as the city walls, or one of the Olympian gods may meddle; Apollo Shootafar is very fond of them. You must turn back as soon as you have saved the ships, and let them ravage the plain.

"O Father Zeus, Athenaia, Apollo! If only not one single Trojan could be left alive, and not one Achaian, but you and I might be left, that we alone might tear off the sacred diadem of Troy!" . . .

Patroclos lost no time. He put on his legs the greaves with silver anklets, next covered his chest with the star-bespangled corselet of Aiacidês. Over his shoulders he slung the sword, with bronze blade and silver knob, and then the great strong shield. Upon his head he set the helmet with its plume nodding defiance. He took two lances that fitted his grip, but not the spear of Aiacidês; for only Achillês could wield that huge heavy pike, not another man in the Achaian host. . . .

Meanwhile Achillês had got the men under arms and marshalled in their camp. They were like a pack of ravening wolves ready for the hunt. How the savage beasts bring down a great antlered stag in the mountains and tear him to pieces with blood-dripping jaws!—then off goes the whole pack to a brook, and they lap up the clear surface-water with long, thin tongues, belching out clots of gore. Their courage is high as ever, though their bellies are stuffed. So the Myrmidon leaders and captains bustled about Patroclos. . . .

Patroclos and his force marched on until they found the Trojans. They were like a swarm of wasps with a nest by the road, which boys have been teasing and poking in their way. The poor little fools only stir up trouble for everybody; and if a wayfarer disturbs the wasps by accident, they pour out in fury and defend their home. Just as furious were the

Myrmidons when they poured out of their camp with a great noise. Patroclos cried out in a loud voice:

"Myrmidons! Fellow-soldiers of our prince! Be men! remember your old valour! Let us win honour for Peleidês, who is the best man in this army and his soldiers are second to none! Let my lord King Agamemnon know his blind madness, when he made no account of the best man of all our nation!"

Then with courage refreshed they fell on the Trojans in a swarm, and the ships around resounded with the noise of their shouting.

But when the Trojans saw Patroclos and his companions in their shining armour, they were amazed, and the ranks wavered; for they believed that Achilles had thrown off his resentment and made friends again. Every man looked about him for some escape from certain death. . . .

But now the rout and confusion spread from the ships, as when Zeus spreads the tempest and a cloud comes into the open from the upper air. Now they were all pouring back in a rabble. Hector in his galloping car left the Trojan army, as they were trying to get over the moat which was in their way. Many a team galloped off, leaving their masters' chariots in the ditch with broken poles. But Patroclos was close behind, loudly crying "Kill! Kill!" as the broken hordes filled every path with noise and confusion. The dust rose in clouds, the horses tugged and strained to get clear of the camp. Patroclos drove shouting wherever he saw the thickest crowd; men kept falling out of their cars under his axle-trees, the cars tumbled over clittery clattery. Straight over the moat galloped the horses, on and on; "Down with Hector!" was the cry of his heart. To strike down Hector was his one passion; but Hector was far ahead. Panting horses were everywhere running loose, like a roaring torrent, when a thundercloud in the autumn pours heavy cataracts on the black earth, the rivers rise in flood, crundels and dimbles are full and ravines are cut in the mountains: down come the torrents tumbling criss-cross out of the hills, and destroying the works of men, until they fall roaring into the sea. . . .

And then the Achaians would have taken the proud city of Troy by the valour of Patroclos, for he went onwards like a storm: but Apollo stood on the wall to help the Trojans, intent upon his death. Three times did Patroclos set his foot on a corner of the wall, three times Apollo dooled him back, rapping the shield with his immortal hands. When he tried the fourth time like one more than man, Apollo shouted at him and said in plain words:

"Back, prince Patroclos! It is not fated that proud Troy shall fall to your spear, nor to Achillês, who is a much better man than you."

Then Patroclos fell back a long way, in fear of the wrath of Apollo Shootafar.

But Hector checked his horses at the Scaian Gate; for he was in doubt whether to drive into battle again, or recall his army to take shelter within the walls. As he was considering, Apollo appeared by his side, in the form of a lusty young fellow Asios, who was Hector's own uncle, being brother of Hecabê, and the son of Dymas who lived near the Sangarios in Phrygia. Apollo said then, in the shape of this man:

"Why have you left the battle, Hector? You ought not to do it. I wish I were as much better than you as I am worse; you should soon be sorry you shirked. Hurry—make for Patroclos, and you may get him— Apollo may give you victory!"

As Apollo disappeared into the mellay, Hector told Cebrionês to whip the horses into battle. Apollo turned the Argives to flight and made the Trojans prevail; but Hector left the others alone and drove towards Patroclos. Then Patroclos leapt out of his car, holding the spear in his left hand; he picked up with his right a sharp shining stone just large enough to fill his hand. He did not try to keep clear of the fellow now—he threw with all his might, and his shot was not wasted, for it hit Cebrionês (himself a bastard son of Priam) on the forehead, as he held the reins. The stone crushed both brows into one and smashed the bone, and both eyes fell down in the dust in front of him. He rolled out of the car like a tumbler. . . . Patroclos turned upon the Trojans again. Thrice he leapt on them like another god of war with awful shouts, thrice nine men he killed: but at the fourth furious attack—ah then, Patroclos, the end of your life was in sight! for Phoibos was there in all his terrors.

Patroclos did not see him coming, for the god was hidden in mist. He stood behind Patroclos: his eyes rolled in rage, and he slapped him between the shoulders with the flat of the hand. The helmet was knocked from his head, and went rolling and rattling under the horses' feet; the plumes were dabbled in blood and dust. Never before had it been God's will that this plumed helmet should be fouled in the dust, when it covered the head and brows of a man of the blood divine, Achillês. Then Zeus granted that Hector should wear it, yet death was coming near him. Patroclos felt the spear in his hand broken to pieces, the great strong heavy-bladed spear; the tasselled shield with its belt fell from his shoulders; the corselet was stript off his body by the great son of Zeus. His mind was blinded, his knees crickled under him, he stood there dazed.

Then from behind a spear hit him between the shoulders. A Dardanian struck him, Euphorbos Panthoïdês, best of all his yearsmates in spearmanship and horsemanship and fleetness of foot. He had already dismounted twenty since he drove out to

72. **Cebrionês**, Hector's charioteer.

learn his first lesson of war. His was the first blow, but it did not bring down Patroclos, and Euphorbos pulled out the spear and mixed again with the crowd; he could not stand up to Patroclos even when naked and bare. But the god's blow and the spear together were too much for Patroclos, and he sought safety among his friends.

When Hector saw him retreating and wounded, he came near and stabbed him in the belly: the blade ran through, he fell with a dull thud, and consternation took the Achaians. So fell Patroclos, like a wild boar killed by a lion, when both are angry and both are parched with thirst, and they fight over a little mountain pool, until the lion is too strong for the panting boar. Patroclos Menoitiadês had killed many men, but Hector Priamidês killed him: and then he vaunted his victory without disguise:

"So Patroclos, you thought that you could sack our city! you thought you would rob our women of the day of freedom, and carry them off to your own country! Fool! In front of them are the horses of Hector prancing out to battle. My spear is well known among my brave Trojans, for I defend them from the day of fate: here you shall stay and feed the vultures! Ah, poor wretch, your Achillês is a good man, but he was no help to you, although no doubt he warned you earnestly when you started (and he stayed behind)—'Don't come back to me, my brave Patroclos, until you have stript the blood-stained shirt from Hector's body!' No doubt he must have said that, and you thought you could do it—no more sense in you than that!"

Patroclos replied, half fainting:

"For this once, Hector, make your proud boast; for you are the victor, by help of Zeus Cronidês and Apollo, who mastered me—an easy thing: they stript off my armour themselves. But if twenty men like you had confronted me, my spear would have slain them all on the spot. No, it was cruel fate that killed me, and Leto's son, and of men Euphorbos; you come third and take my armour. One thing I tell you, and you should lay it up in your mind: you have yourself not long to live. Already death and fate are beside you, and Achillês Aiacidês shall lay you low."

Even as he spoke, the shadow of death covered him up. His soul left the body and went down to Hadês, bewailing his lot, cut off in his manhood and strength. But Hector answered him though dead:

"What is this prophecy of certain death to me, Patroclos? Achillês may be the son of the divine Thetis, but who knows if I may not strike him with my spear, and he may be the first to die!" . . .

BOOK XVIII

While the battle went on like blazing fire, Antilochos had been running at the top of his speed to Achillês. He found Achillês in front of the ships anxious and thoughtful. He feared what had really happened, and he was saying to himself:

"Ah, what can this mean? Here are our people again rushing in a rabble towards the camp. I fear the gods may bring bitter grief on me, as my mother told me once. She declared that the best man of the Myrmidons would be killed in battle while I yet lived. It must be the brave Menoitiadês who is dead. Headstrong man! I ordered him strictly to come back as soon as he had got rid of the fire, and not to fight with Hector."

As these thoughts were passing through his mind, there was Antilochos. When he was near enough he told his cruel news, with tears running down his cheeks:

"Bad news, my lord prince! I have very bad news for you, I am sorry to say. Patroclos is dead, they are fighting for his body, only the body, for the armour is lost—Hector has it!"

Sorrow fell on Achillês like a cloud. He swept up the dust with both hands, and poured it over his head and smirched his handsome face, till the black dirt stained his fragrant tunic. He tore his hair and fell flat in the dust, grand in his grandeur. The captive women also whom he and Patroclos had taken, wailed in grief, and ran out to where he lay, beating their breasts and half fainting. Antilochos had taken the hands of Achillês and stood weeping beside him, while he moaned heavily; for he feared Achillês might put the steel to his own throat.

His gracious mother heard his terrible cry, sitting by her old father deep down in the sea. She shrieked, . . . "I must go and see my dear child, and hear what trouble has come to him so far from the battle."

She left the cave, and her sisters went with her weeping, through the water, until they came to the Trojan strand. There they stept out upon the beach one after another, not far from the place where the Myrmidons had drawn up their ships, and Thetis sought her son.

She found him groaning, and clasped his head with a sorrowful cry, saying simply:

"My child, why do you weep? What is your trouble? Tell me, don't hide it. Zeus has done all that for you, all you besought him to do, the whole army has been brought to disaster for want of you and huddled up under their ships!"

Achillês said with a deep groan:

"Yes, my dear mother, the Olympian has done all that for me. But what good do I get of all that now, if my dear friend Patroclos is dead? I cared more for him than all my companions, as much as for my own life. He is lost! my armour is Hector's! Hector killed him, Hector stript off that miraculous armour, that beautiful armour, that wonder of wonders, which the gods gave to Peleus on the day when they laid you in a mortal's bed. . . .

"Quick let me die, since it seems my friend was killed and I was not there to help him! He perished far from his native land, and I was not there to defend him!

"But now, since I am never to return home, since I brought no hope to Patroclos or my other comrades whom Hector killed, and how many they are! since I only sit idle beside the ships a burden to the earth, although there is none like me in battle—as for debate, others are better there—O that discord might utterly cease to be in heaven or earth! and anger, that makes even the prudent man take offence—anger that is far sweeter than trickling honey, and grows in men's hearts like smoke—just as I was made angry now by my lord King Agamemnon.

"But I will let bygones be bygones, although I am indignant; I will rule my temper because I must. Now I will go and find the destroyer of that dear life, Hector! Fate I will welcome whenever Zeus and All Gods may choose to bring it. . . . Don't try to keep me from the battle; you love me, I know, but you shall never persuade me."

Silverfoot Thetis answered:

"Yes indeed, my child, that is true, it is no bad thing to defend comrades in distress and danger of death. But your armour is in the enemy's hands. Hector is wearing that fine shining gear on his own shoulders. He is proud enough, yet I don't think he will have it long to boast of, for death is near him! But I do beseech you not to enter the battle until you see me here again. To-morrow I will come back at sunrise, with new armour from Hephaistos himself."

. . . Silverfoot Thetis set out for Olympos, to fetch new armour for her dear boy.

But all the while the Achaian rout went on, as Hector chased the fugitives with a terrible noise, until they came to their ships on the Hellespont. They could not get the body of Patroclos clear away; for Hector was on them again with horses and men like a consuming fire. Three times Hector caught him by the legs to drag him away, calling on his men. . . .

Indeed, he would have dragged it away in triumph, if Iris had not appeared—Hera sent her to Achillês without a word to Zeus or any other god. She gave her message clear and plain:

"Up, Peleidês! Show them your terrors! Go and help Patroclos! His body is the prize of this awful struggle —Trojans charging to drag him away to Troy, Danaäns fighting to hold him, all killing each other! And Hector most of all—he means to cut off his head and fix it upon the stakes! Up with you, don't lie there! You should be ashamed to let Trojan dogs tumble and tear Patroclos. Yours is the disgrace, if the body is brought in mangled and mutilated!" . . .

Achillês answered:

"And how can I go into the maul? My armour is in the hands of those men, and my mother forbids me to arm until I shall see her again between my eyes. She has promised to bring me fine new armour from Hephaistos. I don't know any other that I could use except the great shield of Aias Telamoniadês. But he is there in the front himself, I believe, using his spear to defend Patroclos."

Iris said:

"We know well enough that they hold your armour. But just go and show yourself at the moat, that the Trojans may be startled into quiet, and your people may have a breathing space. There's little time for breath in face of sudden death!"

Away went Iris at speed, and Achillês rose up. Over his broad shoulders Athena draped the tasselled aegis-cape: over his head she spread a golden haze; from his body shone a white-hot glow. We have seen a city on some island far away in the sea, besieged by enemies: all day long as they fight smoke rises to the sky, but when night falls we can see the beacons one after another signalling to the world for help with fires blazing high. So the light rose from the head of Achillês shining up to the sky, as he stepped from the wall and stood beside the moat. He did not mingle with his people, for he remembered his mother's strict command, but there he stood and shouted, and from far away Pallas Athena lifted up her voice; great was the confusion among the Trojans. The voice of Aiacidês sounded loud and clear, like the loud clear voice of a trumpet when fierce enemies beleaguer a city all about.

The Trojans heard the brazen voice of Aiacidês, and their hearts were filled with consternation. The horses turned away, foreboding evil to come. The charioteers were dumbfounded to see that bright and terrible light blazing above his head, the light which Athena had kindled. Thrice did Achillês shout aloud from the brink of the moat; thrice were confounded the Trojans and all their host. There also perished twelve men of their best, speared upon their own chariots by their own spears.

Then the Achaians were glad indeed to draw back the body of Patroclos out of the turmoil and lay it upon a bier. His companions trooped around it mourning; Achillês followed, weeping hot tears, when he saw his faithful friend stretched on the bier and torn with cruel wounds. He had sent him forth to the war with chariots and horses, hoping to welcome a safe return: but what a return was this!

The sun set unwearied, for Hera sent him unwilling down under the Ocean stream, and the Achaians at last had rest from their desperate struggle.

When the Trojans on their part had left the field of battle and unyoked the horses, they gathered in conference before they thought of food. All stood as they held their debate, none could endure to sit; for all were dismayed now Achillês had shown himself, after he had remained so long far from the battlefield.

Polydamas Panthoös' son was the first to speak, for he alone could look both before and behind. He was Hector's close friend. Both were born in one night; but one was first in debate, the other in battle. This man now addressed the assembly.

"Look well about you, my friends," he said. "My advice is to retire now to the city, and not to spend this night in the plain before the enemy camp. We are a long way from our walls. So long as yon man was incensed against King Agamemnon, the Achaians were easier to fight. I was glad myself to sleep near their ships, when I hoped we should take them. But now I am terribly afraid of Peleion. With his overbearing temper, he will never be content to stay in the middle plain where both sides share the battle; for him the stake is our city and our women.

"Then let us retreat to the city; listen to me, for this is what will happen. Just now the blessed night has checked his pursuit; but if he finds us here tomorrow when he sallies forth armed, many a man shall know him well. Many a Trojan shall be gnawed by dogs and vultures, and he that escapes will be glad of a refuge in Ilios—I only pray that the tale may be far from my ears!

"If we do as I say, with regret I am sure, we will keep our forces assembled, and the city will be safe behind walls and lofty gates and high doors well barred. To-morrow at dawn we will arm ourselves and take post along the walls. It will be the worse for him if he comes out and fights for our fortress! Back to the ships he will go, when he has had enough of exercising the horses and careering round the city. That temper of his will not give him leave to assault it, and take it he never shall—dogs shall devour him first!"

Hector frowned at him and said:

"I don't like what you say this time, Polydamas. Go back and huddle up in the city? Haven't you all enough of being cooped in behind walls? There was a time when the whole world talked of Priam's town, Troy the great magazine of gold and bronze! But now all our homes are stript of their treasures; many have been sold and gone to Phrygia or Meionia since Lord Zeus has been displeased. But now, you fool, do not publish those notions of yours any longer, just when the great god has granted me to win success before the enemy camp and to crush up the Achaians against the sea! Not a Trojan will listen to you—I will not allow it!

"Come now, all, do as I shall tell you. First let us take a good meal in our divisions, see after the watch, keep awake every man. If any Trojan is worried overmuch about his goods, let him collect them and distribute them to be mob-gobbled—it is better the people should enjoy them than our enemies! Tomorrow at dawn we will arm ourselves and make a great attack on the ships. If Achillês has really risen up by

Achillês binding the wounds of his friend Patroclos.

the ships, it shall be all the worse for him—just as he likes! I at least will never turn my back on battle! I will stand up to meet him, to win or lose it all. The God of War will see fair play—he's often slain that wants to slay!"

The Trojans cheered this speech, in their folly, for Pallas Athena stole their sense away. Hector's advice was bad, and they praised him: Polydamas offered good counsel, and no one praised him. Then they took their meal where they were.

But the Achaians mourned Patroclos all night long. Achillês led their lamentations, sobbing and pressing on his friend's breast those hands which had slain so many; groaning like a lion, when some hunter has robbed him of his cubs and he has come back too late. . . .

By this time Silverfoot Thetis had come to the house of Hephaistos—that brazen starry house incorruptible, preëminent among the immortals, which old Crookshank himself had made. She found him in a sweat, running about among his bellows, very busy. . . . The bellows he laid away from the fire, and collected all his working tools in a hutch of silver. Then he wiped a sponge over his face and both arms and sturdy neck and hairy chest, and put on his tunic, and limped out leaning on a thick stick, . . . he stumbled to a chair beside Thetis, saying:

"My dear Thetis, in all your finery! What brings you to our humble home? This in an honour, and I am glad to see you, my dear; you don't often pay us a visit. Tell me what you want; I shall be pleased to do it if it is doable, and if I can do it."

Thetis answered with tears running down her cheeks:

"My dear Hephaistos, is there any goddess in

Olympos who has troubles to bear like mine? Zeus Cronidês has chosen me out of all to make me miserable! . . . He gave me a son to bear and bring up, a hero of heroes. He ran up like a slim tree, I tended him like a rare plant in my garden, I let him go with the fleet to Ilios for the war—but I shall never get him back, he will never come home to his father's house! As long as he lives and sees the light of the sun, he has trouble, and I cannot go to help him. . . .

"So now I come to your knees with my prayer for my son, doomed to die so soon—Will you give him spear and helmet and a good pair of greaves with ankle-guards, and a corselet? What he had was lost when the Trojans killed his faithful friend, and there he lies on the ground in misery!"

The famous Crookshank answered:

"Cheer up, don't worry about that. He shall have his fine armour, and every man that sets eyes on it shall be amazed. I wish I could hide him from death as easily when that dreadful doom shall come!"

Without a moment's delay he went off to his bellows, poked them into the fire and told them to get to work. The bellows, twenty in all, blew under their melting-pots, ready to blow or to stop, letting out the blast strong, or weak, or just in any measure he wanted for his work. He put over the fire to melt, hard brass and tin, precious gold and silver. Then he placed a great anvil-stone on the block, and took hammer in one hand and tongs in the other.

First he fashioned a shield large and strong, adorning it with beautiful designs all over. He made a threefold rim round the edge of shining metal, and slung it on a silver baldric. There were five layers of hide in the shield; on the surface he laid his clever designs in metal. . . .

When the shield was finished, he fashioned a corselet that shone brighter than fire, he fashioned a strong helmet with a golden crest, he fashioned greaves of flexible tin.

Then the famous Crookshank craftsman brought all he had made and laid it before Thetis; and she shot like a falcon from snowy Olympos, bearing the bright armour to her son.

BOOK XIX

Dawn in her saffron robe arose out of the ocean stream, bringing light for heaven and earth; and Thetis came to the Achaian camp with the god's gifts for her son.

He lay with Patroclos in his arms, weeping bitterly, while his comrades were mourning around. The goddess clasped his hand and said:

39. greaves. The greaves were not meant to keep off a spear-thrust, but to prevent the edge of the shield from chafing the leg as the man walked. So they were short and pliable.—Translator's note.

"My child, we must let this man be, for all our sorrow. He is dead once for all, since that is God's will. Now for you: accept these fine gifts from Hephaistos. See how fine they are. No man has ever worn them!"

She laid them before Achillês in a rattling pile. The Myrmidons were too much startled to look at them and shrank back; but Achillês looked, and when he saw them, how his anger swelled, how his eyes blazed as if with some inward flame! But he was glad when he held in his own hands the glorious gifts of the god.

When he had enjoyed this pleasure for a while, he told her plainly what he meant to do.

"Mother," he said, "This armour is indeed the work of immortal hands, such as no man could make. Now I will get ready at once. But I am very much afraid the flies may get into my dear friend's wounds; worms will breed and make the flesh nasty—there's no life in it—the body will rot."

Thetis answered:

"Do not trouble about that, my child, I will see what I can do to keep off those savage tribes of flies which batten on those killed in war. Even if he lies here a whole twelvemonth his flesh will be as sound as ever, or sounder. What you must do is to call a meeting of the princes, and denounce your feud against King Agamemnon. Then you may arm yourself at once, and clothe you in your valour!"

Then she dropt into the dead man's nostrils red nectar and ambrosia to keep the flesh wholesome.

Achillês felt new courage after his mother's words. He paced along the shore calling aloud in a great voice, and summoned the Achaian princes. . . . After them came my lord Agamemnon, still suffering from the wound which he owed to Coön Antenor's son.

As soon as the assembly was full, Achillês rose to his feet and spoke.

"Atreidês, what good was it to us both, you and me, to take things to heart so, and to fall into a soul-devouring feud for a girl? I wish Artemis had shot her dead with an arrow on that day when I took Lyrnessos! Then all those brave men would have been saved who bit the dust in battle because I was angry! Hector and the Trojans got all the good there was; and I think the Achaian nation will not soon forget my feud and yours. But we must let bygones be bygones; we must forget our sorrow and control our temper, for we cannot help it. Then here is the end of my resentment, for I must not be angry for ever and ever. Come then, make haste and tell the army to get ready for battle. Let me meet the enemy face to face once more, and see if they would like to spend a quiet night near our ships. But I think there are some who will be glad to bend the knee in rest, if they escape from the battle when my spear shall drive them!"

The assembly was glad indeed to hear Achillês denounce his feud. Then King Agamemnon answered from the place where he was sitting, without coming forward to the front:

"My friends, my brave Danaäns—"

Here he was interrupted by cries and disturbance:

"My friends! it is right to give a hearing to any speaker who rises, it is not fair to break in. That makes it hard for the best of speakers. (Further disturbance.) With all this noise in the crowd how can a man speak? How can you hear? It is too much for the loudest voice.—Peleidês is the man—I want to explain things to him, please listen the rest of you and take note of what I say. (Loud cries: "It was all your fault!") People have said that to me often enough, and reproached me, but it was not *my* fault! Zeus—fate—the Avenger that walketh in darkness— it was *their* fault! *They* put that blind madness in my heart amongst you all, on that day when I robbed Achillês of his prize myself. But what could I do? God bringeth all things to pass! . . . But since I was blinded and Zeus took away my sense, I wish to make amends, and to pay anything in atonement.

"To the battle then, sir, I pray! Lead the army to battle! Treasures in plenty are here, and here am I ready to offer all that Odysseus promised you yesterday in your quarters. If you wish, wait now, though you are so fervent to begin. I will send servants to bring the treasures here, and you shall see that they are enough to content you."

Achillês answered:

"My lord King Agamemnon, as for treasures, they are yours to give, if you will, which is right and proper, or to keep; but now let us think of battle and at once. We must not waste time jabberwinding here. There is a great work yet undone. To see Achillês once more in the field and striking down the battalions of Troy with the spear—let each of you remember what that was, and fight his man!" . . .

Thus he dismissed the assembly, and they were soon dispersing to their ships. The Myrmidons took charge of the treasures and brought them to the ships of Achillês. They put away the goods in his quarters, and found a place for the women, and the grooms drove off the horses to join the rest. . . .

BOOK XX

. . . When Achillês appeared after his long absence, and the Trojans saw him sweep into the field with gleaming armour like a very god of war, their knees trembled beneath them in dismay, and for a long time the Achaians carried all before them. But as soon as the gods showed themselves, up rose Discord the mighty harrier of nations, loud shouted Athena, standing outside the wall on the edge of the moat, or moving upon the seashore; Arês shouted aloud from the other side, black as a stormcloud, crying his commands from the citadel of Troy, or speeding over Callicolonê by Simoeis river.

So the blessed gods drove the two hosts together and made the bitter strife burst forth. The Father of men and gods thundered terribly from on high, Poseidon made the solid earth quake beneath, and the tall summits of the hills; Mount Ida shook from head to foot, and the citadel of Ilios trembled, and the Achaian ships. Fear seized Aïdoneus the lord of the world below; fear made him leap from his throne and cry aloud, lest Poseidon Earthshaker should break the earth above him, and lay open to every eye those gruesome danksome abodes which even the gods abhor—so terrible was the noise when gods met gods in battle. For against Lord Poseidon stood Phoibos Apollo with his winged arrows, against Enyalios glaring Athena stood; Hera was faced by Shootafar's sister, Artemis Archeress, with her rattling golden shafts, Leto was faced by Luckbringer Hermês in his strength; and Hephaistos had before him that deep River, whom the gods call Xanthos, but men Scamandros.

Achillês longed most of all to meet Hector Priamidês. Hector he sought amid the press; with Hector's blood most of all he longed to glut the greedy god of war. . . .

BOOK XXII

. . . The old King Priam was the first to see him speeding over the plain. His armour shone on his breast, like the star of harvest whose rays are most bright among many stars, in the murky night: they call it Orion's Dog. Most brilliant is that star, but he is a sign of trouble, and brings many fevers for unhappy mankind.

The old man groaned, and lifting up his hands beat them upon his head as he groaned, and cried aloud to his son entreating him; but his son was standing before the gates immovable, and determined to meet Achillês face to face.

"O Hector!" the old man cried in piteous tones as he stretched out his hands, "Hector my beloved son! Do not face that man alone, without a friend, or fate will soon find you out! Do not be so hard-hearted! Peleion will destroy you, for he is stronger than you are. O that the gods loved him as I do! Soon would vultures and dogs feast on him lying on the ground! Then this cruel pain would pass from my heart. He has bereaved me of many sons, and good sons, killing and selling to far-off islands. . . .

"Do come within these walls, my son! Save the men and women of our city; life is sweet—do not let Achillês rob you of life and win glory for himself! Pity me also—an old man, but not too old to know, not too old to be unhappy! A miserable portion indeed Father Cronidês will give me then—to perish in my old age, after I have lived to see many troubles, seen my sons destroyed and my daughters dragged into slavery, my house ransacked, little children dashed on the ground in fury, my sons' wives dragged away by Achaian hands! And my self last of all—some one shall strike me down or pierce my body, and leave me dead at my door for carrion dogs to devour; my own table-dogs, my watchdogs, which I have fed with my own hands, will go mad and lap my blood, and lie sated by the door where they used to watch. For a young man all is decent when he is killed in battle; he may be mangled with wounds, all is honourable in his death whatever may come. But a hoary head, and a white beard, and nakedness violated by dogs, when an old man is killed, there is the most pitiable sight that mortal eyes can see."

As the old man spoke he tore the white hairs from his head; but Hector would not listen. His mother stood there also, weeping; she loosened the folds of her dress, and with the other hand bared her breast, and through her tears cried out the secrets of her heart:

"O Hector my own child, by *this* I beseech you, have pity on me, if ever I gave you the soothing breast! Remember this, my love, and come behind these walls—let these walls keep off that terrible man! Do not stand out in front against him, do not be so hard! For if he kill you, never shall I lay you on your bier, never shall I mourn over you, my pretty bud, son of my own body! Nor your precious wife— we shall both be far away, and Danaän dogs will devour you in the Danaän camp!"

But their tears and their prayers availed nothing with Hector's proud spirit. He stood fast, and awaited the coming of his tremendous foe. Like a serpent of the mountains over his hole, fed full of poisons and imbued with bitter hate, who lies in wait coiled about the hole and fiercely glaring, so Hector imbued with unquenchable passion would not retreat, but stood, leaning his shield against a bastion of the wall. Then deeply moved he spoke to his own heart:

"What shall I do? If I retreat behind these walls, Polydamas will be the first to heap reproaches on me, for he advised me to lead the army back to the city on that dread night when Achillês rose up. I would not listen—it would have been better if I had! And now that I have ruined them all by my rashness, I am ashamed to face the men and women of Troy, or some base fellows may say—Hector thought too much of his own strength, and ruined us all! They will say that: and my better part is to face him for life and death. Either I shall kill him and return in triumph, or I shall die with honour before the gate.

"Shall I lay down my shield and helmet and lean my spear against the wall, and go to meet him alone, and promise to yield Helen with all her wealth, all that Alexandros brought with her to Troy?—yield the woman who was the cause of the great war, let the princes of Argos take her away, offer to pay besides half the treasure of our city, make the elders of the city take oath to hide nothing but to divide honestly all we possess? But what good would that be? Suppose I should approach him, and then he would not have pity and would not spare me? Suppose I should strip off my armour, and then he should just kill me naked like a woman? This is no place for fairy tales, or lovers' pretty prattle, the way of a man with a maid, when man and maid prattle so prettily together! Better get to work at once; we'll see which of us the Olympian makes the winner!"

So he mused and stood his ground, while Achillês drew near, like Enyalios the warrior god, shaking over his right shoulder that terrible Pelian ashplant: the armour upon him shone like flaming fire or beams of the rising sun. Hector trembled to see him. He could stand no longer but took to flight, and Peleidês was upon him with a leap: Hector fled swiftly under the walls of Troy and Peleidês flew after him furiously, as a falcon swoops without effort after a timid dove, for he is the swiftest of flying things, and he darts upon her with shrieking cries close behind, greedy for a kill. They passed the look-out and the wind-beaten fig tree, keeping ever away from the wall along the cartroad, until they reached the two fountains which are the sources of eddying Scamandros. One is a spring of hot water, with steam rising above it as if it were boiling over a fire, one even in summer is cold as hail or snow or frozen ice. Near these are the tanks of stone, where the Trojan women and girls used to wash their linen in peace-time, before the Achaians came.

So far they came in their race, fleeing and pursuing, a strong man fleeing and a far stronger in pursuit: they ran hard, for Hector's life was the prize of this race, not such prizes as men run for, a beast or an oxhide shield. Thrice round the city of Priam they ran, like champion racehorses running round the turning-post for a tripod or a woman or some great stake, when a man is dead and the games are given in his honour. All the gods were watching, and the Father of gods and men exclaimed:

"Confound it, I love that man whom I see hunted round those walls! I am deeply grieved for Hector, who has sacrificed many an ox on the heights of Ida or the citadel of Troy! and now there is prince Achillês, chasing him round the city of Priam. What do you think, gods? Just consider, shall we save him from death, or shall we let Achillês beat him now? He is a brave man."

Athena Brighteyes replied:

"O Father Flashingbolt, O Thundercloud, you must never say that! A mortal man, long doomed by fate, and you will save him from death? Do as you please, but the rest of us cannot approve."

Zeus Cloudgatherer answered:

"Never mind, Tritogeneia, my love. I did not really mean it and I want to be kind to you. Wait no longer but do what you wish."

Athena was ready enough, and shot away down the slopes of Olympos.

Achillês was now following at full speed and gave Hector no chance. He watched him like a hound which has put up a hart from his lair, and gives chase through the dingles and the dells; let the hart hide and crouch in the brake, the hound tracks him out till he finds. If Hector going by the road made a dash at the city gates for refuge, hoping his friends might help him with a volley from the walls above, Achillês would take a short cut and get before him, running under the walls and turning him back towards the open ground. It was like some race in a dream, where one chases another, and he cannot catch or the other escape; so Achillês could never catch Hector, or Hector escape Achillês. How indeed could Hector have escaped his fleet pursuer so far, if Apollo had not then for the last time been near, to give him strength and speed? And Achillês had signalled to his own men that no one should let fly a shot at Hector, and take his own credit away if he came in second.

But when the fourth time they drew near the two fountains, see now, the Father laid out his golden scales and placed in them two fates of death, one for Achillês and one for Hector. He grasped the balance and lifted it: Hector's doom sank down, sank down to Hadês, and Apollo left him.

At that moment Athena was by the side of Achillês, and she said in plain words:

"Now you and I will win, my splendid Achillês! Now I hope we shall bring great glory to our camp before the Achaian nation, by destroying Hector, for all his insatiable courage. Now there is no chance that he can escape, not if Apollo Shootafar should fume and fret and roll over and over on the ground before Zeus Almighty! Rest and take breath, and I will go and persuade the man to stand up to you."

Achillês was glad of a rest, and stood still leaning on his barbed ashplant.

Athena now took the form and voice of Deïphobos: she went over to Hector and said to him simply:

"Achillês is giving you a hard time, old fellow, chasing you like this round the city. Let us stand and defend ourselves."

Hector answered:

"O Deïphobos, I always liked you best of all the sons of my father and mother! But now I shall think more of you than ever, for daring to come outside for my sake when you saw me here. All the rest keep inside!"

Athena said:

"My dear old fellow, father and mother and all our friends begged and besought me to stay, they are so terribly afraid of him; but I had not the heart to desert you. Now then let us have at him! No sparing of spears—let us see whether he will kill us both and carry off our bloodstained spoils, or if your spear shall bring him down!"

So the deceiver led him towards Achillês; and when they were near him Hector spoke:

"I will fly from you no more, Peleidês. Three times I raced round the city of Priam and would not await your attack; but now my heart bids me stand and face you, for death or for life. But first come near and let us give our troth; the gods shall be the best witnesses and sentinels of our agreement. If Zeus gives me endurance, and if I take your life, I will do no vile outrage to your body; I will take your armour, Achillês, and your body I will give back to your people. You do the same."

Achillês answered with a frowning face:

"Hector, I cannot forget. Talk not to me of bargains. Lions and men make no truce, wolves and lambs have no friendship—they hate each other for ever. So there can be no love between you and me; and there shall be no truce for us, until one of the two shall fall and glut Arês with his blood. Call up all your manhood; now you surely need to be a spearman and a bold man of war. There is no chance of escape now; this moment Pallas Athena shall bring you low by my spear. Now in one lump sum you shall pay for all my companions, whom you have slain and I have mourned."

With the words he poised and cast his long spear. But Hector saw it coming and crouched down, so that it flew over and stuck in the earth. Pallas Athena pulled it out and gave it back to Achillês, but Hector saw nothing. Then Hector said:

"A miss! I am not dead yet as you thought, most magnificent Achillês! So there was something Zeus did not tell you about me, as it seems. You are only a rattletongue with a trick of words, trying to frighten me and make me lose heart. I am not going to run and let you pierce my back—I will charge you straight, and then you may strike me in the breast if it be God's will, but first see if you avoid *my* spear! I pray that you may take it all into your body! The war would be lighter for Troy if you were dead, for you are our greatest danger."

He poised his spear and cast it, and hit the shield fair in the middle; but the spear rebounded and fell away. Hector was troubled that the cast had failed; he had no second spear, and he stood discomfited. Then he shouted to Deïphobos and called for another, but no Deïphobos was there. Now Hector knew the truth, and cried out:

"All is lost! It is true then, the gods have summoned me to death. Deïphobos was by my side I thought—but he is in the city and I have been deceived by Athena. Now then, death is near me, there can be no delay, there is no escape. All this while such must have been the pleasure of Zeus and his son Shootafar, who have kindly protected me so far: but now fate is upon me. Yet I pray that I may die not without a blow, not inglorious. First may I do some notable thing that shall be remembered in generations to come!"

With these words he drew the sword that hung by his side, sharp and strong, gathered himself and sprang, like an eagle flying high and swooping down from the clouds upon a lamb or cowering hare. Achillês moved to meet him full of fury, covering his chest with the resplendent shield while the thick golden plumes nodded upon his flashing helmet. His right hand held poised the great spear, which gleamed like the finest of all the stars of heaven, the star of evening brilliant in the dark night; he scanned Hector with ruthless heart, to see where the white flesh gave the best opening for a blow. Hector was well covered with that splendid armour which he had stript from Patroclos, but an opening showed where the collar-bones join the neck to the shoulder, the gullet, where a blow brings quickest death. There Achillês aimed, and the point went through the soft neck; but it did not cut the windpipe, and Hector could still answer his foe. He fell in the dust, and Achillês cried in triumph:

"There, Hector! You thought no doubt while you were stripping Patroclos that you would be safe; you cared nothing for me far away. Fool! There was an avenger, a stronger man than Patroclos, waiting far away! I was there behind in the camp, and I have brought you low! Now you shall be mauled by vultures and dogs, and he shall be buried by a mourning nation!"

Hector half-fainting answered:

"I beseech you by your soul and by your knees, by your father and your mother, do not leave me for dogs to mangle among your ships—accept a ransom, my father and my mother will provide gold and treasure enough, and let them carry home my body, that my people may give me the fire, which is the rightful due of the dead."

Achillês said with an angry frowning face:

"Knee me no knees, you cur, and father me no fathers! No man living shall keep the dogs from your head—not if they bring ransom ten times and twenty times innumerable, and weigh it out, and promise more, not if Priamos Dardanidês pay your weight in gold—not for that ransom shall your mother lay you out on the bier and mourn for the son of her womb, but carrion dogs and carrion birds shall devour you up! For what you have done to me I wish from the bottom of my heart that I could cut you to pieces and eat you raw myself!"

Hector answered him dying:

"Ah, I know you well, and I forebode what will be. I was not likely to persuade you, for your heart is made of iron. But reflect! or I may bring God's wrath upon you, on that day when Paris and Phoibos Apollo shall slay you by the Scaian Gate, although you are strong."

As he spoke, the shadow of death encompassed him; and his soul left the body and went down to Hadês, bewailing his fate, bidding a last farewell to manhood and lusty strength. Hector was dead, but even so Achillês again spoke:

"Lie there dead! My fate I will accept, whenever it is the will of Zeus and All Gods to fulfil it."

He drew the spear out of the body and laid it aside. Then he stript off the armour, and the other Achaians came crowding round. How they gazed in wonder at Hector's noble form and looks! Yet no one came near without a stab; they beat him and stabbed him, saying to each other:

"Ha ha! Hector feels very much softer now than when he burnt our ships with his blazing brands!"

Achillês, when he finished stripping the spoils, turned to the crowd, and made them a speech in his downright manner.

"My friends," he said, "princes and captains of the nation, since as you see the gods have granted me to kill this man who has done us more damage than all the rest put together, let us go round the city ready for battle, and find out what they mean to do: whether they will leave their fortress now this man is dead, or whether they will still confront us although they have no Hector.—But stay, what am I thinking about! Patroclos lies beside our ship unmourned, unburied! Patroclos I can never forget so long as I live and move! And even if in the house of Hadês men forget their dead, yet I will remember my dear comrade even there. Come on, my lads, let us march back to our ships singing our hymn of victory, and bring this man with us. We have won a great triumph; we have killed Hector, to whom the Trojans prayed as if he were a god!"

And then he thought of a shameful outrage. He cut behind the sinews of both Hector's feet from ankle to heel and strapt them together with leather thongs, and fastened them to his chariot leaving the head to drag. Then he laid the armour in the car, and got in himself and whipt up the horses. Away they flew: the dust rose as the body was dragged along, the dark hair spread abroad, there in the dirt trailed the head that was once so charming, which now Zeus gave to his enemies to maltreat in his own native land. And as the head was bedabbled thus in the mire, his mother tore her hair and threw away the covering veil, and wailed aloud seeing her son; his father lamented sore, the people wailed, and lamentation filled the city. Such lamentation there might have been, if all frowning Ilios were smouldering in ashes.

The people had much ado to keep the old King in his frenzy from rushing out of the Dardanian Gate. He rolled in the dung-heap and appealed to all, naming each by his name:

"Have done, my friends! I know you love me, but let me go out alone and visit the Achaian camp—let me pray to this terrible violent man! He may have shame before his fellows, and pity an old man—yes, I think he has an old father like me, Peleus, who begat him and bred him to be the ruin of Troy! And for me more than all he has brought trouble—so many of my sons he has killed in their prime! I mourn for them, but not for them all so much as one, who will bring me down with sorrow to the grave, my Hector. Would that he had died in my arms! Then we could have mourned and wept till we could weep no more, the unhappy mother who bore him, and I his father."

As he spoke, he wept, and the people lamented with him. Then Hecabê led the women's lamentation, herself weeping the while:

"My child, I am desolate: how shall I live in sorrow when you are dead? Night and day you were my boast in the city, and a blessing to all, both men and women, who used welcome you as one divine. Truly you were a great glory to them also while you lived, but now death and fate has come upon you!"

But Hector's wife had not yet heard anything of her husband; no messenger had told her the truth, that he remained outside the gate. She was busy with her loom in a far corner of the house, embroidering pretty flowers on a wide purple web. She called to the servants to put a cauldron to boil on the fire, that Hector might have a warm bath when he came in from the battle. Poor creature, she knew not that he was far away from all baths, brought low by the hands of Achillês and the will of Brighteyes Athena.

But when she heard lamentation and wailing from the wall, her limbs quivered and the shuttle fell to the ground out of her hand, and she called to her maids:

"Here, come with me two of you and let me see what has happened. That was the voice of my honoured goodmother! My heart is in my mouth—my knees are turned to stone! Some trouble is at hand for the sons of Priam! Far from my ear be that word! But I am terribly afraid prince Achillês has cut off my rash Hector by himself and driven him away to the plain! Ah, he will put an end to the fatal pride that always possessed him, for Hector would never stay in the crowd—he would always run out in front and yield in courage to no man!"

She tore out like a mad woman with beating heart, and the maids followed. When she came to the crowd of men on the battlements, she stood peering about— then she saw him dragged along in front of the city; the horses were dragging him at full speed towards the Achaian camp, careless what they did. Then the darkness of night came over her eyes, and she fell backwards fainting and gasping; the coverings fell from her head—diadem, coif, braided circlet, and the veil which golden Aphroditê had given her, on the day when Hector paid his rich bride-gifts and led her away from Eëtion's house. Crowding round her were Hector's sisters and goodsisters holding her up, distracted unto death.

When she came to herself and revived, she cried out amid her sobs:

"O Hector, I am unhappy! So we were both born to one fate, you in Troy in the palace of Priam, I in Thebê under woody Placos, in the house of Eëtion who brought me up as a tiny tot—doomed father, doomed child! Would I had never been born! Now you have gone to the house of Hadês deep down under the earth; but I am left in bitter grief a widow in our home. And our son is still only a baby—O doomed father, doomed mother! Never will you be a blessing to him, Hector, or he to you: for you are dead. Even if he escapes from this miserable war, yet his portion shall be always labour and sorrow, for strangers will rob him of his lands.

"The day of orphanhood makes a child wholly friendless. He must always hang his head, his cheeks are slobbered with tears, he goes begging to his father's friends, and plucks one by the cloak, another by the shirt; if one has pity he puts a cup to his mouth for a sip, wets the lips but not the palate. The boy who has both father and mother slaps him and drives him away from the table with unkind words— 'Just get out! Your father does not dine with us.' Then the boy runs crying to his widowed mother—yes, Astyanax, who once sat on his own father's knee and ate only marrow and richest fat of sheep! And when he felt sleepy and did not want to play any more; he slept on a bedstead, with nurse's arms around him, with a soft bed under him, full and satisfied.

"But now he will have plenty to suffer since his father is gone—my Astyanax as they all call him in this city, because you alone saved their gates and walls. And now you are in the enemy camp, far from your father and mother, and when the dogs have had enough, crawling worms will eat your body—naked, although there is nice soft linen in your house made by your own women. But I will make a bonfire of the whole store; it is of no use to you, for your body will not lie out in that, but it will do you honour in the eyes of the people of Troy."

She wept while she spoke, and the women lamented with her.

BOOK XXIV

. . . Thus Achillês maltreated Hector in his rage. But the blessed gods were offended at this pitiable sight, and wished to send Hermês Argeiphontês to steal him away. Most of the gods approved this; but not Hera nor Poseidon nor the bright-eyed Maiden. They continued as they had been, when first they came to hate sacred Troy, and Priam and his people, for the blind delusion of Alexandros: he had affronted those goddesses, when they came to his farmyard and he preferred the one who granted his shameful lust.

But when the twelfth dawn came, Phoibos Apollo said at last:

"You are hard, you gods, you are torturers! Has not Hector in times past burnt you thigh-pieces of bulls and goats without blemish? Yet you can't bear to save his dead body for his wife to see, and his mother and his son, and Priam his father and his people, to let them burn him in the fire, and perform the rites of burial. But that abominable Achillês—he is the man you want to help, gods—the man who has no sense of decency, no mercy in his mind! . . ."

This made Hera angry, and she retorted:

"That might be all very well, Silverbow, if you are going to put Achillês and Hector in the same rank. Hector's a mortal and sucked a woman's pap, but Achillês had a goddess for his mother—I brought her up myself from a little one, and gave her away as a wife to a man, to Peleus, who was in high favour with the immortals. You were all at the wedding, gods—and you too, there you sat with your harp—but you prefer low company and no one can ever trust you!"

Here Zeus broke in:

"My dear Hera, don't go and get spiky with the gods. They shan't be in the same rank at all, but Hector really was a prime favourite with the gods more than any man in Troy,—at least, I thought so, for he never failed in his friendly offerings. . . . Let one of you call Thetis before me, and I will give her some good advice. Achillês must accept ransom from Priam and let him have Hector."

This was no sooner said, than stormfoot Iris was off with her message. Midway between Samothrace and rocky Imbros down she plunged into the dark sea with a splash, plunged into the deep like the leaden plummet on a horn-bait which carries death to the greedy fishes.

She found Thetis in a vaulted cave. . . . Iris stood before her and said:

"Rise up, Thetis, Zeus Allwise summons you before him."

. . . They stept out on the beach and shot up to heaven.

There they found Cronidês Allseeing, and the deathless gods were seated about him in full assembly. . . .

Then the Father of gods and men spoke:

". . . For nine days there has been quarrelling in our family about Hector's body and Achillês. They want Argeiphontês to steal the body away, but I want to keep your respect and affection in time to come, and so I propose to raise your son even higher in men's esteem, and this is how it will be done.

"Go straight to the camp. Tell your son the gods are angry with him, and I most of all have been moved to wrath, because in his mad passion he keeps Hector and has not let him go. I hope he will fear me and let him go. I will send Iris myself to King Priam, and bid him to visit the Achaian camp and ransom his son. He shall bring treasure enough to warm the heart of Achillês."

Thetis lost no time. . . .

Away went stormfoot Iris on her errand. She came to Priam's, and there she found groaning and lamentation. . . .

The messenger drew near to Priam; he fell into a fit of trembling, and she spoke softly to him:

"Fear nothing, Priamos Dardanidês, be not anxious at all. I come here with no evil tidings, but with good in my heart for you. I am a messenger from Zeus, who far away cares for you much and pities you. The Olympian bids you ransom Prince Hector. You are to carry treasure to Achillês, enough to warm his heart. You must be alone; no other Trojan must go with you. . . . You are not to fear death or to be anxious at all. Zeus will provide for that by sending Argeiphontês as your escort, and he shall lead you as far as Achillês. Even when he shall lead you into the hut, neither Achillês nor any one else will kill you, for he will prevent them. Achillês is not stupid or thoughtless or impious, and he will be scrupulous to spare a suppliant man." . . .

Now the old King made haste to mount his car, and drove out of the front gateway from the echoing gallery. The mules went in front drawing their four-wheeled wagon, with Idaios driving, and the horses followed driven by the old King. As they passed quickly through the city, all his kinsfolk followed weeping and wailing as if he were going to his death. But as soon as they had come down from the city upon the plain, these all went back, sons and good-sons together.

Zeus did not fail to see the two men when they appeared upon the plain. He pitied the old King, and said to Hermês his son:

"Hermês, you always like to make friends with a man and have a talk with any one you fancy. Off with you then, and lead Priam to the Achaian camp. Take care that no one sees or takes any notice until you get to Peleion."

Argeiphontês was willing enough. He put on those fine boots, golden, incorruptible, which carry him over moist or dry to the ends of the earth as quick as the wind; and he took the rod that bewitches the eyes of men to sleep, or wakes the sleeping. Holding this, Argeiphontês flew until he reached the Hellespont and the land of Troy. There he took the shape of a young prince with the first down upon his lip, the time when youth is most charming.

The others had just passed beyond the great barrow of Ilos, and they halted by the river to give the animals a drink; for darkness had come by this time. The herald looked out and noticed Hermês not far off, and he said to his master:

" 'Ware man, Dardanidês! a wary mind now is what we want. I spy a man! and I surmise he'll soon tear us to pieces. Come, let us take the horse-car and be off —unless you would have us clasp his knees and beg for mercy."

The old man was all confusion and frightened to death; he felt gooseflesh all over his body and stood dazed, but Hermês Luckbringer came up of himself and said, taking him by the hand:

"Whither away, father, with horses and mules in the dead of night, when mortal men are all asleep but you? Have you no fear of the Achaians breathing fury, your enemies, and bad men to meet? If one of them saw you driving all these commodities through the black night, what would you do then? You are not young yourself, and this your follower is old for defence if some one wants to pick a quarrel. But I will do you no harm, indeed I would protect you. You remind me of my own father."

Then the old King replied:

"Things are very much as you say, dear boy. But there is still some god even for me, who stretched a hand over me when he sent a wayfarer like you to meet me—a good man to meet, if I may judge from your handsome looks and shape, and no unmannerly savage. You must come of a good family."

Argeiphontês answered:

"Quite right, sir, that is true enough. But tell me please if I may ask you, are you exporting all these precious goods to a foreign land just to put them in safety? Or are you all deserting sacred Troy in fear? For the great man has perished, the noblest of them all—your son. He never hung back from the battlefield!"

The old King said:

"And who are you, noble sir, what is your family? How truly you have told me the passing of my ill-fated son!"

Argeiphontês replied:

"You are trying me, sir, when you ask about noble Hector. Often I have seen him with my own eyes in the field of glory—then also when he drove the Achaians upon their ships, and slew and slew, making havoc with his blade! We had to stand and admire, for Achillês would not let us fight because of his rancour against Agamemnon. I am a servant of his, and we came over in the same ship. . . ."

Then old King Priam said:

"If you are really a servant of Achillês Peleidês, pray tell me the whole truth. Is my son still there by the ships, or has Achillês cut him to pieces and thrown him to the dogs?"

Argeiphontês answered:

"Dear sir, no dogs and vultures have touched him yet, but there he lies beside the ship of Achillês as he was. Twelve days he has been lying there, and his flesh is not decayed, nor do the worms eat him as they eat the dead on the battlefield. It is true Achillês drags him callously round his comrade's barrow at dawn every day, but it does him no harm. You would open your eyes if you could come and see how he lies as fresh as dew, washed clean of blood and nowhere nasty. The wounds have all healed up, and there were many who pierced him. See how the gods care for your son even in death, for he was very dear to them!"

This made the old man happy, and he replied:

"My dear boy, it is good indeed to give the immortals their proper due, for my dead son as truly as he lived never forgot the gods who dwell in Olympos. Therefore they have remembered him, although death is now his portion. But pray do accept from me this pretty cup, and protect me and guide me with God's help, that I may find my way to the hut of Peleidês."

Argeiphontês said:

"You are trying me, sir; you are old, and I am young, but I cannot consent, when you ask me to accept a gift behind the back of Achillês. I fear him, and I should be heartily ashamed to defraud him, or something bad might happen to me. But you shall be my charge. I would guide you carefully as far as Argos, by land or by sea, and no one should despise your guide or attack you."

With this, Luckbringer jumped into the car, and took whip and reins into his hands, and filled horses and mules with spirit. So they went on until they reached the wall and moat. The watchmen were then busy about their supper; but Argeiphontês sent them all to sleep, and in a moment ran back the bars, and opened the gates, and brought in Priam and the wagon with its precious cargo.

They came at last to the hut of Achillês. It was a tall building which the men had made for their prince, walls of fir-planks thatched with a downy roofing of reeds which they had gathered from the meadows. In front was a wide courtyard surrounded by thickset stakes. The door was held by one fir-wood bar; it took three men to push home the bar, and three men to pull it open, but Achillês could push it home by himself. This time, Hermês jumped down and opened the door for the old King, and brought in the precious gifts for Achillês. After that he said:

"I must tell you, sir, that I am an immortal god, Hermês, and my Father sent me to be your guide. But I must go back now, and I must not show myself to Achillês. It would be a shocking thing if a mortal should entertain an immortal god for all to see. You go in and clasp his knees, and beseech him in the name of his father and mother and his son, to touch his heart."

So Hermês took his leave and went back to Olympos.

But Priam dismounted and went towards the house, leaving Idaios where he was, to hold the horses and mules. He found Achillês alone: only two were waiting upon him, Automedon and Alcimos, and he had just finished eating and drinking; the table was still beside him. Priam came in, but they did not see him; he came near Achillês and clasped his knees, and kissed the terrible murderous hands which had killed so many of his sons.

Achillês looked with amazement at royal Priam, and the two men also were amazed and stared at each other, as people stare when some one from a foreign land takes refuge in a rich man's house, after he has killed a man in a fit of madness and has to flee the country.

Then Priam made his prayer:

"Remember your own father, most noble prince Achillês, an old man like me near the end of his days. It may be that *he* is distressed by those who live round about him, and there is no one to defend him from peril and death. But *he* indeed, so long as he hears that you still live, is glad at heart and hopes every day that he will see his well-loved son return home from Troy. But I am all-unhappy, since I had the best sons in the broad land of Troy, and I say not one of them has been left. Fifty I had when the men of Achaia came; nineteen born to me of one womb, the others of women in my household. All those many have fallen in battle; and my only one, who by himself was our safeguard, that one you killed the other day fighting for his country, Hector: for him I come now to your camp, to redeem him from you, and I bring a rich ransom. O Achillês, fear God, and pity me, remembering your own father—but I am even more to be pitied—I have endured to do what no other man in the world has ever done, to lift my hand to the lips of the man who slew my son."

As he said it, he lifted his hand to the face of Achillês, and the heart of Achillês ached with anguish at the thought of his father. He took the old man's hand, and pushed him gently away. So the two thought of their dead and wept, one for his Hector while he crouched before the feet of Achillês, and Achillês for his own father and then for Patroclos. When his agony had passed and he could move

again, he got up from his seat and raised the old man by the hand, pitying his white hairs and white beard, and spoke simply from heart to heart:

"Ah, poor man, indeed your heart has borne many sorrows! How could you come to the Achaian camp alone? How could you bear to look on the man who killed all your noble sons, as I have done? Your heart must be made of steel. Come now, sit down upon a seat. We will let our sorrows lie deep in our hearts awhile, for there is no profit in freezing lamentation. This is the way the gods have spun their threads for poor mortals! Our life is all sorrow, but they are untroubled themselves.

"Zeus has two jars of the gifts that he gives, standing upon the floor beside him, one of good things and one of evil things. When the Thunderer mixes and gives, a man meets with good sometimes and bad other times: when he gives all bad, he makes the man despised and rejected; grinding misery drives him over the face of the earth, and he walks without honour from gods or from men. And so with Peleus, the gods gave him glorious gifts from his birth, for he was preëminent in the world for wealth and riches, he was King over the Myrmidons, and although he was mortal they made a goddess his wife. But God gave him evil too, because he got no family of royal princes in his palace, but only one son, to die before his time. And now he is growing old, and I cannot care for him; for I am here in Troy, far from my country, troubling you and your children.

"You also, sir, once were happy, as we hear: upsea as far as Lesbos the seat of Macar, upland to Phrygia, and along the boundless Hellespont, you were paramount with your riches and your sons. But ever since the lords of Heaven brought this calamity upon you, there has been nothing but battle and manslaughter about your city. Endure it, and let not your heart be uncomforted; for you will have no profit by sorrowing for your son. You will never raise him from the dead; before that, some other trouble will come upon you."

The old King answered:

"Tell me not yet to be seated, gracious prince, while Hector lies here uncared-for. I pray you set him free quickly, that I may look upon him; and accept the ransom that we bring, a great treasure. May you live to enjoy it and return to your own country, since you have spared me first."

Achillês frowned and said:

"Tease me no more, sir, I mean myself to set your Hector free. Zeus sent me a message by my mother, the daughter of the Old Man of the Sea. And I understand quite well, sir, that some god brought you into our camp. For no mere man would dare to come among us, let him be ever so young and strong. He

---

43-44. **lift my hand,** the suppliant's gesture, to touch the chin and caress the lower part of the face. It is clear that Priam does so at this moment, although Homer does not say so; but I have no doubt the minstrel raised his hand, as a Greek would do in reciting such a story, and this would take the place of words.—Translator's note.

53-54. **raised . . . hand.** To raise one by the hand implied accepting him into protection.—Translator's note.

could not escape the guards, and he could not easily lever back the bolt of our doors. Then provoke my temper no more in my sorrow, or I may not spare even you, sir, although you are a suppliant, and that would be sin against the commands of Zeus."

The old man was afraid, and said no more; but Peleidês leapt out like a lion, and the two attendants followed, Automedon and Alcimos, the men whom he trusted most after the dead Patroclos. They unharnessed the horses and mules, and led in the old King's crier to a seat. Then they unpacked Hector's ransom from the wagon, except two sheets and a tunic, which they left to wrap up the body for its journey home. Achillês called out women to wash and anoint the body, but first he moved it out of the way. He did not wish Priam to see his son, and perhaps burst into anger from the sorrow of his heart when he saw him, for then he feared that he might be provoked himself to kill him and sin against the commands of Zeus.

After the women had washed the body and anointed it with oil, and put on the tunic and wrapt the sheet around, Achillês himself lifted him, and laid him upon the bier, and his attendants carried him to the mule-car. Then he cried aloud and called on the name of his lost friend:

"Don't be cross with me, Patroclos, if you hear even in Hadês that I have given back Hector to his father, since the ransom he paid is not unworthy. You shall have your due share of this also."

Then Achillês returned into his hut, and sat down on the bench where he had been before, against the opposite wall, and spoke to Priam:

"Your son, sir, has been set free now as you asked, and he lies on his bier. At break of day you shall see him yourself, on your journey. . . .

"Well then, venerable prince, let us two also think of something to eat. After that, you may weep for your son again when you have brought him back to Ilios. Many tears he will cost you!" . . .

When they had eaten and drunk all they wanted, Priamos Dardanidês gazed at Achillês, admiring his fine looks and stature—indeed he seemed like some god come down from heaven. And Achillês gazed at Priamos Dardanidês, admiring his noble face and speech. They looked at each other a long time, and then the old King said:

"Put me to bed now quickly, my prince, let us lie down and sleep quietly and rest; for my eyes have never closed under my eyelids since my son lost his life at your hands. All this time I have mourned and brooded over my endless sorrow, tossing about in the muck of my courtyard. Now I have tasted food, and I have let the wine run down my throat; until now I had touched nothing."

Achillês gave orders at once to lay beds in the porch, and strew on them rugs of fine purple with blankets above and woollen robes to wear. The women torch in hand went to get ready two beds, and Achillês said a light word or two:

"You must lie outside, my dear sir, for I may have a visit from one of the councillors from headquarters —they are for ever coming and sitting here and counselling their counsels as if it were a public meeting! If one of them should spy you here in the middle of the night, he would go at once and report it to his majesty King Agamemnon, and there would be delay in releasing the dead. . . ."

Then he clasped the old man's right wrist, that he might fear nothing, and led him to the porch where he was to sleep with the herald. Achillês himself lay to rest in a corner of the hut, with lovely Briseïs by his side.

All were fast asleep throughout that night both in heaven and on earth, except Hermês, who could not sleep for thinking how he should bring away King Priam out of the camp and keep the watchmen at the gate from seeing. He stood by the old man's bed and said to him:

"Sir! you do not seem to care what happens, sleeping like that in the midst of your enemies because Achillês spared you! Now then: you have redeemed your son, you have paid a heavy ransom: but you alive will cost three times as much for your other sons to get you back, if Agamemnon Atreidês finds out, or the Achaians find out!"

This frightened the old man, and he woke up the herald: Hermês harnessed the horses and mules and drove quickly through the camp, and no one found out.

But when they reached the ford of the Xanthos, Hermês left them and returned to Olympos.

Then the saffron robe of Dawn spread over all the earth, and they drove towards the city mourning and lamenting, while the mules brought the dead. No man and no woman had seen them coming: Cassandra was the first. She had gone up into the citadel, and from there she caught sight of her father standing in his car, and the city-crier, and the other lying on a bier in the mule-wagon. She lifted her voice in wailing, and cried for the whole town to hear:

"Come, all you men and women of Troy! You shall see Hector! Come, if ever you were glad while he lived to welcome his return from battle, for he was a great gladness to the city and all the nation!"

Then grief intolerable came upon every heart. Not a man, not a woman was left behind in the city; all crowded out of the gates and met the dead. First came his wife and his mother tearing their hair; they ran to the wagon and threw their arms over his head, while the people stood mourning around. They would have stayed there all day weeping and wailing, but the old King called out from his car:

"Let the mules pass. When I have brought him

into our house you will have plenty of time to lament."

So the people made a way for the wagon to pass.

When he had been brought home, they laid him out on a bier, and posted beside him mourners to lead the dirge, who sang their lamentable dirge while the women wailed in chorus. Andromachê laid her white arms about the head of her dead warrior, and led the lament:

"My husband, you have perished out of life, still young, and left me a widow in the house! The boy is only a baby, your son and my son, doomed father, doomed mother! and he I think will never grow up to manhood; long before that our city will be utterly laid waste! For you have perished, you our watchman, you our only saviour, who kept safe our wives and little children! They will soon be carried off in ships, and I with them. And you, my child!—you will go with me where degrading tasks will be found for you to do, drudging under a merciless master; or some enemy will catch you by the arm, and throw you over the wall to a painful death, in revenge perhaps for some brother that Hector killed, or father, or son maybe, since many a man bit the dust under the hands of Hector: your father was not gentle in the field of battle! Therefore the people throughout the city lament for him,—and you have brought woe and mourning unspeakable upon your parents, Hector! But for me most of all cruel sorrow shall be left. For you did not stretch out to me your dying hands from your deathbed, you said no precious word to me, which I might always remember night and day with tears!"

So Andromachê spoke weeping, and the women wailed in chorus.

Then Hecabê led the lament amid her sobs:

"Hector, best beloved of all my children, dearest to my heart! Living the gods loved you well, therefore they have cared for you even when death is your lot. Other sons of mine Achillês took, and he would sell them over the barren sea, one to Samos, one to Imbros, or to steaming Lamnos; but you—when he had torn out your soul with his sharp blade, he dragged you again and again round the barrow of his comrade whom you slew; but that did not bring him back from the grave! And now you lie in my house fresh as the morning dew, like one that Apollo Silverbow has visited and slain with his gentle shafts!"

So Hecabê spoke weeping, and the women wailed long in chorus.

Helen came third and led the lament:

"Hector, best beloved of all my goodbrothers, and dearest to my heart! Indeed my husband is prince Alexandros, who brought me to Troy—but would that I had died first! Twenty years have passed since I left my country and came here, but I never heard from you one unkind or one slighting word. If any one else reproached me, a sister or brother of yours, or a brother's wife, or your mother—for your father was always as kind as if he were mine—you would reprove them, you would check them, with your gentle spirit and gentle words. Therefore I weep for you, and with you for my unhappy self. For there is no one else in the length and breadth of Troy who is kind or friendly; they all shudder at me."

So she spoke weeping, and the people wailed long and loud.

Then old King Priam said:

"Now, Trojans, fetch wood into the city, and have no fear of any ambush of our enemies. For Achillês in parting from me promised that he would do us no harm until the twelfth day shall dawn."

Then they put oxen and mules to their wagons and assembled before the city. Nine days they gathered infinite quantities of wood; when the tenth day dawned, they carried out brave Hector weeping, and laid the body on the pile and set it on fire.

When on the next day Dawn showed her rosy fingers through the mists, the people gathered round about the pyre of Hector. First they quenched the flame with wine wherever the fire had burnt; then his brothers and his comrades gathered his white bones, with hot tears rolling down their cheeks. They placed the bones in a golden casket, and wrapt it in soft purple cloth; this they laid in a hollow space and built it over with large stones. Quickly they piled a barrow, with men on the look-out all round in case the Achaians should attack before their time.

This work done they returned to the city, and the whole assemblage had a famous feast in the palace of Priam their King.

That was the funeral of Hector.

The Odyssey

BOOK I

THIS is the story of a man, one who was never at a loss. He had travelled far in the world, after the sack of Troy, the virgin fortress; he saw many cities of men, and learnt their mind; he endured many troubles and hardships in the struggle to save his own life and to bring back his men safe to their homes. He did his best, but he could not save his companions. For they perished by their own madness, because they killed and ate the cattle of Hyperion the Sun-god, and the god took care that they should never see home again.

At the time when I begin, all the others who had not been killed in the war were at home, safe from

The Odyssey. Abridged from *The Odyssey*, translated by W. H. D. Rouse. Copyright, 1937, by W. H. D. Rouse. Used by permission of Thomas Nelson and Sons, Ltd., publishers.

the perils of battle and sea: but he was alone, longing to get home to his wife. He was kept prisoner by a witch, Calypso, a radiant creature, and herself one of the great family of gods, who wanted him to stay in her cave and be her husband. Well then, the seasons went rolling by, and when the year came, in which by the thread that fate spins for every man he was to return home to Ithaca, he had not yet got free of his troubles and come back to his own people. The gods were all sorry for him, except Poseidon, god of the sea, who bore a lasting grudge against him all the time until he returned.

But it happened that Poseidon went for a visit a long way off, to the Ethiopians; who live at the ends of the earth, some near the sunrise, some near the sunset. There he expected a fine sacrifice of bulls and goats, and there he was, feasting and enjoying himself mightily; but the other gods were all gathered in the palace of Olympian Zeus.

Then the Father of gods and men made them a speech; for his heart was angry against a man, Aigisthos, and Agamemnon's son Orestês, as you know, had just killed the man. So he spoke to the company as follows:

"Upon my word, just see how mortal men always put the blame on us gods! We are the source of evil, so they say—when they have only their own madness to thank if their miseries are worse than they ought to be. . . ."

Then up spoke Athena, with her bright eyes glinting: ". . . But what about that clever Odysseus? I am anxious about him, poor fellow, kept from his friends all this while, in trouble and sorrow, in that island covered with trees, and nothing but the waves all round it, in the very middle of the sea! It is the home of one of ourselves, the daughter of Atlas, you remember, that creature of mischief, who knows all the depths of the sea; you know, he holds up the pillars which keep earth and heaven apart. It is his daughter who keeps the wretched man a prisoner. She is always coaxing him with soft deceitful words to forget Ithaca; but Odysseus would be happy to see as much as the smoke leaping up from his native land, and then to die. And you cannot spare him a thought, Olympian. Don't you owe him something for all those sacrifices which he used to offer in their camp on the plain of Troy? Why have you such an odd grudge against him, Zeus?"

Then Zeus Cloudgatherer answered:

"My child, what a word to let out between your teeth! How could I forget that fine fellow Odysseus, after all! He is almost one of us. Wise beyond mortal men, ready beyond all to offer sacrifice to the lords of the broad heavens. But Poseidon Earthholder bears him unrelenting hatred, because of the Cyclops whose eye he put out; I mean Polyphemos, who has our blood in his veins, the most powerful of all the Cyclopians.

"Thoösa was his mother, the daughter of Phorcys prince of the barren brine; Poseidon possessed her in a hollow cave. Ever since then, Poseidon has kept the man wandering about, although he does not kill him outright. Come now, let us all try to think how we can persuade Poseidon to abate his anger and let him go home to his native land. Surely he will not be able to stand out against all the immortals, and keep up a quarrel all by himself!"

Then Athena said:

"Cronidês our Father, King of Kings and Lord of Lords! If all the gods now agree that Odysseus shall return to his own home, then let us dispatch our messenger Hermês Argeiphontês to the island of Ogygia; and let him announce forthwith to the nymph our unchangeable will, that Odysseus, after all he has patiently endured, shall return home. And I will myself go to Ithaca, to put heart into his son and make him do something. He shall call the people to a meeting, and speak his mind to all the would-be bridegrooms who have been butchering his sheep and his cattle in heaps. And I will send him to Sparta and to sandy Pylos to inquire about his beloved father, if he can hear that he is on his way home. That will be some credit to him in the world.". . .

BOOK V

. . . The King's Messenger was ready, as he had been when he brought death to the watcher Argos. He put on his fine shoes, those golden incorruptible shoes which used to carry him over moist and dry to the ends of the earth, swift as the breath of the winds. He took up the staff which lays a spell on men's eyes if he wills, or wakens the sleeping. Holding this, Argeiphontês flew away swift and strong. One step on Pieria, and he swooped from the upper air upon the deep; then he skimmed the waves like a seagull, which hunts fish in the dangerous inlets of the barren sea, and dives into the brine with folded wings. Such was the shape of Hermês as he rode on the rippling waves.

When at last he came to that far-off island, he left the blue sea and passed over the land until he reached the great cave where Calypso lived. He found her in the cave, with her beautiful hair flowing over her shoulders. A great fire blazed on the hearth, and the burning logs of cedar and juniper wafted their fragrant scent far over the island. Calypso sat within by her loom, singing in a lovely voice, and shooting her golden shuttle to and fro. A thick cop-

36. **daughter of Atlas,** Calypso.

78-79. **would-be-bridegrooms,** the wooers of Queen Penelopeia, who assume that her husband Odysseus is dead.

pice of trees grew round the cave, alder and aspen and sweet-smelling cypress. There the birds would sail to rest on their outspread wings, owls and falcons and long-tongued sea-ravens who busy themselves about the waters. Over the gaping mouth of the cave trailed a luxuriant grape-vine, with clusters of ripe fruit; and four rills of clear water ran in a row close together, winding over the ground. Beyond were soft meadows thick with violets and wild celery. That was a sight to gladden the very gods.

King's Messenger Argeiphontês stood still, and gazed about him with deep content. Then he went into the cave, and Calypso knew him as soon as she saw him; for all those of the divine race know one another when they meet, even if they live a long way off. But Odysseus was not there. He was sitting in his usual place on the shore, wearing out his soul with lamentation and tears.

Calypso gave him greeting:

"My dear Hermês, this is an honour! with your golden rod and all! What has brought you here? You do not often pay me a visit, but you are heartily welcome. Tell me what you want: I am glad to do it if I can, and if it is doable. But do come in, and let me entertain my guest."

With these words, she led him to a seat that shone with diligent polishing, and set a table beside him with a dish of ambrosia and a cup of red nectar. The royal messenger ate, he drank, he enjoyed a hearty meal, and then he answered her question:

"You ask me what brings me here, as one god to another. Very well, I will tell you the whole history, as you ask. Zeus sent me here. I did not want to come here; who would want to travel all that distance over the salt water, no end to it? and no city of mortals anywhere near to provide a god with sacrifice and a handsome feast! But no god can shirk or baffle the will of Zeus Almighty; that is quite impossible. He says there's a man here, one of those who were nine years fighting before Priam's town, and the most unlucky of them all. It took them ten years to capture that city: then they set out for home, but on the way they offended Athena, and she raised a bad wind and a heavy sea against them. All his good comrades were drowned, but he as it seems was carried here by winds and waters.

"That's the man, and the orders are to send him away at once; for it is not his fate to perish in this place far from his friends. It is decreed that he shall see his friends again, and return to his tall house and his native land."

Calypso shivered, and she spoke her mind plainly:

"A hard-hearted lot you are, you gods, and as jealous as jealous can be! Why are you shocked if a goddess sleeps with a man and makes no secret of it, when she happens to find one she could love as a husband? . . . I saved the man when he was strad-dling across a ship's keel, all by himself, after Zeus had sent another fiery thunderbolt at him and smashed the ship to pieces in the middle of the sea. All his crew were drowned, and the winds carried him here. I loved him and cherished him, and I did think I would make him immortal like myself. But since it is impossible for any god to shirk or baffle the will of Zeus Almighty, let him go to the devil over the barren sea, if that is the command of his Mightiness. I will not give him a passage home; I have no ships and no sailors to carry him over the broad back of the sea. But I will gladly advise him and help him to get home."

Hermês answered:

"All right, let him go now, and don't forget the wrath of God, or he may be angry with you one fine day."

So Argeiphontês departed, having delivered his message, and Calypso went in search of Odysseus. She found him sitting upon the shore. The tears were never dry in his eyes; life with its sweetness was slowly trickling away. He cared for her no longer; at night he was forced to sleep by her side in the cave, although the love was all on her part, and he spent the days sitting upon the rocks or the sands staring at the barren sea and sorrowing.

Calypso came up to him and said:

"Poor old fellow! please don't sit here lamenting any more, don't let yourself pine away like this. I'm going to send you off at once, and glad to do it. Come along, cut down trees, hew them into shape, make a good broad raft; you can lay planks across it and it shall carry you over the misty sea! I will provide you with bread, water, red wine, as much as you like, you need not starve. I'll give you plenty of clothes and send a fair wind behind you to bring you home safe and sound—if it so please the gods who rule the broad heavens, who are stronger than I am both to will and to do. . . . If you knew what troubles you will have before you get to Ithaca, you would stay where you are and keep this house with me, and be immortal, however much you might want to see your wife whom you long for day in and day out. Is she prettier than me? I think not. I don't think it likely that a mortal woman would set herself up as a model of beauty against a goddess!"

Odysseus knew what to say to that, and he answered at once:

"Gracious goddess, don't be cross with me! I know all that as well as you do. My wife is nothing compared to you for beauty, I can see that for myself. She is mortal, you are immortal and never grow old. But even so, I long for the day of my home-coming. And if some god wrecks me again on the deep, I will endure it, for I have a patient mind. I have suffered already many troubles and hardships in battle and tempest; this will be only one more." . . .

In four days he had finished the whole; and on the fifth Calypso saw him off, after she had bathed him and clothed him in garments scented with juniper. She did not forget a skin of red wine, and another large one full of water, with provisions in a bag, tasty stuff and plenty of it; and she sent with him a fair wind, friendly and soft. Odysseus was glad of that wind as he set his sail, and sat by the stern-oar steering like a seaman. . . .

But the Earthshaker was now on his way back from the Ethiopians, and caught sight of him in the distance from the Solyman Hills. . . .

Then he gathered the clouds, and stirred up the deep with his trident: he roused all the tempestuous winds, and covered in clouds both land and sea; night rushed down from the heavens. East wind and South wind dashed together, West wind blowing hard and North wind from the cold heights, rolling up great billows. Odysseus felt his knees tremble and his heart fail. . . . A great wave rolled up towering above him, and drove his vessel round. He lost hold of the steering-oar, and fell out into the water; the mast snapt in the middle as the fearful tempest of warring winds fell upon it; sail and yard were thrown from the wreck. He was kept long under water, and he could not get clear, for his clothes weighed him down. But at last he came up, spitting the bitter brine out of his mouth, while it ran down streaming off his head. . . .

After that, he tossed about for two nights and two days on the rolling waves, always looking for death. But the third day broke with rosy streaks of dawn, and when the light was full, the wind fell and there came a breathless calm. Odysseus lifted high on a great swell, took a quick look forward, and there close by he saw the land. As a father's life is welcome to his children, when he has been lying tormented by some fell disease, and in his agony long drawn out the hateful hand of death has touched him, but God has given relief from his troubles; no less welcome to Odysseus was the sight of earth and trees, and he swam on, longing to feel his feet on solid ground.

. . . On he swam until he came opposite the mouth of a river, and glad he was to see it. That seemed a good place, as there were no rough stones, and it gave some shelter from the wind. He saw the river pouring into the sea, and prayed to the river-god in his heart:

"Hear me, Lord, whoever thou art! How I have longed for thee, and now I pray to thee, save me from Poseidon's threats! Pity a homeless man! even the immortal gods might pity one who comes, as I come now, to thy stream and thy knees, after much tribulation! Have mercy upon me, Lord, I throw myself upon thee!"

Then the river stayed his flowing, and held back the wave and made calm before him, and brought him safe into the mouth. He sank on his two knees, and let his strong arms fall, for the sea had worn him out. All his body was swollen, and the salt water bubbled from mouth and nostrils; breathless and voiceless he lay in a faint, and awful weariness overcame him. . . .

BOOK VI

So there he lay in his thicket, worn out and heavy with sleep; but Athena made her way to the Phaiacian town. . . . And the king was now Alcinoös, a man full of inspired wisdom.

To the house of Alcinoös Athena made her way, with her grey eyes glinting, as she planned the homecoming of Odysseus. She entered a splendid chamber where the king's daughter lay asleep. This was Nausicaä, a girl tall and divinely beautiful; and in the same room were two attendants, graceful girls, one beside each doorpost; the gleaming doors were shut. Like a breath of wind Athena passed to the girl's bed, and stooping over her head spoke to her; she had made herself look like the daughter of that famous seaman Dymas, a girl of her own age and her particular friend. In this shape Athena spoke:

"Why are you so lazy, Nausicaä, and with such a mother as you have? There is all the fine linen lying soiled, and it is high time for you to marry; you will want a nice frock then for yourself, and the same for your wedding company. That is the kind of thing which gives a girl a good name in the world, and pleases her father and mother. Let us go out and wash the linen as soon as day dawns. I will lend you a hand myself, that you may get it done quickly, for you will not remain a maiden long; you have plenty of admirers, the finest young men in all the nation. Get up and persuade your good father as soon as the morning dawns to get ready the mules, and a wagon to carry sashes and robes and sheets all glossy and shining. Better for yourself to drive rather than walk, for the washing-tanks are a good way off from the town."

When she had said this, Athena sped to Olympos. . . .

In a moment, there was Dawn on her golden throne; and Nausicaä in her dainty robe awoke. She was excited by the dream, and went straight through the house to tell her mother and father. She found them indoors; her mother sat by the hearth with her attendant women, twisting the purple yarn; her father she met just going out to attend a council of the chief princes, to which he had been summoned. She came close to him, and said:

"Daddy dear, couldn't you let me have a good big cart with plenty of room? because I want to take our best clothes to the river and give them a wash; they are all lying in a dirty heap! You know what is proper for yourself when you are with their worships passing resolutions, you must have clean clothes. And you have five sons in the house, two married and three spruce young bachelors; they always demand everything fresh from the wash when they are going to a dance, and only my poor brains to manage it all!"

That is what she said, for she was too shy to mention her happy dreams in her father's presence; but he saw through it, and answered at once:

"Take the mules and welcome, my child, and anything else you want. Go ahead; the servants shall get you ready a good big cart with plenty of room, and a tilt over the top."

Then he called to the servants, and gave his orders. They got ready the mule-cart outside, and fitted it upon a fine set of wheels, and brought up the mules and yoked them in; and a house-maid brought a handsome cloak from her chamber and laid it in the cart. Her mother packed a hamper full of eatables, everything the heart could desire and plenty of it, not forgetting the meat, and a goatskin full of wine. Then the young girl got into the cart, and her mother handed her a golden flask of olive oil to use after the bath with her attendant women. Then the girl picked up the whip and reins, shining with polish, and whipt up the team: the mules went rattling along and did not shirk the pull, so on went load and lady together —but not alone, for the maids were trotting by her side.

In due time they reached a noble river. The washing-tanks were there, never empty, for the water came bubbling up and running through them enough to cleanse the dirtiest stuff. There they took out the mules and let them go free, driving them down to the eddying stream to browse on sweet clover. Then the maids unloaded the wagon and carried the clothes into the deep water, where they trod them out in the pits, all racing for first done. And when the washing was over, and all was spotless, they flew in a long string to the seashore, choosing a place where the sea used to beat upon the beach and wash the pebbles clean. There they bathed, and rubbed themselves all over with olive oil. After that they took their meal on the river-bank, while they waited for the clothes to dry in the sun.

When they had all had enough, both maids and mistress, they threw off their veils and began playing at ball, and Nausicaä led the singing, with her white arms flashing in the sunlight as she threw the ball. . . .

But just as she was about to yoke the mules, and fold up all the fine clothes, and set out for home, Athena decided that Odysseus should awake and see the lovely girl, and let her take him to the city.

So then, the princess threw the ball to one of the maids; the ball missed the maid, and fell in the eddies, and they all shouted at that. The noise wakened Odysseus, and he sat up and began to think:

"What next, I wonder! what sort of people live in this land? Violent, savage, lawless? or kindly men who know right from wrong? I seemed to hear something like women's voices, the cry of girls. Perhaps they are nymphs; there are plenty of them on the mountains; the dells and springs and brooks are full of them. But these seem to be using human speech. Well, I'll just go and see."

So saying, he crawled out of the bushes. He broke off a branch thick with leaves, and held it before him in his hand, to hide his naked body. Then he strode along like a lion of the mountains, proud of his power, who goes on through wind and rain with eyes blazing, as he pounces on cattle and sheep, or chases the wild deer; indeed he is ready to follow belly's bidding, and to invade even a walled close in search of the bleaters. Odysseus felt just as desperate when he resolved to join a party of pretty girls without a rag upon him; but he could not help it. What a vision they saw! Something filthy and caked in sea-salt which fairly terrified them: away they scampered in all directions, to hide behind hillocks of sand. Only the young princess stood her ground; for Athena took all fear away.

So she halted and stood firm; and Odysseus was uncertain what to do. Should he throw his arms round her knees, and crave mercy of the lovely girl? or should he stand where he was, and ask her politely to give him some clothes, and to tell him the way to the city? When he thought over the matter, it seemed best to stand where he was and to speak politely and quietly, in case he might give offence to the girl by embracing her knees. He lost no time, but spoke to her in gentle and persuasive words:

"I kneel to thee, Queen!—Art thou goddess? Are you mortal? If you are a goddess, one of those who rule the broad heavens, I would liken you most to Artemis the daughter of Zeus Almighty, so tall and beautiful and fair. If you are a mortal and one of those who dwell upon earth, thrice blessed are your father and your gracious mother, thrice blessed are your brothers; their hearts must be warm for your sake, when they see such a fresh young creature trippling over the green. But most blessed beyond all these in his heart of hearts is he who shall come laden with bridal gifts and take you to his home. Never in all my life have I seen such another, man or woman: I am amazed as I look upon you. In Delos once I did see something like you, a young palm-spire springing up beside Apollo's altar. For I have travelled even so far; and there were many others with me on that voyage which was to bring me so much tribulation. Even so when I saw that sapling my spirit was dumbfounded for a long time, for no other trees like that grow out of the earth; and so, my lady, I am amazed and dumbfounded at seeing you, and I am awestruck at the thought of touching your knees.

Greek soldiers, returning from the wars, being greeted by patriarchs.

"But I am in deep distress. Yesterday after twenty days on the dark sea, I escaped; all that time sea and storms had been carrying me away from the island of Ogygia; and now fate has cast me ashore here. No doubt I am to suffer more troubles here; I do not think the gods will give over yet, for they have much to work off on me still. Pity me, Queen, I pray; to you first I appeal, after so much misery; not another soul do I know of all those who live in this country. Show me the way to your town, give me a rag to cover me, some wrapper you may have brought with you for the clothes. And may the gods give you the dearest wish of your heart, husband, and home, and one heart between two; for nothing is better and more precious than when two of one heart and mind keep house together, husband and wife. That is a sight to make their friends happy and their enemies miserable; but they know it best themselves."

Nausicaä stood her ground, and replied:

"Stranger, you do not seem like a bad man or a foolish man; but happiness is something which Olympian Zeus above allots to men, whether good or bad, to each according to his will. Your fortune is what he has given you, and you must endure it in any case. But now that you have come to our country, you shall not lack for clothes, or anything else which it is proper that any forlorn wanderer may have for the asking. I will show you the way to town, and I will tell you what this nation is called. This is the country of the Phaiacians: I am the daughter of Prince Alcinoös, their king and ruler."

Then she called to her maids, and said:

"Stand still, my girls! Why do you run off at the sight of this poor fellow? You don't think he's an enemy, do you? There is no man living upon the earth, and never shall be, who would come into the Phaiacian land to do harm to its people; for they are dear to the immortals. Our home lies far away in the sea, out of sight of land, at the end of the earth, and no other mortal men visit us. But here is a poor homeless man, and you must look after him. God sends the stranger and the beggar man; we gladly give, not much, but all we can. Come along, girls, give this stranger something to eat and drink, and a bath in the river, where he can find shelter from the wind."

The girls stood still, calling to one another, and then they brought Odysseus to a sheltered place, as the princess told them to do. They laid a wrap beside him and a tunic, and gave him the golden flask of olive oil, and bade him go into the river for his bath.

Then Odysseus said to the maids, "Just stand a little way off, good maids, while I wash the salt off my shoulders by myself, and give them a rub with the oil: it is long since my skin knew what oil feels like. I will not wash before you, for I am too shy to show myself naked before a lot of pretty girls."

Accordingly they went and told the princess all about it. Then Odysseus waded into the river, and washed himself clean from the salt which covered his back and broad shoulders, and wiped off the scruff of brine from his head. When he had washed all clean and rubbed himself with oil, and put on the clothes which the princess had provided, . . .

Then he walked away to the seashore, shining with comeliness and grace; and the girl gazed at him. She turned to her attendants, and said:

"Listen to me, pretty ones, I have something to say. The hand of the gods is in this; they who rule Olympos have sent this man to visit the Phaiacians, who are of their own kindred. When I saw him I thought him an ugly creature, but now he is like one of the gods who rule the broad heavens. I only wish that I might have one like him for my husband! I wish it might please him to stay here and live with us! Come, my girls, give him something to eat and drink."

They hastened to obey, and set food and drink

before Odysseus; and Odysseus ate and drank heartily after all his tribulations, for it was long since he
had had anything to eat.

But Nausicaä had other things to think of. She
folded up the clothes, and packed them into the
wagon, and yoked the sturdy mules, and got in
herself. Then she called to Odysseus that they must
be going. She said:

"Now then, stranger, up with you and let us go on
10   to the town. I will take you to my wise father's house,
where I promise you shall become acquainted with
all the best men of the nation. But this is what you
must do: you seem to have your share of good sense.
So long as we are still in the country among the
farms, you must follow smartly with the maids behind the cart, and I will lead the way. But when we
reach the city,—which has a lofty wall round it, with
a fine harbour on each side, and only a narrow approach: the galleys are drawn up there along the
20   road, and each man has a slip for his own: there is
their meeting-place, round about the precinct of
Poseidon, and it is full of great blocks of stone bedded in the earth. There the men are busy about the
tackle of their black ships, making ropes and sails,
and planing down their oars. For the Phaiacians care
nothing for bow and quiver, but only masts and oars
and the ships with their fine lines, these are their
delight as they cross the hoary sea.

"Well, I want to avoid any unkind gossip among
30   the people, or some one might blame me afterwards.
They are very high and mighty in our town; some evil-
minded person might say, if he met us, 'Who is this
fine big stranger with Nausicaä? where did she pick
him up? Will be a husband for her, no doubt. Some
wandering soul she has brought from his ship, must
be a foreigner from a distance, for there is nobody
near us. Perhaps she had tired out some god with her
prayers, and down he comes from heaven to have her
for ever more! A good job, if she has gone herself and
40   picked up a husband from somewhere else, for she
only turns up her nose at the young men of our
nation, who are all after her, and good men too!'
That's what they will say, and it might bring me into
disgrace. Indeed, I should not approve of any girl
who did such a thing, flying in the face of her friends,
with father and mother to teach her better, if she has
anything to do with men before it comes to marriage
open and above-board.

"Now then, sir, be quick and understand what I
50   say, if you wish to have escort and safe conduct from
my father. You will find a fine grove of Athena close
to the road, poplar trees, with a spring bubbling up
inside and a meadow all round. There is my father's
park, and the orchard, full of fruit, as far from the
city as a man's voice will carry. Sit down there and
wait long enough for us to get into the city and reach
my father's mansion. When you think we have got

there, enter the city yourself and ask the way to the
mansion of Prince Alcinoös. It is easy to know it, a
little child could lead you; for the other houses are   60
not like the house of the royal prince Alcinoös.

"When you are within the house you must enter
the hall, and pass along quickly until you come to my
mother; she is a sight worth seeing! There she sits at
the hearth in the firelight, twisting her purple yarn,
close up to a pillar, and the serving-women sit behind. My father's throne is placed near to hers, and
there he sits quaffing his wine like a god! Pass him by,
and lay your hands on my mother's knees, that you
may see the day of your home-coming, and be happy   70
soon, even if you come from a long way off. If she is
pleased with you, there is good hope that you will
set eyes on your friends, and come to see your own
fine house and your native land."

When she had said this, she touched up the mules
with her shining whip, and they soon left the river
behind them. . . .

BOOKS VII–VIII

. . . Odysseus approached the great mansion.
Again and again he stood still in wonder, before he
set foot on the brazen threshold. For a brightness as   80
of sun or moon filled the whole place. Round the
courtyard, walls of bronze ran this way and that way,
from the threshold to the inner end, and upon them
was a coping of blue enamel; golden doors and silver
doorposts stood on a threshold of bronze, with silver
lintel and golden crowlatch. Golden and silver dogs
were on either side, which Hephaistos had made by
his clever brain to guard the mansion of proud Alcinoös; they were immortal, and never grew old as the
days went by. . . .   90

There Odysseus stood gazing, after all his tribulations. When he had taken it in he crossed the threshold with brisk steps, and entered the hall. He found
the lords and rulers of the Phaiacians dropping the
libation out of their cups in honour of Hermês Argeiphontês, whom they used to honour the last of all
before they went to rest. Odysseus passed through
the hall hidden in the mist which Athena spread
about him. When he came up to Arêtê and King
Alcinoös, he threw his arms about the knees of Arêtê, 100
and in a moment the mist faded away. All fell silent
throughout the hall when they saw him, and they
stared in surprise, while Odysseus put his petition to
the queen:

"Arêtê, daughter of divine Rhexenor! I come in my
distress, a suppliant to your husband and to your
knees. Yes, and to these who sit at meat; may the
gods grant them to be happy while they live, and
may each have children to inherit his wealth and the
honourable place which the people has given him.   110
Now I beseech you to send me home to my native

land without delay, for I have long suffered tribulation far from my friends."

. . . Alcinoös held out his hand to Odysseus and led him from the hearth to a high seat, where his own son was sitting, near himself, for he loved the courteous Laodamas best of all his sons. He moved his son out of that seat, and placed Odysseus there. A servant brought the handwash, and poured it from a golden jug over a silver basin to rinse his hands; then set a table beside him. A dignified housewife brought bread and laid the table with all sorts of food, and plenty of it. . . .

Odysseus was melted, and tears ran over his cheeks. He wept as a woman weeps with her arms about a beloved husband, who has fallen in front of his people, fighting to keep the day of ruin from city and children; when she sees him panting and dying, she throws her arms around him and wails aloud, but the enemies behind her beat her about the back and shoulders with their spears, and drag her away into slavery, where labour and sorrow will be her lot and her cheeks will grow thin with pining. No one else noticed his tears, but Alcinoös saw clearly enough, sitting by his side, and heard his sobs. At once he called out. . . .

". . . Tell me what name you go by at home, what your mother and father call you, and the people of your town, and your neighbors all around. No one on the whole world is without a name, high or low; his parents give him some name as soon as he is born. Tell me your country and people, and your city, that our ships may aim at the right place in their minds. . . ."

BOOK IX

Then Odysseus began his tale:

"What a pleasure it is, my lord," he said, "to hear a singer like this, with a divine voice! I declare it is just the perfection of gracious life: good cheer and good temper everywhere, rows of guests enjoying themselves heartily and listening to the music, plenty to eat on the table, wine ready in the great bowl, and the butler ready to fill your cup whenever you want it. I think that is the best thing men can have.—But you have a mind to hear my sad story, and make me more unhappy than I was before. What shall I begin with, what shall I end with? The lords of heaven have given me sorrow in abundance.

"First of all I will tell you my name, and then you may count me one of your friends if I live to reach my home, although that is far away. I am Odysseus Laertiadês, a name well known in the world as one who is ready for any event. My home is Ithaca, that bright conspicuous isle, with Mount Neriton rising clear out of the quivering forests. Round it lie many islands clustering close, Dulichion and Samê and woody Zacynthos. My island lies low, last of all in the sea to westward, the others away towards the dawn and the rising sun. It is rough, but a nurse of good lads; I tell you there is no sweeter sight any man can see than his own country. Listen now: a radiant goddess Calypso tried to keep me by her in her cave, and wanted me for a husband; Circê also would have had me stay in her mansion, and a clever creature she was, and she also wanted me for a husband, but she never could win my heart. How true it is that nothing is sweeter than home and kindred, although you may have a rich house in a foreign land far away from your kindred! Ah well, but you are waiting to hear of my journey home, and all the sorrows which Zeus laid upon me after I left Troy.

". . . We came next to the Cyclopians, the Goggle-eyes, a violent and lawless tribe. They trust to providence, and neither plant nor plow, but everything grows without sowing or plowing; wheat and barley and vines, which bear grapes in huge bunches, and the rain from heaven makes them grow of themselves. These Cyclopians have no parliament for debates and no laws, but they live on high mountains in hollow caves; each one lays down the law for wife and children, and no one cares for his neighbours. . . .

"Then I told the rest of my men to wait for me and look after the ship, but I picked out twelve of the best men I had, and we set out. I took with me a goatskin of ruby wine. . . . I had filled a skin with this wine, and brought it with me, also a bag of provisions; for from the first I had a foreboding that I should meet a man of mighty strength, but savage, knowing neither justice nor law.

"We walked briskly to the cave, but found him not at home; he was tending his fat flocks on the pasture. So we entered the cave and took a good look all round. There were baskets loaded with cheeses, there were pens stuffed full of lambs and kids. Each lot was kept in a separate place; firstlings in one, middlings in another, yearlings in another. Every pot and pan was swimming with whey, all the pails and basins into which he did the milking. The men begged me first to let them help themselves to the cheeses and be off; next they wanted to make haste and drive the kids and lambs out of the pens and get under sail. But I would not listen—indeed it would have been much better if I had! but I wanted to see himself and claim the stranger's gift. As it turned out, he was destined to be anything but a vision of joy to my comrades.

"So we lit a fire and made our thank-offering, and helped ourselves to as many cheeses as we wanted to eat; then we sat inside till he should come back with his flocks. At last in he came, carrying a tremendous load of dry wood to give light for supper. This he threw down inside the cave with a crash that terrified us, and sent us scurrying into the corners. Then he drove his fat flocks into the cave, that is to say, all he milked, leaving the rams and billy-goats outside the cave but within the high walls of the enclosure. Then he picked up a huge great stone and placed it in the doorway: not two and twenty good carts with four wheels apiece could have lifted it off the ground, such was the size of the precipitous rock which he planted in front of the entrance. Then he sat down and milked the goats and ewes, bleating loudly, all in order, and put her young under each. Next he curdled half of the white milk and packed it into wicker baskets, leaving the other half to stand in bowls, that he might have some to drink for supper or whenever he wanted. At last after all this busy work, he lighted the fire and saw us.

"'Who are you?' he called out. 'Where do you come from over the watery ways? Are you traders, or a lot of pirates ready to kill and be killed, bringing trouble to foreigners?'

"While he spoke, our hearts were wholly broken within us to see the horrible monster, and to hear that beastly voice. But I managed to answer him:

"'We are Achaians from Troy, driven out of our course over the broad sea by all the winds of heaven. We meant to sail straight home, but we have lost our way altogether: such was the will of Zeus, I suppose. We have the honour to be the people of King Agamemnon Atreidês, whose fame is greatest of all men under the sky, for the strong city he sacked and the many nations he conquered. But we have found you, and come to your knees, to pray if you will give us the stranger's due or anything you may think proper to give to a stranger. Respect the gods, most noble sir; we are your suppliants! Strangers and suppliants have their guardian strong, God walks with them to see they get no wrong.'

"He answered me with cruel words: 'You are a fool, stranger, or you come from a long way off, if you expect me to fear gods. Zeus Almighty be damned and his blessed gods with him. We Cyclopians care nothing for them, we are stronger than they are. I should not worry about Zeus if I wanted to lay hands on you or your companions. But tell me, where did you moor your ship—far off or close by? I should be glad to know that.'

"He was just trying it on, but I knew something of the world, and saw through it; so I answered back, 'My ship was wrecked by Poseidon Earthshaker, who cast us on the rocks near the boundary of your country; the wind drove us on a lee shore. But I was saved with these others.'

"The cruel monster made no answer, but just jumped up and reached out towards my men, grabbed two like a pair of puppies and dashed them on the ground: their brains ran out and soaked into the earth. Then he cut them up limb by limb, and made them ready for supper. He devoured them like a mountain lion, bowels and flesh and marrow-bones,

and left nothing. We groaned aloud, lifting our hands to Zeus, when we saw this brutal business; but there was nothing to be done.

"When Goggle-eye had filled his great belly with his meal of human flesh, washed down with a draught of milk neat, he lay and stretched himself among the sheep. But I did not lose heart. I considered whether to go near and draw my sharp sword and drive it into his breast; I could feel about till I found the place where the midriff encloses the liver. But second thoughts kept me back. We should have perished ourselves in that place, dead and done for; we could never have moved the great stone which he had planted in the doorway. So we lay groaning and awaited the dawn.

"Dawn came. He lit the fire, milked his flocks, all in order, put the young under each, then he grabbed two more men and prepared his breakfast. That done, he drove out the fat flocks, moving away the great stone with ease; but he put it back again, just as you fit cover to quiver. With many a whistle Goggle-eye turned his fat flocks to the hills; but I was left brooding and full of dark plans, longing to have my revenge if Athena would grant my prayer.

"Among all my schemes and machinations, the best plan I could think of was this. A long spar was lying beside the pen, a sapling of green olive-wood; Goggle-eye had cut it down to dry it and use as a staff. It looked to us about as large as the mast of a twenty-oar ship, some broad hoy that sails the deep sea; it was about that length and thickness. I cut off a fathom of this, and handed it over to my men to dress down. They made it smooth, then I sharpened the end and charred it in the hot fire, and hid it carefully under the dung which lay in a great mass all over the floor. Then I told the others to cast lots who should help me with the pole and rub it into his eye while he was sound asleep. The lot fell on those four whom I would have chosen myself, which made five counting me.

"In the evening, back he came with his flocks. This time he drove them all into the cave, and left none outside in the yard; whether he suspected something, or God made him do it, I do not know. Then he lifted the great stone and set it in place, sat down and milked his ewes and nannies bleating loudly, all in order, put her young under each, and when all this was done, grabbed two more men and made his meal.

"At this moment I came near to Goggle-eye, holding in my hand an ivy-wood cup full of the red wine, and I said:

"'Cyclops, here, have a drink after that jolly meal of mansmutton! I should like to show you what drink we had on board our ship. I brought it as a drink-offering for you, in the hope that you might have pity and help me on my way home. But you are mad beyond all bearing! Hard heart, how can you expect any other men to pay you a visit? For you have done what is not right.'

"He took it and swallowed it down. The good stuff delighted him terribly, and he asked for another drink:

"'Oh, please give me more, and tell me your name this very minute! I will give you a stranger's gift which will make you happy! Mother earth does give us wine in huge bunches, even in this part of the world, and the rain from heaven makes them grow; but this is a rivulet of nectar and ambrosia!'

"Then I gave him a second draught. Three drinks I gave him; three times the fool drank. At last, when the wine had got into his head, I said to him in the gentlest of tones:

"'Cyclops, do you ask me my name? Well, I will tell you, and you shall give me the stranger's due, as you promised. Noman is my name; Noman is what mother and father call me and all my friends.'

"Then the cruel monster said, 'Noman shall be last eaten of his company, and all the others shall be eaten before him! that shall be your stranger's gift.'

"As he said this, down he slipt and rolled on his back. His thick neck drooped sideways, and all-conquering sleep laid hold on him; wine dribbled out of his gullet with lumps of human flesh, as he belched in his drunken slumbers. Then I drove the pole deep under the ashes to grow hot, and spoke to hearten my men that no one might fail me through fear.

"As soon as the wood was on the point of catching fire, and glowed white-hot, green as it was, I drew it quickly out of the fire while my men stood round me: God breathed great courage into us then. The men took hold of the stake, and thrust the sharp point into his eye; and I leaned hard on it from above and turned it round and round. As a man bores a ship's timber with an auger, while others at the lower part keep turning it with a strap which they hold at each end, and round and round it runs: so we held the fire-sharpened pole and turned it, and the blood bubbled about its hot point. The fumes singed eyelids and eyelashes all about as the eyeball burnt and the roots crackled in the fire. As a smith plunges an axe or an adze in cold water, for that makes the strength of steel, and it hisses loud when he tempers it, so his eye sizzled about the pole of olivewood.

"He gave a horrible bellow till the rocks rang again, and we shrank away in fear. Then he dragged out the post from his eye dabbled and dripping with blood, and threw it from him, wringing his hands in wild agony, and roared aloud to the Cyclopians who lived in caves round about among the windy hills. They heard his cries, and came thronging from all directions, and stood about the cave, asking what his trouble was:

"'What on earth is the matter with you, Polyphemos?' they called out. 'Why do you shout like this through the night and wake us all up? Is any man driving away your flocks against your will? Is any one trying to kill you by craft or main force?'

"Out of the cave came the voice of mighty Polyphemos: 'O my friends, Noman is killing me by craft and not by main force!'

"They answered him in plain words:

"'Well, if no man is using force, and you are alone, there's no help for a bit of sickness when heaven sends it; so you had better say your prayers to Lord Poseidon your father!'

"With these words away they went, and my heart laughed within me, to think how a mere nobody had taken them all in with my machinomanations!

"But the Cyclops, groaning and writhing in agony, fumbled about with his hands until he found the stone and pushed it away from the entrance. There he sat with his hands outspread to catch any one who tried to go out with the animals. A great fool he must have thought me! But I had been casting about what to do for the best, if I could possibly find some escape from death for my comrades and myself. All kinds of schemes and machinations I wove in my wits, for it was life or death, and perdition was close by. The plan that seemed to me best was this. The rams were well grown, large and fine, with coats of rich dark wool. In dead silence I tied them together with twisted withies, which the monster used for his bed. I tied them in threes, with a man under the middle one, while the two others protected him on each side. So three carried each of our fellows; but for myself—there was one great ram, the finest of the whole flock; I threw my arms over his back, and curled myself under his shaggy belly, and there I lay turned upwards, with only my hands to hold fast by the wonderful fleece in patience. So we all waited anxiously for the dawn.

"At last the dawn came. The rams and billies surged out to pasture, but the nannies and ewes unmilked went bleating round the pens; for their udders were full to bursting. Their master still tormented with pain felt over the backs of all the animals as they passed out; but the poor fool did not notice how my men were tied under their bellies. Last of all the great ram stalked to the door, cumbered with the weight of his wool and of me and my teeming mind. Polyphemos said as he pawed him over:

"'Hullo, why are you last to-day, you lazy creature? It is not your way to let them leave you behind! No, no, you go first by a long way to crop the fresh grass, stepping high and large, first to drink at the river, first all eagerness to come home in the evening; but now last! Are you sorry perhaps for your master's eye, which a damned villain has blinded with his cursed companions, after he had fuddled me with wine? Noman! who hasn't yet escaped the death in store for him, I tell him that! If you only had sense like me, if you could only speak, and tell me where the man is skulking from my vengeance! Wouldn't I beat his head on the ground, wouldn't his brains go splashing all over the place! And then I should have some little consolation for the trouble which this nobody of a Noman has brought upon me!'

"So he let the ram go from him out of the cave. A little way from the cave and its enclosure, I shook myself loose first from under my ram; then I freed my companions, and with all speed we drove the fat animals trotting along, often looking round, until we reached our ship. Glad indeed our friends were to see us, all of us that were left alive; they lamented the others, and made such a noise that I had to stop it, frowning at them and shaking my head. I told them to look sharp and throw on board a number of the fleecy beasts, and get away. Soon they were in their places paddling along; but when we were about as far off from the shore as a man can shout, I called out in mockery:

"'I say, Cyclops! He didn't turn out to be such a milksop after all, did he, when you murdered his friends, and gobbled them up in your cave? Your sins were sure to find you out, you cruel brute! You had no scruple to devour your guests in your own house, therefore vengeance has fallen upon you from Zeus and the gods in heaven!'

"This made him more furious than ever. He broke off the peak of a tall rock and threw it; the rock fell in front of the ship; the sea splashed and surged up as it fell; it raised a wave which carried us back to the land, and the rolling swell drove the ship right upon the shore. I picked up a long quant and pushed her off, and nodded to the men as a hint to row hard and save their lives. You may be sure they put their backs into it! When we were twice as far as before, I wanted to shout again to Goggle-eye, although my comrades all round tried to coax me not to do it—

"'Foolhardy man! Why do you want to provoke the madman? Just now he threw something to seaward of us and drove back the ship to land, and we thought all was up with us. And if he had heard one of us speaking or making a sound, he would have thrown a jagged rock and smashed our timbers and our bones to smithereens! He throws far enough!'

"But I was determined not to listen, and shouted again in my fury:

"'I say, Cyclops! if ever any one asks you who put out your ugly eye, tell him your blinder was Odysseus, the conqueror of Troy, the son of Laërtês, whose address is in Ithaca!'

"When he heard this he gave a loud cry, and said, 'Upon my word, this is the old prophecy come true! There was a soothsayer here once, a fine tall fellow,

Telemos Eurymedês, a famous soothsayer who lived to old age prophesying amongst our people. He told me what was to happen, that I should lose my sight at the hands of Odysseus. But I always expected that some tall handsome fellow would come this way, clothed in mighty power. Now a nobody, a weakling, a whippersnapper, has blinded my eye after fuddling me with wine! Come to me, dear Odysseus, and let me give you the stranger's gift, let me beseech the worshipful Earthshaker to grant you a happy voyage! For I have the honour to be his son, and he declares he is my father. He will cure me, if he chooses, all by himself, without the help of blessed gods or mortal man.'

"I answered at once, 'I wish I could kill you and send you to hell as surely as no one will ever unblind your eye, not even the Earthshaker!'

"At this he held out his hand to heaven, and prayed to Lord Poseidon:

"'Hear me, Poseidon Earthholder Seabluehair! If I am truly thy son, and thou art indeed my father, grant that Odysseus the conqueror of Troy—the son of Laërtês—whose address is in Ithaca, may never reach his home! But if it is his due portion to see his friends and come again to his tall house and his native land, may he come there late and in misery, in another man's ship, may he lose all his companions, and may he find tribulation at home!'

"This was his prayer, and Seabluehair heard it. Then once again he lifted a stone greater than the other, and circled it round his head, gathering all his vast strength for the blow, and flung it; down it fell behind our ship, just a little, just missed the end of the steering-oar. The sea splashed and surged up as it fell, and the wave carried her on and drove her to shore on the island.

"When we came safe to the island, where the other ships were waiting for us, we found our companions in great anxiety, hoping against hope. We drew up our ship on the sand, and put the sheep of old Goggle-eye ashore, and divided them so as to give every one a fair share. But by general consent the great ram was given to me. I sacrificed him on the beach to Zeus Cronidês; clouds and darkness are round about him, and he rules over all. I made my burnt-offering, but Zeus regarded it not; for as it turned out, he intended that all my tight ships and all my trusty companions should be destroyed.

"We spent the rest of the day until sunset in feasting, eating full and drinking deep; and when the sun set and darkness came on, we lay to rest on the seashore. Then at dawn I directed the men in all haste to embark and throw off the moorings. They

79-80. **Odysseus . . . Ithaca.** Odysseus introduced himself in the proper Greek way, name, family, and address; the reader will notice how carefully the Cyclops repeats it to his divine father, that there may be no mistake—Translator's note.

were soon aboard and rowing away in good fettle over the sea.

"So we fared onwards, thankful to be alive, but sorrowing for our comrades whom we had lost.

BOOK XI

". . . We made all shipshape aboard, and sat tight: wind and helmsman kept her on her course. All day long we ran before the wind, with never a quiver on the sail; then the sun set, and all the ways grew dark.

"We came at last to the deep stream of Oceanos which is the world's boundary. There is the city of the Cimmerian people, wrapt in mist and cloud. Blazing Helios never looks down on them with his rays, not when he mounts into the starry sky nor when he returns from sky to earth; but abominable night is for ever spread over those unhappy mortals. There we beached our ship and put the animals ashore. . . .

"Perimedès and Eurylochos held fast the victims, while I drew my sword and dug the pit, a cubit's length along and across. I poured out the drink-offering for All Souls, first with honey and milk, then with fine wine, and the third time with water, and I sprinkled white barley-meal over it. Earnestly I prayed to the empty shells of the dead, and promised that when I came to Ithaca, I would sacrifice to them in my own house a farrow cow, the best I had, and heap fine things on the blazing pile; to Teiresias alone in a different place I would dedicate the best black ram among my flocks.

"When I had made prayer and supplication to the company of the dead, I cut the victims' throats over the pit, and the red blood poured out. Then the souls of the dead who had passed away came up in a crowd from Erebos: young men and brides, old men who had suffered much, and tender maidens to whom sorrow was a new thing; others killed in battle, warriors clad in bloodstained armour. All this crowd gathered about the pit from every side, with a dreadful great noise, which made me pale with fear.

"Then I told my men to take the victims which lay there slaughtered, to flay them and burn them, and to pray to mighty Hadès and awful Persephoneia; I myself with drawn sword sat still, and would not let the empty shells of the dead come near the blood until I had asked my questions of Teiresias. . . .

"Then came the soul of my dead mother, Anticleia, daughter of the brave Autolycos; she was alive when I left Ithaca on my voyage to sacred Ilion. My tears fell when I saw her, and I was moved with pity; but all the same, I would not let her come near the blood before I had asked my questions of Teiresias.

"Then came the soul of Theban Teiresias, holding a golden rod. He knew me, and said, 'What brings

18. **victims,** the animals for sacrifice.

you here, unhappy man, away from the light of the sun, to visit this unpleasing place of the dead? Move back from the pit, hold off your sharp sword, that I may drink of the blood and tell you the truth.'

"As he spoke, I stept back from the pit, and pushed my sword into the scabbard. He drank of the blood, and only then spoke as the prophet without reproach:

" 'You seek to return home, mighty Odysseus, and home is sweet as honey. But God will make your voyage hard and dangerous; for I do not think the Earthshaker will fail to see you, and he is furious against you because you blinded his son. Nevertheless, you may all get safe home still, although not without suffering much, if you can control yourself and your companions when you have traversed the sea as far as the island of Thrinacia. There you will find the cattle and sheep of Helios, who sees all things and hears all things.

" 'If you sail on without hurting them you may come safe to Ithaca, although not without suffering much. But if you do them hurt, then I foretell destruction for your ship and your crew; and if you can escape it yourself, you will arrive late and miserable, all your companions lost, in the ship of a stranger. You will find trouble in your house, proud blustering men who devour your substance and plague your wife to marry and offer their bridal gifts. But you shall exact retribution from these men.

" 'When you have killed them in your hall, whether by craft or open fight with the cold steel, you must take an oar with you, and journey until you find men who do not know the sea nor mix salt with their food; they have no crimson-cheeked ships, no handy oars, which are like so many wing-feathers to a ship. I will give you an unmistakable token which you cannot miss. When a wayfarer shall meet you and tell you that is a winnowing shovel on your shoulder, fix the oar in the ground, and make sacrifice to King Poseidon, a ram, a bull, and a boar-pig; then return home and make solemn sacrifice to the immortal gods who rule the broad heavens, every one in order. Death shall come to you from the sea, death ever so peaceful shall take you off when comfortable old age shall be your only burden, and your people shall be happy round you. That which I tell you is true.'

"I answered him, 'Ah well, Teiresias, that is the thread which the gods have spun, and I have no say in the matter. But here is something I want to ask, if you will explain it to me. I see over there the soul of my dead mother. She remains in silence near the blood, and she would not look at the face of her own son or say a word to him. Tell me, prince, how may she know me for what I am?'

"He answered, 'I will give you an easy rule to remember. If you let any one of the dead come near the blood, he will tell you what is true; if you refuse, he will go away.'

"When he had said this, the soul of Prince Teiresias returned into the house of Hadês, having uttered his oracles. But I stayed where I was until my mother came near and drank the red blood. At once she knew me, and made her meaning clear with lamentable words:

"'My love, how did you come down to the cloudy gloom, and you alive? It is hard for the living to see this place. There are great rivers between, and terrible streams, Oceanos first of all, which no one can ever cross by walking but only if he has a well-found ship. Are you on your way from Troy, have you been wandering about with ship and crew all this time? Haven't you ever been back to Ithaca, and seen your wife in your own house?'

"I answered, 'Dear mother, necessity has brought me to the house of Hadês, for I had to consult the soul of Teiresias the Theban. I have not been near Achaia nor set foot in our country. I have been driven about incessantly in toil and trouble, ever since I first sailed with King Agamemnon for Troy, to see its fine horses and to fight with its people.

"'But do tell me, really and truly, what was the cause of your death? how did you die? Was it a long disease? or did Artemis Archeress kill you with her gentle shafts? And tell me about my father and the son I left behind me: do they still hold my honours and my possessions, or have they passed to some other man because people think I will never return? And tell me of my own wedded wife, what she thinks and what she means to do. Does she remain with the boy and keep all safe, or has she already married the best man who offered?'

"My beloved mother answered at once, 'Aye indeed, she does remain in your house. She has a patient heart; but her nights and days are consumed with tears and sorrow. Your honours and your possessions have not yet been taken away by any man, but Telemachos holds your demense and attends the public banquets as a ruling prince ought to do, for they all invite him.

"'But your father stays there in the country and never comes to town. His bedding is not glossy rugs and blankets on a bedstead, but in winter he sleeps among the hinds in the house, in the dust beside the fire, and wears poor clothes: when summer comes and blooming autumn, he lies on the ground anywhere about the slope of his vineyard, on a heap of fallen leaves. There he lies sorrowing and will not be comforted, longing for your return; old age weighs heavy upon him.

"'And this is how I sickened and died. The Archeress did not shoot me in my own house with those gentle shafts that never miss; it was no disease that made me pine away; but I missed you so much, and your clever wit and your gay merry ways, and life was sweet no longer, so I died.'

"When I heard this, I longed to throw my arms round her neck. Three times I tried to embrace the ghost, three times it slipt through my hands like a shadow or a dream. A sharp pang pierced my heart, and I cried out straight from my heart to hers:

"'Mother dear! Why don't you stay with me when I long to embrace you? Let us relieve our hearts, and have a good cry in each other's arms. Are you only a phantom which awful Persephoneia has sent to make me more unhappy than ever?'

"My dear mother answered:

"'Alas, alas, my child, most luckless creature on the face of the earth! Persephoneia is not deceiving you, she is the daughter of Zeus; but this is only what happens to mortals when one of us dies. As soon as the spirit leaves the white bones, the sinews no longer hold flesh and bones together—the blazing fire consumes them all; but the soul flits away fluttering like a dream. Make haste back to the light; but do not forget all this, tell it to your wife by and by.'

"As we were talking together, a crowd of women came up sent by awful Persephoneia, wives and daughters of great men. They gathered about the red blood, and I wondered how I should question them. This seemed to be the best plan. I drew my sword and kept off the crowd of ghosts; and then I let them form in a long line and come up one by one. Each one declared her lineage, then I questioned them all.

". . . As soon as dread Persephoneia had dispersed the ghosts of the women, the ghost of Agamemnon Atreidês came near full of sorrow: there was a crowd of others round him, those who died with him in the house of Aigisthos. The king knew me as soon as he had drunk the red blood; he cried aloud and wept, stretching out his hands towards me and trying to reach me. But there was no strength or power left in him such as there used to be in that body so full of life. I shed tears of pity myself when I saw him, and spoke plainly as I called him by name:

"'My lord Atreidês, Agamemnon king of men! What fate of dolorous death brought you low? Did Poseidon raise a terrible tempest and drown you in the sea? Or did the hand of an enemy strike you down on dry land, in some foray or cattle-raid, or fighting for conquest and captives?'

"He answered, 'Prince Laertiadês, Odysseus ever ready! Poseidon did not drown me in the sea, no enemy struck me down on dry land; but Aigisthos plotted my death with my accursed wife—invited me to his house, set me down to a banquet, butchered me as if I were an ox at the manger! That was how I died, and a shameful death it was: my friends were falling, falling all round me, like a lot of tusker pigs that a rich man slaughters for a wedding or a banquet or a butty-meal! You have seen men fall in battle often enough, killed man to man or in the thick melée; but you never saw a sight so pitiable as that, as

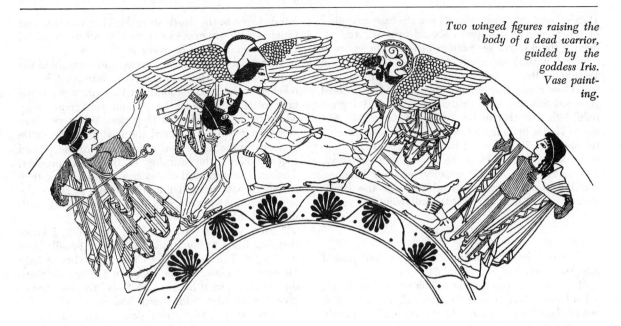

Two winged figures raising the body of a dead warrior, guided by the goddess Iris. Vase painting.

we lay about the wine-bowl, and the tables were piled with meats, and the floor running with blood.

" 'Most frightful of all was the shriek of Cassandra, and she a king's daughter! I heard it when the traitress Clytaimnestra killed her over my body. I tried to lift my hands, but dropt them again on the ground, as I lay dying with a sword through my body: the bitch turned her back, she would not take the trouble to draw down my eyelids or to close my mouth in death.

" 'True it is, there is nothing so cruel and shameless as a woman: that woman proved it to be true, when she plotted that shameful deed and murdered her lawful husband. Ah me, I did think to find welcome with my children and household when I came back to my home; but she had set her mind upon outrageous wickedness, she had brought shame on herself and all women for ever, even if one of them is honest.'

"I cried out:

" 'Mercy upon us! Indeed there is no doubt that Zeus Allseeing has been the deadly foe of the house of Atreus from the beginning, and he has always used the schemes of women. For Helen's sake how many of us fell! and for you, Clytaimnestra was laying her plot while you were far away!'

"He answered:

" 'Then take warning now yourself, and never be too kind even to your wife. Never tell her all you have in your mind; you may tell something, but keep something to yourself. However, *you* will not be murdered by your wife, Odysseus. She is full of intelligence, and her heart is sound, your prudent and modest Penelopeia.

" 'Ah, she was a young bride when we left her and went to the war; there was a baby boy at her breast, and I suppose by this time he counts himself a man. Happy boy! His father will see him when he comes, sure enough, and he will give his father a kiss as a good boy should. But my wife would not even let me delight my eyes with the sight of my son; she killed the father first. . . .'

"As we two stood talking together of our sorrows in this mournful way, other ghosts came up: Achillês and Patroclos, and Antilochos, the man without stain and without reproach, and Aias, who was most handsome and noble of all next to the admirable Achillês. The ghost of Achillês knew me, and said in plain words:

" 'Here is Prince Odysseus who never fails! O you foolhardy man! Your ingenious brain will never do better than this. How did you dare to come down to Hadês, where dwell the dead without sense or feeling, phantoms of mortals whose weary days are done?'

"I answered him, 'My lord Achillês Peleïdês, our chief and our champion before Troy! I came to ask Teiresias if he had any advice or help for me on my way to my rugged island home. For I have not yet set foot in my own country, since trouble has ever been my lot. But you, Achillês, are most blessed of all men who ever were or will be. When you lived, we honoured you like the gods; and now you are a potentate in this world of the dead. Then do not deplore your death, Achillês.'

"He answered at once, 'Don't bepraise death to me, Odysseus. I would rather be plowman to a yeoman farmer on a small holding than lord Paramount in the kingdom of the dead.' . . .

"With these words he strode back into the house of

Hadês; but I remained where I was, in case any other of the heroes of past times should appear. And indeed, I should have seen others of those ancient men whom I wished especially to see, as Theseus and Peirithoös, those famous sons of gods; but before I could see them, the innumerable hosts of the dead gathered together with deafening cries, and I grew pale with fear that awful Persephoneia might send out of Hadês upon me a Gorgon-head of some dreadful monster. Then I went back at once to the ship, and told my men to loose the hawser and get away. They were soon rowing steadily on their benches, and the current bore us steadily down the ocean stream; oars at first, afterwards a following breeze.

BOOK XII

"Our ship left the stream of Oceanos, and passed into the open sea. . . .

"I saw smoke, and a great rolling wave, and heard a loud noise. The men were terrified, the oars flew out of their hands and fell in the sea with a splash, dragging down at the ship's sides by their loops; she made no way, now the oars drove no longer. I walked down the whole length of the ship, pausing by each man, and coaxing them not to lose heart:

"'. . . Keep your seats and row away like men, and then we may hope that Zeus will save and deliver us out of this danger. Now for you, steersman, pay careful heed, for you hold our helm in your hands. Keep her well away from the smoke and surge, and hug the cliffs; whatever you do, don't let her run off in that direction, or we shall all be drowned.' . . .

"We passed up the strait, groaning loudly; for on one side was Scylla, on the other Charybdis swallowed up the salt water in terrible fashion. When she spouted, like a cauldron over a great fire she seethed up in a swirling mess, and the spray rose high in the air till it fell on the tops of the two cliffs: when she swallowed up the salt sea, she showed deep down in her swirling whirlpool black sand at the bottom, and the rocks all round echoed a bellowing boom. Every man was pale with fear. As we gazed in our fear at the death on this side, at the same moment Scylla grabbed six of my men out of the ship, the best and strongest of the crew. I turned, took a glance at the ship, looked for my men, saw their hands and feet already in the air swinging aloft in the clutches of Scylla; while they called aloud on my name, for the last time, in despair. As a fisherman stands on a projecting rock with a long rod, and throws in ground-bait to attract the little fishes, then drops in hook and line with its horn-bait, and at last gets a bite and whips him out gasping, so Scylla swung them gasping up to the rock; there in the cave she devoured them, shrieking and stretching out their hands to me in the death-struggle. That was the most pitiable sight my eyes ever beheld in all my toils and troubles on the weary ways of the sea.

"When we were past the rocks, and away from the terrors of Charybdis and Scylla, immediately we reached a delectable island; in that place were the fine cattle with broad brows and the great sheep which belonged to Helios Hyperion. While we were still a long way off I heard the lowing of the cattle penned for the night, and the bleating of sheep; and I remembered the warning of the blind prophet, Theban Teiresias, and of Aiaian Circê, and how they strictly forbade me to land on the island of Helios the joy of man. At once I said to my companions, with my mind full of foreboding:

"'Men, you are having a hard time of it, I know that, but listen to me a moment; I want to tell you a warning of Teiresias and of Circê also. They strictly forbade us to land on the island of Helios; for there they said an awful danger awaits us. You had better give the island a wide berth and row on.'

"This fairly broke them down, and Eurylochos answered at once angrily:

'You are a hard man, Odysseus, never downhearted and never tired! You must be made of iron! Here are your men, tired to death and scarce able to keep awake, and you won't let us go ashore on this island and cook a square meal. No, you make us go trapesing along the whole blessed night. We must give the island a wide berth and toss about in the dark! Night is the time for dangerous squalls, that's the way ships are lost! How can we expect to get off with our lives if a sudden squall comes out of the south or west? Damned bad winds, that send a ship to the bottom, God willing or not! I vote we take our orders from black Madam Night, pull up the vessel and cook a meal. Then in the morning in we get, and it's over the sea we go!'

"That was the proposal of Eurylochos, and the others applauded. Then I understood that heaven had trouble in store for us, and I gave it him straight:

"'Eurylochos, I must give way to force. I am one against many. But you must swear a solemn oath, that if we find a herd of cattle or a flock of sheep no one shall dare to kill one cow or one sheep. You must keep quiet, and eat the food that Circê gave us.'

"They all swore the oath accordingly; and when that business was done, we brought the ship into a land-locked harbour close to a spring of sweet water. They all went ashore, and prepared their meal in proper style. When they had taken all they wanted, they had time to remember their lost comrades, whom Scylla had caught and eaten out of the ship; and they lamented their dead until welcome sleep

61. **cattle,** the sacred oxen of Helios, for the killing of which the companions of Odysseus and his ships are to be destroyed by Zeus.

overcame them. But when it was the third watch of the night and the stars had moved south, Zeus Cloudgatherer sent out a furious wind in a regular tempest, and covered earth and sea with clouds; night rushed down from the heavens. As soon as the dawn showed ruddy through the mist, we hauled the ship ashore into a cave, in which the Nymphs had their thrones and dancing-rings. Then I called the men together and addressed them:

10 " 'My friends, we have food and drink in the ship, so we must keep our hands off these cattle or we may suffer for it. For an awful god is the owner of these cattle and great sheep—Helios, who sees all and hears all.'

"They were quite willing to agree. But the south wind blew for a whole month without changing, and after that, never a breath of any wind we had but east and south. So long as the food and red wine lasted, they kept their hands off the cattle, for they 20 did not want to die; but when all the provisions on board were consumed, and they had to go about hunting for game, birds, or fish, or whatever fell to their hands or their hooks, and they were half starved, I made my way up into the island to offer prayer to the gods and try whether one would help us. I slipt away from the men and found a place with shelter from the wind; there I washed my hands, and prayed to all the gods who dwell in Olympos, but they made me fall into a deep sleep.

30 "Meanwhile, Eurylochos was making a fatal speech to his companions. 'My friends,' he said, 'you are in a bad way; but let me say a word to you. All deaths are hateful to miserable mortals, but the most pitiable death of all is to starve. Come along, let us drive off the best of these cattle, and sacrifice them to the immortal gods who rule the broad heavens. If we ever return home to Ithaca, we will build a rich temple to Helios Hyperion, and set up there many handsome offerings; but if the god is angry about his 40 straighthorns, and wants to destroy our ship, and if the other gods agree, I choose rather to die once with a mouthful of salt water than to be slowly squeezed out in a desert island.'

"The others applauded this speech. They wasted no time, but drove off the best of the cattle of Helios close by, for the fine beasts with their wide foreheads and crumpled horns used to graze not far off. The men stood round the cattle and prayed to the gods, but they had no barley-meal to sprinkle upon their 50 victims, so they used tender young oak-leaves which they picked from a tree. They had no wine to pour over the burnt offering, but they sprinkled water before they cooked the tripes. Then they chopt up the rest and put the pieces on the spits.

"At that moment I awoke and came back to the seashore. As I came near to the ship a sweetish odour of burning fat was diffused around me. . . .

"As soon as I came down to the seashore, I reproached them one and all, though we could do nothing to help it now: the cattle were already dead. 60 But awful portents were seen in that place: the skins crawled, the meat bellowed on the spits, both raw and roast; it was like the noise of cattle.

"Six days my companions feasted on the best of the cattle of Helios; but when the seventh day came, the furious tempest ceased; we embarked and went sailing away over the sea.

"When the island was far astern and no other land to be seen, nothing but sea and sky, Cronion brought a black cloud over our ship and darkened the deep. 70 Then she did not run long, for suddenly came the west wind screeching and blowing with a furious tempest, the gale broke both the forestays, the mast fell aft, and all the tackle tumbled into the hold, the mast hit the steersman's head and crushed the skull to splinters, he took a header from his deck and was drowned. Zeus at the same time thundered and struck our ship with his bolt; she shivered in all her timbers at the blow, and the place was full of sulphur. The men were cast out, there they were 80 bobbing up and down on the waves like so many crows. So God ended the homeward voyage for them.

"I kept pacing up and down the ship, until the sea tore the sides from the keel. A rolling wave carried her along dismantled, and snapt off the mast close to the keel, but the backstay had fallen upon it; this was made of stout oxhide, so I used it to lash together keel and mast, and I rode upon these drifting before those terrible winds. 90

"Now the furious tempest of the west wind was lulled, and the south quickly followed, bringing anxiety for me, for it was sure to carry me back again to the terrors of Charybdis. All night long I drifted, and by sunrise Scylla and dreadful Charybdis were before me. Charybdis swallowed up the salt water; but I had been carried high up, and caught the wild fig-tree; and I stuck to it like a bat and held tight. I had nothing to plant my feet upon for support and no way to climb; for the roots were far below, and the branches far 100 above, those thick long branches which overshadowed Charybdis. But I held tight without slackening until my mast and keel should be spouted up again. How I longed for them! and they came at last. At the time when a judge gets up from court for his dinner, after settling the morning's disputes among quarrelsome young men, just at that time my spars appeared out of Charybdis. I spread out hands and feet and let go, and came down plump in the water alongside the spars, and then clambered up and lay on them, 110 paddling with my hands. What of Scylla? The Father of gods and men would not allow her to set eyes on me, or I should not have escaped with my life.

"From that place I drifted for nine days, and on

the tenth at night the gods brought me to the island of Ogygia. There dwells Calypso, that goddess so beautiful and so terrible, who can speak the language of man; and she loved me and cared for me. But why go on with my story? . . ."

BOOK XIII

He finished, and all were silent as if spellbound in the shadowy hall. At last Alcinoös spoke:

"Well, Odysseus, since you have come as far as my brazen walls and lofty roof, I don't think you will look a foiled adventurer when you get home, even if you have had plenty of trouble.

"And now, gentlemen, I have a bolt in my quiver for you, who have always been welcome to drink my best company-wine and to hear my musician. The clothes are all packed in that coffer for our guest, with the fine gold plate and all the other gifts which our councillors have brought. I propose now that we offer him a large tripod and a cauldron apiece. We will collect the cost afterwards in the town: it would be too bad to let each man bear it all himself."

They were quite content with this proposal, and dispersed to their homes for the night.

As soon as the first rosy fingers of Dawn appeared, they made haste to the ship with the useful brass-ware. . . . Then the givers went on to the royal mansion and made ready for their banquet.

The King's Grace sacrificed an ox to our Lord Zeus Cronidès, who dwells in clouds and darkness. When they had burnt the thigh-slices, they had a famous feast and enjoyed it mightily, while Demodocos made music for them such as they always loved to hear.

Odysseus turned his head ever and anon to the shining sun, impatient for his setting, for he was eager to be gone. As a man longs for his meal when all through the day his brown oxen draw the plow over the fallow field, until his knees fail under him while he plods along, and he is glad to see the sun set and leave him to his dinner, so Odysseus was glad to see the sun set. At once he addressed the company, Alcinoös in particular, and said:

"My lord Alcinoös, most illustrious prince! now pour out your libations and let me go in peace, and good be with you all. For what my heart desired has been now brought to pass, a friendly escort and friendly gift; which may the gods in heaven bless! May I return to my home and find my faithful wife and my dear ones safe and sound! May you who remain make happy your own wives and children, and may the gods grant you success of every sort, and may no evil thing befall your people!"

All applauded this prayer, and urged the King to speed their guest on his way after his admirable words. Then King Alcinoös said to the herald:

"Pontonoös, mix a bowl and serve round to all in hall, that every one may offer a prayer to Father Zeus, and speed our guest on his way to his native land."

Then Pontonoös mixed the honey-hearted wine, and served it to all in turn: they poured the sacred drops to the blessed gods who rule the broad heavens, each man from his own seat. But Odysseus rose, and passed the two-handled cup to Arêtê, saying to her:

"May it be well with you, Queen, for ever, until old age and death shall come, as they come to all men. Now I depart: a blessing on you in this house, and your children, and your people, and their King Alcinoös!"

With these words Odysseus stept over the thresh-old. King Alcinoös sent the herald with him to lead him to the seashore where the ship lay; and Arêtê sent with him three of her women, one bearing a tunic and a robe newly washed, another to convey the coffer, a third with a supply of bread and red wine.

At the seaside where the ship lay, the young men of his escort received all this and stowed it away on board with the food and drink; and they laid a blanket and sheet on the deck of the poop for Odysseus, that he might sleep soundly. Odysseus went on board in silence and laid himself down, while the crew took their places, and cast off the hawser, drawing it through the hole in the stone pillar. Then they paddled away with a good swing back; blessed sleep fell on his eyelids, deep, sound and most sweet, the very image of death. And the ship! . . . She cut swiftly through the waves, and she carried a man whose mind was as wise as the gods: long years he had suffered great tribulation and sorrow of heart, wars on land and voyages over the stormy seas, and now he slept quietly forgetting all his troubles.

When that brightest of stars rose, which comes to tell us that the dawn is near, the travelling ship was drawing close to an island.

There is a harbour of Phorcys, the Old Man of the Sea, in the island of Ithaca. Two headlands enclose it, with steep sides sloping down to the harbour mouth, to shelter it from the waves which boisterous winds may raise outside: once inside, ships of good size can lie without mooring when they come within mooring-distance. . . .

In that harbour they sailed, for they knew it well. The ship ran up on the beach half her length with a dash—for the oarsmen put a good pace on her; the men leapt on the shore, and carried Odysseus out rolled up in his blanket and white sheet, and laid him down on the sand still heavy with sleep. All his goods were brought out by the sturdy fellows from the places where they had been packed by the fore-thought of Athena. These were piled in a heap under the olive tree, off the road, so that no chance wayfar-er might pilfer before Odysseus awoke. Then the ship went home again. . . .

[Upon awakening, Odysseus disguised himself as a beggar and learned from the faithful swineherd Eumaios of the shocking behavior of the wooers. He revealed himself to his son Telemachos, newly returned from inquiring after his father at the court of Menelaos in Sparta, and together they planned the slaughter of the wooers. His old dog recognized his master, as did his old nurse Eurycleia while bathing his scarred legs, but Odysseus withheld his identity from his wife Penelopeia, who was on the point of abandoning hope of his return.]

BOOK XXI

You remember Penelopeia's plan to bring her husband's great bow into the hall, and the axes, and to propose a shooting-match. Death was the prize, though they knew it not! Now she climbed the stair to her room and got out the key of the store-room, a fine key of bronze with a curving catch and an ivory handle. She passed on with her waiting-women into the innermost store-room, where her husband's treasures were kept, bronze and gold and wrought iron.

There was the great bow with a double back-springing curve, and a quiver full of arrows. . . . Then she sat down and laid it across her knees, weeping bitterly as she handled her husband's bow. But after she had enjoyed a good cry, she descended to the boisterous company in the great hall, holding in her hand the bow and the quiver with its arrows of sorrow. The attendants followed, carrying the tray with the master's iron gear for the contest.

Penelopeia stood by the doorpost of the great hall, holding her soft veil in front of her cheeks, and spoke out before them all:

"Hear me, you proud men that seek my hand, you who have laid siege to this house, eating and drinking day after day all this long time while my husband has been absent: and not one word could you say for yourselves, but that you wished to make me your wife! Now then, here is the prize before your eyes, and, here I lay my noble husband's bow. Whoever shall be able most easily to string the bow with his own hands, and shoot through the openings of twelve axes set in a line, he shall win me: I will leave this house of my young married days, so fine and so full of all good things, which I think I shall always remember even in my dreams."

Then she called Eumaios, and told him to carry round the bow and iron stuff. Eumaios took the bow from his mistress and tears came into his eyes as he laid it down; tears came into the drover's eyes where he stood, as he saw his master's bow. . . .

Then . . . [Telemachos] stood up, and threw off his purple cloak and the sword from his shoulders. First he drew a long trench in the floor, straight to the line, and set up the axes, stamping down the earth to hold them. All were surprised to see how neatly he did it, although he had never seen them

before. Then he returned to the doorway and tried the bow. Three times he moved the upper end forward as he strove to string it, three times he gave up. He felt sure he could bend the bow and shoot the shot; but when he had tried the third time, Odysseus made him a sign and he desisted, much against his will. . . .

The first man who came was Leiodês, their diviner, the son of Wineface Oinops, Leiodês, who always sat up at the very end of the hall beside the great mixing-bowl. He was a man who hated all kinds of violence, and resented their doings. He was the first to take up the bow and arrow; he stood at the threshold and tried the bow, but he could not bend it. His soft unpractised hands soon grew tired as he pulled and pulled. . . .

Then he called to Melanthios the goatherd: "Hurry up, you, light a fire in hall and put a good big seat near it with a fleece to sit on, and then fetch a good chunk of fat from the pantry. The young fellows can warm the bow and grease it well, and then we'll finish our game."

Melanthios lost no time in lighting a fire; he set the seat in place with its fleece, and brought out a good chunk of fat from the pantry. The young men warmed the bow and had their try, but no one could bend it, they were far too weak. . . .

Now the swineherd had taken up the bow; but as he was carrying it along there was a great outcry among the intruders, shouts and protests—"Where are are you taking that bow, you crazy swineherd, confound you? Your dogs shall tear you to pieces, all alone among your pigs! You bred them, and soon you shall feed them, if Apollo and All Gods are gracious to us!"

The swineherd dropt the bow on the spot; he was terrified by all these men shouting at him. But Telemachos called out from the other side in a threatening voice:

"Daddy, take that bow along; soon you'll be sorry if you listen to these people—or I'll chase you out into the country with a shower of stones; I may be younger, but I am stronger! I wish I were as much stronger than all these gentry. I could soon send them out of the house in a way they wouldn't like, for they are a wicked lot."

This made them all laugh heartily, and put them into a better temper; so the swineherd carried the bow along and put it into the hands of Odysseus. Then he went out and called Eurycleia the nurse, and said to her:

"My good Eurycleia, the young master says tha must shut the doors of your rooms; and if any one hears any noise or riot where we are, they must not come out, but mind their own business."

She did not understand the meaning of his words, but she shut the doors of their quarters.

Quietly Philoitios ran out and locked the courtyard gate. There was a strong ship's hawser under the porch, and he used this to fasten the gate; then he came in again and returned to his seat, with his eyes ever on Odysseus. By this time Odysseus was handling the bow, turning it round and round, and feeling every part, to see if the worms had got into it while its master was abroad. The others were watching him, and one would say with a look at his neighbour: "He seems a bit of a bow-fancier! He knows the points of a bow! I wonder if he has things like that at home. Maybe he thinks of making one: see how he handles it and poises it, the clever old rascal!" Or another, again: "He's welcome to all he'll get by stringing that bow!"

Amid all this talk Odysseus balanced the bow and scanned it over. Then as easily as a skilful musician stretches a new string on his harp, fastening the sheepgut over the pegs at each end, so without an effort Odysseus strung the great bow. Then he took the bow in his right hand, and twanged the string; at his touch it sang a clear note like a swallow. The gallants were dumbfounded, and their skin paled: Zeus gave a loud thunderclap, a manifest sign. And Odysseus was glad that after all his troubles Zeus had shown him a portent, Zeus, the son of Cronos the master-deceiver. He took one sharp arrow, which lay out on the table before him; the others were still in the quiver, but those present were soon to feel them. This he laid on the bridge of the bow, and drew back the string and notches together; still sitting upon his chair as he was, he took aim and let fly. He did not miss: right through the tops of all the axes went the shaft, and clean out at the other end. Then he turned to Telemachos and said:

"Telemachos, your guest is no discredit to you, I wasted no time in stringing the bow, and I did not miss the mark. My strength is yet unbroken, not as these men taunt me in their scorn. But now it is time to prepare supper for the company while the light lasts; after that there will be time for other sport with music and song, for these are the graces of a feast."

Then he signalled with a nod to Telemachos; and Telemachos slung on his sharp sword, and grasped his spear, and took his stand by the seat, the son armed by his father's side.

BOOK XXII

Now Odysseus stript off his rags, and leapt upon the great doorstone, holding the bow and the quiver full of arrows. He spread the arrows before his feet, and called aloud to the company:

"So the great game is played! and now for another mark, which no man has ever hit: I will see if Apollo will hear my prayer and let me strike it."

Then he let fly straight at Antinoös: he was holding a large golden goblet in both hands, and about to lift it for a drink. Bloodshed was not in his thoughts; who could imagine at the festal board, that one man amongst many, even if he were very strong, would bring certain death upon his own head? The arrow struck him in the throat, and the point ran through the soft neck. He sank to the other side, and the goblet dropt from his hands. In an instant a thick jet of blood spouted from his nostrils; he pushed the table away with a quick jerk of his feet, spilling all the vittles on the ground—meat and bread in a mess.

Then there was a great uproar all through the place as they saw the man fall; they leapt up from their seats in excitement and looked all round at the walls, but there was neither shield nor spear to be seen. They shouted angrily at Odysseus—

"You shall pay for shooting a man! No more games for you: now your death is a safe thing! You have killed the best fellow in Ithaca, and so the vultures shall eat you here!"

They were just guessing—they never dreamt that he intended to kill the man. Poor fools! they did not know that the cords of death were made fast about them all. But Odysseus said with a frowning face:

"Dogs! you thought I would never come back from Troy, so you have been carving up my substance, forcing the women to lie with you, courting my wife before I was dead, not fearing the gods who rule the broad heavens, nor the execration of man which follows you for ever. And now the cords of death are made fast about you all!"

Then pale fear seized upon them. Eurymachos alone dared to answer:

"If you are really Ithacan Odysseus come back, what you have said is just and right. Plenty of wild doings here, plenty more on your farms! But there lies the guilty man, Antinoös, who is answerable for everything. He was the ringleader; a wife was not what he wanted, not so much as something else, which Cronion has not allowed him to do. He wished to murder your son by a secret assault, and to be sole lord and master in this fine country of Ithaca. Now he has his deserts and lies dead. Sir, spare your own people! We will make it all good, all that has been consumed, all the wine that has been drunk in this hall; there shall be a public collection, and each man severally will pay twenty oxen in compensation, and bring gold and bronze to your heart's content. Till that is done no one could blame you for being angry."

Odysseus answered with a frowning face:

"Eurymachos, not if you would give me your whole estates, all you now possess, and more if you could get it, not even so would I stay my hand from killing until every man of you shall have paid in full for his outrageous violence. Now the choice lies before you, fight or flight, if you wish to save your lives; but I do not think any one of you will escape sudden death."

As they listened, their knees gave way beneath them and despair entered their hearts. But Eurymachos once more spoke:

"My friends," he cried out, "this man will not hold his hands—he thinks he is invincible. He has bow and arrows, and he will shoot from the doorway until he has killed us all! Let us fight for it! Draw your swords and put up the tables to fend off his arrows; have at him all together; see if we can't push him away from the door, and get out and make a hue and cry in the town! Then this man will soon shoot his last shot!"

With this he drew a good sharp blade from his side, and leapt at Odysseus with a yell; but on the instant Odysseus let fly an arrow and struck him in the chest by the nipple. The sharp point pierced his liver; down fell the sword from his hand, he doubled up and fell sprawling over a table, vittles and cup went scattering over the floor; he beat his brow on the ground in agony, his feet kicked out and knocked over the chair, and a mist came over his eyes.

Then Amphinomos ran straight at Odysseus, sword in hand, to force his way out of the door. But Telemachos was too quick for him; he cast his spear from behind and struck him between the shoulders—the point came out through his chest, and his face crashed on the ground with a thud. Telemachos leapt back and left the spear in the body; he feared that some one might stab him with a sword, or strike a blow, if he stooped to pull it out. He ran quickly up to his father, and said without wasting words:

"Father, I'll go at once and fetch you a shield and a couple of spears and a helmet to fit your head, and I'll arm myself, and do the same for the drover and the swineherd. We ought to be armed!"

Odysseus answered: "Run and bring them while I have arrows left, or they may crowd me away from the door."

Telemachos went promptly to the store where the arms were kept. He chose four shields and eight spears and four good helmets of bronze with horsehair plumes; these he brought back at full speed to his father. First he armed himself, then the two men fitted themselves out, and they stood by the indomitable Odysseus.

As long as the arrows lasted Odysseus went on bringing them down one after another. But when the arrows came to an end and he could shoot no more, he leaned his bow on the doorpost and left it standing, then slung the stout shield over his shoulders, and fitted the helmet on his head, where the nodding plume seemed to threaten those who saw it. Lastly, he picked up two sharp-pointed spears.

. . . But now Athena came near to them in the likeness of Mentor. Odysseus was cheered by the sight; he guessed it was Athena Captain of Hosts, but he said to her:

"Mentor, stand by me and remember your old comrade who always did the right thing by you. We are yearsmates!"

Then the others raised a loud shout in the hall, and Agelaos Damastoridês called out threateningly:

"Mentor! don't let Odysseus cajole you to fight on his side against us! If you do, I promise you that when we have settled father and son we will kill you too! You will pay with your life for what you mean to do! We will wipe out your people if they try to avenge you, and seize your goods indoors and out and throw them in with the rest. Your sons and daughters shall not live in your house, your worthy wife shall not walk in the town of Ithaca!"

Athena grew hot with anger at this, and taunted Odysseus with angry words:

"You are not the man you were, Odysseus! Where is the courage and strength you showed in that endless conflict, those nine years of battles for beautiful Helen! Many a man you killed in open fight, and by your device the great city of Priam was taken! Now you have come back to hearth and home, why do you grumble to show your strength before a pack of young men in love? Lazy man, stand by my side and see a masterpiece! I will teach you in the face of the enemy what means the gratitude of Mentor Strongi'th'arm!"

But she did not give him overwhelming victory at once, for she wished to prove still further the strength and courage of Odysseus and his doughty son. In the shape of a swallow she flew up to the smoky rafters, and perched there. . . .

On his way back to Greece, Odysseus forced his sailors to tie him to the mast of his ship in order to succeed in passing the land of the Sirens. From a Greek vase painting.

Another volley came from the crowd in fury, but Athena made most of them miss. One stuck in the doorpost, one in the door, and a third fell heavily against the wall. However, at last Amphimedon grazed the wrist of Telemachos, cutting the skin. . . .

Then they came to close fighting. Odysseus wounded Damastoridês with a spearthrust. Telemachos struck Leocritos, running him through the groin and out at the other side, and he fell flat on his face. At that moment Athena lifted her man-shattering ægis-cape, and held it against them from on high: they fell into a panic, and scampered along the hall like a herd of cows, when the darting gadfly attacks them and scatters them in the long days of springtime. The four were after them like vultures that swoop down out of the mountains with curving beaks and hooked claws on a flock of birds; hide as they will, flying low under the clouds, the vultures are on them, a pounce and a kill, there is no help and no refuge, and the onlookers think it fine sport. So these four rushed upon their enemies spearing men right and left; to every blow a dreadful groan, and the ground ran with blood. . . .

But the minstrel had escaped death so far. This was Phemios Terpiadês, the tuneful son of harmony as his name denotes; but he had been dragged in by compulsion to sing for the roistering crew. He was standing close to the back door, harp in hand, hesitating whether to run out of the hall and take refuge at the great altar of Zeus built in the courtyard, where both Laërtês and Odysseus used to sacrifice, or to run up and clasp the knees of Odysseus Laërtês' son. He thought it better to throw himself on the mercy of Odysseus. So he set down his harp on the ground between the mixing-bowl and the seat of state, and running quickly, clasped the master's knees and besought him in plain and simple words:

"Spare me, Odysseus, I pray! Have mercy upon me! You will be sorry afterwards if you kill a singer like me, one who can sing before God and man! I am self-taught, but God has planted all manner of songs in my mind. I am fit to sing before you as before God; then do not be eager to cut my throat. Your own son Telemachos can tell you that no will of my own made me come into this house, no desire for gain: I had to sing to these men at supper because they were too many for me and too strong, because they compelled me!"

Telemachos was close by his father, and heard this; he said at once:

"Spare him, father, he is innocent, don't strike him; and let us spare Medon the marshal, who used to look after me here when I was a little boy—unless Philoitios or the swineherd has killed him, or he may have come in your way as you went raging through the hall."

Medon heard him! He was there, smart lad, huddled under a chair, rolled up in a new-flayed cowhide, where he had crawled to escape if he could. Now he was out with one leap from under that chair, threw off the hide, dashed up to Telemachos, grasped his knees, cried out simply:

"Here I am, my dear—spare me, sir!—tell the master not to hurt me with that sharp sword! he's almighty now—and those brutes, no wonder a was angry with 'em, devouring his goods in his own house, and thought nothing of thee, like the fools they were!"

Odysseus smiled, and said:

"Cheer up, my son has saved your life. So you shall know, and tell other men, that doing well is far better than doing ill. Now then, you two had better go out of this carnage into the yard, and stay there until I have finished what is left for me to do in this house."

They both went out and sat down by the altar of Zeus, gazing about them and every moment expecting death.

Odysseus looked carefully in every part of the hall, in case any one were still alive and hiding himself from death. But he saw them all lying in heaps amid blood and dust. They were like a great haul of fishes which the fishermen have drawn into a bay with a wide net; they lie on the sand panting for the salt water, while the blazing sun takes away their life. Then at last Odysseus said to Telemachos:

"Go and call Nurse Eurycleia. I have something I want to tell her."

Telemachos went to the women's room, and shaking the door called Eurycleia:

"Wake up now, grandam wife! Wake up, keeper of all the women in this great house! Come this way; my father calls you. He has something which he wants to tell you!"

She had no notion what he meant, but she opened the door and followed him. There she found Odysseus, smothered in blood and filth, cheeks and chest, from head to foot, with a terrible look on his face; like a lion which has just chawed up a bullock in the farmyard. When she saw the piles of dead bodies and streams of blood, she stretched her body for the women's alleluia at this great victory; but Odysseus checked her and stopt it, not without difficulty, as he said plainly:

"Keep your joy in your heart, woman; quiet now, no cries of triumph. It is not decent to boast over slain men. These have been brought low by God's decree and their own wicked deeds. They respected none of those who walk on the earth, neither good men nor bad; therefore their recklessness has brought them to a dreadful end. Now tell over the names of the women in this house, and say which disgrace me and which are innocent."

The old nurse answered:

"Aye, my love, I'll tell thee the truth of it. Fifty women there are in this house; we have taught 'em all their work, to card wool and to put up with what a slave must bear. A dozen of 'em are shameless huzzies, and pay no respect to me or my lady herself. The young master has but now grown up, and the mistress wadn't let him give orders to the women. But I'll just go up the stairs and tell her the news; she's haven a bit of sleep, thank God!"

Odysseus answered:

"Don't wake her yet. Tell all the women to come here who have been disgracing themselves."

Then the old woman went out of the hall to summon the women at once. He called Telemachos and the drover and swineherd, and told them plainly what they had to do:

"The first thing is to carry out these bodies, and tell the women to help you, then wipe clean all the chairs and tables with sponge and water. When you have put the place in order, drive out the women between the domed house and the courtyard wall, and run your sword through them; kill them all, and teach them to forget their secret bussing and cuddling with these brave gallants."

The women now came in with dreadful wailing and floods of tears. First they had to carry out the dead bodies, and lay them along the courtyard wall, packed close together under the gallery. Odysseus gave them directions and let them waste no time—they had to obey. Then they cleaned up the tables and seats with sponges and water. Telemachos and the two men scraped over the floor with shovels, and the women cleared out the scrapings. When the great hall was quite in order, they drove the women outside, and cooped them up in a narrow space between the domed house and the wall so that they could not get out. Telemachos had been thinking, and now he said:

"I should not care to give a clean death to these women who have heaped insults on my head, and upon my mother, and slept by the side of those who pretended to her hand."

So he rigged up a ship's hawser, fastening one end to a tall pillar and throwing the other round the dome. A noose was looped round the neck of each, and he pulled it up tight so that their feet would not touch the ground. They were strung up with their heads in a row—a pitiable death to die, no lover's bed indeed! They looked like a lot of thrushes or doves caught in a net when they come to roost in the bushes. Their feet jerked for a little while, but not long. . . .

The work was done. They washed their hands and feet and went into the great house. Then Odysseus called his nurse Eurycleia, and said:

"Bring sulphur and fire, to cleanse the hall and sweeten the air. Then request Penelopeia to come here with her waiting-women; and tell all the other women in the house to come." . . .

BOOK XXIII

Away went the old woman with her news that the master was in the house. She climbed the stairs chuckling to herself, her knees trotted along, her feet tumbled over each other. She leant down over her mistress, and said:

"Wake up, dear love; wake up, Penelopeia! Come and see with thi own eyes what tha's prayed for many a long day! The master has come, he's in the house, better late than never! and he's killed the whole lot of come-marry-me-quicks, who have made themselves a nuisance, and eaten thi vittles, and plagued thi boy!"

Penelopeia was too cautious to believe this. She replied:

"Nanny dear, the gods have made you mad. They can make the wisest of men foolish, and they can give good sense to the weakest mind. They have upset even you, and you are generally sound enough. Why do you mock me? I have trouble as it is, and here you come to tell me this crazy tale, and wake me out of a lovely sleep when my poor eyes were fast closed! I have not had such a sleep since Odysseus went on his voyage to Ilion the accursed, which I cannot endure to name! Go away, do, and get back to your room. If any of my other women had waked me up and told me this tale, I should have sent her off in disgrace, but your age shall protect you."

The old woman answered:

"I don't mock tha, my love, 'tis the truth! The master has come, he's in the house, as I say—that stranger man, the one they all sneered at in hall. Telemachos knew that he was here, so it turned out, but he's a prudent one, hid his father's notions. Punish the men who were above themselves, make 'em pay for their violence, that was his mind!"

How glad was Penelopeia! She sprang out of bed, and flung her arms round the old woman's neck: the tears ran down her cheeks. . . . She went down the stairs with a heart full of perplexity. Should she keep aloof and question her husband? Should she go to his side and cover head and hands with her kisses?

She passed over the great doorstone into the hall, and seated herself opposite to Odysseus by the wall on one side of the bright fire. He was sitting against a pillar looking down, and wondering whether his brave wife would speak to him when she saw him. But she sat silent a long time as if struck dumb. Again and again she turned her eager eyes and looked hard at his face, but then again she could not know him in those dirty rags. At last Telemachos burst out impatiently:

"My mother—a devil of a mother you are, with your hard heart! Why do you keep all that way from father? Why won't you sit beside him and ask some question or say something? I'm sure no other woman could be so cold and keep her husband at a distance, now he has come home after twenty years and all those terrible dangers! But your heart was always harder than flint."

Penelopeia, still doubtful, answered:

"My boy, my heart is numbed. I cannot speak to him, or ask questions, or look into his face. If he is indeed Odysseus, and this is his house, we shall know each other well enough; there are secrets that we two know and no one else."

. . . Eurynomê bathed Odysseus and rubbed him down and gave him good clothes. Then he seemed another man, taller and stronger than before, and splendid from head to foot by grace of Athena; his head covered with a thick curly crop like the thick clustering petals of the hyacinth. He was a noble and brilliant figure; you might think of some perfect work of art made by one who is inspired by the divine artists, Hephaistos and Pallas Athena, brilliant with gold over silver. He came out of the bathroom looking more like a god than a man, and returned to his former seat facing his wife. Then he said to her:

"Strange woman! The inscrutable will of God has made your heart unfeeling beyond mortal women. No other wife could endure to keep her husband at a distance, when he has just returned after twenty years of dreadful perils. Very well. Come, Nanny, lay me a bed and I will sleep alone. She has a heart of steel, it is clear."

His clever wife replied:

"Strange man, I am not proud, or contemptuous, or offended, but I know what manner of man you were when you sailed away from Ithaca. Come, Eurycleia, make the bed outside the room which he built himself; put the fine bedstead outside, and lay out the rugs and blankets and fleeces."

This was a little trap for her husband. He burst into a rage:

"Wife, that has cut me to the heart! Who has moved my bed? That would be a difficult job for the best workman, unless God himself should come down and move it. It would be easy for God, but no man could easily prize it up, not the strongest man living! There is a great secret in that bed. I made it myself, and no one else touched it. There was a strong young olive tree in full leaf growing in an enclosure, the trunk as thick as a pillar. Round this I built our bridal chamber; I did the whole thing myself, laid the stones and built a good roof over it, jointed the doors and fitted them in their places. After that I cut off the branches and trimmed the trunk from the root up, smoothed it carefully with the adze and made it straight to the line. This tree I made the bedpost.

That was the beginning of my bed; I bored holes through it, and fitted the other posts about it, and inlaid the framework with gold and silver and ivory, and I ran through it leather straps coloured purple. Now I have told you my secret. And I don't know if it is still there, wife, or if some one has cut the olive at the root and moved my bed!"

She was conquered, she could hold out no longer when Odysseus told the secret she knew so well. She burst into tears and ran straight to him, throwing her arms about his neck. She kissed his head, and cried:

"Don't be cross with me, my husband, you were always a most understanding man! The gods brought affliction upon us because they grudged us the joy of being young and growing old together! Don't be angry, don't be hurt because I did not take you in my arms as soon as I saw you! My heart has been frozen all this time with a fear that some one would come and deceive me with a false tale; there are so many impostors! But now you have told me the secret of our bed, that settles it. No one else has seen it, only you and I, and my maid Actoris, the one my father gave me when I came to you, who used to keep the door of our room. You have convinced your hard-hearted wife!"

Odysseus was even more deeply moved, and his tears ran as he held her in his arms, the wife of his heart, so faithful and so wise. She felt like a ship-wrecked mariner, when the stout ship has been driven before the storm and smashed by the heavy waves, but a few have escaped by swimming. How glad they are to see land at last, to get out of the water and stand upon solid ground all caked with brine! So glad was Penelopeia to see her husband at last; she held her white arms close round his neck, and could not let him go. Dawn would have risen upon their tears of joy, but Athena had a thought for them. She held the night in its course and made it long; she kept Dawn on her golden throne at the end of Ocean, so that she could not yoke up her swift pair, Flasher and Flamer, the colts who bring Dawn with her light to mortal men. . . .

Aeschylus

525–456 B.C.

Aeschylus was born during the lifetime of Thespis, the "inventor" of tragedy. To the single actor that Thespis had drawn from the older chorus Aeschylus added a second, which at last made possible mature dramatic dialogue. The seven extant plays of Aeschylus, the oldest preserved of Greek dramas, reveal in themselves an extraordinary development from the choral lyrics of *The Suppliant Women* (c. 490 B.C.) to the full-scale tragedy of *Agamemnon* (458 B.C.).

Yet the man who brought Western drama to maturity was more than a playwright. Born into an ancient noble family in Eleusis, a religious center of Attica, Aeschylus fought at Marathon and Salamis and prided himself on his prowess as a soldier. In the theater he directed and acted in his own plays, and is said to have written as many as seventy tragedies and numerous satyr plays. He first won the prize for tragedy in the contest of 484 B.C. and gained it, in all, thirteen times. His epitaph, however, preserved his military rather than his literary reputation: "Here lies the Athenian Aeschylus, son of Euphorion, who died in grain-growing Gela. The plain of Marathon could tell his great courage, and the long-haired Mede who discovered it there."

The world of Aeschylus was democratic, vigorous Athens rising to hegemony over the Greek states. As he was growing up, Attica rid herself of the last of her tyrants and established a democratic constitution that Aeschylus supports by implication. *Prometheus Bound* (c. 479 B.C.) studies the conflict between brute power and human rights, between the authoritarian rule of Zeus and the courageous independence of the last of the Titans. *The Persians* (472 B.C.) not only glorifies the victory of the Greeks over their Eastern enemies but warns against the evils of Oriental despotism. As a member of a conservative old family in a town sacred to the earth-goddess, Demeter, Aeschylus reveals the conventional religious views of the older generation, and his plays usually turn on moral or theological issues—the right of sanctuary in *The Suppliant Women*, the punishment of pride in *The Persians*, the inheritance of crime in the *Oresteia*, and the power of Fate everywhere.

His dramatic technique is old-fashioned, though he made great strides beyond his predecessors. In his plays the chorus, though reduced, is still an organic element, advising the characters, interpreting their actions, and drawing moral lessons. His limitation to two actors, though they might represent more than two characters, restricted the scope of his action. Any one play, confined by these conventions, had to have a very simple plot; but Aeschylus developed the scheme of presenting a more extended story through a trilogy, or series of three related plays (of which the *Oresteia* is our only extant example). Violent action and any considerable movement were still outlawed as sacrilegious, but he compensated for the restriction by using spectacular stage effects and rich costumes. Although his plays are more dignified than those of Euripides, his is a theatrical dignity. It reposes in the grand style of his lines, sometimes close to bombast, but more often animated by a cosmic vision and lofty poetic inspiration. The titanic majesty of his themes and his verse revives an age in which men were not afraid to be noble.

Agamemnon, the masterpiece of Aeschylus, is the first play in the *Oresteia* trilogy, which relates a grim tale of vengeful crimes within one famous family. As the responsibility for avenging crime passes through the generations of the ill-fated House of Atreus, we see in operation the Greek doctrine of punishment in kind. Atreus, King of Mycenae, had committed an initial crime

when, finding that his brother Thyestes had seduced Aethra, his wife, he served him a dish containing the flesh of Thyestes' own children. Placing a curse on the House of Atreus, Thyestes dedicated his only surviving son, Aegisthus, to revenge on his brother and his brother's sons, Agamemnon and Menelaus.

Agamemnon of Mycenae married the charming Clytemnestra, half-sister of Helen of Troy, who bore him two daughters, Electra and Iphigenia, and a son, Orestes. When Helen was snatched from her husband, Menelaus, by the Trojan prince Paris, Menelaus induced his brother Agamemnon to recruit the Greek princes for the expedition against Troy. But the Greek ships lay becalmed at Aulis because the goddess Artemis demanded the sacrifice of a princess before they might sail. Agamemnon, the leader of the host, lured his daughter Iphigenia to Aulis and offered her as sacrifice, although, unknown to anyone, Artemis rescued her at the last moment and made her a priestess among the savage Tauri. Agamemnon's act sped the Greek ships to Troy, but it won him the undying hatred of his wife Clytemnestra, who made common cause with the vengeful Aegisthus and plotted her husband's murder as they waited out the long years of the war. The play *Agamemnon* portrays the return of the triumphant king with his captive prize, the Trojan princess Cassandra, and Clytemnestra's savage murder of them both.

But the vengeful crimes continue in the next generation. Electra had saved her young brother from her mother, who feared his revenge. While he was being reared by his uncle in a nearby kingdom, Electra frequently reminded him of his duty to avenge his father's death. When the Delphic oracle confirmed this duty, Orestes returned to Mycenae and, egged on by the bloodthirsty Electra, murdered his mother and Aegisthus. At last the family crimes were ended, but for a time the divine punishers, the Furies, pursued the haggard Orestes—even to the land of the savage Tauri, where he rescued his sister, Iphigenia the priestess. Only a formal trial before Athena freed Orestes from his punishment, when it was established that he had acted in obedience to the Delphic oracle. So peace finally came to the House of Atreus.

As *Agamemnon* tells of the murder of the king, the second play in the trilogy, *The Libation-Bearers* (*Choephoroe*), relates Orestes' murder of Clytemnestra and Aegisthus, and the third, *The Furies* (*Eumenides*), completes the story with the punishment and trial of Orestes. Although each of the *Oresteia* plays rises to its own climax, the three form a tightly knit unit, so that the dramatic resolution of the hateful conflict does not come until the end of the third play. Taken together, they are somewhat like a modern play in three acts. As the general title suggests, Orestes is the leading character in this drama, even though he does not appear in the first play. Like Siegfried in Wagner's *Ring* operas, he gradually emerges in the cycle and eventually carries the whole action to its peaceful resolution.

The *Oresteia* is the supreme achievement of Aeschylus. Though the dramatic conventions of his day required a simpler plot and less action than appear in the later plays of Sophocles, he makes use of the trilogy scheme to give a magnificent and terrifying spectacle of human hate and suffering and the inexorable operation of divine law in the affairs of men. His favorite theme—pride goeth before a fall—is grimly illustrated in the career of Agamemnon. Although the style is sometimes inflated, the effect is generally lofty and poetic. A testimony to the enduring influence of this masterpiece is Eugene O'Neill's psychoanalytic interpretation of the same characters and plot in his modern version of the trilogy, *Mourning Becomes Electra*.

Agamemnon

CHARACTERS IN THE PLAY

WATCHMAN
CHORUS OF OLD MEN OF THE CITY
CLYTEMNESTRA
HERALD
AGAMEMNON
CASSANDRA
AEGISTHUS

(SCENE: *A space in front of the palace of* AGA-MEMNON *in Argos. Night. A* WATCHMAN *on the roof of the palace.*)

WATCHMAN.

THE gods it is I ask to release me from this watch
A year's length now, spending my nights like a dog,
Watching on my elbow on the roof of the sons of Atreus
So that I have come to know the assembly of the nightly stars
Those which bring storm and those which bring summer to men,   5
The shining Masters riveted in the sky—
I know the decline and rising of those stars.
And now I am waiting for the sign of the beacon,
The flame of fire that will carry the report from Troy,
News of her taking. Which task has been assigned me   10
By a woman of sanguine heart but a man's mind.
Yet when I take my restless rest in the soaking dew,
My night not visited with dreams—
For fear stands by me in the place of sleep

That I cannot firmly close my eyes in sleep—   15
Whenever I think to sing or hum to myself
As an antidote to sleep, then every time I groan
And fall to weeping for the fortunes of this house
Where not as before are things well ordered now.
But now may a good chance fall, escape from pain,
The good news visible in the midnight fire.   21

(*Pause. A light appears, gradually increasing, the light of the beacon.*)

Ha! I salute you, torch of the night whose light
Is like the day, an earnest of many dances
In the city of Argos, celebration of Peace.
I call to Agamemnon's wife; quickly to rise   25
Out of her bed and in the house to raise
Clamour of joy in answer to this torch
For the city of Troy is taken—
Such is the evident message of the beckoning flame.
And I myself will dance my solo first   30
For I shall count my master's fortune mine
Now that this beacon has thrown me a lucky throw.
And may it be when he comes, the master of this house,
That I grasp his hand in my hand.
As to the rest, I am silent. A great ox, as they say,
Stands on my tongue. The house itself, if it took voice,   36
Could tell the case most clearly. But I will only speak
To those who know. For the others I remember nothing.

(*Enter* CHORUS OF OLD MEN. *During the following chorus the day begins to dawn.*)

CHORUS.

The tenth year it is since Priam's high
Adversary, Menelaus the king   40
And Agamemnon, the double-throned and sceptred
Yoke of the sons of Atreus
Ruling in fee from God,
From this land gathered an Argive army
On a mission of war a thousand ships,   45
Their hearts howling in boundless bloodlust
In eagles' fashion who in lonely
Grief for nestlings above their homes hang
Turning in cycles
Beating the air with the oars of their wings,   50
Now to no purpose
Their love and task of attention.

But above there is One,
Maybe Pan, maybe Zeus or Apollo,
Who hears the harsh cries of the birds   55

Agamemnon. From *The Agamemnon of Aeschylus* translated by Louis MacNeice. Used by permission of Harcourt Brace and Company, Inc., and Faber and Faber Ltd.
8. **beacon,** the last in the series of signal fires, lighted in succession to announce the Greeks' victory at Troy. 11. **woman,** Clytemnestra.

36. **tongue.** The ox signified silence in an old Greek proverb. 47. **eagles'.** This simile, likening Menelaus and Agamemnon to rapacious eagles, will be elaborated later in the omen of the eagles killing the hare, interpreted by the prophet Calchas as the destruction of Troy.

Guests in his kingdom,
Wherefore, though late, in requital
He sends the Avenger.
Thus Zeus our master
Guardian of guest and of host   60
Sent against Paris the sons of Atreus
For a woman of many men
Many the dog-tired wrestlings
Limbs and knees in the dust pressed—
    For both the Greeks and Trojans   65
    An overture of breaking spears.

Things are where they are, will finish
In the manner fated and neither
Fire beneath nor oil above can soothe
The stubborn anger of the unburnt offering.   70
As for us, our bodies are bankrupt,
The expedition left us behind
And we wait supporting on sticks
Our strength—the strength of a child;
For the marrow that leaps in a boy's body   75
Is no better than that of the old
For the War God is not in his body;
While the man who is very old
And his leaf withering away
Goes on the three-foot way   80
No better than a boy, and wanders
A dream in the middle of the day.

But you, daughter of Tyndareus,
Queen Clytemnestra,
What is the news, what is the truth, what have you
    learnt,   85
On the strength of whose word have you thus
Sent orders for sacrifice round?
All the gods, the gods of the town,
Of the worlds of Below and Above,
By the door, in the square,   90
Have their altars ablaze with your gifts,
From here, from there, all sides, all corners.
Sky-high leap the flame-jets fed
By gentle and undeceiving
Persuasion of sacred unguent,   95
Oil from the royal stores.
Of these things tell
That which you can, that which you may,
Be healer of this our trouble
Which at times torments with evil   100
Though at times by propitiations
A shining hope repels
The insatiable thought upon grief
Which is eating away our hearts.

Of the omen which powerfully speeded   105
That voyage of strong men, by God's grace even I
Can tell, my age can still
Be galvanized to breathe the strength of song,

To tell how the kings of all the youth of Greece
Two-throned but one in mind   110
Were launched with pike and punitive hand
Against the Trojan shore by angry birds.
Kings of the birds to our kings came,
One with a white rump, the other black,
Appearing near the palace on the spear-arm side 115
Where all could see them,
Tearing a pregnant hare with the unborn young
Foiled of their courses.
    Cry, cry upon Death; but may the good prevail.

But the diligent prophet of the army seeing the sons
Of Atreus twin in temper knew   121
That the hare-killing birds were the two
Generals, explained it thus—
"In time this expedition sacks the town
Of Troy before whose towers   125
By Fate's force the public
Wealth will be wasted.
Only let not some spite from the gods benight the
    bulky battalions,
The bridle of Troy, nor strike them untimely;
For the goddess feels pity, is angry   130
With the winged dogs of her father
Who killed the cowering hare with her unborn
    young;
Artemis hates the eagles' feast."
    Cry, cry upon Death; but may the good prevail.

"But though you are so kind, goddess,   135
To the little cubs of lions
And to all the sucking young of roving beasts
In whom your heart delights,
Fulfil us the signs of these things,
The signs which are good but open to blame,   140
And I call on Apollo the Healer
That his sister raise not against the Greeks
Unremitting gales to baulk their ships,
Hurrying on another kind of sacrifice, with no feast-
    ing,
Barbarous building of hates and disloyalties   145
Grown on the family. For anger grimly returns
Cunningly haunting the house, avenging the death
    of a child, never forgetting its due."
So cried the prophet—evil and good together,
Fate that the birds foretold to the king's house. 150
In tune with this
    Cry, cry upon Death; but may the good prevail.

Zeus, whoever He is, if this
Be a name acceptable,

133. **feast.** As goddess of childbirth, Artemis pities the mother hare, slain by the eagles as she is about to give birth to her young. 143. **ships,** as Artemis had becalmed their ships at Aulis to prevent them from reaching Troy. 153–155. **Zeus . . . him.** Aeschylus spiritualizes Zeus into a concept of divinity broader than the Zeus of Homer.

By this name I will call him.   155
There is no one comparable
When I reckon all of the case
Excepting Zeus, if ever I am to jettison
The barren care which clogs my heart.

Not He who formerly was great   160
With brawling pride and mad for broils
Will even be said to have been.
And He who was next has met
His match and is seen no more,
But Zeus is the name to cry in your triumph-song
And win the prize for wisdom.   166

Who setting us on the road
Made this a valid law—
    "That men must learn by suffering."
Drop by drop in sleep upon the heart   170
Falls the laborious memory of pain,
Against one's will comes wisdom;
The grace of the gods is forced on us
    Throned inviolably.

So at that time the elder   175
Chief of the Greek ships
Would not blame any prophet
Nor face the flail of fortune;
For unable to sail, the people
Of Greece were heavy with famine,   180
Waiting in Aulis where the tides
    Flow back, opposite Chalcis.

But the winds that blew from the Strymon,
Bringing delay, hunger, evil harbourage,
Crazing men, rotting ships and cables,   185
By drawing out the time
Were shredding into nothing the flower of Argos,
When the prophet screamed a new
Cure for that bitter tempest
And heavier still for the chiefs,   190
Pleading the anger of Artemis so that the sons of
    Atreus
Beat the ground with their sceptres and shed tears.

Then the elder king found voice and answered:
"Heavy is my fate, not obeying,
And heavy it is if I kill my child, the delight of my
    house,   195
And with a virgin's blood upon the altar
Make foul her father's hands.
Either alternative is evil.
How can I betray the fleet

And fail the allied army?   200
It is right they should passionately cry for the winds
    to be lulled
By the blood of a girl. So be it. May it be well."

But when he had put on the halter of Necessity
Breathing in his heart a veering wind of evil   204
Unsanctioned, unholy, from that moment forward
He changed his counsel, would stop at nothing.
For the heart of man is hardened by infatuation,
A faulty adviser, the first link of sorrow.
Whatever the cause, he brought himself to slay
His daughter, an offering to promote the voyage   210
To a war for a runaway wife.

Her prayers and her cries of father,
Her life of a maiden,
Counted for nothing with those militarists;
But her father, having duly prayed, told the attend-
    ants   215
To lift her, like a goat, above the altar
With her robes falling about her,
To lift her boldly, her spirit fainting,
And hold back with a gag upon her lovely mouth
By the dumb force of a bridle   220
The cry which would curse the house.
Then dropping on the ground her saffron dress,
Glancing at each of her appointed
Sacrificers a shaft of pity,
Plain as in a picture she wished   225
To speak to them by name, for often
At her father's table where men feasted
She had sung in celebration for her father
With a pure voice, affectionately, virginally,
The hymn for happiness at the third libation.   230
The sequel to this I saw not and tell not
But the crafts of Calchas gained their object.
To learn by suffering is the equation of Justice; the
    Future
Is known when it comes, let it go till then.
To know in advance is to sorrow in advance.   235
The facts will appear with the shining of the dawn.
            (*Enter* CLYTEMNESTRA.)
But may good, at the least, follow after
As the queen here wishes, who stands
Nearest the throne, the only
    Defence of the land of Argos.   240
LEADER OF THE CHORUS.
I have come, Clytemnestra, reverencing your au-
    thority.
For it is right to honour our master's wife
When the man's own throne is empty.
But you, if you have heard good news for certain,
    or if
You sacrifice on the strength of flattering hopes,   245
I would gladly hear. Though I cannot cavil at si-
    lence.

160–163. He . . . . He. Zeus had been preceded as ruler of all by
Uranus and Cronos, each deposed by force. 177. **prophet**. Agamemnon did not blame Calchas, the seer, for his hateful prophecy.
183. **Strymon**, a river in Macedonia.

CLYTEMNESTRA.

Bearing good news, as the proverb says, may Dawn
Spring from her mother Night.
You will hear something now that was beyond your
        hopes.
The men of Argos have taken Priam's city.   250

LEADER.

What! I cannot believe it. It escapes me.

CLYTEMNESTRA.

Troy in the hands of the Greeks. Do I speak plain?

LEADER.

Joy creeps over me, calling out my tears.

CLYTEMNESTRA.

Yes. Your eyes proclaim your loyalty.

LEADER.

But what are your grounds? Have you a proof of
        it?   255

CLYTEMNESTRA.

There is proof indeed—unless God has cheated us.

LEADER.

Perhaps you believe the inveigling shapes of dreams?

CLYTEMNESTRA.

I would not be credited with a dozing brain!

LEADER.

Or are you puffed up by Rumour, the wingless flyer?

CLYTEMNESTRA.

You mock my common sense as if I were a child.   260

LEADER.

But at what time was the city given to sack?

CLYTEMNESTRA.

In this very night that gave birth to this day.

LEADER.

What messenger could come so fast?

CLYTEMNESTRA.

Hephaestus, launching a fine flame from Ida,
Beacon forwarding beacon, despatch-riders of fire,
Ida relayed to Hermes' cliff in Lemnos   266
And the great glow from the island was taken over
        third
By the height of Athos that belongs to Zeus,
And towering then to straddle over the sea
The might of the running torch joyfully tossed   270
The gold gleam forward like another sun,
Herald of light to the heights of Mount Macistus,
And he without delay, nor carelessly by sleep
Encumbered, did not shirk his intermediary role,
His farflung ray reached the Euripus' tides   275
And told Messapion's watchers, who in turn
Sent on the message further
Setting a stack of dried-up heather on fire.
And the strapping flame, not yet enfeebled, leapt
Over the plain of Asopus like a blazing moon   280
And woke on the crags of Cithaeron
Another relay in the chain of fire.
The light that was sent from far was not declined
By the look-out men, who raised a fiercer yet,
A light which jumped the water of Gorgopis   285

And to Mount Aegiplanctus duly come
Urged the reveille of the punctual fire.
So then they kindle it squanderingly and launch
A beard of flame big enough to pass
The headland that looks down upon the Saronic
        gulf,   290
Blazing and bounding till it reached at length
The Arachnaean steep, our neighbouring heights;
And leaps in the latter end on the roof of the sons of
        Atreus
Issue and image of the fire on Ida.
Such was the assignment of my torch-racers,   295
The task of each fulfilled by his successor,
And victor is he who ran both first and last.
Such is the proof I offer you, the sign
My husband sent me out of Troy.

LEADER.

To the gods, queen, I shall give thanks presently.
But I would like to hear this story further,   301
To wonder at it in detail from your lips.

CLYTEMNESTRA.

The Greeks hold Troy upon this day.
The cries in the town I fancy do not mingle.
Pour oil and vinegar into the same jar,   305
You would say they stand apart unlovingly;
Of those who are captured and those who have
        conquered
Distinct are the sounds of their diverse fortunes,
For *these* having flung themselves about the bodies
Of husbands and brothers, or sons upon the bod-
        ies   310
Of aged fathers from a throat no longer
Free, lament the fate of their most loved.
But *those* a night's marauding after battle
Sets hungry to what breakfast the town offers
Not billeted duly in any barracks order   315
But as each man has drawn his lot of luck.
So in the captive homes of Troy already
They take their lodging, free of the frosts
And dews of the open. Like happy men
They will sleep all night without sentry.   320
But if they respect duly the city's gods,
Those of the captured land and the sanctuaries of
        the gods,
They need not, having conquered, fear reconquest.
But let no lust fall first upon the troops
To plunder what is not right, subdued by gain,   325
For they must still, in order to come home safe,
Get round the second lap of the doubled course.
So if they return without offence to the gods
The grievance of the slain may learn at last
A friendly talk—unless some fresh wrong falls.   330
Such are the thoughts you hear from me, a woman.
But may the good prevail for all to see.
We have much good. I only ask to enjoy it.

LEADER.

Woman, you speak with sense like a prudent man.

I, who have heard your valid proofs, prepare   335
To give the glory to God.
Fair recompense is brought us for our troubles.
    (CLYTEMNESTRA *goes back into the palace.*)
  CHORUS.
O Zeus our king and Night our friend
Donor of glories,
Night who cast on the towers of Troy   340
A close-clinging net so that neither the grown
Nor any of the children can pass
The enslaving and huge
Trap of all-taking destruction.
Great Zeus, guardian of host and guest,   345
I honour who has done his work and taken
A leisured aim at Paris so that neither
Too short nor yet over the stars
  He might shoot to no purpose.

From Zeus is the blow they can tell of,   350
This at least can be established,
They have fared according to his ruling. For some
Deny that the gods deign to consider those among
    men
Who trample on the grace of inviolate things;
It is the impious man says this,   355
For Ruin is revealed the child
Of not to be attempted actions
When men are puffed up unduly
And their houses are stuffed with riches.
Measure is the best. Let danger be distant,   360
This should suffice a man
With a proper part of wisdom.
  For a man has no protection
  Against the drunkenness of riches
  Once he has spurned from his sight   365
  The high altar of Justice.

Sombre Persuasion compels him,
Intolerable child of calculating Doom;
All cure is vain, there is no glozing it over
But the mischief shines forth with a deadly light
And like bad coinage   371
By rubbings and frictions
He stands discoloured and black
Under the test—like a boy
Who chases a winged bird   375
He has branded his city for ever.
His prayers are heard by no god;
Who makes such things his practice
The gods destroy him.
  This way came Paris   380
  To the house of the sons of Atreus
  And outraged the table of friendship
  Stealing the wife of his host.

Leaving to her countrymen clanging of
Shields and of spears and   385

Launching of warships
And bringing instead of a dowry destruction to
    Troy
Lightly she was gone through the gates daring
Things undared. Many the groans
Of the palace spokesmen on this theme—   390
"O the house, the house, and its princes,
O the bed and the imprint of her limbs;
One can see him crouching in silence
Dishonoured and unreviling."
Through desire for her who is overseas, a ghost   395
Will seem to rule the household.
  And now her husband hates
  The grace of shapely statues;
  In the emptiness of their eyes
  All their appeal is departed.   400

But appearing in dreams persuasive
Images come bringing a joy that is vain,
Vain for when in fancy he looks to touch her—
Slipping through his hands the vision
Rapidly is gone   405
Following on wings the walks of sleep.
Such are his griefs in his house on his hearth,
Such as these and worse than these,
But everywhere through the land of Greece which
    men have left
Are mourning women with enduring hearts   410
To be seen in all houses; many
Are the thoughts which stab their hearts;
  For those they sent to war
  They know, but in place of men
  That which comes home to them   415
  Is merely an urn and ashes.

But the money-changer War, changer of bodies,
Holding his balance in the battle
Home from Troy refined by fire
Sends back to friends the dust   420
That is heavy with tears, stowing
A man's worth of ashes
In an easily handled jar.
And they wail speaking well of the men how that
    one
Was expert in battle, and one fell well in the
    carnage—   425
But for another man's wife.
Muffled and muttered words;
And resentful grief creeps up against the sons
Of Atreus and their cause.
  But others there by the wall   430
  Entombed in Trojan ground
  Lie, handsome of limb,
  Holding and hidden in enemy soil.

Heavy is the murmur of an angry people
Performing the purpose of a public curse;   435

There is something cowled in the night
That I anxiously wait to hear.
For the gods are not blind to the
Murderers of many and the black
Furies in time 440
When a man prospers in sin
By erosion of life reduce him to darkness,
Who, once among the lost, can no more
Be helped. Over-great glory
Is a sore burden. The high peak 445
Is blasted by the eyes of Zeus.
    I prefer an unenvied fortune,
    Not to be a sacker of cities
    Nor to find myself living at another's
    Ruling, myself a captive. 450

AN OLD MAN.

From the good news' beacon a swift
Rumour is gone through the town.
Who knows if it be true
Or some deceit of the gods?

ANOTHER O.M.

Who is so childish or broken in wit 455
To kindle his heart at a new-fangled message of
    flame
And then be downcast
At a change of report?

ANOTHER O.M.

It fits the temper of a woman 459
To give her assent to a story before it is proved.

ANOTHER O.M.

The over-credulous passion of women expands
In swift conflagration but swiftly declining is gone
The news that a woman announced.

LEADER OF THE CHORUS.

Soon we shall know about the illuminant torches,
The beacons and the fiery relays, 465
Whether they were true or whether like dreams
That pleasant light came here and hoaxed our wits.
Look: I see, coming from the beach, a herald
Shadowed with olive shoots; the dust upon him,
Mud's thirsty sister and colleague, is my witness
That he will not give dumb news nor news by
    lighting 471
A flame of fire with the smoke of mountain timber;
In words he will either corroborate our joy—
But the opposite version I reject with horror.
To the good appeared so far may good be added.

ANOTHER SPEAKER.

Whoever makes other prayers for this our city, 476
May he reap himself the fruits of his wicked heart.

(*Enter the* HERALD, *who kisses the ground before
speaking.*)

HERALD.

Earth of my fathers, O the earth of Argos,
In the light of the tenth year I reach you thus
After many shattered hopes achieving one, 480

For never did I dare to think that here in Argive
    land
I should win a grave in the dearest soil of home;
But now hail, land, and hail, light of the sun,
And Zeus high above the country and the Pythian
    king—
May he no longer shoot his arrows at us 485
(Implacable long enough beside Scamander)
But now be saviour to us and be healer,
King Apollo. And all the Assembly's gods
I call upon, and him my patron, Hermes,
The dear herald whom all heralds adore, 490
And the Heroes who sped our voyage, again with
    favour
Take back the army that has escaped the spear.
O cherished dwelling, palace of royalty,
O august thrones and gods facing the sun,
If ever before, now with your bright eyes 495
Gladly receive your king after much time,
Who comes bringing light to you in the night time,
And to all these as well—King Agamemnon.
Give him a good welcome as he deserves,
Who with the axe of judgment-awarding God 500
Has smashed Troy and levelled the Trojan land;
The altars are destroyed, the seats of the gods,
And the seed of all the land is perished from it.
Having cast this halter round the neck of Troy
The King, the elder son of Atreus, a blessed man,
Comes, the most worthy to have honour of all 506
Men that are now. Paris nor his guilty city
Can boast that the crime was greater than the atone-
    ment.
Convicted in a suit for rape and robbery
He has lost his stolen goods and with consummate
    ruin 510
Mowed down the whole country and his father's
    house.
The sons of Priam have paid their account with
    interest.

LEADER OF THE CHORUS.

Hail and be glad, herald of the Greek army.

HERALD.

Yes. Glad indeed! So glad that at the gods' demand
I should no longer hesitate to die. 515

LEADER.

Were you so harrowed by desire for home?

HERALD.

Yes. The tears come to my eyes for joy.

LEADER.

Sweet then is the fever which afflicts you.

HERALD.

What do you mean? Let me learn your drift. 519

LEADER.

Longing for those whose love came back in echo.

HERALD.

Meaning the land was homesick for the army?

486. **Scamander,** a river beside Troy.

LEADER.

Yes. I would often groan from a darkened heart.

HERALD.

This sullen hatred—how did it fasten on you?

LEADER.

I cannot say. Silence is my stock prescription.

HERALD.

What? In your masters' absence were there some
    you feared?   525

LEADER.

Yes. In your phrase, death would now be a gratifi-
    cation.

HERALD.

Yes, for success is ours. These things have taken
    time.
Some of them we could say have fallen well,
While some we blame. Yet who except the gods
Is free from pain the whole duration of life?   530
If I were to tell of our labours, our hard lodging,
The sleeping on crowded decks, the scanty blankets,
Tossing and groaning, rations that never reached
    us—
And the land too gave matter for more disgust,
For our beds lay under the enemy's walls.   535
Continuous drizzle from the sky, dews from the
    marshes,
Rotting our clothes, filling our hair with lice.
And if one were to tell of the bird-destroying winter
Intolerable from the snows of Ida
Or of the heat when the sea slackens at noon   540
Waveless and dozing in a depressed calm—
But why make these complaints? The weariness is
    over;
Over indeed for some who never again
Need even trouble to rise.
Why make a computation of the lost?   545
Why need the living sorrow for the spites of
    fortune?
I wish to say a long goodbye to disasters.
For us, the remnant of the troops of Argos,
The advantage remains, the pain can not outweigh
    it;
So we can make our boast to this sun's light,   550
Flying on words above the land and sea:
"Having taken Troy the Argive expedition
Has nailed up throughout Greece in every temple
These spoils, these ancient trophies."
Those who hear such things must praise the city
And the generals. And the grace of God be
    honoured   556
Which brought these things about. You have the
    whole story.

LEADER.

I confess myself convinced by your report.
Old men are always young enough to learn.

539. **Ida,** a mountain range near Troy.

(*Enter* CLYTEMNESTRA *from the palace.*)

This news belongs by right first to the house   560
And Clytemnestra—though I am enriched also.

CLYTEMNESTRA.

Long before this I shouted at joy's command
At the coming of the first night-messenger of fire
Announcing the taking and capsizing of Troy.
And people reproached me saying, "Do mere
    beacons   565
Persuade you to think that Troy is already down?
Indeed a woman's heart is easily exalted."
Such comments made me seem to be wandering
    but yet
I began my sacrifices and in the women's fashion
Throughout the town they raised triumphant cries
And in the gods' enclosures   571
Lulling the fragrant, incense-eating flame.
And now what need is there for you to tell me
    more?
From the King himself I shall learn the whole story.
But how the best to welcome my honoured lord
I shall take pains when he comes back—For what
Is a kinder light for a woman to see than this,   577
To open the gates to her man come back from war
When God has saved him? Tell this to my husband,
To come with all speed, the city's darling;   580
May he returning find a wife as loyal
As when he left her, watchdog of the house,
Good to *him* but fierce to the ill-intentioned,
And in all other things as ever, having destroyed
No seal or pledge at all in the length of time.   585
I know no pleasure with another man, no scandal,
More than I know how to dye metal red.
Such is my boast, bearing a load of truth,
A boast that need not disgrace a noble wife.

(*Exit.*)

LEADER.

Thus has she spoken; if you take her meaning,   590
Only a specious tale to shrewd interpreters.
But do you, herald, tell me; I ask after Menelaus
Whether he will, returning safe preserved,
Come back with you, our land's loved master.

HERALD.

I am not able to speak the lovely falsehood   595
To profit you, my friends, for any stretch of time.

LEADER.

But if only the true tidings could be also good!
It is hard to hide a division of good and true.

HERALD.

The prince is vanished out of the Greek fleet,
Himself and ship. I speak no lie.   600

LEADER.

Did he put forth first in the sight of all from Troy,
Or a storm that troubled all sweep him apart?

HERALD.

You have hit the target like a master archer,
Told succinctly a long tale of sorrow.

LEADER.
Did the rumours current among the remaining ships
Represent him as alive or dead?   606
HERALD.
No one knows so as to tell for sure
Except the sun who nurses the breeds of earth.
LEADER.
Tell me how the storm came on the host of ships
Through the divine anger, and how it ended.   610
HERALD.
Day of good news should not be fouled by tongue
That tells ill news. To each god his season.
When, despair in his face, a messenger brings to a
    town
The hated news of a fallen army—
One general wound to the city and many men   615
Outcast, outcursed, from many homes
By the double whip which War is fond of,
Doom with a bloody spear in either hand,
One carrying such a pack of grief could well
Recite this hymn of the Furies at your asking.   620
But when our cause is saved and a messenger of
    good
Comes to a city glad with festivity,
How am I to mix good news with bad, recounting
The storm that meant God's anger on the Greeks?
For they swore together, those inveterate enemies,
Fire and sea, and proved their alliance, destroying
The unhappy troops of Argos.   627
In night arose ill-waved evil,
Ships on each other the blasts from Thrace
Crashed colliding, which butting with horns in the
    violence   630
Of big wind and rattle of rain were gone
To nothing, whirled all ways by a wicked shepherd.
But when there came up the shining light of the sun
We saw the Aegean sea flowering with corpses
Of Greek men and their ships' wreckage.   635
But for us, our ship was not damaged,
Whether someone snatched it away or begged it
    off,
Some god, not a man, handling the tiller;
And Saving Fortune was willing to sit upon our
    ship
So that neither at anchor we took the tilt of waves
Nor ran to splinters on the crag-bound coast.   641
But then having thus escaped death on the sea,
In the white day, not trusting our fortune,
We pastured this new trouble upon our thoughts,
The fleet being battered, the sailors weary,   645
And now if any of *them* still draw breath,
They are thinking no doubt of us as being lost
And we are thinking of them as being lost.
May the best happen. As for Menelaus
The first guess and most likely is a disaster.   650
But still—if any ray of sun detects him
Alive, with living eyes, by the plan of Zeus

Not yet resolved to annul the race completely,
There is some hope then that he will return home.
So much you have heard. Know that it is the truth.
                        (*Exit.*)
CHORUS.
Who was it named her thus   656
In all ways appositely
Unless it was Someone whom we do not see,
Fore-knowing fate
And plying an accurate tongue?   660
Helen, bride of spears and conflict's
Focus, who as was befitting
Proved a hell to ships and men,
Hell to her country, sailing
Away from delicately-sumptuous curtains,   665
Away on the wind of a giant Zephyr,
And shielded hunters mustered many
On the vanished track of the oars,
Oars beached on the leafy
Banks of a Trojan river   670
For the sake of bloody war.

But on Troy was thrust a marring marriage
By the Wrath that working to an end exacts
In time a price from guests
Who dishonoured their host   675
And dishonoured Zeus of the Hearth,
From those noisy celebrants
Of the wedding hymn which fell
To the brothers of Paris
To sing upon that day.   680
But learning this, unlearning that,
Priam's ancestral city now
Continually mourns, reviling
Paris the fatal bridegroom.
The city has had much sorrow,   685
Much desolation in life,
From the pitiful loss of her people.

So in his house a man might rear
A lion's cub caught from the dam
In need of suckling,   690
In the prelude of its life
Mild, gentle with children,
For old men a playmate,
Often held in the arms
Like a new-born child,   695
Wheedling the hand,
Fawning at belly's bidding.

But matured by time he showed
The temper of his stock and payed
Thanks for his fostering   700
With disaster of slaughter of sheep
Making an unbidden banquet
And now the house is a shambles,
Irremediable grief to its people,

Calamitous carnage: 705
For the pet they had fostered was sent
By God as a priest of Ruin.

So I would say there came
To the city of Troy
A notion of windless calm,   710
Delicate adornment of riches,
Soft shooting of the eyes and flower
Of desire that stings the fancy.
But swerving aside she achieved
A bitter end to her marriage,   715
Ill guest and ill companion,
Hurled upon Priam's sons, convoyed
By Zeus, patron of guest and host,
Dark angel dowered with tears.

Long current among men an old saying   720
Runs that a man's prosperity
When grown to greatness
Comes to the birth, does not die childless—
His good luck breeds for his house
Distress that shall not be appeased.   725
I only, apart from the others,
Hold that the unrighteous action
Breeds true to its kind,
Leaves its own children behind it.
But the lot of a righteous house   730
Is a fair offspring always.

Ancient self-glory is accustomed
To bear to light in the evil sort of men
A new self-glory and madness,
Which sometime or sometime finds   735
The appointed hour for its birth,
And born therewith is the Spirit, intractable, un-
    holy, irresistible,
The reckless lust that brings black Doom upon the
    house,
A child that is like its parents.

But Honest Dealing is clear   740
Shining in smoky homes,
Honours the god-fearing life.
Mansions gilded by filth of hands she leaves,
Turns her eyes elsewhere, visits the innocent house,
Not respecting the power   745
Of wealth mis-stamped with approval,
But guides all to the goal.

(Enter AGAMEMNON *and* CASSANDRA *on chariots.)*
    CHORUS.
Come then my King, stormer of Troy,
Offspring of Atreus,
How shall I hail you, how give you honour   750
Neither overshooting nor falling short
    Of the measure of homage?

737. **Spirit**, Atë, goddess of guilt and revenge.

There are many who honour appearance too much
Passing the bounds that are right.
To condole with the unfortunate man   755
Each one is ready but the bite of the grief
    Never goes through to the heart.
And they join in rejoicing, affecting to share it,
Forcing their face to a smile.
But he who is shrewd to shepherd his sheep   760
Will fail not to notice the eyes of a man
Which seem to be loyal but lie,
    Fawning with watery friendship.
Even you, in my thought, when you marshalled the
    troops
For Helen's sake, I will not hide it,   765
Made a harsh and ugly picture,
Holding badly the tiller of reason,
Paying with the death of men
    Ransom for a willing whore.
But now, not unfriendly, not superficially,   770
I offer my service, well-doers' welcome.
In time you will learn by inquiry
Who has done rightly, who transgressed
    In the work of watching the city.
    AGAMEMNON.
First to Argos and the country's gods   775
My fitting salutations, who have aided me
To return and in the justice which I exacted
From Priam's city. Hearing the unspoken case
The gods unanimously had cast their vote
Into the bloody urn for the massacre of Troy;   780
But to the opposite urn
Hope came, dangled her hand, but did no more.
Smoke marks even now the city's capture.
Whirlwinds of doom are alive, the dying ashes
Spread on the air the fat savour of wealth.   785
For these things we must pay some memorable
    return
To Heaven, having exacted enormous vengeance
For wife-rape; for a woman
The Argive monster ground a city to powder,
Sprung from a wooden horse, shield-wielding folk,
Launching a leap at the setting of the Pleiads,   791
Jumping the ramparts, a ravening lion,
Lapped its fill of the kingly blood.
To the gods I have drawn out this overture
But as for your concerns, I bear them in my mind
And say the same, you have me in agreement.   796
To few of men does it belong by nature
To congratulate their friends unenviously,
For a sullen poison fastens on the heart,
Doubling the pain of a man with this disease;   800
He feels the weight of his own griefs and when
He sees another's prosperity he groans.
I speak with knowledge, being well acquainted
With the mirror of comradeship—ghost of a shadow
Were those who seemed to be so loyal to me.   805
Only Odysseus, who sailed against his will,

Proved, when yoked with me, a ready tracehorse;
I speak of him not knowing if he is alive.
But for what concerns the city and the gods
Appointing public debates in full assembly   810
We shall consult. That which is well already
We shall take steps to ensure it remain well.
But where there is need of medical remedies,
By applying benevolent cautery or surgery
We shall try to deflect the dangers of disease.   815
But now, entering the halls where stands my hearth,
First I shall make salutation to the gods
Who sent me a far journey and have brought me
    back.
And may my victory not leave my side.

(*Enter* CLYTEMNESTRA, *followed by women slaves
carrying purple tapestries.*)
CLYTEMNESTRA.
Men of the city, you the aged of Argos,   820
I shall feel no shame to describe to you my love
Towards my husband. Shyness in all of us
Wears thin with time. Here are the facts first hand.
I will tell you of my own unbearable life
I led so long as this man was at Troy.   825
For first that the woman separate from her man
Should sit alone at home is extreme cruelty,
Hearing so many malignant rumours—First
Comes one, and another comes after, bad news to
    worse,
Clamour of grief to the house. If Agamemnon   830
Had had so many wounds as those reported
Which poured home through the pipes of hearsay,
    then—
Then he would be gashed fuller than a net has
    holes!
And if only he had died . . . as often as rumour
    told us,
He would be like the giant in the legend,   835
Three-bodied. Dying once for every body,
He should have by now three blankets of earth
    above him—
All that above him; I care not how deep the mat-
    tress under!
Such are the malignant rumours thanks to which
They have often seized me against my will and
    undone   840
The loop of a rope from my neck.
And this is why our son is not standing here,
The guarantee of your pledges and mine,
As he should be, Orestes. Do not wonder;
He is being brought up by a friendly ally and host,
Strophius the Phocian, who warned me in advance
Of dubious troubles, both your risks at Troy   847
And the anarchy of shouting mobs that might
Overturn policy, for it is born in men
To kick the man who is down.   850
This is not a disingenuous excuse.

For me the outrushing wells of weeping are dried
    up,
There is no drop left in them.
My eyes are sore from sitting late at nights
Weeping for you and for the baffled beacons,   855
Never lit up. And, when I slept, in dreams
I have been waked by the thin whizz of a buzzing
Gnat, seeing more horrors fasten on you
Than could take place in the mere time of my
    dream.
Having endured all this, now, with unsorrowed
    heart   860
I would hail this man as the watchdog of the farm,
Forestay that saves the ship, pillar that props
The lofty roof, appearance of an only son
To a father or of land to sailors past their hope,
The loveliest day to see after the storm,   865
Gush of well-water for the thirsty traveller.
Such are the metaphors I think befit him,
But envy be absent. Many misfortunes already
We have endured. But now, dear head, come down
Out of that car, not placing upon the ground   870
Your foot, O King, the foot that trampled Troy.
Why are you waiting, slaves, to whom the task is
    assigned
To spread the pavement of his path with tapestries?
At once, at once let his way be strewn with purple
That Justice lead him toward his unexpected home.
The rest a mind, not overcome by sleep   876
Will arrange rightly, with God's help, as destined.
AGAMEMNON.
Daughter of Leda, guardian of my house,
You have spoken in proportion to my absence.
You have drawn your speech out long. Duly to
    praise me,   880
That is a duty to be performed by others.
And further—do not by women's methods make
    me
Effeminate nor in barbarian fashion
Gape ground-grovelling acclamations at me   884
Nor strewing my path with cloths make it invidious.
It is the gods should be honoured in this way.
But being mortal to tread embroidered beauty
For me is no way without fear.
I tell you to honour me as a man, not god.
Footcloths are very well—Embroidered stuffs   890
Are stuff for gossip. And not to think unwisely
Is the greatest gift of God. Call happy only him
Who has ended his life in sweet prosperity.
I have spoken. This thing I could not do with con-
    fidence.
CLYTEMNESTRA.
Tell me now, according to your judgment.   895
AGAMEMNON.
I tell you you shall not override my judgment.
CLYTEMNESTRA.
Supposing you had feared something . . .

Could you have vowed to God to do this thing?
AGAMEMNON.
Yes. If an expert had prescribed that vow.   899
CLYTEMNESTRA.
And how would Priam have acted in your place?
AGAMEMNON.
He would have trod the cloths, I think, for certain.
CLYTEMNESTRA.
Then do not flinch before the blame of men.
AGAMEMNON.
The voice of the multitude is very strong.
CLYTEMNESTRA.
But the man none envy is not enviable.
AGAMEMNON.
It is not a woman's part to love disputing.   905
CLYTEMNESTRA.
But it is a conqueror's part to yield upon occasion.
AGAMEMNON.
You think such victory worth fighting for?
CLYTEMNESTRA.
Give way. Consent to let me have the mastery.
AGAMEMNON.
Well, if such is your wish, let someone quickly loose
My vassal sandals, underlings of my feet,   910
And stepping on these sea-purples may no god
Shoot me from far with the envy of his eye.
Great shame it is to ruin my house and spoil
The wealth of costly weavings with my feet.
But of this matter enough. This stranger woman here   915
Take in with kindness. The man who is a gentle master
God looks on from far off complacently.
For no one of his will bears the slave's yoke.
This woman, of many riches being the chosen
Flower, gift of the soldiers, has come with me.   920
But since I have been prevailed on by your words
I will go to my palace home, treading on purples.

(*He dismounts from the chariot and begins to walk up the tapestried path. During the following speech he enters the palace.*)

CLYTEMNESTRA.
There is the sea and who shall drain it dry? It breeds
Its wealth in silver of plenty of purple gushing
And ever-renewed, the dyeings of our garments.
The house has its store of these by God's grace, King.   926
This house is ignorant of poverty
And I would have vowed a pavement of many garments
Had the palace oracle enjoyed that vow
Thereby to contrive a ransom for his life.   930
For while there is root, foliage comes to the house
Spreading a tent of shade against the Dog Star.

So now that you have reached your hearth and home
You prove a miracle—advent of warmth in winter;
And further this—even in the time of heat   935
When God is fermenting wine from the bitter grape,
Even then it is cool in the house if only
Its master walk at home, a grown man, ripe.
O Zeus the Ripener, ripen these my prayers;
Your part it is to make the ripe fruit fall.   940

(*She enters the palace.*)

CHORUS.
Why, why at the doors
Of my fore-seeing heart
Does this terror keep beating its wings?
And my song play the prophet
Unbidden, unhired—   945
Which I cannot spit out
Like the enigmas of dreams
Nor plausible confidence
Sit on the throne of my mind?
It is long time since   950
The cables let down from the stern
Were chafed by the sand when the seafaring army
started for Troy.

And I learn with my eyes
And witness myself their return;   955
But the hymn without lyre goes up,
The dirge of the Avenging Fiend,
In the depths of my self-taught heart
Which has lost its dear
Possession of the strength of hope.   960
But my guts and my heart
Are not idle which seethe with the waves
Of trouble nearing its hour.
But I pray that these thoughts
May fall out not as I think   965
And not be fulfilled in the end.

Truly when health grows much
It respects not limit; for disease,
Its neighbour in the next door room,
Presses upon it.   970
A man's life, crowding sail,
Strikes on the blind reef:
But if caution in advance
Jettison part of the cargo
With the derrick of due proportion,   975
The whole house does not sink,
Though crammed with a weight of woe
The hull does not go under.
The abundant bounty of God
And his gifts from the year's furrows   980
Drive the famine back.

But when upon the ground there has fallen once

The black blood of a man's death,
Who shall summon it back by incantations?
Even Asclepius who had the art   985
To fetch the dead to life, even to him
Zeus put a provident end.
But, if of the heaven-sent fates
One did not check the other,
Cancel the other's advantage,   990
My heart would outrun my tongue
In pouring out these fears.
But now it mutters in the dark,
Embittered, no way hoping
To unravel a scheme in time   995
　　From a burning mind.
　　(CLYTEMNESTRA *appears in the door of the palace*.)
　　CLYTEMNESTRA.
Go in too, you; I speak to you, Cassandra,
Since God in his clemency has put you in this
　　house
To share our holy water, standing with many slaves
Beside the altar that protects the house,   1000
Step down from the car there, do not be overproud.
Heracles himself they say was once
Sold, and endured to eat the bread of slavery.
But should such a chance inexorably fall,
There is much advantage in masters who have long
　　been rich.   1005
Those who have reaped a crop they never expected
Are in all things hard on their slaves and overstep
　　the line.
From us you will have the treatment of tradition.
　　LEADER OF CHORUS.
You, it is you she has addressed, and clearly.
Caught as you are in these predestined toils   1010
Obey her if you can. But should you disobey . . .
　　CLYTEMNESTRA.
If she has more than the gibberish of the swallow,
An unintelligible barbaric speech,
I hope to read her mind, persuade her reason.
　　LEADER.
As things now stand for you, she says the best. 1015
Obey her; leave that car and follow her.
　　CLYTEMNESTRA.
I have no leisure to waste out here, outside the door.
Before the hearth in the middle of my house
The victims stand already, wait the knife.
You, if you will obey me, waste no time.   1020
But if you cannot understand my language—
　　(*To* CHORUS LEADER)
You make it plain to her with the brute and voice-
　　less hand.
　　LEADER.
The stranger seems to need a clear interpreter.
She bears herself like a wild beast newly captured.

985. **Asclepius**, the god of medicine.

　　CLYTEMNESTRA.
The fact is she is mad, she listens to evil thoughts,
Who has come here leaving a city newly captured
Without experience how to bear the bridle   1027
So as not to waste her strength in foam and blood.
I will not spend more words to be ignored.
　　　　(*She re-enters the palace*.)
　　CHORUS.
But I, for I pity her, will not be angry.   1030
Obey, unhappy woman. Leave this car.
Yield to your fate. Put on the untried yoke.
　　CASSANDRA.
Apollo! Apollo!
　　CHORUS.
Why do you cry like this upon Apollo?
He is not the kind of god that calls for dirges.   1035
　　CASSANDRA.
Apollo! Apollo!
　　CHORUS.
Once more her funereal cries invoke the god
Who has no place at the scene of lamentation.
　　CASSANDRA.
Apollo! Apollo!
God of the Ways! My destroyer!   1040
Destroyed again—and this time utterly!
　　CHORUS.
She seems about to predict her own misfortunes.
The gift of the god endures, even in a slave's mind.
　　CASSANDRA.
Apollo! Apollo!
God of the Ways! My destroyer!   1045
Where? To what house? Where, where have you
　　brought me?
　　CHORUS.
To the house of the sons of Atreus. If you do not
　　know it,
I will tell you so. You will not find it false.
　　CASSANDRA.
No, no, but to a god-hated, but to an accomplice
In much kin-killing, murdering nooses,   1050
Man-shambles, a floor asperged with blood.
　　CHORUS.
The stranger seems like a hound with a keen scent,
Is picking up a trail that leads to murder.
　　CASSANDRA.
Clues! I have clues! Look! They are these.
These wailing, these children, butchery of children;
Roasted flesh, a father sitting to dinner.   1056
　　CHORUS.
Of your prophetic fame we have heard before
But in this matter prophets are not required.
　　CASSANDRA.
What is she doing? What is she planning?

1033. **Apollo.** Cassandra enters the trance of prophecy. Because she spurned his love, Apollo condemned Cassandra to prophesy truth that no one would believe.

What is this new great sorrow?   1060
Great crime . . . within here . . . planning
Unendurable to his folk, impossible
Ever to be cured. For help
   Stands far distant.
    CHORUS.
This reference I cannot catch. But the children
I recognized; that refrain is hackneyed.   1066
    CASSANDRA.
Damned, damned, bringing this work to comple-
      tion—
Your husband who shared your bed
To bathe him, to cleanse him, and then—
How shall I tell of the end?   1070
Soon, very soon, it will fall.
   The end comes hand over hand
   Grasping in greed.
    CHORUS.
Not yet do I understand. After her former riddles
Now I am baffled by these dim pronouncements.
    CASSANDRA.
Ah God, the vision! God, God, the vision!   1076
A net, is it? Net of Hell!
But herself is the net; shared bed; shares murder.
O let the pack ever-hungering after the family
Howl for the unholy ritual, howl for the victim.
    CHORUS.
What black Spirit is this you call upon the house—
To raise aloft her cries? Your speech does not
      lighten me.   1082
Into my heart runs back the blood
Yellow as when for men by the spear fallen
The blood ebbs out with the rays of the setting life
   And death strides quickly.   1086
    CASSANDRA.
Quick! Be on your guard! The bull—
Keep him clear of the cow.
Caught with a trick, the black horn's point,
She strikes. He falls; lies in the water.   1090
Murder; a trick in a bath. I tell what I see.
    CHORUS.
I would not claim to be expert in oracles
But these, as I deduce, portend disaster.
Do men ever get a good answer from oracles?
No. It is only through disaster   1095
That their garrulous craft brings home
The meaning of the prophet's panic.
    CASSANDRA.
And for me also, for me, chance ill-destined!
My own now I lament, pour into the cup my own.
Where is this you have brought me in my misery?
Unless to die as well. What else is meant?   1101
    CHORUS.
You are mad, mad, carried away by the god,
Raising the dirge, the tuneless
Tune, for yourself. Like the tawny
Unsatisfied singer from her luckless heart   1105

Lamenting "Itys, Itys," the nightingale
Lamenting a life luxuriant with grief.
    CASSANDRA.
Oh the lot of the songful nightingale!
The gods enclosed her in a winged body,
Gave her a sweet and tearless passing.   1110
But for me remains the two-edged cutting blade.
    CHORUS.
From whence these rushing and God-inflicted
Profitless pains?
Why shape with your sinister crying
The piercing hymn—fear-piercing?   1115
How can you know the evil-worded landmarks
   On the prophetic path?
    CASSANDRA.
Oh the wedding, the wedding of Paris—death to his
      people!
O river Scamander, water drunk by my fathers!
When I was young, alas, upon your beaches   1120
I was brought up and cared for.
But now it is the River of Wailing and the banks of
      Hell
   That shall hear my prophecy soon.
    CHORUS.
What is this clear speech, too clear?
A child could understand it.   1125
I am bitten with fangs that draw blood
By the misery of your cries,
Cries harrowing the heart.
    CASSANDRA.
Oh trouble on trouble of a city lost, lost utterly!
My father's sacrifices before the towers,   1130
Much killing of cattle and sheep,
No cure—availed not at all
To prevent the coming of what came to Troy,
And I, my brain on fire, shall soon enter the trap.
    CHORUS.
This speech accords with the former.   1135
What god, malicious, over-heavy, persistently press-
      ing,
Drives you to chant of these lamentable
Griefs with death their burden?
But I cannot see the end.
   (CASSANDRA *now steps down from the car.*)
    CASSANDRA.
The oracle now no longer from behind veils   1140
Will be peeping forth like a newly-wedded bride;
But I can feel it like a fresh wind swoop
And rush in the face of the dawn and, wave-like,
      wash
Against the sun a vastly greater grief
Than this one. I shall speak no more conundrums.
And bear me witness, pacing me, that I   1146
Am trailing on the scent of ancient wrongs.

1104–1107. **Like . . . grief.** Procné, transformed into a nightingale, mourned for her son Itys, whom she had killed and served as a dish to her husband in revenge for his infidelity.

For this house here a choir never deserts,
Chanting together ill. For they mean ill,
And to puff up their arrogance they have drunk
Men's blood, this band of revellers that haunts the
    house, 1151
Hard to be rid of, fiends that attend the family.
Established in its rooms they hymn their hymn
Of that original sin, abhor in turn
The adultery that proved a brother's ruin. 1155
A miss? Or do my arrows hit the mark?
Or am I a quack prophet who knocks at doors, a
    babbler?
Give me your oath, confess I have the facts,
The ancient history of this house's crimes.

    LEADER.

And how could an oath's assurance, however finely
    assured, 1160
Turn out a remedy? I wonder, though, that you
Being brought up overseas, of another tongue,
Should hit on the whole tale as if you had been
    standing by.

    CASSANDRA.

Apollo the prophet set me to prophesy.

    LEADER.

Was he, although a god, struck by desire? 1165

    CASSANDRA.

Till now I was ashamed to tell that story.

    LEADER.

Yes. Good fortune keeps us all fastidious.

    CASSANDRA.

He wrestled hard upon me, panting love.

    LEADER.

And did you come, as they do, to child-getting?

    CASSANDRA.

No. I agreed to him. And I cheated him. 1170

    LEADER.

Were you already possessed by the mystic art?

    CASSANDRA.

Already I was telling the townsmen all their future
    suffering.

    LEADER.

Then how did you escape the doom of Apollo's
    anger?

    CASSANDRA.

I did not escape. No one ever believed me.

    LEADER.

Yet to us your words seem worthy of belief. 1175

    CASSANDRA.

Oh misery, misery!
Again comes on me the terrible labour of true
Prophecy, dizzying prelude; distracts . . .
Do you see these who sit before the house,
Children, like the shapes of dreams? 1180
Children who seem to have been killed by their
    kinsfolk,
Filling their hands with meat, flesh of themselves,
Guts and entrails, handfuls of lament—

Clear what they hold—the same their father tasted.
For this I declare someone is plotting vengeance—
A lion? Lion but coward, that lurks in bed, 1186
Good watchdog truly against the lord's return—
My lord, for I must bear the yoke of serfdom.
Leader of the ships, overturner of Troy,
He does not know what plots the accursed hound
With the licking tongue and the pricked-up ear will
    plan 1191
In the manner of a lurking doom, in an evil hour.
A daring criminal! Female murders male.
What monster could provide her with a title?
An amphisbaena or hag of the sea who dwells 1195
In rocks to ruin sailors—
A raving mother of death who breathes against her
    folk
War to the finish. Listen to her shout of triumph,
Who shirks no horrors, like men in a rout of battle.
And yet she poses as glad at their return. 1200
If you distrust my words, what does it matter?
That which will come will come. You too will soon
    stand here
And admit with pity that I spoke too truly.

    LEADER.

Thyestes' dinner of his children's meat
I understood and shuddered, and fear grips me
To hear the truth, not framed in parables. 1206
But hearing the rest I am thrown out of my course.

    CASSANDRA.

It is Agamemnon's death I tell you you shall
    witness.

    LEADER.

Stop! Provoke no evil. Quiet your mouth! 1209

    CASSANDRA.

The god who gives me words is here no healer.

    LEADER.

Not if this shall be so. But may some chance avert it.

    CASSANDRA.

You are praying. But others are busy with murder.

    LEADER.

What man is he promotes this terrible thing?

    CASSANDRA.

Indeed you have missed my drift by a wide margin!

    LEADER.

But I do not understand the assassin's method.

    CASSANDRA.

And yet too well I know the speech of Greece! 1216

    LEADER.

So does Delphi but the replies are hard.

    CASSANDRA.

Ah what a fire it is! It comes upon me.
Apollo, Wolf-Destroyer, pity, pity . . .
It is the two-foot lioness who beds 1220
Beside a wolf, the noble lion away,
It is she will kill me. Brewing a poisoned cup

1184. **tasted.** Thyestes unknowingly ate his sons' flesh, served by
his brother Atreus. 1221. **wolf,** Aegisthus.

She will mix my punishment too in the angry
    draught
And boasts, sharpening the dagger for her husband,
To pay back murder for my bringing here.   1225
Why then do I wear these mockeries of myself,
The wand and the prophet's garland round my
    neck?
My hour is coming—but you shall perish first.
Destruction! Scattered thus you give me my
    revenge;
Go and enrich some other woman with ruin.   1230
See: Apollo himself is stripping me
Of my prophetic gear, who has looked on
When in this dress I have been a laughing-stock
To friends and foes alike, and to no purpose;
They called me crazy, like a fortune-teller,   1235
A poor starved beggar-woman—and I bore it.
And now the prophet undoing his prophetess
Has brought me to this final darkness.
Instead of my father's altar the executioner's block
Waits me the victim, red with my hot blood.   1240
But the gods will not ignore me as I die.
One will come after to avenge my death,
A matricide, a murdered father's champion.
Exile and tramp and outlaw he will come back
To gable the family house of fatal crime;   1245
His father's outstretched corpse shall lead him
    home.
Why need I then lament so pitifully?
For now that I have seen the town of Troy
Treated as she was treated, while her captors
Come to their reckoning thus by the gods' verdict,
I will go in and have the courage to die.   1251
Look, these gates are the gates of Death. I greet
    them.
And I pray that I may meet a deft and mortal stroke
So that without a struggle I may close
My eyes and my blood ebb in easy death.   1255

LEADER.

Oh woman very unhappy and very wise,
Your speech was long. But if in sober truth
You know your fate, why like an ox that the gods
Drive, do you walk so bravely to the altar?

CASSANDRA.

There is no escape, strangers. No; not by postpone-
    ment.   1260

LEADER.

But the last moment has the privilege of hope.

CASSANDRA.

The day is here. Little should I gain by flight.

LEADER.

This patience of yours comes from a brave soul.

CASSANDRA.

A happy man is never paid that compliment.

LEADER

But to die with credit graces a mortal man.   1265

1242. **One,** Orestes.

CASSANDRA.

Oh my father! You and your noble sons!
    (*She approaches the door, then suddenly recoils.*)

LEADER.

What is it? What is the fear that drives you back?

CASSANDRA.

Faugh.

LEADER.

Why faugh? Or is this some hallucination?

CASSANDRA.

These walls breathe out a death that drips with
    blood.   1270

LEADER.

Not so. It is only the smell of the sacrifice.

CASSANDRA.

It is like a breath out of a charnel-house.

LEADER.

You think our palace burns odd incense then!

CASSANDRA.

But I will go to lament among the dead
My lot and Agamemnon's. Enough of life!   1275
Strangers,
I am not afraid like a bird afraid of a bush
But witness you my words after my death
When a woman dies in return for me a woman
And a man falls for a man with a wicked wife.   1280
I ask this service, being about to die.

LEADER.

Alas, I pity you for the death you have foretold.

CASSANDRA.

One more speech I have; I do not wish to raise
The dirge for my own self. But to the sun I pray
In face of his last light that my avengers   1285
May make my murderers pay for this my death,
Death of a woman slave, an easy victim.
    (*She enters the palace.*)

LEADER.

Ah the fortunes of men! When they go well
A shadow sketch would match them, and in ill-
    fortune
The dab of a wet sponge destroys the drawing.
It is not myself but the life of man I pity.   1291

CHORUS.

Prosperity in all men cries
For more prosperity. Even the owner
Of the finger-pointed-at palace never shuts
His door against her, saying "Come no more."   1295
So to our king the blessed gods had granted
To take the town of Priam, and heaven-favoured
He reaches home. But now if for former bloodshed
    He must pay blood
And dying for the dead shall cause   1300
    Other deaths in atonement
What man could boast he was born
    Secure, who heard this story?

AGAMEMNON.

(*Within*) Oh! I am struck a mortal blow—within!

LEADER.

Silence! Listen. Who calls out, wounded with a
mortal stroke?   1305

AGAMEMNON.

Again—the second blow—I am struck again.

LEADER.

You heard the king cry out. I think the deed is done.
Let us see if we can concert some sound proposal.

2ND OLD MAN.

Well, I will tell you my opinion—
Raise an alarm, summon the folk to the palace.

3RD OLD MAN.

I say burst in with all speed possible.   1311
Convict them of the deed while still the sword is
wet.

4TH OLD MAN.

And I am partner to some such suggestion.
I am for taking some course. No time to dawdle.

5TH OLD MAN.

The case is plain. This is but the beginning.   1315
They are going to set up dictatorship in the state.

6TH OLD MAN.

We are wasting time. The assassins tread to earth
The decencies of delay and give their hands no
sleep.

7TH OLD MAN.

I do not know what plan I could hit on to propose.
The man who acts is in the position to plan.   1320

8TH OLD MAN.

So I think, too, for I am at a loss
To raise the dead man up again with words.

9TH OLD MAN.

Then to stretch out our life shall we yield thus
To the rule of these profaners of the house?

10TH OLD MAN.

It is not to be endured. To die is better.   1325
Death is more comfortable than tyranny.

11TH OLD MAN.

And are we on the evidence of groans
Going to give oracle that the prince is dead?

12TH OLD MAN.

We must know the facts for sure and *then* be angry.
Guesswork is not the same as certain knowledge.

LEADER.

Then all of you back me and approve this plan—
To ascertain how it is with Agamemnon.   1332

(*The doors of the palace open, revealing the
bodies of* AGAMEMNON *and* CASSANDRA. CLYTEMNES-
TRA *stands above them.*)

CLYTEMNESTRA.

Much having been said before to fit the moment,
To say the opposite now will not outface me.
How else could one serving hate upon the hated,
Thought to be friends, hang high the nets of doom
To preclude all leaping out?   1337
For me I have long been training for this match,

I tried a fall and won—a victory overdue.
I stand here where I struck, above my victims;
So I contrived it—this I will not deny—   1341
That he could neither fly nor ward off death;
Inextricable like a net for fishes
I cast about him a vicious wealth of raiment
And struck him twice and with two groans he
loosed   1345
His limbs beneath him, and upon him fallen
I deal him the third blow to the God beneath the
earth,
To the safe keeper of the dead a votive gift,
And with that he spits his life out where he lies
And smartly spouting blood he sprays me with
The sombre drizzle of bloody dew and I   1351
Rejoice no less than in God's gift of rain
The crops are glad when the ear of corn gives birth.
These things being so, you, elders of Argos,
Rejoice if rejoice you will. Mine is the glory.   1355
And if I could pay this corpse his due libation
I should be right to pour it and more than right;
With so many horrors this man mixed and filled
The bowl—and, coming home, has drained the
draught himself.

LEADER.

Your speech astonishes us. This brazen boast   1360
Above the man who was your king and husband!

CLYTEMNESTRA.

You challenge me as a woman without foresight
But I with unflinching heart to you who know
Speak. And you, whether you will praise or blame,
It makes no matter. Here lies Agamemnon,   1365
My husband, dead, the work of this right hand,
An honest workman. There you have the facts.

CHORUS.

Woman, what poisoned
Herb of the earth have you tasted
Or potion of the flowing sea   1370
To undertake this killing and the people's curses?
You threw down, you cut off—The people will cast
you out,
Black abomination to the town.

CLYTEMNESTRA.

Now your verdict—in my case—is exile
And to have the people's hatred, the public curses,
Though then in no way you opposed this man   1376
Who carelessly, as if it were a head of sheep
Out of the abundance of his fleecy flocks,
Sacrificed his own daughter, to me the dearest
Fruit of travail, charm for the Thracian winds.   1380
He was the one to have banished from this land,
Pay off the pollution. But when you hear what I
Have done, you judge severely. But I warn you—
Threaten me on the understanding that I am ready
For two alternatives—Win by force the right   1385
To rule me, but, if God brings about the contrary,
Late in time you will have to learn self-discipline.

CHORUS.
You are high in the thoughts,
You speak extravagant things,
After the soiling murder your crazy heart   1390
Fancies your forehead with a smear of blood.
Unhonoured, unfriended, you must
Pay for a blow with a blow.

CLYTEMNESTRA.
Listen then to this—the sanction of my oaths:
By the Justice totting up my child's atonement,
By the Avenging Doom and Fiend to whom I
          killed this man,   1396
For me hope walks not in the rooms of fear
So long as my fire is lit upon my hearth
By Aegisthus, loyal to me as he was before.
The man who outraged me lies here,   1400
The darling of each courtesan at Troy,
And here with him is the prisoner clairvoyante,
The fortune-teller that he took to bed,
Who shares his bed as once his bench on shipboard,
A loyal mistress. Both have their deserts.   1405
He lies so; and she who like a swan
Sang her last dying lament
Lies his lover, and the sight contributes
An appetiser to my own bed's pleasure.

CHORUS.
Ah would some quick death come not overpainful,
Not overlong on the sickbed,   1411
Establishing in us the ever-
Lasting unending sleep now that our guardian
Has fallen, the kindest of men,
Who suffering much for a woman   1415
By a woman has lost his life.
     O Helen, insane, being one
     One to have destroyed so many
     And many souls under Troy,
     Now is your work complete, blossomed not for
          oblivion,   1420
     Unfading stain of blood. Here now, if in any
          home,
     Is Discord, here is a man's deep-rooted ruin.

CLYTEMNESTRA.
Do not pray for the portion of death
Weighed down by these things, do not turn
Your anger on Helen as destroyer of men,   1425
One woman destroyer of many
Lives of Greek men,
     A hurt that cannot be healed.

CHORUS.
O Evil Spirit, falling on the family,
On the two sons of Atreus and using   1430
Two sisters in heart as your tools,
A power that bites to the heart—

1429. **Spirit,** the evil genius in the race of Tantalus, the grandfather of Atreus, which was ultimately responsible for placing
the fate of the race in the hands of women, Helen and Clytemnestra.

See on the body
Perched like a raven he gloats
Harshly croaking his hymn.   1435

CLYTEMNESTRA.
Ah, now you have amended your lips' opinion,
Calling upon this family's three times gorged
Genius—demon who breeds
Blood-hankering lust in the belly:
Before the old sore heals, new pus collects.   1440

CHORUS.
It is a great spirit—great—
You tell of, harsh in anger,
A ghastly tale, alas,
Of unsatisfied disaster
Brought by Zeus, by Zeus,   1445
Cause and worker of all.
For without Zeus what comes to pass among us?
Which of these things is outside Providence?
     O my king, my king,
     How shall I pay you in tears,   1450
     Speak my affection in words?
     You lie in that spider's web,
     In a desecrating death breathe out your life,
     Lie ignominiously
     Defeated by a crooked death   1455
     And the two-edged cleaver's stroke.

CLYTEMNESTRA.
You say this is *my* work—mine?
Do not cozen yourself that I am Agamemnon's wife.
Masquerading as the wife
Of the corpse there the old sharp-witted Genius
Of Atreus who gave the cruel banquet   1461
Has paid with a grown man's life
The due for children dead.

CHORUS.
That you are not guilty of
This murder who will attest?   1465
No, but you may have been abetted
By some ancestral Spirit of Revenge.
Wading a millrace of the family's blood
The black Manslayer forces a forward path
To make the requital at last   1470
For the eaten children, the blood-clot cold with
          time.
     O my king, my king,
     How shall I pay you in tears,
     Speak my affection in words?
     You lie in that spider's web,   1475
     In a desecrating death breathe out your life,
     Lie ignominiously
     Defeated by a crooked death
     And the two-edged cleaver's stroke.

CLYTEMNESTRA.
Did he not, too, contrive a crooked   1480
Horror for the house? My child by him,
Shoot that I raised, much-wept-for Iphigeneia,
He treated her like this;

So suffering like this he need not make
Any great brag in Hell having paid with death   1485
Dealt by the sword for work of his own beginning.
    CHORUS.
I am at a loss for thought, I lack
All nimble counsel as to where
To turn when the house is falling.
I fear the house-collapsing crashing   1490
Blizzard of blood—of which these drops are earnest.
Now is Destiny sharpening her justice
On other whetstones for a new infliction.
    O earth, earth, if only you had received me
    Before I saw this man lie here as if in bed   1495
      In a bath lined with silver.
    Who will bury him? Who will keen him?
    Will you, having killed your own husband,
    Dare now to lament him
    And after great wickedness make   1500
      Unamending amends to his ghost?
    And who above this godlike hero's grave
    Pouring praises and tears
      Will grieve with a genuine heart?
    CLYTEMNESTRA.
It is not your business to attend to that.   1505
By my hand he fell low, lies low and dead,
And I shall bury him low down in the earth,
And his household need not weep him
For Iphigeneia his daughter
Tenderly, as is right,   1510
Will meet her father at the rapid ferry of sorrows,
Put her arms round him and kiss him!
    CHORUS.
Reproach answers reproach,
It is hard to decide,
The catcher is caught, the killer pays for his
    kill.   1515
But the law abides while Zeus abides enthroned
That the wrongdoer suffers. That is established.
Who could expel from the house the seed of the
    Curse?
The race is soldered in sockets of Doom and Venge-
    ance.
    CLYTEMNESTRA.
In this you say what is right and the will of
    God.   1520
But for my part I am ready to make a contract
With the Evil Genius of the House of Atreus
To accept what has been till now, hard though it is,
But that for the future he shall leave this house
And wear away some other stock with deaths   1525
Imposed among themselves. Of my possessions
A small part will suffice if only I
Can rid these walls of the mad exchange of murder.
    (Enter AEGISTHUS, *followed by soldiers.*)

    AEGISTHUS.
O welcome light of a justice-dealing day!

From now on I will say that the gods, avenging
    men,   1530
Look down from above on the crimes of earth,
Seeing as I do in woven robes of the Furies
This man lying here—a sight to warm my heart—
Paying for the crooked violence of his father.
For his father Atreus, when he ruled the coun-
    try,   1535
Because his power was challenged, hounded out
From state and home his own brother Thyestes.
My father—let me be plain—was this Thyestes,
Who later came back home a suppliant,
There, miserable, found so much asylum   1540
As not to die on the spot, stain the ancestral floor.
But to show his hospitality godless Atreus
Gave him an eager if not a loving welcome,
Pretending a day of feasting and rich meats
Served my father with his children's flesh.   1545
The hands and feet, fingers and toes, he hid
At the bottom of the dish. My father sitting apart
Took unknowing the unrecognizable portion
And ate of a dish that has proved, as you see, ex-
    pensive.
But when he knew he had eaten worse than poi-
    son   1550
He fell back groaning, vomiting their flesh,
And invoking a hopeless doom on the sons of Pelops
Kicked over the table to confirm his curse—
So may the whole race perish!
Result of this—you see this man lie here.   1555
I stitched this murder together; it was my title.
Me the third son he left, an unweaned infant,
To share the bitterness of my father's exile.
But I grew up and Justice brought me back,
I grappled this man while still beyond his door,   1560
Having pieced together the programme of his ruin.
So now would even death be beautiful to me
Having seen Agamemnon in the nets of Justice.
    LEADER.
Aegisthus. I cannot respect brutality in distress.
You claim that you deliberately killed this
    prince   1565
And that you alone planned this pitiful murder.
Be sure that in your turn your head shall not escape
The people's volleyed curses mixed with stones.
    AEGISTHUS.
Do you speak so who sit at the lower oar
While those on the upper bench control the
    ship?   1570
Old as you are, you will find it is a heavy load
To go to school when old to learn the lesson of tact.
For old age, too, gaol and hunger are fine
Instructors in wisdom, second-sighted doctors.
You have eyes. Cannot you see?   1575
Do not kick against the pricks. The blow will hurt
    you.

1552. **Pelops,** the father of Atreus and Thyestes.

LEADER.
You woman waiting in the house for those who re-
turn from battle
While you seduce their wives! Was it you devised
The death of a master of armies?
AEGISTHUS.
And these words, too, prepare the way for tears.   1580
Contrast your voice with the voice of Orpheus: he
Led all things after him bewitched with joy, but you
Having stung me with your silly yelps shall be
Led off yourself, to prove more mild when mastered.
LEADER.
Indeed! So you are now to be king of Argos,   1585
You who, when you had plotted the king's death,
Did not even dare to do that thing yourself!
AEGISTHUS.
No. For the trick of it was clearly woman's work.
I was suspect, an enemy of old.
But now I shall try with Agamemnon's wealth   1590
To rule the people. Any who is disobedient
I will harness in a heavy yoke, no tracehorse work
for him
Like barley-fed colt, but hateful hunger lodging
Beside him in the dark will see his temper soften.
LEADER.
Why with your cowardly soul did you yourself   1595
Not strike this man but left that work to a woman
Whose presence pollutes our country and its gods?
But Orestes—does he somewhere see the light
That he may come back here by favour of fortune
And kill this pair and prove the final victor?   1600
AEGISTHUS. (Summoning his guards.)
Well, if such is your design in deeds and words, you
will quickly learn—
Here my friends, here my guards, there is work for
you at hand.
LEADER.
Come then, hands on hilts, be each and all of us
prepared.
(The old men and the guards threaten each
other.)

AEGISTHUS.
Very well! I too am ready to meet death with sword
in hand.
LEADER.
We are glad you speak of dying. We accept your
words for luck.   1605
CLYTEMNESTRA.
No, my dearest, do not so. Add no more to the train
of wrong.
To reap these many present wrongs is harvest
enough of misery.
Enough of misery. Start no more. Our hands are
red.

1581. Orpheus, the musician whose lyre enchanted not only the
wild beasts, but the trees and rocks upon Olympus.

But do you, and you old men, go home and yield to
fate in time,
In time before you suffer. We have acted as we had
to act.   1610
If only our afflictions now could prove enough, we
should agree—
We who have been so hardly mauled in the heavy
claws of the evil god.
So stands my word, a woman's, if any man thinks
fit to hear.
AEGISTHUS.
But to think that these should thus pluck the blooms
of an idle tongue
And should throw out words like these, giving the
evil god his chance,   1615
And should miss the path of prudence and insult
their master so!
LEADER.
It is not the Argive way to fawn upon a cowardly
man.
AEGISTHUS.
Perhaps. But I in later days will take further steps
with you.
LEADER.
Not if the god who rules the family guides Orestes
to his home.
AEGISTHUS.
Yes. I know that men in exile feed themselves on
barren hopes.   1620
LEADER.
Go on, grow fat defiling justice . . . while you
have your hour.
AEGISTHUS.
Do not think you will not pay me a price for your
stupidity.
LEADER.
Boast on in your self-assurance, like a cock beside
his hen.
CLYTEMNESTRA.
Pay no heed, Aegisthus, to these futile barkings.
You and I,
Masters of this house, from now shall order all
things well.   1625
(They enter the palace.)

Sophocles

c. 495–406 B.C.

Sophocles belonged to Athens at the zenith of
her political power and cultural splendor, and
even in such a day he seemed the supreme embodiment
of noble character and versatile genius. To the Athenians
he was the favorite of the gods. He had been born into a

wealthy and socially prominent family.* He grew up as the model citizen, handsome and sweet-natured, sociable and temperate, pious and intellectual. About 440 B.C. he was elected one of the ten generals of Athens—the highest elective office of the state. His piety and conservative religious views won him priesthoods in several cults. His serenity endeared him to such friends as Herodotus the historian and youthful Aristophanes, who expressed his admiration in his comedy *The Frogs.* He preserved his intellectual powers to the age of ninety, composing one of his masterpieces, *Oedipus at Colonus,* shortly before his death. Phrynichus, his contemporary in comedy, voiced a universal tribute in the words: "Blessed is Sophocles, a happy and fortunate man who died after a long life. Author of many beautiful tragedies, he came to a beautiful end and lived to see no evil day."

Sophocles was much less interested in religious problems than Aeschylus or in social criticism than Euripides. Although as conservative as Aeschylus, he belonged to a new generation, no longer troubled by matters of state important during the Persian Wars. And while he lived the robust life of the typical Greek citizen, he divorced his plays from contemporary issues and concentrated on the timeless problems of well-intentioned men and women striving for happy and honest lives against the odds of fortune. Instead of the theological issues that concerned Aeschylus he emphasizes the human meaning in the tragic operation of eternal laws. To this sympathetic vision of the plight of mankind he brings the technique of a master artist. Turning away from the trilogy scheme of Aeschylus, he gives more plot and action to the single play and freely uses three or four actors at once. A better craftsman than Euripides, he molds his material into a harmonious work of art, with a careful, inevitable construction and a simple, yet noble style that is free from the grandiloquence of Aeschylus.

Although Sophocles wrote at least 120 plays and won the first prize twenty-four times (more than any other playwright), the Alexandrian scholars preserved only seven of his tragedies, of which the three greatest treat one connected story. Though written at different periods of his career and in no sense a trilogy, *Oedipus the King, Oedipus at Colonus,* and *Antigone* give three incidents in the tragic history of the house of Laius, King of Thebes. Laius, married to Jocasta, had been warned by an oracle of Apollo that his newborn son would kill him if he lived to manhood. So the king exposed the baby to death in a barren place, but a kindly shepherd took him to the childless king and queen of Corinth, who named him Oedipus and reared him as their son. Grown to manhood, Oedipus was shocked by a prophecy of the oracle that he would kill his father and marry his mother. Not knowing that the king and queen were his adopted parents, in horror he left Corinth to seek his fortune elsewhere. On the road to Thebes "at a place where three roads met," Oedipus unknowingly encountered his own father, Laius,

driving with an attendant. A dispute arose about the right of the road, and when the attendant killed one of Oedipus' horses, the enraged Oedipus killed the two men, thus fulfilling the first of the prophecies.

At Thebes he found the populace harassed by a monster called the Sphinx, who killed every traveler to the city who could not answer the riddle, "What is it that goes on four feet in the morning, on two at noon, and on three in the evening?" The vacant throne of Laius and the hand of his queen were offered by the desperate people to any man who could solve the riddle. The guess of Oedipus was "man, who creeps on all fours as a child, who walks erect as a man, and who leans on a staff in his old age." The mortified Sphinx killed herself, and the grateful Thebans accepted Oedipus as their king and the husband of Queen Jocasta. So the second prophecy was fulfilled.

In the happy years that followed, Oedipus had two sons, Eteocles and Polynices, and two daughters, Antigone and Ismene, by his wife-mother. Then at last Thebes was afflicted by a great plague, and the earnest king asked the oracle to reveal the cause of the gods' displeasure. In *Oedipus the King* we learn how he was ordered to find the slayer of Laius and how his vigorous pursuit of the criminal gradually proved that he himself was the man. In horror Jocasta killed herself and Oedipus tore out his eyes and banished himself to a life of wandering. In *Oedipus at Colonus* we see the melancholy end of the haggard king. Accompanied by his daughters, he finally reached the spot where the oracle had prophesied that he would die. Learning that his sons were fighting each other for the throne of Thebes, he indignantly laid upon them the curse that they would kill each other. Then as a clap of thunder announced his end, Oedipus blessed his daughters and found peace at last.

The curse of Oedipus upon his sons was fulfilled. Since it was Polynices who had challenged the rule of Eteocles and attacked the city, Creon, the brother of Jocasta, who succeeded to the throne, decreed that the body of Polynices should not be buried. This act was peculiarly shocking to the Greeks, since burial was essential for admission to Hades. In the *Antigone,* the faithful sister, Antigone, defied the decree of Creon and secretly performed a token rite of burial over the corpse of Polynices. The angry Creon, sensitive to any rebellion against his guilty rule, ordered Antigone to be buried alive, even though she was betrothed to his own son. Soon after, he suffered a change of heart and countermanded his order, but too late, for Antigone, his son, and his wife had all committed suicide. With this grim warning against abuse of power in the desolate figure of Creon, Sophocles brings the tragic tale of Thebes to an end.

Oedipus the King, the most famous of Greek plays and the one chosen by Aristotle in his *Poetics* as the model of tragedy, won only the second prize in its competition, behind a now-forgotten work by a nephew of Aeschylus. The date of the competition is unknown. Despite its fame the play is hardly so typical of Greek tragedies as several others, though it is one of the best constructed and most gripping. The relentless prosecution of a single dramatic

*It is convenient to remember that in the year of Salamis (480 B.C.) Aeschylus, a man of forty-five, fought in the battle; Sophocles, a youth of fifteen, was chosen to lead a boys' chorus celebrating the return of the victors; and Euripides was born.

motif, the gradual discovery of the identity and hence the crimes of Oedipus, makes for complete unity. But the final downfall of the hero for crimes committed before the opening of the play is distinctly unusual. Aristotle's description of a tragic hero as an essentially worthy man with one tragic flaw of character that leads him into error is hard for us to apply to this well-intentioned king, who is doomed to disaster before his birth and commits his crimes without knowing that he is doing so. Yet the Greeks' more practical and unquestioning interpretation of divine law found no obstacle here. Man is subject to the whims of Fate, and with a sublime show of irony Fate placed a mark of impurity upon this man from birth which was as inescapable a flaw as pride or obstinacy. In addition, one of the crimes of Oedipus, the murder of Laius, was an impetuous one, which might reflect a further tragic flaw of insolence and hot temper. In any case, the workings of Fate are inscrutable to man, and as the concluding chorus reminds us: "Count no man happy until you witness his final day."

The sardonic operation of fate is reflected in the *dramatic irony* of the play whereby the audience knows at the start the secret that Oedipus is trying to find and follows with terrified fascination his gradual discovery. Not simply the situation but many of the speeches are profoundly ironic as we see in them double meanings that the hero is in no position to grasp. When he vows to track down and punish the slayer of Laius as he would his own father's assassin, we know that it *is* his own father and that *he* is the assassin. Such speeches as these contribute a great deal to our sympathy for the pathetic human being who finds himself so innocently the sport of the gods. Although many playwrights have treated the tragic tale of Oedipus—Aeschylus and Euripides in lost plays, Seneca, Corneille, Dryden, and Voltaire in later imitations—none of the others comes close to the majesty and humanity of Sophocles.

Oedipus the King

PERSONS IN THE PLAY

OEDIPUS, *King of Thebes*
JOCASTA, *wife of* OEDIPUS
ANTIGONE, *daughter of* OEDIPUS
ISMENE, *daughter of* OEDIPUS
CREON, *brother-in-law of* OEDIPUS
TIRESIAS, *a seer*
A PRIEST
MESSENGERS
A HERDSMAN
CHORUS

Oedipus the King. Translated by W. B. Yeats as *Sophocles' King Oedipus.* From *The Collected Plays of W. B. Yeats* by W. B. Yeats. Used by permission of the Macmillan Company, the Macmillan Company of Canada Ltd., and Mrs. W. B. Yeats. Application for the right of performing this play must be made to Messrs. Samuel French Inc., 25 W. 45th St., New York 36, N. Y. or to Samuel French (Canada) Ltd., 27 Grenville St., Toronto 5, Canada, who, upon payment of a fee, will issue a licence for the performance to be given.

(SCENE: *The palace of King Oedipus at Thebes.*)

OEDIPUS.

CHILDREN, descendants of old Cadmus, why do you come before me, why do you carry the branches of suppliants, while the city smokes with incense and murmurs with prayer and lamentation? I would not learn from any mouth but yours, old man, therefore I question you myself. Do you know of anything that I can do and have not done? How can I, being the man I am, being King Oedipus, do other than all I know? I were indeed hard of heart did I not pity such suppliants. 10

PRIEST. Oedipus, King of my country, we who stand before your door are of all ages, some too young to have walked so many miles, some—priests of Zeus such as I—too old. Among us stand the pick of the young men, and behind in the market-places the people throng, carrying suppliant branches. We all stand here because the city stumbles towards death, hardly able to raise up its head. A blight has fallen upon the fruitful blossoms of the land, a blight upon flock and field and upon the bed of marriage 20 —plague ravages the city. Oedipus, King, not God but foremost of living men, seeing that when you first came to this town of Thebes you freed us from that harsh singer, the riddling Sphinx, we beseech you, all we suppliants, to find some help; whether you find it by your power as a man, or because, being near the Gods, a God has whispered you. Uplift our State; think upon your fame; your coming brought us luck, be lucky to us still; remember that it is better to rule over men than over a waste 30 place, since neither walled town nor ship is anything if it be empty and no man within it.

OEDIPUS. My unhappy children! I know well what need has brought you, what suffering you endure; yet, sufferers though you be, there is not a single one whose suffering is as mine—each mourns himself, but my soul mourns the city, myself, and you. It is not therefore as if you came to arouse a sleeping man. No! Be certain that I have wept many tears and searched hither and thither for some remedy. I have 40 already done the only thing that came into my head for all my search. I have sent the son of Menoeceus, Creon, my own wife's brother, to the Pythian House of Phoebus, to hear if deed or word of mine may yet deliver this town. I am troubled, for he is a long time away—a longer time than should be—but when he comes I shall not be an honest man unless I do whatever the God commands.

PRIEST. You have spoken at the right time. They have just signalled to us that Creon has arrived. 50

1. **Cadmus.** Cadmus, the legendary founder of Thebes, had killed a dragon, the son of Ares, which had killed certain followers of Cadmus. Oedipus descended from him through Polydorus, Labdacus, and Laius. 43–44. **Pythian . . . Phoebus**, the Delphic oracle of Phoebus Apollo.

OEDIPUS. O King Apollo, may he bring brighter fortune, for his face is shining!

PRIEST. He brings good news, for he is crowned with bay.

OEDIPUS. We shall know soon. Brother-in-law, Menoeceus' son, what news from the God?

CREON. Good news; for pain turns to pleasure when we have set the crooked straight.

OEDIPUS. But what is the oracle?—so far the news 10 is neither good nor bad.

CREON. If you would hear it with all these about you, I am ready to speak. Or do we go within?

OEDIPUS. Speak before all. The sorrow I endure is less for my own life than these.

CREON. Then, with your leave, I speak. Our lord Phoebus bids us drive out a defiling thing that has been cherished in this land.

OEDIPUS. By what purification?

CREON. King Laius was our King before you came 20 to pilot us.

OEDIPUS. I know—but not of my own knowledge, for I never saw him.

CREON. He was killed; and the God now bids us revenge it on his murderers, whoever they be.

OEDIPUS. Where shall we come upon their track after all these years? Did he meet his death in house or field, at home or in some foreign land?

CREON. In a foreign land: he was journeying to Delphi.

30 OEDIPUS. Did no fellow-traveller see the deed? Was there none there who could be questioned?

CREON. All perished but one man who fled in terror and could tell for certain but one thing of all he had seen.

OEDIPUS. One thing might be a clue to many things.

CREON. He said that they were fallen upon by a great troop of robbers.

OEDIPUS. What robbers would be so daring unless 40 bribed from here?

CREON. Such things were indeed guessed at, but Laius once dead no avenger arose. We were amid our troubles.

OEDIPUS. But when royalty had fallen what troubles could have hindered search?

CREON. The riddling Sphinx put those dark things out of our thoughts—we thought of what had come to our own doors.

OEDIPUS. But I will start afresh and make the dark 50 things plain. In doing right by Laius I protect myself, for whoever slew Laius might turn a hand against me. Come, my children, rise up from the altar steps; lift up these suppliant boughs and let all the children of Cadmus be called hither that I may search out everything and find for all happiness or misery as God wills.

PRIEST. May Phoebus, sender of the oracle, come with it and be our saviour and deliverer!

(*The* CHORUS *enter.*) *Chanting & dancing at same time*

CHORUS.

What message comes to famous Thebes from the 60 Golden House?

What message of disaster from that sweet-throated Zeus?

What monstrous thing our fathers saw do the seasons bring?

Or what that no man ever saw, what new monstrous thing?

Trembling in every limb I raise my loud importunate cry,

And in a sacred terror wait the Delian God's reply. 70

Apollo chase the God of Death that leads no shouting men,

Bears no rattling shield and yet consumes this form with pain.

Famine takes what the plague spares, and all the crops are lost;

No new life fills the empty place—ghost flits after ghost

To that God-trodden western shore, as flit benighted birds. 80

Sorrow speaks to sorrow, but no comfort finds in words.

Hurry him from the land of Thebes with a fair wind behind

Out on to that formless deep where not a man can find

Hold for an anchor-fluke, for all is world-enfolding sea;

Master of the thunder-cloud, set the lightning free,

And add the thunder-stone to that and fling them 90 on his head,

For death is all the fashion now, till even Death be dead.

We call against the pallid face of this God-hated God

The springing heel of Artemis in the hunting sandal shod,

The tousle-headed Maenads, blown torch and drunken sound,

The stately Lysian king himself with golden fillet 100 crowned,

And in his hands the golden bow and the stretched golden string,

And Bacchus' wine-ensanguined face that all the Maenads sing.

OEDIPUS. You are praying, and it may be that your prayer will be answered; that if you hear my words and do my bidding you may find help out of all your trouble. This is my proclamation, children of

70. **Delian God.** Apollo was born on the island of Delos. 98. **Maenads,** frenzied worshipers of Dionysus (Bacchus). 100. **Lysian king,** Apollo, god of light; from Lyceus, a surname of Apollo.

Cadmus. Whoever among you knows by what man Laius, son of Labdacus, was killed, must tell all he knows. If he fear for himself and being guilty denounce himself, he shall be in the less danger, suffering no worse thing than banishment. If on the other hand there be one that knows that a foreigner did the deed, let him speak, and I shall give him a reward and my thanks: but if any man keep silent from fear or to screen a friend, hear all what I will
10 do to that man. No one in this land shall speak to him, nor offer sacrifice beside him; but he shall be driven from their homes as if he himself had done the deed. And in this I am the ally of the Pythian God and of the murdered man, and I pray that the murderer's life may, should he be so hidden and screened, drop from him and perish away, whoever he may be, whether he did the deed with others or by himself alone: and on you I lay it to make—so far as man may—these words good, for my sake, and
20 for the God's sake, and for the sake of this land. And even if the God had not spurred us to it, it were a wrong to leave the guilt unpurged, when one so noble, and he your King, had perished; and all have sinned that could have searched it out and did not: and now since it is I who hold the power which he held once, and have his wife for wife—she who would have borne him heirs had he but lived—I take up this cause even as I would were it that of my own father. And if there be any who do not
30 obey me in it, I pray that the Gods send them neither harvest of the earth nor fruit of the womb; but let them be wasted by this plague, or by one more dreadful still. But may all be blessed for ever who hear my words and do my will!

CHORUS. We do not know the murderer, and it were indeed more fitting that Phoebus, who laid the task upon us, should name the man.

OEDIPUS. No man can make the Gods speak against their will.

40 CHORUS. Then I will say what seems the next best thing.

OEDIPUS. If there is a third course, show it.

CHORUS. I know that our lord Tiresias is the seer most like to our lord Phoebus, and through him we may unravel all.

OEDIPUS. So I was advised by Creon, and twice already have I sent to bring him.

CHORUS. If we lack his help we have nothing but vague and ancient rumours.

50 OEDIPUS. What rumours are they? I would examine every story.

CHORUS. Certain wayfarers were said to have killed the King.

OEDIPUS. I know, I know. But who was there that saw it?

CHORUS. If there is such a man, and terror can move him, he will not keep silence when they have told him of your curses.

OEDIPUS. He that such a deed did not terrify will not be terrified because of a word. 60

CHORUS. But there is one who shall convict him. For the blind prophet comes at last—in whom alone of all men the truth lives.

(*Enter* TIRESIAS, *led by a boy.*)

OEDIPUS. Tiresias, master of all knowledge, whatever may be spoken, whatever is unspeakable, whatever omens of earth and sky reveal, the plague is among us, and from that plague, Great Prophet, protect us and save us. Phoebus in answer to our question says that it will not leave us till we have found the murderers of Laius, and driven them into 70 exile or put them to death. Do you therefore neglect neither the voice of birds, nor any other sort of wisdom, but rescue yourself, rescue the State, rescue me, rescue all that are defiled by the deed. For we are in your hands, and what greater task falls to a man than to help other men with all he knows and has?

TIRESIAS. Aye, and what worse task than to be wise and suffer for it? I know this well; it slipped out of mind, or I would never have come.

OEDIPUS. What now? 80

TIRESIAS. Let me go home. You will bear your burden to the end more easily, and I bear mine—if you but give me leave for that.

OEDIPUS. Your words are strange and unkind to the State that bred you.

TIRESIAS. I see that you, on your part, keep your lips tight shut, and therefore I have shut mine that I may come to no misfortune.

OEDIPUS. For God's love do not turn away—if you have knowledge. We suppliants implore you on our 90 knees.

TIRESIAS. You are fools—I will bring misfortune neither upon you nor upon myself.

OEDIPUS. What is this? You know all and will say nothing? You are minded to betray me and Thebes?

TIRESIAS. Why do you ask these things? You will not learn them from me.

OEDIPUS. What! Basest of the base! You would enrage the very stones. Will you never speak out? Cannot anything touch you? 100

TIRESIAS. The future will come of itself though I keep silent.

OEDIPUS. Then seeing that come it must, you had best speak out.

TIRESIAS. I will speak no further. Rage if you have a mind to; bring out all the fierceness that is in your heart.

OEDIPUS. That will I. I will not spare to speak my thoughts. Listen to what I have to say. It seems to me that you have helped to plot the deed; and, 110 short of doing it with your own hands, have done the deed yourself. Had you eyesight I would declare that you alone had done it.

TIRESIAS. So that is what you say? I charge you to obey the decree that you yourself have made, and from this day out to speak neither to these nor to me. You are the defiler of this land.

OEDIPUS. So brazen in your impudence? How do you hope to escape punishment?

TIRESIAS. I have escaped; my strength is in my truth.

OEDIPUS. Who taught you this? You never got it by your art.

TIRESIAS. You, because you have spurred me to
10 speech against my will.

OEDIPUS. What speech? Speak it again that I may learn it better.

TIRESIAS. You are but tempting me—you understood me well enough.

OEDIPUS. No; not so that I can say I know it; speak it again.

TIRESIAS. I say that you are yourself the murderer that you seek.

OEDIPUS. You shall rue it for having spoken twice
20 such outrageous words.

TIRESIAS. Would you that I say more that you may be still angrier?

OEDIPUS. Say what you will. I will not let it move me.

TIRESIAS. I say that you are living with your next of kin in unimagined shame.

OEDIPUS. Do you think you can say such things and never smart for it?

TIRESIAS. Yes, if there be strength in truth.
30 OEDIPUS. There is; yes—for everyone but you. But not for you that are maimed in ear and in eye and in wit.

TIRESIAS. You are but a poor wretch flinging taunts that in a little while everyone shall fling at you.

OEDIPUS. Night, endless night has covered you up so that you can neither hurt me nor any man that looks upon the sun.

TIRESIAS. Your doom is not to fall by me. Apollo
40 is enough: it is his business to work out your doom.

OEDIPUS. Was it Creon that planned this or you yourself?

TIRESIAS. Creon is not your enemy; you are your own enemy.

OEDIPUS. Power, ability, position, you bear all burdens, and yet what envy you create! Great must that envy be if envy of my power in this town—a power put into my hands unsought—has made trusty Creon, my old friend Creon, secretly long to
50 take that power from me; if he has suborned this scheming juggler, this quack and trickster, this man with eyes for his gains and blindness in his art. Come, come, where did you prove yourself a seer? Why did you say nothing to set the townsmen free when the riddling Sphinx was here? Yet that riddle was not for the first-comer to read; it needed the skill of a seer. And none such had you! Neither found by help of birds, nor straight from any God.

No, I came; I silenced her, I the ignorant Oedipus, it was I that found the answer in my mother-wit, 60 untaught by any birds. And it is I that you would pluck out of my place, thinking to stand close to Creon's throne. But you and the plotter of all this shall mourn despite your zeal to purge the land. Were you not an old man, you had already learnt how bold you are and learnt it to your cost.

CHORUS. Both this man's words and yours, Oedipus, have been said in anger. Such words cannot help us here, nor any but those that teach us to obey the oracle. 70

TIRESIAS. King though you are, the right to answer when attacked belongs to both alike. I am not subject to you, but to Loxias; and therefore I shall never be Creon's subject. And I tell you, since you have taunted me with blindness, that though you have your sight, you cannot see in what misery you stand, nor where you are living, nor with whom, unknowing what you do—for you do not know the stock you come of—you have been your own kin's enemy be they living or be they dead. And one day 80 a mother's curse and father's curse alike shall drive you from this land in dreadful haste with darkness upon those eyes. Therefore, heap your scorn on Creon and on my message if you have a mind to; for no one of living men shall be crushed as you shall be crushed.

OEDIPUS. Begone this instant! Away, away! Get you from these doors!

TIRESIAS. I had never come but that you sent for me. 90

OEDIPUS. I did not know you were mad.

TIRESIAS. I may seem mad to you, but your parents thought me sane. ✱ HINT

OEDIPUS. My parents! Stop! Who was my father?

TIRESIAS. This day shall you know your birth; and it will ruin you.

OEDIPUS. What dark words you always speak!

TIRESIAS. But are you not most skilful in the unravelling of dark words?

OEDIPUS. You mock me for that which made me 100 great?

TIRESIAS. It was that fortune that undid you.

OEDIPUS. What do I care? For I delivered all this town.

TIRESIAS. Then I will go: boy, lead me out of this.

OEDIPUS. Yes, let him lead you. You take vexation with you.

TIRESIAS. I will go: but first I will do my errand. For frown though you may you cannot destroy me. The man for whom you look, the man you have 110 been threatening in all the proclamations about the death of Laius, that man is here. He seems, so far as looks go, an alien; yet he shall be found a native Theban and shall nowise be glad of that fortune. A

73. **Loxias**, Apollo as the god of oracles.

blind man, though now he has his sight; a beggar, though now he is most rich; he shall go forth feeling the ground before him with his stick; so you go in and think on that, and if you find I am in fault say that I have no skill in prophecy.

(TIRESIAS *is led out by the boy.* OEDIPUS *enters the palace.*)

CHORUS.
The Delphian rock has spoken out, now must a
    wicked mind,
Planner of things I dare not speak and of this bloody
10   wrack,
Pray for feet that are as fast as the four hoofs of the
    wind:
Cloudy Parnassus and the Fates thunder at his back.

That sacred crossing-place of lines upon Parnassus'
    head,
Lines that have run through North and South, and
    run through West and East,
That navel of the world bids all men search the
    mountain wood,
20 The solitary cavern, till they have found that in-
    famous beast.

(CREON *enters from the house.*)

CREON. Fellow-citizens, having heard that King Oedipus accuses me of dreadful things, I come in my indignation. Does he think that he has suffered wrong from me in these present troubles, or anything that could lead to wrong, whether in word or deed? How can I live under blame like that? What life would be worth having if by you here, and by my nearest friends, called a traitor through the 30 town?

CHORUS. He said it in anger, and not from his heart out.

CREON. He said it was I put up the seer to speak those falsehoods.

CHORUS. Such things were said.

CREON. And had he his right mind saying it?

CHORUS. I do not know—I do not know what my masters do.

(OEDIPUS *enters.*)

OEDIPUS. What brought you here? Have you a 40 face so brazen that you come to my house—you, the proved assassin of its master—the certain robber of my crown? Come, tell me in the face of the Gods what cowardice, or folly, did you discover in me that you plotted this? Did you think that I would not see what you were at till you had crept upon me, or seeing it would not ward it off? What madness to seek a throne, having neither friends nor followers!

CREON. Now, listen, hear my answer, and then 50 you may with knowledge judge between us.

OEDIPUS. You are plausible, but waste words now that I know you.

CREON. Hear what I have to say. I can explain it all.

OEDIPUS. One thing you will not explain away—that you are my enemy.

CREON. You are a fool to imagine that senseless stubbornness sits well upon you.

OEDIPUS. And you to imagine that you can wrong a kinsman and escape the penalty. 60

CREON. That is justly said, I grant you; but what is this wrong that you complain of?

OEDIPUS. Did you advise, or not, that I should send for that notorious prophet?

CREON. And I am of the same mind still.

OEDIPUS. How long is it, then, since Laius—

CREON. What, what about him?

OEDIPUS. Since Laius was killed by an unknown hand?

CREON. That was many years ago. 70

OEDIPUS. Was this prophet at his trade in those days?

CREON. Yes; skilled as now and in equal honour.

OEDIPUS. Did he ever speak of me?

CREON. Never certainly when I was within earshot.

OEDIPUS. And did you enquire into the murder?

CREON. We did enquire but learnt nothing.

OEDIPUS. And why did he not tell out his story then?

CREON. I do not know. When I know nothing I 80 say nothing.

OEDIPUS. This much at least you know and can say out.

CREON. What is that? If I know it I will say it.

OEDIPUS. That if he had not consulted you he would never have said that it was I who killed Laius.

CREON. You know best what he said; but now, question for question.

OEDIPUS. Question your fill—I cannot be proved 90 guilty of that blood.

CREON. Answer me then. Are you not married to my sister?

OEDIPUS. That cannot be denied.

CREON. And do you not rule as she does? And with a like power?

OEDIPUS. I give her all she asks for.

CREON. And am not I the equal of you both?

OEDIPUS. Yes: and that is why you are so false a friend. 100

CREON. Not so; reason this out as I reason it, and first weigh this: who would prefer to lie awake amid terrors rather than to sleep in peace, granting that his power is equal in both cases? Neither I nor any sober-minded man. You give me what I ask and let me do what I want, but were I King I would have to do things I did not want to do. Is not influence and no trouble with it better than any throne, am I such a fool as to hunger after unprofitable honours? Now all are glad to see me, every one wishes me well, all that want a favour from you ask speech of me—finding in that their hope. Why should I give up these things and take those? No wise mind is treacherous. I am no contriver of plots, and if another took to them he would not come to me for help. And in proof of this go to the Pythian Oracle, and ask if I have truly told what the Gods said: and after that, if you have 10 found that I have plotted with the Soothsayer, take me and kill me; not by the sentence of one mouth only—but of two mouths, yours and my own. But do not condemn me in a corner, upon some fancy and without proof. What right have you to declare a good man bad or a bad good? It is as bad a thing to cast off a true friend as it is for a man to cast away his own life—but you will learn these things with certainty when the time comes; for time alone shows a just man; though a day can show a 20 knave.

CHORUS. King! He has spoken well, he gives himself time to think; a headlong talker does not know what he is saying. *[oed: speak 1st – think later]*

OEDIPUS. The plotter is at his work, and I must counterplot headlong, or he will get his ends and I miss mine.

CREON. What will you do then? Drive me from the land?

OEDIPUS. Not so; I do not desire your banishment 30 —but your death.

CREON. You are not sane.

OEDIPUS. I am sane at least in my own interest.

CREON. You should be in mine also.

OEDIPUS. No, for you are false.

CREON. But if you understand nothing?

OEDIPUS. Yet I must rule.

CREON. Not if you rule badly.

OEDIPUS. Hear him, O Thebes!

CREON. Thebes is for me also, not for you alone.

40 CHORUS. Cease, princes: I see Jocasta coming out of the house; she comes just in time to quench the quarrel.

(JOCASTA *enters.*)

JOCASTA. Unhappy men! Why have you made this crazy uproar? Are you not ashamed to quarrel about your own affairs when the whole country is in trouble? Go back into the palace, Oedipus, and you, Creon, to your own house. Stop making all this noise about some petty thing.

CREON. Your husband is about to kill me—or to 50 drive me from the land of my fathers.

OEDIPUS. Yes: for I have convicted him of treachery against me. *[in oed's own mind.]*

CREON. Now may I perish accursed if I have done such a thing!

JOCASTA. For God's love believe it, Oedipus.

First, for the sake of his oath, and then for my sake, and for the sake of these people here.

CHORUS (*all*). King, do what she asks.

OEDIPUS. What would you have me do?

CHORUS. Not to make a dishonourable charge, 60 with no more evidence than rumour, against a friend who has bound himself with an oath.

OEDIPUS. Do you desire my exile or my death?

CHORUS. No, by Helios, by the first of all the Gods, may I die abandoned by Heaven and earth if I have that thought! What breaks my heart is that our public griefs should be increased by your quarrels.

OEDIPUS. Then let him go, though I am doomed thereby to death or to be thrust dishonoured from 70 the land; it is your lips, not his, that move me to compassion; wherever he goes my hatred follows him.

CREON. You are as sullen in yielding as you were vehement in anger, but such natures are their own heaviest burden. *[Oed's FLAW]*

OEDIPUS. Why will you not leave me in peace and begone?

CREON. I will go away; what is your hatred to me? In the eyes of all here I am a just man. 80

(*He goes.*)

CHORUS. Lady, why do you not take your man in to the house?

JOCASTA. I will do so when I have learned what has happened.

CHORUS. The half of it was blind suspicion bred of talk; the rest the wounds left by injustice.

JOCASTA. It was on both sides?

CHORUS. Yes.

JOCASTA. What was it?

CHORUS. Our land is vexed enough. Let the thing 90 alone now that it is over.

(*Exit leader of* CHORUS.)

JOCASTA. In the name of the Gods, King, what put you in this anger?

OEDIPUS. I will tell you; for I honour you more than these men do. The cause is Creon and his plots against me.

JOCASTA. Speak on, if you can tell clearly how this quarrel arose.

OEDIPUS. He says that I am guilty of the blood of Laius. *[Creon says – Oed thinks Creon plots w/Tires]* 100

JOCASTA. On his own knowledge, or on heresay?

OEDIPUS. He has made a rascal of a seer his mouthpiece.

JOCASTA. Do not fear that there is truth in what he says. Listen to me, and learn to your comfort that nothing born of woman can know what is to come. I will give you proof of that. An oracle came to Laius once, I will not say from Phoebus, but from his ministers, that he was doomed to die by the hand of his own child sprung from him and me. 110

When his child was but three days old, Laius bound its feet together and had it thrown by sure hands upon a trackless mountain; and when Laius was murdered at the place where three highways meet, it was, or so at least the rumour says, by foreign robbers. So Apollo did not bring it about that the child should kill its father, nor did Laius die in the dreadful way he feared by his child's hand. Yet that was how the message of the seers mapped out the future. Pay no attention to such things. What the God would show he will need no help to show it, but bring it to light himself.

OEDIPUS. What restlessness of soul, lady, has come upon me since I heard you speak, what a tumult of the mind!

JOCASTA. What is this new anxiety? What has startled you?

OEDIPUS. You said that Laius was killed where three highways meet.

JOCASTA. Yes: that was the story.

OEDIPUS. And where is the place?

JOCASTA. In Phocis where the road divides branching off to Delphi and to Daulia.

OEDIPUS. And when did it happen? How many years ago?

JOCASTA. News was published in this town just before you came into power.

OEDIPUS. O Zeus! What have you planned to do unto me?

JOCASTA. He was tall; the silver had just come into his hair; and in shape not greatly unlike to you.

OEDIPUS. Unhappy that I am! It seems that I have laid a dreadful curse upon myself, and did not know it.

JOCASTA. What do you say? I tremble when I look on you, my King.

OEDIPUS. And I have a misgiving that the seer can see indeed. But I will know it all more clearly, if you tell me one thing more.

JOCASTA. Indeed, though I tremble I will answer whatever you ask.

OEDIPUS. Had he but a small troop with him; or did he travel like a great man with many followers?

JOCASTA. There were but five in all—one of them a herald; and there was one carriage with Laius in it.

OEDIPUS. Alas! It is now clear indeed. Who was it brought the news, lady?

JOCASTA. A servant—the one survivor.

OEDIPUS. Is he by chance in the house now?

JOCASTA. No; for when he found you reigning instead of Laius he besought me, his hand clasped in mine, to send him to the fields among the cattle that he might be far from the sight of this town; and I sent him. He was a worthy man for a slave and might have asked a bigger thing.

OEDIPUS. I would have him return to us without delay.

JOCASTA. Oedipus, it is easy. But why do you ask this?

OEDIPUS. I fear that I have said too much, and therefore I would question him.

JOCASTA. He shall come, but I too have a right to know what lies so heavy upon your heart, my King.

OEDIPUS. Yes: and it shall not be kept from you now that my fear has grown so heavy. Nobody is more to me than you, nobody has the same right to learn my good or evil luck. My father was Polybus of Corinth, my mother the Dorian Merope, and I was held the foremost man in all that town until a thing happened—a thing to startle a man, though not to make him angry as it made me. We were sitting at the table, and a man who had drunk too much cried out that I was not my father's son— and I, though angry, restrained my anger for that day; but the next day went to my father and my mother and questioned them. They were indignant at the taunt and that comforted me—and yet the man's words rankled, for they had spread a rumour through the town. Without consulting my father or my mother I went to Delphi, but Phoebus told me nothing of the thing for which I came, but much of other things—things of sorrow and of terror: that I should live in incest with my mother, and beget a brood that men would shudder to look upon; that I should be my father's murderer. Hearing those words I fled out of Corinth, and from that day have but known where it lies when I have found its direction by the stars. I sought where I might escape those infamous things—the doom that was laid upon me. I came in my flight to that very spot where you tell me this king perished. Now, lady, I will tell you the truth. When I had come close up to those three roads, I came upon a herald, and a man like him you have described seated in a carriage. The man who held the reins and the old man himself would not give me room, but thought to force me from the path, and I struck the driver in my anger. The old man, seeing what I had done, waited till I was passing him and then struck me upon the head. I paid him back in full, for I knocked him out of the carriage with a blow of my stick. He rolled on his back, and after that I killed them all. If this stranger were indeed Laius, is there a more miserable man in the world than the man before you? Is there a man more hated of Heaven? No stranger, no citizen, may receive him into his house, not a soul may speak to him, and no mouth but my own mouth has laid this curse upon me. Am I not wretched? May I be swept from this world before I have endured this doom!

CHORUS. These things, O King, fill us with terror; yet hope till you speak with him that saw the deed, and have learnt all.

OEDIPUS. Till I have learnt all, I may hope. I await the man that is coming from the pastures.

JOCASTA. What is it that you hope to learn?

OEDIPUS. I will tell you. If his tale agrees with yours, then I am clear.

JOCASTA. What tale of mine?

10 OEDIPUS. He told you that Laius met his death from robbers; if he keeps to that tale now and speaks of several slayers, I am not the slayer. But if he says one lonely wayfarer, then beyond a doubt the scale dips to me.

JOCASTA. Be certain of this much at least, his first tale was of robbers. He cannot revoke that tale— the city heard it and not I alone. Yet, if he should somewhat change his story, King, at least he cannot make the murder of Laius square with prophecy;

20 for Loxias plainly said of Laius that he would die by the hand of my child. That poor innocent did not kill him, for it died before him. Therefore from this out I would not, for all divination can do, so much as look to my right hand or to my left hand, or fear at all.

OEDIPUS. You have judged well; and yet for all that, send and bring this peasant to me.

JOCASTA. I will send without delay. I will do all that you would have of me—but let us come in to

30 the house.   (*They go in to the house.*)

CHORUS.
For this one thing above all I would be praised as
        a man,
That in my words and my deeds I have kept those
        laws in mind
Olympian Zeus, and that high clear Empyrean,
Fashioned, and not some man or people of mankind,
Even those sacred laws nor age nor sleep can blind.

A man becomes a tyrant out of insolence,
40 He climbs and climbs, until all people call him
        great,
He seems upon the summit, and God flings him
        thence;
Yet an ambitious man may lift up a whole State,
And in his death be blessed, in his life fortunate.

And all men honour such; but should a man forget
The holy images, the Delphian Sibyl's trance,
And the world's navel-stone, and not be punished
        for it
50 And seem most fortunate, or even blessed perchance,
Why should we honour the Gods, or join the sacred
        dance?
                (JOCASTA *enters from the palace.*)
JOCASTA. It has come into my head, citizens of

Thebes, to visit every altar of the Gods, a wreath in my hand and a dish of incense. For all manner of alarms trouble the soul of Oedipus, who instead of weighing new oracles by old, like a man of sense, is at the mercy of every mouth that speaks terror. Seeing that my words are nothing to him, I cry to you, Lysian Apollo, whose altar is the first I meet: I 60 come, a suppliant, bearing symbols of prayer; O, make us clean, for now we are all afraid, seeing him afraid, even as they who see the helmsman afraid.

                (*Enter* MESSENGER.)
MESSENGER. May I learn from you, strangers, where is the home of King Oedipus? Or better still, tell me where he himself is, if you know.

CHORUS. This is his house, and he himself, stranger, is within it, and this lady is the mother of his children.

MESSENGER. Then I call a blessing upon her, 70 seeing what man she has married.

JOCASTA. May God reward those words with a like blessing, stranger! But what have you come to seek or to tell?

MESSENGER. Good news for your house, lady, and for your husband.

JOCASTA. What news? From whence have you come?

MESSENGER. From Corinth, and you will rejoice at the message I am about to give you; yet, maybe, 80 it will grieve you.

JOCASTA. What is it? How can it have this double power?

MESSENGER. The people of Corinth, they say, will take him for king.

JOCASTA. How then? Is old Polybus no longer on the throne?

MESSENGER. No. He is in his tomb.

JOCASTA. What do you say? Is Polybus dead, old man? 90

MESSENGER. May I drop dead if it is not the truth.

JOCASTA. Away! Hurry to your master with this news. O oracle of the Gods, where are you now? This is the man whom Oedipus feared and shunned lest he should murder him, and now this man has died a natural death, and not by the hand of Oedipus.

                (*Enter* OEDIPUS.)
OEDIPUS. Jocasta, dearest wife, why have you called me from the house? 100

JOCASTA. Listen to this man, and judge to what the oracles of the Gods have come.

OEDIPUS. And he—who may he be? And what news has he?

JOCASTA. He has come from Corinth to tell you that your father, Polybus, is dead.

OEDIPUS. How, stranger? Let me have it from your own mouth.

MESSENGER. If I am to tell the story, the first thing is that he is dead and gone.

OEDIPUS. By some sickness or by treachery?

MESSENGER. A little thing can bring the aged to their rest.

OEDIPUS. Ah! He died, it seems, from sickness?

MESSENGER. Yes; and of old age.

10 OEDIPUS. Alas! Alas! Why, indeed, my wife, should one look to that Pythian seer, or to the birds that scream above our heads? For they would have it that I was doomed to kill my father. And now he is dead—hid already beneath the earth. And here am I—who had no part in it, unless indeed he died from longing for me. If that were so, I may have caused his death; but Polybus has carried the oracles with him into Hades—the oracles as men have understood them—and they are worth nothing.

20 JOCASTA. Did I not tell you so, long since?

OEDIPUS. You did, but fear misled me.

JOCASTA. Put this trouble from you.

OEDIPUS. Those bold words would sound better, were not my mother living. But as it is—I have some grounds for fear; yet you have said well.

JOCASTA. Yet your father's death is a sign that all is well.

OEDIPUS. I know that: but I fear because of her who lives.

30 MESSENGER. Who is this woman who makes you afraid?

OEDIPUS. Merope, old man, the wife of Polybus.

MESSENGER. What is there in her to make you afraid?

OEDIPUS. A dreadful oracle sent from Heaven, stranger.

MESSENGER. Is it a secret, or can you speak it out?

OEDIPUS. Loxias said that I was doomed to marry 40 my own mother, and to shed my father's blood. For that reason I fled from my house in Corinth; and I did right, though there is great comfort in familiar faces.

MESSENGER. Was it indeed for that reason that you went into exile?

OEDIPUS. I did not wish, old man, to shed my father's blood.

MESSENGER. King, have I not freed you from that fear?

50 OEDIPUS. You shall be fittingly rewarded.

MESSENGER. Indeed, to tell the truth, it was for that I came; to bring you home and be the better for it——

OEDIPUS. No! I will never go to my parents' home.

MESSENGER. Oh, my son, it is plain enough, you do not know what you do.

OEDIPUS. How, old man? For God's love, tell me.

MESSENGER. If for these reasons you shrink from going home.

OEDIPUS. I am afraid lest Phoebus has spoken true. 60

MESSENGER. You are afraid of being made guilty through Merope?

OEDIPUS. That is my constant fear.

MESSENGER. A vain fear.

OEDIPUS. How so, if I was born of that father and mother?

MESSENGER. Because they were nothing to you in blood.

OEDIPUS. What do you say? Was Polybus not my father? 70

MESSENGER. No more nor less than myself.

OEDIPUS. How can my father be no more to me than you who are nothing to me?

MESSENGER. He did not beget you any more than I.

OEDIPUS. No? Then why did he call me his son?

MESSENGER. He took you as a gift from these hands of mine.

OEDIPUS. How could he love so dearly what came from another's hands?

MESSENGER. He had been childless. 80

OEDIPUS. If I am not your son, where did you get me?

MESSENGER. In a wooded valley of Cithaeron.

OEDIPUS. What brought you wandering there?

MESSENGER. I was in charge of mountain sheep.

OEDIPUS. A shepherd—a wandering, hired man.

MESSENGER. A hired man who came just in time.

OEDIPUS. Just in time—had it come to that?

MESSENGER. Have not the cords left their marks upon your ankles? 90

OEDIPUS. Yes, that is an old trouble.

MESSENGER. I took your feet out of the spancel.

OEDIPUS. I have had those marks from the cradle.

MESSENGER. They have given you the name you bear.

OEDIPUS. Tell me, for God's sake, was that deed my mother's or my father's?

MESSENGER. I do not know—he who gave you to me knows more of that than I.

OEDIPUS. What? You had me from another? You 100 did not chance on me yourself?

MESSENGER. No. Another shepherd gave you to me.

OEDIPUS. Who was he? Can you tell me who he was?

MESSENGER. I think that he was said to be of Laius' household.

OEDIPUS. The king who ruled this country long ago?

MESSENGER. The same—the man was herdsman 110 in his service.

94–95. **name you bear.** Oedipus means "swollen feet" in Greek. When he was exposed for death as a baby, his parents had his feet pierced and tied together.

OEDIPUS. Is he alive, that I might speak with him?

MESSENGER. You people of this country should know that.

OEDIPUS. Is there any one here present who knows the herd he speaks of? Any one who has seen him in the town pastures? The hour has come when all must be made clear.

CHORUS. I think he is the very herd you sent for but now; Jocasta can tell you better than I.

JOCASTA. Why ask about that man? Why think about him? Why waste a thought on what this man has said? What he has said is of no account.

OEDIPUS. What, with a clue like that in my hands and fail to find out my birth?

JOCASTA. For God's sake, if you set any value upon your life, give up this search—my misery is enough.

OEDIPUS. Though I be proved the son of a slave, yes, even of three generations of slaves, you cannot be made base-born.

JOCASTA. Yet, hear me, I implore you. Give up this search.

OEDIPUS. I will not hear of anything but searching the whole thing out.

JOCASTA. I am only thinking of your good—I have advised you for the best.

OEDIPUS. Your advice makes me impatient.

JOCASTA. May you never come to know who you are, unhappy man!

OEDIPUS. Go, some one, bring the herdsman here —and let that woman glory in her noble blood.

JOCASTA. Alas, alas, miserable man! Miserable! That is all that I can call you now or for ever.
(She goes out.)

CHORUS. Why has the lady gone, Oedipus, in such a transport of despair? Out of this silence will burst a storm of sorrows.

OEDIPUS. Let come what will. However lowly my origin I will discover it. That woman, with all a woman's pride, grows red with shame at my base birth. I think myself the child of Good Luck, and that the years are my foster-brothers. Sometimes they have set me up, and sometimes thrown me down, but he that has Good Luck for mother can suffer no dishonour. That is my origin, nothing can change it, so why should I renounce this search into my birth?

CHORUS.
Oedipus' nurse, mountain of many a hidden glen,
Be honoured among men;
A famous man, deep-thoughted, and his body strong;
Be honoured in dance and song.
Who met in the hidden glen? Who let his fancy run
Upon nymph of Helicon?
Lord Pan or Lord Apollo or the mountain Lord

55. **mountain Lord.** The mountain Cyllene was sacred to Hermes.

By the Bacchantes adored?

OEDIPUS. If I, who have never met the man, may venture to say so, I think that the herdsman we await approaches; his venerable age matches with this stranger's, and I recognize as servants of mine those who bring him. But you, if you have seen the man before, will know the man better than I.

CHORUS. Yes, I know the man who is coming; he was indeed in Laius' service, and is still the most trusted of the herdsmen.

OEDIPUS. I ask you first, Corinthian stranger, is this the man you mean?

MESSENGER. He is the very man.

OEDIPUS. Look at me, old man! Answer my questions. Were you once in Laius' service?

HERDSMAN. I was: not a bought slave, but reared up in the house.

OEDIPUS. What was your work—your manner of life?

HERDSMAN. For the best part of my life I have tended flocks.

OEDIPUS. Where, mainly?

HERDSMAN. Cithaeron or its neighbourhood.

OEDIPUS. Do you remember meeting with this man there?

HERDSMAN. What man do you mean?

OEDIPUS. This man. Did you ever meet him?

HERDSMAN. I cannot recall him to mind.

MESSENGER. No wonder in that, master; but I will bring back his memory. He and I lived side by side upon Cithaeron. I had but one flock and he had two. Three full half-years we lived there, from spring to autumn, and every winter I drove my flock to my own fold, while he drove his to the fold of Laius. Is that right? Was it not so?

HERDSMAN. True enough; though it was long ago.

MESSENGER. Come, tell me now—do you remember giving me a boy to rear as my own foster-son?

HERDSMAN. What are you saying? Why do you ask me that?

MESSENGER. Look at that man, my friend, he is the child you gave me.

HERDSMAN. A plague upon you! Cannot you hold your tongue?

OEDIPUS. Do not blame him, old man; your own words are more blameable.

HERDSMAN. And how have I offended, master?

OEDIPUS. In not telling of that boy he asks of.

HERDSMAN. He speaks from ignorance, and does not know what he is saying.

OEDIPUS. If you will not speak with a good grace you shall be made to speak.

HERDSMAN. Do not hurt me for the love of God, I am an old man.

OEDIPUS. Some one there, tie his hands behind his back.

HERDSMAN. Alas! Wherefore! What more would you learn?

OEDIPUS. Did you give this man the child he speaks of?

HERDSMAN. I did: would I had died that day!

OEDIPUS. Well, you may come to that unless you speak the truth.

HERDSMAN. Much more am I lost if I speak it.

OEDIPUS. What! Would the fellow make more de-
10 lay?

HERDSMAN. No, no. I said before that I gave it to him.

OEDIPUS. Where did you come by it? Your own child, or another?

HERDSMAN. It was not my own child—I had it from another.

OEDIPUS. From any of those here? From what house?

HERDSMAN. Do not ask any more, master; for
20 the love of God do not ask.

OEDIPUS. You are lost if I have to question you again.

HERDSMAN. It was a child from the house of Laius.

OEDIPUS. A slave? Or one of his own race?

HERDSMAN. Alas! I am on the edge of dreadful words.

OEDIPUS. And I of hearing: yet hear I must.

HERDSMAN. It was said to have been his own
30 child. But your lady within can tell you of these things best.

OEDIPUS. How? It was she who gave it to you?

HERDSMAN. Yes, King.

OEDIPUS. To what end?

HERDSMAN. That I should make away with it.

OEDIPUS. Her own child?

HERDSMAN. Yes: from fear of evil prophecies.

OEDIPUS. What prophecies?

HERDSMAN. That he should kill his father.

40 OEDIPUS. Why, then, did you give him up to this old man?

HERDSMAN. Through pity, master, believing that he would carry him to whatever land he had him-self come from—but he saved him for dreadful misery; for if you are what this man says, you are the most miserable of all men.

OEDIPUS. O! O! All brought to pass! All truth! Now, O light, may I look my last upon you, having been found accursed in bloodshed, accursed in mar-
50 riage, and in my coming into the world accursed!

(He rushes into the palace.)

CHORUS.

What can the shadow-like generations of man attain
But build up a dazzling mockery of delight that
    under their touch dissolves again?
Oedipus seemed blessed, but there is no man blessed
    amongst men.

Oedipus overcame the woman-breasted Fate;
He seemed like a strong tower against Death and
    first among the fortunate;
He sat upon the ancient throne of Thebes, and all   60
    men called him great.

But, looking for a marriage-bed, he found the bed
    of his birth,
Tilled the field his father had tilled, cast seed into
    the same abounding earth;
Entered through the door that had sent him wailing
    forth.

Begetter and begot as one! How could that be hid?
What darkness cover up that marriage-bed? Time
    watches, he is eagle-eyed,   70
And all the works of man are known and every soul
    is tried.

Would you had never come to Thebes, nor to this
    house,
Nor riddled with the woman-breasted Fate, beaten
    off Death and succoured us,
That I had never raised this song, heartbroken
    Oedipus!

SECOND MESSENGER (coming from the house).
Friends and kinsmen of this house! What deeds must   80
you look upon, what burden of sorrow bear, if true
to race you still love the House of Labdacus. For not
Ister nor Phasis could wash this house clean, so
many misfortunes have been brought upon it, so
many has it brought upon itself, and those misfortunes are always the worst that a man brings upon
himself.

CHORUS. Great already are the misfortunes of this
house, and you bring us a new tale.

SECOND MESSENGER. A short tale in the telling: 90
Jocasta, our Queen, is dead.

CHORUS. Alas, miserable woman, how did she die?

SECOND MESSENGER. By her own hand. It cannot
be as terrible to you as to one that saw it with his
eyes, yet so far as words can serve, you shall see it.
When she had come into the vestibule, she ran half
crazed towards her marriage-bed, clutching at her
hair with the fingers of both hands, and once within
the chamber dashed the doors together behind her.
Then called upon the name of Laius, long since   100
dead, remembering that son who killed the father
and upon the mother begot an accursed race. And
wailed because of that marriage wherein she had
borne a two-fold race—husband by husband, children by her child. Then Oedipus with a shriek burst
in and running here and there asked for a sword,
asked where he would find the wife that was no
wife but a mother who had borne his children and
himself. Nobody answered him, we all stood dumb;

83. **Ister nor Phasis,** two rivers.

but supernatural power helped him, for, with a dreadful shriek, as though beckoned, he sprang at the double doors, drove them in, burst the bolts out of their sockets, and ran into the room. There we saw the woman hanging in a swinging halter, and with a terrible cry he loosened the halter from her neck. When that unhappiest woman lay stretched upon the ground, we saw another dreadful sight. He dragged the golden brooches from her dress and 10 lifting them struck them upon his eyeballs, crying out, "You have looked enough upon those you ought never to have looked upon, failed long enough to know those that you should have known; henceforth you shall be dark." He struck his eyes, not once, but many times, lifting his hands and speaking such or like words. The blood poured down and not with a few slow drops, but all at once over his beard in a dark shower as it were hail.

(The CHORUS *wails and he steps further on to the stage.*)

Such evils have come forth from the deeds of 20 those two and fallen not on one alone but upon husband and wife. They inherited much happiness, much good fortune; but to-day, ruin, shame, death, and loud crying, all evils that can be counted up, all, all are theirs.

CHORUS. Is he any quieter?

SECOND MESSENGER. He cries for someone to unbar the gates and to show to all the men of Thebes his father's murderer, his mother's—the unholy word must not be spoken. It is his purpose to cast himself 30 out of the land that he may not bring all this house under his curse. But he has not the strength to do it. He must be supported and led away. The curtain is parting; you are going to look upon a sight which even those who shudder must pity.

(*Enter* OEDIPUS.)

OEDIPUS. Woe, woe is me! Miserable, miserable that I am! Where am I? Where am I going? Where am I cast away? Who hears my words?

CHORUS. Cast away indeed, dreadful to the sight of the eye, dreadful to the ear.

40 OEDIPUS. Ah, friend, the only friend left to me, friend still faithful to the blind man! I know that you are there; blind though I am, I recognize your voice.

CHORUS. Where did you get the courage to put out your eyes? What unearthly power drove you to that?

OEDIPUS. Apollo, friends, Apollo, but it was my own hand alone, wretched that I am, that quenched these eyes.

50 CHORUS. You were better dead than blind.

OEDIPUS. No, it is better to be blind. What sight is there that could give me joy? How could I have looked into the face of my father when I came among the dead, aye, or on my miserable mother, since against them both I sinned such things that no halter can punish? And what to me this spectacle, town, statue, wall, and what to me this people, since I, thrice wretched, I, noblest of Theban men, have doomed myself to banishment, doomed myself when I commanded all to thrust out the unclean thing? 60

CHORUS. It had indeed been better if that herdsman had never taken your feet out of the spancel or brought you back to life.

OEDIPUS. O three roads, O secret glen; O coppice and narrow way where three roads met; you that drank up the blood I spilt, the blood that was my own, my father's blood: remember what deeds I wrought for you to look upon, and then, when I had come hither, the new deeds that I wrought. O marriage-bed that gave me birth and after that gave 70 children to your child, creating an incestuous kindred of fathers, brothers, sons, wives, and mothers. Yes, all the shame and the uncleanness that I have wrought among men.

CHORUS. For all my pity I shudder and turn away.

OEDIPUS. Come near, condescend to lay your hands upon a wretched man; listen, do not fear. My plague can touch no man but me. Hide me somewhere out of this land for God's sake, or kill me, or throw me into the sea where you shall never look 80 upon me more.

(*Enter* CREON *and attendants.*)

CHORUS. Here Creon comes at a fit moment; you can ask of him what you will, help or counsel, for he is now in your place. He is King.

OEDIPUS. What can I say to him? What can I claim, having been altogether unjust to him.

CREON. I have not come in mockery, Oedipus, nor to reproach you. Lead him in to the house as quickly as you can. Do not let him display his misery before strangers. 90

OEDIPUS. I must obey, but first, since you have come in so noble a spirit, you will hear me.

CREON. Say what you will.

OEDIPUS. I know that you will give her that lies within such a tomb as befits your own blood, but there is something more, Creon. My sons are men and can take care of themselves, but my daughters, my two unhappy daughters, that have ever eaten at my own table and shared my food, watch over my daughters, Creon. If it is lawful, let me touch 100 them with my hands. Grant it, Prince, grant it, noble heart. I would believe, could I touch them, that I still saw them.

(ISMENE *and* ANTIGONE *are led in by attendants.*) But do I hear them sobbing? Has Creon pitied me and sent my children, my darlings? Has he done this?

CREON. Yes, I ordered it, for I know how greatly you have always loved them.

OEDIPUS. Then may you be blessed, and may Heaven be kinder to you than it has been to me! My 110

children, where are you? Come hither—hither—come to the hands of him whose mother was your mother; the hands that put out your father's eyes, eyes once as bright as your own; his who, understanding nothing, seeing nothing, became your father by her that bore him. I weep when I think of the bitter life that men will make you live, and the days that are to come. Into what company dare you go, to what festival, but that you shall return home from
10 it not sharing in the joys, but bathed in tears? When you are old enough to be married, what man dare face the reproach that must cling to you and to your children? What misery is there lacking? Your father killed his father, he begat you at the spring of his own being, offspring of her that bore him. That is the taunt that would be cast upon you and on the man that you should marry. That man is not alive; my children, you must wither away in barrenness. Ah, son of Menoeceus, listen. Seeing that you are the
20 only father now left to them, for we their parents are lost, both of us lost, do not let them wander in beggary—are they not your own kindred?—do not let them sink down into my misery. No, pity them, seeing them utterly wretched in helpless childhood if you do not protect them. Show me that you promise, generous man, by touching me with your hand. (CREON *touches him.*) My children, there is much advice that I would give you were you but old enough to understand, but all I can do now is
30 bid you pray that you may live wherever you are let live, and that your life be happier than your father's.

CREON. Enough of tears. Pass into the house.

OEDIPUS. I will obey, though upon conditions.

CREON. Conditions?

OEDIPUS. Banish me from this country. I know that nothing can destroy me, for I wait some incredible fate; yet cast me upon Cithaeron, chosen by my father and my mother for my tomb.

CREON. Only the Gods can say yes or no to that.

40 OEDIPUS. No, for I am hateful to the Gods.

CREON. If that be so you will get your wish the quicker. They will banish that which they hate.

OEDIPUS. Are you certain of that?

CREON. I would not say it if I did not mean it.

OEDIPUS. Then it is time to lead me within.

CREON. Come, but let your children go.

OEDIPUS. No, do not take them from me.

CREON. Do not seek to be master; you won the mastery but could not keep it to the end.

(*He leads* OEDIPUS *into the palace, followed by* ISMENE, ANTIGONE, *and attendants.*)

50 CHORUS. Make way for Oedipus. All people said,
"That is a fortunate man;"
And now what storms are beating on his head!
"That is a fortunate man;"
Call no man fortunate that is not dead.
The dead are free from pain.

Euripides

c. 480–c. 407 B.C.

Although Sophocles is generally considered the greatest Greek tragedian, Euripides has long been the most popular and is certainly the most modern and arresting in point of view. A poorer artist and a more revolutionary thinker than Sophocles or Aeschylus, he was suspiciously received in his day and won the first prize only five times in an active career of nearly fifty years, during which he wrote some ninety plays. But his free-thinking spirit was in tune with a new generation which was philosophically minded rather than religious, and decadent in its radicalism, so that after his death he quickly outdistanced his predecessors in popular esteem. As many as eighteen of his plays have survived, in comparison with seven each of his predecessors. His popularity in the declining years of Greece was due to his veiled but exciting iconoclasm and to the theatrical devices which his predecessors had scorned, as much as to the humanness of his characters and his warm poetic style.

Sometimes called the psychologist among the Greek playwrights, Euripides was himself a challenging subject for a psychologist. Born probably in 480 B.C., the year of Salamis, he was even in childhood an aloof and grim-faced introvert. Although his father trained him as a professional boxer and wrestler, he came to loathe athletics and turned instead to painting, music, and playwriting. His introspective nature often led him to retirement among his many books or in a cave on Salamis, where he is said to have written his plays. He performed his military service, but later took no interest in the army, the Assembly, the religious festivals, or other concerns of the well-rounded Greek citizen. His wife found him a cold, difficult man, but the many searching and sometimes unflattering pictures of women in his tragedies reveal less of a sour attitude toward them than his characteristic urge to analyze personality and to project the pathetic qualities in human life.

As a dispassionate observer of his contemporaries, he won their distrust and hostility by his social criticism and disrespect for tradition. Aristophanes voiced the conservatives' alarm in his brutal satire of Euripides in the *Thesmophoriazusae* and *The Frogs*. But he was enthusiastically accepted in the radical circles of Anaxagoras, Protagoras, and Socrates, the philosophers, and outside Athens he had many admirers. In Sicily, where his works were especially popular, some Athenian prisoners once won freedom because they could recite speeches from his plays. At last the sensitive poet grew weary of censure and misunderstanding at home and accepted the invitation of the King of Macedonia to settle in his northern kingdom, where he probably wrote his final masterpieces, the *Bacchae* and *Iphigenia at Aulis*. After his death in his seventies one of his sons produced his last plays at

Athens and won him a posthumous first prize. Sophocles, who outlived him, made his chorus wear mourning that year in Euripides' honor.

Although Euripides presents the time-honored myths that were still considered the only suitable subjects for a religious theater, he was far from a religious man, if not actually an atheist. He was interested in the old tales, not as holy legends, but as vehicles of character study and social comment. His heroes and heroines, regardless of their traditional sanctity, emerge as strikingly human creations, sympathetically but objectively studied for their weaknesses and even morbid traits. Although he is a moralistic pyschologist rather than a scientific one, his moral outlook was closer to the radical views of Socrates than to the conventional theology of Aeschylus and Sophocles. He took a realistic view of mankind but implied a conception of justice superior to the pragmatic ethics of Homer. As he could reduce an ancient hero like Agamemnon to the level of a vacillating politician, so he could give a sympathetic picture of a traditional villainess, like Phaedra, the faithless wife, or Medea, the murderer of her own children. Like Dante in his *Commedia*, he detested the smug self-satisfaction of an Admetus (in *Alcestis*) or Pentheus (in *Bacchae*) but was lenient toward those who committed crimes while overcome by passion.

Interested primarily in character, Euripides often seemed to consider plot no more than a necessary nuisance and developed theatrical devices to dispose of it and to allow himself freedom to concentrate on his men and women. He frequently used a monologue-prologue to give a rapid review of the background of the plot, and popularized a spectacular device for bringing a quick and usually happy end to the story, called the *deus ex machina*, whereby a god not previously involved in the action would suddenly descend in a magic car (for which actual machinery was provided) to rescue an innocent Iphigenia from slaughter or arrange a marriage for a guilty Medea. To a modern reader this melodramatic device often does violence to the logic of the plot, but for the Greeks it placed a seal of divine approval on the solution. Occasionally it was used to solve an otherwise unsolvable situation, but more often to foretell the future of the characters, as only a god was in a position to do. Again, to concentrate on his central characters, Euripides reduced the status of the traditional chorus to brief interludes between the scenes and predicted the disappearance of the chorus entirely in the centuries to follow. This was in line with the increased realism that he introduced into the conception, dialogue, and staging of his dramas.

Although several other plays challenge its place, the masterpiece of Euripides is probably *Hippolytus*. Even the Athenians recognized its worth by giving it one of his few first prizes in 428 B.C. No other of his works has a better constructed plot or a fuller study of character, and the scenes of Phaedra's confession of love for her stepson and of the final reconciliation of father and son are among the most appealing in Greek tragedy. The same poignant domestic tale was to inspire the later French master, Racine, to write his best play; and both Sophocles and Seneca produced plays of that name. The parallel with the tale of Joseph and Potiphar's wife in Genesis is obvious.

Hippolytus was a startling novelty on the Athenian stage because it was the first work to present sexual passion freely as a source of tragedy. The old legend had long intrigued Euripides, and he had written an earlier play on the same subject, now lost, which apparently concentrated on the illicit desires of Phaedra, as Racine's play was to do. But Hippolytus is the central character of the extant play, and Euripides has given a masterful study of a young man's misguided attempt at sexual adjustment.

Barely out of adolescence, Hippolytus has an exaggerated sense of chastity and has joined the monkish Orphic brotherhood, which leads him to despise women and Aphrodite, the goddess of love, who represents them in his eyes. This fatal show of pride in his purity attracts the malevolence of the goddess, who bewitches Phaedra as an instrument of his undoing. There is no perversion implied in the nature of Hippolytus. He is a rugged youth, devoted to athletics and the hunt (symbolized by Artemis, the virgin goddess of the chase), who errs in being excessively idealistic and prudish. His self-righteousness leads him to be insolent toward a goddess—an unforgivable act in Greek eyes. Only this condones the shabbiness of Aphrodite in making this otherwise innocent youth the victim of a vicious plot. But even after Theseus confronts him with his accusation, Hippolytus maintains his supercilious attitude and seems to justify his father's attack, if not his suspicions. In accepting banishment and death he seems to feel more pity for his misguided father than for himself.

Phaedra is one of the famous women characters of Euripides. As with Medea in his play of that name, her crime is unflinchingly declared, and yet somewhat excused on the ground that she was simply an instrument of divine justice. Born into a family that had suffered much for love, Phaedra fights her passion for her stepson, but its intensity is too great for her. Her situation inspires our sympathy for a decent and modest woman who is wracked against her will by illicit desires. The picture of a woman in love is painted with realistic detail—her irresponsibility, her vanity, her humiliating frustration and hateful accusation after the sting of Hippolytus' rebuff. Though her career in the play is shocking, Euripides convinces us that she, like the others, is merely a fallible human being. In many respects she is more admirable than the loyal but hard-headed nurse who advises her.

This play illustrates the frequent tendency of Greek authors from Homer down to use the gods as mere abstractions, poetic devices, or metaphors to represent human experience. Aphrodite and Artemis symbolize opposite poles of behavior—wanton sex gratification and asceticism, both of which violated the Greek ideal of "nothing to excess." Like the *Bacchae*, *Hippolytus* teaches that no man should inhibit the instinctive urges in his nature. The natural life, led with moderation, is the ideal one.

Hippolytus

CHARACTERS IN THE PLAY

APHRODITE
HIPPOLYTUS, *son of* THESEUS
ATTENDANTS OF HIPPOLYTUS
CHORUS OF TROEZENIAN WOMEN
NURSE OF PHAEDRA
PHAEDRA, *wife of* THESEUS
THESEUS
MESSENGER
ARTEMIS

(SCENE: *Before the royal palace at Troezen. The goddess* APHRODITE *appears.*)

APHRODITE.

WIDE o'er man my realm extends, and proud the name that I, the goddess Cypris, bear, both in heaven's courts and 'mongst all those who dwell within the limits of the sea and the bounds of Atlas, beholding the sungod's light; those that respect my power I advance to honour, but bring to ruin all who vaunt themselves at me. For even in the race of gods this feeling finds a home, even pleasure at the honour men pay them. And the truth of this I soon 10 will show; for that son of Theseus, born of the Amazon, Hippolytus, whom holy Pittheus taught, alone of all the dwellers in this land of Troezen, calls me vilest of the deities. Love he scorns, and, as for marriage, will none of it; but Artemis, daughter of Zeus, sister of Phoebus, he doth honour, counting her the chief of goddesses, and ever through the greenwood, attendant on his virgin goddess, he clears the earth of wild beasts with his fleet hounds, enjoying the comradeship of one too high for mortal ken. 'Tis not 20 this I grudge him, no! why should I? But for his sins against me, I will this very day take vengeance on Hippolytus; for long ago I cleared the ground of many obstacles, so it needs but trifling toil. For as he came one day from the home of Pittheus to witness the solemn mystic rites and be initiated therein in Pandion's land, Phaedra, his father's noble wife, caught sight of him, and by my designs she found her heart was seized with wild desire. And ere she came to this Troezenian realm, a temple did she rear 30 to Cypris hard by the rock of Pallas where it o'erlooks this country, for love of the youth in another land; and to win his love in days to come she called after his name the temple she had founded for the god-

dess. Now, when Theseus left the land of Cecrops, flying the pollution of the blood of Pallas' sons, and with his wife sailed to this shore, content to suffer exile for a year, then began the wretched wife to pine away in silence, moaning 'neath love's cruel scourge, and none of her servants knows what ails her. But this passion of hers must not fail thus. No, 40 I will discover the matter to Theseus, and all shall be laid bare. Then will the father slay his child, my bitter foe, by curses, for the lord Poseidon granted this boon to Theseus; three wishes of the god to ask, nor ever ask in vain. So Phaedra is to die, an honoured death 'tis true, but still to die; for I will not let her suffering outweigh the payment of such forfeit by my foes as shall satisfy my honour. But lo! I see the son of Theseus coming hither—Hippolytus, fresh from the labours of the chase. I will get me hence. 50 At his back follows a long train of retainers, in joyous cries of revelry uniting hymns of praise to Artemis, his goddess; for little he recks that Death hath oped his gates for him, and that this is his last look upon the light.

(APHRODITE *vanishes.* HIPPOLYTUS *and his retinue of hunting* ATTENDANTS *enter, singing. They move to worship at an altar of* ARTEMIS *on one side of the stage.*)

HIPPOLYTUS. Come follow, friends, singing to Artemis, daughter of Zeus, throned in the sky, whose votaries we are.

ATTENDANTS. Lady goddess, awful queen, daughter of Zeus, all hail! hail! child of Latona and of 60 Zeus, peerless mid the virgin choir, who hast thy dwelling in heaven's wide mansions at thy noble father's court, in the golden house of Zeus. All hail! most beauteous Artemis, lovelier far than all the daughters of Olympus!

HIPPOLYTUS. For thee, O mistress mine, I bring this woven wreath, culled from a virgin meadow, where nor shepherd dares to herd his flock nor ever scythe hath mown, but o'er the mead unshorn the bee doth wing its way in spring; and with the dew 70 from rivers drawn purity that garden tends. Such as know no cunning lore, yet in whose nature self-control, made perfect, hath a home, these may pluck the flowers, but not the wicked world. Accept, I pray, dear mistress, mine this chaplet from my holy hand to crown thy locks of gold; for I, and none other of mortals, have this high guerdon, to be with thee, with thee converse, hearing thy voice, though not thy face beholding. So be it mine to end my life as I began. 80

LEADER OF THE ATTENDANTS. My prince! we needs must call upon the gods, our lords, so wilt thou listen to a friendly word from me?

Hippolytus. Translated by E. P. Coleridge. Reprinted by permission of G. Bell and Sons, Ltd.
11. **Pittheus,** grandfather of Theseus and mentor of Hippolytus.
26. **Pandion's land,** Athens, of which Pandion had been king.

34–35. **Now, when . . . sons.** Theseus fled from Athens after killing the sons of Pallas, son of Pandion, for attempting to regain the Athenian throne.

HIPPOLYTUS. Why, that will I! else were I proved a fool.

LEADER. Dost know, then, the way of the world?

HIPPOLYTUS. Not I; but wherefore such a question?

LEADER. It hates reserve which careth not for all men's love.

HIPPOLYTUS. And rightly too; reserve in man is ever galling.

10 LEADER. But there's a charm in courteous affability?

HIPPOLYTUS. The greatest surely; aye, and profit, too, at trifling cost.

LEADER. Dost think the same law holds in heaven as well?

HIPPOLYTUS. I trow it doth, since all our laws we men from heaven draw.

LEADER. Why, then, dost thou neglect to greet an august goddess?

HIPPOLYTUS. Whom speak'st thou of? Keep watch 20 upon thy tongue lest it some mischief cause.

LEADER. Cypris I mean, whose image is stationed o'er thy gate.

HIPPOLYTUS. I greet her from afar, preserving still my chastity.

LEADER. Yet is she an august goddess, far renowned on earth.

HIPPOLYTUS. 'Mongst gods as well as men we have our several preferences.

LEADER. I wish thee luck, and wisdom too, so far 30 as thou dost need it.

HIPPOLYTUS. No god, whose worship craves the night, hath charms for me.

LEADER. My son, we should avail us of the gifts that gods confer.

HIPPOLYTUS. Go in, my faithful followers, and make ready food within the house; a well-filled board hath charms after the chase is o'er. Rub down my steeds ye must, that when I have had my fill I may yoke them to the chariot and give them proper 40 exercise. As for thy Queen of Love, a long farewell to her.

(HIPPOLYTUS *goes into the palace, followed by all the* ATTENDANTS *except the* LEADER, *who prays before a statue of* APHRODITE *on the other side of the stage.*)

LEADER. Meantime I with sober mind, for I must not copy my young master, do offer up my prayer to thy image, lady Cypris, in such words as it becomes a slave to use. But thou should'st pardon all, who, in youth's impetuous heat, speak idle words of thee; make as though thou hearest not, for gods must needs be wiser than the sons of men.

(*The* LEADER *goes into the palace. The* CHORUS OF TROEZENIAN WOMEN *enters.*)

CHORUS. A rock there is, where, as they say, the 50 ocean dew distils, and from its beetling brow it pours a copious stream for pitchers to be dipped therein;

'twas here I had a friend washing robes of purple in the trickling stream, and she was spreading them out on the face of a warm sunny rock; from her I had the tidings, first of all, that my mistress—

Was wasting on the bed of sickness, pent within her house, a thin veil o'ershadowing her head of golden hair. And this is the third day I hear that she hath closed her lovely lips and denied her chaste body all sustenance, eager to hide her suffering and reach 60 death's cheerless bourn.

Maiden, thou must be possessed, by Pan made frantic or by Hecate, or by the Corybantes dread, and Cybele the mountain mother. Or maybe thou hast sinned against Dictynna, huntress-queen, and art wasting for thy guilt in sacrifice unoffered. For she doth range o'er lakes' expanse and past the bounds of earth upon the ocean's tossing billows.

Or doth some rival in thy house beguile thy lord, the captain of Erechtheus' sons, that hero nobly born, 70 to secret amours hid from thee? Or hath some mariner sailing hither from Crete reached this port that sailors love, with evil tidings for our queen, and she with sorrow for her grievous fate is to her bed confined?

Yea, and oft o'er woman's wayward nature settles a feeling of miserable helplessness, arising from labor-pains or passionate desire. I, too, have felt at times this sharp thrill shoot through me, but I would cry to Artemis, queen of archery, who comes from heaven to aid us in our travail, and thanks to heaven's 80 grace she ever comes at my call with welcome help. Look! where the aged nurse is bringing her forth from the house before the door, while on her brow the cloud of gloom is deepening. My soul longs to learn what is her grief, the canker that is wasting our queen's fading charms.

(PHAEDRA *is led out and placed upon a couch by the* NURSE *and attendants.*)

NURSE. O, the ills of mortal men! the cruel diseases they endure! What can I do for thee? from what refrain? Here is the bright sun-light, here the azure sky; lo! we have brought thee on thy bed of sickness 90 without the palace; for all thy talk was of coming hither, but soon back to thy chamber wilt thou hurry. Disappointment follows fast with thee, thou hast no joy in aught for long; the present has no power to please; on something absent next thy heart is set. Better be sick than tend the sick; the first is but a single ill, the last unites mental grief with manual toil. Man's whole life is full of anguish; no respite from his woes he finds; but if there is aught to love beyond this life, night's dark pall doth wrap it round.

62–64. **Maiden . . . mother,** all religious explanations of insanity.
70. **Erechtheus' sons,** the Athenians, after a mythical king of Athens.

And so we show our mad love of this life because its light is shed on earth, and because we know no other, and have naught revealed to us of all our earth may hide; and trusting to fables we drift at random.

PHAEDRA. Lift my body, raise my head! My limbs are all unstrung, kind friends. O handmaids, lift my arms, my shapely arms.
10 The tire on my head is too heavy for me to wear; away with it, and let my tresses o'er my shoulders fall.

NURSE. Be of good heart, dear child; toss not so wildly to and fro. Lie still, be brave, so wilt thou find thy sickness easier to bear; suffering for mortals is nature's iron law.

PHAEDRA. Ah! would I could draw a draught of water pure from some dew-fed spring, and lay me down to rest in the grassy meadow 'neath the poplar's
20 shade!

NURSE. My child, what wild speech is this? O say not such things in public, wild whirling words of frenzy bred!

PHAEDRA. Away to the mountain take me! to the wood, to the pine-trees I will go, where hounds pursue the prey, hard on the scent of dappled fawns. Ye gods! what joy to hark them on, to grasp the barbed dart, to poise Thessalian hunting-spears close to my golden hair, then let them fly.
30 NURSE. Why, why, my child, these anxious cares? What hast thou to do with the chase? Why so eager for the flowing spring, when hard by these towers stands a hill well watered, whence thou may'st freely draw?

PHAEDRA. O Artemis, who watchest o'er sea-beat Limna and the race-course thundering to the horse's hoofs, would I were upon thy plains curbing Venetian steeds!

NURSE. Why betray thy frenzy in these wild whirl-
40 ing words? Now thou wert for hasting hence to the hills away to hunt wild beasts, and now thy yearning is to drive the steed over the waveless sands. This needs a cunning seer to say what god it is that reins thee from the course, distracting thy senses, child.

PHAEDRA. Ah me! alas! what have I done? Whither have I strayed, my senses leaving? Mad, mad! stricken by some demon's curse! Woe is me! Cover my head again, nurse. Shame fills me for the words I have spoken. Hide me then; from my eyes the tear-
50 drops stream, and for very shame I turn them away. 'Tis painful coming to one's senses again, and madness, evil though it be, has this advantage, that one has no knowledge of reason's overthrow.

NURSE. There then I cover thee; but when will death hide my body in the grave? Many a lesson length of days is teaching me. Yea, mortal men should pledge themselves to moderate friendships only, not to such as reach the very heart's core; affection's ties should be light upon them to let them slip 60 or draw them tight. For one poor heart to grieve for twain, as I do for my mistress, is a burden sore to bear. Men say that too engrossing pursuits in life more oft cause disappointment than pleasure, and too oft are foes to health. Wherefore I do not praise excess so much as moderation, and with me wise men will agree.   (PHAEDRA *lies back on the couch.*)

LEADER OF THE CHORUS. O aged dame, faithful nurse of Phaedra, our queen, we see her sorry plight; but what it is that ails her we cannot discern, so fain would learn of thee and hear thy opinion. 70

NURSE. I question her, but am no wiser, for she will not answer.

LEADER. Nor tell what source these sorrows have?

NURSE. The same answer thou must take, for she is dumb on every point.

LEADER. How weak and wasted is her body!

NURSE. What marvel? 'tis three days now since she has tasted food.

LEADER. Is this infatuation, or an attempt to die?

NURSE. 'Tis death she courts; such fasting aims at 80 ending life.

LEADER. A strange story! Is her husband satisfied?

NURSE. She hides from him her sorrow, and vows she is not ill.

LEADER. Can he not guess it from her face?

NURSE. He is not now in his own country.

LEADER. But dost not thou insist in thy endeavour to find out her complaint, her crazy mind?

NURSE. I have tried every plan, and all in vain; yet not even now will I relax my zeal, that thou too, 90 if thou stayest, mayst witness my devotion to my unhappy mistress. Come, come, my darling child, let us forget, the twain of us, our former words; be thou more mild, smoothing that sullen brow and changing the current of thy thought, and I, if in aught before I failed in humouring thee, will let that be and find some better course. If thou art sick with ills thou canst not name, there be women here to help to set thee right; but if thy trouble can to men's ears be divulged, speak, that physicians may pronounce on 100 it. Come, then, why so dumb? Thou shouldst not so remain, my child, but scold me if I speak amiss, or, if I give good counsel, yield assent. One word, one look this way! Ah me! Friends, we waste our toil to no purpose; we are as far away as ever; she would not relent to my arguments then, nor is she yielding now. Well, grow more stubborn than the sea, yet be assured of this, that if thou diest thou art a traitress to thy children, for they will ne'er inherit their father's halls, nay, by that knightly queen the Amazon 110 who bore a son to lord it over thine, a bastard born but not a bastard bred, whom well thou knowest, e'en Hippolytus—

PHAEDRA (*aroused by his name*). Oh! oh!

NURSE. Ha! doth that touch the quick?

PHAEDRA. Thou hast undone me, nurse; I do adjure by the gods, mention that man no more.

NURSE. There now! thou art thyself again, but e'en yet refusest to aid thy children and preserve thy life.

PHAEDRA. My babes I love, but there is another storm that buffets me.

NURSE. Daughter, are thy hands from bloodshed pure?

10 PHAEDRA. My hands are pure, but on my soul there rests a stain.

NURSE. The issue of some enemy's secret witchery?

PHAEDRA. A friend is my destroyer, one unwilling as myself.

NURSE. Hath Theseus wronged thee in any wise?

PHAEDRA. Never may I prove untrue to him!

NURSE. Then what strange mystery is there that drives thee on to die?

PHAEDRA. O, let my sin and me alone! 'tis not 20 'gainst thee I sin.

NURSE. Never willingly! and, if I fail, 'twill rest at thy door.

PHAEDRA. How now? Thou usest force in clinging to my hand.

NURSE. Yea, and I will never loose my hold upon thy knees.

PHAEDRA. Alas for thee! my sorrows, shouldst thou learn them, would recoil on thee.

NURSE. What keener grief for me than failing to 30 win thee?

PHAEDRA. 'Twill be death to thee; though to me that brings renown.

NURSE. And dost thou then conceal this boon despite my prayers?

PHAEDRA. I do, for 'tis out of shame I am planning an honourable escape.

NURSE. Tell it, and thine honour shall the brighter shine.

PHAEDRA. Away, I do conjure thee; loose my hand.

40 NURSE. I will not, for the boon thou shouldst have granted me is denied.

PHAEDRA. I will grant it out of reverence for thy holy suppliant touch.

NURSE. Henceforth I hold my peace; 'tis thine to speak from now.

PHAEDRA. Ah! hapless mother, what a love was thine!

NURSE. Her love for the bull? daughter, or what meanest thou?

PHAEDRA. And woe to thee! my sister, bride of 50 Dionysus.

NURSE. What ails thee, child? speaking ill of kith and kin.

PHAEDRA. Myself the third to suffer! how am I undone!

47. Her love . . . bull. To punish Minos, the father of Phaedra, Poseidon inspired her mother, Pasiphaë, with passion for a bull, by whom she bore the Minotaur. 49-50. bride of Dionysus, Ariadne.

NURSE. Thou strik'st me dumb! Where will this history end?

PHAEDRA. That "love" has been our curse from time long past.

NURSE. I know no more of what I fain would learn.

PHAEDRA. Ah! would thou couldst say for me what 60 I have to tell.

NURSE. I am no prophetess to unriddle secrets.

PHAEDRA. What is it they mean when they talk of people being in "love"?

NURSE. At once the sweetest and the bitterest thing, my child.

PHAEDRA. I shall only find the latter half.

NURSE. Ha! my child, art thou in love?

PHAEDRA. The Amazon's son, whoever he may be— 70

NURSE. Mean'st thou Hippolytus?

PHAEDRA. 'Twas thou, not I, that spoke his name.

NURSE. O heavens! what is this, my child? Thou hast ruined me. Outrageous! friends; I will not live and bear it; hateful is life, hateful to mine eyes the light. This body I resign, will cast it off, and rid me of existence by my death. Farewell, my life is o'er. Yea, for the chaste have wicked passions, 'gainst their will maybe, but still they have. Cypris, it seems, is not a goddess after all, but something greater far, 80 for she hath been the ruin of my lady and of me and our whole family.

CHORUS. O, too clearly didst thou hear our queen uplift her voice to tell her startling tale of piteous suffering. Come death ere I reach thy state of feeling, loved mistress. O horrible! woe, for these miseries! woe, for the sorrows on which mortals feed! Thou art undone! thou hast disclosed thy sin to heaven's light. What hath each passing day and every hour in store for thee? Some strange event will come to 90 pass in this house. For it is no longer uncertain where the star of thy love is setting, thou hapless daughter of Crete.

PHAEDRA. Women of Troezen, who dwell here upon the frontier edge of Pelops' land, oft ere now in heedless mood through the long hours of night have I wondered why man's life is spoiled; and it seems to me their evil case is not due to any natural fault of judgment, for there be many dowered with sense, but we must view the matter in this light: by 100 teaching and experience we learn the right but neglect it in practice, some from sloth, others from preferring pleasure of some kind or other to duty. Now life has many pleasures, protracted talk, and leisure, that seductive evil; likewise there is shame which is of two kinds, one a noble quality, the other a curse to families; but if for each its proper time were clearly known, these twain could not have had the selfsame letters to denote them. So then since I had made up my mind on these points, 'twas not likely 110 any drug would alter it and make me think the contrary. And I will tell thee too the way my judgment went. When love wounded me, I bethought me how I best might bear the smart. So from that day forth I began to hide in silence what I suffered. For I put no faith in counsellors, who know well to lecture others for presumption, yet themselves have countless troubles of their own. Next I did devise noble endurance of these wanton thoughts, striving by continence for victory. And last when I could not succeed in mastering love hereby, methought it best to die; and none can gainsay my purpose. For fain I would my virtue should to all appear, my shame have few to witness it. I knew my sickly passion now; to yield to it I saw how infamous; and more, I learnt to know so well that I was but a woman, a thing the world detests. Curses, hideous curses on that wife who first did shame her marriage-vow for lovers other than her lord! 'Twas from noble families this curse began to spread among our sex. For when the noble countenance disgrace, poor folk of course will think that it is right. Those too I hate who make profession of purity, though in secret reckless sinners. How can these, queen Cypris, ocean's child, e'er look their husbands in the face? do they never feel one guilty thrill that their accomplice, night, or the chambers of their house will find a voice and speak? This it is that calls on me to die, kind friends, that so I may ne'er be found to have disgraced my lord, or the children I have borne; no! may they grow up and dwell in glorious Athens, free to speak and act, heirs to such fair fame as a mother can bequeath. For to know that father or mother has sinned doth turn the stoutest heart to slavishness. This alone, men say, can stand the buffets of life's battle, a just and virtuous soul in whomsoever found. For time unmasks the villain soon or late, holding up to them a mirror as to some blooming maid. 'Mongst such may I be never seen!

LEADER OF THE CHORUS. Now look! how fair is chastity however viewed, whose fruit is good repute amongst men.

NURSE. My queen, 'tis true thy tale of woe, but lately told, did for the moment strike me with wild alarm, but now I do reflect upon my foolishness; second thoughts are often best even with men. Thy fate is no uncommon one nor past one's calculations; thou art stricken by the passion Cypris sends. Thou art in love; what wonder? so are many more. Wilt thou, because thou lov'st, destroy thyself? 'Tis little gain, I trow, for those who love or yet may love their fellows, if death must be their end; for though the Love-Queen's onset in her might is more than man can bear, yet doth she gently visit yielding hearts, and only when she finds a proud unnatural spirit, doth she take and mock it past belief. Her path is in the sky, and mid the ocean's surge she rides; from her all nature springs; she sows the seeds of love, inspires the warm desire to which we sons of earth all owe

our being. They who have aught to do with books of ancient scribes, or themselves engage in studious pursuits, know how Zeus of Semele was enamoured, how the bright-eyed goddess of the Dawn once stole Cephalus to dwell in heaven for the love she bore him; yet these in heaven abide nor shun the gods' approach, content, I trow, to yield to their misfortune. Wilt thou refuse to yield? thy sire, it seems, should have begotten thee on special terms or with different gods for masters, if in these laws thou wilt not acquiesce. How many, prithee, men of sterling sense, when they see their wives unfaithful, make as though they saw it not? How many fathers, when their sons have gone astray, assist them in their amours? 'Tis part of human wisdom to conceal the deed of shame. Nor should man aim at excessive refinement in his life; for they cannot with exactness finish e'en the roof that covers in a house; and how dost thou, after falling into so deep a pit, think to escape? Nay, if thou hast more of good than bad, thou wilt fare exceeding well, thy human nature considered. O cease, my darling child, from evil thoughts, let wanton pride be gone, for this is naught else, this wish to rival gods in perfectness. Face thy love; 'tis heaven's will thou shouldst. Sick thou art, yet turn thy sickness to some happy issue. For there are charms and spells to soothe the soul; surely some cure for thy disease will be found. Men, no doubt, might seek it long and late if our women's minds no scheme devise.

LEADER. Although she gives thee at thy present need the wiser counsel, Phaedra, yet do I praise thee. Still my praise may sound more harsh and jar more cruelly on thy ear than her advice.

PHAEDRA. 'Tis even this, too plausible a tongue, that overthrows good governments and homes of men. We should not speak to please the ear but point the path that leads to noble fame.

NURSE. What means this solemn speech? No need of rounded phrases,—but a man. Straightway must we move to tell him frankly how it is with thee. Had not thy life to such a crisis come, or wert thou with self-control endowed, ne'er would I to gratify thy passions have urged thee to this course; but now 'tis a struggle fierce to save thy life, and therefore less to blame.

PHAEDRA. Accursed proposal! peace, woman! never utter those shameful words again!

NURSE. Shameful, maybe, yet for thee better than honour's code. Better this deed, if it shall save thy life, than that name thy pride will kill thee to retain.

PHAEDRA. I conjure thee, go no further! for thy words are plausible but infamous; for though as yet love has not undermined my soul, yet, if in specious words thou dress thy foul suggestion, I shall be beguiled into the snare from which I am now escaping.

NURSE. If thou art of this mind, 'twere well thou

ne'er hadst sinned; but as it is, hear me; for that is the next best course; I in my house have charms to soothe thy love,—'twas but now I thought of them;— these shall cure thee of thy sickness on no disgraceful terms, thy mind unhurt, if thou wilt be but brave. But from him thou lovest we must get some token, a word or fragment of his robe, and thereby unite in one love's twofold stream.

PHAEDRA. Is thy drug a salve or potion?

10 NURSE. I cannot tell; be content, my child, to profit by it and ask no questions.

PHAEDRA. I fear me thou wilt prove too wise for me.

NURSE. If thou fear this, confess thyself afraid of all; but why thy terror?

PHAEDRA. Lest thou shouldst breathe a word of this to Theseus' son.

NURSE. Peace, my child! I will do all things well; only be thou, queen Cypris, ocean's child, my part-ner in the work! And for the rest of my purpose, it 20 will be enough for me to tell it to our friends within the house. (*Exit* NURSE.)

CHORUS (*singing*). O Love, Love, that from the eyes diffusest soft desire, bringing on the souls of those, whom thou dost camp against, sweet grace, O never in evil mood appear to me, nor out of time and tune approach! Nor fire nor meteor hurls a mightier bolt than Aphrodite's shaft shot by the hands of Love, the child of Zeus.

Idly, idly by the streams of Alpheus and in the 30 Pythian shrines of Phoebus, Hellas heaps the slaugh-tered steers; while Love we worship not, Love, the king of men, who holds the key to Aphrodite's sweet-est bower,—worship not him who, when he comes, lays waste and marks his path to mortal hearts by wide-spread woe.

There was that maiden in Oechalia, a girl unwed, that knew no wooer yet nor married joys; her did the Queen of Love snatch from her home across the sea and gave unto Alcmena's son, mid blood and smoke 40 and murderous marriage-hymns, to be to him a fran-tic fiend of hell; woe! woe for his wooing!

Ah! holy walls of Thebes, ah! fount of Dirce, ye could testify what course the love-queen follows. For with the blazing levin-bolt did she cut short the fatal marriage of Semele, mother of Zeus-born Bacchus. All things she doth inspire, dread goddess, winging her flight hither and thither like a bee.

PHAEDRA. Peace, oh women, peace! I am undone.

LEADER OF THE CHORUS. What, Phaedra, is this 50 dread event within thy house?

29. **Alpheus,** the major river of southern Greece. 36. **maiden,** Iolé, carried away by Heracles. 42. **Dirce,** who mistreated her hus-band's former wife and was thrown into the fountain in punishment. 43-45. **For with . . . Bacchus.** The lightning of Zeus killed Semele as she gave birth to Dionysus.

PHAEDRA. Hush! let me hear what those within are saying.

LEADER. I am silent; this is surely the prelude to evil.

PHAEDRA. Great gods! how awful are my suffer-ings!

CHORUS. What a cry was there! what loud alarm! say what sudden terror, lady, doth thy soul dis-may.

PHAEDRA. I am undone. Stand here at the door and 60 hear the noise arising in the house.

CHORUS. Thou art already by the bolted door; 'tis for thee to note the sounds that issue from within. And tell me, O tell me what evil can be on foot.

PHAEDRA. 'Tis the son of the horse-loving Amazon who calls, Hippolytus, uttering foul curses on my servant.

CHORUS. I hear a noise, but cannot clearly tell which way it comes. Ah! 'tis through the door the 70 sound reached thee.

PHAEDRA. Yes, yes, he is calling her plainly enough a go-between in vice, traitress to her master's honour.

CHORUS. Woe, woe is me! thou art betrayed, dear mistress! What counsel shall I give thee? thy secret is out; thou art utterly undone.

PHAEDRA. Ah me! ah me!

CHORUS. Betrayed by friends!

PHAEDRA. She hath ruined me by speaking of my misfortune; 'twas kindly meant, but an ill way to cure my malady. 80

LEADER OF THE CHORUS. O what wilt thou do now in thy cruel dilemma?

PHAEDRA. I only know one way, one cure for these my woes, and that is instant death.

(HIPPOLYTUS *rushes out of the palace, followed by the* NURSE.)

HIPPOLYTUS. O mother earth! O sun's unclouded orb! What words, unfit for any lips, have reached my ears!

NURSE. Peace, my son, lest some one hear thy out-cry.

HIPPOLYTUS. I cannot hear such awful words and 90 hold my peace.

NURSE. I do implore thee by thy fair right hand.

HIPPOLYTUS. Let go my hand, touch not my robe.

NURSE. O by thy knees I pray, destroy me not ut-terly.

HIPPOLYTUS. Why say this, if, as thou pretendest, thy lips are free from blame?

NURSE. My son, this is no story to be noised abroad.

HIPPOLYTUS. A virtuous tale grows fairer told to many. 100

NURSE. Never dishonour thy oath, my son.

HIPPOLYTUS. My tongue an oath did take, but not my heart.

NURSE. My son, what wilt thou do? destroy thy friends?

HIPPOLYTUS. Friends indeed! the wicked are no friends of mine.

NURSE. O pardon me; to err is only human, child.

HIPPOLYTUS. Great Zeus, why didst thou, to man's sorrow, put woman, evil counterfeit, to dwell where shines the sun? If thou wert minded that the human race should multiply, it was not from women they should have drawn their stock, but in thy temples they should have paid gold or iron or ponderous
10 bronze and bought a family, each man proportioned to his offering, and so in independence dwelt, from women free. But now as soon as ever we would bring this plague into our home we bring its fortune to the ground. 'Tis clear from this how great a curse a woman is; the very father, that begot and nurtured her, to rid him of the mischief, gives her a dower and packs her off; while the husband, who takes the noxious weed into his home, fondly decks his sorry idol in fine raiment and tricks her out in robes, squan-
20 dering by degrees, unhappy wight! his house's wealth. For he is in this dilemma; say his marriage has brought him good connections, he is glad then to keep the wife he loathes; or, if he gets a good wife but useless relations, he tries to stifle the bad luck with the good. But it is easiest for him who has settled in his house as wife a mere cipher, incapable from simplicity. I hate a clever woman; never may she set foot in *my* house who aims at knowing more than women need; for in these clever women Cypris
30 implants a larger story of villainy, while the artless woman is by her shallow wit from levity debarred. No servant should ever have had access to a wife, but men should put to live with them beasts, which bite, not talk, in which case they could not speak to any one nor be answered back by them. But, as it is, the wicked in their chambers plot wickedness, and their servants carry it abroad. Even thus, vile wretch, thou cam'st to make me partner in an outrage on my father's honour; wherefore I must wash that stain
40 away in running streams, dashing the water into my ears. How could I commit so foul a crime when by the very mention of it I feel myself polluted? Be well assured, woman, 'tis only my religious scruple saves thee. For had not I unawares been caught by an oath, 'fore heaven! I would not have refrained from telling all unto my father. But now I will from the house away, so long as Theseus is abroad, and will maintain strict silence. But, when my father comes, I will return and see how thou and thy mis-
50 tress face him, and so shall I learn by experience the extent of thy audacity. Perdition seize you both! I can never satisfy my hate for women, no! not even though some say this is ever my theme, for of a truth they always are evil. So either let some one prove them chaste, or let me still trample on them for ever. (*Exit* HIPPOLYTUS.)

CHORUS. O the cruel, unhappy fate of women!

What arts, what arguments have we, once we have made a slip, to loose by craft the tight-drawn knot?

PHAEDRA. I have met my deserts. O earth, O light 60 of day! How can I escape the stroke of fate? How my pangs conceal, kind friends? What god will appear to help me, what mortal to take my part or help me in unrighteousness? The present calamity of my life admits of no escape. Most hapless I of all my sex!

LEADER OF THE CHORUS. Alas, alas! the deed is done, thy servant's schemes have gone awry, my queen, and all is lost.

PHAEDRA (*to the* NURSE). Accursed woman! traitress to thy friends! How hast thou ruined me! May 70 Zeus, my ancestor, smite thee with his fiery bolt and uproot thee from thy place. Did I not foresee thy purpose, did I not bid thee keep silence on the very matter which is now my shame? But thou wouldst not be still; wherefore my fair name will not go with me to the tomb. But now I must another scheme devise. Yon youth, in the keenness of his fury, will tell his father of my sin, and the aged Pittheus of my state, and fill the world with stories to my shame. Perdition seize thee and every meddling fool who 80 by dishonest means would serve unwilling friends!

NURSE. Mistress, thou may'st condemn the mischief I have done, for sorrow's sting o'ermasters thy judgment; yet can I answer thee in face of this, if thou wilt hear. 'Twas I who nurtured thee; I love thee still; but in my search for medicine to cure thy sickness I found what least I sought. Had I but succeeded, I had been counted wise, for the credit we get for wisdom is measured by our success.

PHAEDRA. Is it just, is it any satisfaction to me, that 90 thou shouldst wound me first, then bandy words with me?

NURSE. We dwell on this too long; I was not wise, I own; but there are yet ways of escape from the trouble, my child.

PHAEDRA. Be dumb henceforth; evil was thy first advice to me, evil too thy attempted scheme. Begone and leave me, look to thyself; I will my own fortunes for the best arrange. (*Exit* NURSE.)

Ye noble daughters of Troezen, grant me the only 100 boon I crave; in silence bury what ye here have heard.

LEADER. By majestic Artemis, child of Zeus, I swear I will never divulge aught of thy sorrows.

PHAEDRA. 'Tis well. But I, with all my thought, can but one way discover out of this calamity, that so I may secure my children's honour, and find myself some help as matters stand. For never, never will I bring shame upon my Cretan home, nor will I, to save one poor life, face Theseus after my disgrace. 110

LEADER. Art thou bent then on some cureless woe?

PHAEDRA. On death; the means thereto must I devise myself.

LEADER. Hush!

PHAEDRA. Do thou at least advise me well. For this very day shall I gladden Cypris, my destroyer, by yielding up my life, and shall own myself vanquished by cruel love. Yet shall my dying be another's curse, that he may learn not to exult at my misfortunes; but when he comes to share the self-same plague with me, he will take a lesson in wisdom. (*Exit* PHAEDRA.)

CHORUS. O to be nestling 'neath some pathless cav-
10 ern, there by god's creating hand to grow into a bird amid the wingèd tribes! Away would I soar to Adria's wave-beat shore and to the waters of Eridanus; where a father's hapless daughters in their grief for Phaethon distil into the glooming flood the amber brilliance of their tears.

And to the apple-bearing strand of those minstrels in the west I then would come, where ocean's lord no more to sailors grants a passage o'er the deep dark main, finding there the heaven's holy bound, upheld
20 by Atlas, where water from ambrosial founts wells up beside the couch of Zeus inside his halls, and holy earth, the bounteous mother, causes joy to spring in heavenly breasts.

O white-winged bark, that o'er the booming ocean-wave didst bring my royal mistress from her happy home, to crown her queen 'mongst sorrow's brides! Surely evil omens from either port, at least from Crete, were with that ship, what time to glorious Athens it sped its way, and the crew made fast its
30 twisted cable-ends upon the beach of Munychus, and on the land stept out.

Whence comes it that her heart is crushed, cruelly afflicted by Aphrodite with unholy love; so she by bitter grief o'erwhelmed will tie a noose within her bridal bower to fit it to her fair white neck, too modest for this hateful lot in life, prizing o'er all her name and fame, and striving thus to rid her soul of passion's sting.

(*The* NURSE *rushes out of the palace.*)

NURSE. Help! ho! To the rescue all who near the
40 palace stand! She hath hung herself, our queen, the wife of Theseus.

LEADER OF THE CHORUS. Woe worth the day! the deed is done; our royal mistress is no more, dead she hangs in the dangling noose.

NURSE. Haste! some one bring a two-edged knife wherewith to cut the knot about her neck.

FIRST SEMI-CHORUS. Friends, what shall we do? think you we should enter the house, and loose the queen from the tight-drawn noose?

50 SECOND SEMI-CHORUS. Why should *we?* Are there

13–15. where . . . tears. The sisters of Phaethon mourned his death after his ill-fated attempt to drive the chariot of the sun. Their tears turned to amber. 30. Munychus, the port of Athens.

not young servants here? To do too much is not a safe course in life.

NURSE. Lay out the hapless corpse, straighten the limbs. This was a bitter way to sit at home and keep my master's house! (*Exit* NURSE.)

LEADER OF THE CHORUS. She is dead, poor lady; so I hear. Already are they laying out the corpse.

(THESEUS *and his retinue have entered.*)

THESEUS. Women, can ye tell me what the uproar in the palace means? There came the sound of serv-ants weeping bitterly to mine ear. None of my house- 60 hold deign to open wide the gates and give me glad welcome as a traveller from prophetic shrines. Hath aught befallen old Pittheus? No. Though he be well advanced in years, yet should I mourn, were he to quit this house.

LEADER. 'Tis not against the old, Theseus, that fate, to strike thee, aims this blow; prepare thy sor-row for a younger corpse.

THESEUS. Woe is me! is it a child's life death robs me of? 70

LEADER. They live; but, cruellest news of all for thee, their mother is no more.

THESEUS. What! my wife dead? By what cruel mis-chance?

LEADER. About her neck she tied the hangman's knot.

THESEUS. Had grief so chilled her blood? or what had befallen her?

LEADER. I know but this, for I am myself but now arrived at the house to mourn thy sorrows, O 80 Theseus.

THESEUS. Woe is me! why have I crowned my head with woven garlands, when misfortune greets my embassage? Unbolt the doors, servants, loose their fastenings, that I may see the piteous sight, my wife, whose death is death to me.

(*The central doors of the palace open, disclosing the corpse.*)

CHORUS. Woe! woe is thee for thy piteous lot! thou hast done thyself a hurt deep enough to overthrow this family. Ah! ah! the daring of it! done to death by violence and unnatural means, the desperate effort 90 of thy own poor hand! Who cast the shadow o'er thy life, poor lady?

THESEUS. Ah me, my cruel lot! sorrow hath done her worst on me. O fortune, how heavily hast thou set thy foot on me and on my house, by fiendish hands inflicting an unexpected stain? Nay, 'tis com-plete effacement of my life, making it impossible; for I see, alas! so wide an ocean of grief that I can never swim to shore again, nor breast the tide of this ca-lamity. How shall I speak of thee, my poor wife, what 100 tale of direst suffering tell? Thou art vanished like a bird from the covert of my hand, taking one head-long leap from me to Hades' halls. Alas, and woe! this is a bitter, bitter sight! This must be a judgment sent by God for the sins of an ancestor, which from some far source I am bringing on myself.

LEADER OF THE CHORUS. My prince, 'tis not to thee alone such sorrows come; thou hast lost a noble wife, but so have many others.

THESEUS. Fain would I go hide me 'neath earth's blackest depth, to dwell in darkness with the dead in misery, now that I am reft of thy dear presence! for thou hast slain me than thyself e'en more. Who can tell me what caused the fatal stroke that reached thy heart, dear wife? Will no one tell me what befell? doth my palace all in vain give shelter to a herd of menials? Woe, woe for thee, my wife! sorrows past speech, past bearing, I behold within my house; myself a ruined man, my home a solitude, my children orphans!

CHORUS. Gone and left us hast thou, fondest wife and noblest of all women 'neath the sun's bright eye or night's star-lit radiance. Poor house, what sorrows are thy portion now! My eyes are wet with streams of tears to see thy fate; but the sequel to this tragedy has long with terror filled me.

THESEUS. Ha! what means this letter? clasped in her dear hand it hath some strange tale to tell. Hath she, poor lady, as a last request, written her bidding as to my marriage and her children? Take heart, poor ghost; no wife henceforth shall wed thy Theseus or invade his house. Ah! how yon seal of my dead wife stamped with her golden ring affects my sight! Come, I will unfold the sealed packet and read her letter's message to me.

CHORUS. Woe unto us! Here is yet another evil in the train by heaven sent. Looking to what has happened, I should count my lot in life no longer worth one's while to gain. My master's house, alas! is ruined, brought to naught, I say. Spare it, O Heaven, if it may be. Hearken to my prayer, for I see, as with prophetic eye, an omen boding ill.

THESEUS. O horror! woe on woe! and still they come, too deep for words, too heavy to bear. Ah me!

LEADER OF THE CHORUS. What is it? speak, if I may share in it.

THESEUS. This letter loudly tells a hideous tale! where can I escape my load of woe? For I am ruined and undone, so awful are the words I find here written clear as if she cried them to me; woe is me!

LEADER. Alas! thy words declare themselves the harbingers of woe.

THESEUS. I can no longer keep the cursed tale within the portal of my lips, cruel though its utterance be. Ah me! Hippolytus hath dared by brutal force to violate my honour, recking naught of Zeus, whose awful eye is over all. O father Poseidon, once didst thou promise to fulfil three prayers of mine; answer one of these and slay my son, let him not escape this single day, if the prayers thou gavest me were indeed with issue fraught.

LEADER. O king, I do conjure thee, call back that prayer; hereafter thou wilt know thy error. Hear, I pray.

THESEUS. Impossible! moreover I will banish him from this land, and by one of two fates shall he be struck down; either Poseidon, out of respect to my prayer, will cast his dead body into the house of Hades; or exiled from this land, a wanderer to some foreign shore, shall he eke out a life of misery.

LEADER. Lo! where himself doth come, thy son Hippolytus, in good time; dismiss thy hurtful rage, King Theseus, and bethink thee what is best for thy family.

(HIPPOLYTUS *enters.*)

HIPPOLYTUS. I heard thy voice, father, and hasted to come hither; yet know I not the cause of thy present sorrow, but would fain learn of thee.

(*He sees* PHAEDRA'S *body.*)

Ha! what is this? thy wife is dead? 'Tis very strange; it was but now I left her; a moment since she looked upon the light. How came she thus? the manner of her death? this would I learn of thee, father. Art dumb? silence availeth not in trouble; nay, for the heart that fain would know all must show its curiosity even in sorrow's hour. Be sure it is not right, father, to hide misfortunes from those who love, ay, more than love thee.

THESEUS. O ye sons of men, victims of a thousand idle errors, why teach your countless crafts, why scheme and seek to find a way for everything, while one thing ye know not nor ever yet have made your prize, a way to teach them wisdom whose souls are void of sense?

HIPPOLYTUS. A very master in his craft the man, who can force fools to be wise! But these ill-timed subtleties of thine, father, make me fear thy tongue is running wild through trouble.

THESEUS. Fie upon thee! man needs should have some certain test set up to try his friends, some touchstone of their hearts, to know each friend whether he be true or false; all men should have two voices, one the voice of honesty, expediency's the other, so would honesty confute its knavish opposite, and then we could not be deceived.

HIPPOLYTUS. Say, hath some friend been slandering me and hath he still thine ear? and I, though guiltless, banned? I am amazed; thy random, frantic words fill me with wild alarm.

THESEUS. O the mind of mortal man! to what lengths will it proceed? What limit will its bold assurance have? for if it goes on growing as man's life advances, and each successor outdo the man before him in villainy, the gods will have to add another sphere unto the world, which shall take in the knaves and villains. Behold this man; he, my own son, hath outraged mine honour, his guilt most clearly proved by my dead wife. Now, since thou hast dared this loathly crime, come, look thy father in the face. Art thou the man who dost with gods consort, as one above the vulgar herd? art thou the chaste and sinless saint? Thy boasts will never persuade me to be guilty of attributing ignorance to gods. Go then, vaunt thyself, and drive thy petty trade in viands formed of lifeless food; take Orpheus for thy chief and go a-revelling, with all honour for the vapourings of many a written scroll, seeing thou now

10 art caught. Let all beware, I say, of such hypocrites! who hunt their prey with fine words, and all the while are scheming villainy. She is dead; dost think that this will save thee? Why this convicts thee more than all, abandoned wretch! What oaths, what pleas can outweigh this letter, so that thou shouldst 'scape thy doom? Thou wilt assert she hated thee, that 'twixt the bastard and the true-born child nature has herself put war; it seems then by thy showing she made a sorry bargain with her life, if to gratify her

20 hate of thee she lost what most she prized. 'Tis said, no doubt, that frailty finds no place in man but is innate in woman; my experience is, young men are no more secure than women, whenso the Queen of Love excites a youthful breast; although their sex comes in to help them. Yet why do I thus bandy words with thee, when before me lies the corpse, to be the clearest witness? Begone at once, an exile from this land, and ne'er set foot again in god-built Athens nor in the confines of my dominion. For if I am tamely to

30 submit to this treatment from such as thee, no more will Sinis, robber of the Isthmus, bear me witness how I slew him, but say my boasts are idle, nor will those rocks Scironian, that fringe the sea, call me the miscreants' scourge.

LEADER. I know not how to call happy any child of man; for that which was first has turned and now is last.

HIPPOLYTUS. Father, thy wrath and the tension of thy mind are terrible; yet this charge, specious

40 though its arguments appear, becomes a calumny, if one lay it bare. Small skill have I in speaking to a crowd, but have a readier wit for comrades of mine own age and small companies. Yea, and this is as it should be; for they, whom the wise despise, are better qualified to speak before a mob. Yet am I constrained under the present circumstances to break silence. And at the outset will I take the point which formed the basis of thy stealthy attack on me, designed to put me out of court unheard; dost see yon

50 sun, this earth? These do not contain, for all thou dost deny it, chastity surpassing mine. To reverence God I count the highest knowledge, and to adopt as friends not those who attempt injustice, but such as

would blush to propose to their companions aught disgraceful or pleasure them by shameful services; to mock at friends is not my way, father, but I am still the same behind their backs as to their face. The very crime thou thinkest to catch me in, is just the one I am untainted with, for to this day have I kept me pure from women. Nor know I aught thereof, 60 save what I hear or see in pictures, for I have no wish to look even on these, so pure my virgin soul. I grant my claim to chastity may not convince thee; well, 'tis then for thee to show the way I was corrupted. Did this woman exceed in beauty all her sex? Did I aspire to fill the husband's place after thee and succeed to thy house? That surely would have made me out a fool, a creature void of sense. Thou wilt say, "Your chaste man loves to lord it." No, no! say I, sovereignty pleases only those whose hearts are 70 quite corrupt. Now, I would be the first and best at all the games in Hellas, but second in the state, for ever happy thus with the noblest for my friends. For there one may be happy, and the absence of danger gives a charm beyond all princely joys. One thing I have not said, the rest thou hast. Had I a witness to attest my purity, and were I pitted 'gainst her still alive, facts would show thee on enquiry who the culprit was. Now by Zeus, the god of oaths, and by the earth, whereon we stand, I swear to thee I never did 80 lay hand upon thy wife nor would have wished to, or have harboured such a thought. Slay me, ye gods! rob me of name and honour, from home and city cast me forth, a wandering exile o'er the earth! nor sea nor land receive my bones when I am dead, if I am such a miscreant! I cannot say if she through fear destroyed herself, for more than this am I forbid. With her discretion took the place of chastity, while I, though chaste, was not discreet in using this virtue.

LEADER. Thy oath by heaven, strong security, suf- 90 ficiently refutes the charge.

THESEUS. A wizard or magician must the fellow be, to think he can first flout me, his father, then by coolness master my resolve.

HIPPOLYTUS. Father, thy part in this doth fill me with amaze; wert thou my son and I thy sire, by heaven! I would have slain, not let thee off with banishment, hadst thou presumed to violate my honour.

THESEUS. A just remark! yet shalt thou not die by the sentence thine own lips pronounce upon thyself; 100 for death, that cometh in a moment, is an easy end for wretchedness. Nay, thou shalt be exiled from thy fatherland, and wandering to a foreign shore drag out a life of misery; for such are the wages of sin.

HIPPOLYTUS. Oh! what wilt thou do? Wilt thou banish me, without so much as waiting for Time's evidence on my case?

THESEUS. Ay, beyond the sea, beyond the bounds of Atlas, if I could, so deeply do I hate thee.

HIPPOLYTUS. What! banish me untried, without

7–10. take Orpheus . . . caught. Hippolytus was apparently associated with the Orphic brotherhood, a kind of monastic order. 32–34. nor . . . scourge. A second robber, Sciron, kicked his victims from a rock into the sea. He too was killed by Theseus.

even testing my oath, the pledge I offer, or the voice of seers?

THESEUS. This letter here, though it bears no seers' signs, arraigns thy pledges; as for birds that fly o'er our heads, a long farewell to them.

HIPPOLYTUS (*aside*). Great gods! why do I not unlock my lips, seeing that I am ruined by you, the objects of my reverence? No, I will not; I should nowise persuade those whom I ought to, and in vain should 10 break the oath I swore.

THESEUS. Fie upon thee! that solemn air of thine is more than I can bear. Begone from thy native land forthwith!

HIPPOLYTUS. Whither shall I turn? Ah me! whose friendly house will take me in, an exile on so grave a charge?

THESEUS. Seek one who loves to entertain as guests and partners in his crimes corrupters of men's wives.

HIPPOLYTUS. Ah me! this wounds my heart and 20 brings me nigh to tears to think that I should appear so vile, and thou believe me so.

THESEUS. Thy tears and forethought had been more in season when thou didst presume to outrage thy father's wife.

HIPPOLYTUS. O house, I would thou couldst speak for me and witness if I am so vile!

THESEUS. Dost fly to speechless witnesses? This deed, though it speaketh not, proves thy guilt clearly.

HIPPOLYTUS. Alas! Would I could stand and face 30 myself, so should I weep to see the sorrows I endure.

THESEUS. Ay, 'tis thy character to honour thyself far more than reverence thy parents, as thou shouldst.

HIPPOLYTUS. Unhappy mother! son of sorrow! Heaven keep all friends of mine from bastard birth!

THESEUS. Ho! servants, drag me hence! You heard my proclamation long ago condemning him to exile.

HIPPOLYTUS. Whoso of them doth lay a hand on me shall rue it; thyself expel me, if thy spirit move 40 thee, from the land.

THESEUS. I will, unless my word thou straight obey; no pity for thy exile steals into my heart.

(THESEUS *goes in. The central doors of the palace are closed.*)

HIPPOLYTUS. The sentence then, it seems, is passed. Ah, misery! How well I know the truth herein, but know no way to tell it! O daughter of Latona, dearest to me of all deities, partner, comrade in the chase, far from glorious Athens must I fly. Farewell, city and land of Erechtheus; farewell, Troezen, most joyous home wherein to pass the 50 spring of life; 'tis my last sight of thee, farewell! Come, my comrades in this land, young like me, greet me kindly and escort me forth, for never will ye behold a purer soul, for all my father's doubts.

(*Exit* HIPPOLYTUS.)

CHORUS. In very deed the thoughts I have about the gods, whenso they come into my mind, do much to soothe its grief, but though I cherish secret hopes of some great guiding will, yet am I at fault when I survey the fate and doings of the sons of men; change succeeds to change, and man's life veers and shifts in endless restlessness. 60

Fortune grant me this, I pray, at heaven's hand,— a happy lot in life and a soul from sorrow free; opinions let me hold not too precise nor yet too hollow; but, lightly changing my habits to each morrow as it comes, may I thus attain a life of bliss!

For now no more is my mind free from doubts, unlooked-for sights greet my vision; for lo! I see the morning star of Athens, eye of Hellas, driven by his father's fury to another land. Mourn, ye sands of my native shores, ye oak-groves on the hills, where with 70 his fleet hounds he would hunt the quarry to the death, attending on Dictynna, awful queen.

No more will he mount his car drawn by Venetian steeds, filling the course round Limna with the prancing of his trained horses. Nevermore in his father's house shall he wake the Muse that never slept beneath his lute-strings; no hand will crown the spots where rests the maiden Latona 'mid the boskage deep; nor ever more shall our virgins vie to win thy love, now thou art banished. 80

While I with tears at thy unhappy fate shall endure a lot all undeserved. Ah! hapless mother, in vain didst thou bring forth, it seems. I am angered with the gods; out upon them! O ye linked Graces, why are ye sending from his native land this poor youth, a guiltless sufferer, far from his home?

LEADER OF THE CHORUS. But lo! I see a servant of Hippolytus hasting with troubled looks towards the palace.

(*A* MESSENGER *enters.*)

MESSENGER. Ladies, where may I find Theseus, 90 king of the country? pray, tell me if ye know; is he within the palace here?

LEADER. Lo! himself approaches from the palace.

(THESEUS *enters.*)

MESSENGER. Theseus, I am the bearer of troublous tidings to thee and all citizens who dwell in Athens or the bounds of Troezen.

THESEUS. How now? hath some strange calamity o'ertaken these two neighbouring cities?

MESSENGER. In one brief word, Hippolytus is dead. 'Tis true one slender thread still links him to the light 100 of life.

THESEUS. Who slew him? Did some husband come to blows with him, one whose wife, like mine, had suffered brutal violence?

MESSENGER. He perished through those steeds that

drew his chariot, and through the curses thou didst utter, praying to thy sire, the ocean-king, to slay thy son.

THESUS. Ye gods and king Poseidon, thou hast proved my parentage by hearkening to my prayer! Say how he perished; how fell the uplifted hand of Justice to smite the villain who dishonoured me?

MESSENGER. Hard by the wave-beat shore were we combing out his horses' manes, weeping the while, for one had come to say that Hippolytus was harshly exiled by thee and nevermore would return to set foot in this land. Then came he, telling the same doleful tale to us upon the beach, and with him was a countless throng of friends who followed after. At length he stayed his lamentation and spake: "Why weakly rave on this wise? My father's commands must be obeyed. Ho! servants, harness my horses to the chariot; this is no longer now city of mine." Thereupon each one of us bestirred himself, and, ere a man could say 'twas done, we had the horses standing ready at our master's side. Then he caught up the reins from the chariot-rail, first fitting his feet exactly in the hollows made for them. But first with outspread palms he called upon the gods, "O Zeus, now strike me dead, if I have sinned, and let my father learn how he is wronging me, in death at least, if not in life." Therewith he seized the whip and lashed each horse in turn; while we, close by his chariot, near the reins, kept up with him along the road that leads direct to Argos and Epidaurus. And just as we were coming to a desert spot, a strip of sand beyond the borders of this country, sloping right to the Saronic gulf, there issued thence a deep rumbling sound, as it were an earthquake, a fearsome noise, and the horses reared their heads and pricked their ears, while we were filled with wild alarm to know whence came the sound; when, as we gazed toward the wave-beat shore, a wave tremendous we beheld towering to the skies, so that from our view the cliffs of Sciron vanished, for it hid the isthmus and the rock of Asclepius; then swelling and frothing with a crest of foam, the sea discharged it toward the beach where stood the harnessed car, and in the moment that it broke, that mighty wall of waters, there issued from the wave a monstrous bull, whose bellowing filled the land with fearsome echoes, a sight too awful as it seemed to us who witnessed it. A panic seized the horses there and then, but our master, to horses' ways quite used, gripped in both hands his reins, and tying them to his body pulled them backward as the sailor pulls his oar; but the horses gnashed the forged bits between their teeth and bore him wildly on, regardless of their master's guiding hand or rein or jointed car. And oft as he would take the guiding rein and steer for softer ground, showed that bull in front to turn him back again, maddening his team with terror; but if in their frantic career they ran towards the rocks, he would draw nigh the chariot-rail, keeping up with them, until, suddenly dashing the wheel against a stone, he upset and wrecked the car; then was dire confusion, axle-boxes and linchpins springing into the air. While he, poor youth, entangled in the reins was dragged along, bound by a stubborn knot, his poor head dashed against the rocks, his flesh all torn, the while he cried out piteously, "Stay, stay, my horses whom my own hand hath fed at the manger, destroy me not utterly. O luckless curse of a father! Will no one come and save me for all my virtue?" Now we, though much we longed to help, were left far behind. At last, I know not how, he broke loose from the shapely reins that bound him, a faint breath of life still in him; but the horses disappeared, and that portentous bull, among the rocky ground, I know not where. I am but a slave in thy house, 'tis true, O king, yet will I never believe so monstrous a charge against thy son's character, no! not though the whole race of womankind should hang itself, or one should fill with writing every pine-tree tablet grown on Ida, sure as I am of his uprightness.

LEADER. Alas! new troubles come to plague us, nor is there any escape from fate and necessity.

THESEUS. My hatred for him who hath thus suffered made me glad at thy tidings, yet from regard for the gods and him, because he is my son, I feel neither joy nor sorrow at his sufferings.

MESSENGER. But say, are we to bring the victim hither, or how are we to fulfil thy wishes? Bethink thee; if by me thou wilt be schooled, thou wilt not harshly treat thy son in his sad plight.

THESEUS. Bring him hither, that when I see him face to face, who hath denied having polluted my wife's honour, I may by words and heaven's visitation convict him. (*Exit* MESSENGER.)

CHORUS. Ah! Cypris, thine the hand that guides the stubborn hearts of gods and men; thine, and that attendant boy's, who, with painted plumage gay, flutters round his victims on lightning wing. O'er the land and booming deep on golden pinion borne flits the god of Love, maddening the heart and beguiling the senses of all whom he attacks, savage whelps on mountains bred, ocean's monsters, creatures of this sun-warmed earth, and man; thine, O Cypris, thine alone the sovereign power to rule them all.

(ARTEMIS *appears above.*)

ARTEMIS. Hearken, I bid thee, noble son of Aegeus: lo! 'tis I, Latona's child, that speak, I, Artemis. Why, Theseus, to thy sorrow dost thou rejoice at these tidings, seeing that thou hast slain thy son most impiously, listening to a charge not clearly proved, but falsely sworn to by thy wife? though clearly has the curse therefrom upon thee fallen. Why dost thou not for very shame hide beneath the dark places of the earth, or change thy human life and soar on wings to escape this tribulation? 'Mongst men of honour thou hast now no share in life.

Hearken, Theseus; I will put thy wretched case. Yet will it naught avail thee, if I do, but vex thy heart; still with this intent I came, to show thy son's pure heart,—that he may die with honour,—as well the frenzy and, in a sense, the nobleness of thy wife; for she was cruelly stung with a passion for thy son by that goddess whom all we, that joy in virgin purity, detest. And though she strove to conquer love by resolution, yet by no fault of hers she fell, thanks to her nurse's strategy, who did reveal her malady unto thy son under oath. But he would none of her counsels, as indeed was right, nor yet, when thou didst revile him, would he break the oath he swore, from piety. She meantime, fearful of being found out, wrote a lying letter, destroying by guile thy son, but yet persuading thee.

THESEUS. Woe is me!

ARTEMIS. Doth my story wound thee, Theseus? Be still awhile; hear what follows, so wilt thou have more cause to groan. Dost remember those three prayers thy father granted thee, fraught with certain issue? 'Tis one of these thou hast misused, unnatural wretch, against thy son, instead of aiming it at an enemy. Thy sea-god sire, 'tis true, for all his kind intent, hath granted that boon he was compelled, by reason of his promise, to grant. But thou alike in his eyes and in mine hast shewn thy evil heart, in that thou hast forestalled all proof or voice prophetic, hast made no inquiry, nor taken time for consideration, but with undue haste cursed thy son even to the death.

THESEUS. Perdition seize me! Queen revered!

ARTEMIS. An awful deed was thine, but still even for this thou mayest obtain pardon; for it was Cypris that would have it so, sating the fury of her soul. For this is law amongst us gods; none of us will thwart his neighbour's will, but ever we stand aloof. For be well assured, did I not fear Zeus, never would I have incurred the bitter shame of handing over to death a man of all his kind to me most dear. As for thy sin, first thy ignorance absolves thee from its villainy, next thy wife, who is dead, was lavish in her use of convincing arguments to influence thy mind. On thee in chief this storm of woe hath burst, yet is it some grief to me as well; for when the righteous die, there is no joy in heaven, albeit we try to destroy the wicked, house and home.

CHORUS. Lo! where he comes, this hapless youth, his fair young flesh and auburn locks most shamefully handled. Unhappy house! what twofold sorrow doth o'ertake its halls, through heaven's ordinance!

(HIPPOLYTUS enters, assisted by his attendants.)

HIPPOLYTUS. Ah! ah! woe is me! foully undone by an impious father's impious imprecation! Undone, undone! woe is me! Through my head shoot fearful pains; my brain throbs convulsively. Stop, let me rest my worn-out frame. Oh, oh! Accursed steeds, that mine own hand did feed, ye have been my ruin and my death. O by the gods, good sirs, I beseech ye, softly touch my wounded limbs. Who stands there at my right side? Lift me tenderly; with slow and even step conduct a poor wretch cursed by his mistaken sire. Great Zeus, dost thou see this? Me thy reverent worshipper, me who left all men behind in purity, plunged thus into yawning Hades 'neath the earth, reft of life; in vain the toils I have endured through my piety towards mankind. Ah me! ah me! O the thrill of anguish shooting through me! Set me down, poor wretch I am; come Death to set me free! Kill me, end my sufferings. O for a sword two-edged to hack my flesh, and close this mortal life! Ill-fated curse of my father! the crimes of bloody kinsmen, ancestors of old, now pass their boundaries and tarry not, and upon me are they come all guiltless as I am; ah! why? Alas, alas! what can I say? How from my life get rid of this relentless agony? O that the stern Death-god, night's black visitant, would give my sufferings rest!

ARTEMIS. Poor sufferer! cruel the fate that links thee to it! Thy noble soul hath been thy ruin.

HIPPOLYTUS. Ah! the fragrance from my goddess wafted! Even in my agony I feel thee near and find relief; she is here in this very place, my goddess Artemis.

ARTEMIS. She is, poor sufferer! the goddess thou hast loved the best.

HIPPOLYTUS. Dost see me, mistress mine? dost see my present suffering?

ARTEMIS. I see thee, but mine eyes no tear may weep.

HIPPOLYTUS. Thou hast none now to lead the hunt or tend thy fane.

ARTEMIS. None now; yet e'en in death I love thee still.

HIPPOLYTUS. None to groom thy steeds, or guard thy shrines.

ARTEMIS. 'Twas Cypris, mistress of iniquity, devised this evil.

HIPPOLYTUS. Ah me! now know I the goddess who destroyed me.

ARTEMIS. She was jealous of her slighted honour, vexed at thy chaste life.

HIPPOLYTUS. Ah! then I see her single hand hath struck down three of us.

ARTEMIS. Thy sire and thee, and last thy father's wife.

HIPPOLYTUS. My sire's ill-luck as well as mine I mourn.

ARTEMIS. He was deceived by a goddess's design.

HIPPOLYTUS. Woe is thee, my father, in this sad mischance!

THESEUS. My son, I am a ruined man; life has no joys for me.

HIPPOLYTUS. For this mistake I mourn thee rather than myself.

THESEUS. O that I had died for thee, my son!

HIPPOLYTUS. Ah! those fatal gifts thy sire Poseidon gave.

10 THESEUS. Would God these lips had never uttered that prayer!

HIPPOLYTUS. Why not? thou wouldst in any case have slain me in thy fury then.

THESEUS. Yes; Heaven had perverted my power to think.

HIPPOLYTUS. O that the race of men could bring a curse upon the gods!

ARTEMIS. Enough! for though thou pass to gloom beneath the earth, the wrath of Cypris shall not, at 20 her will, fall on thee unrequited, because thou hadst a noble righteous soul. For I with mine own hand will with these unerring shafts avenge me on another, who is her votary, dearest to her of all the sons of men. And to thee, poor sufferer, for thy anguish now will I grant high honours in the city of Troezen; for thee shall maids unwed before their marriage cut off their hair, thy harvest through the long roll of time of countless bitter tears. Yea, and for ever shall the virgin choir hymn thy sad memory, nor shall Phae-30 dra's love for thee fall into oblivion and pass away unnoticed. But thou, O son of old Aegeus, take thy son in thine arms, draw him close to thee, for unwittingly thou slewest him, and men may well commit an error when gods put it in their way. And thee Hippolytus, I admonish; hate not thy sire, for in this death thou dost but meet thy destined fate. And now farewell! 'tis not for me to gaze upon the dead, or pollute my sight with death-scenes, and e'en now I see thee nigh that evil.

(ARTEMIS *vanishes.*)

40 HIPPOLYTUS. Farewell, blest virgin queen! leave me now! How easily thou resignest our long friendship! I am reconciled with my father at thy desire, yea, for ever before I would obey thy bidding. Ah me! the darkness is settling even now upon my eyes. Take me, father, in thy arms, lift me up.

THESEUS. Woe is me, my son! what art thou doing to me thy hapless sire!

HIPPOLYTUS. I am a broken man; yes, I see the gates that close upon the dead.

50 THESEUS. Canst leave me thus with murder on my soul!

HIPPOLYTUS. No, no; I set thee free from this bloodguiltiness.

21-22. For I . . . another. Artemis will have a boar give a fatal wound to Adonis, beloved of Aphrodite, in revenge for the death of Hippolytus.

THESEUS. What saye̶ bloodshed?

HIPPOLYTUS. Artemis, the ̶ ness that I do.

THESEUS. My own dear child, ̶ thou show thyself to thy father!

HIPPOLYTUS. Farewell, dear father! ̶ well to thee!

THESEUS. O that holy, noble soul of thine!

HIPPOLYTUS. Pray to have children such as ̶ born in lawful wedlock.

THESEUS. O leave me not, my son; endure awhile.

HIPPOLYTUS. 'Tis finished, my endurance; I die, father; quickly cover my face with a mantle.

THESEUS. O glorious Athens, realm of Pallas, what a splendid hero ye have lost! Ah me, ah me! How 70 oft shall I remember thy evil works, O Cypris!

CHORUS. On all our citizens hath come this universal sorrow, unforeseen. Now shall the copious tear gush forth, for sad news about great men takes more than usual hold upon the heart.

Aristophanes

c. 446–c. 386 B.C.

The social, political, and intellectual changes that beset Athens in the later fifth century were variously received by her citizens. The Sophist philosophers and Cleon, the democratic politician, saw practical advantages in the new liberalism. Euripides and Socrates, though critical of the old tradition, sought a new morality more acceptable to their generation. Thucydides, the detached historian of his day, was caught up in the new intellectual currents and yet was grimly pessimistic about the future of a state that had chosen this very path. It remained for Aristophanes, the archconservative, to voice the militant alarm of the landed aristocracy in an era of atheism, radical democracy, and costly war. It is a tribute to the political freedom of his time that this raucous spokesman for the tory minority was allowed with almost complete impunity to pour abuse on his contemporaries in play after play.

Just why Aristophanes embraced the cause of the conservatives so passionately is hard to determine on the basis of the scanty records of his life. Although his family owned a tract of land in Aegina, he was apparently not of Athenian stock and for a time had to produce his comedies under the names of others. Cleon, the demagogue who succeeded Pericles, tried to prosecute his persistent foe on the technicality of his alien birth, but the great popularity of Aristophanes in Athens guaranteed his immunity. His conservatism was probably an ingrained bias.

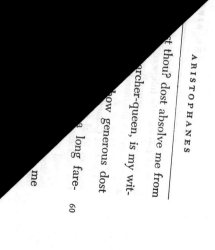

petes with *The Clouds* as Aristophanes' masterpiece, it depends for its delightful effect on literary points difficult for the layman to interpret. The later plays of Aristophanes, such as *Plutus* (388 B.C.), are playful satires on society as a whole, that look toward the inoffensive school of Middle Comedy, divorced from personal satire and brash vulgarity. The New Comedy of Menander in the fourth century completes the transition to an urbane comedy of manners close to our own in spirit.

The Clouds is probably the masterpiece of Aristophanes and certainly his most influential work. Although it was awarded only a third prize in its original version (423 B.C.), he rewrote it into something like its present form, and as such it was his own favorite among his comedies. The reasons are easy to find. It is the most intellectual of his plays, the most divorced from buffoonery, and it attacks what he thought to be the root of social decay in his time: an educational system that was leading to slick cynicism rather than to reform of morals at home and abroad. Socrates was the most conspicuous and most colorful of the teachers of Athens, and Aristophanes chose him as a symbol of the new-style education and philosophy. Actually he was far from being a spokesman for the Sophistic teachings credited to him in this play. The ideas travestied in the dialogue were derived from other, more strictly pragmatic philosophers; and of course Socrates never kept a school and prided himself on never teaching for pay.

Borrowing Socrates' famous name, Aristophanes made him a composite figure, with the master's personal traits for humor but with the ideas and practices of the whole group, most of whom Socrates disliked as heartily as did Aristophanes. Indeed, Plato's *Symposium* indicates that the two men were good friends, and the earlier version of *The Clouds* was certainly more friendly to Socrates than is the present one. The blight of this play on Socrates' reputation was severe and permanent, and at his trial for his life a quarter of a century later Plato reports that Socrates defended himself against this gross misrepresentation of what he stood for.

It is illuminating to place side by side Plato's idealized portrait of his master and Aristophanes' caricature. Somewhere between the two must have lain the real Socrates, who unfortunately left no writing to speak for him directly. Since later generations have followed Plato in sentimentalizing him as the symbol of man's free search for truth, it does no harm to be reminded of a counterview.

Aristophanes' play is shot through with prejudice and pettiness. His attack on the scientific explanation of natural phenomena in the school scene seems embarrassingly unenlightened today, and attributing to Socrates Protagoras' boast to make the unjust argument sound better than the just is a rank libel. But the conservative social critic was right in deciding that the era of speculation was destroying the moral stamina of the Greek people, and Socrates was certainly a leader in the whole movement. Regardless of its fairness or lack of it, this skit is one of the greatest personal satires in literature.

bodying his own common sense... ls, such as Dionysus in *The Frogs*, may be honored as buffoons in this perverse kind of drama, which tries at every point to be the complete antithesis of lofty tragedy. And yet imbedded in the topsy-turvy antics are earnest ideas and some of the most exquisite lyrics in Greek literature. As if anything can be expected here but the expected, Aristophanes sandwiches cheek-and-jowl hilarious farce, serious satire, and the most exalted choral poetry.

Growing up in the early years of the Peloponnesian War, Aristophanes became convinced that this fruitless struggle was bringing ruin to all of Greece. Although begun under the enlightened Pericles, the war was now protracted by Cleon, a democratic imperialist, with his ruthless insistence on total victory. Aristophanes opened his career with a series of comedies satirizing the war and especially Cleon, whom he held responsible for it. *The Babylonians* (426 B.C.), now lost, condemned the cruelty of Athenian rule of lesser states, and *The Acharnians* showed the amusing advantages enjoyed by one Athenian citizen who made a private peace with Sparta. In *The Knights*, the first play produced under the playwright's own name, Cleon—a leather-seller by trade—finds his political chicanery excelled by a sausage-seller, who thereby wins the government. An armistice the next year and the death of Cleon a year later ended this series. In 416 B.C. the government forbade the lampooning of living politicians on the stage.

Aristophanes assumed a milder manner, but in *The Birds* and *Lysistrata* he continued through fantasy and bawdy farce his plea for peace. Eventually he turned his conservative disapproval on yet another intellectual, Euripides, whose sacrilegious versions of hallowed myths he condemned as bad art and a dangerous undermining of the traditions of the state. In *The Frogs* (405 B.C.), written a year after the death of Euripides, the god Dionysus journeys to Hades to bring back a worthy playwright to relight the fires of tragedy. After listening to a debate between Aeschylus and Euripides in which sharp criticism is exchanged, he chooses Aeschylus over the bumptious, opinionated Euripides. Although *The Frogs* com-

The Clouds

CHARACTERS IN THE PLAY

STREPSIADES
PHEIDIPPIDES, *his son*
SERVANT OF STREPSIADES
SOCRATES
DISCIPLES OF SOCRATES
RIGHT LOGIC
WRONG LOGIC
PASIAS, *a money-lender*
AMYNIAS, *another money-lender*
CHORUS OF CLOUDS

SCENE: *A street in Athens with two houses, that of* STREPSIADES *and that of* SOCRATES. *A room in the former is open to view, revealing two beds occupied by* STREPSIADES *and* PHEIDIPPIDES.

STREPSIADES.

O DEAR! O dear!
    O Lord! O Zeus! these nights, how long they are.
Will they ne'er pass? will the day never come?
Surely I heard the cock crow, hours ago.
Yet still my servants snore. These are new customs. 5
O 'ware of war for many various reasons;
One fears in war even to flog one's servants.
And here's this hopeful son of mine wrapped up
Snoring and sweating under five thick blankets.
Come, we'll wrap up and snore in opposition. 10
                              (*Tries to sleep*)
But I can't sleep a wink, devoured and bitten
By ticks, and bugbears, duns, and race-horses,
All through this son of mine. *He* curls his hair,
And sports his thoroughbreds, and drives his tandem;
Even in dreams he rides: while I—I'm ruined, 15
Now that the Moon has reached her twentieths,
And paying-time comes on. Boy! light a lamp,
And fetch my ledger: now I'll reckon up
Who are my creditors, and what I owe them.
Come, let me see then. *Fifty pounds to Pasias!* 20
Why fifty pounds to Pasias? what were they for?
O, for the hack from Corinth. O dear! O dear!
I wish my eye had been hacked out before—
    PHEIDIPPIDES (*in his sleep*). You are cheating,
        Philon; keep to your own side.

STREPSIADES. Ah! there it is! that's what has ruined
        me! 25
Even in his very sleep he thinks of horses.
    PHEIDIPPIDES (*in his sleep*). How many heats do
        the war-chariots run?
    STREPSIADES. A pretty many heats you have run
        your father.
Now then, what debt assails me after Pasias?
A curricle and wheels. Twelve pounds. Amynias. 30
    PHEIDIPPIDES (*in his sleep*). Here, give the horse
        a roll, and take him home.
    STREPSIADES. You have rolled me *out* of house and
        home, my boy,
Cast in some suits already, while some swear
They'll seize my goods for payment.
    PHEIDIPPIDES.   Good, my father,
What makes you toss so restless all night long? 35
    STREPSIADES. There's a bumbailiff from the mattress bites me.
    PHEIDIPPIDES. Come now, I prithee, let me sleep
        in peace.
    STREPSIADES. Well then, you sleep; only be sure of
        this,
These debts will fall on your own head at last.
Alas, alas! 40
For ever cursed be that same match-maker,
Who stirred me up to marry your poor mother.
Mine in the country was the pleasantest life,
Untidy, easy-going, unrestrained,
Brimming with olives, sheepfolds, honey-bees. 45
Ah! then I married—I a rustic—her
A fine town-lady, niece of Megacles.
A regular, proud, luxurious, Coesyra.
This wife I married, and we came together, 49
I rank with wine-lees, fig-boards, greasy woolpacks;
She all with scents, and saffron, and tongue-kissings,
Feasting, expense, and lordly modes of loving.
She was not idle though, she was too fast.
I used to tell her, holding out my cloak, 54
Threadbare and worn; *Wife, you're too fast by half.*
    SERVANT-BOY. Here's no more oil remaining in the
        lamp.
    STREPSIADES. O me! what made you light the tippling lamp?
Come and be whipp'd.
    SERVANT-BOY.   Why, what would you whip me
        for?
    STREPSIADES. Why did you put one of those thick
        wicks in?
Well, when at last to me and my good woman 60
This hopeful son was born, our son and heir,
Why then we took to wrangle on the name.

The Clouds. Translated by B. Bickley Rogers. Reprinted by permission of G. Bell and Sons, Ltd.
17. **And paying-time comes on.** Interest on debts had to be paid on the first of the month. 22. **hack,** horse.

47–48. **A . . . Coesyra.** The aristocratic Megacleid family included Pericles and Alcibiades and was descended from Coesyra, distinguished for her pride and love of luxury. 50. **fig-boards,** boards for drying figs in the sun.

Pheidipp - son of spare of horses (handwritten margin note)

She was for giving him some knightly name,
"Callippides," "Xanthippus," or "Charippus":
I wished "Pheidonides," his grandsire's name.   65
Thus for some time we argued: till at last
We compromised it in Pheidippides.
This boy she took, and used to spoil him, saying,
Oh! when you are driving to the Acropolis, clad
Like Megacles, in your purple; whilst I said   70
Oh! when the goats you are driving from the fells,
Clad like your father, in your sheepskin coat.
Well, he cared nought for my advice, but soon
A galloping consumption caught my fortunes.
Now cogitating all night long, I've found   75
One way, one marvellous transcendent way,
Which if he'll follow, we may yet be saved.
So,—but, however, I must rouse him first;
But how to rouse him kindliest? that's the rub.
Pheidippides, my sweet one.

PHEIDIPPIDES.   Well, my father.   80

STREPSIADES. Shake hands, Pheidippides, shake
hands and kiss me.

PHEIDIPPIDES. There; what's the matter?

STREPSIADES.   Dost thou love me, boy?

PHEIDIPPIDES. Ay! by Poseidon there, the God of
horses.

STREPSIADES. No, no, not that: miss out the God
of horses,
That God's the origin of all my evils.   85
But if you love me from your heart and soul,
My son, obey me.

PHEIDIPPIDES.   Very well: what in?

STREPSIADES. Strip with all speed, strip off your
present habits,
And go and learn what I'll advise you to.

PHEIDIPPIDES. Name your commands.

STREPSIADES.   Will you obey?

PHEIDIPPIDES.   I will, by Dionysus!   90

STREPSIADES. Well then, look this way.
See you that wicket and the lodge beyond?

PHEIDIPPIDES. I see: and prithee what is that, my
father?

STREPSIADES. That is the thinking-house of sapient
souls.
There dwell the men who teach—aye, who persuade
us,   95
That Heaven is one vast fire-extinguisher
Placed round about us, and that we're the cinders.
Aye, and they'll teach (only they'll want some
money),
How one may speak and conquer, right or wrong.

PHEIDIPPIDES. Come, tell their names.

STREPSIADES.   Well, I can't
quite remember,   100
But they're deep thinkers, and true gentlemen.

65. **Pheidonides,** which means "son of thrift."   67. **Pheidippides.**
The composite name ludicrously combined the grandfather's thrift
and the mother's aristocratic squandering.

PHEIDIPPIDES. Out on the rogues! I know them.
Those rank pedants,
Those palefaced, barefoot vagabonds you mean:
That Socrates, poor wretch, and Chaerephon.

STREPSIADES. Oh! Oh! hush! hush! don't use those
foolish words;   105
But if the sorrows of my barley touch you,
Enter their Schools and cut the Turf for ever.

PHEIDIPPIDES. I wouldn't go, so help me Dionysus,
For all Leogoras's breed of Phasians!

STREPSIADES. Go, I beseech you, dearest, dearest
son,   110
Go and be taught.

PHEIDIPPIDES. And what would you have me learn?

STREPSIADES. 'Tis known that in their Schools they
keep two Logics,
The Worse, Zeus save the mark, the Worse and
Better.
This Second Logic then, I mean the Worse one,
They teach to talk unjustly and—prevail.   115
Think then, you only learn that Unjust Logic,
And all the debts, which I have incurred through
you,—
I'll never pay, no, not one farthing of them.

PHEIDIPPIDES. I will not go. How could I face the
knights
With all my colour worn and torn away!   120

STREPSIADES. O! then, by Earth, you have eat your
last of mine,
You, and your coach-horse, and your sigma-brand:
Out with you! Go to the crows, for all I care.

PHEIDIPPIDES. But uncle Megacles won't leave me
long
Without a horse: I'll go to him: good-bye.   125
(He leaves.)

STREPSIADES. I'm thrown, by Zeus, but I won't
long lie prostrate.
I'll pray the Gods and send myself to school:
I'll go at once and try their thinking-house.
Stay: how can I, forgetful, slow, old fool,
Learn the nice hair-splittings of subtle Logic?   130
Well, go I must. 'Twont do to linger here.
Come on, I'll knock the door. Boy! Ho there, boy!
(STREPSIADES *goes to the house of* SOCRATES.)

STUDENT *(within).* O, hang it all! who's knocking
at the door?

STREPSIADES. Me! Pheidon's son: Strepsiades of
Cicynna.

STUDENT. Why, what a clown you are! to kick our
door,   135
In such a thoughtless, inconsiderate way!
You've made my cogitation to miscarry.

104. **Chaerephon,** companion of Socrates for many years.   106. **sorrows of my barley;** as a rustic, Strepsiades thinks of his property in terms of grain.   109. **Leogoras's breed of Phasians,** pheasants bred by the luxurious idler, Leogoras.   119-120. **How . . . away!** He means facing his aristocratic friends with his complexion ruined by study.

STREPSIADES. Forgive me: I'm an awkward country fool.

But tell me, what was that I made miscarry?

STUDENT. 'Tis not allowed: Students alone may hear.   140

STREPSIADES. O that's all right: you may tell *me*: I'm come

To be a student in your thinking-house.

STUDENT. Come then. But they're high mysteries, remember.

'Twas Socrates was asking Chaerephon,

How many feet of its own a flea could jump.   145

For one first bit the brow of Chaerephon,

Then bounded off to Socrates's head.

STREPSIADES. How did he measure this?

STUDENT.   Most cleverly.

He warmed some wax, and then he caught the flea,

And dipped its feet into the wax he'd melted: 150

Then let it cool, and there were Persian slippers!

These he took off, and so he found the distance.

STREPSIADES. O Zeus and king, what subtle intellects!

STUDENT. What would you say then if you heard another,

Our Master's own?

STREPSIADES.   O come, do tell me that.   155

STUDENT. Why, Chaerephon was asking him in turn,

Which theory did he sanction; that the gnats

Hummed through their mouth, or backwards, through the tail?

STREPSIADES. Aye, and what said your Master of the gnat?

STUDENT. He answered thus: the entrail of the gnat   160

Is small: and through this narrow pipe the wind

Rushes with violence straight towards the tail;

There, close against the pipe, the hollow rump

Receives the wind, and whistles to the blast.

STREPSIADES. So then the rump is trumpet to the gnats!   165

O happy, happy in your entrail-learning!

Full surely need he fear nor debts nor duns,

Who knows about the entrails of the gnats.

STUDENT. And yet last night a mighty thought we lost

Through a green lizard.

STREPSIADES.   Tell me, how was that? 170

STUDENT. Why, as Himself, with eyes and mouth wide open,

Mused on the moon, her paths and revolutions,

A lizard from the roof squirted full on him.

STREPSIADES. He, he, he, he. I like the lizard's spattering Socrates.

STUDENT. Then yesterday, poor we, we'd got no dinner.   175

152. found, measured.

STREPSIADES. Hah! what did he devise to do for barley?

STUDENT. He sprinkled on the table—some fine ash—

He bent a spit—he grasped it compass-wise—

And—filched a mantle from the Wrestling School.

STREPSIADES. Good heavens! Why Thales was a fool to this!   180

O open, open, wide the study door,

And show me, show me, show me Socrates.

I die to be a student. Open, open!

(*The interior of Socrates' house is opened to view.*)

O Heracles, what kind of beasts are these!

STUDENT. Why, what's the matter? what do you think they're like?   185

STREPSIADES. Like? why those Spartans whom we brought from Pylus:

What makes them fix their eyes so on the ground?

STUDENT. They seek things underground.   *sarcastic*

STREPSIADES.   O! to be sure,

Truffles! You there, don't trouble about that!

I'll tell you where the best and finest grow.   190

Look! why do those stoop down so very much?

STUDENT. They're diving deep into the deepest secrets.

STREPSIADES. Then why's their rump turned up towards the sky?

STUDENT. It's taking private lessons on the stars.

(*To the other Students*)

Come, come: get in: HE'll catch us presently.   195

STREPSIADES. Not yet! not yet! just let them stop one moment,

While I impart a little matter to them.

STUDENT. No, no: they must go in: 'twould never do

To expose themselves too long to the open air.

STREPSIADES. O! by the Gods, now, what are these? do tell me.   200

STUDENT. This is Astronomy.

STREPSIADES.   And what is this?

STUDENT. Geometry.

STREPSIADES.   Well, what's the use of that?

STUDENT. To mete out lands.

STREPSIADES.   What, for allotment grounds?

STUDENT. No, but all lands.

STREPSIADES.   A choice idea, truly.

Then every man may take his choice, you mean. 205

STUDENT. Look; here's a chart of the whole world. Do you see?

This city's Athens.

179. And . . . Wrestling School. Apparently the supercilious student is mystifying the rustic Strepsiades with nonsense.   180. Thales, the philosopher, here symbolizing wisdom.   186–187. those Spartans . . . Pylus, war-prisoners.   203. allotment grounds, conquered lands allotted to Athenian citizens.

STREPSIADES.   Athens? I like that.
I see no dicasts sitting. That's not Athens.
   STUDENT. In very truth, this is the Attic ground.
   STREPSIADES. And where then are my townsmen of
     Cicynna?   210
   STUDENT. Why, thereabouts; and here, you see,
     Euboea:
Here, reaching out a long way by the shore.
   STREPSIADES. Yes, overreached by us and Pericles.
But now, where's Sparta?
   STUDENT.   Let me see: O, here.
   STREPSIADES. Heavens! how near us. O do please
     manage this,   215
To shove her off from us, a long way further.
   STUDENT. We can't do that, by Zeus.
   STREPSIADES.   The worse for
     you.
Hallo! who's that? that fellow in the basket?
   STUDENT. That's HE.
   STREPSIADES.   Who's HE?
   STUDENT.   Socrates.
   STREPSIADES.   Socrates!
You sir, call out to him as loud as you can.   220
   STUDENT. Call him yourself: I have not leisure
     now.
   STREPSIADES.   Socrates! Socrates!
Sweet Socrates!
   SOCRATES.   Mortal! why call'st thou me?
   STREPSIADES. O, first of all, please tell me what
     you are doing.
   SOCRATES. I walk on air, and contem-plate the
     Sun.   225
   STREPSIADES. O then from a basket you contemn
     the Gods,
And not from the earth, at any rate?
   SOCRATES.   Most true.
I could not have searched out celestial matters
Without suspending judgement, and infusing
My subtle spirit with the kindred air.   230
If from the ground I were to seek these things,
I could not find: so surely doth the earth
Draw to herself the essence of our thought.
The same too is the case with water-cress.
   STREPSIADES. Hillo! what's that?   235
Thought draws the essence into water-cress?
Come down, sweet Socrates, more near my level,
And teach the lessons which I come to learn.
   SOCRATES. And wherefore art thou come?
   STREPSIADES.   To learn to speak.
For owing to my horrid debts and duns,   240
My goods are seized, I'm robbed, and mobbed, and
     plundered.
   SOCRATES. How did you get involved with your
     eyes open?

STREPSIADES. A galloping consumption seized my
     money.
Come now: do let me learn the unjust Logic
That can shirk debts: now do just let me learn it.
Name your own price, by all the Gods I'll pay it. 246
   SOCRATES. The Gods! why you must know the
     Gods with us
Don't pass for current coin.
   STREPSIADES.   Eh? what do you use then?
Have you got iron, as the Byzantines have?
   SOCRATES. Come, would you like to learn celestial
     matters.   250
How their truth stands?
   STREPSIADES.   Yes, if there's any truth.
   SOCRATES. And to hold intercourse with yon bright
     Clouds,
Our virgin Goddesses?
   STREPSIADES.   Yes, that I should.
   SOCRATES. Then sit you down upon that sacred
     bed.
   STREPSIADES. Well, I am sitting.
   SOCRATES.   Here then, take
     this chaplet.   255
   STREPSIADES. Chaplet? why? why? now, never,
     Socrates:
Don't sacrifice poor me, like Athamas.
   SOCRATES. Fear not: our entrance-services require
All to do this.
   STREPSIADES. But what am I to gain?
   SOCRATES. You'll be the flower of talkers, prattlers,
     gossips: 260
Only keep quiet.
   STREPSIADES.   Zeus! your words come true!
I shall be flour indeed with all this peppering.

   SOCRATES. Old man sit you still, and attend to my
     will,
        and hearken in peace to my prayer,
O Master and King, holding earth in your swing, 265
        O measureless infinite Air;
And thou glowing Ether, and Clouds who enwreathe
     her
      with thunder, and lightning, and storms,
Arise ye and shine, bright Ladies Divine,
      to your student in bodily forms.   270
   STREPSIADES. No, but stay, no, but stay, just one
     moment I pray,
      while my cloak round my temples I wrap.
To think that I've come, stupid fool, from my home,
      with never a waterproof cap!
   SOCRATES. Come forth, come forth, dread Clouds,
     and to earth   275
      your glorious majesty show;

208. **I see no dicasts sitting.** It was notorious that a good share of
the Athenian citizenry was constantly doing judicial duty.   213.
overreached, exhausted of tribute by the conquering Athenians.

249. **Have . . . have?** They lacked silver for coins. 257. **Don't**
. . . Athamas. He mistakes the chaplet of initiation for the chaplet
of sacrifice which he has seen on a character in a play by Sophocles.
262. **peppering;** with ceremonial flour.

Whether lightly ye rest on the time-honoured crest
       of Olympus environed in snow,
Or tread the soft dance 'mid the stately expanse
       of Ocean, the nymphs to beguile, 280
Or stoop to enfold with your pitchers of gold,
       the mystical waves of the Nile,
Or around the white foam of Maeotis ye roam,
       or Mimas all wintry and bare,
O hear while we pray, and turn not away 285
       from the rites which your servants prepare.

CHORUS.   Clouds of all hue,
Rise we aloft with our garments of dew.
Come from old Ocean's unchangeable bed, 289
Come, till the mountain's green summits we tread,
Come to the peaks with their landscapes untold.
Gaze on the Earth with her harvests of gold,
Gaze on the rivers in majesty streaming,
   Gaze on the lordly, invincible Sea,
Come, for the Eye of the Ether is beaming, 295
   Come, for all Nature is flashing and free.
     Let us shake off this close-clinging dew
     From our members eternally new,
     And sail upwards the wide world to view.
       Come away! Come away! 300

SOCRATES. O Goddesses mine, great Clouds and
    divine,
      ye have heeded and answered my prayer.
Heard ye their sound, and the thunder around,
      as it thrilled through the tremulous air?
STREPSIADES. Yes, by Zeus, and I shake, and I'm
    all of a quake, 305
      and I fear I must sound a reply,
Their thunders have made my soul so afraid,
      and those terrible voices so nigh:
So if lawful or not, I must run to a pot,
      by Zeus, if I stop I shall die. 310
SOCRATES. Don't act in our schools like those Com-
    edy-fools
      with their scurrilous scandalous ways.
Deep silence be thine: while this Clus⌐ ⌐ divine
      their soul-stirring melody raise.

CHORUS.   Come then with me, 315
Daughters of Mist, to the land of the free.
Come to the people whom Pallas hath blest,
Come to the soil where the Mysteries rest;
Come, where the glorified Temple invites
The pure to partake of its mystical rites: 320
Holy the gifts that are brought to the Gods,
   Shrines with festoons and with garlands are
    crowned,
Pilgrims resort to the sacred abodes,
   Gorgeous the festivals all the year round.

283, 284. **Maeotis, Mimas,** a remote sea and mountain.

And the Bromian rejoicings in Spring, 325
When the flutes with their deep music ring,
And the sweetly-toned Choruses sing
   Come away! Come away!

STREPSIADES. O Socrates pray, by all the Gods,
    say,
      for I earnestly long to be told, 330
Who are these that recite with such grandeur and
    might?
      are they glorified mortals of old?
SOCRATES. No mortals are there, but Clouds of the
    air,
      great Gods who the indolent fill:
These grant us discourse, and logical force, 335
      and the art of persuasion instil,
And periphrasis strange, and a power to arrange,
      and a marvellous judgement and skill.
STREPSIADES. So then when I heard their omnip-
    otent word,
      my spirit felt all of a flutter, 340
And it yearns to begin subtle cobwebs to spin
      and about metaphysics to stutter,
And together to glue an idea or two,
      and battle away in replies:
So if it's not wrong, I earnestly long 345
      to behold them myself with my eyes.
SOCRATES. Look up in the air, towards Parnes out
    there,
      for I see they will pitch before long
These regions about.
STREPSIADES.   Where? point me them out.
SOCRATES.   They are drifting, an infinite throng,
And their long shadows quake over valley and
    brake. 351
STREPSIADES. Why, whatever's the matter to-day?
I can't see, I declare.
SOCRATES.   By the Entrance; look there!
STREPSIADES. Ah, I just got a glimpse, by the way.
SOCRATES. There, now you must see how resplend-
    ent they be, 355
      or your eyes must be pumpkins, I vow.
STREPSIADES. Ah! I see them proceed; I should
    think so indeed:
      great powers! they fill everything now.
SOCRATES. So then till this day that celestials were
    they,
      you never imagined or knew? 360
STREPSIADES. Why, no, on my word, for I always
    had heard
      they were nothing but vapour and dew.
SOCRATES. O, then I declare, you can't be aware
      that 'tis these who the sophists protect,

325. **Bromian rejoicings in Spring,** the spring festival of Dionysus.
347. **Parnes out there,** an Attic mountain, visible to the theater
audience. 353. **Entrance,** opening which admitted the chorus to the
orchestra.

Prophets sent beyond sea, quacks of every degree,
      fops signet-and-jewel-bedecked, 366
Astrological knaves, and fools who their staves
      of dithyrambs proudly rehearse—
'Tis the Clouds who all these support at their ease,
      because they exalt them in verse. 370

STREPSIADES. 'Tis for this then they write of "the on-rushin' might
      o' the light-stappin' rain-drappin' Cloud,"
And the "thousand black curls whilk the Tempest-lord whirls,"
      and the "thunder-blast stormy an' loud,"
And "birds o' the sky floatin' upwards on high," 375
      and "air-water leddies" which "droon
Wi' their saft falling dew the gran' Ether sae blue,"
      and then in return they gulp doon
Huge gobbets o' fishes an' bountifu' dishes
      o' mavises prime in their season. 380

SOCRATES. And is it not right such praise to requite?

STREPSIADES.   Ah, but tell me then what is the reason
That if, as you say, they are Clouds, they to-day
      as women appear to our view?
For the ones in the air are not women, I swear. 385

SOCRATES.   Why, what do they seem then to you?

STREPSIADES. I can't say very well, but they straggle and swell
      like fleeces spread out in the air;
Not like women they flit, no, by Zeus, not a bit,
      but these have got noses to wear. 390

SOCRATES. Well, now then, attend to this question, my friend.

STREPSIADES.   Look sharp, and propound it to me.

SOCRATES. Didst thou never espy a Cloud in the sky,
      which a centaur or leopard might be,
Or a wolf, or a cow?

STREPSIADES.   Very often, I vow: 395
      and show me the cause, I entreat.

SOCRATES. Why, I tell you that these become just what they please,
      and whenever they happen to meet
One shaggy and wild, like the tangle-haired child
      of old Xenophantes, their rule 400
Is at once to appear like Centaurs, to jeer
      the ridiculous look of the fool.

STREPSIADES. What then do they do if Simon they view,
      that fraudulent harpy to shame?

SOCRATES. Why, his nature to show to us mortals below, 405
      a wolfish appearance they frame.

399. tangle-haired child of old Xenophantes, Hieronymus, a dithyrambic poet. 403. Simon, probably a minor Sophist.

STREPSIADES. O, they then I ween having yesterday seen
      Cleonymus quaking with fear,
(Him who threw off his shield as he fled from the field),
      metamorphosed themselves into deer. 410

SOCRATES. Yes, and now they espy soft Cleisthenes nigh,
      and therefore as women appear.

STREPSIADES. O then without fail, All hail! and All hail!
      my welcome receive; and reply
With your voices so fine, so grand and divine, 415
      majestical Queens of the Sky!

CHORUS. Our welcome to thee, old man, who wouldst see
      the marvels that science can show:
And thou, the high-priest of this subtlety feast,
      say what would you have us bestow? 420
Since there is not a sage for whom we'd engage
      our wonders more freely to do,
Except, it may be, for Prodicus; he
      for his knowledge may claim them, but you,
For that sideways you throw your eyes as you go,
      and are all affectation and fuss; 426
No shoes will you wear, but assume the grand air
      on the strength of your dealings with us.

STREPSIADES. O Earth! what a sound, how august and profound!
      it fills me with wonder and awe. 430

SOCRATES. These, these then alone, for true Deities own,
      the rest are all Godships of straw.

STREPSIADES. Let Zeus be left out: He's a God beyond doubt:
      come, that you can scarcely deny.

SOCRATES. Zeus, indeed! there's no Zeus: don't you be so obtuse. 435

STREPSIADES.   No Zeus up aloft in the sky!
Then, you first must explain, who it is sends the rain;
      or I really must think you are wrong.

SOCRATES. Well then, be it known, these send it alone:
      I can prove it by arguments strong. 440
Was there ever a shower seen to fall in an hour
      when the sky was all cloudless and blue?
Yet on a fine day, when the Clouds are away,
      he might send one, according to you.

STREPSIADES. Well, it must be confessed, that chimes in with the rest: 445
      your words I am forced to believe.
Yet before, I had dreamed that the rain-water streamed
      from Zeus and his chamber-pot sieve.

411. soft Cleisthenes, an effeminate debauchee, probably in the theater at the time. 423. Prodicus, the best of the Sophists.

But whence then, my friend, does the thunder descend?

        that does make me quake with affright!

SOCRATES. Why 'tis they, I declare, as they roll through the air.   451

STREPSIADES.   What the Clouds? did I hear you aright?

SOCRATES. Ay: for when to the brim filled with water they swim,

        by Necessity carried along,

They are hung up on high in the vault of the sky,

        and so by Necessity strong   456

In the midst of their course, they clash with great force,

        and thunder away without end.

STREPSIADES. But is it not He who compels this to be?

        does not Zeus this Necessity send?   460

SOCRATES. No Zeus have we there, but a Vortex of air.

STREPSIADES.   What! Vortex? that's something, I own.

I knew not before, that Zeus was no more,

        but Vortex was placed on his throne!

But I have not yet heard to what cause you referred   465

        the thunder's majestical roar.

SOCRATES. Yes, 'tis they, when on high full of water they fly,

        and then, as I told you before,

By Compression impelled, as they clash, are compelled

        a terrible clatter to make.   470

STREPSIADES. Come, how can that be? I really don't see.

SOCRATES.   Yourself as my proof I will take.

Have you never then eat the broth-puddings you get

        when the Panathenaea comes round,

And felt with what might your bowels all night   475

        in turbulent tumult resound?

STREPSIADES. By Apollo, 'tis true, there's a mighty to-do,

        and my belly keeps rumbling about;

And the puddings begin to clatter within

        and kick up a wonderful rout: 480

Quite gently at first, papapax, papapax,

        but soon pappapappax away,

Till at last, I'll be bound, I can thunder as loud,

        papapappappapapappax, as They.

SOCRATES. Shalt thou then a sound so loud and profound   485

        from thy belly diminutive send,

And shall not the high and the infinite Sky

        go thundering on without end?

---

474. **Panathenaea**, festival at which oxen were sacrificed.

For both, you will find, on an impulse of wind

        and similar causes depend.   490

STREPSIADES. Well, but tell me from Whom comes the bolt through the gloom,

        with its awful and terrible flashes;

And wherever it turns, some it singes and burns,

        and some it reduces to ashes!

For this 'tis quite plain, let who will send the rain,

        that Zeus against perjurers dashes.   496

SOCRATES. And how, you old fool of a dark-ages school,

        and an antediluvian wit,

If the perjured they strike, and not all men alike,

        have they never Cleonymus hit?   500

Then of Simon again, and Theorus explain:

        known perjurers, yet they escape.

But he smites his own shrine with his arrows divine,

        and Sunium, Attica's cape,

And the ancient gnarled oaks: now what prompted those strokes?   505

        They never forswore I should say.

STREPSIADES. Can't say that they do: your words appear true.

        Whence comes then the thunderbolt, pray?

SOCRATES. When a wind that is dry, being lifted on high,

        is suddenly pent into these,   510

It swells up their skin, like a bladder, within,

        by Necessity's changeless decrees:

Till, compressed very tight, it bursts them outright,

        and away with an impulse so strong,

That at last by the force and the swing of its course,

        it takes fire as it whizzes along.   516

STREPSIADES. That's exactly the thing that I suffered one Spring,

        at the great feast of Zeus, I admit:

I'd a paunch in the pot, but I wholly forgot

        about making the safety-valve slit.   520

So it spluttered and swelled, while the saucepan I held,

        till at last with a vengeance it flew:

Took me quite by surprise, dung-bespattered my eyes,

        and scalded my face black and blue!

CHORUS. O thou who wouldst fain great wisdom attain,   525

        and comest to us in thy need,

All Hellas around shall thy glory resound,

        such a prosperous life thou shalt lead:

So thou art but endued with a memory good,

        and accustomed profoundly to think,   530

And thy soul wilt inure all wants to endure,

        and from no undertaking to shrink,

And art hardy and bold, to bear up against cold,

        and with patience a supper thou losest:

---

504. **Sunium, Attica's cape**, a promontory in southern Attica.

Nor too much dost incline to gymnastics and wine,
        but all lusts of the body refusest: 536
And esteemest it best, what is always the test
        of a truly intelligent brain,
To prevail and succeed whensoever you plead,
        and hosts of tongue-conquests to gain.
STREPSIADES. But as far as a sturdy soul is con-
    cerned   541
            and a horrible restless care,
And a belly that pines and wears away
        on the wretchedest, frugalest fare,
You may hammer and strike as long as you like; 545
            I am quite invincible there.
SOCRATES. Now then you agree in rejecting
    with me
        the Gods you believed in when young,
And *my* creed you'll embrace *"I believe in wide
    space,*
        in the Clouds, in the eloquent Tongue."
STREPSIADES. If I happened to meet other Gods
    in the street,   551
        I'd show the cold shoulder, I vow.
No libation I'll pour: not one victim more
        on their altars I'll sacrifice now.
CHORUS. Now be honest and true, and say what
    we shall do: 555
        since you never shall fail of our aid,
If you hold us most dear in devotion and fear,
        and will ply the philosopher's trade.
STREPSIADES. O Ladies Divine, small ambition is
    mine:
            I only most modestly seek,   560
Out and out for the rest of my life to be best
        of the children of Hellas to speak.
CHORUS. Say no more of your care, we have
    granted your prayer:
        and know from this moment, that none
More acts shall pass through in the People than
    you: 565
            such favour from us you have won.
STREPSIADES. Not acts, if you please: I want noth-
    ing of these:
            this gift you may quickly withdraw;
But I wish to succeed, just enough for my need,
        and to slip through the clutches of law.
CHORUS. This then you shall do, for your wishes
    are few: 571
        not many nor great your demands,
So away with all care from henceforth, and prepare
        to be placed in our votaries' hands.
STREPSIADES. This then will I do, confiding in you,
        for Necessity presses me sore,   576
And so sad is my life, 'twixt my cobs and my wife,
        that I cannot put up with it more.
So now, at your word, I give and afford
My body to these, to treat as they please,   580
To have and to hold, in squalor, in cold,

In hunger and thirst, yea by Zeus, at the worst,
To be flayed out of shape from my heels to my nape
So along with my hide from my duns I escape,
And to men may appear without conscience or fear,
Bold, hasty, and wise, a concocter of lies,   586
A rattler to speak, a dodger, a sneak,
A regular claw of the tables of law,
A shuffler complete, well worn in deceit,
A supple, unprincipled, troublesome cheat;   590
A hang-dog accurst, a bore with the worst,
In the tricks of the jury-courts thoroughly versed.
If all that I meet this praise shall repeat,
Work away as you choose, I will nothing refuse,
Without any reserve, from my head to my shoes.
You shan't see me wince though my gutlets you
        mince,   596
And these entrails of mine for a sausage combine,
Served up for the gentlemen students to dine.
CHORUS. Here's a spirit bold and high
Ready-armed for any strife.   600
                    (*To* STREPSIADES)
If you learn what I can teach
            Of the mysteries of speech,
Your glory soon shall reach
            To the summit of the sky.
STREPSIADES. And what am I to gain?
CHORUS.   With the Clouds you will obtain
The most happy, the most enviable life.
STREPSIADES. Is it possible for me Such felicity
    to see?   605
CHORUS. Yes, and men shall come and wait
            In their thousands at your gate,
Desiring consultations and advice
On an action or a pleading
        From the man of light and leading,
And you'll pocket many talents in a trice.
                    (*To* SOCRATES)
Here, take the old man, and do all that you can,
        your new-fashioned thoughts to instil, 611
And stir up his mind with your notions refined,
        and test him with judgement and skill.
SOCRATES. Come now, you tell me something of
    your habits:
For if I don't know them, I can't determine   615
What engines I must bring to bear upon you.
STREPSIADES. Eh! what? Not going to storm me,
    by the Gods?
SOCRATES. No, no: I want to ask you a few ques-
    tions.
First: is your memory good?
STREPSIADES.   Two ways, by Zeus:
If I'm owed anything, I'm mindful, very: 620
But if I owe, (Oh, dear!) forgetful, very.
SOCRATES. Well then: have you the gift of speak-
    ing in you?
STREPSIADES. The gift of speaking, no: of cheat-
    ing, yes.

SOCRATES. No? how then can you learn?
STREPSIADES.   Oh, well enough.
SOCRATES. Then when I throw you out some
    clever notion   625
About the laws of nature, you must catch it.
STREPSIADES. What! must I snap up sapience, in
    dog-fashion?
SOCRATES. Oh! why the man's an ignorant old
    savage:
I fear, my friend, that you'll require the whip.
Come, if one strikes you, what do you do?
STREPSIADES.   I'm struck: 630
Then in a little while I call my witness:
Then in another little while I summon him.
SOCRATES. Put off your cloak.
STREPSIADES.   Why, what have I done wrong?
SOCRATES. O, nothing, nothing: all go in here
    naked.
STREPSIADES. Well, but I have not come with a
    search-warrant.   635
SOCRATES. Fool! throw it off.
STREPSIADES.   Well, tell me this one thing;
If I'm extremely careful and attentive,
Which of your students shall I most resemble?
SOCRATES. Why, Chaerephon. You'll be his very
    image.
STREPSIADES. What! I shall be half-dead! O luck-
    less me!   640
SOCRATES. Don't chatter there, but come and fol-
    low me;
Make haste now, quicker, here.
STREPSIADES.   Oh, but do first
Give me a honied cake: Zeus! how I tremble,
To go down there, as if to see Trophonius.
SOCRATES. Go on! why keep you pottering round
    the door?   645

CHORUS. Yes! go, and farewell; as your courage is
    great,
    So bright be your fate.
May all good fortune his steps pursue,
    Who now, in his life's dim twilight haze,
Is game such venturesome things to do,   650
To steep his mind in discoveries new,
    To walk, a novice, in wisdom's ways. . . .
                                                (Later)
SOCRATES. Never by Chaos, Air, and Respiration,
Never, no never have I seen a clown
So helpless, and forgetful, and absurd!   655
Why if he learns a quirk or two he clean
Forgets them ere he has learnt them: all the same,
I'll call him out of doors here to the light.
Take up your bed, Strepsiades, and come!

644. **Trophonius,** the oracle of Trophonius situated in a subterranean
cave whose entryway was lined with demons who could be placated
with cakes.   653. **Chaos, Air, and Respiration,** the new gods of Socrates.

STREPSIADES. By Zeus, I can't: the bugs make such
    resistance.   660
SOCRATES. Make haste. There, throw it down, and
    listen.
STREPSIADES.   Well!
SOCRATES. Attend to me: what shall I teach you
    first
That you've not learnt before? Which will you have,
Measures or rhythms or the right use of words?
STREPSIADES. Oh! measures to be sure: for very
    lately   665
A grocer swindled me of full three pints.
SOCRATES. I don't mean that: but which do you
    like the best
Of all the measures; six feet, or eight feet?
STREPSIADES. Well, I like nothing better than the
    yard.
SOCRATES. Fool! don't talk nonsense.
STREPSIADES.   What will you bet me now   670
That two yards don't exactly make six feet?
SOCRATES. Consume you! what an ignorant clown
    you are!
Still, perhaps you can learn tunes more easily.
STREPSIADES. But will tunes help me to repair my
    fortunes?
SOCRATES. They'll help you to behave in com-
    pany: 675
If you can tell which kind of tune is best
For the sword-dance, and which for finger music.
STREPSIADES. For fingers! aye, but I know that.
SOCRATES.   Say on, then.
STREPSIADES. What is it but this finger? though
    before,
Ere this was grown, I used to play with that.   680
SOCRATES. Insufferable dolt!
STREPSIADES.   Well but, you goose,
I don't want to learn this.
SOCRATES.   What *do* you want then?
STREPSIADES. Teach me the Logic! teach me the
    unjust Logic!
SOCRATES. But you must learn some other matters
    first:
As, what are males among the quadrupeds.   685
STREPSIADES. I should be mad indeed not to know
    that.
The Ram, the Bull, the Goat, the Dog, the Fowl.
SOCRATES. Ah! there you are! there's a mistake at
    once!
You call the male and female fowl the same.
STREPSIADES. How! tell me how.
SOCRATES.   Why fowl and fowl of course.   690
STREPSIADES. That's true though! what then shall
    I say in future?
SOCRATES. Call one a fowless and the other a fowl.
STREPSIADES. A fowless? Good! Bravo! Bravo! by
    Air.

677. **finger music,** the dactyl.

Now for that one bright piece of information
I'll give you a barley bumper in your trough.   695
   SOCRATES. Look there, a fresh mistake; you called
      it trough,
Masculine, when it's feminine.
   STREPSIADES.   How, pray?
How did I make it masculine?
   SOCRATES.   Why "trough,"
Just like "Cleonymus."
   STREPSIADES.   I don't quite catch it.
   SOCRATES. Why "trough," "Cleonymus," both mas-
      culine.   700
   STREPSIADES. Ah, but Cleonymus has got no
      trough,
His bread is kneaded in a rounded mortar:
Still, what must I say in future?
   SOCRATES.   What! why call it
A "troughess," female, just as one says "an actress."
   STREPSIADES. A "troughess," female?
   SOCRATES.   That's the way to call it.   705
   STREPSIADES. O "troughess" then and Miss Cleon-
      ymus.
   SOCRATES. Still you must learn some more about
      these names;
Which are the names of men and women.
   STREPSIADES. Oh, I know which are women.
   SOCRATES.   Well, repeat some.
   STREPSIADES. Demetria, Cleitagora, Philinna.   710
   SOCRATES. Now tell me some men's names.
   STREPSIADES.   O yes, ten thousand.
Philon, Melesias, Amynias.
   SOCRATES. Hold! I said men's names: these are
      women's names.
   STREPSIADES. No, no, they're men's.
   SOCRATES.   They are *not* men's, for how
Would you address Amynias if you met him?   715
   STREPSIADES. How? somehow thus: "Here, here,
      Amynia!"
   SOCRATES. Amynia! a woman's name, you see.
   STREPSIADES. And rightly too; a sneak who shirks
      all service!
But all know this: let's pass to something else.
   SOCRATES. Well, then, you get into the bed.
   STREPSIADES.   And then?   720
   SOCRATES. Excogitate about your own affairs.
   STREPSIADES. Not there: I do beseech, not there:
      at least
Let me excogitate on the bare ground.
   SOCRATES. There is no way but this.
   STREPSIADES.   O luckless me!
How I shall suffer from the bugs to-day.   725

697. **Masculine, when it's feminine.** The mixing of genders satirizes the grammatical subtleties of the sophists.   702. **His . . . mortar.** The meaning of this passage is obscure.   716. **Amynia.** The vocative of Amynias is feminine in form, and Amynias was notoriously effemi-nate.

SOCRATES. Now then survey in every way,
   with airy judgement sharp and quick:
  Wrapping thoughts around you thick:
  And if so be in one you stick,
  Never stop to toil and bother,   730
   Lightly, lightly, lightly leap,
  To another, to another;
   Far away be balmy sleep.
STREPSIADES. Ugh! Ugh! Ugh! Ugh! Ugh!
CHORUS. What's the matter? where's the pain?   735
STREPSIADES. Friends! I'm dying. From the bed
  Out creep bugbears scantly fed,
  And my ribs they bite in twain,
  And my life-blood out they suck,
  And my manhood off they pluck,   740
  And my loins they dig and drain,
  And I'm dying, once again.
CHORUS. O take not the smart so deeply to heart.
STREPSIADES.   Why, what can I do?
  Vanished my skin so ruddy of hue,   745
  Vanished my life-blood, vanished my shoe,
  Vanished my purse, and what is still worse
  As I hummed an old tune till my watch should
    be past,
  I had very near vanished myself at the last.

SOCRATES. Hallo there, are you pondering?
STREPSIADES.   Eh! what? I?   750
Yes to be sure.
   SOCRATES.   And what have your ponderings
      come to?
   STREPSIADES. Whether these bugs will leave a bit
      of me.
   SOCRATES. Consume you, wretch!
   STREPSIADES.   Faith, I'm consumed already.
   SOCRATES. Come, come, don't flinch: pull up the
      clothes again:
Search out and catch some very subtle dodge   755
To fleece your creditors.
   STREPSIADES.   O me, how can I
Fleece any one with all these fleeces on me?
          (*Puts his head under the clothes.*)
   SOCRATES. Come, let me peep a moment what he's
      doing.
Hey! he's asleep!
   STREPSIADES. No, no! no fear of that!
   SOCRATES. Caught anything?
   STREPSIADES.   No, nothing.
   SOCRATES.   Surely, something.   760
   STREPSIADES. Well, I had something in my hand,
      I'll own.
   SOCRATES. Pull up the clothes again, and go on
      pondering.
   STREPSIADES. On what? now do please tell me,
      Socrates.
   SOCRATES. What is it that you want? first tell me
      that.

STREPSIADES. You have heard a million times what
    'tis I want: 765
My debts! my debts! I want to shirk my debts.
  SOCRATES. Come, come, pull up the clothes: refine
    your thoughts
With subtle wit: look at the case on all sides:
Mind you divide correctly.
  STREPSIADES.   Ugh! O me.
  SOCRATES. Hush: if you meet with any diffi-
    culty   770
Leave it a moment: then return again
To the same thought: then lift and weigh it well.
  STREPSIADES. Oh, here, dear Socrates!
  SOCRATES.   Well, my old friend.
  STREPSIADES. I've found a notion how to shirk my
    debts.
  SOCRATES. Well then, propound it.
  STREPSIADES.   What do you think of this? 775
Suppose I hire some grand Thessalian witch
To conjure down the Moon, and then I take it
And clap it into some round helmet-box,
And keep it fast there, like a looking-glass,—
  SOCRATES. But what's the use of that?
  STREPSIADES.   The use, quotha: 780
Why if the Moon should never rise again,
I'd never pay one farthing.
  SOCRATES.   No! why not?
  STREPSIADES. Why, don't we pay our interest by
    the month?
  SOCRATES. Good! now I'll proffer you another
    problem.
Suppose an action: damages, five talents: 785
Now tell me how you can evade that same.
  STREPSIADES. How! how! can't say at all: but I'll
    go seek.
  SOCRATES. Don't wrap your mind for ever round
    yourself,
But let your thoughts range freely through the air,
Like chafers with a thread about their feet. 790
  STREPSIADES. I've found a bright evasion of the
    action:
Confess yourself, 'tis glorious.
  SOCRATES.   But what is it?
  STREPSIADES. I say, haven't you seen in druggists'
    shops
That stone, that splendidly transparent stone,
By which they kindle fire?
  SOCRATES.   The burning-glass? 795
  STREPSIADES. That's it: well then, I'd get me one
    of these,
And as the clerk was entering down my case,
I'd stand, like this, some distance towards the sun,
And burn out every line.

769. **Mind you divide correctly.** This refers to the division of genus
into species in logic. 790. **Like chafers . . . feet.** The thread was
tied by boys to tantalize the insects.

  SOCRATES.   By the Three Graces,
A clever dodge!
  STREPSIADES.   O me, how pleased I am 800
To have a debt like that clean blotted out.
  SOCRATES. Come, then, make haste and snap up
    this.
  STREPSIADES.   Well, what?
  SOCRATES. How to prevent an adversary's suit
Supposing you were sure to lose it; tell me.
  STREPSIADES. O, nothing easier.
  SOCRATES.   How, pray?
  STREPSIADES.   Why thus, 805
While there was yet one trial intervening,
Ere mine was cited, I'd go hang myself.
  SOCRATES. Absurd!

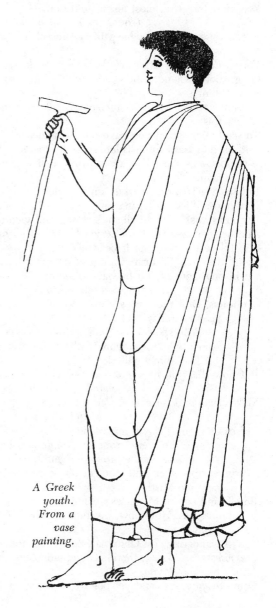

*A Greek
youth.
From a
vase
painting.*

STREPSIADES. No, by the Gods, it isn't though:
They could not prosecute me were I dead.

SOCRATES. Nonsense! Be off: I'll try no more to
teach you. 810

STREPSIADES. Why not? do, please: now, please
do, Socrates.

SOCRATES. Why you forgot all that you learn, directly.
Come, say what you learnt first: there's a chance for
you.

STREPSIADES. Ah! what was first?—Dear me: what-
ever was it?—
Whatever's that we knead the barley in?— 815
Bless us, what was it?

SOCRATES. Be off, and feed the crows,
You most forgetful, most absurd old dolt!
(SOCRATES *enters his house.*)

STREPSIADES. O me! what will become of me, poor
wretch!
I'm clean undone: I haven't learnt to speak.—
O gracious Clouds, now do advise me something. 820

CHORUS. Our counsel, ancient friend, is simply
this,
To send your son, if you have one at home,
And let him learn this wisdom in your stead.

STREPSIADES. Yes! I've a son, quite a fine gentleman:
But he won't learn, so what am I to do? 825

CHORUS. What! is he master?

STREPSIADES. Well: he's strong and vigorous,
And he's got some of the Coesyra blood within him:
Still I'll go for him, and if he won't come
By all the Gods I'll turn him out of doors.
Go in one moment, I'll be back directly. 830
(STREPSIADES *returns to his house.*)

CHORUS. Dost thou not see how bounteous we our
favours free
Will shower on you,
Since whatsoe'er your will prepare
This dupe will do.
But now that you have dazzled and
elated so your man, 835
Make haste and seize whate'er you please
as quickly as you can,
For cases such as these, my friend,
are very prone to change and bend.
(*Enter* STREPSIADES *and* PHEIDIPPIDES.)

STREPSIADES. Get out! you shan't stop here: so
help me Mist!
Be off, and eat up Megacles's columns.

PHEIDIPPIDES. How now, my father? what's i' the
wind to-day? 840
You're wandering; by Olympian Zeus, you are.

STREPSIADES. Look there! Olympian Zeus! you
blockhead you,
Come to *your* age, and yet believe in Zeus!

PHEIDIPPIDES. Why prithee, what's the joke?

STREPSIADES. 'Tis so preposterous
When babes like you hold antiquated notions. 845
But come and I'll impart a thing or two,
A wrinkle, making you a man indeed.
But, mind: don't whisper this to any one.

PHEIDIPPIDES. Well, what's the matter?

STREPSIADES. Didn't you swear by Zeus?

PHEIDIPPIDES. I did.

STREPSIADES. See now, how good a thing is
learning. 850
There is no Zeus, Pheidippides.

PHEIDIPPIDES. Who then?

STREPSIADES. Why Vortex reigns, and he has
turned out Zeus.

PHEIDIPPIDES. Oh me, what stuff.

STREPSIADES. Be sure that this is so.

PHEIDIPPIDES. Who says so, pray?

STREPSIADES. The Melian—Socrates,
And Chaerephon, who knows about the flea-
tracks. 855

PHEIDIPPIDES. And are you come to such a pitch of
madness
As to put faith in brain-struck men?

STREPSIADES. O hush!
And don't blaspheme such very dexterous men
And sapient too: men of such frugal habits
They never shave, nor use your precious ointment,
Nor go to baths to clean themselves: but you 861
Have taken *me* for a corpse and cleaned me out.
Come, come, make haste, do go and learn for me.

PHEIDIPPIDES. What can one learn from them that
is worth knowing?

STREPSIADES. Learn! why, whatever's clever in the
world: 865
And you shall learn how gross and dense you are.
But stop one moment: I'll be back directly.

PHEIDIPPIDES. O me! what must I do with my mad
father?
Shall I indict him for his lunacy,
Or tell the undertakers of his symptoms? 870

STREPSIADES. Now then! you see this, don't you?
what do you call it?

PHEIDIPPIDES. That? why a fowl.

STREPSIADES. Good! now then, what is this?

PHEIDIPPIDES. That's a fowl too.

STREPSIADES. What both! Ridiculous!
Never say that again, but mind you always
Call this a fowless and the other a fowl. 875

PHEIDIPPIDES. A fowless! These then are the
mighty secrets
You have picked up amongst those earth-born fellows.

STREPSIADES. And lots besides: but everything I
learn
I straight forget: I am so old and stupid.

854. **The Melian,** that is, an atheist, like Diagoras of Melos.

PHEIDIPPIDES. And this is what you have lost your
    mantle for? 880

STREPSIADES. It's very absent sometimes: 'tisn't lost.

PHEIDIPPIDES. And what have you done with your
    shoes, you dotard you?

STREPSIADES. Like Pericles, all for the best, I've
    lost them.

Come, come; go with me: humour me in this,
And then do what you like. Ah! I remember 885
How I to humour you, a coaxing baby,
With the first obol which my judgeship fetched me
Bought you a go-cart at the great Diasia.

PHEIDIPPIDES. The time will come when you'll re-
    pent of this.

STREPSIADES. Good boy to obey me. (*They go to
the house of* SOCRATES.) Hallo! Socrates. 890
Come here; come here; I've brought this son of
    mine.
Trouble enough, I'll warrant you. (*Enter* SOCRATES.)

SOCRATES.   Poor infant,
Not yet aware of my suspension-wonders.

PHEIDIPPIDES. You'd make a wondrous piece of
    ware, suspended.

STREPSIADES. Hey! Hang the lad! Do you abuse
    the Master? 895

SOCRATES. And look, "suthspended!" In what fool-
ish fashion
He mouthed the word with pouting lips agape.
How can *he* learn evasion of a suit,
Timely citation, damaging replies?
Hyperbolus, though, learnt them for a talent. 900

STREPSIADES. O never fear! he's very sharp, by
    nature.
For when he was a little chap, *so* high,
He used to build small baby-houses, boats,
Go-carts of leather, darling little frogs
Carved from pomegranates, you can't think how
    nicely! 905
So now, I prithee, teach him both your Logics,
The Better, as you call it, and the Worse
Which with the worse cause can defeat the Better;
Or if not both, at all events the Worse.

SOCRATES. Aye, with his own ears he shall hear
    them argue. 910
I shan't be there.

STREPSIADES.   But please remember this,
Give him the knack of reasoning down all Justice.
(RIGHT LOGIC *and* WRONG LOGIC *enter, quarreling
violently.*)

RIGHT LOGIC. Come show yourself now
               with your confident brow.
    —To the stage, if you dare!

WRONG LOGIC. Lead on where you please:
          I shall smash you with ease, 915
    If an audience be there.

883. Like Pericles . . . best; so Pericles accounted for money spent
on bribing the enemy.

RIGHT LOGIC. *You'll* smash me, you say! And who
    are *you*, pray?

WRONG LOGIC. A Logic, like you.

RIGHT LOGIC.   But the Worst of the two.

WRONG LOGIC. Yet you I can drub whom my Better they dub.

RIGHT LOGIC. By what artifice taught?

WRONG LOGIC.   By original thought. 920

RIGHT LOGIC. Aye, truly your trade so successful
    is made.
By means of these noodles of ours, I'm afraid.

WRONG LOGIC. Not noodles, but wise.

RIGHT LOGIC.   I'll smash you and your lies!

WRONG LOGIC. By what method, forsooth?

RIGHT LOGIC.   By speaking the Truth.

WRONG LOGIC. Your words I will meet, and en-
    tirely defeat: 925
There never *was* Justice or Truth, I repeat.

RIGHT LOGIC. No Justice! you say?

WRONG LOGIC.   Well, where does it stay?

RIGHT LOGIC. With the Gods in the air.

WRONG LOGIC.   If Justice be there,
How comes it that Zeus could his father reduce,
Yet live with their Godships unpunished and loose?

RIGHT LOGIC. Ugh! Ugh! These evils come thick,
            I feel awfully sick, 931
A basin, quick, quick!

WRONG LOGIC. You're a useless old drone with one
    foot in the grave!

RIGHT LOGIC. You're a shameless, unprincipled,
    dissolute knave!

WRONG LOGIC. Hey! a rosy festoon.

RIGHT LOGIC.   And a vulgar
    buffoon! 935

WRONG LOGIC. What! Lilies from *you*?

RIGHT LOGIC.   And a parricide too!

WRONG LOGIC. 'Tis with gold (you don't know it)
    you sprinkle my head.

RIGHT LOGIC. O gold is it now? but it used to be
    lead!

WRONG LOGIC. But now it's a grace and a glory instead.

RIGHT LOGIC. You're a little too bold.

WRONG LOGIC.   You're a good
    deal too old. 940

RIGHT LOGIC. 'Tis through you I well know not a
    stripling will go
To attend to the rules which are taught in the
    Schools;
But Athens one day shall be up to the fools.

WRONG LOGIC. How squalid your dress!

RIGHT LOGIC.   Yours is fine,
    I confess.
Yet of old, I declare, but a pauper you were; 945
And passed yourself off, our compassion to draw
    As a Telephus, (Euripidéan)

Well pleased from a beggarly wallet to gnaw
At inanities Pandeletéan.
    WRONG LOGIC. O me! for the wisdom you've men-
      tioned in jest!   950
    RIGHT LOGIC. O me! for the folly of you, and the
      rest
Who you to destroy their children employ!
    WRONG LOGIC. *Him* you never shall teach: you are
      quite out of date.
    RIGHT LOGIC. If not, he'll be lost, as he'll find to
      his cost:
Taught nothing by you but to chatter and prate.
    WRONG LOGIC. He raves, as you see: let him be, let
      him be.   956
    RIGHT LOGIC. Touch him if you dare! I bid you be-
      ware.
    CHORUS. Forbear, forbear to wrangle and scold!
Each of you show
You what you taught their fathers of old,   960
You let us know
Your system untried, that hearing each side
From the lips of the Rivals the youth may decide
To which of your schools he will go.
    RIGHT LOGIC. This then will I do.   964
    WRONG LOGIC.   And so will I too.
    CHORUS. And who will put in his claim to be-
    gin?
    WRONG LOGIC. If *he* wishes, he may: I kindly give
      way:
And out of his argument quickly will I
Draw facts and devices to fledge the reply
Wherewith I will shoot him and smite and refute
him.   970
And at last if a word from his mouth shall be heard
My sayings like fierce savage hornets shall pierce
His forehead and eyes,
Till in fear and distraction he yields and he—dies!
    CHORUS. With thoughts and words and maxims
      pondered well   975
Now then in confidence let both begin:
Try which his rival can in speech excel:
Try which this perilous wordy war can win,
Which all my votaries' hopes are fondly centred
in.
O Thou who wert born our sires to adorn   980
      with characters blameless and fair,
Say on what you please, say on and to these
      your glorious Nature declare.
    RIGHT LOGIC. To hear then prepare of the Dis-
    cipline rare
      which flourished in Athens of yore   985
When Honour and Truth were in fashion with youth
      and Sobriety bloomed on our shore;

First of all the old rule was preserved in our school
      that "boys should be seen and not heard:"
And then to the home of the Harpist would come
      decorous in action and word   991
All the lads of one town, though the snow peppered
down,
      in spite of all wind and all weather:
And they sang an old song as they paced it along,
      not shambling with thighs glued together:
"O the dread shout of War how it peals from afar,"
      or *"Pallas the Stormer adore,"*   997
To some manly old air all simple and bare
      which their fathers had chanted before.
And should anyone dare the tune to impair   1000
      and with intricate twistings to fill,
Such as Phrynis is fain, and his long-winded train,
      perversely to quaver and trill,
Many stripes would he feel in return for his zeal,
      as to genuine Music a foe.   1005
And every one's thigh was forward and high
      as they sat to be drilled in a row,
So that nothing the while indecent or vile
      the eye of a stranger might meet;
And then with their hand they would smooth down
the sand   1010
      whenever they rose from their seat
To leave not a trace of themselves in the place
      for a vigilant lover to view.
They never would soil their persons with oil
      but were inartificial and true.   1015
Nor tempered their throat to a soft mincing note
      and sighs to their lovers addressed:
Nor laid themselves out, as they strutted about,
      to the wanton desires of the rest:
Nor would anyone dare such stimulant fare   1020
      as the head of the radish to wish:
Nor to make over bold with the food of the old,
      the anise, and parsley, and fish:
Nor dainties to quaff, nor giggle and laugh,
      nor foot within foot to enfold.   1025
    WRONG LOGIC. Faugh! this smells very strong of
    some musty old song,
      and Chirrupers mounted in gold;
And Slaughter of beasts, and old-fashioned feasts.
    RIGHT LOGIC.   Yet these are the precepts
    which taught
The heroes of old to be hardy and bold,   1030
      and the Men who at Marathon fought!
But now must the lad from his boyhood be clad
      in a Man's all-enveloping cloak:
So that, oft as the Panathenaea returns,
      I feel myself ready to choke

948–949. **Well . . . Pandeletéan.** Telephus, wounded by Achilles, sought a cure from him in the disguise of a beggar. In Euripides' lost play on the subject, Aristophanes detected ideas of the Sophist Pandeletus in the beggar's speech.

990. **And . . . come.** Music was a major branch of ancient Greek education. 1002. **Phrynis,** native of Mitylene and leader of a revolutionary school of contemporary music. 1027. **Chirrupers mounted in gold.** Athenians of ancient families wore golden grasshoppers as tokens of their lineage.

When the dancers go by with their shields to their
    thigh, 1036
        not caring for Pallas a jot.
You therefore, young man, choose me while you can;
        cast in with my Method your lot;
And then you shall learn the forum to spurn, 1040
    and from dissolute baths to abstain,
And fashions impure and shameful abjure,
    and scorners repel with disdain:
And rise from your chair if an elder be there,
    and respectfully give him your place, 1045
And with love and with fear your parents revere,
    and shrink from the brand of Disgrace,
And deep in your breast be the Image impressed
    of Modesty, simple and true,
Nor resort any more to a dancing-girl's door, 1050
    nor glance at the harlotry crew,
Lest at length by the blow of the Apple they throw
    from the hopes of your Manhood you fall.
Nor dare to reply when your Father is nigh,
    nor "musty old Japhet" to call 1055
In your malice and rage that Sacred Old Age
    which lovingly cherished your youth.
    WRONG LOGIC. Yes, yes, my young friend, if to
    him you attend,
        by Bacchus I swear of a truth
You will scarce with the sty of Hippocrates vie, 1060
    as a mammy-suck known even there!
    RIGHT LOGIC. But then you'll excel in the games
    you love well,
        all blooming, athletic and fair:
Not learning to prate as your idlers debate
    with marvellous prickly dispute, 1065
Nor dragged into Court day by day to make sport
    in some small disagreeable suit:
But you will below to the Academe go,
    and under the olives contend
With your chaplet of reed, in a contest of speed
    with some excellent rival and friend: 1071
All fragrant with woodbine and peaceful content,
    and the leaf which the lime blossoms fling,
When the plane whispers love to the elm in the
    grove
        in the beautiful season of Spring. 1075
If then you'll obey and do what I say,
And follow with me the more excellent way,
Your chest shall be white, your skin shall be
    bright,
Your arms shall be tight, your tongue shall be
    slight,
And everything else shall be proper and right.
But if you pursue what men nowadays do, 1081

1036–37. **When . . . jot.** In the war-dance the young men show disrespect for Athena by letting their shields hang down listlessly. 1052.
the Apple they throw; as an invitation to love. 1055. **musty old
Japhet,** one of the old Titans, and hence an old fogy. 1060. **sty of
Hippocrates;** the sons of Hippocrates were notoriously piggish and
stupid.

You will have, to begin, a cold pallid skin,
Arms small and chest weak, tongue practised to
    speak,
Special laws very long, and the symptoms all
    strong
Which show that your life is licentious and
    wrong. 1085
And your mind he'll prepare so that foul to be
    fair
And fair to be foul you shall always declare;
And you'll find yourself soon, if you listen to him,
With the filth of Antimachus filled to the brim!

CHORUS. O glorious Sage! with loveliest Wisdom
    teeming! 1090
    Sweet on thy words does ancient Virtue rest!
    Thrice happy they who watched thy Youth's
    bright beaming!
    Thou of the vaunted genius, do thy best;
This man has gained applause: His Wisdom
    stands confessed.
And you with clever words and thoughts must needs
    your case adorn 1095
Else he will surely win the day, and you retreat
    with scorn.

    WRONG LOGIC. Aye, say you so? why I have been
        half-burst; I do so long
To overthrow his arguments
        with arguments more strong. 1100
I am the Lesser Logic? True:
        these Schoolmen call me so,
Simply because I was the first
        of all mankind to show
How old established rules and laws 1105
        might contradicted be:
And this, as you may guess, is worth
        a thousand pounds to me,
To take the feebler cause, and yet
        to win the disputation. 1110
And mark me now, how I'll confute
        his boasted Education!
You said that always from warm baths
        the stripling must abstain:
Why must he? on what grounds do you 1115
        of these warm baths complain?
    RIGHT LOGIC. Why, it's the worst thing possible,
        it quite unstrings a man.
    WRONG LOGIC. Hold there: I've got you round the
    waist:
        escape me if you can. 1120
And first: of all the sons of Zeus
        which think you was the best?
Which was the manliest? which endured
        more toils than all the rest?

1089. **Antimachus,** unknown.

RIGHT LOGIC. Well, I suppose that Heracles   1125
         was bravest and most bold.
WRONG LOGIC. And are the baths of Heracles
         so wonderfully cold?
Aha! you blame warm baths, I think.
    RIGHT LOGIC.   This, this is what they say: 1130
This is the stuff our precious youths
         are chattering all the day!
This is what makes them haunt the baths,
         and shun the manlier Games!
    WRONG LOGIC. Well then, we'll take the Forum
next: 1135
         I praise it, and he blames.
But if it *was* so bad, do you think
         old Homer would have made
Nestor and all his worthies ply
         a real forensic trade?   1140
Well: then he says a stripling's tongue
         should always idle be:
I say it should be used of course:
         so there we disagree.
And next he says you must be chaste.   1145
         A most preposterous plan!
Come, tell me did you ever know
         one single blessed man
Gain the least good by chastity?
         come, prove I'm wrong: make haste.   1150
RIGHT LOGIC. Yes, many, many! Peleus gained
         a sword by being chaste.
    WRONG LOGIC. A sword indeed! a wondrous meed
         the unlucky fool obtained.
Hyperbolus the Lamp-maker   1155
         hath many a talent gained
By knavish tricks which I have taught:
         but not a sword, no, no!
RIGHT LOGIC. Then Peleus did to his chaste life
         the bed of Thetis owe.   1160
    WRONG LOGIC. And then she cut and ran away!
         for nothing so engages
A woman's heart as forward warmth,
         old shred of those dark Ages!
For take this chastity, young man: 1165
         sift it inside and out:
Count all the pleasures, all the joys,
         it bids you live without:
No kind of dames, no kind of games,
         no laughing, feasting, drinking,—   1170
Why, life itself is little worth
         without these joys, I'm thinking.
Well, I must notice now the wants
         by Nature's self implanted;

You love, seduce, you can't help that,   1175
         you're caught, convicted. Granted.
You're done for; you can't say one word:
         while if you follow me
Indulge your genius, laugh and quaff,
         hold nothing base to be.   1180
Why if you're in adultery caught,
         your pleas will still be ample:
You've done no wrong, you'll say, and then
         bring Zeus as your example.
He fell before the wondrous powers   1185
         by Love and Beauty wielded:
And how can you, the Mortal, stand,
         where He, the Immortal, yielded?
RIGHT LOGIC. Aye, but suppose in spite of all,
         he must be wedged and sanded.   1190
Won't he be probed, or else can you
         prevent it? now be candid.
    WRONG LOGIC. And what's the damage if it should
be so?
RIGHT LOGIC. What greater damage can the young
man know?
WRONG LOGIC. What will you do, if this dispute
I win?   1195
RIGHT LOGIC. I'll be for ever silent.
WRONG LOGIC.   Good, begin.
The Counsellor: from whence comes he?
RIGHT LOGIC. From probed adulterers.
WRONG LOGIC.   I agree.
The Tragic Poets: whence are they?
RIGHT LOGIC. From probed adulterers.
WRONG LOGIC.   So I say.   1200
The Orators: what class of men?
RIGHT LOGIC. All probed adulterers.
WRONG LOGIC.   Right again.
You feel your error, I'll engage,
But look once more around the stage,
Survey the audience, which they be,   1205
Probed or not Probed.
RIGHT LOGIC.   I see, I see.
WRONG LOGIC. Well, give your verdict.
RIGHT LOGIC.   It must go
For probed adulterers: him I know,
And him, and him: the Probed are most.
WRONG LOGIC. How stand we then?
RIGHT LOGIC.   I own, I've lost.   1210
O Cinaeds, Cinaeds, take my robe!
Your words have won, to you I run
To live and die with glorious Probe!
      (They go into the house of SOCRATES.*)*

SOCRATES. Well, what do you want? to take away
    your son
At once, or shall I teach him how to speak?   1215

1127–28. **And . . . cold?** Warm springs were called "springs of Her-
cles" after some given him by Athena for refreshment. 1151–52.
Peleus . . . chaste. For repulsing the advances of another's wife
the gods rewarded Peleus with a sword. Later he married Thetis,
who deserted him after the birth of Achilles.

1191. **probed.** This refers to a physical punishment for adultery.
1211. **Cinaeds,** debauchees.

STREPSIADES. Teach him, and flog him, and be
  sure you well
Sharpen his mother wit, grind the one edge
Fit for my little law-suits, and the other,
Why, make that serve for more important matters.
  SOCRATES. Oh, never fear! He'll make a splendid
    sophist.   1220
  STREPSIADES. Well, well, I hope he'll be a poor
    pale rascal.
(SOCRATES *retires with* PHEIDIPPIDES *into his
house, and* STREPSIADES *into his.*)

  CHORUS. Go: but in us the thought is strong,
              you will repent of this ere long.
Now we wish to tell the Judges
              all the blessings they shall gain 1225
If, as Justice plainly warrants,
              we the worthy prize obtain.
First, whenever in the Season
              ye would fain your fields renew,
All the world shall wait expectant   1230
              till we've poured our rain on you:
Then of all your crops and vineyards
              we will take the utmost care
So that neither drought oppress them,
              nor the heavy rain impair.   1235
But if anyone amongst you
              dare to treat our claims with scorn,
Mortal he, the Clouds immortal,
              better had he ne'er been born!
He from his estates shall gather   1240
              neither corn, nor oil, nor wine,
For whenever blossoms sparkle
              on the olive or the vine
They shall all at once be blighted:
              we will ply our slings so true.   1245
And if ever we behold him
              building up his mansions new,
With our tight and nipping hailstones
              we will all his tiles destroy.
But if he, his friends or kinsfolk,   1250
              would a marriage-feast enjoy,
All night long we'll pour in torrents:
              so perchance he'll rather pray
To endure the drought of Egypt,
              than decide amiss to-day!   1255
        (*Enter* STREPSIADES.)
  STREPSIADES. The fifth, the fourth, the third, and
    then the second,
And then that day which more than all the rest
I loathe and shrink from and abominate,
Then comes at once that hateful Old-and-New day.

And every single blessed dun has sworn   1260
He'll stake his gage, and ruin and destroy me.
And when I make a modest small request,
"O my good friend, part don't exact at present,
And part defer, and part remit," they swear
So they shall never touch it, and abuse me   1265
As a rank swindler, threatening me with actions.
Now let them bring their actions! Who's afraid?
Not I: if these have taught my son to speak.
But here's the door: I'll knock and soon find out.
Boy! Ho there, boy! (*Enter* SOCRATES.)
  SOCRATES.   I clasp Strepsiades.   1270
  STREPSIADES. And I clasp you: but take this meal-
    bag first.
'Tis meet and right to glorify one's Tutors.
But tell me, tell me, has my son yet learnt
That Second Logic which he saw just now?
  SOCRATES. He hath.
  STREPSIADES.   Hurrah! great Sovereign Knav-
    ery!   1275
  SOCRATES. You may escape whatever suit you
    please.
  STREPSIADES. What, if I borrowed before wit-
    nesses?
  SOCRATES. Before a thousand, and the more the
    merrier.
  STREPSIADES. Then shall my song be loud and
    deep.
Weep, obol-weighers, weep, weep, weep,   1280
Ye, and your principals, and compound interests,
For ye shall never pester me again.
  Such a son have I bred,
  (He is within this door),
Born to inspire my foemen with dread,   1285
  Born his old father's house to restore:
Keen and polished of tongue is he,
He my Champion and Guard shall be,
He will set his old father free,
Run you, and call him forth to me.   1290
"O my child! O my sweet! come out, I entreat;
  'Tis the voice" of your sire. (*Enter* PHEIDIPPIDES)
  SOCRATES. Here's the man you require.
  STREPSIADES. Joy, joy of my heart!
  SOCRATES. Take your son and depart.   1295
  STREPSIADES. O come, O come, my son, my son,
O dear! O dear!
O joy, to see your beautiful complexion!
Aye now you have an aspect Negative
And Disputative, and our native query   1300
Shines forth there: "What d'ye say?" You've the
    true face
Which rogues put on, of injured innocence.

1222–23. **Go . . . long.** The chorus now turns to the audience for a
second parabasis. 1256. **The fifth . . . second.** The days of the last
third of the Attic month were reckoned backwards. 1259. **Old-and-
New day,** the day when the moon was old for part of the day and new
for part.

1261. **stake his gage,** deposit the cost of legal procedure in summoning
the debtor to court. 1271. **meal-bag,** the reward he had promised.
1291–92. **"O . . . voice."** These and other lines in this scene parody
passages from Euripides. 1301. **"What d'ye say?"** This is an impudent question to intimidate an opponent.

You have the regular Attic look about you.
So now, you save me, for 'twas you undid me.

PHEIDIPPIDES. What is it ails you?

STREPSIADES.   Why the Old-and-
New day.   1305

PHEIDIPPIDES. And is there such a day as Old-
and-New?

STREPSIADES. Yes: that's the day they mean to
stake their gages.

PHEIDIPPIDES. They'll lose them if they stake
them. What! do you think
That one day can be two days, both together?

STREPSIADES. Why, can't it be so?

PHEIDIPPIDES.   Surely not; or else   1310
A woman might at once be old and young.

STREPSIADES. Still, the law says so.

PHEIDIPPIDES.   True: but I believe
They don't quite understand it.

STREPSIADES.   You explain it.

PHEIDIPPIDES. Old Solon had a democratic turn.

STREPSIADES. Well, but that's nothing to the Old-
and-New.   1315

PHEIDIPPIDES. Hence then he fixed that sum-
monses be issued
For these two days, the old one and the new one,
So that the gage be staked on the New-month.

STREPSIADES. What made him add "the old" then?

PHEIDIPPIDES.   I will tell you.
He wished the litigants to meet on *that* day   1320
And compromise their quarrels: if they could not,
Then let them fight it out on the New-month.

STREPSIADES. Why then do Magistrates receive
the stakes
On the Old-and-New instead of the New-month?

PHEIDIPPIDES. Well, I believe they act like the
Foretasters.   1325
They wish to bag the gage as soon as possible,
And thus they gain a whole day's foretaste of it.

STREPSIADES. Aha! poor dupes, why sit ye moon-
ing there,
Game for us Artful Dodgers, you dull stones,
You ciphers, lambkins, butts piled up together!   1330
Oh! my success inspires me, and I'll sing
Glad eulogies on me and thee, my son.
    "Man, most blessed, most divine,
      What a wondrous wit is thine,
      What a son to grace thy line,"   1335
    Friends and neighbours day by day
      Thus will say,
When with envious eyes my suits they see you win:
But first I'll feast you, so come in, my son, come in.
    (*They retire into the house. Enter* PASIAS *and a
witness.*)

PASIAS. What! must a man lose his own property!

1314. Old Solon . . . turn. Solon had named the "Old-and-New
day." 1325. Foretasters, those appointed to taste beforehand food
served at a public banquet.

No: never, never. Better have refused   1341
With a bold face, than be so plagued as this.
See! to get paid my own just debts, I'm forced
To drag you to bear witness, and what's worse
I needs must quarrel with my townsman here.   1345
Well, I won't shame my country, while I live,
I'll go to law, I'll summon him . . .
         (*Enter* STREPSIADES.)

STREPSIADES.   Hallo!

PASIAS. To the next Old-and-New.

STREPSIADES.   Bear witness, all!
He named two days. You'll summon me; what for?

PASIAS. The fifty pounds I lent you when you
bought   1350
That iron-grey.

STREPSIADES. Just listen to the fellow!
The whole world knows that I detest all horses.

PASIAS. I swear you swore by all the Gods to
pay me.

STREPSIADES. Well, now I swear I won't: Pheidippides
Has learnt since then the unanswerable Logic.   1355

PASIAS. And will you therefore shirk my just demand?

STREPSIADES. Of course I will: else why should he
have learnt it?

PASIAS. And will you dare forswear it by the
Gods?

STREPSIADES. The Gods indeed! What Gods?

PASIAS. Poseidon, Hermes, Zeus.

STREPSIADES.   By Zeus I would,   1360
Though I gave twopence halfpenny for the privilege.

PASIAS. O then confound you for a shameless
rogue!

STREPSIADES. Hallo! this butt should be rubbed
down with salt.

PASIAS. Zounds! you deride me!

STREPSIADES.   Why 'twill hold four gallons.

PASIAS. You 'scape me not, by Mighty Zeus, and
all   1365
The Gods!

STREPSIADES. I wonderfully like the Gods;
An oath by Zeus is sport to knowing ones.

PASIAS. Sooner or later you'll repent of this.
Come do you mean to pay your debts or don't you?
Tell me, and I'll be off.

STREPSIADES.   Now do have patience;   1370
I'll give you a clear answer in one moment.
    (*He fetches a kneading-trough from his house.*)

PASIAS. What do you think he'll do?

WITNESS.   I think he'll pay you.

STREPSIADES. Where is that horrid dun? O here:
now tell me
What you call this.

PASIAS.   What I call that? a trough.

STREPSIADES. Heavens! what a fool: and do *you*
    want your money? 1375
I'd never pay one penny to a fellow
Who calls my troughess, trough. So there's your
    answer.
    PASIAS. Then you won't pay me?
    STREPSIADES.   No, not if I know it.
Come put your best foot forward, and be off:
March off, I say, this instant!
    PASIAS.   May I die 1380
If I don't go at once and stake my gage!
              (*Exit* PASIAS *and witness.*)
    STREPSIADES. No don't: the fifty pounds are loss
    enough:
And really on my word I would not wish you
To lose this too just for one silly blunder.
        (*Enter* AMYNIAS.)

    AMYNIAS. Ah me! Oh! Oh! Oh! 1385
    STREPSIADES. Hallo! who's that making that hor-
    rible noise?
Not one of Carcinus's snivelling Gods?
    AMYNIAS. Who cares to know what I am? what
    imports it?
An ill-starred man.
    STREPSIADES.   Then keep it to yourself.
    AMYNIAS. "O heavy fate!" "O Fortune, thou hast
    broken 1390
My chariot wheels!" "Thou hast undone me,
    Pallas!"
    STREPSIADES. How! has Tlepolemus been at you,
    man?
    AMYNIAS. Jeer me not, friend, but tell your worthy
    son
To pay me back the money which I lent him:
I'm in a bad way and the times are pressing. 1395
    STREPSIADES. What money do you mean?
    AMYNIAS.   Why, what he borrowed.
    STREPSIADES. You *are* in a bad way, I really think.
    AMYNIAS. Driving my four-wheel out I fell, by
    Zeus.
    STREPSIADES. You rave as if you'd fall'n times
    out-of-mind. 1399
    AMYNIAS. I rave? how so? I only claim my own.
    STREPSIADES. You can't be quite right, surely.
    AMYNIAS.   Why, what mean you?
    STREPSIADES. I shrewdly guess your brain's re-
    ceived a shake.
    AMYNIAS. I shrewdly guess that you'll receive a
    summons
If you don't pay my money.
    STREPSIADES.   Well then, tell me,
Which theory do you side with, that the rain 1405

1387. **Carcinus's snivelling Gods,** characters in the lost tragedies of
Carcinus. 1390–91. "O . . . Pallas!" These lines are from a play
about Licymnius and Tlepolemus by a son of Carcinus.

Falls fresh each time, or that the Sun draws back
The same old rain, and sends it down again?
    AMYNIAS. I'm very sure I neither know nor care.
    STREPSIADES. Not care! good heavens! And do *you*
    claim your money,
So unenlightened in the Laws of Nature? 1410
    AMYNIAS. If you're hard up then, pay me back the
    Interest
At least.
    STREPSIADES. Int-er-est? what kind of a beast is
    that?
    AMYNIAS. What else than day by day and month
    by month
Larger and larger still the silver grows
As time sweeps by?
    STREPSIADES.   Finely and nobly said. 1415
What then! think you the Sea is larger now
Than 'twas last year?
    AMYNIAS.   No surely, 'tis no larger:
It is not right it should be.
    STREPSIADES.   And do you then,
Insatiable grasper! when the Sea,
Receiving all these Rivers, grows no larger, 1420
Do you desire your silver to grow larger?
Come now, you prosecute your journey off!
Here, fetch the whip.
    AMYNIAS.   Bear witness, I appeal.
    STREPSIADES. Be off! what, won't you? Gee up,
    sigma-brand! 1424
    AMYNIAS. I say! a clear assault!
    STREPSIADES.   You won't be off?
I'll stimulate you; Zeus! I'll goad your haunches.
Aha! you run: I thought I'd stir you up
You and your phaetons, and wheels, and all!
(AMYNIAS *runs off.* STREPSIADES *enters his house.*)

    CHORUS. What a thing it is to long for matters
    which are wrong!
        For you see how this old man 1430
        Is seeking, if he can
        His creditors trepan:
        And I confidently say
        That he will this very day
          Such a blow 1435
Amid his prosperous cheats receive,
          that he will deeply grieve.

For I think that he has won what he wanted for his
    son,
        And the lad has learned the way
        All justice to gainsay, 1440
        Be it what or where it may:
        That he'll trump up any tale,
        Right or wrong, and so prevail.
        This I know.
Yea! and perchance the time will come 1445
        when he shall wish his son were dumb.

(STREPSIADES *rushes onstage, followed by* PHEIDIP-
PIDES.)

STREPSIADES.   Oh! Oh!
Help! Murder! Help! O neighbours, kinsfolk,
    townsmen,
Help, one and all, against this base assault,
Ah! Ah! my cheek! my head! O luckless me!   1450
Wretch! do you strike your father?

PHEIDIPPIDES.   Yes, Papa.

STREPSIADES. See! See! he owns he struck me.

PHEIDIPPIDES.   To be sure.

STREPSIADES. Scoundrel! and parricide! and house-
    breaker!

PHEIDIPPIDES. Thank you: go on, go on: do please
    go on.
am quite delighted to be called such names!   1455

STREPSIADES. O probed Adulterer.

PHEIDIPPIDES.   Roses from your lips.

STREPSIADES. Strike you your father?

PHEIDIPPIDES.   O dear yes; what's more,
I'll prove I struck you justly.

STREPSIADES.   Struck me justly!
Villain! how can you strike a father justly?

PHEIDIPPIDES. Yes, and I'll demonstrate it, if you
    please.   1460

STREPSIADES. Demonstrate this?

PHEIDIPPIDES.   O yes, quite easily.
Come, take your choice, which Logic do you choose?

STREPSIADES. Which what?

PHEIDIPPIDES.   Logic: the Better or the Worse?

STREPSIADES. Ah, then, in very truth I've had you
    taught
To reason down all Justice, if you think   1465
You can prove this, that it is just and right
That fathers should be beaten by their sons!

PHEIDIPPIDES. Well, well, I think I'll prove it, if
    you'll listen,
So that even you won't have one word to answer.

STREPSIADES. Come, I should like to hear what
    you've to say.   1470

CHORUS. 'Tis yours, old man, some method to con-
    trive
    This fight to win:
He would not without arms wherewith to strive
    So bold have been.
He knows, be sure, whereon to trust.   1475
His eager bearing proves he must.
So come and tell us from what cause
              this sad dispute began;
Come, tell us how it first arose:
              do tell us if you can.   1480

STREPSIADES. Well from the very first I will
              the whole contention show:
'Twas when I went into the house
              to feast him, as you know,
I bade him bring his lyre and sing,   1485
              the supper to adorn,

Some lay of old Simonides,
              as, how the Ram was shorn:
But he replied, to sing at meals
              was coarse and obsolete;   1490
Like some old beldame humming airs
              the while she grinds her wheat.

PHEIDIPPIDES. And should you not be thrashed
              who told   your son, from food abstaining
To SING! as though you were, forsooth   1495
              cicalas entertaining.

STREPSIADES. You hear him! so he said just now
              or e'er high words began:
And next he called Simonides
              a very sorry man.   1500
And when I heard him, I could scarce
              my rising wrath command;
Yet so I did, and him I bid
              take myrtle in his hand
And chant some lines from Aeschylus,   1505
              but he replied with ire,
"Believe me, I'm not one of those
              who Aeschylus admire,
That rough, unpolished, turgid bard,
              that mouther of bombast!"   1510
When he said this, my heart began
              to heave extremely fast;
Yet still I kept my passion down,
              and said, "Then prithee you,
Sing one of those new-fangled songs   1515
              which modern striplings do."
And he began the shameful tale
              Euripides has told
How a brother and a sister lived
              incestuous lives of old.   1520
Then, then I could no more restrain,
              but first I must confess
With strong abuse I loaded him,
              and so, as you may guess,
We stormed and bandied threat for threat: 1525
              till out at last he flew,
And smashed and thrashed and thumped and
    bumped
              and bruised me black and blue.

PHEIDIPPIDES. And rightly too, who coolly dared
              Euripides to blame,   1530
Most sapient bard.

STREPSIADES.   Most sapient bard!
              you, what's your fitting name?
Ah! but he'll pummel me again.

PHEIDIPPIDES.   He will: and justly too.

STREPSIADES. What! justly, heartless villain! when
              'twas I who nurtured you.   1536
I knew your little lisping ways,
              how soon, you'd hardly think,

1496. cicalas entertaining; they supposedly lived on dew. 1519–20.
How . . . old. This refers to Macareus and Canache in the lost
play, *Aeolus.*

If you cried "bree!" I guessed your wants,
   and used to give you drink: 1540
If you said "mamm!" I fetched you bread
   with fond discernment true,
And you could hardly say "Cacca!"
   when through the door I flew
And held you out a full arm's length 1545
   your little needs to do:
  But now when I was crying
  That I with pain was dying,
  You brute! you would not tarry
  Me out of doors to carry, 1550
  But choking with despair
  I've been and done it there.

CHORUS. Sure all young hearts are palpitating now
   To hear him plead,
  Since if those lips with artful words avow
   The daring deed, 1556
  And once a favouring verdict win,
  A fig for every old man's skin.
O thou! who rakest up new thoughts
   with daring hands profane. 1560
Try all you can, ingenious man,
   that verdict to obtain.
PHEIDIPPIDES. How sweet it is these novel arts,
   these clever words to know
And have the power established rules 1565
   and laws to overthrow.
Why in old times when horses were
   my sole delight, 'twas wonder
If I could say a dozen words
   without some awful blunder! 1570
But now that he has made me quit
   that reckless mode of living,
And I have been to subtle thoughts
   my whole attention giving,
I hope to prove by logic strict 1575
   'tis right to beat my father.
STREPSIADES. O! buy your horses back, by Zeus,
   since I would ten times rather
Have to support a four-in-hand,
   so I be struck no more. 1580
PHEIDIPPIDES. Peace. I will now resume the thread
   where I broke off before.
And first I ask: when I was young,
   did you not strike me then?
STREPSIADES. Yea: for I loved and cherished you.
PHEIDIPPIDES. Well, solve me this again, 1586
Is it not just that I your son
   should cherish you alike,
And strike you, since, as you observe,
   to cherish means to strike? 1590
What! must my body needs be scourged
   and pounded black and blue

And yours be scathless? was not I
   as much freeborn as you?
"Children are whipped, and shall not sires be
  whipped?" 1595
Perhaps you'll urge that children's minds
   alone are taught by blows:—
Well: Age is Second Childhood then:
   that everybody knows.
And as by old experience Age 1600
   should guide its steps more clearly,
So when they err, they surely should
   be punished more severely.
STREPSIADES. But Law goes everywhere for me:
   deny it, if you can. 1605
PHEIDIPPIDES. Well was not he who made the law,
   a man, a mortal man,
As you or I, who in old times
   talked over all the crowd?
And think you that to you or me 1610
   the same is not allowed,
To change it, so that sons by blows
   should keep their fathers steady?
Still, we'll be liberal, and blows
   which we've received already 1615
We will forget, we'll have no ex-
   post-facto legislation.
—Look at the game-cocks, look at all
   the animal creation,
Do not *they* beat their parents? Aye: 1620
   I say then, that in fact
They are as we, except that they
   no special laws enact.
STREPSIADES. Why don't you then, if always where
   the game-cock leads you follow, 1625
Ascend your perch to roost at night,
   and dirt and ordure swallow?
PHEIDIPPIDES. The case is different there, old man,
   as Socrates would see.
STREPSIADES. Well then you'll blame yourself at
  last, 1630
   if you keep striking me.
PHEIDIPPIDES. How so?
STREPSIADES. Why, if it's right for me to
  punish you my son,
You can, if you have got one, yours.
PHEIDIPPIDES. Aye, but suppose I've none.
Then having gulled me you will die, 1635
   while I've been flogged in vain.
STREPSIADES. Good friends! I really think he has
   some reason to complain.
I must concede he has put the case
   in quite a novel light: 1640
I really think we should be flogged
   unless we act aright!
PHEIDIPPIDES. Look to a fresh idea then.

1539. **bree**, a baby word for drink.

1595. "**Children . . . whipped?**" The line is quoted from the *Alcestis* of Euripides.

STREPSIADES. He'll be my death I vow.

PHEIDIPPIDES. Yet then perhaps you will not grudge 1645
ev'n what you suffer now.

STREPSIADES. How! will you make me like the blows
which I've received to-day?

PHEIDIPPIDES. Yes, for I'll beat my mother too.

STREPSIADES. What! What is that you say! 1650
Why, this is worse than all.

PHEIDIPPIDES. But what, if as I proved the other,
By the same Logic I can prove
'tis right to beat my mother?

STREPSIADES. Aye! what indeed! if this you plead,
If this you think to win, 1656
Why then, for all I care, you may
To the Accursed Pit convey
Yourself with all your learning new,
Your master, and your Logic too, 1660
And tumble headlong in.
O Clouds! O Clouds! I owe all this to you!
Why did I let you manage my affairs!

CHORUS. Nay, nay, old man, you owe it to yourself.
Why didst thou turn to wicked practices? 1665

STREPSIADES. Ah, but ye should have asked me that before,
And not have spurred a poor old fool to evil.

CHORUS. Such is our plan. We find a man
On evil thoughts intent,
Guide him along to shame and wrong,
Then leave him to repent. 1671

STREPSIADES. Hard words, alas! yet not more hard than just.
It was not right unfairly to keep back
The money that I borrowed. Come, my darling,
Come and destroy that filthy Chaerephon 1675
And Socrates; for they've deceived us both!

PHEIDIPPIDES. No. I will lift no hand against my Tutors.

STREPSIADES. Yes do, come, reverence Paternal Zeus.

PHEIDIPPIDES. Look there! Paternal Zeus! what an old fool.
Is there a Zeus?

STREPSIADES. There is.

PHEIDIPPIDES. There is *no* Zeus. 1680
Young Vortex reigns, and he has turned out Zeus.

1658. **Accursed Pit,** the Barathrum, a thirty-foot pit into which criminals or their remains were sometimes cast.

STREPSIADES. No Vortex reigns. That was my foolish thought
All through this vortex here. Fool that I was,
To think a piece of earthenware a God.

PHEIDIPPIDES. Well, rave away, talk nonsense to yourself. 1685
(*He returns into the house of* STREPSIADES.)

STREPSIADES. Oh! fool, fool, fool, how mad I must have been
To cast away the Gods, for Socrates.
Yet Hermes, gracious Hermes, be not angry
Nor crush me utterly, but look with mercy
On faults to which his idle talk hath led me. 1690
And lend thy counsel; tell me, had I better
Plague them with lawsuits, or how else annoy them
(*Affects to listen.*)
Good: your advice is good: I'll have no lawsuits,
I'll go at once and set their house on fire,
The prating rascals. Here, here, Xanthias, 1695
Quick, quick here, bring your ladder and your pitchfork,
Climb to the roof of their vile thinking-house,
Dig at their tiles, dig stoutly, an' thou lovest me,
Tumble the very house about their ears.
And someone fetch me here a lighted torch, 1700
And I'll soon see if, boasters as they are,
They won't repent of what they've done to me.
(*He sets fire to the house of* SOCRATES.)

STUDENT 1 (*from within*). O dear! O dear!

STREPSIADES. Now, now, my torch, send out a lusty flame.

STUDENT 1. Man! what are you at there?

STREPSIADES. What am I at? I'll tell you. 1705
I'm splitting straws with your house-rafters here.

STUDENT 2. Oh me! who's been and set our house on fire?

STREPSIADES. Who was it, think you, that you stole the cloak from?

STUDENT 3. O Murder! Murder!

STREPSIADES. That's the very thing,
Unless this pick prove traitor to my hopes, 1710
Or I fall down, and break my blessed neck.

SOCRATES. Hallo! what are you at, up on our roof?

STREPSIADES. I walk on air, and contemplate the Sun.

SOCRATES. O! I shall suffocate. O dear! O dear!

CHAEREPHON. And I, poor devil, shall be burnt to death. 1715

STREPSIADES. For with what aim did ye insult the Gods,
And pry around the dwellings of the Moon?
Strike, smite them, spare them not, for many reasons,
BUT MOST BECAUSE THEY HAVE BLASPHEMED THE GODS!

CHORUS. Lead out of the way: for I think we may say 1720
We have acted our part very fairly to-day.

Thucydides

c. 460–c. 400 B.C.

The Greeks considered history a fine art, as worthy in its way as epic and tragedy, and dedicated one of their nine Muses, Clio, to its care. Certainly few modern historians combine the objective inquiry into fact and the imaginative re-creation of the past that distinguish Thucydides, their greatest master. He had predecessors, of course, who gradually shaped this ideal through their own experiments, but even the *History* of Herodotus (c. 484–c. 425 B.C.) seems primitive and naïve when compared with Thucydides' *History of the Peloponnesian War.*

Yet Thucydides was not so much a research historian as a chronicler of contemporary events, in some of which he took an active part. He lived in the discouraging days of city-state wars when the national unity and democratic ideals that had inspired Herodotus were disintegrating and the decline of faith in tradition and of hope for the future was undermining the Greek way of life. Stoically he watched this beginning of Greek suicide and set down the facts about the ruinous wars for later generations to read.

He was born into a rich Athenian family, and, narrowly escaping death in the great plague of 429 B.C. that killed Pericles, lived to assume command of a naval expedition to Thrace in 425. The failure of his efforts there to prevent the Spartans from capturing an Athenian city led him into voluntary exile, since he suspected that the democratic leader in Athens, Cleon, would victimize him as an aristocrat. During the twenty years of war that followed, he traveled widely, especially in the realm of the Spartans and their allies, who welcomed him because of his exile and gave him a knowledge of their activities that contributed to the impartiality of his later history. With the end of the war in 404 B.C., victorious Sparta deposed the democratic party in Athens, and Thucydides returned under the hateful rule of the Thirty Tyrants. From the very start of the war he had been keeping his records of events, but not until the end of it, apparently, did he set about his *History* in earnest. He was still engaged on it when he died (or was murdered) around 400 B.C.

The incomplete *History* carries the story of the war from 431 B.C. to the Revolution of the Four Hundred in 411 B.C. It is preceded by a sketch of Greek military history from Minoan times, obviously much less trustworthy than the chronicle Thucydides recorded at first hand, though his method even here invites our confidence. With great pride in his undertaking he makes a stern promise of accuracy and sets forth the first real historical method in Western literature. The hearsay and miracles that had charmed Herodotus are severely ruled out. His silence about the gods and his cynical mention of oracles assure us that Thucydides belonged to the new philosophical order; for him the age of faith and the old religion was a thing of the past.

Yet the most famous episodes in the *History* are the very ones where, as he explains, he has taken liberty with his text—namely, the speeches of statesmen and emissaries on great occasions. No text existed for the Funeral Oration of Pericles, but Thucydides has re-created it as he actually heard it spoken. He explained his procedure as follows: "As to the words spoken by orators it was hard for me and for others from whom I received them at secondhand to remember the exact words that were spoken. But I have made each orator speak as befitted the occasion and as I thought he would have spoken, keeping nevertheless as closely as possible to the general sense of what was really spoken." If the speech of Pericles sounds more finished and rhetorical than the homely utterances of a straightforward man of affairs, we must still be grateful to the artist in Thucydides that preserved his noble sentiments on that occasion in such vivid and tangible form.

In the grim sequence of martial events that form the *History* it is refreshing to come upon two of the great political documents of Greece, which give us our most direct insight into the meaning of Greek democracy to the Greeks themselves. The Funeral Oration of Pericles, which is the Greek counterpart of Lincoln's Gettysburg Address, was delivered at a celebration for the Athenians who had died in the first year of war. It is not a militant address, but a magnificent tribute to the democratic Athens that had been Pericles' ideal. It is an inspirational talk that proudly reviews the free institutions and enlightened culture for which the Athenians were fighting. This enkindling speech, which remains alive for democratic people everywhere, takes on a melancholy cast when we realize that the very features of Athenian culture honored here were to suffer a mortal blow in the long war that lay ahead.

The Melian Dialogue, associated with a political incident fifteen years later (416 B.C.), gives a much less flattering view of the Athenians. Far from tolerant abroad, they had sent envoys supported by troops to demand that the Spartan colony of Melos surrender and join the Athenian confederacy. Although in a hopeless military position, the Melians pleaded for political justice and civic honor, since they desired only to remain neutral in the war. The cynical, or realistic, Athenians argued that the Melians' honor would be more disgraced by the fall of their city than by renunciation of their tie with Sparta. But the Melians chose the road of principle, dismissed the Athenian envoys, and were soon annihilated. Thucydides does not represent them as foolish, however. In our century more than one nation has had to choose whether to live in slavery or die for freedom and honor. Thucydides was gravely concerned about the decline of political morality in his day. Without swerving from his objective approach to his material, he has made the Melian Dialogue a noble plea for justice among nations, regardless of their strength. This is only one of many passages in his *History* that rise to the heights of inspiration and art.

Funeral Speech of Pericles

DURING the same winter, in accordance with an old national custom, the funeral of those who first fell in this war was celebrated by the Athenians at the public charge. The ceremony is as follows: Three days before the celebration they erect a tent in which the bones of the dead are laid out, and every one brings to his own dead any offering which he pleases. At the time of the funeral the bones are placed in chests of cypress wood, which are conveyed on hearses; there is one chest for each tribe. They also carry a single empty litter decked with a pall for all whose bodies are missing, and cannot be recovered after the battle. The procession is accompanied by anyone who chooses, whether citizen or stranger, and the female relatives of the deceased are present at the place of interment and make lamentation. The public sepulchre is situated in the most beautiful spot outside the walls; there they always bury those who fall in war; only after the battle of Marathon the dead, in recognition of their pre-eminent valor, were interred on the field. When the remains have been laid in the earth, some man of known ability and high reputation, chosen by the city, delivers a suitable oration over them; after which the people depart. Such is the manner of interment; and the ceremony was repeated from time to time throughout the war. Over those who were the first buried Pericles was chosen to speak. At the fitting moment he advanced from the sepulchre to a lofty stage, which had been erected in order that he might be heard as far as possible by the multitude, and spoke as follows:—

"Most of those who have spoken here before me have commended the lawgiver who added this oration to our other funeral customs; it seemed to them a worthy thing that such an honor should be given at their burial to the dead who have fallen on the field of battle. But I should have preferred that, when men's deeds have been brave, they should be honored in deed only, and with such an honor as this public funeral, which you are now witnessing. Then the reputation of many would not have been imperilled on the eloquence or want of eloquence of one, and their virtues believed or not as he spoke well or ill. For it is difficult to say neither too little nor too much; and even moderation is apt not to give the impression of truthfulness. The friend of the dead who knows the facts is likely to think that the words of the speaker fall short of his knowledge and of his wishes; another who is not so well-informed, when he hears of anything which surpasses his own powers, will be envious and will suspect exaggeration. Mankind are tolerant of the praises of others so long as each hearer thinks that he can do as well or nearly as well himself, but, when the speaker rises above him, jealousy is aroused and he begins to be incredulous. However, since our ancestors have set the seal of their approval upon the practice, I must obey, and to the utmost of my power shall endeavor to satisfy the wishes and beliefs of all who hear me.

"I will speak first of our ancestors, for it is right and seemly that now, when we are lamenting the dead, a tribute should be paid to their memory. There has never been a time when they did not inhabit this land, which by their valor they have handed down from generation to generation, and we have received from them a free state. But if they were worthy of praise, still more were our fathers, who added to their inheritance, and after many a struggle transmitted to us their sons this great empire. And we ourselves assembled here today, who are still most of us in the vigor of life, have carried the work of improvement further, and have richly endowed our city with all things, so that she is sufficient for herself both in peace and war. Of the military exploits by which our various possessions were acquired, or of the energy with which we or our fathers drove back the tide of war, Hellenic or Barbarian, I will not speak; for the tale would be long and is familiar to you. But before I praise the dead, I should like to point out by what principles of action we rose to power, and under what institutions and through what manner of life our empire became great. For I conceive that such thoughts are not unsuited to the occasion, and that this numerous assembly of citizens and strangers may profitably listen to them.

"Our form of government does not enter into rivalry with the institutions of others. We do not copy our neighbors, but are an example to them. It is true that we are called a democracy, for the administration is in the hands of the many and not of the few. But while the law secures equal justice to all alike in their private disputes, the claim of excellence is also recognized; and when a citizen is in any way distinguished, he is preferred to the public service, not as a matter of privilege, but as the reward of merit. Neither is poverty a bar, but a man may benefit his country whatever be the obscurity of his condition. There is no exclusiveness in our public life, and in our private intercourse we are not suspicious of one another, nor angry with our neighbor if he does what he likes; we do not put on sour looks at him which, though harmless, are not pleas-

Funeral . . . Pericles. Translated by Benjamin Jowett. Published by The Clarendon Press, Oxford.
3. **war,** the Peloponnesian War, a 27-year-old struggle between Athens and Sparta and their respective allies.

ant. While we are thus unconstrained in our private intercourse, a spirit of reverence pervades our public acts; we are prevented from doing wrong by respect for the authorities and for the laws, having an especial regard to those which are ordained for the protection of the injured as well as to those unwritten laws which bring upon the transgressor of them the reprobation of the general sentiment.

10 "And we have not forgotten to provide for our weary spirits many relaxations from toil; we have regular games and sacrifices throughout the year; our homes are beautiful and elegant; and the delight which we daily feel in all these things helps to banish melancholy. Because of the greatness of our city the fruits of the whole earth flow in upon us; so that we enjoy the goods of other countries as freely as of our own.

"Then, again, our military training is in many respects superior to that of our adversaries. Our city is 20 thrown open to the world, and we never expel a foreigner or prevent him from seeing or learning anything of which the secret if revealed to an enemy might profit him. We rely not upon management or trickery, but upon our own hearts and hands. And in the matter of education, whereas they from early youth are always undergoing laborious exercises which are to make them brave, we live at ease, and yet are equally ready to face the perils which they face. And here is the proof. The Lacedaemonians 30 come into Attica not by themselves, but with their whole confederacy following; we go alone into a neighbor's country; and although our opponents are fighting for their homes and we on a foreign soil, we have seldom any difficulty in overcoming them. Our enemies have never yet felt our united strength; the care of a navy divides our attention, and on land we are obliged to send our own citizens everywhere. But they, if they meet and defeat a part of our army, are as proud as if they had routed us all, and when 40 defeated they pretend to have been vanquished by us all.

"If then we prefer to meet danger with a light heart but without laborious training, and with a courage which is gained by habit and not enforced by law, are we not greatly the gainers? Since we do not anticipate the pain, although, when the hour comes, we can be as brave as those who never allow themselves to rest; and thus too our city is equally admirable in peace and in war. For we are lovers of 50 the beautiful, yet simple in our tastes, and we cultivate the mind without loss of manliness. Wealth we employ, not for talk and ostentation, but when there is a real use for it. To avow poverty with us is no disgrace; the true disgrace is in doing nothing to avoid it. An Athenian citizen does not neglect the

29. **Lacedaemonians,** the Spartans.

state because he takes care of his own household; and even those of us who are engaged in business have a very fair idea of politics. We alone regard a man who takes no interest in public affairs, not as a harmless, but as a useless character; and if few of 60 us are originators, we are all sound judges of a policy. The great impediment to action is, in our opinion, not discussion, but the want of that knowledge which is gained by discussion preparatory to action. For we have a peculiar power of thinking before we act and of acting too, whereas other men are courageous from ignorance, but hesitate upon reflection. And they are surely to be esteemed the bravest spirits who, having the clearest sense both of the pains and pleasures of life, do not on that account shrink 70 from danger. In doing good, again, we are unlike others; we make our friends by conferring, not by receiving favors. Now he who confers a favor is the firmer friend, because he would fain by kindness keep alive the memory of an obligation; but the recipient is colder in his feelings, because he knows that in requiting another's generosity he will not be winning gratitude but only paying a debt. We alone do good to our neighbors not upon a calculation of interest, but in the confidence of freedom and in a 80 frank and fearless spirit. To sum up: I say that Athens is the school of Hellas, and that the individual Athenian in his own person seems to have the power of adapting himself to the most varied forms of action with the utmost versatility and grace. This is no passing and idle word, but truth and fact; and the assertion is verified by the position to which these qualities have raised the state. For in the hour of trial Athens alone among her contemporaries is superior to the report of her. No enemy who comes 90 against her is indignant at the reverses which he sustains at the hands of such a city; no subject complains that his masters are unworthy of him. And we shall assuredly not be without witnesses; there are mighty monuments of our power which will make us the wonder of this and of succeeding ages; we shall not need the praises of Homer or of any other panegyrist whose poetry may please for the moment, although his representation of the facts will not bear the light of day. For we have compelled every land 100 and every sea to open a path for our valor, and have everywhere planted eternal memorials of our friendship and of our enmity. Such is the city for whose sake these men nobly fought and died; they could not bear the thought that she might be taken from them; and every one of us who survive should gladly toil on her behalf.

"I have dwelt upon the greatness of Athens because I want to show you that we are contending for a higher prize than those who enjoy none of 110 these privileges, and to establish by manifest proof the merit of these men whom I am now commemorating. Their loftiest praise has been already spoken. For in magnifying the city I have magnified them, and men like them whose virtues made her glorious. And of how few Hellenes can it be said as of them, that their deeds when weighed in the balance have been found equal to their fame! Methinks that a death such as theirs has been gives the true measure of a man's worth; it may be the first revelation of his virtues, but is at any rate their final seal. For even those who come short in other ways may justly plead the valor with which they have fought for their country; they have blotted out the evil with the good, and have benefited the state more by their public services than they have injured her by their private actions. None of these men were enervated by wealth or hesitated to resign the pleasures of life; none of them put off the evil day in the hope, natural to poverty, that a man, though poor, may one day become rich. But, deeming that the punishment of their enemies was sweeter than any of these things, and that they could fall in no nobler cause, they determined at the hazard of their lives to be honorably avenged, and to leave the rest. They resigned to hope their unknown chance of happiness; but in the face of death they resolved to rely upon themselves alone. And when the moment came they were minded to resist and suffer, rather than to fly and save their lives; they ran away from the word of dishonor, but on the battle-field their feet stood fast, and in an instant, at the height of their fortune, they passed away from the scene, not of their fear, but of their glory.

"Such was the end of these men; they were worthy of Athens, and the living need not desire to have a more heroic spirit, although they may pray for a less fatal issue. The value of such a spirit is not to be expressed in words. Anyone can discourse to you forever about the advantages of a brave defence, which you know already. But instead of listening to him I would have you day by day fix your eyes upon the greatness of Athens, until you become filled with the love of her; and when you are impressed by the spectacle of her glory, reflect that this empire has been acquired by men who knew their duty and had the courage to do it, who in the hour of conflict had the fear of dishonor always present to them, and who, if ever they failed in an enterprise, would not allow their virtues to be lost to their country, but freely gave their lives to her as the fairest offering which they could present at her feast. The sacrifice which they collectively made was individually repaid to them; for they received again each one for himself a praise which grows not old, and the noblest of all sepulchres—I speak not of that in which their remains are laid, but of that in which their glory survives, and is proclaimed always and on every fitting

occasion both in word and deed. For the whole earth is the sepulchre of famous men; not only are they commemorated by columns and inscriptions in their own country, but in foreign lands there dwells also an unwritten memorial of them, graven not on stone but in the hearts of men. Make them your examples, and, esteeming courage to be freedom and freedom to be happiness, do not weigh too nicely the perils of war. The unfortunate who has no hope of a change for the better has less reason to throw away his life than the prosperous who, if he survive, is always liable to a change for the worse, and to whom any accidental fall makes the most serious difference. To a man of spirit, cowardice and disaster coming together are far more bitter than death striking him unperceived at a time when he is full of courage and animated by the general hope.

"Wherefore I do not now commiserate the parents of the dead who stand here; I would rather comfort them. You know that your life has been passed amid manifold vicissitudes; and that they may be deemed fortunate who have gained most honor, whether an honorable death like theirs, or an honorable sorrow like yours, and whose days have been so ordered that the term of their happiness is likewise the term of their life. I know how hard it is to make you feel this, when the good fortune of others will too often remind you of the gladness which once lightened your hearts. And sorrow is felt at the want of those blessings, not which a man never knew, but which were a part of his life before they were taken from him. Some of you are of an age at which they may hope to have other children, and they ought to bear their sorrow better; not only will the children who may hereafter be born make them forget their own lost ones, but the city will be doubly a gainer. She will not be left desolate, and she will be safer. For a man's counsel cannot have equal weight or worth, when he alone has no children to risk in the general danger. To those of you who have passed their prime, I say: 'Congratulate yourselves that you have been happy during the greater part of your days; remember that your life of sorrow will not last long, and be comforted by the glory of those who are gone. For the love of honor alone is ever young, and not riches, as some say, but honor is the delight of men when they are old and useless.'

"To you who are the sons and brothers of the departed, I see that the struggle to emulate them will be an arduous one. For all men praise the dead, and, however pre-eminent your virtue may be, hardly will you be thought, I do not say to equal, but even to approach them. The living have their rivals and detractors, but when a man is out of the way, the honor and good-will which he receives is unalloyed. And, if I am to speak of womanly virtues to those of you who will henceforth be widows, let me sum them up in one short admonition: To a woman not to show more weakness than is natural to her sex is a great glory, and not to be talked about for good or for evil among men.

"I have paid the required tribute, in obedience to the law, making use of such fitting words as I had. The tribute of deeds has been paid in part; for the dead have been honorably interred, and it remains only that their children should be maintained at the public charge until they are grown up: this is the solid prize with which, as with a garland, Athens crowns her sons living and dead, after a struggle like theirs. For where the rewards of virtue are greatest, there the noblest citizens are enlisted in the service of the state. And now, when you have duly lamented, every one his own dead, you may depart."

Such was the order of the funeral celebrated in this winter, with the end of which ended the first year of the Peloponnesian War.

The Melian Dialogue

THE Athenians next made an expedition against the island of Melos with thirty ships of their own, six Chian, and two Lesbian, twelve hundred hoplites and three hundred archers besides twenty mounted archers of their own, and about fifteen hundred hoplites furnished by their allies in the islands. The Melians are colonists of the Lacedaemonians who would not submit to Athens like the other islanders. At first they were neutral and took no part. But when the Athenians tried to coerce them by ravaging their lands, they were driven into open hostilities. The generals, Cleomedes the son of Lycomedes and Tisias the son of Tisimachus, encamped with the Athenian forces on the land. But before they did the country any harm they sent envoys to negotiate with the Melians. Instead of bringing these envoys before the people, the Melians desired them to explain their errand to the magistrates and to the dominant class. They spoke as follows:—

"Since we are not allowed to speak to the people, lest, forsooth, a multitude should be deceived by seductive and unanswerable arguments which they would hear set forth in a single uninterrupted oration (for we are perfectly aware that this is what you mean in bringing us before a select few), you who are sitting here may as well make assurance yet surer. Let us have no set speeches at all, but do you reply to each several statement of which you disapprove, and criticize it at once. Say first of all how you like this mode of proceeding."

The Melian representatives answered:—"The quiet

The Melian Dialogue. Translated by Benjamin Jowett. Published by The Clarendon Press, Oxford.

interchange of explanations is a reasonable thing, and we do not object to that. But your warlike movements, which are present not only to our fears but to our eyes, seem to belie your words. We see that, although you may reason with us, you mean to be our judges; and that at the end of the discussion, if the justice of our cause prevail and we therefore refuse to yield, we may expect war; if we are convinced by you, slavery."

ATHENIANS. "Nay, but if you are only going to argue from fancies about the future, or if you meet us with any other purpose than that of looking your circumstances in the face and saving your city, we have done; but if this is your intention we will proceed."

MELIANS. "It is an excusable and natural thing that men in our position should neglect no argument and no view which may avail. But we admit that this conference has met to consider the question of our preservation; and therefore let the argument proceed in the manner which you propose."

ATHENIANS. "Well, then, we Athenians will use no fine words; we will not go out of our way to prove at length that we have a right to rule, because we overthrew the Persians; or that we attack you now because we are suffering any injury at your hands. We should not convince you if we did; nor must you expect to convince us by arguing that, although a colony of the Lacedaemonians, you have taken no part in their expeditions, or that you have never done us any wrong. But you and we should say what we really think, and aim only at what is possible, for we both alike know that into the discussion of human affairs the question of justice only enters where there is equal power to enforce it, and that the powerful exact what they can, and the weak grant what they must."

MELIANS. "Well, then, since you set aside justice and invite us to speak of expediency, in our judgment it is certainly expedient that you should respect a principle which is for the common good; that to every man when in peril a reasonable claim should be accounted a claim of right, and that any plea which he is disposed to urge, even if failing of the point a little, should help his cause. Your interest in this principle is quite as great as ours, inasmuch as you, if you fall, will incur the heaviest vengeance, and will be the most terrible example to mankind."

ATHENIANS. "The fall of our empire, if it should fall, is not an event to which we look forward with dismay; for ruling states such as Lacedaemon are not cruel to their vanquished enemies. With the Lacedaemonians, however, we are not now contending; the real danger is from our many subject states, who may of their own motion rise up and overcome their masters. But this is a danger which you may leave to us. And we will now endeavor to show that we have come in the interests of our empire, and that in what we are about to say we are only seeking the preservation of your city. For we want to make you ours with the least trouble to ourselves, and it is for the interests of us both that you should not be destroyed."

MELIANS. "It may be your interest to be our masters, but how can it be ours to be your slaves?"

ATHENIANS. "To you the gain will be that by submission you will avert the worst; and we shall be all the richer for your preservation."

MELIANS. "But must we be your enemies? Will you not receive us as friends if we are neutral and remain at peace with you?"

ATHENIANS. "No, your enmity is not half so mischievous to us as your friendship; for the one is in the eyes of our subjects an argument of our power, the other of our weakness."

MELIANS. "But are your subjects really unable to distinguish between states in which you have no concern, and those which are chiefly your own colonies, and in some cases have revolted and been subdued by you?"

ATHENIANS. "Why, they do not doubt that both of them have a good deal to say for themselves on the score of justice, but they think that states like yours are left free because they are able to defend themselves, and that we do not attack them because we dare not. So that your subjection will give us an increase of security, as well as an extension of empire. For we are masters of the sea, and you who are islanders, and insignificant islanders too, must not be allowed to escape us."

MELIANS. "But do you not recognize another danger? For, once more, since you drive us from the plea of justice and press upon us your doctrine of expediency, we must show you what is for our interest, and, if it be for yours also, may hope to convince you:—Will you not be making enemies of all who are now neutrals? When they see how you are treating us they will expect you some day to turn against them; and if so, are you not strengthening the enemies whom you already have, and bringing upon you others who, if they could help, would never dream of being your enemies at all?"

ATHENIANS. "We do not consider our really dangerous enemies to be any of the peoples inhabiting the mainland who, secure in their freedom, may defer indefinitely any measures of precaution which they take against us, but islanders who, like you, happen to be under no control, and all who may be already irritated by the necessity of submission to our empire—these are our real enemies, for they are the most reckless and most likely to bring themselves as well as us into a danger which they cannot but foresee."

MELIANS. "Surely then, if you and your subjects will brave all this risk, you to preserve your empire and they to be quit of it, how base and cowardly would it be in us, who retain our freedom, not to do and suffer anything rather than be your slaves."

ATHENIANS. "Not so, if you calmly reflect: for you are not fighting against equals to whom you cannot yield without disgrace, but you are taking counsel whether or no you shall resist an overwhelming force. The question is not one of honor but of prudence."

MELIANS. "But we know that the fortune of war is sometimes impartial, and not always on the side of numbers. If we yield now, all is over; but if we fight, there is yet a hope that we may stand upright."

ATHENIANS. "Hope is a good comforter in the hour of danger, and when men have something else to depend upon, although hurtful, she is not ruinous. But when her spendthrift nature has induced them to stake their all, they see her as she is in the moment of their fall, and not till then. While the knowledge of her might enable them to be wary of her, she never fails. You are weak and a single turn of the scale might be your ruin. Do not you be thus deluded; avoid the error of which so many are guilty, who, although they might still be saved if they would take the natural means, when visible grounds of confidence forsake them, have recourse to the invisible, to prophecies and oracles and the like, which ruin men by the hopes which they inspire in them."

MELIANS. "We know only too well how hard the struggle must be against your power, and against fortune, if she does not mean to be impartial. Nevertheless we do not despair of fortune; for we hope to stand as high as you in the favor of heaven, because we are righteous, and you against whom we contend are unrighteous; and we are satisfied that our deficiency in power will be compensated by the aid of our allies the Lacedaemonians; they cannot refuse to help us, if only because we are their kinsmen, and for the sake of their own honor. And therefore our confidence is not so utterly blind as you suppose."

ATHENIANS. "As for the Gods, we expect to have quite as much of their favor as you: for we are not doing or claiming anything which goes beyond common opinion about divine or men's desires about human things. For of the Gods we believe, and of men we know, that by a law of their nature wherever they can rule they will. This law was not made by us, and we are not the first who have acted upon it; we did but inherit it, and shall bequeath it to all time, and we know that you and all mankind, if you were as strong as we are, would do as we do. So much for the Gods; we have told you why we expect to stand as high in their good opinion as you. And then as to the Lacedaemonians—when you imagine that out of very shame they will assist, we admire the innocence of your idea, but we do not envy you the folly of it. The Lacedaemonians are exceedingly virtuous among themselves and according to their national standard of morality. But, in respect of their dealings with others, although many things might be said, they can be described in a few words—of all men whom we know they are the most notorious for identifying what is pleasant with what is honorable, and what is expedient with what is just. But how inconsistent is such a character with your present blind hope of deliverance!"

MELIANS. "That is the very reason why we trust them; they will look to their interest, and therefore will not be willing to betray the Melians, who are their own colonists, lest they should be distrusted by their friends in Hellas and play into the hands of their enemies."

ATHENIANS. "But do you not see that the path of expediency is safe, whereas justice and honor involve danger in practice, and such dangers the Lacedaemonians seldom care to face?"

MELIANS. "On the other hand, we think that whatever perils there may be, they will be ready to face them for our sakes, and will consider danger less dangerous where we are concerned. For if they need our aid we are close at hand, and they can better trust our loyal feeling because we are their kinsmen."

ATHENIANS. "Yes, but what encourages men who are invited to join in a conflict is clearly not the goodwill of those who summon them to their side, but a decided superiority in real power. To this no men look more keenly than the Lacedaemonians; so little confidence have they in their own resources, that they only attack their neighbors when they have numerous allies, and therefore they are not likely to find their way by themselves to an island, when we are masters of the sea."

MELIANS. "But they may send their allies: the Cretan sea is a large place; and the masters of the sea will have more difficulty in overtaking vessels which want to escape than the pursued in escaping. If the attempt should fail they may invade Attica itself, and find their way to allies of yours whom Brasidas did not reach; and then you will have to fight, not for the conquest of a land in which you have no concern, but nearer home, for the preservation of your confederacy and of your own territory."

ATHENIANS. "Help may come from Lacedaemon to you as it has come to others, and should you ever have actual experience of it, then you will know that never once have the Athenians retired from a siege through fear of a foe elsewhere. You told us that the safety of your city would be your first care, but we remark that, in this long discussion, not a word has been uttered by you which would give a reasonable man expectation of deliverance. Your strongest grounds are hopes deferred, and what power you have is not to be compared with that which is already arrayed against you. Unless after we have withdrawn you mean to come, as even now you may, to a wiser conclusion, you are showing a great want of sense. For surely you cannot dream of flying to that false sense of honor which has been the ruin of so many when danger and dishonor were staring them in the face. Many men with their eyes still open to the consequences have found the word 'honor' too much for them, and have suffered a mere name to lure them on, until it has drawn down upon them real and irretrievable calamities; through their own folly they have incurred a worse dishonor than fortune would have inflicted upon them. If you are wise you will not run this risk; you ought to see that there can be no disgrace in yielding to a great city which invites you to become her ally on reasonable terms, keeping your own land, and merely paying tribute; and that you will certainly gain no honor if, having to choose between two alternatives, safety and war, you obstinately prefer the worse. To maintain our rights against equals, to be politic with superiors, and to be moderate toward inferiors is the path of safety. Reflect once more when we have withdrawn, and say to yourselves over and over again that you are deliberating about your one and only country, which may be saved or may be destroyed by a single decision."

The Athenians left the conference: the Melians, after consulting among themselves, resolved to persevere in their refusal, and made answer as follows: —"Men of Athens, our resolution is unchanged; and we will not in a moment surrender that liberty which our city, founded seven hundred years ago, still enjoys; we will trust to the good fortune which, by the favor of the Gods, has hitherto preserved us, and for human help to the Lacedaemonians, and endeavor to save ourselves. We are ready however to be your friends, and the enemies neither of you nor of the Lacedaemonians, and we ask you to leave our country when you have made such a peace as may appear to be in the interest of both parties."

Such was the answer of the Melians; the Athenians, as they quitted the conference, spoke as follows:—"Well, we must say, judging from the decision at which you have arrived, that you are the only men who deem the future to be more certain than the present, and regard things unseen as already realized in your fond anticipation, and that the more you cast yourselves upon the Lacedaemonians and fortune and hope, and trust them, the more complete will be your ruin."

Plato

c. 427–348 B.C.

If the portrait of Socrates in *The Clouds* is ridiculously unfair, the counterpicture in Plato's dialogues sometimes comes close to idolatry. Socrates numbered among his followers some of the best and most diverse minds of the new generation—Antisthenes the Cynic, Aristippus the Cyrenaic, Eucleides the Skeptic, Alcibiades the reckless politician. But only two set themselves the grateful task of recording their master's words and personality for future ages. Xenophon was more a man of action than a philosopher, and his *Memorabilia* of Socrates are superficial, though reverent and honest. It remained for Plato, the greatest of the disciples, to create our traditional portrait of the Great Gadfly.

Socrates was already in his sixties when Aristocles (later called Plato) came to him for instruction as an earnest youth not yet twenty. The slovenly person of Socrates was often seen at rich men's tables and he drew most of his followers from the aristocratic youth of the day. Plato was no exception, for his family was one of the most ancient and distinguished in Athens. In his youth he approached, like Sophocles, the Greek ideal—handsome, skilled in athletics, brave in battle, and talented in mathematics, politics, music, poetry, and drama. Although the influence of Socrates led him to renounce the theater for philosophy, the dramatic form of the dialogue that he chose to convey his ideas gave him a happy opportunity to express his dramatic talent.

For ten formative years he absorbed the teachings of Socrates. Then in rapid succession came the collapse of Athens in the Peloponnesian War, the year's rule of the Thirty Tyrants, the restoration of the democratic party, and the trial and execution of Socrates. Completely disillusioned with politics and the democratic system of Athens, Plato left to travel for over ten years in Egypt, Italy, and Sicily. In 387 B.C. he returned to Athens and with the financial help of his friends founded his Academy in an olive grove sacred to the hero Academus, not the first of ancient universities, but the most famous and enduring. The Academy charged no tuition fee, but was supported by the donations of wealthy patrons, and attracted some of the greatest minds of the next generation—Aristotle, Demosthenes, Xenocrates. Although the lectures and discussions at the Academy included such technical subjects as mathematics, astronomy, and music, Plato's personal interests were in ethics, politics, and law—in general, the subjects of his dialogues.

Following the bent of Socrates more closely than any other of the disciples, Plato perfected his theory of Ideas as the ultimate reality underlying individual things. The material objects that we perceive by the senses are perpetually changing and eventually disappear. Only the generalized images, or ideas of these things, which are made by divinity, can be perceived in the mind, remain constant, and constitute the true reality. Knowledge lies in grasping these ideas rather than in knowing specific things. The highest of all the ideas is goodness, the moving principle of the world and hence undistinguishable from divinity itself. All education, then, is ultimately ethical in design, aspiring to the knowledge of goodness; and Plato represents Socrates, the great teacher, as drawing out of his disciples by questions the true definition of such moral ideas as temperance, courage, beauty, and love. Through understanding these ideas they are led to virtue.

It can readily be seen that Plato's ethics was the core of his philosophy; and even his metaphysics was a kind of ethical idealism. We should not be surprised that in aesthetics too, he should tolerate only that art and literature that lead to an understanding of goodness. In the last excerpt from the *Republic* given here he illustrates his general theory of Ideas by opposing the objects called bed and table to the ideas of bed and table—the ultimate reality in this instance. But he proceeds to a third possibility in the artist's depiction, or imitation, of the bed or table, and draws his famous conclusion that all art is imitation of reality. As such it provides deception rather than knowledge and must be ruled out of the philosopher's education. It can be tolerated at all only when it concentrates on ethical objectives and inspires men to that search for knowledge which is goodness. This theory of art as the servant of the philosopher's state leads to a propagandistic view of art and is opposed to the doctrine of "art for art's sake."

Yet Plato was as much artist as philosopher and, in his only known writings, chose one of the most charming of literary forms to expound and popularize his ideas. He did not invent the philosophical dialogue, but in perfecting it he made it his own. It appealed to him originally as the ideal medium for representing the question-and-answer teaching of Socrates, and later, as in the *Symposium,* it could embody the round-table discussion of an idea in the search for truth. In the most artistic of the dialogues there is genuine give-and-take, and the speakers are adroitly differentiated like character creations in drama. In the later dialogues, when the artist in Plato succumbs to the philosopher, the dialogue is sheer pretense, and the lesser characters are allowed to interpolate mere yes and no in the monologues of Socrates (become himself a thin disguise for Plato). Of course the conversations are intended to be idealized versions of reality, synthesized in the early period from recollections or written notes, but eventually quite fictitious. The philosophers whom he presented expressed amazement at the words Plato put into their mouths. But he remains true to the spirit of his personalities and, like Thucydides in his speeches, represents what they at least might have said. And the details of setting and stage business give a dramatic reality to the best of the dialogues, a reality which is heightened by the rambling turns of the discussions and the inconclusive ends of many of them.

The dialogues of Plato are conventionally grouped by the three periods in which they are supposed to have been written. Shortly after the death of Socrates, before Plato had reached a secure philosophy of his own, he completed eight or nine short dialogues to record the personality, method, and characteristic ideas of his master. These are the most dramatic and popular of all and apparently the most faithful to the person and philosophy of Socrates. The best known are the three in which Plato recounts the actual trial and death of Socrates in an effort to vindicate him before the Athenian public. Of these, the *Apology* is not a dialogue but the substance of a speech made by Socrates at his trial. The bravery and independence of the man, as well as his jocularity and insolence, are masterfully conveyed in the artistic prose of Plato. The *Crito* reveals the efforts of his friends to save Socrates from execution and his insistence on living and dying by the laws of the state.

In middle life Plato composed about a dozen dialogues still built around the personality of his teacher but certainly embodying much more of his own thinking. Both the art and the philosophy of the man reach their zenith here. The *Phaedo* returns to the scene of his master's death and reveals him discoursing on the immortality of the soul just before he heroically drinks the hemlock. The *Phaedrus* and the *Symposium* discuss the controversial subject of Platonic love. But it is the monumental *Republic* that is best remembered from his entire career. He returned to writing late in life with a half-dozen dialogues, notably the *Parmenides* and *Laws,* but his art had declined and his philosophy was settling into an authoritarianism that completely repudiated Athenian democracy.

Actually this was not new with Plato. His aristocratic background and training were early reflected in his theory of Ideas, which subordinated the world of beds and tables so important to the democratic merchant class to those virtues—temperance, courage, wisdom, and justice—that belonged to the aristocratic ideal of the Greeks. In the *Republic* he defined an aristocratic utopia in which ideal goodness is achieved by paternalistic rule over the unenlightened working classes by a cultured minority, carefully chosen and educated, and living according to a Spartan communism. Indeed, the Spartan state came closest to the ideal of Plato, and his own effort to persuade Dionysius I and II, tyrants of Syracuse, to bring his ideal state to reality produced less of it than had the code of Lycurgus in Sparta. Clearly Plato is not a reassuring thinker for a democratic state as we know it, but his art and his idealism have made him an enduring force in Western thought. His Academy survived till the sixth century A.D., and through the Neoplatonists of the third century A.D. he helped to shape the ethics of Christianity.

Apology

How you, O Athenians, have been affected by my accusers, I cannot tell; but I know that they almost made me forget who I was—so persuasively did they speak; and yet they have hardly uttered a word of truth. But of the many falsehoods

Apology. Translated by Benjamin Jowett. Published by The Clarendon Press, Oxford. Plato's version of Socrates' speech of defense at his trial in 399 B.C. is much idealized.

told by them, there was one which quite amazed me; —I mean when they said that you should be upon your guard and not allow yourselves to be deceived by the force of my eloquence. To say this, when they were certain to be detected as soon as I opened my lips and proved myself to be anything but a great speaker, did indeed appear to me most shameless—unless by the force of eloquence they mean the force of truth; for if such is their meaning, I admit that I am eloquent. But in how different a way from theirs! Well, as I was saying, they have scarcely spoken the truth at all; but from me you shall hear the whole truth: not, however, delivered after their manner in a set oration duly ornamented with words and phrases. No, by heaven! but I shall use the words and arguments which occur to me at the moment; for I am confident in the justice of my cause: at my time of life I ought not to be appearing before you, O men of Athens, in the character of a juvenile orator—let no one expect it of me. And I must beg of you to grant me a favour:—If I defend myself in my accustomed manner, and you hear me using the words which I have been in the habit of using in the agora, at the tables of the money-changers, or anywhere else, I would ask you not to be surprised, and not to interrupt me on this account. For I am more than seventy years of age, and appearing now for the first time in a court of law, I am quite a stranger to the language of the place; and therefore I would have you regard me as if I were really a stranger, whom you would excuse if he spoke in his native tongue, and after the fashion of his country:—Am I making an unfair request of you? Never mind the manner, which may or may not be good; but think only of the truth of my words, and give heed to that: let the speaker speak truly and the judge decide justly.

And first, I have to reply to the older charges and to my first accusers, and then I will go on to the later ones. For of old I have had many accusers, who have accused me falsely to you during many years; and I am more afraid of them than of Anytus and his associates, who are dangerous, too, in their own way. But far more dangerous are the others, who began when you were children, and took possession of your minds with their falsehoods, telling of one Socrates, a wise man, who speculated about the heaven above, and searched into the earth beneath, and made the worse appear the better cause. The disseminators of this tale are the accusers whom I dread; for their hearers are apt to fancy that such enquirers do not believe in the existence of the gods. And they are many, and their charges against me are of ancient date, and they were made by them in the days when you were more impressible than you are now—in childhood, or it may have been in

47. **Anytus,** a wealthy politician and chief prosecutor of Socrates.

youth—and the cause when heard went by default, for there was none to answer. And hardest of all, I do not know and cannot tell the names of my accusers; unless in the chance case of a comic poet. All who from envy and malice have persuaded you— some of them having first convinced themselves— all this class of men are most difficult to deal with; for I cannot have them up here, and cross-examine them, and therefore I must simply fight with shadows in my own defence, and argue when there is no one who answers. I will ask you then to assume with me, as I was saying, that my opponents are of two kinds; one recent, the other ancient: and I hope that you will see the propriety of my answering the latter first, for these accusations you heard long before the others, and much oftener.

Well, then, I must make my defence, and endeavour to clear away in a short time, a slander which has lasted a long time. May I succeed, if to succeed be for my good and yours, or likely to avail me in my cause! The task is not an easy one; I quite understand the nature of it. And so leaving the event with God, in obedience to the law I will now make my defence.

I will begin at the beginning, and ask what is the accusation which has given rise to the slander of me, and in fact has encouraged Meletus to prefer this charge against me. Well, what do the slanderers say? They shall be my prosecutors, and I will sum up their words in an affidavit: "Socrates is an evil-doer, and a curious person, who searches into things under the earth and in heaven, and he makes the worse appear the better cause; and he teaches the aforesaid doctrines to others." Such is the nature of the accusation: it is just what you have yourselves seen in the comedy of Aristophanes, who has introduced a man whom he calls Socrates, going about and saying that he walks in air, and talking a deal of nonsense concerning matters of which I do not pretend to know either much or little—not that I mean to speak disparagingly of any one who is a student of natural philosophy. I should be very sorry if Meletus could bring so grave a charge against me. But the simple truth is, O Athenians, that I have nothing to do with physical speculations. Very many of those here present are witnesses to the truth of this, and to them I appeal. Speak then, you who have heard me, and tell your neighbours whether any of you have ever known me hold forth in few words or in many upon such matters. . . . You hear their answer. And from what they say of this part of the charge you will be able to judge of the truth of the rest.

As little foundation is there for the report that I am a teacher and take money; this accusation has

4. a comic poet; an allusion to *The Clouds* of Aristophanes.
27. Meletus, a minor tragic poet.

no more truth in it than the other. Although, if a man were really able to instruct mankind, to receive money for giving instruction would, in my opinion, be an honour to him. There is Gorgias of Leontium, and Prodicus of Ceos, and Hippias of Elis, who go the round of the cities, and are able to persuade the young men to leave their own citizens by whom they might be taught for nothing, and come to them whom they not only pay, but are thankful if they may be allowed to pay them. There is at this time a Parian philosopher residing in Athens, of whom I have heard; and I came to hear of him in this way: —I came across a man who has spent a world of money on the Sophists, Callias, the son of Hipponicus, and knowing that he had sons, I asked him: "Callias," I said, "if your two sons were foals or calves, there would be no difficulty in finding some one to put over them; we should hire a trainer of horses, or a farmer, probably, who would improve and perfect them in their own proper virtue and excellence; but as they are human beings, whom are you thinking of placing over them? Is there any one who understands human and political virtue? You must have thought about the matter, for you have sons; is there any one?" "There is," he said. "Who is he?" said I; "and of what country? and what does he charge?" "Evenus the Parian," he replied; "he is the man, and his charge is five minae." Happy is Evenus, I said to myself, if he really has this wisdom, and teaches at such a moderate charge. Had I the same, I should have been very proud and conceited; but the truth is that I have no knowledge of the kind.

I dare say, Athenians, that some one among you will reply, "Yes, Socrates, but what is the origin of these accusations which are brought against you; there must have been something strange which you have been doing? All these rumours and this talk about you would never have arisen if you had been like other men: tell us, then, what is the cause of them, for we should be sorry to judge hastily of you." Now, I regard this as a fair challenge, and I will endeavour to explain to you the reason why I am called wise and have such an evil fame. Please to attend then. And although some of you may think that I am joking, I declare that I will tell you the entire truth. Men of Athens, this reputation of mine has come of a certain sort of wisdom which I possess. If you ask me what kind of wisdom, I reply, wisdom such as may perhaps be attained by man, for to that extent I am inclined to believe that I am wise; whereas the persons of whom I was speaking have a superhuman wisdom, which I may fail to describe, because I have it not myself; and he who says that I have, speaks falsely, and is taking away my character. And here, O men of Athens, I must beg you not to interrupt me, even if I seem to say something extravagant. For the word which I will speak is not mine. I will refer you to a witness who is worthy of credit; that witness shall be the god of Delphi—he will tell you about my wisdom, if I have any, and of what sort it is. You must have known Chaerephon; he was early a friend of mine, and also a friend of yours, for he shared in the recent exile of the people, and returned with you. Well, Chaerephon, as you know, was very impetuous in all his doings, and he went to Delphi and boldly asked the oracle to tell him whether—as I was saying, I must beg you not to interrupt—he asked the oracle to tell him whether any one was wiser than I was, and the Pythian prophetess answered, that there was no man wiser. Chaerephon is dead himself; but his brother, who is in court, will confirm the truth of what I am saying.

Why do I mention this? Because I am going to explain to you why I have such an evil name. When I heard the answer, I said to myself, What can the god mean? and what is the interpretation of his riddle? for I know that I have no wisdom, small or great. What then can he mean when he says that I am the wisest of men? And yet he is a god, and cannot lie; that would be against his nature. After long consideration, I thought of a method of trying the question. I reflected that if I could only find a man wiser than myself, then I might go to the god with a refutation in my hand. I should say to him, "Here is a man who is wiser than I am; but you said that I was the wisest." Accordingly I went to one who had the reputation of wisdom, and observed him—his name I need not mention; he was a politician whom I selected for examination—and the result was as follows: When I began to talk with him, I could not help thinking that he was not really wise, although he was thought wise by many, and still wiser by himself; and thereupon I tried to explain to him that he thought himself wise, but was not really wise, and the consequence was that he hated me, and his enmity was shared by several who were present and heard me. So I left him, saying to myself, as I went away: Well, although I do not suppose that either of us knows anything really beautiful and good, I am better off than he is,—for he knows nothing, and thinks that he knows; I neither know nor think that I know. In this latter particular, then, I seem to have slightly the advantage of him. Then I went to another who had still higher pretensions to wisdom, and my conclusion was exactly the same. Whereupon I made another enemy of him, and of many others besides him.

Then I went to one man after another, being not unconscious of the enmity which I provoked, and I lamented and feared this: but necessity was laid upon me,—the word of God, I thought, ought to be considered first. And I said to myself, Go I must to all who appear to know, and find out the meaning of the oracle. And I swear to you, Athenians, by the dog I swear!—for I must tell you the truth—the result of my mission was just this: I found that the men most in repute were all but the most foolish; and that others less esteemed were really wiser and better. I will tell you the tale of my wanderings and of the "Herculean" labours, as I may call them, which I endured only to find at last the oracle irrefutable. After the politicians, I went to the poets; tragic, dithyrambic, and all sorts. And there, I said to myself, you will be instantly detected; now you will find out that you are more ignorant than they are. Accordingly I took them some of the most elaborate passages in their own writings, and asked what was the meaning of them—thinking that they would teach me something. Will you believe me? I am almost ashamed to confess the truth, but I must say that there is hardly a person present who would not have talked better about their poetry than they did themselves. Then I knew that not by wisdom do poets write poetry, but by a sort of genius and inspiration, they are like diviners or soothsayers who also say many fine things, but do not understand the meaning of them. The poets appeared to me to be much in the same case; and I further observed that upon the strength of their poetry they believed themselves to be the wisest of men in other things in which they were not wise. So I departed, conceiving myself to be superior to them for the same reason that I was superior to the politicians.

At last I went to the artisans. I was conscious that I knew nothing at all, as I may say, and I was sure that they knew many fine things; and here I was not mistaken, for they did know many things of which I was ignorant, and in this they certainly were wiser than I was. But I observed that even the good artisans fell into the same error as the poets; —because they were good workmen they thought that they also knew all sorts of high matters, and this defect in them overshadowed their wisdom; and therefore I asked myself on behalf of the oracle, whether I would like to be as I was, neither having their knowledge nor their ignorance, or like them in both; and I made answer to myself and to the oracle that I was better off as I was.

This inquisition has led to my having many enemies of the worst and most dangerous kind, and has given occasion also to many calumnies. And I am called wise, for my hearers always imagine that I myself possess the wisdom which I find wanting in others: but the truth is, O men of Athens, that God only is wise; and by his answer he intends to show that the wisdom of men is worth little or nothing; he is not speaking of Socrates, he is only using my name by way of illustration, as if he said, He, O men, is the wisest, who, like Socrates, knows that his wisdom is in truth worth nothing. And so I go about the world obedient to the god, and search and make enquiry into the wisdom of any one, whether citizen or stranger, who appears to be wise; and if he is not wise, then in vindication of the oracle I show him that he is not wise; and my occupation quite absorbs me, and I have no time to give either to any public matter of interest or to any concern of my own, but I am in utter poverty by reason of my devotion to the god.

10 There is another thing:—young men of the richer classes, who have not much to do, come about me of their own accord; they like to hear the pretenders examined, and they often imitate me, and proceed to examine others; there are plenty of persons, as they quickly discover, who think that they know something, but really know little or nothing; and then those who are examined by them instead of being angry with themselves are angry with me: This confounded Socrates, they say; this villainous mis-

20 leader of youth!—and then if somebody asks them, Why, what evil does he practise or teach? they do not know, and cannot tell; but in order that they may not appear to be at a loss, they repeat the ready-made charges which are used against all philosophers about teaching things up in the clouds and under the earth, and having no gods, and making the worse appear the better cause; for they do not like to confess that their pretence of knowledge has been detected—which is the truth; and as they

30 are numerous and ambitious and energetic, and are drawn up in battle array and have persuasive tongues, they have filled your ears with their loud and inveterate calumnies. And this is the reason why my three accusers, Meletus and Anytus and Lycon, have set upon me; Meletus, who has a quarrel with me on behalf of the poets; Anytus, on behalf of the craftsmen and politicians; Lycon, on behalf of the rhetoricians: and, as I said at the beginning, I cannot expect to get rid of such a mass of

40 calumny all in a moment. And this, O men of Athens, is the truth and the whole truth; I have concealed nothing, I have dissembled nothing. And yet, I know that my plainness of speech makes them hate me, and what is their hatred but a proof that I am speaking the truth? Hence has arisen the prejudice against me; and this is the reason of it, as you will find out either in this or in any future enquiry.

I have said enough in my defence against the first class of my accusers; I turn to the second class.

50 They are headed by Meletus, that good man and true lover of his country as he calls himself. Against these, too, I must try to make a defence:—Let their affidavit be read: it contains something of this kind: It says that Socrates is a doer of evil, who corrupts the youth; and who does not believe in the gods of the State, but has other new divinities of his own. Such is the charge; and now let us examine the par-

ticular counts. He says that I am a doer of evil, and corrupt the youth; but I say, O men of Athens, that Meletus is a doer of evil, in that he pretends 60 to be in earnest when he is only in jest, and is so eager to bring men to trial from a pretended zeal and interest about matters in which he really never had the smallest interest. And the truth of this I will endeavour to prove to you.

Come hither, Meletus, and let me ask a question of you. You think a great deal about the improvement of youth?

Yes, I do.

Tell the judges, then, who is their improver; for 70 you must know, as you have taken the pains to discover their corrupter, and are citing and accusing me before them. Speak, then, and tell the judges who their improver is.—Observe, Meletus, that you are silent, and have nothing to say. But is not this rather disgraceful, and a very considerable proof of what I was saying, that you have no interest in the matter? Speak up, friend, and tell us who their improver is.

The laws. 80

But that, my good sir, is not my meaning. I want to know who the person is, who, in the first place, knows the laws.

The judges, Socrates, who are present in court.

What, do you mean to say, Meletus, that they are able to instruct and improve youth?

Certainly they are.

What, all of them, or some only and not others?

All of them.

By the goddess Here, that is good news! There 90 are plenty of improvers, then. And what do you say of the audience,—do they improve them?

Yes, they do.

And the senators?

Yes, the senators improve them.

But perhaps the members of the assembly corrupt them?—or do they improve them?

They improve them.

Then every Athenian improves and elevates them; all with the exception of myself; and I alone 100 am their corrupter? Is that what you affirm?

That is what I stoutly affirm.

I am very unfortunate if you are right. But suppose I ask you a question: How about horses? Does one man do them harm and all the world good? Is not the exact opposite the truth? One man is able to do them good, or at least not many;—the trainer of horses, that is to say, does them good, and others who have to do with them rather injure them? Is not that true, Meletus, of horses, or of any other 110 animals? Most assuredly it is; whether you and Anytus say yes or no. Happy indeed would be the condition of youth if they had one corrupter only, and all the rest of the world were their improvers.

But you, Meletus, have sufficiently shown that you never had a thought about the young: your carelessness is seen in your not caring about the very things which you bring against me.

And now, Meletus, I will ask you another question—by Zeus I will: Which is better, to live among bad citizens, or among good ones? Answer, friend, I say; the question is one which may be easily answered. Do not the good do their neighbours good, and the bad do them evil?

Certainly.

And is there any one who would rather be injured than benefited by those who live with him? Answer, my good friend, the law requires you to answer—does any one like to be injured?

Certainly not.

And when you accuse me of corrupting and deteriorating the youth, do you allege that I corrupt them intentionally or unintentionally?

Intentionally, I say.

But you have just admitted that the good do their neighbours good, and the evil do them evil. Now, is that a truth which your superior wisdom has recognized thus early in life, and am I, at my age, in such darkness and ignorance as not to know that if a man with whom I have to live is corrupted by me, I am very likely to be harmed by him; and yet I corrupt him, and intentionally, too—so you say, although neither I nor any other human being is ever likely to be convinced by you. But either I do not corrupt them, or I corrupt them unintentionally; and on either view of the case you lie. If my offence is unintentional, the law has no cognizance of unintentional offences: you ought to have taken me privately, and warned and admonished me; for if I had been better advised, I should have left off doing what I only did unintentionally—no doubt I should, but you would have nothing to say to me and refused to teach me. And now you bring me up in this court, which is a place not of instruction, but of punishment.

It will be very clear to you, Athenians, as I was saying, that Meletus has no care at all, great or small, about the matter. But still I should like to know, Meletus, in what I am affirmed to corrupt the young. I suppose you mean, as I infer from your indictment, that I teach them not to acknowledge the gods which the State acknowledges, but some other new divinities or spiritual agencies in their stead. These are the lessons by which I corrupt the youth, as you say.

Yes, that I say emphatically.

Then, by the gods, Meletus, of whom we are speaking, tell me and the court, in somewhat plainer terms, what you mean! For I do not as yet understand whether you affirm that I teach other men to acknowledge some gods, and therefore that I do believe in gods, and am not an entire atheist—this you do not lay to my charge,—but only you say

that they are not the same gods which the city recognizes—the charge is that they are different gods. Or, do you mean that I am an atheist simply, and a teacher of atheism?

I mean the latter—that you are a complete atheist.

What an extraordinary statement! Why do you think so, Meletus? Do you mean that I do not believe in the godhead of the sun, or moon, like other men?

I assure you, judges, that he does not: for he says that the sun is stone, and the moon earth.

Friend Meletus, you think that you are accusing Anaxagoras: and you have but a bad opinion of the judges, if you fancy them illiterate to such a degree as not to know that these doctrines are found in the books of Anaxagoras the Clazomenian, which are full of them. And so, forsooth, the youth are said to be taught them by Socrates, when there are not infrequently exhibitions of them at the theatre (price of admission one drachma at the most); and they might pay their money, and laugh at Socrates if he pretends to father these extraordinary views. And so, Meletus, you really think that I do not believe in any god?

I swear by Zeus that you believe absolutely in none at all.

Nobody will believe you, Meletus, and I am pretty sure that you do not believe yourself. I cannot help thinking, men of Athens, that Meletus is reckless and impudent, and that he has written this indictment in a spirit of mere wantonness and youthful bravado. Has he not compounded a riddle, thinking to try me? He said to himself:—I shall see whether the wise Socrates will discover my facetious contradiction, or whether I shall be able to deceive him and the rest of them. For he certainly does appear to me to contradict himself in the indictment as much as if he said that Socrates is guilty of not believing in the gods, and yet of believing in them—but this is not like a person who is in earnest.

I should like you, O men of Athens, to join me in examining what I conceive to be his inconsistency; and do you, Meletus, answer. And I must remind the audience of my request that they would not make a disturbance if I speak in my accustomed manner:

Did ever man, Meletus, believe in the existence of human things, and not of human beings? . . . I wish, men of Athens, that he would answer, and not be always trying to get up an interruption. Did ever any man believe in horsemanship, and not in horses? or in flute-playing, and not in flute-players? No, my

71. **Anaxagoras,** an Ionian philosopher, the first to propose the atomic theory of matter, and to suggest that the sun and moon were not gods but matter. Expelled from Athens 450 B.C. 77. **exhibitions . . . theatre.** Euripides and others incorporated the ideas of Anaxagoras in their plays.

friend; I will answer to you and to the court, as you refuse to answer for yourself. There is no man who ever did. But now please to answer the next question: Can a man believe in spiritual and divine agencies, and not in spirits or demigods?

He cannot.

How lucky I am to have extracted that answer, by the assistance of the court! But then you swear in the indictment that I teach and believe in divine
10 or spiritual agencies (new or old, no matter for that); at any rate, I believe in spiritual agencies,— so you say and swear in the affidavit; and yet if I believe in divine beings, how can I help believing in spirits or demigods;—must I not? To be sure I must; and therefore I may assume that your silence gives consent. Now what are spirits or demigods? are they not either gods or the sons of gods?

Certainly they are.

But this is what I call the facetious riddle in-
20 vented by you: the demigods or spirits are gods, and you say first that I do not believe in gods, and then again that I do believe in gods; that is, if I believe in demigods. For if the demigods are the illegitimate sons of gods, whether by the nymphs or by any other mothers, of whom they are said to be the sons— what human being will ever believe that there are no gods if they are the sons of gods? You might as well affirm the existence of mules, and deny that of horses and asses. Such nonsense, Meletus, could
30 only have been intended by you to make trial of me. You have put this into the indictment because you had nothing real of which to accuse me. But no one who has a particle of understanding will ever be convinced by you that the same men can believe in divine and superhuman things, and yet not believe that there are gods and demigods and heroes.

I have said enough in answer to the charge of Meletus: any elaborate defence is unnecessary; but I know only too well how many are the enmities
40 which I have incurred, and this is what will be my destruction if I am destroyed;—not Meletus, nor yet Anytus, but the envy and detraction of the world, which has been the death of many good men, and will probably be the death of many more; there is no danger of my being the last of them.

Some one will say: And are you not ashamed, Socrates, of a course of life which is likely to bring you to an untimely end? To him I may fairly answer: There you are mistaken: a man who is good for any-
50 thing ought not to calculate the chance of living or dying; he ought only to consider whether in doing anything he is doing right or wrong—acting the part of a good man or of a bad. Whereas, upon your view, the heroes who fell at Troy were not good for much, and the son of Thetis above all, who altogether despised danger in comparison with dis-

55. son of Thetis, Achilles.

grace; and when he was so eager to slay Hector, his goddess mother said to him, that if he avenged his companion Patroclus, and slew Hector, he would die
60 himself—"Fate," she said, in these or the like words, "waits for you next after Hector"; he, receiving this warning, utterly despised danger and death, and instead of fearing them, feared rather to live in dishonour, and not to avenge his friend. "Let me die forthwith," he replies, "and be avenged of my enemy, rather than abide here by the beaked ships, a laughing stock and a burden of the earth." Had Achilles any thought of death and danger? For wherever a man's place is, whether the place which
70 he has chosen or that in which he has been placed by a commander, there he ought to remain in the hour of danger; he should not think of death or of anything but of disgrace. And this, O men of Athens, is a true saying.

Strange, indeed, would be my conduct, O men of Athens, if I, who, when I was ordered by the generals whom you chose to command me at Potidaea and Amphipolis and Delium, remained where they placed me, like any other man, facing death—if now,
80 when, as I conceive and imagine, God orders me to fulfil the philosopher's mission of searching into myself and other men, I were to desert my post through fear of death, or any other fear; that would indeed be strange, and I might justly be arraigned in court for denying the existence of the gods, if I disobeyed the oracle because I was afraid of death, fancying that I was wise when I was not wise. For the fear of death is indeed the pretence of wisdom, and not real wisdom, being a pretence of knowing the un-
90 known; and no one knows whether death, which men in their fear apprehended to be the greatest evil, may not be the greatest good. Is not this ignorance of a disgraceful sort, the ignorance which is the conceit that a man knows what he does not know? And in this respect only I believe myself to differ from men in general, and may perhaps claim to be wiser than they are:—that whereas I know but little of the world below, I do not suppose that I know: but I do know that injustice and disobedience to a better,
100 whether God or man, is evil and dishonourable, and I will never fear or avoid a possible good rather than a certain evil. And therefore if you let me go now, and are not convinced by Anytus, who said that since I had been prosecuted I must be put to death; (or if not that I ought never to have been prosecuted at all); and that if I escape now, your sons will all be utterly ruined by listening to my words—if you say to me, Socrates, this time we will not mind Anytus, and you shall be let off, but upon one condition, that you are not to enquire and speculate in this
110 way any more, and that if you are caught doing so again you shall die;—if this was the condition on which you let me go, I should reply: Men of Athens,

I honour and love you; but I shall obey God rather than you, and while I have life and strength I shall never cease from the practice and teaching of philosophy, exhorting any one whom I meet and saying to him after my manner: You, my friend,—a citizen of the great and mighty and wise city of Athens,—are you not ashamed of heaping up the greatest amount of money and honour and reputation, and caring so little about wisdom and truth and the greatest improvement of the soul, which you never regard or heed at all? And if the person with whom I am arguing, says: Yes, but I do care; then I do not leave him or let him go at once; but I proceed to interrogate and examine and cross-examine him, and if I think that he has no virtue in him, but only says that he has, I reproach him with undervaluing the greater, and overvaluing the less. And I shall repeat the same words to every one whom I meet, young and old, citizen and alien, but especially to the citizens, inasmuch as they are my brethren. For know that this is the command of God; and I believe that no greater good has ever happened in the State than my service to the God. For I do nothing but go about persuading you all, old and young alike, not to take thought for your persons or your properties, but first and chiefly to care about the greatest improvement of the soul. I tell you that virtue is not given by money, but that from virtue comes money and every other good of man, public as well as private. This is my teaching, and if this is the doctrine which corrupts the youth, I am a mischievous person. But if any one says that this is not my teaching, he is speaking an untruth. Wherefore, O men of Athens, I say to you, do as Anytus bids or not as Anytus bids, and either acquit me or not; but whichever you do, understand that I shall never alter my ways, not even if I have to die many times.

Men of Athens, do not interrupt, but hear me; there was an understanding between us that you should hear me to the end: I have something more to say, at which you may be inclined to cry out; but I believe that to hear me will be good for you, and therefore I beg that you will not cry out. I would have you know, that if you kill such an one as I am, you will injure yourselves more than you will injure me. Nothing will injure me, not Meletus nor yet Anytus—they cannot, for a bad man is not permitted to injure a better than himself. I do not deny that Anytus may, perhaps, kill him, or drive him into exile, or deprive him of civil rights; and he may imagine, and others may imagine, that he is inflicting a great injury upon him: but there I do not agree. For the evil of doing as he is doing—the evil of unjustly taking away the life of another—is greater far.

And now, Athenians, I am not going to argue for my own sake, as you may think, but for yours, that you may not sin against the God by condemning me, who am his gift to you. For if you kill me you will not easily find a successor to me, who, if I may use such a ludicrous figure of speech, am a sort of gadfly, given to the State by God; and the State is a great and noble steed who is tardy in his motions owing to his very size, and requires to be stirred into life. I am that gadfly which God has attached to the State, and all day long and in all places am always fastening upon you, arousing and persuading and reproaching you. You will not easily find another like me, and therefore I would advise you to spare me. I dare say that you may feel out of temper (like a person who is suddenly awakened from sleep), and you think that you might easily strike me dead as Anytus advises, and then you would sleep on for the remainder of your lives, unless God in his care of you sent you another gadfly. When I say that I am given to you by God, the proof of my mission is this:—if I had been like other men, I should not have neglected all my own concerns or patiently seen the neglect of them during all these years, and have been doing yours, coming to you individually like a father or elder brother, exhorting you to regard virtue; such conduct, I say, would be unlike human nature. If I had gained anything, or if my exhortations had been paid, there would have been some sense in my doing so; but now, as you will perceive, not even the impudence of my accusers dares to say that I have ever exacted or sought pay of any one; of that they have no witness. And I have a sufficient witness to the truth of what I say—my poverty.

Some one may wonder why I go about in private giving advice and busying myself with the concerns of others, but do not venture to come forward in public and advise the State. I will tell you why. You have heard me speak at sundry times and in divers places of an oracle or sign which comes to me, and is the divinity which Meletus ridicules in the indictment. This sign, which is a kind of voice, first began to come to me when I was a child; it always forbids but never commands me to do anything which I am going to do. This is what deters me from being a politician. And rightly, as I think. For I am certain, O men of Athens, that if I had engaged in politics, I should have perished long ago, and done no good either to you or to myself. And do not be offended at my telling you the truth: for the truth is, that no man who goes to war with you or any other multitude, honestly striving against the many lawless and unrighteous deeds which are done in a State, will save his life; he who will fight for the right, if he would live even for a brief space, must have a private station and not a public one.

I can give you convincing evidence of what I say, not words only, but what you value far more—actions. Let me relate to you a passage of my own life which will prove to you that I should never have yielded to injustice from any fear of death and that "as I should have refused to yield" I must have died at once. I will tell you a tale of the courts, not very interesting perhaps, but nevertheless true. The only office of State which I ever held, O men of Athens, was that of senator: the tribe Antiochis, which is my tribe, had the presidency at the trial of the generals who had not taken up the bodies of the slain after the battle of Arginusae, and you proposed to try them in a body, contrary to law, as you all thought afterwards; but at the time I was the only one of the Prytanes who was opposed to the illegality, and I gave my vote against you; and when the orators threatened to impeach and arrest me, and you called and shouted, I made up my mind that I would run the risk, having law and justice with me, rather than take part in your injustice because I feared imprisonment and death. This happened in the days of the democracy. But when the oligarchy of the Thirty was in power, they sent for me and four others into the rotunda, and bade us bring Leon the Salaminian from Salamis, as they wanted to put him to death. This was a specimen of the sort of commands which they were always giving with the view of implicating as many as possible in their crimes; and then I showed, not in word only but in deed, that, if I may be allowed to use such an expression, I cared not a straw for death, and that my great and only care was lest I should do an unrighteous or unholy thing. For the strong arm of that oppressive power did not frighten me into doing wrong; and when we came out of the rotunda the other four went to Salamis and fetched Leon, but I went quietly home. For which I might have lost my life, had not the power of the Thirty shortly afterwards come to an end. And many will witness to my words.

Now, do you really imagine that I could have survived all these years, if I had led a public life, supposing that like a good man I had always maintained the right and had made justice, as I ought, the first thing? No, indeed, men of Athens, neither I nor any other man. But I have been always the same in all my actions, public as well as private, and never have I yielded any base compliance to those who are slanderously termed my disciples, or to any other. Not that I have any regular disciples. But if any one likes to come and hear me while I am pursuing my mission, whether he be young or old, he is not excluded. Nor do I converse only with those who pay; but any one, whether he be rich or poor, may ask and answer me and listen to my words; and whether he turns out to be a bad man or a good one, neither result can be justly imputed to me; for I never taught or professed to teach him anything. And if any one

14. **Prytanes,** a committee on public affairs.

says that he has ever learned or heard anything from me in private which all the world has not heard, let me tell you that he is lying.

But I shall be asked, Why do people delight in continually conversing with you? I have told you already, Athenians, the whole truth about this matter: they like to hear the cross-examination of the pretenders to wisdom; there is amusement in it. Now, this duty of cross-examining other men has been imposed upon me by God; and has been signified to me by oracles, visions, and in every way in which the will of divine power was ever intimated to any one. This is true, O Athenians; or, if not true, would be soon refuted. If I am or have been corrupting the youth, those of them who are now grown up and have become sensible that I gave them bad advice in the days of their youth should come forward as accusers, and take their revenge; or if they do not like to come themselves, some of their relatives, fathers, brothers, or other kinsmen, should say what evil their families have suffered at my hands. Now is their time. Many of them I see in the court. There is Crito, who is of the same age and of the same deme with myself, and there is Critobulus his son, whom I also see. Then again there is Lysanias of Sphettus, who is the father of Aeschines—he is present; and also there is Antiphon of Cephisus, who is the father of Epigenes; and there are the brothers of several who have associated with me. There is Nicostratus the son of Theosdotides, and the brother of Theodotus (now Theodotus himself is dead, and therefore he, at any rate, will not seek to stop him); and there is Paralus the son of Demodocus, who had a brother Theages; and Adeimantus the son of Ariston, whose brother Plato is present; and Aeantodorus, who is the brother of Apollodorus, whom I also see. I might mention a great many others, some of whom Meletus should have produced as witnesses in the course of his speech; and let him still produce them, if he has forgotten—I will make way for him. And let him say, if he has any testimony of the sort which he can produce. Nay, Athenians, the very opposite is the truth. For all these are ready to witness on behalf of the corrupter, of the injurer of their kindred, as Meletus and Anytus call me; not the corrupted youth only—there might have been a motive for that—but their uncorrupted elder relatives. Why should they too support me with their testimony? Why, indeed, except for the sake of truth and justice, and because they know that I am speaking the truth, and that Meletus is a liar.

Well, Athenians, this and the like of this is all the defence which I have to offer. Yet a word more. Perhaps there may be some one who is offended at me, when he calls to mind how he himself on a similar, or even a less serious occasion, prayed and entreated

91. **Plato;** one of Plato's very few allusions to himself in his works.

the judges with many tears, and how he produced his children in court, which was a moving spectacle, together with a host of relations and friends; whereas I, who am probably in danger of my life, will do none of these things. The contrast may occur to his mind, and he may be set against me, and vote in anger because he is displeased at me on this account. Now, if there be such a person among you,—mind, I do not say that there is,—to him I may fairly reply: My friend, I am a man, and like other men, a creature of flesh and blood, and not "of wood or stone," as Homer says; and I have a family, yes, and sons, O Athenians, three in number, one almost a man, and two others who are still young; and yet I will not bring any of them hither in order to petition you for an acquittal. And why not? Not from any self-assertion or want of respect for you. Whether I am or am not afraid of death is another question, of which I will not now speak. But, having regard to public opinion, I feel that such conduct would be discreditable to myself, and to you, and to the whole State. One who has reached my years, and who has a name for wisdom, ought not to demean himself. Whether this opinion of me be deserved or not, at any rate the world has decided that Socrates is in some way superior to other men. And if those among you who are said to be superior in wisdom and courage, and any other virtue, demean themselves in this way, how shameful is their conduct! I have seen men of reputation, when they have been condemned, behaving in the strangest manner: they seemed to fancy that they were going to suffer something dreadful if they died, and that they could be immortal if you only allowed them to live; and I think that such are a dishonour to the State, and that any stranger coming in would have said of them that the most eminent men of Athens, to whom the Athenians themselves give honour and command, are no better than women. And I say that these things ought not to be done by those of us who have a reputation; and if they are done, you ought not to permit them; you ought rather to show that you are far more disposed to condemn the man who gets up a doleful scene and makes the city ridiculous, than him who holds his peace.

But, setting aside the question of public opinion, there seems to be something wrong in asking a favour of a judge, and thus procuring an acquittal, instead of informing and convincing him. For his duty is, not to make a present of justice, but to give judgment; and he has sworn that he will judge according to the laws, and not according to his own good pleasure; and we ought not to encourage you, nor should you allow yourselves to be encouraged, in this habit of perjury—there can be no piety in that. Do not then require me to do what I consider dishonourable and impious and wrong, especially now, when I am being tried for impiety on the indictment of Meletus. For if, O men of Athens, by force of persuasion and entreaty I could overpower your oaths, then I should be teaching you to believe that there are no gods, and in defending should simply convict myself of the charge of not believing in them. But that is not so— far otherwise. For I do believe that there are gods, and in a sense higher than that in which any of my accusers believe in them. And to you and to God I commit my cause, to be determined by you as is best for you and me.

———

There are many reasons why I am not grieved, O men of Athens, at the vote of condemnation. I expected it, and am only surprised that the votes are so nearly equal; for I had thought that the majority against me would have been far larger; but now, had thirty votes gone over to the other side, I should have been acquitted. And I may say, I think, that I have escaped Meletus. I may say more; for without the assistance of Anytus and Lycon, any one may see that he would not have had a fifth part of the votes, as the law requires, in which case he would have incurred a fine of a thousand drachmae.

And so he proposes death as the penalty. And what shall I propose on my part, O men of Athens? Clearly that which is my due. And what is my due? What returns shall be made to the man who has never had the wit to be idle during his whole life; but has been careless of what the many care for— wealth, and family interests, and military offices, and speaking in the assembly, and magistracies, and plots, and parties. Reflecting that I was really too honest a man to be a politician and live, I did not go where I could do no good to you or to myself; but where I could do the greatest good privately to every one of you, thither I went, and sought to persuade every man among you that he must look to himself, and seek virtue and wisdom before he looks to his private interests, and look to the State before he looks to the interests of the State; and that this should be the order which he observes in all his actions. What shall be done to such an one? Doubtless some good thing, O men of Athens, if he has his reward; and the good should be of a kind suitable to him. What would be a reward suitable to a poor man who is your benefactor, and who desires leisure that he may instruct you? There can be no reward so fitting as maintenance in the Prytaneum, O men of Athens, a reward which he deserves far more than the citizen who has won the prize at Olympia in the horse or chariot race, whether the chariots were

67–68. . . . is best for you and me. A vote was taken at this point and Socrates was condemned by a small majority. He was then asked to propose his own penalty. 105. as maintenance . . . Prytaneum; that is, at public expense in the council hall.

drawn by two horses or by many. For I am in want, and he has enough; and he only gives you the appearance of happiness, and I give you the reality. And if I am to estimate the penalty fairly, I should say that maintenance in the Prytaneum is the just return.

Perhaps you think that I am braving you in what I am saying now, as in what I said before about the tears and prayers. But this is not so. I speak rather because I am convinced that I never intentionally wronged any one, although I cannot convince you —the time has been too short; if there were a law at Athens, as there is in other cities, that a capital cause should not be decided in one day, then I believe that I should have convinced you. But I cannot in a moment refute great slanders; and, as I am convinced that I never wronged another, I will assuredly not wrong myself. I will not say of myself that I deserve any evil, or propose any penalty. Why should I? Because I am afraid of the penalty of death which Meletus proposes? When I do not know whether death is a good or an evil, why should I propose a penalty which would certainly be an evil? Shall I say imprisonment? And why should I live in prison, and be the slave of the magistrate of the year —of the Eleven? Or shall the penalty be a fine, and imprisonment until the fine is paid? There is the same objection. I should have to lie in prison, for money I have none, and cannot pay. And if I say exile (and this may possibly be the penalty which you will affix), I must indeed be blinded by the love of life if I am so irrational as to expect that when you, who are my own citizens, cannot endure my discourses and words, and have found them so grievous and odious that you will have no more of them, others are likely to endure me. No, indeed, men of Athens, that is not very likely. And what a life should I lead, at my age, wandering from city to city, ever changing my place of exile, and always being driven out! For I am quite sure that wherever I go, there, as here, the young men will flock to me; and if I drive them away, their elders will drive me out at their request; and if I let them come, their fathers and friends will drive me out for their sakes.

Some one will say: Yes, Socrates, but cannot you hold your tongue, and then you may go into a foreign city, and no one will interfere with you? Now, I have great difficulty in making you understand my answer to this. For if I tell you that to do as you say would be a disobedience to the God, and therefore that I cannot hold my tongue, you will not believe that I am serious; and if I say again that daily to discourse about virtue, and of those other things about which you hear me examining myself and others, is the greatest good of man, and that the unexamined life is not worth living, you are still less likely to believe me. Yet I say what is true, although a

thing of which it is hard for me to persuade you. Also, I have never been accustomed to think that I deserve to suffer any harm. Had I money I might have estimated the offence at what I was able to pay, and not have been much the worse. But I have none, and therefore I must ask you to proportion the fine to my means. Well, perhaps I could afford a mina, and therefore I propose that penalty: Plato, Crito, Critobulus, and Apollodorus, my friends here, bid me say thirty minae, and they will be the sureties. Let thirty minae be the penalty; for which sum they will be ample security to you.

————

Not much time will be gained, O Athenians, in return for the evil name which you will get from the detractors of the city, who will say that you killed Socrates, a wise man; for they will call me wise, even although I am not wise, when they want to reproach you. If you had waited a little while, your desire would have been fulfilled in the course of nature. For I am far advanced in years, as you may perceive, and not far from death. I am speaking now not to all of you, but only to those who have condemned me to death. And I have another thing to say to them: You think that I was convicted because I had no words of the sort which would have procured my acquittal—I mean, if I had thought fit to leave nothing undone or unsaid. Not so; the deficiency which led to my conviction was not of words—certainly not. But I had not the boldness or impudence or inclination to address you as you would have liked me to do, weeping and wailing and lamenting, and saying and doing many things which you have been accustomed to hear from others, and which, as I maintain, are unworthy of me. I thought at the time that I ought not to do anything common or mean when in danger: nor do I now repent of the style of my defence; I would rather die having spoken after my manner, than speak in your manner and live. For neither in war nor yet at law ought I or any man to use every way of escaping death. Often in battle there can be no doubt that if a man will throw away his arms, and fall on his knees before his pursuers, he may escape death; and in other dangers there are other ways of escaping death, if a man is willing to say and do anything. The difficulty, my friends, is not to avoid death, but to avoid unrighteousness; for that runs faster than death. I am old and move slowly, and the slower runner has overtaken me, and my accusers are keen and quick, and the faster runner, who is unrighteousness, has overtaken them. And now I depart hence condemned by you to suffer the penalty of death,—they too go their ways condemned by the truth to suffer the penalty of vil-

69. . . . **ample security to you.** The insolence of this speech led the judges to condemn Socrates to death.

lainy and wrong; and I must abide by my award—let them abide by theirs. I suppose that these things may be regarded as fated,—and I think that they are well.

And now, O men who have condemned me, I would fain prophesy to you; for I am about to die, and in the hour of death men are gifted with prophetic power. And I prophesy to you who are my murderers, that immediately after my departure punishment far heavier than you have inflicted on me will surely await you. Me you have killed because you wanted to escape the accuser, and not to give an account of your lives. But that will not be as you suppose: far otherwise. For I say that there will be more accusers of you than there are now; accusers whom hitherto I have restrained: and as they are younger they will be more inconsiderate with you, and you will be more offended at them. If you think that by killing men you can prevent some one from censuring your evil lives, you are mistaken; that is not a way of escape which is either possible or honourable; the easiest and the noblest way is not to be disabling others, but to be improving yourselves. This is the prophecy which I utter before my departure to the judges who have condemned me.

Friends, who would have acquitted me, I would like also to talk with you about the thing which has come to pass, while the magistrates are busy, and before I go to the place at which I must die. Stay then a little, for we may as well talk with one another while there is time. You are my friends, and I should like to show you the meaning of this event which has happened to me. O my judges—for you I may truly call judges—I should like to tell you of a wonderful circumstance. Hitherto the divine faculty of which the internal oracle is the source has constantly been in the habit of opposing me even about trifles, if I was going to make a slip or error in any matter; and now as you see there has come upon me that which may be thought, and is generally believed to be, the last and worst evil. But the **oracle made no sign of opposition, either when I was** leaving my house in the morning, or when I was on my way to the court, or while I was speaking, at anything which I was going to say; and yet I have often been stopped in the middle of a speech, but now in nothing I either said or did touching the matter in hand has the oracle opposed me. What do I take to be the explanation of this silence? I will tell you. It is an intimation that what has happened to me is a good, and that those of us who think that death is an evil are in error. For the customary sign would surely have opposed me had I been going to evil and not to good.

Let us reflect in another way, and we shall see that there is great reason to hope that death is a good; for one of two things—either death is a state of nothingness and utter unconsciousness, or, as men say, there is a change and migration of the soul from this world to another. Now, if you suppose that there is no consciousness, but a sleep like the sleep of him who is undisturbed even by dreams, death will be an unspeakable gain. For if a person were to select the night in which his sleep was undisturbed even by dreams, and were to compare with this the other days and nights of his life, and then were to tell us how many days and nights he had passed in the course of his life better and more pleasantly than this one, I think that any man, I will not say a private man, but even the great king will not find many such days or nights, when compared with the others. Now, if death be of such a nature, I say that to die is gain; for eternity is then only a single night. But if death is the journey to another place, and there, as men say, all the dead abide, what good, O my friends and judges, can be greater than this? If, indeed, when the pilgrim arrives in the world below, he is delivered from the professors of justice in this world, and finds the true judges who are said to give judgment there, Minos and Rhadamanthus and Aeacus and Triptolemus, and other sons of God who were righteous in their own life, that pilgrimage will be worth making. What would not a man give if he might converse with Orpheus and Musaeus and Hesiod and Homer? Nay, if this be true, let me die again and again. I myself, too, shall have a wonderful interest in there meeting and conversing with Palamedes, and Ajax the son of Telamon, and any other ancient hero who has suffered death through an unjust judgment; and there will be no small pleasure, as I think, in comparing my own sufferings with theirs. Above all, I shall then be able to continue my search into true and false knowledge; as in this world, so also in the next; and I shall find out who is wise, and who pretends to be wise, and is not. What would not a man give, O judges, to be able to examine the leader of the great Trojan expedition; or Odysseus or Sisyphus, or numberless others, men and women too! What infinite delight would there be in conversing with them and asking them questions! In another world they do not put a man to death for asking questions: assuredly not. For besides being happier than we are, they will be immortal, if what is said is true.

Wherefore, O judges, be of good cheer about death, and know of a certainty, that no evil can happen to a good man, either in life or after death. He and his are not neglected by the gods; nor has my own approaching end happened by mere chance. But I see clearly that the time had arrived when it was better for me to die and be released from trouble: wherefore the oracle gave no sign. For which reason, also, I am not angry with my condemners, or with my accusers; they have done me no harm, although they did not mean to do me any good; and for this I may gently blame them.

Still, I have a favour to ask of them. When my sons are grown up, I would ask you, O my friends, to punish them; and I would have you trouble them, as I have troubled you, if they seem to care about riches, or anything, more than about virtue; or if they pretend to be something when they are really nothing,—then reprove them, as I have reproved you, for not caring about that for which they ought to care, and thinking that they are something when they are really nothing. And if you do this, both I and my sons will have received justice at your hands.

The hour of departure has arrived, and we go our ways—I to die, and you to live. Which is better God only knows.

Crito

Persons of the Dialogue:
Socrates *and* Crito

Scene: *The Prison of Socrates.*

socrates.

WHY have you come at this hour, Crito? it must be quite early?

CRITO. Yes, certainly.

SOCRATES. What is the exact time?

CRITO. The dawn is breaking.

SOCRATES. I wonder that the keeper of the prisoner would let you in.

CRITO. He knows me, because I often come, Socrates; moreover, I have done him a kindness.

SOCRATES. And are you only just arrived?

CRITO. No, I came some time ago.

SOCRATES. Then why did you sit and say nothing, instead of at once awakening me?

CRITO. I should not have liked myself, Socrates, to be in such great trouble and unrest as you are—indeed I should not: I have been watching with amazement your peaceful slumbers; and for that reason I did not awake you, because I wished to minimize the pain. I have always thought you to be of a happy disposition; but never did I see anything like the easy, tranquil manner in which you bear this calamity.

SOCRATES. Why, Crito, when a man has reached my age he ought not to be repining at the approach of death.

CRITO. And yet other old men find themselves in similar misfortunes, and age does not prevent them from repining.

Crito. Translated by Benjamin Jowett. Published by The Clarendon Press, Oxford. Crito is a faithful follower of Socrates, who here receives his master's instructions on the duty of obedience to the laws.

SOCRATES. That is true. But you have not told me why you come at this early hour.

CRITO. I come to bring you a message which is sad and painful; not, as I believe, to yourself, but to all of us who are your friends, and saddest of all to me.

SOCRATES. What? Has the ship come from Delos, on the arrival of which I am to die?

CRITO. No, the ship has not actually arrived, but she will probably be here to-day, as persons who have come from Sunium tell me that they left her there; and therefore to-morrow, Socrates, will be the last day of your life.

SOCRATES. Very well, Crito; if such is the will of God, I am willing; but my belief is that there will be a delay of a day.

CRITO. Why do you think so?

SOCRATES. I will tell you. I am to die on the day after the arrival of the ship.

CRITO. Yes; that is what the authorities say.

SOCRATES. But I do not think that the ship will be here until to-morrow; this I infer from a vision which I had last night, or rather only just now, when you fortunately allowed me to sleep.

CRITO. And what was the nature of the vision?

SOCRATES. There appeared to me the likeness of a woman, fair and comely, clothed in bright raiment, who called to me and said: O Socrates,

"The third day hence to fertile Phthia shalt thou go."

CRITO. What a singular dream, Socrates!

SOCRATES. There can be no doubt about the meaning, Crito, I think.

CRITO. Yes; the meaning is only too clear. But, oh! my beloved Socrates, let me entreat you once more to take my advice and escape. For if you die I shall not only lose a friend who can never be replaced, but there is another evil: people who do not know you and me will believe that I might have saved you if I had been willing to give money, but that I did not care. Now, can there be a worse disgrace than this —that I should be thought to value money more than the life of friend? For the many will not be persuaded that I wanted you to escape, and that you refused.

SOCRATES. But why, my dear Crito, should we care about the opinion of the many? Good men, and they are the only persons who are worth considering, will think of these things truly as they occurred.

CRITO. But you see, Socrates, that the opinion of the many must be regarded, for what is now happening shows that they can do the greatest evil to any one who has lost their good opinion.

SOCRATES. I only wish it were so, Crito; and that

50–51. **Has the ship . . . die.** Every year a sacred embassy was sent to the island of Delos. From the time this ship left Athens until it returned, the city was in a state of purification, and no public execution could take place. Since the embassy departed during Socrates' trial, his death had to be delayed until its return.

the many could do the greatest evil; for then they would also be able to do the greatest good—and what a fine thing this would be! But in reality they can do neither; for they cannot make a man either wise or foolish; and whatever they do is the result of chance.

CRITO. Well, I will not dispute with you; but please to tell me, Socrates, whether you are not acting out of regard to me and your other friends: are you not afraid that if you escape from prison we may get into trouble with the informers for having stolen you away, and lose either the whole or a great part of our property; or that even a worse evil may happen to us? Now, if you fear on our account, be at ease; for in order to save you, we ought surely to run this, or even a greater risk; be persuaded, then, and do as I say.

SOCRATES. Yes, Crito, that is one fear which you mention, but by no means the only one.

CRITO. Fear not—there are persons who are willing to get you out of prison at no great cost; and as for the informers, they are far from being exorbitant in their demands—a little money will satisfy them. My means, which are certainly ample, are at your service, and if you have a scruple about spending all mine, here are strangers who will give you the use of theirs; and one of them, Simmias the Theban, has brought a large sum of money for this very purpose; and Cebes and many others are prepared to spend their money in helping you to escape. I say, therefore, do not hesitate on our account, and do not say, as you did in the court, that you will have a difficulty in knowing what to do with yourself anywhere else. For men will love you in other places to which you may go, and not in Athens only; there are friends of mine in Thessaly, if you like to go to them, who will value and protect you, and no Thessalian will give you any trouble. Nor can I think that you are at all justified, Socrates, in betraying your own life when you might be saved; in acting thus you are playing into the hands of your enemies, who are hurrying on your destruction. And further I should say that you are deserting your own children; for you might bring them up and educate them; instead of which you go away and leave them, and they will have to take their chance; and if they do not meet with the usual fate of orphans, there will be small thanks to you. No man should bring children into the world who is unwilling to persevere to the end in their nurture and education. But you appear to be choosing the easier part, not the better and manlier, which would have been more becoming in one who professes to care for virtue in all his actions, like yourself. And, indeed, I am ashamed not only of you, but of us who are your friends, when I reflect that the whole business will be attributed entirely to our want of courage. The trial need never have come on, or might have been managed differently; and this last act, or crowning folly, will seem to have occurred through our negligence and cowardice, who might have saved you, if we had been good for anything; and you might have saved yourself, for there was no difficulty at all. See now, Socrates, how sad and discreditable are the consequences, both to us and you. Make up your mind, then, or rather have your mind already made up, for the time of deliberation is over, and there is only one thing to be done, which must be done this very night, and if we delay at all will be no longer practicable or possible; I beseech you therefore, Socrates, be persuaded by me, and do as I say.

SOCRATES. Dear Crito, your zeal is invaluable, if a right one; but if wrong, the greater the zeal the greater the danger; and therefore we ought to consider whether I shall or shall not do as you say. For I am and always have been one of those natures who must be guided by reason, whatever the reason may be which upon reflection appears to me to be the best; and now that this chance has befallen me, I cannot repudiate my own words: the principles which I have hitherto honoured and revered I still honour, and unless we can at once find other and better principles, I am certain not to agree with you; no, not even if the power of the multitude could inflict many more imprisonments, confiscations, deaths, frightening us like children with hobgoblin terrors. What will be the fairest way of considering the question? Shall I return to your old argument about the opinions of men?—we were saying that some of them are to be regarded, and others not. Now, were we right in maintaining this before I was condemned? And has the argument which was once good now proved to be talk for the sake of talking—mere childish nonsense? That is what I want to consider with your help, Crito:—whether, under my present circumstances, the argument appears to be in any way different or not; and is to be allowed by me or disallowed. That argument, which, as I believe, is maintained by many persons of authority, was to the effect, as I was saying, that the opinions of some men are to be regarded, and of other men not to be regarded. Now you, Crito, are not going to die to-morrow—at least, there is no human probability of this—and therefore you are disinterested and not liable to be deceived by the circumstances in which you are placed. Tell me, then, whether I am right in saying that some opinions, and the opinions of some men only, are to be valued, and that other opinions, and the opinions of other men, are not to be valued. I ask you whether I was right in maintaining this?

CRITO. Certainly.

SOCRATES. The good are to be regarded, and not the bad?

CRITO. Yes.

SOCRATES. And the opinions of the wise are good, and the opinions of the unwise are evil?

CRITO. Certainly.

SOCRATES. And what was said about another matter? Is the pupil who devotes himself to the practice of gymnastics supposed to attend to the praise and blame and opinion of every man, or of one man only —his physician or trainer, whoever he may be?

CRITO. Of one man only.

SOCRATES. And he ought to fear the censure and welcome the praise of that one only, and not of the many?

CRITO. Clearly so.

SOCRATES. And he ought to act and train, and eat and drink in the way which seems good to his single master who has understanding, rather than according to the opinion of all other men put together?

CRITO. True.

SOCRATES. And if he disobeys and disregards the opinion and approval of the one, and regards the opinion of the many who have no understanding, will he not suffer?

CRITO. Certainly he will.

SOCRATES. And what will the evil be, whither tending and what affecting, in the disobedient person?

CRITO. Clearly, affecting the body; that is what is destroyed by the evil.

SOCRATES. Very good; and is not this true, Crito, of other things which we need not separately enumerate? In questions of just and unjust, fair and foul, good and evil, which are the subjects of our present consultation, ought we to follow the opinion of the many and to fear them; or the opinion of the one man who has understanding? ought we not to fear and reverence him more than all the rest of the world: and if we desert him shall we not destroy and injure that principle in us which may be assumed to be improved by justice and deteriorated by injustice; —there is such a principle?

CRITO. Certainly there is, Socrates.

SOCRATES. Take a parallel instance:—if, acting under the advice of those who have no understanding, we destroy that which is improved by health and is deteriorated by disease, would life be worth having? And that which has been destroyed is—the body?

CRITO. Yes.

SOCRATES. Could we live, having an evil and corrupted body?

CRITO. Certainly not.

SOCRATES. And will life be worth having, if that higher part of man be destroyed, which is improved by justice and depraved by injustice? Do we suppose that principle, whatever it may be in man, which has to do with justice and injustice, to be inferior to the body?

CRITO. Certainly not.

SOCRATES. More honourable than the body?

CRITO. Far more.

SOCRATES. Then, my friend, we must not regard what the many say of us: but what he, the one man who has understanding of just and unjust, will say. and what the truth will say. And therefore you begin in error when you advise that we should regard the opinion of the many about just and unjust, good and evil, honourable and dishonourable.—"Well," some one will say, "but the many can kill us."

CRITO. Yes, Socrates; that will clearly be the answer.

SOCRATES. And it is true: but still I find with surprise that the old argument is unshaken as ever. And I should like to know whether I may say the same of another proposition—that not life, but a good life, is to be chiefly valued?

CRITO. Yes, that also remains unshaken.

SOCRATES. And a good life is equivalent to a just and honourable one—that holds also?

CRITO. Yes, it does.

SOCRATES. From these premises I proceed to argue the question whether I ought or ought not to try to escape without the consent of the Athenians: and if I am clearly right in escaping, then I will make the attempt; but if not, I will abstain. The other considerations which you mention, of money and loss of character and the duty of educating one's children, are, I fear, only the doctrines of the multitude, who would be as ready to restore people to life, if they were able, as they are to put them to death— and with as little reason. But now, since the argument has thus far prevailed, the only question which remains to be considered is, whether we shall do rightly either in escaping or in suffering others to aid in our escape and paying them in money and thanks, or whether in reality we shall not do rightly; and if the latter, then death or any other calamity which may ensue on my remaining here must not be allowed to enter into the calculation.

CRITO. I think that you are right, Socrates; how then shall we proceed?

SOCRATES. Let us consider the matter together, and do you either refute me if you can, and I will be convinced; or else cease, my dear friend, from repeating to me that I ought to escape against the wishes of the Athenians: for I highly value your attempts to persuade me to do so, but I may not be persuaded against my own better judgment. And now please to consider my first position, and try how you can best answer me.

CRITO. I will.

SOCRATES. Are we to say that we are never intentionally to do wrong, or that in one way we ought and in another way we ought not to do wrong, or is doing wrong always evil and dishonourable, as I was

just now saying, and as has been already acknowledged by us? Are all our former admissions which
were made within a few days to be thrown away?
And have we, at our age, been earnestly discoursing
with one another all our life long only to discover
that we are no better than children? Or, in spite of
the opinion of the many, and in spite of consequences whether better or worse, shall we insist on
the truth of what was then said, that injustice is
10 always an evil and dishonour to him who acts unjustly? Shall we say so or not?

CRITO. Yes.

SOCRATES. Then we must do no wrong?

CRITO. Certainly not.

SOCRATES. Nor when injured injure in return, as
the many imagine; for we must injure no one at all?

CRITO. Clearly not.

SOCRATES. Again, Crito, may we do evil?

CRITO. Surely not, Socrates.

20 SOCRATES. And what of doing evil in return for
evil, which is the morality of the many—is that just
or not?

CRITO. Not just.

SOCRATES. For doing evil to another is the same as
injuring him?

CRITO. Very true.

SOCRATES. Then we ought not to retaliate or render evil for evil to any one, whatever evil we may
have suffered from him. But I would have you con-
30 sider, Crito, whether you really mean what you are
saying. For this opinion has never been held, and
never will be held, by any considerable number of
persons; and those who are agreed and those who
are not agreed upon this point have no common
ground, and can only despise one another when they
see how widely they differ. Tell me, then, whether
you agree with and assent to my first principle, that
neither injury nor retaliation nor warding off evil
by evil is ever right. And shall that be the premiss of
40 our argument? Or do you decline and dissent from
this? For so I have ever thought, and continue to
think; but, if you are of another opinion, let me hear
what you have to say. If, however, you remain of the
same mind as formerly, I will proceed to the next step.

CRITO. You may proceed, for I have not changed
my mind.

SOCRATES. Then I will go on to the next point,
which may be put in the form of a question:—
Ought a man to do what he admits to be right, or
50 ought he to betray the right?

CRITO. He ought to do what he thinks right.

SOCRATES. But if this is true, what is the application? In leaving the prison against the will of the
Athenians, do I wrong any? or rather do I not wrong
those whom I ought least to wrong? Do I not desert
the principles which were acknowledged by us to
be just—what do you say?

CRITO. I cannot tell, Socrates; for I do not know.

SOCRATES. Then consider the matter in this way:
—Imagine that I am about to play truant (you may
call the proceeding by any name which you like),
and the laws and the government come and interrogate me: "Tell us, Socrates," they say; "what are
you about? are you not going by an act of yours to
overturn us—the laws, and the whole State, as far
as in you lies? Do you imagine that a State can subsist and not be overthrown, in which the decisions of
law have no power, but are set aside and trampled
upon by individuals?" What will be our answer,
Crito, to these and the like words? Any one, and
especially a rhetorician, will have a good deal to say
on behalf of the law which requires a sentence to be
carried out. He will argue that this law should not
be set aside; and shall we reply, "Yes; but the State
has injured us and given an unjust sentence." Suppose I say that?

CRITO. Very good, Socrates.

SOCRATES. "And was that our agreement with
you?" the law would answer; "or were you to abide
by the sentence of the State?" And if I were to express my astonishment at their words, the law would
probably add: "Answer, Socrates, instead of opening your eyes—you are in the habit of asking and
answering questions. Tell us,—What complaint have
you to make against us which justifies you in attempting to destroy us and the State? In the first
place did we not bring you into existence? Your
father married your mother by our aid and begat
you. Say whether you have any objection to urge
against those of us who regulate marriage?" None,
I should reply. "Or against those of us who after
birth regulate the nurture and education of children,
in which you also were trained? Were not the laws,
which have the charge of education, right in commanding your father to train you in music and
gymnastic?" Right, I should reply. "Well, then, since
you were brought into the world and nurtured and
educated by us, can you deny in the first place that
you are our child and slave, as your fathers were
before you? And if this is true, you are not on equal
terms with us; nor can you think that you have a
right to do to us what we are doing to you. Would
you have any right to strike or revile or do any other
evil to your father or your master, if you had one,
because you have been struck or reviled by him, or
received some other evil at his hands?—you would
not say this? And because we think right to destroy
you, do you think that you have any right to destroy
us in return, and your country as far as in you lies?
Will you, O professor of true virtue, pretend that
you are justified in this? Has a philosopher like you
failed to discover that our country is more to be
valued and higher and holier far than mother or
father or any ancestor, and more to be regarded in

the eyes of the gods and of men of understanding? also to be soothed, and gently and reverently entreated when angry, even more than a father, and either to be persuaded, or if not persuaded, to be obeyed? And when we are punished by her, whether with imprisonment or stripes, the punishment is to be endured in silence; and if she lead us to wounds or death in battle, thither we follow as is right; neither may any one yield or retreat or leave his rank, but whether in battle or in a court of law, or in any other place, he must do what his city and his country order him; or he must change their view of what is just: and if he may do no violence to his father or mother, much less may he do violence to his country." What answer shall we make to this, Crito? Do the laws speak truly, or do they not?

CRITO. I think that they do.

SOCRATES. Then the laws will say: "Consider, Socrates, if we are speaking truly that in your present attempt you are going to do us an injury. For, having brought you into the world, and nurtured and educated you, and given you and every other citizen a share in every good which we had to give, we further proclaim to any Athenian by the liberty which we allow him, that if he does not like us when he has become of age and has seen the ways of the city, and made our acquaintance, he may go where he pleases and take his goods with him. None of us laws will forbid him or interfere with him. Any one who does not like us and the city, and who wants to emigrate to a colony or to any other city, may go where he likes, retaining his property. But he who has experience of the manner in which we order justice and administer the State, and still remains, has entered into an implied contract that he will do as we command him. And he who disobeys us is, as we maintain, thrice wrong; first, because in disobeying us he is disobeying his parents; secondly, because we are the authors of his education; thirdly, because he has made an agreement with us that he will duly obey our commands; and he neither obeys them nor convinces us that our commands are unjust; and we do not rudely impose them, but give him the alternative of obeying or convincing us;— that is what we offer, and he does neither.

"These are the sort of accusations to which, as we were saying, you, Socrates, will be exposed if you accomplish your intentions; you, above all other Athenians." Suppose now I ask, why I rather than anybody else? they will justly retort upon me that I above all other men have acknowledged the agreement. "There is clear proof," they will say, "Socrates, that we and the city were not displeasing to you. Of all Athenians you have been the most constant resident in the city, which, as you never leave, you may be supposed to love. For you never went out of the city either to see the games, except once when you went to the Isthmus, or to any other place unless when you were on military service; nor did you travel as other men do. Nor had you any curiosity to know other States or their laws: your affections did not go beyond us and our State; we were your special favourites, and you acquiesced in our government of you; and here in this city you begat your children, which is a proof of your satisfaction. Moreover, you might in the course of the trial, if you had liked, have fixed the penalty at banishment; the State which refuses to let you go now would have let you go then. But you pretended that you preferred death to exile, and that you were not unwilling to die. And now you have forgotten these fine sentiments, and pay no respect to us, the laws, of whom you are the destroyer; and are doing what only a miserable slave would do, running away and turning your back upon the compacts and agreements which you made as a citizen. And, first of all, answer this very question: Are we right in saying that you agreed to be governed according to us in deed, and not in word only? Is that true or not?" How shall we answer, Crito? Must we not assent?

CRITO. We cannot help it, Socrates.

SOCRATES. Then will they not say: "You, Socrates, are breaking the covenants and agreements which you made with us at your leisure, not in any haste or under any compulsion or deception, but after you have had seventy years to think of them, during which time you were at liberty to leave the city, if we were not to your mind, or if our covenants appeared to you to be unfair. You had your choice, and might have gone either to Lacedaemon or Crete, both which States are often praised by you for their good government, or to some other Hellenic or foreign State. Whereas you, above all other Athenians, seemed to be so fond of the State, or, in other words, of us, her laws (and who would care about a State which has no laws?), that you never stirred out of her; the halt, the blind, the maimed were not more stationary in her than you were. And now you run away and forsake your agreements. Not so, Socrates, if you will take our advice; do not make yourself ridiculous by escaping out of the city.

"For just consider, if you transgress and err in this sort of way, what good will you do either to yourself or to your friends? That your friends will be driven into exile and deprived of citizenship, or will lose their property, is tolerably certain; and you yourself, if you fly to one of the neighbouring cities, as, for example, Thebes or Megara, both of which are well governed, will come to them as an enemy, Socrates, and their government will be against you, and all patriotic citizens will cast an evil eye upon you as a subverter of the laws, and you will confirm in the minds of the judges the justice of their own condemnation of you. For he who is a corrupter of the laws is more than likely to be a corrupter of the young and foolish portion of mankind. Will you then flee from well-ordered cities and virtuous men? and is existence worth having on these terms? Or will you go to them without shame, and talk to them, Socrates? And what will you say to them? What you say here about virtue and justice and institutions and laws being the best things among men? Would that be decent of you? Surely not. But if you go away from well-governed States to Crito's friends in Thessaly, where there is great disorder and licence, they will be charmed to hear the tale of your escape from prison, set off with ludicrous particulars of the manner in which you were wrapped in a goatskin or some other disguise, and metamorphosed as the manner is of runaways; but will there be no one to remind you that in your old age you were not ashamed to violate the most sacred laws from a miserable desire of a little more life? Perhaps not, if you keep them in a good temper; but if they are out of temper you will hear many degrading things; you will live, but how?—as the flatterer of all men, and the servant of all men; and doing what?—eating and drinking in Thessaly, having gone abroad in order that you may get a dinner. And where will be your fine sentiments about justice and virtue? Say that you wish to live for the sake of your children—you want to bring them up and educate them—will you take them into Thessaly and deprive them of Athenian citizenship? Is this the benefit which you will confer upon them? Or are you under the impression that they will be better cared for and educated here if you are still alive, although absent from them; for your friends will take care of them? Do you fancy that if you are an inhabitant of Thessaly they will take care of them, and if you are an inhabitant of the other world that they will not take care of them? Nay; but if they who call themselves friends are good for anything, they will—to be sure they will.

"Listen, then, Socrates, to us who have brought you up. Think not of life and children first, and of justice afterwards, but of justice first, that you may be justified before the princes of the world below. For neither will you nor any that belong to you be happier or holier or juster in this life, or happier in another, if you do as Crito bids. Now you depart in innocence, a sufferer and not a doer of evil; a victim, not of the laws but of men. But if you go forth, returning evil for evil, and injury for injury, breaking the covenants and agreements which you have made with us, and wronging those whom you ought least of all to wrong, that is to say, yourself, your friends, your country, and us, we shall be angry with you while you live, and our brethren, the laws in the world below, will receive you as an enemy; for they will know that you have done your best to destroy us. Listen, then, to us and not to Crito."

This, dear Crito, is the voice which I seem to hear murmuring in my ears, like the sound of the flute in the ears of the mystic; that voice, I say, is humming in my ears, and prevents me from hearing any other. And I know that anything more which you may say will be vain. Yet speak, if you have anything to say.

CRITO. I have nothing to say, Socrates.

SOCRATES. Leave me then, Crito, to fulfil the will of God, and to follow whither he leads.

Phaedo

. . . OF THAT upper earth which is under the heaven, I can tell you a charming tale, Simmias, which is well worth hearing.

And we, Socrates, replied Simmias, shall be charmed to listen to you.

The tale, my friend, he said, is as follows:—In the first place, the earth, when looked at from above, is in appearance streaked like one of those balls which have leather coverings in twelve pieces, and is decked with various colours, of which the colours used by painters on earth are in a manner samples. But there the whole earth is made up of them, and they are brighter far and clearer than ours; there is a purple of wonderful lustre, also the radiance of gold, and the white which is in the earth is whiter than any chalk or snow. Of these and other colours the earth is made up, and they are more in number and fairer than the eye of man has ever seen; the very hollows (of which I was speaking) filled with air and water have a colour of their own, and are seen like light gleaming amid the diversity of the other colours, so that the whole presents a single and continuous appearance of variety in unity. And in this fair region everything that grows—trees, and flowers, and fruits—are in a like degree fairer than any here; and there are hills, having stones in them in a like degree smoother, and more transparent, and fairer in colour than our highly valued emeralds and sardonyxes and jaspers, and other gems, which are but minute fragments of them: for there all the stones are like our precious stones, and fairer still. The reason is, that they are pure, and not, like our precious stones, infected or corroded by the corrupt briny elements which coagulate among us, and which breed foulness and disease both in earth and stones, as well as in animals and plants. They are the jewels of the upper earth which also shines with gold and silver and the like, and they are set in the light of day and are large and abundant and in all places, making the earth a sight to gladden the beholder's

*Phaedo.*⁵ Translated by Benjamin Jowett. Published by The Clarendon Press, Oxford. Phaedo, a disciple of Socrates, tells a friend how Socrates, shortly before he drank the hemlock, discoursed with his disciples on the immortality of the soul and the nature of the other world.

eye. And there are animals and men, some in a middle region, others dwelling about the air as we dwell about the sea; others in islands which the air flows round, near the continent; and, in a word, the air is used by them as the water and the sea are by us, and the ether is to them what the air is to us. Moreover, the temperament of their seasons is such that they have no disease, and live much longer than we do, and have sight and hearing and smell, and all the other senses, in far greater perfection, in the same proportion that air is purer than water or the ether than air. Also they have temples and sacred places in which the gods really dwell, and they hear their voices and receive their answers, and are conscious of them and hold converse with them; and they see the sun, moon, and stars as they truly are, and their other blessedness is of a piece with this.

Such is the nature of the whole earth, and of the things which are around the earth; and there are divers regions in the hollows on the faces of the globe everywhere, some of them deeper and more extended than that which we inhabit, others deeper but with a narrower opening than ours, and some are shallower and also wider. All have numerous perforations, and there are passages broad and narrow in the interior of the earth, connecting them with one another; and there flows out of and into them, as into basins, a vast tide of water, and huge subterranean streams of perennial rivers, and springs hot and cold, and a great fire, and great rivers of fire, and streams of liquid mud, thin or thick (like the rivers of mud in Sicily, and the lava streams which follow them), and the regions about which they happen to flow are filled up with them. And there is a swinging or seesaw in the interior of the earth which moves all this up and down, and is due to the following cause:—There is a chasm which is the vastest of them all, and pierces right through the whole earth; this is that chasm which Homer describes in the words,—

"Far off, where is the inmost depth beneath the
    earth";

and which he in other places, and many other poets, have called Tartarus. And the seesaw is caused by the streams flowing into and out of this chasm, and they each have the nature of the soil through which they flow. And the reason why the streams are always flowing in and out, is that the watery element has no bed or bottom, but is swinging and surging up and down, and the surrounding wind and air do the same; they follow the water up and down, hither and thither, over the earth—just as in the act of respiration the air is always in process of inhalation and exhalation,—and the wind swinging with the water in and out produces fearful and irresistible blasts: when the waters retire with a rush into the lower parts of the earth, as they are called, they flow through the earth in those regions, and fill them up like water raised by a pump, and then when they leave those regions and rush back hither, they again fill the hollows here, and when these are filled, flow through subterranean channels and find their way to their several places, forming seas, and lakes, and rivers, and springs. Thence they again enter the earth, some of them making a long circuit into many lands, others going to a few places and not so distant; and again fall into Tartarus, some at a point a good deal lower than that at which they rose, and others not much lower, but all in some degree lower than the point from which they came. And some burst forth again on the opposite side, and some on the same side, and some wind round the earth with one or many folds like the coils of a serpent, and descend as far as they can, but always return and fall into the chasm. The rivers flowing in either direction can descend only to the centre and no further, for opposite to the rivers is a precipice.

Now these rivers are many, and mighty, and diverse, and there are four principal ones, of which the greatest and outermost is that called Oceanus, which flows round the earth in a circle; and in the opposite direction flows Acheron, which passes under the earth through desert places into the Acherusian lake: this is the lake to the shores of which the souls of the many go when they are dead, and after waiting an appointed time, which is to some a longer and to some a shorter time, they are sent back to be born again as animals. The third river passes out between the two, and near the place of outlet pours into a vast region of fire, and forms a lake larger than the Mediterranean Sea, boiling with water and mud; and proceeding muddy and turbid, and winding about the earth, comes, among other places, to the extremities of the Acherusian lake, but mingles not with the waters of the lake, and after making many coils about the earth plunges into Tartarus at a deeper level. This is that Pyriphlegethon, as the stream is called, which throws up jets of fire in different parts of the earth. The fourth river goes out on the opposite side, and falls first of all into a wild and savage region, which is all of a dark blue colour, like lapis lazuli; and this is that river which is called the Stygian river, and falls into and forms the Lake Styx, and after falling into the lake and receiving strange powers in the waters, passes under the earth, winding round in the opposite direction, and comes near the Acherusian lake from the opposite side to Pyriphlegethon. And the water of this river too mingles with no other, but flows round in a circle and falls into Tartarus over against Pyriphlegethon; and the name of the river, as the poets say, is Cocytus.

Such is the nature of the other world; and when

the dead arrive at the place to which the genius of each severally guides them, first of all, they have sentence passed upon them, as they have lived well and piously or not. And those who appear to have lived neither well nor ill, go to the river Acheron, and embarking in any vessels which they may find, are carried in them to the lake, and there they dwell and are purified of their evil deeds, and having suffered the penalty of the wrongs which they have done to others, they are absolved, and receive the rewards of their good deeds, each of them according to his deserts. But those who appear to be incurable by reason of the greatness of their crimes—who have committed many and terrible deeds of sacrilege, murders foul and violent, or the like—such are hurled into Tartarus which is their suitable destiny, and they never come out. Those again who have committed crimes, which, although great, are not irremediable—who in a moment of anger, for example, have done some violence to a father or a mother, and have repented for the remainder of their lives, or, who have taken the life of another under the like extenuating circumstances—these are plunged into Tartarus, the pains of which they are compelled to undergo for a year, but at the end of the year the wave casts them forth—mere homicides by way of Cocytus, parricides and matricides by Pyriphlegethon—and they are borne to the Acherusian lake, and there they lift up their voices and call upon the victims whom they have slain or wronged, to have pity on them, and to be kind to them, and let them come out into the lake. And if they prevail, then they come forth and cease from their troubles; but if not, they are carried back again into Tartarus and from thence into the rivers unceasingly, until they obtain mercy from those whom they have wronged: for that is the sentence inflicted upon them by their judges. Those too who have been preeminent for holiness of life are released from this earthly prison, and go to their pure home which is above, and dwell in the purer earth; and of these, such as have duly purified themselves with philosophy live henceforth altogether without the body, in mansions fairer still which may not be described, and of which the time would fail me to tell.

Wherefore, Simmias, seeing all these things, what ought not we to do that we may obtain virtue and wisdom in this life? Fair is the prize, and the hope great!

A man of sense ought not to say, nor will I be very confident, that the description which I have given of the soul and her mansions is exactly true. But I do say that, inasmuch as the soul is shown to be immortal, he may venture to think, not improperly or unworthily, that something of the kind is true. The venture is a glorious one, and he ought to comfort himself with words like these, which is the reason why I lengthen out the tale. Wherefore, I say, let a man be of good cheer about his soul, who having cast away the pleasures and ornaments of the body as alien to him and working harm rather than good, has sought after the pleasures of knowledge; and has arrayed the soul, not in some foreign attire, but in her own proper jewels, temperance, and justice, and courage, and nobility, and truth—in these adorned she is ready to go on her journey to the world below, when her hour comes. You, Simmias and Cebes, and all other men, will depart at some time or other. Me already, as a tragic poet would say, the voice of fate calls. Soon I must drink the poison; and I think that I had better repair to the bath first, in order that the women may not have the trouble of washing my body after I am dead.

When he had done speaking, Crito said: And have you any commands for us, Socrates—anything to say about your children, or any other matter in which we can serve you?

Nothing particular, Crito, he replied: only, as I have always told you, take care of yourselves; that is a service which you may be ever rendering to me and mine and to all of us, whether you promise to do so or not. But if you have no thought for yourselves, and care not to walk according to the rule which I have prescribed for you, not now for the first time, however much you may profess or promise at the moment, it will be of no avail.

We will do our best, said Crito: And in what way shall we bury you?

In any way that you like; but you must get hold of me, and take care that I do not run away from you. Then he turned to us, and added with a smile: —I cannot make Crito believe that I am the same Socrates who have been talking and conducting the argument; he fancies that I am the other Socrates whom he will soon see, a dead body—and he asks, How shall he bury me? And though I have spoken many words in the endeavour to show that when I have drunk the poison I shall leave you and go to the joys of the blessed,—these words of mine, with which I was comforting you and myself, have had, as I perceive, no effect upon Crito. And therefore I want you to be surety for me to him now, as at the trial he was surety to the judges for me: but let the promise be of another sort; for he was surety for me to the judges that I would remain, and you must be my surety to him that I shall not remain, but go away and depart; and then he will suffer less at my death, and not be grieved when he sees my body being burned or buried. I would not have him sorrow at my hard lot, or say at the burial, Thus we lay out Socrates, or, Thus we follow him to the grave or bury him; for false words are not only evil in themselves, but they inflict the soul with evil. Be of good cheer then, my dear Crito, and say that you are burying my body only, and do with that whatever is usual, and what you think best.

When he had spoken these words, he arose and went into a chamber to bathe; Crito followed him and told us to wait. So we remained behind, talking and thinking of the subject of discourse, and also of the greatness of our sorrow; he was like a father of whom we were being bereaved, and we were about to pass the rest of our lives as orphans. When he had taken the bath his children were brought to him (he had two young sons and an elder one); and the women of his family also came, and he talked to them and gave them a few directions in the presence of Crito; then he dismissed them and returned to us.

Now the hour of sunset was near, for a good deal of time had passed while he was within. When he came out, he sat down with us again after his bath, but not much was said. Soon the jailer, who was the servant of the Eleven, entered and stood by him, saying:—To you, Socrates, whom I know to be the noblest and gentlest and best of all who ever came to this place, I will not impute the angry feeling of other men, who rage and swear at me, when, in obedience to the authorities, I bid them drink the poison —indeed, I am sure that you will not be angry with me; for others, as you are aware, and not I, are to blame. And so fare you well, and try to bear lightly what must needs be—you know my errand. Then bursting into tears he turned away and went out.

Socrates looked at him and said: I return your good wishes, and will do as you bid. Then turning to us, he said, How charming the man is: since I have been in prison he has always been coming to see me, and at times he would talk to me, and was as good to me as could be, and now see how generously he sorrows on my account. We must do as he says, Crito; and therefore let the cup be brought, if the poison is prepared: if not, let the attendant prepare some.

Yet, said Crito, the sun is still upon the hill-tops, and I know that many a one has taken the draught late, and after the announcement has been made to him, he has eaten and drunk, and enjoyed the society of his beloved: do not hurry—there is time enough.

Socrates said: Yes, Crito, and they of whom you speak are right in so acting, for they think that they will be gainers by the delay; but I am right in not following their example, for I do not think that I should gain anything by drinking the poison a little later; I should only be ridiculous in my own eyes for sparing and saving a life which is already forfeit. Please then to do as I say, and not to refuse me.

Crito made a sign to the servant, who was stand-ing by; and he went out, and having been absent for some time, returned with the jailer carrying the cup of poison. Socrates said: You, my good friend, who are experienced in these matters, shall give me directions how I am to proceed. The man answered: You have only to walk about until your legs are heavy, and then to lie down, and the poison will act. At the same time he handed the cup to Socrates, who in the easiest and gentlest manner, without the least fear or change of colour or feature, looking at the man with all his eyes, as his manner was, took the cup and said: What do you say about making a libation out of this cup to any god? May I, or not? The man answered: We only prepare, Socrates, just so much as we deem enough. I understand, he said: but I may and must ask the gods to prosper my journey from this to the other world—even so—and so be it according to my prayer. Then raising the cup to his lips, quite readily and cheerfully he drank off the poison. And hitherto most of us had been able to control our sorrow; but now when we saw him drinking, and saw too that he had finished the draught, we could no longer forbear, and in spite of myself my own tears were flowing fast; so that I covered my face and wept, not for him, but at the thought of my own calamity in having to part from such a friend. Nor was I the first; for Crito, when he found himself unable to restrain his tears, had got up, and I followed; and at that moment, Apollodorus, who had been weeping all the time, broke out in a loud and passionate cry which made cowards of us all. Socrates alone retained his calmness: What is this strange outcry? he said. I sent away the women mainly in order that they might not misbehave in this way, for I have been told that a man should die in peace. Be quiet then, and have patience. When we heard his words we were ashamed, and refrained our tears; and he walked about until, as he said, his legs began to fail, and then he lay on his back, according to directions, and the man who gave him the poison now and then looked at his feet and legs; and after a while he pressed his foot hard, and asked him if he could feel; and he said, No; and then his leg, and so upwards and upwards, and showed us that he was cold and stiff. And he felt them himself, and said: When the poison reaches the heart, that will be the end. He was beginning to grow cold about the groin, when he uncovered his face, for he had covered himself up, and said—they were his last words—he said: Crito, I owe a cock to Asclepius; will you remember to pay the debt? The debt shall be paid, said Crito; is there anything else? There was no answer to this question; but in a minute or two a movement was heard, and the attend-

106. **I owe a cock.** . . . A cock was the usual sacrifice to Asclepius, god of healing, for recovery from an illness.

---

ants uncovered him; his eyes were set, and Crito closed his eyes and mouth.

Such was the end, Echecrates, of our friend; concerning whom I may truly say, that of all men of his time whom I have known, he was the wisest and justest and best.

Republic

BOOK VII

And now, I said, let me show in a figure how far our nature is enlightened or unenlightened:—Behold! human beings living in an underground den, which has a mouth open towards the light and reaching all along the den; here they have been from their childhood, and have their legs and necks chained so that they cannot move, and can only see before them, being prevented by the chains from turning round their heads. Above and behind them a fire is blazing at a distance, and between the fire and the prisoners there is a raised way; and you will see, if you look, a low wall built along the way, like the screen which marionette players have in front of them, over which they show the puppets.

I see.

And do you see, I said, men passing along the wall carrying all sorts of vessels, and statues and figures of animals made of wood and stone and various materials, which appear over the wall? Some of them are talking, others silent.

You have shown me a strange image, and they are strange prisoners.

Like ourselves, I replied; and they see only their own shadows, or the shadows of one another, which the fire throws on the opposite wall of the cave.

True, he said; how could they see anything but the shadows if they were never allowed to move their heads?

And of the objects which are being carried in like manner they would only see the shadows?

Yes, he said.

And if they were able to converse with one another, would they not suppose that they were naming what was actually before them?

Very true.

And suppose further that the prison had an echo which came from the other side, would they not be sure to fancy when one of the passers-by spoke that the voice which they heard came from the passing shadow?

No question, he replied.

To them, I said, the truth would be literally nothing but the shadows of the images.

That is certain.

And now look again, and see what will naturally follow if the prisoners are released and disabused of their error. At first, when any of them is liberated and compelled suddenly to stand up and turn his neck round and walk and look towards the light, he will suffer sharp pains; the glare will distress him, and he will be unable to see the realities of which in his former state he had seen the shadows; and then conceive someone saying to him, that what he saw before was an illusion, but that now, when he is approaching nearer to being and his eye is turned towards more real existence, he has a clearer vision,—what will be his reply? And you may further imagine that his instructor is pointing to the objects as they pass and requiring him to name them,—will he not be perplexed? Will he not fancy that the shadows which he formerly saw are truer than the objects which are now shown to him?

Far truer.

And if he is compelled to look straight at the light, will he not have a pain in his eyes which will make him turn away to take refuge in the objects of vision which he can see, and which he will conceive to be in reality clearer than the things which are now being shown to him?

True, he said.

And suppose once more, that he is reluctantly dragged up a steep and rugged ascent, and held fast until he is forced into the presence of the sun himself, is he not likely to be pained and irritated? When he approaches the light his eyes will be dazzled, and he will not be able to see anything at all of what are now called realities.

Not all in a moment, he said.

He will require to grow accustomed to the sight of the upper world. And first he will see the shadows best, next the reflections of men and other objects in the water, and then the objects themselves; then he will gaze upon the light of the moon and the stars and the spangled heaven; and he will see the sky and the stars by night better than the sun or the light of the sun by day?

Certainly.

Last of all he will be able to see the sun, and not mere reflections of him in the water, but he will see him in his own proper place, and not in another; and he will contemplate him as he is.

Certainly.

He will then proceed to argue that this is he who gives the season and the years, and is the guardian of all that is in the visible world, and in a certain way the cause of all things which he and his fellows have been accustomed to behold?

Republic. Translated by Benjamin Jowett. Published by The Clarendon Press, Oxford.
7. **I said.** . . . Plato has Socrates present the famous apologue of the cave of Glaucon.

1 : 267

Clearly, he said, he would first see the sun and then reason about him.

And when he remembered his old habitation, and the wisdom of the den and his fellow-prisoners, do you not suppose that he would felicitate himself on the change, and pity them?

Certainly, he would.

And if they were in the habit of conferring honours among themselves on those who were quickest to observe the passing shadows and to remark which of them went before, and which followed after, and which were together; and who were therefore best able to draw conclusions as to the future, do you think that he would care for such honours and glories, or envy the possessors of them? Would he not say with Homer,

'Better to be the poor servant of a poor master,'

and to endure anything, rather than think as they do and live after their manner?

Yes, he said, I think that he would rather suffer anything than entertain these false notions and live in this miserable manner.

Imagine once more, I said, such an one coming suddenly out of the sun to be replaced in his old situation; would he not be certain to have his eyes full of darkness?

To be sure, he said.

And if there were a contest, and he had to compete in measuring the shadows with the prisoners who had never moved out of the den, while his sight was still weak, and before his eyes had become steady (and the time which would be needed to acquire this new habit of sight might be very considerable), would he not be ridiculous? Men would say of him that up he went and down he came without his eyes; and that it was better not even to think of ascending; and if any one tried to loose another and lead him up to the light, let them only catch the offender, and they would put him to death.

No question, he said.

This entire allegory, I said, you may now append, dear Glaucon, to the previous argument; the prison-house is the world of sight, the light of the fire is the sun, and you will not misapprehend me if you interpret the journey upwards to be the ascent of the soul into the intellectual world according to my poor belief, which, at your desire, I have expressed— whether rightly or wrongly God knows. But, whether true or false, my opinion is that in the world of knowledge the idea of good appears last of all, and is seen only with an effort; and, when seen, is also inferred to be the universal author of all things beautiful and right, parent of light and of the lord of light in this visible world, and the immediate source of reason and truth in the intellectual; and that this is the power upon which he who would act

rationally either in public or private life must have his eye fixed.

I agree, he said, as far as I am able to understand you.

Moreover, I said, you must not wonder that those who attain to this beatific vision are unwilling to descend to human affairs; for their souls are ever hastening into the upper world where they desire to dwell; which desire of theirs is very natural, if our allegory may be trusted.

Yes, very natural.

And is there anything surprising in one who passes from divine contemplations to the evil state of man, misbehaving himself in a ridiculous manner; if, while his eyes are blinking and before he has become accustomed to the surrounding darkness, he is compelled to fight in courts of law, or in other places, about the images or the shadows of images of justice, and is endeavouring to meet the conceptions of those who have never yet seen absolute justice?

Anything but surprising, he replied.

Anyone who has common sense will remember that the bewilderments of the eyes are of two kinds, and arise from two causes, either from coming out of the light or from going into the light, which is true of the mind's eye, quite as much as of the bodily eye; and he who remembers this when he sees anyone whose vision is perplexed and weak, will not be too ready to laugh; he will first ask whether that soul of man has come out of the brighter life, and is unable to see because unaccustomed to the dark, or having turned from darkness to the day is dazzled by excess of light. And he will count the one happy in his condition and state of being, and he will pity the other; or, if he have a mind to laugh at the soul which comes from below into the light, there will be more reason in this than in the laugh which greets him who returns from above out of the light into the den.

That, he said, is a very just distinction.

But then, if I am right, certain professors of education must be wrong when they say that they can put a knowledge into the soul which was not there before, like sight into blind eyes.

They undoubtedly say this, he replied.

Whereas, our argument shows that the power and capacity of learning exists in the soul already; and that just as the eye was unable to turn from darkness to light without the whole body, so too the instrument of knowledge can only by the movement of the whole soul be turned from the world of becoming into that of being, and learn by degrees to endure the sight of being, and of the brightest and best of being, or in other words, of the good.

Very true.

And must there not be some art which will effect

conversion in the easiest and quickest manner; not implanting the faculty of sight, for that exists already, but has been turned in the wrong direction, and is looking away from the truth?

Yes, he said, such an art may be presumed.

And whereas the other so-called virtues of the soul seem to be akin to bodily qualities, for even when they are not originally innate they can be implanted later by habit and exercise, the virtue of wisdom more than anything else contains a divine element which always remains, and by this conversion is rendered useful and profitable; or, on the other hand, hurtful and useless. Did you never observe the narrow intelligence flashing from the keen eye of a clever rogue—how eager he is, how clearly his paltry soul sees the way to his end; he is the reverse of blind, but his keen eye-sight is forced into the service of evil, and he is mischievous in proportion to his cleverness?

Very true, he said.

But what if there had been a circumcision of such natures in the days of their youth; and they had been severed from those sensual pleasures, such as eating and drinking, which, like leaden weights, were attached to them at their birth, and which drag them down and turn the vision of their souls upon the things that are below—if, I say, they had been released from these impediments and turned in the opposite direction, the very same faculty in them would have seen the truth as keenly as they see what their eyes are turned to now. . . .

BOOK III

. . . You are aware, I suppose, that all mythology and poetry is a narration of events, either past, present, or to come?

Certainly, he replied.

And narration may be either simple narration, or imitation, or a union of the two?

That again, he said, I do not quite understand.

I fear that I must be a ridiculous teacher when I have so much difficulty in making myself apprehended. Like a bad speaker, therefore, I will not take the whole of the subject, but will break a piece off in illustration of my meaning. You know the first lines of the Iliad, in which the poet says that Chryses prayed Agamemnon to release his daughter, and that Agamemnon flew into a passion with him; whereupon Chryses, failing of his object, invoked the anger of the God against the Achaeans. Now as far as these lines,

32. **You are aware.** . . . Socrates is supposedly presenting to Adeimantus his (actually Plato's) theory of art and its place in an ideal republic.

'And he prayed all the Greeks, but especially the two sons of Atreus, the chiefs of the people,' the poet is speaking in his own person; he never leads us to suppose that he is any one else. But in what follows he takes the person of Chryses, and then he does all that he can to make us believe that the speaker is not Homer, but the aged priest himself. And in this double form he has cast the entire narrative of the events which occurred at Troy and in Ithaca and throughout the Odyssey.

Yes.

And a narrative it remains both in the speeches which the poet recites from time to time and in the intermediate passages?

Quite true.

But when the poet speaks in the person of another, may we not say that he assimilates his style to that of the person who, as he informs you, is going to speak?

Certainly.

And this assimilation of himself to another, either by the use of voice or gesture, is the imitation of the person whose character he assumes?

Of course.

Then in this case the narrative of the poet may be said to proceed by way of imitation?

Very true.

Or, if the poet everywhere appears and never conceals himself, then again the imitation is dropped, and his poetry becomes simple narration. However, in order that I may make my meaning quite clear, and that you may no more say, 'I don't understand,' I will show how the change might be effected. If Homer had said, 'The priest came, having his daughter's ransom in his hands, supplicating the Achaeans, and above all the kings'; and then if, instead of speaking in the person of Chryses, he had continued in his own person, the words would have been, not imitation, but simple narration. The passage would have run as follows (I am no poet, and therefore I drop the metre), 'The priest came and prayed the gods on behalf of the Greeks that they might capture Troy and return safely home, but begged that they would give him back his daughter, and take the ransom which he brought, and respect the God. Thus he spoke, and the other Greeks revered the priest and assented. But Agamemnon was wroth, and bade him depart and not come again, lest the staff and chaplets of the God should be of no avail to him—the daughter of Chryses should not be released, he said—she should grow old with him in Argos. And then he told him to go away and not to provoke him, if he intended to get home unscathed. And the old man went away in fear and silence, and, when he had left the camp, he called upon Apollo by his many names, reminding him of everything which he had done pleasing to him, whether in building his temples, or in offering sacrifice, and praying that his good deeds might be returned to him, and that the Achaeans might expiate his tears by the arrows of the god,'—and so on. In this way the whole becomes simple narrative.

I understand, he said.

Or you may suppose the opposite case—that the intermediate passages are omitted, and the dialogue only left.

That also, he said, I understand; you mean, for example, as in tragedy.

You have conceived my meaning perfectly; and if I mistake not, what you failed to apprehend before is now made clear to you, that poetry and mythology are, in some cases, wholly imitative—instances of this are supplied by tragedy and comedy; there is likewise the opposite style, in which the poet is the only speaker—of this the dithyramb affords the best example; and the combination of both is found in epic, and in several other styles of poetry. Do I take you with me?

Yes, he said; I see now what you meant.

I will ask you to remember also what I began by saying, that we had done with the subject and might proceed to the style.

Yes, I remember.

In saying this, I intended to imply that we must come to an understanding about the mimetic art,—whether the poets, in narrating their stories, are to be allowed by us to imitate, and if so, whether in whole or in part, and if the latter, in what parts; or should all imitation be prohibited?

You mean, I suspect, to ask whether tragedy and comedy shall be admitted into our State?

Yes, I said; but there may be more than this in question: I really do not know as yet, but whither the argument may blow, thither we go.

And go we will, he said.

Then, Adeimantus, let me ask you whether our guardians ought to be imitators; or rather, has not this question been decided by the rule already laid down that one man can only do one thing well, and not many; and that if he attempt many, he will altogether fail of gaining much reputation in any?

Certainly.

And this is equally true of imitation; no one man can imitate many things as well as he would imitate a single one?

He cannot.

Then the same person will hardly be able to play a serious part in life, and at the same time to be an imitator and imitate many other parts as well; for even when two species of imitation are nearly allied, the same persons cannot succeed in both, as, for example, the writers of tragedy and comedy—did you not just now call them imitations?

Yes, I did; and you are right in thinking that the same persons cannot succeed in both.

Any more than they can be rhapsodists and actors at once?

True.

Neither are comic and tragic actors the same; yet all these things are but imitations.

They are so.

And human nature, Adeimantus, appears to have been coined into yet smaller pieces, and to be as incapable of imitating many things well, as of performing well the actions of which the imitations are copies.

Quite true, he replied. . . .

And therefore when any one of these pantomimic gentlemen, who are so clever that they can imitate anything, comes to us, and makes a proposal to exhibit himself and his poetry, we will fall down and worship him as a sweet and holy and wonderful being; but we must also inform him that in our State such as he are not permitted to exist; the law will not allow them. And so when we have anointed him with myrrh, and set a garland of wool upon his head, we shall send him away to another city. For we mean to employ for our souls' health the rougher and severer poet or story-teller, who will imitate the style of the virtuous only, and will follow those models which we prescribed at first when we began the education of our soldiers. . . . We would not have our guardians grow up amid images of moral deformity, as in some noxious pasture, and there browse and feed upon many a baneful herb and flower day by day, little by little, until they silently gather a festering mass of corruption in their own soul. Let our artists rather be those who are gifted to discern the true nature of the beautiful and graceful; then will our youth dwell in a land of health, amid fair sights and sounds, and receive the good in everything; and beauty, the effluence of fair works, shall flow into the eye and ear, like a health-giving breeze from a purer region, and insensibly draw the soul from earliest years into likeness and sympathy with the beauty of reason. . . .

BOOK X

Can you tell me what imitation is? for I really do not know.

A likely thing, then, that I should know.

Why not? for the duller eye may often see a thing sooner than the keener.

Very true, he said; but in your presence, even if I had any faint notion, I could not muster courage to utter it. Will you enquire yourself?

Well then, shall we begin the enquiry in our usual manner: Whenever a number of individuals have a

101. **Can you tell me.** . . . Plato has Socrates enlarge upon his theory of art to Glaucon.

common name, we assume them to have also a corresponding idea or form:—do you understand me?

I do.

Let us take any common instance; there are beds and tables in the world—plenty of them, are there not?

Yes.

But there are only two ideas or forms of them—one the idea of a bed, the other of a table.

True.

And the maker of either of them makes a bed or he makes a table for our use, in accordance with the idea—that is our way of speaking in this and similar instances—but no artificer makes the ideas themselves: how could he?

Impossible.

And there is another artist,—I should like to know what you would say of him.

Who is he?

One who is the maker of all the works of all other workmen.

What an extraordinary man!

Wait a little, and there will be more reason for your saying so. For this is he who is able to make not only vessels of every kind, but plants and animals, himself and all other things—the earth and heaven, and the things which are in heaven or under the earth; he makes the god also.

He must be a wizard and no mistake.

Oh! you are incredulous, are you? Do you mean that there is no such maker or creator, or that in one sense there might be a maker of all these things but in another not? Do you see that there is a way in which you could make them all yourself?

What way?

An easy way enough; or rather, there are many ways in which the feat might be quickly and easily accomplished, none quicker than that of turning a mirror round and round—you would soon enough make the sun and the heavens, and the earth and yourself, and other animals and plants, and all the other things of which we were just now speaking, in the mirror.

Yes, he said; but they would be appearances only.

Very good, I said, you are coming to the point now. And the painter too is, as I conceive, just such another—a creator of appearances, is he not?

Of course.

But then I suppose you will say that what he creates is untrue. And yet there is a sense in which the painter also creates a bed?

Yes, he said, but not a real bed.

And what of the maker of the bed? were you not saying that he too makes, not the idea which, according to our view, is the essence of the bed, but only a particular bed?

Yes, I did.

Then if he does not make that which exists he cannot make true existence, but only some semblance of existence; and if any one were to say that the work of the maker of the bed, or of any other workman, has real existence, he could hardly be supposed to be speaking the truth.

At any rate, he replied, philosophers would say that he was not speaking the truth.

No wonder, then, that his work too is an indistinct expression of truth.

No wonder.

Suppose now that by the light of the examples just offered we enquire who this imitator is?

If you please.

Well then, here are three beds: one existing in nature, which is made by God, as I think that we may say—for no one else can be the maker?

No.

There is another which is the work of the carpenter?

Yes.

And the work of the painter is a third?

Yes.

Beds, then, are of three kinds, and there are three artists who superintend them: God, the maker of the bed, and the painter?

Yes, there are three of them.

God, whether from choice or from necessity, made one bed in nature and one only; two or more such ideal beds neither ever have been nor ever will be made by God.

Why is that?

Because even if He had made but two, a third would still appear behind them which both of them would have for their idea, and that would be the ideal bed and not the two others.

Very true, he said.

God knew this, and He desired to be the real maker of a real bed, not a particular maker of a particular bed, and therefore He created a bed which is essentially and by nature one only.

So we believe.

Shall we, then, speak of Him as the natural author or maker of the bed?

Yes, he replied; inasmuch as by the natural process of creation He is the author of this and of all other things.

And what shall we say of the carpenter—is not he also the maker of the bed?

Yes.

But would you call the painter a creator and maker?

Certainly not.

Yet if he is not the maker, what is he in relation to the bed?

I think, he said, that we may fairly designate him as the imitator of that which the others make.

Good, I said; then you call him who is third in the descent from nature an imitator?

Certainly, he said.

And the tragic poet is an imitator, and therefore, like all other imitators, he is thrice removed from the king and from the truth?

That appears to be so.

Then about the imitator we are agreed. And what about the painter?—I would like to know whether he may be thought to imitate that which originally exists in nature, or only the creations of artists?

The latter.

As they are or as they appear? you have still to determine this.

What do you mean?

I mean, that you may look at a bed from different points of view, obliquely or directly or from any other point of view, and the bed will appear different, but there is no difference in reality. And the same of all things.

Yes, he said, the difference is only apparent.

Now let me ask you another question: Which is the art of painting designed to be—an imitation of things as they are, or as they appear—of appearance or of reality?

Of appearance.

Then the imitator, I said, is a long way off the truth, and can do all things because he lightly touches on a small part of them, and that part an image. For example: A painter will paint a cobbler, carpenter, or any other artist, though he knows nothing of their arts; and, if he is a good artist, he may deceive children or simple persons, when he shows them his picture of a carpenter from a distance, and they will fancy that they are looking at a real carpenter.

Certainly.

And whenever any one informs us that he has found a man who knows all the arts, and all things else that anybody knows, and every single thing with a higher degree of accuracy than any other man— whoever tells us this, I think that we can only imagine him to be a simple creature who is likely to have been deceived by some wizard or actor whom he met, and whom he thought all-knowing, because he himself was unable to analyze the nature of knowledge and ignorance and imitation.

Most true.

And so, when we hear persons saying that the tragedians, and Homer, who is at their head, know all the arts and all things human, virtue as well as vice, and divine things too, for that the good poet cannot compose well unless he knows his subject, and that he who has not this knowledge can never be a poet, we ought to consider whether here also there may not be a similar illusion. Perhaps they may have come across imitators and been deceived by them; they may not have remembered when they saw their works that these were but imitations thrice removed from the truth, and could easily be made without any knowledge of the truth, because they are appearances only and not realities? Or, after all, they may be in the right, and poets do really know the things about which they seem to the many to speak so well?

The question, he said, should by all means be considered.

Now do you suppose that if a person were able to make the original as well as the image, he would seriously devote himself to the image-making branch? Would he allow imitation to be the ruling principle of his life, as if he had nothing higher in him?

I should say not.

The real artist, who knew what he was imitating, would be interested in realities and not in imitations; and would desire to leave as memorials of himself works many and fair; and, instead of being the author of encomiums, he would prefer to be the theme of them. . . .

But we have not yet brought forward the heaviest count in our accusation:—the power which poetry has of harming even the good (and there are very few who are not harmed), is surely an awful thing?

Yes, certainly, if the effect is what you say.

Hear and judge: The best of us, as I conceive, when we listen to a passage of Homer, or one of the tragedians, in which he represents some pitiful hero who is drawling out his sorrows in a long oration, or weeping, and smiting his breast—the best of us, you know, delight in giving way to sympathy, and are in raptures at the excellence of the poet who stirs our feelings most.

Yes, of course I know.

But when any sorrow of our own happens to us, then you may observe that we pride ourselves on the opposite quality—we would fain be quiet and patient; this is the manly part, and the other which delighted us in the recitation is now deemed to be the part of a woman.

Very true, he said.

Now can we be right in praising and admiring another who is doing that which any one of us would abominate and be ashamed of in his own person?

No, he said, that is certainly not reasonable.

Nay, I said, quite reasonable from one point of view.

What point of view?

If you consider, I said, that when in misfortune we feel a natural hunger and desire to relieve our sorrow by weeping and lamentation, and that this feeling which is kept under control in our own calamities is satisfied and delighted by the poets;—the

better nature in each of us, not having been sufficiently trained by reason or habit, allows the sympathetic element to break loose because the sorrow
is another's; and the spectator fancies that there can
be no disgrace to himself in praising and pitying any
one who comes telling him what a good man he is,
and making a fuss about his troubles; he thinks that
the pleasure is a gain, and why should he be supercilious and lose this and the poem too? Few persons
ever reflect, as I should imagine, that from the evil
of other men something of evil is communicated to
themselves. And so the feeling of sorrow which has
gathered strength at the sight of the misfortunes of
others is with difficulty repressed in our own. .

How very true!

And does not the same hold also of the ridiculous?
There are jests which you would be ashamed to
make yourself, and yet on the comic stage, or indeed in private, when you hear them, you are
greatly amused by them, and are not at all disgusted at their unseemliness;—the case of pity is
repeated;—there is a principle in human nature
which is disposed to raise a laugh, and this which
you once restrained by reason, because you were
afraid of being thought a buffoon, is now let out
again; and having stimulated the risible faculty at
the theatre, you are betrayed unconsciously to yourself into playing the comic poet at home.

Quite true, he said.

And the same may be said of lust and anger and
all the other affections, of desire and pain and pleasure, which are held to be inseparable from every
action—in all of them poetry feeds and waters the
passions instead of drying them up; she lets them
rule, although they ought to be controlled, if mankind are ever to increase in happiness and virtue.

I cannot deny it.

Therefore, Glaucon, I said, whenever you meet
with any of the eulogists of Homer declaring that he
has been the educator of Hellas, and that he is profitable for education and for the ordering of human
things, and that you should take him up again and
again and get to know him and regulate your
whole life according to him, we may love and honour those who say these things—they are excellent
people, as far as their lights extend; and we are
ready to acknowledge that Homer is the greatest of
poets and first of tragedy writers (but we must remain firm in our conviction that hymns to the gods
and praises of famous men are the only poetry
which ought to be admitted into our State). For if
you go beyond this and allow the honeyed muse to
enter, either in epic or lyric verse, not law and reason of mankind, which by common consent have
ever been deemed best, but pleasure and pain will
be the rulers in our State. . . .

Aristotle

384–322 B.C.

Little of Aristotle's work belongs to literature,
and yet he was the most influential of all ancient
philosophers from his day until the seventeenth century
of Christian Europe. Only the rise of modern scientific
method undermined the prestige of his contributions to
knowledge. In ancient times he was known also as a man
of letters, on the strength of philosophical dialogues similar to Plato's. But only one of his literary works, *The Constitution of Athens,* has been preserved, and it is a minor
achievement. His reputation as a thinker and scientist
rests on bare lecture notes written for his conferences at
the Lyceum in Athens. Though they were long accepted
as the very foundation of human knowledge, they have
no literary value.

Aristotle was a student and teacher at the Academy
during the last twenty years of Plato's life. Unlike his
master, he was much less interested in mathematics, metaphysics, and ethics than in biological and physical science. His father, physician to the king of Macedonia, had
fostered his curiosity about science from childhood. Rumors of friction between Plato and Aristotle are probably
exaggerated, but it is clear that their views diverged
sharply. Plato was a poet and idealist, given to speculation and even mysticism. Aristotle was a hard-headed,
practical man, content to record facts with accuracy and
good sense.

After Plato's death Aristotle lived for three years with
Hermeias, tyrant of Atarneus, whose niece he married,
and later served as tutor to Alexander the Great through
the years preceding the youth's accession to the Macedonian throne. To his influence may be ascribed Alexander's
enthusiastic dissemination of Greek science and culture
through his Eastern empire. But Aristotle returned to
Athens and, when the headship of the Academy was not
offered to him, founded a rival university, the Lyceum,
in the grove of Apollo Lyceius. It was an enclosed place
with gardens between the buildings, and since much of
the instruction was given on walks around the enclosure,
Aristotle and his followers came to be called the Peripatetics. Here he taught for eighteen years and composed
the majority of his works, until the death of Alexander
forced him into exile as a Macedonian. He died a year
later.

Aristotle was the first Western scholar to attempt an
encyclopedic classification of human knowledge. Indeed,
he was also the last, because in clarifying the divisions of
science and philosophy and indicating the channels that
later research would follow, he began the specialization
of learning that soon made encyclopedic knowledge impossible for one man. He was conscious of the highly
tentative nature of his pioneer work and would hardly
have approved the later elevation of his findings to the
sacrosanct position of law. In the Christian era his works

were widely known in the Latin translation of Boethius and were gradually grafted with all their errors upon Christian doctrine. Although a source of enlightenment, his works impeded scientific progress because of their hallowed status.

The breadth of Aristotle's interests is reflected in his forty-seven extant treatises, in themselves only a fraction of the hundreds attributed to him. By far the most extensive, if also the least valuable today, are the treatises on various sciences—physics, mechanics, astronomy, meteorology, psychology, and especially biology. But it is his philosophical writings that have endured. His many works on logic are still the conventional authority, though they have been severely challenged in our century by "non-Aristotelian" logicians. His *Metaphysics* presents his familiar distinction between matter and form in opposition to Plato's doctrine of Ideas. In the *Politics* he comes close to Plato's *Republic* in his picture of an ideal city-state founded on aristocratic principles and state education. The lay reader knows Aristotle best through his treatises on ethics (the *Nichomachean Ethics* and *Eudemian Ethics*) and aesthetics (the *Rhetoric* and *Poetics*).

The *Nichomachean Ethics,* named for his son Nichomachus, is the most famous of all books on morals and our best source for the Greek ideal of conduct. According to Aristotle, the good life is the happy life, but happiness does not spring from mere pleasure, health, fame, or money. These important things are only means to an end. Happiness results from acting in harmony with one's nature and one's circumstances, as intelligence dictates. Right action leading to happiness is usually a mean between two extremes of possible action; in other words, the right path of virtue lies between two wrong paths. Intelligence is needed to determine this sensible mean of conduct, but eventually right action becomes a habit with the virtuous man, who is consequently happy. Aristotle illustrates his celebrated doctrine of the Golden Mean with numerous applications to everyday living, but for the best examples we should turn to Roman Horace and our eighteenth-century classicists, who made it their law of life.

The influence of the *Poetics* too was strongest in the Classical Age two thousand years after Aristotle. He intended it as an analysis of Greek tragedy (together with comedy and epic) as practice had molded it, but the authoritarian critics of the later era made it a canon of right composition with which to condemn as heretics any playwrights who violated its laws. The section on comedy is lost, and the allusions to the epic are brief; the *Poetics* is primarily a handbook of tragedy.

Aristotle accepts Plato's view of art as imitation and does not condemn it for being such. Indeed, the whole purpose of tragedy, according to Aristotle, is to call forth the emotions of pity and fear by a spectacle that imitates tragic reality and thus purge the spectator of his accumulation of these upsetting emotions. This is Aristotle's famous doctrine of the *catharsis* (purging effect) of tragedy. The classical doctrine of the dramatic unities of time, place, and action is merely inferred from Aristotle, because he prescribes only unity of action (or a single plot). His definition of the proper hero for tragedy as an essentially good man possessed of a tragic fault that proves his undoing * is readily applied to Shakespeare's heroes as well as to Oedipus and is still substantially true of tragic characters in modern drama. Indeed, despite the different theater that inspired Aristotle's treatise, it is surprising to observe how much of his advice is still illustrated in the drama of our day, not through conscious imitation but merely as sound practice in reaching an audience. Of course many other ideas in Aristotle's works are outmoded, but his career and his logic and his actual contributions to knowledge are an abiding inspiration to those who seek the truth.

Nicomachean Ethics

BOOK TWO

VIRTUE, being of two kinds, intellectual and moral, intellectual virtue in the main owes both its birth and its growth to teaching (for which reason it requires experience and time), while moral virtue comes about as a result of habit, whence also its name *ethike* is one that is formed by a slight variation from the word *ethos* (habit). From this it is also plain that none of the moral virtues arises in us by nature; for nothing that exists by nature can form a habit contrary to its nature. For instance 10 the stone which by nature moves downwards cannot be habituated to move upwards, not even if one tries to train it by throwing it up ten thousand times; nor can fire be habituated to move downwards, nor can anything else that by nature behaves in one way be trained to behave in another. Neither by nature, then, nor contrary to nature do the virtues arise in us; rather we are adapted by nature to receive them, and are made perfect by habit.

Again, of all the things that come to us by nature 20 we first acquire the potentiality and later exhibit the activity (this is plain in the case of the senses; for it was not by often seeing or often hearing that we got these senses, but on the contrary we had them before we used them, and did not come to have them by using them); but the virtues we get by first exercising them, as also happens in the case of the arts as well. For the things we have to learn before we can do them, we learn by doing them, e.g., men become builders by building and 30 lyre-players by playing the lyre; so too we become just by doing just acts, temperate by doing temperate acts, brave by doing brave acts.

* This traditional interpretation of Aristotle's idea has been challenged by some recent scholars, who speak rather of the character's fatal mistake, a wrong decision that leads to tragedy.
Nicomachean Ethics.△ Translated by W. D. Ross. From *The Oxford Student Aristotle.* Reprinted by permission of The Clarendon Press, Oxford.

This is confirmed by what happens in states; for legislators make the citizens good by forming habits in them, and this is the wish of every legislator, and those who do not effect it miss their mark, and it is in this that a good constitution differs from a bad one.

Again, it is from the same causes and by the same means that every virtue is both produced and destroyed, and similarly every art; for it is from playing the lyre that both good and bad lyre-players are produced. And the corresponding statement is true of builders and of all the rest; men will be good or bad builders as a result of building well or badly. For if this were not so, there would have been no need of a teacher, but all men would have been born good or bad at their craft. This, then, is the case with the virtues also; by doing the acts that we do in our transactions with other men we become just or unjust, and by doing the acts that we do in the presence of danger, and being habituated to feel fear or confidence, we become brave or cowardly. The same is true of appetites and feelings of anger; some men become temperate and good-tempered, others self-indulgent and irascible, by behaving in one way or the other in the appropriate circumstances. Thus, in one word, states of character arise out of like activities. This is why the activities we exhibit must be of a certain kind; it is because the states of character correspond to the differences between these. It makes no small difference, then, whether we form habits of one kind or of another from our very youth; it makes a very great difference, or rather *all* the difference. . . .

4. The question might be asked, what we mean by saying that we must become just by doing just acts, and temperate by doing temperate acts; for if men do just and temperate acts, they are already just and temperate, exactly as, if they do what is in accordance with the laws of grammar and of music, they are grammarians and musicians.

Or is this not true even of the arts? It is possible to do something that is in accordance with the laws of grammar, either by chance or at the suggestion of another. A man will be a grammarian, then, only when he has both done something grammatical and done it grammatically; and this means doing it in accordance with the grammatical knowledge in himself.

Again, the case of the arts and that of the virtues are not similar; for the products of the arts have their goodness in themselves, so that it is enough that they should have a certain character, but if the acts that are in accordance with the virtues have themselves a certain character it does not follow that they are done justly or temperately. The agent also must be in a certain condition when he does them; in the first place he must have knowledge, secondly he must choose the acts, and choose them for their own sakes, and thirdly his action must proceed from a firm and unchangeable character. These are not reckoned in as conditions of the possession of the arts, except the bare knowledge; but as a condition of the possession of the virtues knowledge has little or no weight, while the other conditions count not for a little but for everything, i.e. the very conditions which result from often doing just and temperate acts.

Actions, then, are called just and temperate when they are such as the just or the temperate man would do; but it is not the man who does these that is just and temperate, but the man who also does them as just and temperate men do them. It is well said, then, that it is by doing just acts that the just man is produced, and by doing temperate acts the temperate man; without doing these no one would have even a prospect of becoming good.

But most people do not do these, but take refuge in theory and think they are being philosophers and will become good in this way, behaving somewhat like patients who listen attentively to their doctors, but do none of the things they are ordered to do. As the latter will not be made well in body by such a course of treatment, the former will not be made well in soul by such a course of philosophy.

5. Next we must consider what virtue is. Since things that are found in the soul are of three kinds—passions, faculties, states of character, virtue must be one of these. By passions I mean appetite, anger, fear, confidence, envy, joy, friendly feeling, hatred, longing, emulation, pity, and in general the feelings that are accompanied by pleasure or pain; by faculties the things in virtue of which we are said to be capable of feeling these, e.g. of becoming angry or being pained or feeling pity; by states of character the things in virtue of which we stand well or badly with reference to the passions, e.g. with reference to anger we stand badly if we feel it violently or too weakly, and well if we feel it moderately; and similarly with reference to the other passions.

Now neither the virtues nor the vices are *passions,* because we are not called good or bad on the ground of our passions, but are so called on the ground of our virtues and our vices, and because we are neither praised nor blamed for our passions (for the man who feels fear or anger is not praised, nor is the man who simply feels anger blamed, but the man who feels it in a certain way), but for our virtues and our vices we are praised or blamed.

Again, we feel anger and fear without choice, but the virtues are modes of choice or involve choice. Further, in respect of the passions we are said to be moved, but in respect of the virtues and the vices we are said not to be moved but to be disposed in a particular way.

For these reasons also they are not *faculties;* for we are neither called good nor bad, nor praised nor blamed, for the simple capacity of feeling the passions; again, we have the faculties by nature, but we are not made good or bad by nature.

If, then, the virtues are neither passions nor faculties, all that remains is that they should be *states of character.* Thus we have stated what virtue is in respect of its genus.

10   6. We must, however, not only describe virtue as a state of character, but also say what sort of state it is. We may remark, then, that every virtue or excellence both brings into good condition the thing of which it is the excellence and makes the work of that thing be done well; e.g. the excellence of the eye makes both the eye and its work good; for it is by the excellence of the eye that we see well. Similarly the excellence of the horse makes a horse both good in itself and good at running and at carrying 20 its rider and at awaiting the attack of the enemy. Therefore, if this is true in every case, the virtue of man also will be the state of character which makes a man good and which makes him do his own work well.

How this is to happen we have stated already, but it will be made plain also by the following consideration of the specific nature of virtue. In everything that is continuous and divisible it is possible to take more, less, or an equal amount, and that 30 either in terms of the thing itself or relatively to us; and the equal is an intermediate between excess and defect. By the intermediate in the object I mean that which is equidistant from each of the extremes, which is one and the same for all men; by the intermediate relatively to us that which is neither too much nor too little—and this is not one, nor the same for all. For instance, if ten is many and two is few, six is the intermediate, taken in terms of the object; for it exceeds and is exceeded by an equal 40 amount; this is intermediate according to arithmetical proportion. But the intermediate relatively to us is not to be taken so; if ten pounds are too much for a particular person to eat and two too little, it does not follow that the trainer will order six pounds; for this also is perhaps too much for the person who is to take it, or too little—too little for Milo, too much for the beginner in athletic exercises. The same is true of running and wrestling. Thus a master of any art avoids excess and defect, but seeks the 50 intermediate and chooses this—the intermediate not in the object but relatively to us.

If it is thus, then, that every art does its work well—by looking to the intermediate and judging its works by this standard (so that we often say of good works of art that it is not possible either to take away or to add anything, implying that excess and defect destroy the goodness of works of art, while the mean preserves it; and good artists, as we say, look to this in their work), and if, further, virtue is more exact and better than any art, as 60 nature also is, then virtue must have the quality of aiming at the intermediate. I mean moral virtue; for it is this that is concerned with passions and actions, and in these there is excess, defect, and the intermediate. For instance, both fear and confidence and appetite and anger and pity and in general pleasure and pain may be felt both too much and too little, and in both cases not well; but to feel them at the right times, with reference to the right objects, towards the right people, with the right 70 motive, and in the right way, is what is both intermediate and best, and this is characteristic of virtue. Similarly with regard to actions also there is excess, defect, and the intermediate. Now virtue is concerned with passions and actions, in which excess is a form of failure, and so is defect, while the intermediate is praised and is a form of success; and being praised and being successful are both characteristics of virtue. Therefore virtue is a kind of 80 mean, since, as we have seen, it aims at what is intermediate.

Again, it is possible to fail in many ways (for evil belongs to the class of the unlimited, as the Pythagoreans conjectured, and good to that of the limited), while to succeed is possible only in one way (for which reason also one is easy and the other difficult—to miss the mark easy, to hit it difficult); for these reasons also, then, excess and defect are characteristic of vice, and the mean of 90 virtue;

For men are good in but one way, but bad in many.

Virtue, then, is a state of character concerned with choice, lying in a mean, i.e. the mean relative to us, this being determined by a rational principle, and by that principle by which the man of practical wisdom would determine it. Now it is a mean between two vices, that which depends on excess and that which depends on defect; and again it is a mean because the vices respectively fall short of or 100 exceed what is right in both passions and actions, while virtue both finds and chooses that which is intermediate. Hence in respect of its substance and the definition which states its essence virtue is a mean, with regard to what is best and right an extreme.

But not every action nor every passion admits of a mean; for some have names that already imply badness, e.g. spite, shamelessness, envy, and in the case of actions adultery, theft, murder; for all of 110 these and suchlike things imply by their names that they are themselves bad, and not the excesses or

---

46. **Milo,** a famous wrestler.

deficiencies of them. It is not possible, then, ever to be right with regard to them; one must always be wrong. Nor does goodness or badness with regard to such things depend on committing adultery with the right woman, at the right time, and in the right way, but simply to do any of them is to go wrong. It would be equally absurd, then, to expect that in unjust, cowardly, and voluptuous action there should be a mean, an excess, and a deficiency; for at that rate there would be a mean of excess and of deficiency, an excess of excess, and a deficiency of deficiency. But as there is no excess and deficiency of temperance and courage because what is intermediate is in a sense an extreme, so too of the actions we have mentioned there is no mean nor any excess and deficiency, but however they are done they are wrong; for in general there is neither a mean of excess and deficiency, nor excess and deficiency of a mean.

7. We must, however, not only make this general statement, but also apply it to the individual facts. For among statements about conduct those which are general apply more widely, but those which are particular are more genuine, since conduct has to do with individual cases, and our statements must harmonize with the facts in these cases. We may take these cases from our table. With regard to feelings of fear and confidence courage is the mean; of the people who exceed, he who exceeds in fearlessness has no name (many of the states have no name), while the man who exceeds in confidence is rash, and he who exceeds in fear and falls short in confidence is a coward. With regard to pleasures and pains—not all of them, and not so much with regard to the pains—the mean is temperance, the excess self-indulgence. Persons deficient with regard to the pleasures are not often found; hence such persons also have received no name. But let us call them 'insensible.'

With regard to giving and taking of money the mean is liberality, the excess and the defect prodigality and meanness. In these actions people exceed and fall short in contrary ways; the prodigal exceeds in spending and falls short in taking, while the mean man exceeds in taking and falls short in spending. With regard to money there are also other dispositions—a mean, magnificence (for the magnificent man differs from the liberal man; the former deals with large sums, the latter with small ones), and excess, tastelessness and vulgarity, and a deficiency, niggardliness; these differ from the states opposed to liberality.

With regard to honour and dishonour the mean is proper pride, the excess is known as a sort of 'empty vanity' and the deficiency is undue humility; and as liberality was related to magnificence, differing from it by dealing with small sums, so there is a state similarly related to proper pride, being concerned with small honours while that is concerned with great. For it is possible to desire honour as one ought, and more than one ought, and less, and the man who exceeds in his desires is called ambitious, the man who falls short unambitious, while the intermediate person has no name. The dispositions also are nameless, except that that of the ambitious man is called ambition. Hence the people who are at the extremes lay claim to the middle place; and we ourselves sometimes call the intermediate person ambitious and sometimes unambitious, and sometimes praise the ambitious man and sometimes the unambitious.

With regard to anger also there is an excess, a deficiency, and a mean. Although they can scarcely be said to have names, yet since we call the intermediate person good-tempered let us call the mean good temper; of the persons at the extremes let the one who exceeds be called irascible, and his vice irascibility, and the man who falls short an inirascible sort of person, and the deficiency inirascibility.

There are also three other means, which have a certain likeness to one another, but differ from one another: for they are all concerned with intercourse in words and actions, but differ in that one is concerned with truth in this sphere, the other two with pleasantness; and of this one kind is exhibited in giving amusement, the other in all the circumstances of life. We must therefore speak of these too, that we may the better see that in all things the mean is praiseworthy, and the extremes neither praiseworthy nor right, but worthy of blame. Now most of these states also have no names, but we must try, as in the other cases, to invent names ourselves so that we may be clear and easy to follow. With regard to truth, then, the intermediate is a truthful sort of person and the mean may be called truthfulness, while the pretence which exaggerates is boastfulness and the person characterized by it a boaster, and that which understates is mock modesty and the person characterized by it mock-modest. With regard to pleasantness in the giving of amusement the intermediate person is ready-witted and the disposition ready wit, the excess is buffoonery and the person characterized by it a buffoon, while the man who falls short is a sort of boor and his state is boorishness. With regard to the remaining kind of pleasantness, that which is exhibited in life in general, the man who is pleasant in the right way is friendly and the mean is friendliness, while the man who exceeds is an obsequious person if he has no end in view, a flatterer if he is aiming at his own advantage, and the man who falls short and is unpleasant in all circumstances is a quarrelsome and surly sort of person.

There are also means in the passions and concerned with the passions; since shame is not a virtue, and yet praise is extended to the modest man. For even in these matters one man is said to be intermediate, and another to exceed, as for instance the bashful man who is ashamed of everything; while he who falls short or is not ashamed of anything at all is shameless, and the intermediate person is modest. Righteous indignation is a mean between envy and spite, and these states are concerned with the pain and pleasures that are felt at the fortunes of our neighbours; the man who is characterized by righteous indignation is pained at undeserved good fortune, the envious man, going beyond him, is pained at all good fortune, and the spiteful man falls so far short of being pained that he even rejoices.

8. There are three kinds of disposition, then, two of them vices, involving excess and deficiency respectively, and one a virtue, viz. the mean, and all are in a sense opposed to all; for the extreme states are contrary both to the intermediate state and to each other, and the intermediate to the extremes; as the equal is greater relatively to the less, less relatively to the greater, so the middle states are excessive relatively to the deficiencies, deficient relatively to the excesses, both in passions and in actions.

Poetics

A TRAGEDY is the imitation of an action that is serious and also, as having magnitude, complete in itself; in language with pleasurable accessories, each kind brought in separately in the parts of the work; in a dramatic, not in a narrative form; with incidents arousing pity and fear, where-with to accomplish its catharsis of such emotions. Here by 'language with pleasurable accessories' I mean that with rhythm and harmony or song superadded; and by 'the kinds separately' I mean that some portions are worked out with verse only, and others in turn with song.

I. As they act the stories, it follows that in the first place the Spectacle (or stage-appearance of the actors) must be some part of the whole; and in the second Melody and Diction, these two being the means of their imitation. Here by 'Diction' I mean merely this, the composition of the verses; and by 'Melody,' what is too completely understood to require explanation. But further: the subject represented also is an action; and the action involves agents, who must necessarily have their distinctive qualities both of character and thought, since it is

Poetics. (Chapters 6-18.) [A] Translated by Ingram Bywater. From *The Oxford Student Aristotle.* Reprinted by permission of The Clarendon Press, Oxford.

from these that we ascribe certain qualities to their actions. There are in the natural order of things, therefore, two causes, Thought and Character, of their actions, and consequently of their success or failure in their lives. Now the action (that which was done) is represented in the play by the Fable or Plot. The Fable, in our present sense of the term, is simply this, the combination of the incidents, or things done in the story; whereas Character is what makes us ascribe certain moral qualities to the agents; and Thought is shown in all they say when proving a particular point or, it may be, enunciating a general truth. There are six parts consequently of every tragedy, as a whole (that is) of such or such quality, viz. a Fable or Plot, Characters, Diction, Thought, Spectacle, and Melody; two of them arising from the means, one from the manner, and three from the objects of the dramatic imitation, and there is nothing else besides these six. Of these, its formative elements, then, not a few of the dramatists have made due use, as every play, one may say, admits of Spectacle, Character, Fable, Diction, Melody, and Thought.

II. The most important of the six is the combination of the incidents of the story. Tragedy is essentially an imitation not of persons but of action and life, of happiness and misery. All human happiness or misery takes the form of action; the end for which we live is a certain kind of activity, not a quality. Character gives us qualities, but it is in our actions —what we do—that we are happy or the reverse. In a play accordingly they do not act in order to portray the Characters; they include the Characters for the sake of the action. So that it is the action in it, i.e. its Fable or Plot, that is the end and purpose of the tragedy; and the end is everywhere the chief thing. Besides this, a tragedy is impossible without action, but there may be one without Character. . . . And again: one may string together a series of characteristic speeches of the utmost finish as regards Diction and Thought, and yet fail to produce the true tragic effect; but one will have much better success with a tragedy which, however inferior in these respects, has a Plot, a combination of incidents, in it. . . . A further proof is in the fact that beginners succeed earlier with the Diction and Characters than with the construction of a story; and the same may be said of nearly all the early dramatists. We maintain, therefore, that the first essential, the life and soul, so to speak, of Tragedy is the Plot; and that the Characters come second—compare the parallel in painting, where the most beautiful colours laid on without order will not give one the same pleasure as a simple black-and-white sketch of a portrait. We maintain that Tragedy is primarily an imitation of action, and that it is mainly for the sake of the action that it imitates the personal agents.

Third comes the element of Thought, i.e. the power of saying whatever can be said, or what is appropriate to the occasion. This is what, in the speeches in Tragedy, falls under the arts of Politics and Rhetoric; for the older poets make their personages discourse like statesmen, and the modern like rhetoricians. One must not confuse it with Character. Character in a play is that which reveals the moral purpose of the agents, i.e. the sort of thing they seek or avoid, where that is not obvious—hence there is no room for Character in a speech on a purely indifferent subject. Thought, on the other hand, is shown in all they say when proving or disproving some particular point, or enunciating some universal proposition. Fourth among the literary elements is the Diction of the personages, the expression of their thoughts in words, which is practically the same thing with verse as with prose. As for the two remaining parts, the Melody is the greatest of the pleasurable accessories of Tragedy. The Spectacle, though an attraction, is the least artistic of all the parts, and has least to do with the art of poetry. The tragic effect is quite possible without a public performance and actors; and besides, the getting-up of the Spectacle is more a matter for the costumier than the poet.

Having thus distinguished the parts, let us now consider the proper construction of the Fable or Plot, as that is at once the first and the most important thing in Tragedy. We have laid it down that a tragedy is an imitation of an action that is complete in itself, as a whole of some magnitude; for a whole is that which has beginning, middle, and end. A beginning is that which is not itself necessarily after anything else, and which has naturally something else after it; an end is that which is naturally after something itself, either as its necessary or usual consequent, and with nothing else after it; and a middle, that which is by nature after one thing and has also another after it. A well-constructed Plot, therefore, cannot either begin or end at any point one likes; beginning and end in it must be of the forms just described. Again: to be beautiful, a living creature, and every whole made up of parts, must not only present a certain order in its arrangement of parts, but also be of a certain definite magnitude. Beauty is a matter of size and order, and therefore impossible either (1) in a very minute creature, since our perception becomes indistinct as it approaches instantaneity; or (2) in a creature of vast size—one, say, 1,000 miles long—as in that case, instead of the object being seen all at once, the unity and wholeness of it is lost to the beholder. Just in the same way, then, as a beautiful whole made up of parts, or a beautiful living creature, must be of some size, but a size to be taken in by the eye, so a story or Plot must be of some length, but of a length to be taken in by the memory. As for the limit of its length, so far as that is relative to public performances and spectators, it does not fall within the theory of poetry. If they had to perform a hundred tragedies, they would be timed by water-clocks, as they are said to have been at one period. The limit, however, set by the actual nature of the thing is this: the longer the story, consistently with its being comprehensible as a whole, the finer it is by reason of its magnitude. As a rough general formula, 'a length which allows of the hero passing by a series of probable or necessary stages from misfortune to happiness, or from happiness to misfortune,' may suffice as a limit for the magnitude of the story.

The Unity of a Plot does not consist, as some suppose, in its having one man as its subject. An infinity of things befall that one man, some of which it is impossible to reduce to unity; and in like manner there are many actions of one man which cannot be made to form one action. One sees, therefore, the mistake of all the poets who have written a *Heracleid*, a *Theseid*, or similar poems; they suppose that, because Heracles was one man, the story also of Heracles must be one story. Homer, however, evidently understood this point quite well, whether by art or instinct, just in the same way as he excels the rest in every other respect. In writing an *Odyssey*, he did not make the poem cover all that ever befell his hero—it befell him, for instance, to get wounded on Parnassus and also to feign madness at the time of the call to arms, but the two incidents had no necessary or probable connection with one another—instead of doing that, he took as the subject of the *Odyssey*, as also of the *Iliad*, an action with a Unity of the kind we are describing. The truth is that, just as in the other imitative arts one imitation is always of one thing, so in poetry the story, as an imitation of action, must represent one action, a complete whole, with its several incidents so closely connected that the transposal or withdrawal of any one of them will disjoin and dislocate the whole. For that which makes no perceptible difference by its presence or absence is no real part of the whole.

From what we have said it will be seen that the poet's function is to describe, not the thing that has happened, but a kind of thing that might happen, i.e. what is possible as being probable or necessary. The distinction between historian and poet is not in the one writing prose and the other verse—you might put the work of Herodotus into verse, and it would still be a species of history; it consists really in this, that the one describes the thing that has been, and the other a kind of thing that might be.

80. *Heracleid, Theseid;* that is, epics of such heroes as Hercules and Theseus.

Hence poetry is something more philosophic and of graver import than history, since its statements are of the nature rather of universals, whereas those of history are singulars. By a universal statement I mean one as to what such or such a kind of man will probably or necessarily say or do—which is the aim of poetry, though it affixes proper names to the characters; by a singular statement, one as to what, say, Alcibiades did or had done to him. In Comedy this has become clear by this time; it is only when their plot is already made up of probable incidents that they give it a basis of proper names, choosing for the purpose any names that may occur to them, instead of writing like the old iambic poets about particular persons. In Tragedy, however, they still adhere to the historic names; and for this reason: what convinces is the possible; now whereas we are not yet sure as to the possibility of that which has not happened, that which has happened is manifestly possible, else it would not have come to pass. Nevertheless even in Tragedy there are some plays with but one or two known names in them, the rest being inventions; and there are some without a single known name, e.g. Agathon's *Antheus,* in which both incidents and names are of the poet's invention; and it is no less delightful on that account. So that one must not aim at a rigid adherence to the traditional stories on which tragedies are based. It would be absurd, in fact, to do so, as even the known stories are only known to a few, though they are a delight none the less to all.

It is evident from the above that the poet must be more the poet of his stories or Plots than of his verses, inasmuch as he is a poet by virtue of the imitative element in his work, and it is actions that he imitates. And if he should come to take a subject from actual history, he is none the less a poet for that; since some historic occurrences may very well be in the probable and possible order of things; and it is in that aspect of them that he is their poet.

Of simple Plots and actions the episodic are the worst. I call a Plot episodic when there is neither probability nor necessity in the sequence of its episodes. Actions of this sort bad poets construct through their own fault, and good ones on account of the players. His work being for public performance, a good poet often stretches out a Plot beyond its capabilities, and is thus obliged to twist the sequence of incident.

Tragedy, however, is an imitation not only of a complete action, but also of incidents arousing pity and fear. Such incidents have the very greatest effect on the mind when they occur unexpectedly and at the same time in consequence of one another; there is more of the marvellous in them then than if they

happened of themselves or by mere chance. Even matters of chance seem most marvellous if there is an appearance of design as it were in them; as for instance the statue of Mitys at Argos killed the author of Mitys' death by falling down on him when a looker-on at a public spectacle; for incidents like that we think to be not without a meaning. A Plot, therefore, of this sort is necessarily finer than others.

Plots are either simple or complex, since the actions they represent are naturally of this twofold description. The action, proceeding in the way defined, as one continuous whole, I call simple, when the change in the hero's fortune takes place without Peripety or Discovery; and complex, when it involves one or the other, or both. These should each of them arise out of the structure of the Plot itself, so as to be the consequence, necessary or probable, of the antecedents. There is a great difference between a thing happening *propter hoc* and *post hoc.*

A Peripety is the change of the kind described from one state of things within the play to its opposite, and that too in the way we are saying, in the probable or necessary sequence of events; as it is for instance in *Oedipus*: here the opposite state of things is produced by the Messenger, who, coming to gladden Oedipus and to remove his fears as to his mother, reveals the secret of his birth. And in *Lynceus*: just as he is being led off for execution, with Danaus at his side to put him to death, the incidents preceding this bring it about that he is saved and Danaus put to death. A Discovery is, as the very word implies, a change from ignorance to knowledge, and thus to either love or hate, in the personages marked for good or evil fortune. The finest form of Discovery is one attended by Peripeties, like that which goes with the Discovery in Oedipus. There are no doubt other forms of it; what we have said may happen in a way in reference to inanimate things, even things of a very casual kind; and it is also possible to discover whether some one has done or not done something. But the form most directly connected with the Plot and the action of the piece is the first-mentioned. This, with a Peripety, will arouse either pity or fear —actions of that nature being what Tragedy is assumed to represent; and it will also serve to bring about the happy or unhappy ending. The Discovery, then, being of persons, it may be that of one party only to the other, the latter being already known; or both the parties may have to discover themselves. Iphigenia, for instance, was discovered to Orestes

---

24. **Agathon,** Greek tragic poet, friend to Euripides and Plato.

74–75. **There . . .** *post hoc.* That is, the difference between a thing happening *in consequence* of something else and merely *after* something else. 84. *Lynceus,* by Theodectes. 92. **Peripeties,** complete reversals of fortune. 107. **Iphigenia . . .** This occurred in *Iphigenia among the Taurians* by Euripides.

by sending the letter; and another Discovery was required to reveal him to Iphigenia.

Two parts of the Plot, then, Peripety and Discovery, are on matters of this sort. A third part is Suffering; which we may define as an action of a destructive or painful nature, such as murders on the stage, tortures, woundings, and the like. The other two have been already explained. . . .

The next points after what we have said above will be these: (1) What is the poet to aim at, and what is he to avoid, in constructing his Plots? and (2) What are the conditions on which the tragic effect depends?

We assume that, for the finest form of Tragedy, the Plot must be not simple but complex; and further, that it must imitate actions arousing fear and pity, since that is the distinctive function of this kind of imitation. It follows, therefore, that there are three forms of Plot to be avoided. (1) A good man must not be seen passing from happiness to misery, or (2) a bad man from misery to happiness. The first situation is not fear-inspiring or piteous, but simply odious to us. The second is the most untragic that can be; it has no one of the requisites of Tragedy; it does not appeal either to the human feeling in us, or to our fears. Nor, on the other hand, should (3) an extremely bad man be seen falling from happiness into misery. Such a story may arouse the human feeling in us, but it will not move us to either pity or fear; pity is occasioned by undeserved misfortune, and fear by that of one like ourselves; so that there will be nothing either piteous or fear-inspiring in the situation. There remains, then, the intermediate kind of personage, a man not pre-eminently virtuous and just, whose misfortune, however, is brought upon him not by vice and depravity but by some error of judgement, of the number of those in the enjoyment of great reputation and prosperity; e.g. Oedipus, Thyestes, and the men of note of similar families. The perfect Plot, accordingly, must have a single, and not (as some tell us) a double issue; the change in the hero's fortunes must be not from misery to happiness, but on the contrary from happiness to misery; and the cause of it must lie not in any depravity, but in some great error on his part; the man himself being either such as we have described, or better, not worse, than that.

Fact also confirms our theory. Though the poets began by accepting any tragic story that came to hand, in these days the finest tragedies are always on the story of some few houses, on that of Alcmeon, Oedipus, Orestes, Meleager, Thyestes, Telephus, or any others that may have been involved, as either agents or sufferers, in some deed of horror. The theoretically best tragedy, then, has a Plot of this description. The critics, therefore, are wrong who

blame Euripides for taking this line in his tragedies, and giving many of them an unhappy ending. It is, as we have said, the right line to take. The best proof is this: on the stage, and in the public performances, such plays, properly worked out, are seen to be the most truly tragic; and Euripides, even if his execution be faulty in every other point, is seen to be nevertheless the most tragic certainly of the dramatists. After this comes the construction of Plot which some rank first, one with a double story (like the *Odyssey*) and an opposite issue for the good and the bad personages. It is ranked as first only through the weakness of the audiences; the poets merely follow their public, writing as its wishes dictate. But the pleasure here is not that of Tragedy. It belongs rather to Comedy, where the bitterest enemies in the piece (e.g. Orestes and Aegisthus) walk off good friends at the end, with no slaying of any one by any one.

The tragic fear and pity may be aroused by the Spectacle; but they may also be aroused by the very structure and incidents of the play—which is the better way and shows the better poet. The Plot in fact should be so framed that, even without seeing the things take place, he who simply hears the account of them shall be filled with horror and pity at the incidents; which is just the effect that the mere recital of the story in Oedipus would have on one. To produce this same effect by means of the Spectacle is less artistic, and requires extraneous aid. Those, however, who make use of the Spectacle to put before us that which is merely monstrous and not productive of fear, are wholly out of touch with Tragedy; not every kind of pleasure should be required of a tragedy, but only its own proper pleasure.

The tragic pleasure is that of pity and fear, and the poet has to produce it by a work of imitation; it is clear, therefore, that the causes should be included in the incidents of his story. Let us see, then, what kinds of incident strike one as horrible, or rather as piteous. In a deed of this description the parties must necessarily be either friends, or enemies, or indifferent to one another. Now when enemy does it on enemy, there is nothing to move us to pity either in his doing or in his meditating the deed, except so far as the actual pain of the sufferer is concerned; and the same is true when the parties are indifferent to one another. Whenever the tragic deed, however, is done within the family —when murder or the like is done or meditated by brother on brother, by son on father, by mother on son, or son on mother—these are the situations the poet should seek after. The traditional stories, accordingly, must be kept as they are, e.g. the murder of Clytaemnestra by Orestes. At the same time even with these there is something left to the poet himself; it is for him to devise the right way of treating them. Let us explain more clearly what we mean by 'the right way.' The deed of horror may be done by the doer knowingly and consciously, as in the old poets, and in Medea's murder of her children in Euripides. Or he may do it, but in ignorance of his relationship, and discover that afterwards, as does the Oedipus in Sophocles. Here the deed is outside the play; but it may be within it. . . . A third possibility is for one meditating some deadly injury to another, in ignorance of his relationship, to make the discovery in time to draw back. These exhaust the possibilities, since the deed must necessarily be either done or not done, and either knowingly or unknowingly.

The worst situation is when the personage is with full knowledge on the point of doing the deed, and leaves it undone. It is odious and also (through the absence of suffering) untragic· hence it is that no one is made to act thus except in some few instances, e.g. Haemon and Creon in *Antigone*. Next after this comes the actual perpetration of the deed meditated. A better situation than that, however, is for the deed to be done in ignorance, and the relationship discovered afterwards, since there is nothing odious in it, and the Discovery will serve to astound us. But the best of all is the last; what we have in *Cresphontes*, for example, where Merope, on the point of slaying her son, recognizes him in time; in *Iphigenia*, where sister and brother are in a like position; and in *Helle*, where the son recognizes his mother, when on the point of giving her up to her enemy.

This will explain why our tragedies are restricted to such a small number of families. It was accident rather than art that led the poets in quest of subjects to embody this kind of incident in their Plots. They are still obliged, accordingly, to have recourse to the families in which such horrors have occurred.

On the construction of the Plot, and the kind of Plot required for Tragedy, enough has now been said.

In the Characters there are four points to aim at. First and foremost, that they shall be good. There will be an element of character in the play, if (as has been observed) what a personage says or does reveals a certain moral purpose; and a good element of character, if the purpose so revealed is good. Such goodness is possible in every type of personage; even in a woman or a slave, though the one is perhaps an inferior, and the other wholly a worthless being. The second point is to make them appropriate. The Character before us may be, say, manly; but it is not appropriate in a female Character to be manly,

or clever. The third is to make them like the reality, which is not the same as their being good and appropriate, in our sense of the term. The fourth is to make them consistent and the same throughout; even if inconsistency be part of the man before one for imitation as presenting that form of character, he should still be consistently inconsistent. We have an instance of . . . inconsistency in *Iphigenia at Aulis*, where Iphigenia the suppliant is utterly unlike the later Iphigenia. The right thing, however, is in the Characters just as in the incidents of the play to endeavour always after the necessary or the probable; so that whenever such-and-such a personage says or does such-and-such a thing, it shall be the necessary or probable outcome of his character; and whenever this incident follows on that, it shall be either the necessary or the probable consequence of it. From this one sees (to digress for a moment) that the Dénouement also should arise out of the plot itself, and not depend on a stage-artifice. . . . The artifice must be reserved for matters outside the play—for past events beyond human knowledge, or events yet to come, which require to be foretold or announced; since it is the privilege of the Gods to know everything. There should be nothing improbable among the actual incidents. If it be unavoidable, however, it should be outside the tragedy, like the improbability in the *Oedipus* of Sophocles. But to return to the Characters. As Tragedy is an imitation of personages better than the ordinary man, we in our way should follow the example of good portrait-painters, who reproduce the distinctive features of a man, and at the same time, without losing the likeness, make him handsomer than he is. The poet in like manner, in portraying men quick or slow to anger, or with similar infirmities of character, must know how to represent them as such, and at the same time as good men as Agathon and Homer have represented Achilles. . . .

There is a further point to be borne in mind. Every tragedy is in part Complication and in part Dénouement; the incidents before the opening scene, and often certain also of those within the play, forming the Complication; and the rest the Dénouement. By Complication I mean all from the beginning of the story to the point just before the change in the hero's fortunes; by Dénouement, all from the beginning of the change to the end. . . . Now it is right, when one speaks of a tragedy as the same or not the same as another, to do so on the ground before all else of their Plot, i.e. as having the same or not the same Complication and Dénouement. Yet there are many dramatists who, after a good Complication, fail in the Dénouement. But it is necessary for both points of construction to be always duly mastered.

21. *Antigone*, a play by Sophocles. 28, 30, 31. *Cresphontes, Iphigenia, Helle;* the first two plays are by Euripides, the third by an unknown author.

62–63. *Iphigenia at Aulis,* play by Euripides.

Lucian

125–c. 200 A.D.

The last major figure in Greek literature, Lucian of Samosata, is also the wittiest and most entertaining of its prose writers. A product of the so-called Greek Renaissance, which came centuries after the Golden Age, he left some eighty brief works which provide a kind of cynical summary of the Greeks' achievements from Homer down. Lucian is not a creative writer but a critical one, not a constructive thinker but a destructive satirist who reduces the gods and heroes, the statesmen and philosophers of the past to the level of petty but pretentious mortals in order to amuse lesser folk with their foibles and false pride.

By the time of the Greek Renaissance—an artificial revival of Hellenistic culture stimulated by the Roman emperor Hadrian in the second century A.D.—Socrates and Plato were as remote as Chaucer is to us. The traditional religion had been decaying for centuries. All the schools of philosophy, which Lucian passes in contemptuous review in his *Sale of the Philosophers*, had said their say, and the world seemed no better for them. Christianity was growing as a spiritual force underground, but as yet it had barely touched the jaded Graeco-Roman world, and its leaders still suffered martyrdom. Lucian was the cynical spokesman for this age without faith, keenly intellectual, brilliantly artistic, and devoid of serious belief in anything. But underneath his playful irreverence he was a moralist too and satirized humbug and cant out of a healthy respect for truth and right living.

Typical of his cosmopolitan era, Lucian was neither Greek nor Roman, but a Syrian of Samosata on the Euphrates, who was reared in the Roman provinces of Asia Minor and adopted Greek as his literary tongue. Apprenticed to his uncle, a sculptor, he quickly shifted to the professions of law and rhetoric. In maturity he was an itinerant professor, lecturing his way through Greece, Italy, and Gaul. But he eventually settled in Athens around 164 A.D. and probably wrote his major works there. Still the wanderlust was in his blood, and at the time of his death he held a legal position in Egypt. This restless, inquisitive man had covered a good part of the Empire in his quest for knowledge of people and ideas, and if he inclined to the Cynic philosophy of skepticism and asceticism, his wholesome writings suggest that he led a robust life and could laugh at himself as well as at others.

Although Lucian wrote philosophical essays, rhetorical exercises, and comic narratives, his forte was the satiric dialogue, which he developed especially in his later years. Unlike the graceful Platonic dialogues with their long and serious speeches ascribed to the author's friends, the dialogues of Lucian are generally brief fragments of witty conversation between mythical or long-dead characters in short, racy speeches close to the give and take of actual talk. An outgrowth of the ancient *mimes* and reminiscent of the satiric comedies of Aristophanes, they burlesque the hallowed personalities of the past with their rational attack on religion and philosophy. In the *Dialogues of the Gods* the dignitaries of Olympus are politely lampooned as idle aristocrats given to jealous backbiting, catty argument, and free love. The *Dialogues of the Dead* carry underneath their playful picture of Hades the insistent reminder that human ambition and pride are ultimately futile.

Dialogues of the Gods

THE TRICKS OF HERMES

HEPHAESTUS.

HAVE you seen Maia's baby, Apollo? Such a pretty little thing, with a smile for everybody; you can see it is going to be a treasure.

APOLLO. That baby a treasure? Well, in mischief Iapetus is young beside it.

HEPHAESTUS. Why, what harm can it do, only just born?

APOLLO. Ask Posidon; it stole his trident. Ask Ares; he was surprised to find his sword gone out of the scabbard. Not to mention myself, disarmed of bow and arrows. 10

HEPHAESTUS. Never! That infant? He has hardly found his legs yet; he is not out of his baby-linen.

APOLLO. Ah, you will find out, Hephaestus, if he gets within reach of you.

HEPHAESTUS. He has been.

APOLLO. Well? all your tools safe? None missing?

HEPHAESTUS. Of course not.

APOLLO. I advise you to make sure.

HEPHAESTUS. Zeus! where are my pincers? 20

APOLLO. Ah, you will find them among the baby-linen.

HEPHAESTUS. So light-fingered? One would swear he had practiced petty larceny in the womb.

APOLLO. Ah, and you don't know what a glib young chatterbox he is; and, if he has his way, he is to be our errand-boy! Yesterday he challenged Eros —tripped up his heels somehow, and had him on his back in a twinkling; before the applause was over,

Dialogues of the Gods. "The Tricks of Hermes" and "Cupid's Exceptions" translated by H. W. Fowler, "The Birth of Athena" and "The Judgement of Paris" translated by F. G. Fowler. From *The Works of Lucian of Samosata* by H. W. and F. G. Fowler. Reprinted by permission of The Clarendon Press, Oxford.
1. **Maia's baby.** Hermes, the precocious and tricky son of Maia by Zeus, was notorious for his thieving in infancy. 5. **Iapetus,** the mischievous Titan, imprisoned in Tartarus.

he had taken the opportunity of a congratulatory hug from Aphrodite to steal her girdle; Zeus had not done laughing before—the sceptre was gone. If the thunderbolt had not been too heavy, and very hot, he would have made away with that too.

HEPHAESTUS. The child has some spirit in him, by your account.

APOLLO. Spirit, yes—and some music, moreover, young as he is.

HEPHAESTUS. How can you tell that?

APOLLO. He picked up a dead tortoise somewhere or other, and contrived an instrument with it. He fitted horns to it, with a cross-bar, stuck in pegs, inserted a bridge, and played a sweet tuneful thing that made an old harper like me quite envious. Even at night, Maia was saying, he does not stay in Heaven; he goes down poking his nose into Hades— on a thieves' errand, no doubt. Then he has a pair of wings, and he has made himself a magic wand, which he uses for marshalling souls—convoying the dead to their place.

HEPHAESTUS. Ah, I gave him that, for a toy.

APOLLO. And by way of payment he stole—

HEPHAESTUS. Well thought on; I must go and get them; you may be right about the baby-linen.

THE BIRTH OF ATHENA

HEPHAESTUS. What are your orders, Zeus? You sent for me, and here I am; with such an edge to my axe as would cleave a stone at one blow.

ZEUS. Ah; that's right, Hephaestus. Just split my head in half, will you?

HEPHAESTUS. You think I am mad, perhaps? . . . Seriously, now, what can I do for you?

ZEUS. What I say: crack my skull. Any insubordination, now, and you shall taste my resentment; it will not be the first time. Come, a good lusty stroke, and quick about it. I am in the pangs of travail; my brain is in a whirl.

HEPHAESTUS. Mind you, the consequences may be

serious: the axe is sharp, and will prove but a rough midwife.

ZEUS. Hew away, and fear nothing. I know what I am about.

HEPHAESTUS. H'm. I don't like it: however, one must obey orders. . . . Why, what have we here? A maiden in full armor! This is no joke, Zeus. You might well be waspish, with this great girl growing up beneath your *pia mater;* in armor, too! You have been carrying a regular barracks on your shoulders all this time. So active too! See, she is dancing a war-dance, with shield and spear in full swing. She is like one inspired; and (what is more to the point) she is extremely pretty, and has come to marriageable years in these few minutes; those grey eyes, even, look well beneath a helmet. Zeus, I claim her as the fee for my midwifery.

ZEUS. Impossible! She is determined to remain a maid for ever. Not that *I* have any objection, personally.

HEPHAESTUS. That is all I want. You can leave the rest to me. I'll carry her off this moment.

ZEUS. Well, if you think it so easy. But I am sure it is a hopeless case.

CUPID'S EXCEPTIONS

APHRODITE. Eros, dear, you have your victories over most of the gods—Zeus, Posidon, Rhea, Apollo, nay, your own mother; how is it you make an exception for Athene? Against her your torch has no fire, your quiver no arrows, your right hand no cunning.

EROS. I am afraid of her, mother; those awful flashing eyes! She is like a man, only worse. When I go against her with my arrow on the string, a toss of her plume frightens me; my hand shakes so that it drops the bow.

APHRODITE. I should have thought Ares was more terrible still; but you disarmed and conquered him.

EROS. Ah, he is only too glad to have me; he calls me to him. Athene always eyes me so! Once when I flew close past her, quite by accident, with my torch, 'If you come near me,' she called out, 'I swear by my father, I will run you through with my spear, or take you by the foot and drop you into Tartarus, or tear you in pieces with my own hands'—and more such dreadful things. And she has such a sour look; and then on her breast she wears that horrid face with the snaky hair; that frightens me worst of all; the nasty bogy—I run away directly I see it.

APHRODITE. Well, well, you are afraid of Athene and the Gorgon; at least so you say, though you do not mind Zeus's thunderbolt a bit. But why do you let the Muses go scot free? Do *they* toss their plumes and hold out Gorgons' heads?

The birth of Athena from the brain of Zeus. Hephaestus at right holds his double axe, with which he clave the skull of Zeus. From an early Greek vase.

87. the Gorgon, the terrible Medusa, whose hair was changed to snakes by Athena and whose head Athena placed in the center of her breastplate.

EROS. Ah, mother, they make me bashful; they are so grand, always studying and composing; I love to stand there listening to their music.

APHRODITE. Let them pass too, because they are grand. And why do you never take a shot at Artemis?

EROS. Why, the great thing is that I cannot catch her; she is always over the hills and far away. But besides that, her heart is engaged already.

APHRODITE. Where, child?

EROS. In hunting stags and fawns; she is so fleet, she catches them up, or else shoots them; she can think of nothing else. Her brother, now, though he is an archer too, and draws a good arrow—

APHRODITE. I know, child, you have hit *him* often enough.

THE JUDGEMENT OF PARIS

ZEUS. Hermes, take this apple, and go with it to Phrygia; on the Gargaran peak of Ida you will find Priam's son, the herdsman. Give him this message: "Paris, because you are handsome, and wise in the things of love, Zeus commands you to judge between the Goddesses, and say which is the most beautiful. And the prize shall be this apple."—Now, you three, there is no time to be lost: away with you to your judge. I will have nothing to do with the matter: I love you all exactly alike, and I only wish you could all three win. If I were to give the prize to one of you, the other two would hate me, of course. In these circumstances, I am ill qualified to be your judge. But this young Phrygian to whom you are going is of the royal blood—a relation to Ganymede's, —and at the same time a simple countryman; so that we need have no hesitation in trusting his eyes.

APHRODITE. As far as I am concerned, Zeus, Momus himself might be our judge; *I* should not be afraid to show myself. What fault could he find with *me?* But the others must agree too.

HERA. Oh, we are under no alarm, thank you,— though your admirer Ares should be appointed. But Paris will do; whoever Paris is.

ZEUS. And my little Athene; have we 'er approval? Nay, never blush, nor hide your face. Well, well, maidens will be coy; 'tis a delicate subject. But there, she nods consent. Now, off with you; and mind, the beaten ones must not be cross with the judge; I will not have the poor lad harmed. The prize of beauty can be but one.

HERMES. Now for Phrygia. I will show the way; keep close behind me, ladies, and don't be nervous. I know Paris well: he is a charming young man; a great gallant, and an admirable judge of beauty. Depend on it, he will make a good award.

14–15. I know . . . enough. The handsome Apollo had many affairs. 30. Ganymede, the beautiful shepherd boy beloved of Zeus and carried away by him in the guise of an eagle to become cupbearer to the king of the gods. 33–34. Momus, the god of censure.

APHRODITE. I am glad to hear that; I ask for nothing better than a just judge.—Has he a wife, Hermes, or is he a bachelor?

HERMES. Not exactly a bachelor.

APHRODITE. What do you mean?

HERMES. I believe there is a wife, as it were; a good enough sort of girl—a native of those parts— but sadly countrified! I fancy he does not care very much about her.—Why do you ask?

APHRODITE. I just wanted to know.

ATHENE. Now, Hermes, that is not fair. No whispering with Aphrodite.

HERMES. It was nothing, Athene; nothing about you. She only asked me whether Paris was a bachelor.

ATHENE. What business is that of hers?

HERMES. None that I know of. She meant nothing by the question; she just wanted to know.

ATHENE. Well, and is he?

HERMES. Why, no.

ATHENE. And does he care for military glory? Has he ambition? Or is he a *mere* neatherd?

HERMES. I couldn't say for certain. But he is a young man, so it is to be presumed that distinction on the field of battle is among his desires.

APHRODITE. There, you see; *I* don't complain; I say nothing when you whisper with *her*. Aphrodite is not so particular as some people.

HERMES. Athene asked me almost exactly the same as you did; so don't be cross. It will do you no harm, my answering a plain question.—Meanwhile, we have left the stars far behind us, and are almost over Phrygia. There is Ida: I can make out the peak of Gargarum quite plainly; and if I am not mistaken, there is Paris himself.

HERA. Where is he? I don't see him.

HERMES. Look over there to the left, Hera: not on the top, but down the side, by that cave where you see the herd.

HERA. But I *don't* see the herd.

HERMES. What, don't you see them coming out from between the rocks,—where I am pointing, look —and the man running down from the crag, and keeping them together with his staff?

HERA. I see him now; if he it is.

HERMES. Oh, that is Paris. But we are getting nearer; it is time to alight and walk. He might be frightened, if we were to descend upon him so suddenly.

HERA. Yes; very well. And now that we are on the earth, you might go on ahead, Aphrodite, and show us the way. You know the country, of course, having been here so often to see Anchises; or so I have heard.

57. I believe . . . were. Paris was married to Oenone, the daughter of the river god Cebren.

APHRODITE. Your sneers are thrown away on me, Hera.

HERMES. Come; I'll lead the way myself. I spent some time on Ida, while Zeus was courting Ganymede. Many is the time that I have been sent here to keep watch over the boy; and when at last the eagle came, I flew by his side, and helped him with his lovely burden. This is the very rock, if I remember; yes, Ganymede was piping to his sheep, when down swooped the eagle behind him, and tenderly, oh, so tenderly, caught him up in those talons, and with the turban in his beak bore him off, the frightened boy straining his neck the while to see his captor. I picked up his pipes—he had dropped them in his fright—and—ah! here is our umpire, close at hand. Let us accost him.—Good-morrow, herdsman!

PARIS. Good-morrow, youngster. And who may you be, who come thus far afield? And these dames? They are over comely to be wandering on the mountain-side.

HERMES. "These dames," good Paris, are Hera, Athene, and Aphrodite; and I am Hermes, with a message from Zeus. Why so pale and tremulous? Compose yourself; there is nothing the matter. Zeus appoints you the judge of their beauty. "Because you are handsome, and wise in the things of love" (so runs the message), "I leave the decision to you; and for the prize,—read the inscription on the apple."

PARIS. Let me see what it is about. FOR THE FAIR, it says. But, my lord Hermes, how shall a mortal and a rustic like myself be judge of such unparalleled beauty? This is no sight for a herdsman's eyes; let the fine city folk decide on such matters. As for me, I can tell you which of two goats is the fairer beast; or I can judge betwixt heifer and heifer;—'tis my trade. But here, where all are beautiful alike, I know not how a man may leave looking at one, to look upon another. Where my eyes fall, there they fasten, —for there is beauty: I move them, and what do I find? More loveliness! I am fixed again, yet distracted by neighboring charms. I bathe in beauty: I am enthralled: ah, why am I not *all* eyes like Argus? Methinks it were a fair award, to give the apple to all three. Then again: one is the wife and sister of Zeus; the others are his daughters. Take it where you will, 'tis a hard matter to judge.

HERMES. So it is, Paris. At the same time—Zeus's orders! There is no way out of it.

PARIS. Well, please point out to them, Hermes, that the losers must not be angry with me; the fault will be in my eyes only.

HERMES. That is quite understood. And now to work.

PARIS. I must do what I can; there is no help for it. But first let me ask,—am I just to look at them as they are, or must I go into the matter thoroughly?

HERMES. That is for you to decide, in virtue of your office. You have only to give your orders; it is as you think best.

PARIS. As I think best? Then I will be thorough.

HERMES. Get ready, ladies. Now, Mr. Umpire.— I will look the other way.

HERA. I approve your decision, Paris. I will be the first to submit myself to your inspection. You will see that I have more to boast of than white arms and large eyes: nought of me but is beautiful.

PARIS. Aphrodite, will you also prepare?

ATHENE. Oh, Paris,—make her take off that girdle, first; there is magic in it; she will bewitch you. For that matter, she has no right to come thus tricked out and painted,—just like a courtesan! She ought to show herself unadorned.

PARIS. They are right about the girdle, madam; it must go.

APHRODITE. Oh, very well, Athene: then take off that helmet, and show your head bare, instead of trying to intimidate the judge with that waving plume. I suppose you are afraid the color of your eyes may be noticed, without their formidable surroundings.

ATHENE. Oh, here is my helmet.

APHRODITE. And here is my girdle.

HERA. Now then.

PARIS. God of wonders! What loveliness is here! Oh, rapture! How exquisite these maiden charms! How dazzling the majesty of Heaven's true queen! And oh, how sweet, how enthralling is Aphrodite's smile! 'Tis too much, too much of happiness.—But perhaps it would be well for me to view each in detail; for as yet I doubt, and know not where to look; my eyes are drawn all ways at once.

APHRODITE. Yes, that will be best.

PARIS. Withdraw then, you and Athene; and let Hera remain.

HERA. So be it; and when you have finished your scrutiny, you have next to consider, how you would like the present which I offer you. Paris, give me the prize of beauty, and you shall be lord of all Asia.

PARIS. I will take no presents. Withdraw. I shall judge as I think right. Approach, Athene.

ATHENE. Behold. And, Paris, if you will say that I am the fairest, I will make you a great warrior and conqueror, and you shall always win, in every one of your battles.

PARIS. But I have nothing to do with fighting, Athene. As you see, there is peace throughout all Lydia and Phrygia, and my father's dominion is uncontested. But never mind: I am not going to take your present, but you shall have fair play. You can robe again and put on your helmet; I have seen. And now for Aphrodite.

APHRODITE. Here I am; take your time, and examine carefully; let nothing escape your vigilance. And I have something else to say to you, handsome

Paris. Yes, you handsome boy, I have long had an eye on you; I think you must be the handsomest young fellow in all Phrygia. But it is such a pity that you don't leave these rocks and crags, and live in a town: you will lose all your beauty in this desert. What have you to do with mountains? What satisfaction can your beauty give to a lot of cows? You ought to have been married long ago; not to any of these dowdy women hereabouts, but to some Greek girl; an Argive, perhaps, or a Corinthian, or a Spartan; Helen, now, is a Spartan, and such a pretty girl—quite as pretty as I am—and so susceptible! Why, if she once caught sight of *you*, she would give up everything, I am sure, to go with you, and a most devoted wife she would be. But you have heard of Helen, of course.

PARIS. No, ma'am; but I should like to hear all about her now.

APHRODITE. Well, she is the daughter of Leda, the beautiful woman, you know, whom Zeus visited in the disguise of a swan.

PARIS. And what is she like?

APHRODITE. She is fair, as might be expected from the swan, soft as down (she was hatched from an egg, you know), and such a lithe, graceful figure; and only think, she is so much admired, that there was a war because Theseus ran away with her; and she was a mere child then. And when she grew up, the very first men in Greece were suitors for her hand, and she was given to Menelaus, who is descended from Pelops.—Now, if you like, she shall be your wife.

PARIS. What, when she is married already?

APHRODITE. Tut, child, you are a simpleton: *I* understand these things.

PARIS. I should like to understand them too.

APHRODITE. You will set out for Greece on a tour of inspection: and when you get to Sparta, Helen will see you; and for the rest—her falling in love, and going back with you—that will be my affair.

PARIS. But that is what I cannot believe,—that she will forsake her husband to cross the seas with a stranger, a barbarian.

APHRODITE. Trust me for that. I have two beautiful children, Love and Desire. They shall be your guides. Love will assail her in all his might, and compel her to love you: Desire will encompass you about, and make you desirable and lovely as himself; and I will be there to help. I can get the Graces to come too, and between us we shall prevail.

PARIS. How this will end, I know not. All I do know is, that I am in love with Helen already. I see her before me—I sail for Greece—I am in Sparta—I am on my homeward journey, with her at my side! Ah, why is none of it true?

APHRODITE. Wait. Do not fall in love yet. You have first to secure my interest with the bride, by your award. The union must be graced with my victorious presence: your marriage-feast shall be my feast of victory. Love, beauty, wedlock; all these you may purchase at the price of yonder apple.

PARIS. But perhaps after the award you will forget all about *me*?

APHRODITE. Shall I swear?

PARIS. No; but promise once more.

APHRODITE. I promise that you shall have Helen to wife; that she shall follow you, and make Troy her home; and I will be present with you, and help you in all.

PARIS. And bring Love, and Desire, and the Graces?

APHRODITE. Assuredly; and Passion and Hymen as well.

PARIS. Take the apple: it is yours.

Dialogues of the Dead

HERMES AND CHARON

HERMES.

Ferryman, what do you say to settling up accounts? It will prevent any unpleasantness later on.

CHARON. Very good. It does save trouble to get these things straight.

HERMES. One anchor, to your order, five shillings.

CHARON. That is a lot of money.

HERMES. So help me Pluto, it is what I had to pay. One rowlock-strap, fourpence.

CHARON. Five and four; put that down.

HERMES. Then there was a needle, for mending the sail; ten-pence.

CHARON. Down with it.

HERMES. Caulking-wax; nails; and cord for the brace. Two shillings the lot.

CHARON. They were worth the money.

HERMES. That's all; unless I have forgotten anything. When will you pay it?

CHARON. I can't just now, Hermes; we shall have a war or a plague presently, and then the passengers will come shoaling in, and I shall be able to make a little by jobbing the fares.

HERMES. So for the present I have nothing to do but sit down, and pray for the worst, as my only chance of getting paid?

CHARON. There is nothing else for it;—very little business doing just now, as you see, owing to the peace.

Dialogues of the Dead. Translated by H. W. and F. G. Fowler. From *The Works of Lucian of Samosata*, Vol. I., by H. W. and F. G. Fowler. Reprinted by permission of The Clarendon Press, Oxford.

HERMES. That is just as well, though it does keep me waiting for my money. After all, though, Charon, in old days men were men; you remember the state they used to come down in,—all blood and wounds generally. Nowadays, a man is poisoned by his slave or his wife; or gets dropsy from overfeeding; a pale, spiritless lot, nothing like the men of old. Most of them seem to meet their end in some plot that has money for its object.

CHARON. Ah; money is in great request.

HERMES. Yes; you can't blame me if I am somewhat urgent for payment.

MENIPPUS AND HERMES

MENIPPUS. Where are all the beauties, Hermes? Show me round; I am a new-comer.

HERMES. I am busy, Menippus. But look over there to your right, and you will see Hyacinth, Narcissus, Nireus, Achilles, Tyro, Helen, Leda,—all the beauties of old.

MENIPPUS. I can only see bones, and bare skulls; most of them are exactly alike.

HERMES. Those bones, of which you seem to think so lightly, have been the theme of admiring poets.

MENIPPUS. Well, but show me Helen; I shall never be able to make her out by myself.

HERMES. This skull is Helen.

MENIPPUS. And for this a thousand ships carried warriors from every part of Greece; Greeks and barbarians were slain, and cities made desolate.

HERMES. Ah, Menippus, you never saw the living Helen; or you would have said with Homer,

Well might they suffer grievous years of toil
Who strove for such a prize.

We look at withered flowers, whose dye is gone from them, and what can we call them but unlovely things? Yet in the hour of their bloom these unlovely things were things of beauty.

MENIPPUS. Strange, that the Greeks could not realize what it was for which they laboured; how short-lived, how soon to fade.

HERMES. I have no time for moralizing. Choose your spot, where you will, and lie down. I must go to fetch new dead.

MENIPPUS AND CERBERUS

MENIPPUS. My dear coz—for Cerberus and Cynic are surely related through the dog—I adjure you by the Styx, tell me how Socrates behaved during the descent. A God like you can doubtless articulate instead of barking, if he chooses.

CERBERUS. Well, while he was some way off, he seemed quite unshaken; and I thought he was bent on letting the people outside realize the fact too. Then he passed into the opening and saw the gloom; I at the same time gave him a touch of the hemlock, and a pull by the leg, as he was rather slow. Then he squalled like a baby, whimpered about his children, and, oh, I don't know what he didn't do.

MENIPPUS. So he was one of the theorists, was he? his indifference was a sham?

CERBERUS. Yes; it was only that he accepted the inevitable, and put a bold face on it, pretending to welcome the universal fate, by way of impressing the bystanders. All that sort are the same, I tell you—bold resolute fellows as far as the entrance; it is inside that the real test comes.

MENIPPUS. What did you think of my performance?

CERBERUS. Ah, Menippus, you were the exception; you are a credit to the breed, and so was Diogenes before you. You two came in without any compulsion or pushing, of your own free will, with a laugh for yourselves and a curse for the rest.

MENIPPUS AND CHIRON

MENIPPUS. I have heard that you were a god, Chiron, and that you died of your own choice?

CHIRON. You were rightly informed. I am dead, as you see, and might have been immortal.

MENIPPUS. And what should possess you, to be in love with Death? He has no charm for most people.

CHIRON. You are a sensible fellow; I will tell you. There was no further satisfaction to be had from immortality.

MENIPPUS. Was it not a pleasure merely to live and see the light?

CHIRON. No; it is variety, as I take it, and not monotony, that constitutes pleasure. Living on and on, everything always the same; sun, light, food, spring, summer, autumn, winter, one thing following another in unending sequence,—I sickened of it all. I found that enjoyment lay not in continual possession; that deprivation had its share therein.

MENIPPUS. Very true, Chiron. And how have you got on since you made Hades your home?

CHIRON. Not unpleasantly. I like the truly republican equality that prevails; and as to whether one is in light or darkness, that makes no difference at all. Then again there is no hunger or thirst here; one is independent of such things.

MENIPPUS. Take care, Chiron! You may be caught in the snare of your own reasonings.

CHIRON. How should that be?

MENIPPUS. Why, if the monotony of the other world brought on satiety, the monotony here may do the same. You will have to look about for a further change, and I fancy there is no third life procurable.

CHIRON. Then what is to be done, Menippus?

MENIPPUS. Take things as you find them, I suppose, like a sensible fellow, and make the best of everything.

Sappho

Sixth century B.C.

The Tenth Muse, as Plato ecstatically called Sappho, is a legend of literature built from ancient tradition and a few extant poems into the greatest of all women poets. As late as 1073 a large collection of her verse still existed but in that year it was publicly burned by church dignitaries of Rome and Constantinople. The biographies of Sappho surviving from antiquity were probably derived from her poems and are far from trustworthy.

Sappho belongs to Mitylene, a brilliant city on the Aegean island of Lesbos, and to the sixth century B.C., when a social revolution there was replacing the old landed aristocracy with an upstart bourgeoisie. Along with the poet Alcaeus, she was banished as an aristocrat to Pyrrha, where Alcaeus paid romantic attention to her, at least in verse. But she was indifferent to his proposals, and after further exile to distant Sicily she married a wealthy merchant and probably had a daughter. We know too that she had a younger brother who won his sister's resentment by marrying a courtesan while on a business trip in Egypt.

Sappho's songs, which she herself set to the music of the lyre, are passionate love poems addressed to younger women whom she may have taught in a kind of finishing school. As her disciples left her to marry, she expressed her feelings in sorrowful laments and graceful epithalamia, or wedding songs. The personal note is strong, as in all the Aeolian school, and the simplicity of her style burns her feelings into the reader's mind. Sappho helped to raise her Aeolian dialect to the level of literary expression and perfected several distinctive meters, of which one still bears the name "Sapphic."

Ode to Aphrodite

DEATHLESS Aphrodite, throned in flowers,
  Daughter of Zeus, O terrible enchantress,
With this sorrow, with this anguish, break my spirit,
    Lady, not longer!

Hear anew the voice! O hear and listen!   5
Come, as in that island dawn thou camest,
Billowing in thy yoked car to Sappho
    Forth from thy father's

Ode to Aphrodite. Translated by William Ellery Leonard. From *A Son of Earth* by William Ellery Leonard. Copyright 1928 by The Viking Press, Inc. Reprinted by permission of The Viking Press, Inc., New York.

Golden house in pity! . . . I remember:
Fleet and fair thy sparrows drew thee, beating   10
Fast their wings above the dusky harvests,
    Down the pale heavens,

Lighting anon! And thou, O blest and brightest,
Smiling with immortal eyelids, asked me:
"Maiden, what betideth thee? Or wherefore   15
    Callest upon me?

"What is here the longing more than other,
Here in this mad heart? And who the lovely
One beloved thou wouldst lure to loving?
    Sappho, who wrongs thee?   20

"See, if now she flies, she soon must follow;
Yes, if spurning gifts, she soon must offer;
Yes, if loving not, she soon must love thee,
    Howso unwilling. . . ."

Come again to me! O now! Release me!   25
End the great pang! And all my heart desireth
Now of fulfillment, fulfill! O Aphrodite,
    Fight by my shoulder!

Ode to Anactoria

PEER of gods he seemeth to me, the blissful
  Man who sits and gazes at thee before him,
Close beside thee sits, and in silence hears thee
    Silverly speaking,

Laughing love's low laughter. Oh this, this only   5
Stirs the troubled heart in my breast to tremble!
For should I but see thee a little moment,
    Straight is my voice hushed;

Yea, my tongue is broken, and through and through
    me
'Neath the flesh impalpable fire runs tingling;   10
Nothing see mine eyes, and a noise of roaring
    Waves in my ear sounds;

Sweat runs down in rivers, a tremor seizes
All my limbs, and paler than grass in autumn,
Caught by pains of menacing death, I falter,   15
    Lost in the love-trance.

Ode to Anactoria. Translated by John Addington Symonds. This translation follows the "Sapphic meter" of the original.

Farewell
To Anactoria

NEVER the tramp of foot or horse,
  Nor lusty cries from ships at sea,
Shall I call loveliest on the dark earth—
  My heart moves lovingly.

I say that what one loves is best—   5
The midnight fastness of the heart. . . .
Helen, you filched the beauty of men
  With unpitying art!

White Paris from Idean hills
For you the Trojan towers razed—   10
Who swiftly plowed the black seas
  Had on your white arms gazed!

Oh, how loving from afar
Led you to grief, for in your mind
The present was too light, as ever   15
  Among fair womankind. . . .

So, Anactoria, you go away
With what calm carelessness of sorrow!
Your gleaming footstep and your grace,
  When comes another morrow,   20

Much would I rather then behold
Than Lydian cars or infantry.
I ask the lot of blessedness,
  Beloved, in memory.

(Fragments)

ROUND about me hum the winds of autumn,
  Cool between the apple boughs: and slumber,
Flowing from the quivering leaves to earthward,
  Spreads as a river.

Love, like a mountain-wind upon an oak,
Falling upon me, shakes me leaf and bough.

The moon and seven Pleiades have set;
It is the midnight now; the hours go by;
And still I'm lying in my bed alone.

Farewell to Anactoria. Translated by Allen Tate. From *Mr. Pope and Other Poems*, by Allen Tate. Copyright 1928 by Minton, Balch & Co. Courtesy of G. P. Putnam's Sons.
Fragments. Translated by William Ellery Leonard. From *A Son of Earth* by William Ellery Leonard. Copyright 1928 by The Viking Press, Inc. Reprinted by permission of The Viking Press, Inc., New York.

Off in the twilight hung the low full moon,
And all the women stood before it grave,
As round an altar. Thus at holy times
The Cretan damsels dance melodiously
With delicate feet about the sacrifice,   5
Trampling the tender bloom of the soft grass.

A Bride

I

LIKE the sweet apple which reddens upon the topmost bough,
A-top on the topmost twig,—which the pluckers forgot somehow,—
Forgot it not, nay, but got it not, for none could get it till now.

II

Like the wild hyacinth flower which on the hills is found,
Which the passing feet of the shepherds forever tear and wound,   5
Until the purple blossom is trodden in the ground.

Forgotten

DEAD shalt thou lie; and nought
  Be told of thee or thought,
For thou hast plucked not of the Muses' tree:
  And even in Hades' halls
  Amidst thy fellow-thralls
No friendly shade thy shade shall company!   5

A Girl

I HAVE a child; so fair
  As golden flowers is she,
My Cleïs, all my care.
I'd not give her away
For Lydia's wide sway   5
Nor lands men long to see.

A Bride. Translated by Dante Gabriel Rossetti.
Forgotten. Translated by Thomas Hardy. From *Collected Poems* by Thomas Hardy. By permission of The Macmillan Company, publishers. This savage poem was addressed to a wealthy but uneducated woman.
A Girl. Translated by C. M. Bowra. From *The Oxford Book of Greek Verse in Translation*, by T. F. Higham and C. M. Bowra. Reprinted by permission of The Clarendon Press, Oxford.
5. **Lydia,** an ancient kingdom in Asia Minor.

Mother, I Cannot
Mind My Wheel

MOTHER, I cannot mind my wheel;
  My fingers ache, my lips are dry;
Oh! if you felt the pain I feel!
But oh, who ever felt as I!

Hesperus
the Bringer

O HESPERUS, thou bringest all good things—
  Home to the weary, to the hungry cheer,
To the young bird the parent's brooding wings,
  The welcome stall to the o'erlabored steer;
Whate'er of peace about our hearthstone clings,   5
  Whate'er our household gods protect of dear,
Are gathered round us by thy look of rest;
Thou bringest the child too to its mother's breast.

The Dust of Timas

THIS dust was Timas; and they say
  That almost on her wedding day
She found her bridal home to be
The dark house of Persephone.

And many maidens, knowing then   5
That she would not come back again,
Unbound their curls; and all in tears,
They cut them off with sharpened shears.

Mother, I Cannot. . . . Translated by Walter Savage Landor.
Hesperus the Bringer. Translated by Lord Byron. "Hesperus the
Bringer" is the evening star.
The Dust of Timas. Translated by Edwin Arlington Robinson. From
Captain Craig by Edwin Arlington Robinson. By permission of The
Macmillan Company, publishers.

*Women with water jars at the Athenian fountain of
Callirrhoe. From a Greek vase.*

Anacreon

Sixth century B.C.

Anacreon was an Ionian of Teos in Asia Minor,
but his curiosity about the world led him to visit
many parts of Hellas—especially Samos and Athens. As
individualistic as Sappho, he lacked her seriousness and
devoted his long life to an incessant round of pleasure.
He detested physical exertion and in his youth threw
away his shield on the battlefield and literally ran out of
the army. As he grew older, he worked hard at staying
young and was still the life of the party in his eighties.
Wine and love were his favorite themes, though he was
always moderate in both, mixing his wine with two parts
water and his love with the common sense that kept him
from getting too involved in any affairs of the heart. His
language is as simple and his style as delicate as Sappho's,
so that the two are complementary spirits of earnest and
frivolous in a common lyric tradition. He was beloved
after his death as during his life, and his jolly example
inspired in the Hellenistic era a host of anonymous imitators whose convivial poems are now lumped together as
the "Anacreontic" tradition. Most of the following lyrics
belong to this category.

The Wounded Cupid

CUPID, as he lay among
  Roses, by a bee was stung.
Whereupon in anger flying
To his mother, said, thus crying,
Help! O help! your boy's a-dying.   5
And why, my pretty lad? said she.
Then blubbering replièd he,
A wingèd snake has bitten me,
Which country people call a bee.
At which she smiled, then with her hairs   10
And kisses, drying up his tears,
Alas! said she, my wag, if this
Such a pernicious torment is;
Come, tell me then how great's the smart
Of those thou woundest with thy dart!   15

The Cheat of Cupid

OR, THE UNGENTLE GUEST

ONE silent night of late,
  When every creature rested,
Came one unto my gate,
  And knocking, me molested.

The Wounded Cupid. Translated by Robert Herrick.
The Cheat of Cupid. Translated by Robert Herrick.

Who's that, said I, beats there, 5
  And troubles thus the sleepy?
Cast off, said he, all fear,
  And let not locks thus keep ye.

For I am a boy who
  By moonless nights have swervèd, 10
And all with showers wet through,
  And e'en with cold have starvèd.

I pitiful arose,
  And soon a taper lighted,
And did myself disclose 15
  Unto the lad benighted.

I saw he had a bow,
  And wings too, which did shiver;
And looking down below,
  I spied he had a quiver. 20

I to my chimney's shine
  Brought him, as love professes,
And chafed his hands with mine,
  And dried his dropping tresses.

But when he felt him warmed, 25
  Let's try this bow of ours
And string, if they be harmed,
  Said he, with these late showers.

Forthwith his bow he bent,
  And wedded string and arrow, 30
And struck me that it went
  Quite through my heart and marrow.

Then laughing loud, he flew
  Away, and thus said, flying,
Adieu, mine host, adieu, 35
  I'll leave thy heart a-dying.

Love

I'LL sing of heroes and of kings,
  In mighty numbers, mighty things.
Begin, my Muse!—but lo! the strings
To my great song rebellious prove;
The strings will sound of nought but love. 5
—I broke them all, and put on new;
—'Tis this, or nothing, now will do.
"These, sure," said I, "will me obey;
These, sure, heroic notes will play."
Straight I began with thundering Jove 10
And all th' immortal powers; but Love,
Love smiled; and from my enfeebled lyre
Came gentle airs, such as inspire

Love. Translated by Abraham Cowley.

Melting love and soft desire.—
Farewell, then, heroes! farewell, kings! 15
And mighty numbers, mighty things!
Love tunes my heart just to my strings.

The Combat

Now will I a lover be;
  Love himself commanded me.
Full at first of stubborn pride,
To submit my soul denied;
He his quiver takes and bow, 5
Bids defiance, forth I go,
Arm'd with spear and shield, we meet;
On he charges, I retreat:
Till perceiving in the fight
He had wasted every flight, 10
Into me, with fury hot,
Like a dart himself he shot,
And my cold heart melts; my shield
Useless, no defense could yield;
For what boots an outward screen 15
When, alas, the fight's within!

The Epicure

UNDERNEATH this myrtle shade,
  On flowery beds supinely laid,
With odorous oils my head o'erflowing,
And around it roses growing,
What should I do but drink away 5
The heat and troubles of the day?
In this more than kingly state,
Love himself shall on me wait.
Fill to me, Love; nay, fill it up;
And mingled cast into the cup 10
Wit, and mirth, and noble fires,
Vigorous health, and gay desires.
The wheel of life no less will stay
In a smooth than rugged way:
Since it equally doth flee, 15
Let the motion pleasant be.
Why do we precious ointments shower,
Nobler wines why do we pour,
Beauteous flowers why do we spread,
Upon the monuments of the dead? 20
Nothing they but dust can show,
Or bones that hasten to be so.
Crown me with roses whilst I live,—
Now your wines and ointments give;
After death I nothing crave, 25
Let me alive my pleasures have!
All are Stoics in the grave.

The Combat. Translated by Thomas Stanley.
The Epicure. Translated by Abraham Cowley.

Beauty

Horns to bulls wise Nature lends;
  Horses she with hoofs defends;
Hares with nimble feet relieves;
Dreadful teeth to lions gives;
Fishes learn through streams to slide;   5
Birds through yielding air to glide;
Men with courage she supplies;
But to women these denies.
What then gives she? Beauty, this
Both their arms and armor is: 10
She that can this weapon use,
Fire and sword with ease subdues.

The Grasshopper

Happy insect! what can be
  In happiness compar'd to thee?
Fed with nourishment divine,
The dewy morning's gentle wine!
Nature waits upon thee still,   5
And thy verdant cup does fill;
'Tis filled wherever thou dost tread,
Nature self's thy Ganymede.
Thou dost drink, and dance, and sing;
Happier than the happiest king!   10
All the fields which thou dost see,
All the plants belong to thee;
All that summer hours produce;
Fertile made with early juice.
Man for thee does sow and plow;   15
Farmer he, and landlord thou!
Thou dost innocently joy;
Nor does thy luxury destroy;
The shepherd gladly heareth thee,
More harmonious than he.   20
Thee country-hinds with gladness hear,
Prophet of the ripen'd year!
Thee Phoebus loves, and does inspire;
Phoebus is himself thy sire.
To thee, of all things upon earth,   25
Life's no longer than thy mirth.
Happy insect, happy, thou
Dost neither age nor winter know;
But, when thou'st drunk and danc'd and sung
Thy fill, the flowery leaves among,   30
(Voluptuous and wise withal,
Epicurean animal!)—
Sated with thy summer feast,
Thou retir'st to endless rest.

Beauty. Translated by Thomas Stanley.
The Grasshopper. Translated by Abraham Cowley.

All Things Drink

Fruitful earth drinks up the rain;
  Trees from earth drink that again;
The sea drinks the air, the sun
Drinks the sea, and him the moon.
Is it reason then, d'ye think,   5
I should thirst when all else drink?

The Cup

Make me a bowl, a mighty bowl,
  Large as my capacious soul,
Vast as my thirst is. Let it have
Depth enough to be my grave.
I mean the grave of all my care,   5
For I intend to bury't there.
Let it of silver fashioned be,
Worthy of wine! worthy of me!
Worthy to adorn the spheres
As that bright Cup among the stars!   10

Yet draw no shapes of armor there,
No casque nor shield nor sword nor spear
Nor wars of Thebes nor wars of Troy,
Nor any other martial toy.
For what do I vain armor prize,   15
Who mind not such rough exercise?
For gentle sieges, softer wars,
Fights that cause no wounds or scars.
I'll have not battles on my plate,
Lest sight of them should brawls create, 20
Lest that provoke to quarrels too,
Which wine itself enough can do.

Old I Am

Old I am, yet can (I think)
  Those that younger are out-drink.
When I dance no staff I take,
But a well-fill'd bottle shake.
He that doth in war delight,   5
Come, and with these arms let's fight.
Fill the cup, let loose a flood
Of the rich grape's luscious blood.
Old I am, and therefore may,
Like Silenus, drink and play.

All Things Drink. Translated by Thomas Stanley.
The Cup. Translated by John Oldham.
Old I Am. Translated by Thomas Stanley.   10. Silenus, the jolly
old satyr who spent his life drinking wine and playing the flute.

Youthful Age

YOUNG men dancing, and the old
   Sporting I with joy behold;
But an old man gay and free
Dancing most I love to see.
Age and youth alike he shares,   5
For his heart belies his hairs.

Age

OFT am I by the women told,
   "Poor Anacreon! thou grow'st old.
Look! how thy hairs are falling all;
Poor Anacreon, how they fall!"—
Whether I grow old or no,   5
By the effects I do not know;
But this I know, without being told,
'Tis time to live, if I grow old.
'Tis time short pleasures now to take,
Of little life the best to make,   10
And manage wisely the last stake.

Old Age

SWEET Youth no more will tarry,
   My friend a while ago;
Now white's the head I carry,
   And grey my temples grow,
   My teeth—a ragged row.   5

To taste the joy of living
   But little space have I,
And torn with sick misgiving
   I can but sob and sigh,
   So deep the dead men lie.   10

So deep their place and dismal,
   All means, be sure, they lack
Down in the murk abysmal
   To scale the upward track
   And win their journey back.

Youthful Age. Translated by Thomas Stanley.
Age. Translated by Abraham Cowley.
Old Age. Translated by T. F. Higham. From *The Oxford Book of Greek Verse in Translation,* by T. F. Higham and C. M. Bowra. Reprinted by permission of The Clarendon Press, Oxford.

Theocritus

Flourished 260 B.C.

The best of the Alexandrine poets, Theocritus, was also the founder of the pastoral tradition in world poetry with his ten charming rustic idylls. His total output was slight—twenty-odd idylls and twenty brief epigrams—but its influence on later poetry down to the last century has been prodigious. Theocritus apparently invented the idyll as a little picture of life, usually with some slight dramatic action. Half of his idylls have the beautiful countryside of Sicily for background and turn on the dainty love affairs of poetic shepherds or their contests in wrestling and song for the favor of a ladylove.

Theocritus was born in Sicily, in the fair city of Syracuse, and knew in childhood the charm of its hilly slopes. But ambition took him away to study medicine at Cos and then to seek the favor of the Ptolemies at Alexandria a few years later. His success in this brilliant capital did not satisfy him long, because we hear of him thereafter at Cos again and at Miletus, where he may have died. But wherever he went, he seems to have retained a nostalgia for the simple life of rustic Sicily, and his pastoral idylls are his tribute to his birthplace. Sentimental and unrealistic as they are, these sweet, lively vignettes delighted the sophisticates of Alexandria and other aristocratic societies of later centuries. The sensitive little shepherds with poetic names like Thyrsis, Corydon, and Menalcas, their delicate loves for demure damsels like Amaryllis and Simaetha, and the Arcadian simplicity of a land where there was always sun by day and moon by night hardened into an artificial pastoral tradition. Virgil re-created it in his *Eclogues* for the elegant court of Augustus. It produced Spenser's *Shepheardes Calender* at the English court of Elizabeth. Pope, Ambrose Philips, and John Gay were among the pastoral poets who regaled the aristocratic eighteenth century; and the tradition reached its most insipid depths in the circle of Marie Antoinette, decked out in ribbons with shepherd's crooks. It was applied to the novel in Sidney's *Arcadia* and to the drama in the pastoral plays of Jonson, Fletcher, and Ramsay. And in its loftiest metamorphosis the dirges in Theocritus inspired the great pastoral elegies of Milton, Shelley, and Arnold.

Despite the artificiality of his imitators there is freshness and vivacity in the originals of Theocritus. Moreover, he varied the form of the idyll to include other types of material. The half-pathetic, half-absurd whimpering of Polyphemus, the ugly Cyclops, for love of the nymph Galatea is one of several on mythological subjects. But the most famous and amusing of all is *The Syracusan Ladies,* a realistic dialogue between two housewives on their way to a festival of Adonis in Alexandria. The feminine chatter about fashions and husbands is as modern as today, and nearly every allusion in it can be translated into the terms of our century. This is not the greatest poetry, to be sure, but within his modest limits Theocritus was a true artist.

The Two Workmen

(IDYLL X)

This charming dialogue contrasts the rugged, earthy reaper, Milo, with his melancholy, lovelorn companion, Battus. Their songs reflect their opposite characters.

MILO.

WHAT now, poor o'erworked drudge, is on thy
    mind?
No more in even swathe thou layest the corn:
Thy fellow-reapers leave thee far behind,
    As flocks a ewe that's footsore from a thorn.
By noon and midday what will be thy plight   5
If now, so soon, thy sickle fails to bite?
    BATTUS. Hewn from hard rocks, untired at set of
      sun,
Milo, didst ne'er regret some absent one?
    MILO. Not I. What time have workers for regret?
    BATTUS. Hath love ne'er kept thee from thy slum-
      bers yet?   10
    MILO. Nay, heaven forbid! If once the cat taste
      cream!
    BATTUS. Milo, these ten days love hath been my
      dream.
    MILO. You drain your wine, while vinegar's scarce
      with me.
    BATTUS.—Hence since last spring untrimmed my
      borders be.
    MILO. And what lass flouts thee?
    BATTUS.   She whom we heard
    play   15
Amongst Hippocoön's reapers yesterday.
    MILO. Your sins have found you out—you're e'en
      served right:
You'll clasp a corn-crake in your arms all night.
    BATTUS. You laugh: but headstrong Love is blind
      no less
Than Plutus: talking big is foolishness.   20
    MILO. I talk not big. But lay the corn-ears low,
And trill the while some love-song—easier so
Will seem your toil: you used to sing, I know.
    BATTUS. Maids of Pieria, of my slim lass sing!
One touch of yours ennobles everything.   25
                              (Sings)

Fairy Bombyca! thee do men report
    Lean, dusk, a gipsy: I alone nut-brown.
Violets and pencilled hyacinths are swart,
    Yet first of flowers they're chosen for a crown.
As goats pursue the clover, wolves the goat,   30
And cranes the ploughman, upon thee I dote.

The Two Workmen. Translated by C. S. Calverley. **19–20. Love
. . . Plutus.** The god of wealth was thought to be blind, because he
dispensed riches to the undeserving as well as to the deserving. **24.
Maids of Pieria,** the Muses.

Had I but Croesus' wealth, we twain should stand
    Gold-sculptured in Love's temple; thou, thy lyre
(Ay or a rose or apple) in thy hand,
    I in my brave new shoon and dance-attire.   35
Fairy Bombyca! twinkling dice thy feet,
Poppies thy lips, thy ways none knows how sweet!
    MILO. Who dreamed what subtle strains our
      bumpkin wrought?
How shone the artist in each measured verse!
Fie on the beard that I have grown for naught!   40
Mark, lad, these lines by glorious Lytierse.
                              (Sings)

O rich in fruit and cornblade: be this field
Tilled well, Demeter, and fair fruitage yield!

Bind the sheaves, reapers: lest one, passing, say—
'A fig for these; they're never worth their pay.'   45

Let the mown swathes look northward, ye who mow,
Or westward—for the ears grow fattest so.

Avoid a noontide nap, ye threshing men:
The chaff flies thickest from the corn-ears then.

Wake when the lark wakes; when he slumbers,
    close   50
Your work, ye reapers: and at noontide doze.

Boys, the frogs' life for me! They need not him
Who fills the flagon, for in drink they swim.

Better boil herbs, thou toiler after gain,
Than, splitting cummin, split thy hand in twain.   55

Strains such as these, I trow, befit them well
    Who toil and moil when noon is at its height:

Thy meager love-tale, bumpkin, thou shouldst tell
    Thy grandam as she wakes up ere 'tis light.

The Cyclops

(IDYLL XI)

The sweet love-complaint of Polyphemus to the sea-nymph Galatea is charmingly absurd when one recalls him as the cannibal giant of the *Odyssey*.

AND so an easier life our Cyclops drew,
    The Ancient Polyphemus, who in youth
Loved Galatea while the manhood grew
    Adown his cheeks, and darkened round his mouth.
No jot he cared for apples, olives, roses;   5
    Love made him mad; the whole world was neg-
      lected,
The very sheep went backward to their closes

The Cyclops. Translated by Elizabeth Barrett Browning.

From out the fair green pastures, self-directed.
And singing Galatea, thus, he wore
The sunrise down along the weedy shore, 10
    And pined alone, and felt the cruel wound
Beneath his heart, which Cypris' arrow bore,
    With a deep pang: but, so, the cure was found;
And sitting on a lofty rock, he cast
His eyes upon the sea, and sang at last: 15
"O whitest Galatea, can it be
    That thou shouldst spurn me off who love thee
        so?
More white than curds, my girl, thou art to see,
More meek than lambs, more full of leaping glee
    Than kids, and brighter than the early glow 20
On grapes that swell to ripen,—sour like thee!
Thou comest to me with the fragrant sleep,
    And with the fragrant sleep thou goest from me;
Thou fliest . . . fliest as a frightened sheep
    Flies the gray wolf!—yet love did overcome me,
So long!—I loved thee, maiden, first of all, 26
    When down the hills (my mother fast beside
        thee)
I saw thee stray to pluck the summer-fall
Of hyacinth-bells, and went myself to guide thee;
And since my eyes have seen thee, they can leave
    thee 30
    No more, from that day's light! But thou . . . by
        Zeus,
Thou wilt not care for *that*, to let it grieve thee!
    I know thee, fair one, why thou springest loose
From my arm round thee. Why? I tell thee, dear!
    One shaggy eyebrow draws its smudging road 35
Straight through my ample front, from ear to ear;
    One eye rolls underneath; and yawning, broad,
Flat nostrils feel the bulging lips too near.
Yet . . . ho, ho!—I,—whatever I appear,—
    Do feed a thousand oxen! When I have done, 40
I milk the cows, and drink the milk that's best!
    I lack no cheese, while summer keeps the sun;
And after, in the cold, it's ready prest!
    And then, I know to sing, as there is none
Of all the Cyclops can, . . . a song of thee, 45
Sweet apple of my soul, on love's fair tree,
And of myself who love thee . . . till the West
Forgets the light, and all but I have rest.
I feed for thee, besides, eleven fair does,
    And all in fawn; and four tame whelps of bears.
Come to me, sweet! thou shalt have all of those 51
    In change for love! I will not halve the shares.
Leave the blue sea, with pure white arms extend-
    ed
    To the dry shore; and, in my cave's recess,
Thou shalt be gladder for the noon-light ended; 55
    For here be laurels, spiral cypresses,
Dark ivy, and a vine whose leaves infold

Most luscious grapes; and here is water cold,
    The wooded Aetna pours down thro the trees
From the white snows, which gods were scarce too
    bold 60
    To drink in turn with nectar. Who with these
Would choose the salt wave of the lukewarm
    seas?
Nay, look on me! If I am hairy and rough,
    I have an oak's heart in me; there's a fire
In these grey ashes which burns hot enough; 65
    And, when I burn for *thee*, I grudge the pyre
No fuel . . . not my soul, nor this one eye,—
Most precious thing I have, because thereby
I see thee, fairest! Out, alas! I wish
My mother had borne me finnèd like a fish, 70
That I might plunge down in the ocean near thee,
    And kiss thy glittering hand beneath the weeds,
If still thy face were turned; and I would bear thee
    Each lily white, and poppy fair that bleeds
Its red heart down its leaves!—one gift, for hours 75
    Of summer,—one for winter; since to cheer
        thee,
I could not bring at once all kinds of flowers.
Even now, girl, now, I fain would learn to swim,
If stranger in a ship sailed nigh, I wis,
    That I may know how sweet a thing it is 80
To live down with you in the deep and dim!
Come up, O Galatea, from the ocean,
    And, having come, forget again to go!
As I, who sing out here my heart's emotion,
    Could sit forever. Come up from below! 85
Come, keep my flocks beside me, milk my kine;
    Come, press my cheese, distrain my whey and
        curd!
Ah, mother! she alone . . . that mother of mine . . .
    Did wrong me sore! I blame her! Not a word
Of kindly intercession did she address 90
Thine ear with for my sake; and ne'ertheless
    She saw me wasting, wasting, day by day:
    Both head and feet were aching, I will say,
All sick for grief, as I myself was sick.
    O Cyclops, Cyclops! whither hast thou sent 95
    Thy soul on fluttering wings? If thou wert bent
On turning bowls, or pulling green and thick
    The sprouts to give thy lambkins, thou wouldst
        make thee
    A wiser Cyclops than for what we take thee.
Milk dry the present! Why pursue too quick 100
That future which is fugitive aright?
Thy Galatea thou shalt haply find,
Or else a maiden fairer and more kind;
For many girls do call me thro the night,
    And, as they call, do laugh out silvery.. 105
    I, too, am something in the world, I see!"

While thus the Cyclops love and lambs did fold,
Ease came with song, he could not buy with gold.

12. Cypris, Aphrodite.

The Syracusan Ladies

(IDYLL XV)

Modeled perhaps on an older work by Sophron, this delightful dialogue of two chattering housewives on their way to a festival of Adonis gives a realistic picture of everyday life in Alexandria. Since the festival was given by Arsinoë, sister-queen to Ptolemy Philadelphus, the idyll is dated sometime after their marriage in 266 B.C.

GORGO.

Is Praxinoë at home?

PRAXINOË. Dear Gorgo, how long it is since you have been here! Yes she *is* at home. The wonder is that you have got here at last! Eunoë, see that she has a chair. Throw a cushion on it too.

GORGO. It does most charmingly as it is.

PRAXINOË. Do sit down.

GORGO. Oh, what a thing spirit is! I have scarcely got to you alive, Praxinoë! What a huge crowd,
10 what hosts of four-in-hands! Everywhere cavalry boots, everywhere men in uniform! And the road is endless: yes, you really live *too* far away!

PRAXINOË. It is all the fault of that madman of mine. Here he came to the ends of the earth and took—a hole, not a house, and all that we might not be neighbors. The jealous wretch, always the same, anything for spite!

GORGO. Don't talk of your husband Dinon like that, my dear, before your little boy,—look how he
20 is staring at you! Never mind, Zopyrion, sweet child, she is not speaking about papa.

PRAXINOË. Our Lady! The child does notice.

GORGO. Nice papa!

PRAXINOË. That papa of his the other day went to get soap and rouge at the shop, and came back to me with salt—the great big oaf!

GORGO. Mine is the same—a perfect spendthrift, Diocleides! Yesterday he got what he took for five fleeces, and paid seven drachmas a piece for—what
30 do you suppose?—dog-skins, shreds of old leather wallets, mere trash. But come, take your coat and shawl. Let us be off to the palace of rich Ptolemy the King, to the Adonis. I hear the Queen has provided something splendid!

PRAXINOË. Yes, fine folks do everything finely.

GORGO. What a tale you will have to tell about the things you have seen, to anyone who has not seen them! It is nearly time to go.

PRAXINOË. It's always holiday for idlers, Eunoë,
40 bring the water and put it down in the middle of the room, lazy creature that you are. You cats always like to sleep soft! Come, hurry, bring the water; quicker! I want water first; and how she carries it! Give it to me all the same; don't pour out so much, you extravagant thing. Stupid girl! Why are you wetting my dress? There, stop; I have washed my hands, as heaven would have it. Where is the key to the big chest? Bring it here.

GORGO. Praxinoë, that full dress becomes you
50 wonderfully. Tell me, how much did the stuff cost you off the loom?

PRAXINOË. Don't speak of it, Gorgo! More than eight pounds in good silver money,—and the work on it! I nearly slaved my soul out over it!

GORGO. Well, it is *most* successful, I must say.

PRAXINOË. Thanks for the pretty speech! (*To Eunoë*) Bring my shawl, and set my hat on my head properly.—No, child, I'm not going to take you. Boo! Bogies! There's a horse that bites little boys!
60 You may cry as much as you please, but I am not going to have you lamed.—Let us be moving. Phrygia, take the child, and keep him amused. Call in the dog, and shut the door. (*They go into the street.*) Ye gods, what a crowd! How on earth are we ever to get through this crush? They are like numberless ants. Many a good deed have you done, Ptolemy! Since your father joined the immortals, there's never a thug to maul the pedestrian, creeping up on him in Egyptian fashion. Oh! the tricks those rascals used
70 to play. Birds of a feather, rascals all!—Dear Gorgo, what will become of us? Here come the King's horses!—My dear man, don't trample on me. Look, the bay's rearing; see, what temper!—Eunoë, you foolhardy girl, will you never keep out of the way? The beast will be the death of the man that's leading him. What a good thing it is that I left my brat safe at home.

GORGO. Courage, Praxinoë. We are safe behind them now, and they have got in line.

PRAXINOË. There! I begin to be myself again.
80 Ever since I was a child I have feared nothing so much as horses and slimy snakes. Come along; a huge mob is pouring after us.

GORGO (*to an old woman*). Are you from the court, Mother?

OLD WOMAN. I am, my child.

PRAXINOË. Is it easy to get there?

OLD WOMAN. The Achaeans got into Troy by trying, my pretty. Trying will do everything in the long run.
90

GORGO. The old wife has spoken her oracles, and off she goes.

The Syracusan Ladies. Translated by Andrew Lang. Reprinted by permission of Macmillan & Co., Ltd. (Revised)

69. **Egyptian fashion.** The ladies are proud Greeks of Syracuse living in the Greek city of Alexandria established in conquered Egypt. Hence they look with disdain on the native Egyptian population.

PRAXINOË. Women know everything, even how Zeus married Hera!

GORGO. See, Praxinoë, what a crowd there is about the doors.

PRAXINOË. Monstrous, Gorgo! Give me your hand, and you, Eunoë, take hold of Eutychis. Don't lose hold of her, Eutychis, or you will get lost. Let us all go in together; Eunoë, clutch tight to me. Oh dear, Gorgo, my muslin dress is torn in two already!—
10 For heaven's sake, sir, if you wish to be fortunate, look out for my shawl!

STRANGER. I can hardly help myself, but I will be as careful as I can.

PRAXINOË. How close-packed the mob is! They push like a lot of pigs.

STRANGER. Courage, lady, all is well now.

PRAXINOË. Both this year and forever may all be well with you, dear sir, for the care you've taken of us.—What a nice, kind man! We're letting Eunoë
20 get squeezed—come, wretched girl, push your way through. That's the way. Now we are all on the right side of the door, as the bridegroom said when he had shut himself in with his bride.

GORGO. Do come here, Praxinoë. Look at these embroideries. How light and how lovely! You might call them the garments of the gods.

PRAXINOË. Lady Athene! what spinning women wrought them, what painters designed these drawings, so true they are? How naturally they stand and
30 move, like living creatures, not woven patterns. What a clever thing man is! Ah, and himself— Adonis—how beautiful to behold on his silver couch, with the first down on his cheeks, the thrice beloved Adonis—Adonis beloved even among the dead.

A STRANGER. You tiresome women, stop your endless cooing!—They bore one to death with their eternal broad vowels!

GORGO. Indeed! And where may this person come from? What is to you if we are chatter-boxes! Give
40 orders to your own servants, sir. Do you pretend to command ladies of Syracuse? If you must know, we are Corinthians by descent, and we speak Peloponnesian. Dorian women may lawfully speak Doric, I presume?

PRAXINOË. Lady Persephone! never may we have more than one master. I am not afraid of *your* orders.

GORGO. Hush, hush, Praxinoë—the Argive woman's daughter, the great singer, is beginning the
50 *Adonis;* she that won the prize last year for dirge-singing. I am sure she will give us something lovely. See, she is making her bow.

(The idyll ends with the dirge to Adonis, which is omitted here.)

The Greek Anthology

From the days of the Alexandrian scholars, collections of short poems, or epigrams, were made in order to preserve the fugitive Greek verse of older ages. The most famous was compiled by the poet Meleager of Gadara in the first century B.C. and represented forty-six poets ranging in time from Sappho to himself. This collection, which he called the *Stephanos,* or garland, in a charming preface likening his poets to flowers in a wreath, was expanded and reworked by later scholars, until Constantinus Cephalas in the tenth century A.D. prepared what is now known as the Palatine Anthology, containing the verse of 320 poets. With the addition of other poems in recent centuries, it became our *Greek Anthology,* a compilation of over six thousand short poems representing seventeen centuries of Greek and Roman culture and arranged in sixteen books according to subject.

The general tone of this collection of little gems is bright and cynical, with frequent surprises. Although a few major poets are well represented—Simonides, Callimachus, Meleager, and Palladas—most of the authors are minor figures known only through the *Anthology.* It is the poems, not the poets, that are remembered.

Not Such Your Burden

Not such your burden, happy youths, as
    ours—
Poor women—children nurtured daintily—
For ye have comrades when ill-fortune lours,
    To hearten you with talk and company;
And ye have games for solace, and may roam   5
    Along the streets and see the painters' shows.
But woe betide us if we stir from home—
    And there our thoughts are dull enough, God
        knows!   ——*Agathias*

Undying Thirst

This rudely sculptured porter-pot
    Denotes where sleeps a female sot;
Who passed her life, good easy soul,
In sweetly chirping o'er her bowl.
Not for her friends or children dear   5
She mourns, but only for her beer.
E'en in the very grave, they say,
She thirsts for drink to wet her clay;
And, faith, she thinks it very wrong
This jug should stand unfilled so long.——*Antipater*

Not Such Your Burden. Translated by William H. Hardinge.
Undying Thirst. Translated by Robert Bland.

Sea Dirge

CRUSHED by the waves upon the crag was I,
  Who still must hear these waves among
    the dead,
Breaking and brawling on the promontory,
  Sleepless; and sleepless is my weary head!
For me did strangers bury on the coast   5
  Within the hateful hearing of the deep,
Nor Death, that lulleth all, can lull my ghost,
  One sleepless soul among the souls that sleep!
                    ——*Archias of Byzantium*

To Archinus

IF I did come of set intent
  Then be thy blame my punishment;
But if by love a capture made
Forgive my hasty serenade.
Wine drew me on, Love thrust behind,   5
I was not master of my mind.
And when I came I did not cry
My name aloud, my ancestry;
Only my lips thy lintel pressed;
If this be crime, the crime's confessed.
                    ——*Callimachus*

Saon of Acanthus

HERE lapped in hallowed slumber Saon lies,
  Asleep, not dead; a good man never dies.
                    ——*Callimachus*

Heraclitus

THEY told me, Heraclitus, they told me you
    were dead;
They brought me bitter news to hear and bitter tears
    to shed.
I wept as I remembered how often you and I
Had tired the sun with talking and sent him down
    the sky.
And now that thou art lying, my dear old Carian
    guest,   5
A handful of gray ashes, long, long ago at rest,
Still are thy pleasant voices, thy nightingales, awake;
For Death, he taketh all away, but them he cannot
    take.   ——*Callimachus*

Sea Dirge. Translated by Andrew Lang. From *The Poetical Works of Andrew Lang*. Reprinted by permission of Longmans, Green & Co., Ltd. and the representatives of the late Andrew Lang.
To Archinus. Translated by F. A. Wright. From *Poets of the Greek Anthology*. Reprinted by permission of Routledge and Kegan Paul, Ltd.
Saon of Acanthus. Translated by J. A. Symonds.
Heraclitus. Translated by William Cory.

Timon's Epitaph

HERE lie I, Timon; who, alive, all living men
    did hate.
Pass by, and curse thy fill; but pass and stay not here
    thy gait.   ——*Callimachus*

Crethis

FOR Crethis' store of tales and pleasant chat
  Oft sigh the Samian maidens, missing that
Which cheered their tasks, but she, beyond their
    call,
Sleeps here the sleep that must be slept by all.
                    ——*Callimachus*

An Inscription
By the Sea

NO dust have I to cover me,
    My grave no man may show;
My tomb is this unending sea,
    And I lie far below.
My fate, O stranger, was to drown;   5
And where it was the ship went down
    Is what the sea-birds know.   ——*Glaucus*

Stay in Town

STAY in town, little wight,
    Safe at home.
  If you roam,
The cranes who delight
Upon pygmies to sup,   5
Will gobble you up.
    Stay at home.   ——*Julianus Antecessor*

A Dinner Gift

THE Muses to Herodotus one day
    Came, nine of them, and dined;
And in return, their host to pay,
    Left each a book behind.   4
                    ——*Leonidas of Alexandria*

Timon's Epitaph. Translated by William Shakespeare.
Crethis. Translated by Richard Garnett.
An Inscription By the Sea. Translated by Edwin Arlington Robinson. From *Captain Craig* by Edwin Arlington Robinson. By permission of The Macmillan Company, publishers.
Stay in Town. Translated by Henry Wellesley.
A Dinner Gift. Translated by De Teissier.   4. Left . . . behind. The *History* of Herodotus contains nine books.

Old Age

THESE shriveled sinews and this bending frame
The workmanship of Time's strong hand pro-
    claim,
Skilled to reverse whate'er the gods create,
And make that crooked which they fashion straight.
Hard choice for man: to die—or else to be   5
That tottering, wretched, wrinkled thing you see.
Age then we all prefer; for age we pray,
And travel on to life's last lingering day;
Then sinking slowly down from worse to worse,
Find heaven's extorted boon our greatest curse.
                                        ——Crates

The Spinning Woman

MORNING and evening, sleep she drove away,
    Old Platthis,—warding hunger from the
    door.
And still to wheel and distaff hummed her lay
    Hard by the gates of Eld, and bent and hoar;
Plying her loom until the dawn was gray,   5
    The long course of Athene did she tread:
With withered hand by withered knee she spun
    Sufficient for the loom of goodly thread,
Till all her work and all her days were done.
    And in her eightieth year she saw the wave   10
Of Acheron,—old Platthis,—kind and brave.
                            ——Leonidas of Tarentum

The Last Journey

WITH courage seek the kingdom of the dead;
    The path before you lies.
It is not hard to find, nor tread;
No rocks to climb, no lanes to thread;
But broad, and straight, and even still,   5
And ever gently slopes down-hill;
    You cannot miss it, though you shut your eyes.
                            ——Leonidas of Tarentum

On An Old Woman

MYCILLA dyes her locks, 'tis said,
    But 'tis a foul aspersion.
She buys them black; they therefore need
    No subsequent immersion.   ——Lucilius

Old Age. Translated by Richard Cumberland.
The Spinning Woman. Translated by Andrew Lang. From *The Poeti-
cal Works of Andrew Lang.* Reprinted by permission of Longmans,
Green and Co., Ltd. and the representatives of the late Andrew Lang.
The Last Journey. Translated by Charles Merivale.
On An Old Woman. Translated by William Cowper.

Treasure

THEY call thee rich; I deem thee poor;
    Since, if thou darest not use thy store,
But savest only for thine heirs,
The treasure is not thine, but theirs.   ——*Lucilius*

A Heavyweight

CHAEREMON, lighter than a wisp of straw,
    Sailed once uplifted on a summer's flaw
Sky-high, and might be spinning still through air,
But that his foot caught in a spider's snare.
Five days he downwards dangled there his head,   5
But on the sixth clomb down the spider's thread.
                                        ——*Lucilius*

Spring

NOW the bright crocus flames, and now
    The slim narcissus takes the rain,
And, straying o'er the mountain's brow,
    The daffodillies bud again.
The thousand blossoms wax and wane   5
    On wold, and heath, and fragrant bough,
    But fairer than the flowers art thou,
Than any growth of hill or plain.

Ye gardens, cast your leafy crown,
That my Love's feet may tread it down,   10
    Like lilies on the lilies set;
My Love, whose lips are softer far
Than drowsy poppy petals are,
    And sweeter than the violet!   ——*Meleager*

Upon a Maid That Died the Day She Was Married

THAT morn which saw me made a bride,
    The evening witnessed that I died.
Those holy lights, wherewith they guide
Unto the bed the bashful bride,
Served but as tapers, for to burn,   5
And light my relics to their urn.
This epitaph, which here you see,
Supplied the epithalamy.   ——*Meleager*

Treasure. Translated by William Cowper.
A Heavyweight. Translated by Alexander Lothian. Published by
Basil Blackwell & Mott, Ltd., 1920.
Spring. Translated by Andrew Lang. From *The Poetical Works of
Andrew Lang.* Reprinted by permission of Longmans, Green & Co.,
Ltd. and the representatives of the late Andrew Lang.
Upon a Maid That Died. . . . Translated by Robert Herrick.

A Garland for Heliodora

I'LL frame, my Heliodora, a garland for thy hair,
    Which thou, in all thy beauty's pride, mayst
        not disdain to wear;
For I with tender myrtles white violets will twine,
White violets, but not so pure as that pure breast of
    thine.
With laughing lilies I will twine narcissus, and the
    sweet   5
Crocus shall, in its yellow hue, with purple hyacinth
    meet.
And I will twine with all the rest, and all the rest
    above,
Queen of them all, the red red rose, the flower which
    lovers love.   ——*Meleager*

Love at the Door

COLD blows the winter wind: 'tis Love,
    Whose sweet eyes swim with honeyed
        tears,
That bears me to thy doors, my love,
    Tossed by the storm of hopes and fears.
Cold blows the blast of aching Love;   5
    But be thou for my wandering sail,
Adrift upon these waves of love,
    Safe harbor from the whistling gale!
                                            ——*Meleager*

Lost Desire

LOVE brought by night a vision to my bed,
    One that still wore the vesture of a child
But eighteen years of age—who sweetly smiled
Till of the lovely form false hopes were bred
    And keen embraces wild.   5
Ah! for the lost desire that haunts me yet,
Till mine eyes fail in sleep that finds no more
That fleeting ghost! Oh, lovelorn heart, give o'er—
Cease thy vain dreams of beauty's warmth—forget
    The face thou longest for!   ——*Meleager*

A Garland for Heliodora. Translated by Christopher North.
Love at the Door. Translated by John Addington Symonds.
Lost Desire. Translated by William M. Hardinge.

The Old Story

LIKE many a one, when you had gold
    Love met you smiling, we are told;
But now that all your gold is gone,
Love leaves you hungry and alone.

And women who have called you more   5
Sweet names than ever were before
Will ask another now to tell
What man you are and where you dwell.

Was ever anyone but you
So long in learning what is true?   10
Must you find only at the end
That who has nothing has no friend?
                                    ——*Marcus Argentarius*

Vanity of Vanities

NAKED to earth was I brought—naked to earth
        I descend.
Why should I labor for naught, seeing how naked
    the end?   ——*Palladas*

United

HOW long must we two hide the burning gaze,
    And look by stealth in one another's eyes?
Let us proclaim our love; and whoso stays
The sweet embrace that lulls all miseries—
The sword's our doctor: best that you and I   5
Should live together, or together die.
                                    ——*Paul the Silentiary*

An Unknown Grave

MY name, my country, what are they to thee?
    What, whether proud or base my ped-
        igree?
Perhaps I far surpassed all other men;
Perhaps I fell below them all. What then?
Suffice it, stranger, that thou seest a tomb.   5
Thou knowest its use. It hides—no matter whom.
                                    ——*Paul the Silentiary*

The Old Story. Translated by Edwin Arlington Robinson. From
Captain Craig by Edwin Arlington Robinson. By permission of The
Macmillan Company, publishers.
Vanity of Vanities. Translated by William M. Hardinge.
United. Translated by W. H. D. Rouse in *An Echo of Greek Song*,
1899. Reprinted by permission of Mr. Philip G. Rouse as represent-
ative of the executors.
An Unknown Grave. Translated by William Cowper.

Life a Boon

IN every way of life true pleasure flows:
  Immortal fame from public action grows;
Within the doors is found appeasing rest;
In fields the gifts of nature are expressed.
The sea brings gain, the rich abroad provide   5
To blaze their names, the poor their wants to hide.
All households best are governed by a wife;
His cares are light who leads a single life.
Sweet children are delights which marriage bless;
He that hath none disturbs his thoughts the less.   10
Strong youth can triumph in victorious deeds;
Old age the soul with pious motion feeds.
All states are good, and they are falsely led
Who wish to be unborn or quickly dead.
                              ——Metrodorus

Life a Bane

WHAT course of life should wretched mortals
              take?
In courts hard questions large contention make;
Care dwells in houses, labor in the field;
Tumultuous seas affrighting dangers yield.
In foreign lands thou never canst be blessed: 5
If rich, thou art in fear; if poor, distressed.
In wedlock frequent discontentments swell;
Unmarried persons as in deserts dwell.
How many troubles are with children born;
Yet he that wants them counts himself forlorn.   10
Young men are wanton, and of wisdom void;
Gray hairs are cold, unfit to be employed.
Who would not one of these two offers choose:
Not to be born, or breath with speed to lose?
                              ——Posidippus

The Lover's Posy

I SENT a garland to my love
  Which with my own hands I wove:
Rose and lily here there be
Twined with cool anemone,
White narcissus, dewy wet,   5
And the purple violet.
Take and bind it on your brow,
Nor be proud, as you are now,
As the flowers bloom and fade,
So must you too, haughty maid.   ——Rufinus

On Archaeanassa

To Archaeanassa, on whose furrow'd brow
  Love sits in triumph, I my service vow.
If her declining graces shine so bright,
What flames felt you who saw her noon of light?
                              ——Plato

A Farewell

VENUS, take my votive glass,
  Since I am not what I was:
What from this day I shall be,
Venus, let me never see.   ——Plato

Resourcefulness

THE blind man bears the lame, and onward
      hies,
Made right by lending feet and borrowing eyes.
                              ——Plato

To Amyntor

TAKE old Amyntor to thy heart, dear soil,
  In kind remembrance of his former toil;
Who first enriched and ornamented thee
With many a lovely shrub and branching tree,
And lured a stream to fall in artful showers   5
Upon thy thirsting herbs and fainting flowers.
First in the spring he knew the rose to rear,
First in the autumn culled the ripened pear.
His vines were envied all the country round,
And favoring heaven showered plenty on his ground.
Therefore, kind earth, reward him in thy breast   11
With a green covering and an easy rest.
                              ——Simmias of Thebes

Grapes

WHILE yet the grapes were green, thou didst
        refuse me,
  When they were ripe, didst proudly pass me by;
But do not grudge me now a single cluster,
  Now that the grapes are withering and dry.
                              ——Anonymous

Life a Boon. Translated by Sir John Beaumont. Compare with the poem of Posidippus that follows.
Life a Bane. Translated by Sir John Beaumont.
The Lover's Posy. Translated by W. H. D. Rouse in An Echo of Greek Song, 1899. Reprinted by permission of Mr. Philip G. Rouse as representative of the executors.

On Archaeanassa. Translated by Thomas Stanley.
A Farewell. Translated by Matthew Prior.
Resourcefulness. Translated by Charles Neaves.
To Amyntor. Translated by Robert Bland.
Grapes. Translated by Alma Strettell.

Not of Itself But Thee

I SEND thee myrrh, not that thou mayest be
By it perfumed, but it perfumed by thee.
——*Anonymous*

Dion of Tarsus

DION of Tarsus, here I lie, who sixty years
        have seen.
I was not ever wed, and would my father had not
        been!   ——*Anonymous*

Riches

POOR in my youth, and in life's later scenes
        Rich to no end, I curse my natal hour,
Who nought enjoyed while young, denied the
        means:
And nought when old enjoyed, denied the power.
——*Anonymous*

A Grecian runner in the Olympic games wearing a helmet and carrying a decorated shield. A red-figured vase painting.

The Persian Peril

WHEN on a razor's edge all Hellas stood,
        We who lie here preserved her with our
blood.   ——*Anonymous*

Not of Itself But Thee. Translated by Richard Garnett.
Dion of Tarsus. Translated by Alma Strettell.
Riches. Translated by William Cowper.
The Persian Peril. Translated by Charles Neaves.

This Stone

THIS stone, beloved Sabinus, on thy grave
        Memorial small of our great love shall be.
I still shall seek thee lost; from Lethe's wave,
        Oh, drink not thou forgetfulness of me.
——*Anonymous*

This Stone. Translated by Goldwin Smith. From *Bay Leaves* by
Goldwin Smith. Published by The Macmillan Company.

THE WEST
UNDER
ROMAN SWAY

300 B.C. TO 300 A.D.

I F Greece was the mother of the West, Rome
was its stern and vigorous father. The genius
of Greece lay in the warm humanity of its literature,
art, and philosophy. The genius of Rome lay in the
engineering skill with which it built and equipped
an empire and the discipline of law by which it
ruled it.

Rome followed Greece by about four hundred
years. In the Golden Age of Athens, Rome was a
struggling city-state on the Tiber river. During the
conquests of Alexander Rome was beginning its own
conquest of Italy. Three centuries later it was to add
Alexander's eastern domains with their Hellenistic
culture to its empire in the West. Rome's own
Golden Age is so influenced by Greek culture that
the matrimonial metaphor is not far-fetched. The
warmth and charm of Greece eventually conquered
the matter-of-fact Roman soul * and maintained a
continuous tradition from Homer to the Christian
overthrow of paganism.

The Romans called the Mediterranean *mare
nostrum*—our sea—and it is easy to see in the boot-
shaped peninsula of Italy a Roman foot thrust down
into the center of this area of many races to claim it
all from Gibraltar to Jerusalem. Yet the Romans were
not such seafarers as the Greeks. As late as the first
Punic War (264 B.C.) Rome had no navy. Italy
lacked the many harbors of the Greek peninsula, and
her fertile valleys led the Romans to hug the earth
and to build their empire first by overland fighting.
The sea-loving Greeks, on the other hand, maintained
the separate independence of their city-states and
their colonies overseas as well.

* As Horace put it in his famous epigram, *Graecia capta ferum
victorem cepit*—"Conquered Greece took captive her fierce conqueror" (*Epistles*, II, 1.156).

Augustus, the first of the Roman emperors.

Down Italy from the north run the Apennine
Mountains, much closer to the east coast than to the
west. The thin strip of land along the cold, stormy
Adriatic shore did not attract settlers. As the Greeks
had faced east, the Romans faced west where their
fruitful plains sloped gradually to the sea. It is still
a beautiful region of olive groves and vine-clad
hills with small rivers like the Tiber, to which Rome
was to bring fame. The soft climate and volcanic
soil made this west coast the great grain-producer
of southern Europe. The upland pastures were ideal
for cattle-grazing, and the blue and peaceful Mediterranean attracted fishermen. To the north between
the Apennines and the Alps is the vast plain watered
by the river Po, but this fertile region, so important
to modern Italy, was in ancient times a land apart,
Cisalpine Gaul, and was not Romanized until the
time of the Punic Wars (222 B.C.).

Into the sunny land of Italy came several races in ancient times to form the mongrel Roman. Mysterious aborigines were absorbed by successive invasions from the north of peoples speaking Indo-European tongues. The Latins and Sabines settled central Italy, and their state of Latium (now Lazio) was to beget Rome and the Latin language that bears their name. Less numerous but more powerful at first were the alien Etruscans, who settled to the north in Etruria (now Toscana, or Tuscany) around 800 B.C. and for a time controlled much of the peninsula.

Greeks had built cities along the central coast in early times, but the chief Greek colonization came in the eighth century B.C., when they converted extreme southern Italy into *Magna Graecia* with its beautiful cities. Finally, there were Celtic barbarians called the Gauls, who swarmed down from their homeland north of the Alps and conquered Rome briefly in 390 B.C. The Latins were far from the strongest of these nations in the centuries of restless settlement, but time held for them the destiny of welding these peoples into the Italians of the empire.

THE REPUBLIC OF ROME

BECAUSE the Gauls destroyed the old records of Rome, only vague and often poetic tradition preserved the ancient past. Virgil was one of many poets to tell how Aeneas, a Trojan prince, supposedly escaped the Greeks at the fall of Troy and found refuge and a wife at Latium. His son Ascanius (or Iulus, the supposed ancestor of Julius Caesar) founded the city of Alba Longa, twenty miles southeast of the site of Rome. Nine generations later, as a usurper tried to exterminate the line of Aeneas, the twins Romulus and Remus were born to the last surviving daughter and the god Mars and suckled by a she-wolf. Grown to manhood, they killed the usurper and seized the women of some Sabine visitors to provide wives for their own settlers. It was Romulus who supposedly founded Rome in 753 B.C. and, killing his brother, named the city for himself.

As myth turns into history at the end of the sixth century B.C., the little state of Latium with its growing city of Rome was fretting under a hundred years of rule by Etruscan kings. The last of these despots, Tarquin the Proud, whose son figures as the villain in Shakespeare's *Rape of Lucrece*, was deposed by the Roman Senate in 510 B.C.

The Romans replaced the monarchy with a "republic," * actually an oligarchy ruled by a Senate of patricians (*patres*) and wealthy businessmen (*equites*), though the executive power was in the hands of two consuls elected for one year by the people of Rome voting by *centuries*, or groups, according to the property they owned. Gradually the plebeians, or *plebs,* came to demand a direct voice in the government alongside the aristocratic classes and twice marched out of the city on strike before their Assembly achieved legislative powers and their two (later ten) tribunes a "veto" power over the Senate's actions. The struggle of the *plebs* against the Senate was long and bloody. For two centuries and more the commoners fought for a more democratic system and eventually won the right to be ruled by elected officers and to hold the offices of *quaestor, aedile, praetor,* and *consul,* along with such social reforms as limitation of estates and a public dole of grain to the needy. One of the earliest of their victories, important as the beginning of Roman law, was the conversion of the old secret records of the tribal priests into the Twelve Tables of public law (450 B.C.), available for all to see in the Forum of Rome.

Meanwhile, the power of Rome was spreading out over the Italian peninsula. The sack of the city by the Gauls was followed by a century of warfare with her neighbors. The defeat of the powerful Samnites in 290 B.C. gave Rome control of central Italy. Next she forced the Greek cities of the south into an alliance that amounted to annexation. By 272 B.C. Rome controlled all of Italy from the Arno River in the north to the tip of the boot.

This brought Rome into direct conflict with her powerful rival in the western Mediterranean, the Phoenician city of Carthage, in north Africa, associated in Virgil's *Aeneid* with the tragic Queen Dido. Because the Carthaginian threat was the greatest danger that Rome had ever faced, the Roman Senator Cato ended every speech with the famous words, "Also, I move that Carthage must be destroyed." Yet Carthage had great generals—Hamilcar and his son, Hannibal—and instead nearly destroyed Rome until Scipio defeated Hannibal in Africa. The first two Punic Wars (264–201 B.C.) lost Carthage her empire, but the third (150–146 B.C.) led to the utter annihilation of the city and a grim fulfillment of Cato's demand. Sicily, Sardinia, Corsica, and the riches of Spain now belonged to Rome, and imperialism became the settled policy of the republic.

In the same year (146 B.C.), growing impatient after a half century of gentlemanly penetration in Greece, Rome formally annexed the city-states and savagely destroyed Corinth as an ominous lesson to Athens and Sparta. One by one the eastern domains of Alexander fell to the Roman legions, and became

---

* The term "republic," or *res publica* (the public affairs), meant simply the commonwealth to the Romans, and was applied later to the Imperial government.

A Roman relief depicting a fierce battle between Roman troops and "barbarians," who are being badly defeated.

provinces or protectorates—Egypt in 168 B.C., Macedonia in 146 B.C., "Asia" in 133 B.C. In the last days of the republic, Julius Caesar subdued Gaul (modern France), and Pompey finally pushed Roman rule to the distant Euphrates in the east.

This unique conquest of the western and near-eastern world was carried on from the city of Rome, and largely by a Senate of rugged aristocrats, who thrived on the plunder and tribute that poured in from the provinces. Jealous of their prerogatives and prosperity, they bitterly opposed the extension of political power to lower classes or of citizenship to men outside their little city-state. The whole world was to be exploited for the benefit of one community, which was gradually to lapse into dissipation and cynicism because of the fantastic luxury that these riches provided. The republic tried to govern an empire with the constitution of a city-state. But the republic was dying, and a true empire was to be born out of the personal ambitions of two remarkable men.

Both Pompey and Julius Caesar were first-rate generals supported by personal armies of professional soldiers, and both became contemptuous of the Senate that tried to curb them. The egotistical Pompey began his career with brilliant conquests of Spain and the eastern kingdoms of Alexander, while the no less dashing Caesar thrilled the Roman populace with his nine-year conquest of Gaul. Both realized that the republic had outlived its usefulness, but each wanted to be dictator. At first they worked

together (with Crassus) in the First Triumvirate (60 B.C.) to force reforms upon the unwilling Senate. But eventually Pompey took advantage of Caesar's absence in Gaul to become sole dictator in Rome, whereupon Caesar with one of his legions crossed the Rubicon River, part of the northern boundary of Italy (the occasion for his famous "The die is cast") and accumulated a personal army for his march on Rome. In the battles that followed, Pompey showed bad judgment and irresolution and was destroyed by the superior generalship of Caesar at Pharsalia (48 B.C.).

Dictator now, Caesar spent most of the four short years left to him in military campaigns and tarried nine months in Egypt under the spell of the young queen Cleopatra of the Greek Ptolemies. But upon his return to Italy, which he found in chaos after a century of revolution and bad government, he showed generosity toward his enemies and the qualities of great statesmanship. He enlarged the Senate with men from all classes and pursued the land reforms which had been earlier attempted. He stimulated a revival of morality by bolstering the state religion and tried to legislate political corruption away. He relieved unemployment by public works and renovated the dole system. He extended Roman citizenship even to some barbarians in remote provinces and envisioned a united empire functioning for the good of all the far-flung lands that he had seen, rather than for the profit of the city of Rome that bounded the Senators' world. His assassination in 44 B.C. by disgruntled aristocrats and high-minded patriots led by Cassius and Brutus plunged the empire into fourteen years of civil war until the rise of his nephew Octavian to power assured the good government and many reforms that Caesar had projected. These were achieved under a new form of government, an imperial one, in place of the moribund republic.

THE ROMAN POINT OF VIEW

THE world empire of Rome challenges the imagination. We may well ask what traits in the Roman led him to achieve or even to desire a world conquest that the freedom-loving Greeks never dreamed of. We will find the answer in his philosophy and the social pattern of his culture that produced it—perhaps still further back in the geography that influenced his history at every point.

The seafaring Greek felt secure in his sea-girdled homeland and developed without the constant fear of hostile barbarian neighbors, whereas from the start the Roman had to battle enemies on all sides for survival. With war a daily possibility, he organized his society on a military pattern and stood ever ready to lay down the plough for the sword. The bundle of rods, called the *fasces*, that symbolized the judges' authority to punish symbolized also the collective security of the community against threat from outside. The empire grew by successive attempts to insure the safety of the commonwealth from border menace, and in its growth not simply the army but a society built on the military principle of command and obedience carried the day. Such a rule appears not simply in the Roman's public life but in his family career that conditioned him in youth to accept law and discipline outside the home.

In Greece all the forces of the market place and the gymnasium combined to defeat the power of the family in the life of the citizen; in Rome the family was the indestructible nucleus of society, a

Excavation of Pompeii revealed fine examples of Roman buildings. This is the peristyle of the house of the Vettii, partly restored.

microcosm which contained in miniature the structure of the empire itself. The Greek stands forth as an individual, the Roman as a member of a family, a clan, a nation. The family was ruled by the father, the *paterfamilias* in a thoroughly paternalistic society, whose *familia* included not only his children but the servant slaves and the *clientes,* his free dependents, as well. To these must be added the *manes,* or ancestral spirits, and the *lares* and *penates,* the family gods peculiar to each *familia.* In the father were concentrated the traditions of the clan, the laws of his forbears, and the grave responsibilities of family leadership, so that he wielded a traditional and legal power over his household unthinkable today. He owned all the property. He could divorce his wife with a letter or even condemn her to death, though Roman women, unlike the Greek, had a respected social position and shared the government of the family through moral influence, if not legal right. He had a life-and-death power over his dependents and could kill a son for a crime or sell him into slavery, though such drastic uses of authority were uncommon. The Roman son was ever conscious of his father's will and prepared himself seriously for the power that he would someday wield in his father's stead. His very name revealed his absorption in the family—Marcus, his personal name; Tullius, his clan name; Cicero, his family name. The tight, strict organization of the family gave him a stern discipline and unreasoning loyalty far removed from the free individualism of the Greek.

Like the family, the state religion worked to mould a sturdy, practical, unquestioning citizen. Although the Greek pantheon was later identified with Roman deities, Rome had an older and more characteristic religion of its own that persevered with the populace through the coming of Christianity. Primitive fears of nature led to primitive superstitions and taboos and eventually to a myriad of spirits, hardly gods, associated with particular places, seasons, and experiences of men. These deities were not thought to have human form but to dwell as spirits in trees, groves, hills, and rocks— within the Roman earth, not in the sky to which most religions look. Literally thousands of these local divinities peopled the landscape and were a part of the daily life of the Roman. Each family had its spirits for protection—a *lar* to watch over its land and buildings, *penates* to guard the possessions indoors, and the *manes* of male ancestors to guide the new generations. A religion that surrounded the citizen with watchful spirits deprived him of individual freedom and forced upon him a conventional and dutiful behavior. Eventually more universal deities—Jupiter, Juno, Venus, and Mars—emerged and were honored through public ritual and festivals provided by the state. When Greek influence grew strong in Italy, Zeus, Hera, Aphrodite, and Ares were merged with them to provide an expanded and more attractive theology. Cults from the East continued to find favor in Rome for centuries, though the state frowned on their romantic excesses and did what it could to curb them. Priestly officials, serving under a *pontifex maximus,* superintended the state religion and tended to standardize orthodox belief into law. The stern rigidity of Roman religion is in contrast with the aesthetic variation in the Greek.

Roman religion tended to mould the citizen's behavior according to traditional practice, but did it affect his spiritual life? Certainly on the surface it was like the Greek in emphasizing the legal contract between gods and men implied in ritual and sacrifice. Its *quid-pro-quo* basis suggested that the gods were pleased with gifts rather than morality, and they were themselves as irresponsible and unethical as their Greek counterparts. They did not inspire goodness by their example, nor did they value it in dispensing rewards. For example, Venus exasperates even her son Aeneas by her frivolous deceptions, and when she demands a just reward for Aeneas' *pietas* from Jupiter, she has in mind his faithful performance of sacrifices and other religious rites and his unswerving concern for his mission, not any innate virtue such as we might admire. Yet pious obedience to the gods did promote devotion to duty and the sacrifice of selfish ends to the good of the whole. Religion may not have taught virtue, but it was a part of virtue to care for the gods. They underlay the corporate life of the community and supported the institutions of marriage, family, war, and the state. They inspired piety and justified patriotism, for the real Roman god behind all the gods was Rome itself. In this strictly Roman sense the state religion touched the roots of the Roman's spiritual being—his fanatical love of country and his stoic willingness to sacrifice himself without question for the safety or glory of the state.

Out of such a society and such a religion emerged the peculiarly Roman view of virtue, which is best summarized in the Latin names for the four ideal qualities. *Pietas* was actually a divinity, but an abstraction as well, to which the Roman aspired. Though it gives us the word "piety," it meant for him duty, or dutiful conduct toward his parents, relatives, ancestors, gods, and country. *Pietas* was the supreme virtue, acquired in the family and expressed in action throughout the good Roman's life. *Gravitas* means seriousness, and for the Roman, life was an intensely serious affair. Responsibilities destroy the carefree experimentation so dear to the Greeks, and the Roman had the individual responsibility of family leadership as well as the corporate responsibility of an empire to govern. The Roman's seriousness expressed itself in the formality of his

This small rural sanctuary with a sacrificial altar is from a Roman stucco relief. A garland is being offered here.

life and his intense conservatism. A kind of gloomy earnestness surrounds much of Roman literature, a heaviness that makes the Greeks seem skittish and reckless by comparison. *Simplicitas* comes close to plainness or even bluntness in English. It suggests singleness of purpose and directness in achieving one's ends. At its highest it stands for frankness and honesty, qualities which the Roman esteemed much more than the Greek with his admiration for the cleverness and sly duplicity of an Odysseus. *Virtus* originally meant manliness, but came to suggest physical courage and eventually virtue in our sense, though associated more with the battlefield than with the council chamber. A sober and unimaginative outlook, a strong sense of duty, and courage in performing it—these, then, are the moral qualities in the Roman point of view, and it is not hard to relate them to success in war, efficiency in government, and the stoic acceptance of a god-given destiny to rule the world.

In the intellectual realm the Roman is less satisfactory. Basically he was a prosy, practical man who built an empire without thinking too much about it. He was content to do what had to be done without asking why. The impractical Greek was forever exploring and inquiring into the nature of things. The Roman was suspicious of speculation as

being dangerous to order and a status quo in which he had been taught to believe. He was an efficiency expert, concerned with facts rather than theories and demanding of everything that it should be useful first of all. The Latin language that he developed illustrated his practical turn of mind—compact rather than beautiful, elegant rather than noble. Intellectual things are not obviously useful, and consequently played no part in the rapid growth of the empire. The Roman had a serviceable philosophy of life that supplied his needs, but he had no interest in philosophies. He approved of education so long as it was practical and reverent. He was a masterful engineer but never a creative scientist.

All of these things apply to the Roman in the formative years of the empire before alien influences from his own provinces to the east began to corrupt his soul. The conquest of Greece brought to Roman life a Hellenistic veneer which eventually infected upper-class circles with philosophy. As the unphilosophical Roman surveyed the schools of Greece, he passed over the metaphysical Eleatics, the idealistic Platonists, the scientific Peripatetics to the one school that seemed to give voice to his national point of view. Stoicism originated with the Greek Zeno of Citium (fl. 300 B.C.), who preached that the highest virtue is manliness, which expresses itself in the power to endure hardship and to repress feeling and the demands of the body. He exalted self-denial and impassive reserve as a means of subordinating oneself to the will of the Supreme Deity. This rugged philosophy reached Rome through Panaetius of Rhodes (c. 180–c. 110 B.C.), who taught a modified version to his friend and pupil, Scipio Aemilianus, the Roman general. Man, he said, is part of the physical whole and must function within it, cooperating with his family, his state, and his God. He must act according to his duty without question and with the temperance of the Golden Mean. This gentlemanly code, so completely in harmony with the traditional ideal of Roman conduct, gradually replaced for educated Romans the naïve state religion. Cicero modeled his *De Officiis* on Panaetius' treatise of the same name. Seneca accepted Stoicism as a religion. Epictetus the slave (c. 50–130 A.D.) and Marcus Aurelius the emperor (121–180 A.D.) remind us of the enduring influence of this national philosophy throughout the Silver Age. Aeneas, the Roman hero of Virgil, is a Stoic in his dutiful renunciation of his love for Dido and in his calm resignation to his fate to found Rome. In the English language the word "stoic" still connotes intellectual control of feeling and a resolute indifference to pleasure and pain.

Yet the stoic view of life that built an empire was eventually corrupted by the luxury and cynicism that empire produced. In the last years of the republic, many who thought of themselves as Stoics lived like

Epicureans, and the opposed philosophy of Epicurus (341–270 B.C.) developed its own school in Rome. Although in modern English "epicurean" suggests a luxurious pursuit of physical pleasure, this debased extension of the term does injustice to the wise and moderate founder of the school and his devoted Roman follower, Lucretius. Outlawing all belief in the supernatural and immortality, the Epicureans were materialists who conceived of the universe in terms of ever-moving atoms. Man is tied to this system by his senses but has also a rational self that chooses a way of life. The sole end of this life is the achievement of pleasure, but not merely physical pleasures; these should only assist us to the supreme pleasure of a peaceful and happy mind. Physical excess produces pain, as does too rigorous self-denial. Prudence shows us how to attain a maximum of enjoyment with a minimum of distress. Virtue, therefore, is only a means to an end—happiness. This pleasant doctrine was far removed from the Roman view of life in the robust years of the republic, but it came more and more to explain the practice of many latter-day Romans. Although seemingly opposed to Stoicism, it was actually combined with it in a curiously consistent harmony. Horace illustrates this in his undisguised pursuit of the pleasures of life tempered always by moderation and self-control. In the aesthetic excesses of a Nero, on the other hand, Epicureanism passes into hedonism, and responsible citizens bemoan the decay of the old Roman virtues. A natural stoicism came closest to the Roman point of view. Whether a simple evolution of her community life or an asssimilation of a foreign philosophy, this stern, unimaginative outlook made Rome great and steeled her to resist the barbarian.

LITERATURE OF THE REPUBLIC

LITERATURE came late to Rome, and then as a deliberate importation from the Greeks. Of course there had been folk poetry—hymns and ballads in prehistoric times—but almost none of it has survived and Roman references to it are surprisingly meager. The practical-minded Romans, bent at first upon survival, later upon security through conquest, lacked the warm imagination and sensitivity to beauty that made the Greeks evolve literature and other arts as necessary expressions of their community life. Like many Americans living also in a materialistic culture, the Romans were suspicious of the arts as unmanly and dangerous to the vigor of the state. Only after the Punic Wars, when empire brought wealth and luxury to some classes, did a leisured aristocracy begin to enjoy them without shame and decide that national pride demanded national poets and playwrights. The Greeks had taught them the art of writing; they were now to teach them the art of literature.

So we should not be surprised that the first known Latin poet was a Greek, Livius Andronicus (fl. 240 B.C.), who had been brought as a slave to Rome, or that the first Roman who became a poet, Cnaeus Naevius (fl. 200 B.C.), modeled his Latin verses on Greek meters. These pioneers are now little more than names. Not only were their works to be superseded by later masters, but the early Latin that they used was so uncouth and unliterary in comparison with the melodious Greek that later generations found it unpleasant to recall. The man who refined this coarse speech into a flexible and elegant instrument of expression was the poet Ennius (239–169 B.C.), who prepared the way for Lucretius and Catullus. This exuberant pathfinder wrote twenty tragedies (all lost) in the manner of Euripides, and an epic history of Rome from Aeneas down, called the *Annales,* which was the Roman national poem till the time of Virgil's *Aeneid.*

To the period of Ennius belong the first two important figures of Roman literature, the comic playwrights Plautus and Terence. Drama of a sort, especially in the form of vulgar mimes, had been popular in Italy from the early days of the republic, but literary drama in the Greek style dates from the first works of Livius Andronicus. Rome had no permanent theater until 55 B.C., largely because of Senate opposition to the drama as a frivolous and immoral entertainment, but the populace crowded around their wooden stages nevertheless to applaud noisily the robust and sometimes obscene plays of their early favorites, which the state did provide. This mob in holiday mood often jeered the tragedies of Ennius and demanded broad farce and obvious satire that they could understand. The man who satisfied them best of all was Plautus (c. 254–184 B.C.), a commoner like themselves, who had lost his earnings in commerce and then wrote plays to keep alive. This robust and jovial fellow had the only sure sense of theater among surviving Roman playwrights.

The comedies of Plautus, totally unlike the satiric Old Comedy of Aristophanes, are derived from the New Comedy of fourth-century Greece and in many instances are frank adaptations of actual plays of Menander and Philemon, though Roman in spirit. Gone is the chorus of birds or frogs and the religious meaning of the occasion. Gone is the satire of famous men and the comment on the politics of the day.

The New Comedy is a harmless comedy of manners involving social types from the Roman scene—an irate father, a spendthrift son, a pompous soldier, a bawdy-house madam, a cunning slave or parasite—in a farcical mix-up that is straightened out in the last scene. As likely as not, the plot is some variation on Terence's *Phormio:* A young Athenian falls in love with a girl of unknown parentage and despite his father's enraged objections maneuvers himself with the aid of the lying parasite Phormio into a legal position where he must marry her. The father is reconciled to the match when the girl turns out to be the long-lost daughter of his brother by a secret early marriage. Everyone is happy except the brother, whose wife berates him for his bigamy. Terence (c. 190–159 B.C.), a freed slave of Carthage who rose to social prominence at Rome in the intellectual coterie of Scipio Africanus, wrote six comedies of this sort. They have a more restrained and finished style than Plautus' but lack the robust humor of the earlier comedian.

The greatest republican literature belongs to the period of Caesar and the revolution that prepared the way for the Augustan empire. We think of it as the Ciceronian era, because the commanding personality of Marcus Tullius Cicero (106–43 B.C.), statesman, orator, and master of prose, gives it stature and continuity. Cicero's long career in the Senate tied his literary work to contemporary politics, and even his philosophical writings, which echo his Greek masters, are most satisfactory when they are prescribing a practical code of conduct for the Roman citizen. His many personal letters reveal the charming, mellow personality of the old Senator of this period, surveying with stoic calm the decline of republican Rome. But perhaps his greatest achievement lies in bringing the Latin language to magnificent maturity as a flexible instrument for expressing thought. The fluent grace and elegant diction of his style first showed the power of Latin as a precise, urbane, and eloquent vehicle for ideas. Down to an age just before our own, Cicero represented an ideal of literary prose for writers in all of western Europe.

To the age of Cicero belong the first great poets of Rome—Lucretius, the superb spokesman for Epicurean philosophy, and Catullus, the greatest of her

Cicero, rugged statesman of the Roman republic.

love poets. The atomic theory of Epicurus does not seem at first sight to be a suitable subject for poetry, but Lucretius expounded it with such an enkindling earnestness and enlivened it with such imaginative illustrations and figures of speech that he created in *Of the Nature of Things* the world's great didactic poem. In our age, when Cicero and Virgil are out of fashion, many critics consider Lucretius Rome's most modern writer, if not her greatest poet as well.

Catullus is the only survivor from a group of Roman lyricists of the Ciceronian era who imitated the graceful Alexandrians in love poems to contemporary ladies. His beloved was the fascinating but dissolute daughter of an old Roman house. To her, Catullus gave a youthful devotion, which he lived to despise, and to us he has left blazing lyric records of both his moods. He is the bridge to Horace and the Augustan Age of Roman poetry.

THE EMPIRE OF ROME

THE dictatorship of Julius Caesar had not established an empire. His assassination left the way open for the Senate to reassert its power under the old Constitution, but by this time the Senate was so weakened by the deaths of old families and the in-flux of the many new ones that it wanted no rule of its own but a new leader who would support its monied interests. Caesar had adopted as his son and heir his nephew Octavian (63 B.C.–14 A.D.), but this stripling of nineteen seemed less fit for command than Caesar's capable general, Mark Antony (83–30 B.C.), who promptly plotted to seize power. His skillful funeral oration over Caesar's body won him popular support against the Senators, some of whom had helped to assassinate Caesar, but he avoided an outright breach with the Senate while using the popular Assembly to sanction his rule.

Meanwhile, Octavian, reverencing the memory of his great-uncle Caesar, was shocked to find that Antony had granted amnesty to his assassins; and with the support in the Senate of the orator Cicero, who had held the favor of Caesar, Octavian led out two legions to defeat Antony and then, as consul, had the conspirators sentenced to death. At once Cicero and the Senate turned against this dictator as they had against Antony, so that Octavian retaliated by inviting Antony and the treacherous general Lepidus to form the Second Triumvirate (43–33). A reign of terror followed as the three leaders coolly sanctioned the murder of all their enemies, including Cicero, and defeated the armies of Caesar's assassins, Cassius and Brutus, at Philippi. Octavian and Antony thereupon divided the empire between themselves, and Antony proceeded to establish his eastern capital at Alexandria, where he fell captive to the charms of that same Cleopatra who had beguiled Caesar. Soon after, he divorced his wife Octavia, the virtuous sister of Octavian, in favor of the Greek-Egyptian siren. While Antony succumbed to Oriental pleasures, Octavian brought order to his western half of the empire, and then set out to avenge his sister's humiliation by depriving Antony of his eastern command. The issue was decided in a naval battle at Actium (31 B.C.), after which Cleopatra followed her devoted Antony to death. Octavian was now sole commander of the Roman world and in a position to carry out the projects of his uncle Caesar.

The servile Senate was delighted to hear that he shunned the title of king as Caesar had done and was content to be called *princeps senatus* (chief in the Senate) and *imperator* (commander of the army, but an army which he bound to himself by oaths of personal loyalty). He had become king and emperor in fact, if not in name, and founded a dynasty that continued for fifty years after his death. In gratitude for his tact, the Senate gave him the title of *Augustus*, which has come to be thought of as his name, and Octavian strove through the forty years of his reign (27 B.C.–14 A.D.) to justify it. Physically weak as he was, his success in war had been a tour de force, but nearly a half century of peace gave his intellectual capacity and strong will the chance to show themselves in wise statesmanship. The Golden Age, predicted by Virgil in his *Fourth Eclogue* ten years before, came to Rome and the empire; and literature was only one phase of life that felt the inspiration of his just and tolerant rule.

Augustus ministered to the needs of all classes with laws favoring each. He encouraged trade by suppressing piracy and maintaining peace throughout the realm. Using the wealth of the Egyptian treasury, he gave employment to the poor by public works, not simply temples, a theater, and a new senate-house, but roads for travel and commerce in the Roman tradition of road building that had been linking the empire overland for two hundred years. His ascetic nature made him attempt to curb the rising immorality of the city with the puritanical Julian Laws, but here he went too far and was ultimately defeated by the cynicism of a populace that had lost the old Roman virtues in luxury and venality. His own daughter and granddaughter shamed him with their flagrant immorality; the one he imprisoned for adultery, the other he exiled, along with the poet Ovid, who was involved in her misconduct. Worn out with disappointment and physical ills, he died at seventy-six, having preserved his frail body by abstemious living for four decades of remarkable service to the empire he created. He had long been worshiped in the east as a god, and his work was to endure in the two centuries of *Pax Romana* that followed.

It is a tribute to the statesmanship of Augustus that the empire functioned prosperously to the end of his dynasty fifty years later, even under the bad rulers who succeeded him. His stepson Tiberius lacked his tact and skill and retired into a morbid seclusion, leaving the government to a treacherous favorite. The notorious psychopaths Caligula and Nero remain in the popular imagination as prototypes of the depraved Roman emperor, cruel, debauched, reckless, and extravagant. The forced suicide of Nero brought the terrible year of the Four Emperors (68–69 A.D.) and civil war. But the Augustan machine of government weathered all these attacks upon its stability, and the empire as a whole continued in peace.

Out of the struggle emerged a new dynasty, the despotic Flavians, who brought sound but unimaginative rule to their vast domain for nearly thirty years. The last of them, Domitian, fostered a revival of art and literature which became the focal point of Rome's Silver Age. The poets Statius and Martial flattered him shamelessly, and the historian Tacitus, the essayist Pliny the Younger, and the satirist Juvenal dissented as immoderately. This glittering galaxy made his reign brilliant with the last great flowering of Roman literary talent. Still the Senate was happy to see the assassination of Domitian in 96 A.D. and the end of the dynastic principle of succession to the throne.

It replaced him with the first of the five Good Emperors who gave the empire its longest period, eighty-four years, of uninterrupted peace and prosperity.

Each of these rulers was chosen by his predecessor to rule, regardless of family connections. They were a varied lot of striking personalities, but all capable and conscientious sovereigns. Hadrian (76–138), the most attractive of them all, was a man of culture, who enthusiastically encouraged the Greek renaissance of literature and philosophy that produced the satires of Lucian and yet found time to reorganize the civil service and supervise the codification of Roman law. The empire reached its greatest extent under Hadrian, and he spent much of his reign in delighted travel from one end of it to the other. Peaceful rule continued under Marcus Aurelius (121–180), the philosopher-king, who did not allow his Stoic asceticism to interfere with a vigorous prosecution of government. His quiet *Meditations* on duty and happiness, written in Greek according to the contemporary fashion, have been a source of inspiration to many of our day.

The Good Emperors made the second century A.D. the most glorious in Roman history. The boundaries of the empire came to include Britain and Dacia (modern Rumania) in the north, Mauretania (Morocco) in the south, and Armenia, Mesopotamia, and northern Arabia to the east. The whole western world and much of the east felt the unifying hand of Roman rule. The *Pax Romana* brought industry and commerce to far-flung provinces, where miniature Romes were built as prosperous outposts of Western civilization. Roman roads provided an easy, safe communication that the world was not to see again until the nineteenth century. Roman architecture flourished in the forums, the triumphal arches, the public baths and aqueducts, the theaters and temples that still dot the Mediterranean world. Portrait sculpture reached new heights of realism and preserved for us the likenesses of many prominent men of the day. Literature declined sharply, but philosophy held its own with Epictetus and Marcus Aurelius, the most famous of the Stoics. The state religion persevered among the lower classes, but the intellectuals merely tolerated it as an instrument of political control. Oriental cults, including Christianity, flourished, and deification and worship of the emperor was encouraged as a bond of political unity throughout the realm. However repugnant to us the imperial system of Rome may be, we should try to judge it at its best by the fruits of prosperity and contentment that it brought to its conquered lands.

From its very founding the empire had within it the seeds of its decay. It evolved as the easiest substitution for an obsolete political system when social unrest fomented civil war. The principate of Augustus gave political stability to the far-flung realm, but it did not eliminate the social inequalities that were destroying the old unity of the nation. For generations Rome had been a place of very rich and very poor, with a huge slave population to compete with poor citizens as a labor supply. Wars took free farmers away from the land into the army and often laid waste their farms. Service in the army sophisticated the country folk and left them eager for city life and content to live on the grain dole in Rome. Their small farms were added to the large estates of the wealthy, who sought secure investments for their new riches and the power that comes from land ownership. The large estates might be farmed by slaves, but were more often converted to grazing land, since new and cheaper sources of grain in the provinces made cattle-raising more profitable. Wine and olive oil were also produced on a large scale by city capital. The result was to destroy the reliable, hard-working farmer class, the stable backbone of the nation. The evil was not new. Even under the republic, the vested interests had blocked attempts at land reform. Caesar planned to carry out such reforms, and Augustus vainly encouraged a back-to-the-farm movement with land distribution.

Large-scale industry was unknown to the ancient world, and even in the heyday of empire, clothing, furniture, building materials, and household implements were made by artisans, often within the *familia* itself. There were factories for objects that could not readily be produced by individual workers —glassware, metalware, paper, and simple machinery—but these like agriculture enlisted slave labor more often than free. Nearly half the one million population of Rome in the first century A.D. was slave, but the practice of freeing slaves for ability or special services had grown common. Freedmen began to swell the plebeian class of citizens, alongside freeborn artisans, artists, and professional men, and some rose to political power in the imperial palace. A freedman's son, like Horace, had full rights of citizenship; his grandson could become a senator, or even, like Pertinax in the second century A.D., an emperor. Yet in general the freedmen merely augmented the plebeian class and increased the social pressure upon the upper classes. Wealthy men sometimes appeased them with gifts of money to all citizens, and the dole of grain to *clientes*, or parasites, was a common and demoralizing practice which played a major and often sinister role in Roman politics.

Still more vicious were the public games, provided by the state to keep the populace amused and tractable, and multiplied lavishly by demagogues and emperors who sought the favor of the *plebs*. They were presented in connection with religious festivals, military triumphs, political elections, and the like. These were no athletic contests of citizens in friendly rivalry, such as the Greeks had enjoyed at Olympia and Delphi, but bloody struggles of slaves and condemned prisoners. Least objectionable were the

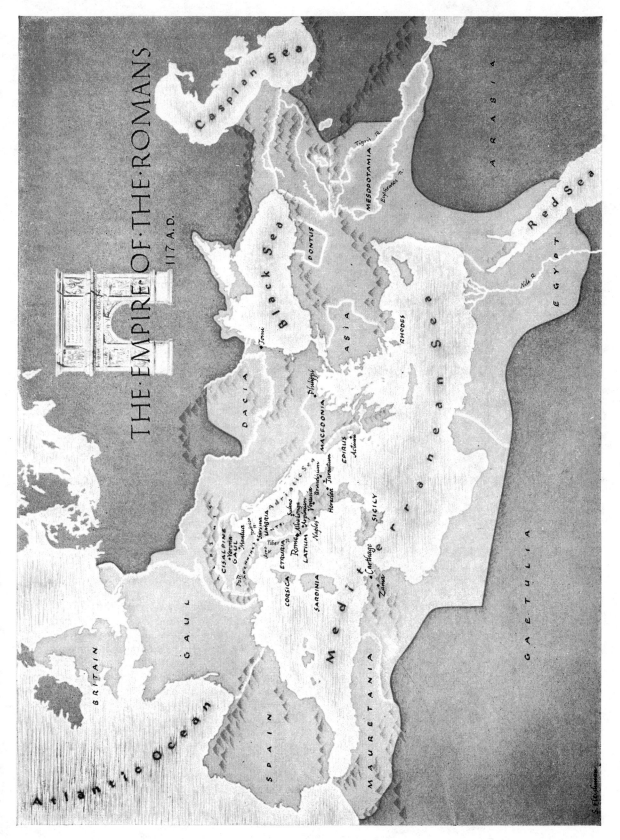

THE·EMPIRE·OF·THE·ROMANS

117 A.D.

Caspian Sea

Black Sea

Tigris R.

MESOPOTAMIA

Euphrates R.

Red Sea

ARABIA

EGYPT

Nile R.

PONTUS

Ioni

ASIA

RHODES

Mediterranean Sea

DACIA

Philippi

MACEDONIA

EPIRUS

Actium

Adriatic Sea

Sulmo

ILLYRIA

Aquileia

Venusia

Brundisium

Naples

Horatii Tarentum

Rome Alba Longa

LATIUM

Tiber R.

Arno R.

Po R.

ETRURIA

CISALPINE GAUL

Mantua

Verona

Pro R.

SICILY

Carthage

Zama

CORSICA

SARDINIA

SPAIN

GAUL

BRITAIN

MAURETANIA

GAETULIA

Atlantic Ocean

S. Fleischmann

Men wearing tunics and armored vests
fight lions in the arena before the
spectators of the circus "games." At
the bottom of this carved diptych
one gladiator indicates victory over
the beast.

horse races and the chariot races at the Circus Maximus, which combined the functions of our race tracks and professional ball games in the social life of Rome. The competition of rival stables, jockeys, and drivers inspired endless conversation for the populace; gambling ran riot before the races, and the excitement of the events themselves knew no bounds. Most notorious of the entertainments were the fights of the gladiators and of men with wild animals. All classes of Rome turned out in gayest attire to assume their favored places in the Colosseum and watch the shocking spectacle of death. Tigers fought elephants; men hunted lions and panthers; bulls fought men; but worst of all were the contests of men with men to the death. Romans condoned these grisly shows on the ground that most of the gladiators were criminals and war prisoners condemned to death anyway and that they stood the chance of winning freedom by success in combat. A few thoughtful citizens, such as Cicero and Seneca, deplored such brutalizing exhibitions, but most men accepted them as deterrents of crime and examples of stoic courage.

Though the upper classes enjoyed these spectacles with the *plebs*, their special amusement came from private luxuries. When Horace speaks of the modesty of his way of life, we must remember that his Sabine farm was a magnificent affair of twenty-eight rooms with three bathing pools and three slaves to serve him dinner. Yet it seemed humble in comparison with the huge palace of his friend Maecenas on the Esquiline. Maecenas was a middle-class businessman, and to his "equestrian" class the riches of Rome were gravitating in the money-mad era of trade and exploitation of the empire. The laissez-faire economy of Rome put few restrictions on moneymaking.

The *nouveau riche* attitude of the millionaires is reflected in the crude display of wealth in grandiose palaces stocked with legions of slaves, in country estates and villas for vacations at fashionable Baiae, in rare furniture and bric-a-brac imported from eastern provinces, and in gourmet dinners of exotic dishes costing $10,000 or more. With thousands of the *plebs* living on the dole, such sumptuous living among the privileged reflected the cleavage between the classes and the fatal disintegration of Roman society that had come with the decline of Spartan living and stoic thinking. The *familia* was breaking down; celibacy and divorce were common; the suicide of the race was well under way. It appears as an ominous background in the literature of the empire, in the playful cynicism of Horace's satires, in Ovid's decadent absorption in sex, in Juvenal's unpleasant picture of social life in the Imperial City, in the satire of bourgeois splendor and vice in the writings of Petronius.

LITERATURE OF THE EMPIRE

THE enlightened patronage of Augustus and the prosperity of his reign inspired the great period of Roman poetry as a climax to the era of Cicero. Together they form Rome's Golden Age (70 B.C.–14 A.D.). Rich men, of whom the best known was Maecenas, encouraged authors by magnificent gifts, and the writers responded with graceful poetic tributes. It was not a free literature of self-supporting, independently speaking men, but an imperial literature dedicated to Rome and the fashionable society of the city. It glittered with aristocratic sophistication and modeled itself deliberately on the Greeks, who were now extravagantly popular with the intellectuals. Homer reappeared in Virgil's *Aeneid*, Hesiod in his *Georgics*, Theocritus in his *Eclogues*. Anacreon and the Alexandrians inspired the graceful lyrics of Horace and Propertius and the legends of Ovid. Euripides found a stiff reflection in Seneca. But the imitation was not exact, and the Romans substituted for the youthful vigor and nobility of the Greeks their own worldly cynicism and elegant polish.

The great writers who produced this literature were not originally of the city of Rome, but provincials who gravitated to the capital for education, advancement, or a life of urban amusement. Virgil, Horace, Propertius, and Tibullus had all lost their ancestral lands in the civil wars and came to Rome out of necessity to seek their fortunes. But Ovid was a man of means who shocked his middle-class father by sacrificing a promising political career to enjoy the idle pleasures of the town. All disliked war and politics through temperament or rough experience and were embarrassed by the Emperor's insistence on poetry to glorify the Roman military spirit and the ancient institutions of the state. Horace and Propertius occasionally obliged; Ovid celebrated the religious feasts of the Roman calendar in his *Fasti;* but the gentle, retiring Virgil accepted his duty most cheerfully of them all and assisted the back-to-the-farm movement in his *Georgics* and the exaltation of the empire and the Caesars in his *Aeneid.*

All but Ovid lived on the bounty of rich patrons in the luxurious but dignified society of which Augustus approved. Virgil, Horace, and Propertius were of the circle of Maecenas; Tibullus of the circle of Messala; and the historian Livy was only one of many writers befriended by the Emperor himself.

The stamp of patronage is on their work in their fulsome gratitude and their deference to the imperial person and principle. Yet Ovid was the exception. He was the voice for another stratum of Rome's high society, the world of flaming youth and fashionable debauchees who sneered at the seriousness of the inner circle and lived for elegant idleness and cynical lovemaking. The Emperor's stern disapproval of this demimonde eventually forced Ovid into a bitter exile.

Poetry was the special glory of the Augustan Age, and the variety of its themes and types is surprising. Most characteristic of the period and of Rome itself is the stately *Aeneid,* for Virgil was the national poet of the empire. The majestic role was far from natural to this sensitive, mystical writer, the shyest and least heroic of men. But he loved the soil of Italy and had revealed in his *Eclogues* and *Georgics* a nostalgia for the simple country life of his youth. Augustus marked his wholesome devotion to the land and may have remembered the poet's enthusiastic prediction in his *Fourth Eclogue,* written in the midst of civil war ten years before, that the world was on the eve of a new era of peace and prosperity. The Emperor chose Virgil to glorify this new world of empire in an epic about the founding of the state. The martial poem was a tour de force for the gentle poet, and the middle-aged stoicism of its hero, caught up in a conflict of love and duty, fighting a weary war, reveals the remoteness of Homer's world from Virgil's. But this spirit is also the spirit of Rome, resigned to greatness, obediently accepting the call of history. And despite its sedate quality and intellectual cast, the *Aeneid* rings with beautiful melody and patriotic devotion. The effect may be studied, the background moralistic, but the perfection of its style and the dramatic interest of its great scenes justify its extraordinary influence in later literature. Because of the general understanding of Latin in the Renaissance, Virgil rather than Homer was the inspiration of later epics from Dante and Camoëns to Pope and Voltaire.

The prolific Ovid was also a master of the long poem, but of a vastly different character. The profligate poet of pleasure fell short of the high seriousness of the epic strain and aspired, not to glorify his race for posterity, but to entertain the smart set of his time with piquant tales and cynical advice to the lovelorn. His *Art of Love* is a systematic guide to flirtation and lechery, and the *Amores* telescope several of his own affairs in an account of his adulterous love for the fanciful Corinna. He even composed a manual of cosmetics in elegant meters.

These racy poems delighted the jaded tastes of his fashionable friends but won him the severe disapproval of Augustus and his circle. Certainly the temperament of Ovid and the spirit of his works are far from the stoicism and *virtus* of Cicero and the Romans who built the empire. He is the soft epicurean, genial, amiable, and light-hearted. His vivacity and downright levity are infectious; he was a man of abundant personality but no character, though we may still admire his unenvious regard for his fellow-poets, his literary ambition, and his persistent devotion to his art. To his contemporaries and many later generations he brought the spirit of romance through his endless inventiveness, his sensitivity to color and life, and his fluent and graceful style. His love poems were to make him the idol of the Wandering Scholars of the Middle Ages as well as a chief source of the courtly love tradition in the age of chivalry. But it is his masterpiece, the *Metamorphoses*, that has had the most lasting influence on world literature. His marvelous retelling of the most picturesque myths of Greece and Rome has delighted young people for generations and inspired such a wide circle of poets as Chaucer, Boccaccio, Spenser, Shakespeare, Milton, and Dryden. The *Metamorphoses* makes Ovid Rome's great storyteller.

Virgil and Ovid excelled in narrative verse; Horace's province was the lyric, of which he was the undisputed master in the Augustan Age. He could command as well the longer poem in his mellow epistles and his *Art of Poetry*, but we meet him at his most engaging in his graceful odes and songs. Horace left the mighty line to Virgil, his friend and literary twin, and, secure on the Sabine farm outside Rome given to him by Maecenas, he lived in happy contempt for ambition and worldly wealth, and casually preached the Golden Mean of Aristotle as the avenue to contentment. His sprightly love lyrics court a galaxy of literary ladies of doubtful virtue. His polished satires poke fun at fools and bores. But no matter where we meet him, Horace is the good companion who enjoyed life as an epicurean and feared death no more than the best of stoics.

His effortless union of the two philosophies makes him the perfect spokesman for the private morality of the imperial Roman. He is cynical but not pessimistic; no passion clouds his realistic eye. He is abundantly aware of the pleasures of life, yet unwilling to wear them out through excess. Horace thought of himself as the laureate of Rome, and in a sense he was. But he has been the laureate as well of a cultured minority in many ages, with a mellow understanding of experience and a sensitivity to his exquisite art. His philosophy put him under a cloud during the Christian Middle Ages, but the Renaissance rediscovered him, and in the Age of Reason he achieved his greatest popularity of all. The modern Augustans of seventeenth-century France and eighteenth-century England found in his common sense and refinement a kinship over nearly twenty centuries.

Although the empire continued strong for two centuries after Augustus, literature began a gradual decline almost immediately. The Silver Age (15–140 A.D.) that followed the Golden had writers of keen intellect and graceful appeal, but the hardness of their outlook and the superficial brilliance of their style betray the corruption of society and the drying up of the Roman soul. Seneca (4 B.C.–65 A.D.) is the most typical and inclusive figure of them all. The tutor and adviser of Nero in some of the most shameful of his crimes, he grew wealthy and tried to retire from the treacherous political scene to a life of study and writing in his handsome villa, but Nero had him pursued and forced him to a stoic suicide. Despite his venality and his complicity in malodorous politics, Seneca thought of himself as a philosopher and wrote voluminously and seriously. His nine closet-dramas, of which the *Medea* is best known, are our only surviving Roman tragedies. But the most readable of his works are the little *Moral Epistles,* or informal essays, which are an urbane and delightful application of Stoicism to everyday life. It is perhaps an indictment of the empire that this brilliant but derivative thinker whose life reflects so little the pious morality of his preaching should have been its greatest philosopher.

Prose flourished in the Silver Age. The patriotic history of Livy (59 B.C.–17 A.D.) in the Augustan era gave way to the savage exposure of the evils of empire in the *Histories* and *Annals* of Tacitus (c. 55– c. 115 A.D.). Our grim impression of the irresponsible brutality of the imperial system stems very largely from this gloomy republican, who had the misfortune to live through the worst years of the Emperor Domitian. But the epigrammatic brilliance of his concentrated style makes Tacitus a master of prose. His condemnation of the Rome of his day is confirmed in the harsh verse satires of Juvenal, who also suffered through the last years of Domitian. Forced to grovel before wealthy patrons, Juvenal became a bitter pessimist and gives an appalling picture of the vices and cruelty of latter-day Rome. He is the undisputed master of verse satire, the one literary invention of Rome, and was widely imitated in our classical eighteenth century. His acquaintance, Martial, chose the neat and witty epigram for his picture of Roman life and presents in delightful snatches an equally cynical appraisal of his times.

Despite the rewards that his obsequious eulogies brought from Domitian, Martial remained discontented, and his impression of his age is no more trustworthy than the jaundiced views of Tacitus and Juvenal.

These were the last major writers of pagan Rome. The decline of her greatness in the chaotic third century is reflected in the decay of her artistic and intellectual life. But the period is one of confused transition to the Christian era of the fourth century, and the first Christian authors of Rome, Tertullian (c. 160–230) and St. Cyprian (c. 200–258), prepare the way for the great St. Augustine a century later. Much of classical Roman literature was to fall quickly into disrepute. St. Jerome in the fourth century scourged himself for his sinful interest in the writers of pagan Rome and dreamed that Christ appeared to deny him heaven because of his fondness for Cicero. Though the energetic Tertullian's mind is surprisingly reminiscent of Cicero, Tacitus, and even Juvenal, he attacked all of Roman literature as idolatrous and eventually rejected even the orthodox Church as insufficiently puritanical. The materialism of Lucretius, the eroticism of Catullus and Ovid, even the moderate epicureanism of Horace were to be eclipsed through many centuries of Christian orthodoxy. But one by one they reappeared in the Middle Ages, the Renaissance, and the Enlightenment to inspire new generations with their vigorous message out of the past.

ROME AND THE WESTERN TRADITION

THE Macedonian conquest did not destroy Greece. It had already grown weary and disillusioned before Alexander arrived, and yet it was to outlive him to Hellenize the Roman world for centuries. Nor was Rome destroyed by the Goths and Vandals who overran the empire in the fifth century. She too had been declining for three hundred years, if not indeed from the last years of the republic. But the Roman accomplishments had already merged with the rising tradition of Christianity, officially with Constantine's edict of 313 A.D., and were to be transmitted in a hundred ways through the Christian era to us.

From the Greeks Christianity absorbed the cult of the martyred and resurrected Dionysus, the mystical ethics of the Platonists, and Aristotle's system of knowledge. But Christian connections with Rome are still more striking. The Latin language became the Church Latin of the Roman Church and remains her universal medium of ritual and communication. The government of the pagan religion is duplicated in the organization of the Church to the very title and vestments of the *pontifex maximus*. Local cults throughout the Mediterranean world were countenanced by the Church in its early years and survive as Christian today. But most important is the continuing symbol of the city of Rome, which lost its political power to the barbarians but conquered their souls in return, and established its spiritual sway over a wider empire than Hadrian had ever dreamed of.

Though the Church may be the only place where Latin itself survives, the ancient tongue was corrupted through the Dark Ages into a half-dozen living languages—Italian, French, Spanish, Portuguese, Rumanian. Even the vocabulary of our Anglo-Saxon English owes a great deal to Latin. And our physicians, scientists, and lawyers find much of their special jargons in Latin phraseology. Throughout the Middle Ages and Renaissance, Latin was the universal speech of educated men in Europe, and when antiquity was rediscovered in its own terms

The Romans constructed aqueducts like this one at Segovia, Spain, throughout the empire.

in the fourteenth century, it was the Roman poets and philosophers who were first read and who first inspired imitation. The Greeks whom they in turn had imitated slumbered still in a language few could read. So we think of Mars, not Ares; Venus, not Aphrodite; Vulcan, not Hephaestus; Cupid, not Eros—reminders that Latin mythology honeycombs our poetry and is as much a part of Western heritage as the stories of the Bible. Imitation of Virgil, Plautus, and Juvenal may not be so common in our time as in the days of Spenser, Ben Jonson, and Pope, but their spirits have found a permanent place in English letters. In literature as in philosophy, architecture, and science, Rome was the carrier from Greece and the East, not the inspired inventor.

But transmitting culture is also a worthy service. In the field of law alone Rome was the great inventor. Through the thousand years from the birth of the republic to the Code of Justinian (529 A.D.) she experimented with democracy and monarchy and evolved a system of checks and balances through legislative and executive branches that survives in our own constitution. Law codes in Italy and France, Spain and Latin America, and our own Louisiana and Puerto Rico are still based on Roman law. Less directly it appears throughout the British Empire and the Mohammedan lands of the East. The law is the greatest glory of Rome, and with it she brought to the world a peace which we have long sought to revive.

Symbolic of the decay of Roman civilization is the ruined interior of the Colosseum at Rome. In the days of Rome's imperial greatness her citizens gathered here to greet their friends and to witness the circus entertainments.

Cicero

106–43 B.C.

The great Stoic philosophers, Epictetus and Marcus Aurelius, belong to the second century A.D., when the empire had begun to decay and Stoicism had become a kind of religion to be merged two centuries later with Christianity. But the stoic moral outlook had grown up with the republic and was well defined as the national ethics long before the Greek founders of Stoicism were known in Rome. Cicero, the perfect philosopher for the unphilosophical republic, thought of himself as the Roman Plato, but was really an eclectic whose moral outlook was chiefly Stoic. He rejected the violent metaphysics of Stoicism, as Romans in general ignored it, but his life and death illustrate the Roman brand of Stoic morality as clearly as his treatise on duty, De Officiis, summarizes it.

Marcus Tullius Cicero represents the dignified, able, conscientious Roman senator who built the empire by a stern but practical policy. Yet he was an equestrian, or middle-class man, born in the provincial town of Arpinum, seventy-five miles from Rome, and he won his way to the patrician class only by the force of his talent and integrity. After the military service required of every Roman citizen he studied philosophy with an Epicurean, a Stoic, and a Platonist, but his philosophical interests were always superficial, and his real abilities lay in rhetoric and law, which he mastered under Apollonius Molo of Rhodes. His ambitious wife, Terentia, urged him into public practice, where his oratory and honesty carried him through each step in the round of political offices—quaestor in 76, aedile in 69, praetor in 66, and consul in 63, in which year he reached the height of his career as leader of the state.

But these were troubled times for the republic, and Cicero's effort to unite all that was good in the opposed parties—his "concord of the orders"—was a conservative's dream that ignored the obvious decay of the old order that he idealized. He vacillated between Pompey and Caesar, eventually favored Pompey, but was later pardoned by Caesar. Under the dictatorship he retired from public life to pursue study and writing. His divorce of Terentia for a frivolous young woman, and the death of his beloved daughter, Tullia, clouded his later years and tried his stoic calm. The death of Caesar recalled him to public life as head of the government for one last year, but his fiery opposition to Mark Antony (preserved in fourteen speeches) cost him his life. Antony's soldiers overtook him as slaves were hurrying him to safety on a ship, and true to his stoic code he not only submitted but stretched his head out of his litter so that they might more easily behead him.

The works of Cicero were the best loved of classical prose until our grandfathers' day. Today he is less popular. His 58 surviving orations are admitted to be the greatest of their kind and perfect illustrations of his own treatises on public speaking; but oratory is out of fashion, and the rhetorical tricks and pragmatic insincerity of their rolling periods make them fall short of the greatest literature. His philosophical works are not of the first order. Cicero was, as he readily admitted, an industrious compiler of Greek philosophies rather than a creative thinker, and his great influence on later thought was as transmitter of the teachings of others. Being a typical Roman, he wrote much on political philosophy, but his *Republic* is merely an idealized picture of the Roman state modeled on the dialogue of Plato. His *Laws* applies the Stoic doctrine that reason sanctions law to existing Roman laws and others that Cicero favored. *On the Nature of the Gods* reviews the theology of various schools of philosophy, and the *De Finibus* does the same for their concepts of good and evil. *The Tusculan Disputations* treat superficially death and immortality.

The most readable and characteristic of his philosophical works, *De Officiis*, composed in 44 B.C., a year before his death, was written to strengthen the character of his worthless son. It is a collection of practical rules of conduct based on a lost treatise of the Stoic Panaetius and amounts to a code of behavior for the Roman gentleman. Book I treats duties as virtuous action, Book II considers expedient action, and Book III tries to reconcile the two. The ideal of Roman conduct is brilliantly summarized in this practical work on Stoic ethics, written in Cicero's most elegant style.

But we come closest to the man himself in his informal essays on friendship and old age and, above all, in his 800 surviving letters, carefully collected by his devoted freedman, Tiro. Written to his family, to his brother Quintus, to the conspirators Brutus and Cassius, to the millionaire philosopher Atticus, and other friends, they cover the last twenty-five years of his life but especially the last nine. They treat a wide variety of subjects, from national affairs to troubles in his own household. We get a day-to-day picture of Roman politics tempered with philosophical comments and literary criticism. Although some are formal in tone, the best are surprisingly intimate and reveal the true Cicero as a decent, human sort of man trying to preserve his integrity in a dangerous and chaotic age, a man sometimes cowardly, insufferably vain, yet industrious, honest, and able withal.

The Offices

DEAR Son Marcus. . . .
Having resolved to write something at present, and a great many others hereafter to you, I thought I could begin on no better argument than that which is fittest for your age, and most becoming my authority as a father; for, of all those useful and important subjects, which philosophers have handled so largely and accurately, the precepts they have delivered about Offices or Duties seem of the largest

*The Offices.*⁸ Translated by Thomas Cockman.

extent and comprehension; for they take in every part of our lives, so that whatever we go about, whether of public or private affairs, whether at home or abroad, whether considered barely by ourselves, or as we stand in relation to other people, we lie constantly under an obligation to some duties: and as all the virtue and credit of our lives proceed from the due discharge of this, so all the baseness and turpitude of them result from the non-observance of the same. Now, though this be a subject which all philosophers have employed themselves about (for, who ever dared to assume that name without laying down some instructions about duty?), yet have some sects of them given such accounts of man's happiness and misery, as destroy the very being of virtue and honesty: for he that makes any thing his chiefest good, wherein justice or virtue does not bear a part, and sets up profit, not honesty, for the measure of his happiness; as long as he acts in conformity with his own principles, and is not overruled by the mere dictates of reason and humanity, can never do the offices of friendship, justice, or liberality: nor can he ever be a man of courage, who thinks that pain is the greatest evil; or he of temperance, who imagines pleasure to be the sovereign good. Which things are all so obvious and plain, that one would think they could never stand in need of a dispute. . . . These sects, therefore, unless they are resolved to be inconsistent with themselves, ought wholly to abstain from speaking anything about duties; nor indeed can any constant, unalterable, rational rules of them at all be given, unless it be by those who go on this principle—that it is virtue alone, or at least that chiefly, which ought to be desired for its own sake. So that only the Stoics, Academics, and Peripatetics, have a right to lay down any rules on this subject. . . . I shall follow therefore at this time, and on this subject more especially, the Stoics; not as a bare translator of them, but, according to my usual custom, shall take out of their stores so much, and after such a manner, as in my own judgement I shall think most convenient. . . .

III. The whole subject of duties, in its greatest latitude, comprehends under it these two parts: the first is taken up in explaining what is good, and what our greatest good; the second in certain directions and precepts, according to which on all occasions it is our duty to govern our lives and actions. To the first part belong such questions as these, whether all duties are perfect or not? and, whether one can be greater or less than another? with several others to the same purpose. Not but that the duties of this second part, the rules and precepts of which are laid down, have some tendency and relation to our chiefest good; but only it does not so plainly appear, because they seem to concern more immediately the government of our lives and regulation of our manners; and these are they which I design to explain in the following treatise. . . .

IV. The first thing to be taken notice of is this, that every creature doth by nature endeavour to preserve its own self, its life and body; and to shun and avoid those things which appear prejudicial and hurtful to it; but to seek and procure whatever is necessary for the support of its being, and advancement of its happiness, such as food, shelter, and the like. There is likewise common to all sorts of animals a desire for the continuance and propagation of their several species; together with a love and concern for their young ones. Now there is this special difference between men and brutes; that the latter are governed by nothing but their senses, never look any farther than just to what strikes and affects them at present, and have a very little, or hardly any concern, for what is past or to come: but the former are creatures endowed with reason, which gives them a power to carry their thoughts to the consequences of things, to discover causes before they have yet produced their effects; to see the whole progress, and even the first seeds, as it were, and appearances of them; to compare like occurrences with like, and by joining what is past and what is to come together, to make a just estimate of the one from the other; whereby they are able at once to take a view of their whole lives, and accordingly to make provision for the necessities of them. . . . But of all the properties and inclinations of men, there is none more natural and peculiar to them than an earnest desire and search after truth. Hence it is that our minds are no sooner free from the thoughts and engagements of necessary business, but we presently long to be either seeing, or hearing, or learning of something; and esteem the knowledge of things secret and wonderful as a necessary ingredient of a happy life. Whence it appears that nothing is more agreeable and suited to the nature and minds of men than undisguised openness, truth, and sincerity. Next to this love and affection for truth, there follows in the soul an impatient desire and inclination to pre-eminence; so that whoever has the genuine nature of a man in him, will never endure to be subject to another, unless he be one that instructs or advises, or is invested with a just and lawful authority for the benefit of the public: whence there arises a greatness of soul, which sets it above all the petty concerns and trifling enjoyments of this present world. It is another, and that too no mean prerogative of our reasonable nature, that man alone can discern all the beauties of order and decency, and knows how to govern his words and actions in conformity to them. It is he alone that, of all the creatures, observes and is pleased with the beauty, gracefulness, and symmetry of parts in the objects of sense; which nature and reason observing in them, from thence take occasion to apply the same also to those of the mind; and to conclude that beauty, consistency, and regularity, should be much more kept up in our words and actions; and therefore command us, that nothing be done that is effeminate or unbecoming; and that so strict a guard be kept over every thought and action, as that no indecency be either conceived or practised by us. From these inclinations and instincts of nature arises and results that honesty we are seeking for; which, however little valued and esteemed it may be, is nevertheless virtuous and amiable in itself; and which we may justly say, though it were commended by no one, is yet in its own nature truly commendable.

V. Thus, son Marcus, have I given you a rough draught, and just the outlines, as it were, of honesty; which, could she be seen in her full beauty with mortal eye, would make the whole world (as Plato has said) be in love with wisdom. Now whatever is contained under the notion of honesty arises from one of these four heads; first, a sagacious inquiry and observation for the finding out of truth, which may be called by the general name of prudence: secondly, a care to maintain that society and mutual intercourse which is between them; to render to every man what is his due; and to stand to one's words in all promises and bargains; which we call justice: thirdly, the greatness and unshaken resolution of a truly brave and invincible mind, which goes by the name of magnanimity or fortitude: and lastly, a keeping of our words and actions within the due limits of order and decency; under which are comprehended temperance and moderation. . . .

VI. First, of Prudence, which is wholly taken up in the knowledge of truth, and has the nearest affinity of any with the reasonable nature of man. For how are we all of us drawn and enticed with the desire of wisdom! how noble and glorious a thing do we imagine it to excel in knowledge! and how mean and reproachful do we count it, on the other hand, to slip, to be in error, to be ignorant, or to be imposed on? In gratifying this so natural and virtuous inclination in the mind of man, there are two grand faults to be carefully avoided: the first is an over-great hastiness and rashness in giving up our assent, presuming that we know things before we really do so. Whoever desires (as I am sure all ought) to avoid this error, must in all his inquiries allow himself time, and diligently consider the matter with himself, before he proceeds to pass his judgement on it. The second fault is, that a great many men bestow abundance of study, and a world of pains, on very difficult and obscure subjects; and such as, perhaps, when they are found out, are of but very little, or no concernment. Would men but be careful to shun these two mistakes, whatever study or pains they might spend on virtuous, worthy,

or profitable subjects, it would not without reason be highly commended. . . . In a word, the general aim and design of our thought, and application of mind, is either the attainment of such things as are honest, and tend to a virtuous and happy way of life, or else the improvement of our reason and understanding in wisdom and knowledge. And this may suffice for the first of our general heads of duty.

VII. Of the other remaining three, that which consists in upholding society, and keeping up mutual love and good nature amongst mankind, seems of the largest and most diffusive extent. It comprehends under it these two parts: first, justice, which is much the most glorious and splendid of all virtues, and alone entitles us to the name and appellation of good men; and, secondly, beneficence, which may also be called either bounty or liberality. Now the first thing that justice requires of us is this; that no one should do any hurt to another, unless by way of reasonable and just retribution for some injury received from him: and whatever belongs either to all in common, or particular persons as their own property, should not be altered, but made use of accordingly. Now no man can say that he has anything his own by a right of nature; but either by an ancient immemorial seizure, as those who first planted uninhabited countries; or, secondly, by conquest, as those who have got things by the right of the sword; or else by some law compact, agreement, or lot. It is by some of these means that the people inhabiting Arpinum and Tusculum came to have those lands, which are now called theirs; and the same may be said as to private men's estates. However, since at present, by some of these ways, each particular man has his personal possessions, out of that which by nature was common to all, it is but just that each should hold what is now his own; which, if any one endeavour to take away from him, he directly breaks in on common justice, and violates the rights of human society. . . .

Now the great foundation of justice is faithfulness, which consists in being constantly firm to your word, and a conscientious performance of all compacts and bargains. The vice that is opposite to justice is injustice, of which there are two sorts: the first consists in the actual doing an injury to another; the second, in tamely looking on while he is injured, and not helping and defending him though we are able: for he that injuriously falls on another, whether prompted by rage or other violent passion, does as it were leap at the throat of his companion; and he that refuses to help him when injured, and to ward off the wrong if it lies in his power, is as plainly guilty of baseness and injustice as though he had deserted his father, his friends, or his native country. Now that former injustice, which consists in the wilful and actual wronging another, has oftentimes no other cause but fear; when he, who designedly does a man an injury, is afraid lest himself should be forced to undergo one, if he does not secure himself by doing it beforehand. But, generally speaking, the great source and fountain of all such injustice is the satisfying some irregular and exorbitant appetite; and in a more especial manner, the desire of riches; of which we shall therefore say something in particular.

10 VIII. Riches then are most commonly desired, either to supply us with the necessaries of life, or furnish us with the pleasures and conveniences of it; or else, as it often is observed to happen in persons of great and aspiring minds, as a means of obtaining an interest in the public, and a power of obliging and gratifying one's friends; to which purpose was that saying of the late Marcus Crassus, that whoever designed to be a leading man in the commonwealth, ought never to think he had estate enough, till he 20 could maintain an army with its yearly revenue. Others take pleasure in splendour and magnificence, in a handsome, noble, and plentiful way of living: all which things have begot an insatiable greediness after money, without which they can never be supported and maintained. Not but that a moderate desire of riches, and bettering a man's estate, so long as it abstains from oppressing of others, is allowable enough; but a very great care ought always to be taken that we be not drawn to any injustice by it. 30 There is another desire that makes men as apt to be forgetful of justice, as that after riches; the thirst, I mean, of empire, glory, honours, etc. For that saying of Ennius, "There is no inviolable faith or friendship in the matter of a kingdom;" though applied by him to that one case only, is yet fully as true in a great many others; for wherever the subject of contention is such, as that only one party can meet with success, and the rest must fall short of what they desire; things are usually carried to so great 40 a height, as that it is very difficult not to break in on faith and friendship. This hath appeared but too manifestly of late, in that rash and most impudent attempt of Caesar's; who has broken through all those ties and obligations, that either by gods or men could be laid on him, for the compassing and getting of that dominion to himself, which he had vainly proposed in his depraved imagination. But in this case, it is one very great unhappiness, that the thirst after honour, empire, power, etc., falls most on men 50 of the greatest souls and most exalted natures; wherefore the greater care ought to be taken that nothing of offence be committed in this kind. Now it makes a great difference in all acts of justice, whether they proceed from some violent passion, which is for the most part of short continuance, or

17. **Marcus Crassus,** the third member of the first Triumvirate, notorious for his love of wealth.

are done with design and previous deliberation: for those that are the effects of a sudden gust of passion ought not to be esteemed of so heinous a nature, as those that proceed from premeditated malice. And this may suffice for the first sort of injustice, which 60 consists in the actual doing of wrong, and the causes of it.

IX. As for the second, which only consists in seeing another injured, and being wanting to our duty, by not defending him; the causes of that are wont to be several: for some are afraid of offending others, or of bringing a trouble and charge on themselves: others are negligent, idle, or mean-spirited: and a third sort there is, who are so taken up with their own concerns, that they have no time left to regard 70 the oppressed, whom yet it is their duty to save and protect. I am therefore of opinion, that Plato's consequence will hardly hold good where, speaking about the philosophers, he says, "They are wholly taken up in the seeking out of truth, and perfectly neglect and make light of those things which the rest of the world are so eager after, and so contend about; and that therefore they are just." This, I say, I am afraid is a bad consequence; for though, it is true, they keep the first sort of justice, inasmuch as 80 they actually do no wrong; yet they run perfectly counter to the other; for being engaged in their learning and studies, they abandon their friends to be injured by others, whom in justice they ought to have protected and defended. So that it is believed they hardly ever trouble themselves so far, as at all to intermeddle with the business of the public, if it was not altogether, as it were, forced on them. But it were a great deal better would they do it voluntarily; for an action, though honest, is not therefore 90 truly virtuous, unless it be done out of choice, and with a good will. There are others yet, who out of a desire of improving their own estates, or else a morose and unsociable sort of temper, cry, they meddle with nobody's business but their own, that so they may seem to be men of strict honesty, and to injure nobody; and they do indeed avoid the one sort of injustice, but directly run themselves into the other; for they desert the common good and society of mankind, while they bestow neither study, pains, 100 nor money toward the preservation of it. . . .

XI. There are certain duties also to be strictly observed, even towards those that have injured us; for we ought not to go beyond certain bounds, in exacting revenge and punishment of another: in which particular it may, perhaps, be enough to make him that has wronged us repent of the wrong done; so that both he himself may abstain from the like, and others may be discouraged from injuring us for the future. There are certain peculiar laws of war 110 also, which are of all things most strictly to be observed in the commonwealth; for there being two sorts of disputing in the world, the one by reason, and the other by open force; and the former of these being that which is agreeable to the nature of man, and the latter to that of brutes; when we cannot obtain what is our right by the one, we must of necessity have recourse to the other. It is allowable therefore to undertake wars, but it must always be with design of obtaining a secure peace: and when we have got the better of our enemies, we should rest content with the victory alone, and show ourselves merciful and kind to them afterwards, unless they are such as have been very cruel, and committed inhuman barbarities in the war. Thus our forefathers took into their city the Aequians, Volscians, Sabines, and others whom they had subdued; whereas Carthage and Numantia they entirely destroyed. I could wish I might not add Corinth too; but I believe they had something in their eye when they did it, and more especially the situation of the place; which, being so very convenient as it was, they were afraid lest it might be at one time or other an encouragement to revolt. In my opinion it is always our duty to do what we can for a fair and safe peace; in which thing, if people would have hearkened unto me, we might at this time have seen the republic, though, it is true, I cannot say in a flourishing condition, yet certainly not as at present we perceive it, entirely subverted and fallen into ruins. As we are bound to be merciful to those whom we have actually conquered; so should those also be received into favour, who have laid down their arms, and thrown themselves wholly on the general's mercy; and that even though the breach be made in their city walls. . . .

XII. We have told you already what previous causes and conditions there should be, before any war can be lawful and just; the same are required even in those wars also, which are undertaken merely for glory and empire; but then all contests of this latter sort should be carried on with less heat and animosities; for as in the differences that happen among citizens, we make a distinction between a violent enemy and a generous rival, in one case nothing but a title of honour, in the other our lives and reputations being concerned; so did our ancestors do in their wars. That which they waged with the Cimbers and Celtibers, was managed as with hateful and implacable enemies; the question then being, not whether of the two should remain a conqueror, but whether should remain a people at all; whereas those with the Latins, Carthaginians, Pyrrhus, etc., were only quarrels about honour and dominion. The Carthaginians were perfidious and treacherous; Hannibal, their great commander, cruel; but all the rest more faithful and merciful. . . .

XIII. It is also the duty of particular persons, if at any time forced by the necessity of their circumstances, they have made any promise or oath to an enemy, afterwards to see that they perform it faithfully. Thus Regulus was taken in the first Punic war by the Carthaginians, and sent by them to Rome about an exchange of prisoners, on solemn oath given that he would return to them again: first, then, as soon as he was come to Rome, he advised the senate against making such an exchange, and when he had done so, though begged on to stay by his friends and relations, rather returned to a certain punishment than his oath should be broken, though made to an enemy. . . . But the greatest example of justice to an enemy was shown by our ancestors towards king Pyrrhus. There came a deserter out of Pyrrhus' camp, and offered the senate to despatch him with poison; which they and Fabricius were so far from accepting of, that they gave him up again as a traitor to his master. Thus we may see, that they would not allow any unjust way of dealing, though for the death of a powerful and invading adversary: and so much for the duties required in war. There is one part of justice remaining behind, and which ought by no means to be forgotten by us; I mean that towards the lowest and meanest sort of people: and these are more especially those we call our slaves; in relation to whom, it is a very good rule that is given by some men, that we should use them no otherwise than we do our day-labourers, make them first do their work, and then pay them honestly what they have earned. In fine, to close up this discourse of justice, there are two ways or methods whereby one man may injure or oppress another; the one is fraud and subtlety, the other open force and violence; the former of which is esteemed the part of a fox, and the latter of a lion; both of them certainly very unworthy of a reasonable creature, though fraud, I think, is the more odious of the two. But of all injustice, theirs is certainly of the deepest die, who make it their business to appear honest men, even whilst they are practising the greatest of villainies.

XIV. We have now gone through with the subject of justice; it remains, in the next place, to go on according to our method proposed, that we say something likewise of bounty and liberality, than which there is nothing more nearly allied to the nature of man. But then we must observe these following cautions—first, that we take care in all acts of bounty, that they be not prejudicial to those we would oblige by them, nor to any other body; secondly, that we do not in our bounty and liberality go beyond our estates; and, thirdly, that we duly proportion our kindness, according to every man's merit and deserts. And first of the former, which is grounded on the great and fundamental principle of all justice, to which this duty in all its particular instances should be referred—for he who, pretending

to do one a kindness, does that which is really a prejudice to him, is indeed so far from being kind and obliging, as that he ought to be counted a most pernicious flatterer; and to do any manner of injury to one, that you may show your generosity and bounty to another, is just one and the same sort of roguery and injustice, as to enrich yourself by the spoils of your neighbour. . . . That action therefore of Caesar and Sylla's, in taking away estates from
10 the rightful proprietors, and giving them to others, who had no right to them, ought by no means to be accounted liberal; for nothing can ever be truly such that is not at the same time just and honest. A second caution to be observed was this: that our bounty be not suffered to exceed our abilities; for they who give more than their estates will allow of, are, in the first place, injurious to their own relations, by spending that wealth on other people which should rather have been given or left to them. Beside that
20 this over-great bounty in giving is usually accompanied with an answerable desire and greediness of getting; which often proceeds even to downright oppression, that so men may have wherewithal to supply this extravagant humour. One may also observe in a great many people, that they take a sort of pride in being counted magnificent, and give very plentifully, not from any generous principle in their natures, but only to appear great in the eye of the world; so that all their bounty is resolved into noth-
30 ing but mere outside pretence, and is nearer of kin to vanity and folly, than it is to either liberality or honesty. The third caution was, that our bounty should be proportioned to the merits of the receiver; in judging of which, we are first to consider the man's honesty or manners; secondly, the good-will he bears towards us; thirdly, the nearness of relation, or society that is between us; and, lastly, the benefits we have formerly received from him. It is desirable that all these inducements might concur in the same
40 person; but when they do not, we should bestow our kindness more especially on him, in whom we find the most and weightiest of them. . . .

Roman politicians. From a painting from Pompeii.

XVI. There is such a thing as a fellowship or society between all men in general: the bond or cement that holds this together is reason and discourse, which, by teaching, learning, communicating one with another, etc., easily make men agree together, and unite them all in one natural sort of conjunction and community: nor does anything set us at a greater distance from the nature of beasts; for we 50 oftentimes talk of the courage of them, such as lions and horses; but never a word of their equity, justice, or goodness: and why is this, but because they are destitute of reason and discourse? This is then the largest and most comprehensive of all societies, being made up of men considered barely as such, and so taking in even the whole race and kind of them one with another; the duties of which are, to let every one have a share in those things which by nature were produced for the common advantage 60 and benefit of all; to let what is already determined by laws and civil constitutions remain as it is, without breaking in on any man's rights; as to which things, however, we should remember a rule, which is now among the Greeks become a usual proverb, "All things in common amongst friends.". . .

XVII. But there are several degrees of society and fellowship amongst mankind; for to take now our leave of that general and universal one already mentioned, there is a nearer among those who are all of 70 the same country, nation, or language, than which nothing more knits and unites men to one another. There is a closer yet among those who are all of the same city; for a great many things are in common to fellow-citizens, such as markets, temples, walks, ways, laws, privileges, courts of justice, freedom of votes, besides common meetings and familiarities, and abundance of business and intercourse with one another. But there is a stricter bond of alliance still between those who belong to the same family, as 80 taking into it but a very small part of that vast and immense one of all mankind. The closest and nearest of all societies is between man and wife; then follows that between them and their children, and afterwards that of the whole family, who inhabit together and have all things in common; which is, as it were, the first beginning of a city, and ground or seed-plot of a whole commonwealth. . . . But when we have gone over all the relations that are in the world, and thoroughly considered the nature of each, 90 we shall find that there is no one of greater obligation, no one that is dearer and nearer to us, than that which we all of us bear to the public. We have a tender concern and regard for our parents, for our children, our kindred, and acquaintance, but the love which we have for our native country swallows up all other loves whatsoever; for which there is no honest man but would die, if by his death he could do it any necessary service. How detestable, then, must the wickedness and barbarity of those people be, who have mangled and rent this their native country by all manner of villanies, and have made it their business (nay, and still do so) to bring it to ruin and utter desolation. Now if there should happen any contest or competition between these relations, which of them should have the greatest share of our duty, we should pay the first regard to our country and parents, from whom we have received the most endearing obligations; the next to our children and family, who all have their eyes on us alone, and have nobody else on whom they can depend; next in order to these come our kindred and relations, whose fortune is generally the same with our own. . . .

XVIII. It is to be observed, that whereas there were laid down four general heads, from which all virtue and honesty is derived, whatever proceeds from a brave and exalted mind, that is raised above fortune and all the little chances and accidents of the world, is usually made most account of amongst men. . . .

XIX. Fortitude is very well defined by the Stoic philosophers, when they call it "a virtue contending for justice and honesty." No man, by baseness and treachery, has ever got the name and reputation of true courage; for nothing can ever be virtuous or creditable that is not just. . . . The first thing therefore I would have in a truly courageous man is, that he be a follower of goodness and fair dealing, of truth and sincerity; which are the principal and constituent parts of justice. But here it is one very unhappy thing, that, most times, these great and exalted minds are naturally ungovernable and desirous of rule: so that what Plato observed of the Spartans, that all their customs had no other aim but to get the superiority, may fitly enough be applied to these persons: for the more any man has of this greatness of soul, the more eager he is of being a sharer in the government, or rather of obtaining it wholly to himself: and it is no easy matter to be fair and equitable in all one's actions, which is the proper and peculiar office of justice, while one is endeavoring to make himself uppermost. Hence it comes to pass, that they never will be conquered in any debates, nor overruled by the laws and constitutions of the public; but make it their business, by factions and bribery, to get a strong party and interest in the republic; and rather choose to be uppermost by force and injustice, than equal to others by fair and upright dealing. But the difficulty of it can only serve to make it more honourable, but never its contrary more excusable: for no sort of case or circumstance whatever can excuse any man for be-

ing guilty of injustice. Those are therefore your truly brave and courageous men, not who rob, plunder, and injure others, but those who secure and protect them from injuries. But that greatness of mind which is truly such, and, under the direction of wisdom and prudence, makes that honour and credit, which we naturally desire, not consist in the outward imaginary applause, but in the real intrinsic goodness of its actions; and is not so eager of appearing to be greater and better than others, as of really being so: for he that is so mean as to depend on the giddy and ignorant multitude, ought never to be accounted of a truly great and exalted spirit; besides that, there is nothing so easily draws men to acts of injustice as a loftiness of mind, when joined with this foolish desire of applause. This is indeed a very dangerous place, and requires our greatest concern and watchfulness; because you shall hardly find any man, who, when he has gone through labours and difficulties, does not expect this honour and applause, as a kind of reward for his courage and achievements.

XX. . . . The desire of glory, robs a man wholly of his freedom and liberty, which generous spirits ought of all things in the world to maintain and contend for. Neither ought places of power to be sought after; but at some times rather to be refused when offered, at others to be laid down if they can conveniently. We should free ourselves, in short, from all vehement passions and disorders of mind, not only those of desire and fear, but also of sorrow, of joy, and anger; that so the state of the mind may be calm and undisturbed; which will make the whole life become graceful and uniform. Now there both are and have been many, who, to gain this repose of which I am speaking, have betaken themselves to a life of retirement, and wholly withdrawn from all business of the public. Among these the noblest and most eminent of the philosophers; and some men of rigid and severe lives, who disliked the manners of the people or their governors; others have withdrawn themselves into the country, being pleased with the management of their own private fortunes. These men proposed the same end to themselves that kings and princes do, viz. the living so as to want for nothing; to be under the power and control of none, but to enjoy a full and perfect freedom; which consists in living so as one's self best pleases.

XXI. . . . One can hardly condemn them, in that they despise, and make little account of glory and applause; but their true reason seems to be rather this, that they do not care to suffer the labour and fatigue of them, and are afraid of encountering with rubs and repulses, as things that are attended with some shame and dishonour: for you shall often find there are a great many men, who are very inconsistent with themselves in things of a contrary nature: as for pleasure, they despise it with all the severity of a

1–5. those people . . . desolation, an allusion to Julius Caesar and Marc Antony.

Stoic; but yet are so effeminate, as not to be able to bear the least trouble; are mighty contemners of fame and applause; but extremely concerned at anything of disgrace: which are things that do not very well agree together. Those people then, whom Nature has endowed with abilities for that purpose, should forthwith endeavour to procure themselves places, and manage the business of the commonwealth; otherwise how should the city be well governed, or the greatness of their endowments be made known to the world? But that greatness of soul, and contempt of all human things, which we have often mentioned, together with that calmness and serenity of mind, is requisite in those of a public station, as much, if not more than it is in philosophers, if ever they hope to be free from anxieties, and arrive at any steadiness or uniformity in their lives. Now these things are easier to philosophers than to them; forasmuch as their lives being led in private, require for their support a less number of things, and have fewer within the power and reach of fortune: and if any ill accident should befall them, it is impossible their sufferings can be very considerable. Those men, therefore, that are in public stations, having things of more weight and importance to be taken care of, must in reason be supposed to lie much more open to the assaults of the passions than those who spend their days in privacy and retirement. On which account they should take the more care to fortify themselves with this greatness of spirit. . . .

XXIII. On the whole, that virtue which consists in greatness and elevation of soul, and makes up the subject of our present inquiry, is obtained by the strength of the mind, not the body: however, the body ought not to be neglected, but by exercise brought to such a frame and condition, as that it may be able to obey the prescriptions of the mind, in performing that business, and bearing those fatigues which are required of it. But still the nature of the virtue we are seeking for, consists in due care and application of mind; in which particular, the public receives as much benefit from gownmen, who manage and take care of its civil concerns, as it doth from soldiers, who are generals of its armies: for they by their prudence have often either hindered the breaking out of wars, or else have occasioned their speedy conclusion; and sometimes too have been the cause of their being undertaken, as the third with Carthage was entered into on the advice of Cato, whose credit and authority prevailed in that case even after he was dead. Wisdom, therefore, and skill in determining civil affairs, is more to be desired than courage in fighting: but then we must always be careful in this case that our design be not the avoiding of war, but the being more useful and serviceable to the public. . . .

XXV. Those who design to be partakers in the government should be sure to remember those two precepts of Plato; first, to make the safety and interest of their citizens the great aim and design of all their thoughts and endeavours, without ever considering their own personal advantage; and, secondly, so to take care of the whole collective body of the republic, as not to serve the interest of any one party, to the prejudice or neglect of all the rest: for the government of a state is much like the office of a guardian or trustee; which should always be managed for the good of the pupil, and not of the persons to whom he is entrusted; and those men who, whilst they take care of one, neglect or disregard another part of the citizens, do but occasion sedition and discord, the most destructive things in the world to a state: whence it comes to pass, that while some take part with the popular faction, and others make their court to every great one, there are but very few left who are concerned for the benefit and good of the whole. From this root have sprung many grievous dissensions amongst the Athenians; and not only tumults, but even destructive civil wars in our own republic; things which a worthy and truly brave citizen, and one who deserves to hold the reins of the government, will shun and detest; and will give himself so to the service of the public, as to aim at no riches or power for himself; and will so take care of the whole community, as not to pass over any one part of it. . . .

XXVI. Another great duty of fortitude is, not to be haughty, disdainful, and arrogant when Fortune favours us, and all things go forward according to our wishes: for it shows as much meanness and poorness of spirit to be transported with good, as it does with ill fortune; whereas, on the other hand, nothing is more brave than an evenness of temper in every condition, and (as is reported of Socrates and Laelius) a constant retaining the same air in one's countenance, without ever seeming puffed up or dejected. I find that Philip, the king of Macedonia, was inferior to his son in the outward glory and splendour of his achievements, but very far above him in good nature and condescension: therefore the father kept always the character of a great person, whereas the son often was guilty of base and dishonourable actions. It is a good rule therefore, I think, which is given by some men, that the higher our station in the world is, the more care we should take of our lives and actions, that they be kept within the compass of lowliness and humility. . . . Whoever observes these measures laid down, let his way of life be either public or private, may perform all the duties of magnanimity, constancy, and greatness of soul, as well as of sincerity, fidelity, and doing good to mankind.

XXVII. We are now in the next place to speak of the fourth, and only remaining part of virtue or honesty, under which are comprehended temperance, modesty, government of the passions, and the observing a just order as to time and place in our words and actions; from all which arises a certain engaging kind of beauty and gracefulness, which serves to set off and adorn our lives. Under this head is contained that becomingness, which is in its nature so closely united and riveted to honesty, that there is no way left of pulling them asunder; for whatever is becoming is likewise honest, and whatever is honest is likewise becoming. The difference between them is so very small, that we may better conceive what it is, than explain it; for whatever becomingness there is in any action, it immediately arises from the honesty of it. From hence it appears that becomingness does not peculiarly belong to this one part of honesty, whereof we are now undertaking to discourse, but shows itself also in each of the three former. To reason, for instance, and discourse according to the rules of prudence; to go about nothing but after due consideration, and on every occasion to be quick at espying and defending the truth, are things that are becoming; whereas to be deceived, to be in an error or mistake, and to be imposed on, are very unbecoming, as well as to be mad or beside oneself. So again, all actions of justice are becoming; but those of injustice are both scandalous and unbecoming. The same may be said as to the actions of fortitude: whatever is done with a manly courage and bravery of mind, as it is worthy of, so it becomes a man. . . .

XXVIII. Nature has given every one of us a character, by endowing us with that nobleness and excellence of being, whereby we are set above all other creatures; a character of temperance and modesty, of constancy and moderation. And the same Nature having also taught us that we ought to be careful of our carriage and demeanour towards the rest of men, hence it appears of how large an extent that becomingness is, which belongs to the nature of honesty in general, and also that other, which is seen in the exercise of the several kinds of it: for as the beauty and comeliness of the body draws the eyes to it by the fit composure of all its members, and pleases us only on this account, because all its parts correspond with a kind of proportion and harmony; so this decorum, which gives a sort of lustre and grace to our lives, engages the approbation and esteem of all we live with, by that just and due order, consistency, and regularity, which it keeps up and maintains in our words and actions. . . .

XXIX. Every action therefore should be free, as from precipitancy and rashness on the one hand, so from all carelessness and negligence on the other; nor should anything be done, for which we cannot give a sufficient reason; which is almost the very definition of duty. In order to this the passions must be brought under the power of reason, so as neither through hastiness to run before its orders, nor through coldness and heaviness to disregard them when given; but all their motions must be so quieted and restrained, as to bring no uneasiness or disturbance to the mind: and from this calm and peaceable state of the soul arises that constancy and moderation we have mentioned; for when once the passions grow unruly and extravagant, and refuse to be guided in their desires and aversions by the rules of prudence, they will run without question beyond all bounds and measure; for they abandon and cast off their allegiance to reason, which they ought to obey by the constitution of nature. By this means are all things turned topsy-turvy; and not the mind only, but even the body also, put very much into disorder and confusion. Do but mark those who are inflamed with a vehement anger or desire; who are transported with fear, or an over-great joy; and you will see an alteration in their countenances, voices, gestures, and all their actions; which sufficiently gives us to understand (that we may return again to the duty now before us) how necessary it is to restrain and give check to the movements of the appetite, and to be always watchful and standing on our guard, that so we may neither be careless and inconsiderate, nor do anything rashly and at all adventures: for mankind were never designed by Nature merely to sport and idle away their time, but to follow after grave and serious studies, and business of greater importance than play is. Not but that jesting and diversion are allowable, provided we use them but as we do sleep, and other such necessary refreshments of nature, viz. after the discharge of our serious and more important duties. And even then we must see that our jesting be neither excessive nor immodest, but such as is handsome and becoming a gentleman; for as boys are allowed not all kinds of sports, but only such as have nothing that is vicious or ill in them; so in this jesting we should allow ourselves nothing but what is agreeable to honesty and good manners. We may therefore observe that jesting or merriment is of two sorts: the one clownish, abusive, scandalous, and obscene; the other handsome, genteel, ingenious, and truly pleasant. . . .

XXX. But in all inquiries concerning what becomes us, it is of very great moment to be constantly reflecting how much man's nature excels that of beasts and inferior animals. These have no taste or relish for anything but the pleasures of the body, towards which they are carried with a great deal of eagerness; whereas nothing is more agreeable and nourishing, as it were, to the mind of man, than learning and contemplation. Hence he is always seeking or contriving something that is new, and is greatly delighted with seeing and hearing, for the increase of his knowledge: and if there is any one too much addicted to sensual pleasures, unless he is

transformed into a mere brute; (for some such there are, who are men in name, and not in reality) but if, I say, any one is too much addicted, and suffers himself to be conquered by pleasure; yet, for very shame, he will hide and conceal his propensities towards it as much as possible. And what is this now but a plain indication that sensual pleasures are unbecoming the dignity of a reasonable creature, and ought to be despised and rejected by him? and that whoever sets any value on them should be sure to take care that he keep within the limits of reason and moderation? Hence it follows that we should not have any respect to pleasure, but only to the preservation of our health and strength, in our victuals, clothes, and other conveniences belonging to the body. And does not the consideration of the same dignity and excellence of our natures plainly inform us how base and unworthy a thing it is to dissolve in luxury, softness, and effeminacy; and how brave and becoming it is, on the other hand, for a man to lead a life of frugality and temperance, of strictness and sobriety? And here we must observe that Nature has given us, as it were, a double part to be acted in the world: the first is extended to all men in common, forasmuch as we are all of us partakers of reason, and that prerogative of our nature, whereby we are exalted above other animals; it is this that conducts us in the finding out our duty, and from it all honesty and becomingness arises: the second is appropriate to each in particular; for as there is a great deal of difference in bodies, some being nimble and proper for running, others more lusty, and fitter for wrestling; some of a noble and majestic air, others of a sweet and engaging kind of beauty: so there is no less, or rather a far greater variety in humours. . . .

XXXI. The more easily then to arrive at that decorum of which we are speaking, let every one stick to his own peculiar character and humour, provided it has nothing that is vicious in it: I say, provided it has nothing that is vicious in it; for we should always take particular care to do nothing that is contrary to that universal character which Nature has imprinted on every one of us; but, saving the reverence we owe to that, then to live according to our own particular one, so as to follow after that kind of study, and apply ourselves to that course of life which is most suitable and agreeable to our own inclinations, though others perhaps may be more useful and important; for it is in vain to struggle against the bias of your nature, or to engage in that sort of business in which you can never arrive at any perfection. From what has been said it more fully appears what that is which we call becoming; since nothing can be such that is done, as we say, in despite of nature, *i.e.* contrary to the bent and tendency of a man's genius. Now it is certain, if anything

in the world is becoming, it is a constant uniformity in our whole lives and particular actions; which it is utterly impossible we should ever maintain, so long as we run counter to our own inclinations, and foolishly follow after those of other people: for as we should use our own native language, which all are supposed to understand best, and not lard our talk, as a great many do, with expressions out of Greek, who are therefore deservedly laughed at by others; so we should keep to one constant tenor and regular conduct in our lives and actions, so that nothing may be in them which is not well suited and of a piece with the rest.

Lucretius

c. 99–c. 55 B.C.

Epicurean philosophy was never so popular in Rome as Stoicism, but in the first century B.C. it did produce a modest school, and the greatest of all philosophical poets, Lucretius. Epicurus himself (341–270 B.C.) wrote voluminously, but only three of his philosophical letters, a brief summary of his doctrines, and some fragments have survived. It was his passionate Roman disciple, Lucretius, who converted his matter-of-fact prose into the persuasive form of magnificent poetry.

Titus Lucretius Carus is known to us through only one work. His birth and death dates are doubtful; yet it is clear from his poem that he lived through the chaotic last years of the republic and turned for spiritual peace to nature and philosophy. He apparently came from an obscure branch of an ancient family and addressed his poem as a social inferior to a minor political figure named Memmius. This great work received next to no recognition until centuries later.

It is the metaphysical system of Epicurus that Lucretius sets forth in *Of the Nature of Things*, although his ethical view of pleasure as the end of living can be inferred from the tone and details of the whole. He tells us with a disorderly enthusiasm how epicureanism has enabled him to live happily without religion in the harsh and disillusioning world of men. Although he begins with a beautiful invocation of Venus, he promptly denounces religion as superstition and proposes to show how a philosophical understanding of the universe can free men from fear of the gods and death and make them happy.

His view of things is materialistic, and Books I and II expound the atomic theory of Democritus and Epicurus in terms surprisingly suggestive of modern science. Nothing exists but atoms and space. The atoms are ceaselessly moving, not in straight lines but by "swerves," and are accidentally forming endless combinations that we recognize as the elements of air, fire, earth, and water, and all the things of the universe from the stars to the smallest objects on earth. Since atoms and space alone exist, the disasters of nature that breed fear in men and make them create gods to be placated are mere phenomena of the moving atoms—thunderstorms from clashing clouds, not Jupiter; earthquakes from expanding gases under the earth, not Vulcan.

Book III discusses the place of the soul in such a system. Living things are part of the material system, simply combinations of inert atoms that function for a while as living units. The mind is an organ (situated in the chest), while the soul is spread finely through the body. Both die with the body, though all the atoms of body, mind, and soul move into new combinations with other atoms as indestructible parts of the material system. Therefore we should not fear death, for it cannot come until we have ceased to exist. In Book IV Lucretius applies his materialism to sense-perception, sexual passion, and the mind in general. Book V, the most interesting of the six, gives his theory of the history of the universe and man, discussing sometimes naïvely yet always intelligently, astronomy, biology, and the growth of human institutions. The last book, which is obviously unfinished, applies his theory to a variety of specific phenomena.

Through all of the inaccuracy of Lucretius' speculation shines a courageous attempt to explain the universe and the world of man in rational terms. We need not agree with him to admit the modernity of his outlook and his anticipations of modern science. Nor should we let his cold materialism obscure the vigor of his poem and his Wordsworthian sensitivity to the beauties of the world, however atomic it may be in structure. His whole point is that denying religion and accepting science leads him not to despair but to happiness founded on freedom from fear. In his expression of this satisfaction he proved himself a great artist.

Of the Nature of Things

BOOK I

PROEM

WHILST human kind
    Throughout the lands lay miserably crushed
Before all eyes beneath Religion—who
Would show her head along the region skies,
Glowering on mortals with her hideous face—   5
A Greek it was who first opposing dared
Raise mortal eyes that terror to withstand,
Whom nor the fame of Gods nor lightning's stroke
Nor threatening thunder of the ominous sky
Abashed; but rather chafed to angry zest   10

*Of the Nature of Things.*ᴬ Translated by William Ellery Leonard. Taken from *Of the Nature of Things* by Lucretius. Published and copyrighted by E. P. Dutton & Co., Inc., New York, 1922 (Everyman's Lib. Ed.). Reprinted by permission of E. P. Dutton & Co., Inc. and J. M. Dent & Sons, Ltd.
6. **A Greek,** Epicurus.

His dauntless heart to be the first to rend
The crossbars at the gates of Nature old.
And thus his will and hardy wisdom won;
And forward thus he fared afar, beyond
The flaming ramparts of the world, until   15
He wandered the unmeasurable All.
Whence he to us, a conqueror, reports
What things can rise to being, what cannot,
And by what law to each its scope prescribed,
Its boundary stone that clings so deep in Time.   20
Wherefore religion now is under foot,
And us his victory now exalts to heaven. . . .
    I fear perhaps thou deemest that we fare
An impious road to realms of thought profane;
But 'tis that same religion oftener far   25
Hath bred the foul impieties of men:
As once at Aulis, the elected chiefs,
Foremost of heroes, Danaan counsellors,
Defiled Diana's altar, virgin queen,
With Agamemnon's daughter, foully slain.   30
She felt the chaplet round her maiden locks
And fillets, fluttering down on either cheek,
And at the altar marked her grieving sire,
The priests beside him who concealed the knife,
And all the folk in tears at sight of her.   35
With a dumb terror and a sinking knee
She dropped; nor might avail her now that first
'Twas she who gave the king a father's name.
They raised her up, they bore the trembling girl
On to the altar—hither led not now   40
With solemn rites and hymeneal choir,
But sinless woman, sinfully foredone,
A parent felled her on her bridal day,
Making his child a sacrificial beast
To give the ships auspicious winds for Troy: 45
Such are the crimes to which religion leads. . . .
Then be it ours with steady mind to clasp
The purport of the skies—the law behind
The wandering courses of the sun and moon;
To scan the powers that speed all life below;   50
But most to see with reasonable eyes
Of what the mind, of what the soul is made,
And what it is so terrible that breaks
On us asleep, or waking in disease,
Until we seem to mark and hear at hand   55
Dead men whose bones earth bosomed long ago.

SUBSTANCE IS ETERNAL

This terror, then, this darkness of the mind,
Not sunrise with its flaring spokes of light,
Nor glittering arrows of morning can disperse,
But only Nature's aspect and her law,   60
Which, teaching us, hath this exordium:
Nothing from nothing ever yet was born.
Fear holds dominion over mortality

30. **Agamemnon's daughter,** Iphigenia.

Only because, seeing in land and sky
So much the cause whereof no wise they know, 65
Men think Divinities are working there.
Meantime, when once we know from nothing still
Nothing can be create, we shall divine
More clearly what we seek: those elements
From which alone all things created are, 70
And how accomplished by no tool of Gods. . . .
Confess then, naught from nothing can become,
Since all must have their seeds, wherefrom to grow,
Wherefrom to reach the gentle fields of air.

Hence too it comes that Nature all dissolves 75
Into their primal bodies again, and naught
Perishes ever to annihilation.
For, were aught mortal in its every part,
Before our eyes it might be snatched away
Unto destruction; since no force were needed 80
To sunder its members and undo its bands. . . .
Nothing returns to naught; but all return
At their collapse to primal forms of stuff.
Lo, the rains perish which Ether-father throws
Down to the bosom of Earth-mother; but then 85
Upsprings the shining grain, and boughs are green
Amid the trees, and trees themselves wax big
And lade themselves with fruits; and hence in turn
The race of man and all the wild are fed;
Hence joyful cities thrive with boys and girls; 90
And leafy woodlands echo with new birds. . . .

CHARACTER OF THE ATOMS

Bodies, again,
Are partly primal germs of things, and partly
Unions deriving from the primal germs.
And those which are the primal germs of things 95
No power can quench; for in the end they conquer
By their own solidness; though hard it be
To think that aught in things has solid frame;
For lightnings pass, no less than voice and shout,
Through hedging walls of houses, and the iron 100
White-dazzles in the fire, and rocks will burn
With exhalations fierce and burst asunder.
Totters the rigid gold dissolved in heat;
The ice of bronze melts conquered in the flame;
Warmth and the piercing cold through silver seep,
Since, with the cups held rightly in the hand, 106
We oft feel both, as from above is poured
The dew of waters between their shining sides:
So true it is no solid form is found. . . .
But powerful in old simplicity, 110
Abide the solid, the primeval germs;
And by their combinations more condensed,
All objects can be tightly knit and bound
And made to show unconquerable strength.
Again, since all things kind by kind obtain 115
Fixed bounds of growing and conserving life;
Since nature hath inviolably decreed
What each can do, what each can never do;

Since naught is changed, but all things so abide
That ever the variegated birds reveal 120
The spots or stripes peculiar to their kind,
Spring after spring: thus surely all that is
Must be composed of matter immutable.
For if the primal germs in any wise
Were open to conquest and to change, 'twould be
Uncertain also what could come to birth 126
And what could not, and by what law to each
Its scope prescribed, its boundary stone that clings
So deep in Time. Nor could the generations
Kind after kind so often reproduce 130
The nature, habits, motions, ways of life,
Of their progenitors. . . .

THE INFINITY OF THE UNIVERSE

But since I've taught that bodies of matter, made
Completely solid, hither and thither fly
Forevermore unconquered through all time, 135
Now come, and whether to the sum of them
There be a limit or be none, for thee
Let us unfold; likewise what has been found
To be the wide inane, or room, or space
Wherein all things soever do go on, 140
Let us examine if it finite be
All and entire, or reach unmeasured round
And downward an illimitable profound.

Thus, then, the All that is is limited
In no one region of its onward paths, 145
For then 'tmust have forever its beyond.
And a beyond 'tis seen can never be
For aught, unless still further on there be
A somewhat somewhere that may bound the same—
So that the thing be seen still on to where 150
The nature of sensation of that thing
Can follow it no longer. Now because
Confess we must there's naught beside the sum,
There's no beyond, and so it lacks all end.
It matters nothing where thou post thyself, 155
In whatsoever regions of the same;
Even any place a man has set him down
Still leaves about him the unbounded all
Outward in all directions; or, supposing
A moment the all of space finite to be, 160
If some one farthest traveller runs forth
Unto the éxtreme coasts and throws ahead
A flying spear, is't then thy wish to think
It goes, hurled off amain, to where 'twas sent
And shoots afar, or that some object there 165
Can thwart and stop it? For the one or other
Thou must admit and take. Either of which
Shuts off escape for thee, and does compel
That thou concede the all spreads everywhere,
Owning no confines. . . . 170
In endless motion everything goes on
Forevermore; out of all regions, even
Out of the pit below, from forth the vast,

Are hurtled bodies evermore supplied.
The nature of room, the space of the abyss   175
Is such that even the flashing thunderbolts
Can neither speed upon their courses through,
Gliding across eternal tracts of time,
Nor, further, bring to pass, as on they run,
That they may bate their journeying one whit: 180
Such huge abundance spreads for things around—
Room off to every quarter, without end.
Lastly, before our very eyes is seen
Thing to bound thing: air hedges hill from hill,
And mountain walls hedge air; land ends the sea,
And sea in turn all lands; but for the All   186
Truly is nothing which outside may bound. . . .

BOOK II
PROEM

'Tis sweet, when, down the mighty main, the winds
Roll up its waste of waters, from the land
To watch another's labouring anguish far,   190
Not that we joyously delight that man
Should thus be smitten, but because 'tis sweet
To mark what evils we ourselves be spared;
'Tis sweet, again, to view the mighty strife
Of armies embattled yonder o'er the plains,   195
Ourselves no sharers in the peril; but naught
There is more goodly than to hold the high
Serene plateaus, well fortressed by the wise,
Whence thou may'st look below on other men
And see them ev'rywhere wand'ring, all dispersed
In their lone seeking for the road of life;   201
Rivals in genius, or emulous in rank,
Pressing through days and nights with hugest toil
For summits of power and mastery of the world.
O wretched minds of men! O blinded hearts!   205
In how great perils, in what darks of life
Are spent the human years, however brief!—
O not to see that nature for herself
Barks after nothing, save that pain keep off,
Disjoined from the body, and that mind enjoy   210
Delightsome feeling, far from care and fear!
Therefore we see that our corporeal life
Needs little, altogether, and only such
As takes the pain away, and can besides
Strew underneath some number of delights.   215
More grateful 'tis at times (for nature craves
No artifice nor luxury), if forsooth
There be no golden images of boys
Along the halls, with right hands holding out
The lamps ablaze, the lights for evening feasts, 220
And if the house doth glitter not with gold
Nor gleam with silver, and to the lyre resound
No fretted and gilded ceilings overhead,
Yet still to lounge with friends in the soft grass
Beside a river of water, underneath   225

A big tree's boughs, and merrily to refresh
Our frames, with no vast outlay—most of all
If the weather is laughing and the times of the year
Besprinkle the green of the grass around with
    flowers.
Nor yet the quicker will hot fevers go,   230
If on a pictured tapestry thou toss,
Or purple robe, than if 'tis thine to lie
Upon the poor man's bedding. Wherefore, since
Treasure, nor rank, nor glory of a reign
Avail us naught for this our body, thus   235
Reckon them likewise nothing for the mind:
Save then perchance, when thou beholdest forth
Thy legions swarming round the Field of Mars,
Rousing a mimic warfare—either side
Strengthened with large auxiliaries and horse,   240
Alike equipped with arms, alike inspired;
Or save when also thou beholdest forth
Thy fleets to swarm, deploying down the sea:
For then, by such bright circumstance abashed,
Religion pales and flees thy mind; O then   245
The fears of death leave heart so free of care.
But if we note how all this pomp at last
Is but a drollery and a mocking sport,
And of a truth man's dread, with cares at heels,
Dreads not these sounds of arms, these savage
    swords,   250
But among kings and lords of all the world
Mingles undaunted, nor is overawed
By gleam of gold nor by the splendour bright
Of purple robe, canst thou then doubt that this
Is aught, but power of thinking?—when, besides 255
The whole of life but labours in the dark.
For just as children tremble and fear all
In the viewless dark, so even we at times
Dread in the light so many things that be
No whit more fearsome than what children feign,
Shuddering, will be upon them in the dark.   261
This terror then, this darkness of the mind,
Not sunrise with its flaring spokes of light,
Nor glittering arrows of morning can disperse,
But only nature's aspect and her law.   265

ATOMIC MOTIONS

Now come: I will untangle for thy steps
Now by what motions the begetting bodies
Of the world-stuff beget the varied world. . . .
For far beneath the ken of senses lies
The nature of those ultimates of the world;   270
And so, since those themselves thou canst not see,
Their motion also must they veil from men—
For mark, indeed, how things we *can* see, oft
Yet hide their motions, when afar from us
Along the distant landscape. Often thus,   275
Upon a hillside will the woolly flocks
Be cropping their goodly food and creeping about
Whither the summons of the grass, begemmed

With the fresh dew, is calling, and the lambs,
Well filled, are frisking, locking horns in sport: 280
Yet all for us seem blurred and blent afar—
A glint of white at rest on a green hill. . . .
When first the dawn is sprinkling with new light
The lands, and all the breed of birds abroad
Flit round the trackless forests, with liquid notes
Filling the regions along the mellow air, 286
We see 'tis forthwith manifest to man
How suddenly the risen sun is wont
At such an hour to overspread and clothe
The whole with its own splendour; but the sun's
Warm exhalations and this sérene light 291
Travel not down an empty void; and thus
They are compelled more slowly to advance,
Whilst, as it were, they cleave the waves of air;
Nor one by one travel these particles 295
Of the warm exhalations, but are all
Entangled and enmassed, whereby at once
Each is restrained by each, and from without
Checked, till compelled more slowly to advance.
But the primordial atoms with their old 300
Simple solidity, when forth they travel
Along the empty void, all undelayed
By aught outside them there, and they, each one
Being one unit from nature of its parts,
Are borne to that one place on which they strive
Still to lay hold, must then, beyond a doubt, 306
Outstrip in speed, and be more swiftly borne
Than light of sun, and over regions rush,
Of space much vaster, in the self-same time 309
The sun's effulgence widens round the sky. . . .
The atoms, as their own weight bears them down
Plumb through the void, at scarce determined times,
In scarce determined places, from their course
Decline a little—call it, so to speak,
Mere changèd trend. For were it not their wont 315
Thuswise to swerve, down would they fall, each one,
Like drops of rain, through the unbottomed void;
And then collisions ne'er could be nor blows
Among the primal elements; and thus
Nature would never have created aught. 320
But, if perchance be any that believe
The heavier bodies, as more swiftly borne
Plumb down the void, are able from above
To strike the lighter, thus engendering blows
Able to cause those procreant motions, far 325
From highways of true reason they retire.
For whatsoever through the waters fall,
Or through thin air, must quicken their descent,
Each after its weight—on this account, because
Both bulk of water and the subtle air 330
By no means can retard each thing alike,
But give more quick before the heavier weight;
But contrariwise the empty void cannot,
On any side, at any time, to aught
Oppose resistance, but will ever yield, 335

True to its bent of nature. Wherefore all,
With equal speed, though equal not in weight,
Must rush, borne downward through the still inane.
Thus ne'er at all have heavier from above 339
Been swift to strike the lighter, gendering strokes
Which cause those divers motions, by whose means
Nature transacts her work. And so I say,
The atoms must a little swerve at times—
But only the least, lest we should seem to feign
Motions oblique, and fact refute us there. . . . 345

ATOMIC FORMS
AND THEIR COMBINATIONS

Thus the long war, from everlasting waged,
With equal strife among the elements
Goes on and on. . . . This, too, in these affairs
'Tis fit thou hold well sealed, and keep consigned
With no forgetting brain: nothing there is 350
Whose nature is apparent out of hand
That of one kind of elements consists—
Nothing there is that's not of mixèd seed.
And whatsoe'er possesses in itself
More largely many powers and properties 355
Shows thus that here within itself there are
The largest number of kinds and differing shapes
Of elements. And, chief of all, the earth
Hath in herself first bodies whence the springs,
Rolling chill waters, renew forevermore 360
The unmeasured main; hath whence the fires
    arise—
For burns in many a spot her flamèd crust,
Whilst the impetuous Aetna raves indeed
From more profounder fires—and she, again,
Hath in herself the seed whence she can raise 365
The shining grains and gladsome trees for men;
Whence, also, rivers, fronds, and gladsome pastures
Can she supply for mountain-roaming beasts.
Wherefore great mother of gods, and mother of
    beasts,
And parent of man hath she alone been named. . . .
So great in any sort of herb thou wilt, 371
So great again in any river of earth
Are the distinct diversities of matter.
Hence, further, every creature—any one
From out them all—compounded is the same 375
Of bones, blood, veins, heat, moisture, flesh, and
    thews—
All differing vastly in their forms, and built
Of elements dissimilar in shape. . . .
Thus unlike forms into one mass combine,
And things exist by inter-mixèd seed. . . . 380
Now, too: whate'er we see possessing sense
Must yet confessedly be stablished all
From elements insensate. And those signs,
So clear to all and witnessed out of hand,
Do not refute this dictum nor oppose; 385

But rather themselves do lead us by the hand,
Compelling belief that living things are born
Of elements insensate, as I say.
Sooth, we may see from out the stinking dung   389
Live worms spring up, when, after soaking rains,
The drenched earth rots; and all things change the
  same:
Lo, change the rivers, the fronds, the gladsome pas-
  tures
Into the cattle, the cattle their nature change
Into our bodies, and from our body, oft   394
Grow strong the powers and bodies of wild beasts
And mighty-wingèd birds. Thus nature changes
All foods to living frames, and procreates
From *them* the senses of live creatures all,
In manner about as she uncoils in flames
Dry logs of wood and turns them all to fire.   400
And seest not, therefore, how it matters much
After what order are set the primal germs,
And with what other germs they all are mixed,
And what the motions that they give and get?

 But now, what is't that strikes thy sceptic mind,
Constraining thee to sundry arguments   406
Against belief that from insensate germs
The sensible is gendered?—Verily,
'Tis this: that liquids, earth, and wood, though
  mixed,
Are yet unable to gender vital sense.   410
And, therefore, 'twill be well in these affairs
This to remember: that I have not said
Senses are born, under conditions all,
From all things absolutely which create
Objects that feel; but much it matters here   415
Firstly, how small the seeds which thus compose
The feeling thing, then, with what shapes endowed,
And lastly what they in *positions* be,
In motions, in arrangements. Of which facts
Naught we perceive in logs of wood and clods;   420
And yet even these, when sodden by the rains,
Give birth to wormy grubs, because the bodies
Of matter, from their old arrangements stirred
By the new factor, then combine anew
In such a way as genders living things. . . .   425

INFINITE WORLDS

Off to all regions round, on either side,
Above, beneath, throughout the universe
End is there none—as I have taught, as too
The very thing of itself declares aloud,
And as from nature of the unbottomed deep   430
Shines clearly forth. . . . Thus, I say,
Again, again, 'tmust be confessed there are
Such congregations of matter otherwhere,
Like this our world which vasty ether holds
In huge embrace. . . .   435
    If store of seeds there is
So great that not whole life-times of the living

Can count the tale . . .
And if their force and nature abide the same,
Able to throw the seeds of things together   440
Into their places, even as here are thrown
The seeds together in this world of ours,
'Tmust be confessed in other realms there are
Still other worlds, still other breeds of men,
And other generations of the wild.   445
 Hence too it happens in the sum there is
No one thing single of its kind in birth,
And single and sole in growth, but rather it is
One member of some generated race,
Among full many others of like kind.   450
First, cast thy mind abroad upon the living:
Thou'lt find the race of mountain-ranging wild
Even thus to be, and thus the scions of men
To be begot, and lastly the mute flocks
Of scalèd fish and wingèd frames of birds.   455
Wherefore confess we must on grounds the same
That earth, sun, moon, and ocean, and all else,
Exist not sole and single—rather in number
Exceeding number. Since that deeply set
Old boundary stone of life remains for them   460
No less, and theirs a body of mortal birth
No less, than every kind which here on earth
Is so abundant in its members found.
 Which well perceivèd if thou hold in mind,
Then Nature, delivered from every haughty lord,
And forthwith free, is seen to do all things   466
Herself and through herself of own accord,
Rid of all gods. For—by their holy hearts
Which pass in long tranquillity of peace
Untroubled ages and a sérene life!—   470
Who hath the power (I ask), who hath the power
To rule the sum of the immeasurable,
To hold with steady hand the giant reins
Of the unfathomed deep? Who hath the power
At once to roll a multitude of skies,   475
At once to heat with fires ethereal all
The fruitful lands of multitudes of worlds,
To be at all times in all places near,
To stablish darkness by his clouds, to shake
The sérene spaces of the sky with sound,   480
And hurl his lightnings,—ha, and whelm how oft
In ruins his own temples, and to rave,
Retiring to the wildernesses, there
At practice with that thunderbolt of his,
Which yet how often shoots the guilty by,   485
And slays the honourable blameless ones! . . .

BOOK III

THE SOUL IS MORTAL

 Now come: that thou mayst able be to know
That minds and the light souls of all that live
Have mortal birth and death, I will go on
Verses to build meet for thy rule of life,   490

Sought after long, discovered with sweet toil.
But under one name I'd have thee yoke them both;
And when, for instance, I shall speak of soul,
Teaching the same to be but mortal, think
Thereby I'm speaking also of the mind—   495
Since both are one, a substance inter-joined.

First, then, since I have taught how soul exists
A subtle fabric, of particles minute,
Made up from atoms smaller much than those
Of water's liquid damp, or fog, or smoke,   500
So in mobility it far excels,
More prone to move, though strook by lighter cause,
Even moved by images of smoke or fog—
As where we view, when in our sleeps we're lulled,
The altars exhaling steam and smoke aloft—   505
For, beyond doubt, these apparitions come
To us from outward. Now, then, since thou seest,
Their liquids depart, their waters flow away,
When jars are shivered, and since fog and smoke
Depart into the winds away, believe   510
The soul no less is shed abroad and dies
More quickly far, more quickly is dissolved
Back to its primal bodies, when withdrawn
From out man's members it has gone away.
For, sure, if body (container of the same   515
Like as a jar), when shivered from some cause,
And rarefied by loss of blood from veins,
Cannot for longer hold the soul, how then
Thinkst thou it can be held by any air—
A stuff much rarer than our bodies be?   520
    Besides we feel that mind to being comes
Along with body, with body grows and ages.
For just as children totter round about
With frames infirm and tender, so there follows
A weakling wisdom in their minds; and then,   525
Where years have ripened into robust powers,
Counsel is also greater, more increased
The power of mind; thereafter, where already
The body's shattered by master-powers of eld,
And fallen the frame with its enfeebled powers,   530
Thought hobbles, tongue wanders, and the mind
          gives way;
All fails, all's lacking at the selfsame time.
Therefore it suits that even the soul's dissolved,
Like smoke, into the lofty winds of air;
Since we behold the same to being come   535
Along with body and grow, and, as I've taught,
Crumble and crack, therewith outworn by eld.
    Then, too, we see, that, just as body takes
Monstrous diseases and the dreadful pain,
So mind its bitter cares, the grief, the fear;   540
Wherefore it tallies that the mind no less
Partaker is of death; for pain and disease
Are both artificers of death,—as well
We've learned by the passing of many a man ere
          now.
Nay, too, in diseases of body, often the mind   545

Wanders afield; for 'tis beside itself,
And crazed it speaks, or many a time it sinks,
With eyelids closing and a drooping nod,
In heavy drowse, on to eternal sleep;
From whence nor hears it any voices more,   550
Nor able is to know the faces here
Of those about him standing with wet cheeks
Who vainly call him back to light and life. . . .

FOLLY OF THE FEAR
OF DEATH

                    Therefore death to us
Is nothing, nor concerns us in the least,   555
Since nature of mind is mortal evermore.
And just as in the ages gone before
We felt no touch of ill, when all sides round
To battle came the Carthaginian host,
And the times, shaken by tumultuous war,   560
Under the aery coasts of arching heaven
Shuddered and trembled, and all humankind
Doubted to which the empery should fall
By land and sea, thus when we are no more,   564
When comes that sundering of our body and soul
Through which we're fashioned to a single state,
Verily naught to us, us then no more,
Can come to pass, naught move our senses then—
No, not if earth confounded were with sea,
And sea with heaven. But if indeed do feel   570
The nature of mind and energy of soul,
After their severance from this body of ours,
Yet nothing 'tis to us who in the bonds
And wedlock of the soul and body live,
Through which we're fashioned to a single state.
And, even if time collected after death   576
The matter of our frames and set it all
Again in place as now, and if again
To us the light of life were given, O yet
That process too would not concern us aught,   580
When once the self-succession of our sense
Has been asunder broken. And now and here,
Little enough we're busied with the selves
We were aforetime, nor, concerning them,
Suffer a sore distress. For shouldst thou gaze   585
Backwards across all yesterdays of time
The immeasurable, thinking how manifold
The motions of matter are, then couldst thou well
Credit this too: often these very seeds
(From which we are to-day) of old were set   590
In the same order as they are to-day—
Yet this we can't to consciousness recall
Through the remembering mind. For there hath
          been
An interposèd pause of life, and wide
Have all the motions wandered everywhere   595
From these our senses. For if woe and ail
Perchance are toward, then the man to whom
The bane can happen must himself be there

At that same time. But death precludeth this,
Forbidding life to him on whom might crowd   600
Such irk and care; and granted 'tis to know:
Nothing for us there is to dread in death,
No wretchedness for him who is no more,
The same estate as if ne'er born before,
When death immortal hath ta'en the mortal
    life. . . .   605
But ask the mourner what's the bitterness
That man should waste in an eternal grief,
If, after all, the thing's but sleep and rest?
For when the soul and frame together are sunk
In slumber, no one then demands his self   610
Or being. Well, this sleep may be forever,
Without desire of any selfhood more,
For all it matters unto us asleep.
Yet not at all do those primordial germs
Roam round our members, at that time, afar   615
From their own motions that produce our senses—
Since, when he's startled from his sleep, a man
Collects his senses. Death is, then, to us
Much less—if there can be a less than that
Which is itself a nothing: for there comes   620
Hard upon death a scattering more great
Of the throng of matter, and no man wakes up
On whom once falls the icy pause of life. . . .

BOOK V

Thus far we've gone; the order of my plan
Hath brought me now unto the point where I   625
Must make report how, too, the universe
Consists of mortal body, born in time,
And in what modes that congregated stuff
Establishèd itself as earth and sky,
Ocean, and stars, and sun, and ball of moon;   630
And then what living creatures rose from out
The old telluric places, and what ones
Were never born at all; and in what mode
The human race began to name its things
And use the varied speech from man to man;   635
And in what modes hath bosomed in their breasts
That awe of gods, which halloweth in all lands
Fanes, altars, groves, lakes, idols of the gods. . . .

FORMATION OF THE WORLD

In that long-ago
The wheel of the sun could nowhere be discerned
Flying far up with its abounding blaze,   641
Nor constellations of the mighty world,
Nor ocean, nor heaven, nor even earth nor air.
Nor aught of things like unto things of ours
Could then be seen—but only some strange storm
And a prodigious hurly-burly mass   646
Compounded of all kinds of primal germs,
Whose battling discords in disorder kept
Interstices, and paths, coherencies,

And weights, and blows, encounterings, and mo-
    tions,   650
Because, by reason of their forms unlike
And varied shapes, they could not all thuswise
Remain conjoinèd nor harmoniously
Have interplay of movements. But from there
Portions began to fly asunder, and like   655
With like to join, and to block out a world,
And to divide its members and dispose
Its mightier parts—that is, to set secure
The lofty heavens from the lands, and cause
The sea to spread with waters separate,   660
And fires of ether separate and pure
Likewise to congregate apart. . . .

ORIGINS OF VEGETABLE
AND ANIMAL LIFE

In the beginning, earth gave forth, around
The hills and over all the length of plains,
The race of grasses and the shining green;   665
The flowery meadows sparkled all aglow
With greening colour, and thereafter, lo,
Unto the divers kinds of trees was given
An emulous impulse mightily to shoot,
With a free rein, aloft into the air.   670
As feathers and hairs and bristles are begot
The first on members of the four-foot breeds
And on the bodies of the strong-y-winged,
Thus then the new Earth first of all put forth
Grasses and shrubs, and afterward begat   675
The mortal generations, there upsprung—
Innumerable in modes innumerable—
After diverging fashions. For from sky
These breathing-creatures never can have dropped,
Nor the land-dwellers ever have come up   680
Out of sea-pools of salt. How true remains,
How merited is that adopted name
Of earth—"The Mother!"—since from out the earth
Are all begotten. And even now arise
From out the loams how many living things—   685
Concreted by the rains and heat of the sun.
Wherefore 'tis less a marvel, if they sprang
In Long Ago more many, and more big,
Matured of those days in the fresh young years
Of earth and ether. First of all, the race   690
Of the wingèd ones and parti-coloured birds,
Hatched out in spring-time, left their eggs behind;
As now-a-days in summer tree-crickets
Do leave their shiny husks of own accord,
Seeking their food and living. Then it was   695
This earth of thine first gave unto the day
The mortal generations; for prevailed
Among the fields abounding hot and wet.
And hence, where any fitting spot was given,
There 'gan to grow womb-cavities, by roots   700
Affixed to earth. And when in ripened time
The age of the young within (that sought the air

And fled earth's damps) had burst these wombs, O
  then
Would Nature thither turn the pores of earth
And make her spurt from open veins a juice   705
Like unto milk; even as a woman now
Is filled, at child-bearing, with the sweet milk,
Because all that swift stream of aliment
Is thither turned unto the mother-breasts.
There earth would furnish to the children food;   710
Warmth was their swaddling cloth, the grass their
  bed
Abounding in soft down. Earth's newness then
Would rouse no dour spells of the bitter cold,
Nor éxtreme heats nor winds of mighty powers—
For all things grow and gather strength through
  time   715
In like proportions; and then earth was young.
  Wherefore, again, again, how merited
Is that adopted name of Earth—the Mother!—
Since she herself begat the human race,
And at one well-nigh fixèd time brought forth   720
Each beast that ranges raving round about
Upon the mighty mountains and all birds
Aerial with many a varied shape.
But, lo, because her bearing years must end,
She ceased, like to a woman worn by eld.   725
For lapsing aeons change the nature of
The whole wide world, and all things needs must
  take
One status after other, nor aught persists
Forever like itself. All things depart;
Nature she changeth all, compelleth all   730
To transformation. Lo, *this* moulders down,
A-slack with weary eld, and *that,* again,
Prospers in glory, issuing from contempt.
In suchwise, then, the lapsing aeons change
The nature of the whole wide world, and earth   735
Taketh one status after other. And what
She bore of old, she now can bear no longer,
And what she never bore, she can to-day. . . .

ORIGINS AND SAVAGE PERIOD
OF MANKIND

              But mortal man
Was then far hardier in the old champaign,   740
As well he should be, since a hardier earth
Had him begotten; builded too was he
Of bigger and more solid bones within,
And knit with stalwart sinews through the flesh,
Nor easily seized by either heat or cold,   745
Or alien food or any ail or irk.
And whilst so many lustrums of the sun
Rolled on across the sky, men led a life
After the roving habit of wild beasts.   749
Not then were sturdy guiders of curved ploughs,
And none knew then to work the fields with iron,
Or plant young shoots in holes of delvèd loam,

Or lop with hookèd knives from off high trees
The boughs of yester-year. What sun and rains
To them had given, what earth of own accord   755
Created then, was boon enough to glad
Their simple hearts. Mid acorn-laden oaks
Would they refresh their bodies for the nonce;
And the wild berries of the arbute-tree,
Which now thou seest to ripen purple-red   760
In winter time, the old telluric soil
Would bear then more abundant and more big.
And many coarse foods, too, in long ago
The blooming freshness of the rank young world
Produced, enough for those poor wretches there.
And rivers and springs would summon them of old
To slake the thirst, as now from the great hills
The water's down-rush calls aloud and far
The thirsty generations of the wild.   769
So, too, they sought the grottos of the Nymphs—
The woodland haunts discovered as they ranged—
From forth of which they knew that gliding rills
With gush and splash abounding laved the rocks,
The dripping rocks, and trickled from above
Over the verdant moss; and here and there   775
Welled up and burst across the open flats.
As yet they knew not to enkindle fire
Against the cold, nor hairy pelts to use
And clothe their bodies with the spoils of beasts;
But huddled in groves, and mountain-caves, and
  woods,   780
And 'mongst the thickets hid their squalid backs,
When driven to flee the lashings of the winds
And the big rains. Nor could they then regard
The general good, nor did they know to use
In common any customs, any laws: 785
Whatever of booty fortune unto each
Had proffered, each alone would bear away,
By instinct trained for self to thrive and live.
And Venus in the forests then would link
The lovers' bodies; for the woman yielded   790
Either from mutual flame, or from the man's
Impetuous fury and insatiate lust,
Or from a bribe—as acorn-nuts, choice pears,
Or the wild berries of the arbute-tree.
And trusting wondrous strength of hands and legs,
They'd chase the forest-wanderers, the beasts;   796
And many they'd conquer, but some few they fled,
A-skulk into their hiding-places . . .
With the flung stones and with the ponderous heft
Of gnarlèd branch. And by the time of night   800
O'ertaken, they would throw, like bristly boars,
Their wildman's limbs naked upon the earth,
Rolling themselves in leaves and fronded boughs.
Nor would they call with lamentations loud
Around the fields for daylight and the sun,   805
Quaking and wand'ring in shadows of the night;
But, silent and buried in a sleep, they'd wait
Until the sun with rosy flambeau brought

The glory to the sky. From childhood wont
Ever to see the dark and day begot   810
In times alternate, never might they be
Wildered by wild misgiving, lest a night
Eternal should possess the lands, with light
Of sun withdrawn forever. But their care
Was rather that the clans of savage beasts   815
Would often make their sleep-time horrible
For those poor wretches; and, from home y-driven,
They'd flee their rocky shelters at approach
Of boar, the spumy-lipped, or lion strong,
And in the midnight yield with terror up   820
To those fierce guests their beds of out-spread
          leaves.

    And yet in those days not much more than now
Would generations of mortality
Leave the sweet light of fading life behind.
Indeed, in those days here and there a man,   825
More oftener snatched upon, and gulped by fangs,
Afforded the beasts a food that roared alive,
Echoing through groves and hills and forest-trees,
Even as he viewed his living flesh entombed
Within a living grave; whilst those whom flight   830
Had saved, with bone and body bitten, shrieked,
Pressing their quivering palms to loathsome sores,
With horrible voices for eternal death—
Until, forlorn of help, and witless what   834
Might medicine their wounds, the writhing pangs
Took them from life. But not in those far times
Would one lone day give over unto doom
A soldiery in thousands marching on
Beneath the battle-banners, nor would then
The ramping breakers of the main seas dash   840
Whole argosies and crews upon the rocks.
But ocean uprisen would often rave in vain,
Without all end or outcome, and give up
Its empty menacings as lightly too;
Nor soft seductions of a sérene sea   845
Could lure by laughing billows any man
Out to disaster: for the science bold
Of ship-sailing lay dark in those far times.
Again, 'twas *then* that lack of food gave o'er
Men's fainting limbs to dissolution: now   850
'Tis plenty overwhelms. Unwary, they
Oft for themselves themselves would then outpour
The poison; now, with nicer art, themselves
They give the drafts to others.

BEGINNINGS OF CIVILIZATION

                              Afterwards,   855
When huts they had procured and pelts and fire,
And when the woman, joined unto the man,
Withdrew with him into one dwelling place,
    . . . and when they saw an offspring born
From out themselves, then first the human race   860
Began to soften. For 'twas now that fire
Rendered their shivering frames less staunch to bear,

Under the canopy of the sky, the cold;
And Love reduced their shaggy hardiness;
And children, with the prattle and the kiss,   865
Soon broke the parents' haughty temper down.
Then, too, did neighbours 'gin to league as friends,
Eager to wrong no more or suffer wrong,
And urged for children and the womankind
Mercy, of fathers, whilst with cries and gestures
They stammered hints how meet it was that all   871
Should have compassion on the weak. And still,
Though concord not in every wise could then
Begotten be, a good, a goodly part
Kept faith inviolate—or else mankind   875
Long since had been unutterably cut off,
And propagation never could have brought
The species down the ages. . . .
                              And now what cause
Hath spread divinities of gods abroad   880
Through mighty nations, and filled the cities full
Of the high altars, and led to practices
Of solemn rites in season—rites which still
Flourish in midst of great affairs of state
And midst great centres of man's civic life,   885
The rites whence still in poor mortality
Is grafted that quaking awe which rears aloft
Still the new temples of gods from land to land
And drives mankind to visit them in throngs
On holy days—'tis not so hard to give   890
Reason thereof in speech. Because, in sooth,
Even in those days would the race of man
Be seeing excelling visages of gods   893
With mind awake; and in his sleeps, yet more,—
Bodies of wondrous growth. And, thus, to these
Would men attribute sense, because they seemed
To move their limbs and speak pronouncements
          high,
Befitting glorious visage and vast powers.
And men would give them an eternal life,
Because their visages forevermore   900
Were there before them, and their shapes remained,
And chiefly, however, because men would not think
Beings augmented with such mighty powers
Could well by any force o'ermastered be.
And men would think them in their happiness   905
Excelling far, because the fear of death
Vexèd no one of them at all, and since
At same time in men's sleeps men saw them do
So many wonders, and yet feel therefrom
Themselves no weariness. Besides, men marked   910
How in a fixèd order rolled around
The systems of the sky, and changèd times
Of annual seasons, nor were able then
To know thereof the causes. Therefore 'twas
Men would take refuge in consigning all   915
Unto divinities, and in feigning all
Was guided by their nod. And in the sky
They set the seats and vaults of gods, because

Across the sky night and the moon are seen
To roll along—moon, day, and night, and night's
Old awesome constellations evermore,   921
And the night-wandering fireballs of the sky,
And flying flames, clouds, and the sun, the rains,
Snow and the winds, the lightnings, and the hail,
And the swift rumblings, and the hollow roar   925
Of mighty menacings forevermore.

    O humankind unhappy!—when it ascribed
Unto divinities such awesome deeds,
And coupled thereto rigours of fierce wrath!
What groans did men on that sad day beget   930
Even for themselves, and O what wounds for us,
What tears for our children's children! Nor, O man,
Is thy true piety in this: with head
Under the veil, still to be seen to turn
Fronting a stone, and ever to approach   935
Unto all altars; nor so prone on earth
Forward to fall, to spread upturnèd palms
Before the shrines of gods, nor yet to dew
Altars with prófuse blood of four-foot beasts,
Nor vows with vows to link. But rather this: 940
To look on all things with a master eye
And mind at peace. For when we gaze aloft
Upon the skiey vaults of yon great world
And ether, fixèd high o'er twinkling stars,
And into our thought there come the journeyings
Of sun and moon, O then into our breasts,   946
O'erburdened already with their other ills,
Begins forthwith to rear its sudden head
One more misgiving: lest o'er us, percase,
It be the gods' immeasurable power   950
That rolls, with varied motion, round and round
The far white constellations. For the lack
Of aught of reasons tries the puzzled mind:
Whether was ever a birth-time of the world,
And whether, likewise, any end shall be   955
How far the ramparts of the world can still
Outstand this strain of ever-rousèd motion,
Or whether, divinely with eternal weal
Endowed, they can through endless tracts of age
Glide on, defying the o'er-mighty powers   960
Of the immeasurable ages. Lo,
What man is there whose mind with dread of gods
Cringes not close, whose limbs with terror-spell
Crouch not together, when the parchèd earth
Quakes with the horrible thunderbolt amain,   965
And across the mighty sky the rumblings run?
Do not the peoples and the nations shake,
And haughty kings do they not hug their limbs,
Strook through with fear of the divinities,
Lest for aught foully done or madly said   970
The heavy time be now at hand to pay?
When, too, fierce force of fury-winds at sea
Sweepeth a navy's admiral down the main
With his stout legions and his elephants,
Doth he not seek the peace of gods with vows,   975

And beg in prayer, a-tremble, lullèd winds
And friendly gales?—in vain, since, often up-caught
In fury-cyclones, is he borne along,
For all his mouthings, to the shoals of doom.
Ah, so irrevocably some hidden power   980
Betramples forevermore affairs of men,
And visibly grindeth with its heel in mire
The lictors' glorious rods and axes dire,
Having them in derision! Again, when earth
From end to end is rocking under foot,   985
And shaken cities ruin down, or threaten
Upon the verge, what wonder is it then
That mortal generations abase themselves,
And unto gods in all affairs of earth
Assign as last resort almighty powers   990
And wondrous energies to govern all? . . .
                   In those days
Copper it was that was the thing of price;
And gold lay useless, blunted with dull edge.
Now lies the copper low, and gold hath come   995
Unto the loftiest honours. Thus it is
That rolling ages change the times of things:
What erst was of a price, becomes at last
A discard of no honour; whilst another
Succeeds to glory, issuing from contempt,   1000
And day by day is sought for more and more,
And, when 'tis found, doth flower in men's praise,
Object of wondrous honour. . . .
                  Nature herself,
Mother of things, was the first seed-sower   1005
And primal grafter; since the berries and acorns,
Dropping from off the trees, would there beneath
Put forth in season swarms of little shoots;
Hence too men's fondness for ingrafting slips
Upon the boughs and setting out in holes   1010
The young shrubs o'er the fields. Then would they
    try
Ever new modes of tilling their loved crofts,
And mark they would how earth improved the taste
Of the wild fruits by fond and fostering care.
And day by day they'd force the woods to move
Still higher up the mountain, and to yield   1016
The place below for tilth, that there they might,
On plains and uplands, have their meadow-plats,
Cisterns and runnels, crops of standing grain,
And happy vineyards, and that all along   1020
O'er hillocks, intervales, and plains might run
The silvery-green belt of olive-trees,
Marking the plotted landscape; even as now
Thou seest so marked with varied loveliness
All the terrain which men adorn and plant   1025
With rows of goodly fruit-trees and hedge round
With thriving shrubberies sown.
                 But by the mouth
To imitate the liquid notes of birds
Was earlier far 'mongst men than power to make,
By measured song, melodious verse and give   1030

Delight to ears. And whistlings of the wind
Athrough the hollows of the reeds first taught
The peasantry to blow into the stalks
Of hollow hemlock-herb. Then bit by bit
They learned sweet plainings, such as pipe out-
    pours,   1035
Beaten by finger-tips of singing men,
When heard through unpathed groves and forest
    deeps
And woodsy meadows, through the untrod haunts
Of shepherd folk and spots divinely still.
Thus time draws forward each and everything   1040
Little by little unto the midst of men,
And reason uplifts it to the shores of light.
These tunes would soothe and glad the minds of
    mortals
When sated with food,—for songs are welcome
    then.
And often, lounging with friends in the soft grass
Beside a river of water, underneath   1046
A big tree's branches, merrily they'd refresh
Their frames, with no vast outlay—most of all
If the weather were smiling and the times of the
    year
Were painting the green of the grass around with
    flowers.   1050
Then jokes, then talk, then peals of jollity
Would circle round; for then the rustic muse
Was in her glory; then would antic Mirth
Prompt them to garland head and shoulders about
With chaplets of intertwinèd flowers and leaves,
And to dance onward, out of tune, with limbs 1056
Clownishly swaying, and with clownish foot
To beat our mother earth—from whence arose
Laughter and peals of jollity, for, lo,
Such frolic acts were in their glory then,   1060
Being more new and strange. And wakeful men
Found solaces for their unsleeping hours
In drawing forth variety of notes,
In modulating melodies, in running
With puckered lips along the tunèd reeds,   1065
Whence, even in our day do the watchmen guard
These old traditions, and have learnèd well
To keep true measure. And yet they no whit
Do get a larger fruit of gladsomeness
Than got the woodland aborigines   1070
In olden times. For *what* we have at hand—
If theretofore naught sweeter we have known—
That chiefly pleases and seems best of all;
But then some later, likely better, find
Destroys its worth and changes our desires   1075
Regarding good of yesterday.
                            And thus
Began the loathing of the acorn; thus
Abandoned were those beds with grasses strewn
And with the leaves beladen. Thus, again,
1077. loathing of the acorn; as food.

Fell into new contempt the pelts of beasts—   1080
Erstwhile a robe of honour, which, I guess,
Aroused in those days envy so malign
That the first wearer went to woeful death
By ambuscades,—and yet that hairy prize,
Rent into rags by greedy foemen there   1085
And splashed by blood, was ruined utterly
Beyond all use or vantage. Thus of old
'Twas pelts, and of to-day 'tis purple and gold
That cark men's lives with cares and weary with
    war.   1089
Wherefore, methinks, resides the greater blame
With us vain men to-day: for cold would rack,
Without their pelts, the naked sons of earth;
But us it nothing hurts to do without
The purple vestment, broiderèd with gold
And with imposing figures, if we still   1095
Make shift with some mean garment of the Plebs.
So man in vain futilities toils on
Forever and wastes in idle cares his years—
Because, of very truth, he hath not learnt
What the true end of getting is, nor yet   1100
At all how far true pleasure may increase.
And 'tis desire for better and for more
Hath carried by degrees mortality
Out onward to the deep, and rousèd up
From the far bottom mighty waves of war.   1105
    But sun and moon, those watchmen of the world,
With their own lanterns traversing around
The mighty, the revolving vault, have taught
Unto mankind that seasons of the years
Return again, and that the Thing takes place   1110
After a fixèd plan and order fixed.
    Already would they pass their life, hedged round
By the strong towers; and cultivate an earth
All portioned out and boundaried; already
Would the sea flower with sail-wingèd ships;   1115
Already men had, under treaty pacts,
Confederates and allies, when poets began
To hand heroic actions down in verse;
Nor long ere this had letters been devised—
Hence is our age unable to look back   1120
On what has gone before, except where reason
Shows us a footprint.
                        Sailings on the seas,
Tillings of fields, walls, laws, and arms, and roads,
Dress and the like, all prizes, all delights
Of finer life, poems, pictures, chiselled shapes 1125
Of polished sculptures—all these arts were learned
By practice and the mind's experience,
As men walked forward step by eager step.
Thus time draws forward each and everything
Little by little into the midst of men,   1130
And reason uplifts it to the shores of light.
For one thing after other did men see
Grow clear by intellect, till with their arts
They've now achieved the súpreme pinnacle.

Plautus

c. 254–184 B.C.

Our best view of Roman society under the republic comes from Plautus, who was inspired by the New Comedy of fourth-century Athens to develop a Roman comedy of manners. He was born into a lower-class family in the Umbrian town of Sarsina and came in his youth to Rome, where he learned the playwright's craft through producing or acting in plays. After he lost his earnings in a trading venture, he is said to have worked as a humble baker's assistant until the success of his first comedies freed him to write. In any case we do know that he began writing late in life and rose to a popularity that continued beyond his death to the time of Cicero.

His business failure and the poverty that resulted made Plautus write with money in mind, and that meant writing to the taste of the motley Roman audiences, who were a rough and rowdy lot with a fondness for broad farce. He followed the Greek Menander in holding up the mirror to his society and amusing the populace with satiric portraits of the social types they knew—the blustering father, the shrewish wife, the romantic son, the mock-innocent damsel, the foolish miser, the pompous soldier, the shifty-eyed parasite, the clever slave. Sometimes, as in *The Pot of Gold*, he gives us a serious study of character, but more often he is content with carefree farce often crudely constructed and full of indecent puns, local allusions, comic surprises, and slapstick humor. His dialogue is racy and exuberant in contrast to the suave elegance of later Roman writers. Particularly in his later plays he interrupts his metrical speech with popular songs in the manner of our musical comedies, but eliminates the Greek chorus entirely. In these and other ways Plautus placed his Roman stamp on Greek originals, for each of his plays began as an adaptation of a Greek comedy of Menander, Philemon, or Apollodorus. Despite this close imitation we feel everywhere the earthy, hearty personality of a distinctly lower-class man.

Tradition credits Plautus with over a hundred comedies, but only twenty survive. These show great variety of mood, subject matter, and worth. *Amphitryon* travesties the myth of Jupiter's amour with Alcmene so wittily that it has inspired endless imitations in later times from Molière to Giraudoux and Behrman.

The Captives is a mild and moral play that unites a family after various vicissitudes. *The Menaechmi Twins*, an absurd farce about mistaken identity, inspired Shakespeare's *Comedy of Errors*. The long play, *The Rope*, is a romantic comedy of shipwreck. But none excels in power or influence the *Aulularia*, or *The Pot of Gold*, which Molière was to adapt into his own comedy of *The Miser*. This brilliant play, probably based on Menander, is built around the subtle character of a miser who loses his treasure because of his own fear that he will do so. With this are interwoven the minor plot of his daughter's seduction and the low-comedy characters of the cooks. Although the last scene is lost, the ending of the play is obvious enough.

The Pot of Gold

CHARACTERS IN THE PLAY

HOUSEHOLD GOD
EUCLIO, *an aged Athenian*
STAPHYLA, *an old woman, slave of* EUCLIO
EUNOMIA, *a lady of Athens*
MEGADORUS, *brother of* EUNOMIA
STROBILUS, *his slave*
CONGRIO, *a cook*
ANTHRAX, *another cook*
PYTHODICUS, *a slave*
LYCONIDES, *a young man, son of* EUNOMIA
SLAVE *of* LYCONIDES
PHAEDRIA, *daughter of* EUCLIO
Music Girls

(SCENE: *A street in Athens on which are the houses of* EUCLIO *and* MEGADORUS *and the temple of Faith.*)

PROLOGUE

HOUSEHOLD GOD.

Lest any wonder who in the world I am,
I'll tell you shortly. I'm the household God
Of this house, which you see me leaving now;
These many years I have it in my care;
Grandfather, father, son who has it now,   5
Have all been friends; the grandfather himself
Intrusted to me secretly a hoard
Of gold, which he within the hearth had buried,
Beseeching me to keep it safe for him.
He died, and was of such a greedy soul   10
He never would reveal it to his son,
But wished to leave him poor and penniless
Rather than show him where the treasure was.
He left him just a bit of ground, on which
With pain and labour he could make his living.   15
And when he died, who gave the trust to me,
I watched with care whether his son would show
More reverence to me than his father had.
But he, it seemed, spent less and less upon me,
And paid me less of honour. So he died;   20
And I revenged myself. And next in line
Is he who has it now, like-mannered too
With those who went before. He has a child,
A daughter, who with incense or with wine
Pays daily worship to me, crowning me   25
With wreaths. And for the sake of her it was
That I to Euclio disclosed the treasure,
That he more easily might marry her;

The Pot of Gold. Translated by Sir Robert Allison. Reprinted by permission of Hatchards, Ltd., London.

A youth of high position had led her
Astray; he knew her who she was, but she   30
Did not know him; nor did the father know
What had taken place. Today I will arrange
That an old man, a neighbour, shall demand
Her for his wife; more gladly will I do it,
That the young man, who was the first to love her
(He met her on the night of Ceres' festival),   36
May marry her more easily. The old man
Who wants to do so is the young man's uncle.
But Euclio's calling out, as is his wont;
He's turned the old woman out of doors, lest she   40
Should know where the treasure is; he wants to see
That the hoard of gold has not been carried off.

(*The* HOUSEHOLD GOD *departs.*)

ACT ONE

(*Enter* EUCLIO *from his house, pushing* STAPHYLA
in front of him.)

EUCLIO. Go out; go out, I say, and get you gone,
You that are looking round with prying eyes!
    STAPHYLA. Why beat a miserable wretch like me?
    EUCLIO. That you may be more miserable still,
And lead the wretched life you well deserve.   5
    STAPHYLA. Pray, why have you thus thrust me
        from the house?
    EUCLIO. Am I to argue with a wretch like you,
Whose back is scored with stripes; go from the door,
Be off, I say; how leisurely she goes!
See to yourself, for if I take in hand   10
A stick or goad, I will increase the pace
Of that old tortoise.
    STAPHYLA.   Would the gods would bring
Me to the gallows than to serve you thus!
    EUCLIO. How the old wretch is murmuring to
        herself!
I'll dig your eyes out that you may not see   15
What I am doing; now away, away,
And further yet; stand there; if from that place
You stir by the width of a finger or the breadth
Of a nail, or if you look back till such time
I give you leave, I'll hand you over straight   20
To torture. (*Aside*) Never surely did I see
A wickeder old woman; much I fear
Lest she may gather from some words of mine
Too rashly said, where the gold is hidden away.
Wretch, she has eyes, too, in the back of her head.   25
Now I will go and see if the gold is there.
Just as I hid it, gold which has become
A constant source of trouble to myself.

(EUCLIO *goes into his house.*)

    STAPHYLA (*to herself*). I can't think what has
        happened to my master,
Nor why he is so mad; he beats me so,   30
And thrusts me out of doors ten times a day
I don't know what has put him out of tune;

He wakens all the night, and then by day,
Like a lame cobbler, sits for hours at home.
Nor can I tell how best I can conceal   35
His daughter's state; and nothing more remains
Than to make one long letter of myself—
The letter I—and hang myself full length.

(*Re-enter* EUCLIO *from the house.*)

    EUCLIO (*aside*). And now with mind at ease I
        leave the house,
As soon as I have seen all's safe within.   40
(*To* STAPHYLA) Return now to your work.
    STAPHYLA.   Why should
        I go?
Is some one going to take the house away?
There is nothing here for thieves; nor aught indeed
But emptiness and spider webs.
    EUCLIO.   D'ye think
That for your sake the gods would make me rich,   45
As Philip or Darius, sorceress?
I like to keep those cobwebs; I am poor,
I do admit; and bear it. I'm content
With what the gods may give. Go in and close
The door; I'll come again; let no one enter.   50
If any ask a light, see that the fire
Is quite put out; that none may ask for it;
If it is not, you'll be put out yourself.
Say that the pump is dry, if any seek
For water. If a spade, an axe, a mortar,   55
Or a pestle, things which neighbours always borrow,
Say that the thieves have come and stolen them.
No one's to enter, while I am away.
These are my orders; if Good Fortune comes,
Please say I am not at home.
    STAPHYLA.   No fear of that;   60
That never comes, however near it be.
    EUCLIO. Be quiet and go within.
    STAPHYLA.   I'll go at once.
    EUCLIO. Draw both the bolts. I will be back anon.

(*To himself, as* STAPHYLA *goes into the house*)

I'm vexed because I have to leave the house;
I go unwillingly; yet what to do   65
I know not; for the master of our guild
Has said he will divide the funds amongst us.
If I don't go and take my share, they'll think
That I have gold at home; for 'tis not likely
A poor man would despise a dole, though small.   70
For now, although I keep the secret to myself,
All seem to know it, and pay greater court
Than they used to do before; they come, they stay,
They give me their right hands; ask how I am,
And what I'm doing, what my business.   75
Now I'll be off where I was going; and
Return as soon as possible again. (EUCLIO *departs.*)

37–38. **Than . . . The letter I**; because the letter "I" resembles a
hanging body.   46. **Philip or Darius.** Philip of Macedonia and Darius
of Persia were obvious examples of wealthy kings.   59–60. **if Good
Fortune . . . home.** Even good luck may not enter in his absence.

ACT TWO

(*Enter* EUNOMIA *and* MEGADORUS *from the house of the latter.*)

EUNOMIA. I wish, my brother, you would think
    that I
Am acting in your interest, for your sake,
As well becomes a sister; though I know
We women are not held in much esteem.
We all are told we talk by far too much,   5
And never in the world they say was found
A silent woman. But remember, brother,
How near you are to me, and I to you.
'Tis right that we should one another help.
You should advise and counsel me, I you;   10
Nor keep it secret, nor be afraid to speak,
Make me your confidant, and I the same.
So now I brought you out of doors to speak
In private, as to your and mine concerns.
    MEGADORUS. Your hand, my best of women!
    EUNOMIA.   Who is
    she?   15
Where is such woman?
    MEGADORUS.   You!
    EUNOMIA.   Do you say so?
    MEGADORUS. If you deny it, I will do the same.
    EUNOMIA. Well, one must speak the truth. There
    is no best;
For one, I fear, is only worse than other.
    MEGADORUS. I think the same; it needs no argu-
    ment.   20
    EUNOMIA. Lend me your ear.
    MEGADORUS.   'Tis yours! Do as you
    like.
    EUNOMIA. I come to advise—what is the best for
    you.
    MEGADORUS. You do as you have always done
    to me.
    EUNOMIA. I wish—
    MEGADORUS.   What, sister?
    EUNOMIA.   What will be to you
An everlasting blessing, that you may   25
Have many children.
    MEGADORUS.   May the gods forfend!
    EUNOMIA. I would that you should marry.
    MEGADORUS.   I'm undone!
    EUNOMIA. How so?
    MEGADORUS. Your speech nigh splits my head in
    two!
Poniards you speak, and every word's a stab.   30
    EUNOMIA. Do as your sister wishes.
    MEGADORUS.   If you wish, I
    will.
    EUNOMIA. It is for your advantage.
    MEGADORUS.   May I die
Before I marry, or on this condition,
That she I marry, on the morrow may,

Or the day after that, be carried out   35
To burial. This being settled, get the bride,
Prepare the marriage.
    EUNOMIA.   I will get for you
The largest fortune that I can; but she
Is older, of the middle age, and if
You like, I'll ask her hand.
    MEGADORUS.   One question first.   40
    EUNOMIA. Ask what you will!
    MEGADORUS. You see when one has passed
Mid-life, and marries one who's passed it too,
If there should be a child, his name would be,
What could it be but Posthumus? Now I,
Dear sister, will relieve you of this care.   45
I by the goodness of the gods, and our forbears,
Am rich; great family, high spirit, wealth,
Applause, position, splendid equipage,
Dresses and purple, these which oft reduce
A man to slavery, do not appeal   50
At all to me.
    EUNOMIA. Then who d'ye wish to marry?
    MEGADORUS. Know you poor Euclio who lives next
    door?
    EUNOMIA. I know him; he is quite a decent man.
    MEGADORUS. I wish his daughter for my wife. I
    know
What you are going to say; that she is poor.   55
Don't say a word; I like her poverty.
    EUNOMIA. The gods direct things well!
    MEGADORUS.   I hope so too.
Farewell. (EUNOMIA *departs.*) I'll see if Euclio is at
    home.
Ah! There he is! I do not know from whence he
    comes.
    (*Enter* EUCLIO.)
    EUCLIO (*to himself*). I thought 'twas all in vain
    when I went out   60
And so I went unwillingly; for none
Belonging to the guild has ever come;
Nor yet the master, who should give to us
Our share of the funds; so now I hasten home,
For though I'm here myself, my heart is there.   65
    MEGADORUS. Good morning, Euclio, good luck to
    you!
    EUCLIO. The blessing of the gods!
    MEGADORUS.   And are you well?
And as you wish?
    EUCLIO (*aside*). It is not without cause,
When a rich man addresses thus the poor.
He knows I've gold; and hence his kindly words.   70
    MEGADORUS. You say you're well?
    EUCLIO.   I am, but not too well
In point of money.
    MEGADORUS.   If you are content,
You have enough for life and all its needs.
    EUCLIO (*aside*). The old woman's told him of the
    gold; that's clear.

I will cut out her tongue, and gouge out too   75
Her eyes, when I get home.

MEGADORUS.   What say you now,
Thus muttering to yourself?

EUCLIO.   I do bemoan
My poverty; I have a grown-up daughter
Without a dowry whom I cannot wed
Nor give to any.

MEGADORUS. Pray be still. Take courage!   80
I'll help you, you shall have enough and more.
What do you want?

EUCLIO (aside). His promises are fair;
But still there's something that he wants himself.
He gapes for gold to swallow it; he brings
Bread in one hand, a stone within the other.   85
I never trust the man who shows himself
So generous to the poor; he gives his hand
So kindly, but behind there is some hurt.
I know those polyps, with their tentacles,
Clinging to all they touch.

MEGADORUS.   Euclio, a word   90
Respecting what concerns yourself and me.

EUCLIO (aside). Alas! My gold is stolen; he wants,
    I know,
To come to some arrangement. I will have
A look at home.

MEGADORUS. Where are you going, Euclio?

EUCLIO. I will return; there's something that I
    want   95
To see about at home. (Hurries into house.)

MEGADORUS (to himself). I do believe
When I make mention of his daughter that
I wish to marry her, that he will think
I'm laughing at him; nor is any one
More niggardly in poverty than he.   100
        (Re-enter EUCLIO.)

EUCLIO (aside). All, all is safe! Nothing at all is
    gone.
I was too much afraid before I went,
Half mad with fear. (To MEGADORUS) Now, Mega-
    dorus, I
Return to thee, if there is aught you want.

MEGADORUS. Thanks. Now please answer what I
    ask of you.   105

EUCLIO. So be it you ask not what I cannot grant.

MEGADORUS. What think you of my family?

EUCLIO.   'Tis good!

MEGADORUS. My reputation?

EUCLIO.   Good!

MEGADORUS.   My conduct, then?

EUCLIO. Why, that I think is neither bad nor good.

MEGADORUS. You know my age?

EUCLIO.   I know it is advanced,   110
As great as is your fortune.

MEGADORUS.   As to you
I've always thought, and think you are a man
Quite without guile.

Actors wearing masks and performing a comedy.

EUCLIO (aside). Alas! He smells my gold.
(Aloud) What want you now?

MEGADORUS.   Well, as we know each other,
That all may turn out well for me and you,   115
And for your daughter, I do ask for her
In marriage. Promise me her hand.

EUCLIO.   Alas!
That which you do is unworthy of your acts;
To mock at one who's poor, and has never given
Offence to you or yours; in word or deed   120
I have done naught, that you should treat me so.

MEGADORUS. I do not come to mock, nor do I so;
I would not think it fitting.

EUCLIO.   Then why ask
My daughter's hand?

MEGADORUS.   That you, through me,
May be the better off, and I through you.   125

EUCLIO. But I do bear in mind that you are rich,
Eager for power; while I am very poor;
So poor, and if I give my daughter's hand
To you, you are a mighty ox, and I
A humble ass; and when I'm joined with you,   130
Unequal to the load that you can bear,
I, the poor ass, shall founder in the mire;
While you, proud ox, will not acknowledge me.

I'll find you worse than heretofore you were,
While those of my own order will deride; 135
If we should separate, there'll be no stall
Left for me; while the asses with their teeth
Are rending me, the oxen will proceed
To butt me with their horns. This is the danger
Of climbing from one class into another, 140
And being an ass, to try to be an ox.

MEGADORUS. The main thing is still to ally your-
self
With honest men. Hear me; accept my terms,
And give your daughter to me.

EUCLIO. But I have
No dowry.

MEGADORUS. Give her none; as long as she 145
Is well conducted, that's enough for me.

EUCLIO. I name it, lest you think I've found a
treasure.

MEGADORUS. I know; don't tell me; only give her
hand.

EUCLIO. Well, be it so. But stay, by Jove, I'm
ruined!

MEGADORUS. What is it?

EUCLIO. I heard some iron weapon strike. 150
(He runs into his house.)

MEGADORUS. It was my gardener digging. Where's
the man?
He's gone without an answer; he scorns me,
Because he sees I seek his friendship, just
As men often do; for if a rich man seeks
A favour from a poor one, he's afraid 155
To grant it, and, through fear, misses his chance;
And when the occasion's past, he's sorry for it.
(Re-enter EUCLIO.)

EUCLIO (to STAPHYLA within): If I don't have
your tongue taken out by the roots,
You may have me mauled and damaged as you like.

MEGADORUS. I see you think that I'm an old man
now, 160
Who may be mocked, although I don't deserve it.

EUCLIO. It is not so, nor could I, if I would.

MEGADORUS. Then do you give me your daughter?

EUCLIO. Yes, I do;
Upon the terms I said, without a dowry.

MEGADORUS. You promise?

EUCLIO. Yes.

MEGADORUS. And may the gods
bless it! 165

EUCLIO. I wish they may. Only remember this:
My daughter brings no dowry.

MEGADORUS. I remember.

EUCLIO. I know that sometimes men mislike a bargain;
The bargain's on or off, just as they please.

MEGADORUS. There shall be no dispute. Now, can
we have 170
The marriage for today?

EUCLIO. Most certainly.

MEGADORUS. I'll go and get me ready. Want you
aught?

EUCLIO. No, only that!

MEGADORUS. 'Tis done. Farewell. (Call-
ing at his door) Now, slave,
Follow me to the market; now, at once.
(MEGADORUS departs.)

EUCLIO (to himself). He's gone. Ye gods immortal,
what can gold 175
Achieve! He must have heard I think there is
Some treasure here; he's gaping for it now,
And that is the reason he persists in this proposal.

EUCLIO (calling at his door). Where are you, who
has blabbed to all our neighbours,
Gone chitter-chattering to all the town, 180
That I would give a dowry to my daughter?
Hi! Staphyla! I call! D'ye hear? Bring in
The sacred dishes; wash them well. Today
I have betrothed my daughter; she will wed
Today.

STAPHYLA (as she enters). The gods direct it well;
but stay, 185
It cannot be; it is too sudden, sure.

EUCLIO. Begone! Be quiet! See these things are
done
When I return; shut to the door at once;
I will be here anon.
(EUCLIO departs.)

STAPHYLA (to herself). What must I do?
Destruction waits me and my master's daughter. 190
Her state must now be known; I'll go within
And see my master's orders carried out.
I fear some evil; and of such a kind
That I must drink the poison to the dregs.
(STAPHYLA goes into the house.)

ACT THREE

(Enter STROBILUS bringing the cooks, ANTHRAX
and CONGRIO, and music girls; attendants follow
with provisions.)

STROBILUS. After my master had laid in his stores,
And hired his cooks and flute players at the market,
He bid, that I divide the feast in two.

ANTHRAX. Most certainly you shall not divide me;
But if you wish the whole of me, I'll help. 5

STROBILUS. My master weds today.

ANTHRAX. Whose daughter
is it?

STROBILUS. Our neighbour Euclio's here; he bid
me give
Him half the dinner, and a cook as well,
And one flute player.

ANTHRAX. Half that is for here,
And half for the other house.

STROBILUS. Just as you say. 10

ANTHRAX. Could this old man not find his own provisions
To grace his daughter's wedding?

STROBILUS. Bosh!

ANTHRAX. What is't?

STROBILUS. What is't you ask? A pumice-stone is not
So hard and dry as is this old man's heart.

ANTHRAX. Is't so indeed?

STROBILUS. Why, judge him for yourself.   15
He's always calling upon gods and men
To witness that he's ruined and undone,
If but a puff of smoke come from his chimney.
Why, when he sleeps, he binds the bellows to his throat—

ANTHRAX. Why that?

STROBILUS. For fear in sleep he'll lose his breath.   20

ANTHRAX. And does he close the lower outlet too,
Lest he lose wind?

STROBILUS. You might believe my tale,
As I do yours.

ANTHRAX. I do indeed believe.

STROBILUS. And when he washes, he bewails the waste
Of water.

ANTHRAX. Do you think there could be begged   25
A good round sum from this man for to buy
Our liberty?

STROBILUS. By Jove! He would not give
Starvation, if you asked him. The other day
The barber cut his nails; he gathered all
The parings up, and carried them away.   30

ANTHRAX. He is indeed a stingy soul you tell of.

STROBILUS. And can you think indeed he lived so sparely?
A hawk, it seems, once carried off his dinner.
So, full of tears, he goes before the judge;
Howling and plaining there, begins to ask   35
That the hawk should be bound over to appear.
If I had time I'd tell a thousand tales.
But which of you is nimblest?

ANTHRAX. I, by far.

STROBILUS. A cook I want, and not a thief.

ANTHRAX. I am one.

STROBILUS. And what say you?

CONGRIO. I am as you can see.   40

ANTHRAX. He's only fit to cook a funeral feast;
That's all he does.

CONGRIO. Five letters would describe
What you are; you're a thief.

ANTHRAX. Trebly a thief.

STROBILUS. Be still! Which is the fatter lamb of these?

ANTHRAX. This. (Departs to house of MEGADORUS with lamb.)   45

STROBILUS. You, Congrio, take this one straight within.
(To some of the attendants) You follow him; the rest will come with me.

CONGRIO. It is not fair, they have the fatter lamb.

STROBILUS. But you shall have the fatter music girl.
Go with him, Phrygia; you, Eleusium,   50
You come with us. (ELEUSIUM and attendants go into house of MEGADORUS.)

CONGRIO. O clever Strobilus!
You've put me off upon a mean old man,
From whom ev'n if I cried myself all hoarse
I should not get a shilling.

STROBILUS. You're a fool,
And most ungrateful.

CONGRIO. How is that?

STROBILUS. D'ye ask?   55
Why first there'll be no crowd of servants there.
If you want aught, you get it for yourself,
Lest you should waste your time in asking for it;
With us there'll be a large establishment,
A crowd of servants, gold and silver plate,   60
Dresses and furniture; if any one
Should something lose (and you I know could not,
If none were by, prevent yourself from theft),
They say at once: "The cooks have taken it;
Catch him and bind him, put him in the well,   65
And beat him!" None of these will happen there,
For there is naught to steal. Come, follow me.
(They approach the house of EUCLIO.)

STROBILUS (knocking). Hi! Staphyla, come out, open the door!

STAPHYLA. (opening the door cautiously). Who calls?

STROBILUS. 'Tis Strobilus.

STAPHYLA. And what d'ye want?

STROBILUS. Here, take these cooks, this music girl, the food   70
To serve the wedding. Megadorus sends
All these for Euclio.

STAPHYLA. I suppose it is
For Ceres' marriage?

STROBILUS. Why?

STAPHYLA. Because I see
You bring no wine.

STROBILUS. That will be brought anon
When he comes from the market.

STAPHYLA. We've no wood.   75

CONGRIO. Are there no doors?

STAPHYLA. There are.

CONGRIO. Then you have wood.
You need not go outside.

74. **You bring no wine.** In the festivals called "the marriage of Ceres," the use of wine was forbidden.

STAPHYLA. What, wretch, although
Vulcan you serve, are we, to cook your dinner
That you may get your wage, are we to burn
Our dwelling to the ground?
CONGRIO. I don't ask that. 80
STROBILUS. Then take them in at once. (*Goes into
house of* MEGADORUS.)
STAPHYLA (*opening wide the door*). Come, follow
me! (CONGRIO *and others go inside*.)
(*Enter* PYTHODICUS *from the house of* MEGA-
DORUS.)
PYTHODICUS (*to himself*). Well now, I'll see to
what the cooks are doing;
And that today's a pretty heavy job.
They ought to do it in the cellar; thence
To take it up in baskets; if they eat 85
Below what they have cooked, then those above
Will go without their dinner, those below
Will get it. I am talking just as if
I had no business; when there's in the house
Such a crowd of harpies as is here today. (*Goes into
the house*.) 90
(*Enter* EUCLIO *from the forum with some flowers
and a small package*.)
EUCLIO (*to himself*). I wished today to brace my-
self a little,
To make a show at this my daughter's wedding;
I go to market; ask the price of fish;
They say they're dear, the lamb and beef are dear;
The veal, the dogfish, and the pork are dear; 95
And all the dearer, that I had no money.
Full vexed I come away; there's nought to buy;
To all this unclean herd I said adieu.
Then as I walked I thought thus to myself;
If, on a festal day like this, you spend 100
Your money freely, nothing spare, then you
Will want tomorrow; and this reasoning
My stomach and my heart approved, so I
Intend to celebrate this wedding here
At the smallest possible expense I can. 105
So I have bought a little frankincense,
And a few flowers; these shall now be placed
Around our household god, that he may grant
A happy issue. But do I really see
My house-door open? Such a noise within! 110
What, am I robbed?
CONGRIO (*within*). Go fetch a larger pot
If you can get one; this is far too small.
EUCLIO (*in great alarm*). I am undone; and all my
gold is taken!
The pot is sought; unless I run within
At once I'm good as dead. Oh! Help me now, 115
Apollo! help, and with your arrows slay
These treasure-laden thieves, as you have done
Before. Here must I rush and see what's taking
place.
(EUCLIO *runs into his house*.)

(*Enter* ANTHRAX *from the house of* MEGADORUS.)
ANTHRAX (*to servants within*). Here, Dromo,
clean the fish; Machaerio, you
Bone if you can the lamprey and the eel, 120
That all may be prepared when I return.
I go to seek a bread pan; see that cock
Is plucked e'en smoother than a player's chin.
But what's this noise next door? It is the cooks
At work. I'll go within and try to stop 125
Them making like confusion in this house.
(*He returns to the house of* MEGADORUS.)
(CONGRIO *and his assistants rush in haste from the
house of* EUCLIO.)
CONGRIO. Dear citizens, and fellow-countrymen,
Dwellers or strangers, whosoe'er ye be,
Make room for me to fly; let the whole street
Be open to my path. I never came 130
Before today to cook at such a place;
'Tis like a Bacchic orgy; they have beaten
My pupils and myself with sticks and staves.
I'm sore all over, and indeed quite dead!
That old boy took me for a boxing school; 135
I never saw posts come in handier
Than these; he beat us all and turned us out.
Alas! I am undone! Here comes again
The Bacchanalian orgy; he is here;
He follows. I know what to do; I'll go 140
The way my master went before today.
(*Enter* EUCLIO *from his house, stick in hand*.)
EUCLIO. Hallo! Why fly? Return, return, I say!
CONGRIO. Why are you shouting, fool?
EUCLIO. I'll lay your name
Before the magistrates.
CONGRIO. I pray you why?
EUCLIO. Because you wear a knife.
CONGRIO. As well becomes 145
A cook.
EUCLIO. Ay, and because you threatened me.
CONGRIO. The wrong was that I did not sheath it
in you.
EUCLIO. There's not a man more wicked than you
are,
Nor one I'd rather do an injury to.
CONGRIO. No need to say so; it is clear enough; 150
You've made me supple as a dancer is,
Wretch that I am! Why did you touch me thus,
And for what reason?
EUCLIO. Do you ask me why?
Have I done something less than was your due?
CONGRIO. You'll suffer for it, if my head can feel.
EUCLIO. I don't know what may come; but yours
feels now. 156
But pray what business had you in my house
When I was absent, without my commands?
I wish to know.
CONGRIO. Be quiet, then; we came
To cook your wedding-feast.

EUCLIO.   What matters it 160
To you if I eat meat that's cooked or raw?
Are you my master?
    CONGRIO.   Well, I want to know
Whether you wish the dinner cooked or not.
    EUCLIO. And I whether my things are safe with
        you
Or not.
    CONGRIO. I only hope that I may take   165
The things away, that I have brought with me
All safe and sound. The rest it matters not,
For I want none of yours.
    EUCLIO.   I know, I know.
    CONGRIO. But why prevent us cook your dinner
        here?
What have we done or said you do not like?   170
    EUCLIO. D'ye ask, you wretch, who thus have made
        your way
Through all the corners of my house and rooms?
If you had stopped beside the hearth, which is
Your proper place, your head had not been split.
You well deserved it. Now that you may know   175
My sentiments, if you come nearer to
My door than I shall order, you shall be
The most unhappy man that is. D'ye hear?
             (EUCLIO *goes into his house.*)
    CONGRIO. Art going? Pray come back! And may
        Laverna,
Who watches over thieves, be kind to me!   180
If you don't order all my cooking things
To be returned to me, I'll make a row
Before the house. What am I now to do?
An evil day it was that brought me here;
The money that I got won't pay the doctor.   185
    (*Re-enter* EUCLIO *from the house, with the pot of
gold under his cloak.*)
    EUCLIO (*to himself*). Ah! This at all events,
        where'er I go,
I'll carry with me, as my constant friend,
Nor e'er expose it to like perils again.
(*To* CONGRIO *and others*) Go now within, cooks and
        flute-players all,
Bring if you like the whole vile venal herd,   190
And cook, and act, and bustle as you please.
    CONGRIO. Most timely, after you have split our
        heads.
    EUCLIO. Go in! You came to work, and not to talk.
    CONGRIO. Old gentleman, for this I'll make you
        pay;
I was engaged to cook, not to be beaten.   195
    EUCLIO. Don't bother! Go to law! But first to cook,
Or else go and be hanged.
    CONGRIO.   Pray go yourself.
    (CONGRIO *and the assistants go into the house of*
EUCLIO.)
    EUCLIO (*to himself*). He's gone within. Immortal
        gods, he who,

Though poor, does business with wealthy men
Needs a brave heart to have. Thus Megadorus   200
Tries me in every way, pretends to send
His cooks to do me honour; sent this one
To steal this treasure from me. And to match him
Even my cock, that was the special friend
Of that old woman's, nearly ruined me,   205
And with his claws began to dig a hole
Where this was buried. Further need I say?
My heart was cut to the very quick; I seized
A stick, I kill the cock, in the very act
Of thieving. I believe the cooks themselves   210
Promised that cock a rich reward if he
Disclosed the treasure. Anyhow, I spoiled
Their little game. No more; the cock is dead.
But see, my neighbour Megadorus comes;
I dare not pass him; I must stop and speak.   215
    (*Enter* MEGADORUS *from the forum.*)
    MEGADORUS (*to himself, not seeing* EUCLIO). To
        many friends I've told that I propose
To marry Euclio's daughter; they approve;
They think it wise and excellently done.
I would, I think, if others did the same;
If wealthy people married in this way   220
The daughters of the poor, nor asked a dower,
The state would be more happy than it is,
With less of jealousy than now we have;
Our wives would treat us with the more respect,
And we should live at less expense ourselves.   225
'Twould benefit the greater part of men;
A few old misers would object to it,
Whose greedy and insatiable souls
Nor law nor governor can hold in check.
But some may say, if marriage is for the poor,   230
Whom can the wealthy wed? Why, whom they
        choose,
If but their fortune has been left behind.
And in the place of fortune they would bring
A better disposition; I would make
Mules, which are dearer now than any horse,   235
Cheaper by far than any horse can be.
    EUCLIO (*aside*). How gladly here I hearken to
        this man
Who speaks such pleasant things of narrow means!
    MEGADORUS. No wife could say: "I brought to you
        a dower
Much larger than your fortune; therefore I   240
Must live in gold and purple, and have maids,
Pages and lackeys, mules and muleteers,
And carriages to ride in."
    EUCLIO (*aside*).   Ah! How well he knows
Fine ladies' ways; I wish he was their tutor.
    MEGADORUS. But now where'er you go, at your
        town house   245

233–236. **And in the place of fortune . . . be.** In this attack on the institution of the dowry Plautus was supporting reforms proposed at the time by Cato the censor.

You'll find more waggons waiting than you will
Ev'n at your country seat. But that's a trifle
To what it is when they present their bills.
There stands the fuller and embroiderer,
The goldsmith and the man who curls your hair, 250
The tailor and the hosier, and the host
Who dye your bridal veils in red or yellow,
Who sell you muffs, and perfumed slippers too,
Hucksters in linen, showmakers galore,
Clogs, slippers, sandals, all are here to sell, 255
To dye or mend your garments as you wish;
Sellers of stays and girdles swell the train.
You think them all; three hundred go and come.
Outside the duns are watching in the hall,
The weavers and the men who caskets make; 260
They've reckoned up; the money paid; 'tis all,
You fancy; when once more these come in view,
Dyers in something else, some wretched thing
That makes still further levies on your purse.

    EUCLIO (*aside*). I would address him, but I fear
        to stop 265
This nice recital of our ladies' ways.
Let him proceed.

    MEGADORUS.   And when at length you've paid
For all this female rubbish, comes in view
The taxgatherer, presents his bill; you go
And reckon with your banker, while he waits 270
Undined, expecting to receive his pay.
When the account is furnished, then you find
You've overdrawn; the tax-man has to wait
Another day. These are the cares that wait,
The inconveniences and vast expense, 275
On these huge dowries; she who's none at all
Is in her husband's power; and dowered wives
Bring loss and trouble to their husband's lives.
But, see, my neighbour comes. Euclio, good day!

    EUCLIO. Most gladly have I listened to your
        words. 280

    MEGADORUS. Didst hear them?

    EUCLIO.   Ay. I did from the
        very first.

    MEGADORUS. Methinks it would be better still if
        you
Looked rather sprucer for your daughter's wedding.

    EUCLIO. According to our means and circum-
        stances,
Our wealth and show should still proportioned be.
Let those who have, think of their high estate. 286
But I, and such as me, no more of wealth
Possess than public rumour gives to us.

    MEGADORUS. Surely you have; may the gods make
        it more.

    EUCLIO (*aside*). I do not like his words: "surely
        you have;" 290
He knows as well as I do what I have;
The old woman's told him.

    MEGADORUS.   Why d'ye speak apart?

    EUCLIO. I thought of making a complaint to you.

    MEGADORUS. On what?

    EUCLIO.   On what, d'ye ask? You
        who have filled
Nigh every corner of my house with thieves; 295
Who've sent into it five hundred cooks at least,
With six hands each, like Geryon of old.
Argus himself who was all eyes, to whom
Jove once entrusted Io, he could not
Keep watch upon them, even if he would. 300
A music girl, who by herself could drink
The famous fountain of Pirene dry,
If bubbling over with wine! And then their food—

    MEGADORUS. I've sent as much as would a legion
        feed;
Aye, and a lamb beside.

    EUCLIO.   I've never seen 305
A more curious beast than that.

    MEGADORUS.   How curious?

    EUCLIO. All bone and skin; so thin with toil and
        trouble;
You can see right through it in the light of day;
'Tis as transparent as an ivory lamp.

    MEGADORUS. I bought it to be butchered.

    EUCLIO.   A splendid bargain,
For 'tis already dead.

    MEGADORUS.   Euclio, I wish 311
To drink with you today.

    EUCLIO.   I cannot do so.

    MEGADORUS. But I will bid a cask of rich old wine
To be brought from my cellar.

    EUCLIO.   I can drink
But water only.

    MEGADORUS. If I live today, 315
I'll send you back as drunk as any lord—
You who drink only water.

    EUCLIO (*aside*).   Ah! I see
What is his aim; to get quit of me with wine,
That is his plan, and what I have, annex.
But I'll take care; I'll put it out of doors. 320
And he shall lose his wine and trouble too.

    MEGADORUS. Unless you want me further, I
        shall go
To get me ready for the sacrifice. (*Goes into his
        house.*)

    EUCLIO (*to object under cloak*). Ah, little pot,
        how many foes you have,
You and the gold entrusted to your care. 325
And now the best that I can do is this,
To take you to the temple of Good Faith
And hide you there. Good Faith, you know me well,
And I know you; so take good care to yourself,

297. Geryon, a three-bodied monster in Greek mythology. 298–299.
Argus himself . . . Io. Actually it was Juno who set the many-eyed
Argus to watching her husband's mistress day and night. 302. foun-
tain of Pirene; at Corinth in Greece.

And see you do not change the name you bear, 330
If I trust you with this. Relying on
Your honesty, Good Faith, I come to you.
                    (*He goes into the temple of Faith.*)

ACT FOUR

(*Enter the* SLAVE *of* LYCONIDES.)

SLAVE (*to himself*). This is the office of a useful
            slave
To do as I do, nor to grumble at
Nor yet oppose a master's bidding. For
The slave who wants to serve his master well,
Does first his master's work and then his own, 5
And if he sleeps, why let him sleep, as if
He were a slave. Who serves a loving master
Like my own, if he should chance to see
That he's in love, that is the slave's concern:
To bring him back to safety, not to drive 10
Him further on the path he wants to go.
Just as to boys who learn to swim is given
A raft of rushes to make less their toil,
That they may use their hands more easily;
In the same way a slave should be a raft, 15
To bear his master up, when he's in love.
His master's will he studies, and his eyes
Note what is on his brow; his last command,
Swifter than courser's flight, he hastes to obey.
Who takes this care, escapes the censuring thong;
Nor keeps his fetters bright by constant wear. 21
My master is in love with Euclio's daughter;
And now we hear that she is to be married
To Megadorus; he has sent me now
To spy about, and learn what is going on. 25
Here by this sacred altar I will stand
All unsuspected, and from hence can judge
What here or there is being carried on.
            (*Enter* EUCLIO *from the temple of faith.*)
EUCLIO (*not seeing* SLAVE). Take care, Good
            Faith, you do not indicate
To a single soul that all my gold is there. 30
I do not fear lest any find the place,
It is so hidden away; still, he would have
A pretty booty who should find the pot
Laden with gold. See to it then, Good Faith.
Now I will wash me for the sacrifice 35
And not delay my neighbour when he comes
To take my daughter home. And so, Good Faith,
Again and yet again, I say, that I
May carry off the pot all sound and safe,
To you I so entrust it. In your shrine 40
And grove it lies securely hidden away.
                    (*He goes into his house.*)
SLAVE. Ye gods immortal, what is this I hear
This man to say, that he has hidden away

---

1. *Slave of Lyconides*. The manuscripts mistakenly assign the slave's
speeches to Strobilus.

A heavy pot of gold within this shrine?
Good Faith, see to it that you're not more kind 45
To him than me. This man, methinks, is father
To her my master loves. I will go in
And spy around the temple; if I find
The gold, when this man's back is turned; then if
I do, I'll brew a stoup of wine for you, 50
And, when I do it, drink the same myself.
                    (*He goes into the temple.*)
            (EUCLIO *hurries from his house.*)
EUCLIO (*to himself*). 'Twas not for nothing that
            the raven cried
At my left hand, and flew close to the ground
And croaked anon; my heart began to play
A curious game, and leaped into my throat. 55
I am all shaking; I must run and run.
(*He rushes into the temple and drags out the*
SLAVE.)
EUCLIO. Out, out of doors, vile worm, that just
            has crept
Out of the ground! But now, you were not here,
And now you are, you die! You wretched cheat,
I'll treat you as you well deserve to be. 60
SLAVE. What demon troubles you? Or what
            have I
To do with you? Why do you trouble me?
Why drag me thus? Why beat me as you do?
EUCLIO. Most worthy of a beating of all men!
Still asking questions, you, who are a thief, 65
Or even more than that, a triple thief.
SLAVE. What have I stolen?
EUCLIO.   Bring it back to me.
SLAVE. What should I bring?
EUCLIO.   D'ye want to know what 'tis?
SLAVE. I've taken nothing.
EUCLIO.   Give it back to me.
SLAVE. What must I do?
EUCLIO.   You shall not take it hence.
SLAVE. What do you want?
EUCLIO.   Now put it down at once.
SLAVE. I think, old gentleman, you're wont to
            jest. 72
EUCLIO. Be done with jesting; put it down, I say.
SLAVE. And put what down? Pray tell me what
            it is
By its own name; I've touched and taken nothing.
EUCLIO. Show me your hands!
SLAVE.   Look there!
EUCLIO.   And yet again!
SLAVE. See there!
EUCLIO.   And show the third hand now, I pray!
SLAVE. Distempered dreams and wild illusions vex
This old man's soul. D'ye want to do mischief?
EUCLIO. Ay, marry, all I can, not hanging you;
And that will come if you do not confess. 81
SLAVE. Confess to what?
EUCLIO.   What you have taken away.

SLAVE. The gods destroy me if I have taken
    aught,
Or even wished to do so.
EUCLIO.   Shake your cloak.
SLAVE. Yes, as you will.
EUCLIO.   Lest there be something hidden
Between the folds.
SLAVE.   Try any way you like.   86
EUCLIO. You wretch, how smooth you speak, that
    I may not
Detect you in the theft. I know your dodges.
Show me your right hand now.
SLAVE.   Well, there it is.
EUCLIO. And now your left.
SLAVE.   You see, I proffer both.
EUCLIO. I do not care to search. Restore the
    things.   91
SLAVE. And what restore?
EUCLIO.   You jest, for you must have it.
SLAVE. Have what?
EUCLIO.   I need not say, you know full well.
Restore me what you've had of mine.
SLAVE.   You're mad.
You've searched me as you like, and nothing
    found.   95
EUCLIO. Stay, who is that who was inside with
    you?
(Aside) I am undone; that other is inside.
If I lose sight of this one, he'll be off.
Yet I have searched him; he has nothing on him.
(Aloud) Go where you like.
SLAVE.   You be completely damned!
EUCLIO. He is not thankful. I will go inside   101
And wring the neck of your companion.
Are you away? Art off? And out of sight?
SLAVE. I am.
EUCLIO. Take care you never see me more.
          (Goes into the temple.)
SLAVE. I'd rather perish by some foul disease   105
Than not contrive to play some nasty trick
On this old man today. He will not dare
To hide away his gold in this place now.
He'll take it out and change the hiding-place.
I hear the door. And see, he brings the gold!   110
I'll stand aside behind the door and watch.
    (Enter EUCLIO from the temple, with the pot of
gold.)
    EUCLIO (to himself). I thought Good Faith was
      fairly to be trusted,
But cruelly she's disappointed me.
But for the raven I had been undone.
I wish to see him once again and make   115
Some small return—a compliment, not meat.
And now I know a solitary place
Where I may hide this pot; it is the grove
Of our god Silvanus, stretching far beyond
The city wall, with willows planted round.   120

There I will choose a spot; for I am sure
I had rather trust Silvanus than Good Faith.
          (EUCLIO departs.)
    SLAVE. Good luck! The gods are full of kindness
      to me.
I'll run before and climb into a tree,
And watch from thence where he may hide the
    gold.   125
For, though my master bid me to stay here,
That gain is worth a blow doth still appear.
          (The SLAVE departs.)
    (Enter LYCONIDES and EUNOMIA.)
    LYCONIDES. I've told you, mother, and you know
      the story
Of what has taken place between myself
And Euclio's daughter. Now I pray you tell   130
My uncle all; once more I do beseech you
As I have done before.
EUNOMIA.   Your wish is mine.
And this I hope my brother will consent
To grant; and, if things be as you assert,
Your cause is just. You say it did take place   135
When you were overcome with use of wine?
    LYCONIDES. And think you, mother, I'd impose on
      you?
    PHAEDRIA (inside EUCLIO's house). Help me, dear
      nurse! Juno Lucina,
Help!
    LYCONIDES. The thing is clear enough; she has a
      child.
    EUNOMIA. Then come within with me, and see
      my brother,   140
That he at my request may grant your prayer.
        (She goes into the house of MEGADORUS.)
    LYCONIDES. I follow you. (To himself) But now
      I wonder where
My servant Strobilus can be. I bid
Him wait me here. Yet now I think on it,
It were unfair to blame him, as he may   145
Be helping me elsewhere. I'll come within;
The meeting's one of life or death to me.
        (He goes into the house of MEGADORUS.)
    (Enter SLAVE of LYCONIDES, with the pot of gold.)
    SLAVE (to himself). Myself I do surpass in stores
      of wealth
The fabled griffins, who are said to dwell
Upon the golden mountains; mighty kings   150
I scarce do notice; they are beggars all.
Philip himself I am. Oh! Blessed day,
On which I went from here, and was the first,
And placed myself in hiding on the tree,
And watched from thence where he would place
    the gold.   155
When he was gone, I creep along the tree,

138. **Juno Lucina.** Juno with the attribute of Lucina was goddess of
childbirth. **149. fabled griffins.** Half eagle and half lion, the griffins
guarded gold mines and hidden treasures.

And disinter a pot quite full of gold.
I see the old man go; he sees not me;
I leaned aside a little from the road.
But see, he comes, I'll hide the gold at home.   160
                                    (*Departs.*)
        (*Enter* EUCLIO *frantic.*)
EUCLIO (*to himself*). I'm ruined, slaughtered,
        quite undone! Oh, where
Am I to go? Or not to go? Stay! Stop!
But whom? Or what? I cannot see, I'm blind!
I cannot say for certain where I go,
Nor where, nor who I am. (*To audience*) I pray
        your help   165
To point me out the man who stole the gold.
Ay, there they sit in white like honest men.
What say you? I can trust you; and I know
An honest man by sight. What is it now?
Why do you laugh? There are thieves enough, I
        know,   170
And many thieves. What, none of these have it?
You kill me! Don't you know? Say who it is.
Alas, alas, I am undone! I'm killed!
A pretty state of things! So much of woe,
So much of grief has this day brought to me!   175
Hunger and poverty, most wretched man!
What hope of life to one who's lost so much,
So much that I have guarded? I denied
Myself all pleasure; others now will joy,
At my expense, my loss. I cannot bear it!   180
    LYCONIDES (*entering from the house of* MEGADO-
        RUS).
Who is this man who howls before our doors,
Lamenting loudly? Euclio 'tis, I think.
Ah, I am ruined! Everything is known.
He knows what's happened to his daughter now.
What must I do? Stay here, or go away?   185
Approach him, or fly from him? I know not.
    EUCLIO. Who is 't who speaks?
    LYCONIDES.   A most unhappy man!
    EUCLIO. And I not less so, for to me has chanced
Such ills and sorrow.
    LYCONIDES.   Nay, be of good heart.
    EUCLIO. How can I?
    LYCONIDES.   'Cause the deed that troubles you
Is mine. I do admit it.
    EUCLIO.   What is this?   191
    LYCONIDES. The truth.
    EUCLIO.   What have I done, young
        man, to you,
That you should ruin me, and leave forlorn
My children and myself?
    LYCONIDES.   God was my guide;
'Twas he who led me on.
    EUCLIO.   And how was that?   195
    LYCONIDES. I do admit my sin, and know that I
Deserve your blame. Therefore I come to you
And ask your pardon.

EUCLIO.   But why did you dare
To touch what was not yours?
    LYCONIDES.   What do you want?
It cannot be undone. I think the gods   200
Have willed it, or it never could have been.
    EUCLIO. I think the gods have willed that I should
        kill you.
    LYCONIDES. Nay, say not so.
    EUCLIO.   But why against my will
Have you laid hands on that which was my own?
    LYCONIDES. 'Twas wine and love that made me.
    EUCLIO.   Daring man!
To come to me with such a tale as that!   206
If that is law, then might we just as well
In open daylight take a woman's jewels,
And say when caught that we were drunk, and
        did it
For the sake of love; too vile are wine and love   210
If they excuse whate'er we choose to do.
    LYCONIDES. I come to ask your pardon for my folly.
    EUCLIO. I like not those who first do ill, and then
Excuse themselves. You know it was not yours;
And you should not have touched it.
    LYCONIDES.   Well, I did it.
And now I will not argue more about it.   216
    EUCLIO. Keep mine against my will?
    LYCONIDES.   I do not ask
To have it so, but think it should be mine.
And now, O Euclio, I'm sure you'll realize
It should be mine.
    EUCLIO.   I'll take you to the judge,   220
And serve a writ, until you bring it back.
    LYCONIDES. And bring what back?
    EUCLIO.   Why, what
        you stole from me.
    LYCONIDES. I stole? Whence? And what is it?
    EUCLIO.   May great Jove
Himself so love you in the same degree,
As you are ignorant!
    LYCONIDES.   Unless you tell me   225
What 'tis you seek.
    EUCLIO.   A pot of gold it is
I ask, which you admit that you have stolen.
    LYCONIDES. I never said so, and I never did it.
    EUCLIO. What, you deny?
    LYCONIDES.   Most certainly I do.
I know no gold, nor any pot at all.   230
    EUCLIO. Give me the pot you stole from Silvan's
        grove.
Go, bring it back; I'll give to you a third.
Although a thief, I won't deal hardly with you.
    LYCONIDES. You are not sane, in calling me a
        thief.
I thought that you had spoke of something else,   235
Which close concerns me. If you have the time,
There is a most important thing I want
To speak of to you.

EUCLIO.   Tell me on your word
You have not stolen it.
LYCONIDES.   Upon my honour!
EUCLIO. Nor know who did'st so?
LYCONIDES.   No, upon my word!
EUCLIO. And if you know, you'll tell me.
LYCONIDES.   That I swear.
EUCLIO. And will not ask a share, nor shield the
          thief?   242
LYCONIDES. Most certainly.
EUCLIO.   And what if you play false?
LYCONIDES. May Jupiter do with me what he will.
EUCLIO. Enough! Now tell me what you want
          of me.   245
LYCONIDES. Well, if you do not know my family,
This Megadorus here, he is my uncle;
Antimachus my father was, and I
Lyconides am called; my mother is Eunomia.
EUCLIO. The family I know.   250
But what d'ye want with me?
LYCONIDES.   You have a daughter?
EUCLIO. I have, at home.
LYCONIDES.   Betrothed to my uncle?
EUCLIO. You know it all.
LYCONIDES.   He bid me tell you he
Renounces now her hand.
EUCLIO (angrily).   Renounces now
When all is ready and the wedding furnished?   255
May all the gods and goddesses destroy
This man for whom I've lost so much today.
LYCONIDES. Be of good cheer. May all yet turn
          out well
For you and for your daughter; pray it be so.
EUCLIO. May the gods do it!
LYCONIDES.   And the same to me!
Now listen. There's not a man who's sinned,   261
But is ashamed and sorry, if he's worth
A straw. Now I beseech you, Euclio,
In this misfortune my imprudence caused
You and your daughter, you should pardon me   265
And give her me for wife as the law permits.
I do confess I did her grievous wrong
On Ceres' night, through wine and youthful impulse.
EUCLIO. Alas! Alas! And what is this I hear?
LYCONIDES. Why should you mourn, when at your
          daughter's wedding   270
You will at once as grandfather appear.
She bare a child just ten months after it;
Pray reckon for yourself; and therefore 'tis
My uncle has renounced her hand for me.
Go in, and you will hear that it is so.   275
EUCLIO. Ah me! I am quite ruined! Evils come
One on the top of others, clinging fast.
I'll go within and see if this is so.
          (Goes into his house.)
LYCONIDES. And I will follow. (To himself) My
affairs appear

To have reached shoal waters, where my safety lies.
But now I cannot find where he should be,   281
My servant Strobilus; I'll wait for him,
And then will follow this man; I will give
Him time to make enquiries from his daughter
And from the nurse; for she at least knows all.   285

ACT FIVE

(Enter SLAVE of LYCONIDES.)

SLAVE (to himself). Ye gods immortal, with what
          joys have you
Presented me; how great the sum of them!
I have a four pound pot that is full of gold!
Who now more rich than me? What man at Athens
To whom the gods are kinder?
LYCONIDES (to himself).   Sure, I thought,   5
I heard the voice of some one speaking here.
SLAVE (aside). Ah! Do I see my master?
LYCONIDES (aside).   And is it
My servant coming here I see?
SLAVE (aside).   It is.
LYCONIDES (aside). And not another.
SLAVE (aside).   I'll advance
          to meet him.
LYCONIDES (aside). And I'll draw nearer. I be-
          lieve that he   10
Has, as I ordered, seen this lady's nurse.
SLAVE (aside). And why not tell him I have found
          this treasure?
I will that he may set me free. I'll go.
(To LYCONIDES) I've found—
LYCONIDES.   What have you found?
SLAVE.   Why, not that which
Boys look for in a bean and shout with joy,   15
When they have found it nestling there inside.
LYCONIDES. You're jesting, as you're wont.
SLAVE.   Stay, master, hear.
LYCONIDES. Speak then.
SLAVE.   Today I found a hoard of wealth,
Too much for me.
LYCONIDES.   And where, I pray, was that?
SLAVE. A four pound pot of gold.
LYCONIDES.   What crime is this?
SLAVE. I stole it from this old man Euclio.   21
LYCONIDES. Where is the gold?
SLAVE.   Why, in a chest at home.
And now I wish my freedom at your hand.
LYCONIDES. I make you free, most scoundrellest
          of knaves?
SLAVE. Off with you, master! I know what you
          want.   25
And cleverly I laid a bait for you.
You were prepared to take it. What if I
Myself had found it?

282. **My servant Strobilus,** that is, his slave, not the Strobilus of Act Three.

LYCONIDES.   Now we want no trifling.
Bring me the gold.
   SLAVE.   Must I return the gold?
   LYCONIDES. Yes, that it may be given to him.
   SLAVE.   And whence?
   LYCONIDES. Just now you did confess 'twas in
      your chest.   31
   SLAVE. Yes, I was joking, as I'm wont to do.
   LYCONIDES. But how, I pray?
   SLAVE.   Then kill me if you like;
Of this be sure, you shall not take it hence.

(The remainder of the play is lost. Lyconides apparently returned the pot of gold to Euclio and received permission to marry his daughter; Euclio gave the gold to the young couple, saying as he did so, "I never had a minute's peace day or night watching it; now I will sleep.")

Virgil

70–19 B.C.

The arrival of empire with Augustus coincided with a sharp break in Roman literary tradition. The generation of Cicero died out in the forties, and with it that freedom of self-expression characteristic of Lucretius, Catullus, and Cicero himself. In its place came a new school, patronized by Maecenas, Pollio, and the Emperor, which owed its support to the Empire and industriously set about deserving it. Literature took on a new restraint and new brilliance, and authors vied with each other in venerating Augustus, the Julian line, and the empire that it had created. The chief of these new writers was Virgil, the national poet of Rome.

Publius Vergilius Maro of Mantua in Cisalpine Gaul was intended for the law by his ambitious peasant father, but one experience in court convinced the shy and sensitive youth that he should apply his excellent education to philosophy and poetry. Always happiest in peaceful seclusion, he found his studies interrupted by a succession of civil wars. In 41 B.C. his family farm was confiscated in favor of one of Antony's soldiers, but he supposedly applied to Octavian in Rome for redress and thus came to the notice of the future emperor. He had already begun to compose the *Eclogues,* his earliest notable work, and included in the first of them a graceful mention of the incident. The *Eclogues* (39 B.C.), ten little pastorals that the painstaking Virgil took three years to write, seem artificial and cold in comparison with the writings of his model, Theocritus, but they established his reputation and were immensely popular in the centuries to follow. The famous Fourth Eclogue, dedicated to the consul Pollio, passes from the world of playful shepherds to salute the impending birth to a glorious father of a child in whose lifetime the Golden Age of peace and prosperity would be restored to the earth. Though variously interpreted now as referring to a child soon to be born to his patron, Pollio, or Antony, or even Octavian, it was accepted in the Middle Ages as a prophecy of the imminent coming of Christ and accounts for Virgil's inclusion among the Prophets in medieval religious plays.

Securely entrenched in the esteem of Maecenas and Octavian, he next wrote at their request the *Georgics* (30 B.C.), a slender work which occupied him for seven years. It was designed to assist the back-to-the-farm movement of Octavian through painting a fresh and alluring picture of the farmer's occupation. The four books of this magnificent didactic poem treat, in turn, crops and the weather, the culture of grapes and olives, cattle-breeding, and bee-keeping, but the agricultural information is transformed by poetic treatment and enlivened by digressions on the wholesome simplicity of farm-life, myths associated with the earth, and even praise of Augustus. John Dryden called the *Georgics* "the best poem of the best poet."

Modern readers know Virgil largely through his magnum opus, the *Aeneid.* It was begun at the request of Augustus but was left unfinished when Virgil died of a fever at Brundisium in 19 B.C.* Rome had at this time no folk epic comparable to those of Greece and had long since outgrown the crude *Annales* of Ennius. Augustus wanted a literary epic that would do justice to the Empire and emphasize his own part in founding it. Other poets were approached, but only Virgil rose to the task. And although the last eleven years of his life went to the slow composition of its twelve books, this perfectionist was still so dissatisfied with its lack of finish that he requested on his deathbed that it be burned. Augustus prevented this and carried out his alternative wish that two of his friends should edit it. The *Aeneid* was finally published two years later.

Instead of building his epic around the contemporary empire or the personality of Augustus, Virgil showed his good taste in electing to retell and elaborate the traditional legend of the settlement of Aeneas in Latium and the establishment of the Julian line. Superficially, the *Aeneid* imitates the Homeric epics. The meter is once more the hexameter, and the opening "Arms and the man I sing" recalls Homer's beginnings. The epic commonplaces reappear in *pius Aeneas* (dutiful Aeneas) and *fidus Achates* (faithful Achates, his friend). The first six books are reminiscent of the *Odyssey* in telling how the Trojan prince fled from his burning city and, by the spiteful will of the goddess Juno, wandered for years through the Mediterranean. In Books II and III Aeneas tells Dido of his adventures, as Odysseus had told his story at the court of King Alcinoüs. In Book V Aeneas describes the funeral games for his father's memory, comparable to the games in the *Iliad* to honor the dead Patroclus; and in Book VI the descent of Aeneas into Hades recalls the similar experience of Odysseus. But the tragic love of Dido in Book IV is the invention of Virgil and the most famous

---

* Virgil's tomb at Naples became a kind of shrine in the Middle Ages and a Mecca of literary pilgrims down to our day.

and appealing episode in a work not generally distinguished for its warmth.

The last six books recounting the arrival of Aeneas in Italy and his war with the hero Turnus for the hand of Lavinia, daughter of King Latinus of Latium, are intended to suggest Homer's epic of war, the *Iliad*. The struggle for a woman reminds us of the Trojan War for Helen, and the final combat of the heroes in Book XII recalls Achilles and Hector. Again, the roll of the Italian armies in Book VII is modeled on the catalog of the ships in the *Iliad*. Perhaps the weariest Homeric imitation appears in the supernatural machinery, for the struggle of Juno and Venus over the destiny of Aeneas, the son of Venus, is an empty convention without religious conviction or poetic value.

Yet Virgil was in his way a religious man, looking beyond paganism to a mysticism inspired by Greek philosophy and prophetic of Christian teachings. In Hades, Anchises tells his son that all creation is animated by a great spirit, which wars in man against material things that entice him to evil. Hence in the world to come, man's soul must be purified in a kind of Purgatory before it is free to enter the Elysian Fields. If the purification is incomplete the soul is reincarnated in a new body to continue the process. This doctrine made a strong appeal to Dante, who incorporated Virgil's Hades in his *Inferno* and made Virgil himself a leading character in the *Commedia*. Akin to Virgil's mysticism is his romanticism, which appears in the tragic tale of Dido and in the array of fantastic creatures and places in Book VI. The poetic imagination in such episodes as these helps to temper the intellectual cast of the poem as a whole and the weary quality that betrays how inconsistent were the heroic theme and the gory battlefield with the quiet, retiring nature of the poet. The *Aeneid* was written by plan and often with stoic effort, and hence lacks the robustness, simplicity, and spontaneity of Homer. *Pius Aeneas* is a middle-aged man weighed down with stoic duties and denied by his fate and by the gods of any power to act for himself. He is the embodiment of Rome and the prophecy of Augustus, and he must deny his heart, even to abandoning disgracefully the woman he loves, in order to fulfill his high destiny. He is at bottom a Roman senator forced to exchange the toga for the leather tunic of the warrior. Only contrast this reserved and thoughtful man with the passionate youth, Achilles, full of ardor and high spirits and unrestrained in expressing them, and you will sense the difference between the youthful, extravagant Greeks and the stoic, sophisticated Romans.

Virgil's appeal is unlike Homer's, but it is still unmistakable. Though he has lost the refreshing youth of the vigorous Greek, he knows more, and speaks with the wisdom and humanity of a mature mind. He has thought seriously of life and death and feels tenderness for simple people. He is a magnificent poet, with the capacity to express in lovely images his awareness of beauty, and with a sweet and sonorous style—one of the most uniformly polished in all literature. For centuries after his death the *Aeneid* was considered the greatest of all poems, and it has not lost its charm.

The Messiah
(*Eclogue IV*)

SICILIAN Muse, begin a loftier strain!
  Tho' lowly shrubs, and trees that shade the
    plain,
Delight not all; Sicilian Muse, prepare
To make the vocal woods deserve a consul's care.
The last great age, foretold by sacred rhymes,   5
Renews its finished course: Saturnian times
Roll round again; and mighty years, begun
From their first orb, in radiant circles run.
The base, degenerate iron offspring ends;
A golden progeny from heaven descends.   10
O chaste Lucina, speed the mother's pains,
And haste the glorious birth! thy own Apollo reigns!
The lovely boy, with his auspicious face,
Shall Pollio's consulship and triumph grace;
Majestic months set out with him to their appointed
    race.   15
The father banished virtue shall restore,
And crimes shall threat the guilty world no more.
The son shall lead the life of gods, and be
By gods and heroes seen, and gods and heroes see.
The jarring nations he in peace shall bind,   20
And with paternal virtues rule mankind.
Unbidden Earth shall wreathing ivy bring,
And fragrant herbs (the promises of spring),
As her first offerings to her infant king.
The goats with strutting dugs shall homeward speed,
And lowing herds secure from lions feed.   26
His cradle shall with rising flowers be crowned:
The serpent's brood shall die; the sacred ground
Shall weeds and poisonous plants refuse to bear;
Each common bush shall Syrian roses wear.   30
But when heroic verse his youth shall raise,
And form it to hereditary praise,
Unlabored harvests shall the fields adorn,
And clustered grapes shall blush on every thorn;
The knotted oaks shall showers of honey weep,   35
And thro' the matted grass the liquid gold shall
    creep.
Yet of old fraud some footsteps shall remain:
The merchant still shall plow the deep for gain;
Great cities shall with walls be compassed round,
And sharpened shares shall vex the fruitful
    ground. . . .

The Messiah. Translated by John Dryden.
1. **Sicilian Muse,** the muse of pastoral verse, associated with Sicily, the birthplace of Theocritus. 4. **consul,** Pollio, apparently the father of the child whose birth is predicted here. 6. **Saturnian times,** the ancient age of gold, when civilization was supposed to have been introduced into Italy by Saturnus, a mythical king identified with the Greek Cronos as the father of Jupiter, Juno, and other gods. 11. **chaste Lucina,** the goddess of childbirth. 18. **The son shall lead the life of gods.** . . . The parallel of this whole passage with the Christian tradition of the life of Christ is striking.

But when to ripened manhood he shall grow,
The greedy sailor shall the seas forego;
No keel shall cut the waves for foreign ware,
For every soil shall every product bear.
The laboring hind his oxen shall disjoin;   45
No plough shall hurt the glebe, no pruning hook the
          vine;
Nor wool shall in dissembled colors shine.
But the luxurious father of the fold,
With native purple, or unborrowed gold,
Beneath his pompous fleece shall proudly sweat;
And under Tyrian robes the lamb shall bleat.   51
The Fates, when they this happy web have spun,
Shall bless the sacred clew, and bid it smoothly run.
Mature in years, to ready honors move,
O of celestial seed! O foster son of Jove!   55
See, laboring Nature calls thee to sustain
The nodding frame of heaven, and earth, and main!
See to their base restored, earth, seas, and air;
And joyful ages, from behind, in crowding ranks ap-
          pear.
To sing thy praise, would Heaven my breath pro-
          long,   60
Infusing spirits worthy such a song. . . .
Begin, auspicious boy, to cast about
Thy infant eyes, and, with a smile, thy mother single
          out:
Thy mother well deserves that short delight,
The nauseous qualms of ten long months and travail
          to requite.   65
Then smile: the frowning infant's doom is read;
No god shall crown the board, nor goddess bless the
          bed.

The Aeneid

BOOK I

I TELL about war and the hero who first from
   Troy's frontier,
Displaced by destiny, came to the Lavinian shores,
To Italy—a man much travailed on sea and land
By the powers above, because of the brooding anger
          of Juno,
Suffering much in war until he could found a city   5
And march his gods into Latium, whence rose the
          Latin race,
The royal line of Alba and the high walls of Rome.
Where lay the cause of it all? How was her godhead
          injured?
What grievance made the queen of heaven so harry a
          man

Renowned for piety, through such toils, such a cycle
          of calamity?   10
Can a divine being be so persevering in anger?
There was a town of old—men from Tyre colonised
          it—
Over against Italy and Tiber mouth, but afar off,
Carthage, rich in resources, fiercely efficient in war-
          fare.
This town, they say, was Juno's favourite dwelling,
          preferred   15
To all lands, even Samos: here were her arms, her
          chariot:
And even from the long-ago time she cherished the
          aim that this
Should be, if fate allowed, the metropolis of all
          nations.
Nevertheless, she had heard a future race was form-
          ing
Of Trojan blood, which one day would topple that
          Tyrian stronghold—   20
A people arrogant in war, born to be everywhere
          rulers
And root up her Libyan empire—so the Destiny-
          Spinners planned.
Juno, afraid of this, . . . tossed all over the sea
The Trojans, the few that the Greeks and relentless
          Achilles had left,
And rode them off from their goal, Latium. Many
          years   25
They were wandering round the seven seas, moved
          on by destiny.
So massive a task it was to found the Roman race.
They were only just out of sight of Sicily, towards
          deep water
Joyfully crowding on sail and driving the foam-flocks
          before them,
When Juno, who under her heart nursed that inveter-
          ate wound,   30
Soliloquised thus:—Shall I give up? own myself
          beaten?
. . . I, who walk in majesty, queen of heaven, Jove's
Sister and consort, I must feud with a single nation
For all these years. Does anyone worship my divinity
After this, or pay my altar a suppliant's homage?   35
   Such were the thoughts milling round in her angry
          heart as the goddess
Came to the storm-cloud country, the womb-land of
          brawling siroccos,
Aeolia. Here in a huge cavern King Aeolus
Keeps curbed and stalled, chained up in durance to
          his own will,
The heaving winds and far-reverberating tempests.   40
Behind the bars they bellow, mightily fretting: the
          mountain is

---

*The Aeneid.*ᴬ Copyright 1952 by C. Day Lewis. Reprinted by permission of the Harold Matson, Co., Inc.
2. **Lavinian.** Lavinium, a town in Latium, was supposedly founded
by Aeneas and named for his wife Lavinia.

16. **Samos,** where stood one of the most splendid temples of Juno.

One immense murmur. Aeolus, aloft on his throne of
    power,
Sceptre in hand, gentles and disciplines their fierce
    spirits.
Otherwise, they'd be bolting off with the earth and
    the ocean
And the deep sky—yes, brushing them all away into
    space.   45
But to guard against this the Father of heaven put
    the winds
In a dark cavern and laid a heap of mountains upon
    them,
And gave them an overlord who was bound by a firm
    contract
To rein them in or give them their head, as he was
    ordered.
Him Juno now petitioned. Here are the words she
    used:—   50
    Aeolus, the king of gods and men has granted
You the rule of the winds, to lull the waves or lift
    them.
A breed I have no love for now sails the Tyrrhene
    sea,
Transporting Troy's defeated gods to Italy.
Lash fury into your winds! Whelm those ships and
    sink them!   55
Flail the crews apart! Litter the sea with their frag-
    ments!
Fourteen nymphs I have—their charms are quite out
    of the common—
Of whom the fairest in form, Deiopea, I'll join
To you in lasting marriage and seal her yours for
    ever,
A reward for this great favour I ask, to live out
    all   60
The years with you, and make you the father of
    handsome children.
    Aeolus answered thus:—
                  O queen, it is for you to
Be fully aware what you ask: my duty is but to obey.
Through you I hold this kingdom, for what it's worth,
    as Jove's   64
Viceroy; you grant the right to sit at the gods' table;
You are the one who makes me grand master of cloud
    and storm.
    Thus he spoke, and pointing his spear at the
    hollow mountain,
Pushed at its flank: and the winds, as it were in a
    solid mass,
Hurl themselves through the gates and sweep the
    land with tornadoes.
They have fallen upon the sea, they are heaving it
    up from its deepest   70
Abysses, the whole sea—East wind, South, Sou'-
    wester
Thick with squalls—and bowling great billows at the
    shore.

There follows a shouting of men, a shrilling of stays
    and halyards.
All of a sudden the storm-clouds are snatching the
    heavens, the daylight
From the eyes of the Trojans; night, black night is
    fallen on the sea.   75
The welkin explodes, the firmament flickers with
    thick-and-fast lightning,
And everything is threatening the instant death of
    men.
At once a mortal chill went through Aeneas and
    sapped him;
He groaned, and stretching out his two hands toward
    the stars,
Uttered these words:—
                Oh, thrice and four times blessèd you
Whose luck it was to fall before your fathers' eyes   81
Under Troy's battlements! . . .
    Even as he cried out thus, a howling gust from the
    North
Hit the front of the sail, and a wave climbed the
    sky.
Oars snapped; then the ship yawed, wallowing
    broadside on   85
To the seas: and then, piled up there, a precipice of
    sea hung.
One vessel was poised on a wave crest; for another
    the waters, collapsing,
Showed sea-bottom in the trough: the tide-race
    boiled with sand.
Three times did the South wind spin them towards an
    ambush of rocks
(Those sea-girt rocks which Italians call by the name
    of "The Altars"),   90
Rocks like a giant spine on the sea. . . .
    Meanwhile Neptune has felt how greatly the sea
    is in turmoil,
Felt the unbridled storm disturbing the water even
Down to the sea-bed, and sorely troubled has broken
    surface;
He gazes forth on the deep with a pacific mien.   95
He sees the fleet of Aeneas all over the main, dis-
    membered,
The Trojans crushed by waves and the sky in
    ribbons about them:
Juno's vindictive stratagems do not escape her
    brother.
He summons the East and the West winds, and . . .
    the insurgent sea was calmed,
The mob of cloud dispersed and the sun restored to
    power. . . .   100
Just as so often it happens, when a crowd collects,
    and violence
Brews up, and the mass mind boils nastily over, and
    the next thing
Firebrands and brickbats are flying (hysteria soon
    finds a missile),

That then, if they see some man whose goodness of
heart and conduct
Have won their respect, they fall silent and stand
still, ready to hear him;   105
And he can change their temper and calm their
thoughts with a speech:
So now the crash of the seas died down, when Nep-
tune gazed forth
Over their face, and the sky cleared, and the Father
of ocean,
Turning his horses, wheeled away on an easy course.
Aeneas' men, worn out, with a last effort, make for
The nearest landing place; somewhere on the coast of
Libya.   111
A spot there is in a deep inlet, a natural harbour
Formed by an island's flanks upon which the swell
from the deepsea
Breaks and dividing runs into the land's recesses.
At either end of the lofty cliffs a peak towers up   115
Formidably to heaven, and under these twin sum-
mits
The bay lies still and sheltered: a curtain of over-
hanging
Woods with their shifting light and shadow forms the
backdrop;
At the seaward foot of the cliffs there's a cave of
stalactites,
Fresh water within, and seats which nature has hewn
from the stone—   120
A home of the nymphs. Here, then, tired ships could
lie, and need
No cable nor the hooking teeth of an anchor to hold
them.
Here, with seven ships mustered, all that was left of
his convoy,
Aeneas now put in: and the Trojans, aching for dry
land,
Tumbled out of their ships onto the sands they
craved so,   125
And laid their limbs, crusted with brine, upon the
shore.
Then first of all Achates struck a spark from flint,
Nursed the spark to a flame on tinder, gave it to feed
on
Dry fuel packed around it and made the flame blaze
up there.
Sick of mischance, the men got ready the gifts and
gear of   130
Ceres, setting themselves to roast on the fire and
grind,
Though tainted it was with the salt water, what
grain they had salvaged.
While this was going forward, Aeneas scaled a
crag
To get an extensive view of the sea. . . .

Ship there was none in view; but on the shore three
stags   135
Caught his eye as they wandered with a whole herd
behind them,
A straggling drove of deer which browsed along the
valley.
Aeneas, where he stood, snatched up the bow and
arrows—
The weapons he had borrowed just now from faithful
Achates—
And aiming first at the leaders of the herd, which
carried their heads high   140
With branching antlers, he laid them low; then shot
at the herd,
And his arrows sent it dodging all over the leafy
woods.
Nor would he stop shooting until triumphantly
He had brought down seven beasts, one for each of
his ships.
Then he returned to the harbour and shared them
among his comrades.   145
And then he shared out the wine which good Acestes
had casked
In Sicily and given them—a generous parting
present,
And spoke these words of comfort to his sad-hearted
friends:—
Comrades, we're well acquainted with evils, then
and now.
Worse than this you have suffered. God will end all
this too.   150
You, who have risked the mad bitch, Scylla, risked
the cliffs
So cavernously resounding, and the stony land of the
Cyclops,
Take heart again, oh, put your dismal fears away!
One day—who knows?—even these will be grand
things to look back on.
Through chance and change, through hosts of dan-
gers, our road still   155
Leads on to Latium: there, destiny offers a home
And peace; there duty tells us to build the second
Troy.
Hold on, and find salvation in the hope of better
things!
Thus spoke Aeneas; and though his heart was sick
with anxiety,
He wore a confident look and kept his troubles to
himself.   160
. . . Jupiter from high heaven
Looked down at the flights of sails on the sea, and
the earth beneath him,
Its shores and its far-flung peoples: so, at the top of
the morning

127. **Achates,** the close friend of Aeneas.

146. **Acestes,** the king of Sicily, who had entertained Aeneas hos-
pitably.

He stood, and presently focussed his gaze on the
    Libyan realm.
Now, as he deeply pondered the troubles there,
    came Venus,   165
Sadder than is her wont, her eyes shining with tears,
And spoke to him:—
              Sir, you govern the affairs of
    gods and men
By law unto eternity, you are terrible in the light-
    ning:
Tell me, what wrong could my Aeneas or his Trojans
Have done you, so unforgivable that, after all these
    deaths,   170
To stop them reaching Italy they are locked out from
    the whole world?
Verily you had promised that hence, as the years
    rolled on,
Troy's renaissance would come, would spring the
    Roman people
And rule as sovereigns absolute over earth and sea.
You promised it. Oh, my father, why have you
    changed your mind?   175
That knowledge once consoled me for the sad fall of
    Troy:
I could balance fate against fate, past ills with luck to
    come.
But still the same ill fortune dogs my disaster-ridden
Heroes. Oh when, great king, will you let their ordeal
    end? . . .
    The begetter of gods and men inclined towards her
    the smiling   180
Countenance which calms the sky and makes fair
    weather,
Gently kissed his daughter's mouth, and began to
    speak:—
    Fear no more, Cytherea. Take comfort, for your
    people's
Destiny is unaltered; you shall behold the
    promised
City walls of Lavinium, and exalt great-hearted
    Aeneas   185
Even to the starry skies. I have not changed my
    mind.
I say it now—for I know these cares constantly gnaw
    you—
And show you further into the secret book of fate:
Aeneas, mightily warring in Italy, shall crush   189
Proud tribes, to establish city walls and a way of life,
Till a third summer has seen him reigning in Latium
And winter thrice passed over his camp in the con-
    quered land.
His son Ascanius, whose surname is now Iulus—
Ilus it was, before the realm of Ilium fell—
Ascanius for his reign shall have full thirty years   195

193. **Ascanius,** the son of Aeneas by his wife Creusa, who was lost at
the fall of Troy.

With all their wheeling months; shall move the
    kingdom from
Lavinium and make Long Alba his sure stronghold.
Here for three hundred years shall rule the dynasty
Of Hector, until a priestess and queen of Trojan
    blood,
With child by Mars, shall presently give birth to twin
    sons.   200
Romulus, then, gay in the coat of the tawny she-
    wolf
Which suckled him, shall succeed to power and
    found the city
Of Mars and with his own name endow the Roman
    nation.
To these I set no bounds, either in space or time;
Unlimited power I give them. Even the spiteful Juno,
Who in her fear now troubles the earth, the sea and
    the sky,   206
Shall think better of this and join me in fostering
The cause of the Romans, the lords of creation, the
    togaed people.
Thus it is written. An age shall come, as the years
    glide by,
When the children of Troy shall enslave the children
    of Agamemnon,   210
Of Diomed and Achilles, and rule in conquered
    Argos.
From the fair seed of Troy there shall be born a
    Caesar—
Julius, his name derived from great Iulus—whose
    empire
Shall reach to the ocean's limits, whose fame shall
    end in the stars.
He shall hold the East in fee; one day, cares ended,
    you shall   215
Receive him into heaven; him also will mortals pray
    to.
Then shall the age of violence be mellowing into
    peace:
Venerable Faith, and the Home, with Romulus and
    Remus,
Shall make the laws; the grim, steel-welded gates of
    War
Be locked; and within, on a heap of armaments, a
    hundred   220
Bronzen knots tying his hands behind him, shall sit
Growling and bloody-mouthed the godless spirit of
    Discord.
    So Jupiter spoke, and sent Mercury down from on
    high
To see that the land and the new-built towers of
    Carthage offered
Asylum to the Trojans, for otherwise might queen
    Dido,   225
Blind to destiny, turn them away. He aerially wafted,
Feathering his wings, and post-haste came down on
    Libyan soil.

Now he performs his mission; at the god's will that
    people
Puts by its haughty temper, the queen at once re-
    sponds to
An intimation of peace and goodwill towards the
    Trojans.   230
True-hearted Aeneas, after a night spent on a tread-
    mill
Of cares, when kindly dawn came, determined to
    reconnoitre
The strange terrain, find out to what land the storm
    had brought them
And who lived there—was it men or only beasts—for
    it looked like
A wilderness, and bring back a full report to his
    friends.   235
He saw that the ships were concealed in a woody
    creek, beneath
The overhang of the cliff, with trees and shifting
    shadows
About them; and then set forth, accompanied by
    Achates
Only, swinging a couple of broad-tipped spears in his
    hand.
There, from the heart of the woodland, his mother
    came to meet him   240
Guised as a maiden in face and dress, with a girl's
    weapons—
A Spartan girl, as it might be. . . .
In huntress wise she had handily slung her bow from
    her shoulder,
And her hair was free to blow in the wind, and she
    went bare-kneed
With the flowing folds of her dress kilted up and
    securely knotted.   245
She spoke first:—

      Hullo there, young men! If you have seen
One of my sisters roving hereabouts or in full cry
After a foaming boar—she carries a slung quiver
And wears a spotted lynx-skin—please tell me where
    she went.

    Thus Venus spoke; and the son of Venus began to
    reply thus:—   250
    No sight or sound have I had of any of your sisters,
O—but what shall I call you, maiden? for your face
    is
Unmortal, and your speech rings not of humankind.
Goddess surely you are. A nymph? The sister of
    Phoebus?
Give luck, whoever you be! Lighten, I pray, our
    ordeal!   255
Tell me in what clime, upon what shores of the world
We are cast up: for, driven here by wind and wave,
We have no clue to the peoples or places of our
    wandering.
Tell this, and we will offer sacrifice at your altar.   259
    Then Venus said:—

Believe me, such titles are not my due:
It is the fashion for Tyrian girls to carry a quiver
And wear like this the high-laced, crimson hunting
    boot.
The kingdom you see is Carthage, the Tyrians, the
    town of Agenor;
But the country around is Libya, no folk to meet in
    war.   264
Dido, who left the city of Tyre to escape her brother,
Rules here—a long and labyrinthine tale of wrong
Is hers, but I will touch on its salient points in order.
Her husband was Sychaeus, a man of great estates
Among the Phoenicians and greatly loved by the ill-
    starred Dido
Whose father had given her in marriage to Sychaeus,
A virgin bride. Now the throne of Tyre was held by
    her brother,   271
Pygmalion, a monster who had no rival in wicked-
    ness.
Maniac evil stepped in. Pygmalion, blinded by love
    for
Gold, godlessly murdered the unsuspecting Sychaeus
In secret before the altar—no pang of compunction
    for her love;   275
And kept the deed dark for a long time, vilely inven-
    tive of fictions
To cheat with hollow hope her pining, loving heart.
But there came, one night as she slept, the phantom
    of her unburied
Husband, weirdly floating its clay-white face up to
    her,
Exposed the atrocious altar, the breast spitted with
    steel,   280
And took the cover off that crime hidden in the
    house.
Then the phantom urged her swiftly to fly the coun-
    try,
And told her where she could find in the earth an old
    treasure, a secret
Hoard of gold and silver to help her on her way.
Dido, in great disquiet, organised her friends for
    escape.   285
They met together, all those who harshly hated the
    tyrant
Or keenly feared him: they seized some ships which
    chanced to be ready
And loaded them with the gold: so was that treasure
    sailed
Out of Pygmalion's grasp: a woman led the exploit.
They came to this spot, where to-day you can behold
    the mighty   290
Battlements and the rising citadel of New Carthage,
And purchased a site, which was named "Bull's
    Hide" after the bargain

263. **Agenor.** Dido was descended from Agenor, a king of Phoenicia.

By which they should get as much land as they could
    enclose with a bull's hide.
But now, tell me who you are, what land you have
    come from, and whither
Your journey leads.
              So Venus questioned him; and Aeneas,
Sighing, drew up his voice as it were from the heart's
    depth:—   296
    Goddess, if I were to tell our tale right through
    from the start
And leisure there was to hear the chronicles of our
    labours,
Evening would close the sky and the day be asleep
    ere I finished.
We from old Troy (if ever the name of Troy has come
    to   300
Your ears) were voyaging, when the weather's caprice
    drove us
Off our course and piled us onto the Libyan shore.
I am true-hearted Aeneas; my fame has been heard
    of in heaven:
I carry my gods of Home which I rescued from the
    enemy.
I go to my own land, Italy, where Jove began our
    line.   305
With twenty ships I embarked on the Phrygian sea,
    my mother,
A goddess, showing the way, I following destiny's
    bidding:
But seven ships now are left us, battered by wind and
    wave.
I, a stranger and needy, now roam the Libyan desert,
Driven from Europe and Asia.
                          Venus could bear no longer
To hear him grieve, and so she broke in on his an-
    guish, saying:—   311
    Whoever you are, you cannot breathe and live, I
    am sure,
Hateful to heaven, for soon you'll have reached the
    Tyrian city.
Do but fare on, press on from here to the queen's
    palace.
Unless what my parents taught me of signs and
    omens is meaningless,   315
I can declare your friends rallied to you, your miss-
    ing
Ships brought back to haven here by a shift of the
    wind. . . .
    She spoke. She turned away; and as she turned,
    her neck
Glowed to a rose-flush, her crown of ambrosial hair
    breathed out
A heavenly fragrance, her robe flowed down, down
    to her feet,   320
And in gait she was all a goddess. Aeneas recognised
His mother, and as she passed from him, sent these
    words in her wake:—

Must you too be cruel? Must you make game of
    your son
With shapes of sheer illusion? Oh, why may we not
    join   324
Hand to hand, or ever converse straightforwardly?
    Thus he reproached her, and turned his steps
    toward the battlements.
But Venus folded them as they went in an opaque
    mist,
Magically poured round them an ample cloak of
    cloud,
Lest any should spy or encounter Aeneas and
    Achates,
Attempt to delay them or demand to know their
    business. . . .   330
    Meanwhile the two pressed on apace, where the
    track pointed.
And now they were climbing a hill whose massive
    bulk looms over
The city and commands a prospect of soaring tow-
    ers.
Aeneas marvels at great buildings, where once were
    shanties,
Marvels at city gates and the din of the paved
    streets. . . .   335
"Ah, fortunate you are, whose town is already build-
    ing!"
Aeneas said, and gazed up at the city's heights.
Then, in his cloak of darkness he went—a miraculous
    thing—
Into their midst and joined the crowds, but none
    perceived him.
    There was a grove, most genial its shade, at the
    city centre,   340
Just where the Carthaginians, after their rough
    passage,
First dug and found the sign which royal Juno had
    promised—
The skull of a spirited horse; it was a sign that hence-
    forth
Their nation would thrive in wealth and war through-
    out the ages.
Dido was building here, in Juno's honour, a huge 345
Temple, made rich by offerings and the indwelling
    presence of Juno:
Bronze was its threshold, approached by a flight of
    steps; the door-posts
Were braced with bronze, and the door with its
    grinding hinges was bronze.
This grove had seen Dido's fear allayed by a chance
    of renewal
For the first time; and here Aeneas first dared to hope
    for   350
Salvation and believe that at last his luck was turn-
    ing.
For, while he awaited the queen and his eyes roved
    over the detail

Of that immense facade, amazed by the town's good
    fortune,
Admiring the skill of the rival craftsmen, the scope of
    their work,
He noticed a series of frescoes depicting the Trojan
    war,   355
Whose fame had already gone round the world; the
    sons of Atreus
Were there, and Priam, Achilles too, hostile to both.
Aeneas stood; wept:—
            Oh, Achates, is there anywhere,
Any place left on earth unhaunted by our sorrows?
Look!—Priam. Here too we find virtue somehow
    rewarded,   360
Tears in the nature of things, hearts touched by
    human transience.
Then cast off fear; the fame of our deeds will ensure
    your welfare.
    He spoke, and fed his soul on those insubstantial
    figures,
Heavily sighing, the large tears rivering down his
    cheeks. . . .
    Now while Aeneas viewed with wonder all these
    scenes,   365
And stood at gaze, rooted in a deep trance of atten-
    tion,
There came in royal state to the temple, a crowd of
    courtiers
Attending her, queen Dido, most beautiful to
    see. . . .
So Dido was, even so she went her radiant way
Through the crowds, eager to forward the work and
    growth of her realm.   370
Now, at the holy doors, under the temple porch,
Hedged by the spears of her guard, she throned
    herself on high;
Gave laws and ordinances, appointed the various
    tasks
In equitable proportions or else by drawing lots.
Just then, all of a sudden, Aeneas saw approaching
Amid the multitude Antheus, Sergestus, valiant
Cloanthus and other Trojans, whom the black hurri-
    cane
Had sundered at sea and driven afar to different
    beaches.
He and Achates together were thrilled through, were
    dumbfounded
With anxious joy: they eagerly yearned to join hands
    with their friends,   380
But the mystery of the whole affair disquieted
    them.
So they keep dark, and peering out from their womb
    of cloud,
Speculate what befell these friends, where their ships
    are beached,
Why they are here: for spokesmen from each of the
    ships were coming

To sue the queen's favour, and shouting aloud as
    they neared the temple.   385
    When they had entered and Dido had granted to
    them an audience,
The eldest, Ilioneus, began in collected tones:—
    O queen, who, under God, have founded a new
    city
And curbed the arrogance of proud clans with your
    justice,
We hapless Trojans, wanderers over a world of
    seas,   390
Implore you, stop your people from wickedly burning
    our ships.
God-fearing men we are. Incline your heart to spare
    us. . . .
Aeneas was our king: never was a man more just,
More duteous of heart, more adept in warlike arts,
    than he.
If destiny has preserved him, if still he breathes the
    air   395
Of day, and is not sleeping in death's unwelcome
    shade,
We need not fear; and you should have no cause to
    regret
That you were prompt to aid us. . . .
    Ilioneus stopped speaking. A shout of assent rose
    from
The Trojans all. . . .   400
Then Dido, with her eyes downcast, addressed them
    briefly:—
    Trojans, put fear away from your hearts and forget
    your troubles!
Mine's a hard task, with a young country: that's why
    I have to
Do such things, to guard my frontiers everywhere.
Who has not heard of Troy and the men of Aeneas—
    their manly   405
Virtues, and all that famous conflagration of
    war? . . .
I will give you an escort there and what provision
    you need.
Or would you like to share my kingdom, on equal
    terms?
This city I am building—it's yours: draw up your
    ships, then;
There shall be no preference, I say, between you and
    us.   410
    Oh, if only your king, Aeneas himself, could come
    here,
Fetched by the same storm. Well, I will send couriers
    abroad
With orders to comb the furthest corners of Libya, in
    case
He is wandering somewhere, in woods or towns, a
    castaway. . . .
    These words were hardly spoken, when in a flash
    the cloud-cloak   415

They wore was shredded and purged away into pure
air.
Aeneas was standing there in an aura of brilliant
light,
Godlike of face and figure: for Venus herself had
breathed
Beauty upon his head and the roseate sheen of youth
on 419
His manhood and a gallant light into his eyes;
As an artist's hand adds grace to the ivory he works
on,
As silver or marble when they're plated with yellow
gold.
So then Aeneas addressed the queen, and startling
them all
At once began:—
     I am here, before you, the one you look for,
Trojan Aeneas, saved from the Libyan sea. 425
O lady, you alone have pitied the tragic ordeal
Of Troy, and now you offer to share your home and
city
With us, the remnant of Troy—men utterly spent by
Every disaster on land and sea, deprived of every-
thing.
Dido, we have not the means to repay your goodness,
nor have 430
Any of our kin, wherever they are, scattered over the
world.
If angels there be who look after the good, if indeed
just dealing
And minds informed with the right mean anything to
heaven,
May God reward you as you deserve! What happy
age,
What great parentage was it gave life to the like of
you? 435
So long as rivers run to the sea, and shadows wheel
round
The hollows of the hills, and star-flocks browse in the
sky,
Your name, your fame, your glory shall perish not
from the land
Wherever I am summoned to go.
                He spoke: he stretched out
His right hand to Ilioneus, his friend, and his left to
Serestus, 440
Then to others, brave Gyas and brave Cloanthus.
    Sidonian Dido, amazed first by the man's appear-
ance
Then by the magnitude of his downfall, thus ad-
dressed him:—
   O goddess-born, what doom is pursuing you
through so many
Hazards? What violent fate casts you on this harsh
coast? 445
Are *you* the famed Aeneas, whom gentle Venus bore
To Trojan Anchises by the waters of Simois? . . .

So, gentlemen, do not hesitate to come under my
roof.
I too have gone through much; like you, have been
roughly handled
By fortune; but now at last it has willed me to settle
here. 450
Being acquainted with grief, I am learning to help
the unlucky.
   She spoke: she led Aeneas into the royal palace,
And ordered a thanksgiving service to be held in the
gods' temples.
Besides, she sent to his companions on the shore
Twenty bulls, a hundred head of bristle-backed
swine, 455
A hundred fatted lambs together with their ewes,
And the good cheer of the Wine-god.
Within, the palace was being arrayed in all the glitter
Of regal luxury, and a banquet being made ready:
Richly embroidered the hangings of princely purple;
a service 460
Of solid silver on the tables; and golden vessels
chased
With the legends of family history—a long lineage of
glory
Traced through many heroes right from its earliest
source.
   Aeneas, whose love for his son would not allow a
moment's 464
Delay, now sent Achates running down to the ships,
Bade him tell Ascanius the news and return with
him,
Aeneas being always thoughtful for his dear son,
Ascanius.
They were to bring back also some gifts, which had
been salvaged
From Troy's ruins—a robe of stiff golden brocade
And a veil with a pattern of yellow acanthus round its
border; 470
Argive Helen had worn them once, had brought
them with her
Out of Mycenae when she eloped to Troy for that
lawless
Marriage; they were a marvellous gift from her
mother, Leda.
In addition to these, a sceptre which Ilione, the eldest
Daughter of Priam, had carried once, a pearl neck-
lace, 475
And a double coronet of gold and precious stones.
With this commission Achates hurried down to the
ships.
   But Venus was meditating a new and artful
scheme,
Which was to substitute, for little Ascanius, Cupid
Changed into his likeness, and let Cupid inflame 480
The queen with those gifts and set a match to her
very marrow:
For Venus felt uneasy about her hospitality

And Tyrian equivocation; the thought of Juno irked
    her,
Recurring at nightfall. So she talks to her winged
    Cupid:—
   My son, my only strength, sole agent of my pow-
     ers,   485
My son, who laugh at the bolts of giant-killing Jove,
To you I come for a favour, petitioning your god-
    head.
Your own brother, Aeneas, is being tossed about
From shore to shore, a victim of Juno's brutal resent-
    ment—
This you know well and often have shared my grief
    at it.   490
Now Carthaginian Dido clings to him and delays him
With flattery. I fear the results of kindness inspired
    by
Juno: she'll not give up, when so much hinges on this.
Her I mean to forestall by rusefully taking the
    queen's heart
And throwing a cordon of fire round it: no deity   495
May swerve her if she is mine, possessed by love for
    Aeneas.
Now listen to my plan, how you can do this thing.
Sent for by his dear father, the royal child, the apple
Of my own eye, makes ready to go to Dido's city,
With gifts for her—things that escaped the sea and
    the blaze of Troy: 500
Him I shall hide away, drugged with sleep, in one of
My holy places, on high Cythera or on Idalium,
Lest he should figure out my plot or stumble upon it.
Do you impersonate him, for the space of one night
    only;   504
A boy yourself, put on that boy's familiar features,
So that, when Dido takes you joyfully into her lap
There at the banquet table with the wine passing
    round,
And when she hugs you close and pours sweet kisses
    upon you,
Then you may secretly fire her heart and inject your
    magic.
   Cupid obeyed the words of his dear mother: he
    took off   510
His wings, and walked rejoicing in the gait of young
    Ascanius.
But Venus showered a dew of peaceful sleep on the
    limbs of
Ascanius, snuggled him in her breast, and divinely
    bore him
Up to Idalian groves, where the tender marjoram
    puts him
To bed in a cradle of flowers and shade and entranc-
    ing fragrance.   515
And now, as his mother had bade him, Cupid was on
    his way
Carrying the kingly gifts and delighted to walk with
    Achates.

When he arrived, the queen had taken her place in
    the midst
And reclined on her golden couch beneath a mag-
    nificent awning.   519
Aeneas and his Trojan followers now assembled,
Disposed themselves upon the purple-upholstered
    couches.
Manservants brought round water to wash their
    hands, and offered
Bread in baskets, and gave out napkins of fine wool.
Within there were fifty maids, whose task it was by
    rote
To keep up the kitchen fire and a good supply of
    victuals: 525
A hundred maids and a hundred manservants, all of
    the same age,
Were there to load the banqueting tables and set
    the wine cups.
Carthaginians too, great numbers of them, were met
In the festive hall, invited to sit at the painted
    couches.
They admire the gifts of Aeneas, admire the boy
    Ascanius—   530
Or rather the radiant looks and plausible speech of
    Cupid—
Admire the robe and the veil with its pattern of
    yellow acanthus.
But above all poor Dido, fated to be destroyed,
Can't slake her soul with gazing, and in the gazing
    grows
Ever more ardent, moved alike by the boy and the
    gifts.   535
Cupid, when he had put his arms round Aeneas' neck
And been embraced, appeasing the love of his
    feigned father,
Went to the queen. With her eyes, with all her heart
    she devoured him,
Fondled him oft in her bosom—poor Dido, little she
    knew
The strength of him who was settling insidiously
    there. But Cupid,   540
Obeying his mother, began to efface little by little
The memory of Sychaeus from Dido's mind and
    tempt her
Disused, long-slumbering heart to awake to a living
    love.
   When first there was a lull in the feast, and a
    course was removed,
Great bowls of wine were brought to the tables and
    garlanded.   545
A rumble of talk went up, the wide hall surged with
    voices:
The chandeliers that hung from the gold-fretted
    ceiling
Were lit, and cressets of torches subdued the night
    with their flames.
. . . Dido poured a libation of wine on the table,

And after the toast was first to touch her lips to the
goblet;   550
Then passed it to Bitias with a challenge, who eager-
ly drained
The foaming golden cup and swilled the wine down
without heeltaps.
Next, other chieftains drank. Then the long-haired
Iopas,
A pupil of Atlas, made the hall hum with his golden
zither:
He sang of the travelling moon and the sun's mani-
fold labours;   555
. . . ill-starred Dido talked on into the small hours,
Talked over many things as she drank deep of love,
Asking over and over again about Priam and Hector,
Asking about the armour the son of Aurora had come
in,
The points of Diomed's horses and the stature of
great Achilles.   560
    But no, dear guest, tell us, please tell us from the
beginning
The story of Greek stratagems, and how your comrades fell,
And your own wanderings; for now is the seventh
summer
That over land and sea you have been widely wandering.

BOOK II

    All fell silent now, and their faces were all atten-
tion
When from his place of honour Aeneas began to
speak:—
    . . . If you want so much to know what happened
to us
And hear in brief a recital of Troy's last agony,
Although the memory makes me shudder, and shrink
from its sadness,   5
I will attempt it.
                        Broken in war and foiled by fate,
With so many years already slipping away, the Greek
staff
Constructed a horse, employing the craft of the
goddess Athene—
It was high as a hill, and its ribs were made from
planks of pinewood—
To pay for their safe return to Greece, they pretended:
this rumour   10
Got round. But, choosing warriors by lot, they
secretly
Put them in on the blind side of the horse, until its
vast
And cavernous belly was crammed with a party of
armed men.
    In sight of Troy there's an island, a well-known
island, Tenedos—

Rich and powerful it was, while Priam's empire
stood;   15
Now, little but a bay, a roadstead unsafe for ship-
ping.
Thither the Greeks sailed out, and hid on its desolate
coast.
This was evacuation, we thought—they had sailed
for Greece.
So all Troy threw off the chains of her long anguish.
We opened the gates, we enjoyed visiting the Greek
camp,   20
Viewing the derelict positions on the abandoned
beaches.
Here the Dolopes camped; there, ferocious Achilles:
Here was beached their navy, and here the battle
raged.
Some of us gaped at the gift—so deadly—the Greeks
had left for
Minerva, and its stupendous bulk. Thymoetes first, 25
Either from treachery or because Troy's fate now was
sealed,
Urged that the horse be brought through the walls
and placed in our citadel.
But Capys and all those of sounder views recom-
mended
Hurling it into the sea or setting fire to it, as some
Booby-trap of the Greeks and not to be trusted—or
else   30
Boring holes in its belly to see what might be inside
it.
So the rank and file were violently torn between
contraries.
Then out in front of them all, hundreds straggling
behind him,
In a great temper Laocoon came tearing down from
the citadel,   34
Crying from far:—
                        Citizens, are you all stark mad?
Do you really believe our foes are gone? Do you
imagine
Any Greek gift is guileless? Is that your idea of
Ulysses?
This thing of wood conceals Greek soldiers, or else it
is
A mechanism designed against our walls—to pry into
Our homes and to bear down on the city; sure, some
trick   40
Is there. No, you must never feel safe with the horse,
Trojans.
Whatever it is, I distrust the Greeks, even when they
are generous.
    He spoke: he put forth his strength, and spun his
huge great spear
At the flank of the monster, right into its belly's
rounded frame.
The spear stuck quivering; the hollow womb of the
creature   45

Grunted at the concussion and rumbled hollowly.
If destiny, if our own will had not been so contrary,
Laocoon would have made us rip open that cache of
  Greek troops—
There'd still be a Troy—O topless towers, you'd be
  standing now!
    But listen, just at this moment some Trojan shep-
    herds were noisily   50
Dragging a young man, handcuffed, into our king's
  presence.
The fellow had quite deliberately put himself in their
  path. . . .
Eager to stare at him, the youth of Troy came mob-
  bing
All round the man, and vied in jeering at him for
  being captured.
Now hear how the Greeks tricked us; learn from one
  case of their wickedness   55
What every Greek is like.
Well then, he came to a halt—stared at, worried,
  unarmed—
Stood there, and ran his eyes round the Trojan
  spectators, and spoke:—
    O god! Is there now a single land or sea to accept
    me?
What awaits me now at the latter end? Oh, it is
  hopeless!   60
I have no foothold at all with the Greeks, and now
  the Trojans
Are my vindictive foes and they will have my blood.
    His pitiable tones produced a revulsion of feeling;
    our violence
Was checked: we encouraged him to tell us who he
  was,
What he could say for himself, and what he relied on
  in letting   65
Himself be taken. Finally, he laid aside fear, and
  spoke:—
    Sir, I will tell you all, of course, come what come
    may,
And tell you the whole truth. I will not deny that I
  am a Greek;
This first: if Fortune has cast Sinon for tragedy,
She shall not wantonly shape me into a liar as
  well. . . .   70
    Often, sick of the way the war dragged on, the
    Greeks
Longed to withdraw from Troy, to sail home and be
  shut of fighting.
If only they'd done it! But always a stormy, vicious
  mood
Of the sea intervened and the South wind frightened
  them off sailing.
Especially when that horse, that fabric of maple,
  already   75
Was standing here, did the whole sky reverberate
  with storm clouds.

In this quandary, we sent Eurypylus to enquire
Of Phoebus' oracle; who brought back this message
  of gloom from the shrine:—
    "With human sacrifice, O Greeks, with a young girl's
    blood
Did you appease the winds when first you sailed to
  Troy: 80
With human blood, with a Greek life, you must make
  sacrifice
If you're to get safe home." The words went round:
  our people's
Spirits were paralysed; an icy shuddering coursed
  through
Their bones—whom would fate fix on? whom does
  Apollo require?
At this stage Ulysses made a great scene, pulling the
  seer   85
Calchas into our midst, pestering him to tell us
The god's will. Yes, and already many surmised that I
  was
That heartless schemer's victim, and silently saw
  what was coming.
For ten days Calchas was dumb, stayed in retreat,
  and would not
Name or commit to death anyone by his utter-
  ance.   90
But at long last, as Ulysses got ever more importu-
  nate,
According to plan he broke silence and smelt me out
  for the altar.
They all approved: what each had feared for himself,
  was easy
To tolerate when it became the death of this one poor
  scapegoat.
And now the hideous day was here; the last rites
  made ready   95
For me—the salted meal, the headband to go round
  my temples.
I dodged away then from death, I confess it; I broke
  prison,
And lay all night concealed in the mud of a lake,
  among reeds,
Giving them time to sail, on the chance that indeed
  they would sail.
No more hope have I now of seeing the old country,
  seeing   100
My little sons or the father I yearn for: on them the
  Greeks
Maybe will exact reprisals because of my escape
And make them pay, poor things, with their life for
  what I have done.
Yet by the gods I beg you, by the high powers that
  are witness
To Truth, by Fidelity—if anywhere upon earth   105
She still can be found inviolate—I beg you to pity so
  dreadful
An ordeal, pity one who has too much to bear.

We gave him his life for those tears: they even aroused our compassion.

Priam himself at once ordered the handcuffs, the cramping

Chains to be struck off the fellow, and spoke him a friendly word:— 110

Whoever you are, from now on give up the Greeks, you are clear of them:

Be one of us, and answer these questions of mine truthfully.

Why did they build this huge monster of a horse? Who advised it?

Is their object religious? or was it to be some engine of war?

So Priam spoke. Sinon, well up in the Greek art of trickery, 115

Raised to heaven his hands, free of the fetters, crying:—

All the hope of the Greeks, their assurance in starting the war,

Was sustained by the backing of Pallas Athene. But when the godless

Diomed and that master-craftsman of crime, Ulysses,

Set out to steal Troy's luck, Athene's image, away from 120

Her holy place, massacred the sentries high on the citadel,

Snatched up the sacred image, and dared to lay their bloodstained

Hands on her virginal headband—from that day forth, the hopes

Of the Greeks were caught in an undertow and carried away, their strength

Was shattered, for the goddess hardened her heart against them. 125

Unmistakeable were the signs of anger she gave us.

The image was hardly set up in our camp, when its eyes glared

Balefully glittering fire, salt sweat broke out all over it,

And thrice—oh, supernatural—did the statue, untouched, dart forth

From her base, the spear and shield she carried quivering. 130

Straightaway, Calchas pronounced we must dare the sea and be gone,

For Troy would never now be destroyed by Greek weapons

Unless we sailed back home to fetch new luck, and returned with

The gods' blessing as when we first sailed here in our fine ships.

So at this moment they're running free towards Mycenae 135

To get fresh force and the gods on their side again: but they'll be back

Unexpectedly over the sea. So Calchas interprets the omens.

Thus advised, they built this horse to dispel the curse of

Guilt for stealing Athene's image and wounding her godhead.

But Calchas bade them build the horse of enormous size 140

With strong oak planks, a real sky-scraping monster, so that

It could not get through your gates or be towed within the walls,

And thus become your guardian, serving the old cult.

For if your hands had outraged this offering to Minerva,

It would be quite disastrous (may the omen sooner recoil 145

On its own prophet!) for Priam's rule and for the Trojans:

But if your hands should have got the horse up into the city,

Then would you carry Asia in war right up to the Grecian

Strongholds; such is the fate that is reserved for our children.

Such was the artful, treacherous perjury Sinon used 150

To impose on us. We were tricked by cunning and crocodile tears—

We whom neither Diomed nor Larissaean Achilles

Could conquer, not in ten years, not with a thousand warships.

Just then another event, the most alarming yet,

Befell us wretches, muddling still further our hooded minds. 155

Laocoon, whom we'd elected by lot as Neptune's priest,

Was sacrificing a great bull at the official altar,

When over the tranquil deep, from Tenedos, we saw—

Telling it makes me shudder—twin snakes with immense coils

Thrusting the sea and together streaking towards the shore: 160

Rampant they were among the waves, their blood-red crests

Reared up over the water; the rest of them slithered along

The surface, coil after coil sinuously trailing behind them.

We heard a hiss of salt spray. Next, they were on dry land,

In the same field—a glare and blaze of bloodshot eyes, 165

Tongues flickering like flame from their mouths, and the mouths hissing.

Our blood drained away at the sight; we broke and
    ran. The serpents
Went straight for Laocoon. First, each snake knotted
    itself
Round the body of one of Laocoon's small sons,
    hugging him tight
In its coils, and cropped the piteous flesh with its
    fangs. Next thing,   170
They fastened upon Laocoon, as he hurried, weapon
    in hand,
To help the boys, and lashed him up in their giant
    whorls.
With a double grip round his waist and his neck, the
    scaly creatures
Embrace him, their heads and throats powerfully
    poised above him.
All the while his hands were struggling to break their
    knots,   175
His priestly headband is spattered with blood and
    pitchy venom;
All the while, his appalling cries go up to heaven—
A bellowing, such as you hear when a wounded bull
    escapes from
The altar, after it's shrugged off an ill-aimed blow at
    its neck.
But now the twin monsters are gliding away and
    escaping towards   180
The shrine of relentless Minerva, high up on our
    citadel,
Disappearing behind the round of the goddess'
    shield, at her feet there.
Then, my god! a strange panic crept into our people's
    fluttering
Hearts: they argued Laocoon had got what he de-
    served
For the crime, the sacrilege of throwing his spear at
    the wooden   185
Horse and so profaning its holiness with the
    stroke. . . .
We cut into our walls, laid open the heart of the
    city.
Everyone set about the task: we inserted rollers
Under its hooves, put hawsers of hemp around its
    neck,
And strained. The disastrous engine was jockeyed
    over our walls,   190
An army in its womb. Boys and unmarried maidens
Escorted it, singing psalms, joyfully gripping the
    traces.
The menace mounts, comes trundling into the city
    centre.
O, my country! O Ilium, home of the gods! O Troy
    town,
Famous through war! Four times the monster
    stopped, just where the entrance   195
Was, and every time the accoutrements clanged in its
    belly.

Yet we persevered, with never a thought—we were
    madly blind—
Until we had lodged the ominous thing in our holy
    place.
Then, to cap all, Cassandra opened her mouth for
    prophecy—
She whom her god had doomed to be never believed
    by the Trojans.   200
But we poor fools, whose very last day it was, fes-
    tooned
The shrines of the gods with holiday foliage all over
    the city.
    So now the sky rolled round, and night raced up
    from the ocean
Voluminously shrouding the earth and heaven's vault
And the villainous scheme of the Greeks. Not a sound
    from the Trojans, supine   205
Along the walls, tired out, in the embrace of sleep.
And now the main Greek army was moving from
    Tenedos
In fleet formation, under the favouring silences
Of a quiet moon, towards the coast they knew so
    well.
Their leading galley had signalled with flame: Sinon,
    protected   210
By fate's injustice, stealthily unlocked the wooden
    horse
And let the Greeks out from its belly. The horse
    disgorged, the men
Burst revelling forth from its hollow flank into the
    fresh air—
Thessander and Sthenelus in the lead, with Ulysses
    the terrible,
Sliding down a rope they had lowered—Acamas,
    Thoas,   215
Neoptolemus son of Peleus, Machaon and Mene-
    laus,
And Epeus—the man who had actually built the
    clever contraption.
They broke out over a city drowned in drunken
    sleep;
They killed the sentries and then threw open the
    gates, admitting
Their main body, and joined in the pre-arranged plan
    of attack.   220
    It was the hour when worn-out men begin to get
Some rest, and by god's grace genial sleep steals over
    them.
I dreamt, I seemed to behold our Hector standing
    before me,
Most woebegone and shedding great tears, just as
    he'd looked once
In death, after being dragged by the chariot, black
    with the dirt   225

200. **god had doomed.** Apollo condemned the prophetess for spurning
his love.

And blood, his swollen feet pierced where the thongs
    had been threaded. . . .
He . . . spoke out:—
  Goddess-born, you must go, you must save your-
    self from these flames.
The enemy's within the gates. Troy's tower is falling,
    falling.
You owe no more to your country or Priam: if strong
    right hands   230
Could save our town, this hand of mine would have
    saved it long ago.
Her holy things, her home-gods Troy commends to
    your keeping:
Take these as partners in your fate, for these search
    out
The walls you are destined to build after long roam-
    ing the seaways.
  He spoke, he picked up the holy headbands, the
    puissant Vesta   235
And her undying fire from out the temple sanctu-
    ary.
  Meantime, Troy was shaken through and through
    by her last pangs—
Yes, more and more, although the house of my father,
    Anchises,
Lay far back from the street, detached, and screened
    by trees,
The sounds of death came clearly, the battle alarum
    swelled.   240
I shook myself out of sleep, and clambering onto the
    ridge
Of the roof, I stood up there, on the *qui vive*,
    listening.
You know how it is when southerly gales are fanning
    a fire through
A cornfield, or when a torrent in spate with mountain
    water
Smears flat the fields, flattens the crops which the
    oxen have worked for,   245
Drags forests down in its course—how then a shep-
    herd, perched on
A rock, hearing the noise, is bemused and quite at a
    loss.
Now what I saw in my dream came true, and the
    Greeks' treachery
Was plain to behold. . . .
Everywhere rose the shouting of men, the braying of
    trumpets.   250
Madly I snatch up my arms, beyond thinking how
    best to employ them;
Only I'm wild to rally some fighters and counter-
    attack
To relieve the citadel: blind rage and desperation
Drive me; one thought comes—that death in battle is
    a fine thing. . . .
That night!—what words can render its deaths and
    its disaster?   255

What tears can rise to the level of all that was
    suffered then?
An ancient city is falling, after long years of power:
So many motionless bodies prostrated everywhere
Along the streets, in the houses, on the gods' holy
    thresholds.
Not the Trojans alone paid their account in blood: 260
There were times when courage returned even
    though we knew we were beaten,
And then the conquering Greeks fell. All over the
    town you saw
Heart-rending agony, panic, and every shape of
    death.
. . . But soon myself,
Iphitus and Pelias were drawn away—Iphitus   265
Being old, and Pelias slowed down by a wound
    Ulysses had given him—
Urgently summoned by war-cries we heard from the
    palace of Priam.
Here we beheld so tremendous a struggle as made it
    seem that
Nowhere else in the city could men be fighting and
    dying—   269
A bitter battle, the Greeks trying to scale the walls
And ramming a compact wedge of shields at the door
    they assaulted.
They advance ladders to the walls; hard by the very
    doorposts
They climb the rungs, with left hands holding their
    shields above them
To ward off missiles, and grasping the battlements
    with their right hands.
The Trojans for their part are stripping the turrets
    and rooftops,   275
Ready, since now the end is in sight, to use the
    material
For missiles, to put up a stern defence though death
    is upon them:
Yes, they throw down even the gilded beams, the
    pride of
Their ancestors; while others cluster to guard the
    doors
Below with a thick-set hedge of naked swords. Our
    courage   280
Rekindled now. We would seek to succour the king's
    palace,
Reinforce the defenders and lend our strength to the
    conquered.
  There was a door, a secret entrance by which you
    went
From one block to another, a postern out of the way
Behind the palace: by this, while our empire stood,
    Andromache—   285
Poor soul—would often come unattended to visit her
    husband's
Parents, bringing her child, Astyanax, to his grand-
    sire.

Using this door, I got out onto the rooftop whence
The luckless Trojans were raining missiles, all to no
    purpose.
A tower stood over the sheer of the wall, its apex
    soaring   290
Skyward: this tower commanded a long-familiar
    prospect
Across Troyland to the Greek ships and the Achaean
    lines.
This we attacked with crowbars all round, where the
    weak joints of
Its flooring offered a purchase, prised it off from its
    deep bed
And pushed hard at it: the tower tottered and fell
    full length   295
With a sudden crash, bursting all over the massed
    attackers.
But still, others came on; still it rained spears and
    arrows
And stones and every missile unceasingly . . .
    Right on the very threshold of the entrance hall
    was Pyrrhus
In all his insolent glory, aglitter with bronze accoutre-
    ments.   300
So a snake comes out, full fed on malignant herbs—a
    snake
Which winter had kept underground sullenly brew-
    ing its poison,
But now it has sloughed its old skin, is young again
    and glistening;
It coils along on its slithering belly, and lifts to the
    sunlight
Its vertical throat and flickers a tongue like forked
    lightning. . . .   305
Pyrrhus himself, in the lead, seized an axe, and
    battering the stout door
Smashed through it, and wrenched it away from its
    hinges, though it was strengthened
With bronze: now he had hewed out a panel, and
    made a hole
In the tough wood, opening up a gap the size of a
    window.
Through this they are able to see the interior, the
    long gallery;   310
The private rooms of Priam and Troy's old kings are
    exposed,
And they see the armed defenders packing the
    doorway within.
    Inside the palace, all was confusion, groans, agony.
The echoing halls resounded through and through
    with the keening
Of women, whose wails and shrieks beat at the golden
    stars.   315
Mothers, distracted with fear, were wandering about

    the palace,
Clinging tight to its doorposts and kissing them
    goodbye.
Pyrrhus attacks, with his father's *élan*: neither the
    bolts
Nor the guards have the strength to withstand it:
    stroke upon stroke, a ram
Weakens the door, till it's torn away from its hinges
    and falls in.   320
Brute force has made a breach; the Greeks go storm-
    ing through,
Massacre those in their way, and the place overflows
    with soldiery.
More violent it was than when, banks broken, a
    foaming river
Pours through: the dykes have gone down to the
    thrust of the water, and now
In a mass it raves forth over the fields, swirling the
    herds and   325
Their shippons across the plain. I had to watch
    Pyrrhus crazed with
Blood-lust, and the brothers Atrides, there on the
    threshold,
Hecuba with her hundred princesses, and Priam
    sullying
All over with blood the altar whose fire he had conse-
    crated.
Those fifty bridal rooms, that promised a rich pos-
    terity—   330
Fallen flat were their doors, proudly adorned with
    eastern
Gold and with spoils. Wherever there was no fire, the
    Greeks were.
    I daresay you are wondering what happened to
    Priam then.
Once he had seen how the captured city was faring,
    seen
His doors were hacked away and the enemy deep in
    the palace,   335
Priam, though tremulous with old age, donned the
    armour
He had not worn for years—a pathetic gesture—
    strapped on
His useless sword, and was moving deathwards
    against the foe.
In the central court, beneath the uncovered sweep of
    the sky,
Stood a massive altar, and near it a very old laurel
    tree   340
Leaned over the altar, enfolding the home-gods with
    its shade.
Here Hecuba and her daughters, like a flock of doves
    dashed down
By a black storm, were sitting huddled about the
    altars
That would not protect them, and clasping the
    images of the gods.

Now, when she saw Priam dressed up in his youthful
    armour,   345
She cried:—
        Oh, my poor husband, what fatal inten-
    tion has made you
Take up arms like this? Where are you running? Our
    present
Predicament is beyond such aid. Weapons won't save
    us,
Nor would they save us even if my own Hector was
    here now.
Please come back, over here: this altar shall guard us
    all,   350
Or else we will die together.
    This did she say, and taking
The old king to her, made him sit down in sanctuary.
    But picture it, Priam's son, Polites, had just avoid-
    ed
A death-blow from Pyrrhus, and wounded was
    running the enemy gauntlet,   355
Running away down the long colonnades and across
    the great hall
Alone. Pyrrhus hotly pursued him, always about to
    strike,
Each moment seeming to have him, so close did the
    spearpoint come.
Just when Polites emerged before his parents' eyes,
He fell, and his life ebbed out in a deep river of
    blood.   360
Priam, though death now ringed him round, could
    not be passive,
Could not refrain from uttering his indignation. He
    cried:—
    Hear me, you criminal! If there is any justice in
    heaven,
Any eye for such things, may the gods pay you the
    due reward
And unstintingly show their gratitude for this most
    monstrous crime   365
You have committed—making me witness my son's
    death,
Fouling a father's eyes like this with the sight of
    murder!
You are poles apart from Achilles—your father, you
    lyingly claim.
He treated me differently far, though I was his foe;
    he respected
A suppliant's rights, gave up the bloodless remains of
    Hector   370
For burial, and gave me safe conduct back to my
    city.
    So saying, the old man flung his weapon, but
    harmlessly—
No strength behind it: a clang when the shield of
    Pyrrhus parried it,
And then the spear was dangling impotently from its
    centre.

Pyrrhus replied:—
        All right, you shall go and carry
    a message   375
To my father Achilles. Remember to tell him how
    soft a milksop
His son has become, and what shocking deeds he has
    committed.
Now die!
    Even as he spoke, he dragged the old man,
    trembling,
And sliding in the pool of his son's blood, right to the
    altar;
Twined Priam's hair in his left hand, raised with his
    right the flashing   380
Sword, and sank it up to the hilt between his ribs.
Such was Priam's end, the close decreed by des-
    tiny—
That in his dying hour he should see Troy blazing,
    falling—
His Troy which boasted once such a wealth of lands
    and subjects,
The mistress of Asia once. A great trunk lies on the
    shore,   385
A head torn from the shoulders, a body without a
    name.
    Then first the full horror of it all was borne in upon
    me. I stood
In a daze: the picture of my dear father came to
    mind,
As I watched king Priam, a man of the same age,
    cruelly wounded,
Gasping his life away; I pictured my Creusa   390
Deserted, my home pillaged, and the fate of my little
    Ascanius.
I glanced round, wishing to see what force of men
    was left me.
All were gone: utter exhaustion and sickness of heart
Had made them drop from the roof to the ground or
    into the flames.
    Yes, I was now the one man left of my party. But
    just then,   395
Hugging close to the threshold of Vesta, speechlessly
    hiding there,
I noticed the daughter of Tyndareus, Helen. The
    blaze lit up
The whole scene as I wandered, peering this way and
    that.
Helen, the scourge of Troy and her own land alike,
In dread anticipation of Trojan wrath at Troy's
Downfall, of Greek revenge, of her cuckolded hus-
    band's anger,—   401
Helen, that hateful creature, was crouched by the
    altar, in hiding.
A fire broke out in my heart, a passion of rage to
    avenge
My country's fall and punish her crime by a crime
    upon her.

Was she going to get away with it? see Sparta again
    and her homeland? 405
Return as a queen, in triumph? be once more reunit-
    ed
With husband, home, parents and children? use our
    Trojan
Ladies for her attendants and Trojan men for slaves?—
All this, with Priam put to the sword, and Troy in
    ashes,
And Troy's shore time and again bathed in a sweat of
    blood? 410
Not so, I said. For although to kill a woman earns
    one
No fame, and victory over a female wins no decora-
    tions,
I shall be praised for stamping out an iniquity, pun-
    ishing
One who so richly deserves it; and I shall enjoy
    fulfilling
My soul with a flame of vengeance, appeasing my
    people's ashes. 415
Such were my thoughts, the insensate fury that drove
    me onward,
When to my view—and never before had I seen her
    so clear—
My gentle mother appeared: all glowing with light
    she came
Through the gloom, a goddess manifest, oh, high and
    handsome as
The heaven-dwellers know her. She laid a hand on
    mine, 420
Restraining me, then shaped these words with her
    rosy lips:—
  My son, what anguish spurs you to this ungov-
    erned rage?
What madness has driven all thought for love out of
    your heart?
Will you not first find out if your aged father, An-
    chises,
Is where you left him, and whether your wife, Creu-
    sa, be still 425
Alive, and little Ascanius? A whole Greek army is
    surging
Round them on every side, and but for my guardian
    care
The flames would have got them by now, the fell
    sword drained their blood.
It is not the beauty of hated Helen, it is not Paris,
Though you hold him to blame—the gods, the gods,
    I tell you, are hostile, 430
It's they who have undermined Troy's power and
    sent it tumbling.
Look! I shall wipe away the cloud which now oc-
    cludes
And dulls your mortal vision, even as you gaze, the
    dank mist
Befogging you. Fear not to do whatever your mother

Tells you, and willingly be guided by me. Now, look
    at 435
That litter of masonry there, huge blocks, stone torn
    from stone,
And the dust-laden smoke billowing up from the
    debris—
It's Neptune's work: he gores and tosses with his
    great trident
The walls, the foundations, until the whole city is
    disembowelled. 439
Look over there! At the Scaean gate, panoplied Juno
Heads the shock-troops, and in a vindictive fury calls
    up
Her allies from the ships.
Look round! See Pallas Athene planted upon the
    citadel—
The storm-cloud is lurid about her, the Gorgon glares
    from her shield. 444
Jove supplies fresh courage and a victorious strength
To the Greeks, inciting the gods against the Trojan
    cause.
Escape then, while you may, my son, and end this
    ordeal.
I shall be with you, seeing you safe to your father's
    house.
  She had spoken; and now she was vanished into
    the night's thick darkness.
Terrible shapes loom up, set against Troy, the shapes
    of 450
Heaven's transcendent will.
  Then indeed I saw that all Ilium was subsiding
Into the flames, and Neptune's Troy quite over-
    thrown.
Imagine a veteran ash-tree upon some mountain top,
When woodsmen are working to fell it, with blow
    upon blow of their axes 455
Vigorously hacking: the tree seems always about to
    fall;
It nods, and the topmost leaves are shivered by each
    concussion:
Little by little their blows master it, till at last
With a great groan it snaps off and falls full length on
    the hillside.
Well, I went down from the roof, and divinely guided
    pressed on 460
Through flame and foe: the weapons gave way, the
    flames drew back for me.
  But when I reached the door of my father's house,
    the ancestral
Home, my father Anchises, whom first I looked for,
    wishing
To get him away first to the safety of the hills—
    Anchises
Flatly refused to prolong his life, now Troy was
    finished, 465
Or to endure exile. He said:—
                   O you, whose blood

Is in the prime, who are strong enough to stand on
  your own feet,
Do you try for escape!
But as for me, if the gods had meant me to go on
  living,
They'd have preserved this place. Enough, more than
  enough   470
To have seen Troy ruined once and once have sur-
  vived her capture.
Bid me farewell and leave, O leave this body of mine
Where it is! I shall find death in action. The foe will
  slay me
For pity, or spoils. And to bury me—that will not
  cost them much.
For years now I have been lingering, obnoxious to
  heaven and useless   475
To mankind, ever since the ruler of gods and men
Blasted me with the searing breath of his levin-
  flash. . . .
  My sword was at my side again; I was fitting my
    left arm
Through the strap of my shield, and on my way out
  of the house,
When Creusa clung to me at the door, gripping my
  ankles,   480
Holding little Ascanius up to his father, and
  crying:—
  If it's deathwards you go, take us with you! O take
    us, and come what may!
But if your experience tells you that something is to
  be gained by
Fighting, protect this house first! Think what you're
  leaving us to—
Ascanius, your father, and me who loved to be called
  your wife once!   485
  Loudly she cried these words, and filled the house
    with her crying.
Just then a miracle happened, a wonderful miracle.
Imagine it!—our hands and our sad eyes were upon
Ascanius, when we beheld a feathery tongue of flame
Luminously alight on his head, licking the soft
  curls   490
With fire that harmed them not, and playing about
  his temples.
Anxious, in great alarm, his mother and I hurried to
Beat out, put out with water, that holy blaze on his
  hair.
But father Anchises, greatly heartened, lifted his eyes
  up,
Stretched up his hands to heaven, with words of
  prayer, saying:—   495
  O god omnipotent, if any prayers can sway you,
Give ear to mine. One thing I ask: if by our goodness
We have deserved it, grant your aid, confirm this
  omen!
  The old man had hardly spoken when from our left
    hand came

A sudden crash of thunder, and a shooting star slid
  down   500
The sky's dark face, drawing a trail of light behind
  it.
We watched that star as it glided high over the
  palace roof,
And blazing a path, buried its brightness deep in the
  woods of
Ida; when it was gone, it left in its wake a long
  furrow
Of light, and a sulphurous smoke spread widely over
  the terrain.   505
That did convince my father. He drew himself
  upright,
Addressed the gods above, and worshipped the
  heaven-sent star:—
  No more, no more lingering! I follow, I'm there,
    where you guide me!
Gods of our fathers, guard this family, guard my
  grandson!
This sign is yours, and Troy is still in your heavenly
  keeping.   510
Yea, I consent. I refuse no longer, my son, to go with
  you.
  He had spoken; and now more clearly over the
    town the fire's roar
Was heard, and nearer rolled the tide of its
  conflagration.
"Quick, then, dear father," I said, "climb onto my
  back, and I will
Carry you on my shoulders—that's a burden will not
  be burdensome.   515
However things turn out, at least we shall share one
  danger,
One way of safety, both of us. Let little Ascanius
  walk
Beside me, and Creusa follow my steps at a distance.
And you, servants, pay careful attention to what I
  shall tell you.
As you go out of the city, you come to a mound with
  an ancient   520
Temple of Ceres upon it, secluded; nearby, an old
  cypress
Stands, which for many years our fathers preserved
  in reverence.
Let this be our rendezvous: we'll get there by
  different routes.
Do you, my father, carry the sacred relics and home-
  gods:
Sinful for me to touch them, when I have just with-
  drawn   525
From battle, with blood on my hands, until in run-
  ning water
I am purified."
  With these words, I laid the pelt of a tawny lion
For covering over my broad shoulders and bowed
  neck;

Then stooped to lift my burden: Ascanius twined his
 fingers   530
In mine, hurrying to keep up with his father's longer
 stride.
My wife came on behind. We fared on, hugging the
 shadows.
I, who just now had faced the enemy volleys, the
 Greeks'
Concentrated attack, without turning a hair—I was
 scared by   534
Every breeze, alarmed by every sound, so strung up
Was I with anxiety for my burden and my compan-
 ion.
 And now I was nearing the gates and thinking that
 we had made it,
When on a sudden there came to my ears the sound
 of many
Footsteps—or so it seemed. Then, peering into the
 gloom,   539
My father exclaimed:—
 Run! They're upon us! Run, Aeneas!
I can see the shine of their shields and the bronze
 accoutrements winking.
 Well, I panicked. My wits were fuddled, were
 snatched away
By some malignant prompting. For even as I darted
 off
Into byways, off my course among streets I knew not
 —O god,
The anguish of it!—my wife Creusa, fate took her—
 did she   545
Stop there? or lose her way? Did she sink down in
 exhaustion?
We never knew. We never set eyes on her again.
I did not look back for the lost one, I did not give her
 a thought
Until we had reached the mound, the ancient, hal-
 lowed place
Of Ceres. Here at last, when all were assembled, one
 was   550
Missing, one had denied husband and son her compa-
 ny.
I was out of my mind. What mortal, what god did I
 not curse?
In all the city's ruin what bitterer thing did I see?
Commending Ascanius, Anchises and the Teucrian
 home-gods
To my friends' care, and hiding them deep in the
 hollow vale,   555
I put on my shining armour, I made for the city once
 more.
To reconstruct those events, to retrace our path
 through Troy
And expose my life to its perils again—that was my
 purpose.

554. Teucrian, Trojan, after Teucer, first king of Troy.

For a start, I returned to the shadowed gate in the
 city wall
By which I had sallied forth, noting my tracks and
 following them   560
Back through the night, straining my eyes to scan
 them. Everywhere
Dread and the sheer silence reduced my courage to
 nothing.
Next, I went home, in case—just on the chance that
 she might have
Gone there. The Greeks had broken in, the whole
 house was occupied.
That instant, gluttonous fire was fanned by the
 draught right up to   565
The roof top; flames burst out there, the blast of the
 heat roared skywards.
I went on, to revisit Priam's house and the citadel.
Here, in the empty colonnades of Juno's sanctuary,
Phoenix and fell Ulysses were engaged on the duty
 allotted them,
Guarding the loot. To this point from all over Troy
 had plunder,   570
Salvaged from burning shrines, been brought: tables
 of gods,
Solid gold bowls and looted vestments were being
 piled up here
In heaps. Children and frightened mothers were
 standing about
In a long queue.
I dared (you will hardly believe it) to call out loud
 through the gloom   575
And fill the streets with shouting: sadly I cried "Creu-
 sa!"—
Called to her over and over again, but it was no good.
As I roamed on that endless, frenzied search through
 the city buildings,
There appeared before my eyes a piteous phantom,
 yes,
The very ghost of Creusa—a figure larger than
 life.   580
I was appalled: my hair stood on end, and my voice
 stuck
In my throat. It was she who spoke then, and thus
 relieved my pain:—
 Darling husband, it's madness of you to indulge
 your grief
Like this. These happenings are part of the divine
Purpose. It was not written that you should bring
 Creusa   585
Away with you; the great ruler of heaven does not
 allow it.
For you, long exile is destined, broad tracts of sea to
 be furrowed;
Then you will reach Hesperia, where Lydian Tiber
 flows
Gently through a land in good heart, and good men
 live.

There, your affairs will prosper; a kingdom, a royal
  bride   590
Await you. No more tears now for your heart's love,
  Creusa:
I shall not see the proud halls of the Myrmidons or
  Dolopes,
Nor work as a slave for Greek women—I, who am
  Dardan
And daughter-in-law to the goddess Venus.
No, the great Mother of the gods is going to keep me
  here.   595
Goodbye, Aeneas. Cherish our love in the son it gave
  us.

  With these words, though I wept and had so much
    to say
To her, she left me, fading out into thin air.
Three times I tried to put my arms round her neck,
  and three times
The phantom slipped my hands, my vain embrace: it
  was like   600
Grasping a wisp of wind or the wings of a fleeting
  dream.
So in the end I went back to my friends, the night
  being over.
I was astonished to find, when I got there, a great
  number
Of new arrivals come in, both women and men, a
  sorry
Concourse of refugees assembled for exile. From all
  sides   605
They'd rendezvous'd, their minds made up, their
  belongings ready
For me to lead them wherever I wished across the
  sea.
And now was the dawn star rising over the ridges of
  Ida,
Bringing another day. The Greeks were holding the
  gates of   609
The city in force. Troy was beyond all hope of aid.
I accepted defeat, picked up my father and made for
  the mountains.

[Book III, describing the seven years' wandering
of Aeneas, is omitted.]

BOOK IV

But now for some while the queen had been growing
  more grievously love-sick,
Feeding the wound with her life-blood, the fire biting
  within her.
Much did she muse on the hero's nobility, and much
On his family's fame. His look, his words had gone to
  her heart
And lodged there: she could get no peace from love's
  disquiet.   5
  The morrow's morn had chased from heaven the
    dewy darkness,

Was carrying the sun's torch far and wide over earth,
When almost beside herself, she spoke to her sister,
  her confidante:—
  Anna, sister, why do these nerve-racking dreams
    haunt me?
This man, this stranger I've welcomed into my house
  —what of him?   10
How gallantly he looks, how powerful in chest and
  shoulders!
I really do think, and have reason to think, that he is
  heaven-born.
Mean souls convict themselves by cowardice. Oh,
  imagine
The fates that have harried him, the fight to a finish
  he told of!
Were it not that my purpose is fixed irrevocably   15
Never to tie myself in wedlock again to anyone,
Since that first love of mine proved false and let
  death cheat me;
Had I not taken a loathing for the idea of marriage,
For him, for this one man, I could perhaps have
  weakened.
Anna, I will confess it, since poor Sychaeus, my
  husband,   20
Was killed and our home broken up by my brother's
  murderous act,
This man is the only one who has stirred my senses
  and sapped
My will. I feel once more the scars of the old flame.
But no, I would rather the earth should open and
  swallow me
Or the father of heaven strike me with lightning
  down to the shades—   25
The pale shades and deep night of the Underworld—
  before
I violate or deny pure widowhood's claim upon me.
He who first wedded me took with him, when he
  died,
My right to love: let him keep it, there, in the tomb,
  for ever.
  So Dido spoke, and the rising tears flooded her
    bosom.   30
Anna replied:—
            You are dearer to me than the light
  of day.
Must you go on wasting your youth in mourning and
  solitude,
Never to know the blessings of love, the delight of
  children?
Do you think that ashes, or ghosts underground, can
  mind about such things?
I know that in Libya, yes, and in Tyre before it, no
  wooers   35
Could touch your atrophied heart: Iarbas was rejected

36. **Iarbas,** king of the Getulians, whose attentions Dido had spurned.

And other lords of Africa, the breeding-ground of the
    great.
Very well: but when love comes, and pleases, why
    fight against it? . . .
I hold it was providential indeed, and Juno willed it,
That hither the Trojan fleet should have made their
    way. Oh, sister,   40
Married to such a man, what a city you'll see, what a
    kingdom
Established here! With the Trojans as our comrades
    in arms,
What heights of glory will not we Carthaginians soar
    to! . . .
    These words blew to a blaze the spark of love in
    the queen's heart,
Set hope to her wavering will and melted her modes-
    ty's rigour.   45
So first they went to the shrines, beseeching at every
    altar
For grace: as religion requires, they sacrificed chosen
    sheep to
Ceres, giver of increase, to Phoebus, and to the
    Wine-god;
To Juno, chief of all, for the marriage-bond is her
    business.
Dido herself, most beautiful, chalice in hand, would
    pour   50
Libations between the horns of a milk-white heifer,
    and slowly
Would pace by the dripping altars, with the gods
    looking on,
And daily renew her sacrifice, poring over the vic-
    tims'
Opened bodies to see what their pulsing entrails
    signified.
Ah, little the soothsayers know! What value have
    vows or shrines   55
For a woman wild with passion, the while love's
    flame eats into
Her gentle flesh and love's wound works silently in
    her breast?
So burns the ill-starred Dido, wandering at large
    through the town
In a rage of desire, like a doe pierced by an arrow—
    a doe which
Some hunting shepherd has hit with a long shot while
    unwary   60
She stepped through the Cretan woods, and all
    unknowing has left his
Winged weapon within her: the doe runs fleetly
    around the Dictaean
Woods and clearings, the deathly shaft stuck deep in
    her flank.
Now she conducts Aeneas on a tour of her city, and
    shows him
The vast resources of Carthage, the home there ready
    and waiting;   65

Begins to speak, then breaks off, leaving a sentence
    unfinished.
Now, as the day draws out, she wants to renew that
    first feast,
In fond distraction begs to hear once again the Trojan
Story, and hangs on his words as once again he tells
    it.
Then, when the company's broken up, when the
    moon is dimming   70
Her beams in turn and the dipping stars invite to
    sleep,
Alone she frets in the lonely house, lies down on her
    bed,
Then leaves it again: he's not there, not there, but
    she hears him and sees him.
Or charmed by his likeness to his father, she keeps
    Ascanius
Long in her lap to assuage the passion she must not
    utter.   75
Work on the half-built towers is closed down mean-
    while; the men
Of Carthage have laid off drilling, or building the
    wharves and vital
Defences of their town; the unfinished works are
    idle—
Great frowning walls, head-in-air cranes, all at a
    standstill.
    Now as soon as Jupiter's consort perceived that
    Dido was mad   80
With love and quite beyond caring about her reputa-
    tion,
She, Juno, approached Venus, making these over-
    tures:—
    A praiseworthy feat, I must say, a fine achievement
    you've brought off,
You and your boy; it should make a great, a lasting
    name for you—   84
One woman mastered by the arts of two immortals!
It has not entirely escaped me that you were
    afraid of my city
And keenly suspicious of towering Carthage's hospi-
    tality.
But how will it all end? Where is our rivalry taking
    us?
Would it not be far better, by arranging a marriage,
    to seal
A lasting peace? You have got the thing you had set
    your heart on: 90
Dido's afire with love, wholly infatuated.
Well then, let us unite these nations and rule them
    with equal
Authority. Let Dido slave for a Trojan husband,
And let the Tyrians pass into your hand as her dowry.
    Venus, aware that this was double-talk by which
Juno aimed at basing the future Italian empire   96
On Africa, countered with these words:—
                   Senseless indeed to reject

Such terms and prefer to settle the matter with you
    by hostilities,
Provided fortune favour the plan which you propose.
But I'm in two minds about destiny, I am not sure if
    Jupiter   100
Wishes one city formed of Tyrians and Trojan exiles,
Or would approve a pact or miscegenation between
    them.
You are his wife: you may ask him to make his policy
    clearer.
Proceed. I will support you.
                     Queen Juno replied thus:—
   That shall be my task. Now, to solve our immedi-
    ate problem,   105
I will briefly put forward a scheme—pray give me
    your attention.
Aeneas and his unfortunate Dido plan to go
A-hunting in the woods to-morrow, as soon as the sun
Has risen and unshrouded the world below with his
    rays.
On these two, while the beaters are scurrying about
    and stopping   110
The coverts with cordon of nets, I shall pour down a
    darkling rain-storm
And hail as well, and send thunder hallooing all over
    the sky.
Dispersing for shelter, the rest of the hunt will be
    cloaked in the mirk:
But Dido and lord Aeneas, finding their way to the
    same cave,
Shall meet. I'll be there: and if I may rely on your
    goodwill,   115
There I shall join them in lasting marriage, and seal
    her his,
With Hymen present in person.
                     Venus made no opposition
To Juno's request, though she smiled at the ingenuity
    of it.
So now, as Aurora was rising out of her ocean bed
And the day-beam lofted, there sallied forth the *élite*
    of Carthage: 120
With fine-meshed nets and snares and the broad
    hunting lances
Massylian riders galloped behind a keen-nosed pack.
The queen dallies: the foremost Carthaginians await
    her
By the palace door, where stands her horse, capari-
    soned
In purple and gold, high-spirited, champing the
    foam-flecked bit.   125
At last she comes, with many courtiers in attendance:
She wears a Phoenician habit, piped with bright-
    coloured braid:
Her quiver is gold, her hair bound up with a golden
    clasp,
A brooch of gold fastens the waist of her brilliant
    dress.

Her Trojan friends were there too, and young Ascani-
    us   130
In high glee. But by far the handsomest of them all
Was Aeneas, who came to her side now and joined
    forces with hers. . . .
When they had reached the mountains, the trackless
    haunt of game,
Wild goats—picture the scene!—started from crags
    up above there,
Ran down the slopes: from another direction stags
    were galloping   135
Over the open ground of a glen, deserting the
    heights—
A whole herd jostling together in flight, with a dust-
    cloud above it.
But young Ascanius, proud of his mettlesome horse,
    was riding
Along the vale, outstripping group after group of
    hunters,
And praying hard that, instead of such tame quarry,
    a frothing   140
Boar might come his way or a sand-coloured mountain
    lion.
   At this stage a murmur, a growling began to be
    heard
In the sky: soon followed a deluge of rain and hail
    together.
The Trojan sportsmen, their Carthaginian friends and
    the grandson   144
Of Venus, in some alarm, scattered over the terrain
Looking for shelter. Torrents roared down from the
    mountain-tops.
Now Dido and the prince Aeneas found themselves
In the same cave. Primordial Earth and presiding
    Juno
Gave the signal. The firmament flickered with fire, a
    witness
Of wedding. Somewhere above, the Nymphs cried
    out in pleasure.   150
That day was doom's first birthday and that first day
    was the cause of
Evils: Dido recked nothing for appearance or repu-
    tation:
The love she brooded on now was a secret love no
    longer;
Marriage, she called it, drawing the word to veil her
    sin.
   Straightaway went Rumour through the great
    cities of Libya—   155
Rumour, the swiftest traveller of all the ills on earth,
Thriving on movement, gathering strength as it goes;
    at the start
A small and cowardly thing, it soon puffs itself up,
And walking upon the ground, buries its head in the
    cloud-base.
The legend is that, enraged with the gods, Mother
    Earth produced   160

This creature, her last child, as a sister to Enceladus
And Coeus—a swift-footed creature, a winged angel
    of ruin,
A terrible, grotesque monster, each feather upon
    whose body—
Incredible though it sounds—has a sleepless eye
    beneath it,
And for every eye she has also a tongue, a voice and
    a pricked ear.   165
At night she flits midway between earth and sky,
    through the gloom
Screeching, and never closes her eyelids in sweet
    slumber:
By day she is perched like a look-out either upon a
    roof-top
Or some high turret; so she terrorises whole cities
Loud-speaker of truth, hoarder of mischievous false-
    hood, equally.   170
This creature was now regaling the people with
    various scandal
In great glee, announcing fact and fiction indiscrimi-
    nately:
Item, Aeneas has come here, a prince of Trojan
    blood,
And the beauteous Dido deigns to have her name
    linked with his;
The couple are spending the winter in debauchery,
    the whole long   175
Winter, forgetting their kingdoms, rapt in a trance of
    lust.
Such gossip did vile Rumour pepper on every mouth.
Not long before she came to the ears of king Iarbas,
Whispering inflammatory words and heaping up his
    resentment.
    He, the son of Ammon by a ravished African
    nymph,   180
Had established a hundred shrines to Jove in his
    ample realm,
A hundred altars, and consecrated their quenchless
    flames
And vigils unceasing there; the ground was richly
    steeped in
Victims' blood, and bouquets of flowers adorned the
    portals.
He now, driven out of his mind by that bitter blast of
    rumour,   185
There at the altar, among the presences of the gods,
Prayed, it is said, to Jove, with importunate, humble
    entreaty:—
    Almighty Jove, whom now for the first time the
    Moorish people
Pledge with wine as they banquet on ornamental
    couches,
Do you observe these things? Or are we foolish to
    shudder   190
When you shoot fire, O Father, foolish to be dis-
    mayed

By lightning which is quite aimless and thunder
    which growls without meaning?
That woman who, wandering within our frontiers,
    paid to establish
Her insignificant township, permitted by us to plough
    up
A piece of the coast and be queen of it—that woman,
    rejecting my offer   195
Of marriage, has taken Aeneas as lord and master
    there.
And now that philanderer, with his effeminate follow-
    ing—
His chin and oil-sleeked hair set off by a Phrygian
    bonnet—
That fellow is in possession; while we bring gifts to
    your shrine,
If indeed you are there and we do not worship a vain
    myth.   200
    Thus did Iarbas pray, with his hands on the altar;
    and Jove
Omnipotent, hearing him, bent down his gaze upon
    Dido's
City and on those lovers lost to their higher fame.
Then he addressed Mercury, entrusting to him this
    errand:—
    Go quick, my son, whistle up the Zephyrs and
    wing your way   205
Down to the Trojan leader, who is dallying now in
    Carthage
Without one thought for the city which fate has
    assigned to be his.
Carry my dictate along the hastening winds and tell
    him,
Not for such ways did his matchless mother guaran-
    tee him
To us, nor for such ends rescue him twice from the
    Greeks;   210
Rather, that he should rule an Italy fertile in leader-
    ship
And loud with war, should hand on a line which
    sprang from the noble
Teucer and bring the whole world under a system of
    law.
If the glory of such great exploits no longer fires his
    heart   214
And for his own renown he will make no effort at all,
Does he grudge his son, Ascanius, the glory of Rome
    to be?
What aim, what hope does he cherish, delaying there
    in a hostile
Land, with no thought for posterity or his Italian
    kingdom?
Let him sail. That is the gist. Give him that message
    from me.   219
    Jove spake. Mercury now got ready to obey
His father's command. So first he bound on his feet
    the sandals,

The golden sandals whose wings waft him aloft over
    sea
And land alike with the hurrying breath of the
    breezes. Then
He took up his magic wand (with this he summons
    wan ghosts
From Orcus and consigns others to dreary Tarta-
    rus,   225
Gives sleep or takes it away, seals up the eyes of dead
    men).
Now, with that trusty wand, he drove the winds and
    threshed through
The cloud-wrack. . . .
As soon as his winged feet had carried him to the
    shacks there,
He noticed Aeneas superintending the work on
    towers   230
And new buildings: he wore a sword studded with
    yellow
Jaspers, and a fine cloak of glowing Tyrian purple
Hung from his shoulders—the wealthy Dido had
    fashioned it,
Interweaving the fabric with threads of gold, as a
    present for him.   234
Mercury went for him at once:—
                  So now you are laying
Foundations for lofty Carthage, building a beautiful
    city
To please a woman, lost to the interests of your own
    realm?
The king of the gods, who directs heaven and earth
    with his deity,
Sends me to you from bright Olympus: the king of
    the gods
Gave me this message to carry express through the
    air:—What do you   240
Aim at or hope for, idling and fiddling here in Libya?
If you're indifferent to your own high destiny
And for your own renown you will make no effort at
    all,
Think of your young hopeful, Ascanius, growing to
    manhood,
The inheritance which you owe him—an Italian
    kingdom, the soil of   245
Rome.
        Such were the words which Mercury delivered;
And breaking off abruptly, was manifest no more,
But vanished into thin air, far beyond human ken.
    Dazed indeed by that vision was Aeneas, and
    dumbfounded:
His hair stood on end with terror, the voice stuck in
    his throat.   250
Awed by this admonition from the great throne
    above,
He desired to fly the country, dear though it was to
    him.
But oh, what was he to do? What words could he find

to get round
The temperamental queen? How broach the matter
    to her?
His mind was in feverish conflict, tossed from one
    side to the other,   255
Twisting and turning all ways to find a way past his
    dilemma.
So vacillating, at last he felt this the better deci-
    sion:—
Sending for Mnestheus, Sergestus and brave Seres-
    tus, he bade them
Secretly get the ships ready, muster their friends on
    the beach,
Be prepared to fight: the cause of so drastic a change
    of plan   260
They must keep dark: in the meanwhile, assuming
    that generous Dido
Knew nothing and could not imagine the end of so
    great a love,
Aeneas would try for a way to approach her, the
    kindest moment
For speaking, the best way to deal with this delicate
    matter. His comrades
Obeyed the command and did as he told them with
    cheerful alacrity.   265
    But who can ever hoodwink a woman in love? The
    queen,
Apprehensive even when things went well, now
    sensed his deception,
Got wind of what was going to happen. That mis-
    chievous Rumour,
Whispering the fleet was preparing to sail, put her in
    a frenzy.
Distraught, she witlessly wandered about the city,
    raving. . . .   270
Finding Aeneas at last, she cried, before he could
    speak:—
    Unfaithful man, did you think you could do such a
    dreadful thing
And keep it dark? yes, skulk from my land without
    one word?
Our love, the vows you made me—do these not give
    you pause,
Nor even the thought of Dido meeting a painful
    death?   275
Now, in the dead of winter, to be getting your ships
    ready
And hurrying to set sail when northerly gales are
    blowing,
You heartless one! Suppose the fields were not for-
    eign, the home was
Not strange that you are bound for, suppose Troy
    stood as of old,
Would you be sailing for Troy, now, in this stormy
    weather?   280
Am I your reason for going? By these tears, by the
    hand you gave me—

They are all I have left, to-day, in my misery—I
    implore you,
And by our union of hearts, by our marriage hardly
    begun,
If I have ever helped you at all, if anything
About me pleased you, be sad for our broken home,
    forgo   285
Your purpose, I beg you, unless it's too late for
    prayers of mine!
Because of you, the Libyan tribes and the Nomad
    chieftains
Hate me, the Tyrians are hostile: because of you I
    have lost
My old reputation for faithfulness—the one thing
    that could have made me
Immortal. Oh, I am dying! To what, my guest, are
    you leaving me?   290
"Guest"—that is all I may call you now, who have
    called you husband.
Why do I linger here? Shall I wait till my brother,
    Pygmalion,
Destroys this place, or Iarbas leads me away captive?
If even I might have conceived a child by you before
You went away, a little Aeneas to play in the palace
And, in spite of all this, to remind me of you by his
    looks, oh then   296
I should not feel so utterly finished and desolate.
    She had spoken. Aeneas, mindful of Jove's words,
    kept his eyes
Unyielding, and with a great effort repressed his
    feeling for her.
In the end he managed to answer:—
                      Dido, I'll never pretend
You have not been good to me, deserving of every-
    thing   301
You can claim. I shall not regret my memories of
    Elissa
As long as I breathe, as long as I remember my own
    self.
For my conduct—this, briefly: I did not look to make
    off from here
In secret—do not suppose it; nor did I offer you
    marriage   305
At any time or consent to be bound by a marriage
    contract.
If fate allowed me to be my own master, and gave
    me
Free will to choose my way of life, to solve my
    problems,
Old Troy would be my first choice: I would restore it,
    and honour
My people's relics—the high halls of Priam perpetu-
    ated,   310
Troy given back to its conquered sons, a renaissant
    city,
Had been my task. But now Apollo and the Lycian
Oracle have told me that Italy is our bourne.

There lies my heart, my homeland. You, a Phoeni-
    cian, are held by
These Carthaginian towers, by the charm of your
    Libyan city: 315
So can you grudge us Trojans our vision of settling
    down
In Italy? We too may seek a kingdom abroad.
Often as night envelops the earth in dewy darkness,
Often as star-rise, the troubled ghost of my father,
    Anchises,
Comes to me in my dreams, warns me and frightens
    me.   320
I am disturbed no less by the wrong I am doing
    Ascanius,
Defrauding him of his destined realm in Hesperia.
What's more, just now the courier of heaven, sent by
    Jupiter—
I swear it on your life and mine—conveyed to me,
    swiftly flying,
His orders: I saw the god, as clear as day, with my
    own eyes,   325
Entering the city, and these ears drank in the words
    he uttered.
No more reproaches, then—they only torture us both.
God's will, not mine, says "Italy."
    All the while he was speaking she gazed at him
    askance,
Her glances flickering over him, eyes exploring the
    whole man   330
In deadly silence. Now, furiously, she burst out:—
    Faithless and false! No goddess mothered you, no
    Dardanus
Your ancestor! I believe harsh Caucasus begat you
On a flint-hearted rock and Hyrcanian tigers suckled
    you.
Why should I hide my feelings? What worse can
    there be to keep them for?   335
Not one sigh from him when I wept! Not a softer
    glance!
Did he yield an inch, or a tear, in pity for her who
    loves him?
I don't know what to say first. It has come to this,—
    not Juno,
Not Jove himself can view my plight with the eye of
    justice.
Nowhere is it safe to be trustful. I took him, a casta-
    way,   340
A pauper, and shared my kingdom with him—I must
    have been mad—
Rescued his lost fleet, rescued his friends from death.
Oh, I'm on fire and drifting! And now Apollo's proph-
    ecies,
Lycian oracles, couriers of heaven sent by Jupiter
With stern commands—all these order you to betray
    me.   345
Oh, of course this is just the sort of transaction that
    troubles the calm of

The gods. I'll not keep you, nor probe the dishonesty
    of your words.
Chase your Italy, then! Go, sail to your realm over-
    seas!
I only hope that, if the just spirits have any power,
Marooned on some mid-sea rock you may drink the
    full cup of agony   350
And often cry out for Dido. I'll dog you, from far,
    with the death-fires;
And when cold death has parted my soul from my
    body, my spectre
Will be wherever you are. You shall pay for the evil
    you've done me.
The tale of your punishment will come to me down in
    the shades.
    With these words Dido suddenly ended, and sick
    at heart   355
Turned from him, tore herself away from his eyes,
    ran indoors,
While he hung back in dread of a still worse scene,
    although
He had much to say. Her maids bore up the fainting
    queen
Into her marble chamber and laid her down on the
    bed.
    But the god-fearing Aeneas, much as he longed to
    soothe   360
Her anguish with consolation, with words that would
    end her troubles,
Heavily sighing, his heart melting from love of her,
Nevertheless obeyed the gods and went off to his
    fleet.
Whereupon the Trojans redoubled their efforts, all
    along
The beach dragging down the tall ships, launching
    the well-tarred bottoms,   365
Fetching green wood to make oars and baulks of
    unfashioned timber
From the forest, so eager they were to be gone.
You could see them on the move, hurrying out of the
    city.
It looked like an army of ants when, provident for
    winter,
They're looting a great big corn-heap and storing it
    up in their own house;   370
Over a field the black file goes, as they carry the
    loot
On a narrow track through the grass; some are
    strenuously pushing
The enormous grains of corn with their shoulders,
    while others marshal
The traffic and keep it moving: their whole road
    seethes with activity.
Ah, Dido, what did you feel when you saw these
    things going forward?   375
What moans you gave when, looking forth from your
    high roof-top,

You beheld the whole length of the beach aswarm
    with men, and the sea's face
Alive with the sound and fury of preparations for
    sailing!
Excess of love, to what lengths you drive our human
    hearts!
Once again she was driven to try what tears and
    entreaties   380
Could do, and let love beggar her pride—she would
    leave no appeal
Untried, lest, for want of it, she should all needlessly
    die.
    Anna, you see the bustle down there on the beach;
    from all sides
They have assembled; their canvas is stretched to the
    winds already,   384
And the elated mariners have garlanded their ships.
If I was able to anticipate this deep anguish,
I shall be able to bear it. But do this one thing, Anna,
For your poor sister. You were the only confidante
Of that faithless man: he told you even his secret
    thoughts:
You alone know the most tactful way, the best time
    to approach him.   390
Go, sister, and make this appeal to my disdainful
    enemy:—
Say that *I* never conspired with the Greeks at Aulis to
    ruin
The Trojan people, nor sent squadrons of ships
    against Troy;
I never desecrated the ashes of dead Anchises,
So why must Aeneas be deaf and obdurate to my
    pleading?   395
Why off so fast? Will he grant a last wish to her who
    unhappily
Loves him, and wait for a favouring wind, an easier
    voyage?
Not for our marriage that was do I plead now—he
    has forsworn it,
Nor that he go without his dear Latium and give up
    his kingdom.
I ask a mere nothing—just time to give rein to de-
    spair and thus calm it,   400
To learn from ill luck how to grieve for what I have
    lost, and to bear it.
This last favour I beg—oh, pity your sister!—and if
    he
Grants it, I will repay him; my death shall be his
    interest.
    Such were her prayers, and such the tearful en-
    treaties her agonised
Sister conveyed to Aeneas again and again. But
    unmoved by   405
Tearful entreaties he was, adamant against all plead-
    ings:
Fate blocked them, heaven stopped his ears lest he
    turn complaisant.

As when some stalwart oak-tree, some veteran of the
  Alps,
Is assailed by a wintry wind whose veering gusts tear
  at it,
Trying to root it up; wildly whistle the branches,   410
The leaves come flocking down from aloft as the bole
  is battered;
But the tree stands firm on its crag, for high as its
  head is carried
Into the sky, so deep do its roots go down towards
  Hades:
Even thus was the hero belaboured for long with
  every kind of
Pleading, and his great heart thrilled through and
  through with the pain of it;   415
Resolute, though, was his mind; unavailingly rolled
  her tears.
    But hapless Dido, frightened out of her wits by her
      destiny,
Prayed for death: she would gaze no more on the
  dome of daylight.
And now, strengthening her resolve to act and to
  leave this world,
She saw, as she laid gifts on the incense-burning
  altars—   420
Horrible to relate—the holy water turn black
And the wine she poured changing uncannily to
  blood.
She told no one, not even her sister, of this phenome-
  non.
Again, she had dedicated a chantry of marble within
The palace to her first husband; held it in highest
  reverence;   425
Hung it with snow-white fleeces and with festoons of
  greenery:
Well, from this shrine, when night covered the earth,
  she seemed
To be hearing words—the voice of that husband
  calling upon her.
There was something dirge-like, too, in the tones of
  the owl on the roof-top
Whose lonely, repeated cries were drawn out to a
  long keening.   430
Besides, she recalled with horror presages, dread
  forewarnings
Of the prophets of old. Aeneas himself pursued her
  remorselessly
In dreams, driving her mad; or else she dreamed of
  unending
Solitude and desertion, of walking alone and eternally
Down a long road, through an empty land, in search
  of her Tyrians. . . .   435
    So when, overmastered by grief, she conceived a
      criminal madness
And doomed herself to death, she worked out the
  time and method

In secret; then, putting on an expression of calm
  hopefulness
To hide her resolve, she approached her sorrowing
  sister with these words:—
    I have found out a way, Anna—oh, wish me joy
      of it—   440
To get him back or else get free of my love for him.
Near Ocean's furthest bound and the sunset is Ae-
  thiopia,
The very last place on earth, where giant Atlas
  pivots
The wheeling sky, embossed with fiery stars, on his
  shoulders.
I have been in touch with a priestess from there, a
  Massylian, who once,   445
As warden of the Hesperides' sacred close, was used
  to
Feed the dragon which guarded their orchard of
  golden apples,
Sprinkling its food with moist honey and sedative
  poppy-seeds.
Now this enchantress claims that her spells can
  liberate
One's heart, or can inject love-pangs, just as she
  wishes;   450
Can stop the flow of rivers, send the stars flying
  backwards,
Conjure ghosts in the night: she can make the earth
  cry out
Under one's feet, and elm trees come trooping down
  from the mountains.
Dear sister, I solemnly call to witness the gods and
  you whom   454
I love, that I do not willingly resort to her magic arts.
You must build up a funeral pyre high in the inner
  courtyard,
And keep it dark: lay on it the arms which that
  godless man
Has left on the pegs in our bedroom, all relics of him,
  and the marriage-bed
That was the ruin of me. To blot out all that reminds
  me
Of that vile man is my pleasure and what the enchan-
  tress directs.   460
    So Dido spoke, and fell silent, her face going
      deadly white.
Yet Anna never suspected that Dido was planning
  her own death
Through these queer rites, nor imagined how frantic
  a madness possessed her,
Nor feared any worse would happen than when
  Sychaeus had died.   464
So she made the arrangements required of her.
    When in the innermost court of the palace the pyre
      had been built up
To a great height with pinewood and logs of ilex, the
  queen

Festooned the place with garlands and wreathed it
    with funereal
Foliage: then she laid on it the clothes, the sword
    which Aeneas
Had left, and an effigy of him; she well knew what
    was to happen.   470
Altars are set up all round. Her hair unloosed, the
    enchantress
Loudly invokes three hundred deities—Erebus,
    Chaos,
Hecate, three in one, and three-faced Diana, the
    virgin.
She had sprinkled water which came, she pretended,
    from Lake Avernus;
Herbs she had gathered, cut by moonlight with a
    bronze knife—   475
Poisonous herbs all rank with juices of black venom;
She has found a love charm, a gland torn from the
    forehead of a new-born
Foal before its mother could get it.
Dido, the sacramental grain in her purified hands,
One foot unsandalled, her dress uncinctured, stood
    by the altars   480
Calling upon the gods and the stars that know fate's
    secrets,
Death at her heart, and prayed to whatever power it
    is
Holds unrequited lovers in its fair, faithful keeping.
    Was night. All over the earth, creatures were
    plucking the flower
Of soothing sleep, the woods and the wild seas fallen
    quiet—   485
A time when constellations have reached their mid-
    career,
When the countryside is all still, the beasts and the
    brilliant birds
That haunt the lakes' wide waters or the tangled
    undergrowth
Of the champain, stilled in sleep under the quiet
    night—
Cares are lulled and hearts can forget for a while
    their travails.   490
Not so the Phoenician queen: death at her heart, she
    could not
Ever relax in sleep, let the night in to her eyes
Or mind: her agonies mounted, her love reared up
    again
And savaged her, till she writhed in a boiling sea of
    passion.
So thus she began, her thoughts whirling round in a
    vicious circle:—   495
    What shall I do? Shall I, who've been jilted, return
    to my former
Suitors? go down on my knees for marriage to one of
    the Nomads
Although, time and again, I once rejected their
    offers?

Well, then am I to follow the Trojan's fleet and bow
    to
Their lightest word? I helped them once. Will that
    help me now?   500
Dare I think they remember with gratitude my old
    kindness?
But even if I wished it, who would suffer me, wel-
    come me
Aboard those arrogant ships? They hate me. Ah,
    duped and ruined!—
Surely by now I should know the ill faith of Laome-
    don's people?
So then? Shall I sail, by myself, with those exulting
    mariners,   505
Or sail against them with all my Tyrian folk about
    me—
My people, whom once I could hardly persuade to
    depart from Sidon—
Bidding them man their ships and driving them out
    to sea again?
Better die—I deserve it—end my pain with the
    sword.
Sister, you started it all: overborne by my tears, you
    laid up   510
These evils to drive me mad, put me at the mercy of
    a foe.
Oh, that I could have been some child of nature and
    lived
An innocent life, untouched by marriage and all its
    troubles!
I have broken the faith I vowed to the memory of
    Sichaeus.
    Such were the reproaches she could not refrain
    from uttering.   515
High on the poop of his ship, resolute now for depar-
    ture,
Aeneas slept; preparations for sailing were fully
    completed.
To him in a dream there appeared the shape of the
    god, returning
Just as he'd looked before, as if giving the same
    admonitions—
Mercury's very image, the voice, the complexion, the
    yellow   520
Hair and the handsome youthful body identical:—
    Goddess-born, can you go on sleeping at such a
    crisis?
Are you out of your mind, not to see what dangers
    are brewing up
Around you, and not to hear the favouring breath of
    the West wind?
Being set upon death, her heart is aswirl with
    conflicting passions,   525
Aye, she is brooding now some trick, some desperate
    deed.
Why are you not going, all speed, while the going is
    good?

If dawn finds you still here, delaying by these shores,
You'll have the whole sea swarming with hostile
　　ships, there will be
Firebrands coming against you, you'll see this beach
　　ablaze.　　　　　　　　　　　　　　530
Up and away, then! No more lingering! Woman was
　　ever
A veering, weathercock creature.
　　　　　　　He spoke, and vanished in the darkness.
Then, startled by the shock of the apparition, Aeneas
Snatched himself out of sleep and urgently stirred up
　　his comrades:—
　　Jump to it, men! To your watch! Get to the rowing
　　　　benches!　　　　　　　　　　　　535
Smartly! Hoist the sails! A god from heaven above
Spurs me to cut the cables, make off and lose not a
　　moment:
This was his second warning. O blessed god, we
　　follow you,
God indeed, and once more we obey the command
　　joyfully!
Be with us! Look kindly upon us! Grant us good
　　sailing weather!　　　　　　　　　540
　　Thus did Aeneas cry, and flashing his sword from
　　　its scabbard,
With the drawn blade he severed the moorings. The
　　same sense of
Urgency fired his comrades all; they cut and ran for
　　it.
The shore lay empty. The ships covered the open sea.
The oarsmen swept the blue and sent the foam flying
　　with hard strokes.　　　　　　　545
　　And now was Aurora, leaving the saffron bed of
　　　Tithonus,
Beginning to shower upon earth the light of another
　　day.
The queen, looking forth from her roof-top, as soon
　　as she saw the sky
Grow pale and the Trojan fleet running before the
　　wind,
Aware that the beach and the roadstead were empty,
　　the sailors gone,　　　　　　　　550
Struck herself three times, four times, upon her lovely
　　breast,
Tore at her yellow hair, and exclaimed:—
　　　　　　　　In god's name! shall that foreigner
Scuttle away and make a laughing-stock of my
　　country?
Will not my people stand to arms for a mass pursuit?
Will some not rush the warships out of the docks?
　　Move, then!　　　　　　　　　　555
Bring firebrands apace, issue the weapons, pull on the
　　oars!
What am I saying? Where am I? What madness
　　veers my mind?
Poor Dido, the wrong you have done—is it only now
　　coming home to you?

You should have thought of that when you gave him
　　your sceptre. So this is
The word of honour of one who, men say, totes round
　　his home-gods　　　　　　　　　560
Everywhere, and bore on his back a doddering
　　father!
Why could I not have seized him, torn up his body
　　and littered
The sea with it? finished his friends with the sword,
　　finished his own
Ascanius and served him up for his father to banquet
　　on?
The outcome of battle had been uncertain?—Let it
　　have been so:　　　　　　　　　565
Since I was to die, whom had I to fear? I should have
　　stormed
Their bulwarks with fire, set alight their gangways,
　　gutted the whole lot—
Folk, father and child—then flung myself on the
　　conflagration.
O sun, with your beams surveying all that is done on
　　earth!　　　　　　　　　　　569
Juno, the mediator and witness of my tragedy!
Hecate, whose name is howled by night at the city
　　crossroads!
Avenging Furies, and you, the patrons of dying
　　Elissa!—
Hear me! Incline your godheads to note this wicked-
　　ness
So worthy of your wrath! And hear my prayer! If he,
That damned soul, must make port and get to land, if
　　thus　　　　　　　　　　　　575
Jove destines it, if that bourne is fixed for him irrevo-
　　cably,
May he be harried in war by adventurous tribes, and
　　exiled
From his own land; may Ascanius be torn from his
　　arms; may he have to
Sue for aid, and see his own friends squalidly dying.
Yes, and when he's accepted the terms of a harsh
　　peace,　　　　　　　　　　　580
Let him never enjoy his realm or the allotted span,
But fall before his time and lie on the sands, unbur-
　　ied.
That is my last prayer. I pour it out, with my life-
　　blood.
Let you, my Tyrians, sharpen your hatred upon his
　　children
And all their seed for ever: send this as a present
　　to　　　　　　　　　　　　　585
My ghost. Between my people and his, no love, no
　　alliance!
Rise up from my dead bones, avenger! Rise up, one
To hound the Trojan settlers with fire and steel
　　remorselessly,
Now, some day, whenever the strength for it shall be
　　granted!

Shore to shore, sea to sea, weapon to weapon opposed—   590
I call down a feud between them and us to the last generation!
  These things she said; then tried to think of every expedient,
Seeking the quickest way out of the life she hated.
Briefly now she addressed Barce, the nurse of Sychaeus,
Her own being dust and ashes, interred in her native land:—   595
  Dear nurse, please will you get my sister, Anna. She must
Hasten to purify herself with living water, and fetch
The cattle, tell her—the atonement offerings, as directed;
Then let her come. And do you go and put on the holy headband.
These rites to Jove of the Underworld, duly made ready and started,   600
I mean to go through with now, and put an end to my troubles,
Committing to the flames the funeral pyre of that Trojan.
  She spoke. The nurse hurried off with senile officiousness.
But Dido, trembling, distraught by the terrible thing she was doing,
Her bloodshot eyes all restless, with hectic blotches upon   605
Her quivering cheeks, yet pale with the shade of advancing death,
Ran to the innermost court of the palace, climbed the lofty
Pyre, frantic at heart, and drew Aeneas' sword—
Her present to him, procured once for a far different purpose.
Then, after eyeing the clothes he had left behind, and the memoried   610
Bed, pausing to weep and brood on him for a little,
She lay down on the bed and spoke her very last words:—
  O relics of him, things dear to me while fate, while heaven allowed it,
Receive this life of mine, release me from my troubles!
I have lived, I have run to the finish the course which fortune gave me: 615
And now, a queenly shade, I shall pass to the world below.
I built a famous city, saw my own place established,
Avenged a husband, exacted a price for a brother's enmity.
Happy I would have been, ah, beyond words happy,
If only the Trojan ships had never come to my shore!
  These words; then, burying her face in the bed:—
          Shall I die unavenged?

At least, let me die. Thus, thus! I go to the dark, go gladly.
May he look long, from out there on the deep, at my flaming pyre,
The heartless! And may my death-fires signal bad luck for his voyage!
  She had spoken; and with these words, her attendants saw her falling   625
Upon the sword, they could see the blood spouting up over
The blade, and her hands spattered. Their screams rang to the roofs of
The palace; then rumour ran amok through the shocked city.
All was weeping and wailing, the streets were filled with a keening
Of women, the air resounded with terrible lamentations.   630
It was as if Carthage or ancient Tyre should be falling,
With enemy troops breaking into the town and a conflagration
Furiously sweeping over the abodes of men and of gods.
Anna heard it: half dead from extreme fear, she ran through
The crowd, tearing her cheeks with her nails, beating her breast   635
With her fists, and called aloud by name on the dying woman:—
  So this was your purpose, Dido? You were making a dupe of me?
That pyre, those lighted altars—for me, they were leading to this?
How shall I chide you for leaving me? Were you too proud to let your
Sister die with you? You should have called me to share your end: 640
One hour, one pang of the sword could have carried us both away.
Did I build this pyre with my own hands, invoking our family gods,
So that you might lie on it, and I, the cause of your troubles, not be there?
You have destroyed more than your self—me, and the lords
And commons and city of Sidon. Quick! Water for her wounds!   645
Let me bathe them, and if any last breath is fluttering from her mouth,
Catch it in mine!
          So saying, she had scaled the towering pyre,
Taken the dying woman into her lap, was caressing her,
Sobbing, trying to staunch the dark blood with her own dress.

Dido made an effort to raise her heavy eyes, 650
Then gave it up: the sword-blade grated against her
    breast bone.
Three times she struggled to rise, to lift herself on an
    elbow,
Three times rolled back on the bed. Her wandering
    gaze went up
To the sky, looking for light: she gave a moan when
    she saw it.
    Then did almighty Juno take pity on her long-
    drawn-out 655
Sufferings and hard going, sent Iris down from
    Olympus
To part the agonised soul from the body that still
    clung to it.
Since she was dying neither a natural death nor from
    others'
Violence, but desperate and untimely, driven to it
By a crazed impulse, not yet had Proserpine clipped
    from her head 660
The golden tress, or consigned her soul to the Under-
    world.
So now, all dewy, her pinions the colour of yellow
    crocus,
Her wake a thousand rainbow hues refracting the
    sunlight,
Iris flew down, and over Dido hovering, said:—
    As I was bidden, I take this sacred thing, the
    Death-god's 665
Due: and you I release from your body.
                   She snipped the tress.
Then all warmth went at once, the life was lost in air.

BOOK VI

. . . Aeneas, in tears, then gave the ships their head,
And at long last they slid to the shores of Euboean
    Cumae.
The bows are swung round to face the sea, the
    vessels made fast with
The biting hook of their anchors, and the sheer sterns
    are lining
The beach. Now, full of excitement, the heroes
    tumble out 5
On the Hesperian shore: some look for the seeds of
    fire
Hidden in veins of flint, some scour the woods, the
    tangled
Haunts of wild beasts, for fuel, and point to the
    springs they have found.
But the god-fearing Aeneas made for the shrine
    where Apollo
Sits throned on high, and that vasty cave—the
    deeply-recessed 10

2. **Cumae,** in central Italy.

Crypt of the awe-inspiring Sibyl, to whom the god
    gives
The power to see deep and prophesy what's to
    come. . . .
    There's a huge cave hollowed out from the flank of
    Cumae's hill;
A hundred wide approaches it has, a hundred mouths
From which there issue a hundred voices, the Sibyl's
    answers. 15
They had reached its threshold. . . .
    An icy shudder ran through their very bones
And Aeneas poured out a prayer from the bottom of
    his heart:—
. . . O most holy Sibyl,
Foreseer of future things, grant—I but ask for the
    kingdom
Owed by my destiny—grant that we Trojans may
    settle in Latium, 20
We and our wandering gods, the hard-driven deities
    of Troy.
Then will I found a temple of solid marble to Phoe-
    bus
And Trivia, appointing festival days in Phoebus'
    honour.
You too shall have your holy place in the realm to
    be. . . .
I have one request: since here is reputed to be the
    gateway 25
Of the Underworld and the dusky marsh from Acher-
    on's overflow,
May it befall me to go into my dear father's
Presence—open the hallowed gates and show me the
    way!
Him through the flames, through a thousand pursu-
    ing missiles I rescued
Out of the enemy's midst and bore him away on
    these shoulders: 30
He voyaged with me, enduring sea after sea, endur-
    ing
All menace of sea and storm, weak as he was—great
    ordeals
Beyond his strength, exceeding the normal lot of old
    age.
Yes, and he himself most earnestly bade me, more
    than once,
To come to you here and make this appeal. I pray
    you, kind one, 35
Take pity on father and son. You have the power: it
    was not
For nothing that Hecate put you in charge of the
    grove of Avernus. . . .
    Thus he was making petition, his hands upon the
    altar,
When the Sibyl began to speak:—
                 O child of a goddess' womb,
Trojan son of Anchises, the way to Avernus is
    easy; 40

Night and day lie open the gates of death's dark
    kingdom:
But to retrace your steps, to find the way back to
    daylight—
That is the task, the hard thing. A few, because of
    Jove's
Just love, or exalted to heaven by their own flame of
    goodness,
Men born from gods, have done it. Between, there
    lies a forest,   45
And darkly winds the river Cocytus round the place.
But if so great your love is, so great your passion to
    cross
The Stygian waters twice and twice behold black
    Tartarus,
If your heart is set on this fantastic project,
Here's what you must do first. Concealed in a tree's
    thick shade   50
There is a golden bough—gold the leaves and the
    tough stem—
Held sacred to Proserpine: the whole wood hides this
    bough
And a dell walls it round as it were in a vault of
    shadow.
Yet none is allowed to enter the land which earth
    conceals
Save and until he has plucked that gold-foil bough
    from the tree.   55
Fair Proserpine ordains that it should be brought to
    her
As tribute. When a bough is torn away, another
Gold one grows in its place with leaves of the same
    metal.
So keep your eyes roving above you, and when you
    have found the bough
Just pull it out: that branch will come away quite
    easily ·   60
If destiny means you to go; otherwise no amount of
Brute force will get it, nor hard steel avail to hew it
    away.
Also—and this you know not—the lifeless corpse of a
    friend
Is lying unburied, a dead thing polluting your whole
    expedition,
While you are lingering here to inquire about fate's
    decrees.   65
Before anything else, you must give it proper burial
    and make
Sacrifice of black sheep: only when you are thus
Purified, shall you see the Stygian groves and the
    regions
Not viable to the living.
                She spoke, then closed her lips.
Aeneas, eyes downcast, countenance full of sorrow,

46. **Cocytus,** the "river of wailing," a tributary of Acheron. 48.
Tartarus, the underworld. 52 **Proserpine,** queen of the underworld.

Moved off, leaving the cave, pondering much in his
    heart   71
On the cryptic issues the Sibyl had raised. Loyal
    Achates
Walked with him, his tread heavy beneath the same
    load of trouble.
Many were the conjectures they threw out, one to the
    other,
As to which of their dead friends the Sibyl had
    meant, and whose body   75
Must be interred. Now when they drew near the
    beach, they saw there
The body of Misenus, cut off by cruel death—
Misenus, son of Aeolus, whom none had excelled in
    firing
The warrior passions of men with thrilling trumpet
    calls.
He had been a comrade of mighty Hector, at Hec-
    tor's side   80
Had fought and won great fame as a trumpeter and a
    spearman.
After Achilles had defeated Hector and killed him,
This valiant hero, Misenus, attached himself to
    Dardan
Aeneas' company, following now no lesser a man.
But to-day, as he sent his horn's notes ringing over
    the sea,   85
Mostly rashly challenging the gods to a musical
    contest,
Jealous Triton caught him off guard—if we may
    credit
The story—and plunged him down in the surf among
    those rocks.
Now they were all standing around him, lamenting
    loudly,
Not least the good-hearted Aeneas. And now at once
    they hasten   90
Weeping to carry out the Sibyl's instructions, piling
Timber up with a will for a towering funeral altar.
Into the age-old forest, where only wild things lurk,
They go: spruces are felled, the holm oak rings with
    axe blows,
Wedges are used to split ash logs and the cleavable
    wood   95
Of oaks, immense rowans are rolled down from the
    heights.
Aeneas himself, in the middle of these activities,
Carrying the same tools as they, encouraged his
    friends.
But also, sad at heart, gazing up at the huge forest,
He brooded; and then he uttered his thoughts aloud
    in a prayer:—   100
    If only I might glimpse that golden bough on its
    tree
In the great wood this very moment! for all that the
    Sibyl
Said about you, Misenus, was true, too sadly true.

The words were hardly out when it befell that two doves
Came planing down from above before his very eyes   105
And alighted upon the green turf. The hero recognised
His mother's birds. His heart leapt up and he said a prayer:—
  Show me the way, if way there is! Oh, wing your flight
To that part of the forest where the precious bough overshadows
The fruitful soil. Do not forsake me, heavenly mother,   110
At this most crucial hour!
                  He spoke; froze in his tracks
To note what signs they gave and in what direction they'd move.
Now the doves, as they fed, flitted on from spot to spot, but never
So far ahead that one who followed lost sight of them.
Then, when they came to the mouth of foul-breathing Avernus,   115
Swiftly they soared, went gliding through the soft air and settled,
The pair of them, on a tree, the wished-for place, a tree
Amid whose branches there gleamed a bright haze, a different colour—
Gold. Just as in depth of winter the mistletoe blooms
In the woods with its strange leafage, a parasite on the tree,   120
Hanging its yellow-green berries about the smooth round boles:
So looked the bough of gold leaves upon that ilex dark,
And in a gentle breeze the gold-foil foliage rustled.
Aeneas at once took hold of the bough, and eagerly breaking
It off with one pull, he bore it into the shrine of the Sibyl.   125
Meantime upon the shore the Trojans were still lamenting
Misenus, and paying the last rites to his oblivious dust. . . .
  This done, Aeneas hastened to follow the Sibyl's directions.
A deep, deep cave there was, its mouth enormously gaping,
Shingly, protected by the dark lake and the forest gloom: 130
Above it, no winged creatures could ever wing their way
With impunity, so lethal was the miasma which
Went fuming up from its black throat to the vault of heaven:

Wherefore the Greeks called it Avernus, the Birdless Place.
Here the Sibyl first lined up four black-skinned bullocks,   135
Poured a libation of wine upon their foreheads, and then,
Plucking the topmost hairs from between their brows, she placed
These on the altar fires as an initial offering,
Calling aloud upon Hecate, powerful in heaven and hell.
While others laid their knives to these victims' throats, and caught   140
The fresh warm blood in bowls, Aeneas sacrificed
A black-fleeced lamb to Night, the mother of the Furies,
And her great sister, Earth, and a barren heifer to Proserpine.
Then he set up altars by night to the god of the Underworld,
Laying upon the flames whole carcasses of bulls   145
And pouring out rich oil over the burning entrails.
But listen!—at the very first crack of dawn, the ground
Underfoot began to mutter, the woody ridges to quake,
And a baying of hounds was heard through the half-light: the goddess was coming,
Hecate. The Sibyl cried:—
               Away! Now stand away,
You uninitiated ones, and clear the whole grove!   151
But you, Aeneas, draw your sword from the scabbard and fare forth!
Now you need all your courage, your steadfastness of heart.
  So much she said and, ecstatic, plunged into the opened cave mouth:
Unshrinking went Aeneas step for step with his guide.   155
  You gods who rule the kingdom of souls! You soundless shades!
Chaos, and Phlegethon! O mute wide leagues of Nightland!—
Grant me to tell what I have heard! With your assent
May I reveal what lies deep in the gloom of the Underworld!
  Dimly through the shadows and dark solitudes they wended,   160
Through the void domiciles of Dis, the bodiless regions:
Just as, through fitful moonbeams, under the moon's thin light,
A path lies in a forest, when Jove has palled the sky
With gloom, and the night's blackness has bled the world of colour.

161. **Dis,** the underworld.

See! At the very porch and entrance way to Orcus 165
Grief and ever-haunting Anxiety make their bed:
Here dwell pallid Diseases, here morose Old Age,
With Fear, ill-prompting Hunger, and squalid Indigence,
Shapes horrible to look at, Death and Agony;
Sleep, too, which is the cousin of Death; and Guilty Joys, 170
And there, against the threshold, War, the bringer of Death:
Here are the iron cells of the Furies, and lunatic Strife
Whose viperine hair is caught up with a headband soaked in blood. . . .
    From here is the road that leads to the dismal waters of Acheron.
Here a whirlpool boils with mud and immense swirlings 175
Of water, spouting up all the slimy sand of Cocytus.
A dreadful ferryman looks after the river crossing,
Charon: appallingly filthy he is, with a bush of unkempt
White beard upon his chin, with eyes like jets of fire;
And a dirty cloak draggles down, knotted about his shoulders. 180
He poles the boat, he looks after the sails, he is all the crew
Of that rust-coloured wherry which takes the dead across—
An ancient now, but a god's old age is green and sappy.
This way came fast and streaming up to the bank the whole throng:
Matrons and men were there, and there were greatheart heroes 185
Finished with earthly life, boys and unmarried maidens,
Young men laid on the pyre before their parents' eyes;
Multitudinous as the leaves that fall in a forest
At the first frost of autumn, or the birds that out of the deepsea
Fly to land in migrant flocks, when the cold of the year 190
Has sent them overseas in search of a warmer climate.
So they all stood, each begging to be ferried across first,
Their hands stretched out in longing for the shore beyond the river.
But the surly ferryman embarks now this, now that group,
While others he keeps away at a distance from the shingle. 195
Aeneas, being astonished and moved by the great stir, said:—

Tell me, O Sibyl, what means this rendezvous at the river?
What purpose have these souls? By what distinction are some
Turned back, while other souls sweep over the wan water?
    To which the long-lived Sibyl uttered this brief reply:— 200
    O son of Anchises' loins and true-born offspring of heaven,
What you see is the mere of Cocytus, the Stygian marsh
By whose mystery even the gods, having sworn, are afraid to be forsworn.
All this crowd you see are the helpless ones, the unburied:
That ferryman is Charon: the ones he conveys have had burial. 205
None may be taken across from bank to awesome bank of
That harsh-voiced river until his bones are laid to rest.
Otherwise, he must haunt this place for a hundred years
Before he's allowed to revisit the longed-for stream at last. . . .
    And look! yonder was roaming the helmsman, Palinurus, 210
Who, on their recent voyage, while watching the stars, had fallen
From the afterdeck, thrown off the ship there in midpassage.
A sombre form in the deep shadows, Aeneas barely
Recognised him; then accosted:—
                    Which of the gods, Palinurus,
Snatched you away from us and made you drown in the midsea? 215
Oh, tell me! For Apollo, whom never before had I found
Untruthful, did delude my mind with this one answer,
Foretelling that you would make your passage to Italy
Unharmed by sea. Is it thus he fulfils a sacred promise?
    Palinurus replied:—
    The oracle of Phoebus has not tricked you,
My captain, son of Anchises; nor was I drowned by a god. 221
It was an accident: I slipped, and the violent shock
Of my fall broke off the tiller to which I was holding firmly
As helmsman, and steering the ship. By the wild seas I swear
That not on my own account was I frightened nearly so much as 225
Lest your ship, thus crippled, its helmsman overboard,

Lose steerage-way and founder amid the mountainous
waves.
Three stormy nights did the South wind furiously
drive me along
Over the limitless waters: on the fourth day I just
Caught sight of Italy, being lifted high on a wave
crest. 230
Little by little I swam to the shore. I was all but safe,
When, as I clung to the rough-edged cliff top, my
fingers crooked
And my soaking garments weighing me down, some
barbarous natives
Attacked me with swords, in their ignorance thinking
that I was a rich prize.
Now the waves have me, the winds keep tossing me
up on the shore again. 235
So now, by the sweet light and breath of heaven
above
I implore you, and by your father, by your hopes for
growing Ascanius
Redeem me from this doom, unconquered one!
Please sprinkle
Dust on my corpse—you can do it and quickly get
back to port Velia:
Or else, if way there is, some way that your heavenly
mother 240
Is showing you (not, for sure, without the assent of
deity
Would you be going to cross the swampy Stygian
stream),
Give poor Palinurus your hand, take me with you
across the water
So that at least I may rest in the quiet place, in death.
Thus did the phantom speak, and the Sibyl began
to speak thus:— 245
This longing of yours, Palinurus, has carried you
quite away.
Shall you, unburied, view the Styx, the austere river
Of the Infernal gods, or come to its bank unbidden?
Give up this hope that the course of fate can be
swerved by prayer.
But hear and remember my words, to console you in
your hard fortune. 250
I say that the neighbouring peoples, compelled by
portents from heaven
Occurring in every township, shall expiate your
death,
Shall give you burial and offer the solemn dues to
your grave,
And the place shall keep the name of Palinurus for
ever.
Her sayings eased for a while the anguish of his
sad heart; 255
He forgot his cares in the joy of giving his name to a
region.
So they resumed their interrupted journey, and
drew near

The river. Now when the ferryman, from out on the
Styx, espied them
Threading the soundless wood and making fast for
the bank,
He hailed them, aggressively shouting at them before
they could speak:— 260
Whoever you are that approaches my river, carry-
ing a weapon,
Halt there! Keep your distance, and tell me why you
are come!
This is the land of ghosts, of sleep and somnolent
night:
The living are not permitted to use the Stygian
ferry. . . .
The priestess of Apollo answered him shortly,
thus:— 265
There is no such duplicity here, so set your mind at
rest;
These weapons offer no violence. . . .
Trojan Aeneas, renowned for war and a duteous heart,
Comes down to meet his father in the shades of the
Underworld.
If you are quite unmoved by the spectacle of such
great faith, 270
This you must recognise—
And here she disclosed the golden
Bough which was hid in her robe. His angry mood
calms down.
No more is said. Charon is struck with awe to see
After so long that magic gift, the bough fate-given;
He turns his sombre boat and poles it towards the
bank. 275
Then, displacing the souls who were seated along its
benches
And clearing the gangways, to make room for the big
frame of Aeneas,
He takes him on board. The ramshackle craft creaked
under his weight
And let in through its seams great swashes of muddy
water.
At last, getting the Sibyl and the hero safe across, 280
He landed them amidst wan reeds on a dreary mud
flat.
Huge Cerberus, monstrously couched in a cave
confronting them,
Made the whole region echo with his three-throated
barking.
The Sibyl, seeing the snakes bristling upon his neck
now,
Threw him for bait a cake of honey and wheat infused with 285
Sedative drugs. The creature, crazy with hunger,
opened
Its three mouths, gobbled the bait; then its huge
body relaxed
And lay, sprawled out on the ground, the whole
length of its cave kennel.

Aeneas, passing its entrance, the watch-dog neutral-
ised,
Strode rapidly from the bank of that river of no
return.   290
　At once were voices heard, a sound of mewling
and wailing,
Ghosts of infants sobbing there at the threshold,
infants
From whom a dark day stole their share of delicious
life,
Snatched them away from the breast, gave them sour
death to drink.
Next to them were those condemned to death on a
false charge.   295
Yet every place is duly allotted and judgment is
given.
Minos, as president, summons a jury of the dead: he
hears
Every charge, examines the record of each; he shakes
the urn.
Next again are located the sorrowful ones who killed
Themselves, throwing their lives away, not driven by
guilt   300
But because they loathed living: how they would like
to be
In the world above now, enduring poverty and hard
trials!
God's law forbids: that unlovely fen with its glooming
water
Corrals them there, the nine rings of Styx corral them
in.
Not far from here can be seen, extending in all
directions,   305
The vale of mourning—such is the name it bears: a
region
Where those consumed by the wasting torments of
merciless love
Haunt the sequestered alleys and myrtle groves that
give them
Cover; death itself cannot cure them of love's disease. . . .
Amongst them, with her death-wound still bleeding,
through the deep wood   310
Was straying Phoenician Dido. Now when the Trojan
leader
Found himself near her and knew that the form he
glimpsed through the shadows
Was hers—as early in the month one sees, or imagines he sees,
Through a wrack of cloud the new moon rising and
glimmering—
He shed some tears, and addressed her in tender,
loving tones:—   315
　Poor, unhappy Dido, so the message was true that
came to me
Saying you'd put an end to your life with the sword
and were dead?

Oh god! was it death I brought you, then? I swear by
the stars,
By the powers above, by whatever is sacred in the
Underworld,
It was not of my own will, Dido, I left your
land.   320
Heaven's commands, which now force me to traverse
the shades,
This sour and derelict region, this pit of darkness,
drove me
Imperiously from your side. I did not, could not
imagine
My going would ever bring such terrible agony on
you.   324
Don't move away! Oh, let me see you a little longer!
To fly from me, when this is the last word fate allows
us!
　Thus did Aeneas speak, trying to soften the wild-
eyed,
Passionate-hearted ghost, and brought the tears to his
own eyes.
She would not turn to him; she kept her gaze on the
ground,
And her countenance remained as stubborn to his
appeal   330
As if it were carved from recalcitrant flint or a crag of
marble.
At last she flung away, hating him still, and vanished
Into the shadowy wood where her first husband,
Sychaeus,
Understands her unhappiness and gives her an equal
love.
None the less did Aeneas, hard hit by her piteous
fate,   335
Weep after her from afar, as she went, with tears of
compassion.
　Then he passed on the appointed way. They came
to the last part
Of Limbo, the place set apart for men famous in
war. . . .
To right and left the spirits press thickly around
Aeneas.
Not enough just to have seen him once—they want
to detain him,   340
To pace along beside him and find out why he has
come there.
But the Greek generals and the regiments of Aga-
memnon,
When they beheld his armour glinting through the
gloom,
Were seized with fear and trembling; some turned
tail, even as
In the old days they had run for their ships; some
uttered a wraith of   345
A war cry—they tried to shout, but their wide
mouths only whimpered.
. . . Aurora, driving her rosy chariot,

Had passed the midway point of the sky in her flying
    course;
And indeed they might have used up all the allotted
    time thus,
Had not his guide, the Sibyl, spoken a few words of
    warning:—   350
   Night comes apace, Aeneas; yet we spend the
    hours in grieving.
Here is the spot where the way forks, going in two
    directions;
The right-hand leads beneath the battlements of
    great Dis,
And is our route to Elysium; the left-hand takes the
    wicked
To Tartarus, their own place, and punishment con-
    dign. . . .   355
   Aeneas looked back on a sudden: he saw to his left
    a cliff
Overhanging a spread of battlements, a threefold
    wall about them,
Girdled too by a swift-running stream, a flaming
    torrent—
Hell's river of fire, whose current rolls clashing rocks
    along.
In front, an enormous portal, the door-posts columns
    of adamant,   360
So strong that no mortal violence nor even the heaven-
    dwellers
Can broach it: an iron tower stands sheer and soaring
    above it,
Whereupon Tisiphone sits, wrapped in a bloodstained
    robe,
Sleeplessly, day-long, night-long, guarding the fore-
    court there.
From within can be heard the sounds of groaning
    and brutal lashing,   365
Sounds of clanking iron, of chains being dragged
    along.
Scared by the din, Aeneas halted; he could not
    move:—
   What kinds of criminals are these? Speak, lady!
    What punishments
Afflict them, that such agonised sounds rise up from
    there?   369
   Then the Sibyl began:—
                O famous lord of the Trojans,
No righteous soul may tread that threshold of the
    damned:
But, when Hecate appointed me to the Avernian
    grove,
She instructed me in heaven's punishments, showed
    me all.
Here Rhadamanthus rules, and most severe his rule
    is,

Trying and chastising wrongdoers, forcing confes-
    sions   375
From any who, on earth, went gleefully undetect-
    ed—
But uselessly, since they have only postponed till
    death their atonement.
At once Tisiphone, the avenger, scourge in hand,
Pounces upon the guilty, lashing them, threatening
    them
With the angry snakes in her left hand, and calls up
    her bloodthirsty sisters.   380
Then at last the hinges screech, the infernal gates
Grind open. Do you see the sentry, who she is,
Posted over the forecourt? the shape that guards the
    threshold?
Within, there dwells a thing more fierce—the fifty-
    headed
Hydra, with all its black throats agape. Then Tar-
    tarus   385
Goes sheer down under the shades, an abyss double
    in depth
The height that Olympus stands above a man gazing
    skyward.
Here Earth's primaeval offspring, the breed of Titans,
    who
Were hurled down by Jove's lightning, writhe in the
    bottomless pit. . . .   389
Here are those who in life hated their own brothers,
Or struck their parents; those who entangled their
    dependants
In fraudulent dealing; and those who sat tight on the
    wealth they had won,
Setting none aside for their own kin—most numerous
    of all are these;
Then such as were killed for adultery, took part in
    militant treason,
Men who made bold to break faith with their mas-
    ters:—all such await   395
Punishment, mewed up here. And seek not to know
    what punishment,
What kind of destined torment awaits each one in the
    Pit.
Some have to roll huge rocks; some whirl round,
    spreadeagled
On spokes of wheels: the tragic Theseus sits, con-
    demned to
Spend eternity in that chair: the poor wretch, Phle-
    gyas,   400
Admonishes all, crying out through the mirk in
    solemn avowal,
"Be warned by me! Learn justice, and not to belittle
    the gods!"
One sold his country for gold, putting her under the
    yoke of

---

363. **Tisiphone,** one of the Furies. 374. **Rhadamanthus,** a judge in
Hades because of his reputation for justice while on earth.

399. **Theseus,** who assisted in a plot to carry off Proserpine from the
underworld. 400. **Phlegyas,** who burned a temple of Apollo.

Dictatorship, and corruptly made and unmade her
    laws;
One entered the bed of his daughter, forced an
    unholy mating: 405
All dared some abominable thing, and what they
    dared they did.
No, not if I had a hundred tongues, a hundred
    mouths
And a voice of iron, could I describe all the shapes of
    wickedness,
Catalogue all the retributions inflicted here.
    Thus spoke the long-lived priestess of Phoebus,
        then added this:—   410
    But come, resume your journey, finish the task in
        hand!
Let us go quickly on. I can see the bastions, forged in
The Cyclops' furnaces, and the arch of the gateway
    yonder,
Where we are bidden to put down your passport, the
    golden bough.
    She had spoken. Side by side they went the twi-
        light way,   415
Rapidly covering the space between, and approached
    the gateway.
Aeneas stopped at the entrance, sprinkled himself
    with holy
Water, and placed the bough right at the doorway
    there.
    Now this was done at last, and Proserpine had her
        offering,
They went on into the Happy Place, the green and
    genial   420
Glades where the fortunate live, the home of the
    blessed spirits.
What largesse of bright air, clothing the vales in
    dazzling
Light, is here! This land has a sun and stars of its
    own.
Some exercise upon the grassy playing-fields   424
Or wrestle on the yellow sands in rivalry of sport;
Some foot the rhythmic dances and chant poems
    aloud. . . .
Aeneas noticed others to left and right on the green-
    sward
Feasting and singing a jovial paean in unison
Amidst a fragrant grove of bay trees, whence the
    river
Eridanus springs, to roll grandly through woods of
    the world above.   430
Here were assembled those who had suffered wounds
    in defence of
Their country; those who had lived pure lives as
    priests; and poets
Who had not disgraced Apollo, poets of true integ-
    rity;
Men who civilised life by the skills they discovered,
    and men whose

Kindness to other people has kept their memory
    green—   435
All these upon their temples wore headbands white
    as snow. . . .
    Deep in a green valley stood father Anchises,
        surveying
The spirits there confined before they went up to the
    light of
The world above; he was musing seriously, and
    reviewing
His folk's full tally, it happened, the line of his loved
    children,   440
Their destinies and fortunes, their characters and
    their deeds.
Now, when he saw Aeneas coming in his direction
Over the grass, he stretched out both hands, all
    eagerness,
And tears poured down his cheeks, and the words
    were tumbling out:—
    So you have come at last? The love that your
        father relied on   445
Has won through the hard journey? And I may gaze,
    my son,
Upon your face, and exchange the old homely talk
    with you?
Thus indeed I surmised it would be, believed it must
    happen,
Counting the days till you came: I was not deceived
    in my hopes, then.
Over what lands, what wide, wide seas you have
    made your journey!   450
What dangers, my son, have beset you! And now you
    are here with me.
How I dreaded lest you should come to some harm at
    Carthage!
    Aeneas replied:—
                        Your image it was, your troubled
        phantom
That, often rising before me, has brought me to this
    place, father.
Our ships are riding at anchor in the Tyrrhene Sea.
    Oh, let me   455
Take your hand and embrace you, father! Let me!
    Withdraw not!
    Even as he spoke, his cheeks grew wet with a flood
        of tears.
Three times he tried to put his arms round his father's
    neck,
Three times the phantom slipped his vain embrace—
    it was like
Grasping a wisp of wind or the wings of a fleeting
    dream.   460
    Now did Aeneas descry, deep in a valley retiring,
A wood, a secluded copse whose branches soughed in
    the wind,
And Lethe river drifting past the tranquil places.
Hereabouts were flitting a multitude without number,

Just as, amid the meadows on a fine summer day,
The bees alight on flowers of every hue, and brim
the   466
Shining lilies, and all the lea is humming with them.
Aeneas, moved by the sudden sight, asked in his
ignorance
What it might mean, what was that river over there
And all that crowd of people swarming along its
banks.   470
Then his father, Anchises, said:—
                    They are souls who are destined for
Reincarnation; and now at Lethe's stream they are
drinking
The waters that quench man's troubles, the deep
draught of oblivion.
Long, long have I wanted to tell you of these and
reveal them
Before your eyes, to count them over, the seed of my
seed,   475
That you might the more rejoice with me in the
finding of Italy.
  But father, must it be deemed that some souls
ascend from here
To our earthly scene? re-enter our dull corporeal
existence?
Why ever should so perverse a craving for earth
possess them?
  I will tell you, my son, certainly; I will not keep
you in doubt,   480
  Answered Anchises, and then enlarged on each
point successively:—
  First, you must know that the heavens, the earth,
the watery plains
Of the sea, the moon's bright globe, the sun and the
stars are all
Sustained by a spirit within; for immanent Mind,
flowing
Through all its parts and leavening its mass, makes the
universe work.   485
This union produced mankind, the beasts, the birds
of the air,
And the strange creatures that live under the sea's
smooth face.
The life-force of those seeds is fire, their source
celestial,
But they are deadened and dimmed by the sinful
bodies they live in—
The flesh that is laden with death, the anatomy of
clay: 490
Whence these souls of ours feel fear, desire, grief,
joy,
But encased in their blind, dark prison discern not
the heavenlight above.
Yes, not even when the last flicker of life has left us,
Does evil, or the ills that flesh is heir to, quite
Relinquish our souls; it must be that many a taint
grows deeply,   495

Mysteriously grained in their being from long contact
with the body.
Therefore the dead are disciplined in purgatory, and
pay
The penalty of old evil: some hang, stretched to the
blast of
Vacuum winds; for others, the stain of sin is washed
Away in a vast whirlpool or cauterised with fire.   500
Each of us finds in the next world his own level: a few
of us
Are later released to wander at will through broad
Elysium,
The Happy Fields; until, in the fullness of time, the
ages
Have purged that ingrown stain, and nothing is left
but pure
Ethereal sentience and the spirit's essential flame. 505
All these souls, when they have finished their thou-
sand-year cycle,
God sends for, and they come in crowds to the river
of Lethe,
So that, you see, with memory washed out, they may
revisit
The earth above and begin to wish to be born again.
  When Anchises had finished, he drew his son and
the Sibyl   510
Into the thick of the murmuring concourse assembled
there
And took his stand on an eminence from which he
could scan the long files
Over against him, and mark the features of those who
passed.
  Listen, for I will show you your destiny, setting
forth
The fame that from now shall attend the seed of
Dardanus,   515
The posterity that awaits you from an Italian mar-
riage—
Illustrious souls, one day to come in for our Trojan
name.
That young man there—do you see him? who leans
on an untipped spear,
Has been allotted the next passage to life, and first of
All these will ascend to earth, with Italian blood in
his veins;   520
He is Silvius, an Alban name, and destined to be your
last child,
The child of your late old age by a wife, Lavinia,
who shall
Bear him in sylvan surroundings, a king and the
father of kings
Through whom our lineage shall rule in Alba
Longa. . . .
Further, a child of Mars shall go to join his grand-
sire—   525
Romulus, born of the stock of Assaracus by his
mother,

Ilia. Look at the twin plumes upon his helmet's crest,
Mars' cognisance, which marks him out for the world
    of earth!
His are the auguries, my son, whereby great Rome
Shall rule to the ends of the earth, shall aspire to the
    highest achievement,   530
Shall ring the seven hills with a wall to make one
    city,
Blessed in her breed of men. . . .
Now bend your gaze this way, look at that people
    there!
They are *your* Romans. Caesar is there and all As-
    canius'
Posterity, who shall pass beneath the arch of day.   535
And here, here is the man, the promised one you
    know of—
Caesar Augustus, son of a god, destined to rule
Where Saturn ruled of old in Latium, and there
Bring back the age of gold: his empire shall expand
Past Garamants and Indians to a land beyond the
    zodiac   540
And the sun's yearly path, where Atlas the sky-bearer
    pivots
The wheeling heavens, embossed with fiery stars, on
    his shoulder.
Even now the Caspian realm, the Crimean country
Tremble at oracles of the gods predicting his ad-
    vent,
And the seven mouths of the Nile are in a lather of
    fright. . . .   545
Let others fashion from bronze more lifelike, breath-
    ing images—
For so they shall—and evoke living faces from mar-
    ble;
Others excel as orators, others track with their instru-
    ments
The planets circling in heaven and predict when stars
    will appear.
But, Romans, never forget that government is your
    medium!   550
Be this your art:—to practise men in the habit of
    peace,
Generosity to the conquered, and firmness against
    aggressors. . . .
They wandered through that region, those broad and
    hazy plains.
After Anchises had shown his son over the whole
    place
And fired his heart with passion for the great things
    to come,   555
He told the hero of wars he would have to fight one
    day,
Told of the Laurentines and the city of Latinus,
And how to evade, or endure, each crisis upon his
    way.

540. **Garamants.** Garamant was the southernmost land in Africa
known in antiquity.

There are two gates of Sleep: the one is made of
    horn,
They say, and affords the outlet for genuine appari-
    tions: 560
The other's a gate of brightly-shining ivory; this way
The Shades send up to earth false dreams that impose
    upon us.
Talking, then, of such matters, Anchises escorted his
    son
And the Sibyl as far as the ivory gate and sent them
    through it.
Aeneas made his way back to the ships and his
    friends with all speed,   565
Then coasted along direct to the harbour of Caieta.
The ships, anchored by the bows, line the shore with
    their sterns.

BOOK VII

. . . Now was the sea's face blushing with dawn
    rays, and in heaven
Rosily charioted shone crocus-yellow Aurora,
When the wind dropped—all of a sudden not one
    breath
Was blowing—and the oars toiled in water slow as
    syrup.
Now, looking forth from the deep, Aeneas sighted a
    big wood: 5
Through this wood the genial stream of Tiber flow-
    ing,
Yellow with racing eddies that stir up sand galore,
Debouches into the sea. Around and above, bright-
    plumaged
Birds whose habitat is the river banks and channel
Charmed the air with their song, flitted about the
    wood.   10
Aeneas ordered his squadron to change course to-
    wards the land.
Soon in high spirits he entered the shady mouth of
    the river.
    Come, Muse of Love, let me rehearse the kings,
    the phase of
History, and the conditions that reigned in antique
    Latium   14
When first that expedition arrived upon the beaches
Of Italy: I'll recall what first led to the war there.
. . . An old man now, Latinus
Was king of the towns and country, his reign being
    long and peaceful. . . .
Latinus, by fate's decree, had no son now; his male
Succession was no more, cut off in the bloom of first
    youth.   20
One daughter he had, sole prop of his house and heir
    of his ample
Estate, a girl fully budded now and ripe for marriage.

566. **Caieta,** a town in Latium.

Many sought her hand, from all over Latium, from all
Italy: the handsomest by far of these wooers was
    Turnus—
He had the prestige of a splendid pedigree and the
    backing   25
Of the queen, who had set her heart on getting him
    as a son-in-law:
But various alarming portents from heaven were
    proving an obstacle.
. . . while the maiden Lavinia stood beside
Her father, who with ritual taper was lighting the
    altar—   29
Sinister thing—they beheld her long hair set on fire
And all her head-dress burning with crackling flames;
    they saw
Those queenly tresses ablaze, ablaze her coronet
Of precious stones: before long, enshrouded in golden-
    glowering
Smoky flame, she was fountaining sparks all over the
    palace.
It was counted, of course, as a dreadful, miraculous
    manifestation: 35
The maiden herself, they foretold, was singled out for
    a famous
Destiny, but for the people it meant a widespread
    war.
    The king, greatly disturbed by this portent, goes to
    visit
The oracle of Faunus, his prophet father, and ques-
    tions
The grove where Albunea towers over the forest,
    resounding   40
With hallowed cascade and darkly exhaling a deadly
    vapour. . . .
This was where Latinus now went to consult the
    oracle;
After the ritual sacrifice of a hundred wool-bearing
    sheep
He lay down and reclined upon the hides, the out-
    spread
Fleeces: and at once from the depths of the wood a
    voice came:—   45
    Seek not, my son, to marry your daughter to a man
    of
The Latin race. Embark not upon a native alliance.
From abroad shall sons-in-law come, to wed our
    women and make
Our name illustrious: to their descendents the whole
Spinning globe shall be a footstool and an empire—
All that the sun looks down on, even to the ends of
    the earth.   51
    The oracle of his father, Faunus, the counsel given
Thus in the stilly night, Latinus kept not secret;
But rumour had already flown it far and wide
Throughout the towns of Ausonia, when the Trojan
    expedition   55
Lay with their vessels moored to the grassy bank of

the Tiber. . . .
    But look! from Argos, city of Inachus, now return-
    ing
And well on her way through the sky, the vindictive
    consort of Jupiter
Saw from the air above Pachynus in Sicily,
At a great distance, Aeneas triumphant, his fleet all
    there.   60
She notes they have disembarked from their ships
    and are busily building
Habitations already, feeling quite safe in that land.
Bitter resentment checked her. Shaking her head,
. . . Juno came down to earth, horrific,
And haled forth from the infernal regions, the home
    of the terrible
Deities, Allecto, maker of grief, who revels   65
In war, in open and underhand violence, in damaging
    quarrels.
Even her father, Pluto, and her hellish sisters loathe
That fiend, Allecto, so manifold her aspects and so
    ferocious
Each form she takes, such a nest of vipers swarms in
    her black hair.
Now Juno began to speak, whetting this creature's
    appetite:—   70
    Maiden, daughter of Night, do me this favour—
    it's your kind—
This service, so that our honour and reputation may
    not be
Diminished, so that the Trojans fail to wheedle
    Latinus
By means of this marriage or to take possession of
    Italy.
You can set brothers of one mind at one another's
    throats,   75
Torment a home with hatred, bringing your whips
    and destructive
Firebrands to lash a house: you have a thousand
    titles,
A thousand tricks for making mischief. Stir up your
    teeming
Ideas! Disrupt the peace they have made! Sow seeds
    of war!
Let them wish for weapons, demand them and use
    them, all in an instant.   80
    At once Allecto went, steeped in her viperish
    venom,
And sought out first the high walls of the Laurentine
    monarch
In Latium. There she pickets Amata's quiet thresh-
    old—
The queen, whose motherly heart is seething with
    grief and chagrin
Over the Trojans' coming and the marriage with
    Turnus cancelled.   85

65. **Allecto,** one of the Furies.

On her the fiend now casts a serpent, one of her snake-blue
Tresses, and thrusts it into her bosom, deep into her heart,
So that the queen may discharge through the household its maniac infection.
Gliding between her dress and her smooth breasts, that serpent
Coils—she feels not its touch nor notices it in her madness—   90
Breathing its morbid breath into her: swelling, it turns
Into a golden necklace, into the head-dress binding
Her hair, and its pendant ribbon, and slithers over her body.
Now, while that moist and magic contagion was but beginning
To work upon her mind and twine her bones with fire,   95
The queen, whose thoughts were not yet wholly possessed by the flame in
Her breast, quite gently spoke, as soft-hearted mothers do,
Greatly upset at the idea of her daughter wedding a Trojan:—
    Father, must our Lavinia be wed to a Trojan, an outcast?
Have you no feeling for her? no sense of your own interests?   100
No pity for her mother?—that false-hearted pirate will leave me
As soon as a fair wind blows, and sail away with my daughter.
It's Paris all over again—just so did Paris steal into
Sparta, then carried Ledaean Helen away to Troy.
What of your solemn pledge? the love you had in the old days   105
For your own people? the promise given so often to Turnus,
Your kinsman? . . .
    But when she saw these arguments had no effect on Latinus
And he was firmly opposed; when the serpent's frenzying poison
Had worked its way into her marrow and spread all over her being;   110
Then, overwrought by monstrous hallucinations, the poor queen
Went uncontrollably raving, beside herself, round the city. . . .
The louring Allecto mounted at once on her sombre wings
And made for the walls of hot-headed Turnus. . . .
    Here, in the lofty palace,   114
Turnus was taking his rest at the mid-hour of night.
Allecto now sloughed off her grim looks and diabolical

Form, changing herself to the likeness of an old crone,
Uncannily furrowing her brow with wrinkles; she assumed
White hair and a headband, wreathed her head with a chaplet of olive:
So, as the aged priestess of Juno's temple, Calybe,   120
Coming before the young man's eyes, she spoke as follows:—
    Turnus, will you tolerate that all your efforts should run
To waste, the dominion you've worked for pass into the hands of foreigners?
The king denies you your bride and the marriage-portion you've bought with
Bloodshed: an alien now is called in to be his successor.   125
Go then, you laughing-stock, face dangers, mow down the Tuscans,
Ensure peace for the Latins!—this is the thanks you get.
Indeed, almighty Juno appeared in person and bade me
Speak to you even thus, while you lay in the quiet of night.
Up, then! Take heart of grace! Mobilise the army! March   130
Out of the gates to war! Those Trojan ships and leaders
That occupy our beautiful river—burn them to ashes!
These are orders from the heavenly powers. Let king Latinus,
Unless he agree to stand by his word and allow your marriage,
Suffer for it, and discover what Turnus is like as an enemy.   135
    Here the young man in his turn began to speak, deriding
Her prophecy:—
                I am not, as you seem to think, unaware that
A fleet has sailed into the Tiber; the news did come to my ears.
Do not be such an alarmist, I beg you. Queen Juno is not
Indifferent to me and mine.   140
As for you, mother—it's old age, clogging the mind and impairing its
Sense of reality, that haunts you with bogey-man worries,
And scares your prophetic soul with the delusions of civil war.
Your job's to look after the temple and the images of the gods:
Leave making war and peace to men, whose business is warfare.   145

These words of Turnus made Allecto explode into
  anger.
As the young prince still spoke, a sudden palsy shook
  him,
And his eyes went stiff with fear; for the Fury,
  hissing-snake-tressed,
Was hideously revealed at her full height. She rolled
Her flaming eyes, she flung him back as he tried to
  falter   150
A few more words; two snakes stood up like horns on
  her head,
And she cracked her whip, and spoke again, her
  mouth like a mad dog's:—
  So! My mind is clogged? Old age, impairing my
    sense of
Reality, scares me with delusions of civil war?
Look at me, then! I am come from the place where
  the Furies are.   155
War and death I bear in this hand.
So saying, she hurled an incendiary brand at Turnus,
  which buried
Itself deep in his heart, blazing and pitchily smok-
  ing.
Extreme terror awoke him from sleep; a sweat broke
  out
All over the young man's body, soaked him from
  head to foot.   160
Madly yelling for arms, by his bed, through his house
  he hunts for them;
Crazy with bloodlust he is, with the criminal mania
  for fighting,
Still more, with resentment. So, when a fire of wood,
  loud crackling,
Is stoked up high beneath the belly of a boiling
  cauldron,
The water dances in the heat; within the cauldron
  the water   165
Seethes and fumes, bubbling, spitting up foam, till it
  cannot
Contain itself any more and a cloud of dense steam
  rises.
Breaking the peace, then, Turnus ordered his army
  commanders
To get on a war footing and march against king
  Latinus:
Italy must be protected, the foe thrown back from its
  frontiers;   170
He would be more than a match for Trojans and
  Latins together.
So Turnus proclaimed, and called the gods to witness
  his vow.
The Rutuli egg one another on to war with enthusi-
  asm,
Some being stirred by the youthful, handsome pres-
  ence of Turnus,
Some by his royal lineage, some by his notable
  deeds. . . .   175

BOOK VIII

When Turnus hoisted the ensign of war from the
  Laurentine
Citadel, and the trumpets blared out their husky
  calls;
When Turnus lashed his mettlesome horses and
  clashed his weapons,
Instantly men were excited: the alarm brought about
  a feverish
Uprising and leaguing-together in Latium: war
  hysteria   5
Gripped the youth. . . . Aeneas, seed of Laomedon,
Seeing them so, was much agitated by surging wor-
  ries,
His mind in feverish conflict, tossed from one side to
  the other,
Twisting and turning all ways to find a way past his
  dilemma. . . .
It was night, and throughout the earth deep slumber
  lay upon   10
All weary creatures, lay on bird and beast alike.
Bedded upon the river-bank under the chilly vault
Of heaven, his heart much exercised by sombre
  thoughts
About war, Aeneas at last yielded himself to sleep.
Before his face there appeared now, rising amidst the
  leaves of   15
The poplars out of that pleasant river, its deity, old
Tiberinus: a veil of grey and gauzy stuff was draped
About him, a coronal of reeds shadowed his brow.
He spoke to Aeneas, relieving his troubled heart like
  this:—
  O prince of divine lineage, who out of the enemy's
    clutches   20
Bring Troy town back to us, preserving it for all time.
. . . Now pay heed while I tell you briefly
How you may best unravel the urgent problem
  before you.
Arcadians, a people descended from Pallas, followers
  now
Of king Evander in peace and war, having chosen a
  site   25
Within this country, have built a township on the
  hills
And named it Pallanteum after their ancestor, Pallas.
This people wages war persistently with the Latins:
Make a treaty with them, and get them onto your
  side.
I for my part will conduct you straight up my water-
  way   30
That, rowing against the current, you may achieve a
  passage. . . .
All that night the Tiber smoothed down its popply
  stream
And the current beneath its quietened surface came
  to a standstill,

So that the face of the waters was flat as a gentle pool
Or a calm mere, and rowing cost no strenuous effort.
So with the river helping they sped on the trip they
    had started.   36
The well-tarred ships glide on; waters and woods
    admire
A spectacle new to them—shields of warriors shining
Afar down the river and painted hulls floating upon
    it.
All night and the following day the Trojans rowed
    without respite,   40
Up the long loops of the river, under the shade of
    diverse
Trees, through the green reflection of woods in the
    glass-calm water.
The blazing sun had climbed to the midway of
    heaven
When they saw in the distance walls, a citadel, and a
    few
Scattered roofs: Rome's dominion has since exalted
    that place   45
To the skies; but then Evander was lord of a meagre
    realm.
Quickly the Trojans steered to the bank and ap-
    proached the settlement.
    It happened that day the Arcadian king was
    holding a festival
Honouring Hercules, heir of Amphitryon, and the
    gods   49
In a grove outside the city. With him his son, Pallas,
The younger notables all and the plain-living senators
Burnt incense, while the warm blood of victims
    steamed at the altars.
Now when they saw the tall ships come gliding up
    amid
The trees, through the wood's dim vistas, and the
    oars quietly moving,
Alarmed by so unexpected a sight, they started up
    from   55
The banquet as one man. But Pallas, undaunted,
    forbade them
To leave the rites unfinished; seizing a weapon, he
    hurried
Towards the Trojans and hailed them from a vantage-
    point at a distance:—
    Strangers, whither away, taking a route so strange
    to you?
Who are you? Where do you come from? Do you
    bring peace or war?   60
    Then, where he stood high up on the poop, Aeneas
    answered,
Holding out in his hand an olive branch, emblem of
    peace:—
    We are sons of Troy that you see here, and no
    friends to the Latins
Who have driven us out of their land by a cynical act
    of aggression.

We're looking for king Evander. Tell him a deputa-
    tion   65
Of Trojan leaders has come to plead for his alliance.
    Pallas, struck with awe by so famous a name,
    called out:—
    Come ashore, whoever you are, sir. Come, and talk
    to my father
Yourself. Do us the honour of being a guest in our
    house.
    He extended a welcoming hand and clasped
    Aeneas' right hand.   70
Leaving the river-bank they went forward into the
    wood.
Before long, Aeneas was making a friendly speech to
    the king:—
    Best of the sons of Greece, it is fortune's will that
    to you
I should come for a favour, extending the formal
    olive branch.
I do so without misgivings, although you are an
    Arcadian,   75
A leader of Greeks, and related by blood to the twin
    Atridae.
My own merit, the sacred oracles of the gods,
The kinship between our fathers, your own far-
    reaching fame
Have bound me to you, and I follow the bidding of
    fate most gladly. . . .
Relying on this, I launched no professional-diplomatic
Overtures, to make a compact with you: I have
    come   81
In person to ask your aid and have put my life in
    your hands.
We are bitterly menaced in war by that same Dauni-
    an people
Which persecutes you: they believe they have only to
    drive us out
And nothing will stop them from subjugating the
    whole of Hesperia   85
And getting control of the Adriatic and Tuscan
    seaboards.
Let us exchange guarantees. My men are stout-
    hearted fighters,
And their morale is high; as soldiers, their deeds
    speak for them.
    Thus spoke Aeneas. The king for some time had
    been watching intently
His face and eyes, scrutinising the whole man while
    he talked.   90
Now he replied briefly:—
                Most glad am I, bravest of Trojans,
To welcome and get to know you. How vividly you
    remind me
Of your great father Anchises in speech, in accent
    and feature!
For I remember how Priam, Laomedon's son, when
    he travelled

To visit his sister Hesione's kingdom, *en route* for
    Salamis,   95
Came on from there and crossed the borders of cold
    Arcadia.
I was a young man then, in the first flush of youth:
I used to hero-worship your Trojan chiefs and their
    prince,
The son of Laomedon; but taller than any, strode
Anchises. I recollect in boyish enthusiasm   100
Longing to speak to the hero and shake him by the
    hand.
I went up to him, eagerly brought him into the city of
    Pheneus.
He gave me, when he left, a very fine quiver contain-
    ing
Lycian arrows, a gold-embroidered scarf, and a pair
    of
Golden bridles which now are owned by my son,
    Pallas.   105
And so, the hand you ask for in friendship—here, it is
    yours!
To-morrow, as soon as the earth grows light, I will
    send you away
With an escort to gladden your heart, and will aid
    you from my resources.
Meantime, this annual feast which we cannot rightly
    defer—
Since you have come here as friends, do us the
    kindness of sharing it   110
With us, begin straight away to get used to the board
    of your comrades.
    So saying, he has the dishes and wine cups put
    back, which had been
Removed, and himself arranges the Trojans on grassy
    seats,
Inviting Aeneas, as guest of honour, to take his place
    on
A maple chair which is draped with the shaggy pelt
    of a lion.   115
Then picked young men and the priest of the altar,
    promptly attentive,
Bring on the roast meat of bulls, and baskets loaded
    high with
Cereal food expertly prepared, and serve the wine.
Aeneas and his Trojan comrades all are feeding
On a whole chine of beef, and the meat left from the
    sacrifice.   120
    Hunger being satisfied, the desire for eating
    checked now,
King Evander began. . . .
    Great captain of the Teucrians—believe me, I'll
    never admit
The cause of Troy is lost, or its hope of dominion,
    while you
Are alive—though our reputation is high, we are
    short in the sinews   125
Of war to aid you, confined as we are on this side by

the Tiber,
Hard pressed on that by the Rutuli, whose arms
    clang round our walls.
But I propose to bring to your side a confederation
Of rich and numerous peoples: an unforeseen chance
    has offered
This reinforcement. It must have been fate that
    brought you here.   130
Not far away lies Caere, a populous city, founded
On ancient rock: a tribe from Lydia, renowned in
    war,
Settled it long ago upon a hill of Etruria.
For many years they flourished; but there rose a king,
    Mezentius,
Who with insolent tyranny and cruel force oppressed
    them.   135
I will not enlarge on that despot's brutish acts or his
    damnable
Massacres—may the gods keep such things for him-
    self and his breed!
Why, he would even have live men bound to dead
    bodies,
Clamping them hand to hand and face to face—a
    horrible
Method of torture—so that they died a lingering
    death   140
Infected with putrefaction in that most vile embrace.
At last the townsfolk could stand it no more: they
    rose in arms
Against the criminal maniac, besieged him in his
    palace,
Put his friends to the sword and set the place alight.
But Mezentius somehow escaped through the slaugh-
    ter into Rutulian   145
Territory, and asked his guest-friend, Turnus, for
    protection.
So all Etruria has risen in righteous anger, demand-
    ing
His extradition for punishment, or else they'll make
    war at once.
Thousands they are, Aeneas, and I'll put you at their
    head. . . .
Besides, you shall have my son here, my hope and
    consolation,   150
Pallas, that under your tuition he may be trained
In soldiering, the rough work of war—to endure its
    rigours,
And watching your deeds, to model himself on you
    from the start.
Him will I give two hundred Arcadian horsemen, the
    flower of
Our youth, and Pallas shall give you two hundred in
    his own name.   155
    He had barely finished speaking; Aeneas, son of
    Anchises,
And his confidant, Achates, their eyes downcast,
    were reflecting

Sadly on the hard trials before them, and long would
  have done so
But that Venus sent them a sign out of the clear
  sky.
All of a sudden the heavens shook with a flash of
  lightning   160
And thunder pealed: it seemed as if the whole uni-
  verse suddenly
Tottered and Etruscan trumpets were bawling above
  them.
They looked up: again and again a terrific crash
  resounded.
Up there among the fleecy clouds in the fair-weather
  sky
Were arms, red-glinting and thunderously clashing
  through the clear air.   165
The rest were stunned with amazement: but the
  Trojan hero heard
In the sound his divine mother keeping a promise
  she'd given.
So then he exclaimed:—
              My friend, do not, oh, do not ask
What issue these portents may bring! They're a call
  from above, and the call is
For me. My goddess mother foretold she would send
  this sign   170
If war was looming close, and would come to my
  help through the air
With arms of Vulcan's making.
Ah, what terrible slaughter awaits the Laurentines
  now!
What a price you will pay me, Turnus! How many
  shields and helmets
And corpses of gallant men shall the Tiber roll be-
  neath   175
Its waves! Now let them clamour for war and break
  their treaties.
    When he'd said this, Aeneas got up from where he
      was sitting,
And at once rekindling the drowsy fire on the altar of
  Hercules,
Cheerfully paid his respects to the guardian angel of
  the house
And its humble gods. . . .   180
    And now the gates had been opened and the
      horsemen had sallied forth,
Aeneas with his close friend, Achates, among the
  leaders;
Next, other Trojan princes; Pallas himself was riding
In the middle of the column, his tunic and blazoned
  armour conspicuous—
Just like the Morning Star, beloved by Venus above
  all   185
The stars of heaven, when it rises from bathing in
  ocean deeps, and
Puts forth its holy light from the sky and melts the
  darkness.

On the city wall stand the mothers, trembling; their
  eyes follow
Those squadrons—flashes of bronze and a dust cloud
  rolling about them. . . .
[Fierce battles ensue.]

BOOK X

. . . Equal in force and leadership, the armies close.
  Support troops
Press up to strengthen the front line: so thick the
  mêlée, they can hardly
Move weapon or hand. Here Pallas strains and
  shoves, here Lausus
Struggles to meet him: the two are of much the same
  age, and both
Uncommonly handsome; but fate had forbidden that
  they should ever   5
Return to their own homelands. The ruler of great
  Olympus
Did not, however, allow these two to confront each
  other:
Their fates await them—how near!—at the hands of
  greater foes.
    Meanwhile Turnus was warned by his guardian
      sister to hurry
To Lausus' aid; so he cut through the fray in his
  speeding chariot.   10
When he got there, he called out:—
              You can stop fighting now.
I am going alone against Pallas: he is my meat, and
  mine
Alone. I wish his father was here to witness the duel.
    He spoke; and his comrades withdrew from the
      field of battle, as bidden.
But when the Rutulians moved back, young Pallas,
  amazed by that arrogant   15
Order, stood tongue-tied a moment, surveying the
  mighty bulk of
Turnus, and truculent, looking him up and down at a
  distance,
Then he hurled back these words in the teeth of that
  haughty prince:—
    I shall soon be renowned for winning the arms of
      an enemy general   19
Or dying a glorious death: my father can take either.
To hell with your threats!
              So saying, he moved out onto the field.
The blood of his Arcadians grew chill, and their
  hearts numb.
Leaping down from his chariot, Turnus prepares for
  close combat
On foot. As a lion who has espied, from some high
  point of   24
Vantage, far off on the plain a bull spoiling for battle,

3. **Lausus,** an Etruscan prince in the army of Turnus. 9. **sister,**
Juturna, a nymph.

He bounds forward; yes, that was what Turnus'
  oncoming looked like.
Pallas, as soon as he reckoned his foe was in range of
  a spearcast,
Was first to move, hoping that luck would side with
  one who dared
To take on a powerfuller man, and praying thus to
  high heaven:—
  Hercules, I implore you, by the welcome my father
    gave you,   30
The table you shared, though a stranger, help me in
  this great enterprise!
Let Turnus, dying, behold me strip off his blood-
  stained armour,
And let his closing eyes acknowledge me as his
  conqueror!
  Hercules heard the lad. He repressed a terrible
    groan
That rose from deep in his heart, gave way to hope-
  less tears.   35
Then the Father of heaven spoke these kindly words
  to his son:—
  Every man's hour is appointed. Brief and unaltera-
    ble
For all, the span of life. To enlarge his fame by great
  deeds
Is what the brave man must aim at. . . . Turnus too is
  summoned
By his fate, and is nigh to the destined finish of his
  life.   40
  So Jupiter spoke, then averted his eyes from the
    land of Italy.
But Pallas hurled a spear, putting all his strength
  behind it,
And plucked his sword, flashing, out of the hollow
  scabbard.
That skimming spear went home high up, where
  shield and armour
Protect the shoulder, and actually piercing the rim of
  the shield,   45
Just managed to graze in the end the mighty body of
  Turnus.
Turnus now gave himself plenty of time to poise and
  aim at
Pallas his steel-tipped, oaken spear; as he threw it, he
  shouted:—
  Watch out, and see if my spear does not go deeper
    than his went!   49
Pallas' shield, for all its layers of iron and bronze,
For all the protective layers of bull's hide that rein-
  forced it,
Was broken through in the centre by the impact of
  Turnus' quivering
Spearpoint, which drove on to pierce the breastplate
  and then the breast.
Pallas wrenched out the weapon warm from the
  wound: it was no good;

His blood and his life ebbed, through the same
  channel, at once.   55
Hunched over the wound, he fell, his armour clang-
  ing above him—
Fell with his bleeding mouth to the enemy soil,
  dying.
Turnus straddled above him and spoke:—
  Remember well what I say, you Arcadians, and tell
    your king
I send him back his Pallas, a dead man; Evander
  deserved it.   60
What compensation there is in a tomb, what comfort
  in burial,
He can have. He'll find he has paid dear enough for
  making friends with
Aeneas.
  So saying, he pressed his left foot hard on the
    back of
The corpse, and tore off the sword-belt, a thing of
  immense weight. . . .
This belt was now taken by Turnus for spoils, and
  delighted his heart.   65
Ah, mind of man, so ignorant of fate, of what shall
  befall him,
So weak to preserve moderation when riding the crest
  of good fortune!
For Turnus a time is coming when he'd give anything
To have left Pallas unharmed, and will loathe this
  day and the spoils
It brought him. But Pallas' comrades clustered
  around him, laid   70
His corpse on a shield and bore it away, lamenting
  and weeping.
What grief, what pride his father would feel at his
  homecoming!
To-day had been his baptism in war, to-day his end;
Still, he had left behind him a trail of Italian
  dead. . . .

BOOK XI

. . . Old Acoetes watched over the lifeless body of
  Pallas
Which had been laid there: Acoetes had served as
  squire to Evander
In the old days in Arcadia; but then, beneath a less
  fortunate
Star, he went as an aide to his dear foster-son, Pallas.
All the servants were gathered round, and a crowd of
  Trojans,   5
With Trojan women whose hair streamed loose in the
  manner of mourning.
But when Aeneas entered the lofty door, they raised
To heaven a loud, long sound of keening, and beat
  their breasts;
The royal tent was one great moan of grief and
  wailing.

Aeneas, looking at Pallas' head on the pillow there, 10
The snow-white face, the open wound in his young
    breast
Made by the spear of Turnus, spoke amid rising
    tears:—
    Poor lad, alas that Fortune, in the hour she smiled
        on me,
Grudged me one thing—your life—and would not let
    you behold
My kingdom or ride back to your father's home in
    triumph! 15
How different from all I promised Evander to do for
    you,
That day I left him, when he embraced me and sent
    me forth
To my imperial destiny! He felt some fear, and
    warned me
How dangerous was the foe, how tough the people
    I'd fight with.
This very moment—who knows!—quite beguiled by
    a groundless hope, 20
He may be paying his vows and loading the altars
    with offerings;
While we, with mourning tributes useless to him,
    attend
Dead Pallas, who now owes nothing to any of the
    gods in heaven.
Evander, poor man, shall see his son buried, and
    break his heart. 24
So much for our triumphal return that he is awaiting!
So much for my solemn promise! But at least Evan-
    der will not
Look on a son wounded in cowardly flight, or pray for
A death made accursed by the son's living on in
    dishonour. Alas,
What a tower of strength is lost to Italy, lost to
    Ascanius!
    When he had made lamentation, Aeneas bade
    them lift up 30
The piteous corpse, and choosing a thousand men
    from his whole
Army, detailed them to form the solemn cortege and
    to share in
The tears of the bereaved Evander—small consola-
    tion
In such great grief, but one that was due to a sorrow-
    ing father. 34
Others quickly construct a resilient wickerwork bier,
Wattling switches of oak and shoots from the arbutus
    tree,
Then shade the built-up bier with a canopy of foli-
    age.
Now they are laying young Pallas aloft on that
    country bed;
And he resembles a flower plucked by a girl's fin-
    gers— 39
A gentle violet, perhaps, or a fainting hyacinth—

Whose sheen and shape are not yet lost, not yet
    departed,
Though mother earth no longer can give it sap or
    strength.
Aeneas now brought out two purple robes that were
    richly
Brocaded in golden thread: Sidonian Dido had made
    them
With her own hands, in the old days, interweaving
    the fabric 45
With threads of gold, and giving all her heart to the
    work.
In one of these robes he sadly wrapped Pallas—a
    farewell gesture,
Hooding with it the hair that would soon be burned
    to ashes:
He made a great heap, as well, of spoil they had won
    in the battle
Against the Laurentines, and had it borne in a long
    procession— 50
Horses and weapons, too, they had taken from the
    enemy.
Manacled captives there were, consigned to be gifts
    to the dead—
Victims whose blood would be sprinkled upon the
    altar flames.
He bade the leaders themselves to carry tree-trunks
    adorned with
Enemy armour, the names of the fallen foes attached
    to them. 55
. . . Now followed a phalanx
Of mourners—Trojans, all the Etruscans, Arcadians
    bearing
Their arms reversed. When the files of his comrades
    had gone some distance
Forward, Aeneas stopped, sighed heavily, then
    spoke:—
    The same dread fate of war summons me hence to
    weep 60
For the other dead. Brave Pallas, salute for ever-
    more!
For evermore, farewell!
                  Aeneas said nothing further,
But turned towards the ramparts and made his way
    into camp. . . .
    And now winged Rumour came, first herald of
    great grief,
To Evander's ears, to his palace and all his city—
    Rumour 65
Which only just now was reporting that Pallas had
    beaten the Latins.
Hurriedly seizing funeral torches—an antique
    custom—
The Arcadians ran to their gates: the long, torchlight
    procession
They formed shone like a broad parting across the
    fields.

The Trojan cortege moved on to meet them: the
    mourning columns   70
Merged into one. When the mothers saw it enter the
    city,
Their shrieking ran like wildfire through the afflicted
    streets.
No force on earth could restrain Evander now. He
    rushed out
Into the crowds, and as soon as the bier was set
    down, prostrated
Himself upon Pallas, clung to the body, weeping and
    moaning.   75
For a while grief choked him: at last he just managed
    to find his voice:—
    Oh, Pallas, this was not the promise you gave your
      father—
That you'd be careful how you ventured into the
    grim fight!
But I knew too well how great is the lure of glory in
    battle
For a young man, how sweet to win fame in his first
    engagement.   80
Bitter your youth's first-fruits, harsh your initiation
Into this war so near home! Alas that not one of the
    gods
Gave ear to my vows and prayers! My blessed wife,
    how lucky
You were to die before such anguish could come
    upon you!
But I have lived on, exceeding my natural term—
    lived on   85
For what?—to survive my own son. Why didn't I
    march with our Trojan
Allies, and fall to the enemy's fire? Would *I* had
    perished,
And this cortege was carrying me, not Pallas, home!
Yet, Trojans, don't think I am blaming you, or our
    pact, or the joining
Of our right hands in friendship. What has happened
    —fate surely had it   90
In store for my old age. But though an untimely
    death
Was awaiting my son, I'll be proud that he died
    leading the Teucrians
Into Latium, with thousands of enemy dead to his
    credit.
Besides, I could not grace you with a worthier funer-
    al, Pallas,
Than this which Aeneas the true, the mighty Trojans,
    the generals   95
Of the Etruscans and their whole army are giving
    you.
They bear great trophies, symbols of those who fell
    by your hand.
You too, Turnus, would be here—a trophy, a giant
    tree-trunk
Adorned with arms—had your age and the strength

of your years been no more than
My son's. But why do I let my own tragedy keep you
    Trojans   100
From war? Go forth, and forget not to take back
    these words to your king;
Tell him I linger on, though I care not for life now
    Pallas
Is gone, to receive the debt which he knows is owing
    to father
And son—vengeance on Turnus: it's the sole task
    that remains for
His courage and luck to accomplish. I ask it, not to
    gladden   105
My life—that were wrong—but to bring the good
    news to my son in the underworld. . . .

BOOK XII

. . . Then did his lovely mother put into the head
    of Aeneas
That he should move on the city, divert his men to a
    sudden
Assault on its walls, and surprising the Latins, disor-
    ganise
And defeat them. Scouring the various battle sectors
    for Turnus,
And looking all round him, this way and that, he
    viewed the city   5
Untouched by all this fighting, peaceful and undis-
    turbed.
At once his imagination was lit by the thought of a
    greater
Battle. He called up Mnestheus, Sergestus and brave
    Serestus,
His staff, and took his stand on a hillock: the rest of
    the Trojan
Force gathered to him, tight-packed, but did not
    ground their shields   10
Or spears. Then, standing above the ring of warriors,
    he said:—
    I want my orders obeyed instantly. Jupiter's with
      us.
My plan may surprise you, but that must be no
    excuse for half-heartedness.
Look at the city, the cause of this war, the seat of
    Latinus'
Power!—unless they admit they are beaten and owe
    us obedience,   15
This day I'll destroy it and raze its smoking roofs to
    the ground.
Do I have to wait until Turnus feels like facing the
    ordeal
Of combat? is willing to meet me again, after once
    being beaten?
Here is the heart, the centre of this cursed war, my
    men.
Get torches! Hurry! Fire shall exact the terms of the
    treaty.   20

Upon these words, they all are seized by an equal
    enthusiasm,
Get into wedge formation, drive solidly at the walls.
In a moment ladders appear, incendiaries the same
    instant.
Some of them run to the several gates, cut down the
    guards there;
While others darken the sky with a covering fire of
    arrows.   25
Aeneas, in the forward party, stretches his right hand
Up at the battlements, loudly rebukes Latinus, and
    calls
The gods to witness that once again a fight is forced
    on him,
Twice the Italians have broken a treaty and been the
    aggressors.
The citizens' nervous excitement bursts out into
    violent dissension,   30
One party demanding the gates be unbarred, the
    town thrown open
To the Trojans, and Latinus himself haled onto the
    walls:
The others took arms and ran to the defence of their
    city.
So, when a shepherd has traced a swarm of bees to
    their chamber
Deep in some porous rock, and filled it with acrid
    smoke,   35
The bees within, alarmed for their community, scurry
About the wax castle, and raise their temper with
    high-pitched buzzing:
Black, pungent smoke rolls through their cells; the
    hollow rock
Is all one inward humming; smoke trickles out from
    its crannies.
    A further calamity now befell the war-weary
    Latins,   40
Shaking the town to its very foundations, and causing
    great grief.
The queen, looking forth from her roof-top, saw the
    advance of the foe,
Their assault on the walls, the flaming material flung
    at the houses,
But nowhere the Rutuli, no opposition from Turnus.
She believed, alas, that her warrior had lost his life in
    the desperate   45
Fighting. The shock and anguish of this unsettled her
    mind:
Crying out that she was the cause, she only to blame
    for disaster,
Talking wildly, distracted by paroxysms of grief,
Death in her heart, she tore the crimson gown she
    was wearing
And hung from a beam the noose that would horribly
    make an end of her.   50
When the poor Latin women got word of this calam-
    ity,

Led by the queen's daughter, who tore at her flower-
    bright tresses
And rose-petal cheeks, they soon were all of them in
    a frenzy
Of grief around her: the palace resounded with
    lamentations.
From there the appalling story spread through the
    city everywhere.   55
All were dismayed: Latinus, rending his clothes, went
    about
In a daze at the tragic end of his wife and his city's
    downfall,
Sprinkling upon his grey head handfuls of unclean
    dust. . . .
    The picture of their changed fortunes struck
    Turnus dumb, bewildered him.
Speechless and staring, he stood there, his heart in a
    violent conflict,   60
Torn by humiliation, by grief shot through with
    madness,
By love's tormenting jealousy and a sense of his own
    true courage.
As soon as the mists parted and he could think again
    clearly,
He turned his blazing eyes upon the walls, in great
Distress of mind, looked back at the city there from
    his chariot.   65
He saw a whirling spire of flame which was leaping
    upwards,
Wave after wave, through the floors of a turret, had
    got a firm grip on it:
Turnus had built this turret himself, a solid construc-
    tion
Of planking, with wheels to move on, and gangways
    rigged aloft:—
    The fates are too strong for me, sister—I see it
    now. Don't hold me back;   70
Let me go where God and my own unmerciful for-
    tune call me.
I am resolved to fight Aeneas, to bear whatever
Bitterness death holds for me. You shall not see me
    disgraced
Any longer. Just let me indulge this madness of mine
    ere I die.
    So saying, Turnus at once leapt down to the
    ground from his chariot,   75
And leaving his sister sorrowing, dashed through the
    enemy, ran
The gauntlet of fire, his impetus breaking a way
    through their midst.
Even as a boulder that rolls straight down from a
    mountain summit,
Dislodged by a gust of wind—a cloudburst has
    washed away
The soil it was fast in, perhaps, or the passage of time
    has loosened it;   80
Down, with terrific momentum, the huge thing

insensately bounces
Over the ground, steep down, carrying trees, flocks, men
Before it: just like this did Turnus speed to the city,
Scattering the foe from his path, and run to the walls where the earth was
Most deeply drenched with blood and the air screeched with missiles. 85
He held up his hand as a signal, shouted for all to hear:—
   Rutuli, put up your weapons! Cease fire, you Latins! Whatever
The issue is, I shoulder it. Better that I redeem
For you the breaking of the treaty, and decide all, in a duel.
   So then they drew apart, leaving a space in the midst for the combat. 90
But lord Aeneas, as soon as he heard the name of Turnus,
Hurried away from the walls, from the towers he was then attacking,
Broke off the whole engagement, impatient of any delay,
Overjoyed at the prospect of meeting Turnus; and terribly clashed his
Sword on his shield. Gigantic as Athos he looked, as Eryx, 95
As our own Apennine range when a storm roars in its oak trees
Dancing their leaves, and its snowy peaks soar joyfully skywards.
Now did the Rutuli, the Trojans and all the Italians
Excitedly gaze at their two champions—those who were up on
The battlements, and those who were thumping the walls below 100
With a ram. All laid down their shields. Latinus himself marvelled
To see those giants, born in different parts of the world,
Now met together to fight it out in single combat. . . .
   Meantime the king of all-powerful Olympus addresses Juno
As she looks down at the combat out of a golden cloud:— 105
   My wife, how shall it end now? What more is there you can do?
For you know, and admit the knowledge, that Aeneas is called of heaven
As a national hero, and fate is exalting him to the stars.
What are you planning? Why do you linger here in the chill clouds? . . .
This is the end, I say. You had power to harry the Trojans 110
All over lands and seas, to kindle accursed war,

Bring tragic disgrace on a king's home and drape a betrothal in mourning.
I forbid you to carry the feud any further.
                So Jupiter spoke.
Juno, the daughter of Saturn, with lowered eyes, replied:—
   It is because your wishes, great consort, were known to me, 115
That I have reluctantly given up Turnus and quit the earth.
Otherwise I'd not be sitting apart here and putting up with
Every humiliation: no, armed with flame, I'd be there
In action, dragging the Trojans into a fatal fight.
I admit I encouraged Juturna to go and help her unfortunate 120
Brother, approved of her acting more boldly still to preserve him;
But not that she should use her bow and shoot at the Trojans:
This I swear by the source of the inexorable river,
Styx—the one dreadful and binding oath for us heaven-dwellers.
And now I do truly yield; I give up the fight—I am sick of it. 125
One thing, and no ruling of fate forbids you to grant it, I do
Entreat, for Latium's sake and the dignity of your own kin:
When they make peace through a prosperous—aye, let it be so—a prosperous
Marriage, and when they are making agreements and laws to unite them,
Do not command the indigenous Latins to change their ancient 130
Name, to become Trojans and to be called the Teucrians:
Allow them to keep the old language and their traditional dress:
Let it be Latium for ever, and the kings be Alban kings;
Let the line be Roman, the qualities making it great be Italian.
Troy's gone; may it be gone in name as well as reality. 135
   The creator of man and of all things replied to her with a smile:—
   Jove's sister you are indeed and the second child of Saturn,
So powerful the tides of wrath sweeping within your breast!
But come, there was no need for this violent emotion; calm yourself.
Willingly I grant what you ask: you have won me over. 140
The Italians shall keep their native tongue and their old traditions;

Their name shall not be altered. The Trojans will but
    sink down in
The mass and be made one with them. I'll add the
    rites and usage
Of Trojan worship to theirs. All will be Latins, speak-
    ing
One tongue. From this blend of Italian and Trojan
    blood shall arise   145
A people surpassing all men, nay even the gods, in
    godliness.
No other nation on earth will pay such reverence to
    Juno.
    The goddess bowed and agreed, glad now to
    change her whole policy,
Passed forthwith from the sky, leaving her place in
    the clouds.
    Aeneas moved up on his enemy, hefting and flash-
    ing his spear   150
Which was huge as a tree, and shouted out with
    extreme ferocity:—
    Turnus, you'll get no more reprieves. Are you still
    recoiling?
It's cold steel now, hand to hand, not fleetness of
    foot, that will tell.
Try all the transformations of Proteus! Summon up
Your powers, whether of courage or magic! Take
    wings, if you like,   155
And shoot straight up to the stars, or go to ground in
    the deep earth!
    Turnus, shaking his head, replied:—
                It's the gods' and Jupiter's
Enmity frighten me, not your sneers or your blood-
    thirsty speeches.
    Without a word more he looked round and his eyes
    alit on a huge stone—
A huge old stone which for years had been lying
    there on the plain   160
As a boundary mark between fields, to prevent
    disputes about ownership.
Hardly could twelve strong men, of such physique as
    the earth
Produces nowadays, pick up and carry it on their
    shoulders.
Well, Turnus pounced on it, lifted it, and taking a
    run to give it
More impetus, hurled this stone from his full height
    at Aeneas.   165
But as he moved, as he ran, as he raised his hands, as
    he threw
That boulder, for him it was just as if somebody else
    were doing it.
Ice-bound were his veins, and his legs felt like water.
So too the stone he hurled, flying through empty air,
Failed to make the distance, fell short of its objective.
But, as it is in a nightmare, when sleep's narcotic
    hand   171
Is leaden upon our eyes, we seem to be desperately

trying
To run and run, but we cannot—for all our efforts,
    we sink down
Nerveless; our usual strength is just not there, and our
    tongue
Won't work at all—we can't utter a word or produce
    one sound: 175
So with Turnus, each move he bravely attempted to
    make,
The unearthly demon brought it to nothing. Now did
    his feelings
Veer this way and that in distraction: he gazed at the
    city, the Rutuli;
Faltered with fear; trembled at the weapon menacing
    him.
He could see no way to escape and no way to get at
    Aeneas;   180
His chariot, his sister who drove it, were nowhere to
    be seen.
So Turnus faltered: the other brandished his fateful
    spear,
And watching out for an opening, hurled it with all
    his might
From a distance. The noise it made was louder than
    that of any   184
Great stone projected by siege artillery, louder than
A meteorite's explosion. The spear flew on its sinister
Mission of death like a black tornado, and piercing
    the edge of
The seven-fold shield, laid open the corselet of
    Turnus, low down.
Right through his thigh it ripped, with a hideous
    sound. The impact
Brought giant Turnus down on bent knee to the
    earth.   190
The Italians sprang to their feet, crying out: the hills
    all round
Bayed back their howl of dismay, far and wide the
    deep woods echoed it.
Turnus, brought low, stretched out a pleading hand,
    looked up at
His foe in appeal:—
              I know, I've deserved it. I'll not
    beg life.
Yours was the luck. Make the most of it. But if the
    thought of a father's   195
Unhappiness can move you—a father such as you
    had
In Anchises—I ask you, show compassion for aged
    Daunus
And give me back to him; or if that is the way it
    must be,
Give back my dead body. You have won. The Ital-
    ians have seen me
Beaten, these hands outstretched. Lavinia is yours to
    wed.   200
Don't carry hatred further.

                                Aeneas stood over him, poised
On the edge of the stroke; but his eyes were restless,
    he did not strike.
And now what Turnus had said was taking effect,
    was making him
More and more indecisive, when on his enemy's
    shoulder
He noticed the fatal baldric, the belt with its glitter-
    ing studs—   205
How well he knew it!—which Turnus had stripped
    from young Pallas after
He'd killed him, and put on himself—a symbol of
    triumph and doom.
Aeneas fastened his eyes on this relic, this sad
    reminder
Of all the pain Pallas' death had caused. Rage shook
    him. He looked
Frightening. He said:—
                    Do you hope to get off now,
    wearing the spoils   210
You took from my Pallas? It's he, it's Pallas who
    strikes this blow—
The victim shedding his murderer's blood in retribu-
    tion!
  So saying, Aeneas angrily plunged his sword full
    into
Turnus' breast. The body went limp and cold. With a
    deep sigh
The unconsenting spirit fled to the shades below.   215

Horace

65–8 B.C.

Horace too could sing the patriotic strain, and he vied with Virgil in respectful praise of Augustus and Maecenas, his patrons. But national propaganda was not to his taste, and he produced it only because his security depended on it. Close friend to Virgil, he was quite unlike that shy, rustic spirit in being a man of the world, equally at home in the court circles of Rome or on his Sabine farm some forty miles away. His philosophy of life was a practical rationalism, lacking totally the melancholy mysticism of Virgil, and he avoided the long verse forms of Virgil to compose lyrics and brief satires that are among the most finished and exquisite in all literature. He resembled his friend only in being a thoroughly genial and generous man, who, indeed, excelled Virgil as a jovial companion and witty conversationalist.

Quintus Horatius Flaccus was the son of an ambitious freedman who had retired to a small farm at Venusia in the south and devoted his life to educating his son for an important career. At Rome young Horace studied under the grammarian Orbilius, whom the poet later nicknamed

"plagosus" (flogging) because of his generous application of the rod. His father, whom Horace revered all his life, taught him the stoic morality that was to mature into the mellow philosophy of his later years. Toward twenty Horace went to Athens to complete his education and there became embroiled in civil war on the side of Brutus. But when Octavian's army routed Brutus' forces at Philippi in 42, Horace fled from the field and returned to Rome with the general amnesty, there to find his father dead and their farm confiscated. In poverty he took a small government post and began writing poetry as an avenue to patronage and security. The satires and epodes of this early period betray a bitterness that was to disappear with his later success.

Virgil was the first to recognize the talent of young Horace and introduced him to Maecenas. In time his work and his friendly personality won him a secure place in the circle. For thirty years he was the close intimate of Maecenas, who gave him his Sabine farm around 34 B.C. and on his deathbed asked Augustus to "be mindful of Horatius Flaccus as of myself." With Maecenas and Virgil he made a diplomatic jaunt by boat, coach, and foot across Italy to Brundisium in 37, which he immortalized amusingly in the fifth satire of Book I. Together they spent many evenings over gourmet dinners and the intellectual conversation that they loved—"the feasts of the gods," as he called them. But in his later years, having learned the evils as well as the pleasures of the capital, he retired more frequently to his Sabine farm, where Maecenas insured him the modest comforts and the leisure that he needed to pursue his writing at his own speed. Here his philosophy ripened, and his works are full of gratitude to Maecenas and the Empire that had given his life stability and peace. He devoutly predicted that he would not long outlive Maecenas, and this prediction proved true, for he died a few months after his patron.

Although in youth Horace had been a dark-haired, attractive fellow who philandered a good deal with the courtesans of the town, we think of him especially as the roly-poly little man turned forty who had grown prematurely gray and middle-aged. The romantic Catullus was at his best in his passionate twenties; the classical Horace reached his zenith in his mellow forties. His life was a long experiment in the art of living, for which he was equipped with a singularly detached, tolerant, and serene mind. He had a natural love for the simple things of life —a mountain stream and the sky at night, a winter fire and a jug of peasant wine beside him, his little farm, which was at least little for his day—but he could enjoy also the pleasures of luxury—the boulevards and rich men's houses, the conversation of statesmen and the companionship of courtesans, the feasts of a Lucullus and the feel of fine clothes. He was a true epicurean; experience had sharpened his taste, but had made him independent of luxury. His pleasures entailed no hangover or heartache. He never drank to excess and thought of love as only one kind of enjoyment, to be abandoned when it threatened to become tragic. His ladies entertained him with their charms, as he entertained them with his wit and good nature, but if we can trust his verses, he passed quickly from one to another—Phyllis, Cinara, Lydia, and Chloe, to mention a few.

As his shrewd common sense interpreted his experience, he evolved a philosophy that is half Stoic, half Epicurean. All men, he decided, are ruled by two opposing drives—emotion and reason. Many fluctuate violently from one of these extremes to the other, now expend themselves in passion, now regret it with reason. The secret of happiness is to preserve the balance between them, to indulge one's emotions up to a point for pleasurable experience, but to keep a rational check on them always to ward off failure and despair. So the golden mean of Aristotle becomes the "Golden Mediocrity" of Horace, as it is often called. One's ambition should be to possess enough for happiness; more brings only responsibility and pain. Desire should be kept under rational control, for happiness lies in our response to what fate brings us, not in the things themselves. Hence, we should, like Lucretius, rise above hope and fear to a perfect equanimity, appreciative of life but indifferent to death. So Horace became the preacher of moderation.

Such a detached attitude does not make for emotional or highly imaginative poetry, and Horace is as aware of that as he is sure of his lasting fame. He is the spokesman for hard work, not mystical inspiration, in poetry, and he polished every line of his verse to a perfection that defies translation. Tearing up far more than he published, he strove for the inevitable word and the perfect technique. The result is one thin volume of poems, the perfect essence and no more, of what he had to say. These are thought of in groups according to literary type. The eighteen *Sermones,* or "little talks," usually called his *Satires,* are the earliest and most uneven of his works and betray the bitterness of his outlook during his years of poverty in Rome. The best are charming discussions of many subjects—the foibles and vices of mankind, or incidents in the poet's own life. The fifth relates his Brundisium jaunt with Virgil and Maecenas. The sixth extolls his father and his patron. The ninth is the amusing satire of a bore. The sixteenth contrasts town life and country life and contains the fable of the town mouse and the country mouse. The seventeen *Epodes,* so-named from a Greek meter of Archilochus which they imitated, were culled from ten years of writing in this form, but they are still the least satisfactory of all his work.

He reached his peak in his *Carmina,* or "songs," usually called his *Odes,* which imitate a number of Greek meters with consummate success. These are his true lyrics, 103 gems issued in four books and covering a wide variety of themes—politics and patriotism (especially the famous "Ship of State"), hymns and prayers, his friends and their journeys (especially his address to Virgil's ship to Greece), their love affairs and his, the joys of wine and the brevity of life (especially *Carpe diem,* "snatch the day"), and of course his doctrine of the Golden Mean. His final works were his twenty-three *Epistles,* a forbidding title for a collection of delightful literary letters to his friends, discoursing familiarly on subjects that interested him—the joys of his farm, the state of Latin literature, the

value of personal freedom. The last of these, now called *The Art of Poetry,* is his charming advice to authors on the pursuit of their craft, by no means intended as the writer's bible that it became in the classical seventeenth century. Yet it is studded with famous literary concepts and phrases, such as "Homer nods," "in medias res" to signify Homer's beginning his tales in the middle, and "purple patches." Horace exerted little influence on the Middle Ages or early Renaissance, but with the sixteenth century he came into his own again, and his perfection of style, his urbane humor, and his common sense had an unparalleled appeal for the intellectual age of reason.

To the Ship in Which Virgil Sailed to Athens

So may the auspicious Queen of Love,
    And the twin Stars (the seed of Jove),
And he who rules the raging wind,
To thee, O sacred ship, be kind,
And gentle breezes fill thy sails,   5
Supplying soft Etesian gales,
As thou, to whom the Muse commends
The best of poets and of friends,
Dost thy committed pledge restore,
And land him safely on the shore;   10
And save the better part of me
From perishing with him at sea.

Sure he who first the passage tried,
In harden'd oak his heart did hide,
And ribs of iron arm'd his side!   15
Or his at least, in hollow wood
Who tempted first the briny flood;
Nor fear'd the winds' contending roar,
Nor billows beating on the shore;
Nor Hyades portending rain;   20
Nor all the tyrants of the main.
What form of death could him affright
Who, unconcern'd, with steadfast sight,
Could view the surges mounting steep,
And monsters rolling in the deep?   25
Could through the ranks of ruin go,
With storms above and rocks below?
In vain did Nature's wise command
Divide the waters from the land,
If daring ships and men profane   30
Invade the inviolable main,
The eternal fences overleap,

To the Ship in Which Virgil Sailed to Athens. Translated by John Dryden.
·2. **the seed of Jove,** Castor and Pollux, the Dioscuri. 20. **Hyades portending rain.** The Hyades, or Rainers, were sea-nymphs forming a constellation.

And pass at will the boundless deep.
No toil, no hardship can restrain
Ambitious man inured to pain;   35
The more confin'd, the more he tries,
And at forbidden quarry flies.
Thus bold Prometheus did aspire,
And stole from heaven the reed of fire:
A train of ills, a ghastly crew,   40
The robber's blazing track pursue;
Fierce Famine, with her meager face,
And fevers of the fiery race,
In swarms the offending wretch surround,
All brooding on the blasted ground;   45
And limping Death, lash'd on by Fate,
Comes up to shorten half our date.
This made not Dedalus beware,
With borrow'd wings to sail in air:
To hell Alcides forced his way,   50
Plunged through the lake, and snatch'd the prey.
Nay, scarce the gods or heavenly climes
Are safe from our audacious crimes:
We reach at Jove's imperial crown,
And pull the unwilling thunder down.

The Love-Sick
Athlete

WHY, Lydia, why,
    I pray, by all the gods above,
Art so resolved that Sybaris should die,
And all for love?

    Why doth he shun   5
The Campus Martius' sultry glare,
    He that once recked of neither dust nor sun?
Why rides he there,

    First of the brave,
Taming the Gallic steed no more?   10
    Why doth he shrink from Tiber's yellow wave?
Why thus abhor

    The wrestler's oil
As 't were from viper's tongue distilled?
    Why do his arms no livid bruises soil,   15
He, once so skilled

    The disk or dart
Far, far beyond the mark to hurl?
    And tell me, tell me, in what nook apart
Like baby-girl,   20

50. **Alcides,** Hercules, grandson of Alcaeus. 51. **prey,** Cerberus, the three-headed dog guarding the entrance to Hades, whom Hercules had to bring to the uppcr world as the last of his twelve labors.
The Love-Sick Athlete. From *Horace,* translated by Sir Theodore Martin. Reprinted by permission of J. B. Lippincott Company and Wm. Blackwood & Sons Ltd.

Lurks the poor boy,
Veiling his manhood, as did Thetis' son
    To 'scape war's bloody clang, while fated Troy
Was yet undone.

To Pyrrha,
a Flirt

WHAT slender youth, with perfumed locks,
    In some sweet nook beneath the rocks,
Pyrrha, where clustering roses grow,
Bends to thy fatal beauty now?
For whom is now that golden hair   5
Wreathed in a bank so simply fair?
How often will he weep to find
Thy pledges frail, Love's power unkind?
And start to see the tempest sweep
With angry blast the darkening deep;   10
Though sunned by thy entrancing smile,
He fears no change, suspects no guile.
A sailor on bright summer seas,
He wots not of the fickle breeze.
For me—yon votive tablet scan;   15
It tells that I, a shipwrecked man,
Hung my dank weeds in Neptune's fane
And ne'er will tempt those seas again.

"Fair and Colder"

How snowy white Soracte stands!
    How still the streams with cold!
Pile the logs higher upon the fire!
Decant that four-year old!

Leave to the gods the other things!   5
The ash and cypress trees
Shall fall asleep when on the deep
Blows not the battling breeze.

Ask not about the morrow morn;
Take what the gods may give,   10
Nor scorn the dance and sweet romance—
Life is not long to live.

Come seek the Campus and the squares,
As fall the shades of night
Where many a maid, all unafraid,   15
Laughs absolute delight.

22. **Thetis' son,** Achilles.
To Pyrrha, a Flirt. Translated by Goldwin Smith. From *Bay Leaves,* by Goldwin Smith. Published by The Macmillan Company, 1893.
"Fair and Colder." Translated by Franklin P. Adams. From *The Melancholy Lute* by Franklin P. Adams, copyright 1936 by Franklin P. Adams. Reprinted by permission of The Viking Press, Inc.
1. **Soracte,** a snow-capped peak in Etruria, visible in Rome.

Ad Leuconoen

IT is not right for you to know, so do not ask,
    Leuconoë,
How long a life the gods may give or ever we are
    gone away;
Try not to read the Final Page, the ending colo-
    phonian,
Trust not the gypsy's tea-leaves, nor the prophets
    Babylonian.
Better to have what is to come enshrouded in ob-
    scurity   5
Than to be certain of the sort and length of our
    futurity.
Why, even as I monologue on wisdom and longevity
How Time has flown! Spear some of it!
    The longest life is brevity.

The Ship of State

SHIP of State, beware!
    Hold fast the port. Cling to the friendly
    shore
Lest sudden storms and whirling eddies bear
Thy shattered hull to faithless seas once more.

See how the rower faints upon his oar!   5
    Hark to the groaning of the mast,
    Sore stricken by the Libyan blast!
Thy shrouds are burst; thy sails are torn;
And through thy gaping ribs forlorn
    The floods remorseless pour.   10

Dare not to call for aid on powers divine;
    Dishonored once, they hear no more:
    Nor boast, majestic pine,
Daughter of Pontic forests, thy great name,
    Old lineage, well-earned fame,   15
    The honors of this sculptured prow—
Sport of the mocking winds, nor feared nor trusted
    now.

Alas! my country, long my anxious care,
Source now of bitter pain and fond regret!
    Thy stars obscured, thy course beset   20
    By rocks unseen, beware!
Trust not soft winds and treacherous seas
Or the false glitter of the Cyclades.

Ad Leuconoen (*Carpe Diem*). Translated by Franklin P. Adams. From *Tobogganing on Parnassus* by Franklin P. Adams, copyright 1911 by Doubleday & Company, Inc.
The Ship of State. Translated by Stephen Edward De Vere. Horace may have borrowed his famous figure of the Roman state as a hard-pressed ship from a speech of Maecenas urging Augustus not to resign his leadership of the government. He uses the figure to warn his countrymen against reviving the civil war.
23. Cyclades, a group of islands in the Aegean Sea.

Lalage

THAT happy man whose virtuous heart
    Is free from guilt and conscious fear
Needs not the poisoned Moorish dart,
    Nor bow, nor sword, nor deadly spear.

Whether on shores that Ganges laves,   5
    Or Syrtes' quivering sands among,
Or where the Hydaspes' fabled waves
    In strange meanders wind along.

When free from care I dared to rove,
    And Lalage inspired my lay,   10
A wolf within the Sabine grove
    Fled wild from his defenceless prey.

Such prodigy the Daunian bands
    In their drear haunts shall never trace,
Nor barren Libya's arid sands,   15
    Rough parent of the lion race.

O place me where no verdure smiles,
    No vernal zephyrs fan the ground
No varied scene the eye beguiles,
    Nor murmuring rivulets glide around.   20

Place me on Thracia's frozen lands,
    Uncheered by genial light of day!
Place me on Afric's burning sands,
    Scorched by the sun's inclement ray!

Love in my heart shall pain beguile,   25
    Sweet Lalage shall be my song,
The gentle beauties of her smile,
    The gentle music of her tongue.

To Chloë

YOU shun me, Chloë, wild and shy,
    As some stray fawn that seeks its mother
Through trackless woods. If spring winds sigh
    It vainly strives its fears to smother.

Its trembling knees assail each other   5
    When lizards stir the brambles dry;—
You shun me, Chloë, wild and shy,
    As some stray fawn that seeks its mother.

Lalage. Translated by W. Herbert.
6. **Syrtes' quivering sands.** The Syrtes was a great gulf on the northern coast of Africa, notoriously dangerous because of its quicksands. 7. **Hydaspes,** one of the great tributaries of the Indus River in India, remote and mysterious. 13. **Daunian bands,** the people of southeastern Italy.
To Chloë. Translated by Austin Dobson. Reprinted by permission of Oxford University Press, London, and Mr. A. T. A. Dobson as representative of the Executors.

And yet no Libyan lion I,—
　　No ravening thing to rend another;　　10
Lay by your tears, your tremors dry,
　　A husband's better than a brother;
Nor shun me, Chloë, wild and shy,
　　As some stray fawn that seeks its mother.

Past Her Prime

Swains in numbers
　　Break your slumbers,
Saucy Lydia, now but seldom,
Ay, though at your casement nightly,
Tapping loudly, tapping lightly,　　5
By the dozen once you held them.

　　Ever turning,
　　Night and morning
Swung your door upon its hinges;
Now, from dawn till evening's closing,　　10
Lone and desolate reposing,
Not a soul its rest infringes.

　　Serenaders,
　　Sweet invaders,
Scanter grow, and daily scanter,　　15
Singing, "Lydia, art thou sleeping?
Lonely watch thy love is keeping!
Wake, O wake, thou dear enchanter!"

　　Lone and faded,
　　You, as they did,　　20
Woo, and in your turn are slighted,
Worn and torn by passion's fret.
You, the pitiless coquette,
Waste by fires yourself have lighted,

　　Late relenting,　　25
　　Left lamenting,—
"Withered leaves strew wintry brooks!
Ivy garlands greenly darkling,
Myrtles brown with dew-drops sparkling,
Best beseem youth's glowing looks!"

Faith Renewed

Wise in the love of philosophic fools
　　I strayed perplexed amid conflicting
　　　　schools:
O worshipped not, believed not, hoped not! Now
To long-neglected gods perforce must bow,
Reverse my shattered sail, and turn once more,　　5
Repentant, to the course I steered of yore;

For Jove, whose lightnings from Olympus hurled
Erewhile through rifted storm-clouds smote the
　　　　world,
Through cloudless skies and azure depths afar
Drove now his fiery steeds and thunder-winged car.
Trembled the solid earth, the ocean floor,　　11
The wandering rivers, and the Stygian shore,
Dark Taenarus accurst and Atlas hoar.

There is a god: his justice and his might
Adjust the balance of the world aright;　　15
Abase the proud; exalt and glorify
The lowly grace of true humility.
Fortune at his command plucks monarchs down,
And on the humble outcast lays the crown.

Persian Fopperies

Boy, I hate their empty shows,
　　Persian garlands I detest,
Bring me not the late-blown rose
　　Lingering after all the rest:

Plainer myrtle pleases me　　5
　　Thus outstretched beneath my vine,
Myrtle more becoming thee,
　　Waiting with thy master's wine.

Ad Xanthiam
Phoceum

Nay, Xanthias, feel unashamed
　　That she you love is but a servant.
Remember, lovers far more famed
　　Were just as fervent.

Achilles loved the pretty slave　　5
　　Briseïs for her fair complexion;
And to Tecmessa Ajax gave
　　His young affection.

Why, Agamemnon at the height
　　Of feasting, triumph, and anointment,　　10
Left everything to keep, one night,
　　A small appointment.

And are you sure the girl you love—
　　This maid on whom you have your heart set—
Is lowly—that she is not of　　15
　　The Roman smart set?

13. **Dark Taenarus accurst**, a cave-entrance to the underworld.
Persian Fopperies. Translated by William Cowper.
Ad Xanthiam Phoceum (*Xanthias Jollied*). Translated by Franklin P. Adams. From *Tobogganing on Parnassus* by Franklin P. Adams, copyright 1911 by Doubleday & Company, Inc.

Past Her Prime. From *Horace*, translated by Sir Theodore Martin. Reprinted by permission of J. B. Lippincott Company and Wm. Blackwood & Sons Ltd.
Faith Renewed. Translated by Stephen Edward De Vere.

A maiden modest as is she,
    So full of sweetness and forbearance,
Must be all right; her folks must be
    Delightful parents.   20

Her arms and face I can commend,
    And, as the writer of a poem,
I fain would compliment, old friend,
    The limbs below 'em.

Nay, be not jealous. Stop your fears.   25
    My tendencies are far from sporty.
Besides, the number of my years
    Is over forty.

To Licinius

RECEIVE, dear friend, the truths I teach;
    So shalt thou live beyond the reach
      Of adverse Fortune's power;
Not always tempt the distant deep,
Nor always timorously creep   5
      Along the treacherous shore.

He that holds fast the golden mean
And lives contentedly between
      The little and the great,
Feels not the wants that pinch the poor,   10
Nor plagues that haunt the rich man's door,
      Embittering all his state.

The tallest pines feel most the power
Of wintry blasts; the loftiest tower
      Comes heaviest to the ground;   15
The bolts that spare the mountain's side,
His cloud-capt eminence divide,
      And spread the ruin round.

The well-inform'd philosopher
Rejoices with a wholesome fear,   20
      And hopes, in spite of pain;
If winter bellow from the north,
Soon the sweet spring comes dancing forth,
      And Nature laughs again.

What if thine heaven be overcast?   25
The dark appearance will not last;
      Expect a brighter sky.
The god that strings the silver bow
Awakes sometimes the Muses too,
      And lays his arrows by.   30

If hindrances obstruct thy way,
Thy magnanimity display,
      And let thy strength be seen;
But oh! if Fortune fill thy sail
With more than a propitious gale,   35
      Take half thy canvas in.

To Licinius. Translated by William Cowper.

To Postumus

SWIFTLY fly the rolling years, my friend!
    Nor can your anxious prayers extend
      The fleeting joys of youth.
The trembling hand, the wrinkled cheek,
Too plainly life's decay bespeak,   5
      With sad but silent truth.

What though your daily offerings rise
In fragrant clouds of sacrifice
      To Jove's immortal seat;
You cannot fly death's cold embrace,   10
Where peasants—chiefs of kingly race
      An equal welcome meet.

In vain, from battlefields afar
You gently dream of waging war,
      Secure in peace and wealth: 15
In vain you shun the stormy wave,
The scorching breeze that others brave,
      Profuse of vigorous health.

Though zealous friends your portals throng,
They cannot still your life prolong   20
      By one short lingering hour;
Whate'er our plans, whate'er our state,
We mortals own one common fate,
      One stern, unbending power.

When your parched lips shall faintly press   25
On your fond wife their faint caress,
      And farewell murmurs breathe,
Your wandering eyes shall feebly rove
O'er each loved wood and well-trained grove,
      To seek a funeral wreath.   30

The purple vineyard's luscious stores,
Secured by trebly bolted doors,
      Excite, in vain, your care;
Soon shall the rich and sparkling hoard
Flow largely o'er the festive board   35
      Of your unsparing heir.

To Postumus. Translated by Ralph Bernal.
32. **trebly bolted doors,** the doors of his wine cellar.

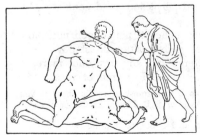

Wrestlers
and referee.
From
a Roman
painting.

Extremum Tanain

BEFORE thy door too long of late,
  O Lyce, I bewail my fate;
    Not Don's barbarian maids, I trow,
    Would treat their luckless lovers so;
Thou,—thou alone art obstinate.   5
Hast thou nor eyes nor ears, Ingrate!
Hark! how the NORTH WIND shakes thy gate!
    Look! how the laurels bend with snow
      Before thy doors!

Lay by thy pride,—nor hesitate,   10
Lest Love and I grow desperate;
    If prayers, if gifts for naught must go,
    If naught my frozen pallor show,—
Beware! . . . I shall not always wait
      Before thy doors!

To the Fountain
of Bandusia

O FOUNTAIN of Bandusia!
    Whence crystal waters flow,
With garlands gay and wine I'll pay
    The sacrifice I owe;
A sportive kid with budding horns   5
    I have, whose crimson blood
Anon shall dye and sanctify
    Thy cool and babbling flood.

O fountain of Bandusia!
    The Dog-star's hateful spell   10
No evil brings into the springs
    That from thy bosom well;
Here oxen, wearied by the plow,
    The roving cattle here
Hasten in quest of certain rest,   15
    And quaff thy gracious cheer.

O fountain of Bandusia!
    Ennobled shalt thou be,
For I shall sing the joys that spring
    Beneath yon ilex-tree.   20
Yes, fountain of Bandusia,
    Posterity shall know
The cooling brooks that from thy nooks
    Singing and dancing go.

Extremum Tanain. Translated by Austin Dobson. Reprinted by permission of Oxford University Press, London, and Mr. A. T. A. Dobson as representative of the Executors.
To the Fountain of Bandusia. Translated by Eugene Field. From *Echoes from the Sabine Farm*, by Eugene and R. M. Field, copyright 1893 by Eugene Field, 1921 by Julia Sutherland Field; used by permission of the publishers, Charles Scribner's Sons.

Holiday

WHAT celebration should there be? . . .
    Quick, Lyde, bring a jar!
Against a dull sobriety
    We'll wage a lusty war.

The festive sun is setting low,   5
    The dusk is almost there;
And yet you scarcely move, as though
    We both had time to spare!

Let's pour the wine and sing in turns
    Of Neptune in his lair,   10
Of mermaids in the water-ferns,
    And of their sea-green hair.

And you, upon your curving lyre,
    Shall spend a tuneful hour,
Singing Diana's darts of fire   15
    And her benignant power.

Hymns shall arise to Her who sends
    Fresh laughter and delight,
Until our weary singing ends
    In lullabies tonight.

The Immortality
of Verse

LEST you should think that verse shall die,
    Which sounds the silver Thames along,
Taught on the wings of truth to fly
    Above the reach of vulgar song;

Though daring Milton sits sublime,   5
    In Spenser native Muses play;
Nor yet shall Waller yield to time,
    Nor pensive Cowley's Mortal lay.

Sages and chiefs long since had birth
    Ere Caesar was, or Newton named;   10
These raised new empires o'er the earth,
    And those, new heavens and systems framed.

Vain was the chief's, the sage's pride!
    They had no poet, and they died.
In vain they schemed, in vain they bled!   15
    They had no poet, and are dead.

Holiday. From *Including Horace*, copyright, 1919, by Harcourt, Brace & World, Inc.; copyright, 1947, by Louis Untermeyer. Reprinted by permission of the publishers.
The Immortality of Verse. Translated by Alexander Pope.
2. **silver Thames.** Pope has replaced Horace's Roman allusions with English counterparts.

The Noble Soul

THE man of firm and noble soul
  No factious clamors can control;
No threat'ning tyrant's darkling brow
  Can swerve him from his just intent.
Gales the warring waves which plough   5
  By Auster on the billows spent,
To curb the Adriatic main,
Would awe his fix'd, determin'd mind in vain.

  Ay, and the red right arm of Jove,
Hurtling his lightnings from above,   10
With all his terrors then unfurl'd,
  He would unmoved, unawed behold.
The flames of an expiring world
  Again in crashing chaos roll'd,
In vast promiscuous ruin hurl'd,   15
Might light his glorious funeral pile:
Still dauntless mid the wreck of earth he'd smile.

Rain Tomorrow

UNLESS yon old soothsaying crow
  Deceive me, from the East shall blow
    Tomorrow such a blast
As will with leaves the forest strew,
And heaps of useless sea-weed, too,   5
    Upon the sea-beach cast.

Dry faggots, then, house while you may;
Give all your household holiday
    Tomorrow, and with wine
Your spirits cheer; be blithe and bold,   10
And on a pigling two moons old
    Most delicately dine!

To a Jar of Wine

O PRECIOUS crock, whose summers date,
  Like mine, from Manlius' consulate,
I wot not whether in your breast
Lie maudlin wail or merry jest,
Or sudden choler, or the fire   5
Of tipsy Love's insane desire,
Or fumes of soft caressing sleep,
Or what more potent charms you keep;
But this I know, your ripened power
Befits some choicely festive hour!   10

The Noble Soul. Translated by Lord Byron.
6. **Auster,** the sultry south wind, called *sirocco* in modern Italy.
Rain Tomorrow and *To a Jar of Wine.* From *Horace,* translated by
Sir Theodore Martin. Reprinted by permission of J. B. Lippincott
Company and Wm. Blackwood & Sons Ltd.

A cup peculiarly mellow
Corvinus asks; so come, old fellow,
From your time-honored bin descend,
And let me gratify my friend!
No churl is he, your charms to slight,   15
Though most intensely erudite:
And even old Cato's worth, we know,
Took from good wine a nobler glow.

  Your magic power of wit can spread
The halo round a dullard's head   20
Can make the sage forget his care,
His bosom's inmost thoughts unbare,
And drown his solemn-faced pretense
Beneath your blithesome influence.
Bright hope you bring and vigor back   25
To minds outworn upon the rack,
And put such courage in the brain
As makes the poor be men again
Whom neither tyrants' wrath affrights,
Nor all their bristling satellites.   30

  Bacchus and Venus, so that she
Bring only frank festivity,
With sister Graces in her train,
Twining close in lovely chain,
And gladsome tapers' living light,   35
Shall spread your treasures o'er the night,
Till Phoebus the red East unbars,
And puts to rout the trembling stars.

Renouncing Love

FOR ladies' love I late was fit,
  And good success my warfare blest;
But now my arms, my lyre I quit,
  And hang them up to rust or rest.
Here, where arising from the sea   5
  Stands Venus, lay the load at last,
Links, crowbars, and artillery,
  Threatening all doors that dared be fast.
O goddess! Cyprus owns thy sway,
  And Memphis, far from Thracian snow: 10
Raise high thy lash, and deal me, pray,
  That haughty Chloë just one blow!

To Venus

VENUS, again thou mov'st a war
  Long intermitted, pray thee, pray thee,
    spare!
I am not such as in the reign
  Of the good Cynara I was; refrain,

Renouncing Love. Translated by John Conington.
To Venus. Translated by Ben Jonson.

Sour mother of sweet Loves, forbear   5
  To bend a man, now at his fiftieth year.
Too stubborn for commands so slack:
  Go where youth's soft entreaties call thee back.
More timely hie thee to the house
  (With thy bright swans) of Paulus Maximus: 10
There jest and feast, make him thine host
  If a fit liver thou dost seek to toast.
For he's both noble, lovely, young,
  And for the troubled client files his tongue:
Child of a hundred arts, and far   15
  Will he display the ensigns of thy war.
And when he, smiling, finds his grace
  With thee 'bove all his rivals' gifts take place,
He'll thee a marble statue make,
  Beneath a sweet-wood roof, near Alba lake;   20
There shall thy dainty nostril take
  In many a gum, and for thy soft ear's sake
Shall verse be set to harp and lute,
  And Phrygian hau'boy, not without the flute.
There twice a day in sacred lays,   25
  The youths and tender maids shall sing thy
     praise!
And in the Salian manner meet
  Thrice 'bout thy altar, with their ivory feet.
Me now, nor girl, nor wanton boy
  Delights, nor credulous hope of mutual joy;   30
Nor care I now health to propound
  Or with fresh flowers to gird my temples round.
But why, oh why, my Ligurine,
  Flow my thin tears down these pale cheeks of
     mine?
Or why my well-graced words among,   35
  With an uncomely silence, fails my tongue?
Hard-hearted, I dream every night
  I hold thee fast! but fled hence with the light,
Whether in Mars his field thou be,
  Or Tiber's winding streams, I follow thee.

Revenge!

THE gods have heard me, Lyce,
  The gods have heard my prayer.
Now you, who were so icy,
  Observe with cold despair
  Your thin and snowy hair.   5

Your cheeks are lined and sunken;
  Your smiles have turned to leers;
But still you sing, a drunken
  Appeal to Love, who hears
  With inattentive ears.   10

Young Chia, with her fluty
  Caressing voice compels.
Love lives upon her beauty;
  Her cheeks, in which He dwells,
  Are His fresh citadels.   15

He saw the battered ruin,
  This old and twisted tree;
He marked the scars, and flew in
  Haste that He might not see
  Your torn senility.   20

No silks, no purple gauzes
  Can hide the lines that last.
Time, with his iron laws, is
  Implacable and fast.
  You cannot cheat the past.   25

Where now are all your subtle
  Disguises and your fair
Smile like a gleaming shuttle?
  Your shining skin, your rare
  Beauty half-breathless—where?   30

Only excelled by Cinara,
  Your loveliness ranked high.
You even seemed the winner, a
  Victor as years went by,
  And she was first to die.   35

But now—the young men lightly
  Laugh at your wrinkled brow.
The torch that burned so brightly
  Is only ashes now;
  A charred and blackened bough.

To His Book

YOU vain, self-conscious little book,
  Companion of my happy days,
How eagerly you seem to look
For wider fields to spread your lays;
  My desk and locks cannot contain you,   5
  Nor blush of modesty restrain you.

Well, then, begone, fool that thou art!
But do not come to me and cry,
  When critics strike you to the heart:
"Oh, wretched little book am I!"
  You know I tried to educate you
  To shun the fate that must await you.

27. **Salian manner.** The Salii, or "jumpers," were priests of Mars. *Revenge!* From *Including Horace*, copyright, 1919, by Harcourt, Brace & World, Inc.; copyright, 1947, by Louis Untermeyer. Reprinted by permission of the publishers.

To His Book (Epistle xx). Translated by R. M. Field. Reprinted from *Echoes from the Sabine Farm* by Eugene and R. M. Field; copyright 1893 by Eugene Field, 1921 by Julia Sutherland Field; used by permission of the publishers, Charles Scribner's Sons.

In youth you may encounter friends
(Pray this prediction be not wrong),
　　But wait until old age descends　　15
And thumbs have smeared your gentlest song;
　　Then will the moths connive to eat you
　　And rural libraries secrete you.

However, should a friend some word
Of my obscure career request,　　20
　　Tell him how deeply I was stirred
To spread my wings beyond the nest;
　　Take from my years, which are before you,
　　To boom my merits, I implore you.

Tell him that I am short and fat,　　25
Quick in my temper, soon appeased,
　　With locks of gray,—but what of that?
Loving the sun, with nature pleased.
　　I'm more than four and forty, hark you,—
　　But ready for a night off, mark you!

Satires

CONTENTMENT

How comes it, say, Maecenas, if you can,
　　That none will live like a contented man
Where choice or chance directs, but each must praise
The folk who pass through life by other ways?
'Those lucky merchants!' cries the soldier stout,　　5
When years of toil have well-nigh worn him out:
What says the merchant, tossing o'er the brine?
'Yon soldier's lot is happier, sure, than mine:
One short, sharp shock, and presto! all is done:
Death in an instant comes, or victory's won.'　　10
The lawyer lauds the farmer, when a knock
Disturbs his sleep at crowing of the cock:
The farmer, dragged to town on business, swears
That only citizens are free from cares.
I need not run through all: so long the list,　　15
Fabius himself would weary and desist:
So take in brief my meaning: just suppose
Some God should come, and with their wishes close:
'See, here am I, come down of my mere grace
To right you: soldier, take the merchant's place!　　20
You, counsellor, the farmer's! go your way,
One here, one there! None stirring? all say nay?
How now? you won't be happy when you may.'
Now, after this, would Jove be aught to blame
If with both cheeks he burst into a flame,　　25
And vowed, when next they pray, they shall not find
His temper easy, or his ear inclined?
　　Well, not to treat things lightly (though, for me,

*Roman painting
of a
city merchant.*

Why truth may not be gay, I cannot see:
Just as, we know, judicious teachers coax　　30
With sugar-plum or cake their little folks
To learn their alphabet):—still, we will try
A graver tone, and lay our joking by.
The man that with his plough subdues the land,
The soldier stout, the vintner sly and bland,　　35
The venturous sons of ocean, all declare
That with one view the toils of life they bear,
When age has come, and labour has amassed
Enough to live on, to retire at last:
E'en so the ant (for no bad pattern she),　　40
That tiny type of giant industry,
Drags grain by grain, and adds it to the sum
Of her full heap, foreseeing cold to come:
Yet she, when winter turns the year to chill,
Stirs not an inch beyond her mounded hill,　　45
But lives upon her savings: you, more bold,
Ne'er quit your gain for fiercest heat or cold:
Fire, ocean, sword, defying all, you strive
To make yourself the richest man alive.
Yet where's the profit, if you hide by stealth　　50
In pit or cavern your enormous wealth?
'Why, once break in upon it, friend, you know,
And, dwindling piece by piece, the whole will go.
But, if 'tis still unbroken, what delight
Can all that treasure give to mortal wight?'　　55
Say, you've a million quarters on your floor:
Your stomach is like mine: it holds no more:
Just as the slave who 'neath the bread-bag sweats
No larger ration than his fellows gets.
What matters it to reasonable men　　60
Whether they plough a hundred fields or ten?
'But there's a pleasure, spite of all you say,
In a large heap from which to take away.'
If both contain the modicum we lack,
Why should your barn be better than my sack?　　65
You want a draught of water: a mere urn,
Perchance a goblet, well would serve your turn:
You say, 'The stream looks scanty at its head;
I'll take my quantum where 'tis broad instead.'
But what befalls the wight who yearns for more　　70

Satires: "Contentment." Translated by John Conington.
16. **Fabius . . . desist.** The patient Fabius, known for his delay and
caution in prosecuting the war against Hannibal, is here meant.

Than Nature bids him? down the waters pour,
And whelm him, bank and all; while he whose greed
Is kept in check, proportioned to his need,
He neither draws his water mixed with mud,
Nor leaves his life behind him in the flood.   75

But there's a class of persons, led astray
By false desires, and this is what they say:
'You cannot have enough: what you possess,
That makes your value, be it more or less.'
What answer would you make to such as these?   80
Why, let them hug their misery if they please,
Like the Athenian miser, who was wont
To meet men's curses with a hero's front:
'Folks hiss me,' said he, 'but myself I clap
When I tell o'er my treasures on my lap.'   85
So Tantalus catches at the waves that fly
His thirsty palate—Laughing, are you? why?
Change but the name, of you the tale is told:
You sleep, mouth open, on your hoarded gold;
Gold that you treat as sacred, dare not use,   90
In fact, that charms you as a picture does.
Come, will you hear what wealth can fairly do?
'Twill buy you bread, and vegetables too,
And wine, a good pint measure: add to this
Such needful things as flesh and blood would miss.
But to go mad with watching, nights and days   96
To stand in dread of thieves, fires, runaways
Who filch and fly,—in these if wealth consist,
Let me rank lowest on the paupers' list.

'But if you suffer from a chill attack,   100
Or other chance should lay you on your back,
You then have one who'll sit by your bed-side,
Will see the needful remedies applied,
And call in a physician, to restore
Your health, and give you to your friends once more.'
Nor wife nor son desires your welfare: all   106
Detest you, neighbours, gossips, great and small.
What marvel if, when wealth's your one concern,
None offers you the love you never earn?
Nay, would you win the kinsmen Nature sends   110
Made ready to your hand, and keep them friends,
'Twere but lost labour, as if one should train
A donkey for the course by bit and rein.

Make then an end of getting: know, the more
Your wealth, the less the risk of being poor;   115
And, having gained the object of your quest,
Begin to slack your efforts and take rest;
Nor act like one Ummidius (never fear,
The tale is short, and 'tis the last you'll hear).
So rich, his gold he by the peck would tell,   120
So mean, the slave that served him dressed as well;
E'en to his dying day he went in dread
Of perishing for simple want of bread,
Till a brave damsel, of Tyndarid line
The true descendant, clove him down the chine. 125

86-87. **So Tantalus . . . palate.** This was his punishment in Hades
for divulging the secrets of Jupiter.

'What? would you have me live like some we
    know,
Maenius or Nomentanus?' There you go!
Still in extremes! in bidding you forsake
A miser's ways, I say not, Be a rake.
'Twixt Tanais and Visellius' sire-in-law   130
A step there is, and broader than a straw.
Yes, there's a mean in morals: life has lines,
To north or south of which all virtue pines.

Now to resume our subject: why, I say,
Should each man act the miser in his way,   135
Still discontented with his natural lot,
Still praising those who have what he has not?
Why should he waste with very spite, to see
His neighbour has a milkier cow than he,
Ne'er think how much he's richer than the mass, 140
But always strive this man or that to pass?
In such a contest, speed we as we may,
There's some one wealthier ever in the way.
So from their base when vying chariots pour,
Each driver presses on the car before,   145
Wastes not a thought on rivals overpast,
But leaves them to lay on among the last.
Hence comes it that the man is rarely seen
Who owns that his a happy life has been,
And, thankful for past blessings, with good will 150
Retires, like one who has enjoyed his fill.
Enough: you'll think I've rifled the scrutore
Of blind Crispinus, if I prose on more.

ABOUT MYSELF

Now on myself, the freedman's son, I touch,
    The freedman's son, by all condemned as
    such,
Once, when a legion followed my command,
Now, when Maecenas takes me by the hand.
But this and that are different: some stern judge   5
My military rank with cause might grudge,
But not your friendship, studious as you've been
To choose good men, not pushing, base, or mean.
In truth, to luck I care not to pretend,
For 'twas not luck that mark'd me for your friend: 10
Virgil at first, that faithful heart and true,
And Varius after, named my name to you.
Brought to your presence, stammeringly I told
(For modesty forbade me to be bold)
No vaunting tale of ancestry of pride,   15
Of good broad acres and sleek nags to ride,
But simple truth: a few brief words you say,
As is your wont, and wish me a good day.
Then, nine months after, graciously you send,
Desire my company, and hail me friend.   20
O, 'tis no common fortune, when one earns

130. **Tanais,** unidentified.
"**About Myself.**" Translated by John Conington.
12. **Varius,** Lucius Varius Rufus, epic poet and friend to Horace
and Virgil.

A friend's regard, who man from man discerns,
Not by mere accident of lofty birth
But by unsullied life, and inborn worth!
    Yet, if my nature, otherwise correct,   25
But with some few and trifling faults is flecked,
Just as a spot or mole might be to blame
Upon somebody else of comely frame,
If none can call me miserly and mean
Or tax my life with practices unclean,   30
If I have lived unstained and unreproved
(Forgive self-praise), if loving and beloved,
I owe it to my father, who, though poor,
Passed by the village school at his own door,
The school where great tall urchins in a row,   35
Sons of great tall centurions, used to go,
With slate and satchel on their backs, to pay
Their monthly quota punctual to the day,
And took his boy to Rome, to learn the arts
Which knight or senator to *his* imparts.   40
Whoe'er had seen me, neat and more than neat,
With slaves behind me, in the crowded street,
Had surely thought a fortune fair and large,
Two generations old, sustained the charge.
Himself the true tried guardian of his son,   45
Whene'er I went to class, he still made one.
Why lengthen out the tale? he kept me chaste,
Which is the crown of virtue, undisgraced
In deed and name: he feared not lest one day
The world should talk of money thrown away,   50
If after all I plied some trade for hire,
Like him, a tax-collector, or a crier:
Nor had I murmured: as it is, the score
Of gratitude and praise is all the more.
No: while my head's unturned, I ne'er shall need 55
To blush for that dear father, or to plead
As men oft plead, 'tis Nature's fault, not mine,
I came not of a better, worthier line.
Not thus I speak, not thus I feel: the plea
Might serve another, but 'twere base in me.   60
Should Fate this moment bid me to go back
O'er all my length of years, my life retrack
To its first hour, and pick out such descent
As man might wish for e'en to pride's content,
I should rest satisfied with mine, nor choose   65
New parents, decked with senatorial shoes.
Mad, most would think me, sane, as you'll allow,
To waive a load ne'er thrust on me till now.
More gear 'twould make me get without delay,
More bows there'd be to make, more calls to pay, 70
A friend or two must still be at my side,
That all alone I might not drive or ride,
More nags would want their corn, more grooms their
        meat,
And waggons must be bought, to save their feet.
Now on my bobtailed mule I jog at ease,   75
As far as e'en Tarentum, if I please,
A wallet for my things behind me tied,

Which galls his crupper, as I gall his side,
And no one rates my meanness, as they rate
Yours, noble Tillius, when you ride in state   80
On the Tiburtine road, five slaves *en suite*,
Wineholder and et-ceteras all complete.
'Tis thus my life is happier, man of pride,
Than yours and that of half the world beside.
When the whim leads, I saunter forth alone,   85
Ask how are herbs, and what is flour a stone,
Lounge through the Circus with its crowd of liars,
Or in the Forum, when the sun retires,
Talk to a soothsayer, then go home to seek
My frugal meal of fritter, vetch, and leek: 90
Three youngsters serve the food: a slab of white
Contains two cups, one ladle, clean and bright:
Next, a cheap basin ranges on the shelf,
With jug and saucer of Campanian delf:
Then off to bed, where I can close my eyes   95
Not thinking how with morning I must rise
And face grim Marsyas, who is known to swear
Young Novius' looks are what he cannot bear.
I lie a-bed till ten: then stroll a bit,
Or read or write, if in a silent fit,   100
And rub myself with oil, not taken whence
Natta takes his, at some poor lamp's expense.
So to the field and ball; but when the sun
Bids me go bathe, the field and ball I shun:
Then eat a temperate luncheon, just to stay   105
A sinking stomach till the close of day,
Kill time in-doors, and so forth. Here you see
A careless life, from stir and striving free,
Happier (O be that flattering unction mine!)
Than if three quaestors figured in my line.

CITY LIFE
AND COUNTRY LIFE

THIS used to be my wish: a bit of land,
    A house and garden with a spring at hand,
And just a little wood. The gods have crowned
My humble vows; I prosper and abound:
Nor ask I more, kind Mercury, save that thou   5
Wouldst give me still the goods thou giv'st me now:
If crime has ne'er increased them, nor excess
And want of thrift are like to make them less;
If I ne'er pray like this, 'O might that nook
Which spoils my field be mine by hook or crook! 10
O for a stroke of luck like his, who found
A crock of silver, turning up the ground,
And, thanks to good Alcides, farmed as buyer
The very land where he had slaved for hire!'
If what I have contents me, hear my prayer: 15
Still let me feel thy tutelary care,
And let my sheep, my pastures, this and that,
My all, in fact, (except my brains), be fat.

86. **stone,** fourteen pounds, English weight.
"City Life and Country Life." Translated by John Conington.
13. **Alcides,** Hercules.

*From
a Roman
painting.*

Now, lodged in my hill-castle, can I choose
Companion fitter than my homely Muse?   20
Here no town duties vex, no plague-winds blow,
Nor Autumn, friend to graveyards, works me woe.
Sire of the morning (do I call thee right,
Or hear'st thou Janus' name with more delight?)
Who introducest, so the gods ordain,   25
Life's various tasks, inaugurate my stain.
At Rome to bail I'm summoned. 'Do your part,'
Thou bidd'st me; 'Quick, lest others get the start.'
So, whether Boreas roars, or winter's snow
Clips short the day, to court I needs must go.   30
I give the fatal pledge, distinct and loud,
Then pushing, struggling, battle with the crowd.
'Now, madman!' clamours some one, not without
A threat or two, 'just mind what you're about:
What? you must knock down all that's in your way,
Because you're posting to Maecenas, eh?'   36
This pleases me, I own; but when I get
To black Esquiliae, trouble waits me yet:
For other people's matters in a swarm
Buzz round my head and take my ears by storm.   40
'Sir, Roscius would be glad if you'd arrange
By eight a.m. to be with him on 'Change.'
'Quintus, the scribes entreat you to attend
A meeting of importance, as their friend.'
'Just get Maecenas' seal attached to these.'   45
'I'll try.' 'O, you can do it, if you please.'
Seven years, or rather eight, have well-nigh passed
Since with Maecenas' friends I first was classed,
To this extent, that, driving through the street,
He'd stop his car and offer me a seat,   50
Or make such chance remarks as 'What's o'clock?'
'Will Syria's champion beat the Thracian cock?'
'These morning frosts are apt to be severe';
Just chit-chat, suited to a leaky ear.
Since that auspicious date, each day and hour   55
Has placed me more and more in envy's power:
'He joined his play, sat next him at the games:
A child of Fortune!' all the world exclaims.
From the high rostra a report comes down,

24. **Janus,** god of the threshold and hence of beginnings. 29. **Boreas,** the north wind.

And like a chilly fog, pervades the town: 60
Each man I meet accosts me 'Is it so?
You live so near the gods, you're sure to know:
What news about Dacians? have you heard
No secret tidings?' 'Not a single word.'
'O yes! you love to banter us poor folk.'   65
'Nay, if I've heard a tittle, may I choke!'
'Will Caesar grant his veterans their estates
In Italy, or t'other side of the straits?'
I swear that I know nothing, and am dumb:
They think me deep, miraculously mum.   70
And so my day between my fingers slips,
While fond regrets keep rising to my lips:
O my dear homestead in the country! when
Shall I behold your pleasant face again;
And, studying now, now dozing and at ease,   75
Imbibe forgetfulness of all this tease?
O when, Pythagoras, shall thy brother bean,
With pork and cabbage, on my board be seen?
O happy nights and suppers half divine,
When, at the home-gods' altar, I and mine   80
Enjoy a frugal meal, and leave the treat
Unfinished for my merry slaves to eat!
Not bound by mad-cap rules, but free to choose
Big cups or small, each follows his own views:
You toss your wine off boldly, if you please,   85
Or gently sip, and mellow by degrees.
We talk of—not our neighbour's house or field,
Nor the last feat of Lepos, the light-heeled—
But matters which to know concerns us more,
Which none but at his peril can ignore: 90
Whether 'tis wealth or virtue makes men blest,
What leads to friendship, worth or interest,
In what the good consists, and what the end
And chief of goods, on which the rest depend:
While neighbour Cervius, with his rustic wit,   95
Tells old wives' tales, this case or that to hit.
Should some one be unwise enough to praise
Arellius' toilsome wealth, he straightway says:
'One day a country mouse in his poor home

63. **Dacians,** the troublesome people of Dacia, a Roman province north of the lower Danube. 77. **brother bean,** the humble bean named for the philosopher Pythagoras, whose ascetic followers forbade the eating of beans.

Merchants and clients. From a Roman painting.

Country scene. From a Roman mosaic.

Received an ancient friend, a mouse from Rome: 100
The host, though close and careful, to a guest
Could open still: so now he did his best.
He spares not oaks or vetches: in his chaps
Raisins he brings and nibbled bacon-scraps,
Hoping by varied dainties to entice   105
His town-bred guest, so delicate and nice,
Who condescended graciously to touch
Thing after thing, but never would take much,
While he, the owner of the mansion, sate
On threshed-out straw, and spelt and darnels ate. 110
At length the townsman cries: "I wonder how
You can live here, friend, on this hill's rough brow:
Take my advice, and leave these ups and downs,
This hill and dale, for humankind and towns.
Come now, go home with me: remember, all   115
Who live on earth are mortal, great and small:
Then take, good sir, your pleasure while you may;
With life so short, 'twere wrong to lose a day."
This reasoning made the rustic's head turn round;
Forth from his hole he issues with a bound,   120
And they two make together for their mark,
In hopes to reach the city during dark.
The midnight sky was bending over all,
When they set foot within a stately hall,
Where couches of wrought ivory had been spread
With gorgeous coverlets of Tyrian red,   126
And viands piled up high in baskets lay,
The relics of a feast of yesterday.
The townsman does the honours, lays his guest
At ease upon a couch with crimson dressed,   130
Then nimbly moves in character of host,
And offers in succession boiled and roast;
Nay, like a well-trained slave, each wish prevents,
And tastes before the tit-bits he presents.
The guest, rejoicing in his altered fare,   135
Assumes in turn a genial diner's air,
When hark! a sudden banging of the door:

Each from his couch is tumbled on the floor;
Half dead, they scurry round the room, poor things,
While the whole house with barking mastiffs rings.
Then says the rustic: "It may do for you,   141
This life, but I don't like it; so adieu:
Give me my hole, secure from all alarms,
I'll prove that tares and vetches still have charms." '

The Art of Poetry

Good authors, take a brother bard's advice:
  Ponder your subject o'er not once nor twice,
And oft and oft consider, if the weight
You hope to lift be or be not too great.
Let but our theme be equal to our powers,   5
Choice language, clear arrangement, both are ours.
Would you be told how best your pearls to thread?
Why, say just now what should just now be said,
But put off other matter for to-day,
To introduce it later by the way.   10
  In words again be cautious and select,
And duly pick out this, and that reject.
High praise and honour to the bard is due
Whose dexterous setting makes an old word new.
Nay more, should some recondite subject need 15
Fresh signs to make it clear to those who read,
A power of issuing terms till now unused,
If claimed with modesty, is ne'er refused.
New words will find acceptance, if they flow
Forth from the Greek, with just a twist or so.   20
But why should Rome capriciously forbid
Our bards from doing what their fathers did? . . .
To utter words stamped current by the mill
Has always been thought right and always will. . . .
  Why hail me poet, if I fail to seize   25
The shades of style, its fixed proprieties?
Why should false shame compel me to endure
An ignorance which common pains would cure?
A comic subject steadily declines
To be related in high tragic lines.   30
The Thyestean feast no less disdains
The vulgar vehicle of comic strains.
Each has its place allotted; each is bound
To keep it, nor invade its neighbour's ground. . . .
Mere grace is not enough: a play should thrill 35
The hearer's soul, and move it at its will.
Smiles are contagious; so are tears; to see
Another sobbing, brings a sob from me.
No, no, good Peleus; set the example, pray,
And weep yourself; then weep perhaps I may: 40

The Art of Poetry. Translated by John Conington.
31. **Thyestean feast,** the feast at which Atreus served his brother
Thyestes the flesh of Thyestes' own murdered sons.

But if no sorrow in your speech appear,
I nod or laugh; I cannot squeeze a tear.
Words follow looks: wry faces are expressed
By wailing, scowls by bluster, smiles by jest,
Grave airs by saws, and so of all the rest.   45
For nature forms our spirits to receive
Each bent that outward circumstance can give:
She kindles pleasure, bids resentment glow,
Or bows the soul to earth in hopeless woe;
Then, as the tide of feeling waxes strong,   50
She vents it through her conduit-pipe, the
          tongue. . . .
     In painting characters, adhere to fame,
Or study keeping in the type you frame:
If great Achilles figure in the scene,
Make him impatient, fiery, ruthless, keen;   55
All laws, all covenants let him still disown,
And test his quarrel by the sword alone. . . .
     If you would be original still, and seek
To frame some character ne'er seen in Greek,
See it be wrought on one consistent plan,   60
And end the same creation it began.
'Tis hard, I grant, to treat a subject known
And hackneyed so that it may look one's own;
Far better turn the Iliad to a play
And carve out acts and scenes the readiest way,   65
Than alter facts and characters, and tell
In a strange form the tale men know so well.
But with some few precautions, you may set
Your private mark on public chattels yet:
Avoid careering and careering still   70
In the old round, like carthorse in a mill;
Nor, bound too closely to the Grecian Muse,
Translate the words whose soul you should transfuse,
Nor act the copyist's part, and work in chains
Which, once put on by rashness, shame retains. . . .
     Now listen, dramatists, and I will tell   76
What I expect, and all the world as well.
If you would have your auditors to stay
Till curtain-rise and plaudit end the play,
Observe each age's temper, and impart   80
To each the grace and finish of your art.
     Note first the boy who just knows how to talk
And feels his feet beneath him in his walk:
He likes his young companions, loves a game,
Soon vexed, soon soothed, and not two hours the
          same.   85
     The beardless youth, at last from tutor freed,
Loves playing-field and tennis, dog and steed:
Pliant as wax to those who lead him wrong,
But all impatience with a faithful tongue;
Imprudent, lavish, hankering for the moon,   90
He takes things up and lays them down as soon.
     His nature revolutionized, the man
Makes friends and money when and how he can:
Keen-eyed and cool, though on ambition bent,
He shuns all acts of which he may repent.   95

     Grey hairs have many evils: without end
The old man gathers what he dares not spend,
While, as for action, do he what he will,
'Tis all half-hearted, spiritless, and chill:
Inert, irresolute, his neck he cranes   100
Into the future, grumbles, and complains,
Extols his own young years with peevish praise,
But rates and censures these degenerate days.
     Years, as they come, bring blessings in their train;
Years, as they go, take blessings back again: 105
Yet haste or chance may blink the obvious truth,
Make youth discourse like age, and age like youth:
Attention fixed on life alone can teach
The traits and adjuncts which pertain to each.
     Sometimes 'tis done elsewhere, and there made
          known.   110
A thing when heard, remember, strikes less keen
On the spectator's mind than when 'tis seen.
Yet 'twere not well in public to display
A business best transacted far away,
And much may be secluded from the eye   115
For well-graced tongues to tell of by and by.
Medea must not shed her children's blood,
Nor savage Atreus cook man's flesh for food,
Nor Philomel turn bird or Cadmus snake,
With people looking on and wide awake.   120
If scenes like these before my eyes be thrust,
They shock belief and generate disgust.
     Would you your play should prosper and endure?
Then let it have five acts, nor more nor fewer.
Bring in no god save as a last resource,   125
Nor make four speakers join in the discourse.
     An actor's part the chorus should sustain
And do their best to get the plot in train:
And whatsoe'er between the acts they chant
Should all be apt, appropriate, relevant.   130
Still let them give sage counsel, back the good,
Attemper wrath, and cool impetuous blood,
Praise the spare meal that pleases but not sates,
Justice, and law, and peace with unbarred gates,
Conceal all secrets, and the gods implore   135
To crush the proud and elevate the poor. . . .
     My friends, make Greece your model when you
          write,
And turn her volumes over day and night.
'But Plautus pleased our sires, the good old folks;
They praised his numbers, and they praised his
          jokes.'   140
They did: 'twas mighty tolerant in them
To praise where wisdom would perhaps condemn;
That is, if you and I and our compeers
Can trust our tastes, our fingers, and our ears,
Know polished wit from horse-play, and can tell   145
What verses do, and what do not, run well.
     Thespis began the drama: rumour says
In travelling carts he carried round his plays,
Where actors, smeared with lees, before the throng

Performed their parts with gesture and with song. 150
Then Aeschylus brought in the mask and pall,
Put buskins on his men to make them tall,
Turned boards into a platform, not too great,
And taught high monologue and grand debate.
The elder Comedy had next its turn, 155
Nor small the glory it contrived to earn:
But freedom passed into unbridled spite,
And law was soon invoked to set things right;
And (shame to say) thenceforth refused to sing.

Our poets have tried all things; nor do they 160
Deserve least praise, who follow their own way,
And tell in comedy or history-piece
Some story of home growth, not drawn from Greece.
Nor would the land we love be now more strong
In warrior's prowess than in poet's song, 165
Did not her bards with one consent decline
The tedious task, to alter and refine.
Dear Pisos! as you prize old Numa's blood,
Set down that work, and that alone, as good,
Which, blurred and blotted, checked and counter-
        checked, 170
Has stood all tests, and issued forth correct. . . .

Of writing well, be sure, the secret lies
In wisdom: therefore study to be wise.
The page of Plato may suggest the thought,
Which found, the words will come as soon as sought.
The man who once has learned to comprehend 176
His duty to his country and his friend,
The love that parent, brother, guest may claim,
The judge's, senator's, or general's aim,
That man, when need occurs, will soon invent 180
For every part its proper sentiment.
Look too to life and manners, as they lie

168. **Dear Pisos,** the father and two sons to whom this Epistle was
addressed. **Numa,** the legendary second king of Rome.

City workers in Rome.

Before you: these will living words supply.
A play, devoid of beauty, strength, and art,
So but the thought and morals suit each part, 185
Will catch men's minds and rivet them when caught
More than the clink of verses without thought. . . .

Some faults may claim forgiveness: for the lyre
Not always gives the note that we desire;
We ask a flat; a sharp is its reply; 190
And the best bow will sometimes shoot awry.
But when I meet with beauties thickly sown,
A blot or two I readily condone,
Such as may trickle from a careless pen,
Or pass unwatched: for authors are but men. 195
What then? the copyist who keeps stumbling still
At the same word had best lay down his quill:
The harp-player, who for ever wounds the ear
With the same discord, makes the audience jeer:
So the poor dolt who's often in the wrong 200
I rank with Choerilus, that dunce of song,
Who, should he ever deviate into sense,
Moves but fresh laughter at his own expense:
While e'en good Homer may deserve a tap,
If, as he does, he drop his head and nap. 205
Yet, when a work is long, 'twere somewhat hard
To blame a drowsy moment in a bard. . . .

But here occurs a question some men start,
If good verse comes from nature or from art.
For me, I cannot see how native wit 210
Can e'er dispense with art, or art with it.
Set them to pull together, they're agreed,
And each supplies what each is found to need.

The youth who runs for prizes wisely trains,
Bears cold and heat, is patient and abstains: 215
The flute-player at a festival, before
He plays in public, has to learn his lore.
Not so our bardlings: they come bouncing in—
'I'm your true poet: let them laugh that win:
Plague take the last! although I ne'er was taught, 220
Is that a cause for owning I know nought?' . . .

Read verses to Quintilius, he would say,
'I don't like this and that: improve it, pray':
Tell him you found it hopeless to correct;
You'd tried it twice or thrice without effect: 225
He'd calmly bid you make the three times four,
And take the unlicked cub in hand once more.
But if you chose to vindicate the crime,
Not mend it, he would waste no further time,
But let you live, untroubled by advice, 230
Sole tenant of your own fool's paradise.

A wise and faithful counsellor will blame
Weak verses, note the rough, condemn the lame,
Retrench luxuriance, make obscureness plain,

201. **Choerilus, that dunce of song,** a mediocre epic poet, friend to
Alexander the Great. 204–205. **While e'en good Homer . . . nap.**
This is another translation of the familiar "Homer nods." 222.
Quintilius, Quintilius Varus, the poet and critic, a friend of Virgil.

Cross-question this, bid that be writ again: 235
A second Aristarch, he will not ask,
'Why for such trifles take my friend to task?'
Such trifles bring to serious grief ere long
A hapless bard, once flattered and led wrong. . . .

Catullus

87–54 B.C.

Romantic love was a subject of little interest to Greeks of the Golden Age because of the inferior social position of women and a system of education and marriage that discouraged it. In Rome women enjoyed almost complete emancipation, but the formality of marital arrangements and a stoic training that subjected the emotions to reason and duty discouraged romantic love here as well. The love poetry of Horace and Ovid is *vers de société*, celebrating casual affairs with a variety of rather dubious ladies. Tibullus (54?– 19 B.C.) with his Delia, and Propertius (50?–15 B.C.) with his Cynthia are more convincing, but the only great love poetry of Rome is that of Catullus, inspired by an authentic devotion to a worthless woman. It too was a blighted product of the fashionable, reckless circles of the capital in the days of its sophistication.

Gaius Valerius Catullus came of a distinguished family in the northern city of Verona and was probably of warm Celtic blood. His father's wealth provided him a gentleman's education and took him to Rome in his early twenties. Here he was caught up in the youthful smart set which was emulating the cultured society of Alexandria with its free love and idle living, and the poets of Alexandria with their gay love ditties. He adopted the fashionable policy of lampooning Caesar but otherwise took no part in politics. He spent his time in his town house with its fine library or at one of his two country estates, where his extravagance led him to complain of an empty purse. In a misguided effort to recoup his finances, he accompanied Memmius, the governor of Bithynia, to that province and visited Greece en route. Debonair and dissipated, he squandered his life in a decade and died the Romantic's early death at thirty.

Lovemaking was a favorite pastime of the young blades of the capital, but Catullus was unconventional in devoting himself to a depraved and heartless woman. She was Clodia, the sister of Cicero's enemy, Publius Clodius, and the wife of Metellus Celer, who was away governing Cisalpine Gaul in the year 62, when Catullus probably arrived in Rome and began his attachment to her. Cicero has left us a blistering account of this bold and libidinous siren in defending another of her lovers, Caelius Rufus, from her charge that he tried to poison her. She was older than Catullus and saw in this naïve youth from the provinces a refreshing interlude in her

236. **Aristarch**, Aristarchus (fl. 150 B.C.), considered the greatest critic of antiquity.

round of amours. For him it was love at first sight, and he wooed her with exquisite verses of passionate and innocent devotion. All the stages of an ill-fated love are there: his first attraction, his jealousy of her pet bird and tender grief at its death, the frenzy of passion in which he abandoned all reserves, his final recoil from her infidelities in bitter revenge. He stoops to obscenity in his last revulsion, and eventually turns to other poetic themes.

The trembling lyrics that preserve the anguished love of this great poet are partially in the contemporary tradition of the polished Alexandrians, partially in the old Greek tradition of Sappho of Lesbos, whose memory Catullus recalled in the poetic name Lesbia, with which he addressed Clodia. The meters of his 116 poems are varied, and their subjects go beyond his love affair to shocking obscenities, charming wedding songs, myths retold, poems of tender friendship, and the salute to his brother's grave with its *ave atque vale* (Hail and farewell!). Nearly all are brief and fervent, and their light grace, warm color, and frenzied abandonment to joy and despair stamp them as more modern than Roman. Catullus in his untrammeled moods has been variously compared to Sappho, Shelley, and Robert Burns. His poems were completely forgotten in the Middle Ages, but returned in the fourteenth century with the accidental discovery of the one surviving manuscript. They have had a profound effect on modern poets from Petrarch down.

To Lesbia's Sparrow

SPARROW, the plaything of my fair,
    Whom in her lap she loves to bear,
Or with raised finger-tip excites
Till wickedly he pecks and bites;
When the bright lady of my yearning   5
To some dear dainty play is turning,
Sweet solace for love's pain, I trow,
Or in the lull of passion's glow,—
Oh! might I play with you as she,
And my heart's burden lighter be.

On the Death of Lesbia's Sparrow

MOURN Loves and Graces all, and you
    Of men the lovelier chosen few.
The sparrow of my love is dead,
The playmate of my love is sped,
Her sparrow, prized beyond her eyes,   5
So honey-sweet was he, and wise

To Lesbia's Sparrow; On the Death of Lesbia's Sparrow. Translated by Hugh MacNaghton. From *The Poems of Catullus* by Hugh MacNaghton. Reprinted by permission of The University Press, Cambridge, England.

To know her as a girl her mother.
He would not leave her for another,
Would on her lap be still astir
And chirping still for none but her. 10
And now he journeys whence they say
No steps retrace the darkling way.
Cursed shades, I curse you, swallowing
In Orcus every dainty thing:
The dainty pet ye ravished here! 15
Fie, fie for shame! ah, birdie dear!
Flushed, heavy eyelids are the due
My love is paying, all for you.

Catullus Contrasts Quintia with Lesbia

MANY say Quintia is "lovely." I
    Say "fair" and "straight" and "tall."
    Each single claim
I grant, but not the sum of "lovely." Why?
    Sparkles nor wit nor grace in all her frame. 5
But Lesbia is lovely, cap-à-pie,
And from all others takes all charm away.

On Lesbia

LESBIA forever on me rails.
    To talk of me she never fails.
Now, hang me, but for all her art,
I find that I have gained her heart.
My proof is this: I plainly see 5
The case is just the same with me;
I curse her every hour sincerely,
Yet, hang me, but I love her dearly.

"Love Is Best"

O! LET us love and have our day,
    All that the bitter greybeards say
Appraising at a single mite.
My Lesbia, suns can set and rise:
For us the brief light dawns and dies 5
Once only, and the rest is night.
A thousand kisses, then five score,
A thousand and a hundred more,
Then one for each you gave before.
Then, as the many thousands grow, 10
We'll wreck the counting lest we know,
Or lest an evil eye prevail
Through knowledge of the kisses' tale.

14. **In Orcus**; that is, in the abode of Orcus or Pluto, god of the underworld. Roman poets called him either Dis or Orcus.
Catullus Contrasts Quintia . . . ; "Love Is Best." Translated by Hugh MacNaghton. From *The Poems of Catullus* by Hugh Mac-Naghton. Reprinted by permission of The University Press, Cambridge, England.
On Lesbia. Translated by Jonathan Swift.

Of Metellus, Husband of Clodia

LESBIA reviles me when her husband's by.
    This throws the booby into ecstasy.
You senseless ass! Were I unnamed, forgot,
She were heart-whole: who snarls, forgets me not;
Who rails is angry. Sure, the wound is sore: 5
'Tis "The heart flames, the mouth proclaims" once
    more.

After a Quarrel

IF that which is the heart's desire be told
    Unhoped for, it is joy beyond the rest;
Therefore I count it joy more dear than gold
That, love, you turn again and make me blest;
You turn, my heart's desire so long denied, 5
Unasked, unhoped for. Oh! the white, bright day!
What happiness in all the world beside
Is like to mine? The rapture who shall say?

Doubt

THOUGH Jupiter himself should court her,
    My lady vows she'd marry only me.
She vows—but what a lady vows her lover
    Write on the wind and in the shifting sea.

True or False

NONE could ever say that she,
    Lesbia! was so loved by me.
Never all the world around
Faith so true as mine was found.
If no longer it endures 5
(Would it did!) the fault is yours.
I can never think again
Well of you: I try in vain.
But . . . be false . . . do what you will.—
Lesbia! I must love you still.

Odi et Amo

I LOVE and hate. Ah! never ask why so!
    I hate and love . . . and that is all I know.
I see 'tis folly; but I feel 'tis woe.

Of Metellus, Husband of Clodia; After a Quarrel. Translated by Hugh MacNaghton. From *The Poems of Catullus* by Hugh Mac-Naghton. Reprinted by permission of The University Press, Cambridge, England.
Doubt. Translated by Robert Warnock.
True or False. Translated by Walter Savage Landor.
Odi et Amo. Translated by Walter Savage Landor.

The Undying Fire

ONCE you would say to me: 'Your heart has
found me
And yours alone.
I would not have the arms of Jove around me
More than your own.'
Saying it, you became no more the fashion   5
Of cheap desire,
But wife and child and home, loved with the pas-
sion
Of life-long fire.

I know you now. Yet my soul goes on burning,
As burn it must,   10
When you and all I gave to you are turning
To death and dust.
Strange, do you say? How strange that love should
cherish
Light that is gone!
That every kindly thought of you should perish,   15
Yet love last on.

Journey's End

THEY say that benefits to others rendered
Win in our memories their late reward.
They say that love, once it is loyally tendered,
Stays sweet and keeps the lover's heart unscarred.

If it is true that faith promised and given   5
Is profit, and a guileless heart is gain,
How surely shall I profit, who hath striven
So long with pain.

The gentle word, the generous intent,
The decent things that men can do or say,   10
All these to gladden her I freely spent
But could not touch her when she turned away.

Why then, you fool, cherish your long affliction?
Why fight against the thing that must prevail?
Put her away from you. Need resolution   15
Forever fail?

"It is impossible to lay aside forever
In one brief point of time the love of years."
Then do th' impossible. Steel yourself. Sever
This knot, and wring relief from bitter tears.   20

The Undying Fire. Translated by E. A. Havelock. From *The Lyric Genius of Catullus* by E. A. Havelock. Reprinted by permission of Basil Blackwell & Mott, Ltd.
Journey's End; The Office of My Heart. Translated by E. A. Havelock. From *The Lyric Genius of Catullus* by E. A. Havelock. Reprinted by permission of Basil Blackwell & Mott, Ltd.

O gods, if yours be pity, yours compassion
Given to failing men even on the road
Leading to death, dispel this black obsession,
Rescue my soul from hell. Support its load—

How like a stupor every sense pervading   25
My sorrow steals! How faint I grow with grief!
How swift the sunlight of my life is fading,
My bliss how brief!

I look no more for her to be my lover
As I love her. That thing could never be.   30
Nor pray I for her purity—that's over.
Only this much I pray, that I be free,

Free from insane desire myself, and guarded
In peace at last. O heaven, grant that yet
The faith by which I've lived may be rewarded.   35
Let me forget.

Catullus Struggles to Be Free

CATULLUS, hapless one, be sane at last,
Believe your eyes, confess the past is past.
So bright, so white the suns that shone before!
Then where your lady led you followed fain,
And loved her as none else shall love again.   5
Ah! then the glad surprises and the play—
You wished it so, nor said your lady nay.
So white, so bright the suns that shine no more!
Now she says nay: ah! weakling, say it too,
Nor live to grieve, nor one who flies pursue,   10
But stubborn stand and bear the purpose through.
Lady, good-bye! now stands Catullus fast,
Nor woos against your will nor mourns the past:
But surely you shall mourn when wooed no more.
Poor culprit! ah, the days for you in store!   15
Who will now heed your beauty, take your hand?
Whom will you fondle? who will call you his?
Whose lips will you devour with kiss on kiss?
But thou, Catullus, stubborn, steadfast stand.

The Office of My Heart

THE office of my heart is still to love
When I would hate.
Time and again your faithlessness I prove
Proven too late.
Your ways might mend, yet my contempt could
never   5
Be now undone.
Yet crimes repeated cannot stop this fever
From burning on.

Catullus Struggles to Be Free. Translated by Hugh MacNaghton. From *The Poems of Catullus* by Hugh MacNaghton. Reprinted by permission of The University Press, Cambridge, England.

She That I Loved

SHE that I loved, that face,
   Those hands, that hair,
Dearer than all my race,
   As dear as fair—
See her where throngs parade   5
   Th' imperial route,
Plying her skill unpaid—
   Rome's prostitute.

At the Grave of His Brother

BY ways remote and distant waters sped,
   Brother, to thy sad graveside am I come,
That I may give the last gifts to the dead,
   And vainly parley with thine ashes dumb;
Since She who now bestows and now denies   5
   Have ta'en thee, hapless brother, from mine
      eyes.
But lo! These gifts, the heirlooms of past years,
   Are made sad things to grace thy coffin-shell;
Take them, all drenchèd with a brother's tears,
   And, brother, for all time, hail and farewell.

Sirmio

GEM of all isthmuses and isles that lie
   Fresh or salt water's children, in clear lake
Or ampler ocean: with what joy do I
Approach thee, Sirmio! Oh! am I awake,
Or dream that once again my eye beholds   5
Thee, and has looked its last on Thynian wolds?
Sweetest of sweets to me that pastime seems,
When the mind drops her burden: when—the pain
Of travel past—our own cot we regain,
And nestle on the pillow of our dreams!   10
'Tis this one thought that cheers us as we roam.
Hail, O fair Sirmio! Joy, thy lord is here!
Joy too, ye waters of the Garda Mere!
And ring out, all ye laughter-peals of home.

She That I Loved. Translated by E. A. Havelock. From *The Lyric Genius of Catullus* by E. A. Havelock. Reprinted by permission of Basil Blackwell & Mott, Ltd.
At the Grave of His Brother. Translated by Aubrey Beardsley. The grave was at Rhoetum, which Catullus visited on his journey to Bithynia in Asia Minor in 57 B.C.
5. **She,** the goddess Fortuna. 10. **hail and farewell,** *Ave atque vale,* a common grave inscription.
Sirmio. Translated by Charles Stuart Calverley. Catullus's "all-but-island," since it was connected to the mainland by a narrow strip of land which was at times covered by water. In 56 B.C. Catullus was returning to his villa there from his journey to Bithynia. This fourteen-line poem has been called the first sonnet, though its resemblance to the later form is purely accidental.
13. **Garda Mere,** the lake of Garda, into which Sirmio stretched.

To Varus

SUFFENUS, whom so well you know,
   My Varus, as a wit and beau,
Of smart address and smirking smile,
Will write you verses by the mile.
You cannot meet with daintier fare   5
Than title-page and binding are;
But when you once begin to read
You find it sorry stuff indeed,
And you are ready to cry out
Upon this beau—"O what a lout!"   10
No man on earth so proud as he
Of his own precious poetry,
Or knows such perfect bliss as when
He takes in hand that nibbled pen.
Have we not all some faults like these?   15
Are we not all Suffenuses?
In others the defect we find,
But cannot see our sack behind.

Ovid

43 B.C.–17 A.D.

The most scandalous of Roman love poets was Ovid, another playboy of the city smart set, who lacked entirely the emotional depths of Catullus and converted his many love affairs into fashionable erotic verse. Coming more than a generation after Catullus, he belonged to the empire in the glorious days of Augustus, but turned from the intellectual circles of Horace and Propertius to the demimonde that carried on the traditions of Clodia's salon. Publius Ovidius Naso (or Ovid, as we call him) was intended by his ambitious equestrian father for a career in the government and was sent from his provincial birthplace at Sulmo to schools in Rome and Athens. But when he settled in the capital, his attentions quickly shifted from law to poetry, for which he had shown a natural talent since childhood. Most of all, he enjoyed idleness and play and was to become Rome's poet of pleasure, especially amorous pleasure. These interests endeared him to the jaded fast set, whose poet laureate he was for thirty years.

Despite the questionable taste of much of his work and the frivolous insincerity of his mind, Ovid is a thoroughly charming writer of endless facility and bright grace. Unlike the studied verses of Virgil and Horace, his bubble on delightfully without effort or strain on the intellect. Even his most decadent love poems have an insidious effervescence that makes them highly entertaining. His *Amores,* 49 short lyrics, pretend to record an affair of his

To Varus. Translated by Walter Savage Landor.

own with a certain Corinna, who has eluded identification. Probably she is a composite figure made out of numerous mistresses; certainly the passion is feigned, as the sprightly mood and dainty style betray. Alexandrian influence is strong here as in the *Heroides*, a series of imaginary letters from mythical heroines like Penelope and Dido condemning their husbands or lovers for deserting them. The most notorious of his love poems is the *Art of Love*, a lively treatise giving instruction in the first two books to men, in the last one to women. But the "love" alluded to is mere physical conquest inspired by Ovid's own liaisons with Roman courtesans. A sequel provided instructions for falling out of love and into marriage; but whether it is love or marriage that he is discussing, his attitude is as amoral as it is amusing. However much it may entertain us, we must agree with Augustus that it does not conduce to sincere and lofty sentiment, a substantial family life, or even good citizenship.

As Ovid turned forty, his interests shifted to a larger sphere and a more serious theme, though he knew that he had not the seriousness of mind to attempt an epic. The fifteen books of the *Metamorphoses* display his endless ingenuity and great narrative skill in a kind of poetic summary of ancient myths. The old tales were of course familiar to his audience and in his time considered no more religious than we consider them. But he arranged them by a clever chronology according to the four ages of man—gold, silver, bronze, and iron—and built almost every one around a transformation of some kind, as the title indicates—the changing of Pygmalion's statue into a beautiful woman, the metamorphosis of the weeping Niobe into a column of stone and a spring. But it is the brilliant style and fanciful beauty of his world of fable that make the *Metamorphoses*, not simply our best compendium of classical myths, but a source of endless entertainment.

In 8 A.D. Ovid's career in Rome ended abruptly with his exile by Augustus to the barbarous town of Tomi on the Black Sea coast for reasons that are still obscure— "a poem and an error," he tells us: probably the *Art of Love*, written ten years before, and his complicity in an immoral affair of Augustus' granddaughter. The sentence was abrupt and cruel, for the gay poet of fashionable society was now lost in an uncultured wilderness; but his unmanly response to his misfortune does not inspire our pity. His work declined, and the *Tristia* in five books are wearisome complaints of his desolation. His whimpering betrays his fatal lack of character. It is best to remember Ovid in the gay and cynical capital of his youthful success.

The Art of Love

BOOK I

IF any here be ignorant of love,
  Let him read this, he shall a lover prove.
To sail swift ships, in chariots to ride,
Require an art; no less is art love's guide. . . .
Love raging is, he struggles oft with me,   5

*The Art of Love.*ᴬ Translated by Francis Wolferston.

But he's a boy and must directed be. . . .
So I can Love subdue, my heart though he
Wound with his bow, and dart his flames at me;
The more he doth vindictive torments make,
Greater shall be the vengeance that I take. . . .   10
Experience is my muse; the truths I know,
I sing; Venus, grace my beginnings now. . . .
  You who a soldier in this war would prove
Must labour first to find out whom to love,
And next, the girl that pleases you to gain,   15
And last that constant may her love remain.
This way, this manner to our course assign,
Nor must our chariot-wheel this goal decline.
  With out-cast lures, go round about, choose one
Of whom to say, 'She pleaseth me alone.'   20
Heaven will not drop one down; then look about
Until you find a pleasing beauty out.
The huntsman knows where best his toils to lay,
And in what dale the foaming boar to slay;
The fowler knows the trees, the angler's taught   25
To know the places where most fish are caught;
So you that would a lover be must walk
In groves where maidens love to meet and talk.
To find these out I would not bid you go
Afar, nor plough the ocean to and fro. . . .   30
But Rome so many beauties offers you—
None better though you search the wide world
    through.
As corn on Ida, grapes on Lesbos found,
As seas with fish, as trees with birds abound,
As heaven with stars, of maids so full is Rome: 35
The city of her son is Venus' home.
If that a tender growing age you prize,
Unstained virgins are before your eyes.
If one mature you seek, here thousands are;
You cannot choose one than the rest more fair.   40
If a grave matron do delight you much,
No trouble will you have in finding such.
  You in the theatre must a-hunting go—
Choice beauties there will best repay your vow.
There you will find with whom you may make bold
In dalliance, or perhaps for longer hold.   46
As busy ants in troops march to and fro—
With mouths full-stored with wonted food they go—
Or as the bee from grove to meadow hies,
There from one flower to another flies;   50
So thick the ladies to the stage repair:
Oft have I wondered at their numbers there.
Hither they come to see and to be seen—
Here modesty hath oft neglected been. . . .
And at the horse-race in the Circus too   55
Here opportunity will wait on you.
With look and nod you need not here beseech
Your mistress, nor with finger's silent speech,
But go straight to her, here by none denied,

36. her son, Aeneas.

The god Eros.

And gently join yourself unto her side.　60
If she refuse that you should sit so near,
The custom of the place allows it here.
Here you must ask (for 'tis the readiest way
To gain discourse) things in the present play:
Whose horse is this comes up? And then must you,
Whatever she commends, commend it too. . . .　66
Or if the dust raised high fall on her, then
You with your hand must brush it off again.
If none light on her, yet brush off that none;
Action in such a case becometh one.　70
If her loose mantle's trailing down, you must
Catch up the hem and keep it from the dust,
And when you stoop, observe with nimble eye
If you can there a dainty leg espy.
Take care lest they that sit behind should push,　75
Or with their knees her tender back should crush.
'Tis profitable—slight things please her oft—
With ready hand to make her cushions soft.
Some fanning cool air do their mistress move,
Or with a foot eased give a birth to love.　80
The Circus yields such opportunities;
The Forum too whereon the grim sand lies.
Cupid has oft in the arena fought,
And the spectator then has worse wounds caught
Than those he looks on; while he lays his bet　85
And asks his mistress who she thinks will get
The prize that day, himself is struck to the heart
And cries out, wounded with Love's cruel dart. . . .
Then if your mistress ask a prince's name,
O lover, or from where the captives came,　90
Her questions answer—whether she ask or not;
Pretend to knowledge which thou hast not got—
Name him Euphrates with his reedy crown;
That one is Tigris whose dark hair hangs down!
Call these Armenians, those Persians are,　95
Say 'tis a city in Achaemenia.
Some were once chieftains; these by right name call
If well you can; if not, feign names for all.
　Chance waits on you whene'er the banquet's
　　spread
And something besides wine is to be had. . . .　100
Wine often will our private thoughts declare,
And by its means concealments banished are.

It often will young men with love inspire—
Love joined with wine is putting fire to fire.
Choose not in wine nor do so when 'tis night;　105
One injures judgment, and the other sight.
Paris by day the goddesses did see
When Venus was the fairest judged to be.
Night imperfection hides, will no fault show,
Makes them that are not fair seem to be so.　110
Rich gems and purple cloth by day peruse,
And in the sun a good complexion choose. . . .
　The several places where choice beauties be—
Thus far hath my Thalia sung to thee.
The fair one which thou most dost fancy, how　115
To obtain—the top of art—I'll teach thee now. . . .
Doubt not to gain what beauty e'er you choose;
'Mongst many you'll not find one to refuse.
They grant or they deny, yet love to be
Entreated; so no harm is done if she　120
Refuses. But why should she? Your love's new;
What's new is welcome—to the old adieu.
The corn is riper in adjacent fields;
Your neighbour's cow a larger udder yields.
　Before the mistress you must win the maid,　125
For she will help you in your escapade.
It is the handmaid that all secrets knows,
To whom the mistress will her thoughts disclose.
With gifts and promises corrupt her: she
Will bring you to her mistress willingly.　130
Like a physician, she a time will choose
When she you love is least apt to refuse.
At times of joy she won't from love recoil:
So standing corn thrives best in fatting soil.
When mirth she entertains, no griefs molest,　135
Venus is soon admitted to her breast.
Ilion, when sad, with arms defended sits;
When glad, the foe-containing horse admits.
Try when some rival steals her husband, too;
For her revenge on him she'll pleasure you.　140
The handmaid while she combs her mistress' hair
May further this, your faithfulness declare,
Suggest the husband should be made to rue:
'He takes elsewhere his pleasure; why not you?'
Your name she'll mention then and urge your praise,
Swear, if you have her not you'll end your days.　146
Make haste then and go to her lest she may
Be angry, and grow cold through your delay. . . .
　Times are appointed when to sow and reap,
And times when sailors venture on the deep:　150
So in your courting be not overlong;
For love there is a right time and a wrong.
When she her birthday keeps, or when the Queen
Of Love with Mars is in conjunction seen,
Or at those times when costly merchandise　155
Is in the Circus spread before your eyes,
Desist: when storms come with the Pleiades
And when the Goat is swallowed in the seas,
'Tis best leave off; then they which trust the deep

Scarce any part of their torn sails can keep.   160
Begin such time as Allia heretofore
Ran red, its waters stained with Roman gore;
Or on that feast begin to court again,
Which Syrians of Palestine ordain.
But let her birthday solemnly be spent;   165
A black day when you must a gift present:
Women for gifts will always find excuses
And put their lover's wealth to many uses.
The milliner will to your mistress go—
While you look on, to her his wares will show;   170
She'll your opinion ask and something try,
Then with a kiss solicit you to buy.
She'll say it will for long her uses fit—
'Tis very cheap and she hath need of it.
Then if you say you can't so much expend,   175
She'll bid you write for money from a friend.
Give her upon her birthday what you will—
Whate'er she wants, it is her birthday still;
Perhaps her jewelled ear-ring's dropped, she'll feign,
And then you must buy one for her again.   180
She'll borrow many things, yet none restore,
Nor shall your loss of them gain favour more.
Ten mouths, as many tongues, too little are
For me the arts of women to declare.

   First must a letter sealed an entrance find;   185
Let your wax bear the impress of your mind.
And let your letter love-expressions bear,
To which you must add an imploring prayer.
Achilles at the king's request did send
Back Hector; Heaven will to prayers bend.   190
A promise hurts you not; then promise much;
It makes those that are not rich seem to be such.
Your letter wins her, if she credit it;
Hope's a false goddess, yet for you most fit.
Give her not much, for fear that you should part;
She only gains then; thou the loser art.   196
Be always giving, yet let nothing go:
Swains are with barren soil deluded so.
Thus gamblers fear to lose, yet losing more
Clutch at the dice that was their loss before.   200
You may her favour without gifts procure;
If she loves gratis, it will long endure.
With handsome words you must prepare her mind;
First try if those will entertainment find. . . .

   I'd have young men to learn to plead a cause:
For them, not for their clients, is th' applause.   206
Women to him their pleasing glances send
Whom the grave judge and senators commend.
But wear your learning gracefully and well;
Let not your lips on tedious stories dwell.   210
Whoever to his mistress would declaim?
Lengthy epistles only bring you blame.
Use smooth and taking words, a handsome style,
That she may on your pleading language smile.

161–162. **Begin such time . . . gore;** that is, July 16, when the
Gauls defeated the Romans on the Allia in 390 B.C.

Should she your letter back unopened send,   215
Proceed and hope she'll read it in the end. . . .
The softest drops by constant falling on
Will make impression on the hardest stone.
Persist; were she Penelope you'd gain;
Troy's towers late, but yet at last were ta'en.   220
Ere you ask her to write I bid you pause:
'Tis grace enough if she but look on yours.
If once she read she will write back, but these
Great favours she bestoweth by degrees.
Perhaps no pleasure her first letter brings—   225
Bids you not trouble her with such fond things;
But yet she hopes that you may fixed remain:
Pursue and fear not but you will obtain.

   If you should see your mistress in the street
On litter borne, be wary when you meet;   230
Be sure that none o'erhear lest they defame
And add a scandal to your mistress' name.
If in the porch you chance to see her loiter,
Walk at a distance while you reconnoitre;
Sometimes before, sometimes behind her go,   235
Now you may walk apace, and then walk slow.
When you shall overtake her, don't divide,
But go as close as may be to her side.
Perchance if to the theatre she has gone,
There follow her, observe what she hath on;   240
There you may boldly look on her attire,
Commend her eyes and every part admire.
Applaud the woman in the mummer's art,
And favour him who acts a lover's part.
When she stands, stand; when she sits, do not stir,
And gladly spend your time observing her.   246

   Do not use instruments to curl your hair,
Nor make your legs with pumice smooth and
     bare. . . .
Neatness delights; the fields won't tan too much;
Be sure your clothes are handsome, without smutch.
Keep shoe-straps smooth and let your teeth be fair;
And see they're not too big, the shoes you wear;   252
And then your hair in order neatly put,
And let your beard by skillful hands be cut.
Look that your nails be clean and keep them low,
Nor let the hairs within your nostrils grow.   256
Lest your presence should be known by other sense
Than sight, let your breath be without offence.
Leave other things for shameless maids to use,
And men that basely their own sex abuse. . . .   260

   When Bacchus has presented gifts to you,
And should a lady share your banquet too,
The gods nocturnal you must beg to lend
Their aid, that wine may not your head offend.
You in a covert way may speak things so   265
That she, 'tis only she you mean, may know.
Let sweet discourse wait on your wine, that she
May mistress of your table choose to be;
And that your flame may be acknowledged, you
Must teach your looks as well as lips to woo.   270

First take the cup and kiss the very place
Which with her lips she did in drinking grace.
The food her fair hand touches, ask for, and
As you receive it, gently touch her hand.
Take care to please her husband also; such   275
A friend will expedite your business much.
When you drink, first to him your cup direct;
In keeping your head bare, show him respect.
Whether he be your equal or below,
Yet still a like respect unto him show.   280
Through friendship to deceive is saf'st of all;
Yet he that so deceives is criminal.
If friendship does some liberty permit,
You may take more as you've a mind to it.

   Observe to keep a mean in drinking, so   285
Your tongue and feet their office best will know.
Chiefly beware of quarrelling in wine,
For then your hands too much to blows incline. . . .
Have you a voice, then sing; if nimble, dance;
What pleasing part soe'er you have, advance.   290
Real drunkenness is harm, but so to feign
I think is good; pretend you can't speak plain,
Then if you speak or do what is unfit
The wine is judged to be the cause of it.
Say the man she'll sleep with shall most happy be,
But pray not for him if she means not thee.   296
The banquet ended and the table moved,
Then is your chance to show her she is loved.
The crowd itself allows that you should press
Her close; foot touches foot, fingers caress.   300
Now is the time to speak; what fears you have,
Banish: Venus and Fortune aid the brave.
Art cannot eloquence on you bestow:
Only begin, and you shall find it so.
You must act love, and feeling wounds must feign;
By all means try a promise to obtain.   306
Say she is lovely, and she will believe:
No woman thinks her looks are cause to grieve.
Oft a dissembler I have seen in love;
What first he feigned, at length did real prove.   310
Then, ladies, use men kindly; in the end
Their love proves true, which they at first pretend.
With praises you may captivate her mind,
So banks are with soft water undermined.
Her face admire, her lovely hair commend,   315
Her little slender foot, her dainty hand:
The chastest maids with praise delighted are,
A virgin's beauty is her love and care. . . .
   Fear not to promise—promises will move—
And call the gods as witness to your love.   320
Jove from above laughs at love's perjuries,—
Bidding Aeolus blow away such tricks,
For he himself to Juno swore by Styx
Falsely, and he our great exemplar is.
'Tis fit there should be gods; then gods there be;
In wine and incense let us pay their fee.   326
Be sure they do not bind themselves in sleep,

All seeing they; your life then harmless keep.
Restore what you have borrowed, none delude,
Nor have your hand in human blood imbrued.   330
Only to maids does falsehood go unblamed;
Break faith with women and be not ashamed.
Only deceive those who deceivers are,
And let them fall into their self-made snare. . . .
So perjury its own reward must earn,   335
And women who wrong us are wronged in turn.
   Shed tears, for they a stony heart will move;
By your wet eyes let her perceive your love.
If tears are lacking (for men cannot cry
At need), with a wet finger rub your eye.   340
Wise men mix kisses with the words they speak;
If they're not given, those ungiven take;
But she'll perhaps refuse and anger feign,
Yet wishes her resistance be in vain.
Take heed that when upon her lips you seize,   345
You press them not too hard lest it displease.
Who gains a kiss and other sweets get not,
Deserves to lose that kiss which he hath got.
If after kisses further pleasures were
Forgone, 'twas clownishness, not bashful fear.   350
She who is forced will find that forcing sweet:
Unwilling, willingly she will it meet.
She that's of Venus will no rape forsake,
But let her wantonness full pleasure take.   354
And she who might, yet doth untouched depart,
Although she may seem pleased, is sad at heart. . . .
They're bashful till the first time's over; then
Having once tried, they must be tried again.
   Too confident is he who doth expect
His mistress to ask first and him select.   360
First let the man approach her, and beseech;
A woman hearkens to a handsome speech.
Speak if you would obtain, she would be asked;
And your desire with words shall be unmasked.
Jove suppliant went unto the maids of old,   365
Deny his suit no maiden ever could.
If you perceive her scorn at and disdain
Your prayers, forbear; from her a while abstain.
They love what's not, at what is theirs they scoff,
Take their disdain away by keeping off.   370
Be always wooing and she'll never bend,
Sometimes a simple friendliness pretend.
I have known one this strategy display,
Come an adviser, and a lover stay.
   Sailors should not pale faces have, but be   375
Made swarthy by the sun and storms at sea. . . .
But lovers with a pining look excel;
Though some say not, yet it becomes them well. . . .
Thin looks a lover argue; sometimes wear
A hood and cover up your gleaming hair.   380
Sorrows and griefs immense with watchings late—
The effects of love—young men attenuate.
By looking melancholy, you will prove
Successful; all will say, 'This man's in love.'

And must I warn you now that wrong and right
Mean nothing? Truth and friendship turn to spite;
And if you praise your mistress to a friend,   387
His love for her begins and yours will end. . . .
Men nowadays are selfish, lost to shame;
To hurt another is their favourite game.   390
Ah, wicked times! Fear not an open foe;
Shun whom you trust and you may safely go.
Nor brother, nor a friend confide in; just
Occasion they will give you to mistrust.

   I'd almost done; but women are diverse,   395
And each one's heart doth take a different course.
One kind of produce suits each piece of ground,
Here vines, there olives, elsewhere corn is found.
Hearts are so various, alike are none,
That a wise man prepares for every one. . . .   400
Some fish with darts are caught, others with hook,
And some within a hollow net are took.
With various ages various ways agree:
The older a woman grows, more wary she.
If learned to the rude you seem, or wanton to   405
The chaste, she will mistrust herself and you.
Hence timid women honest husbands lose;
Instead, a man of meaner sort they choose.
   Part of my work remains, part now is made,
And here my ship is by her anchor stayed.

Metamorphoses

NARCISSUS

Thus did the nymphs in vain caress the boy,
He still was lovely, but he still was coy;
When one fair virgin of the slighted train
Thus pray'd the gods, provok'd by his disdain,
"Oh may he love like me, and love like me in vain!"
Rhamnusia pity'd the neglected fair,   6
And with just vengeance answer'd to her pray'r.
   There stands a fountain in a darksome wood,
Nor stain'd with falling leaves nor rising mud;
Untroubled by the breath of winds it rests,   10
Unsully'd by the touch of men or beasts;
High bow'rs of shady trees above it grow,
And rising grass and cheerful greens below.
Pleas'd with the form and coolness of the place,
And over-heated by the morning chase,   15
Narcissus on the grassy verdure lies:
But whilst within the crystal fount he tries
To quench his heat, he feels new heats arise.
For as his own bright image he survey'd,
He fell in love with the fantastic shade;   20

Metamorphoses. "Narcissus," translated by Joseph Addison;
"Pyramus and Thisbe," translated by Laurence Eusden; "Daedalus
and Icarus," translated by Samuel Croxall; "Baucis and Philemon,"
translated by John Dryden; "Orpheus and Eurydice," translated by
William Congreve.
1. boy, Narcissus. 6. Rhamnusia, Nemesis, goddess of divine vengeance.

And o'er the fair resemblance hung unmov'd,
Nor knew, fond youth! it was himself he lov'd.
The well-turn'd neck and shoulders he descries,
The spacious forehead, and the sparkling eyes;
The hands that Bacchus might not scorn to show,
And hair that round Apollo's head might flow;   26
With all the purple youthfulness of face,
That gently blushes in the wat'ry glass;
By his own flames consum'd the lover lies,
And gives himself the wound by which he dies.   30
To the cold water oft he joins his lips,
Oft catching at the beauteous shade he dips
His arms, as often from himself he slips.
Nor knows he who it is his arms pursue
With eager clasps, but loves he knows not who.   35
   What could, fond youth, this helpless passion
         move?
What kindle in thee this unpity'd love?
Thy own warm blush within the water glows,
With thee the colour'd shadow comes and goes,
Its empty being on thy self relies;   40
Step thou aside, and the frail charmer dies.
   Still o'er the fountain's wat'ry gleam he stood,
Mindless of sleep, and negligent of food.
Still view'd his face, and languish'd as he view'd.
At length he rais'd his head, and thus began   45
To vent his griefs, and tell the woods his pain.
"You trees," says he, "and thou surrounding grove,
Who oft have been the kindly scenes of love,
Tell me, if e'er within your shades did lie
A youth so tortur'd, so perplex'd as I?   50
I, who before me see the charming fair,
Whilst there he stands, and yet he stands not there:
In such a maze of love my thoughts are lost;
And yet no bulwark'd town, nor distant coast,
Preserves the beauteous youth from being seen,   55
No mountains rise, nor oceans flow between,
A shallow water hinders my embrace;
And yet the lovely mimic wears a face
That kindly smiles, and when I bend to join
My lips to his, he fondly bends to mine.   60
Hear, gentle youth, and pity my complaint,
Come from thy well, thou fair inhabitant.
My charms an easy conquest have obtain'd
O'er other hearts, by thee alone disdain'd.
But why should I despair? I'm sure he burns   65
With equal flames, and languishes by turns.
Whene'er I stoop he offers at a kiss,
And when my arms I stretch, he stretches his.
His eye with pleasure on my face he keeps,
He smiles my smiles, and when I weep he weeps.
Whene'er I speak, his moving lips appear   71
To utter something, which I cannot hear.
"Ah wretched me! I now begin too late
To find out all the long-perplex'd deceit:
It is myself I love, myself I see;   75
The gay delusion is a part of me.

I kindle up the fires by which I burn,
And my own beauties from the well return.
Whom should I court? how utter my complaint!
Enjoyment but produces my restraint,   80
And too much plenty makes me die for want.
How gladly would I from myself remove!
And at a distance set the thing I love.
My breast is warm'd with such unusual fire,
I wish him absent whom I most desire.   85
And now I faint with grief; my fate draws nigh;
In all the pride of blooming youth I die.
Death will the sorrows of my heart relieve:
Oh might the visionary youth survive,
I should with joy my latest breath resign!   90
But oh! I see his fate involv'd in mine."
This said, the weeping youth again return'd
To the clear fountain, where again he burn'd;
His tears defac'd the surface of the well,
With circle after circle, as they fell: 95
And now the lovely face but half appears,
O'er-run with wrinkles, and deform'd with tears.
"Ah whither," cries Narcissus, "dost thou fly?
Let me still feed the flame by which I die;
Let me still see, tho' I'm no further blest."   100
Then rends his garment off, and beats his breast:
His naked bosom redden'd with the blow,
In such a blush as purple clusters show,
Ere yet the sun's autumnal heats refine
Their sprightly juice, and mellow it to wine.   105
The glowing beauties of his breast he spies,
And with a new redoubled passion dies.
As wax dissolves, as ice begins to run,
And trickle into drops before the sun;
So melts the youth, and languishes away,   110
His beauty withers, and his limbs decay;
And none of those attractive charms remain,
To which the slighted Echo su'd in vain.

    She saw him in his present misery,
Whom, spight of all her wrongs, she griev'd to see.
She answer'd sadly to the lover's moan,   116
Sigh'd back his sighs, and groan'd to ev'ry groan:
"Ah youth! belov'd in vain," Narcissus cries;

Narcissus
watching
his image
with Eros
in the background.
From a
Roman painting.

"Ah youth! belov'd in vain," the nymph replies.
"Farewell," says he; the parting sound scarce fell
From his faint lips, but she reply'd, "Farewell."   121
Then on th' unwholesome earth he gasping lies,
Till death shuts up those self-admiring eyes.
To the cold shades his flitting ghost retires,
And in the Stygian waves itself admires.   125
    For him the Naiads and the Dryads mourn,
Whom the sad Echo answers in her turn,
And now the sister-nymphs prepare his urn:
When, looking for his corpse, they only found
A rising stalk, with yellow blossoms crown'd.   130

PYRAMUS AND THISBE

IN Babylon, where first her queen, for state
    Rais'd walls of brick magnificently great,
Liv'd Pyramus and Thisbe, lovely pair!
He found no eastern youth his equal there,
And she beyond the fairest nymph was fair.   5
A closer neighbourhood was never known:
Tho' two the houses, yet the roof was one.
Acquaintance grew, th' acquaintance they improve
To friendship, friendship ripen'd into love:
Love had been crown'd, but impotently mad,   10
What parents could not hinder, they forbade.
For with fierce flames young Pyramus still burn'd,
And grateful Thisbe's flames as fierce return'd.
Aloud in words their thoughts they dare not break
But silent stand, and silent looks can speak.   15
The fire of love the more it is supprest,
The more it glows, and rages in the breast.
    When the division-wall was built, a chink
Was left, the cement unobserv'd to shrink.
So slight the cranny, that it still had been   20
For centuries unclos'd, because unseen.
But oh! what thing so small, so secret lies,
Which 'scapes, if form'd for love, a lover's eyes?
Ev'n in this narrow chink they quickly found
A friendly passage for a trackless sound.   25
Safely they told their sorrows and their joys,
In whisper'd murmurs, and a dying noise.
By turns to catch each other's breath they strove,
And suck'd in all the balmy breeze of love.
Oft as on diff'rent sides they stood, they cry'd,   30
"Malicious wall, thus lovers to divide!
Suppose, thou should'st awhile to us give place
To lock, and fasten in a close embrace:
But if too much to grant so sweet a bliss,
Indulge at least the pleasure of a kiss.   35
We scorn ingratitude: To thee, we know,
This safe conveyance of our minds we owe."
    Thus they their vain petition did renew
Till night, and then they softly sigh'd adieu.
But first they strove to kiss, and that was all;   40
Their kisses dy'd untasted on the wall.

130. **A rising stalk . . . crown'd,** the narcissus flower.

Soon as the morn had o'er the stars prevail'd,
And warn'd by Phoebus, flow'rs their dews exhal'd,
The lovers to their well-known place return,
Alike they suffer, and alike they mourn.   45
At last their parents they resolve to cheat,
(If to deceive in love be call'd deceit)
To steal by night from home, and thence unknown
To seek the fields, and quit th' unfaithful town.
But to prevent their wand'ring in the dark,   50
They both agree to fix upon a mark;
A mark that could not their designs expose:
The tomb of Ninus was the mark they chose;
There they might rest secure beneath the shade,
Which boughs, with snowy fruit encumber'd, made:
A wide-spread mulberry its rise had took   56
Just on the margin of a gurgling brook.
Impatient for the friendly dusk they stay;
And chide the slowness of departing day;
In western seas down sank at last the light,   60
From western seas up-rose the shades of night.
The loving Thisbe ev'n prevents the hour,
With cautious silence she unlocks the door,
And veils her face, and marching thro' the gloom
Swiftly arrives at th' assignation tomb.   65
For still the fearful sex can fearless prove;
Boldly they act, if spirited by love.
When lo! a lioness rush'd o'er the plain,
Grimly besmear'd with blood of oxen slain:
And what to the dire sight new horrors brought,   70
To slake her thirst the neighb'ring spring she sought.
Which, by the moon, when trembling Thisbe spies,
Wing'd with her fear, swift as the wind, she flies;
And in a cave recovers from her fright,
But dropp'd her veil, confounded in her flight.   75
When sated with repeated draughts, again
The queen of beasts scour'd back along the plain.
She found the veil, and mouthing it all o'er
With bloody jaws the lifeless prey she tore.
    The youth, who could not cheat his guards so
        soon,   80
Late came, and noted by the glimm'ring moon
Some savage feet, new printed on the ground,
His cheeks turn'd pale, his limbs no vigour found:
But, when advancing on, the veil he spied
Distain'd with blood, and ghastly torn, he cried, 85
"One night shall death to two young lovers give,
But she deserv'd unnumber'd years to live!
'Tis I am guilty, I have thee betray'd,
Who came not early, as my charming maid.
Whatever slew thee, I the cause remain,   90
I nam'd, and fix'd the place, where thou wast slain.
Ye lions from your neighb'ring dens repair,
Pity the wretch, this impious body tear!
But cowards thus for death can idly cry;
The brave still have it in their pow'r to die."   95
Then to th' appointed tree he hastes away,
The veil first gather'd, tho' all rent it lay:

The veil all rent, yet still itself endears,
He kist, and kissing, wash'd it with his tears.
"Tho' rich," he cry'd, "with many a precious stain,
Still from my blood a deeper tincture gain."   101
Then in his breast his shining sword he drown'd,
And fell supine, extended on the ground.
As out again the blade he dying drew,
Out spun the blood, and streaming upwards flew.
So if a conduit pipe e'er burst you saw,   106
Swift spring the gushing waters through the flaw:
Then spouting in a bow, they rise on high,
And a new fountain plays amid the sky.
The berries, stain'd with blood, began to show   110
A dark complexion, and forgot their snow;
While fatten'd with the flowing gore, the root
Was doom'd forever to a purple fruit.
    Meantime poor Thisbe fear'd, so long she stay'd,
Her lover might suspect a perjur'd maid.   115
Her fright scarce o'er, she strove the youth to find
With ardent eyes, which spoke an ardent mind.
Already in his arms, she hears him sigh
At her destruction, which was once so nigh.
The tomb, the tree, but not the fruit she knew,   120
The fruit she doubted for its alter'd hue.
Still as she doubts, her eyes a body found
Quiv'ring in death, and gasping on the ground.
She started back, the red her cheeks forsook,
And ev'ry nerve with thrilling horrors shook.   125
So trembles the smooth surface of the seas,
If brush'd o'er gently with a rising breeze.
But when her view her bleeding love confest,
She shriek'd, she tore her hair, she beat her breast;
She rais'd the body, and embrac'd it round,   130
And bath'd with tears unfeign'd the gaping wound.
Then her warm lips to the cold face apply'd.
"And is it thus, ah! thus we meet!" she cry'd.
"My Pyramus! whence sprung thy cruel fate?
My Pyramus!—ah! speak, e'er 'tis too late.   135
I, thy own Thisbe, but one word implore,
One word thy Thisbe never ask'd before."
At Thisbe's name, awak'd, he open'd wide
His dying eyes; with dying eyes he try'd
On her to dwell, but clos'd them slow, and dy'd.
    The fatal cause was now at last explor'd;   141
Her veil she knew, and saw his sheathless sword:
"From thy own hand thy ruin thou hast found,"
She said, "but love first taught that hand to wound
Ev'n I for thee as bold a hand can show,   145
And love, which shall as true direct the blow.
I will against the woman's weakness strive,
And never thee, lamented youth, survive.
The world may say, I caus'd, alas! thy death,
But saw thee breathless, and resign'd my breath.
Fate, tho' it conquers, shall no triumph gain,   151
Fate, that divides us, still divides in vain.
    "Now, both our cruel parents, hear my pray'r,
My pray'r to offer for us both I dare;

Oh! see our ashes in one urn confin'd,   155
Whom love at first, and fate at last has join'd.
The bliss you envy'd is not our request;
Lovers, when dead, may sure together rest.
Thou, tree, where now one lifeless lump is laid,
Ere long o'er two shalt cast a friendly shade.   160
Still let our loves from thee be understood,
Still witness in thy purple fruit our blood."
She spoke, and in her bosom plung'd the sword,
All warm and reeking from its slaughter'd lord.

The pray'r, which dying Thisbe had preferr'd,
Both gods and parents with compassion heard.   166
The whiteness of the mulberry soon fled,
And rip'ning sadden'd in a dusky red:
While both their parents their lost children mourn,
And mix their ashes in one golden urn.   170

DAEDALUS AND ICARUS

IN tedious exile now too long detain'd,
Daedalus languish'd for his native land:
The sea foreclos'd his flight; yet thus he said:
"Tho' earth and water in subjection laid,
O cruel Minos, thy dominion be,   5
We'll go thro' air; for sure the air is free."
Then to new arts his cunning thought applies,
And to improve the work of nature tries.
A row of quills in gradual order plac'd,
Rise by degrees in length from first to last;   10
As on a cliff th' ascending thicket grows,
Or different reeds the rural pipe compose.
Along the middle runs a twine of flax,
The bottom stems are join'd by pliant wax.
Thus, well compact, a hollow bending brings   15
The fine composure into real wings.

His boy, young Icarus, that near him stood,
Unthinking of his fate, with smiles pursu'd
The floating feathers, which the moving air
Bore loosely from the ground, and wafted here and
        there.   20
Or with the wax impertinently play'd,
And with his childish tricks the great design delay'd.

The final master-stroke at last impos'd,
And now, the neat machine completely clos'd;
Fitting his pinions on, a flight he tries,   25
And hung self-balanc'd in the beaten skies.
Then thus instructs his child: "My boy, take care
To wing your course along the middle air;
If low, the surges wet your flagging plumes,
If high, the sun the melting wax consumes: 30
Steer between both: nor to the northern skies,
Nor south Orion turn your giddy eyes;
But follow me: Let me before you lay
Rules for the flight, and mark the pathless way."
Then teaching, with a fond concern, his son,   35
He took the untry'd wings, and fix'd 'em on,
But fix'd with trembling hands; and, as he speaks,
The tears roll gently down his aged cheeks.

*The fall of Icarus.
From a Roman painting.*

Then kiss'd, and in his arms embrac'd him fast,
But knew not this embrace must be the last.   40
And mounting upward, as he wings his flight,
Back on his charge he turns his aching sight,
As parent birds, when first their callow care
Leave the high nest to tempt the liquid air;
Then cheers him on, and oft, with fatal art,   45
Reminds the stripling to perform his part.

These, as the angler at the silent brook,
Or mountain-shepherd leaning on his crook,
Or gaping ploughman from the vale descries,
They stare, and view 'em with religious eyes,   50
And straight conclude 'em gods; since none, but
        they,
Thro' their own azure skies could find a way.

Now Delos, Paros, on the left are seen,
And Samos, favour'd by Jove's haughty queen;
Upon the right, the isle Lebynthos nam'd,   55
And fair Calymne for its honey fam'd.
When now the boy, whose childish thoughts aspire
To loftier aims, and make him ramble high'r,
Grown wild, and wanton, more embolden'd flies
Far from his guide, and soars among the skies.   60
The soft'ning wax, that felt a nearer sun,
Dissolv'd apace, and soon began to run.
The youth in vain his melting pinions shakes,
His feathers gone, no longer care he takes:
"Oh! father, father," as he strove to cry,   65
Down to the sea he tumbled from on high,
And found his fate; yet still subsists by fame,
Among those waters that retain his name.

The father, now no more a father, cries,
"Ho, Icarus! where are you?" as he flies;   70
"Where shall I seek my boy?" he cries again,
And saw his feathers scatter'd on the main.
Then curs'd his art; and fun'ral rites conferr'd,
Naming the country from the youth interr'd.

A partridge, from a neighb'ring stump, beheld

The sire his monumental marble build; 76
Who, with peculiar call, and flutt'ring wing,
Chirpt joyful, and malicious seem'd to sing:
The only bird of all its kind, and late
Transform'd in pity to a feather'd state: 80
From whence, O Daedalus, thy guilt we date.

BAUCIS AND PHILEMON

Heav'n's pow'r is infinite: earth, air, and sea,
The manufactur'd mass, the making pow'r obey
By proof to clear your doubt: in Phrygian ground
Two neighb'ring trees, with walls encompass'd round,
Stand on a mod'rate rise, with wonder shown, 5
One a hard oak, a softer linden one. . . .
Not far from thence is seen a lake, the haunt
Of coots, and of the fishing cormorant:
Here Jove with Hermes came; but in disguise
Of mortal men conceal'd their deities; 10
One laid aside his thunder, one his rod;
And many toilsome steps together trod:
For harbour at a thousand doors they knock'd,
Not one of all the thousand but was lock'd.
At last an hospitable house they found, 15
A homely shed; the roof, not far from ground,
Was thatch'd with reeds, and straw together bound.
There Baucis and Philemon liv'd, and there
Had liv'd long marry'd, and a happy pair:
Now old in love, though little was their store, 20
Inur'd to want, their poverty they bore,
Nor aim'd at wealth, professing to be poor.
For master or for servant here to call,
Was all alike, where only two were all.
Command was none, where equal love was paid,
Or rather both commanded, both obey'd. 26
   From lofty roofs the gods repuls'd before,
Now stooping, enter'd through the little door:
The man (their hearty welcome first express'd)
A common settle drew for either guest, 30
Inviting each his weary limbs to rest.
But ere they sat, officious Baucis lays
Two cushions stuff'd with straw, the seat to raise;
Coarse, but the best she had; then rakes the load
Of ashes from the hearth, and spreads abroad 35
The living coals; and, lest they should expire,
With leaves, and bark she feeds her infant fire:
It smokes; and then with trembling breath she blows,
Till in a cheerful blaze the flames arose.
With brush-wood and with chips she strengthens these, 40
And adds at last the boughs of rotten trees.
The fire thus form'd, she sets the kettle on,
(Like burnish'd gold the little seether shone)
Next took the coleworts which her husband got 44
From his own ground (a small well-water'd spot);

She stripp'd the stalks of all their leaves; the best
She cull'd, and them with handy care she drest.
High o'er the hearth a chine of bacon hung;
Good old Philemon seiz't it with a prong,
And from the sooty rafter drew it down, 50
Then cut a slice, but scarce enough for one;
Yet a large portion of a little store,
Which for their sakes alone he wish'd were more.
This in the pot he plung'd without delay,
To tame the flesh, and drain the salt away. 55
The time between, before the fire they sat,
And shorten'd the delay by pleasing chat.
   A beam there was, on which a beechen pail
Hung by the handle, on a driven nail:
This fill'd with water, gently warm'd, they set 60
Before their guests; in this they bath'd their feet,
And after with clean towels dry'd their sweat.
This done, the host produc'd the genial bed,
Sallow the feet, the borders, and the sted,
Which with no costly coverlet they spread, 65
But coarse old garments; yet such robes as these
They laid alone, at feasts or holidays.
The good old housewife, tucking up her gown,
The table sets; th' invited gods lie down.
The trivet-table of a foot was lame, 70
A blot which prudent Baucis overcame,
Who thrusts beneath the limping leg a sherd,
So was the mended board exactly rear'd:
Then rubb'd it o'er with newly gather'd mint,
A wholesome herb, that breath'd a grateful scent.
Pallas began the feast, where first was seen 76
The party-colour'd olive, black, and green:
Autumnal cornels next in order serv'd,
In lees of wine well pickled and preserv'd.
A garden salad was the third supply, 80
Of endive, radishes, and succory:
Then curds, and cream, the flow'r of country fare,
And new-laid eggs, which Baucis' busy care
Turn'd by a gentle fire, and roasted rare.
All these in earthen ware were serv'd to board; 85
And next in place, an earthen pitcher stor'd,
With liquor of the best the cottage could afford.
This was the table's ornament, and pride,
With figures wrought: like pages at his side
Stood beechen bowls; and these were shining clean,
Varnish'd with wax without, and lin'd within. 91
By this the boiling kettle had prepar'd,
And to the table sent the smoking lard;
On which with eager appetite they dine,
A sav'ry bit, that serv'd to relish wine: 95
The wine itself was suiting to the rest,
Still working in the must, and lately press'd.
The second course succeeds like that before,
Plums, apples, nuts, and of their wintry store
Dry figs, and grapes, and wrinkled dates were set
In canisters, t' enlarge the little treat: 101
All these a milk-white honey-comb surround,

Which in the midst the country banquet crown'd:
But the kind hosts their entertainment grace
With hearty welcome, and an open face: 105
In all they did, you might discern with ease,
A willing mind, and a desire to please.
   Meantime the beechen bowls went round, and
     still,
Though often empty'd, were observ'd to fill;
Fill'd without hands, and of their own accord   110
Ran without feet, and danc'd about the board.
Devotion seiz'd the pair, to see the feast
With wine, and of no common grape, increas'd;
And up they held their hands, and fell to pray'r,
Excusing, as they could, their country fare,   115
   One goose they had ('twas all they could allow),
A wakeful sentry, and on duty now,
Whom to the gods for sacrifice they vow:
Her with malicious zeal the couple view'd;
She ran for life, and limping they pursu'd: 120
Full well the fowl perceiv'd their bad intent,
And would not make her master's compliment;
But persecuted, to the pow'rs she flies,
And close between the legs of Jove she lies:
He with a gracious ear the suppliant heard,   125
And sav'd her life; then what he was declar'd,
And own'd the god. "The neighbourhood," said he,
"Shall justly perish for impiety:
You stand alone exempted; but obey   129
With speed, and follow where we lead the way:
Leave these accurs'd; and to the mountain's height
Ascend; nor once look backward in your flight."
   They haste, and what their tardy feet deny'd,
The trusty staff (their better leg) supply'd.
An arrow's flight they wanted to the top,   135
And there secure, but spent with travel, stop;
Then turn their now no more forbidden eyes;
Lost in a lake the floated level lies:
A wat'ry desert covers all the plains,
Their cot alone, as in an isle, remains.   140
Wond'ring with weeping eyes, while they deplore
Their neighbours' fate, and country now no more,
Their little shed, scarce large enough for two,
Seems, from the ground increas'd, in height and bulk
    to grow.
A stately temple shoots within the skies,   145
The crotchets of their cot in columns rise:
The pavement polish'd marble they behold,
The gates with sculpture grac'd, the spires and tiles
    of gold.
   Then thus the sire of gods, with looks serene:
"Speak thy desire, thou only just of men;   150
And thou, O woman, only worthy found
To be with such a man in marriage bound."
   Awhile they whisper; then, to Jove address'd,
Philemon thus prefers their joint request:
"We crave to serve before your sacred shrine,   155
And offer at your altars rites divine:

And since not any action of our life
Has been polluted with domestic strife;
We beg one hour of death, that neither she
With widow's tears may live to bury me,   160
Nor weeping I, with wither'd arms may bear
My breathless Baucis to the sepulchre."
   The godheads sign their suit. They run their race
In the same tenour all th' appointed space:
Then, when their hour was come, while they relate
These past adventures at the temple gate,   166
Old Baucis is by old Philemon seen
Sprouting with sudden leaves of spritely green:
Old Baucis look'd where old Philemon stood,
And saw his lengthen'd arms a sprouting wood;   170
New roots their fasten'd feet begin to bind,
Their bodies stiffen in a rising rind:
Then, ere the bark above their shoulders grew,
They give, and take at once their last adieu.   174
At once, "Farewell, O faithful spouse," they said;
At once th' incroaching rinds their closing lips in-
    vade.
Ev'n yet, an ancient Tyanaean shows
A spreading oak, that near a linden grows;
The neighbourhood confirm the prodigy,
Grave men, not vain of tongue, or like to lie.   180
I saw myself the garlands on their boughs,
And tablets hung for gifts of granted vows;
And off'ring fresher up, with pious pray'r,
The good, said I, are God's peculiar care,
And such as honour heav'n, shall heav'nly honour
    share.

ORPHEUS AND EURYDICE

THENCE, in his saffron robe, for distant Thrace,
   Hymen departs, thro' air's unmeasur'd space;
By Orpheus call'd, the nuptial pow'r attends,
But with ill-omen'd augury descends;   4
Nor cheerful look'd the god, nor prosp'rous spoke,
Nor blaz'd his torch, but wept in hissing smoke.
In vain they whirl it round, in vain they shake,
No rapid motion can its flames awake.
   With dread these inauspicious signs were view'd,
And soon a more disastrous end ensu'd;   10
For as the bride, amid the Naiad train,
Ran joyful, sporting o'er the flow'ry plain,
A venom'd viper bit her as she pass'd;
Instant she fell, and sudden breath'd her last.
   When long his loss the Thracian had deplor'd,   15
Not by superior pow'rs to be restor'd;
Inflam'd by love, and urg'd by deep despair,
He leaves the realms of light, and upper air;
Daring to tread the dark Tenarian road,
And tempt the shades in their obscure abode;   20
Thro' gliding spectres of th' interr'd to go,
And phantom people of the world below:
Persephone he seeks, and him who reigns
O'er ghosts, and hell's uncomfortable plains.

Arriv'd, he, tuning to his voice his strings,   25
Thus to the king and queen of shadows sings:
     "Ye pow'rs, who under earth your realms extend,
To whom all mortals must one day descend:
If here 'tis granted sacred truth to tell;
I come not curious to explore your hell;   30
Nor come to boast (by vain ambition fir'd)
How Cerberus at my approach retir'd.
My wife alone I seek; for her lov'd sake
These terrors I support, this journey take.
She, luckless wand'ring, or by fate misled,   35
Chanc'd on a lurking viper's crest to tread;
The vengeful beast, enflam'd with fury, starts,
And thro' her heel his deathful venom darts.
Thus was she snatch'd untimely to her tomb;
Her growing years cut short, and springing bloom.
Long I my loss endeavour'd to sustain,   41
And strongly strove, but strove, alas, in vain:
At length I yielded, won by mighty love;
Well known is that omnipotence above!
But here, I doubt, his unfelt influence fails;   45
And yet a hope within my heart prevails,
That here, ev'n here, he has been known of old;
At least, if truth be by tradition told;
If fame of former rapes belief may find,
You both by love, and love alone were join'd.   50
Now, by the horrors which these realms surround,
By the vast chaos of these depths profound;
By the sad silence which eternal reigns
O'er all the waste of these wide-stretching plains;
Let me again Eurydice receive,   55
Let fate her quick-spun thread of life re-weave.
All our possessions are but loans from you,
And soon, or late, you must be paid your due;
Hither we haste to human-kind's last seat,
Your endless empire, and our sure retreat.   60
She too, when ripen'd years she shall attain,
Must, of avoidless right, be yours again:
I but the transient use of that require,
Which soon, too soon, I must resign entire.
But if the destines refuse my vow,   65
And no remission of her doom allow;
Know, I'm determin'd to return no more;
So both retain, or both to life restore."
     Thus, while the bard melodiously complains,
And to his lyre accords his vocal strains,   70
The very bloodless shades attention keep,
And silent, seem compassionate to weep;
Ev'n Tantalus his flood unthirsty views,
Nor flies the stream, nor he the stream pursues;
Ixion's wond'ring wheel its whirl suspends,   75
And the voracious vulture, charm'd, attends . . .
     Then first ('tis said) by sacred verse subdu'd,
The Furies felt their cheeks with tears bedew'd:
Nor could the rigid king, or queen of hell,
Th' impulse of pity in their hearts repel.   80
     Now, from a troop of shades that last arriv'd,

Eurydice was call'd, and stood reviv'd.
Slow she advanc'd, and halting seem'd to feel
The fatal wound, yet painful in her heel.
Thus he obtains the suit so much desir'd,   85
On strict observance of the terms requir'd:
For if, before he reach the realms of air,
He backward cast his eyes to view the fair,
The forfeit grant, that instant, void is made,
And she forever left a lifeless shade.   90
     Now thro' the noiseless throng their way they
          bend,
And both with pain the rugged road ascend;
Dark was the path, and difficult, and steep,
And thick with vapours from the smoky deep.
They well-nigh now had pass'd the bounds of night,
And just approach'd the margin of the light,   96
When he, mistrusting lest her steps might stray,
And gladsome of the glimpse of dawning day,
His longing eyes, impatient, backward cast
To catch a lover's look, but look'd his last;   100
For, instant dying, she again descends,
While he to empty air his arms extends.
Again she dy'd, nor yet her lord reprov'd;
What could she say, but that too well he lov'd?
One last farewell she spoke, which scarce he heard;
So soon she dropp'd, so sudden disappear'd.   106
     All stunn'd he stood, when thus his wife he
          view'd
By second fate, and double death subdu'd . . .
Now to repass the Styx in vain he tries,
Charon averse, his pressing suit denies.   110
Sev'n days entire, along th' infernal shores,
Disconsolate, the bard Eurydice deplores;
Defil'd with filth his robe, with tears his cheeks,
No sustenance but grief, and cares he seeks;
Of rigid fate incessant he complains,   115
And hell's inexorable gods arraigns.
This ended, to high Rhodope he hastes,
And Haemus' mountain, bleak with northern blasts.
     And now his yearly race the circling sun
Had thrice compleat thro' wat'ry Pisces run,   120
Since Orpheus fled the face of womankind,
And all soft union with the sex declin'd. . . .
     A hill there was, and on that hill a mead,
With verdure thick, but destitute of shade.
Where, now, the Muses' son no sooner sings,   125
No sooner strikes his sweet resounding strings,
But distant groves the flying sounds receive,
And list'ning trees their rooted stations leave;
Themselves transplanting, all around they grow,
And various shades their various kinds bestow.   130
Here, tall Chaonian oaks their branches spread,
While weeping poplars there erect their head. . . .
Here, brittle hazels, laurels here advance,
And there tough ash to form the hero's lance;
Here silver first with knotless trunks ascend,   135
There, scarlet oaks beneath their acorns bend.

That spot admits the hospitable plain,
On this, the maple grows with clouded grain;
Here wat'ry willows are with lotus seen,
There, tamarisk, and box forever green.   140
With double hue here myrtles grace the ground,
And laurestines, with purple berries crown'd.
With pliant feet, now, ivies this way wind,
Vines yonder rise, and elms with vines entwin'd.
Wild Ornus now, the pitch-tree next takes root,   145
And arbutus adorn'd with blushing fruit.
Then easy bending palms, the victor's prize,
And pines erect with bristly tops arise.
To Rhea grateful still the pine remains,
For Atys still some favour she retains;   150
He once in human shape her breast had warm'd,
And now is cherish'd to a tree transform'd.

Juvenal

60–140 A.D.

In the Silver Age the stoic intellectualism of the Romans hardened into a cold and cynical aloofness and produced the formal satire as the one literary invention of Rome. The first Roman satirist, Lucilius (180–102 B.C.), survives only in fragments. Horace wrote playful satires on men and manners, and Persius (34–62 A.D.) used the satire to dispense Stoic morality. It remained for Juvenal, Rome's master of the form, to apply it to the social evils of his day and to show how a vitriolic pen can annihilate one's enemies. Certainly Rome in its decline offered abundant material for attack, but the savage invective of Juvenal springs from a personal pessimism close to misanthropy.

Decimus Junius Juvenalis, to give him his full name, is known chiefly through his works; the many medieval biographies of the man are largely fictitious. Born in Aquinum in central Italy he became a rhetorician in Rome. There he attached himself to several wealthy patrons, but the humiliation of such a situation and his persistent poverty soured his nature, and he vented his spleen against the rich and successful in a series of moralistic satires. A doubtful tradition adds that his lampoon of the actor Paris was later misunderstood as an attack on an actor close to the throne and that Juvenal was consequently exiled to a military post in distant Egypt or possibly Britain.

His sixteen satires, written between 100 and 128 A.D., are the venomous outpourings of a middle-aged man, grown disgruntled with failure and self-righteous in his stoic morality. His hatred of vice and love of simple living sound genuine, but the shocking picture of conditions in Rome in the Third Satire is certainly exaggerated. Yet it has contributed heavily to our grim impression of the city in its decline and inspired Dr. Johnson's satire of another city, *London*, many centuries later. The Sixth Satire is the bitterest diatribe against woman ever penned, and the Tenth is the source of Johnson's *Vanity of Human Wishes* with its noble pessimism about human hopes and ambitions. Everywhere in Juvenal we meet the same indignant censure of a world lost to the vilest corruption; no hopeful rays illuminate the sordid picture. Granted the unfairness of his jaundiced eye, we can still enjoy the incessant lash of his attack and the stately rhetoric in which he phrased it.

Third Satire

Umbritius, a friend of the author, disgusted at the prevalence of vice and the disregard of unassuming virtue, is on the point of quitting Rome; and when a little way from the city, stops short to acquaint the poet, who has accompanied him, with the causes of his retirement. These may be arranged under the following heads: that flattery and vice are the only thriving arts at Rome; in these, especially the first, foreigners have a manifest superiority over the natives, and consequently engross all favor; that the poor are universally exposed to scorn and insult; that the general habits of extravagance render it difficult for them to subsist; that the want of a well-regulated police subjects them to numberless miseries and inconveniences, aggravated by the crowded state of the capital, from all which a country life is happily free: on the tranquillity and security of which he dilates with great beauty.

GRIEVED though I am to see the man depart,
    Who long has shared, and still must share,
        my heart,
Yet (when I call my better judgment home)
I praise his purpose: to retire from Rome
And give, on Cumae's solitary coast,   5
The Sibyl one inhabitant to boast!
    Full on the road to Baiae, Cumae lies,
And many a sweet retreat her shore supplies—
Though I prefer ev'n Prochyta's bare strand
To the Suburra; for what desert land,   10
What wild, uncultured spot, can more affright
Than fires wide blazing through the gloom of night,
Houses, with ceaseless ruin, thundering down,
And all the horrors of this hateful town?
Where poets, while the dog-star glows, rehearse   15
To gasping multitudes their barbarous verse!
    Now had my friend, impatient to depart,
Consigned his little all to one poor cart:
For this, without the town he chose to wait;   19
But stopped a moment at the Conduit-gate. . . .

Third Satire. Translated by William Gifford.
7. **Baiae,** a fashionable watering-place. 9–10. **Prochyta's bare strand . . . Suburra.** Prochyta was a desolate volcanic island; the Suburra, the busiest and most questionable section of Rome.

Gladiators.
From a Roman
Mosaic.

Umbritius here his sullen silence broke,
And turned on Rome, indignant, as he spoke.
Since virtue droops, he cried, without regard,
And honest toil scarce hopes a poor reward;
Since every morrow sees my means decay,   25
And still makes less the little of today;
I go where Daedalus, as poets sing,
First checked his flight and closed his weary wing:
While something yet of health and strength remains,
And yet no staff my faltering step sustains;   30
While few grey hairs upon my head are seen,
And my old age is vigorous still and green.
Here, then, I bid my much-loved home farewell—
Ah, mine no more!—there let Arturius dwell,
And Catullus, knaves who, in truth's despite,   35
Can white to black transform, and black to white,
Build temples, furnish funerals, auctions hold,
Farm rivers, ports, and scour the drains for gold!
    Once they were trumpeters, and always found
With strolling fencers in their annual round,   40
While their puffed cheeks, which every village knew,
Called to "high feats of arms" the rustic crew.
Now they give shows themselves, and, at the will
Of the base rabble, raise the sign—to kill,
Ambitious of their voice; then turn once more   45
To their vile gains, and farm the common shore!
And why not everything?—since Fortune throws
Her more peculiar smiles on such as those
Whene'er, to wanton merriment inclined,
She lifts to thrones the dregs of humankind!   50
    But why, my friend, should I at Rome remain?
I cannot teach my stubborn lips to feign;
Nor, when I hear a great man's verses, smile,
And beg a copy, if I think them vile.
A sublunary wight, I have no skill   55
To read the stars. I neither can nor will
Presage a father's death. I never pried
In toads for poison, nor—in aught beside.
Others may aid the adulterer's vile design,
And bear the insidious gift and melting line,   60
Seduction's agents! I such deeds detest;

And, honest, let no thief partake my breast.
For this, without a friend, the world I quit;
A palsied limb, for every use unfit.   64
    Who now is loved, but he whose conscious breast
Swells with dark deeds, still, still to be supprest?
He pays, he owes, thee nothing (strictly just),
Who gives an honest secret to thy trust.
But a dishonest!—there he feels thy power,
And buys thy friendship high from hour to hour.   70
But let not all the wealth which Tagus pours
In Ocean's lap, not all his glittering stores,
Be deemed a bribe sufficient to requite
The loss of peace by day, of sleep by night.
O take not, take not, what thy soul rejects,   75
Nor sell the faith which he who buys suspects!
    The nation, by the great admired, carest,
And hated, shunned by me above the rest,
No longer now restrained by wounded pride,
I haste to show (nor thou my warmth deride),   80
I cannot rule my spleen and calmly see
A Grecian capital in Italy!
Grecian? O no! With this vast sewer compared,
The dregs of Greece are scarcely worth regard.
Long since, the stream that wanton Syria laves   85
Has disembogued its filth in Tiber's waves,
Its language, arts; o'erwhelmed us with the scum
Of Antioch's streets, its minstrel, harp, and drum.
Hie to the Circus! There in crowds they stand,   89
Tires on their head and timbrels in their hand. . . .
    For lo! where versed in every soothing art,
The wily Greek assails his patron's heart,
Finds in each dull harangue an air, a grace,
And all Adonis in a Gorgon face;
Admires the voice that grates upon the ear   95
Like the shrill scream of amorous chanticleer;
And equals the crane neck and narrow chest
To Hercules, when, straining to his breast
The giant son of Earth, his every vein
Swells with the toil and more than mortal pain.   100
    We too can cringe as low and praise as warm,
But flattery from the Greeks alone can charm.
See! They step forth and figure to the life
The naked nymph, the mistress, or the wife,
So just, you view the very woman there,   105
And fancy all beneath the girdle bare!
No longer now the favourites of the stage
Boast their exclusive power to charm the age;
The happy art with them a nation shares:
Greece is a theatre, where all are players.   110
For lo! their patron smiles—they burst with mirth;

27. **Daedalus.** Escaping from the labyrinth of Crete, Daedalus flew
on wings of wax and descended to earth at Cumae, where he built a
temple to Apollo.

71. **Tagus,** a river in central Spain, renowned as a bearer of gold.
83. **Grecian? O no!** The Greeks had long since been conquered by the
Romans and were now despised at Rome for their Oriental ways.
85. **the stream . . . laves,** the Orontes, largest river in Syria. 88.
minstrel, harp, and drum. Greek and Oriental street-musicians were
hired to play at Roman banquets. 99. **giant son of Earth,** Antaeus.
104. **The naked nymph . . . wife.** So the debased Greek can play
the woman's role offstage.

He weeps—they droop, the saddest souls on earth;
He calls for fire—they court the mantle's heat;
'Tis warm, he cries—and they dissolve in sweat.
Ill-matched!—secure of victory they start,   115
Who, taught from youth to play a borrowed part,
Can with a glance the rising passion trace
And mould with their own to suit their patron's
          face;
At deeds of shame their hands admiring raise,
And mad debauchery's worst excesses praise.   120

Besides, no mound their raging lust restrains;
All ties it breaks, all sanctity profanes;
Wife, virgin-daughter, son unstained before—
And where these fail, they tempt the grandam hoar.
They notice every word, haunt every ear,   125
Your secrets learn, and fix you theirs from fear. . . .

Produce at Rome your witness: let him boast
The sanctity of Berecynthia's host,
To search his rent-roll first the bench prepares;
His honesty employs their latest cares.   130
What table does he keep, what slaves maintain,
And what, they ask, and where, is his domain?
These weighty matters known, his faith they rate,
And square his probity to his estate.
The poor may swear by all the immortal powers,
By the great gods of Samothrace and ours;   136
His oaths are false, they cry; he scoffs at heaven
And all its thunders; scoffs—and is forgiven!
Add that the wretch is still the theme of scorn
If the soiled cloak be patched, the gown o'erworn;
If through the bursting shoe the foot be seen,   141
Or the coarse seam tell where the rent has been.
O Poverty, thy thousand ills combined
Sink not so deep into the generous mind
As the contempt and laughter of mankind! . . .

There's many a part of Italy, 'tis said,   146
Where none assumes the toga but the dead.
There, when the toil foregone and annual play
Mark from the rest some high and solemn day,
To theatres of turf the rustics throng,   150
Charmed with the farce that charmed their sires so
          long;
While the pale infant, of the mask in dread,
Hides in his mother's breast his little head.
No modes of dress high birth distinguish there:
All ranks, all orders, the same habit wear,   155
And the dread aedile's dignity is known,
O sacred badge! by his white vest alone.
But here, beyond our power arrayed we go,
In all the gay varieties of show;
And when our purse supplies the charge no more,
Borrow, unblushing, from our neighbor's store.   161

128. **Berecynthia's host.** Berecynthia was a surname of Cybele, the
Great Mother. Hence, an unquestionable proof of the honesty of the
witness.   147. **Where none assumes . . . dead.** This is an indication of the simplicity of country life in contrast to the city of Rome,
where a gentleman had to buy several new togas each year.

Such is the reigning vice, and so we flaunt,
Proud in distress and prodigal in want!
Briefly, my friend, here all are slaves to gold;
And words, and smiles, and everything is sold. . . .

O! may I live where no such fears molest,   166
No midnight fires burst on my hour of rest!
For here 'tis terror all; midst the loud cry
Of "water! water!" the scared neighbors fly,
With all their haste can seize. The flames aspire,   170
And the third floor is wrapt in smoke and fire
While you, unconscious, doze. Up, ho! and know,
The impetuous blaze which spreads dismay below,
By swift degrees will reach the aerial cell   174
Where, crouching, underneath the tiles you dwell,
Where your tame doves their golden couplets rear,
"And you could no mischance but drowning fear!"
"Codrus had but one bed, and that too short
For his short wife;" his goods of every sort
Were else but few: six little pipkins graced   180
His cupboard head; a little can was placed
On a snug shelf beneath, and near it lay
A Chiron, of the same cheap marble—clay.
And was this all? O no: he yet possest
A few Greek books, shrined in an ancient chest,   185
Where barbarous mice through many an inlet crept
And fed on heavenly numbers while he slept.
"Codrus, in short, had nothing." You say true;
And yet poor Codrus lost that nothing too!
One curse alone was wanting to complete   190
His woes: that, cold and hungry, through the street
The wretch should beg, and in the hour of need
Find none to lodge, to clothe him, or to feed!

But should the raging flames on grandeur prey,
And low in dust Asturius' palace lay,   195
The squalid matron sighs, the senate mourns,
The pleaders cease, the judge the court adjourns;

*A mother
and daughter
before the
Roman judges.*

All join to wail the city's hapless fate
And rail at fire with more than common hate.   199
Lo! while it burns, the obsequious courtiers haste,
With rich materials to repair the waste.
This brings him marble, that a finished piece,
The far-famed boast of Polyclete and Greece;
This, ornaments which graced of old the fane

183. **A Chiron.** A clay statue of Chiron, the noble Centaur, was one
of the few possessions of humble Codrus.   203. **Polyclete,** the great
Greek sculptor.

Of Asia's gods; that, figured plate and plain; 205
This, cases, books, and busts the shelves to grace,
And piles of coin his specie to replace.
So much the childless Persian swells his store
(Though deemed the richest of the rich before)
That all ascribe the flames to thirst of pelf 210
And swear, Asturius fired his house himself.

O, had you, from the Circus, power to fly,
In many a halcyon village might you buy
Some elegant retreat for what will here
Scarce hire a gloomy dungeon through the year! 215
There wells, by nature formed, which need no rope,
No laboring arm, to crane their waters up,
Around your lawn their facile streams shall shower
And cheer the springing plant and opening flower.
There live, delighted with the rustic's lot, 220
And till with your own hands the little spot;
The little spot shall yield you large amends
And glad with many a feast your Samian friends.
And sure—in any corner we can get,
To call one lizard ours, is something yet. 225

Flushed with a mass of indigested food,
Which clogs the stomach and inflames the blood,
What crowds, with watching wearied and o'erprest,
Curse the slow hours and died for want of rest!
For who can hope his languid lids to close 230
Where brawling taverns banish all repose?
Sleep, to the rich alone, "his visits pays:"
And hence the seeds of many a dire disease.
The carts loud rumbling through the narrow way,
The drivers' clamors at each casual stay, 235
From drowsy Drusus would his slumber take,
And keep the calves of Proteus broad awake!

If business calls, obsequious crowds divide,
While o'er their heads the rich securely ride,
By tall Illyrians borne, and read or write, 240
Or (should the early hour to rest invite)
Close the soft litter and enjoy the night.
Yet reach they first the goal; while, by the throng
Elbowed and jostled, scarce we creep along;
Sharp strokes from poles, tubs, rafters, doomed to feel, 245
And plastered o'er with mud from head to heel;
While the rude soldier gores us as he goes,
Or marks in blood his progress on our toes!

See, from the Dole a vast tumultuous throng,
Each followed by his kitchen, pours along! 250
Huge pans, which Corbulo could scarce uprear,

223. **Samian friends,** followers of Pythagoras of Samos, who ate nothing but vegetables. 225. **To call one lizard ours.** According to Dr. Johnson, this means to own "as much ground as one may have a chance to find a lizard upon." 236–237. **From drowsy Drusus . . . awake!** Both the Emperor Tiberius (Drusus) and seals in the sea (the calves of Proteus) were thought to sleep soundly. 249–250. **See, from the Dole . . . pours along!** The Roman dole, a feature of Roman life throughout the empire, often consisted of food rather than money, in which case the needy citizens might have their slaves bring along portable kitchens to cook the food in the street. 251. **Corbulo,** a famous strong man.

With steady neck a puny slave must bear,
And, lest amid the way the flames expire,
Glide nimbly on and, gliding, fan the fire; 254
Through the close press with sinuous efforts wind,
And piece by piece leave his botched rags behind.

Hark! groaning on, the unwieldy wagon spreads
Its cumbrous load, tremendous! o'er our heads,
Projecting elm or pine, that nods on high
And threatens death to every passerby. 260
Heavens! should the axle crack, which bears a weight
Of huge Ligurian stone, and pour the freight
On the pale crowd beneath, what would remain,
What joint, what bone, what atom of the slain?
The body, with the soul, would vanish quite, 265
Invisible as air to mortal sight!—
Meanwhile, unconscious of their fellow's fate,
At home they heat the water, scour the plate,
Arrange the strigils, fill the cruse with oil,
And ply their several tasks with fruitless toil. 270
For he who bore the dole, poor mangled ghost,
Sits pale and trembling on the Stygian coast,
Scared at the horrors of the novel scene,
At Charon's threatening voice and scowling mien;
Nor hopes a passage, thus abruptly hurled 275
Without his farthing to the nether world

Pass we these fearful dangers, and survey
What other evils threat our nightly way.
And first, behold the mansion's towering size,
Where floors on floors to the tenth story rise; 280
Whence heedless garretteers their potsherds throw,
And crush the unwary wretch that walks below!
Clattering, the storm descends from heights unknown,
Ploughs up the street, and wounds the flinty stone!
'Tis madness, dire improvidence of ill, 285
To sup abroad before you sign your will,
Since fate in ambush lies and marks his prey
From every wakeful window in the way.
Pray, then—and count your humble prayer well sped
If pots be only—emptied on your head. 290

The drunken bully, ere his man be slain,
Frets through the night and courts repose in vain,
And while the thirst of blood his bosom burns,
From side to side in restless anguish turns, 294
Like Peleus' son when, quelled by Hector's hand,
His loved Patroclus pressed the Phrygian strand.

There are, who murder as an opiate take,
And only when no brawls await them wake.
Yet even these heroes, flushed with youth and wine,
All contest with the purple robe decline; 300
Securely give the lengthened train to pass,
The sun-bright flambeaux and the lamps of brass.
Me, whom the moon or candle's paler gleam,

262. **Ligurian stone,** marble. 299–302. **Yet even these heroes . . . lamps of brass.** The impudent street-bully still is wise enough not to attack the rich man, with his large retinue of attendants.

Whose wick I husband to the last extreme,
Guides through the gloom, he braves, devoid of
  fear. 305
The prelude to our doughty quarrel, hear—
If that be deemed a quarrel where, heaven knows,
He only gives, and I receive, the blows!
Across my path he strides, and bids me stand!
I bow, obsequious to the dread command; 310
What else remains where madness, rage combine
With youth and strength superior far to mine?
  "Whence come you, rogue?" he cries; "whose
    beans tonight
Have stuffed you thus? What cobbler clubbed his
    mite
For leeks and sheep's-head porridge? Dumb! quite
    dumb! 315
Speak, or be kicked. —Yet once again! Your home?
Where shall I find you? At what beggar's stand
(Temple or bridge) whimp'ring with outstretched
    hand?"
  Whether I strive some humble plea to frame
Or steal in silence by, 'tis just the same: 320
I'm beaten first, then dragged in rage away;
Bound to the peace or punished for the fray!
  Mark here the boasted freedom of the poor!
Beaten and bruised, that goodness to adore,
Which, at their humble prayer, suspends its ire 325
And sends them home with yet a bone entire.
  Nor this the worst; for when deep midnight reigns,
And bolts secure our doors, and massy chains,
When noisy inns a transient silence keep,
And harassed nature woos the balm of sleep, 330
Then thieves and murderers ply their dreadful trade,
With stealthy steps our secret couch invade.
Roused from the treacherous calm, aghast we start,
And the fleshed sword—is buried in our heart!
  Hither from bogs, from rocks, and caves pursued
(The Pontine marsh and Gallinarian wood), 336
The dark assassins flock, as to their home,
And fill with dire alarm the streets of Rome.
Such countless multitudes our peace annoy
That bolts and shackles every forge employ, 340
And cause so wide a waste, the country fears
A want of ore for mattocks, rakes, and shares.
  O! happy were our sires, estranged from crimes;
And happy, happy, were the good old times,
Which saw, beneath their kings', their tribunes' reign,
One cell the nation's criminals contain! 346
  Much could I add, more reasons could I cite,
If time were ours, to justify my flight;
But see! the impatient team is moving on,
The sun declining; and I must be gone. 350
Long since, the driver murmured at my stay
And jerked his whip to beckon me away.

336. **Pontine marsh and Gallinarian wood,** two notorious haunts of bandits. 346. **One cell . . . contain!** This refers to the Mamertine prison, for many years the only one in Rome.

Farewell, my friend! with this embrace we part;
Cherish my memory ever in your heart.
And when from crowds and business you repair 355
To breathe at your Aquinum freer air,
Fail not to draw me from my loved retreat
To Elvine Ceres and Diana's seat.
For your bleak hills my Cumae I'll resign,
And (if you blush not at such aid as mine) 360
Come well equipped to wage in angry rhymes
Fierce war with you on follies and on crimes.

Martial

c. 40–c. 104 A.D.

Though considerably older than Juvenal, Martial was apparently his close friend and saluted him in three of his epigrams. Their friendship seems appropriate, for both were caustic, dissatisfied men who have left equally sinister impressions of their age. Marcus Valerius Martialis was born and educated in Roman Spain, but gravitated to the capital in 64 A.D. to seek his fortune. His first patrons, Seneca and Lucan, were also Spaniards, but their fall from power under Nero cast a shadow over Martial's career. His later success was modest at best, but in his search for it he accumulated many acquaintances and a cynical understanding of city people.

Martial specialized in the tiniest of literary forms, the epigram. Each of his 1561 epigrams (arranged in fifteen books) is a brief, pithy poem with its own unity and a sting or surprise at the end. Imported from Greece, the type became completely Roman in Martial through the force of his mordant wit and spicy humor.

At bottom, Martial is a keen social critic who brings Imperial Rome to life with less exaggeration than Juvenal. He has an ever-watchful eye for meaningful details, and from his many little observations we can build a fairly accurate picture of the city. His approach is straightforward and free from Juvenal's rhetoric. Friends appear for direct tribute, but his enemies are disguised, since his satiric purpose is to attack vices, not persons. We must overlook the cringing sycophancy of his poems to patrons and his gross vulgarity in many places. What remains is the ironic or sportive jests of a highly original talent that seems ever fresh and vigorous.

Post-Obits and the Poets

HE unto whom thou art so partial
  Oh, reader! is the well-known Martial,
The Epigrammatist: while living,
Give him the fame thou wouldst be giving;
So shall he hear, and feel, and know it— 5
  Post-obits rarely reach a poet.

356–358. **Aquinum . . . Diana's seat.** Juvenal was probably born in Aquinum near the shrine of Ceres and Diana.
Post-Obits and the Poets. Translated by Lord Byron.

To His Book

To read my book, the virgin shy
　　May blush, while Brutus standeth by;
But when he's gone, read through what's writ,
And never stain a cheek for it.

"'Tis Wise to Forget"

I MAY have asked you here to dine,
　　But that was late at night,
And none of us had spared the wine
　　If I remember right.
You thought the invitation meant,　　　　　5
　　Though wine obscured my wit!
And—O most parlous precedent—
　　You made a note of it!
The maxim that in Greece was true
　　Is true in Rome to-day—　　　　　　10
"I hate a fellow-toper who
　　Remembers what I say."

On Acerra

He reeks, you might think, of his yesterday's
　　drink;
　　But knowing his customs and ways,
You are wrong, I'll be sworn, for he drank till the
　　morn,
　　So the savor is truly to-day's.

To Diaulus

A SURGEON once, you now begin
　　As undertaker's man,
To earn a bedside practice in
　　The only way you can.

Moderation

You bid me say what kind of maid
　　Can draw me or repel?
My friend, I hate a forward jade
　　But loathe a prude as well.
I love the mean: extremes are vain　　　　5
　　And never bring me joy;
Love long denied is grief and pain,
　　While easy favors cloy.

Non Amo Te

I DO not love thee, Doctor Fell,
　　The reason why I cannot tell;
But this alone I know full well,
I do not love thee, Doctor Fell.

On Charinus

His health is good, yet he is always pale;
　　He drinks but little, 'tis of no avail,
So wan his face no sun can darken it,
And good digestion aids him not a whit,
Not even rouge that pallid cheek can flush—　　5
And e'en his vices do not make him blush!

To Bithynicus

Though you hope that her cough will soon
　　carry her off,
　　For gasping and swooning is she,
Do not flatter yourself that you'll finger her pelf;
　　For her faint is a feint with an "e."

To Naevia

You would not carve the hare: it was not
　　basted,
So you declared: the mullet went untasted:
The boar was more than high—our senses proved
　　it—
You called it "over-fresh," and then removed it.
"Uneatable and raw," you kept repeating;　　　5
In proof whereof you gave your cook a beating.
A vain excuse; we're safe beyond all question.
A meal of nothing gives no indigestion.

To Apicius

You had spent sixty thousand on gorging your
　　fill,
And there only remained a poor ten thousand still.
That to you was starvation; so into your cup
You poured deadly poison and drank the lot up.
You were always a gourmet, of that I am sure;　　5
But by death you were proved the complete epicure.

To His Book. Translated by Robert Herrick.
"'*Tis Wise to Forget*"; *On Acerra; To Diaulus; Moderation.* Translated by J. A. Pott. From *The Epigrams* of *Martial* by J. A. Pott and F. A. Wright. Reprinted by permission of Routledge and Kegan Paul, Ltd.

Non Amo Te. Translated by Tom Brown.
On Charinus; To Bithynicus; To Naevia; To Apicius. Translated by J. A. Pott. From *The Epigrams of Martial* by J. A. Pott and F. A. Wright. Reprinted by permission of Routledge and Kegan Paul, Ltd.

On a Bas-Relief

THEY'RE Pheidias' fish, engraved by him,
Add water—and behold they swim.

To Ligurinus

Book is Long & Boring

YOU never your friends, sir, to dinner invite
Except when you have some bad verse to
recite.
We have scarcely sat down when on our weary ears
Comes the sound of "Book One," ere the *hors-
d'oeuvre* appears.
You read through Book Two while the entrée we
wait;   5
Book Three makes dessert and the savory late.
Then comes Number Four and at last Number Five:
Even dainties so frequent a surfeit would give.
If you won't to the waste-paper merchant consign
Your poems, in future alone you must dine.

To Chloë

(Chloe is a tease)

I COULD resign that eye of blue
Howe'er its splendor used to thrill me;
And even that cheek of roseate hue,—
To lose it, Chloë, scarce would kill me.
That snowy neck I ne'er should miss,   5
However much I've raved about it;
And sweetly as that lip can kiss,
I *think* I could exist without it.
In short, so well I've learned to fast,
That, sooth my love, I know not whether   10
I might not bring myself at last,
To—do without you altogether.

To Polla

LEAVE off thy paint, perfumes, and youthful
dress,
And nature's failing honestly confess;
Double we see those faults which art would mend,
Plain downright ugliness would less offend.

A Total Abstainer

THOUGH you serve richest wines,
Paulus, Rumor opines
That they poisoned your four wives, I think.
It's of course all a lie;
None believes less than I—   5
No, I really don't care for a drink.

The Author's Reward

'TIS my fifth book of merry verse,
Yet no man has protested,
Or said he is one whit the worse,
So gently I have jested.
But many a reader finds his name   5
Is honored in my pages,
And these rejoice to know their fame
Will last throughout the ages.
"Such tributes all are profitless,
For no one will requite them"—   10
They bring no money, I confess,
And yet I love to write them.

Procrastination

TO-MORROW you will live, you always cry;
In what far country does this morrow lie,
That 'tis so mighty long ere it arrive?
Beyond the Indies does this morrow live?
'Tis so far fetched, this morrow, that I fear   5
'Twill be both very old and very dear.
To-morrow I will live, the fool does say;
To-day itself's too late: the wise lived yesterday.

To Maximus

SYRISCUS a full hundred thousand received
From his patron, and though it will scarce be
believed,
He managed at taverns to squander the lot
About the four baths, drinking pot after pot.
What a thirst he must have such a fortune to drown,
And to do it too standing, without sitting down.   6

On a Bas-Relief. Translated by J. A. Pott. From *The Epigrams of
Martial* by J. A. Pott and F. A. Wright. Reprinted by permission of
Routledge and Kegan Paul, Ltd.
1. **Pheidias**, the great Greek sculptor.
To Ligurinus. Translated by F. A. Wright. From *The Epigrams of
Martial* by J. A. Pott and F. A. Wright. Reprinted by permission
of Routledge and Kegan Paul, Ltd.
To Chloë. Translated by Thomas Moore.
To Polla. Translated by Sir Charles Sedley.

A Total Abstainer. Translated by Paul Nixon. From *A Roman Wit*
by Paul Nixon. Reprinted by permission of Houghton Mifflin Company.
The Author's Reward. Translated by J. A. Pott. **To Maximus.** Translated by F. A. Wright. From *The Epigrams of Martial* by J. A. Pott
and F. A. Wright. Reprinted by permission of Routledge and Kegan
Paul, Ltd.
Procrastination. Translated by Abraham Cowley.

Return Favors

WHY don't I send my book to you
    Although you often urge me to?
The reason's good, for if I did
You'd send me yours—which God forbid!

Galla's Hair

THE golden hair that Galla wears
    Is hers: who would have thought it?
She swears 'tis hers, and true she swears,
    For I know where she bought it.

On an Ant
in Amber

THE amber dripped from Phaethon's fair tree
    And whelmed a petty ant that wandered there,
And, though of little worth in life was she,
    Now in her death she is a treasure rare.

Respectability

Now, a suspected past to cover,
    You make a husband of your lover,
Lest law should visit your transgression;
This is not marriage but confession!

A Promising Youth

AT sixty years of age is he
    A man of promise still:
Methinks he needs eternity
    That promise to fulfill.

To Quintus

YOUR birthday I wished to observe with a gift;
    You forbade, and your firmness is known.
    Every man to his taste:
    I remark with some haste,
May the third is the date of my own.

Return Favors; On an Ant in Amber; Respectability; A Promising Youth. Translated by J. A. Pott. From The Epigrams of Martial, by Pott and Wright. Reprinted by permission of Routledge and Kegan Paul, Ltd.
Galla's Hair. Translated by Sir John Harington.
To Quintus; Union Labor. Translated by Paul Nixon. From A Roman Wit by Paul Nixon. Reprinted by permission of Houghton Mifflin Company.

To a Rival Poet

YOUR verses are full of a sugary grace,
    As spotless and pure as a well-powdered
        face,
Not an atom of salt or suspicion of gall,
So how can they but on an audience pall!
Even food does not please if the cooking's too
        simple,   5
And cheeks lack in charm when they haven't a dim-
        ple.
A child may like apples and figs without savor;
But give me the sort that have got a sharp flavor.

Presentation Copies

PRESENT you with my books? Not I indeed.
    I know you want to sell them, not to read.

Union Labor

BY the time the Barber Eurus
    Had circled Lupo's face,
A second beard had sprouted
    In the first one's place.

False Appearances

HE makes parade of poverty—a plot
    To make us think him rich when he is not.

The Cook

BECAUSE I beat my cook who spoilt the dinner
    You say, "Oh cruel wretch, oh greedy sinner,
Such penalties for greater faults are fit."
What greater crime, I ask, can cooks commit?

On Picentinus' Marriage
with Galla

SEVEN husbands she got,
    Made away with the lot
    And has buried them all—but I know
That as you're number eight,
She has not long to wait   5
    Before she rejoins them—below.

To a Rival Poet. Translated by F. A. Wright. Presentation Copies; False Appearances; The Cook; On Picentinus' Marriage with Galla. Translated by J. A. Pott. From The Epigrams of Martial by Pott and Wright. Reprinted by permission of Routledge and Kegan Paul, Ltd.

A Productive Estate

Seven wives you've had and all of them lie
    buried in your field;
I don't suppose that any land could boast more rich
    a yield.

What Makes
a Happy Life

What makes a happy life, dear friend,
    If thou wouldst briefly learn, attend—
An income left, not earned by toil;
Some acres of a kindly soil;
The pot unfailing on the fire;   5
No lawsuits, seldom town attire;
Health, strength with grace; a peaceful mind;
Shrewdness with honesty combined;
Plain living; equal friends and free;
Evenings of temperate gayety;   10
A wife discreet yet blithe and bright;
Sound slumber that lends wings to night.
With all thy heart embrace thy lot,
Wish not for death, and fear it not.

To Lupus

You gave me a farm—so you called it, at least,
    In a sort of rhetorical turn—
But I'm forced to relate that the total estate
    Doesn't hold as much dirt as an urn.

A grove of Diana, you told me, I think,   5
    Was a notable sight on the place:
But beyond one poor beet, overcome by the heat,
    Of grove I deny there's a trace.

The wing of a cricket would cover that farm,
    And an overfed ant with the gout   10
Couldn't find enough crops to tickle his chops
    To last till the sun flickered out.

Moreover that garden you bragged so about
    Proves a worm-eaten rose with one leaf,
And the lawn's yield of grass doesn't greatly sur-
        pass   15
    Its produce of gravy and beef.

A cucumber hasn't got room to lie straight,
    And a snake's bound to live there in pieces.
A grasshopper hopped just one day and then
        stopped—
    Starved to death, with its stomach in creases. 20

A mole is the sole agriculturist there,
    And he's hardly got room to turn around.
Why, a mushroom can't spread, or a flower wave its
        head
    Sans trespass on my neighbor's ground.

An undergrown mouse when he gets at that farm
    Makes it look as though hit by the plague,   26
And my whole crop of hay was carried away
    By a thrush hardly out of the egg.

A statue of Pan—minus head, legs, and trunk—
    Casts its shade over all the domain: 30
And the shell of a clam, without sign of a jam,
    My harvest complete can contain.

Now pardon, my friend, if my praise has been
        faint—
    We can seldom express what we feel:
So I merely will add that I'd be mighty glad   35
    To swap farm for a thirty-cent meal.

To Fabullus

Of all the guests you ask to dine
    I know not one, so I decline;
Why should you grumble? 'Tis not rude
To hate a crowded solitude.

A Hinted Wish

You told me, Maro, whilst you live
    You'd not a single penny give,
But that, whene'er you chanct to die,
You'd leave a handsome legacy:
You must be mad beyond redress,   5
If my next wish you cannot guess!

A Pretty Pair

Says your wife with a sneer, "You're the lady-
        maid's dear,"
    And she mocks at your conduct as shady;
But well-matched you must be; 'tis notorious that
        she
    Is the gentleman's gentleman's lady!

A Productive Estate. Translated by J. A. Pott. From *The Epigrams of Martial* by Pott and Wright. Reprinted by permission of Routledge and Kegan Paul, Ltd.
What Makes a Happy Life. Translated by Goldwin Smith. From *Bay Leaves*, by Goldwin Smith. Published by The Macmillan Company, 1893.
To Lupus. Translated by Paul Nixon. From *A Roman Wit* by Paul Nixon. Reprinted by permission of Houghton Mifflin Company.
To Fabullus; A Pretty Pair. Translated by J. A. Pott. From *The Epigrams of Martial* by Pott and Wright. Reprinted by permission of Routledge and Kegan Paul, Ltd.
A Hinted Wish. Translated by Samuel Johnson.

CENTURIES OF TRANSITION

CHRISTENDOM, ISLAM, AND THE MIDDLE AGES

300 TO 1350

THE Middle Ages in Europe constituted that long era of transition between the civilization of imperial Rome and the complicated modern world which has been developing for the past five hundred years. The Middle Ages was indeed a long era, covering as it did a full thousand years and a trifle more, from about 300 to about 1350. Essentially what characterizes this enormous span of years is the fact that men's efforts throughout these eleven centuries were directed toward the establishment of a new system of life after the older system had col-lapsed amid the ruins of the classical world of **Greece** and Rome. The breaking up of the mighty Roman empire opened a chasm across the road which the Western world was traveling. And although this Western world had no clearer idea of the future at that time than is ever vouchsafed blundering man-kind, still it had instinctively to move on, because the one great eternal verity is change. In order for Occidental man to continue along his appointed road, the chasm had somehow to be bridged. What we choose to call medieval civilization was the bridge which was eventually built.

A notable integration of life and thought remains the prime characteristic of this age. This unity is best illustrated by the power over the individual man wielded by the two great institutions of the Middle Ages—the Holy Catholic Church in the realm of the spiritual and religious life, and the feudal system in the secular sphere. Of these two institutions it is obvious that the Church was for the time the greater; it was able to partake of feudalism and yet rise above feudalism. It could bring kings and em-perors to heel. When cracks began to appear in the central structures of these two institutions, the Mid-dle Ages was nearing its end, and the modern era was about to begin. Although it is not possible to examine here the bricks and blocks which went to make up these two magnificent edifices, the Church and the feudal system, it is important to realize that both assumed the supremacy of a central authority —that of the Pope in the Church and that of the royal sovereign in the feudal system—and, further, that the authoritarian tendency is the leading motif in medieval culture and medieval learning.

RELIGIOUS HIERARCHY AND FEUDAL STRUCTURE

THE Church had emerged from the collapse of the Roman empire as the one universally ac-cepted center of authority. Christianity, made the sole and official religion of the state by the emperor Theodosius in 395, had gradually developed an or-ganized hierarchy. A basic doctrine, that the bishop at Rome was the heir to the power of Peter, the dis-ciple whom Christ had appointed His successor, resulted in the acceptance of the Pope as head of the Church, at least in the West. Conversion by the Church of the various "barbarian" tribes accom-panied the development of its dogma, so that in the Middle Ages the people of Europe and their various rulers were Christian. What did such a status entail?

The Church took the position from the very be-ginning that it was the sole means which Christianity had at hand for the furtherance of God's plan on earth. No other plan, it maintained, was possible.

Salvation for the individual could be obtained only through the offices of the Church and by active par-ticipation in its ceremonies. The clergy administered the sacraments, by means of which Christians achieved grace necessary for happiness in the next world. The threat (implicit in interdict and excom-munication) of being barred from the sacraments and from grace was equivalent to the threat of being barred from Heaven. The Devil, or Antichrist, was the perennial adversary; the world was a perpetual battleground in the momentous conflict between the Kingdom of God and the Kingdom of the Devil. The Holy Father in Rome was the spiritual and moral sovereign of Christendom, the exponent of divine affirmation. He was also the champion of mortal man against the onslaughts of the world, the flesh, and the devil—the very essence of the Antichrist. The vast and imposing hierarchy of the Church must administer the affairs of the Kingdom of God in this world; but to God Himself was due all the homage, the glory, and the wonder for the greatness of His manifold works.

The hierarchy of the medieval Church was an organization at once complex and compact. First there was God Himself in the Trinity. Then came the various orders of angels and then man, "a little lower than the angels"; and the relation of man to his superiors formed the pattern on which was planned the whole institution of the Church. Each official of the Church bore a direct responsibility to the official above him in the hierarchy—priest to bishop, bishop to archbishop, archbishop to cardinal, cardinal to pontiff. Eventually, of course, all responsibility was laid upon the shoulders of the Pope, who was the representative of God on earth, the spiritual ruler of Christendom—and, it should be added, in view of the tremendous material wealth of the medieval Church, a temporal ruler also who wielded immense power.

Such was the essential sameness of the design in the organization of medieval life, moreover, that the pattern from which the religious phases of this life were shaped served also as the design which determined the secular life of the time. In a more earthy way—as Caesar is earthier than God—the feudal system was the secular counterpart of the medieval Church. To be sure, the king of a country was not the vicar of Christ; he had no right to the keys of Heaven. Nevertheless, according to the social and political philosophies of the era, the sovereign was considered the material owner of every square inch of land within his domain, except for the estates of the Church. This ownership was his by divine consent and privilege granted; therefore, in spite of its material nature, it assumed also a spiritual significance. In the mind of a patriotic liegeman, at least, it might be called a spiritual entity. For the sovereign theoretically embodied his country.

To speak in more material terms, we may simplify the matter, admittedly to the danger point, by observing that the land was leased by its medieval sovereign to his hierarchy of nobility or vassals, who in turn subleased it; the nobility owed the sovereign, in return for the privilege of occupying and exploiting this land, homage and the tangible obligations of certain money payments and the defense of his realm, usually in the form of military service. Moreover, always keeping in mind the hierarchical aspect of the whole arrangement, we see that each lesser nobleman was responsible, in paying for his privileges, to the nobleman next above him in social rank. Thus a baron would owe an earl or a count; an earl would owe a duke; a duke would owe the king or emperor. It is impossible to consider here all the details of feudal returns or all the niceties of feudal

French peasants plowing and sowing on a strip of land with the lord's castle in the background. From the Très Riches Heures du Duc de Berry, *illuminated before 1416.*

organization, a complex study in itself; but the presence of the system in the social life of the Middle Ages must always be kept in mind, along with the submissive habits of thought and conduct which such a system must engender.

Obviously the feudal system worked to the benefit of the relatively infinitesimal number of the privileged aristocracy. The people as a whole, the masses of the population, had but little power until the Middle Ages had outlived its potency. Underneath the superstructure of feudalism labored the villein, or serf, as part of an economic unit called the manor. The serf was bound to the land allotted him by the local noble. He worked his own half-acre when he could and tilled the land of the noble, so that the lord of the manor could subsist on his expected higher level and pay his due to his superior. For the feudal system was based primarily on agricul-

This relief over the central doorway of the Cathedral of Bourges depicts the Last Judgment as the medieval mind pictured it. At the center St. Michael weighs and separates the souls. The good souls are being received

ture, not on industry or commerce. The general effect was that the Middle Ages in its most characteristic aspects recognized but two classes of society—the nobility (among whom we must include members of the Church organization) and the people as a whole. Only among the freemen, who had been re-leased from serfdom for special services signally rendered, was there a substantial foundation for a future middle class, and such freemen were extremely rare before the year 1000. When a middle class became truly discernible, the Middle Ages had entered its terminal stage.

MEDIEVAL THOUGHT, SPIRITUAL AND SECULAR

IN theory there was the understanding that one should render unto Caesar the things that were Caesar's and unto God the things that were God's. Yet, where the religious and secular powers were not distinct, since the Church's higher clergy were feudal lords as well, there were inevitable frictions, jealousies, and contentions. The eventual outcome of such jostlings and collisions, however, would in this era be usually a foregone conclusion. The Church, as the divine instrument of God, created to advance His purposes on earth, could brook no assumption of unauthorized power by a mere monarch, who, in the final analysis, was only a sinful mortal. No sovereign during the true ascendancy of the Middle Ages was ever able to combat successfully the power of the Holy Father. The Pope being the true overlord of all Christendom, the might of the Church would always, in the final test,

be victorious over the forces of the State. The Holy Roman Emperor himself, Henry IV, was obliged in 1077 to humble himself before Pope Gregory VII at Canossa after having been defeated in a controversy over the investiture of ecclesiastics with office by lay rulers. Archbishop Thomas à Becket, although martyred, won his battle with King Henry II of England; and Archbishop Stephen Langton humiliated King John.

Now what of the position taken by the medieval Church in reference to man's relation to man and his relation to God? While no complete exegesis can be compressed into a few sentences, still it is necessary for anyone interested in the Middle Ages to keep in mind some fundamental points about this attitude, since an understanding of the literature of the age is otherwise difficult if not impossible. The Church took the world in which we live for what it

by Abraham at the left as they enter heaven. The damned, being carried off by devils for suitable punishment, are shown at the right.

was, dominated by the struggle between the Kingdom of God and the Kingdom of the Devil, and demonstrated how, by adhering to a particular belief and to a particular code of conduct, the world could be accepted and understood, against a final terrible Judgment Day. This coming of the Lord, this day of final ordeal, was inevitable; it awaited only God's pleasure. Certain interpreters of Holy Writ thought it likely that He would come at a particular time—in the year 1000, for example. The majority, however, preferred to think of the date of this divine event as indeterminate and indeterminable. At any rate, the belief in the body of doctrine established by century-old tradition and the code of conduct which served as the outward sign of this doctrine were both enforced under the strictest penalties for lack of faith or disobedience or too free subjective interpretation—heresy in the eyes of the Church.

And what of the world, which was man's immediate environment? There was some curiosity of varying degrees about the physical world. Most of the information about it was derived ultimately from sources which were either pre-Christian or non-Christian, such as the ancient Greek mathematicians, astronomers, and geographers, or the Arab scientists of contemporaneous fame. All this information, together with its dissemination, was monopolized by the Church. In the Middle Ages there was, to the

twentieth-century mind, an appalling unwillingness even to test or question this information or to speculate about the physically unknown except to relate it to the firmly established doctrine of the Church. It was deemed altogether sufficient to demonstrate that human reason would lead one inevitably to God, and this reconciliation of faith and reason is perhaps the greatest intellectual contribution of the Middle Ages.

As for the rest, the implication expressed in medieval teaching—and it is often far more than a mere implication—is that this world is at best temporary. Humanity, to take the long view necessary in all abiding faiths, philosophies, and religions, is therefore on its way to Heaven or to Hell, as the case may be. The world is a road of pilgrimage to the appointed lodging place. Certainly the world to come, for better or for worse, is a far more important consideration than this transitory life on earth. If the medieval teacher seems to think of man as more likely than not to end in Hell, that is because of his fundamental belief in man's sinfulness, an evil state that is attributable to the seduction by the Devil of man's first parents. Heaven is for the tried, the true, the privileged in God's sight; and before man can attain to Heaven, he must be put through the refining process of Purgatory—which is in itself no trifling ordeal—unless a man be so saintly that he can be borne away from this world direct to Heaven, as happened to a few saints and prophets. As a consequence of this attitude in so much of the moral and spiritual literature of the Middle Ages, it is the Other World, in contradistinction to the world in which man must live out his earthly span, that is the true end of existence.

At this point, however, a word of warning is due. To say that the world to come was more important in the eyes of the Middle Ages than the world of the present can be maintained, but only with some qualifications. Such was indeed the message of its moralists and teachers. But it cannot be believed, for instance, that men during this thousand-year period passed through life with hearts and minds fixed only on the Celestial City or on the lurid infernos conjured up by their poets and prophets. The mere experience of living is altogether too important to the average man and woman for such a way of life to be possible. The relation of man to man could never be made tolerable on such a basis. It is therefore proper to assume that the daily problems of life faced by the man and woman of the Middle Ages were then, as always, the usual familiar ones that were nevertheless immediate and urgent, and that human nature was basically the same then as it is now. There is ample evidence in the surviving works of Chaucer, Dante, the romance writers, and the tale tellers that such was the case, because, contrary to superficial impressions, the literature of the Middle Ages was not all didactic. It is true that the men of the Middle Ages did not invent the steam engine or the airplane; but they ate and drank and propagated themselves, transacted business, made homes and broke them up, practiced obstetrics, and buried their dead, as now.

Each significant age in the history of humanity has appreciated the world in which it lived; and the Middle Ages was no exception to this general rule. And so the sovereign, with all his advisers, agents,

and sycophants, conducted the administration of his kingdom. The villein laboriously cultivated his master baron's strips of land, with a care for the soil which could teach some farmers of today a great deal; the tradesman, when he finally appeared, went about his needful occupations in the congested, dark, unsanitary towns, whose streets were crowded with domestic animals by day and infested by bandits at night; the housewife occupied herself with the usual meals and household tasks that have been the lot of women since time immemorial; the nobleman exercised his privilege of hunting, rode with his hawks and hounds or chatted with his ladies. There were always feast days, religious as well as secular, town fairs and market days, as well as days when nothing much occurred. There were violence, poverty, and filth beyond what a modern can easily imagine. There were also superstition, cruelty, treachery, selfishness, greed, and a numbing passivity which defies belief. There were hate and love and friendship as well. It is impossible that people in such an environment and with such matters to keep them busy should go about continually preoccupied with their immortal souls.

Still, most of the literature produced throughout the Middle Ages—a literature which was always the responsibility of the churchman or the teacher, since they controlled learning and literacy—is a stern reminder of the power of the pen. It is truly unfortunate that the commoners did not possess more vocal spokesmen. We might have now a much more accurate picture of the Middle Ages if they had been rather more articulate and more willing to speak out without fear or favor. The fact remains, nevertheless, that medieval teaching laid emphasis upon the life to come far more than did the teachers of the ancient world on the one hand or of the modern world on the other; and this emphasis assuredly colored medieval literature to a great extent.

PHASES OF THE MEDIEVAL LITERARY TRADITION

So much for suggestions concerning the social and intellectual fiber of the Middle Ages; what of the literature produced? The bastions of this literature are the Church and the feudal system, as they grew through the centuries of strife that went into their building. From the time of the permanent division of the Roman empire into two parts (395) until the coronation of Charlemagne by the pope as "Emperor of the Romans" (800), the Church had managed to hold together the remnants of the older civilization, in both the secular and the spiritual sense, spreading the word of God through missionaries and evangelists, defending itself against here-

sies which might split its unity, and preserving whatever learning it could salvage. In those earlier centuries of the Middle Ages, feudalism was only beginning; those were the days of absolute rule only, when a kingdom was scarcely more complex in its structure or its geographical extent than a mere barbaric tribe. In one sense, then, the ecclesiastical structure, as it developed through the first four centuries of the medieval era, was the predecessor of the feudal system.

As it happens, however, the years from 400 to 800 are not important to us as years of literary production in Western Europe. Epics and sagas un-

The beauty and religious conviction of medieval Gothic architecture is embodied in this thirteenth-century double lancet window from La Tricherie church, Vienne, France, now in the Cloisters, New York.

doubtedly flourished in oral tradition, very likely in much greater profusion than we realize today. In this type of literature the English took the lead, for the Anglo-Saxon epic poems, represented by *Beowulf* and the Caedmonian and Cynewulfian epic cycles,* all of which were originally composed by the end of the eighth century or shortly thereafter, are head and shoulders above contemporaneous continental literature. The superiority of these poems lies in the fact that their authors were men of talent belonging to a literary tradition both of artistic possibilities and of rigid standards; the Anglo-Saxon bard, or *scop,* had developed the potentialities of the Old Germanic alliterative verse to the point where it was expressive, elastic, and often extremely impressive. In addition to the writers of these epic poems, Anglo-Saxon England produced at least one unusual scholarly talent in the Venerable Bede, who died in 735. Bede's *Ecclesiastical History of the English People* was a model of historiography for centuries to come. On the continent before 800, on the other hand, the writing was almost exclusively of an ecclesiastical or academic nature—works on ecclesiastical policy; on doctrine; on the combatting of heresy; on the chronicling of historical events and the observation of basic natural phenomena, including geography, natural history, medicine, botany, and astronomy. Except for theological works, however, the total literary output of the continent until the year 800 is both highly derivative and essentially pallid. The single important exception is the work of Boethius, a Roman philosopher (d. 524), who wrote on music and rhetoric but is most valuable as a gifted transmitter of Platonic philosophy in his *De Consolatione Philosophiae,* which, translated into all the languages of Western Europe, exerted an influence of a diffused and secular kind as long as the Middle Ages lasted.

The unusual unifying power which was Charlemagne's introduces a second phase of development in the medieval tradition. From a political viewpoint, Charlemagne created a Frankish empire which was recognized by the Church as the heritage of the Roman empire,† and as duly sanctioned by God. With the strife which followed the death of Charlemagne, feudalism received its most powerful single impulse. But even more important to the history of Occidental civilization was Charlemagne's sincere desire to encourage learning in all of its

accepted forms. The founding of his Palace School was the first great milestone along the road which was to lead to the establishment of the University of Paris and thence to the spread of the Renaissance into Western Europe. It was an Englishman, Alcuin of York, who was his most useful and effective teacher. Unfortunately for the political harmony of the age, Charlemagne's empire after his death, becoming a bone of contention among his sons, was broken up. The struggles for leadership among its parts tormented the continent for centuries.

The years from 800 to about 1200 represent a second phase of the medieval tradition. To this period belongs the evolution of monasticism and Scholasticism.** Regardless of other developments, it was these particular manifestations of the medieval intellect which dominated the scene during these four centuries. During this time there came a revivifying of and stricter obedience to the monastic rules, as typified in particular by the reform of the Benedictine Rule in various parts of Europe during the ninth, tenth, and eleventh centuries. The monk in his cloister examined God's inventory and recorded the course of human events in chronicles, interpreted the Word of God as manifested in the Scriptures, pointed out the obvious superiority of the world to come over the world that was, preached how both reason and natural affection would draw men to God. This was the age of teaching by catechistic devices, dialogues, and debates; by the rigid application of logic, dialectics, and practical persuasion. In this age the orders of friars went forth to help found seats of learning in such widely separated places as Bologna, Paris, Oxford, Cambridge, and elsewhere; in this age were sown the seeds which bore fruit later in the lonely eminence of such theologians as Thomas Aquinas or Duns Scotus; such a talented investigating scholar, born before his time, as Roger Bacon; such possessors of "all knowledge" as Albertus Magnus or Vincent of Beauvais. This was the age of the churchman near the threshold of the Supreme, which he would approach but never quite cross.

Then came the thirteenth century, which many have regarded as the peak of medieval culture. Never again would there reign a Pope so absolute in his authority; never again would the Holy Roman Emperor be so potent in secular matters. Actually, in many quarters, the feudal edifice was being subjected to intense strain. The barons were becoming restive; the full prerogatives of the sovereign were in question. In England, early in this century, King John

---

* Caedmon was the earliest English Christian poet and his poems on Biblical themes date from about 1000. Cynewulf is the only Old English vernacular poet of whom we have undisputed extant works, written in the ninth century. The poetry of both is referred to as Old English Christian Epics.

† More than a century after the collapse of this "Roman Empire" of Charlemagne a new empire, ruled over by a German king, replaced it, 962. This came to be called the Holy Roman Empire, and lasted until 1806.

** Scholasticism was the study of philosophy aimed basically at reconciling Church dogma with Aristotelian logic, or faith with reason. It reached its zenith in the thirteenth century and then began to degenerate into formalistic arguing over minute points of dogma; as such it was ridiculed by many Humanist writers of the Renaissance.

was obliged to sign Magna Charta (1215), which was the opening wedge to weaken and destroy royal privilege. On the continent, the struggle continued between Pope and Emperor, as illustrated in Italy by the fierce local internecine warfare between Guelphs and Ghibellines;* and although the Pope, then at the height of his secular powers, was still supreme, the taint of worldliness was upon him, and the succeeding centuries were to prove that even his high office could become of the earth earthy. Yet it is entirely appropriate that Innocent III, the superb, should be the author of *De Contemptu Mundi*, a thoroughly characteristic document which states the medieval definition of this world as well as any.

This was the century of the great Scholastics, who continued to argue with infinite zeal and patience that the Kingdom of God was ascertainable through human reason, that it was essentially the reflection of God's relationship to man—the relationship of eternal love and well-being—and that man was truly blessed only when he withdrew himself from the temptations of the world, the flesh, and the devil, and regarded the present world as evil in contrast to the New Jerusalem flowing with milk and honey. And, in a narrower and more human way, it was dimly recognized that man, submitting to the decrees of omnipotent God, was blessed also when in the simplest terms he took comfort in the lesser things of nature, as was preached by Saint Francis of Assisi.

Still, side by side with the monasticism of the twelfth and thirteenth centuries, there was a secular compensation with more than one outlet. There was the chivalric movement, which gave prominence in fiction, as well as in courtly manners, to the aristocratic lady, giving her reverence and homage and joining the secular ideas of love to the divine concept of heavenly bliss. And while the thirteenth century produced Magna Charta and the revolt of the barons, thereby widening the base of the ruling power, it produced something else, the guildsman. Here was the first recognition of the social importance of the man of industry, the ancestor of the modern middle class, or *bourgeoisie;* and as this man's political and social position was enhanced—a process unquestionably helped along by the social, recreational, and religious organization of laborers called the guild— so much were medieval traditions weakened.

The advance of the guildsman to a position of importance in the medieval municipality coincided in the fourteenth century with early signs of weakness in the medieval Church—a confusion of authority, a

schism, which prevailed through a large part of the century (the Babylonian Captivity, 1305–1376). One faction professed spiritual obedience to a Pope in Rome; another to a Pope in Avignon while the courts of both Popes were remarkable chiefly for a cynical worldliness and luxurious display. Even when the Papacy returned to Rome, it was clear that the damage had been done. Almost immediately there-

A monk, one of the figures by Claus Sluter from the tomb of Philip the Bold of Burgundy, who died in 1404.

* These were two factions in the Italian city-states, the Ghibellines supporting the Holy Roman Emperors and the Guelphs backing the claims of the Popes.

after John Wycliffe in England began to preach what were termed heresies by the medieval Church and John Huss of Bohemia paid with his life (1415) for his revolt against the dicta of Rome. The Reformation was not officially recognized until a century later, but the essence of its thought can be found at this period.

If the twelfth and thirteenth centuries came to mean the greatest achievements of medieval theology and philosophy, then in comparison the fourteenth century, which happened to produce the greatest writers, if not the greatest thinkers, of the Middle Ages, was an era of transition to the Renaissance. Dante, who died in 1321, was the last and in every way the most typical great exponent of medievalism, with his rigid cosmography; his harsh, almost pedantic preoccupation with the sinful and the virtuous; his inspiration derived from the worlds still to come. Yet Dante had a noble admiration for poetry as poetry; and the later fourteenth-century authors like Boccaccio, Petrarch, and Chaucer have little to anchor them to the Middle Ages except their dates and the fact that they observed certain medieval conventions—an occasional concession to abstract teaching, allegory, and esoteric symbolism; a routine deference to the tenets if not the institution of the medieval Church. Yet these conventions, as these writers honor them, are not likely to strike one as anything more than external. By 1400 the Renaissance was already in the ascendant almost everywhere save in England, which suffered a temporary intellectual and literary stagnation during most of the fifteenth century.

We may safely conclude that the Middle Ages was primarily a period of constant struggle, both covert and overt, between the Church and outer paganism, or between the Church and the State. If Europe, from the eleventh to the thirteenth century, was split down the middle in the conflict between Pope and Emperor, Guelph and Ghibelline, what were the consequences of the conflict? For one thing, the growing city-states of medieval Italy, Venice, Florence, Genoa, for all their internal strife, cast off the restraints of the Middle Ages and became the birthplace of the individualism of the Renaissance; and here is an illustration of the truism that each age contains within itself the seeds of that which will later bring about its passing.

FROM EARLY EPIC TO CHAUCER

I T is a simple matter to ignore the literature produced in Europe before the year 800, for that is the interest of the confirmed specialist only. Its nature has already been briefly described; its expression was neither original enough nor powerful enough to stand the test of time. However, the epic tradition from non-Christian times and places, which is more vital than any other literary tradition in existence between the fall of Rome and the days of Charlemagne, showed itself in writing first in Anglo-Saxon England, as we have seen, and gradually emerged—as evidenced in their extant literature—among the continental nations and outlying Celtic lands, always, to be sure, under the auspices of an indulgent Christendom. This early epic tradition was first expressed compellingly in the true heroic style of *Beowulf*, from the eighth or ninth century; of the *Hildebrandslied*, in a mixture of Low and High German from about the same time; and of the Irish Finn and Cuchulain sagas, which were composed probably about a century later. The French *chansons de geste*, short epic poems, culminated in *The Song of Roland* in the eleventh century. In all these works, the hero is primarily a masculine hero; he typifies the ideals of his tribe or nation; he performs marvelous feats; he dies in the odor of sanctity. The English and Germans, in particular, carried over their epic traditions into heroic poems about Biblical characters; these survive as the poems of the Caedmonian and Cynewulfian cycles in Anglo-Saxon England and the Low German *Heliand*, from the late eighth and early ninth centuries.

During the eleventh and twelfth centuries— partly as a result of the revival of interest in the fiction of ancient Greece and Rome (typified, let us say, by the works of Ovid); partly as a result of the cult of the Virgin Mary which emerged during the later tenth century; partly as a result of the adventurous spirit which prompted the First Crusade; and partly because the feudal system had developed strength all over Europe—there evolved a type of epic poem in which the hero became a lover as well as a warrior and assumed the duties of a feudal servant to his lady love. From this type, which originated generally in Provence and southern France and spread thence throughout western Europe, grew the so-called medieval romance in all its varieties. Underlying most of these from the first was the concept of chivalry, in which the knight on horseback did valiant deeds for his sovereign lady. Although woman had appeared at times in the older heroic epic, she was now placed on a far higher pedestal than she had hitherto occupied and was looked up to as an ideal inspiration for a knight's greatest feats. Blending themselves with Celtic and general Germanic legendary narrative material, these new

Chivalric love as depicted on a Swiss wool tapestry. The words, translated freely, read: "In our sport will I be true; that indeed ye'll never rue." The tapestry is now in the Art Institute of Chicago.

epic poems, henceforth to be called romances, generated a powerful and pervasive influence over the whole of European literature. Therefore Lancelot loved and served Guinevere, and Tristan must follow Isoude, and Aucassin could think of no other woman but Nicolete. Older epic sagas, such as the famous *Volsungasaga* of Scandinavian origin, were integrated with a chivalric background into the famous *Nibelungenlied* of the thirteenth or fourteenth century. On the other hand, most of the Norse sagas themselves, relatively free from chivalric atmosphere because of their geographical remoteness, were written down about this same time and stand forth as epics in isolated grandeur.

The medieval romances represent the antithesis of the otherworldly literature which emanated from religious sources, because they glorified, in terms which none could fail to understand, the world in which we live, with its hopes and aspirations, its

dreams, its appetites, its disappointments, and its successes. These were love stories which signified an escape from reality, portraying the feudal world (in which most marriages were actually political) as a glamorous place where loving, handsome knights and loving, beautiful ladies lived together in amorous happiness amid infinite riches. To the medieval lady, who now had become an important segment of the audience and reading public, these romances no doubt satisfied a longing for an emotional outlet in real life, regardless of technical marriage ties. The illicit relationships so prominent in these chivalric narratives are doubtless explicable because even state marriages cannot quench love. These courtly, aristocratic romances and the ancillary lyrics following in their wake—the creations of the gifted Chrestien de Troyes or Gottfried von Strasbourg in the narrative poem and of Walther von der Vogelweide in the love lyric—were designed for women

A late medieval statue of the Virgin from Troyes, France.

Isoude were adulterers. Yet the Church was shrewd enough to know that prohibition is a poor way to stop the gratification of a human appetite. Instead, the clergy were encouraged to write their own romances, or to inspire the composition of romances by others, which would convey a moral message while at the same time they conformed to the aristocratic forms and frameworks of the true chivalric romance. And so we come to another type of medieval romance, with moral preachment sometimes couched in highly allegorical or esoteric terms, which produced such masterpieces as the cycle of the Holy Grail (later attached to the Arthurian saga) and the celebrated thirteenth-century French allegorical poem, the *Roman de la Rose*, which taught not only sacred love but a love of nature as well. In fact, the finest single example of a romance in medieval England, *Sir Gawain and the Green Knight*, of about 1370, is distinctly a "moral" rather than a "chivalric" romance. Ultimately, however, these two types of romance, originally quite different in purpose, were blended into a prose type of dissimilar elements—the original romances had been written in verse—and in this prose composition was achieved a compromise between the worldly and the didactic, with the moralistic element tending to predominate. By the fifteenth century, the prose romance was more and more the common form; and the type tended to go to seed in a prolix as well as pedestrian style.

All such fiction, whether secular or relgious, whether for a moral purpose only or for the sake of entertainment and solace alone, was of a type originating among and belonging to the traditions of the feudal aristocracy and the clergy. What of the commoners? Unhappily, as we have seen, they were at this time relatively inarticulate. Enough has come down to us, however, to demonstrate that the ordinary individual in the Middle Ages could be entertained by tales, in verse or in prose, sometimes cruder interpretations of aristocratic romance, sometimes animal stories or beast fables of shrewd satirical import, sometimes flat narratives of the barrack room or the tavern. Among all these secular tales, the short, anecdotal type which was based upon either the sex intrigue or the practical joke, or on both—the so-called *fabliau*—was undoubtedly extremely popular. But so also were the innumerable little stories intended to illustrate some moral teaching—the *exempla*—which embellished virtually every kind of didactic writing and were especially common as teaching devices in the medieval sermons. The general basis for all of these tales of popular origin was their essential realism, often presented with savage satirical intent.

Beginning undoubtedly in the later Middle Ages among the Celtic and Germanic peoples, and to a

as much as for men, and they called to the flesh as freshly and sincerely as does *The Song of Songs*.

The Church, however, did not approve of these romantic and erotic glorifications of human passion, for when all is said and done, it could legitimately insist that Lancelot and Guinevere or Tristan and limited extent also on French soil, were the so-called popular ballads, the true origins of which have never been fully explained. Their development at this time is obscure; nearly all surviving versions date from 1400 or later. It is clear that they come from the common people, but older theories about their actual genesis have now been largely cast aside. It is now generally agreed that they are the creations of village Miltons and rustic Homers; that they are of single authorship; that some employ a technique which suggests that they were originally intended for performance in a folk group, but that others are obviously of a more "literary" flavor. Yet all are primarily narrative, rather than lyric, and all were doubtless intended to be sung. In some there are clear indications not only of choral but also of choreographic elements of some sort. It seems reasonably evident that more than one type of narrative song has been included in this category, yet all are referred to as "ballads." At any rate, whatever their origin, they represent the fictional and epic instincts of the people as a whole rather than of the aristocracy or of the clergy, even though some are religious in subject matter; they are fascinating to the folklorist, but, although some possess an eloquence and a dramatic effectiveness altogether beyond the ordinary, they are to be referred to the backwaters rather than to the main stream of literature.

Also developing in western Europe during the Middle Ages was a native drama. There was a slight carry-over of classical drama through clerical channels during the early centuries of the era, but these surviving imitations of Roman comedy, for example, are isolated and altogether atypical. The most celebrated imitation of the classical is evident in the works of the German nun, Hrostvitha, of the tenth century. We may, however, dismiss the influence of Greece and Rome in this period and concentrate instead on the development of the new drama. Like Greek drama, medieval plays originated in religious observances, but there is no direct continuity from classical days. The theater made a fresh start. Certain dramatic and mimetic interpolations were made in the readings of the scriptures on special Church festivals, such as Christmas and Easter. This first ritualistic stage of medieval drama is usually assigned to the tenth century. It is a hazardous business to state categorically that the miracle or mystery plays grew directly out of the liturgical drama, yet such is most likely the case.

Unfortunately there is a gap of two or three centuries, from the tenth to the thirteenth, which cannot be filled in satisfactorily. It seems probable that the Christmas and Easter representations were followed by representations of other sacred material from the scriptures and that the dramatic business involved became more and more extensive and popular, until the representations themselves overflowed the church, pushed out into the church enclosure, and finally debouched into the market place. At this point in the thirteenth or fourteenth century, the guilds assumed the production of plays devoted to incidents from the Bible—usually to miracles or to the lives of saints. It was found both convenient and desirable to give these plays on feast days when there was good weather; and the presentation of these plays by the guildsmen therefore tended to group them together into cycles. An entire cycle of these miracle plays would then be performed by various guilds in a town on a given holy day; in the fourteenth and fifteenth centuries, the period of our surviving miracle plays, Corpus Christi Day, celebrated in June, became a favorite. The plays, well salted with lusty yeoman's humor, were then staged on floats or pageants, which moved about through the town. The actors were amateurs at first, but we hear of wages eventually paid them. Sooner or later the performances were held at a fixed place, such as the center of the town, perhaps the steps of the local church or cathedral or the courtyard of the local inn; but this is hardly likely to have happened before the fifteenth century.

During the later decades of this fifteenth century there emerged another type of play, in which the characters were abstract personages and in which the central theme was likely to be the struggle between God and the Devil for the possession of a human soul. The origin of these so-called morality plays, however, is most obscure. It seems probable that they arose independently of the miracle plays and that their authors were primarily clerics and teachers rather than laymen. Their messages are often ponderous and platitudinous and only occasionally endowed with the lusty humor of the miracle plays. By 1500, which is approximately the time of the most famous of morality plays, the Dutch *Elckerlijk* (translated into English as *Everyman*), it is evident that the miracle play as a type had died out except in isolated places. The Renaissance was to borrow elements from the moralities, from the slapstick of the older miracle plays, from the still more venerable folk drama (about which we know virtually nothing before 1500 at the earliest), and was to fuse these different elements with humanistic borrowings from classical drama, to achieve from this complex blend a modern European drama which was far advanced beyond anything produced in the dramatic field during the Middle Ages.

Even if the ballads, the tales, and the medieval plays owe their chief vitality to the common people, it still remains basically true that the stewardship over all writing in the Middle Ages, whatever the type might be, lay in the hands of the

"The Morris Dance," an engraving by Israhel van Meckenem, shows that medieval life was not entirely serious.

Church. These hands wrought sermons, homilies, commentaries on the scriptures, interpretations of monastic rule, and religious lyrics—some of which, such as the medieval Latin hymns like the *Te Deum,* the *Dies Irae,* the *Stabat Mater,* and the *Hora Novissima,* are of permanent value.

The scribe was, generally speaking, a cleric, either in a monastery or among the Church's secular clergy; and churchly tradition determined in the main what was to be written and what was to be cast into outer darkness. Furthermore, the survival to the present day of any piece of

medieval writing is a matter of the workings of Fortune. On a liberal estimate, it is probable that we have in our possession today only about one half of what was actually produced during the Middle Ages. From the earlier centuries of this era we doubtless know about much less than half. Was the lost half more worldly than otherwise? Possibly so, for the Church would naturally prefer to save only that which suited its purposes. As it is, the medieval Church has bequeathed to us a truly staggering amount of Christian commentary, monitory literature, precept, proverb, and the like. Some of all this

—that which represents common sense and the wisdom of the ages—may have come also from the people as a whole. But much of it originated in the monastery or the consistory. Little of it has any further appeal today than to the specialist who makes the Middle Ages his particular field of endeavor or to the enthusiast who sees the monastic and scholastic tradition as inherently superior to the modern.

This is all doubtless to be expected. It means in general, however, that the kind of medieval literature most deserving to live in the ages to come, on which we, for better or worse, are most apt to base our estimate of the net achievement of medieval civilization and traditions, is that literature which was produced during the later thirteenth century and the fourteenth century as a whole. Yet, as we have seen, it is the fourteenth century which foreshadows the collapse of the Middle Ages. Here at the beginning of the 1300's stands the great figure of Dante; at the end of the century stands another figure, Chaucer, who is fully as great in a different way. Between these two giants come Boccaccio, Petrarch, Gower, the Piers Plowman Poet, and the Pearl Poet. Shortly thereafter appear the distinguished poet and chronicler Froissart, the romantic vagabond Villon, and the most readable today of the many writers in the tradition of medieval theology, scholasticism, and moral preachment—Thomas à Kempis.

To be sure, if we are to give the medieval Church its proportion just and due, we must still read Anselm and Thomas Aquinas and Bonaventura and Albertus Magnus and Duns Scotus and even Vincent of Beauvais and John of Salisbury. But they are a forbidding and—again except to the enthusiast—a strangely inhuman group of writers. On the other hand, the unknown authors of the Book of Lancelot and the *Conte del Graal;* the romantic and somewhat tedious Guillaume de Lorris and the sardonic Jean de Meun (sometimes known as the medieval

Grimly fortified strongholds testify to the constant feudal wars which endangered medieval life. This is Carcassonne.

CHRISTENDOM, ISLAM, AND THE MIDDLE AGES II:17

A portrait of Chaucer now in the National Portrait Gallery, London. It is probably an early copy from a miniature.

Voltaire), who between them were responsible for the *Roman de la Rose*; and such worldlings as Walter Map and the mysterious "Sir John Mandeville," to say nothing of the remarkable list of first-rate writers mentioned in the preceding paragraph —these are the men to whom we refer all the vital, abiding medieval literature of which we have knowledge. Which of these two groups represents the characteristically medieval?

The answer is, of course, that both groups are representative. Whatever the integration of thought in the Middle Ages—an integration adored in certain quarters today—the fact remains that no truly great period of human history is simple or uncomplicated, and the Middle Ages is no exception. It is equally true that while the theological and the scholastic held sway during the heart of the Middle Ages, still they are the most definitely limited by place and time. The more secular is the more nearly universal.

As an example, when the true medieval teacher, and he who is under his immediate influence, wishes to convey a piece of doctrine, what is the form he prefers? The dialogue, fresh from the center of the scholastic symposium. Perhaps he can secularize the matter into a debate between the body and the soul or between an owl and a nightingale, yet a dialogue it remains—the discussion between master and pupil or the controversy between master and master. Even in the courtly French love poetry the dialogue represents an influence from the teacher in love. But when Petrarch dedicates a new poetic form, the son-net, to his Laura's beauty; when Boccaccio turns over his narrative to the churls Calandrino and Bufal-macco; when Chaucer creates what is fundamentally a modern English novel, *Troilus and Criseyde,* and the first dramatic monologue of extensive self-anal-ysis, the *Prologue to The Wife of Bath's Tale*—then we have reached a stage of sophisticated literature which shows that the Middle Ages, in its last his-torical phases, cannot well be dissociated from the Renaissance.

THE IMPACT OF ISLAM

WE must remember that the terms "Middle Ages" and "medieval" can apply only to the world of western Europe. China, India, Per-sia, and the Moslem world in general would not be concerned with them. China and India were at that time proceeding unperturbed along their highly conservative courses. Persia was undergoing a true renaissance of arts and letters during these same centuries. The contributions of the Mohammedan civilizations to the sciences alone put them far ahead of European medieval culture in an intellectual sense. Indeed, the Near East in this period was an-ticipating the European Renaissance in most of the activities of the human mind. The obvious but sel-dom recognized fact remains that, except in the fields of theology and religious philosophy, medie-val Europe was relatively backward until near the close of the thousand-year era under consideration; and it may well be added that Dante and particu-larly Chaucer—by all odds the greatest writers of the Middle Ages—were as much a part of the Ren-aissance as of the European Middle Ages.

Before our final evaluation of the actual litera-ture of this age, therefore, we must turn our atten-tion eastward. The Byzantine Empire, during the approximately thousand years of its existence, be-came a symbol both of Eastern Christianity * and of high artistic achievements. These achievements were confined to the fine arts, however, for Byzantine literature, as such, was of little worth except in so far as it served as a repository for the great contri-butions of ancient Greece and Rome. The greatest individual among the Eastern emperors, Justinian, left as early as 500 the reputation of a jurist, not of a man of letters.

The great factor in a versatile culture in Eastern lands throughout this era was the Mohammedan religion, whose influence from the seventh to the

fifteenth century was enormous. The teachings of Mohammed were in themselves fundamentally sim-ple. They were first preached among nomadic tribes-men in a bare and austere environment, but they spread like a forest fire over a huge territory, into all walks of life, and eventually came to be centered in a luxurious, opulent capital which gave the great-est possible encouragement to what we choose to call civilized thought. Mohammed (570–632) was him-self a builder of immense energy in the history of religions, and the *Koran* is important solely as a religious document, not as a work of literary art. As time went on, the rigor of Mohammed's teachings was blended with the worldly philosophies of other schools of Oriental thought, and the net resultant of these various forces was a civilization for which teeming, vivid Bagdad became the symbol. It was a world of practical living and idealistic thought, of commerce and trade, of materialism as well as mys-ticism. Haroun al-Raschid, Caliph of Bagdad, and Charlemagne communicated with each other, it is true, but there was little else in common between Moslems and Christians in the year 800. For in knowledge of the world and in knowledge of mankind, to say nothing of intellectual range and elasticity, the Moslem world was far ahead of the Christian world until the dawn of the thirteenth century.

It was not only the kind of work accomplished by Averroës or Avicenna, who in the eleventh and twelfth centuries pushed Arabic science and mathe-matics to the highest peak of development, that ac-counted for the difference between the Moslem and the Christian worlds. The Middle East had never dropped so far below the artistic and intellec-tual standards of Greece and Rome as had the west-ern world of Europe. On the contrary, it was in most respects, though perhaps not consciously, continuing the true classical traditions. Its literary achievement in particular culminated in the work of that re-markable quartet of Persian poets—Firdousi, Omar Khayyam, Sadi, and Hafiz—a group of writers of high

* The long-standing split between the Eastern and Western Churches became official in 1054. Constantinople (Byzantium) was the religious capital of the Eastern Orthodox Church as Rome was of the Western Catholic.

order, who coincide approximately in time with the peak of Moslem scientific contributions. All of these men had passed away before the death of Chaucer in 1400, and in most ways the finest accomplishments of this neo-Persian literature had been completed by the middle of the fourteenth century.

From the time of Mohammed to the time of Haroun al-Raschid is nearly two centuries; and no religious faith, however simple, can remain either simple or unsophisticated for so long a time, especially when it has in the meantime become a world issue. The Bagdad of the days of Haroun al-Raschid was the locale of most of those remarkable narratives, partly satirical, partly erotic, partly adventurous and fantastic, which were ultimately collected and translated into European literature as *The Arabian Nights' Entertainment* or *The Thousand and One Nights*. It is manifestly unjust to think of these superb stories as mere juvenile fare—a fate which has overtaken both them and *Gulliver's Travels*, for example—because in their original and native state they combine the worldliness of Persius and Juvenal with the urbanity of Horace, the clarity of Ovid, and an exotic imagination which is in no way Roman or even Occidental.

After the close of the first Christian millennium the scene shifts from Bagdad to Shiraz. Now the romanticism of *The Arabian Nights* is mingled with the skepticism, the melancholy and world-weariness, and the paradoxical mysticism inspired by the Persian garden, the desert, the sun, moon, and cosmic universe—still romantic in essentials, but touched now with the restless, inquiring spirit of doubt questing after the unknown mystery of life and impregnated with fatalism. Here Omar Khayyam pondered his vision of the lion and the lizard in the ruined courts of Jamshyd, reflected upon the ineluctable moving finger of Time, begged God to forgive him for his carnality and then magnanimously returned that forgiveness, urged a stoical preparation for death, and mused in unforgettable words on how youth must pass forever. In this same kind of setting arose the vast epic by Firdousi, the *Shah Nameh*, the mighty songs of arms and the man—not Achilles, not Aeneas, but Rustum. Here the satirist Sadi, in his *Gulistan*, took his Moslem world for his province, seeing life steadily and as completely as one man can see it. And here Hafiz, the last of the great Shirazists and perhaps the most versatile poet of later Oriental literature, wrote odes to his mistress' eyebrows in precisely the same vein as that made famous centuries later by the courtly French poets of the Renaissance and the gifted singers of Elizabethan England.

Philosophically, the contrast between the Oriental and the Christian points of view at this stage of world history is not necessarily achieved by balancing the work of Omar Khayyam or Sadi against that of Thomas Aquinas, startling as the comparative study of such men will be. In any event, this contrast would have to be supplemented by a juxtaposition of the *Koran* with the New Testament—the naïve, austere, fanatical, yet at the same time sensual teachings of the *Koran* beside the poetic, subtle, withdrawing, yet practical Sermon on the Mount or Pauline Epistles. Compare and contrast, for example, the description of Paradise in the *Koran* with the New Jerusalem in the book of *Revelation*. The essential fact, in any thorough comparative study, will be that in the writings of Omar Khayyam and Hafiz we find a polish, a sense of life in this world, with all its strengths and weaknesses, and a *laissez-faire* attitude toward living which is altogether "modern" and not to be found in European literature until the fourteenth century. The reason for this is not that medieval Europe was essentially more inexperienced or more idealistic than contemporary Islam; it is only that Europe, due to historical circumstances, had developed a different approach, to cope with problems peculiarly its own.

At the same time, the Oriental mind from Haroun al-Raschid to Hafiz was by no means merely materialistic. The Persian writers in particular were powerfully influenced by a special brand of mysticism known as Sufism—a mysticism which, unlike the medieval vision of the New Jerusalem, affords the modern reader a remarkably liberal kind of spiritual experience. Sufism depends upon the character of the believer's mind and is equally at home in all doctrines and dogmas. It assumes that God, the nameless, undefinable core of being, is to be revered above all things, because He alone is worthy of adoration; and everything here below is to be subordinated, even sacrificed if necessary, to attain a recognition of God.

So far this is but little different from the medieval Christian point of view, except that the Christian insisted upon a personal kind of divinity, obviously anthropomorphic. Both points of view are clearly related to the Platonic theory of God as Love. The Persian Sufists, however, could at the same time express themselves in worldly and skeptical thoughts, which was not possible for a medieval Christian; religiously speaking, therefore, they were far more liberal than otherwise. The most that even so emancipated an individual as Chaucer could do, on the other hand, was to commit himself to a mild agnosticism about philosophical or religious matters— "I know not; such I leave to the divines." And this agnosticism would never be applied among medieval Christians to fundamental matters of Christian doctrine, except in the case of radicals like Wycliffe and Huss, who were obviously ahead of their times. The conclusion to be drawn from these comparisons is that the Persian of the year 1000 was able to make his transition to the modern era far more comfortably than his contemporary Christian enemy, who at that time was even fearful of the end of the world. It might well be argued that the Oriental had no transition to make. But, on the other hand, the European Christian was able to advance on seven-league boots after the fourteenth century, whereas Persian literature after the death of Hafiz in 1388 has remained fundamentally unchanged.

Crescent or Cross—until the eighth century it was a burning question which would dominate Europe, for Mohammedanism had penetrated from North Africa far into Spain. Charles Martel, ancestor of Charlemagne, settled this matter, as we can see now, on the fields about Tours in France in the year 732; and so the question as to what would have happened if the Universities of Paris, Bologna, and Oxford had been founded by Moslems remains a purely speculative matter. One must not, therefore, yield to Oriental literature at this stage of history any more than its just deserts, for the Western world has since passed it by.

To be sure, the inevitable impress of the Oriental upon European literature could never be lost, particularly in certain areas. The Crusades began in western Europe about 1100; they started as holy wars to wrest from the Moslems the Holy Sepulchre in Jerusalem, and they achieved a temporary success in the attaining of that immediate objective; but they ended as opportunistic junkets designed to increase the worldly power of Christian princes and the Christian Church. They often produced disillusioning spectacles like the Fourth Crusade of 1204 or the ghastly inhumanity of the fanatical Children's Crusade of 1212. But they brought western Europe into closer contact with the East than ever before; from the hated Saracen the European grudgingly and reluctantly learned much, for the Crusaders brought back with them to Europe fascinating Oriental stories and legends, and some few Europeans, at least, came to realize the importance of Arabic science.

In the meantime, the Orient was preparing a counterattack. The Ottoman Turks debouched upon the eastern extremities of Europe; they captured Constantinople (Byzantium) in 1453; they penetrated to the gates of Vienna as late as the seventeenth century. The Moors remained in Spain until nearly 1500. Interrelations between Crescent and Cross were therefore inevitable, in spite of the bigotry of the Christian and the fanatical intolerance of the Moslem. The plain fact remains, however, that from the later thirteenth century on it is medieval European literature which counts chiefly in the main sum. And after the Middle Ages had passed away, it was still European literature which was fulfilling a dynamic, penetrating role in the history of civilization.

THE MEANING OF THE MIDDLE AGES

I N summary, we see now that the Middle Ages before 800 were, intellectually, comparatively barren everywhere in the European world. It is now out of fashion to refer to these centuries as "The Dark Ages"; and yet if there is any period of recorded history which deserves this epithet, it is still the period between 400 and 800. In the last analysis, we know of little that was contributed to the future during those uncertain years. Of course, if there is any special preëminence to be granted any segment of this early medieval literature, it should go to the Anglo-Saxons in England. During this monastic age, the most typical and withal the best examples of medieval literature are in Latin and therefore international in scope. The Scandinavian Eddic Poems came into being at the very end of this period, as did the continental and English romances, to say nothing of the Welsh and Irish legends; but these are grand examples of fundamentally isolated literature, with some of the virtues that derive from originality and yet with the parochialism that comes from their very isolation.

The significant literature of the later Middle Ages, at least after the year 800, is still in western Europe the work of the great Scholastics and the clerical writings on real and legendary history, as well as on the struggle between the Kingdom of God and the Kingdom of Satan. Near the year 1200 the romances of chivalric nature were flourishing, followed closely in time by the moral antiromances of clerical origins. At the same time there were outpourings of popular tales, generally in oral tradition, the beginnings of drama, the germs of balladry. In all these fields of literature, except for the ballad, France unquestionably assumed leadership; indeed, French influence is clearly the greatest in medieval literature. At this same time, too, came the full tide of Moslem science and belles-lettres.

During the thirteenth century, the massive contributions of Scholastic philosophy and theology, on the side of the otherworldly, were balanced by the continuous and increasing flow of romance material and popular fiction. Significant events, the rise of an industrial middle class, the growth of cities, and the ascendancy of a bourgeoisie, during this century and later, portended the end of the medieval era.

A hunt at the court of Philip the Good, a French painting of the Bourgogne school, fifteenth century.

In the fourteenth century, which witnessed clearly both a decay of the medieval and a promise of the Renaissance, the honors in literature were divided fairly between the Italians and the English; and, indeed, the honors in Renaissance art and literature were to be divided in similar fashion. If Italy produced her Dante and her Petrarch and her Boccaccio, England produced her Chaucer and her Piers Plowman Poet and her Pearl Poet. Chaucer looms more and more, as time goes by, a greater figure than Petrarch or Boccaccio and a formidable rival of Dante and the medieval mystics. Which of the two titans, Chaucer or Dante, by our twentieth-century standards is the more characteristically medieval? Probably Dante. Which is the greater poet as poet? Again, probably Dante. Which is the more comprehensive interpreter of humanity and critic of life? Unquestionably Chaucer. At this point we may leave the medievalists to wrangle among themselves.

As for the fifteenth century, which is already the time of the Renaissance in Italy, there can be little dispute. England went into a temporary eclipse; France, Spain, and Germany were not yet ready for this profound experience in the history of human civilization. But it was the century when Villon, Erasmus, Machiavelli, Ariosto, Rabelais, Cellini, Michelangelo, Raphael, and Leonardo da Vinci— to say nothing of Columbus and Copernicus—were born and bred, and the European mind at this time was entering one of the most brilliant periods in its development.

There is a certain tendency for some thinkers in our twentieth century to turn to the Middle Ages with something approaching veneration, as if this thousand-year period would be a desirable era to imitate. To some extent this feeling is the instinct of the latter-day orthodox Christian, standing embattled against new, urgent forces in the twentieth century which threaten the integrity of the Christian pattern. To others not thus religiously inclined, there remains still the fascination exerted by a unified program of living which the Middle Ages may seem to hold out. To such as these it will appear that no effective kind of civilization can exist without a culture, that this culture must depend upon a pattern, that a pattern necessarily assumes a hierarchy, and that the Middle Ages furnished a hierarchy in both Church and State. The fallacy in such reasoning lies in the assumption that a workable pattern must necessarily include a hierarchy. But more misguided than such an assumption is the hope that a return to the medieval way of life is either possible or profitable. The hands of the clock can never be turned back, and no self-respecting modernist could possibly be content in the Middle Ages, which was, after all, merely a transitional stage in the history of the world. The Middle Ages, to be candid, was an era of much ignorance, intolerance, and unquestioning acceptance of authority; no looking through rose-colored glasses, no plea for unity, no mystic communion with the saints and a personal divinity can alter those inescapable facts. If some deplore the coming of the Reformation and the releasing of powerful intellectual forces difficult to control, then they are a thousand years behind the times, or else they are gazing in wistful nostalgia at a bygone age which it would be impracticable and obstructive to renew; the Middle Ages died once and for all when Martin Luther nailed on the door of the church his theses and when it was finally realized that the world is too much with us, no matter how much we may prefer simple thinking and simple doing. A vast distance separates the Middle Ages from the Atomic Age.

The Koran

The *Koran* is the sacred book of Islam. It is a prose work in Arabic—the first important body of Arabic prose—consisting of one hundred and fourteen chapters, or *suras,* of varying length. Mohammedans accept it as the word of Allah or God, who established it in Heaven, where it is preserved in perfect, immortal form, and revealed it to his greatest prophet, Mohammed. Objective criticism insists that it was composed largely by Mohammed, who, though probably unable to read or write, had the undoubted talents of a brilliant prophet, as well as an oral knowledge of the Pentateuch and the Psalms from the Hebrew Old Testament, the New Testament, and other Oriental religious works, particularly those of the Persian Magians. It is therefore to be presumed that the *Koran* came into being during the active years of Mohammed as prophet, or between 610 and 632.

The *suras* of the *Koran* were very likely first written down in isolated pieces by Mohammed's scribe or scribes. Shortly after the death of the prophet in 632, a collection was undertaken by Zaid ibn Tabit, secretary to Mohammed—or so it is believed—under the guidance of Abu Bekr, Mohammed's father-in-law. To remove all possible dispute about sources and originals, the Caliph Othman in 650 sanctioned an authorized version. All previous copies of the *Koran* were then destroyed, and so the book as we have it in Othman's version is a remarkable example of a great religious source of authority which has remained intact to the present day.

Although it is a work in formal prose, the *Koran* in many of its *suras* has an unusually strong emotional and lyrical spirit, which is further enhanced by the frequent use of rhyme effects and refrains. The chronological order of the one hundred and fourteen *suras,* however, has never been satisfactorily determined. The speaker in virtually all of them is God. The tone of all is strikingly dogmatic and absolute. But in the varying degrees of this dogmatic quality some have seen a clue to the date of the composition of a given *sura*—the more assured and intolerant the tone, the greater the likelihood that the *sura* was written at Medina rather than at Mecca (that is, after 622, when Mohammed was established as the leader of a powerful political party). The whole matter is, of course, still open to liberal conjecture.

The *Koran* is, in any event, the great book of authority for the morals, laws, theological doctrines, and social ethics of the Moslem world. It is given more than is usual in such works to a consideration of the life to come. It is austere, unyielding, passionate as well as noble, fierce and cruel as well as sympathetic. From first to last it preaches the Unity and Soleness of the Most High, the Most Merciful and Most Compassionate God, Allah; to serve him and to die for him are the greatest of privileges, to neglect him and to disregard his commandments

are the unforgivable sins. The imagery of the *Koran* is the imagery of the desert, of the lonely places of body and soul, of the unsophisticated pastoral and rural scene rather than of the crowded bazaar and teeming Oriental city streets. It entertains the promise of an idyllic sensual existence for the Faithful after the great Day of Judgment. By its words billions have lived and died.

The Koran

CHAPTER 47. *In the Name of the Most Merciful God*

GOD will render of none effect the works of those who believe not, and who turn away men from the way of God: but as to those who believe, and work righteousness, and believe the revelation which hath been sent down unto Mohammed (for it is the truth from their Lord), he will expiate their evil deeds from them, and will dispose their heart aright. This will he do, because those who believe not follow vanity, and because those who believe follow the truth from their Lord. Thus God [10] propoundeth unto men their examples. When ye encounter the unbelievers, strike off their heads, until ye have made a great slaughter among them; and bind them in bonds; and either give them a free dismission afterwards, or exact a ransom; until the war shall have laid down its arms. This shall ye do. Verily if God pleased he could take vengeance on them, without your assistance; but he commandeth you to fight his battles, that he may prove the one of you by the other. And as to those who fight in [20] defence of God's true religion, God will not suffer their works to perish; he will guide them, and will dispose their heart aright; and he will lead them into paradise, of which he hath told them.

O true believers, if ye assist God, by fighting for his religion, he will assist you against your enemies; and will set your feet fast: but as for the infidels, let them perish; and their works shall God render vain. This shall befall them, because they have rejected with abhorrence that which God hath revealed, [30] wherefore their works shall become of no avail. Do they not travel through the earth, and see what hath been the end of those who were before them? God utterly destroyed them, and the like awaiteth the unbelievers. This shall come to pass, for that God is the patron of the true believers, and for that the infidels have no protector. Verily God will introduce those who believe, and do good works, into gardens beneath which rivers flow; but the unbelievers indulge themselves in pleasures, and eat as the beasts

The Koran. [s] Translated by George Sale.
39–40. indulge . . . eat. Unbelievers, intoxicated with purely animal pleasures, will live in a merely animal state; the believers, whatever their physical pleasures, will have a spiritual euphoria as well.

eat, and their abode shall be hell fire. How many cities were more mighty in strength than thy city which hath expelled thee; yet have we destroyed them, and there was none to help them? Shall he therefore, who followeth the plain declaration of his Lord, be as he whose evil works have been dressed up for him by the devil, and who follow their own lusts? The description of paradise, which is promised unto the pious: therein are rivers of in-
10 corruptible water, and rivers of milk, the taste whereof changeth not, and rivers of wine, pleasant unto those who drink, and rivers of clarified honey, and therein shall they have plenty of all kinds of fruits, and pardon from their Lord. Shall the man for whom these things are prepared be as he who must dwell forever in hell fire; and will have the boiling water given him to drink, which shall burst his bowels? Of the unbelievers there are some who give ear unto thee, until, when they go out from
20 thee, they say, by way of derision unto those to whom knowledge hath been given, "What hath he said now?" These are they whose hearts God hath sealed up, and who follow their own lusts; but as to those who are directed, God will grant them a more ample direction, and he will instruct them what to avoid. Do the infidels wait for any other than the last hour, that it may come upon them suddenly? Some signs thereof are already come: and when it shall actually overtake them, how can they then re-
30 ceive admonition? Know therefore, that there is no god but God: and ask pardon for thy sin, and for the true believers, both men and women. God knoweth your busy employment in the world, and the place of your abode hereafter. . . .

CHAPTER 55. *In the Name of the Most Merciful God*

The Merciful hath taught his servant the Koran. He created man; he hath taught him distinct speech. The sun and the moon run their courses according to a certain rule, and the vegetables which creep on the ground, and the trees submit to his disposi-
40 tion. He also raised the heaven, and he appointed the balance, that ye should not transgress in respect to the balance: wherefore observe a just weight, and diminish not the balance. And the earth hath he prepared for living creatures: therein are various fruits, and palm-trees bearing sheaths of flowers, and grain having chaff, and leaves. Which, therefore,

of your Lord's benefits will you ungratefully deny? He created man of dried clay like an earthen vessel, but he created the genii of fire clear from smoke. Which, therefore, of your Lord's benefits will you 50 ungratefully deny? He is Lord of the east and the Lord of the west. Which, therefore of your Lord's benefits will you ungratefully deny? He hath let loose the two seas, that they meet each another; between them is placed a bar which they cannot pass. Which, therefore, of your Lord's benefits will you ungratefully deny? From them are taken forth unions and lesser pearls. Which, therefore, of your Lord's benefits will you ungratefully deny? His also are the ships, carrying their sails aloft in the sea 60 like mountains. Which, therefore, of your Lord's benefits will you ungratefully deny?

Every creature which liveth on the earth is subject to decay; but the glorious and honorable countenance of thy Lord shall remain forever. Which, therefore, of your Lord's benefits will you ungratefully deny? Unto him do all creatures which are in heaven and earth make petition; every day is he employed in some new work. Which, therefore, of your Lord's benefits will you ungratefully deny? We will 70 surely attend to judge you, O men and genii, at the last day. Which, therefore, of your Lord's benefits will you ungratefully deny? O ye collective body of genii and men, if ye be able to pass out of the confines of heaven and earth, pass forth; you shall not pass forth but by absolute power. Which, therefore, of your Lord's benefits will you ungratefully deny? A flame of fire without smoke, and a smoke without flame shall be sent down upon you, and you shall not be able to defend yourselves therefrom. Which, 80 therefore, of your Lord's benefits will you ungratefully deny? And when the heaven shall be rent in sunder, and shall become red as a rose, and shall melt like ointment, which, therefore, of your Lord's benefits will you ungratefully deny? On that day neither man nor genii shall be asked concerning his sin. Which, therefore, of your Lord's benefits will you ungratefully deny? The wicked shall be known by their marks, and they shall be taken by the forelocks and the feet and shall be cast into hell. Which, therefore, 90 of your Lord's benefits will you ungratefully deny? This is hell, which the wicked deny as a falsehood; they shall pass to and fro between the same and hot boiling water. Which, therefore, of your Lord's benefits will you ungratefully deny? But for him who

---

28. **Some signs . . . come.** These include particularly the splitting in two of the moon, a grievous pestilence, and a peculiar smoke which will cover both the heavens and the earth. 31. **pardon . . . sin.** "Though Mohammed here and elsewhere acknowledges himself to be a sinner, yet several Mohammedan doctors pretend he was wholly free from sin, and suppose he is here commanded to ask forgiveness, not that he wanted it, but that he might set an example to his followers . . ." (Translator's note). 41. **balance,** justice and equity in dealings among human beings.

46–47. **Which . . . deny?** This refrain is addressed to men and *genii;* that is, to human and supernatural beings. 54. **two seas,** the Persian Gulf and the Mediterranean. 68–69. **every . . . work.** "In executing those things which he hath decreed from eternity, by giving life and death, raising one and abasing another, hearing prayers and granting petitions, etc." (Translator's note). 78–79. **smoke without flame;** possibly this signifies molten brass, which will be poured over the heads of the sinful. 85–86. **On that day . . . sin.** They will not be asked because their sins will be known by different marks stamped upon their bodies.

dreadeth the tribunal of his Lord are prepared two gardens (which, therefore, of your Lord's benefits will you ungratefully deny?) planted with shady trees. Which, therefore, of your Lord's benefits will you ungratefully deny? In each of them shall be two fountains flowing. Which, therefore, of your Lord's benefits will you ungratefully deny? In each of them shall there be of every fruit two kinds. Which, therefore, of your Lord's benefits will you ungratefully
10 deny? They shall repose on couches, the linings whereof shall be of thick silk interwoven with gold; and the fruit of the two gardens shall be near at hand to gather. Which, therefore, of your Lord's benefits will you ungratefully deny? Therein shall receive them beauteous damsels, refraining their eyes from beholding any besides their spouses, whom no man shall have deflowered before them, neither any genii (which, therefore, of your Lord's benefits will you ungratefully deny?) having com-
20 plexions like rubies and pearls. Which, therefore, of your Lord's benefits will you ungratefully deny? Shall the reward of good works be any other good? Which, therefore, of your Lord's benefits will you ungratefully deny? And besides these there shall be two other gardens (which, therefore, of your Lord's benefits will you ungratefully deny?) of a dark green. Which, therefore, of your Lord's benefits will you ungratefully deny? In each of them shall be two fountains pouring forth plenty of water. Which,
30 therefore, of your Lord's benefits will you ungratefully deny? In each of them shall be fruits, and palm-trees, and pomegranates. Which, therefore, of your Lord's benefits will you ungratefully deny? Therein shall be agreeable and beauteous damsels (which, therefore, of your Lord's benefits will you ungratefully deny?), having fine black eyes and kept in pavilions from public view (which, therefore, of your Lord's benefits will you ungratefully deny?) whom no man shall have deflowered before their
40 destined spouses, nor any genii. Which, therefore, of your Lord's benefits will you ungratefully deny? Therein shall they delight themselves, lying on green cushions and beautiful carpets. Which, therefore, of your Lord's benefits will you ungratefully deny? Blessed be the name of thy Lord, possessed of glory and honor!

CHAPTER 56. *In the Name of the Most Merciful God*

When the inevitable day of judgment shall suddenly come, no soul shall charge the prediction of

An Arabic miniature showing Mohammed besieging a fortress, from a fourteenth-century universal history now in London.

its coming with falsehood; it will abase some, and exalt others. When the earth shall be shaken with a 50 violent shock, and the mountains shall be dashed in pieces, and shall become as dust scattered abroad, then shall ye be separated into three classes: the companions of the right hand (how happy shall the companions of the right hand be!), and the companions of the left hand (how miserable shall the companions of the left hand be!), and those who have preceded others in the faith shall precede them to paradise. These are they who shall approach near unto God; they shall dwell in gardens of delight, 60 reposing on couches adorned with gold and precious stones, sitting opposite to one another thereon. Youths who shall continue in their bloom forever shall go round about to attend them, with goblets and beakers and a cup of flowing wine; their heads shall not ache by drinking the same, neither shall their reason be disturbed; and with fruits of the sorts which they shall choose, and the flesh of birds of the kind which they shall desire. And there shall accompany them fair damsels having large black eyes, 70 resembling pearls hidden in their shells, as a reward for that which they shall have wrought. They shall not hear therein any vain discourse, or any charge of sin, but only the salutation, "Peace! Peace!" And the companions of the right hand (how happy shall the companions of the right hand be!) shall have their abode among lotus-trees free from thorns, and trees of mauz loaded regularly with their fruits from top to bottom, under an extended shade, near a flowing water, and amidst fruits in abundance, which 80 shall not fail, nor shall be forbidden to be gathered; and they shall repose themselves and enjoy damsels upon lofty couches. Verily we have created the damsels of paradise by a special creation, and we have

---

1–2. **two gardens.** The duality here and below is explained by the fact that one set of benefits will be decreed for men and another for *genii.* 47. **inevitable.** "The original word, the force whereof cannot well be expressed by a single one in English, signifies a calamitous accident, which falls surely, and with sudden violence; and is therefore made use of here to designate the Day of Judgment" (Translator's note).

55–56. **right hand . . . left hand.** Compare Matthew, 25:33 ff. The *Koran* often acknowledges Moses and David as the authors of the Pentateuch and the Psalms, but makes no such acknowledgment of material to be found in the New Testament. Yet there is ample reason to believe that Mohammed was acquainted with the teachings of Jesus. 57–59. **those who . . . paradise,** possibly the first converts to Mohammedanism, or the prophets, or persons who were spiritual leaders through piety. 78. **trees of mauz,** acacia-trees. 84. **special creation,** created of finer materials than the females of the earth, and subject to none of those inconveniences natural to the sex.

made them virgins, beloved by their husbands, of equal age with them, for the delight of the companions of the right hand. And the companions of the left hand (how miserable shall the companions of the left hand be!) shall dwell amidst burning winds and scalding water, under the shade of a black smoke, neither cool nor agreeable. For they enjoyed the pleasures of life before this, while on earth, and obstinately persisted in a heinous wickedness; and they said, "After we shall have died, and become dust and bones, shall we surely be raised to life? Shall our forefathers also be raised with us?" Say, "Verily both the first and the last shall surely be gathered together to judgment, at the predestined time of a known day. Then ye, O men, who have erred and denied the resurrection as a falsehood, shall surely eat of the fruit of the tree of al Zakkum, and shall fill your bellies therewith; and ye shall drink thereon boiling water, and ye shall drink as a thirsty camel drinketh. This shall be their entertainment on the Day of Judgment.

We have created you; will you not therefore believe that we can raise you from the dead? What think you? The seed which you emit, do you create the same, or are we the creators thereof? We have decreed death unto you all, and we shall not be prevented. We are able to substitute others like unto you in your stead and to produce you again in the condition and form which you know not. You know the original birth by creation; will you not therefore consider that we are able to produce you by resuscitation? What think you? The grain which you sow, do you cause the same to spring forth, or do we cause it to spring forth? If we pleased, verily we could render the same dry and fruitless, so that you would not cease to wonder, saying, "Verily we have contracted debts for seed and labor, but we are not permitted to reap the fruit thereof." What think you? The water which you drink, do you send down the same from the clouds, or are we the senders thereof? If we pleased, we could render the same brackish; will you not therefore give thanks? What think you? The fire which you strike, do you produce the tree whence you obtain the same, or are we the producers thereof? We have ordained the same for an admonition, and an advantage to those who travel through the deserts.

Wherefore praise the name of thy Lord, the great God. Moreover I swear by the setting of the stars (and it is surely a great oath, if you knew it) that this is the excellent Koran, the original whereof is written in the preserved book; none shall touch the same, except those who are clean. It is a revelation from the Lord of all creatures. Will you, therefore, despise this new revelation? And do you make this return for your food which you receive from God, that you deny yourselves to be obliged to him for the same? When the soul of a dying person cometh up to his throat, and you at the same time are looking on (and we are nigher unto him than you, but you see not his true condition), would you not, if you are to be rewarded for your actions hereafter, cause the same to return into the body, if you speak the truth? And whether he be of those who shall approach near unto God, his reward shall be rest and mercy and a garden of delights; or whether he be of the companions of the right hand, he shall be saluted with the salutation, "Peace be unto thee!" by the companions of the right hand, his brethren; or whether he be of those who have rejected the true faith, and gone astray, his entertainment shall consist of boiling water, and the burning of hell fire. Verily this is a certain truth. Wherefore praise the name of thy Lord, the great God.

The Arabian Nights

The huge collection of Oriental tales known in English as *The Arabian Nights' Entertainment,* or *The Thousand and One Nights,* has probably been in existence since at least the tenth century, but its actual origins are obscure. There is good reason to believe that it came into being among the Persians rather than among the Arabs, but, for that matter, much of its material can be referred to the folklore of ancient India. It is clear, however, that in its present form it belongs to the Moslem world, even if the Mohammedans themselves have never regarded the collection as constituting, on the whole, polite literature.

The Arabian Nights was first introduced to Europe through the French translation (1704–1717) by Antoine Galland and was an enormous success from the beginning. This version was translated into other European languages, including the English; but the best-known modern English versions are derived from a compilation found in Egypt in the later eighteenth century. It should be insisted that there is no authoritative text of this collection, only a kind of well-established tradition. Obviously nothing can be discovered about the authors of the many tales, who must have been legion. Several tales of precisely the same nature as those found in the traditional collection, such as the famous stories of "Aladdin and His Lamp" or of "Ali Baba and the Forty Thieves,"

---

1. **virgins,** perpetual virgins, no matter how much they may have to do with men. 17. **tree . . . Zakkum,** possibly the sycamore. 45–46. **admonition,** to put men in mind of the resurrection.

61–64. **would you not . . . truth?** This passage is obscure; one reasonable explanation would be that it means, "If you are not obliged to give an account of your actions on the Day of Judgment, as you seem to believe by denying the resurrection—you could as easily put the soul back into a dying man as avoid judgment." 64–65. **of those . . . God,** a leader or one of the first to profess the faith.

do not appear in either Galland's collection or the Egyptian version from which the modern English translations have been made. Such omissions, however, merely confirm the theory that *The Arabian Nights* is but a portion of the virtually limitless field of Oriental fiction.

This great collection comprises direct, fast-moving narratives of the greatest variety, clearly drawn from many different levels of society. Some are adventurous and fabulous (such as the most famous of them all, the tales of Sindbad the Sailor), some are supernatural, some are bawdy, some are romantic in a chivalric and aristocratic vein, some are trenchantly satirical. Quite apart from their intrinsic value as narratives, however, these tales serve as remarkable mirrors of the life of Islam during the past thousand years. The earthiness, the sensuality, and the sights and smells of the Orient must always be assumed here, no matter how much they may have been filtered out in polite modern English translations. All in all, they constitute the most celebrated single collection of popular fiction in the history of literature.

As is the case with many other similar collections, *The Arabian Nights* is integrated by means of the so-called "framework" device—that is, there exists a central story which is the frame on which the many canvases are stretched. Here the framework narrative has to do with a certain Sultan Shahriar, who caught his wife in adultery and killed her. In further revenge on womankind, he adopted the rather wasteful procedure of marrying a woman each night and then executing her the following morning. His realm was rapidly being depleted of marriageable females until the Princess Sheherezade, daughter of the Sultan's Grand Vizier, became his wife and entertained him on their wedding night with a marvelous narrative. So artfully did she contrive to have dawn interrupt her story at its most interesting stage that Shahriar postponed her execution for the moment to discover the end of the tale. Having finished one in daylight, she proceeded without a break to another and after a thousand and one nights, the Sultan abandoned his sanguinary program altogether, and he and Sheherezade remained married happily until the intervention of "the Separator of Friends and the Terminator of Delights."

The Arabian Nights

SINDBAD THE SEAMAN
AND SINDBAD THE LANDSMAN

THERE lived in the city of Baghdad, during the reign of the Commander of the Faithful Haroun Al-Rashid, a man named Sindbad the Hammal, one in poor case who bore burdens on his head for hire. It happened to him one day of great heat that whilst he was carrying a heavy load, he became ex-

The Arabian Nights.[8] Translated by William Lane.
2–3. **Haroun Al-Rashid,** Caliph of Bagdad from 786 to 809.
3. **Hammal,** a porter.

ceeding weary and sweated profusely, the heat and the weight alike oppressing him. Presently, as he was passing the gate of a merchant's house, before which the ground was swept and watered and there the air was temperate, he sighted a broad bench beside the door; so he set his load thereon, to take rest and smell the air,—And Sheherezade was surprised by the dawn of day and ceased saying her permitted say.

NOW WHEN IT WAS THE FIVE HUNDRED AND
THIRTY-SEVENTH NIGHT,

She said, It hath reached me, O auspicious King, that when the Hammal set his load upon the bench to take rest and smell the air, there came out upon him from the court-door a pleasant breeze and a delicious fragrance. He sat down on the edge of the bench, and at once heard from within the melodious sound of lutes and other stringed instruments, and mirth-exciting voices singing and reciting, together with the song of birds warbling and glorifying Almighty Allah in various tunes and tongues; turtles, mocking-birds, merles, nightingales, cushats, and stone-curlews, whereat he marvelled in himself and was moved to mighty joy and solace. Then he went up to the gate and saw therein a great flower-garden wherein were pages and black slaves and such a train of servants and attendants and so forth as is found only with Kings and Sultans; and his nostrils were greeted with the savory odors of all manner meats rich and delicate, and delicious and generous wines. So he raised his eyes heavenwards and said, "Glory to Thee, O Lord, O Creator and Provider, who providest whomever Thou wilt without count or stint! O mine Holy One, I cry Thee pardon for all sins and turn to Thee repenting of all offences! O Lord, there is no gainsaying Thee in Thine ordinance and Thy dominion, neither wilt Thou be questioned of that Thou dost, for Thou indeed over all things art Almighty! Extolled be Thy perfection; whom Thou willest Thou makest poor and whom Thou willest Thou makest rich! Whom Thou willest Thou exaltest and whom Thou willest Thou abasest and there is no god but Thee! How mighty is Thy majesty and how enduring Thy dominion and how excellent Thy government! Verily, Thou favorest whom Thou willest of Thy servants, whereby the owner of this place abideth in all joyance of life and delighteth himself with pleasant scents and delicious meats and exquisite wines of all kinds. For indeed Thou appointest unto Thy creatures that which Thou willest and that which Thou hast foreordained unto them; wherefore are some weary and others are at rest and some enjoy fair fortune and affluence, whilst others suffer the extreme of travail and misery, even as I do." And he fell to reciting:

The luxurious interior of an Arabic palace; the harem.

How many by my labors, that evermore endure—
  All goods of life enjoy and in cooly shade recline?
Each morn that dawns I wake in travail and in woe
  —And strange is my condition and my burden
    gars me pine;
Many others are in luck and from miseries are free—
  And Fortune never loads them with loads the
    like o' mine;
They live their happy days in all solace and delight
10   —Eat, drink and dwell in honor 'mid the noble
    and the digne;
All living things were made of a little pinch of dust
  —Thine origin is mine and my provenance is
    Thine;
Yet the difference and the distance 'twixt the twain
  of us are far—As the difference of savor 'twixt
    vinegar and wine;
But at Thee, O God All-wise! I venture not to rail—
  Whose ordinance is just and whose justice cannot
20   fail.

When Sindbad the Porter had made an end of reciting his verses, he took up his burden and was

about to trudge onwards, when there came forth to
him from the gate a little foot-page, fair of face and
shapely of shape and dainty of dress who caught
him by the hand, saying, "Come in and speak with
my lord, for he calleth for thee." The Porter would
have excused himself to the page but the lad would
take no refusal; so he left his load with the door-
keeper in the vestibule, and followed the boy into 30
the house, which he found to be a goodly mansion,
radiant and full of majesty, till he brought him to a
grand sitting-room wherein he saw a company of
nobles and great lords, seated at tables garnished
with all manner of flowers and sweet-scented herbs,
besides great plenty of dainty viands and fruits dried
and fresh and confections and wines of the choicest
vintages. There were also instruments of music and
mirth and lovely slave-girls playing and singing.
All the company was ranged according to rank; and 40
in the highest place sat a man of worshipful and
noble aspect whose beard-sides hoariness had
stricken; and he was stately of stature and fair of
favor, agreeable of aspect and full of gravity and
dignity and majesty. So Sindbad the Porter was
confounded at that which he beheld and said in
himself, "By Allah, this must be either a piece of
Paradise or some King's palace!" Then he saluted
the company with much respect, praying for their
prosperity; and, kissing the ground before them, 50
stood with his head bowed down in humble attitude.
—And Sheherezade perceived the dawn of day and
ceased to say her permitted say.

Now when it was the five hundred and
    thirty-eighth night,

She said, It hath reached me, O auspicious King,
that Sindbad the Porter, after kissing ground between their hands, stood with his head bowed down
in humble attitude. The master of the house bade
him draw near and be seated and bespoke him 60
kindly, bidding him welcome. Then he set before
him various kinds of viands, rich and delicate and
delicious, and the Porter, after saying his Bismillah,
fell to and ate his fill, after which he exclaimed,
"Praised be Allah whatever be our case!" and, washing his hands, returned thanks to the company for
his entertainment. Quoth the host, "Thou art welcome and thy day is a blessed. But what is thy name
and calling?" Quoth the other, "O my lord, my name
is Sindbad the Hammal, and I carry folk's goods on 70
my head for hire." The house-master smiled and
rejoined, "Know, O Porter, that thy name is even
as mine, for I am Sindbad the Seaman; and now, O
Porter, I would have thee let me hear the couplets
thou recitedest at the gate anon." The Porter was
abashed and replied, "Allah upon thee! Excuse me,
65. "**Praised . . . case!**" This formula was supposed to avert the
evil eye.

for toil and travail and lack of luck when the hand is empty teach a man ill manners and boorish ways." Said the host, "Be not ashamed; thou art become my brother; but repeat to me the verses, for they pleased me whenas I heard thee recite them at the gate." Hereupon the Porter repeated the couplets and they delighted the merchant, who said to him: "Know, O Hammal, that my story is a wonderful one, and thou shalt hear all that befell me and all I underwent ere I rose to this state of prosperity and became the lord of this place wherein thou seest me; for I came not to this high estate save after travails sore and perils galore, and how much toil and trouble have I not suffered in days of yore! I have made seven voyages, by each of which hangeth a marvellous tale, such as confoundeth the reason, and all this came to pass by doom of fortune and fate; for from what destiny doth write there is neither refuge nor flight. "Know, then, good my lords," continued he, "that I am about to relate

THE FIRST VOYAGE
OF SINDBAD HIGHT THE SEAMAN

My father was a merchant, one of the notables of my native place, a monied man and ample of means, who died whilst I was yet a child, leaving me much wealth in money and lands and farmhouses. When I grew up, I laid hands on the whole and ate of the best and drank freely and wore rich clothes and lived lavishly, companioning and consorting with youths of my own age, and considering that this course of life would continue forever and know no change. Thus did I for a long time, but at last I awoke from my heedlessness and, returning to my senses, I found my wealth had become unwealth and my condition ill-conditioned and all I once held had left my hand. And recovering my reason I was stricken with dismay and confusion and bethought me of a saying of our lord Solomon, son of David (on whom be peace!), which I had heard aforetime from my father, "Three things are better than other three: the day of death is better than the day of birth, a live dog is better than a dead lion, and the grave is better than want." Then I got together my remains of estates and property and sold all, even my clothes, for three thousand dirhams, with which I resolved to travel to foreign parts, remembering the saying of the poet:

By means of toil man shall scale the height—Who
    to fame aspires must not sleep of nights;
Who seeketh pearls in the deep must dive—Winning
    weal and wealth by his main and might;
And who seeketh Fame without toil and strife—Th'
    impossible seeketh and wasteth life.

So taking heart I bought me goods, merchandise and all needed for a voyage and, impatient to be at sea, I embarked, with a company of merchants, on board a ship bound for Bassorah. There we again embarked and sailed many days and nights, and we passed from isle to isle and sea to sea and shore to shore, buying and selling and bartering everywhere the ship touched, and continued our course till we came to an island as it were a garth of the gardens of Paradise. Here the captain cast anchor and making fast to the shore put out the landing planks. So all on board landed and made furnaces, and lighting fires therein, busied themselves in various ways, some cooking and some washing, whilst some others walked about the island for solace, and the crew fell to eating and drinking and playing and sporting. I was one of the walkers but, as we were thus engaged, behold the master who was standing on the gunwale cried out to us at the top of his voice, saying, "Ho there! passengers, run for your lives and hasten back to the ship and leave your gear and save yourselves from destruction, Allah preserve you! For this island whereon you stand is no true island, but a great fish stationary a-middlemost of the sea, whereon the sand hath settled and trees have sprung up of old time, so that it is become like unto an island; but, when ye lighted fires on it, it felt the heat and moved; and in a moment it will sink with you into the sea and ye will all be drowned. So leave your gear and seek your safety ere ye die!"—And Sheherezade was surprised by the dawn of day and ceased saying her permitted say.

Now WHEN IT WAS THE FIVE HUNDRED AND THIRTY-NINTH NIGHT,

She said, It hath reached me, O auspicious King, that when the ship-master cried to the passengers, "Leave your gear and seek safety, ere you die," all who heard him left gear and goods, clothes washed and unwashed, fire pots and brass cooking-pots, and fled back to the ship for their lives, and some reached it while others (amongst whom was I) did not, for suddenly the island shook and sank into the abysses of the deep, with all that were thereon, and the dashing sea surged over it with climbing waves. I sank with the others down, down into the deep, but Almighty Allah preserved me from drowning and threw in my way a great wooden tub of those that had served the ship's company for tubbing. I gripped it for the sweetness of life and bestriding it like one riding, paddled with my feet like oars, whilst the waves tossed me as in sport right and left. Mean-

39–42. **"Three . . . want."** Compare wording of Ecclesiastes, 7:1 and 9:4.

64. **furnaces,** more properly braziers, pots full of charcoal sunk in the ground, or a little hearth of clay shaped like a horseshoe and opening down wind (Editor's note). 75–76. **For this island . . . fish stationary.** Popular lore is full of examples of great fishes or whales mistaken for islands, on which the luckless seafarers may land to their own destruction.

while the captain made sail and departed with those who had reached the ship, regardless of the drowning and the drowned; and I ceased not following the vessel with my eyes, till she was hid from sight and I made sure of death. Darkness closed in upon me while in this plight and the winds and waves bore me on all that night and the next day, till the tub brought to with me under the lee of a lofty island, with trees overhanging the tide. I caught hold of a branch and by its aid clambered up on to the land, after coming nigh upon death; but when I reached the shore, I found my legs cramped and numbed and my feet bore traces of the nibbling of fish upon their soles; though I had felt nothing for excess of anguish and fatigue. I threw myself down on the island-ground, like a dead man, and drowned in desolation swooned away, nor did I return to my senses till next morning, when the sun rose and revived me. But I found my feet swollen, so made shift to move by shuffling and crawling on my hands and knees, for in that island were found store of fruits and springs of sweet water. I ate of the fruits which strengthened me; and thus I abode days and nights, till my life seemed to return and my spirits began to revive and I was better able to move about. So, after due consideration, I fell to exploring the island and diverting myself with gazing upon all things that Allah Almighty had created there; and rested under the trees from which I cut me a staff to lean upon. One day as I walked along the shore, I caught sight of some object in the distance and thought it a wild beast or one of the monster-creatures of the sea; but, as I drew near it, looking hard the while, I saw that it was a noble mare, tethered on the beach. Presently I went up to her, but she cried out against me with a great cry, so that I trembled for fear and turned to go away, when there came forth a man from under the earth and followed me, crying out and saying, "Who and whence art thou, and what caused thee to come hither?" "O my lord," answered I, "I am in very sooth, a waif, a stranger, and was left to drown with sundry others by the ship we voyaged in; but Allah graciously sent me a wooden tub; so I saved myself thereon and it floated with me, till the waves cast me up on this island." When he heard this, he took my hand and saying, "Come with me," carried me into a great Sardab, or underground chamber, which was spacious as a saloon. He made me sit down at its upper end; then he brought me somewhat of food and, being hungered, I ate till I was satisfied and refreshed; and when he had put me at mine ease he questioned me of myself, and I told him all that had befallen me from first to last; and, as he wondered at my adventure, I

said, "By Allah, O my lord, excuse me; I have told me the truth of my case and the accident which betided me; and now I desire that thou tellest me who thou art and why thou abidest here under the earth and why thou hast tethered yonder mare on the brink of the sea." Answered he, "Know that I am one of the several who are stationed in different parts of this island, and we are of the grooms of King Mihrjan and under our hand are all his horses. Every month, about new-moon tide we bring hither our best mares for the purpose of having a breed between them and the sea-horses. The sea-horses try to drag them away with them, but cannot, by reason of the leg-ropes; so they cry out at them and butt at them and kick them, which we hearing, know that we must run out and shout at them, whereupon they are startled and return in fear to the sea. Their colts and fillies are worth a mint of money, nor is their like to be found on the earth's face. This is the time of the coming forth of the sea-horses; and Inshallah! I will bear thee to King Mihrjan," —And Sheherezade perceived the dawn of day and ceased to say her permitted say.

Now when it was the five hundred and for- tieth night,

She continued, It hath reached me, O auspicious King, that the Syce said to Sindbad the Seaman, "I will bear thee to King Mihrjan and show thee our country. And know that hadst thou not happened on us thou hadst perished miserably and none had known of thee; but I will be the means of the saving of thy life and of thy return to thine own land." I called down blessings on him and thanked him for his kindness and courtesy; and, while we were yet talking, behold, the horse came up out of the sea; and would have carried the mare away with him, but could not by reason of the tether. Thereupon the groom took a sword and target and ran out of the underground saloon, smiting the buckler with the blade and calling to his company, who came up shouting and brandishing spears; and the sea-horse took fright at them and plunging into the sea, like a buffalo, disappeared under the waves. After this we sat awhile, till the rest of the grooms came up, each leading a mare, and seeing me with their fellow-Syce, questioned me of my case and I re- peated my story to them. Thereupon they drew near me and spreading the table ate and invited me to eat; so I ate with them, after which they took horse and mounting me on one of the mares, set out with me and fared on without ceasing till we came to the capital city of King Mihrjan, and going in to him acquainted him with my story. Then he sent for me, and when they set me before him and salams had

---

42–43. **ship we voyaged in.** Note that Sindbad does not say that he was shipwrecked; in accordance with the tales of fabulous trav- elers, he often tells the truth when an untruth would not serve him.

63. **Mihrjan,** probably a corruption of *Maharajah*, the Hindu word for "Great King." 81. **Syce,** a groom. 92. **target,** shield.

been exchanged, he gave me a cordial welcome and wishing me long life bade me tell him my tale. So I related to him all that I had seen and all that had befallen me from first to last, whereat he marvelled and said to me, "By Allah, O my son, thou hast indeed been miraculously preserved! Were not the term of thy life a long one, thou hadst not escaped from these straits; but praised be Allah for safety!" Then he spoke cheerily to me and entreated me with kindness and consideration; moreover, he made me his agent for the port and registrar of all ships that entered the harbor. I attended him regularly, to receive his commandments, and he favored me and did me all manner of kindness and invested me with costly and splendid robes. Indeed, I was high in credit with him, as an intercessor for the folk and an intermessary between them and him, when they wanted aught of him. I abode thus a great while and, as often as I passed through the city to the port, I questioned the merchants and travelers and sailors of the city of Baghdad; so haply I might hear of an occasion to return to my native land, but could find none who knew it or knew any who resorted thither. At this I was chagrined, for I was weary of long strangerhood; and my disappointment endured for a time till one day, going in to King Mihrjan, I found him with a company of Indians. I saluted them and they returned my salam; and politely welcomed me and asked me of my country.—And Sheherezade was surprised by the dawn of day and ceased saying her permitted say.

Now WHEN IT WAS THE FIVE HUNDRED AND FORTY-FIRST NIGHT,

She continued, It hath reached me, O auspicious King, that Sindbad the Seaman said: "When they asked me of my country, I questioned them of theirs and they told me that they were of various castes, some being called Shakiriyah, who are the noblest of their castes, and neither oppress nor offer violence to any, and others Brahmans, a folk who abstain from wine, but live in delight and solace and merriment and own camels and horses and cattle. Moreover, they told me that the people of India are divided into two-and-seventy castes, and I marvelled at this with exceeding marvel. Amongst other things that I saw in King Mihrjan's dominions was an island called Kasil, wherein all night is heard the beating of drums and tabrets; but we were told by the neighboring islanders and by travelers that the inhabitants are people of diligence and judgment. In this sea I saw also a fish two hundred cubits long and the fishermen fear it; so they strike together pieces of wood and put it to flight. I saw also another fish, with a head like that of an owl, besides many other wonders and rarities, which it would be

38. **Shakiriyah,** the second, or warrior, caste of Hindu society.

tedious to recount. I occupied myself thus in visiting the island till, one day, as I stood in the port, with a staff in my hand, according to my custom, behold, a great ship, wherein were many merchants, came sailing for the harbor. When it reached the small inner port where ships anchor under the city, the master furled his sails and making fast to the shore, put out the landing-planks, whereupon the crew fell to breaking bulk and landing cargo whilst I stood by, taking written note of them. They were long in bringing the goods ashore, so I asked the master, "Is there aught left in thy ship?" and he answered, "O my lord, there are divers bales of merchandise in the hold, whose owner was drowned from amongst us at one of the islands on our course; so his goods remained in our charge by way of trust and we purpose to sell them and note their price, that we may convey it to his people in the city of Baghdad, the Palace of Peace." "What was the merchant's name?" quoth I, and quoth he, "Sindbad the Seaman;" whereupon I straightly considered him and knowing him, cried out to him with a great cry, saying, "O captain, I am that Sindbad the Seaman who traveled with other merchants; and when the fish heaved and thou calledst to us, some saved themselves and others sank, I being one of them. But Allah Almighty threw in my way a great tub of wood, of those the crew had used to wash withal, and the winds and waves carried me to this island, where by Allah's grace, I fell in with King Mihrjan's grooms and they brought me hither to the King their master. When I told him my story, he entreated me with favor and made me his harbor-master, and I have prospered in his service and found acceptance with him. These bales, therefore, are mine, the goods which God hath given me."— And Sheherezade perceived the dawn of day and ceased to say her permitted say.

Now WHEN IT WAS THE FIVE HUNDRED AND FORTY-SECOND NIGHT,

She continued, It hath reached me, O auspicious King, that when Sindbad the Seaman said to the captain, These bales are mine, the goods which Allah hath given me, the other exclaimed, "There is no majesty and there is no might save in Allah, the Glorious, the Great! Verily, there is neither conscience nor good faith left among men!" Said I, "O Rais, what mean these words, seeing that I have told thee my case?" And he answered, "Because thou heardest me say that I had with me goods whose owner was drowned, thou thinkest to take them without right; but this is forbidden by law to thee, for we saw him drown before our eyes, together with many other passengers, nor was one of them saved. So how canst thou pretend that thou

103. **Rais,** the captain of the vessel.

art the owner of the goods?" "O captain," said I, "listen to my story and give heed to my words, and my truth will be manifest to thee; for lying and leasing are the letter-marks of the hypocrites." Then I recounted to him all that had befallen me since I sailed from Baghdad with him to the time when we came to the fish-island where we were nearly drowned; and I reminded him of certain matters which had passed between us; whereupon both he and the merchants were certified of the truth of my story and recognized me and gave me joy of my deliverance, saying, "By Allah, we thought not that thou hadst escaped drowning! But the Lord hath granted thee new life." Then they delivered my bales to me, and I found my name written thereon, nor was aught thereof lacking. So I opened them and making up a present for King Mihrjan of the finest and costliest of the contents, caused the sailors to carry it up to the palace, where I went in to the King and laid my present at his feet, acquainting him with what had happened, especially concerning the ship and my goods; whereat he wondered with exceeding wonder and the truth of all that I had told him was made manifest to him. His affection for me redoubled after that and he showed me exceeding honor and bestowed on me a great present in return for mine. Then I sold my bales and what other matters I owned, making a great profit on them, and bought me other goods and gear of the growth and fashion of the island-city. When the merchants were about to start on their homeward voyage, I embarked on board the ship all that I possessed, and going in to the King thanked him for all his favors and friendship and craved his leave to return to my own land and friends. He farewelled me and bestowed on me great store of the country-stuffs and produce; and I took leave of him and embarked. Then we set sail and fared on nights and days, by the permission of Allah Almighty; and Fortune served us and Fate favored us, so that we arrived in safety at Bassorah City, where I landed rejoicing at my safe return to my natal soil. After a short stay, I set out for Baghdad, the Palace of Peace, with store of goods and commodities of great price. Reaching the city in due time, I went straight to my own quarter and entered my house, where all my friends and kinsfolk came to greet me. Then I bought me eunuchs and concubines, servants and negro-slaves till I had a large establishment, and I bought me horses, and lands and gardens, till I was richer and in better case than before, and returned to enjoy the society of my friends and familiars more assiduously than ever, forgetting all I had suffered of fatigue and hardship and strangerhood and every peril of travel; and I applied myself to all manner joys and solaces and delights, eating the daintiest

viands and drinking the most delicious wines; and my wealth allowed this state of things to endure. This, then, is the story of my first Voyage, and tomorrow, Inshallah! I will tell you the tale of my second voyage. (Saith he who telleth the tale).

Then Sindbad the Seaman made Sindbad the Landsman sup with him and bade give him an hundred gold pieces, saying, "Thou hast cheered us with thy company this day." The Porter thanked him and, taking the gift, went his way, pondering that which he had heard and marvelling mightily at what things betide mankind. He passed the night in his own place and with early morning repaired to the abode of Sindbad the Seaman, who received him with honor and seated him by his side. As soon as the rest of the company was assembled, he set meat and drink before them and, when they had well eaten and drunken and were merry and in cheerful case, he took up his discourse and recounted to them in these words the narrative of

THE SECOND VOYAGE
OF SINDBAD THE SEAMAN

Know, O my brother, that I was living a most comfortable and enjoyable life, in all solace and delight, as I told you yesterday.—And Sheherezade was surprised by the dawn of day and ceased saying her permitted say.

NOW WHEN IT WAS THE FIVE HUNDRED AND FORTY-THIRD NIGHT,

She continued, It hath reached me, O auspicious King, that when Sindbad the Seaman's guests were all gathered together, he thus bespake them:—I was living a most enjoyable life until one day my mind became possessed with the thought of travelling about the world of men and seeing their cities and islands; and a longing seized me to traffic and to make money by trade. Upon this resolve I took a great store of cash and, buying goods and gear fit for travel, bound them up in bales. Then I went down to the river-bank, where I found a noble ship and brand-new about to sail, equipped with sails of fine cloth and well-manned and provided; so I took passage on her, with a number of other merchants, and after embarking our goods we weighed anchor the same day. Right fair was our voyage and we sailed from place to place and from isle to isle; and whenever we anchored we met a crowd of merchants and notables and customers, and we took to buying and selling and bartering. At last Destiny brought us to an island, fair and verdant, in trees abundant, with yellow-ripe fruits luxuriant, and flowers fragrant and birds warbling soft descant; and streams crystalline and radiant; but no sign of man showed to the descrier, no, not a blower of the fire.

109. **blower . . . fire,** a popular Arabic phrase to express desolation.

The captain made fast with us to this island, and the merchants and sailors landed and walked about, enjoying the shade of the trees and the songs of the birds, that chanted the praises of the One, the Victorious, and marvelling at the works of the Omnipotent King. I landed with the rest; and, sitting down by a spring of sweet water that welled up among the trees, took out some food I had with me and ate of that which Allah Almighty had allotted unto me. And so sweet was the zephyr and so fragrant were the flowers, that presently I waxed drowsy and lying down in that place was soon drowned in sleep. When I awoke, I found myself alone, for the ship had sailed and left me behind, nor had one of the merchants or sailors bethought himself of me. I searched the island right and left, but found neither man nor Jinn, whereat I was beyond measure troubled, and my heart was like to break for stress of chagrin and anguish and concern, because I was left quite alone, without aught of worldly gear or meat or drink, weary and heart-broken. So I gave myself up for lost and said, "Not always doth the crock escape the shock. I was saved the first time by finding one who brought me from the desert island to an inhabited place, but now there is no hope for me." Then I fell to weeping and wailing and gave myself up to an excess of rage, blaming myself for having again ventured upon the perils and hardships of voyage, whenas I was at my ease in mine own house in mine own land, taking my pleasure, with good meat and good drink and good clothes and lacking nothing, neither money nor goods. And I repented me of having left Baghdad, and this the more after all the travails and dangers I had undergone in my first voyage, wherein I had so narrowly escaped destruction, and exclaimed, "Verily we are Allah's and unto Him we are returning!" I was indeed even as one mad and Jinn-struck, and presently I rose and walked about the island, right and left and every whither, unable for trouble to sit or tarry in any one place. Then I climbed a tall tree and looked in all directions, but saw nothing save sky and sea and trees and birds and isles and sands. However, after a while my eager glances fell upon some great white thing, afar off in the interior of the island; so I came down from the tree and made for that which I had seen; and behold, it was a huge white dome rising high in air and of vast compass. I walked all around it, but found no door thereto, nor could I muster strength or nimbleness by reason of its exceeding smoothness and slipperiness. So I marked the spot where I stood and went round about the dome to measure its circumference, which I found fifty good paces. And as I stood, casting about how to gain an entrance, behold, the sun was suddenly hidden from me and the air be-

came dull and dark. Methought a cloud had come over the sun, but it was the season of summer; so I marvelled at this and lifting my head looked steadfastly at the sky, when I saw that the cloud was none other than an enormous bird, of gigantic girth and inordinately wide of wing, which, as it flew through the air, veiled the sun and hid it from the island. At this sight my wonder redoubled and I remembered a story—And Sheherezade perceived the dawn of day and ceased to say her permitted say.

NOW WHEN IT WAS THE FIVE HUNDRED AND FORTY-FOURTH NIGHT,

She said, It hath reached me, O auspicious King, that Sindbad the Seaman continued in these words: —My wonder redoubled and I remembered a story I had heard aforetime of pilgrims and travellers, how in a certain island dwelleth a huge bird, called the Roc, which feedeth its young on elephants; and I was certified that the dome which caught my sight was none other than a Roc's egg. As I looked and wondered at the marvellous works of the Almighty, the bird alighted on the dome and brooded over it with its wings covering it and its legs stretched out behind it on the ground, and in this posture it fell asleep, glory be to Him who sleepeth not! When I saw this, I arose and, unwinding my turban from my head, doubled it and twisted it into a rope, with which I girt my middle and bound my waist fast to the legs of the Roc, saying to myself, "Peradventure, this bird may carry me to a land of cities and inhabitants, and that will be better than abiding in this desert island." I passed the night watching and fearing to sleep, lest the bird should fly away with me unawares; and, as soon as the dawn broke and the morn shone, the Roc rose off its egg and spreading its wings with a great cry flew up into the air dragging me with it; nor ceased it to soar and to tower till I thought it had reached the limit of the firmament; after which it descended, earthwards, little by little, till it lighted on the top of a high hill. As soon as I found myself on the hard ground, I made haste to unbind myself, quaking with fear of the bird, though it took no heed of me nor even felt me; and, loosing my turban from its feet, I made off with my best speed. Presently I saw it catch up in its huge claws something from the earth and rise with it high in air, and observing it narrowly I saw it to be a serpent big of bulk and gigantic of girth, wherewith it flew away clean out of sight. I marvelled at this and faring forwards found myself on a peak overlooking a valley, exceeding great and wide and deep, and bounded by vast mountains that spired high in air; none could descry their summits for the excess of their height, nor was any able to climb up thereto. When I saw this, I blamed myself for that which I had done and said, "Would Heaven I had tarried in the island! It was better than this wild desert, for there I had at least fruits to eat and water to drink, and here are neither trees nor fruits nor streams. But there is no Majesty and there is no Might save in Allah, the Glorious, the Great! Verily, as often as I am quit of one peril, I fall into a worse danger and a more grievous."

However, I took courage and walking along the wady found that its soil was of diamond, the stone wherewith they pierce minerals and precious stones and porcelain and the onyx, for that it is a dense stone and a stubborn, whereon neither iron nor hardhead hath effect, neither can we cut off aught therefrom nor break it, save by means of leadstone. Moreover, the valley swarmed with snakes and vipers, each big as a palm-tree, that would have made but one gulp of an elephant; and they came out by night, hiding during the day, lest the rocs and eagles pounce on them and tear them to pieces, as was their wont—why I wot not. And I repented of what I had done and said, "By Allah, I have made haste to bring destruction upon myself!" The day began to wane as I went along and I looked about for a place where I might pass the night, being in fear of the serpents; and I took no thought of meat and drink in my concern for my life. Presently I caught sight of a cave near at hand, with a narrow doorway; so I entered and seeing a great stone close to the mouth, I rolled it up and stopped at the entrance, saying to myself, "I am safe here for the night; and as soon as it is day, I will go forth and see what destiny will do." Then I looked within the cave and saw at the upper end a great serpent brooding on her eggs, at which my flesh quaked and my hair stood on end; but I raised my eyes to Heaven and, committing my case to fate and lot, abode all that night without sleep till daybreak, when I rolled back the stone from the mouth of the cave and went forth, staggering like a drunken man and giddy with watching and fear and hunger. As in this sore case I walked along the valley, behold, there fell down before me a slaughtered beast; but I saw no one, whereat I marvelled with great marvel and presently remembered a story I had heard aforetime of traders and pilgrims and travellers: how the mountains where are the diamonds are full of perils and terrors, nor can any fare through them; but the merchants who traffic in diamonds have a device by which they obtain them, that is to say, they take a sheep and slaughter and skin it and cut it in pieces and cast them down from the mountain-tops into the valley-floor, where the meat being fresh and sticky with blood, some of the gems cleave to it. There they leave it till midday, when the eagles and

vultures swoop down upon it and carry it in their claws to the mountain summits, whereupon the merchants come and shout at them and scare them away from the meat. Then they come and, taking the diamonds which they find sticking to it, go their ways with them and leave the meat to the birds and beasts; nor can any come at the diamonds but by this device.—And Sheherezade was surprised by the dawn of day and ceased saying her permitted say.

NOW WHEN IT WAS THE FIVE HUNDRED AND FORTY-
FIFTH NIGHT,

She said, It hath reached me, O auspicious King, that Sindbad the Seaman continued his relation of what befell him in the Mountain of Diamonds, and informed them that the merchants cannot come at the diamonds save by the device aforesaid. So, when I saw the slaughtered beast fall (he pursued) and bethought me of the story, I went up to it and filled my pockets and shawl-girdle and turban and the folds of my clothes with the choicest diamonds; and, as I was thus engaged, down fell before me another great piece of meat. Then with my unrolled turban and lying on my back, I set the bit on my breast so that I was hidden by the meat, which was thus raised above the ground. Hardly had I gripped it, when an eagle swooped down upon the flesh and, seizing it with his talons, flew up with it high in air and me clinging thereto, and ceased not its flight till it alighted on the head of one of the mountains where, dropping the carcass, he fell to rending it; but, behold, there arose behind him a great noise of shouting and clattering of wood, whereat the bird took fright and flew away. Then I loosed off myself the meat, with clothes dabbled with blood therefrom and stood up by its side; whereupon up came the merchant, who had cried out at the eagle, and seeing me standing there, bespoke me not, but was affrighted at me and shook with fear. However, he went up to the carcass and turning it over, found no diamonds sticking to it, whereat he gave a great cry and exclaimed, "Alack, my disappointment! There is no Majesty and there is no Might save in Allah with whom we seek refuge from Satan the stoned!" And he bemoaned himself and beat hand upon hand, saying, "Alas, the pity of it! How cometh this?"

Then I went up to him and he said to me, "Who art thou and what causeth thee to come hither?" And I, "Fear not, I am a man and a good man and a merchant. My story is a wondrous and my adventures are marvellous and the manner of my coming hither is prodigious. So be of good cheer, thou shalt receive of me what shall rejoice thee, for I have with me great plenty of diamonds and I will give thee thereof what shall suffice thee; for each is better than aught thou couldst get otherwise. So fear nothing." The man rejoiced thereat and thanked and blessed me; then we talked together till the other merchants, hearing me in discourse with their fellow, came up and saluted me, for each of them had thrown down his piece of meat. And as I went off with them I told them my whole story, how I had suffered hardships at sea and the fashion of my reaching the valley. But I gave the owner of the meat a number of the stones I had by me, so they all wished me joy of my escape, saying, "By Allah, a new life hath been decreed to thee, for none ever reached yonder valley and came off thence alive before thee; but praised be Allah for thy safety!" We passed the night together in a safe and pleasant place, beyond measure rejoiced at my deliverance from the Valley of Serpents and my arrival in an inhabited land; and on the morrow we set out and journeyed over the mighty range of mountains, seeing many serpents in the valley, till we came to a fair great island, wherein was a garden of huge camphor trees under each of which an hundred men might take shelter. When the folk have a mind to get camphor, they bore into the upper part of the bole with a long iron, whereupon the liquid camphor, which is the sap of the tree, floweth out and they catch it in vessels, where it concreteth like gum; but, after this, the tree dieth and becometh firewood. Moreover, there is in this island a kind of wild beast, called Rhinoceros, that pastureth as do steers and buffaloes with us; but it is a huge brute, bigger of body than the camel and like it feedeth upon the leaves and twigs of trees. It is a remarkable animal with a great and thick horn, ten cubits long, amiddleward its head; wherein, when cleft in twain, appeareth the likeness of a man. Voyagers and pilgrims and travelers declare that this beast, called Karkadan, will carry off a great elephant on its horn and graze about the island and the sea-coast therewith and take no heed of it, till the elephant dieth and its fat, melting in the sun, runneth down into the rhinoceros's eyes and blindeth him, so that he lieth down upon the shore. Then cometh the bird Roc and carrieth off both the rhinoceros and that which is on its horn to feed its young withal.

Moreover, I saw in this island many kinds of oxen and buffaloes, whose like are not found in our country. Here I sold some of the diamonds which I had by me for gold dinars and silver dirhams and bartered others for the produce of the country; and, loading them upon beasts of burden, fared on with the merchants from valley to valley and town to town, buying and selling and viewing foreign countries and the works and creatures of Allah, till we came to Bassorah-City, where we abode a few days, after which I continued my journey to Baghdad,—

And Sheherezade perceived the dawn of day and ceased to say her permitted say.

NOW WHEN IT WAS THE FIVE HUNDRED AND FORTY-SIXTH NIGHT,

She said, It hath reached me, O auspicious King, that when Sindbad the Seaman returned from his travel to Baghdad, the House of Peace, he arrived at home with great store of diamonds and money and goods. (Continued he) I foregathered with my friends and relations and gave alms and largesse and bestowed curious gifts and made presents to all my friends and companions. Then I betook myself to eating well and drinking well and wearing fine clothes and making merry with my fellows, and forgot all my sufferings in the pleasures of return to the solace and delight of life, with light heart and broadened breast. And everyone who heard of my return came and questioned me of my adventures and of foreign countries, and I related to them all that had befallen me, and the much I had suffered, whereat they wondered and gave me joy of my safe return. This, then, is the end of the story of my second Voyage; and tomorrow, Inshallah! I will tell you what befell me in my third Voyage.

Omar Khayyam

The remarkable impact of the poetry of Omar Khayyam upon the English-speaking peoples, thanks to the gifted translation and adaptation of many of his verses by the Englishman Edward Fitzgerald (1809–1883), has tended to obscure the fact that Omar was a celebrated mathematician. He was born, probably in the sixth or seventh decade of the eleventh century (although the exact year is not known), at Nishapur, one of the principal towns of the Province of Khorasan in Persia. By nature a retiring individual, he devoted himself to the study of astronomy and attained such eminence in that field that he was raised to the post of Astronomer Royal. In this capacity he worked upon a reform of the calendar. He was noted also for a brilliant treatise on algebra. But during his lifetime he was also the author of more than five hundred quatrains of an epigrammatic nature, and it is on these quatrains, or *rubaiyat*, that his fame in the Western world will always depend.

There is no accepted text of these quatrains; and, indeed, it is debatable whether all are to be accredited to Omar Khayyam, but there is no doubt about most of them. In substance the *rubaiyat* comprise: (1) complaints against Fate, or the spirit of necessity; (2) satires on the pious, the learned, and the reputedly good people of the times; (3) love lyrics on the sorrows of separation and the joys of reunion; (4) poems in praise of gardens, flowers, and the springtime; (5) poems of rebellion against the prevailing conceptions of God, Heaven, and Hell, balancing their promise of an afterlife against the certainty or reality of the joys of the moment; and (6) addresses to the Deity, of a strongly mystical nature.

Undoubtedly Omar Khayyam was, even for his day, a freethinker and a liberal, one to live and let live, with a hard core of scientific objectivity in most of his intellectual outlook. There is some evidence to show that his liberalism made it hard for him at Nishapur. In any case, however, it remains a question whether the epicurean nature of some of the quatrains is to be taken literally. The poet preaches the joys of the vine and of the body; he implies, however, the joys of the mind and of the soul as well. At the same time, he is not to be regarded as a pure mystic, for his scientific turn of mind counteracts this tendency.

It is more likely that Omar, a man who adopted the life of the observer and the spectator, was moved to poetic expression of his skepticism, his cynicism, and his regrets at the contemplation of that which is beautiful but which either does not last or is tainted with the commonplace and the thwarting of the ideal. His *rubaiyat* were probably written during the course of a long life, and the conflicting points of view they show— a religiousness on the one hand and a worldliness on the other—may be accounted for on the grounds that his philosophy changed as he grew older. But on the other hand, he may well have had the common failings of a liberal: he may have been a hesitator, one whose practice backslid while his ideals soared aloft. In this respect he is one of the most human and understandable of all poets.

In the essentially contradictory nature of Omar Khayyam's poetry lies one of his greatest sources of appeal. But this dichotomy is not peculiar to him. For example, he admits the problem of evil and then takes to task God, the only real "agent" of evil. Still, God was similarly taken to task by Job in the Old Testament and again in sublime fashion by the poet of Ecclesiastes, who observed that there is one event to all, to him that sacrificeth and to him that sacrificeth not. The author of Job counsels resignation; the poet of Ecclesiastes tells us to make the most of time. Omar Khayyam, in effect, does both, albeit in more flippant and perhaps insolent manner. Even so, Omar wrote many quatrains of deep religious feeling; he cannot be called another Lucretius or another Voltaire, for his faith in a God, whatever His nature and His sense of justice, is unshaken.

The translation of Omar Khayyam's *rubaiyat* by Edward Fitzgerald is admittedly selective; it emphasizes the sybaritic and the rebellious more than did the original and passes lightly over the devotional quatrains. Yet no reader of Omar Khayyam in the original could well deny that Fitzgerald has caught the essence of Omar—his world-weariness, his love of ease and comfort, his skepticism and sophistication, his romantic yearning and passionate regret, his fatalism, his inquisitiveness, and his love of beauty—all couched in phrases that, for all the popular overuse to which they have been put, come close

to the immortal. Omar Khayyam told his friend and pupil, Nizami of Samarkand, "My tomb shall be in a certain place where each breath of the north wind shall shower down roses upon it." His verses have been given imperishable form by Fitzgerald's quatrains, which are the rose petals he desired.

The Rubaiyat

WAKE! For the Sun, who scatter'd into flight
The Stars before him from the Field of Night,
   Drives Night along with them from Heav'n, and strikes
The Sultan's Turret with a Shaft of Light.

Before the Phantom of False Morning died,   5
Methought a Voice within the Tavern cried,
   "When all the Temple is prepared within,
"Why nods the drowsy Worshipper outside?"

And, as the Cock crew, those who stood before
The Tavern shouted—"Open then the Door!   10
   "You know how little while we have to stay,
"And, once departed, may return no more."

Now the New Year reviving old Desires,
The thoughtful Soul to Solitude retires,
   Where the White Hand of Moses on the Bough
Puts out, and Jesus from the Ground suspires.   16

Iram indeed is gone with all his Rose,
And Jamshyd's Sev'n-ring'd Cup where no one knows;
   But still a Ruby kindles in the Vine,
And many a Garden by the Water blows.   20

And David's lips are locked; but in divine
High-piping Pehleví, with "Wine! Wine! Wine!
   "Red Wine!"—the Nightingale cries to the Rose
That sallow cheek of hers to incarnadine.

Come, fill the Cup, and in the fire of Spring   25
Your Winter-garment of Repentance fling:
   The Bird of Time has but a little way
To flutter—and the Bird is on the Wing.

The Rubaiyat. Translated by Edward Fitzgerald.
15. **White Hand of Moses.** Moses, at the command of the Lord, put his hand into his bosom, and he took it out as white as snow. The metaphor is used here for the blooming of flowers in the spring. 16. **Jesus . . . suspires.** The Persians believed Jesus healed by his breath. 17. **Iram,** an ancient Persian garden, now disappeared. 18. **Jamshyd,** a legendary Persian king, whose seven-ringed cup symbolized the seven heavens, the seven seas, etc. 21. **David's . . . locked;** King David's actual language is forgotten. 22. **Pehleví,** the ancient literary language of Persia.

Whether at Nishápúr or Babylon,
Whether the Cup with sweet or bitter run, 30
   The Wine of Life keeps oozing drop by drop,
The Leaves of Life keep falling one by one.

Each Morn a thousand Roses brings, you say;
Yes, but where leaves the Rose of Yesterday?
   And this first Summer month that brings the Rose
Shall take Jamshyd and Kaí-kobád away. 36

Well, let it take them! What have we to do
With Kaí-kobád the Great, or Kai-khosrú?
   Let Zál and Rustum bluster as they will,
Or Hátim call to Supper—heed not you. 40

With me along the strip of Herbage strewn
That just divides the desert from the sown,
   Where name of Slave and Sultan is forgot—
And peace to Mahmúd on his golden Throne!

A Book of Verses underneath the Bough, 45
A Jug of Wine, a Loaf of Bread—and Thou
   Beside me singing in the Wilderness—
Ah, Wilderness were Paradise enow!

Some for the Glories of This World; and some
Sigh for the Prophet's Paradise to come; 50
   Ah, take the Cash, and let the Credit go,
Nor heed the rumble of a distant Drum!

Look to the blowing Rose about us—"Lo,
"Laughing," she says, "into the world I blow,
   "At once the silken tassel of my Purse 55
Tear, and its Treasure on the Garden throw."

And those who husbanded the Golden Grain,
And those who flung it to the winds like Rain,
   Alike to no such aureate Earth are turn'd
As, buried once, Men want dug up again. 60

The Worldly Hope men set their Hearts upon
Turns Ashes—or it prospers; and anon,
   Like Snow upon the Desert's dusty Face,
Lighting a little hour or two—is gone.

Think, in this batter'd Caravanserai 65
Whose Portals are alternate Night and Day,
   How Sultan after Sultan with his Pomp
Abode his destined Hour, and went his way.

29. **Nishápúr,** a town in Persia and Omar's own birthplace. 38.
Kaí-kobád . . . Kai-khosrú. Kaí-kobád, a celebrated Persian hero,
was the founder of an important Persian dynasty; Kai-khosrú has
been tentatively identified with Cyrus the Great of the sixth century B.C. 39. **Zál and Rustum.** Zal was the father of Rustum;
Rustum is perhaps the greatest of Persian epic heroes. 44. **Mahmúd,**
presumably Sultan Mahmud the Great (970?–1030), the Persian
conqueror of the Punjab and Afghanistan. 57. **Golden Grain,** to
be taken here symbolically as "wealth." 65. **Caravanserai,** an inn
where Oriental caravans put up.

Portrait of a physician, by a 16th-century Persian painter.

They say the Lion and the Lizard keep 69
The Courts where Jamshyd gloried and drank deep:
   And Bahrám, that great Hunter—the Wild Ass
Stamps o'er his Head, but cannot break his Sleep.

I sometimes think that never blows so red
The Rose as where some buried Caesar bled;
   That every Hyacinth the Garden wears 75
Dropt in her Lap from some once lovely Head.

And this reviving Herb whose tender Green
Fledges the River-Lip on which we lean—
   Ah, lean upon it lightly! for who knows
From what once lovely Lip it springs unseen! 80

Ah, my Belovéd, fill the Cup that clears
Today of past Regrets and future Fears:

70. **Courts . . . deep,** Persepolis, capital of Jamshyd. 71. **Bahrám,**
a legendary Persian hero who lost his life while hunting a wild ass.

Tomorrow!—Why, Tomorrow I may be
Myself with Yesterday's Sev'n thousand Years.

For some we loved, the loveliest and the best   85
That from his Vintage rolling Time hath prest,
    Have drunk their Cup a Round or two before,
And one by one crept silently to rest.

And we, that now make merry in the Room
They left, and Summer dresses in new bloom,   90
    Ourselves must we beneath the Couch of Earth
Descend—ourselves to make a Couch—for whom?

Ah, make the most of what we yet may spend,
Before we too into the Dust descend;
    Dust into Dust, and under Dust to lie,   95
Sans Wine, sans Song, sans Singer, and—sans End!

Alike for those who for TODAY prepare
And those that after some TOMORROW stare,
    A Muezzin from the Tower of Darkness cries,
"Fools! your Reward is neither Here nor There."

Why, all the Saints and Sages who discuss'd   101
Of the Two Worlds so wisely—they are thrust
    Like foolish Prophets forth; their Words to Scorn
Are scatter'd, and their Mouths are stopt with Dust.

Myself when young did eagerly frequent   105
Doctor and Saint, and heard great argument
    About it and about: but evermore
Came out by the same door where in I went.

With them the seed of Wisdom did I sow,   109
And with mine own hand wrought to make it grow;
    And this was all the Harvest that I reap'd—
"I came like Water, and like Wind I go."

Into this Universe, and *Why* not knowing
Nor *Whence*, like Water willy-nilly flowing;
    And out of it, as Wind along the Waste,   115
I know not *Whither*, willy-nilly blowing.

What, without asking, hither hurried *Whence?*
And, without asking, *Whither* hurried hence!
    Oh, many a Cup of this forbidden Wine
Must drown the memory of that insolence!   120

Up from Earth's Centre through the Seventh Gate
I rose, and on the Throne of Saturn sate,
    And many a Knot unravel'd by the Road;
But not the Master-knot of Human Fate.

99. **Muezzin,** the Mohammedan summoner of the Faithful to Prayer.
119. **forbidden Wine;** because the teachings of Mohammed strictly
forbid the use of alcohol in any form.

There was the Door to which I found no Key;   125
There was the Veil through which I might not see:
    Some little talk awhile of ME and THEE
There was—and then no more of THEE and ME.

Earth could not answer; nor the Seas that mourn
In flowing Purple, of their Lord forlorn;   130
    Nor rolling Heaven, with all his Signs reveal'd
And hidden by the sleeve of Night and Morn.

Then of the THEE IN ME who works behind
The Veil, I lifted up my hands to find
    A Lamp amid the Darkness; and I heard,   135
As from Without—"THE ME WITHIN THEE BLIND!"

Then to the Lip of this poor earthen Urn
I lean'd, the Secret of my Life to learn:
    And Lip to Lip it murmur'd—"While you live,
Drink!—for, once dead, you never shall return."

I think the Vessel, that with fugitive   141
Articulation answer'd, once did live,
    And drink; and Ah! the passive Lip I kiss'd,
How many Kisses might it take—and give!

For I remember stopping by the way   145
To watch a Potter thumping his wet Clay:
    And with its all-obliterated Tongue
It murmur'd—"Gently, Brother, gently, pray!"

And has not such a story from of Old
Down Man's successive generations roll'd   150
    Of such a clod of saturated Earth
Cast by the Maker into Human Mould?

And not a drop that from our Cups we throw
For Earth to drink of, but may steal below
    To quench the fire of Anguish in some Eye   155
There hidden,—far beneath, and long ago.

As then the Tulip for her morning sup
Of Heav'nly Vintage from the soil looks up;
    Do you devoutly do the like, till Heav'n
To Earth invert you—like an empty Cup.   160

Perplext no more with Human or Divine,
Tomorrow's tangle to the winds resign,
    And lose your fingers in the tresses of
The Cypress-slender Minister of Wine.

And if the Wine you drink, the Lip you press,   165
End in what All begins and ends in—Yes;
    Think then you are Today what Yesterday
You were—Tomorrow you shall not be less.

So when that Angel of the darker Drink
At last shall find you by the river-brink   170

131. **Signs,** constellations of the Zodiac.

And, offering his Cup, invite your Soul
Forth to your Lips to quaff—you shall not shrink.

Why, if the Soul can fling the Dust aside,
And naked on the Air of Heaven ride,
    Were't not a Shame—were't not a Shame for him
In this clay carcase crippled to abide?   176

'Tis but a Tent where takes his one day's rest
A Sultan to the realm of Death addrest;
    The Sultan rises, and the dark Ferrásh
Strikes, and prepares it for another Guest.   180

And fear not lest Existence closing your
Account, and mine, should know the like no more;
    The Eternal Sákí from the Bowl has pour'd
Millions of Bubbles like us, and will pour.

When You and I behind the Veil are past,   185
Oh, but the long, long while the World shall last
    Which of our Coming and Departure heeds
As the Sea's self should heed a pebble-cast.

A Moment's Halt—a momentary taste
Of Being from the Well amid the Waste—   190
    And Lo!—the phantom Caravan has reach'd
The Nothing it set out from—Oh, make haste!

Would you that spangle of Existence spend
About THE SECRET—quick about it, Friend!
    A Hair perhaps divides the False and True—   195
And upon what, prithee, may life depend?

A Hair perhaps divides the False and True;
Yes; and a single Alif were the clue—
    Could you but find it—to the Treasure-House,
And peradventure to THE MASTER too;   200

Whose secret Presence, through Creation's veins
Running Quicksilver-like, eludes your pains;
    Taking all shapes from Máh to Máhi; and
They change and perish all—but He remains;

A moment guess'd—then back behind the Fold   205
Immerst of Darkness round the Drama roll'd
    Which, for the Pastime of Eternity,
He doth Himself contrive, enact, behold.

But if in vain, down on the stubborn floor
Of Earth, and up to Heav'n's unopening Door,   210
    You gaze Today, while You are You—how then
Tomorrow, when You shall be You no more?

Waste not your Hour, nor in the vain pursuit
Of This and That endeavor and dispute;
    Better be jocund with the fruitful Grape   215
Than sadden after none, or bitter, Fruit.

You know, my Friends, with what a brave Carouse
I made a Second Marriage in my house;
    Divorced old barren Reason from my Bed,
And took the Daughter of the Vine to Spouse.   220

For "Is" and "Is-not" though with Rule and Line
And "Up-and-down" by Logic I define,
    Of all that one should care to fathom, I
Was never deep in anything but—Wine.

Ah, but my Computations, People say,   225
Reduced the Year to better reckoning?—Nay,
    'Twas only striking from the Calendar
Unborn Tomorrow, and dead Yesterday.

And lately, by the Tavern Door agape,   229
Came shining through the Dusk an Angel Shape
    Bearing a Vessel on his Shoulder; and
He bid me taste of it; and 'twas—the Grape!

The Grape that can with Logic absolute
The Two-and-Seventy jarring Sects confute:
    The Sovereign Alchemist that in a trice   235
Life's leaden metal into Gold transmute:

The mighty Mahmúd, Allah-breathing Lord,
That all the misbelieving and black Horde
    Of Fears and Sorrows that infest the Soul
Scatters before him with his whirlwind Sword.   240

Why, be this Juice the growth of God, who dare
Blaspheme the twisted tendril as a Snare?
    A Blessing, we should use it, should we not?
And if a Curse—why, then, Who set it there?

I must abjure the Balm of Life, I must,   245
Scared by some After-reckoning ta'en on trust,
    Or lured with Hope of some Diviner Drink,
To fill the Cup—when crumbled into Dust!

Oh threats of Hell and Hopes of Paradise!
One thing at least is certain—*This* Life flies; 250
    One thing is certain and the rest is Lies;
The Flower that once has blown forever dies.

Strange, is it not? that of the myriads who
Before us pass'd the door of Darkness through,

179. **Ferrásh,** a camp-follower and military servant. 183. **Sákí,** a
wine-bearer (see line 401 below). 198. **Alif,** the first letter of the
Arabic alphabet. 203. **Máh to Máhi,** fish to moon.

225–228. **Computations . . . Yesterday.** Omar, as we have seen,
was a distinguished astronomer noted for his treatise on algebra
and for the reform of the calendar undertaken under the auspices
of Shah Malik of Persia. 234. **Two-and-Seventy . . . Sects,** according to Arabic lore, the number of religious faiths in the world.
237. **Allah-breathing,** worshiping Allah. 252. **blown,** blossomed.

Pastoral scene, from a Persian manuscript illumination, c. 1540.

Not one returns to tell us of the Road, 255
Which to discover we must travel too.

The Revelations of Devout and Learn'd
Who rose before us, and as Prophets burn'd,
Are all but Stories, which, awoke from Sleep
They told their comrades, and to Sleep return'd.

I sent my Soul through the Invisible, 261
Some letter of that After-life to spell:
And by and by my Soul return'd to me,
And answer'd, "I Myself am Heav'n and Hell:"

Heav'n but the Vision of fulfill'd Desire, 265
And Hell the Shadow from a Soul on fire,
Cast on the Darkness into which Ourselves,
So late emerged from, shall so soon expire.

We are no other than a moving row
Of Magic Shadow-shapes that come and go 270
Round with the Sun-illumined Lantern held
In Midnight by the Master of the Show;

But helpless Pieces of the Game He plays
Upon this Checker-board of Nights and Days;

Hither and thither moves, and checks, and slays,
And one by one back in the Closet lays. 276

The Ball no question makes of Ayes and Noes,
But Here or There, as strikes the Player, goes;
And He that toss'd you down into the Field,
He knows about it all—HE knows—HE knows! 280

The Moving Finger writes; and, having writ,
Moves on: nor all your Piety nor Wit
Shall lure it back to cancel half a Line,
Nor all your Tears wash out a Word of it.

And that inverted Bowl they call the Sky, 285
Whereunder crawling coop'd we live and die,
Lift not your hands to *It* for help—for It
As impotently moves as you or I.

With Earth's first Clay They did the Last Man
knead,
And there of the Last Harvest sow'd the Seed: 290
And the first Morning of Creation wrote
What the Last Dawn of Reckoning shall read.

Yesterday This Day's Madness did prepare;
Tomorrow's Silence, Triumph, or Despair:
Drink! for you know not whence you came, nor
why; 295
Drink! for you know not why you go, nor where.

I tell you this—When, started from the Goal,
Over the flaming shoulders of the Foal
Of Heav'n Parwín and Mushtarí they flung,
In my predestined Plot of Dust and Soul, 300

The Vine had struck a fibre: which about
If clings my Being—let the Dervish flout;
Of my Base metal may be filed a Key,
That shall unlock the Door he howls without.

And this I know: whether the one True Light 305
Kindle to Love, or Wrath-consume me quite,
One Flash of It within the Tavern caught
Better than in the Temple lost outright.

What! out of senseless Nothing to provoke
A conscious Something to resent the yoke 310
Of unpermitted Pleasure, under pain
Of Everlasting Penalties, if broke!

What! from his helpless Creature be repaid
Pure Gold for what he lent him dross-allay'd—
Sue for a Debt he never did contract, 315
And cannot answer—Oh the sorry trade!

277. **The Ball,** in a game of polo. 298. **the Foal,** the equatorial constellation of Equulus (little Horse). 299. **Parwín and Mushtarí.** Parwín refers to the Pleiades; Mushtarí is Arabic for the planet Jupiter. 302. **Dervish,** any Mohammedan zealot.

Oh Thou, who didst with pitfall and with gin
Beset the Road I was to wander in,
　　Thou wilt not with Predestined Evil round
Enmesh, and then impute my Fall to Sin!　　320

O Thou, who Man of baser Earth didst make,
And ev'n with Paradise devise the Snake:
　　For all the Sin wherewith the Face of Man
Is blacken'd—Man's forgiveness give—and take!

———

As under cover of departing Day　　325
Slunk hunger-stricken Ramazán away,
　　Once more within the Potter's house alone
I stood, surrounded by the Shapes of Clay.

Shapes of all Sorts and Sizes, great and small,
That stood along the floor and by the wall;　　330
　　And some loquacious Vessels were; and some
Listen'd perhaps, but never talk'd at all.

Said one among them—"Surely not in vain
My substance of the common Earth was ta'en
　　And to this Figure moulded, to be broke,　　335
Or trampled back to shapeless Earth again."

Then said a Second—"Ne'er a peevish Boy
Would break the Bowl from which he drank in joy;
　　And He that with his hand the Vessel made
Will surely not in after Wrath destroy."　　340

After a momentary silence spake
Some Vessel of a more ungainly Make;
　　They sneer at me for leaning all awry:
"What! did the Hand then of the Potter shake?"

Whereat some one of the loquacious Lot—　　345
I think a Súfi pipkin—waxing hot—
　　"All this of Pot and Potter—Tell me, then,
Who is the Potter, pray, and who the Pot?"

"Why," said another, "some there are who tell
Of one who threatens he will toss to Hell　　350
　　The luckless Pots he marr'd in making—Pish!
He's a Good Fellow, and 't will all be well."

"Well," murmur'd one, "let whoso make or buy,
My Clay with long Oblivion is gone dry:
　　But fill me with the old familiar Juice,　　355
Methinks I might recover by and by."

So, while the Vessels one by one were speaking,
The little Moon look'd in that all were seeking:

326. **Ramazán,** the Mohammedan fasting month. 346. **Súfi.** See p. 44, Hafiz headnote.

And then they jogg'd each other, "Brother!
　　Brother!
Now for the Potter's shoulder-knot a-creaking!"

———

Ah, with the Grape my fading Life provide,　　361
And wash the Body whence the Life has died,
　　And lay me, shrouded in the living Leaf,
By some not unfrequented Garden-side.

That ev'n my buried Ashes such a snare　　365
Of Vintage shall fling up into the Air
　　As not a True-believer passing by
But shall be overtaken unaware.

Indeed the Idols I have loved so long
Have done my credit in this World much wrong:
　　Have drown'd my Glory in a shallow Cup,　　371
And sold my Reputation for a Song.

Indeed, indeed, Repentance oft before
I swore—but was I sober when I swore?
　　And then and then came Spring, and Rose-in-
　　　　hand　　375
My threadbare Penitence apieces tore.

And much as Wine has play'd the Infidel,
And robb'd me of my Robe of Honor—Well,
　　I wonder often what the Vintners buy
One half so precious as the stuff they sell.　　380

Yet ah, that Spring should vanish with the Rose!
That Youth's sweet-scented manuscript should close!
　　The Nightingale that in the branches sang,
Ah whence, and whither flown again, who knows!

Would but the Desert of the Fountain yield　　385
One glimpse—if dimly, yet indeed, reveal'd,
　　To which the fainting Traveller might spring
As springs the trampled herbage of the field!

Would but some wingéd Angel ere too late
Arrest the yet unfolded Roll of Fate,　　390
　　And make the stern Recorder otherwise
Enregister, or quite obliterate!

Ah, Love! could you and I with Him conspire
To grasp this sorry Scheme of Things entire,
　　Would we not shatter it to bits—and then　　395
Remould it nearer to the Heart's Desire!

———

Yon rising Moon that looks for us again—
How oft hereafter will she wax and wane;
　　How oft hereafter rising look for us
Through this same Garden—and for *one* in vain!

And when like her, O Sákí, you shall pass   401
Among the Guests Star-scatter'd on the Grass,
   And in your joyous errand reach the spot
Where I made One—turn down an empty Glass!

Hafiz

c. 1300–c. 1388

Friend of Shah and Sultan, religious teacher and mystic, lover of love and worshiper of all that is beautiful in living, Hafiz (Shemsuddin Mohammed) stands as the last of the distinguished group of Persian poets whose preëminence coincides with the intellectual and artistic preëminence of their Moslem world. Hafiz spent his life in Shiraz, Persia, a city as peculiarly identified with him as Nishapur was with Omar Khayyam and Bagdad with Haroun al-Raschid. His life span covered the greater part of the fourteenth century, for he died at a great age in 1388 or very soon thereafter. He was born about the time that Dante wrote *The Divine Comedy* and was a mature writer at the time of Chaucer's birth.

No poet of the Oriental world is more often quoted by Orientals, and none has had such a long-lasting international reputation, although among English-speaking peoples Omar Khayyam is far better known, partly because of Fitzgerald's magnificent English version of Omar's *rubaiyat*. Actually there are many points in common between Hafiz and Omar Khayyam. Both celebrate the joys of the flesh and the joys of the vine, and both imply that these joys are to be received not only in the physical but also in the spiritual sense. But Hafiz, living more than two hundred years after Omar, was clearly caught up in Sufism—the philosophy of a particular mystical sect which Omar Khayyam regarded satirically rather than otherwise. The Sufists preached oneness with God, who was the source of all truth and beauty. It is impossible to read the poetry of Hafiz, as exemplified by *The Divan* (or *Collected Odes*), without sensing sooner or later these Sufistic tendencies; but these tendencies, which show marked affinity with the Platonic writings, are left both vague and diffuse. Perhaps it is this vagueness, which is after all inherent in the very nature of Sufistic teachings, that made Omar Khayyam impatient with the sect; at any rate, his was an instinctively scientific mind, whereas that of Hafiz was by nature transcendental.

There is no doubt, however, that Hafiz was a man of the world as well as a mystic. It is difficult for the Occidental (though not for the Oriental) to comprehend this seeming paradox. None other than the illustrious Sherlock Holmes has borne witness that "there is as much sense in Hafiz as in Horace, and as much knowledge of the world." It was the conqueror Timur (Tamerlane) who sternly reproached Hafiz for having dared to put the eyebrow of the poet's mistress above Tamer-

lane's glory in capturing Shiraz; but Hafiz had the more profound wisdom when he smiled in the assurance that the poet was right. It was Hafiz who expressed the hope that his tomb might be the shrine for all drunkards, very much as Omar Khayyam wished to be identified in death with rose petals and the grape. And in the sense that one can be drunk not only on wine but also on love and on religion—which is precisely the interpretation that Hafiz would put upon the idea of drunkenness —his wish has been fulfilled.

The Divan (Odes)

V

Up, sákí!—let the goblet flow;
   Strew with dust the head of our earthly woe!

Give me thy cup; that, joy-possessed,
I may tear this azure cowl from my breast.

The wise may deem me lost to shame,   5
But no care have I for renown or name.

Bring wine!—how many a witless head
By the wind of pride has with dust been spread!

My bosom's fumes, my sighs so warm,
Have inflamed yon crude and unfeeling swarm.   10

This mad heart's secret, well I know,
Is beyond the thoughts of both high and low.

E'en by that sweetheart charmed am I,
Who once from my heart made sweetness fly.

Who that my Silvern Tree hath seen,   15
Would regard the cypress that decks the green?

    In grief be patient,
      Night and day,
    Till thy fortune, Hafiz,
      Thy wish obey.

XII

Oh! where are deeds of virtue and this frail spirit
   where?
How wide the space that sunders the bounds of
   Here and There!

The Divan (Odes).[5] Translated by H. Bicknell. Reprinted by permission of P. F. Collier and Son Corporation.
4. **azure cowl,** the cloak of deceit and false humility. Hafiz is here attacking the members of Sheikh Hazan's Order of Dervishes, who were hostile to the poet through most of his career. 10. **yon . . . swarm,** another hostile reference to Sheikh Hazan's Order of Dervishes. 15–16. **Silvern Tree . . . green?** By a silver tree Hafiz is referring to the precious quality of his own way of life, for in many parts of the Orient silver is more highly regarded than gold.

Can toping aught in common with works and wor-
    ship own?
Where is regard for sermons, where is the rebeck's
    tone?

My heart abhors the cloister, and the false cowl its
    sign: 5
Where is the Magian's cloister, and where is his pure
    wine?

'Tis fled: may memory sweetly mind me of union's
    days!
Where is that voice of anger, where those coquettish
    ways?

Can a foe's heart be kindled by the friend's face so
    bright?
Where is a lamp unlighted, and the clear Day-star's
    light?   10

As dust upon thy threshold supplies my eyes with
    balm,
If I forsake thy presence, where can I hope for calm?

Turn from that chin's fair apple; a pit is on the way.
To what, O heart, aspirest thou? Whither thus
    quickly? Say!

    Seek not, O friend, in Hafiz   15
    Patience, nor rest from care;
    Patience and rest—what are they?
    Where is calm slumber? Where?

XLII

'TIS a deep charm which wakes the lover's flame,
Not ruby lip, nor verdant down its name.

Beauty is not the eye, lock, cheek, and mole;
A thousand subtle points the heart control.

XLV

O BREEZE of morn! where is the place which guards
    my friend from strife?
Where is the abode of that sly Moon who lovers
    robs of life?

The night is dark, the Happy Vale in front of me I
    trace.   3
Where is the fire of Sinai, where is the meeting
    place?

Here jointly are the wine-filled cup, the rose, the
    minstrel; yet   5
While we lack love, no bliss is here: where can my
    Loved be met?

Of the Sheikh's cell my heart has tired, and of the
    convent bare:
Where is my friend, the Christian's child, the vint-
    ner's mansion? Where?

    Hafiz, if o'er the glade of earth
    The autumn blast is borne,   10
    Grieve not, but musing ask thyself:
    "Where has the rose no thorn?"

LXIII

MY HEART has of the world grown weary and all
    that it can lend:
The shrine of my affection holds no Being but my
    friend.

If e'er for me thy love's sweet garden a fragrant
    breath exhale,
My heart, expansive in its joy, shall bud-like burst
    its veil.

Should I upon love's path advise thee, when now
    a fool I've grown,   5
'Twould be the story of the fool, the pitcher, and
    the stone.

Go! say to the secluded zealot: "Withhold thy
    blame; for know,
I find the Arch of the Mihrab but in an eyebrow's
    bow."

Between the Ka'bah and the wine-house, no differ-
    ence I see:
Whate'er the spot my glance surveys, there equally
    is He.   10

'Tis not for beard, hair, eyebrow only, Kalandarism
    should care:
The Kalandar computes the Path by adding hair to
    hair.

    The Kalandar who gives a hair's head
    An easy path doth tread:
    The Kalandar of genuine stamp,   15
    As Hafiz gives his head.

4. rebeck, an old stringed instrument and ancestor of the violin.
7. union's days, that is, the days when the lovers were together.
13. chin's . . . apple. A favorite "conceit" of Oriental love poetry
in this era is the belief that a cleft in the chin was a prime indication
of beauty. 3. Happy Vale. The Valley of Aiman ("Happiness")
was where God appeared to Moses—metaphorically, then, the abode
of the beloved.

8. Arch of the Mihrab. The *mihrab* is the niche in a mosque, facing
which all Mohammedans pray. 9. Ka'bah, the Palladium, the
"Holy of Holies," of the Moslem faith, located in the holy city of
Mecca. 11-16. Kalandarism . . . head. The Kalenders are an
order of Mohammedan dervishes who wander about and beg. Hafiz
is making the point that the worthless kalender will observe ex-
ternals by shaving off his beard and by tonsuring but will neglect
his fundamental spiritual duty; the true kalender, like the poet, will
sacrifice anything, even his head, for the scrupulous observance of
his religious duty.

LXIX

MY HEART desires the face so fair of Farrukh;
It is perturbed as is the hair of Farrukh.

No creature but that lock, that Hindu swart,
Enjoyment from the cheek has sought of Farrukh.

A blackamoor by Fortune blest is he,   5
Placed at the side, and near the knee of Farrukh.

Shy as the aspen is the cypress seen,
Awed by the captivating mien of Farrukh.

Sákí, bring syrtis-tinted wine to tell
Of those narcissi, potent spell of Farrukh.   10

Bent as the archer's bow my frame is now,
From woes continuous as the brow of Farrukh.

E'en Tartar gales which musky odors whirl,
Faint at the amber-breathing curl of Farrukh.

If leans the human heart to any place,   15
Mine has a yearning to the grace of Farrukh.

> That lofty soul
> Shall have my service true,
> That serves, as Hafiz,
> The Hindu of Farrukh.   20

LXXXVII

WHEN beamed thy beauty on creation's morn,
The world was set on fire by love new-born.

Thy cheeks shone bright, yet angels' hearts were
    cold:
Then flashed it fire, and turned to Adam's mould.

The lamp of Reason from this flame had burned,   5
But lightning jealousy the world o'erturned.

The enemy Thy secret sought to gain;
A hand unseen repelled the beast profane.

The die of Fate may render others glad:
My own heart saddens, for its lot is sad.   10

Thy chin's deep pit allures the lofty mind:
The hand would grasp thy locks in twines entwined.

> Hafiz his love-scroll
> To Thyself addressed,
> When he had cancelled   15
> What his heart loved best.

1. **Farrukh,** obviously a beloved.   3. **Hindu swart,** Farrukh's servant.

CXV

LOST Joseph shall return to Kanaan's land—Despair
    not;
Affliction's cell of gloom with flowers shall bloom:
> Despair not.

Sad heart, thy state shall mend; repel despondency;
Thy head confused with pain shall sense regain;   5
> Despair not.

When life's fresh spring returns upon the dais mead,
O night-bird! o'er thy head the rose shall spread.
> Despair not.

Hope on, though things unseen may baffle thy re-
    search;   10
Mysterious sports we hail beyond the veil:
> Despair not.

Has the revolving Sphere two days opposed thy
    wish,
Know that the circling Round is changeful found:
> Despair not.   15

If on the Ka' bah bent, thou brave the desert sand,
Though from the acacias' thorns thy foot be torn,
> Despair not.

Heart, should the flood of death life's fabric sweep
    away,
Noah shall steer the Ark o'er billows dark: 20
> Despair not.

Though perilous the stage, though out of sight the
    goal,
Whithersoe'er we wend, there is an end:
> Despair not.

If Love evades our grasp, and rivals press our suit,
God, Lord of every change, surveys the range: 26
> Despair not.

> Hafiz, in thy poor nook—
> Alone, the dark night through—
> Prayer and the Koran's page   30
> Shall grief assuage—
> > Despair not.

CXXXV

I TRIED my fortune in this city lorn:
From out its whirlpool must my pack be borne.

1. **Lost Joseph.** The Biblical Joseph became in the legendry of the Near East the symbol of a lover; the story of Joseph and Potiphar's wife (Zuleika) was considered a deathless romance. 13–14. **Sphere . . . Round.** The spheres of Heaven in the Ptolemaic system move daily around the stationary Earth; the Round refers to their astrological influence.

I gnaw my hand, and, heaving sighs of ire,
I light in my rent frame the rose's fire.

Sweet sang the bulbul at the close of day   5
The rose attentive on her leafy spray:

"O heart! be joyful, for thy ruthless Love
Sits down ill-tempered at the sphere above.

"To make the false, harsh world thyself pass o'er,
Ne'er promise falsely and be harsh no more.   10

"If beat misfortune's waves upon heavens roof,
Devout men's fate and gear bide ocean-proof.

> "Hafiz, if lasting
> Were enjoyment's day,
> Jem's throne would never   15
> Have been swept away."

CLXXX

O THOU who art unlearned still, the quest of love
    essay:
Canst thou who hast not trod the path guide others
    on the way?

While in the school of Truth thou stay'st, from
    Master Love to learn,
Endeavor, though a son today, the father's grade to
    earn.

Slumber and food have held thee far from Love's
    exalted good: 5
Wouldst thou attain the goal of love, abstain from
    sleep and food.

If with the rays of love of truth thy heart and soul
    be clear,
By God! thy beauty shall outshine the sun which
    lights the sphere.

Wash from the dross of life thy hands, as the Path's
    men of old,
And winning Love's alchemic power, transmute thy-
    self to gold.   10

On all thy frame, from head to foot, the light of God
    shall shine,
If on the Lord of Glory's path nor head nor foot be
    thine.

An instant plunge into God's sea, nor e'er the truth
    forget
That the Seven Seas' o'erwhelming tide, no hair of
    thine shall wet.

15. Jem, Jamshyd; see notes, pp. 38, 39. 9. Path's men of old,
old and orthodox believers.

If once thy glancing eye repose on the Creator's
    face,   15
Thenceforth among the men who glance shall doubt-
    less be thy place.

When that which thy existence frames all upside-
    down shall be,
Imagine not that up and down shall be the lot of
    thee.

> Hafiz, if ever in thy head
>   Dwell Union's wish serene,   20
> Thou must become the threshold's dust
>   Of men whose sight is keen.

The New Testament

The New Testament evangelical Book of Matthew was probably written somewhere between
the years 65 and 68, although some scholars have thought
that the passage in Chapter 22:6–7 ("But when the king
heard thereof, he was wroth; and he sent forth his armies,
and destroyed these murderers, and burned up their
city") refers to the destruction of Jerusalem by the
Romans in 70. The author of this Gospel was presumably
a Greek-speaking or Hellenistic Jewish Christian, who
wrote with the definite purpose of confirming others of
his race and religious profession in the view that Jesus
Christ was the true Messiah, whose coming was prophesied in the Old Testament. This Gospel is therefore much
more closely connected than the other three (Mark,
Luke, and John) with the traditions of the Old Testament—a fact which appears evident from the very first
chapter, with its long genealogy from Abraham to Christ,
from the attention given in Matthew to Hebrew prophets
and their sayings (which are to be fulfilled in the words
and deeds of Christ), and from the constant reference to
Christ as the "Son of David."

The source of this Gospel is in part the earlier Book
of Mark and in part a lost Gospel, possibly in Aramaic
and possibly by the disciple Matthew himself. It contains
also, of course, the usual increments of Jewish or Semitic
folklore, as well as the permeating atmosphere of Greek
and Oriental idealistic philosophies, which can be traced
throughout Christian teachings. Although it may be assumed that the author was a Palestinian, it is not certain
whether he actually composed the Gospel in Palestine;
and localities as far apart as Syria in the north and
Alexandria in the south have been suggested for the
geographical origin of the work.

One fact, however, is indisputable. The Gospel according to St. Matthew is not only the longest of the four
gospels, but it contains also more of the longer discourses
of Christ. It seems most likely that these longer discourses
represent a culling by the author of various shorter sayings of Christ and the gathering of them into groups of

16. men who glance, lovers.

precepts and admonitions. or, as the product has been rather happily described, into "bouquets of discourse." There are five of these: (1) The Sermon on the Mount (5:1 to 7:27); (2) The Address to the Apostles (10:5–42); (3) The Kingdom of Heaven Parables (13:1–52); (4) On Humility and Forgiveness (18:1–35); and (5) The Apocalyptic Utterances (24:4 to 25:46). In these five great passages, especially in the Sermon on the Mount, lies the quintessence of the Christian ideal of conduct. But no less arresting to the general reader and student are the shrewd grasp of human relationships and the insight into human nature, the poetic didacticism of the parables, the otherworldliness of the kernels of Christian faith, the almost rhapsodic picture of ruin and desolation to be encountered in the Latter Day, and the magnificent human wisdom shown throughout. Apart from these longer discourses, there is portrayed the true personality and life of Christ, from His birth to the unforgettable drama of His Passion and Crucifixion; and although Luke's account of His birth and John's account of His Passion are more moving, neither of these Gospels is more comprehensive in a biographical sense. The impact of all this upon Christian minds since the inception of the Faith need not be dwelt upon here; virtually every chapter of Matthew has contributed to the phraseology and the religious and ethical imagination of the Christian world.

The establishment of the early Christian Church and the part played by Saul of Tarsus, who was converted into the missionary apostle Paul, make up together the most important part of the New Testament Book of Acts. The labors of Paul as the spokesman for Christianity and as the organizer of the Church and queller of factions within the Church are nothing less than monumental; and his various epistles to members of the Church in the many localities of Asia Minor and the Roman world, known as the Pauline Epistles, constitute an extremely influential body of Christian doctrine which does much to explain the structure of modern Christian ecclesiasticism.

Some fifteen years before his death in the year 67, Paul spent more than a year and a half (50–51) in Corinth, Greece, working on the ironing out of a serious factional dispute among the Christians of that city. The result of his efforts was a pair of epistles, in the nature of pastoral letters, to the members of the Church in Corinth, discussing tactfully their points of dispute and stating here and there some of the cardinal tenets of the Christian belief. The first of these two, I Corinthians, written shortly after 50 A.D., is more philosophical than the second, and in the thirteenth and fifteenth chapters reaches perhaps the most eloquent of the many eloquent peaks achieved by Paul in his missionary and administrative career. For the thirteenth chapter, with its noble exaltation of the Love of Mankind, is perhaps the most famous section of the Pauline Epistles; and the fifteenth chapter, with its towering words on immortality, has become an integral part of the Christian burial service, particularly among the many modern Protestant sects.

A twelfth-century manuscript shows St. Matthew writing his gospel, inspired by his traditional symbol, the angel.

The Gospel
ACCORDING TO
Saint Matthew

CHAPTER I

. . . Now the birth of Jesus Christ was on this wise: When as his mother Mary was espoused to Joseph, before they came together, she was found with child of the Holy Ghost.

Then Joseph her husband, being a just man, and not willing to make her a public example, was minded to put her away privily.

But while he thought on these things, behold, the angel of the Lord appeared unto him in a dream, saying, 'Joseph, thou son of David, fear not to take unto thee Mary thy wife; for that which is conceived in her is of the Holy Ghost.

'And she shall bring forth a son, and thou shalt

*The Gospel according to Saint Matthew.*⁴ From the King James Version of the Bible.

call his name JESUS: for he shall save his people from their sins.'

Now all this was done, that it might be fulfilled which was spoken of the Lord by the prophet, saying:

'Behold, a virgin shall be with child, and shall bring forth a son, and they shall call his name Emmanuel, which being interpreted is, God with us.'

Then Joseph, being raised from sleep, did as the angel of the Lord had bidden him, and took unto him his wife:

And knew her not till she had brought forth her firstborn son: and he called his name JESUS.

CHAPTER II

Now when Jesus was born in Bethlehem of Judaea in the days of Herod the king, behold, there came wise men from the east to Jerusalem,

Saying, 'Where is he that is born King of the Jews? for we have seen his star in the east, and are come to worship him.'

When Herod the king had heard these things, he was troubled, and all Jerusalem with him.

And when he had gathered all the chief priests and scribes of the people together, he demanded of them where Christ should be born.

And they said unto him, 'In Bethlehem of Judaea, for thus it is written by the prophet:

"And thou, Bethlehem, in the land of Juda, art not the least among the princes of Juda, for out of thee shall come a Governor, that shall rule my people Israel."'

Then Herod, when he had privily called the wise men, inquired of them diligently what time the star appeared.

And he sent them to Bethlehem, and said, 'Go and search diligently for the young child; and when ye have found him, bring me word again, that I may come and worship him also.'

When they had heard the king, they departed; and, lo, the star, which they saw in the east, went before them, till it came and stood over where the young child was.

When they saw the star, they rejoiced with exceeding great joy.

And when they were come into the house, they saw the young child with Mary his mother, and fell down, and worshipped him; and when they had opened their treasures, they presented unto him gifts: gold, and frankincense, and myrrh.

And being warned of God in a dream that they should not return to Herod, they departed into their own country another way.

And when they were departed, behold, the angel of the Lord appeareth to Joseph in a dream, saying, 'Arise, and take the young child and his mother, and flee into Egypt, and be thou there until I bring thee word, for Herod will seek the young child to destroy him.'

When he arose, he took the young child and his mother by night, and departed into Egypt;

And was there until the death of Herod, that it might be fulfilled which was spoken of the Lord by the prophet, saying: 'Out of Egypt have I called my son.'

Then Herod, when he saw that he was mocked of the wise men, was exceeding wroth, and sent forth, and slew all the children that were in Bethlehem, and in all the coasts thereof, from two years old and under, according to the time which he had diligently inquired of the wise men.

Then was fulfilled that which was spoken by Jeremy the prophet, saying:

'In Rama was there a voice heard, lamentation and weeping, and great mourning; Rachel weeping for her children, and would not be comforted, because they were not.'

But when Herod was dead, behold, an angel of the Lord appeareth in a dream to Joseph in Egypt,

Saying, 'Arise, and take the young child and his mother, and go into the land of Israel, for they are dead which sought the young child's life.'

And he arose, and took the young child and his mother, and came into the land of Israel.

But when he heard that Archelaus did reign in Judaea in the room of his father Herod, he was afraid to go thither; notwithstanding, being warned of God in a dream, he turned aside into the parts of Galilee;

And he came and dwelt in a city called Nazareth, that it might be fulfilled which was spoken by the prophets, 'He shall be called a Nazarene.'

CHAPTER III

In those days came John the Baptist, preaching in the wilderness of Judaea,

And saying, 'Repent ye, for the kingdom of Heaven is at hand.

For this is he that was spoken of by the prophet Esaias, saying, "The voice of one crying in the wilderness, 'Prepare ye the way of the Lord, make his paths straight.'"'

And the same John had his raiment of camel's hair, and a leathern girdle about his loins; and his meat was locusts and wild honey.

Then went out to him Jerusalem, and all Judaea, and all the region about Jordan,

1. JESUS, that is, the Savior. 6–8. 'Behold . . . us.' See Isaiah, 7:14 and 9:6. 50. Herod, known as Herod the Great, King of Judaea (appointed by the Roman Senate) from 40 B.C. until his death in 4 B.C. He was known as a servile cringer before Rome, as a builder of cities, and as a despotic and bloody tyrant given to massacres.

72. Rama. See Jeremiah, 31:15. The name is applied to several places in Palestine and used here to refer to the whole country. 90. Nazarene. See Judges, 13:5 and I Samuel, 1:11. 96–98. "The voice . . . straight." See Isaiah, 11:3.

And were baptized of him in Jordan, confessing their sins.

But when he saw many of the Pharisees and Sadducees come to his baptism, he said unto them, 'O generation of vipers, who hath warned you to flee from the wrath to come?

'Bring forth therefore fruits meet for repentance,

'And think not to say within yourselves, "We have Abraham to our father," for I say unto you, that God is able of these stones to raise up children unto Abraham.

'And now also the axe is laid unto the root of the trees; therefore every tree which bringeth not forth good fruit is hewn down, and cast into the fire.

'I indeed baptize you with water unto repentance, but he that cometh after me is mightier than I, whose shoes I am not worthy to bear; he shall baptize you with the Holy Ghost, and with fire:

'Whose fan is in his hand, and he will thoroughly purge his floor, and gather his wheat into the garner; but he will burn up the chaff with unquenchable fire.'

Then cometh Jesus from Galilee to Jordan unto John, to be baptized of him.

But John forbad him, saying, 'I have need to be baptized of thee, and comest thou to me?'

And Jesus answering said unto him, 'Suffer it to be so now, for thus it becometh us to fulfill all righteousness.' Then he suffered him.

And Jesus, when he was baptized, went up straightway out of the water; and, lo, the heavens were opened unto him, and he saw the Spirit of God descending like a dove, and lighting upon him;

And, lo, a voice from Heaven, saying, 'This is my beloved Son, in whom I am well pleased.'

CHAPTER IV

Then was Jesus led up of the spirit into the wilderness to be tempted of the devil.

And when he had fasted forty days and forty nights, he was afterward a-hungred.

And when the tempter came to him, he said, 'If thou be the Son of God, command that these stones be made bread.'

But he answered and said, 'It is written, "Man shall not live by bread alone, but by every word that proceedeth out of the mouth of God."'

Then the devil taketh him up into the holy city, and setteth him on a pinnacle of the temple,

And saith unto him, 'If thou be the Son of God, cast thyself down, for it is written, "He shall give his angels charge concerning thee; and in their hands they shall bear thee up, lest at any time thou dash thy foot against a stone."'

Jesus said unto him, 'It is written again, "Thou shalt not tempt the Lord thy God."'

Again, the devil taketh him up into an exceeding high mountain, and showeth him all the kingdoms of the world, and the glory of them,

And saith unto him, 'All these things will I give thee, if thou wilt fall down and worship me.'

Then saith Jesus unto him, 'Get thee hence, Satan, for it is written, "Thou shalt worship the Lord thy God, and him only shalt thou serve."'

Then the devil leaveth him, and, behold, angels came and ministered unto him.

Now when Jesus had heard that John was cast into prison, he departed into Galilee;

And leaving Nazareth, he came and dwelt in Capernaum, which is upon the sea coast, in the borders of Zabulon and Nepthalim,

That it might be fulfilled which was spoken by Esaias the prophet, saying:

'The land of Zabulon, and the land of Nepthalim, by the way of the sea, beyond Jordan, Galilee of the Gentiles;

'The people which sat in darkness saw great light; and to them which sat in the region and shadow of death light is sprung up.'

From that time Jesus began to preach, and to say, 'Repent; for the kingdom of heaven is at hand.'

And Jesus walking by the sea of Galilee, saw two brethren, Simon called Peter, and Andrew his brother, casting a net into the sea, for they were fishers.

And he saith unto them, 'Follow me, and I will make you fishers of men.'

And they straightway left their nets, and followed him.

And going on from thence, he saw other two brethren, James the son of Zebedee, and John his brother, in a ship with Zebedee their father, mending their nets; and he called them.

And they immediately left their ship and their father and followed him.

And Jesus went about all Galilee, teaching in their synagogues, and preaching the gospel of the Kingdom, and healing all manner of sickness and all manner of disease among the people.

And his fame went throughout all Syria; and they brought unto him all sick people that were taken with divers diseases and torments, and those which were possessed with devils, and those which were lunatic, and those that had the palsy; and he healed them.

3-4. **Pharisees and Sadducees,** two important sects of Jews in Jerusalem of the time of Christ. The chief contribution of the Pharisees was to make the synagogue the center of social, intellectual, and religious life; they were formalistic and insisted on fundamentalistic links with Hebrew religious traditions, as represented not only by the Old Testament but by the *Talmud* and rabbinical lore. The Sadducees accepted only the written word of the scriptures and not the mass of oral tradition and ritual as well.

69. **Zabulon . . . Nepthalim,** names of two of the original twelve tribes of Israel.

And there followed him great multitudes of people from Galilee, and from Decapolis, and from Jerusalem, and from Judaea, and from beyond Jordan.

CHAPTER V

And seeing the multitudes, he went up into a mountain; and when he was set, his disciples came unto him;

And he opened his mouth, and taught them, saying:

'Blessed are the poor in spirit, for theirs is the kingdom of Heaven.

'Blessed are they that mourn, for they shall be comforted.

'Blessed are the meek, for they shall inherit the earth.

'Blessed are they which do hunger and thirst after righteousness, for they shall be filled.

'Blessed are the merciful, for they shall obtain mercy.

'Blessed are the pure in heart, for they shall see God.

'Blessed are the peacemakers, for they shall be called the children of God.

'Blessed are they which are persecuted for righteousness' sake, for theirs is the kingdom of Heaven.

'Blessed are ye, when men shall revile you, and persecute you, and shall say all manner of evil against you falsely, for my sake.

'Rejoice, and be exceeding glad, for great is your reward in Heaven, for so persecuted they the prophets which were before you.

'Ye are the salt of the earth, but if the salt have lost his savor, wherewith shall it be salted? It is thenceforth good for nothing, but to be cast out, and to be trodden under foot of men.

'Ye are the light of the world. A city that is set on a hill cannot be hid.

'Neither do men light a candle, and put it under a bushel, but on a candlestick; and it giveth light unto all that are in the house.

'Let your light so shine before men that they may see your good works, and glorify your Father which is in Heaven.

'Think not that I am come to destroy the law, or the prophets; I am not come to destroy, but to fulfill.

'For verily I say unto you, Till Heaven and earth pass, one jot or one tittle shall in no wise pass from the law, till all be fulfilled.

'Whosoever therefore shall break one of these least commandments, and shall teach men so, he shall be called the least in the kingdom of Heaven; but whosoever shall do and teach them, the same shall be called great in the Kingdom of Heaven.

'For I say unto you, that except your righteousness shall exceed the righteousness of the scribes and Pharisees, ye shall in no case enter into the kingdom of Heaven.

'Ye have heard that it was said by them of old time, "Thou shalt not kill"; and whosoever shall kill shall be in danger of the judgment:

'But I say unto you, that whosoever is angry with his brother without a cause shall be in danger of the judgment; and whosoever shall say to his brother, "Raca," shall be in danger of the council; but whosoever shall say, "Thou fool," shall be in danger of hell-fire.

'Therefore if thou bring thy gift to the altar, and there rememberest that thy brother hath ought against thee,

'Leave there thy gift before the altar, and go thy way; first be reconciled to thy brother, and then come and offer thy gift.

'Agree with thine adversary quickly whiles thou are in the way with him, lest at any time the adversary deliver thee to the judge, and the judge deliver thee to the officer, and thou be cast into prison.

'Verily I say unto thee, thou shalt by no means come out thence, till thou hast paid the uttermost farthing.

'Ye have heard that it was said by them of old time, "Thou shalt not commit adultery,"

'But I say unto you, that whosoever looketh on a woman to lust after her hath committed adultery with her already in his heart.

'And if thy right eye offend thee, pluck it out, and cast it from thee, for it is profitable for thee that one of thy members perish, and not that thy whole body should be cast into Hell.

'And if thy right hand offend thee, cut it off, and cast it from thee, for it is profitable for thee that one of thy members should perish, and not that thy whole body should be cast into Hell.

'It hath been said, "Whosoever shall put away his wife, let him give her a writing of divorcement,"

'But I say unto you, that whosoever shall put away his wife, saving for the cause of fornication, causeth her to commit adultery; and whosoever shall marry her that is divorced committeth adultery.

'Again, ye have heard that it hath been said by them of old time, "Thou shalt not forswear thyself, but shalt perform unto the Lord thine oaths,"

'But I say unto you, swear not at all, neither by Heaven, for it is God's throne;

'Nor by the earth, for it is his footstool; neither by Jerusalem, for it is the city of the great King.

---

2. **Decapolis,** the name of a loose confederation of largely non-Jewish states lying both east and west of the River Jordan. 39. **bushel,** originally a basket or any kind of vessel holding the amount known by the name of the unit.

65. **"Raca,"** vain man.

'Neither shalt thou swear by thy head, because thou canst not make one hair white or black.

'But let your communication be, "Yea, yea; nay, nay!" for whatsoever is more than these cometh of evil.

'Ye have heard that it hath been said, "An eye for an eye, and a tooth for a tooth":

'But I say unto you, that ye resist not evil; but whosoever shall smite thee on thy right cheek, turn to him the other also.

'And if any man will sue thee at the law, and take away thy coat, let him have thy cloak also.

'And whosoever shall compel thee to go a mile, go with him twain.

'Give to him that asketh thee, and from him that would borrow of thee turn thou not away.

'Ye have heard that it hath been said, "Thou shalt love thy neighbor and hate thine enemy."

'But I say unto you, love your enemies, bless them that curse you, do good to them that hate you, and pray for them which despitefully use you, and persecute you,

'That ye may be the children of your Father which is in Heaven, for he maketh his sun to rise on the evil and on the good, and sendeth rain on the just and on the unjust.

'For if ye love them which love you, what reward have ye? Do not even the publicans the same?

'And if ye salute your brethren only, what do ye more than others? Do not even the publicans so?

'Be ye therefore perfect, even as your Father which is in Heaven is perfect.

CHAPTER VI

'Take heed that ye do not your alms before men, to be seen of them; otherwise ye have no reward of your Father which is in Heaven.

'Therefore when thou doest thine alms, do not sound a trumpet before thee, as the hypocrites do in the synagogues and in the streets, that they may have glory of men. Verily I say unto you, they have their reward.

'But when thou doest alms, let not thy left hand know what thy right hand doeth,

'That thine alms may be in secret, and thy Father which seeth in secret himself shall reward thee openly.

'And when thou prayest, thou shalt not be as the hypocrites are, for they love to pray standing in the synagogues and in the corners of the streets, that they may be seen of men. Verily I say unto you, they have their reward.

'But thou, when thou prayest, enter into thy closet, and when thou hast shut thy door, pray to thy Father which is in secret; and thy Father which seeth in secret shall reward thee openly.

'But when ye pray, use not vain repetitions, as the heathen do, for they think that they shall be heard for their much speaking.

'Be not ye therefore like unto them, for your Father knoweth what things ye have need of, before you ask him.

'After this manner therefore pray ye: "Our Father, which art in Heaven, hallowed be thy name.

' "Thy kingdom come. Thy will be done in earth, as it is in Heaven.

' "Give us this day our daily bread,

' "And forgive us our debts, as we forgive our debtors.

' "And lead us not into temptation, but deliver us from evil, for thine is the kingdom and the power and the glory, for ever. Amen."

'For if ye forgive men their trespasses, your heavenly Father will also forgive you;

'But if ye forgive not men their trespasses, neither will your Father forgive your trespasses.

'Moreover, when ye fast, be not, as the hypocrites, of a sad countenance, for they disfigure their faces, that they may appear unto men to fast. Verily I say unto you, they have their reward.

'But thou, when thou fastest, anoint thine head, and wash thy face,

'That thou appear not unto men to fast, but unto thy Father which is in secret; and thy Father, which seeth in secret, shall reward thee openly.

'Lay not up for yourselves treasures upon earth, where moth and rust doth corrupt, and where thieves break through and steal;

'But lay up for yourselves treasures in Heaven, where neither moth nor rust doth corrupt, and where thieves do not break through nor steal.

'For where your treasure is, there will your heart be also.

'The light of the body is the eye; if therefore thine eye be single, thy whole body shall be full of light.

'But if thine eye be evil, thy whole body shall be full of darkness. If therefore the light that is in thee be darkness, how great is that darkness!

'No man can serve two masters, for either he will hate the one and love the other, or else he will hold to the one, and despise the other. Ye cannot serve God and Mammon.

'Therefore I say unto you, take no thought for your life, what ye shall eat, or what ye shall drink; nor yet for your body, what ye shall put on. Is not the life more than meat, and the body than raiment?

'Behold the fowls of the air, for they sow not, neither do they reap, nor gather into barns; yet your heavenly Father feedeth them. Are ye not much better than they?

79–80. **when . . . face;** in other words, go about your outward business in a normal fashion.   100. **Mammon,** a Syriac word used here (and here only) as a personification of riches and material possessions.

'Which of you by taking thought can add one cubit unto his stature?

'And why take ye thought for raiment? Consider the lilies of the field, how they grow; they toil not, neither do they spin;

'And yet I say unto you, that even Solomon in all his glory was not arrayed like one of these.

'Wherefore, if God so clothe the grass of the field, which today is, and tomorrow is cast into the oven, shall he not much more clothe you, O ye of little faith?

'Therefore take no thought, saying, "What shall we eat?" or "What shall we drink?" or "Wherewithal shall we be clothed?"

'(For after all these things do the Gentiles seek;) for your heavenly Father knoweth that ye have need of all these things.

'But seek ye first the kingdom of God, and his righteousness; and all these things shall be added unto you.

'Take therefore no thought for the morrow, for the morrow shall take thought for the things of itself. Sufficient unto the day is the evil thereof.

CHAPTER VII

'Judge not, that ye be not judged.

'For with what judgment ye judge, ye shall be judged; and with what measure ye mete, it shall be measured to you again.

'And why beholdest thou the mote that is in thy brother's eye, but considerest not the beam that is in thine own eye?

'Or how wilt thou say to thy brother, "Let me pull out the mote out of thine eye"; and, behold, a beam is in thine own eye?

'Thou hypocrite, first cast out the beam out of thine own eye; and then shalt thou see clearly to cast out the mote out of thy brother's eye.

'Give not that which is holy unto the dogs, neither cast ye your pearls before swine, lest they trample them under their feet, and turn again and rend you.

'Ask, and it shall be given you; seek, and ye shall find; knock, and it shall be opened unto you.

'For every one that asketh receiveth, and he that seeketh findeth; and to him that knocketh it shall be opened.

'Or what man is there of you, whom if his son ask bread, will he give him a stone?

'Or if he ask a fish, will he give him a serpent?

'If ye then, being evil, know how to give good gifts unto your children, how much more shall your Father which is in Heaven give good things to them that ask him?

2. **cubit,** an ancient measure, from eighteen to twenty inches. 28–29. **mote . . . beam.** A mote is a minute particle or speck of dirt; a beam is theoretically a splinter. Here the two are used virtually interchangeably.

'Therefore all things whatsoever ye would that men should do to you, do ye even so unto them, for this is the law and the prophets.

'Enter ye in at the strait gate, for wide is the gate, and broad is the way that leadeth to destruction, and many there be which go in thereat,

'Because strait is the gate, and narrow is the way, which leadeth unto life, and few there be that find it.

'Beware of false prophets, which come to you in sheep's clothing, but inwardly they are ravening wolves.

'Ye shall know them by their fruits. Do men gather grapes of thorns, or figs of thistles?

'Even so every good tree bringeth forth good fruit, but a corrupt tree bringeth forth evil fruit.

'A good tree cannot bring forth evil fruit, neither can a corrupt tree bring forth good fruit.

'Every tree that bringeth not forth good fruit is hewn down, and cast into the fire.

'Wherefore by their fruits ye shall know them.

'Not every one that saith unto me, "Lord, Lord," shall enter into the kingdom of Heaven, but he that doeth the will of my Father which is in Heaven.

'Many will say to me in that day, "Lord, Lord; have we not prophesied in thy name? and in thy name have cast out devils? and in thy name done many wonderful works?"

'And then will I profess unto them, "I never knew you; depart from me, ye that work iniquity."

'Therefore whosoever heareth these sayings of mine, and doeth them, I will liken him unto a wise man, which built his house upon a rock;

'And the rain descended, and the floods came, and the winds blew, and beat upon that house; and it fell not, for it was founded upon a rock.

'And every one that heareth these sayings of mine, and doeth them not, shall be likened unto a foolish man, which built his house upon the sand.

'And the rain descended, and the floods came, and the winds blew, and beat upon that house; and it fell; and great was the fall of it.'

And it came to pass, when Jesus had ended these sayings, the people were astonished at his doctrine,

For he taught them as one having authority, and not as the scribes.

CHAPTER IX

And he entered into a ship, and passed over, and came into his own city.

And behold, they brought to him a man sick of the palsy, lying on a bed; and Jesus, seeing their faith, said unto the sick of the palsy, 'Son, be of good cheer; thy sins be forgiven thee.'

And behold, certain of the scribes said within themselves, 'This man blasphemeth.'

And Jesus knowing their thoughts said, 'Wherefore think ye evil in your hearts?

'For whether is easier: to say, "Thy sins be forgiven thee?" or to say, "Arise and walk?"'

'But that ye may know that the Son of man hath power on earth to forgive sins' (then saith he to the sick of the palsy), "Arise, take up thy bed, and go unto thine house.'

And he arose, and departed to his house.

10 But when the multitudes saw it, they marvelled, and glorified God, which had given such power unto men.

And as Jesus passed forth from thence, he saw a man named Matthew, sitting at the receipt of custom; and he saith unto him, 'Follow me.' And he arose and followed him.

And it came to pass, as Jesus sat at meat in the house, behold, many publicans and sinners came and sat down with him and his disciples.

20 And when the Pharisees saw it, they said unto his disciples, 'Why eateth your Master with publicans and sinners?'

But when Jesus heard that, he said unto them, 'They that be whole need not a physician, but they that are sick.

'But go ye and learn what that meaneth, "I will have mercy, and not sacrifice; for I am not come to call the righteous, but sinners to repentance."'

Then came to him the disciples of John, saying,
30 'Why do we and the Pharisees fast oft, but thy disciples fast not?'

And Jesus said unto them, 'Can children of the bridechamber mourn, as long as the bridegroom is with them? But the days will come, when the bridegroom shall be taken from them, and then shall they fast.

'No man putteth a piece of new cloth unto an old garment, for that which is put in to fill it up taketh from the garment, and the rent is made worse.

40 'Neither do men put new wine into old bottles, else the bottles break, and the wine runneth out, and the bottles perish; but they put new wine into new bottles, and both are preserved.'

While he spake these things unto them, behold, there came a certain ruler, and worshipped him, saying, 'My daughter is even now dead; but come and lay thy hand upon her, and she shall live.'

And Jesus arose, and followed him, and so did his disciples.

50 And, behold, a woman, which was diseased with an issue of blood twelve years, came behind him, and touched the hem of his garment,

For she said within herself, 'If I may but touch his garment, I shall be whole.'

But Jesus turned him about, and when he saw

her, he said, 'Daughter, be of good comfort; thy faith hath made thee whole.' And the woman was made whole from that hour.

And when Jesus came into the ruler's house, and saw the minstrels and the people making a noise, 60

He said unto them, 'Give place, for the maid is not dead, but sleepeth.' And they laughed him to scorn.

But when the people were put forth, he went in, and took her by the hand, and the maid arose.

And the fame hereof went abroad into all that land.

And when Jesus departed thence, two blind men followed him, crying, and saying, 'Thou son of David, have mercy on us.' 70

And when he was come into the house, the blind men came to him; and Jesus said unto them, 'Believe ye that I am able to do this?' They said unto him, 'Yea, Lord.'

Then touched he their eyes, saying, 'According to your faith be it unto you.'

And their eyes were opened, and Jesus straitly charged them, saying, 'See that no man know it.'

But they, when they were departed, spread abroad his fame in all that country. 80

As they went out, behold, they brought to him a dumb man possessed with a devil.

And when the devil was cast out, the dumb spake; and the multitudes marvelled, saying, 'It was never so seen in Israel.'

But the Pharisees said, 'He casteth out devils through the prince of the devils.'

And Jesus went about all the cities and villages, teaching in their synagogues, and preaching the gospel of the Kingdom, and healing every sickness 90 and every disease among the people.

But when he saw the multitudes, he was moved with compassion on them, because they fainted, and were scattered abroad, as sheep having no shepherd.

Then saith he unto his disciples, 'The harvest truly is plenteous, but the laborers are few;

'Pray ye therefore the Lord of the harvest, that he will send forth laborers into his harvest.'

CHAPTER XII

At that time Jesus went on the sabbath day through the corn, and his disciples were a-hungred, 100 and began to pluck the ears of corn, and to eat.

But when the Pharisees saw it, they said unto him, 'Behold, thy disciples do that which is not lawful to do upon the sabbath day.'

But he said unto them, 'Have ye not read what David did, when he was a-hungred, and they that were with him;

'How he entered into the house of God, and did eat the shewbread, which was not lawful for him to

18. **publicans**, tax-collectors.

109. **shewbread**, loaves of unleavened bread shown in the sanctuary.

eat, neither for them which were with them, but only for the priests?

'Or have ye not read in the law, how that on the sabbath days the priests in the temple profane the sabbath, and are blameless?

'But I say unto you, that in this place is one greater than the temple.

'But if ye had known what this meaneth, "I will have mercy, and not sacrifice," ye would not have condemned the guiltless.

'For the Son of man is Lord even of the sabbath day.'

And when he was departed thence, he went into their synagogues;

And behold, there was a man which had his hand withered. And they asked him, saying, 'Is it lawful to heal on the sabbath days?' that they might accuse him.

And he said unto them, 'What man shall there be among you, that shall have one sheep, and if it fall into a pit on the sabbath day, will he not lay hold on it, and lift it out?

'How much then is a man better than a sheep? Wherefore it is lawful to do well on the sabbath days.'

Then saith he to the man, 'Stretch forth thine hand.' And he stretched it forth, and it was restored whole, like as the other.

Then the Pharisees went out and held a council against him, how they might destroy him.

But when Jesus knew it, he withdrew himself from thence; and great multitudes followed him, and he healed them all;

And charged them that they should not make him known,

That it might be fulfilled which was spoken by Esaias the prophet, saying:

'Behold my servant, whom I have chosen; my beloved, in whom my soul is well pleased; I will put my spirit upon him, and he shall show judgment to the Gentiles.

'He shall not strive, nor cry; neither shall any man hear his voice in the streets.

'A bruised reed shall he not break, and smoking flax shall he not quench, till he send forth judgment unto victory.

'And in his name shall the Gentiles trust.'

Then was brought unto him one possessed with a devil, blind, and dumb; and he healed him, insomuch that the blind and dumb both spake and saw.

And all the people were amazed and said, 'Is not this the son of David?'

But when the Pharisees heard it, they said, 'This fellow doth not cast out devils, but by Beelzebub the prince of the devils.'

And Jesus knew their thoughts, and said unto them, 'Every kingdom divided against itself is brought to desolation; and every city or house divided against itself shall not stand;

'And if Satan cast out Satan, he is divided against himself; how shall then his kingdom stand?

'And if I by Beelzebub cast out devils, by whom do your children cast them out? Therefore they shall be your judges.

'But if I cast out devils by the Spirit of God, then the kingdom of God is come unto you.

'Or else how can one enter into a strong man's house, and spoil his goods, except he first bind the strong man? And then he will spoil his house.

'He that is not with me is against me; and he that gathereth not with me scattereth abroad.

'Wherefore I say unto you, all manner of sin and blasphemy shall be forgiven unto men; but the blasphemy against the Holy Ghost shall not be forgiven unto men.

'And whosoever speaketh a word against the Son of man, it shall be forgiven him; but whosoever speaketh against the Holy Ghost, it shall not be forgiven him, neither in this world, neither in the world to come.

'Either make the tree good, and his fruit good; or else make the tree corrupt, and his fruit corrupt, for the tree is known by his fruit.

'O generation of vipers, how can ye, being evil, speak good things? For out of the abundance of the heart the mouth speaketh.

'A good man out of the good treasure of his heart bringeth forth good things; and an evil man out of the evil treasure bringeth forth evil things.

'But I say unto you, that every idle word that men shall speak, they shall give account thereof in the day of judgment.

'For by thy words thou shalt be justified, and by thy words thou shalt be condemned.'

Then certain of the scribes and of the Pharisees answered, saying, 'Master, we would see a sign from thee.'

But he answered and said unto them, 'An evil and adulterous generation seeketh after a sign; and there shall no sign be given to it, but the sign of the prophet Jonas.

'For as Jonas was three days and three nights in the whale's belly, so shall the Son of man be three days and three nights in the heart of the earth.

'The men of Nineveh shall rise in judgment with this generation, and shall condemn it, because they repented at the preaching of Jonas; and behold, a greater than Jonas is here.

'The queen of the south shall rise up in the judgment with this generation, and shall condemn it, for

109. queen of the south, the Queen of Sheba, who visited Solomon for counsel and teaching, as told in I Kings, 10:1 ff. and II Chronicles, 9:1 ff.

she came from the uttermost parts of the earth to hear the wisdom of Solomon; and behold, a greater than Solomon is here.

'When the unclean spirit is gone out of a man, he walketh through dry places, seeking rest, and findeth none.

'Then he saith, "I will return into my house from whence I came out," and when he is come, he findeth it empty, swept, and garnished.

'Then goeth he, and taketh with himself seven other spirits more wicked than himself, and they enter in and dwell there; and the last state of that man is worse than the first. Even so shall it be also unto this wicked generation.'

While he yet talked to the people, behold, his mother and his brethren stood without, desiring to speak with him.

Then one said unto him, 'Behold, thy mother and thy brethren stand without, desiring to speak with thee.'

But he answered and said unto him that told him, 'Who is my mother? and who are my brethren?'

And he stretched forth his hand toward his disciples, and said, 'Behold my mother and my brethren!

'For whosoever shall do the will of my Father which is in Heaven, the same is my brother, and sister, and mother.'

CHAPTER XVIII

At the same time came the disciples unto Jesus, saying, 'Who is the greatest in the kingdom of Heaven?'

And Jesus called a little child unto him, and set him in the midst of them,

And said, 'Verily I say unto you, except ye be converted, and become as little children, ye shall not enter into the kingdom of Heaven.

'Whosoever therefore shall humble himself as this little child, the same is greatest in the kingdom of Heaven.

'And whoso shall receive one such little child in my name receiveth me.

'But whoso shall offend one of these little ones which believe in me, it were better for him that a millstone were hanged about his neck, and that he were drowned in the depth of the sea.

'Woe unto the world because of offences! For it must needs be that offences come; but woe to that man by whom the offence cometh!

'Wherefore, if thy hand or thy foot offend thee, cut them off, and cast them from thee; it is better for thee to enter into life halt or maimed, rather than having two hands or two feet to be cast into everlasting fire.

'And if thine eye offend thee, pluck it out, and cast it from thee; it is better for thee to enter into life with one eye, rather than having two eyes to be cast into hell-fire.

'Take heed that ye despise not one of these little ones, for I say unto you, that in Heaven their angels do always behold the face of my Father which is in Heaven.

'For the Son of man is come to save that which was lost.

'How think ye? If a man have a hundred sheep, and one of them be gone astray, doth he not leave the ninety and nine, and goeth into the mountains, and seeketh that which is gone astray?

'And if so be that he find it, verily I say unto you, he rejoiceth more of that sheep, than of the ninety and nine which went not astray.

'Even so it is not the will of your Father which is in Heaven, that one of these little ones should perish.

'Moreover, if thy brother shall trespass against thee, go and tell him his fault between thee and him alone; if he shall hear thee, thou hast gained thy brother.

'But if he will not hear thee, then take with thee one or two more, that in the mouth of two or three witnesses every word may be established.

'And if he shall neglect to hear them, tell it unto the church; but if he neglect to hear the church, let him be unto thee as a heathen man and a publican.

'Verily I say unto you, whatsoever ye shall bind on earth shall be bound in Heaven; and whatsoever ye shall loose on earth shall be loosed in Heaven.

'Again, I say unto you, that if two of you shall agree on earth touching anything that they shall ask, it shall be done for them of my Father which is in Heaven.

'For where two or three are gathered together in my name, there am I in the midst of them.'

Then came Peter to him, and said, 'Lord, how oft shall my brother sin against me, and I forgive him? Till seven times?'

Jesus saith unto him, 'I say not unto thee, until seven times; but, until seventy times seven.

'Therefore is the kingdom of Heaven likened unto a certain king, which would take account of his servants.

'And when he had begun to reckon, one was brought unto him, which owed him ten thousand talents.

'But forasmuch as he had not to pay, his lord commanded him to be sold, and his wife, and children, and all that he had, and payment to be made.

'The servant therefore fell down and worshipped him, saying, "Lord, have patience with me, and I will pay thee all."

'Then the lord of that servant was moved with compassion, and loosed him, and forgave him the debt.

'But the same servant went out, and found one of his fellow-servants which owed him an hundred pence; and he laid hands on him, and took him by the throat, saying, "Pay me that thou owest."

'And his fellow-servant fell down at his feet, and besought him, saying, "Have patience with me, and I will pay thee all."

'And he would not, but went and cast him into prison, till he should pay the debt.

'So when his fellow-servants saw what was done, they were very sorry, and came and told unto their lord all that was done.

'Then his lord, after that he had called him, said unto him, "O thou wicked servant, I forgave thee all that debt, because thou desiredst me;

'"Shouldest not thou also have had compassion on thy fellow-servant . . . ?"'

CHAPTER XXIV

And Jesus went out, and departed from the temple; and his disciples came to him for to show him the buildings of the temple.

And Jesus said unto them, 'See ye not all these things? Verily I say unto you, there shall not be left here one stone upon another, that shall not be thrown down.'

And as he sat upon the Mount of Olives, the disciples came unto him privately, saying, 'Tell us, when shall these things be? And what shall be the sign of thy coming, and of the end of the world?'

And Jesus answered and said unto them, 'Take heed that no man deceive you.

'For many shall come in my name, saying, "I am Christ"; and shall deceive you.

'And ye shall hear of wars and rumors of wars; see that ye be not troubled, for all these things must come to pass, but the end is not yet.

'For nation shall rise against nation, and kingdom against kingdom; and there shall be famines, and pestilences, and earthquakes, in divers places.

'All these are the beginning of sorrows.

'Then shall they deliver you up to be afflicted, and shall kill you; and ye shall be hated of all nations for my name's sake.

'And then shall many be offended, and shall betray one another, and shall hate one another.

'And many false prophets shall rise and shall deceive many.

'And because iniquity shall abound, the love of many shall wax cold.

'But he that shall endure to the end, the same shall be saved.

'And the gospel of the kingdom shall be preached in all the world for a witness unto all nations; and then shall the end come.

'When ye therefore shall see the abomination of desolation, spoken of by Daniel the prophet, stand in the holy place, (whoso readeth, let him understand:)

'Then let them which be in Judaea flee into the mountains;

'Let him which is on the housetop not come down to take anything out of his house;

'Neither let him which is in the field return back to take his clothes.

'And woe unto them that are with child, and to them that give suck in those days!

'But pray ye that your flight be not in the winter, neither on the sabbath day;

'For then shall be great tribulation, such as was not since the beginning of the world to this time, no, nor ever shall be.

'And except those days should be shortened, there should no flesh be saved; but for the elect's sake those days shall be shortened.

'Then if any man shall say unto you, "Lo, here is Christ, or there," believe it not.

'For there shall arise false Christs, and false prophets, and shall show great signs and wonders, insomuch that, if it were possible, they shall deceive the very elect.

'Behold, I have told you before.

'Wherefore if they shall say unto you, "Behold, he is in the desert"; go not forth; "Behold, he is in the secret chambers"; believe it not.

'For as the lightning cometh out of the east, and shineth even unto the west, so shall also the coming of the Son of man be.

'For wheresoever the carcass is, there will the eagles be gathered together.

'Immediately after the tribulation of those days shall the sun be darkened, and the moon shall not give her light, and the stars shall fall from Heaven, and the powers of the heavens shall be shaken;

'And then shall appear the sign of the Son of man in Heaven; and then shall all the tribes of the earth mourn, and they shall see the Son of man coming in the clouds of Heaven with power and great glory.

'And he shall send his angels with a great sound of a trumpet, and they shall gather together his elect from the four winds, from one end of Heaven to the other.

'Now learn a parable of the fig tree. When his branch is yet tender and putteth forth leaves, ye know that summer is nigh;

'So likewise ye, when ye shall see all these things, know that it is near, even at the doors.

'Verily I say unto you, this generation shall not pass, till all these things be fulfilled.

'Heaven and earth shall pass away, but my words shall not pass away.

'But of that day and hour knoweth no man, no, not the angels of Heaven, but my Father only.

'But as the days of Noah were, so shall also the coming of the Son of man be.

'For as in the days before the Flood they were eating and drinking, marrying and giving in marriage, until the day that Noah entered into the Ark,

'And knew not until the Flood came, and took them all away, so shall also the coming of the Son of man be.

10 'Then shall two be in the field; the one shall be taken, and the other left.

'Two women shall be grinding at the mill; the one shall be taken, and the other left.

'Watch therefore, for ye know not what hour your Lord doth come.

'But know this, that if the good man of the house had known in what watch the thief would come, he would have watched, and would not have suffered his house to be broken up.

'Therefore be ye also ready, for in such an hour as 20 ye think not the Son of man cometh.

'Who then is a faithful and wise servant, whom his lord hath made ruler over his household, to give them meat in due season?

'Blessed is that servant, whom his lord, when he cometh, shall find so doing.

'Verily I say unto you, that he shall make him ruler over all his goods.

'But and if that evil servant shall say in his heart, "My lord delayeth his coming";

30 'And shall begin to smite his fellow-servants, and to eat and drink with the drunken;

'The lord of that servant shall come in a day when he looketh not for him, and in an hour that he is not aware of,

'And shall cut him asunder, and appoint him his portion with the hypocrites; there shall be weeping and gnashing of teeth.

CHAPTER XXV

'Then shall the kingdom of Heaven be likened unto ten virgins, which took their lamps, and went 40 forth to meet the bridegroom.

'And five of them were wise, and five were foolish.

'They that were foolish took their lamps, and took no oil with them;

'But the wise took oil in their vessels with their lamps.

'While the bridegroom tarried, they all slumbered and slept.

'And at midnight there was a cry made, "Behold, 50 the bridegroom cometh; go ye out to meet him."

'Then all those virgins arose, and trimmed their lamps.

'And the foolish said unto the wise, "Give us of your oil, for our lamps are gone out."

'But the wise answered, saying, "Not so, lest there be not enough for us and you; but go ye rather to them that sell, and buy for yourselves."

'And while they went to buy, the bridegroom came; and they that were ready went in with him to the marriage, and the door was shut. 60

'Afterward came the other virgins, saying, "Lord, Lord, open to us."

'But he answered and said, "Verily I say unto you, I know you not."

'Watch therefore, for ye know neither the day nor the hour wherein the Son of man cometh.

'For the kingdom of Heaven is as a man travelling into a far country, who called his own servants, and delivered unto them his goods.

'And unto one he gave five talents, to another 70 two, and to another one; and to every man according to his several ability; and straightway took his journey.

'Then he that had received the five talents went and traded the same, and made them other five talents.

'And likewise he that had received two, he also gained other two.

'But he that had received one went and digged in the earth, and hid his lord's money. 80

'After a long time the lord of those servants cometh, and reckoneth with them.

'And so he that had received five talents came and brought other five talents, saying, "Lord, thou deliveredst unto me five talents; behold, I have gained beside them five talents more."

'His lord said unto him, "Well done, thou good and faithful servant; thou hast been faithful over a few things; I will make thee ruler over many things. Enter thou into the joy of thy lord." 90

'He also that had received two talents came and said, "Lord, thou deliveredst unto me two talents; behold, I have gained two other talents beside them."

'His lord said unto him, "Well done, good and faithful servant; thou hast been faithful over a few things, I will make thee ruler over many things; enter thou into the joy of thy lord."

'Then he which had received the one talent came and said, "Lord, I knew thee that thou art a hard 100 man, reaping where thou hast not sown, and gathering where thou hast not strawed:

'"And I was afraid, and went and hid thy talent in the earth: lo, there thou hast that is thine."

'His lord answered and said unto him, "Thou wicked and slothful servant, thou knewest that I reap where I sowed not, and gather where I have not strawed;

70. **talents,** an ancient monetary weight of greatly varying value; the Hebraic talent was roughly equal to two thousand dollars.

' "Thou oughtest therefore to have put my money to the exchangers, and then at my coming I should have received mine own with usury.

' "Take therefore the talent from him, and give it unto him which hath ten talents.

' "For unto every one that hath shall be given, and he shall have abundance; but from him that hath not shall be taken away even that which he hath.

10 ' "And cast ye the unprofitable servant into outer darkness; there shall be weeping and gnashing of teeth."

'When the Son of man shall come in his glory, and all the holy angels with him, then shall he sit upon the throne of his glory:

'And before him shall be gathered all nations; and he shall separate them one from another, as a shepherd divideth his sheep from the goats:

'And he shall set the sheep on his right hand, but the goats on the left.

20 'Then shall the King say unto them on his right hand, "Come, ye blessed of my Father, inherit the kingdom prepared for you from the foundation of the world;

' "For I was a hungred, and ye gave me meat; I was thirsty, and ye gave me drink; I was a stranger, and ye took me in;

' "Naked, and ye clothed me; I was sick, and ye visited me; I was in prison, and ye came unto me."

'Then shall the righteous answer him, saying,
30 "Lord, when saw we thee a hungred, and fed thee? Or thirsty, and gave thee drink?

' "When saw we thee a stranger, and took thee in? Or naked, and clothed thee?

' "Or when saw we thee sick, or in prison, and came unto thee?"

'And the King shall answer and say unto them, "Verily I say unto you, inasmuch as ye have done it unto one of the least of these my brethren, ye have done it unto me."

40 'Then shall he say also unto them on the left hand, "Depart from me, ye cursed, into everlasting fire, prepared for the devil and his angels,

' "For I was a hungred, and ye gave me no meat; I was thirsty, and ye gave me no drink;

' "I was a stranger, and ye took me not in; naked, and ye clothed me not; sick, and in prison, and ye visited me not."

'Then shall they also answer him, saying, "Lord, when saw we thee a hungred, or athirst, or a
50 stranger, or naked, or sick, or in prison, and did not minister unto thee?"

'Then shall he answer them saying, "Verily I say unto you, inasmuch as ye did it not to one of the least of these, ye did it not to me."

'And these shall go away into everlasting punishment; but the righteous into life eternal.'

CHAPTER XXVI

And it came to pass, when Jesus had finished all these sayings, he said unto his disciples:

'Ye know that after two days is the feast of the Passover, and the Son of man is betrayed to be 60 crucified.'

Then assembled together the chief priests, and the scribes, and the elders of the people, unto the palace of the high priest, who was called Caiaphas,

And consulted that they might take Jesus by subtlety, and kill him.

But they said, 'Not on the feast-day, lest there be an uproar among the people.'

Now when Jesus was in Bethany, in the house of Simon the leper, 70

There came unto him a woman having an alabaster box of very precious ointment, and poured it on his head, as he sat at meat.

But when his disciples saw it, they had indignation, saying, 'To what purpose is this waste?

'For this ointment might have been sold for much, and given to the poor.'

When Jesus understood it, he said unto them, 'Why trouble ye the woman? For she hath wrought a good work upon me. 80

'For ye have the poor always with you; but me ye have not always.

'For in that she hath poured this ointment on my body, she did it for my burial.

'Verily I say unto you, wheresoever this gospel shall be preached in the whole world, there shall also this, that this woman hath done, be told for a memorial of her.'

Then one of the twelve, called Judas Iscariot, went unto the chief priests. 90

And said unto them, 'What will ye give me, and I will deliver him unto you?' And they covenanted with him for thirty pieces of silver.

And from that time he sought opportunity to betray him.

Now the first day of the feast of unleavened bread the disciples came to Jesus, saying unto him, 'Where wilt thou that we prepare for thee to eat the passover?'

And he said, 'Go into the city to such a man, and 100 say unto him, "The Master saith, 'My time is at hand; I will keep the passover at thy house with my disciples.' " '

And the disciples did as Jesus had appointed them; and they made ready the passover.

Now when the even was come, he sat down with the twelve.

And as they did eat, he said, 'Verily I say unto you, that one of you shall betray me.'

And they were exceeding sorrowful, and began

every one of them to say unto him, 'Lord, is it I?'

And he answered and said, 'He that dippeth his hand with me in the dish, the same shall betray me.

'The Son of man goeth as it is written of him; but woe unto that man by whom the Son of man is betrayed! It had been good for that man if he had not been born.'

Then Judas, which betrayed him, answered and said, 'Master, is it I?' He said unto him, 'Thou hast said.'

And as they were eating, Jesus took bread, and blessed it, and brake it, and gave it to the disciples, and said, 'Take; eat. This is my body.'

And he took the cup, and gave thanks, and gave it to them, saying, 'Drink ye all of it;

'For this is my blood of the new testament, which is shed for many for the remission of sins.

'But I say unto you, I will not drink henceforth of this fruit of the vine, until that day when I drink it new with you in my Father's kingdom.'

And when they had sung a hymn, they went out into the Mount of Olives.

Then saith Jesus unto them, 'All ye shall be offended because of me this night; for it is written, "I will smite the shepherd, and the sheep of the flock shall be scattered abroad."

'But after I am risen again, I will go before you into Galilee.'

Peter answered and said unto him, 'Though all men shall be offended because of thee, yet will I never be offended.'

Jesus said unto him, 'Verily I say unto thee, that this night, before the cock crow, thou shalt deny me thrice.'

Peter said unto him, 'Though I should die with thee, yet will I not deny thee.' Likewise also said all the disciples.

Then cometh Jesus with them unto a place called Gethsemane, and saith unto the disciples, 'Sit ye here, while I go and pray yonder.'

And he took with him Peter and the two sons of Zebedee, and began to be sorrowful and very heavy.

Then saith he unto them, 'My soul is exceeding sorrowful, even unto death; tarry ye here, and watch with me.'

And he went a little farther, and fell on his face, and prayed, saying, 'O my Father, if it be possible, let this cup pass from me; nevertheless not as I will, but as thou wilt.'

And he cometh unto the disciples, and findeth them asleep, and saith unto Peter, 'What, could ye not watch with me one hour?

'Watch and pray, that ye enter not into temptation; the spirit indeed is willing, but the flesh is weak.'

He went away again the second time, and prayed, saying, 'O my Father, if this cup may not pass away from me, except I drink it, thy will be done.'

And he came and found them asleep again, for their eyes were heavy.

And he left them, and went away again, and prayed the third time, saying the same words.

Then cometh he to his disciples, and saith unto them, 'Sleep on now, and take your rest; behold, the hour is at hand, and the Son of man is betrayed into the hands of sinners.

'Rise, let us be going; behold, he is at hand that doth betray me.'

And while he yet spake, lo, Judas, one of the twelve, came, and with him a great multitude with swords and staves, from the chief priests and elders of the people.

Now he that betrayed him gave them a sign, saying, 'Whomsoever I shall kiss, that same is he; hold him fast.'

And forthwith he came to Jesus, and said, 'Hail, master'; and kissed him.

And Jesus said unto him, 'Friend, wherefore art thou come?' Then came they, and laid hands on Jesus, and took him.

And behold, one of them which were with Jesus stretched out his hand, and drew his sword, and struck a servant of the high priest's, and smote off his ear.

Then said Jesus unto him, 'Put up again thy sword into his place, for all they that take the sword shall perish with the sword.

'Thinkest thou that I cannot now pray to thy Father, and he shall presently give me more than twelve legions of angels?

'But how then shall the scriptures be fulfilled, that thus it must be?'

In that same hour said Jesus to the multitudes, 'Are ye come out as against a thief, with swords and staves for to take me? I sat daily with you teaching in the temple, and ye laid no hold on me.'

But all this was done, that the scriptures of the prophets might be fulfilled. Then all the disciples forsook him, and fled.

And they that had laid hold on Jesus led him away to Caiaphas the high priest, where the scribes and the elders were assembled.

But Peter followed him afar off unto the high priest's palace, and went in, and sat with the servants, to see the end.

Now the chief priests, and elders, and all the council, sought false witness against Jesus, to put him to death;

But found none; yea, though many false witnesses came, yet found they none. At the last came two false witnesses

And said, 'This fellow said, "I am able to destroy the temple of God, and to build it in three days."'

And the high priest arose, and said unto him, 'Answerest thou nothing? What is it which these witness against thee?'

But Jesus held his peace. And the high priest answered and said unto him, 'I adjure thee by the living God, that thou tell us whether thou be the Christ, the Son of God.'

Jesus saith unto him, 'Thou hast said; nevertheless I say unto you, hereafter shall ye see the Son of man sitting on the right hand of power, and coming in the clouds of Heaven.'

Then the high priest rent his clothes, saying, 'He hath spoken blasphemy; what further need have we of witnesses? Behold, now ye have heard his blasphemy.

'What think ye?' They answered and said, 'He is guilty of death.'

Then did they spit in his face, and buffeted him; and others smote him with the palms of their hands,

Saying, 'Prophesy unto us, thou Christ. Who is he that smote thee?'

Now Peter sat without in the palace; and a damsel came unto him, saying, 'Thou also wast with Jesus of Galilee.'

But he denied before them all, saying, 'I know not what thou sayest.'

And when he was gone out into the porch, another maid saw him, and said unto them that were there, 'This fellow was also with Jesus of Nazareth.'

And again he denied with an oath, 'I do not know the man.'

And after awhile came unto him they that stood by, and said to Peter, 'Surely thou also art one of them, for thy speech bewrayeth thee.'

Then began he to curse and to swear, saying, 'I know not the man.' And immediately the cock crew.

And Peter remembered the word of Jesus, which said unto him, 'Before the cock crow, thou shalt deny me thrice.' And he went out, and wept bitterly.

CHAPTER XXVII

When the morning was come, all the chief priests and elders of the people took counsel against Jesus to put him to death:

And when they had bound him, they led him away, and delivered him to Pontius Pilate the governor.

Then Judas, which had betrayed him, when he saw that he was condemned, repented himself, and brought again the thirty pieces of silver to the chief priests and elders,

Saying, 'I have sinned in that I have betrayed the innocent blood.' And they said, 'What is that to us? See thou to that.'

And he cast down the pieces of silver in the temple, and departed, and went and hanged himself.

And the chief priests took the silver pieces, and said, 'It is not lawful for to put them into the treasury, because it is the price of blood.'

And they took counsel, and bought with them the potter's field, to bury strangers in.

Wherefore that field was called the Field of Blood, unto this day.

Then was fulfilled that which was spoken by Jeremiah the prophet, saying, 'And they took the thirty pieces of silver, the price of him that was valued, whom they of the children of Israel did value;

'And gave them for the potter's field, as the Lord appointed me.'

And Jesus stood before the governor; and the governor asked him, saying, 'Art thou the King of the Jews?' And Jesus said unto him, 'Thou sayest.'

And when he was accused of the chief priests and elders, he answered nothing.

Then said Pilate unto him, 'Hearest thou not how many things they witness against thee?'

And he answered him to never a word, insomuch that the governor marvelled greatly.

Now at that feast the governor was wont to release unto the people a prisoner, whom they would.

And they had then a notable prisoner, called Barabbas.

Therefore when they were gathered together, Pilate said unto them, 'Whom will ye that I release unto you? Barabbas, or Jesus which is called Christ?'

For he knew that for envy they had delivered him.

When he sat down on the judgment seat, his wife sent unto him, saying, 'Have thou nothing to do with that just man, for I have suffered many things this day in a dream because of him.'

But the chief priests and elders persuaded the multitude that they should ask Barabbas, and destroy Jesus.

The governor answered and said unto them, 'Whether of the twain will ye that I release unto you?' They said, 'Barabbas.'

Pilate saith unto them, 'What shall I do then with Jesus which is called Christ?' They all say unto him, 'Let him be crucified.'

And the governor said, 'Why, what evil hath he done?' But they cried out the more, saying, 'Let him be crucified.'

When Pilate saw that he could prevail nothing, but that rather a tumult was made, he took water and washed his hands before the multitude, saying, 'I am innocent of the blood of this just person; see ye to it.'

Then answered all the people and said, 'His blood be on us, and on our children.'

Then released he Barabbas unto them; and when he had scourged Jesus, he delivered him to be crucified.

Then the soldiers of the governor took Jesus into

the common hall, and gathered unto him the whole band of soldiers.

And they stripped him, and put on him a scarlet robe.

And when they had platted a crown of thorns, they put it upon the head, and a reed in his right hand; and they bowed the knee before him and mocked him, saying, 'Hail! King of the Jews!'

And they spit upon him, and took the reed, and 10 smote him on the head.

And after they had mocked him, they took the robe off from him, and put his own raiment on him, and led him away to crucify him.

And as they came out, they found a man of Cyrene, Simon by name; him they compelled to bear his cross.

And when they were come unto a place called Golgotha, that is to say, a place of a skull,

They gave him vinegar to drink mingled with 20 gall; and when he had tasted thereof, he would not drink.

And they crucified him and parted his garments, casting lots, that it might be fulfilled which was spoken by the prophet, 'They parted my garments among them, and upon my vesture did they cast lots.'

And sitting down they watched him there;

And set up over his head his accusation written, THIS IS JESUS THE KING OF THE JEWS.

30 Then were there two thieves crucified with him, one on the right hand, and another on the left.

And they that passed by reviled him, wagging their heads,

And saying, 'Thou that destroyedest the temple, and buildest it in three days, save thyself. If thou be the Son of God, come down from the cross.'

Likewise also the chief priests mocking him, with the scribes and elders, said,

'He saved others; himself he cannot save. If he be 40 the King of Israel, let him now come down from the cross, and we will believe him.

'He trusted in God; let him deliver him now, if he will have him; for he said, "I am the Son of God."'

The thieves also, which were crucified with him, cast the same in his teeth.

Now from the sixth hour there was darkness over all the land unto the ninth hour.

And about the ninth hour Jesus cried with a loud voice, saying, 'Eli, Eli, lama sabachthani?', that is 50 to say, 'My God, my God, why hast thou forsaken me?'

Some of them that stood there when they heard that, said, 'This man calleth for Elias.'

And straightway one of them ran, and took a sponge, and filled it with vinegar, and put it on a reed, and gave him to drink.

The rest said, 'Let be, let us see whether Elias will come to save him.'

Jesus, when he had cried again with a loud voice, yielded up the ghost. 60

And behold, the vail of the temple was rent in twain from the top to the bottom; and the earth did quake; and the rocks rent;

And the graves were opened; and many bodies of the saints which slept arose,

And came out of the graves after his resurrection, and went into the holy city, and appeared unto many.

Now when the centurion, and they that were with him, watching Jesus, saw the earthquake, and those 70 things that were done, they feared greatly, saying, 'Truly this was the Son of God.'

And many women were there beholding afar off, which followed Jesus from Galilee, ministering unto him:

Among which was Mary Magdalene, and Mary the mother of James and Joses, and the mother of Zebedee's children.

When the even was come, there came a rich man of Arimathea, named Joseph, who also himself was 80 Jesus' disciple;

He went to Pilate, and begged the body of Jesus. Then Pilate commanded the body to be delivered.

And when Joseph had taken the body, he wrapped it in a clean linen cloth,

And laid it in his own new tomb, which he had hewn out in the rock; and he rolled a great stone to the door of the sepulchre, and departed.

And there was Mary Magdalene, and the other Mary, sitting over against the sepulchre. 90

Now the next day, that followed the day of the preparation, the chief priests and Pharisees came together unto Pilate,

Saying, 'Sir, we remember that that deceiver said, while he was yet alive, "After three days I will rise again."

'Command therefore that the sepulchre be made sure until the third day, lest his disciples come by night, and steal him away, and say unto the people, "He is risen from the dead." So the last error shall 100 be worse than the first.'

Pilate said unto them, 'Ye have a watch; go your way, make it as sure as ye can.'

So they went, and made the sepulchre sure, sealing the stone, and setting a watch.

CHAPTER XXVIII

In the end of the sabbath, as it began to dawn toward the first day of the week, came Mary Magdalene and the other Mary to see the sepulchre.

And behold, there was a great earthquake, for the angel of the Lord descended from Heaven, and came and rolled back the stone from the door, and sat upon it.

His countenance was like lightning, and his raiment white as snow;

And for fear of him the keepers did shake, and became as dead men.

And the angel answered and said unto the women, 'Fear not ye, for I know that ye seek Jesus, which was crucified.

10 'He is not here, for he is risen, as he said. Come, see the place where the Lord lay.

'And go quickly, and tell his disciples that he is risen from the dead; and behold, he goeth before you into Galilee; there shall ye see him. Lo, I have told you.'

And they departed quickly from the sepulchre with fear and great joy, and did run to bring his disciples word.

And as they went to tell the disciples, behold,
20 Jesus met them, saying, 'All hail!' And they came and held him by the feet, and worshipped him.

Then said Jesus unto them, 'Be not afraid; go, tell my brethren that they go into Galilee, and there shall they see me.'

Now when they were going, behold, some of the watch came into the city, and showed unto the chief priests all the things that were done.

And when they were assembled with the elders, and had taken counsel, they gave large money unto
30 the soldiers,

Saying, 'Say ye, his disciples came by night, and stole him away while we slept.

'And if this come to the governor's ears, we will persuade him, and secure you.'

So they took the money, and did as they were taught; and this saying is commonly reported among the Jews until this day.

Then the eleven disciples went away into Galilee, into a mountain where Jesus had appointed them.

40 And when they saw him, they worshipped him; but some doubted.

And Jesus came and spake unto them, saying, 'All power is given me in Heaven and in earth.

'Go ye therefore, and teach all nations, baptizing them in the name of the Father, and of the Son, and of the Holy Ghost,

'Teaching them to observe all things whatsoever I have commanded you. And lo, I am with you alway, even unto the end of the world. AMEN.'

An Italian mosaic of Saint Peter, c. 600.

First Epistle of Paul to the Corinthians

CHAPTER XIII

T HOUGH I speak with the tongues of men and 50 of angels, and have not charity, I am become as sounding brass, or a tinkling cymbal.

And though I have the gift of prophecy, and understand all mysteries, and all knowledge; and though I have all faith, so that I could remove mountains, and have not charity, I am nothing.

And though I bestow all my goods to feed the poor, and though I give my body to be burned, and have not charity, it profiteth me nothing.

Charity suffereth long, and is kind; charity en- 60 vieth not; charity vaunteth not itself, is not puffed up,

Doth not behave itself unseemly, seeketh not her own, is not easily provoked, thinketh no evil;

Rejoiceth not in iniquity, but rejoiceth in the truth;

Beareth all things, believeth all things, hopeth all things, endureth all things.

Charity never faileth; but whether there be prophecies, they shall fail; whether there be tongues, they 70 shall cease; whether there be knowledge, it shall vanish away.

For we know in part, and we prophesy in part,

But when that which is perfect is come, then that which is in part shall be done away.

When I was a child, I spake as a child, I understood as a child, I thought as a child; but when I became a man, I put away childish things.

For now we see through a glass, darkly; but then face to face. Now I know in part, but then shall I 80 know even as also I am known.

And now abideth faith, hope, charity—these three; but the greatest of these is charity.

CHAPTER XV

Moreover, brethren, I declare unto you the gospel which I preached unto you, which also ye have received, and wherein ye stand;

By which also ye are saved, if ye keep in memory what I preached unto you, unless ye have believed in vain.

For I delivered unto you first of all that which 90 I also received, how that Christ died for our sins according to the scriptures;

First Epistle of Paul to the Corinthians.[8] From the King James Version of the Bible.
69. whether, if.

And that he was buried, and that he rose again the third day according to the scriptures;

And that he was seen of Cephas, then of the twelve;

After that, he was seen of above five hundred brethren at once; of whom the greater part remain unto this present, but some are fallen asleep.

After that, he was seen of James, then of all the apostles.

10 And last of all he was seen of me also, as of one born out of due time.

For I am the least of the apostles, that am not meet to be called an apostle, because I persecuted the church of God.

But by the grace of God I am what I am, and His grace which was bestowed upon me was not in vain; but I labored more abundantly than they all. Yet not I, but the grace of God which was with me.

Therefore whether it were I or they, so we preach, 20 and so ye believed.

Now if Christ be preached that he rose from the dead, how say some among you that there is no resurrection of the dead?

But if there be no resurrection of the dead, then is Christ not risen;

And if Christ be not risen, then is our preaching vain, and your faith is also vain.

Yea, and we are found false witnesses of God, because we have testified of God that he raised up 30 Christ; whom he raised not up, if so be that the dead rise not.

For if the dead rise not, then is not Christ raised;

And if Christ be not raised, your faith is vain; ye are yet in your sins.

Then they also which are fallen asleep in Christ are perished.

If in this life only we have hope in Christ, we are of all men most miserable.

But now is Christ risen from the dead, and be- 40 come the firstfruits of them that slept.

For since by men came death, by man came also the resurrection of the dead.

For as in Adam all die, even so in Christ shall all be made alive.

But every man in his own order: Christ the first-fruits; afterward they that are Christ's at his coming.

Then cometh the end, when he shall have delivered up the kingdom to God, even the Father; 50 when he shall have put down all rule and all authority and power.

For he must reign, till he hath put all enemies under his feet.

The last enemy that shall be destroyed is death.

For he hath put all things under his feet. But when he saith all things are put under him, it is manifest that he is excepted, which did put all things under him.

And when all things shall be subdued unto him, then shall the Son also himself be subject unto him 60 that put all things under him, that God may be all in all.

Else what shall they do which are baptized for the dead, if the dead rise not at all? Why are they then baptized for the dead?

And why stand we in jeopardy every hour?

I protest by your rejoicing which I have in Christ Jesus our Lord, I die daily.

If after the manner of men I have fought with beasts at Ephesus, what advantageth it me, if the 70 dead rise not? Let us eat and drink, for tomorrow we die.

Be not deceived; evil communications corrupt good manners.

Awake to righteousness, and sin not; for some have not the knowledge of God. I speak this to your shame.

But some man will say, 'How are the dead raised up? and with what body do they come?'

Thou fool, that which thou sowest is not quick- 80 ened, except it die;

And that which thou sowest, thou sowest not that body that shall be, but bare grain, it may chance of wheat, or of some other grain;

But God giveth it a body as it hath pleased him, and to every seed his own body.

All flesh is not the same flesh; but there is one kind of flesh of men, another flesh of beasts, another of fishes, and another of birds.

There are also celestial bodies, and bodies ter- 90 restrial; but the glory of the celestial is one, and the glory of the terrestrial is another.

There is one glory of the sun, and another glory of the moon, and another glory of the stars, for one star differeth from another star in glory.

So also is the resurrection of the dead. It is sown in corruption; it is raised in incorruption;

It is sown in dishonor; it is raised in glory; it is sown in weakness; it is raised in power;

It is sown a natural body; it is raised a spiritual 100 body. There is a natural body, and there is a spiritual body.

And so it is written, 'The first man Adam was made a living soul; the last Adam was made a quickening spirit.'

Howbeit that was not first which is spiritual, but that which is natural; and afterward that which is spiritual.

3. **Cephas,** Simon, the son of Jonah. 10–11. **And last of all . . . time.** See Acts, 9:4. Paul, known as Saul of Tarsus before his conversion, had been a violent anti-Christian. In the ninth chapter of Acts we are told of his conversion by divine intervention.

69–70. **fought . . . Ephesus,** an incident in Paul's career hinted at in II Corinthians, 1:8–9.

The first man is of the earth, earthy; the second man is the Lord from Heaven.

As is the earthy, such are they also that are earthy; and as is the heavenly, such are they also that are heavenly.

And as we have borne the image of the earthy, we shall also bear the image of the heavenly.

Now this I say, brethren, that flesh and blood cannot inherit the kingdom of God; neither doth 10 corruption inherit incorruption.

Behold, I tell you a mystery: We shall not all sleep, but we shall all be changed,

In a moment, in the twinkling of an eye, at the last trumpet. For the trumpet shall sound, and the dead shall be raised incorruptible, and we shall be changed.

For this corruptible must put on incorruption, and this mortal must put on immortality.

So when this corruptible shall have put on incorruption, and this mortal shall have put on immortality, then shall be brought to pass the saying that 20 is written, 'Death is swallowed up in victory.'

O death, where is thy sting? O grave, where is thy victory?

The sting of death is sin; and the strength of sin is the law.

But thanks be to God, which giveth us the victory through our Lord Jesus Christ.

Therefore, my beloved brethren, be ye steadfast, unmoveable, always abounding in the work of the 30 Lord, for as much as ye know that your labor is not in vain in the Lord.

A 15th-century English drawing of a Canterbury bishop.

The Nicaean Creed

The Roman Emperor Constantine the Great in the year 323 defeated the Byzantine tyrant Licinius and thereby assured the Roman state a period of tranquillity. The effect of this victory, considering the sympathy felt by Constantine toward the Christians, was the collapse of opposition to Christianity in any kind of official way within the empire. As is well known, Constantine was himself baptized a few years later on his deathbed and so established the Roman empire as a Christian realm. But in spite of this long-sought victory over its external foes, the Christian Church was in the early fourth century plagued by a fundamental controversy, the first great heresy. This controversy was brought to a head by the stated opinions of Arius, a presbyter under Bishop Alexander of Alexandria, who believed in the essential unity of the Deity rather than in the orthodox Trinity. The resulting conflict was decided officially in 325 by the Council of Nicaea, held in the city of that name in Bithynia, Asia Minor, which denied the teachings of Arius, formulated an official *Credo,* and drove Arius and his followers into banishment, at the same time thrusting into the foreground as a champion of Trinitarian faith a deacon of Alexandria by the name of Athanasius.

This official *Credo,* known as the Nicaean Creed, states the premises on which the orthodox position of the Catholic Church is based.

But Arianism, obviously a forerunner of present-day Unitarianism, persisted for a long time within the Church in spite of the Council of Nicaea; although it had no recognized status, it was particularly attractive to the young and forthright Germanic nations at the time of their conversions to Christianity. It is indeed a beautiful irony of history that Constantine the Great himself should have been baptized by Eusebius of Nicomedia, a powerful Arian spokesman.

The Nicaean Creed

WE BELIEVE in one God, the Father Almighty, Maker of all things, visible and invisible; and in one Lord Jesus Christ, the Son of God, the only begotten of the Father, that is, of the substance of the Father; God of God, light of light, true God of true God; begotten, not made, consubstantial with the Father, by whom all things were made, both in Heaven and in earth; who for us men, and for our salvation, descended, was incarnate, and was made man, and suffered, and rose again the third day; he ascended into Heaven, and shall come to judge the living and the dead; And in the HOLY SPIRIT. But the holy catholic and apostolic Church of God anathematizes those who affirm that there was a time when the Son was not, or that he was not before he was begotten, or that he was made of things not existing; or who say, that the Son of God was of any other substance or essence, or created, or liable to change or conversion.

Thomas à Kempis

c. 1380–1471

Thomas Hammerken was born at Kempen, near Düsseldorf, Germany, whence his monastic name of Thomas à Kempis. A dreamy, shy kind of boy of humble peasant birth, he grew into a retiring young man of pronounced mystical inclinations and, after some education at Deventer, in the Netherlands, he entered the Augustinian Order and went to the monastery at Mount Saint Agnes, near Zwolle, Holland, where his elder brother was prior. He spent all the remaining many years of his life at Mount Saint Agnes, was chosen subprior on two occasions, and ultimately became prior. He was the author of a large number of somewhat pedestrian tracts on the monastic life, and the reputed author of the *Imitatio Christi,* or *Imitation of Christ,* which might have been more properly called "The Following of Christ."

The authorship of this, probably the most famous and influential of all medieval ascetic and monastic writings, is still, however, very much in dispute. The conclusion, in one of the most important of its manuscripts, declares that it was "finished and completed in the year of Our Lord 1441 by the hands of Brother Thomas à Kempis in Mount Saint Agnes near Zwolle." But there are no less than twenty-two manuscripts of the work which can be dated before 1441. In view of the amazing difference in power and inspiration between the *Imitation of Christ* and the other works by Thomas à Kempis, it is altogether likely that he was not the actual author, but rather the redactor or editor of a work by someone else—John

Gersen and Saint Bernard have both been suggested. Yet the *Imitation of Christ* is so characteristic of the temperament of the highly ascetic, self-effacing, and even self-abasing Thomas à Kempis, who could not stay in a room where the conversation was too sprightly, that it may be ascribed to him in spirit if not in actual fact. For no work, not even the writings of the great Scholastics of the twelfth and thirteenth centuries, catches more truly the otherworldliness which was so integral a part of the medieval intellect, exhibited here to an almost psychopathological degree. It is notably unscholarly and unacademic, for that matter, but its style is austere and simple; its awareness of the contemporary world is virtually nil and it seems drenched in the flood of divinity. These very qualities, however, have made it a work of great appeal to all minds of an enthusiastically religious nature; it is not remarkable, therefore, that the *Imitation of Christ* should have been translated from its original Latin into all the languages of the Christian world, and that the work should have retained its hold now for nearly five hundred years.

The Imitation of Christ

BOOK II

Here beginneth concerning the admonitions drawing greatly inward.
Of inward conversation

OUR Lord saith that the kingdom of Heaven is within you. Turn thyself to God with all thine heart and forsake this wretched world and thy soul shall find rest.

Learn to despise outward things and to turn thee to inward things and thou shalt see the kingdom come into thee; for the kingdom of God is peace and joy in the Holy Ghost the which is not given to wicked men.

Christ shall come to thee showing thee His consolation if thou make for him within thee a worthy ·dwelling place; all His glory and honor is within and there is His plesaunce. 10

His visitation is common and oft with an inward man; with Him is His sweet talking, gracious consolation, much wonderful familiarity.

Ah, thou true soul, array thy soul for thy spouse that He may vouchsafe to come to thee and to dwell in thee; for thus He saith, 'Whoso loveth me shall keep my word and to him we shall come and in him make our dwelling place.' Wherefore give Christ place and as to all other hold them out. 20

When thou hast Christ, thou art rich and it sufficeth thee; He shall be thy provisor, thy true proc-

The Imitation of Christ.[8] First English translation, sixteenth century, anonymous.

urator, in all things, so that thou shalt not need to trust in man. Men are soon changed and fail soon; Christ abideth for ever and standeth steadfastly unto the end.

Great trust is not to be put in a mortal and frail man though he be profitable and well beloved; nor great sorrow to be felt though sometimes he withstand thee and is contrary. They that are this day with thee, tomorrow they may be contrary; and in contrary wise they be ofttimes turned as the wind.

Put all thy trust in God; let Him be thy dread; let Him be thy love; He shall answer for thee and do well and as is best.

Thou hast here no dwelling-city and wherever thou be thou art as a stranger and a pilgrim; here gettest thou no rest, unless thou be inwardly one with Christ.

Why lookest thou about here, since this is not the place of thy resting? In heavenly things ought to be thine habitation, and all earthly things are to be considered as in a manner of passing; for all things pass, and thou also with them. Look that thou cleave not to them, lest thou be taken with them and perish.

Let thy thinking be on the high God and let thy prayer be lifted up unto Christ without intermission. If thou canst not behold high celestial things, rest in the passion of Christ and dwell gladly in His holy wounds; for if thou flee devoutly to the wounds and the precious prints of Christ, thou shalt find great comfort in tribulation, nor thou shalt not greatly care for men's despisings, and thou shalt lightly bear backbiting words; for Christ was despised of men in this world, and in His greatest need suffered reproofs, forsaken of His friends and of his known men.

Christ would suffer and be despised; and thou wilt have all men friends and benefactors?

Christ had adversaries, and suffered shrewd speakers; and thou darest complain on any body?

How shall thy patience be crowned if there come no adversity? If thou wilt suffer no contrary, how shalt thou be the friend of Christ? Suffer for Christ and with Christ if thou wilt reign with Christ.

If thou hadst once perfectly entered into the innerness of Jesus and hast savored a little of his burning love, thou wouldst have set naught by thine own profit or harm but rather thou wouldst rejoice of reproof done to thee; for the love of Jesus maketh a man to set naught of himself.

A lover of Jesus and a very inward man and free from inordinate affections may freely turn himself to God and lift himself above himself in spirit and there rest joyously.

The man to whom all things taste as they be, not as they are said or thought to be, he is very wise and taught more by God than by men.

He that can go within and praise things without but little, he seeketh no place, nor abideth for no times to have devout exercises. The inward man soon gathereth himself together, for he never poureth himself out wholly over outward things. Outward labor hindereth him not nor needful occupation of the day, but so as things come, so he giveth himself to them.

He that is well disposed and ordained within, he careth not for the wicked and wonderful conduct and bearing of men.

Just so much is a man hindered and distracted as things are drawn to him.

If it were well with thee and thou wert well purged, all should turn for thee to good and profit.

Many things as yet trouble thee and displease thee, for thou art not yet dead to thyself nor parted from all earthly things; nothing so defouleth and entangleth men's hearts as impure love in created things.

If thou forsake outward comfort, thou shalt be able to behold heavenly things and ofttimes have jubilation within.

Of meek submission

Set not much by this—who is against thee or with thee, but so do and care that God be with thee.

In every thing that thou dost, have a good conscience, and God shall defend thee; for him that God will help no man's overthwartness shall be able to annoy.

If thou canst be still and suffer, thou shalt see without any doubt the help of our Lord; he knoweth the time and manner of helping thee, and therefore thou oughtest to reserve thyself for him.

To God it belongeth to help and to deliver from all confusion.

Ofttimes it availeth to the keeping of greater meekness that other men should know our faults and reprove them.

When a man humbleth himself for his faults, then he appeaseth others lightly and easily maketh satisfaction to them that were displeased.

The meek man God defendeth and delivereth; the meek man He loveth and comforteth; to the meek man He bareth Himself; to the meek man He granteth great grace, and after his humbling He lifteth him in glory; to the meek man He showeth His secrets and draweth him and calleth him sweetly.

The meek man receiving reproofs or wrong or confusion is in peace well enough, for he standeth in God and not in the world.

Account thyself never to have profited till thou feel thee lower than all others.

Of a good peaceable man

Set thyself first in peace, and then shalt thou be able to set others at peace.

A peaceable man availeth more than a great learned man.

A passionate man turneth good into evil and soon believeth evil; a good peaceable man draweth all things to good.

He that is well in peace hath suspicion against no man; he that cannot be content, but is moved, he is shaken with many suspicions; neither can he be in rest nor suffer others to be in rest. Ofttimes he saith that he should not say and leaveth that which were more expedient to do; he considereth what other men ought to do and taketh no heed to his own charge.

Have therefore first zeal to better thyself and then mayst thou have zeal to thy neighbor.

Thou canst well excuse and color thine own deeds, but other men's excuses thou wilt not receive. It were more righteous first to accuse thyself and to excuse thy brother.

If thou wilt be borne, bear thou another.

See how far thou art yet from true charity and meekness the which cannot be wroth, nor have indignation with no man, but only with itself.

It is not a great thing for a man to be conversant with good men and mild men, for that pleaseth all men naturally, and every man gladly hath peace with them that feel as he doth; and such he loveth.

But for a man to live peaceably with hard and overthwart men indisciplined and contrarious is a great grace and a commendable and a manly deed.

There are some that keep themselves at peace and have peace with others also; and there be some also that neither have peace themselves nor suffer others to have peace; to others they be grievous, but most grievous to themselves. And there be that keep their peace in themselves and study to reduce other men to peace.

Nevertheless all our peace in this wretched life is rather to be set in meek suffering than in not feeling what goes contrary.

He that can well suffer shall find most peace; he is an overcomer of himself, lord of the world, the friend of Christ and the heir of Heaven.

Of pure and simple intention

A man is lifted up from earthly things with two wings—they are simplicity and purity; simplicity ought to be in intention; purity in affection. Simplicity intendeth God; purity taketh Him and tasteth Him.

There shall no good deed hinder thee if thou be free within from inordinate affection.

If thou intend not nor seek nothing else but the pleasing of God and the profit of thy neighbor, thou shalt have inward liberty. If thine heart were right, then every creature should be to thee a mirror of life and a book of holy doctrine. There is no creature so little nor so vile but it represents the goodness of God.

If thou wert inward, good and pure, then shouldest thou see all things without impediment and understand them.

A pure heart pierceth Heaven and Hell.

Such as every man is inwardly, so he judgeth outwardly.

If there be any joy in this world, the man of pure heart hath it; and if there be in any place tribulation and anguish, an idle conscience knoweth it best.

Like as iron put in the fire loseth his rust and shall be made bright, so a man turning him wholly to God is freed and taken from sloth and changed into a new man.

When a man beginneth to wax lukewarm, then he dreadeth a little labor and receiveth gladly outward consolation; but when he beginneth perfectly to overcome himself and to go manly in the way of God, then he setteth little by those things that before seemed to him right grievous.

Of consideration of oneself

We ought not to believe ourselves overmuch, for ofttimes grace is lacking in us, and understanding. Little light is in us, and ofttimes we lose that by negligence. And also ofttimes we perceive not how blind we are within.

Ofttimes we do evil, and worse—we excuse it.

Ofttimes we be moved to anger and think that it is zeal.

We reprove small things in others and pass over our own faults that are greater.

We feel and weigh soon enough what we suffer from others; but how much others suffer from us, of this we take no heed.

He that would ponder well and truly his own faults, he should find naught to judge in others grievously. An inward man before all other things taketh care of himself; and he that diligently taketh heed of himself holdeth his peace of others. Thou shalt never be an inward and devout man unless thou keep silence of other men and specially behold thyself. If thou take heed only to God and to thyself, what thou perceivest outside thee shall little move thee.

Where art thou when thou art not present to thyself? And when thou hast run over all things, taking no heed of thyself, what hast thou profited?

If thou wilt have peace and very unity, thou must set all aside and only have thyself before thine eyes; and then thou shalt profit much if thou keep holiday and rest from every temporal care.

Thou shalt greatly fail if thou set great store by any temporal thing. Let nothing be great or high or acceptable to thee but purely God. All things deem as vain comfort that come from any creature—the soul that loveth God, let her despise all things but God alone.

God alone, everlasting and great, without any measure, fulfilling all things; he is the solace of man's soul and true gladness of heart.

Of the gladness of a good conscience

The joy of a good man is the witness of a good conscience; have a good conscience and thou shalt ever have gladness.

A good conscience may bear right many, very many, things and is right glad among adversities; an evil conscience is ever dreadful and out of quiet.

Thou shalt rest sweetly if thine heart reprehend thee not.

Be not glad but when thou hast done well.

Evil men have never true gladness nor never feel inward peace; for, as our Lord saith, there is no peace to wicked men; and if they say, 'we are in peace, there shall none evils come upon us,' believe them not, for the wrath of God shall arise suddenly, and their deeds shall be brought to naught, and their thoughts shall perish.

For a man to rejoice in tribulation is not grievous to him who loves; for so to joy is to joy in the Cross of Christ.

Short is the glory that is given and taken by men; and sorrow followeth ever the glory of the world.

The glory of good men is in their conscience and not in the mouths of men.

The gladness of righteous men is of God and in God; and their joy is of truth.

He that desireth everlasting and true glory setteth no care on that which is temporal; and he that seeketh not temporal glory but despiseth it from his heart, he must needs love heavenly glory. He hath great tranquility of heart that setteth nothing by praisings or blamings.

He whose conscience is clean, he will soon be content and pleased. Thou art not the holier though thou be praised, nor the more vile though thou be blamed or dispraised.

What thou art, that thou art, that God knoweth thee to be and thou canst be said to be no greater.

If thou take heed what thou art within, thou shalt not reck what men say of thee; man looketh on the visage and God on the heart; man considereth the deeds and God praiseth the thoughts.

For a man ever to do well and to think little of himself is token of a meek soul.

For a man not to wish to be comforted by any creature is a token of great purity and of inward trust.

He that seeketh no outward witness for himself, it appeareth openly that he hath committed himself all wholly to God; for, as the apostle saith, he that commendeth himself is not approved, but only he whom God commendeth.

The state of the inner man is to walk with God and to be held by no outward affection.

Of the love of Jesus above all things

Blissful is he that understandeth what it is to love Jesus and to despise himself for Jesus.

It behooveth thee to forsake all things for the loved one, for Jesus would be loved alone above all things: the love of a creature is failing and unstable; the love of Jesus is true and persevering.

He that cleaveth to a creature shall fall with the sliding creature; he that embraceth Jesus shall be made steadfast forever.

Love him and hold him fast as a friend which, when all goeth away, shall not forsake thee nor shall not suffer thee to perish at the end.

From all things thou must be departed some time, whether thou wilt or not. Hold thee with Jesus living and dying and commit thee to His trust, who, all other failing, alone may help thee.

Thy beloved is of such nature that He will admit no stranger, but He alone will have thy heart and there sit as a king on His own throne.

If thou couldest well free thee from every creature, Jesus would gladly dwell with thee.

Thou shalt find almost all lost, whatever trust thou settest in creatures; trust not nor lean not upon a windy reed, for every flesh is grass and all his glory shall fall as the flower of grass.

Thou shalt soon be deceived if thou look only to the outer appearance of men. If thou seek thy solace and thy lucre in others, thou shalt ofttimes find hindrances to thee.

If thou seek Jesus in all things, thou shalt find Jesus; and if thou seek thyself, thou shalt find thyself but—to thine own harm.

A man hurteth himself more, if he seeketh not Jesus, than all the world and all his adversaries can hurt him.

Of the familiar friendship of Jesus

When Jesus is nigh, all goodness is nigh, and nothing seemeth hard; but when Jesus is not nigh, all things are hard.

When Jesus speaketh not within, the comfort is of little price; but if Jesus speak one word, there is found great comfort.

Did not Mary Magdalene rise out of her place wherein she wept, anon as Martha said, 'Our master is nigh and calleth thee'?

Blissful is that man whom, when Jesus cometh, he calleth from tears to the joy of the spirit.

How dry and how hard thou art without Jesus; how unsavory, how vain, if thou covet anything without Jesus; whether is it not more harm than if thou lost all the world?

What may the world avail without Jesus? to be

without Jesus is a grievous Hell, and to be with Jesus is a sweet Paradise.

If Jesus be with thee, there may no enemy hurt thee.

He that findeth Jesus findeth a good treasure; yea, good above all good; and he that loseth Jesus he loseth over much and more than if he lost all the world.

It is a great craft for a man to be conversant with Jesus, and to know how to hold Jesus is a great prudence.

Be meek and peaceable, and Jesus shall be with thee; be devout and restful, and Jesus shall abide with thee; thou mayest soon chase out Jesus and lose his grace if thou wilt decline to outer things; and if thou chase out Jesus and lose him, to whom shalt thou flee? and what friend shalt thou seek? Without a friend thou canst not well live, and save Jesus be thy friend before all other, thou shalt be over sorry and over desolate; wherefore thou dost foolishly if thou trust or art glad in any other.

It is more to be chosen for a man to have all the world contrary to him than to have Jesus offended.

Among all therefore that are dear to thee, let Jesus be solely thy darling and thy special friend.

Let all men be loved for Jesus and Jesus for himself.

Only Jesus Christ is singly to be loved, who only is found good and true before all other friends; for Him and in Him let both friends and enemies be dear to thee; and for all them He is to be prayed that they may know Him and love Him.

Desire never to be singularly praised or loved, for that belongeth to God alone, that hath none like Him.

Nor desire not that any man be occupied in his mind about love of thee, nor be not thou occupied about no other love: be pure and free within, without impediment or encumbrance of any creature.

Thou must be bare and bear to God a pure heart if thou wilt taste and see how sweet God is; and verily thereto shalt thou never come unless thou be prevented and nourished with His grace, that all things being voided and left, thou alone be united with Him.

For when the grace of God cometh to a man, then is he mighty to all things; and when it goeth away, then shall he be poor and unmighty and as a man left only to scourgings and beatings and pains.

In these things be not thrown down, nor despair not, but stand simply at the will of God, and suffer all things that come to thee praising our Lord Jesus Christ; for after winter cometh summer, and after even cometh day, and after tempest cometh clearness.

Of lacking of all manner of solace

It is not grievous for a man to set no price as man's solace when God is nigh; but it is great, and right great, for a man to lack both God's solace and man's and for the honor of God gladly to suffer exile of heart and in nothing to seek himself and trust not to his own merit.

What great thing is it, when grace comes, that thou be glad and devout? For that hour is desirable to all men: he rideth easily and merrily whom the grace of God beareth.

And what wonder that he feel no burden, who is borne of the Almighty and led of the sovereign leader?

Gladly we take somewhat by way of solace, and hard it is for a man to be drawn out of himself.

Saint Laurence overcame the world with his priest, for he despised all things delectable in the world and for the love of God suffered benignly the high priest Sextus, whom he most loved, to be taken away from him.

The love therefore of the Creator overcame the love of man, and he chose the well-willing of God before man's solace.

So learn thou to forsake for the love of God some dear friend that is necessary to thee, nor bear it heavily when thou art forsaken of thy friend, knowing that at last we must all depart from each other.

It behooveth a man long time and mightily to strive with himself before a man shall be able perfectly to overcome himself and draw all his affection unto God.

When a man standeth upon himself, he slideth lightly to man's consolations, but the very true lover of Christ and studious follower of virtue slideth not to consolations nor seeketh such sensible sweetness, but rather would suffer for Christ mighty trials and hard labors.

Wherefore, when spiritual consolation is given of God, receive it with great thanks and understand it to be the gift of God and not thy merit.

Be not proud nor rejoice not too much nor presume not vainly; but be the more meek for the gift and the more aware and the more anxious in all thy deeds; for that hour shall pass and temptation shall follow.

And when the consolation is taken away, despair not anon, but with meekness and patience abide the heavenly visitation; for God is mighty enough to give thee greater consolation.

This is no new nor strange thing to them that are expert in the way of God; for ofttimes in great saints and holy prophets hath been this manner of alterna-

70–74. **Saint Laurence . . . him.** The martyred Saint Laurence, a native of Huesca, Spain, went to Rome at an early age and was chosen archdeacon by Pope Sextus II, who intrusted to him the treasures of the Church. Later, in the reign of the Emperor Valerian, Sextus was persecuted, imprisoned, and sentenced to death (258 A.D.), whereupon Laurence addressed to him the words: "Whither goest thou, O my father! without thy son and servant."

tion. Wherefore one, grace being present, said, 'I said in mine abundance I shall never be moved.' And, when grace was absent, he rehearsed what he felt, saying, 'Thou hast turned away, and I was troubled.' Nevertheless among these things he despaired not, but prayed more heartily, saying, 'Lord, to thee shall I cry, and I shall pray to my God.' And then he reported the fruit of his prayer, confessing himself to be heard of God, saying, 'Our Lord hath heard and hath pity on me and is made my helper.' But wherein? 'Thou hast,' he said, 'turned my sorrow into joy, and clothed me with gladness.'

If it were done then with great saints, we, feeble and poor, ought not to despair, if some time we be in fervor and some time in coldness; for the holy spirit goeth and cometh after the well pleasing of His will. Wherefore Job saith, 'Thou visitest Him betimes or in the twilight, and suddenly thou provest Him.'

Upon what, therefore, shall I hope, or in whom shall I trust but in the great mercy of God and only in hope of heavenly grace?

Whether good men be nigh thee or devout brethren or true friends or holy books or fair treatises or sweet songs and melodious hymns; all these help but little, savor but little.

When I am forsaken of grace and left in my poverty, then is there no better remedy than patience and denying of myself in the will of God.

I have found no man so religious or devout that feeleth not some time withdrawing of grace or diminution of fervor. There was never saint so highly ravished or illumined but that later or earlier he was tempted; for he is not high in the contemplation of God who is not tried for God in some tribulation; and tribulation going before is wont to be a token of consolation following. For to them that are proved in temptations is promised heavenly comfort.

'He that overcometh,' saith our Lord, 'I shall give him to eat of the tree of life.' Heavenly comfort is given that a man should be stronger to sustain adversities; temptation also followeth lest man be proud of the gift; the devil sleepeth never and the flesh is not dead.

Wherefore, cease not to array thee to battle, for both on the right hand and on the left are enemies that never cease.

Of thanks for the Grace of God

Why seekest thou rest, since thou are born to labor? Put thee to patience more than to consolations, and to bear the cross more than to gladness.

What secular man is there that would not gladly have spiritual consolations and gladness if he might have it for ever? For spiritual consolations pass all the delights of the world and all fleshly pleasures.

For all the delights of the world, either they are vain or foul, but spiritual delights are jocund and honest, engendered of gentle virtues and infused into pure minds by God.

But no man may use these divine consolations at his own will, for the time of temptation ceaseth not for long.

False liberty and trust in self are much contrary to heavenly visitation.

God doth well in giving grace of consolation, but man doth evil, not giving all to God with thanks; and the gifts of God cannot flow in on us, for we be ungrateful to the giver, and we refund not again all to the original will.

Grace is ever due to him that thinketh worthily, and that shall be taken away from the proud man which is wont to be given to meek men.

I wish not that consolation which shall take away from me compunction, nor do I desire that contemplation which shall bring me into elation, for not every high thing is holy, nor every sweet thing good, nor every desire pure, nor every dear thing acceptable to God.

I receive gladly that grace whereby I am found the more meek, the more anxious, and the more ready to forsake myself.

He that is taught with the gift of grace and learned with the beatings of its withdrawal dare ascribe nothing to himself but rather will acknowledge himself poor and naked.

Give to God that is His, and ascribe to thyself that is thine; give God thanks for His grace and to thyself guilt and pain known to be due to thee for thy guilt.

Put thee ever at the lowest, and the highest shall be given to thee, for the highest cannot stand without the lowest.

The highest saints before God are lowest before themselves, and the more glorious that they be, the more meek they are in themselves.

They that are full of truth and heavenly glory are not desirous of vain glory.

They that are grounded and confirmed in God are not proud;

And they that ascribe all to God whatever good they receive, they seek not glory each of the other but they wish the glory that is only of God; and they desire God to be praised in Himself and in His saints above all things, and to that evermore they tend.

Be thankful, therefore, for a little thing, and thou shalt be worthy to take a greater; let also the least thing be to thee as the greatest, and the least of price as a special gift.

If the dignity of the giver be considered, there shall no gift appear little that is given of the high God; yea, if He give pains and beatings, it ought to be taken gladly, for all is done for our help, whatever he suffereth to come to us.

He that desireth to keep the grace of God, let him be thankful for the grace given and patient when it is taken away; let him pray that it come again, and be aware and meek that he lose it not.

Of the fewness of the lovers of the cross of Christ

Jesus hath many lovers of the kingdom of Heaven but few bearers of the cross; he hath many who desire consolations and few desiring tribulations; he findeth many fellows of the table and few of abstinence.

All desire to joy with Him; but few will suffer any pain for Him.

Many follow Jesus unto the breaking of the bread, but few unto the drinking of the cup of the passion.

Many worship His miracles, but few follow the reproof of the Cross.

Many love Jesus when no adversity happeneth.

Many praise Him and bless Him while they take any consolations from Him; but if Jesus hide Himself and forsake them a little, they fall into a complaining or into over great dejection.

But they that love Jesus for Jesus, and not for any consolations, they bless Him in every tribulation and anguish of heart as in the highest consolation; and if He would never give them consolation, yet would they ever praise Him and ever thank Him.

O how mighty is the pure love of Jesus when it is mingled with no love of self nor profit of self!

Whether all they that always seek consolations are not to be called mercenaries and hired men?

Whether are they not proved lovers of themselves and not of Christ who think of their own lucre and profit? where is found one that will serve God freely?

Seldom shall there be any man found so spiritual that will be naked from all worldly things. And who shall find a man very poor in spirit and bare from every creature? his price is from the uttermost coasts.

If a man give all his substance, it is as naught; and if he do great penance, yet it is but little; and if he apprehend all manner of science, yet is he far; and if he have great virtue and right fervent devotion, yet him lacketh much; but one thing is sovereignly necessary to him. What is that? that, all things forsaken, he forsake himself and go wholly out of himself and retain nothing of self-love.

When he hath done all things that he knoweth how to do, let him feel himself to have done naught.

Let him not weigh as great all that may be esteemed great; but let him in truth pronounce himself

an unprofitable servant, as the truth saith, when ye have done all things that are commanded to you, say that we are unprofitable servants.' For such a one may say with the prophet that 'I am sole and poor' when he beginneth verily to be bare and poor in spirit.

Nevertheless no man is richer, no man is mightier, no man more free than he that can forsake himself and all things and put himself at the lowest.

Of the King's Highway of the cross

This word, 'deny thyself and take thy cross and follow me,' seemeth a hard word to many men; but much harder it shall be to hear this word, 'Go from me, ye cursed people, into the fire everlasting.'

They that gladly hear and follow the word of the cross shall not dread the word of everlasting damnation.

This sign of the cross shall be in Heaven when our Lord shall come to judgment.

Then all the servants of the cross that have conformed them to Christ in their life shall come nigh unto Christ the judge with great trust.

Why dreadest thou therefore to take the cross whereby men go to the kingdom?

In the cross is health, in the cross is life, in the cross is protection from enemies, in the cross is infusion of heavenly sweetness, in the cross is strength of mind, in the cross is joy of spirit, in the cross is the sum of virtue, in the cross is perfection of holiness; there is no health of soul nor hope of everlasting life, but in the cross. Take thy cross therefore and follow Jesus, and thou shalt go into life everlasting.

He that bare His own cross is gone before and died for thee on the cross, that thou shouldest bear thy cross and desire to die on the cross; and if thou be fellow in pain, thou shalt be fellow in glory.

Lo, in the cross standeth all things, and in dying lieth all; and there is none other way to life and to very inward peace but the way of the holy cross and of daily mortifying, for if thou be dead with Him, thou shalt also live with Him.

Walk therefore where thou wilt; seek wherever it pleaseth thee, and thou shalt find no higher way above nor surer way beneath than the way of the cross.

Dispose and ordain all things after thy will and thy seeming, and thou shalt not find it anything but a duty to suffer somewhat either willingly or against thy will, and thou shalt ever find the cross.

Thou shalt either suffer sorrow in thy body or tribulation of spirit in the soul.

Sometimes thou shalt be forsaken of God and sometimes thou shalt be stirred by thy neighbor and, what is more, sometimes thou shalt be grievous to thyself.

39–40. his price . . . coasts, that is, as a gem that is brought from afar (Author's note). 43. science, knowledge.

And yet it shall not lie in thy power to be eased or delivered with no remedy and with no solace; but, while God will, thou must needs suffer and bear.

God willeth that thou shalt learn to suffer tribulation without comfort, for thou shouldest subdue all things to Him and be the meeker for tribulation.

No man so heartily feeleth the passion of Christ as he that suffereth like things.

The cross therefore is ever ready, and over all things it abideth for thee; thou canst not flee it, wherever thou run; and wherever thou come, thou bearest thyself with thee, and ever thou shalt find thyself.

Turn thyself above, turn thyself below, turn thyself outward, turn thyself inward; and in all these thou shalt find the cross; and everywhere it is needful for thee to keep patience, if thou wilt have inward peace and deserve a crown everlasting.

If thou bear the cross gladly, it shall bear thee, and lead thee to a desirable end, where an end shall be of suffering—though it be not here.

If thou bear it against thy will, thou makest for thyself a heavy burden and grievest thyself more; and yet must thou needs sustain it.

If thou put away one cross, doubtless thou shalt find another and peradventure a more grievous one.

Thinkest thou to escape what never mortal man might escape? What saint in this world was without cross and tribulation? Not our Lord Jesus Christ was without sorrow of passion one hour in all his life. The evangelist saith, 'It behooved Christ to suffer and to rise from death and so to enter into his glory.' And how seekest thou another way than the king's highway, the cross way? All Christ's life was a cross and a martyrdom; and thou seekest to thyself rest and joy?

Thou errest, thou goest out of the way if thou seek other thing to thee than tribulation, for all this mortal life is full of miseries and marked all about with crosses; and the higher that a man profiteth in spirit, the higher crosses ofttimes he findeth; for the pain of his exile groweth more through love.

Nevertheless this man, thus pained, is not without some manner of comfort, for he feeleth great fruit to grow to him through the sufferance of his cross; for while he gladly subdueth him thereto, all burden of tribulation is turned into trust of divine consolation; and the more that the flesh is thrown down by affliction, the more the spirit is strengthened by inward grace.

And ofttimes he is so greatly comforted and strengthened that for desire of tribulation and adversity, for love of conformity to the cross of Christ, he would not be without sorrow and tribulation; for the more acceptable he accounteth himself to God, the more and the greater are the pains that he must suffer for God.

This is not man's might, but the grace of Christ, that man doeth so great things in his frail flesh, that through fervor of spirit he can take upon him and love that thing which the flesh ever naturally fleeth and abhorreth.

It is not like man to bear the cross, to love the cross, to chastise the body, to bring it to thralldom, to flee honor, gladly to sustain reproofs and wrongs, to despise himself and to will to be despised, to suffer all manner of adversities with harms and to desire no manner of prosperity in this world.

If thou look to thyself, thou canst do no such thing of thyself; but, if thou trust in our Lord, strength shall be given to thee from Heaven, and the world and the flesh shall be made subject to thy commandment; nor shalt thou dread thine enemy the devil, if thou be armed with faith and marked with the cross.

Put thee therefore forward as a good and true servant of Christ, to bear manly the cross of thy Lord crucified for thee through love. Make thee ready to suffer many contrary things and diverse incommodities in this wretched life; for so he shall be with thee wherever thou be, and so thou shalt find him wherever thou be hid.

It must be so; for there is no remedy of escaping from tribulation of evil men and sorrow—except that thou suffer.

Drink the chalice of our Lord lovingly, if thou desire to be His friend and to have part with Him. Consolations commit thou to God; let Him do therewith as it pleaseth Him.

Put thou thyself forward to suffer tribulations and account them as greatest consolations, for there are no passions of this time worthy to deserve the glory that is to come; yea, though thou mightest suffer all alone.

When thou comest to this, that tribulation is sweet to thee and is savory to thee for Christ, then deem it well with thee, for thou hast found Paradise on earth.

As long as it is grievous to thee to suffer, and thou seekest to flee it, so long shall it be evil with thee, and fleeing after thee, tribulation shall follow thee everywhere.

If thou puttest thee forward, as thou oughtest to do, to suffer and to die, it shall soon be better and thou shalt find peace.

Yea, if thou be ravished into the third heaven with Paul, thou art not yet sure to suffer no contrary

108–109. Yea, if thou . . . Paul. There was a tradition that Paul, on the occasion of his martyrdom, was translated immediately into the third Heaven. This is, according to medieval astronomy, the sphere of Venus, or Love. The legend probably grew out of the conception of Paul as the apostle of divine love.

thing: for Jesus said, 'I shall show him how great things he must suffer for my name.'

To suffer, therefore, remaineth to thee if thou wilt love and ever please Him.

Would God that thou wert worthy to suffer any thing for the name of Jesus; how great glory should be to thee, how great exultation to all the saints of Heaven, how great edification of thy neighbor; for all men commend patience, though few will suffer it.

Thou shouldest gladly suffer for Christ, since men suffer much more grievous things for the world.

Know for certain that thou must lead a dying life, and the more that a man dieth to himself, the more he beginneth to live to God; there is no man fit to take heavenly things unless he submit himself to bear adversities for Christ.

There is nothing more acceptable to God, nothing more wholesome to thee in this world than gladly to suffer for Christ; and if it lay in thy choice, thou shouldest rather desire to suffer contrary things for Christ than to be refreshed with many consolations, for thou wouldest be more like unto Christ and be more conformed to all saints.

For our merit and the profiting of our estate standeth not in sweetness and consolations, but rather in suffering of grievous things and tribulations; for if there had been any thing more better or more profitable to man than to suffer, Christ would verily have shown it by word and example. But He exhorted all His disciples and all them that desired to follow Him openly to bear the cross, saying, 'Who that will come after me, let him deny himself, and take his cross, and follow me.'

All things therefore being read over and searched, be this the final conclusion, that by many tribulations it behooveth us to enter into the kingdom of Heaven.

Saint Francis of Assisi

c. 1182–1226

Of all the great saints of the Christian Church in the Middle Ages, Saint Francis of Assisi could most properly be called popular. He was the son of a rather well-to-do independent merchant of Assisi, a small town near Perugia, Italy. We have no record of any particular amount of formal education given him, yet he became a great spiritual leader of the people, a man of remarkable personal appeal, which more than seven centuries have not been able to dim. To him all living things, man or beast, were the sacred vessels of God's spirit; yet it is altogether inadequate to think of him as only a gentle, unworldly, devoted soul who preached to the birds and flowers. For it happens that,

although born with mundane comforts at hand, he chose to espouse poverty while still hardly more than an adolescent; and his supreme achievement in life was the founding of the great Order of Franciscan Friars—an order which typifies the very spirit incarnate of the mendicant friars of the later Middle Ages—servants of the Lord and the souls of the people, whose lives were completely dedicated to the triplex vow of poverty, chastity, and obedience.

Saint Francis established this Order, it is believed, in either 1208 or 1209. There were only some half-dozen original members of the group, but the number increased slowly and steadily as the marvelous reputation of the eloquent ascetic of Assisi became known throughout the Christian world. The original center of the Order was a small church near Assisi, known as the Church of Santa Maria degli Angeli, or as the Porziuncula, or simply as The Place. The plan of religious life envisaged by Francis was simple and austere in the extreme, as can be seen from the following:

"Provide neither gold nor silver nor brass in your purses, nor scrip for your journey, neither two coats, nor yet staves . . . Sell all that thou hast, and give to the poor; then thou shalt have treasure in Heaven . . . Fear not because you are small and seem foolish. Have confidence in the Lord who has vanquished the world. Some will receive you. Many proud ones will resist you. Bear all with sweetness and patience. Soon the wise and the noble will be with us. The Lord hath given me to see this . . . Go and preach by two and two. Preach peace and patience; tend the sick and wounded; relieve the distressed; reclaim the erring; bless them which persecute you, and pray for them that despitefully use you."

The strong scriptural influence on Saint Francis is obvious without further comment, for many of the phrases in these instructions are identical with those in the Holy Gospels.

The great initial victory of Saint Francis was the securing of the sanction of the Pope, for the incumbent at that time was none other than the formidable Innocent III, perhaps the most arrogant and absolute in power of any of the medieval popes. Thenceforth the Franciscan Order (often called in English literature the Gray Friars) moved about all over Christendom. In addition, Francis founded an Order of Sisters, known as the Clarisses, or Poor Claras, named after Saint Clara, a woman of Assisi, whom Francis had persuaded to adopt a life of poverty and ascetic devotion and who remained his steadfast friend, even his confidante, throughout her life. Unusual indeed was the third Order of Tertiaries or Brethren of Penitence, which Saint Francis established in 1221. This comprised lay men and women who desired austerity in life but who wished to retain their secular social position and employment. In founding this third Order, Saint Francis demonstrated a shrewdness and an insight into human nature which are quite sufficient by themselves to indicate his effectiveness as a religious leader.

But there are other qualities which show equally well the power of Saint Francis as a spiritual influence.

Saint Francis and a companion, from a painting by Giotto (1276–1337) in the Louvre.

or folkbook, of tales about Saint Francis, which remains the most attractive and moving of all medieval biographical writings. The legendary nature of all works relating to the life of Saint Francis is illustrated by the tradition adhering to his death. Saint Francis died in 1226; according to report, his corpse exhibited the same wounds, or marks of wounds, as those suffered by Christ on the Cross. These, the celebrated Stigmata of Saint Francis, were explained by some as marks of wounds self-inflicted during the lifetime of Saint Francis; such an explanation would be entirely credible in the case of one who followed so closely the life of Christ. According to others, of course, they were miraculous indications of the oneness with Christ. In any case, they combined with the saintliness of Saint Francis' character and works to bring about his early canonization (1228). And it is altogether appropriate that such a legend should have arisen, for no man in the long history of Christianity has served better as a living exemplar of the teachings of Christ and His ideals.

The Little Flowers of Saint Francis

CHAPTER X

How Friar Masseo, as if in raillery, said to St. Francis that all the world followed after him; and he replied that that was to the confusion of the world and the grace of God

ONCE while St. Francis dwelt in the place of Porziuncula with Friar Masseo of Marignano, a man of great sanctity, discretion, and grace in speaking of God (wherefore St. Francis loved him much), it came to pass that, one day, when St. Francis was returning from the wood and from prayer, and was already come to the place of egress from the wood, the said Friar Masseo desired to prove how great was his humility and drew nigh unto him and, as if in raillery, said: "Why after thee? why after thee? why after thee?" St. Francis answered: "What is this that thou wouldst say?" Said Friar Masseo: "I say, why doth all the world follow after thee, and why doth every man seem to desire to see thee and to hear thee and to obey thee? Thou art not a man beautiful of body, thou art not greatly learned, thou art not noble; wherefore then should all the world follow after thee?" Hearing this St. Francis rejoiced greatly in spirit, and raising his face to Heaven, stood for a long time with his mind uplifted in God, and thereafter, returning to himself, kneeled down and gave praise and thanks to

10

20

The Little Flowers of Saint Francis.[8] Translated by W. Heywood. Reprinted by permission of Methuen and Co., Ltd., Publishers.

One was his boundless energy; he traveled extensively and was in words and deeds an indefatigable missionary. Tradition has it that he converted the "Sultan of Babylon," although this seems to be apocryphal; but there is no gainsaying the useful work of Saint Francis among Moslems, Hebrews, Levantines, and Byzantines abroad, as well as among sinners at home. Furthermore, his Christian charity was of the most convincing sincerity, as was his essential humanity. The complete antithesis of Chaucer's Friar, he worked willingly among lepers and madmen, among the poor and barren, even preferring them as subjects of his labors to the wealthy and powerful. It is scarcely surprising, then, that he attained something of the preëminence of an epic hero among Christian workers; so many legends gathered about him that it is now virtually impossible, in dealing with the career of Saint Francis, to disentangle fact and fiction.

It has been forgotten also that Saint Francis was a religious poet of great sincerity though of limited poetic accomplishments—an honorable forerunner, however, in the field of religious verse, of the Italian lyricists of the thirteenth century; a well-defined foothill to the towering mountain range of Dante. However, there are many who insist that Saint Francis' poetry is at its best dependent entirely upon his personality and his works of good report.

The *Fioretti di San Francesco,* or *Little Flowers of Saint Francis,* tells the whole story of the saint as it appeared in the popular Italian imagination of the early fourteenth century, about a hundred years after his death. Its authorship is unknown, although Ugolino Brunforte, a member of the Order who died in 1348, is sometimes named in tradition. Actually it is a *Volksbuch,*

God, and then with great fervor of spirit turned to Friar Masseo and said: "Wouldst know why after me? wouldst know why after me? why all the world follows after me? This have I from those eyes of the most high God, which in every place behold the good and the wicked; because these most holy eyes have not seen among sinners any more vile, or more insufficient, or a greater sinner than I am; and since to do that marvelous work which He meaneth to do,
10 He hath not found a viler creature upon earth, therefore hath He chosen me to confound the nobility and the pride and the strength and the beauty and wisdom of the world, to the end that it may know that every virtue and every good thing is of Him and not of the creature, and that no one may be able to glory in His sight; but whosoever shall glory, let him glory in the Lord, to whom is all honor and glory for ever." Then Friar Masseo, at so lowly an answer, spoken with so much fervor, was
20 afraid and knew of a surety that St. Francis was established in humility.

CHAPTER XI

How St. Francis made Friar Masseo turn round and round many times, and thereafter gat him to Siena

One day, while St. Francis journeyed with Friar Masseo, the said Friar Masseo went a little before; and arriving at a certain place where three roads meet which led to Florence, to Siena, and to Arezzo, Friar Masseo said: "Father, by which way must we go?" St. Francis made answer: "By that which God shall will." Said Friar Masseo: "And how shall we be able to know the will of God?" St. Francis
30 answered: "By the sign which I shall show thee. Wherefore I command thee by the duty of holy obedience, that in this place where three roads meet, on the spot where now thy feet are set, thou turn round and round, as children do, and stop not from turning thyself unless I bid thee to do so." Then Friar Masseo began to turn himself round, and so much did he turn that, by reason of the dizziness of the head which is wont to be generated by such turning, he fell divers times to the ground;
40 but, in that St. Francis did not bid him stop, he, desiring to obey faithfully, gat him up again and resumed the said turning. At the last, while he was turning round manfully, St. Francis said: "Stand still, and move not," and he stood; and St. Francis asked him: "Toward which part is thy face set?" Friar Masseo answered: "Toward Siena." St. Francis said: "That is the way whereby God wills that we go." Now, as they went by that way, Friar Masseo marvelled that St. Francis had made him do even as
50 children do, before the worldly folk who were passing by; nevertheless, for the sake of reverence, he

ventured not to say anything to the holy father. As they drew nigh unto Siena, the people of the city heard of the coming of the saint, and went forth to meet him; and for devotion they bare him and his companion even unto the bishop's house, so that they touched no ground with their feet. In that hour certain men of Siena fought together, and already two of them were slain; but when St. Francis
60 arrived there, he preached to them so devoutly and holily that he brought them all to peace and to great unity and concord. For the which thing the Bishop of Siena, hearing of that holy work which St. Francis had done, invited him to his house and lodged him with great honor that day and also that night. And, on the morning of the following day, St. Francis, who, with true humility, in all his actions sought only God's glory, rose up early with his companion and got him thence without the
70 knowledge of the bishop. For which cause the said Friar Masseo went by the way murmuring within himself, and saying: "What is it that this good man hath done? He made me turn round like a child, and to the bishop who hath shown him so much honor he hath spoken never a word nor thanked him;" and it seemed to Friar Masseo that therein St. Francis had borne himself indiscreetly. But afterward, returning to his right mind by Divine inspiration, and reproaching himself in his heart, he said: "Friar Masseo, too proud art thou who judgest
80 Divine works, and thou art worthy of Hell for thy indiscreet pride; for yesterday Friar Francis wrought such holy deeds that if an angel of God had done them they could not have been more marvelous; wherefore, if he should bid thee throw stones, thou oughtest so to do and to obey him; and that which he did upon the way proceeded from Divine inspiration, as is shown by the good result which followed thereupon; in that if he had not made peace between them who fought together, not only would
90 the sword have devoured the bodies of many, even as it had already begun to do, but also the devil would have carried away many souls to Hell; and therefore art thou very foolish and proud who murmurest against that which manifestly proceedeth from the will of God." And all these things which Friar Masseo said in his heart, as he went before, were revealed of God to St. Francis. Wherefore St. Francis drew nigh unto him and spake thus: "Hold fast to those things which now thou thinkest,
100 in that they are good and useful and inspired of God; but the first murmuring which thou madest was blind and vain and proud, and was put in thy mind by the demon." Then Friar Masseo perceived clearly that St. Francis knew the secrets of his heart, and he understood certainly that the spirit of Divine wisdom guided the holy father in all his actions.

CHAPTER XII

How St. Francis laid upon Friar Masseo the service of the gate, of almsgiving, and of the kitchen; and thereafter, at the prayer of the other friars, relieved him of them

St. Francis, desiring to humble Friar Masseo, to the end that he might not become puffed up by reason of the many gifts and graces which God was giving him, but by virtue of humility might increase thereby from virtue to virtue; once when he was dwelling in a solitary place with those true saints, his first companions, among whom was the said Friar Masseo, he spake on a day to Friar Masseo before all his companions, saying: "O Friar Masseo, all these thy companions have the grace of preaching the Word of God to the satisfying of the people; and therefore, to the end that these thy companions may be able to give themselves to contemplation, I will that thou perform the office of the gate and of almsgiving and of the kitchen; and when the other friars shall eat, thou shalt eat without the gate of the Place, so that thou mayest satisfy those who come to the Place with some good words of God or ever they have knocked; thus it will not be necessary for any other to go forth save thee alone; and this do thou for the merit of holy obedience." Thereupon, Friar Masseo drew back his cowl and bowed his head and humbly received this obedience and persevered therein for many days, performing the office of the gate, of almsgiving, and of the kitchen. Wherefore his companions, as men illuminated of God, began to feel great remorse in their hearts, considering that Friar Masseo was a man of great perfection even as they or more so, and upon him was laid all the burthen of the Place and not on them. For which cause they were all moved with one desire and went to beseech the holy father that he would be pleased to distribute among them those offices; inasmuch as their consciences might in no wise bear that Friar Masseo should endure so great labor. Hearing this, St. Francis inclined his ear unto their counsels and consented unto their wish. Calling Friar Masseo, he spake to him after this manner: "Friar Masseo, thy companions desire to share the offices which I have given thee; and therefore I will that they be divided among them." Said Friar Masseo, with great humility and patience: "Father, that which thou layest upon me, whether in whole or in part, I esteem it altogether done of God." Then St. Francis, beholding the charity of those others and the humility of Friar Masseo, preached unto them a marvelous sermon touching most holy humility; teaching them that the greater the gifts and graces which God bestows upon us, the greater should our humility be, because without humility

no virtue is acceptable to God. And when he had finished preaching, he distributed the offices with very great love.

CHAPTER XIII

How St. Francis and Friar Masseo placed the bread which they had begged upon a stone hard by a fountain, and St. Francis praised Poverty much. Thereafter, he prayed God and St. Peter and St. Paul, that He would cause him to be enamored of holy Poverty; and how St. Peter and St. Paul appeared to him

The marvelous servant and follower of Christ, Messer St. Francis, to the end that in everything he might conform himself to Christ, who, according to the Gospel, sent His disciples by two and two to all those cities and places whither He Himself was about to go; inasmuch as after the example of Christ he had gathered together twelve companions, sent them through the world to preach by two and two. And, to set them an ensample of true obedience, he himself was the first to go, after the ensample of Christ, who began to do before He began to teach. Wherefore, having assigned to his companions the other regions of the world, he, taking Friar Masseo as his companion, journeyed toward the province of France. And coming one day to a village and being very hungry, they went, according to the Rule, begging bread for the love of God; and St. Francis went through one street and Friar Masseo through another. But because St. Francis was a man too despicable and small of body, and was esteemed a vile mendicant therefor by those who knew him not, he got only some mouthfuls and fragments of dry bread; whereas to Friar Masseo, because he was tall and beautiful of body, were given good pieces and large and in plenty and fresh cut from the loaf. And so when they had finished begging, they met together to eat outside the village in a place where there was a beautiful fountain with a fair large stone beside it, whereupon each of them laid all the bread which he had begged; and when St. Francis saw that Friar Masseo's pieces of bread were more plentiful and better and larger than his, he showed very great joy thereat, and spake after this manner: "O Friar Masseo, we are not worthy of so great treasure;" and when he had repeated these words many times, Friar Masseo replied: "Father, how is it possible to speak of treasure where there is such great poverty and lack of all things needful? Here is neither tablecloth, nor knife, nor trencher, nor porringer, nor house, nor table, nor man-servant, nor maid-servant." Said St. Francis: "And this is

58–59. **He himself . . . to go.** Here, as elsewhere, it is to be noted how closely St. Francis follows the precepts of Christ.

that which I esteem great treasure, where there is nothing prepared by human industry; but that which there is, is prepared by the Divine Providence, as may be manifestly seen in the bread which we have begged, in this beautiful table of rock and in this clear spring. Wherefore I will that we pray God that He make us to love with our whole heart the so noble treasure of holy Poverty, which hath God to servitor." And when he had said these words and had prayed and partaken for bodily sustenance of these fragments of bread and of that water, they rose up to journey into France; and coming to a church, St. Francis got him behind the altar and betook himself to prayer; and in that prayer he received by Divine visitation such exceeding fervor, the which kindled his soul so mightily to love of holy Poverty, that by the heat of his face and by the unwonted gaping of his mouth it seemed that he breathed forth flames of love. And coming thus enkindled to his companion, he spake to him on this wise: "Ah! Ah! Ah! Friar Masseo, give me thyself"; and so spake he three times; and the third time St. Francis raised Friar Masseo into the air with his breath, and cast him before him a great spear's length. Thereat was Friar Masseo filled with very great wonder; and thereafter, he related to his companions that when St. Francis thus lifted him up and cast him from him with his breath, he experienced such great sweetness of spirit and consolation of the Holy Ghost, that never in his life had he felt the like. And when this was done, St. Francis said: "Companion mine, let us go to St. Peter and St. Paul and pray them that they will teach us and aid us to possess the immeasurable treasure of most holy Poverty; for she is a treasure so surpassing and so Divine that we are not worthy to possess it in our most vile vessels; for this is that celestial virtue whereby all earthly things and transitory are trodden under foot, and every barrier is removed which might hinder the soul from freely uniting itself to the eternal God. This is that virtue which enableth the soul, while yet on earth, to hold converse in Heaven with the angels; this is she, who bare Christ company upon the Cross, with Christ was buried, with Christ was raised again, and with Christ ascended into Heaven; who even in this life grants to the souls which are enamored of her nimbleness to fly to Heaven, seeing that it is she who guards the weapons of true humility and charity. Therefore, pray we the most holy Apostles of Christ, who were perfect lovers of this evangelic pearl, that they may beg this grace for us from our Lord Jesus Christ that, of His most holy pity, He may grant us to be worthy to be true lovers, observers, and humble disciples of most precious, most beloved and evangelic Poverty." And thus discoursing, they came to Rome and entered into the Church of St. Peter; and St. Francis betook

himself to prayer in one corner of the church and Friar Masseo in another; and they abode long time in prayer with great devotion and many tears, until, at the last, the most holy Apostles Peter and Paul appeared to St. Francis in great splendor, and said: "Because thou askest and desirest to observe that which Christ and His Apostles observed, the Lord Jesus Christ sends us to thee to make known unto thee that thy prayer is heard, and that the treasure of most holy Poverty is granted unto thee of God in fullest perfection, to thee and to thy followers. And further we tell thee in His name that whosoever, after thy example, shall perfectly follow this desire, he is assured of the beatitude of life eternal; and thou and all thy followers shall be blessed of God." And when they had thus spoken, they vanished away, leaving St. Francis full of consolation. Thereafter, he rose up from prayer and returned to his companion and asked him if God had revealed aught unto him; and he answered, "No." Then St. Francis told him how the holy Apostles had appeared to him and what they had revealed unto him. Wherefore each of them was fulfilled with joy; and they determined to return to the Val di Spoleto and to leave their journeying into France.

CHAPTER XIV

How while St. Francis and his friars spake of God,
He appeared in the midst of them

In the beginning of the Religion, what time St. Francis and his companions were gathered together to speak of Christ, he, in fervor of spirit, commanded one of them that, in the name of God, he should open his mouth and speak of God that which the Holy Ghost inspired him. Now, while the friar was fulfilling that commandment and was discoursing marvelously of God, St. Francis imposed silence upon him and bade another friar speak in like manner. He, yielding obedience and discoursing subtly of God, St. Francis, in like manner, imposed silence upon him, and commanded a third to speak of God, who, in his turn, began to speak so profoundly of the secret things of God that, of a verity, St. Francis knew that he, like the other two, spake through inspiration of the Holy Ghost; and this also was shown by example and by a clear sign: in that, while they were thus speaking, Christ the blessed appeared in the midst of them in the likeness and form of a youth, exceeding beautiful, and, blessing them, fulfilled them all with so much grace and sweetness, that they were all rapt away out of themselves and lay like dead men, wholly insensible to the things of this world. And thereafter, when they had come to themselves, St. Francis said unto them: "My dearest brethren, let us thank God, who hath

83. **Religion,** the way of life prescribed in the Order of the Franciscans.

willed to reveal the treasures of Divine wisdom through the mouths of the simple; for it is God who openeth the mouth of the dumb and maketh the tongues of the simple to talk very wisely."

CHAPTER XV

How St. Clare ate with St. Francis and with the friars, his companions, in Santa Maria degli Angeli

St. Francis, when he abode at Assisi, ofttimes visited St. Clare and gave her holy admonishments; and she having very great longings to eat once with him, and thereto beseeching him many times, he was never willing to give her this consolation; wherefore his companions perceiving the desire of St. Clare, said to St. Francis: "Father, to us it seems that this severity is not in accordance with Divine charity, in that thou hearkenest not to Sister Clare, a virgin so holy and so beloved of God, in so small a matter as is this of eating with thee; and the more so considering that she through thy preaching abandoned the riches and pomps of the world; and, of a surety, if she asked of thee a greater boon than this is, thou oughtest to grant it to thy spiritual offspring." Then St. Francis made answer: "Doth it seem to you that I ought to grant her prayer?" The companions replied: "Yea, father; it is a fitting thing that thou grant her this grace and consolation." Then St. Francis said: "Since it seemeth so to you, it seemeth so also to me. But to the end that she may have the greater consolation, I desire that this meal be eaten in St. Mary of the Angels, because she hath been long shut up in St. Damian, and thus will she have joy in beholding the Place of St. Mary, where she was shorn and made the bride of Jesus Christ; and there will we eat together in the name of God." Accordingly, the day thereunto appointed being come, St. Clare went forth from the convent with one companion, and, accompanied by the companions of St. Francis, came to St. Mary of the Angels, and after she had devoutly saluted the Virgin Mary before her altar, where she had been shorn and veiled, they took her to see the Place until the dinner hour was come. And, in the meantime, St. Francis caused the table to be set upon the bare ground, as he was wont to do. And when the dinner hour was come, St. Francis and St. Clare sat down together, and one of the companions of St. Francis with the companion of St. Clare; and thereafter all the other companions sat them humbly down at the table. And, at the first dish, St. Francis began to speak of God so sweetly, so highly and so marvelously, that abundance of Divine grace descended upon them and they were all rapt in God. And while they were thus rapt, with eyes and hands raised to Heaven, the men of Assisi and of Bettona, and they of the district round about, saw that St. Mary of the Angels, and all the Place, and the wood which was

hard by the Place, were burning fiercely; and it seemed to them that there was a great fire which encompassed the church and the monastery and the wood together; for the which cause the men of Assisi ran down thither with great haste to quench the fire, believing that verily everything was burning. But when they reached the Place, they saw that there was no fire at all, and they went in and found St. Francis and St. Clare and all their company rapt in God through contemplation, and sitting about that lowly board. Whereby they understood of a surety that that had been Divine fire and not material, the which God had made to appear miraculously to show forth and signify the fire of Divine love wherewith were enkindled the souls of those holy friars and holy nuns; wherefore they departed thence with great consolation of heart and holy edification. Then, after a long while, St. Francis and St. Clare, together with the others, returned to themselves and being greatly comforted with spiritual food they gave but little thought to bodily food; and so, that blessed meal being ended, St. Clare, well accompanied, returned to St. Damian; whereof, when they beheld her, the nuns had great joy, in that they feared lest St. Francis should have sent her to rule some other convent, even as he had aforetime sent Sister Agnes, her holy sister, to be abbess of Montecelli in Florence; and St. Francis had once said to St. Clare: "Hold thyself in readiness, that, if need be, I may send thee to some other Place;" whereto she as a daughter of holy obedience had made answer: "Father, I am ready to go whithersoever you shall send me;" and therefore the nuns rejoiced greatly when they received her back again; and from thenceforward St. Clare abode in much consolation.

CHAPTER XVI

How St. Francis received the counsel of St. Clare, and of the holy Friar Sylvester, that he ought by preaching to convert much folk; and how St. Francis founded the Third Order and preached to the birds and made the swallows keep silence

Shortly after his conversion, the humble servant of Christ, St. Francis, having already gathered many companions and received them into the Order, stood in great anxiety and in great doubt as to that which he ought to do; whether to devote himself wholly to prayer or sometimes also to preaching; and touching that matter he desired greatly to know the will of God; and because the holy humility which was in him suffered him not to trust to himself nor to his own prayers, he bethought him to inquire of the Divine will through the prayers of others; wherefore he called Friar Masseo and said: "Go thou to Sister Clare and tell her in my name that, together with certain of the most spiritual of her companions, she should devoutly pray God that He may vouch-safe to show me whether it be better that I give my-self to preaching or to prayer alone. And thereafter go to Friar Sylvester and tell him to do the like." Now, in the world, this had been that Messer Sylvester who had seen a cross of gold proceeding out of the mouth of St. Francis, the which was high even unto Heaven and wide even unto the ends of the earth; and this Friar Sylvester was of so great devotion and of so great sanctity that by prayer he prevailed with God and all that he asked was granted him, and ofttimes he talked with God; and therefore St. Francis had great devotion toward him. Friar Masseo departed and, according to the bidding of St. Francis, did his embassage first to St. Clare and thereafter to Friar Sylvester; who, as soon as he had received it, forthwith got himself to prayer, and while he was yet praying he obtained the Divine answer, and turned him to Friar Masseo and said: "Thus doth God bid thee say to Friar Francis: that God hath not called him to this estate for himself alone, but that he may have much fruit of souls, and that many through him may be saved." And when he had heard this, Friar Masseo returned to St. Clare, to know what answer she had received from God; and she replied that she and the other companions had had the selfsame answer from God which Friar Sylvester had had. Therewith Friar Masseo returned to St. Francis; and St. Francis wel-comed him with very great charity, washing his feet and setting food before him. And when he had eaten, St. Francis called Masseo into the wood; and there he kneeled down before him, and drew back his cowl, and making a cross of his arms, asked him, "What doth my Lord Jesus Christ bid me do?" Friar Masseo made answer: "To Friar Sylvester as to Sister Clare and to her companion, Christ hath made answer and revealed that His will is that thou go through the world to preach, because He hath not chosen thee for thyself alone but also for the salva-tion of others." Then St. Francis, when he had had this answer and knew thereby the will of Jesus Christ, rose up with exceeding great fervor and said: "Let us go, in the name of God;" and he took as his companion Friar Masseo and Friar Agnolo, holy men. And going with impetuosity of spirit, taking thought neither of way nor path, they came to a walled place which is called Savurniano; and St. Francis began to preach; but first he bade the swal-lows which were twittering to keep silence until such time as he should finish preaching; and the swallows obeyed him; and there he preached with so great fervor that for devotion all the men and women of that town were minded to follow him and to abandon the town; but St. Francis suffered them not, saying: "Be not over hasty to depart; and I will ordain that which it behooves you to do for the sal-

vation of your souls;" and then he bethought him to institute the Third Order for the universal salva-tion of all men; and so, leaving them greatly com-forted and with minds turned to repentance, he got him thence and came betwixt Cannaio and Bevagno. And passing on, full of fervor, he lifted up his eyes and saw certain trees hard by the road, whereupon was an almost infinite number of birds; whereat St. Francis marveled, and said to his companions: "Ye shall await me here on the road, and I will go and preach to the birds my sisters;" and he went into the field and began to preach to the birds which were upon the ground; and anon those which were in the trees came to him, and all of them stood still together until St. Francis finished preaching; and even then they departed not until he gave them his blessing; and according to that which Friar Masseo afterward related to Friar James of Massa, when St. Francis went about among them, touching them with his mantle, none of them moved therefor. Now the preaching of St. Francis was on this wise: "My sisters the birds, much are ye beholden unto God your creator, and always and in every place ought ye to praise Him, because He hath given you liberty to fly wheresoever ye will, and hath clothed you on with twofold and threefold raiment. Moreover, He preserved your seed in the Ark of Noah, that your race might not be destroyed. Again, ye are beholden unto Him for the element of the air which He hath appointed for you; furthermore, ye sow not, neither do ye reap; yet God feedeth you and giveth you rivers and fountains wherefrom to drink; He giveth you mountains and valleys for your refuge, and high trees wherein to build your nests; and, in that ye know not how to sew nor spin, God clothed you and your little ones; wherefore doth your Creator love you, seeing that He giveth you so many benefits. Guard yourselves, therefore, my sisters the birds, from the sin of ingratitude and be ye ever mindful to give praise to God." And, as St. Francis spake these words unto them, all those birds began to open their beaks, and to stretch out their necks, and to open their wings, and reverently to bow their heads even unto the ground, and to show by their motions and by their songs that the holy father gave them very great delight; and St. Francis rejoiced with them and was glad and marveled much at so great a multitude of birds, and at the most beautiful diversity of them, and at their attention and fearless-ness; for which cause he devoutly praised the Cre-ator in them. Finally, when he had made an end of preaching, St. Francis made over them the sign of the Cross and gave them leave to depart; whereupon all those birds rose into the air with wondrous songs;

59. **Third Order.** See headnote to St. Francis. 62. **Cannaio and Bevagno,** two villages in Perugia near Assisi.

and thereafter, according to the form of the Cross which St. Francis had made over them, they divided themselves into four bands; and one band flew towards the East, and one towards the West, and one towards the South and the fourth towards the North, and each company went singing marvelous songs; signifying thereby that, even as St. Francis, the Standard-bearer of the Cross, had preached to them, and made over them the Sign of the Cross, according whereunto they separated themselves toward the four quarters of the world, so the preaching of the Cross of Christ, renewed by St. Francis, was about to be carried through all the world by him and by his friars; the which friars, like unto the birds, possess nothing of their own in this world but commit their lives wholly to the providence of God.

CHAPTER XVII

How a boy friar, while St. Francis was praying by night, saw Christ and the Virgin Mary and very many other saints hold converse with him

While St. Francis yet lived, a boy very pure and innocent was received into the Order; and he abode in a little Place; wherein the friars, of necessity, slept on rugs. Once St. Francis came to the said Place, and, in the evening, when compline had been said, betook himself to sleep to the end that he might be able to rise up at night and pray, while the other friars slept, as he was wont to do. Now the said boy settled it in his heart to observe carefully the ways of St. Francis, if so be he might know his sanctity and especially that which he did at night when he rose up. Wherefore, that sleep might not betray him, that boy laid down to sleep close to St. Francis and tied his cord to the cord of St. Francis, that he might perceive when he rose up. And of this St. Francis felt nothing. But during the night, in the first watch, while all the other friars slept, he rose up and found his cord thus tied, and he loosed it gently that the boy might not perceive it, and so St. Francis got him alone to the wood which was hard by the Place, and entered into a little cell which was there and betook himself to prayer; and, after a certain time, the boy awoke and finding the cord untied and St. Francis gone away, he rose up and went to seek him; and finding the gate which led into the wood open, he bethought him that St. Francis might have gone thither, and he entered into the wood. And coming nigh unto the place where St. Francis was praying, he began to hear a sound as of many folk talking, and drawing nearer to see and to understand that which he heard, he beheld a wonderful light which encompassed St. Francis round about, and in the midst thereof he saw Christ

and the Virgin Mary and St. John the Baptist and the Evangelist and a very great multitude of angels who spake with St. Francis. When he saw and heard this, the boy fell to the ground in a swoon. Thereafter, the mystery of that holy vision being ended, St. Francis, as he returned to the Place, stumbled upon the said boy, lying as if dead; and for compassion he lifted him up and carried him in his arms, even as the good shepherd carrieth his lambs. And then, learning from him how he had beheld the said vision, he commanded him to tell no man as long as he lived. Afterward the boy, increasing in great grace with God and in devotion to St. Francis, became a worthy man in the Order; and after the death of St. Francis, he revealed the said vision to the friars.

CHAPTER XVIII

Of the marvelous chapter which St. Francis held at Santa Maria degli Angeli, where there were more than five thousand friars

Once the faithful servant of Christ, Francis, held a general chapter at Santa Maria degli Angeli, to which chapter were gathered more than five thousand friars; and thither came St. Dominic, head and founder of the Order of Preaching Friars, the which at that time was journeying from Burgundy to Rome. And hearing of the congregation of the chapter which St. Francis was holding in the plain of Santa Maria degli Angeli, he betook himself thither to see the same, with seven friars of his Order. There was then at the said chapter a cardinal who was greatly devoted to St. Francis, who had prophesied to him that he would be Pope, and so thereafter it befell; the which cardinal had come specially from Perugia, where was the court, to Assisi; every day he came to see St. Francis and his friars, and sometimes he sang mass and sometimes he preached to the friars in chapter; and the said cardinal took very great delight and was filled with devotion when he came to visit that holy college. And seeing the friars seated round about Santa Maria, company by company, here forty, there a hundred, and there eighty together, all employed in speaking of God, in prayers, in tears, and in exercises of charity, behaving themselves with so great silence and with such sobriety that no clamor was heard there, nor any disturbance, he marveled to behold so great discipline in so vast a multitude, and, with tears and great devotion, said: "Verily this is the camp of the army of the knights of God!" In all the great multitude no one was heard to tell stories or to jest; but, wherever a company of

---

21. **compline,** the last service of prayer during the day, held after vespers.

51. **the Evangelist,** the Apostle John. 69–70. **St. Dominic . . . Friars.** Dominic of Calahorra (1170–1221), a Spanish cleric, was the founder of the Order of Dominican Friars (Blackfriars). Their aims were the same as those of the Franciscans but their appeal was more intellectual and less emotional.

friars was gathered together, they either prayed, or said the office, or bewailed their own sins or those of their benefactors, or reasoned of the salvation of souls. In that encampment were booths made of withes and of rushes, separate for each company, according to the diverse provinces of the friars; and therefore that chapter was called the Chapter of the Withes or of the Rushes. Their beds were the bare ground, and some had a little straw; their bolsters were of stone or wood. For which cause, whoever heard or saw them had so great devotion toward them, and such was the fame of their sanctity that, from the court of the Pope, which was then in Perugia, and from other places in the Val di Spoleto, there came many counts, barons, knights and other gentlemen, and many common folk, and cardinals, and bishops and abbots, with many other clerks, to see that so holy and great and humble congregation of so many holy men, the like whereof the world had never; and chiefly they came to see the head and most holy father of that holy folk, who had robbed the world of so fair a prey, and gathered so goodly and devout a flock to follow in the footsteps of the true Shepherd Jesus Christ. All this general chapter, then, being gathered together, the holy father of all and minister-general, St. Francis, in fervor of spirit, expounded the word of God and preached unto them in a loud voice that which the Holy Spirit made him say; and he set forth the argument of his sermon in these words: "My sons, great things have we promised unto God; but greater are the promises of God to us-ward, if we observe these promises which we have made unto Him; and we await with confidence those things which are promised unto us. Short is the pleasure of the world; the pain which follows it is eternal; small is the pain of this life, but the glory of the other life is infinite." And most devoutly preaching upon these words, he comforted and urged the friars to obedience and reverence of Holy Mother Church, and to fraternal love, and to pray God for all men, to have patience in the adversities of the world and temperance in its prosperities, and to hold fast purity and angelic chastity, and to be at peace and concord with God, and with men, and with their own consciences, and to love and observe most holy Poverty. And touching the same he said: "I command you, for the merit of holy obedience, all of you who are here met together, that not one of you take any thought or care of anything to eat or to drink, or of things necessary for the body, but give yourselves wholly to prayer and to praising God; and all the care of your bodies leave ye to Him, for of you He hath peculiar care." And all of them received this commandment with joyful hearts and happy faces; and when St. Francis had finished his sermon, they all with one accord betook themselves to prayer. Wherefore, St. Domi-

nic, who was present while all these things were done, marveled greatly at the commandment of St. Francis, and deemed him indiscreet, being unable to think how so great a multitude could be provided for, without taking any thought of the things necessary for the body. But the Chief Shepherd, Christ the Blessed, willing to show that He careth for His sheep and hath singular love for His poor, presently inspired the inhabitants of Perugia, of Spoleto, of Foligno, of Spello and of Assisi, and of the other places round about, to bring food and drink to that holy congregation. And lo! immediately, from the aforesaid towns came men with pack-animals, horses and carts laden with bread and wine and beans and cheese and other good things to eat, according to that which was necessary for the poor of Christ. Besides this, they brought tablecloths, pitchers, bowls, glasses, and other vessels which were needful for so great a multitude; and blessed was he esteemed who could bring the most, or who could serve most diligently; so that even knights, barons, and other gentlemen, who came to see, waited upon them at table with great humility and devotion. For the which cause, St. Dominic, beholding these things and knowing of a surety that Divine Providence showed forth itself therein, humbly acknowledged that he had wrongly judged St. Francis to have given an indiscreet commandment, and going before him, he kneeled down and humbly confessed his fault, and said: "Verily God hath special care of these holy mendicants, and I knew it not; and from henceforward I promise to observe the holy gospel poverty; and in the name of God do I curse all the friars of my Order who in the said Order shall presume to have private property." Thus was St. Dominic greatly edified by the faith of the most holy Francis, and by the obedience and poverty of so great and ordered an assembly, and by the Divine Providence and by the great abundance of every good thing. In that same chapter, St. Francis was told that many friars wore a mail-shirt next the skin and iron rings whereby many fell sick and died and many were hindered from prayer. Wherefore St. Francis, as a most discreet father, commanded in the name of holy obedience that whosoever had either mail-shirt or iron ring should take it off and place it before him, and they did so; and there were counted more than five hundred iron shirts, and many more rings, both for the arms and for the belly; so that they made a great heap; and St. Francis caused them to be left there. Thereafter, the chapter being ended, St. Francis, exhorting them all to well doing, and teaching them how they ought to keep themselves unspotted from this evil world, sent them back to their provinces, with God's blessing and with his, full of consolation and of spiritual joy.

CHAPTER XIX

How from the vineyard of the priest of Rieti, in whose house St. Francis prayed, the grapes were taken away and gathered by the much folk which came unto him, and how thereafter that priest miraculously made more wine than ever before, even as St. Francis had promised him. And how God revealed to St. Francis that he would have Paradise for his portion

Upon a time, St. Francis being grievously diseased in his eyes, Messer Ugolino, Cardinal Protector of the Order, for the great love which he had toward him, wrote to him that he should go to him at Rieti, where were very excellent physicians for the eyes. Then St. Francis, having received the letter of the Cardinal, betook himself first to St. Damian, where was St. Clare, the most devoted bride of Christ, to give her some consolation; and afterward to go to
10 the cardinal. Now, the night after St. Francis came thither, his eyes became so much worse, that he saw no light at all. Wherefore, in that he could not depart, St. Clare made for him a little cell of reeds, wherein he might the better rest himself. But St. Francis, through the pain of his infirmity and by reason of the multitude of mice, which caused him very great annoyance, was not able on anywise to find rest, either by day or by night. And enduring for much time that pain and tribulation, he began
20 to think and to know that that was a scourge from God for his sins; and he began to thank God with all his heart and with his mouth, and thereafter he cried with a loud voice and said: "My Lord, I am worthy of this and much worse. My Lord Jesus Christ, the Good Shepherd, who showest forth Thy mercy to us sinners through divers pains and bodily afflictions, grant grace and virtue to me, Thy little sheep, that by no infirmity or anguish or pain I may depart from Thee." And, while he was thus praying, there came
30 unto him a voice from Heaven, saying: "Francis, answer Me: if all the earth were gold, and all the seas and fountains and rivers were balm, and all the mountains and hills and rocks were precious stones; and thou shouldst find another treasure more excellent than these things are, even as gold is more excellent than earth, and balm than water, and precious stones than mountains and rocks; and if instead of this infirmity that most excellent treasure were given to thee, wouldst thou not be well con-
40 tent therewith and full of mirth?" St. Francis answered: "Lord, I am not worthy of so precious a treasure." And the voice of God said unto him: "Rejoice, Francis, because that is the treasure of life eternal which I keep for thee, and from this very hour I invest thee therewith, and this infirmity and affliction is the earnest of that blessed treasure." Then St. Francis, full of very great joy at so glorious a promise, called his companion and said: "Let us

go to the Cardinal." And having first consoled St. Clare with holy words, and having humbly taken 50 leave of her, he set out towards Rieti, and when he drew nigh thereto, so great a multitude of people came forth to meet him that he did not wish to enter the city, but betook himself to a church which was distant from the city peradventure two miles. The citizens, knowing that he was in the said church, thronged it round about to look upon him, on such wise that the vineyard of the church was laid waste and all the grapes thereof were carried away; whereat the priest was sore grieved in his heart, 60 and repented him that he had received St. Francis into his church. The thought of the priest being revealed of God to St. Francis, he sent to call him and said unto him: "Most dear father, how many measures of wine doth this vineyard yield thee a year, when it yieldeth its best?" He made answer: "Twelve measures." St. Francis said: "I pray thee, father, bear patiently my sojourning here for certain days, because I find here much repose; and do thou permit every man to take the grapes of this thy vine- 70 yard, for the love of God and of me a mendicant; and I promise thee in the name of my Lord Jesus Christ that it shall yield thee this year twenty measures." And this St. Francis did in return for his sojourn there, by reason of the great salvation of souls which was manifestly being wrought among the folk which came thither, of whom many departed drunk with Divine love, and abandoned the world. The priest, trusting to the promise of St. Francis, abandoned his vineyard freely to those who came to 80 him. When, behold a marvel! Albeit the vineyard was wholly wasted and despoiled so that scarcely were there left therein any bunches of grapes; yet when the time of the vintage was come, the priest gathered those few bunches and put them in the winepress and trod upon them; and, according to the promise of St. Francis, drew therefrom twenty measures of excellent wine. By which miracle it was made manifest that, as, by the merits of St. Francis, the vineyard despoiled of grapes abounded in wine, 90 so likewise the Christian people, barren of virtue through their sins, through the merits and doctrine of St. Francis, abounded in the good fruits of repentance.

CHAPTER XX

Of a very beautiful vision which was seen by a young friar, who held the cowl in so great abomination that he was minded to put off the habit and to leave the Order

A young man very noble and dainty entered the Order of St. Francis; the which, after certain days, by the instigation of the demon, began to hold the habit that he wore in such abomination, that it seemed to him that he wore a most base sack; he

had a horror of the sleeves, he abominated the cowl, and in the length and roughness of the habit appeared to him an intolerable burden. And his disgust for the Religion ever increasing, he finally resolved to abandon the habit and return to the world. Now he had already accustomed himself, according to that which his master had taught him, whenever he passed before the altar of the convent, wherein was kept the Body of Christ, to kneel with great
10 reverence and to draw back his cowl and with his arms crossed upon his breast to bow himself down. It befell that, on the night on which he was about to depart and leave the Order, it was necessary for him to pass before the altar of the convent, and, according to his custom, he kneeled him down and did reverence. And, anon, he was rapt in spirit and a marvelous vision was showed him by God: for he saw before him an almost infinite number of saints, after the fashion of a procession, two and two, clad
20 in very beautiful and precious vestments of silken stuffs; and their faces and hands shone like the sun, and they moved to the sound of angelic songs and music; among which saints were two more nobly clad and adorned than all the rest; and they were encompassed round about by so bright a light that whosoever looked on them was filled with very great amaze; and, almost at the end of the procession, he saw one adorned with so great glory that he seemed a new-made knight, more honored than his peers.
30 Beholding the aforesaid vision, this young man marveled thereat and knew not what that procession might mean, and he dared not ask but stood dazed with keen delight. Nevertheless, when all the procession had passed by, he took courage and ran after the last of them and with great dread inquired of them, saying: "O most dear ones, I beseech you that it may please you to tell me, who are these so marvelous folk which go in this procession so majestical?" They made answer: "Know, son, that we be all
40 minor friars, who now are coming from Paradise." Whereupon he asked: "Who are those two who are more resplendent than the rest?" They answered: "These be St. Francis and St. Anthony; and he who goeth last, whom thou seest so highly honored, is a holy friar who is newly dead, whom, because he fought valiantly against temptations and persevered even unto the end, we are leading in triumph to the glory of Paradise; and these beautiful silken vestments which we wear, are given us of God in ex-
50 change for the rough habits which we wore patiently in the Religion; and the glorious resplendence which thou seest in us, is given us of God for the humility and patience, and for the holy poverty and obedience and chastity which we observed even unto the end. Wherefore, son, deem it not a hard thing to wear the sackcloth of the Religion which bringeth

so great a reward; because if, with the sackcloth of St. Francis, for the love of Christ, thou shalt despise the world and mortify the flesh, and shalt fight valiantly against the demon, thou, together with us, 60 shalt have like vestments, brightness and glory." And when these words had been spoken, the young man came to himself, and, comforted by the vision, drove away from him every temptation and confessed his fault before the guardian and the friars: from thenceforward he desired the roughness of penance and of raiment, and ended his life in the Order in great sanctity.

CHAPTER XXI

Of the most holy miracle which St. Francis wrought when he converted the very fierce wolf of Agobio

During the time that St. Francis dwelt in the city of Agobio, there appeared in the territory of Agobio 70 a very great wolf, terrible and fierce, the which not only devoured animals but also men and women, so that all the citizens stood in great fear, because ofttimes he came nigh unto the city; and all men went armed when they went forth from the city, as if they were going to battle; and therewithal they were not able to defend themselves from him, when haply any man encountered him alone; and for dread of this wolf things came to such a pass that no one dared to leave the city. Wherefore, St. Francis, 80 having compassion on the men of the city, was minded to go forth to meet this wolf, albeit the citizens altogether counselled him not to do so; and, making the sign of the cross, he went forth from the city with his companions, putting all his trust in God. And because the others feared to go farther, St. Francis alone took the road toward the place where the wolf was. And lo! while many citizens who had come out to behold this miracle were looking on, the said wolf made at St. Francis with open 90 mouth. Whereupon St. Francis advanced toward him, and making over him the sign of the most holy Cross, called him unto him and spake to him after this manner: "Come hither, friar wolf, I command thee in Christ's name that thou do no harm to me nor to any other." O marvelous thing! Scarcely had St. Francis made the sign of the cross than the terrible wolf instantly closed his mouth and stayed his running; and, in obedience to that command, came, gentle as a lamb, and laid himself down at the feet 100 of St. Francis. Then St. Francis spake unto him thus: "Friar wolf, thou dost much damage in these parts, and thou hast committed great crimes, destroying and slaying the creatures of God without His license; and not only hast thou slain and devoured beasts,

70. **Agobio,** another town of north-central Italy.

but thou hast also had the hardihood to slay men, made in the image of God; for the which cause thou dost merit the gallows as a thief and most iniquitous murderer; and all men cry out against thee and complain, and all this city is thine enemy. But I desire, friar wolf, to make peace between thee and them; to the end that thou mayest no more offend them and that they may forgive thee all thy past offences and neither men nor dogs may pursue thee any more." At these words, the wolf, by movements of his body and tail and eyes, and by bowing his head, showed that he accepted that which St. Francis said and was minded to observe the same. Thereupon St. Francis spake unto him again, saying: "Friar wolf, inasmuch as it seemeth good unto thee to make and keep this peace, I promise thee that, so long as thou shalt live, I will cause thy food to be given thee continually by the men of the city, so that thou shalt no more suffer hunger; for I know full well that whatever of evil thou hast done, thou hast done it through hunger. But seeing that I beg for thee this grace, I desire, friar wolf, that thou shouldst promise me that never from henceforward wilt thou injure any human being or any animal. Dost thou promise me this?" And the wolf, by bowing its head, gave evident token that he promised it. And St. Francis said: "Friar wolf, I desire that thou swear me fealty touching this promise, to the end that I may trust thee utterly." Then St. Francis held forth his hand to receive his fealty, and the wolf lifted up his right fore-foot and put it with friendly confidence in the hand of St. Francis, giving thereby such token of fealty as he was able. Thereupon St. Francis said: "Friar wolf, I command thee in the name of Jesus Christ to come now with me, nothing doubting, and let us go and stablish this peace in the name of God." And the wolf went with him obediently, like a gentle lamb; wherefore the citizens beholding the same marveled greatly. And anon, the fame thereof was noised abroad through all the city, and all the people, men and women, great and small, young and old, thronged to the piazza to see the wolf with St. Francis. And when all the folk were gathered together, St. Francis rose up to preach unto them, saying, among other things, how, by reason of sin, God permits such pestilences; and far more perilous is the fire of Hell, the which must forever torment the damned, than is the fury of a wolf which can only kill the body; how much then are the jaws of Hell to be feared when the jaws of a little beast can hold so great a multitude in fear? "Turn ye then, most dear ones, turn ye to God, and do befitting penance for your sins, and God will save you from the wolf in this present world and from the fire of Hell in that which is to come." And when he had done preach-ing, St. Francis said: "Hear ye, my brethren. Friar wolf, who is here before you, hath promised and sworn fealty to me, that he will make peace with you and never more offend you in anything; do ye now promise him to give him every day that whereof he hath need; and I become surety unto you for him that he will faithfully observe this covenant of peace." Then all the people with one voice promised to provide him food continually, and St. Francis spake unto the wolf before them all, saying: "And thou, friar wolf, dost thou promise to observe the covenant of peace which thou hast made with this folk, that thou wilt offend neither men nor beasts nor any creature?" And the wolf kneeled him down and bowed his head, and, with gentle movements of his body and tail and ears, showed as far as he was able his determination to keep that covenant wholly. Said St. Francis: "Friar wolf, as thou didst me fealty touching this promise, without the gate, so now I desire that thou do me fealty, before all the people, touching thy promise, and that thou wilt not deceive me concerning my promise and surety which I have given for thee." Then the wolf, lifting up its right foot, put it in the hand of St. Francis. By which act, and by the other acts aforesaid, all the people were fulfilled with so great joy and wonder, alike for devotion toward the saint, and for the strangeness of the miracle, and for the peace with the wolf, that they all began to shout to Heaven, praising and blessing God who had sent them St. Francis, who, by his merits, had freed them from the jaws of the cruel beast. And thereafter, the said wolf lived two years in Agobio, and entered familiarly into the houses, going from door to door, neither doing injury to any one nor receiving any; and he was courteously nourished by the people; and, as he thus went through the town and through the houses, never did any dog bark after him. Finally, after two years, friar wolf died of old age; whereat the citizens lamented much, because as long as they saw him going so gently through their city, they recalled the better the virtue and sanctity of St. Francis.

CHAPTER XXII
How St. Francis tamed the wild turtle-dove

One day, a youth had taken many turtle-doves, and as he was carrying them to sell them, St. Francis, who ever had singular compassion for gentle creatures, chanced to meet him, and looking upon those turtle-doves with compassionate eye, said to the youth: "Good youth, I pray thee give them to me, that birds so gentle, which in the Scriptures are likened unto chaste and humble and faithful souls, come not into the hands of cruel men who would slay them." Whereupon, inspired of God, he forthwith gave them all to St. Francis; and he receiving

them in his bosom, began to speak to them sweetly: "O my sisters, simple, innocent, chaste turtle-doves, why do you let yourselves be taken? Now I desire to save you from death and to make nests for you, so that ye may bring forth fruit and multiply, according to the commandments of our Creator." And St. Francis went and made nests for them all, and they resorted thereunto, and began to lay eggs and hatch forth their young, in the presence of the friars;
10 and so tame were they and so familiar with St. Francis and with the other friars that they might have been domestic fowls which had always been fed by them; and never did they depart until St. Francis with his blessing gave them leave to do so. And to the young man, which had given them unto him, St. Francis said: "Son, thou wilt yet be a friar in this Order, and thou wilt serve Jesus Christ with all thy heart;" and so it came to pass, for the said youth became a friar and lived in the Order in great sanc-
20 tity.

CHAPTER XXIII
How St. Francis set free the friar who was in sin with the demon

Once when St. Francis was praying in the Place of Porziuncula, he saw by Divine revelation, the whole Place encompassed about and besieged by the demons after the fashion of a great army; but none of them could enter into the Place, inasmuch as these friars were of so great sanctity that the demons found none into whom they might enter. But while they thus persisted, it fell upon a day that one of those friars was offended with another, and thought
30 within his heart how he could accuse and avenge himself on him; for the which cause, while yet he cherished this evil thought, the devil, the door being opened, entered into the Place and set himself upon the neck of that friar. Thereupon the compassionate and careful shepherd, who ever watched over his flock, seeing that the wolf had entered in to devour his little sheep, immediately caused that friar to be called to him, and bade him forthwith reveal the poison of hatred conceived against his neighbor,
40 through the which he had come into the hands of the enemy. Wherefore, he, full of fear at seeing himself thus discovered by the holy father, disclosed all the venom and rancor of his heart, and confessed his fault and humbly besought penance and mercy; and when he had so done, and was absolved of his sin, and had received penance, anon, in the presence of St. Francis, the demon departed; and the friar, thus delivered from the hands of the cruel beast, through the loving kindness of the good shepherd,
50 gave thanks to God, and returning, corrected and admonished, to the flock of the holy shepherd, lived afterward in great sanctity.

CHAPTER XXIV
How St. Francis converted the Soldan of Babylon to the faith

St. Francis, urged thereto by zeal for the faith of Christ and by the desire of martyrdom, went once across the seas with his twelve most holy companions, to betake himself straight to the Soldan of Babylon; and being come unto a country of the Saracens, where the passes were guarded by certain cruel men to the end that no Christian who went thereby might be able to escape death; they, as it 60 pleased God, were not slain, but taken, beaten, and bound, and so led into the presence of the Soldan. And being in his presence, St. Francis, taught by the Holy Ghost, preached so divinely of the faith of Christ, that for the faith he even wished to enter into the fire. Wherefore the Soldan began to have very great devotion toward him, alike for the constancy of his faith and for the contempt of the world which he saw in him (inasmuch as he would receive no gift from him, albeit he was exceeding poor), 70 and also for the zeal of martyrdom which he saw in him. From thenceforward the Soldan heard him gladly and prayed him that he would often return to him; granting to him and his companions leave to preach wherever they pleased; and he gave them a token to the end that they might not be offended by any man. Having this leave then, St. Francis sent his chosen companions, two by two, into divers regions of the Saracens to preach the faith of Christ. . . . At last St. Francis, seeing that he could have 80 no more fruit in those parts, prepared, by Divine revelation, to return with all his companions to the land of the faithful; and, having gathered them all together, he returned to the Soldan and took leave of him. Then the Soldan said unto him: "Friar Francis, I would willingly be converted to the faith of Christ, but I fear to be so now, because, if these heard thereof, they would slay both thee and me, with all thy companions; and seeing that thou canst yet do much good and that I have certain matters 90 of great moment to conclude, I would not now bring about thy death and mine; but do thou teach me how I may save myself; I am ready to do that which thou mayest lay upon me." Then St. Francis said: "Sir, I now go from thee; but after I shall be come into my own country and, through the grace of God, shall have ascended into Heaven, after my death, according as it shall please God, I will send thee two of my friars from whom thou mayest receive the holy baptism of Christ, and thou shalt be saved, 100 as my Lord Jesus Christ hath revealed unto me. And do thou, in the meantime, free thyself from every hindrance, to the end that, when the grace of God shall come unto thee, it may find thee prepared to faith and to devotion." And this he promised to do, and so did he. Now when this was done, St. Francis returned with that venerable college of his holy companions; and after certain years, St. Francis by bodily death rendered his soul to God. And the Soldan, falling sick, awaited the fulfillment of the promise of St. Francis, and set guards at certain passes and ordered that, if two friars should appear in the habit of St. Francis, they should immediately be brought to him. At that time, St. Francis appeared to two friars, and commanded them to go without delay to the Soldan to provide for his salvation, according as he had promised him; the which friars set out immediately, and crossing the sea, were led before the Soldan by the aforesaid guard; and when the Soldan saw them, he was exceeding glad and said: "Now know I of a truth that God hath sent me His servants for my salvation, according to the promise which St. Francis made me by Divine revelation." And, when he had been instructed in the faith of Christ and baptised by the said friars, thus born again in Christ, he died of that sickness and his soul was saved through the merits and prayers of St. Francis.

CHAPTER XXV

How St. Francis miraculously healed one who was a leper both in soul and body; and that which the soul said unto him as it went into Heaven

The true disciple of Christ, Messer St. Francis, while he lived in this miserable life, sought with all his strength to follow Christ, the perfect Master; whence it ofttimes befell, through Divine operation, that, in the selfsame hour that he healed men's bodies, their souls were healed by God, even as we read of Christ. And, inasmuch as he not only himself willingly served lepers, but, furthermore, had commanded that the friars of his Order, wheresoever they went or sojourned throughout the world, should serve lepers for the love of Christ, who for our sake willed to be accounted leprous; it came to pass upon a time that, in a certain Place, near to that wherein St. Francis then dwelt, the friars served the lepers and the sick in a hospital; wherein was a leper so impatient and so intolerable and so froward, that every one believed most certainly that he was possessed of the devil, and so in truth he was; for not only did he revile and shamefully belabor whomsoever served him, but (what is far worse) he blasphemously railed upon Christ the blessed and His most holy Mother the Virgin Mary, so that on no wise could any one be found who was able or willing to serve him. And albeit the friars strove to endure patiently the insults and injuries to themselves, that they might increase the merit of patience; nevertheless, because their consciences were

unable to bear those which were uttered against Christ and His Mother, they resolved to abandon the said leper altogether; but they were unwilling to do so until they had duly given notice to St. Francis, who was then dwelling in a Place near at hand. And when they had told him thereof, St. Francis betook himself to this perverse leper, and coming unto him saluted him, saying: "God give thee peace, my dearest brother." The leper made answer: "What peace can I have from God, who hath taken from me peace and every good thing, and hath made me all rotten and stinking?" And St. Francis said: "Son, have patience; for the infirmities of our bodies are given us of God, in this world, for the salvation of our souls, because they are of great merit when they are borne with patience." The sick man answered: "And how can I bear patiently the continual pain which torments me day and night? And not only am I afflicted by my sickness, but yet worse by the friars whom thou gavest me that they might serve me, for they do not serve me as they ought." Then St. Francis, knowing by revelation that this leper was possessed by an evil spirit, departed and betook himself to prayer and devoutly besought God for him. And when he had done praying he returned and spake thus: "Son, I would serve thee myself, since thou art not satisfied with the others." "I am content," said the sick man, "but what canst thou do for me more than the others?" Said St. Francis: "That which thou desirest I will do." Said the leper: "I desire that thou wash me all over, because I stink so greatly that I cannot endure my own self." Then St. Francis forthwith caused water to be heated with many sweet-smelling herbs; thereafter he undressed him and began to wash him with his own hands, while another friar poured on the water; and by Divine miracle, where St. Francis touched him with his holy hands, the leprosy departed and the flesh remained perfectly sound. And even as the flesh began to heal, so the soul began to heal also; wherefore the leper, seeing that he was beginning to be made whole, began to feel great remorse and repentance for his sins, and to weep very bitterly; so that, while the body was cleansed outwardly of the leprosy by washing of water, so the soul was cleansed inwardly of sin by amendment and by tears. And when he was completely cured, both in body and in soul, he humbly confessed his fault and said, weeping aloud: "Woe is me, for I am worthy of Hell for the injuries and revilings which I have done and spoken against the friars, and for my impatience against God and the blasphemies which I have uttered;" wherefore, for fifteen days he continued to weep bitterly for his sins, beseeching mercy of God, and confessing himself wholly to a priest. And St. Francis beholding so clear a miracle,

which God had wrought by his hands, gave thanks to God and got him thence, going to countries very far away; because by reason of humility he desired to flee every glory, and in all his works sought only the honor and glory of God and not his own. Afterward, as it pleased God, the said leper, healed in body and soul, after his fifteen days of penance, fell sick of another sickness, and, fortified with the sacraments of the Church, died a holy death; and, as
10 his soul went into Paradise, it appeared in the air to St. Francis, who was praying in a wood, and said unto him: "Knowest thou me?" "Who art thou?" said St. Francis. "I am that leper whom Christ the blessed healed through thy merits, and today I go to eternal life; wherefore I give thanks to God and to thee. Blessed be thy soul and thy body, and blessed thy holy works and words; because through thee many souls shall be saved in the world; and know that there is no day in the world, whereon
20 the holy angels and the other saints thank not God for the holy fruits which thou and thy Order bring forth in divers parts of the world; and therefore do thou take comfort and thank God, abiding always in His benediction." And when he had said these words he went into Heaven; and St. Francis remained much consoled.

Sir Gawain and the Green Knight

A single manuscript in fourteenth-century English literature contains four poems, the resemblances of which one to another are so great that the entire group has been assigned to one author, known simply as the Pearl Poet. Many attempts have been made to identify this author, attempts often showing the greatest ingenuity, but no general agreement has ever been reached, only the belief that there was such a poet, not yet identified, and that he wrote the four poems somewhere around the year 1370.

The Pearl, the first of the four, which has given the poet his mythical name, is a beautiful and elaborate elegy on a little girl. The second and third poems, *Purity (Cleanness)* and *Patience,* are didactic religious poems notable for their generous poetic talent. The last piece, *Sir Gawain and the Green Knight,* however, has been regarded generally as the cream of Middle English metrical romances. It is told with a unity of narrative effect, a vigorous style, a masterly control of suspense, and a highly poetic coloring that are most unusual for the romance, which was inclined to be rather stereotyped. Instead of the usual manifold adventures which befall the hero, there are in this romance only two, and these two are made to depend one upon the other.

These two central incidents, as will be seen, serve as tests for Gawain's character as a knight. One, the beheading incident, tests his physical courage and his fidelity to his word; the other, the incident of the lady in the castle of the Green Knight, makes a trial of Gawain's chastity and moral purpose. The ultimate objective of the romance, therefore, apart from the obvious narrative entertainment, is clearly didactic; *Sir Gawain and the Green Knight,* for that reason, cannot be considered a true example of the chivalric romance, however thoroughly the Pearl Poet may know the usages of chivalric courtesy and conduct. The poem is, rather, a fine and artistic example of the moral romance. But it is to be noted further that Gawain's conduct, exemplary as it is, will not strike the reader as impossibly idealized. He flinches quite naturally under the first terrifying blow of the Green Knight's ax, and he does not emerge unscathed from the ordeal of the bedchamber. The drop of humanity which the Pearl Poet injects into his treatment of Gawain puts him head and shoulders above the mass of moral romance writers in the Middle Ages.

The two incidents are known elsewhere in medieval legendry, but they are combined in this poem only, unless one counts two later romances in Middle English clearly derived from *Sir Gawain and the Green Knight;* that is, *The Green Knight* and *The Turk and Gawain.* The episode of the beheading is paralleled in a medieval Irish romance, *The Feast of Bricriu,* even down to the detail of the three strokes aimed at Gawain in the climactic scene with the Green Knight. The figure of Gawain is a Welsh divinity, and all the important names in the story are also Celtic. Such matters of resemblance suggest a definitely Celtic origin for the story and a possible Celtic ancestry for the Pearl Poet himself, although it is probable that he had as his immediate source a French romance based on Celtic legendry.

At the end of *Sir Gawain and the Green Knight* is the motto, "Honi soit qui mal y pense," made famous by King Edward III, ruler of England during the Pearl Poet's lifetime. Some have seen in this the possibility that the poem was written in honor of some particular knightly order, such as the Order of the Garter, which adopted this French motto. The fifteenth-century derivative romance, *The Green Knight,* actually names the Knights of the Bath, but this Order was not in existence at the time of the Pearl Poet. Some have gone so far as to assume that the green color of the knight and of the girdle is symbolic of spring, and that the poem was a spring poem intended for a celebration of Saint George's Day (April 23), the holiday of the patron saint of the Order of the Garter and of English chivalry in general. Furthermore, the color green is invariably associated in Celtic legendry with the supernatural and magical.

The possibility that *Sir Gawain and the Green Knight* is a Garter poem is, however, something to be inferred but not proved. The presence of the motto may signify merely that the Pearl Poet was a courtier of Edward III. This fact can be reasonably accepted: if he was not a courtier, he was at least acquainted with the court and wrote the poem with his royal sovereign in mind. But all such inferences are playthings for the academic. What is truly important about *Sir Gawain and the Green Knight* is that it is a superb example of the art of the medieval storyteller; it pictures the favorite English chivalric hero, Gawain, in his best and most attractive aspects, before he was debased to make room for the French hero, Lancelot; it is a clear exposition of the ideals of physical and moral integrity demanded of the medieval knight; it combines powerful and vigorous narrative with a deep feeling for nature; it is sophisticated but neither cynical nor oversentimental.

Sir Gawain and the Green Knight

I

AFTER the siege and assault of Troy after the city had been shattered and burnt to brands and ashes, and the man who had wrought stratagems of treason had been tried for his trickery— the veriest upon earth—it was Aeneas the noble and his exalted family who then vanquished nations and became sovereigns of well nigh all the lands in the Western Isles. So proud Romulus turned to Rome and with great pomp built that city (and 10 named it with his name, which it bears today); Ticius moved to Tuscany and began there his habitation; Langobard in Lombardy raised up homes for himself; and far over the French flood Felix Brutus established on many a shore broad Britain with joy, where wars and waste and wonder by turns have dwelt therein, and often bliss as well as bale have followed one another quickly enow.

And when Britain had been built by this mighty man, brave warriors flourished who loved strife, and 20 many a time they wrought woe. Since that time more wonders have come to pass in this land than in any other of which I have knowledge. But of all the kings of Britain who lived here, Arthur was ever the most gracious, as I have heard tell. And so I desire to make known an adventure that befell in the land (many men consider it a marvel), most surprising even among the many wonders of Arthur's reign. If ye will listen to this lay for a little while, I shall tell it to you straightway, as I heard it told 30 with tongue, and as it has been set forth in story

stout and strong, fixed with true letters, as it has long been known in the land.

King Arthur lay at Camelot of a Christmas tide, with many a splendid lord, the best men in the world. With him in princely fashion was all the mighty brotherhood of the Round Table. There was many a rich revel and careless joy; there folk tourneyed again and again; the noble knights jousted fairly, then repaired to the court to sing carols. For full fifteen days the feast lasted, with all the food 40 and merriment that man could devise, such riotous glee glorious to hear, sounding forth by day, and lovesome dancing by night. There was good fortune everywhere in halls and chambers among lords and ladies, as they most desired. With all the joy in the world they lived there together: the most famous knights in Christendom and the loveliest ladies that ever lived, and the comeliest king that ever held court. For this fair people was in its youth, the happiest under Heaven; their king the greatest on 50 earth; it would be hard now to name so brave a hero in all the land.

The New Year was so recently come that it had barely arrived. The people on the dais were served double that day. The king had come with all his knights into the hall; the ceremony in the chapel had been brought to a close. Loud were the cries raised by clerks and by others; Noel was celebrated anew and named full often. Gallant men hastened to give their gifts—gave them and asked for them 60 both—admired and talked about the gifts one to another. Ladies laughed aloud, even when they were overlooked (and those that received were not wroth, ye may well believe!). All this revelry they kept until meal-time. When they had washed, full worthily they went to their seats; the best knights above, as befitted their rank. Then came Guinevere gay, in royal attire, and sat on the dais amid pomp and pleasure. Of fine silk was the seat; above her a canopy of costly Toulouse, hung with tapestries 70 from Tars that were embroidered and embossed with the fairest of gems that could be bought with money and be proved of value. She was the fairest of all to behold; her gray eyes shone; no man could say truthfully that he ever saw one more beautiful.

But Arthur would not eat till all were served; he was so glad in his joy, even as a child; his desire was for an easy life; he could abide neither to lie long

---

Sir Gawain . . . ^ Translated by George K. Anderson.
5. Aeneas the noble. It was a medieval tradition that Troy had been taken through the machinations of Aeneas. **8. Western Isles,** probably "the three islands of Britain" of antiquity—England, with Scotland; the Hebrides; and Ireland—as well as the adjacent islands —Wight, Man, the Orkneys and Shetlands, and probably the Scilly Isles. **11–12. Ticius . . . Lombardy.** It is likely that Ticius, like Langobard, is the name of a fictitious descendant of Aeneas. Langobard is also the name of the traditional ancestor of the Langobardi, or Lombards. **13. Felix Brutus,** according to legend, the grandson of Aeneas and the founder of Britain (Brutlond, the land of Brutus).

31. fixed . . . letters. This probably signifies, "written in alliterative verse." **33. Camelot.** This was identified by many medieval writers with Winchester; other possibilities are Colchester, Cadbury (Somersetshire), and Carlisle. But the frequent mention of Logres suggests that Camelot was in the southern portion of England. **36. Round Table,** a motif of Welsh legendry. The story goes that Arthur's guests once quarreled because of the order in which they had been seated at table. A round table was devised because there could then be no question of "high" or "low." **39. carols,** in reality dances accompanied by song; originally ring-dances. **71. Tars,** the usual Middle English form of Tharsia, the old name for Turkestan.

nor to sit; his young blood and impetuous brain so worked upon him. And also another habit was fast upon him, which came from his nobility: he would never eat on such a delightful day until some strange kind of wondrous tale had been recounted, some story of mighty marvel, which he could believe, of his ancestors, or of arms and other adventures; or until some strange knight should ask of him that he might join him in a joust and lay his life in jeopardy, life against life, one against another, as fortune might favor them. This was the king's wont when he was holding court, at every high feast among his noble retinue in the hall. And so, fair of face, he was sitting straight in his seat, making great mirth against the New Year.

Thus the valiant king sat there before the high table, talking of light trifles; there good Gawain was seated by Guinevere, and Agravayne *à la dure main* was sitting on the other side. Both were sons of the King's sister and full courageous knights. Bishop Bawdewyne was at the end of the table; and Ywain, son of Urien, sat eating by himself. These were all worthily served on the dais, and at the lower tables many a valiant retainer. Then in came the first course amid the crackling of trumpets, and many a bright banner waving, the rolling noise of drums with shrill pipes, wild music and melody awakened. Many a heart leaped high at those sounds; dainties were brought forth, full costly meats, abundance of fresh foods, and on so many dishes that it was difficult to find a place before the people to set the silver vessels with their savory viands. Each man took what he liked best; by every two were twelve dishes, good beer and bright wine.

Now I will tell you no more about their table-service, for all can understand that there was no lack of good things. For another sound was heard, and a new wonder that folk might well have left their labor to gaze upon. Scarcely had the hum of the banquet dwindled and the first course been served royally in the court, when there rushed in through the hall-door a terrible knight, the greatest in the world as to stature. From neck to loin he was so square and thickset, and his back and limbs were so long and broad that I think he must have been half giant. Certainly I believe he must have been the tallest of men and the lustiest in size that could ride on horse. His back and breast were sturdy and stout, but his belly and waist were nobly slender; and all his features alike clean-cut. But for his color men stood in wonder, as his semblance appeared clear: he came as a hostile knight, and was green all over.

16–17. **high table;** on a dais at one end of the hall, reserved for the lord of the castle, his family, and his nobles. 19–20. **sons . . . sister.** Gawain is Arthur's nephew. 52–53. **green all over.** Green was a fairy color, hence quite appropriate to this particular knight (see headnote).

This man was, indeed, clad all in green; a green cloak clung to his sides, and a simple mantle over it, worthily lined with fur showing clearly and with cloth full clean. Of bright fur, too, was the hood that was thrown back from his locks and lay on his shoulders. Beautifully trimmed was the hem of his coat, and he wore hose of that same green, fastened neatly to the calves of his leg, and clean spurs attached of bright gold, with silken clasps striped most regally, and neat pads under his legs to protect him from galling. All his vesture, in truth, was of pure green, and the ornaments of his belt and fair stones in his girdle, that were nobly arrayed in neat order about his waist and his saddle, on a silk cloth. It would be too tedious to tell of half the adornments that were woven thereon—birds and insects in gay gauds of green, with gold amid them. There were trappings on the neck of his steed and on the crupper; all the ornaments there were of metal and enamel. The stirrups that he stood in were stained green; and the pommel of his saddle, like the stirrups, gleamed and shone with green jewels. The horse that he rode upon, forsooth, was of that same hue, a steed hard to restrain, strong and powerful, in embroidered bridle, full meet for his rider.

Gaily was this knight attired in green, as was the hair of his fine steed. Fair-flowing hair fell over the knight's shoulders; a beard as great as a bush hung over his breast, which, together with his lordly hair on his head, was clipped round about above his elbows, and half his sleeves were clasped in the same manner as a king's mantle, which encloses the neck. The mane of the horse was curled and twisted with many a knot folded in with gold thread over that fair green; here a twist of hair; there a flash of gold. Both the mane and the tail were tied in like manner and bound around with a band of bright green, decked with precious stones to the very end of the tail, and tied aloft with a very subtle knot. There many bells of shining gold rang out full bright. Such a horse or such a knight to ride him had never been seen before in that hall by man's eye; he flashed like lightning, so that men who looked upon him said it appeared that no man could survive the stroke of the knight.

But the knight had no helmet nor hauberk, no gorget, nor armor to cover his arms, no spear or shield to fend or to smite with. Only in his hand he carried a holly-bough, that is greenest when the groves are bare. In the other hand he bore an ax, huge and monstrous, a cruel battle-weapon if one could but describe it. The head of the ax was a full ell long; the grain of green steel and of gold; the blade burnished bright, with a broad edge, as able to shear as the sharpest of razors. The strong man held it set on a stout staff which was braced with

iron down to the edge of the wood, and all engraved with green in cunning work. A lace was
wrapped about it, that was looped over the head
and then fastened to the handle; attached to it were
costly tassels hanging from buttons of bright green
full richly bedecked.

The knight rode in through the entrance of the
hall, pushing his way up to the dais, fearing no
harm. He saluted never a one, but looked over them
all. The first word that he uttered was, "Where is
the ruler of this company? Gladly would I see that
man with my eyes, and speak with him in very
truth." On the knights he cast his glance and swag-
gered up and down, then stopped still and studied
them to see who was the most renowned.

Then there was long looking to gaze upon that
knight, for every man marveled what it might mean,
that a hero and a horse should have such a hue, as
green as grown grass and perhaps greener even
than green enamel shining on gold. All that stood
there gazed upon him and stepped nearer, with all
the wonder in the world, to see who he might be.
Many a strange sight had they seen, but never such
a one as this; therefore the people thought it a
phantasm or faerie. Many were afraid to give him
answer, and were astounded at his voice; they sat
stone-still in a heavy silence through that noble
hall; their talking ceased as if they had been struck
with slumber. I believe it was not so much for fear
as for courtesy; they would let him whom all should
defer to speak himself to that knight.

So Arthur beheld this marvel before his high dais;
he greeted the stranger in knightly fashion (never
was he rash), and said: "Knight, welcome in truth
to this place! My name is Arthur, lord of this hall;
light down, fair sir, and tarry; we shall know later
what thy will is." "Nay, so help me," quoth the
knight, "He that sits on high; to stay any time in
this dwelling was not my errand. But because
the renown of this people has been so exalted, because thy castle and thy warriors are esteemed the
best and the bravest to ride on steeds under steel
harness, the strongest and worthiest of all mankind and proven of excellence in knightly sports—
therefore courtesy has flourished here, as I have
heard tell; and that has drawn me hither, forsooth,
at this time. Ye may be sure by this branch that I
bear here that I come in peace and seek no strife. For
if I had come in warlike manner with a band beside
me—well, I have a hauberk at home and a helmet
also; a shield and a sharp spear, shining bright, and
other weapons to wield, as I can vouchsafe. But
because I desire no war, my garments are softer! If
thou art as bold as all men say, thou wilt grant me
by rights the sport that I ask." Arthur answered
and said: "Sir courteous knight, if thou cravest
a mere battle, thou shalt not fail to fight here!"

"Nay," said the knight, "I seek no fight, in faith;
about this bench I see naught but beardless children. If I were enclosed in armor upon a lofty steed,
there would be no man here to match me, so weak
is their strength. And so I crave in this court a
Christmas-game, for it is Yule and New Year, and
here are many active men. If any one in this hall
considers himself so hardy, be his blood so bold or
the brain in his head, that he dare strike one stroke
for another, I shall give him as a gift this mighty
ax, which is heavy enough for him to handle as he
pleases; and I will abide the first blow, unarmed as
I sit here. If any man be so fierce as to try what I
propose, let him leap swiftly upon me, and take his
weapon. I quit claim to it; he may keep it as his
own. I shall stand his stroke, firm on this floor. If
so, thou shalt grant me the right to deal him another,
in faith; and yet I shall give him respite for a year
and a day. Now hasten, and let us see whether any
one here say aught!"

If he had astonished them at first, now all were
more silent than ever—all Arthur's followers in the
hall, high and low. The warrior on his steed fixed
himself in his saddle, and rolled his red eyes about
most violently, bent his beetling brows, glittering
green; he twisted his beard about while he waited
for whoever would rise. When none would retort
to him, he coughed loudly and spoke to them in
loud mockery: "What? Is this Arthur's house, whose
fame runs through so many realms? Where is your
haughtiness and your conquests, your fierceness and
your anger and your mighty words? Now the glory
and renown of the Round Table has been overturned by the words of one man; for all fear out of
dread, and not a blow seen!" With that he laughed
so loud that it grieved the king: the blood rushed
for shame into his fair face; he was as angry as the
blast of winter—so were all that were there. The
king so brave by nature stepped near to that stern
knight, and said: "Knight, by Heaven, thy request
is strange; and since thou hast sought folly, thou
must in truth find it! I know of no man here that is
afraid of thy big words! Give me now thine ax, in
God's name, and I shall grant thy boon which thou
hast demanded."

Lightly he leaped at the knight and caught at his
hand; then fiercely the knight dismounted. Now
Arthur had taken the ax and grasped it by the handle
and stoutly brandished it, thinking to strike. The
sturdy knight towered over the king, higher than
any in the house by a head or more; with grisly
cheer he stood there and stroked his beard with immovable countenance, drawing aside his coat, no
more frightened or dismayed at the king's threatened
blows than if some man on the benches had brought
him a draught of wine. Then Gawain, who was sitting by the king, leaned toward him and spoke: "I

beseech thee now, of a truth, that this affair be mine."

"Would ye, noble lord," said Gawain to the king, "but bid me rise from this bench and stand by you there, that I without discourtesy may leave the table and not displease my liege-lady, I would come to your counsel before your royal court. For it seems to me not fitting, if the truth be known, when such a demand be raised high in your hall, that you should be desirous of taking it upon yourself, while many men so bold are sitting about on the benches—there are not, I hope, men of more precious courage under the heavens, nor better bodies for fighting when strife is lifted up. I know that I am the weakest of them and the feeblest of understanding; and less would be the loss of my life, if the truth were told. Save that you are my uncle there is little to praise in me; I know no virtue in my body save your blood. And since this business is so strange that it is not seemly for you to assume it, and since I have asked it of you first, grant it to me, and if I speak not in comely fashion, let all this court still be without blame." Then the mighty knights all counseled with one accord that the crowned king withdraw and give Gawain the venture.

Then the king commanded the knight to arise; and he rose up full quickly and fixed him fair. Then he knelt down again before the king and grasped the weapon; the king graciously relinquished it to Gawain, and lifted up his hand and gave him God's blessing and was fain to pray that his heart and his hand should both be valiant. "Keep thyself, nephew," said the king, "and set thyself for one blow; if thou hast heard him aright, I think that thou must abide a blow that he will give thee in return." Gawain advanced against the stranger with the ax in his hand; the stranger boldly awaited him, no whit abashed. Then the knight in green said to Sir Gawain: "Let us renew our agreement ere we proceed further. First I ask thee, Sir Knight, what thy name is; thou must tell me truly, so I may trust it." "In good faith," said the good knight, "Gawain I call myself, who offer thee this buffet, whatsover may befall later. And this time twelvemonth I shall take from thee another, with whatsoever weapon thou wilt, and with none other to help me, none in the world." The other replied: "Sir Gawain, so may I prosper, I am fair and fain to receive the blow that thou shalt direct."

"By God," quoth the Green Knight, "Sir Gawain, it pleases me that I shall take from thy fist what I have asked for here. Thou hast readily rehearsed, correctly indeed, the covenant that I requested of the king; but thou must assure me, knight, by thy troth, that thou shalt seek thyself, wheresoever thou dost believe I am to be found on the earth, and shalt get for thyself such rewards as thou dealest to me

today in the presence of this mighty troop." "Where am I to seek thee," asked Gawain; "where is thy home? I know not where thou dwellest, by Him that made me; nor do I know thy court, O knight, nor thy name. But teach me truly thereto, and tell me thy name, and I shall use all my wits to get myself thither. That I swear of a truth, and by my firm troth." "That is enough on the New Year; we need no more," quoth the warrior in green to Gawain the gracious. "If I tell thee truly, after I have received the stroke, and thou hast struck me in all honor, quickly I will tell thee of my house and my home and mine own name; then thou canst ask my business and keep covenant. And if I waste no speech, so much the better for thee, for thou canst stay longer in thy land, and seek no farther. But enough, take now thy grim weapon and let us see how thou canst strike." "Gladly, sir, forsooth," quoth Gawain, stroking his ax.

The Green Knight quickly made him ready on the ground; he bowed his head a little and uncovered his countenance; his long fair locks he laid over his head and let the naked neck show for the ax. Gawain gripped his weapon and gathered it aloft; his left foot he placed forward on the earth, then let the blade fall quickly on the bare neck. The sharp edge shattered the bones of the stranger, bit through the fair skin and sheared it in two, so that the brown-steeled blade ate into the ground. The fair head fell from the neck to earth; many kicked it with their feet as it rolled about; the blood spurted from the body and glistened on the green. Yet the strange warrior never faltered or fell, but stoutly leaped upon sturdy legs, rushed forth and reached out where the warriors were standing, caught up his fair head and lifted it up. Then he turned to his steed, caught the bridle, stepped into the stirrup and mounted; he held his head by the hair with his hand. And he settled himself in his saddle as calmly as if no accident had befallen him there, although he was headless. He turned his horse about—his ugly body bleeding all the while; many were in terror of him and greatly distrusted the covenant.

For he held up his head in his hand, raising the face toward the most valiant king on the dais. And the head raised its eyelids and looked full about and spoke these words with its mouth, as you may now hear: "Look, Gawain, that thou be ready to go as thou didst promise and seek faithfully, O knight, until thou dost find me, as thou didst promise in this hall in the presence of these knights. Take thy way to the Green Chapel, I charge thee, to get such a blow deservedly as thou hast dealt, to be yielded thee promptly next New Year's Morn. Many men know me as the knight of the Green Chapel; therefore, if thou dost ask to find me, thou wilt never fail. So come, or be called recreant and coward!" Then the stranger turned his bridle and rushed out in a gallop, so that sparks flew up from the hooves of his horse. To what land he went, none there could tell any more than they knew whence he had come. And then? The king and Gawain laughed and joked at that Green Knight; yet it assuredly had been a marvel for those knights to behold.

Then King Arthur was astounded at heart, although he let no hint be given of his wonder, but said aloud to the comely queen in fair speech: "Dear lady, be never dismayed today; such a marvel well becomes Christmas-tide, when we lack entertainment, laughing or singing, or fair carols sung by knights and ladies. But now I can turn to my food, for I have seen a miracle I can never forget." He looked at Sir Gawain and quickly said: "Now, sir, hang up thine ax; it has hewn enough." So it was placed above the dais, hanging on the back of a seat, where all men could look upon it as a marvel, and by its true evidence tell of the wonder. Then they bowed them to bench, did these warriors together, the king and the good knight, and brave men served them a double portion of all dainties, as was the share of the most valiant—with all manner of meats and minstrelsy as well. In well-being they spent that day on earth, until it came to an end.

Now bethink thee well, Sir Gawain, that thou delay not to seek the harm-fraught adventure which thou hast taken upon thee.

II

THIS beginning of adventures befell Arthur on the New Year, for he yearned to hear of deeds of glory, though his words were few when he sat at his feasts. But now their hands were filled aplenty with grim work. Gawain was glad to begin the game in the hall, but ye need have no wonder that the end was hard. For though a man be merry in mind when he has had strong drink, a year passes full quickly and never brings again its like; the beginning and the ending accord full seldom. And so this Yule departed, and the year after, and each season in turn followed upon another. After Christmas came crabbed Lent, that tries flesh with fish and simpler foods; then the weather of the world struggles against winter; the cold shrinks away, the clouds uplift themselves; bright pours the rain down in warm showers and falls on the fair fields; flowers peep forth; green are the garments of earth and grove; birds make them ready to build and sing with passion for the solace of soft summer that comes down from the heights. Then bursting blossoms burgeon forth in rich and rank hedgerows, and noble notes enow are heard in the fair woodlands.

After the season of summer with its soft winds, when Zephirus breathes on seeds and grasses—very joyous are the roots that grow thereout—then the moistening dew drips from the leaves, awaiting a blissful glance from the bright sun. But autumn approaches and hardens the seeds, warning them to grow full ripe before winter; in drought he drives the dust in clouds; it whirls aloft over the face of the earth. Angry winds in the heavens wrestle with the sun; leaves drop from the linden and alight on earth; the grass turns gray that once was green. Then all that at first was blooming ripens and rots. So the year passes away into many yesterdays, and winter winds are returned, for which no man need wonder.

When the Michaelmas moon had come with its warnings of winter, Gawain bethought him of his wearisome journey. But he lingered with Arthur until All Souls' Day. And Arthur partook of that feast for the sake of his nephew amid all the rich revel of the Round Table, with knights full courteous and comely ladies. Yet all were in sorrow for the knight Gawain; but nevertheless they spoke of naught but mirth, although many who made there courtly play were joyless. For after the feast, Gawain sadly spoke to his uncle, and mentioned his departure, saying aloud: "Now, liege-lord of my life, I ask your leave. You know the matter of this affair; I need not tell you of the trouble. I am ready unconditionally for the blow; tomorrow I go to seek the man in green, as God will make him known to me." Then gathered together all the best in the castle: Ywain, and Erec, and full many another, Sir Dodinel le Sauvage, the Duke of Clarence, Lancelot, and Lionel, and Lucan the good, Sir Bors and Sir Bedivere, both mighty men, and many other honorable knights, with Mador de la Port. All this company of the court approached the king to counsel the knight, with care in their hearts. In that hall there was much secret grief pressing at their hearts that so worthy a knight as Gawain should go on that adventure, to endure a grievous blow and not be able to return it with his sword. But the knight kept good cheer and said: "Why should I shrink? What can a man do but try his fate, whether stern or pleasant?"

He dwelt there all that day, and arose in the morning and asked for his arms. They were all brought him. First a royal carpet was stretched over the floor, and great was the gold gear that glittered upon it. The valiant knight stepped thereon, and handled his steel. He was dressed in a doublet of precious silk from Tars, and then in a close hood of crafty design that was lined within with a bright-

---

69. **Michaelmas moon,** the moon which would come to the full about Michaelmas (September 29), hence the harvest moon.   85–90. **Ywain . . . Mador de la Port.** From the standpoint of Middle English romances, the most important of these are Lancelot, Lucan, Bors, and Bedivere. All but Lucan participated in the Quest of the Holy Grail.

Two knights fighting, from a North French sketchbook, c. 1400.

colored fur. Then they set steel shoes upon the knight's feet; his legs they lapped in steel with ornamented greaves and knee-pieces fastened thereto, brightly polished; about his knees they were riveted with knots of gold. Well-fitting cuisses closed with thongs firmly encased his stout and brawny thighs; then the woven corslet of bright steel rings sewn on a fair stuff they fitted upon the knight; and well-burnished braces on both his arms, with good and
10 gay elbow-pieces, and gloves of mail, and all the goodly gear that would help him in his time of trouble. Thus Gawain stood forth in rich coat-of-mail, his gold spurs proudly added, girt with a trusty brand, and a silk girdle about his waist.

When he was clad in arms, his war-harness was costly—the smallest latchet or loop gleamed of gold. And harnessed as he was, he heard mass celebrated, and made his offering at the high altar. Then he came to the king and his companions of the court,
20 took fairly his leave of lords and ladies; and they kissed him and escorted him forth, committing him to Christ. By that time Gringolet was ready, and girded with a saddle that gleamed full gay with its many gold hangings, richly studded anew for that adventure; the bridle was barred about and braced with bright gold thread; the adornment of the neck-piece and of the sweeping saddle-skirts, the crupper and coverture, all matched the saddle-bow; all were bordered with rich, red-gold buttons that glittered
30 and gleamed like the light of the sun. Then Gawain caught up his helmet and hastily kissed it; that helmet was stoutly braced and stuffed within. It towered high on his head, fastened behind with a light linen kerchief over the aventail, embroidered and bedecked with the best of gems and having a broad silken border and designs of birds; preening parrots, turtle-doves, and true-loves so closely inter-woven as many a maiden in the town had wrought seven years in the making. The circle atop his

helmet was of still greater cost; it was a device of diamonds, that were both light and dark. 40

Then they showed him his shield, that was of bright red, with the pentangle painted thereon in pure gold color. He seized it by the baldric and cast it about his neck; it became the knight wondrous fair. And why the pentangle pertained to that noble knight I purpose to tell you, though it delay my story. It is a sign that Solomon set erewhile, as betokening truth; it has its name because it is a figure that has five points, and each line overlaps 50 and is locked in another; ever it is endless, and the English call it everywhere, so I have heard, "the endless knot." Therefore it was fitting for this knight and for his shining arms; for Gawain was known before God as faithful ever in five and many times five various ways, and as refined gold, void of every impurity, and adorned with all virtue in the assemblage. And so this fresh pentangle he bore on shield and coat, the knight truest of speech and noblest of form. 60

For first he was faultless in his five senses; and the knight had never failed in his five fingers; and all his faith on this earth was in the five wounds that Christ got on the Cross, as the creed tells. And wheresoever this knight was beset in conflict, his earnest thought was in this above all other things: that all his vigor he received from the five joys that the gracious Queen of Heaven had in her Child. For this reason the knight had in the greater part of his shield the image of Our Lady painted, so 70 that, when he looked upon it, his courage could never flag. The fifth five that I find Gawain used were frankness, and fellowship above all; in cleanness and courtesy he was never found wanting; nor in pity that surpasses everything—these virtues five were more firmly wrapped about the hero than about any other. All these, fivefold, forsooth, were linked together in this knight, and each but attached to the other; but they never ended; and were fixed at five points, which never failed. Nor did they ever 80 merge, neither were they ever sundered; everywhere, at all points, they were endless and without a beginning as well. Wherefore on his bright shield this knot was shaped, red-gold upon red; that is the pure pentangle; the people call it so by tradition. Now Sir Gawain was gaily armed; he caught up his lance, and gave them all good-day—he thought, forever.

---

22. **Gringolet,** with Roland's Veillantif perhaps the most famous steed of medieval legendry. The French form Guingalet suggests that he was a white horse (from Welsh *gwen,* "white"). 34. **aventail,** the movable front of the helmet, sometimes called the "beaver."

43. **pentangle,** a five-pointed star, an ancient symbol believed to have the power to repel demons. 48. **Solomon set erewhile.** Solomon's seal consisted of a pentangle circumscribed by a circle. The symbol is still to be found in synagogues and in Freemasonry, which is supposed to have originated in the building of the Temple of Solomon. 67. **five joys.** The five joys of the Virgin Mary were usually considered to be the joys in the Annunciation, the Nativity, the Resurrection, the Ascension, and the Assumption, although the list varied slightly among medieval writers.

He smote his steed with the spurs and sprang on his way, so sternly that he struck fire from the stones. All that saw that seemly sight sighed in their hearts; all folk said truly to each other, in care for that comely knight: "By Christ, it is a pity, that thou, O knight, shouldst be lost, that art of such a pure life! To find his equal in the world, in faith, will not be easy. It would have been wiser to have acted more warily; yonder brave knight should have become a duke; a shining leader of men he is worthy to be, and would have been that more fittingly than cut to pieces or brought low by an elvish man with the pride of arrogance. Whoever knew a king to take such counsel as to put his knights to a venture as a Christmas jest!" Many were the warm tears that were shed when that seemly knight departed from the court that day. But he did not tarry; he went on his way swiftly over many a wild road, as I heard say in the book.

Now the knight was riding through the realm of Logres, Sir Gawain in a good cause, though it seemed to him no sport. Often he lay companionless, alone in the night, nor did he find there the fare that would have been pleasing to him. He had no comrade but his horse, over the woodlands and downs; and there was no one but God with whom he could take counsel. At length he drew full near to North Wales; he kept all the isles of Anglesey on his left and crossed over the fords by the foreland at Holyhead, until he finally passed into the wilderness of Wirral. There dwelt few who loved either God or good men in their hearts. But as Gawain went along, he kept asking folk that he met if they had heard any talk of a green knight anywhere about, or of the Green Chapel. All answered him nay; never in their lives had they seen any such man of such a green hue. Gawain took strange paths over many an impassable height; full often was his mood to change before he could find the Green Chapel.

Many a cliff he climbed over in strange countries; far away from his friends he rode along as a stranger. At every water-ford and stream that the knight passed he found a foe before him, and one so marvelous and so foul and fierce that it behooved Gawain to fight. It would be too tedious to tell the tenth part of all his adventures; so many wonders befell the knight on his journeyings. Sometimes he fought with dragons and with wolves; sometimes with wild men that lived in the stone cliffs; with bulls and bears, and sometimes with boars; with giants of the high moorlands who were wont to attack him. Had he not been doughty and stern and a servant of the Lord, doubtless he had been dead,

for he was often near to being slain. Yet the fighting troubled him not so much; the winter was worse, when cold clear water was shed from the clouds and froze ere it could fall upon the fallow earth. Nearly slain by the sleet he slept in his armor; on more nights than enow on bare rocks, where the cold brook rushed down bubbling from the hillcrest and hung high over his head in hard icicles. Thus in peril and pain and plights full hard, Gawain toiled over the countryside all alone, until Christmas Eve, and on that night he made his prayer to Mary, that she should guide him to some dwelling.

In the morning he rode merrily by a hill into a full deep forest that was fearsome and wild; high hills were on each side of it, and thick woods below them, huge hoary oaks a hundred or more. The hazel and the hawthorn stood there intertwined, with rough ragged moss trailing everywhere and many birds sitting unhappily upon bare twigs, piping piteously for pain of the cold. The knight rode beneath them on Gringolet through many a marsh and quagmire, alone and fearful lest he should not be able to perform the service of our Lord, who on that selfsame night was born of a maiden to allay all our woe. And sighing therefore he said: "I beseech Thee, Lord, and Thee, Mary, that is most mild and precious of mothers, that You grant me some lodging, that I may fittingly hear mass, and Your matins tomorrow. Meekly I ask it and thereto I pray my paternoster and creed." He rode praying and lamenting his misdeeds, blessing himself many times and saying: "May the cross of Christ speed me!"

He had not crossed himself, that knight, more than three times before he was aware of a dwelling in the wood, surrounded by a moat, above a lawn on a hill, enclosed by many a burly oak-tree that grew above the moat. There was a castle, the comeliest that lord ever possessed, built in a meadow with a park about it; a spiked palisade closely driven enclosed the trees for more than two miles. The knight saw the castle from one side, as its lights gleamed through the bright oaks. He seized hold of his helmet in joy, and uttered thanks to Jesus and Saint Julian (both are noble), who had courteously made known to him this abode and had hearkened to his prayer. "Now I beseech You yet," quoth the warrior, "that I may have good lodging!" Then he pricked Gringolet with his gilded heels; he

21. **Logres,** the term applied in Welsh legendry to England south of the river Humber. Since the knight's course is northerly, it is to be assumed that Camelot is in the southern portion of England.

67. **deep forest . . .** From the direction taken by Gawain in his travels, it would appear that he traveled north or northwest. Wirral in Cheshire, near present Liverpool, was a forest as late as the sixteenth century. It is apparent that Gawain traveled for some time past Wirral; the older theory, therefore, that the castle of the lord and lady near the Green chapel was in Wirral has since been abandoned. It is more likely that the Green Knight lived in Cumberland, not far from Carlisle, where many stories of adventure about Arthur and his knights have collected. 98. **Saint Julian,** the patron saint of travelers and hospitality.

rode casually up to the main gate, and came soon to the end of the bridge. The drawbridge had been raised, and the gates were shut fast. The walls were strong; no blast of wind need they fear.

The knight waited on the bank of the deep double ditch that surrounded the place. As he sat on his charger, he saw that the walls were set in the water wondrous deep; and the building towered aloft to a tremendous height. It was of hard hewn stone up 10 to the corbels, which were adorned under the battlements with excellent taste; many fair watchtowers were placed in between with many well-made loopholes. Never had the knight seen a better barbican. Within he could see the high hall and the tower built with thick cornices; fair turrets marvelously high, with carved capitals, cunningly wrought. He could see chalk-white chimneys on the turreted roofs that shone full white. Many pinnacles were scattered everywhere among the battlements, so thick and 20 white that they seemed to be cut out of paper. The noble knight on his steed thought it all fair enow; he wanted to gain the shelter within, to take lodging in that castle, until pleasant Holy-day had passed. He called, and straightway there came a kindly-faced porter, who stood on the wall, and asked the knight-errant in his greeting, what his errand might be.

"Good sir," said Gawain, "wilt thou take my message to the high lord of this house, and crave 30 for me shelter?" "Yea, by Peter," quoth the porter, "truly, I think, O sir knight, you are welcome to stay here while it pleases you." Then the servant went quickly and with him many folk to receive the knight. They let down the great drawbridge, and came forth graciously, and knelt down upon the cold earth, to welcome Gawain as was fitting. They opened for him the broad gate; when it was ready, he bade them rise, and rode over the bridge. Many men held his saddle-horse while he dismounted; and 40 bold men enow then stabled his steed. Knights and squires came down to bring the warrior with honor into the hall. When he raised up his helmet, there were many to take it from his hand and serve the gracious knight; his sword and his shield they also received. Then Gawain greeted full graciously each one of the retinue and praised there many a proud man in order to honor their prince. In his noble armor they escorted him to the hall, where a fair fire on the hearth was briskly burning. Then the lord 50 of the castle came down from his chambers to meet with ceremony the knight in the hall; he said, "You are welcome to do here as it pleases you. What is here is all your own, to have and wield at your will." "Gramercy," said Gawain, "may Christ it requite

10. **corbels,** the cornice-moldings. 13. **barbican,** the outer fortification of a castle.

you." As friends that were fain each one embraced the other.

Gawain gazed upon the lord that had greeted him in thus goodly fashion; and thought him a brave warrior who owned the castle—a mighty hero for the nonce, and of high age. Broad and shining was 60 his beard and hued like a beaver; stern and stout was the stride of his stalwart legs. His face was as fierce as fire, but his speech was noble; and he seemed altogether able, so it seemed to Gawain, to be a lord and protector of full valiant men.

The lord led Gawain to a chamber and ordered a retinue to serve his guest in loyal manner. At his bidding came men enow to escort Gawain to a fair bower. There the bedding was royal; the curtains of clean silk and clear gold hems; the counterpanes 70 comely and of fairly embroidered linen. These curtains were run on ropes with red-gold rings; there were tapestries of Toulouse and Tars hung on the walls and carpets underfoot of the same material. There, with many a merry speech, Gawain was relieved of his byrnie and of his bright armor, while alert servants brought him costly garments for him to wear, fair, radiant, and most choice. When he donned these clothes, he saw that they were seemly and fitted him well; the skirts of his mantle flowed 80 gracefully. Truly that hero seemed to outtop all other knights in the fair complexion of his countenance, shining and radiant. It seemed to all that beheld him that Christ had never made a comelier knight. Whatever his origin, they thought that he must be a prince without peer in the field where brave men fight.

Before the fireplace, where a charcoal fire was burning, a chair was placed for Sir Gawain, accoutered with fair cushions and hassocks that were 90 of subtle artistry; and then a simple mantle was offered the knight, of a brown samite, richly embroidered, and lined with skins of ermine, and a hood of the same stuff. So Gawain sat him down in that seemly regal chair and warmed himself first of all, and then his mood lightened. Straightway a table was raised up on trestles, covered with a clean cloth that shone clear white; and there were set on the table salt-cellar and napkin and silver spoons. The knight washed at his will and then sat down 100 before his meat. Men enow served him appropriately with several sweet viands, seasoned well, double portions, as it happened, and several kinds of fishes— some baked in bread, some broiled on the fire, some boiled, some in sauce, savored with spices, with all kinds of subtle devices to please the knight's palate. Gawain called it a feast, full graciously and often, while all the retinue entertained him with gaiety, for they said: "Now take this penance, and it shall be for your amendment." The knight made much 110 mirth of that, for the wine had gone to his head.

Then they questioned Gawain in most temperate fashion, with skilfully chosen questions put to the knight himself, so that he acknowledged in courteous wise the court whence he had come; that noble Arthur the gracious, who was the rich royal king of the Round Table, considered him one of his own knights; that it was Gawain himself who was sitting in that spot, come there on the Christmas, as chance would have it. When the lord heard that he was entertaining that knight, he laughed aloud; it seemed to him glad news indeed. And all the men in the place made great joy, to be able to appear ready in his presence, for all worth and prowess and pure customs pertained to Gawain's person, and he had ever been praised. Before all men on earth his virtue had been the greatest. Each man said softly to his comrade: "Now we shall see seemly manners and customs and the blameless terms of courtly talk; what charm lies in speech, we can learn without asking, for we have received in our midst the very father of courtesy. God has given us His goodly grace, forsooth, since He has granted us to have a goodly guest like Gawain, when men sit and sing with pleasure and joy of His birth. The true meaning of simple courtesy this knight will now bring us. I think that he who hears him will learn the subtle speech of love."

By that time the dinner was finished and Gawain had risen. It was near nightfall. Chaplains took their way to the chapel; the bells were rung loudly, even as they should be, for the devout evensong of Yule-tide. The lord went thither, and the lady also; she entered into a comely closet; Gawain gaily followed and straightway went thither. The lord caught him by the sleeve and led him to a seat and called him by his name, and told him he was the most welcome person in the world. Gawain thanked him truly, and each saluted the other and sat together in dignity during the time of the service. Then the lady was pleased to look upon the knight; she came forth from her closet with many a fair maiden. But she herself was the fairest of countenance and complexion, of figure and hue and all other charms—even more beautiful than Guinevere, as the knight thought. She passed through the chancel to greet Gawain the gracious; another lady held her by the left hand and was older than she—a dowager, it appeared, with many nobles about her. But the two ladies were unlike in looks; for if the younger was fair, the older was sallow. Rich red was the bloom on the cheeks of the one; rough wrinkled were the cheeks of the other. Kerchiefs with many a lucent pearl adorned the breast and bright throat of the one, and shone more dazzling than snow that falls on the hills. But the other wore on her neck a gorget, wimpling over her pale chin in milk-white folds; her forehead wrapped in silk worked in knots and bordered with trifling decorations. Only the black brows of the dowager were bare, and her two eyes and nose and naked lips—and these were all sour to see and strangely bleared, though one could fairly call her an honorable lady. Her body was short and thick; her buttocks round and broad; far more pleasing to gaze upon was she who walked beside her.

When Gawain saw that gay lady who looked so gracious, he walked towards her, with full permission of the lord. He greeted the elder, bowing full low; but he took the younger lightly in his arms and kissed her in seemly fashion, and spoke to her as became a knight. They hailed him as friend, and he quickly asked to be her servant in truth if it should please her. And so the two ladies escorted him, leading him, while talking, to the hall, before the hearth, and straightway called for spices, which men brought them without stint and right speedily, also good wine to be drunk at this season. The lord sprang to his feet and bade them make merry; he caught off his hood and hung it on a spear, and said he should win the worship thereof who could make most mirth on that Christmas-tide. "And I shall try, by my faith, to contend with the rest, with the help of my friends, before I lose all my raiment!" So with laughing words the lord bestirred him to gladden Sir Gawain that night with games in the hall, until it was time to bid them light the hall. Then Sir Gawain took leave of them and prepared for rest.

On the morrow, when every man calls to mind that Our Lord for our destiny was born to die, joy is breathed into every dwelling in the world for His sake—so it was there on that day amid many delights. Brave men on the dais were dressed in their best, and there was many a feast and many a cunningly cooked dish. The old dowager sat highest; the lord respectfully was seated beside her. Gawain and the gay lady were together, even in the midst of the board, as the feast was worthily served to each man according to his rank. There were meat and mirth and great joy; it would take me too long to speak thereof, and to describe it I could not though I might try. But I know that Gawain and the lovely lady found great pleasure in each other's company through her sweet words and courteous conversation, her gentle talk free from uncleanness, and her vivacious play charming and pure, fit for a prince. Trumpets and drums and merry piping sounded forth; each man hearkened to his minstrel; and they too hearkened to theirs.

High feast they held there that day and the next, and the third day that came in thereafter. The joy on St. John's Day was noble to hear; it was the last of the feast as the folk there intended. The guests

111. **St. John's Day,** December 27.

were to depart on the gray morning; and so they woke early and drank wine, and danced with vigor to the sound of carols. At last, when it was late, they took their leave, each one departing on his way—that was a brave lord! Gawain gave him good-day; the bold lord took him by the hand, and led him to his own chamber, beside the fireplace, and there he thanked him privately for the great honor that Gawain had bestowed upon him in coming to his

10 castle at that high season, and in adorning his home with his fair countenance. "Surely, sir, while I live, I shall be held the better because Gawain has been my guest at God's own feast." "Gramercy, sir," replied Gawain, "in good faith, all yours is the honor. May the High King grant it to you. I am a knight at your will, to do your behest, as I am beholden to you by rights in things both great and small." The lord then endeavored to keep the knight longer; but Gawain answered him that he could nowise tarry.

20 Then the lord asked him full fairly what stern mission had driven him, at that sacred feast, to depart all alone from his king's court so boldly, ere the holiday's holly had been carried from the town. "Forsooth, sir," quoth Gawain, "you say but the truth; it was a lofty mission and a pressing one that drove me from my home, for I myself am summoned to seek a certain place—I know not where in the world to find it. So help me the Lord, I would give all the land in Logres to find it before New Year's

30 Morn. Therefore, sir, I make this request of you here, that you tell me truly, if you ever heard tell of the Green Chapel or where it stands, or of the knight who keeps it, so green of color? There was established by agreement a compact between us; I must meet that man at that appointed place if I can do so; and of that same New Year there lacks little or no time. I would look on that knight, if God but let me, more gladly, by God's Son, than on any fair sight! Therefore, ywis, by your will, it

40 behooves me to go; I have now but barely three days for the business; I had liefer fall doomed as fail in my errand." Then the lord said, laughing: "Now indeed you must stay; for I shall show you that place by the appointed time, that Green Chapel forsooth. So grieve you no longer. You can take your ease, knight, in your bed till the fourth day; then you can ride on the first of the year and come to the appointed place at mid-morn, to do what you like at that time. Dwell here till New Year's Day;

50 then rise and ride thither. We shall set you on your way; it is not two miles hence."

Then Gawain was full glad, and laughed merrily. "Now I thank you heartily for every thing. Now my quest is achieved; I shall linger here at your service,

39. **ywis,** certainly, indeed.

and do aught else you desire." Then the lord took him and set him beside him; he had the ladies fetched in to please them the better, though they had solace between themselves. The lord for his joy made merry jests, as a man who knew not what to do for his delight. Then he spoke to Gawain, crying 60 aloud: "You have decided to do what I bid you. Will you keep that promise here for the nonce?" "Yea, my lord, forsooth," said Gawain the true, "while I stay in your castle, I shall be obedient to your behests." "Now since you have traveled," said the lord, "from a far-off land, and then watched with me, you have not been refreshed either by rest or by sleep, as I truly perceive. You shall stay in your chamber and lie at your ease tomorrow at mass-tide, and go to meat when you will with my wife. 70 She shall sit with you and console you with her company. Tarry here until I return home; I shall rise early and go a-hunting." To all this Gawain agreed, keeping his word as a gracious man should.

"Yet further," said the lord, "we shall make a covenant. Whatsoever I win in the wood, it shall be yours; and whatever fortune you achieve, give it to me in exchange. Good friend, let us so exchange, and swear it by oath, whether our fortunes, sir knight, be for better or for worse." "By God," 80 said Gawain the good, "I agree; and whatever it pleases you to propose; I shall do thy bidding." "Bring us the wine-cup; the bargain is made," said the lord of the castle. They laughed each one, they drank and made merry and passed the time of day until night, did these lords and ladies, as it pleased them. Then with gay talk and many a merry jest they arose and stood and spoke softly, kissed full sweetly, and took leave of each other. With many a graceful serving-man and gleaming torches, each 90 knight retired at last to his bed full soft. But before they went to bed they rehearsed the covenant, for the old lord of the castle knew well how to make sport.

III

VERY early before daybreak the folk rose up; the guests who would go called their grooms and made themselves quickly ready; they saddled their steeds and arranged the harness, set the girths in order, and packed up their bags. The knights dressed themselves and came forth arrayed for rid- 100 ing; they leaped lightly to horse, took up their bridles, and each man went on his way as he pleased. The noble lord of the land was not the last to prepare for riding, nor the many men with him. He ate a sop hastily, after he had heard mass. With a blast of the bugle he fared forth to the uplands. Before any daylight shone upon earth, he and his

retine were mounted on their lofty steeds. Then those huntsmen who knew the sport well coupled their hounds, unclosed the kennel-doors, and called them out. Three blasts were blown gaily on the bugle; the hounds bayed at the sound, and made a great racket; and those that were going on the hunt turned and chastised them—at least a hundred hunters, as I have been told. The trackers went to their stations and released the hounds; the forest re-
10 sounded again with their lusty blasts. . . .

[A description of the day-long hunt follows here.]

So the lord of the castle sported on the edge of the linden-woods. But Gawain the good knight lay in his fair bed, resting, till the daylight gleamed on the walls, under a coverlet radiant and closely be-curtained. And as he slipped into slumbering, he heard a soft little noise at his door. So he lifted his head out of the bedclothes and lifted a little the corner of the bedcurtains, and looked out warily to see what it might be. It was the lady, most lovely
20 to behold, that closed the door after her full softly and still, and moved towards the bed. The knight was ashamed and laid him down quickly, pretending to sleep. But she stepped quietly and stole up to his bed, cast up the curtain and crept within, seating herself softly upon the bedside, and stayed there wondrous long, to see when he should awaken. A very long time the knight lay there and considered in his mind what this coming might amount to; he was in great wonder. But finally he said to himself:
30 "It would be more seemly if I asked her in words what she wants here." So he awoke and moved about, and turning towards her unlocked his eyelids, and pretended to marvel, crossing himself with his hand, as if to be safer in speech. The lady, sweet of chin and cheek, looked at him winsomely, her small lips smiling.

"Good morrow, Sir Gawain," said the fair lady, "you are a heavy sleeper, since one can enter hither.
40 Now you are taken unawares, but lest you escape us, I shall bind you in your bed, of that you may be sure." All laughing, the lady thus fell into jesting. "Good morrow, fair lady," said Gawain the blithe, "I will do your will, and that pleases me well. I will yield me promptly and beseech grace; and that will be best, I believe, for I needs must do so!" And so he joked in return with much happy laughter. "But would you, lovely lady, grant me leave; release your prisoner, and pray him to rise. I would get up from this bed and array myself. I should then have more
50 comfort to talk to you better." "Nay, forsooth, fair sir," said that sweet one, "you shall not rise from your bed; I shall direct you better. I shall keep you

8. **trackers,** keepers of the hounds.

here even longer, and then talk with my knight which I have captured. For I know well, of a surety, Sir Gawain the noble—whom all the world worships, wheresoever you ride—your honor and courtesy have been graciously praised among lords and ladies and all that are alive. And now you are here, ywis, and we are alone. My lord and his men are far off; other servants in their beds, and my maidens 60 also; the door is drawn and fastened with a strong bolt. And since I have in this house him whom everyone likes, I shall take good care of my time in speech, as long as it lasts. You are welcome to my body, at the wish of your will; it is proper for me, out of courtesy, to be your servant; so will I be."

"In good faith," quoth Gawain, "it seems unfitting for me—though I am not what you were speaking of—to attain to such an honor as you have just mentioned. I am an unworthy man; I know it my- 70 self. By God, I should be glad, if it seemed good to you, to please you with words or with service; verily, it would be pure joy!" "In good faith, Sir Gawain," quoth the fair lady, "the prowess and worth that pleases all other women—if I lacked it, or set it at naught, it were sad courtesy! But there are ladies enow that had liefer now hold a knight in their power, as I hold you here, to dally with the charm of your courteous words, to show them comfort and lighten their cares, than much of the treasure or gold 80 that they possess. But as I love that same Lord who rules the heavens, I have through His grace gotten wholly in my hands that which they all desire." She that was so fair of face made him good cheer; and he with modest speech answered all her sallies.

"Madam," said the happy knight, "Mary requite you, for I have found, in good faith, your frankness noble. Other folk have shown me much courtesy, in truth, but the honor that they have shown me for my poor deserts seems foolish; what is important is 90 the worship of yourself, who know naught but good." "By Mary," said the lady, "it seems to me otherwise; for were I worth all the riches of women alive, and had all the weal of the world in my power, and if I should bargain and choose to get me a lord, then, for the virtues that I have seen in you, Sir Gawain, of beauty, and mildness, and blithe sem-blance, or have heard of you and consider true—no man in the world would be chosen rather than you!" "Certes, my lady," replied Gawain, "you could have 100 chosen a better; but I am proud of the value that you put on me, and humbly as servant I acknowl-edge you my sovereign, and am become your knight. Christ requite you." So they talked of many things until mid-morn passed; and ever the lady made as if she loved him, and the knight was cautious and turned the talk aside. Though she were the most radiant of women, the one most in his mind, yet he would show the less love in his bearing, because of the adventure that he sought so near at hand—the blow that must confound him and yet must needs be done. The lady then took her leave, and Sir Gawain straightway granted it.

She gave him good-day, and with a laughing glance; but as she stood before him, she astonished him with full stern words: "Now He that speeds fair speech reward you for this disport! But that you are Gawain I sorely mistrust!" "Wherefore?" asked the knight, and repeated the question, afraid lest he had failed somehow in his courtesy. But the lady blessed him, and spoke thus: "As good as Gawain is held among men, with courtesy so pure enclosed within him, he could not easily have tarried so long with a lady without asking a kiss out of courtesy, or some token or trifle at the end of the story." Then said Gawain: "Surely; let it be as you will; I shall kiss under orders, as befits a knight who fears lest he displease you. So ask it no more." She came near at those words, and caught him in her arms, bent down in her beauty and kissed the knight. Then they fairly commended each other to Christ; she went out of the door without any sound; and he hastened to rise forthwith. He called to his chamberlain and chose his garments and went forth, when he was ready, blithely to mass. Then he went to his meal that had been graciously kept for him, and made merry with mirth all day until the moon was rising. Never was a knight more fairly lodged; he sat between the two worthy ladies, the older and the younger; in merriment and comfort.

Meanwhile the lord of the castle was occupied with his sport, hunting in holt and heath and chasing the hinds. Such a number he slew, before the sun declined, of does and other deer, that it was a wonder. Then happily they returned in a group at last, and quickly made a quarry of all the killed deer. . . . Boldly they sounded the bugle that broke up the hunt; their hounds bayed. Then they took their trussed booty home, blowing stoutly many a stirring measure. Before daylight was done, the troop were all within the comely castle, where Gawain abode quietly. Amid the warmth of a kindled fire, the lord had come home, and Gawain met him with all the joy in the world.

Then the lord had all his retainers gathered together in the hall; and both the happy ladies joined them with their maidens. Before all that folk in the hall he had the venison brought in, and called to Gawain in jest and counted to him all the tails of the beasts and showed him the glistening fat shorn from the ribs. "How does this sport please you? Have I not won praise? Have I not earned hearty thanks for my craft in the hunt?" "Yea, assuredly,"

38. **quarry,** a collection of game slain during the hunt.

answered Gawain, "here is the fairest game that I have seen these seven years in the winter season." "And all I give to you, Gawain," said the lord, "for by the terms of our agreement you can claim it as your own." "That is true," said the knight, "I say the same to you, and this I have honorably won within these walls; and with as good will I yield it to you." So he clasped the lord's neck within his arms, and kissed him as courteously as he might. "Take here my booty; I gained no more. I vouchsafe it wholly, though it were greater than this." "It is good," quoth the fair lord, "gramercy therefore. So be it; but were it not better that you tell me where you won this booty, and if it were by your own wit?" "That was not our covenant," replied Gawain, "ask me no more; for you have taken what belongs to you; you can look for no more." They laughed and made them blithe and spoke low to each other; straightway they went to a supper of fresh dainties enow.

And later they sat by the hearth in the chamber. Men bore them excellent wine more than once. And still in their jesting they agreed on the morrow to carry out the same compact that they had made before; for chance might bring it about that their gains might be different; but what new things they won they would exchange when they met at night in the presence of the court—such was their covenant. The night-drink was served amid merriment; and in friendly wise they took leave of each other at last, and each knight prepared himself for bed. Scarcely had the cock crowed and cackled but thrice before the lord of the castle had left his bed and each of his followers. The meal was served and mass heard quickly; the retainers turned once more to the wood, to begin the hunt before day broke. Hunters and horns sounded forth as they passed over the meadows; the hounds uncoupled ran racing among the thorny brakes.

Straightway they struck a scent in a field; the huntsmen cheered on the hounds that had first come upon it; wild shouts were cast forth in a noisy din. The hounds heard it and hastened up and fell fast to the chase, forty at once. Then such a yelping clamor of packing hounds arose that the very rocks rang out; hunters urged them on with horn and mouth. All came together beside a pool in the woods, before a rugged crag; in a knot, by a cliff, at the side of a bluff. There rough boulders had tumbled in jagged heaps. The huntsmen fared to the finding and looked about them; the men surrounded the rocky crag, till they knew for certain that the beast they had uncovered with their blood-hounds was within their circle. Then they beat about the bushes and bade him spring up. Suddenly he rushed fiercely across the path of the men, a most marvelous boar. Long since he had grown old and departed from his herd. Surely he was the greatest of wild swine-kind; and every time he grunted, he caused trouble to many, for he thrust three to earth at the first rush, and then raced forth with great speed, without further injury. Then they hallooed loudly and cried out "Hay! Hay!" and put their horns to their mouth to blow the recheat. Great was the rout of men and of hounds that rushed with boast and noise after the boar to make the kill. Long he stood at bay, however, and maimed the pack of hounds pressing upon him, hurting them so badly that they most mournfully yowled and yelled.

The men then turned to shooting; they aimed their arrows at him and hit him often enow; but the arrow-heads were blunted by the strength of his shield-like hide, and the barbs would not bite on his brow, for the smooth shafts splintered in pieces, and the arrow-head fell back wherever it struck. But when the blows of their mighty strokes began to hurt him, then, mad from strife, he rushed upon the huntsmen once more, hurting them sorely wherever he attacked, so that many waxed fearful and drew back a little. But the lord on a swift horse darted after him; like the brave man he was, he swung over the meadow, blowing his horn. He recheated and rode through thick underbrush, ever pursuing this wild boar until the sun sank low.

All the day the huntsmen spent in this wise, while our gracious knight lay in his bed, Gawain the noble, at home in rich gear so fair of hue. The lady did not forget, but came in to greet him; full early she was at his side to cheer his mood.

She came to the curtain and looked at the knight. And Gawain welcomed her fittingly at that time, and she yielded him good morrow, with eager and ready words. Softly she sat down at his side, and laughed much, and with a lovesome look spoke to him thus: "Sir, if you be Gawain, it is a wonder to me—a man that is so turned to God and does not bother with the courtesies of companionship; and if one teaches you how to recognize these courtesies, you cast them forthwith from your mind. You have forgotten promptly what I showed you yesterday, by all the truest tokens of which I have knowledge." "What is that?" asked the knight. "I know, forsooth, nothing of all this; if what you say is true, the blame is all mine." "And yet I taught you of kissing," said the beautiful lady; "wherever a fair face is shown him, it becomes every knight quickly to claim courtly usage." "My dear," said the strong knight, "do away that speech, for that I dare not do, lest I be denied. If I were refused, surely I would be in the wrong if I still proffered a kiss." "My faith,"

said the sweet woman, "you cannot be denied; you are strong enough to force it with your strength, if it pleased you—if, perchance, any were so churlish as to deny you." "Yea, by God," said Gawain, "your speech is fair; but threats are not profitable in the land where I live; nor any gift that is not given with good will. I am at your command, to kiss you when you please; you may take them when you wish and leave them when it seems the best time." The lady then bent down and kissed his face in comely wise. Much talk they made there of the woes and charms of secret love.

"I would know from you, sir knight," said the noble lady, "if you will not be angry, what the reason may be that you, so young and so active, as you are at this moment, so courteous and so knightly, as you are known abroad, and choicest of all chivalry and most praised of all in the faithful joys of love and the science of arms—I know not. For to tell all the troubles of a true knight is the beginning, the title, and the text of all works: how ladies for their loyal loves have risked their very lives and endured for their loved one doleful hours; and how their lovers avenged them by their valor and eased all their care and brought bliss into the bower and raptures all their own. Now you are a knight, fairest of renown in your age; your words and your worship have gone everywhere. Yet I have sat by your side two separate times, and never have I heard you utter any words that pertained to love, small or great. And you, that are so courteous and careful of your promises, should be willing to show a young thing like me some token of true love's craft. Why are you so unlearned who have all men's praise? Is it that you deem me too foolish to listen to your teaching? For shame! I came hither single, and sit beside you to learn from you some skill; come, teach me of your knowledge while my lord is away."

"In good faith," replied Gawain, "God requite you! Good glee is a great thing; and a wondrous pleasure it is to me that such a beautiful one as you should come hither and bother yourself with so poor a man and pretend that he is your knight with such a sweet countenance; truly it brings me heart's ease! But to take the task upon myself to expound true love, to turn to the stories of love and tales of arms and relate them to you who, I know well, have more skill in the sweet art than a hundred such as I am or ever shall be on earth where I live—truly, my sweet, it would be manifold folly! I would gladly do your desires as best I can, as I am bound to do, and evermore I will be servant to you, so may God save me!" Thus she tried the knight and tempted him oft to have won him to wrong, whatever else her purpose. But he defended himself so well that no fault appeared and no evil on either side—naught but happiness and jest. They laughed and joked forsooth;

7. **recheat.** Originally the recheat was sounded to call back the hounds from a wrong scent, but later, as used here, to call them to the hunters or to urge them on.

at last she kissed him, that fair one, and then took her leave and went her way.

Then Gawain bestirred him and rose to mass; and then their dinner was prepared and richly served. The knight amused himself all day with the ladies. But the lord of the castle meanwhile rushed over the land in pursuit of the wild boar that went hurtling through the brush and biting the best of his hounds in two. Finally the beast stopped at bay; the bow-men caught up with him and made him, in spite of himself, take to flight again. Many an arrow flew through the air, when those folk gathered. But even the bravest of them the boar made to spring back, until at last he was so wearied that he could run no longer, but with all the haste possible, he hid in a hole in a mound by a rock where the brook ran by. He got the mound over his back and began to dig; the froth foamed at his mouth and dismayed the hunters. He gnashed his white tusks, while the bold hunters that stood near him all exhausted came on toward him. But none yet dared come too near him for fear of harm. He had hurt many before, which all thought was a pity; all the more they were afraid of him and his rending tusks; he was both coura-geous and frenzied.

But the lord of the castle came up and reined in his steed. Seeing the boar at bay and his men near by, he alighted and left his courser, snatched out his bright brand, and strode forth boldly. Quickly he stalked through the brook to where the fierce creature was standing. The wild beast caught sight of the man with the weapon in his hand. He set his bristles high and snorted so violently that many feared for the lord, lest the monster should crush him. The boar made a lunge at the man; and both knight and swine were thrown in a heap full in the water. But the boar had the worst of it, for the man took good aim when they first met, and plunged the sharp blade fair in the pit of the animal's stomach, driving it up to the hilt, so that the boar's heart was shivered, and snarling he gave up the ghost and was swept down to the water. A hundred hounds leaped upon him and chewed him famously; the hunters dragged him to the bank, and the dogs completed his death.

Then came a notable blowing of many a famous horn, the hallooing of huntsmen on the heights, the baying of the best of hounds, as their masters urged them on—those who were the chief hunters in that dangerous chase. Then a man who was wise in woodcraft began to flay the boar. First he hewed off the head and set it aloft and then rent the shaggy hide along the backbone, snatched out the entrails and burnt them in a fire, later rewarding his hounds with bread mixed therewith. Next he broke out the muscles from the bright broad flanks and removed the heart and lights, as was fit and proper. Then he

bound the two sides of the beast all whole together and hung the carcass bravely on a stiff, strong pole. And then with this boar they came marching home; the boar's head was borne before the huntsman himself—he who had destroyed it in the brook, through the force of his hand so strong. It seemed long to that lord before he caught sight of Gawain in the hall; he called, and Gawain came towards him to receive his reward.

In jesting manner the lord laughed full loud and merry, when he saw Sir Gawain; with kind words he spoke to him. The good ladies were summoned, and the retinue gathered; he showed them the boar's flanks and told them the tale of its largeness and length and fierceness also, and of the fight the wild swine offered in the wood where he had fled. The other knight commended his deeds in comely wise and praised them as great feats and well proving his courage. For such a brawny beast, bold Gawain said, nor such flanks of a boar he had never seen before. Then they felt of the huge head, and the gracious knight praised it, and courteously spoke it so that the lord of the castle might hear. "Now, Ga-wain," quoth that good man, "this game is all yours, by a nice covenant and a firm, as you very well know." "That is true," said Gawain, "of a surety; all I have won I shall give back to you, by my troth." He took the lord about the neck and gave him gra-cious kisses, two of them. "Now we are even," said Gawain, "for this time, in all the covenants that we sealed by law, since I came hither." The lord said, "By Saint Giles; you are the best that I know; you will be rich in a short time if you drive such bar-gains!"

Then they set up the tables on trestles, cast cloths over them; a clear light shone over the walls, for men had set waxen torches whereby they might serve in the hall. Much noise and laughter rose up therein, about the fire and over the floor, in all manner wise. At the supper and after there were many lovely songs, lays of Christmas-tide and new carols, with all the mirth that a man could imagine. And ever our fair knight sat beside the lady; such a semblant of love she made to Gawain, with still demure coun-tenance to please that stalwart man, that Gawain was all wonder and wroth with himself. But he would not out of courtesy proffer her aught in re-turn, but treated her in all deference, howsoever she might try to twist the words awry. When they had played in the hall as long as it was their will, she called them all to the inner chamber; they turned to the hearth.

And there they drank and dallied and discoursed

98. lays of Christmas-tide, probably motets, or songs for many voices, sung while the priest was proceeding to the altar. It is from these medieval songs that the modern Christmas carol has been derived. The carols mentioned here were dancing-songs.

anew, conversing on a like covenant for the day of
New Year's Eve. But Gawain craved leave to depart
on the morrow, for it was near to term-time, when
he should meet his appointment with the Green
Knight. The lord forbade him to go and constrained
him to linger and said, "As I am a truthful man, I
swear by my troth, that thou shalt reach the Green
Chapel and do thy task, sir knight, at the daybreak
of the New Year, long before prime. So lie in thy
tower, and take thine ease; I shall hunt in the wood
and keep the covenant to exchange with thee my
winnings, such as I may bring back hither. For I
have tried thee twice, and I find thee faithful; now
tomorrow will be the third time and the best. Let
us make merry while we can, and think of naught
but joy. A man can always find misfortune when he
so desires!" This Gawain agreed to in courtesy;
therefore he tarried. Sweet drink was brought to
him, and then they were all lighted to bed. Sir
Gawain lay and slept still and soft all night long;
the lord of the castle kept to his woodcraft—full
early he was all ready.

After mass he and his men had a morsel or two
to eat. Fair was the morning, as he called for his
mount. All the hunters on horse followed after him:
fairly accoutered were their steeds before the hall-
gates. Very fair shone the earth to which the frost
still clung; all streaked with red the majestic sun
rose on a rack of clouds; soft and clear were the
clouds in the heavens. The huntsmen scattered by
the wood-side; the rocks beneath the boughs of
hanging trees echoed to the voice of the hunting-
horn. Some came upon the scent of the wily fox,
carried often across the path, true to the beast's
tricks. A hound cried out thereat; the hunter called
to him; his fellows joined him, panting hard; they
ran forth in a rabble, as was their habit. The fox
flitted before them; they espied him straightway;
and as they caught sight of him they followed him
fast, driving after him savagely with a horrid noise.
And the fox tricked and turned through many a rough
copse; crossed over and stopped to listen in hedgerows. Finally he leaped a little ditch near one of
those hedges and then stole forth quietly by a
rugged path, thinking to escape by his wiles from
the wood—and from the hounds. Then he came,
ere he knew it, to a skilful tracker; indeed, three
men at one rush pressed upon the gray little beast
together. He drew back quickly and stoutly leaped
to one side; in the utmost anguish he turned back
to the wood.

Then was it a pleasure indeed to listen to the
hounds, when all the hunters had met together in
counsel. Such a tumult they made when they caught
sight of him once more, as if all the clustering cliffs
had crashed down at once. Here the fox was hallooed, when the huntsmen met him; loud was he

cried upon with snarling yells. Often was he threatened and called a thief, and ever there were hounds
at his tail, so that he could not linger; often was he
run at, when he darted out of covert, and often
forced back again. But Reynard was wily, and led
them low and high, the lord and his huntsmen; now
over the hills, now down, over, and under.

Meanwhile gracious Gawain at home slept most
wholesomely, beneath comely coverlets on that cold
morning. But the lady for love cared not to sleep,
and thus spoil the purpose that was set in her heart.
She rose up early, and hurried to Gawain, in a lovely
mantle that reached to the ground, furred fine with
costly furs, well cared for. No gems wore she on
her hair, but the precious stones were all bordering
her head-dress, in clusters of twenty. Her beautiful
face and her throat she showed all bare, and her
breast bare, and her back as well. She came through
the chamber door, and closed it after her. Opening
a window, she called to Gawain, and thus readily
greeted him with cheerful sweet words: "Ah, man,
how canst thou sleep, on this morning so clear?" He
was in a deep drowse; nevertheless he did hear her.

In a fierce fitful slumber that knight was disturbed, as a man often is in the morning from many
bold thoughts. He was dreaming of the destiny that
should next day prepare his fate at the Green
Chapel, when he was to meet the Green Knight and
must abide his buffet without further fight. But
when comely Sir Gawain had recovered his wits and
awakened from his dreams, he answered the lady
in haste. She came towards him laughing in sweet
loving manner, bent over his fair face, and featly
did kiss him. He welcomed her fondly, with fair
good cheer. He saw her so glorious and beautifully
attired, so faultless of feature, and so fine of complexion that welling joy warmed his heart. With
gentle smiles they fell into mirthful speech, and all
was bliss and gaiety and joy that passed between
them. They uttered sweet words and exchanged
much happiness. Truly, great peril was there for
both of them, unless the knight was ware of it!

For the princely Gawain was so hard borne down;
so tense was his feeling, that it behooved him by
need either to take her love on the spot or hatefully
refuse it. He cared for his courtesy, lest he be deemed
craven, and even more for his honor if he should
sin and be a traitor to the lord of the castle. "God
forbid!" said the knight, "that shall never happen!"
With laughter in love, he turned aside all the special
speeches that came from her mouth. Said the lady
to the knight: "You should be blamed, if you do not
love the life that lies next to you, above all the
creatures in the world wounded as she is in heart,
unless you have a mistress or true-love that pleases
you better, and unless you have pledged faith to that
lady, fixed so firm that you will not loosen it. Indeed,

that is what I believe. Now I pray you, tell me this truly. For all the love in the world, do not keep the truth a secret, out of guile." The knight replied, "By Saint John," and softly smiled. "In faith, I possess not such a one, nor will I possess one for a time."

"That," said the lady, "is the worst thing you could have said; but at least I have been answered, though it is a vexation to me. Now kiss me in courtly wise, and I shall go hence; I can but mourn
10 and weep as a maiden who loves much." Sighing she bent down and gave him a seemly kiss; and then left his embrace and said as she stood beside him: "Now, dear, at our parting give me at least this comfort; yield me some sort of gift, thy glove mayhap, that I may remember the man and lessen my mourning." "Now truly," replied Gawain, "I would that I had here the most precious thing I owned, that I might give it you for your love. Forsooth, you have deserved far more reward, and
20 rightly, than I could ever give. But alas, I would then be giving you a keepsake of a love that profited little or nothing. Indeed, it would not be honorable to give you at this time my glove for a recompense, a glove of Gawain, as I am here on an errand the strangest in the world and have with me no retainers bearing bags brimful of precious things. That displeases me greatly, lady, at this time. But every man must fare as he is taken, even for sorrow or ill." "Nay, gracious knight of high honor," said that
30 lovely lawn-clad lady, "though I have naught of yours, yet you shall have something of mine."

She caught up a rich ring worked in red gold with a staring gem standing out of it, that cast beams as dazzling as the bright sun; know ye well, it was of immense worth. But the knight refused it and said forthwith: "I will have no gifts even for good, fair lady, at this time. I have none to offer you, and I will take none." She prayed him eagerly to receive it, and he denied her prayer, and swore firmly by
40 his truth that he would not take it. And she was grieved that he refused it and spoke thus: "If you refuse my ring because it seems to you too costly and you do not wish to be obligated to me, I shall at least give you my girdle that will be a lesser gift." She loosened a lace here and there, which encircled her waist, fastened at her side under the bright mantle. The girdle was of green silk and decorated with gold thread worked about by the fingers; this she offered to the knight and blithely besought him to
50 take it though it were unworthy. But he denied that he would accept in any wise either gold or gift, before God sent him grace to achieve the adventure that he had undertaken there. "And so, I pray you, do not be displeased, and let the matter go, for I cannot at all grant your request. I am dearly beholden to you because of your beauty, and will ever be your true servant in hot and cold alike."

"Well, do you refuse this silken piece," then asked the lady, "because it is too simple, as it well
60 seems? Indeed, it seems little, and therefore of less value. But whoever knew the virtues that are hidden therein would appraise it more highly, peradventure. For whatever man is wrapped in this green lace, while he has it tied about him, no hero under the heavens could hew him down; he could not be slain or struck to earth." Truly then Gawain thought, when he pondered in his heart, that it would be a jewel in the jeopardy which had been decreed him when he went to the Green Chapel to receive his
70 blow; might he escape unslain, this were a noble stratagem! So he endured her chiding and suffered her to speak. She carried the girdle to him and offered it to him again. He accepted it, and she handed it over with a good will, and besought him for her sake never to reveal it, but to conceal it faithfully from the lord of the castle. The knight agreed that no wight should know it, for certain, but the two of them. He thanked her again and again, earnestly, with heart and mind. By that time
80 the lady had kissed the gracious knight three times.

Then she took her leave and left him there, for she could not get more pleasure from the knight. When she had gone, Sir Gawain got him ready, rose, and arrayed himself in rich attire, caught up the love-lace which the lady had bestowed upon him, and hid it loyally where he might find it again. Then he took his way fairly to the chapel; there he privily approached a priest and prayed him to forgive his life and teach him better how his soul might be
90 saved when he should go hence. There he was sweetly shriven and confessed his misdeeds both more and less, and besought mercy, and called on the priest for absolution. And he was assoiled in certainty and was made as pure as if Doomsday had been appointed for that morning. And after that he made merry among the noble ladies, with comely carols and all kinds of mirth (as he never had done but that one day with such bliss) even till dark night. Each man had great and marvelous respect
100 for him there and said, of a truth, that he had never been thus joyful before that time, since he had come hither.

Now let Gawain linger in the castle where love had befallen him. But the lord was still abroad, leading his huntsmen. He had destroyed the fox that he had followed long. As he rushed over a spinney to catch sight of the rascal (for he heard the hounds hastening in that direction), Reynard came running through a bushy grove, and all the rabble of hounds
110 in a rush at his heels. The knight saw the wild animal and bided his time, and snatched out his bright sword and struck at the beast. He shrank from the

106. **spinney,** a thorny hedge.

blow and tried to retreat, but a hound seized him before he could reach safety, and they all fell upon him right at the horse's feet and worried him to death with a horrid noise. The lord quickly alighted and caught the fox, raising him quickly out of the mouth of a dog, and holding him high aloft, hallooed loudly. Many a brave hound bayed in return; the hunters all hurried thither with many a horn, re-cheating aright till they caught sight of their lord. By that time his whole noble retinue had assembled; all that had bugles blew at one and the same time; and those that had no horns hallooed—it was the merriest meet that men ever heard, and the noisiest uproar that was lifted up in jest for Reynard's soul. The hounds had their reward; their heads were stroked and patted; and then they took Reynard and stripped off his coat.

So then they turned homeward, for it was nearly night, blowing most loudly on their mighty horns. The lord at last alighted at his beloved castle; he found fire on the hearth and the knight beside it, Sir Gawain the good, who was fain withal and was having much joy out of love for the ladies. He wore a robe of blue that reached to the earth; his surcoat fitted him well and was beautifully furred; and his hood of the same material hung down to his shoul-ders, blended with fine linen all about. He met the good lord in the middle of the floor and greeted him in all mirth and said fairly: "Now I shall be the first to fulfill our covenant which we made most happily when there was no lack of wine." So he embraced the lord of the castle and kissed him thrice, as care-fully and soberly as he could. "By Christ," said the lord, "you had great fortune in the obtaining of this bargain, if the exchange be good!" "Yea, of the ex-change no matter," said the other knight, "since what I owe has been openly paid." "Marry," quoth the lord, "mine is behind, for I have hunted all this day and have got naught but this foul fox-skin— the devil take it—for it is very poor to pay for such precious things as you have given me here—three such kisses so fair!" "Enough!" replied Sir Gawain, "I thank you, by the rood!" Then the lord told him, as they were standing there, how the fox was slain.

With mirth and minstrelsy and dainties at their will, with laughing of the ladies and jests along the board, they made as merry as any men could. Ga-wain and the good lord were both as high-spirited as if the band had gone mad or become over-drunk. Both the men and the retainers joked and jested un-til the time came when they should depart, when the knights must retire to their beds. Then Gawain the noble humbly took his leave of the lord and thanked him fairly: "For all this happy sojourn that I have had here at this high feast, may the great King repay your worship! I yield myself here as one of yours, if it so please you; now I must needs,

as you know, move on the morrow; and you will give me, as you promised, a man to show me the way to the Green Chapel, where God will suffer me to partake on New Year's Day of the destiny decreed me." "In good faith," said the noble lord, "with a good will; all that I ever promised you I shall ful-fill with good intent." So he assigned Gawain a serv-ant to set him on his way, and to lead him over the downs, that he might have no trouble in riding through the woods and passing most speedily through the groves. Gawain thanked the lord for the honor he had done him; then the knight took leave of the two noble ladies; with sorrow he kissed them and spoke to them and begged them to have his sincere thanks for everything. And they gave him back a like reply; they commended him to Christ with many cold sighs.

Then Gawain departed from the company in cour-tesy; each man that he met he thanked for his serv-ice and his comfort and his many little pains that he had made for Gawain's sake, to treat him well. And each man was as sorry to part from him as if he had dwelt in the castle forever. Then the servants led him with torches to his chamber and he happily laid down on the bed, to be at rest. Whether he slept soundly I dare not say, for he had much to think about on the morrow, if he would turn his thoughts thereto. Let him lie there still; he was near what he had sought. Now if you will be still a while, I shall tell you what happened.

IV

Now New Year's Day drew nigh, and the night passed; the day put the darkness to flight, as the Lord had commanded. But stormy weather awak-ened the world that day; clouds hurled sharp cold down on the earth, hard enow from the north for those who lacked clothing. The snow lay about in heaps and nipped the wild animals of the wood; the howling wind swooped down from on high and piled each valley full of great drifts. Gawain, ly-ing in bed, listened to the storm; though he closed his eyes, full little he had slept; he knew the voice of every cock that had crowed. Quickly he rose ere day broke, for there was light from a lamp that burned in his chamber. He called to his chamberlain, who speedily answered him, and bade him fetch his byrnie and saddle his steed. The chamberlain arose and brought the knight's armor, and got Gawain ready in knightly fashion. First he put on his clothes to protect him from the cold, and then his armor that was nobly cared for, his coat of mail and his hauberk, burnished and shining. The rust had been polished away from the ringed mail on his rich byrnie. All was as fresh as at first, and Gawain was fain to thank the chamberlain, for each piece of armor was wiped well and clean—it was the gayest armor from here to Greece. Gawain then called for his steed.

Meanwhile he cast upon himself the proudest garments; his coat with the badge of famous deeds, adorned with precious stones on velvet, the borders worked and embroidered and lined fairly with costly furs. Nor did he forget the girdle, the lady's gift; that, you may be sure, he did not leave behind, for the good it might do him. When he had belted his sword over his round and smooth waist, he wrapped the love-token doubly about him, closely and sweetly folded over his loins, a girdle of green silk that became him very well on the background of royal red cloth, that was gorgeous to behold. But the knight wore the girdle not for its value in treasure or for the glory of its pendants, although they were polished, and although glittering gold-thread gleamed brightly on the ends, but rather to save himself, when it was necessary for him to suffer, to await destruction without fighting back, to guard him against brand or knife. With that the hero, all ready, marched forth quickly, thanking full often the renowned retinue of the lord of the castle.

Then Gringolet the great and strong was ready; he had been lodged with care in a safe place; that proud horse was in good condition for his journey. The knight went up to him and looked on Gringolet's coat, and said soberly to himself, swearing by his truth: "There is a band in this castle that think upon honor; joy may they have, and the lord who maintains them; the dear lady, may love befall her all her life long. Since they for charity cherish a guest and hold honor in their hands, may the Lord, who holds the heavens on high, requite them and all of you! And if I might lead my life anywhere on earth, I would bring you full reward in truth if I could." Then he stepped to the stirrup and bestrode the horse; his servant handed him his shield, and he laid it on his shoulder. He struck Gringolet with his golden spurs, and the steed started to prance on the stones and abide still no longer. His servant was mounted on horse then, bearing Gawain's spear and lance. "This castle I commend to Christ; may He give it ever good chance!"

The drawbridge was let down and the broad gates unbarred and opened on both sides. The knight crossed himself and passed beyond the limits of the castle. He praised the porter, who knelt before the knight, and gave him good-day and commended him to God, that he should pray for Gawain. Then he went on his way, alone with his man, who should show him where to turn to come to that place of woe where he was to receive that rueful blow. They passed by banks and trees with bare boughs; they climbed along cliffs, where the cold clung fast. Naught fell from the heavens, but it was ugly un-

derfoot; mist hovered over the moorlands and dissolved on the mountains. Every hill wore a hat and a huge cloak of haze; the brooks boiled and foamed between their banks, dashed sparkling against the shores where they shelved downwards. Exceeding lonesome was the road as they passed through the wood, until it was the time when the sun should rise on that day of the New Year. They found themselves on a very high hill, covered over with the whitest of snow. The servant riding beside Gawain bade his master halt.

"Well, I have brought you hither, sir knight, this time; and now you are not far from that noted place that you have sought and inquired for so particularly. But I will tell you in truth, since I know you, and you are a knight in the world that I greatly love, that if you follow my counsel you would fare the better. The place to which you proceed is esteemed full perilous. There dwells a creature in that desolation, the worst on earth, for he is brave and stern and loves to strike, and he is greater in size than any man in the world, and his body bigger than those of the best four in Arthur's house or of Hector himself or of any other. He brings it to pass at the Green Chapel that no man can go by that place, be he never so proud in his arms, that this creature does not strike him dead with a blow from his hand. For he is a man without pity and practices no mercy; for be it churl or chaplain that ride by the Chapel, monk or mass-priest, or any other man, it is as pleasant for him to slay them as to pass alive himself. Therefore I say to you, as truly as you are sitting in that saddle, that if you go there, you will be killed. I can counsel you truly, knight, though you had twenty lives to spend. He has lived here full long, and has brought about much violence. Against his terrible blows you cannot defend yourself.

"Therefore, good Sir Gawain, let that man alone, and depart some other way, for the sake of Christ. Turn home by some other land, where Christ may speed you; and I shall hie me home again, and promise you, moreover, that I shall swear by God and all His good saints—so help me God and all the saints—oaths enow that I shall faithfully conceal it and never tell tale that you ever took to flight, for fear of the man I described to you."

"Gramercy," quoth Gawain, and said in ill humor, "Good fortune for the man who wishes me good; I believe well that thou wouldst conceal my shame loyally! But though thou didst keep my secret ever so truly, and I passed by here, and took to flight out of fear, in the manner you spoke of, I should be a

81. **Hector himself.** The manuscript reads *Hestor*, a reading which occurs in several French romances, but refers without doubt to the great Trojan hero, one of the Nine Worthies of the World.

coward knight and could never be forgiven. Therefore I will go on to the Chapel, whatever chance
may befall, and tell that fellow there whatever tale I
please, be it for weal or for woe, or as fate will be
pleased to have it. Though he be a strong knave to
control or rule by the rod, still the Lord knows full
well how to save His servants."

"Marry," said the retainer, "since thou talkest so
much and will take this danger upon thyself, and
10 since it pleases thee to lose thy life, I shall not stop
thee. Take here thy helmet on thy head and thy
spear in thy hand, and ride down this very path by
yonder rocks till thou hast come to the bottom of
this rugged valley; then look about a little on thy
left hand, and thou shalt see in a grove the very
Chapel, and the burly warrior that guards it. Now
farewell in God's name, noble Gawain; I would not
go with thee for all the gold in the ground, nor
bear thee fellowship further on foot through this
20 woodland." With that the man in the wood turned
his bridle, hit his horse over his heel as hard as he
could, leapt quickly over the land, and left the
knight there alone. "By God's self," quoth Gawain,
"I shall neither wail nor groan aloud; I am full
obedient to God's will, and I have committed myself to Him."

Then he spurred on Gringolet, and followed the
path, which inclined down through the woods to
the edge of a grove. He rode through the rough land
30 right down to the valley, and then looked about him.
It was wild country; he saw no sign of a resting-
place anywhere about, nothing but towering banks
on both sides and rough craggy rocks with jagged
stones strewn about. The clouds seemed to him
grazed by the cliffs. Then he halted, reining in his
horse for the moment, and changed his gaze now
and again, to find the Green Chapel. He saw no such
Chapel in any direction, and it seemed strange to
him. Then he saw as it were on a rise near by, a
40 little round mound by a bank, near a stream—near
the ford of a stream, indeed, that rushed past. The
brook bubbled away as if it were boiling. The knight
reined his steed and came to the mound, gracefully
dismounted, and fastened the reins to a linden-
branch and tied his noble horse likewise. Then he
turned to the mound and walked about it, debating
within himself what it might be. It had an opening
in the end and on each side, and was overgrown
everywhere with clumps of grass; it was all hollow
50 within, as an old cave, or the crevice of an old crag.
He could not tell what it was. "Ah," said the gentle
knight, "can this be the Green Chapel? Here the
devil may pray his matins at midnight!"

"Now truly," continued Gawain, "it is desolate
here. This is an ugly oratory overgrown with herbs;
indeed a fitting place for the man clad in green to
perform his devotions in devil's worship. In my five

wits I feel that it is the fiend that has appointed for
me this meeting that he may destroy me here. This
is a chapel of mischance, ill fortune befall it; it is 60
the cursedest kirk that ever I came upon!" With his
high helmet on his head and his lance in his hand,
he wandered up the wall of the rude rocky dwelling.
Then he heard from that hill, aloft in a towering
rock beyond the brook and above the bank, a
wondrous fierce noise. Lo! it echoed about the cliffs
so loud that it seemed wild enough to cleave the
rocks—as if one were grinding a scythe upon a
grindstone. Lo! it whirred and grated like water on
a mill-wheel; truly, it rumbled and rang out that it 70
was terrible to hear. Then, "By God!" exclaimed
Gawain, "that gear is being prepared, so I think, for
the use of the warrior who is to meet me here according to our agreement. But let God do his will.
Well, it helps me not a whit even though I lose my
life. But no mere sound shall affright me."

Then the brave knight called aloud: "Who dwells
in this place, let him hold discourse with me. For
now brave Gawain has come hither; if any man
would have anything of him now, let him get his 80
business done now or never." "Stay," answered one
on the bank above Gawain's head, "and thou shalt
have all in haste that I promised thee." Yet for a
while the loud noise went on with its jarring sound
of whetting before the man appeared. Then he descended from a craggy boulder; he had come out
of a cave in the rock, out of some obscure corner,
and now stepped forth brandishing a wicked weapon
—a Danish ax new burnished, with which to give a
mighty blow. The powerful blade bent back in line 90
with the handle; it had been freshly sharpened on
a grindstone and was at least four feet wide, no less,
and bound to the handle with thongs that shone
bright. And the warrior in green was attired as at
first as to complexion and limbs, locks, and beard,
save that now he walked fair on the ground. He set
the handle to the ground and stalked along. When
he came to the brookside, he would not wade
through, but vaulted over with the help of his ax,
and strode along with vigor, fierce and angry in the 100
snow-covered field that stretched far around them.
Sir Gawain met the Green Knight without any kind
of obeisance; the other said, "Now, fair sir, one may
trust thee to keep an agreement."

"Gawain," said the Green Knight, "may God protect thee! Truly thou art welcome, knight, to my
place; and thou hast timed thy travel as well as a
true man could; and thou knowest the covenant
drawn up between us: at this time twelvemonth
thou wouldst take what befell thee; and I should

89. **Danish ax,** the long-bladed battle-ax without the spike at the end
of the shaft, so called because it was a favorite weapon of the Norse
Vikings.

on this New Year quickly repay thee. Now we are in this valley verily alone; here are no henchmen to separate us; we may meet as we please. Take thy helmet off thy head, and receive here thy reward; make no more talk now than I offered thee when thou didst strike off my head with one blow." "Nay, by God," replied Gawain, "who didst give me soul; I shall not murmur in ill-will for any mischief that shall be my lot; now settle thyself for the stroke, and I shall stand still and cast no refusal in thy teeth, but let thee do as thou wilt." He stretched forth his neck and bowed, showing his bright skin all bare, and made as if he did not fear, for he would not tremble out of dread.

Then the knight in green got him ready and gathered up the grim weapon to smite Gawain; with all the power in his body he lifted it on high with a mighty feint to slay him. Had the blow fallen as violently as he seemed to intend, Gawain would have been dead from the stroke, doughty as he may have been. But our bold knight caught a glimpse of that ax as it came swishing downward to destroy him there on the hill, and he flinched a little from that sharp iron, moving his shoulders slightly. The Green Knight let the blow swerve and withheld the ax, and then reproved Gawain with many haughty words: "Thou art not Gawain," said the warrior, "who is esteemed so good, who never waxed timid before any band on either hill or dale; and now thou dost shrink for fear before thou dost feel any hurt. Such cowardice I never knew in that knight. Nor did I shrink nor flee, sir knight, when thou didst swing thy stroke over me, nor did I cast any trifling objection in the way there in King Arthur's court. My head rolled at my feet, and yet I never fled. And thou, ere any harm has befallen thee, art fearful in heart; wherefore I ought to be called the better knight." Said Gawain then: "I flinched once, but I will not do so again; but if my head drops down on the stones, I shall not be able to restore it.

"But, sir knight, by thy faith, hasten and bring me to the point; deal out to me my destiny, and do it out of hand; for I will stand thee a stroke and start no more until thine ax has struck me. Here is my troth!" "Have at thee then," said the Green Knight, and heaved the ax aloft and looked as fierce and grim as if he were beside himself. He aimed a mighty blow, but did not cut Gawain; he held quickly his hand before the weapon could hurt him. Gawain bravely awaited it, and did not flinch in any part of him, but stood as still as a stone or rather the stock of a tree that is fixed in rocky ground with a hundred roots. Then the Green Knight spoke in merry tones: "So now that thou hast thy heart whole, it behooves me to hit. Hold up thy noble hood, that Arthur gave thee, and keep thy neck with this blow,

if perchance it survive!" But Gawain in full wrathful anger spoke thus: "Why smite further, thou fierce man; thou hast threatened too long. I believe that thine own heart has grown timid." "Forsooth," retorted the Green Knight, "so boldly thou hast spoken; I will no longer hold back thine adventure. Here it is right now!" So he spread his legs far apart to strike and frowned horribly with lips and brow; it was no marvel that it pleased him little who hoped for no rescue.

Lightly he lifted his ax and let it fall fair, with the cutting edge of the blade against the bare neck. But though he swung mightily, he hurt him no more than before, but nicked him slightly on the side, so that he broke the skin. The sharp blade bit through the flesh and the swelling muscle, so that the bright blood ran over his shoulders and dropped on the ground. And when the knight saw the blood flow on the snow, he sprang forth, swift of foot, more than a spear's length, quickly seized his helmet and set it on his head, threw the fair shield in front of his shoulders, snatched out his bright sword, and spoke fiercely (never since he had been born of his mother had he been so joyous): "Cease, knight, of thy blows; give me no more. I have received a blow in this place without combat; and if thou dost yield me any more, I shall readily repay you and yield you back still more forbidding blows; thou mayest be sure of that! But one stroke is my lot here; the covenant we shaped just so in Arthur's hall. Therefore, sir knight, halt!"

The Green Knight drew off and rested on his ax, setting the shaft on earth, and leaning against the blade. He looked at Sir Gawain, who was in a clearing, and saw how that doughty warrior stood there fearless, armed, and dangerous; in his heart he was pleased. Then in a loud voice he addressed Gawain gaily, and said to the knight in a mighty rumble: "Bold warrior, be not so wroth in the field; no man here has offered thee wrong, nor will do so, except according to the covenant drawn up at the king's court. I promised thee a stroke, and thou hast received it—consider thyself well paid. I release thee of all other claims. If I had been active, peradventure I could have dealt thee a buffet more harshly and have stirred thee to frenzy. First I menaced thee jestingly with a feigned blow, and did not rend thee with a gash or a wound which in justice I should offer thee according to the covenant that we bound on that first night, and that thou faithfully didst hold in keeping with thy faith and troth. All thy gains thou didst yield me, as a good man should. The second blow, sir knight, I gave thee for that morn. Thou didst kiss my lovely wife; those kisses thou didst give to me. For both those days I offered thee here but two more feints without harm to thee: true man, true return—he need fear no harm. But the third day thou didst fail me, and therefore hadst thou the real blow, though slight.

"For it is my weed that thou art wearing, that same woven girdle; my own wife wove it; I know it well forsooth. Now I know thy kisses, and thy virtues as well, and the wooing of my wife—I brought it all about. I sent her to try thee; in truth I think that thou art the most faultless knight that ever walked on earth. As a pearl among white peas is of more value than they, so is Gawain, in good faith, beside other knights. But yet thou wert lacking in a little, sir, and wert wanting in loyalty; but that was not for any base intrigue or lustful wooing, but because you loved your life. So I blame you the less." Gawain stood for a great while in silent thought, so grieved and angry he trembled within; all the blood from his breast poured into his face, and he shrank back for very shame at what the Green Knight had said. The first words that Gawain spoke were: "Cursed be cowardice and covetousness alike! In you both are villainy and vice that destroy virtue." Then he caught at the knot and loosened the twist and angrily hurled the belt at the Green Knight himself: "Lo! there is the breaking of faith, evil befall it! For fear of thy blow, cowardice taught me to be reconciled with covetousness, to forsake my own nature, which is the generosity and loyalty that pertain to knights. Now I am faulty and false and have been afraid from the beginning; from treachery and untruth come both sorrow and care! I acknowledge to thee once again, sir knight, I have done wrong. Do then thy will; hereafter I shall be more wary."

Then the Green Knight laughed and spoke in friendly manner: "I believe it is all whole now, the hurt that I had. Thou art so cleanly confessed and hast acknowledged thy sins and hast borne open penance through the edge of my weapon, that I esteem thee cleansed of that fault and pure and clean withal as if thou hadst never done ill since the time thou wast born. And I give thee, sir knight, this girdle all gold-hemmed; for it is green like my raiment, Sir Gawain. You can think upon this contest when thou goest forth among great princes of worth; it shall be a pure token of the adventure of the Green Chapel, as it befell among chivalrous knights. And in this New Year you shall come back to my castle, and we shall revel for the remnant of this high season in mirth and joy." And the Green Knight invited Gawain further and said: "We shall make peace between you and my wife, I ween, for she was your bitter enemy."

"Nay, forsooth," said Gawain, and seized his helmet and doffed it courteously as he thanked the Green Knight, "I have sojourned ill, but may bliss betide you, and may He that dispenses all honor reward you fittingly. Commend me to that noble lady, your comely wife, both to her and to that other lady,

both honored, who have thus cleverly beguiled their knight with their trick. But it is no wonder if a man be made a fool of and be brought to sorrow through the wiles of a woman. For so was Adam beguiled by one, and Solomon by a great many, and Samson also—Delilah dealt him his doom—and David thereafter was deluded by Bathsheba and suffered much woe. All these were brought to disaster by women's wiles; if a knight could love them well and believe them not, it were a great gain! And these were of old the noblest that lived for a time in all worldly prosperity, preëminent among all in the kingdoms of this earth, and all bemused by love, all beguiled by women with whom they had dealings. And so if I have now been deceived, I may well be excused.

"But as for your girdle," said Gawain, "God be with you! I will accept it with pleasure, not for the gain of the gold, nor for the silk or the samite, nor for the costly pendants, neither for weal nor for worship nor for pride of workmanship; but as a sign of my fault I shall often look upon it. When I ride in pomp, I shall see it as a rebuke to myself for the sin and faintness of crabbed flesh—how likely it is to entice to the desire for evil. And thus when pride shall spur me on in prowess of arms, the sight of this lovely girdle will humble my heart. But one thing I would ask of you, if it displease you not: since you are lord of yonder land, where I have dwelt with you in happiness (may the Lord who upholds the heavens and sits on the high throne ever keep it for you)—what, indeed, is your rightful name? Pray tell me, and I will ask no more." "That I shall truly," said the Green Knight. "I am called Bernlak de Hautdesert in this my home. Morgan le Fay dwells in my house, and through the power and knowledge of clerkly works, well learned in craft, she, the pupil of Merlin, has taken many. For she has long since been the paramour of the excellent magician Merlin, who knows all the knights in Arthur's court. Morgain the goddess is she called therefore; none has so great haughtiness of spirit that she cannot tame him.

"She sent me in this manner to your joyous hall, to test the pride, if there be pride, that comes from the great renown of the Round Table. She taught me this marvel to take away your wits and to grieve Guinevere and frighten her to death with the fear of the man who spoke in ghostly fashion before the high dais, with his head in his hand. That is she at my home, the dowager lady; she is even thine aunt, Arthur's half-sister, the daughter of the Duchess of Tintagel, on whom great Uther begat Arthur, who

96–97. **Morgain the goddess,** sister of Arthur, and an evil figure in Arthurian legend. Her hatred of Guenevere is due to the fact that Morgain had an affair which Guenevere discovered and made known. 107–108. **Duchess . . . Arthur.** Uther Pendragon had fallen in love with Ygerne, Duchess of Tintagel and wife of Gorlois. Gorlois died in battle, and, helped by Merlin, Uther visited Ygerne in the guise of her husband. The child of this union was Arthur.

now is so famous. Therefore I ask thee, sir knight, to come to thine aunt; make merry in my house; my retinue loves thee; and I myself, sir knight, by my faith, I wish thee as well as any man under Heaven, because of thy great devotion to faith." But Gawain shook his head in refusal; he would not return. They embraced and kissed and commended each other to the Prince of Paradise, and parted right there on the cold ground. Gawain on his fair steed turned away

10 boldly to King Arthur's castle; and the knight in bright green turned whither he would.

Through many a wild path now rode Gawain on Gringolet—Gawain who had thus won grace of his life. Often he lodged in a house, and often outside, and had many adventures by the way and vanquished many men, things that I do not intend to recount in this tale. The wound in his neck healed; he bore the shining belt about him; the badge of his fault he wore as a baldric bound at his side, knotted under

20 his left arm, in token of the fact that he had been found remiss; and so he came to Arthur's court, a knight strong and whole. Joy was lifted up in that castle when great Arthur knew that Gawain had come, for he deemed it gain. The king kissed the knight, and the queen also, and many another trusty knight who hurried up to greet him. They asked him of his adventure, and he told them all the wondrous happenings—the chance of the chapel, the actions of the Green Knight, the love of the lady, and last of

30 all the girdle. He showed them the scar in his bare neck that he had won from the hands of the Green Knight as a reproach for his lack of loyalty. He suffered torment when he had to tell of that last adventure; he groaned aloud for very grief and shame; the blood rushed into his face in chagrin, but he told of his humiliation.

"Lo, my lords and ladies," said knight Gawain, and handled the girdle, "this is the bond of the blame that I bear on my neck; this is the offense and

40 the loss that I have got for myself, the cowardice and the covetousness that I felt there; this is the token of my disloyalty, in which I was taken; and I must needs wear this as long as I live. For none can hide his fault, but some mishap will reveal it; for if it once has clung to thee, it will never be severed from thee." The king comforted Gawain, and all the court as well, laughing loudly at the whole story. With general accord the lords and the ladies who belonged to the Round Table agreed that each knight

50 of the brotherhood should wear a baldric, a band of bright green as a badge, following Gawain's example. And with this was the renown of the Round Table

52–53. **Round Table in accord.** As suggested in the headnote above, *Sir Gawain and the Green Knight* may have been written in honor of the Knights of the Garter, though the Garter, so far as is known, never used a green collar or band as a badge. The decision of the Round Table here certainly suggests the founding of some order, but the evidence as to a particular one is so vague as to be unconvincing.

in accord; and he was honored ever after who wore the badge, as the best book of romance tells the tale.

Thus the adventure of Gawain and the Green Knight befell in Arthur's day, as the book of Brutus bears witness. For since Brutus, that brave knight, first came hither, after the siege and assault of Troy had ceased, forsooth,

Many adventures herebefore 60
Have fallen such as this;
He that the crown of thorns once bore
Now bring us to His bliss!
AMEN.

Honi Soit Qui Mal Y Pense.

The Song of Roland

In the year 777 some Saracens of Spain, irked by what they considered their unrewarded fealty to the Caliph of Cordova, and impressed by the great power and liberality of the King of the Franks, later the Emperor of the Romans, came to Charlemagne at Paderborn and offered to transfer their allegiance to him. In order to make the best of the opportunity thus offered to spread his influence and the influence of Christianity south of the Pyrenees, Charlemagne in the next year (778), still a young man, advanced into Spain as far south as the river Ebro. His imperialistic aims satisfied for the time, he returned to France. On his way back through the Pyrenees, his rear guard was attacked and destroyed by a raiding force of Basque mountaineers, known in the old chronicles as Gascons. To quote the contemporary biographer of Charlemagne, one Einhard: "In the struggle that ensued, the Gascons cut them off to a man; they then plundered the baggage, and dispersed with all speed in every direction under the cover of approaching night . . . Eggihard, the King's steward; Anselm, Count Palatine; and Roland, Governor of the March of Brittany, with very many others, fell in this engagement. This ill turn could not be avenged for the nonce, because the enemy scattered so widely after carrying out their plan that not the least clue could be had to their whereabouts."

So much for history. But the inscrutable process of hero making has decreed that Eggihard and Anselm, who doubtless fought most valiantly, have been forgotten, whereas Roland has become a great epic champion. Perhaps the fact that he came from Brittany had something to do with the development; perhaps his personality was in any case more memorable; perhaps it was merely that he was blessed with more articulate friends and publicity agents. At any rate, Roland became in the following centuries the subject of more than one French epic lay, or *cantilene*. These epic lays were circulated in oral tradition, taking on with the passing of time various increments and elaborations from the mouths of successive bards, until they combined to give an extended account of the hero's progress. At this point the assembled lays about Roland were brought into an artistic whole by some interested individual, probably a cleric, who no doubt gave them literary embellishment and a more orderly arrangement than they had possessed while in oral tradition. The resulting epic poem now constituted a *chanson de geste*, a form of aristocratic narrative in verse which flourished during the ninth, tenth, and eleventh centuries in France and adjacent parts.

The Song of Roland, most celebrated of the *chansons de geste*, probably came into being in its present form during the latter half of the eleventh century. Tradition has it that the Norman Taillefer sang it at the Battle of Hastings in 1066; but whether this was the epic we now have, or some earlier form thereof, is not known. At any rate, reference is made in *The Song of Roland* to England's being subject to Charlemagne; while this was never historically true, it might have been suggested by the contemporary Norman Conquest of England by William, Duke of Normandy. The poem consistently refers to Jerusalem as being in heathen hands, whence the assumption that it was composed before the First Crusade established the Christian Kingdom of Jerusalem in 1099.

There is no question, however, about the significance of *The Song of Roland* as a national epic. Its glorification and idealization of "sweet France" can never leave the reader in doubt as to its patriotic viewpoint. Roland is in all respects a complete exemplar of the epic hero. He is physically overwhelming; courageous to the point of contempt for his adversary; intensely loyal to his comrades-at-arms, his king, his country, and his God; proud in his achievements past and present; jealous of the reputation of his great sphere of activity; a bulwark to all who need him in an emergency; a champion of champions. He has been exalted above everyone else in the poem. Charlemagne, also exalted, is nevertheless made vaguely glorious and venerable in a fictitious old age conferred upon him; his true radiance shines in his mighty *comitatus*, or knightly retinue: Roland, Oliver, the fighting Archbishop Turpin, and the Twelve Peers.

The general absence of any significant female characters or of any important love elements is remarkable; it stamps the poem as distinct from a medieval romance. Although Roland is affianced to Aude, Oliver's sister, she is a mere concession to feudal perpetuity and conveniently dies at once when she hears of Roland's demise. The society in *The Song of Roland* is military and feudal; the action is largely a series of personal encounters on the battlefield. The tone of the poem is that of aggressive, intolerant medieval Christianity; such chivalrousness as it possesses is directed only toward those who profess the Christian faith. Most noteworthy is, therefore, the formidable power of Archbishop Turpin of Rheims, who survives the disaster of Roncevals longer than any Frank except Roland himself. And Roland, be it observed, does not fall by the blows of Saracen warriors; he wounds himself mortally in blowing the ivory horn to summon aid from Charlemagne—something he should have done long before but which in his epic pride he postponed until too late. Such is his tragic flaw, if flaw there must be in an epic hero. But his fame is secure; no other heroes of medieval epic or romance, with the exceptions of Lancelot, Gawain, and Siegfried, have had a more lasting international renown.

The Song of Roland

[Charlemagne has made himself master of all Spain, except for Saragossa, whose king, Marsila, vows vengeance upon the Franks. Marsila sends envoys to Charlemagne, ostensibly to sue for peace, but actually to give Marsila opportunity for a treacherous assault on the Franks. Charlemagne offers Marsila peace—the price being Marsila's conversion to Christianity. At the suggestion of the great champion Roland, Charlemagne sends his terms to Marsila by Count Ganelon, stepfather of Roland. Ganelon, envious of Roland and his select comrades, the Twelve Peers of Charlemagne, and feeling that he has been sent through Roland's machinations upon an unnecessarily dangerous mission, plots with Marsila to fall upon the rear guard of Charlemagne's army, commanded by Roland, while it is passing through the vale of Roncevals. The dire event is consummated; Roland and his group are attacked while Charles is too far forward to be of any immediate use.]

THEN Oliver goes up into a high mountain, and looks away to the right, all down a grassy valley, and sees the host of the heathen coming on, and he called to Roland, his comrade, saying: "From the side of Spain I see a great light coming, thousands of white hauberks and thousands of gleaming helms. They will fall upon our Franks with great wrath. Ganelon the felon has done this treason, and he it was adjudged us to the rear guard, before the Emperor." "Peace, Oliver," saith Count Roland, "he is my mother's husband, speak thou no ill of him." 10

Oliver has fared up the mountain, and from the summit thereof he sees all the kingdom of Spain and the great host of the Saracens. Wondrous is the shine of helmets studded with gold, of shields and broidered hauberks, of lances and gonfanons. The battles are without number, and no man may give count thereof, so great is the multitude. Oliver was all astonied at the sight; he got him down the hill as best he might, and came to the Franks, and gave them his tidings. 20

"I have seen the paynims," said Oliver; "never was so great a multitude seen of living men. Those of the vanguard are upon a hundred thousand, all

The Song of Roland▲ Translated by Isabella Butler. Reprinted by permission of and arrangement with Houghton Mifflin Company, the authorized publishers.
16. **gonfanons,** battle standards, sometimes known as gonfalons.

armed with shields and helmets, and clad in white hauberks; right straight are the shafts of their lances, and bright the points thereof. Such a battle we shall have as was never before seen of man. Ye lords of France, may God give you might! and stand ye firm that we be not overcome." "Foul fall him who flees!" then say the Franks, "for no peril of death will we fail thee."

"Great is the host of the heathen," saith Oliver, "and few is our fellowship. Roland, fair comrade, I pray thee sound thy horn of ivory that Charles may hear it and return again with all his host." "That were but folly," quoth Roland, "and thereby would I lose all fame in sweet France. Rather will I strike good blows and great with Durendal, that the blade thereof shall be blooded even unto the hilt. Woe worth the paynims that they come into the passes! I pledge thee my faith, short life shall be theirs."

"Roland, comrade, blow now thy horn of ivory, and Charles shall hear it, and bring hither his army again, and the King and his barons shall succor us." But Roland answers him, saying: "Now God forfend that through me my kinsman be brought to shame, or aught of dishonor befall fair France. But first I will lay on with Durendal, the good sword that is girded here at my side, and thou shalt see the blade thereof all reddened. Woe worth the paynims when they gathered their hosts! I pledge me they shall all be given over to death."

"Roland, comrade, blow thy horn of ivory, that Charles may hear it as he passes the mountains, and I pledge me the Franks will return hither again." But Roland saith: "Now God forfend it be said of any living man that I sounded my horn for dread of paynims. Nay, that reproach shall never fall upon my kindred. But when I am in the stour I will smite seven hundred blows, or mayhap a thousand, and thou shalt see the blade of Durendal all crimson. The Franks are goodly men, and they will lay on right valiantly, nor shall those of Spain have any surety from death."

Saith Oliver, "I see no shame herein. I have seen the Saracens of Spain; they cover the hills and the valleys, the heaths and the plains. Great are the hosts of this hostile folk, and ours is but a little fellowship." And Roland makes answer: "My desire is the greater thereby. May God and His most holy angels forfend that France should lose aught of worship through me. Liefer had I die than bring dishonor upon me. The Emperor loves us for dealing stout blows."

Roland is brave, and Oliver is wise; and both are good men of their hands; once armed and a-horseback, rather would they die than flee the battle. Hardy are the Counts and high their speech. The felon paynims ride on in great wrath. Saith Oliver:

36. **stour,** the onset of battle.

"Roland, prithee look. They are close upon us, but Charles is afar off. Thou wouldst not deign to sound thy horn of ivory; but were the King here we should suffer no hurt. Look up towards the passes of Aspre and thou shalt see the woeful rear guard; they who are of it will do no more service henceforth." But Roland answers him: "Speak not so cowardly. Cursed be the heart that turns coward in the breast! Hold we the field, and ours be the buffets and the slaughter."

When Roland sees that the battle is close upon them, he waxes fiercer than lion or leopard. He calls to the Franks, and he saith to Oliver: "Comrade, friend, say not so. When the Emperor left us his Franks, he set apart such a twenty thousand of men that, certes, among them is no coward. For his liege lord a man ought to suffer all hardship, and endure great heat and great cold, and give both his blood and his body. Lay on with thy lance, and I will smite with Durendal, my good sword that the King gave me. If I die here, may he to whom it shall fall say, 'This was the sword of a goodly vassal.' "

Nigh at hand is Archbishop Turpin; he now spurs his horse to the crest of a knoll, and speaks to the Franks, and this is his sermon: "Lords, barons, Charles left us here, and it is a man's devoir to die for his King. Now help ye to uphold Christianity. Certes, ye shall have a battle, for here before you are the Saracens. Confess your sins and pray God's mercy, and that your souls may be saved I will absolve you. If ye are slain, ye will be holy martyrs, and ye shall have seats in the higher Paradise." The Franks light off their horses and kneel down, and the Archbishop blesses them, and for a penance bids them that they lay on with their swords.

The Franks get upon their feet, freed and absolved from sin; and the Archbishop blesses them in the name of God. Then they mounted their swift horses, and armed themselves after the manner of knights, and made them ready for battle. Count Roland calls to Oliver, saying: "Sir comrade, rightly thou saidst Ganelon hath betrayed us all, and hath received gold and silver and goods therefor; but the Emperor will well revenge us. King Marsila hath bought and sold us, but he shall pay for it with the sword."

Roland rides through the passes of Spain on Veillantif, his good horse and swift. He is clad in his harness; right well it becomes him, and as he rides he brandishes his spear, turning its point towards Heaven; and to its top is bound a gonfanon of pure

78. **Archbishop Turpin,** the reputed author of a history of the reign of Charlemagne. Turpin may have been the name of an authentic Frankish warrior confused with Tilpin, Archbishop of Rheims, who did not participate in the battle of Roncevals. 102. **Veillantif.** Compare Gawain and his great steed Gringolet. The celebrated swords named—Roland's Durendal, Oliver's Hauteclere, and Turpin's Almace—are also to be compared to the Arthurian Excalibur.

white, whereof the golden fringes fall down even unto his hands. Well fashioned is his body, and his face fair and laughing; close behind him rides his comrade; and all the Franks claim him as their champion. Full haughtily he looks on the Saracens, but gently and mildly on the Franks, and he speaks to them courteously, saying: "Lords, barons, ride on softly. The paynims come seeking destruction, and this day we shall have plunder so goodly and great that no King of France hath ever taken any of so great price." At these words the two hosts come together.

Saith Oliver: "I have no mind for more words. Thou wouldst not deign to sound thy horn of ivory, and no help shalt thou get from Charles; naught he knows of our case, nor is the wrong his, the baron's. They who are beyond the mountains are no wise to blame. Now ride on with what might ye may. Lords, barons, hold ye the field! And in God's name I pray you bethink you both how to deal good blows and how to take them. And let us not forget the device of our King." At these words all the Franks cried out together, and whosoever may have heard that cry of Montjoy must call to mind valor and worth. Then they rode forward—God! how proudly—spurring their horses for the more speed, and fell a-smiting—how else should they do? But no whit adread were the Saracens. And lo you! Franks and paynims come together in battle.

The nephew of Marsila, who was called Aelroth, rides before all his host, and foul are his words to our Franks: "Ye Frankish felons, today ye shall do battle with us. He who should have been your surety has betrayed you; mad is the King who left you behind in the passes. Today shall fair France lose her fame, and the right arm of Charles shall be smitten off from his body." When Roland hears this, God! how great is his wrath. He spurs as fast as his horse may run, and with all the might he hath he smites Aelroth, and breaks his shield, and rends apart his hauberk, that he cleaves his breast and breaks the bone, and severs the spine from the back; with his lance he drives out the soul from the body, for so fierce is the blow that Aelroth wavers, and with all the force of his lance Roland hurls him from his horse dead, his neck broken in two parts. Yet Roland still chides him, saying: "Out, coward! Charles is not mad, nor loves he treason. He did well and knightly to leave us in the passes. Today shall France lose naught of her fame. Franks, lay on! Ours is the first blow. Right is with us, and these swine are in the wrong."

Among the paynims is a Duke, Falsaron by name,

A French warrior of the Carolingian period.

who was brother to King Marsila, and held the land of Dathan and Abiram; there is no more shameless felon on all the earth; so wide is his forehead that the space between his eyes measures a full half foot. When he sees his nephew slain, he is full of dole, and he drives through the press as swift as he may, and cries aloud the paynim war-cry. Great is his hatred of the Franks. "Today shall fair France lose her fame!" Oliver hears him and is passing wroth; with his golden spurs he pricks on his horse and rides upon him like a true baron; he breaks the shield, tears asunder the hauberk, and drives his lance into the body up to the flaps of his pennon, and with the might of his blow hurls him dead from the saddle. He looks to earth where lies the felon, and speaks him haughtily: "Coward, naught care I for thy threats. Lay on, Franks, certes, we shall overcome them." And he cries out Montjoy, the war-cry of Charles.

A King there is, Corsablis by name; he is of Barbary, a far-off land, and he spoke to the Saracens, saying: "We shall win a fair day on these Franks, for few is their fellowship. And such as be here shall prove themselves of small avail, nor shall one be saved alive for Charles; the day has come whereon they must die." Archbishop Turpin hears him right well, and to no man under Heaven has he ever borne such hate; with his spurs of fine gold he pricks on his horse, and rides upon the King with great might, cleaves his shield and rends his hauberk, and

---

24. **Montjoy.** The obscure etymology of this war cry is partially cleared up in the final section (Book III) of *The Song of Roland*. The word seems to be a corruption of "mon joie," an ungrammatical form of "ma joie"—"my joy."

55–58. **shameless felon . . . foot.** It is an old medieval belief that moral turpitude is reflected in a grotesque physical appearance. 58. **nephew.** It is a commonplace of the Western epic that the relationship of nephew to uncle is the closest possible tie, for fathers and sons might be hostile to one another.

thrusts his great lance into his body, and so drives home the blow that sorely the King wavers, and with all the force of his lance Turpin hurls him dead into the path. He looks on the ground where he sees the glutton lie, nor doth he withhold him from speech, but saith: "Coward and heathen, thou hast lied! Charles, my liege lord, is ever our surety, and our Franks have no mind to flee; and we shall have a care that thy comrades go not far hence; yea, and a

10 second death must ye suffer, Lay on, ye Franks, let no man forget himself! This first blow is ours, thanks be to God." And he cries out Montjoy, to hold the field.

And Gerin smites Malprimis de Brigal, that his good shield no whit avails; he shatters the jewelled boss thereof, and half of it falls to earth; he pierces the hauberk to the flesh, and drives his good lance into the body; the paynim falls down in a heap, and his soul is carried away by Satan.

20 And Gerier, the comrade of Gerin, smites the Emir, and shatters his shield and unmails his hauberk, and thrusts his good lance into his heart; so great is the blow his lance drives through the body, and with all the force of the shaft he throws him to the ground dead. "Ours is a goodly battle," quoth Oliver.

Samson the Duke rides upon the Almaçur, and breaks his shield all flowered and set with gold, nor doth his good hauberk give him any surety, but

30 Samson pierces him through heart and liver and lungs, and fells him dead, whether any one grieves for him or no. Saith the Archbishop, "That was knightly stricken."

And Anseis urges on his horse and encounters with Turgis of Tortosa, cleaves his shield below the golden boss, rends asunder his twofold hauberk, and sets the point of his good lance in his body, and thrusts so well that the iron passes sheer through him, that the might of the blow hurls him to the

40 ground dead. "That was the buffet of a man of good prowess," saith Roland.

And Engelier, the Gascon of Bordeaux, spurs his horse, slackens his rein, and encounters with Escremis of Valtierra, breaks and carves the shield from his shoulder, rends apart the ventail of his hauberk, and smites him in his breast between his two collarbones, and with the might of the blow hurls him from the saddle, saying: "Ye are all given over to destruction."

50 And Oton smites the paynim Esturgant upon the leathern front of his shield, marring all the blue and white thereof, breaks through the sides of his hauberk, and drives his good spear and sharp into his body, and casts him from his swift horse, dead. "Naught may save thee," saith Oliver thereat.

27. **Almaçur,** an honorary title bestowed upon a Saracen chieftain, from the Arabic al mansur, "the victorious."

And Berengier rides on Estramaris, shatters his shield, rends asunder his hauberk, and drives his stout lance into his body, and smites him dead amid a thousand Saracens. Of the Twelve Peers ten are 60 now slain and but two are still living men, to wit, Chernuble and Count Margaris.

Margaris is a right valiant knight, strong and goodly, swift and keen; he spurs his horse and rides on Oliver, breaks his shield below the boss of pure gold, that the lance passed along his side, but by God's help, it did not pierce the body; the shaft grazes him but doth not overthrow him, and Margaris drives on, in that he has no hindrance, and sounds his horn to call his men about him. 70

Now the battle waxes passing great on both sides. Count Roland spares himself no whit, but smites with his lance as long as the shaft holds, but by fifteen blows it is broken and lost; thereupon he draws out Durendal his good sword, all naked, spurs his horse and rides on Chernuble, breaks his helm whereon the carbuncles blaze, cleaves his mail-coif and the hair of his head so that the sword cuts through eyes and face, and the white hauberk of fine mail, and all the body to the fork of the legs, 80 sheer into the saddle of beaten gold, nor did the sword stint till it had entered the horse and cleft the backbone, never staying for joint, that man and horse fell dead upon the thick grass. Thereupon Roland cried: "Coward, woe worth the day thou camest hither! no help shalt thou get from Mahmoud; nor by such swine as thou shalt today's battle be achieved."

Count Roland rides through the press; in his hand he hath Durendal, right good for hacking and 90 hewing, and doth great damage upon the Saracens. Lo, how he hurls one dead upon another, and the bright blood flows out on the field. All reddened are his hauberk and his arms, and the neck and shoulders of his good horse. Nor doth Oliver hold back from the battle; the Twelve Peers do not shame themselves, and all the Franks smite and slay, that the paynims perish or fall swooning. Then saith the Archbishop, "Our barons do passing well," and he cries out Montjoy, the war-cry of Charles. 100

Oliver drives through the stour; his lance is broken and naught is left him but the truncheon; yet he smites the paynim Malsaron that his shield patterned with gold and flowers is broken, and his two eyes fly out from his head, and his brains fall at his feet; among seven hundred of his fellows Oliver smites him dead. Then he slew Turgin and Esturgus, and

60. **Twelve Peers,** here the Saracen champions; the French poet has evidently assigned the Saracen leader a *comitatus* of twelve nobles exactly similar to that which surrounded Charlemagne. The Twelve Peers of France are perhaps the most famous of the set *comitatus* groups in European legendry. 77. **mail-coif,** a skull-cap worn under the mail hood, which in turn lay beneath the helmet. 96. **Twelve Peers,** in this case clearly the twelve of France.

thereby broke his lance that it splintered even unto the pommel. Thereat Roland saith: "Comrade, what dost thou? I have no mind for a staff in so great battle, rather a man hath need of iron and steel. Where is thy sword Halteclere?" "I may not draw it," Oliver answered him. "So keen am I to smite."

But now the lord Oliver hath drawn his good sword, even as his comrade had besought him, and hath shown it to him in knightly wise; and therewith he smites the paynim Justin de Val Ferrée that he severs his head in twain, cuts through his broidered hauberk and his body, through his good saddle set with gold, and severs the backbone of his steed, that man and horse fall dead on the field before him. Then said Roland: "Now I hold you as my brother, and 'tis for such buffets the Emperor loves us." And on all sides they cry out Montjoy.

Count Gerin rides his horse Sorel, and Gerier, his comrade, rides Passecerf; both slacken rein, and spurring mightily set upon the paynim Timosel; one smites him on the shield, and the other on the hauberk, that both their lances break in his body; and he falls dead in the field. I wot not, nor have I ever heard man say, which of the twain was the more swift. Then Esperveris, son of Borel, died at the hand of Engelier of Bordeaux. And the Archbishop slew Siglorel, that enchanter who of old had passed down into Hell, led thither by the spells of Jupiter. "Of him we are well rid," quoth Turpin. And Roland answered him: "Yea, the coward is overthrown. Oliver, my brother, such buffets please me right well."

Meantime the battle waxes passing hard, and both Franks and paynims deal such blows that it is wonder to see; here they smite, and there they make what defence they may; and many a lance is broken and reddened, and there is great rending of pennons and ensigns. Many a good Frank loses his youth, and will never again see wife or mother, or the men of France who await him in the passes. Charles the Great weeps for them, and makes great sorrow; but what avails it? No help shall they get therefrom. An ill turn Ganelon did them the day he sold his own kindred in Saragossa. Thereafter he lost both life and limb therefor; in the council at Aix, he was condemned to hang, and with him upon thirty of his kindred to whom death left no hope.

Dread and sore is the battle. Roland and Oliver lay on valiantly, and the Archbishop deals more than a thousand buffets, nor are the Twelve Peers backward, and all the Franks smite as a man. The paynims are slain by hundreds and thousands, whosoever does not flee has no surety from death, but will he, nill he, must take his end. But the Franks lose their goodliest arms; lances adorned with gold, and trenchant spears, and gonfanons red and white and blue, and the blades of their good swords are broken, and thereto they lose many a valiant knight. Never again shall they see father or kindred, or Charles their liege lord who abides for them in the passes.

Meantime, in France, a wondrous tempest broke forth, a mighty storm of wind and lightning, with rain and hail out of all measure, and bolts of thunder that fell ever and again; and verily therewith came a quaking of the earth that ran through all the land from Saint Michael of the Peril, even unto Xanten, and from Besançon to the port of Guitsand; and there was not a dwelling whose walls were not rent asunder. And at noon fell a shadow of great darkness, nor was there any light save as the heavens opened. They that saw these things were sore afraid, and many a one said: "This is the Day of Judgment, and the end of the world is at hand." But they were deceived, and knew not whereof they spoke; it was the great mourning for the death of Roland.

Meantime the Franks smote manfully and with good courage, and the paynims were slain by thousands and by multitudes; of a hundred thousand not two may survive. Then said the Archbishop: "Our Franks are of good prowess, no man under Heaven hath better; it is written in the annals of France that valiant they are for our Emperor." And the Franks fare through the field seeking their fellows, and weeping from dole and pity for their kin, in all love and kindness. But even now King Marsila is upon them with his great host.

Count Roland is a knight of much worship, so likewise are Oliver and the Twelve Peers, and all the Franks are good warriors. By their great might they have made such slaughter of paynims that of a hundred thousand only one hath escaped, Margaris, to wit. Blame him not that he fled, for in his body he bore the wounds of four lances. Back he fared in haste towards Spain, and came to Marsila and gave him tidings. And in a loud voice he cried: "Good King of Spain, now ride on with all speed, the Franks are weary and spent with the smiting and

53–54. will he, nill he, the modern "willy-nilly." 61. Meantime, in France. . . . The ensuing effective section is an illustration of the extremely common folklore motif which associates the passing of a hero with storm, earthquake, or some perturbation of nature. 66–67. Saint Michael . . . Guitsand. The monastery of Mont Saint Michel, off the coast of France at the boundary line of Brittany and Normandy, was founded in the ninth century as Saint Michael "in periculo maris," or "of the peril of the sea." Xanten, a town in the northeastern area of the French domain, in present Cleves, is not mentioned in some manuscripts, which give the reading Senz, a town not precisely identifiable. Besançon is an important city in extreme central eastern France of today. Guitsand, or Wissant, was a famous medieval Flemish port. 72–73. "This is . . . hand." It was a widespread belief in Western Christendom that the world was to come to an end in the year 1000.

28–29. spells of Jupiter. To the medieval Christian writer Jupiter was merely a pagan god, and that was enough to give him a claim on the Saracens' worship. 44–46. Thereafter . . . to hang. Actually, however, the later passages explain that Ganelon, having been arrested by Charles and his knights, was first humiliated and then executed by being torn to pieces by horses.

slaying of our Saracens; they have lost their lances and spears, and a good half of their men, and those who yet live are weakened, and the more part of them maimed and bleeding, nor have they more arms wherewith to help themselves."

Marsila comes on down the valley with the mighty host that he has assembled; full twenty battles the King has arrayed. There is a great shining of helmets, set with gold and precious stones, and of shields and of broidered hauberks. Trumpets to the number of seven thousand sound the onset, and the din thereof runs far and wide. Then saith Roland: "Oliver, comrade and brother, Ganelon the felon has sworn our death. The treason is manifest, and great vengeance shall the Emperor take therefor. The battle will be sore and great, such a one as was never before fought of man. I will smite with Durendal my sword, and do thou, comrade, lay on with Halteclere. Through many lands have we carried them, and with them have we conquered many a battle; no ill song must be sung of them."

When the Franks see how great is the multitude of the paynims, that on all sides they cover the field, they call upon Roland, and Oliver, and the Twelve Peers, that they may be their defence. Then the Archbishop tells them his mind, saying: "Lords, barons, put from you all cowardly thoughts; and in God's name I pray you give not back. Better it were that we die in battle than that men of worship should speak foully of us in their songs. Certain it is we shall straightway take our end, nor shall we from today be living men; yet there is a thing I can promise you, blessed Paradise shall be opened to you, and ye shall take your place among the innocent." At his words, the Franks take heart, and every man cries out Montjoy.

Wily and cunning is King Marsila, and he saith to the paynims: "Now set your trust in me; this Roland is of wondrous might, and he who would overcome him must strive his uttermost; in two encounters he will not be vanquished, methinks; and if not, we will give him three. Then Charles the King shall lose his glory, and shall see France fall into dishonor. Ten battles shall abide here with me, and the remaining ten shall set upon the Franks." Then to Grandonie he gave a broidered banner that it might be a sign unto the rest, and gave over to him the commandment.

King Marsila abides on the mountain, and Grandonie comes on down the valley. By three golden nails he has made fast his gonfanon; and he cries aloud: "Now ride on, ye barons!" And for the more goodly noise he bids them sound a thousand trumpets. Say the Franks: "God our Father, what shall we do? Woe worth the day we saw Count Ganelon! he hath sold us by foul treason. Now help us, ye Twelve Peers!" But the first to answer them is the Archbishop, saying: "Good knights, this day great honor shall be yours, for God will give you crowns and flowers in Paradise among the glorious; but therein the coward shall not enter." And the Franks make answer: "We will lay on as one man, and though we die we will not betray him." Then they spur on with their golden spurs to smite the miscreant felons.

Among the paynims is a Saracen of Saragossa; lord he is of half the city, and Climborin he hight; never will he flee from any living man. He it was who swore fellowship with Count Ganelon, kissed him in all friendship upon the lips, and gave him his helm and his carbuncle. And he hath sworn to bring the Great Land to shame, and to strip the Emperor of his crown. He rides his horse whom he calls Barbamusche, that is swifter than falcon or swallow; and slackening his rein, he spurs mightily, and rides upon Engelier of Gascony that neither shield nor byrnie may save him, but he drives the head of his lance into his body, thrusting so manfully that the point thereof passes through to the other side, and with all the might of his lance hurls him in the field dead. Thereafter he cries: "These folk are good to slay!" But the Franks say: "Alack, that so good a knight should take his end."

And Count Roland speaks to Oliver, saying: "Sir comrade, now is Engelier slain, nor have we any knight of more valor." And the Count answers him, saying: "Now God grant me to avenge him." He pricks on his horse with spurs of pure gold, and he grasps Halteclere—already is the blade thereof reddened—and with all his strength he smites the paynim; he drives the blow home that the Saracen falls; and the devils carry away his soul. Then Oliver slew Duke Alphaien, and cut off the head of Escababi, and unhorsed seven Arabs—never again shall they do battle. Then said Roland: "Wroth is my comrade, and now at my side he wins great worship; for such blows Charles holds us the more dear." And he cried aloud: "To battle, knights, to battle!"

Hard by is the paynim Valdabrun, that had stood godfather to King Marsila; on the sea he is lord of four hundred dromonds, and well honored of all shipmen. He it was who aforetime took Jerusalem by treason, violated the Temple of Solomon, and slew the Patriarch before the baptismal fonts. And he had sworn fellowship with Ganelon, and had given him a sword and a thousand mangons. He rides a horse called Gramimond, swifter than any

102. **dromonds,** large and swift sea-going galleys. 103–105. **He it was . . . fonts.** According to the chronicler Adhemar of Chabannes, Jews and Saracens in the year 1010 sacked the Church of the Holy Sepulchre in Jerusalem and killed the Patriarch. France of the militant eleventh century doubtless accepted this story. Actually, however, the raid was led by a fanatical Caliph, did not destroy the Church, and happened over two centuries after the battle of Roncevals.

falcon; he spurs him well with his sharp spurs, and rides upon Samson the mighty Duke, breaks his shield, and rends his hauberk, and drives the flaps of his gonfanon into his body, and with all the force of his lance, hurls him from the saddle dead. "Lay on, paynims, for hardily we shall overthrow them!" But the Franks say: "God, woe worth the good baron!"

When Roland sees that Samson is dead, ye may guess he is sore stricken; he spurs his horse and lets him run as fast as he may; in his hand he holds Durendal, of greater worth than is pure gold, and with all the might he hath, he smites the paynim on the helm set with gold and gems, and cuts through head and hauberk and body, and through the good saddle set with gold and jewels, deep into the back of the horse, and slays both him and his rider, whosoever has dole or joy thereof. Cry the paynims: "That was a woeful blow for us." Then quoth Roland: "No love have I for any one of you, for yours is the pride and the iniquity."

Among the paynims is an African, Malquiant, son of King Malcud; his armor is all of the beaten gold, and brighter than all the rest it shines to Heaven. His horse, which he calls Salt-Perdut, is so swift that he has not his fellow in any four-footed beast. And now Malquiant rode on Anseis, and smote him full on the shield that its scarlet and blue were hewn away, and he rent the sides of his hauberk, and drove his lance into his body, both point and shaft. Dead is the Count and done are his life-days. Thereat cry the Franks: "Alack for thee, good baron!"

Through the press rides Turpin the Archbishop —never did another priest say mass who did with his own strength so great deeds of arms—and he saith to the paynim: "Now may God bring all evil upon thee! for thou hast slain one for whom my heart is sore stricken." Then he set his good horse at a gallop, and smote Malquiant on his shield of Toledo, that he fell dead upon the green grass.

Hard by is the paynim Grandonie, son of Capuel, King of Cappadocia; he rides a horse called Marmorie, swifter than any bird that flies; he now slackens rein, and spurring well, thrusts mightily upon Gerin, breaks his crimson shield that it falls from his shoulder, and rends all asunder his hauberk, and thereafter drives all his blue gonfanon into his body that he falls dead beside a great rock. Then he slays Gerier, Gerin's comrade, and Berengier, and Guyon of Saint-Antonie; and thereafter he smote Austor, the mighty Duke that held Valence and the land along the Rhône, and felled him dead that the paynims had great joy thereof. But the Franks cry: "How many of ours are stricken."

Roland holds his ruddied sword in his hand; he has heard the Franks make lament, and so great is his sorrow that his heart is nigh to bursting, and he saith to the paynims: "Now may God bring all evil upon thee! Methinks thou shalt pay me dear for him thou hast slain." And he spurs his horse, which springs forward eagerly; and let whoso will pay the price, the two knights join battle.

Grandonie was a man of good prowess, of much valor and hardiness, and amid the way he encounters with Roland, and albeit before that time he had never set eyes upon him, he none the less knew him of a certainty by his look and countenance; and he could not but be sore adread at the sight, and fain would he have fled, but he could not. The Count smites him mightily, so that he rends all his helm down to the nasal, cleaves through nose and mouth and teeth, through the hauberk of fine mail, and all the body, splits the silver sides from off the golden saddle, and cuts deep into the back of the horse, that both he and the rider are slain beyond help. Thereat those of Spain make great lament, but the Franks cry: "That was well stricken of our captain."

Wondrous and fierce is the battle; the Franks lay on in their wrath and their might, that hands and sides and bones fall to earth, and garments are rent off to the very flesh, and the blood runs down to the green grass. The paynims cry: "We may not longer endure. May the curse of Mahmoud fall upon the Great Land, for its folk have not their fellows for hardiness." And there was not a man but cried out: "Marsila! haste, O King, for we are in sore need of thy help."

Wondrous and great is the battle. And still the Franks smite with their burnished lances. There is great dolor of folk, and many a man is slain and maimed and bleeding, and one lies on another, or on his back, or face down. The Saracens may not longer endure, but howsoever unwillingly they must give back. And eagerly the Franks pursue after them.

Marsila sees the slaughter of his people, and lets sound his horns and bussynes, and gets to horse with all his vassal host. In the foremost front rides the Saracen Abisme, the basest knight of his fellowship, all compact of evil and villainy. He believes not in God the son of Mary; and he is black as melted pitch. Dearer than all the gold of Galicia he loves treachery and murder, nor did any man ever see him laugh or take disport. But he is a good man of arms, and bold to rashness, wherefore he is well beloved of the felon King Marsila, and to him it is given to bear the Dragon, around which the paynims gather. The Archbishop hath small love for Abisme, and so soon as he sees him, he is all desirous to smite him, and quietly, within himself, he saith: "This Saracen seems a misbelieving felon; I had liefer die than not set upon him to slay him; never shall I love coward or cowardice."

97. **bussynes,** an old French trumpet.

Whereupon the Archbishop begins the battle. He rides the horse that he won from Grossaille, a King whom he slew in Denmark; the good steed is swift and keen, featly fashioned of foot, and flat of leg; short in the thigh and large of croupe, long of flank and high of back; his tail is white and yellow his mane, his head is the color of the fawn, and small are his ears; of all four-footed beasts none may outstrip him. The Archbishop spurs mightily, and will
10 not fail to meet with Abisme and smite him on his shield, a very marvel, set with gems,—topaz and amethysts, and precious crystals, and blazing carbuncles; the gift it was of Galafré the Amiral, who had received it of a devil in Val-Metas. Now Turpin smites it and spares it not, so that after his buffet it has not the worth of a doit. And he pierces Abisme through the body, and hurls him dead in the open field. And the Franks say: "That was a good deed of arms; in the hands of our Archbishop safe is the
20 crozier."

And Count Roland speaks to Oliver, saying: "Sir comrade, what say ye, is not the Archbishop a right good knight, that there is no better under Heaven? For well he knows how to smite with lance and spear." "Now let us aid him," the Count makes answer. And at these words the Franks go into battle again; great are the blows and grievous the slaughter, and great is the dolor of the Christians.

The Franks have lost much of their arms, yet still
30 there are a good four hundred of naked swords, with which they smite and hew on shining helmets. God! how many a head is cleft in twain; and there is great rending of hauberks and unmailing of byrnies; and they smite off feet and hands and heads. The paynims cry: "These Franks sore mishandle us; whoso doth not defend himself hath no care for his life." King Marsila hears them make lament, and saith in his wrath: "Terra Major, now may Mahmoud destroy thee, for thy folk hath discomfited mine, and
40 hath destroyed and spoiled me of many cities which Carles of the white beard now holds; he hath conquered Rome and Apulia and Calabria, Constantinople, and Saxony the wide, liefer had I die than flee before him. Paynims, now lay on that the Franks may have no surety. If Roland dies, Charles loses the life of his body; if he lives, we shall all take our end."

The felon paynims again smite with their lances upon shields and bright helmets; so great is the
50 shock of iron and steel that the flame springs out towards Heaven; and lo, how the blood and brains run down! Great is the dolor and grief of Roland when he sees so many good knights take their end; he calls to remembrance the land of France, and his

uncle, Charlemagne the good King, and he cannot help but be heavy.

Yet still he thrust through the press and did not leave from smiting. In his hand he held Durendal, his good sword, and rent hauberks, and broke helmets, and pierced hands and heads and trunks that he threw a hundred paynims to ground, they who had held themselves for good men of arms.

And on his side the lord Oliver drove forward, smiting great blows; in his hand he held Halteclere, his good and trusty sword that had not its fellow under Heaven, save only Durendal, and with it he fought valorously; all stained he was with blood even to his arms. "God!" saith Roland, "that is a goodly baron. O gentle Count, all courage and all loyalty, this day our friendship must have an end, for today, though great, woe we twain must part! Never again shall we see the Emperor; never again shall there be such lamentation in fair France. The Frankish folk will pray for us, and in holy churches orisons will be offered; certes, our souls will come into Paradise." Oliver slackens rein and spurs his horse, and in the thick of the press comes nigh unto Roland, and one saith unto the other: "Comrade, keep near me; so long as death spares me I will never fail thee."

Would ye had seen Roland and Oliver hack and hew with their swords, and the Archbishop smite with his lance! We can reckon those that fell by their hands, for the number thereof is written in charter and record; the Geste says more than four thousand. In four encounters all went well with the Franks, but the fifth was sore and grievous to them, for in this all their knights were slain save only sixty, spared by God's mercy. Before they die they will sell their lives dear.

When Count Roland is ware of the great slaughter of his men, he turns to Oliver, saying: "Sir comrade, as God may save thee, see how many a good man of arms lies on the ground; we may well have pity on sweet France, the fair, that must now be desolate of such barons. Ah, King and friend, would thou wert here! Oliver, my brother, what shall we do? How shall we send him tidings?" "Nay, I know not how to seek him," saith Oliver; "but liefer had I die than bring dishonor upon me."

Then saith Roland: "I will sound my horn of ivory, and Charles, as he passes the mountains, will hear it; and I pledge thee my faith the Franks will return again." Then saith Oliver: "Therein would be great shame for thee, and dishonor for all thy kindred, a reproach that would last all the days of their life. Thou wouldst not sound it when I bid thee, and now thou shalt not by my counsel. And if thou dost sound it, it will not be hardily, for now

---

16. **doit,** a penny.   38. **Terra Major.** The "Great Land," mentioned several times in the course of the poem, refers to Charlemagne's empire as a whole.

85. **Geste;** that is, the Latin chronicles.

both thy arms are stained with blood." "Yea," the Count answers him, "I have dealt some goodly blows."

Then saith Roland: "Sore is our battle; I will blow a blast, and Charles the King will hear it." "That would not be knightly," saith Oliver; "when I bid thee, comrade, thou didst disdain it. Had the King been here, we had not suffered this damage; but they who are afar off are free from all reproach. By this my beard, an I see again my sister, Aude the Fair, never shalt thou lie in her arms."

Then saith Roland: "Wherefore art thou wroth with me?" And Oliver answers him, saying: "Comrade, thou thyself art to blame. Wise courage is not madness, and measure is better than rashness. Through thy folly these Franks have come to their death; nevermore shall Charles the King have service at their hands. Hadst thou taken my counsel, my liege lord had been here, and this battle had been ended, and King Marsila had been taken or slain. Woe worth thy prowess, Roland! Henceforth Charles shall get no help of thee; never till God's Judgment Day shall there be such another man; but thou must die, and France shall be shamed thereby. And this day our loyal fellowship shall have an end; before this evening grievously shall we be parted."

The Archbishop, hearing them dispute together, spurs his horse with his spurs of pure gold, and comes unto them, and rebukes them, saying: "Sir Roland, and thou, Sir Oliver, in God's name I pray you, let be this strife. Little help shall we now have of thy horn; and yet it were better to sound it; if the King come, he will revenge us, and the paynims shall not go hence rejoicing. Our Franks will light off their horses, and find us dead and maimed, and they will lay us on biers, on the backs of sumpters, and will weep for us with dole and pity; and they will bury us in the courts of churches, that our bones may not be eaten by wolves and swine and dogs." "Sir, thou speakest well and truly," quoth Roland.

And therewith he sets his ivory horn to his lips, grasps it well and blows it with all the might he hath. High are the hills, and the sound echoes far, and for thirty full leagues they hear it resound. Charles and all his host hear it, and the King saith: "Our men are at battle." But Count Ganelon denies it, saying: "Had any other said so, we had deemed it great falsehood."

With dolor and pain, and in sore torment, Count Roland blows his horn of ivory, that the bright blood springs out of his mouth, and the temples of his brain are broken. Mighty is the blast of the horn, and Charles, passing the mountains, hears it; and Naymes hears it, and all the Franks listen and hear. Then saith the King: "I hear the horn of Roland; never would he sound it, an he were not at battle." But Ganelon answers him, saying: "Battle is there

none; thou art old and white and hoary, and thy words are those of a child. Well thou knowest the great pride of Roland—a marvel is it that God hath suffered it thus long. Aforetime he took Noples against thy commandment, and when the Saracens came out of the city and set upon Roland the good knight (he slew them with Durendal his sword), thereafter with water he washed away the blood which stained the meadow, that none might know of what he had done. And for a single hare he will blow his horn all day long; and now he but boasts among his fellows, for there is no folk on earth would dare do him battle. I prithee ride on. Why tarry we? The Great Land still lies far before us."

Count Roland's mouth has burst out a-bleeding, and the temples of his brain are broken. In dolor and pain he sounds his horn of ivory; but Charles hears it and the Franks hear it. Saith the King: "Long drawn is the blast of that horn." "Yea," Naymes answers, "for in sore need is the baron who blows it. Certes, our men are at battle; and he who now dissembles hath betrayed Roland. Take your arms and cry your war-cry, and succor the men of your house. Dost thou not hear Roland's call?"

The Emperor has commanded that his trumpets be sounded, and now the Franks light down from their horses and arm themselves with hauberks and helms and swords adorned with gold; fair are their shields, and goodly and great their lances, and their gonfanons are scarlet and white and blue. Then all the barons of the host get them to horse, and spur through the passes; and each saith to other: "An we may but see Roland a living man, we will strike good blows at his side." But what avails it? For they have abode too long.

Clear is the evening as was the day, and all their armor glistens in the sun, and there is great shining of hauberks, and helms, and shields painted with flowers, and lances, and gilded gonfanons. The Emperor rides on in wrath, and the Franks are full of care and foreboding; and not a man but weeps full sore and hath great fear for Roland. Then the King let take Count Ganelon, and gave him over to the cooks of his household; and he called Besgon their chief, saying: "Guard him well, as beseems a felon who hath betrayed my house." Besgon took him, and set a watch about him of a hundred of his fellows of the kitchen, both best and worst. They plucked out the hairs of Ganelon's beard and moustache, and each one dealt him four blows with his fist, and hardily they beat him with rods and staves; then they put about his neck a chain, and bound him even as they would a bear, and in derision they set him upon a sumpter. So they guard him until they return him unto Charles.

61. **Noples,** a good example of one of the unknown Spanish towns so often mentioned in *The Song of Roland.*

A Carolingian coin showing the head of Charlemagne.

High are the hills and great and dark, deep the valleys, and swift the waters. To answer Roland's horn all the trumpets are sounded, both rear and van. The Emperor rides on in wrath, and the Franks are full of care and foreboding; there is not a man but weepeth and maketh sore lament, praying to God that he spare Roland until they come unto the field, that at his side they may deal good blows. But what avails it? They have tarried too long, and may
10 not come in time.

Charles the King rides on in great wrath, and over his hauberk is spread his white beard. And all the barons of France spur mightily, not one but is full of wrath and grief that he is not with Roland the captain who is at battle with the Saracens of Spain. If he be wounded, what hope that one soul be left alive? God! what a sixty he still hath in his fellowship; no king or captain ever had better.

Roland looks abroad over hill and heath and sees
20 the great multitude of the Frankish dead, and he weeps for them as beseems a gentle knight, saying: "Lords and barons, now may God have mercy upon you, and grant Paradise to all your souls, that ye may rest among the blessed flowers. Man never saw better men of arms that ye were. Long and well, year in and year out, have ye served me, and many wide lands have ye won for the glory of Charles. Was it to such an end that he nourished you? O France, fair land, today art thou made
30 desolate by rude slaughter. Ye Frankish barons, I see you die through me, yet can I do naught to save you or defend you. May God, who knows no lie, aid you! Oliver, brother, I must not fail thee; yet I shall die of grief, an I be not slain by the sword. Sir comrade, let us get us into battle."

So Count Roland falls a-smiting again. He holds Durendal in his hand, and lays on right valiantly, so that he cleaves in twain Faldron de Pui, and slays four and twenty of the most worshipful of the
40 paynims. Never shall you see a man more desirous to revenge himself. And even as the hart flies before the hounds, so flee the heathen from before Roland. "Thou dost rightly," then said the Archbishop; "such valor well beseems a knight who bears arms and sits a good horse; in battle such a one should be fell and mighty, or he is not worth four deniers, and it behooves him to turn monk and get him into a monastery to pray the livelong day for our sins." And Roland answered him, saying: "Smite and spare not." And at these words the Franks go into 50 battle again; but great is the slaughter of the Christians.

That man who knows he shall get no mercy defends himself savagely in battle. Wherefore the Franks are fierce as lions. Marsila like a true baron sits his horse Gaignon; he spurs him well and rides on Bevon—lord he was of Beaune and Dijon—and breaks his shield, and rends his hauberk, that without other hurt he smites him dead to ground. And thereafter he slew Ivon and Ivory, and with them 60 Gerard the Old of Roussillon. Now nigh at hand is Count Roland, and he saith to the paynim: "May the Lord God bring thee to mishap! And because thou hast wrongfully slain my comrades, thou shalt thyself get a buffet before we twain dispart, and this day thou shalt learn the name of my sword." And therewith he rides upon him like a true baron, and smites off his right hand, and thereafter he takes off the head of Jurfaleu the Fair, the son of King Marsila. Thereat the paynims cry: "Now help us, 70 Mahound! O ye our gods, revenge us upon Charles! He has sent out against us into our marches men so fierce that though they die they will not give back." And one saith to another: "Let us fly." At these words a hundred thousand turn and flee, and let whosoever will call them, they will not return again.

King Marsila has lost his right hand; and now he throws his shield on earth, and pricks on his horse with his sharp spurs, and with slackened rein, flees away towards Spain. Upon twenty thousand Sara- 80 cens follow after him, nor is there one among them who is not maimed or hurt of body, and they say one to another; "The nephew of Charles has won the field."

But alack, what avails it? For though Marsila be fled, his uncle the Caliph yet abides, he who ruled Aferne, Carthage, Garmalie, and Ethiopia, a cursed land; under his lordship he has the black folk; great are their noses and large their ears, and they are with him to the number of fifty thousand. And now 90 they come up in pride and wrath, and cry aloud the war-cry of the paynims. Then saith Roland: "Now must we needs be slain, and well I know we have but a little space to live; but cursed be he who does not sell himself right dear. Lay on, lords, with your burnished swords, and debate both life and death; let not sweet France be brought to shame
46. **deniers,** pennies.

through us. When Charles, my liege lord, shall come into this field, he will see such slaughter of the Saracens, that he shall find fifteen of them dead over against each man of ours, and he will not fail to bless us."

When Roland sees the cursed folk whose skin is blacker than any ink, and who have naught of white about them save their teeth, he saith: "Now I know in very sooth that we shall die this day. Lay on, lords, and yet again I bid thee, smite." "Now foul fall him who lags behind," quoth Oliver. And at this word the Franks haste into the fray.

Now when the paynims see how few are the Franks, they have great pride and joy thereof; and one saith to another: "Certes, the Emperor is in the wrong." The Caliph bestrides a sorrel horse; he pricks him on with his spurs of gold, and smites Oliver from behind, amid the back, so that he drives the mails of his white hauberk into his body, and his lance passes out through his breast. "Now hast thou got a good buffet," quoth the Caliph. "On an ill day Charles the Great left thee in the passes; much wrong hath he done us, yet he shall not boast thereof, for on thee alone have I well revenged us."

Oliver feels that he is wounded unto death; in his hand he holds Halteclere; bright was its blade, and with it he smites the Caliph on his golden pointed helmet, that its flowers and gems fall to earth, and he cleaves the head even unto the teeth, and with the force of the blow smote him dead to earth, and said: "Foul fall thee, paynim! *Say not that I am come to my death through Charles;* and neither to thy wife, nor any other dame, shalt thou ever boast in the land from which thou art come, that thou hast taken from me so much as one farthing's worth, or hast done any hurt to me or to others." And thereafter he called to Roland for succor.

Oliver feels that he is wounded unto death; never will he have his fill of vengeance. In the thick of the press he smites valiantly, cleaving lances and embossed shields, and feet and hands and flanks and shoulders. Whoever saw him thus dismember the Saracens, and hurl one dead upon another, must call to mind true valiance; nor did he forget the war-cry of Charles, but loud and clear he cries out Montjoy! And he calls to Roland, his friend and peer: "Sir comrade, come stand thou beside me. In great dolor shall we twain soon be disparted."

Roland looks Oliver in the face; pale it is and livid and all discolored; the bright blood flows down from amid his body and falls in streams to the ground. "God!" saith the Count, "now I know not what to do. Sir comrade, woe worth thy valor! Never shall the world see again a man of thy might. Alas, fair France, today art thou stripped of goodly vassals, and fallen and undone. The Emperor will suffer great loss thereby." And so speaking he swoons upon his horse.

Lo! Roland has swooned as he sits his horse, and Oliver is wounded unto death; so much has he bled that his sight is darkened, and he can no longer distinguish any living man whether far off or near at hand; and now, as he meets his comrade, he smites him upon the helm set with gold and gems, and cleaves it down to the nasal, but does not come unto the head. At the blow Roland looks up at him, and asks him full softly and gently: "Comrade, dost thou this wittingly? I am Roland, who so loves thee. Never yet hast thou mistrusted me." Then saith Oliver: "Now I hear thee speak, but I cannot see thee; may the Lord God guard thee. I have struck thee, but I pray thy pardon." "Thou hast done me no hurt," Roland answers him; "I pardon thee before God, as here and now." So speaking each leans forward towards other, and lo! in such friendship they are disparted.

Oliver feels the anguish of death come upon him; his two eyes turn in his head; and his hearing goes from him, and all sight. He lights down from his horse and lies upon the ground, and again and again he confesses his sins; he holds out his clasped hands towards Heaven and prays God that He grant him Paradise, and he blesses Charles and sweet France, and Roland, his comrade, above all men. Then his heart fails him, and his head sinks upon his breast, and he lies stretched at all his length upon the ground. Dead is the Count and gone from hence. Roland weeps for him and is sore troubled; never on the earth shall ye see a man so sorrowful.

When Count Roland sees his friend lie prone and dead, facing the East, gently he begins to lament him: "Sir comrade, woe worth thy hardiness! We twain have held together for years and days; never didst thou me wrong or I thee. Since thou art dead, alack that I yet live." So speaking, the Count swoons as he sits Veillantif his steed, but his golden spurs hold him firm, and let him go where he will, he cannot fall.

So soon as Roland comes to his senses, and is restored from his swoon, he is ware of the great slaughter about him. Slain are the Franks; he has lost them all save only Gualter del Hum and the Archbishop. Gualter has come down from the mountains where he fought hardily with those of Spain; the paynims conquered, and his men are slain, and howsoever unwillingly, he must perforce flee down into the valley and call upon Roland for succor. "O gentle Count, brave captain, where art thou? For where thou art, I have no fear. It is I, Gualter, who conquered Maelgut, I the nephew of Droon the old, the hoary, I whom thou wert wont to love for my hardihood. Now my shield is pierced, and the shaft of my lance is broken, and my hauberk rent and unmailed; I have the wounds of eight lances in my body, and I must die, but dear have I sold myself."

So he saith, and Roland hears him, and spurs his horse and rides towards him.

"Sir Gualter," then saith Roland, "thou hast, as I know, done battle with the paynims, and thou art a hardy and valiant warrior. A thousand good knights thou didst take with thee; my men they were, and now I would ask them of thee again; give them over to me, for sore is my need." But Gualter makes answer: "Never again shall ye see one of them alive. I left them on the dolorous field. We encountered a great host of Saracens, Turks and Armenians, Persians, and men of Canaan and of Lude, warriors of the best, mounted on swift Arabian horses. And we fought a battle so fierce that never a paynim shall boast thereof; sixty thousand lie dead and bleeding; and we, on our part, lost all our Franks, but vengeance we took therefor with our swords of steel. Rent and torn is my hauberk, and deadly wounds I have in side and flank, and from all my body flows out the bright blood, and takes from me my strength; certes, my time is nigh spent. Thy man am I, and I look to thee as protector. Blame me not, that I fled." "Nay, I blame thee no whit," quoth Count Roland. "But now do thou aid me, so long as thou art a living man."

Full sorrowful is Roland and of great wrath; he falls a-smiting in the thick of the press, and of those of Spain he cast twenty to the ground dead, and Gualter slew six, and the Archbishop five. Then say the paynims: "Fierce and fell are these men. Take ye heed, lords, that they go not hence alive. He who doth not set upon them is traitor, and recreant he who lets them go hence." Then the hue and cry begins again, and from all sides they close about the three Franks.

Count Roland is a full noble warrior, and a right good knight is Gualter del Hum; the Archbishop is of good valor and well tried; not one would leave aught to his fellows, and together, in the thick of the press, they smite the paynims. A thousand Saracens get them to foot, and there are still forty thousand on horseback, yet in sooth they dare not come nigh unto the three, but they hurl upon them lances and spears, arrows and darts and sharp javelins. In the first storm they slew Gualter, and sundered the shield of Turpin of Rheims, broke his helmet and wounded him in his head, and rent and tore his hauberk that he was pierced in the body by four spears; and his horse was slain under him. The Archbishop falls; great is the pity thereof.

But so soon as Turpin of Rheims finds himself beaten down to earth with the wounds of four lances in his body, he right speedily gets him afoot again; he looks toward Roland, and hastes to him, and saith: "I am nowise vanquished; no good vassal yields him so long as he is a living man." And he draws Almace, his sword of brown steel, and in the thick of the press he deals well more than a thousand buffets. Afterwards Charles bore witness that Turpin spared himself no whit, for around him they found four hundred dead, some wounded, some cut in twain amid the body, and some whose heads had been smitten off; so saith the Geste and he who was on the field, the valiant Saint Gilles, for whom God wrought miracles; he it was who wrote the annals of the monastery of Laon. And he who knows not this, knows naught of the matter.

Count Roland fights right nobly, but all his body is a-sweat and burning hot, and in his head he hath great pain and torment, for when he sounded his horn, he rent his temples. But he would fain know that Charles were coming, and he takes his horn of ivory, and feebly he sounds it. The Emperor stops to listen: "Lords," he saith, "now has great woe come upon us; this day shall we lose Roland my nephew; I wot from the blast of his horn that he is nigh to death. Let him who would reach the field ride fast. Now sound ye all the trumpets of the host." Then they blew sixty thousand, so loud that the mountains resound and the valleys give answer. The paynims hear them and have no will to laugh, but one saith to another; "We shall have ado with Charles anon."

Say the paynims: "The Emperor is returning; we hear the trumpets of France; if Charles come hither, we shall suffer sore loss. Yet if Roland live, our war will begin again, and we shall lose Spain our land." Then four hundred, armed in their helmets, and of the best of those on the field, gather together, and on Roland they make onset fierce and sore. Now is the Count hard bestead.

When Count Roland sees them draw near he waxes hardy and fierce and terrible; never will he yield as long as he is a living man. He sits his horse Veillantif, and spurs him well with his spurs of fine gold, and rides into the stour upon them all; and at his side is Archbishop Turpin. And the Saracens say one to another: "Now save yourselves, friends. We have heard the trumpets of France; Charles the mighty King is returning."

Count Roland never loved the cowardly, or the proud, or the wicked, or any knight who was not a good vassal, and now he calls to Archbishop Turpin, saying: "Lord! thou art on foot and I am a-horseback, for thy love I would make halt, and together we will take the good and the ill; I will not leave thee for any living man; the blows of Almace and of Durendal shall give back this assault to the paynims." Then saith the Archbishop: "A traitor is he who doth not smite; Charles is returning, and well will he revenge us."

64–66. **the valiant Saint Gilles . . . Laon.** Saint Giles (Aegidius) was not mentioned in the chronicles as present with Charlemagne's army as it came upon the battlefield of Roncevals; perhaps the poet meant that Saint Giles was present in spirit only.

"In an evil hour," say the paynims, "were we born; woeful is the day that has dawned for us! We have lost our lords and our peers. Charles the valiant cometh hither again with his great host; we hear the clear trumpets of those of France, and great is the noise of their cry of Montjoy. Count Roland is of such might he cannot be vanquished by any mortal man. Let us hurl our missiles upon him, and then leave him." Even so they did; and cast upon him many a dart and javelin, and spears and lances and feathered arrows. They broke and rent the shield of Roland, tore open and unmailed his hauberk, but did not pierce his body; but Veillantif was wounded in thirty places, and fell from under the Count, dead. Then the paynims flee, and leave him; Count Roland is left alone and on foot.

The paynims flee in anger and wrath, and in all haste they fare toward Spain. Count Roland did not pursue after them, for he has lost his steed Veillantif, and whether he will or no, is left on foot. He went to the help of Archbishop Turpin, and unlaced his golden helm from his head, and took off his white hauberk of fine mail, and he tore his tunic into strips and with the pieces bound his great wounds. Then he gathers him in his arms, and lays him down full softly upon the green grass, and gently he beseeches him: "O gracious baron, I pray thy leave. Our comrades whom we so loved are slain, and it is not meet to leave them thus. I would go seek and find them, and range them before thee." "Go and return again," quoth the Archbishop. "Thank God, this field is thine and mine."

Roland turns away and fares on alone through the field; he searches the valleys and the hills; and there he found Ivon and Ivory, and Gerier his comrade, and he found Engelier the Gascon, and Berengier, and Oton, and he found Anseis and Samson, and Gerard the Old of Rousillon. One by one he hath taken up the barons, and hath come with them unto the Archbishop, and places them in rank before him. The Archbishop cannot help but weep; he raises his hand and gives them benediction, and thereafter saith: "Alas for you, lords! May God the Glorious receive your souls, and bring them into Paradise among the blessed flowers. And now my own death torments me sore; never again shall I see the great Emperor."

Again Roland turned away to search the field; and when he found Oliver his comrade, he gathered him close against his breast, and as best he might returned again unto the Archbishop, and laid his comrade upon a shield beside the others; and the Archbishop absolved and blessed him. Then their sorrow and pity broke forth again, and Roland saith: "Oliver, fair comrade, thou wert son of the great Duke Reinier, who held the marches of Rivier and Genoa; for the breaking of lances or the piercing of shields, for vanquishing and affrighting the proud, for upholding and counselling the good, never in any land was there a better knight."

When Roland sees the peers, and Oliver whom he so loved, lying dead, pity takes him and he begins to weep; and his face is all discolored; so great is his grief he cannot stand upright, but will he, nill he, falls to the ground in a swoon. Saith the Archbishop: "Alack for thee, good baron!"

When the Archbishop sees Roland swoon, he has such dole as he has never known before. He stretches out his hand and takes the horn of ivory, for in Roncevals there is a swift streamlet, and he would go to it to bring of its water to Roland. Slowly and falteringly he sets forth, but so weak is he that he cannot walk; his strength has gone from him; too much blood has he lost, and before a man might cross an acre his heart faileth, and he falls forward upon his face, and the anguish of death comes upon him.

When Count Roland recovers from his swoon, he gets upon his feet with great torment; he looks up and he looks down, and beyond his comrades, on the green grass, he sees that goodly baron, the Archbishop, appointed of God in His stead. Turpin saith his *mea culpa*, and looks up, and stretches out his two hands towards Heaven, and prays God that He may grant him Paradise. And so he dies, the warrior of Charles. Long had he waged strong war against the paynims, both by his mighty battling and his goodly sermons. May God grant him His holy benison.

Count Roland sees the Archbishop upon the ground; his bowels have fallen out of his body, and his brains are oozing out of his forehead; Roland takes his fair, white hands and crosses them upon his breast between his two collar-bones; and lifting up his voice, he mourns for him, after the manner of his people: "Ah, gentle man, knight of high parentage, now I commend thee to the heavenly Glory; never will there be a man who shall serve Him more willingly; never since the day of the apostles hath there been such a prophet to uphold the law, and win the hearts of men; may thy soul suffer no dole or torment, but may the doors of Paradise be opened to thee."

Now Roland feels that death is near him, and his brains flow out at his ears; he prays to the Lord God for his peers, that He will receive them, and he prays to the Angel Gabriel for himself. That he may be free from all reproach, he takes his horn of ivory in the one hand, and Durendal, his sword, in the other, and farther than a cross-bow can cast an arrow, through a cornfield he goeth on towards Spain. At the crest of a hill, beneath two fair trees, are four stairs of marble; there he falls down on the green grass in a swoon, for death is close upon him.

High are the hills, and very tall are the trees; the four stones are of shining marble; and there Count Roland swoons upon the green grass. Meantime a Saracen is watching him; he has stained his face and his body with blood, and feigning death, he lies still among his fellows; but now he springs to his feet and hastens forward. Fair he was, and strong, and of good courage; and in his pride he breaks out into mighty wrath, and seizes upon Roland, both him and his arms, and he cries: "Now is the nephew of Charles overthrown. This his sword will I carry into Arabia." But at his touch the Count recovered his senses.

Roland feels that his sword hath been taken from him; he opens his eyes, and saith: "Certes, thou art not one of our men." He holds his horn of ivory, which he never lets out of his grasp, and he smites the Saracen upon the helm, which was studded with gold and gems, and he breaks steel and head and bones, so that his two eyes start out, and he falls down dead at his feet. Then saith Roland: "Coward, what made thee so bold as to lay hands upon me, whether right or wrong? No man shall hear it but shall hold thee a fool. Now is my horn of ivory broken in the bell, and its gold and its crystals have fallen."

Now Roland feels that his sight is gone from him. With much striving he gets upon his feet; the color has gone from his face; before him lies a brown stone, and in his sorrow and wrath he smites ten blows upon it. The sword grates upon the rock, but neither breaks nor splinters; and the Count saith: "Holy Mary, help me now! Ah, Durendal, alas for your goodness! *Now am I near to death, and have no more need of you.* Many a fight in the field have I won with you; many a wide land have I conquered with you, lands now ruled by Charles with the white beard. May the man who would flee before another never possess you. For many a day have you been held by a right good lord; never will there be such another in France the free."

Roland smote upon the block of *hard stone,* and the steel grates, but neither breaks nor splinters. And when he sees that he can in nowise break it, he laments, saying: "O Durendal, how fair and bright thou art, in the sunlight how thou flashest and shinest! Charles was once in the Valley of Moriane, when God commanded him by one of His angels that he should give thee to a chieftain Count; then the great and noble King girded thee upon me; and with thee I won for him Anjou and Bretagne, and I conquered Poitou and Maine for him, and for him I conquered Normandy the free, and Provence, and Aquitaine; and Lombardy, and all of Romagna; and I conquered for him Bavaria, and Flanders, and Bulgaria, and all of Poland; Constantinople, which now pays him fealty, and Saxony, where he may

work his will. And I conquered for him Wales, and Scotland, and Ireland, and England, which he holds as his demesne. Many lands and countries have I won with thee, lands which Charles of the white beard rules. And now am I heavy of heart because of this sword; rather would I die than that it should fall into the hands of the paynims. Lord God our Father, let not this shame fall upon France."

And again Roland smote upon the brown stone, and beyond all telling shattered it; the sword grates, but springs back again into the air and is neither dinted nor broken. And when the Count sees that he may in nowise break it, he laments, saying: "O Durendal, how fair and holy a thing thou art! In thy golden hilt is many a relic—a tooth of Saint Peter, and some of the blood of Saint Basil, and hairs from the head of my lord, Saint Denis, and a bit of the raiment of the Virgin Mary. It is not meet that thou fall into the hands of the paynims; only Christians should wield thee. May no coward ever possess thee! Many wide lands have I conquered with thee, lands which Charles of the white beard rules; and thereby is the Emperor great and mighty."

Now Roland feels that death has come upon him, and that it creeps down from his head to his heart. In all haste he fares under a pine tree, and hath cast himself down upon his face on the green grass. Under him he laid his sword and his horn of ivory; and he turned his face toward the paynim folk, for he would that Charles and all his men should say that the gentle Count had died a conqueror. Speedily and full often he confesses his sins, and in atonement he offers his glove to God.

Roland lies on a high peak looking towards Spain; he feels that his time is spent, and with one hand he beats upon his breast: "O God, I have sinned; forgive me through Thy might the wrongs, both great and small, which I have done from the day I was born even to this day on which I was smitten." With his right hand he holds out his glove to God; and lo! the angels of Heaven come down to him.

Count Roland lay under the pine tree; he has turned his face toward Spain, and he begins to call many things to remembrance—all the lands he had won by his valor, and sweet France, and the men of his lineage, and Charles, his liege lord, who had brought him up in his household; and he cannot help but weep. But he would not wholly forget himself, and again he confesses his sins and begs forgiveness of God: "Our Father, who art truth, who raised up Lazarus from the dead, and who defended Daniel from the lions, save Thou my soul from the perils to which it is brought through the sins I

58–60. And . . . demesne. Charlemagne never conquered Britain, of course; but William the Conqueror's successful expedition may have led the poet to transfer this feat to Roland. 90. offers . . . God. To hand the glove to someone was to submit to him.

wrought in my life-days." With his right hand he offers his glove to God, and Saint Gabriel has taken it from his hand. Then his head sinks on his arm, and with clasped hands he hath gone to his end. And God sent him His cherubim, and Saint Michael of the Seas, and with them went Saint Gabriel, and they carried the soul of the Count into Paradise.

Knight's tournament costume of the fifteenth century in France.

The Nibelungenlied

In what is now Austria there was written about the middle of the twelfth century an epic poem which has ever since been recognized as the German contribution to the literature of the national epic. *The Nibelungenlied* is actually a blending of more than one ancient Germanic saga into one medieval epic poem of German feudal aristocracy. The poem falls clearly into two parts: the first part, culminating in the death and burial of Siegfried, is based upon the celebrated *Volsungasaga* of Scandinavian legendry; the second, recounting the story of Kriemhild's revenge for the killing of her husband, Siegfried, is derived chiefly from the only slightly less renowned *Dietrich Saga* of Continental origin. The *Volsungasaga*, except for a passing reference in the Anglo-Saxon epic *Beowulf* of the eighth or ninth century, is first told in the *Poetic* or *Elder Edda* of the Scandinavian countries, dating from some time near 900. An independent Norse version survives from about 1200;

this is a long epic poem based upon the account in the *Poetic Edda*. The *Prose* or *Younger Edda* of about 1230, however, contains an epitome of the Norse version of the saga, which is extremely useful as a means of understanding some of the details in *The Nibelungenlied*.

Even in this epitome the early deeds of Sigurd (Siegfried) are given more fully than in *The Nibelungenlied*. Indeed, the German poem seems to know very little about these, for it presents Siegfried as a warrior of great, established reputation, with a few legendary and mythical attributes (particularly his cloak of invisibility, his fabulous physical strength, and his spot of vulnerability), who wins Brunhild for King Gunther and then falls through the treacherous acts of Brunhild, Gunther, and Hagen. The intimacy between Siegfried and Brunhild implied in the Norse version has been somewhat diluted in *The Nibelungenlied*, and Brunhild herself tends to fade out of the story.

The entire second part of *The Nibelungenlied*, which follows the burial of Siegfried, has drawn upon an extensive amount of material from other Germanic legends, notably, as has been said, from the *Dietrich Saga*. It is concerned primarily with Kriemhild, widow of Siegfried and later wife of King Etzel (the Hun Attila of history). Kriemhild corresponds to Gudrun in the Norse versions; her name has evidently been suggested by that of the Norse Gudrun's mother—an interesting example of simple "contamination" of details in different versions of what was originally the same story. Kriemhild plans and achieves a notable revenge upon the slayers of Siegfried, although she loses her own life in doing so. Since, in *The Nibelungenlied*, Gunther and Hagen thrive and prosper after Siegfried's murder, it is necessary for Kriemhild to revenge herself against them rather than against her second husband Etzel (the Norse Atli), as Gudrun did in the *Volsungasaga*. In any event, the poem ends in a grand slaughter.

Certain characters in *The Nibelungenlied* are based upon historical personages: King Gunther of the Burgundians was defeated and killed by the Huns in the year 437, although the famous Attila (Etzel or Atli) was not actually involved in this battle. Dietrich of Bern is Theodoric the Great, the Ostrogothic conqueror of Italy, who lived from 475 to 526. The natural implication is that other characters have a historical basis; such an implication arises in the study of any epic. But the four other chief characters in the poem—Siegfried, Brunhild, Kriemhild, and Hagen—are not at present identifiable with any specific historical figures; theirs seems to be clearly a legendary origin, and in the cases of Siegfried and Brunhild there is every reason to suppose that they belong to Germanic mythology.

At any rate *The Nibelungenlied* is more important as fiction than as fact. It glows on almost every page with the glamor and pomp of medieval feudal aristocracy, yet this encrustation of feudalism is not in the slightest degree worthy of the chivalric age. No more savage succession of incidents will be found in the entire field of the epic. If, as some maintain, this is not only the great epic of Germany but in its widest sense the epic of the Germanic people as well, it implies a certain amount of brutality in the Germanic imagination. Not a character in the story, save perhaps Dietrich of Bern—a wayfarer from another saga—is in any way attractive. Treachery, cruelty, childishness, vindictive bloodthirstiness of motive, greed, and a kind of cosmic destructiveness fill the lines of the whole poem. Here is none of the knightly fealty of the Frankish Roland, nor the sober steadiness and loyalty of the "English" Scandinavian Beowulf (either of whom would be a more admirable representative of the Germanic race). The same moral strictures can be expressed in regard to the Norse saga, of course; but in the Norse saga there is little of the pride and circumstance of what is presumed to be medieval Christian chivalric feudalism, and therefore there is more excuse for its having the qualities we deplore in *The Nibelungenlied*. For, despite the medieval atmosphere of *The Nibelungenlied*, the gore-caked warriors at King Etzel's castle are not fighting paynim infidels as Roland was or monstrous incarnations of evil as was Beowulf. It is, rather, internecine warfare of the crudest kind, although described in extremely talented narrative verse.

The Nibelungenlied

ADVENTURE 2. *Of Siegfried*

IN the Netherlands there grew the child of a noble king (his father had for name, Siegmund, his mother Siegelind), in a mighty castle, known far and wide, in the lowlands of the Rhine: Xanten, men called it. Of this hero I sing, how fair he grew. Free he was of every blemish. Strong and famous he later became, this valiant man. Ho! what great worship he won in this world! Siegfried hight this good and doughty knight. Full many kingdoms did he put to the test through his warlike mood. Through his strength of body he rode into many lands. Ho! what bold warriors he after found in the Burgundian land! Mickle wonders might one tell of Siegfried in his prime, in youthful days; what honors he received and how fair of body he. The most stately women held him in their love; with the zeal which was his due men trained him. But of himself what virtues he attained! Truly his father's lands were honored, that he was found in all things of such right lordly mind. Now was he become of age that he might ride to court. Gladly the people saw him, many a maid wished that his desire might ever bear him hither. Enow gazed on him with favor; of this

the prince was well aware. Full seldom was the youth allowed to ride without a guard of knights. Siegmund and Siegelind bade deck him out in brave attire. The older knights who were acquaint with courtly custom, had him in their care. Well therefore might he win both folk and land.

Now he was of the strength that he bare weapons well. Whatever he needed thereto, this he had enow. With purpose he began to woo fair ladies; these bold Siegfried courted well in proper wise. Then bade Siegmund have cried to all his men, that he would hold a feasting with his loving kindred. The tidings thereof men brought into the lands of other kings. To the many strangers and the home-folk he gave steeds and armor. Wheresoever any was found who, because of his birth, should become a knight, these noble youths were summoned to the land for the feasting. Here with the youthful prince they gained the knightly sword. Wonders might one tell of this great feast; Siegmund and Siegelind wist well how to gain great worship with their gifts, of which their hands dealt out great store. Wherefore one beheld many a stranger riding to their realm. Four hundred sword-thanes were to put on knightly garb with Siegfried. Many a fair maid was aught but idle with the work, for he was beloved of them all. Many precious stones the ladies inlaid on the gold, which together with the edging they would work upon the dress of the proud young warriors, for this must be done.

The host bade make benches for the many valiant men, for the midsummer festival, at which Siegfried should gain the name of knight. Then full many a noble knight and many a high-born squire did hie them to the minster. Right were the elders in that they served the young, as had been done to them afore. Pastimes they had and hope of much good cheer. To the honor of God a mass was sung; then there rose from the people full great a press, as the youths were made knights in courtly wise, with such great honors as might not ever lightly be again. Then they ran to where they found saddled many a steed. In Siegmund's court the hurtling waxed so fierce that both palace and hall were heard to ring; the high-mettled warriors clashed with mighty sound. From young and old one heard many a shock, so that the splintering of the shafts reëchoed to the clouds. Truncheons were seen flying out before the palace from the hand of many a knight. This was done with zeal. At length the host bade cease the

The Nibelungenlied ▲ Translated by Daniel Shumway. Reprinted by permission of and arrangement with Houghton Mifflin Company, the authorized publishers.
The Nibelungenlied means the song or lay of the Nibelungs. These were a legendary Germanic people whose name is believed to mean "Children of the Mist." 2. **Siegmund**, originally the hero of an independent legend, as told in the *Volsungasaga* of Norse tradition. 5. **Xanten**, Santen, a town in Germany near Düsseldorf.

47. **sword-thanes**, young squires who were eligible for the knighthood. 55. **midsummer festival**, the summer solstice (about June 21), originally a pagan German festival which the medieval church brought into agreement with St. John's Eve (June 23), a day celebrated by merry-making and bonfires. 66. **hurtling**, a form of jousting, featuring head-on clashes of armed knights. 67. **palace**, as used in medieval romances, a large hall standing alone and used for audiences and receptions. 71. **Truncheons**, originally, as here, fragments of lances or spears.

A tournament, as sketched in a late fifteenth-century German manuscript.

tourney and the steeds were led away. Upon the turf one saw all to-shivered many a mighty buckler and great store of precious stones from the bright spangles of the shields. Through the hurtling this did hap.

Then the guests of the host betook them to where men bade them sit. With good cheer they refreshed them and with the very best of wine, of which one bare full plenty. To the strangers and the home-folk was shown worship enow. Through much pastime they had throughout the day, many of the strolling folk forsware all rest. They served for the largess, which men found there richly, whereby Siegmund's whole land was decked with praise. Then bade the king enfeoff Siegfried, the youth, with land and castles, as he himself had done. Much his hand bestowed upon the sword-companions. The journey liked them well, that to this land they were come. The feasting lasted until the seventh day. Siegelind, the noble queen, for the love of her son, dealt out ruddy gold in time-honored wise. Full well she wot how to make him beloved of the folk. Scarce could a poor man be found among the strolling mimes. Steeds and raiment were scattered by their hand, as if they were to live not one more day. I trow that never did serving folk use such great bounty. With worshipful honors the company departed hence. Of the mighty barons the tale doth tell that they desired the youth unto their lord, but of this the stately knight, Sir Siegfried, listed naught. Forasmuch as both Siegmund and Siegelind were still alive, the dear child of them twain wished not to wear a crown, but fain would he become a lord against all the deeds of force within his lands, whereof the bold and daring knight was sore adread.

[So Siegfried, hearing reports of the beauty of Kriemhild, goes to Worms, seat of King Gunther of Burgundy.

He makes a tremendous impression and fights successfully against the Saxons, winning the favor of his Kriemhild, to whom he is ultimately married. Meanwhile Gunther has become enamored of the peerless princess Brunhild of Isenland; he manages to win her theoretically, but in the contest to establish his right to this Amazon-at-arms, he is obliged to call upon the most spectacular Siegfried. Siegfried, relying upon a cloak of invisibility, substitutes for Gunther in a spear-throwing contest. And later, though married to Kriemhild, he helps Gunther once more in a more intimate way. Gunther is unable to consummate his marriage with Brunhild, but Siegfried subdues her. Unfortunately for all, he takes from the hand of Brunhild a ring, the famous Ring of the Nibelungs, and gives it to his wife, Kriemhild. At first all goes well; then—]

ADVENTURE 14. *How the queens reviled each other*

On a day before the vesper tide a great turmoil arose, which many knights made in the court, where they plied their knightly sports for pastime's sake, and a great throng of men and women hasted there to gaze. The royal queens had sat them down together and talked of two worshipful knights.

Then spake the fair Kriemhild: 'I have a husband who by right should rule over all these kingdoms.'

Quoth Lady Brunhild: 'How might that be? If none other lived but he and thou, then might these kingdoms own his sway, but the while Gunther liveth, this may never hap.'

Kriemhild replied: 'Now dost thou see, how he standeth, how right royally he walketh before the knights, as the moon doth before the stars? Therefore must I needs be merry of mood.'

Said Lady Brunhild: 'However stately be thy husband, howso worthy and fair, yet must thou grant the palm to Knight Gunther, the noble brother of thine. Know of a truth, he must be placed above all kings.'

Then Kriemhild spake again: 'So doughty is my husband, that I have not lauded him without good cause. His worship is great in many things. Dost thou believe it, Brunhild, he is easily Gunther's peer.'

'Forsooth thou must not take it amiss of me, Kriemhild, for I have not spoken thus without good reason. I heard them both aver, when I saw them first of all, and the king was victor against me in the games, and when he won my love in such knightly wise, that he was liegeman to the king, and Siegfried himself declared the same. I hold him therefore as my vassal, sith I heard him speak thus himself.'

Then spake fair Kriemhild: 'Ill had I then sped. How could my noble brothers have so wrought, that I should be a mere vassal's bride? Therefore I do beseech thee, Brunhild, in friendly wise, that for my sake thou kindly leave off this speech.'

'I'll not leave it off,' quoth the king's wife. 'Why

should I give up so many a knight, who with the warrior doth owe us service?'

Kriemhild, the passing fair, waxed wroth out of wit. 'Thou must forego that he ever do you a vassal's service; he is worthier than my brother Gunther, the full noble man. Thou must retract what I have heard thee say. Certes, it wondereth me, sith he be thy vassal and thou hast so much power over us twain, why he hath rendered thee no tribute so long a time.
10 By right I should be spared thy overweening pride.'

'Thou bearest thee too high,' spake the king's wife. 'I would fain see whether men will hold thee in such high honor as they do me.'

The ladies both grew wonderly wroth of mood. Then spake the Lady Kriemhild: 'This must now hap. Sith thou hast declared my husband for thy liegeman, now must the men of the two kings perceive today whether I durst walk before the queen to church. Thou must see today that I am noble and
20 free and that my husband is worthier than thine; nor will I myself be taxed therewith. Thou shalt mark today how thy liegewoman goeth to court before the knights of the Burgundian land. I myself shall be more worshipful than any queen was known to be, who ever wore a crown.' Great hate enow rose then betwixt the ladies.

Then Brunhild answered: 'Wilt thou not be a liegewoman of mine, so must thou sunder thee with thy ladies from my train when that we go to church.'
30 To this Kriemhild replied: 'In faith that shall be done.'

'Now array you, my maids,' spake Siegfried's wife. 'I must be here without reproach. Let this be seen today, and ye do have rich weeds. Brunhild shall fain deny what she hath here averred.'

They needed not much bidding, but sought rich robes and many a dame and maid attired her well. Then the wife of the noble king went forth with her train. Fair Kriemhild, too, was well arrayed and
40 three and forty maidens with her, whom she had brought hither to the Rhine. They wore bright vesture wrought in Araby, and thus the fair-fashioned maids betook them to the minster. All Siegfried's men awaited them before the house. The folk had marvel whence it chanced that the queens were seen thus sundered, so that they did not walk together as afore. From this did many a warrior later suffer dire distress. Here before the minster stood Gunther's wife, while many a good knight had pastime with
50 the comely dames whom they there espied.

Then came the Lady Kriemhild with a large and noble train. Whatever kind of clothes the daughters of noble knights have ever worn, these were but the wind against her retinue. She was so rich in goods, that what the wives of thirty kings could not purvey, that Kriemhild did. An one would wish to, yet he could not aver that men had ever seen such costly

dresses as at this time her fair-fashioned maidens wore. Kriemhild had not done it, save to anger Brunhild. They met before the spacious minster. 60 Through her great hate the mistress of the house in evil wise bade Kriemhild stand: 'Forsooth no vassaless should ever walk before the queen.'

Then spake the fair Kriemhild (angry was her mood): 'Couldst thou have held thy peace, 'twere well for thee. Thou hast disgraced thee and the fair body of thine. How might a vassal's leman ever be the wife of any king?'

'Whom callest thou here leman?' spake the queen.

'That call I thee,' quoth Kriemhild. 'Thy fair per- 70 son was first caressed by Siegfried, my dear husband. Certes, it was not my brother who won thy maidhood. Whither could thy wits have wandered? It was an evil trick. Wherefore didst thou let him love thee, sith he be thy vassal? I hear thee make plaint without good cause,' quoth Kriemhild.

'I' faith,' spake then Brunhild, 'Gunther shall hear of this.'

'What is that to me?' said Kriemhild. 'Thy pride hath bewrayed thee. With words thou hast claimed 80 me for thy service. Know, by my troth, it will ever grieve me, for I shall be no more thy faithful friend.'

Then Brunhild wept. Kriemhild delayed no longer, but entered the minster with her train before the queen. Thus there rose great hatred, from which bright eyes grew dim and moist.

Whatso men did or sang to God's service there, the time seemed far too long for Brunhild, for she was sad of heart and mood. Many a brave knight and a good must later rue this day. Brunhild with 90 her ladies now went forth and stopped before the minster. Her thought: 'Kriemhild must tell me more of what this word-shrewd woman hath so loudly charged me. Hath Siegfried made boast of this, 'twill cost his life.'

Now the noble Kriemhild came with many a valiant liegeman. Lady Brunhild spake: 'Stand still a while. Ye have declared me for a leman; that must ye let be seen. Know, that through thy speech, I have fared full ill.' 100

Then spake the Lady Kriemhild: 'Ye should have let me pass. I'll prove it by the ring of gold I have upon my hand, and which my lover brought me when he first lay at your side.'

Brunhild had never seen so ill a day. She spake: 'This costly hoop of gold was stolen from me, and hath been hid full long a time from me in evil wise. I'll find out yet who hath ta'en it from me.'

Both ladies now had fallen into grievous wrath.

Kriemhild replied: 'I'll not be called a thief. Thou 110 hadst done better to have held thy peace, an thou hold thine honor dear. I'll prove it by the girdle

67. leman, paramour or mistress.

which I wear about my waist, that I lie not. Certes, my Siegfried became thy lord.'

She wore the cord of silk of Nineveh, set with precious stones; in sooth 't was fair enow. When Brunhild spied it, she began to weep. Gunther and all the Burgundian men must needs now learn of this.

Then spake the queen: 'Bid the prince of the Rhineland come hither. I will let him hear how his sister hath mocked me. She saith here openly that I be Siegfried's wife.'

The king came with knights, and when he saw his love a-weeping, how gently he spake: 'Pray tell me, dear lady, who hath done you aught?'

She answered to the king: 'I must stand unhappy; thy sister would fain part me from all mine honors. I make here plaint to thee, she doth aver that Siegfried, her husband, hath had me as his leman.'

Quoth King Gunther: 'Then hath she done ill.'

'She weareth here my girdle, which I have lost, and my ring of ruddy gold. It doth repent me sore that I was ever born, unless be thou clearest me of this passing great shame; for that I'll serve thee ever.'

King Gunther spake: 'Have him come hither. He must let us hear if he hath made boast of this, or he must make denial, the hero of Netherland.' One bade fetch at once Kriemhild's love.

When Siegfried saw the angry dames (he wist not of the tale), how quickly that he spake: 'I fain would know why these ladies weep, or for what cause the king hath had me fetched.'

Then King Gunther spake: 'It doth rue me sore, forsooth. My Lady Brunhild hath told me here a tale, that thou hast boasted thou wast the first to clasp her lovely body in thine arms; this Lady Kriemhild, thy wife, doth say.'

Then spake Lord Siegfried: 'An she hath told this tale, she shall rue it sore, or ever I turn back, and I'll clear me with solemn oaths in front of all thy men, that I have not told her this.'

Quoth the king of the Rhineland: 'Let that be seen. The oath thou dost offer, and let it now be given, shall free thee of all false charges.' ·

They bade the proud Burgundians form a ring. Siegfried, the bold, stretched out his hand for the oath; then spake the mighty king: 'Thy great innocence is so well known to me, that I will free thee of that of which my sister doth accuse thee, and say, thou hast never done this thing.'

Siegfried replied: 'If it boot my lady aught to have thus saddened Brunhild, that will surely cause me boundless grief.'

Then the lusty knights and good gazed one upon the other. 'One should so train women,' spake again Siegfried, the knight, 'that they leave haughty words unsaid. Forbid it to thy wife, and I'll do the same to mine. In truth, I do shame me of her great discourtesie.'

Many fair ladies were parted by the speech. Brunhild mourned so sore, that it moved King Gunther's men to pity. Then came Hagen of Troneg to his sovran lady. He found her weeping, and asked what grief she had. She told him then the tale. On the spot he vowed that Kriemhild's lord should rue it sore, or he would nevermore be glad. Ortwin and Gernot joined their parley and these heroes counseled Siegfried's death. Gieselher, the son of the noble Uta, came hither too. When he heard the talk, he spake full true: 'Ye trusty knights, wherefore do ye this? Siegfried hath not merited forsooth such hate, that he should therefore lose his life. Certes, women oft grow angry over little things.'

'Shall we then raise cuckolds?' answered Hagen; 'such good knights would gain from that but little honor. Because he hath boasted of my liege lady, I will rather die, an it cost him not his life.'

Then spake the king himself: 'He hath shown us naught but love and honor, so let him live. What booteth it, if I now should hate the knight? He was ever faithful to us, and that right willingly.'

Knight Ortwin of Metz then spake: 'His great prowess shall not in sooth avail him aught. If my lord permit, I'll do him every evil.'

So without cause the heroes had declared a feud against him. In this none followed, save that Hagen counseled all time Knight Gunther that if Siegfried no longer lived, then many knightly lands would own his sway. At this the king grew sad, so they let it rest.

Jousting was seen once more. Ho! what stout shafts they splintered before the minster in the presence of Siegfried's wife, even down to the hall! Enow of Gunther's men were now in wrath. The king spake: 'Let be this murderous rage; he is born to our honor and to our joy. Then, too, the wonderly bold man is so fierce of strength, that none durst match him, if he marked it.'

'No, not he,' spake Hagen then. 'Ye may well keep still; I trow to bring it to pass in secret, that he rue Brunhild's tears. Certes, Hagen hath broken with him for all time.'

Then spake King Gunther: 'How might that chance?'

3. silk of Nineveh. Oriental materials were introduced into Europe extensively at the time of the Crusades, although the name given them did not necessarily correspond to their place of origin. Here "Nineveh" merely indicates a general locality in the Near East.

63. Troneg, the corrupted name of an ancient Roman colony, Colonia Trajana, on the Lower Rhine. Hagen would therefore seem to be a Frank rather than a Burgundian. 67-68. Ortwin and Gernot. Ortwin is merely another knight in the story, but Gernot (Godomar, Gutthormr) is described in the first Adventure as the brother of Gunther and Kriemhild. 69. Gieselher, the youngest brother of Kriemhild and Gunther. 70. Uta, the mother of Kriemhild.

To this Hagen made answer: 'I'll let you hear. We'll bid messengers, that be not known to any here, ride into our land, to declare war upon us openly. Then do ye say before your guests that ye and your men will take the field. When that is done, he will vow to serve you then, and from this he shall lose his life, an I learn the tale from the bold knight's wife.'

The king followed his liegeman in evil wise. These chosen knights gan plan great faithlessness, or ever any one was ware. From two women's quarreling full many a hero lost his life.

ADVENTURE 15. *How Siegfried was betrayed*

Upon the fourth morning two and thirty men were seen to ride to court and the tale was brought to mighty Gunther that war had been declared. The very direst woes befell fair women from a lie. They gained leave to come before the king and say that they were Liudeger's men, whom Siegfried's hand had conquered afore and had brought as hostages to Gunther's land. He greeted then the messengers and bade them go and seat them. One among them spake: 'My lord, pray let us stand till we have told the message we do bear you. This know, ye have of a truth many a mother's son as foe. Liudegast and Liudeger, whom ye one time gave grievous sores, declare a feud against you and are minded to ride with an army to this land.' The king waxed wroth when he heard this tale.

Men bade lead the perjurers to their lodgings. How might Siegfried, or any else against whom they plotted, ware himself against their wiles? This later brought great sorrow to them all. The king walked whispering with his friends; Hagen of Troneg never let him rest. Enow of the king's liegemen would fain have parted the strife, but Hagen would not give up his plan. On a day Siegfried found them whispering. The hero of Netherland gan ask: 'How go the king and his men so sadly? I'll help avenge it, hath any done you aught.'

Then spake King Gunther: 'I am rightly sad. Liudegast and Liudeger have challenged me to war; they are minded to ride openly into my land.'

At this the bold knight said: 'Siegfried's hand shall hinder that with zeal, as beseemeth all your honors. I'll do yet to these knights as I did before; I'll lay waste their lands, or ever I turn again. Be my head your pledge of this. Ye and your warriors shall stay at home and let me ride to meet them with those I have. I'll let you see how fain I serve you. This know, through me it shall go evil with your foes.'

'Well is me of these tidings,' spake then the king, as though he were glad in earnest of this aid. With guile the faithless man bowed low.

Quoth Lord Siegfried: 'Ye shall have small care.'

Then they made ready for the journey hence with the men-at-arms. This was done for Siegfried and his men to see. He, too, bade those of Netherland get them ready. Siegfried's warriors sought out warlike weeds. Then the stalwart Siegfried spake: 'My father Siegmund, ye must stay here. We shall return in short space hither to the Rhine, and God give us luck. Ye must here make merry with the king.'

They tied fast their banners, as though they would away, and there were enow of Gunther's men who wist not wherefore this was done. Great rout of men was seen at Siegfried's side. They bound their helmets and their breastplates upon the steeds, and many a stout knight made ready to quit the land. Then Hagen of Troneg went to find Kriemhild and asked for leave, sith they would void the land.

'Now well is me,' spake Kriemhild, 'that I have won a husband who dare protect so well my loving kinsfolk, as my Lord Siegfried doth here. Therefore,' spake the queen, 'will I be glad of heart. Dear friend Hagen, think on that, that I do serve you gladly and never yet did bear you hate. Requite this now to me in my dear husband. Let him not suffer, if I have done to Brunhild aught. I since have rued it,' spake the noble wife. 'Moreover, he since hath beaten me black and blue; the brave hero and a good hath well avenged that ever I spake what grieved her heart.'

'Ye'll be friends once more after some days, Kriemhild, dear lady, pray tell me how I may serve you in your husband Siegfried. Liefer will I do this for you than for any else.'

'I should be without all fear,' quoth the noble dame, 'that any one would take his life in the fray, if he would not follow his overweening mood; then the bold knight and a good were safe.'

'Lady,' spake then Hagen, 'an ye do think that men might wound him, pray let me know with what manner of arts I can prevent this. On foot, on horse, will I ever be his guard.'

She spake: 'Thou art my kinsman and I am thine. I'll commend to thee trustingly the dear lover of mine, that thou mayst guard him well, mine own dear husband.' She made him acquaint with tales which had been better left unsaid. She spake: 'My husband is brave and strong enow. When he slew the dragon on the hill, the lusty warrior bathed him of a truth in the blood, so that since then no weapon ever cut him in the fray. Yet am I in fear, whenever he standeth in the fight and many javelins are cast by heroes' hands, that I may lose this dear husband

18–20. **Siegfried's hand . . . land.** This deed of Siegfried is narrated in Adventure Four, and is the only prominent military feat of the hero to be told in detail in *The Nibelungenlied*.

100–101. **When . . . dragon.** This, because of the Wagnerian influence, is the best known of Siegfried's achievements. It occupies a central position in the career of the hero as told in the *Volsungasaga*.

of mine. Alas, how oft I suffer sore for Siegfried's sake! Dear kinsman, in the hope that thou wilt hold thy troth with me, I'll tell thee where men may wound the dear lord of mine. I let thee hear this, 't is done in faith. When the hot blood gushed from the dragon's wounds and the bold hero and a good bathed him therein, a broad linden leaf did fall betwixt his shoulder blades. Therefore am I sore afraid that men may cut him there.'

10 Then spake Hagen of Troneg: 'Sew a small mark upon his coat, whereby I may know where I must guard him, when we stand in battle.'

She weened to save her knight, but 't was done unto his death. She spake: 'With fine silk I'll sew a secret cross upon his vesture. There, knight, thy hand must guard my husband, when the strife is on and he standeth in the battle before his foes.'

'That will I well, dear my lady,' Hagen then replied.

20 The lady weened that it would boot him aught, but Kriemhild's husband was thereby betrayed. Hagen then took leave; merrily he hied him hence. The king's liegeman was blithe of mood. I ween that nevermore will warrior give such false counsel, as was done by him when Kriemhild trusted in his troth.

Next morning Siegfried with a thousand of his men rode merrily forth. He weened he should avenge the grievance of his kinsmen. Hagen rode so near
30 him that he could eye his clothes. When he saw the sign, he sent in secret twain of his men, who should tell another tale; that Gunther's land should still have peace and that Liudeger had sent them to the king. How loth Siegfried now rode home again, or ever he had avenged his kinsmen's wrongs! Gunther's men could hardly turn him back. He rode then to the king; the host gan thank him. 'Now God requite you of your will, friend Siegfried, that ye do so willingly what I bid you. For this I'll ever serve you, as I
40 rightly should. I trust you more than all my friends. Now that we be rid of this foray, I am minded to ride a-hunting for bears and boars to the Vosges forest, as I have done oft-time.' That Hagen, the faithless knight, had counseled. 'Let it be told to all my guests, that we ride betimes. Those that would hunt with me must make them ready. If any choose to stay at home to court the ladies, that liketh me as well.'

Then spake Sir Siegfried in lordly wise: 'An ye
50 would a-hunting, I'd fain go with you. Pray lend me a huntsman and some brach, and I will ride to the pines.'

'Will ye have but one?' spake the king anon. 'I'll lend you, an ye will, four men to whom both wood

51. brach, a hunting dog; later it was applied to the female of the species only.

and paths be known where the game is wont to go, and who will not let you miss the camp.'

Then rode the full lusty warrior to his wife, whilst Hagen quickly told the king how he thought to trap the doughty knight. A man should never use such faithlessness. 60

ADVENTURE 16. *How Siegfried was slain*

Gunther and Hagen, the passing bold knights, faithlessly let cry a-hunting in the woods, that with sharp spears they would hunt boars and bears and bison. What might be braver? With them rode Siegfried in lordly guise; many kinds of victual did they take along. At a cool spring he later lost his life, the which Brunhild, King Gunther's wife, had counseled. The bold knight then went to where he found Kriemhild. His costly hunting garb and those of his fellowship were already bound upon the 70 sumpters, for they would cross the Rhine. Never could Kriemhild have been more sorrowful. He kissed his love upon her mouth. 'God let me see thee, lady, still in health and grant that thine eyes may see me too. Thou shalt have pastime with thy loving kinsmen. I may not stay at home.'

Then she thought of the tale she had told to Hagen, though she durst not say a whit. The noble queen began to rue that she was ever born. Lord Siegfried's wife wept out of measure. She spake to 80 the knight: 'Let be your hunting. I had an evil dream last night, how two wild boars did chase you across the heath; then flowers grew red. I have in truth great cause to weep so sore. I be much adread of sundry plans and whether we have not misserved some who might bear us hostile hate. Tarry here, dear my lord, that I counsel by my troth.'

He spake: 'Dear love, I'll come back in a few short days. I wot not here of people who bear me aught of hate. Each and all of thy kinsmen be my 90 friends, nor have I deserved it other of the knights.'

'No, no, Sir Siegfried; in truth I fear thy fall. I had last night an evil dream, how two mountains fell upon thee. I saw thee nevermore. It doth cut me to the heart, that thou wilt part from me.'

In his arms he clasped his courteous wife and kissed her tenderly. Then in a short space he took his leave and parted hence. Alas, she never saw him in health again.

Then they rode from thence into a deep wood for 100 pastime's sake. Many bold knights did follow Gunther and his men, but Gernot and Gieselher stayed at home. Many laden sumpters were sent before them across the Rhine, the which bare for the hunting fellowship bread and wine, meat and fish, and great store of other things, which so mighty a king might rightly have. They bade the proud huntsmen and bold halt before a green wood over against the courses of the game, upon a passing broad glade where they should hunt. The king was told that Siegfried, too, was come. The hunting fellowship now took their stand on every side. Then the bold knight, the sturdy Siegfried, asked: 'Ye heroes bold and brave, who shall lead us to the game within the wood?'

'Let us part,' spake Hagen, 'ere we begin the chase. Thereby my lords and I may know who be the best hunter on this woodland journey. Let us divide the folk and hounds and let each turn whithersoever he list. He who doth hunt the best shall have our thanks.' Short time the huntsmen bided by another after that.

Then spake Lord Siegfried: 'I need no dogs save one brach that hath been trained that he can tell the track of the beasts through the pine woods.' Quoth Kriemhild's husband: 'We'll find the game.'

Then an old huntsman took a good sleuth-hound and in a short space brought the lord to where many beasts were found. Whatso rose from its lair the comrades hunted as good hunters still are wont to do. Whatever the brach started, bold Siegfried, the hero of Netherland, slew with his hand. His horse did run so hard that none escaped him. In the chase he gained the prize above them all. Doughty enow he was in all things. The beast which he slew with his hands was the first, a mighty boar; after which he found full soon a monstrous lion. When the brach started this from its lair, he shot it with his bow, in which he had placed a full sharp arrow. After the shot the lion ran the space of but three bounds. The hunting fellowship gave Siegfried thanks. Thereafter he speedily slew a bison and an elk, four strong ure-oxen, and a savage shelk. His horse bare him so swiftly that naught escaped him, nor could hart or hind avoid him. Then the sleuth hound found a mighty boar; when he began to flee, at once there came the master of the hunt and encountered him upon his path. Wrathfully the boar did run against the valiant hero, but Kriemhild's husband slew him with his sword. Another huntsman might not have done this deed so lightly. When he had felled him, they leashed the sleuth-hound; his rich booty was soon well known to the Burgundian men.

Then spake his huntsman: 'Sir Siegfried, if might so be, let us leave a deal of the beasts alive. Ye'll empty both our hills and woods today.'

At this the brave knight and a bold gan smile. Then the calls of men and the baying of hounds were heard on every side; so great was the noise that both hill and pine woods echoed with the sound. The huntsmen had let loose full four and twenty packs.

Then passing many beasts must needs lose their lives. Each man weened to bring it to pass that men should give him the prize of the hunt; that might not be, for the stalwart Siegfried was already standing by the fire. The chase was over, and yet not quite. Those who would to the campfire brought with them thither hides of many beasts and game in plenty. Ho! how much the king's meiny bare then to the kitchen!

Then bade the king announce to the huntsmen that he would dismount. A horn was blown full loud just once, that all might know that one might find the noble prince in camp. Spake then one of Siegfried's huntsmen: 'My lord, I heard by the blast of a horn that we must now hie to the quarters; I'll now give answer.'

Thus by many blasts of horns they asked about the hunters. Then spake Sir Siegfried: 'Now let us leave the pine wood!' His steed bare him smoothly and with him they hasted hence. With their rout they started up a savage beast; a wild bear it was. Quoth then the knight to those behind: 'I'll give our fellowship a little pastime. Let loose the brach. Forsooth I spy a bear which shall journey with us to the camp. Flee he never so fast, he shall not escape us.'

The brach was loosed, the bear sprang hence; Kriemhild's husband would fain overtake him. He reached a thicket, where none could follow. The mighty beast weened now to escape from the hunter with his life, but the proud knight and a good leaped from his steed and began to chase him. The bear was helpless and could not flee away. At once the hero caught it and bound it quickly with not a wound, so that it might neither scratch nor bite the men. The doughty knight then tied it to his saddle and horsed him quickly. Through his overweening mood the bold warrior and a good brought it to the camp-fire as a pastime. In what lordly wise he rode to the quarters! Mickle was his boar-spear, strong and broad. A dainty sword hung downward to his spurs. The lord bare also a fair horn of ruddy gold. Never heard I tale of better hunting weeds. One saw him wear a coat of black and silky cloth and a hat of sable: rich enow it was. Ho! what costly bands he wore upon his quiver! A panther's skin was drawn over it for the sake of its sweet fragrance. He bare a bow, which any but the hero must needs draw back with a windlass, an he would bend it. His vesture was befurred with otter skin from head to toe. From the bright fur shone out on both sides of the bold master of the hunt many a bar of gold. Balmung he also bare, a good broad sword, that was

28. lion; a good example of embroidery with the fabulous to which the medieval romancer often resorted. 34. ure-oxen, the aurochs or European bison, now extinct in Europe, although specimens may be found in Siberia. shelk, a giant deer, possibly akin to the moose.

61. meiny, retinue. 98–99. panther's skin . . . fragrance. According to medieval legend, the panther's breath was so sweet as to enable it to lure its prey through that alone, and the fragrance permeated its whole body. 102. otter. It is not known whether this means the familiar fish-otter or a mythical faun-like beast. 105. Balmung, the famous sword of Siegfried.

so sharp that it never failed when 'twas wielded 'gainst a helmet; its edge was good. In high spirits was the lordly huntsman. Sith I must tell you all the tale, his costly quiver was full of goodly darts, the heads a full hand's breadth, on golden shafts. What he pierced therewith must needs die soon.

Thus the noble knight rode hence in hunter's garb. Gunther's men espied him coming and ran out to meet him and took his horse in charge. On his sad-
10 dle he carried a large bear and a strong. When he had dismounted, he loosed the bonds from feet and snout. Those of the pack bayed loudly, that spied the bear. The beast would to the woods; the serving folk had fear. Dazed by the din, the bear made for the kitchen. Ho! how he drove the scullions from the fire! Many a kettle was upset and many a firebrand scattered. Ho! what good victual men found lying in the ashes! Then the lordings and their liegemen sprang from their seats. The bear grew furious and
20 the king bade loose the pack that lay enleashed. Had all sped well, they would have had a merry day. No longer the doughty men delayed, but ran for the bear with bows and pikes. There was such press of dogs that none might shoot, but from the people's shouts the whole hill rang. The bear began to flee before the dogs; none could follow him but Kriem-hild's husband, who caught and slew him with his sword. Then they bore the bear again to the fire. Those that saw it, averred he was a mighty man.
30 Men bade now the proud hunting fellowship seat them at the tables. Upon a fair mead there sate a goodly company. Ho! what rich viands they bare there to the noble huntsmen! The butlers who should bring the wine delayed; else might never heroes have been better served. Had they not been so falsely minded, then had the knights been free of every blame.

Now the Lord Siegfried spake: 'Me wondereth, since men do give us such great store from the
40 kitchen, why the butlers bring us not the wine. Un-less men purvey the hunters better, I'll be no more your hunting-fellow. I have well deserved that they regard me, too.'

The king addressed him from his seat with guile: 'We fain would do your remedy of what we lack. It is Hagen's fault, who is willed to let us die of thirst.'

Then spake Hagen: 'Dear my lord, I weened that the hunt should be in the Spessart wood, therefore sent I thither the wine. Though we may not drink
50 today, how well will I avoid this in the future!'

At this Lord Siegfried spake: 'Small thanks ye'll get for that. One should have brought me hither seven sumpter loads of mead and mulled wine. If

that might not be, then men should have placed our benches nearer to the Rhine.'

Then spake Hagen of Troneg: 'Ye noble knights and bold, I wot nearby a good spring. Let us go thither, that ye wax not wroth.'

To the danger of many a knight was this counsel
60 given. The pangs of thirst now plagued the warrior Siegfried. He bade the tables be borne away the sooner, for he would go to the spring in the moun-tains. With false intent the counsel was then given by the knights. They bade the game which Sieg-fried's hand had slain, be carried home on wains. Whoever saw it gave him great laud. Hagen of Troneg now foully broke his troth to Siegfried. When they would hence to the broad linden, he spake: 'It hath oft been told me, that none can keep pace with
70 Kriemhild's husband when he be minded for to race. Ho! if he would only let us see it here!'

Bold Siegfried from Netherland then answered: 'Ye can well test that, an ye will run a race with me to the spring. When that is done, we can give the prize to him who winneth.'

'So let us try it then,' quoth Hagen, the knight.

Spake the sturdy Siegfried: 'Then will I lay me down on the greensward at your feet.'

How lief it was to Gunther, when he heard these
80 words! Then the bold knight spake again: 'I'll tell you more. I'll take with me all my trappings, my spear and shield and all my hunting garb.' Around him he quickly girded his quiver and his sword.

Then they drew the clothes from off their limbs; men saw them stand in two white shifts. Like two wild panthers through the clover they ran, but men spied bold Siegfried first at the spring. In all things he bare away the prize from many a man. Quickly he ungirt his sword and laid aside his quiver and
90 leaned the stout spear against a linden bough. The lordly stranger stood now by the flowing spring. Passing great was Siegfried's courtesie. He laid down his shield where the spring gushed forth, but the hero drank not, albeit he thirsted sore, until the king had drunk, who gave him evil thanks. Cool, clear, and good was the spring. Gunther stooped down then to the flowing stream, and when he had drunken straightened up again. Bold Siegfried would fain also have done the same, but now he paid for his courtesie. Hagen bare quite away from him both
100 bow and sword and bounded then to where he found the spear; then he looked for the mark on bold Sieg-fried's coat. As Lord Siegfried drank above the spring, he pierced him through the cross, so that his heart's blood spurted from the wounds almost on Hagen's clothes. Nevermore will hero do so foul a

---

48. **Spessart wood,** a forest about fifty miles east of Worms, consid-erably farther than an ordinary day's hunt would carry the knights.
53. **mulled wine,** a claret mixed with spices and herbs and allowed to clear.

77–78. **'Then will I . . . feet.'** Siegfried arrogantly suggests this in order to enhance his assumed victory over Hagen. In other words, Hagen will start from a standing position while Siegfried will first have to rise to his feet. Hagen had not requested this handicap.

deed. Hagen left the spear a-sticking in his heart and fled more madly than he ever in the world had run from any man.

When Lord Siegfried felt the mighty wound, up from the spring he started in a rage. From betwixt his shoulder blades a long spear-shaft towered. He weened to find his bow or his sword, and then had Hagen been repaid as he deserved. But when the sorely wounded hero found no trace of his sword, then had he naught else but his shield. This he snatched from the spring and ran at Hagen; nor could King Gunther's man escape him. Albeit he was wounded unto death, yet he smote so mightily that a plenty of precious stones were shaken from the shield. The shield itself burst quite apart. Fain would the lordly stranger have avenged him. Now was Hagen fallen to the ground at his hands, and from the force of the blow the glade rang loudly. Had he had a sword in hand, then had it been Hagen's death, so sore enraged was the wounded man. Forsooth he had good cause thereof. His hue grew pale, he could not stand; his strength of body melted quite away, for in bright colors he bore the signs of death. Thereafter he was bewailed by fair dames enow.

Kriemhild's husband fell now among the flowers. Fast from his wounds blood was seen to gush. He began to rail, as indeed he had great cause, at those who had planned this treacherous death. The deadly wounded spake: 'Forsooth, ye evil cowards, what avail my services now that ye have slain me? This is my reward that I was always faithful to you. Alas, ye have acted ill against your kinsmen. Those of them who are born in after days will be disgraced. Ye have avenged your wrath too sore upon me. With shame shall ye be parted from all good warriors!'

The knights all ran to where he lay slain. For enow of them it was a hapless day. He was bewailed by those who had aught of loyalty, and this the brave and lusty knight had well deserved. The king of the Burgundians bemoaned his death. Quoth the deadly wounded: 'There is no need that he should weep who hath done the damage; he doth merit mickle blame. It had been better left undone.'

Then spake the fierce Hagen: 'Forsooth I wot not what ye now bewail. All our fear and all our woe have now an end. We shall find scant few who dare withstand us now. Well is me, that to his rule I have put an end.'

'Ye may lightly boast you,' Siegfried then replied. 'Had I wist your murderous bent, I had well guarded my life against you. None doth rue me so sore as Lady Kriemhild, my wife. Now may God have pity that I ever had a son to whom the reproach will be made in after days, that his kindred have slain a man with murderous intent. If I might,' so spake Siegfried, 'I should rightly make complaint of this.'

Piteously the deadly wounded spake again: 'Noble king, if ye will keep your troth to any in the world, then let my dear love be commended to your grace and let it avail her that she be your sister. For the sake of your princely courtesie, protect her faithfully. My father and my men must wait long time for me. Never was woman sorer wounded in a loving friend.'

The flowers on every side were wet with blood. With death he struggled, but not for long, sith the sword of death had cut him all too sorely. Then the lusty warrior and a brave could speak no more.

When the lordings saw that the knight was dead, they laid him on a shield of ruddy gold and took counsel how they might conceal that Hagen had done the deed. Enow of them spake: 'Ill hath it gone with us. Ye must all aver alike that robbers slew Kriemhild's husband as he rode alone a-hunting through the pine wood.'

Then Hagen of Troneg spake: 'I'll bring him home; I care not if it be known to her, for she hath saddened Brunhild's heart. Little doth it trouble me however much she weep.'

ADVENTURE 17. *How Kriemhild mourned her husband and how he was buried*

Then they waited for the night and crossed the Rhine. Never had heroes hunted worse. Noble maids bewept the game they slew. Forsooth many good warriors must needs atone for this in after days. Now ye may hear a tale of great overweening and dire revenge. Hagen bade carry Siegfried of the Nibelungland, thus dead, before the bower where Kriemhild lodged. He bade place him stealthily against the door, that she might find him when she went forth before the break of day to matins, which Lady Kriemhild full seldom missed through sleep.

Men rang the minster bells according to their custom. Lady Kriemhild, the fair, now waked her many maids and bade them bring a light and her vesture, too. Then came a chamberlain and found Siegfried there. He saw him red with blood, his clothes all wet. He wist not it was his lord, but with the light in his hand he hasted to the bower and through this Lady Kriemhild learned the baneful tale. As she would set out with her ladies for the minster, the chamberlain spake: 'Pray stay your feet, there doth lie before the chamber a knight, slain unto death.'

Kriemhild gan make passing sore wail, or ever she heard aright that it was her husband. She began to think of Hagen's question, of how he might protect him. Then first she suffered dole; she renounced all pleasure at his death. To the earth she sank, not a word she spake, and here they found lying the hapless fair. Passing great grew Kriemhild's woe. After her faint, she shrieked, that all the chamber rang. Then her meiny said: 'Perchance it is a stranger knight.'

The blood gushed from her mouth, from dole of heart; she spake: 'Tis Siegfried, mine own dear husband. Brunhild hath counseled this and Hagen hath done the deed.'

The lady bade them lead her to where the hero lay. With her white hand she raised his head, and though it was red with blood, she knew him soon. There lay the hero of the Nibelungland in piteous guise. The gracious queen cried sadly: 'Oh, woe is me of my sorrow! Thy shield is not carved with swords; thou liest murdered here. Wist I who hath done the deed, I'd ever plot his death.'

All her maids made mourn and wailed with their dear lady, for they grieved full sore for their noble lord whom they had lost. Hagen had cruelly avenged the wrath of Brunhild.

Then spake the grief-stricken dame: 'Go now and wake with haste all Siegfried's men. Tell Siegmund also of my grief, mayhap he'll help me bewail brave Siegfried.'

A messenger ran quickly to where lay Siegfried's warriors from the Nibelungland, and with his baleful tidings stole their joy. They could scarcely believe it, till they heard the weeping. Right soon the messenger came to where the king did lie. Siegmund, the lord, was not asleep. I trow his heart did tell him what had happed. Never again might he see his dear son alive.

'Awake, Sir Siegmund! Kriemhild, my lady, bade me go to fetch you. A wrong hath been done her that doth cut her to the heart, more than all other ills. Ye must help her mourn, for much it doth concern you.'

Siegmund sat up; he spake: 'What are fair Kriemhild's ills, of which thou tellest me?'

Weeping the messenger spake: 'I cannot hide them from you; alas, bold Siegfried of Netherland is slain.'

Quoth Siegmund: 'For my sake let be this jesting and such evil tales, that thou shouldst tell any that he be dead, for I might never bewail him fully before my death.'

'If ye will believe naught of what ye hear me say, then ye may hear yourself Kriemhild and all her maids bewailing Siegfried's death.'

Siegmund then was sore affrighted, as indeed he had great need. He and a hundred of his men sprang from their beds and grasped with their hands their long sharp swords. In sorrow they ran toward the sound of wail. Then came a thousand men-at-arms, bold Siegfried's men. When they heard the ladies wail so pitifully, some first grew ware that they should dress them. Forsooth they lost their wits

for very sorrow. Great heaviness was buried in their hearts.

Then King Siegmund came to where he found Kriemhild. He spake: 'Alas for the journey hither to this land! Who hath so foully bereft me of my child and you of your husband among such good friends?'

'Oh, if I knew him,' spake the noble wife, 'neither my heart nor soul would ever wish him well. I would plan such ill against him that his kin must ever weep because of me.'

Around the prince Lord Siegmund threw his arms. So great grew the sorrow of his kin, that the palace, the hall, and the town of Worms resounded from the mighty wail and weeping. None might now comfort Siegfried's wife. They stripped off the clothes from his fair body; they washed his wounds and laid him on the bier. Woe were his people from their mighty grief. Then spake his warriors from the Nibelungland: 'Our hands be ever ready to avenge him; he liveth in this castle who hath done the deed.'

All of Siegfried's men hasted then to arms. These chosen knights came with their shields, eleven hundred men-at-arms, whom Lord Siegfried had in his troop. He would fain avenge the death of his son, as indeed he had great need. They wist not to whom they should address their strife, unless it be to Gunther and his men, with whom Lord Siegfried had ridden to the hunt.

Kriemhild saw them armed, which rued her sore. However great her grief and how dire her need, yet she did so mightily fear the death of the Nibelungs at the hands of her brothers' liegemen, that she tried to hinder it. In kindly wise she warned them, as kinsmen do to loving kin. The grief-stricken woman spake: 'My Lord Siegmund, what will ye do? Ye wot naught aright; forsooth King Gunther hath so many valiant men, ye will all be lost, and ye would encounter these knights.'

With their shields uncovered, the men stood eager for the fight. The noble queen both begged and bade that the lusty knights avoid it. When they would not give it over, sorely it grieved her. She spake: 'Lord Siegmund, ye must let it be until more fitting time, then I'll avenge my husband with you. An I receive proof who hath bereft me of him, I'll do him scathe. There be too many haughty warriors by the Rhine, wherefore I will not counsel you to fight. They have full well thirty men to each of ours. Now God speed them, as they deserve of us. Stay ye here and bear with me my dole. When it beginneth to dawn, help me, ye lusty knights, to coffin the dear husband of mine.'

Quoth the knights: 'That shall be done.'

None might tell you all the marvel of knights and

ladies, how they were heard to wail, so that even in the town men marked the sound of weeping. The noble burghers hasted hither. With the guests they wept, for they, too, were sore aggrieved. None had told them of any guilt of Siegfried, or for what cause the noble warrior lost his life. The wives of the worthy burghers wept with the ladies of the court. Men bade smiths haste to work a coffin of silver and gold, mickle and strong, and make it firm with
10 strips of good hard steel. Sad of heart were all the folk.

The night was gone, men said the day was dawning. Then the noble lady bade them bear Lord Siegfried, her loved husband, to the minster. Whatever friends he had there were seen weeping as they went. Many bells were ringing as they brought him to the church. On every side one heard the chant of many priests. Then came King Gunther with his men and grim Hagen also toward the sound of wail.
20 He spake: 'Alas for thy wrongs, dear sister, that we may not be free from this great scathe. We must ever lament for Siegfried's death.'

'That ye do without cause,' spake the sorrow-laden wife. 'Were this loath to you, it never would have happed. I may well aver, ye thought not on me, when I thus was parted from my dear husband. Would to God,' quoth Kriemhild, 'that it had happed to me.'

Firmly they made denial. Kriemhild gan speak:
30 'Whoso declareth him guiltless, let him show that now. He must walk to the bier before all the folk; thereby one may know the truth eftsoon.'

This is a great marvel, which oft doth hap: whenever the blood-stained murderer is seen to stand by the dead, the latter's wounds do bleed, as indeed happed here, whereby one saw the guilt was Hagen's. The wounds bled sore, as they had done at first. Much greater grew the weeping of those who wailed afore.
40 Then spake King Gunther: 'I'd have you know that robbers slew him; Hagen did not do the deed.'

'I know these robbers well,' quoth she. 'Now may God yet let his friends avenge it. Certes, Gunther and Hagen, 'twas done by you.'

Siegfried's knights were now bent on strife. Then Kriemhild spake again: 'Now share with me this grief.'

Gernot, her brother, and young Gieselher, these twain now came to where they found him dead.
50 They mourned him truly with the others; Kriemhild's men wept inly. Now should mass be sung, so on every side, men, wives, and children did hie them to the minster. Even those who might lightly bear his loss, wept then for Siegfried. Gernot and Gieselher spake: 'Sister mine, now comfort thee after this

33–35. whenever . . . bleed. This is an age-old superstition, as defined in the text.

death, as needs must be. We'll try to make it up to thee, the while we live.'

Yet none in the world might give her comfort. His coffin was ready well towards midday. From the bier whereon he lay they raised him. The lady would 60 not have that he be buried, so that all the folk had mickle trouble. In a rich cloth of silk they wound the dead. I ween, men found none there that did not weep. Uta, the noble dame, and all her meiny mourned bitterly the stately man. When it was noised abroad that men sang in the minster and had encoffined him, then rose a great press of folk. What offerings they made for his soul's sake! He had good friends enow among these foes. Poor Kriemhild spake to her chamberlains: 'Ye must now be put to 70 trouble for my sake, ye who wished him well and be my friends. For Siegfried's soul shall ye deal out his gold.'

No child, however small, that had its wits, but must go to service, or ever he was buried. Better than a hundred masses were sung that day. Great throng were there of Siegfried's friends.

When that mass was sung, the folk went hence. Then Lady Kriemhild spake: 'Pray let me not hold vigil over the chosen knight this night alone. With 80 him all my joys have come to fall. I will let him lie in state three days and nights, until I sate me with my dear lord. What if God doth bid that death should take me too. Then had ended well the grief of me, poor Kriemhild.'

The people of the town returned now to their lodgings. She begged the priests and monks and all his retinue, that served the knight, to stay. They spent full evil nights and toilsome days; many a man remained without all food and drink. For those who 90 would partake, it was made known that men would give them to the full. This Sir Siegmund purveyed. Then were the Nibelungs made acquaint with mickle toil. During the three days, as we hear tell, those who knew how to sing, were made to bear a deal of work. What offerings men brought them! Those who were very poor, grew rich enow. Whatever of poor men there were, the which had naught, these were bid go to mass with gold from Siegfried's treasure chamber. Since he might not live, many thousand 100 marks of gold were given for his soul. She dealt out well-tilled lands, wherever cloisters and pious folk were found. Enow of gold and silver was given to the poor. By her deeds she showed that she did love him fondly.

Upon the third morning at time of mass, the broad churchyard by the minster was full of weeping country folk. They served him after death, as one should do to loving kin. In the four days, as hath been told, full thirty thousand marks or better still were 110 given to the poor for his soul's sake. Yet his great beauty and his life lay low. When God had been served and the chants were ended, many people fought against monstrous grief. Men bade bear him from the minster to the grave. Those were seen to weep and wail who missed him most. With loud laments the people followed hence; none was merry, neither wife nor man. They sang and read a service before they buried him. Ho, what good priests were present at his burial! Ere Siegfried's wife was come to the grave, her faithful heart was wrung with grief, so that they must needs oft sprinkle her with water from the spring. Her pain was passing great; a mickle wonder it was that she ever lived. Many a lady helped her in her plaint.

Then spake the queen: 'Ye men of Siegfried, by your loyalty must ye prove your love to me. Let me receive this little favor after all my woe, that I may see once more his comely head.'

She begged so long, with grief's strong will, that they must needs break open the lordly casket. Then men brought the lady to where he lay. With her white hand she raised his fair head and kissed the noble knight and good, thus dead. Tears of blood her bright eyes wept from grief. Then there happed a piteous parting. Men bare her hence, she could not walk, and soon they found the high-born lady lying senseless. Fain would the lovely fair have died of grief.

When they had now buried the noble lord, those who were come with him from the Nibelungland were seen to suffer from unmeasured grief. Men found Siegmund full seldom merry then. There were those that for three days would neither eat nor drink for passing grief. Yet might they not so waste away their bodies, but that they recovered from their sorrows, as still happeneth oft enow.

A German prince in tourney costume, the early fifteenth century.

Aucassin and Nicolete

Some time near the middle of the twelfth century a gifted Frenchman composed *Aucassin and Nicolete*. Nothing is known about him, however, except through surmise. He appears to have been a man of popular rather than of clerical mold, entirely secular in his outlook, a man of delightful fancy and delicately satirical expression, but thoroughly in love with love, albeit with a somewhat middle-aged tolerance. The tale of the two naïve young lovers he told in the so-called *chantefable* form, with alternating prose and verse sections to the narrative, garnished with interspersed lyrics. This form is known in early literature from Scotland to India and the Far East, but *Aucassin and Nicolete* is the unique surviving example of the type from medieval France, and it is quite possible that the poet was seeking (and seeking successfully) a fresh form of narrative for the sake of variety.

The name of the hero, Aucassin, which could be a French form of an Arabic Al-Kassim, as well as the fact that Nicolete is by birth a Saracen princess, suggests that the story was of Oriental origin. Indeed, the theme of the separation and reuniting of devoted lovers is commonplace in Mediterranean and Oriental tales. The matter is academic, however, and immaterial for the general reader, for the story of two young lovers who in their simple, sensuous, and passionate way refuse to remain separated is a universal one. What is more important is the manner in which the poet treats this familiar material.

The knightly young hero, Aucassin, is so bemused by love that he neglects his knightly duties and talks back to his father when reminded of them; and his ideas about Paradise and Hell are refreshingly frank and unecclesiastical. There is more than a hint, in fact, that the poet is satirizing not only the institution of knighthood but also the narrow insistence of the more evangelical members of the clergy that the world to come is more important than the world that is. On the contrary, in *Aucassin and Nicolete* the world that is strikes one as a thoroughly charming place for the noble and the beloved. Although there are sieges and stours, they are touched upon but lightly and then in jocose fashion; although there is humanitarian sympathy for the loathly churl whom Aucassin meets, the poet solves the problem quickly. More significant are the rose-covered lodge of Nicolete in the woods, the charming picture of Nicolete in flight from Biaucaire, the ride of Aucassin and Nicolete to Torelore, and the final reunion of the lovers. The bizarre episode of Torelore anticipates the fantastic satire of Rabelais written centuries later. But whether the purpose of the poet is satirical or merely imaginative, the result is nothing if not entertaining, affording a delightful contrast to the more serious and rugged specimens of courtly narrative of which the age was full.

Aucassin
and Nicolete

Tis of Aucassin and Nicolete.
Who would list to the good lay,
Gladness of the captive grey?
'Tis how two young lovers met,
Aucassin and Nicolete,
Of the pains the lover bore
And the sorrows he outwore,
For the goodness and the grace
Of his love, so fair of face.

10 Sweet the song, the story sweet.
There is no man hearkens it,
No man living 'neath the sun,
So outwearied, so fordone,
Sick and woful, worn and sad,
But is healed, but is glad
    'Tis so sweet.

So say they, speak they, tell they the Tale:
How the Count Bougars de Valence made war
on Count Garin de Biaucaire, war so great, and so
20 marvellous, and so mortal that never a day dawned,
but always he was there, by the gates and walls, and
barriers of the town with a hundred knights, and ten
thousand men at arms, horsemen and footmen; so
burned he the Count's land, and spoiled his country,
and slew his men. Now the Count Garin de Biaucaire was old and frail, and his good days were gone
over. No heir had he, neither son nor daughter, save
one young man only; such an one as I shall tell you.
Aucassin was the name of the damoiseau; fair was
30 he, goodly, and great, and featly fashioned of his
body, and limbs. His hair was yellow, in little curls,
his eyes blue and laughing, his face beautiful and
shapely, his nose high and well set, and so richly
seen was he in all things good that in him was none
evil at all. But so suddenly overtaken was he of
Love, who is a great master, that he would not, of
his will, be dubbed knight, nor take arms, nor follow
tourneys, nor do whatsoever him beseemed. Therefore his father and mother said to him:
40 "Son, go take thine arms, mount thy horse, and
hold thy land, and help thy men, for if they see thee
among them, more stoutly will they keep in battle
their lives and lands and thine and mine."
"Father," said Aucassin, "I marvel that you will

be speaking. Never may God give me aught of my
desire if I be made knight, or mount my horse, or
face stour and battle wherein knights smite and are
smitten again, unless thou give me Nicolete, my true
love, that I love so well."
"Son," said the father, "this may not be. Let Nico- 50
lete go, a slave girl she is, out of a strange land, and
the captain of this town bought her of the Saracens,
and carried her hither, and hath reared her and let
christen the maid, and took her for his daughter in
God, and one day will find a young man for her,
to win her bread honorably. Herein hast thou naught
to make or mend, but if a wife thou wilt have, I
will give thee the daughter of a King, or a Count.
There is no man so rich in France, but if thou desire
his daughter, thou shalt have her." 60
"Faith! my father," said Aucassin, "tell me where
is the place so high in all the world, that Nicolete,
my sweet lady and love, would not grace it well? If
she were Empress of Constantinople or of Germany,
or Queen of France or England, it were little enough
for her; so gentle is she and courteous and debonaire
and compact of all good qualities."

Here singeth one:

Aucassin was of Biaucaire,
Of a goodly castle there, 70
But from Nicolete the fair
None might win his heart away,
Though his father, many a day,
And his mother said him nay,
"Ha! fond child, what wouldest thou?
Nicolete is glad enow!
Was from Carthage cast away,
Paynims sold her on a day!
Wouldst thou win a lady fair,
Choose a maid of high degree, 80
Such an one is meet for thee."
"Nay, of these have I no care,
Nicolete is debonaire,
Her body sweet and the face of her
Take my heart as in a snare,
Loyal love is but her share
    That is so sweet."

Then speak they, say they, tell they the Tale:
When the Count Garin de Biaucaire knew that
he would not avail to withdraw Aucassin his son 90
from the love of Nicolete, he went to the Captain
of the city, who was his man, and spake to him,
saying:
"Sir Count; away with Nicolete thy daughter in
God; cursed be the land whence she was brought

Aucassin and Nicolete. Translated by Andrew Lang.
19. **Biaucaire.** The setting of this poem is in general the lower Rhone
Valley in southern France. Beaucaire is about fifteen miles from the
mouth of the Rhone; Valence, mentioned in the preceding line, is
some sixty miles farther up the river. 29. **damoiseau,** a young unmarried man of superior birth.

47. **stour,** the onset of battle. 54. **christen the maid.** In *Aucassin
and Nicolete* the traditional course is reversed, for it is much more
common in medieval romances for a hero to be of Saracen birth and
then to be converted and baptized. A Saracen heroine is not unknown,
however.

into this country, for by reason of her do I lose Aucassin, that will neither be dubbed knight, nor do aught of the things that fall to him to be done. And wit ye well," he said, "that if I might have her at my will, I would burn her in a fire, and yourself might well be sore adread."

"Sir," said the Captain, "this is grievous to me that he comes and goes and hath speech with her. I had bought the maiden at mine own charges, and nour-
10 ished her, and baptized, and made her my daughter in God. Yea, I would have given her to a young man that should win her bread honorably. With this had Aucassin thy son naught to make or mend. But, sith it is thy will and thy pleasure, I will send her into that land, and that country, where never will he see her with his eyes."

"Have a heed to thyself," said the Count Garin, "thence might great evil come on thee."

So parted they each from other. Now the Captain
20 was a right rich man; so had he a rich palace with a garden in face of it; in an upper chamber thereof he let place Nicolete, with one old woman to keep her company, and in that chamber put bread and meat and wine and such things as were needed. Then he let seal the door, that none might come in or go forth, save that there was one window, over against the garden, and strait enough, wherethrough came to them a little air.

Here singeth one:

30 Nicolete, as ye heard tell
Prisoned is within a cell
That is painted wondrously
With colors of a far country,
And the window of marble wrought,
There the maiden stood in thought,
With straight brows and yellow hair,
Never saw ye fairer fair!
On the wood she gazed below,
And she saw the roses blow,
40 Heard the birds sing loud and low,
Therefore spoke she wofully:
"Ah me, wherefore do I lie
Here in prison wrongfully;
Aucassin, my love, my knight,
Am I not thy heart's delight,
Thou that lovest me aright!
'Tis for thee that I must dwell
In the vaulted chamber cell,
Hard beset and all alone!
50 By our Lady Mary's Son
Here no longer will I wonn,
    If I may flee!"

Then speak they, say they, tell they the Tale:
Nicolete was in prison, as ye have heard soothly, in the chamber. And the noise and bruit of it went through all the country and all the land, how that

Nicolete was lost. Some said she had fled the country, and some that the Count Garin de Biaucaire had let slay her. Whosoever had joy thereof, Aucas-
60 sin had none, so he went to the Captain of the town and spoke to him, saying:

"Sir Captain, what hast thou made of Nicolete, my sweet lady and love, the thing that best I love in all the world? Hast thou carried her off or ravished her away from me? Know well that if I die of it, the price shall be demanded of thee, and that will be well done, for it shall be even as if thou hadst slain me with thy two hands, for thou hast taken from me the thing that in this world I loved the
70 best."

"Fair Sir," said the Captain, "let these things be. Nicolete is a captive that I did bring from a strange country. Yea, I bought her at my own charges of the Saracens, and I bred her up and baptized her, and made her my daughter in God. And I have cherished her, and one of these days I would have given her a young man, to win her bread honorably. With this hast thou naught to make, but do thou take the daughter of a King or a Count. Nay more,
80 what wouldst thou deem thee to have gained, hadst thou made her thy leman, and taken her to thy bed? Plentiful lack of comfort hadst thou got thereby, for in Hell would thy soul have lain while the world endures, and into Paradise wouldst thou have entered never."

"In Paradise what have I to win? Therein I seek not to enter, but only to have Nicolete, my sweet lady that I love so well. For into Paradise go none but such folk as I shall tell thee now: thither go
90 these same old priests, and halt old men and maimed, who all day and night cower continually before the altars, and in the crypts; and such folk as wear old amices and old clouted frocks, and naked folk and shoeless, and covered with sores, perishing of hunger and thirst, and of cold, and of little ease. These be they that go into Paradise; with them have I naught to make. But into Hell would I fain go; for into Hell fare the goodly clerks, and goodly knights that fall in tourneys and great wars, and
100 stout men at arms, and all men noble. With these would I liefly go. And thither pass the sweet ladies and courteous that have two lovers, or three, and their lords also thereto. Thither goes the gold, and the silver, and cloth of vair, and cloth of gris, and harpers, and makers, and the prince of this world. With these I would gladly go, let me but have with me Nicolete, my sweetest lady."

86. **"In Paradise . . ."** This passage, probably the most celebrated in *Aucassin and Nicolete*, is an excellent corrective to the prevailing concept of the Middle Ages as altogether priest-ridden. 93. **amices,** vestments consisting of a rectangular piece of fine white linen on which a small cross is embroidered. **clouted,** ragged. 104. **vair . . . gris,** two kinds of fur; vair is believed to have been used only by the nobility and may have been ermine; gris was presumably less costly, and, as the name implies, gray in color.

"Certes," quoth the Captain, "in vain wilt thou speak thereof, for never shalt thou see her; and if thou hadst word with her, and thy father knew it, he would let burn in a fire both her and me, and thyself might well be sore adread."

"That is even what irketh me," quoth Aucassin. So he went from the Captain sorrowing.

Here singeth one:

Aucassin did so depart
10 Much in dole and heavy at heart
For his love so bright and dear,
None might bring him any cheer,
None might give good words to hear,
To the palace doth he fare,
Climbeth up the palace-stair,
Passeth to a chamber there,
Thus great sorrow doth he bear
For his lady and love so fair.

"Nicolete, how fair art thou,
20 Sweet thy foot-fall, sweet thine eyes,
Sweet the mirth of thy replies,
Sweet thy laughter, sweet thy face,
Sweet thy lips and sweet thy brow,
And the touch of thine embrace,
All for thee I sorrow now,
Captive in an evil place,
Whence I ne'er may go my ways,
    Sister, sweet friend!"

So say they, speak they, tell they the Tale:
30   While Aucassin was in the chamber sorrowing for Nicolete his love, even then the Count Bougars de Valence, that had his war to wage, forgot it no whit, but had called up his horsemen and his footmen, so made he for the castle to storm it. And the cry of battle arose, and the din, and knights and men at arms, busked them, and ran to walls and gates to hold the keep. And the townsfolk mounted to the battlements, and cast down bolts and pikes. Then while the assault was great; even at its height, the
40 Count Garin de Biaucaire came into the chamber where Aucassin was making lament, sorrowing for Nicolete, his sweet lady that he loved so well.

"Ha! son," quoth he, "how caitiff art thou, and cowardly, that canst see men assail thy goodliest castle and strongest. Know thou that if thou lose it, thou losest all. Son, go to, take arms, and mount thy horse, and defend thy land, and help thy men, and fare into the stour. Thou needst not smite nor be smitten. If they do but see thee among them, better
50 will they guard their substance, and their lives, and thy land and mine. And thou art so great, and hardy of thy hands, that well mightst thou do this thing, and to do it is thy devoir."

"Father," said Aucassin, "what is this thou sayest

The siege of a medieval city, from a manuscript history.

now? God grant me never aught of my desire, if I be dubbed knight, or mount steed, or go into the stour where knights do smite and are smitten, if thou givest me not Nicolete, my sweet lady, whom I love so well."

"Son," quoth his father, "this may never be; rather 60 would I be quite disinherited and lose all that is mine, than that thou shouldst have her to thy wife, or to love *par amours.*"

So he turned him about. But when Aucassin saw him going, he called to him again, saying,

"Father, go to now; I will make with thee fair covenant."

"What covenant, fair son?"

"I will take up arms, and go into the stour, on this covenant, that, if God bring me back sound and 70 safe, thou wilt let me see Nicolete my sweet lady, even so long that I may have of her two words or three, and one kiss."

"That will I grant," said his father.

At this was Aucassin glad.

Here one singeth:

Of the kiss heard Aucassin
That returning he shall win.
None so glad would he have been 80
Of a myriad marks of gold
Of a hundred thousand told.
Called for raiment brave of steel,
Then they clad him, head to heel,
Twyfold hauberk doth he don,
Firmly braced the helmet on.
Girt the sword with hilt of gold,

63. *par amours,* as a paramour or mistress.

Horse doth mount, and lance doth wield,
Looks to stirrups and to shield,
Wondrous brave he rode to field.
Dreaming of his lady dear
Setteth spurs to the destrere,
Rideth forward without fear,
Through the gate and forth away
　　To the fray.

So speak they, say they, tell they the Tale:

10　Aucassin was armed and mounted as ye have heard tell. God! how goodly sat the shield on his shoulder, the helm on his head, and the baldric on his left haunch! And the damoiseau was tall, fair, featly fashioned, and hardy of his hands, and the horse whereon he rode swift and keen, and straight had he spurred him forth of the gate. Now believe ye not that his mind was on kine, nor cattle of the booty, nor thought he how he might strike a knight, nor be stricken again; nor no such thing. Nay, no
20　memory had Aucassin of aught of these; rather, he so dreamed of Nicolete, his sweet lady, that he dropped his reins, forgetting all there was to do, and his horse that had felt the spur, bore him into the press and hurled him among the foe, and they laid hands on him all about, and took him captive, and seized away his spear and shield, and straightway they led him off a prisoner, and were even now discoursing of what death he should die.

And when Aucassin heard them,

30　"Ha! God," said he, "sweet Saviour. Be these my deadly enemies that have taken me, and will soon cut off my head? And once my head is off, no more shall I speak with Nicolete, my sweet lady that I love so well. Natheless have I here a good sword, and sit a good horse unwearied. If now I keep not my head for her sake, God help her never, if she love me more!"

The damoiseau was tall and strong, and the horse whereon he sat was right eager. And he laid hand
40　to sword, and fell a-smiting to right and left, and smote through helm and nasal, and arm and clenched hand, making a murder about him, like a wild boar when hounds fall on him in the forest, even till he struck down ten knights, and seven he hurt, and straightway he hurled out of the press, and rode back again at full speed, sword in hand. The Count Bougars de Valence heard say they were about hanging Aucassin, his enemy, so he came into that place, and Aucassin was ware of him, and gat
50　his sword into his hand, and lashed at his helm with such a stroke that he drove it down on his head, and he being stunned, fell grovelling. And Aucassin laid hands on him, and caught him by the nasal of his helmet, and gave him to his father.

"Father," quoth Aucassin, "lo, here is your mortal foe, who hath so warred you with all malengin. Full twenty years did this war endure, and might not be ended by man."

"Fair son," said his father, "thy feats of youth shouldst thou do, and not seek after folly."　60

"Father," saith Aucassin, "sermon me no sermons, but fulfill my covenant."

"Ha! what covenant, fair son?"

"What, father, hast thou forgotten it? By mine own head, whosoever forgets, will I not forget it, so much it hath me at heart. Didst thou not covenant with me when I took up arms, and went into the stour, that if God brought me back safe and sound, thou wouldst let me see Nicolete, my sweet lady, ever so long that I may have of her two words or　70 three, and one kiss? So didst thou covenant, and my mind is that thou keep thy word."

"I!" quoth the father, "God forsake me when I keep this covenant! Nay, if she were here, I would let burn her in the fire, and thyself shouldst be sore adread."

"Is this thy last word?" quoth Aucassin.

"So help me God," quoth his father, "yea!"

"Certes," quoth Aucassin, "this is a sorry thing, meseems, when a man of thine age lies!"　80

"Count of Valence," quoth Aucassin, "I took thee?"

"In sooth, Sir, thou didst," saith the Count.

"Give me thy hand," saith Aucassin.

"Sir, with good will."

So he set his hand in the other's.

"Now givest thou me thy word," saith Aucassin, "that never whilst thou art living man wilt thou avail to do my father dishonor, or harm him in body, or in goods, but do it thou wilt?"　90

"Sir, in God's name," saith he, "mock me not, but put me to my ransom; ye cannot ask of me gold nor silver, horses nor palfreys, vair nor gris, hawks nor hounds, but I will give you them."

"What," quoth Aucassin, "Ha! knowest thou not it was I that took thee?"

"Yea, sir," quoth the Count Bougars.

"God help me never, but I will make thy head fly from thy shoulders, if thou makest not troth," said Aucassin.　100

"In God's name," said he, "I make what promise thou wilt."

So they did the oath, and Aucassin let mount him on a horse, and took another and so led him back till he was in all safety.

Here one singeth:

When the Count Garin doth know
That his child would ne'er forego

---

41. **nasal**, nose-guard.

56. **malengin**, evil intent.

Love of her that loved him so,
Nicolete, the bright of brow,
In a dungeon deep below
Childe Aucassin did he throw.
Even there the Childe must dwell
In a dun-walled marble-cell.
There he waileth in his woe
Crying thus as ye shall know.

"Nicolete, thou lily white,
10 My sweet lady, bright of brow,
Sweeter than the grape art thou,
Sweeter than sack posset good
In a cup of maple wood!
Was it not but yesterday
That a palmer came this way,
Out of Limousin came he,
And at ease he might not be,
For a passion him possessed
That upon his bed he lay,
20 Lay and tossed and knew not rest
In his pain discomforted.
But thou camest by the bed,
Where he tossed amid his pain,
Holding high thy sweeping train,
And thy kirtle of ermine,
And thy smock of linen fine,
Then these fair white limbs of thine,
Did he look on, and it fell
That the palmer straight was well,
30 Straight was hale—and comforted,
And he rose up from his bed,
And went back to his own place,
Sound and strong, and full of face!
My sweet lady, lily white,
Sweet thy footfall, sweet thine eyes,
And the mirth of thy replies.
Sweet thy laughter, sweet thy face,
Sweet thy lips and sweet thy brow,
And the touch of thine embrace.
40 Who but doth in thee delight?
I for love of thee am bound
In this dungeon under ground,
All for loving thee must lie
Here where loud on thee I cry,
Here for loving thee must die
          For thee, my love."

    Then say they, speak they, tell they the Tale:
    Aucassin was cast into prison as ye have heard
tell, and Nicolete, of her part, was in the chamber.
50 Now it was summer time, the month of May, when
days are warm, and long, and clear, and the night
still and serene. Nicolete lay one night on her bed,
and saw the moon shine clear through a window,
yea, and heard the nightingale sing in the garden,
so she minded her of Aucassin her lover, whom she

loved so well. Then fell she to thoughts of Count
Garin de Biaucaire, that hated her to the death;
therefore deemed she that there she would no longer
abide, for that, if she were told of, and the Count
knew whereas she lay, an ill death would he make 60
her die. Now she knew that the old woman slept
who held her company. Then she arose, and clad
her in a mantle of silk she had by her, very goodly,
and took napkins, and sheets of the bed, and knotted
one to the other, and made therewith a cord as long
as she might, so knitted it to a pillar in the window,
and let herself slip down into the garden, then
caught up her raiment in both hands, behind and
before, and kilted up her kirtle, because of the dew
that she saw lying deep on the grass, and so went 70
her way down through the garden.
    Her locks were yellow and curled, her eyes blue
and smiling, her face featly fashioned, the nose high
and fairly set, the lips more red than cherry or rose
in time of summer, her teeth white and small; her
breasts so firm that they bore up the folds of her
bodice as they had been two apples; so slim was she
in the waist that your two hands might have clipped
her, and the daisy flowers that brake beneath her
as she went tip-toe, and that bent above her instep, 80
seemed black against her feet, so white was the
maiden. She came to the postern-gate, and unbarred
it, and went out through the streets of Biaucaire,
keeping always on the shadowy side, for the moon
was shining right clear, and so wandered she till she
came to the tower where her lover lay. The tower
was flanked with buttresses, and she cowered under
one of them, wrapped in her mantle. Then thrust
she her head through a crevice of the tower that
was old and worn, and so heard she Aucassin wail- 90
ing within, and making dole and lament for the
sweet lady he loved so well. And when she had
listened to him, she began to say;
    Here one singeth:

Nicolete the bright of brow
On a pillar leanest thou,
All Aucassin's wail dost hear
For his love that is so dear,
Then thou spakest, shrill and clear,
"Gentle knight withouten fear, 100
Little good befalleth thee,
Little help of sigh or tear,
Ne'er shalt thou have joy of me.
Never shalt thou win me; still
Am I held in evil will
Of thy father and thy kin,
Therefore must I cross the sea,
And another land must win."
Then she cut her curls of gold,

76–77. breasts . . . apples. "*Nois gauges* in the original. But 'wal-
nuts' sound inadequate." (Translator's note.)

Cast them in the dungeon bold,
Aucassin doth clasp them there,
Kissed the curls that were so fair,
Them doth in his bosom bear,
Then he wept, even as of old,
    All for his love!

Then say they, speak they, tell they the Tale:
When Aucassin heard Nicolete say that she would
pass into a far country, he was all in wrath.

10 "Fair sweet friend," quoth he, "thou shalt not go,
for then wouldst thou be my death. And the first
man that saw thee and had the might withal, would
take thee straightway into his bed to be his leman.
And once thou camest into a man's bed, and that
bed not mine, wit ye well that I would not tarry till
I had found a knife to pierce my heart and slay
myself. Nay, verily, wait so long I would not; but
would hurl myself on it so soon as I could find a
wall, or a black stone, thereon would I dash my head
20 so mightily that the eyes would start and my brain
burst. Rather would I die even such a death than
know thou hadst lain in a man's bed, and that bed
not mine."

"Aucassin," she said, "I trow thou lovest me not
so much as thou sayest, but I love thee more than
thou lovest me."

"Ah, fair sweet friend," said Aucassin, "it may not
be that thou shouldst love me even as I love thee.
Woman may not love man as man loves woman,
30 for a woman's love lies in the glance of her eye, and
the bud of her breast, and her foot's tip-toe; but the
love of man is in his heart planted, whence it can
never issue forth and pass away."

Now while Aucassin and Nicolete held this parley
together, the town's guards came down a street, with
swords drawn beneath their cloaks, for the Count
Garin had charged them that if they could take her
they should slay her. But the sentinel that was on
the tower saw them coming, and heard them speak-
40 ing of Nicolete as they went, and threatening to slay
her.

"God!" quoth he, "this were great pity to slay so
fair a maid! Right great charity it were if I could
say aught to her, and they perceive it not, and she
should be on her guard against them, for if they slay
her, then were Aucassin, my damoiseau, dead, and
that were great pity."

Here one singeth:

Valiant was the sentinel,
50 Courteous, kind, and practised well,
So a song did sing and tell

51. **song did sing.** This warning song of the sentinel belongs to the
tradition of the *aubade*, or "dawn-song," a French courtly lyric poem
lamenting the necessity for lovers to separate but urging them to do
so in the face of danger, usually from an oncoming husband.

Of the peril that befell.
"Maiden fair that lingerest here,
Gentle maid of merry cheer,
Hair of gold, and eyes as clear
As the water in a mere,
Thou, meseems, hast spoken word
To thy lover and thy lord,
That would die for thee, his dear;
Now beware the ill accord,   60
Of the cloaked men of the sword,
These have sworn and keep their word,
They will put thee to the sword
    Save thou take heed!"

Then speak they, say they, tell they the Tale:
"Ha!" quoth Nicolete, "be the soul of thy father
and the soul of thy mother in the rest of Paradise,
so fairly and courteously hast thou spoken me!
Please God, I will be right ware of them, God keep
me out of their hands."   70

So she shrank under her mantle into the shadow
of the pillar till they had passed by, and then took
she farewell of Aucassin, and so fared till she came
unto the castle wall. Now that wall was wasted and
broken, and some deal mended, so she clomb
thereon till she came between wall and fosse, and
so looked down, and saw that the fosse was deep
and steep, whereat she was sore adread.

"Ah God," saith she, "sweet Saviour! If I let myself fall hence, I shall break my neck, and if here I 80
abide, tomorrow they will take me, and burn me in
a fire. Yet liefer would I perish here than that
tomorrow the folk should stare on me for a gazing-
stock."

Then she crossed herself, and so let herself slip
into the fosse, and when she had come to the
bottom, her fair feet, and fair hands that had not
custom thereof, were bruised and frayed, and the
blood springing from a dozen places, yet felt she
no pain nor hurt, by reason of the great dread 90
wherein she went. But if she were in cumber to win
there, in worse was she to win out. But she deemed
that there to abide was of none avail, and she found
a pike sharpened, that they of the city had thrown
out to keep the hold. Therewith made she one stepping place after another, till, with much travail, she
climbed the wall. Now the forest lay within two
crossbow shots, and the forest was of thirty leagues
this way and that. Therein also were wild beasts,
and beasts serpentine, and she feared that if she 100
entered there, they would slay her. But anon she
deemed that if men found her there they would hale
her back into the town to burn her.

Here one singeth:

Nicolete, the fair of face,
Climbed upon the coping-stone,

There made she lament and moan,
Calling on our Lord alone
For His mercy and His grace.

"Father, king of Majesty,
Listen, for I nothing know
Where to flee or whither go.
If within the wood I fare,
Lo, the wolves will slay me there,
Boars and lions terrible,
10 Many in the wild wood dwell,
But if I abide the day,
Surely worse will come of it,
Surely will the fire be lit
That shall burn my body away,
Jesus, lord of Majesty,
Better seemeth it to me,
That within the wood I fare,
Though the wolves devour me there
Than within the town to go,
20   Never be it so!"

Then speak they, say they, tell they the Tale:
Nicolete made great moan, as ye have heard; then
commended she herself to God, and anon fared till
she came unto the forest. But to go deep into it she
dared not, by reason of the wild beasts, and beasts
serpentine. Anon crept she into a little thicket, where
sleep came upon her, and she slept till prime next
day, when the shepherds issued forth from the town
and drove their beasts between wood and water.
30 Anon came they all into one place by a fair fountain
which was on the fringe of the forest; thereby spread
they a mantle, and thereon set bread. So while they
were eating, Nicolete wakened, with the sound of
the singing birds, and the shepherds, and she went
unto them, saying, "Fair boys, our Lord keep you!"
"God bless thee," quoth he that had more words
to his tongue than the rest.
"Fair boys," quoth she, "know ye Aucassin, the
son of Count Garin de Biaucaire?"
40 "Yea, well we know him."
"So may God help you, fair boys," quoth she,
"tell him there is a beast in this forest, and bid him
come chase it, and if he can take it, he would not
give one limb thereof for a hundred marks of gold,
nay, for five hundred, nor for any ransom."
Then looked they on her, and saw her so fair that
they were all astonied.
"Will I tell him thereof?" quoth he that had more
words to his tongue than the rest, "foul fall him who
50 speaks of the thing or tells him the tidings. These
are but visions ye tell of, for there is no beast so
great in this forest, stag, nor lion, nor boar, that
one of his limbs is worth more than two deniers, or
three at the most, and ye speak of such great ransom. Foul fall him that believes your word, and

him that telleth Aucassin. Ye be a Fairy, and we
have no liking for your company; nay, hold on your
road."
"Nay, fair boys," quoth she, "nay, ye will do my
bidding. For this beast is so mighty of medicine that 60
thereby will Aucassin be healed of his torment. And
lo! I have five sols in my purse, take them, and tell
him; for within three days must he come hunting it
hither, and if within three days he find it not, never
will he be healed of his torment."
"My faith," quoth he, "the money will we take,
and if he come hither we will tell him, but seek
him we will not."
"In God's name," quoth she; and so took farewell
of the shepherds, and went her way.   70
Here singeth one:

Nicolete the bright of brow
From the shepherds doth she pass
All below the blossomed bough
Where an ancient way there was,
Overgrown and choked with grass,
Till she found the cross-roads where
Seven paths do all way fare,
Then she deemeth she will try,
Should her lover pass thereby,   80
If he love her loyally.
So she gathered white lilies,
Oak-leaf, that in green wood is,
Leaves of many a branch I wis,
Therewith built a lodge of green,
Goodlier was never seen,
Swore by God who may not lie,
"If my love the lodge should spy,
He will rest awhile thereby
If he love me loyally."   90
Thus his faith she seemed to try,
"Or I love him not, not I,
        Nor he loves me!"

Then speak they, say they, tell they the Tale:
Nicolete built her lodge of boughs, as ye have
heard, right fair and feteously, and wove it well,
within and without, of flowers and leaves. So lay
she hard by the lodge in a deep coppice to know
what Aucassin will do. And the cry and the bruit
went abroad through all the country and all the land, 100
that Nicolete was lost. Some told that she had fled,
and some that the Count Garin had let slay her.
Whosoever had joy thereof, no joy had Aucassin.
And the Count Garin, his father, had taken him out
of prison, and had sent for the knights of that land,
and the ladies, and let make a right great feast, for
the comforting of Aucassin his son. Now at the
high time of the feast, was Aucassin leaning from a

62. **sols,** sous, the modern French coin; its value in the twelfth century is altogether problematical. 96. **feteously,** neatly.

gallery, all woful and discomforted. Whatsoever men might devise of mirth, Aucassin had no joy thereof, nor no desire, for he saw not her that he loved. Then a knight looked on him, and came to him, and said:

"Aucassin, of that sickness of thine have I been sick, and good counsel will I give thee, if thou wilt hearken to me——"

"Sir," said Aucassin, "gramercy, good counsel would I fain hear."

"Mount thy horse," quoth he, "and go take thy pastime in yonder forest; there wilt thou see the good flowers and grass, and hear the sweet birds sing. Perchance thou shalt hear some word, whereby thou shalt be the better."

"Sir," quoth Aucassin, "gramercy; that will I do."

He passed out of the hall, and went down the stairs, and came to the stable where his horse was. He let saddle and bridle him, and mounted, and rode forth from the castle, and wandered till he came to the forest, so rode till he came to the fountain and found the shepherds at the point of noon. And they had a mantle stretched on the grass, and were eating bread, and making great joy.

Here one singeth:

There were gathered shepherds all,
Martin, Esmerie, and Hal,
Aubrey, Robin, great and small.
Saith the one, "Good fellows all,
God keep Aucassin the fair,
And the maid with yellow hair,
Bright of brown and eyes of vair.
She that gave us gold to ware,
Cakes therewith to buy, ye know,
Goodly knives and sheaths also,
Flutes to play, and pipes to blow,
    May God him heal!"

Here speak they, say they, tell they the Tale:
When Aucassin heard the shepherds, anon he bethought him of Nicolete, his sweet lady whom he loved so well, and he deemed that she had passed thereby; then set he spurs to his horse, and so came to the shepherds.

"Fair boys, God be with you."

"God bless you," quoth he that had more words to his tongue than the rest.

"Fair boys," quoth Aucassin, "say the song again that anon ye sang."

"Say it again we will not," quoth he that had more words to his tongue than the rest, "foul fall him who will sing it again for you, fair sir!"

"Fair boys," quoth Aucassin, "know ye me not?"

"Yea, we know well that you are Aucassin, our damoiseau, natheless we be not your men, but the Count's."

"Fair boys, yet sing it again, I pray you."

"Hearken! by the Holy Heart," quoth he, "wherefore should I sing it for you, if it likes me not? Lo, there is no such rich man in this country, saving the body of Garin the Count, that dare drive forth my oxen, or my cows, or my sheep, if he finds them in his fields, or his corn, lest he lose his eyes for it, and wherefore should I sing for you, if it likes me not?"

"God be your aid, fair boys, sing it ye will, and take ye these ten sols I have here in a purse."

"Sir, the money will we take, but never a note will I sing, for I have given my oath; but I will tell thee a plain tale, if thou wilt."

"By God," saith Aucassin, "I love a plain tale better than naught."

"Sir, we were in this place, a little time agone, between prime and tierce, and were eating our bread by this fountain, even as now we do, and a maid came past, the fairest thing in the world, whereby we deemed that she should be a fay, and all the wood shone round about her. Anon she gave us of that she had, whereby we made covenant with her, that if ye came hither we would bid you hunt in the forest, wherein is such a beast that, an ye might take him, ye would not give one limb of him for five hundred marks of silver, nor for no ransom; for this beast is so mighty of medicine, that, an ye could take him, ye should be healed of your torment, and within three days must ye take him, and if ye take him not then, never will ye look on him. So chase ye the beast, an ye will, or an ye will let be, for my promise have I kept with her."

"Fair boys," quoth Aucassin, "ye have said enough. God grant me to find this quarry."

Here one singeth:

Aucassin when he had heard,
Sore within his heart was stirred,
Left the shepherds on that word,
Far into the forest spurred,
Rode into the wood; and fleet
Fled his horse through paths of it,
Three words spoke he of his sweet,
"Nicolete the fair, the dear,
'Tis for thee I follow here
Track of boar, nor slot of deer,
But thy sweet body and eyes so clear,
All thy mirth and merry cheer,
That my very heart have slain,
So please God to me maintain
I shall see my love again,
    Sweet sister, friend!"

Then speak they, say they, tell they the Tale:
Aucassin fared through the forest from path to path after Nicolete, and his horse bore him furiously. Think ye not that the thorns him spared, nor the briars, nay, not so, but tore his raiment, that

scarce a knot might be tied with the soundest part thereof, and the blood sprang from his arms, and flanks, and legs, in forty places, or thirty, so that behind the Childe men might follow on the track of his blood in the grass. But so much he went in thoughts of Nicolete, his lady sweet, that he felt no pain nor torment, and all the day hurled through the forest in this fashion nor heard no word of her. And when he saw Vespers draw nigh, he began to weep for that he found her not. All down an old road, and grassgrown, he fared, when anon, looking along the way before him, he saw such an one as I shall tell you. Tall was he, and great of growth, laidly and marvellous to look upon; his head huge, and black as charcoal, and more than the breadth of a hand between his two eyes, and great cheeks, and a big nose and broad, big nostrils and ugly, and thick lips redder than a collop, and great teeth yellow and ugly, and he was shod with hosen and shoon of bull's hide, bound with cords of bark over the knee, and all about him a great cloak twyfold, and he leaned on a grievous cudgel, and Aucassin came unto him, and was afraid when he beheld him.

"Fair brother, God aid thee."

"God bless you," quoth he.

"As God he helpeth thee, what makest thou here?"

"What is that to thee?"

"Nay, naught, naught," saith Aucassin, "I ask but out of courtesy."

"But for whom weepest thou," quoth he, "and makest such heavy lament? Certes, were I as rich a man as thou, the whole world should not make me weep."

"Ha, know you me?" saith Aucassin.

"Yea, I know well that ye be Aucassin, the son of the Count, and if ye tell me for why ye weep, then will I tell you what I make here."

"Certes," quoth Aucassin, "I will tell you right gladly. Hither came I this morning to hunt in this forest; and with me a white hound, the fairest in the world; him have I lost, and for him I weep."

"By the Heart our Lord bore in His breast," quoth he, "are ye weeping for a stinking hound? Foul fall him that holds thee high henceforth! for there is no such rich man in the land, but if thy father asked it of him, he would give thee ten, or fifteen, or twenty, and be the gladder for it. But I have cause to weep and make dole."

"Wherefore so, brother?"

"Sir, I will tell thee. I was hireling to a rich villain, and drove his plough; four oxen had he. But three days since came on me great misadventure, whereby I lost the best of mine oxen, Roger, the best of my team. Him go I seeking, and have neither eaten nor drunken these three days, nor may I go to the town, lest they cast me into prison, seeing that I have not wherewithal to pay. Out of all the wealth of the world have I no more than ye see on my body. A poor mother bore me, that had no more but one wretched bed; this have they taken from under her, and she lies in the very straw. This ails me more than mine own case, for wealth comes and goes; if now I have lost, another time will I gain, and will pay for mine ox whenas I may; never for that will I weep. But you weep for a stinking hound. Foul fall whoso thinks well of thee!"

"Certes thou art a good comforter, brother, blessed be thou! And of what price was thine ox?"

"Sir, they ask me twenty sols for him, whereof I cannot abate one doit."

"Nay, then," quoth Aucassin, "take these twenty sols I have in my purse, and pay for thine ox."

"Sir," saith he, "gramercy. And God give thee to find that thou seekest."

So they parted each from other, and Aucassin rode on; the night was fair and still, and so long he went that he came to the lodge of boughs, that Nicolete had builded and woven within and without, over and under, with flowers, and it was the fairest lodge that might be seen. When Aucassin was ware of it, he stopped suddenly, and the light of the moon fell therein.

"God!" quoth Aucassin, "here was Nicolete, my sweet lady, and this lodge builded she with her fair hands. For the sweetness of it, and for love of her, will I alight, and rest here this night long."

He drew forth his foot from the stirrup to alight, and the steed was great and tall. He dreamed so much on Nicolete his right sweet lady, that he slipped on a stone, and drove his shoulder out of its place. Then knew he that he was hurt sore; natheless he bore him with what force he might, and fastened with the other hand the mare's son to a thorn. Then turned he on his side, and crept backwise into the lodge of boughs. And he looked through a gap in the lodge and saw the stars in Heaven, and one that was brighter than the rest; so began he to say:

Here one singeth:

"Star, that I from far behold,
Star, the Moon calls to her fold,
Nicolete with thee doth dwell,
My sweet love with locks of gold,
God would have her dwell afar,
Dwell with him for evening star,
Would to God, whate'er befall,
Would that with her I might dwell.

---

4. **Childe,** young knight. 13. **Tall was he . . .** The man represented here is the loathly (laidly) churl, who is a convention of medieval legend. To be noted here is his forthrightness in the presence of Aucassin (matched by that of the shepherds some lines above) and particularly his tender regard for his mother, since sentimentality about mothers was not a common feature of medieval literature. 18. **collop,** a large piece of meat for stewing.

I would clip her close and strait;
Nay, were I of much estate,
Some king's son desirable,
Worthy she to be my mate,
Me to kiss and clip me well,
     Sister, sweet friend!"

So speak they, say they, tell they the Tale:
When Nicolete heard Aucassin, right so came she
unto him, for she was not far away. She passed
within the lodge, and threw her arms about his
neck, and clipped and kissed him.

"Fair sweet friend, welcome be thou."

"And thou, fair sweet love, be thou welcome."

So either kissed and clipped the other, and fair
joy was between them.

"Ha! sweet love," quoth Aucassin, "but now was
I sore hurt, and my shoulder wried, but I take no
force of it, nor have no hurt therefrom since I have
thee."

Right so felt she his shoulder and found it was
wried from its place. And she so handled it with
her white hands, and so wrought in her surgery, that
by God's will who loveth lovers, it went back into
its place. Then took she flowers, and fresh grass,
and leaves green, and bound these herbs on the
hurt with a strip of her smock, and he was all
healed.

"Aucassin," saith she, "fair sweet love, take counsel what thou wilt do. If thy father let search this
forest tomorrow, and men find me here, they will
slay me, come to thee what will."

"Certes, fair sweet love, therefore should I sorrow
heavily, but, an if I may, never shall they take
thee."

Anon got he on his horse, and his lady before
him, kissing and clipping her, and so rode they at
adventure.

Here one singeth:

Aucassin the frank, the fair,
Aucassin of the yellow hair,
Gentle knight, and true lover,
From the forest doth he fare,
Holds his love before him there,
Kissing cheek, and chin, and eyes,
But she spoke in sober wise,
"Aucassin, true love and fair,
To what land do we repair?"
Sweet my love, I take no care,
Thou art with me everywhere!
So they pass the woods and downs,
Pass the villages and towns,
Hills and dales and open land,
Came at dawn to the sea sand,
Lighted down upon the strand,
     Beside the sea.

1. **clip,** embrace.

Then say they, speak they, tell they the Tale:
Aucassin lighted down and his love, as ye have
heard sing. He held his horse by the bridle, and his
lady by the hands; so they went along the sea shore,
and on the sea they saw a ship, and he called unto
the sailors, and they came to him. Then held he
such speech with them, that he and his lady were
brought aboard that ship, and when they were on
the high sea, behold a mighty wind and tyrannous
arose, marvellous and great, and drove them from
land to land, till they came unto a strange country,
and won the haven of the castle of Torelore. Then
asked they what this land might be, and men told
them that it was the country of the King of Torelore.
Then he asked what manner of man was he, and
was there war afoot, and men said,

"Yea, and mighty!"

Therewith took he farewell of the merchants, and
they commended him to God. Anon Aucassin
mounted his horse, with his sword girt, and his lady
before him, and rode at adventure till he was come
to the castle. Then asked he where the King was,
and they said that he was in childbed.

"Then where is his wife?"

And they told him she was with the army, and
had led with her all the force of that country.

Now when Aucassin heard that saying, he made
great marvel, and came into the castle, and lighted
down, he and his lady, and his lady held his horse.
Right so went he up into the castle, with his sword
girt, and fared hither and thither till he came to the
chamber where the King was lying.

Here one singeth:

Aucassin the courteous knight
To the chamber went forthright,
To the bed with linen dight
Even where the King was laid.
There he stood by him and said:
"Fool, what makest thou here abed?"
Quoth the King: "I am brought to bed
Of a fair son, and anon
When my month is over and gone,
And my healing fairly done,
To the Minster will I fare
And will do my churching there,
As my father did repair,
Then will sally forth to war,
Then will drive my foes afar
     From my countrie!"

Then speak they, say they, tell they the Tale:
When Aucassin heard the King speak on this wise,

78. **he was in childbed.** This is an old folklore motif, known as the
Couvade, that a man lay in childbirth while his wife assumed his
manly and military duties. "The feigned lying-in of the father may
have been either a recognition of paternity . . . or may have been
caused by the belief that the health of the father at the time of a
child's birth affected that of the child . . ." (Translator's note.)

he took all the sheets that covered him, and threw them all abroad about the chamber. Then saw he behind him a cudgel, and caught it into his hand, and turned, and took the King, and beat him till he was well-nigh dead.

"Ha, fair sir," quoth the King, "what would you with me? Art thou beside thyself, that beatest me in mine own house?"

"By God's heart," quoth Aucassin, "thou ill son of an ill wench, I will slay thee if thou swear not that never shall any man in all thy land lie in of child henceforth for ever."

So he did that oath, and when he had done it, "Sir," said Aucassin, "bring me now where thy wife is with the army."

"Sir, with good will," quoth the King.

He mounted his horse, and Aucassin got on his own, and Nicolete abode in the Queen's chamber. Anon rode Aucassin and the King even till they came to that place where the Queen was, and lo! men were warring with baked apples, and with eggs, and with fresh cheeses, and Aucassin began to look on them, and made great marvel.

Here one singeth:

Aucassin his horse doth stay,
From the saddle watched the fray,
All the stour and fierce array;
Right fresh cheeses carried they,
Apples baked, and mushrooms gray,
Whoso splasheth most the ford
He is master called and lord.
Aucassin doth gaze awhile,
Then began to laugh and smile
⠀⠀⠀And made game.

Then speak they, say they, tell they the Tale:
When Aucassin beheld these marvels, he came to the King, and said: "Sir, be these thine enemies?"

"Yea, Sir," quoth the King.

"And will ye that I should avenge you of them?"

"Yea," quoth he, "with all my heart."

Then Aucassin put hand to sword, and hurled among them, and began to smite to the right hand and the left, and slew many of them. And when the King saw that he slew them, he caught at his bridle and said,

"Ha, fair sir! Slay them not in such wise."

"How?" quoth Aucassin. "Will ye not that I should avenge you of them?"

"Sir," quoth the King, "overmuch already hast thou avenged me. It is nowise our custom to slay each other."

Anon turned they and fled. Then the King and Aucassin betook them again to the castle of Torelore, and the folk of that land counselled the King to put Aucassin forth, and keep Nicolete for his son's wife, for that she seemed a lady high of lineage.

And Nicolete heard them, and had no joy of it, so began to say:

Here singeth one:

Thus she spoke, the bright of brow:
"Lord of Torelore and king,
Thy folk deem me a light thing.
When my love doth me embrace,
Fair he finds me, in good case,
Then am I in such derray,
Neither harp, nor lyre, nor lay,
Dance nor game, nor rebeck-play
⠀⠀⠀Were so sweet."

Then speak they, say they, tell they the Tale:
Aucassin dwelt in the castle of Torelore, in great ease and great delight, for that he had with him Nicolete his sweet love, whom he loved so well. Now while he was in such pleasure and such delight, came a troop of Saracens by sea, and laid siege to the castle and took it by main strength. Anon took they the substance that was therein and carried off the men and maidens captives. They seized Nicolete and Aucassin, and bound Aucassin hand and foot, and cast him into one ship, and Nicolete into another. Then rose there a mighty wind over sea, and scattered the ships. Now that ship wherein was Aucassin went wandering on the sea, till it came to the castle of Biaucaire, and the folk of the country ran together to wreck her, and there found they Aucassin, and they knew him again. So when they of Biaucaire saw their damoiseau, they made great joy of him, for Aucassin had dwelt full three years in the castle of Torelore, and his father and mother were dead. So the people took him to the castle of Biaucaire, and there were they all his men. And he held the land in peace.

Here singeth one:

Lo ye, Aucassin hath gone
To Biaucaire that is his own,
Dwelleth there in joy and ease
And the kingdom is at peace.
Swears he by the Majesty
Of our Lord that is most high,
Rather would he they should die
All his kin and parentry,
So that Nicolete were nigh.

"Ah sweet love, and fair of brow,
I know not where to seek thee now,
God made never that countrie,
Not by land, and not by sea,
Where I would not search for thee,
⠀⠀⠀If that might be!"

65. **derray**, distraction.

Then speak they, say they, tell they the Tale:

Now leave we Aucassin, and speak we of Nicolete. The ship wherein she was cast pertained to the King of Carthage, and he was her father, and she had twelve brothers, all princes or kings. When they beheld Nicolete, how fair she was, they did her great worship, and made much joy of her, and many times asked her who she was, for surely seemed she a lady of noble line and high parentry. But she
10 might not tell them of her lineage, for she was but a child when men stole her away. So sailed they till they won the City of Carthage, and when Nicolete saw the walls of the castle, and the country-side, she knew that there had she been nourished and thence stolen away, being but a child. Yet was she not so young a child but that well she knew she had been daughter of the King of Carthage; and of her nurture in that city.

Here singeth one:

20 Nicolete the good and true
To the land hath come anew,
Sees the palaces and walls,
And the houses and the halls!
Then she spoke and said, "Alas!
That of birth so great I was,
Cousin of the Amiral
And the very child of him
Carthage counts King of Paynim,
Wild folk hold me here withal;
30 Nay, Aucassin, love of thee,
Gentle knight, and true, and free,
Burns and wastes the heart of me.
Ah, God grant it of His grace,
That thou hold me, and embrace,
That thou kiss me on the face,
　　　Love and lord!"

Then speak they, say they, tell they the Tale:

When the King of Carthage heard Nicolete speak in this wise, he cast his arms about her neck.
40 "Fair sweet love," saith he, "tell me who thou art, and be not adread of me."

"Sir," said she, "I am daughter to the King of Carthage, and was taken, being then a little child, it is now fifteen years gone."

When all they of the court heard her speak thus, they knew well that she spoke sooth: so made they great joy of her, and led her to the castle in great honor, as the King's daughter. And they would have given her to her lord a King of Paynim, but she had
50 no mind to marry. There dwelt she three days or four. And she considered by what means she might seek for Aucassin. Then she got her a viol, and learned to play on it, till they would have married her on a day to a great King of Paynim, and she stole forth by night, and came to the sea-port, and dwelt with a poor woman thereby. Then took she

This French donjon *was built in the twelfth century at Château-Gaillard by Richard Coeur de Lion. Since restored.*

a certain herb, and therewith smeared her head and her face, till she was all brown and stained. And she let make coat, and mantle, and smock, and hose, and attired herself as if she had been a harper. So she 60 took the viol and went to a mariner, and so wrought on him that he took her aboard his vessel. Then hoisted they sail, and fared on the high seas even till they came to the land of Provence. And Nicolete went forth and took the viol, and went playing through all that country, even till she came to the castle of Biaucaire, where Aucassin lay.

Here singeth one:

At Biaucaire below the tower
Sat Aucassin, on an hour, 70
Heard the bird, and watched the flower,
With his barons him beside,
Then came on him in that tide,
The sweet influence of love
And the memory thereof;
Thought of Nicolete the fair,
And the dainty face of her
He had loved so many years,
Then was he in dule and tears!
Even then came Nicolete, 80
On the stair a foot she set,
And she drew the viol-bow
Through the strings and chanted so:
"Listen, lords and knights, to me,

Lords of high or low degree,
To my story list will ye,
All of Aucassin and her
That was Nicolete the fair?
And their love was long to tell,
Deep woods through he sought her well;
Paynims took them on a day
In Torelore and bound they lay.
Of Aucassin naught know we,
10 But fair Nicolete the free
Now in Carthage doth she dwell,
There her father loves her well,
Who is king of that countrie.
Her a husband hath he found,
Paynim lord that serves Mahound!
Ne'er with him the maid will go,
For she loves a damoiseau,
Aucassin, that ye may know,
Swears to God that never mo
20 With a lover will she go
Save with him she loveth so
    In long desire."

So speak they, say they, tell they the Tale:
When Aucassin heard Nicolete speak in this wise,
he was right joyful, and drew her on one side, and
spoke, saying:
"Sweet fair friend, know ye nothing of this Nicolete, of whom ye have thus sung?"
"Yea, Sir, I know her for the noblest creature, and
30 the most gentle, and the best that ever was born on
earth. She is daughter to the King of Carthage, that
took her there where Aucassin was taken, and
brought her into the City of Carthage, till he knew
that verily she was his own daughter, whereon he
made right great mirth. Anon wished he to give her
for her lord one of the greatest kings of all Spain,
but she would rather let herself be hanged or
burned than take any lord, how great soever."
"Ha! fair sweet friend," quoth the Count Aucassin,
40 "if thou wilt go into that land again, and bid her
come and speak to me, I will give thee of my substance, more than thou wouldst dare to ask or take.
And know ye, that for the sake of her, I have no
will to take a wife, howsoever high her lineage. So
wait I for her, and never will I have a wife, but her
only. And if I knew where to find her, no need
would I have to seek her."
"Sir," quoth she, "if ye promise me that, I will
go in quest of her for your sake, and for hers, that
50 I love much."
So he swore to her, and anon let give her twenty
livres, and she departed from him, and he wept for
the sweetness of Nicolete. And when she saw him
weeping, she said:
"Sir, trouble not thyself so much withal. For in a

little while shall I have brought her into this city,
and ye shall see her."
When Aucassin heard that, he was right glad
thereof. And she departed from him, and went into
the city to the house of the Captain's wife, for the 60
Captain her father in God was dead. So she dwelt
there, and told all her tale; and the Captain's wife
knew her, and knew well that she was Nicolete that
herself had nourished. Then she let wash and bathe
her, and there rested she eight full days. Then took
she an herb that was named *Eyebright* and anointed
herself therewith, and was as fair as ever she had
been all the days of her life. Then she clothed herself in rich robes of silk whereof the lady had great
store, and then sat herself in the chamber on a 70
silken coverlet, and called the lady and bade her go
and bring Aucassin her love, and she did even so.
And when she came to the Palace she found Aucassin
weeping, and making lament for Nicolete his love,
for that she delayed so long. And the lady spoke
unto him and said:
"Aucassin, sorrow no more, but come thou on
with me, and I will show thee the thing in the world
that thou lovest best; even Nicolete thy dear love,
who from far lands hath come to seek of thee." And 80
Aucassin was right glad.
Here singeth one:

When Aucassin heareth now
That his lady bright of brow
Dwelleth in his own countrie,
Never man was glad as he.
To her castle doth he hie
With the lady speedily,
Passeth to her chamber high, 90
Findeth Nicolete thereby.
Of her true love found again
Never maid was half so fain.
Straight she leaped upon her feet;
When his love he saw at last,
Arms about her did he cast,
Kissed her often, kissed her sweet,
Kissed her lips and brows and eyes.
Thus all night do they devise,
Even till the morning white.
Then Aucassin wedded her, 100
Made her Lady of Biaucaire.
Many years abode they there,
Many years in shade or sun,
In great gladness and delight.
Ne'er hath Aucassin regret
Nor his lady Nicolete.
Now my story all is done,
    Said and sung!

66. *Eyebright*. ". . . a fanciful rendering of *Esclaire*." (Translator's
note.)

The Minnesingers

When the great vogue of chivalric literature spread from France into Germany, it had for its representatives and missionaries in Germany the talented and numerous group of poets known ever since as the Minnesingers, or singers of courtly love. These poets flourished in the twelfth and thirteenth centuries, and the peak of their achievement was reached close to the year 1200. Although for a time they remained relatively independent of the metrical forms developed by the French courtly poets and troubadours, in spirit they were dedicated to the established traditions of *courtoisie*. Their work was sometimes epic in spirit, as in the fine medieval chivalric romances composed by Wolfram von Eschenbach and Gottfried von Strassburg, but it was more often lyrical. The emotion universally expressed was that of an admiring, worshipful love, addressed nearly always to a married woman or to one who had already been spoken for. The poet was customarily of the lesser nobility, and his patroness was above him in station; consequently much of this love poetry was both fulsome and artificial. In some instances the passion expressed was Platonic, in others altogether carnal; but in every case the lady was placed upon a pedestal from which she could either gaze scornfully or beam amiably upon the poet, depending upon circumstances.

Later the subject matter of these poems acquired greater range, and their forms became experimental. More than a few came to contain political or satirical implications; some were even antireligious and discreetly hostile to the tyrannies of feudalism. But the majority were usually assignable to one of a handful of types. There was, for instance, the *Spruch*, a poem in a single strophe of pure lyric outburst or of philosophical utterance. More commonly, however, the poems were in three strophes—or at least of a threefold structure—in which the first two strophes served to state and develop the theme, and the last, the so-called *Abgesang*, gave the conclusion and allowed the poet to take his leave in a manner appropriate to the court. Of this sort was the *Tagelied*, the blood-cousin of the French *aubade*, which lamented the call of the sentinel or warder who warned the lovers of the approach of daylight and danger. The *Leiche*, or lays, were more extensively narrative and were often virtually religious odes in essence. Many of the individual Minnesingers were known chiefly for writing Crusaders' Hymns, which were obviously religious in both a militant and chivalric manner. Apart from the chivalric romances like Wolfram von Eschenbach's *Parzival* or Gottfried von Strassburg's *Tristan*, which are not, strictly speaking, to be classed among the *Minnelieder*, there were many ballads of somewhat popular cast. By and large, however, the poetry of the Minnesingers is to be referred most properly to the great library of amoristic poetry, of which, it must be insisted, shades and variations are innumerable. It is a mistake to think of this poetry as a matter of formula alone, and it is equally erroneous to demand the strict categorization of each and every one of these poems as *Sprüche, Tagelieder, Leiche,* or Crusader Hymns.

These poems were probably first delivered orally in open court, the poet himself singing the verses to a melody (the *Weise*), accompanying himself on a small harp or a lute. Their vogue in the courtly society of central Europe during the later Middle Ages was enormous; the more successful entertainers among the Minnesingers became personally so celebrated as to assume in later years a legendary status which often had no correspondence to fact. Good examples of such treatment are the cases of Tannhäuser and Walther von der Vogelweide, the latter of whom, all things considered, is the finest lyric poet of the group. Medieval European literature owes much to the Minnesingers. Leaving aside the matter of their obvious talents, we can see in them ample testimony to the perennial existence of love poetry and an excellent check upon the point of view that medieval lyricism was inspired only by religious or political considerations.

The Minnesingers

O LADY, long have I been fain
    To set my love on thee,
And made good use of all I was:
Thou hast ennobled me.
May all that I from thee have won   5
To my advantage tell;
And if it ends as it begun,
You have done all things well.

—*Dietmar von Aist*

To MY lady's bower I crept
    By the watchers unsuspected.
"Sir, the bounds you have o'erstepped!
You surprise me unprotected."
"Lady, now committed is the sin."   5
"Tell me, Sir, what bringeth you my bower within?"
"Once again to swear the truth:
I for love of you am dying."
"Out upon thee, foolish youth!
Save the effort of thy sighing."   10
"You will kill me sweet, if so you gird."
"Sigh a thousand years, you never shall be heard."
    "And is this my recompense:
Chiding in such cruel fashion?"

The Minnesingers ⁶ Translated by Jethro Bithell. From *The Minnesingers* by Jethro Bithell, published by Longmans Green and Co., Ltd.
4. **Thou . . . me.** This is the basic idea of all chivalric love poetry, or, in the terms of the Minnesingers, the *Minnedienst*, or service of love.

"Sir, you have but little sense, 15
Wantonly to stir my passion."
"Mistress, my existence you have blighted."
"You're an arrant fool to love me uninvited."
"Could I other than adore you
When I looked upon your beauty?" 20
"You insult me! I implore you
To respect my wifely duty."
"To insult you never came into my mind."
"You would boast of my dishonor, were I kind."
"I am faithful and discreet; 25
My deserts you still have scanted."
"I forbid you to entreat
Favors that can ne'er be granted."
"Of love's long servitude is this the fee?"
"Others may accord you what you seek of me." 30
"Then my singing must remain,
And true service, unrewarded?"
"Nay, your pains were not in vain:
(Guerdon) good shall be accorded."
"I entreat you, make your meaning plain!" 35
"You are happier now and nobler in the grain."
                              —*Albrecht von Johannsdorf*

WHAT sweetness into that old word *woman*
          grew!
How soothing is it both to speak and hear!
There is no other word rings half so true;
It is the seal of noble things and dear.
Not even he thou lovest, none on earth, 5
O woman, praises thee to thy full worth.
Thou dost enrich the soul
Of all: and shall I lack my dole?
                              —*Reinmar von Hagenau*

WILL you take this wilding wreath?"
          I murmured to a maiden fair,
"To grace the dance on the heath
When you wear it on your shining hair,
If I had many a precious jewel, 5
Yourself should wear them all
In one bright coronal—
Believe it, dearest maid, and be not cruel!

     You are so exquisite,
I culled the garland but for you: 10
Think not too mean of it.
I know where flowers of brightest hue

Are growing in the distant heather:
Birds are singing
Where they are springing— 15
There let us go to gather them together!"

     She took the gift; and said
Her thanks in maiden's manner, shy.
Her cheeks grew red
Like roses that by lilies lie. 20
She veiled her eyes as she were frightened;
The curtsy that she made
My trouble all repaid.
And was that all? Ye shall not be enlightened.

     Methought as then so fain 25
My mind had never been before:
The trees did rain
Their blossoms down upon us more and more.
Then laughed I so my sides were shaken—
Such joy it seemed 30
The while I dreamed;
And then it dawned and I was forced to awaken.

     And thus it did arise
The girls I meet these summer days
I peep into their eyes 35
Hoping my dream-maiden meet my gaze.
Is she dancing here with you, I wonder?
Lassie, just bend back
Your bonnet brim! Alack!
Could I but find her out my garland under!
                              —*Walther von der Vogelweide*

WHATEVER be my faults, one quality
          I have been fain from childhood's days to
          keep:
I can join in not unseemly jollity,
And I am loth to laugh when others weep.
For others' sake I grieve: 5
For others' sake I sorrow;
Though sorrow to me cleave,
What matter? joy I borrow.
As others are, so will I be,
That they grow not tired of me. 10
Some there are with no compassion
For others' pains; let them be treated in like fashion.
     In the good old days, when love and honor ruled,
My youthful songs were ever smooth and cheery:
But now that love and honor are befooled, 15
My songs, alas! are rugged grown and dreary.
According as things be,
The real poet sings:
Not till boorishness shall flee
Will I sing of courtly things. 20

29. **"Of . . . fee."** This is a commonplace of all chivalric love-poetry, even down to the Renaissance. 1. **What . . . grew** . . . This little poem, a typical example of the Minnesingers' *Spruch*, was considered by Walther von der Vogelweide as Reinmar's masterpiece. Few of the Minnesingers' poems can summarize so well the essential spirit of the genre. 1. **"Will . . . wreath."** This is classed as a dancing song of the sort made famous by Reinmar von Hagenau. It is also, however, a dream song; none of the Minnesingers was capable of more beautiful lyric effects in this typical medieval medium.

39. **Your . . . brim.** Large hats were at the time especially the fashion in Austria, the home of Walther von der Vogelweide.

Joy will return and a day for song;
Happy who can wait so long.
If you will only take my word,
I know the way and when a poet should be heard.
    For a bare greeting I did praise the ladies,   25
And took it as the payment of my praise:
But now I wait in vain till my song paid is—
Let another laud, if any lady pays.
Since I no more can earn
With all my songs their smile,   30
A proud man I will turn
My back on them the while:
Which signifies: "As thou to me,
Lady, so am I to thee."
Grateful ladies, not the crowd   35
My song shall praise: what profit me the overproud?
    I will tell you of my common harm and shame—
Ladies compare with scant discrimination.
For them the good and bad men are the same:
So the good men are debased from their high sta-
        tion.   40
When dames again shall learn
To sort the men, that they
Be sorted in their turn,
Love will the more repay.
What were bad, and what were good,   45
If none distinguish could?
Noble ladies, pray you think:
If women all are equal, then your worth will sink.
            —*Walther von der Vogelweide*

Spruch

Who slays the lion, who slays the dragon?
    He that can leave the cork in the flagon.
He that from passion's storm and strife
Can pilot his soul to a quiet life.
Virtue false, and hypocrite shame,   5
May shine awhile, like the candle's flame,
That flickers, splutters, dies out quick,
Smothered on its own muddy wick.
            —*Walther von der Vogelweide*

Tagelied

Went a maid fair to behold
    To the warder on the castle wall:
"Warder, be thou glad and bold!
If any creep, when shadows fall,
To thee, then whisper: 'Who goes there?'   5
But with a humble voice and low.
If 'yes' be answer, have no care:
That he is welcome, thou mayst know;
To the bower-window guide my lord:
Our châtelaine should well reward."   10

In the wall's shadow, very soon,
The well-beloved holds his breath:

1. **Who . . . dragon,** another fine example of the *Spruch.*
1. **Went . . . behold,** an elaborate example of the *Tageslied.*

Keen is the warder on his boon,
And, "Who is there?" he whispereth.
"It is I who am Love's paladin: 15
Keep thou thy watch upon thy tower."
"I will not stay to guide you in!
You are of courtesy the flower."
Soon to the bower the knight was led:
He kissed the lady's lips so red.   20

    "The sun is at the heaven's brim,"
Sang a warder o'er the window-sill:
"Who sleepeth long, the worse for him;
I warn you with a right good will.
And I am innocent of all   25
If aught should hap to lovers twain.
No man the darkness can recall:
The morning star is bright again
Over the cradle of the day.
Thou trusty knight, up and away."   30

    Tears filled the gentle lady's eyes,
When such shrill song her dreams awoke:
"My knight, it dawns, thou must arise!"
In frightened loveliness she spoke.
"Let me be dearest unto thee,   35
As thou to me my dearest art,
And, as I hold thy heart with me,
I grudge thee not to hold my heart.
To the highest God I thee confide;
O woe that thou must leave my side!"   40

    With many a rich and tender word
He comforts her who fills his soul;
Such speech as is of lovers heard
Comes quick from love beyond control.
Sweet interchange of agonies,   45
With many a kiss and long delay;
Her heart did break a way to his,
As closely in his arms she lay.
After joys come often woes:
From her embrace the hero goes.
            —*The Burgrave of Lüenz*

leich & ballad

THE BALLAD
OF SIR TANNHÄUSER

Now I begin another song,
    Of Tannhäuser for to tell,
And of his leman, fair Venus,
With whom he long did dwell.

    Tannhäuser was, as men do say,   5
A goodly knight of pride.

The Ballad of Sir Tannhäuser, a good example of the ballad which
was attached to the name of a prominent Minnesinger. It serves as
a basis for Wagner's famous opera.

He has wended his way to the women gay,
Through the mountain side.

"Sir Tannhäuser, I love thee still!
Thou sworest here to one;
To love thy fill in the hollow hill,   10
And never to get thee gone."

"Now I were loth to swear such oath:
I give you back the lie.
And if it were not you who spoke,   15
Then he should surely die."

"Sir Tannhäuser, hold thy tongue!
Yet shalt thou with me tarry;
And one of these my maidens young
I give thee now to marry."   20

"If another wife I take to me
Than her I love so well,
Then may I everlastingly
Burn in the fire of Hell!"

"Thou speakest of the fire of Hell,   25
Which never yet hath burned thee!
Bethink thee of my red, red mouth
And that I never spurned thee."

"O what avails your red, red mouth,
That I have come to hate?   30
Let me be gone from thee, sweet Venus,
Ere that it be too late."

"Tannhäuser, wouldst thou fain depart?
Thou shalt not go from me!
O stay with me here, my Tannhäuser dear,   35
In ravishment and glee."

"O I am growing thin and wan,
And ready for my shroud.
Let me e'en hie before I die,
All by thy body proud."   40

"Sir Tannhäuser, speak no more!
Your mind is all distraught.
But in my bower we'll go for an hour,
If love can help you aught."

"The love of your limbs is a loathsome snare!   45
I am persuaded well,
Beneath your hair and skin so fair
You are a fiend from Hell!"

"Sir Tannhäuser, thy words are ill,
And ye are bold to chide!   50
In this my hill ye must tarry still,
And dear those words abide."

"Whate'er you say, I will not stay,
I may no longer bide!
Sweet Mother of God, now help me away   55
From this evil witch's side!"

"Now will I give you leave to fare;
And only this I pray you!
To sing my praises everywhere.
The graybeard will not stay you."   60

Tannhäuser from the hill is boun,
In ruth and yet in hope.
"I will to Rome, the holy town;
My trust is in the Pope.

"Now I set out with heart so stout,   65
And Jesus' guidance crave,
Unto a Pope is Urban hight,
If haply he will save.

"Sir Pope, thou ghostly Father of mine,
My sins lie hard on me!   70
But since I truly do repine,
Let me confess to thee.

"I lingered for a long, long year
With Venus, a fair lady,
And now I seek some penance here,   75
That I my God may see."

The Pope he has a staff so stout,
The dry bough of a tree:
"Lo, when this staff shall green and sprout,
Thy sins are forgiven thee."   80

"Though I lived no more than short, short year,
To suffer away my sin,
I thought my penance to endure,
God's mercy for to win."

He has gone forth from the city gates,   85
In grief and agony.
"Mary Mother, Thou pure Virgin,
Since Thou wilt none of me,

"Then I will to the mountain go,
And ever there remain,   90
Since God has sent me to my sweet
Lady love again."

"O welcome, thou good Tannhäuser,
Whom I have missed so sore!

60. "The graybeard . . . you." The graybeard is taken to refer to
one Eckhart, a sentinel who was stationed at the entrance to the
Venusberg, the unsanctified abode of Venus.

O welcome now, my dearest lord,   95
Never to leave me more!"

And ere the third day was gone by,
The staff began to green,
And messengers rode to every land
Where Tannhäuser had been seen.   100

But he was in the mountain den,
With his sweet love to be;
And Urban that fourth Pope is damned
To all eternity.

—*Author Unknown*

LIFE AND DEATH OF THE NOBLE BRENNENBERGER

FIT I

IN VIENNA town at the Austrian court
A thousand tongues are ringing
With what the Brennenberger hath
To the noble Duchess been singing.

"O Brennenberger, dear vassal of mine,   5
Art thou indeed in earnest,
To sing there is no lady so fair
Whithersoever thou turnest?"

"Yea, lady, the fairest of women are you!
These fables that men weave   10
Of the beauty of the Queen of France
I never can believe."

"Yet will I rest not till this skein
Of lies some man unravels.
Take thou my gold, and jewels sheen,   15
And get thee on thy travels.

"And when thou seest the Queen of France,
Be judge between us twain:
And she who winneth beauty's prize,
Shall pay thee for thy pain."   20

"O lady, if ill news I bring,
I lose my hopes of Heaven;
But I am sure I shall tell you a tale
With a merry heart and steven."

FIT II

Now he has come to Paris town,   25
With jewels and with gold;

And there to the innkeeper's wife
He hath his purpose told.

"Sit in a huckster-woman's weeds,
The castle-gate before,   30
And cry, when the Queen comes forth to church:
'Come buy my jewels' store!' "

Now he became a huckster-wife,
And spread his wares to view;
And it was bruited at the Court,   35
And when the fair Queen knew,

She called her page, and charged him so:
"Before my face go summon—
With stealth and care, lest the King should know—
This wealthy huckster-woman."   40

The huckster came into the Queen's bright bower;
She could not trust her eyes.
"God sain you, most noble Queen," she said;
"Your noble ladies likewise."   44

The Queen she took her by the hand,
With snow-white hands and tender;
She bought her bracelets, she bought her rings;
There was no end of the splendor.

Now this went on till the evening came,
The huckster was in sorrow: 50
"Where shall I lie this night?" she said;
"Good store is left for tomorrow."

Brennenberger thought: "I would I were at home;
I am not made of stone.
If you vouchsafe, most noble Queen,   55
I fain would sleep alone."

The Queen spoke out: "That may not be;
Thou must be bedded meetly.
For thy necklaces and rings of price
We must with honor treat thee.   60

"Now I have here twelve maidens dear:
Lie with the youngest together;
Lie close and warm, and fear no harm
From this inclement weather."

It was about the time of Yule,   65
The longest nights of the year:
Brennenberg lay with the youngest maid,
He lay in dule and fear.

Sore dismayed by the gentle maid,
His elbow out he bent;   70

Life and Death of the Noble Brennenberger. Brennenberger was
a Minnesinger of repute but of mediocre talent. This poem probably
was of the fifteenth century and popular not at court but among the
people.

43. **sain,** bless.

*The costume worn by noble women in
the second half of the fifteenth century.*

Had he not called upon the Saints,
The Devil him had shent.

FIT III

The huckster rose at break of day;
She was in evil plight;
Twelve days the Queen there kept her pent,   75
With another maid each night.

The thirteenth day out spoke the Queen:
"With all my maids ye lay;
Now lie with me this last night of all,
We will part at the break of day."   80

He was afeared of such rich meed,
His face did blood-red burn!
"Most noble Queen, O let it wait
Till I again return.

"I will return with richer wares,   85
Which, if they you delight—
And O, if the King, your noble Lord,
Should come to you at night!"

"The King comes not to me at night;
He is to me a stranger.   90
The King has shunned me ever so long,
Thy honor will be in no danger.

"And warders three in my service stand,
Of his approach to warn:

We will of knights and heroes talk,   95
Until the break of morn."

Brennenberg was in sore distress:
"With the Queen so close to me,
She is so fair, it would be my death;
Worsted I should be.   100

"And if I harmed the lady fair,
I should forever rue;
Hers of Austria is my heart,
I will to her be true."

FIT IV

And when they went to bed that night,   105
They sought for the huckster in vain;
Brennenberg never rested an hour,
Till he came to Vienna again.

"Brennenberg, thou dear vassal of mine,
How hath it gone with thee, say?"   110
"O lady, ill and well, and I
Twelve days a prisoner lay.

"Twelve nights with tender virgins twelve;
A youth distressed was I!
And the last night of all the Queen herself   115
Desired with me to lie.

"My huckster's heart was ill bestead,
This had I not withstood;
I slunk out of the city-gate,
And fled as fast as I could."   120

"Alas, that ever I counselled thee
On her to cast thine eyes!
But say, my love, to whom wouldst thou
Adjudge all beauty's prize?"

"O lady, she is Heaven on earth,   125
None can be peer to her;
Her face was like a sun; it seemed
As if in Heaven I were."

"And if thou deemest her fairer than I,
Sing thou thy songs to her;   130
Go back to France again forthwith,
To be her servitor."

"Nay, noble lady, I say not so,
You dwell in my heart's core;
I know no fairer woman than you,   135
For whom I suffer sore."

"Yet didst thou say, a fairer dame
Thine eyes did never see."

"Yea, verily; it must have been
Her beauty blinded me.   140

"Yet you have fairer neck and chin,
And nobler is your mien;
But after you no woman is
So lovely as the Queen.   144

"And if she were twenty times fairer than you,
You is it I would praise;
For to you belong my heart and mind,
To you belong my lays."

FIT V

Now had the noble Brennenberg
Sung song on song abounding   150
In praises of his mistress high,
From land to land resounding.

The Duke he was an angry man,
And to suspicion prone:
"Ye woo my wife so much, ye yet   155
May with your life atone."

He hired three murderers with red gold,
That never pity knew;
They tore his heart hot out of his breast,
And mocked him while they slew.   160

At eve the cook, in a golden dish,
Did serve it, spiced sweet:
And her red mouth did eat the heart,
That but for her had beat.

"And do ye know what now you ate,   165
The larks baked in the pie?"
"I do not know, it tasted sweet,
And fain to know were I."

"It was the heart of Brennenberg,
Who often you delighted;   170
He brought you ever much joy and glee;
So is false love requited."

The Duchess waxed as pale as death,
As pale as death waxed she:
"And if I have eaten the heart of the knight,   175
Who brought me joy and glee,

"Thereafter I will drain a draught,
Such draught I straight will drain,
That food or drink shall nevermore
Pass my lips again."   180

Then did the noble Duchess rise,
And to her chamber go:

"Mary, Queen of Heaven, to thee
I cry my anguished woe.

"I must forever grieve for him;   185
For my sake he was killed;
My anguish for his guiltless death
Can but by death be stilled.

"Thou knowest, he never came so near
That he might me embrace;   190
And he had rather, for noble fear,
Fled a hundred miles from my face.

"To thee I cry, my heart is sore;
I die in agony;
For Thy Son's Passion's sake, give thou   195
Eternal peace to me."

Merciful Mary lifted her up,
And in her bosom cherished;
The Duke was put to the Empire's ban,
And soon repentant perished.
                                          —*Author Unknown*

HIDDEN lovers' woes
      Thou wert wont to sing ere dawn arose:
Bitter parting after raptured meeting.
Whosoever love and lady's greeting
So received that he was torn   5
From her breast by fear of men,
Thou wouldst sing him counsel, when
Shone the star of morn.
Warder, sing it now no more, lay by thy bugle-horn!

He to whom is given   10
Not to be from love by morning riven—
Whom the watchers think not to beleaguer,
Hath no need to be alert and eager
To avert the peril rife
In the day; his rest is pure,   15
Nor a warder makes secure
His unhappy life.
Love so sweet bestows in all men's sight his own
      true wife!
                                  —*Wolfram von Eschenbach*

Dante Alighieri

1265–1321

The Middle Ages culminate in Dante's *Commedia*. Produced as Europe stood on the brink of a new era, this magnificent epic poem summarized nine hundred years in the evolution of Christian thought and chivalric idealism. It is shot through with an affectionate awareness of pagan antiquity, but its world is still the neat, enclosed, assured world of medieval theology, not the new world of limitless space and conflicting creeds that the Renaissance was soon to usher in.

The vast scope of Dante's masterpiece and its elaborate and intricate plan reflect the towering intellect, immense erudition, and lofty poetic vision of the man. We might assume from his learning and intense mysticism that Dante was a scholarly recluse of monkish inclinations, but nothing could be further from the truth. Only the accident of exile from his native Florence forced him into retirement from the life of action and power to which he first aspired. His family was ancient but impoverished, and had adhered to the Guelph party against the Ghibellines in the city's bitter political strife. In the rivalry of the Pope and the Holy Roman Emperor for control of the states of Italy, the Guelphs held that the Pope was supreme in both the temporal and spiritual spheres, and hence that the Emperor was his vassal. But the Ghibellines contended that the Emperor was responsible only to God and hence that he was supreme in the temporal sphere as the Pope was in the spiritual. For half a century the political power shifted from one party to the other through violent contest, but in 1289 the Ghibellines were decisively defeated at Campaldino, where young Dante served gallantly in the Guelph cavalry.

The Guelphs, now in control, soon split into two new factions—the aristocratic Blacks, who continued the Guelph support of papal authority, and the more democratic Whites, who revived some of the policies of the Ghibellines. Favoring the Whites' position, Dante served as one of the six Priors who ruled Florence in 1300, so that when the city fell to the Blacks two years later, he and other newly appointed officials were exiled and threatened with a sentence of death by fire if they returned. Thus began Dante's years of wandering through various Italian cities—Verona, Lunigiana, Lucca, Ravenna—where he made his living as a tutor and political adviser in the households of great lords. He expounded his political convictions in a Latin treatise, *De Monarchia*, setting forth the Ghibelline contention for the division of supreme power in the temporal and spiritual realms between the Emperor and the Pope. He pictured a unification of the Italian states under the peaceful rule of the Emperor, and argued for it earnestly again in the *Commedia*. But his idealistic vision was never to materialize. Although he was nostalgic for Florence in his later years, he indignantly refused to return under the humiliating conditions that he pay a fine to the state and do penance for his opposition to the Pope. At the time of his death he was at Ravenna under the protection of Guido da Polenta, a nephew of Francesca da Rimini, whose tragic love story he had told in Canto V of the *Inferno*.

Dante married Gemma Donati, of an aristocratic family, to whom he was probably betrothed in childhood. She bore him four children, but played no part in his emotional life, as far as we know from his works. It was another woman that he idealized as his symbol of romantic love, a shadowy figure in his works whom he called simply Beatrice but whom his biographer Boccaccio identified as Bice Portinari, the daughter of a prominent Florentine and eventually the wife of another, Simone de' Bardi. More important than her actual life is her life in Dante's imagination, which he set forth in brief introductions to a series of exquisite sonnets and other love poems written in 1292 as the *Vita Nuova* (New Life). According to his account, "at the beginning of her ninth year, the Glorious Lady of my mind, who was called Beatrice by many who knew not what to call her, appeared to me, and I near the end of my ninth year saw her. She appeared to me clothed in a most noble color, a modest and becoming crimson, and she was girt and adorned in such wise as befitted her very youthful age. At that instant I say truly that the spirit of life, which dwells in the most secret chamber of the heart, began to tremble with such violence that it appeared fearfully in the least pulses, and, trembling, said these words: 'Behold a god stronger than I, who coming shall rule over me!'" So began Dante's intense idealization of Beatrice, which eventually exalted her to the symbol of divine revelation in the *Commedia*. Their acquaintance seems to have been slight and confined to large social gatherings; indeed, she may never have known of his worship, because he made efforts to shield it so as to protect her reputation. Some critics see in her simply the ideal of Platonic love, a love convention that Dante inherited from older poets, especially Guido Guinicelli, his immediate master. Following this tradition, Dante's passion for Beatrice is the path to virtue and an understanding of God's love. After her early death, what personality she had for Dante in the *Vita Nuova* was gradually lost, and she became in the *Commedia* little more than the sweet embodiment of a theological idea.

But it was for her that he wrote the *Commedia*, as he had predicted he would in the closing lines of the *Vita Nuova*. He had completed seven cantos of the hundred at the time of his banishment in 1302 and apparently finished the work just before his death. Through the years he did not deviate from the mammoth plan that he had first worked out for it. Into it he poured all of the spiritual experience of his life, all of the knowledge and philosophy of his time, so that the modern reader may approach the work on at least three levels of interpretation.

On the most obvious and literal of these levels, the *Commedia* is the narrative of a journey that Dante made in a vision through hell, purgatory, and paradise, the three realms of departed spirits, which he projects in highly specific terms. Dante's conception of the universe amplified and particularized the orthodox view of the medieval Church, but he had certainly no notion that all of the geography was literally as his imagination pictured it. Several conflicting theories of the universe were current in late antiquity, but the medieval Church accepted the geocentric theory of Ptolemy because it harmonized best with Biblical tradition and Christian doctrine. If God created man as the climax of creation, it was only reasonable to suppose that the earth man inhabited was at the center of the universe.

Dante pictured the earth as a sphere floating in space, whose northern hemisphere consisted primarily of land extending from Gibraltar in the west to the Ganges in the east with the holy city of Jerusalem in its center. Beneath this inhabited hemisphere is hell, a vast pit in the shape of a funnel or inverted cone, having its apex at the center of the earth. When Satan and the rebellious angels were driven from heaven, they fell to earth, which opened this great pit to receive them. Hell has nine circles, corresponding to the seriousness of the sins of the damned souls, at the lowest of which is Satan himself, frozen forever in ice. In the center of the southern hemisphere of water, directly opposite Jerusalem, is the island mountain of Purgatory, with the Garden of Eden, the earthly paradise, at its top. On the nine ledges on its side repenting souls purify themselves for eventual worthiness of the pristine state of Eden and the actual Paradise above. Paradise consists of nine concentric circles of heavens revolving about the earth and corresponding to the moon, the sun, the planets, and the stars. Enclosing them all is the Empyrean, the motionless heaven where God and the Virgin Mary reside. It is this long way that Dante in his vision travels through the days immediately preceding and following Easter in 1300, a holy year of Papal Jubilee.

On a second plane, the *Commedia* is the spiritual autobiography of Dante himself, stripped of references to his external experiences. His parents, his wife, his children, his years of wandering find no place here, but his spiritual struggle and the divine inspiration of Beatrice are clearly set forth in symbolic terms. He informs us more than once of the evil habits into which he fell in the decade after Beatrice's death. At last at 35, a mid-point in his career, Dante finds himself lost in the dark forest of worldly sin and prevented from escaping to the hill of salvation by the three beasts of ambition, pride, and physical desire. But Beatrice as the symbol of revelation sees his plight from her abode in heaven and sends him human understanding in the form of his beloved Virgil to lead him out of the evil of hell to the purification of purgatory. He is made aware of the sins of hell one by one and then of the penances that bring him to salvation. But human understanding can lead him only to the threshold of redemption, and so Virgil, the sorrowful pagan, must leave Dante at the gate of Eden to return to his fellow heathen in Limbo. At this point revelation embodied in Beatrice appears to conduct him to the ecstasy of paradise. Human reason has guided him out of sin to temporal happiness, but the higher judgments of God he can understand only through revelation (Beatrice), grace (St. Lucy), and divine mercy (The Virgin Mary). With this assistance he at last achieves the vision of God.

But Dante's experience is every Christian's experience, and on a third level the *Commedia* is, like *Pilgrim's Progress*, a gigantic allegory of the life of a Christian in this world. Hell is the error into which every man falls, a grotesque panorama of the ugliness in human nature. In the hopelessness of the sad souls there we see the depths of sin and despair into which man may fall. Purgatory points the way to salvation through repentance and penance. It is a happy place, though tinged with melancholy, as the contrite souls renounce their unworthy past with a joyful knowledge of the infinite happiness beyond. Paradise is the climax of human bliss, as the Christian exults in the surety of salvation and a sense of his spiritual perfection. This is the triumph of his better self aided by God's revelation and mercy. Dante called his work *Commedia* to signify that it is not a tragedy, nor composed in a tragic style, but a story with a happy ending, the spiritual salvation that God holds out to every man.*

This account of the *Commedia* will suggest that it is built on layers of symbols. More baffling to the understanding than the allegory are the numerical symbols that reflect Dante's complete absorption in the medieval outlook. The mystical number that honeycombs the *Commedia* is three, the most common of all in an age that saw God in three persons, the blessed Trinity. The epic describes three great realms in three long books. Each of these books has thirty-three cantos, which with one introductory canto add up to a round one hundred. Three beasts stand in the way of Dante's salvation, and three guides lead him to it. Three ladies intercede for him. Even the metrical form of the poem embodies the mystical number, because Dante developed for the *Commedia* the *terza rima*, whereby units of three lines of iambic pentameter are rhymed *aba, bcb*, etc. On the other hand, nine is the number that Dante associates with Beatrice, since her root is the Trinity as the root of nine is three. No feature of the poem is more remote from us than this medieval notion of the mystical properties of numbers.

Indeed, a reader in our century must overlook many medieval trappings in Dante to get at his perennial message for all mankind. His view of the universe is patently obsolete in an age that calls our earth a lesser planet revolving around a lesser sun in an infinite universe. The pagans of antiquity often seem closer to us in their intellectual sophistication than the sober Florentine hedged in by severe restrictions of knowledge and point of view. But the limits of his knowledge should not obscure the universal meaning of his work on other planes. His exquisite flights of poetry must touch even the most skeptical reader. His vigorous narrative, as in the account of the giants and demons, is first-rate storytelling. The humanity of the man shines through his warm account of Virgil. And his vision itself is ultimately the vision of every thoughtful, well-intentioned human being, whatever his creed may be. However much we may accept intellectually the insignificance of our planet, it is still all of the universe that really concerns us, and on the surface of this planet nothing is more important to us than the spiritual life of man. Few can be so completely absorbed in material affairs as to lose sight of their aspi-

---

* The term "Divine" was added to its title two hundred years after Dante's time and gives it a highly misleading slant.

ration toward a worthier life. Many poets and thinkers have pointed the way, but none more compellingly than **Dante.**

The Divine Comedy

HELL

CANTO I. *The Dark Wood: Virgil*

IN THE middle of the journey of our life I came to myself in a dark wood where the straight way was lost. Ah! how hard a thing it is to tell what a wild, and rough, and stubborn wood this was, which in my thought renews the fear! So bitter is it, that scarcely more is death: but to treat of the good that I there found, I will relate the other things that I discerned. I cannot rightly tell how I entered it, so full of sleep was I about the moment that I left the true way. But after I had reached the foot of a Hill there, where that valley ended, which had pierced my heart with fear, I looked up and saw its shoulders already clothed with the rays of the Planet that leads men straight on every road. Then the fear was somewhat calmed, which had continued in the lake of my heart the night that I passed so piteously. And as he, who with panting breath has escaped from the deep sea to the shore, turns to the dangerous water and gazes: so my mind, which still was fleeing, turned back to see the pass that no one ever left alive.

After I had rested my wearied body a short while, I took the way again along the desert strand. And behold, almost at the commencement of the steep, a Leopard, light and very nimble, which was covered with spotted hair. And it went not from before my face; nay, so impeded my way, that I had often turned to go back. The time was at the beginning of the morning; and the sun was mounting up with those stars, which were with him when Divine Love first moved those fair things: so that the hour of time and the sweet season caused me to have good hope of that animal with the gay skin; yet not so, but that I feared at the sight, which appeared to me, of a Lion. He seemed coming upon me with head erect, and furious hunger; so that the air seemed to have fear thereat; and a She-wolf, that looked full of all cravings in her leanness; and has ere now made many live in sorrow. She brought such

heaviness upon me with the terror of her aspect, that I lost the hope of ascending. And as one who is eager in gaining, and, when the time arrives that makes him lose, weeps and afflicts himself in all his thoughts: such that restless beast made me, which coming against me, by little and little drove me back to where the Sun is silent.

Whilst I was rushing downwards, there appeared before my eyes one who seemed hoarse from long silence. When I saw him in the great desert, I cried: "Have pity on me, whate'er thou be, whether shade or veritable man!" He answered me: "Not man, a man I once was; and my parents were Lombards, and both of Mantua by country. I was born *sub Julio*, though it was late; and lived at Rome under the good Augustus, in the time of the false and lying Gods. A poet I was; and sang of that just son of Anchises, who came from Troy after proud Ilium was burnt. But thou, why returnest thou to such disquiet? why ascendest not the delectable mountain, which is the beginning and the cause of all gladness?"

"Art thou then that Virgil, and that fountain which pours abroad so rich a stream of speech?" I answered him, with bashful front. "O glory, and light of other poets! May the long zeal avail me, and the great love, that made me search thy volume. Thou art my master and my author; thou alone art he from whom I took the good style that hath done me honour. See the beast from which I turned back; help me from her, thou famous sage; for she makes my veins and pulses tremble."

"Thou must take another road," he answered, when he saw me weeping, "if thou desirest to escape from this wild place: because this beast, for which thou criest, lets not men pass her way; but so entangles that she slays them; and has a nature so perverse and vicious, that she never satiates her craving appetite; and after feeding, she is hungrier than before. . . . Wherefore I think and discern this for thy best, that thou follow me; and I will be thy guide, and lead thee hence through an eternal place, where thou shalt hear the hopeless shrieks, shalt see the ancient spirits in pain, so that each calls for a second death; and then thou shalt see those who are contented in the fire: for they hope to come, whensoever it be, amongst the blessed; then to these, if thou desirest to ascend, there shall be a spirit worthier than I to guide thee; with her will I leave thee at my parting: for that Emperor who reigns above, because I was rebellious to his law, wills not that I come into his city. In all parts he rules and there holds sway; there is his city, and his high seat: O happy whom he chooses for it!"

The Divine Comedy▲ Translated by J. A. Carlyle, Thomas Okey, and Philip H. Wicksteed. From *The Divine Comedy* by Dante, published by E. P. Dutton and Co., Inc., New York. By permission of E. P. Dutton and Co., Inc. and J. M. Dent and Sons.

1. In the middle . . . life. The poem opens on the night before Good Friday, 1300, when Dante was 35. **10. a Hill,** the Hill of Salvation in the Bible. **13. Planet,** the sun. **24. Leopard.** The leopard, the lion, and the she-wolf represent worldly pleasure, pride, and avarice.

52. born *sub Julio*. Virgil, Dante's guide through Hell and Purgatory, represents the highest wisdom of man. He was born in the time of Julius Caesar. **85. a spirit,** Beatrice, who represents heavenly wisdom.

And I to him: "Poet, I beseech thee by that God whom thou knowest not: in order that I may escape this ill and worse, lead me where thou now hast said, so that I may see the Gate of St. Peter, and those whom thou makest so sad." Then he moved; and I kept on behind him.

CANTO II. *Virgil's Explanation and Promise*

The day was departing, and the brown air taking the animals, that are on earth, from their toils; and I, one alone, was preparing myself to bear the war both of the journey and the pity, which memory, that errs not, shall relate. O Muses, O high Genius, now help me! O Memory, that hast inscribed what I saw, here will be shown thy nobleness.

I began: "Poet, who guidest me, look if there be worth in me sufficient, before thou trust me to the arduous passage. Thou sayest that the father of Sylvius, while subject to corruption, went to the immortal world, and was there in body. But if the Adversary of all evil was propitious to him, considering the high effect, and who and what should come from him, it seems not unfitting to an understanding mind: for in the empyreal heaven, he was chosen to be the father of generous Rome, and of her Empire; both these, to say the truth, were established for the holy place, where the Successor of the greatest Peter sits. . . . But I, why go? or who permits it? I am not Æneas, am not Paul; neither myself nor others deem me worthy of it. Wherefore, if I resign myself to go, I fear my going may prove foolish; thou art wise, and understandest better than I speak." And as one who unwills what he willed, and with new thoughts changes his purpose, so that he wholly quits the thing commenced, such I made myself on that dim coast: for with thinking I wasted the enterprise, that had been so quick in its commencement.

"If I have rightly understood thy words," replied that shade of the Magnanimous, "thy soul is smit with coward fear, which oftentimes encumbers men, so that it turns them back from honoured enterprise; as false seeing does a startled beast. To free thee from this dread, I will tell thee why I came, and what I heard in the first moment when I took pity of thee. I was amongst them who are in suspense and a Lady, so fair and blessed that I prayed her to command, called me. Her eyes shone brighter than the stars; and she began soft and gentle to tell me with angelic voice, in her language: 'O courteous Mantuan Spirit, whose fame still lasts in the world, and

will last as long as Time! my friend, and not the friend of fortune, is so impeded in his way upon the desert shore, that he has turned back for terror; and I fear he may already be so far astray, that I have risen too late for his relief, from what I heard of him in Heaven. Now go, and with thy ornate speech, and with what is necessary for his escape, help him so, that I may be consoled thereby. I am Beatrice who send thee; I come from a place where I desire to return; love moved me, that makes me speak. When I shall be before my Lord, I oft will praise thee to him.'

"She was silent then, and I began: 'So grateful to me is thy command, that my obeying, were it done already, seems tardy; it needs not that thou more explain to me thy wish. But tell me the cause, why thou forbearest not to descend into this centre here below from the spacious place, to which thou burnest to return.'

"'Since thou desirest to know thus far, I will tell thee briefly,' she replied, 'why I fear not to come within this place. Those things alone are to be feared that have the power of hurting; the others not, which are not fearful. I am made such by God, in his grace, that your misery does not touch me; nor the flame of this burning assail me. There is a noble Lady in Heaven who has such pity of this hindrance, for which I send thee, that she breaks the sharp judgment there on high. She called Lucia, in her request, and said: 'Now thy faithful one has need of thee; and I commend him to thee.' Lucia, enemy of all cruelty, arose and came to the place where I was sitting with the ancient Rachel. She said: "Beatrice, true praise of God; why helpest thou not him who loved thee so, that for thee he left the vulgar crowd? Hearest not thou the misery of his plaint? Seest thou not the death which combats him upon the river over which the sea has no boast?" None on earth were ever swift to seek their good, or flee their hurt, as I, after these words were uttered, to come down from my blessed seat; confiding in thy noble speech, which honours thee, and them who have heard it.'

"After saying this to me, she turned away her bright eyes weeping; by which she made me hasten more to come; and thus I came to thee, as she desired; took thee from before that savage beast, which bereft thee of the short way to the beautiful mountain. What is it then? why, why haltest thou? why lodgest in thy heart such coward fear? why art thou not bold and free, when three such blessed Ladies care for thee in the court of Heaven, and my words promise thee so much good?"

As flowerets, by the nightly chillness bended down

---

4. **Gate of St. Peter,** the Gate of Purgatory. 16–17. **father of Sylvius,** Aeneas. 44. **amongst them . . . suspense,** among the virtuous pagans in Limbo, where Beatrice came to him.

75–76. **noble Lady in Heaven,** the Virgin Mary, representing Divine Mercy. 78. **Lucia,** St. Lucy, representing Illuminating Grace. 82. **Rachel;** Rachel represents the Contemplative Life.

II : 161

and closed, erect themselves all open on their stems when the sun whitens them: thus I did, with my fainting courage; and so much good daring ran into my heart, that I began as one set free: "O compassionate she, who succoured me! and courteous thou, who quickly didst obey the true words that she gave thee! Thou hast disposed my heart with such desire to go, by what thou sayest, that I have returned to my first purpose. Now go, for both have one will; 10 thou guide, thou lord and master." Thus I spake to him; and he moving, I entered on the arduous and savage way.

CANTO III. *The Gate of Hell, Ante-hell, and Acheron*

"Through me is the way into the doleful city; through me the way into the eternal pain; through me the way among the people lost. Justice moved my High Maker; Divine Power made me, Wisdom Supreme, and Primal Love. Before me were no things created, but eternal; and eternal I endure: leave all hope, ye that enter." These words, of colour 20 obscure, saw I written above a gate; whereat I: "Master, their meaning to me is hard."

And he to me, as one experienced: "Here must all distrust be left; all cowardice must here be dead. We are come to the place where I told thee thou shouldst see the wretched people, who have lost the good of the intellect." And placing his hand on mine, with a cheerful countenance that comforted me, he led me into the secret things.

Here sighs, plaints, and deep wailings resounded 30 through the starless air: it made me weep at first. Strange tongues, horrible outcries, words of pain, tones of anger, voices deep and hoarse, and sounds of hands amongst them, made a tumult, which turns itself unceasing in that air for ever dyed, as sand when it eddies in a whirlwind. And I, my head begirt with horror, said: "Master, what is this that I hear? and who are these that seem so overcome with pain?"

And he to me: "This miserable mode the dreary 40 souls of those sustain, who lived without blame, and without praise. They are mixed with that caitiff choir of the angels, who were not rebellious, nor were faithful to God; but were for themselves. Heaven chased them forth to keep its beauty from impair; and the deep Hell receives them not, for the wicked would have some glory over them."

And I: "Master, what is so grievous to them, that makes them lament thus bitterly?" He answered: "I will tell it to thee very briefly. These have no hope 50 of death; and their blind life is so mean, that they

are envious of every other lot. Report of them the world permits not to exist; Mercy and Justice disdains them: let us not speak of them; but look, and pass."

And I, who looked, saw an ensign, which whirling ran so quickly that it seemed to scorn all pause; and behind it came so long a train of people, that I should never have believed death had undone so many. Forthwith I understood and felt assured, that this was the crew of caitiffs, hateful to God and to 6 his enemies. These unfortunates, who never were alive, were naked, and sorely goaded by hornets and by wasps that were there. These made their faces stream with blood, which mixed with tears was gathered at their feet by loathsome worms.

And then, as I looked onwards, I saw people on the Shore of a great River: whereat I said: "Master, now grant that I may know who these are; and what usage makes them seem so ready to pass over, as I discern by the faint light." And he to me: "The 7 things shall be known to thee, when we stay our steps upon the joyless strand of Acheron." Then, with eyes ashamed and downcast, fearing my words might have offended him, I kept myself from speaking till we reached the stream. And lo! an old man, white with ancient hair, comes towards us in a bark, shouting: "Woe to you, depraved spirits! hope not ever to see Heaven: I come to lead you to the other shore; into the eternal darkness; into fire and into ice. And thou who art there, alive, depart 8 thee from these who are dead." But when he saw that I departed not, he said: "By other ways, by other ferries, not here, shalt thou pass over: a lighter boat must carry thee."

And my guide to him: "Charon, vex not thyself: thus it is willed there, where what is willed can be done; and ask no more." Then the woolly cheeks were quiet of the steersman on the livid marsh, who round his eyes had wheels of flame. But those spirits, who were foreworn and naked, changed colour and 9 chattered with their teeth, soon as they heard the bitter words. They blasphemed God and their parents; the human kind; the place, the time, and origin of their seed, and of their birth. Then all of them together, sorely weeping, drew to the accursed shore, which awaits every man that fears not God. Charon the demon, with eyes of glowing coal, beckoning them, collects them all; smites with his oar whoever lingers. As the leaves of autumn fall off one after the other, till the branch sees all its spoils upon 10 the ground: so one by one the evil seed of Adam cast themselves from that shore at signals, as the bird at its call. Thus they depart on the brown water; and ere they have landed on the other shore, again a fresh crowd collects on this.

45–46. **for the wicked . . . over them,** because the wicked could at least make up their minds.

55. **an ensign;** this represents the uncertainty of these souls.

"My son," said the courteous Master, "those who die under God's wrath, all assemble here from every country; and they are prompt to pass the river, for Divine Justice spurs them so, that fear is changed into desire. By this way no good spirit ever passes; and hence, if Charon complains of thee, thou easily now mayest know the import of his words." When he had ended, the dusky champaign trembled so violently, that the remembrance of my terror bathes me still with sweat. The tearful ground gave out wind, which flashed forth a crimson light that conquered all my senses; and I fell, like one who is seized with sleep.

CANTO IV. *Circle I, Limbo: the unbaptized and the virtuous heathen*

A heavy thunder broke the deep sleep in my head; so that I started like one who is awaked by force; and, having risen erect, I moved my rested eyes around, and looked steadfastly to know the place in which I was. True is it, that I found myself upon the brink of the dolorous Valley of the Abyss, which gathers thunder of endless wailings. It was so dark, profound, and cloudy, that, with fixing my look upon the bottom, I there discerned nothing.

"Now let us descend into the blind world here below," began the Poet all pale; "I will be first, and thou shalt be second." And I, who had remarked his colour, said: "How shall I come, when thou fearest, who are wont to be my strength in doubt?" And he to me: "The anguish of the people who are here below, on my face depaints that pity, which thou takest for fear. Let us go; for the length of way impels us."

Thus he entered, and made me enter, into the first circle that girds the abyss. Here there was no plaint, that could be heard, except of sighs, which caused the eternal air to tremble; and this arose from the sadness, without torment, of the crowds that were many and great, both of children, and of women and men.

The good Master to me: "Thou askest not what spirits are these thou seest? I wish thee to know, before thou goest farther, that they sinned not; and though they have merit, it suffices not: for they had not Baptism, which is the portal of the faith that thou believest; and seeing they were before Christianity, they worshipped not God aright; and of these am I myself. For such defects, and for no other fault, are we lost; and only in so far afflicted, that without hope we live in desire." Great sadness took me at the heart on hearing this; because I knew men of much worth, who in that Limbo were suspense. . . .

Our way was not yet far since my slumber, when I saw a fire, which conquered a hemisphere of the darkness. We were still a little distant from it; yet not so distant, that I did not in part discern what honourable people occupied that place. "O thou, that honourest every science and art; who are these, who have such honour, that it separates them from the manner of the rest?" And he to me: "The honoured name, which sounds of them, up in that life of thine, gains favours in heaven which thus advances them."

Meanwhile a voice was heard by me: "Honour the great Poet! His shade returns that was departed." After the voice had paused, and was silent, I saw four great shadows come to us; they had an aspect neither sad nor joyful. The good Master began to speak: "Mark him with that sword in hand, who comes before the three as their lord: that is Homer, the sovereign Poet; the next who comes is Horace the satirist; Ovid is the third, and the last is Lucan. Because each agrees with me in the name, which the one voice sounded, they do me honour: and therein they do well." Thus I saw assembled the goodly school of those lords of highest song, which, like an eagle, soars above the rest.

After they had talked a space together, they turned to me with a sign of salutation; and my Master smiled thereat. And greatly more besides they honoured me for they made me of their number, so that I was a sixth amid such intelligences. Thus we went onwards to the light, speaking things which it is well to pass in silence, as it was well to speak there where I was.

We came to the foot of a Noble Castle, seven times circled with lofty Walls, defended round by a fair Rivulet. This we passed as solid land; through seven gates I entered with those sages; we reached a meadow of fresh verdure. On it were people with eyes slow and grave, of great authority in their appearance; they spoke seldom, with mild voices. Thus we retired on one of the sides, into a place open, luminous, and high, so that they could all be seen.

There direct, upon the green enamel, were shown to me the great spirits, so that I glory within myself for having seen them. I saw Electra with many companions: amongst whom I knew both Hector and Æneas; Cæsar armed, with the falcon eyes. I saw Camilla and Penthesilea on the other hand, and saw the Latian King, sitting with Lavinia his daughter. I saw that Brutus who expelled the Tarquin.

When I raised my eyelids a little higher, I saw the Master of those that know, sitting amid a philosophic family. All regard him; all do him honour; here I saw Socrates and Plato, who before the rest stand nearest to him; Democritus, who ascribes the world to chance: Diogenes, Anaxagoras, and Thales; Emped-

---

70. **Lucan**, Roman poet (39–65 A.D.), author of the heroic poem, *Pharsalia.* 95. **Electra**, the mother of Dardanus, the founder of Troy. Caesar, as descendant of Aeneas, belongs in the Trojan company. 102. **Master . . . that know**, Aristotle.

ocles, Heraclitus, and Zeno; and I saw the good collector of the qualities, Discorides I mean; and saw Orpheus, Tully, Linus, and Seneca the moralist; Euclid the geometer, and Ptolemæus; Hippocrates, Avicenna, and Galen; Averroës, who made the great comment. I may not paint them all in full: for the long theme so chases me, that many times the word comes short of the reality.

10 The company of six diminishes to two; by another road the sage guide leads me, out of the quiet, into the trembling air; and I come to a part where there is naught that shines.

CANTO V. *Circle II: the carnal sinners*

Thus I descended from the first circle down into the second, which encompasses less space, and so much greater pain, that it stings to wailing. There Minos sits horrific, and grins: examines the crimes upon the entrance; judges, and sends according as he girds himself. I say, that when the ill-born spirit comes before him, it confesses all; and that sin-dis-
20 cerner sees what place in hell is for it, and with his tail makes as many circles round himself as the degrees he will have it to descend. Always before him stands a crowd of them; they go each in its turn to judgment; they tell, and hear; and then are whirled down.

"O thou who comest to the abode of pain!" said Minos to me, when he saw me leaving the act of that great office; "look how thou enterest, and in whom thou trustest; let not the wideness of the en-
30 trancy deceive thee." And my guide to him: "Why criest thou too? Hinder not his fated going; thus it is willed there where what is willed can be done: and ask no more."

Now begin the doleful notes to reach me; now am I come where much lamenting strikes me. I came into a place void of all light, which bellows like the sea in tempest, when it is combated by warring winds. The hellish storm, which never rests, leads the spirits with its sweep; whirling, and smiting it
40 vexes them. When they arrive before the ruin, there the shrieks, the moanings, and the lamentation; there they blaspheme the divine power. I learnt that to such torment are doomed the carnal sinners, who subject reason to lust. And as their wings bear along the starlings, at the cold season, in large and crowded troop: so that blast, the evil spirits; hither, thither, down, up, it leads them. No hope ever comforts them, not of rest but even of less pain. And as the cranes go chanting their lays, making a long
50 streak of themselves in the air: so I saw the shadows come, uttering wails, borne by that strife of winds.

Whereat I said: "Master, who are those people, whom the black air thus lashes?" "The first of these concerning whom thou seekest to know," he then replied, "was Empress of many tongues. With the vice of luxury she was so broken, that she made lust and law alike in her decree, to take away the blame she had incurred. She is Semiramis, of whom we read that she succeeded Ninus, and was his spouse; she held the land which the Soldan rules. That other 6 is she who slew herself in love, and broke faith to the ashes of Sichæus; next comes luxurious Cleopatra. Helena see, for whom so long a time of ill revolved; and see the great Achilles, who fought at last with love; see Paris, Tristan"; and more than a thousand shades he showed to me, and pointing with his finger, named to me those whom love had parted from our life.

After I had heard my teacher name the olden dames and cavaliers, pity came over me, and I was 7 as if bewildered. I began: "Poet, willingly would I speak with those two that go together, and seem so light upon the wind." And he to me: "Thou shalt see when they are nearer to us; and do thou then entreat them by that love, which leads them; and they will come."

Soon as the wind bends them to us, I raised my voice: "O wearied souls! come to speak with us, if none denies it." As doves called by desire, with raised and steady wings come through the air to 8 their loved nest, borne by their will: so those spirits issued from the band where Dido is, coming to us through the malignant air; such was the force of my affectuous cry.

"O living creature, gracious and benign; that goest through the black air, visiting us who stained the earth with blood: if the King of the Universe were our friend, we would pray him for thy peace; seeing that thou hast pity of our perverse misfortune. Of that which it pleases thee to hear and to speak, we 9 will hear and speak with you, whilst the wind, as now, is silent for us. The town, where I was born, sits on the shore, where Po descends to rest with his attendant streams. Love, which is quickly caught in gentle heart, took him with the fair body of which I was bereft; and the manner still afflicts me. Love, which to no loved one permits excuse for loving, took me so strongly with delight in him, that, as thou seest, even now it leaves me not. Love led us to one death; Caïna waits for him who quenched our life." 10 These words from them were offered to us.

After I had heard those wounded souls, I bowed my face, and held it low until the Poet said to me: "What art thou thinking of?" When I answered, I

61–62. she . . . Sichaeus, Dido. 72. those two, Paolo and Francesca, the famous lovers. Francesca of Ravenna, married for political reasons to the deformed Gianciotto of Rimini, accepted the love of his younger brother, Paolo, and was killed with her lover by the outraged husband. 100. Caïna, the section of the ninth hell reserved for those who had killed relatives, as Cain his brother Abel.

began: "Ah me! what sweet thoughts, what longing led them to the woeful pass!" Then I turned again to them; and I spoke, and began: "Francesca, thy torments make me weep with grief and pity. But tell me: in the time of the sweet sighs, by what and how love granted you to know the dubious desires?"

And she to me: "There is no greater pain than to recall a happy time in wretchedness; and this thy teacher knows. But if thou hast such desire to learn the first root of our love, I will do like one who weeps and tells. One day, for pastime, we read of Lancelot, how love constrained him; we were alone, and without all suspicion. Several times that reading urged our eyes to meet, and changed the colour of our faces; but one moment alone it was that overcame us. When we read how the fond smile was kissed by such a lover, he, who shall never be divided from me, kissed my mouth all trembling: the book, and he who wrote it, was a Galeotto. That day we read in it no farther." Whilst the one spirit thus spake, the other wept so, that I fainted with pity, as if I had been dying; and fell, as a dead body falls.

CANTO VI. *Circle III: the gluttons*

On sense returning, which closed itself before the pity of the two kinsfolk that stunned me all with sadness, I discern new torments, and new tormented souls, whithersoever I move, and turn, and gaze. I am in the Third Circle, that of the eternal, accursed, cold, and heavy rain; its law and quality is never new. Large hail, and turbid water, and snow, pour down through the darksome air; the ground, on which it falls, emits a putrid smell. Cerberus, a monster fierce and strange, with three throats, barks dog-like over those that are immersed in it. His eyes are red, his beard greasy and black, his belly wide, and clawed his hands; he clutches the spirits, flays, and piecemeal rends them. The rain makes them howl like dogs; with one side they screen the other; they often turn themselves, the impious wretches.

When Cerberus, the great Worm, perceived us, he opened his mouths and showed his tusks: no limb of him kept still. My Guide, spreading his palms, took up earth; and, with full fists, cast it into his ravening gullets. As the dog, that barking craves, and grows quiet when he bites his food, for he strains and battles only to devour it: so did those squalid visages of Cerberus, the Demon, who thunders on the spirits so, that they would fain be deaf. We passed over the shadows whom the heavy rain subdues; and placed our soles upon their emptiness, which seems a body. . . .

Thus passed we through the filthy mixture of the shadows and the rain, with paces slow, touching a

19. a Galeotto, a pander.

little on the future life. Wherefore I said: "Master, shall these torments increase after the great Sentence, or grow less, or remain as burning?" And he to me: "Return to thy science, which has it, that the more a thing is perfect, the more it feels pleasure and likewise pain. Though these accursed people never attain to true perfection, yet they look to be nearer it after than before."

We went round along that road, speaking much more than I repeat; we reached the point where the descent begins; here found we Plutus, the great enemy.

CANTO VII. *Circle IV: Misers and Prodigals; Circle V, Styx: the angry and sullen*

"Pape Satan! pape Satan, aleppe!" began Plutus, with clucking voice; and that gentle Sage, who knew all, said, comforting me: "Let not thy fear hurt thee: for, whatever power he have, he shall not hinder thee from descending this rock." Then he turned himself to that inflated visage, and said: "Peace, cursed Wolf! consume thyself internally with thy greedy rage. Not without cause is our journey to the deep: it is willed on high." As sails, swelled by the wind, fall entangled when the mast breaks: so fell that cruel monster to the ground. Thus we descended into the fourth concavity, taking in more of the dismal bank, which shuts up all the evil of the universe.

Ah, Justice Divine! who shall tell in few the many fresh pains and travails that I saw? and why does guilt of ours thus waste us? As does the surge, there above Charybdis, that breaks itself against the surge wherewith it meets: so have the people here to counter-dance. Here saw I too many more than elsewhere, both on the one side and on the other, with loud howlings, rolling weights by force of chests; they smote against each other, and then each wheeled round just there, rolling aback, shouting "Why holdest thou?" and "Why throwest thou away?" Thus they returned along the gloomy circle, on either hand, to the opposite point, again shouting at each other their reproachful measure. Then every one, when he had reached it, turned through his half-circle towards the other joust. And I, who felt my heart as it were stung, said: "My Master, now show me what people these are, and whether all those tonsured on our left were of the clergy."

And he to me: "In their first life, all were so squint-eyed in mind, that they made no expenditure in it with moderation. Most clearly do their voices

63. **Plutus.** Dante probably meant Pluto, the god of the underworld, rather than Plutus, the god of wealth. 65. "**Pape . . . aleppe!**" The meaning of the words is unknown. 82. **Charybdis,** the whirlpool encountered by Odysseus (Odyssey, XI).

bark out this, when they come to the two points of the circle, where contrary guilt divides them. These were Priests, that have not hairy covering on their heads, and Popes and Cardinals, in whom avarice does its utmost."

And I: "Master, among this set, I surely ought to recognize some that were defiled by these evils." And he to me: "Vain thoughts combinest thou: their undiscerning life, which made them sordid, now makes them too obscure for any recognition. To all eternity they shall continue butting one another; these shall arise from their graves with closed fists; and these with hair shorn off. Ill-giving, and ill-keeping, has deprived them of the bright world, and put them to this conflict; what a conflict it is, I adorn no words to tell. But thou, my Son, mayest now see the brief mockery of the goods that are committed unto Fortune, for which the human kind contend with one another. For all the gold that is beneath the moon, or ever was, could not give rest to a single one of these weary souls."

"Master," I said to him, "now tell me also: this Fortune, of which thou hintest to me; what is she, that has the good things of the world thus within her clutches?" And he to me: "O foolish creatures, how great is this ignorance that falls upon ye! Now I wish thee to receive my judgment of her. He whose wisdom is transcendent over all, made the heavens and gave them guides, so that every part shines to every part, equally distributing the light; in like manner, for worldly splendours, he ordained a general minister and guide, to change betimes the vain possession, from people to people, and from one kindred to another, beyond the hindrance of human wisdom: hence one people commands, another languishes; obeying her sentence, which is hidden like the serpent in the grass. Your knowledge cannot understand her: she provides, judges, and maintains her kingdom, as the other Gods do theirs. Her permutations have no truce; necessity makes her be swift; thus he comes oft who doth a change obtain. This is she, who is so much reviled, even by those who ought to praise her, when blaming her wrongfully, and with evil words. . . . But let us now descend to greater misery; already every star is falling, that was ascending when I set out, and to stay too long is not permitted."

We crossed the circle, to the other bank, near a fount, that boils and pours down through a cleft, which it has formed. The water was darker far than perse; and we, accompanying the dusky waves, entered down by a strange path. This dreary streamlet makes a Marsh, that is named Styx, when it has descended to the foot of the grey malignant shores. And I, who stood intent on looking, saw muddy people in that bog, all naked and with a look of anger. They were smiting each other, not with hands only,

but with head, and with chest, and with feet; maiming one another with their teeth, piece by piece.

The kind Master said: "Son, now see the souls of those whom anger overcame; and also I would have thee to believe for certain, that there are people underneath the water, who sob, and make it bubble at the surface; as thy eye may tell thee, whichever way it turns. Fixed in the slime, they say: 'Sullen were we in the sweet air, that is gladdened by the Sun, carrying lazy smoke within our hearts; now lie we sullen here in the black mire.' This hymn they gurgle in their throats, for they cannot speak it in full words."

Thus, between the dry bank and the putrid fen, we compassed a large arc of that loathly slough, with eyes turned towards those that swallow of its filth; we came to the foot of a tower at last.

CANTO VIII. *The Entrance to the City of Dis: the fallen angels*

I say continuing, that, long before we reached the foot of the high tower, our eyes went upwards to its summit, because of two flamelets, that we saw put there, and another from far give signal back, so far that the eye could scarcely catch it. And I turned to the Sea of all intelligence; I said: "What says this? and what replies yon other fire? And who are they that made it?" And he to me: "Over the squalid waves, already thou mayest discern what is expected, if the vapour of the fen conceal it not from thee."

Never did cord impel from itself an arrow, that ran through the air so quickly, as a little bark which I saw come towards us then through the water, under the guidance of a single steersman, who cried: "Now art thou arrived, fell spirit?" "Phlegyas, Phlegyas," said my Lord, "this time thou criest in vain; thou shalt not have us longer than while we pass the wash." As one who listens to some great deceit which has been done to him, and then sore resents it: such grew Phlegyas in his gathered rage. My Guide descended into the skiff, and then made me enter after him; and not till I was in, did it seem laden. Soon as my Guide and I were in the boat, its ancient prow went on, cutting the water. . . .

The kind Master said: "Now, Son, the city that is named of Dis draws nigh, with its grave citizens, with its great company." And I: "Master, already I discern its mosques, distinctly there within the valley, red as if they had come out of fire." And to me he said: "The eternal fire, which causes them to glow within, shows them red, as thou seest, in this low Hell."

74. **a tower;** from which signals are sent to Phlegyas, the ferryman, to indicate that passengers await the ferry across the marsh.

We now arrived in the deep fosses, which moat that joyless city; the walls seemed to me as if they were of iron. Not before making a long circuit, did we come to a place where the boatman loudly cried to us: "Go out: here is the entrance." Above the gates I saw more than a thousand spirits, rained from the Heavens, who angrily exclaimed: "Who is that, who, without death, goes through the kingdom of the dead?" And my sage Master made a sign of wish-10 ing to speak with them in secret. Then they some-what shut up their great disdain, and said: "Come thou alone; and let that one go, who has entered so daringly into this kingdom. Let him return alone his foolish way; try, if he can: for thou shalt stay here, that hast escorted him through so dark a country."

Judge, Reader, if I was discouraged at the sound of the accursed words: for I believed not that I ever should return hither. "O my loved Guide, who more than seven times hast restored me to safety, and res-20 cued from deep peril that stood before me, leave me not so undone," I said, "and if to go farther be de-nied us, let us retrace our steps together rapidly." And that Lord, who had led me thither, said to me: "Fear not, for our passage none can take from us: by Such has it been given to us. But thou, wait here for me; and comfort and feed thy wearied spirit with good hope: for I will not forsake thee in the low world."

Thus the gentle Father goes, and leaves me here, 30 and I remain in doubt: for yes and no contend within my head. I could not hear that which was offered to them; but he had not long stood with them, when they all, vying with one another, rushed in again. These our adversaries closed the gates on the breast of my Lord who remained without; and turned to me with slow steps. He had his eyes upon the ground, and his eyebrows shorn of all boldness, and said with sighs: "Who hath denied me the doleful houses?" And to me he said: "Thou, be not dis-40 mayed, though I get angry: for I will master the trial, whatever be contrived for hindrance." . . .

CANTOS IX–X. *Circle VI, the City of Dis:*
the heretics

And more he said, but I have it not in memory: for my eye had drawn me wholly to the high tower with glowing summit, where all at once had risen up three Hellish Furies, stained with blood; who had the limbs and attitude of women, and were girt with greenest hydras; for hair, they had little serpents and cerastes, wherewith their horrid temples were bound. And he, knowing well the handmaids of the 50 Queen of everlasting lamentation, said to me: "Mark

the fierce Erinnyes! This is Megæra on the left hand; she, that weeps upon the right, is Alecto; Tisiphone is in the middle"; and therewith he was silent. With her claws each was rending her breast; they were smiting themselves with their palms, and crying so loudly, that I pressed close to the Poet for fear. "Let Medusa come, that we may change him into stone," they all said, looking downwards.

"Turn thee backwards, and keep thy eyes closed: for if the Gorgon show herself, and thou shouldst 60 see her, there would be no returning up again." Thus said the Master, and he himself turned me, and trusted not to my hands, but closed me also with his own.

And now there came, upon the turbid waves, a crash of fearful sound, at which the shores both trembled; a sound as of a wind, impetuous for the adverse heats, which smites the forest without any stay; shatters off the boughs, beats down, and sweeps away; dusty in front, it goes superb, and makes the 70 wild beasts and the shepherds flee. He loosed my eyes, and said: "Now turn thy nerve of vision on that ancient foam, there where the smoke is harsh-est." As frogs, before their enemy the serpent, run all asunder through the water, till each squats upon the bottom: so I saw more than a thousand ruined spirits flee before one, who passed the Stygian ferry with soles unwet. He waved that gross air from his countenance, often moving his left hand before him; and only of that trouble seemed he weary. 80

Well did I perceive that he was a Messenger of Heaven; and I turned to the Master; and he made a sign that I should stand quiet, and bow down to him. Ah, how full he seemed to me of indignation! He reached the gate, and with a wand opened it: for there was no resistance. "O outcasts of Heaven! race despised!" began he, upon the horrid threshold, "why dwells this insolence in you? Why spurn ye at that Will, whose object never can be frustated, and which often has increased your pain?" . . . Then he re- 90 turned by the filthy way, and spake no word to us; but looked like one whom other care urges and in-cites than that of those who stand before him.

And we moved our feet towards the city, secure after the sacred words. We entered into it without any strife; and I, who was desirous to behold the condition which such a fortress encloses, as soon as I was in, sent my eyes around; and saw, on either hand, a spacious plain full of sorrow and of evil tor-ment. . . . The sepulchres make all the place un- 100 even: so did they here on every side, only the man-ner here was bitterer: for amongst the tombs were scattered flames, whereby they were made all over so glowing-hot, that iron more hot no craft requires.

5–7. Above the gates . . . Heavens; at the time that Satan fell from Heaven.   49–50. the Queen, Proserpine, Queen of the Underworld.

56–57. Let Medusa come . . . stone. The terrible head of the Gor-gon Medusa would turn its beholder to stone.

Their covers were all raised up; and out of them proceeded moans so grievous, that they seemed indeed the moans of spirits sad and wounded.

And I: "Master, what are these people who, buried within those chests, make themselves heard by their painful sighs?" And he to me: "Here are the Arch-heretics with their followers of every sect; and much more, than thou thinkest, the tombs are laden. Like with like is buried here; and the monuments
10 are more and less hot." Then, after turning to the right hand, we passed between the tortures and the high battlements.

Now by a secret path, between the city-wall and the torments, my Master goes on, and I behind him. "O Virtue supreme! who through the impious circles thus wheelest me, as it pleases thee," I began; "speak to me, and satisfy my wishes. Might these people, who lie within the sepulchres, be seen? the covers are all raised, and none keeps guard." And he to me:
20 "All shall be closed up, when, from Jehosaphat, they return here with the bodies which they have left above. In this part are entombed with Epicurus all his followers, who make the soul die with the body." . . .

CANTO XII. *Circle VII, the River Phlegethon: tyrants and murderers*

The place to which we came, in order to descend the bank, was alpine, and such, from what was there besides, that every eye would shun it, for from the summit of the mountain, whence it moved, to the plain, the rock is shattered so, that it might give
30 some passage to one that were above: such of that rocky steep was the descent. . . . Thus we took our way downwards on the ruin of those stones, which often moved beneath my feet, from the unusual weight.

I went musing, and he said: ". . . Fix thy eyes upon the valley: for the river of blood draws nigh, in which boils every one who by violence injures others." O blind cupidity both wicked and foolish, which so incites us in the short life, and then, in the
40 eternal, steeps us so bitterly!

I saw a wide fosse bent arcwise, as embracing all the plain, according to what my Guide had told me; and between it and the foot of the bank were Centaurs, running one behind the other, armed with arrows, as they were wont on earth to go in hunting. Perceiving us descend, they all stood still; and from the band three came forth with bows and javelins chosen first. And one of them cried from far: "To what torment come ye, ye that descend the coast?
50 Tell from thence; if not, I draw the bow."

22–24. **In this part . . . body.** See Lucretius, *Of the Nature of Things*, Book III.

My Master said: "Our answer we will make to Chiron, there near at hand; unhappily thy will was always thus rash." Then he touched me and said: "This is Nessus, who died for the fair Dejanira, and of himself took vengeance for himself; he in the middle, who is looking down upon his breast, is the great Chiron, he who nursed Achilles; that other is Pholus, who was so full of rage. Around the foss they go by thousands, piercing with their arrows whatever spirit wrenches itself out of the blood farther 60 than its guilt has allotted for it."

We drew near those rapid beasts; Chiron took an arrow, and with the notch put back his beard upon his jaws. When he had uncovered his great mouth, he said to his companions: "Have ye perceived that the one behind moves what he touches? The feet of the dead are not wont to do so." And my good Guide, who was already at the breast of him, where the two natures are consorted, replied: "Indeed he is alive, and solitary thus have I to show him the 70 dark valley; necessity brings him to it, and not sport. From singing Alleluiah, came She who gave me this new office; he is no robber, nor I a thievish spirit. But by that virtue through which I move my steps on such a wild way, give us some one of thine whom we may follow, that he may show us where the ford is, and carry over him upon his back, for he is not a spirit to go through the air." Chiron bent round on his right breast, and said to Nessus: "Turn, and guide them then; and if another troop encounter 80 you, keep it off."

We moved onwards with our trusty guide, along the border of the purple boiling, wherein the boiled were making loud shrieks. I saw people down in it even to the eyebrows; and the great Centaur said: "These are tyrants who took to blood and plunder. Here they lament their merciless offences; here is Alexander; and fierce Dionysius, who made Sicily have years of woe." . . .

A little farther on, the Centaur paused beside a 90 people which, as far as the throat, seemed to issue from that boiling stream. . . . Then some I saw, who kept the head and likewise all the chest out of the river; and of these I recognized many. Thus more and more that blood grew shallow, until it cooked the feet only; and here was our passage through the fosse. "As thou seest the boiling stream, on this side, continually diminish," said the Centaur, "so I would have thee to believe that, on this other, it lowers its bottom more and more, till it comes 100 again to where tyranny is doomed to mourn." . . .

CANTO XIII. *Circle VII, the Wood of the Harpies: the suicides*

Nessus had not yet reached the other side, when we moved into a wood, which by no path was

marked. Not green the foliage, but of colour dusky;
not smooth the branches, but gnarled and warped;
apples none were there, but withered sticks with
poison. . . . Here the unseemly Harpies make their
nests. . . . Wide wings they have, and necks and
faces human, feet with claws, and their large belly
feathered; they make rueful cries on the strange
trees. The kind Master began to say to me: "Before
thou goest farther, know that thou art in the second
10 round; and shalt be, until thou comest to the horrid
sand. Therefore look well, and thou shalt see things
which would take away belief from my speech."

Already I heard wailings uttered on every side,
and saw no one to make them: wherefore I, all bewildered, stood still. I think he thought that I was
thinking so many voices came, amongst those
stumps, from people who hid themselves on our account. Therefore the Master said: "If thou breakest
off any little shoot from one of these plants, the
20 thoughts, which thou hast, will all become defective."

Then I stretched my hand a little forward, and
plucked a branchlet from a great thorn; and the
trunk of it cried, "Why dost thou rend me?" And
when it had grown dark with blood, it again began
to cry: "Why dost thou tear me? hast thou no breath
of pity? Men we were, and now are turned to trees:
truly thy hand should be more merciful, had we
been souls of serpents." As a green brand, that is
30 burning at one end, at the other drops, and hisses
with the wind which is escaping: so from that
broken splint, words and blood came forth together:
whereat I let fall the top, and stood like one who is
afraid. . . .

The Poet then said to me: "Since he is silent, lose
not the hour; but speak, and ask him, if thou wouldst
know more." Whereat I to him: "Do thou ask him
farther, respecting what thou thinkest will satisfy
me; for I could not, such pity is upon my heart."
40 He therefore resumed: "So may the man do freely
for thee what thy words entreat him, O imprisoned
spirit, please thee tell us farther, how the soul gets
bound up in these knots; and tell us, if thou mayest,
whether any ever frees itself from such members."
Then the trunk blew strongly, and soon that wind
was changed into these words: "Briefly shall you be
answered. When the fierce spirit quits the body,
from which it has torn itself, Minos sends it to the
seventh gulf. It falls into the wood, and no place is
50 chosen for it; but wherever fortune flings it, there it
sprouts, like grain of spelt; shoots up to a sapling,
and to a savage plant; the Harpies, feeding then
upon its leaves, give pain, and to the pain an outlet.
Like the others, we shall go for our spoils, but not
to the end that any may be clothed with them again:
for it is not just that a man have what he takes from
himself. Hither shall we drag them, and through the

mournful wood our bodies shall be suspended, each
on the thorny tree of its tormented shade." . . .

CANTO XIV. *Circle VII, the Burning
Sands: blasphemers, sodomists, and usurers*

The love of my native place constraining me, I
gathered up the scattered leaves; and gave them
back to him, who was already hoarse. Then we came
to the limit, where the second round is separated
from the third, and where is seen a fearful device of
justice. To make the new things clear, I say we
reached a plain which from its bed repels all plants.
The dolorous wood is a garland to it round about, as
to the wood the dismal fosse; here we stayed our
steps close to its very edge.

I saw many herds of naked souls, who were all
lamenting very miserably; and there seemed imposed upon them a diverse law. Some were lying
supine upon the ground; some sitting all crouched
up; and others roaming incessantly. Those that
moved about were much more numerous; and those
that were lying in the torment were fewer, but uttered louder cries of pain. Over all the great sand,
falling slowly, rained dilated flakes of fire, like those
of snow in Alps without a wind . . . so fell the
eternal heat, by which the sand was kindled, like
tinder under flint and steel, redoubling the pain.
Ever restless was the dance of miserable hands, now
here, now there, shaking off the fresh burning.

I began: "Master, thou who conquerest all things,
save the hard Demons, that came forth against us
at the entrance of the gate, who is that great spirit,
who seems to care not for the fire, and lies disdainful
and contorted, so that the rain seems not to ripen
him?" And he himself, remarking that I asked my
Guide concerning him, exclaimed: "What I was living, that am I dead." . . .

Then my Guide spake with a force such as I had
not heard before: "O Capaneus! in that thy pride
remains unquenched, thou art punished more: no
torture, except thy own raving, would be pain proportioned to thy fury." Then to me he turned with
gentler lip, saying: "That was the one of the seven
kings who laid siege to Thebes; and he held, and
seems to hold, God in defiance and prize him lightly;
but, as I told him, his revilings are ornaments that
well befit his breast. Now follow me, and see thou
place not yet thy feet upon the burning sand; but
always keep them back close to the wood."

In silence we came to where there gushes forth
from the wood a little rivulet, the redness of which
still makes me shudder. . . . Its bottom and both
its shelving banks were petrified, and also the margins near it: whereby I discerned that our passage
lay there. . . . Then he said: "Now it is time to quit

the wood; see that thou follow me; the margins which are not burning, form a path and over them all fire is quenched." . . .

CANTOS XVI–XVII. *The Descent to Circle VIII*

I followed him; and we had gone but little, when the sound of the water was so near us, that in speaking we should scarce have heard each other. . . . I had a cord girt round me; and with it I thought some time to catch the Leopard of the painted skin. After I had quite unloosed it from me, as my
10 Guide commanded me, I held it out to him coiled and wound up. Then he bent himself toward the right side, and threw it, some distance from the edge, down into that steep abyss. "Surely," said I within myself, "something new must answer this new signal, which my Master thus follows with his eye." Ah! how cautious ought men to be with those who see not only the deed, but with their sense look through into the thoughts! He said to me: "What I expect will soon come up; and what thy thought dreams of,
20 soon must be discovered to thy view."

Always to that truth which has an air of falsehood, a man should close his lips, so far as he is able, for, though blameless, he incurs reproach; but here keep silent I cannot; and, Reader, I swear to thee, by the notes of this my Comedy—so may they not be void of lasting favour—that I saw, through that air gross and dark, come swimming upwards, a figure marvellous to every steadfast heart; like as he returns, who on a time goes down to loose the anchor, which grap-
30 ples a rock or other thing that in the sea is hid, who spreads the arms and gathers up the feet.

"Behold the savage beast with the pointed tail, that passes mountains, and breaks through walls and weapons; behold him that pollutes the whole world." Thus began my Guide to speak to me; and beckoned him to come ashore, near the end of our rocky path; and that uncleanly image of Fraud came onward, and landed his head and bust, but drew not his tail upon the bank. His face was the face of a just man,
40 so mild an aspect had it outwardly; and the rest was all a reptile's body. He had two paws, hairy to the armpits; the back and the breast, and both the flanks, were painted with knots and circlets. . . . In the void glanced all his tail, twisting upwards the venomed fork, which, as in scorpions, armed the point.

My Guide said: "Now must we bend our way a little, to that wicked brute which couches there." Then we descended on the right, and made ten paces

towards the edge, that we might quite avoid the 50 sand and flames. . . . I found my Guide, who had already mounted on the haunch of the dreadful animal; and he said to me: "Now be stout and bold! Now by such stairs must we descend; mount thou in front: for I wish to be in the middle, that the tail may not do hurt to thee."

As one who has the shivering of the quartan so near, that he has his nails already pale and trembles all, still keeping the shade, such I became when these words were uttered; but his threats excited in 60 me shame, which makes a servant brave in presence of a worthy master. I placed myself on those huge shoulders; I wished to say, only the voice came not as I thought: "See that thou embrace me." But he, who at other times assisted me in other difficulties, soon as I mounted, clasped me with his arms, and held me up; then he said: "Geryon, now move thee! be thy circles large, and gradual thy descent: think of the unusual burden that thou hast."

As the bark goes from its station backwards, back- 70 wards, so the monster took himself from thence; and when he felt himself quite loose, there where his breast had been he turned his tail, and stretching moved it, like an eel, and with his paws gathered the air to him. Greater fear there was not, I believe, . . . than was mine, when I saw myself in the air on all sides, and saw extinguished every sight, save of the beast. He goes on swimming slowly, slowly; wheels and descends; but I perceive it not, otherwise than by a wind upon my face and from below. 80 Already, on the right hand, I heard the whirlpool make a hideous roaring under us; whereat, with eyes downwards, my head I stretched.

Then was I more timorous as regards dismounting: for I saw fires and heard lamentings, so that I cower all trembling. And then I saw—for I had not seen it before—the sinking and the wheeling, through the great evils which drew near on diverse sides. As the falcon, that has been long upon his wings—that, without seeing bird or lure, makes the 90 falconer cry, "Ah, ah! thou stoopest"—descends weary; then swiftly moves himself with many a circle, and far from his master sets himself disdainful and sullen: so at the bottom Geryon set us, close to the foot of the ragged rock; and, from our weight relieved, he bounded off like an arrow from the string.

CANTOS XVIII–XX. *Circle VIII, Malebolge: the fraudulent*

There is a place in Hell called Malebolge, all of stone, and of an iron colour, like the barrier which winds round it. Right in the middle of the malignant

---

8. **Leopard of the painted skin.** A monk's severe life would destroy the thirst for worldly pleasure. 27. **a figure,** Geryon, the monster guarding Circle VIII.

98. **Malebolge,** Italian for "evil pouches," since there are ten pouches or regions in Circle VIII.

field yawns a well exceeding wide and deep, whose structure I shall tell in its own place. The border therefore that remains, between the well and the foot of the high rocky bank, is round; and it has its bottom divided into ten valleys. As is the form that ground presents, where to defend the walls successive ditches begird a castle: such image made here; and as, from the thresholds of the fortress, there are bridges to the outward bank: so from the basis of the rock proceeded cliffs that crossed the embankments and the ditches, down to the well which truncates and collects them. In this place, shaken from the back of Geryon, we found ourselves; and the Poet kept to the left, and I moved behind.

On the right hand I saw new misery, new torments, and new tormentors, wherewith the first chasm was filled. In its bottom the sinners were naked; on our side of the middle they came facing us; and, on the other side, along with us, but with larger steps. . . . On this side, on that, along the hideous stone, I saw horned Demons with large scourges, who smote them fiercely from behind. Ah! how they made them lift their legs at the first strokes! truly none waited for the second or the third. . . . We had already come to where the narrow pathway crosses the second bank, and makes of it a buttress for another arch. Here we heard people whining in the other chasm, and puffing with mouth and nostrils, and knocking on themselves with their palms. The banks were crusted over with a mould from the vapour below, which concretes upon them, which did battle with the eyes and with the nose. The bottom is so deep, that we could see it nowhere without mounting to the ridge of the arch, where the cliff stands highest. We got upon it; and thence in the ditch beneath, I saw a people dipped in excrement, that seemed as it had flowed from human privies. . . .

And through the circular valley I saw a people coming silent and weeping, at the pace which the Litanies make in this world. When my sight descended lower on them, each seemed wondrously distorted, between the chin and the commencement of the chest: for the face was turned towards the loins; and they had to come backward, for to look before them was denied. Perhaps by force of palsy some have been thus quite distorted; but I have not seen, nor do believe it to be so. Reader, so God grant thee to take profit of thy reading, now think for thyself how I could keep my visage dry, when near at hand I saw our image so contorted, that the weeping of the eyes bathed the hinder parts at their division? Certainly I wept, leaning on one of the rocks of the hard cliff, so that my Escort said to me: "Art thou,

1–2. a well . . . its own place, Circle IX.

too, like the other fools? Here pity lives when it is altogether dead. Who more impious than he that sorrows at God's judgment?" . . .

CANTOS XXI–XXII. *Encounter with the Demons*

Thus from bridge to bridge we came, with other talk which my Comedy cares not to recite; and held the summit, when we stood still to see the other cleft of Malebolge and the other vain lamentings; and I found it marvellously dark. As in the arsenal of the Venetians boils the clammy pitch in winter, to caulk their damaged ships, which they cannot navigate; and, instead thereof, one builds his ship anew, one plugs the ribs of that which hath made many voyages; some hammer at the prow, some at the stern; some make oars, and some twist ropes; one mends the jib, and one the mainsail: so, not by fire but by art Divine, a dense pitch boiled down there, and overglued the banks on every side. It I saw; but saw naught therein, except the bubbles which the boiling raised, and the heaving and compressed subsiding of the whole.

Whilst I was gazing fixedly down on it, my Guide, saying, "Take care, take care!" drew me to him from the place where I was standing. Then I turned round, like one who longs to see what he must shun, and who is dashed with sudden fear, so that he puts not off his flight to look; and behind us I saw a black Demon come running up the cliff. Ah, how ferocious was his aspect! and how bitter he seemed to me in gesture, with his wings outspread, and light of foot! His shoulders that were sharp and high, a sinner with both haunches laded; and of each foot he held the sinew grasped. . . . Down he threw him, then wheeled along the flinty cliff; and never was mastiff loosed with such a haste to follow thief. The sinner plunged in, and came up again writhing convolved; but the Demons, who were under cover of the bridge, cried: "Unless thou wishest to make trial of our drags, come not out above the pitch." Then they struck him with more than a hundred prongs, and said: "Covered thou must dance thee here; so that, if thou canst, thou mayest pilfer privately." Not otherwise do the cooks make their vassals dip the flesh into the middle of the boiler with their hooks, to hinder it from floating.

The kind Master said to me: "That it may not be seen that thou art here, cower down behind a jag, so that thou mayest have some screen for thyself; and whatever outrage may be done to me, fear not thou: for I know these matters, having once before been in the like affray." Then he passed beyond the head of the bridge; and when he arrived on the sixth bank, it was needful for him to have a steadfast front. With that fury and that storm, wherewith the dogs rush forth upon the poor man who where he stops suddenly seeks alms, rushed those Demons from beneath the bridge, and turned against him all their crooks; but he cried: "Be none of ye outrageous! Before ye touch me with your forks, let one of you come forth to hear me, and then take counsel about hooking me."

All cried: "Let Malacoda go"; thereat one moved himself, the other standing firm, and came to him, 10 saying: "What will this avail him?" "Dost thou expect, Malacoda," said my Master, "to find I have come here, secure already against all your hindrances, without will Divine and fate propitious? Let me pass on: for it is willed in Heaven that I show another this savage way." Then was his pride so fallen, that he let the hook drop at his feet, and said to the others: "Now strike him not!"

And my Guide to me: "O thou that sittest cowering, cowering amongst the great splinters of the 20 bridge, securely now return to me!" Whereat I moved, and quickly came to him; and the Devils all pressed forward, so that I feared they might not hold the compact. . . . I drew near my Guide with my whole body, and turned not away my eyes from the look of them, which was not good. They lowered their drag-hooks, and kept saying to one another: "Shall I touch him on the rump?" and answering: "Yes, see thou nick it for him."

But that Demon, who was speaking with my 30 Guide, turned instant round, and said: "Quiet, quiet, Scarmiglione!" Then he said to us: "To go farther by this cliff will not be possible: for the sixth arch lies all in fragments at the bottom; and if it please you still to go onward, go along this ridge: near at hand is another cliff which forms a path. . . . Thitherward I send some of these my men, to look if anyone be out airing himself; go with them, for they will not be treacherous. Draw forward, Alichino and Calcabrina," he then began to say, "and 40 thou, Cagnazzo; and let Barbariccia lead the ten. Let Libicocco come besides, and Draghignazzo, tusked Ciriatto, and Graffiacane, and Farfarello, and furious Rubicante. Search around the boiling glue; be these two safe as far as the other crag, which all unbroken goes across the dens."

"Oh me! Master, what is this that I see?" said I; "ah, without escort let us go alone, if thou knowest the way; for as to me, I seek it not! If thou beest so wary, as thou art wont, dost thou not see how they 50 grind their teeth, and with their brows threaten mischief to us?" And he to me: "I would not have thee be afraid; let them grind on at their will: for they do it at the boiled wretches." . . .

We went with the ten Demons: ah, hideous company! but, "In church with saints, and with guzzlers in the tavern." Yet my intent was on the pitch, to see each habit of the chasm and of the people that were

burning in it. As dolphins, when with the arch of the back they make sign to mariners that they may prepare to save their ship: so now and then, to ease the 60 punishment, some sinner showed his back and hid in less time than it lightens. And as at the edge of the water of a ditch, the frogs stand only with their muzzles out, so that they hide their feet and other bulk: thus stood on every hand the sinners; but as Barbariccia approached, they instantly retired beneath the seething.

I saw, and my heart still shudders thereat, one linger so, as it will happen that one frog remains while the other spouts away; And Graffiacane, who 70 was nearest to him, hooked his pitchy locks and hauled him up, so that to me he seemed an otter. I already knew the name of everyone, so well I noted them as they were chosen, and when they called each other, listened how. "O Rubicante, see thou plant thy clutches on him, and flay him!" shouted together all the accursed crew.

And I: "Master, learn if thou canst, who is that piteous wight, fallen into the hand of his adversaries." My Guide drew close to his side and asked 80 him whence he came; and he replied: "I was born in the kingdom of Navarre. My mother placed me as a servant of a lord; for she had borne me to a ribald waster of himself and of his substance. Then I was domestic with the good king Thibault; here I set myself to doing barratry, of which I render reckoning in this heat."

And Ciriatto, from whose mouth on either side came forth a tusk as from a hog, made him feel how one of them did rip. Amongst evil cats the mouse 90 had come; but Barbariccia locked him in his arms, and said: "Stand off whilst I enfork him!" . . . And Libicocco cried: "Too much have we endured!" and with the hook seized his arm, and mangling carried off a part of brawn. Draghignazzo, he too, wished to have a catch at the legs below; whereat their Decurion wheeled around with evil aspect. . . .

O Reader, thou shalt hear new sport! All turned their eyes toward the other side, he first who had been most unripe for doing it. The Navarrese chose 100 well his time; planted his soles upon the ground, and in an instant leapt and from their purpose freed himself. Thereat each was stung with guilt; but he most who had been cause of the mistake; he therefore started forth, and shouted: "Thou'rt caught!" But little it availed him; for wings could not outspeed the terror the sinner went under; and he, flying, raised up his breast: not otherwise the duck suddenly dives down, when the falcon approaches, and he returns up angry and defeated. 110

Calcabrina, furious at the trick, kept flying after him, desirous that the sinner might escape, to have a quarrel. And, when the barrator had disappeared, he turned his talons on his fellow, and was clutched with him above the ditch. But the other was indeed a sparrowhawk to claw him well; and both dropt down into the middle of the boiling pond. The heat at once unclutched them; but rise they could not, their wings were so beglued. Barbariccia with the rest lamenting, made four of them fly over to the other coast with all their drags; and most rapidly on this side, on that, they descended to the stand; they stretched their hooks towards the limed pair, who were already scalded within the crust; and we left them thus embroiled. . . .

CANTOS XXIV–XXV. *The Punishment of Thieves*

When we reached the shattered bridge, my Guide turned to me with that sweet aspect which I saw first at the foot of the mountain. He opened his arms after having chosen some plan within himself, first looking well at the ruin, and took hold of me. And as one who works, and calculates, always seeming to provide beforehand: so, lifting me up towards the top of one big block, he looked out another splinter, saying: "Now clamber over that, but try first if it will carry thee."

It was no way for one clad with cloak of lead: for scarcely we, he light and I pushed on, could mount up from jag to jag. And were it not on that precinct the ascent was shorter than on the other, I know not about him, but I certainly had been defeated. But as Malebolge all hangs towards the entrance of the lowest well, the site of every valley imports that one side rises and the other descends; we, however, came at length to the point from which the last stone breaks off. The breath was so exhausted from my lungs, when I was up, that I could no farther; nay, seated me at my first arrival.

"Now it behoves thee thus to free thyself from sloth," said the Master: "for sitting on down, or under coverlet, men come not into fame; without which whoso consumes his life, leaves such vestige of himself on earth, as smoke in air or foam in water; and therefore rise! conquer thy panting with the soul, that conquers every battle, if with its heavy body it sinks not down. A longer ladder must be climbed: to have quitted these is not enough; if thou understandest me, now act so that it may profit thee." I then rose, showing myself better furnished with breath than I felt, and said: "Go on; for I am strong and confident." We took our way up the cliff, which was rugged, narrow, and difficult, and greatly steeper than the former. . . .

We went down the bridge, at the head where it joins with the eighth bank; and then the chasm was manifest to me: and I saw within it a fearful throng of serpents, and of so strange a look, that even now the recollection scares my blood. . . . Amid this cruel and most dismal swarm were people running, naked and terrified, without hope of lurking hole or heliotrope. They had their hands tied behind with serpents; these through their loins fixed the tail and the head, and were coiled in knots before.

And lo! at one, who was near our shore, sprang up a serpent, which transfixed him there where the neck is bound upon the shoulders. Neither "O" nor "I" was ever written so quickly as he took fire, and burnt, and dropt down all changed to ashes; and after he was thus dissolved upon the ground, the powder reunited of itself and at once resumed the former shape: thus by great sages 'tis confest the Phœnix dies, and then is born again, when it approaches the five-hundredth year; in its life it eats no herb or grain, but only tears of incense and amomum; and nard and myrrh are its last swathings. And as one who falls, and knows not how, through force of Demon which drags him to the ground, or of other obstruction that fetters men; who, when he rises, looks fixedly round him, all bewildered by the great anguish he has undergone, and looking sighs: such was the sinner when he rose. Power of God! O how severe, that showers such blows in vengeance! . . .

Under us there came three spirits, whom neither I nor my Guide perceived, until they cried: "Who are ye?" Our story therefore paused and we then gave heed to them alone. . . .

Whilst I kept gazing on them, lo! a serpent with six feet darts up in front of one, and fastens itself all upon him. With its middle feet it clasped his belly, with the anterior it seized his arms; then fixed its teeth in both his cheeks. The hinder feet it stretched along his thighs; and put its tail between the two, and bent it upwards on his loins behind. Ivy was never so rooted to a tree, as round the other's limbs the hideous monster entwined its own; then they stuck together, as if they had been of heated wax, and mingled their colours; neither the one, nor the other, now seemed what it was at first: as up before the flame on paper, goes a brown colour which is not yet black, and the white dies away.

The other two looked on, and each cried: "O me! Agnello, how thou changest! lo, thou art already neither two nor one!" The two heads had now become one, when two shapes appeared to us mixed in one face, where both were lost. Two arms were made of the four lists; the thighs with the legs, the belly, and the chest, became such members as were never seen. The former shape was all extinct in them: both, and neither the perverse image seemed; and such it went away with languid step.

As the lizard, beneath the mighty scourge of the canicular days, going from hedge to hedge, appears

56. heliotrope, a stone, supposed to make its wearer invisible.

a flash of lightning, if it cross the way: so, coming towards the bowels of the other two, appeared a little reptile burning with rage, livid and black as peppercorn. And it pierced that part, in one of them, at which we first receive our nourishment; then fell down stretched out before him. The pierced thief gazed on it but said nothing; nay, with his feet motionless, yawned only as if sleep or fever had come upon him. He eyed the reptile, the reptile him; the
10 one from his wound, the other from its mouth, smoked violently, and their smoke met. . . .

They mutually responded in such a way, that the reptile cleft its tail into a fork, and the wounded spirit drew his steps together. The legs and the thighs along with them so stuck to one another, that soon their juncture left no mark that was discernible. The cloven tail assumed the figure that was lost in the other; and its skin grew soft, the other's hard. I saw the arms enter at the armpits, and the two feet
20 of the brute, which were short, lengthen themselves as much as those arms were shortened. Then the two hinder feet, twisted together, became the member which man conceals; and the wretch from his had two thrust forth.

Whilst the smoke with a new colour veils them both, and generates on one part hair, and strips it from another, the one rose upright, and prostrate the other fell, not therefore turning the impious lights, under which they mutually exchanged visages. He
30 that was erect, drew his towards the temples; and from the too much matter that went thither, ears came out of the smooth cheeks; that which went not back, but was retained, of its superfluity formed a nose, and enlarged the lips to a fit size. He that lay prone, thrusts forward his sharpened visage, and draws back his ears into the head, as the snail does its horns; and his tongue, which was before united and apt for speech, cleaves itself; and in the other the forked tongue recloses; and the smoke now rests.
40 The soul that had become a brute, fled hissing along the valley, and after it the other talking and sputtering. . . .

CANTOS XXVI–XXVII. *The Meeting with Odysseus*

We departed thence; and, by the stairs which the curbstones had made for us to descend before, my Guide remounted and drew me up; and pursuing our solitary way among the jags and branches of the cliff, the foot without the hand sped not. I sorrowed then, and sorrow now again when I direct my memory to what I saw; and curb my genius more
50 than I am wont, lest it run where Virtue guides it not; so that, if kindly star or something better have given to me the good, I may not grudge myself that gift.

As many fireflies as the peasant who is resting on the hill—at the time that he who lights the world least hides his face from us, when the fly yields to the gnat—sees down along the valley, there perchance where he gathers grapes and tills: with flames thus numerous the eighth chasm was all gleaming, as I perceived, so soon as I came to where
60 the bottom showed itself, and every flame steals a sinner. I stood upon the bridge, having risen so to look, that if I had not caught a rock, I should have fallen down without being pushed. And the Guide, who saw me thus attent, said: "Within those fires are the spirits; each swathes himself with that which burns him."

"Master," I replied, "from hearing thee I feel more certain; but had already discerned it to be so, and already wished to say to thee: who is in that fire,
70 which comes so parted at the top, as if it rose from the pyre where Eteocles with his brother was placed?"

He answered me: "Within it there Ulysses is tortured, and Diomed; and thus they run together in punishment, as erst in wrath." . . . "If they within those sparks can speak," said I, "Master! I pray thee much, and repray that my prayer may equal a thousand, deny me not to wait until the horned flame comes hither; thou seest how with desire I
80 bend me towards it." And he to me: "Thy request is worthy of much praise, and therefore I accept it; but do thou refrain thy tongue. Let me speak: for I have conceived what thou wishest; and they, perhaps, because they were Greeks, might disdain thy words."

After the flame had come where time and place seemed fitting to my Guide, I heard him speak in this manner: "O ye, two in one fire! if I merited of you whilst I lived, if I merited of you much or little,
90 when on earth I wrote the High Verses, move ye not; but let the one of you tell where he, having lost himself, went to die."

The greater horn of the ancient flame began to shake itself, murmuring, just like a flame that struggles with the wind. Then carrying to and fro the top, as if it were the tongue that spake, threw forth a voice, and said: "When I departed from Circe, who beyond a year detained me there near Gaeta, ere Æneas thus had named it, neither fondness for my
100 son, nor reverence for my aged father, nor the due love that should have cheered Penelope, could conquer in me the ardour that I had to gain experience of the world, and of human vice and worth; I put forth on the deep open sea, with but one ship, and with that small company, which had not deserted me. Both the shores I saw as far as Spain, far as Mo-

---

72. **Eteocles with his brother,** the sons of Oedipus, parted on their funeral pyre as they were opposed in life.

rocco; and saw Sardinia and the other isles which that sea bathes round.

"I and my companions were old and tardy, when we came to that narrow pass, where Hercules assigned his landmarks to hinder man from venturing farther; on the right hand, I left Seville; on the other, had already left Ceuta. 'O brothers!' I said, 'who through a hundred thousand dangers have reached the West, deny not, to this the brief vigil of your senses that remains, experience of the unpeopled world behind the Sun. Consider your origin: ye were not formed to live like brutes, but to follow virtue and knowledge.'

"With this brief speech I made my companions so

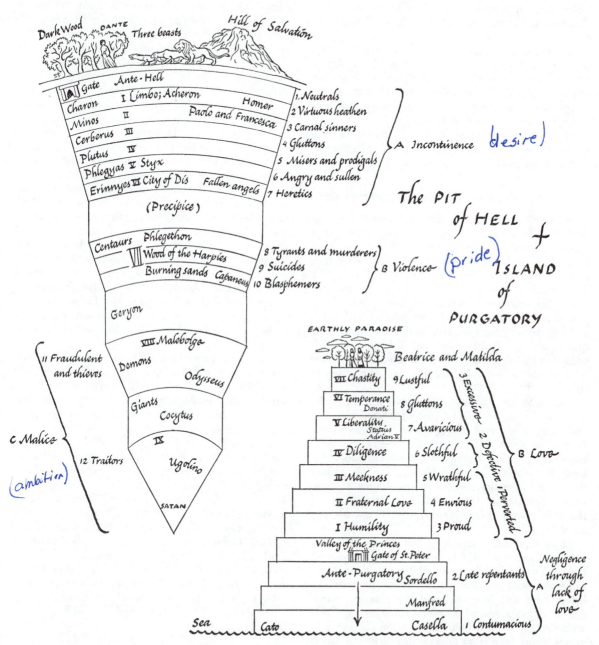

The complex structures of Dante's Hell and Purgatory are shown in the above diagrams. Hell, the Inferno, extends from the surface of the earth to its center in nine concentric circles diminishing in circumference to the abode of Satan. Purgatory Dante pictures as an island mountain rising to the Earthly Paradise of Eden at its summit.

eager for the voyage, that I could hardly then have checked them; and, turning the poop towards morning, we of our oars made wings for the foolish flight, always gaining on the left. Night already saw the other pole, with all its stars; and ours so low, that it rose not from the ocean floor. Five times the light beneath the Moon had been rekindled and quenched as oft, since we had entered on the arduous passage,
10 when there appeared to us a Mountain, dim with distance; and to me it seemed the highest I had ever seen.

"We joyed, and soon our joy was turned to grief: for a tempest rose from the new land, and struck the forepart of our ship. Three times it made her whirl round with all the waters; at the fourth, made the poop rise up and prow go down, as pleased Another, till the sea was closed above us."

The flame was now erect and quiet, having ceased to speak, and now went away from us with license
20 of the sweet Poet. . . .

CANTO XXXI. *The Meeting with the Giants*

We turned our back to the wretched valley, up by the bank that girds it round, crossing without any speech. Here was less than night and less than day, so that my sight went little way before me; but I heard a high horn sound so loudly, that it would have made any thunder weak; which directed my eyes, that followed its course against itself, all to one place: after the dolorous rout, when Charlemain had lost the holy emprise, Roland did not sound with
30 his so terribly. Short while had I kept my head turned in that direction, when I seemed to see many lofty towers; whereat I: "Master! say, what town is this?"

And he to me: "Because thou traversest the darkness too far off, it follows that thou errest in thy imagining. Thou shalt see right well, if thou arrivest there, how much the sense at distance is deceived: therefore spur thee somewhat more." Then lovingly he took me by the hand, and said: "Ere we go far-
40 ther, that the reality may seem less strange to thee, know, they are not towers, but Giants; and are in the well, around its bank, from the navel downwards all of them."

As when a mist is vanishing, the eye by little and little reshapes that which the air-crowding vapour hides; so whilst piercing through that gross and darksome air, more and more approaching towards the brink, error fled from me, and my fear increased. For as on its round wall Montereggione crowns itself
50 with towers: so with half their bodies, the horrible giants whom Jove from heaven still threatens when

he thunders, turreted the bank which compasses the pit.

And already I discerned the face of one, the shoulders and the breast, and great part of the belly, and down along his sides both arms. Nature certainly, when she left off the art of making animals like these, did very well, in taking away such executioners from Mars; and if she repents her not of Elephants and Whales, whoso subtly looks, therein re-60 gards her as more just and prudent: for where the instrument of the mind is joined to evil will and potency, men can make no defence against it. His face seemed to me as long and large as the pine of St. Peter's at Rome, and his other bones were in proportion to it; so that the bank, which was an apron from his middle downwards, showed us certainly so much of him above, that three Frieslanders had vainly boasted to have reached his hair: for downwards from the place where a man buckles on 70 his mantle, I saw thirty large spans of him.

"Rafel mai amech zabi almi," began to shout the savage mouth, for which no sweeter psalmody was fit. And towards him my Guide: "Stupid soul! keep to thy horn; and vent thyself with that, when rage or other passion touches thee. Search on thy neck, and thou wilt find the belt that holds it tied, O soul confused, and see the horn itself that girdles thy huge breast." Then he said to me: "He accuses himself; this is Nimrod, through whose ill thought one lan-80 guage is not still used in the world. Let us leave him standing, and not speak in vain: for every language is to him as to others his which no one understands.". . .

We then proceeded farther on, and reached Antæus, who full five ells, besides the head, forth issued from the cavern. "O thou! who in the fateful valley, which made Scipio heir of glory when Hannibal retreated with his hosts, didst take of old a thousand lions for thy prey; and through whom, 90 hadst thou been at the high war of thy brethren, it seem yet to be believed that the sons of earth had conquered; set us down—and be not shy to do it—where the cold locks up Cocytus.". . . Thus spake the Master; and he in haste stretched forth the hands, whence Hercules of old did feel great stress, and took my Guide. Virgil, when he felt their grasp, said to me: "Come here, that I may take thee"; then of himself and me he made one bundle. . . . It was so terrible a moment, that I should have wished to go 100 by other road; but gently on the deep, which swallows Lucifer with Judas, he set us down; nor lingered there thus bent, but raised himself as in a ship the mast. . . .

9. **a Mountain,** Purgatory. 49. **Montereggione,** a castle near Siena.

80–81. **Nimrod . . . in the world;** Nimrod supposedly built the Tower of Babel. 94. **where the cold . . . Cocytus;** Circle IX.

CANTOS XXXII–XXXIII. *Circle IX: the traitors*

When we were down in the dark pit, under the Giant's feet, much lower, and I still was gazing at the high wall, I heard a voice say to me: "Look how thou passest: take care that with thy soles thou tread not on the heads of thy weary wretched brothers." Whereat I turned myself, and saw before me and beneath my feet a lake, which through frost had the semblance of glass and not of water. . . . And as the frog to croak, sits with his muzzle out of the water, when the peasant-woman oft dreams that she is gleaning: so, livid, up to where the hue of shame appears, the doleful shades were in the ice, sounding with their teeth like storks. Each held his face turned downwards; by the mouth their cold, and by the eyes the sorrow of their hearts is testified amongst them. . . .

I saw two frozen in one hole so closely, that the one head was a cap to the other; and as bread is chewed for hunger, so the uppermost put his teeth into the other there where the brain joins with the nape. "O thou! who by such brutal token showest thy hate on him whom thou devourest, tell me why," I said; "on this condition, that if thou with reason complainest of him, I, knowing who ye are and his offence, may yet repay thee in the world above, if that, wherewith I speak, be not dried up."

From the fell repast that sinner raised his mouth, wiping it upon the hair of the head he had laid waste behind. Then he began: "Thou willest that I renew desperate grief, which wrings my heart, even at the very thought, before I tell thereof. But if my words are to be a seed, that may bear fruit of infamy to the traitor whom I gnaw, thou shalt see me speak and weep at the same time. I know not who thou mayest be, nor by what mode thou hast come down here; but, when I hear thee, in truth thou seemest to me a Florentine.

"Thou hast to know that I was Count Ugolino, and this the Archbishop Ruggieri; now I will tell thee why I am such a neighbour to him. That by the effect of his ill devices I, confiding in him, was taken and thereafter put to death, it is not necessary to say. But that which thou canst not have learnt, that is, how cruel was my death, thou shalt hear and know if he has offended me.

"A narrow hole within the mew, which from me has the title of Famine, and in which others yet must be shut up, had through its opening already shown me several moons, when I slept the evil sleep that rent for me the curtain of the future. This man seemed to me lord and master, chasing the wolf and his whelps, upon the mountain for which the Pisans cannot see Lucca. . . . After short course, the father and his sons seemed to me weary; and methought I saw their flanks torn by the sharp teeth.

"When I awoke before the dawn, I heard my sons who were with me, weeping in their sleep, and asking for bread. Thou art right cruel, if thou dost not grieve already at the thought of what my heart foreboded; and if thou weepest not, at what art thou used to weep? They were now awake, and the hour approaching at which our food used to be brought us, and each was anxious from his dream, and below I heard the outlet of the horrible tower locked up: whereat I looked into the faces of my sons, without uttering a word. I did not weep: so stony grew I within; they wept; and my little Anselm said: 'Thou lookest so, father, what ails thee?' But I shed no tear, nor answered all that day, nor the next night, till another sun came forth upon the world.

"When a small ray was sent into the doleful prison, and I discerned in their four faces the aspect of my own, I bit on both my hands for grief. And they, thinking that I did it from desire of eating, of a sudden rose up, and said: 'Father, it will give us much less pain, if thou wilt eat of us: thou didst put upon us this miserable flesh, and do thou strip it off.' Then I calmed myself, in order not to make them more unhappy; that day and the next we all were mute. Ah, hard earth! why didst thou not open?

"When we had come to the fourth day, Gaddo threw himself stretched out at my feet, saying: 'My father! why don't you help me?' There he died; and even as thou seest me, saw I the three fall one by one, between the fifth day and the sixth: whence I betook me, already blind, to groping over each, and for three days called them, after they were dead; then fasting had more power than grief." When he had spoken this, with eyes distorted he seized the miserable skull again with his teeth, which as a dog's were strong upon the bone. . . .

CANTO XXXIV. *Satan*

"*Vexilla regis prodeunt inferni* towards us: therefore look in front of thee," my Master said, "if thou discernest him." As, when a thick mist breathes, or when the night comes on our hemisphere, a mill, which the wind turns, appears at distance: such an edifice did I now seem to see; and, for the wind, shrunk back behind my Guide, because no other shed was there. Already I had come (and with fear I put it into verse) where the souls were wholly covered, and shone through like straw in glass. Some are ly-

88. **then fasting . . . than grief.** This cryptic clause means that Ugolino died of hunger, not that hunger forced him to eat the bodies. 92. "*Vexilla regis prodeunt inferni*, "The standards of the King of Hell advance"—from an old Latin hymn.

ing; some stand upright, this on its head, and that upon its soles; another, like a bow, bends face to feet.

When we had proceeded on so far, that it pleased my Guide to show to me the Creature which was once so fair, he took himself from before me, and made me stop, saying: "Lo Dis! and lo the place where it behoves thee arm thyself with fortitude." How icy chill and hoarse I then became, ask not, O Reader! for I write it not, because all speech would fail to tell. I did not die, and did not remain alive; now think for thyself, if thou hast any grain of ingenuity, what I became, deprived of both death and life.

The Emperor of the dolorous realm, from mid breast stood forth out of the ice; and I in size am liker to a giant, than the giants are to his arms: mark now how great that whole must be, which corresponds to such a part. If he was once as beautiful as he is ugly now, and lifted up his brows against his Maker, well may all affliction come from him. Oh how great a marvel seemed it to me, when I saw three faces on his head! The one in front, and it was fiery red; the others were two, that were adjoined to this, above the very middle of each shoulder; and they were joined at his crest; and the right seemed between white and yellow; the left was such to look on, as they who come from where the Nile descends. Under each there issued forth two mighty wings, of size befitting such a bird: sea-sails I never saw so broad. No plumes had they; but were in form and texture like a bat's: and he was flapping them, so that three winds went forth from him. Thereby Cocytus all was frozen; with six eyes he wept, and down three chins gushed tears and bloody foam.

In every mouth he champed a sinner with his teeth, like a brake; so that he thus kept three of them in torment. To the one in front, the biting was nought, compared with the tearing: for at times the back of him remained quite stript of skin. "That soul up there, which suffers greatest punishment," said the Master, "is Judas Iscariot, he who has his head within, and outside plies his legs. Of the other two, who have their heads beneath, that one, who hangs from the black visage, is Brutus: see how he writhes himself, and utters not a word; and the other is Cassius, who seems so stark of limb. But night is reascending; and now must we depart: for we have seen the whole."

As he desired, I clasped his neck; and he took opportunity of time and place; and when the wings were opened far, applied him to the shaggy sides, and then from shag to shag descended down, between the tangled hair and frozen crusts. When we

46-47. . . . the other is Cassius. As Judas betrayed the founder of Christianity, Brutus and Cassius betrayed the founder of the Roman empire.

had come to where the thigh revolves just on the swelling of the haunch, my Guide with labour and with difficulty turned his head where he had had his feet before, and grappled on the hair, as one who mounts; so that I thought we were returning into Hell again. "Hold thee fast! for by such stairs," said my Guide, panting like a man forspent, "must we depart from so much ill."

Thereafter through the opening of a rock he issued forth, and put me on its brim to sit; then towards me he stretched his wary step. I raised my eyes, and thought to see Lucifer as I had left him; and saw him with the legs turned upwards; and the gross people who see not what that point is which I had passed, let them judge if I grew perplexed then. "Rise up!" said the Master, "upon thy feet: the way is long, and difficult the road." . . . The Guide and I entered by that hidden road, to return into the bright world; and, without caring for any rest, we mounted up, he first and I second, so far that I distinguished through a round opening the beauteous things which Heaven bears; and thence we issued out, again to see the Stars.

PURGATORY

CANTO I. *The Shore of the Island of Purgatory*

To course o'er better waters now hoists sail the little bark of my wit, leaving behind her a sea so cruel. And I will sing of that second realm, where the human spirit is purged and becomes worthy to ascend to Heaven. . . .

Sweet hue of orient sapphire which was gathering on the clear forehead of the sky, pure even to the first circle, to mine eyes restored delight, soon as I issued forth from the dead air which had afflicted eyes and heart. . . . I saw near me an old man solitary, worthy of such great reverence in his mien, that no son owes more to a father. Long he wore his beard and mingled with white hair, like unto his locks of which a double list fell on his breast. The rays of the four holy lights adorned his face so with brightness, that I beheld him as were the sun before him.

"Who are ye that against the dark stream have fled the eternal prison?" said he, moving those venerable plumes. "Who hath guided you? or who was a lamp unto you issuing forth from the deep night that ever maketh black the infernal vale? Are the laws of the pit thus broken, or is there some new counsel changed in Heaven that being damned ye come to my rocks?"

83-84. Sweet hue . . . the sky; it is dawn of Easter Sunday. 87. an old man. Cato of Utica (95-46 B.C.), the stern Roman statesman who committed suicide rather than surrender to Caesar, is the guardian of Purgatory.

Then did my Leader lay hold on me, and with words, and with hand, and with signs, made reverent my knees and brow. Then answered him: "Of myself I came not. A lady came down from Heaven through whose prayers I succoured this man with my company. But since it is thy will that more be unfolded of our state, how it truly is, my will it cannot be that thou be denied. He hath ne'er seen the last hour, but by his madness was so near to it, that very short time there was to turn. Even as I said, I was sent to him to rescue him, and no other way there was but this along which I have set me. I have shown him all the guilty people, and now do purpose showing those spirits that purge them under thy charge. How I have brought him, 'twere long to tell thee: Virtue descends from on high which aids me to guide him to see thee and to hear thee. Now may it please thee to be gracious unto his coming: he seeketh freedom, which is so precious, as he knows who giveth up life for her. Thou knowest it; since for her sake death was not bitter to thee in Utica, where thou leftest the raiment which at the great day shall be so bright.". . .

"Go then," said he, "and look that thou gird this man with a smooth rush, and that thou bathe his face so that all filth may thence be wiped away: for 'twere not meet with eye obscured by any mist to go before the first minister of those that are of Paradise. This little isle all round about the very base, there, where the wave beats it, bears rushes on the soft mud. No other plant that would put forth leaf or harden can live there, because it yields not to the buffetings. Then be not this way your return; the sun, which now is rising, will show you how to take the mount at an easier ascent." So he vanished; and I uplifted me without speaking, and drew me all back to my Leader, and directed mine eyes to him. He began: "Son, follow thou my steps: turn we back, for this way the plain slopes down to its low bounds."

The dawn was vanquishing the breath of morn which fled before her, so that from afar I recognized the trembling of the sea. We paced along the lonely plain, as one who returns to his lost road, and, till he reach it, seems to go in vain. When we came there where the dew is striving with the sun, being at a place where, in the cool air, slowly it is scattered; both hands outspread, gently my Master laid upon the sweet grass; wherefore I who was ware of his purpose, raised towards him my tear-stained cheeks: there made he all revealed my hue which Hell had hidden. We came then on to the desert shore, that never saw man navigate its waters who thereafter knew return. There he girded me even as it pleased Another: O marvel! that such as he plucked the lowly plant, even such did it forthwith spring up again, there whence he tore it. . . .

CANTO II. *The Meeting with Casella*

We were alongside the ocean yet, like folk who ponder o'er their road, who in heart do go and in body stay; and lo, as on the approach of morn, through the dense mists Mars burns red, low in the West o'er the ocean-floor; such to me appeared—so may I see it again!—a light coming o'er the sea so swiftly, that no flight is equal to its motion; from which, when I had a while withdrawn mine eyes to question my Leader, I saw it brighter and bigger grown. Then on each side of it appeared to me a something white; and from beneath it, little by little, another whiteness came forth.

My Master yet did speak no word, until the first whitenesses appeared as wings; then, when well he knew the pilot, he cried: "Bend, bend thy knees: behold the Angel of God: fold thy hands: henceforth shalt thou see such ministers. Look how he scorns all human instruments, so that oar he wills not, nor other sail than his wings, between shores so distant. See how he has them heavenward turned, plying the air with eternal plumes, that are not mewed like mortal hair."

Then as more and more towards us came the bird divine, brighter yet he appeared, wherefore mine eye endured him not near: but I bent it down, and he came on to the shore with a vessel so swift and light that the waters nowise drew it in. On the stern stood the celestial pilot, such, that blessedness seemed writ upon him, and more than a hundred spirits sat within. "*In exitu Israel de Ægypto*," sang they all together with one voice, with what of that psalm is thereafter written. Then made he to them the sign of Holy Cross, whereat they all flung them on the strand and quick even as he came he went his way.

The throng that remained there seemed strange to the place, gazing around like one who assayeth new things. On every side the sun, who with his arrows bright had chased the Goat from midst of heaven, was shooting forth the day, when the new people lifted up their faces towards us, saying to us: "If ye know show us the way to go to the mount." And Virgil answered: "Ye think perchance that we have experience of this place, but we are strangers even as ye are. We came but now, a little while before you, by other way which was so rough and hard, that the climbing now will seem but play to us."

The souls who had observed me by my breathing that I was yet alive, marvelling grew pale; and as to a messenger, who bears the olive, the folk draw nigh to hear the news, and none shows himself shy at trampling; so on my face those souls did fix their gaze, fortunate every one, well nigh forgetting to go and make them fair.

88–89. that psalm, Psalm 114.

I saw one of them draw forward to embrace me with such great affection, that he moved me to do the like. O shades empty save in outward show! thrice behind it my hands I clasped, and as often returned with them to my breast. With wonder methinks I coloured me, whereat the shade smiled and drew back, and I, following it, flung me forward. Gently it bade me pause: then knew I who it was, and did pray him that he would stay a while to speak to me. He answered me: "Even as I loved thee in the mortal body so do I love thee freed; therefore I stay: but wherefore goest thou?"

"Casella mine, to return here once again where I am, make I this journey," said I, "but if a new law take not from thee memory or skill in that song of love which was wont to calm my every desire, may it please thee therewith to solace awhile my soul, that, with its mortal form journeying here, is sore distressed." "*Love that in my mind discourseth to me,*" began he then so sweetly, that the sweetness yet within me sounds.

My Master and I and that people who were with him, seemed so glad as if to aught else the mind of no one of them gave heed. We were all fixed and intent upon his notes; and lo the old man venerable, crying: "What is this, ye laggard spirits? what negligence, what tarrying is this? Haste to the mount and strip you of the slough, that lets not God be manifest to you." As doves when gathering wheat or tares, all assembled at their repast, quiet and showing not their wonted pride, if aught be seen whereof they have fear, straightway let stay their food, because they are assailed by greater care; so saw I that new company leave the singing, and go towards the hillside, like one who goes, but knoweth not where he may come forth; nor was our parting less quick. . . .

CANTOS III–VIII. *Ante-Purgatory and the Valley of the Princes: the late repentants*

On the left hand appeared to me a throng of souls, who moved their feet towards us, and yet seemed not *to advance,* so slow they came. "Master," said I, "lift up thine eyes, behold there one who will give us counsel; if of thyself thou mayest have it not." He looked at them, and with gladsome mien answered: "Go we thither, for slowly they come, and do thou confirm thy hope, sweet son.". . .

As sheep come forth from the pen, in ones, in twos, in threes, and the others stand all timid, casting eye and nose to earth, and what the first one doeth, the others do also, huddling up to her if she stand still, silly and quiet, and know not why, so saw I then

the head of that happy flock move to come on, modest in countenance, in movement dignified. . . . He began: "Whoever thou art, thus while going turn thy face, give heed if e'er thou sawest me yonder."

I turned me to him, and steadfastly did look: golden-haired was he, and fair, and of noble mien; but one of his eyebrows a cut had cleft. When I humbly had disclaimed ever to have seen him, he said: "Now look"; and he showed me a wound above his breast. Then smiling said: "I am Manfred, grandson of Empress Constance; wherefore I pray thee, that when thou returnest, thou go to my fair daughter, parent of the glory of Sicily and of Aragon, and tell her sooth, if other tale be told. After I had my body pierced by two mortal stabs, I gave me up weeping to him who willingly doth pardon. Horrible were my transgressions; but infinite goodness hath such wide arms that it accepteth all that turn to it. . . .

"True is it, that he who dies in contumacy of Holy Church, even though at the last he repent, needs must stay outside this bank thirtyfold for all the time that he hath lived in his presumption, if such decree be not shortened by holy prayers. Look now, if thou canst make me glad, by revealing to my good Constance how thou hast seen me, and also this ban: for here, through those yonder, much advancement comes.". . .

And I: "My Lord, go we with greater haste; for already I grow not weary as before, and look, the hillside doth now a shadow cast." "We with this day will onward go," answered he, "so far as yet we may; but the fact is other than thou deemest. Ere thou art above, him shalt thou see return that now is being hidden by the slope, so that thou makest not his rays to break. But see there a soul which, placed alone, solitary, looketh towards us; it will point out to us the quickest way."

We came to it: O Lombard soul, how wast thou haughty and disdainful, and in the movement of thine eyes majestic and slow! Naught it said to us, but allowed us to go on, watching only after the fashion of a lion when he couches. Yet did Virgil draw on towards it, praying that it would show to us the best ascent; and that spirit answered not his demand, but of our country and of our life did ask us. And the sweet Leader began: "Mantua,". . . and the shade, all rapt in self, leapt towards him from the place where first it was, saying: "O Mantuan, I am Sordello of thy city." And one embraced the other. . . .

After the greetings dignified and glad had been repeated three and four times, Sordello drew him back, and said: "Who art thou?". . .

13. **Casella,** a musician friend of Dante, who probably set to music the poem *Love that in my mind discourseth to me,* included by Dante in his *Convito.*

59. **Manfred,** (c. 1231–1266), usurping king of Sicily, was excommunicated and died in battle. 99. **Sordello,** a medieval Italian poet.

"I am Virgil; and for no other sin did I lose heaven than for not having faith": thus answered then my Leader. As one who seeth suddenly a thing before him whereat he marvels, who believes, and believes not, saying: "It is, it is not"; such seemed he, and forthwith bent his brow, and humbly turned back towards my Leader, and embraced him where the inferior clasps.

"O glory of the Latins," said he, "by whom our tongue showed forth all its power, O eternal praise of the place whence I sprang, what merit or what favour showeth thee to me? If I am worthy to hear thy words, tell me if thou comest from Hell, and from what cloister."

"Through all the circles of the woeful realm," answered he him, "came I here. A virtue from heaven moved me, and with it I come. Not for doing, but for not doing, have I lost the vision of the high Sun, whom thou desirest, and who too late by me was known. Down there is a place not sad with torments, but with darkness alone, where the lamentations sound not as wailings, but as sighs. There do I abide with the innocent babes, bitten by the fangs of death, ere they were exempt from human sin. There dwell I with those who clad them not with the three holy virtues, and without offence knew the others and followed them all. But if thou knowest and canst, give us some sign whereby we may most quickly come there where Purgatory has right beginning."

He answered: "No fixed place is set for us: 'tis permitted to me to go up and around; so far as I may go, as guide I place me beside thee. But see now how the day is declining, and ascend by night we cannot; therefore 'tis well to think of some fair resting-place. Here are souls on the right apart; if thou allow it I will lead thee to them, and not without joy will they be known to thee.". . .

There, seated on the grass and on the flowers, singing *Salve Regina,* saw I souls who because of the valley were not seen from without. "Ere the little sun now sinks to his nest," began the Mantuan who had led us aside, "desire not that I guide you among them. From this terrace ye will better know the acts and faces of them all, than if received among them down in the hollow.". . .

I saw that noble army thereafter silently gaze upward, as if in expectancy, pale and lowly; and I saw two angels come forth from on high and descend below with two flaming swords, broken short and deprived of their points. Green, as tender leaves just born, was their raiment, which they trailed behind, fanned and smitten by green wings. One came and alighted a little above us, and the other descended on the opposite bank, so that the people were contained in the middle. Clearly I discerned the fair hair of them; but in their faces the eye was dazed, like a faculty which by excess is confounded. "Both come from Mary's bosom," said Sordello, "as guard of the vale, because of the serpent that straightway will come."

Whereat I, who knew not by what way, turned me around, and placed me all icy cold close to the trusty shoulders. . . . And Night, in the place where we were, had made two of the steps wherewith she climbs, and the third was already down-stooping its wings; when I, who with me had somewhat of Adam, vanquished by sleep, sank down on the grass.

CANTO IX. *The Gate of St. Peter*

At the hour when the swallow begins her sad lays nigh unto the morn, perchance in memory of her former woes, and when our mind, more of a wanderer from the flesh and less prisoned by thoughts, in its visions is almost prophetic; in a dream methought I saw an eagle poised in the sky, with plumes of gold, with wings outspread, and intent to swoop. . . . Then meseemed that, having wheeled awhile, terrible as lightning, he descended and snatched me up far as the fiery sphere. There it seemed that he and I did burn, and the visionary flame so scorched that needs was my slumber broken. . . . I startled, soon as sleep fled from my face, and I grew pale even as a man who freezes with terror.

Alone beside me was my Comfort, and the sun was already more than two hours high, and mine eyes were turned to the sea. "Have no fear," said my Lord, "make thee secure, for we are at a good spot: hold not back, but put out all thy strength. Thou art now arrived at Purgatory; see there the rampart that compasseth it around; see the entrance there where it seems cleft. Erewhile, in the dawn which precedes the day, when thy soul was sleeping within thee upon the flowers wherewith down below is adorned, came a lady and said: 'I am Lucy, let me take this man who sleepeth, so will I prosper him on his way.' Sordello remained and the other noble forms. She took thee, and as day was bright, came on upward, and I followed in her track. Here she placed thee, and first her fair eyes did show to me that open entrance; then she and sleep together went away." As doth a man who in dread is reassured, and who changes his fear to comfort after the truth is revealed to him, I changed me; and when my Leader saw me

40-41. souls who . . . from without; these are the kings who neglected duty for selfish war or luxury. 50. swords, broken . . . ; to symbolize justice tempered with mercy.

65-67. two of the steps . . . wings; it was the third hour of night. 78-81. There it seemed . . . broken; the dream symbolized moral purification. 94. Lucy, symbol of Illuminating Grace. See Inferno II.

freed from care, he moved up by the rampart, and I following, towards the height.

Reader, well thou seest how I exalt my subject, therefore marvel thou not if with greater art I sustain it. We drew nigh, and were at a place, whence there where first appeared to me a break just like a fissure which divides a wall, I espied a gate, and three steps beneath to go to it, of divers colours, and a warder who as yet spake no word. And as more I opened mine eyes there, I saw him seated upon the topmost step, such in his countenance that I endured him not; and in his hand he held a naked sword which reflected the rays so towards us, that I directed mine eyes to it oft in vain.

"Tell, there where ye stand, what would ye?" he began to say; "where is the escort? Beware lest coming upward be to your hurt!" "A heavenly lady who well knows these things," my Master answered him, "even now did say to us: 'Go ye thither, there is the gate.'" "And may she speed your steps to good," again began the courteous door-keeper; "come then forward to our stairs."

There where we came, at the first step, was white marble so polished and smooth that I mirrored me therein as I appear. The second darker was then perse, of a stone, rugged and calcined, cracked in its length and in its breadth. The third, which is massy above, seemed to me of porphyry so flaming red as blood that spurts from a vein. Upon this God's angel held both his feet, sitting upon the threshold, which seemed to me adamantine stone. Up by the three steps, with my good will, my Leader brought me, saying: "Humbly ask that the bolt be loosed." Devoutly I flung me at the holy feet; for mercy I craved that he would open to me; but first on my breast thrice I smote me.

Seven P's upon my forehead he described with the point of his sword and: "Do thou wash these wounds when thou art within," he said. Ashes, or earth which is dug out dry, would be of one colour with his vesture, and from beneath it he drew forth two keys. One was of gold and the other was of silver; first with the white and then with the yellow he did so to the gate that I was satisfied. "Whensoever one of these keys fails so that it turns not aright in the lock," said he to us, "this passage opens not. More precious is one, but the other requires exceeding art and wit ere it unlocks, because it is the one which unties the knot. From Peter I hold them; and he told me to err rather in opening, than in keeping it locked, if only the people fell prostrate at my feet."

Then he pushed the door of the sacred portal, saying: "Enter, but I make you ware that he who look-eth behind returns outside again.". . . I turned me intent for the first sound, and *Te Deum laudamus* meseemed to hear in a voice mingled with sweet music. Just such impression gave me that which I heard, as we are wont to receive when people are singing with an organ, and now the words are clear, and now are not.

CANTO X–XII. *Terrace I: Pride vs. Humility*

When we were within the threshold of the gate, which the evil love of souls disuses, because it makes the crooked way seem straight, by the ringing sound I heard it was shut again; and had I turned mine eyes to it what would have been a fitting excuse for the fault? We climbed through a cleft rock, which was moving on one side and on the other, even as a wave that recedes and approaches. "Here we must use a little skill," began my Leader, "in keeping close, now hither now thither, to the side that is receding." And this made our steps so scant, that the waning orb of the moon regained its bed to sink again to rest ere we were forth from that needle's eye. But when we were free and on the open above, where the mount is set back, I wearied and both uncertain of our way, we stood still on a level place more solitary than roads through deserts. From its edge where it borders on the void, to the foot of the high bank which sheer ascends, a human body would measure in thrice; and so far as mine eye could wing its flight, now on the left now on the right side, such this cornice appeared to me.

Thereon our feet had not yet moved, when I discerned that circling bank (which, being upright, lacked means of ascent) to be of pure white marble, and adorned with sculptures so that not only Polycletus, but Nature there would be put to shame. The angel that came to earth with the decree of peace wept for since many a year, which opened heaven from its long ban, before us appeared so vividly graven there in gentle mien, that it seemed not an image which is dumb. One would have sworn that he was saying: *Ave*, for there she was fashioned who turned the key to open the supreme love. . . .

While I was rejoicing to look on the images of humilities so great and for their Craftsman's sake precious to see, "Lo here," murmured the Poet, "much people, but few they make their steps; these will send us on to the high stairs." Mine eyes, that were intent on gazing to see new things whereof they are fain, were not slow in turning towards him. I would not, reader, that thou be scared from a good purpose through hearing how God wills that the

---

8–9. **a warder,** the angel-confessor with his sword of divine justice. 37. **Seven P's,** the seven deadly sins (peccata), corresponding to the seven terraces of Purgatory where they are expiated.

86–87. **Polycletus,** ancient Greek sculptor. 93–94. **she . . . who turned the key,** the Angel of the Annunciation.

debt be paid. Heed not the form of the pain; think what followeth, think that at worst beyond the great judgment it cannot go.

I began: "Master, that which I see moving towards us seems not persons to me, yet I know not what, so wanders my sight." And he to me: "The grievous state of their torment doubles them down to earth so that mine eyes at first thereat were at strife. But look steadily there and disentwine with thy sight what is coming beneath those stones; already thou canst discern how each one beats his breast."

O ye proud Christians, wretched and weary, who, sick in mental vision, put trust in backward steps, perceive ye not that we are worms, born to form the angelic butterfly that flieth to judgment without defence? Why doth your mind soar on high, since ye are as 'twere imperfect insects, even as the grub in which full form is wanting? As to support ceiling or roof is sometimes seen for corbel a figure joining knees to breast, which of unreality begetteth real discomfort in him who beholds it; in such wise saw I these when I gave good heed. True it is that more and less were they contracted, according as they had more or less upon them, and he who had most patience in his bearing, weeping seemed to say: "I can no more.". . .

Already more of the mount was circled by us, and of the sun's path much more spent, than the mind, not set free, esteemed; when he, whoever in front of me alert was going, began: "Lift up thy head, this is no time to go thus engrossed. See there an angel who is making ready to come towards us; look how the sixth handmaiden is returning from the day's service. Adorn with reverence thy bearing and thy face, so that it may delight him to send us upward; think that this day never dawns again." Right well was I used to his monitions never to lose time, so that in that matter he could not speak to me darkly.

To us came the beauteous creature, robed in white, and in his countenance, such as a tremulous star at morn appears. His arms he opened and then outspread his wings; he said: "Come; here nigh are the steps, and easily now is ascent made." To this announcement few be they who come. O human folk, born to fly upward, why at a breath of wind thus fall ye down? He led us where the rock was cut; there he beat his wings upon my forehead, then did promise me my journey secure. . . . While we were turning there our persons, *"Beati pauperes spiritu"* voices so sweetly sang, that no speech would tell it. Ah! how different are these openings from those in Hell! for here we enter through songs, and down there through fierce wailings.

40. the **beauteous creature**, the Angel of Humility. 50. **"Beati** *pauperes spiritu,"* "Blessed are the poor in spirit." (Matthew 5:3)

Now were we mounting up by the sacred steps, and meseemed I was exceeding lighter, than meseemed before on the flat; wherefore I: "Master, say, what heavy thing has been lifted from me, that scarce any toil is perceived by me in journeying?" He answered: "When the P's which have remained still nearly extinguished on thy face, shall, like the one, be wholly rased out, thy feet shall be so vanquished by good will, that not only will they feel it no toil, but it shall be a delight to them to be urged upward." Then did I, like those who go with something on their head unknown to them, save that another's signs make them suspect; wherefore the hand lends its aid to make certain, and searches, and finds, and fulfils that office which cannot be furnished by the sight; and with the fingers of my right hand outspread, I found but six the letters, which he with the keys had cut upon me over the temples: whereat my Leader looking did smile.

CANTOS XIII–XV. *Terrace II: Envy vs. Fraternal Love*

We were at the top of the stairway where a second time the mount is cut away which, by our ascent, frees us from evil. . . . As far as here counts for a mile, so far there had we already gone, in short time, by reason of our ready will; and, flying towards us were heard, but not seen, spirits, speaking courteous invitations to the table of love. . . .

"O Father," said I, "what voices are these?" and as I was asking, lo one of them saying: "Love them from whom ye have suffered evil." And the good Master: "This circle doth scourge the sin of envy, and therefore the cords of the whip are drawn from love. . . . But fix thine eyes through the air full steadily, and thou shalt see people sitting down in front of us, and each one along the cliff is seated."

Then wider than before mine eyes I opened; I looked before me, and saw shades with cloaks not different from the hue of the stone. And after we were a little further forward, I heard a cry: "Mary, pray for us"; a cry: "Michael, and Peter, and all Saints." I believe not that on earth there goeth this day a man so hardened, who were not pierced with compassion at what I then saw; for when I had reached so nigh to them that their features came distinctly to me, heavy grief was running from mine eyes.

With coarse haircloth they seemed to me covered, and one was supporting the other with the shoulder, and all were supported by the bank. Even so the blind, to whom means are lacking, sit at Pardons begging for their needs; and one sinks his head upon the other, so that pity may quickly be awakened in others, not only by the sound of their words, but by their appearance which pleads not less. And as to the blind the sun profits not, so to the shades there where I was now speaking, heaven's light will not be bounteous of itself; for all their eyelids an iron wire pierces and stitches up, even as is done to a wild hawk because it abideth not still. . . .

As when a ray of light leaps from the water or from the mirror to the opposite direction, ascending at an angle similar to that at which it descends, and departs as far from the line of the falling stone in an equal space, even as experiment and science shows, so I seemed to be smitten by reflected light in front of me, wherefore mine eyes were swift to flee. "What is that, sweet Father, from which I cannot screen my sight so that it may avail me," said I, "and seems to be moving towards us?"

"Marvel thou not if the heavenly household yet dazes thee," he answered me, " 'tis a messenger that cometh to invite us to ascend. Soon will it be that to behold these things shall not be grievous to thee, but shall be a joy to thee, as great as nature hath fitted thee to feel." When we had reached the blessed angel, with gladsome voice, he said: "Enter here to a stairway far less steep than the others." We were mounting, already departed thence, and *"Beati misericordes"* was sung behind, and "Rejoice thou that overcomest.". . .

CANTOS XV–XVII. *Terrace III: Anger vs. Meekness*

We were journeying on through the evening, straining our eyes forward, as far as we could, against the evening and shining rays; and lo, little by little, a smoke, dark as night, rolling towards us, nor any room was there to escape from it. This reft us of sight and the pure air. Gloom of hell and of a night bereft of every planet under a meagre sky, darkened by cloud as much as it can be, made not to my sight so thick a veil, nor of a pile so harsh to the feel, as that smoke which there covered us; for it suffered not the eye to stay open: wherefore my wise and trusty Escort closed up to me, and offered me his shoulder. Even as a blind man goeth behind his guide in order not to stray, and not to butt against aught that may do him hurt, or perchance kill him, so went I through the bitter and foul air, listening to my Leader who was saying ever: "Look that thou be not cut off from me."

I heard voices, and each one seemed to pray for peace and for mercy, to the Lamb of God that taketh away sins. Only *"Agnus Dei"* were their beginnings; one word was with them all, and one measure; so that full concord seemed to be among them. "Are those spirits, Master, that I hear?" said I. And he

to me: "Thou apprehendest truly, and they are untying the knot of anger."

"Now who art thou that cleavest our smoke, and speakest of us even as if thou didst still measure time by calends?" Thus by a voice was said.

And I: "Hide not from me who thou wast before death, but tell it me, and tell me if I am going aright for the pass; and thy words shall be our escort." "A Lombard was I and was called Mark; I had knowledge of the world, and loved that worth at which now every one hath unbent his bow; for mounting up thou goest aright." Thus answered he, and added: "I pray thee that thou pray for me, when thou art above."

And I to him: "By my faith I bind me to thee to do that which thou askest of me, but I am bursting within at a doubt, if I free me not from it. First 'twas simple, and now is made double by thy discourse, which makes certain to me, both here and elsewhere, that whereto I couple it. The world is indeed so wholly desert of every virtue, even as thy words sound to me, and heavy and covered with sin; but I pray that thou point the cause out to me, so that I may see it, and that I may show it to others; for one places it in the heavens and another here below."

A deep sigh, which grief compressed to "Alas!" he first gave forth, and then began: "Brother, the world is blind, and verily thou comest from it. Ye who are living refer every cause up to the heavens alone, even as if they swept all with them of necessity. Were it thus, Free Will in you would be destroyed, and it were not just to have joy for good and mourning for evil. The heavens set your impulses in motion; I say not all, but suppose I said it, a light is given you to know good and evil, and Free Will, which, if it endure the strain in its first battlings with the heavens, at length gains the whole victory, if it be well nurtured. Ye lie subject, in your freedom, to a greater power and to a better nature; and that creates in you mind which the heavens have not in their charge.

"Therefore, if the world to-day goeth astray, in you is the cause, in you be it sought, and I now will be a true scout to thee therein. From his hands who fondly loves her ere she is in being, there issues, after the fashion of a little child that sports, now weeping, now laughing, the simple, tender soul, who knoweth naught save that, sprung from a joyous maker, willingly she turneth to that which delights her. First she tastes the savour of a trifling good; there she is beguiled and runneth after it, if guide or curb turn not her love aside. Wherefore 'twas needful to put law as a curb, needful to have a ruler who might discern at least the tower of the true city.

21–22. **the blessed angel,** the Angel of Fraternal Love. 25. *"Beati misericordes,"* "Blessed are the merciful." (Matthew 5:7)

59. **Mark,** Marco Lombardo, a learned courtier of thirteenth-century Venice.

"Laws there are, but who putteth his hand to them? None. . . . Wherefore the people, that see their guide aiming only at that good whereof he is greedy, feed on that and ask no further. Clearly canst thou see that evil leadership is the cause which hath made the world sinful, and not nature that may be corrupted within you. Rome, that made the good world, was wont to have two suns, which made plain to sight the one road and the other; that of the world, and that of God. One hath quenched the other; and the sword is joined to the crook; and the one together with the other must perforce go ill; because, being joined, one feareth not the other. . . .

"God be with you, for no further I come with you. See the light, that beams through the smoke, now waxing bright; the angel is there, and it behooves me to depart ere I am seen of him." So turned he back and no more would hear me. . . .

I turned me to see where I was, when a voice which removed me from every other intent, said: "Here one ascends"; and it gave my desire to behold who it was that spake, such eagerness as never rests until it sees face to face. But, as at the sun which oppresses our sight, and veils his form by excess, so my virtue there was failing me. "This is a divine spirit, that directs us to the way of ascent without our prayer, and conceals itself with its own light.". . . Thus spake my Leader, and I with him did turn our footsteps to a stairway; and soon as I was at the first step, near me I felt as 'twere the stroke of a wing, and my face fanned, and heard one say: "*Beati pacifici* who are without evil wrath."

CANTOS XVII–XIX. *Terrace IV: Sloth vs. Diligence*

Now were the last rays whereafter night followeth so far risen above us that the stars were appearing on many sides. . . . The moon, almost retarded to midnight, made the stars appear more thin to us, fashioned like a bucket all burning; wherefore I, who had garnered clear and plain reasons to my questionings, stood like one who is rambling drowsily.

But this drowsiness was taken from me on a sudden, by people who behind our backs had already come round to us. . . . Soon were they upon us, because all that great throng was moving at a run; and two in front were shouting in tears. "Haste! Haste! let no time be lost through little love," cried the others afterwards, "that striving to do well may renew grace.". . . We are so filled with desire to speed us, that stay we cannot; therefore forgive, if thou hold our penance for rudeness.". . .

Then, when those shades were so far parted from us, that they could be seen no more, a new thought was set within me, wherefrom many and divers others sprang; and so from one to another I rambled, that I closed mine eyes for very wandering, and thought I transmuted into dream. . . . There came to me in a dream, a stuttering woman, with eyes asquint, and crooked on her feet, with maimed hands, and of sallow hue. I gazed upon her; and as the sun comforteth the cold limbs which night weighs down, so my look made ready her tongue, and then set her full straight in short time, and her pallid face even as love wills did colour. When she had her tongue thus loosed, she began to sing, so that with difficulty should I have turned my attention from her.

"I am," she sang, "I am the sweet Siren, who leads mariners astray in mid-sea, so full am I of pleasantness to hear. I turned Ulysses from his wandering way with my song, and whoso liveth with me rarely departs, so wholly do I satisfy him." Her mouth was not yet shut, when a lady appeared holy and alert alongside me, to put her to confusion. "O Virgil, Virgil, who is this?" angrily she said; and he came with eyes ever fixed on that honest one. He seized the other, and, rending her clothes, laid her open in front and showed me her belly; that awakened me with the stench which issued therefrom.

I turned my eyes, and the good Virgil said: "At least three calls have I uttered to thee; arise and come, find we the opening by which thou mayst enter." Up I lifted me, and all the circles of the holy mount were now filled with the high day, and we journeyed with the new sun at our backs. Following him, I was bearing my brow like one that hath it burdened with thought, who makes of himself half an arch of a bridge, when I heard: "Come, here is the pass," spoken in a tone so gentle and kind as is not heard in this mortal confine. With outspread wings which swanlike seemed, he who thus spoke to us did turn us upward, between the two walls of the hard stone. He stirred his pinions then, and fanned us, affirming *qui lugent* to be blessed, for they shall have their souls rich in consolation.

CANTOS XIX–XXI. *Terrace V: Avarice vs. Liberality*

When I was in the open, on the fifth circle, I saw people about it who wept, lying on the ground all turned downwards. "*Adhæsit pavimento anima mea*," I heard them say with such deep sighs that hardly

7–10. **Rome . . . that of God.** The clearest statement of Dante's view of temporal and spiritual power. 30–32. **near me . . . "*Beati pacifici.*** The Angel of Meekness said, "Blessed are the peace-makers." (Matthew 5:9)

75–78. **He seized . . . therefrom.** Dante's dream of the Siren contrasts the superficial attractiveness and the essential loathsomeness of the three sins of sense that follow. 92–93. **He stirred . . . *qui lugent*.** The Angel of Diligence said, "Blessed are they that mourn." (Matthew 5:4) 97. **"*Adhaesit pavimento anima mea*,"** "My spirit cleaveth unto the dust." (Psalms 119: 25)

were the words understood. "O chosen of God, whose sufferings both justice and hope make less hard, direct us towards the high ascents." "If ye come secure from lying prostrate, and desire to find the way most quickly, let your right hands be ever to the outside." Thus prayed the poet, and thus a little in front of us was answer made; wherefore I noted what else was concealed in the words, and turned mine eyes then to my Lord; whereat he gave
10 assent with glad sign to what the look of my desire was craving.

When I could do with me according to my own mind, I drew forward above that creature whose words before made me take note, saying: "Spirit, in whom weeping matures that without which one cannot turn to God, stay a while for me thy greater care. Who thou wast, and why ye have your backs turned upward, tell me, and if thou wouldst that I obtain aught for thee yonder, whence living I set
20 forth."

And he to me: "Wherefore heaven turneth our backs to itself shalt thou know; but first, *scias quod ego fui successor Petri.* Between Sestri and Chiaveri flows down a fair river, and from its name the title of my race takes origin. One month, and little more, I learned how the great mantle weighs on him who keeps it from the mire, so that all other burdens seem feathers. My conversion, ah me! was late; but when I was made Pastor of Rome, so I discovered
30 the life which is false. I saw that there the heart was not at rest, nor could one mount higher in that life; wherefore love of this was kindled within me. Up to that moment, I was a soul wretched and parted from God, wholly avaricious; now, as thou seest, here am I punished for it.

"What avarice works, here is declared in the purgation of the down-turned souls, and no more bitter penalty hath the mount. Even as our eye, fixed on earthly things, did not lift itself on high, so
40 here justice hath sunk it to earth. As avarice quenched our love for every good, wherefore our works were lost, so justice here doth hold us fast, bound and seized by feet and hands; and so long as it shall be the pleasure of the just Lord, so long shall we lie here motionless and outstretched."

I had kneeled down, and was about to speak; but as I began, and he perceived my reverence merely by listening, "What reason," he said, "thus bent thee down?" And I to him: "Because of your dignity
50 my conscience smote me for standing." "Make straight thy legs, uplift thee, brother," he answered; "err not, a fellow-servant am I with thee and with the others unto one Power. . . . Now get thee hence; I desire not that thou stay longer, for thy

tarrying disturbs my weeping, whereby I mature that which thou didst say.". . .

A shade appeared to us, and came on behind us, gazing at its feet on the prostrate crowd, nor did we perceive it until it first spake, saying: "My brothers, God give you peace." Quickly we turned us, and 60 Virgil gave back to him the sign that is fitting thereto. Then began: "May the true court, which binds me in eternal exile, bring thee in peace to the council of the blest." "How," said he, and meantime we went sturdily, "if ye are shades that God deigns not above, who hath escorted you so far by his stairs?"

And my Teacher: "If thou lookest at the marks which this man bears, and which the angel outlines, clearly wilt thou see 'tis meet he reign with the 70 good. But since she who spins day and night, had not yet drawn for him the fibre which Clotho charges and packs on the distaff for each one, his spirit, which is thy sister and mine, coming up, could not come along, because it sees not after our fashion: wherefore I was brought forth from Hell's wide jaws to guide him, and I will guide him onward, so far as my school can lead him.". . .

Answered that spirit, "I was yonder, great in fame, but not yet with faith. So sweet was the music 80 of my words, that me, a Toulousian, Rome drew to herself, where I did merit a crown of myrtle for my brow. Statius folk yonder still do name me; I sang of Thebes, and then of the great Achilles; but I fell by the way with the second burden. The sparks, which warmed me, from the divine flame whence more than a thousand have been kindled, were the seeds of my poetic fire: of the Æneid I speak, which was a mother to me, and was to me a nurse in poesy; without it I had not stayed the weight of a drachm. 90 And to have lived yonder, when Virgil was alive, I would consent to one sun more than I owe to my coming forth from exile."

These words turned Virgil to me with a look that silently said: "Be silent." But the virtue which wills is not all powerful; for laughter and tears follow so closely the passion from which each springs, that they least obey the will in the most truthful. I did but smile, like one who makes a sign: whereat the shade was silent and looked at me in the eyes, where 100 most the soul is fixed.

And he said: "So may such great toil achieve its end; wherefore did thy face but now display to me a flash of laughter?" Now am I caught on either side; one makes me keep silence, the other conjures me to speak; wherefore I sigh and am understood by my Master, and he said to me, "Have no fear of

3–6. "If ye come . . . the outside." The words are spoken by a pope, Adrian v, who later identifies himself.

57. A shade, the Roman poet Statius, author of the *Thebaid*, allegedly converted to Christianity. Hence he represents the human wisdom of Virgil enlightened by the Christianity that Virgil never knew. 72. Clotho, the fate who prepared the thread of life.

speaking, but speak, and tell him that which he asketh with so great desire."

Wherefore I: "Perchance thou dost marvel, O ancient spirit, at the laugh I gave, but I desire that yet greater wonder seize thee. He who guideth mine eyes on high, is that Virgil from whom thou drewest power to sing of men and gods. If thou didst believe other cause for my laughter, set it aside as untrue, and believe it was those words which thou spakest of him."

Already was he stooping to embrace my Teacher's feet; but he said: "Brother, do not so, for thou art a shade and a shade thou seest." And he, rising: "Now canst thou comprehend the measure of the love which warms me toward thee, when I forget our nothingness, and treat shades as a solid thing."

CANTOS XXII–XXIV. *Terrace VI: Gluttony vs. Temperance*

Already was the angel left behind us, the angel that had turned us to the sixth circle, having erased a scar from my face, and had said to us that those who have their desire to righteousness were blessed, and his words accomplished that with *sitiunt*, and naught else. And I, lighter than by the other passages, went on so that without any toil I was following the fleet spirits upward. . . . They journeyed on in front, and I, solitary, behind; and I hearkened to their discourse which gave me understanding in poesy. . . .

Even as musing wayfarers do, who on overtaking strange folk by the way, turn round to them and stay not, so behind us, moving more quickly, coming, and passing by, a throng of spirits, silent and devout, was gazing upon us in wonder. Dark and hollow-eyed was each one, pallid of face, and so wasted away that the skin took form from the bones. . . . Who, not knowing the reason, would believe that the scent of fruit and that of water had thus wrought, by begetting desire?

Already I was in astonishment at what thus famishes them, because of the reason not yet manifest, of their leanness, and of their sad scurf, when lo, from the hollow of the head a shade turned its eyes to me and fixedly did gaze; then cried aloud: "What grace is this to me?" Never had I recognized him by the face, but in his voice, was revealed to me, that which was blotted out in his countenance. This spark rekindled within me all my knowledge of the changed features, and I recognized the face of Forese.

"Ah stare not," he prayed, "at the dry leprosy which discolours my skin, nor at any default of flesh that I may have, but tell me sooth of thyself, and who those two spirits are that there make thy escort; abide thou not without speaking to me." "Thy face," answered I him, "which in death I wept for once, gives me now not less grief, even unto tears, seeing it so disfigured. Therefore tell me, in God's name, what strips you so; make me not talk while I am marvelling, for ill can he speak who is full of other desire."

And he to me: "From the eternal counsel virtue descends into the water, and into the tree left behind, whereby I thus do waste away. All this people, who weeping sing, sanctify themselves again in hunger and thirst, for having followed appetite to excess. The scent which issues from the fruit, and from the spray that is diffused over the green, kindles within us a desire to eat and to drink. . . . But pray, brother, look that thou hide thee no longer from me; thou seest that not only I, but all this people are gazing where thou veilest the sun."

Wherefore I to him: "If thou bring back to mind what thou hast been with me and what I have been with thee, the present memory will still be grievous. From that life he who goeth before me did turn me, the other day."

Neither did our speech make the going, nor the going, more slow; but, talking we went bravely on, even as a ship driven by a fair wind. And the shades, that seemed things twice dead, drew in wonderment at me through the pits of their eyes, aware of my being alive. . . . Thus we passed close against one of the two margins, hearing sins of gluttony, once followed by woeful gains. Then, spread out along the solitary way, full a thousand paces and more bore us onward, each in contemplation without a word.

"What go ye thus pondering on, ye lone three," a sudden voice did say; wherefore I startled as frightened and timid beasts do. I raised my head to see who it was, and never in a furnace were glasses or metals seen so glowing and red, as I saw one who said: "If it please you to mount upward, here must a turn be given; hence goeth he who desires to go for peace." His countenance had bereft me of sight; wherefore I turned me back to my Teachers, like one who goeth according as he listens. And as the May breeze, herald of the dawn, stirs and breathes forth sweetness, all impregnate with grass and with flowers, such a wind felt I give on the middle of my brow, and right well I felt the pinions move which wafted ambrosial fragrance to my senses; and I heard say: "Blessed are they who are illumined by

19–22. **and had said . . . naught else.** The Angel of Justice said, "Blessed are they which do thirst after righteousness." (Matthew 5:6) 48. **Forese**, Forese Donati, a friend of Dante.

74. **From that life he . . . did turn me . . . ;** clear indication that Dante had fallen into actual dissipation after the death of Beatrice. 88 **a sudden voice,** the voice of the Angel of Temperance.

so much grace, that the love of taste kindleth not too great desire in their breasts, and who hunger always so far as is just.". . .

[Cantos XXV–XXVI, describing the journey through Terrace VII: Lust vs. Chastity, are omitted.]

CANTO XXVII. *The Steps to Eden, the Earthly Paradise*

The day was passing away when God's glad angel appeared to us. Outside the flames on the bank he was standing and singing *"Beati mundo corde"* in a voice more piercing far than ours. Then: "No farther may ye go, O hallowed souls, if first the fire bite not; enter therein and to the singing beyond
10 be not deaf," he said to us when we were nigh to him; wherefore I became when I heard him, such as one who is laid in the grave. I bent forward over my clasped hands, gazing at the fire, and vividly imagining human bodies once seen burnt.

The kindly escorts turned them toward me, and Virgil said to me: "My son, here may be torment but not death. Remember thee, remember thee, . . . and if on Geryon I guided thee safely, what shall I do now nearer to God? Of a surety believe, that if
20 within the womb of these flames thou didst abide full a thousand years, they could not make thee bald of one hair; and if perchance thou thinkest that I beguile thee, get thee toward them, and get credence with thy hands on the hem of thy garments. Put away now, put away all fear; turn thee hither, and onward come securely." And I, yet rooted, and with accusing conscience.

When he saw me stand yet rooted and stubborn, troubled a little he said: "Now look, my son, 'twixt
30 Beatrice and thee is this wall." As at Thisbe's name Pyramus opened his eyes at the point of death, and gazed at her, when the mulberry became red, so, my stubbornness being softened, I turned me to my wise Leader on hearing the name which ever springs up in my mind. Whereupon he shook his head, and said: "What? do we desire to stay this side?" then smiled as one does to a child that is won by an apple.

Then he entered into the fire in front of me, pray-
40 ing Statius that he would come behind; who for a long way before had separated us. When I was within, I would have flung me into molten glass to cool me, so immeasurable there was the burning. My sweet Father, to encourage me, went on discoursing ever of Beatrice, saying: "Already I seem to behold her eyes." A voice guided us, which was singing on the other side, and we, intent only on it, came forth, there where the ascent began. . . .

Straight the way mounted through the rock, to-
50 ward such a quarter, that in front of me I stayed the rays of sun who already was low. And of few steps made we assay, when I and my sages perceived that the sun had set behind us, because of the shadow which had vanished. And ere the horizon in all its stupendous range had become of one hue, and night held all her dominion, each of us made a bed of a step; for the law of the mount took from us the power, rather than the desire, to ascend. . . . Little of the outside could there be seen, but through
60 that little I saw the stars brighter and bigger than their wont. As I was thus ruminating, and thus gazing at them, sleep fell on me, sleep which oft doth know the news ere the fact come to pass. . . .

And now, at the brightness ere dayspring born, which rises the gratefuler to wayfarers as on their return they lodge less far from home, the shades of night were fleeing on every side, and my sleep with them; wherefore I arose, seeing the great Masters already risen. "That sweet fruit whereof the care of mortals goeth in search on so many boughs, this day
70 shall give thy hungerings peace." Words such as these did Virgil use to me, and never have there been gifts that were equal in sweetness to these. So greatly did desire upon desire come over me to be above, that at every step after I felt my pinions grow for the flight.

When the stairway was all sped beneath us, and we were upon the topmost step, on me did Virgil fix his eyes, and said: "Son, the temporal fire and the eternal, hast thou seen, and art come to a place
80 where I, of myself, discern no further. Here have I brought thee with wit and with art; now take thy pleasure for guide; forth art thou from the steep ways, forth art from the narrow. Behold there the sun that shineth on thy brow; behold the tender grass, the flowers, and the shrubs, which the ground here of itself alone brings forth. While the glad fair eyes are coming, which weeping made me come to thee, thou canst sit thee down and canst go among them. No more expect my word, nor my sign. Free,
90 upright, and whole, is thy will, and 'twere a fault not to act according to its prompting; wherefore I do crown and mitre thee over thyself."

CANTO XXVIII. *Eden, the Earthly Paradise*

Now eager to search within and around the divine forest dense and verdant, which to mine eyes was tempering the new day, without waiting more I left the mountain-side, crossing the plain with lingering

---

6–7. *"Beati mundo corde."* The Angel of Chastity said, "Blessed are the pure in heart." (Matthew 5:8)

90. **No more expect my word.** . . . Virgil the pagan, who can never enter Eden or Paradise, has brought Dante as far as human wisdom alone can do. Beatrice, symbolizing revelation, will be his new guide.

step, over the ground which gives forth fragrance on every side. A sweet breeze, itself invariable, was striking on my brow with no greater force than a gentle wind, before which the branches, responsively trembling, were all bending toward that quarter, where the holy mount casts its first shadow. . . .

And lo, a stream took from me further passage which, toward the left with its little waves, bent the grass which sprang forth on its bank. All the waters which here are purest, would seem to have some mixture in them, compared with that, which hideth nought; albeit full darkly it flows beneath the ever-lasting shade, which never lets sun, nor moon, beam there.

With feet I halted and with mine eyes did pass beyond the rivulet, to gaze upon the great diversity of the tender blossoms; and there to me appeared, even as on a sudden something appears which, through amazement, sets all other thought astray, a lady solitary, who went along singing, and culling flower after flower, wherewith all her path was painted. "Pray, fair lady, who at love's beams dost warm thee, if I may believe outward looks, which are wont to be a witness of the heart, may it please thee to draw forward," said I to her, "towards this stream, so far that I may understand what thou singest.". . .

As a lady who is dancing turns her round with feet close to the ground and to each other, and hardly putteth foot before foot, she turned toward me upon the red and upon the yellow flowerets, not otherwise than a virgin that droppeth her modest eyes; and made my prayers satisfied, drawing so near that the sweet sound reached me with its meaning. Soon as she was there, where the grass is already bathed by the waves of the fair river, she vouchsafed to raise her eyes to me. I do not believe that so bright a light shone forth under the eyelids of Venus, pierced by her son, against all his wont. . . .

"New-comers are ye," she began, "and perchance, because I am smiling in this place, chosen for nest of the human race, some doubt doth hold you mar-velling. . . . I will tell from what cause that arises which makes thee marvel, and I will purge away the mist that offends thee. The highest Good, who him-self alone doth please, made man good and for goodness, and gave this place to him as an earnest of eternal peace. Through his default, small time he sojourned here; through his default, for tears and sweat he exchanged honest laughter and sweet play. . . .

"The water which thou seest wells not from a spring that is fed by moisture which cold condenses, like a river that gains and loses volume, but issues from a fount, constant and sure, which regains by God's will, so much as it pours forth freely on either side. On this side it descends with a virtue which takes from men the memory of sin; on the other it restores the memory of every good deed. On this side Lethe, as on the other Eunoë 'tis called, and works not except first it is tasted on this side and on that. This exceedeth all other savours; and albeit thy thirst may be full sated, even tho' I reveal no more to thee, I will give thee yet a corollary as a grace; nor do I think that my words will be less precious to thee if they extend beyond my promise to thee. They who in olden times sang of the golden age and its happy state, perchance dreamed in Parnassus of this place. Here the root of man's race was innocent; here spring is everlasting, and every kind of fruit; this is the nectar whereof each one tells." Then did I turn me right back to my poets, and saw that with smiles they had heard the last interpretation. . . .

CANTOS XXX–XXXI. *The Meeting with Beatrice*

As the saints at the last trump shall rise ready each one from his tomb, with re-clad voice singing Halleluiah, such on the divine chariot rose up a hundred ministers and messengers of life eternal. . . . Ere now have I seen, at dawn of day, the eastern part all rosy red, and the rest of heaven adorned with fair clear sky, and the face of the sun rise shadowed, so that by the tempering of the mists the eye long time endured him: so within a cloud of flowers, which rose from the angelic hands and fell down again within and without, olive-crowned over a white veil, a lady appeared to me, clad, under a green mantle, with hue of living flame. And my spirit, that now so long a time had passed, since, trembling in her presence, it had been broken down with awe, without having further knowledge by mine eyes through hidden virtue which went out from her, felt the mighty power of ancient love.

Soon as on my sight the lofty virtue smote, which already had pierced me ere I was out of my boy-hood, I turned me to the left with the trust with which the little child runs to his mother when he is frightened or when he is afflicted, to say to Virgil: "Less than a drachm of blood is left in me that trembleth not; I recognize the tokens of the ancient flame." But Virgil had left us bereft of himself, Virgil sweetest Father, Virgil to whom for my weal I gave me up; nor did all that our ancient mother lost, avail to keep my dew-washed cheeks from turning dark again with tears. "Dante, for that Virgil

---

5. **toward that quarter . . .** , the west.   7. **a stream,** Lethe, whose waters brought forgetfulness of the past.   19–20. **a lady,** Matilda, symbolizing the original purity of Eden.

102. **our ancient mother,** Eve.

goeth away, weep not yet, weep not yet, for thou must weep for other sword."

Even as an admiral, who at stern and at bow, comes to see the folk that man the other ships, and heartens them to brave deeds, so on the left side of the car, when I turned me at sound of my name, which of necessity here is recorded, I saw the lady, who first appeared to me veiled beneath the angelic festival, directing her eyes to me on this side the stream. Albeit the veil which fell from her head, crowned with Minerva's leaves, did not let her appear manifest, queenlike, in bearing yet stern, she continued, like one who speaks and holdeth back the hottest words till the last: "Look at me well; verily am I, verily am I Beatrice. How didst thou deign to draw nigh the mount? knewest thou not that here man is happy?"

Mine eyes drooped down to the clear fount; but beholding me therein, I drew them back to the grass, so great a shame weighed down my brow. So doth the mother seem stern to her child, as she seemed to me; for the savour of harsh pity tasteth of bitterness. She was silent, and straightway the angels sang. . . . But when I heard in their sweet harmonies their compassion on me, more than if they had said "Lady, why dost thou so shame him?" The ice which had closed about my heart became breath and water, and with anguish through mouth and eyes issued from my breast.

She, standing yet fixed on the said side of the car, then turned her words to the pitying angels thus: . . . "This man was such in his new life potentially, that every good talent would have made wondrous increase in him. But so much the more rank and wild the ground becomes with evil seed and untilled, the more it hath of good strength of soil. Some time I sustained him with my countenance; showing my youthful eyes to him I led him with me turned to the right goal. So soon as I was on the threshold of my second age, and I changed life, he forsook me, and gave him to others. When I was risen from flesh to spirit, and beauty and virtue were increased within me, I was less precious and less pleasing to him; and he did turn his steps by a way not true, pursuing false visions of good, that pay back no promise entire. Nor did it avail me to gain inspirations, with which in dream and otherwise, I called him back; so little recked he of them. so low sank he, that all means for his salvation were already short, save showing him the lost people. For this I visited the portal of the dead, and to him who has guided him up hither, weeping my prayers were borne. God's high decree would be broken, if Lethe were passed, and such viands were tasted, without some scot of penitence that may shed tears."

"O thou that art yon side the sacred stream," her speech directing with the point towards me, which

even with the edge had seemed sharp to me, she began again, continuing without delay, "say, say, if this is true; to such accusation thy confession must be joined.". . . Confusion and fear, together mingled, drove forth from my mouth a "Yea" such that to understand it the eyes were needed. As a crossbow breaks, when shot at too great tension, both its string and bow, and with less force the bolt hits the mark, so burst I under this heavy charge, pouring forth a torrent of tears and sighs, and my voice died away in its passage. . . . And she: "If thou wert silent, or if thou hadst denied what thou confessest, not less noted were thy fault; by such a judge 'tis known. But when self-accusation of sin bursts from the cheeks in our Court, the grindstone is turned back against the edge. . . . Put away the seed of weeping.". . . Then when my heart restored to me the sense of outward things, the lady whom I had found alone I saw above me; and she said: "Hold me! Hold me!" She had drawn me into the river up to my neck, and, pulling me after her, went along over the water light as a shuttle. . . . The fair lady opened her arms, clasped my head, and dipped me where I must needs swallow of the water; then drew me forth, and led me bathed within the dance of the four fair ones, and each did cover me with her arm.

"Here we are nymphs and in heaven are stars; ere Beatrice descended to the world we were ordained to her for her handmaids. We will lead thee to her eyes; but the three on the other side who deeper gaze, will sharpen thine eyes to the joyous light that is within." Thus singing they began; and then did lead me with them up to the breast of the griffin, where Beatrice stood turned towards us. . . . O glory of living eternal, who that so pale hath grown beneath the shade of Parnassus, or hath drunk at its well, that would not seem to have mind encumbered, on trying to render thee as thou appearedest, when in the free air thou didst disclose thee, where heaven in its harmony shadows thee forth?

Then she placed them all seven in front of her, and, merely by her nod, motioned behind her, me and the Lady and the Sage who had stayed. . . . Both more refulgent, and with slower steps, the sun was holding the meridian circle, which varies hither and thither as positions vary, when did halt, even as he halts who goes for escort before folk, if he finds aught that is strange or the traces thereof, those seven ladies at the margin of a pale shadow, such as beneath green leaves and dark boughs, the Alp casts over its cool streams. In front of them I seemed to behold Euphrates and Tigris welling up from one spring, and parting like friends that linger. "O light,

72. the grindstone is turned . . . ; and blunts the sword of justice. 82–83. the four fair ones, the four cardinal virtues—prudence, justice, temperance, and fortitude. 87. the three on the other side, the three theological virtues—faith, hope, and charity.

O glory of human kind, what water is this that here pours forth from one source, and self from self doth wend away?"

At such prayer was said to me: "Pray Matilda that she tell it thee"; and here made answer, as he doth who frees him from blame, the fair Lady: "This and other things have been told him by me, and sure am I that Lethe's water hid them not from him." And Beatrice: "Haply a greater care that oft bereaves of memory hath dimmed his mind's eyes. But behold Eunoë, which there flows on; lead him to it, and as thou art wont, requicken his fainting virtue."

As a gentle soul that maketh no excuse, but makes her will of the will of another, soon as it is disclosed by outward sign, so the fair Lady, after I was taken by her, set forth, and to Statius with queenly mien did say: "Come with him." If, reader, I had greater space for writing, I would sing, at least in part, of the sweet draught which never would have sated me; but forasmuch as all the pages ordained for this second canticle are filled, the curb of art no further lets me go. I came back from the most holy waves, born again, even as new trees renewed with new foliage, pure and ready to mount to the stars.

PARADISE

CANTOS I–VI. *Sphere I, the Moon: breakers of vows; Sphere II, Mercury: seekers of fame*

O YE who in your little skiff longing to hear, have followed on my keel that singeth on its way, turn to revisit your own shores; commit you not to the open sea; for perchance, losing me, ye would be left astray. The water which I take was never coursed before; Minerva bloweth, Apollo guideth me, and the nine Muses point me to the Bears. . . .

Beatrice was gazing upward, and I on her; and perchance in such space as an arrow stays and flies and is discharged from the nocking point, I saw me arrived where a wondrous thing drew my sight to it; and therefore she from whom my doing might not be hidden turning to me as much in joy as beauty, "Direct thy mind to God in gratitude," she said, "who hath united us with the first star." Meseemed a cloud enveloped us, shining, dense, firm and polished, like diamond smitten by the sun. Within itself the eternal pearl received us, as water doth receive a ray of light, though still itself uncleft. . . .

But there appeared to me a sight which so straitly held me to itself, to look upon it, that I bethought

me not of my confession. In such guise as, from glasses transparent and polished, or from waters clear and tranquil, not so deep that the bottom is darkened, come back the notes of our faces, so faint that a pearl on a white brow cometh not slowlier upon our pupils; so did I behold many a countenance, eager to speak; wherefore I fell into the counter error of that which kindled love between the man and fountain.

No sooner was I aware of them, than, thinking them reflected images, I turned round my eyes to see of whom they were; and I saw naught, and turned them forward again straight on the light of my sweet guide, whose sacred eyes glowed as she smiled. "Wonder not that I smile," she said, "in presence of thy child-like thought, since it trusts not its foot upon the truth, but turneth thee after its wont, to vacancy. True substances are they which thou beholdest, relegated here for failure of their vows. Wherefore speak with them, and listen and believe; for the true light which satisfieth them, suffereth them not to turn their feet aside from it."

And I to the shade who seemed most to long for converse turned me and began, as one whom too great longing doth confound: "O well-created spirit, who in the rays of eternal life dost feel the sweetness which, save tasted, may ne'er be understood; it were acceptable to me, wouldst thou content me with thy name and with your lot." Whereat she, eager and with smiling eyes: "Our love doth no more bar the gate to a just wish, than doth that love which would have all its court like to itself. In the world I was a virgin sister; and if thy memory be rightly searched, my greater beauty will not hide me from thee, but thou wilt know me again for Piccarda, who, placed here with these other blessed ones, am blessed in the sphere that moveth slowest. Our affections, which are aflame only in the pleasure of the Holy Spirit, rejoice to be informed after his order. And this lot, which seemeth so far down, therefore is given us because our vows were slighted, and on some certain side were not filled in.". . .

Thus did she speak to me, and then began to sing *Ave Maria*, and vanished as she sang, like to a heavy thing through the deep water. My sight, which followed her far as it might, when it had lost her turned to the target of a greater longing, and bent itself all upon Beatrice; but she so flashed upon my look, that at the first my sight endured it not; and this made me the slower with my questioning. . . .

So Beatrice began this chant, and, as one who interrupteth not his speech, continued thus the sacred progress: "The greatest gift God of his largess

31–32. **the Bears,** the constellation of the Bears, since Dante now leaves the earth to rise through the nine revolving heavens. 40. **the first star,** the moon.

53–54. **the counter error.** . . . Dante mistook the real spirits for reflections, unlike Narcissus, who fell in love with his own reflection in the water.

made at the creation, and the most conformed to his own excellence, and which he most prizeth, was the will's liberty, wherewith creatures intelligent, both all and only, were and are endowed. . . . Ye Christians, be more sedate in moving, not like a feather unto every wind; nor think that every water cleanseth you. Ye have the Old and the New Testament and the shepherd of the Church to guide you; let this suffice you, unto your salvation. If sorry greed proclaim aught else to you, be men, not senseless sheep, lest the Jew in your midst should scoff at you. Do not ye as the lamb who leaves his mother's milk, silly and wanton, fighting with himself for his disport." Her ceasing and her transmuted semblance enjoined silence on my eager wit, which already had new questionings before it.

And even as an arrow which smiteth the targe ere the cord be still, so fled we to the second realm. . . . As in a fish-pool still and clear, the fishes draw to aught that so droppeth from without as to make them deem it somewhat they may feed on, so did I see more than a thousand splendours draw towards us, and in each one was heard: . . . "This little star adorneth her with good spirits who were active that honour and that fame might come to them; and when hereon desire, thus swerving, leaneth, needs must the rays of the true love mount upward with less life. But in the commeasuring of our rewards to our desert is part of our joy, because we see them neither less nor more. Whereby the living justice so sweeteneth our affection that it may ne'er be warped to any malice. Divers voices upon earth make sweet harmony, and so the divers seats in our life render sweet harmony amongst these wheels.". . .

CANTOS VIII–XIV. *Sphere III, Venus:*
lovers; Sphere IV, the Sun: religious
teachers

The world was wont to think in its peril that the fair Cyprian rayed down mad love, rolled in the third epicycle; and from her from whom I take my start, they took the name of the star which courts the sun, now from the nape, now from the brow. I had no sense of rising into her, but my Lady gave me full faith that I was there, because I saw her grow more beautiful. And as we see a spark within a flame, and as a voice within a voice may be distinguished, if one stayeth firm, and the other cometh and goeth; so in that light itself I perceived other torches moving in a circle more and less swift, after the measure, I suppose, of their eternal vision. . . . And within those who most in front appeared, Hosannah sounded in such wise that never since have I been free from longing to re-hear it.

Then one drew himself more nigh to us, and alone began: "All we are ready at thy will, that thou mayst have thy joy of us. We roll with those celestial Princes in one circle and in one circling and in one thirst, to whom thou from the world didst sometime say: *Ye who by understanding give the third heaven motion,* and so full of love are we that, to pleasure thee, a space of quiet shall be no less sweet to us. . . . Here we not repent, but smile; not at the sin, which cometh not again to mind, but at the Worth that ordered and provided. Here gaze we on the Art that beautifieth its so great effect, and here discern the Good which bringeth back the world below unto the world above.". . .

Now stay thee, reader, on thy bench, back thinking on this foretaste, wouldst thou have good joyance ere that thou be weary. I have set before thee; now feed thou thyself, for that matter whereof I have made me scribe, now wresteth to itself my total care. The greatest minister of Nature, who with the worth of heaven stampeth the world, and with his light measureth the time for us, united with that part now called to mind, was circling on the spirals whereon he doth present him ever earlier. And I was with him; but of my ascent I was no more aware than is a man, ere his first thought, aware that it is coming. 'Tis Beatrice who leadeth thus from good to better, so instantly that her act doth not expatiate through time. How shining in itself must that needs be which in the sun, whereinto I had entered, itself revealeth not by hue, but light! . . . Such, there, was the fourth household of the exalted Father who ever satisfieth it, showing how he doth breathe, and how beget.

And Beatrice began: "Give thanks, give thanks to the sun of the Angels, who of his grace hath to this sun of sense exalted thee." Never was heart of mortal so disposed unto devotion, and so keen to give itself to God with all its will, as to those words was I; and so wholly was my love committed unto him, it eclipsed Beatrice in oblivion. Her it displeased not; but she so smiled thereat, the splendour of her laughing eyes parted my erst united mind amongst things multiform.

Then saw I many a glow, living and conquering, make of us a centre, and of themselves a crown; sweeter in voice than shining in appearance. . . . When, so singing, those burning suns had circled round us thrice, like stars neighbouring the fixed poles, they seemed as ladies, not from the dance released, but pausing, silent, listening till they catch the notes renewed. And within one I heard begin: . . ."Thou wouldst know with what plants this garland is enflowered, which amorously doth circle

---

35–36. **the fair Cyprian,** Venus. 45–46. **other torches.** The spirits in Paradise are no longer represented with human features.

70. **greatest minister of Nature,** the sun. 74. **. . . . doth present him ever earlier;** that is, from midwinter to midsummer.

round the beauteous lady who strengtheneth thee for heaven. I was of the lambs of the sacred flock that Dominic leadeth upon the way where is good fattening if there be no straying. This, who most neighboureth me upon the right, brother and master was to me, and he was Albert of Cologne, I Thomas of Aquino. . . .

"The providence which governeth the world,— with counsel wherein every creature's gaze must
10 stay, defeated, e'er it reach the bottom,—in order that the spouse of him, who with loud cries espoused· her with the blessed blood, might go toward her delight, secure within herself and faithfuller to him, two Princes did ordain on her behalf, who on this side and that should be for guides. The one was all seraphic in his ardour, the other by his wisdom was on earth a splendour of cherubic light. Of one will I discourse, because of both the two he speaketh who doth either praise, which so he will; for to one
20 end their works. . . .

"Not yet was he far distant from his rising when he began to make the earth to feel from his great power a certain strengthening; for in his youth for such a lady did he rush into war against his father, to whom, as unto death, not one unbars the gate of his good pleasure; and in the spiritual court that had rule over him, and in his father's presence he was united to her, and then from day to day loved her more strongly. She, reft of her first husband, a
30 thousand and a hundred years and more, despised, obscure, even till he stood without invitation. . . . But, lest I should proceed too covertly, Francis and Poverty as these two lovers now accept in speech outspread. Their harmony and joyous semblance, made love and wonder and tender looks the cause of sacred thoughts; so that the venerable Bernard first cast off his sandals and ran to follow so great peace, and as he ran him thought him all too slow. . . .

"Thence took his way, this father and this master,
40 together with his lady, and with the household already binding on the humble cord; nor abjectness of heart weighed down his brow, that he was Pietro Bernadone's son, nor that he seemed so marvellous despised. But royally his stern intent to Innocent revealed he, and from him had the first imprint upon his Order. . . . And when, in thirst of martyrdom, in the proud presence of the Soldan, he preached Christ and his followers; and because he found the folk too crude against conversion,—not to stay in
50 vain,—returned to gather fruit from the Italian herbage. . . . When it pleased him who for such good ordained him, to draw him up to his reward

6–7. Albert of Cologne, Thomas of Aquino, Albertus Magnus and Thomas Aquinas, the great theologians. 15–16. The one . . . the other. . . . St. Francis and St. Dominic, founders of holy orders emphasizing love and knowledge respectively. 17. Of one; St. Francis. 29. her first husband, Jesus. 41. the humble cord, the rope girdle of the Franciscans.

which he had earned in making himself lowly, to his brethren; as to his right heirs, his dearest lady he commended, and bade that they should love her faithfully; and from her bosom the illustrious soul willed to depart, turning to its own realm, and for its body would no other bier. Think now what he was, who was a worthy colleague to maintain the bark of Peter in deep sea towards the right sign! 60 And such was our patriarch; wherefore who followeth him as he commandeth, thou must perceive, loadeth him with good wares.". . .

Into my mind this thought dropped sudden, just as the glorious life of Thomas held its peace, because of the resemblance that sprang from his discourse, and then from Beatrice's, whom to begin thus after him it pleased: "This man hath need, and telleth it you not, neither with voice, nor as yet with his thought, to track another truth unto its root. Tell if 70 the light wherewith your being blossometh, eternally will cleave to you as now, and if it doth remain, tell how, when ye grow visible again, it may not grieve your vision.". . .

And I heard in the divinest light of the smaller circle an unassuming voice, perchance such as the Angel's unto Mary, answering: "Whenas the garment of the glorified and sainted flesh shall be resumed, our person shall be more acceptable by being all complete. Whereby shall grow that which 80 the highest Good giveth to us of unearned light, light which enableth us him to see; wherefore the vision must needs wax, and wax the ardour which is kindled by it, and wax the ray which goeth forth from it. But like the coal which giveth forth the flame, and by its living glow o'ercometh it, so that its own appearance is maintained, so shall this glow which doth already swathe us, be conquered in appearance by the flesh which yet and yet the earth o'ercovereth; nor shall such light have power to 90 baffle us, for the organs of the body shall be strong to all that may delight us." So swift and eager to cry *Amen*, meseemed, was the one and the other chorus, that verily they showed desire for their dead bodies. . . .

CANTOS XIV–XVIII. *Sphere V, Mars: holy warriors*

Therefrom my eyes regained their power to uplift them, and I saw me transported, only with my Lady, to more exalted weal. Surely did I perceive that I was more uplifted by the enkindled smile of the star which seemed to me more ruddy than his wont. 100 . . . for with such shining, and so ruddy, within two rays, splendours appeared to me, that I ex-

58. . . . would no other bier; than the earth. 76. an unassuming voice, Solomon.

claimed: "O God! who thus dost glorify them!" As, pricked out with less and greater lights, between the poles of the universe the Milky Way so gleameth white as to set very sages questioning, so did those rays, star-decked, make in the depth of Mars the venerable sign which crossing quadrant lines make in a circle. . . .

From horn to horn, from summit unto base, were moving lights that sparkled mightily in meeting one another and in passing. . . . And as viol and harp tuned in harmony of many cords, make sweet chiming to one by whom the notes are not apprehended, so from the lights that there appeared to me was gathered on the cross a strain that rapt me albeit I followed not the hymn. Well I discerned it was of lofty praise, for there came to me "Rise thou up and conquer," as to who understandeth not, but heareth. And so was I enamoured there, that up till then there had been naught that me had bound with so sweet chains.

As through the tranquil and pure skies darteth, from time to time, a sudden flame setting a-moving eyes that erst were steady, seeming a star that changeth place, save that from where it kindleth no star is lost, and that itself endureth but a little; such from the horn that stretcheth to the right unto that cross's foot, darted a star of the constellation that is there a-glow; nor did the gem depart from off its riband, but coursed along the radial line, like fire burning behind alabaster. With such-like tenderness Anchises' shade proffered itself, if our greatest Muse deserveth credit, when in Elysium he perceived his son. "Oh blood of mine! oh grace of God poured o'er thee! to whom, was ever twice, as unto thee, heaven's gate thrown open?". . . Then said he "He from whom thy kindred hath its name, and who a hundred years and more hath circled round the Mount on the first terrace, was son to me, and thy grandfather's father; meet it is, that with thy works thou shouldst abate his long-stretched toil for him. Florence, within the ancient circling wherefrom she still receiveth tierce and nones, abode in peace, sober and chaste. . . . To so reposeful and so fair a life among the citizens, to so faithful cityhood, to so sweet abode, Mary—with deep wailings summoned—gave me; and, in your ancient Baptistery, at once a Christian I became and Cacciaguida. Moronto was my brother and Eliseo; my wife came to me from Po valley, and from her was thy surname derived. Then followed I the Emperor Conrad, who girt me with his knighthood, so much by valiant work did I advance me in his grace. In his train I marched against the infamy of that Law whose people doth usurp, shame to the pastors,

what is yours by right. There by that foul folk was I unswathed of the deceitful world, whose love befouleth many a soul, and came from martyrdom unto this peace."

Ah puny blood-nobility of ours! If thou makest folk glory in thee here below, where our affections sicken, it shall be marvel to me never more; for there, where appetite is unwarped, I mean in heaven, I gloried me therein. Yet verily thou art a mantle that soon shrinketh, so that, if day by day there be nought added, time goeth round with the shears. . . . I began: "Ye are my father, ye give me full boldness to speak, ye so uplift me, that I am more than I. . . . Thou dost see contingent things, or ere themselves exist, gazing upon the point whereto all times are present; whilst I was companioned by Virgil along the mount which cureth souls, and down-going through the world defunct, heavy words were said to me anent my future life; albeit I feel me squarely set against the blows of fortune; wherefore my will were well content to hear what the disaster drawing nigh to me; for the arrow seen before cometh less rudely." So spake I unto that same light which had before addressed me, and, as Beatrice willed, was my wish confessed.

In no dark sayings, such as limed the foolish folk of old, before the Lamb of God who taketh sins away, was slain, but in clear words, and with precise discourse, answered that love paternal, hidden and revealed by his own smile: ". . . Thou shalt abandon everything beloved most dearly; this is the arrow which the bow of exile shall first shoot. Thou shalt make trial of how salt doth taste another's bread, and how hard the path to descend and mount upon another's stair. And that which most shall weigh thy shoulders down, shall be the vicious and ill company with which thou shalt fall down into this vale, for all ungrateful, all mad and impious shall they become against thee; but, soon after, their temples and not thine shall redden for it. . . . Yet would I not have thee envious of thy neighbours, since thy life shall be prolonged far beyond falling of the penalty upon their perfidies."

When by his silence the sacred soul showed he had finished setting of the woof across the warp I had held out in readiness to him, I began, as he who longeth in doubt for counsel from one who seeth and willeth straight, and loveth: "Well do I see, my father, how time cometh spurring toward me to give me such a buffet as is heaviest to whoso most abandoneth himself; wherefore with foresight it were well to arm me, that if the dearest place be reft from me, I lose not all the rest by reason of my songs.". . .

The light wherein was smiling my treasure which I there had found, first coruscated as at the sun's rays doth a golden mirror; then answered: "Con-

---

23. **a star,** Cacciaguida, an ancestor of Dante.   42. **tierce and nones,** the canonical hours, sounded from the belfry of the Badia church.

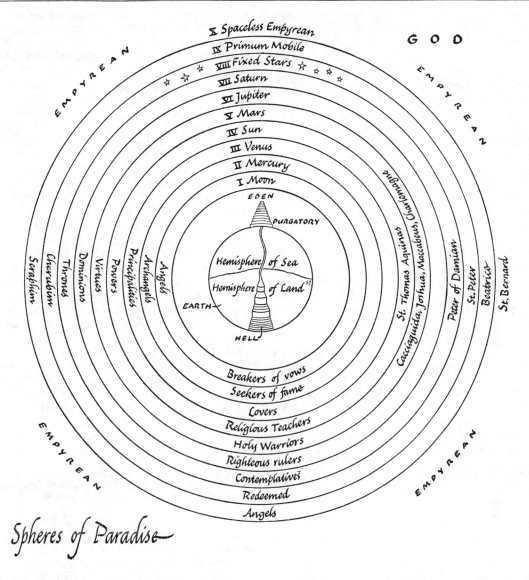

Spheres of Paradise

science darkened, or by its own or by another's shame, will in truth feel thy utterance grating. But none the less, every lie set aside, make thy entire vision manifest, and let them scratch wherever is the scab; for if thy voice be grievous at first taste, yet vital nutriment shall it leave thereafter when digested. This cry of thine shall do as doth the wind, which smiteth most upon the loftiest summits; and this shall be no little argument of honour. Therefore have been displayed to thee, in these wheels, upon the mount, and in the dolorous vale, only souls known to fame; for the soul of him who heareth resteth not nor fixeth faith by an example which hath its root unknown and hidden, nor other unconspicuous argument.". . .

As here sometimes we read the affection in the countenance, if it be so great that all the mind is taken up by it, so in the flaming of the sacred glow to which I turned me, I recognized the will in him yet further somewhat to discourse with me. He began: "In this fifth range of the tree which liveth from the summit, and ever beareth fruit, and never sheddeth leaf, are spirits blessed, who below, ere they came unto heaven, were of a great name, so that every Muse would be enriched by them. Wherefore gaze upon the horns of the cross; he whom I shall name shall there do the act which in a cloud its swift flame doth."

I saw a light drawn along the cross at the naming of Joshua, as it was done; nor was the word known to me ere the fact. And at the name of the lofty Maccabee I saw another move, wheeling, and glad-

ness was the lash unto the top. Thus for Charlemagne and for Orlando two more were followed by
my keen regard, as the eye followeth its falcon flying. . . . Thereon amongst the other lights, moving
and mingling, the soul which had discoursed to me
showed me his artist quality among heaven's singers.
I turned to my right side to see in Beatrice my duty,
whether by speech or gesture indicated, and I saw
her eyes so clear, so joyous, that her semblance sur-
10 passed all former usage and the last.

CANTOS XVIII–XX. *Sphere VI, Jupiter*: *righteous rulers*

As by feeling more delight in doing well, man
from day to day perceiveth that his virtue gaineth
ground; so did I perceive that my circling round together with the heaven had increased its arc, seeing
this miracle yet more adorned. And such change as
cometh in short passage of time over a fair dame,
when her countenance unburdeneth shame's burden,
was presented to my eyes, when I turned me, because of the white glow of the temperate sixth star
20 which had received me into it. I saw in that torch
of Jove the sparkling of the love which was therein
signalling to my eyes our speech. . . .
As at the smiting of burnt brands there rise innumerable sparks, wherefrom the foolish ones use
to draw augury, meseemed there rose thence more
than thousand lights, and mounted some much,
some little, even as the sun which kindleth them,
ordained them; and when each one had stilled it in
its place, an eagle's head and neck I saw presented
30 by that pricked-out fire. . . . With outstretched
wings appeared before me the fair image which
those enwoven souls, rejoicing in their sweet fruition,
made. Each one appeared as a ruby whereon the
sun's ray should burn, enkindled so as to re-cast it
on mine eyes. And that which I must now retrace,
nor ever voice conveyed, nor ink did write, nor ere
by fantasy was comprehended; for I saw and eke I
heard the beak discourse and utter in its voice both
I and *Mine*, when in conception it was *We* and *Our*.
40 And it began: "In that I was just and duteous am I
here exalted to this glory which suffereth not itself
to be surpassed by longing; and upon earth have I
left a memory, so fashioned that there the evil folk
commend it, though they follow not the tale." So do
we feel one glow from many coals as from those
many loves there issued forth one only sound out of
that image.
Whereon straightway I: "O perpetual flowers of
the eternal gladness, ye who make all your odours

seem to me but one, solve, as ye breathe, the great 50
fast which long hath held me hungering, because on
earth I found no food for it. Well do I know that if
the divine justice maketh any other realm of heaven
its mirror, yours apprehendeth it without a veil. Ye
know how eager I prepare me to hearken; ye know
what is that question which hath been to me a fast
of so long date.". . .
Then it began: "Thou didst say: 'A man is born
upon the bank of Indus and there is none to tell of
Christ, nor none to read, nor none to write; and all 60
his volitions and his deeds are good so far as human
reason seeth, sinless in life or in discourse. He dieth
unbaptized and without faith; where is that justice
which condemneth him? where is his fault, in that
he not believes?' Now who art thou who wouldst
sit upon the seat to judge at a thousand miles away
with the short sight that carries but a span? Truly
to him who goeth subtly to work with me, were not
the Scripture over you, there were marvellous
ground for questioning. O animals of earth, minds 70
gross! the primal Will, good in itself, never departed
from its own self which is the highest good. All is
just which doth harmonize with it; no created good
draweth it to itself, but it by raying forth giveth rise
to it. . . . To this realm ne'er rose one who believed not in Christ, neither before nor after he was
nailed unto the tree. But see, many cry Christ,
Christ, who at the judgment shall be far less near to
him than such as know not Christ.". . . So by this
divine image to clear my curtailed vision was given 80
me sweet medicine. . . .

CANTOS XXI–XXII. *Sphere VII, Saturn*: *the contemplatives*

Already were mine eyes fixed on my Lady's
countenance again, and my mind with them, from
all other intent removed; and she smiled not, but:
"Were I to smile," she began, "thou wouldst be such
as was Semele, when she turned to ashes; for my
beauty, which, along the steps of the eternal palace
kindleth more, as thou hast seen, the higher the
ascent, were it not tempered, so doth glow as that
thy mortal power, at its flash, would be like foliage 90
that the thunder shattereth. We have arisen to the
seventh splendour, which, underneath the bosom of
the glowing Lion, downrayeth now mingling with
its power. Fix thy mind after thine eyes, and make
of them mirrors to the figure which in this mirror
shall be shown unto thee.". . .
I saw a ladder erected upward so far that my
sight might not follow it. I saw, moreover, descend
upon the steps so many splendours that methought

---

14. **had increased its arc**; because they were now farther from the
earth. 19. **temperate sixth star**. Jupiter is temperate between hot
Mars and cold Saturn. 29. **an eagle's head and neck**. The eagle is
the symbol of justice.

86. **Semele . . . ashes**. Jove's undisguised presence turned Semele
to ashes.

every light which shineth in the heaven had been thence poured down. And as, after their nature's way, the daws at the beginning of the day set out in company to warm their chilled feathers; then some go off without return, others come again to whence they started, and others make a wheeling sojourn; such fashion, meseemed, was in that sparkling which came in company, soon as it smote upon a certain step, and the one which abode nighest to us became so bright that in my thought I said: "I do perceive the love which thou art signalling unto me. But she from whom I wait the how and when of speech and silence, pauses, and therefore I, counter to my desire, do well not to demand."

Whereat she, who saw my silence in his sight who seeth all, said to me: "Loose thy warm desire." And I began: "My merit maketh me not worthy of thy response, but for her sake who granteth me to make request, O blessed life, who abidest hidden in thy gladness, make known to me the cause which so nigh to me hath placed thee; and say, wherefore in this wheel the sweet symphony of Paradise keepeth silence, which below throughout the others soundeth so devoutly."

"Thou hast the hearing, as the sight, of mortals," he answered me; "wherefore here is no song for that same reason for which Beatrice hath not smiled. Down by the steps of the sacred ladder I so far descended only to do thee joyance with speech and with the light which mantleth me; nor was it greater love that made me swifter; for more and so much love up there doth burn, as the flashing maketh plain to thee; but the deep love which holdeth us prompt servants of the counsel which governeth the world, maketh assignment here as thou observest. . . . I, Peter of Damian, was. Little of mortal life was left to me when I was called and drawn unto the hat which doth but change from bad receptacle to worse. Now the modern pastors must needs be buttressed on this side and on that, and have one to lead them on, so heavy are they, and one to hoist behind. With their mantles they o'erspread their palfreys, so that two beasts travel beneath one hide; O patience, that so much endureth!"

At this voice I saw more flames from step to step descend and whirl, and every whirl made them more beauteous. Around this one they came and stayed themselves and raised a cry of so deep sound that here it may not find similitude; nor did I understand it, so vanquished me the thunder. . . . The assembly drew close; then like a whirlwind was all gathered upward. The sweet Lady thrust me after them, only with a sign, up by that ladder, so did her power overcome my nature; nor ever here below, where we

9. **the one,** Peter of Damian (d. 1072), a stern cardinal who attacked the loose morals of monks in his day.

mount and descend by nature's law, was so swift motion as might compare unto my wing.

"Thou art so nigh to the supreme weal," began Beatrice, "that thou shouldst have thine eyes clear and keen. And therefore, ere thou further wend thereinto, look down and see how great a universe I have already put beneath thy feet; so that thy heart, rejoicing to its utmost, may be presented to the throng triumphant which cometh glad through this sphered ether." With my sight I turned back through all and every of the seven spheres, and saw this globe such that I smiled at its sorry semblance; and that counsel I approve as best which holdeth it for least; and he whose thoughts are turned elsewhither may be called truly upright. . . . And all the seven were displayed to me, how great they are and swift, and how distant each from other in repair. . . .

CANTOS XXIII–XXVII. *Sphere VIII, the Fixed Stars: the redeemed*

As the bird amidst the loved foliage who hath brooded on the nest of her sweet offspring through the night which hideth things from us, who, to look upon their longed-for aspect and to find the food wherewith to feed them, wherein her heavy toils are pleasant to her, foreruns the time, upon the open spray, and with glowing love awaiteth the sun, fixedly gazing for the dawn to rise; so was my Lady standing, erect and eager, turned toward the region beneath which the sun showeth least speed; so that, as I looked on her in her suspense and longing, I became like him who, desiring, would fain have other than he hath, and payeth him with hope. But short the space 'twixt one and the other *when,* of fixing my attent I mean, and of seeing the heaven grow brilliant more and more. And Beatrice said: "Behold the hosts of Christ's triumph, and all the fruit gathered by the circling of these spheres.". . .

I saw, thousands of lamps surmounting, one sun which all and each enkindled, as doth our own the things we see above; and through the living light outglowed the shining substance so bright upon my vision that it endured it not. O Beatrice, sweet guide and dear! She said to me: "That which o'ercometh thee is power against which nought hath defence. Therein is the wisdom and the might which oped the pathways betwixt heaven and earth, for which there erst had been so long desire." Even as fire is unbarred from the cloud, because it so dilateth that it hath not space within, and counter to its nature dasheth down to earth, so my mind, grown greater 'mid these feasts, forth issued from itself, and what it then became knoweth not to recall. . . .

"Open thine eyes and look on what I am; thou hast seen things by which thou art made mighty to sustain my smile." I was as one who cometh to himself from a forgotten vision, and doth strive in vain to bring it back unto his mind, when I heard this proffer, worthy of so great gratitude, as never to be blotted from the book that doth record the past. . . . As under the sun's ray, which issueth pure through a broken cloud, ere now mine eyes have seen a meadow full of flowers, when themselves covered by the shade; so beheld I many a throng of splendours, glowed on from above by ardent rays, beholding not the source whence came the glowings. O benign power which dost so imprint them! thou hadst thyself uplifted to yield place there for mine eyes that lacked in power. The name of the beauteous flower which I ever invoke, morning and evening, drew all my mind together to look upon the greatest flame.

And when on both mine eyes had been depicted the quality and greatness of the living star which conquereth up there, e'en as down here it conquered, from within the heaven descended a torch circle-formed, in fashion of a crown, and girt her and wheeled round her. Whatever melody soundeth sweetest here below, and most doth draw the soul unto itself, would seem a rent cloud thundering, compared unto the sound of that lyre whereby was crowned the beauteous sapphire by which the brightest heaven is ensapphired. "I am the angelic love who circles the lofty gladness that doth breathe from out the womb which was the hostelry of our desire; and I will circle, Lady of heaven, until thou followest thy son, and dost make yet more divine the supreme sphere in that thou enterest it."

Thus the circling melody impressed itself, and all the other lights made sound the name of Mary. . . . And as the infant who toward his mother stretcheth up his arms when he hath had the milk, because his mind flameth forth even into outward gesture; so each one of these glowings up-stretched with its flame, so that the deep love which they had for Mary was made plain to me. Then they stayed there within my sight, singing *O Queen of heaven* so sweetly that ne'er hath parted from me the delight. . . .

"O fellowship elect to the great supper of the blessed Lamb, who feedeth you in such fashion that your desire ever is fulfilled; if by the grace of God this man foretasteth of that which falleth from your table ere death prescribe the time to him, give heed to his unmeasured yearning and bedew him somewhat: ye drink ever of the fountain whence floweth that on which his thought is fixed." Thus Beatrice: and those glad souls made themselves spheres upon fixed poles, outflaming mightily like unto comets. And even as wheels in harmony of clock-work so turn that the first, to whoso noteth it, seemeth still,

and the last to fly, so did these carols with their differing whirl, or swift or slow, make me deem of their riches.

Should it e'er come to pass that the sacred poem to which both heaven and earth so have set hand, that it hath made me lean through many a year, should overcome the cruelty which doth bar me forth from the fair sheepfold wherein I used to sleep, a lamb, foe to the wolves which war upon it; with changed voice now, and with changed fleece shall I return, a poet, and at the font of my baptism shall I assume the chaplet; because into the Faith which maketh souls known of God, 'twas there I entered; and afterward Peter, for its sake, circled thus my brow. . . .

All Paradise took up the strain, "To the Father, to the Son, to the Holy Spirit, glory!" so that the sweet song intoxicated me. Meseemed I was beholding a smile of the universe; wherefore my intoxication entered both by hearing and by sight. O joy! O gladness unspeakable! O life compact of love and peace! O wealth secure that hath no longing!

CANTO XXVII–XXIX. *Sphere IX, Primum Mobile: the angels*

My enamoured mind, which held amorous converse ever with my Lady, burned more than ever to bring back my eyes to her; and whatsoever food nature or art e'er made, to catch the eyes and so possess the mind, be it in human flesh, be it in pictures, if all united, would seem nought towards the divine delight which glowed upon me when that I turned me to her smiling face. And the power of which that look made largest to me, from the fair nest of Leda plucked me forth, and into the swiftest heaven thrust me. Its parts most living and exalted are so uniform that I know not to tell which Beatrice chose for my position.

But she, who saw my longing, smiling began—so glad that God seemed joying in her countenance— "The nature of the universe which stilleth the centre and moveth all the rest around, hence doth begin as from its starting point. And this heaven hath no other *where* than the divine mind wherein is kindled the love which rolleth it and the power which it sheddeth. Light and love grasp it in one circle, as doth it the others, and this engirdment he only who doth gird it understandeth. Its movement by no other is marked out; but by it all the rest are measured, as ten by half and fifth. And how Time in this same vessel hath its roots, and in the rest its leaves, may now be manifest to thee.". . .

57. these carols; in the old sense of groups of singing dancers. 87–88. from the . . . Leda, the constellation of the Twins, Castor and Pollux, children of Leda and Jupiter.

A point I saw which rayed forth light so keen, needs must the vision that it flameth on be closed because of its strong poignancy; and whatever star from here appeareth smallest, were seen a moon neighboured with it, as star with star is neighboured. Perhaps as close as the halo seemeth to gird the luminary that doth paint it, whenso the vapour which supporteth it is thickest, at such interval around the point there wheeled a circle of fire so rapidly it had surpassed the motion which doth swiftest gird the universe; and this was by a second girt around, that by a third, and the third by a fourth, by a fifth the fourth, then by a sixth the fifth. Thereafter followed the seventh, already in its stretch so far outspread that were the messenger of Juno made complete, it were too strait to hold it. And so the eighth and ninth; and each one moved slower according as in number it was more remote from unity; and that one had the clearest flame, from which the pure spark was least distant; because, I take it, it sinketh deepest into the truth thereof.

My Lady, who beheld me in toil of deep suspense, said: "From that point doth hang heaven and all nature. Look on that circle which is most conjoint thereto, and know its movement is so swift by reason of the enkindled love whereby 'tis pierced. The first circles have revealed to thee the Seraphs and the Cherubs. So swift they follow their withies that they may liken them unto the point as most they may; and they may in measure as they are sublime in vision. Those other loves which course around them are named Thrones of the divine aspect, because they brought to its completion the first ternary. And thou shouldst know that all have their delight in measure as their sight sinketh more deep into the truth wherein every intellect is stilled. . . . The second ternary which thus flowereth in this eternal spring. . . . In that hierarchy are the three divinities, first Dominations, and then Virtues; the third order is of Powers. Then in the two last-save-one upleapings, Principalities and Archangels whirl; the last consisteth all of Angelic sports.

"These orders all gaze upward, and downward have such conquering might that toward God all are drawn and all draw. . . . These substances, since first they gathered joy from the face of God, have never turned their vision from it wherefrom nought is concealed; wherefore their sight is never intercepted by a fresh object, and so behoveth not to call aught back to memory because thought hath been cleft. . . . See now the height and breadth of the eternal worth, since it hath made itself so many mirrors wherein it breaketh, remaining in itself one as before."

CANTOS XXX–XXXIII. *Sphere X, the Empyrean: the Saints, the Virgin, and God*

Love constrained me to turn with mine eyes to Beatrice. If that which up till here is said of her were all compressed into one act of praise 'twould be too slight to serve this present turn. The beauty I beheld transcendeth measure, not only past our reach, but surely I believe that only he who made it enjoyeth it complete. At this pass I yield me vanquished more than e'er yet was overborne by his theme's thrust comic or tragic poet. For as the Sun in sight that most trembleth, so the remembrance of the sweet smile sheareth my memory of its very self. From the first day when in this life I saw her face, until this sight, my song hath ne'er been cut off from the track.

But now needs must my tracking cease from following her beauty further forth in poesy, as at his utmost reach must every artist. Such as I leave her for a mightier proclamation than of my trumpet, which draweth its arduous subject to a close, with alert leader's voice and gesture, did she again begin: "We have issued forth from the greatest body into the heaven which is pure light, light intellectual fullcharged with love, love of true good full-charged with gladness, gladness which transcendeth every sweetness. Here shalt thou see the one and the other soldiery of Paradise, and the one in those aspects which thou shalt see at the last judgment."

As a sudden flash of lightning which so shattereth the visual spirits as to rob the eye of power to realize e'en strongest objects; so there shone around me a living light, leaving me swathed in such a web of its glow that naught appeared to me. "Ever doth the love which stilleth heaven, receive into itself with such like salutation, duly to fit the taper for its flame." So soon as these brief words came into me I felt me to surmount my proper power; and kindled me with such new-given sight that there is no such brightness unalloyed that mine eyes might not hold their own with it.

And I saw a light, in river form, glow tawny betwixt banks painted with marvellous spring. From out this river issued living sparks, and dropped on every side into the blossoms, like rubies set in gold. Then as inebriated with the odours they plunged themselves again into the marvellous swirl, and as one entered issued forth another. "The lofty wish that now doth burn and press thee to have more

---

1. **A point.** The point is God, and the nine circles are the nine orders of angels, corresponding to the nine heavens that Dante has come through. 15–16. **messenger of Juno,** Iris, the rainbow. 33. **the first ternary;** that is, the first of the three groups of angelic orders.

79–80. **the one and . . . Paradise,** the redeemed and the angels.

knowledge of the things thou seest, pleaseth me more the more it swelleth. But of this water needs thou first must drink, ere so great thirst in thee be slaked." So spoke mine eyes' sun unto me; then added: "The river and the topaz-gems that enter and go forth, and the smiling of the grasses are the shadowy prefaces of their reality. Not that such things are harsh as in themselves; but on thy side is the defect, in that thy sight not yet exalteth it so
10 high."

Never doth child so sudden rush with face turned to the milk, if he awake far later than his wont, as then did I, to make yet better mirrors of mine eyes, down bending to the wave which floweth that we may better us. And no sooner drank of it mine eyelids' rim than into roundness seemed to change its length. Then—as folk under masks seem other than before, if they do off the semblance not their own wherein they hid them,—so changed before me
20 into ampler joyance the flowers and the sparks, so that I saw both the two courts of heaven manifested.

O splendour of God whereby I saw the lofty triumph of the truthful realm, give me the power to tell how I beheld it. A light there is up yonder which maketh the Creator visible unto the creature, who only in beholding him hath its own peace; and it so far outstretcheth circle-wise that its circumference would be too loose a girdle for the sun. All its appearance is composed of rays reflected from the top
30 of the First Moved, which draweth thence its life and potency. And as a hill-side reflect itself in water at its foot, as if to look upon its own adornment when it is rich in grasses and in flowers, so, mounting o'er the light, around, around, casting reflection in more than thousand ranks I saw all that of us hath won return up yonder.

And if the lowest step gathereth so large a light within itself, what then the amplitude of the rose's outmost petals? My sight in the breath and height
40 lost itself not, but grasped the scope and nature of that joyance. Near and far addeth not nor subtracteth there, for where God governeth without medium the law of nature hath no relevance. Within the yellow of the eternal rose, which doth expand, rank upon rank, and reeketh perfume of praise unto the Sun that maketh spring for ever, me—as who doth hold his peace yet fain would speak—Beatrice drew, and said: "Behold how great the white-robed concourse! See how large our city sweepeth! See our
50 thrones so filled that but few folk are now awaited there.". . .

In form, then, of a white rose displayed itself to me that sacred soldiery which in his blood Christ made his spouse; but the other, which as it flieth seeth and doth sing his glory who enamoureth it, and the excellence which hath made it what it is, like to a swarm of bees which doth one while plunge

into the flowers and another while wend back to where its toil is turned to sweetness, ever descended into the great flower adorned with so many leaves, and reascended thence to where its love doth ceaseless make sojourn. They had their faces all of living flame, and wings of gold, and the rest so white that never snow reacheth such limit. When they descended into the flower, from rank to rank they proffered of the peace and of the ardour which they acquired as they fanned their sides, nor did the interposing of so great a flying multitude, betwixt the flower and that which was above, impede the vision nor the splendour; for the divine light so penetrateth through the universe, in measure of its worthiness, that nought hath power to oppose it. . . .

As the pilgrim who doth draw fresh life in the temple of his vow as he gazeth, and already hopeth to tell again how it be placed, so, traversing the living light, I led mine eyes along the ranks, now up, now down, and now round circling. I saw countenances suasive of love, adorned by another's light and their own smile, and gestures graced with every dignity. The general form of Paradise my glance had already taken in, in its entirety, and on no part as yet had my sight paused; and I turned me with rekindled will to question my Lady concerning things whereanent my mind was in suspense.

One thing I purposed, and another answered me; I thought to see Beatrice, and I saw an elder clad like the folk in glory. His eyes and cheeks were overpoured with benign gladness, in kindly gesture as befits a tender father. And: "Where is she?" all sudden I exclaimed; whereunto he: "To bring thy desire to its goal Beatrice moved me from my place; and if thou look up to the circle third from the highest rank, thou shalt re-behold her, on the throne her merits have assigned to her."

Without answering I lifted up mine eyes and saw her, making to herself a crown as she reflected from her the eternal rays. From that region which thundereth most high, no mortal eye is so far distant, though plunged most deep within the sea, as there from Beatrice was my sight; but that wrought not upon me, for her image descended not to me mingled with any medium. "O Lady, in whom my hope hath vigour, and who for my salvation didst endure to leave in Hell thy footprints; of all the things which I have seen I recognize the grace and might, by thy power and by thine excellence. Thou hast drawn me from a slave to liberty by all those paths, by all those methods by which thou hadst the power so to do. Preserve thy munificence in me, so that my soul which thou hast made sound, may unloose it from the body, pleasing unto thee." So did I pray;

87. **an elder**, St. Bernard, symbolizing intuition.

and she, so distant as she seemed, smiled and looked on me, then turned her to the eternal fountain.

And the holy elder said: "That thou mayest consummate thy journey perfectly—whereto prayer and holy love dispatched me,—fly with thine eyes throughout this garden; for gazing on it will equip thy glance better to mount through the divine ray."

. . . I lifted up mine eyes, and as at morn the oriental regions of the horizon overcome that where the sun declineth, so, as from the valley rising to the mountain; with mine eyes I saw a region at the boundary surpass all the remaining ridge in light. . . . And at that mid point, with out-stretched wings, I saw more than a thousand Angels making festival, each one distinct in glow and art. I saw there, smiling to their sports and to their songs, a beauty which was gladness in the eyes of all the other saints. And had I equal wealth in speech as in conception, yet dared I not attempt the smallest part of her delightsomeness. Bernard, when he saw mine eyes fixed and eager towards the glowing source of his own glow, turned his eyes to her, with so much love that he made mine more ardent to regaze.

With his Love fixed on his Delight, that contemplating saint took the free office of the teacher on him, and began these sacred words: "Virgin Mother, daughter of thy son, lowly and uplifted more than any creature, fixed goal of the eternal counsel, thou art she who didst human nature so ennoble that its own Maker scorned not to become its making. In thy womb was lit again the love under whose warmth in the eternal peace this flower hath thus unfolded. Here art thou unto us the meridian torch of love and there below with mortals art a living spring of hope. Lady, thou art so great and hast such worth, that if there be who would have grace yet betaketh not himself to thee, his longing seeketh to fly without wings. Thy kindliness not only succoureth whoso requesteth, but doth oftentimes freely forerun request. In thee is tenderness, in thee is pity, in thee munificence, in thee united whatever in created being is of excellence. Now he who from the deepest pool of the universe even to here hath seen the spirit lives one after one imploreth thee, of grace, for so much power as to be able to uplift his eyes more high towards final bliss.". . .

And I, who to the goal of all my longings was drawing nigh, even as was meet the ardour of the yearning quenched within me. Bernard gave me the sign and smiled to me that I should look on high, but I already of myself was such as he would have me; because my sight, becoming purged, now more and more was entering through the ray of the deep light which in itself is true. . . . And so I was the bolder, as I mind me, so long to sustain it as to unite my glance with the Worth infinite.

16. **a beauty,** the Virgin Mary.   56. **the Worth infinite,** God.

O grace abounding, wherein I presumed to fix my look on the eternal light so long that I consumed my sight thereon! Within its depths I saw ingathered, bound by love in one volume, the scattered leaves of all the universe; substance and accidents and their relations, as though together fused, after such fashion that what I tell of is one simple flame. The universal form of this complex I think that I beheld, because more largely, as I say this, I feel that I rejoice. . . .

Thus all suspended did my mind gaze fixed, immovable, intent, ever enkindled by its gazing. Such at that light doth man become that to turn thence to any other sight could not by possibility be ever yielded. For the good, which is the object of the will, is therein wholly gathered, and outside it that same thing is defective which therein is perfect. . . . In the profound and shining being of the deep light appeared to me three circles, of three colours and one magnitude; one by the second as Iris by Iris seemed reflected, and the third seemed a fire breathed equally from one and from the other. Oh but how scant the utterance, and how faint, to my conceit! and it, to what I saw, is such that it sufficeth not to call it little.

O Light eternal who only in thyself abidest, only thyself dost understand, and to thyself, self-understood self-understanding, turnest love and smiling! That circling which appeared in thee to be conceived as a reflected light, by mine eyes scanned some little, in itself, of its own colour, seemed to be painted with our effigy, and thereat my sight was all committed to it. As the geometer who all sets himself to measure the circle and who findeth not, think as he may, the principle he lacketh; such was I at this new-seen spectacle; I would perceive how the image consorteth with the circle, and how it settleth there; but not for this were my proper wings, save that my mind was smitten by a flash wherein its will came to it. To the high fantasy here power failed; but already my desire and will were rolled—even as a wheel that moveth equally—by the Love that moves the sun and the other stars.

Geoffrey Chaucer

c. 1340–1400

The greatest English poet of the Middle Ages was born in London, the son of a wine-merchant, sometime between the years 1340 and 1343. Entering the service of the nobility at the court of Edward III of England, Chaucer spent his life as a busy and efficient servant of the Crown. His formal education was apparently limited to some legal studies, but we cannot be sure even of that detail, and the general fact remains that we know as little about Chaucer's life as we do about Shakespeare's, and far less than we know about Dante's. There is no doubt, however, that Chaucer was all his life a man of letters, for he gives clear evidence of being a widely, though not phenomenally, read man, seizing every possible opportunity which presented itself to cultivate literature, if only as an avocation. This is one of the two inescapable facts which every reader of Chaucer must bear in mind at all times.

The other fact is Chaucer's professional career at court just mentioned, which accounts for his unquestionably courtly or aristocratic attitude toward humanity and his equally objective view of life as a whole. His abilities as a servant of his government were evidently noteworthy; his tasks ranged from administration, such as a comptrollership of customs and a supervisorship of royal works and forests, to ambassadorial duties, the latter often involving such delicate matters as the negotiation of a royal marriage, although the details of these embassies, probably secret at the time, are necessarily obscure today. There is ample evidence, however, that Chaucer was all his life a successful man in worldly affairs, regardless of the various ups and downs which would be inevitable at the court of a Plantagenet king of England. (The reign of Richard II, from 1377 to 1399, is particularly notorious as a period of intrigue and counter-intrigue in royal feudal society.) It is scarcely likely that Chaucer was ever seriously in want, although he was of course dependent upon royal favor; and while it is true that we know little of his life during the decade of the 1390's, at which time he wrote some of his most distinguished works, it is not to be supposed that he was then much less fortunate in circumstances than he had been before. His death took place in 1400.

For most general purposes, it is best to concentrate on Chaucer as a man of affairs who wrote as an avocation, for if we do this, we do much to explain Chaucer's work. Being a success and a courtier at one and the same time, Chaucer developed an independence of outlook, an obvious social snobbishness, a typical superior spectator's point of view, which, combined with his truly remarkable human insight, made him one of the most effective reporters of society who ever lived. By instinct Chaucer's major interest lay in humanity alive and breathing, not in philosophical abstractions or mystical visions of the Other World. As a philosopher, indeed, Chaucer is negligible; aside from the Platonic philosophy of Boethius, whose magnum opus, *De Philosophiae Consolatione* (c. 520), he translated somewhere in the early 1380's, he has no regard for sheer dialectics. If a knotty intellectual or spiritual problem poses itself, Chaucer is inclined to leave it to the "clerkes," for he seems always to imply that the world is served best by personal integrity, a fidelity to principles, and in addition by a practical viewpoint and a rational approach to living, since he believes that it is useless to kick against the pricks and essential to co-operate with the inevitable. The important thing for him, it would seem, is to take life as one finds it.

Such an idea is no different from that held by millions of people both before and after Chaucer's time, and so we must look farther to see what makes Chaucer's empirical attitude so unusual as to place him in the very top rank of interpreters of life. The reason for this is not far to seek. For one thing, Chaucer has an uncanny gift of putting an individual in his place, in his proper pigeonhole, neatly wrapped up; his talents for decisive portraiture, especially on a small canvas, have never been surpassed. Moreover, he is a superbly direct and economical storyteller; some of his masterpieces of narrative, such as *The Pardoner's Tale*, can literally be said to contain not a single waste word or phrase. His inescapable sense of humor—a gift most rare among famous writers—can be either kindly or malicious, but in either case it cannot long be suppressed; it is, in its most characteristic vein, of a deft, Puckish type. Still, Chaucer can wage stern warfare upon the social parasite, the hypocrite, and the pretender to knowledge not possessed; then his battery of satire is formidable.

In his earlier career—that is, until the middle of the 1380's—Chaucer's poetry was rather derivative. He wrote short lyrics, some of them of much grace and finish, in the manner of the contemporary courtly poets of France like Deschamps, Machaut, and Froissart. He was, in a manner typical of the Middle Ages, prone to allegory—explicit, as in the case of *The Book of the Duchess* (c. 1370), or implicit, as in the case of *The Parliament of Fowls* (c. 1380)—and very much under the influence of the thirteenth-century French allegorical romance, the *Roman de la Rose*. It was in *Troilus and Criseyde* (c. 1385–86), however, that Chaucer's genius reached full stature. This long narrative poem, beautifully integrated in structure, has all the requirements of a modern novel except possibly for its poetic form. The characterization of its major figures is complex, subtle, and completely human; only the hero, Troilus, who is anchored in the tradition of the chivalric knight, strikes the present-day reader as "medieval," and even Troilus can be recognized as a human being. This work alone, a study of a triangular situation which affects nearly all men and women at some time in their lives, would have been sufficient to make Chaucer a great writer in the judgment of posterity. It is, incidentally, the only long work that Chaucer ever completed.

As for the famous *Canterbury Tales*, it was probably written over a considerable number of years. Some of these tales were probably composed early in Chaucer's career and then were incorporated into the collection. *The Second Nun's Tale* or *The Prioress's Tale* are examples. Others, like *The Knight's Tale*, probably existed in some early form and then were revised before they were included among *The Canterbury Tales*. Most of them, however, sprang full-fledged from the author with no previous incarnation. Conservative estimates date different parts of *The Canterbury Tales* anywhere from 1386 to 1398; Chaucer may even have been working on them at the time of his death in 1400. It is unnecessary to discuss at any length either these multifarious tales or the brilliant *Prologue*, the most celebrated of all Chaucerian pieces, except to remark that as a gallery of portraits of medieval types of society as well as of individual men and women, it is absolutely unrivaled in medieval literature. The tales told by these characters are all appropriate to the tellers. They cover every type of medieval literature with the exception of the drama. They are arranged, by means of the plausible, realistic, and dramatic framework of the Canterbury Pilgrimage, in a delightfully informal way. Although a few are grouped by the fact that they discuss various aspects of married life (the so-called Marriage Group), and others are connected as part of a quarrel between members of the company, there is no overall plan of arrangement in evidence, as is the case with most other medieval story collections. Incomplete as Chaucer's design may be, it only serves to illustrate his characteristically frank acceptance of life as he finds it—as it is instead of as it ought to be.

The Canterbury Tales

PROLOGUE

W HAN that Aprille with his shoures soote *
  The droghte of Marche hath percéd to
  the roote,
And bathed every veyne in swich licour,
Of which vertu engendred is the flour;
Whan Zephirus eek with his swete breeth   5
Inspiréd hath in every holt and heeth
The tendre croppes, and the yonge sonne
Hath in the Ram his halfe cours y-ronne,
And smale fowles maken melodye,
That slepen al the night with open yë,   10

The Canterbury Tales. Text prepared by George K. Anderson, with the exception of *The Reeve's Tale*, which is from the Tyrwhitt edition revised in the light of present-day Chaucerian scholarship.
* In *The Canterbury Tales* Chaucer makes use chiefly (1) of the iambic pentameter riming couplet and (2) of the seven-line iambic pentameter stanza (riming *a b a b b c c*), known as the Chaucerian stanza or Rime Royal. The iambic pentameter couplet is the "heroic" or "closed" couplet of neo-classical fame, except that the writers of the seventeenth and eighteenth centuries preferred to "close" it to a greater degree; that is, to bring the thought to a more definite conclusion at the end of the second line.
1. **soote**, sweet. 3. **swich**, such. **licour**, "moisture," not "liquor." 4. **vertu**, power, efficacy, magical influence. **flour**, flower. 5. **eek**, also. 6. **holt and heeth.** A *holt* is a cultivated tract, or plantation; *heeth* is the modern *heath*. No doubt the combining of these two words in such a phrase is to be attributed in part to the popularity of alliterative formulas in Middle English poetry—a popularity which is in some degree found in all English literature. 7. **sonne**, sun—"young" in the sense that it is early in the year. The medieval calendar started the year at the vernal equinox in March rather than on the first of January. 8. **Ram**, the constellation of Aries, one of the constellations of the zodiac, along the path of the sun. Aries is the spot on the celestial map at which the sun is located at the time of the vernal equinox; hence it is the first constellation of the year. There are twelve such zodiacal constellations.

(So priketh hem nature in hir corages),
Than longen folk to goon on pilgrimages
(And palmers for to seken straunge strondes)
To ferne halwes, couthe in sondry londes;
And specially, from every shires ende   15
Of Engelond, to Caunterbury they wende,
The holy blisful martir for to seke,
That hem hath holpen, whan that they were seke.
    Bifel that, in that sesoun on a day,
In Southwerk at the Tabard as I lay   20
Redy to wenden on my pilgrimage
To Caunterbury with ful devout corage,
At night was come in-to that hostelrye
Wel nyne and twenty in a companye,
Of sondry folk, by aventure y-falle   25
In felawshipe, and pilgrims were they alle,
That toward Caunterbury wolden ryde;
The chambres and the stables weren wyde,
And wel we weren esed atte beste.
And shortly, whan the sonne was to reste,   30
So hadde I spoken with hem everichon,
That I was of hir felawshipe anon,
And made forward erly for to ryse,
To take our wey, ther as I yow devyse.
    But natheles, whyl I have tyme and space,   35
Ere that I ferther in this tale pace,
Me thinketh it acordaunt to resoun,

---

11. **hem,** them. The modern forms of the third person plural pronoun probably to be traced to the Norse, were beginning to come into general use during Chaucer's lifetime (note *they* in l. 18), but they had not yet been accepted for the oblique cases. So *hem* for *them*, *hir(e)* for *their*. **corages.** This word may be either singular or plural, and its meanings may be many. The modern meaning of "courage" is usually the last to be thought of in Middle English literature. "Disposition," "temperament," "sexual desire," "will" are some of the more common meanings. Here the sense of the line can be construed thus: "the small birds make melody; Nature so prompts them (priketh hem) in their desires or instincts." 13. **strondes,** strands, shores. 14. **ferne halwes,** distant shrines or hallowed places. **couthe,** famous, well-known. 17. **The holy . . . seke.** The "holy martyr" is Thomas à Becket, Archbishop of Canterbury, slain during the course of a Church and Crown dispute during the reign of Henry II of England. His assassination took place in 1170, and he was canonized in 1173. His position in the quarrel with Henry could be interpreted by the commoners as in their favor, and he was immensely popular after his death; his tomb became the most famous shrine in medieval England. 18. **seke,** sick. Note that this actually forms an identical rime with *seke* (seek) in the preceding line. Identical rimes of this sort were not only not avoided as unharmonious and inadequate, but were even sought at times. 20. **Southwerk,** the bustling suburb of London, on the south bank of the Thames River, the beginning of the Canterbury road. **the Tabard.** A *tabard* was a short, sleeveless coat, and was here the "sign" of the inn. 22. **corage.** See note to l. 11. "Full devout will" would be the modern equivalent. 25. **y-falle,** befallen, taken place—here, happened along. The prefix *y-* is frequently found on past participles in Middle English; it is a development of the older form *ge-*, which students of Modern German would at once recognize. 29. **esed,** entertained, set at ease. **atte beste,** at the best, in the best possible way. 31. **everichon,** every (each) one. 33. **forward,** agreement. 34. **ther . . . devyse,** where I describe it to you. In Chaucer *ther* and *wher* are virtually interchangeable. 36. **pace,** pass. 37. **acordaunt to resoun,** according to right, in keeping with the right thing to do. Note the meaning of the Modern French *raison*. But the word may here have the meaning of "order," "arrangement."

To telle yow al the condicioun
Of ech of hem, so as it semed me,
And whiche they weren, and of what degree; 40
And eek in what array that they were inne:
And at a knight than wol I first biginne.

A KNIGHT ther was, and that a worthy man,
That fro the tyme that he first bigan
To ryden out, he loved chivalrye, 45
Trouthe and honour, fredom and curteisye.
Ful worthy was he in his lordes werre,
And therto hadde he riden (no man ferre)
As wel in cristendom as hethenesse,
And ever honoured for his worthinesse. 50
At Alisaundre he was, whan it was wonne;
Ful ofte tyme he hadde the bord bigonne
Aboven alle naciouns in Pruce.
In Lettow hadde he reysed and in Ruce,
No cristen man so ofte of his degree. 55
In Gernade at the sege eek hadde he be
Of Algezir, and riden in Belmarye.
At Lyeys was he, and at Satalye,
Whan they were wonne; and in the Grete See
At many a noble aryve hadde he be. 60
At mortal batailles hadde he been fiftene,
And foughten for our feith at Tramissene
In listes thryes, and ay slayn his foo.
This ilke worthy knight hadde been also

Sometyme with the lord of Palatye, 65
Ageyn another hethen in Turkye:
And everemore he hadde a sovereyn prys,
And though that he were worthy, he was wys,
And of his port as meek as is a mayde.
He nevere yet no vileinye ne sayde 70
In al his lyf, un-to no maner wight.
He was a verray parfit gentil knight.
But for to tellen yow of his array,
His hors were goode, but he was nat gay.
Of fustian he weréd a gipoun 75
Al bismoteréd with his habergeoun,
For he was late y-come from his viage,
And wente for to doon his pilgrimage.
With him there was his sone, a yong SQUYER,
A lovyere, and a lusty bacheler, 80
With lokkes crulle, as they were leyd in presse.
Of twenty yeer of age he was, I gesse.
Of his stature he was of evene lengthe,
And wonderly deliver, and greet of strengthe.
And he had been somtyme in chivachye, 85
In Flaundres, in Artoys, and Picardye,
And born him wel, as of so litel space,
In hope to stonden in his lady grace.
Embrouded was he, as it were a mede
Al ful of fresshe floures, whyte and rede. 90
Singinge he was, or floytinge, al the day;
He was as fresh as is the month of May.
Short was his goune, with sleves longe and wyde.
Wel coude he sitte on hors, and faire ryde.
He coude songes make and wel endyte, 95
Juste and eek daunce, and wel purtreye and wryte.
So hote he lovede, that by nightertale
He sleep namore than doth a nightingale.
Curteys he was, lowly, and servisable,

47. **worthy.** See also l. 43. Here, as elsewhere in Chaucer, the word has a much stronger meaning (with no connotation of condescension) than in Modern English. **werre,** war. 48. **ferre,** farther. 51. ff. **Alisaundre,** etc. The knight, as a soldier of fortune and a mercenary, is a veteran of many wars of the fourteenth century. His service is the feudal service to his immediate lord, whose political interests were doubtless many; and the Knight could often change his lord. (Compare the issue in the Danish ballad, *Niels Ebbeson*, p. II:252.) 52. **hadde . . . bigonne.** "To begin the board" was to sit at the head of the table, the obvious place of honor. 53. **Pruce,** Prussia. The line means undoubtedly that the Knight was a member of the Teutonic Order of Knights, one of the great chivalric associations of the Middle Ages, and a powerful preserver of the old Germanic warrior spirit; it looks forward to the Prussian military tradition. 54. **Lettow,** Lithuania. The Lithuanians were converted to Christianity in 1386, largely through the instrumentality of the Teutonic Order of Knights. If the date of this conversion meant the earliest possible time at which the Knight could have returned to England, this would be a valuable detail in dating the *Prologue.* The conversion, however, was preceded by much campaigning, and the evidence may not be very convincing. **reysed,** made expeditions (compare the German *reisen*). **Ruce,** Russia. The Teutonic Order was a strong buffer between Western Christendom and pagan nations in the East, particularly the Tartars, who had made several incursions into Russia during the Middle Ages. 56–57. **Gernade,** Granada, Spain. **sege . . . Algezir,** modern Algeciras, captured by the English under the Earl of Derby in 1344. **Belmarye,** Benmarin, Morocco. There were several raids upon the Moorish inhabitants during the forties, sixties, and eighties of the fourteenth century; it is consequently impossible to tell in which the Knight was involved. 58. **Lyeys,** Lyas in Armenia, harried by Pierre de Lusignan (see note to l. 65) in 1367. **Satalye,** Atalia, on the coast of Asia Minor, captured by Pierre de Lusignan in 1361. 59. **Grete See,** the Mediterranean. 62. **Tramissene,** Tlemcen in Algeria; as in the case of *Belmarye* in l. 57, the allusion is too vague to help us much; there was fighting along the Moroccan and Algerian coasts all through the middle of the fourteenth century. 64. **ilke,** same.

65. **Palatye,** probably the Turkish *Balat;* the "lord of Palatye" was, then, a heathen allied to Pierre de Lusignan—further evidence of the difference between the chivalric adventurer like Pierre in the dying days of knighthood, and the chivalric idealist of the medieval romances; or perhaps it is merely the difference between fact and romance. But it is difficult to imagine Lancelot or Roland fighting on the same side as a Saracen. 67. **sovereyn prys,** noble or sovereign worth. 68. **though that he . . . wys,** though he was brave, he was prudent. 69. **port,** bearing, behavior. 72. **verray parfit,** "true and perfect," not "very perfect." 74. **hors.** This word was in Old English a neuter noun (compare the Modern German *Kind,* "child," or *Weib,* "woman"), and as such had no ending in the plural, as here. 75. **fustian,** a thick cotton cloth. **gipoun,** a tunic. 76. **bismoteréd,** smutted, marked with dirt. **habergeoun,** hauberk, coat of mail. 77. **viage,** voyage, expedition. 79. **SQUYER,** a young candidate for knighthood. In *The Canterbury Tales* the squire is the type of the young courtly lover. 81. **crulle,** curled. 84. **deliver,** active, agile. 85. **chivachye,** cavalry-raids. 87. **as . . . space,** considering the small opportunity, or short period of time the Squire had been training for knighthood. 88. **lady.** Many Old English feminine nouns had no ending in the genitive case, so *lady* instead of *lady's.* 89. **Embrouded,** decorated with embroidery; but it is altogether possible that Chaucer is thinking of the young man's pink-and-white complexion. **mede,** meadow. 91. **floytinge,** playing the flute. 95. **make,** write in poetry. **endyte,** compose, in particular, the words of a song (as differentiated from *make*). 96. **Juste,** joust (in a tournament). **purtreye,** draw pictures. 97. **nightertale,** nighttime.

And carf biforn his fader at the table. 100

A YEMAN hadde he, and servaunts namo
At that tyme, for him liste ryde so;
And he was clad in cote and hood of grene;
A sheef of pecok-arwes brighte and kene
Under his belt he bar ful thriftily; 105
(Wel coude he dresse his takel yemanly:
His arwes drouped noght with fetheres lowe),
And in his hand he bar a mighty bowe.
A not-heed hadde he, with a broun visage.
Of wode-craft wel coude he al the usage. 110
Upon his arm he bar a gay bracer,
And by his syde a swerd and a bokeler,
And on that other syde a gay daggere,
Harneised wel and sharp as point of spere;
A Cristofre on his brest of silver shene. 115
An horn he bar, the bawdrik was of grene;
A forster was he, soothly, as I gesse.

Ther was also a Nonne, a PRIORESSE,
That of hir smyling was ful simple and coy,
Hir gretteste ooth was but by seÿnt Loy; 120
And she was cleped madame Eglentyne.
Ful wel she song the service divyne,
Entuned in hir nose ful semely;
And Frensh she spak ful faire and fetisly,
After the scole of Stratford atte Bowe, 125
For Frensh of Paris was to hir unknowe.
At mete wel y-taught was she with-alle;
She leet no morsel from hir lippes falle,
Ne wette hir fingres in hir sauce depe.
Wel coude she carie a morsel, and wel kepe, 130
That no drope ne fille up-on hir brest.
In curteisye was set ful muche hir lest.
Hir over lippe wyped she so clene,
That in hir coppe was no ferthing sene
Of grece, whan she dronken hadde hir draughte.
Ful semely after hir mete she raughte, 136
And sikerly she was of greet disport,
And ful plesaunt, and amiable of port,

And peyned hir to countrefete chere
Of court, and been estatlich of manere, 140
And to ben holden digne of reverence.
But, for to speken of hir conscience,
She was so charitable and so pitous,
She wolde wepe, if that she sawe a mous
Caught in a trappe, if it were deed or bledde. 145
Of smale houndes had she, that she fedde
With rosted flesh, or milk and wastel breed.
But sore weep she if oon of hem were deed,
Or if men smoot it with a yerde smerte:
And al was conscience and tendre herte. 150
Ful semely hir wimpel pinched was;
Hir nose tretys; hir eyen greye as glas;
Hir mouth ful smal, and ther-to softe and reed;
But sikerly she hadde a fair forheed;
It was almost a spanne brood, I trowe; 155
For, hardily, she was nat undergrowe.
Ful fetis was hir cloke, as I was war.
Of smal coral aboute hir arm she bar
A peire of bedes, gauded al with grene;
And ther-on heng a broche of gold ful shene, 160
On which ther was first write a crowned A,
And after, *Amor vincit omnia.*

Another NONNE with hir hadde she,
That was hir chapeleyne, and PREESTES three.

A MONK ther was, a fair for the maistrye, 165
An out-rydere, that lovede venerye;
A manly man, to been an abbot able.
Ful many a deyntee hors hadde he in stable:
And, whan he rood men mighte his brydel here
Ginglen in a whistling wynd as clere, 170
And eek as loude as doth the chapel-belle
Ther as this lord was keper of the celle.
The reule of seint Maure or of seint Beneit,

100. **carf . . . table.** It was a regular duty of a squire to do the carving before a meal. 101. **YEMAN,** yeoman. Strictly speaking, he should be ranked in military service below the Squire (because he as a mere freeman would have no pretensions to chivalric knighthood), but above the groom. **namo,** no more. 102. **him liste,** it pleased him to. 106. **takel,** tackle; that is, equipment. 109. **not-heed,** head with hair cropped short or shaved. 111. **bracer,** an arm-guard worn just above the wrist to protect the archer from the impact of the string. 114. **Harneised,** armored, sheathed. 115. **Cristofre,** an emblem or image of Saint Christopher, the patron saint of foresters, whose protection he desired. 116. **bawdrik,** baldric, the cord or belt by which the horn was attached to its owner. 117. **forster,** a forester. 119. **simple,** naïve, unsophisticated. **coy,** quiet. 120. **seÿnt Loy,** St. Eloi, St. Eligius, chosen here partly for the sake of the rime, partly for the ladylike sound of the name, and possibly for some other reasons which are now obscure. 121. **cleped,** called. 124. **fetisly,** neatly, accurately. 125. **Stratford atte Bowe,** a nunnery of St. Leonard's in Bromley, Middlesex. The implication is, therefore, clear: the Prioress spoke the kind of French one would hear in a nunnery-*cum*-finishing-school of medieval England, not the true French of Paris. 132. **lest,** pleasure, joy. 134. **ferthing,** bit, trace. 136. **raughte,** reached. 137. **sikerly,** surely, certainly.

139-140. **countrefete . . . court,** a satirical thrust at the elegant manners of the Prioress, and possibly her aping of courtly custom. The word *countrefete,* unlike our modern *counterfeit,* does not suggest dishonesty or insincerity or falseness, rather mere imitation. 141. **digne,** worthy; cf. Latin *dignus.* 142. **conscience,** sensibility, tender feelings. 143. **pitous,** having pity, tender-hearted. 147. **wastel breed,** a fine white wheat-bread. 149. **yerde,** rod, stick. The *smerte* immediately following is the adverb *smartly.* 151. **pinched,** pleated, fluted. 152. **tretys,** well-formed. 156. **hardily,** surely, certainly, without need for hesitation. 159. **peire of bedes,** apparently a rosary, although *peire* is still obscure. **gauded,** covered with large beads. 161. **crowned A,** evidently a large *A* surmounted by a crown. To some this is a reference to Queen Anne, first wife of Richard II, and hence a means of dating the *Prologue,* since Anne died in 1394. 162. *Amor . . . omnia,* "Love conquers all"—proverbial. 164. **chapeleyne,** a secretary and personal assistant. **PREESTES three.** Possibly this is an error on Chaucer's part; three nun's priests would bring the total of Canterbury pilgrims up to 31, instead of the 29 mentioned in l. 24. 165. **for the maistrye,** for the mastery (of all others), hence "surpassing all others"; then loosely as an adverb, "extremely," and finally as a weak pleonastic phrase, "all right." 166. **out-rydere,** a monk who had the duty of inspecting the estates of the monastery, which were often of considerable extent. 168. **deyntee,** from the Latin *dignus;* here, "worthy," "fine." 172. **celle,** a subordinate monastery. 173. **seint Maure or of seint Beneit.** St. Benedict was the founder of monasticism in Western Europe. St. Maurus was his follower.

By-cause that it was old and som-del streit,
This ilke monk leet olde thinges pace,   175
And held after the newe world the space.
He yaf nat of that text a pulled hen,
That seith, that hunters been nat holy men;
Ne that a monk, whan he is cloisterlees,
Is lykned til a fish that is waterlees;   180
This is to seyn, a monk out of his cloystre.
But thilke text heeld he nat worth an oystre.
And I seyde his opinion was good.
What sholde he studie, and make hymselven wood,
Upon a book in cloystre alwey to poure,   185
Or swynken with his handes, and laboure,
As Austyn bit? How shal the world be served?
Lat Austyn have his swynk to him reserved.
Therfore he was a prikasour aright;
Grehoundes he hadde, as swift as fowel in flight;
Of prikyng and of huntyng for the hare   191
Was al his lust, for no cost wolde he spare.
I seigh his sleves y-purfiled at the hond
With grys, and that the fyneste of a lond;
And, for to festne his hood under his chyn,   195
He hadde of gold y-wroght a ful curious pyn:
A love-knotte in the gretter ende ther was.
His heed was balled, that shoon as any glas,
And eek his face, as it hadde been anoynt.
He was a lord ful fat and in good poynt;   200
Hise eyen stepe, and rollynge in his heed,
That stemed as a forneys of a leed;
His botes souple, his hors in greet estat.
Now certeinly he was a fair prelat;
He was nat pale as a for-pyned goost.   205
A fat swan loved he best of any roost.
His palfrey was as broun as is a berye.

    A FRERE ther was, a wantown and a merye,
A limitour, a ful solempne man.
In alle the ordres foure is noon that can   210
So muche of daliaunce and fair langage.

He hadde maad ful many a mariage
Of yonge wommen, at his owne cost.
Un-to his ordre he was a noble post.
Ful wel biloved and famulier was he   215
With frankeleyns over-al in his contree,
And eek with worthy wommen of the toun:
For he had power of confessioun,
As seyde him-self, more than a curat,
For of his ordre he was licentiat.   220
Ful swetely herde he confessioun,
And plesaunt was his absolucioun;
He was an esy man to yeve penaunce
Ther as he wiste to han a good pitaunce;
For unto a povre ordre for to yive   225
Is signe that a man is wel y-shrive.
For if he yaf, he dorste make avaunt,
He wiste that a man was repentaunt.
For many a man so hard is of his herte,
He may nat wepe al-thogh him sore smerte.   230
Therfore, in stede of weping and preyeres,
Men moot yeve silver to the povre freres.
His tipet was ay farsed ful of knyves
And pinnes, for to yeven faire wyves.
And certeinly he hadde a mery note;   235
Wel coude he singe and pleyen on a rote.
Of yeddinges he bar utterly the prys.
His nekke whyt was as the flour-de-lys;
There-to he strong was as a champioun.
He knew the tavernes wel in every toun,   240
And everich hostiler and tappestere
Bet than a lazar or a beggestere;
For un-to swich a worthy man as he
Acorded nat, as by his facultee,
To have with seke lazars aqueyntaunce.   245
It is nat honest, it may nat avaunce
For to delen with no swich poraille,
But al with riche and sellers of vitaille.
And over-al, ther as profit sholde aryse,
Curteys he was, and lowly of servyse.   250
Ther nas no man nowher so vertuous.
He was the beste beggere in his hous;
For thogh a widwe hadde noght a sho,

174. **som-del streit,** somewhat strict. 176. **the space.** This phrase is probably purely adverbial, and can be translated "meanwhile," "for the time (he held after the new ways)." 177. **yaf,** gave. **pulled hen,** plucked hen, another one of the endless symbols of the time for worthlessness. 180. **til,** to. 184. **What,** why? **wood,** mad, out of his wits. 187. **Austyn bit.** Austyn is the shortened form of Augustine, the great Church Father (354–430). *Bit* is the third person singular present indicative of *bid*, a contracted form of *biddeth*. 188. **swynk,** labor. 189. **prikasour,** a hunter on horseback. 191. **prikyng,** tracking an animal by its footprints (pricks). 193. **seigh,** saw. **y-purfiled,** trimmed at the edges. 194. **grys,** an expensive gray fur, possibly of squirrel. 197. **love-knotte,** cloth or brooch in an intertwined pattern. 200. **in good poynt,** *en bon point*, in good condition, but implying plumpness or even fatness. 202. **stemed . . . leed,** glistened or gleamed like a furnace or fire under a cauldron—a somewhat strained simile. 203. **greet estat,** fine condition. 205. **for-pyned,** tormented, wasted by torture. 208. **wantown,** gay. This description of the Friar, however, is full of sly insinuations, and the probability that he was "wanton" in the later Elizabethan sense of "sexually irregular" is more than likely to be inferred here. 209. **limitour,** a friar licensed, in return for a rental, to beg within assigned limits. **solempne,** formal, even pompous. 210. **ordres foure,** Dominicans, Franciscans, Carmelites, and Augustinians. 211. **daliaunce,** social conversation, chat; but again, the word veers here into the chivalric and modern use of the term to mean "love-caresses."

212–213. **mariage . . . cost,** he found husbands or dowries, at his own expense, for women whom he himself had seduced with embarrassing results. 214. **post,** pillar; compare the modern "pillar of the church." Note the bitter sarcasm of this line. 216. **frankeleyns,** landholders of free but not of noble birth. **over-al,** everywhere. 220. **licentiat.** The Friar had received from his Order a license to hear confession and to give absolution and penance. This practice led to considerable rivalry between mendicant friars and parish priests. The friars were often accused of making shrift altogether too easy if their palms had been acceptably greased. 223. **yeve,** give. 224. **pitaunce,** allowance, especially of food, to religious folk. 227. **make avaunt,** boast. 233. **tipet,** cape. **farsed,** stuck through, stuffed. 236. **rote,** a stringed instrument. 237. **yeddinges,** songs or ballads, originally in alliterative verse. By Chaucer's time, however, the term had been generalized to refer to any type of ballad or song. 241. **hostiler,** inn-keeper. **tappestere,** female tapster, barmaid. 242. **lazar,** leper. **beggestere,** female beggar or tramp. 246. **honest,** a good thing. **avaunce,** be helpful, advance one—apparently intransitive here. 247. **poraille,** poor folk, trash. 248. **vitaille,** victuals. 253. **sho,** shoe.

So plesaunt was his *"In principio,"*
Yet wolde he have a ferthing, er he wente.   255
His purchas was wel bettre than his rente.
And rage he coude, as it were right a whelpe.
In love-dayes ther coude he muchel helpe.
For ther he was nat lyk a cloisterer,
With a thredbar cope as is a povre scoler,   260
But he was lyk a maister or a pope.
Of double worsted was his semi-cope,
That rounded as a belle out of the presse.
Somwhat he lipsed, for his wantownesse,
To make his English swete up-on his tonge;   265
And in his harping, whan that he had songe,
His eyen twinkled in his heed aright,
As doon the sterres in the frosty night.
This worthy limitour was cleped Huberd.

A MARCHANT was ther with a forked berd,   270
In mottelee, and hye on horse he sat,
Up-on his heed a Flaundrish bever hat;
His botes clasped faire and fetisly.
His resons he spak ful solempnely,
Souninge alway th'encrees of his winning.   275
He wolde the see were kept for any thing
Bitwixe Middelburgh and Orewelle.
Wel coude he in eschaunge sheeldes selle.
This worthy man ful wel his wit bisette;
Ther wiste no wight that he was in dette,   280
So estatly was he of his governaunce,
With his bargaynes, and with his chevisaunce.
For sothe he was a worthy man with-alle,
But sooth to seyn, I noot how men him calle.

A CLERK ther was of Oxenford also,   285
That un-to logik hadde longe y-go.

As lene was his hors as is a rake,
And he nas nat right fat, I undertake;
But loked holwe, and ther-to soberly.
Ful thredbar was his overest courtepy;   290
For he had geten him yet no benefyce,
Ne was so worldly for to have offyce.
For him was lever have at his beddes heed
Twenty bokes, clad in blak or reed,
Of Aristotle and his philosophye,   295
Than robes riche, or fithele, or gay sautrye.
But al be that he was a philosophre,
Yet hadde he but litel gold in cofre;
But al that he mighte of his freendes hente,
On bokes and on lerninge he it spente,   300
And bisily gan for the soules preye
Of hem that yaf him wher-with to scoleye.
Of studie took he most cure and most hede.
Noght o word spak he more than was nede,
And that was seyd in forme and reverence,   305
And short and quik, and ful of hy sentence.
Souninge in moral vertu was his speche,
And gladly wolde he lerne, and gladly teche.

A SERGEANT OF THE LAWE, war and wys,
That often hadde been at the parvys,   310
Ther was also, ful riche of excellence.
Discreet he was, and of greet reverence:
He semed swich, his wordes weren so wyse,
Iustyce he was ful often in assyse,
By patente and by pleyn commissioun;   315
For his science, and for his heigh renoun
Of fees and robes hadde he many oon.
So greet a purchasour was nowher noon.
Al was fee simple to him in effect,

254. *"In principio,"* "in the beginning (was the Word, etc.)"—John 1: 1. These opening words of the Gospel of John were believed to have special saving, almost magical, value. 256. **His purchas . . . his rente.** What he picked up on the side (his *purchas*) amounted to more than his lawful income (his *rente*). The term *purchas* seems always to have had a somewhat sinister connotation in Middle English, applying particularly to what one comes by illegally. 257. **as it . . . whelpe,** as if he were a pup or cub. The line is unquestionably contemptuous. 258. **love-dayes,** special days set aside for the arbitration of all disputes; the clergy usually took a firm hand in the proceedings. 260. **cope,** cape, cloak. 262. **semi-cope,** short over-cloak or cape. 264. **lipsed,** lisped. 271. **mottelee,** motley, cloth with a figured design, often of more than one color. The material was frequently used for distinctive liveries among the different guildsmen. 275. **Souninge,** pertaining to, in keeping with, proclaiming. **th'encrees,** the increase or profit. 277. **Middelburgh and Orewelle.** Middelburgh is a port on the island of Walcheren on the coast of the Low Countries; Orewelle is the old port of Orwell, near Harwich, almost directly opposite Middelburgh. Here would be, in other words, a direct line for the wool trade between England and the Low Countries. Obviously, then, the Merchant would want this sea path kept free from pirates and smugglers at all costs. 278. **sheeldes,** the French *écu.* This selling of *écus* to Englishmen for profit was distinctly illegal, according to a statute of King Edward III. 279. **bisette,** used. 281. **governaunce,** demeanor. **estatly,** stately, dignified. In other words, the Merchant put up an impressive front. 282. **chevisaunce,** a term referring to borrowing and lending; it was used also loosely for any illicit income, particularly from usury. Such is its meaning here, for the Merchant is a slippery individual. 284. **noot,** *ne* plus *woot,* I know not. 286. **y-go,** gone. Here the verb is to be construed with *un-to* in the same line. "To go to logic" would mean "to study logic."

290. **courtepy,** short-coat. 291. **geten . . . benefyce,** been given no religious office. The Clerk, be it noted, is a man of clerical training preparing for the priesthood. 293. **him was lever,** he would rather. 295. **Aristotle . . . philosophye.** The amount of Aristotle's work available to the Middle Ages through Latin channels to Englishmen could easily have filled twenty volumes, but it is not sensible to assume that Chaucer meant his statement to be taken literally. Indeed, Aristotle was often a convenient name to represent all the sages of antiquity. 296. **fithele,** fiddle, violin. **sautrye,** a zither-like stringed instrument, psaltery. 299. **hente,** get, seize, acquire. 302. **to scoleye,** to go to school, to receive learning. 303. **cure,** care. 306. **hy sentence,** lofty thoughts, sentiments, or meaning. 309. SERGEANT OF THE LAWE, a legal servant of the Crown, chosen from barristers of at least sixteen years' experience. Those who were not chosen to serve as judges of the King's courts or of the Exchequer went about on circuit as justices of the assizes. In short, The Man of Law is a jurist rather than a practicing lawyer. **war and wys,** a common alliterative formula: discreet and prudent. 310. **parvys,** the porch of old St. Paul's Church in London, where members of the legal profession were accustomed to consult with their clients. 315. **patente,** letters patent from the King, making the appointment as judge. **pleyn commissioun,** the more common certificates of appointment made in the form of letters sealed and addressed to the appointee, giving him full jurisdiction. 316. **science,** knowledge (of the law). The Sergeant of the Law should certainly be considered among the heads of his profession. 318. **purchasour.** Note again the implication of this word, in reference to l. 256. But on its face value, we can take this to mean, "Such a getter never was." 319. **Al . . . in effect,** all things were in effect fee simple to him. In other words, he always got property in unrestricted possession, with a clear title (fee simple).

His purchasing mighte nat been infect.   320
No-wher so bisy a man as he ther nas,
And yet he semed bisier than he was.
In termes hadde he caas and domes alle,
That from the tyme of King William were falle.
Thereto he coude endyte, and make a thing,   325
Ther coude no wight pinche at his wryting;
And every statut coude he pleyn by rote
He rood but hoomly in a medlee cote
Girt with a ceint of silk, with barres smale;
Of his array telle I no lenger tale.   330

A FRANKELEYN was in his companye;
Whyt was his berd, as is the dayesye.
Of his complexioun he was sangwyn.
Wel loved he by the morwe a sop in wyn.
To liven in delyt was ever his wone,   335
For he was Epicurus owne sone,
That heeld opinioun, that pleyn delyt
Was verraily felicitee parfyt.
An housholdere, and that a greet, was he;
Seynt Iulian he was in his contree.   340
His breed, his ale, was alwey after oon;
A bettre envyned man was nowher noon.
With-oute bake mete was never his hous,
Of fish and flesh, and that so plentevous,
It snewed in his hous of mete and drinke,   345
Of alle deyntees that men coude thinke.
After the sondry sesons of the yeer,
So chaunged he his mete and his soper.
Ful many a fat partrich hadde he in mewe,
And many a breem and many a luce in stewe.   350
Wo was his cook, but-if his sauce were
Poynaunt and sharp, and redy al his gere

His table dormant in his halle alway
Stood redy covered al the longe day.
At sessiouns ther was he lord and sire;   355
Ful ofte tyme he was knight of the shire.
An anlas and a gipser al of silk
Heng at his girdel, whyt as morne milk.
A shirreve hadde he been, and a countour;
Was nowher such a worthy vavasour.   360
AN HABERDASSHER and a CARPENTER,
A WEBBE, a DYERE, and a TAPICER,
Were with us eek, clothed in o liveree,
Of a solempne and greet fraternitee,
Ful fresh and newe hir gere apyked was;   365
Hir knyves were y-chaped noght with bras,
But al with silver, wroght ful clene and weel.
Hir girdles and hir pouches every-deel.
Wel semed ech of hem a fair burgeys,
To sitten in a yeldhalle on a deys.   370
Everich, for the wisdom that he can,
Was shaply for to been an alderman.
For catel hadde they y-nogh and rente,
And eek hir wyves wolde it wel assente;
And elles certein were they to blame.   375
It is ful fair to been y-clept "ma dame,"
And goon to vigilyës al bifore,
And have a mantel royalliche y-bore.
A COOK they hadde with hem for the nones,
To boille chiknes with the mary-bones,   380
And poudre-marchant tart, and galingale.
Wel coude he knowe a draughte of London ale.
He coude roste, and sethe, and broille, and frye,
Maken mortreux, and wel bake a pye.
But greet harm was it, as it thoughte me,   385

320. **purchasing . . . infect,** no defect (*nat . . . infect*) could be found in his title to his possessions. 323. **caas and domes,** cases and judgments. He knew statutes and court decisions (common law) as well. Nouns ending in *s*, like *caas*, if of foreign origin, were in many instances not given plural endings. 324. **King William,** William the Conqueror (William I of England), whose passion for orderly codification of the law resulted in the famous Doomsday Book. 325. **endyte.** to write out a legal document (see note to l. 95). 326. **pinche,** object to, cavil at. 327. **coude,** knew. **by rote,** on basic principles. 328. **medlee,** cloth of mixed weave and often of many colors. The official robes of the Sergeant of Law had the colors brown and green. 329. **ceint,** girdle, sash. 330. **telle . . . tale,** I shall not tell a longer story. 333. **sangwyn,** etc. According to the older conception of the human body, before Harvey's discovery of the circulation of the blood in 1610, there were four component *humours*: blood, phlegm, bile, and black bile. These humours were held in a kind of harmony or balance, known as the *complexioun.* But all *complexiouns* showed a tendency on the part of some particular *humour* to dominate, with the result that we hear of sanguine, phlegmatic, bilious, and melancholy *complexiouns* or temperaments, according as to whether blood, phlegm, bile, or black bile predominated. The Franklin, then, was of sanguine complexion or temperament: blood predominated in his make-up; he was ruddy, cheerful, and a hearty liver. 334. **sop in wyn,** bread soaked in wine. 335. **wone,** habit, custom. 336. **Epicurus owne sone.** In other words, he was an epicure. 340. **Seynt Iulian . . . contree.** St. Julian was the patron saint of hospitality. 342. **bettre envyned,** with a better stock of wine. 348. **So chaunged . . . soper,** so did he vary his meals and his supper. 349. **mewe,** the coop or pen for birds. 350. **breem,** bream, a fish with arched back. **luce,** a luce, a pickerel. **stewe,** fish-pool. 351. **but-if,** unless. 352. **gere,** equipment, furnishings.

353. **table dormant,** a table fixed in the floor, instead of movable, intended for unexpected guests. This would be in keeping with the Franklin's noted hospitality. 355. **sessiouns,** sessions of the local courts, which were presided over by local justices of the peace, of which the Franklin was one. 356. **knight of the shire,** member of Parliament for his county. 357. **anlas,** a short, two-edged knife or dagger, sometimes referred to as an *anlace.* **gipser,** purse or pouch. 359. **shirreve,** sheriff, king's administrator in a county or shire. **countour.** This term is very vague; it might mean "accountant," or it might be a "sergeant at law" (see note to l. 309). From the mention of the Franklin's position as sheriff, it would seem that the sergeant at law is denoted here. 360. **vavasour,** a substantial landholder, not of the nobility. 362. **WEBBE,** weaver. **TAPICER,** a tapestry-maker. 365. **apyked,** adorned. 366. **y-chaped,** capped; that is, the tops of the handles of the knives were crowned with a metal piece. 368. **every-deel,** every bit, entirely. 369. **burgeys,** burgess, townsman, citizen. 370. **yeldhalle,** guild-hall. **deys,** dais, raised platform. In all town councils the mayor and his aldermen sat on the dais; the common councilors on the floor. 372. **shaply,** suitable, fitted. 373. **catel,** property in general, rather than cattle in particular. 377. **vigilyës.** Each guild had a certain day in the year dedicated to it, usually the saint's day of its patron saint. The *vigilyë* was the celebration held on the eve of the feast-day. 378. **y-bore,** carried, borne. 379. **for the nones,** for that one time, for the occasion, but often a rather meaningless expletive like the modern "all right." "They had a cook with them for the occasion," however, makes fairly good sense as it stands. 380. **mary-bones,** marrowbones. 381. **poudre-marchant tart,** a tart made with a heavy coating of a sweetish flavoring-powder. **galingale,** the extract of sweet cyperus. 384. **mortreux.** The *x* was probably pronounced as an *s.* This was a thick soup or stew.

That on his shine a mormal hadde he;
For blankmanger, that made he with the beste.

A SHIPMAN was ther, woning fer by weste:
For aught I woot, he was of Dertemouthe.
He rood up-on a rouncy as he couthe,   390
In a gowne of falding to the knee.
A daggere hanging on a laas hadde he
Aboute his nekke under his arm adoun.
The hote somer had maad his hewe al broun;
And, certeinly, he was a good felawe.   395
Ful many a draughte of wyn had he y-drawe
From Burdeux-ward, whyl that the chapman sleep.
Of nyce conscience took he no keep.
If that he faught, and hadde the hyer hond,
By water he sente hem hoom to every lond.   400
But of his craft to rekene wel his tydes,
His stremes and his daungers him bisydes,
His herberwe and his mone, his lodemenage,
Ther nas noon swich from Hulle to Cartage.
Hardy he was, and wys to undertake;   405
With many a tempest hadde his berd been shake.
He knew wel alle the havenes, as they were,
From Gootlond to the cape of Finistere,
And every cryke in Britayne and in Spayne;
His barge y-cleped was the Maudelayne.   410

With us ther was a DOCTOUR OF PHISYK,
In al this worlde ne was ther noon him lyk
To speke of phisik and of surgerye;
For he was grounded in astronomye.
He kepte his pacient a ful greet del   415
In houres, by his magik naturel.

Wel coude he fortunen the ascendent
Of his images for his pacient.
He knew the cause of everich maladye,
Were it of hoot or cold, or moiste, or drye,   420
And where engendred, and of what humour;
He was a verray parfit practisour.
The cause y-knowe, and of his harm the roote,
Anon he yaf the seke man his boote.
Ful redy hadde he his apothecaries,   425
To sende him drogges, and his letuaries,
For ech of hem made other for to winne;
Hir frendschipe nas nat newe to biginne.
Wel knew he th'olde Esculapius,
And Deiscorides, and eek Rufus,   430
Old Ypocras, Haly, and Galien;
Serapion, Razis, and Avicen;
Averrois, Damascien, and Constantyn;
Bernard, and Gatesden, and Gilbertyn.
Of his diete mesurable was he,   435
For it was of no superfluitee,
But of greet norissing and digestible.
His studie was but litel on the bible.
In sangwin and in pers he clad was al,
Lyned with taffata and with sendal;   440
And yet he was but esy of dispence;
He kepte that he wan in pestilence.
For gold in phisik is a cordial,
Therfor he lovede gold in special.

A good WYF was ther of bisyde BATHE,   445
But she was som-del deef, and that was scathe.

386. **mormal,** an ulcer, a running sore. 387. **blankmanger,** creamed meat stewed with rice, eggs, sugar, and sometimes nuts; not the modern "blanc-mange." 388. SHIPMAN, a seafaring man, but here the captain of a ship. **woning,** dwelling. 390. **rouncy.** This word, strangely enough, appears in the equivocal meanings of (1) a broken-down nag, and (2) a good strong horse. The reader can take his choice. **as he couthe,** as best he knew how; the sailor would not be expected to ride like a knight. 391. **falding,** a coarse woolen cloth. 392. **laas,** a string or cord; compare the modern shoe*lace.* 397. **whyl . . . sleep,** while the merchant napped. The Shipman stole much of the wine which he was carrying for a merchant; he extracted, in other words, some of the cargo which had been entrusted to him. 398. **nyce conscience,** foolish scruples or tender feelings. 400. **By water . . . every lond.** Presumably the Shipman could turn to piracy and sink his victim's ship or drown his prisoners. 402. **daungers,** here a kind of generic term for which tides, currents, moons, and compass-bearings would be specific details; in short, factors governing his business of navigation. The word *daunger* in Middle English is always close to its Latin source, the verb *dominare,* to rule or control. 403. **herberwe,** lodgings as applied to a shipman, his harbor or anchorage. **lodemenage,** pilotage. 404. **Cartage,** not ancient Carthage, but one of the Spanish ports, Cartagena. 408. **Gootlond,** the island of Gothland, off the coast of Sweden in the Baltic. **Finistere,** the westernmost point in the Iberian Peninsula, in Spain. 414. **astronomye.** The science which the scholars of the Middle Ages called astronomy is nearer what we would call today the pseudoscience of astrology than modern astronomy, inasmuch as all natural phenomena observable in the heavens were supposed to have direct bearing upon the lives of men. Even a physician, therefore, would in the Middle Ages have to be cognizant of the natural laws of astronomy, as they were then understood. 415–416. **kepte . . . In houres . . . magik naturel.** The physician watched his patient for the times most advantageous to his treatment. "Magik naturel" is what we would today term the doctor's scientific medical knowledge.

417. **fortunen,** place in a favorable position. **ascendent,** that degree of the ecliptic (the celestial path of the sun) which is rising at any given time. It would have to lie in one of the twelve constellations (signs) of the zodiac, since the zodiacal constellations are those through which the ecliptic runs. The Physician, then, was skillful at picking ascendants that showed a favorable grouping of beneficent planets and constellations, and an arrangement of malefic constellations and planets at points where they would do the least harm to the patient. 418. **images,** either representations of the patient in wax or clay figures, or talismans representing the different signs of the zodiac, which any astrological chart will furnish to the modern reader. By exposing these images to the firmament when there was a favorable ascendant, the Physician was supposed to work wonders with the patient's condition. 420. **hoot . . . drye.** There were four elementary "qualities," consisting of contrary attributes, which in combinations produced the four elements: (1) cold and dry (Earth); (2) hot and moist (Air); (3) cold and moist (Water); (4) hot and dry (Fire). 421. **humour.** See note to l. 333. The humours were similarly produced by the combination of contrary attributes: (1) hot and moist (Blood); (2) cold and moist (Phlegm); (3) hot and dry (Bile); (4) cold and dry (Black Bile). This conception goes back to Hippocrates and Galen. 424. **boote,** remedy. 426. **letuaries,** electuaries, remedies. 429–434. **Esculapius . . . Gilbertyn.** This is a noteworthy list of the great names in medicine prior to and contemporaneous with Chaucer. 435. **mesurable,** moderate. 439. **sangwin,** a cloth of blood-red color. **pers,** a cloth of Persian blue or azure. 440. **sendal,** a thin kind of silk. 441. **esy of dispence,** slow (easy-going) about spending. 442. **pestilence,** not necessarily the Black Death, although such an allusion is certainly possible here, but simply any kind of epidemic. 443. **gold . . . cordial.** Gold in solution, *aurum potabile,* was a sovereign remedy for desperate diseases, but the word "cordial" means specifically a heart stimulant, and Chaucer may therefore imply that gold in his profession was a heart-warming thing to the Physician, perhaps more heart-warming than his Hippocratic oath called for. 446. **som-del,** somewhat. **scathe,** a pity.

Of clooth-making she hadde swiche an haunt,
She passed hem of Ypres and of Gaunt.
In al the parisshe wyf ne was ther noon
That to th' offring bifore hir sholde goon;   450
And if ther dide, certeyn, so wrooth was she,
That she was out of alle charitee.
Hir coverchiefs ful fyne were of ground;
I dorste swere they weyeden ten pound
That on a Sonday were upon hir heed.   455
Hir hosen weren of fyn scarlet reed.
Ful streite y-teyd, and shoos ful moiste and newe.
Bold was hir face, and fair, and reed of hewe.
She was a worthy womman al hir lyve,
Housbondes at chirche-dore she hadde fyve,   460
Withouten other companye in youthe;
But thereof nedeth nat to speke as nouthe.
And thryes hadde she been at Jerusalem;
She hadde passed many a straunge streem;
At Rome she hadde been, and at Boloigne,   465
In Galice at seint Jame, and at Cologne.
She coude muche of wandring by the weye:
Gat-tothed was she, soothly for to seye.
Up-on an amblere esily she sat,
Y-wimpled wel, and on hir heed an hat   470
As brood as is a bokeler or a targe;
A foot-mantel aboute hir hipes large,
And on hir feet a paire of spores sharpe.
In felawschip wel coude she laughe and carpe.
Of remedyes of love she knew perchaunce,   475
For she coude of that art the olde daunce.

A good man was ther of religioun,
And was a povre PERSOUN of a toun;
But riche he was of holy thoght and werk.
He was also a lerned man, a clerk,   480
That Cristes gospel trewely wolde preche;
His parisshens devoutly wolde he teche.
Benigne he was, and wonder diligent,
And in adversitee ful pacient;
And swich he was y-preved ofte sythes.   485
Ful looth were him to cursen for his tythes,

But rather wolde he yeven, out of doute,
Un-to his povre parisshens aboute
Of his offring, and eek of his substaunce.
He coude in litel thing han suffisaunce.   490
Wyd was his parisshe, and houses fer a-sonder,
But he ne lafte nat, for reyn ne thonder,
In siknes nor in meschief, to visyte
The ferreste in his parisshe, muche and lyte,
Up-on his feet, and in his hand a staf.   495
This noble ensample to his sheep he yaf,
That first he wroghte, and afterward he taughte;
Out of the gospel he tho wordes caughte;
And this figure he added eek ther-to,
That if gold ruste, what shal yren do?   500
For if a preest be foul, on whom we truste,
No wonder is a lewed man to ruste;
And shame it is, if a preest take keep,
A shiten shepherde and a clene sheep.
Wel oghte a preest ensample for to yive,   505
By his clennesse, how that his sheep shold live.
He sette nat his benefice to hyre,
And leet his sheep encombred in the myre,
And ran to London, un-to seynt Poules,
To seken him a chaunterie for soules,   510
Or with a bretherhed to been withholde;
But dwelte at hoom, and kepte wel his folde,
So that the wolf ne made it nat miscarie;
He was a shepherde and no mercenarie.
And though he holy were, and vertuous,   515
He was to sinful man nat despitous,
Ne of his speche daungerous ne digne,
But in his teching discreet and benigne.
To drawen folk to heven by fairnesse
By good ensample, was his bisinesse: 520
But if were any persone obstinat,
What so he were, of heigh or lowe estat,
Him wolde he snibben sharply for the nones.
A bettre preest, I trowe that nowher noon is.
He wayted after no pompe and reverence,   525
Ne maked him a spyced conscience,
But Cristes lore, and his apostles twelve,
He taughte, but first he folwed it him-selve.

447. **swiche an haunt,** such a skill or practice. 448. **Ypres . . .
Gaunt.** Ypres and Ghent were two important centers of the Flemish
textile trade. 453. **coverchiefs,** kerchiefs, head-scarves. **ground,**
texture. 454–455. **they weyeden . . . hir heed.** Women of fashion
in England during the late fourteenth and early fifteenth centuries
wore extremely elaborate and heavy headdress. 462. **as nouthe,** as
now, at this moment. 466. **seint Jame,** etc. The places mentioned
in reference to the pilgrimages of the Wife of Bath were the choicest
shrines in the Western world of the time. *Seint Jame* is the shrine
of Saint James of Compostella in Spain. 468. **Gat-tothed,** with teeth
set far apart, "gap-toothed" or "gate-toothed." The medieval mind
associated this characteristic with sensuality. 469. **amblere,** an
ambling or easy-paced horse. 471. **targe,** a large round shield. 472.
foot-mantel, an outer riding-skirt. 474. **carpe,** discourse greatly.
475. **remedyes of love,** cures for love; the conduct of the suitor and
of the rejected lover, and the discussion of all other features of lovemaking, so far as the Middle Ages went, were to be found in Ovid's
Ars Amoris, one section of which, the *Remedia Amoris,* was devoted
to the question of remedies. 478. **PERSOUN,** parson, parish priest.
482. **parisshens,** parishioners. 485. **y-preved,** proved. **ofte sythes,**
oftentimes, many times. 486. **cursen,** to curse in the sense of ex-
communicate for nonpayment of tithes.

493. **meschief,** misfortune. 494. **ferreste** farthest, most remote.
muche and lyte, high and low (in social rank). 500. **if gold . . .
yren do?** This expression is proverbial, particularly in the medieval
French didactic romances. 502. **lewed,** ignorant, unlearned; hence,
a layman. The modern meaning, highly specialized in a moral sense,
is comparatively recent. 507. **sette . . . to hyre,** he did not rent
his churchly office to someone else, while he went up to London, etc.
510. **chaunterie,** a provision whereby a priest was to sing a daily
mass for the repose of a soul. There were many such at St. Paul's in
London, whither the more self-seeking clergymen tried to go, but
after 1391 only minor canons of the Cathedral were allowed to sing
chantries, and the abuse diminished. 511. **a bretherhed . . . withholde,** to be retained by a guild as a chaplain—an additional source of
income for a worldly priest. 513. **wolf,** "the world, the flesh, and the
Devil." 516. **despitous,** spiteful and contemptuous. 517. **daungerous,** arrogant, arbitrary (see note to l. 402). **digne,** haughty. 523.
snibben, snub, chide, rebuke. **for the nones,** here loosely used; an
expletive, "all right." See note to l. 379. 526. **spyced conscience,**
oversweetened feelings.

With him ther was a PLOWMAN, was his brother,
That hadde y-lad of dong ful many a fother,   530
A trewe swinker and a good was he,
Livinge in pees and parfit charitee.
God loved he best with al his hole herte
At alle tymes, thogh him gamed or smerte,
And thanne his neighebour right as him-selve.   535
He wolde thresshe, and ther-to dyke and delve,
For Cristes sake, for every povre wight,
Withouten hyre, if it lay in his might.
His tythes payed he full faire and wel,
Bothe of his propre swink and his catel.   540
In a tabard he rood upon a mere.

   Ther was also a Reve and a Millere,
A Somnour and a Pardoner also,
A Maunciple, and my-self; ther were namo.

   The MILLER was a stout carl, for the nones,   545
Ful big he was of braun, and eek of bones;
That proved wel, for over-al ther he cam,
At wrastling he wolde have alwey the ram.
He was short-sholdred, brood, a thikke knarre,
Ther nas no dore that he nolde heve of harre,   550
Or breke it, at a renning, with his heed.
His berd as any sowe or fox was reed,
And ther-to brood, as though it were a spade.
Up-on the cop right of his nose he hade
A werte, and ther-on stood a tuft of heres,   555
Reed as the bristles of a sowes eres;
His nose-thirles blake were and wyde.
A swerd and bokeler bar he by his syde;
His mouth as greet was as a greet forneys.

He was a janglere and a goliardeys,   560
And that was most of sinne and harlotryes.
Wel coude he stelen corn, and tollen thryes,
And yet he hadde a thombe of gold, pardee.
A whyt cote and blew hood wered he.
A baggepype wel coude he blowe and sowne,   565
And therwithal he broghte us out of towne.

   A gentil MAUNCIPLE was ther of a temple,
Of which achatours mighte take exemple
For to be wyse in bying of vitaille.
For whether that he payde, or took by taille,   570
Algate he wayted so in his achat,
That he was ay biforn and in good stat.
Now is nat that of God a ful fair grace,
That swich a lewed mannes wit shal pace
The wisdom of an heep of lerned men?   575
Of maistres hadde he mo than thryes ten,
That were of lawe expert and curious;
Of which ther were a doseyn in that hous
Worthy to been stiwardes of rente and lond
Of any lord that is in Engelond,   580
To make him live by his propre good,
In honour dettelees, but he were wood,
Or live as scarsly as him list desire;
And able for to helpen al a shire
In any cas that mighte falle or happe;   585
And yit this maunciple sette hir aller cappe.

   The REVE was a sclendre colerik man,
His berd was shave as ny as ever he can.
His heer was by his eres round y-shorn.
His top was dokked lyk a preest biforn.   590
Ful longe were his legges, and ful lene,
Y-lyk a staf, ther was no calf y-sene.
Wel coude he kepe a gerner and a binne;
Ther was noon auditor coude on him winne.
Wel wist he, by the droghte, and by the reyn,   595
The yeldyng of his seed, and of his greyn.

530. **y-lad**, led, pulled. **fother**, load. 531. **swinker**, laborer. 533–535. **God loved . . . neighebour . . . him-selve.** This "eleventh" commandment is found expressed most completely in Matthew, 22: 37–39. 534. **him gamed or smerte**, he was pleased to or was reluctant to. Note the impersonal construction, extremely common in Middle English. The general effect of the clause is "under all circumstances." 536. **dyke**, dig, make a ditch. The phrase dyke and delve is an alliterative formula, both words meaning almost the same thing. 541. **tabard.** See note to l. 20. 542. **Reve.** This official's duties were many and vague. If the steward (or seneschal) was the manager of a feudal estate, his immediate subordinate would be the bailiff, who would enforce the statutes of the estate and collect taxes, etc. The Reeve was apparently subordinate to the bailiff, but in some cases he was superior, as in the case of Chaucer's Reeve. 543. **Somnour**, an officer of the ecclesiastical courts; in effect, a policeman for all offenses involving a breach of ecclesiastical law (rather than civil law). **Pardoner.** Pardoners were distributors of papal indulgences, sometimes for money. In many instances, pardoners were not even ordained clergymen, and were itinerant and irresponsible in consequence. Their capacity for dishonesty is vouched for unanimously by the writers of the time. Some, however, like Chaucer's Pardoner, were even allowed to preach. 544. **Maunciple**, the purchasing agent for a college of law or any similar institution, such as an Inn of Court or a college at Oxford or Cambridge; note *The Reeve's Tale*, p. II:216, l. 73. **namo**, no more. 545. **carl**, fellow, churl. **for the nones.** See note to l. 523. 548. **wrastling . . . the ram.** At country fairs, wrestling was one of the favorite diversions. The prize for the winner of a contest was often some livestock, such as a ram or goat. 549. **knarre**, literally, a knot of wood; hence, a tough individual. There may be a trace of our contemptuous *blockhead* present in the meaning of the word. 550. **of harre**, from the hinge. Note the original sense of *of*. 551. **renning.** The Miller could break down any door by running at it with his head in the role of battering ram. 554. **cop**, top. 557. **nose-thirles**, nostrils.

560. **janglere**, a chatterbox, one who talks incessantly and to little purpose. **goliardeys**, a retailer of smutty stories. By Chaucer's time the word had come to signify merely a coarse buffoon. 562. **tollen thryes**, take toll three times; that is, charge excessively. 563. **a thombe of gold**, referring to the skill of the Miller in testing the fineness of flour with his thumb, thereby learning its value. English bakers still know how to do this. There was an old proverb, "An honest miller has a thumb of gold," indicating that the miller's thumb, thus used honestly, was worth money to him. On the other hand, taken satirically, this proverb might indicate that there was no such thing as an honest miller. 565. **sowne**, sound forth, play. 567. **MAUNCIPLE.** See note to l. 544. **temple**, possibly the Inner or Middle Temple near the Strand in London, occupied in Chaucer's time by societies of lawyers. 568. **achatours**, buyers, caterers. 570. **took by taille**, took by tally, took on credit. The "tally" was a stick on which the amount of the debt was notched. 571. **Algate**, always, any way, in any case. **achat**, purchase, buying. 572. **in good stat**, in good financial standing. 577. **curious**, having care for, diligent, skillful. 586. **sette hir aller cappe**, "set the cap of them all," a slang expression of the time for "made fools of them all." 587. **colerik**, choleric, one in whom the humour *choler* (bile) predominated; see notes to ll. 333 and 421. Such a man would be "hot and dry"—the lean, sallow, wiry, nervous type. 590. **dokked**, docked, shorn. This was a sign of his servile station, one relic of which is the old practice of shaving the heads of convicts. 593. **gerner**, garner, granary. 594. **on him winne**, get any profit with him around.

His lordes sheep, his neet, his dayerye,
His swyn, his hors, his stoor, and his pultrye,
Was hoolly in this reves governing,
And by his covenaunt yaf the rekening, 600
Sin that his lord was twenty yeer of age;
Ther coude no man bringe him in arrerage.
Ther nas baillif, ne herde, ne other hyne,
That he ne knew his sleighte and his covyne,
They were adrad of him, as of the deeth. 605
His woning was ful fair up-on an heeth,
With grene treës shadwed was his place.
He coude bettre than his lord purchace.
Ful riche he was astored prively,
His lord wel coude he plesen subtilly, 610
To yeve and lene him of his owne good,
And have a thank, and yet a cote, and hood.
In youthe he lerned hadde a good mister;
He was a wel good wrighte, a carpenter.
This reve sat up-on a ful good stot, 615
That was al pomely grey, and highte Scot.
A long surcote of pers up-on he hade,
And by his syde he bar a rusty blade.
Of Northfolk was this reve, of which I telle,
Bisyde a toun men clepen Baldeswelle. 620
Tukked he was, as is a frere, aboute,
And ever he rood the hindreste of our route.

A Somnour was ther with us in that place,
That hadde a fyr-reed cherubinnes face,
For sawceflem he was, with eyen narwe. 625
As hoot he was, and lecherous, as a sparwe;
With scalled browes blake, and piled berd;
Of his visage children were aferd.
Ther nas quik-silver, litarge, ne brimstoon,
Boras, ceruce, ne oille of tartre noon, 630
Ne oynement that wolde clense and byte,

That him mighte helpen of his whelkes whyte,
Ne of the knobbes sittinge on his chekes.
Wel loved he garleek, oynons, and eek lekes,
And for to drinken strong wyn, reed as blood. 635
Thanne wolde he speke, and crye as he were wood.
And whan that he wel dronken hadde the wyn,
Than wolde he speke no word but Latyn.
A fewe termes hadde he, two or thre,
That he had lerned out of som decree; 640
No wonder is, he herde it al the day;
And eek ye knowen wel, how that a jay
Can clepen "Watte," as well as can the pope.
But who-so coude in other thing him grope,
Thanne hadde he spent al his philosophye; 645
Ay "Questio quid iuris" wolde he crye.
He was a gentil harlot and a kynde;
A bettre felawe sholde men noght fynde.
He wolde suffre, for a quart of wyn,
A good felawe to have his concubyn 650
A twelf-month, and excuse him atte fulle;
And prively a finch eek coude he pulle.
And if he fond o-wher a good felawe,
He wolde techen him to have non awe,
In swich cas, of the erchedeknes curs, 655
But-if a mannes soule were in his purs;
For in his purs he sholde y-punisshed be.
"Purs is the erchedeknes helle," seyde he.
But wel I woot he lyed right in dede;
Of cursing oghte ech gilty man him drede— 660
For curs wol slee, right as assoilling saveth—
And also war him of a significavit.
In daunger hadde he at his owne gyse
The yonge girles of the diocyse,
And knew hir counseil, and was al hir reed. 665
A gerland hadde he set up-on his heed,
As greet as it were for an ale-stake;
A bokeler hadde he maad him of a cake.
    With him ther rood a gentil Pardoner
Of Rouncival, his freend and his compeer, 670
That streight was comen fro the court of Rome.

597. **neet,** domestic animals, but usually specifying cattle. 598. **stoor,** general possessions, but possibly specialized to livestock. 601. **Sin,** since. 602. **bringe . . . arrerage,** no man could catch him in arrears; his books were always up to the minute. 603. **herde,** herdsman, shepherd. **hyne,** servant. 604. **covyne,** etc. The Reeve knew all their tricks (*sleights*) and their deceits (*covyne*). 605. **adrad,** afraid of, in dread of. **the deeth.** With the definite article before it, this word usually signifies in Middle English plague or pestilence. 606. **woning,** dwelling. 609. **astored,** provided for. 613. **mister,** trade, profession; see the French *métier*. 615. **stot,** stallion. 616. **pomely,** dappled, with spots like an apple; note the French *pomme.* **highte,** was called. 617. **surcote,** outer coat, overcoat. 620. **Baldeswelle,** Bawdswell in northern Norfolkshire, the property of the Pembroke family, whom Chaucer may have once served as deputy. The specific locality mentioned leads us to suspect that here, as often in other instances, Chaucer had a real person in mind for the prototype of the Reeve, but the matter is still speculative. 621. **Tukked,** with his coat hitched up and held with a girdle. 622. **hindreste,** farthest behind, the last in line. Since the Reeve later has a violent quarrel with the Miller, who led the way playing his bagpipe (note l. 566), it is significant that the two men are as far apart as possible. 625. **sawceflem,** pimpled, erupted. The Summoner was suffering from a skin disease akin to leprosy. 627. **scalled,** scaly, scabby. **piled,** scanty, moth-eaten, with hair falling out in patches. 629. **litarge,** the protoxide of lead used in an ointment. The remedies mentioned in these lines were the stock remedies for skin diseases during the Middle Ages; some of them, the mercury and sulphur particularly, still are of value. 630. **ceruce,** white lead.

632. **whelkes,** pustules, blotches. 643. "**Watte,**" the diminutive of Walter. Parrots were evidently taught to call out (*clepen*) "Watte!" instead of our traditional "Polly!" 644. **grope,** question, test. 646. "*Questio quid iuris,*" "the question is, what (part) of the law (applies)?"—apparently a familiar piece of legalistic jargon. 647. **harlot,** rascal, not necessarily limited to the female of the species. 651. **atte fulle,** at the full, fully; the same formation as *atte beste* (see note to l. 29). 652. **prively . . . pulle,** secretly . . . pluck a finch, a slang phrase of highly indecent nature. 653. **o-wher,** anywhere. 661. **assoilling,** absolution. 662. *significavit,* the first word in the writ which sent a person to prison following excommunication, the gravest penalty which an ecclesiastical court could impose. 663. **daunger.** Here, as is usual in Chaucer, the meaning is "power," "control." **at his owne gyse,** at his own discretion. 664. **girles,** young people of either sex, not young females only. 667. **ale-stake.** As a sign, every inn had a stake projecting horizontally over the door, on which was suspended a hoop (or *gerland,* l. 666) decorated with ivy leaves—a symbol of festivity. The Summoner's wreath of flowers was not unusual among church people on special occasions, such as an ecclesiastical procession or a pilgrimage. 670. **Rouncival,** the hospital of the Blessed Mary of Rouncivale, near Charing Cross, London. **compeer,** comrade.

Ful loude he song, "Com hider, love, to me."
This somnour bar to him a stif burdoun,
Was nevere trompe of half so greet a soun.
This pardoner hadde heer as yelow as wex, 675
But smothe it heng, as doth a strike of flex;
By ounces henge his lokkes that he hadde,
And there-with he his shuldres overspradde;
But thinne it lay, by colpons oon and oon;
But hood, for jolitee, ne wered he noon, 680
For it was trussed up in his walet.
Him thoughte, he rood al of the newe jet;
Dischevele, save his cappe, he rood al bare.
Swiche glaringe eyen hadde he as an hare.
A vernicle hadde he sowed on his cappe. 685
His walet lay biforn him in his lappe,
Bret-ful of pardoun come from Rome al hoot.
A voys he hadde as smal as hath a goot.
No berd hadde he, ne never sholde have.
As smothe it was as it were late y-shave; 690
I trowe he were a gelding or a mare.
But of his craft, fro Berwik into Ware,
Ne was ther swich another pardoner.
For in his male he hadde a pilwe-beer,
Which that, he seyde, was our lady veyl: 695
He seyde, he hadde a gobet of the seyl
That seynt Peter hadde, whan that he wente
Up-on the see, til Jesu Crist him hente.
He hadde a croys of latoun, ful of stones,
And in a glas he hadde pigges bones. 700
But with thise relikes, whan that he fond
A povre person dwelling up-on lond,
Up-on a day he gat him more moneye
Than that the person gat in monthes tweye.
And thus with feyned flaterye and japes, 705
He made the person and the peple his apes.
But trewely to tellen, atte laste,
He was in chirche a noble ecclesiaste.
Wel coude he rede a lessoun or a storie,
But alderbest he song an offertorie; 710
For wel he wiste, whan that song was songe,

He moste preche, and wel affyle his tonge,
To winne silver, as he ful wel coude;
Therefore he song so meriely and loude.
    Now have I told you shortly, in a clause, 715
Th'estat, th'array, the nombre, and eek the cause
Why that assembled was this companye
In Southwerk, at this gentil hostelrye,
That highte the Tabard, faste by the Belle.
But now is tyme to yow for to telle 720
How that we baren us that ilke night,
Whan we were in that hostelrye alight.
And after wol I telle of our viage,
And al the remenaunt of our pilgrimage.
But first I pray yow, of your curteisye, 725
That ye n'arette it nat my vileinye,
Though that I pleynly speke in this matere,
To telle yow hir wordes and hir chere;
Ne thogh I speke hir wordes proprely.
For this ye knowen al-so wel as I, 730
Who-so shal telle a tale after a man,
He moot reherce, as ny as ever he can,
Everich a word, if it be in his charge,
Al speke he never so rudeliche and large;
Or elles he moot telle his tale untrewe, 735
Or feyne thing, or finde wordes newe.
He may nat spare, al-though he were his brother;
He moot as wel seye o word as another.
Crist spak him-self ful brode in holy writ,
And wel ye woot, no vileinye is it. 740
Eek Plato seith, who-so that can him rede,
The wordes mote be cosin to the dede.
Also I prey yow to foryeve it me,
Al have I nat set folk in hir degree
Here in this tale, as that they sholde stonde; 745
My wit is short, ye may wel understonde.
    Greet chere made our hoste us everichon,
And to the soper sette he us anon;
And served us with vitaille at the beste.

672. "Com . . . to me," probably the first line of a current popular song.   673. stif burdoun, a stout "burden," or basic ground-melody (bass).   676. strike, a bunch (of flax).   677. ounces, small tufts or bunches.   679. colpons, shreds, strips.   681. trussed up, packed up, stuffed.   682. al of the newe jet, all in the new manner or style. 685. vernicle, a little "veronica," a copy of the handkerchief which tradition says St. Veronica lent to Christ during the march to Calvary, and which was said to bear the imprint of His face.   687. Bret-ful, brimful.   692. Berwik into Ware. Berwik is undoubtedly Berwick, at the mouth of the River Tweed in Northumberland, the town at the northeastern extremity of England. Ware is in Hertfordshire and is hardly the southernmost town of importance in England. Chaucer merely wishes to say that there was not another Pardoner like him in all England.   694. male, bag. pilwe-beer, pillow-case. 696. gobet, piece, fragment.   698. hente, caught. The episode referred to is to be found in Matthew, 14: 22–33.   699. croys of latoun, a cross of latten, an alloy of copper and zinc.   702–704. person, parson. This is a direct reference to the friction that arose between parish priests and mendicant friars and pardoners; see note to l. 220.   705. japes, japes, jests, jokes.   707. atte laste, at the last, finally; see atte beste (l. 29) and atte fulle (l. 651).   710. alderbest, best of all; for alder- (aller-) see note to l. 586.

712. affyle, file, smooth off and sharpen.   719. the Tabard . . . the Belle. For the Tabard and its general location in Southwark, see note to l. 20; the Belle has not been identified certainly, although several inns by that name have been located in Southwark—none, however, authentically dated before 1600.   726. n'arette, etc., do not impute or ascribe. Chaucer's disclaimer of responsibility here is extremely interesting, since he is deliberately telling the reader or listener of his intention to be as realistic as a true reporter should be.   734. Al, although. The inverted word order in a clause introduced by a concessive conjunction (Al speke he instead of Al he speke) is characteristic of Chaucer's syntax.   735. moot, must.   741. Plato. The great Greek philosopher (p. 1:258) and his works were probably known to Chaucer not through the original work, but through Latin derivatives, such as Boethius' Consolation of Philosophy.   747. our hoste. The Host, whose description begins with this line, is certainly one of the most important figures in the Canterbury pilgrimage, although he appears only in the framework of The Canterbury Tales. He serves as interlocutor and as master of ceremonies, and his reactions to the different stories seem to have been intended by Chaucer as the reactions of a typical English fourteenth-century middle-class burgeys. His identity with Henry or Harry Bailly, an actual innkeeper of Southwark, who appears in historical documents, has been reasonably well established. Undoubtedly he is the most "historical" member of the pilgrimage except Chaucer himself. everichon, every one.

Strong was the wyn, and wel to drinke us leste. 750
A semely man our hoste was with-alle
For to han been a marshal in an halle;
A large man he was with eyen stepe,
A fairer burgeys was ther noon in Chepe:
Bold of his speche, and wys, and wel y-taught, 755
And of manhood him lakkede right naught.
Eek thereto he was right a mery man,
And after soper pleyen he bigan,
And spak of mirthe amonges othere thinges,
Whan that we hadde maad our rekeninges; 760
And seyde thus: "Now, lordinges, trewely,
Ye ben to me right welcome hertely:
For by my trouthe, if that I shal nat lye,
I ne saught this yeer so mery a companye
At ones in this herberwe as is now. 765
Fayn wolde I doon yow mirthe, wiste I how.
And of a mirthe I am right now bithoght,
To doon yow ese, and it shal coste noght.
"Ye goon to Caunterbury; God yow spede,
The blisful martir quyte yow your mede. 770
And wel I woot, as ye goon by the weye,
Ye shapen yow to talen and to pleye;
For trewely, confort ne mirthe is noon
To ryde by the weye doumb as a stoon;
And therfore wol I maken yow disport, 775
As I seyde erst, and doon yow som confort.
And if yow lyketh alle, by oon assent,
Now for to stonden at my jugement,
And for to werken as I shal yow seye,
To-morwe, whan ye ryden by the weye, 780
Now, by my fader soule, that is deed,
But ye be merye, I wol yeve yow myn heed.
Hold up your hond, withouten more speche."
Our counseil was nat longe for to seche;
Us thoughte it was noght worth to make it wys, 785
And graunted him withouten more avys,
And bad him seye his verdit, as him leste.
"Lordinges," quod he, "now herkneth for the
            beste;
But tak it not, I prey yow, in desdeyn;
This is the poynt, to speken short and pleyn, 790
That ech of yow, to shorte with your weye,
In this viage, shal telle tales tweye,
To Caunterbury-ward, I mene it so,
And hom-ward he shal tellen othere two,

Of aventures that whylom han bifalle. 795
And which of yow that bereth him best of alle,
That is to seyn, that telleth in this cas
Tales of best sentence and most solas,
Shal have a soper at our aller cost
Here in this place, sitting by this post, 800
Whan that we come agayn fro Caunterbury.
And for to make yow the more mery,
I wol my-selven gladly with yow ryde,
Right at myn owne cost, and be your gyde.
And who-so wol my jugement withseye 805
Shal paye al that we spenden by the weye.
And if ye vouche-sauf that it be so,
Tel me anon, with-outen wordes mo,
And I wol erly shape me therfore."
This thing was graunted, and our othes swore
With ful glad herte, and preyden him also 811
That he wold vouche-sauf for to do so,
And that he wolde been our governour,
And of our tales juge and reportour,
And sette a soper at a certeyn prys; 815
And we wold reuled been at his devys,
In heigh and lowe; and thus, by oon assent,
We been acorded to his jugement
And ther-up-on the wyn was fet anoon;
We dronken, and to reste wente echon, 820
With-outen any lenger taryinge.
A-morwe, whan that day bigan to springe,
Up roos our host, and was our aller cok,
And gadrede us togidre, alle in a flok,
And forth we riden, a litel more than pas, 825
Un-to the watering of seint Thomas.
And there our host bigan his hors areste,
And seyde; "Lordinges, herkneth if yow leste.
Ye woot your forward, and I it yow recorde.
If even-song and morwe-song acorde, 830
Lat se now who shal telle the firste tale.
As ever mote I drinke wyn or ale,
Who-so be rebel to my jugement
Shal paye for al that by the weye is spent.
Now draweth cut, er that we ferrer twinne, 835
He which that hath the shortest shal beginne.
Sire knight," quod he, "my maister and my lord,
Now draweth cut, for that is myn acord.
Cometh neer," quod he, "my lady prioresse;
And ye, sir clerk, lat be your shamfastnesse, 840
Ne studieth noght; ley hond to, every man."
Anon to drawen every wight bigan,

750. **us leste,** it pleased us. 752. **marshal in an halle;** that is, the Host was imposing enough in personality to have been a marshal in any assembly of people. 754. **Chepe,** Cheapside, one of the principal London streets of the time. 758. **pleyen,** a very vague word, not as definite even as our modern *play.* Here the meaning is simply "waxed merry," "disported himself," "joked," etc. 765. **At ones,** at one time. **herberwe,** inn. 770. **quyte,** requite, reward. **mede,** meed, reward. 772. **shapen,** plan. **talen,** talk and tell stories. 776. **erst,** first, before. 781. **fader soule.** *Fader* (father) is often undeclined in Middle English. 785. **make it wys,** to play the wise man, to deliberate. 786. **avys,** consideration, argument. 787. **verdit,** verdict, decision. **him leste,** he wished. 789. **in desdeyn,** in contempt. 794. **tellen othere two.** This would call for four stories from each pilgrim. Chaucer never completed this design.

795. **whylom,** formerly. 798. **solas,** amusement, entertainment. 799. **our aller cost,** at the expense of us all. (On *aller* or *alder,* see note to l. 586.) 805. **withseye,** deny, gainsay. 813. **governour,** guide and leader. 814. **reportour,** commentator or referee. 816. **at his devys,** at his discretion. 817. **heigh and lowe,** in high and low, in every respect. 819. **fet,** fetched. 823. **our aller cok,** cock for all! of us, our reveille. 825. **more than pas,** at a trot. 826. **watering of seint Thomas,** a brook at the second milestone out of London on the old Kent road. 829. **forward,** agreement. 835. **ferrer twinne,** get farther away (from London). 840. **shamfastnesse,** not our shamefacedness, but rather shyness, bashfulness, overmodesty.

And shortly for to tellen, as it was,
Were it by aventure, or sort, or cas,
The sothe is this, the cut fil to the knight,   845
Of which ful blythe and glad was every wight;
And telle he moste his tale, as was resoun,
By forward and by composicioun,
As ye han herd; what nedeth wordes mo?
And whan this gode man saugh it was so,   850
As he that wys was and obedient
To kepe his forward by his free assent,
He seyde: "Sin I shal beginne the game,
What, welcome be the cut, a Goddes name!
Now lat us ryde, and herkneth what I seye."   855
    And with that word we riden forth our weye;
And he bigan with right a mery chere
His tale anon, and seyde in this manere.

THE REEVE'S TALE

The medieval *fabliau*, the nature of which has already
been outlined, appears in more than one form. But it is
clear that the handling of this type of fiction must be
either strictly popular or strictly literary, in the academic
sense of the word. It is not easy to find written records
of this, the secular tale of masculine amusement, for the
medieval Church would not look with lenity upon the
mundane stories of husbands deceived, mere practical
jokes, or blasphemous *divertissements*. A few collections
of such narrative material have come down to us, chiefly
through the French. Nevertheless, the student will be
better informed and edified by an artistic treatment of
the *fabliau* as it is told by Geoffrey Chaucer than by its
more popular and vulgar representatives. *The Reeve's
Tale* illustrates all the characteristics of the *fabliau*—the
theme of the biter bit, the sex motif, the horseplay, the
rough realism and humor of the age.

The Knight, as we will see, is the first of the Canterbury pilgrims to tell a tale; his choice is a long and
eminently correct romance. Although the pilgrims as a
group applaud his effort, the Miller, who is drunk, interrupts to tell a tale of scabrous adventure involving a
carpenter, his young wife, a star boarder in their house,
and a lecherous ·clerk of the local parish. Since the
carpenter husband is the butt of this brilliant *fabliau*,
Chaucer's Reeve, who was once a carpenter (see 1. 614
of the *Prologue* to *The Canterbury Tales*), takes issue
with the Miller, and in retaliation tells the following
tale, almost as brilliant as that of the Miller. Especially
noteworthy in *The Reeve's Tale* is the use of the northern
Middle English dialect for the purposes of local color—

844. **aventure . . . cas.** There is no clear distinction here in the use
of these three nouns, although they originally had separate meanings.
All seem to be synonymous with *luck* or *chance*. 845. **cut . . .
knight.** The Knight, as a representative of chivalric society, is treated
by Chaucer with the greatest respect. In the mind of its author,
The Knight's Tale was the obvious choice to begin the collection of
stories. 848. **By forward . . . composicioun,** according to the agreement and the arrangement. 850. **saugh,** saw. 854. **What,** an old
interjection, approximately the equivalent of our *Lo!* or *Well!* a
Goddes name! in God's name! The weakened form of *on* (*in*) appears
as *a*.

the first good example of this in English literature, for
the two young students at Cambridge come from the
north of England. The situations arising in this tale are
altogether typical of the *fabliau*.

THE REEVE'S TALE

At TROMPINGTON, not fer fro Cantebrigge,
    Ther goth a brook, and over that a brigge,
Upon the whiche brook there stent a melle:
And this is veray sothe, that I you telle.
A miller was ther dwelling many a day,   5
As any peacok he was proude and gay:
Pipen he coude, and fishe, and nettes bete,
And turnen cuppes, and wrastlen wel, and shete.
Ay by his belt he bare a long panade,
And of a swerd ful trenchant was the blade.   10
A joly popper bare he in his pouche;
Ther nas no man for peril dorst him touche.
A Shefeld thwitel bare he in his hose.
Round was his face, and camuse was his nose.
As piled as an ape was his skull.   15
He was a market-beter at the full.
Ther dorste no wight hond upon him legge,
That he ne swore he shuld anon abegge.
    A thefe he was forsooth, of corn and mele,
And that a slye, and usant for to stele.   20
His name was hoten deinous Simekin.
A wif he hadde, comen of noble kin:
The persoun of the toun hire fader was.
With hire he yaf ful many a panne of bras,
For that Simkin shuld in his blood allye.   25
She was yfostered in a nonnerie:
For Simkin wolde no wif, as he sayde,
But she were wel ynourished, and a mayde,
To saven his estat of yemanrie:
And she was proud, and pert as is a pie.   30
A ful faire fight was it upon hem two.
On holy dayes before hire wolde he go
With his tipet ybounde about his hed;
And she came after in a gite of red,
And Simkin hadde hosen of the same.   35
Ther dorste no wight clepen hire but dame:

3. **stent,** stands. 7. **bete,** mend, repair. 8. **turnen cuppes,** make
wooden cups in a lathe. 9. **panade,** cutlass. Note that the miller,
for a supposedly orderly citizen, was armed to the teeth. 11. **popper,**
a short dagger, probably the same as the bodkin (bodekin) of l. 40.
13. **Shefeld thwitel,** a whittling-knife from Sheffield, then, as now,
noted for its cutlery. 14. **camuse,** pug-nosed; his daughter had
the same characteristic (l. 54). 15. **piled,** here "bald" rather than
"moth-eaten." 16. **market-beter,** one who frequents markets and
fairs, generally to no good purpose. 17. **legge,** lay. 18. **abegge,**
pay for it. 19. **corn,** the customary English meaning of grain in
general. 20. **usant,** accustomed to, in the habit of. 21. **hoten,**
called. **deinous,** haughty and spiteful. It is something of a fixed
epithet like *hende* for Nicholas in *The Miller's Tale*, a regular nick-
name, which in many instances produced family surnames in later
years. 23. **persoun,** parish priest. 29. **estat of yemanrie,** status of a
free yeoman; the snobbishness of Simkin and his wife is a particular
motive for bringing them low. 30. **pie,** magpie. 34. **gite,** dress,
robe (?).

Was non so hardy, that went by the way,
That with hire dorste rage or ones play,
But if he wold be slain of Simekin
With panade, or with knif, or bodekin.   40
(For jalous folk ben perilous evermo:
Algate they wold hir wives wenden so).
And eke for she was somdel smoterlich,
She was as digne as water in a dich,
And also ful of hoker and of bismare.   45
Hire thoughte that a ladie shuld hire spare,
What for hire kinrede, and hire nortelrie,
That she had lerned in the nonnerie.

A doughter hadden they betwix hem two
Of twenty yere, withouten any mo,   50
Saving a child that was of half yere age;
In cradle it lay, and was a propre page.
This wenche thikke and wel ygrowen was,
With camuse nose, and eyen grey as glas;
With buttokes brode, and brestes round and hie; 55
But right faire was hire here, I wol nat lie.

The person of the toun, for she was faire,
In purpos was to maken hire his haire
Both of his catel, and of his mesuage,
And strange he made it of hire mariage.   60
His purpos was for to bestowe hire hie
Into som worthy blood of ancestrie.
For holy chirches good mote ben despended
On holy chirches blood that is descended.
Therfore he wolde his holy blood honoure,   65
Though that he holy chirche shuld devoure.

Gret soken hath this miller, out of doute,
With whete and malt, of all the land aboute;
And namely ther was a gret college
Men clepe the Soler Hall at Cantebregge,   70
Ther was hir whete and eke hir malt yground.
And on a day it happed in a stound,
Sike lay the manciple on a maladie,
Men wenden wisly that he shulde die.
For which this miller stale both mele and corn   75
An hundred times more than beforn.
For ther beforn he stale but curteisly,
But now he was a thefe outrageously.
For which the wardein chidde and made fare,
But therof set the miller not a tare;   80
He craked bost, and swore it nas not so.

Than were ther yonge poure scoleres two,
That dwelten in the halle of which I say;
Testif they were, and lusty for to play;
And only for hir mirth and revelrie   85
Upon the wardein besily they crie,
To yeve hem leve but a litel stound
To gon to mille, and seen hir corn yground:
And hardily they dorsten lay hir nekke,
The miller shuld not stele hem half a pekke   90
Of corn by sleighte, ne by force hem reve.

And at the last the wardein yave hem leve.
John highte that oon, and Alein highte that other,
Of o toun were they born, that highte Strother,
Fer in the North, I can not tellen where.   95
This Alein maketh redy all his gere,
And on a hors the sak he cast anon:
Forth goth Alein the clerk, and also John,
With good swerd and with bokeler by hir side.
John knew the way, him neded not no guide,   100
And at the mille the sak adoun he laith.

Alein spake first: "All haile, Simond, in faith,
How fares thy faire doughter, and thy wif?"
"Alein, welcome," quod Simkin, "by my lif,
And John also: how now, what do ye here?"   105
"By God, Simond," quod John, "nede has na pere.
Him behoves serve himself that has na swain,
Or elles he is a fool, as clerkes sain.
Our manciple, I hope he wol be ded,
Swa werkes ay the wanges in his hed;   110
And therfore is I come, and eke Alein,
To grind our corn and cary it hame agein;
I pray you, spede us hethen that ye may."
"It shal be don," quod Simkin, "by my fay.
What wol ye don while that it is in hand?"   115
"By God, right by the hopper wol I stand,"
Quod John, "and seen how that the corn gas in.
Yet saw I never by my fader kin,
How that the hopper wagges til and fra."
Alein answered: "John, and wolt thou swa?   120
Than wol I be benethe, by my croun,
And see how that the mele falles adoun
In til the trogh, that shal be my disport;
For, John, in faith I may ben of your sort;
I is as ill a miller as ar ye."   125
This miller smiled at hir nicetee,
And thought, "All this nis don but for a wile.
They wenen that no man may hem bigile,
But by my thrift, yet shal I blere hir eie,
For all the sleighte in hir philosophie.   130

38. **rage,** make over her amorously. 42. **wenden,** thought, supposed.
43. **smoterlich,** besmirched in reputation because of her illegitimacy
(l. 23). 44. **digne . . . dich,** as worthy as ditch water. 45. **hoker,**
scorn, snobbishness. **bismare,** shrewishness, abusiveness. 46. **spare,**
overlook (her illegitimacy). 52. **page,** little boy. 59. **mesuage,** or
mansuage, dwelling; see the modern *manse.* 60. **strange . . .
mariage,** made difficulties about marrying the girl. 63. **mote,** must.
67. **soken,** toll, receipts. 69. **namely,** particularly, specifically. 70.
the Soler Hall, King's Hall at Cambridge, founded by Edward III
in 1337, and later merged with Trinity College, Cambridge; the early
name was apparently derived from a solarium in the building. 72.
stound, occasion, hour. 73. **manciple,** the purchasing agent of the
college. 79. **wardein,** the warden or head of the institution. **made
fare,** made some trouble (unsuccessfully). 81. **craked bost,** boasted
loudly and with coarse wit.

84. **Testif,** headstrong, impulsive. 89. **lay,** wager, bet. 94. **Strother.**
There is no longer a town by this name in England, but the name
belongs to an old family of Northumberland. In any event, it is to
be assumed that the two young men are both from the north of
England, for Chaucer puts into their mouths an unmistakable northern dialect. Incidentally, this is the first effective use of dialect in
English literature for the purpose of portraying local color. 106.
nede has na pere, necessity has no equal. 109. **hope,** expect. 110.
werkes ay the wanges, his molars ache so. 113. **hethen,** hence.
123. **disport,** recreation or diversion. 129. **blere hir eie,** cheat them.

The more queinte krakkes that they make,
The more wol I stele whan that I take.
In stede of flour yet wol I yeve hem bren.
The gretest clerkes ben not the wisest men,
As whilom to the wolf thus spake the mare;   135
Of all hir art ne count I not a tare."

  Out at the dore he goth ful prively,
Whan that he saw his time softely.
He loketh up and doun, til he hath found
The clerkes hors, ther as he stood ybound   140
Behind the mille, under a levesell;
And to the hors he goth him faire and well,
And stripeth of the bridel right anon.

  And whan the hors was lous, he gan to gon
Toward the fen, ther wilde mares renne,   145
And forth, with "wehee," thurgh thick and thinne.
This miller goth again, no word he said,
But doth his note, and with these clerkes plaid,
Till that hir corn was faire and wel yground.
And whan the mele is sacked and ybound,   150
This John goth out, and fint his hors away,
And gan to crie, "Harow and Wala wa!
Our hors is lost; Alein, for Goddes banes,
Step on thy feet; come of, man, al at anes!
Alas! our wardein has his palfrey lorn!"   155

  This Alein al forgat both mele and corn;
Al was out of his mind his husbandrie:
"What! whilke way is he gon?" he gan to crie.

  The wif came leping inward at a renne;
She sayd: "Alas! youre hors goth to the fenne   160
With wilde mares, as fast as he may go.
Unthank come on his hand that bond him so,
And he that better shuld have knit the rein."

  "Alas!" quod John, "Alein, for Cristes pein,
Lay doun thy swerd, and I shal min alswa.   165
I is ful wight, God wat, as is a ra.
By Goddes saule, he shal not scape us bathe.
Why ne had thou put the capel in the lathe?
Ill haile, Alein, by God! thou is a fonne!"

  These sely clerkes han ful fast yronne   170
Toward the fen, bothe Alein and eke John;
And whan the miller saw that they were gon,
He half a bushel of hir flour hath take,
And bad his wif go knede it in a cake.
He sayd: "I trow, the clerkes were aferde.   175
Yet can a miller make a clerkes berde,

For all his art. Ye, let hem gon hir wey.
Lo! wher they gon! Ye, let the children play;
They get him not so lightly, by my croun!"

  These sely clerkes rennen up and doun   180
With "Kepe, kepe! stand, stand! jossa! warderere!
Ga whistle thou, and I shal kepe him here."
But shortly, til that it was veray night,
They coude not, though they did all hir might,
Hir capel catch; he ran alway so fast: 185
Til in a diche they caught him at the last.

  Wery and wet, as bestes in the rain,
Cometh sely John, and with him cometh Alein.
"Alas!" quod John, "the day that I was borne!
Now are we driven til hething and til scorne.   190
Our corn is stolne, men wol us fonnes calle,
Both the wardein, and eke our felawes alle,
And namely the miller, wala wa!"

  Thus plaineth John, as he goth by the way
Toward the mille, and Bayard in his hond.   195
The miller sitting by the fire he fond,
For it was night, and forther might they nought,
But for the love of God they him besought
Of herberwe and of ese, as for hir peny.

  The miller saide agen, "If ther be any,   200
Swiche as it is, yet shull ye have your part.
Myn hous is streit, but ye have lerned art;
Ye can by arguments maken a place
A mile brode, of twenty foot of space.
Lat see now if this place may suffice,   205
Or make it roume with speche, as if your gise."
"Now, Simond," said this John, "by Seint Cuthberd,
Ay is thou mery, and that is faire answerd.
I have herd say, man sal take of twa thinges,
Slike as he findes, or slike as he bringes.   210
But specially I pray thee, hoste dere,
Gar us have mete and drinke, and make us chere,
And we sal paien trewely at the full;
With empty hand, men may na haukes tull.
Lo! here our silver, redy for to spend."   215

  This miller to the toun his doughter send
For ale and bred, and rosted hem a goos,
And bond hir hors, he shuld no more go loos:
And in his owen chambre hem made a bedde,
With shetes and with chalons faire yspredde,   220
Nat from his owen bed ten foot or twelve:
His doughter had a bed all by hire selve,
Right in the same chambre by and by:
It mighte be no bet, and cause why?

---

131. **queinte krakkes**, subtly arrogant remarks. 133. **bren**, bran. 135. **wolf . . . mare.** In the old beast fables of the Middle Ages, the Wolf once wished to buy the Mare's foal, and was told by her that the price was written on her hind foot, and that if he had learning enough, he could come and read it. When the unwary Wolf went to look, he received a kick that knocked him out completely. The Fox, who, as usual, had brought about this disaster to the Wolf, hypocritically remarked that clerks are not always the wisest men. 141. **levesell**, an arbor formed of branches or foliage. 144. **lous**, loose. 148. **note**, job. 154. **at anes**, at once, in a hurry. 159. **renne**, run. 162. **Unthank . . . hand**, "Bad luck come to his hand who, etc." 166. **I . . . ra**, "I am as fast, God knows, as a roe." 167. **bathe**, both. 168. **capel**, a sturdy horse. **lathe**, barn. 169. **fonne**, fool. 176. **make . . . berde**, cheat, make a fool of.

181. **jossa!** from an Old French cry of direction, "Down here!" **warderere**, "Look out for the rear!" 190. **hething**, scorn, contempt. 193. **namely**, particularly, especially. 199. **herberwe**, lodging. 202. **streit**, narrow and small. 206. **roume**, roomy, spacious. **gise**, manner, practice. 207. **Cuthberd**, St. Cuthbert, Bishop of Lindisfarne in Northumbria, who died in 686. It is appropriate that John, as a man from that part of England, should swear by a Northumbrian saint. 209–210. **man sal take . . . he bringes**, "A man must take one of two things—what he finds or what he brings." In other words, a man must put up with what he can get. 214. **tull**, lure, entice. 220. **chalons**, blankets.

Ther was no roumer herberwe in the place. 225
They soupen, and they speken of solace,
And drinken ever strong ale at the best.
Abouten midnight wente they to rest.
 Wel hath this miller vernished his hed,
Ful pale he was, for dronken, and nought red. 230
He yexeth, and he speketh thurgh the nose,
As he were on the quakke, or on the pose.
To bed he goth, and with him goth his wif;
As any jay she light was and jolif,
So was hire joly whistle wel ywette. 235
The cradel at hire beddes feet was sette,
To rokken, and to yeve the child to souke.
And whan that dronken was all in the crouke,
To bedde went the doughter right anon,
To bedde goth Alein, and also John. 240
Ther nas no more; it nedeth hem no dwale.
This miller hath so wisly bibbed ale,
That as an hors he snorteth in his slepe,
Ne of his tail behind he toke no kepe.
His wif bare him a burdon, a ful strong; 245
Men might hir routing heren a furlong.
The wenche routeth eke *par compagnie*.
 Alein the clerk, that herd this melodie,
He poketh John, and sayde: "Slepest thou?
Herdest thou ever slike a sang er now? 250
Lo! whilke a complin is ymell hem alle.
A wilde fire upon hir bodies falle!
Wha herkned ever slike a ferly thing?
Ye, they sall have the flour of yvel ending.
This lange night ther tides me no reste. 255
But yet na fors; all sal be for the beste.
For John," sayd he, "as ever mote I thrive,
If that I may, yon wenche wol I swive.
Som esement has lawe yshapen us.
For John, ther is a lawe that saieth thus, 260
That if a man in o point be agreved,
That in another he sal be releved.
Our corn is stolen, sothly it is na nay,
And we han had an yvel fit today.
And sin I sal have nan amendement 265
Again my losse, I wol have an esement;
By Goddes saule, it sal nan other be!"
 This John answered: "Alein, avise thee!
The miller is a perilous man," he sayde.
"And if that he out of his slepe abrayde, 270
He mighte don us bathe a vilanie."
Alein answered: "I count him nat a flye!"
And up he rist, and by the wenche he crepte.

This wenche lay upright, and faste slepte,
Til he so nigh was, or she might espie, 275
That it had ben to late for to crie.
And, shortly for to say, they were at on.
Now play, Alein, for I wol speke of John.
 This John lith still a furlong way or two,
And to himself he maketh routh and wo: 280
"Alas!" quod he, "this is a wikked jape;
Now may I say that I is but an ape.
Yet has my felaw somwhat for his harme;
He has the millers doughter in his arme;
He auntred him, and hath his nedes spedde, 285
And I lie as a draf-sak in my bedde;
And whan this jape is told another day,
I sal be halden a daffe or a cokenay;
I wol arise, and auntre it, by my fay;
Unhardy is unsely, thus men say." 290
 And up he rose, and softely he wente
Unto the cradel, and in his hand it hente,
And bare it soft unto his beddes fete.
Sone after this the wif hir routing lete,
And gan awake, and went hire out to pisse, 295
And came again, and gan the cradel misse,
And groped here and ther, but she fond non.
"Alas!" quod she, "I had almost misgon.
I had almost gon to the clerkes bedde.
Ey! *benedicite!* than had I foule yspedde." 300
And forth she goth, til she the cradel fond.
She gropeth alway forther with hire hond,
And fond the bed, and thoughte nat but good,
Because that the cradel by it stood,
And niste wher she was, for it was derk, 305
But faire and wel she crepte in by the clerk,
And lith ful still, and wold han caught a slepe.
Within a while this John the clerk up lepe,
And on this goode wif he layeth on sore;
So mery a fit ne had she nat ful yore. 310
He priketh hard and depe, as he were mad.
 This joly life han these two clerkes lad,
Til that the thridde cok began to sing.
Alein wex werie in the morwening,
For he had swonken all the longe night, 315
And sayd: "Farewel, Malkin, my swete wight.

---

229. **vernished his hed,** "varnished his head," become drunk.   231. **yexeth,** hiccoughs.   232. **quakke,** asthma. **on the pose,** suffering from a head cold.   235. **whistle wel ywette,** well drunk. The expression "to wet one's whistle" is still found in Modern English.   238. **crouke,** crock, jug, pitcher.   241. **dwale,** sedative, sleeping-potion.   245. **burdon,** refrain.   246. **routing,** snoring.   247. *par compagnie,* in concert.   250. **slike,** such (northern form).   252. **wilde fire,** the vicious skin disease known as erysipelas.   253. **ferly,** weird and fearsome.   255. **tides,** betides, happens to.   256. **na fors,** no matter.   258. **swive,** have intercourse with.   270. **abrayde,** started up.

274. **upright,** straight on her back.   277. **at on,** agreed.   279. **a furlong way or two,** the time it would take one to go a furlong, or an eighth of a mile.   285. **auntred,** ventured, risked.   286. **draf-sak,** a sack full of draff or chaff.   288. **daffe,** fool. **cokenay.** There was an old folk belief that all imperfect eggs were laid by the cock rather than by the hen. Hence a *cokenay* or "cock's egg," is the equivalent of a half-formed creature, an effeminate weakling. In addition, it carries the idea of freakishness. The term, as the slang term for the inhabitants of a certain part of London, *cockney*, is of modern development; see the *New English Dictionary*.   290. **Unhardy is unsely;** that is, the coward has no luck; nothing ventured, nothing gained.   294. **lete,** stopped, ceased.   300. *benedicite!* This mild oath, "Bless us!" is usually pronounced in three syllables, as if spelled *bencite*.   310. **nat ful yore,** not for a long time past.   313. **thridde cok.** In British folklore, the first cockcrow comes shortly after midnight, the second about three in the morning, and the third between five and six A.M.

The day is come, I may no longer bide,
But evermo, wherso I go or ride,
I is thin awen clerk, so have I hele."
"Now, dere lemman," quod she, "go, farewele;   320
But or thou go, o thing I wol thee telle.
Whan that thou wendest homeward by the melle,
Right at the entree of the dore behinde
Thou shalt a cake of half a bushel finde,
That was ymaked of thin owen mele,   325
Which that I halpe my fader for to stele.
And, good lemman, God thee save and kepe."
And with that word she gan almost to wepe.
    Alein uprist and thought, "Er that it dawe
I wol go crepen in by my felawe";   330
And fond the cradel at his hand anon.
"By God," thought he, "all wrang I have misgon;
My hed is tottie of my swink tonight,
That maketh me that I go nat aright.
I wot wel by the cradel I have misgo;   335
Here lith the miller and his wif also."
And forth he goth, a twenty divel way
Unto the bed, ther as the miller lay.
He wend have cropen by his felaw John,
And by the miller in he crept anon,   340
And caught him by the nekke, and gan him shake,
And sayd: "Thou John, thou swinesshed, awake!
For Cristes saule, and here a noble game;
For, by that lord that called is Seint Jame,
As I have thries as in this shorte night   345
Swived the millers doughter bolt upright,
While thou hast as a coward ben agast."
    "Ye, false harlot," quod the miller, "hast?
A, false traitour, false clerk," quod he,
"Thou shalt be ded, by Goddes dignitee,   350
Who dorste be so bold to disparage
My doughter, that is come of swiche linage."
And by the throte-bolle he caught Alein,
And he him hent despitously again,
And on the nose he smote him with his fist;   355
Doun ran the blody streme upon his brest;
And in the flore, with nose and mouth tobroke,
They walwe, as done two pigges in a poke.
And up they gon, and doun again anon,
Til that the miller sporned at a ston,   360
And doun he fell backward upon his wif,
That wiste nothing of this nice strif;
For she was fall aslepe a litel wight
With John the clerk, that waked had all night;
And with the fall out of hire slepe she brayde.   365
"Helpe, holy crois of Bromeholme!" she sayde,

"*In manus tuas*, Lord, to thee I calle.
Awake, Simond, the fend is on me falle;
Myn herte is broken; helpe! I nam but ded!
Ther lith on up my wombe and up myn hed.   370
Helpe, Simkin, for the false clerkes fighte!"
This John sterte up as fast as ever he might,
And graspeth by the walles to and fro
To find a staf; and she sterte up also,
And knew the estres bet than did this John,   375
And by the wall she toke a staf anon;
And saw a litel shemering of a light,
For at an hole in shone the mone bright,
And by that light she saw hem bothe two,
But sikerly she niste who was who,   380
But as she saw a white thing in hire eye.
And whan she gan this white thing espie,
She wend the clerk had wered a volupere;
And with the staf she drow ay nere and nere,
And wend han hit this Alein atte fulle,   385
And smote the miller on the piled skulle,
That doun he goth, and cried, "Harrow! I die!"
Thise clerkes bete him wel, and let him lie,
And greithen hem, and take hir hors anon,
And eke hir mele, and on hir way they gon;   390
And at the mille dore eke they toke hir cake
Of half a bushel flour, ful wel ybake.
    Thus is the proude miller wel ybete,
And hath ylost the grinding of the whete,
And payed for the souper every del   395
Of Alein and of John, that bete him wel;
His wif is swived, and his doughter als;
Lo! swiche it is a miller to be fals.
And therfore this proverbe is sayd ful soth:
Him thar not winnen wel that evil doth;   400
A gilour shal himself begiled be;
And God that siteth hie in magestee
Save all this compagnie, grete and smale.
Thus have I quit the miller in my tale.

THE FRANKLIN'S TALE

The Franklin's Tale is generally accepted as the concluding tale in the so-called Marriage Group of *The Canterbury Tales*; this is an old designation for a handful of stories which are designed to illustrate divergent points of view about the problem of who should rule in the married state. Perhaps Chaucer had no such group actually in mind, and the Marriage Group may be, as some scholars would have it, a myth; but if so, it is a convenient myth, because it seems obvious enough that

320. **lemman**, sweetheart, beloved. 322. **melle**, mill. 333. **tottie**, dizzy, muddled. 337. **twenty divel way**, with extremely bad luck. 342. **swinesshed**, pig's head. 346. **bolt upright**; see note to l. 274. **bolt**; that is, "like a bolt," calls attention to the extreme rectilinear quality of the girl's position. 352. **come . . . linage**; that is, descended from the parish priest. 353. **throte-bolle**, Adam's apple. 360. **sporned**, kicked, stumbled. 366. **Bromeholme**, a celebrated shrine in Norfolk, alleged to have housed a piece of the Cross of Christ.

367. *In manus tuas*, "into Thy hands (I commend my spirit)," a formula to be recited by all those who stand in the imminence of death. 370. **wombe**, belly. 375. **estres**, interior. 383. **volupere**, night-cap. 384. **nere and nere**, nearer and nearer. 389. **greithen**, dressed themselves and prepared to return. 400. **thar**, need. The meaning of the proverb is, "He need not expect good who does evil." 401. **gilour**, beguiler, deceiver. The idea of a deceiver deceived is one of the cardinal points in the medieval *fabliau*. 404. **quit**, repaid with satisfaction.

there *are* different stories in the collection which serve as *exempla*—if the term is admissible in this case—of different attitudes toward marriage.

Assuming the reality of the Marriage Group as a talking point, we note that the Wife of Bath begins the forum (in the long, extremely brilliant and satirical *Prologue* to *The Wife of Bath's Tale*) by expressing her violent prejudices in favor of a wife's complete supremacy over the husband. The Clerk implies, at least, the directly opposite position, and his tale of Griselda converts the wife into a figurative door mat for a domineering husband. The Merchant is sour and disillusioned on the whole subject of matrimony, and the Squire is wildly romantic. But the Franklin wishes at least to present the tempered outlook that marriage is successful only when it rests upon mutual respect and when the partners are both persons of "gentilesse" who are true to their obligations and responsibilities. Unfortunately Chaucer, as a medievalist, makes his colors too much black and white in this story; in any event it is the complex, realistic, human experience of *The Wife of Bath's Prologue* and *The Merchant's Tale* that raises these pieces above the others in the Marriage Group; and as between the Wife of Bath and the Merchant, further human experience shows that the Wife of Bath will always win.

But *The Franklin's Tale* has another special point of interest. In the *Prologue* to this tale Chaucer indicates that the story is based upon an old Breton *lai*. The *lai* was a type of short, imaginative chivalric romance which seems to be best represented by the brilliant little narratives of Marie de France (c. 1200). In spite of the assertion in lines 1–6 of this *Prologue*, there is little historical evidence that these *lais* were ever composed in the Breton tongue, although there may well have been Celtic Breton tales corresponding to the type. Indeed, in the color and imagination displayed in these Breton *lais*—which were in French or English—there is ample suggestion of the Celtic spirit. It is probable that Chaucer imitated the type in *The Franklin's Tale*, either from the *lais* of Marie de France herself or, more probably, from those of her imitators and followers, who were many during the thirteenth and fourteenth centuries. Whatever its source, however, *The Franklin's Tale* is a pleasant story of generosity and moral sanity, entirely appropriate to the Franklin, the sanguine, hospitable, kindly *bon vivant* of wealth and social standing.

THE PROLOGUE
OF THE FRANKELEYNS TALE

T HISE olde gentil Britons in hir dayes
    Of diverse aventures maden layes,
Rymeyed in hir firste Briton tonge;
Which layes with hir instruments they songe,
Or elles redden hem for hir plesaunce;   5
And oon of hem have I in remembraunce,

1. gentil, aristocratic, cultivated. hir, their. 3. Rymeyed, put into rime. Briton, here, as in l. 1, "Breton."

Which I shal seyn with good wil as I can.
    But, sires, by-cause I am a burel man,
At my biginning first I yow biseche
Have me excused of my rude speche;   10
I lerned never rethoryk certeyn;
Thing that I speke, it moot be bare and pleyn.
I sleep never on the mount of Pernaso,
Ne lerned Marcus Tullius Cithero.
Colours ne knowe I none, with-outen drede,   15
But swiche colours as growen in the mede,
Or elles swiche as men dye or peynte.
Colours of rethoryk ben me to queynte;
My spirit feleth noght of swich matere.
But if yow list, my tale shul ye here.   20

THE FRANKELEYNS TALE

In Armorik, that called is Britayne,
Ther was a knight that loved and dide his payne
To serve a lady in his beste wyse;
And many a labour, many a greet empryse
He for his lady wroghte, er she were wonne.   25
For she was oon the faireste under sonne,
And eek therto come of so heigh kinrede,
That wel unnethes dorste this knight, for drede,
Telle hir his wo, his peyne, and his distresse.
But atte laste, she, for his worthinesse,   30
And namely for his meke obeysaunce,
Hath swich a pitee caught of his penaunce,
That prively she fil of his accord
To take him for hir housbonde and hir lord,
Of swich lordshipe as men han over hir wyves;   35
And for to lede the more in blisse hir lyves,
Of his free wil he swoor hir as a knight,
That never in al his lyf he, day ne night,
Ne sholde upon him take no maistrye
Agayn hir wil, ne kythe hir jalousye,   40
But hir obeye, and folwe hir wil in al
As any lovere to his lady shal;
Save that the name of soveraynetee,
That wolde he have for shame of his degree.

8. burel. Burel, or borel, was a coarse woolen cloth; hence *burel man* was one who wore burel, a humble, ignorant layman; compare our modern "homespun," with its connotations. The deprecating tone of the Franklin's *Prologue* is something of a commonplace, not only in *The Canterbury Tales* but also in medieval literature generally. It is hardly in keeping with the high-flown sentiments of *The Franklin's Tale*. 13. Pernaso, Parnassus, the mountain in Greece on which the Muses were traditionally supposed to dwell. Note the apparently Italian form of the word here. This is actually due to a following by Chaucer of the ablative form of the Latin, because he is here quoting from the Latin satirist, Persius (34–62). 14. Cithero, Cicero. 15. Colours, rhetorical figures. drede, doubt. 18. queynte, subtle, complicated. 21. Armorik, Armorica, the ancient name for Brittany. Britayne, Brittany. 25. were, might be (the subjunctive mood). 26. oon the faireste. The preposition *of*, necessary in the Modern English construction, was not used in Early English, although the modern idiom was beginning to appear in Chaucer; see l. 224. 28. unnethes, without ease, with difficulty, uneath (arch.). 30. atte laste, the early form of Modern English *at last*. 31. namely, particularly. 33. fil . . . accord, agreed with him. 39. maistrye, mastery, assumption of power over. 40. kythe, make known, show. 44. shame . . . degree, respect for his social position and rank as a husband.

She thanked him, and with ful greet humblesse
She seyde, "Sire, sith of your gentillesse 46
Ye profre me to have so large a reyne,
Ne wolde never God bitwixe us tweyne,
As in my gilt, were outher werre or stryf.
Sir, I wol be your humble trewe wyf, 50
Have heer my trouthe, til that myn herte breste."
Thus been they bothe in quiete and in reste.

For o thing, sires, saufly dar I seye,
That frendes everich other moot obeye,
If they wol longe holden companye. 55
Love wol nat ben constreyned by maistrye;
Whan maistrie comth, the god of love anon
Beteth hise winges, and farewel! he is gon!
Love is a thing as any spirit free;
Wommen of kinde desiren libertee, 60
And nat to ben constreyned as a thral;
And so don men, if I soth seyen shal.
Loke who that is most pacient in love,
He is at his avantage al above.
Pacience is an heigh vertu certeyn; 65
For it venquisseth, as thise clerkes seyn,
Thinges that rigour sholde never atteyne.
For every word men may nat chyde or pleyne.
Lerneth to suffre, or elles, so moot I goon,
Ye shul it lerne, wher-so ye wole or noon. 70
For in this world, certein, ther no wight is,
That he ne dooth or seith som-tyme amis.
Ire, siknesse, or constellacioun,
Wyn, wo, or chaunginge of complexioun
Causeth ful ofte to doon amis or speken. 75
On every wrong a man may nat be wreken;
After the tyme, moste be temperaunce
To every wight that can on governaunce.
And therfore hath thise wyse worthy knight,
To live in ese, suffrance hir bihight, 80
And she to him ful wisly gan to swere
That never sholde ther be defaute in here.

Heer may men seen an humble wys accord;
Thus hath she take hir servaunt and hir lord,
Servant in love, and lord in mariage; 85
Than was he bothe in lordship and servage;

Servage? nay, but in lordshipe above,
Sith he hath bothe his lady and his love;
His lady, certes, and his wyf also,
The which that lawe of love acordeth to, 90
And whan he was in this prosperitee,
Hoom with his wyf he gooth to his contree,
Nat fer fro Penmark, ther his dwelling was,
Wher-as he liveth in blisse and in solas.

Who coude telle, but he had wedded be, 95
The joye, the ese, and the prosperitee
That is bitwixe an housbonde and his wyf?
A yeer and more lasted this blisful lyf,
Til that the knight of which I speke of thus,
That of Kayrrud was cleped Arveragus, 100
Shoop him to goon, and dwelle a yeer or tweyne
In Engelond, that cleped was eek Briteyne,
To seke in armes worship and honour;
For al his lust he sette in swich labour;
And dwelled ther two yeer, the book seith thus. 105

Now wol I stinte of this Arveragus,
And speken I wole of Dorigene his wyf,
That loveth hir housbonde as hir hertes lyf.
For his absence wepeth she and syketh,
As doon thise noble wyves whan hem lyketh. 110
She moorneth, waketh, wayleth, fasteth, pleyneth;
Desyr of his presence hir so distreyneth,
That al this wyde world she sette at noght.
Hir frendes, whiche that knewe hir hevy thoghte,
Conforten hir in al that ever they may; 115
They prechen hir, they telle hir night and day,
That causelees she sleeth hir-self, allas!
And every confort possible in this cas
They doon to hir with al hir bisinesse,
Al for to make hir leve hir hevinesse. 120

By proces, as ye knowen everichoon,
Men may so longe graven in a stoon,
Til som figure ther-inne emprented be.
So longe han they conforted hir, til she
Receyved hath, by hope and by resoun, 125
Th' emprenting of hir consolacioun,
Thurgh which hir grete sorwe gan aswage;
She may nat alwey duren in swich rage.
And eek Arveragus, in al this care,
Hath sent hir lettres hoom of his welfare, 130
And that he wol come hastily agayn
Or elles hadde this sorwe hir herte slayn.

---

48. **God.** There is a curious blend of Christian and pagan deities in this tale. But the Christian God appears only in oaths and asseverations, such as might occur anywhere in Middle English speech; the pagan divinities, on the other hand, are appealed to as important factors in the story. 49. **As . . . gilt,** through my fault. **werre,** war. The entire sentence beginning with l. 48 might be translated: "Would God there may never be war or strife between us through my fault." 53. **saufly,** safely. 60. **of kinde,** by nature. 64. **He . . . avantage,** he has an advantage. 69. **suffre,** tolerate, be tolerant. **so . . . goon,** a mild asseveration, "as I can walk," "as I live and breathe," etc. 70. **wher-so ye . . . noon,** whether you will or not. 73. **constellacioun.** This has reference to the influence of heavenly bodies and their celestial positions on human affairs. 74. **complexioun,** the harmony or balance of the humours in the body; see the *Prologue* to *The Canterbury Tales,* p. II:209, l. 421 and note; also *The Nun's Priest's Tale,* l. 104 and note. 76. **wreken,** avenged. 77. **After the tyme,** according to the time and situation. 78. **can on governaunce,** knows how to control himself. 80. **bihight,** promised. 86. **servage,** service, used here in the sense of chivalric love.

93. **Penmark,** Pedmark in some of the manuscripts. It was probably Penmarch, a commune in the southwestern portion of the Department of Finisterre, France. This section of the Brittany peninsula is still noted for its dangerously rocky coast. 95. **he,** he who. 100. **Kayrrud,** the modern Breton Kerru, the name of several places in Brittany. None of these, however, exactly fits the geographical situation indicated here. 101. **Shoop,** shaped, planned. 104. **lust,** pleasure. 105. **book,** the obscure source of Chaucer's tale. Perhaps he has made up this book out of whole cloth in order to give his story the "authority" which the medieval public loved. 109. **syketh,** sighs. 111. **waketh,** either "lies awake" or "watches"; probably both meanings are intended. 112. **distreyneth,** afflicts. 121. **proces,** due course. 128. **duren,** endure. **rage,** distemper, abnormal state.

Hir frendes sawe hir sorwe gan to slake,
And preyede hir on knees, for Goddes sake,
To come and romen hir in companye,   135
Awey to dryve hir derke fantasye.
And finally, she graunted that requeste;
For wel she saugh that it was for the beste.
    Now stood hir castel faste by the see,
And often with hir freendes walketh she   140
Hir to disporte up-on the bank an heigh,
Wher-as she many a ship and barge seigh
Seilinge hir cours, wher-as hem liste go;
But than was that a parcel of hir wo.
For to hir-self ful ofte "allas!" seith she,   145
"Is ther no ship, of so manye as I see,
Wol bringen hom my lord? than were myn herte
Al warisshed of his bittre peynes smerte."
    Another tyme ther wolde she sitte and thinke,
And caste hir eyen dounward fro the brinke.   150
But whan she saugh the grisly rokkes blake,
For verray fere so wolde hir herte quake,
That on hir feet she might hir noght sustene.
Than wolde she sitte adoun upon the grene,
And pitously into the see biholde,   155
And seyn right thus, with sorweful sykes colde:
    "Eterne God, that thurgh thy purveyaunce
Ledest the world by certein governaunce,
In ydel, as men seyn, ys no-thing make;
But, Lord, thise grisly feendly rokkes blake,   160
That semen rather a foul confusioun
Of werk than any fair creacioun
Of swich a parfit wys God and a stable,
Why han ye wroght this werk unresonable?
For by this werk, south, north, ne west, ne est,   165
Ther nis y-fostred man, ne brid, ne beest;
It dooth no good, to my wit, but anoyeth.
See ye nat, Lord, how mankinde it destroyeth?
An hundred thousand bodies of mankinde
Han rokkes slayn, al be they nat in minde,   170
Which mankinde is so fair part of thy werk
That thou it madest lyk to thyn owene merk.
Than semed it ye hadde a greet chiertee
Toward mankinde; but how than may it be
That ye swiche menes make it to destroyen,   175
Whiche menes do no good, but ever anoyen?
I woot wel clerkes wol seyn, as hem leste,
By arguments, that al is for the beste,
Though I ne can the causes nat y-knowe.
But thilke God, that made wind to blowe,   180
As kepe my lord! this my conclusioun;
To clerkes lete I al disputisoun.
But wolde God that alle thise rokkes blake

Were sonken in-to Helle for his sake!
Thise rokkes sleen myn herte for the fere."   185
Thus wolde she seyn, with many a pitous tere.
    Hir freendes sawe that it was no disport
To romen by the see, but disconfort;
And shopen for to pleyen somwher elles.
They leden hir by riveres and by welles,   190
And eek in othere places delitables;
They dauncen, and they pleyen at ches and tables.
    So on a day, right in the morwe-tyde,
Un-to a gardin that was ther bisyde,
In which that they had maad hir ordinaunce   195
Of vitaille and of other purveyaunce,
They goon and pleye hem al the longe day.
And this was on the sixte morwe of May,
Which May had peynted with his softe shoures
This gardin ful of leves and of floures;   200
And craft of mannes hand so curiously
Arrayed hadde this gardin, trewely,
That never was ther gardin of swich prys,
But-if it were the verray paradys.
Th'odour of floures and the fresshe sighte   205
Wolde han maad any herte for to lighte
That ever was born, but-if to gret siknesse,
Or to gret sorwe helde it in distresse;
So ful it was of beautee with plesaunce.
At after-diner gonne they to daunce,   210
And singe also, save Dorigen allone,
Which made alwey hir compleint and hir mone;
For she ne saugh him on the daunce go,
That was hir housbonde and hir love also.
But nathelees she moste a tyme abyde,   215
And with good hope lete hir sorwe slyde.
    Up-on this daunce, amonges othere men,
Daunced a squyer biforen Dorigen,
That fressher was and jolyer of array,
As to my doom, than is the monthe of May.   220
He singeth, daunceth, passinge any man
That is or was, sith that the world bigan.
Ther-with he was, if men sholde him discryve,
Oon of the beste faringe man on-lyve;
Yong, strong, right vertuous, and riche and wys,   225
And wel biloved, and holden in gret prys.
And shortly, if the sothe I tellen shal,
Unwiting of this Dorigen at al,
This lusty squyer, servant to Venus,
Which that y-cleped was Aurelius,   230
Had loved hir best of any creature
Two yeer and more, as was his aventure,
But never dorste he telle hir his grevaunce;

135. **romen,** walk about, wander. 142. **seigh,** saw (v.). 148. **warisshed,** cured. 156. **sykes,** sighs. 157. **purveyaunce,** Providence, foresight. 159. **In ydel,** in vain, to no purpose. 173. **chiertee,** love. 177. **as hem leste,** as it pleases them, as they will. 180. **thilke,** that same. 182. **lete,** leave. The sentiment of this line is typical of Chaucer when a knotty problem of human thought or conduct presents itself.

190. **welles,** springs, fountains. 191. **delitables,** delectable, delightful. The *-s* is an indication that the word was originally a French adjective, agreeing in number and form with the noun it modified. 192. **tables,** backgammon. 195. **ordinaunce,** arrangements. 196. **purveyaunce,** provisions. 201. **curiously,** carefully, with skill and pains. 204. **But-if,** unless. 210. **after-diner,** the period of relaxation following the midday meal. 219–220. **That fressher . . . May.** Compare the description of the Squire as given in the *Prologue* to *The Canterbury Tales*, ll. 91–92. 232. **aventure,** chance.

Chaucer, from a manuscript of The Canterbury Tales *written c. 1400 and now in the University of Chicago Library.*

With-outen coppe he drank al his penaunce.
He was despeyred, no-thing dorste he seye,   235
Save in his songes somwhat wolde he wreye
His wo, as in a general compleyning;
He seyde he lovede, and was biloved nothing.
Of swich matere made he manye layes,
Songes, compleintes, roundels, virelayes,   240
How that he dorste nat his sorwe telle,
But languisseth, as a furie dooth in Helle;
And dye he moste, he seyde, as dide Ekko
For Narcisus, that dorste nat telle hir wo.
In other manere than ye here me seye,   245
Ne dorste he nat to hir his wo biwreye;
Save that, paraventure, som-tyme at daunces,
Ther yonge folk kepen hir observaunces,
It may wel be he loked on hir face
In swich a wyse, as man that asketh grace;   250
But no-thing wiste she of his entente.

Nathelees, it happed, er they thennes wente,
By-cause that he was hir neighebour,
And was a man of worship and honour,
And hadde y-knowen him of tyme yore,   255
They fille in speche; and forth more and more
Un-to his purpos drough Aurelius,
And whan he saugh his tyme, he seyde thus:
    "Madame," quod he, "by God that this world made,
So that I wiste it mighte your herte glade,   260
I wolde, that day that your Arveragus
Wente over the see, that I, Aurelius,
Had went ther never I sholde have come agayn;
For wel I woot my service is in vayn.
My guerdon is but bresting of myn herte;   265
Madame, reweth upon my peynes smerte;
For with a word ye may me sleen or save,
Heer at your feet God wolde that I were grave!
I ne have as now no leyser more to seye;
Have mercy, swete, or ye wol do me deye!"   270
    She gan to loke up-on Aurelius:
"Is this your wil," quod she, "and sey ye thus?
Never erst," quod she, "ne wiste I what ye mente.
But now, Aurelie, I knowe your entente,
By thilke God that yaf me soule and lyf,   275
Ne shal I never been untrewe wyf
In word ne werk, as fer as I have wit:
I wol ben his to whom that I am knit;

234. **With-outen coppe.** This rather obscure expression, *without a cup,* seems to mean either "under difficulties" or possibly "in full draught," "in abundance." 236. **wreye,** reveal. 238. **nothing,** not at all. 240. **compleintes . . . virelayes,** names of common French courtly lyrical forms of the period. Chaucer wrote several of these in his earlier career. The *compleinte* is a lament expressing the sorrows of unrequited love. The *roundel* was a rather rigid form for a short lyric of love or nature. The *virelay* was a poem characterized by the presence of only two sets of rime in the rime-scheme. 243–244. **Ekko . . . Narcisus.** According to the old classical legend, the nymph Echo was madly in love with the beautiful youth Narcissus, but he was so absorbed in the contemplation of his own beauty that he paid no attention to Echo. She pined away until she became nothing but a voice, and Narcissus was transformed into a flower. 248. **observaunces,** customary social attentions and duties.

257. **drough,** drew. 263. **ther,** where. 268. **grave,** buried. 273. **erst,** before.

Tak this for fynal answer as of me."
But after that in pley thus seyde she: 280
    "Aurelie," quod she, "by heighe God above,
Yet wolde I graunte yow to been your love,
Sin I yow see so pitously complayne;
Loke what day that, endelong Britayne,
Ye remoeve alle the rokkes, stoon by stoon,   285
That they ne lette ship ne boot to goon—
I seye, whan ye han maad the coost so clene
Of rokkes, that ther nis no stoon y-sene,
Than wol I love yow best of any man;
Have heer my trouthe in al that ever I can."   290
"Is ther non other grace in yow?" quod he.
"No, by that Lord," quod she, "that maked me!
For wel I woot that it shal never bityde.
Lat swiche folies out of your herte slyde.
What deyntee sholde a man han in his lyf   295
For to go love another mannes wyf,
That hath hir body whan so that him lyketh?"
    Aurelius ful ofte sore syketh;
Wo was Aurelie, whan that he this herde,
And with a sorweful herte he thus answerde: 300
    "Madame," quod he, "this were an inpossible!
Than moost I dye of sodein deth horrible."
And with that word he turned him anoon.
Tho come hir othere freendes many oon,
And in the aleyes romeden up and doun,   305
And no-thing wiste of this conclusioun,
But sodeinly bigonne revel newe
Til that the brighte sonne lost his hewe;
For th'orisonte hath reft the sonne his light;
This is as muche to seye as it was night.   310
And hoom they goon in joye and in solas,
Save only wrecche Aurelius, allas!
He to his hous is goon with sorweful herte;
He seeth he may nat fro his deeth asterte.
Him semed that he felte his herte colde;   315
Up to the hevene his handes he gan holde,
And on his knowes bare he sette him doun,
And in his raving seyde his orisoun.
For verray wo out of his wit he breyde.
He niste what he spak, but thus he seyde;   320
With pitous herte his pleynt hath he bigonne
Un-to the goddes, and first un-to the sonne:
    He seyde, "Appollo, god and governour
Of every plaunte, herbe, tree and flour,
That yevest, after thy declinacioun,   325

To ech of hem his tyme and his sesoun,
As thyn herberwe chaungeth lowe or hye,
Lord Phebus, cast thy merciable yë
On wrecche Aurelie, which that am but lorn.
Lo, lord! my lady hath my deeth y-sworn   330
With-oute gilt, but thy benignitee
Upon my dedly herte have som pitee!
For wel I woot, lord Phebus, if yow lest,
Ye may me helpen, save my lady, best.
Now voucheth sauf that I may yow devyse   335
How that I may been holpe and in what wyse.
    "Your blisful suster, Lucina the shene,
That of the see is chief goddesse and quene,
Though Neptunus have deitee in the see,
Yet emperesse aboven him is she;   340
Ye knowen wel, lord, that right as hir desyr
Is to be quiked and lightned of your fyr,
For which she folweth yow ful bisily,
Right so the see desyreth naturelly
To folwen hir, as she that is goddesse   345
Bothe in the see and riveres more and lesse.
Wherfore, lord Phebus, this is my requeste—
Do this miracle, or do myn herte breste—
That now, next at this opposicioun,
Which in the signe shal be of the Leoun,   350
As preyeth hir so greet a flood to bringe,
That fyve fadme at the leeste it overspringe
The hyeste rokke in Armorik Britayne;
And lat this flood endure yeres tweyne;
Than certes to my lady may I seye: 355
'Holdeth your heste, the rokkes been aweye.'
    "Lord Phebus, dooth this miracle for me;
Preye hir she go no faster cours than ye;
I seye, preyeth your suster that she go
No faster cours than ye thise yeres two.   360
Than shal she been evene atte fulle alway,
And spring-flood laste bothe night and day.
And, but she vouche-sauf in swiche manere
To graunte me my sovereyn lady dere,
Prey hir to sinken every rok adoun   365
In-to hir owene derke regioun
Under the ground, ther Pluto dwelleth inne,
Or never-mo shal I my lady winne.
Thy temple in Delphos wol I barefoot seke;

327. **herberwe,** lodging, dwelling-place. 335. **voucheth sauf,** vouchsafe. **devyse,** describe. 337. **Lucina,** Diana in her aspect of goddess of the Moon, which governs the tides. **shene,** beautiful, fair. 342. **quiked,** made alive, quickened. 348. **do . . . breste,** make my heart break. 349. **opposicioun,** when the moon and the sun are on opposite sides of the earth, all three bodies being approximately in line. This is the occasion of full moon, which, with the time of new moon, is the period of highest tides on the earth. 350. **the Leoun,** Leo, one of the major constellations of the zodiac. The sun is in this constellation during most of July, and the constellation is "favorable" to the sun; it is, therefore, one of the sun's "mansions." 351. **As,** a pleonastic particle that can be omitted entirely from the translation of the line. 356. **heste,** promise. 367. **Pluto,** in classical mythology, the god of the underworld and the ruler of Hades. 369. **Delphos,** Delphi, a town in Phocis, Greece, near the base of Mount Parnassus, the seat of a famous shrine sacred to Apollo. The priestess of this shrine had the power of effective though ambiguous prophecy.

284. **endelong,** all along. 286. **lette,** hinder, prevent. 295. **deyntee,** dignity, honor. 302. **dye . . . horrible.** The lover tormented by an unrequited and unsatisfied love was likely to fall into a wasting sickness, which would inevitably prove fatal unless the beloved should relent. This conception of love-sickness (*care-bed*) is a commonplace in all medieval romances of chivalric nature (see *Aucassin and Nicolete*). 305. **aleyes,** pathways or walks. 309. **th'orisonte,** the horizon. 314. **asterte,** escape. 317. **knowes,** knees. 319. **breyde,** started up. 320. **niste,** knew not. 323. **Appollo.** Apollo is here invoked as the god of vegetation and hence regeneration (see, however, note to l. 48). As such, he was also god of the sun (*Phebus,* l. 328) and is considered as the solar body in the next line. 325. **declinacioun,** the distance of the sun north or south of the celestial equator.

Lord Phebus, see the teres on my cheke,   370
And of my peyne have som compassioun."
And with that word in swowne he fil adoun,
And longe tyme he lay forth in a traunce.
    His brother, which that knew of his penaunce,
Up caughte him and to bedde he hath him broght.
Dispeyred in this torment and this thoght   376
Lete I this woful creature lye;
Chese he, for me, whether he wol live or dye.
    Arveragus, with hele and greet honour,
As he that was of chivalrye the flour,   380
Is comen hoom, and othere worthy men.
O blisful artow now, thou Dorigen,
That hast thy lusty housbonde in thyne armes,
The fresshe knight, the worthy man of armes
That loveth thee, as his owene hertes lyf.   385
No-thing list him to been imaginatyf
If any wight had spoke, whyl he was oute,
To hire of love; he hadde of it no doute.
He noght entendeth to no swich matere,
But daunceth, justeth, maketh hir good chere;   390
And thus in joye and blisse I lete hem dwelle,
And of the syke Aurelius wol I telle.
    In langour and in torment furious
Two yeer and more lay wrecche Aurelius,
Er any foot he mighte on erthe goon;   395
Ne confort in this tyme hadde he noon,
Save of his brother, which that was a clerk;
He knew of al this wo and al this werk.
For to non other creature certeyn
Of this matere he dorste no word seyn.   400
Under his brest he bar it more secree
Than ever dide Pamphilus for Galathee.
His brest was hool, with-oute for to sene,
But in his herte ay was the arwe kene.
And wel ye knowe that of a sursanure   405
In surgerye is perilous the cure,
But men mighte touche the arwe, or come therby.
His brother weep and wayled prively,
Til atte laste him fil in remembraunce,
That whyl he was at Orliens in Fraunce,   410
As yonge clerkes, that been likerous
To reden artes that been curious,
Seken in every halke and every herne
Particuler sciences for to lerne,
He him remembred that, upon a day,   415
At Orliens in studie a book he say

Of magik naturel, which his felawe,
That was that tyme a bacheler of lawe,
Al were he ther to lerne another craft,
Had prively upon his desk y-laft;   420
Which book spak muchel of the operaciouns,
Touchinge the eighte and twenty mansiouns
That longen to the mone, and swich folye,
As in our dayes is nat worth a flye;
For holy chirches feith, in our bileve,   425
Ne suffreth noon illusion us to greve.
And whan this book was in his remembraunce,
Anon for joye his herte gan to daunce,
And to him-self he seyde prively,
"My brother shal be warissed hastily;   430
For I am siker that ther be sciences,
By whiche men make diverse apparences
Swiche as thise subtile tregetoures pleye.
For ofte at festes have I wel herd saye,
That tregetours, with-inne an halle large,   435
Have maad come in a water and a barge,
And in the halle rowen up and doun.
Somtyme hath semed come a grim leoun;
And somtyme floures springe as in a mede;
Somtyme a vyne, and grapes whyte and rede;   440
Somtyme a castel, al of lym and stoon;
And whan hem lyked, voyded it anoon.
Thus semed it to every mannes sighte.
    "Now than conclude I thus, that if I mighte
At Orliens som old felawe y-finde,   445
That hadde this mones mansions in minde,
Or other magik naturel above,
He shulde wel make my brother han his love.
For with an apparence a clerk may make
To mannes sighte, that alle the rokkes blake   450
Of Britaigne weren y-voyded everichon,
And shippes by the brinke comen and gon,
And in swich forme endure a day or two;
Than were my brother warissed of his wo.
Than moste she nedes holden hir biheste,   455
Or elles he shal shame hir atte leste."
    What sholde I make a lenger tale of this?
Un-to his brotheres bed he comen is,
And swich confort he yaf him for to gon
To Orliens, that he up stirte anon,   460
And on his wey forthward thanne is he fare,
In hope for to ben lissed of his care.
    Whan they were come almost to that citee,
But-if it were a two furlong or three,

378. **Chese,** let him choose. 379. **hele,** health, well-being. 386. **to been imaginatyf,** to imagine things. 388. **doute,** fear, suspicion. 402. **Pamphilus for Galathee.** Pamphilus was the hero of a medieval Latin poem, *De Amore*, well known in Chaucer's time. He was in love with the beautiful Galatea. 404. **arwe,** arrow. 405. **sursanure,** in medieval medicine, the name given to a deep wound which had healed superficially but not beneath the surface. 407. **But,** unless. 410. **Orliens,** Orleans, the seat of a famous old French university, which had something of a reputation in the Middle Ages as the seat of scientific learning; to the popular mind this suggested that it was the home of practitioners of magic, black as well as white. 411. **likerous,** avid for, eager for, lusting after. 413. **halke . . . herne,** nook and corner.

417. **magik naturel.** "Natural magic" was generally what we should call today scientific information, knowledge, and procedure; it is virtually the same as "white magic" and hence is diametrically opposed to "black magic," or necromancy. At the same time, it should be remarked that the magician's feat of making the rocks disappear from the coast of Brittany is more necromancy than otherwise. 422. **eighte and twenty mansiouns** were the positions of the moon at noon on each of the twenty-eight days of the lunar month. 423. **longen,** belong. 433. **tregetoures,** jugglers, magicians, sleight-of-hand men. 451. **y-voyded,** removed. 462. **lissed,** relieved. 464. **But-if,** except for.

A yong clerk rominge by him-self they mette,   465
Which that in Latin thriftily hem grette,
And after that he seyde a wonder thing:
"I knowe," quod he, "the cause of your coming";
And er they ferther any fote wente,
He tolde hem al that was in hir entente.   470
  This Briton clerk him asked of felawes
The whiche that he had knowe in olde dawes;
And he answerde him that they dede were,
For which he weep ful ofte many a tere.
  Doun of his hors Aurelius lighte anon,   475
And forth with this magicien is goon
Hoom to his hous, and made hem wel at ese.
Hem lakked no vitaille that mighte hem plese;
So wel arrayed hous as ther was oon
Aurelius in his lyf saugh never noon.   480
  He shewed him, er he wente to sopeer,
Forestes, parkes ful of wilde deer;
Ther saugh he hertes with hir hornes hye,
The gretteste that ever were seyn with yë.   484
He saugh of hem an hondred slayn with houndes,
And somme with arwes blede of bittre woundes.
He saugh, whan voided were thise wilde deer,
Thise fauconers upon a fair river,
That with hir haukes han the heron slayn.
Tho saugh he knightes justing in a playn;   490
And after this, he dide him swich plesaunce,
That he him shewed his lady on a daunce
On which him-self he daunced, as him thoughte.
And whan this maister, that this magik wroughte,
Saugh it was tyme, he clapte his handes two,   495
And farewel! al our revel was ago.
And yet remoeved they never out of the hous,
Whyl they saugh al this sighte merveillous,
But in his studie, ther-as his bookes be,
They seten stille, and no wight but they three.   500
  To him this maister called his squyer,
And seyde him thus: "Is redy our soper?
Almost an houre it is, I undertake,
Sith I yow bad our soper for to make,
Whan that thise worthy men wenten with me   505
In-to my studie, ther-as my bookes be."
  "Sire," quod this squyer, "whan it lyketh yow,
It is al redy, though ye wol right now."
"Go we than soupe," quod he, "as for the beste;
This amorous folk som-tyme mote han reste."   510
  At after-soper fille they in tretee,
What somme sholde this maistres guerdon be,
To remoeven alle the rokkes of Britayne,

466. thriftily, heartily and suitably.   472. dawes, days.   483. hertes, harts, deer.   496. And farewel! . . . ago. Compare the speech by Prospero in Shakespeare's *The Tempest*, IV, i, 148 ff., beginning "Our revels now are ended." There are other echoes of lines from Chaucer in lines by Shakespeare, which suggest to some that Shakespeare knew the work of Chaucer to some extent, which is altogether likely, for that matter; but such echoes are also explained by two men of poetic ability expressing the same idea in the same felicitous words though altogether independently.   511. after-soper, the period of relaxation immediately following the evening meal.

And eek from Gerounde to the mouth of Sayne.
  He made it straunge, and swoor, so God him
   save,   515
Lasse than a thousand pound he wolde nat have,
Ne gladly for that somme he wolde nat goon.
  Aurelius, with blisful herte anoon,
Answerde thus, "Fy on a thousand pound!
This wyde world, which that men saye is round,
I wolde it yeve, if I were lord of it.   521
This bargayn is ful drive, for we ben knit.
Ye shal be payed trewely, by my trouthe!
But loketh now, for no necligence or slouthe,
Ye tarie us heer no lenger than to-morwe."   525
  "Nay," quod this clerk, "have heer my feith to
   borwe."
  To bedde is goon Aurelius whan him leste,
And wel ny al that night he hadde his reste;
What for his labour and his hope of blisse,
His woful herte of penaunce hadde a lisse.   530
  Upon the morwe, whan that it was day,
To Britaigne toke they the righte way,
Aurelius, and this magicien bisyde,
And been descended ther they wolde abide;
And this was, as the bookes me remembre,   535
The colde frosty seson of Decembre.
  Phebus wex old, and hewed lyk latoun,
That in his hote declinacioun
Shoon as the burned gold with stremes brighte;
But now in Capricorn adoun he lighte,   540
Wher-as he shoon ful pale, I dar wel seyn.
The bittre frostes, with the sleet and reyn,
Destroyed hath the grene in every yerd.
Janus sit by the fyr, with double berd,
And drinketh of his bugle-horn the wyn.   545
Biforn him stant braun of the tusked swyn,
And "Nowel!" cryeth every lusty man.
  Aurelius, in al that ever he can,
Doth to his maister chere and reverence,

514. Gerounde . . . Sayne. The river Seine in France, on which the city of Paris is situated, needs no comment beyond the fact that it empties into the western end (extended) of the English Channel. The *Gerounde* is the Garonne, the large river of western France on which Bordeaux is located; it empties into the Bay of Biscay. The stretch of coast between the mouths of these two rivers would include all of northwestern maritime France.   515. made it straunge, found or made difficulties.   520. This wyde world . . . round. Note the reference to the roundness of the earth, which is often met with in the learned literature of the fourteenth century, a century and a half before Columbus or Magellan.   526. borwe, pledge, promise.   530. lisse, stop, cessation.   534. descended, that is, from their horses.   537. latoun, latten, an alloy of copper and zinc.   538. declinacioun. See note to l. 325. But here the reference is to the fact that in December the sun was south of the celestial equator, in the zodiacal constellation of Capricornus (l. 540). There was an erroneous idea that the farther south one went, even below the equator, the hotter it became.   544. Janus, an old Roman solar god, who watched both the rising and the setting sun, and hence was regarded as having two faces looking in opposite directions (note the *double berd*). He has given his name to the month of January.   546. braun, brawn, roasted flesh of the boar. This entire passage, lines 536–547, is a striking English medieval scene, and one of the happiest of such descriptive touches in English literature.

And preyeth him to doon his diligence 550
To bringen him out of his peynes smerte,
Or with a swerd that he wolde slitte his herte.

This subtil clerk swich routhe had of this man,
That night and day he spedde him that he can,
To wayte a tyme of his conclusioun; 555
This is to seye, to make illusioun,
By swich an apparence or jogelrye
(I ne can no termes of astrologye),
That she and every wight sholde wene and seye,
That of Britaigne the rokkes were aweye, 560
Or elles they were sonken under grounde.
So atte laste he hath his tyme y-founde
To maken his japes and his wrecchednesse
Of swich a supersticious cursednesse.
His tables Toletanes forth he broght, 565
Ful wel corrected, ne ther lakked noght,
Neither his collect ne his expans yeres,
Ne his rotes ne his othere geres,
As been his centres and his arguments,
And his proporcionels convenients 570
For his equacions in every thing.
And, by his eighte spere in his wirking,
He knew ful wel how fer Alnath was shove
Fro the heed of thilke fixe Aries above

That in the ninthe speere considered is; 575
Ful subtilly he calculed al this.

Whan he had founde his firste mansioun,
He knew the remenant by proporcioun;
And knew the arysing of his mone weel,
And in whos face, and terme, and everydeel; 580
And knew ful weel the mones mansioun
Acordaunt to his operacioun,
And knew also his othere observaunces
For swiche illusiouns and swiche meschaunces
As hethen folk used in thilke dayes; 585
For which no lenger maked he delayes,
But thurgh his magyk, for a wyke or tweye,
It semed that alle the rokkes were aweye.

Aurelius, which that yet despeired is
Wher he shal han his love or fare amis, 590
Awaiteth night and day on this miracle;
And whan he knew that ther was noon obstacle,
That voided were thise rokkes everichon,
Doun to his maistres feet he fil anon,
And seyde, "I, woful wrecche, Aurelius, 595
Thanke yow, lord, and lady myn Venus,
That me han holpen fro my cares colde."
And to the temple his wey forth hath he holde,
Wher-as he knew he sholde his lady see.
And whan he saugh his tyme, anon-right he, 600
With dredful herte and with ful humble chere,
Salewed hath his soveryn lady dere:

"My righte lady," quod this woful man,
"Whom I most drede and love as I best can,
And lothest were of al this world displese, 605
Nere it that I for yow have swich disese,
That I moste dyen heer at your foot anon,
Noght wolde I telle how me is wo bigon;
But certes outher moste I dye or pleyne;
Ye slee me giltelees for verray peyne. 610
But of my deeth, thogh that ye have no routhe,
Avyseth yow, er that ye breke your trouthe.
Repenteth yow, for thilke God above,
Er ye me sleen by-cause that I yow love.
For, madame, wel ye woot what ye han hight; 615
Nat that I chalange any thing of right
Of yow my sovereyn lady, but your grace;
But in a gardin yond, at swich a place,
Ye woot right wel what ye bihighten me;
And in myn hand your trouthe plighten ye 620
To love me best, God woot, ye seyde so,

555. wayte, watch for. 558. can, know. Perhaps the Franklin knew no astronomical terms, although he does pretty well in the ensuing lines, but Chaucer was a master of the science and actually wrote a textbook on the use of an astronomical instrument, the astrolabe. 563. japes . . . wrecchednesse, wretched tricks; an interesting example of the old rhetorical figure of hendiadys. The Franklin, as a good orthodox Christian, is occasionally distressed by the suggestion that there should be a belief in magic. 565. tables Toletanes, Toledo tables, astronomical tables drawn up under the supervision of King Alphonso x of Castile, and based upon the position of the city of Toledo, Spain; they date from the thirteenth century. 567. collect . . . yeres. Collect yeres are the computations of the changes in a planet's position over a long period of time—from twenty to three thousand years; expans yeres computed the changes in a planet's position for single years and short periods up to twenty years. 568. rotes, roots, data for a given year which must serve as the basis for computations. geres, gear, equipment for computation. 569. centres . . . arguments. Centres refers to the small brass projection on an astrolabe, the instrument then used for ascertaining the astronomical position of a fixed star. Arguments denotes the mathematical material from which other mathematical material is to be deduced, or on which its calculation depends. 570. proporcionels convenients, tables of proportional parts, as in a modern table of logarithms, to be used for computing the changes in a planet's position during the fractions of a year. For the -s on convenients, see note to l. 191. 572. eighte spere. According to Ptolemaic astronomy, there were seven concentric spheres which rotated around the earth, one to each of the seven planets (Sun, Moon, Mercury, Venus, Mars, Jupiter, and Saturn). The eighth sphere, beyond that of Saturn, was the sphere of the fixed stars. 573. Alnath, the chief star in the zodiacal constellation of Aries, the Ram. 574. Aries is called fixed (fixe) because it was in Aries that the vernal equinox was located; that is, the sun was in that constellation when it crossed the celestial equator in March coming northward and bringing spring. For several centuries after Chaucer's time the year began officially not on January 1 but on March 21. The vernal equinox was the starting point for all measurements of the positions of celestial bodies; it still is in respect to right ascension and azimuth. It was, in short, a focal point in the heavens and was believed to attach the eighth sphere of the fixed stars to the vague ninth sphere, or Primum Mobile, which made the entire works go round; hence the reference in l. 575.

577. firste mansioun, the first mansion of the moon (see note to l. 422) was named Alnath, after the brightest star in Aries. 578. by proporcioun, that is, by the use of his proporcionels convenients of l. 570. 580. face, and terme. Each constellation (sign) of the zodiac, to which was assigned thirty degrees along the celestial equator, was for purposes of calculation divided into three equal parts of ten degrees each (faces). Fractions of these equal parts were called termes. Each face and terme of a constellation had, of course, a particular relation to one or more of the planets. 585. thilke, those (same). Note the rather contemptuous tone of the Franklin in these lines. 601. dredful, timid, full of fear. 604. drede, respect; literally, fear. 606. disese, lack of comfort and ease. 609. outher, either. 615. hight, promised. 619. bihighten, promised.

Al be that I unworthy be therto.
Madame, I spake it for the honour of yow,
More than to save myn hertes lyf right now;
I have do so as ye comanded me; 625
And if ye vouche-sauf, ye may go see.
Doth as yow list, have your biheste in minde,
For quik or deed, right ther ye shul me finde;
In yow lyth al, to do me live or deye;—
But wel I woot the rokkes been aweye!" 630

    He taketh his leve, and she astonied stood,
In al hir face nas a drope of blood;
She wende never han come in swich a trappe:
"Allas!" quod she, "that ever this sholde happe!
For wende I never, by possibilitee, 635
That swich a monstre or merveille mighte be!
It is agayns the process of nature."
And hoom she gooth a sorweful creature.
For verray fere unnethe may she go,
She wepeth, wailleth, al a day or two, 640
And swowneth, that it routhe was to see;
But why it was, to no wight tolde she;
For out of toune was goon Arveragus.
But to hir-self she spak, and seyde thus,
With face pale and with ful sorweful chere, 645
In hir compleynt, as ye shul after here:
"Allas," quod she, "on thee, Fortune, I pleyne,
That unwar wrapped hast me in thy cheyne;
For which, t'escape, woot I no socour
Save only deeth or elles dishonour; 650
Oon of thise two bihoveth me to chese.
But nathelees, yet have I lever lese
My lyf than of my body have a shame,
Or knowe my-selven fals, or lese my name,
And with my deth I may be quit, y-wis. 655
Hath ther nat many a noble wyf, er this,
And many a mayde y-slayn hir-self, allas!
Rather than with hir body doon trespas?
"Yis, certes, lo, thise stories beren witnesse;
Whan thretty tyraunts, ful of cursednesse, 660
Had slayn Phidoun in Athenes, atte feste,
They comanded his doghtres for t'areste,
And bringen hem biforn hem in despyt
Al naked, to fulfille hir foul delyt,
And in hir fadres blood they made hem daunce 665
Upon the pavement, God yeve hem mischaunce!
For which thise woful maydens, ful of drede,
Rather than they wolde lese hir maydenhede,
They prively ben stirt into a welle,
And dreynte hem-selven, as the bokes telle. 670
"They of Messene lete enquere and seke

Of Lacedomie fifty maydens eke,
On whiche they wolden doon hir lecherye;
But was ther noon of al that companye
That she nas slayn, and with a good entente 675
Chees rather for to dye than assente
To been oppressed of hir maydenhede.
Why sholde I thanne to dye been in drede?
    "Lo, eek, the tiraunt Aristoclides
That loved a mayden, heet Stimphalides, 680
Whan that hir fader slayn was on a night,
Un-to Dianes temple goth she right,
And hente the image in hir handes two,
Fro which image wolde she never go.
No wight ne mighte hir handes of it arace, 685
Til she was slayn right in the selve place.
Now sith that maydens hadden swich despyt
To been defouled with mannes foul delyt,
Wel oghte a wyf rather hir-selven slee
Than be defouled, as it thinketh me. 690
    "What shal I seyn of Hasdrubales wyf,
That at Cartage birafte hir-self hir lyf?
For whan she saugh that Romayns wan the toun,
She took hir children alle, and skipte adoun
In-to the fyr, and chees rather to dye 695
Than any Romayn dide hir vileinye.
    "Hath nat Lucresse y-slayn hir-self, allas!
At Rome, whanne she oppressed was
Of Tarquin, for hir thoughte it was a shame
To liven whan she hadde lost hir name? 700
    "The sevene maydens of Milesie also
Han slayn hem-self, for verray drede and wo,
Rather than folk of Gaule hem sholde oppresse.
Mo than a thousand stories, as I gesse,
Coude I now telle as touchinge this matere. 705
    "Whan Habradate was slayn, his wyf so dere
Hirselven slow, and leet hir blood to glyde
In Habradates woundes depe and wyde,
And seyde, 'my body, at the leeste way,
Ther shal no wight defoulen, if I may,' 710
    "What sholde I mo ensamples heer-of sayn,
Sith that so manye han hem-selven slayn
Well rather than they wolde defouled be?
I wol conclude, that it is bet for me
To sleen my-self, than been defouled thus. 715
I wol be trewe un-to Arveragus,
Or rather sleen my-self in som manere,

627. **biheste**, promise. 633. **wende**, weened, thought, expected. 639. **unnethe**, uneath, with difficulty. 660. **thretty tyraunts**. The following lines (670–748), characteristic of Chaucer's annoying tendency to parade his knowledge of classical or other "authorities," cite a number of *exempla* of women who died for the sake of their chastity. They are taken from the *Epistle of St. Jerome against Jovinian*, a work which Chaucer evidently knew very well. 669. **stirt**, leaped, jumped. 670. **dreynte**, drowned. 671. **Messene**, the city of Messenia, in ancient Greece.

672. **Lacedomie**, Lacedemonia, Sparta, in Greece. 677. **oppressed**, threatened. 679. **Aristoclides**, tyrant of Orchomenos in Arcadia, Greece. 680. **heet**, called, named. 683. **hente**, seized. 685. **arace**, tear away. 687. **sith**, since. 691. **Hasdrubales wyf**. Hasdrubal was a leader of the Carthaginians in the Third Punic War. Historically, Hasdrubal eventually surrendered to Scipio Africanus, and his wife, upbraiding him for cowardice, killed herself and her children. 697. **Lucresse**, Lucretia, in ancient Roman history the wife of Collatinus, was raped by Tarquinius Sextus. She later killed herself; and public opinion was so aroused against the Tarquins that they were expelled, and the Roman republic was founded. 701. **Milesie**, Miletus, a city in Asia Minor. It was sacked by the Gauls in 276 B.C. 706. **Habradate**, Abradates, King of the Susi, a tribe who once constituted a part of the mighty Persian empire.

As dide Demociones doghter dere,
By-cause that she wolde nat defouled be.
    "O Cedasus! it is ful greet pitee,   720
To reden how thy doghtren deyde, allas!
That slowe hem-selven for swich maner cas.
    "As greet a pitee was it, or wel more,
The Theban mayden, that for Nichanore
Hir-selven slow, right for swich maner wo.   725
    "Another Theban mayden dide right so;
For oon of Macedoine hadde hir oppressed,
She with hir deeth hir maydenhede redressed.
    "What shal I seye of Nicerates wyf,
That for swich cas birafte hir-self hir lyf?   730
    "How trewe eek was to Alcebiades
His love, that rather for to dyen chees
Than for to suffre his body unburied be!
Lo, which a wyf was Alceste," quod she.
    "What seith Omer of gode Penalopee?   735
Al Grece knoweth of hir chastitee.
    "Pardee, of Laodomya is writen thus,
That whan at Troye was slayn Protheselaus,
No lenger wolde she live after his day.
    "The same of noble Porcia telle I may;   740
With-oute Brutus coude she nat live,
To whom she hadde al hool hir herte yive.
    "The parfit wyfhood of Arthemesye
Honoured is thurgh al the Barbarye.
    "O Teuta, queen! thy wyfly chastitee   745
To alle wyves may a mirour be.
The same thing I seye of Bilia,
Of Rodogone, and eek Valeria."

Thus pleyned Dorigene a day or tweye,
Purposinge ever that she wolde deye.   750
    But nathelees, upon the thridde night,
Hom cam Arveragus, this worthy knight,
And asked hir why that she weep so sore.
And she gan wepen ever lenger the more.
    "Allas!" quod she, "that ever was I born!   755
Thus have I seyd," quod she, "thus have I sworn—"
And told him al as ye han herd bifore;
It nedeth nat reherce it yow na-more.
    This housbond with glad chere, in freendly
        wyse,
Answerde and seyde as I shal yow devyse: 760
"Is ther oght elles, Dorigen, but this?"
    "Nay, nay," quod she, "God help me so, as wis;
This is to muche, and it were Goddes wille."
    "Ye, wif," quod he, "lat slepen that is stille;
It may be wel, paraventure, yet to-day   765
Ye shul your trouthe holden, by my fay!
For God so wisly have mercy on me,
I hadde wel lever y-stiked for to be,
For verray love which that I to yow have,
But-if ye sholde your trouthe kepe and save.   770
Trouthe is the hyeste thing that man may kepe."
But with that word he brast anon to wepe,
And seyde, "I yow forbede, up peyne of deeth,
That never, whyl thee lasteth lyf ne breeth,
To no wight tel thou of this aventure.   775
As I may best, I wol my wo endure,
Ne make no contenance of hevinesse,
That folk of yow may demen harm or gesse."
    And forth he cleped a squyer and a mayde:
"Goth forth anon with Dorigen," he sayde,   780
"And bringeth hir to swich a place anon."
They take hir leve, and on hir wey they gon;
But they ne wiste why she thider wente.
He nolde no wight tellen his entente.
    Paraventure an heep of yow, y-wis,   785
Wol holden him a lewed man in this,
That he wol putte his wyf in jupartye;
Herkneth the tale, er ye up-on hir crye.
She may have bettre fortune than yow semeth;
And whan that ye han herd the tale, demeth.   790
    This squyer, which that highte Aurelius,
On Dorigen that was so amorous,
Of aventure happed hir to mete
Amidde the toun, right in the quikkest strete,
As she was boun to goon the wey forthright   795
Toward the gardin ther-as she had hight.
And he was to the gardinward also;
For wel he spyed, whan she wolde go

---

718. **Demociones doghter.** Demotion, a member of the famous court of the Areopagus at Athens, had a daughter who, when she heard of the death of the man she was engaged to marry, killed herself because she felt that she was married only to this man. 720. **Cedasus.** The two daughters of Scedasus of Boeotia, Greece, were violated, and killed themselves rather than face dishonor. 724. **Nichanore,** an officer of Alexander the Great at the capture of Thebes (336 B.C.). **Another Theban mayden** (l. 726) has reference to the same circumstances. 729. **Nicerates wyf.** Nicerates of Athens was put to death by the Thirty Tyrants (see l. 660), and his wife killed herself lest she fall into their hands. 731. **Alcebiades.** The mistress of Alcibiades, leader of the Athenians in the Peloponnesian War, was Timandra. 734. **Alceste.** Alcestis was the wife of Admetus, King of Pherae in Thessaly, Greece. She consented to die in his place in order to prolong his life. Later Hercules brought her back from Hades. 735. **Penalopee.** Penelope, wife of Odysseus (Ulysses) in *The Odyssey*, fended off innumerable suitors until the return of her husband after his wanderings. She did not, however, sacrifice herself in death, yet she has always been a symbol of conjugal fidelity. 737. **Laodomya.** Protesilaus was reputedly the first Greek to fall in the Trojan War. 740. **Porcia.** The story of Portia is no doubt familiar from Shakespeare and his *Julius Caesar.* When her husband, Brutus, departed from Rome in the civil war following the assassination of Caesar, Portia committed suicide by swallowing live coals. 743. **Arthemesye,** Artemisia, wife of King Mausolus of Caria, Asia Minor; it was she whose magnificent tomb has given us the word *mausoleum.* 745. **Teuta,** a queen of Illyria, along the eastern coast of the Adriatic Sea. She was noted for her chastity. 747. **Bilia,** wife of Duellius, a famous Roman naval commander who won a victory over the Carthaginians in 260 B.C. 748. **Rodogone,** daughter of Emperor Darius of Persia. When her nurse tried to persuade her to a second marriage, she killed her. **Valeria,** wife of Servius, the ancient king of Rome; she refused to marry a second time.

754. **lenger the more,** the longer the more. 762. **as wis,** as (is) certain. 763. **and,** even if. 764. **stille,** quiet. The phrase is the equivalent of the old "let sleeping dogs lie." 768. **lever y-stiked,** rather be stabbed. 773. **up peyne of,** on pain of. 779. **cleped,** called. 786. **lewed,** ignorant, foolish. 787. **jupartye,** jeopardy. 790. **demeth,** judge (the imperative of the verb). 794. **quikkest,** liveliest, busiest.

Out of hir hous to any maner place.
But thus they mette, of aventure or grace; 800
And he saleweth hir with glad entente
And asked of hir whiderward she wente.

And she answerde, half as she were mad,
"Unto the gardin, as myn housbond bad,
My trouthe for to holde, allas! allas!" 805

Aurelius gan wondren on this cas,
And in his herte had greet compassioun
Of hir and of hir lamentacioun,
And of Arveragus, the worthy knight,
That bad hir holden al that she had hight, 810
So looth him was his wyf sholde breke hir trouthe;
And in his herte he caught of this greet routhe,
Consideringe the beste on every syde,
That fro his lust yet were him lever abyde
Than doon so heigh a cherlish wrecchednesse 815
Agayns franchyse and alle gentillesse;
For which in fewe wordes seyde he thus:

"Madame, seyth to your lord Arveragus,
That sith I see his grete gentillesse
To yow, and eek I see wel your distresse, 820
That him were lever han shame (and that were routhe)
Than ye to me sholde breke thus your trouthe,
I have wel lever ever to suffre wo
Than I departe the love bitwix yow two.
I yow relesse, madame, in-to your hond 825
Quit every surement and every bond,
That ye han maad to me as heer-biforn,
Sith thilke tyme which that ye were born.
My trouthe I plighte, I shal yow never repreve
Of no biheste, and here I take my leve, 830
As of the treweste and the beste wyf
That ever yet I knew in al my lyf.
But every wyf be-war of hir biheste,
On Dorigene remembreth atte leste.
Thus can a squyer doon a gentil dede, 835
As well as can a knight, with-outen drede."

She thonketh him up-on hir knees al bare,
And hoom un-to hir housbond is she fare,
And tolde him al as ye han herd me sayd;
And be ye siker, he was so weel apayd, 840
That it were inpossible me to wryte;
What sholde I lenger of this cas endyte?

Arveragus and Dorigene his wyf
In sovereyn blisse leden forth hir lyf.
Never eft ne was ther angre hem bitwene; 845
He cherisseth hir as though she were a quene;
And she was to him trewe for evermore.
Of thise two folk ye gete of me na-more.

Aurelius, that his cost hath al forlorn,
Curseth the tyme that ever he was born; 850

"Allas!" quod he, "allas! that I bihighte
Of pured gold a thousand pound of wighte
Un-to this philosophre! how shal I do?
I see na-more but that I am fordo.
Myn heritage moot I nedes selle, 855
And been a begger; heer may I nat dwelle,
And shamen al my kinrede in this place,
But I of him may gete bettre grace.
But nathelees, I wol of him assaye,
At certeyn dayes, yeer by yeer, to paye, 860
And thanke him of his grete curteisye;
My trouthe wol I kepe, I wol nat lye."

With herte soor he gooth un-to his cofre,
And broghte gold un-to this philosophre,
The value of fyve hundred pound, I gesse, 865
And him bisecheth, of his gentillesse,
To graunte him dayes of the remenaunt,
And seyde, "Maister, I dar wel make avaunt,
I failled never of my trouthe as yit;
For sikerly my dette shal be quit 870
Towardes yow, how-ever that I fare
To goon a-begged in my kirtle bare.
But wolde ye vouche-sauf, up-on seurtee,
Two yeer or three for to respyten me,
Than were I wel; for elles moot I selle 875
Myn heritage; ther is na-more to telle."

This philosophre sobrely answerde,
And seyde thus, whan he thise wordes herde:
"Have I nat holden covenant un-to thee?"
"Yes, certes, wel and trewely," quod he. 880
"Hastow nat had thy lady as thee lyketh?"
"No, no," quod he, and sorwefully he syketh.
"What was the cause? tel me if thou can."
Aurelius his tale anon bigan,
And tolde him al, as ye han herd bifore; 885
It nedeth nat to yow reherce it more.

He seide, "Arveragus, of gentillesse,
Had lever dye in sorwe and in distresse
Than that his wyf were of hir trouthe fals."
The sorwe of Dorigen he tolde him als, 890
How looth hir was to been a wikked wyf,
And that she lever had lost that day hir lyf,
And that hir trouthe she swoor, thurgh innocence:
"She never erst herde speke of apparence;
That made me han of hir so greet pitee, 895
And right as frely as he sente hir me,
As frely sente I hir to him ageyn.
This al and som, ther is na-more to seyn."

This philosophre answerde, "Leve brother,
Everich of yow dide gentilly til other. 900
Thou art a squyer, and he is a knight;
But God forbede, for His blisful might,
But-if a clerk coude doon a gentil dede
As wel as any of yow, it is no drede!

"Sire, I relesse thee thy thousand pound, 905

800. of aventure or grace, by chance or by (God's) grace. 811. him; that is, Arveragus. 816. franchyse, nobleness. 826. surement, surety. 842. endyte, write. 849. forlorn, completely lost.

852. pured, refined. wighte, weight. 853. philosophre, wise man, magician. 872. a-begged, a-begging.

As thou right now were cropen out of the ground,
Ne never er now ne haddest knowen me.
For, sire, I wol nat take a peny of thee
For al my craft, ne noght for my travaille.
Thou hast y-payed wel for my vitaille;   910
It is y-nogh, and farewel, have good day!"
And took his hors, and forth he gooth his way.

    Lordinges, this question wolde I aske now,
Which was the moste free, as thinketh yow?
Now telleth me, er that ye ferther wende.   915
I can na-more, my tale is at an ende.

THE NUN'S PRIEST'S TALE

There were three priests mentioned in the *Prologue* as convoying the Prioress and her companion (the Second Nun), but only one of these three is ever mentioned again. He is the narrator of the vigorous *exemplum* on flattery—and other things—presented in the form of a beast-story. But the most effective quality of *The Nun's Priest's Tale* is its satire—on husbands, on wives, on husbands and wives together, on people who believe in dreams, on people who do not believe in dreams, on the medieval weakness for quoting authorities. The bumbling Chantecleer and his sprightly favorite wife, Pertelote, are portrayed with unfailing good humor, and the end of the story rises to a full frenzy of mock-heroic action.

THE NUN'S PRIEST'S TALE

A POVRE widwe, somdel stape in age,
Was whylom dwelling in a narwe cotage,
Bisyde a grove, stonding in a dale.
This widwe, of which I telle yow my tale,
Sin thilke day that she was last a wyf,   5
In pacience ladde a ful simple lyf,
For litel was hir catel and hir rente;
By housbondrye, of such as God hir sente,
She fond hir-self, and eek hir doghtren two.
Three large sowes hadde she, and namo,   10
Three kyn, and eek a sheep that highte Malle.
Ful sooty was hir bour, and eek hir halle,
In which she eet ful many a sclendre meel.
Of poynaunt sauce hir neded never a deel.
No deyntee morsel passed thurgh hir throte;   15
Hir dyete was accordant to hir cote.

Repleccioun ne made hir nevere syk;
Attempree dyete was al hir phisyk,
And exercyse, and hertes suffisaunce.
The goute lette hir no-thing for to daunce,   20
N'apoplexye shente nat hir heed;
No wyn ne drank she, neither whyt ne reed;
Hir bord was served most with whyt and blak,
Milk and broun breed, in which she fond no lak,
Seynd bacoun, and somtyme an ey or tweye,   25
For she was as it were a maner deye.

    A yerd she hadde, enclosed al aboute
With stikkes, and a drye dich with-oute,
In which she hadde a cok, hight Chauntecleer,
In al the land of crowing nas his peer.   30
His vois was merier than the merye orgon
On messe dayes that in the chirche gon;
Wel sikerer was his crowing in his logge,
Than is a clokke, or an abbey orlogge.
By nature knew he ech ascencioun   35
Of equinoxial in thilke toun;
For whan degrees fiftene were ascended,
Thanne crew he, that it mighte nat ben amended.
His comb was redder than the fyn coral,
And batailed as it were a castel-wal.   40
His bile was blak, and as the jeet it shoon;
Lyk asur were his legges, and his toon;
His nayles whytter than the lilie flour,
And lyk the burned gold was his colour.
This gentil cok hadde in his governaunce   45
Sevenne hennes, for to doon al his pleasaunce,
Whiche were his sustres and his paramours,
And wonder lyk to him, as of colours.
Of whiche the faireste hewed on hir throte
Was cleped faire damoysele Pertelote.   50
Curteys she was, discreet, and debonaire,
And compaignable, and bar hir-self so faire,
Sin thilke day that she was seven night old,
That trewely she hath the herte in hold
Of Chauntecleer loken in every lith,   55
He loved hir so, that wel him was therwith.
But such a joye was it to here hem singe,
Whan that the brighte sonne gan to springe,

17. **Repleccioun,** repletion, overeating. 18. **Attempree,** temperate, moderate. 20. **goute lette,** etc., the gout did not prevent her from dancing. 21. **shente,** injured, harmed. 23. **whyt and blak,** light and dark ale. 25. **Seynd,** singed, crisped. **ey,** egg. 26. **deye,** dairyman or dairywoman; note the modern English surname Day. 30. **nas,** "ne" and "was," was not. 32. **messe dayes,** feast-days, church holidays. 33. **sikerer,** more certain, more dependable. 34. **orlogge,** horologe, large clock. 35–36. **ascencioun . . . equinoxial.** The *equinoxial* is the great circle made in the heavens by the extended plane of the earth's equator. It makes a complete revolution in twenty-four hours; consequently fifteen degrees would pass, or "ascend," every hour. In short, Chauntecleer knew by instinct every hour of the day when it came around, and proclaimed by crowing the arrival of each new hour. 38. **it . . . amended,** it could not be improved upon. 40. **batailed,** with battlements (the cock's wattles). 41. **jeet,** jet. 42. **toon,** toes. This word has both the *n*-plural and the *s*-plural in Chaucer's English; see l. 509 below. 45. **governaunce,** control, power. 51. **debonaire,** meek. 54. **in hold,** in her grasp, in her possession. 55. **loken,** locked. **lith,** limb.

906. **As thou . . . ground,** as if you had just crawled out of the ground; that is, as if I had just seen you for the first time. 914–916. **Which . . . ende.** The closing question is a common device in medieval courtly fiction, and has here the additional point of sharpening the marriage problem for the concluding tale in what most Chaucerians call the "marriage group" in *The Canterbury Tales*. 1. **stape,** "stepped," advanced. 7. **catel . . . rente.** *Catel* is any kind of property (note our modern chattel); *rente* is simply income. 9. **fond,** provided for. **doghtren,** daughters. 11. **kyn,** kine, cows. 16. **dyete . . . cote,** her diet was in keeping with her garments.

In swete accord, "my lief is faren in londe."
For thilke tyme, as I have understonde, 60
Bestes and briddes coude speke and singe.
     And so bifel, that in a dawenynge,
As Chauntecleer among his wyves alle
Sat on his perche, that was in the halle,
And next him sat this faire Pertelote, 65
This Chauntecleer gan gronen in his throte,
As man that in his dreem is drecched sore.
And whan that Pertelote thus herde him rore,
She was agast, and seyde, "O herte dere,
What eyleth yow, to grone in this manere? 70
Ye been a verray sleper, fy for shame!"
And he answerde and seyde thus, "Madame,
I pray yow, that ye take it nat a-grief:
By God, me mette I was in swich meschief
Right now, that yet myn herte is sore afright. 75
Now God," quod he, "my swevene recche aright,
And keep my body out of foul prisoun!
Me mette, how that I romed up and doun
Withinne our yerde, wher-as I saugh a beste,
Was lyk an hound, and wolde han maad areste 80
Upon my body, and wolde han had me deed.
His colour was bitwixe yelwe and reed;
And tipped was his tail, and bothe his eres,
With blak, unlyk the remenant of his heres;
His snowte smal, with glowinge eyen tweye. 85
Yet of his look for fere almost I deye;
This caused me my groning, douteles.
     "Avoy!" quod she, "fy on yow, herteles!
Allas!" quod she, "for, by that God above,
Now han ye lost myn herte and al my love; 90
I can nat love a coward, by my feith.
For certes, what so any womman seith,
We alle desyren, if it mighte be,
To han housbonds hardy, wyse, and free,
And secree, and no nigard, ne no fool, 95
Ne him that is agast of every tool,
Ne noon avauntour, by that God above!
How dorste ye seyn for shame unto your love,
That any thing mighte make yow aferd?
Have ye no mannes herte, and han a berd? 100

Allas! and conne ye been agast of swevenis?
No-thing, God wot, but vanitee, in sweven is.
Swevenes engendren of replecciouns
And ofte of fume, and of complecciouns,
Whan humours been to habundant in a wight. 105
Certes this dreem, which ye han met to-night,
Cometh of the grete superfluitee
Of youre rede *colera*, pardee,
Which causeth folk to dremen in here dremes
Of arwes, and of fyr with rede lemes, 110
Of grete bestes, that they wol hem byte,
Of contek, and of whelpes grete and lyte;
Right as the humour of malencolye
Causeth ful many a man, in sleep, to crye,
For fere of blake beres, or boles blake, 115
Or elles, blake develes wole hem take.
Of othere humours coude I telle also,
That werken many a man in sleep ful wo;
But I wol passe as lightly as I can.
     "Lo Catoun, which that was so wys a man, 120
Seyde he nat thus, ne do no fors of dremes?
Now, sire," quod she, "whan we flee fro the bemes,
For goddes love, as tak som laxatyf;
Up peril of my soule, and of my lyf,
I counseille yow the beste, I wol nat lye, 125
That both of colere, and of malencolye
Ye purge yow; and for ye shul nat tarie,
Though in this toun is noon apotecarie,
I shal my-self to herbes techen yow,
That shul ben for your hele, and for your prow; 130
And in our yerd tho herbes shal I fynde,
The whiche han of hir propretee, by kynde,
To purgen yow binethe, and eek above.
Forget not this, for goddes owene love!
Ye been ful colerik of compleccioun. 135
Ware the sonne in his ascencioun
Ne fynde yow nat repleet of humours hote;

60–61. **For thilke . . . singe,** "For in that same time . . . birds and beasts could speak and sing"—the usual trick of the writer of fables, who thereby colors his satire with the harmless tints of unreality. 67. **drecched,** troubled, afflicted. 73. **a-grief,** amiss. 74. **me mette,** "it met me"—a common circumlocution for "dreamt." 76. **swevene,** dream. **recche,** interpret. Chaucer in his works frequently shows us his interest in dreams, and although the careful reader will probably decide that Chaucer believed in the physiological explanation of dreams (as does Dame Pertelote in this story), it still is true that he gives plenty of space to the premonitory element which is dear to the common people. In reference to this premonitory element, *The Nun's Priest's Tale* is an interesting commentary upon the medieval attitude toward dreams, in that the two main characters, Chauntecleer and Pertelote, represent in a sense the two fundamentally different approaches to the question of dreams. 87. **douteles,** doubtless, "never fear." 88. **"Avoy!"** "Fie!," an expression of contemptuous reproach. **herteles,** "heartless" in the sense of "lacking courage or heart." 97. **avauntour,** "boaster," "braggart," which often connotes cowardice and indiscretion.

101–102. **swevenis . . . sweven is.** Identical rimes, common enough in modern humorous verse, are not considered out of place in serious verse of the Middle Ages. See note to l. 18 of the *Prologue* to *The Canterbury Tales.* 103. **engendren,** have their source in, come about from. 104. **fume,** air or gas on the stomach. **complecciouns,** the combination and balance of the four "humours" of the body; see the *Prologue* to *The Canterbury Tales* (p. 11:203), and note to l. 333. 106. **Certes,** surely, certainly. 108. **rede colera.** The *colera* would be the bile. The belief was held in medical quarters that a serious overbalance of one humour in respect to the others would give a corresponding tinge to all objects seen by the patient. Too much bile was supposed to make all things appear red; note in this connection ll. 113 ff. below. 110. **lemes,** flames. 112. **contek,** conflict. 115. **boles,** bulls. 120. **Catoun,** Dionysius Cato, the name given to the unknown author of a Latin work, probably of about the fourth century, called the *Dionysii Catonis Disticha de Moribus ad Filium,* "The Couplets of Dionysius Cato to his Son on the Subject of Morals." The collection was extremely popular in the Middle Ages and well illustrates the incurable Anglo-Saxon predilection for didactic epigrams—pithy statements of the laws underlying human nature. 121. **do no fors of,** make no account of, attach no importance to. 123. **as,** a superfluous particle here; translate, if at all, as "now (go)". 124. **Up,** upon, on. 126. **colere,** choler, bile. **malencolye,** another humour, "black bile." 130. **hele,** health. **prow,** benefit, profit. 132. **by kynde,** by nature.

And if it do, I dar wel leye a grote,
That ye shul have a fevere terciane,
Or an agu, that may be youre bane. 140
A day or two ye shul have digestyves
Of wormes er ye take your laxatyves,
Of lauriol, centaure, and fumetere,
Or elles of ellebor, that groweth there,
Of catapuce, or of gaytres beryis, 145
Of erbe yve, growing in our yerd, that mery is;
Pekke hem up right as they growe, and ete hem in.
Be mery, housbond, for your fader kyn!
Dredeth no dreem; I can say yow namore."
"Madame," quod he, "graunt mercy of your lore.
But natheles, as touching daun Catoun, 151
That hath of wisdom such a gret renoun,
Though that he had no dremes for to drede,
By God, men may in olde bokes rede
Of many a man, more of auctoritee 155
Than ever Catoun was, so mote I thee,
That al the revers seyn of this sentence,
And han wel founden by experience,
That dremes ben significaciouns,
As wel of joye as tribulaciouns 160
That folk enduren in this lyf present.
Ther nedeth make of this noon argument;
The verray preve sheweth it in dede.
"Oon of the gretteste auctours that men rede
Seith thus, that whylom two felawes wente 165
On pilgrimage, in a ful good entente;
And happed so, thay came into a toun,
Wher as ther was swich congregacioun
Of peple, and eek so streit of herbergage,
That they ne founde as muche as o cotage, 170
In which they bothe mighte y-logged be.
Wherfor thay mosten, of necessitee,
As for that night, departen compaignye;
And ech of hem goth to his hostelrye,
And took his logging as it wolde falle. 175
That oon of hem was logged in a stalle,

Fer in a yerd, with oxen of the plough;
That other man was logged wel y-nough,
As was his aventure, or his fortune,
That us governeth alle as in commune. 180
"And so bifel, that, long er it were day,
This man mette in his bed, ther as he lay,
How that his felawe gan up-on him calle,
And seyde, 'Allas! for in an oxes stalle
This night I shal be mordred ther I lye. 185
Now help me, dere brother, er I dye;
In alle haste com to me,' he sayde.
This man out of his sleep for fere abrayde;
But whan that he was wakned of his sleep,
He turned him, and took of this no keep; 190
Him thoughte his dreem nas but a vanitee.
Thus twyës in his sleping dremed he.
And atte thridde tyme yet his felawe
Cam, as him thoughte, and seide, 'I am now slawe,
Bihold my blody woundes, depe and wyde! 195
Arys up erly in the morwe-tyde,
And at the west gate of the toun,' quod he,
'A carte ful of donge ther shaltow see,
In which my body is hid ful prively;
Do thilke carte aresten boldely. 200
My gold caused my mordre, sooth to sayn',
And tolde him every poynt how he was slayn,
With a ful pitous face, pale of hewe.
And truste wel, his dreem he fond ful trewe;
For on the morwe, as sone as it was day, 205
To his felawes in he took the way;
And whan that he cam to this oxes stalle,
After his felawe he bigan to calle.
"The hostiler answerde him anon,
And seyde, 'Sire, your felawe is agon, 210
As sone as day he wente out of the toun.'
This man gan fallen in suspecioun,
Remembring on his dremes that he mette,
And forth he goth, no lenger wolde he lette,
Unto the west gate of the toun, and fond 215
A dong-carte, as it were to donge lond,
That was arrayed in that same wyse
As ye han herd the dede man devyse;
And with an hardy herte he gan to crye
Vengeaunce and justice of this felonye: 220
'My felawe mordred is this same night,

---

138. **leye a grote,** wager a groat. A groat was a Low German coin from the trading ports of Holland and North Germany, notably from Bremen, worth about four silver pennies. 139. **fevere terciane,** a tertian fever, one that recurs every third day. The medieval authorities attributed the disease to a superabundance of bile or black bile; it would seem to be, according to present-day diagnosis, a malarial infection. 140. **youre bane.** The original meaning of *bane* is "slayer," "killer." 143–146. **lauriol . . . erbe yve.** The drugs mentioned in this list include the common cathartics in use during the Middle Ages. *Lauriol* is the spurge-laurel. *centaure,* the century plant, a common remedy for pain in the abdomen. *fumetere,* fumitory. *ellebor,* hellebore. *catapuce,* the caperberry. *gaytres beryis,* berries of the dogwood. *erbe yve,* ground ivy. 151. **daun.** Here, as elsewhere, the shortened form of the Latin *dominus* ("lord") is used as a title of respect. (Note the Spanish *Don.*) *Daun Catoun* is therefore Lord Cato. So Tennyson in his *Palace of Art* speaks of Dan Chaucer, and there is also the familiar Dan Cupid. 156. **so mote I thee,** a mild asseveration meaning literally "so may I prosper." 157. **sentence,** statement, opinion. 163. **verray preve,** etc., "the true test (of the statement) proves it in fact." 166. **ful good entente,** the best of intentions. 169. **streit,** "narrow"; here used in the sense of "crowded." **herbergage,** lodgings. 173. **departen,** part (company).

182. **ther as,** where. 188. **abrayde,** started up. The word is used for any kind of violent motion. 191. **Him thoughte,** not "he thought" but "it seemed to him," an impersonal construction. The same is true of the more common "methinks," which means "it seems to me." This is not the verb "to think," but the verb seen in the German *es dünkt mir* ("it seems to me"). *nas,* "ne" plus "was," therefore "was not." The construction with *but* means simply: "It seemed to him that his dream was nothing but a foolish thing." 194. **slawe,** slain. 203. **pitous,** pitiful, awakening pity. 206. **in,** inn. 214. **lette,** literally "hinder" (compare the legal phrase "without let or hindrance" or a "let" ball in tennis); then the meaning here of "linger," "loiter." 216. **to donge lond,** to cover land with dung. Raw sewage was carried outside the city gates and dumped. 218. **devyse,** describe.

And in this carte he lyth gapinge upright.
I crye out on the ministres,' quod he,
'That sholden kepe and reulen this citee;
Harrow! allas! her lyth my felawe slayn!'   225
What sholde I more un-to this tale sayn?
The peple out-sterte, and caste the cart to grounde,
And in the middel of the dong they founde
The dede man, that mordred was al newe.

    "O blisful God, that art so just and trewe!   230
Lo, how that thou biwreyest mordre alway!
Mordre wol out, that se we day by day.
Mordre is so wlatsom and abhominable
To God, that is so just and resonable,
That he ne wol nat suffre it heled be;   235
Though it abyde a yeer, or two, or three,
Mordre wol out, this my conclusioun.
And right anoon, ministres of that toun
Han hent the carter, and so sore him pyned,
And eek the hostiler so sore engyned,   240
That thay biknewe hir wikkednesse anoon,
And were an-hanged by the nekke-boon.

    "Here may men seen that dremes been to drede.
And certes, in the same book I rede,
Right in the nexte chapitre after this,   245
(I gabbe nat, so have I joye or blis,)
Two men that wolde han passed over see,
For certeyn cause, in-to a fer contree,
If that the wind ne hadde been contrarie,
That made hem in a citee for to tarie,   250
That stood ful mery upon an haven-syde.
But on a day, agayn the even-tyde,
The wind gan chaunge, and blew right as hem leste.
Jolif and glad they wente un-to hir reste,
And casten hem ful erly for to saille;   255
But to that oo man fel a greet mervaille.
That oon of hem, in sleping as he lay,
Him mette a wonder dreem, agayn the day;
Him thoughte a man stood by his beddes syde,
And him comaunded, that he sholde abyde,   260
And seyde him thus, 'If thou to-morwe wende,

Thou shalt be dreynt; my tale is at an ende.'
He wook, and tolde his felawe what he mette,
And preyde him his viage for to lette;
As for that day, he preyde him to abyde.   265
His felawe, that lay by his beddes syde,
Gan for to laughe, and scorned him ful faste.
'No dreem,' quod he, 'may so myn herte agaste,
That I wol lette for to do my thinges.
I sette not a straw by thy dreminges,   270
For swevenes been but vanitees and japes.
Men dreme al-day of owles or of apes,
And eek of many a mase therwithal;
Men dreme of thing that never was ne shal.
But sith I see that thou wolt heer abyde,   275
And thus for-sleuthen wilfully thy tyde,
God wot it reweth me; and have good day.'
And thus he took his leve, and wente his way.
But er that he hadde halfe his cours y-seyled,
Noot I nat why, ne what mischaunce it eyled,   280
But casuelly the shippes botme rente,
And ship and man under the water wente
In sighte of othere shippes it byside,
That with hem seyled at the same tyde.
And therfor, faire Pertelote so dere,   285
By swiche ensamples olde maistow lere,
That no man sholde been to recchelees
Of dremes, for I sey thee, doutelees,
That many a dreem ful sore is for to drede.

    "Lo, in the lyf of seint Kenelm, I rede,   290
That was Kenulphus sone, the noble king
Of Mercenrike, how Kenelm mette a thing;
A lyte er he was mordred, on a day,
His mordre in his avisioun he say.
His norice him expounded every del   295
His sweven, and bad him for to kepe him wel
For traisoun; but he nas but seven yeer old,
And therefore litel tale hath he told
Of any dreem, so holy was his herte.

---

222. **upright.** This word does not necessarily refer to a vertical or perpendicular position, as in Modern English, so much as to straightness or rigidity of posture. One can lie "upright" in Middle English, meaning to lie straight, stretched out in a horizontal position. One can also stand "upright." The murdered man here was lying stretched out and gaping up at the light of day. 225. **Harrow! allas!** The two cries of distress are usually found in combination. The first, *Harrow!*, may originally have had some relation to the idea of "raking," "harrowing," hence "distressing" (we can still speak of a "harrowing" experience), but no doubt the original meaning had long since faded. 231. **biwreyest,** uncoverest, makest known. 233. **wlatsom,** disgusting, horrible. 235. **heled,** concealed. 239. **hent,** seized. **pyned,** tortured (to force a confession). 240. **engyned,** put on the rack or some other instrument of torture. 241. **biknewe,** acknowledged, confessed. 242. **an-hanged,** hanged. 246. **gabbe,** speak idly. It is amusing to see how consistently Chaucer has portrayed Chauntecleer as the pompous, self-important husband. 252. **agayn,** toward, just before. 254. **Jolif,** jolly, merry, with the Old French *-if* suffix still seen in "active," "pensive," etc. 255. **hem,** them. 256. **oo,** one.

262. **dreynt,** drowned. 264. **lette,** put off; see note to l. 214 above. 271. **vanitees and japes,** follies and jokes. 273. **mase,** confusion, bewilderment. 274. **shal,** shall (be). 275. **sith,** since. 276. **forsleuthen,** waste in sloth. **tyde,** time; see the alliterative formula, "time and tide," or combinations like "Yuletide," "Christmastide," "Eventide," etc. 277. **it reweth me,** "it rues me," "I am sorry"—still another in the long list of Middle English impersonal constructions. 281. **casuelly,** by accident. 287. **recchelees,** not caring for, not heeding. 290. **seint Kenelm,** etc. The story is told in one of the many collections of medieval English saints' lives. Kenulphus (Cenwulf), mentioned in the next line, had a son Kenelm (Cenhelm). Kenulphus was King of Mercia, one of the important Anglo-Saxon kingdoms in England before King Alfred (d. 901); he died in 821. The boy Kenelm was but seven years of age at the time, and was put under the care of his aunt, who conspired to murder him. Before his death the child dreamt that he climbed into a lofty tree; one of his friends came and cut it down, whereupon the boy flew to Heaven as a bird. As a symbol of martyred childhood and innocence, Kenelm was later canonized. 294. **avisioun,** vision, dream. **say,** saw. 295. **norice,** nurse. 298. **tale,** importance, account. **told,** ascribed, attributed.

By God, I hadde lever than my sherte   300
That ye had rad his legende, as have I.
Dame Pertelote, I sey yow trewely,
Macrobeus, that writ th'avisioun
In Affrike of the worthy Cipioun,
Affermeth dremes, and seith that they been   305
Warning of thinges that men after seen.

    "And forther-more, I pray yow loketh wel
In th'olde testament, of Daniel,
If he held dremes any vanitee.
Reed eek of Joseph, and ther shul ye see   310
Wher dremes ben somtyme (I set nat alle)
Warning of thinges that shul after falle.
Loke of Egipt the king, daun Pharao,
His bakere and his boteler also,
Wher they ne felte noon effect in dremes.   315
Who-so wol seken actes of sondry remes,
May rede of dremes many a wonder thing.

    "Lo Cresus, which that was of Lyde king,
Mette he nat that he sat upon a tree;
Which signified he sholde anhanged be?   320
Lo heer Andromacha, Ectores wyf,
That day that Ector sholde lese his lyf,
She dremed on the same night biforn,
How that the lyf of Ector sholde be lorn,
If thilke day he wente in-to bataille;   325
She warned him, but it mighte nat availle;
He wente for to fighte nathelees,
But he was slayn anoon of Achilles.
But thilke tale is al to long to telle,
And eek it is ny day, I may nat dwelle.   330

Shortly I seye, as for conclusioun,
That I shal han of this avisioun
Adversitee; and I seye forther-more,
That I ne telle of laxatyves no store,
For they ben venimous, I woot it wel;   335
I hem defye, I love hem nevere a del.

    "Now let us speke of mirthe, and stinte al this;
Madame Pertelote, so have I blis,
Of o thing God hath sent me large grace;
For whan I see the beautee of your face,   340
Ye ben so scarlet-reed about youre yën,
It maketh al my drede for to dyen;
For, also siker as *In principio*,
Mulier est hominis confusio;
Madame, the sentence of this Latin is—   345
Womman is mannes joye and al his blis.
For whan I feele anight your softe syde,
Al be it that I may nat on yow ryde,
For that oure perche is maad so narwe, allas!
I am so ful of joye and of solas   350
That I defye bothe sweven and dreem."
And with that word he fley doun fro the beem,
For it was day, and eek his hennes alle;
And with a chuk he gan hem for to calle,
For he had founde a corn, lay in the yerd.   355
Royal he was, he was namore aferd;
He fethered Pertelote twenty tyme,
And trad as ofte, er that it was pryme.
He loketh as it were a grim leoun,
And on his toos he rometh up and doun,   360
Him deyned not to sette his foot to grounde.
He chukketh, whan he hath a corn y-founde,
And to him rennen thanne his wyves alle.
Thus royal, as a prince is in his halle,
Leve I this Chauntecleer in his pasture;   365
And after wol I telle his aventure.

    Whan that the month in which the world bigan,
That highte March, whan God first maked man,
Was complet, and [y]-passed were also,
Sin March bigan, thritty dayes and two,   370
Bifel that Chauntecleer, in al his pryde,
His seven wyves walking by his syde,
Caste up his eyen to the brighte sonne,
That in the signe of Taurus hadde y-ronne

---

300. **lever,** "liefer," rather. 303. **Macrobeus,** the "authority" on dreams during the Middle Ages. His accredited importance is hardly fair to another greater writer, Cicero, who, by the way, is probably "oon of the gretteste auctours" of l. 164 above, since the story of the murdered traveler is found in Cicero's *De Divinatione*. Macrobeus, a Latin writer of about the fifth century, made an elaborate commentary to that section of Cicero's *De Republica* known as the *Somnium Scipionis* or "Dream of Scipio," in which commentary there appears a discussion of the various kinds of dreams and their application to human life. It is worth noting that Macrobeus is certainly the leading champion of the "portentous" or "premonitory" interpretation of dreams as opposed to the physiological interpretation (see note to l. 76 above). 308. **Daniel,** the Old Testament prophet. The passage in the Bible relevant to this line is Daniel, 7:1, 1 ff. 310. **Joseph.** The manner in which Joseph interpreted dreams is told in Genesis 37:40–41. The marshaling of authorities (Macrobeus, Daniel, Joseph, and the classical folk) is absolutely typical of the method of reasoning in the Middle Ages. 311. **Wher,** whether. Chauntecleer is, after all, a citizen of the late fourteenth century in Europe, which produces its Chaucer and its Mandeville. The little caution that he assumes here is symptomatic of the growing caution of the age in asserting all statements of authority as truth; this tendency is a definite indication of the coming of the Renaissance. 316. **remes,** realms. 318. **Cresus.** The story is told in *The Romance of the Rose*. Croesus, King of Lydia (603–546 B.C.) was defeated and killed by Cyrus the Great (d. 529 B.C.). 321. **Andromacha,** Andromache, the wife of Hector in Homer's *Iliad*. There is nothing in Homer about her dream; it is a fiction of the medieval authors in the development of the Legend of Troy. 322. **lese,** lose. 324. **lorn,** lost.

335. **venimous,** venomous, poisonous. 337. **stinte,** stop, cease. 343. **siker,** sure, surely. **In principio,** the beginning of the first verse of the Gospel of John or of the Book of Genesis. 344. **Mulier . . . confusio,** "woman is man's confusion," more or less of a proverb of the time. 355. **corn,** grain (of any kind). 359. **leoun,** lion. 370. **bigan,** passed, went by (not "began"). In other words, this means thirty-two days after March 31, which would be May 2–3. 374. **signe of Taurus,** the second of the twelve Signs of the Zodiac, constellations through which the sun must pass in its annual journey through the heavens. The sun would be in Taurus from about April 20 to May 20. The reference in the next line to the "twenty-one or more degrees" would put the date of Chauntecleer's adventure later than May 3; in other words Chaucer's astronomical data is a little out of line, a most unusual error for him.

Twenty degrees and oon, and somwhat more;   375
And knew by kynde and by noon other lore,
That it was pryme, and crew with blisful stevene.
"The sonne," he sayde, "is clomben up on hevene
Fourty degrees and oon, and more, y-wis.
Madame Pertelote, my worldes blis,   380
Herkneth thise blisful briddes how they singe,
And see the fresshe floures how they springe;
Ful is myn hert of revel and solas."
But sodeinly him fil a sorweful cas;
For ever the latter ende of joye is wo.   385
God woot that worldly joye is sone ago;
And if a rethor coude faire endyte,
He in a cronique saufly mighte it write,
As for a sovereyn notabilitee.
Now every wys man, lat him herkne me;   390
This storie is al-so trewe, I undertake,
As is the book of Launcelot de Lake,
That wommen holde in ful gret reverence.
Now wol I torne agayn to my sentence.
    A col-fox, ful of sly iniquitee,   395
That in the grove hadde woned yeres three,
By heigh imaginacioun forn-cast,
The same night thurgh-out the hegges brast
Into the yerd, ther Chauntecleer the faire
Was wont, and eek his wyves, to repaire;   400
And in a bed of wortes stille he lay,
Til it was passed undern of the day,
Wayting his tyme on Chauntecleer to falle
As gladly doon thise homicydes alle,
That in awayt liggen to mordre men.   405
O false mordrer lurking in thy den!
O newe Scariot, newe Genilon!
False dissimilour, O Greek Sinon
That broghtest Troye al outrely to sorwe!

O Chauntecleer, acursed be that morwe,   410
That thou into that yerd flough fro the bemes!
Thou were ful wel y-warnéd by thy dremes,
That thilke day was perilous to thee.
But what that God forwoot mot nedes be,
After the opinioun of certeyn clerkis.   415
Witnesse on him, that any perfit clerk is,
That in scole is gret altercacioun
In this matere, and greet disputisoun,
And hath ben of an hundred thousand men.
But I ne can not bulte it to the bren,   420
As can the holy doctour Augustyn,
Or Boëce, or the bishop Bradwardyn,
Whether that Goddes worthy forwiting
Streyneth me nedely for to doon a thing,
(Nedely clepe I simple necessitee);   425
Or elles, if free choys be graunted me
To do that same thing, or do it noght,
Though God forwoot it, er that it was wroght;
Or if his witing streyneth nevere a del
But by necessitee condicionel.   430
I wol not han to do of swich matere;
My tale is of a cok, as ye may here,
That took his counseil of his wyf, with sorwe,
To walken in the yerd upon that morwe
That he had met the dreem, that I yow tolde.   435
Wommennes counseils been ful ofte colde;
Wommannes counseil broghte us first to wo,
And made Adam fro paradys to go,
Ther-as he was ful mery, and wel at ese.—
But for I noot, to whom it mighte displese,   440
If I counseil of wommen wolde blame,
Passe over, for I seyde it in my game.
Rede auctours, wher they trete of swich matere,
And what thay seyn of wommen ye may here.
Thise been the cokkes wordes, and nat myne;   445

---

376. **by kynde**, by nature, by instinct. 377. **pryme**, the first hour of the day (6 A.M.), or roughly, from 6 to 9 in the morning. **stevene**, voice. 379. **y-wis**, indeed, in truth, surely. Forty-one degrees would be almost halfway to the zenith. In May this would be shortly after nine o'clock in the morning. 381. **briddes**, birds. 384. **sorweful cas**, sad event. 386. **ago**, gone. 387. **rethor**, rhetorician. 389. **sovereyn**, mighty superior. 392. **Launcelot de Lake**, the great chivalric hero of the Arthurian saga; the reference here is probably to the French romance (book) of the thirteenth century, which was the source of all English treatments of this non-English hero. 396. **woned**, dwelt. 397. **heigh imaginacioun forn-cast**, by divine foreknowledge (*imaginacioun*) foreordained. 398. **brast**, burst. 401. **wortes**, herbs. 402. **undern**, early morning. The usual hour conveyed by this term is nine o'clock in the morning, but it is quite possible that, as in the case of *pryme* (see note to l. 377 above), the word expresses a two- or three-hour period following the precise original hour. On this analogy, *undern* could mean anywhere from nine o'clock in the morning until noon. 405. **liggen**, lie. 407. **Scariot**, Judas Iscariot, the disciple who betrayed Christ; see Matthew, 26:14–25 and 47–56. **Genilon**, Ganelon, the traitor in *The Song of Roland* (p. 11:110), who betrayed Roland's command to the Saracens. 408. **Sinon**, the man who persuaded the Trojans to admit the Wooden Horse to Troy, by which stratagem the city was captured. The story was probably familiar to medieval readers through Virgil's *Aeneid*, Book 11 (p. 1:375).

411. **flough**, flew. 414. **forwoot**, foreknows, has foreknowledge of; see note to l. 397 above. The question of Providence vs. Free Will was one of the favorite points of discussion among medieval theologians and philosophers. 418. **disputisoun**, argument, dispute. 420. **bulte . . . bren**, "sift it to the bran," "analyze the question thoroughly and leave nothing behind but immaterial or irrelevant facts." Chaucer's attitude, here as elsewhere, is that of the casual spectator and observer whenever weighty or insoluble problems of philosophy happen to get in his way. 421. **Augustyn**, St. Augustine of Hippo, the Church Father (354–430), who was the great representative of orthodox doctrine. 422. **Boëce**, Boethius (480?–524), whose *Consolation of Philosophy* was the great book on philosophy in the Middle Ages. **bishop Bradwardyn**, lecturer at Oxford and Archbishop of Canterbury at the time of his death in 1349. His treatment of the problem was conservative and orthodox—he relied chiefly upon Providence. 424. **Streyneth**, constrains, forces. **nedely**, of necessity, by necessity. 425. **clepe**, call. 430. **necessitee condicionel**, necessity conditioned by God's foreknowledge as contrasted to simple necessity, whereby a thing happens because it must happen. 440. **noot**, "ne" plus "woot," therefore "know not." 442. **game**, joke, sport. 443. **auctours**, authors and authorities. Once more there appears the medieval love of authority (*magister dixit*) motif; see note to l. 310 above.

I can noon harm of no womman divyne.

Faire in the sond, to bathe hir merily,
Lyth Pertelote, and alle hir sustres by,
Agayn the sonne; and Chauntecleer so free
Song merier than the mermayde in the see;   450
For Phisiologus seith sikerly,
How that they singen wel and merily.
And so bifel that, as he caste his yë,
Among the wortes, on a boterflyë,
He was war of this fox that lay ful lowe.   455
No-thing ne liste him thanne for to crowe,
But cryde anon, "cok, cok," and up he sterte,
As man that was affrayed in his herte.
For naturelly a beest desyreth flee
Fro his contrarie, if he may it see,   460
Though he never erst had seyn it with his yë.

This Chauntecleer, whan he gan him espyë,
He wolde han fled, but that the fox anon
Seyde, "Gentil sire, allas! wher wol ye gon?
Be ye affrayed of me that am your freend?   465
Now certes, I were worse than a feend,
If I to yow wolde harm or vileinye.
I am nat come your counseil for t'espye;
But trewely, the cause of my cominge
Was only for to herkne how that ye singe.   470
For trewely ye have as mery a stevene,
As eny aungel hath, that is in hevene;
Therwith ye han in musik more felinge
Than hadde Boëce, or any that can singe.
My lord your fader (God his soule blesse!),   475
And eek your moder, of hir gentilesse,
Han in myn hous y-been, to my gret ese;
And certes, sire, ful fayn wolde I yow plese.
But for men speke of singing, I wol saye,
So mote I brouke wel myn eyen tweye,   480

Save yow, I herde never man so singe,
As dide your fader in the morweninge;
Certes, it was of herte, al that he song.
And for to make his voys the more strong,
He wolde so peyne him, that with both his yën   485
He moste winke, so loude he wolde cryen,
And stonden on his tiptoon ther-with-al,
And strecche forth his nekke long and smal.
And eek he was of swich discrecioun,
That ther nas no man in no regioun   490
That him in song or wisdom mighte passe.
I have wel rad in daun Burnel the Asse,
Among his vers, how that there was a cok,
For that a preestes sone yaf him a knok
Upon his leg, whyl he was yong and nyce,   495
He made him for to lese his benefyce.
But certeyn, ther nis no comparisoun
Bitwix the wisdom and discrecioun
Of youre fader, and of his subtiltee.
Now singeth, sire, for seinte Charitee,   500
Let see, conne ye your fader countrefete?"
This Chauntecleer his winges gan to bete,
As man that coude his tresoun nat espye,
So was he ravisshed with his flaterye.

Allas! ye lordes, many a fals flatour   505
Is in your courtes, and many a losengeour,
That plesen yow wel more, by my feith,
Than he that soothfastnesse unto yow seith.
Redeth Ecclesiaste of flaterye;
Beth war, ye lordes, of hir trecherye.   510

This Chauntecleer stood hye up-on his toos,
Strecching his nekke, and heeld his eyen cloos,
And gan to crowe loude for the nones;
And daun Russel the fox sterte up at ones,
And by the gargat hente Chauntecleer,   515
And on his bak toward the wode him beer,
For yet ne was ther no man that him sewed.
O destinee, that mayst nat been eschewed!

---

446. I . . . devyne, "I can guess (or imagine) no harm of any woman,"
probably to be taken as sarcastic. The double negative, a feature of
Early English, is purely for emphasis. In no case do two negatives
cancel each other out to make a positive. 451. Phisiologus . . .
sikerly. *Sikerly* means *certainly*. The *Physiologus* is the Latin Physiologus or Bestiary, a collection of verses treating of the habits of
certain animals and drawing therefrom moral lessons of Christian
import. 460. contrarie, opposite (sb.). According to medieval belief,
every creature had another creature that was its contrary, toward
which it felt a natural dislike or fear (dog to cat, snake to bird, etc.).
461. erst, before, first. The antipathy would be instinctive. 474.
Boëce. Boethius (see note to l. 422 above) was also an authority on
the music of his time. 476. gentilesse. The word *gentilesse*, a combination in sense of "gentleness" and "gentility," has a variety of
meanings, which, when blended together, come close to producing
the ideal of chivalry either for man or for woman. Nobility or aristocracy of birth, nobility of character according to the Christian or
knightly codes, courtesy, good breeding, delicacy, tact, and even
slenderness of body—all come at one time or another under this one
word *gentilesse*. But most important of all considerations here is the
matter of innate virtuous qualities. In consequence, no one translation of the word can fit any one occurrence thereof, and the reader
must choose for himself. 480. So . . . brouke, another extremely
mild oath, of the same kind as "So mote I thee" of l. 156 above, "as
I may enjoy my eyes!"

486. winke, to close the eyes, not to blink them momentarily, as in
Modern English. 488. smal, narrow, slender. 492. daun Burnel the
Asse. There was an Anglo-Latin poem of the twelfth century, satirical
in nature, by Nigel Wireker, called *Burnellus, seu Speculum Stultorum*
(Burnell, or the Mirror of Fools). A young man named Gundulfus was
annoyed by a cock, and upon throwing a stone broke the bird's leg.
Later Gundulfus was to be ordained, but the injured cock delayed his
crowing, so that Gundulfus overslept and lost his benefice, or church
living. 495. nyce. As usual before the seventeenth century, this
word means here "ignorant," "foolish." 501. countrefete, imitate
and match. This word does not have in Middle English the suggestion
of falseness or criminality that it has assumed in Modern English.
505. flatour, flatterer. 506. losengeour, flatterer. 508. soothfastnesse, truth. 509. Ecclesiaste of flaterye. The reference is to the
Apocryphal Book of Ecclesiasticus, not to the Poetic Book of Ecclesiastes in the Old Testament. The specific passages in Ecclesiasticus, which are too long to quote here, are to chapters 12: 10 ff.
and 27: 26. 514. Russel. This, in the medieval Beast Epic, was the
name of one of the sons of Reynard the Fox. 515. gargat, throat.
hente, seized. 517. sewed, pursued, followed.

Allas, that Chauntecleer fleigh fro the bemes!
Allas, his wyf ne roghte nat of dremes! 520
And on a Friday fil al this meschaunce.
O Venus, that art goddesse of plesaunce,
Sin that thy servant was this Chauntecleer,
And in thy service dide al his poweer,
More for delyt, than world to multiplye, 525
Why woldestow suffre him on thy day to dye?
O Gaufred, dere mayster soverayn,
That, whan thy worthy king Richard was slayn
With shot, compleynedest his deth so sore,
Why ne hadde I now thy sentence and thy lore, 530
The Friday for to chide, as diden ye?
(For on a Friday soothly slayn was he.)
Than wolde I shewe yow how that I coude pleyne
For Chauntecleres drede, and for his peyne.
　　Certes, swich cry ne lamentacioun 535
Was never of ladies maad, whan Ilioun
Was wonne, and Pirrus with his streite swerd,
Whan he hadde hent king Priam by the berd,
And slayn him (as saith us *Eneydos*),
As maden alle the hennes in the clos, 540
Whan they had seyn of Chauntecleer the sighte.
But sovereynly dame Pertelote shrighte,
Ful louder than dide Hasdrubales wyf,
Whan that hir housbond hadde lost his lyf,
And that the Romayns hadde brend Cartage; 545
She was so ful of torment and of rage,
That wilfully into the fyr she sterte,
And brende hir-selven with a stedfast herte.
O woful hennes, right so cryden ye,
As, whan that Nero brende the citee 550
Of Rome, cryden senatoures wyves,
For that hir housbondes losten alle hir lyves;
Withouten gilt this Nero hath hem slayn.
Now wol I torne to my tale agayn:
　　This sely widwe, and eek hir doghtres two, 555
Herden thise hennes crye and maken wo,
And out at dores sterten they anoon,
And syen the fox toward the grove goon,
And bar upon his bak the cok away;

And cryden, "Out! harrow! and weylaway! 560
Ha, ha, the fox!" and after him they ran,
And eek with staves many another man;
Ran Colle our dogge, and Talbot, and Gerland,
And Malkin, with a distaf in hir hand;
Ran cow and calf, and eek the verray hogges 565
So were they fered for berking of the dogges
And shouting of the men and wimmen eke,
They ronne so, hem thoughte hir herte breke.
They yolleden as feendes doon in helle;
The dokes cryden as men wolde hem quelle; 570
The gees for fere flowen over the trees;
Out of the hyve cam the swarm of bees;
So hidous was the noyse, a! *benedicite!*
Certes, he Jakke Straw, and his meynee,
Ne made never shoutes half so shrille, 575
Whan that they wolden any Fleming kille,
As thilke day was maad upon the fox.
Of bras thay broghten bemes, and of box,
Of horn, of boon, in whiche they blewe and pouped,
And therwithal thay shryked and they houped; 580
It seemed as that heven sholde falle.
Now, gode men, I pray yow herkneth alle!
　　Lo, how fortune turneth sodeinly
The hope and pryde eek of hir enemy!
This cok, that lay upon the foxes bak, 585
In al his drede, un-to the fox he spak,
And seyde, "Sire, if that I were as ye,
Yet sholde I seyn (as wis God helpe me):
'Turneth agayn, ye proude cherles alle!
A verray pestilence up-on yow falle! 590
Now am I come un-to this wodes syde,
Maugree your heed, the cok shal heer abyde;
I wol him ete in feith, and that anon.'"
The fox answerde, "In feith, it shal be don"—
And as he spak that word, al sodeinly 595
This cok brak from his mouth deliverly,
And heighe up-on a tree he fleigh anon.
And whan the fox saugh that he was y-gon,
"Allas!" quod he, "O Chauntecleer, allas!
I have to yow," quod he, "y-doon trespas, 600
In-as-muche as I maked yow aferd,
Whan I yow hente, and broghte out of the yerd;
But, sire, I dide it in no wikke entente;
Com doun, and I shal telle yow what I mente.

---

520. **roghte,** recked, heeded, took account of.　527. **Gaufred,** Geoffrey de Vinsauf, a writer on the art of poetry. His great work, the *Poetria Nova,* appeared shortly after the death of Richard I (the Lion-Heart) of England, near 1200. Geoffrey's model for an elegy consists of some lines of lament on the death of Richard.　532. **on a Friday.** Friday has been a traditionally unlucky day because it has been associated with the goddess of love (Venus, Freya), who is notoriously fickle and changeable. The death of the Saviour on Friday has stimulated the superstition most powerfully. 533. **pleyne,** complain, lament for. 539. **Eneydos,** Virgil's *Aeneid* (p. I:357). 540. **clos,** close (sb.), yard. 542. **sovereynly,** more than anyone else. **shrighte,** shrieked. 543–545. **louder . . . Cartage.** Hasdrubal was ruler of Carthage when the Romans sacked it (146 B.C.). **brend,** burned. 546. **rage,** not "wrath" or "anger" in our modern sense, but "madness." 550. **Nero . . . citee,** a reference to the disastrous fire at Rome during the reign of Nero (37–68) in the year 64. Nero was popularly supposed to have set the fire himself, but modern historians disbelieve the story. 555. **sely,** good.

565. **verray hogges,** even the hogs. 570. **dokes,** ducks. **quelle,** kill. 574. **Jakke Straw . . . meynee,** Jack Straw and his followers. This passage is virtually the only one in Chaucer's works having reference to an important event in England during his lifetime. The Peasants' Revolt of 1381 was featured by rioting against the Flemish (Flemings) who had settled in London and adjacent parts to pursue their occupation of weaving, at which they were expert. The competition with native workers offered by the Flemish in the textile industry was the chief reason for the bad feeling toward them on the part of the English. 578. **bemes,** trumpets, horns. **box,** box-wood; there were wooden as well as metal trumpets. 579. **pouped,** puffed. 580. **houped,** whooped. 592. **Maugree your heed,** "in spite of your head," "in spite of you." 596. **deliverly,** quickly. 603. **wikke,** wicked, evil.

I shal seye sooth to yow, God help me so." 605
"Nay than," quod he, "I shrewe us bothe two,
And first I shrewe my-self, bothe blood and bones,
If thou bigyle me ofter than ones.
Thou shalt namore, thurgh thy flaterye
Do me to singe and winke with myn yë. 610
For he that winketh, whan he sholde see,
Al wilfully, God lat him never thee!"
"Nay," quod the fox, "but God yive him mes-
        chaunce,
That is so undiscreet of governaunce,
That jangleth whan he sholde holde his pees." 615
    Lo, swich it is for to be recchelees,
And necligent, and truste on flaterye.
But ye that holden this tale a folye,
As of a fox, or of a cok and hen,
Taketh the moralitee, good men. 620
For seint Paul seith, that al that writen is,
To our doctryne it is y-write, y-wis.
Taketh the fruyt, and lat the chaf be stille.
    Now, gode God, if that it be Thy wille,
As seith my Lord, so make us alle good men; 625
And bringe us to His heighe blisse. Amen.

THE PARDONER'S TALE

The Pardoner, hypocrite, swindler, winebibber, and
eunuch, is a repulsive figure among the Canterbury
pilgrims. In his portrait he appeared as an unattractive
physical specimen, but he obviously had a personality of
some kind beyond the average, for he boasts of his success as an orator and a wielder of words. His tale bears
him out on that point, for it is one of the most effective
pieces of writing in all medieval literature—powerful,
dramatic, economical to the point of terseness, unforgettable.

The pilgrims pause beside the road, and the Pardoner,
asked for a story, requests that he be allowed some
liquid refreshment first. Warmed by his drink, he proceeds to a remarkable prologue in which he exposes
himself and all the frauds and deceits which he practices
upon the populace, what with his pig's bones and rags
which he palms off as holy relics. He then launches upon
his moral tale, which is in reality a medieval sermon on
the evils of avarice and self-indulgence. Imbedded in
the sermon is the characteristic *exemplum*—in this case
The Pardoner's Tale itself. At the conclusion the Pardoner
shamelessly bids the pilgrims step up and take out spiritual insurance against the perils of their expedition by

buying some of his relics; with equal shamelessness he
bids the Host to be the first to acquiesce, for he has considered the Host's inveterate swearing and profanity to
be a heinous sin. Unfortunately the Host is too much of
a fighter, and the result is disastrous for the Pardoner,
who retires in disorder.

It is not known where Chaucer got this particular version, but the story itself has been traced to the Orient.
The setting of the pestilence must have been suggested
to Chaucer and his contemporaries by the Black Death
and all its horrors; indeed, *The Pardoner's Tale* is unusual
for Chaucer, in that it makes an allusion, however remote, to events of contemporary or near-contemporary
interest. The terse style and rushing pace of the narrative,
in combination with the impressive dramatic force, make
the tale one of the most remarkable of Chaucer's achievements.

THE PROLOGUE
OF THE PARDONER'S TALE

LORDYNGES (quod he), in chirches whan I
        preche,
I peyne me to han an hauteyn speche,
And rynge it out as round as gooth a belle,
For I kan al by rote that I telle.
My theme is alwey oon and ever was, 5
"Radix malorum est Cupiditas."
    First I pronounce whennes that I come,
And thanne my bulles shewe I, alle and some;
Oure lige lordes seel on my patente,
That shewe I first, my body to warente, 10
That no man be so boold, ne preest ne clerk,
Me to destourbe of Cristes hooly werk.
And after that thanne telle I forth my tales,
Bulles of popes and of cardynales,
Of patriarkes and bishopes I shewe, 15
And in Latyn I speke a wordes fewe,
To saffron with my predicacioun,
And for to stire hem to devocioun.
Thanne shew I forth my longe cristal stones,
Ycrammed ful of cloutes and of bones; 20
Relikes been they, as wenen they echoon.
Thanne have I in latoun a sholder-boon
Which that was of an hooly Jewes sheepe.
"Goode men," I seye, "taak of my wordes keepe:

606. **shrewe,** curse. 612. **God . . . thee,** "God let him never prosper," a malediction parallel to the "So mote I thee" of l. 156 above.
614. **governaunce,** self-control, behavior. 615. **jangleth,** chatter,
babble. 616. **recchelees,** reckless, careless. 621–622. **seint Paul
. . . y-write.** "For whatever things were written aforetime were
written for our learning." (Romans, 15: 4). The doctrine is implicit
in all medieval literature until an idea of art for art's sake began to
emerge in the Rennaisance.

2. **hauteyn,** exalted, eloquent. 6. **"Radix . . . Cupiditas.",** "The
root of evil is greed." 8. **bulles,** bulls not from the Pope, in all probability, but rather from the local bishop (the *lige lorde* in l. 9 below),
although, since the Pardoner's pardons had come hot from Rome (see
Prologue to The Canterbury Tales, p. II:213, l. 687), the Pope may be
actually the source. 9. **patente,** an "open" document conferring the
rights and privileges of the Pardoner. 10. **warente,** guarantee, safeguard. 17. **saffron . . . predicacioun,** to color my sermon; saffron
is a yellow dye newly brought to Europe from the Middle East. 19.
cristal stones, hollow glass cases for the preservation of relics. 20.
cloutes, rags. 22. **latoun,** an alloy of copper and zinc. 23. **hooly
Jewes sheepe,** the sheep of a Jewish patriarch of the Old Testament;
Jews after the incarnation of Christ would never be called holy in the
Middle Ages.

If that this boon be wasshe in any welle, 25
If cow, or calf, or sheep, or oxe swelle,
That any worm hath ete, or worm ystonge,
Taak water of that welle, and wassh his tonge,
And it is hool anon; and forthermoor,
Of pokkes and of scabbe and every soor 30
Shal every sheepe be hool that of this welle
Drynketh a draughte; taak kepe eek what I telle,
If that the goode man that the beestes oweth,
Wol every wyke, er that the cok hym croweth,
Fastynge, drinken of this welle a draughte, 35
As thilke hooly Jew oure eldres taughte,
Hise beestes and his stoor shal multiplie.
And, sire, also it heeleth jalousie;
For though a man be falle in jalous rage,
Lat maken with this water his potage, 40
And nevere shal he moore his wyf mistriste,
Though he the soothe of hir defaute wiste,
Al had she taken preestes two or thre.
   Heere is a miteyn, eek, that ye may see:
He that his hand wol putte in this mitayn, 45
He shal have multipliyng of his grayn
What he hath sowen, be it whete or otes,
So that he offre pens, or elles grotes.
Goode men and wommen, o thyng warne I yow,
If any wight be in this chirche now, 50
That hath doon synne horrible, that he
Dar nat for shame of it yshryven be,
Or any womman, be she yong or old,
That hath ymaad hir housbonde cokewold,
Swich folk shal have no power ne no grace 55
To offren to my relikes in this place.
And who so fyndeth hym out of swich fame,
He wol come up and offre, on Goddes name,
And I assoille him, by the auctoritee
Which that by bulle ygraunted was to me." 60
   By this gaude have I wonne, yeer by yeer,
An hundred mark, sith I was pardoner.
I stonde lyk a clerk in my pulpet,
And whan the lewed peple is doun yset,
I preche so, as ye han herd bifoore, 65
And telle an hundred false japes moore.
Thanne peyne I me to strecche forth the nekke,
And est and west upon the peple I bekke,
As doth a dowve sittyng on a berne.
Myne handes and my tonge goon so yerne 70
That it is joye to se my bisynesse.
Of avarice and of swich cursednesse
Is al my prechyng, for to make hem free
To yeven hir pens; and namely unto me!

For myn entente is nat but for to wynne, 75
And no thyng for correccioun of synne.
I rekke nevere, whan that they been beryed,
Though that hir soules goon a-blakeberyed,
For certes, many a predicacioun
Comth ofte tyme of yvel entencioun. 80
Som for plesance of folk, and flaterye,
To ben avaunced by ypocrisye,
And som for veyne glorie, and som for hate.
For whan I dar noon oother weyes debate,
Thanne wol I stynge hym with my tonge smerte 85
In prechyng, so that he shal not asterte
To been defamed falsely, if that he
Hath trespased to my bretheren, or to me.
For though I telle noght his propre name,
Men shal wel knowe that it is the same 90
By signes, and by othere circumstances.
Thus quyte I folk that doon us displesances,
Thus spitte I out my venym, under hewe
Of hoolynesse, to semen hooly and trewe.
   But shortly, myn entente I wol devyse; 95
I preche of no thyng but for coveityse.
Therfore my theme is yet, and evere was,
"Radix malorum est Cupiditas."
Thus kan I preche agayn that same vice
Which that I use, and that is avarice. 100
But though myself be gilty in that synne,
Yet kan I maken oother folk to twynne
From avarice, and soore to repente;
But that is nat my principal entente.
I preche no thyng but for coveitise; 105
Of this mateere it oghte ynogh suffise.
Thanne telle I hem ensamples many oon
Of olde stories longe tyme agoon,
For lewed peple loven tales olde;
Swiche thynges kan they wel reporte and holde.
What? trowe ye, the whiles I may preche, 111
And wynne gold and silver for I teche,
That I wol lyve in poverte wilfully?
Nay, nay, I thoghte it nevere, trewely.
For I wol preche and begge in sondry landes, 115
I wol nat do no labour with myne handes,
Ne make baskettes, and lyve thereby,
Because I wol nat beggen ydelly.
I wol non of the apostles counterfete;
I wol have money, wolle, chese, and whete, 120
Al were it yeven of the povrest page,
Or of the povrest widwe in a village,
Al sholde hir children sterve for famyne.
Nay! I wol drinke licour of the vyne,
And have a joly wenche in every toun. 125

25. **welle,** water-spring. 33. **oweth,** owns, possesses. 34. **wyke,** week. 37. **stoor,** possessions. 42. **defaute,** fault, offense. 43. **Al,** although. 44. **miteyn,** mitten, glove. 48. **So that,** provided that. 58. **offre,** make his offering. 61. **gaude,** trickery. 62. **mark.** The mark was in Chaucer's time about the equivalent of fourteen shillings. 64. **lewed,** laymen, or perhaps also in the secondary sense of ignorant folk. 66. **japes,** tricks. 68. **bekke,** nod, glance. 69. **dowve,** dove, pigeon. 70. **yerne,** eagerly, quickly.

76. **no thyng,** not at all. 77–78. I . . . **a-blakeberyed,** "after they have been buried, I don't care if their souls go a-blackberrying (that is, wandering off)." 82. **avaunced,** advanced. 96. **for,** concerning, in reference to. 102. **twynne,** part from. 113. **poverte wilfully?** Willful, or voluntary, poverty is that kind assumed by the holy Orders. 119. **counterfete,** imitate, emulate. 121. **page,** little boy.

But herkneth, lordings, in conclusioun;
Your lyking is that I shal telle a tale.
Now have I dronke a draughte of corny ale,
By God, I hope I shal yow telle a thing
That shal, by resoun, been at your lyking.   130
For, thogh myself be a ful vicious man,
A moral tale yet I yow telle can,
Which I am wont to preche, for to winne.
Now holde your pees, my tale I wol beginne.

THE PARDONER'S TALE

In Flaundres whylom was a companye   135
Of yonge folk, that haunteden folye,
As ryot, hasard, stewes, and tavernes,
Wher-as, with harpes, lutes, and giternes,
They daunce and pleye at dees bothe day and
        night,
And ete also and drinken over hir might,   140
Thurgh which they doon the devel sacrifyse
With-in that develes temple, in curséd wyse,
By superfluitee abhominable;
Hir othes been so grete and so dampnable,
That it is grisly for to here hem swere;   145
Our blisséd Lordes body they to-tere;
Hem thoughte that Jewes rente hym noght ynough,
And ech of hem at otheres synne lough.
And right anon thanne comen tombesteres,
Fetys and smale, and yonge frutesteres,   150
Syngeres with harpes, baudes, wafereres,
Whiche been the verray develes officeres
To kyndle and blowe the fyr of lecherye,
That is annexed unto glotonye.
The hooly writ take I to my witnesse,   155
That luxurie is in wyn and dronkenesse.

Lo, how that dronken Looth unkyndely
Lay by hise doghtres two unwityngly;
So dronke he was, he nyste what he wroghte.
Herodes, whoso wel the stories soghte,   160
Whan he of wyn was repleet at his feeste,

Right at his owene table he yaf his heeste
To sleen the Baptist John, ful giltelees.
Senec seith a good word, doutelees;
He seith, he kan no difference fynde   165
Bitwix a man that is out of his mynde,
And a man which that is dronkelewe,
But that woodnesse fallen in a shrewe
Persevereth lenger than dooth dronkenesse.
O glotonye, ful of cursednesse!   170
O cause first of oure confusioun!
O original of oure dampnacioun
Til Crist hadde boght us with his blood agayn!
Lo, how deere, shortly for to sayn,
Aboght was thilke cursed vileynye!   175
Corrupt was al this world for glotonye!
Adam oure fader, and his wyf also,
Fro Paradys to labour and to wo
Were dryven for that vice, it is no drede;
For whil that Adam fasted, as I rede,   180
He was in Paradys, and whan that he
Eet of the fruyt deffended on the tree,
Anon he was out-cast to wo and peyne.
O glotonye, on thee wel oghte us pleyne!
O, wiste a man how manye maladyes   185
Folwen of excesse and of glotonyes,
He wolde been the moore mesurable
Of his diete, sittynge at his table.
Allas! the shorte throte, the tendre mouth
Maketh that est and west and north and south   190
In erthe, in eir, in water, man to swynke
To gete a glotoun deyntee mete and drynke!
Of this matiere, O Paul! wel kanstow trete,
"Mete unto wombe and wombe eek unto mete
Shal God destroyen bothe," as Paulus seith.   195
Allas, a foul thyng is it, by my feith!
To seye this word, and fouler is the dede,
Whan man so drinketh of the whyte and rede,
That of his throte he maketh his privee,
Thurgh thilke cursed superfluitee.   200
    The apostel weping seith ful pitously,
"Ther walken many of whiche yow told have I,
I seye it now weping with pitous voys,
That they been enemys of Cristes croys,
Of whiche the ende is deeth, wombe is her god."   205
O wombe! O bely! O stinking cod,
Fulfild of donge and of corrupcioun!
At either ende of thee foul is the soun.

128. corny ale, ale with plenty of grain or body to it. 130. by resoun, rightfully. 137. hasard, gambling, games of chance. 138. giternes, citherns, small stringed instruments. 139. dees, dice. 140. over hir might, beyond their powers, with disastrous effect. 146. to-tere, a reference to the "tearing" or "rending" of Christ's body through ill-advised oaths like "By God's bones," "By God's blood!" God in all such oaths is Christ. 148. lough, laugh. 149. tombesteres, female tumblers, dancing-girls. 150. frutesteres, women who sell fruit; they were traditionally prostitutes. 151. wafereres, sellers of cakes and wafers, pastry and confectionery. 153–154. lecherye . . . glotonye. These two of the Seven Deadly Sins were nearly always bracketed in the medieval treatment of sin. 155–156. The hooly writ . . . dronkenesse. "And be not drunk with wine, wherein is excess."—Ephesians, 5:18; "Wine is a mocker, strong drink is raging; and whosoever is deceived thereby is not wise."—Proverbs, 20:1. 157. dronken Looth. The story of Lot's incest is told in Genesis, 19:30–36. unkyndely, unnaturally. 160. Herodes. The basis for the stories about Herod, Herodias, the daughter of Herodias (Salome), and John the Baptist is in Matthew, 14:3–12, and Mark, 6:17–29.

162. yaf his heeste, gave his commands. 164. Senec, Seneca (3 B.C.– 65 A.D.), the Roman philosopher and writer of tragedies. 168. woodnesse, madness, insanity. 173. boght, bought and paid for, redeemed. 182. deffended, forbidden. For the story, see Genesis, 3. 191. swynke, labor. 195. as Paulus seith: "Meats for the belly (wombe), and the belly for meats; but God shall destroy both it and them."—I Corinthians, 6:13. 202–205. "Ther walken . . . her god." "For many walk, of whom I have told you often, and now tell you even weeping, that they are the enemies of the cross of Christ; whose end is destruction, whose God is their belly," etc.—Philippians, 3:18–19. 206. cod, gut, stomach, intestines. 207. Fulfild, filled full.

How greet labour and cost is thee to finde!
Thise cokes, how they stampe, and streyne, and
    grinde, 210
And turnen substance into accident,
To fulfille al thy likerous talent!
Out of the harde bones knokke they
The mary, for they caste noght a-wey
That may go thurgh the golet softe and swote; 215
Of spicerye of leef, and bark, and rote
Shal been his sauce y-maked by delyt,
To make him yet a newer appetyt.
But certes, he that haunteth swich delyces
Is deed, whyl that he liveth in tho vyces. 220
    A lecherous thing is wyn, and dronkenesse
Is ful of stryving and of wrecchednesse.
O dronke man, disfigured is thy face,
Sour is thy breeth, foul artow to embrace,
And thurgh thy dronke nose semeth the soun 225
As though thou seydest ay "Sampsoun, Sampsoun!"
And yet, God wot, Sampsoun drank never no wyn.
Thou fallest, as it were a stiked swyn;
Thy tonge is lost, and al thyn honest cure;
For dronkenesse is verray sepulture 230
Of mannes wit and his discrecioun.
In whom that drinke hath dominacioun,
He can no conseil kepe, it is no drede.
Now kepe yow fro the whyte and fro the rede,
And namely, fro the white wyn of Lepe, 235
That is to selle in Fysshstrete, or in Chepe.
This wyn of Spaigne crepeth subtilly
In othere wynes, growynge faste by,
Of which ther ryseth swich fumositee,
That whan a man hath dronken draughtes three 240
And weneth that he be at hoom in Chepe,
He is in Spaigne, right at the toune of Lepe,
Nat at the Rochele, ne at Burdeux toun,
And thanne wol he seye "Sampsoun, Sampsoun!"
But herkneth, lordes, o word, I yow preye, 245
That alle the sovereyn actes, dar I seye,
Of victories in the Olde Testament,
Thurgh verray God that is omnipotent,
Were doon in abstinence and in preyere.
Looketh the Bible, and ther ye may it leere. 250
Looke, Attila, the grete conquerour,

209. **How greet . . . finde!** How great a labor and cost it is to provide for (*finde*) thee! 211. **substance into accident.** In a sense peculiar to medieval philosophy, the "substance" of a thing is its real
essence; the "accident" comprises the external qualities (color,
weight, shape, etc.). The cooks, then, must take an edible and labor
to change its "accident" in such a way as to tickle the palate afresh.
212. **likerous talent**, lecherous or gluttonous appetite. 214. **mary**,
marrow. 229. **honest cure**, care for one's honor, self-respect. 235.
Lepe, a town near Cadiz, Spain. 236. **Fysshstrete . . . Chepe.**
Fishstreet was a very busy mercantile street near London Bridge.
Chaucer's father had been a wine-dealer in the immediate vicinity of
Fishstreet. *Chepe*, Cheapside, was another. 239. **fumositee**, fumes,
gas. 243. **the Rochele**, La Rochelle, France. **Burdeux toun**, Bordeaux, France. 251. **Attilla**, Attila, the great leader of the Huns,
whose disastrous inroads into Western Europe threatened the foundations of Occidental culture, died in 453, according to story, as a
result of overdissipation on his wedding night.

Deyde in his sleepe, with shame and dishonour,
Bledynge ay at his nose in dronkenesse.
A capitayn sholde lyve in sobrenesse;
And over al this avyseth yow right wel, 255
What was comaunded unto Lamuel,
Nat Samuel, but Lamuel, seye I;
Redeth the Bible and fynde it expresly,
Of wyne-yevyng to hem that han justise.
Namoore of this, for it may wel suffise. 260
    And now that I have spoken of glotonye,
Now wol I yow deffenden hasardrye.
Hasard is verray moder of lesynges,
And of deceite and cursed forswerynges,
Blasphemyng of Crist, manslaughtre and wast also 265
Of catel and of tyme, and forthermo
It is repreeve and contrarie of honour
For to ben holde a commune hasardour.
And ever the hyer he is of estaat,
The more is he holden desolaat. 270
If that a prince useth hasardrye,
In alle governaunce and policye
He is, as by commune opinioun,
Y-holde the lasse in reputacioun.
    Stilbon, that was a wys embassadour, 275
Was sent to Corinthe, in ful greet honour,
Fro Lacedomie, to make hir alliaunce.
And whan he cam, him happede, par chaunce,
That alle the grettest that were of that lond,
Pleyinge atte hasard he hem fond. 280
For which, as sone as it mighte be,
He stal him hoom agayn to his contree,
And seyde, "ther wol I nat lese my name;
N' I wol nat take on me so greet defame,
Yow for to allye un-to none hasardours. 285
Sendeth othere wyse embassadours;
For, by my trouthe, me were lever dye,
Than I yow sholde to hasardours allye.
For ye that been so glorious in honours
Shul nat allyen yow with hasardours 290
As by my wil, ne as by my tretee."
This wyse philosophre thus seyde he.
    Loke eek that, to the king Demetrius
The king of Parthes, as the book seith us,
Sente him a paire of dees of gold in scorn, 295
For he hadde used hasard ther-biforn;
For which he heeld his glorie or his renoun
At no value or reputacioun.
Lordes may finden other maner pley

256. **Lamuel**, Lemuel. Note the words of Lemuel in Proverbs, 30,
notably the passage beginning in verse 4 on the evils of strong drink.
264. **deceite and cursed forswerynges**, swearing falsely, taking "the
name of the Lord thy God in vain." 267. **repreeve and contrarie of
honour**, a shame and a foe to honor. 270. **holden desolaat**, considered debased. 275. **Stilbon**, etc. The story is told in a late Greek
chronicle, but the ambassador's name there was *Chilon*. 293. **Demetrius**, etc. This story is taken from the same source as that of
Stilbon's legend (see preceding note); we are uncertain as to which
of several kings by the name of Demetrius the incident treats.

Honeste y-nough to dryve the day awey.   300
   Now wol I speke of othes false and grete
A word or two, as olde bokes trete.
Gret sweryng is a thyng abhominable
And fals sweryng is yet moore reprevable.
The heighe God forbad sweryng at al,   305
Witnesse on Mathew; but in special
Of sweryng seith the hooly Jeremye,
"Thou shalt seye sooth thýne othes, and nat lye,
And swere in doom, and eek in rightwisnesse,"
But ydel sweryng is a cursednesse.   310
Bihoold and se, that in the firste table
Of heighe Goddes heestes honurable
How that the seconde heeste of Hym is this:
"Take nat my name in ydel or amys."
Lo, rather He forbedeth swich sweryng   315
Than homycide, or any cursed thyng!
I seye, that as by ordre thus it stondeth,
This knowen that Hise heestes understondeth
How that the seconde heeste of God is that.
And forther-over I wol thee telle al plat,   320
That vengeance shal nat parten from his hous
That of hise othes is to outrageous—
"By Goddes precious herte and by His nayles,
And by the blood of Crist that is in Hayles,
Sevene is my chaunce and thyn is cynk and treye.   325
By Goddes armes, if thou falsly pleye,
This dagger shal thurghout thyn herte go!"
This fruyt cometh of the bicched bones two,
Forsweryng, ire, falsnesse, homycide!
Now for the love of Crist, that for us dyde,   330
Lete youre othes bothe grete and smale.
But, sires, now wol I telle forth my tale.

————

   Thise ryotoures three, of whiche I telle,
Longe erst er pryme rong of any belle,
Were set hem in a taverne for to drinke;   335
And as they satte, they herde a belle clinke
Biforn a cors was caried to his grave;
That oon of hem gan callen to his knave,
   "Go bet," quod he, "and axe redily,

What cors is this that passeth heer forby;   340
And look that thou reporte his name wel."
   "Sir," quod this boy, "it nedeth never-a-del.
It was me told, er ye cam heer, two houres;
He was, pardee, an old felawe of youres;
And sodeynly he was y-slayn to-night,   345
For-dronke, as he sat on his bench upright;
Ther cam a privee theef, men clepeth Deeth,
That in this contree al the peple sleeth,
And with his spere he smoot his herte atwo,
And wente his wey with-outen wordes mo.   350
He hath a thousand slayn this pestilence:
And, maister, er ye come in his presence,
Me thinketh that it were necessarie
For to be war of swich an adversarie:
Beth redy for to mete him evermore.   355
Thus taughte me my dame, I sey namore."
   "By seinte Marie," seyde this taverner,
"The child seith sooth, for he hath slayn this yeer,
Henne over a myle, within a greet village,
Both man and womman, child and hyne and page.
I trowe his habitacioun be there;   361
To been avyséd greet wisdom it were,
Er that he dide a man a dishonour."
   "Ye, Goddes armes," quod this ryotour,
"Is it swich peril with him for to mete?   365
I shal him seke by wey and eek by strete,
I make avow to Goddes digne bones!
Herkneth, felawes, we three been al ones;
Lat ech of us holde up his hond til other,
And ech of us bicomen otheres brother,   370
And we wol sleen this false traytour Deeth;
He shal be slayn, which that so many sleeth,
By Goddes dignitee, er it be night."
   Togidres han thise three her trouthes plight,
To live and dyen ech of hem for other,   375
As though he were his owene y-boren brother.
And up they sterte al dronken, in this rage,
And forth they goon towardes that village,
Of which the taverner had spoke biforn;
And many a grisly ooth than han they sworn,   380
And Cristes blesséd body they to-rente—
Deeth shal be deed, if that they may him hente!
   Whan they han goon nat fully half a myle,
Right as they wolde han troden over a style,
An old man and a povre with hem mette.   385
This olde man ful mekely hem grette,
And seyde thus, "Now, lordes, God yow see!"
   The proudest of thise ryotoures three

306. **Witnesse on Mathew.** "Swear not at all; neither by Heaven, for it is God's throne."—Matthew, 5:34. 308–309. **"Thou . . . right- wisnesse,"** see Jeremiah, 4:2. 320. **plat,** flatly. 322. **outrageous,** immoderate, raging, excessive. 324. **in Hayles,** etc. Some of Christ's blood, shed at the time of the Crucifixion, was believed to be con- tained in a vessel at the noted shrine in Hayles, Gloucestershire. 325. **Sevene . . . treye.** This is a clear reference to the game of *hazard,* which has a close resemblance to the modern game of craps. The man throwing the dice chooses a number—any number from five to nine, but usually seven. "If he then throws either seven or eleven, he wins; if he throws aces or deuce-ace or twelve, he loses. If he throws some other number, that number is called the caster's chance and he goes on throwing until either his 'main' or his 'chance' turns up. In the first case he loses; in the second he wins." **cynk,** the number five; **treye,** the number three. 328. **bicched bones,** the perfect descrip- tion of a pair of dice. 334. **pryme,** the first hour of the day; later, the period between six and nine in the morning; see *The Nun's Priest's Tale* (p. 11:236, l. 377 and note). 339. **"Go bet,"** a hunting term: the call to the hounds.

342. **ʒever-a-del,** never a bit, not at all. 346. **For-dronke,** very drunk. 347. **privee,** secret, stealthy. 359. **Henne,** hence, from here. 360. **hyne,** servant; specifically, a farm laborer. **page,** boy. 362. **avyséd,** forewarned. 367. **digne,** worthy, honorable. 368. **al ones,** all of one mind. 373. **dignitee,** worthiness, honor. 387. **God yow see!** It should be noted that the name of the Deity is not capitalized in a Chaucer text, unless some modern editor has done it. The phrase means literally, "God see you!"; that is, "God behold you!" or "God protect you!"

Answerde agayn, "What? carl, with sory grace,
Why artow al forwrappéd save thy face? 390
Why livestow so longe in so greet age?"

This olde man gan loke in his visage,
And seyde thus, "For I ne can nat finde
A man, though that I walkéd into Inde,
Neither in citee nor in no village, 395
That wolde chaunge his youthe for myn age;
And therefore moot I han myn age stille,
As longe time as it is Goddes wille.
Ne deeth, allas! ne wol nat han my lyf;
Thus walke I, lyk a restelees caityf, 400
And on the ground, which is my modres gate,
I knokke with my staf, bothe erly and late,
And seye, 'Leve moder, leet me in!
Lo, how I vanish, flesh, and blood, and skin!
Allas! whan shul my bones been at reste? 405
Moder, with yow wolde I chaunge my cheste,
That in my chambre longe tyme hath be,
Ye! for an heyre clowt to wrappe me!'
But yet to me she wol nat do that grace,
For which ful pale and welkéd is my face. 410

"But, sirs, to yow it is no curteisye
To speken to an old man vileinye,
But he trespasse in worde, or elles in dede.
In holy writ ye may your-self wel rede,
'Agayns an old man, hoor upon his heed, 415
Ye sholde aryse'; wherfor I yeve yow reed,
Ne dooth un-to an old man noon harm now;
Na-more than ye wolde men dide to yow
In age, if that ye so longe abyde;
And God be with yow, wher ye go or ryde. 420
I moot go thider as I have to go."
"Nay, olde cherl, by God, thou shalt nat so,"
Seyde this other hasardour anon;
"Thou partest nat so lightly, by seint John!
Thou spak right now of thilke traitour Deeth, 425
That in this contree alle our frendes sleeth.
Have heer my trouthe, as thou art his aspye,
Tel wher he is, or thou shalt it abye,
By God, and by the holy sacrament!
For soothly thou art oon of his assent, 430
To sleen us yonge folk, thou false theef!"
"Now, sirs," quod he, "if that yow be so leef
To finde Deeth, turne up this crokéd wey,
For in that grove I lafte him, by my fey,
Under a tree, and ther he wol abyde; 435
Nat for your boost he wol him no-thing hyde.
See ye that ook? right ther ye shul him finde.
God save yow, that boghte agayn mankinde,
And yow amende!"—thus seyde this olde man.

And everich of thise ryotoures ran, 440
Til he cam to that tree, and ther they founde
Of florins fyne of golde y-coynéd rounde
Wel ny an eighte busshels, as hem thoughte.
No lenger thanne after Deeth they soughte,
But ech of hem so glad was of that sighte, 445
For that the florins been so faire and brighte,
That doun they sette hem by this precious hord.
The worste of hem he spak the firste word.

"Brethren," quod he, "tak kepe what I seye;
My wit is greet, though that I bourde and pleye. 450
This tresor hath Fortune un-to us yiven,
In mirthe and jolitee our lyf to liven,
And lightly as it comth, so wol we spende.
Ey! Goddes precious dignitee! who wende
Today, that we sholde han so faire a grace? 455
But mighte this gold be caried fro this place
Hoom to myn hous, or elles un-to youres—
For wel ye woot that al this gold is oures—
Than were we in heigh felicitee.
But trewely, by daye it may nat be; 460
Men wolde seyn that we were theves stronge,
And for our owene tresor doon us honge.
This tresor moste y-caried be by nighte
As wysly and as slyly as it mighte.
Wherfore I rede that cut among us alle 465
Be drawe, and lat se wher the cut wol falle;
And he that hath the cut with herte blythe
Shal renne to the toune, and that ful swythe,
And bringe us breed and wyn ful prively.
And two of us shul kepen subtilly 470
This tresor wel; and, if he wol nat tarie,
Whan it is night, we wol this tresor carie
By oon assent, wher-as us thinketh best."
That oon of hem the cut broughte in his fest,
And bade hem drawe, and loke wher it wol falle; 475
And it fil on the yongeste of hem alle;
And forth toward the toun he wente anon.
And al-so sone as that he was gon,
That oon of hem spak thus un-to that other,
"Thou knowest wel thou art my sworne brother, 480
Thy profit wol I telle thee anon.
Thou woost wel that our felawe is agon;
And heer is gold, and that ful greet plentee,
That shal departed been among us three.
But natheles, if I can shape it so 485
That it departed were among us two,
Hadde I nat doon a frendes torn to thee?"
That other answerde, "I noot how that may be:
He woot how that the gold is with us tweye,

389. **carl,** churl, old fellow—a term of disrespect. 390. **forwrappéd,**
excessively wrapped up. 408. **heyre clowt,** a hair shirt, the garment
for repentants. 410. **welkéd,** withered. 415–416. **'Agayns an old
man . . . aryse.'** "Thou shalt rise up before the hoary head, and
honor the face of the old man."—Leviticus, 19:32. 420. **go,** walk.
428. **abye,** pay for it. 432. **leef,** lief, glad, eager.

450. **bourde,** jest, joke. 454. **wende,** (would have) weened, supposed, expected. 462. **doon us honge,** make us hang, have us
hanged. 465–466. **cut . . . drawe,** lots be drawn. 468. **swythe,**
quickly; the word is a general intensifying adverb. 474. **fest,** fist.
The lot was chosen, presumably, by plucking grass—the shortest
blade determined the choice. 476. **fil on,** fell to. 479. **other.** The
original meaning of this word was always *second;* it was the regular
ordinal numeral for *two.* 484. **departed,** divided, shared. 487.
frendes torn, a friendly turn.

What shal we doon, what shal we to him seye?" 490
"Shal it be conseil?" seyde the firste shrewe,
"And I shal tellen thee, in wordes fewe,
What we shal doon, and bringe it wel aboute."
"I graunte," quod that other, "out of doute,
That, by my trouthe, I wol thee nat biwreye." 495
"Now," quod the firste, "thou woost wel we be
    tweye,
And two of us shul strenger be than oon.
Look whan that he is set, and right anoon
Arys, as though thou woldest with him pleye;
And I shal ryve him thurgh the sydes tweye 500
Whyl that thou strogelest with him as in game,
And with thy dagger look thou do the same;
And than shal al this gold departed be,
My dere freend, bitwixen me and thee;
Than may we bothe our lustes al fulfille, 505
And pleye at dees right at our owene wille."
And thus accorded been thise shrewes tweye
To sleen the thridde, as ye han herd me seye.

This yongest, which that wente un-to the toun,
Ful ofte in herte he rolleth up and doun
The beautee of thise florins newe and brighte. 510
"O lord!" quod he, "if so were that I mighte
Have al this tresor to my-self allone,
Ther is no man that liveth under the trone
Of God, that sholde live so mery as I!" 515
And atte laste the feend, our enemy,
Putte in his thought that he shold poyson beye,
With which he mighte sleen his felawes tweye;
For-why the feend fond him in swich lyvinge,
That he had leve him to sorwe bringe, 520
For this was outrely his fulle entente
To sleen hem bothe, and never to repente.
And forth he gooth, no lenger wold he tarie,
Into the toun, un-to a pothecarie,
And preyéd him, that he him wolde selle 525
Some poyson, that he mighte his rattes quelle,
And eek ther was a polcat in his hawe,
That, as he seyde, his capouns hadde y-slawe,
And fayn he wolde wreke him, if he mighte,
On vermin, that destroyéd him by nighte. 530

The pothecarie answerde, "and thou shalt have
A thing that, al-so God my soule save,
In al this world ther nis no creature,
That ete or dronke hath of this confiture
Noght but the mountance of a corn of whete, 535
That he ne shal his lyf anon forlete;
Ye, sterve he shal, and that in lasse whyle
Than thou wolt goon a paas nat but a myle;

This poyson is so strong and violent."
This curséd man hath in his hond y-hent 540
This poyson in a box, and sith he ran
In-to the nexte strete, un-to a man,
And borwed [of] him large botels three;
And in the two his poyson pouréd he;
The thridde he kepte clene for his drinke. 545
For all the night he shoop him for to swinke
In caryinge of the gold out of that place.
And whan this ryotour, with sory grace,
Had filled with wyn his grete botels three,
To his felawes agayn repaireth he. 550

What nedeth it to sermone of it more?
For right as they had cast his deeth bifore,
Right so they han him slayn, and that anon.
And whan that this was doon thus spak that oon,
"Now lat us sitte and drinke, and make us merie, 555
And afterward we wol his body berie."
And with that word it happéd him, par cas,
To take the botel ther the poyson was,
And drank, and yaf his felawe drinke also,
For which anon they storven bothe two. 560
But certes, I suppose that Avicen
Wroot nevere in no canoun, ne in no fen,
Mo wonder signes of empoisonyng
Than hadde thise wrecches two, er hir endyng.
Thus ended been thise homycides two, 565
And eek the false empoysoner also.

O cursed synne ful of cursednesse!
O traytours homycide! O wikkednesse!
O glotonye, luxurie, and hasardrye!
Thou blasphemour of Crist, with vileynye, 570
And othes grete, of usage and of pride,
Allas, mankynde! how may it bitide
That to thy Creatour which that the wroghte,
And with His precious herte-blood thee boghte,
Thou art so fals and so unkynde, allas! 575
Now, goode men, God foryeve yow youre trespas,
And ware yow fro the synne of avarice;
Myn hooly pardoun may yow alle warice,
So that ye offre nobles or sterlynges,
Or elles silver broches, spoones, rynges; 580
Boweth youre heed under this hooly bulle,
Com up, ye wyves, offreth of youre wolle;
Youre names I entre heer in my rolle anon,
Into the blisse of hevene shul ye gon.
I yow assoille by myn heigh power, 585
Yow that wol offre, as clene and eek as cleer

---

491. **conseil,** a secret. 495. **biwreye,** betray. 519. **For-why,** because.
520. **leve,** leave, permission. God permitted the Devil to bring this
man to sorrow. The idea lies back of Job, 1:12 and 2:6. 526. **quelle,**
kill. 527. **hawe,** yard; the original meaning is *hedge* or *fence.* 528.
y-slawe, slain. 529. **wreke him,** avenge himself. 534. **confiture,**
concoction, mixture; the apothecary is obviously being ironical. 535.
mountance, amount. 536. **forlete,** leave, abandon, give up. 537.
sterve, die (from any cause); not specifically our modern *starve.*

541. **sith,** afterwards. 551. **nedeth . . . sermone,** why is it necessary to make a sermon? 557. **par cas,** by chance. 560. **storven**
died. 561. **Avicen,** Avicenna, the famous Arab philosopher and
physician of the eleventh century, particularly famous for his studies
of toxicology; cf. the *Prologue* to *The Canterbury Tales,* p. II:209,
l. 432. 562. **fen,** chapter, book; **canoun** signifies the chapter heading.
568. **traytours,** a possessive form serving as an adjective, *traitorous.*
575. **unkynde,** unnatural, monstrous. 578. **warice,** cure. 579. **So
that,** provided that. **nobles or sterlynges.** The *noble* was a coin first
used in the fourteenth century, worth six shillings eight pence; the
sterlyng was probably a silver penny rather than the pound sterling.

As ye were born—and lo, sires, thus I preche;
And Jesu Crist, that is oure soules leche,
So graunte yow His pardoun to receyve,
For that is best, I wol yow nat deceyve.   590

But sires, o word forgat I in my tale,
I have relikes and pardoun in my male
As faire as any man in Engelond,
Whiche were me yeven by the popes hond.
If any of yow wole, of devocioun,   595
Offren and han myn absolucioun,
Com forth anon, and kneleth heere adoun,
And mekely receyveth my pardoun,
Or elles taketh pardoun as ye wende,
Al newe and fressh at every miles ende,   600
So that ye offren alwey newe and newe
Nobles or pens, whiche that be goode and trewe.
It is an honour to everich that is heer,
That ye mowe have a suffisant pardoneer
Tassoille yow, in contree as ye ryde,   605
For aventures whiche that may bityde.
Paraventure ther may fallen oon or two
Doun of his hors, and breke his nekke atwo.
Look, which a seuretee is it to yow alle
That I am in youre felaweship yfalle,   610
That may assoille yow, bothe moore and lasse,
Whan that the soule shal fro the body passe.
I rede that oure Hoost heere shal bigynne,
For he is moost envoluped in synne.
Com forth, sire Hoost, and offre first anon,   615
And thou shalt kisse my relikes everychon,
Ye, for a grote, unbokele anon thy purs—
    "Nay, nay," quod he, "thanne have I Cristes curs!"
"Lat be," quod he, "it shal nat be, so theech,
Thou woldest make me kisse thyn olde breech,   620
And swere it were a relyk of a seint,
Though it were with thy fundement depeint!
But, by the croys which that Seint Eleyne fond,
I wolde I hadde thy coillons in myn hond
In stide of relikes or of seintuarie.   625
Lat kutte hem of, I wol thee helpe hem carie;
They shul be shryned in an hogges toord!"
    This pardoner answerde nat a word;

So wrooth he was, no word ne wolde he seye.
    "Now," quod our host, "I wol no lenger pleye   630
With thee, ne with noon other angry man."
But right anon the worthy Knight bigan,
Whan that he saugh that al the peple lough,
"Na-more of this, for it is right y-nough;
Sir Pardoner, be glad and mery of chere;   635
And ye, sir Host, that been to me so dere,
I prey yow that ye kisse the Pardoner.
And Pardoner, I prey thee, drawe thee neer.
And, as we diden, lat us laughe and pleye."
Anon they kiste, and riden forth hir weye.

British and Danish Popular Ballads

The term "popular ballad" has been applied to narrative songs which originated among the people rather than at the courts of kings or in the parlors of the aristocratic and educated. The process of making such ballads is many centuries old, and may take place at any time where a state of general illiteracy obtains. The ballads of Denmark, England, and Scotland—to take the three most famous collections—lived in oral tradition for hundreds of years. Some of them were brought to the New World by emigrants. They can be found today in many of the less sophisticated communities in the United States. They are a part of the spontaneous heritage of Western Europe. But, as has been noted again and again, to commit these ballads to writing has a curiously blighting effect upon them. To appreciate the full value of a popular ballad, one must hear it sung by an authentic ballad singer.

The first great modern assemblage of these ballads was the repository of Danish ballads assembled by Svend Grundtvig, the publication of which was begun in 1853. This served as a model for the impressive collection of English and Scottish popular ballads published under the editorship of Francis J. Child in the 1860's and stamped in definitive style in his great five-volume edition of 1882–1898. Child gathered over three hundred of these ballads. The Danish ballads collected are somewhat fewer in number, but statistics mean little here, for there must be hundreds of ballads, even those of modern vintage, which have never found their way into the pages of Grundtvig or Child. Many of these ballads have an origin in the later Middle Ages, though scarcely before. The great majority of them, however, were not written down until the sixteenth and seventeenth centuries; in Britain, for example, less than a dozen survive in a form older than that of the celebrated Percy Manuscript of about 1650. The most ancient English ballad is

---

592. **male,** bag; see *Prologue* to *The Canterbury Tales*, p. II:213, l. 694 and note. 602. **pens,** pence, pennies. 605. **Tassoille,** to absolve; the elision here is of the preposition *to*. 613–614. **oure Hoost . . . envoluped in synne.** It is clear that the Host is one of those men who can hardly open his mouth without uttering some sort of profanity. The Pardoner is obviously objecting to this habit in the Host, which certainly cuts across the lines of the homily which he has just completed; see especially ll. 169–170. That the Pardoner may be completely hypocritical in his objection is beside the point. But the Host seems to sense insincerity in the Pardoner, which is probably the chief reason for his rage. 619. **so theech,** "so may I prosper!"—a rather mild asseveration, considering the general ferocity of the Host's retort. The southern form of the first personal pronoun, *ich,* has been suffixed to the verb *thee(n),* "to prosper." 622. **with thy fundement depeint!** daubed with thy excrement! 623. **croys . . . fond.** St. Helen, the mother of Constantine the Great, was believed to have been the finder of the True Cross. 624. **coillons,** cullions, testicles. 626. **of,** off.

Judas (Child #23), which survives from the thirteenth century; the next extant ballad was not written down until the middle of the fifteenth century. Most of the Robin Hood ballads, most famous of all, exist in a text from well past 1500. And yet the Middle English vision-satire, *Piers Plowman*, originating in the latter half of the fourteenth century, makes a reference to the "rimes of Robin Hood" so casual that it is possible to assume the currency of Robin Hood ballads long before 1350. Besides, many of the stock situations in the popular ballads belong to the province of Germanic and Celtic folklore and as such know not the limits of time.

The problem of the authorship of the popular ballads has vexed scholars since Bishop Percy wrote his memorable preface to his *Reliques of Ancient English Poetry* (1765). Since that time three main schools of thought have emerged: (1) the ballads were composed by individual authors; (2) the ballads were composed by a community as a whole (communal authorship); (3) the ballads were composed by an individual who made, as George Lyman Kittredge so aptly observed, "an improvisation in the presence of a sympathetic company which may even, at times, participate in the process."

It is essential for us to realize that there are two distinct types of popular ballad, which we may designate as the folk ballad and the minstrel ballad. The *folk ballad*, much the older type, is characterized by much dialogue; refrains of marked rhythmic or choral value; and repetition, at least of a single word or phrase, and usually of a more subtle nature called "incremental repetition," by which the story is made to "hitch along" through small variations on a repetitive element. The true folk ballad is notably objective; the very presence of the words "I" or "my," except in direct discourse, should render it suspect as a folk ballad. There is also a minimum of descriptive or atmospheric material; the folk ballad, indeed, is further characterized by notable simplicity of thought, situation, and metrical style. The importance of the repetitive elements, the implication of a chorus or a dance in the refrain material, the strong suggestion of possible dramatic or mimetic interpretation in the interchanging dialogue—all this lends weight to the argument that the folk ballad is in some sense a communal affair. One or more individuals could have composed the narrative portions, and even acted out the story, while the community group, assembled for some special occasion, could have roared the refrain, perhaps dancing as they did so. In fact, such a process is familiar to any folklorist who observes similar gatherings in the present age. Knowing as we do that improvisation was not regarded as out of the ordinary on the part of any intelligent person of earlier times, we may well accept the theory that several members had a hand in the composition of the main body of the folk ballad. Their number would be small, however, because one must reckon always with the obvious fact that every gathering has its few guiding spirits. Song is to be assumed for the ballad; choral dancing may have entered into it as well; indeed, the choreographic element seems to have been especially prominent in the early Danish ballads.

On the other hand, a number of ballads show no traces of the many peculiar characteristics of the folk ballad, or exhibit at most only feeble, imitative suggestions of these. They proceed to the business of the story after a brief, "Come, all ye, and listen" formula; and they possess often a special "literary" flavor, such as comes from a description of the countryside or an analysis of the thoughts and feelings of the characters in the story. In other words, they are more subjective than the folk ballads; and to say that they are subjective implies an individual originator and an individual only. Such ballads we call *minstrel ballads*. The minstrel was simply a bard of the people, and as such he had to possess a keen insight into the tastes of the people and had to have at his command an extensive repertory of popular song. Perhaps he may have had some experience at the court of a nobleman and in that way have become familiar with romance materials. This possibility would explain how some of the minstrel ballads have to do with shreds of medieval romances. In the British collection there are even a few Arthurian ballads. The minstrel could be responsible for the creation of Robin Hood, that great popular hero of epic proportions; he might be fighting in the armies of My Lords Douglas and Percy and so create the ballads of border warfare; he might participate in the assassination of Count Gert by Niels Ebbeson. But however much he might imitate the manner and even the language and style of the older folk ballad—even to the point of throwing in a few rhythmic devices in the form of meaningless words and a few faint echoes of incremental repetition—still his work was entirely his own. He was the author of the entire ballad. To put *Edward* or *Sir Luno and the Mermaid* beside *Robin Hood's Death and Burial* is to see at once the basal differences between the two types, the folk ballad and the minstrel ballad. Moreover, some of the Danish ballads, according to the researches of Grundtvig and Olrik, originated from the pens of lords and ladies of Denmark during the sixteenth and seventeenth centuries, just as some of the English ballads came from writers of established reputation in England from the Renaissance to the present time.

It is possible, then, to argue that the folk ballad was composed by individuals with the assistance of the community in varying degrees; the minstrel ballad, on the other hand, is the work of an individual who is catering to the tastes of the people and conforming in a measure to the style of the older folk ballad. The theory of Grimm that the community as a whole was responsible for a ballad ("das Volk dichtet") has been generally discredited; taken literally it would be impossible. But the community was certainly the fertile soil in which the folk ballad could grow, and in that sense at least, "communal authorship" has meaning.

The subject matter of the popular ballad was, of course, extremely varied. The ballads in their older aspects dealt with mortals of a dateless age, when contact with the supernatural was not considered in the least miraculous. They are rich in folklore and the expression of folkways, but they may give their attention wholly to tragic family or clan relationships (cf. *Edward* and

Young Engel. Historical ballads of all kinds, as well as ballads of the outlaw, are of the minstrel ballad variety (cf. the Robin Hood ballad and *Niels Ebbeson*).

It has been pointed out that musical settings are the rule for all ballads. Many of these melodies have been recovered, but many others are lost forever. Careful usage, however, should limit the term "ballad" to *narrative* rather than *lyric* verse set to music, although in the "coronach," or song of lamentation, it is often difficult to tell whether the narrative or the lyric predominates (cf. *Bonnie George Campbell*). Similarly, the ballad often veers toward the didactic or satirical in that ancient type called the "riddle" ballad (cf. *Riddles Wisely Expounded*). Finally, there is to be recognized a burlesque or farcical type of ballad (cf. *The Bride of Ribe*), which is usually of later date, and which moves all the way from slapstick and horseplay to a fairly sophisticated type of humor.

Because the ballad was the unwritten product of peasant and commoner, it was not considered highly by scholars and critics of literature until the interest in antiquities that was a feature of the later eighteenth century resulted in the printing of as many of these ancient songs as were accessible. But it should be remembered that ballads appeared in print almost as soon as the art of printing became current; these were usually put out in the form of single sheets, or broadsides, and often in cheap little pamphlets, or "chap-books." The romantic writers of the late eighteenth and early nineteenth century, such as Burger, Goethe, Schiller, Burns, and Scott, undertook many imitations of the ballad. The nineteenth-century writers all over Europe emulated them most industriously and often brilliantly. But none of the imitations of the folk ballad have been quite so effective as the better examples of the original type—the simple and grim domestic tragedy of *Edward*, like the naïve and gripping course of many a folk tune, is virtually impossible for the sophisticate to render with equal sincerity and appeal.

Riddles Wisely Expounded

(BRITISH)

The riddle or enigma is of frequent occurrence in all folk literatures. It is extremely ancient and remarkably vital; riddle tales, of which this ballad is an illustration, can still be found, in much the same form as the following, among primitive European and Asiatic peoples. It should be observed that one person has to guess another person's riddle, with a severe penalty, usually death, in case he fails.

In this ballad appears also the theme of the devil in the shape of a man, come down to try a human being, who will be carried away to Hell unless he or she survives the test by answering the riddle. This device was often used in the Middle Ages for didactic purposes.

THERE was a knicht riding frae the east,
  Sing the Cather banks, the bonnie brume,
Wha had been wooing at monie a place,
  And ye may beguile a young thing sune.

He came unto a widow's door,   5
And speired whare her three dochters were.

The auldest ane's to a washing gane,
The second's to a baking gane.

The youngest ane's to a wedding gane,
And it will be nicht or she be hame.   10

He set him doun upon a stane,
Till thir three lasses came tripping hame.

The auldest ane's to the bed making,
And the second ane's to the sheet spreading.

The youngest ane's was bauld and bricht,   15
And she was to lye with this unco knicht.

"Gin ye will answer me questions ten,
The morn ye sall be made my ain.

"O what is heigher nor the tree?
And what is deeper nor the sea?   20

"Or what is heavier nor the lead?
And what is better nor the breid?

"O what is whiter nor the milk?
Or what is safter nor the silk?

"Or what is sharper nor a thorn?   25
Or what is louder nor a horn?

"Or what is greener nor the grass?
Or what is waur nor a woman was?"

"O Heaven is higher nor the tree,
And Hell is deeper nor the sea.   30

"O sin is heavier nor the lead,
The blessing's better nor the bread.

2. **Sing . . . brume.** This is the characteristic refrain, made up of words chosen for sound rather than sense, although if we could trace the ballad back far enough the significance of the lines might be plainer. The localities appearing in these refrains are definite ones, such as the Cather banks, and suggest the possible place of origin of the ballad. On the other hand it would be simple for some ballad minstrel to transfer a rhythmical refrain from one ballad to another. This line is repeated as the second line of each ensuing stanza. **And . . . sune** (l. 4) is the fourth and final line of each stanza. Again, it is a refrain, but this time it serves as a kind of motif to sound the theme of the whole ballad. *Sune* is modern "soon." 6. **speired,** asked; still common in Anglo-Scottish. 10. **or,** ere, before. 12. **thir,** these. 15. **bauld,** bold, sharp, brisk. 16. **unco knicht,** the devil. 18. **sall,** shall. 22. **breid,** bread. 28. **waur,** worse.

"The snaw is whiter nor the milk,
And the down is safter nor the silk.

"Hunger is sharper nor a thorn, 35
And shame is louder nor a horn.

"Poison is greener nor the grass,
And Clootie's waur nor a woman was."

As sune as she the fiend did name,
He flew away in a blazing flame.

Edward

(BRITISH)

This fine folk ballad should be studied not only for its story, a characteristic tragedy of the "domestic relations" group of ballads, but also for its structure. The tale is told in typical hitching, though highly dramatic, fashion through the skillful use of incremental repetition. Refrains like "Edward, Edward" or "Mither, Mither," which are not incremental, are spoken of as "parallel repetition."

WHY dois your brand sae drap wi bluid,
        Edward, Edward,
Why dois your brand sae drap wi bluid,
    And why sae sad gang yee O?"
"O I hae killed my hauke sae guid, 5
        Mither, mither,
O I hae killed my hauke sae guid,
    And I had nae mair bot hee O."

"Your haukis bluid was nevir sae reid,
        Edward, Edward, 10
Your haukis bluid was nevir sae reid,
    My dear son I tell thee O."
"O I hae killed my reid-roan steid,
        Mither, mither,
O I hae killed my reid-roan steid, 15
    That erst was sae fair and frie O."

"Your steid was auld, and ye hae gat mair,
        Edward, Edward,
Your steid was auld, and ye hae gat mair,
    Sum other dule ye drie O." 20
"O I hae killed my fadir deir,
        Mither, mither,
O I hae killed my fadir deir,
    Alas, and wae is mee O!"

"And whatten penance wul ye drie for that, 25
        Edward, Edward?

And whatten penance wul ye drie for that?
    My deir son, now tell me O."
"Ile set my feit in yonder boat,
        Mither, mither, 30
Ile set my feit in yonder boat,
    And Ile fare ovir the sea O."

"And what wul ye doe wi your towirs and your ha,
        Edward, Edward?
And what wul ye doe wi your towirs and your ha, 35
    That were sae fair to see O?"
"Ile let them stand tul they doun fa,
        Mither, mither,
Ile let them stand tul they doun fa,
    For here nevir mair maun I bee O." 40

"And what wul ye leive to your bairns and your wife,
        Edward, Edward?
And what wul ye leive to your bairns and your wife,
    Whan ye gang ovir the sea O?"
"The warldis room, late them beg thrae life, 45
        Mither, mither,
The warldis room, late them beg thrae life,
    For thame nevir mair wul I see O."

"And what wul ye leive to your ain mither deir,
        Edward, Edward? 50
And what wul ye leive to your ain mither deir,
    My deir son, now tell me O."
"The curse of Hell fram me sall ye beir,
        Mither, mither,
The curse of Hell fram me sall ye beir, 55
    Sic counseils ye gave to me O."

Aage and Else

(DANISH)

This ballad deals with one of the most common themes of the supernatural ballads—the love of a dead man for a mortal woman. In most versions, as typified for example by the British *Sweet William's Ghost*, the mortal woman rides off with her dead lover and is carried irretrievably to the grave and damnation. In *Aage and Else* the dead lover averts this melancholy end for his mortal sweetheart by bidding her at the last minute look up to the stars. The theme of these ballads is known in folklore simply as the theme of the Demon Lover; but, from the many excellent German versions of the ballad, culminating in the *Lenore* of Gottfried Bürger (1748–1794)—much the most famous "literary" treatment of the subject—it is sometimes known as the "Lenore" theme. The demon lover, to be sure, may not cause the maiden's death, but

---

38. **Clootie**, the devil. A cloot is the half-hoof of a cloven-footed animal.
8. **mair**, more. 9. **reid**, red. 16. **erst**, once. 20. **dule**, sorrow, anguish. **drie**, suffer. 25. **whatten**, what a?—what kind of?

29. **feit**, feet. 33. **ha**, hall. This "satirical legacy," as it is called, is a feature of popular literature. 37. **fa**, fall. 45. **thrae**, through.

at least does irreparable damage to her soul. The same is true of the obverse of this tale—the love of a mortal man for a supernatural woman, illustrated by the Tann-häuser ballad (p. II:153) and in English literature by the ballad of *Thomas Rymer.*

THREE maidens sit in a bower,
Two broider with gold,
The third she weeps her own true-love
Under darksome mould,
For her troth to him was plighted.　　　　5

It was the knight Sir Aage
That rode by land and lea,
He loved the lady Elselil,
So fair was she.

He wooed the lady Elselil　　　　10
With gifts and gold,
On Monday thereafter
He lay in the mould.

Sore wept the lady Elselil
With wellaway,　　　　15
That heard the knight Sir Aage,
Low where he lay.

Up stood the knight Sir Aage,
His coffin black he bore,
With mickle toil and trouble　　　　20
He sought her door.

He knocked there with his coffin,
No cloak had he:
"Rise up, thou lady Elselil,
Open to me!"　　　　25

Up spake the lady Elselil,
With tears spake she:
"Canst thou name the name of Jesu
I'll open to thee!"

"Rise up, thou lady Elselil,　　　　30
Open thy door!
I can name the name of Jesu
As ever I could of yore."

Up stood the lady Elselil
In dule and dread.　　　　35
So opened she the bower door,
Let in the dead.

She took her golden comb
To smooth his hair,
For every lock she ordered　　　　40
Down fell a tear.

"Now lithe and list, Sir Aage,
Dearest love mine,
How goes it under murk and mould
In grave of thine?"　　　　45

"So goes it under darksome mould
Where I am laid,
As in the happy realm of Heaven,
Therefore be glad."

"Lithe and list, Sir Aage,　　　　50
Dearest love mine,
Fain would I lie 'neath murk and mould
In grave of thine."

"So goes it under darksome mould
There where I rest,　　　　55
As in the blackest depths of Hell!
Cross thou thy breast.

"For every tear thou lettest fall
In mournful mood,
Adown into my grave doth drip　　　　60
A drop of blood.

"Up above my head
The green grass grows,
Down about my feet
The dark worm goes.　　　　65

"But when a song thou singest
All in delight,
Then all my darksome grave is hung
With roses red and white.

"Now in the darksome entry　　　　70
The black cocks crow,
And all the doors are opening,
Forth must I go.

"And now the white cock croweth
In the high hall,　　　　75
To earth I now betake me
With dead men all.

"Now croweth on the high-loft
The cock so red,
And I must back to earth again　　　　80
With all the dead."

Aage and Else. Translated by E. M. Smith-Dampier. From *Book of Danish Ballads,* edited by Axel Obrick, published by Princeton University Press, 1939. Reprinted by permission of the American-Scandinavian Foundation.
8. **Elselil.** The suffix "-lil" implies that Else was both fair and small.
14–16. **Sore wept . . . heard.** It is a common belief in folklore that when someone weeps for a dead person, the corpse will not lie easily in the grave. Note ll. 58–62 below.

71. **The black cocks . . .** For the general significance of cocks in this situation, see *The Wife of Usher's Well,* note to l. 33; but the color combination of black, white (l. 74), and red (l. 79) is suggestive of the old tricolor of the Germanic or Teutonic Knights of the Middle Ages—white for purity, black for death, and red for courage.

Up stood the knight Sir Aage,
His coffin took once more,
Forth fared he to the kirkyard
With travail sore.   85

Up stood the lady Elselil,
In mournful mood,
To follow him, her own true-love,
Through the greenwood.

And when they came to the kirkyard   90
With toil and care,
Wan it grew and faded,
His goodly golden hair.

"Behold now up in Heaven
The stars so bright!   95
There mayst thou see full surely
How goes the night."

She saw the stars a-shining
In Heaven so blue
Down in the earth the dead man sank   100
Or e'er she knew.

Home went the lady Elselil
With care so cold,
And when a moon was over
Lay she in the mould.

Thomas Rymer

(BRITISH)

TRUE Thomas lay oer yon grassy bank,
  And he beheld a ladie gay,
A lady that was brisk and bold,
  Come riding oer the fernie brae.

Her skirt was of the grass-green silk,   5
  Her mantel of the velvet fine,
And ilka tett of her horse's mane
  Hung fifty silver bells and nine.

True Thomas he took off his hat,
  And bowed him low down till his knee: 10
"All hail, thou mighty Queen of Heaven!
  For your peer on earth I never did see."

"O no, O no, True Thomas," she says,
  "That name does not belong to me;
I am but the queen of fair Elfland,   15
  And I'm come here for to visit thee.

7. **ilka tett,** each lock; the preposition "from" should be read before *ilka.* 16. **I'm come . . . visit thee.** In the present version there is here a gap in the ballad, but other versions indicate that at this point the lady granted Thomas her love.

"But ye maun go wi me now, Thomas,
  True Thomas, ye maun go wi me,
For ye maun serve me seven years,
  Thro weel or wae as may chance to be."   20

She turned about her milk-white steed,
  And took True Thomas up behind,
And aye wheneer her bridle rang,
  The steed flew swifter than the wind.

For forty days and forty nights   25
  He wade through red blude to the knee,
And he saw neither sun nor moon,
  But heard the roaring of the sea.

O they rade on, and further on,
  Until they came to a garden green: 30
"Light down, light down, ye ladie free,
  Some of that fruit let me pull to thee."

"O no, O no, True Thomas," she says,
  "That fruit maun not be touched by thee,
For a' the plagues that are in Hell   35
  Light on the fruit of this countrie.

"But I have a loaf here in my lap,
  Likewise a bottle of claret wine,
And now ere we go farther on,
  We'll rest a while, and ye may dine."   40

When he had eaten and drunk his fill,
  "Lay down your head upon my knee,"
The lady said, "ere we climb yon hill,
  And I will show you fairlies three.

"O see not ye yon narrow road,   45
  So thick beset wi thorns and briers?
That is the path of righteousness,
  Tho after it but few enquires.

"And see not ye that braid braid road,
  That lies across yon lillie leven?   50
That is the path of wickedness,
  Tho some call it the road to Heaven.

"And see not ye that bonny road,
  Which winds about the fernie brae?
That is the road to fair Elfland,   55
  Where you and I this night maun gae.

"But Thomas, ye maun hold your tongue,
  Whatever you may hear or see,
For gin ae word you should chance to speak,
  You will neer get back to your ain countrie." 60

19. **serve me seven years.** Thomas must serve the traditional period of apprenticeship, so to speak. 44. **fairlies,** wonders, marvels. 50. **lillie leven,** lovely glades.

He has gotten a coat of the even cloth,
  And a pair of shoes of velvet green,
And till seven years were past and gone
  True Thomas on earth was never seen.

Sir Patrick Spens

(BRITISH)

In spite of the fine atmospheric quality of this ballad, which bespeaks a gifted minstrel author whose talents resemble those of a poet like Coleridge, this is probably to be classed as a historical ballad. It is believed that Sir Patrick Spens, himself difficult to identify, was lost at sea while returning from the expedition which conducted Margaret, daughter of King Alexander III of Scotland, to her husband, King Eric of Norway. The marriage took place in 1281.

THE king sits in Dunfermline toune
  Drinking the blude-red wine:
"O whar will I get guid sailor,
  To sail this schip of mine?"

Up and spak an eldern knicht,   5
  Sat at the kings richt kne:
"Sir Patrich Spens is the best sailor
  That sails upon the se."

The king has written a braid letter,
  And signed it wi his hand,   10
And sent it to Sir Patrick Spens,
  Was walking on the sand.

The first line that Sir Patrick red,
  A loud lauch lauched he;
The next line that Sir Patrick red,   15
  The teir blinded his ee.

"O wha is this has don this deid,
  This ill deid don to me,
To send me out this time o' the yeir,
  To sail upon the se!   20

"Mak haste, mak haste, my mirry men all,
  Our guid schip sails the morne:"
"O say na sae, my master deir,
  For I feir a deadlie storme.

"Late late yestreen I saw the new moone, 25
  Wi the auld moone in his arme,
And I feir, I feir, my deir master,
  That we will cum to harme."

64. **True Thomas . . . seen;** because of his breaking bread, drinking wine, and having intercourse with the fairy queen.
9. **braid letter,** a letter written on a long or broad sheet. 25-26. **Late . . . arme.** The bad omen in such a sight lay in the fact that the new moon was seen *late* in the evening.

O our Scots nobles wer richt laith
  To weet their cork-heild schoone;   30
But lang owre a' the play wer playd,
  Their hats they swam aboone.

O lang, lang may their ladies sit,
  Wi their fans into their hand,
Or eir they se Sir Patrick Spens   35
  Cum sailing to the land.

O lang, lang may the ladies stand,
  Wi their gold kems in their hair,
Waiting for their ain deir lords,
  For they'll se thame na mair.   40

Haf owre, haf owre to Aberdour,
  It's fiftie fadom deip,
And thair lies guid Sir Patrick Spens,
  Wi the Scots lords at his feit.

Niels Ebbeson

(DANISH)

In the year 1340 in Denmark, King Christian had died, the young prince Valdemar was absent from the country, and the unscrupulous barons of Holstein were making merry in the North Jutland section of Denmark. A certain Niels Ebbeson, a Danish patriot of whom little is known beyond his major feat, got the help of a group of like-minded citizens, and on a raiding expedition directed against Count Gert, or Gerhardt, assassinated the count and thus disposed of one of the most obnoxious of these tyrannous barons. Niels Ebbeson as a result became a popular hero of major dimensions, and the balladry about him has some of the outlaw flavor that characterizes the approximately contemporary Robin Hood ballads; at any rate, there is in these ballads the same championing of the people against the aristocracy.

THE Count to Denmark took his way,
  And would not be gainsaid,
What though the spaeman told him true
  That there should he lie dead.

Was none could cross his wilful mind   5
  His fate to put to test,
Yeoman and boor, and knight and squire,
  Must have him for their guest.

29. **laith,** loath. 30. **cork-heild schoone,** shoes with heels of cork, much affected by the nobility. 31. **owre,** ere, before. 32. **hats . . . aboone.** Their hats were floating above their bodies. 35. **Or eir,** ere ever. 41. **Haf . . . Aberdour,** halfway on the return journey to Aberdour (Aberdeen); that is, halfway home.
Niels Ebbeson. Translated by E. M. Smith-Dampier. From *Book of Danish Ballads,* edited by Axel Obrick, published by Princeton University Press, 1939. Reprinted by permission of the American-Scandinavian Foundation.
3. **spaeman,** fortune-teller.

The Count has called Niels Ebbeson
To come and meet with him,   10
And peace should reign whilst the hour endured,
With truce for life and limb.

The Count he met Niels Ebbeson
Northward beside the sea:
"Now be thou welcome, Niels Ebbeson,   15
Right welcome unto me!

"Blithe is thy cheer, Niels Ebbeson,
Retainer dear of mine!
Now what is the mind of the Northern Jutes,
And what of kinsfolk thine?"   20

"Yea, kinsfolk enow are mine, I trow,
And my wife hath kin also,
And all of them shall do thy will
If they thy will may know."

"Niels Ebbeson, thou art a valiant man,   25
And a man of wit beside,
And canst thou not ride straightforward
The long way round thou'lt ride.

"Now lithe and listen, Niels Ebbeson,
Wilt thou mine errand speed,   30
Then say how many swains hast thou
Will stand by thee at need?"

"Some five and forty swains have I,
Such as they well may be,
And are they many or are they few   35
Right dear they are to me."

"And hast thou five and forty carles,
Well art thou served, I ween—
But last night wert thou in Sir Bugge's hold
With a hundred mail-clad men!"   40

Niels Ebbeson he stamped his foot,
And straight made answer high:
"Is any man here, or knight or knave,
That dares maintain that lie?

"Is any man here, or knight or knave,   45
Who dares that lie maintain,
Never a foot will I retreat
Till I answer him back again!"

"Now lithe and list, Niels Ebbeson,
Of this we'll make an end,   50
Go, ask of him, Sir Bugge,
If he will be my friend.

"Sir Bugge and Povl Glob the young
To do my will did swear,
And Sir Anders Frost is one with them,   55
And foremost in counsel there.

"Yea, more have sworn to do my will
That now would work me woe,
So hear and heed Sir Bugge's rede,
And see how the thing will go!"   60

"Oh, nought know I of Sir Bugge's mind,
What he may say or do,
But Anders has kept his troth with thee
As all men will tell thee true.

"Anders hath kept his faith with thee,   65
As all men will tell thee true,
But would he take leave of thy service
Such leave is a free man's due.

"For this is the Danish custom,
And hath been since days of yore,   70
If a swain would change his service
He should have leave therefor."

Up and spake Lord Gert the Count
That liked his words right ill:
"Nay, never a vassal may leave his Lord   75
Save with his Lord's good will."

"Oh, none is bound with a holy vow
Save a monk to his cowl of grey!
Let chieftains come and chieftains go,
Men serve them as best they may."   80

"Overbold is his speech, Niels Ebbeson,
That bandies words with me!
Or thou shalt depart from Denmark,
Or I'll hang thee to a tree!"

"And must I depart from Denmark,   85
From wife's and bairns' embrace,
Oh, thou shalt call it a luckless hour
That e'er thou sawest my face!"

"Get hence, get hence, Niels Ebbeson,
And let thy prating be,   90
Or I will do what well I may
And break my truce with thee!"

"Oh, ne'er hast thou seen me so sore afraid
As to tremble for curse and ban,
Look well to thyself, Count Gert, I say,   95
And defend thy head like a man!"

69–72. For this . . . therefor. This is a reference to the ancient Danish Law of Commutation, which gave every retainer the right to take his leave every year and find service with another lord. It is a difference of opinion between Niels and Count Gert on this question which precipitates the action of the ballad.

29. lithe, listen

"Niels Ebbeson, thy words are hard,
As oft ere this was shown,
But I will hold truce with thee today,
E'en till the sun goes down."   100

Niels Ebbeson waved his lily-white hand,
And turned his steed on the shore:
"Farewell, Count Gert, with all thy men!
Soon shall we meet once more!"

Niels Ebbeson he fled full fast,   105
Nor spur was fain to spare,
And the Count held back with all his men,
Was none durst follow there.

It was he, Niels Ebbeson,
That home to hold did win,   110
And it was his own dear lady
Went forth to lead him in.

"Now lithe thou and listen, wife, I pray,
Some counsel give to me,
For the Count will make me an outlawed man,   115
Or hang me on gallows-tree!"

"What counsel can I give to thee
That have but a woman's wit?
The worst of rede were here the best,
Could we but light on it.   120

"The worst of rede were here the best,
All in this evil hour,
The Count to slay whilst yet we may,
Or burn him in his bower.

"Now take thy steeds to the smithy,   125
(This is my counsel true),
And turn their shoon the backward way
When they are shod anew.

"Turn thou their shoon the backward way,
So the foeman thy track shall miss,   130
And take heed and tell to no man
That a woman taught thee this!"

Up and spake Niels Ebbeson,
Unto his men spake he:
"Now which of you will follow,   135
And which take leave of me?

"Let him that now will follow
Reach forth his hand to me,
And he that now will take his leave
Speak up right speedily!"   140

Up they stood, his Danish squires,
And answered their lord so free:

"Now all of us will follow
And risk our lives for thee!"

Now up they rode to Ladywood,   145
And there their steeds did bind,
And into Randers Town they went,
Count Gert to seek and find.

And when to Randers Bridge he came
He spake to his squires anew: 150
"Now let him take his leave and go
Who will not stand me true!"

Up and spake the little lad Trust,
The truest of them all:
"Now give me leave, my master,   155
And saddle and steed withal."

He gave him leave, his master,
And saddle and steed withal,
And or ever the day was over
He served him best of all.   160

It was he, Niels Ebbeson,
Through cloak that smote the door:
"Rise up, rise up, Lord Gert the Count,
For thou must sleep no more!

"Stand up, Lord Gert the Count,   165
And lend to me thine ear!
Duke Henrik's messenger am I,
And he hath sent me here.

"Rise up, Lord Gert the Count,
Nor longer lay thee down!   170
Kolding is beleaguered
And burnt is Ribe Town."

"And dost thou tell me tidings true,
Then good are they to hear!
Free in my hold whilst yet we live   175
Thou shalt have steed and gear."

Oh, they have opened wide the door
More of that news to know,
And it was he, Niels Ebbeson,
To the Count's bedside did go.   180

"Now thou and I, Niels Ebbeson,
Can league us far and wide,
Word will we send to Duke Henrik,
And Sir Klaus his friend beside."

Up and spake the swarthy swain: 185
"Now waste no further word!
Let be, let be thy tedious tale,
And hearken to the sword!"

They've seized him, Gert the Count,
All by his golden hair,
Body from head they've sundered
Over his bedside there.

Now when the Count was done to death 195
All on the drums they beat,
Forth fared he, Niels Ebbeson,
And hastened down the street.

It was he, Niels Ebbeson,
That fain would flee away,
But Sir Ove Haas he barred the road, 200
And strove to say him nay.

"Now lithe and listen, Sir Ove Haas,
And seek not to hinder me,
For thou art wed to my kinswoman,
As well is known to thee."

"Yea, he that has wed thy kinswoman 205
Is kin to thee, I trow,
But thou hast slain my Lord this day,
And thou shalt not pass me now!"

Niels Ebbeson he drew his blade,
He would not flee the strife, 210
Sir Ove and many a German foe
Must there lay down their life.

It was he, Niels Ebbeson,
To Randers Bridge did ride,
And the little page that took his leave 215
Was standing there beside.

Over the bridge rode Niels Ebbeson,
For his foes came like the wind,
And it was the little foot-page
Broke down the bridge behind. 220

Niels Ebbeson rode to Noringsris,
And fast he spurred his steed,
Sore, good sooth, was his anguish,
And sorer still his need.

She sheltered him, an old good-wife, 225
Of loaves that had but two,
And she's given one to Niels Ebbeson,
Because Count Gert he slew.

The Wife of Usher's Well

(BRITISH)

Like *Aage and Else* or the British *Sweet William's Ghost*, this ballad typifies the common theme of the return of the dead, or the revenant, but the ghosts in *The Wife of Usher's Well* are benevolent ghosts. This particular ballad has had a very long and complicated history and still exists among English-speaking peoples in the United States. In fact, in the American version, *The Blue and the Gray*, a widow has three sons, killed respectively in the Mexican, the Civil, and the Spanish Wars (!), who return to visit her.

THERE lived a wife at Usher's well,
And a wealthy wife was she;
She had three stout and stalwart sons,
And sent them o'er the sea.

They hadna been a week from her, 5
A week but barely ane,
When word came to the carline wife
That her three sons were gane.

They hadna been a week from her,
A week but barely three, 10
When word came to the carline wife
That her sons she'd never see.

"I wish the wind may never cease,
Nor fashes in the flood,
Till my three sons come hame to me 15
In earthly flesh and blood!"

It fell about the Martinmas,
When nights are lang and mirk,
The carline's wife's three sons came hame,
And their hats were o' the birk. 20

It neither grew in syke nor ditch,
Nor yet in ony sheugh;
But at the gates o' Paradise
That birk grew fair enugh.

"Blow up the fire, my maidens! 25
Bring water from the well!
For a' my house shall feast this night,
Since my three sons are well."

And she has made to them a bed,
She's made it large and wide; 30
And she's ta'en her mantle her about,
Sat down at the bedside.

Up then crew the red, red cock,
And up and crew the gray;

7. **carline wife,** old woman. 14. **fashes,** trouble, turbulence. 17. **Martinmas,** the feast of St. Martin which fell on November 11. 20. **hats . . . birk,** hats of birch. There is an old tradition that a man returning from the dead wears some form of vegetation on his head to prevent the wind on earth from having power over him. The herbs of Paradise are his protection. 21. **syke,** trench. 22. **sheugh,** furrow. 33. **Up then crew . . . cock.** The dead arose from their graves at midnight and remained above ground until the cock crowed.

The eldest to the youngest said,   35
    " 'Tis time we were away."

The cock he hadna crawed but once,
    And clapped his wings at a',
When the youngest to the eldest said,
    "Brother, we must awa'."   40

"The cock doth craw, the day doth daw,
    The channerin' worm doth chide;
Gin we be missed out o' our place,
    A sair pain we maun bide."

"Lie still, lie still but a little wee while,   45
    Lie still but if we may;
Gin my mother should miss us when she wakes,
    She'll go mad ere it be day."

"Fare ye weel, my mother dear!
    Fareweel to barn and byre!   50
And fare ye weel, the bonny lass
    That kindles my mother's fire."

Bonny Barbara Allan

(BRITISH)

Here is the familiar old theme of "lovesickness," this
time carried to a fatal conclusion. The maiden, resenting
a slight, real or fancied, spurns the suddenly enamored
lover. He takes to his bed ("care-bed") and dies the
wasting death of a rejected lover. The maiden then dies
in sympathy. Few ballads in the entire Child collection
have had a greater vitality in America.

It was in and about the Martinmas time,
    When the green leaves were a-falling,
That Sir John Graeme, in the West Country,
    Fell in love with Barbara Allan.

He sent his man down through the town,   5
    To the place where she was dwelling;
"O haste and come to my master dear,
    Gin ye be Barbara Allan."

O hooly, hooly rose she up,
    To the place where he was lying,   10
And when she drew the curtain by,
    "Young man, I think you're dying."

"O it's I'm sick, and very, very sick,
    And 'tis a' for Barbara Allan;"
"O 'tis better for me ye's never be,   15
    Tho your heart's blood were a-spilling."

38. **at a',** at all. The phrase apparently means that the cock had
crowed but once and had not yet flapped his wings.   42. **channerin',**
devouring.   50. **byre,** a shed for cattle.
9. **hooly,** slowly and softly.

He turned his face unto the wall,
    And death was with him dealing:
"Adieu, adieu, my dear friends all,
    And be kind to Barbara Allan."   20

"O dinna ye mind, young man," said she,
    "When ye was in the tavern a-drinking,
That ye made the healths gae round and round,
    And slighted Barbara Allan?"

And slowly, slowly raise she up,   25
    And slowly, slowly left him,
And sighing said, she could not stay,
    Since death of life had reft him.

She had not gane but a mile or twa,
    When she heard the dead-bell ringing,   30
And every jow that the dead-bell geid,
    It cryed "Woe to Barbara Allan!"

"O mother, mother, make my bed!
    O make it soft and narrow!
My love has died for me today,   35
    I'll die for him tomorrow."

The Bride of Ribe

(DANISH)

This ballad represents the tradition of the shrewish,
churlish woman, so formidable to mankind that neither
saint nor devil can control her. A similar representative
in British balladry is *The Farmer's Curst Wife.*

There dwelt a man in Ribe Town
    So rich and full of pride,
He gave his daughter a silken sark
Was fifteen fathoms wide.
She swept the dew from all the earth.   5

And fifteen tailors sewed the sark
That were of great renown,
And some dwelt up in Ribe
If they dwelt not in Ribe Town.

And fifteen maids of good repute   10
That sark must wash and dry,
And some got cramp in every limb,
While some lay down to die.

21. **mind,** remember. 31. **jow,** stroke of a bell. **geid,** gave (from
"gived").
The Bride of Ribe. Translated by E. M. Smith-Dampier. From *Book
of Danish Ballads,* edited by Axel Obrick, published by Princeton
University Press, 1939. Reprinted by permission of the American-
Scandinavian Foundation.
3. **sark,** here a blouse rather than a coat of mail.

And fifteen were the carpenters
That hung it out to air,   15
Some broke their arms and some their legs,
And some lay sick a year.

And now the bride went forth to kirk
All wrappen in cloak of skin,
Full fifteen fathom must they unfurl   20
Ere she could enter in.

And when she entered in the kirk
Loud did she rage and roar
She struck adown the holy Cross
That stood therein of yore.   25

A penny was all the bridal-fee
That she in pouch did find,
She threw one deacon off his legs,
And struck another blind.

Before the altar stood the priest,   30
And by Saint Knud he cried:
"No bridal can be hallowed here
Till ye remove the bride!"

With nose in air that maiden fair
From kirk returned again,   35
And all the kine in field that fed
Went galloping home again.

And when she sat at bridal feast
She laughed both loud and high:
"A penny we spent and to kirk we went,   40
As nobody can deny!"

Robin Hood's Death and Burial

(BRITISH)

As Child, the great authority on the British popular ballads, has so aptly observed, "Robin Hood is absolutely a creation of the ballad-muse." Attempts to associate Robin Hood, most celebrated of all ballad characters, with a historical personage have thus far failed completely. Nor is it possible to get far with the theory that he is a medieval popularization of Woden, the god of the Germanic peoples. Instead, he is a fictitious yeoman, idealized, with a kingly courtesy and courage, the defender of the poor and the champion of womanhood, the avowed enemy of the organized Church. But he is devout and reverent to the Virgin. He is an epic figure in the greenwood; his followers—Little John, Scarlet, and Friar Tuck—are analogous to the retainers of Roland or Beowulf or even to the knights of King Arthur, but they are nevertheless as much yeomen as Robin Hood himself.

The most extensive and withal the best treatment of the entire career of Robin Hood is *A Gest of Robyn Hode*, a long minstrel ballad of the later Middle English or early Modern English period. So close does the *Gest* come to an epic that it might be called a heroic epic, except that Robin Hood was not created by any poet of the court. Later isolated ballads make Robin Hood less impressive than his associates; he suffers a debasement comparable to that suffered by King Arthur or Charlemagne. But *Robin Hood's Death and Burial* shows the hero still in a heroic light.

The betrayal of Robin Hood by his cousin is reminiscent of the tragic "domestic relations" ballad, in which one relative either kills another or does him a great wrong.

WHEN Robin Hood and Little John
    Down a down a down a down
Went oer yon bank of broom,
    Said Robin Hood bold to Little John,
We have shot for many a pound.   5
    Hey down a down a down a down!

But I am not able to shoot one shot more,
    My broad arrows will not flee;
But I have a cousin lives down below,
    Please God, she will bleed me.   10

Now Robin he is to fair Kirkly gone,
    As fast as he can win;
But before he came there, as we do hear,
    He was taken very ill.

And when he came to fair Kirkly Hall,   15
    He knocked all at the ring,
But none was so ready as his cousin herself
    For to let Bold Robin in.

"Will you please to sit down, cousin Robin," she said,
    "And drink some beer with me?"   20
"No, I will neither eat nor drink,
    Till I am blooded by thee."

"Well, I have a room, cousin Robin," she said,
    "Which you did never see,
And if you please to walk therein,   25
    You blooded by me shall be."

She took him by the lily-white hand,
    And led him to a private room,
And there she blooded bold Robin Hood,
    While one drop of blood would run down.   30

2. **Down . . . down.** The refrain, the second line of each stanza, is repeated to make the sixth and last line of most of the stanzas, though not of the second and third stanzas from the end. 2. **broom,** the broom-plant. 8. **broad arrows,** arrows with a forked or barbed head. 11. **Kirkly,** Kirklees, not clearly identified. Some of the versions mention Bricklies (in Yorkshire) and others Bricklies (in Scotland).

She blooded him in a vein of the arm,
    And locked him up in the room;
There did he bleed all the live-long day,
    Until the next day at noon.

He then bethought him of a casement there,   35
    Thinking for to get down;
But was so weak he could not leap,
    He could not get him down.

He then bethought him of his bugle-horn,
    Which hung low down to his knee;   40
He set his horn upon his mouth,
    And blew out weak blasts three.

Then Little John, when hearing him,
    As he sat under a tree,
"I fear my master is now near dead,   45
    He blows so wearily."

Then Little John to fair Kirkly is gone,
    As fast as he can dree;
But when he came to Kirkly Hall,
    He broke locks two or three;   50

Until he came bold Robin to see,
    Then he fell on his knee;
"A boon, a boon," cries Little John,
    "Master, I beg of thee."

"What is that boon," said Robin Hood,   55
    "Little John, thou begs of me?"
"It is to burn fair Kirkly Hall,
    And all their nunnery."

"Now nay, now nay," quoth Robin Hood,
    "That boon I'll not grant thee;   60
I never hurt woman in all my life,
    Nor men in woman's company.

"I never hurt fair maid in all my time,
    Nor at mine end shall it be;
But give me my bent bow in my hand,   65
    And a broad arrow I'll let flee,
And where this arrow is taken up,
    There shall my grave digged be.

"Lay me a green sod under my head,
    And another at my feet;   70
And lay my bent bow by my side,
    Which was my music sweet;
And make my grave of gravel and green,
    Which is most right and meet.

"Let me have length and breadth enough,   75
    With a green sod under my head;

48. **dree,** literally "endure," to be interpreted here as "be able."
Contrast the word here with *drie* in *Edward*, l. 25 and note.

Then they may say, when I am dead
    'Here lies bold Robin Hood.'"

These words they readily granted him,
    Which did bold Robin Hood please;   80
And there they buried bold Robin Hood,
    Within the fair Kirkleys.

Bonnie George Campbell

(SCOTTISH)

This ballad is a characteristic example of the Scottish
coronach, or ballad of lamentation.

Hie upon Hielands,
    And laigh upon Tay,
Bonnie George Campbell
    Rode out on a day.

He saddled, he bridled,   5
    And gallant rode he,
And hame cam his guid horse,
    But never cam he.

Out cam his mother dear,
    Greeting fu sair,   10
And out cam his bonnie bryde,
    Riving her hair.

"The meadow lies green,
    The corn is unshorn,
But Bonnie George Campbell   15
    Will never return."

Saddled and bridled
    And booted rode he,
A plume in his helmet,
    A sword at his knee.   20

But toom cam his saddle,
    All bloody to see,
Oh, hame cam his guid horse,
    But never cam he!

Young Engel

(DANISH)

Although *Young Engel* has generally been classified
by Danish scholars as historical, its central situation—
that of the interrupted elopement—is essentially a com-

2. **laigh,** low.
Young Engel. Translated by E. M. Smith-Dampier. From *Book of
Danish Ballads*, edited by Axel Obrick, published by Princeton University Press, 1939. Reprinted by permission of the American-Scandinavian Foundation.

monplace motif in the "domestic relation" type of ballad. The couple, in this situation, will be pursued by angry relatives bent on punishing the man in the case.

IT WAS the swain young Engel
   That was both free and fair,
Up did he ride in the countryside
And seized a maiden there.
   Will the day ne'er be dawning?   5

Now Malfred hight the maiden,
   Was honest as the day,
And on the night of their luckless flight
In greenwood wild they lay.

It was the swain young Engel   10
   At midnight did awake,
And of his dream so dreary
To her he up and spake:

"A wolf methought was on me,
   A wolf so grim and grey,   15
That tore my heart with bloody teeth
E'en when I waking lay."

"Small marvel if thus thou dreamest,
   Nor doth thy dream deceive,
When thou by force hast taken me   20
Lacking my kinsfolk's leave."

In he came, the little foot-page,
   And stood beside the board,
Both swift of wit and sharp of tongue,
He well could speak his word.   25

"Now hearken thou, young Engel,
   And be for flight well boun,
For Gode Lovmand and his host
By four ways come to town!"

"Oh, not for four I tremble,   30
   Nor do I fear for five,
I reck not of Gode Lovmand,
Nor any man alive!"

"Nay, more of five the number,
   And a greater tale than ten!   35
Here cometh Gode Lovmand
With an hundred weaponed men."

It was the swain young Engel
   That kissed his fair lady:
"If aught thou know'st of counsel   40
In God's name counsel me!"

"Now call thy squires together
   To saddle each his steed,
And seek we the kirk of Our Lady
So long as endures our need!"   45

And now round the kirk of Our Lady
   Was laid a leaguer close,
And ever Gode Lovmand
Was foremost among the foes.

Up spake the mother of Malfred   50
   Of mood so grim and cold:
"An ye fire the kirk of Saint Mary
Ye can build it again for gold.

"Now cast we our gold and silver
   Till it brims o'er a lordly cup;   55
An ye level the kirk of Our Lady,
I trow ye can build it up!"

Oh, they fired the kirk of Saint Mary,
   And fast the flames leapt on,
And 'twas the lady Malfred   60
Must needs grow pale and wan.

Now heat like a fiery furnace
   Did in the kirkyard glow,
But 'twas hotter within the walls, I ween,
When the lead dripped down below.   65

Up spake the swain young Engel
   That was so bold of mood:
"Now let us slay our coursers
And cool us in their blood!"

Up spake the little horse-boy   70
   That loved the steeds so free:
"Slay rather the lady Malfred,
More worthy of death is she!"

It was the swain young Engel
   That took her in his arm: 75
"Thou art not worthy death, dear love,
And none shall do thee harm!"

Oh, they've set her on a shining shield
   To lift her with glaive and spear,
They've hoisted her out of the kirk-window,   80
A-weeping full many a tear.

With many a tear young Malfred
   Did through the kirkyard fare,
Blackened were all her garments
And burnt her golden hair.   85

Sore wept the lady Malfred
   Came in the meads so green:
"Now burneth the kirk of Our Lady,
And a gallant swain therein!"

'Twas so soon thereafter,   90
Ere harvest time was done,
The lady sought her bower,
And bore so fair a son.

Born was he at even,
And christened the selfsame night;   95
They gave him the name of his father,
And fostered him while they might.

She fostered him seven winters,
And ever these words did say:
"My brother slew thy father,   100
And this must thou learn today."

She fostered him for a winter,
And for nine winters yet:
"My brother slew thy father,
And never shalt thou forget!"   105

And now her son, young Engel,
Unto his kinsfolk saith:
"Fain would I seek my father's foes
All to avenge his death."

It was Gode Lovmand   110
Sat drinking at the board,
And in he came, the little page,
So ready with his word.

"Now hearken, Gode Lovmand,
Ye may to flight be boun,   115
Here come young Engel and his men
By four ways to the town!

"Young Engel and his merry men
Upon the town advance,
And wrathful is his mood, I ween,   120
So high he shakes his lance."

"To Thing and meeting-place afar
My way I oft have won,
But the name of this young Engel
Was spoken of by none!"   125

It was Gode Lovmand
That clapped his cheek so white:
"Now canst thou give me counsel,
Then counsel thou me aright!"

"And if thou ask me counsel   130
This will I give to thee,
Seek we our stone-built tower
So long as need there be.

"The doors are all of the lead so grey,
And the walls of marble stone,   135

And a wondrous lot will be ours, I wot,
If ever that hold be won!"

And now that stone-built tower
On four sides they beset,
And 'twas the swain young Engel   140
That would be foremost yet.

It was Gode Lovmand
From loophole looked below:
"Who be ye that come hither
To make so proud a show?"   145

Up spake the swain young Engel,
Decked all in scarlet gear:
"Engel the name men call me,
Son of thy sister dear."

Up spake Gode Lovmand   150
All with a darkening brow:
"Of that needs little boasting,
For a bastard bairn wert thou!"

"And was I born of love, Godsooth,
The better is my breed!   155
And I have gold and liegemen bold,
And many a gallant steed.

"And was I but a bastard bairn
The fault was thine, I trow,
Yet am I lord of lands so broad,   160
With towers and holds enow."

It was the swain young Engel
Would sooner fight than fly;
He fired the stone-built tower
Till the flames leapt to the sky.   165

It was the swain young Engel
That would not ride his way,
Till he saw the stone-built tower
Lie low in ashes grey.

It was the swain young Engel   170
That clapped his lily-white hands,
When he saw his father's slayer
Lie dead 'mid burning brands.

It was the swain young Engel
Did home to hold repair,   175
And met by the gate his mother
Wrapped in her cloak of vair.

"Now greetings, greetings, mother dear,
Let all thy sorrow be!
My father's death have I avenged,   180
And bring the news to thee."

It was the lady Malfred
Wrung hands in dule and pain:
"I had one daily sorrow,
And thou hast made it twain!"   185

It was the swain young Engel
That turned and rode away:
"Strange are the ways of women,
And that for sooth I say!"

Now lieth Gode Lovmand   190
All under darksome mould,
But Engel serves before the King
For goods and red, red gold.

Sir Luno
and the Mermaid

(DANISH)

As in the ballad of *Riddles Wisely Expounded*, we are
dealing here with the case of a mortal who, confronted
by a supernatural creature and threatened with disaster,
is able to save himself by solving a riddle or reading a
secret message (a *rune*).

S IR Luno built him a ship so great
    That ne'er on sea did sail its mate.
So they gained their red, red gold all up in Green-
    land.

A ship so great
That ne'er on sea did sail its mate.   5
On either side the red gold shone,
And Our Lady's name was written thereon.

The red gold shone,
Our Lady's name was written thereon.
On stem and stern did the red gold flame,   10
And thereon was written Our Saviour's name.

Did the red gold flame,
And thereon was written Our Saviour's name.
Of silk so fine the sails were spread,
And pied with stripes of blue and red.   15

The sails were spread,
And pied with stripes of blue and red.
The yards were all of silver white,
And with red gold the mast was dight.

Of silver white,   20
And with red gold the mast was dight.

Sir Luno and the Mermaid. Translated by E. M. Smith-Dampier.
From *Book of Danish Ballads*, edited by Axel Obrick, published by
Princeton University Press, 1939. Reprinted by permission of the
American-Scandinavian Foundation.

Down to the strand they bore
Both anchor stout and oar.

They bore
Both anchor stout and oar.   25
Swiftly Sir Luno sailed the sea,
And there met a Mermaid, and grim was she.

Sailed the sea,
And there met a Mermaid, and grim was she.
"Turn back now, Sir Luno, and get thee gone,   30
Or thy ship will I straightway change to stone!

"Get thee gone,
Or thy ship will I straightway change to stone!"
"Ne'er shalt thou live to see the day
When for a Mermaid I turned from my way.   35

"To see the day
When for a Mermaid I turned from my way."
With the first blue billow the Mermaid sent,
Both mast and yard were asunder rent.

The Mermaid sent,   40
Both mast and yard were asunder rent.
With the second she sent against the boat
The silken sail on the sea did float.

Against the boat,
The silken sail on the sea did float.   45
Up spake the steersman and said this word:
"Is there no man who knoweth the runes aboard?"

Said this word:
"Is there no man who knoweth the runes aboard?"
Up spake Sir Luno, the well-born knight: 50
" 'Tis I that can rist the runes aright."

The well-born knight:
" 'Tis I that can rist the runes aright."
On a linden-twig did he rist the spell,
And there as a stone must the Mermaid dwell.   55

Rist the spell,
And there as a stone must the Mermaid dwell.
He risted the runes on a linden-bough,
And bound the Mermaid with power enow.

On a linden-bough,   60
And bound the Mermaid with power enow.
"Sir Luno, Sir Luno, now loose thou me!
Seven barrels of silver I'll give to thee.

"Loose thou me,
Seven barrels of silver I'll give to thee,   65
And another of gold will I bestow
Wilt thou have mercy and let me go.

"Will I bestow,
Wilt thou have mercy and let me go."
"Sit thou a stone and starve for aye,   70
I'll loose thee not till the Judgment Day!

"Starve for aye,
I'll loose thee not till the Judgment Day.
Tell all who come hither by sea or land
Thou wert bound by Sir Luno's lily-white hand.   75

"By sea or land,
Thou wert bound by Sir Luno's lily-white hand."
He sailed back to Greenland, that knight so bold,
And there sits the Mermaid, a stone so cold.

Kemp Owyne

(BRITISH)

The common folklore themes here are (1) the "loathly
lady" and (2) the magic transformation. Perhaps it could
be said that one grows out of the other. The lady is made
hideous through the working of magic, but can be released from her spell through the courage and love of a
mortal who is willing to kiss her even in her hideous
form. There is, moreover, a test of the knight's physical
courage and endurance. On the magic ring, for example,
see *Hind Horn*.

HER mother died when she was young,
    Which gave her cause to make great moan;
Her father married the warst woman
    That ever lived in Christendom.

She served her with foot and hand,   5
    In every thing that she could dee,
Till once, in an unlucky time,
    She threw her in ower Craigy's sea.

Says, "Lie you there, dove Isabel,
    And all my sorrows lie with thee;   10
Till Kemp Owyne come ower the sea,
    And borrow you with kisses three,
Let all the world do what they will,
    Oh, borrowed shall you never be!"

Her breath grew strang, her hair grew lang,   15
    And twisted thrice about the tree,
And all the people, far and near,
    Thought that a savage beast was she.

6. **dee,** do. 8. **Craigy's sea.** Although this body of water has not been
identified, there is known a Craigie Wood, a hill south of Perth,
Scotland, on the shores of the River Tay. Possibly, then, Craigy's
Sea is the Tay itself.   9. **dove,** a helpless or innocent young woman.
11. **Kemp Owyne.** A *kemp* is a champion fighting man. *Owyne* is very
likely the Owain of the Arthurian romance-cycles; if so, there is
here another instance of a figure taken from the chivalric romances
appearing in a popular ballad.   12. **borrow,** ransom, release.

These news did come to Kemp Owyne,
    Where he lived, far beyond the sea;   20
He hasted him to Craigy's sea,
    And on the savage beast looked he.

Her breath was strang, her hair was lang,
    And twisted was about the tree,
And with a swing she came about: 25
    "Come to Craigy's sea, and kiss with me.

"Here is a royal belt," she cried,
    "That I have found in the green sea;
And while your body it is on,
    Drawn shall your blood never be;   30
But if you touch me, tail or fin,
    I vow my belt your death shall be."

He stepped in, gave her a kiss,
    The royal belt he brought him wi;
Her breath was strang, her hair was lang,   35
    And twisted twice about the tree,
And with a swing she came about:
    "Come to Craigy's sea, and kiss with me.

"Here is a royal ring," she said,
    "That I have found in the green sea;   40
And while your finger it is on,
    Drawn shall your blood never be;
But if you touch me, tail or fin,
    I swear my ring your death shall be."

He stepped in, gave her a kiss,   45
    The royal ring he brought him wi;
Her breath was strang, her hair was lang,
    And twisted ance about the tree,
And with a swing she came about:
    "Come to Craigy's sea, and kiss with me.   50

"Here is a royal brand," she said,
    "That I have found in the green sea;
And while your body it is on,
    Drawn shall your blood never be;
But if you touch me, tail or fin,   55
    I swear my brand your death shall be."

He stepped in, gave her a kiss,
    The royal brand he brought him wi;
Her breath was sweet, her hair grew short,
    And twisted nane about the tree,   60
And smilingly she came about,
    As fair a woman as fair could be.

27, 39, 51. **belt . . . ring . . . brand.** These three acouterments are
the commonest talismans against wounds. One would have been
enough, but three kisses are necessary to redeem the loathly lady,
and so three talismans come into the story. For the magic ring in
another use, see *Hind Horn*, line 9 ff.

Johnie Armstrong

(BRITISH)

The Armstrongs were a powerful Scottish family living near the Border, for many centuries the debatable land between England and Scotland. John Armstrong, the hero of this ballad, appears about 1525. He was an independent nobleman, paying little respect either to the English or to the Scots, and consequently making frequent border raids on both. Finally, in 1530, King James v of Scotland got possession of John Armstrong and had him executed. The suggestion here is that James captured Armstrong through treachery, but such suggestions are frequently made in outlaw ballads, where the sympathy is always with the outlaw.

THERE dwelt a man in faire Westmerland,
　Ionne Armstrong men did him call,
He had nither lands nor rents coming in,
　Yet he kept eight score men in his hall.

He had horse and harness for them all,　　　　5
　Goodly steeds were all milke-white;
O the golden bands an about their necks,
　And their weapons, they were all alike.

Newes then was brought unto the king
　That there was sicke a won as hee,　　　　10
That lived lyke a bold outlaw,
　And robbed all the north country.

The king he writt an a letter then,
　A letter which was large and long;
He signed it with his owne hand,　　　　15
　And he promised to doe him no wrong.

When this letter came Ionne untill,
　His heart it was as blythe as birds on the tree:
"Never was I sent for before any king,
　My father, my grandfather, nor none but mee.　20

"And if wee goe the king before,
　I would we went most orderly;
Every man of you shall have his scarlet cloak,
　Laced with silver laces three.

"Every one of you shall have his velvett coat,　25
　Laced with sillver lace so white;
O the golden bands an about your necks,
　Black hatts, white feathers, all alyke."

By the morrow morninge by ten of the clock,
　Towards Edenburough gon was hee,　　　　30
And with him all his eight score men;
　Good Lord, it was a goodly sight for to see!

When Ionne came befower the king,
　He fell downe on his knee:
"O pardon, my soveraine leige," he said,　　　35
　"O pardon my eight score men and mee!"

"Thou shalt have no pardon, thou traytor strong,
　For thy eight score men nor thee;
For tomorrow morning by ten of the clock,
　Both thou and them shall hang on the gallow-
　　tree."　　　　40
But Ionne looked over his left shoulder,
　Good Lord, what a grievous look looked hee!
Saying, "Asking grace of a graceles face—
　Why there is none for you nor me."

But Ionne had a bright sword by his side,　　　45
　And it was made of the mettle so free,
That had not the king stept his foot aside,
　He had smitten his head from his faire boddë.

Saying, "Fight on, my merry men all,
　And see that none of you be taine;　　　　50
For rather then men shall say we were hanged,
　Let them report how we were slaine."

Then, God wot, faire Eddenburrough rose,
　And so besett poore Ionne rounde,
That fowerscore and tenn of Ionnes best men　55
　Lay gasping all upon the ground.

Then like a mad man Ionne laid about,
　And like a mad man then fought hee,
Until a falce Scot came Ionne behinde,
　And runn him through the faire boddee.　　　60

Saying, "Fight on, my merry men all,
　And see that none of you be taine;
For I will stand by and bleed but awhile,
　And then will I come and fight againe."

Newes then was brought to young Ionne **Arm-**
　　strong,　　　　65
　As he stood by his nurse's knee,
Who vowed if ere he lived for to be a man,
　O the treacherous Scots revenged hee'd be.

1. **Westmerland,** Westmoreland, the county in northwest England. 7. **an,** a superfluous word, inserted to fill out the meter. 10. **sicke a won,** such a one. 17. **untill,** unto. The preposition is put after the word in many instances.

59. **falce Scot.** It is a commonplace of the outlaw ballads to have the death of the outlaw encompassed by "treachery" of some sort. 65. **young Ionne Armstrong,** the little son of the outlaw.

REBIRTH
AND
DISCOVERY

1350 TO 1650

Lorenzo de' Medici, patron of art and letters and ruthless Renaissance ruler, by the sculptor Verrocchio.

T HE Middle Ages reached their climax in the thirteenth century, when all the faith and spirituality of Christian Europe, united in the fold of a common Church, expressed themselves in lofty masterpieces of literature and Gothic building. It was the century of Albertus Magnus, Thomas Aquinas, Roger Bacon, and Duns Scotus, of St. Francis and St. Dominic, of the Minnesingers and *Roman de la Rose* and the Dante of *La Vita Nuova*. In the hundred years that followed, the medieval synthesis began to disintegrate under the pressure of new forces in the life of Europe, and with the fifteenth century a new era supplanted it. The change did not come quickly nor to all countries at the same time. The first focal point of the new movement was the Italian city of Florence in the mid-fourteenth century, and from there it spread to the rest of Italy, Germany, and France in the next hundred years. The new movement did not affect England and Spain significantly until the sixteenth century, and it was still animating Spain as late as the mid-seventeenth century, when the rest of western Europe had already passed beyond it.

As this period cannot be exactly dated, so it cannot be briefly defined. For some historians it is simply an elaborate transition from the Middle Ages to modern times without a special name or integrity of its own. But for the classical French of the eighteenth century it had come to seem the time of Renaissance, or rebirth, after the long night of the Middle Ages, the time when ancient learning, literature, and architecture were rediscovered and the continuity of antiquity and modern times was re-established. By rights, the term Renaissance should be confined to the art and philosophy of the period, though even here it carries with it a classical prejudice against the hardy culture of the later Middle Ages. But no more accurate term has risen to identify this whole age, and we fall back on it because the distinctness of the period in literature cannot be denied.

The great cultural activity of the thirteenth century brought with it no radical changes in the intellectual outlook or social life of Europe. It simply carried to their most articulate and striking expression the forces of the medieval Church and Scholasticism, of feudalism and chivalry, which had prevailed for centuries. But the Renaissance brought a basic change in men's attitude toward themselves and the world. A new spirit gradually permeated every phase of life—a spirit of exploration and adventure that pushed back the limits of the physical and intellectual world in which medieval men had lived. Little by little, men became aware of a new interest in themselves and in the world around them. They awoke from the medieval dream of a snug universe centered upon man and neatly ordered to enable him to work out his destiny in this life and in the life to come. They opened their eyes to a challenging new reality which intoxicated the youthful pioneers but sobered the Montaignes and the Francis Bacons at the end of the period. Yet all felt a new excitement in the actual things of everyday experience and the actual life they were sharing, and they found among the ancient Romans and Greeks kindred spirits who had felt the same curiosity centuries before.

If antiquity was reborn in this age, it was not because it had been unknown to the Middle Ages, but because a gigantic barrier of spiritual concentration and intellectual orthodoxy stood between the medieval mind and the ancient classics. This wall gradually crumbled in the atmosphere of cosmopolitanism and sophistication that the fourteenth and fifteenth centuries ushered in. Independent thinking and self-expression invited back the Greeks of ancient Athens and their belief in the freedom of the individual. Eventually we will see that literature was exchanging one authority for another, but the new tyranny of the classics did not become complete until the age beyond the Renaissance. This is a time of creative adventure and discovery in all the realms of mind and spirit.

COMMERCE AND COSMOPOLITANISM

No phase of the Renaissance—economic, political, social, religious, or artistic—can be understood apart from the total complex of changes that were converting the medieval world into the modern world. But the starting point would seem to be the sphere of trade and finance. In the Middle Ages, Christian Europe had lapsed into a purely agricultural economy, cut off from trade as it was by Arab conquests to the east and south and by Norse piracy to the west and north. The powerful middle class of Roman days gradually disappeared as the sources of wealth dried up. With it went the large cities and the ready communication over open roads so essential to commerce. The cosmopolitanism of ancient times vanished with the cities, and the map of Europe broke up into a myriad of little self-contained feudal cells, where the money economy of antiquity was replaced by the simple barter of a still older day. Land, labor on the land, and the produce of the land were the chief forms of wealth under the feudal system, and the provincial conservatism of rural life condemned education as useless and new ideas as heresy.

The coastal towns of northern Italy, Venice and Genoa especially, best survived the decay of commerce, and, when trade with the East was resumed in the eleventh century through the decline of Arab power and the early Crusades, Italian merchants were the first to establish sea routes in the eastern Mediterranean and land routes to the Low Countries in the north. Italy was the natural center for the exchange of Oriental luxuries for raw materials from the primitive northern lands, and in time the Italian cities developed export industries, fashioning products of their own out of the goods they handled. Venice and Genoa grew rapidly in size, wealth, and political power, and eventually accumulated eastern empires to insure unhampered trade monopolies. In the thirteenth century a third city, Florence, rose to challenge the commercial position of Venice and Genoa as well as to lead the intellectual movement of the Renaissance.

Wealth flowed into the Italian cities and attracted population away from the land, so that in the thirteenth century feudalism disappeared in northern Italy, taking with it the rural provincialism of medieval society. The barter system was replaced by gold coins, especially the Venetian ducat and Florentine florin, which became the standard media of exchange. Modern capitalism was born as the great merchants invested their earnings from trade in well-organized industries, such as the Florentine textile manufacture, and competed with each other in building vast fortunes. Despite the formal prohibition of the church, moneylending and banking flourished, and the great Florentine houses, such as the Bardi, the Peruzzi, and later the Medici, not only established agencies beyond Italy in the Low Countries, France, and England, but handled the Pope's finances as well. When cities north of the Alps began to challenge the preëminence of Italy in commerce, a great financial center arose in the south-German city of Augsburg, and with it the wealthiest of all the Renaissance banking houses, the Fuggers, who built a huge fortune on mine exploitation. Farther north the Low Countries, and especially Antwerp, enjoyed enormous prosperity. But the vigorous Italian cities retained their economic leadership of Europe until the late fifteenth century.

One might well ask why the great nations along the Atlantic seaboard, England, France, and Spain, allowed the small city-states of northern Italy, southern Germany, and the Low Countries to monopolize this lucrative trade for three centuries. In the western lands feudalism had achieved a more complete domination of economic life than in the Italian states, so that they were not so immediately respon-

"The Banker and His Wife," by a Flemish painter, Matsys.

sive to the revival of trade. Moreover, all three were involved in costly wars that consumed their attention and energy—England and France in the Hundred Years' War (1339–1453) that devastated France; England in the civil Wars of the Roses (1455–1485); Spain in the long struggle to oust the Moors. But most important was their remote geographical situation at a time when the chief trade was with the East, and Italy was the natural center of exchange.

The geographical discoveries of the fifteenth century that opened up the Americas and Africa to exploitation shifted the center of commerce from the Mediterranean to the Atlantic seaboard and brought a rapid decline in the prosperity of Italy and the south-German cities. The explorations that led to these discoveries were sponsored by the At-

lantic powers in an effort to gain commercial advantages over the Italians and Germans. Portugal pioneered, and her great hero, Vasco da Gama, found a new and cheaper route to India around Africa in 1498, shortly after the Ottoman Turks conquered the Byzantine Empire and absorbed the colonies of Venice in the eastern Mediterranean. Meanwhile, Spain had financed the expedition of Columbus and Pinzón to find a third route to India, which instead opened up the Americas to Spanish galleons. Magellan's circumnavigation of the globe in 1519–1522 proved the distinctness of the Americas from India and challenged the Renaissance imagination with the undreamed-of size of the earth. The Netherlands were quick to turn their attention from the eastern overland route to the western sea. Antwerp and all of Flanders declined under Spanish rule in the sixteenth century, while the Dutch of the northern Netherlands freed themselves from Spain and, at the expense of the Portuguese, carved out an empire in the East Indies around 1600. England too entered the race and supplanted Portugal in India. More important, however, was her colonization of the Atlantic seaboard of North America in the seventeenth century, where she soon came in conflict with Dutch and even Swedish colonies and with French settlements farther north.

So geographical discovery led to a commercial revolution as the big nations of the Atlantic seaboard scrambled to exploit the new worlds overseas. The economic movement that brought fabulous prosperity to the Italian cities in the fourteenth century shifted westward in the sixteenth. A new capitalism of national proportions outstripped the power of city-states, and their decline was insured when Spain and France made Italy a battleground of empire. In the shifting fortunes of central and western Europe during the Renaissance we may see one explanation of why the Italian cities, Florence, Venice, and Rome, led the early and middle periods of the Renaissance in literature and art, while France, England, and Spain dominated its last century.

MONARCHY AND NATIONALISM

THE agricultural economy of the Middle Ages with its barter of goods and services worked against the power of national sovereigns and in favor of the barons living in close contact with their retainers on feudal estates. Without a money economy the kings could not readily collect taxes, and without the power of wealth they could not force their rule on the nation as a whole. The self-sufficient and virtually independent estates that dotted the map of Europe discouraged the rise of national feel-

ing among the people as well as any strong national rule.

But the revival of trade in the late Middle Ages restored the money economy of the ancient world, and there emerged a powerful merchant class, which, in order to pursue its farflung trading, demanded a more stable government than the petty feudal rulers could provide with their limited resources. Money enabled the national sovereign to collect taxes, develop a national army, and assert a personal rule over his country as a whole. The merchants readily supported the power of the throne in return for a stable national law and uniform conditions of trade throughout the land. But the national monarchies of the Renaissance rose out of bitter civil struggles in which the kings finally destroyed the power of feudal nobles and the entire system of feudalism.

ITALY. In Italy, the first area to feel the force of the Renaissance, special conditions produced a peculiar political evolution. During the thirteenth and fourteenth centuries the Italian cities in the north formed part of the Holy Roman Empire, the international agglomeration of many little states that was theoretically ruled by a German royal house. There was no native king of Italy in the Middle Ages comparable to the feudal kings of England and France. Consequently, when the authority of the emperors declined in Italy in the thirteenth and fourteenth centuries, the Italian city-states were bent on securing independence from imperial rule rather than union under an Italian sovereign. The growth of their wealth through commerce owed nothing to the protection of a king, and they used it to strengthen their independence. The presence in Italy of the Church and the Pope also discouraged a national spirit, since the Church was an international force and the Pope laid claim to being an international ruler, who was therefore in frequent conflict with the Emperor. Moreover, the temporal rule of the Pope over large states of his own in central Italy discouraged the unification of the northern, central, and southern sections of the peninsula.

Except for the southern Kingdom of Naples, Italy was cut up into numerous small states, each focused on a large city—Venice, Genoa, Pisa, Florence, Milan, Bologna—which controlled its politics and sought through ultimately disastrous little wars to extend its power over its neighbors. The turbulent political history of the oligarchic city-states during this period recalls the tumultuous careers of the Greek cities of antiquity. This internal strife interfered with the commercial prosperity of the states and led the ruling classes in the fourteenth century to sacrifice their power to despots who would guarantee peace and orderly government for a period of years. Since the dictator was often a *condottiere*, or leader of an army of mercenary soldiers, he might continue his rule indefinitely and bequeath it to a member of his family. Thus remarkable dynasties of despots were established in several Italian states and eventually took on the magnificence of royalty in other countries. The famous Medici rule of Florence was founded by Cosimo de' Medici in 1434 and produced in his grandson, Lorenzo the Magnificent (1449–1492), the greatest patron of scholarship, art, and literature in Renaissance Italy. Men did not inquire into the morality of dictatorship but assumed

the pragmatic view that any means, however dishonest or inhumane, was justified if it achieved the end of increasing the prosperity and power of the state. This cynical, if realistic, view of state dictatorship was brilliantly enunciated by Machiavelli in his treatise, *The Prince*. Yet, though it might carry the states to remarkable prosperity in the fourteenth century, this sordid philosophy destroyed patriotism and the citizen's sense of responsibility for the welfare of the state, so that in the sixteenth the states were an easy prey to the imperialistic designs of France and Spain.

GERMANY. Germany too failed to achieve unification under a national monarchy, and for somewhat similar reasons. The many small German states were theoretically united under the Holy Roman Emperor, but since he was elected by seven local rulers called Electors, his office until 1438 lacked the dynastic continuity of the kingships of France and England and did not inspire ambitions to effective monarchy. Moreover, the Holy Roman Emperor was usually more interested in pursuing his international claims or advancing his family holdings than in unifying the German states. The decline of the Empire in the thirteenth century enfeebled central government still further. Nevertheless, some states were gradually consolidated in clusters, as the powerful ones absorbed the weaker, so that several large states emerged from the medieval confusion, although there were still over three hundred states until the nineteenth century. There undoubtedly was national feeling in Germany of the Renaissance, but it expressed itself in the religious Reformation of Luther rather than in a national monarchy, and was thereafter weakened by the religious differences engendered by the Reformation.

ENGLAND. It was in the countries along the Atlantic seaboard that the great monarchies of the Renaissance developed. The time was the fifteenth century, when the little Italian states were enjoying their last period of commercial supremacy. England was the first to evolve a strong central government, perhaps because the power of the king had been stronger in England since the days of William the Conqueror (1028–1087) than in France and elsewhere. The greater power of the king explains why England was the first to achieve a strong monarchy; the importance of the parliament of nobles, church dignitaries, and commoners explains why the English monarchy was never so absolute as the French. When the authority of the king weakened, as in the fourteenth century, the national parliament rather than individual nobles assumed his powers. Yet the fifteenth century brought a civil struggle in which the nobles supporting the rival houses of Lancaster and York fought the War of the Roses (1455–1485) to decide the kingship and in the process dissipated their own authority and paved the way for a dynasty of strong monarchs, who temporarily eclipsed the power of parliament.

After a long period of war and devastation the populace welcomed the firm rule of the Tudors. Henry VII established the line in 1485 and quickly shaped the national monarchy that England was to become. But it was the last of the dynasty, Queen Elizabeth (who reigned from 1558 to 1603), that brought its greatest glory and presided over the Golden Age of the English Renaissance. Personal loyalty to Elizabeth was strong throughout her long and enlightened reign, and as a result her great authority was seldom questioned. Loyalty to the crown inspired national feeling as well, and the chronicle plays of Shakespeare, re-creating the past history of England, are evidence of the patriotic fervor that made England a world power under Elizabeth.

FRANCE. The rise of national monarchy in France was at first inhibited by the claim of the English kings to huge sections of the land. In the Hundred Years' War (1339–1453) the English, using new methods of warfare unknown to the backward French, won brilliant victories at Crécy, Poitiers, and Agincourt and even secured the aid of the Dukes of Burgundy, the most powerful of the feudal nobles in France, against the French king. But in 1429 a naïve peasant girl, Joan of Arc, inspired by what she thought to be divine voices, rallied the French and led an army herself to relieve the siege of Orleans and restore the prestige of the French crown. Soon after, the English evacuated nearly all of France and left that unhappy country to fifty years of slow revival. The process of unifying France as a strong nation was begun by Louis XI, the ugly but able king from 1461 to 1483 who finally established the authority of the French crown over Burgundy. But his successors interrupted French recovery by four expensive and unsuccessful wars with Spain for control of Italy. In the later sixteenth century these were followed by eight civil wars, most of which turned on the religious antagonism of Catholic extremists and the Protestant Huguenots.

Not until the accession of Henry IV, the first Bourbon, in 1589, did France settle down to repair its ravaged land, develop domestic prosperity, and enter competition with the other powers for empires abroad. Henry brought peace and wealth to France by making himself absolute over the nobles and the rival religious factions, and thus laid the foundation of the unlimited monarchy that ruled France for two centuries. The nobility challenged the royal power twice during the seventeenth century, but in the reign of Louis XIV (1661–1715) the monarchy justified its absolute authority over every phase of national life by an efficient domestic policy, successful wars abroad that made France the most

powerful nation in Europe, and a stimulation of culture that gave France her Golden Age of art and literature.

SPAIN. Early in the eighth century the Arabs of the East had extended their power from northern Africa over virtually all of the Iberian peninsula (which contains modern Spain and Portugal). The history of this region for the seven centuries that followed is chiefly the gradual liberation of the land from the Moslems by the dogged persistence of the Christians in pushing them ever farther south toward Gibraltar. By the twelfth century the Moslems controlled merely the southern third, and four powerful feudal states had emerged in the north—Portugal, Leon, Castile, and Aragon. In the thirteenth century the Moslems were reduced to the kingdom of Granada, and Castile had absorbed Leon to become the largest state in the peninsula. The marriage of King Ferdinand of Aragon and Queen Isabella of Castile in 1469 and their conquest of Granada in 1492 completed the political unification. But little Portugal remained an independent kingdom, except for a brief Spanish conquest, and in the late fifteenth and early sixteenth centuries amassed a fantastic empire in South America, Africa, and Asia. Her national poet, Camoëns, preserved the glory of her great century in his magnificent epic, The Lusiads (1572), which told in heroic fashion of the voyage of Vasco da Gama around Africa to India in 1498.

The long struggle with the Moslems gave Spain a unique national fervor in the Renaissance that blended with the Christian ardor of her holy wars. Catholic mysticism was nowhere so intense as in the land of St. John of the Cross and St. Teresa. Spain led the Catholic Reformation with the militant zeal of the Jesuits under Ignatius Loyola and the heresy hunts of the Inquisition. When the national monarchy appeared under Ferdinand and Isabella, the absolute authority of the Spanish monarchs was enforced for several generations by their profound piety, so that the Spaniard's devotion to "dios y el rey" (God and the king) was centered in his Most Catholic Majesty. Ferdinand's grandson, Charles I, became Holy Roman Emperor as Charles V and ruled (1516–1558), not simply the Spanish empire, but the Hapsburg territories in Germany and the Low Countries as well. Throughout his vast realm he thought of himself as the chosen defender of Catholic Christianity against Moslems, Jews, and Protestants. Under his son, Philip II, emperor from 1558 to 1598, religious zeal and absolute rule reached their climax on the Spanish throne. The imperialistic exploitation of America, upon which Spain had been engaged for half a century, was blended with a religious crusade to convert the heathen natives. Spain amassed a great empire in the Americas during the sixteenth century, and their plundered wealth made

Renaissance Europe 1559

her for a short time the leading power in Europe. To this period of her imperial splendor (1500–1650) belongs her Golden Age of art and letters.

NATIONALISM AND INTERNATIONALISM. The rise of aggressive national states and the decline of chivalry, with its idealistic codes of warfare, destroyed for a time the moral basis of international law as the new nations competed in a ruthless struggle for empire. War took on a new horror with more deadly weapons, and respect for treaties and moral obligations declined. The Hundred Years' War ended without a treaty. The English crown actually sanctioned piracy against Spain on the high seas. But humanitarian forces gradually came to demand a regulation of warfare, and even the grasping monarchies began to realize that they all stood to gain from some recognized control of their savage competition.

The Dutch jurist, Hugo Grotius, experiencing the horrors of the Thirty Years' War, provided the first set of rules for an international law in his *Rights of War and Peace* (1625). Assuming that the very nature of man, which had naturally evolved a system of law for his civil life, demanded a similar natural code among nations, Grotius argued that kings should deal with each other as ordinary men are bound by moral law to do, neither stealing nor assaulting nor violating contract. Wars are justified, he insisted, only as a means of enforcing law or punishing international criminals. The work of Grotius did not lead to any moral revolution in the practice of nations, nor have we yet achieved the international law that this idealist prefigured. But he gave voice to the perennial longing of modern man for a curb on the repeated horrors of war that nationalism has brought with it.

FROM KNIGHT TO COURTIER

ALTHOUGH the social changes of the Renaissance did not take place evenly in all of the emerging nations, the general pattern of change was almost universal. Medieval society had been dominated by two powerful classes: the clergy, who controlled the spiritual and intellectual forces of Europe under a divinely inspired authority, and the knightly class of feudal nobles, who controlled the temporal sphere under an international code of chivalry. Both classes gave a universal cast to medieval society and opposed the power of national government, as it was nominally embodied in national sovereigns. The middle class of artisans and shopkeepers was small and only in the towns enjoyed a life apart from the feudal system. The peasant foundation of medieval society was a submerged majority, conservative, illiterate, and inarticulate.

The Renaissance was to see almost everywhere a shift of power from clergy and nobility to absolute national monarchs and a new middle class of wealthy merchants. The clergy, of course, continued its power within the spiritual realm, but the scope of its authority declined sharply, as the Church ceased to embrace the totality of men's lives and the new national churches, whether Catholic in Spain and France or Protestant in Germany and England, became independent, relatively or completely, from the power of Rome. The new economic and social interests of a worldly society challenged religion's enveloping control of men's minds, and the new nationalism weakened everywhere the international power of the Church. As a result, the literature of the Renaissance was to be predominantly secular.

The feudal nobility suffered a decline close to extermination. In a word, the haughty medieval knight became the dependent courtier of the Renaissance. As international commerce revived and national monarchy emerged, the feudal noble discovered that society had no longer a place for him. For centuries he had held his power by monopolizing the art of war. In an age of simple and unorganized military tactics the medieval knight, resplendent on horseback with his flashing armor, deadly lance, and trusty sword, was the supreme embodiment of military glory and protection to his vassals, who in time of danger could crowd within the impregnable walls of their liege lord's stone castle. But the new use of gunpowder in the fourteenth century destroyed the invulnerable strength of these strongholds, and the invention of effective infantry weapons raised the prestige of the common foot-soldier over the knight on horseback. In vain did the knights increase the thickness of their armor against the crossbow and longbow, for the cumbersome weight merely forced them to take the defensive. The doom of the individual knight, fighting picturesquely rather than effectively by the code of chivalry, was sealed when the Italian cities began to employ mercenary armies, drilled to coordinated action by professional soldiers. National armies, fighting for king and country, supplanted the chaotic feudal aggregations, and nobles, if they continued to fight, did so as warriors of the king.

Moreover, the rise of a money economy overturned the barter economy of feudalism and fixed rents and pay for services. Peasants were freed from their anchorage to the land and might even assert their independence of their noble masters by aban doning work on the farm for the new industries of the cities. Ill-equipped by training to cope with the new money economy, the nobles often squandered their resources on new luxuries and then relied on shrewd moneylenders, to whom they gradually lost their estates.

Thus, necessity or the superior sophistication of urban life might lead them to move to the capital, where they lacked roots and were forced to depend on the king for support through sinecures, pensions, and positions in the army, ministry, or church. The king welcomed them, at first because their dependence on the crown made them impotent to oppose it, later because of their ornamental value, since an aristocratic court formed a glamorous setting for the royal presence. Indeed, the actual refinement of the nobility increased greatly as they moved from their isolated country estates to the brilliant capital. The medieval knight, whose exalted code of courtesy did not free him from coarseness and brutality, evolved at the capital into the polished courtier who sought to make himself worthy of his king and the ladies by his charming manners, intellectual culture, sharp wit, and skill with the rapier to defend his personal honor. The code of chivalry did not die with feudalism; it was adapted to the new conditions of the royal court, from which it was to descend to us in our concept of the gentleman, with his romantic deference to women and his personal ideals of loyalty, truth to his word, generosity, and courtesy. Castiglione's *Book of the Courtier* (1514) epitomized the ideal gentleman of the Renaissance, but we must suspect that the usual courtier fell short of the perfect combination of good breeding, character, and intellect that he described. Nevertheless, the polished literature of the Renaissance resulted from the patronage of this aristocracy and was often written by gifted members of such a court. Spenser's *Faerie Queene* and the exquisite lyrics of Ronsard reflect the immaculate ideals for which the courtier stood.

Although the snobbish nobility disdained the money-making of the middle class, it could not indefinitely remain aloof from the wealthy merchants. In some of the Italian cities the two classes eventually cooperated in politics and fell together as the upper class. In England the tradition of primogeniture converted younger sons into commoners and often forced them into trade to support themselves, so that the separation between the nobility and the upper bourgeoisie was never so rigid there as in France and Spain. But the wealthy merchants suffered from a sense of social inferiority and imitated the manners and code of the aristocracy rather than developing new standards of their own. Hence, though they often achieved a culture equal to that of the nobility and patronized art and learning munificently, they created no separate literary tradition. We must wait until the eighteenth century for a socially conscious literature of a militant middle class. Still lower classes, the petty bourgeoisie and the commoners of farm and city, exerted no influence on art and letters, and when they appeared as characters, for example in Shakespeare's Roman rabble in *Julius Caesar* or his artisans in *A Midsummer-Night's Dream*, they were usually ridiculed as dull buffoons. But Lope de Vega's picture of a proud and self-respecting Spanish peasantry in *The Sheep Well* assures us that even at this early time the proletariat of Europe was developing a consciousness of its human rights.

HUMANISM AND THE NEW LEARNING

THE economic, social, and political changes of the Renaissance produced a profound revolution in European thought and culture. Although the feudal courts had developed a secular literature in the twelfth and thirteenth centuries, the learning of the Middle Ages was entirely in the hands of the clergy, and architecture, sculpture, and painting were generally commissioned by the Church and involved a religious purpose or religious subject matter. As the growth of private wealth in the fourteenth century produced generous private patrons, learning and art took on a secular character such as Europe had not known since the Silver Age of Rome. The horizon of this secular culture broadened immensely as it lost the provincial outlook of the feudal estates and came to reflect the cosmopolitanism of the new cities, born of commercial contact with far corners of the world. As it expanded in space, so it reached backward in time and found a new inspiration in the rediscovery of ancient Greece and Rome and a way of life that excited the exploring imagination of the Renaissance.

A knowledge of antiquity and ancient philosophy and literature had never died completely, though it nearly expired in the darkest of the Dark Ages. Because of his *Fourth Eclogue,* Virgil survived as a prophet of Christ's coming and the *Aeneid* was religiously interpreted as a parable of man's search for perfection and peace. Ovid's love poetry was incorporated in the courtly love tradition, and other Latin poets were dimly known. Homer and Aristotle were read only in Latin epitomes. The Greek language and hence its literature were practically forgotten in the West, and not only the classical drama but the very concept of acting and the stage were lost. Even the few ancients who struggled through were largely misunderstood, because the religious mind of the Middle Ages, bound up in mystical symbols and lacking historical perspective, interposed a barrier of Christian theology between itself and the ancient past. Achilles and Aeneas became chivalrous knights with armor and lance, and the Hades of Virgil was transformed into a Christian hell. Hence the "renaissance" of the ancients was not simply a recovery of the ancient classics from oblivion. It was the rebirth of an understanding of the ancients in their own terms, freed from the veil of medieval mysticism. Only the revival of secular culture made possible this new perspective divorced from theology and symbolism.*

The bond between secular culture and the revival of the classics was important to both. If the poets and philosophers of Greece and Rome had to wait for lay scholars to rediscover them, they repaid their benefactors by showing them a new way of life that was basically opposed to the dogma of medieval Christianity. The Church had taught that, because of the fall of Adam, human nature is fundamentally bad, and that within man there is an endless conflict between the flesh and the spirit. The good Christian, recognizing the evil of the flesh, would renounce this world and the enjoyment of life in which the body delights. For the surest salvation of his soul, he would choose the life of the ascetic. But the Greeks had believed precisely the opposite. Aspiring toward an ideal of general perfection, they had sought a rounded development of all human faculties—body, mind, and spirit. The joy of this life was their compensation for grim death to come. Platonists, Stoics, and Epicureans differed widely in their views of how this life should be lived, but they were united in insisting on the dignity of all phases of human nature and in prescribing for a life in this world. In rediscovering the ancients, the Humanistic scholars rediscovered what they thought of as the dignity of man and the ancients' belief in the general perfectability of human nature. It was Leonardo Bruni (1370–1444) who named this new, dynamic learning Humanism after Cicero's *humanitas,* a term for the education that exalts the full worth of man— those liberal arts, literature and philosophy, which are called the humanities to this day.

Rallying behind Terence's claim that "nothing human is alien to me," the Humanists renounced asceticism and eagerly embraced the world and its pleas-

ures, emancipating the body as well as the spirit. Accepting the Greek view of a well-rounded life, the Renaissance produced the fantastic versatility of a Leonardo da Vinci, a Michelangelo, and a Cellini. As the new learning inspired a new way of life, nominal Christians embraced the worldliness of epicureans and stoics, and the liberation of the flesh from the restraints of Christian morality led in time to license and depravity, especially in the Italian cities of the sixteenth century. But such excesses do not concern us here; the rediscovery of "human nature" through the rediscovery of the ancient classics revolutionized the Renaissance outlook on the world and reshaped education and literature.

Although the beginnings of Humanism cannot be exactly dated, Petrarch of fourteenth-century Florence is usually thought of as the first scholar and writer of the new type. A secular man of letters, he divided his life between the enthusiastic unearthing and study of ancient manuscripts and the pursuit of literary fame. His example inspired his friend Boccaccio to turn from the earthy storytelling of the *Decameron* to classical scholarship. The physical gusto running through Boccaccio's hundred tales also implies the new freedom with which the Renaissance man expressed himself. From a wandering Greek scholar of Constantinople Boccaccio learned Greek and labored at translating Homer. His studies predicted the Greek Renaissance in Italy, which dates from the lectures of Emanuel Chrysoloras at Florence in 1397–1400 and the Platonic Academy founded by Cosimo de' Medici. Most of the Italian Humanists, such as Lorenzo Valla and Marsilio Ficino, belong to scholarship rather than literature, but Pico della Mirandola gave eloquent voice to their ideals in his *Oration on the Dignity of Man.*

Humanism was an international movement which, because of the freemasonry of scholars, found its way to the northern countries before other phases of the Renaissance. It was greatly accelerated by the invention of printing in the fifteenth century, which freed learning from dependence on scribes for the laborious reproduction of manuscripts, rapidly increased the circulation of book knowledge, and destroyed the Church monopoly of libraries. Significantly, the new learning did not reach Germany, France, and England until the second half of the fifteenth century, the first era of the printing press.

Of all the continental Humanists who carried the movement through its golden century (1450–1550), none was better known nor more universally esteemed than the wise and gentle Dutch scholar who called himself Desiderius Erasmus. This restless seeker after knowledge moved from one end of western Europe to the other and was greeted everywhere as the bearer of a new enlightenment. He at first entered a monastery but soon rebelled against the

* The term "Revival of Learning" is so ambiguous that it is omitted from this discussion of Humanism. The first revival of learning took place in the twelfth and thirteenth centuries when the first European universities were founded, but the term is generally applied to the revival of classical scholarship in the fourteenth and fifteenth centuries and hence carries with it, like the term "Renaissance," a classical prejudice against the Middle Ages.

austere discipline and the empty formalism of the monk's activities, though he retained deep religious convictions throughout his life and remained loyal to Catholicism after the Protestant Reformation. His classical studies made him crusade against the narrow horizon of the medieval Church, but his mild and peaceful spirit argued for reform from within. The treatises of Erasmus cover a wide variety of Humanist interests—the enlightened use of the classics, the art of writing, the stupidity of the monastic life, the moral education of a Christian king. But the best known of all his works is the delightful satire on human foibles called *The Praise of Folly*, supposedly delivered by a female personification of folly itself, who argues that, for all his blundering, man should follow his human impulses unafraid and guide himself by the natural discipline of moderation.

Humanism began in the universities but soon spread to the court, where the new learning and the new outlook on life became part of the courtier's education. Indeed, it worked a revolution in Renaissance schooling during the sixteenth century as the control of teaching passed from ecclesiastical to lay hands and the subject matter and objectives of the curriculum were completely reoriented. The most boisterous statement of the Renaissance revolt against the medieval disciplines appears in the *Gargantua and Pantagruel* of Rabelais. In famous sections of his extravaganza the emancipated Frenchman satirizes the useless pedantry of the old methods and demands a new type of education designed to produce, not a bookish scholar, but a well-rounded man (or woman). In Ponacrates' instruction of Gargantua, we see the pedagogy that Rabelais had in mind—the emphasis upon the matter rather than the form of knowledge, the constant application of book learning to the world of nature, and the cultivation of all sides of human personality. This Renaissance faith in the trustworthiness of human nature and instinct is revealed in the motto of Rabelais' utopian Abbey of Theleme—"Do what you want to." Only trust men to follow their natural inclinations, he believed, and they will reach inevitably a healthy and worthy goal.

A generation later the last great Renaissance thinker about education, Montaigne, extended Rabelais's radicalism to an attack upon the new tyranny of the ancient classics which had supplanted the medieval tyranny of church rule. Surveying the effects of Humanism, both good and bad, he decided that the ancients had emancipated men from one discipline only to enslave them to another. Attacking knowledge as an end in itself, he insisted that the only end of learning is to contribute to man's understanding of himself and his success in leading a useful, moderate, and upright life. Admittedly Humanism had its evil effects, not the least of which was the pedantic encouragement of literature in Latin at the expense of the vernacular tongues. But its influence endured in European and American education down to the beginning of our century, and the English schools have hardly yet abandoned the idea that the Greek and Latin classics are the cornerstone of a liberal education.

REFORMATION AND COUNTER-REFORMATION

THE various changes that formed the Renaissance were not slow in affecting the status of the Church and the medieval Christianity that had bound all of Europe in one empire of the spirit. The ascetic ideal of the medieval Church and its strictures against moneylending and finance were out of harmony with the economic ambitions of the aggressive and powerful merchant aristocracy, which pursued luxury and worldly culture with a new sophistication. The secularization of learning and art which they sponsored challenged the domination of men's minds and spirits that the Church had enjoyed for a thousand years. Humanism as a movement developed partially within and partially outside the Church, but its objectives ran counter to medieval Christianity at every point. It set a revival of pagan philosophy against a declining Scholasticism; it set the Greek ideal against the ascetic ideal of the medieval churchman; it preferred classical Latin over Church Latin; it sought to emancipate the individual from the dogma and discipline of the Middle Ages that had stifled personality within a general mold.

The growth of national monarchies opposed the claims of the papacy to international temporal power. At its height in the late Middle Ages the Church had conceived of Christendom as a single realm ruled by the Pope, who had the God-given right to depose kings and choose their successors, determine the boundaries of their lands, and appoint a clergy to function within these lands. This clergy should owe its loyalty to Rome, be immune to taxation by the king, and be required to send tribute to the Pope from the kings' realms. Under feudalism the papacy had gradually codified this theory of its temporal power and used it successfully against the rival Holy Roman Emperor. But the new kings of the Renaissance wielded a growing authority that was to force the papacy to relinquish its international claims and content itself with governing the

Papal States. The decisive contest was that between Pope Boniface VIII and King Philip IV of France in which the king met the Pope's sentence of deposition and excommunication by moving the papacy from Rome to Avignon, where for seventy-three years (1305–1378) it functioned under the close supervision of the French throne. The papacy never recovered its temporal prestige after this so-called Babylonian Captivity and the Great Schism (1378–1415) that followed, during which rival popes attacked each other from Avignon and Rome. In the following century most Christian countries asserted their new nationalism against papal power in one way or another: Portugal, Spain, and France secured virtually independent administration for their national churches and so remained loyal to Rome. Northern Germany, Switzerland, Holland, England, and the Scandinavian states seceded entirely in the Protestant Reformation.

In some respects the Reformation movement of the sixteenth century was a continuation of the Renaissance; in others it had the character of a countermovement. In so far as the Renaissance attacked the empty ceremonies and sterile scholasticism of the medieval Church, it was in line with the religious revival. Erasmus, the greatest of the Humanists, was also the greatest harbinger of the Reformation. In his *The Praise of Folly* he denounced the ignorance of the religious orders, the greed and vulgarity of the lower ecclesiastics, and the lack of piety and humility among cardinals and popes. The Reformation, too, was one expression of the new national feeling that resulted from the political unification of Renaissance states. Most important, it reflected the new importance of the layman in Renaissance life, since it took the Bible out of Church Latin into vernacular tongues where every man might read it, encouraged lay interpretation of the Bible against church monopoly of enlightenment, removed education from the hands of the clergy, and sanctified a new middle-class morality that exalted over monastic asceticism the virtues of thrift and hard work for profit.

On the other hand, the intellectual enlightenment of the Renaissance had already saturated the papacy by the sixteenth century. The popes of this period were often classical scholars and patrons of art and humanistic learning, who had strayed far from the simple piety of the medieval Church into secular cosmopolitanism and pagan morality. Increasingly Italian in outlook, the papacy fell into the enlightened depravity of the Italian aristocracy, and reached its nadir in a succession of five popes between 1471 and 1521, notorious for their worldliness, political ambition, avarice, and, in some cases, lust. The infamous Alexander VI was a Borgia; the cultured Leo X was of the Medici. The Italian Renaissance had cap-

Pope Julius II (1503–1513), by Raphael. He patronized artists and beautified Rome while ruling with much skill.

tivated the papacy, and the dissolute papal circles infuriated many northern churchmen and led them to support separation from Rome when the papal court seemed beyond spiritual regeneration. Many Italian ecclesiastics deplored the declining prestige of the papacy and its failure in spiritual leadership. Girolamo Savonarola (1452–1498) inspired the degenerate city of Florence to a brief spiritual revival with his impassioned eloquence and his bold denunciation of the worldliness of Rome, but Pope Alexander VI had him convicted of heresy and executed.

The Reformation of Luther and Calvin was preceded by numerous forerunners of the Protestant movement, which the Church dismissed as heresies. The Waldensians who followed Peter Waldo (fl. 1170) in southern France, the Lollards who rallied around John Wycliffe (d. 1384) in England, and the Hussites who supported John Huss (d. 1415) in Bohemia were national sects aiming at reform of the Church, but all were persecuted out of existence. Something like accident made the German monk Martin Luther the founder of an enduring Protestantism, for his original purpose in nailing his 95 Theses to the door of the Wittenberg Church in 1517 was simply to attack the sale of papal indulgences in Germany which Leo X was authorizing in order to raise funds for building St. Peter's in Rome. But conditions were right for the establishment of a national church in the German states, and when Luther found himself pushed by papal persecution into the leadership of an independent church, he had the protection of many German princes and the support of militant German peasants. With the formulation of the Augsburg Confession in 1530 the Lutheran Church was established as the official Protestant Church in most German states (and eventually Scandinavia), though some states, especially in the west and south, remained loyal to Catholicism, and others turned to Calvinism. In his later years Luther's outlook hardened into a dogmatic provincialism and prevented an international union of Lutheranism with the Swiss reform movement of the same period.

The Lutheran creed established the general Protestant pattern by insisting on the direct and personal relationship of every Christian soul to God without any intermediary of church or priest. Thus with one stroke it tried to sweep away the huge hierarchy of the Roman Church and destroy the separateness of the priestly caste, committed to celibacy and a special religious life. Every human vocation was dignified, and the workman at his bench, the merchant in the market place, and the mother in her home achieved a status before God equal to the minister's in the community church. In a word, Luther secularized the church as he nationalized it.

Similar movements were not slow in getting under way in other countries. John Calvin (1509–1564), a French refugee, set the character of Swiss Protestantism in the direction of rigorous puritanism and fiery intolerance during his twenty-year rule in Geneva. This narrow, austere view of religious reform raised the Bible as a stern master over men's lives and worked against the broad intellectuality and worldly enlightenment of the Renaissance. Calvin's influence shaped the Huguenot movement in France and strongly influenced the strict codes of the English Puritans and Scotch Covenanters in the following century. The Dutch Republic and some German states accepted this form of Protestantism.

England secured a national church separate from Rome in 1534, when Henry VIII forced his parliament to declare him head of the Church in England because the Pope refused to grant him an annulment of his first marriage. But Henry was thoroughly orthodox in his religious views and persecuted heretics and Protestants as vigorously as any Catholic sovereign. Hence, although the Catholic church still sought to gain control of England from the national Anglican church through the reign of James II (1685–1688), the real Protestant movement centered in the stern Puritan group which strove to convert the Anglican church into a Calvinist church by purging church ritual of Roman splendor and national life of worldliness and luxury. Though persecuted by Queen Elizabeth and James I, the Puritans increased their numbers and staged a successful revolution in 1642–1649; they ruled England under Oliver Cromwell for the following ten years, and gave English literature one of its greatest poets—John Milton. Transplanted to the New England colonies of North America, Puritanism exerted an enduring influence on American life and produced a brilliant school of stern divines, of whom Jonathan Edwards the elder was probably the most eloquent. His sermon, *Sinners in the Hands of an Angry God,* terrified his congregation with its grisly warning of divine vengeance.

The Protestant Reformation quickly inspired a Counter-Reformation in the Roman Church, as a reawakened Catholic world recognized the abuses within its hierarchy and set about reviving the pious and militant spirit of medieval Christianity. Catholic Spain took the lead in this vigorous movement and contributed the Jesuit army of Ignatius Loyola (1491–1556) to the Church's war against the heathens and the Protestants. The Council of Trent (1545–1563), which brought representatives from the whole Catholic world to a council of war, produced some reform of ecclesiastical government but in general reinforced the conservative theology and church practice of the Middle Ages. Its lack of a conciliatory attitude toward the Protestants strengthened the breach between northern and southern Europe, so that, by the end of the Renaissance, the unified medieval Church had split into four major churches—Catholic, Lutheran, Calvinist, and Anglican—with a growing background of minor sects.

THE RISE OF MODERN SCIENCE

HUMANISM had only an indirect influence on the religious reformation and almost none on the birth of modern science. Its concern was with the cultural life of man, his individuality and integrity as a human being; it found in ancient literature no stimulus to explore the world by scientific method. Yet the age of the Renaissance saw the first major discoveries of modern science and ended with the articulation of the experimental method that was to expand man's knowledge of his world immeasurably in the next period.

At first sight the later Middle Ages seem much more important to science than does the Renaissance. Beginning in the second half of the eleventh century, a stream of scientific knowledge born of the ancient Greeks, translated into Arabic terms, and combined with the Arabic discoveries of Avicenna and Averroës found its way into Europe via the cultural contacts of the Moslem and Christian worlds in Sicily and Spain. In the thirteenth century it inspired Albertus Magnus and especially Roger Bacon to an enlightened study of the natural sciences, chemistry, physics, and geography. Bacon used the experimental method to reach natural explanations of natural phenomena, such as rainbows and earthquakes, and to understand the magnifying properties of convex lenses and the explosive propensities of gunpowder. But he was as much philosopher as scientist, and susceptible to the superstitions and mysticism of his day. His attacks on the inane activities of the later Scholastics won him the suspicion of his fellow churchmen and twenty years' confinement for the novelty of his ideas. Later generations thought of him as a wizard in league with the devil, and the Church classified him with the magicians and alchemists as a practitioner of forbidden arts. In general, the outlook of the Middle Ages could not comprehend science any more than classical literature, and outlawed new discoveries as a threat to Aristotle and the absolute truth of Christian theology.

The new intellectual horizon of the Renaissance was bound to touch science in time. As medieval restraints on speculation were thrust aside, the biological approach to the world for which Aristotle stood was challenged by a new mathematical interpretation inspired by Plato and the Pythagoreans. Aristotle's conception of a limited universe of concentric spheres was gradually supplanted by the idea of an infinite universe animated by interrelated forces which could be understood only by the application of mathematics. The most brilliant argument for this theory was pronounced by Giordano Bruno. Accepting the new Copernican astronomy, this fiery monk argued that there are innumerable worlds extending into infinity, but that all the phenomena of the universe gain coherence and order by the unifying animation of God.

The conception of an infinite universe paralleled the rise of modern astronomy. Although ancient astronomers had debated whether the earth or the sun was the center of our universe, the geocentric theory of the Alexandrian Ptolemy was accepted by the medieval Church because the idea of an immovable earth around which moved the planets, moon, sun, and stars confirmed the Christian conception of man as the climax of creation and the chief concern of God. Several astronomers of the Renaissance questioned the geocentric theory, but it remained for Nicolaus Copernicus, a Pole, to publish a formal challenge in his *Revolutions of the Heavenly Bodies*

(1543). He long delayed announcement of his heliocentric theory, fearing church persecution as a heretic, but even ecclesiastical condemnation could not prevent the spread of his theory and its acceptance under his name as the starting point of modern astronomy. The Italian Galileo Galilei (1564–1642) strengthened the Copernican theory by perfecting the first useful telescope and proved by observing the spots on the sun's surface that it turned on its axis.

Other modern sciences got their start during the Renaissance. The amazing Leonardo da Vinci began a study of human anatomy and the mathematics of perspective, partially to improve his painting and sculpture, partially out of an enlightened interest in pure science. Andreas Vesalius, a Flemish physician, applied the experimental method to anatomy and produced in 1543 a revolutionary study of the human body. Georg Agricola, a German scholar, founded modern metallurgy and mineralogy.

Clearly, the scientific method was being used by Galileo, Vesalius, and Agricola and had even been identified in part by Roger Bacon, Leonardo da Vinci, and others. But though the metaphysical speculation of ancient science might give way to actual observation and experiment, Renaissance science was still obsessed by the notion of final causes and the supernatural significance of natural facts. In part, it was motivated by the practical urge to gain mastery over nature, even to exploit it as alchemy had tried to do; in part, by the view of nature as the key to human destiny, inherited from

A study of the muscles of torso and legs by Leonardo da Vinci shows his scientific approach to anatomy.

astrology. It remained for Francis Bacon, the English chancellor of James I, to formulate a scientific method freed from medieval objectives and prejudices and to lend to it the weight of his learning and his political prestige. In the *Novum Organum* (1620) Bacon denounced the deductive method of Aristotle, long used by the Scholastics, because it ignored the facts of observation except when they confirmed a preconceived truth or a priori statement. He argued that knowledge must originate in the careful observation of natural facts and unprejudiced experiment with them. The scientist must begin with what is, not with what he has been told there is or what he believes there should be. Neither bookish authority, nor our own speculation, nor any prejudice must stand in the way of our objective observation of nature. Bacon summarized the progress of scientific method to the end of the Renaissance and led to the greater achievements of Descartes and Newton in the next generation.

RENAISSANCE BELLES-LETTRES

ALL of the dynamic forces of Renaissance life are reflected in the magnificent literature of this extravagant period. As the preoccupation of medieval man with theology and Scholastic metaphysics dissolved under the pressure of new intellectual forces, literature lost its absorption in the problems of Christian salvation, its didactic purpose, and its obsession with symbols and allegory. The Middle Ages had had its secular literature in the chivalric romances and commoners' fabliaux, but they were appendages to the religious writings of the time and further illustrated the cultural synthesis of medieval life within the ideology of the Church. A broad secular literature that eagerly returned to nature and exalted every phase of human life was reborn with Boccaccio and Rabelais, as Renaissance man grew inquisitive about his present world and set out in eager pursuit of new experience. Urges long checked by the universal orthodoxy gained free expression under the new sanction of pagan philosophy.

The lay spirit of Renaissance literature is reflected in its passionate individualism. Personality emerged from its long regimentation in the ranks of the theologians and Scholastics, the troubadours and trouvères, the Minnesingers and Mastersingers. The emancipation of the intellect and senses from official sanctions invited divergent responses to the world. As Platonism inspired a new realization of personality in a vast new realm of experience, men developed a consuming interest in themselves, and literature grew subjective and varied in attitude. Autobiography reappeared in Benvenuto Cellini; biography in the hands of Vasari and Pérez de Guzmán reflected the new curiosity about people as individuals. The conventional love poetry of the troubadours took on a personal realism in Petrarch and Ronsard. The familiar essay was reborn as a medium of self-revelation with Montaigne.

Humanism, through exalting the dignity of man, stimulated this new individualism and inspired literature in other directions as well. As ancient classics were rediscovered, old types of literature—the epic, the pastoral, the satire, tragedy, and comedy—reappeared as fresh areas for men of letters. The polished Latin of Cicero and Seneca made men ashamed of the vagaries of Church Latin and the crudities of the vernacular tongues, and a new passion for form and style sprang up. But these fruits of Humanism were mixed blessings. The scorn that Renaissance writers came to feel for all the achievements of the Middle Ages led to a slavish imitation of the classics by which they hoped to regain finesse and dignity. Gradually what had begun as a healthy stimulus from the ancient past became an oppressive deterrent to any deviation from classical models. Latin prosody was forced upon vernacular verse which, in the case of English and German, might be founded on a totally different principle. Form as an end in itself all but swamped the substance of literature. In a misguided application of Ciceronian rhetoric, prose was subjected to artificial laws and led to the excesses of Góngorism in Spain and Euphuism in England.

Most unfortunate of all was the snobbish preference of the Humanists for Latin composition, that interrupted for a century the development of vernacular literatures. The achievements of Dante, Petrarch, and Boccaccio in the vigorous Italian speech of the fourteenth century were contemptuously set aside in the fashionable worship of Virgil and Cicero, and not until the sixteenth did Italian poetry revive with Ariosto and Tasso. The Humanists as an international aristocracy of scholars thought of Latin as the one enduring medium of expression and the only tongue capable of the supreme elegance of the Augustan Romans. The vast Renaissance literature in Latin is little read today, for we have a prejudice against its artificial refinement quite as great as the Humanists' prejudice against the vernacular. Petrarch, Boccaccio, Politian, Sannazaro, Vida, Erasmus, Calvin, More, and Bacon cast what they thought to be their greatest works in Latin, and as late as the time of Milton and Addison the fashion had not died out. But the social and political forces of the Renaissance ultimately worked in favor of the vernacular tongues. The wealthy middle class that patronized men of letters could seldom enjoy Latin prose and verse. The ladies of the courts who became an increasing power in the shaping of taste rarely understood Latin. And the rise of national monarchies undermined the international brotherhood of letters and encouraged the growth of national schools of literature in Italian, French, English, and Spanish as cultural aspects of national life began to emerge.

THE RENAISSANCE THEATER

THOUGH the transition from the medieval to the Renaissance theater was very gradual, so that provincial productions of the religious folk plays were still common in Shakespeare's early years, the true Renaissance stage can be dated from the first modern performances of ancient Roman comedies soon after 1450 and the discovery of a treatise by the Augustan architect, Vitruvius, containing an account of ancient stage arrangements. Italy was naturally the first center of this development, and threaters in strict imitation of the supposed classical models were soon built in Ferrara, Rome, and Florence, though the influence of the medieval stage filled in the gaps in the ancient record. The historic Teatro Olimpico, planned by Palladio in 1580 and completed four years later, still stands in Vicenza as a monument to the classical tradition of the Renaissance theater. With its semi-elliptical arrangement of seats, its orchestra space between the stage and spectators, its long, narrow, rectangular stage, and its elaborate proscenium and sculptured doorways facing the audience, it is a faithful imitation of a Roman theater. But the Italians also pioneered in spectacular scenery and stage effects, extraordinary lighting devices and machines to represent thunder and lightning or even the fiery destruction of whole cities. Lacking great original playwrights at this time, the Italian theater was to assert its originality in striking productions.

France, always friendly to the classical tradition, followed Italy in careful imitation of the ancient, but in Spain and England different theatrical conditions produced a much freer theater and drama. In contrast to the elaborate staging and conventional playwriting of Italy and France, these two countries developed a magnificent literary drama with far simpler productions. The folk plays of the Middle Ages exerted a powerful influence on the more democratic theater of London and especially Madrid, so that there was not here the great cleavage between the aristocrats' neo-classical stage and the plebians' *commedia dell' arte* that appeared in Florence, Rome, and Paris. And like other Renaissance movements, the influence of the ancients on the drama came later to Spain and England. The year 1576 saw the opening of the first public playhouse in London, while the first in Madrid came three years later.

Until the closing of the London theaters in 1642, the theatrical histories of the two capitals were to run parallel courses.

In both countries court shows had been presented for some years before the first public theaters were built. The earliest actors in these graceful entertainments were choir-boys and courtly gentlemen, and in England even after the establishment of professional acting companies, boys continued to play the women's roles. In Spain there was no such taboo against women on the stage, and it has been conjectured that their refining influence encouraged the early development of the graceful cloak and sword *comedias* of Lope de Vega. Still, the glory of the English and Spanish stages of the Renaissance lay always in the plays themselves, the masterworks of Marlowe and Shakespeare, Lope de Vega and Calderón, which gained boldness and power from the very freedom offered by the simple stages on which they were performed.

James Burbage built the first public theater in London (called merely *The Theater*) in 1576, on a site beyond the limits of the city proper so as to avoid the interference of the municipal authorities, who still viewed the shows with disapproval and suspicion. Indeed, theater folk long continued to be frowned on in the more sober quarters, especially by the church, with a prejudice that linked their calling with the buffoonery and bohemianism of medieval showmen. But Queen Elizabeth's enthusiastic support of the stage and the cultured background of numerous figures in the Elizabethan theater were fast diminishing this prejudice. Shakespeare was typical of the respectable burghers who now found their way into the theater and, in his case, retired from it to a country house and even a coat of arms. In Spain too, though the stage was even more popular and more democratic, its leading personages were often highly respected. This was in part because the Spanish theaters were generally operated for the benefit of hospitals and other charitable institutions, which conferred a moral vindication on those who worked in them. In England, on the other hand, actors depended on the personal patronage of the king or queen and members of the nobility.

In both countries the repertory system of production prevailed, though popular plays might run for a number of nights in a row. Since the plays were written for permanent companies, the playwrights had to bear in mind the personnel of the companies and necessarily developed stock parts to suit the special talents of the leading actors. This was particularly true in Spain, where Lope de Vega established the type characters to be used by his successors for over half a century. But even Shakespeare's dramatic output shows a clear relationship to the changing personnel of his company.

The costuming of actors was far from being so realistic as in our day. Greek and Roman characters, such as Timon of Athens and Julius Caesar, wore a conventionalized ancient costume, and Eastern characters such as Othello had their distinctive dress. So would such special characters as lawyers, pedants, ancient deities, ghosts, animals, and those with marked physical traits, like the obese Falstaff.

But such characters as Hamlet, who had no distinctive appearance, always wore the ordinary dress of the actors' time, regardless of the period in which they were supposed to have lived. This convention the audience accepted without question. Indeed, in the early period of this drama a company lacking the means for realistic staging might further tax the imagination of the audience through merely indicating by signboards what the various objects on the stage were supposed to represent. Reared on a realistic stage and cinema tradition, we must prod our lazy imaginations today to appreciate the meaning of the dramatic occasion for a Renaissance audience. Above all, it was the poetry of the great dramatists declaimed by lordly actors that the audiences crowded the theaters of Spain and England in 1600 to hear.

NATIONAL SCHOOLS OF THOUGHT

ITALY. In the fourteenth century Italy regained the leadership of European literature from France with a magnificent triumvirate of writers. Though all three were of the Florentine school and flourished within a period of about sixty years (1293–1353), Dante is in spirit the culmination of the Middle Ages, while Petrarch and Boccaccio transform medieval literary forms with a new awareness of the world that points to the Renaissance and modern times.

Petrarch, variously called "the Father of the Renaissance," "the first Humanist," and "the first modern man," was born Francesco Petracco but Latinized his surname to Petrarca to express his devotion to the new study of classical antiquity which he in large measure initiated. His reverence for the literary form of Roman authors led him to turn from vernacular writing to the imitation of Cicero in his Latin letters and Virgil in his Latin epic, Africa, which won him the homage of the learned world. But his many Latin works are unread today, and his popular reputation rests on a slender volume of Italian love poems with which he celebrated his idealistic love for Laura, an acquaintance of his youth. Though inspired by the troubadour tradition of Dante's Vita Nuova, Petrarch's exquisite sonnets breathe a new humanity and psychological insight into a medieval convention.

His close friend Boccaccio had a similar experience. In his youth he penned elegant sonnets to a faithless lady whom he called Fiammetta and produced his masterpiece, the Decameron, a collection of one hundred lively prose tales. Occasionally pathetic or even tragic, more often humorous, frequently satiric and bawdy, these vigorous tales spring from the earth and revitalize medieval story types with the new freedom of the Renaissance. As

a complement to Dante, they bring us down from the eternal worlds of the Commedia to the world of everyday reality. But Boccaccio's friendship with the learned Petrarch turned his attention from the salon and the market place to the library, to Latin and Greek scholarship and a reverent study of Dante. Immersed in Humanistic endeavors he came to consider it an indiscretion of his youth that he wrote the first great monument of Italian prose and one of the most influential works in all literature.

After 1350 the passion of the Humanists for classical Latin virtually submerged vernacular literature in Italy for about a hundred years. The fifteenth century saw the spread of Humanism from an embattled cult to a broad movement saturating the Roman church as well as the lay society in which it began. The rediscovery and reinterpretation of ancient literature now occupied the leading minds of the land, who came to view Italian as a vulgar medium of the unenlightened. A reversal of taste in later centuries was to discredit these elegant imitators of Virgil, Ovid, and Catullus, but the best of them did not deserve the general oblivion that has overtaken the school. By the second half of the fifteenth century the scholarly labors of the Italian Humanists were largely completed, and both Latin and vernacular literature showed the effect of a new philosophical outlook absorbed from the ancient classics, a revival of Neoplatonic idealism fused with Christian doctrine. Florence remained the center of literary activity, especially because of the Platonic Academy founded there by Cosimo de' Medici as an intellectual center of the Humanists. His grandson, Lorenzo the Magnificent (1448–1492), continued his patronage of art and letters and attracted to Florence a brilliant assemblage of talents, such as Ficino and Pico della Mirandola, the Platonic phi-

Wealthy Italians of the Renaissance encouraged all the arts, including interior decoration. The Ducal Palace at Gubbio, Italy, contained this room which in its splendid carving and ornamentation typifies the period.

losophers, and Poliziano the poet. Lorenzo was himself an excellent poet who admired Petrarch and the older Italian school and began a movement for the revival of vernacular literature. His influence more than any other accounts for the remarkable flowering of Italian poetry in the sixteenth century.

The favorite literary form in this revival was the romantic epic, a long poem which treated the traditional material of medieval romance on a grand scale with the sophisticated outlook of the new age. The influence of Virgil is strong in this form. As deliberate imitations of a popular type, these literary epics were admittedly artificial, and yet their courtly idealism and polished style gave them a subtle charm for their urbane public. Ariosto's romantic epic, *Orlando Furioso* (Insane Roland), of which he published forty cantos in 1516 and others in later years, weaves into a loose pattern a number of chivalric tales of Christian-Moslem struggle in the days of

Charlemagne, but the love stories of the knights, such as Roland's hapless passion for the fickle Angelica that drives him insane, dominate the lively action. Epitomizing the romantic idealism and courtly sophistication of the later Renaissance in Italy, this popular poem remains readable for its sprightly narrative and colorful style.

Ariosto's literary twin, Torquato Tasso, continued the tradition of the romantic epic in the second half of the sixteenth century. Precocious but morbidly sensitive, he completed his great romantic epic, *Jerusalem Delivered*, by the age of thirty-one but betrayed already the mental instability that was to harass his later years, destroy his genius, and lead him at last to a madhouse. Modeled on Virgil, Tasso's pious epic of the First Crusade is now remembered for its charming pagan heroines, Armida, Clorinda, Erminia, and their disrupting amours with the Christian knights. Thoroughly romantic by nature, the poet is at his best in his tender interpretations of courtly love affairs, while his routine treatment of battles and religious themes reveals the synthetic character of the Renaissance epic. We will meet it in the delicate pages of Spenser's *Faerie Queene*.

Italian prose of the Renaissance was long impeded by imitation of classical Latin style. Involved sentence construction, heavy diction, and studied figures of speech raised a wall of rhetoric between author and audience. But the sixteenth century saw some improvement in the direction of greater freedom and clarity. Niccolò Machiavelli, the outstanding political theorist of the age, was also its most influential prose stylist. Typical of Renaissance Italy in his dazzling versatility and his frankly amoral attitude toward life, he gave a brilliant picture of cuckoldry in his excellent comedy, *Mandragola*, and an equally cynical, if realistic, defense of political expediency in his famous treatise, *The Prince*. Though *The Prince* made his name forever a symbol of sinister statecraft, the vigorous prose of the little book has made it also an enduring work of literature.

The romantic counterpart of the realistic Machiavelli was that perfect courtier, Baldassare Castiglione, whose delightful dialogue, *The Courtier*, prescribed for Renaissance social life as *The Prince* had done for its politics. Castiglione's model gentleman is the master of courtesy and refined conversation who makes an art of good manners and whose classical learning has taught him the Ciceronian virtue of *humanitas*. As the Renaissance adaptation of medieval chivalry, this ideal penetrated to such remote lands as England, where Sir Philip Sidney deliberately embodied it in his own life and Spenser illustrated it in the courteous knights of his *Faerie Queene*. Closer to the typical Italian courtier of the Renaissance, however, was that reckless rascal, Benvenuto Cellini (1500–71), whose swaggering *Autobiography* is the most popular work of Renaissance prose. Sculptor, engraver, and goldsmith by profession, he crammed his turbulent life with political intrigue, free-style lovemaking, and incessant quarrels that often led to bloodshed, and wrote of his adventures with brazen exaggeration and an utter indifference to conventional morality. This last great work of the Italian Renaissance summarizes the whole brilliant but ultimately extravagant age.

FRANCE. The Renaissance reached France at least a century after its arrival in Italy. The fourteenth century of Petrarch and Boccaccio was a dismal desert in French history when the Hundred Years' War with England laid waste the land and literature reached its lowest ebb. The proud leadership of France in medieval culture was lost in a period of painful transition from feudalism to national monarchy. Just when the Renaissance spirit

from Italy began to revitalize French culture it is difficult to say. But the slow process of revival may be conveniently dated from the end of the Hundred Years' War in 1453 and the final expulsion of the English from French soil. In the decade that followed there appeared in the exhausted capital of Paris a colorful vagabond poet, François Villon, whose reckless career in crime and literature expressed both the disorderly state of post-war France and the new spirit of adventure that was about to infect the intellectual life of the rejuvenated country. The beautiful lyrics tossed off by this colorful scamp in his spare moments look backward to a medieval school of Provençal poetry, but in his contempt for authority and tradition, his instinctive love of freedom, Villon is the forerunner of Rabelais and the harbinger of the French Renaissance.

With the sixteenth century the movement got unmistakably under way. The French invasions of Italy under Charles VIII and his successors suddenly revealed the new learning and culture to French noblemen, who enthusiastically imported ideas and art works to stimulate a great national revival. Erasmus had taught in Paris and Louvain, but France was to develop a great Humanist of her own in Guillaume Budé. The court of the new monarchs of France became the great center of literary patronage and remained such well into the eighteenth century. Poetry was the first type to reflect the new spirit, and in the transitional career of Clément Marot (1495?–1544), who threw off both the conventional poetic forms and the traditional religious views, we see a new burst of freedom in literature.

In the next generation the influence of Italy and the ancients in French poetry became pronounced in the militant circle of seven poets who called themselves the Pleiades after the constellation that had given a name also to seven ancient Greek poets. In the manifesto of this school Joachim du Bellay declared that their purpose was to elevate the French language by borrowings from Latin and Greek so that it should become a fit medium for a literature based on ancient models. The Pleiades' deep respect for the ancients brought a new finish to French poetry but led as well to a servile imitation that ultimately strangled inspiration. The greatest of them, Pierre de Ronsard, combined a Humanist's devotion to the classics with a deep love of natural beauty, so that, while his imitations of Pindar, Horace, and Ovid seem studied and cold today, his nature poems and love songs to Hélène and Marie retain a freshness and charm unique in this school.

But it was in prose that the French best expressed the Renaissance spirit of intellectual emancipation and self-scrutiny. The movement had two phases that are clearly summarized in the personalities of Rabelais in the first half of the sixteenth century and

Montaigne in the second. François Rabelais, as reckless and merry a figure as Villon before him, became the literary spokesman for revolt against church domination of man's intellectual life. Since his radical views brought him into constant danger of persecution by churchmen, Rabelais conceived the scheme of presenting his attack upon medievalism within a rough-and-tumble narrative about two giants, *Gargantua and Pantagruel,* father and son. This merry mélange is an unpredictable extravanganza of vulgar humor, realistic pictures of social types, obscure learning, and shrewd sense. Rabelais had the boundless faith of the early Renaissance in the goodness and perfectability of human nature, the new-found hope that, once freed from the discipline of the medieval church, it would naturally find its way to right behavior and glorious achievement.

Michel de Montaigne belonged to the dying years of the Renaissance, when these high hopes were sinking into disillusionment and skepticism. The more knowledge Montaigne accumulated, the less he felt he knew about human nature and himself as a specimen of it. Distrusting the reason that had given confidence to so many before him, he returned repeatedly after his studies to the question, "What do I know?" Skeptical of Rabelais's trust in the instincts and questioning the value of the Humanists' learning, he fell back upon a plan of life within the established order as the most sensible after all. Despite his doubts, Montaigne was one of the great sages of all time, and the charm of his intimate style in his *Essays* makes him the most readable prose writer of the French Renaissance.

ENGLAND. The English Renaissance followed the French by about fifty years. Although Chaucer in the fourteenth century had been personally inspired by Boccaccio, the new spirit did not reach English learning and literature until the arrival of the scholars William Grocyn and John Colet at Oxford and Erasmus at Cambridge shortly before 1500. The reign of Henry VIII (1509–1547), a magnificent, ruthless prince on the Italian model, saw a strong national monarchy in England and the establishment of a national church, both of which encouraged the development of a national literature. The first fruit of these influences was Sir Thomas More's *Utopia* (1516), a political romance in Latin reminiscent of Plato's *Republic,* which described an ideal state operated by the laws of reason. Like Rabelais's abbey, More's *Utopia* revealed the ardent hopes of the Renaissance for a better world to come from man's new-found freedom, and prepared the way for Bacon's *New Atlantis* a century later.

The English poets who first felt the challenge of the Italian Renaissance were Wyatt and Surrey. Sir Thomas Wyatt, a favorite of Henry VIII, visited Italy in his youth and was inspired by the love sonnets of Petrarch to write some of his own, frankly imitative but still sincere, and probably the first English poems in sonnet form. The Earl of Surrey, another favorite of Henry until he was suspected of treason and executed, also traveled in Italy and wrote sonnets, but with a new rhyme scheme more appealing to the English ear, which was adopted by many later poets, especially Shakespeare, and became known as the English sonnet. Surrey also introduced blank verse into England, a form that was to be quickly accepted as the most appropriate for serious drama and narrative poetry.

The English Renaissance reached its climax in the reign of Elizabeth (1558–1603), the proud and determined, yet masterful and enlightened daughter of Henry VIII, who realized her father's dream of a strong England ruled by a strong sovereign. Herself a mistress of learning in many languages, Elizabeth approved of her poets' imitation of ancient classics and Italian writers, but encouraged as well a national drama freed from the classical restraints that ruled the Italian and French theater. The genius that her patronage unearthed among her subjects produced a golden age comparable only to the fifth century B.C. in Athens.

Most of the new writers were gentleman amateurs, cultured courtiers like Spenser and Sidney, who wrote to please their fancies and their friends rather than to earn a living by publication. Often addressed hopefully to powerful patrons, their works might be rewarded by gifts or preferment. The court atmosphere in which this literature flourished is reflected in the extravagant style, the classical allusions, the elaborate "conceits" of language, the colorful and bizarre vocabulary better adapted to verse than to prose. Romantic in outlook, it idealizes rather than mirrors the society for which it was written.

The beginnings made by Wyatt and Surrey flowered in a magnificent school of courtly lyric poets. A sudden burst of song rang through the Elizabethan court and countryside. The sonnet, whether in the Italian form of Petrarch or the English form of Surrey, became the vehicle of the love sentiments of Sidney, Spenser, Daniel, Drayton, Shakespeare, and others. Eventually, John Donne showed in his *Holy Sonnets* that it could be used for subjects other than love and pointed the way to its later popularity as a medium of poetic reflection. The exalted woman-worship of the Elizabethan sonneteers gave way to a whimsical view of woman in Donne's love songs, where his satiric and even perverse attitude toward the sex is reflected in cynical irony. Robert Herrick added a playful, pagan quality to his treatment of love and rounded out the Renaissance tradition with some of the most graceful and melodious poems in the language.

Narrative verse of the English Renaissance also

Francis I of France, like Henry VIII of England, was one of the strong monarchs of the national states emerging during the Renaissance period. He is here portrayed by the well-known painter of the French nobility, François Clouet. The painting, done in oil on a panel, is now in the Uffizi Gallery, Florence. It is sometimes ascribed to Jean Clouet.

owed much to the ancients and the new Italian school. Edmund Spenser, the greatest Elizabethan poet, became saturated with Platonic philosophy during his years at Cambridge, and imitated the pastorals of the Greek Theocritus, the Roman Virgil, and the Italian Sannazaro in his *Shepheardes Calender*. On the model of Ariosto, Spenser's masterpiece, *The Faerie Queene*, is a romantic epic each of whose books was to represent one of the twelve virtues of Aristotle in the career of a knight who embodied it. The archaic style of the long poem suggests a strong inspiration as well from older English literature, especially Chaucer. This exquisite work, so delightful in small doses, so tiresome in long draughts, is a Renaissance epitome of chivalry interpreted with the new awareness that the ancients had brought.

But the supreme glory of Elizabethan literature is its drama. In no other country of Europe had the medieval theater of mystery and miracle plays been more popular, and when the Renaissance grafted the secular tradition of the ancients upon the lively Christian tradition, English playwrights experimented with imitations of Plautan comedy and Senecan tragedy. As English drama matured in Elizabethan London, one group of playwrights who had been well schooled in classical tradition continued to demand that modern drama model itself strictly on the ancients. Ben Jonson, a brilliant scholar despite his brief schooling, spent his life in the thick of critical controversy and illustrated his theory of a classical drama in dull, regular tragedies, such as *Sejanus*, and brilliant comedies, such as *Volpone*.

Fortunately the tradition of classical imitation was never so widespread in England as in Italy and France, and a popular tradition of dramatic freedom competed with it throughout the Renaissance, blissfully ignoring the Aristotelian unities and other conventions of the ancient stage. The brilliant but ill-fated Christopher Marlowe (1564–1593), one of the so-called University Wits, reflected his own reckless life in tavern and court in a series f epic plays about unrestrained men misled by extravagant ambition. The boundless energy and aspiration of the Renaissance motivate Tamburlaine and Doctor Faustus in their thirst for power, the Jew of Malta in his lust for money. Loosely constructed and often rhetorical in style, Marlowe's tragedies are also full of poetic fire and titanic force, so that they speak for that school of Elizabethan playwrights who gained confidence from the classics to throw off classical restraints.

William Shakespeare avoided the critical controversy of Jonson and his camp, but allowed no ancient conventions to hamper the full and natural expression of his genius. Inconspicuous in the society of his day, mediocre as a professional actor, he was still the great master of Elizabethan drama, whose reputation has since become second to none in world literature. His life was modest and unexciting; during the twenty years that he spent in London its most important events were the thirty-seven plays by which he gained fame and sufficient fortune to retire to a comfortable home in his native town of Stratford-on-Avon. A quiet and conventional man, he revealed his passionate nature and masterful study of human character only in his plays, his exquisite sonnets, and charming minor poems. His forte in the structure of his plays was not originality; he borrowed all but two of his plots from earlier works and followed the patterns of construction used by other playwrights of his time. His greatness lay in his rich versatility, ranging from the fairyland of *A Midsummer-Night's Dream* to the city streets of *The Comedy of Errors*, from the romantic treatment of love in *Romeo and Juliet* to a cynical contempt for it in *Troilus and Cressida*, from the study of a passionate man of action in *Coriolanus* to the sympathetic portrayal of an introvert bound down by thought in *Hamlet*, perhaps his greatest creation of all. Regardless of his mood or his material, Shakespeare was everywhere a poet with a poet's mastery of language. The profusion of imagery, the lavish use of verbal color, and the restless vigor of his style spring from the extravagant energy of the Renaissance period and yet reveal the unique mind of England's greatest writer.

In comparison with its verse, whether lyric or dramatic, the prose of the English Renaissance is a poor thing, cluttered up with Latin pedantry or ornate figures of speech that reveal the contempt of its courtly practitioners for a natural prose inspired by everyday speech. Fired by the example of Castiglione's *Courtier*, John Lyly sought in his prose romance, *Euphues, or the Anatomy of Wit* (1579), to instruct his readers in courtly language and developed an affected style of elaborately balanced constructions easy for them to imitate. Although it contributed to the refinement of Renaissance prose, the gross artificiality of "euphuistic" style, as it came to be called, perpetuated the misguided notion that prose should have as exact laws as verse and be somehow poetic rather than "prosaic." Support for this came from the ancients, especially Cicero; and the Italians from Boccaccio down had favored ponderous constructions and elegant ornament.

Best loved of all English prose works in this period were the wise and witty *Essays* written by the philosopher-statesman, Sir Francis Bacon. Though his more ambitious works are unfortunately composed in the heavy manner of *The Advancement of Learning* or even the scholarly Latin of the *Novum Organum*, Bacon used a clear-cut, epigrammatic style in his little essays that accounts in very large measure for their perennial popularity as practical guides to conduct.

Toward the end of the Renaissance the religious Reformation exerted a powerful influence on English letters through the nonconformist sect of Puritans. During Elizabeth's reign these extremists suffered legal restrictions because they disapproved of the queen's conception of the royal power, but by 1640 they had increased their numbers to the point where they precipitated a civil war and established a national government of their own under Oliver Cromwell.

The literature of the seventeenth century reflected the religious war of the time, with a militant Puritan school alongside their opponents, the Cavaliers. Drama declined under Puritan opposition to its Royalist outlook and supposed immorality, and with the closing of the theaters by the Puritan Parliament in 1642 playwriting went underground for nearly twenty years. Yet the Puritans produced two great literary spokesmen for their cause in John Bunyan and John Milton. Bunyan was a humble craftsman whose reading was confined to the Bible. His zeal in preaching Puritan doctrine during the Commonwealth led, with the restoration of the monarchy in 1660, to his imprisonment for twelve years. In Bedford jail Bunyan searched his soul to discover his sins and conceived the mission of preaching to a larger audience through personal confessions and allegorical revelations in print. His masterpiece, *The Pilgrim's Progress from this World to that Which is to Come* (1678–1679), is a simple but compelling tale of the spiritual trials of a well-intentioned Christian. This great Protestant allegory appeals to children with its tale of giants and warrior knights and to adults with its underlying symbolism of Christian doctrine. Long popular only with the middle and lower classes, it is written in a direct and vigorous prose that finally influenced the style of more polite literature.

But the supreme Puritan master was John Milton, one of the world's great poets. Unlike Bunyan, Milton was an aristocrat, with a Humanist's familiarity with the ancients reflected in the classical allusions that stud his verse. His early works, such as the masque *Comus* and the pastoral elegy *Lycidas*, show clearly his contact with the Italian Renaissance. During the Cromwell regime Milton forsook poetry for service to the state, but with the restoration of the monarchy he retired into poverty as a still unregenerate rebel, now totally blind. His last years were sustained by the composition of his masterpiece, *Paradise Lost* (1667), and the Christian tragedy in Greek form, *Samson Agonistes* (1671). The epic majesty of the first of these and its sublime vision of the celestial heights make it one of the world's classics of poetry. But in the latter we come closer to Milton himself, spiritually isolated by the Royalist Restoration, in the defiant character of the blind Samson, destroying the alien and sinful Philistines with his own death. The Puritan Reformation was not killed in England by political defeat, but in Milton's last years it was being blended with other social forces to produce a new era in intellectual history. By 1660 the movement of Renaissance and Reformation had run its course, and Milton's work is a final summary of its achievements.

SPAIN. Spain had her Golden Age during the Renaissance, when Spanish seadogs sailed the Spanish Main, and far-flung colonies poured their riches into the imperial coffers of Charles v and Philip II. Humanism arrived early in the sixteenth century, but the study of Latin and Greek classics was never so important here as in Italy and was more successfully harmonized with traditional Christianity in Catholic Spain than in the rest of Europe. It coincided with the religious Reformation in Germany and Switzerland, a movement that only strengthened the orthodox faith in Spain and inspired the Catholic Counter-Reformation of the Jesuits. Hence the resurrection of the ancients reinforced the authority of Aristotle in philosophy and science, and revived Plato in the Christian tradition of Plotinus rather than in the pagan spirit of the Medici Platonic Academy.

But the influence of the new outlook was clearer and stronger in less austere quarters. In Spain the idealistic tradition of medieval chivalry had lingered longer than in other lands, so that as late as 1508 there was first published the most popular of all its chivalric romances, *Amadis of Gaul*. The Christian knight riding through the countryside in quest of wrongs to right, defending his honor and his lady's with his trusty lance, still challenged the Spanish imagination as a living symbol, whereas in Italy and England he had become picturesquely archaic beside the new figure of the Renaissance courtier. Yet even in Spain social conditions were changing, and it remained for a Spaniard, Miguel de Cervantes, to write the great satire of chivalry that finally exposed the inadequacy of its idealism in a changing world. It was the time of Montaigne, when the self-assurance and high hopes of the early Humanists were also dissolving in a new skepticism. As Montaigne applied the devastating test of reason to the claims of Pico and Rabelais, Cervantes applied it to the outmoded social codes of feudalism.

Cervantes began *Don Quixote* as a literary satire of chivalric romance, but as he wrote, the character of his Knight of the Woeful Countenance, so well-intentioned in his noble enterprise, so ignominiously frustrated at every point by a coarse and heartless reality, became a pathetic figure pursuing his high mission on the open road. He became the embodi-

An example of Spanish religious painting is this work by El Greco, "Crucifixion," with a view of Toledo in the background. The elongation and somber atmosphere are characteristic of El Greco.

ment of human aspiration after justice and noble conduct, and in his repeated defeats Cervantes represented the tragic compromise with his better nature that the world forces on every man. Cervantes himself had learned this lesson through a lifetime of defeat and tragedy. The unchecked idealism of the Don is contrasted with the earthy realism of his peasant-squire, Sancho, the voice of common sense through his endless adages and folk wisdom. *Don Quixote* can be read as a comic novel of an absurd old man tilting with windmills and flocks of sheep, but like all really great comedies it carries as well a profound comment on human nature and human society.

Don Quixote sounded the death knell of chivalric romance, but the romantic idealism that it unmasked was too ingrained in Spanish temperament and the whole Renaissance movement not to withstand this exposure. It gives the characteristic flavor to the great school of drama that flourished in this *siglo del oro,* or "golden century," as the Spaniards call the period 1554–1681. Like the English, the Spanish drama of the period ignored the classical code of Aristotle and developed a free form of its own that would allow full range to the romantic imagination of a passionate people. The Spanish *comedia* was not necessarily a comedy, but rather a play that combined serious and comic elements within its three-act structure, usually with a happy ending. Humorous comments on the romantic affairs of the gallant and his lady were generally entrusted to a clownish servant or peasant called the *gracioso,* spokesman for the realistic common sense with which the Spaniards have always tempered their flamboyant romanticism. The *comedias* are classified according to subject matter: historical, religious, mythological, pastoral, and so forth, but all reveal the Renaissance Spaniards' unquestioning devotion to *dios, el rey, y mi dama* (God, the king, and my lady). The fanatical insistence on personal honor that makes every character, from the king to the lowliest peasant, ever ready to defend it gives a high-strung quality to Spanish drama. Although the school flourished at the time of the Elizabethans (1590–1660), its plays seem superficial and repetitious in comparison with Shakespeare and betray the fantastic speed with which Lope de Vega and Calderón turned them out.

Lope led an extravagant and tumultuous life as reckless student, soldier with the Spanish Armada, boastful libertine and faithless husband, finally an unconventional priest. Yet he found time to surpass all other authors in productivity. Despite his careless haste, Lope's endless imagination gave great variety to his dramas and their lively action and brilliant poetic style compensate in part for their shallow thinking and conventionalized characters. *The Sheep Well* is a startling play of proletarian revolt in which Lope's favorite types—the tyrannical feudal lord, the proud peasant and burgher, the noble king, the romantic lovers, and the witty *gracioso*—all appear. Behind its violent conflict lies the war of Renaissance monarchy on the feudal system, and the robust nationalism that animated the playwright in this great period of Spanish power.

Pedro Calderón de la Barca, who preserved the glory of the Spanish Renaissance through the midseventeenth century, followed the example of Lope the pioneer in his two hundred *comedias,* using the same themes and sometimes the same plots. A devoutly religious man, he specialized in such religious studies as *The Devotion to the Cross* and gave us in *Life Is a Dream* the only famous philosophical play of the Spanish Renaissance. With the death of Calderón and the rapid decline of the Spanish empire, Spain virtually disappeared from world literature for two hundred years. The Renaissance had already been dead for half a century in France, which was leading Europe into a new era.

The Wandering Scholars

The Wandering Scholars, or *vagantes,* are our link between medieval Church learning and the Humanism of the Renaissance. In France, Germany, and England of the twelfth and thirteenth centuries they formed a distinct order dedicated to the revival of pagan learning and, especially, pagan morality in the very midst of the Christian renascence. Uninterested in church careers as they were, these young men lacked the economic protection of the church and wandered from university to university, homeless and generally penniless, more familiar with low taverns than with lecture halls. With a strong sense of brotherhood born of their contempt for churchmen and laymen alike, they came to constitute an informal guild with a mythical patron called "Bishop Golias," a Rabelaisian character whom they jokingly thought of as their father and master. He was generally pictured as a reckless foe of the Pope, frankly devoted to free love and riotous living. Hence the wandering scholars were the "Goliards," and their lusty Latin songs in praise of wine, women, and poetry are the so-called Goliardic verse.

As found in the manuscript of the *Carmina Burana,* these student songs are anonymous and reveal no individual personalities but a single type of scholar-tramp singing the pleasures of this world, preferring Ovid to the churchmen, and wine and lovemaking in the springtime to musty scholarship. Sober clerics are frequently the butt of their satire. The pleasures of the country, the beauties of woods and pasture lands in May, flood these poems with a wholesome air from out-of-doors, and the love described is lusty and sensual. Unlike formal classical verse based on long and short syllables, the best of these rollicking stanzas give a new melody to Latin through recurrent accents and ingenious rhymes in tune with English prosody. At least one of them, *Gaudeamus Igitur,* has survived on the Continent as a universal student song.

A Song of the Open Road

WE in our wandering,
    Blithesome and squandering,
        Tara, tantara, teino!

Eat to satiety,
Drink with propriety;   5
        Tara, tantara, teino!

Laugh till our sides we split,

A Song of the Open Road. Translated by John Addington Symonds.

Rags on our hides we fit;
        Tara, tantara, teino!

Jesting eternally,   10
Quaffing infernally:
        Tara, tantara, teino!

Craft's in the bone of us,
Fear 'tis unknown of us:
        Tara, tantara, teino!   15

When we're in neediness,
Thieve we with greediness:
        Tara, tantara, teino!

Brother catholical,
Man apostolical,   20
        Tara, tantara, teino!

Say what you will have done,
What you ask 'twill be done!
        Tara, tantara, teino! . . .

License and vanity   25
Pamper insanity:
        Tara, tantara, teino!

As the Pope bade us do,
Brother to brother's true:
        Tara, tantara, teino!   30

Brother, best friend, adieu!
Now, I must part from you!
        Tara, tantara, teino!

When will our meeting be ?
Glad shall our greeting be!   35
        Tara, tantara, teino!

Vows valedictory
Now have the victory;
        Tara, tantara, teino!

Clasped on each other's breast,   40
Brother to brother pressed,
        Tara, tantara, teino!

The Confessions of Golias

BOILING in my spirit's veins
    With fierce indignation,
From my bitterness of soul
    Springs self-revelation:
Framed am I of flimsy stuff,   5
    Fit for levitation,

The Confessions of Golias. Translated by John Addington Symonds.

Like a thin leaf which the wind
    Scatters from its station. . . .

Down the broad road do I run,
    As the way of youth is;   10
Snare myself in sin, and ne'er
    Think where faith and truth is,
Eager far for pleasure more
    Than soul's health, the sooth is,
For this flesh of mine I care,   15
    Seek not ruth where ruth is.

Prelate, most discreet of priests,
    Grant me absolution!
Dear's the death whereof I die,
    Sweet my dissolution;   20
For my heart is wounded by
    Beauty's soft suffusion;
All the girls I come not nigh,
    Mine are in illusion.

'Tis most arduous to make   25
    Nature's self surrender;
Seeing girls, to blush and be
    Purity's defender!
We young men our longings ne'er
    Shall to stern law render,   30
Or preserve our fancies from
    Bodies smooth and tender. . . .

In the second place I own
    To the vice of gaming:
Cold indeed outside I seem,   35
    Yet my soul is flaming:
But when once the dice-box hath
    Stripped me to my shaming,
Make I songs and verses fit
    For the world's acclaiming.   40

In the third place, I will speak
    Of the tavern's pleasure;
For I never found nor find
    There the least displeasure;
Nor shall find it till I greet   45
    Angels without measure,
Singing requiems for the souls
    In eternal leisure.

In the public-house to die
    Is my resolution;   50
Let wine to my lips be nigh
    At life's dissolution:
That will make the angels cry,
    With glad elocution,
"Grant this toper, God on high,   55
    Grace and absolution!" . . .

Nature gives to every man
    Gifts as she is willing;

I compose my verses when
    Good wine I am swilling,   60
Wine the best for jolly guest
    Jolly hosts are filling;
From such wine rare fancies fine
    Flow like dews distilling.

Such my verse is wont to be   65
    As the wine I swallow;
No ripe thoughts enliven me
    While my stomach's hollow;
Hungry wits on hungry lips
    Like a shadow follow,   70
But when once I'm in my cups,
    I can beat Apollo. . . .

There are poets, worthy men,
    Shrink from public places,
And in lurking-hole or den   75
    Hide their pallid faces;
There they study, sweat, and woo
    Pallas and the Graces,
But bring nothing forth to view
    Worth the girls' embraces.   80

Fasting, thristing, toil the bards,
    Swift years flying o'er them;
Shun the strife of open life,
    Tumults of the forum;
They, to sing some deathless thing,   85
    Lest the world ignore them,
Die the death, expend their breath,
    Drowned in dull decorum. . . .

I have uttered openly
    All I knew that shamed me,   90
And have spued the poison forth
    That so long defamed me;
Of my old ways I repent,
    New life hath reclaimed me;
God beholds the heart—'twas man   95
    Viewed the face and blamed me.

The Invitation
to Youth

TAKE your pleasure, dance and play,
    Each with other while ye may:
Youth is nimble, full of grace;
Age is lame, of tardy pace.

We the wars of love should wage,   5
Who are yet of tender age;

The Invitation to Youth. Translated by John Addington Symonds.
78. **Pallas,** Athena.

'Neath the tents of Venus dwell
All the joys that youth loves well.

Young men kindle heart's desire;
You may liken them to fire: 10
Old men frighten love away
With cold frost and dry decay.

There's No Lust Like to Poetry

SWEET in goodly fellowship
Tastes red wine and rare O!
But to kiss a girl's ripe lip
Is a gift more fair O!
Yet a gift more sweet, more fine,   5
Is the lyre of Maro!
While these three good gifts were mine,
I'd not change with Pharaoh.

Bacchus wakes within my breast
Love and love's desire,   10
Venus comes and stirs the blessed
Rage of Phoebus' fire;
Deathless honour is our due
From the laurelled sire:
Woe should I turn traitor to   15
Wine and love and lyre!

Should a tyrant rise and say,
"Give up wine!" I'd do it;
"Love no girls!" I would obey,
Though my heart should rue it.   20
"Dash thy lyre!" suppose he saith,
Naught should bring me to it;
"Yield thy lyre or die!" my breath,
Dying, should thrill through it!

Gaudeamus Igitur

LET us live, then, and be glad,
While young life's before us!
After youthful pastime had,
After old age hard and sad,
Earth will slumber o'er us.   5

Where are they who in this world,
Ere we kept, were keeping?
Go ye to the gods above;
Go to hell; inquire thereof:
They are not; they're sleeping.   10

There's No Lust Like to Poetry. Translated by John Addington Symonds.
6. **Maro,** Virgil.   12. **Phoebus,** Apollo.
Gaudeamus Igitur. Translated by John Addington Symonds.

Brief is life, and brevity
Briefly shall be ended:
Death comes like a whirlwind strong,
Bears us with his blast along;
None shall be defended.   15

Live this university,
Men that learning nourish;
Live each member of the same,
Long live all that bear its name;
Let them ever flourish!   20

Live the commonwealth also,
And the men that guide it!
Live our town in strength and health,
Founders, patrons, by whose wealth
We are here provided!   25

Live all girls! A health to you,
Melting maids and beauteous!
Live the wives and women too,
Gentle, loving, tender, true,
Good, industrious, duteous!   30

Perish cares that pule and pine!
Perish envious blamers!
Die the Devil, thine and mine!
Die the starch-necked Philistine!
Scoffers and defamers!

Pico della Mirandola

1463–1494

The new discovery by the Humanists of the beauty and perfectability of human nature is nowhere more enthusiastically expressed than in Pico's *Oration on the Dignity of Man.* Pico della Mirandola, the youngest son of a petty Italian prince, was a child prodigy, who was already at sixteen an eager student at the University of Ferrara. His thirst for learning exposed him to the Aristotelian tradition and the oriental tradition of Averroës at Padua, the Platonic tradition in Lorenzo de' Medici's Platonic Academy at Florence, and the scholastic tradition of the Middle Ages at Paris. From the four he attempted to synthesize a philosophy that reconciled the ancient schools of Plato and Aristotle with a revitalized Christianity. But his passion for Humanism brought him into a dangerous conflict with the Church when two of his major works were declared heretical by the Pope. His early death from a fever at the age of thirty cut short his masterpiece, the *Symphonia Platonis et Aristotelis,* and probably saved him from more serious embroilment with Rome.

His famous *Oration on the Dignity of Man* proclaims the worth of human nature in an almost unconscious revolt against the humility of Christian ethics. With his divine gift of reason, man gains a self-reliance that can carry him to the heights of intellectual achievement. The free, confident spirit of this Humanistic document predicts the more earthy emancipation of Rabelais and his Abbey of Theleme.

Of the Dignity of Man

I HAVE read in the records of the Arabians, worshipful Fathers, that Abdala the Saracen, when questioned as to what on this stage of the world, as it were, should be considered most worthy of wonder, replied: "There is nothing to be seen more wonderful than Man," with which opinion the saying of Hermes Trismegistus agrees: "A great miracle, Asclepius, is Man." But when I weighed the reason for these maxims, the many excellences reported of human nature by many men did not satisfy me—that Man is the intermediary between creatures, the intimate of the gods, king of the lower beings, by the acuteness of his senses, by the discernment of his reason and the light of his intelligence the interpreter of nature, the interval between fixed eternity and fleeting time, and (as the Persians say), the bond, nay rather the marriage-song of the world, on David's testimony but little lower than the angels. Admittedly great though these be, they are not the principal reasons, that is to say, those which may rightfully claim for themselves the privilege of the highest admiration. For why should we not admire more the angels themselves and the blessed choirs of Heaven? At last, it seems to me, I have come to understand why Man is the most fortunate of beings, and consequently worthy of all admiration, and what precisely is that rank which is his lot in the universal chain of Being, and which is to be envied not only by brutes but even by the stars, by minds more than earthly. It is a matter past faith, and a wondrous one. Why should it not be? For on this very account Man is rightly both called a great miracle, and judged a wonderful being indeed.

But hear, Fathers, exactly what is this rank, and, as kindly auditors, conformably to your cultivation, forbear to punish me for this work. God the Father, the Supreme Architect, had already built this earthly home we behold of his Godhead, as his most sacred temple, by the laws of his mysterious wisdom. The supercelestial region He had adorned with intelligences, the heavenly spheres He had quickened with eternal souls, and the excrementary and filthy parts of the lower world He had filled with a multitude of creatures of every kind. But when the work was finished the Artist kept wishing that there were someone to ponder the rationality of so great a work, to love its beauty, and to wonder at its vastness. Therefore when everything was done (as Moses and Timaeus bear witness) He finally took thought concerning the creation of Man. But there was not among his archetypes that from which He could fashion a new offspring, nor was there in his treasure-houses anything He might bestow on his new son as an inheritance, nor was there in the courts of all the world a place where the latter might sit as contemplator of the universe. All was now complete, all things had been assigned to the highest, the middle, and the lowest orders. But in its final creation it was not the part of the Father's power to fail as though exhausted. It was not the part of his wisdom to waver in a case of need through poverty of counsel. It was not the intention of his kindly love that he who was to praise God's divine generosity in regard to others, should be compelled to condemn it in regard to himself.

At last the Best of Artisans ordained that that creature to whom he had been able to give nothing proper to himself should have joint possession of whatever had been the peculiar characteristics of the different creatures. He therefore accorded to Man the function of a form not set apart, and a place in the middle of the world, and addressed him thus: "I have given thee neither a fixed abode nor a form that is thine alone nor any function peculiar to thyself, Adam, to the end that, according to thy longing and according to thy judgment, thou mayest have and possess that abode, that form, and those functions which thou thyself shalt desire. The nature of all other things is limited and constrained within the bounds of laws prescribed by me: thou, coerced by no necessity, shalt ordain for thyself the limits of thy nature in accordance with thine own free will, in whose hand I have placed thee. I have set thee at the world's center, that thou mayest from thence more easily observe whatever is in the world. I have made thee neither of heaven nor of earth, neither mortal nor immortal, so that thou mayest with greater freedom of choice and with more honor, as though the maker and moulder of thyself, fashion thyself in whatever shape thou shalt prefer. Thou shalt have the power to degenerate into the lower forms of life, which are animal; thou shalt have the power, out of thy soul's judgment, to be reborn into the higher forms of life, which are divine."

*Of the Dignity of Man.*ᴬ Translated by Elizabeth L. Forbes. Reprinted from the *Journal of the History of Ideas,* III (1942), by permission of the editors.
2. **Abdala the Saracen,** a learned and pious Moor. 7. **Hermes Trismegistus,** the assumed author of a body of ancient Egyptian Neoplatonic literature, including the dialogue *Asclepius* (ref. I, 294). 18–19. but little . . . angels. Psalms, 8:5.

49. **Timaeus,** a Pythagorean philosopher, to whom Plato credits in *Timaeus* an account of the origin of man.

O supreme generosity of God the Father, O highest and most marvellous felicity of Man! to whom it is granted to have that which he chooses, to be that which he wills. Beasts as soon as they are born (so says Lucilius) bring with them from their mother's womb that which they will possess for ever; spiritual beings, either from the beginning or soon thereafter, become what they are to be for ever and ever. On Man when he came into life the Father conferred the seeds of all good and the germs of every form of life. Whatever seeds each man cultivates, those seeds will grow to maturity and bear in him their own fruit. If they be vegetative, he will be like a plant. If sensual, he will become brutish. If rational, he will issue as a heavenly being. If intellectual, he will be an angel and the son of God. And if, happy in the lot of no created thing, he withdraws into the center of his own unity, his spirit made one with God in the solitary darkness of God who is set above all things, he shall surpass them all. Who will not admire this our chameleon? Or who could more greatly admire aught else whatever? It is Man who Asclepius of Athens, arguing from his mutability of character and from his self-transforming nature, on just grounds says was symbolized by Proteus in the mysteries. Hence those metamorphoses renowned among the Hebrews and the Pythagoreans. . . .

Are there any who would not admire Man, who is, in the sacred writings of Moses and the Christains, not without reason described sometimes by the name of "all flesh," sometimes by that of "every creature," in as much as he himself moulds, fashions, and changes himself into the form of all flesh and into the character of every creature? For this reason the Persian Euanthes, in describing the Chaldaean religion, writes that Man has no semblance that is inborn and his very own, but many that are external and foreign to him; whence this saying of the Chaldaeans: "Hanorish tharah sharinas," that is, Man is a being of varied, manifold, and inconstant nature. But to what end is this so? To the end that, after we have been born to this condition, we may understand that we may become that which we will to be. We should have especial care to this, that it should never be said against us, that although born to a privileged position, we failed to recognize it and became like unto wild animals and senseless beasts of burden; but that rather the saying of Asaph the Prophet should apply: "Ye are all angels and sons of the Most High"; and that we may not by abusing

the most indulgent generosity of the Father, that freedom of choice He has given, make for ourselves something harmful out of what is salutary. Let a certain holy ambition invade our souls, so that, not content with the mediocre, we shall pant after the highest, and (since we may if we wish) toil with all our strength to follow it.

Desiderius Erasmus

1466–1536

The best known of the Humanists was a Hollander by birth, but he thought of Latin as his natural tongue. He Latinized and Hellenized his Dutch name Gerhard into Desiderius Erasmus, and during a long life traveled restlessly back and forth through the scholarly circles of France, England, Italy, the Netherlands, and Switzerland, spreading the gospel of the new learning to a host of eager pupils. His love of literature appeared early in youth, but the death of both his parents before he had completed his schooling forced him into training for the priesthood. Though he became learned in theology, he was unhappy under the severe discipline of a monastic life, so that when his reputation for classical scholarship brought him wealthy English pupils in Paris, he was glad to accept patronage from one of them, Lord Mountjoy, and to make the first (1499–1500) of three visits to England.

At Oxford he found a kindred spirit in John Colet, the English Humanist, and he was later to number Linacre, Grocyn, Sir Thomas More, and even Henry VIII among his good friends. He taught Greek and theology at Oxford for a time, but refused to settle permanently in England, as his friends desired. He was by turns in Paris, Padua, Venice, Rome, Louvain, and Basel and everywhere won patrons, friends, and disciples through his charming manners, stimulating conversation, and enlightened scholarship. Although he severely criticized church dogma and the arrogant ignorance of churchmen of his day, he generally retained the good will of the Church and at the time of Luther's split with Rome refused to declare himself for or against the Reformation. Protestants criticized him for not joining a movement that his critical writings had done much to bring about, but he was true to himself in his neutrality.

Erasmus was a pillar of common sense in an era of warring creeds. Although he was opposed to the elaborate theology of Catholicism, he was no friendlier toward the new theology of the Reformation. His urbane rationalism kept him aloof from party strife; his was a detached and independent spirit, interested primarily in the spread of learning, both classical and Christian, and in the liberation of mankind from superstition and entrenched tradition. Strongly interested in ethical problems, he worked for a rational Christianity, freed from dogma and mystical faith and enlightened by the clear common sense of the

5. **Lucilius,** Roman satirist of second century B.C., here quoted in Nonius Marcellus, *De Compendiosa Doctrina* (Lindsay edition, I, 109). 23. **Asclepius of Athens,** supposed author of a Greek dialogue between Hermes and himself on God, Man, and the World. 25. **Proteus,** the legendary Greek prophetic sea god, capable of changing his form at will. 48–49. **Asaph the Prophet,** the Hebrew musician, to whom many of the Psalms are traditionally attributed, as here: Psalms 82:6.

ancients, especially the stoic Romans. This innate conservatism made him look backward to a revived antiquity and a Christianity revived on what he thought of as the original message of the great teacher, Jesus. Resolute in his opposition to the medieval world, he advocated a fusion of two older schools of thought in a new intellectual outlook, liberal with the tolerance born of knowledge.

But his horizon was limited by the characteristic outlook of the Humanists. Indifferent to the new art, opposed to the new science, skeptical of the Reformation, he could not point the way to a new horizon. Although he wrote much about religion and churchmen, he was at heart a literary scholar, whose contacts with the civilized Horace and Cicero of ancient Rome were most congenial with his own rational temperament. Like Voltaire over two centuries later, he was for his age the symbol of intellectual enlightenment, wittily attacking ignorance and dogmatism as he found them exalted in the Middle Ages.

The most famous work of Erasmus, *The Praise of Folly*, was written in the house of Sir Thomas More, to which he had come from Italy in 1509 upon learning of the accession of Henry VIII, his friend and expected patron. This brilliant satire, probably inspired by the *Ship of Fools* (1494) of the German Humanist, Sebastian Brant, is a witty attack on stupidity and corruption in both secular and religious circles, ironically disguised as a praise of ignorance and evil from the lips of Folly herself. Scholars and men of letters, philosophers and men of the Church, popes and kings are all tainted with her touch. The criticism of simony and other ecclesiastical abuses aroused churchmen to indignation, and Erasmus' satire undoubtedly influenced Luther and other spokesmen for the Reformation. But his purpose was merely reform within the establishment, and his work shares with that of Horace and Juvenal the attitude of the armchair observer of the follies committed by men when they are not guided by the cool light of reason.

The Praise of Folly

FOLLY SPEAKS

A T what rate soever the world talks of me (for I am not ignorant what an ill report Folly hath got, even among the most foolish), yet that I am that She, that only She, whose deity recreates both gods and men, even this is a sufficient argument, that I no sooner stepped up to speak to this full assembly than all your faces put on a kind of new and unwonted pleasantness. So suddenly have you cleared your brows and with so frolic and hearty a laughter given me your applause that in truth, as many of you as I behold on every side of me seem

The Praise of Folly.[A] Translation by John Wilson, revised.

to me no less than Homer's gods drunk with nectar and nepenthe; whereas before you sat as lumpish and pensive as if you had come from consulting an oracle. And as it usually happens when the sun begins to show his beams, or when after a sharp winter the spring breathes afresh on the earth, all things immediately get a new face, new color, and recover a certain kind of youth again: in like manner, by but beholding me, you have in an instant gotten another king of countenance; and so what the otherwise great rhetoricians with their tedious and long-studied orations can hardly effect, to wit, to remove the trouble of the mind, I have done at once with my single look. . . .

And therefore, I think it high time to look down a little on the earth, wherein you'll find nothing frolic or fortunate that it owes not to me. So provident has that great parent of mankind, Nature, been that there should not be anything without its mixture and, as it were, seasoning of folly. For since according to the definition of the Stoics, wisdom is nothing else than to be governed by reason, and on the contrary folly to be given up to the will of our passions; that the life of man might not be altogether disconsolate and hard to bear, of how much more passion than reason has Jupiter composed us? Besides, he has confined reason to a narrow corner of the brain and left all the rest of the body to our passions; as also set up against this one two masterless tyrants—anger, that possesses the region of the heart, and consequently the very fountain of life, the heart itself, and lust, that stretches its empire everywhere. Against which double force how powerful reason is, let common experience declare, inasmuch as she, which yet is all she can do, may call out to us till she be hoarse again and tell us the rules of honesty and virtue, while they give up the reins to their governor and make a hideous clamor, till at last being wearied, he suffer himself to be carried whither they please to hurry him.

But forasmuch as such as are born to the business of the world have some little sprinklings of reason more than the rest, yet that they may the better manage it, even in this as well as in other things, they call me to counsel; and I give them such as is worthy of myself, to wit, that they take to them a wife—a silly thing, God wot, and foolish, yet wanton and pleasant, by which means the roughness of the masculine temper is seasoned and sweetened by her folly. For in that Plato seems to doubt under which genus he should put woman, to wit that of rational creatures or brutes, he intended nothing else than to show the apparent folly of the sex. For if perhaps any of them goes about to be thought wiser than the rest, what else does she do but play the fool twice, as if a man should teach a cow to dance, a thing quite against nature. For as it doubles the crime if anyone should put a disguise upon nature, or endeavor to bring her to that which she will in no wise bear, according to that proverb of the Greeks, "An ape is an ape, though clad in scarlet;" so a woman is a woman still, that is to say foolish, let her put on whatever vizard she please. . . .

THE FOLLY OF FRIENDSHIP
AND MARRIAGE

But perhaps there are some that neglect this way of pleasure and rest satisfied in the enjoyment of their friends, calling friendship the most desirable of all things, more necessary than air, fire, or water, so delectable that he that shall take it out of the world had as good put out the sun, and so commendable that not even the philosophers themselves doubted to reckon it among their chiefest good. But what if I show you that I am both the beginning and end of this so great good also? And now tell me if to wink, slip over, be blind at, or deceived in the vices of our friends, nay, to admire and esteem them for virtues, be not at least the next degree to folly? What is it when one kisses his mistress's freckled neck, another the wart on her nose? When a father shall swear his squint-eyed child is more lovely than Venus? What is this, I say, but mere folly? And so, perhaps you'll cry, it is; and yet it is this only that joins friend together and continues them so joined. . . .

And what has been said of friendship may more reasonably be presumed of matrimony, which in truth is no other than an inseparable conjunction of life. Good God! What divorces, or what not worse than that, would daily happen, were not the converse between a man and his wife supported and cherished by flattery, apishness, gentleness, ignorance, dissembling—certain retainers of mine also! How few marriages should we have if the husband should but examine thoroughly how many tricks his pretty little mop of modesty has played before she was married! And how fewer of them would hold together, did not most of the wife's actions escape the husband's knowledge through his neglect or sottishness! And for this also you are beholden to me, by whose means it is that the husband is pleasant to his wife, the wife to her husband, and the house kept in quiet. A man is laughed at when, seeing his wife weeping, he licks up her tears. But how much happier is it to be thus deceived than by being troubled with jealousy, not only to torment himself, but set all things in a hubbub!

In fine, I am so necessary to the making of all society and manner of life both delightful and lasting that neither would the people long endure their governors, nor the servant his master, nor the master his footman, nor the pupil his tutor, nor one friend another, nor the wife her husband, nor the usurer the borrower, nor a soldier his commander, nor one

One of the most famous pictures of Erasmus of Rotterdam is this engraving by Albrecht Dürer made in 1526.

companion another, unless all of them had their interchangeable failings, one while flattering, another while prudently conniving, and generally sweetening one another with some small relish of folly. . . .

SOLDIERS AND PHILOSOPHERS

Is not war the very root and matter of all famed enterprises? And yet what more foolish than to undertake it for I know not what trifles, especially when both parties are sure to lose more than they get by the bargain? For of those that are slain, not a word of them; and for the rest, when both sides are closely engaged and the trumpets make an ugly noise, what use are those wise men, I pray, that are so exhausted with study that their thin cold blood has scarcely any spirits left? No, it must be those blunt fat fellows that by how much the more they exceed in courage fall short in understanding. Unless perhaps one had rather choose Demosthenes for a soldier, who threw away his arms and betook him to his heels ere he had scarce seen his enemy; as ill a soldier, as happy an orator.

But counsel, you will say, is not of least concern in matters of war. In a general I grant it, but this thing of warring is no part of philosophy, but managed by parasites, panders, thieves, cut-throats,

plowmen, sots, spendthrifts, and such other dregs of
mankind, not philosophers; who how unapt they are
even for common converse, let Socrates, whom the
oracle of Apollo judged "the wisest of all men living," be witness; who stepping up to speak in public
was forced to come down again well laughed at for
his pains. Though yet in this he was not altogether
a fool, because he refused the appellation of wise,
and returning it to the oracle, delivered his opinion
that a wise man should abstain from meddling with
public business; unless perhaps he should have rather
admonished us to beware of wisdom if we intended
to be reckoned among the number of men, there being nothing but his wisdom that first accused and
afterwards sentenced him to the drinking of his
poisoned cup. For while as you find him in Aristophanes philosophizing about clouds and ideas, measuring how far a flea could leap, and admiring that so
small a creature as a fly should make so great a buzz,
he meddled not with anything that concerned common life. . . .

Invite a wise man to a feast and he'll spoil the
company, either with morose silence or troublesome
disputes. Take him out to a dance and you'll swear a
cow would have done it better. Bring him to the
theater and his very looks are enough to spoil all,
till like Cato he take an occasion of withdrawing
rather than put off his supercilious gravity. Let him
fall into discourse and he shall make more sudden
stops than if he had a wolf before him. Let him buy
or sell or, in short, go about any of those things
without which there is no living in this world, and
you'll say this piece of wisdom were rather a stock
than a man, of so little use is he to himself, country,
or friends; and all because he is wholly ignorant of
common things and lives a course of life quite different from the people. . . .

WITHOUT FOLLY, WISDOM
WOULD LEAD TO SUICIDE

Suppose a man in some lofty tower, and that he
could look round him, as the poets say Jupiter was
now and then wont. To how many misfortunes
would he find the life of man subject! How miserable, to say no worse, our birth, how difficult our
education; to how many wrongs our childhood exposed, to what pains our youth; how unsupportable
our old age and grievous our unavoidable death, as
also what troops of diseases beset us, how many
casualties hang over our heads, how many troubles
invade us, and how little there is that is not steeped
in gall. To say nothing of those evils that one man
brings upon another, as poverty, imprisonment,
infamy, dishonesty, racks, snares, treachery, reproaches, actions, deceits—but I'm got into as endless a work as numbering the sands. For what offenses mankind have deserved these things, or what

angry god compelled them to be born into such
miseries is not my present business. Yet he that shall
diligently examine it with himself, would he not,
think you, kill himself?

But I, partly through ignorance, partly unad-
visedness, and sometimes through forgetfulness of
evil, do now and then so sprinkle pleasure with the
hopes of good, and sweeten men up in their greatest
misfortunes that they are not willing to leave this
life, even when according to the account of the
destinies this life has left them; and by how much
the less reason they have to live, by so much the
more they desire it; so far are they from being sensible of the least wearisomeness of life. Of my gift it
is that you have so many old Nestors everywhere,
that have scarce left them the shape of a man: stut-
terers, dotards, toothless, gray-haired, bald—or
rather, to use the words of Aristophanes, nasty,
miserable, shriveled, bald, toothless, and wanting
their baubles—yet so delighted with life and to be
thought young that one dyes his gray hair, another
covers his baldness with a periwig, another gets a set
of new teeth, another falls desperately in love with
a young wench and keeps more flickering about her
than a young man would have been ashamed of. For
to see such an old crooked piece, with one foot in
the grave, to marry a plump young wench, and that
too without a portion, is so common that men almost
expect to be commended for it. But the best sport of
all is to see our old women, even dead with age, and
such skeletons that one would think they had stolen
out of their graves, and ever mumbling in their
mouths, "Life is sweet;" and as old as they are, still
catterwauling, daily plastering their faces, scarcely
ever from the glass, gossiping, dancing, and writing
love letters. These things are laughed at as foolish,
as indeed they are; yet they please themselves, live
merrily, swim in pleasure, and in a word are happy,
by my courtesy. But I would have them to whom
these things seem ridiculous consider whether it be
not better to live so pleasant a life in such kind of
follies than, as the proverb goes, "to take a halter
and hang themselves." Besides, though these things
may be subject to censure, it concerns not my fools
in the least, in as much as they take no notice of it,
or if they do, they easily neglect it. If a stone fall
upon a man's head, that's evil indeed; but dishonesty, infamy, villainy, ill reports carry no more
hurt in them than a man is sensible of, and if a man
have no sense of them, they are no longer evils. What
are you the worse if the people hiss at you, so long
as you applaud yourself? And that a man be able to
do so, he must owe it only to folly.

FOOLS ARE NOT UNHAPPY

But methinks I hear the philosophers opposing it
and saying it is a miserable thing for a man to be

foolish, to err, mistake, and know nothing truly. Nay rather, this is to be a man. And why they should call it miserable, I see no reason; forasmuch as we are so born, so bred, so instructed, such is the common condition of us all. And nothing can be called miserable that suits with its kind, unless perhaps you'll think a man such because he can neither fly with birds, nor walk on all fours with beasts, and is not armed with horns as a bull. For by the same reason he would call the warlike horse unfortunate because he understood not grammar, nor ate cheesecakes; and the bull miserable because he'd make so ill a wrestler. And therefore, as a horse that has no skill in grammar is not miserable, no more is man in this respect, for that they agree with his nature. . . .

When fools have passed over this life with a great deal of pleasantness and without so much as the least fear or sense of death, they go straight forth into the Elysian Field to recreate their pious and careless souls with such sports as they used here. Let's proceed then and compare the condition of your wise men with that of this fool. Fancy to me now some example of wisdom you'd set up against him, one that had spent his childhood and youth in learning the sciences and lost the sweetest part of his life in watchings, cares, studies, and for the remaining part of it never so much as tasted the least of pleasure, ever sparing, poor, sad, sour, unjust and rigorous to himself, and troublesome and hateful to others; broken with paleness, leanness, craziness, sore eyes, and an old age and death contracted before their time (though yet, what matter is it when he dies who never lived?); and such is the picture of this great wise man. . . .

THE SUPERSTITIOUS

There is no doubt that that kind of men are wholly ours who love to hear or tell feigned miracles and strange lies, and are never weary of any tale, though never so long, if it be of ghosts, spirits, goblins, devils, or the like; which the farther they are from truth, the more readily they are believed and the more do they tickle their itching ears. And these serve not only to pass away time, but bring profit, especially to mass priests and pardoners. And next to these are they who have gotten a foolish but pleasant persuasion that if they can but see a wooden or painted Polypheme Christopher, they shall not die that day, or do but salute a carved Barbara in the usual set form, that they shall return safe from battle, or make their application to Erasmus on certain days with some small wax candles and proper prayers, that they shall quickly be rich. Or what should I say of them that hug themselves with their

46. **Polypheme Christopher.** Since St. Christopher, the patron saint of travelers, was painted with only one eye showing, Erasmus likens him to the Cyclops.

counterfeit pardons, that have measured purgatory by an hour glass and can without the least mistake demonstrate its ages, years, months, days, hours, minutes, and seconds, as it were in a mathematical table? Or what of those who, having confidence in certain magical charms and short prayers invented by some pious imposter, either for his soul's health or profit's sake, promise to themselves everything: wealth, honor, pleasure, plenty, good health, long life, lively old age, and the next place to Christ in the other world, which yet they desire may not happen too soon, that is to say before the pleasures of this life have left them?

And now suppose some merchant, soldier, or judge, out of so many rapines, parts with some small piece of money. He straight conceives all that sink of his whole life quite cleansed; so many perjuries, so many lusts, so many debaucheries, so many contentions, so many murders, so many deceits, so many breaches of trust, so many treacheries bought off that they may begin upon a new score. But what is more foolish than those, or rather more happy, who daily reciting those seven verses of the Psalms promise to themselves more than the top of felicity? And these are so foolish that I am half ashamed of them myself, and yet they are approved, and that not only by the common people but even the professors of religion. And what, are not they also almost the same where several countries avouch to themselves their peculiar saint, and as every one of them has his particular gift, so also his particular form of worship? As, one is good for the toothache, another for groaning women, a third for stolen goods, a fourth for making a voyage prosperous, and a fifth to cure sheep of the rot; and so of the rest, for it would be too tedious to run over all. And some there are that are good for more things than one, but chiefly the Virgin Mother, to whom the common people do in a manner attribute more than to the Son. . . .

But why do I launch into this ocean of superstitions? Had I a hundred tongues, as many mouths, and a voice never so strong, yet were I not able to run over the several sorts of fools or all the names of folly, so thick do they swarm everywhere. And yet our priests make no scruple to receive and cherish them, as proper instruments of profit, whereas if some scurvy wise fellow should step up and speak things as they are, as, To live well is the way to die well; The best way to get quit of sin is to add to the money thou givest, the hatred of sin, tears, watchings, prayers, fastings, and amendment of life; Such or such a saint will favor thee if thou imitatest his life—these, I say, and the like should this wise man chat to the people, from what happiness into how great troubles would he draw them?

Of this college also are they who in their lifetime appoint with what solemnity they'll be buried, and particularly set down how many torches, how many mourners, how many singers, how many almsmen they will have at it; as if any sense of it could come to them, or that it were a shame to them that their corpse were not honorably interred. . . .

THE SAD THING IS NOT TO BE DECEIVED

But it is a sad thing, they say, to be mistaken. Nay rather, he is most miserable that is not so. For they are quite beside the mark that place the happiness of men in things themselves, since it only depends upon opinion. . . .

And now at how cheap a rate is this happiness purchased! Forasmuch as to the thing itself a man's whole endeavor is required, be it never so inconsiderable, but the opinion of it is easily taken up, which yet conduces as much or more to happiness. For suppose a man were eating rotten stockfish, the very smell of which would choke another, and yet believed it a dish for the gods, what difference is there as to his happiness? Whereas, on the contrary, if another's stomach should turn at a sturgeon, wherein, I pray, is he happier than the other? If a man have a crooked, ill-favored wife, who yet in his eye may stand in competition with Venus, is it not the same as if she were truly beautiful? Or if seeing an ugly, ill-painted piece, he should admire the work as believing it some great master's hand, were he not much happier, think you, than they that buy such things at vast rates and yet perhaps reap less pleasure from them than the other? I know one of my name that gave his new married wife some counterfeit jewels and, as he was a pleasant droll, persuaded her that they were not only right, but of an inestimable price; and what difference, I pray, to her, that was as well-pleased and contented with the glass and kept it as warily as if it had been a treasure? In the meantime the husband saved his money and had this advantage of her folly, that he obliged her as much as if he had bought them at a great rate. Or what difference, think you, between those in Plato's imaginary cave that stand gaping at the shadows and figures of things, so they please themselves and have no need to wish, and that wise man who, being got loose from them, sees things truly as they are? So then there is no difference, or, if there be, the fools have the advantage: first, in that their happiness costs them least, that is to say, only some small persuasion; next, that they enjoy it in common. And the possession of no good can be delightful without a companion. . . .

SCHOLARS AND AUTHORS

Of the same batch are they that hunt after immortality of fame by setting out books. They that write learnedly to the understanding of a few scholars seem to me rather to be pitied than happy, as persons that are ever tormenting themselves, adding, changing, putting in, blotting out, revising, reprinting, showing it to friends, and nine years in correcting, yet never fully satisfied. At so great a rate do they purchase this vain reward, praise, and that too of a very few, with so many watchings, so much sweat, so much vexation and loss of sleep, the most precious of all things. Add to this the waste of health, spoil of complexion, weakness of eyes or blindness, poverty, envy, abstinence from pleasure, over-hasty old age, untimely death, and the like; so highly does this wise man value the approbation of one or two blear-eyed fellows. . . .

But they are the wiser that put out other men's works for their own, and transfer that glory which others with great pains have obtained to themselves, relying on this, that they conceive, though it should so happen that their theft be never so plainly detected, that yet they should enjoy the pleasure of it for the present. And it is worth one's while to consider how they please themselves when they are applauded by the common people, pointed at in a crowd: "This is that excellent person.". . .

But the most pleasant of all is to see them praise one another with reciprocal epistles, verses, and encomiums; fools their fellow-fools, and dunces their brother dunces. And sometimes too they pick out their antagonist and think to raise themselves a fame by writing one against the other, while the giddy multitude are so long divided as to whether of the two they shall determine the victory, till each goes off conqueror and, as if he had done some great action, fancies himself a triumph. And now wise men laugh at these things as foolish, as indeed they are. Who denies it? Yet in the meantime, such is my kindness to them, they live a merry life; while yet those learned men, though they laugh their fill and reap the benefit of the others' folly, cannot without ingratitude deny that even they too are not a little beholden to me themselves.

LAWYERS

And among them our advocates challenge the first place, nor is there any sort of people that please themselves like them; for while they daily quote you a thousand cases as it were in a breath, no matter how little to the purpose, and heap glosses upon glosses and opinions on the neck of opinions, they bring it at last to this pass, that that study of all other seems the most difficult. Add to these our logicians and sophisters, a generation of men more prattling than an echo, and the worst of them able to outchat a hundred of the best-picked gossips. And yet their condition would be much better were they only full of words and not so given to scolding that they must obstinately hack and hew one another about a matter of nothing and make such a sputter about terms and words till they have quite lost the sense. And yet they are so happy in the good opinion of themselves that as soon as they are furnished with two or three syllogisms, they dare boldly enter the lists against any man upon any point, as not doubting to run him down with noise, though the opponent were another Stentor. . . .

MONKS

And next these come those that commonly call themselves the religious and monks, most false in both titles when both a great part of them are farthest from religion and no men swarm thicker in all places than themselves. Nor can I think of anything that could be more miserable, did not I support them so many several ways. For whereas all men detest them to that height that they take it for ill luck to meet one of them by chance, yet such is their happiness that they flatter themselves. For first, they reckon it one of the main points of piety if they are so illiterate that they can't so much as read. And then when they run over their offices, which they carry about them, rather by tale than understanding, they believe the gods more than ordinarily pleased with their braying. And some there are among them that put off their trumperies at vast rates, yet rove up and down for the bread they eat; nay, there is scarce an inn, wagon, or ship into which they intrude not, to the no small damage of the commonwealth of beggars. And yet, like pleasant fellows, with all this vileness, ignorance, rudeness, and impudence, they represent to us, for so they call it, the lives of the apostles. Yet what is more pleasant than that they do all things by rule and, as it were, a kind of mathematics, the least swerving from which were a crime beyond forgiveness; as, how many knots their shoes must be tied with, of what color everything is, what distinction of habits, of what stuff made, how many straws broad their girdles and of what fashion, how many bushels wide their cowl, how many fingers long their hair, and how many hours sleep; which exact equality, how disproportionable it is among such variety of bodies and tempers, who is there that does not perceive it? And yet by reason of these fooleries, they not only set slight by others, but each different order, men otherwise professing apostolical charity, despise one another, and for the different wearing of a habit, or that it is of darker color, they put all things in combustion. And among these there are some so rigidly religious that their upper garment is hair-cloth, their inner of the finest linen; and, on the contrary, others wear linen without and hair next their skins. Others, again, are as afraid to touch money as poison, and yet neither forbear wine nor dallying with women.

21. their offices, the canonical hours.

In a word, it is their only care that none of them come near one another in their manner of living, nor do they endeavor how they may be like Christ, but how they may differ among themselves.

And another great happiness they conceive in their names, while they call themselves Cordeliers, and among these too some are Colletes, some Minors, some Minims, some Crossed; and again, these are Benedictines, those Bernardines; these Carmelites, those Augustines; these Williamites, and those Jacobines; as if it were not worth the while to be called Christians. And of these, a great part build so much on their ceremonies and petty traditions of men that they think one heaven is too poor a reward for so great merit, little dreaming that the time will come when Christ, not regarding any of these trifles, will call them to account for His precept of charity. . . . Christ, interrupting them in their vanities, which otherwise were endless, will ask them, "Whence this new kind of Jews? I acknowledge one commandment, which is truly mine, of which alone I hear nothing. I promised, it is true, my Father's heritage, and that without parables, not to cowls, odd prayers, and fasting, but to the duties of faith and charity. Nor can I acknowledge them that least acknowledge their faults. They that would seem holier than myself, let them if they list possess to themselves those three hundred sixty-five heavens of Basilides the Heretic's invention, or command them whose foolish traditions they have preferred before my precepts, to erect them a new one." When they shall hear these things and see common ordinary persons preferred before them, with what countenance, think you, will they behold one another? In the meantime they are happy in their hopes, and for this also they are beholden to me. . . .

THE CHRISTIAN RELIGION
IS AKIN TO FOLLY

But not to run too far in that which is infinite. To speak briefly, all the Christian religion seems to have a kind of alliance with folly, and in no respect to have any accord with wisdom. Of which if you ask proof, consider first that boys, old men, women, and fools are more delighted with religious and sacred things than others, and to that purpose are ever next the altars; and this they do by mere impulse of nature. And in the next place, you see that those first founders of it were plain, simple persons and most bitter enemies of learning. Lastly, there are no sort of fools that seem more out of the way than are those whom the zeal of the Christian religion has

61. **Colletes,** the order founded by St. Coleta. **Minors,** an order founded by St. Francis of Assisi.
62. **Minims,** an order founded by St. Francis of Paola. **Crossed,** an English order of monks with crosses on their garments. **82. Basilides,** a heretic of the second century.

once swallowed up, so that they waste their estates, neglect injuries, suffer themselves to be cheated, put no difference between friends and enemies, abhor pleasure, are crammed with poverty, watchings, tears, labors, and reproaches, loathe life, and wish death above all things. In short, they seem senseless to common understanding, as if their minds lived elsewhere and not in their own bodies; which, what else is it than to be mad? . . .

Which yet will be more clear if I briefly show you that that great reward they so much fancy is nothing else but a kind of madness. And therefore suppose that Plato dreamed of something like it when he called the madness of lovers the most happy condition of all others. For he that's violently in love lives not in his own body, but in the thing he loves; and by how much the farther he runs from himself into another, by so much the greater is his pleasure. And then, when the mind strives to rove from its body and does not rightly use its own organs, without doubt you may say it is downright madness and not to be mistaken, or otherwise what's the meaning of those common sayings, "Nobody home," "Come to yourself," "He's his own self again"? Besides, the more perfect and true his love is, the more pleasant is his madness. And therefore, what is that life hereafter, after which these holy minds so pantingly breathe, like to be? To wit, the spirit shall swallow up the body, as conqueror and more durable, and this it shall do with the greater ease because heretofore in its lifetime it had cleansed and thinned it into such another nothing as itself. And then the spirit again shall be wonderfully swallowed up by that highest mind, as being more powerful than its infinite parts, so that the whole man is to be out of himself nor to be otherwise happy in any respect but that, being stripped of himself, he shall have some ineffable portion in that chiefest good that draws all things into itself. And this happiness, though it is only then perfected when souls being joined to their former bodies shall be made immortal, yet forasmuch as the life of holy men is nothing but a continued meditation and, as it were, shadow of that life, it so happens that at length they have some taste or relish of it; which, though it be but as the smallest drop in comparison with that fountain of eternal happiness, yet it far surpasses all worldly delight, though all the pleasures of all mankind were all joined together. So much better are things spiritual than things corporeal, and things invisible than things visible; which doubtless is that which the Prophet promises: "The eye hath not seen, nor the ear heard, nor has it entered into the heart of man to consider what God has provided for them that love Him."

52-55. "The eye hath not . . . that love Him." I Corinthians 2:9.

And therefore they that are sensible of it, and few there are to whom this happens, suffer a kind of thing little differing from madness, for they utter many things that do not hang together, and that too not after the manner of men, but make a kind of sound which they neither heed themselves, nor is it understood by others, and change the whole figure of their countenance, one while jocund, another while dejected, now weeping, then laughing, and again sighing. And when they come to themselves, they tell you they know not where they have been, whether in the body or out of the body, or sleeping; nor do they remember what they have heard, seen, spoken, or done, and only know this, as it were in a mist or dream, that they were the most happy while they were so out of their wits. And therefore they are sorry they are come to themselves again, and desire nothing more than this kind of madness, to be perpetually mad. And this is a small taste of that future happiness.

But I forget myself and run beyond my bounds. Though yet, if I seem to have spoken anything more boldly or impertinently than I ought, be pleased to consider that not only Folly but a woman said it, remembering in the meantime that Greek proverb, "Sometimes a fool may speak a word in season," unless perhaps you'll say this concerns not women. I see you expect an epilogue, but give me leave to tell you you are much mistaken if you think I remember anything of what I have said, having foolishly bolted out such a hodge-podge of words. It is an old proverb, "I hate one that remembers what's done over the cup." This is a new one of my own making: I hate a man that remembers what he hears. Wherefore farewell, clap your hands, live and drink lustily, my most excellent disciples of folly.

Giovanni Boccaccio

1313–1375

The fame of the *Decameron* as a collection of racy stories has given Boccaccio an undeserved notoriety in popular fancy and has obscured his powerful role in shaping Italian Humanism and the early Renaissance. The renowned hundred tales, though they remain his chief contribution to world letters, were an incident of his middle years of which he was not proud in later life. Historians remember him today as the founder of the Greek revival and the serious classical scholar who carried forward the pioneer work of his friend, Petrarch.

Boccaccio's life breaks into two quite distinct periods around his meeting with Petrarch in 1351. His scapegrace youth in the social whirl of Naples belongs to literature. His serious later life as Latin writer and professor belongs to Humanistic scholarship. The illegitimate son of a Florentine merchant by his Parisian mistress, Giovanni was brought to Florence in his childhood at a time when that magnificent city had just begun her leadership in European literature. His father intended him for a business career and apprenticed him to another merchant for six years, despite the boy's total lack of interest in trade. Ignoring Giovanni's passionate desire to write poetry, his father next forced him to study canon law for six years as a means to financial security. A bitter friction developed between father and son, and young Boccaccio neglected his law studies to perfect himself in the poet's craft.

A fit subject for his verses appeared around 1338, when his law studies took him to the gay and dissolute city of Naples, then a center of Italian culture under the enlightened King Robert of Anjou. Immediately infatuated with the brilliant social life of the city, Boccaccio soon fell in love with a beautiful siren named Maria d' Aquino, supposedly the natural daughter of King Robert himself and then the wife of a gentleman of the town. It was not his first affair and certainly not hers. Indeed, so sensual and earthy were both the lovers that Boccaccio's efforts to exalt their relationship to the heights of ideality suggest that he was frankly imitating Dante (with his Beatrice) and Petrarch (with his Laura). Fiammetta, as he called Maria, is transformed by his sonnets into the impossible vision of feminine loveliness long familiar in the verse of the troubadours. Actually, she was a jaded product of a worldly society, who could hardly have been faithful for long to her hot-blooded suitor, but she apparently inspired in him the closest thing to overpowering love of which his nature was capable.

For her he wrote a series of impassioned romances, *Il Filocolo, Teseide, Il Filostrato,* and *La Fiammetta,* in the last of which she appears as heroine, telling how her lover betrayed her (although the case was actually reversed). Even after she had forsaken him, she remained the ideal love of his life and the cause of much spiritual anguish. To her he directed exquisite love poems not far below the sonnets of Petrarch. She was still in his mind as he began the *Decameron* and figures as one of the characters in the frame tale of that work. The memory of his agonized love declined only after he completed the *Decameron* (c. 1353), began his close friendship with Petrarch, and entered upon the second period of his career.

Petrarch, enveloped in the Latin spirit of Humanism, dismissed the Italian *Decameron* as a skit, and Boccaccio's humble admiration for his new master led him to turn from it to the study of antiquity. His great service to the Renaissance lay in his revival of Greek studies. With the aid of a crude, ill-tempered Greek named Leontius Pilatus, he made a prose translation of Homer into Italian and thus restored the ancient master to the modern world. Nor were the industrious studies of his later years confined to the ancients. His deep appreciation of Dante led him to write the earliest life of the medieval poet and to hold the first chair of Dante study in any university. Yet the sedate and learned Boccaccio

of his later years, pursuing his researches in poverty, is a sad substitute for the robust, enthusiastic youth who lived a natural, passionate life in the world. Sustained in time of gloom by his friendship for Petrarch, he still shared his master's belief that he had wasted his youth in living and literature and had squandered his talents on what was actually his masterpiece. This sincere, kindly, and self-effacing man survived his friend by only a year, dying on December 21, 1375.

As its Greek title suggests, the *Decameron* (written 1348–1353) is an account of a ten-day sojourn in the countryside near Florence of ten young people, seven ladies and three gentlemen, to avoid the plague that actually ravaged that city and much of Europe in 1348. Three fifths of the population of Florence had died of it, including Petrarch's Laura and probably Fiammetta, though Boccaccio represents his beloved as one of the gay company who dispelled their memory of the harrowing scenes in the city by banqueting, dancing, playing games, and telling stories. As in the case of the *Arabian Nights* and Chaucer's *Canterbury Tales,* this frame tale is merely a device for bringing together a hundred prose stories which are supposedly told by the ten young people on their ten days in the country. Unlike Chaucer's delightful pilgrims, Boccaccio's storytellers are not individualized or interesting in themselves. But the hundred tales which he collected from many sources introduce a wide variety of characters in situations both serious and gay, both moral and ribald. Though the cynicism bred of his youth in Naples reveals itself in these ribald yarns of faithless wives and unholy churchmen, Boccaccio was not favoring immorality or attacking the church, but holding up the glass, like Erasmus, to human folly and lust. As Dante's *Commedia* toured the world to come, the Decameron explored in frankest terms the world that we know in the flesh. The animal spirits and lusty exuberance underlying it predict the emancipation of human instincts in the Renaissance and the new absorption with man as he is rather than man as he should be. The elegant style, inspired by a study of Cicero's Latin constructions, made this the first great monument of Italian prose and a model throughout the Renaissance.

Decameron

THE THREE RINGS

SALADIN was so brave and great a man, that he had raised himself from an inconsiderable person to be Sultan of Babylon, and had gained many victories over both the Saracen and Christian princes. This monarch having in divers wars, and by many extraordinary expenses, run through all his treasure,

Decameron. An old translation revised by various scholars. Reprinted by permission of Pocket Books, Inc.
The Three Rings. This story was used by Lessing as a plea for tolerance in his play, *Nathan the Wise.*

Melchifedech giudeo con una nouella di tre anella, ceſſa un gran perico-
lo dal Saladino apparecchiatogli.   Nouella   III.

Oi che commědata da tutti la nouella di Neiphile, ella ſi
p   tacque, come alla Reina piacque, Philomena coſi comincio-
a parlare. La nouella da Neiphile detta mi ritorna a me-
moria il dubbioſo caſo già a buenuto ad un giudeo, percio che gia-
& di Dio & della uerita della noſtra fede è aſſai bene-ſtato detto, il
diſcen lere hoggimai a glia buenimĕti & a gliatti de glihuomini nõ
ſi doura diſdire, a narrarui quella uero, laquale udita forſe piu caute
diuerreie nelle riſpoſte alle quiſtioni, che fatte ui foſero. Voi douete
Amoroſe compagne ſapere che ſi come la ſciocchezza ſpeſe uolte trahe altrui di felice ſtato, & mette ingran diſſima miſeria, coſi il ſenno-
di grandiſſimi pericoli trahe il ſauio & ponlo in granle & in ſi-
curo ripoſo. Et che uero ſia, che la ſciocchezza di buono ſtato in miſeria alcun conduca, per molti exempli ſi uede, liquali non ſia al pre-
ſente noſtra cura di raccontare, hauendo riguardo, che tutto'l di mille exempli n'appaiano manifeſti. Ma che il ſenno di conſolation ſia
cagione, come promiſi, per una nouelletta moſterro brieuemente.
Il Saladino, il ualore delqual fu tanto, che non ſolamente di piccolo
huomo

A page of the Decameron taken from a 1729 facsimile of the 1527 edition made by an Italian publisher for the British consul at Venice, Joseph Smith. The book is now in the Rare Book Room at the University of Chicago.

some urgent occasion fell out, that he wanted a large sum of money. Not knowing which way he might raise enough to answer his necessities, he at last called to mind a rich Jew of Alexandria, named Melchizedech, who lent out money on interest. Him he believed to have wherewithal to serve him; but then he was so covetous that he would never do it willingly, and he was unwilling to force him. But as necessity has no law, after much thinking which way the matter might best be effected, he at last resolved to use force under some colour of reason. He therefore sent for and received him in a most gracious manner, and making him sit down, he thus addressed him: "Honest man, I hear from divers persons that thou art very wise, and knowing in religious matters; wherefore I would gladly know from thee which religion thou judgest to be the true one—the Jewish, the Mahometan, or the Christian?" The Jew (truly a wise man) found that Saladin had a mind to trap him; and perceiving that he must gain his point should he prefer any one religion, after considering a little how best to avoid the snare, his invention at last supplied him with the following answer:—

"The question which your highness has proposed is very curious; and, that I may give you my sentiments, I must beg leave to tell a short story. I remember often to have heard of a great and rich man, who, among his most rare and precious jewels, had a ring of exceeding great beauty and value; and being proud of possessing a thing of such worth, and desirous that it should continue for ever in his family, he declared, by will, that to whichsoever of his sons he should give this ring, him he designed for his heir, and that he should be respected as the head of the family. That son to whom the ring was given made the same law with respect to his descendants, and the ring passed from one to another in a long succession, till it came to a person who had three sons, all virtuous and dutiful to their father, and all equally beloved by him. And the young men, knowing what depended upon the ring, and ambitious of superiority, began to entreat their father, who was now growing old, every one for himself, that he would give the ring to him. The good man, equally fond of all, was at a loss which to prefer; and as he had promised all, and being willing to satisfy all, privately got an artist to make two others, which were so like the first that he himself scarcely knew the true one, and at his death gave one privately to each of his sons. They afterwards all claimed the honour and estate, each disputing them with his brothers, and producing his ring; and the rings were found so much alike that the true one could not be distinguished. To law then they went, which should succeed, nor is that yet decided. And thus it has happened, my lord, with regard to the three laws given by God the Father to the three peoples concerning which you proposed your question: every one believes he is the true heir of God, has His law, and obeys His commandments; but which is in the right is uncertain in like manner as of the rings."

Saladin perceived that Melchizedech had escaped the net which was spread for him: he therefore resolved to discover his necessity to him, to see if he would lend him money, telling him at the same time what he designed to have done, had not his discreet answer prevented him. The Jew freely supplied him with what he wanted; Saladin afterwards paid him with a great deal of honour, made him large presents, besides maintaining him nobly at his court, and was his friend as long as he lived.

DON FEDERIGO'S FALCON

AT Florence dwelt a young gentleman named Federigo, son of Filippo Alberighi, who, in feats of arms and gentility, surpassed all the youth in Tuscany. This gentleman, as usually happens, fell in love with a lady called Madam Giovanna, one of the most agreeable women in Florence, and, to gain her affection, used to be continually making tilts, balls, and such diversions; lavishing away his money in rich presents, and everything that was extravagant. But she, as careful of her honour as she was fair, made no account either of what he did for her sake or of himself. Living in this manner, his wealth soon began to waste, till at last he had nothing left but a very small farm, the income of which was a most slender maintenance, and a single hawk, one of the best in the world. Yet loving his mistress still more than ever, and finding he could subsist no longer in the city in the manner he would choose to

Don Federigo's Falcon. This famous tale of devotion and self-sacrifice was used by many later authors—La Fontaine, Lope de Vega, Longfellow, and Tennyson.

live, he retired to his farm, where he went out a-fowling, as often as the weather would permit, and bore his distress patiently, and without ever making his necessity known to anybody.

Now, one day it happened that, as he was reduced to the last extremity, this lady's husband, who was very rich, chanced to fall sick, and, feeling the approach of death, made his will, leaving all his substance to an only son, who was almost grown up; and, if he should die without issue, he then ordered that it should revert to his lady, whom he was extremely fond of; and when he had disposed thus of his fortune he died. She now, being left a widow, retired, as our ladies usually do during the summer season, to a house of hers in the country, near to that of Federigo, whence it happened that her son soon became acquainted with him, and they used to divert themselves together with dogs and hawks, when he, having often seen Federigo's hawk fly, and being strangely taken with it, was desirous of having it, though the other valued it to that degree that he knew not how to ask for it. This being so, the lad soon fell sick, which gave his mother great concern, as he was her only child: and she ceased not to attend on and comfort him, often requesting him, if there were any particular thing which he fancied, to let her know it, and promising to procure it for him if it were possible. The young gentleman, after many offers of this kind, at last said, "Madam, if you could contrive for me to have Federigo's hawk, I believe I should soon be well." She was in some suspense at this, and began to consider how best to act. She knew that Federigo had long entertained a liking for her, without the least encouragement on her part; therefore she said to herself, "How can I send or go to ask for this hawk, which I hear is the very best of the kind, and what alone maintains him in the world? Or how can I offer to take away from a gentleman all the pleasure that he has in life?" Being in this perplexity, though she was very sure of having it for the asking, she stood without making any reply; till at last the love of her son so far prevailed that she resolved at all events to make him easy, and not send, but go herself, to bring it. She then replied, "Son, set your heart at rest, and think only of your recovery; for I promise you that the first thing I do to-morrow morning will be to ask for it, and bring it to you." This afforded him such joy that he immediately showed signs of amendment.

The next morning she went, by way of a walk, with another lady in company, to Federigo's little cottage to inquire for him. At that time, as it was too early to go out upon his diversion, he was at work in his garden. Hearing therefore that his mistress inquired for him at the door, he ran thither, surprised and full of joy; whilst she, with a great

"Man with a Falcon." A painting by Titian.

deal of complaisance, went to meet him; and, after the usual compliments, she said, "Good morning, Federigo; I come to give you some recompense for the trouble you have formerly taken on my account, when your love carried you beyond reasonable bounds: it is in this wise,—I mean to dine with you in a homely way, with this lady, my friend." He replied, with a great deal of humility, "Madam, I do not remember ever to have received any hurt or loss by your means, but rather so much good that if I were worth anything at any time it was due to your singular merit and the love I had for you; and most assuredly this courteous visit is more welcome to me than if I had all that I have wasted returned to me to spend over again; but you are come to a very poor host." With these words he showed her into his house, seeming much out of countenance, and from thence they went into the garden, when, having no company for her, he said, "Madam, as I have nobody else, please to admit this honest woman, a labourer's wife, to be with you, whilst I set forth the table."

He, although his poverty was extreme, was never so sensible of his having been extravagant as now; but finding nothing to entertain the lady with, for whose sake he had treated thousands, he was in the utmost perplexity, cursing his evil fortune and running up and down like one out of his wits. At length, having neither money nor anything he could pawn, and being willing to treat her as honourably as he could, at the same time that he would not make his case known, even so much as to his own labourer,

he espied his hawk upon the perch, which he seized, and finding it very fat, judged it might make a dish not unworthy of such a lady. Without further thought, then, he twisted its neck, and gave it to a girl to truss and roast carefully, whilst he laid the cloth and the napkins, having a small quantity of linen yet left; and then he returned, with a smile on his countenance, into the garden, telling her that what little dinner he was able to provide was now ready. She and her friend, therefore, entered and sat down with him, he serving them all the time with great respect, when they ate the hawk. After dinner was over, and they had sat chattering a little together, she thought it a fit time to tell her errand, and she spoke to him courteously in this manner:—

"Sir, if you call to mind your past life, and my resolution, which perhaps you may call cruelty, I doubt not but you will wonder at my presumption, when you know what I am come for: if you had children of your own, whereby you might understand how strong our natural affection is towards them, I am very sure you would excuse me. But, though you have none, I who have am bound by the natural laws of maternity, the force of which is greater than my own will, and indeed my duty: I am therefore constrained to request a thing of you which I know you value extremely, as you have no other comfort or diversion left in the extremity of your fortunes; I mean your hawk, which my son has taken such a fancy to that unless I bring him back with me I very much fear that he will die of his disorder. Therefore I entreat you, not for any regard you have for me (for in that respect you are no way obliged to me), but for that generosity with which you have always distinguished yourself, that you would please to let me have him, by which means you will save my child's life, and lay him under perpetual obligations."

Federigo, hearing the lady's request, and knowing it was out of his power to serve her, began to weep before he was able to make a word of reply. This she first thought was his great concern to part with his favourite bird, and she was about to say that she would not accept it; but she restrained herself, and awaited his reply when he should become more composed. At last he said, "Madam, ever since I have fixed my affections upon you, Fortune has still been contrary to me in many things, and I have often complained of her treatment; but her former harshness has been light and easy compared with what I now endure, which banishes all my peace of mind. You are here to visit me in this my poor mansion, whither in my prosperity you would never deign to come; you also entreat a small present from me, which it is no way in my power to give, as I am going briefly to tell you. As soon as I was acquainted with the great favour you designed me, I thought it proper, considering your superior merit and excellency, to treat you, according to my ability, with something more choice and valuable than is usually given to other persons, when, calling to mind my hawk, which you now request, and his goodness, I judged him a fit repast for you, and you have had him served roasted on your dish. Nor could I have thought him better bestowed, had you not now desired him in a different manner, which is such a grief to me that I shall never be at peace as long as I live;" and upon saying this he produced his feathers, feet, and beak. She began now to blame him for killing such a bird to entertain any woman with, inwardly praising the greatness of his soul, which poverty had no power to abase. Thus, having no farther hopes of obtaining the hawk, she thanked him for the respect and good-will he had showed towards her, and returned full of concern to her son, who, either out of grief for the disappointment or through the violence of his disorder, died within a few days.

She continued sorrowful for some time; but, being left rich and young, her brothers were very pressing with her to marry again; and, though this were against her inclinations, yet, finding them still importunate, and remembering Federigo's great worth and the late instance of his generosity in killing such a bird for her entertainment, she said, "I should rather choose to continue as I am; but, since it is your desire that I take a husband, I will have none save Federigo degli Alberighi." They smiled contemptuously at this, and said, "You simple woman! what are you talking of? He is not worth one farthing in the world." She replied, "I believe it, brothers, to be as you say; but know that I would sooner have a man that stands in need of riches, than riches without a man." They, hearing her resolution, and well knowing his generous temper, gave her to him with all her wealth; and he, seeing himself possessed of a lady whom he had so dearly loved, and such a large fortune, lived in all true happiness with her, and was a better manager of his affairs for the time to come.

FRIAR ONION AND THE RELICS OF THE ANGEL GABRIEL

FOLLOWING your footsteps, I shall show you with what a sudden shift a certain friar, of the order of Saint Antony, most artfully avoided the disgrace which two arch young fellows had prepared for him: and if, to make my story more complete, I spin it out a little in length, I hope it will not be disagreeable, as the sun is yet in the midst of heaven.

Certaldo, as you have all heard, is a village in the vale of Elsa, dependent on the state of Florence; and, though small, was formerly inhabited by many gentlemen and people of substance. Thither a certain friar, known as Friar Onion, of the order of Saint Antony, used to go once a year, as he found pretty good pickings, to receive the contributions of many simple people, and met with great encouragement always—perhaps not through any devotion so much as his name, for that country was famous for the best onions in all Tuscany. Now this friar had a little low person, was red-haired and of a merry countenance, as artful a knave too as any in the world: add to this that, though he was no scholar, yet was he so prompt and voluble of tongue that such as knew him not would not only have considered him as some great orator, but have compared him even to Tully or Quintillian, and yet was he a common gossip-acquaintance to the whole neighborhood.

Coming thither, therefore, in the month of August, according to custom, one Sunday morning, when all the honest people were met together in the principal church to hear mass, as soon as he saw a fit opportunity, he stepped forward and said:—

"Gentlemen and ladies, you know it has been a commendable custom with you to send every year, to the poor brethren of our lord baron Saint Antony, both of your corn and other provisions, some more and some less, according to your several abilities and devotions, to the end that our blessed Saint Antony should be more careful of your oxen, sheep, asses, swine, and other cattle. Moreover, you are accustomed to pay, such especially as have their names registered in our fraternity, those small dues which are paid only once a year, to collect which I am now sent by my superior, namely, our lord abbot. Therefore, with the blessing of God, after twelve o'clock, as soon as you shall hear the bells ring, you may all come to the church-door, when I shall preach a sermon as usual, and you shall all kiss the cross: and, besides this, as I know you all to be devoted to our lord Saint Antony, I intend to show you by special grace a very fair and holy relic, which I myself brought from the Holy Land, that is to say, one of the feathers of the Angel Gabriel, which he dropped at the Annunciation in the Virgin's chamber at Nazareth;" and, having made this speech, he returned to mass.

Whilst he was haranguing upon this subject, there were two arch fellows in the church, one named Giovanni del Bragoniera, and the other Biagio Pizzini, who, after they had laughed together at the father's relics, although they were his friends and acquaintance, resolved to play him a trick with regard to this feather; and, understanding that he was to dine that day with a friend, as soon as they thought he might be set down at table they went to the inn where he lodged, where Biagio was to keep his man in talk, whilst Giovanni ransacked his wallet to steal this feather, that they might see what he would then say to the people.

Now the friar had a lad called by many nicknames —Guccio Balena, Guccio Imbratta, and sometimes Guccio Porco; and even the celebrated Lipotopo could hardly have caricatured his figure; but Father Onion used frequently to say in jest, "My rascal has in him nine qualities, if any one of which belonged either to Solomon, Aristotle, or Seneca, it would baffle and confound all their philosophy, and all their virtue. You may suppose then what sort of creature he must be that has nine such, without either philosophy or virtue to counterbalance." Being asked what those nine qualities were, and having put them into a kind of rhyme, he answered,

"Forgetfulness, lying, and lewdness;
Filching, facing, and nastiness;
Sloth, gracelessness, and worthlessness.

Besides these, he has also many others, and one in particular I cannot help laughing at, which is, that he is for taking a wife and a lodging wherever he goes; and, having a great black greasy beard, he is persuaded that all women must fall in love with him; or, should they take no notice of him, he will burst his belt in running after them. But yet he is a notable fellow to me in one respect, that if anybody has a secret to communicate, he will come in for his share of it; and, should any one ask me a question, he is so fearful that I should not know how to make an answer that he will be sure to say Yes or No before me, just as he thinks most proper."

But to return to our story. This worthy fellow Friar Onion left at the inn, with a particular charge to see that nobody meddled with anything belonging to him, especially his wallet, because the holy relics were contained therein. But the man, whose inclinations stood more for the kitchen than the birds for the branches, and especially if he knew some serving-maid were there, as soon as his master was gone went down thither, where he found a fat, dirty, big-breasted wench, with a face of the Baronci stamp, greasy and grimy, as attractive to him as carrion to a vulture. So, leaving his master's door open, and his things scattered about, and falling into discourse with her, he sat down by the fireside, though it was in August, whilst she was busy in cooking, and began to tell her he was a gentleman who was worth an incredible sum of money, and owed as much more; that he could do and say wonders; and (without considering that his own hat was all over grease and dirt, that his jacket was nothing but a thousand different patches, that his breeches were torn throughout, and his shoes all to pieces) he talked as finely as if he had been some lord, saying that he would buy her new clothes, and take her out of service, and that she should partake of his present posses-

sions, as well as future fortunes, with a great deal more of that kind of stuff, mere froth and wind.

The two young fellows, finding him thus engaged, were very well satisfied, supposing half their work to be done; and, leaving them together, they went upstairs into the friar's chamber, which, thanks to the servant, was open, when the first thing they saw was the wallet: this they opened, and found a cabinet wrapped up in some foldings of fine taffeta, in which was a parroquet's feather, which they supposed to be the same that he had promised to show the people; and surely at that time it was easy enough to impose upon them in that manner, for the vices which have since come from Egypt, and overspread all Italy, had not yet reached them; the ancient simplicity still prevailed, nor was there a person that, so far from seeing, had ever heard of such a thing as a parrot. Not a little pleased at meeting with this feather, they took it away, and, that the box should not be empty, put some coals therein, which they saw lying in a corner of the chamber; and wrapping it up again as before, and making all safe, they walked off, waiting to see how he would behave when he found the coals instead of the feather. The people that were at church, being told that they were to see the Angel Gabriel's feather, went home and acquainted all their neighbours, and the news ran from one to another, so that the moment dinner was over they all crowded to the town, in such manner that every part was full, waiting for the sight.

Accordingly, Friar Onion, having eaten a good dinner and swallowed his wine, and taken his nap, understanding now that there were great multitudes expecting him, sent to the servant to come away with his wallet, and ring to church. The fellow, though loth to leave his mistress and the fireside, did as he ordered him, and fell to chiming the bells. As soon then as the people were all assembled, the friar, not perceiving that anything had been meddled with, entered upon his discourse, running over a thousand things proper to his purpose; and being come to the showing of the feather, he began with a solemn confession, and lighting up two torches, and gently unwrapping the silken cover, having first pulled off his cap, he took out the box, and, making some short ejaculations to the praise and honour of the Angel Gabriel and of that relic, he opened it, when, seeing it full of coals, he could not help secretly blaming himself for leaving such a fellow in trust, who, he imagined, had been imposed upon by somebody or other; but yet, without so much as changing colour, or showing the least concern, he lifted up his eyes and hands to heaven, and said, "O God, blessed for ever be Thy power and might!" Then shutting the box, he turned again to the people, and added—

"Gentlemen and ladies, you must all understand

that, being very young, I was sent by my superior to those parts where the sun first appears, with an express command to inquire into the nature of porcelain, which, though it cost but little in making, affords more profit to others than it does to us. For this purpose I embarked at Venice, and went through the town of Greece; I proceeded thence on horseback through the kingdom of Garbo, and through Baldacca; afterwards I came to Parione, and so to Sardinia. But wherefore need I mention to you all these places? I coasted on still, till I passed the straits of Saint George, into Truffia, and then into Buffia, which are countries much inhabited, and with great people. From thence into the land of Menzogna, where I found many of our order, as well as of other religious, who avoid all labour and trouble, for Heaven's sake, taking no care for other people's sufferings, when their own interest is promoted thereby, and where they spend only uncoined money. Thence I went to the land of Abruzzi, where the men and women go on pattens over the mountains, clothing the swine in their own guts, and in the neighbouring country they carried bread in their staves, and wine in satchels. Parting from thence, I came to the mountains of Bacchus, where the waters all run down hill. Last of all, I arrived in India Pastinaca; where, I swear to you, by the habit I wear, that I saw serpents fly, a thing incredible to such as have never seen it: but, if you doubt the truth of this, ask Maso del Saggio, a great merchant, whom I found cracking nuts, and selling the shells by retail. Nevertheless, not being able to find what I went to look for, and being to pass from thence by water, I returned to the Holy Land, where, in the year of summer, a loaf of cold bread is worth fourpence, and the hot is given away for nothing. There I found the venerable father Blame-me-not-pray, the patriarch of Jerusalem, who, out of reverence to my habit, and love to our lord baron Saint Antony, would have me see all the holy relics which he had in keeping, and which were so many, that were I to recount them, I should never come to an end; but yet, not to leave you altogether disconsolate, I shall mention a few. First, then, he showed me a finger of the Holy Ghost, as whole and perfect as ever; next the muzzle of that seraph which appeared to Saint Francis; with one of the nails of a cherub; also a rib of the Verbum Caro, fastened to one of the windows; some fragments of the vestments of the Holy Catholic Faith; and a few rays of that star which appeared to the three kings who came out of the East; a phial also of Saint Michael's sweat, when he fought with the devil; the jaw-bone of Saint Lazarus, and many others. And because I gave him two of the plains of Mount Morello, in the vulgar edition, and some chapters of Del Caprezio, which he had been long searching after, he let me partake

of his relics. And, first, he gave me a tooth of the Holy Cross; and a little bottle filled with some of the sound of those bells which hung in the Temple of Solomon; a feather also of the Angel Gabriel, as I have told you; with a wooden patten, which the good Saint Gherardo da Villa Magna used to wear in his travels, and which I have lately given to Gherardo di Bonsi, at Florence, who holds it in great veneration. He farther gave me some of the coals on which our blessed martyr, Saint Laurence, was broiled, all which I devoutly received, and do now possess. It is true, my superior would not suffer me to make them public till he was assured that they were genuine; but being now convinced of it by sundry miracles, as well as by letters received from the patriarch, he has given me leave to show them; and these, for fear of trusting any one with them, I always carry with me. Indeed, I have the angel's feather, for its better preservation, in a wooden box, and I have Saint Laurence's coals in another, and these boxes are so like each other, that I have often mistaken them; and so it has happened now, for instead of that with the feather, I have brought the one which contains the coals. This I would not have you call an error; no, I am well assured it was Heaven's particular will, now I call to mind that two days hence is the feast of Saint Laurence. Therefore it was ordered that I should show you the most holy coals on which he was broiled, extinguished by the moisture of his holy body, to kindle in your hearts that true devotion which you ought to have towards him, and not the feather. Approach then, my blessed children, with reverence, and uncover your heads with all due devotion, whilst you behold them. But first I must acquaint you, that whoever is marked with these coals with the sign of the cross may live secure for one whole year that, unless he feel it, no fire shall have any power over him."

So, singing a hymn to the praise of Saint Laurence, he opened the box and showed the coals, which the simple multitude beheld with the utmost zeal and astonishment, and crowded about him with larger offerings than usual, entreating to be signed by them. Then taking the coals in his hand, he began to mark all their white mantles, fine jackets, and veils, with the largest crosses that could be made upon them, affirming that what was consumed of the coals in this manner grew again in the box, as he had frequently experienced. Thus having crossed all the people of Certaldo to his own great benefit, by this dexterous device, he laughed in his sleeve at those who had designed to have made a jest of him. And they being present at his discourse, and hearing this sudden shift of his, and how he had set it off to the multitude, were ready to die with laughter. After the people were all departed, they went and told him, with all the pleasure in the world, what they had done, and returned him his feather, which served him the following year to as good purpose as the coals had done that day.

THE CRADLE

IN the plain of Mugnone, not long since, lived an honest man who kept a little inn for the entertainment of travellers, serving them with meat and drink for their money, but seldom lodging any, unless they were his particular acquaintance. Now, he had a wife, a good comely woman, by whom he had two children, the one an infant, not yet weaned, and the other a pretty girl of about fifteen or sixteen years of age, but unmarried, who had taken the fancy of a young gentleman of our city, one who used to travel much that way; whilst she, proud of such a lover, and endeavouring, by her agreeable carriage, to preserve his good opinion, soon felt the same liking for him: which love of theirs would several times have taken effect, to the desire of both, had not Pinuccio—for that was the young gentleman's name—carefully avoided it, for her credit as well as his own. Till at last, his love growing every day more fervent, he resolved, in order to gain his point, to lie all night at her father's house, judging that the matter might then be effected without any one's privity. Accordingly he let into the secret a friend of his, named Adriano, who had been acquainted with his love; so they hired a couple of horses one evening, and having their portmanteaus behind them, filled with things of no moment, they set out from Florence, and, after taking a circuit, came, as it grew late, to the plain of Mugnone; then turning their horses, as if they had come from Romagna, they rode on to this cottage, and knocking at the door, the landlord, who was always very diligent in waiting upon his guests, immediately went and opened it. Pinuccio then accosted him, and said, "Honest landlord, we must beg the favour of a night's lodging, for we had designed to reach Florence, but have so mistaken that it is now much too late, as you see." The host replied, "Sir, you know very well how ill I can accommodate such gentlemen as yourselves; but, as you are come in at an unseasonable hour, and there is no time for your travelling any farther, I will entertain you as well as I can." So they dismounted, and went into the house, having first taken care of their horses; and, as they had provision along with them, they sat down and invited their host to sup with them.

Now there was only one little chamber in the house, which had three beds in it—namely, two at one end, and the third at the other, opposite to them, with just room to go between. The least bad

The Cradle. This amusing *falliau* was used by Chaucer for his *Reeve's Tale.*

and incommodious of the three the landlord ordered to be prepared for these two gentlemen, and put them to bed. A little time afterwards, neither of them being asleep, though they pretended it, he made his daughter lie in one of the beds that remained, and he and his wife went into the other, whilst she set the cradle with the child by her bedside. Things being so disposed, and Pinuccio having made an exact observation of every particular, as soon as he thought it a proper time, and that every one was asleep, he arose, and went softly to the bed of the daughter, and lay down beside her, she, though very fearful, receiving him joyfully, and so they took what pastime they pleased. In the meantime, a cat happened to throw something down in the house, which awakened the wife, who, fearing it was something else, got up in the dark, and went to find the cause of the noise. Adriano now rose by chance, upon a particular occasion, and finding the cradle in his way, he removed it, without any design, nearer to his own bed, and, having done what he rose for, went to bed again, without putting the cradle in its place. The good woman, finding what was thrown down to be of no moment, never troubled herself to strike a light, to see farther about it, but having driven away the cat, returned to the bed where her husband lay; and, not finding the cradle, "Bless me," she said to herself, "I had like to have made a strange mistake, and gone to bed to my guests!" Going farther then, and finding the cradle, which stood by Adriano, she stepped into bed to him, thinking it had been her husband. He was awake, and treated her very kindly, without saying a word all the time to undeceive her.

At length Pinuccio, fearing lest he should fall asleep, and so be surprised with his mistress, after having made the best use of his time, left her to return to his own bed, when meeting with the cradle, and supposing that was the host's bed, he went farther, and stepped into the host's bed indeed, who immediately awoke. Pinuccio, thinking it was his friend, said to him, "Surely, nothing was ever so sweet as Niccolosa; never man was so blessed as I have been with her; I can assure you that since I left you I have been well employed." The host, hearing this, and not liking it over well, said first to himself, "What the devil does this man mean?" Afterwards, being more passionate than wise, he cried out, "Thou art the greatest of villains to use me in that manner; but I vow to God I will pay thee for it." Pinuccio, who was none of the sharpest men in the world, seeing his mistake, without ever thinking how to amend it, as he might have done, replied, "You pay me? What can you do?" The hostess, imagining that she had been with her husband, said to Adriano, "Alas! dost thou hear our guests? What do they talk of?" He replied, with a laugh, "Let them talk as they will, and be hanged; they drank too much, I suppose, last night."

The woman now distinguishing her husband's voice, and hearing Adriano, soon knew where she was, and with whom. Therefore she very wisely got up, without saying a word, and removed the cradle, though there was no light in the chamber, as near as she could guess to her daughter's bed, and crept in to her; when, seeming as if she had been awak-
10 ened by her husband's noise, she called out to him, to know what was the matter with him and the gentleman. The husband replied, "Do not you hear what he says he has been doing to-night with our daughter?" "He lies in his throat," quoth she; "for he was never in bed with her; it was I, and I assure you I have never closed my eyes since; you are a great fool to think otherwise. You drink to that degree in the evening that you rave all night long, and walk up and down, without knowing anything
20 of the matter, and think you do wonders; it is a pity that you do not break your neck. But what is Pinuccio doing there? why is he not in his own bed?" Adriano, on the other side, perceiving that the good woman had found a very artful evasion both for herself and daughter, said, "Pinuccio, I have told you a hundred times that you should never lie out of your own house; for that great failing of yours, of walking in your sleep and telling your dreams for truth, will be of ill consequence to you some time
30 or other. Come here, then, to your own bed." The landlord hearing what his wife said, and what Adriano had just been speaking, began to think Pinuccio was really dreaming; so he got up and shook him by the shoulders to rouse him, saying, "Awake, and get thee to thine own bed."

Pinuccio, understanding what had passed, began now to ramble in his talk, like a man that was half asleep and dreaming, with which our host made himself vastly merry. At last when daylight came he
40 seemed to awake, after much ado; and, calling to Adriano, he said, "Is it day? what do you wake me for?" "Yes, it is," quoth he; "pray come hither." Then, pretending to be very sleepy, he got up at last, and went to Adriano. And in the morning the landlord laughed very heartily, and was full of jokes about him and his dreams. So they passed from one merry subject to another, whilst their horses were getting ready, and their portmanteaus trussed up, when, taking the host's parting cup, they mounted
50 and went to Florence, no less pleased with the manner in which the thing had happened than the way in which it had been effected.

Afterwards Pinuccio found other means of being with Niccolosa, who still affirmed to her mother that he had been asleep; whilst she, remembering how well she had fared with Adriano, thought herself the only person that had been awake on that occasion.

François Rabelais

c. 1495–1553

The Humanist emancipation of the natural man reaches its climax in the turbulent career, lawless writings, and militant individualism of Rabelais. His life story is one of continuous rebellion against the intellectual restraints of the Middle Ages, as he had known them through church schooling and a restless preparation for the clergy. The youngest son of an apothecary (or possibly an innkeeper), he chose a church career as almost the only one open to a poor boy with a keen desire for education. But his years at the Franciscan monastery of Fontenoy le Comte, where the monks, following the example of St. Francis, frowned upon learning as incompatible with humility, gave him a savage hatred of the order, and he was severely punished for secretly pursuing classical studies, especially Greek. When a powerful friend persuaded the Pope to transfer him to the more liberal Benedictine order, he still chafed under the monastic discipline and eventually freed himself from it entirely to become a secular priest.

His private studies went beyond the ancient classics to medicine, so that after six weeks of official work at the University of Montpellier he secured his medical degree in 1530 and became a lecturer on anatomy. Two years later he published Latin translations of the Greek textbooks on medicine by Hippocrates and Galen. But he neglected his duties on the medical faculty and was dismissed for absence without leave when he accompanied his friend, Jean du Bellay, on a political mission to Rome. He served as city physician in both Lyons and Metz, but apparently was dismissed from both jobs for irresponsibility and had to seek financial aid from Du Bellay, his patron. Eventually, perhaps because he needed funds to support an illegitimate son, he became a parish priest at Meudon, but he was as negligent here as he had been in his medical positions. Rabelais was much too reckless and carefree to submit to professional routine. Throughout his life he demanded complete freedom to pursue his whims and current enthusiasms. No other writer illustrates so well the lusty individualism of the Renaissance. He is said to have made his will in the form of a joke: "I possess nothing; the rest I give to the poor." He died drunk, and his last words were "Draw the curtain; the farce is ended."

But the legend of the great scoffer and laugher that has given the word "rabelaisian" to our language springs from his one important literary work, the huge extravaganza called *Gargantua and Pantagruel*, which he scribbled at odd hours during two stays at Montpellier, perhaps to repay the printer with a broadly popular book for his losses on the translations of Hippocrates and Galen. The result is a unique work, a kind of nonsense novel which half conceals its satire of medieval institutions, especially ecclesiastical education, monastic orders, and feudal wars, under a cloak of ribald fun and personal eccentricity. Like *Tristram Shandy* in a later age, it gushes forth the pranks and prejudices of a literary scalawag, without plan or even connected story. Although it purports to tell the lives of two great giants, father and son, the Pantagruel part was written before the first part, and the careers of the two genial monsters are merely a framework for Rabelais's whimsical learning, playful hoaxes, lists of nonsensical epithets, coarse profanity, parodies, and biting satire. Everything that interested this intense and reckless fellow turns up in his rambling narrative, linked together by a free association of ideas on the conversational level.

Certain characters stand out—the kindly Gargantua, inspired by a gigantic character in French Arthurian story, the benign Grandgousier who is forced into a senseless war with the foolishly arrogant Picrochole, the fighting Friar John of the Choppers, and the cunning, debauched buffoon Panurge, whose search for enlightenment about marriage is the chief theme of the last section. Through all the reckless humor of the piece runs Rabelais's boundless faith in human nature. It lies behind his satiric attack on the stultifying discipline of medieval education and motivates his account of the Abbey of Theleme, an ideal monastery devoted to Humanistic learning, where, instead of the usual monastic restrictions, the only rule is "Do what you want to." Read as a whole, *Gargantua and Pantagruel* is too strong and heaping a dish for modern taste, but the great passages conceal in rollicking, hearty fun a roughly noble plea for the dignity of man.

Gargantua and Pantagruel

BOOK ONE

THE AUTHOR'S PROLOGUE

MOST noble and illustrious drinkers, and you thrice precious pockified blades, (for to you, and none else do I dedicate my writings,) Alcibiades, in that dialogue of Plato's, which is entitled, *The Banquet,* whilst he was setting forth the praises of his schoolmaster, Socrates, (without all question the prince of philosophers,) amongst other discourses to that purpose said, that he resembled the Sileni. Sileni of old were little boxes, like those we now may see in the shops of apothecaries, painted on the outside with wanton toyish figures, as harpies, satyrs, bridled geese, horned hares, saddled ducks, flying goats, thiller harts, and other such counterfeited pictures, at pleasure, to excite people unto laughter, as Silenus himself, who was the foster-father of good Bacchus, was wont to do; but

Gargantua and Pantagruel. ᴬ Translated by Sir Thomas Urquhart.

within those capricious caskets called Sileni, were carefully preserved and kept many rich and fine drugs, such as balm, ambergreese, amomon, musk, civet, with several kinds of precious stones, and other things of great price. Just such another thing was Socrates: for to have eyed his outside, and esteemed of him by his exterior appearance, you would not have given the peel of an onion for him, so deformed he was in body, and ridiculous in his gesture. He had a sharp pointed nose, with the look of a bull, and countenance of a fool; he was in his carriage simple, boorish in his apparel, in fortune poor, unhappy in his wives, unfit for all offices in the commonwealth, always laughing, tippling, and merry, carousing to every one, with continual gibes and jeers, the better by those means to conceal his divine knowledge. Now, opening this box you would have found within it a heavenly and inestimable drug, a more than human understanding, an admirable virtue, matchless learning, invincible courage, inimitable sobriety, certain contentment of mind, perfect assurance, and an incredible disregard of all that for which men commonly do so much watch, run, sail, fight, travel, toil, and turmoil themselves.

Whereunto (in your opinion) doth this little flourish of a preamble tend? For so much as you, my good disciples, and some other jolly fools of ease and leisure, reading the pleasant titles of some books, of our invention, as Gargantua, Pantagruel, Whippot, the Dignity of Codpieces, of Pease and Bacon, with a commentary, &c., are too ready to judge, that there is nothing in them but jests, mockeries, lascivious discourse, and recreative lies; because the outside (which is the title) is usually, without any farther inquiry, entertained with scoffing and derision. But truly it is very unbeseeming to make so slight account of the works of men, seeing yourselves avouch that it is not the habit that makes the monk, many being monasterially accoutred, who inwardly are nothing less than monachal; and that there are of those that wear Spanish caps, who have but little of the valour of Spaniards in them. Therefore is it, that you must open the book, and seriously consider of the matter treated in it. Then shall you find that it containeth things of far higher value than the box did promise; that is to say, that the subject thereof is not so foolish, as by the title at the first sight it would appear to be.

And put the case, that in the literal sense you meet with purposes merry and solacious enough, and consequently very correspondent to their inscriptions, yet must not you stop there as at the melody of the charming Syrens, but endeavour to interpret that in a sublimer sense, which possibly you intended to have spoken in the jollity of your heart. Did you ever pick the lock of a cupboard to steal a bottle of wine out of it? Tell me truly, and, if you did, call to mind the countenance which then you had. Or, did you ever see a dog with a marrow-bone in his mouth,—the beast of all others, says Plato, lib. 2, de Republica, the most philosophical? If you have seen him, you might have remarked with what devotion and circumspectness he wards and watcheth it: with what care he keeps it: how fervently he holds it: how prudently he gobbets it: with what affection he breaks it: and with what diligence he sucks it. To what end all this? What moveth him to take all these pains? What are the hopes of his labour? What doth he expect to reap thereby? Nothing but a little marrow. True it is, that this little is more savoury and delicious than the great quantities of other sorts of meat, because the marrow, (as Galen testifieth, 3, facult. nat. and 11, de usu partium) is a nourishment most perfectly elaboured by nature.

In imitation of this dog, it becomes you to be wise to smell, feel, and have in estimation, these fair, goodly books, stuffed with high conceptions, which though seemingly easy in the pursuit, are in the cope and encounter somewhat difficult. And then, like him, you must, by a sedulous lecture, and frequent meditation, break the bone, and suck out the marrow; that is, my allegorical sense, or the things I to myself propose to be signified by these Pythagorical symbols; with assured hope, that in so doing, you will at last attain to be both well-advised and valiant by the reading of them: for, in the perusal of this treatise, you shall find another kind of taste, and a doctrine of a more profound and abstruse consideration, which will disclose unto you the most glorious doctrines and dreadful mysteries, as well in what concerneth our religion, as matters of the public state and life economical.

Do you believe, upon your conscience, that Homer, whilst he was couching his Iliads and Odysses, had any thought upon those allegories, which Plutarch, Heraclides, Ponticus, Eustathius, Cornutus, squeezed out of him, and which Politian filched again from them? If you trust it, with neither hand nor foot do you come near to my opinion, which judgeth them to have been as little dreamed of by Homer, as the gospel sacraments were by Ovid, in his Metamorphosis; though a certain gulligut friar, and true bacon-picker would have undertaken to prove it, if, perhaps, he had met with as very fools as himself, and as the proverb says, "a lid worthy of such a kettle."

If you give any credit thereto, why do not you the same to these jovial new Chronicles of mine? Albeit, when I did dictate them, I thought thereof no more than you, who possibly were drinking the whilst, as I was. For in the composing of this lordly book, I never lost nor bestowed any more, nor any other time, than what was appointed to serve me for taking of my bodily refection, that is, whilst I was eating and drinking. And, indeed, that is the fittest and most proper hour, wherein to write these high matters and deep sentences: as Homer knew very well, the paragon of all philologues, and Ennius, the father of the Latin poets, as Horace calls him, although a certain sneaking jobbernol alleged that his verses smelled more of the wine than oil.

So saith a Turlupin or a new start-up grub of my books; but a turd for him. The fragrant odour of the wine, oh! how much more dainty, pleasant, laughing, celestial, and delicious it is, than that smell of oil! and I will glory as much when it is said of me, that I have spent more on wine than oil, as did Demosthenes, when it was told him, that his expense on oil was greater than on wine. I truly hold it for an honour and praise to be called and reputed a frolic Gaulter and a Robin Goodfellow; for under this name am I welcome in all choice companies of Pantagruelists. It was upbraided to Demosthenes, by an envious, surly knave, that his Orations did smell like the sarpler, or wrapper of a foul and filthy oil vessel. For this cause interpret you all my deeds and sayings, in the perfectest sense; reverence the cheese-like brain that feeds you with these faire billevezees, and trifling jollities, and do what lies in you to keep me always merry. Be frolic now, my lads, cheer up your hearts, and joyfully read the rest, with all the ease of your body and profit of your reins. But hearken, joltheads, you viedazes, or dickens take ye, remember to drink a health to me for the favour again, and I will pledge you instantly, Tout ares-metys.

CHAPTER VII

After what manner Gargantua had his name given him, and how he tippled, bibbed, and curried the can

The good man Grangousier, drinking and making merry with the rest, heard the horrible noise which his son had made as he entered into the light of this world, when he cried out, Some drink, some drink, some drink; whereupon he said in French, Que *grand tu as* et souple le gousier! that is to say, How great and nimble a throat thou hast. Which the company hearing said, that verily the child ought to be called Gargantua; because it was the first word that after his birth his father had spoke, in imitation,

16. **Galen,** the Greek physician and philosopher (131–201). 40. **Ponticus,** a philosopher of the first century B.C., author of a treatise on Homer. **Eustathius,** twelfth-century author of a commentary on Homer. **Cornutus,** a Stoic philosopher of the first century A.D. 41. **Politian,** Angelo Poliziano (1454–1494), the Italian humanist.

66. **Turlupin,** French for a bad punster. 75. **Gaulter,** good companion. 89–90. **Tout ares-metys,** at once.

and at the example, of the ancient Hebrews; whereunto he condescended, and his mother was very well pleased therewith. In the mean while, to quiet the child, they gave him to drink a tirelarigot, that is, till his throat was like to crack with it; then was he carried to the font, and there baptized, according to the manner of good Christians.

Immediately thereafter were appointed for him seventeen thousand nine hundred and thirteen cows of the towns of Pautille and Brehemond, to furnish him with milk in ordinary, for it was impossible to find a nurse sufficient for him in all the country; considering the great quantity of milk that was requisite for his nourishment; although there were not wanting some doctors of the opinion of Scotus, who affirmed that his own mother gave him suck, and that she could draw out of her breasts one thousand four hundred two pipes, and nine pails of milk at every time.

Which indeed is not probable, and this point hath been found duggishly scandalous and offensive to tender ears, for that it savoured a little of heresy. Thus was he handled for one year and ten months; after which time, by the advice of physicians, they began to carry him, and then was made for him a fine little cart drawn with oxen, of the invention of Jan Denio, wherein they led him hither and thither with great joy; and he was worth the seeing, for he was a fine boy, had a burly physiognomy, and almost ten chins. . . . If he happened to be vexed, angry, displeased, or sorry, if he did fret, if he did weep, if he did cry, and what grievous quarter soever he kept, in bringing him some drink, he would be instantly pacified, reseated in his own temper, in a good humour again, and as still and quiet as ever. One of his governesses told me (swearing by her fig), how he was so accustomed to this kind of way, that, at the sound of pints and flagons, he would on a sudden fall into an ecstasy, as if he had then tasted of the joys of paradise; so that they, upon consideration of this, his divine complexion, would every morning, to cheer him up, play with a knife upon the glasses, on the bottles with their stopples, and on the pottle-pots with their lids and covers, at the sound whereof he became gay, did leap for joy, would loll and rock himself in the cradle, then nod with his head, monocordising with his fingers, and barytonising with his tail.

CHAPTER XII

Of Gargantua's Wooden Horses

Afterwards, that he might be all his lifetime a good rider, they made to him a fair great horse of wood, which he did make leap, curvet, yerk out behind,

15. **Scotus,** the Scottish scholastic theologian of the thirteenth century.

and skip forward, all at a time: to pace, trot, rack, gallop, amble, to play the hobby, the hackney gelding: go the gate of the camel, and of the wild ass. He made him also change his colour of hair, as the Monks of Coultibo (according to the variety of their holidays) use to do their clothes, from bay brown, to sorrel, daple-grey, mouse-dun, deer-colour, roan, cow-colour, gin-gioline, skued colour, piebald, and the colour of the savage elk.

Himself of a huge big post made a hunting nag, and another for daily service of the beam of a winepress: and of a great oak made up a mule, with a foot-cloth, for his chamber. Besides this, he had ten or twelve spare horses, and seven horses for post; and all these were lodged in his own chamber, close by his bed-side. One day the Lord of Breadinbag came to visit his father in great bravery, and with a gallant train: and at the same time, to see him, came likewise the Duke of Freemeale, and the Earl of Wetgullet. The house truly for so many guests at once was somewhat narrow, but especially the stables; whereupon the steward and harbinger of the said Lord Breadinbag, to know if there were any other empty stable in the house, came to Gargantua, a little young lad, and secretly asked him where the stables of the great horses were, thinking that children would be ready to tell all. Then he led them up along the stairs of the castle, passing by the second hall unto a broad great gallery, by which they entered into a large tower, and as they were going up at another pair of stairs, said the harbinger to the steward,—This child deceives us, for the stables are never on the top of the house. You may be mistaken, said the steward, for I know some places at Lyons, at the Basmette, at Chaisnon, and elsewhere, which have their stables at the very tops of the houses; so it may be, that behind the house there is a way to come to this ascent. But I will question with him further. Then said he to Gargantua, my pretty little boy, whither do you lead us? To the stable, said he, of my great horses. We are almost come to it, we have but three stairs to go up at. Then leading them along another great hall, he brought them into his chamber, and, closing the door, said unto them, this is the stable you ask for, this is my gennet, this is my gelding, this is my courser, and this is my hackney, and laid on them with a great lever. I will bestow upon you, said he, this Frizeland horse, I had him from Francfort, yet will I give him you; for he is a pretty little nag, and will go very well, with a tessel of goshawks, half a dozen of spaniels, and a brace of grey-hounds: thus are you king of the hares and partridges for all this winter. By St. John, said they, now we are paid, he hath gleeked us to some pur-

86–87. **which have . . . of the houses;** because here houses were built against the side of a steep hill.

pose, bobbed we are now for ever. I deny it, said he, he was not here above three days. Judge you now, whether they had most cause, either to hide their heads for shame, or to laugh at the jest. As they were going down again thus amazed, he asked them, will you have a whimwham? What is that, said they? It is, said he, five turds to make you a muzzle. To-day, said the steward, though we happen to be roasted, we shall not be burnt, for we are pretty well quipped and larded in my opinion. O my jolly dapper boy, thou has given us a gudgeon, I hope to see thee pope before I die. I think so, said he, myself; and then shall you be a puppy, and this gentle popinjay a perfect papelard, that is, dissembler. . . . Cocksbod, said the steward, we have met with a prater. Farewell, master tatler, God keep you, so goodly are the words which you come out with, and so fresh in your mouth, that it had need to be salted.

Thus going down in great haste, under the arch of the stairs they let fall the great lever, which he had put upon their backs; whereupon Gargantua said, what a devil! you are, it seems, but bad horsemen, that suffer your bilder to fail you, when you need him most. If you were to go from hence to Cahusac, whether had you rather ride on a gosling, or lead a sow in a leash? I had rather drink, said the harbinger. With this they entered into the lower hall, where the company was, and relating to them this new story, they made them laugh like a swarm of flies.

CHAPTER XVI

How Gargantua was sent to Paris, and of the huge Great Mare that he rode on; how she destroyed the Ox-Flies of the Beauce

In the same season Fayoles, the fourth King of Numidia, sent out of the country of Africa to Grangousier, the most hideous great mare that ever was seen, and of the strangest form, for you know well enough how it is said, that Africa always is productive of some new thing. She was as big as six elephants, and had her feet cloven into fingers, like Julius Cæsar's horse, with slouch-hanging ears, like the goats in Languedoc, and a little horn on her buttock. She was of a burnt sorel hue, with a little mixture of daple grey spots, but above all she had a horrible tail; for it was little more or less, than every whit as great as the steeple-pillar of St. Mark, besides Langes: and squared as that is, with tuffs,

and ennicroches or hair-plaits wrought within one another, no otherwise than as the beards are upon the ears of corn.

If you wonder at this, wonder rather at the tails of the Scythian rams, which weighed above thirty pounds each, and of the Surian sheep, who need, if Tenaud say true, a little cart at their heels to bear up their tail, it is so long and heavy. Your female lechers in the plain countries have no such tails. And she was brought by sea in three carricks and a brigantine into the harbour of Olone in Thalmondois. When Grangousier saw her, "Here is," said he "what is fit to carry my son to Paris. So now, in the name of God, all will be well. He will in times coming be a great scholar. If it were not, my masters, for the beasts, we should live like clerks. The next morning, after they drunk, you must understand, they took their journey; Gargantua, his pedagogue Ponocrates, and his train, and with them Eudemon the young page. And because the weather was fair and temperate, his father caused to be made for him a pair of dun boots; Babin calls them buskins. Thus did they merrily pass their time in travelling on their high way, always making good cheer, and were very pleasant till they came a little above Orleans, in which place there was a forest of five-and-thirty leagues long, and seventeen in breadth, or thereabouts. This forest was most horribly fertile and copious in dorflies, hornets, and wasps, so that it was a very purgatory for the poor mares, asses, and horses. But Gargantua's mare did avenge herself handsomely of all the outrages therein committed upon beasts of her kind, and that by a trick whereof they had no suspicion. For as soon as ever they were entered into the said forest, and that the wasps had given the assault, she drew out and unsheathed her tail, and therewith skirmishing, did so sweep them, that she overthrew all the wood alongst and athwart, here and there, this way and that way, longwise and sidewise, over and under, and felled every where the wood with as much ease, as the mower doth the grass, in such sort that never since hath there been there, neither wood, nor dorflies: for all the country was thereby reduced to a plain champagne field. Which Gargantua took great pleasure to behold, and said to his company no more but this, "Je trouve beau ce," I find this pretty; whereupon that country hath been ever since that time called Beauce. But all the breakfast the mare got that day, was but a little yawning and gaping, in memory whereof the gentlemen of Beauce do as yet to this day break their fast with gaping, which they find to be very good, and do spit the better for it. At last they came to Paris, where Gargantua refreshed himself two or three

---

1–2. **I deny it . . . days.** An idiomatic rejoinder, badly translated here. 32. **Fayoles.** Rabelais facetiously uses the names of his friends and acquaintances for his characters. 45. **Langes,** an old brick tower beside the Loire River.

52. **Tenaud;** who wrote of a trip to Cairo. 96. **Beauce;** the name is actually of ancient origin.

days, making very merry with his folks, and inquiring what men of learning there were then in the city, and what wine they drank there.

CHAPTER XVII

How Gargantua paid his welcome to the Parisians, and how he took away the great Bells of Our Lady's Church

Some few days after that they had refreshed themselves, he went to see the city, and was beheld of every body there with great admiration; for the people of Paris are so sottish, so badot, so foolish and fond by nature, that a juggler, a carrier of indulgences, a sumpter-horse, or mule with cymbals, or tinkling bells, a blind fiddler in the middle of a cross lane, shall draw a greater confluence of people together, than an Evangelical preacher. And they pressed so hard upon him, that he was constrained to rest himself upon the towers of Our Lady's Church. . . .

This done, he considered the great bells, which were in the said towers, and made them sound very harmoniously. Which whilst he was doing, it came into his mind, that they would serve very well for tingling Tantans, and ringing Campanels, to hang about his mare's neck, when she should be sent back to his father, as he intended to do, loaded with Brie cheese, and fresh herring. And indeed he forthwith carried them to his lodging. . . .

All the city was risen up in sedition, they being, as you know, upon any slight occasion, so ready to uproars and insurrections, that foreign nations wonder at the patience of the kings of France who do not by good justice restrain them from such tumultuous courses, seeing the manifold inconveniences which thence arise from day to day. Would to God, I knew the shop wherein are forged these divisions and factious combinations, that I might bring them to light in the confraternities of my parish! Believe for a truth, that the place wherein the people gathered together, were thus sulphured, hopurymated, and moiled, was called Nesle, where then was, but now is no more, the Oracle of Leucetia. There was the case proposed, and the inconvenience showed of the transporting of the bells. After they had well ergoted pro and con, they concluded in baralipton, that they should send the oldest and most sufficient of the faculty unto Gargantua, to signify unto him the great and horrible prejudice they sustain'd by the want of those bells. And notwithstanding the good reasons given in by some of the university, why this charge was fitter for an orator than a sophister, there was chosen for this purpose our Master Janotus de Bragmardo.

CHAPTER XVIII

How Janotus de Bragmardo was sent to Gargantua, to recover the Great Bells

Master Janotus, with his hair cut round like a dish à la Cæsarine, in his most antic accoutrement liripipionated with a graduate's hood, and, having sufficiently antidoted his stomach with oven marmalades, that is, bread and holy water of the cellar, transported himself to the lodging of Gargantua, driving before him three red muzzled beadles, and dragging after him five or six artless masters, all thoroughly bedraggled with the mire of the streets. At their entry Ponocrates met them, who was afraid, seeing them so disguised, and thought they had been some maskers out of their wits, which moved him to inquire of one of the said artless masters of the company, what this mummery meant? It was answered him, that they desired to have their bells restored to them. As soon as Ponocrates heard that, he ran in all haste to carry the news unto Gargantua, that he might be ready to answer them, and speedily resolve what was to be done. Gargantua being advertised hereof, called apart his schoolmaster Ponocrates, Philotimus steward of his house, Gymnastes his esquire, and Eudemon, and very summarily conferred with them, both of what he should do, and what answer he should give. They were all of opinion that they should bring them unto the goblet-office, which is the buttery, and there make them drink like roysters, and line their jackets soundly. And that this cougher might not be puft up with vain glory, by thinking the bells were restored at his request, they sent, whilst he was chopining and plying the pot, for the major of the city, the rector of the faculty, and the vicar of the church, unto whom they resolved to deliver the bells, before the sophister had propounded his commission. After that, in their hearing, he should pronounce his gallant oration, which was done; and they being come, the sophister was brought in full hall, and began as followeth, in coughing.

CHAPTER XIX

The Oration of Master Janotus de Bragmardo, for the recovery of the Bells

Hem, hem, gud-day, sirs, gud-day. Et vobis, my masters. It were but reason that you should restore to us our bells; for we have great need of them. Hem, hem, aihfuhash. We have often-times heretofore refused good money for them of those of London, in Cahors, yea and those of Bourdeaux in Brie, who would have bought them for the substantific quality of the elementary complexion, which is intronificated in the terrestreity of their quidditative nature, to extraneize the blasting mists, and whirlwinds upon our vines, indeed not ours, but these round about us. For if we lose the piot and liquor of the grape, we lose all, both sense and law. If you restore them unto us at my request, I shall gain it by six baskets full of sausages, and a fine pair of breeches, which will do my legs a great deal of good, or else they will not keep their promise to me. Ho by gob, Domine, a pair of breeches is good, et vir sapiens non abhorrebit eam. Ha, ha, a pair of breeches is not so easily got; I have experience of it myself. Consider, Domine, I have been these eighteen days in matagrabolising this brave speech. Reddite quæ sunt Cæsaris, Cæsari, et quæ sunt Dei, Deo. Ibi jacet lepus. By my faith, Domine, if you will sup with me in cameris, by cox body, charitatis, nos faciemus bonum cherubin. Ego occidi unum porcum, et ego habet bonum vino: but of good wine we cannot make bad Latin. Well, de parte Dei date nobis bellas nostras. Hold, I give you in the name of the faculty a Sermones de Utino, that utinam you will give us our bells. Vultis etiam pardonos? Per diem vos habebitis, et nihil payabitis.

O Sir, Domine, bellagivaminor nobis; verily, est bonum urbis. They are useful to everybody. If they fit your mare well, so do they do our faculty; quæ comparata est jumentis insipientibus, et similis facta est eis, Psalmo nescio quo. Yet did I quote it in my note-book, et est unum bonum Achilles, a good defending argument. Hem, hem, hem, haikhash! For I prove unto you that you should give me them. Ego sic argumentor. Omnis bella bellabilis in bellerio bellando, bellans bellativo, bellare facit, bellabiliter bellantes. Parisius habet bellas. Ergo gluc. Ha, ha, ha. This is spoken to some purpose. It is in tertio primæ, in Darii, or elsewhere. By my soul, I have seen the time that I could play the devil in arguing, but now I am much failed, and henceforward want nothing but a cup of good wine, a good bed, my back to the fire, my belly to the table, and a good deep dish. Hei, Domine, I beseech you, in nomine Patris, Filii, et Spiritûs Sancti, Amen, to restore unto us our bells: and God keep you from evil, and our Lady from health, qui vivit et regnat per omnia secula seculorum, Amen. Hem, hashchehhawksash, qzrchremhemhash.

Verum enim vero, quandoquidem, dubio procul. Edepol, quoniam, ita certe, meus deus fidius; a town without bells is like a blind man without a staff, an ass without a crupper, and a cow without cymbals. Therefore be assured, until you have restored them unto us, we will never leave crying after you, like a blind man that hath lost his staff, braying like an ass without a crupper, and making a noise like a cow without cymbals. A certain Latinisator, dwelling near the hospital, said once, producing the authority of one Taponus,—I lie, it was one Pontanus the secular poet,—who wished those bells had been made of feathers, and the clapper of a foxtail, to the end that they might have begot a chronicle in the bowels of his brain, when he was about the composing of his carminiformal lines. But nac petetin petetac, tic, torche lorgne, or rot kipipur kipipot put pantse malf, he was declared an heretic. We make them as of wax. And no more saith the dependent. Valete et plaudite. Calepinus recensui.

CHAPTER XX

How the Sophister carried away his cloth

The sophister had no sooner ended, but Ponocrates and Eudemon burst out into a laughing so heartily, that they had almost split with it, and given up the ghost, in rendering their souls to God: even just as Crassus did, seeing a lubberly ass eat thistles; and as Philemon, who, for seeing an ass eat those figs which were provided for his own dinner, died with force of laughing. Together with them Master Janotus fell a-laughing too as fast as he could, in which mood of laughing they continued so long, that their eyes did water by the vehement concussion of the substance of the brain, by which these lachrymal humidities, being prest out, glided through the optic nerves, and so to the full represented Democritus Heraclitising, and Heraclitus Democritising.

When they had done laughing, Gargantua consulted with the prime of his retinue, what should be done. There Ponocrates was of opinion, that they should make this fair orator drink again; and seeing he had showed them more pastime, and made them laugh more than a natural fool could have done, that they should give him ten baskets full of sausages, mentioned in his pleasant speech, with a pair of hose, three hundred great billets of logwood, five and twenty hogsheads of wine, a good large down bed, and a deep capacious dish, which he said were necessary for his old age. All this was done as they did appoint. . . .

CHAPTER XXI

The Study of Gargantua, according to the discipline of his School-masters and Sophisters

The first day being thus spent, and the bells put up again in their own place, the citizens of Paris, in acknowledgment of this courtesy, offered to maintain and feed his mare as long as he pleased, which Gar-

72–73. **Crassus, Philemon**, a Roman politician and an Athenian playwright, both remembered in incidents of laughing. 81–82. **Democritus . . . Democritising.** Democritus was called the laughing philosopher and Heraclitus the weeping philosopher.

gantua took in good part, and they sent her to graze in the forest of Biere. I think she is not there now. This done, he with all his heart submitted his study to the discretion of Ponocrates; who for the beginning appointed that he should do as he was accustomed, to the end he might understand by what means, in so long time, his old masters had made him so sottish and ignorant. He disposed therefore of his time in such fashion, that ordinarily he did awake between eight and nine a clock, whether it was day or not, for so had his ancient governors ordained, alleging that which David saith, Vanum est vobis ante lucem surgere. Then did he tumble and toss, wag his legs, and wallow in the bed some time, the better to stir up and rouse his vital spirits, and appareled himself according to the season: but willingly he would wear a great long gown of thick frieze, furred with fox skins. Afterwards he combed his head with an Alman comb, which is the four fingers and the thumb. For his preceptor said, that to comb himself other ways, to wash and make himself neat, was to lose time in this world. Then he dunged, pist, spued, belched, cracked, yawned, spitted, coughed, yexed, sneezed, and snotted himself like an arch-deacon, and to suppress the dew and bad air, went to breakfast, having some good fried tripe, fair rashers on the coals, excellent gammons of bacon, store of fine minced meat, and a great deal of sippit brewis, made-up of the fat of the beef-pot, laid upon bread, cheese, and chopped parsley stewed together. Ponocrates showed him, that he ought not eat so soon after rising out of his bed, unless he had performed some exercise beforehand. Gargantua answered, what! have not I sufficiently well exercised myself? I have wallowed and rolled myself six or seven turns in my bed, before I rose. Is not that enough? Pope Alexander did so, by the advice of a Jew his physician, and lived till his dying day in despite of his enemies. My first masters have used me to it, saying that to breakfast made a good memory, and therefore they drank first. I am very well after it, and dine but the better. And Master Tubal, who was the first licenciate at Paris, told me, that it was not enough to run a pace, but to set forth betimes: so doth not the total welfare of our humanity depend upon perpetual drinking in a ribble rabble, like ducks, but on drinking early in the morning; unde versus,

> To rise betimes is no good hour,
> To drink betimes is better sure.

After he had thoroughly broke his fast, he went to church, and they carried him in a great basket, a huge impantoufled or thick covered breviary, weigh-

12–13. **Vanum . . . surgere,** "It is vain for you to get up before daylight." (Psalms 127:2) 37–38. **a Jew his physician,** Bonnet de Lates, physician to Alexander VI.

ing, what in grease, clasps, parchment, and cover, little more or less than eleven hundred and six pounds. There he heard six and twenty or thirty masses. This while, to the same place came his orison-mutterer impaletocked, or lapped up about the chin, like a tufted whoop, and his breath antidoted with the store of the vine-tree-sirup. With him he mumbled all his kiriels, and dunsicals breborions, which he so curiously thumbed and fingered, that there fell not so much as one grain to the ground. As he went from the church, they brought him, upon a dray drawn with oxen, a confused heap of pater-nosters and aves of Sanct Claude, every one of them being of the bigness of a hat-block; and thus walking through the cloisters, galleries or garden, he said more in turning them over, than sixteen hermits would have done. Then did he study some paltry half hour with his eyes fixed upon his book; but as the comic saith, his mind was in the kitchen. He sat down at table; and because he was naturally phlegmatic, he began his meal with some dozens of gammons, dried neat's tongues, hard rows of mullet, called botargos, andouilles, or sausages, and such other forerunners of wine. In the mean while, four of his folks did cast into his mouth one after another continually mustard by whole shovels full. Immediately after that, he drank a horrible draught of white-wine for the ease of his kidneys. When that was done, he ate according to the season meat agreeable to his appetite, and then left off eating when his belly began to strout, and was like to crack for fulness. As for his drinking, he had neither end nor rule. For he was wont to say that the limits and bounds of drinking were, when the cork of the shoes of him that drinketh swelleth up half a foot high.

CHAPTER XXIII

How Gargantua was instructed by Ponocrates, and in such sort disciplinated, that he lost not one hour of the day

When Ponocrates knew Gargantua's vicious manner of living, he resolved to bring him up in another kind; but for a while he bore with him, considering that nature cannot endure such a change, without great violence. Therefore to begin his work the better, he requested a learned physician of that time, called Master Theodorus, seriously to perpend, if it were possible, how to bring Gargantua unto a better course. The said physician purged him canonically with Anticyrian-hellebore, by which medicine he cleansed all the alteration, and perverse habitude of his brain. By this means also Ponocrates made him forget all that he had learned under his ancient preceptors, as Timotheus did to his disciples, who had

61. **kiriels,** kyrie eleison, litanies. 102. **Timotheus,** the Greek musician of the fourth century B.C.

been instructed under other musicians. To do this better, they brought him into the company of learned men, which were there, in whose imitation he had a great desire and affection to study otherwise, and to improve his parts. Afterwards he put himself into such a road and way of studying that he lost not any one hour in the day, but employed all his time in learning, and honest knowledge. Gargantua awak'd them about four o'clock in the morning. Whilst they were in rubbing of him, there was read unto him some chapter of the Holy Scripture aloud and clearly, with a pronunciation fit for the matter, and hereunto was appointed a young page born in Basché, named Anagnostes. According to the purpose and argument of that lesson, he oftentimes gave himself to worship, adore, pray, and send up his supplications to that good God, whose word did show his majesty and marvellous judgment. Then went he into the secret places to make excretion of his natural digestions. There his master repeated what had been read, expounding unto him the most obscure and difficult points. In returning, they considered the face of the sky, if it was such as they had observed it the night before, and into what signs the sun was entering, as also the moon for that day. This done, he was appareled, combed, curled, trimmed and perfumed, during which time they repeated to him the lessons of the day before. He himself said them by heart, and upon them would ground some practical cases concerning the estate of man, which he would prosecute sometimes two or three hours, but ordinarily they ceased as soon as he was fully clothed. Then for three good hours he had a lecture read unto him. This done, they went forth, still conferring of the substance of the lecture, either unto a field near the university called the Brack, or unto the meadows where they played at the ball, the long-tennis, and at the pile trigone, most gallantly exercising their bodies, as formerly they had done their minds. All their play was but in liberty, for they left off when they pleased, and that was commonly when they did sweat over all their body, or were otherwise weary. Then were they very well wiped and rubbed, shifted their shirts, and walking soberly, went to see if dinner was ready. Whilst they stayed for that, they did clearly and eloquently pronounce some sentences that they had retained of the lecture. In the meantime Master Appetite came, and then very orderly sat they down at table. At the beginning of the meal, there was read some pleasant history of the warlike actions of former times, until he had taken a glass of wine. Then, if they thought good, they continued reading, or began to discourse merrily together; speaking first of the virtue, propriety, efficacy and nature of all that was served in at that table; of bread, of wine, of water, of salt, of

38. pile trigone, a ball game for three players.

fleshes, fishes, fruits, herbs, roots, and of their dressing. By means whereof, he learned in a little time all the passages competent for this, that were to be found in Pliny, Athenæus, Dioscorides, Julius Pollux, Galen, Porphyrius, Oppian, Polybius, Heliodorus, Aristotle, Ælian, and others. Whilst they talked of these things, many times, to be the more certain, they caused the very books to be brought to the table, and so well and perfectly did he in his memory retain the things above said, that in that time there was not a physician that knew half so much as he did. Afterwards they conferred of the lessons read in the morning, and, ending their repast with some conserve or marmalade of quinces, he picked his teeth with mastic tooth-pickers, washed his hands and eyes with fair fresh water, and gave thanks unto God in some fine canticks, made in praise of the divine bounty and munificence. This done, they brought in cards, not to play, but to learn a thousand pretty tricks, and new inventions, which were all grounded upon arithmetic. By this means he fell in love with that numerical science, and every day after dinner and supper he passed his time in it as pleasantly, as he was wont to do at cards and dice: so that at last he understood so well both the theory and practical part thereof, that Tunstal the Englishman, who had written very largely of that purpose, confessed that verily in comparison of him he had no skill at all. And not only in that, but in the other mathematical sciences, as geometry, astronomy, music, &c. For in waiting on the concoction, and attending the digestion of his food, they made a thousand pretty instruments and geometrical figures, and did in some measure practice the astronomical canons.

After this they recreated themselves with singing musically, in four or five parts, or upon a set theme or ground at random, as it best pleased them. In matter of musical instruments, he learned to play upon the lute, the virginals, the harp, the Allman flute with nine holes, the violin, and the sackbut. This hour thus spent, and digestion finished, he did purge his body of natural excrements, then betook himself to his principal study for three hours together, or more, as well to repeat his matutinal lectures, as to proceed in the book wherein he was, as also to write handsomely, to draw and form the antique and Roman letters. This being done, they went out of their house, and with them a young gentleman of Touraine, named the Esquire Gymnast, who taught him the art of riding. Changing then his clothes, he rode a Naples courser, Dutch roussin, a Spanish gennet, a barbed or trapped steed, then a light fleet horse, unto whom he gave a hundred carieres, made him go the high saults, bounding in the air, free a ditch with a skip, leap over a stile or

82–83. Tunstal the Englishman, sixteenth-century churchman.

pale, turn short in a ring both to the right and left hand. There he broke not his lance; for it is the greatest foolery in the world to say, I have broken ten lances at tilts or in fight. A carpenter can do even as much. But it is a glorious and praiseworthy action, with one lance to break and overthrow ten enemies. Therefore with a sharp, stiff, strong, and well-steeled lance, would he usually force up a door, pierce a harness, beat down a tree, carry away the ring, lift up a cuirassier saddle, with the mail-coat and gauntlet. All this he did in complete arms from head to foot. As for the prancing flourishes, and smacking popisms, for the better cherishing of the horse, commonly used in riding, none did them better than he. The voltiger of Ferrara was but as an ape compared to him. He was singularly skilful in leaping nimbly from one horse to another without putting foot to ground, and these horses were called desultories. He could likewise from either side, with a lance in his hand, leap on horseback without stirrups, and rule the horse at his pleasure without a bridle, for such things are useful in military engagements. Another day he exercised the battle-axe, which he so dexterously wielded, both in the nimble, strong, and smooth management of that weapon, and that in all the feats practiceable by it, that he passed knight of arms in the field, and at all essays.

Then tossed he the pike, played with the two-handed sword, with the back sword, with the Spanish tuck, the dagger, poniard, armed, unarmed, with a buckler, with a cloak, with a target. Then would he hunt the hart, the roebuck, the bear, the fallow deer, the wild boar, the hare, the pheasant, the partridge and the bustard. He played at the balloon, and made it bound in the air, both with fist and foot. He wrestled, ran, jumped, not at three steps and a leap, called the hops, nor at clochepied, called the hare's leap, nor yet at the Almanes; for, said Gymnast, these jumps are for the wars altogether unprofitable, and of no use: but at one leap he would skip over a ditch, spring over a hedge, mount six paces upon a wall, ramp and grapple after this fashion up against a window, of the full height of a lance. He did swim in deep waters on his belly, on his back, sideways, with all his body, with his feet only, with one hand in the air, wherein he held a book, crossing thus the breadth of the River Seine, without wetting, and dragging along his cloak with his teeth, as did Julius Cæsar; then with the help of one hand he entered forcibly into a boat, from whence he cast himself again headlong into the water, sounded the depths, hollowed the rocks, and plunged into the pits and gulfs. Then turned he the boat about, governed it, led it swiftly or slowly with the stream and against the stream, stopped it in his

course, guided it with one hand, and with the other laid hard about him with a huge great oar, hoisted the sail, hied up along the mast by the shrouds, ran upon the edge of the decks, set the compass in order, tackled the bowlines, and steered the helm. Coming out of the water, he ran furiously up against a hill, and with the same alacrity and swiftness ran down again. He climbed up trees like a cat, leaped from the one to the other like a squirrel. He did pull down the great boughs and branches, like another Milo; then with two sharp well-steeled daggers, and two tried bodkins, would he run up by the wall to the very top of a house like a rat; then suddenly come down from the top to the bottom with such an even composition of members, that by the fall he would catch no harm.

He did cast the dart, throw the bar, put the stone, practise the javelin, the boar spear or partisan, and the halbert. He broke the strongest bows in drawing, bended against his breast the greatest cross-bows of steel, took his aim by the eye with the hand-gun, and shot well, traversed and planted the cannon, shot at but-marks, at the papgay from below upwards, or to a height from above downwards, or to a descent; then before him sidewise, and behind him, like the Parthians. They tied a cable-rope to the top of a high tower, by one end whereof hanging near the ground he wrought himself with his hands to the very top; then upon the same tract came down so sturdily and firm that you could not on a plain meadow have run with more assurance. They set up a great pole fixed upon two trees. There would he hang by his hands, and with them alone, his feet touching at nothing, would go back and fore along the aforesaid rope with so great swiftness, that hardly could one overtake him with running; and then, to exercise his breast and lungs, he would shout like all the devils in hell. I heard him once call Eudemon from St. Victor's gate to Montmartre. Stentor never had such a voice at the siege of Troy. Then for the strengthening of his nerves or sinews, they made him two great sows of lead, each of them weighing eight thousand and seven hundred quintals, which they called Alteres. Those he took up from the ground, in each hand one, then lifted them up over his head, and held them so without stirring three quarters of an hour or more, which was an inimitable force. He fought at barriers with the stoutest and most vigorous champions; and when it came to the cope, he stood so sturdily on his feet, that he abandoned himself unto the strongest, in case they could remove him from his place, as Milo was wont to do of old. In whose imitation likewise

15. **Ferrara,** Cesare Fieschi of Ferrara, a celebrated horseman (*voltigeur*).

65. **Milo,** the Greek athlete, famous for his feats of strength. 78. **papgay,** a popinjay, or target in the form of a parrot. 95. **Stentor,** the herald with the loud voice, from whose name the English "stentorian" is derived. 99. **Alteres,** weights like dumbbells.

he held a pomegranate in his hand, to give it unto him that could take it from him. The time being thus bestowed, and himself rubbed, cleansed, wiped, and refreshed with other clothes, he returned fair and softly; and passing through certain meadows, or other grassy places, beheld the trees and plants, comparing them with what is written of them in the books of the ancients, such as Theophrast, Dioscorides, Marinus, Pliny, Nicander, Macer, and Galen, and carried home to the house great handfuls of them, whereof a young page called Rizotomos had charge; together with little mattocks, pickaxes, grubbing hooks, cabbies, pruning knives, and other instruments requisite for herborising. Being come to their lodging, whilst supper was making ready, they repeated certain passages of that which had been read, and then sat down at table. Here remark, that his dinner was sober and thrifty, for he did then eat only to prevent the gnawings of his stomach, but his supper was copious and large; for he took then as much as was fit to maintain and nourish him; which indeed is the true diet prescribed by the art of good and sound physic, although a rabble of loggerheaded physicians, muzzled in the brabbling shop of sophisters, counsel the contrary. During that repast was continued the lesson read at dinner as long as they thought good: the rest was spent in good discourse, learned and profitable. After that they had given thanks, he set himself to sing vocally, and play upon harmonious instruments, or otherwise passed his time at some pretty sports, made with cards and dice, or in practising the feats of legerdemain with cups and balls. There they staid some nights in frolicking thus, and making themselves merry till it was time to go to bed; and on other nights they would go make visits unto learned men, or to such as had been travellers in strange and remote countries. When it was full night before they retired themselves, they went unto the most open place of the house to see the face of the sky, and there beheld the comets, if any were, as likewise the figures, situations, aspects, oppositions and conjunctions of both the fixed stars and planets.

Then with his master did he briefly recapitulate, after the manner of the Pythagoreans, that which he had read, seen, learned, done and understood in the whole course of that day.

Then prayed they unto God the Creator, in falling down before him, and strengthening their faith towards him, and glorifying him for his boundless bounty; and, giving thanks unto him for the time that was past, they recommended themselves to his divine clemency for the future. Which being done, they went to bed, and betook themselves to their repose and rest.

[Gargantua is called home by his father.]

CHAPTER XXXVIII

How Gargantua did eat up six Pilgrims in a sallad

The story requireth, that we relate that which happened unto six pilgrims, who came from Sebastian near to Nantes: and who for shelter that night had hid themselves in the garden upon the chichling peas, among the cabbages and lettuces. Gargantua finding himself somewhat dry, asked whether they could get any lettuce to make him a sallad; and hearing that there were the greatest and fairest in the country, for they were as great as plum-trees, or as walnut-trees, he would go thither himself, and brought thence in his hand what he thought good, and withal carried away the six pilgrims, who were in so great fear, that they did not dare to speak nor cough. Washing them, therefore, first at the fountain, the pilgrims said one to another softly, What shall we do? We are almost drowned here amongst these lettuce, shall we speak? But if we speak he will kill us. And, as they were thus deliberating what to do, Gargantua put them with the lettuce into a platter of the house, as large as the huge tun of the White Friars of the Cistertian order; which done, with oil, vinegar, and salt, he ate them up, to refresh himself a little before supper, and had already swallowed up five of the pilgrims, the sixth being in the platter, totally hid under a lettuce, except his bourbon or staff that appeared, and nothing else. Which Grangousier seeing, said to Gargantua, I think that is the horn of a shell snail, do not eat it. Why not, said Gargantua, they are good all this month: which he no sooner said, but, drawing up the staff, and therewith taking up the pilgrim, he ate him very well, then drank a terrible draught of excellent white wine. The pilgrims, thus devoured, made shift to save themselves as well as they could, by drawing their bodies out of the reach of the grinders of his teeth, but could not escape from thinking they had been put in the lowest dungeon of a prison. And when Gargantua whiffed the great draught, they thought to have drowned in his mouth, and the flood of wine had almost carried them away into the gulf of his stomach. Nevertheless, skipping with their bourbons, as St. Michael's palmers use to do, they sheltered themselves from the danger of that inundation under the banks of his teeth. But one of them by chance, groping or sounding the country with his staff, to try whether they were in safety or no, struck hard against the cleft of a hollow tooth, and hit the mandibulary sinew or nerve of the jaw, which put Gargantua to very great pain, so that he began to cry

75–76. **as large as . . . Cistertian order.** The friars' great tun allegedly had a capacity of 300 hogsheads. 97. **as St. Michael's palmers use to do;** pilgrims to Mont St. Michel had to leap over the quicksands between the mount and the coast.

for the rage that he felt. To ease himself therefore of his smarting ache, he called for his tooth-picker, and rubbing towards a young walnut-tree, where they lay skulking, unnestled you my gentlemen pilgrims.

For he caught one by the legs, another by the scrip, another by the pocket, another by the scarf, another by the band of the breeches, and the poor fellow that had hurt him with the bourbon, him he hooked to him by the codpiece, which snatch never-theless did him a great deal of good, for it pierced unto him a pocky botch he had in the groin, which grievously tormented him ever since they were past Ancenis. The pilgrims thus dislodged, ran away thwart the plain a pretty fast pace, and the pain ceased, even just at the time when by Eudemon he was called to supper. . . .

CHAPTER XXXIX

How the Monk was feasted by Gargantua, and of the jovial discourse they had at supper

There was then in the abbey a claustral monk, called Friar John of the funnels and gobbets, in French, des Entommeures, young, gallant, frisk, lusty, nimbly, quick, active, bold, adventurous, reso-lute, tall, lean, wide-mouthed, long-nosed, a fair

A caricature of Friar John with his breviary. From the "Droll Dreams of Pantagruel" published in Paris in 1565.

despatcher of morning prayers, unbridler of masses, and runner over vigils; and, to conclude summarily in a word, a right monk, if ever there was any, since the monking world monked a monkery: for the rest, a clerk even to the teeth in matter of breviary. . . .

Then Gargantua desired that he might be pres-ently sent for, to the end that with him they might consult of what was to be done. Whereupon, by a joint consent, his steward went for him, and brought him along merrily, with his staff of the cross, upon Grangousier's mule. When he was come, a thousand huggings, a thousand embracements, a thousand good days were given. Ha, Friar John, my friend, Friar John, my brave cousin, Friar John from the devil! Let me clip thee, my heart, about the neck; to me an armsful. I must gripe thee, my ballock, till thy back crack with it. Come, my cod, let me coll thee till I kill thee. And Friar John, the gladdest man in the world, never was man made welcomer, never was any more courteously and graciously received than Friar John. Come, come, said Gargantua, a stool here close by me at this end. I am content, said the monk, seeing you will have it so. Some water, page; fill, my boy, fill, it is to refresh my liver. Give me some, child, to gargle my throat withal. Deposita cappà, said Gymnast, let us pull off this frock. Ho, by G—, gentlemen, said the monk, there is a chapter in Statutis Ordinis, which opposeth my laying of it down. Pish! said Gymnast, a fig for your chapter! This frock breaks both your shoulders, put it off. My friend, said the monk, let me alone with it; for, by G—, I'll drink the better that it is on. It makes all my body jocund. If I should lay it aside, the waggish pages would cut to themselves garters out of it as I was once served at Coulaines. And, which is worse, I shall lose my appetite. But if in this habit I sit down at table, I will drink, by G—, both to thee and to thy horse, and so, courage, frolic, God save the com-pany! I have already supped, yet will I eat never a whit the less for that: for I have a paved stomach, as hollow as a butt of malvasie, or St. Benedictus' boot, and always open like a lawyer's pouch. Of all fishes, but the tench, take the wing of a partridge, or the thigh of a nun. Doth not he die like a good fel-low that dies with a stiff catso? Our prior loves ex-ceedingly the white of a capon. In that, said Gymnast, he doth not resemble the foxes: for of the capons, hens, and pullets, which they carry away, they never eat the white. Why, said the monk? Be-cause, said Gymnast, they have no cooks to dress them; and, if they be not competently made ready, they remain red and not white; the redness of meats being a token that they have not got enough of the fire, whether by boiling, roasting, or otherwise, ex-cept shrimps, lobsters, crabs, and cray-fishes, which

46-47. **Deposita cappà,** a rubric in the ritual, indicating where the priest should take off his cope.

are cardinalised with boiling. By God's feast-gazers, said the monk, the porter of our abbey, then, hath not his head well boiled, for his eyes are as red as a mazer made of an alder-tree. The thigh of this leveret is good for those that have the gout. . . .

Diavolo, is there no more must? No more sweet wine? Germinavit radix Jesse. Je renie ma vie, j'enrage de soif; I renounce my life, I rage for thirst. This wine is none of the worst. What wine drink you at Paris? I give myself to the devil, if I did not once keep open house at Paris for all comers six months together. Do you know Friar Claud of the High Kilderkins? Oh the good fellow that he is! But I do not know what fly hath stung him of late, he is become so hard a student. For my part, I study not at all. In our abbey we never study for fear of the mumps, which disease in horses is called the mourning in the chine. Our late abbot was wont to say, that it is a monstrous thing to see a learned monk. By G——, master, my friend. Magis magnos clericos non sunt magis magnos sapientes. You never saw so many hares as there are this year. I could not any where come by a gosshawk, nor tassel of falcon. My Lord Belloniere promised me a lanner, but he wrote to me not long ago, that he was become pursy. The partridges will so multiply henceforth, that they will go near to eat up our ears. I take no delight in the stalking-horse; for I catch such cold, that I am like to founder myself at that sport. If I do not run, toil, travel, and trot about, I am not well at ease. True it is, that in leaping over the hedges and bushes, my frock leaves always some of its wool behind it. I have recovered a dainty greyhound; I give him to the devil, if he suffer a hare to escape him. A groom was leading him to my Lord Huntlittle, and I robbed him of him. Did I ill? No, Friar John, said Gymnast, no, by all the devils that are, no! So, said the monk, do I attest these same devils so long as they last, or rather, virtue G——, what could that gouty limpard have done with so fine a dog? By the body of G——, he is better pleased, when one presents him with a good yoke of oxen. How now, said Ponocrates, you swear, Friar John; it is only, said the monk, but to grace and adorn my speech. They are colours of a Ciceronian rhetoric.

CHAPTER XL

Why Monks are the outcasts of the World

By the faith of a Christian, said Eudemon, I do wonderfully dote, and enter in a great ecstasy, when I consider the honesty and good fellowship of this monk; for he makes us here all merry. How is it, then, that they exclude the monks from all good companies, calling them feast-troublers, marrers of

One of the monks who, according to Rabelais, are always to be found in the kitchen. From "Droll Dreams."

mirth, and disturbers of all civil conversation, as the bees drive away the drones from their hives? Ignavum fucos pecus, said Maro, à præsepibus arcent. Hereunto, answered Gargantua, there is nothing so true, as that the frock and cowl draw to them the opprobries, injuries, and maledictions of the world, just as the wind called Cecias, attracts the clouds. . . . If you conceive, how an ape in a family is always mocked, and provokingly incensed, you shall easily apprehend how monks are shunned of all men, both young and old. The ape keeps not the house as a dog doth; he draws not in the plough as the ox; he yields neither milk nor wool as the sheep; he carrieth no burthen as a horse doth. That which he doth, is only to conskite, spoil, and defile all, which is the cause wherefore he hath of men mocks, frumperies and bastonadoes.

After the same manner a monk; I mean those lither, idle, lazy monks, doth not labour and work, as do the peasant and artificer; doth not ward and defend the country, as doth the man-of-war; cureth not the sick and diseased, as the physician doth; doth neither preach nor teach, as do the Evangelical doctors and school-masters; doth not import commodities and things necessary for the commonwealth, as

28. **stalking-horse,** catching birds with nets.

53-54. **Ignavum . . . arcent.** The preceding clause translates this quotation from Virgil (*Georgics*, IV, 168). 58. **the wind called Cecias,** the northeast wind.

the merchant doth. Therefore is it, that by and of all men they are hooted at, hated and abhorred. Yea, but, said Grangousier, they pray to God for us. Nothing less, answered Gargantua. True it is, that with a tingle tangle jangling of bells they trouble and disquiet all their neighbours about them. Right, said the monk; a mass, a matin, a vesper well rung is half said. They mumble out great store of legends and psalms, by them not at all understood: they say
10 many pater-nosters, interlarded with Ave-Maries, without thinking upon, or apprehending the meaning of what it is they say, which truly I call mocking of God, and not prayers. But so help them God, as they pray for us, and not for being afraid to lose their victuals, their manchets, and good fat pottage. All true Christians, of all estates and conditions, in all places, and at all times, send up their prayers to God, and the Mediator prayeth and intercedeth for them, and God is gracious to them. Now such a one
20 is our good Friar John, therefore every man desireth to have him in his company. He is no bigot or hypocrite, he is not torn and divided betwixt reality and appearance, no wretch of a rugged and peevish disposition, but honest, jovial, resolute, and a good fellow. He travels, he labours, he defends the oppressed, comforts the afflicted, helps the needy, and keeps the close of the abbey. Nay, said the monk, I do a great deal more than that; for, whilst we are despatching our matins and anniversaries in the
30 quire, I make withal some cross-bow strings, polish glass-bottles and bolts; I twist lines and weave purse nets, wherein to catch coneys. I am never idle. But now, hither come, some drink, some drink here! Bring the fruit. These chesnuts are of the wood of Estrox, and with good new wine are able to make you a fine cracker and composer of bum-sonnets. You are not as yet, it seems, well-moistened in this house with the sweet wine and must. By G——, I drink to all men freely, and at all fords like a proc-
40 tor, or promoter's horse. Friar John, said Gymnast, take away the snot that hangs at your nose. Ha, ha, said the monk, am not I in danger of drowning, seeing I am in water even to the nose? No, no, Quare? Quia, though some water come out from thence, there never goes in any; for it is well antidoted with pot-proof armour, and sirrup of the vine-leaf. . . .

CHAPTER LII

How Gargantua caused to be built for the Monk the Abbey of Theleme

Gargantua would have made the monk Abbot of Sevillé, but he refused it. He would have given him the Abbey of Bourgueil, or of Sanct Florent, which
50 was better, or both, if it pleased him; but the monk gave him a very peremptory answer, that he would never take upon him the charge nor government of

monks. For how shall I be able, said he, to rule over others, that have not full power and command of myself? If you think I have done you, or may hereafter do you any acceptable service, give me leave to found an abbey after my own mind and fancy. The motion pleased Gargantua very well, who thereupon offered him all the country of Theleme by the River of Loire, till within two leagues of the great forest of 60 Port-Huaut. The monk then requested Gargantua to institute his religious order contrary to all others. First then, said Gargantua, you must not build a wall about your convent, for all other abbeys are strongly walled and mured about. See, said the monk, and not without cause, where there is mur before, and mur behind, there is store of murmur, envy, and mutual conspiracy. Moreover, seeing there are certain convents in the world, whereof the custom is, if any women come in, I mean chaste and 70 honest women, they immediately sweep the ground which they had trod upon; therefore was it ordained, that if any man or woman, entered into religious orders, should by chance come within this new abbey, all the rooms should be thoroughly washed and cleansed through which they had passed. And because in all other monasteries and nunneries all is compassed, limited, and regulated by hours, it was decreed that in this new structure there should be neither clock nor dial, but that according to the op- 80 portunities and incident occasions, all their hours should be disposed of; for, said Gargantua, the greatest loss of time that I know, is to count the hours. What good comes of it? Nor can there be any greater dotage in the world than for one to guide and direct his courses by the sound of a bell, and not by his own judgment and discretion.

Item, Because at that time they put no women into nunneries, but such as were either purblind, blinkards, lame, crooked, ill-favoured, mis-shapen, 90 fools, senseless, spoiled, or corrupt; nor encloistered any men, but those that were either sickly, subject to defluxions, ill-bred louts, simple sots, or peevish trouble-houses. But to the purpose, said the monk. A woman that is neither fair nor good, to what use serves she? To make a nun of, said Gargantua. Yea, said the monk, to make shirts and smocks. Therefore was it ordained, that into this religious order should be admitted no women that were not fair, well-featured, and of a sweet disposition; nor men 100 that were not comely, personable, and well conditioned.

Item, Because in the convents of women, men come not but underhand, privily, and by stealth; it was therefore enacted, that in this house there shall be no women in case there be not men, nor men in case there be not women.

Item, Because both men and women, that are received into religious orders after the expiring of their noviciat or probation year, were constrained and forced perpetually to stay there all the days of their life; it was therefore ordered, that all whatever, men or women, admitted within this abbey, should have full leave to depart with peace and contentment, whensoever it should seem good to them so to do.

Item, for that the religious men and women did ordinarily make three vows, to wit, those of chastity, poverty, and obedience; it was therefore constituted and appointed, that in this convent they might be honourably married, that they might be rich, and live at liberty. In regard of the legitimate time of the persons to be initiated, and years under and above which they were not capable of reception, the women were to be admitted from ten till fifteen, and the men from twelve till eighteen.

CHAPTER LIV

The Inscription set upon the great Gate of Theleme

Here enter not vile bigots, hypocrites,
Externally devoted apes, base snites,
Puft up, wry-necked beasts, worse than the Huns,
Or Ostrogots, forerunners of baboons:
Cursed snakes, dissembling varlets, seeming sancts,
Slipshop caffards, beggars pretending wants,
Fat chuffcats, smell-feast knockers, doltish gulls,
Out-strouting cluster-fists, contentious bulls,
Fomenters of divisions and debates,
Elsewhere, not here, make sale of your deceits.
    Your filthy trumperies
    Stuffed with pernicious lies,
      (Not worth a bubble)
      Would only trouble
    Our earthly paradise,
    Your filthy trumperies.

Here enter not attorneys, barristers,
Nor bridle-champing law-practitioners;
Clerks, commissaries, scribes, nor pharisees,
Wilful disturbers of the people's ease:
Judges, destroyers, with an unjust breath,
Of honest men, like dogs, ev'n unto death.
Your salary is at the gibbet-foot:
Go drink there! for we do not here fly out
On those excessive courses, which may draw
A waiting on your courts by suits in law.
    Law-suits, debates, and wrangling
    Hence are exil'd, and jangling.
    Here we are very
    Frolic and merry,
    And free from all entangling,
    Law-suits, debates, and wrangling.

Here enter not base pinching usurers,
Pelf-lickers, everlasting gatherers.
Gold-graspers, coin-gripers, gulpers of mists,

With harpy-griping claws, who, though your chests
Vasts sums of money should to you afford,
Would ne'ertheless add more unto that hoard,
And yet not be content,—you clunchfists dastards,
Insatiable fiends, and Pluto's bastards,
Greedy devourers, chichy sneakbill rogues,
Hell-mastiffs gnaw your bones, you rav'nous dogs,
    You beastly-looking fellows,
    Reason doth plainly tell us,
      That we should not
      To you allot
    Room here, but at the gallows,
    You beastly-looking fellows.

Here enter not fond makers of demurs
In love adventures, peevish jealous curs,
Sad pensive dotards, raisers of garboyles,
Hags, goblins, ghosts, firebrands of household broils,
Nor drunkards, liars, cowards, cheaters, clowns,
Thieves, cannibals, faces o'ercast with frowns,
Nor lazy slugs, envious, covetous,
Nor blockish, cruel, nor too credulous,—
Here mangy, pocky folks shall have no place,
No ugly lusks, nor persons of disgrace.
    Grace, honour, praise, delight,
    Here sojourn day and night.
      Sound bodies lin'd
      With a good mind,
    Do here pursue with might
    Grace, honour, praise, delight.

Here enter you, and welcome from our hearts,
All noble sparks, endow'd with gallant parts.
This is the glorious place, which bravely shall
Afford wherewith to entertain you all.
Were you a thousand, here you shall not want
For anything: for what you'll ask we'll grant.
Stay here you lively, jovial, handsome, brisk,
Gay, witty, frolic, cheerful, merry, frisk,
Spruce, jocund, courteous, furtherers of trades,
And in a word, all worthy, gentle blades.
    Blades of heroic breasts
    Shall taste here of the feasts,
      Both privily
      And civilly
    Of the celestial guests,
    Blades of heroic breasts.

Here enter you, pure, honest, faithful, true,
Expounders of the Scriptures old and new.
Whose glosses do not blind our reason, but
Make it to see the clearer, and who shut
Its passages from hatred, avarice,
Pride, factions, covenants, and all sort of vice.
Come, settle here a charitable faith,
Which neighbourly affection nourisheth.
And whose light chaseth all corrupters hence,

Of the blest word, from the aforesaid sense.
> The Holy Sacred Word,
> May it always afford
> T' us all in common,
> Both man and woman,
> A spiritual shield and sword,
> The Holy Sacred Word.

Here enter you all ladies of high birth,
Delicious, stately, charming, full of mirth,
10 Ingenious, lovely, miniard, proper, fair,
Magnetic, graceful, splendid, pleasant, rare,
Obliging, sprightly, virtuous, young, solacious,
Kind, neat, quick, feat, bright, compt, ripe, choice,
> dear, precious.
Alluring, courtly, comely, fine, complete.
Wise, personable, ravishing, and sweet,
Come joys enjoy. The Lord celestial
Hath given enough, wherewith to please us all.
> Gold give us, God forgive us,
20 > And from all woes relieve us;
> That we the treasure
> May reap of pleasure,
> And shun whate'er is grievous,
> Gold give us, God forgive us.

CHAPTER LVII

How the Thelemites were governed, and of their manner of living

All their life was spent not in laws, statutes, or rules, but according to their own free will and pleasure. They rose out of their beds when they thought good: they did eat, drink, labour, sleep, when they had a mind to it, and were disposed for it. None did 30 awake them, none did offer to constrain them to eat, drink, nor to do any other thing; for so had Gargantua established it. In all their rule, and strictest tie of their order, there was but this one clause to be observed,

DO WHAT THOU WILT.

Because men that are free, well-born, well-bred, and conversant in honest companies, have naturally an instinct and spur that prompteth them unto virtuous actions, and withdraws them from vice, which is 40 called honour. Those same men, when by base subjection and constraint they are brought under and kept down, turn aside from that noble disposition, by which they formerly were inclined to virtue, to shake off and break that bond of servitude, wherein they are so tyrannously enslaved; for it is agreeable with the nature of man to long after things forbidden, and to desire what is denied us.

By this liberty they entered into a very laudable emulation, to do all of them what they saw did 50 please one. If any of the gallants or ladies should say, Let us drink, they would all drink. If any one of them said, Let us play, they all played. If one said, Let us go a walking into the fields, they went all. If it were to go a hawking or a hunting, the ladies mounted upon dainty well-paced nags, seated in a stately palfrey saddle, carried on their lovely fists, miniardly begloved every one of them, either a sparhawk, or a laneret, or a merlin, and the young gallants carried the other kinds of hawks. So nobly were they taught, that there was neither he nor she 60 amongst them, but could read, write, sing, play upon several musical instruments, speak five or six several languages, and composed in them all very quaintly, both in verse and prose. Never were seen so valiant knights, so noble and worthy, so dexterous and skilful both on foot and a horseback, more brisk and lively, more nimble and quick, or better handling all manner of weapons than were there. Never were seen ladies so proper and handsome, so miniard and dainty, less forward, or more ready with their hand, 70 and with their needle, in every honest and free action belonging to that sex, than were there. For this reason, when the time came, that any man of the said abbey, either at the request of his parents, or for some other cause, had a mind to go out of it, he carried along with him one of the ladies, namely her whom he had before that chosen for his mistress, and they were married together. And if they had formerly in Theleme lived in good devotion and amity, they did continue therein and increase it to a 80 greater height in their state of matrimony: and did entertain that mutual love till the very last day of their life, in no less vigour and fervency, than at the very day of their wedding.

Michel de Montaigne
1533–1592

The robust optimism of Rabelais and the early Renaissance gave way in Montaigne to a rational skepticism of the perfectability of human nature and the value of learning as such in the achievement of self-knowledge. Actually, Montaigne was one of the most learned men of his time and interlarded his essays with quotations from his vast reading in the ancient classics. But these ideas of others he had so thoroughly digested that he used them only to illustrate his own thinking and never as the sources of wisdom and hope that they were for the typical Humanists. In a quite different way, Montaigne is as much an individualist as Rabelais, and his quiet skepticism reflects the deep-seated independence of his mind as much as it does the fading hopes of the later Renaissance.

His temperament is revealed in his gentle life. The careful education that his father gave him began that quest for self-knowledge that was the whole aim and end of his career. Montaigne's father, a self-made man whom his son adored as the summary of all the abilities and virtues that he himself lacked, reared his nine children in a palatial château near the thriving city of Bordeaux according to a careful plan that expressed his own wise if also eccentric views on education. Michel, the eldest, had peasant godparents in order that he might not lose touch with the simple life of earthy folk. Corporal punishment was outlawed as injurious to children's nervous systems, and they were awakened in the morning by chamber music rather than by the alarming sound of a gong. A German tutor who knew no French taught them Latin in infancy, so that when Michel went off to school at six he spoke Latin much better than his native tongue. His seven years at the Collège de Guyenne in Bordeaux made him an accomplished classical scholar.

Montaigne was educated as a lawyer, and his father's position as mayor of Bordeaux assured him a thriving practice. But public life did not appeal to him, and after two years in Paris seeking an important post he retired from a political scene dominated by the savage struggle of Catholics and Protestant Huguenots that signalized the coming of the Reformation to France. The bloody Massacre of St. Bartholomew's Day in 1572, in which thousands of Huguenots were butchered, shocked his peaceful nature and enforced his design to seclude himself in his château, which his father's death had left him. After eight years of retirement there he published in 1580 the first two volumes of his *Essays* and then ventured forth on a tourist's trip through Switzerland, Germany, and Italy, during which he kept a careful journal of his observations. Upon his return he served as an able mayor of Bordeaux between 1581 and 1585, but his last years were spent in complete retirement on his estate, pursuing his studies in his magnificent library and revising and augmenting his *Essays*. Although he was happily married in 1565 to an efficient and self-effacing woman and had six daughters by her, he never overcame the sexual wanderlust of his youth and was whimsically devoted in later years to a Parisian girl, Marie de Gournay, thirty-four years younger than himself, who was happy to be called his "adopted daughter." However, the great inspiration of his life was not a woman but the friend of his youth, Étienne de la Boetie, a brilliant lawyer and classical scholar whom Montaigne met in 1559 and whose untimely death four years later cut short an intense friendship. In his fervent essay on *Friendship* Montaigne proclaimed the satisfying nature of their relationship and its enduring effect on his life.

Montaigne's reputation as philosopher and man of letters rests on his three books of *Essays* (published 1580–1595) in which he virtually created a modern literary form to embody his unique role in literature. As a genial skeptic who could discuss human problems better than he could reach conclusions about them, he thought of the essay as a discursive and tentative statement of his personal opinions about such varied subjects as education, social customs, cannibalism, idleness, drunkenness, honesty, old age, repentance, vanity—to mention the

titles of only a few of the ninety-three. His prose style is intimate and informal, according to the literary standards of his day, and reading one of his essays is like listening to his wise, witty, and rambling conversation before a warm fire in the great library of his château.

Yet from the seemingly haphazard pages of the essays emerges a consistent intellectual attitude, if not a formal philosophy. Montaigne is the symbol of the open mind. Lacking the cocksure faith in man's reason assisted by learning that animated Rabelais, he was content to end each discussion with a shrug of the shoulders and his favorite phrase, "Que sçais-je?" ("What do I know?") The objective of all his thinking was to know himself as a specimen of mankind, and upon this study he focused the experiences of his classical education, his public service, his many friendships, his travels in foreign lands, and his years in his library. But knowledge led him at last to agnosticism and the belief that he could do no better in the end than to accept the life that he knew, with all its defects. This amiable note of resignation before the status quo completes a cycle of Renaissance thought and prepares the way for a new kind of rationalism in the next age.

The Author to the Reader

READER, thou hast here an honest book; it doth at the outset forewarn thee that, in contriving the same, I have proposed to myself no other than a domestic and private end: I have had no consideration at all either to thy service or to my glory. My powers are not capable of any such design. I have dedicated it to the particular commodity of my kinsfolk and friends, so that, having lost me (which they must do shortly), they may therein recover some traits of my conditions and humours, and by [10] that means preserve more whole, and more life-like, the knowledge they had of me. Had my intention been to seek the world's favour, I should surely have adorned myself with borrowed beauties: I desire therein to be viewed as I appear in mine own genuine, simple, and ordinary manner, without study and artifice: for it is myself I paint. My defects are therein to be read to the life, and my imperfections and my natural form, so far as public reverence hath permitted me. If I had lived among those nations, [20] which (they say) yet dwell under the sweet liberty of nature's primitive laws, I assure thee I would most willingly have painted myself quite fully and quite naked. Thus, reader, myself am the matter of my book: there's no reason thou shouldst employ thy leisure about so frivolous and vain a subject. Therefore, farewell.

The Author to the Reader. Translated by Charles Cotton.
7. commodity, advantage.

Of Democritus
and Heraclitus

THE judgment is an utensil proper for all subjects, and will have an oar in everything: which is the reason that in these Essays I take hold of all occasions where, though it happen to be a subject I do not very well understand, I try however, sounding it at a distance, and finding it too deep for my stature, I keep me on the shore; and this knowledge that a man can proceed no further is one effect of its virtue, yea, one of those of which it is most proud. One while in an idle and frivolous subject, I try to find out matter whereof to compose a body, and then to prop and support it; another while, I employ it in a noble subject, one that has been tossed and tumbled by a thousand hands, wherein a man can scarce possibly introduce anything of his own, the way being so beaten on every side that he must of necessity walk in the steps of another. In such a case, 'tis the work of the judgment to take the way that seems best, and of a thousand paths, to determine that this or that is the best. I leave the choice of my arguments to fortune, and take that she first presents to me; they are all alike to me. I never design to go through any of them; for I never see all of anything: neither do they who so largely promise to show it others. Of a hundred members and faces that everything has, I take one, onewhile to look it over only, another while to ripple up the skin, and sometimes to pinch it to the bones. I give a stab, not so wide but as deep as I can, and am for the most part tempted to take it in hand by some new light I discover in it. Did I know myself less, I might perhaps venture to handle something or other to the bottom, and to be deceived in my own inability; but sprinkling here one word and there another, patterns cut from several pieces and scattered without design and without engaging myself too far, I am not responsible for them, or obliged to keep close to my subject, without varying at my own liberty and pleasure, and giving up myself to doubt and uncertainty, and to my own governing method, ignorance.

All motion discovers us: the very same soul of Caesar, that made itself so conspicuous in marshalling and commanding the battle of Pharsalia, was also seen as solicitous and busy in the softer affairs of love and leisure. A man makes a judgment of a horse, not only by seeing him when he is showing off his paces, but by his very walk, nay, and by seeing him stand in the stable.

Amongst the functions of the soul, there are some of a lower and meaner form; he who does not see her in those inferior offices as well as in those of nobler note, never fully discovers her; and, peradventure, she is best shown where she moves her simpler pace. The winds of passions take most hold of her in her highest flights; and the rather by reason that she wholly applies herself to, and exercises her whole virtue upon, every particular subject, and never handles more than one thing at a time, and that not according to it, but according to herself. Things in respect to themselves have, peradventure, their weight, measures, and conditions; but when we once take them into us, the soul forms them as she pleases. Death is terrible to Cicero, coveted by Cato, indifferent to Socrates. Health, conscience, authority, knowledge, riches, beauty, and their contraries all strip themselves at their entering into us, and receive a new robe, and of another fashion, from the soul; and of what colour, brown, bright, green, dark, and of what quality, sharp, sweet, deep, or superficial, as best pleases each of them, for they are not agreed upon any common standard of forms, rules, or proceedings; every one is a queen in her own dominions. Let us, therefore, no more excuse ourselves upon the external qualities of things; it belongs to us to give ourselves an account of them. Our good or ill has no other dependence but on ourselves. 'Tis there that our offerings and our vows are due, and to fortune: she has no power over our manners; on the contrary, they draw and make her follow in their train, and cast her in their own mould. Why should not I judge of Alexander at table, ranting and drinking at the prodigious rate he sometimes used to do? Or, if he played at chess? what string of his soul was not touched by this idle and childish game? I hate and avoid it, because it is not play enough, that it is too grave and serious a diversion, and I am ashamed to lay out as much thought and study upon it as would serve to much better uses. He did not more pump his brains about his glorious expedition into the Indies, nor than another in unravelling a passage upon which depends the safety of mankind. To what a degree does this ridiculous diversion molest the soul, when all her faculties are summoned together upon this trivial account! and how fair an opportunity she herein gives every one to know and to make a right judgment of himself? I do not more thoroughly sift myself in any other posture than this: what passion are we exempted from in it? Anger, spite, malice, impatience, and a vehement desire of getting the better in a concern wherein it were more excusable to be ambitious of being over-

Of Democritus and Heraclitus. Translated by Charles Cotton.

75. **excuse ourselves upon,** release ourselves from considering.

come; for to be eminent, to excel above the common rate in frivolous things, nowise befits a man of honour. What I say in this example may be said in all others. Every particle, every employment of man manifests him equally with any other.

Democritus and Heraclitus were two philosophers, of whom the first, finding human condition ridiculous and vain, never appeared abroad but with a jeering and laughing countenance; whereas Heraclitus commiserating that same condition of ours, appeared always with a sorrowful look, and tears in his eyes: "The one always, when he stepped over his threshold, laughed at the world, the other always wept." I am clearly for the first humour; not because it is more pleasant to laugh than to weep, but because it expresses more contempt and condemnation than the other, and I think we can never be despised according to our full desert. Compassion and bewailing seem to imply some esteem of and value for the thing bemoaned; whereas the things we laugh at are by that expressed to be of no moment. I do not think that we are so unhappy as we are vain, or have in us so much malice as folly; we are not so full of mischief as inanity; nor so miserable as we are vile and mean. And therefore Diogenes, who passed away his time in rolling himself in his tub, and made nothing of the great Alexander esteeming us no better than flies, or bladders puffed up with wind, was a sharper and more penetrating, and, consequently in my opinion, a juster judge than Timon, surnamed the Man-hater; for what a man hates he lays to heart. This last was an enemy to all mankind, who passionately desired our ruin and avoided our conversation as dangerous, proceeding from wicked and depraved natures: the other valued us so little that we could neither trouble nor infect him by our example; and left us to herd one with another, not out of fear, but from contempt of our society: concluding us as incapable of doing good as ill.

Of the same strain was Statilius' answer, when Brutus courted him into the conspiracy against Caesar; he was satisfied that the enterprise was just, but he did not think mankind worthy of a wise man's concern; according to the doctrine of Hegesias, who said, that a wise man ought to do nothing but for himself, forasmuch as he only was worthy of it: and to the saying of Theodorus, that it was not reasonable a wise man should hazard himself for his country, and endanger wisdom for a company of fools. Our condition is as ridiculous as risible.

12–13. "The one always . . . always wept." Juvenal, *Satires*, x, 28. 31. **Timon,** of Athens, the noted misanthrope. 43–45. **he was satisfied . . . concern;** quoted in Plutarch's *Life of Brutus*, chapter 12. 45. **Hegesias,** Cyrenaic philosopher, here quoted in Diogenes Laertius, ii, 95. 48. **Theodorus,** another Cyrenaic, here quoted in Diogenes Laertius, ii, 98.

Of the Education of Children

. . . A FRIEND of mine the other day told me that I should a little farther have extended my discourse on the education of children. Now, madam, if I had any sufficiency in this subject, I could not possibly better employ it than to present my best instructions to the little gentleman that threatens you shortly with a happy birth (for you are too generous to begin otherwise than with a male); for having had so great a hand in the treaty of your marriage, I have a certain particular right and interest in the greatness and prosperity of the issue that shall spring from it; besides that, your having had the best of my services so long in possession sufficiently obliges me to desire the honour and advantage of all wherein you shall be concerned. But, in truth, all I understand as to that particular is only this, that the greatest and most important difficulty of human science is the education of children. For as in agriculture, the husbandry that is to precede planting, as also planting itself, is certain, plain, and well known; but after that which is planted comes to life, there is a great deal more to be done, more art to be used, more care to be taken, and much more difficulty to cultivate and bring it to perfection: so it is with men; it is no hard matter to get children; but after they are born, then begins the trouble, solicitude, and care rightly to train, principle, and bring them up. The symptoms of their inclinations in that tender age are so obscure and the promises so uncertain and fallacious that it is very hard to establish any solid judgment or conjecture upon them. Look at Cimon, for example, and Themistocles, and a thousand others, who very much deceived the expectation men had for them. Cubs of bears and puppies readily discover their natural inclination; but men so soon as ever they are grown up, applying themselves to certain habits, engaging themselves in certain opinions, and conforming themselves to particular laws and customs, easily alter, or at least disguise, their true and real disposition; and yet it is hard to force the propension of nature. Whence it comes to pass that, for not having chosen the right course, we often take very great pains and consume a good part of our time in training up children to things for which, by their natural constitution, they are totally unfit. In this difficulty, nevertheless, I am clearly of opinion that they ought to be elemented in the best and most advantageous studies,

*Of the Education of Children.*ᴬ Translated by Charles Cotton. 54. **madam,** the Comtesse de Gurson, to whom the essay is dedicated. 83. **Cimon, Themistocles,** Greek commanders of the fifth century B.C.

without taking too much notice of, or being too superstitious in, those light prognostics they give of themselves in their tender years, and to which Plato in his "Republic" gives, methinks, too much authority.

Madam, science is a very great ornament, and a thing of marvellous use, especially in persons raised to that degree of fortune in which you are. And, in truth, in persons of mean and low condition it cannot perform its true and genuine office, being naturally more prompt to assist in the conduct of war, in the government of peoples, in negotiating the leagues and friendships of princes and foreign nations, than in forming a syllogism in logic, in pleading a process in law, or in prescribing a dose of pills in physic. . . .

For a boy of quality, then, who pretends to letters not upon the account of profit (for so mean an object as that is unworthy of the grace and favour of the Muses, and moreover, in it a man directs his service to and depends upon others), nor so much for outward ornament, as for his own proper and peculiar use, and to furnish and enrich himself within, having rather a desire to come out an accomplished cavalier than a mere scholar or learned man; for such a one, I say, I would also have his friends solicitous to find him out a tutor who has rather a well-made than a well-filled head; seeking, indeed, both the one and the other, but rather of the two to prefer manners and judgment to mere learning, and that this man should exercise his charge after a new method.

'Tis the custom of pedagogues to be eternally thundering in their pupil's ears, as they were pouring into a funnel, whilst the business of the pupil is only to repeat what the others have said. Now I would have a tutor to correct this error, and that at the very first he should, according to the capacity he has to deal with, put it to the test, permitting his pupil himself to taste things and of himself to discern and choose them, sometimes opening the way to him, and sometimes leaving him to open it for himself; that is, I would not have him alone to invent and speak, but that he should also hear his pupil speak in turn. Socrates, and since him Arcesilaus, made first their scholars speak, and then they spoke to them. "The authority of those who teach, is very often an impediment to those who desire to learn." It is good to make him, like a young horse, trot before him, that he may judge of his going and how much he is to abate of his own speed to accommodate himself to the vigour and capacity of the other. For want of which due proportion we spoil all; which also to know how to ad-

just, and to keep within an exact and due measure, is one of the hardest things I know, and 'tis the effect of a high and well-tempered soul to know how to condescend to such puerile motions and to govern and direct them. I walk firmer and more secure up hill than down.

Such as, according to our common way of teaching, undertake with one and the same lesson and the same measure of direction to instruct several boys of differing and unequal capacities are infinitely mistaken; and 'tis no wonder if in a whole multitude of scholars there are not found above two or three who bring away any good account of their time and discipline. Let the master not only examine him about the grammatical construction of the bare words of his lesson, but about the sense and substance of them, and let him judge of the profit he has made, not by the testimony of his memory, but by that of his life. Let him make him put what he has learned into a hundred several forms, and accommodate it to so many several subjects, to see if he yet rightly comprehends it, and has made it his own, taking instruction of his progress by the pedagogic institutions of Plato. 'Tis a sign of crudity and indigestion to disgorge what we eat in the same condition it was swallowed; the stomach has not performed its office unless it has altered the form and condition of what was committed to it to concoct. Our minds work only upon trust when bound and compelled to follow the appetite of another's fancy, enslaved and captivated under the authority of another's instruction. We have been so subjected to the trammel that we have no free nor natural pace of our own; our own vigour and liberty are extinct and gone: "They are ever in wardship." . . .

Let him make him examine and thoroughly sift everything he reads, and lodge nothing in his fancy upon simple authority and upon trust. Aristotle's principles will then be no more principles to him than those of Epicurus and the Stoics. Let this diversity of opinions be propounded to, and laid before him; he will himself choose, if he be able; if not, he will remain in doubt.

"I love to doubt, as well as to know."

For, if he embrace the opinions of Xenophon and Plato by his own reason, they will no more be theirs, but become his own. Who follows another follows nothing, finds nothing, nay, is inquisitive after nothing. "We are under no king; let each look to himself." Let him, at least, know that he knows. It will be necessary that he imbibe their knowledge, not that he be corrupted with their precepts; and no matter if he forget where he had his learning, provided he know how to apply it to his own use. Truth

45–46. **Arcesilaus,** Arcesilas of Pitane (c. 315–240 B.C.), founder of the Second Academy in Athens. 47–49. **"The authority . . . to learn."** Cicero, *De Natura Deorum,* i, 5.

88. **"They are . . . wardship."** Seneca, *Epistles,* 33. 97. **"I love . . . to know."** Dante, *Inferno,* xi, 93. 102–103. **"We are . . . himself."** Seneca, *Epistles,* 33.

and reason are common to every one and are no more his who spake them first than his who speaks them after. 'Tis no more according to Plato than according to me, since both he and I equally see and understand them. Bees cull their several sweets from this flower and that blossom, here and there where they find them, but themselves afterwards make the honey, which is all and purely their own, and no more thyme and marjoram. So the several fragments he borrows from others, he will transform and shuffle together to compile a work that shall be absolutely his own; that is to say, his judgment: his instruction, labour, and study tend to cover whence he got the materials that have assisted him, but only to produce what he has himself done with them. Men that live upon pillage and borrowing expose their purchases and buildings to every one's view: but do not proclaim how they came by the money. We do not see the fees and perquisites of a gentleman of the long robe; but we see the alliances wherewith he fortifies himself and his family, and the titles and honours he has obtained for him and his. No man divulges his revenue; or at least, which way it comes in: but every one publishes his acquisitions. The advantages of our study are to become better and more wise. 'Tis, says Epicharmus, the understanding that sees and hears, 'tis the understanding that improves and reigns: all other faculties are blind, and deaf, and without soul. And certainly we render it timorous and servile in not allowing it the liberty and privilege to do anything of itself. Whoever asked his pupil what he thought of grammar and rhetoric, or of such and such a sentence of Cicero? Our masters stick them, full feathered, in our memories, and there establish them like oracles, of which the letters and syllables are of the substance of the thing.

To know by rote is no knowledge, and signifies no more but only to retain what one has intrusted to our memory. That which a man rightly knows and understands, he is the free disposer of at his own full liberty, without any regard to the author from whence he had it or fumbling over the leaves of his book. A mere bookish learning is a poor, paltry learning; it may serve for ornament, but there is yet no foundation for any superstructure to be built upon it, according to the opinion of Plato, who says that constancy, faith, and sincerity are the true philosophy, and the other sciences, that are directed to other ends, mere adulterate paint. I could wish that Paluel or Pompey, those two noted dancers of my time, could have taught us to cut capers by only seeing them do it, without stirring from our places,

as these men pretend to inform the understanding without ever setting it to work; or that we could learn to ride, handle a pike, touch a lute, or sing without the trouble of practice, as these attempt to make us judge and speak well without exercising us in judging or speaking. Now in this initiation of our studies and in their progress, whatsoever presents itself before us is book sufficient; a roguish trick of a page, a sottish mistake of a servant, a jest at the table are so many new subjects.

And for this reason, conversation with men is of very great use and travel into foreign countries; not to bring back (as most of our young monsieurs do) an account only of how many paces Santa Rotonda is in circuit; or of the richness of Signora Livia's petticoats; or, as some others, how much Nero's face, in a statue in such an old ruin, is longer and broader than that made for him on some medal; but to be able chiefly to give an account of the humours, manners, customs, and laws of those nations where he has been, and that we may whet and sharpen our wits by rubbing them against those of others. I would that a boy should be sent abroad very young, and first, so as to kill two birds with one stone, into those neighbouring nations whose language is most differing from our own, and to which, if it be not formed betimes, the tongue will grow too stiff to bend.

And also 'tis the general opinion of all that a child should not be brought up in his mother's lap. Mothers are too tender, and their natural affection is apt to make the most discreet of them all so overfond that they can neither find in their hearts to give them due correction for the faults they commit, nor suffer them to be inured to hardships and hazards, as they ought to be. They will not endure to see them return all dust and sweat from their exercise, to drink cold drink when they art hot, nor see them mount an unruly horse, nor take a foil in hand against a rude fencer, or so much as to discharge a carbine. And yet there is no remedy; whoever will breed a boy to be good for anything when he comes to be a man must by no means spare him when young and must very often transgress the rules of physic:— "Let him live in the open air, and ever in movement about something." It is not enough to fortify his soul; you are also to make his sinews strong; for the soul will be oppressed if not assisted by the members and would have too hard a task to discharge two offices alone. I know very well to my cost how much mine groans under the burden from being accommodated with a body so tender and indisposed as eternally leans and presses upon her; and often in reading perceive that our masters in their writings make examples pass for magnanimity and fortitude of mind, which really are rather toughness of skin

26. **Epicharmus,** a Greek comic poet of the fifth century B.C., also considered a philosopher because a philosophical poem, probably by another writer, was published under his name.

67. **Santa Rotonda,** the Pantheon of Rome. 97–98. **"Let him live . . . something."** Horace, *Odes,* II, 3, 5.

and hardness of bones; for I have seen men, women, and children naturally born of so hard and insensible a constitution of body that a sound cudgelling has been less to them than a flirt with a finger would have been to me, and that would neither cry out, wince, nor shrink for a good swinging beating; and when wrestlers counterfeit the philosophers in patience, 'tis rather strength of nerves than stoutness of heart. Now to be inured to undergo labour is to be accustomed to endure pain: "Labour hardens us against pain." A boy is to be broken in to the toil and roughness of exercise, so as to be trained up to the pain and suffering of dislocations, cholics, cauteries, and even imprisonment and the rack itself; for he may come, by misfortune, to be reduced to the worst of these, which (as this world goes) is sometimes inflicted on the good as well as the bad. As for proof, in our present civil war whoever draws his sword against the laws threatens the honestest men with the whip and the halter.

And, moreover, by living at home, the authority of this governor, which ought to be sovereign over the boy he has received into his charge, is often checked and hindered by the presence of parents; to which may also be added that the respect the whole family pay him as their master's son, and the knowledge he has of the estate and greatness he is heir to are, in my opinion, no small inconveniences in these tender years.

And yet, even in this conversing with men I spoke of but now, I have observed this vice, that instead of gathering observations from others we make it our whole business to lay ourselves upon them, and are more concerned how to expose and set out our own commodities than how to increase our stock by acquiring new. Silence, therefore, and modesty are very advantageous qualities in conversation. One should, therefore, train up this boy to be sparing and a husband of his knowledge when he has acquired it; and to forbear taking exceptions at or reproving every idle saying or ridiculous story that is said or told in his presence; for it is a very unbecoming rudeness to carp at everything that is not agreeable to our own palate. Let him be satisfied with correcting himself and not seem to condemn everything in another he would not do himself, nor dispute it as against common customs. "Let him be wise without ostentation, without envy." Let him avoid these vain and uncivil images of authority, this childish ambition of coveting to appear better bred and more accomplished than he really will, by such carriage, discover himself to be. And, as if opportunities of interrupting and reprehending were not to be omitted, to desire thence to derive the reputation of something more than ordinary. For as it becomes none but great poets to make use of the poetical licence, so it is intolerable for any but men of great and illustrious souls to assume privilege above the authority of custom; "If Socrates and Aristippus have transgressed the rules of good conduct or custom, let him not imagine that he is licensed to do the same; for it was by great and sovereign virtues that they obtained this privilege." Let him be instructed not to engage in discourse or dispute but with a champion worthy of him, and even there not to make use of all the little subtleties that may seem pat for his purpose, but only such arguments as may best serve him. Let him be taught to be curious in the election and choice of his reasons, to abominate impertinence, and, consequently, to affect brevity; but, above all, let him be lessoned to acquiesce and submit to truth so soon as ever he shall discover it, whether in his opponent's argument or upon better consideration of his own, for he shall never be preferred to the chair for a mere clatter of words and syllogisms and is no further engaged to any argument whatever than as he shall in his own judgment approve it: nor yet is arguing a trade, where the liberty of recantation and getting off upon better thoughts are to be sold for ready money: "Neither is there any necessity upon him that he should defend all things that are recommended to and enjoined him."

If his governor be of my humour, he will form his will to be a very good and loyal subject to his prince, very affectionate to his person and very stout in his quarrel; but withal he will cool in him the desire of having any other tie to his service than public duty. Besides several other inconveniences that are inconsistent with the liberty every honest man ought to have, a man's judgment, being bribed and prepossessed by these particular obligations, is either blinded and less free to exercise its function or blemished with ingratitude and indiscretion. A man that is purely a courtier can neither have power nor will to speak or think otherwise than favourably and well of a master, who, amongst so many millions of other subjects, has picked out him with his own hand to nourish and advance. This favour, and the profit flowing from it, must needs, and not without some show of reason, corrupt his freedom and dazzle him; and we commonly see these people speak in another kind of phrase than is ordinarily spoken by others of the same nation, though what they say in that courtly language is not much to be believed.

Let his conscience and virtue be eminently manifest in his speaking and have only reason for their guide. Make him understand that to acknowledge the error he shall discover in his own argument,

10–11. "Labour . . . pain." Cicero, *Tusculan Disputations*, II, 15. 18. **present civil war**, the Huguenot wars in France. 47–48. "**Let him . . . envy.**" Seneca, *Moral Epistles*, 103.

59–63. "**If Socrates . . . this privilege.**" Cicero, *Offices*, I, 41. 80–83. "**Neither is . . . enjoined him.**" Cicero, *Acad.*, II, 3.

though only found out by himself, is an effect of judgment and sincerity, which are the principal things he is to seek after; that obstinacy and contention are common qualities, most appearing in mean souls; that to revise and correct himself, to forsake an unjust argument in the height and heat of dispute, are rare, great, and philosophical qualities. Let him be advised, being in company, to have his eye and ear in every corner; for I find that the places of greatest honour are commonly seized upon by men that have least in them and that the greatest fortunes are seldom accompanied with the ablest parts. I have been present when, whilst they at the upper end of the chamber have been only commending the beauty of the arras, or the flavour of the wine, many things that have been very finely said at the lower end of the table have been lost and thrown away. Let him examine every man's talent; a peasant, a bricklayer, a passenger: one may learn something from every one of these in their several capacities, and something will be picked out of their discourse whereof some use may be made at one time or another; nay, even the folly and impertinence of others will contribute to his instruction. By observing the graces and manners of all he sees, he will create to himself an emulation of the good and a contempt of the bad.

Let an honest curiosity be suggested to his fancy of being inquisitive after everything; whatever there is singular and rare near the place where he is, let him go and see it; a fine house, a noble fountain, an eminent man, the place where a battle has been anciently fought, the passages of Caesar and Charlemagne: "What country is bound in frost, what land is friable with heat, what wind serves fairest for Italy." Let him inquire into the manners, revenues, and alliances of princes, things in themselves very pleasant to learn, and very useful to know.

In this conversing with men, I mean also, and principally, those who only live in the records of history; he shall, by reading those books, converse with the great and heroic souls of the best ages. 'Tis an idle and vain study to those who make it so by doing it after a negligent manner, but to those who do it with care and observation, 'tis a study of inestimable fruit and value; and the only study, as Plato reports, that the Lacedaemonians reserved to themselves. What profit shall he not reap as to the business of men by reading the lives of Plutarch? But, withal, let my governor remember to what end his instructions are principally directed, and that he do not so much imprint in his pupil's memory the date of the ruin of Carthage as the manners of Hannibal and Scipio; nor so much where Marcellus died as why it was unworthy of his duty that he died

there. Let him not teach him so much the narrative parts of history as to judge them; the reading of them, in my opinion, is a thing that of all others we apply ourselves unto with the most differing measure. I have read a hundred things in Livy that another has not, or not taken notice of at least; and Plutarch has read a hundred more there than ever I could find, or than, peradventure, that author ever wrote. To some it is merely a grammar study, to others the very anatomy of philosophy, by which the most abstruse parts of our human nature penetrate. There are in Plutarch many long discourses very worthy to be carefully read and observed, for he is, in my opinion, of all others the greatest master in that kind of writing; but there are a thousand others which he has only touched and glanced upon, where he only points with his finger to direct us which way we may go if we will, and contents himself sometimes with giving only one brisk hit in the nicest article of the question, whence we are to grope out the rest. As, for example, where he says that the inhabitants of Asia came to be vassals to one only, for not having been able to pronounce one syllable, which is No. Which saying of his gave perhaps matter and occasion to LaBoetie to write his "Voluntary Servitude." Only to see him pick out a light action in a man's life, or a mere word that does not seem to amount even to that, is itself a whole discourse. 'Tis to our prejudice that men of understanding should so immoderately affect brevity; no doubt their reputation is the better by it, but in the meantime we are the worse. Plutarch had rather we should applaud his judgment than commend his knowledge, and had rather leave us with an appetite to read more than glutted with that we have already read. He knew very well that a man may say too much even upon the best subjects, and that Alexandridas justly reproached him who made very good but too long speeches to the Ephori, when he said: "O stranger! thou speakest the things thou shouldst speak, but not as thou shouldst speak them." Such as have lean and spare bodies stuff themselves out with clothes; so they who are defective in matter endeavour to make amends with words.

Human understanding is marvellously enlightened by daily conversation with men, for we are, otherwise, compressed and heaped up in ourselves and have our sight limited to the length of our own noses. One asking Socrates of what country he was, he did not make answer, of Athens, but of the world; he whose imagination was fuller and wider, em-

34–36. "What country . . . for Italy." Propertius, iv, 3, 39.

76. where he says. . . . In his *Essay on False Shame.* 80. LaBoetie, Montaigne's close friend, Étienne de la Boetie, whom he praises in his essay on friendship. 94–96. "O stranger . . . speak them." Plutarch's *Apothegms of the Lacedaemonians.* 104–105. One asking Socrates . . . of the world. Cicero, *Tusculan Disputations,* v, 37.

braced the whole world for his country, and extended his society and friendship to all mankind; not as we do, who look no further than our feet. When the vines of my village are nipped with the frost, my parish priest presently concludes that the indignation of God is gone out against all the human race and that the cannibals have already got the pip. Who is it that, seeing the havoc of these civil wars of ours, does not cry out that the machine of the world is near dissolution and that the day of judgment is at hand; without considering that many worse things have been seen and that, in the meantime, people are very merry in a thousand other parts of the earth for all this? For my part, considering the licence and impunity that always attend such commotions, I wonder they are so moderate and that there is no more mischief done. To him who feels the hailstones patter about his ears, the whole hemisphere appears to be in storm and tempest; like the ridiculous Savoyard who said very gravely that, if that simple king of France could have managed his fortune as he should have done, he might in time have come to have been steward of the household to the duke his master: the fellow could not, in his shallow imagination, conceive that there could be anything greater than a Duke of Savoy. And, in truth, we are all of us, insensibly, in this error, an error of a very great weight and very pernicious consequence. But whoever shall represent to his fancy, as in a picture, that great image of our mother Nature in her full majesty and lustre, whoever in her face shall read so general and so constant a variety, whoever shall observe himself in that figure, and not himself but a whole kingdom, no bigger than the least touch or prick of a pencil in comparison of the whole, that man alone is able to value things according to their true estimate and grandeur.

This great world which some do yet multiply as several species under one genus, is the mirror wherein we are to behold ourselves, to be able to know ourselves as we ought to do in the true bias. In short, I would have this to be the book my young gentleman should study with the most attention. So many humours, so many sects, so many judgments, opinions, laws, and customs teach us to judge aright of our own and inform our understanding to discover its imperfection and natural infirmity, which is no trivial speculation. So many mutations of states and kingdoms and so many turns and revolutions of public fortune will make us wise enough to make no great wonder of our own. So many great names, so many famous victories and conquests drowned and swallowed in oblivion render our hopes ridiculous of eternising our names by the taking of half-a-score of light horse, or a henroost, which only derives its memory from its ruin. The pride and arrogance of so many foreign pomps and ceremonies, the tumorous majesty of so many courts and grandeurs accustom and fortify our sight without astonishment or winking to behold the lustre of our own; so many millions of men, buried before us, encourage us not to fear to go seek such good company in the other world: and so of all the rest. Pythagoras was wont to say that our life resembles the great and populous assembly of the Olympic games, wherein some exercise the body, that they may carry away the glory of the prize, others bring merchandise to sell for profit; there are, also some (and those none of the worst sort) who pursue no other advantage than only to look on, and consider how and why everything is done, and to be spectators of the lives of other men, thereby the better to judge of and regulate their own.

To examples may fitly be applied all the profitable discourses of philosophy, to which all human actions, as to their best rule, ought to be especially directed: a scholar shall be taught to know—"Learn what it is right to wish; what is the true use of coined money; how much it becomes us to give in liberality to our country and our dear relations; whom and what the Deity commanded thee to be; and in what part of the human system thou art placed; what we are and to what purpose engendered"; what it is to know, and what to be ignorant; what ought to be the end and design of study; what valor, temperance, and justice are; the difference betwixt ambition and avarice, servitude and subjection, licence and liberty; by what token a man may know true and solid contentment; how far death, affliction, and disgrace are to be apprehended: "And how you may shun or sustain every hardship"; by what secret springs we move and the reason of our various agitations and irresolutions: for, methinks, the first doctrine with which one should season his understanding ought to be that which regulates his manners and his sense; that teaches him to know himself and how both well to die and well to live. Amongst the liberal sciences, let us begin with that which makes us free; not that they do not all serve in some measure to the instruction and use of life, as all other things in some sort also do; but let us make choice of that which directly and professedly serves to that end. If we are once able to restrain the offices of human life within their just and natural limits, we shall find that most of the sciences in use are of no great use to us, and even in those that are, that there are many very unnecessary cavities and dilations which we had better let alone, and following Socrates' direction, limit the course of our studies to those things only where is a true and real utility: "Dare to be wise; begin: he

63. Pythagoras . . . say. Cicero, *Tusculan Disputations*, v, 3.   77–83. "Learn what . . . purpose engendered." Persius, III, 69. 90–91. "And how . . . hardship." Virgil, *Aeneid*, III, 459.   110. "Dare to be wise. . . ." Horace, *Epistles*, I, 2, 40.

who defers the hour of living well is like the clown, waiting till the river shall have flowed out; but the river still runs on, and will run on, with constant course, to ages without end." 'Tis a great foolery to teach our children—"What influence Pisces have, or the sign of angry Leo, or Capricorn laving in the Hesperian wave."

Anaximenes writing to Pythagoras, "To what purpose," said he, "should I trouble myself in searching out the secrets of the stars, having death or slavery continually before my eyes?" For the kings of Persia· were at that time preparing to invade his country. Every one ought to say thus, "Being assaulted as I am by ambition, avarice, temerity, superstition, and having within so many other enemies of life, shall I go cudgel my brains about the world's revolutions?"

After having taught him what will make him more wise and good, you may then entertain him with the elements of logic, physics, geometry, rhetoric, and the science which he shall then himself most incline to, his judgment being beforehand formed and fit to choose, he will quickly make his own. The way of instructing him ought to be sometimes by discourse and sometimes by reading; sometimes his governor shall put the author himself, which he shall think most proper for him, into his hands, and sometimes only the marrow and substance of it; and if himself be not conversant enough in books to turn to all the fine discourses the books contain for his purpose, there may some man of learning be joined to him that upon every occasion shall supply him with what he stands in need of, to furnish it to his pupil. And who can doubt but that this way of teaching is much more easy and natural than that of Gaza, in which the precepts are so intricate and so harsh and the words so vain, lean, and insignificant that there is no hold to be taken of them, nothing that quickens and elevates the wit and fancy, whereas here the mind has what to feed upon and to digest. This fruit, therefore, is not only without comparison much more fair and beautiful, but will also be much more early ripe.

'Tis a thousand pities that matters should be at such a pass in this age of ours that philosophy, even with men of understanding, should be looked upon as a vain and fantastic name, a thing of no use, no value, either in opinion or effect, of which I think those egotisms and petty sophistries, by prepossessing the avenues to it, are the cause. And people are much to blame to represent it to children for a thing of so difficult access and with such a frowning, grim, and formidable aspect. Who is it that has disguised it thus with this false, pale, and ghostly countenance?

There is nothing more airy, more gay, more frolic, and, I had like to have said, more wanton. She preaches nothing but feasting and jollity; a melancholic, anxious look shows that she does not inhabit there. Demetrius the grammarian finding in the temple of Delphos a knot of philosophers set chatting together, said to them, "Either I am much deceived, or by your cheerful and pleasant countenances, you are engaged in no very deep discourse." To which one of them, Heracleon the Megarean, replied: " 'Tis for such as are puzzled about inquiring whether the future tense of the verb βάλλω be spelt with a double λ, or that hunt after the derivation of the comparatives χεῖρον and βέλτιον, and the superlatives χείριστον and βέλτιστον, to knit their brows whilst discoursing of their science: but as to philosophical discourses, they always divert and cheer up those that entertain them, and never deject them or make them sad." "You may discern the torments of mind lurking in a sick body; you may discern its joys: each habit the face assumes from the mind."

The soul that lodges philosophy ought to be of such a constitution of health as to render the body in like manner healthful too; she ought to make her tranquillity and satisfaction shine so as to appear without, and her contentment ought to fashion the outward behaviour to her own mould and consequently to fortify it with a graceful confidence, an active and joyous carriage, and a serene and contented countenance. The most manifest sign of wisdom is a continual cheerfulness; her state is like that of things in the regions above the moon, always clear and serene. 'Tis Baroco and Baralipton that render their disciples so dirty and illfavoured, and not she; they do not so much as know her but by hearsay. What! It is she that calms and appeases the storms and tempests of the soul, and who teaches famine and fevers to laugh and sing; and that, not by certain imaginary epicycles, but by natural and manifest reasons. She has virtue for her end; which is not, as the schoolmen say, situate upon the summit of a perpendicular, rugged, inaccessible precipice. Such as have approached her find her, quite on the contrary, to be seated in a fair, fruitful, and flourishing plain, from whence she easily discovers all things below; to which place anyone may, however, arrive if he know but the way, through shady, green, and sweetly flourishing avenues, by a pleasant, easy, and smooth descent, like that of the celestial vault. 'Tis for not having frequented this supreme, this beautiful, triumphant, and amiable, this equally delicious and courageous virtue, this so professed and implacable enemy to anxiety, sorrow, fear, and constraint, who, having nature for her guide, has fortune

60

70

80

90

100

5–7. "What influence . . . wave." Propertius, IV, 1, 89. 8–11. Anaximenes . . . before my eyes?" according to Diogenes Laertius, II, 4. 35. Gaza, Theodore Gaza, rector of the Academy of Ferrara.

72–75. "You may discern . . . mind." Juvenal, IX, 18. 87. Baroco and Baralipton, two terms of old scholastic logic.

and pleasure for her companions, that they have gone according to their own weak imagination and created this ridiculous, this sorrowful, querulous, despiteful, threatening, terrible image of it to themselves and others, and placed it upon a rock apart, amongst thorns and brambles, and made of it a hobgoblin to affright people.

But the governor that I would have, that is such a one as knows it to be his duty to possess his pupil with as much or more affection than reverence to virtue, will be able to inform him that the poets have evermore accommodated themselves to the public humour, and make him sensible that the gods have planted more toil and sweat in the avenues of the cabinets of Venus than in those of Minerva. And when he shall once find him begin to apprehend and shall represent to him a Bradamante or an Angelica for a mistress, a natural, active, generous, and not a viragoish, but a manly beauty, in comparison of a soft, delicate, artificial, simpering, and affected form; the one in the habit of a heroic youth, wearing a glittering helmet, the other tricked up in curls and ribbons like a wanton minx; he will then look upon his own affection as brave and masculine when he shall choose quite contrary to that effeminate shepherd of Phrygia.

Such a tutor will make a pupil digest this new lesson, that the height and value of true virtue consists in the facility, utility, and pleasure of its exercise; so far from difficulty that boys as well as men and the innocent as well as the subtle may make it their own: it is by order, and not by force, that it is to be acquired. Socrates, her first minion, is so averse to all manner of violence, as totally to throw it aside, to slip into the more natural facility of her own progress. 'Tis the nursing mother of all human pleasures, who in rendering them just, renders them also pure and permanent; in moderating them, keeps them in breath and appetite; in interdicting those which she herself refuses, whets our desire to those that she allows; and, like a kind and liberal mother, abundantly allows all that nature requires, even to satiety, if not to lassitude: unless we mean to say that the regimen which stops the toper before he has drunk himself drunk, the glutton before he has eaten to a surfeit, and the lecher before he has got the pox is an enemy to pleasure. If the ordinary fortune fail, she does without it and forms another, wholly her own, not so fickle and unsteady as the other. She can be rich, be potent and wise, and knows how to lie upon soft perfumed beds: she loves life, beauty, glory, and health; but her proper and peculiar office is to know how to regulate the use of all these good things, and how to lose them without concern: an office much more noble than troublesome, and with-

out which the whole course of life is unnatural, turbulent, and deformed, and there it is indeed, that men may justly represent those monsters upon rocks and precipices.

If this pupil shall happen to be of so contrary a disposition that he had rather hear a tale of a tub than the true narrative of some noble expedition or some wise and learned discourse; who at the beat of drum that excites the youthful ardour of his companions leaves that to follow another that calls to a morris dance or the bears; who would not wish, and find it more delightful and more excellent, to return all dust and sweat victorious from a battle than from tennis or from a ball, with the prize of those exercises; I see no other remedy but that he be bound prentice in some good town to learn to make minced pies, though he were the son of a duke; according to Plato's precept that children are to be placed out and disposed of, not according to the wealth, qualities, or condition of the father, but according to the faculties and the capacity of their own souls.

Since philosophy is that which instructs us to live, and that infancy has there its lessons as well as other ages, why is it not communicated to children betimes? "The clay is moist and soft: now, now make haste, and form the pitcher on the rapid wheel."

They begin to teach us to live when we have almost done living. A hundred students have got the pox before they have come to read Aristotle's lecture on temperance. Cicero said that though he should live two men's ages, he should never find leisure to study the lyric poets; and I find these sophisters yet more deplorably unprofitable. The boy we would breed has a great deal less time to spare; he owes but the first fifteen or sixteen years of his life to education; the remainder is due to action. Let us, therefore, employ that short time in necessary instruction. Away with the thorny subtleties of dialectics; they are abuses, things by which our lives can never be amended. Take the plain philosophical discourses, learn how rightly to choose, and then rightly to apply them; they are more easy to be understood than one of Boccaccio's novels; a child from nurse is much more capable of them than of learning to read or to write. Philosophy has discourses proper for childhood as well as for the decrepit age of men.

I am of Plutarch's mind that Aristotle did not so much trouble his great disciple with the knack of forming syllogisms or with the elements of geometry as with infusing into him good precepts concerning valor, prowess, magnanimity, temperance, and the contempt of fear; and with this ammunition sent him,

17. a Bradamante or an Angelica, heroines of Ariosto's *Orlando Furioso.* 25-26. that effeminate . . . Phrygia, Paris of Troy.

66. the bears; a reference to bear-baiting, an ugly sport of the time. 81-83. "The clay . . . wheel." Persius, III, 23. 105. his great disciple, Alexander the Great.

whilst yet a boy, with no more than thirty thousand foot, four thousand horse, and but forty-two thousand crowns to subjugate the empire of the whole earth. For the other arts and sciences, he says, Alexander highly indeed commended their excellence and charm and had them in very great honour and esteem, but not ravished with them to that degree as to be tempted to affect the practice of them in his own person. "Young men and old men derive hence a certain end to the mind, and stores for miserable grey hairs."

Epicurus, in the beginning of his letter to Meniceus, says, "That neither the youngest should refuse to philosophize nor the oldest grow weary of it." Who does otherwise seems tacitly to imply that either the time of living happily is not yet come or that it is already past. And yet, for all that, I would not have this pupil of ours imprisoned and made a slave to his book; nor would I have him given up to the morosity and melancholic humour of a sour, ill-natured pedant; I would not have his spirit cowed and subdued by applying him to the rack and tormenting him, as some do, fourteen or fifteen hours a day and so make a packhorse of him. Neither should I think it good when, by reason of a solitary and melancholic complexion, he is discovered to be overmuch addicted to his book, to nourish that humour in him; for that renders him unfit for civil conversation, and diverts him from better employments. And how many have I seen in my time totally brutified by an immoderate thirst after knowledge? Carneades was so besotted with it that he would not find time so much as to comb his head or to pare his nails. Neither would I have his generous manners spoiled and corrupted by the incivility and barbarism of those of another. The French wisdom was anciently turned into proverb: "Early, but of no continuance." And, in truth, we yet see that nothing can be more ingenious and pleasing than the children of France; but they ordinarily deceive the hope and expectation that have been conceived of them; and grown up to be men, have nothing extraordinary or worth taking notice of: I have heard men of good understanding say, these colleges of ours to which we send our young people (and of which we have but too many) make them such animals as they are.

But to our little monsieur, a closet, a garden, the table, his bed, solitude and company, morning and evening, all hours shall be the same, and all places to him a study; for philosophy, who, as the formatrix of judgment and manners, shall be his principal lesson, has that privilege to have a hand in everything. The orator Isocrates, being at a feast entreated to

A portrait of Michel de Montaigne ascribed to the French school of Corneille de Lyon.

speak of his art, all the company were satisfied with and commended his answer: "It is not now a time," said he, "to do what I can do; and that which it is now time to do, I cannot do." For to make orations and rhetorical disputes in a company met together to laugh and make good cheer had been very unseasonable and improper, and as much might have been said of all the other sciences. But as to what concerns philosophy, that part of it at least that treats of man and of his offices and duties, it has been the common opinion of all wise men that, out of respect to the sweetness of her conversation, she is ever to be admitted in all sports and entertainments. And Plato, having invited her to his feast, we see after how gentle and obliging a manner, accommodated both to time and place, she entertained the company, though in a discourse of the highest and most important nature. "It profits poor and rich alike, but, neglected, equally hurts old and young." By this method of instruction, my young pupil will be much more and better employed than his fellows of the college are. But as the steps we take in walking to and fro in a gallery, though three times as many, do not tire a man so much as those we em-

9–11. "Young men . . . grey hairs." Persius, v, 64. 12–14. Epicurus . . . weary of it." Diogenes Laertius, x, 122. 32–34. Carneades . . . pare his nails. Idem, IV, 62.

56–58. "It is not . . . I cannot do." Plutarch, *Symposium*, I, 1. 72–73. "It profits . . . old and young." Horace, *Epistles*, I, 1, 25.

ploy in a formal journey, so our lesson, as it were accidentally occurring without any set obligation of time or place and falling naturally into every action, will insensibly insinuate itself. By which means our very exercises and recreations, running, wrestling, music, dancing, hunting, riding, and fencing, will prove to be a good part of our study. I would have his outward fashion and mien and the disposition of his limbs formed at the same time with his mind. 'Tis not a soul, 'tis not a body that we are training up, but a man, and we ought not to divide him. And, as Plato says, we are not to fashion one without the other, but make them draw together like two horses harnessed to a coach. By which saying of his, does he not seem to allow more time for, and to take more care of, exercises for the body, and to hold that the mind, in a good proportion, does her business at the same time too?

As to the rest, this method of education ought to be carried on with a severe sweetness, quite contrary to the practice of our pedants, who, instead of tempting and alluring children to letters by apt and gentle ways, do in truth present nothing before them but rods and ferules, horror and cruelty. Away with this violence! away with this compulsion! than which, I certainly believe nothing more dulls and degenerates a well-descended nature. If you would have him apprehend shame and chastizement, do not harden him to them: inure him to heat and cold, to wind and sun, and to dangers that he ought to despise; wean him from all effeminacy and delicacy in clothes and lodging, eating and drinking; accustom him to everything, that he may not be a Sir Paris, a carpet-knight, but a sinewy, hardy, and vigorous young man. I have ever, from a child to the age wherein I now am, been of this opinion, and am still constant to it. But amongst other things, the strict government of most of our colleges has evermore displeased me; peradventure they might have erred less perniciously on the indulgent side. 'Tis a real house of correction of imprisoned youth. They are made debauched by being punished before they are so. Do but come in when they are about their lesson and you shall hear nothing but the outcries of boys under execution, with the thundering noise of their pedagogues drunk with fury. A very pretty way this, to tempt these tender and timorous souls to love their book, with a furious countenance and a rod in hand! A cursed and pernicious way of proceeding! Besides what Quintilian has very well observed, that this imperious authority is often attended by very dangerous consequences, and particularly our way of chastising. How much more decent would it be to see their classes strewed with green leaves and fine flowers than with the bloody stumps of birch and willows? Were it left to my ordering, I should paint the school with the pictures of

joy and gladness; Flora and the Graces, as the philosopher Speusippus did his. Where their profit is, let them there have their pleasure too. Such viands as are proper and wholesome for children should be sweetened with sugar, and such as are dangerous to them embittered with gall. 'Tis marvellous to see how solicitous Plato is in his *Laws* concerning the gaiety and diversion of the youth of his city, and how much and often he enlarges upon their races, sports, songs, leaps, and dances: of which, he says, that antiquity has given the ordering and patronage particularly to the gods themselves, to Apollo, Minerva, and the Muses. He insists long upon, and is very particular in, giving innumerable precepts for exercises; but as to the lettered sciences, says very little, and only seems particularly to recommend poetry upon the account of music.

All singularity in our manners and conditions is to be avoided as inconsistent with civil society. Who would not be astonished at so strange a constitution as that of Demophoon, steward to Alexander the Great, who sweated in the shade, and shivered in the sun? I have seen those who have run from the smell of a mellow apple with greater precipitation than from a harquebuss shot; others afraid of a mouse; others vomit at the sight of cream; others ready to swoon at the making of a feather bed; Germanicus could neither endure the sight nor the crowing of a cock. I will not deny but that there may, peradventure, be some occult cause and natural aversion in these cases; but, in my opinion, a man might conquer it if he took it in time. Precept has in this wrought so effectually upon me, though not without some pains on my part, I confess, that beer excepted, my appetite accommodates itself indifferently to all sorts of diet.

Young bodies are supple; one should, therefore, in that age bend and ply them to all fashions and customs: and provided a man can contain the appetite and the will within their due limits, let a young man, in God's name, be rendered fit for all nations and all companies, even to debauchery and excess, if need be; that is, where he shall do it out of complacency to the customs of the place. Let him be able to do everything, but love to do nothing but what is good. The philosophers themselves do not justify Callisthenes for forfeiting the favour of his master Alexander the Great by refusing to pledge him a cup of wine. Let him laugh, play, wench, with his prince: nay, I would have him, even in his debauches, too hard for the rest of the company and to excel his companions in ability and vigour, and that he may not give over doing it, either through defect of power or knowledge how to do it, but for want of will.

58–59. **as the philosopher Speusippus did his**; according to Diogenes Laertius. IV, 1.

"There is a vast difference betwixt forbearing to sin and not knowing how to sin." I thought I passed a compliment upon a lord, as free from those excesses as any man in France, by asking him before a great deal of very good company how many times in his life he had been drunk in Germany in the time of his being there about his majesty's affairs; which he also took as it was intended, and made answer, "Three times;" and withal, told us the whole story
10 of his debauches. I know some who, for want of this faculty, have found a great inconvenience in negotiating with that nation. I have often with great admiration reflected upon the wonderful constitution of Alcibiades, who so easily could transform himself to so various fashions without any prejudice to his health; one while outdoing the Persian pomp and luxury, and another, the Lacedaemonian austerity and frugality; as reformed in Sparta, as voluptuous in Ionia. "Every complexion of life, every station and
20 circumstance, well became Aristippus." I would have my pupil to be such a one: "I should admire him who, with patience bearing a patched garment, bears well a changed fortune, acting both parts equally well." These are my lessons, and he who puts them in practice shall reap more advantage than he who has had them read to him only, and so only knows them. If you see him, you hear him; if you hear him, you see him. God forbid, says one in Plato, that to philosophize were only to read a great many books
30 and to learn the arts. "They have proceeded to this discipline of living well, which of all arts is the greatest, by their lives rather than by their reading." Leo, prince of the Phliasians, asking Heraclides Ponticus of what art or science he made profession; "I know," said he, "neither art nor science, but I am a philosopher." One reproaching Diogenes that, being ignorant, he should pretend to philosophy, "I therefore," answered he, "pretend to it with so much the more reason." Hegesias entreated that he would
40 read a certain book to him; "You are pleasant," said he; "you choose those figs that are true and natural and not those that are painted; why do you not also choose exercises which are naturally true rather than those written?"

The lad will not so much get his lesson by heart as he will practise it: he will repeat it in his actions. We shall discover if there be prudence in his exercises, if there be sincerity and justice in his deportment, if there be grace and judgment in his speak-
50 ing, if there be constancy in his sickness, if there be modesty in his mirth, temperance in his pleasures,

1–2. "There is a vast . . . sin." Seneca, *Epistles*, 90. 19–20. "Every complexion . . . Aristippus." Horace, *Epistles*, XVII, 23. 21–24. "I should . . . well." Idem, 25. 30–32. "They have proceeded . . . reading." Cicero, *Tusculan Disputations*, IV, 3. 35–36. "I know," said he. . . . According to Cotton, Pythagoras (and not Heraclides) made this answer. 40–44. "You are pleasant . . . written?" Diogenes Laertius, VI, 48.

order in his domestic economy, indifference in his palate, whether what he eats or drinks be flesh or fish, wine or water. "Who considers his own discipline, not as a vain ostentation of science, but as a law and rule of life; and who obeys his own decrees, and the laws he has prescribed to himself." The conduct of our lives is the true mirror of our doctrine. Zeuxidamus, to one who asked him why the Lace-
60 daemonians did not commit their constitutions of chivalry to writing and deliver them to their young men to read, made answer that it was because they would inure them to action and not amuse them with words. With such a one, after fifteen or sixteen years' study, compare one of our college Latinists, who has thrown away so much time in nothing but learning to speak. The world is nothing but babble; and I hardly ever yet saw that man who did not rather prate too much than speak too little. And yet
70 half of our age is embezzled this way: we are kept four or five years to learn words only, and to tack them together into clauses; as many more to form them into a long discourse, divided into four or five parts; and other five years at least to learn succinctly to mix and interweave them after a subtle and intricate manner: let us leave all this to those who make a profession of it. . . .

Let but our pupil be well furnished with things, words will follow but too fast; he will pull them
80 after him if they do not voluntarily follow. I have observed some to make excuses that they cannot express themselves and pretend to have their fancies full of a great many very fine things which yet, for want of eloquence, they cannot utter; 'tis a mere shift, and nothing else. Will you know what I think of it? I think they are nothing but shadows of some imperfect images and conceptions that they know not what to make of within, nor consequently bring out. They do not yet themselves understand what they would be at, and if you but observe how they
90 haggle and stammer upon the point of parturition, you will soon conclude that their labour is not to delivery, but about conception, and that they are but licking their formless embryo. For my part, I hold, and Socrates commands it, that whoever has in his mind a sprightly and clear imagination will express it well enough in one kind of tongue or another, and, if he be dumb, by signs. "Once a thing is conceived in the mind, the words to express it soon present themselves."
100 And as another as poetically says in his prose, "When things are once in the mind, the words offer themselves readily:" and this other, "The things themselves force words to express them." He knows

54–57. "Who considers . . . to himself." Cicero, *Tusculan Disputations*, II, 4. 59. Zeuxidamus, a king of Sparta. 98–100. "Once a thing . . . themselves." Horace, *Art of Poetry*, V, 311. 102–103. "When things . . . readily." Seneca, *Controvers.*, III, proem. 103–104. "The things . . . them." Cicero, *De Finibus*, III, 5.

nothing of ablative, conjunctive, substantive, or grammar, no more than his lackey or a fishwife of the Petit Pont; and yet these will give you a bellyful of talk, if you will hear them, and peradventure shall trip as little in their language as the best masters of art in France. He knows no rhetoric, nor how in a preface to bribe the benevolence of the courteous reader; neither does he care to know it. Indeed, all this fine decoration of painting is easily effaced by the lustre of a simple and blunt truth: these fine flourishes serve only to amuse the vulgar, of themselves incapable of more solid and nutritive diet, as Aper very evidently demonstrates in Tacitus. The ambassadors of Samos, prepared with a long and elegant oration, came to Cleomenes, King of Sparta, to incite him to a war against the tyrant Polycrates; who, after he had heard their harangue with great gravity and patience, gave them this answer: "As to the exordium, I remember it not, nor consequently the middle of your speech; and for what concerns your conclusion, I will not do what you desire:" a very pretty answer this, methinks, and a pack of learned orators most sweetly gravelled. And what did the other man say? The Athenians were to choose one of two architects for a very great building they had designed; of these, the first, a pert, affected fellow, offered his service in a long premeditated discourse upon the subject of the work in hand, and by his oratory inclined the voices of the people in his favour; but the other in three words; "O, Athenians, what this man says, I will do." Let it go before or come after, a good sentence or a thing well said is always in season; if it neither suit well with what went before, nor has much coherence with what follows after, it is good in itself. I am none of those who think that good rhyme makes a good poem. Let him make short long and long short if he will, 'tis no great matter; if there be invention and the wit and judgment have well performed their offices, I will say, here's a good poet, but an ill rhymer —"of delicate humour, but of rugged versification." Let a man, says Horace, divest his work of all method and measure, "take away certain rhythms and measures, and change the order of the words, putting that which should be first last, and the last first, still these misplaced members have all the elements of poetry," he will never the more lose himself for that; the very pieces will be fine by themselves. Menander's answer had this meaning, who being reproved by a friend, the time drawing on at which he had promised a comedy, that he had not

yet fallen in hand with it; "It is made and ready," said he, "all but the verses." Having contrived the subject and disposed the scenes in his fancy, he took little care for the rest. Since Ronsard and Du Bellay have given reputation to our French poesy, every little dabbler, for aught I see, swells his words as high and makes his cadences very near as harmonious as they. "More sound than sense." For the vulgar, there were never so many poetasters as now; but though they find it no hard matter to imitate their rhyme, they yet fall infinitely short of imitating the rich descriptions of the one and the delicate invention of the other of these masters. . . .

Words are to serve and to follow a man's purpose; and let Gascon come in play where French will not do. I would have things so excelling and so wholly possessing the imagination of him that hears that he should have something else to do than to think of words. The way of speaking that I love is natural and plain, the same in writing as in speaking, and a sinewy and muscular way of expressing a man's self, short and pithy, not so elegant and artificial as prompt and vehement; rather hard than wearisome; free from affectation; irregular, incontinuous, and bold; where every piece makes up an entire body; not like a pedant, a preacher, or a pleader, but rather a soldier-like style, as Suetonius calls that of Julius Caesar; and yet I see no reason why he should call it so. I have ever been ready to imitate the negligent garb, which is yet observable amongst the young men of our time, to wear my cloak on one shoulder, my cap on one side, a stocking in disorder, which seems to express a kind of haughty disdain of these exotic ornaments and a contempt of the artificial; but I find this negligence of much better use in the form of speaking. All affectation, particularly in the French gaiety and freedom, is ungraceful in a courtier, and in a monarchy every gentleman ought to be fashioned according to the court model; for which reason, an easy and natural negligence does well. I no more like a web where the knots and seams are to be seen than a fine figure, so delicate that a man may tell all the bones and veins. "Let the language that is dedicated to truth be plain and unaffected. . . . For who studies to speak too accurately, that does not at the same time design to perplex his auditory?" That eloquence prejudices the subject it would advance, that wholly attracts us to itself. And as in our outward habit, 'tis a ridiculous effeminacy to distinguish ourselves by a particular and unusual garb or fashion; so in language, to study new phrases and to affect words that are not of current use proceeds from a puerile and scholastic ambition. May I be bound to speak no other language than what is

10–13. these fine flourishes . . . in Tacitus. Tacitus, De Causis Corrputae Eloquentiae. 18–21. "As to the exordium . . . you desire." Plutarch, Apothegms of the Lacedaemonians. 30–31. "O, Athenians . . . will do." Plutarch, Instructions to Statesmen, 4. 41. "of delicate humour . . . versification." Horace, Satires, IV, 8. 43–47. "take away . . . elements of poetry." Horace, Satires, I, 4, 58.

59. "More sound than sense." Seneca, Epistles, 40. 94–98. "Let the language . . . his auditory?" Seneca, Epistles, 40 and 57.

spoken in the market-places of Paris! Aristophanes the grammarian was quite out when he reprehended Epicurus for his plain way of delivering himself, and the design of his oratory, which was only perspicuity of speech. The imitation of words, by its own facility, immediately disperses itself through a whole people; but the imitation of inventing and fitly applying those words is of a slower progress. The generality of readers, for having found a like robe, very mistakenly imagine they have the same body and inside too, whereas force and sinews are never to be borrowed; the gloss and outward ornament, that is, words and elocution, may. Most of those I converse with speak the same language I here write; but whether they think the same thoughts I cannot say. The Athenians, says Plato, study fullness and elegancy of speaking; the Lacedaemonians affect brevity, and those of Crete aim more at the fecundity of conception than the fertility of speech; and these are the best. Zeno used to say that he had two sorts of disciples, one that he called φιλολόγως curious to learn things, and these were his favourites; the other, λογοφίλως that cared for nothing but words. Not that fine speaking is not a very good and commendable quality; but not so excellent and so necessary as some would make it; and I am scandalized that our whole life should be spent in nothing else. I would first understand my own language and that of my neighbours, with whom most of my business and conversation lies.

No doubt but Greek and Latin are very great ornaments, and of very great use, but we buy them too dear. I will here discover one way, which has been experimented in my own person, by which they are to be had better cheap, and such may make use of it as will. My late father, having made the most precise inquiry that any man could possibly make amongst men of the greatest learning and judgment, of an exact method of education, was by them cautioned of this inconvenience then in use, and made to believe that the tedious time we applied to the learning of the tongues of them who had them for nothing was the sole cause we could not arrive to the grandeur of soul and perfection of knowledge of the ancient Greeks and Romans. I do not, however, believe that to be the only cause. However, the expedient my father found out for this was that in my infancy, and before I began to speak, he committed me to the care of a German, who since died a famous physician in France, totally ignorant of our language, but very fluent, and a great critic in Latin. This man, whom he had fetched out of his own country, and whom he entertained with a great salary for this only end, had me continually with

him: to him there were also joined two others, of inferior learning, to attend me and to relieve him; who all of them spoke to me in no other language but Latin. As to the rest of his family, it was an inviolable rule that neither himself, nor my mother, man nor maid, should speak anything in my company but such Latin words as every one had learned only to gabble with me. It is not to be imagined how great an advantage this proved to the whole family; my father and my mother by this means learned Latin enough to understand it perfectly well and to speak it to such a degree as was sufficient for any necessary use; as also those of the servants did who were most frequently with me. In short we Latined it at such a rate, that it overflowed to all the neighbouring villages, where there yet remain, that have established themselves by custom, several Latin appellations of artisans and their tools. As for what concerns myself, I was above six years of age before I understood either French or Perigordin, any more than Arabic; and without art, book, grammar, or precept, whipping, or the expense of a tear, I had, by that time, learned to speak as pure Latin as my master himself, for I had no means of mixing it up with any other. . . .

As to Greek, of which I have but a mere smattering, my father also designed to have it taught me by a device, but a new one, and by way of sport; tossing our declensions to and fro, after the manner of those who, by certain games at tables and chess, learn geometry and arithmetic. For he, amongst other rules, had been advised to make me relish science and duty by an unforced will and of my own voluntary motion and to educate my soul in all liberty and delight without any severity or constraint; which he was an observer of to such a degree, even of superstition, if I may say so, that some being of opinion that it troubles and disturbs the brains of children suddenly to wake them in the morning and to snatch them violently and over-hastily from sleep (wherein they are much more profoundly involved than we), he caused me to be wakened by the sound of some musical instrument and was never unprovided of a musician for that purpose. By this example you may judge of the rest, this alone being sufficient to recommend both the prudence and the affection of so good a father, who is not to be blamed if he did not reap fruits answerable to so exquisite a culture. Of this, two things were the cause: first, a sterile and improper soil; for, though I was a strong and healthful constitution, and of a disposition tolerably sweet and tractable, yet I was, withal, so heavy, idle, and indisposed that they could not rouse me from my sloth, not even to get me out to play. What I saw, I saw clearly enough, and under this heavy complexion nourished a bold imagination and opinions above my age. I had a slow wit, that

1–5. Aristophanes . . . perspicuity of speech. As reported by Diogenes Laertius, X, 13. 16. The Athenians, says Plato. . . . Idem.

would go no faster than it was led; a tardy under-standing, a languishing invention, and, above all, incredible defect of memory; so that it is no wonder if from all these nothing considerable could be extracted. Secondly, like those who, impatient of a long and steady cure, submit to all sorts of prescriptions and recipes, the good man being extremely timorous of any way failing in a thing he had so wholly set his heart upon, suffered himself at last to be overruled by the common opinions, which always follow their leader as a flight of cranes, and complying with the method of the time, having no more those persons he had brought out of Italy and who had given him the first model of education about him, he sent me at six years of age to the College of Guienne, at that time the best and most flourishing in France. And there it was not possible to add anything to the care he had to provide me the most able tutors, with all other circumstances of education, reserving also several particular rules contrary to the college practice; but so it was, that with all these precautions it was a college still. My Latin immediately grew corrupt, of which also by discontinuance I have since lost all manner of use; so that this new way of education served me to no other end than only at my first coming to prefer me to the first forms; for at thirteen years old, that I came out of the college, I had run through my whole course (as they call it), and, in truth, without any manner of advantage that I can honestly brag of in all this time. . . .

To return to my subject, there is nothing like alluring the appetite and affections; otherwise you make nothing but so many asses laden with books; by dint of the lash, you give them their pocketful of learning to keep; whereas, to do well, you should not only lodge it with them, but make them espouse it.

Of Age

I CANNOT allow of the way in which we settle for ourselves the duration of our life. I see that the sages contract it very much in comparison of the common opinion: "What," said the younger Cato to those who would stay his hand from killing himself, "am I now of an age to be reproached that I go out of the world too soon?" And yet he was but eight-and-forty years old. He thought that to be a mature and advanced age, considering how few arrive unto it. And such as, soothing their thoughts with I know not what course of nature, promise to themselves some years beyond it, could they be privileged from the infinite number of accidents to which we are by a natural subjection exposed, they might have some reason so to do. What an idle con-

Of Age. Translated by Charles Cotton.

ceit is it to expect to die of a decay of strength, which is the effect of extremest age, and to propose to ourselves no shorter lease of life than that, considering it is a kind of death of all others the most rare and very seldom seen? We call that only a natural death; as if it were contrary to nature to see a man break his neck with a fall, be drowned in shipwreck, be snatched away with a pleurisy or the plague, and as if our ordinary condition did not expose us to these inconveniences. Let us no longer flatter ourselves with these fine words; we ought rather, peradventure, to call that natural which is general, common, and universal.

To die of old age is a death rare, extraordinary, and singular, and, therefore, so much less natural than the others; 'tis the last and extremest sort of dying: and the more remote, the less to be hoped for. It is, indeed, the bourn beyond which we are not to pass, and which the law of nature has set as a limit not to be exceeded; but it is, withal, a privilege she is rarely seen to give us to last till then. 'Tis a lease she only signs by particular favour, and it may be to one only in the space of two or three ages, and then with a pass to boot, to carry him through all the traverses and difficulties she has strewed in the way of this long career. And therefore my opinion is that when once forty years we should consider it as an age to which very few arrive. For seeing that men do not usually proceed so far, it is a sign that we are pretty well advanced; and since we have exceeded the ordinary bounds, which is the just measure of life, we ought not to expect to go much further; having escaped so many precipices of death, whereinto we have seen so many other men fall, we should acknowledge that so extraordinary a fortune as that which has hitherto rescued us from those eminent perils and kept us alive beyond the ordinary term of living is not likely to continue long.

'Tis a fault in our very laws to maintain this error. These say that a man is not capable of managing his own estate till he be five-and-twenty years old, whereas he will have much ado to manage his life so long. Augustus cut off five years from the ancient Roman standard, and declared that thirty years old was sufficient for a judge. Servius Tullius superseded the knights of above seven-and-forty years of age from the fatigues of war; Augustus dismissed them at forty-five; though methinks it seems a little unreasonable that men should be sent to the fireside till five-and-fifty or sixty years of age. I should be of opinion that our vocation and employment should be as far as possible extended for the public good: I find the fault on the other side, that they do not employ us early enough. This emperor was arbiter of the whole world at nineteen, and yet would have a man to be thirty before he could be fit to determine a dispute about a gutter.

For my part, I believe our souls are adult at twenty as much as they are ever likely to be, and as capable then as ever. A soul that has not by that time given evident earnest of its force and virtue will never after come to proof. The natural qualities and virtues produce what they have of vigorous and fine within that term or never. "If the thorn does not prick at its birth, 'twill hardly ever prick at all," as they say in Dauphiné.

Of all the great human actions I ever heard or read of, of what sort soever, I have observed, both in former ages and our own, more were performed before the age of thirty than after; and this ofttimes in the very lives of the same men. May I not confidently instance in those of Hannibal and his great concurrent Scipio? The better half of their lives they lived upon the glory they had acquired in their youth; great men after, 'tis true, in comparison of others; but by no means in comparison of themselves. As to my own particular, I do certainly believe that since that age, both my understanding and my constitution have rather decayed than improved, and retired rather than advanced. 'Tis possible that with those who make the best use of their time, knowledge and experience may increase with their years; but vivacity, promptitude, steadiness, and other pieces of us, of much greater importance and much more essentially our own, languish and decay. "When once the body's shaken by the violence of time, blood and vigour ebbing away, the judgment then also halts, the tongue trips, and the mind dotes." Sometimes the body first submits to age, sometimes the mind, and I have seen enough who have got a weakness in their brains before either in their legs or stomach; and by how much the more it is a disease of no great pain to the sufferer, and of obscure symptoms, so much greater is the danger. For this reason it is that I complain of our laws, not that they keep us too long to our work, but that they set us to work too late. For the frailty of life considered, and to how many ordinary and natural rocks it is exposed, one ought not to give up so large a portion of it to childhood, idleness, and apprenticeship.

That We Taste Nothing Pure

THE imbecility of our condition is such that things cannot, in their natural simplicity and purity, fall into our use; the elements that we enjoy are changed, and so 'tis with metals; and gold must be debased with some other matter to fit it for our

service. Neither has virtue, so simple as that which Aristo, Pyrrho, and also the Stoics, made the End of life; nor the Cyrenaic and Aristippic pleasure, been without mixture useful to it. Of the pleasure and goods that we enjoy, there is not one exempt from some mixture of ill and inconvenience: "In the very source of our pleasure, there is something that is bitter, and that vexes even the flowers." Our extremest pleasure has some air of groaning and complaining in it; would you not say that it is dying of pain? Nay, when we frame the image of it in its full excellence, we stuff it with sickly and painful epithets and qualities, languor, softness, feebleness, faintness, *morbidezza*: a great testimony of their consanguinity and consubstantiality. The most profound joy has more of severity than gaiety in it. The highest and fullest contentment offers more of the grave than of the merry; "Even felicity, unless it moderate itself, oppresses." Pleasure chews and grinds us; according to the old Greek verse, which says that the gods sell us all the goods they give us; that is to say, that they give us nothing pure and perfect, and that we do not purchase but at the price of some evil.

Labour and pleasure, very unlike in nature, associate, nevertheless, by I know not what natural conjunction. Socrates says, that some god tried to mix in one mass and to confound pain and pleasure, but not being able to do it, he bethought him at least, to couple them by the tail. Metrodorus said that in sorrow there is some mixture of pleasure. I know not whether or no he intended anything else by that saying; but for my part, I am of opinion that there is design, consent, and complacency in giving a man's self up to melancholy. I say, that besides ambition, which may also have a stroke in the business, there is some shadow of delight and delicacy which smiles upon and flatters us even in the very lap of melancholy. Are there not some constitutions that feed upon it? " 'Tis a certain kind of pleasure to weep." And one Attalus in Seneca says that the memory of our lost friends is as grateful to us, as bitterness in wine, when too old, is to the palate— "Boy, when you pour out old Falernian wine, the bitterest put into my bowl"—and as apples that have a sweet tartness.

Nature discovers this confusion to us; painters hold that the same motions and screwings of the

29–32. **"When once . . . the mind dotes."** Lucretius, iii, 452.
That We Taste Nothing Pure. Translated by Charles Cotton.

51. **Aristo,** Stoic philosopher, fl. 260 B.C. **Pyrrho,** founder of the Sceptic school (fourth century B.C.). 52. **Cyrenaic,** the Hedonic school of Aristippus of Cyrene, which made pleasure the end of human life. 55–57. **"In the . . . flowers."** Lucretius, iv, 1130. 63. *morbidezza,* softness. 67–68. **"Even felicity . . . oppresses."** Seneca, *Epistles,* 74. 68–69. **Pleasure . . . Greek verse.** Epicharmus, in Xenophon's *Memorabilia,* ii, 1, 20. 76. **Socrates says. . . .** *Phaedo,* ii, 1, 20. 79. **Metrodorus said. . . .** A disciple of Democritus in the Atomistic school, here quoted by Seneca in *Epistles,* 99. 89–90. **" 'Tis a certain . . . to weep."** Ovid, *Tristia,* iv, 3, 27. 90. **one Attalus in Seneca says. . . .** *Epistles,* 70.

face that serve for weeping, serve for laughter too; and indeed, before the one or the other be finished, do but observe the painter's manner of handling, and you will be in doubt to which of the two the design tends; and the extreme of laughter does at last bring tears. "No evil is without its compensation."

When I imagine man abounding with all the conveniences that are to be desired (let us put the case that all his members were always seized with a pleasure like that of generation, in its most excessive height), I feel him melting under the weight of his delight, and see him utterly unable to support so pure, so continual, and so universal a pleasure.) Indeed, he is running away whilst he is there, and naturally makes haste to escape, as from a place where he cannot stand firm, and where he is afraid of sinking.

When I religiously confess myself to myself, I find that the best virtue I have has in it some tincture of vice; and I am afraid that Plato, in his purest virtue (I, who am as sincere and loyal a lover of virtue of that stamp as any other whatever) if he had listened and laid his ear close to himself, and he did so no doubt, would have heard some jarring sound of human mixture, but faint and only perceptible to himself. Man is wholly and throughout but patch and motley. Even the laws of justice themselves cannot subsist without mixture of injustice; insomuch that Plato says, they undertake to cut off the hydra's head, who pretend to clear the law of all inconveniences. "Every great example has in it some mixture of injustice, which recompenses the wrong done to particular men by the public utility," says Tacitus.

It is likewise true that for the use of life and the service of public commerce, there may be some excesses in the purity and perspicacity of our minds; that penetrating light has in it too much of sublety and curiosity: we must a little stupefy and blunt them to render them more obedient to example and practice, and a little veil and obscure them, the better to proportion them to this dark and earthy life. And therefore common and less speculative souls are found to be more proper for and more successful in the management of affairs; and the elevated and exquisite opinions of philosophy unfit for business. This sharp vivacity of soul, and the supple and restless volubility attending it, disturb our negotiations. We are to manage human enterprises more superficially and roughly, and leave a great part to fortune; it is not necessary to examine

affairs with so much subtlety and so deep: a man loses himself in the consideration of so many contrary lustres, and so many various forms; "Whilst they considered of things so indifferent in themselves, they were astonished, and knew not what to do."

'Tis what the ancients say of Simonides, that by reason his imagination suggested to him, upon the question King Hiero had put to him (to answer which he had had many days to meditate in), several sharp and subtle considerations, whilst he doubted which was the most likely, he totally despaired of the truth.

(He who dives into and in his inquisition comprehends all circumstances and consequences, hinders his election:) a little engine well-handled is sufficient for executions, whether of less or greater weight. The best managers are those who can worst give account how they are so; while the greatest talkers, for the most part, do nothing to purpose. I know one of this sort of men, and a most excellent discourser upon all sorts of good husbandry, who has miserably let a hundred thousand livres yearly revenue slip through his hands. I know another who talks, who better advises than any man of his counsel, and there is not in the world a fairer show of soul and understanding than he has; nevertheless, when he comes to the test, his servants find him quite another thing; not to make any mention of his misfortunes.

Of Three Commerces

WE must not rivet ourselves so fast to our humours and complexions: our chiefest sufficiency is to know how to apply ourselves to divers employments. 'Tis to be, but not to live, to keep a man's self tied and bound by necessity to one only course; those are the bravest souls that have in them the most variety and pliancy. Of this here is an honourable testimony of the elder Cato: "His parts were so pliable to all uses that a man would think he had been born only for precisely that which he was at any time doing." Had I liberty to set myself forth after my own mode, there is no graceful fashion to which I would be so fixed as not to be able to disengage myself from it; life is an unequal, irregular, and multiform motion. 'Tis not to be a friend to one's self, much less a master—'tis to be a slave, incessantly to be led by the nose by

55–58. "Whilst they . . . what to do." Livy, xxxii, 20. 60–61. the question . . . to him. According to Cicero (*De Natura Deorum*, i, 22), King Hiero of Syracuse asked the Greek lyric poet Simonides (556–c. 468 B.C.) what God was.
Of Three Commerces.^A Translated by Charles Cotton.
89. the elder Cato. . . , the Roman statesman (234–149 B.C.) as quoted by Livy, xxxix, 49.

6–7. "No evil . . . compensation." Seneca, *Epistles*, 69. 30. Plato says. . . . *Republic*, iv, 5. 31. the hydra, the many-headed water-serpent in Greek mythology on whom two heads would grow as fast as one was cut off. 35. . . . says Tacitus. *Annals*, xiv, 44.

one's self, and to be so fixed in one's previous inclinations that one cannot turn aside nor writhe one's neck out of the collar. I say this now in this part of my life, wherein I find I cannot easily disengage myself from the importunity of my soul, which cannot ordinarily amuse itself but in things of limited range, nor employ itself otherwise than entirely and with all its force; upon the lightest subject offered it swells and stretches it to that degree as therein to employ its utmost power; wherefore, its idleness is to me a very painful labour, and very prejudicial to my health. Most men's minds require foreign matter to exercise and enliven them; mine has rather need of it to sit still and repose itself. "The vices of sloth are to be shaken off by business," for its chiefest and hardest study is to study itself. Books are to it a sort of employment that debauch it from its study. Upon the first thoughts that possess it, it begins to bustle and make trial of its vigour in all directions, exercises its power of handling, now making trial of force, now fortifying, moderating, and ranging itself by the way of grace and order. It has of its own wherewith to rouse its faculties: nature has given to it, as to all others, matter enough of its own to make advantage of, and subjects proper enough where it may either invent or judge.

Meditation is a powerful and full study to such as can effectually taste and employ themselves; I had rather fashion my soul than furnish it. There is no employment, either more weak or more strong, than that of entertaining a man's own thoughts, according as the soul is; the greatest men make it their whole business; "To whom to live is to think." Nature has therefore favoured it with this privilege, that there is nothing we can do so long, nor any action to which we more frequently and with greater facility addict ourselves. 'Tis the business of the gods, says Aristotle, and from which both their beatitude and ours proceed.

The principal use of reading to me is that by various objects it rouses my reason and employs my judgment, not my memory. Few conversations detain me without force and effort; it is true that beauty and elegance of speech take as much or more with me than the weight and depth of the subject; and forasmuch as I am apt to be sleepy in all other communication and give but the rind of my attention, it often falls out that in such poor and pitiful discourses, mere chatter, I either make drowsy, unmeaning answers, unbecoming a child, and ridiculous, or more foolishly and rudely still, maintain an obstinate silence. I have a pensive way that withdraws me into myself, and, with that, a heavy and childish ignorance of many very ordinary things, by

which two qualities I have earned this, that men may truly relate five or six as ridiculous tales of me as of any other man whatever.

But, to proceed in my subject, this difficult complexion of mine renders me very nice in my conversation with men, whom I must cull and pick out for my purpose; and unfits me for common society. We live and negotiate with the people; if their conversation be troublesome to us, if we disdain to apply ourselves to mean and vulgar souls (and the mean and vulgar are often as regular as those of the finest thread, and all wisdom is folly that does not accommodate itself to the common ignorance), we must no more intermeddle either with other men's affairs or our own; for business, both public and private, has to do with these people. The least forced and most natural motions of the soul are the most beautiful; the best employments, those that are least strained. Good God! how good an office does wisdom to those whose desires it limits to their power! that is the most useful knowledge: "what a man can," was ever the sentence Socrates was so much in love with. A motto of great substance.

We must moderate and adapt our desires to the nearest and easiest to be acquired things. Is it not a foolish humour of mine to separate myself from a thousand to whom my fortune has conjoined me, and without whom I cannot live, and cleave to one or two who are out of my intercourse; or rather a fantastic desire of a thing that I cannot obtain? My gentle and easy manners, enemies of all sourness and harshness, may easily enough have secured me from envy and animosities; to be beloved, I do not say, but never any man gave less occasion of being hated; but the coldness of my conversation has, reasonably enough, deprived me of the goodwill of many, who are to be excused if they interpret it in another and worse sense.

I am very capable of contracting and maintaining rare and exquisite friendships; for, by reason that I so greedily seize upon such acquaintance as fit my liking, I throw myself with such violence upon them that I hardly fail to stick, and to make an impression where I hit; as I have often made happy proof. In ordinary friendships I am somewhat cold and shy, for my motion is not natural, if not with full sail; besides which, my fortune having in my youth given me a relish for one sole and perfect friendship has, in truth, created in me a kind of distaste to others, and too much imprinted in my fancy that it is a beast of company, as the ancient said, but not of the herd. And also I have a natural difficulty of communicating myself by halves, with the modifications and the servile and jealous prudence required in the conversation of numerous and imperfect

14–15. "The vices . . . by business," Seneca, *Epistles*, 56. 33. "To whom . . . to think." Cicero, *Tusculan Disputations*, v, 38. 38. . . . says Aristotle; *Nicomachean Ethics*, x, 8.

105. . . . as the ancient said, Plutarch, *On the Plurality of Friends*, c, 2.

friendships: and we are principally enjoined to these in this age of ours, when we cannot talk of the world but either with danger or falsehood. . . .

There are some particular natures that are private and retired: my natural way is proper for communication, and apt to lay me open; I am all without and in sight, born for society and friendship. The solitude that I love myself and recommend to others is chiefly no other than to withdraw my thoughts and affections into myself; to restrain and check, not my steps, but my own cares and desires, resigning all foreign solicitude, and mortally avoiding servitude and obligation, and not so much the crowd of men, as the crowd of business. Local solitude, to say the truth, rather gives me more room, and sets me more at large; I more readily throw myself upon affairs of state and the world when I am alone. At the Louvre and in the bustle of the court, I fold myself within my own skin; the crowd thrusts me upon myself; and I never entertain myself so wantonly, with so much licence, or so especially, as in places of respect and ceremonious prudence: our follies do not make me laugh, but our wisdom does. I am naturally no enemy to a court life; I have therein passed a good part of my own, and am of a humour cheerfully to frequent great company, provided it be by intervals and at my own time: but this softness of judgment whereof I speak ties me perforce to solitude. Even at home, amidst a numerous family, and in a house sufficiently frequented, I see people enough, but rarely such with whom I delight to converse; and I there reserve both for myself and others an unusual liberty: there is in my house no such thing as ceremony, ushering or waiting upon people down to the coach, and such other troublesome ceremonies as our courtesy enjoins (O servile and importunate custom!) Every one there governs himself according to his own method; let who will speak his thoughts, I sit mute, meditating and shut up in my closet, without any offence to my guests.

The men whose society and familiarity I covet are those they call sincere and able men; and the image of these makes me disrelish the rest. It is, if rightly taken, the rarest of our forms, and a form that we chiefly owe to nature. The end of this commerce is simply privacy, frequentation, and conference, the exercise of souls, without other fruit. In our discourse, all subjects are alike to me; yet there be neither weight nor depth, 'tis all one: there is yet grace and pertinency; all there is tinted with a mature and constant judgment, and mixed with goodness, freedom, gaiety, and friendship. 'Tis not only in talking of the affairs of kings and state that our wits discover their force and beauty, but every whit as much in private conferences. I understand my men even by their silence and smiles; and better

discover them, perhaps, at table than in the council. Hippomachus said very well, "that he could know the good wrestlers by only seeing them walk in the street." If learning pleased to step into our talk, it shall not be rejected, not magisterial, imperious, and importunate, as it commonly is, but suffragan and docile itself. We there only seek to pass away our time; when we have a mind to be instructed and preached to, we will go seek this in its throne. Please let it humble itself to us for the nonce; for, useful and profitable as it is, I imagine that at need we may manage well enough without it and do our business without its assistance. A well-descended soul, and practised in the conversation of men, will of herself render herself sufficiently agreeable; art is nothing but the counterpart and register of what such souls produce.

The conversation also of beautiful and well-bred women is for me a sweet commerce: "For we also have eyes that are versed in the matter." If the soul has not therein so much to enjoy as in the first, the bodily senses, which participate more of this, bring it to a proportion near to, though in my opinion not equal to, the other. But 'tis a commerce wherein a man must stand a little upon his guard, especially those of a warm temperament such as mine. I there scalded myself in my youth, and suffered all the torments that poets say are to befall those who precipitate themselves into love without order and judgment: it is true that the whipping has made me wiser since: "Whoever of the Grecian fleet has escaped the Capharean rocks ever takes care to steer from those of the Euboean sea." 'Tis folly to fix all a man's thoughts upon it and to engage in it with a furious and indiscreet affection; but, on the other hand, to engage there without love and without inclination, like comedians to play a common part, without putting anything to it of his own but words, is indeed to provide for his safety, but, withal, after as cowardly a manner as he who should abandon his honour, profit, or pleasure for fear of ordinary danger; for it is certain that from such a practice they who set it on foot can expect no fruit that can please or satisfy a noble soul. A man must have, in good earnest, desired that which he, in good earnest, expects to have a pleasure in enjoying; I say, though fortune should unjustly favour their dissimulation; which often falls out, because there is none of the sex, let her be as ugly as the devil, who does not think herself well worthy to be beloved, and who does not prefer herself before other women, either for her youth, the colour of her hair, or her graceful motion (for there are no more women universally and throughout ugly than there are women univer-

59–61. Hippomachus said . . . in the street." Plutarch, *Life of Dion,* c, 1. 76–77. "For we also . . . in the matter." Cicero, *Paradox,* v, 2. 88–90. "Whoever . . . sea." Ovid, *Tristia,* i, 1, 83.

sally and throughout beautiful). Consequently, there is not one who does not easily suffer herself to be overcome by the first vow that is made to serve her. Now from this common and ordinary treachery of the men of the present day, that must fall out which we already experimentally see, either that they rally together and separate themselves by themselves to evade us or else form their discipline by the example we give them, play their parts of the farce as we do ours, and give themselves up to the sport, without passion, care, or love: "Incapable of attachment, insensible to that of others:" believing, according to the persuasion of Lysias in Plato, that they may with more utility and convenience surrender themselves up to us the less we love them; where it will fall out, as in comedies, that the people will have as much pleasure or more than the comedians. For my part, I no more acknowledge a Venus without a Cupid than a mother without issue: they are things that mutually lend and owe their essence to one another. . . .

As one who does not desire that men should think me better than I am, I will here say this as to the errors of my youth. Not only from the danger of impairing my health (and yet I could not be so careful but that I had two light mischances), but moreover upon the account of contempt, I have seldom given myself up to common and mercenary embraces. I would heighten the pleasure by the difficulty, by desire, and a certain kind of glory: and was of Tiberius's mind, who in his amours was as much taken with modesty and birth as any other quality; and of the courtesan Flora's humour, who never prostituted herself to less than a dictator, a consul, or a censor, and took pleasure in the dignity of her lovers. Doubtless pearls and gold tissue, titles and train, add something to it.

As to the rest, I had a great esteem for wit, provided the person was not exceptionable; for, to confess the truth, if the one or the other of these two attractions must of necessity be wanting, I should rather have quitted that of the understanding, that has its use in better things; but in the subject of love, a subject principally relating to the senses of seeing and touching, something may be done without the graces of the mind: without the graces of the body, nothing. Beauty is the true prerogative of women, and so peculiarly their own that ours, though naturally requiring another sort of feature, is never in its lustre but when youthful and beardless, a sort of confused image of theirs. 'Tis said, that such as serve the Grand Signior upon the account of beauty, who are an infinite number, are,

at the latest, dismissed at two and twenty years of age. Reason, prudence, and the offices of friendship are better found amongst men, and therefore it is that they govern the affairs of the world.

These two commerces are fortuitous and depending upon others: the one is troublesome by its rarity, the other withers with age, so that they could never have been sufficient for the business of my life. That of books, which is the third, is much more certain, and much more our own. It yields all other advantages to the two first; but has the constancy and facility of its service for its own share. It goes side by side with me in my whole course, and everywhere is assisting me: it comforts me in my old age and solitude; it eases me of a troublesome weight of idleness, and delivers me at all hours from company that I dislike: it blunts the point of griefs, if they are not extreme and have not got an entire possession of my soul. To divert myself from a troublesome fancy, 'tis but to run to my books; they presently fix me to them and drive the other out of my thoughts and do not mutiny at seeing that I have only recourse to them for want of other more real, natural, and lively commodities; they always receive me with the same kindness. He may well go a foot, they say, who leads his horse in his hand; and our James, king of Naples and Sicily, who, handsome, young, and healthy, caused himself to be carried about on a barrow, extended upon a pitiful mattress in a poor robe of grey cloth and a cap of the same, but attended withal by a royal train of litters, led horses of all sorts, gentlemen and officers, did yet herein represent a tender and unsteady authority: "The sick man is not to be pitied, who has his cure in his sleeve." In the experience and practice of this maxim, which is a very true one, consists all the benefit I reap from books; and yet I make as little use of them, almost, as those who know them not. I enjoy them as a miser doth his money, in knowing that I may enjoy them when I please: my mind is satisfied with this right of possession. I never travel without books, either in peace or war; and yet sometimes I pass over several days, and sometimes months, without looking on them. I will read by-and-by, say I to myself, or to-morrow, or when I please; and in the interim, time steals away without any inconvenience. For it is not to be imagined to what degree I please myself and rest content in this consideration that I have them by me to divert myself with them when I am so disposed and to call to mind what a refreshment they are to my life. 'Tis the best viaticum I have yet found out for this human journey, and I very much pity those men of understanding who are unprovided of it. I the rather accept of any other sort of diversion, how light soever, because this can never fail me.

When at home, I a little more frequent my library,

11–12. "Incapable . . . of others." Tacitus, *Annals*, xiii, 45. 13. . . . the persuasion of Lycias in Plato; in the *Phaedo*. 31. of Tiberius's mind . . . ; the Roman emperor (42 B.C.–37 A.D.), as quoted by Tacitus (*Annals*, vi, 1).

whence I overlook at once all the concerns of my family. 'Tis situated at the entrance into my house, and I thence see under me my garden, court, and base-court, and almost all parts of the building. There I turn over now one book, and then another, on various subjects without method or design. One while I meditate, another I record and dictate, as I walk to and fro, such whimsies as these I present to you here. 'Tis in the third storey of a tower, of which the ground room is my chapel, the second storey a chamber with a withdrawing-room and closet, where I often lie, to be more retired; and above is a great wardrobe. This formerly was the most useless part of the house. I there pass away both most of the days of my life and most of the hours of those days. In the night I am never there. There is by the side of it a cabinet handsome enough, with a fireplace very commodiously contrived, and plenty of light: and were I not more afraid of the trouble than the expense—the trouble that frights me from all business—I could very easily adjoin on either side, and on the same floor, a gallery of an hundred paces long and twelve broad, having found walls already raised for some other design to the requisite height. Every place of retirement requires a walk: my thoughts sleep if I sit still; my fancy does not go by itself, as when my legs move it: and all those who study without a book are in the same condition. The figure of my study is round, and there is no more open wall than what is taken up by my table and my chair, so that the remaining parts of the circle present me a view of all my books at once, ranged upon five rows of shelves round about me. It has three noble and free prospects, and is sixteen paces in diameter. I am not so continually there in winter; for my house is built upon an eminence, and no part of it is so much exposed to the wind and weather as this, which pleases me the better, as being of more difficult access and a little remote, as well upon the account of exercise, as also being there more retired from the crowd. 'Tis there that I am in my kingdom, and there I endeavour to make myself an absolute monarch, and to sequester this one corner from all society, conjugal, filial, and civil; elsewhere I have but verbal authority only, and of a confused essence. That man, in my opinion, is very miserable who has not at home where to be by himself, where to entertain himself alone, or to conceal himself from others. Ambition sufficiently plagues her proselytes by keeping them always in show, like the statue of a public square: "A great fortune is a great slavery." They cannot so much as be private in the water-closet. I have thought nothing so severe in the austerity of life that our monks affect as what I have observed in some of their com-

munities; namely, by rule to have a perpetual society of place, and numerous persons present in every action whatever; and think it much more supportable to be always alone than never to be so.

If anyone shall tell me that it is to undervalue the muses, to make use of them only for sport and to pass away the time, I shall tell him that he does not know so well as I the value of the sport, the pleasure, and the pastime; I can hardly forbear to add that all other end is ridiculous. I live from hand to mouth, and, with reverence be it spoken, I only live for myself; there all my designs terminate. I studied, when young, for ostentation; since, to make myself a little wiser; and now for my diversion, but never for any profit. A vain and prodigal humour I had after this sort of furniture, not only for the supplying my own need, but, moreover, for ornament and outward show, I have since quite cured myself of.

Books have many charming qualities to such as know how to choose them; but every good has its ill. 'Tis a pleasure that is not pure and clean, no more than others: it has its inconveniences, and great ones too. The soul indeed is exercised therein, but the body, the care of which I must withal never neglect, remains in the meantime without action and grows heavy and sombre. I know no excess more prejudicial to me, nor more to be avoided in this my declining age.

These have been my three favourite and particular occupations; I speak not of those I owe to the world by civil obligation.

51–52. **"A great fortune . . . great slavery."** Seneca, *De Consolatione ad Polybium*, c, 26.

Miguel de Cervantes
1547–1616

The political and social revolution of the Renaissance that destroyed medieval feudalism disposed as well of the fearless Christian knight on his faithful steed roaming the countryside as the heroic avenger of wrongs. By the sixteenth century knighthood and the code of chivalry were becoming quaint anachronisms in a world of powerful monarchies and wars with gunpowder. They survived as sweet conventions at the courts of the new-style kings, but even here they were attacked by rational observers as ludicrously out of step with the times. Chief among these realists was the Spaniard Cervantes, who began his *Don Quixote* as a satire on chivalric romances but developed it as a timeless commentary on the pathetic aspirations of mankind toward an impossible ideal.

The life of Cervantes was so filled with misfortune and frustration that he may well have presented himself sardonically in the good Don whose noblest ambitions led him to grotesque failure in the unsympathetic world in which he was forced to live. Born as the second son of an itinerant surgeon of Alcalá de Henares, Cervantes later tried to disguise his humble origin by styling himself *hidalgo,* or "gentleman." His desultory education reflected the repeated migrations of his family from one city to another in central Spain. By 1571 he had enlisted as a common soldier, and, at the Battle of Lepanto in the Mediterranean off Greece, he lost the use of his left hand, so that he was styled thereafter "El Manco de Lepanto" (the one-handed man of Lepanto). In 1575 he set out from Italy on leave for Spain, but his ship was captured by Barbary pirates and he endured five years of slavery in Algiers before his repeated efforts to escape were rewarded with a ransom from a religious order.

Back in Spain, he turned to literature to support himself, but his plays, poems, and pastoral romance *Galatea* of this period (1582–1587) had no great success. In desperation he applied to the king for a government post, which turned out to be the uncongenial job of commissary to the Armada. Often destitute, he was several times in prison for debt or for careless bookkeeping in his official position. Down to the age of fifty-seven, he had published no work of enduring worth and had reason to consider himself an abject failure. But in 1605 he issued his resounding masterpiece, *Don Quixote,* which he had conceived in prison and worked at from time to time for five years. His reputation (but not his fortune) was made overnight, and all Spaniards who could read, from King Philip III down, laughed at the droll adventures of the Knight of the Woeful Countenance.

But the book was immediately pirated by unscrupulous publishers, and as Cervantes was at work on a second part in 1614 a mysterious "Avellaneda" beat him to it with a spurious sequel. This imposture may have led him not only to rush his own sequel to completion but to make it superior in art and depth of thought to the first part. The ill-mannered preface of "Avellaneda" maliciously taunted Cervantes with his infirmities, poverty, and loneliness, and these comments were all too true. He lived out his days as a poor but famous author and saw his daughter involved in ugly scandals. His later works —the charming *Exemplary Novels* and especially the conventional *Labors of Persiles and Sigismunda*—reveal his gallant spirit but his weariness of a life that had brought unending hardship. He died on April 23, 1616, the very day on which Shakespeare died in England.

Begun as a parody of the absurdities of romance, *Don Quixote* matured into a thoughtful study of human nature in humorous terms. Like all great comedy, it went beyond the laughter of burlesque to a profound observation about man's efforts to adjust himself to his environment. At the start the Don is a ludicrous figure, a middle-aged bachelor grown insane through reading too much *Amadis of Gaul* and other high-flown romances, who sets out on his bony nag, Rozinante, with his rusty lance to play the medieval knight-errant, righting wrongs in the name of his lady, Dulcinea del Toboso, who proves to be no more than a coarse country wench. All the commonplace things in his path are transfigured by his demented imagination into objects of romance—a wag-

gish innkeeper into a great lord of knights, a windmill into a giant enemy, sheep into an army, and a barber's basin into the helmet of Mambrino. Despite his rebuffs and the derision of those about him, the idealism of the Don remains undiminished.

In time Cervantes came to see in the high-minded lunatic the longing of us all for something nobler than reality. Most of us escape ridicule because we compromise our hopes and finer instincts with conditions as we find them. It is the melancholy message of Cervantes' novel that the idealist who dares to practice what he believes appears to be a fool in a cynical world. Society demands that he should not lose touch with reality and never live so nobly as he would like to live. A prosy foil to the poetic knight is his earthy squire, Sancho Panza, who left home and followed the would-be knight, in part to avoid the dull routine of his peasant existence, in part to gain wealth and power as governor of the island that the Don promised him. The buffoon with his endless proverbs and naïve faith in his master also grows in our esteem, especially when he displays a homely wisdom in managing the affairs of his supposed island. If the Don has his head in the clouds, Sancho has his eyes to the ground, and his very lack of imagination leads him into delusions no less serious than the Don's. Each carries a necessary ingredient of human nature to grotesque extremes. Both idealism and realism are essential to a sound view of life.

But this philosophy is merely implicit in *Don Quixote.* On the surface it is an uproarious comic novel, full of humorous characters and absurd situations. With the pen of a meticulous realist Cervantes brings to life the countryside of La Mancha, its landlords and scullery-maids, its puppet-showmen and talkative barbers, its friendly priests and gracious noblemen. The droll style of the book conveys the infectious mirth in the author's heart as he developed his laughable and yet sympathetic pair of heroes.

THE LIFE AND ACHIEVEMENTS OF

THE RENOWNED

Don Quixote de la Mancha

PART I

The quality and manner of life of the renowned Don Quixote de la Mancha.

AT a certain village in La Mancha, which I shall not name, there lived not long ago one of those old-fashioned gentlemen who are never without a lance upon a rack, an old target, a lean horse, and a greyhound. His diet consisted more of beef than mutton; and with minced meat on most nights,

Don Quixote de la Mancha. Translated by Peter Motteux.

Don Quixote and Sancho Panza, from the title page of the 1605 edition of Don Quixote *printed in Lisbon.*

lentils on Fridays, griefs and groans on Saturdays, and a pigeon extraordinary on Sundays, he consumed three quarters of his revenue: the rest was laid out in a plush coat, velvet breeches, with slippers of the same, for holidays; and a suit of the very best home-spun cloth, which he bestowed on himself for working days. His whole family was a housekeeper something turned of forty, a niece not twenty, and a man that served him in the house and in the field, and could saddle a horse, and handle the pruning-hook. The master himself was nigh fifty years of age, of a hale and strong complexion, lean-bodied, and thin-faced, an early riser, and a lover of hunting. Some say his surname was Quixada, or Quesada (for authors differ in this particular): however, we may reasonably conjecture he was called Quixana (*i.e.* lanthorn-jaws) though this concerns us but little, provided we keep strictly to the truth in every point of this history.

You must know then, that when our gentleman had nothing to do (which was almost all the year round), he passed his time in reading books of knight-errantry; which he did with that application and delight, that at last he in a manner wholly left off his country sports, and even the care of his estate; nay, he grew so strangely besotted with those amusements, that he sold many acres of arable land to purchase books of that kind; by which means he collected as many of them as were to be had. . . .

He would often dispute with the curate of the parish, a man of learning, that had taken his degrees at Ciguenza, who was the better knight, Palmerin of England, or Amadis de Gaul? but master Nicholas, the barber of the same town, would say, that none of them could compare with the Knight of the Sun; and that if any one came near him, it was certainly Don Galaor, the brother of Amadis de Gaul; for he

was a man of a most commodious temper, neither was he so cynical, nor such a puling whining lover as his brother; and as for courage, he was not a jot behind him.

In fine, he gave himself up so wholly to the reading of romances, that a-nights he would pore on until it was day, and a-days he would read on until it was night; and thus, by sleeping little and reading much, the moisture of his brain was exhausted to that degree, that at last he lost the use of his reason. A world of disorderly notions, picked out of his books, crowded into his imagination; and now his head was full of nothing but enchantments, quarrels, battles, challenges, wounds, complaints, amours, torments, and abundance of stuff and impossibilities; insomuch, that all the fables and fantastical tales which he read seemed to him now as true as the most authentic histories. . . .

Having thus lost his understanding, he unluckily stumbled upon the oddest fancy that ever entered into a madman's brain; for now he thought it convenient and necessary, as well for the increase of his own honour, as the service of the public, to turn knight-errant, and roam through the whole world, armed *cap-à-pie* and mounted on his steed, in quest of adventures; that thus imitating those knights-errant of whom he had read, and following their course of life, redressing all manner of grievances, and exposing himself to danger on all occasions, at last, after a happy conclusion of his enterprises, he might purchase everlasting honour and renown. Transported with these agreeable delusions, the poor gentleman already grasped in imagination the imperial sceptre of Trapizonda; and, hurried away by his mighty expectations, he prepared with all expedition to take the field.

The first thing he did was to scour a suit of armour that had belonged to his great-grandfather, and had lain time out of mind carelessly rusting in a corner; but, when he had cleaned and repaired it as well as he could, he perceived there was a material piece wanting; for instead of a complete helmet, there was only a single head-piece: however, his industry supplied that defect; for, with some pasteboard, he made a kind of half-beaver, or vizor, which being fitted to the head-piece, made it look like an entire helmet. Then, to know whether it was cutlass-proof, he drew his sword, and tried its edge upon the pasteboard vizor; but, with the first stroke, he unluckily undid in a moment what he had been a whole week a-doing. He did not like its being broke with so much ease, and therefore to secure it from the like accident, he made it anew, and fenced it with thin plates of iron, which he fixed in the inside of it so artificially, that at last he had reason to be satisfied with the solidity of the work; and so, without any experiment, he resolved it should pass to all intents and purposes for a full and sufficient helmet.

The next moment he went to view his horse, whose bones stuck out like the corners of a Spanish Real; however, his master thought, that neither Alexander's Bucephalus, nor the Cid's Babieca could be compared with him. He was four days considering what name to give him; for, as he argued with himself, there was no reason that a horse bestrid by so famous a knight, and withal so excellent in himself, should not be distinguished by a particular name; and therefore he studied to give him such a one as should demonstrate as well what kind of horse he had been before his master was a knight-errant, as what he was now; thinking it but just, since the owner had changed his profession, that the horse should also change his title, and be dignified with another; a sonorous word, such a one as should fill the mouth, and seem consonant with the quality and profession of his master. And thus after many names which he devised, rejected, changed, liked, disliked, and pitched upon again, he concluded to call him Rozinante; a name, in his opinion, lofty sounding, and significant of what he had been before, and also of what he was now; in a word, a horse before or above all the vulgar breed of horses in the world.

When he had thus given his horse a name so much to his satisfaction, he thought of choosing one for himself; and having seriously pondered on the matter eight whole days more, at last he determined to call himself Don Quixote. Whence the author of this most authentic history draws this inference, that his name was Quixada, and not Quesada, as others obstinately pretend. And observing that the valiant Amadis, not satisfied with the bare appellation of Amadis, added to it the name of his country, that it might grow more famous by his exploits, and styled himself Amadis de Gaul; so he, like a true lover of his native soil, resolved to call himself Don Quixote de la Mancha; which addition, to his thinking, denoted very plainly his parentage and country, and consequently would fix a lasting honour on that part of the world.

And now, his armour being scoured, his head-piece improved to a helmet, his horse and himself new-named, he perceived he wanted nothing but a lady, on whom he might bestow the empire of his heart; for he was sensible that a knight-errant without a mistress was a tree without either fruit or leaves, and a body without a soul. "Should I," said he to himself, "by good or ill fortune chance to encounter some giant, as it is common in knight-errantry, and happen to lay him prostrate on the ground, transfixed with my lance, or cleft in two, or, in short, overcome and have him at my mercy, would

it not be proper to have some lady to whom I may send him as a trophy of my valour? That, when he comes into her presence, throwing himself at her feet, he may thus make his humble submission: 'Lady, I am the giant Caraculiambro, lord of the island of Malindrania, vanquished in single combat by that never-deservedly-enough-extolled knight-errant Don Quixote de la Mancha, who has commanded me to cast myself most humbly at your feet, that it may please your honour to dispose of me according to your will.'" Oh! how elevated was the Knight with the conceit of this imaginary submission of the giant; especially having bethought himself of a person on whom he might confer the title of mistress! which, it is believed, happened thus. Near the place where he lived dwelt a good likely country lass, for whom he had formerly had a sort of an inclination, though it is believed she never heard of it, nor regarded it in the least. Her name was Aldonza Lorenzo, and this was she whom he thought he might entitle to the sovereignty of his heart: upon which he studied to find her out a new name, that might have some affinity with her old one, and yet at the same time sound somewhat like that of a princess, or lady of quality: so at last he resolved to call her Dulcinea, with the addition of del Toboso, from the place where she was born; a name, in his opinion, sweet, harmonious, extraordinary, and no less significative than the others which he had devised.

Of Don Quixote's First Sally

These preparations being made, he found his designs ripe for action, and thought it now a crime to deny himself any longer to the injured world, that wanted such a deliverer; the more when he considered what grievances he was to redress, what wrongs and injuries to remove, what abuses to correct, and what duties to discharge. So one morning before day, in the greatest heat of July, without acquainting any one with his design, with all the secrecy imaginable, he armed himself *cap-à-pie,* laced on his ill-contrived helmet, braced on his target, grasped his lance, mounted Rozinante, and at the private door of his back-yard sallied out into the fields, wonderfully pleased to see with how much ease he had succeeded in the beginning of his enterprise. But he had not gone far ere a terrible thought alarmed him, a thought that had like to have made him renounce his great undertaking; for now it came into his mind that the honour of knighthood had not yet been conferred upon him, and therefore, according to the laws of chivalry, he neither could nor ought to appear in arms against any professed knight: nay, he also considered, that though he were already knighted, it would become him to wear white armour, and not to adorn his shield with any

22–25. **Rozinante . . . in the world.** *Rozin* means a common horse; *ante* before.

device, till he had deserved one by some extraordinary demonstration of his valour.

These thoughts staggered his resolution; but his folly prevailing more than any reason, he resolved to be dubbed a knight by the first he should meet, after the example of several others, who, as his distracting romances informed him, had formerly done the like. . . . He travelled all that day; and, towards the evening, he and his horse being heartily tired, and almost famished, Don Quixote looking about him in hopes to discover some castle, or at least some shepherd's cottage, there to repose and refresh himself; at last, near the road which he kept, he espied an inn, as welcome a sight to his longing eyes, as if he had discovered a star directing him to the gate, nay, to the palace of his redemption. Thereupon hastening towards the inn with all the speed he could, he got thither just at the close of the evening. There stood by chance at the inn-door, two young female adventurers, alias common wenches, who were going to Sevil with some carriers, that happened to take up their lodgings there that very evening; and, as whatever our knight-errant saw, thought, or imagined, was all of a romantic cast, and appeared to him altogether after the manner of the books that had perverted his imagination, he no sooner saw the inn, but he fancied it to be a castle fenced with four towers and lofty pinnacles, glittering with silver, together with a deep moat, drawbridge, and all those other appurtenances peculiar to such kind of places.

Therefore when he came near it, he stopped a while at a distance from the gate, expecting that some dwarf would appear on the battlements, and sound his trumpet to give notice of the arrival of a knight; but finding that nobody came, and that Rozinante was for making the best of his way to the stable, he advanced to the inn-door, where, spying the two young doxies, they seemed to him two beautiful damsels, or graceful ladies, taking the benefit of the fresh air at the gate of the castle. It happened also at the very moment, that a swine-herd, getting together his hogs from the stubble-field, winded his horn; and Don Quixote presently imagined this was the wished-for signal, which some dwarf gave to notify his approach; therefore, with the greatest joy in the world he rode up to the inn. The wenches, affrighted at the approach of a man cased in iron, and armed with a lance and target, were for running into their lodging; but Don Quixote, perceiving their fear by their flight, lifted up the pasteboard beaver of his helmet, and discovering his withered, dusty face, with comely grace and grave delivery accosted them in this manner. "I beseech ye, ladies, do not fly, nor fear the least offence: the order of knighthood, which I profess, does not permit me to countenance or offer injuries to any one in the universe,

and least of all to virgins of such high rank as your presence denotes."

The wenches looked earnestly upon him, endeavouring to get a glimpse of his face, which his ill-contrived beaver partly hid; but when they heard themselves styled virgins, a thing so out of the way of their profession, they could not forbear laughing outright; which Don Quixote resented as a great affront. "Give me leave to tell ye, ladies," cried he, "that modesty and civility are very becoming in the fair sex; whereas laughter without ground is the highest piece of indiscretion: however," added he, "I do not presume to say this to offend you, or incur your displeasure; no, ladies, I assure you I have no other design but to do you service." This uncommon way of expression, joined to the Knight's scurvy figure, increased their mirth; which incensed him to that degree, that this might have carried things to an extremity, had not the innkeeper luckily appeared at that juncture. He was a man whose burden of fat inclined him to peace and quietness, yet when he had observed such a strange disguise of human shape, in his old armour and equipage, he could hardly forbear keeping the wenches company in their laughter; but, having the fear of such a warlike appearance before his eyes, he resolved to give him good words, and therefore accosted him civilly: "Sir Knight," said he, "if your worship be disposed to alight, you will fail of nothing here but of a bed; as for all other accommodations, you may be supplied to your mind." Don Quixote observing the humility of the governor of the castle (for such the innkeeper and inn seemed to him), "Senior Castellano," said he, "the least thing in the world suffices me; for arms are the only things I value, and combat is my bed of repose."

The innkeeper . . . made him this reply: "At this rate, Sir Knight, your bed might be a pavement, and your rest to be still awake; you may then safely alight, and I dare assure you, you can hardly miss being kept awake all the year long in this house, much less one single night." With that he went and held Don Quixote's stirrup, who having not broke his fast that day, dismounted with no small trouble or difficulty. He immediately desired the governor (that is, the innkeeper), to take especial care of his steed, assuring him that there was not a better in the universe; upon which the innkeeper viewed him narrowly, but could not think him to be half so good as Don Quixote said: however, having set him up in the stable, he came back to the Knight to see what he wanted, and found him pulling off his armour by the help of the good natured wenches, who had already reconciled themselves to him; but, though they had eased him of his corslet and back-plate, they could

89. Senior Castellano; that is, governor of a castle.

by no means undo his gorget, nor take off his ill-contrived beaver, which he had tied so fast with green ribbons, that it was impossible to get it off without cutting them; now he would by no means permit that, and so was forced to keep on his helmet all night, which was one of the most pleasant sights in the world; and while his armour was being taken off by the two kind lasses, imagining them to be persons of quality, and ladies of that castle, he very gratefully made them the following compliment: "O Rozinante! for that is my horse's name, ladies, and mine Don Quixote de la Mancha; I never thought to have discovered it, till some feats of arms, achieved by me in your service, had made me better known to your ladyships; but necessity has extorted the secret from me before its time; yet a day will come, when you shall command, and I obey, and then the valour of my arm shall evince the reality of my zeal to serve your ladyships."

The two females, who were not used to such rhetorical speeches, could make no answer to this; they only asked him whether he would eat anything? "That I will with all my heart," cried Don Quixote, "whatever it be, for I am of opinion, nothing can come to me more seasonably." Now, as ill-luck would have it, it happened to be Friday, and there was nothing to be had at the inn but some pieces of fish, which is called Abadexo in Castile, Bacalloa in Andalusia, Curadillo in some places, and in others Truchuela or Little Trout, though, after all, it is but Poor Jack: so they asked him whether he could eat any of that Truchuela, because they had no other fish to give him. Don Quixote, imagining they meant a small trout, told them, that, provided there were more than one, it was the same thing to him, they would serve him as well as a great one, "for," continued he, "it is all one to me whether I am paid a piece of eight in one single piece, or in eight small reals, which are worth as much: besides, it is probable these small trouts may be like veal, which is finer meat than beef; or like the kid, which is better than the goat. In short, let it be what it will, so it comes quickly, for the weight of armour and the fatigue of travel are not to be supported without recruiting food." Thereupon they laid the cloth at the inn-door, for the benefit of the fresh air, and the landlord brought him a piece of that salt fish, but ill-watered and as ill-dressed; and, as for the bread, it was as mouldy and brown as the Knight's armour: but it would have made one laugh to have seen him eat; for, having his helmet on, with his beaver lifted up, it was impossible for him to feed himself without help, so that one of those ladies had that office; but there was no giving him drink that way, and he must have gone without it, had not the innkeeper bored a cane, and setting one end of it to his mouth,

poured the wine in at the other; all which the Knight suffered patiently, because he would not cut the ribbons that fastened his helmet. . . . The only thing that vexed him was, that he was not dubbed a knight; for he fancied he could not lawfully undertake any adventure till he had received the order of knighthood.

An account of the pleasant method taken by Don Quixote to be dubbed a Knight.

Don Quixote's mind being disturbed with that thought, he abridged even his short supper; and as soon as he had done, he called his host, then shut him and himself up in the stable, and falling at his feet, "I will never rise from this place," cried he, "most valorous knight, till you have graciously vouchsafed to grant me a boon, which I will now beg of you, and which will redound to your honour and the good of mankind." The landlord, strangely at a loss to find his guest at his feet, and talking at this rate, endeavoured to make him rise, but all in vain till he had promised to grant him what he asked. "I expected no less from your great magnificence, noble sir," replied Don Quixote, "and therefore I make bold to tell you, that the boon which I beg, and you generously condescend to grant me, is, that tomorrow you will be pleased to bestow the honour of knighthood upon me. This night I will watch my armour in the chapel of your castle, and then in the morning you shall gratify me, as I passionately desire that I may be duly qualified to seek out adventures in every corner of the universe, to relieve the distressed, according to the laws of chivalry, and the inclinations of knights-errant like myself." The innkeeper, who, as I said, was a sharp fellow, and had already a shrewd suspicion of the disorder in his guest's understanding, was fully convinced of it when he heard him talk after this manner; and, to make sport that night, resolved to humour him in his desires. . . .

He said that his castle at present had no chapel, where the Knight might keep his vigil of arms, it being pulled down in order to be new-built; but that he knew they might lawfully be watched in any other place in a case of necessity, and therefore he might do it that night in the court-yard of the castle; and in the morning (God willing) all the necessary ceremonies should be performed, so that he might assure himself he should be dubbed a knight, nay, as much a knight as any one in the world could be. He then asked Don Quixote, whether he had any money? "Not a cross," replied the Knight, "for I never read in any history of chivalry that any knight-errant ever carried money about him." "You are mistaken," cried the innkeeper; "for admit the histories are silent in this matter, the authors thinking it needless to mention things so evidently necessary as money and clean shirts, yet there is no reason to believe the knights went without either; and you may rest assured that all the knights-errant, of whom so many histories are full, had their purses well lined to supply themselves with necessaries, and carried also with them some shirts, and a small box of salves to heal their wounds; for they had not the conveniency of surgeons to cure them every time they fought in fields and deserts, unless they were so happy as to have some sage or magician for their friend, to give them present assistance, sending them some damsel or dwarf through the air in a cloud, with a small bottle of water of so great a virtue, that they no sooner tasted a drop of it, but their wounds were as perfectly cured as if they had never received any. . . . I must therefore advise you," continued he, "nay, I might even charge and command you, as you are shortly to be my son in chivalry, never from this time forwards to ride without money, nor without the other necessaries of which I spoke to you, which you will find very beneficial when you least expect it." Don Quixote promised to perform very punctually all his injunctions; and so they disposed everything in order to his watching his arms in a great yard that adjoined to the inn. To which purpose the Knight, having got them all together, laid them in a cistern close by a well in that yard; then, bracing his target and grasping his lance, just as it grew dark, he began to walk about by the horse-trough with a graceful deportment. . . .

While he was thus employed, one of the carriers who lodged in the inn came out to water his mules, which he could not do without removing the arms out of the trough. With that Don Quixote, who saw him make towards him, cried out to him aloud, "O thou, whoever thou art, rash knight, that prepares to lay thy hands on the arms of the most valorous knight-errant that ever wore a sword, take heed; do not audaciously attempt to profane them with a touch, lest instant death be the too-sure reward of thy temerity." But the carrier never regarded these dreadful threats; and, laying hold on the armour by the straps, without any more ado threw it a good way from him; though it had been better for him to have let it alone: for Don Quixote no sooner saw this, but lifting up his eyes to heaven, and addressing his thoughts, as it seemed, to his lady Dulcinea, "Assist me, lady," cried he, "in the first opportunity that offers itself to your faithful slave; nor let your favour and protection be denied me in this first trial of my valour!" Repeating such like ejaculations, he let slip his target, and lifting up his lance with both his hands, he gave the carrier such a terrible knock on his inconsiderate pate with his lance, that he laid him at his feet in a woeful condition; and, had he backed that blow with another, the fellow would

certainly have had no need of a surgeon. This done, Don Quixote took up his armour, laid it again in the horse-trough, and then walked on, backwards and forwards, with as great unconcern as he did at first.

Soon after another carrier, not knowing what had happened, came also to water his mules, while the first yet lay on the ground in a trance; but, as he offered to clear the trough of the armour, Don Quixote, without speaking a word or imploring any one's assistance, once more dropped his target, lifted up his lance, and then let it fall so heavily on the fellow's pate, that, without damaging his lance, he broke the carrier's head in three or four places. His outcry soon alarmed and brought thither all the people in the inn, and the landlord among the rest; which Don Quixote perceiving, "Thou queen of beauty," cried he, bracing on his shield, and drawing his sword, "thou courage and vigour of my weakened heart, now is the time when thou must enliven thy adventurous slave with the beams of thy greatness, while this moment he is engaging in so terrible an adventure!" With this, in his opinion, he found himself supplied with such an addition of courage, that, had all the carriers in the world at once attacked him, he would undoubtedly have faced them all.

On the other side, the carriers enraged to see their comrades thus used, though they were afraid to come near, gave the Knight such a volley of stones, that he was forced to shelter himself as well as he could under the covert of his target, without daring to go far from the horse-trough, lest he should seem to abandon his arms. The innkeeper called to the carriers as loud as he could to let him alone; that he had told them already that he was mad, and consequently the law would acquit him, though he should kill them. Don Quixote also made yet more noise, calling them false and treacherous villains, and the lord of the castle a base, inhospitable, and discourteous knight, for suffering a knight-errant to be so abused. "I would make thee know," cried he, "what a perfidious wretch thou art, had I but received the order of knighthood; but for you, base, ignominious rabble! fling on, do your worst; come on, draw nearer if you dare, and receive the reward of your indiscretion and insolence." This he spoke with so much spirit and undauntedness, that he struck a terror into all his assailants; so that, partly through fear and partly through the innkeeper's persuasions, they gave over flinging stones at him; and he, on his side, permitted the enemy to carry off their wounded, and then returned to the guard of his arms as calm and composed as before. . . .

Upon this the innkeeper, lest the Knight should proceed to such extremities, fetched the book in which he used to set down the carrier's accounts for straw and barley; and having brought with him the two kind females, already mentioned, and a boy that held a piece of lighted candle in his hand, he ordered Don Quixote to kneel: then reading in his manual, as if he had been repeating some pious oration, in the midst of his devotion, he lifted up his hand, and gave him a good blow on the neck, and then a gentle slap on the back with the flat of his sword, still mumbling some words between his teeth in the tone of a prayer. After this he ordered one of the wenches to gird the sword about the Knight's waist; which she did with much solemnity, and, I may add, discretion, considering how hard a thing it was to forbear laughing at every circumstance of the ceremony. It is true, the thoughts of the Knight's late prowess did not a little contribute to the suppression of their mirth. As she girded on his sword, "Heaven," cried the kind lady, "make your worship a lucky knight, and prosper you wherever you go." Don Quixote desired to know her name, that he might understand to whom he was indebted for the favour she had bestowed upon him, and also make her partaker of the honour he was to acquire by the strength of his arm. To which the lady answered with all humility, that her name was Tolosa, a cobbler's daughter, that kept a stall among the little shops of Sanchobinaya at Toledo; and that, whenever he pleased to command her, she would be his humble servant. Don Quixote begged of her to do him the favour to add hereafter the title of Lady to her name, and for his sake to be called from that time the Lady Tolosa; which she promised to do. Her companion, having buckled on his spurs, occasioned a like conference between them; and, when he had asked her name, she told him she went by the name of Miller, being the daughter of an honest miller of Antequera. Our new Knight entreated her also to style herself the Lady Miller, making her new offers of service. These extraordinary ceremonies (the like never seen before) being thus hurried over in a kind of post-haste, having immediately saddled his Rozinante, and being mounted, he embraced the innkeeper, and returned him so many thanks at so extravagant a rate, for the obligation he had laid upon him in dubbing him a knight, that it is impossible to give a true relation of them all: to which the innkeeper, in haste to get rid of him, returned as rhetorical, though shorter answers; and, without stopping his horse for the reckoning, was glad with all his heart to see him go. . . .

Being highly pleased with himself and what had happened, imagining he had given a most fortunate and noble beginning to his feats of arms, as he went on towards his village, "O most beautiful of beauties," said he with a low voice, "Dulcinea del Toboso! well mayest thou deem thyself most happy, since it was thy good fortune to captivate and hold a willing slave to thy pleasure, so valorous and renowned a knight as is, and ever shall be, Don Quixote de la Mancha.". . . Just as he had said this, he found himself at a place where four roads met. The curate and the barber of the village, both of them Don Quixote's intimate acquaintance, happened to be there at that juncture. Then did they ask the Don a thousand questions, but to every one he made no other answer, but that they should give him something to eat, and then leave him to his repose, a thing which was to him of the greatest importance. . . .

Don Quixote's second sally in quest of adventures.

Full fifteen days did our knight remain quietly at home, without betraying the least sign of his desire to renew his rambling; during which time there passed a great deal of pleasant discourse between him and his two friends, the curate and the barber; while he maintained, that there was nothing the world stood so much in need of as knights-errant; wherefore he was resolved to revive the order. In which disputes Mr. Curate sometimes contradicted him, and sometimes submitted; for had he not now and then given way to his fancies, there would have been no conversing with him.

In the mean time, Don Quixote earnestly solicited one of his neighbours, a country labourer, and a good honest fellow, if we may call a poor man honest, for he was poor indeed, poor in purse, and poor in brains; and, in short, the knight talked so long to him, plied him with so many arguments, and made him so many fair promises, that at last the poor silly clown consented to go along with him, and become his squire. Among other inducements to entice him to do it willingly, Don Quixote forgot not to tell him, that it was likely such an adventure would present itself, as might secure him the conquest of some island, in the time he might be picking up a straw or two, and then the squire might promise himself to be made governor of the place. Allured with these large promises, and many others, Sancho Panca (for that was the name of the fellow) forsook his wife and children to be his neighbour's squire.

This done, Don Quixote made it his business to furnish himself with money; for which purpose, selling one house, mortgaging another, and losing by all, he at last got a pretty good sum together. He also borrowed a target of a friend, and having patched up his headpiece and beaver as well as he could, he gave his squire notice of the day and hour when he intended to set out, that he might also furnish himself with what he thought necessary; but, above all, he charged him to provide himself with a wallet; which Sancho promised him to do, telling him he would also take his ass along with him, which, being a very good one, might be a great ease to him, for he was not used to travel much a-foot. The mentioning of the ass made the noble knight pause a while; he

mused, and pondered whether he had ever read of any knight-errant whose squire used to ride upon an ass; but he could not remember any precedent for it: however, he gave him leave at last to bring his ass, hoping to mount him more honourably with the first opportunity, by unhorsing the next discourteous knight he should meet. He also furnished himself with shirts, and as many other necessaries as he could conveniently carry, according to the innkeep-
10 er's injunctions. Which being done, Sancho Pança, without bidding either his wife or children good-bye; and Don Quixote, without taking any more notice of his housekeeper or of his niece, stole out of the village one night, not so much as suspected by anybody, and made such haste, that by break of day they thought themselves out of reach, should they happen to be pursued. As for Sancho Pança, he rode like a patriarch, with his canvas knapsack, or wallet, and his leathern bottle, having a huge desire to see
20 himself governor of the island, which his master had promised him. . . .

As they jogged on, "I beseech your worship, Sir Knight-errant," quoth Sancho to his master, "be sure you do not forget what you promised me about the island; for, I dare say, I shall make shift to govern it, let it be never so big." "You must know, friend Sancho," replied Don Quixote, "that it has been the constant practice of knights-errant, in former ages, to make their squires governors of the islands or king-
30 doms they conquered: now, I am not only resolved to keep up that laudable custom, but even to improve it, and outdo my predecessors in generosity: for whereas sometimes, or rather most commonly, other knights delayed rewarding their squires till they were grown old, and worn out with service, bad days, worse nights, and all manner of hard duty, and then put them off with some title, either of Count, or at least Marquis of some valley or province of great or small extent; now, if thou and I do but live,
40 it may happen, that before we have passed six days together, I may conquer some kingdom, having many other kingdoms annexed to its imperial crown; and this would fall out most luckily for thee; and then would I presently crown thee king of one of them. Nor do thou imagine this to be a mighty matter; for so strange accidents and revolutions, so sudden and so unforeseen, attend the profession of chivalry, that I might easily give thee a great deal more than I have promised." "Why, should this come to
50 pass," quoth Sancho Pança, "and I be made a king by some such miracle as your worship says, then happy-be-lucky, my Whither-d'ye-go Mary Gutierrez would be at least a queen, and my children infantas and princes, if it like your worship." "Who doubts of that?" cried Don Quixote. "I doubt of it," replied Sancho; "for I cannot help believing, that though it should rain kingdoms down upon the face of the

earth, not one of them would fit well upon Mary Gutierrez's head; for, I must needs tell you, she is not worth two brass jacks to make a queen of: no, Count- 6 ess would be better for her, if it please you; and that too, God help her, will be as much as she can handsomely manage." "Recommend the matter to providence," returned Don Quixote, "it will be sure to give what is most expedient for thee."

Of the good success which the valorous Don Quixote had in the most terrifying and never-to-be-imagined adventure of the wind-mills.

As they were thus discoursing, they discovered some thirty or forty wind-mills that are in that plain; and, as soon as the knight had spied them, "Fortune," cried he, "directs our affairs better than we ourselves could have wished: look yonder, friend Sancho, there 7 are at least thirty outrageous giants, whom I intend to encounter; and, having deprived them of life, we will begin to enrich ourselves with their spoils: for they are lawful prize; and the extirpation of that cursed brood will be an acceptable service to Heaven." "What giants?" quoth Sancho Pança. "Those whom thou seest yonder," answered Don Quixote, "with their long-extended arms; some of that detested race have arms of so immense a size, that sometimes they reach two leagues in length." 8 "Pray, look better, sir," quoth Sancho; "those things yonder are no giants, but wind-mills, and the arms you fancy, are their sails, which, being whirled about by the wind, make the mill go." "It is a sign," cried Don Quixote, "thou art but little acquainted with adventures. I tell thee they are giants; and therefore, if thou art afraid, go aside and say thy prayers, for I am resolved to engage in a dreadful, unequal combat against them all."

This said, he clapped spurs to his horse Rozinante, 9 without giving ear to his squire Sancho, who bawled out to him, and assured him that they were windmills, and no giants. But he was so fully possessed with a strong conceit of the contrary, that he did not so much as hear his squire's outcry, nor was he sensible of what they were, although he was already very near them; far from that. "Stand, cowards," cried he as loud as he could; "stand your ground, ignoble creatures, and fly not basely from a single knight, who dares encounter you all." At the same time the 1ᴏ wind rising, the mill-sails began to move, which, when Don Quixote spied, "Base miscreants," cried he, "though you move more arms than the giant Briareus, you shall pay for your arrogance." He most devoutly recommended himself to his lady Dulcinea, imploring her assistance in this perilous adventure; and so, covering himself with his shield, and couching his lance, he rushed with Rozinante's utmost speed upon the first windmill he could come at, and, running his lance into the sail, the wind whirled

Don Quixote's battle with the windmills as pictured by the famous nineteenth-century illustrator, Gustave Doré.

about with such swiftness, that the rapidity of the motion presently broke the lance into shivers, and hurled away both knight and horse along with it, till down he fell, rolling a good way off in the field.

Sancho Pança ran as fast as his ass could drive to help his master, whom he found lying, and not able to stir, such a blow he and Rozinante had received. "Mercy on me!" cried Sancho, "did I not give your worship fair warning? did not I tell you they were windmills, and that nobody could think otherwise, unless he had also wind-mills in his head?" "Peace, friend Sancho," replied Don Quixote: "there is nothing so subject to the inconstancy of fortune as war. I am verily persuaded, that cursed necromancer Freston has transformed these giants into wind-mills, to deprive me of the honour of the victory; such is his inveterate malice against me; but, in the end, all his pernicious wiles and stratagems shall prove ineffectual against the prevailing edge of my sword." "Amen, say I," replied Sancho. . . .

After many bitter Ohs, and screwed faces, Sancho laid Don Quixote on the ass, tied Rozinante to its tail, and then, leading the ass by the halter, he took the nearest way he could guess to the high road; to which he luckily came before he had travelled a short league, and then he discovered an inn; which,

in spite of all he could say, Don Quixote was pleased to mistake for a castle. Sancho swore bloodily it was an inn, and his master was as positive of the contrary. In short, their dispute lasted so long, that before they could decide it they reached the inn-door, where Sancho straight went in, with all his train, without troubling himself any further about the matter.

What happened to Don Quixote in the inn which he took for a castle.

The innkeeper, seeing Don Quixote lying quite athwart the ass, asked Sancho what ailed him? Sancho answered, it was nothing, only his master had got a fall from the top of a rock to the bottom, and had bruised his sides a little. The innkeeper had a wife very different from the common sort of hostesses, for she was of a charitable nature, and very compassionate of her neighbour's affliction; which made her immediately take care of Don Quixote, and call her daughter (a good handsome girl) to set her helping hand to his cure. One of the servants in the inn was an Asturian wench, a broad-faced, flat-headed, saddle-nosed dowdy, blind of one eye, and the other almost out. However, the activity of her body supplied all other defects. She was not above three feet high from her heels to her head; and her shoulders, which somewhat loaded her, as having too much flesh upon them, made her look downwards oftener than she could have wished. This charming original likewise assisted the mistress and the daughter; and, with the latter, helped to make the Knight's bed, and a sorry one it was; the room where it stood was an old gambling cock-loft, which by manifold signs seemed to have been, in the days of yore, a repository for chopped straw. Somewhat further, in a corner of that garret, a carrier had his lodging; and, though his bed was nothing but the pannels and coverings of his mules, it was much better than that of Don Quixote, which only consisted of four rough-hewn boards laid upon two uneven tressels, a flock-bed, that, for thinness, might well have passed for a quilt, and was full of knobs and bunches, which, had they not peeped out through many a hole, and shown themselves to be of wool, might well have been taken for stones. The rest of that extraordinary bed's furniture was a pair of sheets, which rather seemed to be of leather than of linen-cloth, and a coverlet whose every individual thread you might have told, and never have missed one in the tale.

In this ungracious bed was the Knight laid to rest his belaboured carcase, and presently the hostess and her daughter anointed and plastered him all over, while Maritornes (for that was the name of the Asturian wench) held the candle. The hostess, while she greased him, wondering to see him so bruised all over: "I fancy," said she, "those bumps look much more like a dry beating than a fall." "It was no dry beating, mistress, I promise you," quoth Sancho, "but the rock had I know not how many cragged ends and knobs, whereof every one gave my master a token of his kindness. . . ." "How do you call this same gentleman?" quoth Maritornes. "He is Don Quixote de la Mancha," replied Sancho; "and he is a knight-errant, and one of the primest and stoutest that ever the sun shined on." "A knight-errant," cried the

10 wench, "pray, what is that?" "Heyday!" cried Sancho, "does the wench know no more of the world than that comes to? Why, a knight-errant is a thing which in two words you see well cudgelled, and then an emperor. To-day there is not a more wretched thing upon the earth, and yet to-morrow he will have you two or three kingdoms to give away to his squire." "How comes it to pass, then," quoth the landlady, "that thou, who art this great person's squire, hast not yet got thee at least an earldom?"

20 "Fair and softly goes far," replied Sancho; "why, we have not been a month in our gears, so that we have not yet encountered any adventure worth the naming; besides, many a time we look for one thing, and light on another. But if my lord Don Quixote happens to get well again, and I escape remaining a cripple, I will not take the best title in the land for what I am sure will fall to my share."

Here Don Quixote, who had listened with great attention to all these discourses, raised himself up in

30 his bed with much ado, and taking the hostess in a most obliging manner by the hand, "Believe me," said he, "beautiful lady, you may well esteem it a happiness that you have now the opportunity to entertain my person in your castle. Self praise is unworthy a man of honour, and therefore I shall say no more of myself, but my squire will inform you who I am; only thus much let me add, that I will eternally preserve your kindness in the treasury of my remembrance, and study all occasions to testify

40 my gratitude: and I wish," continued he, "the Powers above had so disposed my fate, that I were not already love's devoted slave, and captivated by the charms of the disdainful beauty who engrosses all my softer thoughts; for then would I be proud to sacrifice my liberty to this beautiful damsel." The hostess, her daughter, and the kind-hearted Maritornes stared on one another, quite at a loss for the meaning of this high-flown language, which they understood full as well as if it had been Greek. Yet, conceiving these

50 were words of compliment and courtship, they looked upon him, and admired him as a man of another world: and so, having made him such returns as innkeeper's breeding could afford, they left him to his rest; only Maritornes stayed to rub down Sancho, who wanted her help no less than his master.

Now you must know, that the carrier and she had agreed to pass the night together; and she had given

him her word that, as soon as all the people in the inn were in bed, she would be sure to come to him, and be at his service. And it is said of this good-na-60 tured thing, that whenever she had passed her word in such cases, she was sure to make it good, though she had made the promise in the midst of a wood, and without any witness at all: for she stood much upon her gentility, though she undervalued herself so far as to serve in an inn; often saying, that nothing but crosses and necessity could have made her stoop to it.

Don Quixote's hard, scanty, beggarly, miserable bed was the first of the four in that wretched apart-70 ment; next to that was Sancho's kennel, which consisted of nothing but a bed-mat and a coverlet, that rather seemed shorn canvas than a rug. Beyond these two beds was that of the carrier, made, as we have said, of the pannels and furniture of two of the best of twelve mules which he kept, every one of them goodly beasts, and in special good case; for he was one of the richest muleteers of Arevalo. . . . After the carrier had visited his mules, and given them their second course, he laid himself down upon his 80 pannels, in expectation of the most punctual Maritornes's kind visit. . . .

And now was every soul in the inn gone to bed, nor any light to be seen, except that of a lamp which hung in the middle of the gate-way. This general tranquillity setting Don Quixote's thoughts at work, offered to his imagination one of the most absurd follies that ever crept into a distempered brain from the perusal of romantic whimsies. Now he fancied 90 himself to be in a famous castle (for, as we have already said, all the inns he lodged in seemed no less than castles to him) and that the innkeeper's daughter (consequently daughter to the lord of the castle) strangely captivated with his graceful presence and gallantry, had promised him the pleasure of her embraces, as soon as her father and mother were gone to rest. This chimera disturbed him, as if it had been a real truth; so that he began to be mightily perplexed, reflecting on the danger to which his honour was exposed. But at last his virtue overcame the 100 powerful temptation, and he firmly resolved not to be guilty of the least infidelity to his lady Dulcinea del Toboso, though Queen Guinever herself, with her trusty Matron Quintaniona, should join to decoy him into the alluring snare.

While these wild imaginations worked in his brain, the gentle Maritornes was mindful of her assignation, and with soft and wary steps, bare-foot, and in her smock, with her hair gathered up in a fustian coif, stole into the room, and felt about for her be-110 loved carrier's bed: but scarce had she got to the door, when Don Quixote, whose ears were on the

80. **their second course**; of fodders.

scout, was sensible that something was coming in: and therefore, having raised himself in his bed, sore and wrapped up in plasters as he was, he stretched out his arms to receive his fancied damsel, and caught hold of Maritornes by the wrist, as she was, with her arms stretched, groping her way to her paramour; he pulled her to him, and made her sit down by his bed's side, she not daring to speak a word all the while. Now, as he imagined her to be the lord of the castle's daughter, her smock, which was of the coarsest canvas, seemed to him of the finest holland; and the glass beads about her wrist, precious oriental pearls; her hair, that was almost as rough as a horse's mane, he took to be soft flowing threads of bright curling gold; and her breath, that had a stronger hogo than stale venison, was to him a grateful compound of the most fragrant perfumes of Arabia. In short, flattering imagination transformed her into the likeness of those romantic beauties, one of whom, as he remembered to have read, came to pay a private visit to a wounded knight, with whom she was desperately in love; and the poor gentleman's obstinate folly had so infatuated his outward sense, that his feeling and his smell could not in the least undeceive him, and he thought he had no less than a balmy Venus in his arms, while he hugged a fulsome bundle of deformities, that would have turned any man's stomach but a sharp-set carrier's.

Therefore clasping her still closer, with a soft and amorous whisper: "Oh! thou most lovely temptation," cried he; "oh! that I now might but pay a warm acknowledgment for the mighty blessing which your extravagant goodness would lavish on me; yes, most beautiful charmer, I would give an empire to purchase your more desirable embraces: but fortune, madam, fortune, that tyrant of my life, that unrelenting enemy to the truly deserving, has maliciously hurried and riveted me to this bed, where I lie so bruised and macerated, that, though I were eager to gratify your desires, I should at this dear unhappy minute be doomed to impotence; nay, to that unlucky bar fate has added a yet more invincible obstacle; I mean my plighted faith to the unrivalled Dulcinea del Toboso, the sole mistress of my wishes, and absolute sovereign of my heart. Oh! did not this oppose my present happiness, I could never be so dull and insensible a knight, as to lose the benefit of this extraordinary favour which you have now condescended to offer me."

Poor Maritornes all this while sweated for fear and anxiety, to find herself thus locked in the Knight's arms; and without either understanding, or willing to understand his florid excuses, she did what she could to get from him, and sheer off without speaking a word. On the other side, the carrier, whose lewd thoughts kept him awake, having heard his trusty Lady when she first came in, and listened ever since to the Knight's discourse, began to be afraid that she had made some other assignation; and so, without any more ado he crept softly to Don Quixote's bed, where he listened a while to hear what would be the end of all this talk, which he could not understand. But perceiving at last, by the struggling of his faithful Maritornes, that it was none of her fault, and that the Knight strove to detain her against her will, he could by no means bear his familiarity; and therefore, taking it in mighty dudgeon, he up with his fist, and hit the enamoured Knight such a swinging blow on the jaws, that his face was all over blood in a moment. And, not satisfied with this, he got on the top of the Knight, and with his splay-feet betrampled him as if he had been trampling a hay-mow. With that the bed, whose foundations were none of the best, sunk under the additional load of the carrier, and fell with such a noise, that it waked the innkeeper, who presently suspects it to be one of Maritornes's nightly skirmishes; and therefore, having called her aloud, and finding that she did not answer, he lighted a lamp, and made to the place where he heard the bustle. The wench, who heard him coming, knowing him to be of a passionate nature, was scared out of her wits, and fled for shelter to Sancho's sty, where he lay snoring to some tune: there she pigged in, and slunk under the coverlet, where she lay snug, and trussed up as round as an egg.

Presently her master came in, in a mighty heat: "Where is this damned whore?" cried he. "I dare say, this is one of her pranks." By this, Sancho awaked; and feeling that unusual lump, which almost overlaid him, he took it to be the night-mare, and began to lay about him with his fists, and thumped the wench so unmercifully, that at last flesh and blood were no longer able to bear it; and, forgetting the danger she was in, and her dear reputation, she paid him back his thumps as fast as her fists could lay them on, and soon roused the drowsy squire out of his sluggishness, whether he would or no: who, finding himself thus pommelled by he did not know who, bustled up in his nest, and catching hold of Maritornes, they began the most pleasant skirmish in the world. When the carrier perceiving, by the light of the innkeeper's lamp, the dismal condition that his dear mistress was in, presently took her part; and leaving the knight, whom he had more than sufficiently mauled, flew at the squire, and paid him confoundedly. On the other hand, the innkeeper, who took the wench to be the cause of all this hurly-burly, cuffed and kicked, and kicked and cuffed her over and over again: and so there was a strange multiplication of fisticuffs and drubbings. The carrier pommelled Sancho, Sancho mauled the wench, the wench belaboured the squire, and the innkeeper thrashed her again: and all of them laid on with such expedition, that you would have thought they had been afraid of losing time. But the jest was, that in the heat of the fray the lamp went out, so that being now in the dark, they plied one another at a venture: they struck and tore, all went to rack, while nails and fists flew about without mercy.

There happened to lodge that night in the inn one of the officers belonging to that society which they call the old holy brotherhood of Toledo, whose chief office is to look after thieves and robbers. Being waked with the heavy bustle, he presently jumped out of his bed, and, with his short staff in one hand, and a tin-box with his commission in it in the other, he groped out his way; and, having entered the room in the dark, cried out, "I charge ye all to keep the peace: I am an officer of the holy brotherhood." The first he popped his hand upon happened to be the poor battered knight, who lay upon his back at his full length, without any feeling, upon the ruins of his bed. The officer, having caught him by the beard, presently cried out, "I charge you to aid and assist me:" but finding he could not stir, though he gripped him hard, he presently imagined him to be dead, and murdered by the rest in the room. With that he bawled out to have the gates of the inn shut. "Here is a man murdered," cried he; "look that nobody makes his escape." These words struck all the combatants with such a terror, that as soon as they reached their ears, they gave over, and left the argument undecided. Away stole the innkeeper to his own room, the carrier to his pannels, and the wench to her kennel; only the unfortunate knight, and his as unfortunate squire, remained where they lay, not being able to stir; while the officer, having let go Don Quixote's beard, went out for a light, in order to apprehend the supposed murderers: but the innkeeper having wisely put out the lamp in the gate-way, as he sneaked out of the room, the officer was obliged to repair to the kitchen-chimney, where, with much ado, puffing and blowing a long while amidst the embers, he at last made shift to get a light.

A further account of the innumerable hardships which the brave Don Quixote, and his worthy squire Sancho, underwent in the inn, which the knight unluckily took for a castle.

Don Quixote, who by this time was come to himself, began to call Sancho with the same lamentable tone as the day before. "Sancho," cried he, "friend Sancho! art thou asleep? art thou asleep, friend Sancho?" "Sleep!" replied Sancho, mightily out of humour, "may Old Nick rock my cradle then: why, how the devil should I sleep, when all the imps of hell have been tormenting me to-night?" "Nay, thou art in the right," answered Don Quixote, "for either I have no skill in these matters, or this castle is enchanted. Hear what I say to thee, but first swear thou wilt never reveal it till after my death." "I swear

it," quoth Sancho. "I am thus cautious," said Don Quixote, "because I hate to take away the reputation of any person." "Why," quoth Sancho, "I tell you again, I swear never to speak a word of the matter while you live; and I wish I may be at liberty to talk on it to-morrow." "Why!" cried Don Quixote, "have I done thee so much wrong, Sancho, that you would have me die so soon?" "Nay, it is not for that neither," quoth Sancho; "because I cannot abide to keep things long, for fear they should grow mouldy." "Well, let it be as thou pleasest," said Don Quixote: "for I dare trust greater concerns to thy courtesy and affection. In short, know, that this very night there happened to me one of the strangest adventures that can be imagined; for the daughter of the lord of this castle came to me, who is one of the most engaging and most beautiful damsels that ever nature has been proud to boast of: what could I not tell thee of the charms of her shape and face, and the perfections of her mind! what could I not add of other hidden beauties, which I condemn to silence and oblivion, lest I endanger my allegiance and fidelity to my lady Dulcinea del Toboso! I will only tell thee, that the Heavens, envying the inestimable happiness which fortune had thrown into my hand; or rather, because this castle is enchanted, it happened, that in the midst of the most tender and passionate discourses that passed between us, the profane hand of some mighty giant, which I could not see, nor imagine whence it came, hit me such a dreadful blow on the jaws, that they are still embrued with blood; after which the discourteous wretch, presuming on my present weakness, did so barbarously bruise me, that I feel myself in a worse condition now than I did yesterday, after the carriers had so roughly handled me for Rozinante's incontinency: from which I conjecture, that the treasure of this damsel's beauty is guarded by some enchanted Moor, and not reserved for me."

"Nor for me neither," quoth Sancho; "for I have been rib-roasted by above four hundred Moors, who have hammered my bones. But, sir, pray tell me, do you call this such a pleasant adventure, when we are so lamentably pounded after it? And yet your hap may well be accounted better than mine, seeing you have hugged that fair maiden in your arms. But I, what have I had, I pray you, but the heaviest blows that ever fell on a poor man's shoulders? Woe is me and the mother that bore me, for I neither am, nor ever mean to be a knight-errant; and yet, of all the misadventures, the greater part falls still to my lot." "What, hast thou been beaten as well as I?" said Don Quixote. "What a plague," cried Sancho, "have not I been telling you so all this while!" "Come, never let it trouble thee, friend Sancho," replied Don Quixote; "for I will immediately make the precious balsam, that will cure thee in the twinkling of an eye."

By this time the officer, having lighted his lamp, came into the room, to see who it was that was murdered. Sancho seeing him enter in his shirt, a napkin wrapped about his head like a turban, and the lamp in his hand, he being also an ugly ill-looked fellow: "Sir," quoth the squire to his master, "pray see whether this be not the enchanted Moor, that is come again to have the other bout with me, and try whether he has not left some place unbruised for him now to maul as much as the rest." "It cannot be the Moor," replied Don Quixote; "for persons enchanted are to be seen by nobody." "If they do not suffer themselves to be seen," quoth Sancho, "at least they suffer themselves to be felt: if not, let my carcase bear witness." "So might mine," cried Don Quixote: "yet this is no sufficient reason to prove, that what we see is the enchanted Moor."

While they were thus arguing, the officer advanced, and wondered to hear two men talk so calmly to one another there: yet finding the unfortunate knight lying in the same deplorable posture as he left him, stretched out like a corpse, bloody, bruised and beplastered, and not able to stir himself, "How is it, honest fellow," quoth he to the champion, "how do you find yourself?" "Were I your fellow," replied Don Quixote, "I would have a little more manners than you have, you blockhead, you; is that your way of approaching knights-errant in this country?" The officer could not bear such a reprimand from one who made so scurvy a figure, and lifting up the lamp, oil and all, hit Don Quixote such a blow on the head with it, that he had reason to fear he had made work for the surgeon, and therefore stole presently out of the room, under the protection of the night. "Well, sir," quoth Sancho, "do you think now it was the enchanted Moor, or no? For my part, I think he keeps the treasure you talk of for others, and reserves only kicks, cuffs, thumps and knocks for your worship and myself." "I am now convinced," answered Don Quixote; "therefore let us waive that resentment of these injuries, which we might otherwise justly show; for considering these enchanters can make themselves invisible when they please, it is needless to think of revenge. But I pray thee rise, if thou canst, Sancho, and desire the governor of the castle to send me some oil, salt, wine and rosemary, that I may make my healing balsam; for truly I want it extremely, so fast the blood flows out of the wound which the phantasm gave me just now."

Sancho then got up as fast as his aching bones would let him, and with much ado made shift to crawl out of the room to look for the innkeeper, and stumbling by the way on the officer, who stood hearkening to know what mischief he had done. "Sir," quoth he to him, "for heaven's sake, do so much as help us to a little oil, salt, wine and rosemary, to make a medicine for one of the best knights-errant that ever trod one shoe of leather, who lies yonder grievously wounded by the enchanted Moor of this inn." The officer hearing him talk at that rate, took him to be one out of his wits; and it beginning to be daylight, he opened the inn-door, and told the innkeeper what Sancho wanted. The host presently provided the desired ingredients, and Sancho crept back with them to his master, whom he found holding his head and sadly complaining of the pain which he felt there; though, after all, the lamp had done him no more harm than only raising of two huge bumps; for that which he fancied to be blood was only sweat, and the oil of the lamp, that had liquored his hair and face.

The knight took all the ingredients, and having mixed them together, he had them set over the fire, and there kept them boiling till he thought they were enough. That done, he asked for a vial to put this precious liquor in: but there being none to be got, the innkeeper presented him with an old earthen jug, and Don Quixote was forced to be contented with that. Then he mumbled over the pot above fourscore *paternosters*, and as many *ave-marias*, *salve reginas*, and *credos*, making the sign of the Cross at every word, by way of benediction. At which ceremony Sancho, the innkeeper, and the officer were present; for, as for the carrier, he was gone to look after his mules, and took no manner of notice of what was passed. This blessed medicine being made, Don Quixote resolved to make an immediate experiment of it on himself; and to that purpose he took off a good draught of the overplus, which the pot would not hold: but he had scarce gulped it down, when it set him a-vomiting so violently, that you would have thought he would have cast up his heart, liver, and guts; and his reaching and straining put him into such a sweat that he desired to be covered up warm, and left to his repose. With that they left him, and he slept three whole hours; and then waking, found himself so wonderfully eased, that he made no question but he had now the right balsam of Fierabrass; and therefore he thought he might safely undertake all the most dangerous adventures in the world, without the least hazard of his person.

Sancho, encouraged by the wonderful effect of the balsam on his master, begged that he would be pleased to give him leave to sip up what was left in the pot, which was no small quantity; and the Don having consented, honest Sancho lifted it up with both his hands, and, with a strong faith and better will, poured every drop down his throat. Now the man's stomach not being so nice as his master's, the drench did not set him a-vomiting after that manner, but caused such a wambling in his stomach, such a bitter loathing, kecking, and reaching, and such grinding pangs, with cold sweats and swoonings, that he verily believed his last hour was come, and in the midst of his agony gave both the balsam and him that made it to the Devil. "Friend," said Don Quixote, seeing him in that condition, "I begin to think all this pain befalls thee, only because thou hast not received the order of knighthood; for, it is my opinion, this balsam ought to be used by no man that is not a professed knight." "What a plague did you mean then by letting me drink it?" quoth Sancho. "A murrain on me and all my generation, why did not you tell me this before?" . . . This dreadful hurricane lasted about two hours; and then, too, instead of finding himself as free from pain as his master, he felt himself as feeble, and so far spent, that he was not able to stand.

But Don Quixote, as we have said, found himself in an excellent temper; and his active soul loathing an inglorious repose, he presently was impatient to depart to perform the duties of his adventurous profession: for he thought those moments that were trifled away in amusements or other concerns, only a blank in life; and all delays a depriving distressed persons, and the world in general, of his needed assistance. The confidence which he reposed in his balsam, heightened, if possible, his resolution; and thus, carried away by his eager thoughts, he saddled Rozinante himself, and then put the pannel upon the ass, and his squire upon the pannel, after he had helped him to huddle on his clothes: that done, he mounted his steed; and, having spied a javelin that stood in a corner, he seized and appropriated it to himself, to supply the want of his lance. Above twenty people that were in the inn stood spectators of all these transactions; and among the rest the inn-keeper's daughter, from whom Don Quixote had not power to withdraw his eyes, breathing out at every glance a deep sigh from the very bottom of his heart; which those who had seen him so mortified the night before, took to proceed from the pain of his bruises.

And now, being ready to set forwards, he called for the master of the house, and with a grave delivery: "My Lord Governor," cried he, "the favours I have received in your castle are so great and extraordinary, that they bind my grateful soul to an eternal acknowledgment: therefore that I may be so happy as to discharge part of the obligation, think if there be ever a proud mortal breathing on whom you desire to be revenged for some affront or other injury, and acquaint me with it now, and by my order of knighthood which binds me to protect the weak, relieve the oppressed, and punish the bad, I promise you I will take effectual care, that you shall have ample satisfaction to the utmost of your wishes." "Sir Knight," answered the innkeeper, with an austere gravity, "I shall not need your assistance to revenge any wrong that may have been offered to

my person; for I would have you to understand, that I am able to do myself justice, whenever any man presumes to do me wrong: therefore all the satisfaction I desire is, that you will pay your reckoning for horse meat and man's meat, and all your expenses in my inn." "How!" cried Don Quixote, "is this an inn?" "Yes," answered the host, "and one of the most noted, and of the best repute upon the road." "How strangely have I been mistaken then!" cried Don Quixote; "upon my honour I took it for a castle, and a considerable one too: but, if it be an inn, and not a castle, all I have to say is, that you must excuse me from paying anything; for I would by no means break the laws which we knights-errant are bound to observe: nor was it ever known, that they ever paid in any inn whatsoever; for this is the least recompense that can be allowed them for the intolerable labours they endure day and night, winter and summer, on foot and on horseback, pinched with hunger, choked with thirst, and exposed to all the injuries of the air, and all the inconveniences in the world." "I have nothing to do with all this," cried the innkeeper: "pay your reckoning, and do not trouble me with your foolish stories of a cock and a bull: I cannot afford to keep house at that rate." "Thou art both a fool and a knave of an innkeeper," replied Don Quixote: and with that, clapping spurs to Rozinante, and brandishing his javelin at his host, he rode out of the inn without any opposition, and got a good way from it, without so much as once looking behind him to see whether his squire came after him.

The Knight being marched off, there remained only the squire, who was stopped for the reckoning. However, he swore bloodily he would not pay a cross; for the self-same law that acquitted the Knight acquitted the squire. This put the innkeeper into a great passion, and made him threaten Sancho very hard, telling him, if he would not pay him by fair means, he would have him laid by the heels that moment. . . . The innkeeper kept his wallet for the reckoning; but the poor squire was so dismayed, and in such haste to be gone, that he never missed it. . . .

Of the discourse between the knight and the squire, with other matters worth relating.

Sancho overtook his master, but so pale, so dead-hearted, and so mortified, that he was hardly able to sit on his ass. "My dear Sancho," said Don Quixote, seeing him in that condition, "I am now fully convinced that this castle, or inn, is enchanted; for what could they be that made themselves such barbarous sport with thee, but spirits and people of the other world? And I the rather believe this, seeing, that when I looked over the wall, I saw thee thus abused, I strove to get over it, but could not stir, nor by any means alight from Rozinante. For, by my honour, could I either have got over the wall or dismounted, I would have revenged thee so effectually on those discourteous wretches, that they should never have forgot the severity of their punishment, though for once I had infringed the laws of chivalry; which, as I have often informed thee, do not permit any knight to lay hands on one that is not knighted, unless it be in his own defence, and in case of great necessity." "Nay," quoth Sancho, "I would have paid them home myself, whether knight or no knight, but it was not in my power; and yet I dare say, those that made themselves so merry with my carcase were neither spirits nor enchanted folks, as you will have it, but mere flesh and blood as we be." . . .

Thus they went on discoursing, when Don Quixote, perceiving a thick cloud of dust arise right before them in the road: "The day is come," said he, turning to his squire, "the day is come, Sancho, that shall usher in the happiness which fortune has reserved for me: this day shall the strength of my arm be signalized by such exploits as shall be transmitted even to the latest posterity. Seest thou that cloud of dust, Sancho? It is raised by a prodigious army marching this way, and composed of an infinite number of nations." "Why then, at this rate," quoth Sancho, "there should be two armies; for yonder is as great a dust on the other side." With that Don Quixote looked, and was transported with joy at the sight, firmly believing that two vast armies were ready to engage each other in that plain. For his imagination was so crowded with those battles, enchantments, surprising adventures, amorous thoughts, and other whimsies which he had read of in romances, that his strong fancy changed everything he saw into what he desired to see; and thus he could not conceive that the dust was only raised by two large flocks of sheep that were going the same road from different parts, and could not be discerned till they were very near. He was so positive that they were two armies that Sancho firmly believed him at last. "Well, sir," quoth the squire, "what are we to do, I beseech you?" "What shall we do," replied Don Quixote, "but assist the weaker and the injured side? For know, Sancho, that the army which now moves toward us is commanded by the great Alifanfaron, emperor of the vast island of Taprobana: the other that advances behind us is his enemy, the king of the Garamantians, Pentapolin with the naked arm; so called, because he always enters into battle with his right arm bare." . . .

Sancho listened to this romantic muster-roll as mute as a fish, with amazement; all that he could do was to turn his head on this side and the other side, to see if he could discern the knights whom his master named. But at length, not being able to discover any: "Why," cried he, "you had as good tell me it snows; the devil of any knight, giant, or man can I see, of all those you talk of now; who knows but all this may be witchcraft and spirits, like yesternight?" "How," replied Don Quixote, "dost thou not hear their horses neigh, their trumpets sound, and their drums beat?" "Not I," quoth Sancho, "I prick up my ears like a sow in the beans, and yet I can hear nothing but the bleating of sheep." Sancho might justly say so indeed, for by this time the two flocks were got very near them. "Thy fear disturbs thy senses," said Don Quixote, "and hinders thee from hearing and seeing right: but it is no matter; withdraw to some place of safety, since thou art so terrified; for I alone am sufficient to give the victory to that side which I shall favour with my assistance." With that he couched his lance, clapped spurs on Rozinante, and rushed like a thunder-bolt from the hillock into the plain. Sancho bawled after him as loud as he could: "Hold, sir," cried Sancho, "for Heaven's sake come back. What do you mean? As sure as I am a sinner, those you are going to maul are nothing but poor harmless sheep. Come back, I say. Woe be to him that begot me! Are you mad, sir? There are no giants, no knights, no cats, no asparagus gardens, no golden quarters, nor what-do-you-call-thems. Does the Devil possess you? You are leaping over the hedge before you come at the stile. You are taking the wrong sow by the ear. Oh, that I was ever born to see this day!"

But Don Quixote, still riding on, deaf and lost to good advice, outroared his expostulating squire. "Courage, brave knights," cried he: "march up, fall on all you who fight under the standard of the valiant Pentapolin with the naked arm: follow me, and you shall see how easily I will revenge him on that infidel Alifanfaron of Taprobana;" and, so saying, he charged the squadron of sheep with that gallantry and resolution, that he pierced, broke, and put it to flight in an instant, charging through and through, not without a great slaughter of his mortal enemies, whom he laid at his feet, biting the ground and wallowing in their blood. The shepherds seeing their sheep go to rack, called out to him; till, finding fair means ineffectual, they unloosed their slings, and began to ply him with stones as big as their fists. But the champion, disdaining such a distant war, spite of their showers of stones, rushed among the routed sheep, trampling both the living and the slain in a most terrible manner, impatient to meet the general of the enemy, and end the war at once. "Where, where art thou," cried he, "proud Alifanfaron? Appear! see here a single knight who seeks thee everywhere, to try now, hand to hand, the boasted force of thy strenuous arm, and deprive thee of life, as a due punishment for the unjust war which thou hast audaciously waged with the valiant Pentapolin." Just as he had said this, while the stones flew about his ears, one unluckily fell upon his small ribs, and had like to have buried two of the shortest deep in the middle of his body. The Knight thought himself slain, or at least desperately wounded; and, therefore, calling to mind his precious balsam, and pulling out his earthen jug, he clapped it to his mouth: but, before he had swallowed a sufficient dose, souse comes another of those bitter almonds that spoiled his draught, and hit him so pat upon the jug, hand and teeth, that it broke the first, maimed the second, and struck out three or four of the last. These two blows were so violent, that the boisterous Knight falling from his horse, lay upon the ground as quiet as the slain; so that the shepherds fearing he was killed, got their flock together with all speed, and carrying away their dead, which were no less than seven sheep, they made what haste they could out of harm's way, without looking any further into the matter.

All this while Sancho stood upon the hill, mortified upon the sight of his mad adventure. There he stamped, swore, and banned his master to the bottomless pit; he tore his beard for madness, and cursed the moment he first knew him: but seeing him at last knocked down, and settled, the shepherds being scampered, he thought he might venture to come down; and found him in a very ill plight, though not altogether senseless. "Ah! master," quoth he, "this comes of not taking my counsel. Did I not tell you it was a flock of sheep, and no army?" "Friend Sancho," replied Don Quixote, "know it is an easy matter for necromancers to change the shapes of things as they please: thus that malicious enchanter, who is my inveterate enemy, to deprive me of the glory which he saw me ready to acquire, while I was reaping a full harvest of laurels, transformed in a moment the routed squadrons into sheep. If thou wilt not believe me, Sancho, yet do one thing for my sake: do but take thy ass, and follow those supposed sheep at a distance, and I dare engage thou shalt soon see them resume their former shapes, and appear such as I described them. But stay, do not go yet, for I want thy assistance: draw near, and see how many cheek-teeth and others I want; for, by the dreadful pain in my jaws and gums, I fear there is a total dilapidation in my mouth."

With that the Knight opened his mouth as wide as he could, while the squire gaped to tell his grinders, with his snout almost in his chops; but just in that fatal moment the balsam that lay wambling and fretting in Don Quixote's stomach, came up with an unlucky hickup; and, with the same violence that the powder flies out of a gun, all that he had in his stomach discharged itself upon the beard, face, eyes, and mouth of the officious squire. "Santa Maria," cried poor Sancho, "what will become of me! my master is a dead man! he is vomiting his very heart's blood!" but he had hardly said this, when the colour, smell, and taste soon undeceived him; and finding it to be his master's loathsome drench, it caused such a sudden rumbling in his maw, that before he could turn his head he unladed the whole cargo of his stomach full in his master's face, and put him in as delicate a pickle as he was himself. Sancho having thus paid him in his own coin, half-blinded as he was, ran to his ass, to take out something to clean himself and his master: but when he came to look for his wallet, and found it missing, not remembering till then that he had unhappily left it in the inn, he was ready to run quite out of his wits. He stormed and stamped, and cursed him worse than before, and resolved with himself to let his master go to the Devil, and even trudge home by himself, though he was sure to lose his wages, and his hopes of being governor of the promised island.

Thereupon Don Quixote got up with much ado, and clapping his left hand before mouth, that the rest of his loose teeth might not drop out, he laid his right hand on Rozinante's bridle; (for such was the good nature of the creature, that he had not budged a foot from his master) then it crept along to squire Sancho, that stood lolling on his ass's pannel, with his face in the hollow of both his hands, in a doleful, moody, melancholy fit. "Friend Sancho," said he, seeing him thus abandoned to sorrow, "learn of me, that one man is no more than another, if he do no more than what another does. All these storms and hurricanes are but arguments of the approaching calm: better success will soon follow our past calamities; good and bad fortune have their vicissitudes; and it is a maxim, that nothing violent can last long; and therefore we may well promise ourselves a speedy change in our fortune, since our afflictions have extended their reign beyond the usual stint; besides, thou oughtest not to afflict thyself so much for misfortunes, of which thou hast no share, but what friendship and humanity bid thee take." "How," quoth Sancho, "have I no other share in them? Did not the wallet, and all that was in it, which I have lost, belong to the son of my mother?" "How," asked Don Quixote, "hast thou lost thy wallet?" "I do not know," said Sancho, "whether it is lost or no, but I am sure I cannot tell what is become of it." "Nay, then," replied Don Quixote, "I find we must fast today." "Ay, marry must we," quoth Sancho, "unless you take care to gather in these fields some of those roots and herbs which I have heard you say you know, and which use to help such unlucky knights-errant as yourself at a dead lift."

"For all that," cried Don Quixote, "I would rather have at this time a good luncheon of bread, or a cake and two pilchards heads, than all the roots and simples in Dioscorides's herbal, and Doctor Laguna's supplement and commentary: I pray thee, therefore, get upon thy ass, good Sancho, and follow me once more; for God's providence, that relieves every creature, will not fail us, especially since we are about a work so much to His service; thou seest He even provides for the little flying insects in the air, the wormlings in the earth, and the spawnlings in the water; and, in His infinite mercy, He makes His sun shine on the righteous and on the unjust, and rains upon the good and the bad." "Many words will not fill a bushel," quoth Sancho, interrupting him; "you would make a better preacher than a knight-errant, or I am plaguedly out." "Knights-errant," replied Don Quixote, "ought to know all things; there have been such in former ages, that have delivered as ingenious and learned a sermon or oration at the head of an army, as if they had taken their degrees at the University of Paris: from which we may infer, that the lance never dulled the pen, nor the pen the lance." "Well then," quoth Sancho, "for once let it be as you would have it; let us even leave this unlucky place, and seek out a lodging; where, I pray God, there may be neither blankets, nor blanket-heavers, nor hobgoblins, nor enchanted Moors; for, before I will be hampered as I have been, may I be cursed with bell, book and candle, if I do not give the trade to the Devil." . . .

How Don Quixote set free many miserable creatures, who were carrying, much against their wills, to a place they did not like.

Cid Hamet Benengeli, an Arabian and Manchegan author, relates in this most grave, high-sounding, minute, soft, and humorous history, that after this discourse between the renowned Don Quixote and his squire, Sancho Pança, the Knight lifting up his eyes, saw about twelve men a-foot, trudging in the road, all in a row, one behind another, like beads upon a string, being linked together by the neck to a huge iron chain, and manacled besides. They were guarded by two horsemen, armed with carabines, and two men a-foot, with swords and javelins. As soon as Sancho spied them, "Look ye, sir," cried he, "here is a gang of wretches hurried away by main force to serve the king in the galleys." "How!" replied Don Quixote, "is it possible the king will force anybody?" "I do not say so," answered Sancho; "I mean these are rogues whom the law has sentenced for their misdeeds, to row in the king's galleys." "However," replied Don Quixote, "they are forced, because they do not go of their own free will." "Sure enough," quoth Sancho. "If it be so," said Don Quixote, "they come within the verge of

my office, which is to hinder violence and oppression, and succour all people in misery." "Ay, sir," quoth Sancho, "but neither the king nor law offer any violence to such wicked wretches, they have but their deserts." By this the chain of slaves came up, when Don Quixote, in very civil terms, desired the guards to inform him why these poor people were led along in that manner? "Sir," answered one of the horsemen, "they are criminals condemned to serve the king in his galleys. That is all that I have to say to you, and you need inquire no further." "Nevertheless, sir," replied Don Quixote, "I have a great desire to know in few words the cause of their misfortune, and I will esteem it an extraordinary favour, if you will let me have that satisfaction." "We have here the copies and certificates of their several sentences," said the other horseman, "but we cannot stand to pull them out and read them now; you may draw near and examine the men yourself: I suppose they themselves will tell you why they are condemned; for they are such honest people, they are not ashamed to boast of their rogueries."

With this permission, which Don Quixote would have taken of himself had they denied it him, he rode up to the chain, and asked the first, for what crimes he was in these miserable circumstances? The galley-slave answered him, that it was for being in love. "What, only for being in love!" cried Don Quixote; "were all those that are in love to be thus used, I myself might have been long since in the galleys." "Ay, but," replied the slave, "my love was not of that sort which you conjecture: I was so desperately in love with a basket of linen, and embraced it so close, that had not the judge taken it from me by force, I would not have parted with it willingly. In short, I was taken in the fact, and so there was no need to put me to the rack, it was proved so plain upon me. So I was committed, tried, condemned, had the gentle lash; and besides that, was sent, for three years, to be an element-dasher, and there is an end of the business." "An element-dasher!" cried Don Quixote, "what do you mean by that?" "A galley-slave," answered the criminal, who was a young fellow, about four-and-twenty years old, and said he was born at Piedra-Hita.

Then Don Quixote examined the second, but he was so sad and desponding, that he would make no answer; however, the first rogue informed the Knight of his affairs. "Sir," said he, "this canary-bird keeps us company for having sung too much." "Is it possible!" cried Don Quixote; "are men sent to the galleys for singing?" "Ay, Mary are they," quoth the arch rogue; "for there is nothing worse than to sing in anguish." "How!" cried Don Quixote, "that contradicts the saying, 'Sing away sorrow, cast away care.' " "Ay, but with us the case is different," replied the slave, " 'he that sings in disaster, weeps all his

Sancho sits patiently on his mule while Don Quixote harangues the prisoners. A Gustave Doré illustration.

life after.'" "This is a riddle which I cannot un-fold," cried Don Quixote. "Sir," said one of the guards, "singing in anguish, among these jail-birds, means to confess upon the rack: this fellow was put to the torture, and confessed his crime, which was stealing of cattle; and because he squeaked, or sung, as they call it, he was condemned to the galleys for six years, besides an hundred jerks with a cat-o'-nine-tails that have whisked and powdered his shoul-
10 ders already. Now the reason why he goes thus mopish and out of sorts, is only because his com-rogues jeer and laugh at him continually for not having had the courage to deny: as if it had not been as easy for him to say No as Yes; or, as if a fellow, taken up on suspicion, were not a lucky rogue, when there is no positive evidence can come in against him but his own tongue; and in my opinion they are somewhat in the right." "I think so too," said Don Quixote.
20 Thence addressing himself to the third, "And you," said he, "what have you done?" "Sir," answered the fellow, readily and pleasantly enough, "I must mow the great meadow for five years together, for want of twice five ducats." "I will give twenty with all my heart," said Don Quixote, "to deliver thee from that misery." "Thank you for nothing," quoth

the slave; "it is just like the proverb, 'After meat comes mustard'; or, like money to a starving man at sea, when there are no victuals to be bought with it. Had I had the twenty ducats you offer me before I 30 was tried, to have greased the clerk's [or recorder's] fist, and have whetted my lawyer's wit, I might have been now at Toledo in the market-place of Zocodover, and not have been thus led along like a dog in a string." . . .

With that the officer held up his staff to strike him; but Don Quixote stepped between them, and desired him not to do it, and to consider, that the slave was the more to be excused for being too free of his tongue, since he had never another member 40 at liberty. Then addressing himself to all the slaves, "My dearest brethren," cried he, "I find, by what I gather from your own words, that though you de-serve punishment for the several crimes of which you stand convicted, yet you suffer execution of the sentence by constraint, and merely because you cannot help it. Now, as Heaven has sent me into the world to relieve the distressed, and free suffering weakness from the tyranny of oppression, according to the duty of my profession of knight-errantry, these 50 considerations induce me to take you under my pro-tection—but, because it is the part of a prudent man not to use violence where fair means may be effectual, I desire you, gentlemen of the guard, to release these poor men, there being people enough to serve his majesty in their places; for it is a hard case to make slaves of men whom God and nature made free; and you have the less reason to use these wretches with severity, seeing they never did you any wrong. Let them answer for their sins in the other world: Heaven is just, you know, and will be sure to punish the wicked, as it will certainly reward the good. Consider besides, gentlemen, that it is neither a Christian-like, nor an honourable action, for men to be the butchers and tormentors of one another; particularly, when no advantage can arise from it. I choose to desire this of you, with so much mildness, and in so peaceable a manner, gentlemen, that I may have occasion to pay you a thankful acknowledgment, if you will be pleased to grant so reasonable a request: but, if you provoke me by refusal, I must be obliged to tell ye, that this lance, and this sword, guided by this invincible arm, shall force you to yield that to my valour which you deny to my civil entreaties."

"A very good jest indeed," cried the officer, "what a devil makes you dote at such a rate? Would you have us set at liberty the king's prisoners, as if we had authority to do it, or you to command it? Go, go about your business, good Sir Errant, and set your basin right upon your empty pate; and pray do not meddle any further in what does not concern you, for those who will play with cats must expect to be scratched."

"Thou art a cat, and rat, and a coward also," cried Don Quixote; and with that he attacked the officer with such a sudden and surprising fury, that before he had any time to put himself into a posture of defence, he struck him down dangerously wounded with his lance, and as fortune had ordered it, this happened to be the horseman who was armed with a carbine. His companions stood astonished at such a bold action, but at last fell upon the champion with their swords and darts, which might have proved fatal to him, had not the slaves laid hold of this opportunity to break the chain, in order to regain their liberty: for, the guards perceiving their endeavours to get loose, thought it more material to prevent them, than to be fighting a madman. But as he pressed them vigorously on one side, and the slaves were opposing them and freeing themselves on the other, the hurly-burly was so great, and the guards so perplexed, that they did nothing to the purpose. . . .

They betook themselves to their heels, leaving Don Quixote and the criminals masters of the field. Sancho, who was always for taking care of the main chance, was not at all pleased with this victory; for he guessed that the guards who were fled would raise a hue and cry, and soon be at their heels with the whole posse of the holy brotherhood, and lay them up for a rescue and rebellion. This made him advise his master to get out of the way as fast as he could, and hide himself in the neighbouring mountains. "I hear you," answered Don Quixote to this motion of his squire, "and I know what I have to do." Then calling to him all the slaves, who by this time had uncased the keeper to his skin, they gathered about him to know his pleasure, and he spoke to them in this manner. "It is the part of generous spirits to have a grateful sense of the benefits they receive, no crime being more odious than ingratitude. You see, gentlemen, what I have done for your sakes, and you cannot but be sensible how highly you are obliged to me. Now all the recompense I require is only, that every one of you, loaded with that chain from which I have freed your necks, do instantly repair to the city of Toboso; and there, presenting yourselves before the Lady Dulcinea del Toboso, tell her, that her faithful votary, the Knight of the Woeful Countenance, commanded you to wait on her, and assure her of his profound veneration. Then you shall give her an exact account of every particular relating to this famous achievement, by which you once more taste the sweets of liberty; which done, I give you leave to seek your fortunes where you please."

To this the ringleader and master-thief, Gines de Passamonte, made answer for all the rest. "What you would have us do," said he, "our noble deliverer, is absolutely impracticable and impossible; for we dare not be seen all together for the world. We must rather part, and skulk some one way, some another, and lie snug in creeks and corners underground, for fear of those damned manhounds that will be after us with a hue and cry; therefore all we can, and ought to do in this case, is to change this compliment and homage which you would have us pay to the Lady Dulcinea del Toboso, into a certain number of Ave Marias and Creeds, which we will say for your worship's benefit; and this may be done by night or by day, walking or standing, and in war as well as in peace: but to imagine we will return to our flesh-pots of Egypt; that is to say, take up our chains again, and lug them the Devil knows where, is as unreasonable as to think it is night now at ten o'clock in the morning. 'Sdeath, to expect this from us, is to expect pears from an elm-tree." "Now, by my sword," replied Don Quixote, "Sir Ginesello de Parapilla, or whatever be your name, you yourself, alone, shall go to Toboso, like a dog that has scalded his tail, with the whole chain about your shoulders." Gines, who was naturally very choleric, judging, by Don Quixote's extravagance in freeing them, that he was not very wise, winked on his companions, who, like men that understood signs, presently fell back to the right and left, and pelted Don Quixote with such a shower of stones, that all his dexterity to cover himself with his shield was now ineffectual, and poor Rozinante no more obeyed the spur, than if he had been only the statue of a horse. As for Sancho, he got behind his ass, and there sheltered himself from the volleys of flints that threatened his bones, while his master was so battered, that in a little time he was thrown out of his saddle to the ground. He was no sooner down, but the student leaped on him, took off his basin from his head, gave him three or four thumps on the shoulders with it, and then gave it so many knocks against the stones, that he almost broke it to pieces. After this, they stripped him of his upper coat, and had robbed him of his hose too, but that his greaves hindered them. They also eased Sancho of his upper coat, and left him in his doublet: then, having divided the spoils, they shifted every one for himself, thinking more how to avoid being taken up, and linked again in the chain, than of trudging with it to my Lady Dulcinea del Toboso. . . . The Knight and the squire continued their journey for the city of Toboso.

PART II

Don Quixote's success in his journey to visit the Lady Dulcinea del Toboso

"Friend Sancho," said Don Quixote, "I find the approaching night will overtake us ere we can reach Toboso, where, before I enter upon any expedition, I am resolved to pay my vows, receive my benediction, and take my leave of the peerless Dulcinea; being assured after that of happy events, in the most dangerous adventures; for nothing in this world inspires a knight-errant with so much valour as the smiles and favourable aspects of his mistress." "I am of your mind," quoth Sancho; "but I am afraid, sir, you will hardly come at her, to speak with her, at least not meet her in a place where she may give you her blessing, unless she throw it you over the mud-wall of the yard, where I first saw her." "Mud-wall, dost thou say!" cried Don Quixote. "Mistaken fool, that wall could have no existence but in thy muddy understanding: it is a mere creature of thy dirty fancy; for that never-duly-celebrated paragon of beauty and gentility was then undoubtedly in some court, in some stately gallery, or walk, or as it is properly called, in a sumptuous and royal palace." "It may be so," said Sancho, "though, so far as I can remember, it seemed to me neither better nor worse than a mud-wall." "It is no matter," replied the Knight, "let us go thither; I will visit my dear Dulcinea; let me but see her, though it be over a mud-wall, through a chink of a cottage, or the pales of a garden, at a lattice, or anywhere; which way soever

the least beam from her bright eyes reaches mine, it will so enlighten my mind, so fortify my heart, and invigorate every faculty of my being, that no mortal will be able to rival me in prudence and valour.". . .

At last, towards evening the next day, they discovered the goodly city of Toboso, which revived the Knight's spirits wonderfully, but had a quite contrary effect on his squire, because he did not know the house where Dulcinea lived, no more than his master. So that the one was mad till he saw her, and the other very melancholic and disturbed in mind, because he had never seen her; nor did he know what to do, should his master send him to Toboso. . . . When Don Quixote was retired into the wood or forest, or rather into the grove of oaks near the grand Toboso, he ordered Sancho to go to the city, and not to return to his presence till he had had audience of his lady; beseeching her that it might please her to be seen by her captive knight, and vouchsafe to bestow her benediction on him, that by the virtue of that blessing he might hope for a prosperous event in all his onsets and perilous attempts and adventures. Sancho undertook the charge, engaging him as successful a return of this as of his former message.

"Go then, child," said the Knight, ". . . thy own better stars, not mine, attend thee; and meet with a more prosperous event, than that which in this doleful desert, tossed between hopes and fears, I dare expect." "I will go, sir," quoth Sancho, "and I will be back in a trice: meanwhile cheer up, I beseech you; come, sir, comfort that little heart of yours, no bigger than a hazelnut! Do not be cast down, I say; remember the old saying, 'Faint heart never won fair lady': where there is no hook, to be sure there will hang no bacon: the hare leaps out of the bush where we least look for her." "Well, Sancho," said the Knight, "thou hast a rare talent in applying thy proverbs; Heaven give thee better success in thy designs!" This said, Sancho turned his back, and switching his Dapple, left the Don on horseback, leaning on his lance, and resting on his stirrups, full of melancholy and confused imaginations. Let us leave him too, to go along with Sancho, who was no less uneasy in his mind.

No sooner was he got out of the grove, but turning about, and perceiving his master quite out of sight, he dismounted, and laying himself down at the foot of a tree, thus began to hold a parley with himself. "Well, there is a remedy for all things but death, which will be sure to lay us flat one time or other. This master of mine, by a thousand tokens I have seen, is a downright madman, and I think I come within an inch of him; nay, I am the greatest cod's-head of the two, to serve and follow him as I do, if the proverb be not a liar, 'Show me thy company, I will tell thee what thou art'; and the other old saw,

'Birds of a feather flock together.' Now then my master being mad, and so very mad as to mistake sometimes one thing for another, black for white, and white for black; as when he took the windmills for giants and the flocks of sheep for armies, and much more to the same tune; I guess it will be no hard matter to pass upon him the first country wench I shall meet with, for the Lady Dulcinea. If he will not believe it, I will swear it; if he swear again, I will outswear him; if he be positive, I will be more positive than he; and stand to it, and out-face him in it, come what will of it: so that when he finds I will not flinch, he will either resolve never to send me more of his sleeveless errands, seeing what a lame account I bring him, or he will think some one of those wicked wizards, who, he says, owes him a grudge, has transmogrified her into some other shape out of spite." This happy contrivance helped to compose Sancho's mind, and now he looked on his grand affair to be as good as done. Having therefore stayed till the evening, that his master might think he had employed so much time in going and coming, things fell out very luckily for him; for as he arose to mount his Dapple, he spied three country wenches coming towards him from Toboso, upon three young asses. . . .

Sancho thereupon made all the haste he could to get to his master, and found him breathing out a thousand sighs and amorous lamentations. "Well, my Sancho," said the Knight, immediately upon his approach, "what news? Are we to mark this day with a white or a black stone?" "Even mark it rather with red oker," answered Sancho, "as they do church chairs, that everybody may know who they belong to." "Why then," said Don Quixote, "I suppose thou bringest good news?" "Ay, marry do I," quoth Sancho, "you have no more to do but to clap spurs to Rozinante, and get into the open fields, and you will see my Lady Dulcinea del Toboso, with a brace of her damsels, coming to see your worship." "Blessed heavens!" cried Don Quixote, "what art thou saying, my dear Sancho? Take heed, and do not presume to beguile my real grief with a delusive joy." "Adsookers! sir," said Sancho, "what should I get by putting a trick upon you, and being found out the next moment? Seeing is believing all the world over. Come, sir, put on, put on, and you will see our Lady Princess coming, dressed up and bedecked like her own sweet self indeed. Her damsels and she are all one spark of gold; all pearls, all diamonds, all rubies, all cloth of gold above ten inches high. Their hair spread over their shoulders like so many sunbeams, and dangling and dancing in the wind; and what is more, they ride upon three flea-bitten gambling hags; there is not a piece of horse-flesh can match them in three kingdoms." " 'Ambling nags' thou meanest, Sancho," said Don Quixote. " 'Ambling

hags' or 'ambling nags,' " quoth Sancho, "there is no such difference methinks; but be they what they will, I am sure, I never set eyes on finer creatures than those that ride upon their backs, especially my Lady Dulcinea; it would make one swoon away but to look upon her." "Let us move, then, my Sancho," said Don Quixote: "and as a gratification for these unexpected happy tidings, I freely bestow on thee the best spoils the next adventure we meet with shall afford; and if that content thee not, take the colts which my three mares thou knowest of, are now ready to foal on our town common." "Thank you for the colts," said Sancho; "but as for the spoils, I am not sure they will be worth anything."

They were now got out of the wood, and discovered the three country lasses at a small distance. Don Quixote casting his eyes towards Toboso, and seeing nobody on the road but the three wenches, was strangely troubled in mind, and turning to Sancho, asked him, whether the princess and her damsels were come out of the city when he left them. "Out of the city," cried Sancho, "why, where are your eyes? are they in your heels, in the name of wonder, that you cannot see them coming towards us, shining as bright as the sun at noon-day?" "I see nothing," returned Don Quixote, "but three wenches upon as many asses." "Now Heaven deliver me from the Devil," quoth Sancho. "Is it possible your worship should mistake three what-d'ye-call-ems, three ambling nags I mean, as white as driven snow, for three ragged ass colts? Body of me! I will even pull off my beard by the roots, if it be so." "Take it from me, friend Sancho," said the Knight, "they are either he or she asses, as sure as I am Don Quixote, and thou Sancho Pança; at least, they appear to be such." "Come, sir," quoth the squire, "do not talk at that rate, but snuff your eyes, and go pay your homage to the mistress of your soul; for she is near at hand"; and so saying, Sancho hastens up to the three country wenches, and alighting from Dapple, took hold of one of the asses by the halter, and falling on his knees, "Queen, and princess, and duchess of beauty," quoth he, "if it please your Haughtiness, and Greatness, vouchsafe to take into your good grace and liking, yonder Knight, your prisoner and captive, who is turned of a sudden into cold marble stone, and struck all of a heap, to see himself before your High and Mightiness. I am Sancho Pança, his squire, and he himself the wandering weather-beaten knight, Don Quixote de la Mancha, otherwise called the Knight of the Woeful Figure." By this time, Don Quixote, having placed himself down on his knees by Sancho, gazed with dubious and disconsolate eyes on the creature, whom Sancho called Queen and Lady; and perceiving her to be no more than a plain country wench, so far from being well-favoured, that she was blubber-cheeked, and flat-nosed, he was lost in astonishment, and could not utter one word. On the other side, the wenches were no less surprised, to see themselves stopped by two men in such different outsides, and on their knees.

But at last she whose ass was held by Sancho took courage, and broke silence in an angry tone. "Come," cried she, "get out of our way with a murrain, and let us go about our business; for we are in haste." "O Princess! and universal Lady of Toboso," answered Sancho, "why does not that great heart of yours melt, to see the post and pillar of knight-errantry fall down before your high and mighty presence?" "Heyday," quoth another of the females, hearing this, "what is here to do? Look how your small gentry come to jeer and flout poor country girls, as if we could not give them as good as they bring. Go, get about your business, and let us go about ours, and speed you well." "Rise, Sancho," said Don Quixote, hearing this, "for I am now convinced, that my malicious stars, not yet satisfied with my past misfortunes, still shed their baleful influence, and have barred all the passages that could convey relief to my miserable soul, in this frail habitation of animated clay. O! thou extremity of all that is valuable, masterpiece of all human perfection, and only comfort of this afflicted heart, thy adorer; though now a spiteful enchanter persecutes me, and fascinates my sight, hiding with mists and cataracts from me, and me alone, those peerless beauties under the foul disguise of rustic deformity, if he has not transformed thy faithful Knight into some ugly shape to make me loathsome to thy sight, look on me with a smiling amorous eye; and in the submission and genuflexion which I pay to thy beauty, even under the fatal cloud that obscures it, read the humility with which my soul adores thee." "Tittle-tattle," quoth the country wench, "spare your breath to cool your porridge, and rid me of your idle gibberish. Get you on, sir, and let us go; and we shall think it a kindness."

This said, Sancho made way for her, and let her pass, overjoyed his plot had succeeded so well. The imaginary Dulcinea was not sooner at liberty, but punching her ass with the end of a staff which she had in her hand, she began to scour along the plain: but the angry beast not being used to such smart instigations, fell a-kicking and wincing at such a rate, that down came my Lady Dulcinea. Presently Don Quixote ran to help her up, and Sancho to re-settle and gird her pack-saddle, that hung under the ass's belly. Which being done, the Knight very courteously was going to take his enchanted mistress in his arms, to set her on her saddle; but she being now got on her legs, took a run, and clapping her hands upon the ass's crupper, at one jump leaped into her pannel, as swift as a hawk, and there she sat with her legs astride like a man. "By the lord Harry!" quoth Sancho, "our lady mistress is as nimble as an eel. Let me be hanged, if I do not think she might teach the best jockey in Cordova or Mexico to mount a horse-back. At one jump she was vaulted into the saddle, and, without spurs, makes her nag smoke it away like a greyhound; her damsels are notable whipsters too; adad! they do not come much short of her, for they fly like the wind." Indeed, he said true, for when Dulcinea was once mounted, they both made after her full speed, without so much as looking behind them for above half a league. Don Quixote followed them as far as he could with his eyes; and when they were quite out of sight, turning to his squire, "Now, Sancho," saith he, "what thinkest thou of this matter? Are not these base enchanters inexorable? How extensive is their spite, thus to deprive me of the happiness of seeing the object of my wishes in her natural shape and glory? Sure I was doomed to be an example of misfortunes, and the mark against which those caitiffs are employed to shoot all the arrows of their hatred. Note, Sancho, that these traitors were not content to turn and transform my Dulcinea, but they must do it into the vile and deformed resemblance of that country wench; nay, they even took from her that sweet scent of flagrant flowers and amber, those grateful odours, so essential to ladies of her rank; for, to tell the truth, when I went to help her upon her nag, as thou callest it (for to me it seemed nothing but an ass), such a whiff, such a rank hogo of raw garlic invaded my nostrils, as had like to have overcome me, and put me into a convulsion." "O ye vile wretches!" cried Sancho. "O ye wicked and ill-minded enchanters! O that I might but once see the whole nest of ye threaded together on one string, and hung up a-smoking by the gills like so many pilchards!" . . .

Where you will find set forth the highest and utmost proof that the great Don Quixote ever gave, or could give of his incredible courage, with the successful issue of the adventure of the lions.

While they were in this conversation, they were overtaken by a gentleman, mounted on a very fine flea-bitten mare. He had on a riding-coat of fine green cloth, faced with murry-coloured velvet, and a hunter's cap of the same. The furniture of his mare was country-like, and after the jennet-fashion, and also murry and green. By his side hung a Moorish scimitar, in a large belt of green and gold. His buskins were of the same work with his belt: his spurs were not gilt, but burnished so well with a certain green varnish, that they looked better to suit with the rest of his equipage, than if they had been of pure gold. As he came up with them, he very civilly saluted them, and clapping spurs to his mare, began to leave them behind. Thereupon Don Quixote called to him: "Sir," cried he, "if you are not in too much haste, we should be glad of the favour of your company, so far as you travel this road." "Indeed," answered the gentleman, "I had not thus rid by you, but that I am afraid your horse may prove unruly with my mare." "If that be all," quoth Sancho, "you may hold in your mare; for our horse here is the honestest and soberest horse in the world; he is not in the least given to do any naughty thing on such occasions. Once upon a time indeed he happened to forget himself, and go astray; but then he, and I, and my master rued for it, with a vengeance. I tell you again, sir, you may safely stay if you please, for if your mare were to be served up to him in a dish, I will lay my life he would not so much as touch her." Upon this the traveller stopped his mare, and did not a little gaze at the figure and countenance of our Knight, who rode without his helmet, which, like a wallet, hung at the saddle-bow of Sancho's ass. If the gentleman in green gazed on Don Quixote, Don Quixote looked no less upon him, judging him to be some man of consequence. His age seemed about fifty; he had some grey hairs, a sharp look, and a grave, yet pleasing aspect. In short, his mien and appearance spoke him a man of quality. When he looked on Don Quixote, he thought he had never beheld before such a strange appearance of a man. He could not but admire at the lankness of his horse; he considered then the long-backed, raw-boned thing that bestrid him; his wan, meagre face, his air, his gravity, his arms, and equipage; such a figure as, perhaps, had not been seen in that country time out of mind. . . .

Don Quixote lifting up his eyes, perceived a wagon on the road, set round with little flags, that appeared to be the king's colours; and believing it to be some new adventure, he called out to Sancho to bring him his helmet. "Give me that helmet, friend," said the Knight, "for if I understand anything of adventures I descry one yonder that obliges me to arm." The gentleman in green hearing this, looked about to see what was the matter, but could perceive nothing but a wagon, which made towards them, and by the little flags about it, he judged it to be one of the King's carriages, and so he told Don Quixote. But his head was too much possessed with notions of adventures to give any credit to what the gentleman said.

The knight-errant having put on the helmet, fixed himself well in the stirrups, tried whether his sword were loose enough in his scabbard, and rested his lance. "Now," cried he, "come what will come; here am I, who dare encounter the Devil himself in *propria persona!*" By this time the wagon was come up with them, attended only by the carter, mounted on

54. *propria persona!* in his own person.

one of the mules, and another man that sat on the fore part of the wagon. Don Quixote making up to them, "Whither go ye, friends?" said he. "What wagon is this? What do you convey in it? And what is the meaning of these colours?" "The wagon is mine," answered the wagoner; "I have there two brave lions, which the General of Oran is sending to the King our master, and these colours are to let people understand that what goes here belongs to him." "And are the lions large?" inquired Don Quixote. "Very large," answered the man in the fore part of the wagon; "there never came bigger from Africa into Spain. I am their keeper," added he, "and have had charge of several others, but I never saw the like of these before. In the foremost cage is a he-lion, and in the other behind, a lioness. By this time they are cruel hungry, for they have not eaten to-day; therefore pray, good sir, ride out of the way, for we must make haste to get to the place where we intend to feed them." "What!" said Don Quixote, with a scornful smile, "lion-whelps against me! Against me those puny beasts! And at this time of day? Well, I will make those gentlemen, that sent their lions this way, know whether I am a man to be scared with lions. Get off, honest fellow; and since you are the keeper, open their cages, and let them both out; for maugre and in despite of those enchanters that have sent them to try me, I will make the creatures know, in the midst of this very field. who Don Quixote de la Mancha is." . . .

"Good sir," cried the wagoner, seeing this strange apparition in armour so resolute, "for mercy's sake do but let me take out our mules first, and get out of harm's way with them as fast as I can, before the lions get out; for if they should once set upon the poor beasts, I should be undone for ever; for alas! that cart and they are all I have in the world to get a living with." "Thou man of little faith," said Don Quixote, "take them out quickly then, and go with them where thou wilt; though thou shalt presently see that thy precaution was needless, and thou mightest have spared thy pains." The wagoner upon this made all the haste he could to take out his mules, while the keeper cried out as loud as he was able, "Bear witness all ye that are here present, that it is against my will I am forced to open the cages and let loose the lions; and that I protest to this gentleman here, that he shall be answerable for all the mischief and damage they may do; together with the loss of my salary and fees. And now, sirs, shift for yourselves as fast as you can before I open the cages: for, as for myself, I know the lions will do me no harm." The gentleman tried to dissuade Don Quixote from doing so mad a thing, telling him, that he tempted Heaven, in exposing himself without reason to so great a danger. To this Don Quixote made no other answer, but that he knew what he had to do. "Consider, however, what you do," replied the gentleman, "for it is most certain that you are very much mistaken." "Well, sir," said Don Quixote, "if you care not to be spectator of an action, which you think is like to be tragical, even set spurs to your mare, and provide for your safety."

Sancho came up to his master with tears in his eyes, and begged him not to go about this fearful undertaking, to which the adventure of the wind-mills, and all the brunts he had ever borne in his life, were but children's play. "Good your worship," cried he, "do but mind, here is no enchantment in the case, nor anything like it. Alack-a-day! sir, I peeped even now through the grates of the cage, and I am sure I saw the claw of a true lion, and such a claw as makes me think the lion that owns it must be as big as a mountain." "Alas, poor fellow!" said Don Quix-ote, "thy fear will make him as big as half the world. Retire, Sancho, and leave me, and if I chance to fall here, thou knowest our old agreement; repair to Dulcinea, I say no more." To this he added some ex-pressions, which cut off all hopes of his giving over his mad design. The gentleman in the green would have opposed him, but considering the other was much better armed, and that it was not prudence to encounter a madman, he even took the opportunity while Don Quixote was storming at the keeper, to march off with his mare, as Sancho did with Dapple, and the carter with his mules, every one making the best of their way to get as far as they could from the wagon, before the lions were let loose. Poor Sancho at the same time made sad lamentations for his mas-ter's death; for he gave him up for lost, not question-ing but the lions had already got him into their clutches. He cursed his ill-fortune, and the hour he came again to his service; but for all his wailing and lamenting, he punched on poor Dapple, to get as far as he could from the lions. The keeper, perceiving the persons who fled to be at a good distance, fell to arguing and entreating Don Quixote as he had done before. But the Knight told him again, that all his reasons and entreaties were but in vain, and bid him say no more, but immediately dispatch. Now while the keeper took time to open the foremost cage, Don Quixote stood debating with himself, whether he had best make his attack on foot or on horseback; and upon mature deliberation, he resolved to do it on foot, lest Rozinante, not used to lions, should be put into disorder. Accordingly he quitted his horse, threw aside his lance, grasped his shield, and drew his sword; then advancing with a deliberate motion, and an undaunted heart, he posted himself just be-fore the door of the cage, commending himself to Heaven, and afterwards to his Lady Dulcinea. . . .

The keeper observing the posture Don Quixote had put himself in, and that it was not possible for him to prevent letting out the lions, without incur-ring the resentment of the desperate knight, set the door of the foremost cage quite open; where, as I have said, the male lion lay, who appeared of a mon-strous bigness, and of a hideous frightful aspect. The first thing he did was to roll and turn himself round in his cage; in the next place he stretched out one of his paws, put forth his claws, and roused himself. After that he gaped and yawned for a good while, and showed his dreadful fangs, and then thrust out half a yard of a broad tongue, and with it licked the dust out of his eyes and face. Having done this, he thrust his head out of his cage, and stared about with his eyes that looked like two live coals of fire; a sight and motion enough to have struck terror into temer-ity itself. But Don Quixote only regarded it with at-tention, wishing his grim adversary would leap out of his hold, and come within his reach, that he might exercise his valour, and cut the monster piecemeal. To this height of extravagance had his folly trans-ported him; but the generous lion, more gentle than arrogant, taking no notice of his vapouring and bra-vadoes, after he had looked about him awhile, turned his tail, and showing Don Quixote his posteriors, very contentedly lay down again in his apartment.

Don Quixote seeing this, commanded the keeper to rouse him with his pole, and force him out whether he would or no. "Not I, indeed, sir," an-swered the keeper; "I dare not do it for my life; for, if I provoke him, I am sure to be the first he will tear to pieces. Let me advise you, sir, to be satisfied with your day's work. It is as much as the bravest he that wears a head can pretend to do. Then pray go no further, I beseech you: the door stands open, the lion is at his choice, whether he will come out or no. You have waited for him, you see he does not care to look you in the face, and since he did not come out at the first, I dare engage he will not stir out this day. You have shown enough the greatness of your courage. No man is obliged to do more than chal-lenge his enemy, and wait for him in the field. If he comes not, that is his own fault, and the scandal is his, as the honour is the challenger's." "It is true," replied Don Quixote. "Come, shut the cage door, honest friend, and give me a certificate under thy hand, in the amplest form thou canst devise, of what thou hast seen me perform; how thou didst open the cage for the lion; how I expected his coming, and he did not come out. How, upon his not coming out then, I stayed his own time, and instead of meeting me, he turned tail and lay down. I am obliged to do no more. So, enchantments avaunt! and Heaven pros-per truth, justice, and knight-errantry! Shut the door, as I bid thee, while I make signs to those that ran away from us, and get them to come back, that they may have an account of this exploit from thy own mouth." The keeper obeyed, and Don Quixote clap-ping on the point of his lance the handkerchief, with which he had wiped off the curds from his face, waved it in the air, and called as loud as he was able to the fugitives, who fled nevertheless, looking behind them all the way, and trooped on in a body with the gentleman in green at the head of them.

At last, Sancho observed the signal of the white flag, and calling out to the rest, "Hold," cried he, "my master calls us; I will be hanged if he has not got the better of the lions." At this they all faced about, and perceived Don Quixote flourishing his ensign; whereupon recovering a little from their fright, they leisurely rode back, till they could plainly distinguish Don Quixote's voice; and then they came up to the wagon. As soon as they were come near it, "Come on, friend," said he to the carter; "put thy mules into the wagon again, and pursue thy journey; and Sancho, do thou give him two ducats for the lion-keeper and himself, to make them amends for the time I have detained them." "Ay, that I will with all my heart," quoth Sancho; "but what is become of the lions? Are they dead or alive?" Then the keeper very formally related the whole action, not failing to exaggerate, to the best of his skill, Don Quixote's courage; how at his sight alone the lion was so terrified, that he neither would nor durst quit his stronghold, though for that end his cage door was kept open for a considerable time; and how at length, upon his remonstrating to the knight, who would have had the lion forced out, that it was presuming too much upon Heaven, he had permitted, though with great reluctancy, that the lion should be shut up again. "Well, Sancho," said Don Quixote to his squire, "what dost thou think of this? Can enchantment prevail over true fortitude? No, these magicians may perhaps rob me of success, but never of my invincible greatness of mind." In short, Sancho gave the wagoner and the keeper the two pieces. The first harnessed his mules, and the last thanked Don Quixote for his noble bounty, and promised to acquaint the king himself with his heroic action when he came to court. "Well," said Don Quixote, "if his majesty should chance to inquire who the person was that did this thing, tell him it was the Knight of the Lions; a name I intend henceforth to take up, in lieu of that which I hitherto assumed, of the Knight of the Woeful Figure; in which proceeding I do but conform to the ancient custom of knights-errant, who changed their names as often as they pleased, or as it suited with their advantage."

After this, the wagon made the best of its way, as Don Quixote, Sancho, and the gentleman in green did of theirs. The latter for a great while was so taken up with making his observations on Don Quixote, that he had not time to speak a syllable; not knowing what opinion to have of a person, in whom he discovered such a mixture of good sense and extravagance. He was a stranger to the first part of his history; for had he read it, he could not have wondered either at his words or actions: but not knowing the nature of his madness, he took him to be wise and distracted by fits, since in his discourse he still expressed himself justly and handsomely enough; but in his actions all was wild, extravagant and unaccountable. "For," said the gentleman to himself, "can there be anything more foolish, than for this man to put on his helmet full of curds, and then believe them conveyed there by enchanters; or anything more extravagant than forcibly to endeavour to fight with lions?" In the midst of this soliloquy, Don Quixote interrupted him. "Without doubt, sir," said he, "you take me for a downright madman, and indeed my actions seem to speak me no less. But for all that, give me leave to tell you, I am not so mad, nor is my understanding so defective, as I suppose you may fancy. What a noble figure does the gallant knight make, who in the midst of some spacious place transfixes a furious bull with his lance in the view of his prince! What a noble figure makes the knight, who before the ladies, at a harmless tournament, comes prancing through the lists enclosed in shining steel; or those court champions, who in exercises of martial kind, or that at least are such in appearance, show their activity: and though all they do is nothing but for recreation, are thought the ornament of a prince's court! But a much nobler figure is the knight-errant, who, fired with the thirst of glorious fame, wanders through deserts, through solitary wildernesses, through woods, through crossways, over mountains and valleys, in quest of perilous adventures, resolved to bring them to a happy conclusion. Yes, I say, a nobler figure is a knight-errant, succouring a widow in some depopulate place, than the court knight making his addresses to the city dames. Every knight has his particular employment. Let the courtier wait on the ladies; let him with splendid equipage adorn his prince's court, and with a magnificent table support poor gentlemen. Let him give birth to feasts and tournaments, and show his grandeur, liberality, and munificence, and especially his piety; in all these things he fulfils the duties of his station.

"But as for the knight-errant, let him search into all the corners of the world, enter into the most intricate labyrinths, and every hour be ready to attempt impossibility itself. Let him in desolate wilds baffle the rigour of the weather, the scorching heat of the sun's fiercest beams, and the inclemency of winds and snow: let lions never fright him, dragons daunt him, nor evil spirits deter him. To go in quest of these, to meet, to dare, to conflict, and to overcome them all, is his principal and proper office. Since then my stars have decreed me to be one of these adventurous knights, I think myself obliged to attempt everything that seems to come within the

verge of my profession. This, sir, engaged me to encounter those lions just now, judging it to be my
immediate business, though I was sensible of the extreme rashness of the undertaking. For well I know,
that valour is a virtue situated between the two
vicious extremes of cowardice and temerity. But
certainly it is not so ill for a valiant man to rise to a
degree of rashness, as it is to fall short and border
upon cowardice. For as it is easier for a prodigal to
become liberal, than a miser; so it is easier for the
hardy and rash person to be reduced to true bravery,
than for the coward ever to rise to that virtue: and
therefore in thus attempting adventures, believe me,
it is better to exceed the bounds a little, and overdo,
rather than underdo the thing; because it sounds
better in people's ears to hear it said, how that
such a knight is rash and hardy, than such a knight
is dastardly and timorous." "For my part, sir," answered the gentleman in green, "I think all you have
said and done is agreeable to the exactest rules of
reason; and I believe, if the laws and ordinances of
knight-errantry were lost, they might be all recovered from you, your breast seeming to be the
safe repository and archive where they are lodged.
But it grows late, let us make a little more haste to
get to our village." . . .

Where you find the grounds of the braying adven-
tures, that of the puppet-player, and the memorable
divining of the fortune-telling ape.

By this time, it began to grow dark, and they
arrived at the inn. Sancho was very well pleased to
be at his journey's end, and the more, that his master
took the house for a real inn, and not for a castle, as
he used to do. . . .
Presently enters a fellow dressed in trowsers and
doublet, all of chamois leather, and calling out as
if he were somebody, "Landlord," cried he, "have
you any lodgings? For here comes the fortune-telling
ape, and the puppet-show of 'Melisandra's deliverance.'" "Body of me," cried the innkeeper, "who is
here, Master Peter? We shall have a merry night,
faith! Honest Master Peter, you are welcome with
all my heart. But where is the ape, and the show,
that I cannot see them?" "They will be here presently," said Peter. "I only came before to see if you
had any lodgings." "Lodging, man," said the innkeeper, "zookers! I would turn out the Duke of Alva
himself, rather than Mr. Peter should want room.
Come, come, bring in your things, for here are guests
in the house to-night that will be good customers to
you, I warrant you." "That is a good hearing," said
Peter, "and to encourage them I will lower my
prices; and if I can but get my charges to-night, I
will look for no more; so I will hasten forward the
cart." This said, he ran out of the door again. . . .

Master Peter came back with his puppet-show
and his ape, in a cart. The ape was pretty lusty,
without any tail, and his buttocks bare as a felt. Yet
he was not very ugly neither. Don Quixote no sooner
saw him, but coming up to him, "Mr. Fortune-teller,"
said he, "will you be pleased to tell us what fish we
shall catch, and what will become of us? and here
is your fee." Saying this, he ordered Sancho to
deliver Mr. Peter two reals. "Sir," answered Peter,
"this animal gives no account of things to come, he
knows something indeed of matters past, and a little
of the present." "Odds bobs!" quoth Sancho, "I
would not give a brass jack to know what is past;
for who knows that better than myself; I am not so
foolish as to pay for what I know already: but since
you say he has such a knack at guessing the present,
let goodman ape tell me what my wife Teresa is
doing, and what she is about, and here is my two
reals." "I will have nothing of you beforehand," said
Master Peter; so clapping himself on his left shoulder, up skipped the ape thither, at one frisk, and
laying his mouth to his ear grated his teeth; and
having made apish grimaces and a chattering noise
for a minute or two, with another skip down he
leaped upon the ground. Immediately upon this,
Master Peter ran to Don Quixote, and fell on his
knees, and embracing his legs, "Oh glorious restorer
of knight-errantry," cried he, "I embrace these legs,
as I would the pillars of Hercules. Who can sufficiently extol the great Don Quixote de la Mancha,
the reviver of drooping hearts, the prop and stay of
the falling, the raiser of the fallen, and the staff of
comfort to the weak and afflicted!"
At these words Don Quixote stood amazed,
Sancho quaked, the page wondered, the innkeeper
stared, all astonished at Master Peter's speech; who
then turning to Sancho, "And thou honest Sancho
Pança," said he, "the best squire to the best knight
in the world, bless thy kind stars, for thy good spouse
Teresa is a good housewife, and is at this instant
dressing a pound of flax, by the same token, she has
standing by her, on her left hand, a large broken-
mouth jug, which holds a pretty scantling of wine,
to cheer up her spirits." "By yea and nay," quoth
Sancho, "that is likely enough, for she is a true soul,
and a jolly soul; were it not for a spice of jealousy
that she has now and then, I would not change her
for the giantess Andondona herself, who, as my
master says, was as clever a piece of woman's flesh
as ever went upon two legs. Well, much good may
it do thee, honest Teresa; thou art resolved to provide for one, I find, though thy heirs starve for it."
"Well," said Don Quixote, "great is the knowledge
procured by reading, travel, and experience; what
on earth but the testimony of my own eyes could
have persuaded me that apes had the gift of divina-

tion! I am indeed the same Don Quixote de la Mancha, mentioned by this ingenious animal, though I must confess somewhat undeserving of so great a character as it has pleased him to bestow on me: but nevertheless I am not sorry to have charity and compassion bear so great a part in my commendation, since my nature has always disposed me to do good to all men, and hurt to none. . . . No more of this at present, let us now see the puppet-show: I fancy we shall find something in it worth seeing."

"Something!" said Master Peter, "sir, you shall see a thousand things worth seeing. I tell you, sir, I defy the world to show such another. I say no more, *Operibus credite, et non verbis.* But now let us begin, for it grows late, and we have much to do, say, and show." Don Quixote and Sancho complied, and went into the room where the show stood, with a good number of small wax-lights glimmering round about, that made it shine gloriously. Master Peter got to his station within, being the man that was to move the puppets; and his boy stood before to tell what the puppets said, and, with a white wand in his hand, to point at the several figures as they came in and out, and explain the mystery of the show. Then all the audience having taken their places, the boy, who was the mouth of the motion, began a story, that shall be heard or seen by those who will take the pains to read or hear the next chapter.

A pleasant account of the puppet-play, with other very good things truly.

The Tyrians and the Trojans were all silent; that is, the ears of all the spectators hung on the mouth of the interpreter of the show, when in the first place they had a loud flourish of kettle-drums and trumpets within the machine, and then several discharges of artillery; which prelude being soon over, "Gentlemen," cried the boy, raising his voice, "we present you here with a true history taken out of the chronicles of France, and the Spanish ballads, sung even by the boys about the streets, and in everybody's mouth; it tells you how Don Gayferos delivered his wife Melisandra, that was a prisoner among the Moors in Spain, in the city of Sansuena, now called Saragossa. Now, gallants, the first figure we present you with is Don Gayferos playing at Tables.

"Gentlemen, in the next place, mark that personage that peeps out there with a crown on his head and a sceptre in his hand. It is the Emperor Charlemagne, fair Melisandra's reputed father, who, vexed at the idleness and negligence of his son-in-law, comes to chide him; and pray observe with what passion and earnestness he rates him, as if he had a mind to lend him half-a-dozen sound raps over the pate with his sceptre. Nay, some authors do not stick to tell ye, he gave him as many, and well laid on too; and after he had told him how his honour lay a-bleeding, till he had delivered his wife out of durance, among many other pithy sayings, 'Look to it,' quoth he to him as he went, 'I will say no more. Mind how the emperor turns his back upon him, and how he leaves Don Gayferos nettled and in the dumps. Now see how he starts up, and in a rage throws the tables one way, and whirls the men another; and calling for his arms with all haste, borrows his cousin-german Orlando's sword, Durindana, who withal offers to go along with him in this difficult adventure, but the valorous enraged knight will not let him, and says, he is able to deliver his wife himself, without his help, though they kept her down in the very centre of the earth. And now he is going to put on his armour in order to begin his journey.

"Now, gentlemen, cast your eyes upon yon tower; you are to suppose it one of the towers of the castle of Saragossa, now called the Aljaferia. That lady, whom you see in the balcony there, in a Moorish habit, is the peerless Melisandra, that casts many a heavy look towards France, thinking of Paris and her husband, the only comfort in her imprisonment. But now, silence, gentlemen, pray silence; here is an accident wholly new, the like perhaps never heard of before: do not you see that Moor who comes a-tiptoe creeping and stealing along with his finger in his mouth behind Melisandra? Hear what a smack he gives on her sweet lips, and see how she spits and wipes her mouth with her white smock sleeve: see how she takes on and tears her lovely hair for very madness, as if it were to blame for this affront. Next pray observe that grave Moor that stands in the open gallery: that is Marsilius, the king of Sansuena, who having been an eye-witness of the sauciness of the Moor, ordered him immediately to be apprehended, though his kinsman and great favourite, to have two hundred lashes given him, then to be carried through the city, with criers before to proclaim his crime, the rods of justice behind. And look how all this is put in execution sooner almost than the fact is committed: for your Moors, you must know, do not use any form of indictment as we do, neither have they any legal trials." "Child, child," said Don Quixote, "go on directly with your story, and do not keep us here with your excursions and ramblings out of the road: I tell you there must be a formal process and legal trial to prove matters of fact." "Boy," said the master from behind the show, "do as the gentleman bids you. Do not run so much upon flourishes, but follow your plain song, without venturing on counter-points, for fear of spoiling all." "I will, sir," quoth the boy, and so proceeding:

"Now, sirs, he that you see there a-horseback, wrapt up in the Gascoigne cloak, is Don Gayferos himself, whom his wife, now revenged on the Moor for his impudence, seeing him from the battlements of the tower, takes him for a stranger, and talks with him as such.

"I omit the rest, not to tire you with a long story. It is sufficient, that he makes himself known to her, as you may guess by the joy she shows; and accordingly now see how she lets herself down from the balcony, to come at her loving husband, and get behind him; but unhappily, alas, one of the skirts of her gown is caught upon one of the spikes of the balcony, and there she hangs and hovers in the air miserably, without being able to get down. But see how Heaven is merciful, and sends relief in the greatest distress! Now Don Gayferos rides up to her, and not fearing to tear her rich gown, lays hold of it, and at one pull brings her down; and then at one lift sets her astride upon his horse's crupper, bidding her to sit fast, and clasp her arms about him, that she might not fall, for the lady Melisandra was not used to that kind of riding.

"Observe now, gallants, how the horse neighs, and shows how proud he is of the burden of his brave master and fair mistress. Look now how they turn their backs, and leave the city, and gallop it merrily away towards Paris. Peace be with you, for a peerless couple of true lovers! may ye get safe and sound into your own country, without any let or ill chance in your journey, and live as long as Nestor in peace and quietness among your friends and relations." "Plainness, boy," cried Mr. Peter, "none of your flights, I beseech you, for affectation is the Devil." The boy answered nothing, but going on: "Now, sirs," quoth he, "some of those idle people, that love to pry into everything, happened to spy Melisandra as she was making her escape, and ran presently and gave Marsilius notice of it: whereupon he straight commanded to sound an alarm; and now mind what a din and hurly-burly there is, and how the city shakes with the ring of the bells backwards in all the mosques!" "There you are out, boy," said Don Quixote: "the Moors have no bells, they only use kettle-drums, and a kind of shawms like our waits or hautboys; so that your ringing of bells in Sansuena is a mere absurdity, good Mr. Peter." "Nay, sir," said Mr. Peter, "giving over ringing; if you stand upon trifles with us, we shall never please you. Do not be so severe a critic: are there not a thousand plays that pass with great success and applause, though they have many greater absurdities, and nonsense in abundance? On, boy, on, let there be as many impertinences as moats in the sun; no matter, so I get the money." "Well said," answered Don Quixote. "And now, sirs," quoth the boy, "observe what a vast company of glittering horse comes pouring out of the city, in pursuit of the Christian lovers; what a dreadful sound of trumpets, and clarions, and drums, and kettle-drums there is in the air. I fear they will overtake them, and then will the poor wretches be dragged along most barbarously at the tails of their horses, which would be sad indeed."

Don Quixote, seeing such a number of Moors, and hearing such an alarm, thought it high time to assist the flying lovers; and starting up, "It shall never be said while I live," cried he aloud, "that I suffered such a wrong to be done to so famous a knight and so daring a lover as Don Gayferos. Forbear then your unjust pursuit, ye base rascals: stop, or prepare to meet my furious resentment." Then drawing out his sword, to make good his threats, at one spring he gets to the show, and with a violent fury lays at the Moorish puppets, cutting and slashing in a most terrible manner; some he overthrows, and beheads others; maims this, and cleaves that in pieces. Among the rest of his merciless strokes, he thundered one down with a mighty force, that had not Mr. Peter luckily ducked and squatted down, it had certainly chopped off his head as easily as one might cut an apple. "Hold, hold, sir," cried the puppet-player, after the narrow escape, "hold for pity's sake. What do you mean, sir? These are no real Moors that you cut and hack so, but poor harmless puppets made of pasteboard. Think of what you do, you ruin me for ever. Oh that ever I was born! you have broke me quite." But Don Quixote, without minding his words, doubled and redoubled his blows so thick, and laid about him so outrageously, that in less than two credos he had cut all the strings and wires, mangled the puppets, and spoiled and demolished the whole motion. King Marsilius was in a grievous condition. The Emperor Charlemagne's head and crown were cleft in two. The whole audience was in a sad consternation. The ape scampered off to the top of the house. Sancho was in a terrible fright, for, as he swore after the hurricane was over, he had never seen his master in such a rage before. . . .

What happened to Don Quixote with the fair huntress.

It happened that the next day about sunset, as they were coming out of a wood, Don Quixote cast his eyes around a verdant meadow, and at the further end of it descried a company, whom upon nearer view he judged to be persons of quality, that were taking the diversion of hawking; approaching nearer yet, he observed among them a very fine lady upon a white pacing mare, in green trappings, and a saddle-cloth of silver. The lady herself was dressed in green, so rich and so gay, that nothing could be finer. She rode with a goss-hawk on her left fist, by which Don Quixote judged her to be of quality, and mistress of the train that attended; as indeed she was. Thereupon calling to his squire, "Son Sancho," cried he, "run and tell that lady on the palfrey with the goss-hawk on her fist, that I the 'Knight of the Lions' humbly salute her highness; and that if she pleases to give me leave, I should be proud to receive her commands, and have the honour of waiting on her, and kissing her fair hands. But take special care, Sancho, how thou deliverest thy message, and be sure do not lard my compliments with any of thy proverbs." "Why this to me?" quoth Sancho. "Marry, you need not talk of larding, as if I had never went ambassador before to a high and mighty dame." "I do not know that ever thou didst," replied Don Quixote, "at least on my account, unless it were when I sent thee to Dulcinea." "It may be so," quoth Sancho; "but a good paymaster needs no surety; and where there is plenty the guests cannot be empty: that is to say, I need none of your telling, nor tutoring about that matter: for, as silly as I look, I know something of everything." "Well, well, I believe it," said Don Quixote; "go then in a good hour, and Heaven inspire and guide thee."

Sancho put on, forcing Dapple from his old pace to a gallop; and approaching the fair huntress, he alighted, and falling on his knees, "Fair lady," quoth he, "that knight yonder, called 'the Knight of the Lions,' is my master: I am his squire, Sancho Pança by name. This same 'Knight of the Lions,' who but the other day was called 'the Knight of the Woeful Figure,' has sent me to tell you, that, so please your Worship's Grace to give him leave, with your good liking, to do as he has a mind; which, as he says, and as I believe, is only to serve your high-flown beauty, and be your 'ternal' vassal; you may chance to do a thing that would be for your own good, and he would take it for a hugeous kindness at your hands." "Indeed, honest squire," said the lady, "you have acquitted yourself of your charge with all the graceful circumstances which such an embassy requires: rise, pray rise; for it is by no means fit the squire to so great a knight as 'the Knight of the Woeful Figure,' to whose name and merit we are no strangers, should remain on his knees. Rise then, and desire your master, by all means to honour us with his company, that my Lord Duke and I may pay him our respects at a house we have hard by." . . . Sancho was overjoyed to find himself so much in the Duchess's favour, for he was ever a cordial friend to a plentiful way of living, and therefore never failed to take such opportunities by the foretop, wherever he met them.

Now the history tells us, that before they got to the castle, the Duke rode away from them, to instruct his servants how to behave themselves towards Don Quixote; so that no sooner did the Knight come near the gates, but he was met by two of the Duke's lacqueys or grooms in long vests, like nightgowns, of fine crimson satin. These suddenly took him in their arms, and lifting him from his horse without any further ceremony, "Go, great and mighty sir," said they, "and help my Lady Duchess down." Thereupon Don Quixote went and offered to do it; and many compliments and much ceremony passed on both sides: but in conclusion the Duchess's earnestness prevailed; for she would not alight from her palfrey but in the arms of her husband, excusing herself from incommoding so great a knight with so insignificant a burden. With that the Duke took her down. And now, being entered into a large courtyard, there came two beautiful damsels, who threw a long mantle of fine scarlet over Don Quixote's shoulders. In an instant, all the galleries about the courtyard were crowded with men and women, the domestics of the Duke, who cried, "Welcome, welcome, the flower and cream of knight-errantry!" Then most, if not all of them, sprinkled bottles of sweet water upon Don Quixote, the Duke, and Duchess: all which agreeably surprised the Don, and this was indeed the first day he knew and firmly believed himself to be a real knight-errant, and that his knighthood was more than fancy; finding himself treated just as he had read the brothers of the order were entertained in former ages.

Sancho was so transported, that he even forsook his beloved Dapple, to keep close to the Duchess, and entered the castle with the company: but his conscience flying in his face for leaving that dear companion of his alone, he went to a reverend old waiting-woman, who was one of the Duchess's retinue, and whispering her in the ear, "Mrs. Gonzales, or Mrs.—pray forsooth may I crave your name?" "Donna Rodriguez de Grijalva is my name," said the old duenna; "what is your business with me, friend?" "Pray now, mistress," quoth Sancho, "do so much as go out at the castle-gate, where you will find a dapple ass of mine; see him into the stable, or else put him in yourself; for, poor thing, it is main fearful and timersome, and cannot abide to be alone in a strange place." . . .

Don Quixote was led up a stately staircase, and then into a noble hall sumptuously hung with rich gold brocade. There his armour was taken off by six young damsels, that served him instead of pages, all of them fully instructed by the Duke and Duchess how to behave themselves so towards Don Quixote, that he might look on his entertainment as conformable to those which the famous knights-errant received of old. . . . They desired he would give them leave to take off his clothes, and put on him a clean shirt. But he would by no means permit it, giving them to understand, that modesty was as commendable a virtue in a knight as valour; and therefore he desired them to leave the shirt. . . .

Don Quixote then dressed himself, put on his belt and sword, threw his scarlet cloak over his shoulders, and clapped on a monteer cap of green velvet, which had been left him by the damsels. Thus accoutred, he entered the stateroom, where he found the damsels ranged in two rows, attending with water, and all necessaries to wash him in state; and having done him that office, with many humble courtesies and solemn ceremonies, immediately twelve pages with the gentleman-sewer at the head of them, came to conduct him to supper, letting him know that the Duke and Duchess expected him. Accordingly, they led him in great pomp, some walking before and some behind, into another room, where a table was magnificently set out.

As soon as he approached, the Duke and the Duchess came as far as the door to receive him, and with them a grave clergyman, one of those that assume to govern great men's houses, and who, not being nobly born themselves, do not know how to instruct those that are, but would have the liberality of the great measured by the narrowness of their own souls, making those whom they govern stingy, when they pretend to teach them frugality. One of these in all likelihood was this grave ecclesiastic, who came with the Duke to receive Don Quixote.

After a thousand courtly compliments on all sides, Don Quixote at last approached the table, between the Duke and the Duchess, and here arose a fresh contest; for the Knight, being offered the upper end of the table, thought himself obliged to decline it However he could not withstand the Duke's pressing importunities, but was forced at last to comply. The parson sat right against him, and the Duke and the Duchess on each side. . . .

The Duchess asked Don Quixote, what news he had of the Lady Dulcinea, and how long it was since he had sent her any giants or robbers for a present, not doubting but that he had lately subdued many such? "Alas! madam," answered he, "my misfortunes have had a beginning, but, I fear, will never have an end. I have vanquished giants, elves, and cut-throats, and sent them to the mistress of my soul, but where shall they find her? She is enchanted, madam, and transformed to the ugliest piece of rusticity that can be imagined." "I do not know, sir," quoth Sancho; "when I saw her last she seemed to be the finest creature in the 'versal' world; thus far, at least, I can safely vouch for her upon my own knowledge, that for activity of body, and leaping, the best tumbler of them all does not go beyond her. Upon my honest word, madam Duchess, she will vault from the ground upon her ass like a cat." "Have you seen her enchanted?" said the Duke. "Seen her!" quoth Sancho; "and who the devil was the first that hit upon this trick of her enchantment,

think you, but I? She is as much enchanted as my father."

The churchman hearing them talk of giants, elves, and enchantments, began to suspect this was Don Quixote de la Mancha, whose history the Duke so often used to read, though he had several times reprehended him for it; telling him, it was a folly to read such follies. Being confirmed in his suspicion, he addressed himself very angrily to the Duke. "My Lord," said he, "your Grace will have a large account to give one day, for soothing this poor man's follies. I suppose this same Don Quixote, or Don Quite Sot, or whatever you are pleased to call him, cannot be quite so besotted as you endeavour to make him, by giving him such opportunities to run on in his fantastical humours." Then, directing his discourse to Don Quixote, "Hark ye," said he; "goodman Addlepate, who has put it into your crown that you are a knight-errant, that you vanquish giants and robbers? Go, go, get you home again, look after your children, if you have any, and what honest business you have to do, and leave wandering about the world, building castles in the air, and making yourself a laughing-stock to all that know you, or know you not. Where have you found, in the name of mischief, that there ever has been, or are now, any such thing as knights-errant? Where will you meet with giants in Spain, or monsters in La Mancha? Where shall one find your enchanted Dulcineas, and all those legions of whimsies and chimeras that are talked of on your account, but in your own empty skull?"

Don Quixote gave this reverend person the hearing with great patience. But at last, seeing him silent, without minding his respect to the Duke and Duchess, up he started with indignation and fury in his looks, and said—but his answer deserves a chapter by itself.

Don Quixote's answer to his reprover, with other grave and merry accidents.

Don Quixote being thus suddenly got up, shaking from head to foot for madness, as if he had quicksilver in his bones, cast an angry look on his indiscreet censor, and with an eager delivery, sputtering and stammering with choler, "This place," cried he, "the presence of these noble persons, and the respect I have always had for your function, check my just resentment, and tie up my hands from taking the satisfaction of a gentleman. For these reasons, and since every one knows that you gownmen, as well as women, use no other weapon but your tongues, I will fairly engage you upon equal terms, and combat you at your own weapon. I should rather have expected sober admonitions from a man of your cloth, than infamous reproaches. Charitable and wholesome correction ought to be managed at another rate, and with more moderation. The least that can be said of this reproof which you have given me here so bitterly, and in public, is, that it has exceeded the bounds of Christian correction, and a gentle one had been much more becoming. Is it fit, that without any insight into the offence which you reprove, you should, without any more ado, call the offender fool, sot, and addlepate? Pray, sir, what foolish action have you seen me do, that should provoke you to give me such ill language, and bid me so magisterially go home to look after my wife and children, before you know whether I have any? Do not you think those deserve as severe a censure, who screw themselves into other men's houses, and pretend to rule the master? A fine world it is truly, when a poor pedant, who has seen no more of it than lies within twenty or thirty leagues about him, shall take upon him to prescribe laws to knight-errantry, and judge of those who profess it! You, forsooth, esteem it an idle undertaking, and time lost, to wander through the world, though scorning its pleasures, and sharing the hardships and toils of it, by which the virtuous aspire to the high seat of immortality. If persons of honour, knights, lords, gentlemen, or men of any birth, should take me for a fool or a coxcomb, I should think it an irreparable affront. But for mere scholars, that never trod the paths of chivalry, to think me mad, I despise and laugh at it. I am a knight, and a knight will I die, if so it please Omnipotence. Some choose the high road of haughty ambition; others the low ways of base servile flattery; a third sort take the crooked path of deceitful hypocrisy; and a few, very few, that of true religion. I, for my own part, guided by my stars, follow the narrow track of knight-errantry; and, for the exercise of it, I despise riches, but not honour. I have redressed grievances, and righted the injured, chastised the insolent, vanquished giants, and trod elves and hobgoblins under my feet! I am in love, but no more than the profession of knight-errantry obliges me to be; yet I am none of this age's vicious lovers, but a chaste Platonic. My intentions are all directed to virtuous ends, and to do no man wrong, but good to all the world. And now let your Graces judge, most excellent Duke and Duchess, whether a person who makes it his only study to practise all this, deserves to be upbraided for a fool."

"Well said, i'faith!" quoth Sancho, "say no more for yourself, my good lord and master, stop when you are well, for there is not the least matter to be added more on your side, either in word, thought, or deed. Besides, since Mr. Parson has had the face to say point-blank as one may say, that there neither are, nor ever were, any knights-errant in the world,

no marvel he does not know what he says." "What," said the clergyman, "I warrant you are that Sancho Pança, to whom they say your master has promised an island?" "Ay, marry am I," answered Sancho, "and I am he that deserves it as well as another body; and I am one of those of whom they say, Keep with good men, and thou shalt be one of them; and of those of whom it is said again, Not with whom thou wert bred, but with whom thou hast fed; as also, Lean against a good tree, and it will shelter thee. I have leaned and stuck close to my good master, and kept him company this many a month; and now he and I are all one; and I must be as he is, if it be Heaven's blessed will; and so he lives and I live, he will not want kingdoms to rule, nor shall I want islands to govern."

"That thou shalt not, honest Sancho," said the Duke; "for I, on the great Don Quixote's account, will now give thee the government of an odd one of my own of no small consequence." "Down, down on thy knees, Sancho," cried Don Quixote, "and kiss his Grace's feet for this favour." Sancho did accordingly: but when the clergyman saw it, he got up in a great heat. . . . The Duchess was ready to die with laughing at Sancho, whom she thought a more pleasant fool, and a greater madman than his master; and she was not the only person at that time of this opinion. In short, Don Quixote being pacified, they made an end of dinner. . . .

The relishing conference which the Duchess and her women held with Sancho Pança, worth your reading and observation.

The story afterwards informs us, that Sancho slept not a wink all that afternoon, but waited on the Duchess as he had promised. Being mightily taken with his comical discourse, she ordered him to take a low chair and sit by her; but Sancho, who knew better things, absolutely declined it, till she pressed him again to sit as he was a governor, and speak as he was a squire; in both which capacities he deserved the very seat of Cid Ruy Dias, the famous champion. Sancho shrugged up his shoulders and obeyed, and all the Duchess's women standing round about her to give her silent attention, she began the conference.

"Now that we are private," said she, "and nobody to overhear us, I would desire you, my Lord Governor, to resolve me of some doubts. . . . I think I hear something whisper me in the ear, and say, if Don Quixote de la Mancha be such a shallow-brain, why does Sancho Pança, who knows him to be so, wait upon this madman, and rely thus upon his vain extravagant promises? I can only infer from this, that the man is more a fool than the master; and if so will not Madam Duchess be thought as mad as either of them, to bestow the government of an island, or the command of others, on one who cannot govern himself?" "By our Lady," quoth Sancho, "your scruple comes in pudding-time. But it need not whisper in your ear, it may even speak plain, and as loud as it will. I am a fool, that is certain, for, if I had been wise, I had left my master many a fair day since; but it was my luck and my vile errantry, and that is all that can be said of it. I must follow him through thick and thin. We are both town-born children; I have eaten his bread, I love him well, and there is no love lost between us. He pays me very well, he has given me three colts, and I am so very true and trusty to him, that nothing but death can part us. And if your High and Mightiness does not think fit to let me have this same government, why, so be it; with less was I born, and with less shall I die; it may be for the good of my conscience to go without it. I am a fool, it is true, but yet I understand the meaning of the saying, The pismire had wings to do her hurt; and Sancho the squire may sooner get to heaven than Sancho the governor. There is as good bread baked here as in France, and Joan is as good as my lady in the dark. In the night all cats are grey. Unhappy is he that wants his breakfast at two in the afternoon. It is always good fasting after a good breakfast. There is no man has a stomach a yard bigger than another, but let it be never so big, there will be hay and straw enough to fill it. A bellyful is a bellyful. The sparrow speeds as well as the sparrowhawk. Good serge is fine, but coarse cloth is warm; and four yards of the one are as long as four yards of the other. When the hour is come we must all be packed off; the prince and the prick-louse go the same way at last: the road is no fairer for the one than the other. The Pope's body takes up no more room than the sexton's, though one be taller; for when they come to the pit, all are alike, and so good-night or good-morrow, which you please. And let me tell you again, if you do not think fit to give me an island, because I am a fool, I will be so wise not to care whether you do or no."

Sancho's proverbial aphorisms were no small diversion to the Duchess. "You know," said she, "honest Sancho, that the promise of a gentleman or knight must be as precious and sacred to him as his life; I make no question, then, but that my Lord Duke, who is also a knight, though not of your master's order, will infallibly keep his word with you in respect of your government. Take courage, then, Sancho, for when you least dream of it, in spite of all the envy and malice of the world, you will suddenly see yourself in full possession of your government, and seated in your chair of state in your rich robes, with all your marks and ornaments of power about you. But be sure to administer true justice to your vassals, who by their loyalty and discretion will merit no less at your hands."

"As for the governing part," quoth Sancho, "let me alone, I was ever charitable and good to the poor, and scorn to take the bread out of another man's mouth. On the other side, by our Lady, they shall play me no foul play. I am an old cur at a crust, and can sleep dog-sleep when I list. I can look sharp as well as another, and let me alone to keep the cob-webs out of my eyes. I know where the shoe wrings me. I will know who and who is together. Honesty is the best policy. I will stick to that. The good shall have my hand and heart, but the bad neither foot nor fellowship. And in my mind, the main point in this post of governing, is to make a good beginning. I will lay my life, that as simple as Sancho sits here, in a fortnight's time he will manage ye this same island as rightly as a sheaf of barley." "You say well, Sancho," said the Duchess, "for time ripens all things. No man is born wise; bishops are made of men, and not of stones." . . .

Sancho kissed the Duchess's hand once more, and begged her Worship's Grace that special care might be taken of his Dapple, for that he was the light of his eyes. "What is that Dapple?" asked the Duchess. "My beast, if it like your honour," answered Sancho; "my ass I would say, saving your presence; but because I will not call him ass, which is so common a name among men, I call him Dapple." . . . "Well," said the Duchess, "your ass may go with you to the government, and there you may feed, and pamper him, and make as much of him as you please." "Adad! my lady," quoth Sancho, "do not let your worship think this will be a strange matter neither. I have seen more asses than one go to a government before now: and if mine goes too, it will be no new thing I trow." . . .

The instructions which Don Quixote gave Sancho Pança, before he went to the government of his island, with other matters of moment.

The day after, the Duke bid Sancho prepare, and be in a readiness to take possession of his government; for now his islanders wished as heartily for him, as they did for rain in a dry summer. . . . "Well then," quoth Sancho, "let me have this island, and I will do my best to be such a governor, that, in spite of rogues, I shall not want a small nook in heaven one day or other. It is not out of covetousness neither, that I would leave my little cot, and set up for somebody, but merely to know what kind of thing it is to be a governor." "Oh! Sancho," said the Duke, "when once you have had a taste of it, you will never leave licking your fingers, it is so sweet and bewitching a thing to command and be obeyed. I am confident, when your master comes to be an Emperor (as he cannot fail to be, according to the course of his affairs) he will never by any consideration be persuaded to abdicate; his only grief will be, that he was one no sooner."

"Troth, sir," replied Sancho, "I am of your mind; it is a dainty thing to command, though it were but a flock of sheep." "Oh! Sancho," cried the Duke, "let me live and die with thee: for thou hast an insight
10 into everything. I hope thou wilt prove as good a governor as thy wisdom bespeaks thee. But no more at this time,—to-morrow, without further delay, you may set forward to your island, and shall be furnished this afternoon with equipage and dress answerable to your post, and all other necessaries for your journey." . . .

By this time Don Quixote arrived, and hearing how suddenly Sancho was to go to his government, with the Duke's permission, he took him aside to
20 give him some good instructions for his conduct in the discharge of his office.

Being entered Don Quixote's chamber, and the door shut, he almost forcibly obliged Sancho to sit by him; and then, with a grave deliberate voice, he thus began.

"First of all, O my son, fear God; for the fear of God is the beginning of wisdom, and wisdom will never let thee go astray.

"Secondly, consider what thou wert, and make it
30 thy business to know thyself, which is the most difficult lesson in the world. Yet from this lesson thou wilt learn to avoid the frog's foolish ambition of swelling to rival the bigness of the ox; else the consideration of your having been a hog-driver, will be, to the wheel of your fortune, like the peacock's ugly feet."

"True," quoth Sancho, "but I was then but a little boy; for when I grew up to be somewhat bigger, I drove geese, and not hogs, but methinks that is
40 nothing to the purpose; for all governors cannot come from kings and princes." . . .

"Be well-pleased with the meanness of thy family, Sancho, nor think it a disgrace to own thyself derived from labouring men; for, if thou art not ashamed of it thyself, nobody else will strive to make thee so. Endeavour rather to be esteemed humble and virtuous, rather than proud and vicious. The number is almost infinite of those who, from low and vulgar births, have been raised to the highest
50 dignities, to the papal chair, and the imperial throne; and this I could prove by examples enough to tire thy patience. . . .

"If thou sendest for thy wife, as it is not fit a man in thy station should be long without his wife, and she ought to partake of her husband's good fortune, teach her, instruct her, polish her the best

thou canst, till her native rusticity is refined to a handsomer behaviour; for often an ill-bred wife throws down all that a good and discreet husband can build up. . . . 60

"Let the tears of the poor find more compassion, though not more justice, than the informations of the rich.

"When the severity of the law is to be softened, let pity, not bribes, be the motive.

"Revile not with words those whom their crimes oblige thee to punish in deed; for the punishment is enough to the wretches, without the addition of ill language.

"If thou observest these rules, Sancho, thy days 70 shall be long, thy fame eternal, thy recompense full, and thy felicity unspeakable. Thou shalt marry thy children and thy grandchildren to thy heart's desire; they shall want no titles: beloved of all men, thy life shall be peaceable, thy death in a good and venerable old age, and the offspring of thy grandchildren, with their soft youthful hands shall close thy eyes." . . .

After dinner Don Quixote gave Sancho, in writing, the copy of his verbal instructions, ordering him 80 to get somebody to read them to him. But the squire had no sooner got them, but he dropped the paper, which fell into the Duke's hands; who, communicating the same to the Duchess, they found a fresh occasion of admiring the mixture of Don Quixote's good sense and extravagance: and so carrying on the humour, they sent Sancho that afternoon, with a suitable equipage, to the place he was to govern, which, wherever it lay, was to be an island to him. . . . 90

How the great Sancho Panca took possession of his island, and in what manner he began to govern.

Sancho, with all his attendants, came to a town that had about a thousand inhabitants, and was one of the best where the Duke had any power: they gave him to understand, that the name of the place was the island of Barataria, either because the town was called Barataria, or because the government cost him so cheap. As soon as he came to the gates (for it was walled) the chief officers and inhabitants, in their formalities, came out to receive him, the bells rung, and all the people gave general demon- 100 strations of their joy. The new governor was then carried in mighty pomp to the great church, to give Heaven thanks; and after some ridiculous ceremonies, they delivered him the keys of the gates, and received him as a perpetual governor of the island of Barataria. In the meantime, the garb, the port, the huge beard, and the short and thick

96–97. or because . . . so cheap. Spanish *borato* means cheap.

shape of the new Governor, made every one who knew nothing of the jest wonder, and even those who were privy to the plot, who were many, were not a little surprised.

In short, from the church they carried him to the court of justice; where, when they had placed him in his seat, "My Lord Governor," said the Duke's steward to him, "it is an ancient custom here, that he who takes possession of this famous island, must
10 answer to some difficult and intricate question that is propounded to him; and by the return he makes, the people feel the pulse of his understanding, and by an estimate of his abilities, judge whether they ought to rejoice, or to be sorry for his coming."

All the while the steward was speaking, Sancho was staring on an inscription in large characters on the wall over against his seat, and as he could not read, he asked, what was the meaning of that which he saw painted there upon the wall. "Sir," said
20 they, "it is an account of the day when your Lordship took possession of this island, and the inscription runs thus: 'This day, being such a day of this month, in such a year, the Lord Don Sancho Pança took possession of this island, which may he long enjoy.' " "And who is he," asked Sancho, "whom they call Don Sancho Pança?" "Your Lordship," answered the steward; "for we know of no other Pança in this island but yourself, who now sits in this chair." "Well, friend," said Sancho, "pray take
30 notice, that Don does not belong to me, nor was it borne by any of my family before me. Plain Sancho Pança is my name; my father was called Sancho, my grandfather Sancho; and all of us have been Panças, without any Don or Donna added to our name. Now do I already guess your Dons are as thick as stones in this island. But it is enough that Heaven knows my meaning; if my government happens but to last four days to an end, it shall go hard but I will clear the island of those swarms of Dons
40 that must needs be as troublesome as so many flesh-flies." . . .

Sancho was conducted from the court of justice to a sumptuous palace; where, in a spacious room, he found the cloth laid, and a most neat and magnificent entertainment prepared. As soon as he entered, the wind music played, and four pages waited on him, in order to the washing his hands; which he did with a great deal of gravity. And now the instruments ceasing, Sancho sat down at the upper
50 end of the table; for there was no seat but there, and the cloth was only laid for one. A certain personage, who afterwards appeared to be a physician, came and stood at his elbow, with a whalebone wand in his hand. Then they took off a curious white cloth that lay over the dishes on the table, and discovered great variety of fruit, and other eatables. One that looked like a student, said grace; a page put a laced

bib under Sancho's chin; and another, who did the office of sewer, set a dish of fruit before him. But he had hardly put one bit into his mouth, before
69 the physician touched the dish with his wand, and then it was taken away by a page in an instant. Immediately another with meat was clapped in the place; but Sancho no sooner offered to taste it, but the doctor with the wand conjured it away as fast as the fruit. Sancho was amazed at this sudden removal, and looking about him on the company, asked them whether they used to tantalize people at that rate, feeding their eyes, and starving their bellies.

"My Lord Governor," answered the physician,
70 "you are to eat here no otherwise than according to the use and custom of other islands where there are governors. I am a doctor of physic, my Lord, and have a salary allowed me in this island, for taking charge of the Governor's health, and I am more careful of it than of my own; studying night and day his constitution, that I may the better know what to prescribe when he falls sick. Now the chief thing I do, is to attend him always at his meals, to let him eat what I think convenient for him, and to
80 prevent his eating what I imagine to be prejudicial to his health, and offensive to his stomach. Therefore I now ordered the fruit to be taken away, because it is too cold and moist; and the other dish, because it is as much too hot, and overseasoned with spices, which are apt to increase thirst; and he that drinks much, destroys and consumes the radical moisture, which is the fuel of life." "So then," quoth Sancho, "this dish of roasted partridges here can do me no manner of harm." "Hold," said the physician, "the
90 Lord Governor shall not eat of them, while I live to prevent it." "Why so?" cried Sancho. "Because," answered the doctor, "our great master, Hippocrates, the north star and luminary of physic, says in one of his aphorisms, *Omnis saturatio mala, perdicis autem pessima*: that is, all repletion is bad, but that of partridges is worst of all." "If it be so," said Sancho, "let Mr. Doctor see which of all these dishes on the table will do me most good and least harm,
100 and let me eat my belly full of that, without having it whisked away with his wand. For, by my hopes, and the pleasures of government, as I live, I am ready to die with hunger; and not to allow me to eat any victuals (let Mr. Doctor say what he will) is the way to shorten my life, and not to lengthen it." "Very true, my Lord," replied the physician. . . . "Therefore what I would advise at present, as a fit diet for the Governor, for the preservation and support of his health, is a hundred of small wafers, and
110 a few thin slices of marmalade, to strengthen his stomach, and help digestion."

Sancho hearing this, leaned back upon his chair, and looking earnestly in the doctor's face, very seriously asked him, what his name was, and where he had studied? "My Lord," answered he, "I am called Doctor Pedro Rezio de Aguero. The name of the place where I was born is Tirteafuera, and lies between Caraquel and Almodabar del Campo, on the right hand; and I took my degree of doctor in the university of Osuna." "Hark you," said Sancho, in a mighty chafe, "Mr. Dr. Pedro Rezio de Aguero, born at Tirteafuera, that lies between Caraquel and Almodabar del Campo, on the right hand, and who took your degree of doctor at the university of Osuna, and so forth, take yourself away! Avoid the room this moment, or by the sun's light, I'll get me a good cudgel, and beginning with your carcase, will so belabour and rib-roast all the physic-mongers in the island, that I will not leave therein one of the tribe of those, I mean that are ignorant quacks; for, as for learned and wise physicians, I will make much of them, and honour them like so many angels.". . . The physician was terrified, seeing the Governor in such a heat, and would that moment have slunk out of the room, had not the sound of a post-horn in the street been heard that moment; whereupon the steward immediately looking out of the window, turned back, and said, there was an express come from the Duke, doubtless with some dispatch of importance.

Presently the messenger entered sweating, with haste and concern in his looks, and pulling a packet out of his bosom, delivered it to the Governor. Sancho gave it to the steward, and ordered him to read the direction, which was this: "To Don Sancho Pança, Governor of the island of Barataria, to be delivered into his own hands, or those of his secretary." "Who is my secretary?" cried Sancho. "It is I, my Lord," answered one that was by, "for I can write and read, and am a Biscainer." "That last qualification is enough to make thee set up for secretary to the emperor himself," said Sancho. "Open the letter then, and see what it says." The new secretary did so, and having perused the dispatch by himself, told the Governor, that it was a business that was to be told only in private: Sancho ordered every one to leave the room except the steward and the carver, and then the secretary read what follows:

"I have received information, my Lord Don Sancho Pança, that some of our enemies intend to attack your island with great fury, one of these nights: You ought therefore to be watchful, and stand upon your guard, that you may not be found unprovided. I have also had intelligence from faithful spies, that there are four men got into the town in disguise, to murder you; your abilities being regarded as a great obstacle to the enemies' designs. Look about you, take heed how you admit strangers to speak with you, and eat nothing that is laid before you. I will take care to send you assistance, if you stand in need of it: And in everything I rely on your prudence. From

our castle, the 16th of August, at four in the morning.

"Your friend,
"THE DUKE."

Sancho was astonished at the news, and those that were with him seemed no less concerned. But at last, turning to the steward, "I will tell you," said he, "what is first to be done in this case, and that with all speed; clap me that same Doctor Rezio in a dungeon; for if anybody has a mind to kill me, it must be he, and that with a lingering death, the worst of deaths, hunger-starving. . . . Secretary, do you send my Lord Duke an answer, and tell him, his order shall be fulfilled in every part without fail. Remember me kindly to my Lady Duchess, . . . and I will be mindful to serve her to the best of my power: and when your hand is in, you may crowd in my service to my Master Don Quixote de la Mancha, that he may see I am neither forgetful nor ungrateful; the rest I leave to you; put in what you will, and do your part like a good secretary, and a staunch Biscainer. Now take away here, and bring me something to eat; and then you shall see I am able to deal with all the spies, wizards, and cut-throat dogs that dare to meddle with me and my island. . . .

"I intend to clear this island of all filth and rubbish, of all rogues and vagrants, idle knaves and sturdy beggars. For I would like you to know, my good friends, that your slothful, lazy, lewd people in a commonwealth, are like drones in a bee-hive, that waste and devour the honey which the labouring bees gather. I design to encourage husbandmen, preserve the privileges of the gentry, reward virtuous persons, and, above all things, reverence religion, and have regard to the honour of religious men. What think you of this, my good friends? Do I talk to the purpose, or do I talk idly?" "You speak so well, my Lord Governor," answered the steward, "that I stand in admiration to hear a man so unlettered as you are (for I believe your Lordship cannot read at all) utter so many notable things, and in every word a sentence; far from what they who sent you hither, and they who are here present, ever expected from your understanding. But every day produces some new wonder, jests are turned into earnest, and those who designed to laugh at others, happened to be laughed at themselves.". . .

A continuation of Sancho Pança's government, with other passages, such as they are.

At last the Lord Governor was pleased to rise; and, by Dr. Pedro Rezio's order, they brought him for his breakfast a little conserve, and a draught of fair water, which he would have exchanged with all his heart for a good luncheon of bread, and a bunch of grapes; but seeing he could not help himself, he was forced to make the best of a bad market, and seem to be content, though full sore against his will and appetite; for the doctor made him believe, that to eat but little, and that which was dainty, enlivened the spirits, and sharpened the wit, and consequently such a sort of diet was most proper for persons in authority and weighty employments, wherein there is less need of the strength of the body than of that of the mind. This sophistry served to famish Sancho, who, half-dead with hunger, cursed in his heart both the government and him that had given it him. However, hungry as he was, by the strength of his slender breakfast, he failed not to give audience that day; and the first that came before him was a stranger, who put the following case to him, the steward and the rest of the attendants being present.

"My Lord," said he, "a large river divides in two parts one and the same lordship. I beg your honour to lend me your attention, for it is a case of great importance, and some difficulty. Upon this river there is a bridge; at one end of which there stands a gallows, and a kind of court of justice, where four judges used to sit, for the execution of a certain law made by the lord of the land and river, which runs thus:

" 'Whoever intends to pass from one end of this bridge to the other, must first upon his oath declare whither he goes, and what his business is. If he swear truth, he may go on; but if he swear false, he shall be hanged, and die without remission upon the gibbet at the end of the bridge.'

"After due promulgation of this law, many people, notwithstanding its severity, adventured to go over this bridge, and as it appeared they swore true, the judges permitted them to pass unmolested. It happened one day that a certain passenger being sworn, declared, that by the oath he had taken, he was come to die upon that gallows, and that was all his business.

"This put the judges to a nonplus; 'for,' said they, 'if we let this man pass freely, he is forsworn, and according to the letter of the law he ought to die; if we hang him, he has sworn truth, seeing he swore he was to die on that gibbet; and then by the same law we should let him pass.'

"Now your Lordship's judgment is desired what the judges ought to do with this man. For they are still at a standing, not knowing what to determine in this case; and having been informed of your sharp wit, and great capacity in resolving difficult questions, they sent me to beseech your Lordship, in their names, to give your opinion in so intricate and knotty a case."

"To deal plainly with you," answered Sancho;

"those worshipful judges that sent you hither might as well have spared themselves the labour; for I am more inclined to dulness I assure you than sharpness: however, let me hear your question once more, that I may thoroughly understand it, and perhaps I may at last hit the nail on the head." The man repeated the question again and again; and when he had done, "To my thinking," said Sancho, "this question may be presently answered, as thus: the man swore he came to die on the gibbet, and if he dies there, he swore true, and according to the law he ought to be free, and go over the bridge. On the other side, if you do not hang him, he swore false, and by the same law he ought to be hanged." "It is as your Lordship says," replied the stranger, "you have stated the case right." "Why then," said Sancho, "even let that part of the man that swore true freely pass; and hang the other part of the man that swore false, and so the law will be fulfilled." "But then, my Lord," replied the stranger, "the man must be divided into two parts, which if we do, he certainly dies, and the law, which must every tittle of it be observed, is not put in execution."

"Well, hark you me, honest man," said Sancho, "either I am a very dunce, or there is as much reason to put this same person you talk of to death as to let him live and pass the bridge; for if the truth saves him, the lie condemns him. Now the case stands thus, I would have you tell those gentlemen that sent you to me, since there is as much reason to bring him off, as to condemn him, that they even let him go free; for it is always more commendable to do good than hurt. And this I would give you under my own hand, if I could write. Nor do I speak this of my own head; but I remember one precept, among many others, that my master Don Quixote gave me the night before I went to govern this island, which was, that when the scale of justice is even, or a case is doubtful, we should prefer mercy before rigour; and it has pleased God I should call it to mind so luckily at this juncture." "For my part," said the steward, "this judgment seems to me so equitable, that I do not believe Lycurgus himself, who gave laws to the Lacedæmonians, could ever have decided the matter better than the great Sancho has done.". . .

The toilsome end and conclusion of Sancho Pança's government.

It was now but the seventh night, after so many days of his government, when the careful Governor had betaken himself to his repose, sated not with bread and wine, but cloyed with hearing causes, pronouncing sentences, making statutes, and putting out orders and proclamations: scarce was sleep, in spite of wakeful hunger, beginning to close his eyes, when, of a sudden, he heard a great noise of bells, and most dreadful out-cries, as if the whole island had been sinking. Presently he started, and sat up in his bed, and listened with great attention, to try if he could learn how far this uproar might concern him. But while he was thus hearkening in the dark, a great number of drums and trumpets were heard, and that sound being added to the noise of the bells and the cries, gave so dreadful an alarm, that his fear and terror increased, and he was in a sad consternation. Up he leaped out of his bed, and put on his slippers, the ground being damp, and without anything else in the world on but his shirt, ran and opened his chamber-door, and saw about twenty men come running along the galleries with lighted links in one hand, and drawn swords in the other, all crying out, "Arm! my Lord Governor, arm! a world of enemies are got into the island, and we are undone, unless your valour and conduct relieve us." Thus bawling and running with great fury and disorder, they got to the door where Sancho stood quite scared out of his senses. "Arm, arm, this moment, my Lord!" cried one of them, "if you have not a mind to be lost with the whole island."

"What would you have me arm for?" quoth Sancho. "Do I know anything of arms or fighting, think ye? why do not ye rather send for Don Quixote, my Master, he will dispatch your enemies in a trice? Alas! as I am a sinner to Heaven, I understand nothing of this hasty service." "For shame, my Lord Governor," said another, "what a faint-heartedness is this! See, we bring you here arms offensive and defensive; arm yourself, and march to the market-place. Be our leader and captain as you ought, and show yourself a Governor." "Why then, arm me, and good luck attend me," quoth Sancho; with that they brought him two large shields, which they had provided, and without letting him put on his other clothes, clapped them over his shirt, and tied the one behind upon his back, and the other before upon his breast, having got his arms through some holes made on purpose. Now the shields being fastened to his body, as hard as cords could bind them, the poor Governor was cased up and immured as straight as an arrow, without being able so much as to bend his knees, or stir a step. Then, having put a lance into his hand for him to lean upon, and keep himself up, they desired him to march, and lead them on, and put life into them all, telling him that they did not doubt of victory, since they had him for their commander. "March!" quoth Sancho, "how do you think I am able to do it, squeezed as I am? These boards stick so plaguy close to me, I cannot so much as bend the joints of my knees; you must even carry me in your arms, and lay me across or set me upright, before some passage, and I will make good that spot of ground, either with this lance or my body." "Fie, my Lord Governor," said another, "it is

more your fear than your armour that stiffens your legs, and hinders you from moving. Move, move, march on, it is high time, the enemy grows stronger, and the danger presses."

The poor Governor, thus urged and upbraided, endeavoured to go forwards; but the first motion he made, threw him to the ground at his full length, so heavily, that he gave over all his bones for broken; and there he lay like a huge tortoise in his shell, or a flitch of bacon clapped between two boards, or like a boat overturned upon a flat, with the keel upwards. Nor had those drolling companions the least compassion upon him as he lay; quite contrary, having put out their lights, they made a terrible noise, and clattered with their swords, and trampled to and again upon the poor Governor's body, and laid on furiously with their swords upon his shields, insomuch, that if he had not shrunk his head into them for shelter, he had been in a woeful condition. Squeezed up in his narrow shell, he was in a grievous fright, and a terrible sweat, praying from the bottom of his heart, for deliverance from the cursed trade of governing islands. Some kicked him, some stumbled and fell upon him, and one among the rest jumped full upon him, and there stood for some time, as on a watch-tower, like a general encouraging his soldiers, and giving orders, crying out, "There boys, there! the enemies charge most on that side, make good that breach, secure that gate, down with those scaling ladders, fetch fire-balls, more granadoes, burning pitch, rosin, and kettles of scalding oil. Intrench yourselves, get beds, quilts, cushions, and barricade the streets;" in short, he called for all the instruments of death, and all the engines used for the defence of a city that is besieged and stormed

Sancho lay snug, though sadly bruised, and while he endured all quietly, "Oh that it would please the Lord," quoth he to himself, "that this island were but taken, or that I were fairly dead, or out of this peck of troubles." At last Heaven heard his prayers; and, when he least expected it, he heard them cry, "Victory! victory! the enemy is routed. Now, my Lord Governor, rise, come and enjoy the fruits of conquest, and divide the spoils taken from the enemy, by the valour of your invincible arms." "Help me up," cried poor Sancho in a doleful tone; and when they had set him on his legs, "Let all the enemy I have routed," quoth he, "be nailed to my forehead: I will divide no spoils of enemies: but if I have one friend here, I only beg he would give me a draught of wine to comfort me, and help me to dry up the sweat that I am in; for I am all over water." Thereupon they wiped him, gave him wine and took off his shields: after that, as he sat upon his bed, what with his fright, and what with the toil he had endured, he fell into a swoon, insomuch that those who acted this scene, began to repent they had carried it so far. But Sancho recovering from his fit in a little time, they also recovered from their uneasiness. Being come to himself, he asked what it was o'clock? They answered, it was now break of day. He said nothing; but, without any words, began to put on his clothes. While this was doing, and he continued seriously silent, all the eyes of the company were fixed upon him, wondering what could be the meaning of his being in such haste to put on his clothes.

At last, he made an end of dressing himself, and creeping along softly (for he was too much bruised to go along very fast), he got to the stable, followed by all the company; and coming to Dapple, he embraced the quiet animal, gave him a loving kiss on the forehead, and, with tears in his eyes, "Come hither," said he, "my friend, thou faithful companion, and fellow-sharer in my travels and miseries; when thee and I consorted together, and all my cares were but to mend thy furniture, and feed thy little carcase, then happy were my days, my months, and years. But since I forsook thee, and clambered up the towers of ambition and pride, a thousand woes, a thousand torments, and four thousand tribulations have haunted and worried my soul." While he was talking thus, he fitted on his pack-saddle, nobody offering to say anything to him. This done, with a great deal of difficulty he mounted his ass, and then addressing himself to the steward, the secretary, the gentleman-waiter, and Dr. Pedro Rezio, and many others that stood by, "Make way, gentlemen," said he, "and let me return to my former liberty. Let me go that I may seek my old course of life, and rise again from that death that buries me here alive. I was not born to be a Governor, nor to defend islands nor cities from enemies that break in upon them. I know better what belongs to ploughing, delving, pruning, and planting of vineyards, than how to make laws, and defend countries and kingdoms. St. Peter is very well at Rome; which is as much as to say, let every one stick to the calling he was born to. A spade does better in my hand than a Governor's truncheon; and I had rather fill my belly with a mess of plain porridge, than lie at the mercy of a coxcombly physic-monger that starves me to death. I had rather solace myself under the shade of an oak in summer, and wrap up my corpse in a double sheep-skin in the winter at my liberty, than lay me down with the slavery of a government in fine holland-sheets, and case my hide in furs and richest sables. Heaven be with you, gentle-folks, and pray tell my Lord Duke from me, that naked I was born, and naked I am at present. I have neither won nor lost, which is as much as to say, without a penny I came to this government, and without a penny I leave it, quite contrary to what governors of islands use to do, when they leave them. Clear the way, then, I beseech you, and let me pass; I must get myself wrapped up all over in cerecloth; for I do not think I have a sound rib left, thanks to the enemies that have walked over me all night long."

"This must not be, my Lord Governor," said Dr. Rezio, "for I will give your Honour a balsamic drink, that is a specific against falls, dislocations, contusions, and all manner of bruises, and that will presently restore you to your former health and strength. And then for your diet, I promise to take a new course with you, and to let you eat abundantly of whatsoever you please." "It is too late, Mr. Doctor," answered Sancho; "you should as soon make me turn Turk, as hinder me from going. No, no, these tricks shall not pass upon me again, you shall as soon make me fly to heaven without wings, as get me to stay here, or ever catch me nibbling at a government again, though it were served up to me in a covered dish. I am of the blood of the Pancas, and we are all wilful and positive. If once we cry Odd, it shall be odd in spite of all mankind, though it be even. Go to, then: let the pismire leave behind him in this stable, those wings that lifted him up in the air to be a prey to martlets and sparrows. Fair and softly. Let me now tread again on plain ground; though I may not wear pinked Cordovan leather-pumps, I shall not want a pair of sandals to my feet. Every sheep to her mate. Let not the cobbler go beyond his last; and so let me go, for it is late." "My Lord Governor," said the steward, "though it grieves us to part with your Honour, your sense and Christian behaviour engaging us to covet your company, yet we would not presume to stop you against your inclination: but you know that every Governor, before he leaves the place he has governed, is bound to give an account of his administration. Be pleased therefore to do so for the ten days you have been among us, and then peace be with you." "No man has power to call me to an account," replied Sancho, "unless it be by my Lord Duke's appointment. Now to him it is that I am going, and to him I will give a fair and square account. And indeed, going away so bare as I do, there needs no greater signs that I have governed like an angel." "In truth," said Dr. Rezio, "the great Sancho is in the right; and I am of opinion, we ought to let him go; for certainly the Duke will be very glad to see him." Thereupon they all agreed to let him pass, offering first to attend him, and supply him with whatever he might want in his journey, either for entertainment or conveniency. Sancho told them, that all he desired was a little corn for his ass, and half a cheese, and half a loaf for himself; having occasion for no other provisions in so short a journey. With that they all embraced him, and he embraced them all, not without tears in

94. **the ten days;** but Sancho governed only seven days.

his eyes, leaving them in admiration of the good sense which he discovered both in his discourse and unalterable resolution. . . .

How Don Quixote took his leave of the Duke.

Don Quixote thought it now time to leave the idle life he led in the castle, believing it a mighty fault, thus to shut himself up, and indulge his sensual appetite among the tempting varieties of dainties and delights, which the Lord and Lady of the place provided for his entertainment, as a knight-errant;
10 and he thought he was to give a strict account to Heaven for a course of life so opposite to his active profession. Accordingly, one day he acquainted the Duke and Duchess with his sentiments, and begged their leave to depart. They both seemed very unwilling to part with him, but yet at last yielded to his entreaties. . . .

Don Quixote, having taken his solemn leave of the Duke and Duchess over-night, left his apartment the next morning, and appeared in his armour in the
20 courtyard, the galleries all round about being filled at the same time with the people of the house; the Duke and Duchess being also got thither to see him: Sancho was upon his Dapple, with his cloak-bag, his wallet, and his provision, very brisk and cheerful. . . . Then Don Quixote bowed his head, and after he had made a low obeisance to the Duke, the Duchess, and all the company, he turned about with Rozinante; and Sancho following him on Dapple, they left the castle, and took the road for Sara-
30 gossa. . . .

Of an unlucky adventure, which Don Quixote laid most to heart of any that had yet befallen him.

Now it happened one morning that Don Quixote going abroad to take the air upon the seashore, armed at all points, according to his custom (his arms, as he said, being his best attire, as combat was his refreshment), he spied a knight riding towards him, armed like himself from head to foot, with a bright moon blazoned on his shield, who coming within hearing, called out to him, "Illustrious, and never-sufficiently extolled Don Quixote de
40 la Mancha, I am the Knight of the White Moon, whose incredible achievements, perhaps, have reached thy ears. Lo, I am come to enter into combat with thee, and to compel thee by dint of sword, to own and acknowledge my mistress, by whatever name and dignity she be distinguished, to be without any degree of comparison, more beautiful than thy Dulcinea del Toboso. Now if thou wilt fairly confess this truth, thou freest thyself from certain death, and me from the trouble of taking or giving
50 thee thy life. If not, the conditions of our combat are these: if victory be on my side, thou shalt be obliged immediately to forsake thy arms, and the

quest of adventures, and to return to thy own home, where thou shalt engage to live quietly and peaceably for the space of one whole year, without laying hand on thy sword, to the improvement of thy estate, and the salvation of thy soul. But if thou comest off conqueror, my life is at thy mercy, my horse and arms shall be thy trophy, and the fame of all my former exploits, by the lineal descent of conquest, 60 be vested in thee as victor. Consider what thou hast to do, and let thy answer be quick, for my dispatch is limited to this very day."

Don Quixote was amazed and surprised as much at the arrogance of the Knight of the White Moon's challenge, as at the subject of it; so with a solemn and austere address, "Knight of the White Moon," said he, "whose achievements have as yet been kept from my knowledge, it is more than probable, that you have never seen the illustrious Dulcinea; for 70 had you ever viewed her perfections, you had there found arguments enough to convince you, that no beauty past, present, or to come, can parallel hers; and therefore, without giving you directly the lie, I only tell thee, knight, thou art mistaken, and this position I will maintain by accepting your challenge on your conditions, except that article of your exploits descending to me; for, not knowing what character your actions bear, I shall rest satisfied with the fame of my own, by which, such as they are, I 80 am willing to abide. And since your time is so limited, choose your ground, and begin your career as soon as you will, and expect to be met with a fair field and no favour: to whom God shall give her, St. Peter give his blessing."

Don Quixote making some short ejaculations to Heaven and his mistress, as he always used upon these occasions, began his career, without either sound of trumpet or any other signal. His adversary was no less forward; for setting spurs to his horse, 90 which was much the swifter, he met Don Quixote before he had run half his career, so forcibly, that without making use of his lance, which it is thought he lifted up on purpose, he overthrew the Knight of la Mancha and Rozinante, both coming to the ground with a terrible fall.

The Knight of the White Moon got immediately upon him, and clapping the point of his lance to his face, "Knight," cried he, "you are vanquished, and a dead man, unless you immediately fulfil the con- 100 ditions of your combat." Don Quixote, bruised and stunned with his fall, without lifting up his beaver, answered in a faint hollow voice, as if he had spoken out of a tomb, "Dulcinea del Toboso is the most beautiful woman in the world, and I the most unfortunate knight upon the earth. It were unjust that such perfection should suffer through my weakness. No, pierce my body with thy lance, Knight, and let my life expire with my honour." "Not so rigorous neither," replied the conqueror, "let the fame of the Lady Dulcinea del Toboso remain entire and unblemished; provided the great Don Quixote return home for a year, as we agreed before the combat, I am satisfied.". . . To which Don Quixote answered, that upon condition he should be enjoined nothing to the prejudice of Dulcinea, he would, upon the faith of a true knight, be punctual in the performance of everything else. This acknowledgment being made, the Knight of the White Moon turned about his horse, and . . . rode at a hand-gallop into the city. . . .

Don Quixote was lifted up, and upon taking off his helmet, they found him pale, and in a cold sweat. As for Rozinante, he was in so bad a plight, that he could not stir for the present. Then, as for Sancho, he was in so heavy a taking, that he knew not what to do, nor what to say; he was sometimes persuaded he was in a dream, sometimes he fancied this rueful adventure was all witchcraft and enchantment. In short, he found his master discomfited in the face of the world, and bound to good behaviour, and to lay aside his arms for a whole year. Now he thought his glory eclipsed, his hopes of greatness vanished into smoke, and his master's promises like his bones, put out of joint by that cursed fall, which he was afraid had at once crippled Rozinante and his master. At last, the vanquished knight was put into a chair, and they carried him into town. . . .

An account of the Knight of the White Moon and other passages.

Don Antonio Moreno followed the Knight of the White Moon to his inn, whither he was attended by a troublesome rabble of boys. The knight being got to his chamber, where his squire waited to take off his armour, Don Antonio came in, declaring he would not be shook off, till he had discovered who he was. The knight finding that the gentleman would not leave him: "Sir," said he, "since I lie under no obligation of concealing myself, if you please, while my man disarms me, you shall hear the whole truth of the story.

"You must know, sir, I am called the Bachelor Carrasco: I live in the same town with this Don Quixote, whose unaccountable frenzy has moved all his neighbours, and me among the rest, to endeavour by some means to cure his madness; in order to which, believing that rest and ease would prove the surest remedy, I bethought myself of this present stratagem. . . . For I know him to be so nicely punctual in whatever his word and honour is engaged for, that he will undoubtedly perform his promise. This, sir, is the sum of the whole story, and I beg the favour of you to conceal me from Don Quixote, that my project may not be ruined, . . .

30. **Don Antonio Moreno;** who had seen the combat.

and that the honest gentleman, who is naturally a man of good parts, may recover his understanding.". . .

Six days did Don Quixote keep his bed, very dejected, sullen, and out of humour, and full of severe and black reflections on his fatal overthrow. Sancho was his comforter, and among other his crumbs of comfort, "My dear master," quoth he, "cheer up, come pluck up a good heart, and be thankful for coming off no worse. Why, a man has broke his neck with a less fall, and you have not so much as a broken rib. Consider, sir, that they that game, sometimes must lose; we must not always look for bacon where we see the hooks. Come, sir, cry a fig for the doctor, since you will not need him this bout; let us jog home fair and softly, without thinking any more of sauntering up and down, nobody knows whither, in quest of adventures and bloody noses. Why, sir, I am the greatest loser, if you go to that, though it is you that are in the worst pickle. It is true, I was weary of being a governor, and gave over all thoughts that way; but yet I never parted with my inclination of being an earl; and now, if you miss being a king, by casting off your knight-errantry, poor I may go whistle for my earldom." "No more of that, Sancho," cried Don Quixote; "I shall only retire for a year, and then reassume my honourable profession, which will undoubtedly secure me a kingdom, and thee an earldom." "Heaven grant it may," quoth Sancho, "and no mischief betide us: Hope well, and have well, says the proverb.". . .

Two days after, Don Quixote, being somewhat recovered . . . and having caused his armour to be laid on Dapple, set forwards on his journey home: Sancho thus being forced to trudge after him on foot. . . .

How Don Quixote fell sick, made his last will, and died.

As all human things, especially the lives of men, are transitory, their very beginnings being but steps to their dissolution; so Don Quixote, who was no way exempted from the common fate, was snatched away by death, when he least expected it. Whether his sickness was the effect of his melancholy reflections, or whether it was so pre-ordained by Heaven, most certain it is, he was seized with a violent fever, that confined him to his bed six days.

All that time his good friends, the curate, bachelor, and barber, came often to see him, and his trusty squire Sancho Pança never stirred from his bedside.

They conjectured that his sickness proceeded from the regret of his defeat, and his being disappointed of Dulcinea's disenchantment; and accordingly they left nothing unessayed to divert him. The bachelor begged him to pluck up a good heart, and rise, that they might begin their pastoral life . . . but this had no effect on Don Quixote, for he still continued dejected. A physician was sent for, who, upon feeling his pulse, did not very well like it; and therefore desired him of all things to provide for his soul's health, for that of his body was in a dangerous condition. Don Quixote heard this with much more temper than those about him; for his niece, his housekeeper, and his squire fell a-weeping as bitterly as if he had been laid out already. The physician was of opinion, that mere melancholy and vexation had brought him to his approaching end. Don Quixote desired them to leave him a little, because he found himself inclinable to rest; they retired, and he had a hearty sleep of about six hours which the maid and niece were afraid had been his last.

At length he waked, and with a loud voice, "Blessed be the Almighty," cried he, "for this great benefit He has vouchsafed to do me! Infinite are His mercies; they are greater, and more in number than the sins of men." The niece hearkening very attentively to these words of her uncle, and finding more sense in them than there was in his usual talk, at least since he had fallen ill: "What do you say, Sir," said she, "has any thing extraordinary happened? What mercies are these you mention?"

"Mercies," answered he, "that Heaven has this moment vouchsafed to show me, in spite of all my iniquities. My judgment is returned clear and undisturbed and that cloud of ignorance is now removed, which the continual reading of those damnable books of knight-errantry had cast over my understanding. Now, I perceive their nonsense and impertinence, and am only sorry the discovery happens so late, when I want time to make amends by those studies that should enlighten my soul, and prepare me for futurity. I find, niece, my end approaches; but I would have it such, that though my life has got me the character of a madman I may deserve a better at my death. Dear child," continued he, "send for my honest friend the curate, the bachelor Carrasco, and Mr. Nicholas the barber, for I intend to make my confession and my will." His niece was saved the trouble of sending, for presently they all three came in; which Don Quixote perceiving, "My good friends," said he, "I have happy news to tell you; I am no longer Don Quixote de la Mancha, but Alonso Quixano, the same whom the world for his fair behaviour has been formerly pleased to call the Good. I now declare myself an enemy to Amadis de Gaul, and his whole generation; all profane stories of knight-errantry, all romances I detest. I have a true sense of the danger of reading them, and of all my past follies, and through Heaven's mercy, and my own experience, I abhor them." His three friends were not a little surprised to hear him talk at this rate, and concluded some new frenzy had possessed

him. "What now?" said Samson to him. "What is all this to the purpose, Signor Don Quixote? We have just had the news that the Lady Dulcinea is disenchanted; and now we are upon the point of turning shepherds, to sing, and live like princes, you are dwindled down to a hermit."

"No more of that, I beseech you," replied Don Quixote; "all the use I shall make of these follies at present, is to heighten my repentance; and though they have hitherto proved prejudicial, yet, by the assistance of Heaven, they may turn to my advantage at my death: I find it comes fast upon me; therefore, pray, gentlemen, let us be serious. I want a priest to receive my confession, and a scrivener to draw up my will. There is no trifling at a time like this; I must take care of my soul; and therefore pray let the scrivener be sent for, while Mr. Curate prepares me by confession."

Don Quixote's words put them all into such admiration, that they stood gazing upon one another; they thought they had reason to doubt of the return of his understanding, and yet they could not help believing him. They were also apprehensive he was near the point of death, considering the sudden recovery of his intellects; and he delivered himself after that with so much sense, discretion, and piety, and showed himself so resigned to the will of Heaven, that they made no scruple to believe him restored to his perfect judgment at last. The curate thereupon cleared the room of all the company but himself and Don Quixote, and then confessed him. In the meantime the bachelor ran for the scrivener, and presently brought him with him; and Sancho Pança being informed by the bachelor how ill his master was, and finding his niece and housekeeper all in tears, began to make wry faces, and fall a-crying. The curate having heard the sick person's confession, came out and told them, that the good Alonso Quixano was very near his end, and certainly in his senses; and therefore, they had best go in, that he might make his will. These dismal tidings opened the sluices of the housekeeper's, the niece's, and the good squire's swollen eyes, so that a whole inundation of tears burst out of those flood-gates, and a thousand sighs from their hearts; for indeed, either as Alonso Quixano, or as Don Quixote de la Mancha, as it has been observed, the sick gentleman had always showed himself such a good-natured man, and of so agreeable a behaviour, that he was not only beloved by his family, but by every one that knew him.

The scrivener, with the rest of the company, then went into the chamber, and the preamble and former part of the will being drawn, and the testator having recommended his soul to Heaven, and bequeathed his body to the earth, according to custom, he came to the legacies, as follows:

"Item, I give and bequeath to Sancho Pança,

whom in my madness I made my squire, whatever money he has, or may have of mine in his hands; and whereas there are reckonings and accounts to be adjusted between us, for what he has received and disbursed; my will and pleasure is, that whatever may remain due to me, which can be but small, be enjoyed by him as my free gift, without any let or molestation, and much good may it do him. And as, when I was mad, he was through my means made governor of an island, I would now, in my right senses, give him the government of a kingdom, were it in my power, in consideration of his integrity and faithfulness. And now, my friend," said he, turning to Sancho, "pardon me that I have brought upon thee, as well as myself, the scandal of madness, by drawing thee into my own errors, and persuading thee that there have been and still are knights-errant in the world." "Woe's me, my dear master's worship!" cried Sancho, all in tears, "do not die this bout, but even take my counsel, and live on many years; it is the maddest trick a man can ever play in his whole life, to let his breath sneak out of his body without any more ado, and without so much as a rap over the pate, or a kick on the guts; to go out like the snuff of a farthing candle, and die merely of the mulligrubs, or the sullens. For shame, sir, do not give way to sluggishness, but get out of your doleful dumps, and rise. Is this a time to lie honing and groaning a-bed, when we should be in the fields in our shepherd's clothing, as we had resolved? Ten to one but behind some bush, or under some hedge, we may find the Lady Madam Dulcinea, stripped of her enchanted rags, and as fine as a queen. Mayhaps you take it to heart, that you were unhorsed, and a little crupper-scratched the other day; but if that be all, lay the blame upon me, and say it was my fault, in not girting Rozinante tight enough. You know too, there is nothing more common in your errantry-books, than for the knights to be every foot jostled out of the saddle. There is nothing but ups and downs in this world, and he that is cast down to-day, may be a cock-a-hoop to-morrow." "Even so," said Samson, "honest Sancho has a right notion of the matter." "Soft and fair, gentleman," replied Don Quixote, "never look for birds of this year in the nests of the last: I was mad, but I am now in my senses; I was once Don Quixote de la Mancha but am now, as I said before, the plain Alonso Quixano, and I hope the sincerity of my words, and my repentance, may restore me to the same esteem you have had for me before; and so, Mr. Scrivener, pray go on."

"Item, I constitute and appoint Antonia Quixano, my niece here present, sole heiress of all my estate both real and personal after all my just debts and legacies, bequeathed by these presents, shall have been payed, satisfied, and deducted, out of the best of my goods and chattels; and the first of that kind to be discharged shall be the salary due to my house-keeper, together with twenty ducats over and above her wages; which said sum I leave and bequeath her to buy her mourning.

"Item, I appoint Mr. Curate, and Mr. Samson Carrasco the bachelor, here present, to be the executors of this my last will and testament.

"Item, it is my will, that if my niece Antonia Quixano be inclinable to marry, it be with none but a person, who, upon strict inquiry, shall be found never to have read a book of knight-errantry in his life; and in case it appears, that he has been conversant in such books, and that she persists in her resolution to marry him, she is then to forfeit all right and title to my bequest, which in such case, my executors are hereby empowered to dispose of to pious uses, as they shall think most proper.

"Item, I entreat the said executors, that if at any time they happen to meet with the author of a book now extant, entitled, 'The Second Part of the Achievements of Don Quixote de la Mancha,' they would from me most heartily beg his pardon for my being undesignedly the occasion of his writing such a parcel of impertinences as is contained in that book; for it is the greatest burthen to my departing soul, that ever I was the cause of his making such a thing public."

Having finished the will he fell into a swooning fit, and extended his body to the full length in the bed. All the company were troubled and alarmed, and ran to his assistance: however, he came to himself at last; but relapsed into the like fits almost every hour, for the space of three days that he lived after he had made his will. . . .

Thus died that ingenious gentleman Don Quixote de la Mancha, whose native place Cid Hamet has not thought fit directly to mention, with design that all the towns and villages in La Mancha should contend for the honour of giving him birth, as the seven cities of Greece did for Homer.

Baldassare Castiglione

1478–1529

Cervantes' satire of the medieval knight and his chivalric code was in part the attack of Renaissance reason on the naïve idealism of the Middle Ages, and in part a sign that knighthood had lost its authority in a world where national monarchies had displaced feudalism. As strong kings destroyed the power of the barons, the nobles flocked to the kings' courts, where they exchanged armor and lance for ruffles and rapier, if not also for the poet's pen. The dashing knight, proud of his independence, became a graceful courtier most valuable as a decoration for his monarch's retinue.

The ideal of the Renaissance gentleman is summarized in *The Courtier* (1514) by the Italian Castiglione. The author was himself a graceful fixture at the elegant court of Guidobaldo, Duke of Urbino. He had enjoyed a classical education at Milan and served as soldier to the Duke of that city, but the Dukes of Urbino employed him as suave ambassador to Henry VII of England and Charles V of Spain. His death in 1529 was said to have been hastened by his shame at being falsely accused of treachery.

Castiglione made himself the arbiter of social elegance for all of Europe through his charming Platonic dialogue, *The Courtier,* in which a group of distinguished ladies and gentlemen of his day supposedly debate the qualities of the perfect courtier in the drawing room of the gracious Duchess of Urbino. The characters, especially the ladies, emerge as witty artistic creations in the lively give-and-take, designed as a model of polite conversation. No phase of aristocratic life from boudoir to throne room is overlooked in their discussions. Born to nobility for noble instincts and to wealth for freedom from toil, Castiglione's gentleman is to realize Cicero's ideal of *humanitas* through a classical education and through service to the state as chivalrous soldier and wise political adviser. Culture of body and mind is to produce the well-rounded aristocrat, whose instincts are further refined by the influence of a good and beautiful woman. Attempting to realize an ideal of beauty in his whole behavior, the courtier is to be the embodiment of grace and virtue, the accomplished swordsman, the exquisite poet or musician, the Platonic lover, the loyal friend. And beside him stands his noble consort, the bright but prudent lady who inspires and complements his stately character. The code of Castiglione was soon accepted as law by the ruder courts to the north, and the Seigneur de Bayard in France and Sir Philip Sidney in England gave Europe living models of the new ideal.*

The Book of the Courtier

BOOK ONE

14.

THIS Courtier of ours should be nobly born and of gentle race; because it is far less unseemly for one of ignoble birth to fail in worthy deeds, than for one of noble birth, who, if he strays from the path of his predecessors, stains his family name, and not only fails to achieve but loses what has been achieved already; for noble birth is like a bright lamp that manifests and makes visible good and evil deeds, and kindles and stimulates to virtue both by fear of shame and by hope of praise. And since

10

* To emphasize the qualities of the courtier and the concept of Platonic love, the dialogue background is omitted from these excerpts. *The Book of the Courtier.*ᴬ Translated by Leonard Opdycke, copyright 1929 by Horace Liveright, New York.

this splendor of nobility does not illumine the deeds of the humbly born, they lack that stimulus and fear of shame, nor do they feel any obligation to advance beyond what their predecessors have done; while to the nobly born it seems a reproach not to reach at least the goal set them by their ancestors. And thus it nearly always happens that both in the profession of arms and in other worthy pursuits the most famous men have been of noble birth, because nature has implanted in everything that hidden seed 20 which gives a certain force and quality of its own essence to all things that are derived from it, and makes them like itself: as we see not only in the breeds of horses and of other animals, but also in trees, the shoots of which nearly always resemble the trunk; and if they sometimes degenerate, it arises from poor cultivation. And so it is with men, who if rightly trained are nearly always like those from whom they spring, and often better; but if there be no one to give them proper care, they 30 become like savages and never reach perfection.

It is true that, by favor of the stars or of nature, some men are endowed at birth with such graces that they seem not to have been born, but rather as if some god had formed them with his very hands and adorned them with every excellence of mind and body. So too there are many men so foolish and rude that one cannot but think that nature brought them into the world out of contempt or mockery. . . . There is a middle state between perfect grace 40 on the one hand and senseless folly on the other; and those who are not thus perfectly endowed by nature, with study and toil can in great part polish and amend their natural defects. Besides his noble birth, then, I would have the Courtier favored in this regard also, and endowed by nature not only with talent and beauty of person and feature, but with a certain grace and (as we say) air that shall make him at first sight pleasing and agreeable to all who see him; and I would have this an ornament 50 that should dispose and unite all his actions, and in his outward aspect give promise of whatever is worthy the society and favor of every great lord.

17. But to come to some details, I am of opinion that the principal and true profession of the Courtier ought to be that of arms; which I would have him follow actively above all else, and be known among others as bold and strong, and loyal to whomsoever he serves. And he will win a reputation for these good qualities by exercising them at all times and in 60 all places, since one may never fail in this without severest censure. And just as among women, their fair fame once sullied never recovers its first lustre, so the reputation of a gentleman who bears arms, if once it be in the least tarnished with cowardice or other disgrace, remains forever infamous before the world and full of ignominy. Therefore the more

our Courtier excels in this art, the more he will be worthy of praise; and yet I do not deem essential in him that perfect knowledge of things and those other qualities that befit a commander; since this would be too wide a sea, let us be content, as we have said, with perfect loyalty and unconquered courage, and that he be always seen to possess them. For the courageous are often recognized even more in small things than in great; and frequently in perils of importance and where there are many spectators, some men are to be found, who, although their hearts be dead within them, yet, moved by shame or by the presence of others, press forward almost with their eyes shut, and do their duty God knows how. While on occasions of little moment, when they think they can avoid putting themselves in danger without being detected, they are glad to keep safe. But those who, even when they do not expect to be observed or seen or recognized by anyone, show their ardor and neglect nothing, however paltry, that may be laid to their charge,—they have that strength of mind which we seek in our Courtier. . . .

Therefore let the man we are seeking, be very bold, stern, and always among the first, where the enemy are to be seen; and in every other place, gentle, modest, reserved, above all things avoiding ostentation and that impudent self-praise by which men ever excite hatred and disgust in all who hear them.

20. Coming to the bodily frame, I say it is enough if this be neither extremely short nor tall, for both of these conditions excite a certain contemptuous surprise, and men of either sort are gazed upon in much the same way that we gaze on monsters. Yet if we must offend in one of the two extremes, it is preferable to fall a little short of the just measure of height than to exceed it, for besides often being dull of intellect, men thus huge of body are also unfit for every exercise of agility, which thing I should much wish in the Courtier. And so I would have him well built and shapely of limb, and would have him show strength and lightness and suppleness, and know all bodily exercises that befit a man of war; whereof I think the first should be to handle every sort of weapon well on foot and on horse, to understand the advantages of each, and especially to be familiar with those weapons that are ordinarily used among gentlemen; for besides the use of them in war, where such sublety in contrivance is perhaps not needful, there frequently arise differences between one gentleman and another, which perhaps result in duels often fought with such weapons as happen at the moment to be within reach: thus knowledge of this kind is a very safe thing. Nor am I one of those who say that skill is forgotten in the hour of need; for he whose skill forsakes him at such

a time, indeed gives token that he has already lost heart and head through fear.

22. There are also many other exercises, which although not immediately dependent upon arms, yet are closely connected therewith, and greatly foster manly sturdiness; and one of the chief among these seems to me to be the chase, because it bears a certain likeness to war: and truly it is an amusement for great lords and befitting a man at court, and furthermore it is seen to have been much cultivated among the ancients. It is fitting also to know how to swim, to leap, to run, to throw stones, for besides the use that may be made of this in war, a man often has occasion to show what he can do in such matters; whence good esteem is to be won, especially with the multitude, who must be taken into account withal. Another admirable exercise, and one very befitting a man at court, is the game of tennis, in which are well shown the disposition of the body, the quickness and suppleness of every member, and all those qualities that are seen in nearly every other exercise. Nor less highly do I esteem vaulting on horse, which although it be fatiguing and difficult, makes a man very light and dexterous more than any other thing; and besides its utility, if this lightness is accompanied by grace, it is to my thinking a finer show than any of the others.

Our Courtier having once become more than fairly expert in these exercises, I think he should leave the others on one side: such as turning summersaults, rope-walking, and the like, which savor of the mountebank and little befit a gentleman.

But since one cannot devote himself to such fatiguing exercises continually, and since repetition becomes very tiresome and abates the admiration felt for what is rare, we must always diversify our life with various occupations. For this reason I would have our Courtier sometimes descend to quieter and more tranquil exercises, and in order to escape envy and to entertain himself agreeably with everyone, let him do whatever others do, yet never departing from praiseworthy deeds, and governing himself with that good judgment which will keep him from all folly; but let him laugh, jest, banter, frolic, and dance, yet in such fashion that he shall always appear genial and discreet, and that everything he may do or say shall be stamped with grace.

26. . . . Having often considered whence this grace springs, laying aside those men who have it by nature, I find one universal rule concerning it, which seems to me worth more in this matter than any other in all things human that are done or said: and that is to avoid affectation to the uttermost and as it were a very sharp and dangerous rock; and, to use possibly a new word, to practice in everything a certain nonchalance that shall conceal design and show that what is done and said is done without

effort and almost without thought. From this I believe grace is in large measure derived, because everyone knows the difficulty of those things that are rare and well done, and therefore facility in them excites the highest admiration; while on the other hand, to strive and as the saying is to drag by the hair, is extremely disgraceful, and makes us esteem everything slightly, however great it be. . . .

27. . . . In nonchalance (which is praiseworthy in itself), I do not think that it is less a vice of affectation to let the clothes fall from one's back, than in care of dress (which also is praiseworthy in itself), to hold the head stiff for fear of disarranging one's locks, or to carry a mirror in the peak of one's cap and a comb in one's sleeve, and to have a valet follow one about the streets with sponge and brush: for such care in dress and such nonchalance both touch upon excess, which is always offensive and contrary to that pure and charming simplicity which is pleasing to the human mind. . . .

33. . . . What is chiefly important for the Courtier, in order to speak and write well, is knowledge; for he who is ignorant and has nothing in his mind that merits being heard, can neither say it nor write it.

Next he must arrange in good order what he has to say or write; then express it well in words, which (if I do not err) ought to be precise, choice, rich, and rightly formed, but above all, in use even among the masses; because such words as these make the grandeur and pomp of speech, if the speaker has good sense and carefulness, and knows how to choose the words most expressive of his meaning, and to exalt them, to mould them like wax to his will, and to arrange them in such position and order that they shall at a glance show and make known their dignity and splendor, like pictures placed in good and proper light.

And this I say as well of writing as of speaking: in which however some things are required that are not needful in writing,—such as a good voice, not too thin and soft like a woman's, nor yet so stern and rough as to smack of the rustic's,—but sonorous, clear, sweet, and well sounding, with distinct enunciation, and with proper bearing and gestures; which I think consist in certain movements of the whole body, not affected or violent, but tempered by a calm face and with a play of the eyes that shall give an effect of grace, accord with the words, and as far as possible express also, together with the gestures, the speaker's intent and feeling.

But all these things would be vain and of small moment, if the thoughts expressed by the words were not beautiful, ingenious, acute, elegant, and grave,—according to the need.

34. . . . Nor would I have him speak always of grave matters, but of amusing things, of games, jests, and waggery, according to the occasion; and in no place let him show vanity or childish folly. And again when he is speaking on an obscure or difficult subject, I would have him carefully explain his meaning with precision of both word and thought, and make every ambiguity clear and plain with a certain touch of unpedantic care. Likewise, where there is occasion, let him know how to speak with dignity and force, to arouse those emotions that are part of our nature, and to kindle them or to move them according to the need. Sometimes, with that simple candor that makes it seem as if nature herself were speaking, let him know how to soften them, and as it were to intoxicate them with sweetness, and so easily withal that the listener shall think that with very little effort he too could reach that excellence, and when he tries, shall find himself very far behind. . . .

41. In this way we avoid and hide affectation, and you can now see how opposed and destructive it is to grace in every office as well of the body as the mind: whereof we have thus far spoken little, and yet we must not omit it, for since the mind is of far more worth than the body, it deserves to be more cultivated and adorned. And as to what ought to be done in the case of our Courtier, we will lay aside the precepts of the many sage philosophers who write of this matter and define the properties of the mind and discuss so subtly about their rank,—and keeping to our subject, we will in a few words declare it to be enough that he be (as we say) an honest and upright man; for in this are included prudence, goodness, strength and temperance of mind, and all the other qualities that are proper to a name so honored. And I esteem him alone to be a true moral philosopher, who wishes to be good; and in this regard he needs few other precepts than that wish. And therefore Socrates was right in saying that he thought his teachings bore good fruit indeed whenever they incited anyone to understand and teach virtue: for they who have reached the goal of desiring nothing more ardently than to be good, easily acquire knowledge of everything needful therefor; so we will discuss this no further.

44. I would have him more than passably accomplished in letters, at least in those studies that are called the humanities, and conversant not only with the Latin language but with the Greek, for the sake of the many different things that have been admirably written therein. Let him be well versed in the poets, and not less in the orators and historians, and also proficient in writing verse and prose, especially in this vulgar tongue of ours; for besides the enjoyment he will find in it, he will by this means never lack agreeable entertainment with ladies, who are usually fond of such things. And if other occupations or want of study prevent his reaching such

perfection as to render his writings worthy of great praise, let him be careful to suppress them so that others may not laugh at him, and let him show them only to a friend whom he can trust: because they will at least be of this service to him, that the exercise will enable him to judge the work of others. For it very rarely happens that a man who is not accustomed to write, however learned he may be, can ever quite appreciate the toil and industry of writers, or taste the sweetness and excellence of style, and those latent niceties that are often found in the ancients. . . .

47. You must know that I am not content with the Courtier unless he be also a musician and unless, besides understanding and being able to read notes, he can play upon divers instruments. For if we consider rightly, there is to be found no rest from toil or medicine for the troubled spirit more becoming and praiseworthy in time of leisure, than this; and especially in courts, where besides the relief from tedium that music affords us all, many things are done to please the ladies, whose tender and gentle spirit is easily penetrated by harmony and filled with sweetness. Thus it is no marvel that in both ancient and modern times they have always been inclined to favor musicians, and have found refreshing spiritual food in music. . . .

52. . . . It is fitting for our Courtier to have knowledge of painting also, as being honorable and useful and highly prized in those times when men were of far greater worth than now they are. And if he should never derive from it other use or pleasure than the help it affords in judging the merit of statues ancient and modern, of vases, buildings, medals, cameos, intaglios, and the like,—it also enables him to appreciate the beauty of living bodies, not only as to delicacy of face but as to symmetry of all the other parts, both in men and in every other creature. Thus you see how a knowledge of painting is a source of very great pleasure. And let those think of this, who so delight in contemplating a woman's beauty that they seem to be in paradise, and yet cannot paint; which if they could do, they would have much greater pleasure, because they would more perfectly appreciate that beauty which engenders such satisfaction in their hearts.

BOOK TWO

17. But not even all these qualities in our Courtier will suffice to win universal favor of lords, cavaliers, and ladies, unless he has also a gentle and amiable manner in daily talk. And I verily believe it to be difficult to give any rule for this, because of the infinite variety of things that arise in conversation, and because among all the men on earth no two are found who have minds quite alike. So whoever has to prepare himself for conversation with many, must needs be guided by his own judgment, and distinguishing the differences between one man and another, must daily change his style and method according to the character of the person with whom he has to converse. . . .

18. I think that the conversation which the Courtier ought most to try in every way to make acceptable, is that which he holds with his prince; and although this word "conversation" implies a certain equality that seems impossible between a lord and his inferior, yet we will call it so for the present. Therefore, besides daily showing everyone that he possesses the worth we have already described, I would have the Courtier strive, with all the thoughts and forces of his mind, to love and almost to adore the prince whom he serves, above every other thing, and mould his wishes, habits, and all his ways to his prince's liking. . . .

Moreover it is possible without flattery to obey and further the wishes of him we serve, for I am speaking of those wishes that are reasonable and right, or of those that in themselves are neither good nor evil, such as would be a liking for play or a devotion to one kind of exercise above another. And I would have the Courtier bend himself to this even if he be by nature alien to it, so that on seeing him his lord shall always feel that he will have something agreeable to say; which will come about if he has the good judgment to perceive what his prince likes, and the wit and prudence to bend himself thereto, and a deliberate purpose to like that which perhaps he by nature dislikes. And adopting these precautions he will never be out of humor or melancholy before his prince, nor so taciturn as many are who seem to bear a grudge against their patrons, which is a truly odious thing. He will not be given to evil speaking, especially against his own lords; which often happens, for in courts there seems to rage a fury of such sort that those who have been most favored by their lord and have been raised to eminence from the lowest estate, are always complaining and speaking ill of him; which is unseemly not only in such as these, but even in those who chance to have been ill used. . . .

20. . . . To have the favor of princes, there is no better way than to deserve it. And when we see another man who is pleasing to a prince for any reason, we must not think to reach the same height ourselves by imitating him, for all things are not proper to all men. Thus there will sometimes be found a man who by nature is so ready at jesting that whatever he may say carries laughter with it, and he seems to have been born solely for that; and if another man, who has a sober habit of mind (however excellently endowed) tries to do the like, it will fall so cold and flat as to disgust those who

hear him, and he will prove exactly like that ass who tried to copy the dogs by frolicking with their master. Hence every man must understand himself and his own powers, and govern himself accordingly, and consider what things he ought to imitate, and what things he ought not.

38. I do not care at present to go more into detail in speaking of things that are too well known, such as that our Courtier ought not avow himself a great eater or drinker, or given to excess in any evil habit, or vile and ungoverned in his life, with certain peasant ways that recall the hoe and plough a thousand miles away; because a man of this kind may not hope to become a good Courtier, but can be set to no more fitting business than feeding sheep. . . . Wherefore the Courtier ought to shun these odious ways, and to praise the fine achievements of other men with kindness and good will; and although he may feel that he is admirable and far superior to all, yet he ought to appear not to think so.

But since such complete perfection as this is very rarely and perhaps never found in human nature, a man who is conscious of being lacking in some particular, ought not to despond thereat or lose hope of reaching a high standard, even though he cannot attain that perfect and supreme excellence to which he aspires. For in every art there are many grades that are honorable besides the highest, and whoever aims at the highest will seldom fail to rise more than half-way.

BOOK FOUR

5. I think that the aim of the perfect Courtier, which has not been spoken of till now, is to win for himself, by means of the accomplishments ascribed to him, the favor and mind of the prince whom he serves, that he may be able to say, and always shall say, the truth about everything which is fitting for the prince to know, without fear or risk of giving offence thereby; and that when he sees his prince's mind inclined to do something wrong, he may be quick to oppose, and gently to make use of the favor acquired by his good accomplishments, so as to banish every bad intent and lead his prince into the path of virtue. . . .

49. . . . By reviewing what has thus far been said, we might conclude that a Courtier who has to allure his prince to virtue by his worth and authority, must almost of necessity be old (because knowledge very rarely comes before years, and especially in those things that are learned by experience),— I do not know how becoming it is for him (being advanced in age) to be in love. For love does not sit well upon old men, and those things which in young men are delights, courtesies, and elegances very pleasing to women, in old men are extrava-gances and ridiculous incongruities, and for him who practices them win hatred from women and derision from others. . . .

51. . . . I say, then, that according to the definition of the ancient sages love is naught but a certain desire to enjoy beauty; and as desire longs only for things that are perceived, perception must needs always precede desire, which by its nature wishes good things, but in itself is blind and does not perceive them. Therefore nature has so ordained that to every faculty of perception there is joined a certain faculty of appetite; and since in our soul there are three modes of perceiving, that is, by sense, by reason, and by intellect: from sense springs appetite, which we have in common with the brutes; from reason springs choice, which is peculiar to man; from the intellect, by which man is able to commune with the angels, springs will. Thus, just as sense perceives only things that are perceptible by the senses, appetite desires the same only; and just as intellect is directed solely to the contemplation of things intellectual, the will feeds only upon spiritual benefits. Being by nature rational and placed as a mean between these two extremes, man can at pleasure (by descending to sense or mounting to intellect) turn his desires now in the one direction and now in the other. In these two ways, therefore, it is possible to desire beauty, which universal name applies to all things (whether natural or artificial) that are framed in good proportion and due measure according to their nature.

52. But speaking of the beauty we have in mind, which is only that which is seen in the bodies and especially in the faces of men, and which excites this ardent desire that we call love,—we will say that it is an effluence of divine goodness, and that although it is diffused like the sun's light upon all created things, yet when it finds a face well proportioned and framed with a certain pleasant harmony of various colors embellished by lights and shadows and by an orderly distance and limit of outlines, it infuses itself therein and appears most beautiful, and adorns and illumines that object whereon it shines with grace and wonderful splendor, like a sunbeam falling on a beautiful vase of polished gold set with precious gems. Thus it agreeably attracts the eyes of men, and entering thereby, it impresses itself upon the soul, and stirs and delights her with a new sweetness throughout, and by kindling her it excites in her a desire for its own self.

Then, being seized with desire to enjoy this beauty as something good, if the soul allows herself to be guided by the judgment of sense, she runs into very grievous errors, and judges that the body wherein the beauty is seen is the chief cause thereof; and hence, in order to enjoy that beauty, she deems it necessary to join herself as closely to that body as she can; which is false: and accordingly, whoever thinks to enjoy the beauty by possessing the body deceives himself, and is moved, not by true perception through reasonable choice, but by false opinion through sensual appetite: wherefore the pleasure also that results therefrom is necessarily false and vicious. . . .

53. The cause, then, of this havoc in the minds of men is chiefly sense, which is very potent in youth, because the vigor of flesh and blood at that period gives to it as much strength as it takes away from reason, and hence easily leads the soul to follow appetite. For, finding herself plunged into an earthly prison and deprived of spiritual contemplation by being set the task of governing the body, the soul cannot of herself clearly comprehend the truth; wherefore, in order to have perception of things, she must needs go begging first notions from the senses, and so she believes them and bows before them and allows herself to be guided by them, especially when they have so much vigor that they almost force her; and as they are fallacious, they fill her with errors and false opinions.

Hence it nearly always happens that young men are wrapped in this love which is sensual and wholly rebellious to reason, and thus they become unworthy to enjoy the graces and benefits which love bestows upon its true subjects; nor do they feel any pleasures in love beyond those which the unreasoning animals feel, but anguish far more grievous.

This premise being admitted then,—and it is most true,—I say that the contrary happens to those who are of maturer age. For if such as these (when the soul is already less weighed down by bodily heaviness and when the natural heat begins to become tepid) are inflamed by beauty and turn thereto a desire guided by rational choice,—they are not deceived, and possess beauty perfectly. Therefore their possession of it always brings them good; because beauty is good, and hence true love of beauty is most good and holy, and always works for good in the mind of those who restrain the perversity of sense with the bridle of reason; which the old can do much more easily than the young.

57. . . . Beauty springs from God, and is like a circle of which goodness is the center. And hence, as there can be no circle without a center, there can be no beauty without goodness. Thus a wicked soul rarely inhabits a beautiful body, and for that reason outward beauty is a true sign of inward goodness. And this grace is impressed upon bodies, more or less, as an index of the soul, whereby she is known outwardly, as in the case of trees, in which the beauty of the blossom gives token of the excellence of the fruit. . . .

58. . . . The ugly are therefore for the most part

wicked too, and the beautiful are good: and we may say that beauty is the pleasant, gay, acceptable, and desirable face of good, and that ugliness is the dark, disagreeable, unpleasant, and sad face of evil. And if you will consider all things, you will find that those which are good and useful always have a charm of beauty also. . . .

62. Therefore, when the gracious aspect of some fair woman meets his view, accompanied with such sweet behavior and gentle manners that he, as an adept in love, feels that his spirit accords with hers: as soon as he finds that his eyes lay hold upon her image and carry it to his heart; and that his soul begins to contemplate her with pleasure and to feel that influence within which stirs and warms it little by little; and that those quick spirits which shine out through the eyes continually add fresh tinder to the fire;—he ought at this first stage to provide a speedy cure, and arouse his reason, and therewith arm the fortress of his heart, and so shut the way to sense and appetite that they cannot enter there by force or trickery. Thus, if the flame is extinguished, the danger is extinguished also; but if it survives or grows, then the Courtier, feeling himself caught, must resolve on shunning wholly every stain of vulgar love, and thus enter on the path of divine love, with reason for guide. And first he must consider that the body wherein this beauty shines is not the fountain whence it springs, but rather that beauty (being an incorporeal thing and, as we have said, a heavenly beam) loses much of its dignity when it finds itself joined to vile and corruptible matter; for the more perfect it is the less it partakes thereof, and is most perfect when wholly separate therefrom. And he must consider that just as one cannot hear with the palate or smell with the ears, so too can beauty in no wise be enjoyed, nor can the desire which it excites in our minds be satisfied, by means of touch, but by that sense of which this beauty is the very object, namely, the power of vision.

Therefore let him shun the blind judgment of sense, and with his eyes enjoy the splendor of his lady, her grace, her amorous sparkle, the laughs, the ways, and all the other pleasant ornaments of her beauty. Likewise with his hearing let him enjoy the sweetness of her voice, the concord of her words, the harmony of her music (if this beloved be a musician). Thus will he feed his soul on sweetest food by means of these two senses—which have little of the corporeal and are ministers of reason—without passing in his desire for the body to any appetite less than seemly.

Next let him obey, please, and honor his lady with all reverence, and hold her dearer than himself, and prefer her conveniences and pleasures to his own, and love in her not less the beauty of mind than that of body. Therefore let him take care not to leave her to fall into any kind of error, but by admonition and good advice let him always seek to lead her on to modesty, to temperance, to true chastity, and see to it that no thoughts find place in her except those that are pure and free from every stain of vice; and by thus sowing virtue in the garden of her fair mind, he will gather fruits of fairest behavior too, and will taste them with wonderful delight. And this will be the true engendering and manifesting of beauty in beauty, which by some is said to be the end of love.

In such fashion will our Courtier be most acceptable to his lady, and she will always show herself obedient, sweet, and affable to him, and as desirous of pleasing him as of being loved by him; and the wishes of both will be most virtuous and harmonious, and they themselves will thus be very happy.

67. But besides these blessings the lover will find another much greater still, if he will employ this love as a step to mount to one much higher; which he will succeed in doing if he continually considers within himself how narrow a restraint it is to be always occupied in contemplating the beauty of one body only; and therefore, in order to escape such close bonds as these, in his thought he will little by little add so many ornaments, that by heaping all beauties together he will form a universal concept, and will reduce the multitude of these beauties to the unity of that single beauty which is spread over human nature at large. In this way he will no longer contemplate the particular beauty of one woman, but that universal beauty which adorns all bodies; and thus, bewildered by this greater light, he will not heed the lesser, and glowing with a purer flame, he will esteem lightly that which at first he so greatly prized. . . .

68. Therefore when our Courtier shall have reached this goal, although he may be called a very happy lover by comparison with those who are plunged in the misery of sensual love, still I would have him not rest content, but press boldly on following along the lofty path after the guide who leads him to the goal of true felicity. And thus, instead of going outside himself in thought (as all must needs do who choose to contemplate bodily beauty only), let him have recourse to himself, in order to contemplate that beauty which is seen by the eyes of the mind, which begin to be sharp and clear when those of the body lose the flower of their loveliness. Then the soul,—freed from vice, purged by studies of true philosophy, versed in spiritual life, and practiced in matters of the intellect, devoted to the contemplation of her own substance,—as if awakened from deepest sleep, opens those eyes which all possess but few use, and sees in herself a ray of that light which is the true image of the angelic beauty

communicated to her, and of which she then communicates a faint shadow to the body. Grown blind to things earthly, the soul thus becomes very keen-sighted to things heavenly; and sometimes, when the motive forces of the body are absorbed by earnest contemplation or fettered by sleep, being unhampered by them, she is conscious of a certain far-off perfume of true angelic beauty, and ravished by the splendor of that light, she begins to kindle and pursues it so eagerly that she almost becomes phrensied with desire to unite herself to that beauty, thinking that she has found God's footstep, in the contemplation of which she seeks to rest as in her beatific end. And thus, glowing in this most happy flame, she rises to her noblest part, which is the intellect; and here, no longer darkened by the gloomy night of things earthly, she sees the divine beauty; but still she does not yet quite enjoy it perfectly, because she contemplates it in her own particular intellect only, which cannot be capable of the vast universal beauty.

Wherefore, not well content with this boon, love gives the soul a greater felicity; for just as from that particular beauty of one body it guides her to the universal beauty of all bodies, so in the highest stage of perfection it guides her from the particular to the universal intellect. Hence the soul, kindled by the most sacred fire of true divine love, flies to unite herself with the angelic nature, and not only quite forsaken sense, but has no longer need of reason's discourse; for, changed into an angel, she understands all things intelligible, and without veil or cloud views the wide sea of pure divine beauty, and receives it into herself, and enjoys that supreme felicity of which the senses are incapable.

Edmund Spenser

c. 1552–1599

It was the English essayist Charles Lamb (1775–1834) who first referred to Spenser as "the poet's poet," and the phrase has come to be the most celebrated cliché ever applied to this fine Renaissance figure. But cliché or not, Lamb's words possess an almost fatal accuracy in determining the limits of Spenser's achievement. There is now no question about Spenser's greatness; he ranks among the first dozen English poets. But his qualities have never made him popular save among the experts, however valiantly his supporters have striven to make him current gold among the people. He is far too complex, too academic, too involved and wordy, too remote, too unemotional, too courtly. Chaucer was even more of a courtier, with a courtier's basic point of view, but he had the common touch that raises him above Spenser as a human artist as well as endearing him to all who can read him. Yet it is difficult to name any other poet in English literature who so happily blended into a finished product of art most of the requirements of poetry: a prodigal poetic imagination; a most sensitively attuned musical perception; a sense of the vivid, the pictorial, the colorful; and an enormous capacity for sheer technical virtuosity. Therefore even if a casual reader of poetry may not essay *The Faerie Queene* or the *Amoretti*, or the *Epithalamion*, any true student of poetry assuredly will.

Beside such positive virtues and sterling achievements the facts of his life seem unimportant, and yet they must be considered as contributing much to his work. He was born about 1552, the son of a clothier in London; he attended the Merchant Taylors' School and then Pembroke Hall in Cambridge University, where he received the master's degree in 1576. At the university his college was very much under Calvinistic influence, an influence which is at once apparent to a reader of *The Faerie Queene*. After his graduation, Spenser retired for a few years to Lancashire, where he lived with relatives. From this period we hear about his love for and possible marriage with a Lancashire girl, known ever since merely as Rosalind, who appears in his first long poem, the collection of ingenious, thoughtful, and often profound pastoral eclogues entitled *The Shepheardes Calender* (1579). To her Spenser addressed his four Platonic *Hymnes in Honor of Love and Beautie*, written early though not published until 1596.

He returned to London in the late 1570's and entered the service of the powerful Earl of Leicester, whose nephew, Sir Philip Sidney—the traditional epitome of the Elizabethan gentleman—was not only a talented poet and critic of the time but also an old university friend of Spenser's. Through Sidney and another friend, the scholar and critic Gabriel Harvey (another college mate), Spenser came into contact with the literary group known as the Areopagus. While it is not clear that Spenser was ever an official member of this group, it is evident that he sympathized with many of the views of these men, who were essentially classicists in poetry, deprecating the crudeness of English prosody. Yet Spenser, for all his classicism, never turned against his native English tongue, whose ancient forms particularly attracted him. Wisely or not, he adopted a pseudo-archaic vocabulary and spelling and grammar, particularly evident in *The Shepheardes Calender* and *The Faerie Queene*. Such a style may have contributed antique charm but assuredly militated against his popularity and readability in quarters which might otherwise have supported him better.

Spenser's association with Leicester brought him into opposition to the faction of Lord Burleigh, the great power behind the throne in Queen Elizabeth's reign; and when Leicester went into political eclipse, Spenser's opportunities for the political preferment he craved were very much lessened, although he continued to seek them through flattery of the Queen in his works. In 1580 he went to Ireland as secretary to Lord Grey de Wilton,

Lord Deputy of Ireland, a Puritan administrator of considerable severity whom Spenser immortalized as Artegal (or Justice) in the fifth book of *The Faerie Queene*. Indeed, Spenser seems to have sympathized with his superior to the extent that he profited by the prevailing English tendency to exploit Ireland in feudal manner, for he became the owner of an estate at Kilcolman in Munster and lived the life of an English landholder in constant conflict with his Irish neighbors. He returned to England in 1589–1590 to gain what advantages he might achieve from the publication of the first three books of *The Faerie Queene*, which, whatever their true poetic excellence, were nevertheless intended to assist Spenser in a political way. They brought fame and a pension but no preferment at court; and so, after writing a lament on the poetry of the times, *The Tears of the Muses*, and a satire on the court, *Prosopopoia*, or *Mother Hubbard's Tale*, he returned to Ireland and celebrated his return in another court satire, *Colin Clout's Come Home Again*. All three of the works just named belong to the years between 1590 and 1593.

After his marriage to Elizabeth Boyle (1594) he published two of his finest works, the sonnet-sequence *Amoretti* and the noble marriage-ode, *Epithalamion*, and went back to London once more to present the second three books of *The Faerie Queene* (1596). But again no preferment was forthcoming, and so in the following year Spenser and his family returned to Ireland. Here in 1598–1599 came a serious rebellion of the Irish, and although Spenser and his family were able to flee, their home was attacked and burned. Spenser himself sickened shortly thereafter and died on January 16, 1599. He was buried in Westminster Abbey not far from the tomb of Geoffrey Chaucer, his most illustrious immediate predecessor in English literature and the English poet who had exerted the greatest influence upon him.

It was Spenser's keenest disappointment that he never had the recognition at court that was bestowed on others much less worthy than he. As we look back at him in the rich setting of the Renaissance, this disappointment is perhaps comprehensible, but it is difficult for us to sympathize with it. Spenser's true calling was, after all, that of poet; and, however incomplete his achievement in terms of the grand plans he had in mind, none today can deny his solid worth and his absolute sincerity as poet supreme. Courtiers come and go, "packs and sects of great ones, that ebb and flow by the moon," but *The Faerie Queene*, the *Amoretti*, and the *Epithalamion* are still fixed in the firmament.

The Faerie Queene

Spenser published the first three books of *The Faerie Queene* in 1590; the second three appeared in 1596. We know, however, that he was working on his poem in the late 1570's. Under the date of January 23, 1589, he wrote an epistle to Sir Walter Raleigh, the famous Elizabethan courtier and man of letters, setting forth in it the plan and purpose of *The Faerie Queene*. The text of this letter is subjoined:

"Sir, knowing how doubtfully all allegories may be construed, and this booke of mine which I have entituled the *Faery Queene*, being a continued allegory, or darke conceit, I have thought good, as well for avoyding of gealous opinions and misconstructions, as also for your better light in reading thereof (being so by you commanded) to discover unto you the general intention and meaning, which in the whole course thereof I have fashioned, without expressing of any particular purposes, or by accidents therein occasioned. The generall end therefore of all the booke is to fashion a gentleman or noble person in vertuous and gentle discipline: which for that I conceived shoulde be most plausible and pleasing, being coloured with an historicall fiction, the which the most part of men delight to read, rather for variety of manner than for profite of the ensample, I chose the historye of King Arthure, as most fitte for the excellency of his person, being made famous by many men's former workes, and also furthest from the daunger of envy, and suspition of present time. In which I have followed all the antique Poets historicall: first Homere, who in the Persons of Agamemnon and Ulysses hath ensampled a good governour and a vertuous man, the one in his Ilias, the other in his Odysseis; then Virgil, whose like intention was to doe in the person of Aeneas; after him Ariosto comprised them both in his Orlando: and lately Tasso dissevered them againe, and formed both parts in two persons, namely that part which they in Philosophy call Ethice, or vertues of a private man, coloured in his Rinaldo; the other named Politice in his Godfredo. By ensample of which excellente poets, I labour to pourtraict in Arthure, before he was king, the image of a brave knight, perfected in the twelve private morall vertues, as Aristotle hath devised; the which is the purpose of these first twelve bookes: which if I finde to be well accepted, I may be perhaps encoraged to frame the other part of polliticke vertues in his person, after that hee came to be king.

"To some, I know, this methode will seeme displesaunt, which had rather have good discipline delivered plainly in way of precepts, or sermoned at large, as they use, then thus clowdily enwrapped in Allegoricall devises. But such, me seeme, should be satisfide with the use of these dayes, seeing all things accounted by their showes, and nothing esteemed of, that is not delightfull and pleasing to commune sence. For this cause is Xenophon preferred before Plato, for that the one, in the exquisite depth of his judgement, formed a commune welth, such as it should be; but the other in the person of Cyrus, and the Persians, fashioned a governement, such as might best be. so much more profitable and gratious is doctrine by ensample, then by rule. So haue I laboured to doe in the person of Arthure: whome I conceive, after his long education by Timon, to whom he was by Merlin delivered to be brought up, so soone as he was borne of the Lady Igrayne, to have seene in a dream or vision the Faery Queene, with whose excellent beauty ravished, he awaking resolved to seeke her out;

and so being by Merlin armed, and by Timon thoroughly instructed, he went to seeke her forth in Faerye land. In that Faery Queene I meane glory in my generall intention, but in my particular I conceive the most excellent and glorious person of our soveraine the Queene, and her kingdome in Faery land. And yet, in some places els, I doe otherwise shadow her. For considering she beareth two persons, the one of a most royall Queene or Empresse, the other of a most vertuous and beautifull Lady, this latter part in some places I doe expresse in Belphoebe, fashioning her name according to your owne excellent conceipt of Cynthia (Phoebe and Cynthia being both names of Diana). So in the person of Prince Arthure I sette forth magnificence in particular, which vertue for that (according to Aristotle and the rest) it is the perfection of all the rest, and conteineth in it them all, therefore in the whole course I mention the deedes of Arthure applyable to that vertue, which I write of in that booke. But of the xii. other vertues, I make xii. other knights the patrones, for the more variety of the history: of which these three bookes contayn three. The first of the knight of the Redcrosse, in whome I expresse holynes: The seconde of Sir Guyon, in whome I sette forth temperaunce: The third of Britomartis, a lady knight, in whom I picture chastity. But, because the beginning of the whole worke seemeth abrupte, and as depending upon other antecedents, it needs that ye know the occasion of these three knights' severall adventures. For the methode of a poet historical is not such, as of an historiographer. For an historiographer discourseth of affayres orderly as they were donne, accounting as well the times as the actions; but a poet thrusteth into the middest, even where it most concerneth him, and there recoursing to the thinges forepaste, and divining of thinges to come, maketh a pleasing analysis of all.

"The beginning therefore of my history, if it were to be told by an historiographer, should be the twelfth booke, which is the last; where I devise that the Faery Queene kept her annuall feaste xii. dayes; upon which xii. severall dayes, the occasions of the xii. several adventures hapned, which, being undertaken by xii. severall knights, are in these xii. books severally handled and discoursed. The first was this. In the beginning of the feast, there presented himselfe a tall clownishe younge man, who, falling before the Queene of Faeries, desired a boone (as the manner then was) which during that feast she might not refuse: which was that hee might have the atchievement of any adventure, which during that feaste should happen: that being graunted, he rested him on the floore, unfitte through his rusticity for a better place. Soone after entred a faire ladye in mourning weedes, riding on a white asse, with a dwarfe behind her leading a warlike steed, that bore the armes of a knight, and his spear in the dwarfes hand. Shee, falling before the Queene of Faeries, complayned that her father and mother, an ancient king and queene, had bene by an huge dragon many years shut up in a brasen castle, who thence suffred them not to yssew; and therefore besought the Faery Queene to assygne her some one of her knights to take on him that exployt. Presently that clownish person, upstarting, desired that adventure: whereat the Queene much wondering, and the lady much gainesaying, yet he earnestly importuned his desire. In the end the lady told him, that unlesse that armour which she brought, would serve him (that is, the armour of a Christian man specified by Saint Paul, vi. Ephes.) that he could not succeed in that enterprise: which being forthwith put upon him, with dewe furnitures thereunto, he seemed the goodliest man in al that company, and was well liked of the lady. And eftesoones taking on him knighthood, and mounting on that straunge courser, he went forth with her on that adventure: where beginneth the first booke, viz.

A gentle knight was pricking on the playne, etc.

"The second day there came in a palmer, bearing an infant with bloody hands, whose parents he complained to have bene slayn by an enchaunteresse called Acrasia; and therefore craved of the Faery Queene, to appoint him some knight to performe that adventure; which being assigned to Sir Guyon, he presently went forth with that same palmer: which is the beginning of the second booke, and the whole subject thereof. The third day there came in a groome, who complained before the Faery Queene, that a vile enchaunter, called Busirane, had in hand a most faire lady, called Amoretta, whom he kept in most grievous torment, because she would not yield him the pleasure of her body. Whereupon Sir Scudamour, the lover of that lady, presently tooke on him that adventure. But being unable to performe it by reason of the hard enchauntments, after long sorrow, in the end met with Britomartis, who succoured him, and reskewed his love.

"But by occasion hereof many other adventures are intermedled; but rather as accidents then intendments: as the love of Britomart, the overthrow of Marinell, the misery of Florimell, the vertuousness of Belphoebe, the lasciviousnes of Hellenora, and many the like.

"Thus much, Sir, I have briefly overronne, to direct your understanding to the welhead of the history, that from thence gathering the whole intention of the conceit ye may, as in a handfull, gripe al the discourse, which otherwise may happily seeme tedious and confused. So, humbly craving the continuance of your honorable favour towards me, and th' eternall establishment of your happines, I humbly take leave."

So much for the plans. Of the twelve projected books of *The Faerie Queene*, Spenser completed only six. Parts of a seventh survive. Book One, of the Red Cross Knight, treats of Holiness; Book Two, of Guyon, represents Temperance; Book Three, of Britomart, Chastity; Book Four, of Cambel and Telamond, Friendship; Book Five, of Artegal, Justice; and Book Six, of Calidore, Courtesy. In all these books, a threefold allegory is discernible, on moral, religious, and political levels; as Spenser is writing in the Elizabethan age, the religious and political implications coincide. But the general reader is probably wise if he adheres to the moral allegory and accepts the other allegories as incidental interpretations only. He will then catch sight of the forest in spite of the trees and will be in a position to admire the warm, colorful nar-

rative, the remarkable ability of the lines to evoke sensuous appeal, and the rich *décor* with which the whole epic is furnished lavishly. Here the Renaissance love of adornment is given its best expression.

BOOK I

CANTO ONE

The patron of true Holinesse
Foule Errour doth defeate:
Hypocrisie, him to entrappe,
Doth to his home entreate.

1

A GENTLE knight was pricking on the plaine,
Ycladd in mightie armes and silver shielde,
Wherein old dints of deepe woundes did remaine,
The cruell markes of many 'a bloudy fielde;
Yet armes till that time did he never wield: 5
His angry steede did chide his foming bitt,
As much disdayning to the curbe to yield:
Full jolly knight he seemd, and faire did sitt,
As one for knightly giusts and fierce encounters fitt.

2

But on his brest a bloodie crosse he bore,   10
The deare remembrance of his dying Lord,
For whose sweete sake that glorious badge he wore,
And dead as living ever him ador'd:
Upon his shield the like was also scor'd,
For soveraine hope, which in his helpe he had: 15
Right faithfull true he was in deede and word,
But of his cheere did seeme too solemne sad;
Yet nothing did he dread, but ever was ydrad.

3

Upon a great adventure he was bond,
That greatest Gloriana to him gave,   20
That greatest glorious queene of Faery Lond,
To winne him worshippe, and her grace to have,
Which of all earthly thinges he most did crave;
And ever as he rode his hart did earne
To prove his puissance in battell brave   25
Upon his foe, and his new force to learne;
Upon his foe, a dragon horrible and stearne.

4

A lovely ladie rode him faire beside,
Upon a lowly asse more white than snow,
Yet she much whiter, but the same did hide   30

8. **jolly,** fair and bold; cf. the French *joli.* 17. **cheere,** countenance, expression. 18. **ydrad,** feared, dreaded. "He feared nothing but was always himself feared." 20–21. **Gloriana . . . Faery Lond;** see Spenser's epistle to Sir Walter Raleigh, p. ɪɪ:397. 27. **dragon,** here the personification of Sin, mentioned in the Apocalypse. 28. **lovely ladie,** Una, the personification of Truth. 29. **asse,** symbolic of humility and, like the "bloodie crosse" (l. 10) belonging to the Red Cross Knight, of Christ's atonement.

Under a vele, that wimpled was full low,
And over all a blacke stole shee did throw:
As one that inly mourned, so was she sad,
And heavie sate upon her palfrey slow:
Seemed in heart some hidden care she had;   35
And by her in a line a milkewhite lambe she lad.

5

So pure and innocent, as that same lambe,
She was in life and every vertuous lore,
And by descent from royall lynage came
Of ancient kinges and queenes, that had of yore   40
Their scepters stretcht from east to westerne shore,
And all the world in their subjection held,
Till that infernall feend with foule uprore
Forwasted all their land, and them expeld:
Whom to avenge, she had this knight from far com-
     peld.   45

6

Behind her farre away a dwarfe did lag,
That lasie seemd, in being ever last,
Or wearied with bearing of her bag
Of needments at his backe. Thus as they past,
The day with cloudes was suddeine overcast,   50
And angry Jove an hideous storme of raine
Did poure into his lemans lap so fast,
That everie wight to shrowd it did constrain,
And this faire couple eke to shroud themselves were
     fain.

7

Enforst to seeke some covert nigh at hand,   55
A shadie grove not farr away they spide,
That promist ayde the tempest to withstand:
Whose loftie trees, yclad with sommers pride,
Did spred so broad, that heavens light did hide,
Not perceable with power of any starr: 60
And all within were pathes and alleies wide,
With footing worne, and leading inward farr:
Faire harbour that them seemes, so in they entred
     ar.

8

And foorth they passe, with pleasure forward led,
Joying to heare the birdes sweete harmony,   65
Which, therein shrouded from the tempest dred,
Seemd in their song to scorne the cruell sky.
Much can they praise the trees so straight and hy,
The sayling pine, the cedar proud and tall,

The vine-propp elme, the poplar never dry,   70
The builder oake, sole king of forrests all,
The aspine good for staves, the cypress funerall,

9

The laurell, meed of mightie conquerours
And poets sage, the firre that weepeth still,
The willow worne of forlorne paramours,   75
The eugh obedient to the benders will,
The birch for shaftes, the sallow for the mill,
The mirrhe sweete bleeding in the bitter wound,
The warlike beech, the ash for nothing ill,
The fruitfull olive, and the platane round,   80
The carver holme, the maple seeldom inward sound.

10

Led with delight, they thus beguile the way,
Untill the blustring storme is overblowne;
When, weening to returne whence they did stray,
They cannot finde that path, which first was showne,
But wander too and fro in waies unknowne,   86
Furthest from end then, when they neerest weene,
That makes them doubt, their wits be not their
     owne:
So many pathes, so many turnings seene,
That which of them to take, in diverse doubt they
     been.   90

11

At last resolving forward still to fare,
Till that some end they finde, or in or out,
That path they take, that beaten seemd most bare,
And like to lead the labyrinth about;
Which when by tract they hunted had throughout,
At length it brought them to a hollowe cave,   96
Amid the thickest woods. The champion stout
Eftsoones dismounted from his courser brave,
And to the dwarfe a while his needlesse spere he
     gave.

12

'Be well aware,' quoth then that ladie milde,   100
'Least suddaine mischiefe ye too rash provoke:
The danger hid, the place unknowne and wilde,
Breeds dreadfull doubts: oft fire is without smoke,
And perill without show: therefore your stroke,
Sir knight, with-hold, till further tryall made.'   105
'Ah, ladie,' sayd he, 'shame were to revoke
The forward footing for an hidden shade:
Vertue gives her selfe light, through darknesse for
     to wade.'

13

'Yea, but,' quoth she, 'the perill of this place
I better wot then you; though nowe too late   110

36. **in a line,** by a cord. 46. **dwarfe,** personifying Prudence. 52. **lemans lap,** lover's lap; that is, the Earth. Jove (l. 51) personifies the heavens in general. 68–81. **praise the trees.** The following catalogue of trees is something of a convention among medieval and classical authors; probably the most famous such passage preceding Spenser is that in Chaucer's *Parliament of Fowls,* ll. 171–182. 69. **sayling;** that is, used in sailing.

76. **eugh,** yew tree. 81. **holme,** a kind of oak, the wood of which was used for knife handles.

To wish you backe returne with foule disgrace,
Yet wisedome warnes, whilest foot is in the gate,
To stay the steppe, ere forced to retrate.
This is the wandring wood, this Errours den,
A monster vile, whom God and man does hate: 115
Therefore I read beware.' 'Fly, fly!' quoth then
The fearefull dwarfe: 'this is no place for living
    men.'

14

But full of fire and greedy hardiment,
The youthfull knight could not for ought be staide,
But forth unto the darksom hole he went,   120
And looked in: his glistring armor made
A little glooming light, much like a shade,
By which he saw the ugly monster plaine,
Halfe like a serpent horribly displaide,
But th' other halfe did womans shape retaine,   125
Most lothsom, filthie, foule, and full of vile disdaine.

15

And as she lay upon the durtie ground,
Her huge long taile her den all overspred,
Yet was in knots and many boughtes upwound,
Pointed with mortall sting. Of her there bred   130
A thousand yong ones, which she dayly fed,
Sucking upon her poisnous dugs, eachone
Of sundrie shapes, yet all ill favored:
Soone as that uncouth light upon them shone,
Into her mouth they crept, and suddain all were
    gone.   135

16

Their dam upstart, out of her den effraide,
And rushed forth, hurling her hideous taile
About her cursed head, whose folds displaid
Were stretcht now forth at length without entraile.
She lookt about, and seeing one in mayle,   140
Armed to point, sought backe to turne againe;
For light she hated as the deadly bale,
Ay wont in desert darknes to remaine,
Where plain none might her see, nor she see any
    plaine.

17

Which when the valiant Elfe perceived, he lept   145
As lion fierce upon the flying pray,
And with his trenchand blade her boldly kept
From turning backe, and forced her to stay:
Therewith enrag'd she loudly gan to bray,
And turning fierce, her speckled taile advaunst,   150
Threatning her angrie sting, him to dismay:

Who, nought aghast, his mightie hand enhaunst:
The stroke down from her head unto her shoulder
    glaunst.

18

Much daunted with that dint, her sence was dazd,
Yet kindling rage her selfe she gathered round,   155
And all attonce her beastly bodie raizd
With doubled forces high above the ground:
Tho, wrapping up her wrethed sterne arownd,
Lept fierce upon his shield, and her huge traine
All suddenly about his body wound,   160
That hand or foot to stirr he strove in vaine:
God helpe the man so wrapt in Errours endless
    traine.

19

His lady, sad to see his sore constraint,
Cride out, 'Now, now, sir knight, shew what ye bee:
Add faith unto your force, and be not faint: 165
Strangle her, els she sure will strangle thee.'
That when he heard, in great perplexitie,
His gall did grate for griefe and high disdaine;
And knitting all his force, got one hand free,
Wherewith he grypt her gorge with so great paine,
That soone to loose her wicked bands did her con-
    straine.   171

20

Therewith she spewd out of her filthie maw
A floud of poyson horrible and blacke,
Full of great lumps of flesh and gobbets raw,
Which stunck so vildly, that it forst him slacke   175
His grasping hold, and from her turne him backe:
Her vomit full of books and papers was,
With loathly frogs and toades, which eyes did lacke,
And creeping sought way in the weedy gras:
Her filthie parbreake all the place defiled has.   180

21

As when old father Nilus gins to swell
With timely pride above the Aegyptian vale,
His fattie waves doe fertile slime outwell,
And overflow each plaine and lowly dale:
But when his later spring gins to avale,   185
Huge heapes of mudd he leaves, wherin there breed
Ten thousand kindes of creatures, partly male
And partly femall, of his fruitful seed;
Such ugly monstrous shapes elswher may no man
    reed.

---

116. read, counsel, advise. 129. boughtes, coils. 136. upstart, started up. 139. entraile, coiling. 141. to point, correctly and completely. 145. Elfe. The Red Cross Knight was of elfin birth.

158. Tho, then. 177. books and papers, the various pamphlets of the time attacking the Church of England, as well as the administration of Elizabeth herself. 180. parbreake, vomit. 185. spring . . . avale, flood begins to subside. The River Nile is here portrayed as a river-god. 189. reed, know about, perceive.

22

The same so sore annoyed has the knight,   190
That, welnigh choked with the deadly stinke,
His forces faile, ne can no lenger fight.
Whose corage when the feend perceivd to shrinke,
She poured forth out of her hellish sinke
Her fruitfull cursed spawne of serpents small,   195
Deformed monsters, fowle, and blacke as inke,
Which swarming all about his legs did crall,
And him encombred sore, but could not hurt at all.

23

As gentle shepheard in sweete eventide,
When ruddy Phebus gins to welke in west,   200
High on an hill, his flocke to vewen wide,
Markes which doe byte their hasty supper best;
A cloud of cumbrous gnattes doe him molest,
All striving to infixe their feeble stinges,
That from their noyance he no where can rest,   205
But with his clownish hands their tender wings
He brusheth oft, and oft doth mar their murmurings.

24

Thus ill bestedd, and fearefull more of shame
Then of the certeine perill he stood in,
Halfe furious unto his foe he came,   210
Resolvd in minde all suddenly to win,
Or soone to lose, before he once would lin;
And stroke at her with more than manly force,
That from her body, full of filthie sin,
He raft her hatefull heade without remorse: 215
A streame of cole black blood forth gushed from her
      corse.

25

Her scattred brood, soone as their parent deare
They saw so rudely falling to the ground,
Groning full deadly, all with troublous feare,
Gathred themselves about her body round,   220
Weening their wonted entrance to have found
At her wide mouth: but being there withstood,
They flocked all about her bleeding wound,
And sucked up their dying mothers bloud,
Making her death their life, and eke her hurt their
      good.   225

26

That detestable sight him much amazde,
To see th'unkindly impes, of heaven accurst,
Devoure their dam; on whom while so he gazd,
Having all satisfide their bloudy thurst,
Their bellies swolne he saw with fulnesse burst,   230

And bowels gushing forth: well worthy end
Of such as drunke her life, the which them nurst!
Now needeth him no lenger labour spend;
His foes have slaine themselves, with whom he
      should contend.

27

His ladie, seeing all that chaunst, from farre,   235
Approcht in hast to greet his victorie,
And saide, 'Faire knight, borne under happie starre,
Who see your vanquisht foes before you lye,
Well worthie be you of that armory,
Wherein ye have great glory wonne this day,   240
And proov'd your strength on a strong enimie,
Your first adventure: many such I pray,
And henceforth ever wish that like succeed it may.'

28

Then mounted he upon his steede againe,
And with the lady backward sought to wend;   245
That path he kept which beaten was most plaine,
Ne ever would to any by way bend,
But still did follow one unto the end,
The which at last out of the wood them brought.
So forward on his way (with God to frend)   250
He passed forth, and new adventure sought:
Long way he traveiled, before he heard of ought.

29

At length they chaunst to meet upon the way
An aged sire, in long blacke weedes yclad,
His feete all bare, his beard all hoarie gray,   255
And by his belt his booke he hanging had;
Sober he seemde, and very sagely sad,
And to the ground his eyes were lowly bent,
Simple in shew, and voide of malice bad,
And all the way he prayed as he went,   260
And often knockt his brest, as one that did repent.

30

He faire the knight saluted, louting low,
Who faire him quited, as that courteous was;
And after asked him, if he did know
Of straunge adventures, which abroad did pas.   265
'Ah! my dear sonne,' quoth he, 'how should, alas!
Silly old man, that lives in hidden cell,
Bidding his beades all day for his trespas,
Tydings of warre and worldly trouble tell?   269
With holy father sits not with such thinges to mell.

31

'But if of daunger, which hereby doth dwell,
And homebredd evil ye desire to heare,

199 ff. **As gentle shepheard,** etc. Note the classical, or Homeric, simile in this stanza. The same thing was observable in Stanza 21 (ll. 181–189). 200. **welke,** fade, decline. 212. **lin,** stop, desist. 227. **th'unkindly impes,** the unnatural young.

239. **armory,** armor bearing the Christian symbol. 256. **his booke,** his prayer-book or Bible. 263. **quited,** returned; that is, the greeting. 270. **With holy . . . mell,** "It is not fitting for a holy father to concern himself with such things."

Of a straunge man I can you tidings tell,
That wasteth all this countrie farre and neare.'
'Of such,' saide he, 'I chiefly doe inquere,   275
And shall you well rewarde to shew the place,
In which that wicked wight his dayes doth weare:
For to all knighthood it is foule disgrace,
That such a cursed creature lives so long a space.'

32

'Far hence,' quoth he, 'in wastfull wildernesse,   280
His dwelling is, by which no living wight
May ever passe, but through great distresse.'
'Now,' saide the ladie, 'draweth toward night,
And well I wote, that of your later fight
Ye all forwearied be: for what so strong,   285
But, wanting rest, will also want of might?
The Sunne, that measures heaven all day long,
At night doth baite his steedes the ocean waves
        emong.

33

'Then with the Sunne take, sir, your timely rest,
And with new day new worke at once begin: 290
Untroubled night, they say, gives counsell best.'
'Right well, sir knight, ye have advised bin,'
Quoth then that aged man; 'the way to win
Is wisely to advise: now day is spent;
Therefore with me ye may take up your in   295
For this same night.' The knight was well content:
So with that godly father to his home they went.

34

A little lowly hermitage it was,
Downe in a dale, hard by a forests side,
Far from resort of people, that did pas   300
In traveill to and froe: a litle wyde
There was an holy chappell edifyde,
Wherein the hermite dewly wont to say
His holy thinges each morne and even-tyde:
Thereby a christall streame did gently play,   305
Which from a sacred fountaine welled forth alway.

35

Arrived there, the little house they fill,
Ne looke for entertainment, where none was:
Rest is their feast, and all thinges at their will;
The noblest mind the best contentment has.   310
With faire discourse the evening so they pas:
For that olde man of plesing wordes had store,
And well could file his tongue as smooth as glas;
He told of saintes and popes, and evermore
He strowd an Ave-Mary after and before.   315

36

The drouping night thus creepeth on them fast,
And the sad humor loading their eye liddes,
As messenger of Morpheus, on them cast
Sweet slombring deaw, the which to sleep them
        biddes:
Unto their lodgings then his guestes he riddes: 320
Where when all drownd in deadly sleepe he findes,
He to his studie goes, and there amiddes
His magick bookes and artes of sundrie kindes,
He seekes out mighty charmes, to trouble sleepy
        mindes.

37

Then choosing out few words most horrible,   325
(Let none them read) thereof did verses frame;
With which and other spelles like terrible,
He bad awake blacke Plutoes griesly dame,
And cursed heven, and spake reprochful shame
Of highest God, the Lord of life and light: 330
A bold bad man, that dar'd to call by name
Great Gorgon, prince of darknes and dead night,
At which Cocytus quakes, and Styx is put to flight.

38

And forth he cald out of deepe darknes dredd
Legions of sprights, the which, like litle flyes   335
Fluttring about his ever damned hedd,
Awaite whereto their service he applyes,
To aide his friendes, or fray his enimies:
Of those he chose out two, the falsest twoo,
And fittest for to forge true-seeming lyes;   340
The one of them he gave a message too,
The other by him selfe staide, other worke to doo.

39

He, making speedy way through spersed ayre,
And through the world of waters wide and deepe,
To Morpheus house doth hastily repaire.   345
Amid the bowels of the earth full steepe,
And low, where dawning day doth never peepe,
His dwelling is; there Tethys his wet bed
Doth ever wash, and Cynthia still doth steepe
In silver deaw his ever-drouping hed,   350
Whiles sad Night over him her mantle black doth
        spred.

40

Whose double gates he findeth locked fast,
The one fair fram'd of burnisht yvory,

317. **sad humor,** heavy moisture. A "dry" brain was not supposed to sleep well; note l. 376.   328. **Plutoes griesly dame,** Proserpine, goddess of Death and the Underworld.   332. **Gorgon,** Demogorgon, a demon of great supernatural powers.   343. **He,** the messenger of Archimago. **spersed,** scattered, rarefied.   348. **Tethys.** In classical mythology Tethys was actually the wife of Oceanus, but here she represents the god himself, and is spoken of as male.

295. **in,** lodging; cf. the modern *inn.*   314-315. **saintes . . . Ave-Mary.** Inasmuch as this "holy man" proves to be Archimago, the symbol of hypocrisy, we may interpret these lines as attacks on the Catholic Church.

II : 402

The other all with silver overcast;
And wakeful dogges before them farre doe lye,   355
Watching to banish Care their enimy,
Who oft is wont to trouble gentle Sleepe.
By them the sprite doth passe in quietly,
And unto Morpheus comes, whom drowned deepe
In drowsie fit he findes: of nothing he takes keepe.

41

And more, to lulle him in his slumber soft,   361
A trickling streame from high rock tumbling downe,
And ever drizling raine upon the loft,
Mixt with a murmuring winde, much like the sowne
Of swarming bees, did cast him in a swowne: 365
No other noyse, nor peoples troublous cryes,
As still are wont t'annoy the walled towne,
Might there be heard: but careless Quiet lyes,
Wrapt in eternall silence farre from enimyes.

42

The messenger approaching to him spake,   370
But his waste wordes retourned to him in vaine:
So sound he slept, that nought mought him awake.
Then rudely he him thrust, and pusht with paine,
Whereat he gan to stretch: but he againe
Shooke him so hard, that forced him to speake.   375
As one then in a dreame, whose dryer braine
Is tost with troubled sights and fancies weake,
He mumbled soft, but would not all his silence
   breake.

43

The sprite then gan more boldly him to wake,
And threatned unto him the dreaded name   380
Of Hecate: whereat he gan to quake,
And, lifting up his lompish head, with blame
Halfe angrie asked him, for what he came.
'Hether,' quoth he, 'me Archimago sent,
He that the stubborne sprites can wisely tame;   385
He bids thee to him send for his intent
A fit false dreame, that can delude the sleepers sent.'

44

The god obayde, and calling forth straight way
A diverse dreame out of his prison darke,
Delivered it to him, and downe did lay   390
His heavie head, devoide of careful carke;
Whose sences all were straight benumbd and starke,
He, backe returning by the yvorie dore,
Remounted up as light as chearefull larke,
And on his little winges the dreame he bore   395
In hast unto his lord, where he him left afore.

45

Who all this while, with charmes and hidden artes,
Had made a lady of that other spright,
And fram'd of liquid ayre her tender partes,
So lively and so like in all mens sight,   400
That weaker sence it could have ravisht quight:
The maker selfe, for all his wondrous witt,
Was nigh beguiled with so goodly sight:
Her all in white he clad, and over it
Cast a black stole, most like to seem for Una fit.   405

46

Now when that ydle dreame was to him brought,
Unto that Elfin knight he bad him fly,
Where he slept soundly, void of evil thought,
And with false shewes abuse his fantasy,
In sort as he him schooled privily: 410
And that new creature, borne without her dew,
Full of the makers guyle, with usage sly
He taught to imitate that lady trew,
Whose semblance she did carrie under feigned hew.

47

Thus well instructed, to their worke they haste,   415
And comming where the knight in slumber lay,
The one upon his hardie head him plaste,
And made him dreame of loves and lustfull play,
That nigh his manly hart did melt away,
Bathed in wanton blis and wicked joy.   420
Then seemed him his lady by him lay,
And to him playnd, how that false winged boy
Her chaste hart had subdewd to learne Dame Pleas-
   ures toy.

48

And she her selfe, of beautie soveraigne queene,
Fayre Venus, seemde unto his bed to bring   425
Her, whom he, waking, evermore did weene
To bee the chastest flowre that aye did spring
On earthly braunch, the daughter of a king,
Now a loose leman to vile service bound:
And eke the Graces seemed all to sing   430
Hymen iö Hymen, dauncing all around,
Whylst freshest Flora her with yvie girlond crownd.

49

In this great passion of unwonted lust,
Or wonted feare of doing ought amis,
He started up, as seeming to mistrust   435
Some secret ill, or hidden foe of his:
Lo! there before his face his ladie is,
Under black stole hyding her bayted hooke,

St. George and the dragon, by the German artist Albrecht Dürer. This is one of a series of woodcuts by Dürer on the same theme.

And as halfe blushing offred him to kis,
With gentle blandishment and lovely looke,   440
Most like that virgin true, which for her knight him
   took.

50

All cleane dismayd to see so uncouth sight,
And halfe enraged at her shameless guise,
He thought have slaine her in his fierce despight;
But hastie heat tempring with sufferance wise,   445
He stayde his hand, and gan himselfe advise
To prove his sense, and tempt her faigned truth.
Wringing her hands in wemens pitteous wise,
Tho can she weepe, to stirre up gentle ruth,   449
Both for her noble blood, and for her tender youth.

51

And sayd, 'Ah sir, my liege lord and my love,
Shall I accuse the hidden cruell fate,
And mightie causes wrought in heaven above,

449. **Tho . . . weepe,** then did she weep. 454. **blind god,** Cupid; see note to l. 422.

Or the blind god, that doth me thus amate,
For hoped love to winne me certaine hate?   455
Yet thus perforce he bids me do, or die.
Die is my dew: yet rew my wretched state
You, whom my hard avenging destinie
Hath made judge of my life or death indifferently.

52

'Your owne deare sake forst me at first to leave   460
My fathers kingdom'—There she stopt with teares;
Her swollen hart her speech seemd to bereave;
And then againe begonne: 'My weaker yeares,
Captiv'd to fortune and frayle worldly feares,
Fly to your fayth for succour and sure ayde: 465
Let me not die in languor and long teares.'
'Why, dame,' quoth he, 'what hath ye thus dismayd?
What frayes ye, that were wont to comfort me affrayd?'

53

'Love of your selfe,' she saide, 'and deare constraint,
Lets me not sleepe, but waste the wearie night   470
In secret anguish and unpittied plaint,
Whiles you in carelesse sleepe are drowned quight.'
Her doubtfull words made that redoubted knight
Suspect her truth: yet since no untruth he knew,
Her fawning love with foule disdainefull spight   475
He would not shend, but said, 'Deare dame, I rew,
That for my sake unknowne such griefe unto you
   grew.

54

'Assure your selfe, it fell not all to ground;
For all so deare as life is to my hart,
I deeme your love, and hold me to you bound;   480
Ne let vaine feares procure your needlesse smart,
Where cause is none, but to your rest depart.'
Not all content, yet seemd she to appease
Her mournefull plaintes, beguiled of her art,
And fed with words, that could not chose but please;
So slyding softly forth, she turnd as to her ease.   486

55

Long after lay he musing at her mood,
Much griev'd to thinke that gentle dame so light,
For whose defence he was to shed his blood.
At last dull wearines of former fight   490
Having yrockt a sleepe his irkesome spright,
That troublous dreame gan freshly tosse his braine
With bowres, and beds, and ladies deare delight:
But when he saw his labour all was vaine,
With that misformed spright he backe returnd
   againe.   495

494. **he,** the dream spirit, who returned to Archimago with the spirit impersonating Una.

CANTO TWO

The guilefull great enchaunter parts
The Redcrosse Knight from Truth:
Into whose stead faire Falsehood steps,
And werkes him woeful ruth.

1

By this the northerne wagoner had set
His sevenfold teme behind the stedfast starre,
That was in ocean waves yet never wet,
But firme is fixt, and sendeth light from farre
To al that in the wide deepe wandring arre: 5
And chearefull Chaunticlere with his note shrill
Had warned once, that Phoebus fiery carre
In hast was climbing up the easterne hill,
Full envious that night so long his roome did fill:

2

When those accursed messengers of hell,   10
That feigning dreame, and that faire-forged spright,
Came to their wicked maister, and gan tel
Their bootelesse paines, and ill succeeding night:
Who, all in rage to see his skilfull might
Deluded so, gan threaten hellish paine   15
And sad Proserpines wrath, them to affright.
But when he saw his threatning was but vaine,
He cast about, and searcht his baleful bokes againe.

3

Eftsoones he tooke that miscreated faire,
And that false other spright, on whom he spred   20
A seeming body of the subtile aire,
Like a young squire, in loves and lustyhed
His wanton daies that ever loosely led,
Without regard of armes and dreaded fight:
Those twoo he tooke, and in a secrete bed,   25
Covered with darkenes and misdeeming night,
Them both together laid, to joy in vaine delight.

4

Forthwith he runnes with feigned faithfull hast
Unto his guest, who, after troublous sights
And dreames, gan now to take more sound repast;   30
Whom suddenly he wakes with fearful frights,
As one aghast with feends or damned sprights,
And to him cals: 'Rise, rise, unhappy swaine,

That here wex old in sleepe, whiles wicked wights
Have knit themselves in Venus shameful chaine;   35
Come, see, where your false lady doth her honor staine.'

5

All in amaze he suddenly up start
With sword in hand, and with the old man went;
Who soone him brought into a secret part,
Where that false couple were full closely ment   40
In wanton lust and leud embracement:
Which when he saw, he burnt with gealous fire,
The eie of reason was with rage yblent,
And would have slaine them in his furious ire,
But hardly was restreined of that aged sire.   45

6

Retourning to his bed in torment great,
And bitter anguish of his guilty sight,
He could not rest, but did his stout heart eat,
And wast his inward gall with deepe despight,
Yrkesome of life, and too long lingring night.   50
At last faire Hesperus in highest skie
Had spent his lampe, and brought forth dawning light;
Then up he rose, and clad him hastily;
The dwarfe him brought his steed: so both away do fly.

7

Now when the rosy fingred Morning faire,   55
Weary of aged Tithones saffron bed,
Had spred her purple robe through deawy aire,
And the high hils Titan discovered,
The royall virgin shooke of drousyhed,
And rising forth out of her baser bowre,   60
Lookt for her knight, who far away was fled,
And for her dwarfe, that wont to wait each howre:
Then gan she wail and weepe, to see that woeful stowre.

8

And after him she rode with so much speede,
As her slowe beast could make; but all in vaine: 65
For him so far had borne his light-foot steede,
Pricked with wrath and fiery fierce disdaine,
That him to follow was but fruitlesse paine;
Yet she her weary limbes would never rest,
But every hil and dale, each wood and plaine,   70
Did search, sore grieved in her gentle brest,
He so ungently left her, whome she loved best.

9

But subtill Archimago, when his guests
He saw divided into double parts,
And Una wandring in woods and forrests,   75
Th' end of his drift, he praisd his divelish arts,
That had such might over true meaning harts:
Yet rests not so, but other meanes doth make,
How he may worke unto her further smarte:
For her he hated as the hissing snake,   80
And in her many troubles did most pleasure take.

10

He then devisde himselfe how to disguise;
For by his mighty science he could take
As many formes and shapes in seeming wise,
As ever Proteus to himselfe could make: 85
Sometime a fowle, sometime a fish in lake,
Now like a foxe, now like a dragon fell,
That of himselfe he ofte for feare would quake,
And oft would flie away. O who can tell
The hidden powre of herbes, and might of magick
      spel?   90

11

But now seemde best, the person to put on
Of that good knight, his late beguiled guest:
In mighty armes he was yclad anon,
And silver shield; upon his coward brest
A bloody crosse, and on his craven crest   95
A bounch of heares discoloured diversly:
Full jolly knight he seemde, and wel addrest,
And when he sate uppon his courser free,
Saint George himselfe ye would have deemed him
      to be.

12

But he, the knight whose semblaunt he did beare,
The true Saint George, was wandred far away,   101
Still flying from his thoughts and gealous feare;
Will was his guide, and griefe led him astray.
At last him chaunst to meete upon the way
A faithlesse Sarrazin, all armde to point,   105
In whose great shield was writ with letters gay
Sans foy; full large of limbe and every joint
He was, and cared not for God or man a point.

13

Hee had a faire companion of his way,
A goodly lady clad in scarlot red,   110

99. **Saint George**, the patron saint of England, with whom the Red Cross Knight is later to be identified. 100. **semblaunt**, semblance or resemblance. 105. **Sarrazin.** The Saracen was originally a follower of Islam, but in the later romances the term is generalized to apply to any heathen warrior. 107. *Sans foy*, without faith. The three brothers Sansfoy, Sansjoy, and Sansloy together typify heathen vices—they are faithless, joyless, and lawless. 110. **goodly lady**, Duessa (Falsehood), who hypocritically assumes the name Fidessa (Faith).

Purfled with gold and pearle of rich assay;
And like a Persian mitre on her hed
Shee wore, with crowns and owches garnished,
The which her lavish lovers to her gave:
Her wanton palfrey all was overspred   115
With tinsell trappings, woven like a wave,
Whose bridle rung with golden bels and bosses
      brave.

14

With faire disport and courting dalliaunce
She intertainde her lover all the way:
But when she saw the knight his speare advaunce,
Shee soone left of her mirth and wanton play,   121
And bad her knight addresse him to the fray:
His foe was nigh at hand. He prickte with pride
And hope to winne his ladies hearte that day,
Forth spurred fast: adowne his coursers side   125
The red blood trickling staind the way, as he did
      ride.

15

The Knight of the Redcrosse, when he him spide
Spurring so hote with rage dispiteous,
Gan fairely couch his speare, and towards ride:
Soone meete they both, both fell and furious,   130
That, daunted with theyr forces hideous,
Their steeds doe stagger, and amazed stand,
And eke themselves, too rudely rigorous,
Astonied with the stroke of their owne hand,
Doe backe rebutte, and ech to other yealdeth land.

16

As when two rams, stird with ambitious pride,   136
Fight for the rule of the rich fleeced flocke,
Their horned fronts so fierce on either side
Doe meete, that, with the terror of the shocke,
Astonied, both stand sencelesse as a blocke,   140
Forgetfull of the hanging victory:
So stood these twaine, unmoved as a rocke,
Both staring fierce, and holding idely
The broken reliques of their former cruelty.

17

The Sarrazin, sore daunted with the buffe,   145
Snatcheth his sword, and fiercely to him flies;
Who well it wards, and quyteth cuff with cuff:
Each others equall puissaunce envies,
And through their iron sides with cruell spies
Does seeke to perce: repining courage yields   150

112. **mitre**, used here in the general sense of a conical-shaped headdress. The epithet *Persian* has reference to its richness of material and brilliance of color. 113. **owches**, jewels, gems. 118. **dalliaunce.** This word is almost never used in the medieval romances without the suggestion of love-play. 123. **prickte**, spurred on, excited. 135. **rebutte**, recoil. 147. **quyteth**, returns. 148. **envies**, imparts hate. 149. **spies**, metaphorically used for "eyes" or perhaps "fingers."

No foote to foe. The flashing fier flies,
As from a forge, out of their burning shields,
And streams of purple bloud new dies the verdant
    fields.

18

'Curse on that Crosse,' quoth then the Sarrazin,
'That keepes thy body from the bitter fitt!   155
Dead long ygoe, I wote, thou haddest bin,
Had not that charme from thee forwarned itt:
But yet I warne thee now assured sitt,
And hide thy head.' Therewith upon his crest
With rigor so outrageous he smitt,   160
That a large share it hewd out of the rest,
And glauncing downe his shield, from blame him
    fairely blest.

19

Who thereat wondrous wroth, the sleeping spark
Of native vertue gan eftsoones revive,
And at his haughty helmet making mark,   165
So hugely stroke, that it the steele did rive,
And cleft his head. He, tumbling downe alive,
With bloudy mouth his mother earth did kis,
Greeting his grave: his grudging ghost did strive
With the fraile flesh; at last it flitted is,   170
Whether the soules doe fly of men that live amis.

20

The lady, when she saw her champion fall,
Like the old ruines of a broken towre,
Staid not to waile his woefull funerall,
But from him fled away with all her powre;   175
Who after her as hastily gan scowre,
Bidding the dwarfe with him to bring away
The Sarrazins shield, signe of the conqueroure.
Her soone he overtooke, and bad to stay,
For present cause was none of dread her to dis-
    may.   180

21

Shee, turning backe with ruefull countenaunce,
Cride, 'Mercy, mercy, sir, vouchsafe to showe
On silly dame, subject to hard mischaunce,
And to your mighty wil!' Her humblesse low,
In so ritch weedes and seeming glorious show,   185
Did much enmove his stout heroicke heart,
And said, 'Deare dame, your suddein overthrow
Much rueth me; but now put feare apart,
And tel, both who ye be, and who that tooke your
    part.'

22

Melting in teares, then gan shee thus lament: 190
'The wreched woman, whom unhappy howre

Hath now made thrall to your commandement,
Before that angry heavens list to lowre,
And Fortune false betraide me to your powre,
Was, (O what now availeth that I was?)   195
Borne the sole daughter of an emperour,
He that the wide west under his rule has,
And high hath set his throne where Tiberis doth pas.

23

'He, in the first flowre of my freshest age,
Betrothed me unto the onely haire   200
Of a most mighty king, most rich and sage;
Was never prince so faithfull and so faire,
Was never prince so meek and debonaire;
But ere my hoped day of spousall shone,
My dearest lord fell from high honors staire,   205
Into the hands of hys accursed fone,
And cruelly was slaine, that shall I ever mone.

24

'His blessed body, spoild of lively breath,
Was afterward, I know not how, convaid
And fro me hid: of whose most innocent death   210
When tidings came to mee, unhappy maid,
O how great sorrow my sad soule assaid!
Then forth I went his woefull corse to find,
And many yeares throughout the world I straid,
A virgin widow, whose deepe wounded mind   215
With love, long time did languish as the striken hind.

25

'At last it chauncéd this proud Sarazin
To meete me wandring; who perforce me led
With him away, but yet could never win
The fort, that ladies hold in soveraigne dread.   220
There lies he now with foule dishonor dead,
Who, whiles he liv'de, was called proud Sansfoy;
The eldest of three brethren, all three bred
Of one bad sire, whose youngest is Sansjoy,
And twixt them both was born the bloudy bold
    Sansloy.   225

26

'In this sad plight, friendlesse, unfortunate,
Now miserable I Fidessa dwell,
Craving of you, in pitty of my state,
To doe none ill, if please ye not doe well.'
He in great passion al this while did dwell,   230
More busying his quicke eies, her face to view,
Then his dull cares, to heare what shee did tell;
And said, 'Faire lady, hart of flint would rew
The undeserved woes and sorrowes which ye shew.

---

155. **bitter fitt,** death-blow. 159. **hide,** shield. 162. **blame . . .
blest,** kept him well from harm.

198. **Tiberis,** the River Tiber in Rome; the reference, however, is to
the papal dominions or Catholicism. 200. **haire,** heir. 206. **fone,**
foes, enemies. 212. **assaid,** assailed, attacked.

27

'Henceforth in safe assuraunce may ye rest, 235
Having both found a new friend you to aid,
And lost an old foe, that did you molest:
Better new friend than an old foe is said.'
With chaunge of chear the seeming simple maid
Let fal her eien, as shamefast, to the earth, 240
And yeelding soft, in that she nought gainsaid,
So forth they rode, he feining seemely merth,
And shee coy lookes: so dainty, they say, maketh
 derth.

28

Long time they thus together traveiled,
Til, weary of their way, they came at last 245
Where grew two goodly trees, that faire did spred
Their armes abroad, with gray mosse overcast,
And their greene leaves, trembling with every blast,
Made a calme shadowe far in compasse round:
The fearfull shepheard, often there aghast, 250
Under them never sat, ne wont there sound
His mery oaten pipe, but shund th'unlucky ground.

29

But this good knight, soone as he them can spie,
For the coole shade him thither hastly got:
For golden Phoebus, now ymounted hie, 255
From fiery wheeles of his faire chariot
Hurled his beame so scorching cruell hot,
That living creature mote it not abide;
And his new lady it endured not.
There they alight, in hope themselves to hide 260
From the fierce heat, and rest their weary limbs a
 tide.

30

Faire seemely plesaunce each to other makes,
With goodly purposes, there as they sit:
And in his falsed fancy he her takes
To be the fairest wight that lived yit; 265
Which to expresse, he bends his gentle wit,
And thinking of those braunches greene to frame
A girlond for her dainty forehead fit,
He pluckt a bough; out of whose rifte there came
Smal drops of gory bloud, that trickled down the
 same. 270

31

Therewith a piteous yelling voice was heard,
Crying, 'O spare with guilty hands to teare
My tender sides in this rough rynd embard;
But fly, ah! fly far hence away, for feare

239. **chear,** expression, countenance. 243. **dainty . . . derth,** apparently a proverb meaning "Coyness or delicacy brings poverty (unsatisfied desire)." 270. **gory,** in this instance probably "clotted." 273. **embard,** confined, enclosed.

Least to you hap that happened to me heare, 275
And to this wretched lady, my deare love;
O too deare love, love bought with death too deare!'
Astond he stood, and up his heare did hove,
And with that suddein horror could no member
 move.

32

At last, whenas the dreadfull passion 280
Was overpast, and manhood well awake,
Yet musing at the straunge occasion,
And doubting much his sence, he thus bespake:
'What voice of damned ghost from Limbo lake,
Or guilefull spright wandring in empty aire, 285
Both which fraile men doe oftentimes mistake,
Sends to my doubtful eares these speaches rare,
And ruefull plaints, me bidding guiltlesse blood to
 spare?'

33

Then groning deep: 'Nor damned ghost,' quoth he,
'Nor guileful sprite to thee these words doth speake,
But once a man, Fradubio, now a tree; 291
Wretched man, wretched tree! whose nature weake
A cruell witch, her cursed wil to wreake,
Hath thus transformd, and plast in open plaines,
Where Boreas doth blow full bitter bleake, 295
And scorching sunne does dry my secret vaines:
For though a tree I seme, yet cold and heat me
 paines.'

34

'Say on, Fradubio, then, or man or tree,'
Quoth then the knight; 'by whose mischievous arts
Art thou misshapen thus, as now I see? 300
He oft finds med'cine who his griefe imparts;
But double griefs afflict concealing harts,
As raging flames who striveth to suppresse.'
'The author then,' said he, 'of all my smarts,
Is one Duessa, a false sorceresse, 305
That many errant knights hath broght to wretched-
 nesse.

35

'In prime of youthly yeares, when corage hott
The fire of love and joy of chevalree
First kindled in my brest, it was my lott
To love this gentle lady, whome ye see 310
Now not a lady, but a seeming tree;
With whome as once I rode accompanyde,
Me chaunced of a knight encountred bee,
That had a like faire lady by his syde;
Lyke a faire lady, but did fowle Duessa hyde. 315

291. **Fradubio,** "Brother Doubt," the symbolizing of uncertainty and skepticism.

36

'Whose forged beauty he did take in hand
All other dames to have exceded farre;
I in defence of mine did likewise stand,
Mine, that did then shine as the morning starre:
So both to batteil fierce arraunged arre;   320
In which his harder fortune was to fall
Under my speare: such is the dye of warre:
His lady, left as a prise martiall,
Did yield her comely person, to be at my call.

37

'So doubly lov'd of ladies unlike faire,   325
Th'one seeming such, the other such indeede,
One day in doubt I cast for to compare,
Whether in beauties glorie did exceede;
A rosy girlond was the victors meede.
Both seemde to win, and both seemde won to bee,
So hard the discord was to be agreede: 331
Fraelissa was as faire as faire mote bee,
And ever false Duessa seemde as faire as shee.

38

'The wicked witch, now seeing all this while
The doubtfull ballaunce equally to sway,   335
What not by right, she cast to win by guile;
And by her hellish science raisd streight way
A foggy mist, that overcast the day,
And a dull blast, that, breathing on her face,
Dimmed her former beauties shining ray,   340
And with foule ugly forme did her disgrace:
Then was she fayre alone, when none was faire in
    place.

39

'Then cride she out, "Fye, fye! deformed wight,
Whose borrowed beautie now appeareth plaine
To have before bewitched all mens sight;   345
O leave her soone, or let her soone be slaine."
Her loathly visage viewing with disdaine,
Eftsoones I thought her such as she me told,
And would have kild her; but with faigned paine
The false witch did my wrathfull hand with-hold:
So left her, where she now is turnd to mould.   351

40

'Thensforth I tooke Duessa for my dame,
And in the witch unweeting joyd long time,
Ne ever wist but that she was the same:
Till on a day (that day is everie prime,   355
When witches wont do penance for their crime)

316. take in hand, maintain, insist. 328. Whether, which one (of
two)? 332. Fraelissa. The name is probably suggested by the adjective *frail*. 339. her, Fraelissa's. 355. everie prime, always
springtime. 356. witches . . . crime. It was an old belief that
spring enforced penance on all witches for crimes committed during
the preceding autumn and winter seasons.

I chaunst to see her in her proper hew,
Bathing her selfe in origane and thyme:
A filthy foule old woman I did vew,
That ever to have toucht her I did deadly rew.   360

41

'Her neather partes misshapen, monstruous,
Were hidd in water, that I could not see,
But they did seeme more foule and hideous,
Then womans shape man would beleeve to bee.
Thensforth from her most beastly companie   365
I gan refraine, in minde to slipp away,
Soone as appeard safe opportunitie:
For danger great, if not assurd decay,
I saw before mine eyes, if I were knowne to stray.

42

'The divelish hag, by chaunges of my cheare,   370
Perceiv'd my thought; and drownd in sleepie night,
With wicked herbes and oyntments did besmeare
My body all, through charmes and magicke might,
That all my senses were bereaved quight:
Then brought she me into this desert waste,   375
And by my wretched lovers side me pight,
Where now enclosd in wooden wals full faste,
Banisht from living wights, our wearie daies we
    waste.'

43

'But how long time,' said then the Elfin knight,
'Are you in this misformed hous to dwell?'   380
'We may not chaunge,' quoth he, 'this evill plight
Till we be bathed in a living well;
That is the terme prescribed by the spell.'
'O how,' sayd he, 'mote I that well out find,
That may restore you to your wonted well?'   385
'Time and suffised fates to former kynd
Shall us restore; none else from hence may us un-
    bynd.'

44

The false Duessa, now Fidessa hight,
Heard how in vaine Fradubio did lament,
And knew well all was true. But the good knight   390
Full of sad feare and ghastly dreriment,
When all this speech the living tree had spent,
The bleeding bough did thrust into the ground,
That from the blood he might be innocent.   394
And with fresh clay did close the wooden wound:
Then turning to his lady, dead with feare her fownd.

45

Her seeming dead he fownd with feigned feare,
As all unweeting of that well she knew,
And paynd himselfe with busie care to reare
Her out of careless swowne. Her eylids blew,   400
And dimmed sight, with pale and deadly hew,

At last she up gan lift: with trembling cheare
Her up he tooke, too simple and too trew,
And oft her kist. At length, all passed feare,
He set her on her steede, and forward forth did
    beare.   405

[The action in Cantos III–VI is concerned with the
separate adventures of Una and the Red Cross Knight,
who meet again, however, in Canto VII. And in Canto
XI Una comes to her native land, in the company of the
Red Cross Knight; but they find their way barred by a
monstrous dragon, which the Red Cross Knight kills after
a terrific two-day struggle in which the Red Cross Knight
is refreshed by fruit from the Tree of Life. We come then
to Canto XII.]

CANTO TWELVE

Fayre Una to the Redcrosse Knight
Betrouthed is with joy:
Though false Duessa, it to barre,
Her false sleightes doe imploy.

1

Behold! I see the haven nigh at hand,
To which I meane my wearie course to bend;
Vere the maine shete, and beare up with the land,
The which afore is fayrly to be kend,
And seemeth safe from storms that may offend: 5
There this fayre virgin, wearie of her way,
Must landed bee, now at her journeyes end;
There eke my feeble barke a while may stay,
Till mery wynd and weather call her thence away.

2

Scarsely had Phoebus in the glooming east 10
Yett harnessed his fyrie-footed teeme,
Ne reard above the earth his flaming creast,
When the last deadly smoke aloft did steeme,
That signe of last outbreathed life did seeme
Unto the watchman on the castle wall; 15
Who thereby dead that balefull beast did deeme,
And to his lord and lady lowd gan call,
To tell, how he had seene the dragons fatall fall.

3

Uprose with hasty joy, and feeble speed,
That aged syre, the lord of all that land, 20
And looked forth, to weet if trew indeed
Those tydinges were, as he did understand:
Which whenas trew by tryall he out fond,
He badd to open wyde his brasen gate,
Which long time had beene shut, and out of hond 25
Proclaymed joy and peace through all his state;
For dead now was their foe, which them forrayed
    late.

4

Then gan triumphant trompets sownd on hye,
That sent to heven the ecchoed report
Of their new joy, and happie victory 30
Gainst him, that had them long opprest with tort,
And fast imprisoned in sieged fort.
Then all the people, as in solemne feast,
To him assembled with one full consort,
Rejoycing at the fall of that great beast, 35
From whose eternall bondage now they were re-
    least.

5

Forth came the auncient lord and aged queene,
Arayd in antique robes downe to the grownd,
And sad habiliments right well beseene:
A noble crew about them waited rownd 40
Of sage and sober peres, all gravely gownd;
Whom far before did march a goodly band
Of tall young men, all hable armes to sownd;
But now they laurell braunches bore in hand,
Glad signe of victory and peace in all their land. 45

6

Unto that doughtie conquerour they came,
And him before themselves prostrating low,
Their lord and patrone loud did him proclame,
And at his feet their lawrell boughes did throw.
Soone after them, all dauncing on a row, 50
The comely virgins came, with girlands dight,
As fresh as flowres in medow greene doe grow,
When morning deaw upon their leaves doth light:
And in their handes sweet timbrels all upheld on
    hight.

7

And them before, the fry of children yong 55
Their wanton sportes and childish mirth did play,
And to the maydens sownding tymbrels song,
In well attuned notes, a joyous lay,
And made delightfull musick all the way,
Untill they came where that faire virgin stood. 60
As fayre Diana, in fresh sommers day,
Beholdes her nymphs enraung'd in shady wood,
Some wrestle, some do run, some bathe in christall
    flood;

8

So she beheld those maydens meriment 64
With chearefull vew; who, when to her they came,
Themselves to ground with gracious humblesse bent,
And her ador'd by honorable name,
Lifting to heven her everlasting fame:
Then on her head they sett a girlond greene,

43. **hable,** able, enabled. **sownd,** make trial of.

And crowned her twixt earnest and twixt game; 70
Who, in her self-resemblance well beseene,
Did seeme, such as she was, a goodly maiden
    queene.

9

And after all the raskall many ran,
Heaped together in rude rablement,
To see the face of that victorious man; 75
Whom all admired, as from heaven sent,
And gazd upon with gaping wonderment.
But when they came where that dead dragon lay,
Stretcht on the ground in monstrous large extent,
The sight with ydle feare did them dismay, 80
Ne durst approach him nigh, to touch, or once assay.

10

Some feard and fledd; some feard, and well it faynd;
One, that would wiser seeme then all the rest,
Warnd him not touch, for yet perhaps remaynd
Some lingering life within his hollow brest, 85
Or in his wombe might lurke some hidden nest
Of many dragonettes, his fruitfull seede;
Another saide, that in his eyes did rest
Yet sparckling fyre, and badd thereof take heed;
Another said, he saw him move his eyes indeed. 90

11

One mother, whenas her foolehardy chyld
Did come to neare, and with his talants play,
Halfe dead through feare, her litle babe revyld,
And to her gossibs gan in counsell say:
'How can I tell, but that his talants may 95
Yet scratch my sonne, or rend his tender hand?'
So diversly them selves in vaine they fray;
Whiles some more bold, to measure him nigh stand,
To prove how many acres he did spred of land.

12

Thus flocked all the folke him rownd about, 100
The whiles that hoarie king, with all his traine,
Being arrived where that champion stout
After his foes defeasaunce did remaine,
Him goodly greetes, and fayre does entertayne
With princely gifts of yvory and gold, 105
And thousand thankes him yeeldes for all his paine;
Then when his daughter deare he does behold,
Her dearely doth imbrace, and kisseth manifold.

13

And after to his pallace he them bringes,
With shaumes, and trompets, and with clarions
    sweet; 110

And all the way the joyous people singes,
And with their garments strowes the paved street;
Whence mounting up, they fynd purveyaunce meet
Of all that royall princes court became,
And all the floore was underneath their feet 115
Bespredd with costly scarlott of great name,
On which they lowly sitt, and fitting purpose frame.

14

What needes me tell their feast and goodly guize,
In which was nothing riotous nor vaine?
What needes of dainty dishes to devize, 120
Of comely services, or courtly trayne?
My narrow leaves cannot in them contayne
The large discourse of roiall princes state.
Yet was their manner then but bare and playne:
For th'antique world excesse and pryde did hate;
Such proud luxurious pompe is swollen up but
    late. 126

15

Then, when with meates and drinkes of every kinde
Their fervent appetites they quenched had,
That auncient lord gan fit occasion finde,
Of straunge adventures, and of perils sad, 130
Which in his travell him befallen had,
For to demaund of his renowned guest:
Who then with utt'rance grave, and count'nance
    sad,
From poynt to poynt, as is before exprest,
Discourst his voyage long, according his request. 135

16

Great pleasure, mixt with pittifull regard,
That godly king and queene did passionate,
Whyles they his pitifull adventures heard,
That oft they did lament his lucklesse state,
And often blame the too importune fate, 140
That heapd on him so many wrathfull wreakes;
For never gentle knight, as he of late,
So tossed was in Fortunes cruell freakes;
And all the while salt teares bedeawed the hearers
    cheaks.

17

Then sayd the royall pere in sober wise: 145
'Dear sonne, great beene the evils which ye bore
From first to last in your late enterprise,
That I note whether praise or pitty more:
For never living man, I weene, so sore
In sea of deadly daungers was distrest; 150
But since now safe ye seised have the shore,
And well arrived are, (High God be blest!)
Let us devize of ease and everlasting rest.'

---

73. **raskall**, rude populace. 86. **wombe**, belly. 92. **talants**, talons,
claws. 94. **gossibs**, close friends or acquaintances. 110. **shaumes**,
shawms, an ancient reed instrument resembling the modern oboe.

120. **devize**, describe. 137. **passionate**, experience with intense feeling. 141. **wreakes**, adventures leading to expeditions in foreign
lands. 148. **note**, do not know. 153. **devize of**, make plans for.

18

'Ah! dearest lord,' said then that doughty knight,
'Of ease or rest I may not yet devize;   155
For by the faith which I to armes have plight,
I bownden am streight after this emprize,
As that your daughter can ye well advize,
Backe to retourne to that great Faery Queene,
And her to serve six yeares in warlike wize,   160
Gainst that proud Paynim King that works her
    teene:
Therefore I ought crave pardon, till I there have
    beene.'

19

'Unhappy falls that hard necessity,'
Quoth he, 'the troubler of my happy peace,
And vowed foe of my felicity;   165
Ne I against the same can justly preace:
But since that band ye cannot now release,
Nor doen undoe, (for vowes may not be vayne)
Soone as the terme of those six yeares shall cease,
Ye then shall hether backe retourne agayne,   170
The marriage to accomplish vowd betwixt you
    twayn.

20

'Which, for my part, I covet to performe,
In sort as through the world I did proclame,
That who so kild that monster most deforme,
And him in hardy battayle overcame,   175
Should have mine onely daughter to his dame,
And of my kingdome heyre apparaunt bee:
Therefore since now to thee perteynes the same,
By dew desert of noble chevalree,
Both daughter and eke kingdome, lo! I yield to
    thee.'   180

21

Then forth he called that his daughter fayre,
The fairest Un', his onely daughter deare,
His onely daughter and his only hayre;
Who forth proceeding with sad sober cheare,
As bright as doth the morning starre appeare   185
Out of the east, with flaming lockes bedight,
To tell that dawning day is drawing neare,
And to the world does bring long wished light:
So faire and fresh that lady shewd her selfe in sight:

22

So faire and fresh, as freshest flowre in May;   190
For she had layd her mournfull stole aside,
And widow-like sad wimple throwne away,
Wherewith her heavenly beautie she did hide,
Whiles on her wearie journey she did ride;
And on her now a garment she did weare   195
All lilie white, withoutten spot or pride,

That seemd like silke and silver woven neare,
But neither silke nor silver therein did appeare.

23

The blazing brightnesse of her beauties beame,
And glorious light of her sunshyny face,   200
To tell, were as to strive against the streame:
My ragged rimes are all too rude and bace,
Her heavenly lineaments for to enchace.
Ne wonder; for her own deare loved knight,
All were she daily with himselfe in place,   205
Did wonder much at her celestiall sight:
Oft had he seene her faire, but never so faire dight.

24

So fairely dight, when she in presence came,
She to her syre made humble reverence,
And bowed low, that he right well became,   210
And added grace unto her excellence:
Who with great wisedome and grave eloquence
Thus gan to say—But eare he thus had sayd,
With flying speede, and seeming great pretence,
Came running in, much like a man dismayd,   215
A messenger with letters, which his message sayd.

25

All in the open hall amazed stood
At suddeinnesse of that unwary sight,
And wondred at his breathlesse hasty mood.
But he for nought would stay his passage right,   220
Till fast before the king he did alight;
Where falling flat, great humblesse he did make,
And kist the ground whereon his foot was pight;
Then he to his handes that writt he did betake,
Which he disclosing, read thus, as the paper spake:

26

'To thee, most mighty king of Eden fayre,   226
Her greeting sends in these sad lines addrest
The wofull daughter and forsaken heyre
Of that great Emperour of all the West;
And bids thee be advized for the best,   230
Ere thou thy daughter linck in holy band
Of wedlocke to that new unknowen guest:
For he already plighted his right hand
Unto another love, and to another land.

27

'To me, sad mayd, or rather widow sad,   235
He was affyaunced long time before,
And sacred pledges he both gave, and had,
False erraunt knight, infamous, and forswore!
Witnesse the burning altars, which he swore,
And guilty heavens of his bold perjury,   240
Which though he hath polluted oft of yore,

218. unwary, unexpected and uncomprehended.

Yet I to them for judgement just doe fly,
And them conjure t'avenge this shamefull inhury.

28

'Therefore since mine he is, or free or bond,
Or false or trew, or living or else dead,   245
Withhold, O soverayne prince, your hasty hond
From knitting league with him, I you aread;
Ne weene my right with strength adowne to tread,
Through weakenesse of my widowhed or woe:
For Truth is strong, her rightfull cause to plead, 250
And shall finde friends, if need requireth soe.
So bids thee well to fare, thy neither friend nor foe,
                                          FIDESSA.'

29

When he these bitter byting wordes had red,
The tydings straunge did him abashed make,
That still he sate long time astonished,   255
As in great muse, ne word to creature spake.
At last his solemne silence thus he brake,
With doubtfull eyes fast fixed on his guest:
'Redoubted knight, that for myne only sake
Thy life and honor late adventurest,   260
Let nought be hid from me, that ought to be ex-
    prest.

30

'What meane these bloody vowes and idle threats,
Throwne out from womanish impatient mynd?
What hevens? what altars? what enraged heates,
Here heaped up with termes of love unkynd,   265
My conscience cleare with guilty bands would bynd?
High God be witnesse, that I guiltlesse ame!
But if your selfe, sir knight, ye faulty fynd,
Or wrapped be in loves of former dame,
With cryme doe not it cover, but disclose the
    same.'   270

31

To whom the Redcrosse Knight this answere sent:
'My lord, my king, be nought hereat dismayed,
Till well ye wote by grave intendiment,
What woman, and wherefore, doth me upbrayd
With breach of love and loialty betrayd.   275
It was in my mishaps, as hitherward
I lately traveild, that unwares I strayd
Out of my way, through perils straunge and hard;
That day should faile me ere I had them all declard.

32

'There did I find, or rather I was fownd   280
Of this false woman, that Fidessa hight;
Fidessa hight the falsest dame on grownd,
Most false Duessa, royall richly dight.

247. aread, counsel you, charge you.

That easy was t'inveigle weaker sight:
Who by her wicked arts and wiely skill,   285
Too false and strong for earthly skill or might,
Unwares me wrought unto her wicked will,
And to my foe betrayd, when least I feared ill.'

33

Then stepped forth the goodly royall mayd,
And on the ground her selfe prostrating low,   290
With sober countenaunce thus to him sayd:
'O pardon me, my soveraine lord, to sheow
The secret treasons, which of late I know
To have been wrought by that false sorceresse.
Shee, onely she, it is, that earst did throw   295
This gentle knight into so great distresse,
That death him did awaite in daily wretchednesse.

34

'And now it seemes, that she suborned hath
This crafty messenger with letters vaine,
To worke new woe and improvided scath,   300
By breaking of the band betwixt us twaine;
Wherein she used hath the practicke paine
Of this false footman, clokt with simplenesse,
Whome if ye please for to discover plaine,
Ye shall him Archimago find, I ghesse,   305
The falsest man alive; who tries, shall find no lesse.'

35

The king was greatly moved at her speach,
And, all with sudden indignation fraight,
Bad on that messenger rude hands to reach.
Eftsoons the gard, which on his state did wait,   310
Attacht that faytor false, and bound him strait:
Who, seeming sorely chauffed at his band,
As chained beare, whom cruell dogs doe bait,
With ydle force did faine them to withstande,
And often semblaunce made to scape out of their
    hand.   315

36

But they him layd full low in dungeon deepe,
And bound him hand and foote with yron chains,
And with continual watch did warely keepe:
Who then would thinke, that by his subtile trains
He could escape fowle death or deadly pains?   320
Thus when that princes wrath was pacifide,
He gan renew the late forbidden bains,
And to the knight his daughter deare he tyde,
With sacred rites and vowes for ever to abyde.

37

His owne two hands the holy knotts did knitt,   325
That none but death for ever can divide;

302. practicke, actual. 308. fraight, fraught, loaded down with
311. faytor, agent, doer. 322. bains, banns (of marriage).

His owne two hands, for such a turne most fitt,
The housling fire did kindle and provide,
And holy water thereon sprinckled wide;
At which the bushy teade a groome did light,   330
And sacred lamp in secret chamber hide,
Where it should not be quenched day nor night,
For feare of evill fates, but burnen ever bright.

38

Then gan they sprinckle all the posts with wine,
And made great feast to solemnize that day: 335
They all perfumde with frankincense divine,
And precious odours fetcht from far away,
That all the house did sweat with great aray:
And all the while sweete musicke did apply
Her curious skill, the warbling notes to play,   340
To drive away the dull melancholy;
The whiles one sung a song of love and jollity.

39

During the which there was an heavenly noise
Heard sownd through all the pallace pleasantly,
Like as it had bene many an angels voice   345
Singing before th' Eternall Majesty,
In their trinall triplicities on hye;
Yett wist no creature, whence that hevenly sweet
Proceeded, yet each one felt secretly,
Himselfe thereby refte of his sences meet,   350
And ravishd with rare impression in his sprite.

40

Great joy was made that day of young and old,
And solemne feast proclayme throughout the land,
That their exceeding merth may not be told:
Suffice it heare by signes to understand   355
The usuall joyes at knitting of loves band.
Thrise happy man the knight himselfe did hold,
Possessed of his ladies hart and hand,
And ever, when his eie did her behold,
His heart did seeme to melt in pleasures manifold.

41

Her joyous presence and sweet company   361
In full content he there did long enjoy,
Ne wicked envy, ne vile gealosy,
His deare delights were hable to annoy:
Yet, swimming in that sea of blisfull joy,   365
He nought forgott, how he whilome had sworne,
In case he could that monstrous beast destroy,
Unto his Faery Queene backe to retourne:
The whice he shortly did, and Una left to mourne.

---

328. **housling**, sacramental. 330. **teade**, torch. 334. **posts**; that is, the posts of the bed. 347. **trinall triplicities**, threefold trinities, a reference to the ninefold arrangement of the angels in Heaven.

42

Now strike your sailes, yee jolly mariners,   370
For we be come unto a quiet rode,
Where we must sand some of our passengers,
And light this weary vessell of her lode.
Here she a while may make her safe abode,
Till she repaired have her tackles spent,   375
And wants supplide; and then againe abroad
On the long voiage whereto she is bent:
Well may she speede, and fairely finish her intent.

Niccolò Machiavelli

1469–1527

The political revolution of the Renaissance brought powerful national monarchies to Western Europe out of the decay of medieval feudalism. In Italy, however, the commercial rivalry of the major cities hindered nationalism and produced instead autocratic princes ruling powerful independent city-states, and it was an Italian, Niccolò Machiavelli, who codified the new philosophy of ruthless power politics in his frankly pragmatic treatise, *The Prince* (1513).

Since the term "machiavellian" in English has become synonymous with unscrupulous cunning, it is important to observe that Machiavelli was no more than a product of his time and that his amoral justification of political expediency sprang from his training and experience. The son of a prominent jurist, he emerged from obscurity at thirty to play an active role in Florentine politics in the era of the Medici. Well schooled in the Latin and Italian classics, he was always more interested in the historians, especially Livy, than in the poets and playwrights. Although he wrote verse and produced in *La Mandragola* (1524) one of the wittiest and most cynical comedies of modern times, the majority of his writings are historical and political. But in them the new, free spirit of Humanism expresses itself through his independent criticism of the feudal nobility, the temporal power of the Church, and the philosophy of scholasticism. His plea for a strong central government reflected his contempt for the political anarchy of the Middle Ages.

Machiavelli entered public life with the expulsion of the Medici from Florence in 1494. Between 1498 and 1512 he was secretary to the Ten of War and Peace, who controlled the military affairs of the city. He worked diligently at diplomatic missions, which took him beyond Italy to the French courts of Louis XII and Louis XIII as well as to Switzerland and Germany. But the embassy most influential in shaping his political views was one to Cesare Borgia, the unscrupulous military dictator who built a brief empire in central Italy by conscienceless murder of his enemies and dubious allies. As the prag-

---

372. **sand**, discharge.

matic philosophy of Machiavelli matured, he came to see Cesare Borgia as the model prince who would allow no moral considerations to impede the growth of his power. Following the example of Borgia, he organized a national militia for Florence and chose a murderous aide of Borgia's to be its leader. But this army was unable to withstand the Medici when they marched on Florence in 1512, and with the fall of the Ten Machiavelli lost his political influence and was even imprisoned for a time. Although he performed minor political duties thereafter, his later years were spent largely in retirement with his wife and children at his villa near San Casciano.

Machiavelli's political philosophy is contained in his monumental *Discourses on the First Ten Books of Livy* and his famous short treatise, *The Prince.* The first builds from an analysis of political elements in the ancient Roman historian a theory of the evolution of a republic, and the second implements autocratic government with a science of statecraft. *The Prince* is the great document of the centralization of government in Renaissance Europe and reveals Machiavelli's longing for a strong leader to unify Italy as England, France, and Spain had been unified. For a time Cesare Borgia seemed about to do this, and even after his fall he seemed to Machiavelli to have pointed the way.

The ideal prince should have the Roman virtue of *virtus,** and the shifts of fortune require that he should be ready to adjust his principles to any necessity. Hence, he should keep his word only if it is expedient and resort to cruelty and even murder if his objective requires it. Being skeptical of the intelligence and worth of common men, Machiavelli places faith in a strong ruler more clever but no more virtuous than his subjects, who justifies his ruthless rise to power by his success in maintaining order. Although the practical truth of *The Prince* has been amply supported by political dictators in our own century, and although its theory may harmonize with a biological explanation of man's social and political behavior, this cold-blooded treatise must shock readers who believe in a moral order in the universe and the rights and integrity of the common man.

The Prince

XIV. Of the Duties of a Prince Relative to His Military Force.

PRINCES ought to make the art of war their sole study and occupation, for it is peculiarly the science of those who govern. War, and the several sorts of discipline and institutions relative to it, should be his only study, the only profession he should follow, and the object he ought always to have in view. By this means princes can maintain possession of their dominions; and private individuals

* This means literally "manliness"; hence the characteristics of a man, such as strength, alertness, courage, and resourcefulness.
*The Prince.*⁸ Translator anonymous.

are sometimes raised thereby to supreme authority; whilst, on the other hand, we frequently see princes shamefully reduced to nothing by suffering themselves to be enfeebled by slothful inactivity. I repeat, therefore, that by a neglect of this art it is that states are lost, and by cultivating it they are acquired. . . .

We cannot establish a comparison between men who are armed and those who are not so; and it would be equally absurd to suppose that the disarmed should command and the others obey. A prince who is ignorant of the art of war can never enjoy repose or safety amongst armed subjects; he will always be to them an object of contempt, as they to him will justly be subjects of suspicion; how is it possible then that they should act in concert? In short, a prince who does not understand the art of war can never be esteemed by his troops, nor can he ever confide in them.

It is necessary therefore that princes should pay their whole attention to the art of war, which includes mental labour and study as well as the military exercise. To begin with the latter, the prince should take the utmost care that his troops be well disciplined and regularly exercised. The chase is well adapted to inure the body of fatigue and to all the intemperances of weather. This exercise will also teach him to observe the sources and situations, as well as the nature of rivers and marshes; to measure the extent of plains and the declivity of mountains. By these means he will acquire a knowledge of the topography of a country which he has to defend, and will easily habituate himself to select the places where war may be best carried on. . . .

As to that part of military science which is learned in the closet, a prince ought to read history and to pay particular attention to the achievements of great generals and the cause of their victories and defeats; but above all he should follow the example of those great men who, when they select a model, resolve to follow in his steps. It was thus that Alexander the Great immortalized himself by following the example of Achilles, Caesar by imitating Alexander, and Scipio by copying Cyrus. . . .

XV. *What Deserves Praise or Blame in Men, and Above All in Princes.* It now remains to show in what manner a prince should behave to his subjects and friends. This matter having been already discussed by others, it may seem arrogant in me to pursue it farther, especially if I should differ in opinion from them; but as I write only for those who possess sound judgment, I thought it better to treat this subject as it really is, in fact, than to amuse the imagination with visionary models of republics and governments which have never existed. For the manner in which men now live is so different from the manner in which they ought to live that he who de-

viates from the common course of practice and endeavours to act as duty dictates necessarily ensures
his own destruction. Thus, a good man, and one who
wishes to prove himself so in all respects, must be
undone in a contest with so many who are evilly
disposed. A prince who wishes to maintain his power
ought therefore to learn that he should not be always
good and must use that knowledge as circumstances
and the exigencies of his own affairs may seem to
require.

Laying aside, then, the false ideas which have
been formed as to princes, and adhering only to
those which are true, I say, that all men, and especially princes, are marked and distinguished by some
quality or other which entails either reputation or
dishonour. For instance, men are liberal or parsimo-
nious, honourable or dishonourable, effeminate or
pusillanimous, courageous or enterprising, humane
or cruel, affable or haughty, wise or debauched, honest or dishonest, good tempered or surly, sedate or
inconsiderate, religious or impious, and so forth.

It would, doubtless, be happy for a prince to unite
in himself every species of good quality; but as our
nature does not allow so great a perfection, a prince
should have prudence enough to avoid those defects
and vices which may occasion his ruin; and as to
those who can only compromise his safety and the
possession of his dominions, he ought, if possible, to
guard against them; but if he cannot succeed in
this, he need not embarrass himself in escaping the
scandal of those vices, but should devote his whole
energies to avoid those which may cause his ruin.
He should not shrink from encountering some blame
on account of vices which are important to the support of his states; for everything well considered,
there are some things having the appearance of
virtues, which would prove the ruin of a prince,
should he put them into practice, and others upon
which, though seemingly bad and vicious, his actual
welfare and security entirely depend.

XVI. *Of Liberality and Economy.* To begin with
the first qualities of the above-mentioned, I must
observe that it is for the interest of a prince to be
accounted liberal, but dangerous so to exercise his
liberality that he is thereby neither feared nor respected. I will explain myself. If a prince be only
liberal as far as it suits his purposes, that is to say,
within certain bounds, he will please but few and
will be called selfish. A prince who wishes to gain
the reputation of being liberal should be regardless
of expense; but then to support this reputation, he
will often be reduced to the necessity of levying
taxes on his subjects and adopting every species of
fiscal resource which cannot fail to make him odious.
Besides exhausting the public treasury by his prodigality, his credit will be destroyed, and he will run
the risk of losing his dominions on the first reverse

of fortune, his liberality, as it always happens, having ensured him more enemies than friends. And
which is worse, he cannot retrace his steps and re-
plenish his finances without being charged with
avarice.

A prince, therefore, who cannot be liberal without
prejudicing his state should not trouble himself
much about the imputation of being covetous; for
he will be esteemed liberal in time, when people see
that by parsimony he has improved his revenue, become able to defend his dominions, and even to
undertake useful enterprises without the aid of new
taxes. Then the many from whom he takes nothing
will deem him sufficiently liberal, and the few only
whose expectations he has failed to realize will accuse him of avarice. In our times we have seen no
great exploits performed except by those who have
been accounted avaricious; all the others have failed.
Julius II attained the pontifical chair by means of
his bounty; but he judged rightly in supposing that
in order to enable him to prosecute the war against
France, it would do him injury to preserve his reputation for liberality. By his parsimony he was able
to support the expense of all his wars without the
imposition of new taxes. The present king of Spain
could never have accomplished all his great enterprises if he had any ambition to be thought liberal.

A prince, then, who would avoid poverty and always be in a condition to defend his dominions without imposing new taxes on his subjects should care
little for being charged with avarice, since the imputed vice may be the very means of securing the
prosperity and stability of his government.

It may however be alleged that Caesar would
never have attained the empire but by his liberality,
and that many others have arrived at the highest
honours by the same means. I answer, you are either
in possession of dominion already, or you are not.
In the first place, liberality would be prejudicial;
in the second, the reputation of it is serviceable and
necessary. Caesar endeavored to appear liberal
whilst he aspired to the empire of Rome. But if he
had lived longer, he would have lost that reputation
for liberality which had paved him the way to empire, or he would have lost himself in the attempt
to preserve it.

There have been, however, some princes who
have performed splendid actions and who have distinguished themselves by their liberality; but then
their prodigality did not come from the public purse.
Such were Cyrus, Alexander, and Caesar. A prince

76. **Julius II.** The great beautifier of Rome was also an able states-
man, who really founded the Papal States and sought to drive the
French from Italy.   82. **The present king of Spain,** Ferdinand of
Aragon (reigned 1479–1516), who unified Spain by his marriage to
Isabella of Castile and drove the Moors from Spain (1492).

ought to be very sparing of his own and his subjects'
property; but he should be equally lavish of that
which he takes from the enemy if he desires to be
popular with his troops; for that will not diminish
his reputation, but rather add to it. He who is too
liberal cannot long continue so; he will become poor
and contemptible unless he grinds his subjects with
new taxes— which cannot fail to render him odious
to them. Now there is nothing a prince ought to
dread so much as his subjects' hatred; unless, indeed, it be their contempt. And both these evils may
be occasioned by over liberality. If he must choose
between extremes, it is better to submit to the imputation of parsimony than to make a show of liberality; since the first, though it may not be productive of honour, never gives birth to hatred and contempt.

XVII. *Of Cruelty and Clemency, and Whether it
is Better to be Loved Than Feared.* To proceed to
other qualities which are requisite in those who
govern. A prince ought unquestionably to be merciful, but should take care how he executes his clemency. Caesar Borgia was accounted cruel; but it was
to that cruelty that he was indebted for the advantage of uniting Romagna to his other dominions and
of establishing in that province peace and tranquillity, of which it had been so long deprived. And,
everything well considered, it must be allowed that
this prince showed greater clemency than the people
of Florence, who, to avoid the reproach of cruelty,
suffered Pistoia to be destroyed. When it is necessary
for a prince to restrain his subjects within the
bounds of duty, he should not regard the imputation
of cruelty, because by making a few examples he
will find that he really showed more humanity in
the end than he who by too great indulgence suffers
disorders to arise, which commonly terminate in rapine and murder. For such disorders disturb a whole
community, whilst punishments inflicted by the
prince affect only a few individuals.

This is particularly true with respect to a new
prince, who can scarcely avoid the reproach of cruelty, every new government being replete with dangers. . . .

A prince, however, should not be afraid of phantoms of his own raising; neither should he lend too
ready an ear to terrifying tales which may be told
him, but should temper his mercy with prudence, in
such a manner that too much confidence may not
put him off his guard, nor causeless jealousies make
him insupportable. There is a medium between a
foolish security and an unreasonable distrust.

It has been sometimes asked whether it is better
to be loved than feared; to which I answer that one
should wish to be both. But as that is a hard matter
to accomplish, I think that, if it is necessary to make
a selection, it is safer to be feared than be loved. For

it may be truly affirmed of mankind in general that
they are ungrateful, fickle, timid, dissembling, and
self-interested; so long as you can serve them, they
are entirely devoted to you; their wealth, their
blood, their lives, and even their offspring are at
your disposal when you have no occasion for them;
but in the day of need they turn their back upon
you. The prince who relies on professions courts his
own destruction, because the friends whom he ac-
quires by means of money alone, and whose attachment does not spring from a regard for personal
merit, are seldom proof against reverse of fortune,
but abandon their benefactor when he most requires
their services. Men are generally more inclined to
submit to him who makes himself dreaded than to
one who merely strives to be beloved; and the reason is obvious, for friendship of this kind, being a
mere moral tie, a species of duty resulting from a
benefit, cannot endure against the calculations of interest: whereas fear carries with it the dread of punishment, which never loses its influence. A prince,
however, ought to make himself feared in such a
manner that, if he cannot gain the love, he may at
least avoid the hatred, of his subjects; and he may
attain this object by respecting his subjects' property
and the honour of their wives. If he finds it absolutely necessary to inflict the punishment of death,
he should avow the reason for it, and, above all
things, he should abstain from touching the property
of the condemned party. For certain it is that men
sooner forget the death of their relations than the
loss of their patrimony. Besides, when he once begins to live by means of rapine, many occasions offer
for seizing the wealth of his subjects; but there will
be little or no necessity for shedding blood.

But when a prince is at the head of his army and
has under his command a multitude of soldiers, he
should make little account of being esteemed cruel;
such a character will be useful to him, by keeping
his troops in obedience and preventing every species
of faction.

Hannibal, among many other admirable talents,
possessed in a high degree that of making himself
feared by his troops; insomuch that, having led a
very large army composed of all kinds of people into
a foreign country, he never had occasion, either in
prosperity or adversity, to punish the least disorder
or the slightest want of discipline: and this can only
be attributed to his extreme severity, and such other
qualities as caused him to be feared and respected
by his soldiers, and without which his extraordinary
talents and courage would have been unavailing. . . .

I conclude, then, with regard to the question
whether it is better to be loved than feared,—that
it depends on the inclinations of the subjects themselves, whether they will love their prince or not;

but the prince has it in his own power to make them fear him, and if he is wise, he will rather rely on his own resources than on the caprice of others, remembering that he should at the same time so conduct himself as to avoid being hated.

XVIII. *Whether a Prince is Obliged by His Promise.* It is unquestionably very praiseworthy in princes to be faithful to their engagements; but among those of the present day, who have been distinguished for great exploits, few indeed have been remarkable for this virtue or have scrupled to deceive others who may have relied on their good faith.

It should, therefore, be known that there are two ways of deciding any contest: the one by laws, the other by force. The first is peculiar to men, the second to beasts; but when laws are not sufficiently powerful, it is necessary to recur to force: a prince ought therefore to understand how to use both these descriptions of arms. This doctrine is admirably illustrated to us by the ancient poets in the allegorical history of the education of Achilles, and many other princes of antiquity, by the centaur Chiron, who, under the double form of man and beast, taught those who were destined to govern that it was their duty to use by turns the arms adapted to both these natures, seeing that one without the other cannot be of any durable advantage. Now, as a prince must learn how to act the part of a beast sometimes, he should make the fox and the lion his patterns. The first can but feebly defend himself against the wolf, and the latter readily falls into such snares as are laid for him. From the fox, therefore, a prince will learn dexterity in avoiding snares; and from the lion, how to employ his strength to keep the wolves in awe. But they who entirely rely upon the lion's strength will not always meet with success: in other words, a prudent prince cannot and ought not to keep his word, except when he can do it without injury to himself, or when the circumstances under which he contracted the engagement still exist.

I should be cautious in inculcating such a precept if all men were good; but as the generality of mankind are wicked and ever ready to break their words, a prince should not pique himself in keeping his more scrupulously, especially as it is always easy to justify a breach of faith on his part. I could give numerous proofs of this and show numberless engagements and treaties which have been violated by the treachery of princes, and that those who enacted the part of the fox have always succeeded best in their affairs. It is necessary, however, to disguise the appearance of craft, and thoroughly to understand the art of feigning and dissembling; for men are generally so simple and so weak that he who wishes to deceive easily finds dupes.

One example, taken from the history of our own times, will be sufficient. Pope Alexander VI played during his whole life a game of deception; and notwithstanding his faithless conduct was extremely well known, his artifices always proved successful. Oaths and protestations cost him nothing; never did a prince so often break his word or pay less regard to his engagements. This was because he so well understood this chapter in the art of government.

It is not necessary, however, for a prince to possess all the good qualities I have enumerated, but it is indispensable that he should appear to have them. I will even venture to affirm that it is sometimes dangerous to use, though it is always useful to seem to possess them. A prince should earnestly endeavour to gain the reputation of kindness, clemency, piety, justice, and fidelity to his engagements. He ought to possess all these good qualities, but still retain such power over himself as to display their opposites whenever it may be expedient. I maintain that a prince, and especially a new prince, cannot with impunity exercise all the virtues, because his own self-preservation will often compel him to violate the laws of charity, religion, and humanity. He should habituate himself to bend easily to the various circumstances which may from time to time surround him. In a word, it will be as useful to him to persevere in the path of rectitude, while he feels no inconvenience in doing so, as to know how to deviate from it when circumstances dictate such a course. He should make it a rule, above all things, never to utter anything which does not breathe of kindness, justice, good faith, and piety. This last quality it is most important for him to appear to possess, as men in general judge more from appearances than from reality. All men have eyes, but few have the gift of penetration. Every one sees your exterior, but few can discern what you have in your heart; and those few dare not oppose the voice of the multitude, who have the majesty of their prince on their side. Now, in forming a judgment of the minds of men, and more especially of princes, as we cannot recur to any tribunal, we must attend only to results. Let it then be the prince's chief care to maintain his authority; the means he employs, be what they may, will for this purpose always appear honourable and meet applause; for the vulgar are ever caught by appearances and judge only by the event. And as the world is chiefly composed of such as are called the vulgar, the voice of the few is seldom or never heard or regarded.

There is a prince now alive (whose name it may

57. **Pope Alexander VI,** a scandalous pope (1492–1503), ruthless and immoral, the father of Cesare Borgia, whose attempted conquest of the Romagna inspired *The Prince.* 107. **a prince now alive,** Ferdinand of Aragon and Castile, who had conquered the kingdoms of Naples and Navarre.

not be proper to mention) who ever preaches the doctrines of peace and good faith; but if he had observed either the one or the other, he would long ago have lost both his reputation and dominions.

XIX. *That it is Necessary to Avoid Being Hated and Despised.* Having distinctly considered the principal qualities with which a prince should be endowed, I shall briefly discuss the rest in a general discourse under the following heads, viz., that a prince ought sedulously to avoid everything which may make him odious or despicable. If he succeed in this, he may fill his part with reasonable success and need not fear danger from the infamy of other vices.

Nothing, in my opinion, renders a prince so odious as the violation of the right of property and a disregard to the honour of married women. Subjects will live contentedly enough under a prince who invades neither their property nor their honour; and then he will only have to contend against the pretensions of a few ambitious persons, whom he can easily find means to restrain.

A prince whose conduct is light, inconstant, pusillanimous, irresolute, and effeminate is sure to be despised. These defects he ought to shun as he would so many rocks, and endeavour to display a character for courage, gravity, energy, and magnificence in all his actions. His decisions in matters between individuals should be irrevocable, so that none may dare to think of abusing or deceiving him. By these means he will conciliate the esteem of his subjects and prevent any attempts to subvert his authority. He will then have less to apprehend from external enemies, who will be cautious in their attacks upon a prince who has secured the affection of his subjects. A prince has two things to guard against, the machinations of his own subjects and the attempts of powerful foreigners. The latter he will be able to repel by means of good friends and good troops; and these he will be sure to have as long as his arms are respectable. Besides, internal peace can only be interrupted by conspiracies, which are only dangerous when they are encouraged and supported by foreign powers. The latter, however, dare not stir if the prince but conform to the rules I have laid down. . . .

With regard to his subjects, if all be at peace without his dominions, a prince has nothing to dread but secret conspiracies, from which he may always secure himself by avoiding whatever can render him odious or contemptible. Conspiracies are seldom formed except against princes whose ruin and death would be acceptable to the people; otherwise men would not expose themselves to the dangers inseparable from such machinations.

History is filled with conspiracies; but how few have been crowned with success? No one can carry on such a design alone, nor trust any accomplices but malcontents. These frequently denounce their confederates and frustrate their designs in the hope of obtaining a large remuneration from him against whom they are leagued; so that those with whom you are necessarily associated in a conspiracy are placed between the temptation of a considerable reward and the dread of a great danger; so that to keep the secret it must either be entrusted to a very extraordinary friend or an irreconcilable enemy of the prince.

In short, conspirators live in continual fear, jealousy, and suspicion, whilst the prince is supported by all the splendour and majesty of the government, the laws, the customs, and the assistance of his friends, not to mention the affection which subjects naturally entertain towards those who govern them. So that conspirators have reason to fear both before and after the execution of their designs, for when the people have been once exasperated, there is no resource left to which they may fly. Of this I might give many examples, but I shall content myself with one only which occurred in the last century.

Hannibal Bentivoglio, the grandfather of the reigning prince of Bologna, had been murdered by the Canneschi, and the only member of the family who survived was John Bentivoglio, then an infant in the cradle. The people rose against the conspirators and massacred the whole family of the murderers; and in order still more strongly to show their attachment to the house of Bentivoglio, as there was none of the family left who was capable of governing the state, the Bolognese, having received information that a natural son of that prince then lived at Florence, sent deputies thither to demand him, though he lived in that city under the name of an artisan who passed for his father, and to him they confided the direction of the state till John Bentivoglio should be of age to govern.

A prince has therefore little to fear from conspiracies when he possesses the affections of the people; but he has no resource left if this support should fail him. Content the people and manage the nobles, and you have the maxim of wise governors.

France holds the first rank amongst well-governed states. One of the wisest institutions they possess is unquestionably that of the parliaments, whose object is to watch over the security of the government and the liberties of the people. The founders of this institution were aware, on the one hand, of the insolence and ambition of the nobles and, on the other, of the excess to which the people are liable to be transported against them, and they endeavoured to restrain both without the intervention of the king, who never could have taken part with the people, as he must thereby render the nobles discontented; nor could he favour the latter, without exciting the hatred of the people. Upon this account they have instituted an authority which, without the interference of the king, may favour the people and repress the insolence of the nobles. It must be confessed that nothing is more likely to give consistency to the government and ensure the tranquillity of the people. And we may learn from hence that princes should reserve to themselves distribution of favours and employments, and leave to the magistrates the care of pronouncing punishments, and, indeed, the general disposal of all things likely to excite discontent. . . .

XXI. *By What Means a Prince May Become Esteemed.* Nothing is more likely to make a prince esteemed than great enterprises and extraordinary actions. Ferdinand, the present king of Spain, may be considered as a new prince, because he has advanced himself from a petty state to be the most renowned monarch in Christendom. Now, if we examine his actions, they all deserve to be accounted great, and some of them indeed are splendid.

Scarcely was this prince seated on the throne when he turned his arms against the kingdom of Granada; and this war laid the foundation of his greatness, in which he met with no impediment, for the nobles of Castile were so intent on the invasion that they wholly disregarded his political innovations. In the meantime he insensibly established a dominion over them by maintaining armies at the expense of the church and people and by disciplining them in such a manner as afterwards made his power irresistible. Afterwards, in order that he might undertake enterprises still more brilliant, he dexterously assumed the mask of religion, and, by a cruel piety, drove the Moors out of his dominions. The means he took for this enterprise were, without doubt, barbarous; yet the exploit was extraordinary and almost unexampled.

Ferdinand, under the same cloak of religion, afterwards attacked Africa, Italy, and France, always having some great design in agitation, the event of which kept his subjects in continual suspense and admiration. And those enterprises succeeded each other so speedily that his subjects had no leisure to think of other matters, much less to engage in conspiracies against him.

It is also of great service to a prince to afford rare examples of civil administration, especially when it is necessary to reward or punish in an exemplary manner, for the extraordinary good or evil his subjects may have done . . . A prince should also invest his actions with a character of greatness, and above all things, avoid weakness and indecision. He must be a firm friend or an open foe; otherwise he will with difficulty conciliate his subjects. Should two powerful neighbours go to war, he must declare

for one of them or he will inevitably become the prey of the conqueror; and the vanquished party will be gratified at his ruin, and thus he will lose all protection; for the conqueror will despise a doubtful friend, who may abandon him on the first reverse of fortune, and the vanquished will never pardon him for remaining a tranquil spectator of his defeat.

When Antiochus marched into Greece on the invitation of the Etolians to drive out the Romans, he sent ambassadors to the Achaians, friends of the latter, to secure their neutrality. The Romans, on the other hand, demanded their assistance. The affair being taken into deliberation in the council of the Achaians, the Roman envoy spoke after the ambassador of Antiochus, and said, "You are advised to remain neutral, as the safest mode of conduct; and I assure you there can be none so bad; for you will inevitably remain at the mercy of the conqueror, whoever he may be, and will thus have two chances to one against you."

They can be no real friends who ask you to stand neuter. This consideration alone ought to open the eyes of a prince to the consequences of such conduct. Irresolute princes frequently embrace a neutrality to avoid some present inconvenience; but they meet their ruin by such a course. A bold adhesion to one party secures friendship by the tie of gratitude and leaves but little to fear from the mercy of the conqueror; first, because men are seldom so wholly destitute of honour as to repay benefits by so revolting ingratitude: secondly, because victory is rarely so very complete as to place the conqueror in a state to violate all the laws of propriety. If, on the other hand, he whose fortune the prince espouses should be vanquished he may in time retrieve his losses and acknowledge this mark of preference and esteem.

A prince ought never, as I have already observed, unless under the pressure of circumstances, to espouse the part of a neighbouring state more powerful than himself, because he lies at the mercy of his neighbour should he be the conqueror. Thus the Venetians were ruined by unnecessarily allying themselves with France against the duke of Milan. The Florentines, on the other hand, could not be blamed for embracing the cause of the pope and the king of Spain, when they marched their forces against Lombardy; because by adopting this step, they yielded to the dictates of necessity. After all, no party can be absolutely sure of success, and sometimes one danger is avoided only to encounter a greater; the utmost human prudence can do in such extremities is to choose the lesser evil.

Princes ought to honour talents and protect the

---

65. Antiochus. Antiochus III, the ancient Seleucid emperor (reigned 223–187 B.C.), was driven from Greece by the Romans in 191 B.C.

arts, particularly commerce and agriculture. It is peculiarly important that those who follow such pursuits should be secure from all dread of being overcharged with taxes and despoiled of their lands after they have improved them by superior cultivation. Finally, they should not neglect to entertain the people at certain periods of the year with festivals and shows, and they should honour with their presence the different trading companies and corporations, and display on such occasions the greatest affability and facility of access, always remembering to support their station with becoming dignity, which should never be lost sight of, under any circumstances.

Hugo Grotius

1583–1645

If nationalistic monarchy found a cynical textbook in Machiavelli, the Renaissance also laid the foundation of international law in the *Rights of War and Peace* (1625) of Hugo Grotius. Grotius (or Huig van Groot, as he was known in his native Holland) is thought of today as a jurist alone, but his life reveals the diversity of interests and abilities characteristic of the titans of the Renaissance. Though his father had served four times as burgomaster of Leyden, the brilliant youth entered the university there at the age of twelve with a thirst for the classics rather than the law and with a talent for writing Latin verses. Later in life he was to vary his legal and diplomatic duties with learned commentaries on classical authors, translations of Greek tragedians, and essays on Christian faith. His achievements as poet and historian were as much admired by his contemporaries as were his legal dissertations.

But he was trained as a lawyer and pleaded his first case at seventeen. On a visit to France the youthful prodigy was dubbed "The Miracle of Holland" by King Henry IV for his theses in jurisprudence. At thirty he was made pensionary (chief magistrate) of Rotterdam, but, becoming involved in the religious controversy of the Remonstrants and Anti-remonstrants that wracked Holland at this time, he was sentenced to life imprisonment by the Anti-remonstrants. Through the ingenuity of his faithful wife he escaped from prison in a chest of linen and thereafter lived abroad in France and Sweden. He served as Swedish ambassador to France between 1635 and the year of his death.

Although Grotius had an active career as advocate and diplomat, he was at heart a theorist about law. Living in an age when the Christian code of medieval warfare and statecraft had given way to the unscrupulous "natural" code of the jungle among the new nations, he had seen the shocking application of Machiavelli's philosophy in the Thirty Years' War in Germany. Convinced that a new code must come to regulate the ambitions and conflicts of nations, he sought his authority in the concept of a rational human nature common to all men which predicates a moral order in the universe older than man himself. Like the Rationalists of the eighteenth century, he appealed to reason rather than religious faith to justify his argument for a universal code and held up the example of ancient lawgivers to prove its permanent truth.

Every man must live in society with other men and hence must observe moral laws that make that society possible. These higher laws demand that men and the groupings of men called nations deny their predatory urges for the good of the whole. The higher law founded upon reason is simply the ethical reflection of the rational principle upon which the whole universe operates. This law of nature is imperfectly embodied in the law of nations (*ius gentium*) because of the variations of custom, but it must lie behind the law of nations and in general motivate their behavior if civilization is to survive. Grotius, then, was no mere idealist, insisting that men and nations should be better than they are. He knew that even the most reckless rulers of his day realized the need to modify Machiavelli in practice and stopped short of the utterly lawless behavior that he condoned, even as they might violate the codes that they could not entirely deny. Upon this sensible basis Grotius set forth his *Rights of War and Peace*.

Rights of War and Peace

I. THE RATIONAL BASIS OF INTERNATIONAL LAW

1.

THE Civil Law, both that of Rome, and that of each nation in particular, has been treated of, with a view either to illustrate it or to present it in a compendious form, by many. But International Law, that which regards the mutual relations of several Peoples, or Rulers of Peoples, whether it proceed from nature, or be instituted by divine command, or introduced by custom and tacit compact, has been touched on by few, and has been by no one treated as a whole in an orderly manner. And yet that this be done concerns the human race.

3. And such a work is the more necessary on this account; that there are not wanting persons in our own time, and there have been also in former times persons, who have despised what has been done in this province of jurisprudence, so far as to hold that no such thing existed, except as a mere name. Every

*Rights of War and Peace.*⁸ Translated by William Whewell.

one can quote the saying of Euphemius in Thucyd-ides;—that for a king or a city which has an em-pire to maintain, nothing is unjust which is useful: and to the same effect is the saying that, for those who have supreme power, the equity is where the strength is: and that other, that state affairs cannot be carried on without doing some wrong. To this we must add that the controversies which arise between peoples and kings have commonly war for their arbiter. And that war is far from having anything to do with rights is not only the opinion of the vulgar, but even learned and prudent men often let fall ex-pressions which favour such an opinion. It is very usual to put rights and arms in opposition to each other.

5. But since our discussion of Rights is worthless if there are no Rights, it will serve both to recom-mend our work and to protect it from objections, if we refute briefly this very grave error. And that we may not have to deal with a mob of opponents, let us appoint them an advocate to speak for them. And whom can we select for this office fitter than Car-neades, who had made such wonderful progress in his suspension of opinion, the supreme aim of his Academical Philosophy, that he could work the ma-chinery of his eloquence for falsehood as easily as for truth. He, then, undertook to argue against jus-tice; and especially the kind of justice of which we here treat; and in doing so, he found no argument stronger than this:—that men had, as utility prompted, established Rights, different as their man-ners differed; and even in the same society often changed with the change of times: but Natural Law there is none: for all creatures, men and animals alike, are impelled by nature to seek their own grati-fication: and thus, either there is no such thing as justice, or if it exist, it is the height of folly, since it does harm to itself in aiming at the good of others.

6. But what the philosopher here says, and what the poet follows:—"By naked nature ne'er was un-derstood what's just and right"—must by no means be admitted. For man is an animal indeed, but an animal of an excellent kind, differing much more from all other tribes of animals than they differ from one another; which appears by the evidence of many actions peculiar to the human species. And among these properties which are peculiar to man is a de-sire for society; that is, a desire for a life spent in common with fellowmen; and not merely spent somehow, but spent tranquilly and in a manner cor-responding to the character of his intellect. This de-sire the Stoics called οἰκείωσις, the domestic in-stinct, or feeling of kindred. And therefore the as-

sertion that by nature every animal is impelled only to seek its own advantage or good, if stated so gen-erally as to include man, cannot be conceded.

7. And indeed even in other animals, as well as in man, their desire of their own individual good is tempered by a regard, partly for their offspring, partly for others of their own species; which in them, indeed, we perceive to proceed from some intelligence outside themselves; because with regard to other acts not at all more difficult than those an equal degree of intelligence does not appear. The same is to be said of infants, in which, previous to all teaching, we see a certain disposition to do good to others, as is sagaciously remarked by Plutarch: as for example, compassion breaks out spontaneously at that age. But inasmuch as a man of full age has the knowledge which enables him to act similarly in similar cases, and along with that, a peculiar and admirable appetite for society, and has also language, an instrument of this desire, given to him alone of all animals, it is reasonable to assume that he has a faculty of knowing and acting according to general principles; and such tendencies as agree with this faculty do not belong to all animals, but are peculiar attributes of human nature.

8. And this tendency to the conservation of so-ciety, which we have now expressed in a rude man-ner, and which tendency is in agreement with the nature of the human intellect, is the source of Jus, or Natural Law, properly so called. To this Jus be-long the rule of abstaining from that which belongs to other persons, and, if we have in our possession anything of another's, the restitution of it, or of any gain which we have made from it, the fulfilling of promises, and the reparation of damage done by fault, and the recognition of certain things as merit-ing punishment among men.

9. From this signification has flowed another larger sense of Jus: for, inasmuch as man is superior to other animals, not only in the social impulse of which we have spoken, but in his judgment and power of estimating advantages and disadvantages; and in these, not only present good and ill, but also future good and ill, and what may lead to each; we may understand that it is congruous to human na-ture to follow, in such matters also, a judgment rightly framed; not to be misled by fear or by the temptation of present pleasure, nor to be carried away by blind and thoughtless impulse; and that what is plainly repugnant to such judgment, is also contrary to Jus, that is, to Natural Human Law.

10. And to this exercise of judgment pertains a reasonable and thoughtful assignment to each indi-vidual and each body of men of the things which peculiarly belong to them; by which exercise of judgment in some cases, the wiser man is preferred to the less wise; in others, our neighbour to a

1-2. **the saying . . . in Thucydides**; in Book VI, 85. 22–23. **Car-neades**, the Skeptic (c. 213–129 B.C.), founder of the Third Academy in Athens. 40–41. **"By naked . . . and right."** Horace, I *Satires*, iii, 113.

stranger; in others, a poor man to a rich man; according as the nature of each act and each thing requires. And this some persons have treated as a part of *Jus* properly and strictly so called; although *Jus* properly so called is really very different in its nature, and has this for its special office; to leave to another what is his, to give to him what we owe.

11. And what we have said would still have great weight, even if we were to grant what we cannot grant without wickedness, that there is no God, or that He bestows no regard on human affairs. But inasmuch as we are assured of the contrary of this, partly by reason, partly by constant tradition, confirmed by many arguments and by miracles attested by all ages, it follows that God, as the author of our being, to Whom we owe ourselves and all that we have, is to be obeyed by us without exception, especially since He has, in many ways, shown Himself both supremely good and supremely powerful: wherefore He is able to bestow upon those who obey Him the highest rewards, even eternal ones, as being Himself eternal; and He must be supposed to be willing as well as able to do this; and the more so, if He have promised such rewards in plain language; which we Christians believe, resting our belief on the indubitable faith of testimonies.

12. And here we are brought to another origin of *Jus,* besides that natural source; namely, the free will of God, to which, as our reason irresistibly tells us, we are bound to submit ourselves. But even that Natural Law of which we have spoken, whether it be that which binds together communities or that looser kind (which enjoins duties), although it do proceed from the internal principles of man, may yet be rightly ascribed to God; because it was by His will that such principles came to exist in us. And in this sense, Chrysippus and the Stoics said that the origin of *Jus,* or Natural Law, was not to be sought in any other quarter than in Jove himself; and it may be probably conjectured that the Latins took the word *Jus* from the name *Jove.*

15. In the next place, since it is comfortable to Natural Law to observe compacts (for some mode of obliging themselves was necessary among men, and no other natural mode could be imagined), Civil Rights were derived from this source, mutual compact. For those who had joined any community or put themselves in subjection to any man or men, either expressly promised or from the nature of the case must have been understood to promise tacitly that they would conform to that which either the majority of the community or those to whom the power was assigned should determine.

16. And therefore what Carneades said (as above), and what others also have said, as Horace, that utility is the mother of justice and right, if we are to speak accurately, is not true. For the Mother of Right, that is, of Natural Law, is Human Nature; for this would lead us to desire mutual society, even if it were not required for the supply of other wants; and the Mother of Civil Laws is Obligation by mutual compact; and since mutual compact derives its force from Natural Law, Nature may be said to be the Grandmother of Civil Laws. But Natural Law (which impels us to society) is reinforced by Utility. For the Author of Nature ordained that we should, as individuals, be weak and in need of many things to make life comfortable, in order that we might be the more impelled to cling to society. But Utility is the occasion of Civil Laws; for the association or subjection by mutual compact, of which we have just spoken, was at the first instituted for the sake of some utility. And accordingly, they who prescribe laws for others, in doing this, aim, or ought to aim at some Utility, to be produced to them for whom they legislate.

17. Further: as the Laws of each Community regard the Utility of that Community, so also between different Communities, Laws might be established, and it appears that Laws have been established, which enjoined the Utility, not of special communities, but of that great aggregate System of Communities. And this is what is called the Law of Nations, or International Law; when we distinguish it from Natural Law. And this part of Law is omitted by Carneades, who divides all Law into Natural Law and the Civil Laws of special peoples; while yet, inasmuch as he was about to treat of that Law which obtains between one people and another (for then follows an oration concerning war and acquisitions by war), he was especially called upon to make mention of Law of this kind.

18. And it is without any good reason that Carneades maintains, as we have said (5), that justice is folly. For since, by his own confession, that Citizen is not foolish who in a Civil Community obeys the Civil Law, although in consequence of such respect for the Law he may lose something which is useful to himself: so too that People is not foolish which does not so estimate its own utility as, on account of that, to neglect the common Laws between People and People. The reason of the thing is the same in both cases. For as a citizen who violates the Civil Law for the sake of present utility destroys that institution in which the perpetual utility of himself and his posterity is bound up; so too a people which violates the Laws of Nature and Nations beats down the bulwark of its own tranquillity for future time. And even if no utility were to arise from the observation of Law, it would be a point, not of folly, but of wisdom, to which we feel ourselves drawn by nature.

19. And therefore neither is that other saying of Horace universally true: "'Twas fear of wrong that

made us make our laws;" an opinion which one of the interlocutors in Plato's *Republic* explains in this way: that Laws were introduced from the fear of receiving wrong, and that men are driven to practise justice by a certain compulsion. For that applies to those institutions and laws only which were devised for the more easy maintenance of rights: as when many, individually feeble, fearing to be oppressed by those who were stronger, combined to establish judicial authorities, and to uphold them by their common strength; that those whom they could not resist singly, they might, united, control. And we may accept in this sense, and in no other, what is also said in Plato, that Right is that which the stronger party likes: namely, that we are to understand that Rights do not attain their external end, except they have force to back them. Thus Solon did great things, as he himself boasted, "by linking Force in the same yoke with Law."

20. But still Rights, even unsupported by force, are not destitute of all effect: for Justice, the observance of Rights, brings security to the conscience; while injustice inflicts on it tortures and wounds, such as Plato describes as assaulting the bosoms of tyrants. The conscience of honest men approves justice, condemns injustice. And what is the greatest point, injustice has for its enemy, justice, for its friend, God, who reserves His judgments for another life, yet in such a manner that He often exhibits their power in this life; of which we have many examples in history.

21. The reason why many persons, while they require justice as necessary in private citizens, commit the error of thinking it superfluous in a People or the Ruler of a People is this: in the first place, that in their regard to rights they look at nothing but the utility which arises from rights, which in the case of private citizens is evident, since they are separately too weak to protect themselves: while great States, which seem to embrace within them all that is requisite to support life in comfort, do not appear to have need of that virtue which regards extraneous parties, and is called justice.

22. But, not to repeat what I have already said, that Rights are not established for the sake of utility alone, there is no State so strong that it may not at some time need the aid of others external to itself, either in the way of commerce or in order to repel the force of many foreign nations combined against it. And hence we see that Leagues of alliance are sought even by the most powerful Peoples and Kings; which can have no force according to the principles of those who confine rights within the boundary of the State alone. It is most true (as Cicero says)

2. in Plato's *Republic*; II, 359 B. 18–19. "by linking . . . with **Law**." Quoted by Plutarch, *Life of Solon*, 86 c.

that everything loses its certainty at once if we give up the belief in rights.

28. I, for the reasons which I have stated, holding it to be most certain that there is among nations a common law of Rights which is of force with regard to war and in war, saw many and grave causes why I should write a work on that subject. For I saw prevailing throughout the Christian world a license in making war of which even barbarous nations would have been ashamed; recourse being had to arms for slight reasons or no reason; and when arms were once taken up, all reverence for divine and human law was thrown away, just as if men were thenceforth authorized to commit all crimes without restraint.

46. Passages of history are of twofold use to us; they supply both examples of our arguments, and judgment upon them with regard to examples; in proportion as they belong to better times and better nations, they have the more authority; and therefore we have preferred those taken from the Greeks and the Romans. Nor are the judgments delivered in such histories to be despised, especially when many of them agree; for Natural Law, as we have said, is in a certain measure, to be proved by such consent; and as to the Law of Nations, there is no other way of proving it.

II. NATURAL LAW AND WAR

1. Natural Law is the Dictate of Right Reason, indicating that any act, from its agreement or disagreement with the rational nature (of man) has in it a moral turpitude or a moral necessity; and consequently that such act is forbidden or commanded by God, the Author of nature.

Acts concerning which there is such a Dictate are obligatory (morally necessary) or are unlawful in themselves, and are therefore understood as necessarily commanded or forbidden by God; and in this character, Natural Law differs, not only from Human Law, but from Positive Divine Law, which does not forbid or command acts which, in themselves and by their own nature, are either obligatory or unlawful; but by forbidding them makes them unlawful, by commanding them makes them obligatory.

In order to understand Natural Law, we must remark that some things are said to be according to Natural Law which are not so properly, but, as the schools love to speak, reductively, Natural Law not opposing them; as we have said that some things are called just which are not unjust. And again, by an abuse of expression, some things are said to be according to Natural Law which reason shows to be decent, or better than their opposites, though not obligatory.

It is to be remarked also that Natural Law deals not only with things made by nature herself, but with things produced by the act of man. Thus property, as it now exists, is the result of human will: but being once introduced, Natural Law itself shows that it is unlawful for me to take what is yours against your will.

Natural Law is so immutable that it cannot be changed by God himself. For though the power of God be immense, there are some things to which it does not extend: because if we speak of those things being done, the words are mere words and have no meaning, being self-contradictory. Thus God Himself cannot make twice two not be four; and, in like manner, He cannot make that which is intrinsically bad, not be bad. For as the essence of things, when they exist and by which they exist, does not depend on anything else, so is it with the properties which follow that essence: and such a property is the baseness of certain actions when compared with the nature of rational beings. And God Himself allows Himself to be judged of by this rule.

Yet sometimes, in acts directed by Natural Law, there is an appearance of change which may mislead the unwary, when in fact it is not Natural Law which is changed, but the thing about which that Law is concerned. Thus, if a creditor gives me a receipt for my debt, I am no longer bound to pay him; not that Natural Law has ceased to command me to pay what I owe, but because I have ceased to owe it. So if God command any one to be slain or his goods to be taken, this does not make lawful homicide or theft, which words involve crime: but the act will no longer be homicide or theft, being authorized by the supreme Lord of life and of goods. . . .

2. In the first principle of nature (Self-preservation) there is nothing which is repugnant to war. Indeed, all things rather favour it: for the end of war, the preservation of life and limb and the retention or acquisition of things useful to life agree entirely with that of principle. And if force be requisite for this purpose, still there is in this nothing at variance with nature; for all animals are provided by nature with means for the very purpose of self-defense. . . .

Again, Right Reason and the nature of Society, which are next to be considered, do not prohibit all force, but that only which is repugnant to Society; that is, that which is used to attack the rights of others. For Society has for its object, that every one may have what is his own in safety, by the common help and agreement. Which consideration would still have place, even if property were not introduced; for even then, each one would have a property in his life, limbs, liberty; and these could not be attacked without wrong done to him. And also to use things which lay in common, and to take as much of them as nature should require, would be the right

of the person who first took occupation of them; and he who should prevent the exercise of this right, would do the occupier wrong. And this is much more easily understood now, when property has taken a shape by law or usage: as Cicero says.

Therefore it is not contrary to the nature of Society to take care of the future for one's self, so that the rights of others be not infringed: and thus, even force which does not violate the right of another is not unjust.

Lope de Vega

1562–1635

The romantic temperament of Spain finds its best expression in the ebullient plays of Lope de Vega. Behind him lay a century of dramatic evolution, but in Lope the Spanish theater reached maturity. His extravagant genius contributed brilliantly to most literary forms of his day, but his best and most voluminous output was reserved for drama, whether the religious *autos sacramentales,* or "cloak-and-sword *comedias*" of manners and intrigue, or the historical plays that revealed his patriotic fervor. His long, teeming life is more romantic and amazing than any single thing he wrote, and through all its inconsistencies shines his passionate faith in the Catholic religion and the high destiny of his beloved Spain.

Lope Felix de Vega Carpio is an almost exact contemporary of Shakespeare, but two more different playwrights in temperament, career, and artistic objectives could hardly be imagined. Beside the modest, thoughtful Englishman with his thirty-odd plays that carefully study human character, set the dashing Spaniard of a thousand plays turned out at breathless speed in oft-repeated molds. Even as a peasant boy, Lope dictated verses before he could write and at twelve completed his first play, which was acted by a prominent company. The youthful prodigy was sent to the University of Alcalá de Henares by a bishop whom he served as page, but it is probable that he left before obtaining his degree to take part in a naval expedition. By 1585 he had established himself as poet and playwright in Madrid, but a disappointment in love and his vengeful libel of the girl's family led to his exile from the city for eight years. He broke this exile only to elope with the daughter of Philip II's King-at-Arms, but cut short his honeymoon to enlist with the Spanish Armada. He dispelled his grief at the defeat of the Armada and at the death of his brother by writing a narrative poem in eleven cantos on the return voyage.

Upon his arrival in Spain, Lope plunged into writing for the stage. The death of his wife in 1595 removed the last barrier to the dissipation to which his passionate nature had long been predisposed. A series of scandalous intrigues was not interrupted by a second marriage for money, and his new wife denounced in vain his liaisons with several mistresses. His illegitimate children were the gossip of his enemies, but no amount of attack could threaten his commanding eminence in literature. In the midst of this wanton life Lope suddenly turned devout and took holy orders in 1614. But this whim did not last long, and a rash of religious writing was followed by more of the libertine. Only in his seventies did a series of misfortunes—the death of his brilliant son, the elopement of a daughter with an older man—lead him to a pious end. Characteristically, he went to extremes in his repentance, beating himself until the walls of his room were spotted with blood. His death soon after was followed by a magnificent funeral.

Lope's total production is almost beyond belief; during nearly seventy years he never stopped writing. His miscellaneous works alone—epics, odes, sonnets, elegies, eclogues, romances, burlesques—fill twenty-one huge volumes. One scholar has estimated that he wrote over twenty-one million lines of verse. Since the majority of his plays have been lost, the exact number of them can never be known. At the age of seventy he claimed to have written fifteen hundred, and a disciple set the figure at eighteen hundred, plus four hundred *autos sacramentales*. Later scholars have reduced this number considerably, but the extant, genuine plays of Lope number 475 —in itself the most amazing dramatic output of all time. No wonder Cervantes, who was not always his friend, called Lope the 'Monster of Nature."

Obviously Lope could not have thought through these plays individually: many are variations on each other, rushed through to appease an insatiable public. His themes are the standard Spanish loyalties—passionate romantic love for a fair lady, unquestioning Catholic faith, undying devotion to king and country. The intensity of these sentiments is revealed in set speeches, often rhetorical to the point of bombast. His characters too are conventionalized—the wise and beneficent king, the haughty and sometimes villainous nobleman whose defeat represents the death of feudalism, the proud peasant, the dashing young hero, his chaste and high-spirited lady, and above all the clever *gracioso*, or clown, whose buffoonery and realistic comments on the romantic characters bring the plays down to earth and comedy. In some respects Lope's plays are surprisingly modern: they are shorter than Shakespeare's, running to three acts rather than five; they are seldom either tragedies or comedies, but tragicomedies essentially serious in tone while relieved by humor and a happy ending; and their respectful treatment of commoners is much more appealing than Shakespeare's aristocratic contempt for the rabble. On the other hand, the high-flown speeches irritate our common sense, and the stock characters and sentiments are poor substitutes for the subtle psychology of Shakespeare and the broad philosophy of Molière. The prodigal Lope appeals through his sheer high spirits and flashes of poetry, not through the force of his ideas.

Of the many classes of his *comedias*, *The Sheep Well* (*Fuente Ovejuna*) excellently represents his chronicle plays. It has been chosen because of its strikingly modern subject—the uprising of a community against injustice and the common loyalty of its members to each other. It has no hero or heroine in the conventional sense; the hero is the town, *Fuente Ovejuna*, victorious over a hateful villain. This grand theme takes on an epic character in the communal solidarity of the last scene. The work was first published in 1619 and was probably written in that decade. Its revival in modern times was due to Russian critics who saw in its theme a parallel with the Soviet Revolution.

The Sheep Well

PERSONS

THE KING, FERDINAND OF ARAGON
QUEEN ISABELLA OF CASTILE
DON MANRIQUE, MASTER OF SANTIAGO
RODRIGO TÉLLEZ GIRÓN, GRAND MASTER OF CALA-
TRAVA
THE COMMANDER FERNÁN GÓMEZ DE GUZMÁN
FLORES ⎱
ORTUÑO ⎰ *his retainers*
CIMBRANOS, *a soldier*
A Judge
Two Regidors of Ciudad Real
ESTEBAN ⎱
ALONSO ⎰ *Alcaldes of Fuente Ovejuna*
JUAN ROJO ⎱
CUADRADO ⎰ *Regidors*
Another Regidor of Fuente Ovejuna
FRONDOSO ⎱
MENGO ⎬ *peasants*
BARRILDO ⎰
LEONELO, *a student*
A Farmer
A Soldier
LAURENCIA ⎱
PASCUALA ⎬ *peasants girls*
JACINTA ⎰
A Boy
Musicians, Soldiers, Farmers, Villagers and Attendants

The scene is laid in Almagro, the village of Fuente Ovejuna (meaning "Sheep Well"), the country round about Ciudad Real, and at the itinerant Royal Court in Castile. Time: 1476.

The Sheep Well. Translated by John Garrett Underhill. Reprinted from *Four Plays of Lope de Vega*, translated by John Garrett Underhill; copyright 1936 by John Garrett Underhill; used by permission of the publishers, Charles Scribner's Sons.

ACT FIRST

SCENE ONE. *A street in Almagro*

(*The* COMMANDER *enters with* FLORES *and* OR-
TUÑO, *servants.*)

COMMANDER.

Does the Master know I have come to town?
    FLORES. He does, sir.
    ORTUÑO. The years will bring discretion.
    COMMANDER. I am Fernán Gómez de Guzmán.
    FLORES. To-day youth may serve as his excuse.
    COMMANDER. If he is ignorant of my name, let him
respect the dignity of the High Commander.
    ORTUÑO. He were ill advised to fail in courtesy.
    COMMANDER. Or he will gain little love. Courtesy
is the key to favor while discourtesy is stupidity that
breeds enmity.
    ORTUÑO. Should a rude oaf hear how roundly he
was hated, with the whole world at his heels not to
bark but to bite, he would die sooner than convict
himself a boor.
    FLORES. Slight no man. Among equals pride is
folly but toward inferiors it becomes oppression.
Here neglect is want of care. The boy has not yet
learned the price of favor.
    COMMANDER. The obligation which he assumed
with the sword the day that the cross of Calatrava
was fixed upon his breast, bound him to humility
and love.
    FLORES. He can intend no despite that his quick
spirit shall not presently make appear.
    ORTUÑO. Return, sir, nor stay upon his pleasure.
    COMMANDER. I have come to know this boy.
(*Enter the* MASTER OF CALATRAVA *and* Attendants.)
    MASTER. A thousand pardons, Fernán Gómez de
Guzmán! I am advised of your arrival in the city.
    COMMANDER. I had just complaint of you, for my
affection and our birth are holy ties, being as we
are the one Master of Calatrava, and the other Commander, who subscribes himself yours wholly.
    MASTER. I had no thought of this purposed honor,
Fernando, hence a tardy welcome. Let me embrace
you once again.
    COMMANDER. Vying in honor. I have staked my
own on your behalf in countless causes, even answering during your minority before the Pope at Rome.
    MASTER. You have indeed. By the holy token that
we bear above our hearts, I repay your love, and
honor you as I should my father.
    COMMANDER. I am well content.
    MASTER. What news of the war at the front?
    COMMANDER. Attend and learn your obligation.
    MASTER. Say I am already in the field.
    COMMANDER. Noble Master
Don Rodrigo Téllez Girón,

To power and rule exalted
Through bravery of a mighty sire
Who eight years since
Renounced the Mastership,
Devising it to you,
As was confirmed by oaths and surety
Of Kings and High Commanders,
Even the Sovereign Pontiff,
Pius the Second,
Concurring by his bull,
And later Paul, succeeding him,
Decreeing holily
That Don Juan Pacheco,
Noble Master of Santiago,
Should co-adjutor be
With you to serve,
Till now, his death recorded,
All government and rule
Descend upon your head,
Sole and supreme
Despite your untried years.
Wherefore take counsel,
Harkening to the voice of honor,
And follow the commitment
Of kin and allies, wisely led.
Henry the Fourth is dead.
Let all his lieges
Bend the knee forthwith
To Alonso, King of Portugal,
Heir by right in Castile
Through his wife
In tie of marriage,
Though Ferdinand,
Lord of Aragon,
Like right maintains
By title of his wife,
Isabella.
Yet to our eyes
The line of her succession is not clear,
Nor can we credit
Shadow of deception
In the right descent
Of Juana, now secure
Under the protection of your cousin,
Who loves you as a brother.
Therefore summon all the Knights
Of Calatrava to Almagro,
Thence to reduce
Ciudad Real,
Which guards the pass
Dividing Andalusia from Castile,
On both
Frowning impartially.
Few men will gain the day.
For want of soldiers
The people mount the walls,
Aided by errant knights

Faithful to Isabella,
And so pledged to Ferdinand
As King.
Strike terror, Rodrigo,
To the hearts of those who say
That this great cross
Rests heavily
Upon the sagging bosom of a child.
Consider the Counts of Ureña,
10 From whom you spring,
Flaunting the laurels of their might
Upon the heights of fame,
Nor neglect to emulate
The Marquises of Villena,
With other gallant captains
Whose names in manifold
Brighten the outstretched wings
Of reputation.
Unsheathe your virgin sword
20 Till in battle, like the cross,
It drip with blood.
Of this red cross,
Blasoned on the breast,
Breathes there no votary
Whose drawn sword flashes white.
At the breast the one,
At the side the other
Must glow and flame with red!
So crown, valiant Girón,
30 With deeds
The immortal temple
Reared stone by stone
By your great ancestors.
    MASTER. Fernan Gómez,
I shall march with you
Because our cause is just,
And with my kin bear arms.
If I must pass,
Then shall I pass at Ciudad Real
40 As a lightning stroke,
Cleaving as I pass,
While my scant years proclaim
To friend and foe alike
That when my uncle died
Was no mortality of valor.
I draw my sword
That men may see it shine,
Livid with the passion of the cross,
Maculately red.
50 Where hold you residence?
Send on your vassals
To combat in my train.
    COMMANDER. Few but faithful serve,
Who will contend like lions
In battle.
Fuente Ovejuna is a town
Of simple folk,

Unskilled in warfare,
Rather with plough and spade
Tilling the fields.   60
    COMMANDER. Favored possession
In these troubled times,
Pastoral, serene!
Gather your men;
Let none remain unarmed.
    MASTER. Today I spur my horse
And level my eager lance.

SCENE TWO. *The Square of Fuente Ovejuna.*

(PASCUALA *and* LAURENCIA *enter.*)

LAURENCIA. I prayed he would never come back.
PASCUALA. When I brought the word I knew it
would grieve you.   70
LAURENCIA. Would to God he had never seen
Fuente Ovejuna!
PASCUALA. Laurencia, many a girl has made a pre-
tense of saying no, yet all the while her heart has
been as soft as butter in her.
LAURENCIA. I am a live-oak, gnarled and twisted.
PASCUALA. Yes, but why refuse a drink of water?
LAURENCIA. I do, be the sun never so hot, though
you may not believe it. Why love Fernando? He's no
husband.   80
PASCUALA. No, woman.
LAURENCIA. And amen! Plenty of girls in the vil-
lage have trusted the Commander to their harm.
PASCUALA. It will be a miracle if you escape.
LAURENCIA. You are blind, because I have avoided
him a full month now, Pascuala, and no quarter.
Flores, who lays his snares, and that villain Ortuño,
offered me a waist, a necklace and a head-dress.
They praised Fernando, their master, and pictured
him so great that I blushed at his very glory, but for 90
all that they could not move me.
PASCUALA. But where was this?
LAURENCIA. Down by the brook there, a week
gone yesterday.
PASCUALA. You're already lost, Laurencia.
LAURENCIA. No, no, no!
PASCUALA. Maybe the priest might believe your
story.
LAURENCIA. I am too innocent for the priest. In
His Name, Pascuala, but of a morning rising early   100
I had rather set me a slice of ham on the fire to
munch with a crust of bread of my own kneading,
filching a glass meanwhile out of the old stopped
butt, once mother's back is turned, to wet my thirst,
and then climb to watch the cow thrash through the
cabbages, all foaming at the mouth come noonday,
while I hearten myself with a bit of eggplant and
a strip of bacon after hard walking, and return
weary toward supper-time to nibble the raisins,

home-grown in our own vineyard, which God fend
the hail from, sitting me down with a dish of salad
and pepper and olive oil, and so to bed tired at
nightfall, in contentment and peace, with a prayer
on my lips to be preserved from the men, devils,
God knows, every one, than I would deliver myself
up to their wiles for all their love and fury. What
they want is to undo us, joy in the night and at
dawning a maid's mourning.

10 PASCUALA. You are right, Laurencia, for a sated
lover flies faster than a farm sparrow. In the winter
when the fields are bare they sing 'tweet' under the
eaves till they come by the crumbs from the farmer's
board, but when the fields are green and frost has
been forgotten, instead of fluttering down to sing
'tweet' they hop up to the roof-tree and cry 'twit,'
and 'twit' it is at you standing down below, make the
most that you can of their twitting. Men are the
same. When they need us we are their very lives,
20 their heart, their soul, their entire being, but their
hunger satisfied off they fly and leave us, too, with
the echo of their twitting. So I say no man can be
trusted.

(MENGO, BARRILDO and FRONDOSO enter.)

FRONDOSO. You defeat yourself, Barrildo.

BARRILDO. Two judges are here who can decide
between us.

MENGO. Agree upon the forfeit and then we'll call
in the girls. If they favor me, you hand me both
your shirts, with whatever else you have on your
30 backs, in need of victory.

BARRILDO. Agreed. But what will you give if you
lose?

MENGO. My rebeck of old box, which is worth
more than a granary, for Gods knows its like cannot
be bought in the village.

BARRILDO. Fairly said and offered.

FRONDOSO. Done!—God save you, ladies.

LAURENCIA. Frondoso calls us ladies.

FRONDOSO. The flattery of the age.
40 The blind we say are one-eyed,
The cross-eyed merely squint,
Pupils equal masters
While cripples barely limp;
The spendthrift fools call "open,"
The dumb now hold their tongues,
Bullies out-vie brave men,
Shouters shame the grave men,
And as for saving
Praise the miser—
50 None so active as the meddler
To promote the common good.
Gossips will "talk freely,"
While concede we must
The quarrelsome are just.

33. old box; that is, boxwood.

Boasters display their courage,
The shrinking coward "retires,"
The impudent grow witty,
The taciturn sit pretty,
All hail the idiot.
Gamblers, pray, "look forward," 60
The bald deserve respect,
Admit the ass is graceful,
That large feet proclaim the faithful,
While a blotched and pimpled face-full
Is a scientific indication
Of a sluggish circulation.
The lie to-day a truth is,
Rudeness clever youth is,
And if you have a hump,
Why follow your bent 70
All the way over,
Without stooping
Moreover,
And so to conclude
I call you ladies,
For otherwise there is no telling what names I might
     call you.

LAURENCIA. In the city praise may be the fashion,
Frondoso, but by my faith we have a contrary custom in the country, where words are sharp and 80
barbed, upon tongues that are calloused to use them.

FRONDOSO. Who speaks knows.

LAURENCIA. Turn all in reverse.
Know and be a bore,
Work and you have luck,
The prudent are faint-hearted,
The upright reek with muck.
Advice to-day spells insult,
Charity rank waste,
Be fair and painted ugly, 90
Be good, what wretched taste!
Truth is made for boobies,
No purity wins rubies,
While as for giving,
'Tis a veil for sinful living,
Fie, fie the hypocrite!
Disparage true worth always.
Dub simple faith imbecility,
Flat cowardice amiability,
Nor ever be fearful 100
Against the innocent
To speak an ear-full.
No woman is honest,
No beauty is chaste,
And as for virtue
There is not enough to hurt you,
For in the country
A curse
Turns merit to reverse.

MENGO. Devil of a girl! 110

BARRILDO. On my soul, she is too quick for us!

MENGO. A pinch of spice plashed into the holy water the day of her christening.

LAURENCIA. Well, well, since you question us, let us have it without delay and judge truly.

FRONDOSO. I'll set out the argument.

LAURENCIA. Plant in season, then, and begin.

FRONDOSO. Attend, Laurencia.

LAURENCIA. Oh, I'll have an answer for you some day.

10 FRONDOSO. Be fair, be just.

LAURENCIA. What is this wager?

FRONDOSO. Barrildo and I oppose Mengo.

LAURENCIA. Mengo is right. So, there!

BARRILDO. A fact is certain and plain which he denies.

MENGO. I deny it because it's a lie and they wander from the mark.

LAURENCIA. Explain.

BARRILDO. He maintains there is no such thing as
20 love.

LAURENCIA. Then it takes hold of one mightily.

BARRILDO. Yes, though it be blind, for without love the world would never go on.

MENGO. I say little, not being able to read, though I could learn, but if the elements make the world and our bodies are made of the elements which war against each other unceasingly, causing anger and discord, then where is love?

BARRILDO. Mengo, the world is love, here and here-
30 after, not discord. Harmony is love. Love is a reaching out.

MENGO. A pulling in, according to nature, which governs all things through the resemblances that are. Love is a looking to its own, it's preservation. I raise my hand to my face to prevent the blow, I move my feet to remove me from danger to my body, my eye-lids close to shield my sight through the attraction of a mutual love.

PASCUALA. He admits it's love, so what then?
40 There's an end.

MENGO. We love ourselves, no one else, that's flat.

PASCUALA. Mengo, what a lie! And God forgive me. The love a man bears for a woman, or a beast for its mate, is a fierce, consuming passion.

MENGO. Self-love, interest, not pure love. What is love?

LAURENCIA. A running after beauty.

MENGO. But why run after beauty?

LAURENCIA. For the thrill and the pleasure, boy.

50 MENGO. True. And the pleasure a man seeks for himself.

LAURENCIA. True again.

MENGO. So that self-love seeks its own delight?

LAURENCIA. Granted.

MENGO. Therefore there is no love, only we like what we like, and we intend in all things to get it, to seek delight, our delight.

BARRILDO. One day the priest preached in the village about a man named Plato who had taught men how to love, but what Plato loved, he said, was the 60 soul and the virtue that was hidden in it.

PASCUALA. So the fathers teach the children in 'cademies and schools.

LAURENCIA. Yes, and don't you listen to any nonsense, either. Mengo, thank God you never knew the curse of love.

MENGO. Were you ever in love?

LAURENCIA. In love with my honor, always.

FRONDOSO. Come, come, ladies! Decide, decide.

BARRILDO. Who wins? 70

PASCUALA. Let the priest or the sacristan cook up a reply, for Laurencia loves too much and I not a little, so how can we, siding both ways, decide?

FRONDOSO. They laugh at us.

(*Enter* FLORES.)

FLORES. God guard the fair!

PASCUALA. This man is from the Commander.

LAURENCIA. Why so brash, old goshawk, in the village?

FLORES. You meet me as a soldier.

LAURENCIA. From Don Fernando? 80

FLORES. The war is done, though it has cost us blood, and armies of our friends.

FRONDOSO. Say what of note our band achieved.

FLORES. I will, and that better than another, having seen it with my own eyes.
Beleaguering the city
Of Ciudad Real,
By charter royal,
The valiant Master mustered in
Two thousand foot, 90
Bravest among his vassals,
Beside three hundred horse,
Churchmen and laymen,
For the crimson cross
Summons to its aid
Those who profess it on their breasts
Though robed and habited for prayer,
Crusading oft in holy cause,
Ruthless to slay the Moor.
Boldly the lad rode forth, 100
His tunic green
Embroidered with golden scrolls,
While silken cords
Caught up his sleeves,
Stayed sixfold
Above his iron gauntlets.
His steed was sturdy stout,
A dappled roan
Bred beside the Betis,
Drinking of the willing stream 110
And pasturing on lush meadows,
But now in panoply of white
Bedecked, patterns of net

Flecking the snowy pools
That gemmed his mottled hide
From plumed crest
Down to the buckskin tail-piece.
At equal pace
The Commander Fernán Gómez
Bestrid a piebald charger,
Black of mane, the tail coal black,
White foaming at the nostril.
10 A Turkish coat of mail he wore,
Breastplate and corselet
Glowing bright orange,
Relieved with pearls and gold.
White plumes
Topped off his helmet,
Pallid plumes wind-blown,
Striking dismay,
The while his puissant arm
Banded now red, now white,
20 Brandished an ash-tree,
Famous as his lance
Even to Granada.
The city flew to arms,
Vain boasts of loyalty
With greed contending,
Some fearful for their homes,
Some of their treasure.
The Master breached those walls,
Flung back those surly churls,
30 And the heads
Of the rebel leaders,
As of those conspiring there
Against his dignity,
With a blow
Severed from the body.
We gagged the common folk,
Then beat them openly,
So in that town
The Master is feared and praised
40 Conjointly.
Though few in years,
By deeds, by valor and by victory
Nature in him has forged
A bolt from heaven
To rive Africa,
Her blue moon senescent
To the red cross bowed,
Obeisant.
Rich the promise
50 Of the rape of this fair city,
With apportionment
Of present gain
To him and the Commander.
Now hear the music sound, for zest in victory adds
    sweetest savor.

45. **Africa;** that is, Moslem Morocco.

(*The* COMMANDER *enters with* ORTUÑO *and* Musicians, *accompanied by* JUAN ROJO, *Regidor*, ESTEBAN *and* ALONSO, *Alcaldes*.)

Song

Welcome, great Commander,
Many times a victor,
Guzmáns, arm, to battle!
Girónes, strike, to battle!
Doves in peace, 60
Mighty in repose.
Forward to the conflict,
Strong of limb as oak-trees,
Drive the Moors before you
From Ciudad Real.
Flaunt your pennons proudly
In Fuente Ovejuna,
Valiant Fernán Gómez,
Glorious Conqueror!

COMMANDER. Acknowledgment and thanks in this 70
    our town
Receive in token of the love you show.
ALONSO. Accept this rustic tribute to renown,
Proffered how simply. These poor meadows grow
Scant sustenance of woe.
ESTEBAN.   Welcome accept
To Fuente Ovejuna, whose elders glow
    With pride, offering homely gifts, yet ept
To please, as pod or sprout or root, in carts
Heaped high with ruddy fruits, the produce rept 80
    From field and orchard, ripening in our hearts,
Mellowed in crib and barnyard. First, car one
Twin hampers bears of jars, baked for these marts,
    Whereto are added geese that sleekly run
Long necks from tangling nets, and shrilly shriek
Cackles of praise, paeans of booty won.
    Ten salted hogs bid the next wagon creak,
Bulging with fatty trimmings and dried meat;
The skins like amber shine, side, haunch and breek.
    A hundred pair of capon follow, treat 90
For the belly, plump hens torn from the cock
Through all the eager farms, tender and meet
    For axing. Arms we lack, nor bring we stock
Of blooded steeds, nor harness for the bold,
For such in rustic hands were cheat and mock
    Of love's pure gold which in our hearts is told.
Twelve wine-skins next appear, with beady wine
Filled full, in winter enemy of cold
    And friendly to the soldier, ally in line
Of battle, or on defense trusty like steel, 100
Tempering courage, for temper springs of wine.
    Unnumbered cheeses, last, jounce past awheel,
With products of the churn and dairy days,
True tokens of the love the people feel
Toward you and yours, harvests of heart-felt praise.
COMMANDER. Thanks and be gone, Alcaldes of
this town. Be gone assured of favor.

ALONSO. Rest, Master, in enjoyment of our love. These cat-tails before the door and this coarse sedge grass should bear pearls to match your deserving, as indeed we pray, and yet fall short of the devotion of the village.

COMMANDER. I accept the gifts right gladly. So get you gone.

ESTEBAN. The singers will repeat the refrain.

Song

Welcome, great Commander,
10 *Many times a victor,*
Men and fields mowed down! (*Exeunt.*)

COMMANDER. The girls stay behind.

LAURENCIA. No, Your Excellency.

COMMANDER. By the Lord you do! No airs nor graces! These are soldiers here.

LAURENCIA. Pascuala, he looks your way.

PASCUALA. Do you teach me to be modest?

COMMANDER. I look your way, little chuck with the crook, and tend to this burr of the pasture, till
20 she open to me.

PASCUALA. We grew here, Master.

COMMANDER. Pass into the house where my men will keep you safe.

LAURENCIA. If the Alcaldes go in so will we, because one is my father, but a girl by herself is just a girl and must be careful.

COMMANDER. A word, Flores.

FLORES. Master?

COMMANDER. How? What mean these green-
30 briers?

FLORES. Walk straight in, girls. Come!

LAURENCIA. You let go!

FLORES. Any fool can walk.

PASCUALA. You'll lock the door if we do go in.

FLORES. Pass and taste the spoils of war. Come!

COMMANDER (*aside to* ORTUÑO). Throw the bolt, Ortuño, once they're inside. (*Exit.*)

LAURENCIA. You hurt us, Flores.

ORTUÑO. These cheeses came in no cart.

40 PASCUALA. No, and we are not for you, either, so get out!

FLORES. What can you do with a girl?

LAURENCIA. Your master has his fill to-day for one stomach.

ORTUÑO. He's a judge of meat and prefers you, though the carts pass.

LAURENCIA. Then let him burst! (*The girls go out.*)

FLORES. What will the Master say with never a sight of a woman for good cheer? They laugh at us.

SCENE THREE. *A tent prepared for audience.*

(*Enter the* KING DON FERDINAND OF ARAGON *and* QUEEN ISABELLA, *accompanied by* DON MANRIQUE *and* Attendants.)

ISABELLA. To prepare is wise. Sire, harry Alonso 50 of Portugal where he has pitched his tents, for a ready offense averts the threatened injury.

THE KING. Navarre and Aragon despatch swift aid and succor. Under my command the Castilian bands shall be reformed. Success lies in prevention.

ISABELLA. Majesty, prevail by strategy.

DON MANRIQUE. Two Regidors of Ciudad Real crave audience.

THE KING. Admit them to our presence.
(*Enter* Two Regidors *of Ciudad Real.*)

FIRST REGIDOR. Great Ferdinand the Catholic our 60
King,
Posting from Aragon to high Castile
On warlike service and the common weal,
Humble petition to thy sword we bring
For vengeance, urging here the patent royal
Bestowed on Ciudad Real, thy city,
Foully wronged. To be thy city was our joy,
Thy will our law, proclaimed in kingly charter;
But blows of fate laid low our fealty.
A froward youth, Rodrigo Téllez Girón, 70
Master of Calatrava, with naked sword
Carves out addition to his wide domain,
Wasting our homes, our lands and revenues.
We met his treacherous assault, and force
Opposed to force, by threat and fear undaunted,
Till blood in rivers ran adown our streets,
Alas but vainly! The day we lost, and he,
Pricked on by the Commander Fernán Gómez,
Cunning in council, governs the city,
While we, enslaved, lament our injuries. 80

THE KING. Where dwells this Fernán Gómez?

FIRST REGIDOR. Sire, Fuente Ovejuna is his seat,
Wherein he rules amid his seignories.
He governs there, there does he his will,
Raining down blows upon his abject thralls
Beyond endurance.

THE KING. Name your captain.

SECOND REGIDOR. Sire,
None lives. Not one, alas, of noble blood
Survives unwounded, untaken or unslain. 90

ISABELLA. This cause demands an instant remedy.
The walls may be surrendered to the foe,
Who thus will boldly dominate the pass,
Entering Extremadura from the side
Of Portugal.

THE KING. Set forth at once, Manrique,
And with two chosen companies chastise
This arrogance, denying let or stay.
The Count of Cabra shall by our command
As swiftly follow, bravest of the house 100
Of Córdoba.
The front of tyranny must bow
And pride lie low
In the presence of our majesty.

ISABELLA. Depart ambassador of victory. (*Exeunt.*)

SCENE FOUR. *A river bank near Fuente Ovejuna. Trees and bushes.*

(LAURENCIA *and* FRONDOSO *enter.*)

LAURENCIA. I had not wrung the sheets, you saucy Frondoso, when you drove me from the river bank with spying. While we gaze the country-side talks and waits on tip-toe. The sturdiest of our lads, your jacket is the gayest and the costliest, so others note what you do, and not a girl in the village nor herdsman on the hills nor down in the river bottoms but swears we are one and of right ought to be joined, while Juan Chamorro, the sacristan, leaves his piping to publish the banns, for love, they say, goes first to church. Ah, wine burst the vaults in August, and burst every pot with must but I heed them not nor attend to their chatter, though it be time, methinks, and time soon for our own good to put an end to all this idle talk and pother.

FRONDOSO. Laughing Laurencia, I die while you smile. Though I say nothing you will not hear me, till at last I have scarcely strength even to mutter. I would be your husband but you repay with taunts my faith and loyalty.

LAURENCIA. I encourage you all I can.

FRONDOSO. It's not enough. When I think of you I cannot eat, drink, or sleep. I starve yet love an angel. God knows I die.

LAURENCIA. Cross yourself, Frondoso, or else bethink you of some charm.

FRONDOSO. There's a charm for two doves at the church, love, that makes them one. God set us beak to beak!

LAURENCIA. Speak to your master, Juan Rojo, if you will, and can summon the courage, else I must, since he is my uncle. Pray for the day, and hope.

FRONDOSO. Look! The Commander!

LAURENCIA. Stalking deer. Hide in the bushes.

FRONDOSO. Big bucks are hard to hide.

(*The* COMMANDER *enters.*)

COMMANDER. Aha! Following the fawn, I hit upon the doe.

LAURENCIA. I was resting from washing and return to the brookside now, Commander.

COMMANDER. Sweet Laurencia, stay, nor obscure the beauty heaven has granted to my sight. If you have escaped my hand till now, the woods and the fields will befriend us, for they are accomplices of love. Bend your pride and let your cheek flush as it has never done yet in the village. Sebastiana, who was Pedro Redondo's wife, has been mine, and so has the chit who wedded Martín del Pozo. I came upon her two nights a bride, and she opened to me fondly.

LAURENCIA. My lord, they had opened to so many that their fondness was no longer in question. Ask the village. God grant you luck with the deer. The cross on your breast proclaims you are no tempter of women.

COMMANDER. You protest too much, lass. I put down my cross-bow. With my hands I will subdue these pretty wiles.

LAURENCIA. No, no! What would you? Let go!

(FRONDOSO *re-enters and seizes the cross-bow.*)

COMMANDER. Struggle is useless.

FRONDOSO. (Aside) I take the bow. Heaven grant I do not shoot.

COMMANDER. Yield! Have done!

LAURENCIA. Heaven help me now!

COMMANDER. We are alone, no one will hear—

FRONDOSO. Noble Commander, loose that girl, or your breast shall be my mark, though the cross shine clear upon it.

COMMANDER. The dog insults me!

FRONDOSO. Here is no dog. Laurencia, flee!

LAURENCIA. Frondoso, you take care.

FRONDOSO. Go! (LAURENCIA *goes.*)

COMMANDER. Only a fool deprives himself of his sword, which I, god or devil, put by, fearing to fright the chase!

FRONDOSO. By God above, Commander, if I loose this string I'll gyve you like a hawk!

COMMANDER. Betrayed! Traitorous hind, deliver up that cross-bow. Dog, set down!

FRONDOSO. To be shot through? Hardly. Love is a warrior that yields his throne to none.

COMMANDER. Shall a knight valiant in battle be foiled by a dumb peasant? Stay, wretch! On guard! —for I forget my rank and station.

FRONDOSO. I do not. I am a swain, but since I will to live, I take the cross-bow with me.

COMMANDER. Ignominy, shame! I will have vengeance to the hilt. Quickly I vanish.

ACT SECOND

SCENE ONE. *Square in Fuente Ovejuna.*

(ESTEBAN *enters with a* Regidor.)

ESTEBAN. Better touch the reserve no further. The year bodes ill with threat of foul weather, so let the grain be impounded though there be mutiny among the people.

REGIDOR. I am of your mind if the village may be governed in peace.

ESTEBAN. Then speak to Fernán Gómez. These astrologers with their harangues pretend they know secrets God only knows. Not a scrap can they read of the future, unholy fabricators of what was and what shall be, when to their eyes even the present is blank,

For their ignorance is rank.

Can they bring the clouds indoors and lay the stars upon the table? How do they peer into heaven and yet come down with such dire disasters? These fellows tell us how and when to sow, here with the grain, there with the barley and the vegetables, the squash, mustard, and cucumber—

As squashes add them to the number.

Next they predict a man will die and one does in Transylvania, or the vineyards shall suffer drought, or people take to beer in far-off Germany; also cherries will freeze and impoverish the neighbors in Gascony, while there will be a plague of tigers in Hyrcania. So or not so, pray remember—

The year ends with December.

(LEONELO, *a student, enters with* BARRILDO.)

LEONELO. I grant this town nothing, upon a review, but as the plain seat of stupidity.

BARRILDO. How did you fare in Salamanca?

LEONELO. That is no simple story.

BARRILDO. By this you must be a complete Bártulo.

LEONELO. Not even a barber by this. In our faculty few trim knowledge from the course.

BARRILDO. You return to us a scholar.

LEONELO. No, but I have learned what it is wise to know.

BARRILDO. With all the printing of books nowadays a man might pick up a few and be wise.

LEONELO. We know less than we did when there was less knowledge, for the bulk of learning is so great no man can compass it. Confusion results from excess, all the stir goes to froth, while those who read befuddle their heads with endless pages and become literal slaves. The art of printing has raised up a thousand geniuses over night. To be sure it spreads and conserves the Holy Scriptures, that they may be known of all and endure, but this invention of Guttenberg, that famous German of Mayence, has in fact devitalized glory. Many a man of repute has proved a very fool when his books have been printed, or else suffered the mortification of having simpletons issue theirs in his name. Others have set down arrant nonsense and credited it to their enemies out of spite, to whose undoing it circulates and appals the world.

BARRILDO. I can find no words to argue with you.

LEONELO. The ignorant have the learned at their mercy.

BARRILDO. Leonelo, on every account printing is a mighty invention.

LEONELO. For centuries the world did very well without it, and to this hour it has not produced one Jerome nor a second Augustine. The men were saints.

BARRILDO. Sit down and rest, for my head is dizzy opposing you.

(JUAN ROJO *and* A Farmer *enter*.)

JUAN ROJO: There is not a dower on four of these farms if the fields continue as they are, and this may be seen on all sides, far and near, for all is one.

FARMER. What word of the Commander?

JUAN ROJO. Would Laurencia had never set foot by the river!

FARMER. I could dangle him gladly from that olive-tree, savage, unbridled and lewd!

(*The* COMMANDER *enters with* ORTUÑO *and* FLORES.)

COMMANDER. Heaven for the just!

REGIDOR. Commander!

COMMANDER. God's body, why do you stand?

ESTEBAN. Señor, where the custom is to sit, we stand.

COMMANDER. I tell you to sit down.

ESTEBAN. As honorable men we cannot do you honor, having none.

COMMANDER. Sit down while I talk with you!

ESTEBAN. Shall we discuss my hound, sir?

COMMANDER. Alcalde, these true men of mine praise the rare virtue of the animal.

ESTEBAN. The beast is swift. In God's name but he can overtake a thief or harry a coward right cruelly.

COMMANDER. I would set him on a graceful hare that these days lopes before me.

ESTEBAN. Done, if you will lead us to the hare.

COMMANDER. Oh, speaking of your daughter—

ESTEBAN. My daughter?

COMMANDER. Yes, why not? The hare.

ESTEBAN. My daughter is not your quarry.

COMMANDER. Alcalde, pray you prevail upon her.

ESTEBAN. How?

COMMANDER. She plumes herself before me. A wife, and a proud one, of a councillor who attends before me now, and listens, at my every look darts kindling glances.

ESTEBAN. She does ill. You, Señor, do ill also, speaking thus freely.

COMMANDER. Oh, what rustic virtue! Here, Flores, get him the book of *Politics*, and let him perfect himself in Aristotle.

ESTEBAN. Señor, the town would live in the reflection of your honor. There be men in Fuente Ovejuna.

LEONELO. I never read of such a tyrant.

COMMANDER. What have I said, in faith, to which you take exception, Regidor?

JUAN ROJO. You have spoken ill. Speak well, for it is not meet you level at our honor.

COMMANDER. Your honor? Good! Are we importing friars to Calatrava?

REGIDOR. There be those that be content to wear the cross, though the heart be not too pure.

COMMANDER. I do not injure you, mingling my blood with yours.

JUAN ROJO. A smirch is no hidden stain.

COMMANDER. In doing my will I accord your wives honor.

ESTEBAN. The very words spell dishonor, while your deeds pass all remedy.

COMMANDER. Obstinate dolt! Ah, better the cities where men of parts and renown wreak their will and their pleasure! There husbands give thanks when their wives sacrifice upon the altar.

ESTEBAN. They do no such service, if with this you would move us. God rules, too, in the cities, and justice is swift.

COMMANDER. Get up and get out.

ESTEBAN. We have said what you have heard.

10 COMMANDER. Out of the square straight! Let not one remain behind!

ESTEBAN. We firmly take our leave.

COMMANDER. What? In company?

FLORES. By the rood, hold your hand!

COMMANDER. These hinds would slander me, de-filing the square with lies, departing together.

ORTUÑO. Pray be patient.

COMMANDER. I marvel that I am so calm! Walk each one by himself, apart. Let no man speak till his 20 door has shut behind him!

LEONELO. Great God, can they stomach this?

ESTEBAN. My path lies this way.

(ESTEBAN, JUAN ROJO, Regidor, LEONELO *and the* Peasants *go out, leaving the* COMMANDER, FLORES *and* ORTUÑO.)

COMMANDER. What shall we do with these knaves?

ORTUÑO. Their speech offends you and you by no means hide your unwillingness to hear it.

COMMANDER. Do they compare themselves with me?

FLORES. Perversity of man.

30 COMMANDER. Shall that peasant retain my cross-bow and not be punished while I live?

FLORES. Last night we took him, as we thought, at Laurencia's door, and I gave an oaf who was his double a slash that married his two ears.

COMMANDER. Can you find no trace of that Fron-doso?

FLORES. They say he remains in these parts still.

COMMANDER. And dares remain, who has at-tempted my life?

40 FLORES. Like a silly bird or a fish, a decoy will tempt him and he will fall into the lure.

COMMANDER. That a laborer, a stripling of the soil should aim a cross-bow at a captain before whose sword Córdoba and Granada tremble! Flores, the end of the world has come!

FLORES. Blame love, for it knows no monopoly of daring.

ORTUÑO. Seeing he lived, I took it as a token of your kindly disposition.

50 COMMANDER. Ortuño, the smile is false. Dirk in hand, within these two hours would I ransack the place, but vengeance yields the rein to reason until the hour shall come. Which of you had a smile of Pascuala?

FLORES. She says she intends to marry.

COMMANDER. How far is she prepared to go?

FLORES. She will advise you anon when she can accept a favor.

COMMANDER. How of Olalla?

60 ORTUÑO. Fair words.

COMMANDER. Buxom and spirited! How far?

ORTUÑO. She says her husband has been uneasy these past days, suspicious of my messages, and of your hovering about, attended. As soon as his fears are allayed, you shall have a sign.

COMMANDER. On the honor of a knight 'tis well! These rustics have sharp eyes and commonly are evil-minded.

ORTUÑO. Evil-minded, ill-spoken and ill-favored.

70 COMMANDER. Say not so of Inés.

FLORES. Which one?

COMMANDER. Antón's wife. Aha!

FLORES. Yes, she will oblige any day. I saw her in the corral, which you can enter secretly.

COMMANDER. These easy girls we requite but poorly. Flores, may women never learn the worth of the wares they sell!

FLORES. No pain wipes out the sweetness wholly. To prevail quickly, cheats the expectation, but, as philosophers agree, women desire the men as they 80 are desired, nor can form be without substance, at which we should not complain, nor wonder.

COMMANDER. A man who is fiercely swept by love finds solace in a speedy yielding to desire, but after-ward despises the object, for the road to forgetful-ness even under the star of honor, is to hold oneself cheap before love's importuning.

(CIMBRANOS, *a soldier, enters, armed.*)

CIMBRANOS. Where is the Commander?

ORTUÑO. Behold him, if you have the faculty of sight. 90

CIMBRANOS. Oh, gallant Fernán Gómez,
Put off the rustic cap
For the morion of steel
And change the cloak
For armor!
The Master of Santiago
And the Count of Cabra,
By the title of the Castilian Queen,
Lay siege to Don Rodrigo Girón
In Ciudad Real, 100
And short his shrift unaided
Before their approaching powers,
Forfeiting the spoils so dearly won
At cost of blood of Calatrava.
Already from the battlements
Our sentinels descry
Pennons and banners,
The castles and the lions,
Quartered with the bars of Aragon.
What though the King of Portugal

Heap on Girón vain honors?
Vanquished, the Master must creep home
To Almagro, wounded,
Abandoning the city.
To horse, to horse, Señor!
At sight of you
The enemy will fly
Headlong into Castile,
Nor pause this side surrender.

10   COMMANDER. Hold and speak no more!
Stay for me.
Ortuño, sound the trumpet
Here in the square.
What soldiers
Are billeted with me?

   ORTUÑO. A troop of fifty men.

   COMMANDER. To horse every one!

   CIMBRANOS. Spur apace or Ciudad Real
Falls to the King

20   COMMANDER. That shall never be.   (*Exeunt.*)

SCENE TWO. *Open country, fields or meadow.*

(MENGO *enters with* LAURENCIA *and* PASCUALA, *running.*)

PASCUALA. Don't leave us.

MENGO. What's the matter?

LAURENCIA. Mengo, we seek the village in groups, when there's no man to go with us, for fear of the Commander.

MENGO. How can the ugly devil torment so many?

LAURENCIA. He is upon us night and day.

MENGO. Oh, would heaven send a bolt to strike him where he stands!

30   LAURENCIA. He's an unchained beast, poison, arsenic and pestilence throughout the land.

MENGO. Laurencia, they say Frondoso pointed an arrow at his breast for your sake, here in this very meadow.

LAURENCIA. Mengo, I hated all men till then, but since that day I relent. Frondoso had courage; it will cost him his life.

MENGO. He must fly these fields, that's sure.

40   LAURENCIA. I love him enough to advise it, but he'll have no counsel of me, storming and raging and turning away. The Commander swears he will hang him feet upward.

PASCUALA. I say hang the Commander.

MENGO. Stone him I say. God knows but I will up and at him with a rock I saved at the sheep-fold that will land him a crack that will crush his skull in! He's wickeder than Gabalus that old Roman.

LAURENCIA. The one that was so wicked was Heliogabalus. He was a man.

50   MENGO. Whoever he was, call him Gab or Gal,

49. **Heliogabalus,** a Roman emperor (218–222 A.D.), distinguished for his debauchery, extravagance, and cruelty.

his scurvy memory yields to this. You know history. Was there ever a man like Fernán Gómez?

PASCUALA. No, he's no man. There must be tigers in him.

(JACINTA *enters.*)

JACINTA. Help in God's name, if you are women!

LAURENCIA. Why, what's this, Jacinta?

PASCUALA. We are all your friends.

JACINTA. The Commander's men, on their way to Ciudad Real, armed with villainy when it should be steel, would seize me and take me to him.   60

LAURENCIA. God help you, Jacinta! With you, pray he be merciful, but I choose rather to die than be taken!   (*Exit.*)

PASCUALA. Jacinta, being no man I cannot save you.   (*Exit.*)

MENGO. I can because I am a man in strength and in name. Jacinta, stand beside me.

JACINTA. Are you armed?

MENGO. Twice. I have two arms.

JACINTA. You will need more.   70

MENGO. Jacinta, the ground bears stones.

(FLORES *and* ORTUÑO *enter.*)

FLORES. Did you think you could run away from us?

JACINTA. Mengo, I am dead with fear!

MENGO. Friends, these are poor peasant girls.

ORTUÑO. Do you assume to defend her?

MENGO. I do, so please you, since I am her relative and must protect her, if that may be.

FLORES. Kill him straightway!

MENGO. Strike me heaven, but I am in a rage! You   80 can put a cord around my neck but, by God, I'll sell my life dear!

(*The* COMMANDER *and* CIMBRANOS *enter.*)

COMMANDER. Who calls? What says this turd?

FLORES. The people of this town, which we should raze for there is no health in it, insult our arms.

MENGO. Señor, if pity can prevail in the face of injustice, reprove these soldiers who would force this peasant girl in your name, though spouse and parents be bred to honor, and grant me license straight   90 to lead her home unharmed.

COMMANDER. I will grant them license straight to harm you for your impudence. Let go that sling.

MENGO. Señor—

COMMANDER. Flores, Ortuño and Cimbranos, it will serve to tie his hands.

MENGO. Is this the voice of honor?

COMMANDER. What do these sheep of Fuente Ovejuna think of me?

MENGO. Señor, have I offended you, or mayhap   100 the village, in anything?

FLORES. Shall we kill him?

COMMANDER. It would soil your arms which we shall stain with redder blood.

ORTUÑO. We wait your orders, sir.

COMMANDER. Flog him without mercy. Tie him to that oak-tree, baring his back, and with the reins—

MENGO. No, no, for you are noble!

COMMANDER. Flog him till the rivets start from the straps!

MENGO. My God, can such things be?

(*They lead him off.*)

COMMANDER. Pretty peasant, draw near daintily.
10 Who would prefer a farmer to a valiant nobleman?

JACINTA. But will you heal my honor, taking me for yourself?

COMMANDER. Truly I do take you.

JACINTA. No, I have an honorable father, sir, who may not equal you in birth, but in virtue he is the first.

COMMANDER. These are troubled days nor will this rude peasantry salve my outraged spirit. Pass with me under the trees.

20 JACINTA. I?

COMMANDER. This way.

JACINTA. Look what you do!

COMMANDER. Refuse and I spurn you. You shall be the slut of the army.

JACINTA. No power of lust can overcome me.

COMMANDER. Silence and go before.

JACINTA. Pity, Señor!

COMMANDER. Pity have I none.

JACINTA. I appeal from your wickedness to God!

(*Exit the* COMMANDER, *haling her out.*)

SCENE THREE. *Room in Juan Rojo's house.*

(LAURENCIA *and* FRONDOSO *enter.*)

30 LAURENCIA. Through fields of danger
My love comes to me.

FRONDOSO. The hazard bear witness
To the love that I bear.
The Commander has vanished
O'er the brow of the hill
And I, the slave of beauty,
Lose all sense of fear,
Seeing him disappear.

LAURENCIA. Speak ill of no man.
40 To pray for his end
Postpones it, my friend.

FRONDOSO. Eternally.
And may he live a thousand years,
And every one bear joy!
I'll pray for his soul also
And may the pious litany
Bite, sear and destroy!
Laurencia, if my love
Live in your heart,
50 Let me enter there, love,

To dwell loyally.
The town counts us one,
Yet by the book we are twain.
Will you, I wonder,
Say yes,
Compulsion under?

LAURENCIA. Say for me to the town
Oh yes, yes and yes
Again and again!

FRONDOSO. I kiss your feet   60
For this new miracle of mercy.
Beauty grants me joy
In words grace conjures.

LAURENCIA. Flatter me no more,
But speak to my father
And win my uncle's praise.
Oh, speak,
Frondoso,
Oh may we marry, oh Frondoso,
It will be heaven   70
To be your wife!

FRONDOSO. In God we trust.   (*Hides himself.*)

(*Enter* ESTEBAN *and* JUAN ROJO, *Regidor.*)

ESTEBAN. His departure outraged the square, and indeed it was most unseemly behavior. Such tyranny stuns as a blow; even poor Jacinta must pay the price of his madness.

JUAN ROJO. Spain turns already to the Catholic Kings, a name by which our rulers have come to be known, and the nation renders obedience to their laws. They have appointed the Master of Santiago   80
Captain General of Ciudad Real, despatching him forthwith against Girón's oppression of the town. But my heart aches for Jacinta, being as she is an honest girl.

ESTEBAN. They beat Mengo soundly.

JUAN ROJO. I never saw dye, black or red, to rival his flesh.

ESTEBAN. Peace and no more, for my blood boils, or else congeals at his name. Have I authority or a staff of office?   90

JUAN ROJO. The man cannot control his servants.

ESTEBAN. On top of all this they chanced on Pedro Redondo's wife one day in the very bottom of the valley, and after he insulted her she was turned over to the men.

JUAN ROJO. Who is listening concealed?

FRONDOSO. I, a petitioner.

JUAN ROJO. Granted, Frondoso. Your father brought you to be, but I have brought you to be what you are, a prop and support, who is my very   100
son in the house.

FRONDOSO. Assured, Alcalde, of permission, I speak as one by birth honorable, and not obscure.

ESTEBAN. You have suffered wrong at the hand of Fernán Gómez?

FRONDOSO. More than a little.

ESTEBAN. My heart records it. The man is surely mad.

FRONDOSO. Señor, appealing to a father,
Serving a daughter,
I beg her hand
Not all a stranger.
Pardon presumption though it be extreme;
Boldly I speak for men shall count me bold.

ESTEBAN. By that word, Frondoso,
10 You renew my life,
Brushing aside
The apprehension of the years.
Now heaven be praised, my son,
For your proposal seals our honor,
Which may love guard jealously.
Apprise your father straight
Of this new promised joy,
For my consent stays
But his approbation,
20 In whose fair prospect
Beams my happiness.

JUAN ROJO. The maid must consent also.

ESTEBAN. Her consent should precede
And has preceded indeed,
Because a faithful lover
Is prophet and recorder.
I have taken an oath to bestow some right good maravedis upon a good young man.

FRONDOSO. I seek no dower. Gold, they say, makes
30 the day dull.

JUAN ROJO. So long as he does not court the wine-skins, you may dower him without stint or mercy.

ESTEBAN. I will speak to my daughter that assurance may be doubly sure.

FRONDOSO. Do, pray, for violence has no part in love.

ESTEBAN. Dearest daughter Laurencia!

LAURENCIA. Oh, father?

ESTEBAN. She approves for she answers before I
40 speak!—Dearest daughter Laurencia, step apart a moment. Frondoso, who is an honest lad, if one there be in Fuente Ovejuna, inquires of me as to your friend Gila, whom he would honor as a wife.

LAURENCIA. Gila a wife?

ESTEBAN. Is she a fitting mate, a proper wife?

LAURENCIA. Yes, father, oh she is! Of course!

ESTEBAN. Of course she is ugly, as ugly as they come, which led me to suggest, Laurencia, that Frondoso look at you.

50 LAURENCIA. Father, be serious as becomes your office.

ESTEBAN. Do you love him?

LAURENCIA. I have favored him and am myself favored. But you knew!

ESTEBAN. Shall I say yes?

LAURENCIA. Yes, father, for me.

28. maravedis, Spanish coins.

ESTEBAN. The yes will do for us both. Come, we will seek his father.

JUAN ROJO. Instantly.

ESTEBAN. My boy, to return to the dower. I can af- 60 ford, yes, and I pledge, four thousand maravedis.

FRONDOSO. Señor, I am your son now and you offend me.

ESTEBAN. A day and pride abates, lad, but if you marry without a dower, by my faith, many a day will succeed and the abatement not be mended.
(*Exeunt* ESTEBAN *and* JUAN ROJO.)

LAURENCIA. Frondoso, bliss!

FRONDOSO. Yes, triply.
In a single moment
I feel so happy 70
I could die with pleasure!
Bliss it must be
Shared among three.
I look at you and laugh,
Laugh my heart out.
Oh, what treasure
I drink in at a glance
Now love comes to me,
Laurencia!   (*Exeunt.*)

SCENE FOUR. *Ciudad Real. The walls.*

(*The* MASTER, *the* COMMANDER, FLORES *and*
ORTUÑO *enter.*)

COMMANDER. Fly, sir! There is no remedy. 80

MASTER. The wall giving way, the weight of the enemy undoes us.

COMMANDER. We have bled them and cost them many lives.

MASTER. The banner of Calatrava shall not trail among their spoils, though it were recompense turning all to glory.

COMMANDER. Our league, Girón, crumbles and lies lifeless.

MASTER. Can we outstrip fortune, though she be 90 blind, favoring us to-day, to-day to leave us?

VOICES (*within*). Hail, Victory! Hail, the Crown of Castile!

MASTER. The pennons show upon the battlements while all the windows of the towers thrust banners forth, proclaiming the victory.

COMMANDER. Much joy may they have of the day! By my soul, a day of slaughter!

MASTER. Fernán Gómez, I'll to Calatrava.

COMMANDER. And I to Fuente Ovejuna. Stay upon 100 your cousin of Portugal, or, weighing adversity, yield allegiance to the Catholic King.

MASTER. I shall apprise you with despatch.

COMMANDER. Time is a hard general.

MASTER. God grant me few years like this, fertile in undeception.   (*Exeunt.*)

SCENE FIVE. *Esteban's house in Fuente Ovejuna.*

(*Enter the wedding-train,* Musicians, MENGO, FRONDOSO, LAURENCIA, PASCUALA, BARRILDO, ESTEBAN *and* JUAN ROJO.)

MUSICIANS. Joy to the bride
And long life beside!
Long life!

MENGO. A clever boy thought that up! Oh, that boy is clever!

BARRILDO. He could troll it out at any wedding.

FRONDOSO. Mengo sings only to the lash because he says it has more tang to it.

MENGO. Yes, and I know a young chap in the val-
10 ley, not meaning you of course, who would make a nice dish for the Commander.

BARRILDO. Enough of gloom and amen, seeing that a ferocious barbarian offers at our honor.

MENGO. I believe a hundred soldiers whipped me that day, and all I had was a sling that I gave up to protect me. However, I know a man, not mentioning names, who was full of honor and pursued with a syringe loaded with dye and some herbs that caused him great pain, and oh my, the pain that they caused
20 him! How that man did suffer!

BARRILDO. By way of jest. It was done as a laugh-ing matter.

MENGO. As it came out afterwards. At the time he never laughed nor even suspected, but felt much better without the dye, though while it was in, death was preferable.

FRONDOSO. A song would be preferable, or any-thing. Come, let it be a good one, Mengo.

MENGO. Good! Do you invite me?
30 *Bride and groom*
Must dwell together.
Pray God neither one of them
Dare fight or row it.
Let both die
Just too tired out to live,
A long time after
They have forgotten all about it—
I mean the wedding.

FRONDOSO. God help the poet who made that up!
40 BARRILDO. He needs more help.

MENGO. Oh, that reminds me! Did you ever see a baker baking buns? He dips the dough into the oil until the pot is full, and then some swell up, some come out askew and twisted, leaning to the right, tumbling to the left, some scorched, some burned, some uneatable. Well, a poet's subject is his dough, he plops a verse onto the paper hoping it will turn out sweet, and his friends all tell him so, but when he tries to sell it he has to eat it himself, for the
50 world is too wise to buy or else hasn't the money.

BARRILDO. You came to the wedding so as not to give the bride and groom a chance to talk.

LAURENCIA. Uncle, you must be kissed. And you, too, Father—

JUAN ROJO. Not on the hand. May your father's hand be your protection, and Frondoso's also, in the hour of need.

ESTEBAN. Rojo, heaven protect her and her hus-band on whom I invoke an everlasting benison.

FRONDOSO. Ever to share with you.   60

JUAN ROJO. Come all now, play and sing, for they are as good as one.

MUSICIANS. *O maiden fair*
With the flowing hair,
Shun Fuente Ovejuna!
A warrior knight
Awaits thee there,
Waits the maid with the flowing hair
With the Cross of Calatrava.
Oh, hide in the shade   70
By the branches made!
Why, lovely maiden,
Why afraid?
Against desire
No wall may aid
'Gainst the Knight of Calatrava.
Thou grim knight spare
Frail beauty there
By Fuente Ovejuna!
No screen can hide,   80
No mountain bare,
No ocean bar love anywhere
'Gainst the Knight of Calatrava.
Here in the shade,
Shall love's debt be paid,
O peerless maiden,
Why afraid?
Against desire
No wall may aid
'Gainst the Knight of Calatrava.   90

(*The* COMMANDER, FLORES, ORTUÑO *and* CIMBRANOS *enter.*)

COMMANDER. Let all in the house stand still on pain of death.

JUAN ROJO. Señor, though this be no play, your command shall be obeyed. Will you sit down? Why all these arms and weapons? We question not, for you bring home victory.

FRONDOSO. I am dead unless heaven helps me.

LAURENCIA. Stand behind me, Frondoso.

COMMANDER. No, seize and bind him.

JUAN ROJO. Surrender, boy, 'tis best.   100

FRONDOSO. Do you want them to kill me?

JUAN ROJO. Why, pray?

COMMANDER. I am no man to take life unjustly, for, if I were, my soldiers would have run him through ere this, forwards or rearwards. Throw him into prison where his own father shall pronounce sentence upon him, chained in his dank cell.

PASCUALA. This is a wedding, Señor.

COMMANDER. What care I for weddings? Is this your occupation in the village?

PASCUALA. Pardon him, Señor, if he has done wrong, being who you are.

COMMANDER. Pascuala, he has done no wrong to me, but offense to the Master, Téllez Girón, whom God preserve. He has mocked his law, scoffed at his rule, and punishment must be imposed as a most dire example, or there will be those to rise against the Master, seeing that one afternoon, but shortly gone, flower of these loyal and faithful vassals, he dared take aim, pointing the cross-bow at the bosom of the High Commander.

ESTEBAN. If a father-in-law may offer a word of excuse, his dudgeon was not strange but manly, taking umbrage as a lover. You would deprive him of his wife. Small wonder the man should defend her!

COMMANDER. Alcalde, the truth is not in you.

ESTEBAN. Be just, Señor.

COMMANDER. I had no thought to deprive him of his wife, nor could so have done, he having none.

ESTEBAN. But you had the thought, which shall suffice. Henceforth enough! A King and Queen rule now in Castile whose firm decrees shall bring this rioting to cease, nor will they stay their hands, these wars once ended, nor suffer arrogance to overpower their towns and villages, crucifying the people cruelly. Upon his breast the King will place a cross, and on that royal breast it shall be the symbol, too, of honor!

COMMANDER. Death to presumption! Wrest the staff from him.

ESTEBAN. Señor, I yield it up, commanded.

COMMANDER. Beat him with it while he capers about this stable. Have at him smartly!

ESTEBAN. Still we suffer your authority. I am ready. Begin!

PASCUALA. They beat an old man?

LAURENCIA. Yes, because he is my father. Beat him, avenging yourself on me!

COMMANDER. Arrest her, and let ten soldiers guard this sinful maid! (Exeunt COMMANDER and Train.)

ESTEBAN. Justice, descend this day from heaven! (Exit.)

PASCUALA. No wedding but a shambles. (Exit.)

BARRILDO. And not a man of us said a word!

MENGO. I have had my beating already and you can still see purple enough on me to outfit a Cardinal, without the trouble of sending to Rome. Try, if you don't believe it, what a thorough job they can do.

JUAN ROJO. We must all take counsel.

MENGO. My counsel, friends, is to take nothing but forget it. I know which side I am on, though I don't say, for it's scaled like a salmon. Never again will any man get me to take it! Nor woman either.

ACT THIRD

SCENE ONE. *A room in the Town Hall at Fuente Ovejuna.*

(ESTEBAN, ALONSO and BARRILDO *enter.*)

ESTEBAN. Is the Town Board assembled?

BARRILDO. Not a person can be seen.

ESTEBAN. Bravely we face danger!

BARRILDO. All the farms had warning.

ESTEBAN. Frondoso is a prisoner in the tower and my daughter Laurencia in such plight that she is lost save for the direct interposition of heaven.

(JUAN ROJO *enters with the* Second Regidor.)

JUAN ROJO. Who complains aloud when silence is salvation? Peace, in God's name, peace!

ESTEBAN. I will shout to the clouds till they re-echo my complaints while men marvel at my silence.

(*Enter* MENGO *and Peasants.*)

MENGO. We came to attend the meeting.

ESTEBAN. Farmers of this village, an old man whose grey beard is bathed in tears, inquires what rites, what obsequies we poor peasants, assembled here, shall prepare for our ravished homes, bereft of honor? And if life be honor, how shall we fare since there breathes not one among us whom this savage has not offended? Speak! Who but has been wounded deeply, poisoned in respect? Lament now, yes, cry out! Well? If all be ill, how then say well? Well, there is work for men to do.

JUAN ROJO. The direst that can be. Since by report it is published that Castile is subject now to a King, who shall presently make his entrance into Córdoba, let us despatch two Regidors to that city to cast themselves at his feet and demand remedy.

BARRILDO. King Ferdinand is occupied with the overthrow of his enemies, who are not few, so that his commitments are warlike entirely. It were best to seek other succor.

REGIDOR. If my voice have any weight, I declare the independence of the village.

JUAN ROJO. How can that be?

MENGO. On my soul, my back tells me the Town Board will be informed as to that directly.

REGIDOR. The tree of our patience has been cut down, the ship of our joy rides storm-tossed, emptied of its treasure. They have rept the daughter from one who is Alcalde of this town in which we dwell, breaking his staff over his aged head. Could a slave be scorned more basely?

JUAN ROJO. What would you have the people do?

REGIDOR. Die or rain death on tyrants! We are many while they are few.

BARRILDO. Lift our hands against our Lord and Master?

ESTEBAN. Only the King is our master, save for

God, never these devouring beasts. If God be with us, what have we to fear?

MENGO. Gentlemen, I advise caution in the beginning and ever after. Although I represent only the very simplest laborers, who bear the most, believe me we find the bearing most unpleasant.

JUAN ROJO. If our wrongs are so great, we lose nothing with our lives. An end, then! Our homes and vineyards burn. Vengeance on the tyrants!

(*Enter* LAURENCIA, *her hair disheveled.*)

LAURENCIA. Open, for I have need of the support of men! Deeds, or I cry out to heaven! Do you know me?

ESTEBAN. Martyr of God, my daughter?

JUAN ROJO. This is Laurencia.

LAURENCIA. Yes, and so changed that, gazing, you doubt still!

ESTEBAN. My daughter!

LAURENCIA. No, no more! Not yours.

ESTEBAN. Why, light of my eyes, why, pride of the valley?

LAURENCIA. Ask not, reckon not,
Here be it known
Tyrants reign o'er us,
We are ruled by traitors,
Justice is there none.
I was not Frondoso's,
Yours to avenge me,
Father, till the night
I was yours
Though he was my husband,
You the defender
Guarding the bride.
As well might the noble pay for the jewel lost in the
     merchant's hand!
I was lost to Fernán Gómez,
Haled to his keep,
Abandoned to wolves.
A dagger at my breast
Pointed his threats,
His flatteries, insults, lies,
To overcome my chastity
Before his fierce desires.

My face is bruised and bloody in this court of honest men. Some of you are fathers, some have daughters. Do your hearts sink within you, supine and cowardly crew? You are sheep, sheep! Oh, well-named, Village of Fuente Ovejuna, the Sheep Well! Sheep, sheep, sheep! Give me iron, for senseless stones can wield none, nor images, nor pillars—jasper though they be—nor dumb living things that lack the tiger's heart that follows him who steals its young, rending the hunter limb from limb upon the very margin of the raging sea, seeking the pity of the angry waves.
But you are rabbits, farmers,
Infidels in Spain,

Your wives strut before you
With the cock upon their train!
Tuck your knitting in your belts,
Strip off your manly swords,
For, God living, I swear
That your women dare
Pluck these fearsome despots,
Beard the traitors there!
No spinning for our girls;
Heave stones and do not blench.
Can you smile, men?
Will you fight?
Caps we'll set upon you,
The shelter of a skirt,
Be heirs, boys, to our ribbons,
The gift of the maidenry,

For now the Commander will hang Frondoso from a merlon of the tower, without let or trial, as presently he will string you all, you race of half-men, for the women will leave this village, nor one remain behind! To-day the age of amazons returns, we lift our arms and strike against this villainy, and the crash of our blows shall amaze the world!

ESTEBAN. Daughter, I am no man to bear names calmly, opprobrious and vile. I will go and beard this despot, though the united spheres revolve against me.

JUAN ROJO. So will I, for all his pride and knavery.

REGIDOR. Let him be surrounded and cut off.

BARRILDO. Hang a cloth from a pike as our banner and cry "Death to Monsters!"

JUAN ROJO. What course shall we choose?

MENGO. To be at them, of course. Raise an uproar and with it the village, for every man will take an oath and be with you that to the last traitor the oppressors shall die.

ESTEBAN. Seize swords and spears, cross-bows, pikes and clubs.

MENGO. Long live the King and Queen!

ALL. Live our lords and masters!

MENGO. Death to cruel tyrants!

ALL. To cruel tyrants, death!

(*Exeunt all but* LAURENCIA.)

LAURENCIA. March on, and heaven march before you! (*At the door.*) Hello! Ho, women of this town! Draw near! Draw near for the salvation of your honor!

(PASCUALA, JACINTA *and various* Women *enter.*)

PASCUALA. Who calls us? Where are the men to-day?

LAURENCIA. Behold them down that street, marching to murder Fernán Gómez. Yes, old men, young men, and troops of eager boys, like furies run to meet him! Shall they share all the glory of this mighty day, when we women can boast wrongs that match and outstrip theirs?

JACINTA. What can we do?

LAURENCIA. Fall in behind me and we will do a deed that shall re-echo round the sphere! Jacinta, you have been most deeply wronged; lead forth a squadron of our girls.

JACINTA. You have borne no less.

LAURENCIA. Oh, Pascuala, for a flag!

PASCUALA. Tie a cloth upon this lance to flourish. We shall have our banner.

10 LAURENCIA. Stay not even for that, for now it comes to me:—Every woman her headdress! Wave, banners, wave!

PASCUALA. Name a captain and march!

LAURENCIA. We need no captain.

PASCUALA. No? Wave, banners!

LAURENCIA. When my courage is up I laugh at the Cid and pale Rodomonte! (*Exeunt.*)

SCENE TWO. *Hall in the Castle of the* COMMANDER.

(FLORES. ORTUÑO, CIMBRANOS *and the* COMMANDER *enter. Also* FRONDOSO, *his hands bound.*)

COMMANDER. And by the cord that dangles from his hands

20 Let him be hung until cut down by death.

FRONDOSO. My Lord, you shame your worth.

COMMANDER. String him up on the battlements without further word.

FRONDOSO. I had no thought, my Lord, against your life.

FLORES. What is this noise outside?

(*Noise and uproar.*)

COMMANDER. I hear voices.

FLORES. Do they threaten your justice, sire?

ORTUÑO. They are breaking down the gates.

(*Knocking and blows.*)

30 COMMANDER. The gate of my castle, the seat of the Commandery?

FLORES. The people fill the court.

JUAN ROJO (*within*). Push, smash, pull down, burn, destroy!

ORTUÑO. I like not their numbers.

COMMANDER. Shall these hinds come against me?

FLORES. Such passing fury sweeps them that all the outer doors are already beaten in!

COMMANDER. Undo this bumpkin. Frondoso, speak

40 to this Alcalde. Warn him of his peril.

FRONDOSO. Sire, what they do, remember is done in love. (*Exit.*)

MENGO (*within*). Hail, Ferdinand and Isabella, and let the last traitor die!

FLORES. Señor, in God's name you had best conceal your person.

COMMANDER. If they persevere we can hold this room, for the doors are strong. They will turn back as quickly as they came.

FLORES. When the people rise and screw their 50 courage to the point, they never stop short of rapine and blood.

COMMANDER. Behind this grating as a barricade we can defend ourselves right stoutly.

FRONDOSO (*within*). Free Fuente Ovejuna!

COMMANDER. What a leader for these swine! I will out and fall upon them.

FLORES. I marvel at your courage.

ESTEBAN. (*Entering.*) Now we meet the tyrant and his minions face to face! Death to the traitor! 60 All for Fuente Ovejuna!

(*Enter the* Peasants.)

COMMANDER. Hold, my people! Stay!

ALL. Wrongs hold not. Vengeance knows no stay!

COMMANDER. Tell your wrongs, and on the honor of a knight I'll requite them, every one.

ALL. Fuente Ovejuna! Long live Ferdinand, our King!

Death to traitors and unbelievers!

COMMANDER. Will you not hear me? I lift my voice. I am your lord and master. 70

ALL. No, our lords and masters are the Catholic Kings!

COMMANDER. Stay a little.

ALL. All for Fuente Ovejuna! Die, Fernán Gómez!

(*Exeunt after breaking through the bars.*)

(*The* Women *enter, armed.*)

LAURENCIA. Stop here and challenge fortune, no women but an army.

PASCUALA. Any that shows herself a woman by mercy, shall swallow the enemy's blood!

JACINTA. We shall spit his body on our pikes.

PASCUALA. As one we stand behind you. 80

ESTEBAN (*within*). Die, traitor though Commander!

COMMANDER. I die! O God, have pity in Thy clemency!

BARRILDO (*within*). Flores next!

MENGO. Have at him, for he landed on me with a thousand whacks.

FRONDOSO. I'll draw his soul out like a tooth!

LAURENCIA. They need us there!

PASCUALA. Let them go on! We guard the door. 90

BARRILDO (*within*). No prayers, no mercy, vermin!

LAURENCIA. Pascuala, I go with my sword drawn, not sheathed! (*Exit.*)

BARRILDO (*within*). Down with Ortuño!

FRONDOSO. Slash him across the cheek.

(FLORES *enters, fleeing, pursued by* MENGO.)

FLORES. Pity, Mengo! I was not to blame.

MENGO. To be a pimp was bad enough, but why the devil lay on me?

16–17. **the Cid and pale Rodomonte,** the bold hero of the Spanish epic and the boastful villain of Ariosto's *Orlando Furioso.*

79. **spit;** that is, thrust the pikes through his body like a spit through a roast.

PASCUALA. Mengo, give this man to the women. Stay, Stay!

MENGO. 'Fore God I will! And no punishment could be worse.

PASCUALA. Be well avenged!

MENGO. Believe me!

JACINTA. Run him through!

FLORES. What? Pity, women!

JACINTA. His courage well becomes him.

PASCUALA. So he has tears?

JACINTA. Kill him, viper of the vile!

PASCUALA. Down, wretch, and die!

FLORES. Pity, women, pity!

(ORTUÑO *enters, pursued by* LAURENCIA.)

ORTUÑO. I am not the man, I was not guilty!

LAURENCIA. In, women, and dye your conquering swords in traitor's blood. Prove all your courage!

PASCUALA. Die dealing death!

ALL. All for Fuente Ovejuna! Hail, King Ferdinand! (*Exeunt.*)

SCENE THREE. *Near Ciudad Real.*

(*Enter the* KING DON FERDINAND OF ARAGON *and* QUEEN ISABELLA OF CASTILE, *accompanied by* DON MANRIQUE, MASTER OF SANTIAGO.)

MANRIQUE. Convenient haste hard following on command,
The victory was gained at little cost,
With show of slight resistance. Eagerly
We crave a fresh assault to try our prowess.
The Count of Cabra consolidates the front
And fends a counter-stroke, keeping the field.

KING. The troops are well disposed. By our decree
He shall continue in his tents, the line
Reforming, holding the pass. An evil wind
Sweeps up from Portugal, where armed Alfonso
Levies further powers. Cabra shall remain
The head and forefront of our valor here,
Watchful as diligent, that men may see
The danger fly before the sentinel
And peace return with plenty to the land.

(*Enter* FLORES, *wounded.*)

FLORES. King Ferdinand the Catholic,
By right acclaim in Castile crowned,
In token of thy majesty
Oh hear the foulest treachery
Done yet by man from where the sun
Springs in the wakening east
To the lands of westering night!

KING. If there be warrant, speak.

FLORES. O thou great King, my wounds speak,
Admitting no delay
To close my story
With my life.
I come from Fuente Ovejuna,
Where the wretched hinds of the village
Have basely murdered their liege lord
In one general mutiny.
Perfidious folk,
They slew Fernán Gómez
As vassals moving upon slight cause,
Fixing upon him
The name of Tyrant,
Thenceforward their excuse.
They broke down his doors,
Closing their ears
To his free knightly pledge
To do each and all
Full justice,
Steeling their hearts against him,
And with unseemly rage
Tearing the cross from his breast,
Inflicting cruel wounds.
After which they cast him from a high window to the ground where he was caught on pikes and swordpoints by the women. They bore him in dead and the most revengeful pulled at his beard and hair, defacing every feature, for their fury waxed to such extremity that they sliced off his ears neatly. They beat down his scutcheon with staves and boast outright that they will set the royal arms above the portal where their lord's should be, full in the square of the village. They sacked the keep as a fallen foe's, and, exulting, raped his goods and properties. These things I saw, hidden—unhappy was my lot!—and so remained till nightfall, escaping to lay my prayer before you. Justice, Sire, that swift penalty may fall upon these offending churls! Bloodshed this day cries out to God and challenges your rigor!

KING. No violence, no cruelty so dire
Escapes the inquest of our royal eye.
I marvel greatly at this villainy,
Wherefore to-day a judge shall be despatched
To verify the tale, and punishment
Mete out unto the guilty as example.
A captain, too, shall march in his escort
Securing the sentence, for mutiny
The bolder grown, bolder the chastisement.
Look to his wounds. (*Exeunt.*)

SCENE FOUR. *The Square in Fuente Ovejuna.*

(*The* Peasants *enter, men and women, bearing the head of* FERNÁN GÓMEZ *on a pike.*)

MUSICIANS. *Hail, Ferdinand!
Isabella, hail!
Death, tyrant band!*

BARRILDO. Let's hear from Frondoso.

FRONDOSO. I've made a song and, if it's wrong,
You correct it as it goes along.
*Hail, Isabella!
'Tis plain to be seen*

Two can make one,
A King and a Queen.
When they die—
This to you, Saint Michael—
Just lift them both up to the sky.
Sweep the land clean,
O King and Queen!

LAURENCIA. See what you can do, Barrildo.

BARRILDO. Silence, then, while I get a rhyme in
10 my head.

PASCUALA. If you keep your head it will be twice
as good.

BARRILDO. *Hail to the King and Queen,*
For they are very famous!
They have won
And so they will not blame us.
May they always win,
Conquer giants
And a dwarf or two.
20 *Down with tyrants!*
And now I'm through.

MUSICIANS. *Hail, Ferdinand!*
Isabella, hail!
Death, tyrant band!

LAURENCIA. Mengo next!

FRONDOSO. Now Mengo!

MENGO. I'm a poet that is one.

PASCUALA. You're the back of the belly.

MENGO. *Oh, one Sunday morning*
30 *The rascal beat me*
From behind!
'Twas no way to treat me,
Most unkind.
How it hurt to seat me!
Glory to the Christian Kings!—
The wife must mind.

MUSICIAN. *Hail, Ferdinand!*
Isabella, hail!
Death, tyrant band!

40 ESTEBAN. You can take the head off the spear now.

MENGO. He might have been hung for his looks.
Phew!

(JUAN ROJO *enters with a shield bearing the royal
arms.*)

REGIDOR. Here come the arms!

ESTEBAN. Let all the people see.

JUAN ROJO. Where shall the arms be set?

REGIDOR. Before the town-hall, here, above the
door.

ESTEBAN. Noble escutcheon, hail!

BARRILDO. That is a coat of arms!

50 FRONDOSO. I see the light to-day, for the sun begins to shine.

ESTEBAN. Hail Castile and hail León!
Hail the bars of Aragon!
May tyrants die!
Hear, Fuente Ovejuna,

Follow counsel of the wise,
Nor hurt shall lie;
King and Queen must needs inquire
Right and wrong as they transpire,
Passing near-by. 60
Loyalty our hearts inspire.

FRONDOSO. That's a problem too. What shall our
story be?

ESTEBAN. Let us all agree to die, if it must be,
crying Fuente Ovejuna, and may no word of this
affair pass beyond that ever.

FRONDOSO. Besides it is the truth, for what was
done, Fuente Ovejuna did it, every man and woman.

ESTEBAN. Then that shall be our answer?

ALL. Yes! 70

ESTEBAN. Now I shall be the Judge and rehearse us
all in what we best had do. Mengo, put you to the
torture first.

MENGO. Am I the only candidate?

ESTEBAN. This is but talk, lad.

MENGO. All the same let's get through with it, and
quickly.

ESTEBAN. Who killed the Commander?

MENGO. Fuente Ovejuna killed him.

ESTEBAN. I'll put you to the torture. 80

MENGO. You will on your life, sir.

ESTEBAN. Confess, conscienceless hind!

MENGO. I do. What of it?

ESTEBAN. Who killed the Commander?

MENGO. Fuente Ovejuna.

ESTEBAN. Rack him again! Turn the wheel once
more.

MENGO. You oblige me.

ESTEBAN. Reduce him to carrion and let him go.

(*Enter* CUADRADO, REGIDOR.)

CUADRADO. What is this meeting? 90

FRONDOSO. Why so grave, Cuadrado?

CUADRADO. The King's Judge is here.

ESTEBAN. All to your homes, and quickly!

CUADRADO. A Captain comes with him also.

ESTEBAN. Let the devil appear! You know what
you are to say?

CUADRADO. They are going through the village prepared to take a deposition of every soul.

ESTEBAN. Have no fear.—Mengo, who killed the
Commander?

MENGO. Fuente Ovejuna. Ask me who! 100

(*Exeunt.*)

SCENE FIVE. *Almagro. A room in the Castle.*

(*The* MASTER *enters with a* Soldier.)

MASTER. Such news cannot be! To end like this?
I have a mind to run you through for your insolence.

SOLDIER. I was sent, Master, without malice.

MASTER. Can a mad handful of louts be moved to
such fury? I will take five hundred men forthwith

and burn the village, leaving no memory of those paths that were so basely trod.

SOLDIER. Master, be not so moved, for they have committed themselves to the King, whose power is not to be gainsaid lightly.

MASTER. How can they commit themselves to the King when they are vassals of Calatrava?

SOLDIER. That, Master, you will discuss with the King.

MASTER. No, for the land is his and all that it contains. I do obeisance to the Crown, and if they have submitted to the King I will subdue my rage and betake me to his presence as to a father's. My fault is grievous, in whose palliation I plead my untried years. I hang my head at this mischance of honor, but again to stumble were clear dishonor, yes, and certain death. *(Exeunt.)*

SCENE SIX. *The Square of Fuente Ovejuna.*
Before the Town Hall.

(Enter LAURENCIA.*)*

LAURENCIA. Loving, that the beloved should suffer pain
A grinding sorrow fastens on the heart,
Fearing the loved must bear alone the smart
 Care weighs the spirit down and hope lies slain.
The firm assurance, watchful to attain,
Doubting falters, and hastens to depart,
Nor is it folly in the brave to start
 And tremble, promised boon transformed to bane.
I love my husband dearly. Now I see
Harpies of Vengeance rise before my sight
 Unshapely, and my hope breathes a faint breath.
Only his good I seek. Oh, set him free
Ever with me to tremble in the night,
 Or take him from me, so you take me, death!

(Enter FRONDOSO.*)*

FRONDOSO. Linger not, Laurencia.

LAURENCIA. My dear husband, fly danger, for I am its very heart.

FRONDOSO. Are you one to reject the homage of a lover?

LAURENCIA. My love, I fear for you, and you are my constant care.

FRONDOSO. Laurencia, I am so happy that surely this moment heaven smiles upon us both.

LAURENCIA. You see what has happened to the others, and how this judge proceeds firmly, with all severity? Save yourself before it is too late. Fly and avoid the danger!

FRONDOSO. What do you expect in such an hour? Shall I disappear and leave the peril to others, besides absenting myself from your sight? No, counsel me courage, for in danger a man betrays his blood, which is as it should be, come what may. *(Cries within.)*

I hear cries. They have put a man to the torture unless my ears deceive me. Listen and be still!

(The Judge *speaks within and Voices are heard in response.)*

JUDGE. Old man, I seek only the truth. Speak!

FRONDOSO. An old man tortured?

LAURENCIA. What barbarity!

ESTEBAN. Ease me a little.

JUDGE. Ease him. Who killed Fernando?

ESTEBAN. Fuente Ovejuna.

LAURENCIA. Good, father! Glory and praise!

FRONDOSO. Praise God he had the strength!

JUDGE. Take that boy there. Speak, you pup, for you know! Who was it? He says nothing. Put on the pressure there.

BOY. Judge, Fuente Ovejuna.

JUDGE. Now by the King, carls, I'll hang you to the last man! Who killed the Commander?

FRONDOSO. They torture the child and he replies like this?

LAURENCIA. There is courage in the village.

FRONDOSO. Courage and heart.

JUDGE. Peasants, be obstinate and this instrument brings death. So prepare! Who killed the Commander?

PASCUALA. Judge, Fuente Ovejuna.

JUDGE. Have no mercy.

FRONDOSO. I cannot think, my mind is blank!

LAURENCIA. Frondoso, Pascuala will not tell them.

FRONDOSO. The very children hold their peace!

JUDGE. They thrive upon it. —More! More!

PASCUALA. Oh, God in heaven!

JUDGE. Again, and answer me! Is she deaf?

PASCUALA. I say Fuente Ovejuna.

JUDGE. Seize that plump lad, half undressed already.

LAURENCIA. It must be Mengo! Poor Mengo!

FRONDOSO. He can never hold out.

MENGO. Oh, oh, oh!

JUDGE. Let him have it.

MENGO. Oh!

JUDGE. Prod his memory.

MENGO. Oh, oh!

JUDGE. Who slew the Commander, slave?

MENGO. Oh, oh! I can't get it out! I'll tell you—

JUDGE. Loosen that hand.

FRONDOSO. We are lost!

JUDGE. Let him have it on the back!

MENGO. No, for I'll give up everything!

JUDGE. Who killed him?

MENGO. Judge, Fuente Ovejuna.

JUDGE. Have these rogues no nerves that they can laugh at pain? The most likely, too, lie by instinct. I will no more to-day. To the street!

FRONDOSO. Now God bless Mengo! I was afraid, transfixed, but that lad is a cure for fear.

*(*BARRILDO *and the* Regidor *enter with* MENGO.*)*

BARRILDO. Good, Mengo, good!

REGIDOR. You have delivered us.

BARRILDO. Mengo, bravo!

FRONDOSO. We cheer you.

MENGO. Oh, oh! Not much.

BARRILDO. Drink, my friend, and eat. Come, come!

MENGO. Oh, oh! What have you got?

BARRILDO. Sweet lemon peel.

MENGO. Oh, oh!

10 FRONDOSA. Drink, drink. Take this.

BARRILDO. He does, too.

FRONDOSO. He takes it well. Down it goes.

LAURENCIA. Give him another bite.

MENGO. Oh, oh!

BARRILDO. Drink this for me.

LAURENCIA. Swallowed without a smile.

FRONDOSO. A sound answer deserves a round drink.

REGIDOR. Another, son?

MENGO. Oh, oh! Yes, yes!

20 FRONDOSO. Drink, for you deserve it.

LAURENCIA. He collects for every pang.

FRONDOSO. Throw a coat around him or he will freeze.

BARRILDO. Have you had enough?

MENGO. No, three more. Oh, oh!

FRONDOSO. He is asking for the wine.

BARRILDO. Yes, let him drink as much as he likes for one good turn begets another. What's the matter now?

30 MENGO. It leaves a taste in my mouth. Oh, I'm catching cold!

FRONDOSO. Another drink will help. Who killed the Commander?

MENGO. Fuente Ovejuna.

(*Exeunt the* Regidor, MENGO *and* BARRILDO.)

FRONDOSO. He has earned more than they give him. Ah, love, as you are mine confess to me. Who killed the Commander?

LAURENCIA. Love, Fuente Ovejuna.

FRONDOSO. Who?

40 LAURENCIA. Don't you think you can torture me. Fuente Ovejuna.

FRONDOSO. It did? How did I get you, then?

LAURENCIA. Love, I got you.   (*Exeunt.*)

SCENE SEVEN. *The open country.*

(*Enter the* KING *and* QUEEN, *meeting.*)

ISABELLA. Meeting, Sire, we crown our fortunes gladly.

KING. In union lies a more enduring glory.
Passing to Portugal the direct path
Leads me to you.

ISABELLA. To my heart, Majesty,
50 Turning away from conquest gratefully.

KING. What news of the war in Castile?

ISABELLA. Peace succeeds and the land lies ready, expecting the plough.

KING. Now my eyes light upon a living miracle, the consummation of a queenly peace.

(*Enter* DON MANRIQUE.)

MANRIQUE. The Master of Calatrava begs audience, having journeyed to your presence from his seat.

ISABELLA. I have a mind to greet this gentleman.

MANRIQUE. Majesty, his years are few, yet they 60 have proved his valor great.   (*Exit.*)

(*Enter the* MASTER.)

MASTER. Rodrigo Téllez Girón,
Master of Calatrava,
Humbly kneels repentant
And pardon begs, foredone.
False counsels proffered one
By one seduced my heart
To deeds disloyal and rash;
Now end all as begun
When a too ready ear 70
In Fernando placed its trust,
That false and unjust knight.
Pardon, Sire, past fear!
In mercy hold me dear,
Oh grant me royal favor,
To pay in loyalty
Forever rendered here!
Upon Granada's plain
When sounds the wild alarm
My valor shall wreak harm, 80
My sword-strokes fall amain
And through that fell champaign
Dart wounds to the enemy
Till the cross of victory
Red o'er the merlons reign.
Five hundred men in steel
I shall lead to smite your foes
Upon my life and oath, or close
My eyes in death! Here I kneel,
Never to displease you more. 90

KING. Rise, Master. Having tendered your allegiance you shall be received royally.

MASTER. Every word is balm.

ISABELLA. Few speak as bravely as they fight.

MASTER. Esther has returned to earth to wed a Christian Xerxes.

(DON MANRIQUE *enters.*)

MANRIQUE. Sire, the Judge that was despatched to Fuente Ovejuna has arrived with the process to report to Your Majesty.

KING (*to the* MASTER). These aggressors, being 100 of the Commandery, fall within your province.

95–96. **Esther has returned . . . Xerxes.** The Jewish maiden became the wife of the Persian king, according to the Biblical account.

MASTER. Sire, I yield to you, else were bloody vengeance taken for the death of the Commander.

KING (*to the* QUEEN). Then the decision rests with me?

ISABELLA. I grant it willingly though the right were mine of God.

(*Enter* Judge.)

JUDGE. I journeyed to Fuente Ovejuna in prosecution of your command probing all with due diligence and care. Having verified the crime, no writ or in-¹⁰dictment has issued, inasmuch as with one accord and most singular fortitude, to all my questions as to the murderer the answer was always Fuente Ovejuna. Three hundred were put to torture, to the degree that forced them each to speak, without profit, Sire, of one word other than I have told you. Boys of ten were delivered to the rack, without yielding so much as a whisper, nor could they be moved by flattery or gold. Wherefore, this is my report, the evidence having failed; either you must ²⁰pardon the village or wipe it out to the last man. They have followed me to your feet that in your own person you may pronounce judgment.

KING. If they seek our presence, let them appear before us, every one.

(*Enter* ESTEBAN *and* ALONSO, *Alcaldes,* JUAN ROJO *and* CUADRADO, *Regidors,* LAURENCIA, FRONDOSO, MENGO *and* Peasants, *both men and women.*)

LAURENCIA. Are those the King and Queen?

FRONDOSO. The power and majesty of Castile!

LAURENCIA. How beautiful, how wonderful! Saint Antonio, bless them both!

ISABELLA. Are these the people of the village?

³⁰ESTEBAN. Majesty, Fuente Ovejuna humbly kneels at your feet in allegiance. The mad tyranny and fierce cruelty of the dead Commander, raining insults through the farms, themselves provoked his death. He ravished our homes, forced our daughters, and knew no heart nor mercy.

FRONDOSO. This simple girl, O Queen, who is mine by rite of heaven, and has brought me all happiness, which surely must be matchless, on my wedding-night, as if it had been his very own, he bore off to ⁴⁰his keep, and but that she is secure in honor, basely that night he had deflowered her.

MENGO. I know something as to that, with your permission, Queen, because you must be anxious to hear from me, seeing the bloody tanning that I got. I stood up for a girl in the village when the Commander went along the way to her undoing, the scurvy Nero, and then he took it out on me, and there never was a more thorough job at bottom. Three men paid it their attention, good pay at all ⁵⁰three, since when, if you ask the explanation, I paid more for balm and ointment, with the powder and the myrtle I applied, than I could sell my sheep-cot for.

ESTEBAN. Sire, we yield ourselves to you. You are our King, and in witness of submission we have placed your arms above our doors. Have mercy, Sire, for our excuse is our extremity, which deserves your clemency.

KING. As no indictment is set down, although the fault be grave, it shall be pardoned. Since you yield ⁶⁰yourselves to me, I further take the town under my protection, for in the Crown henceforth its charter shall abide, under such time as God in His mercy shall vouchsafe you a new Commander.

FRONDOSO. When his Majesty speaks
His voice we obey.
"Fuente Ovejuna" ends.
Friends, approve the play.

William Shakespeare

1564–1616

For an English-speaking person it is virtually impossible to say anything about Shakespeare now that has not already been said, even to excess. About a century after his death he was exalted into the first rank of English writers; and today only a habitual dissident would challenge his right to first place, for Shakespeare's catalog of created men and women is amazing in its scope, his knowledge of human beings uncanny, and his powers of expression, particularly in the dramatic field, unmatched for consistent effectiveness. In the long and distinguished course of English literature, one poet may surpass Shakespeare as a narrative writer, another as a lyric singer, another as a philosopher, another as a symbolist; yet none combines so powerfully a greater number of literary gifts in such an unforgettable medium.

Viewed against the background of world literature, Shakespeare's position is scarcely less high, for, although his range and power may sometimes remain uncomprehended by minds which are controlled by rules and objective standards, his sheer dynamic qualities are enough to inspire awe. It was not always thus, to be sure. Shakespeare was a professional man of the theater at a time when the theater depended upon royal or noble patronage, and he was willing to serve unashamedly the ends of patriotism and nationalism; he was not a man of academic learning and he was not an aristocrat. During the seventeenth century, therefore, even his English fellow countrymen considered him far too irregular and crude in style to bear the stamp of greatness. And even today one finds occasionally a disbeliever who is convinced that the great plays bearing the name of Shakespeare could never have been written by a commoner from a small provincial town, who never saw learning in one of the universities. Such narrow objections we can ignore, for it is an old rule that genius can break out anywhere, and that any man, if he be wise enough, can learn all about the world without benefit of books.

Besides, we know that there was such an individual as William Shakespeare, even if we know very little about the man's true personality. His biography must rest upon a minimum of facts and a maximum of inference and speculation. His parents in Stratford-on-Avon were solid enough citizens, but Shakespeare early contracted what we must regard as an unhappy and unfortunate marriage and may have fallen into difficulties with the local law. At any rate, he came up to London before he was thirty and in one way or another found himself a member of the theatrical profession, where he won the patronage of certain influential people at the court of Queen Elizabeth, served his apprenticeship as playwright, did some acting when the occasion arose, and finally emerged as a master playwright on his own during the early 1590's. His career as playwright and sometimes as actor continued for some twenty years and was clearly a successful one. Near the age of fifty he retired to Stratford, where he died on his fifty-second birthday, the day of St. George, the patron saint of England.

The First Folio edition of Shakespeare's plays, published in 1623, contains thirty-six dramas. Some of these he doubtless wrote in collaboration with other writers, particularly at the beginning and the end of his career. It was thus that he served his apprenticeship and learned his business. In his later years, we think, he sometimes allowed a younger playwright to work with him; it was the approved practice. It is not necessary, however, to consider such details here; it is quite sufficient to observe that the name of Shakespeare, applied to these thirty-six plays, indicates that he had a major interest in all of them, actually composing alone the great majority of them. In all the famous ones, the impress of the master is not to be mistaken. His great period, from *Romeo and Juliet* through *The Tempest*, runs from about 1596 to about 1612. During these years he also wrote a sequence of over one hundred and fifty sonnets of remarkable poetic achievement; and in the early 1590's he was responsible for two long narrative poems. *The Rape of Lucrece* and *Venus and Adonis;* but these lie outside the field of our immediate preoccupation. Taken alone, however, they would in themselves have established their author as one of the great poets of his age.

It is on his dramas, of course, that Shakespeare's position in world literature must rest. As exemplars of one of the greatest ages of dramatic writing anywhere, they brook no rivals. In substance they embrace, as Polonius in *Hamlet* puts it, "tragedy, comedy, history, pastoral, pastoral-comical, historical-pastoral, tragical-historical, tragical-comical-historical-pastoral, scene individable, or poem unlimited: Seneca cannot be too heavy, nor Plautus too light." Their multitudinous characters comprise the greatest single gallery of humanity in the annals of dramatic literature. Their thoughts and passions include all human experience; they pass from the trivial to the earthy, from the earthy to the ideal, from the pathetic to the sublime and back again. Their humor—and Shakespeare was potentially one of the world's great humorists—covers everything from low comedy or farce to the most brittle of courtly witticisms. In portraying these characteristics, Shakespeare is ever ready to exhibit his most priceless gift—the expression of this universality of life in a magnificent language which, whether ugly or beautiful, whether base or noble, is so completely inevitable as to defy either imitation or improvement.

Printed quarto editions of *Hamlet*, the most famous play in the civilized world, appeared in 1602, 1603, 1605, and 1611; and the play of course appeared in the great First Folio edition of 1623, but its composition and production probably took place sometime in 1601 or 1602. The work was based in part on an English revenge-tragedy of some dozen years earlier, most likely by Thomas Kyd; and the ultimate source of the story is the Scandinavian tale of Amlethus or Hamlet told in the chronicle of Saxo Grammaticus, a Danish cleric and scholar of about 1200. The Danish saga was known to Renaissance Europe through a French translation by Belleforest (1570).

An enormous amount of research and scholarship has been expended on the problem of the genesis of *Hamlet*, as well as on the thorny matter of the interpretation of the character of the title role. No single generally satisfactory answer is forthcoming to either of these questions. We cannot tell how much or how little Shakespeare depended upon the earlier English play (the *Ur-Hamlet*); nor, indeed, is it known precisely what was in this play beyond the theme of Hamlet's revenge upon the murderer of his father. A later German dramatic representation of the story, *Der bestrafte Brudermord* (1710), which is supposed to have been based upon an English play (probably, though only probably, the *Ur-Hamlet*), has fratricide instead as the chief motif. Since some doubt has been thrown upon Shakespeare's knowledge of French, it is uncertain to what extent he drew upon Belleforest's version. As to the interpretation of Hamlet's character, it remains to this day an intensely subjective matter; it has been now romantic, now melodramatic, now allegorical, now realistic. The problems of the genesis of the play are, after all, academic problems. But the fascination exerted upon audiences, readers, and players by the role of Hamlet, easily the most celebrated of all modern dramatic roles, has been almost from the beginning a universal matter. Of the tribe of actors it can truly be said, "they all want to play Hamlet." For, whatever else his qualities, Hamlet has always typified the man who would and who would not, the man who tries to sidestep the unpleasant aspects of life and yet knows that he cannot, who hesitates to act but who, despite "the slings and arrows of outrageous fortune," is able to act sufficiently so that the objective of his life is achieved even though he himself is lost. All this even the casual reader of Shakespeare will discern—this, and the magnificent driving dramatic poetry, which has made *Hamlet* for all English-speaking people one of the greatest source-books of quotation.

Hamlet, Prince of Denmark

DRAMATIS PERSONAE

CLAUDIUS, *king of Denmark*

HAMLET, *son to the late, and nephew to the present king*

POLONIUS, *lord chamberlain*

HORATIO, *friend to Hamlet*

LAERTES, *son to Polonius*

VOLTIMAND,
CORNELIUS,
ROSENCRANTZ,
GUILDEN-
STERN,
OSRIC,
A Gentleman } *courtiers*

A Priest

MARCELLUS }
BERNARDO } *officers*

FRANCISCO, *a soldier*

REYNALDO, *servant to Polonius*

Players

Two Clowns, *grave-diggers*

FORTINBRAS, *prince of Norway*

A Captain

English Ambassadors

GERTRUDE, *queen of Denmark, and mother to Hamlet*

OPHELIA, *daughter to Polonius*

Lords, Ladies, Officers, Soldiers, Sailors, Messengers, and other Attendants

Ghost of Hamlet's Father

SCENE: *Denmark*

ACT I

SCENE 1. *Elsinore. A platform before the castle.*

(FRANCISCO *at his post. Enter to him* BERNARDO.)

BERNARDO.

Who's there?

FRANCISCO. Nay, answer me; stand, and unfold yourself.

BERNARDO. Long live the king!

FRANCISCO. Bernardo?

BERNARDO. He.

FRANCISCO. You come most carefully upon your hour.

BERNARDO. 'Tis now struck twelve; get thee to bed, Francisco.

FRANCISCO. For this relief much thanks: 'tis bitter cold,
And I am sick at heart.

BERNARDO. Have you had quiet guard?

FRANCISCO. Not a mouse stirring.

BERNARDO. Well, good night.   11
If you do meet Horatio and Marcellus,
The rivals of my watch, bid them make haste.

FRANCISCO. I think I hear them. Stand, ho!   14
Who's there?

(*Enter* HORATIO *and* MARCELLUS.)

HORATIO. Friends to this ground.

MARCELLUS.   And liegemen to the Dane.

FRANCISCO. Give you good night.

MARCELLUS.   O, farewell, honest soldier:
Who hath relieved you?

FRANCISCO.   Bernardo has my place.
Give you good night.   (*Exit.*)

MARCELLUS.   Holla! Bernardo!

BERNARDO.   Say,
What, is Horatio there?

HORATIO.   A piece of him.

BERNARDO. Welcome, Horatio: welcome, good
Marcellus.   20

MARCELLUS. What, has this thing appeared again tonight?

BERNARDO. I have seen nothing.

MARCELLUS. Horatio says 'tis but our fantasy,
And will not let belief take hold of him
Touching this dreadful sight, twice seen of us:
Therefore I have entreated him along
With us to watch the minutes of this night;
That if again this apparition come,
He may approve our eyes and speak to it.

HORATIO. Tush, tush, 'twill not appear.

BERNARDO.   Sit down awhile;
And let us once again assail your ears,   31
That are so fortified against our story,
What we have two nights seen.

HORATIO.   Well, sit we down,
And let us hear Bernardo speak of this.

BERNARDO. Last night of all,   35
When yond same star that's westward from the pole
Had made his course to illume that part of heaven
Where now it burns, Marcellus and myself,
The bell then beating one,—

(*Enter* Ghost.)

MARCELLUS. Peace, break thee off; look, where it comes again!   40

BERNARDO. In the same figure, like the king that's dead.

Hamlet, Prince of Denmark. The text used here is that of the Globe edition of Shakespeare, with certain emendations by Hardin Craig. Note, too, that the line numbering follows that of the Globe edition. *Act I, Scene I. Stage directions: Elsinore . . . platform.* The platform is a level spot on the battlements of the castle. Elsinore, now Helsingör, was in the Middle Ages a rather important seaport of Denmark, controlling the approaches from the North Sea to the western Baltic. 2. me, emphatic. Evidently Francisco is on guardduty. 3. Long . . . king. This seems to be the pass-word.

16. Give you; that is, God give you. 19. A piece of him, a casual answer. Horatio, like Hamlet, has his moments of flippancy. 29. approve, justify, corroborate. 36. yond same star. It was customary in the Middle Ages to use the constellation of Ursa Major, the "Big Dipper," to calculate time, inasmuch as it was a prominent constellation always to be seen above the horizon in the northern hemisphere.

MARCELLUS. Thou art a scholar; speak to it, Horatio. 42

BERNARDO. Looks it not like the king? mark it, Horatio.

HORATIO. Most like; it harrows me with fear and wonder.

BERNARDO. It would be spoke to.

MARCELLUS. Question it, Horatio. 45

HORATIO. What art thou that usurp'st this time of night,
Together with that fair and warlike form
In which the majesty of buried Denmark
Did sometimes march? by Heaven, I charge thee, speak!

MARCELLUS. It is offended.

BERNARDO. See, it stalks away! 50

HORATIO. Stay! speak, speak! I charge thee, speak!
(*Exit* Ghost.)

MARCELLUS. 'Tis gone, and will not answer.

BERNARDO. How now, Horatio! you tremble and look pale:
Is not this something more than fantasy?
What think you on 't?

HORATIO. Before my God, I might not this believe
Without the sensible and true avouch
Of mine own eyes.

MARCELLUS. Is it not like the king?

HORATIO. As thou art to thyself;
Such was the very armour he had on, 60
When he the ambitious Norway combated;
So frowned he once, when, in an angry parle,
He smote the sledded Polacks on the ice.
'Tis strange.

MARCELLUS. Thus twice before, and just at this dead hour,
With martial stalk hath he gone by our watch.

HORATIO. In what particular thought to work I know not;
But in the gross and scope of my opinion,
This bodes some strange eruption to our state.

MARCELLUS. Good now, sit down, and tell me, he that knows, 70
Why this same strict and most observant watch
So nightly toils the subject of the land,
And why such daily cast of brazen cannon,
And foreign mart for implements of war;
Why such impress of shipwrights, whose sore task
Does not divide the Sunday from the week;
What might be toward, that this sweaty haste 77

Doth make the night joint-laborer with the day:
Who is't that can inform me?

HORATIO. That can I;
At least, the whisper goes so. Our last king, 80
Whose image even but now appeared to us,
Was, as you know, by Fortinbras of Norway,
Thereto pricked on by a most emulate pride,
Dared to the combat; in which our valiant Hamlet—
For so this side of our known world esteemed him—
Did slay this Fortinbras; who, by a sealed compact,
Well ratified by law and heraldry,
Did forfeit, with his life, all those his lands
Which he stood seized of, to the conqueror:
Against the which, a moiety competent 90
Was gaged by our king; which had returned
To the inheritance of Fortinbras,
Had he been vanquisher; as, by the same covenant,
And carriage of the article designed,
His fell to Hamlet. Now, sir, young Fortinbras,
Of unimproved mettle hot and full,
Hath in the skirts of Norway here and there
Sharked up a list of lawless resolutes,
For food and diet, to some enterprise
That hath a stomach in 't; which is no other— 100
As it doth well appear unto our state—
But to recover of us, by strong hand
And terms compulsatory, those foresaid lands
So by his father lost: and this, I take it,
Is the main motive of our preparations,
The source of this our watch and the chief head
Of this post-haste and romage in the land.

BERNARDO. I think it be no other but e'en so:
Well may it sort that this portentous figure
Comes armed through our watch; so like the king 110
That was and is the question of these wars.

HORATIO. A mote it is to trouble the mind's eye.
In the most high and palmy state of Rome,
A little ere the mightiest Julius fell,
The graves stood tenantless and the sheeted dead
Did squeak and gibber in the Roman streets:
As stars with trains of fire and dews of blood,
Disasters in the sun; and the moist star
Upon whose influence Neptune's empire stands
Was sick almost to doomsday with eclipse: 120
And even the like precurse of fierce events,

42. scholar. In the Middle Ages, only clerics or scholars knew Latin, a language which was necessary to exorcise any spirit of the dead. 45. It . . . spoke to. It was the general belief that no ghost would address a living person unless spoken to first. 49. sometimes, now "sometime," meaning "formerly." 57. sensible, perceived by the senses. 62. angry parle, a parley or conference which breaks up in a fight. 63. sledded Polacks, men from Poland on sledges. 68. gross and scope, general range or drift. 70. Good now, a phrase expressing entreaty or argument. 72. toils, causes labor, makes work for. 75. impress, impressment, kidnaping. 77. toward, about to happen.

83. emulate, ambitious. 87. law and heraldry, civil as well as feudal law. 89. seized, possessed, endowed. 90. moiety competent, an adequate or sufficient amount. 91. gaged, pledged. 93. covenant, joint bargain. 94. carriage, substance, import. 96. unimproved, not turned to account or use. hot and full, full of fight. 98. sharked up, collected in hit-or-miss fashion. resolutes, adventurers, desperate men. 99. food and diet, hired only by giving them sustenance, not money. 100. stomach, opportunity for courage, but with a punning reference to "food and diet" in the preceding line. 107. romage, hustle and bustle. 113. palmy state, triumphant sovereignty. 114. Julius, Julius Caesar. 117. As . . . blood. There is probably a loss of some lines between this clause and the preceding. stars . . . fire, comets. 118. Disasters, unfavorable aspects—an astrological term. moist star, the moon, governing tides—hence the reference to Neptune's empire (the sea), in l. 119.

As harbingers preceding still the fates
And prologue to the omen coming on,
Have heaven and earth together demonstrated
Unto our climatures and countrymen.—
But soft, behold! lo, where it comes again!
(*Re-enter* Ghost.)
I'll cross it, though it blast me. Stay, illusion!
If thou hast any sound, or use of voice,
Speak to me:
If there be any good thing to be done,   130
That may to thee do ease and grace to me,
Speak to me: (*Cock crows.*)
If thou art privy to thy country's fate,
Which, happily, foreknowing may avoid,
O, speak!
Or if thou hast uphoarded in thy life
Extorted treasure in the womb of earth,
For which, they say, you spirits oft walk in death,
Speak of it: stay, and speak! Stop it, Marcellus.   139
MARCELLUS. Shall I strike at it with my partisan?
HORATIO. Do, if it will not stand.
BERNARDO.   'Tis here!
HORATIO.   'Tis here!
(*Exit* Ghost.)

MARCELLUS. 'Tis gone!
We do it wrong, being so majestical,
To offer it the show of violence;
For it is, as the air, invulnerable,
And our vain blows malicious mockery.
BERNARDO. It was about to speak, when the cock
crew.
HORATIO. And then it started like a guilty thing
Upon a fearful summons. I have heard,
The cock, that is the trumpet to the morn,   150
Doth with his lofty and shrill-sounding throat
Awake the god of day; and, at his warning,
Whether in sea or fire, in earth or air,
The extravagant and erring spirit hies
To his confine; and of the truth herein
This present object made probation.
MARCELLUS. It faded on the crowing of the cock.
Some say that ever 'gainst that season comes
Wherein our Saviour's birth is celebrated,
The bird of dawning singeth all night long: 160
And then, they say, no spirit dare stir abroad;
The nights are wholesome; then no planets strike,

No fairy takes, nor witch hath power to charm,
So hallowed and so gracious is the time.
HORATIO. So I have heard and do in part believe it.
But, look, the morn, in russet mantle clad,
Walks o'er the dew of yon high eastward hill:
Break we our watch up; and by my advice,
Let us impart what we have seen tonight
Unto young Hamlet; for, upon my life,   170
This spirit, dumb to us, will speak to him.
Do you consent we shall acquaint him with it,
As needful in our loves, fitting our duty?
MARCELLUS. Let's do 't, I pray; and I this morning
know
Where we shall find him most conveniently.
(*Exeunt.*)

SCENE 2. *A room of state in the castle.*

(*Enter the* KING, QUEEN, HAMLET, POLONIUS, LA-
ERTES, VOLTIMAND, CORNELIUS, *Lords, and Attendants.*)

KING. Though yet of Hamlet our dear brother's
death
The memory be green, and that it us befitted
To bear our hearts in grief and our whole kingdom
To be contracted in one brow of woe,
Yet so far hath discretion fought with nature
That we with wisest sorrow think on him,
Together with remembrance of ourselves.
Therefore our sometime sister, now our queen,
The imperial jointress to this warlike state,
Have we, as 'twere with a defeated joy,—   10
With an auspicious and a dropping eye,
With mirth in funeral and with dirge in marriage,
In equal scale weighing delight and dole,—
Taken to wife: nor have we herein barred
Your better wisdoms, which have freely gone
With this affair along. For all, our thanks.
Now follows, that you know, young Fortinbras,
Holding a weak supposal of our worth,
Or thinking by our late dear brother's death
Our state to be disjoint and out of frame,   20
Colleagued with the dream of his advantage,
He hath not failed to pester us with message,
Importing the surrender of those lands
Lost by his father, with all bonds of law,
To our most valiant brother. So much for him.
Now for ourself and for this time of meeting:
Thus much the business is: we have here writ
To Norway, uncle of young Fortinbras,—
Who, impotent and bed-rid, scarcely hears
Of this his nephew's purpose,—to suppress   30

128–129. **If thou . . . speak.** In this passage Horatio mentions the causes for a ghost's walking, as the Elizabethan age believed them to be. Note that the manner of his address is that of an ancient charm. 134. **happily,** by chance, haply. 140. **partisan,** a long-handled spear with a blade projecting laterally. 143. **majestical,** domineering, importunate. 147. **cock crew.** It was the belief that walking ghosts always returned to their graves after the first cock-crow (about one o'clock in the morning). 154. **extravagant,** wandering abroad—the same as erring. 156. **probation,** proof, corroboration. 162. **planets strike.** Planets, particularly certain ones such as Mars, Mercury, and Saturn, were considered malignant to individuals born in an inauspicious hour, and so could bring down pestilence or mortal accidents upon those people, especially at night.

163. **takes,** charms, bewitches. 164. **gracious,** full of grace. *Act I, Scene 2.* 9. **jointress,** dowager, literally a female joiner—a legal term designating a widow who enjoys an estate settled upon her by her husband's death. 17. **that;** as often in Shakespeare, "that which." 18. **weak supposal,** low estimate. 21. **Colleagued,** added to. **dream . . . advantage,** vision of success. 23. **Importing,** referring to.

His further gait herein; in that the levies,
The lists and full proportions, are all made
Out of his subject: and we here dispatch
You, good Cornelius, and you, Voltimand,
For bearers of this greeting to old Norway;
Giving to you no further personal power
To business with the king, more than the scope
Of these delated articles allow.
Farewell, and let your haste commend your duty.

    CORNELIUS AND VOLTIMAND. In that and all things
        will we show our duty.   40

    KING. We doubt it nothing; heartily farewell.

        (*Exeunt* VOLTIMAND *and* CORNELIUS.)

And now, Laertes, what's the news with you?
You told us of some suit; what is 't, Laertes?
You cannot speak of reason to the Dane,
And lose your voice: what wouldst thou beg, Laertes,
That shall not be my offer, not thy asking?
The head is not more native to the heart,
The hand more instrumental to the mouth,
Than is the throne of Denmark to thy father.
What wouldst thou have, Laertes?

    LAERTES.   My dread lord, 50
Your leave and favor to return to France,
From whence though willingly I came to Denmark,
To show my duty in your coronation,
Yet now, I must confess, that duty done,
My thoughts and wishes bend again toward France
And bow them to your gracious leave and pardon.

    KING. Have you your father's leave? What says
        Polonius?

    POLONIUS. He hath, my lord, wrung from me my
        slow leave
By laborsome petition, and at last
Upon his will I sealed my hard consent: 60
I do beseech you, give him leave to go.

    KING. Take thy fair hour, Laertes; time be thine,
And thy best graces spend it at thy will!
But now, my cousin Hamlet, and my son,—

    HAMLET (*aside*). A little more than kin, and less
        than kind.

    KING. How is it that the clouds still hang on you?

    HAMLET. Not so, my lord; I am too much i' the
        sun.

31. **gait,** proceeding. 32. **proportions,** estimate and allocation of forces or supplies for carrying on war, logistics. 38. **delated,** expressly stated. 44. **Dane,** the Danish king. 45. **lose your voice,** speak in vain. 56. **leave and pardon,** permission to leave the country. 62. **Take . . . hour,** enjoy the opportunities and privileges of youth. 65. **A little . . . kind.** There is a play of words in this famous opening line in Hamlet's role. The general sense is, "my relation to you (kith) has become more than a normal kinship; it has become more than natural (kind)." The pun comes largely on the word "kind," which still kept some vestiges of its older meaning of "natural" but which tended to have the meaning of the word at the present time. 67. **too much i' the sun,** another equivocal phrase: "I am too much out of doors"; that is, "I am at sea"; "I am too much in the sun of your grace," definitely ironical; and "I am too much of a son to you." Obviously Hamlet is implying that he is bewildered, discontented at the turn of events, dispossessed of his heritage, and entrapped in an unnatural double relationship of stepson and nephew.

    QUEEN. Good Hamlet, cast thy nighted color off,
And let thine eye look like a friend on Denmark.
Do not for ever with thy vailed lids   70
Seek for thy noble father in the dust:
Thou know'st 'tis common: all that lives must die,
Passing through nature to eternity.

    HAMLET. Ay, madam, it is common.

    QUEEN.   If it be,
Why seems it so particular with thee?

    HAMLET. Seems, madam! nay, it is; I know not
        'seems.'
'Tis not alone my inky cloak, good mother,
Nor customary suits of solemn black,
Nor windy suspiration of forced breath,
No, nor the fruitful river in the eye,   80
Nor the dejected 'havior of the visage,
Together with all forms, moods, shapes of grief,
That can denote me truly: these indeed seem,
For they are actions that a man might play:
But I have that within which passeth show;
These but the trappings and the suits of woe.

    KING. 'Tis sweet and commendable in your nature,
        Hamlet,
To give these mourning duties to your father:
But, you must know, your father lost a father;
That father lost, lost his, and the survivor bound   90
In filial obligation for some term
To do obsequious sorrow: but to persevere
In obstinate condolement is a course
Of impious stubbornness; 'tis unmanly grief:
It shows a will most incorrect to Heaven,
A heart unfortified, a mind impatient,
An understanding simple and unschooled:
For what we know must be and is as common
As any the most vulgar thing to sense,
Why should we in our peevish opposition   100
Take it to heart? Fie! 'tis a fault to Heaven,
A fault against the dead, a fault to nature,
To reason most absurd; whose common theme
Is death of fathers, and who still hath cried,
From the first corse till he that died today,
'This must be so.' We pray you, throw to earth
This unprevailing woe, and think of us
As of a father; for let the world take note,
You are the most immediate to our throne;
And with no less nobility of love   110
Than that which dearest father bears his son,
Do I impart toward you. For your intent

68. **nighted color,** Hamlet is traditionally dressed in black, as befits a mourning son; Queen Gertrude is not. 70. **vailed,** downcast. 74. **common,** a commonplace remark; a frequent situation, and, possibly, a vulgar action on the part of the Queen, though the last meaning is probably a modern interpretation only. 79. **windy suspiration,** loud sighs. **forced breath,** produced by distress of the heart. 92. **obsequious,** dutiful, ceremonially appropriate. 93. **condolement,** sorrowing. 95. **incorrect,** untrained, uncorrected, undisciplined. 99. **vulgar thing,** common experience. 107. **unprevailing,** unavailing. 110. **nobility,** high degree. 112. **impart.** Supply "love" between "impart" and "toward."

In going back to school in Wittenberg,
It is most retrograde to our desire:
And we beseech you, bend you to remain
Here, in the cheer and comfort of our eye,
Our chiefest courtier, cousin, and our son.

QUEEN. Let not thy mother lose her prayers, Ham-
    let:
I pray thee, stay with us; go not to Wittenberg.

HAMLET. I shall in all my best obey you, madam.

KING. Why, 'tis a loving and a fair reply: 121
Be as ourself in Denmark. Madam, come;
This gentle and unforced accord of Hamlet
Sits smiling to my heart: in grace whereof,
No jocund health that Denmark drinks today,
But the great cannon to the clouds shall tell,
And the king's rouse the heavens shall bruit again,
Re-speaking earthly thunder. Come away.
    (Exeunt all but HAMLET.)

HAMLET. O, that this too too solid flesh would melt,
Thaw and resolve itself into a dew!   130
Or that the Everlasting had not fixed
His canon 'gainst self-slaughter! O God! God!
How weary, stale, flat, and unprofitable,
Seem to me all the uses of this world!
Fie on 't! ah fie! 'tis an unweeded garden,
That grows to seed; things rank and gross in nature
Possess it merely. That it should come to this!
But two months dead; nay, not so much, not two:
So excellent a king; that was, to this,
Hyperion to a satyr; so loving to my mother   140
That he might not beteem the winds of Heaven
Visit her face too roughly. Heaven and earth!
Must I remember? why, she would hang on him,
As if increase of appetite had grown
By what it fed on: and yet, within a month—
Let me not think on 't—Frailty, thy name is
    woman!—
A little month, or ere those shoes were old
With which she followed my poor father's body,
Like Niobe, all tears:—why she, even she—
O God! a beast, that wants discourse of reason,   150
Would have mourned longer—married with my
    uncle,
My father's brother, but no more like my father
Than I to Hercules: within a month:

113. **Wittenberg,** the famous university of northern Germany, founded in 1502 and later the center of German Reformation Protestantism.   115. **bend you,** incline yourself.   117. **cousin,** the usual term of courteous address by a king to the nobility of his kingdom.   127. **rouse,** draft of liquor, toast. **bruit again,** echo.   137. **merely,** completely, entirely.   140. **Hyperion,** the god of the sun in the ancient pantheon of Greek mythology (i.e., before the advent of Zeus as king of the gods). In later myth his functions were taken over by Apollo, god of the sun, divine inspiration, and beauty.   141. **beteem,** allow, permit.   149. **Niobe,** daughter of Tantalus, who boasted that she had more sons and daughters than Leto; for this Apollo and Artemis (Diana) slew all her children. Zeus later turned her into a stone. She became in classical myth a symbol of the bereaved mother much as Rachel in Matthew 2:18 is a symbol.   150. **discourse of reason,** process or faculty of reason.

Ere yet the salt of most unrighteous tears
Had left the flushing in her galled eyes,
She married. O, most wicked speed, to post
With such dexterity to incestuous sheets!
It is not nor it cannot come to good:
But break, my heart; for I must hold my tongue.
    (Enter HORATIO, MARCELLUS, and BERNARDO.)

HORATIO. Hail to your lordship!

HAMLET.   I am glad to see you well:
Horatio,—or I do forget myself.   161

HORATIO. The same, my lord, and your poor serv-
    ant ever.

HAMLET. Sir, my good friend; I'll change that
    name with you:
And what make you from Wittenberg, Horatio?
Marcellus?

MARCELLUS. My good lord—

HAMLET. I am very glad to see you. Good even, sir.
But what, in faith, make you from Wittenberg?

HORATIO. A truant disposition, good my lord.

HAMLET. I would not hear your enemy say so,   170
Nor shall you do mine ear that violence,
To make it truster of your own report
Against yourself: I know you are no truant.
But what is your affair in Elsinore?
We'll teach you to drink deep ere you depart.

HORATIO. My lord, I came to see your father's
    funeral.

HAMLET. I pray thee, do not mock me, fellow-
    student;
I think it was to see my mother's wedding.

HORATIO. Indeed, my lord, it followed hard upon.

HAMLET. Thrift, thrift, Horatio! the funeral baked
    meats   180
Did coldly furnish forth the marriage tables.
Would I had met my dearest foe in Heaven
Or ever I had seen that day, Horatio!
My father!—methinks I see my father.

HORATIO. Where, my lord?

HAMLET.   In my mind's eye, Horatio.

HORATIO. I saw him once; he was a goodly king.

HAMLET. He was a man, take him for all in all,
I shall not look upon his like again.

HORATIO. My lord, I think I saw him yesternight.

HAMLET. Saw? who?   190

HORATIO. My lord, the king your father.

HAMLET.   The king my father!

HORATIO. Season your admiration for a while
With an attent ear, till I may deliver,
Upon the witness of these gentlemen,
This marvel to you.

156. **post,** hasten.   163. **I'll . . . you,** "I will be your servant; you will be my friend."   164. **make you,** are you doing?   180. **baked meats,** meat pies; in Shakespeare's time, as always, a favorite English dish.   182. **dearest,** most respected and most cordially hated; according to some, "direst."   192. **Season your admiration,** moderate your wonder and astonishment.   193. **deliver,** reveal.

HAMLET.   For God's love, let me hear.

HORATIO. Two nights together had these gentle-
men,
Marcellus and Bernardo, on their watch,
In the dead vast and middle of the night,
Been thus encountered. A figure like your father,
Armed at point exactly, cap-a-pe,   200
Appears before them, and with solemn march
Goes slow and stately by them: thrice he walked
By their oppressed and fear-surprised eyes,
Within his truncheon's length; whilst they, distilled
Almost to jelly with the act of fear,
Stand dumb and speak not to him. This to me
In dreadful secrecy impart they did;
And I with them the third night kept the watch:
Where, as they had delivered, both in time,   209
Form of the thing, each word made true and good,
The apparition comes: I knew your father;   211
These hands are not more like.

HAMLET.   But where was this?

MARCELLUS. My lord, upon the platform where we
watched.

HAMLET. Did you not speak to it?

HORATIO.   My lord, I did;
But answer made it none: yet once methought
It lifted up it head and did address
Itself to motion, like as it would speak;
But even then the morning cock crew loud,
And at the sound it shrunk in haste away,
And vanished from our sight.

HAMLET.   'Tis very strange.   220

HORATIO. As I do live, my honored lord, 'tis true;
And we did think it writ down in our duty
To let you know of it.

HAMLET. Indeed, indeed, sirs, but this troubles me.
Hold you the watch tonight?

MARCELLUS AND BERNARDO. We do, my lord.

HAMLET. Armed, say you?

MARCELLUS AND BERNARDO. Armed, my lord.

HAMLET. From top to toe?

MARCELLUS AND BERNARDO. My lord, from head to
foot.

HAMLET. Then saw you not his face?   229

HORATIO. O, yes, my lord; he wore his beaver up.

HAMLET. What, looked he frowningly?

HORATIO. A countenance more in sorrow than
anger.   232

HAMLET. Pale or red?

HORATIO.   Nay, very pale.

HAMLET.   And fixed his eyes upon you?

HORATIO. Most constantly.

HAMLET.   I would I had been there.

HORATIO. It would have much amazed you.

HAMLET. Very like, very like. Stayed it long?

HORATIO. While one with moderate haste might tell
a hundred.

MARCELLUS AND BERNARDO. Longer, longer.

HORATIO. Not when I saw it.

HAMLET.   His beard was grizzled,—no?

HORATIO. It was, as I have seen it in his life,   241
A sable silvered.

HAMLET.   I will watch tonight;
Perchance 'twill walk again.

HORATIO.   I warrant it will.

HAMLET. If it assume my noble father's person,
I'll speak to it, though Hell itself should gape
And bid me hold my peace. I pray you all,
If you have hitherto concealed this sight,
Let it be tenable in your silence still;
And whatsoever else shall hap tonight,
Give it an understanding, but no tongue: 250
I will requite your loves. So, fare you well:
Upon the platform, 'twixt eleven and twelve,
I'll visit you.

ALL.   Our duty to your honor.

HAMLET. Your loves, as mine to you; farewell.

             (*Exeunt all but* HAMLET.)

My father's spirit in arms! all is not well;
I doubt some foul play: would the night were come!
Till then sit still, my soul: foul deeds will rise,
Though all the earth o'erwhelm them, to men's eyes.

                        (*Exit.*)

SCENE 3. *A room in Polonius's house.*

       (*Enter* LAERTES *and* OPHELIA.)

LAERTES. My necessaries are embarked: farewell;
And sister, as the winds give benefit
And convoy is assistant, do not sleep,
But let me hear from you.

OPHELIA.   Do you doubt that?

LAERTES. For Hamlet and the trifling of his favor,
Hold it a fashion and a toy in blood,
A violet in the youth of primy nature,
Forward, not permanent, sweet, not lasting,
The perfume and suppliance of a minute;
No more.

OPHELIA. No more but so?

LAERTES.   Think it no more: 10
For nature, crescent, does not grow alone
In thews and bulk, but, as this temple waxes,
The inward service of the mind and soul
Grows wide withal. Perhaps he loves you now,
And now no soil nor cautel doth besmirch

---

200. **at point exactly,** precisely according to etiquette. **cap-a-pe,** from
head to foot.   203. **oppressed,** distressed.   204. **truncheon,** officer's
staff. **distilled,** softened, weakened.   205. **act,** action, effects.   216.
it, its.   230. **beaver,** visor of the helmet.

242. **sable,** in heraldry, the color black.
Act I, Scene 3.   3. **convoy is assistant,** means of transportation are
ready.   6. **fashion,** custom, prevailing usage. **toy in blood,** a passing
amorous fancy.   7. **primy nature,** nature in the prime.   8. **Forward,**
precocious.   9. **suppliance of a minute,** diversion to while away a
minute.   11. **crescent,** growing, waxing.   12. **thews,** sinews, muscles.
temple, the body; cf. I Corinthians, 6:19: "know you not that your
body is the temple of the Holy Ghost?"   15. **soil,** blemish, defile-
ment. **cautel,** trick, deceitful manner.

The virtue of his will: but you must fear,
His greatness weighed, his will is not his own;
For he himself is subject to his birth:
He may not, as unvalued persons do,
Carve for himself; for on his choice depends   20
The safety and health of this whole state;
And therefore must his choice be circumscribed
Unto the voice and yielding of that body
Whereof he is the head. Then if he says he loves you,
It fits your wisdom so far to believe it
As he in his particular act and place
May give his saying deed; which is no further
Than the main voice of Denmark goes withal.
Then weigh what loss your honor may sustain,
If with too credent ear you list his songs,   30
Or lose your heart, or your chaste treasure open
To his unmastered importunity.
Fear it, Ophelia, fear it, my dear sister,
And keep you in the rear of your affection,
Out of the shot and danger of desire.
The chariest maid is prodigal enough,
If she unmask her beauty to the moon:
Virtue itself 'scapes not calumnious strokes:
The canker galls the infants of the spring,
Too oft before their buttons be disclosed,   40
And in the morn and liquid dew of youth
Contagious blastments are most imminent.
Be wary then; best safety lies in fear:
Youth to itself rebels, though none else near.
    OPHELIA. I shall the effect of this good lesson keep,
As watchman to my heart. But, good my brother,
Do not, as some ungracious pastors do,
Show me the steep and thorny way to Heaven;
Whiles, like a puffed and reckless libertine,
Himself the primrose path of dalliance treads,   50
And recks not his own rede.
    LAERTES.   O, fear me not.
I stay too long: but here my father comes.
                (Enter POLONIUS.)
A double blessing is a double grace;
Occasion smiles upon a second leave.
    POLONIUS. Yet here, Laertes! aboard, aboard, for
        shame!
The wind sits in the shoulder of your sail,
And you are stayed for. There; my blessing with thee!
And these few precepts in thy memory
See thou character. Give thy thoughts no tongue,

Nor any unproportioned thought his act.   60
Be thou familiar, but by no means vulgar.
Those friends thou hast, and their adoption tried,
Grapple them to thy soul with hoops of steel;
But do not dull thy palm with entertainment
Of each new-hatched, unfledged comrade. Beware
Of entrance to a quarrel, but being in,
Bear 't that the opposed may beware of thee.
Give every man thy ear, but few thy voice;
Take each man's censure, but reserve thy judgment.
Costly thy habit as thy purse can buy,   70
But not expressed in fancy; rich, not gaudy;
For the apparel oft proclaims the man,
And they in France of the best rank and station
Are of a most select and generous chief in that.
Neither a borrower nor a lender be;
For loan oft loses both itself and friend,
And borrowing dulls the edge of husbandry.
This above all: to thine own self be true,
And it must follow, as the night the day,
Thou canst not then be false to any man.   80
Farewell: my blessing season this in thee!
    LAERTES. Most humbly do I take my leave, my
        lord.
    POLONIUS. The time invites you; go; your servants
        tend.
    LAERTES. Farewell, Ophelia; and remember well
What I have said to you.
    OPHELIA.   'Tis in my memory locked,
And you yourself shall keep the key of it.
    LAERTES. Farewell.   (Exit.)
    POLONIUS. What is 't, Ophelia, he hath said to you?
    OPHELIA. So please you, something touching the
        Lord Hamlet.
    POLONIUS. Marry, well bethought: 90
'Tis told me, he hath very oft of late
Given private time to you; and you yourself
Have of your audience been most free and bounte
    ous:
If it be so, as so 'tis put on me,
And that in way of caution, I must tell you,
You do not understand yourself so clearly
As it behoves my daughter and your honor.
What is between you? Give me up the truth.
    OPHELIA. He hath, my lord, of late made many
        tenders
Of his affection to me.   100
    POLONIUS. Affection! Pooh! You speak like a green
        girl,
Unsifted in such perilous circumstance.
Do you believe his tenders, as you call them?

16. virtue . . . will, good intentions. 19. unvalued persons, persons of no social rank. 23. voice and yielding, support, approval. 27. deed, effect. 32. unmastered, unrestrained. 36. chariest, most scrupuously or painfully modest. 39. canker . . . spring, the canker-worm injures the young plants of spring. 40. buttons, buds. 41. liquid dew, dew that is fresh. 42. blastments, blights. 47. ungracious, graceless. 51. recks . . . rede, heeds not his own advice. 53. double, etc. Laertes has evidently already said good-by to his father. 54. Occasion, opportunity. 58. precepts, etc. It is in keeping with Polonius' penchant for platitudes that the maxims he gives here are age-old. Still, the expression of them is memorable. 59. character, inscribe (v.). The accent of this word came on the second syllable.

60. unproportioned, immoderate, vulgar. 61. familiar, friendly. vulgar, common, cheap. 64. dull thy palm, make thyself less sensitive. 65. unfledged, immature, untried. 69. censure, opinion, criticism. 71. expressed in fancy, fantastic in design. 74. chief, mainly, principally (adv.). 77. husbandry, thrift, economy. 81. season, mature (v.), develop. 94. put on me, impressed on me. 99. tenders, offers. 102. unsifted, untried, untested.

OPHELIA. I do not know, my lord, what I should think.

POLONIUS. Marry, I'll teach you: think yourself a baby;
That you have taken these tenders for true pay,
Which are not sterling. Tender yourself more dearly;
Or—not to crack the wind of the poor phrase,
Running it thus—you'll tender me a fool.

OPHELIA. My lord, he hath importuned me with love   110
In honorable fashion.

POLONIUS. Ay, fashion you may call it; go to, go to.

OPHELIA. And hath given countenance to his speech, my lord,
With almost all the holy vows of Heaven.

POLONIUS. Ay, springes to catch woodcocks. I do know,
When the blood burns, how prodigal the soul
Lends the tongue vows: these blazes, daughter,
Giving more light than heat, extinct in both,
Even in their promise, as it is a-making,
You must not take for fire. From this time,   120
Be somewhat scanter of your maiden presence;
Set your entreatments at a higher rate
Than a command to parley. For Lord Hamlet,
Believe so much in him, that he is young,
And with a larger tether may he walk
Than may be given you: in few, Ophelia,
Do not believe his vows; for they are brokers,
Not of that dye which their investments show,
But mere implorators of unholy suits,
Breathing like sanctified and pious bawds,   130
The better to beguile. This is for all:
I would not, in plain terms, from this time forth,
Have you so slander any moment leisure,
As to give words or talk with the Lord Hamlet.
Look to 't, I charge you; come your ways.

OPHELIA. I shall obey, my lord.   (Exeunt.)

SCENE 4. The platform.

(Enter HAMLET, HORATIO, and MARCELLUS.)

HAMLET. The air bites shrewdly; it is very cold.

HORATIO. It is a nipping and an eager air.

HAMLET. What hour now?

105. Marry, a mild oath by the Virgin Mary. 106. tenders, promises to pay, promissory notes; a pun on *tenders* in l. 99. 107. sterling, legal currency, legal tender. Tender, hold, consider. 108. crack the wind, to run until it is broken-winded. 109. tender . . . fool, show me a fool for a daughter, or possibly, deliver me an illegitimate child. The various uses of the word *tender* (ll. 99, 103, 106, 107, and 109) afford an excellent example of the Elizabethan conceit based upon the pun. 112. fashion, mere form and pretense. go to, a mild term of reproach or teasing. 115. springes, snares. woodcocks, a game-bird noted for the ease with which it can be caught, hence a symbol of stupidity and gullibility. 122. entreatments, conversations, interviews. 123. command to parley, a mere invitation to talk. 124. so much in him, this much concerning him. 126. in few, in a few words, briefly. 127. brokers, go-betweens, bawds. 128. dye, color, hue, kind. investments, clothing. 129. implorators, solicitors of. 130. Breathing, speaking low. 133. slander, debase, bring disgrace upon. Insert "of" between "moment" and "leisure."

HORATIO.   I think it lacks of twelve.

MARCELLUS.   No, it is struck.

HORATIO. Indeed? I heard it not; then it draws near the season
Wherein the spirit held his wont to walk.

(A flourish of trumpets, and ordnance shot off, within.)
What does this mean, my lord?

HAMLET. The king doth wake tonight and takes his rouse,
Keeps wassail, and the swaggering up-spring reels;
And, as he drains his draughts of Rhenish down,   10
The kettle-drum and trumpet thus bray out
The triumph of his pledge.

HORATIO.   Is it a custom?

HAMLET. Ay, marry, is 't:
But to my mind, though I am native here
And to the manner born, it is a custom
More honored in the breach than the observance.
This heavy-headed revel east and west
Makes us traduced and taxed of other nations:
They clepe us drunkards, and with swinish phrase
Soil our addition; and indeed it takes   20
From our achievements, though performed at height,
The pith and marrow of our attribute.
So, oft it chances in particular men,
That for some vicious mole of nature in them,
As, in their birth—wherein they are not guilty,
Since nature cannot choose his origin—
By the o'ergrowth of some complexion,
Oft breaking down the pales and forts of reason,
Or by some habit that too much o'erleavens
The form of plausive manners, that these men,   30
Carrying, I say, the stamp of one defect,
Being nature's livery, or fortune's star,—
Their virtues else—be they as pure as grace,
As infinite as man may undergo—
Shall in the general censure take corruption
From that particular fault: the dram of eale
Doth all the noble substance of a doubt
To his own scandal.

HORATIO.   Look, my lord, it comes!

Act I, Scene 4. 8. wake, stay awake, hold revel. rouse, drinking-bout, carouse. 9. wassail, carousal. up-spring, a wild German folk-dance which generally concluded festivities. reels, reels through. 12. triumph . . . pledge, the glory of his promised achievement. 15. to the manner born, destined by birth to be subject to the custom (manner). 18. taxed of, censured by. 19. clepe, call. with swinish phrase, by calling us swine. 20. addition, title. 22. attribute, reputation. 24. mole of nature, natural blemish. 27. complexion, the particular combination and balance of the four physical humors of medieval physiology which went to constitute a person's temperament and character. 28. pales, palings, fences, stockades of a fortification. 29. o'erleavens, makes too light. 30. plausive, pleasing. 32. nature's livery, endowment from nature. 34. undergo, bear the weight of. 36–38. dram . . . scandal. This difficult passage has had a variety of interpretations, largely because of the obscurity of "eale"; that which makes the best sense is "a dram of evil can by a (mere) doubt put to scandal all noble qualities." It is noteworthy that the entire preceding passage from ll. 17–38 inclusive was omitted from the First Folio of 1623, probably because the then Queen of England was Danish.

HAMLET. Angels and ministers of grace defend us!
Be thou a spirit of health or goblin damned,   40
Bring with thee airs from Heaven or blasts from Hell,
Be thy intents wicked or charitable,
Thou comest in such a questionable shape
That I will speak to thee: I'll call thee Hamlet,
King, father, royal Dane: O, answer me!
Let me not burst in ignorance; but tell
Why thy canonized bones, hearsed in death,
Have burst their cerements; why the sepulchre,
Wherein we saw thee quietly inurned,
Hath oped his ponderous and marble jaws,   50
To cast thee up again. What may this mean,
That thou, dead corse, again in complete steel
Revisitest thus the glimpses of the moon,
Making night hideous; and we fools of nature
So horridly to shake our disposition
With thoughts beyond the reaches of our souls?
Say, why is this? Wherefore? What should we do?
                              (Ghost *beckons* HAMLET.)
HORATIO. It beckons you to go away with it,
As if some impartment did desire
To you alone.
MARCELLUS. Look, with what courteous action   60
It waves you to a more removed ground:
But do not go with it.
HORATIO.   No, by no means.
HAMLET. It will not speak; then I will follow it.
HORATIO. Do not, my lord.
HAMLET.   Why, what should be the fear?
I do not set my life at a pin's fee;
And for my soul, what can it do to that,
Being a thing immortal as itself?
It waves me forth again; I'll follow it.
HORATIO. What if it tempt you toward the flood,
     my lord,
Or to the dreadful summit of the cliff   70
That beetles o'er his base into the sea,
And there assume some other horrible form,
Which might deprive your sovereignty of reason
And draw you into madness? think of it:
The very place puts toys of desperation,
Without more motive, into every brain
That looks so many fathoms to the sea
And hears it roar beneath.
HAMLET.   It waves me still.
Go on; I'll follow thee.   79
MARCELLUS. You shall not go, my lord.

HAMLET.   Hold off your hands.
HORATIO. Be ruled; you shall not go.
HAMLET.   My fate cries out,
And makes each petty artery in this body
As hardy as the Nemean lion's nerve.
Still am I called. Unhand me, gentlemen.
By Heaven, I'll make a ghost of him that lets me!
I say, away! Go on; I'll follow thee.
                              (*Exeunt* Ghost *and* HAMLET.)
HORATIO. He waxes desperate with imagination.
MARCELLUS. Let's follow; 'tis not fit thus to obey
     him.
HORATIO. Have after. To what issue will this come?
MARCELLUS. Something is rotten in the state of
     Denmark.   90
HORATIO. Heaven will direct it.
MARCELLUS.   Nay, let's follow him.
                              (*Exeunt.*)

SCENE 5. *Another part of the platform.*

(*Enter* Ghost *and* HAMLET.)
HAMLET. Where wilt thou lead me? Speak; I'll go
     no further.
GHOST. Mark me.
HAMLET.   I will.
GHOST.   My hour is almost come,
When I to sulphurous and tormenting flames
Must render up myself.
HAMLET.   Alas, poor ghost!
GHOST. Pity me not, but lend thy serious hearing
To what I shall unfold.
HAMLET.   Speak; I am bound to hear.
GHOST. So art thou to revenge, when thou shalt
     hear.
HAMLET. What?
GHOST.   I am thy father's spirit,
Doomed for a certain term to walk the night,   10
And for the day confined to fast in fires,
Till the foul crimes done in my days of nature
Are burnt and purged away. But that I am forbid
To tell the secrets of my prison-house,
I could a tale unfold whose lightest word
Would harrow up thy soul, freeze thy young blood,
Make thy two eyes, like stars, start from their
     spheres,
Thy knotted and combined locks to part
And each particular hair to stand on end,

---

39. **ministers of grace,** messengers bearing the grace (of God). 43. **questionable,** calling for questions and conversation. 47. **canonized,** buried according to the canons and sacraments of the Church. 48. **cerements,** grave-clothes. 53. **glimpses of the moon,** that which the moon sees by night—the earth. 54. **fools of nature,** persons limited in intelligence or perception by nature. 59. **impartment,** communication. 61. **removed,** remote. 65. **fee,** value. 73. **deprive . . . reason.** It was believed that evil spirits, masquerading as the ghost of a loved one, could often produce madness in a human being by luring him to some kind of physical or mental destruction. 75. **toys of desperation,** freakish notions of madness and suicide.

83. **Nemean lion,** one of the monsters slain by the Greek hero Hercules as one of his famous Twelve Labors. **nerve,** sinew, tendon. Arteries, in medieval physiology, were supposed to carry the spirits (animal, vital, and natural) to the appropriate parts of the body. Hamlet is saying that his arteries are tensed as powerfully as the sinews of the fabulous lion. 85. **lets,** hinders. 89. **issue,** outcome. 91. **it,** the outcome.
Act I, Scene 5. 11. **fast,** to do without food, of course; but it is likely that the word was used in Shakespeare's time to denote any kind of penance. 17. **spheres,** orbits, orbs. 18. **knotted,** intricately arranged, a reference to the Elizabethan lord's elaborate coiffure.

Like quills upon the fretful porpentine: 20
But this eternal blazon must not be
To ears of flesh and blood. List, list, O, list!
If thou didst ever thy dear father love—
    HAMLET. O God!
    GHOST. Revenge his foul and most unnatural mur-
        der.
    HAMLET. Murder!
    GHOST. Murder most foul, as in the best it is;
But this most foul, strange and unnatural.
    HAMLET. Haste me to know 't, that I, with wings as
        swift
As meditation or the thoughts of love, 30
May sweep to my revenge.
    GHOST.   I find thee apt;
And duller shouldst thou be than the fat weed
That roots itself with ease on Lethe wharf,
Wouldst thou not stir in this. Now, Hamlet, hear:
'Tis given out that, sleeping in my orchard,
A serpent stung me; so the whole ear of Denmark
Is by a forged process of my death
Rankly abused: but know, thou noble youth,
The serpent that did sting thy father's life
Now wears his crown.
    HAMLET.   O my prophetic soul! 40
My uncle!
    GHOST. Ay, that incestuous, that adulterate beast,
With witchcraft of his wit, with traitorous gifts,—
O wicked wit and gifts, that have the power
So to seduce! won to his shameful lust
The will of my most seeming-virtuous queen:
O Hamlet, what a falling-off was there!
From me, whose love was of that dignity
That it went hand in hand even with the vow
I made to her in marriage, and to decline 50
Upon a wretch whose natural gifts were poor
To those of mine!
But virtue, as it never will be moved,
Though lewdness court it in a shape of Heaven,
So lust, though to a radiant angel linked,
Will sate itself in a celestial bed,
And prey on garbage.
But, soft! methinks I scent the morning air;
Brief let me be. Sleeping within my orchard,
My custom always of the afternoon, 60
Upon my secure hour thy uncle stole,
With juice of cursed hebenon in a vial,
And in the porches of my ears did pour
The leperous distilment; whose effect

Holds such an enmity with blood of man
That swift as quicksilver it courses through
The natural gates and alleys of the body,
And with a sudden vigor it doth posset
And curd, like eager droppings into milk,
The thin and wholesome blood: so did it mine: 70
And a most instant tetter barked about,
Most lazar-like, with vile and loathsome crust,
All my smooth body.
Thus was I, sleeping, by a brother's hand
Of life, of crown, of queen, at once dispatched:
Cut off even in the blossoms of my sin,
Unhouseled, disappointed, unaneled,
No reckoning made, but sent to my account
With all my imperfections on my head:
O, horrible! O, horrible! most horrible! 80
If thou hast nature in thee, bear it not;
Let not the royal bed of Denmark be
A couch for luxury and damned incest.
But, howsoever thou pursuest this act,
Taint not thy mind, nor let thy soul contrive
Against thy mother aught: leave her to Heaven
And to those thorns that in her bosom lodge,
To prick and sting her. Fare thee well at once!
The glow-worm shows the matin to be near,
And 'gins to pale his uneffectual fire: 90
Adieu, adieu! Hamlet, remember me.   (*Exit.*)
    HAMLET. O all you host of Heaven! O earth! what
        else?
And shall I couple Hell? O, fie! Hold, hold, my heart;
And you, my sinews, grow not instant old,
But bear me stiffly up. Remember thee!
Ay, thou poor ghost, while memory holds a seat
In this distracted globe. Remember thee!
Yea, from the table of my memory
I'll wipe away all trivial fond records,
All saws of books, all forms, all pressures past, 100
That youth and observation copied there;
And thy commandment all alone shall live
Within the book and volume of my brain,
Unmixed with baser matter: yes, by Heaven!
O most pernicious woman!
O villain, villain, smiling, damned villain!
My tables,—meet it is I set it down,
That one may smile, and smile, and be a villain;
At least I'm sure it may be so in Denmark:
                      (*Writing.*)
So, uncle, there you are. Now to my word; 110

20. **porpentine**, porcupine. 21. **eternal blazon**, revelation of the hereafter, proclamation of eternity. 25. **unnatural murder**, referring to fratricide. 32. **fat weed**, probably foul weeds that grow along rotting wharves or piles of wood, possibly the asphodel plant. 33. **Lethe wharf**, the bank of the River Lethe, which, in classical mythology, was the river of forgetfulness in the realms of Hades, abode of the dead. 37. **process**, official report. 38. **abused**, deceived. 42. **adulterate**, adulterous. 61. **secure**, unsuspecting, confident. 62. **hebenon**, probably henbane, possibly hemlock or yew-sap. 64. **leperous**, producing leprosy.

68. **posset**, curdle, coagulate. 69. **eager**, sour, acid, bitter; compare the French *aigre*. 71. **tetter barked about**, a weeping eruption encased. *Bark* is a transitive verb. 72. **lazar-like**, leper-like. 77. **Unhouseled . . . unaneled**, without having received the Eucharist, without equipment for my last journey (disappointed), and without having received extreme unction. 83. **luxury**, lechery, lust. 85. **Taint . . . mind**, do not degrade thy character, do nothing unnatural in pursuit of your revenge. 89. **matin**, daybreak. 90. **uneffectual fire**, the cold light of morning. 93. **couple**, add. 97. **distracted globe**, confused head, bewildered brain. 98. **table**, writing-tablet. 100. **saws**, sayings. **pressures**, impressions stamped. 110. **word**, watchword.

It is 'Adieu, adieu! remember me.'
I have sworn 't.
MARCELLUS AND HORATIO (*within*). My Lord, my lord,—
MARCELLUS (*within*). Lord Hamlet,—
HORATIO (*within*). Heaven secure him!
HAMLET. So be it!
HORATIO (*within*). Hillo, ho, ho, my lord!
HAMLET. Hillo, ho, ho, boy! come, bird, come.
(*Enter* HORATIO *and* MARCELLUS.)
MARCELLUS. How is 't, my noble lord?
HORATIO. What news, my lord?
HAMLET. O, wonderful!
HORATIO. Good my lord, tell it.
HAMLET. No; you'll reveal it.
HORATIO. Not I, my lord, by Heaven.
MARCELLUS. Nor I, my lord. 120
HAMLET. How say you, then; would heart of man once think it?
But you'll be secret?
HORATIO AND MARCELLUS. Ay, by Heaven, my lord.
HAMLET. There's never a villain dwelling in all Denmark
But he's an arrant knave.
HORATIO. There needs no ghost, my lord, come from the grave 125
To tell us this.
HAMLET. Why, right; you are i' the right;
And so, without more circumstance at all,
I hold it fit that we shake hands and part:
You, as your business and desire shall point you;
For every man has business and desire, 130
Such as it is; and for mine own poor part,
Look you, I'll go pray.
HORATIO. These are but wild and whirling words, my lord.
HAMLET. I'm sorry they offend you, heartily;
Yes, 'faith, heartily.
HORATIO. There's no offence, my lord.
HAMLET. Yes, by Saint Patrick, but there is, Horatio,
And much offence, too. Touching this vision here,
It is an honest ghost, that let me tell you:
For your desire to know what is between us,
O'ermaster 't as you may. And now, good friends, 140
As you are friends, scholars and soldiers,
Give me one poor request.
HORATIO. What is 't, my lord? we will.
HAMLET. Never make known what you have seen tonight.

MARCELLUS AND HORATIO. My lord, we will not.
HAMLET. Nay, but swear 't.
HORATIO. In faith, My lord, not I.
MARCELLUS. Nor I, my lord, in faith.
HAMLET. Upon my sword.
MARCELLUS. We have sworn, my lord, already.
HAMLET. Indeed, upon my sword, indeed.
GHOST (*beneath*). Swear.
HAMLET. Ah, ha, boy! say'st thou so? art thou there, truepenny? 150
Come on—you hear this fellow in the cellarage—
Consent to swear.
HORATIO. Propose the oath, my lord.
HAMLET. Never to speak of this that you have seen,
Swear by my sword.
GHOST (*beneath*). Swear.
HAMLET. Hic et ubique? then we'll shift our ground.
Come hither, gentlemen,
And lay your hands again upon my sword:
Never to speak of this that you have heard,
Swear by my sword. 160
GHOST (*beneath*). Swear.
HAMLET. Well said, old mole! canst work i' the earth so fast?
A worthy pioner! Once more remove, good friends.
HORATIO. O day and night, but this is wondrous strange!
HAMLET. And therefore as a stranger give it welcome.
There are more things in heaven and earth, Horatio,
Than are dreamt of in your philosophy.
But come;
Here, as before, never, so help you mercy,
How strange or odd soe'er I bear myself, 170
As I perchance hereafter shall think meet
To put an antic disposition on,
That you, at such times seeing me, never shall
With arms encumbered thus, or this headshake,
Or by pronouncing of some doubtful phrase,
As 'Well, well, we know,' or 'We could, an if we would,'
Or 'If we list to speak,' or 'There be, an if they might,'
Or such ambiguous giving out, to note

114. **Hillo, ho, ho!** The falconer's call to his falcon, to bring it back to his wrist. 124. **arrant,** thoroughgoing. 127. **more circumstance,** more beating about the bush. 136. **Saint Patrick.** In early Christian tradition, St. Patrick of Ireland was keeper of Purgatory and patron saint of all errors and confusion. 138. **honest,** real, true.

147. **sword.** In making such an oath, the swearer was to hold the sword upright (point down), so that the blade and the hilt would form an image of the Cross. 150. **truepenny,** a colloquial word meaning "good fellow," "good old man," or something of the sort. 156. **Hic et ubique,** here, there, and everywhere. 163. **pioner,** a military digger, miner, or sapper. 172. **put . . . disposition,** assume a fantastic manner. This passage indicates clearly that Hamlet's madness is feigned. 174. **encumbered,** folded, intertwined. 176. **an if,** if. 178. **giving out,** utterance, expression of information. **note,** indicate, show.

That you know aught of me: this not to do,
So grace and mercy at your most need help you,   180
Swear.

GHOST (*beneath*). Swear.

HAMLET. Rest, rest, perturbed spirit! (*They
swear*). So, gentlemen,
With all my love I do commend me to you:
And what so poor a man as Hamlet is
May do, to express his love and friending to you,
God willing, shall not lack. Let us go in together;
And still your fingers on your lips, I pray.
The time is out of joint: O cursed spite,
That ever I was born to set it right!   190
Nay, come, let's go together.   (*Exeunt.*)

ACT II

SCENE 1. *A room in Polonius's house.*

(*Enter* POLONIUS *and* REYNALDO.)

POLONIUS. Give him this money and these notes,
Reynaldo.

REYNALDO. I will, my lord.

POLONIUS. You shall do marvellous wisely, good
Reynaldo,
Before you visit him, to make inquire
Of his behavior.

REYNALDO.   My lord, I did intend it.

POLONIUS. Marry, well said; very well said. Look
you, sir,
Inquire me first what Danskers are in Paris;
And how, and who, what means, and where they
keep,
What company, at what expense; and finding
By this encompassment and drift of question   10
That they do know my son, come you more nearer
Than your particular demands will touch it:
Take you, as 'twere, some distant knowledge of him;
As thus, 'I know his father and his friends,
And in part him;' do you mark this, Reynaldo?

REYNALDO. Ay, very well, my lord.

POLONIUS. 'And in part him; but', you may say,
'not well:
But, if 't be he I mean, he's very wild;
Addicted so and so:' and there put on him
What forgeries you please; marry, none so rank   20
As may dishonor him; take heed of that;
But, sir, such wanton, wild and usual slips

As are companions noted and most known
To youth and liberty.

REYNALDO.   As gaming, my lord.

POLONIUS. Ay, or drinking, fencing, swearing,
quarrelling,
Drabbing; you may go so far.

REYNALDO. My lord, that would dishonor him.

POLONIUS. 'Faith, no; as you may season it in the
charge.
You must not put another scandal on him,
That he is open to incontinency;   30
That's not my meaning; but breathe his faults so
quaintly
That they may seem the taints of liberty,
The flash and outbreak of a fiery mind,
A savageness in unreclaimed blood,
Of general assault.

REYNALDO.   But, my good lord,—

POLONIUS. Wherefore should you do this?

REYNALDO.   Ay, my lord.
I would know that.

POLONIUS.   Marry, sir, here's my drift;
And, I believe, it is a fetch of wit:
You laying these slight sullies on my son,
As 'twere a thing a little soiled i' the working,   40
Mark you,
Your party in converse, him you would sound,
Having ever seen in the prenominate crimes
The youth you breathe of guilty, be assured
He closes with you in this consequence;
'Good sir,' or so, or 'friend,' or 'gentleman,'
According to the phrase or the addition
Of man and country.

REYNALDO.   Very good, my lord.

POLONIUS. And then, sir, does he this—he does—
what was I about to say? By the mass, I was
about to say something; where did I leave?   51

REYNALDO. At 'closes in the consequence,' at 'friend
or so,' and 'gentleman.'

POLONIUS. At 'closes in the consequence,' ay,
marry;
He closes thus: 'I know the gentleman;
I saw him yesterday, or t'other day,
Or then, or then; with such, or such; and, as you say,
There was a' gaming; there o'ertook in 's rouse;
There falling out at tennis:' or perchance,
'I saw him enter such a house of sale,'   60

---

186. **friending,** friendliness.
Act II, Scene 1. 7. **me,** this so-called "ethical dative," common in Elizabethan English, is to be disregarded in reading. **Danskers,** Danes; but the true meaning is "inhabitants of Dantzig." 8. **keep,** dwell, live. 10. **encompassment,** round-about talking, circumlocution. **drift,** direction, course, trend. 11–12. **come . . . it,** cease direct questioning and come nearer to the facts by assuming an imperfect knowledge of Laertes. 13. **Take,** assume, pretend. 19. **put on,** impute to, ascribe to. 20. **forgeries,** fictions, invented tales. **rank,** excessive. 22. **wanton,** unrestrained, unlicensed.

25. **fencing,** an allusion to the bad reputation of professional fencers and schools of fencing in Elizabethan times. 26. **Drabbing,** whoring, frequenting brothels. 30. **incontinency,** unchastity, sexual unrestraint. 31. **quaintly,** delicately, subtly. 32. **taints of liberty,** defects arising from freedom. 34. **unreclaimed,** tamed. 35. **general assault,** a tendency that attacks all untrained youth. 38. **fetch of wit,** clever trick. 43. **ever,** at any time. **prenominate,** afore-mentioned. 45. **closes . . . consequence,** agrees with you in this conclusion. 47. **addition,** title. 49–51. **And then, sir . . . leave.** Polonius' mind begins to wander at this point, and so Shakespeare reverts to prose. 58. **o'ertook in 's rouse,** overcome by his drinking.

Videlicet, a brothel, or so forth.
See you now;
Your bait of falsehood takes this carp of truth:
And thus do we of wisdom and of reach,
With windlasses and with assays of bias,
By indirections find directions out:
So by my former lecture and advice,
Shall you my son. You have me, have you not?

REYNALDO. My lord, I have.

POLONIUS.   God be wi' you; fare
  you well.

REYNALDO. Good my lord!   70

POLONIUS. Observe his inclination in yourself.

REYNALDO. I shall, my lord.

POLONIUS. And let him ply his music.

REYNALDO.   Well, my lord.

POLONIUS. Farewell!   (*Exit* REYNALDO.)
            (*Enter* OPHELIA.)
                                How now, Ophelia! What's
  the matter?

OPHELIA. O, my lord, my lord, I have been so affrighted!

POLONIUS. With what, i' the name of God?

OPHELIA. My lord, as I was sewing in my closet,
Lord Hamlet, with his doublet all unbraced,
No hat upon his head; his stockings fouled,
Ungartered, and down-gyved to his ancle;   80
Pale as his shirt; his knees knocking each other;
And with a look so piteous in purport
As if he had been loosed out of Hell
To speak of horrors,—he comes before me.

POLONIUS. Mad for thy love?

OPHELIA.   My lord, I do not know;
But truly I do fear it.

POLONIUS.   What said he?

OPHELIA. He took me by the wrist and held me
  hard;
Then goes he to the length of all his arm;
And, with his other hand thus o'er his brow,
He falls to such perusal of my face   90
As he would draw it. Long stayed he so;
At last, a little shaking of mine arm
And thrice his head thus waving up and down,
He raised a sigh so piteous and profound
As it did seem to shatter all his bulk
And end his being: that done, he lets me go;
And, with his head over his shoulder turned,
He seemed to find his way without his eyes;

For out of doors he went without their helps,
And, to the last, bended their light on me.   100

POLONIUS. Come, go with me: I will go seek the
  king.
This is the very ecstasy of love,
Whose violent property fordoes itself
And leads the will to desperate undertakings
As oft as any passion under Heaven
That does afflict our natures. I am sorry.
What, have you given him any hard words of late?

OPHELIA. No, my good lord, but, as you did com-
  mand,
I did repel his letters and denied
His access to me.

POLONIUS.   That hath made him mad.   110
I am sorry that with better heed and judgment
I had not quoted him: I feared he did but trifle,
And meant to wreck thee; but, beshrew my jealousy!
By Heaven, it is as proper to our age
To cast beyond ourselves in our opinions
As it is common for the younger sort
To lack discretion. Come, go we to the king;
This must be known; which, being kept close, might
  move
More grief to hide than hate to utter love. (*Exeunt.*)

SCENE 2. *A room in the castle.*

(*Enter* KING, QUEEN, ROSENCRANTZ, GUILDENSTERN,
and Attendants.)

KING. Welcome, dear Rosencrantz and Guilden-
  stern!
Moreover that we much did long to see you,
The need we have to use you did provoke
Our hasty sending. Something have you heard
Of Hamlet's transformation; so call it,
Sith nor the exterior nor the inward man
Resembles that it was. What it should be,
More than his father's death, that thus hath put him
So much from the understanding of himself,
I cannot dream of: I entreat you both,   10
That, being of so young days brought up with him,
And sith so neighbored to his youth and havior,
That you vouchsafe your rest here in our court
Some little time: so by your companies
To draw him on to pleasures, and to gather,
So much as from occasion you may glean,
Whether aught, to us unknown, afflicts him thus,
That, opened, lies within our remedy.

---

61. Videlicet, namely. 64. reach, capacity, range, ability. 65.
windlasses, round-about paths. assays of bias, attempts resembling
the course of a ball in the old game of bowls. These balls were
weighted on one side and therefore did not travel in a straight line,
but rather on the bias. 66. indirections, devious courses. directions,
straight courses, therefore the truth. 67. lecture, warning, instruction. 68. have me, understand me. 71. Observe . . . yourself, test
his conduct by studying your own. 77. closet, private room or
apartment. 78. doublet, close-fitting coat. unbraced, unfastened.
80. down-gyved, fallen to the ankles, where they seem like gyves or
fetters. 95. bulk, body.

102. ecstasy, the kind of madness arising from a domination by love,
amounting to one's being beside oneself. 103. property, nature,
quality. fordoes, destroys, ruins. 113. beshrew my jealousy, curse
my officious suspicions! 115. cast beyond, overshoot, miscalculate.
118–119. might . . . love, this might cause more grief to others by
hiding the knowledge of Hamlet's love for Ophelia than hatred to
Polonius and his family by revealing it.
Act II, Scene 2. 6. Sith, since. 11. of so young . . . him, from
such early youth. 13. vouchsafe your rest, please to remain.

QUEEN. Good gentlemen, he hath much talked of
you;
And sure I am two men there are not living   20
To whom he more adheres. If it will please you
To show us so much gentry and good will
As to expend your time with us awhile,
For the supply and profit of our hope,
Your visitation shall receive such thanks
As fits a king's remembrance.
    ROSENCRANTZ.   Both your majesties
Might, by the sovereign power you have of us,
Put your dread pleasures more into command
Than to entreaty.
    GUILDENSTERN. But we both obey,
And here give up ourselves, in the full bent   30
To lay our service freely at your feet,
To be commanded.
    KING. Thanks, Rosencrantz and gentle Guilden-
stern.
    QUEEN. Thanks, Guildenstern and gentle Rosen-
crantz:
And I beseech you instantly to visit
My too much changed son. Go, some of you,
And bring these gentlemen where Hamlet is.
    GUILDENSTERN. Heavens make our presence and
our practices
Pleasant and helpful to him!
    QUEEN.   Ay, amen!
    (*Exeunt* ROSENCRANTZ, GUILDENSTERN, *and
some* Attendants.)
    (*Enter* POLONIUS)
    POLONIUS. The ambassadors from Norway, my
good lord,   40
Are joyfully returned.
    KING. Thou still hast been the father of good news.
    POLONIUS. Have I, my lord? I assure my good liege,
I hold my duty, as I hold my soul,
Both to my God and to my gracious king:
And I do think, or else this brain of mine
Hunts not the trail of policy so sure
As it hath used to do, that I have found
The very cause of Hamlet's lunacy.
    KING. O speak of that; that do I long to hear.   50
    POLONIUS. Give first admittance to the ambassa-
dors;
My news shall be the fruit of that great feast.
    KING. Thyself do grace to them, and bring them in.
    (*Exit* POLONIUS.)
He tells me, my dear Gertrude, he hath found
The head and source of all your son's distemper.
    QUEEN. I doubt it is no other but the main;
His father's death, and our o'erhasty marriage.
    KING. Well, we shall sift him.

    (*Re-enter* POLONIUS, *with* VOLTIMAND
and CORNELIUS.)
                 Welcome, my good friends!
Say, Voltimand, what from our brother Norway?
    VOLTIMAND. Most fair return of greetings and de-
sires.   60
Upon our first, he sent out to suppress
His nephew's levies; which to him appeared
To be a preparation 'gainst the Polack;
But, better looked into, he truly found
It was against your highness: whereat grieved,
That so his sickness, age, and impotence
Was falsely borne in hand, sends out arrests
On Fortinbras; which he, in brief, obeys;
Receives rebuke from Norway, and in fine
Makes vow before his uncle never more   70
To give the assay of arms against your majesty.
Whereon old Norway, overcome with joy,
Gives him three thousand crowns in annual fee,
And his commission to employ those soldiers,
So levied as before, against the Polack:
With an entreaty, herein further shown,
    (*Giving a paper,*)
That it might please you to give quiet pass
Through your dominions for this enterprise,
On such regards of safety and allowance
As therein are set down.
    KING.   It likes us well;   80
And at our more considered time we'll read,
Answer, and think upon this business.
Meantime we thank you for your well-took labor;
Go to your rest; at night we'll feast together:
Most welcome home!
    (*Exeunt* VOLTIMAND *and* CORNELIUS.)
    POLONIUS.   This business is well ended.
My liege, and madam, to expostulate
What majesty should be, what duty is,
Why day is day, night night, and time is time,
Were nothing but to waste night, day, and time.
Therefore, since brevity is the soul of wit,   90
And tediousness the limbs and outward flourishes,
I will be brief; your noble son is mad:
Mad call I it; for, to define true madness,
What is 't but to be nothing else but mad?
But let that go.
    QUEEN.   More matter, with less art.
    POLONIUS. Madam, I swear I use no art at all.
That he is mad, 'tis true: 'tis true 'tis pity;
And pity 'tis 'tis true: a foolish figure;
But farewell it, for I will use no art.
Mad let us grant him, then: and now remains   100
That we find out the cause of this effect,

---

22. **gentry,** courtesy. 24. **supply and profit,** aid and successful outcome. 30. **in the full bent,** to the utmost of our abilities. 47.
policy, conduct of public affairs. 56. **main,** chief point, chief concern.

67. **borne in hand,** led on, deluded. 69. **in fine,** finally. 71. **assay,**
trial. 79. **safety and allowance,** pledges of safety to the country and
terms of permission for the troops to pass through. 81. **considered,**
suitable. 90. **wit,** good sense and judgment. 91. **flourishes,** showy
ornament. 98. **figure,** figure of speech.

Or rather say, the cause of this defect,
For this effect defective comes by cause:
Thus it remains, and the remainder thus.
Perpend.
I have a daughter—have while she is mine—
Who, in her duty and obedience, mark,
Hath given me this: now gather, and surmise.   109
                                    (*Reads.*)
'To the celestial and my soul's idol, the most beauti-
fied Ophelia,'—That's an ill phrase, a vile phrase;
'beautified' is a vile phrase: but you shall hear. Thus:
                                    (*Reads.*)
'In her excellent white bosom, these, etc.'
    QUEEN. Came this from Hamlet to her?
    POLONIUS. Good madam, stay awhile; I will be
        faithful.   (*Reads.*)
            'Doubt that the stars are fire;
                Doubt that the sun doth move;
                Doubt truth to be a liar;
                But never doubt I love.   119
'O dear Ophelia, I am ill at these numbers; I have
not art to reckon my groans; but that I love thee best,
O most best, believe it. Adieu.
            'Thine evermore, most dear lady, whilst
                this machine is to him,
                            HAMLET.'
This, in obedience, hath my daughter shown me,
And more above, hath his solicitings,
As they fell out by time, by means and place,
All given to mine ear.
    KING.   But how hath she
Received his love?
    POLONIUS.   What do you think of me?
    KING. As of a man faithful and honorable.   130
    POLONIUS. I would fain prove so. But what might
        you think,
When I had seen this hot love on the wing—
As I perceived it, I must tell you that,
Before my daughter told me—what might you,
Or my dear majesty your queen here, think,
If I had played the desk or table-book,
Or given my heart a winking, mute and dumb,
Or looked upon this love with idle sight;
What might you think? No, I went round to work,
And my young mistress thus I did bespeak: 140
'Lord Hamlet is a prince, out of thy star;
This must not be:' and then I prescripts gave her,
That she should lock herself from his resort,
Admit no messengers, receive no tokens.

Which done, she took the fruits of my advice;
And he, repulsed—a short tale to make—
Fell into a sadness, then into a fast,
Thence to a watch, thence into a weakness,
Thence to a lightness, and, by this declension,
Into the madness wherein now he raves,   150
And all we mourn for.
    KING.   Do you think 'tis this?
    QUEEN. It may be, very likely.
    POLONIUS. Hath there been such a time—I'd fain
        know that—
That I have positively said 'Tis so,'
When it proved otherwise?
    KING.   Not that I know.
    POLONIUS (*pointing to his head and shoulder*).
        Take this from this, if this be otherwise:
If circumstances lead me, I will find
Where truth is hid, though it were hid indeed
Within the centre.
    KING.   How may we try it further?
    POLONIUS. You know, sometimes he walks four
        hours together   160
Here in the lobby.
    QUEEN.   So he does indeed.
    POLONIUS. At such a time I'll loose my daughter
        to him:
Be you and I behind an arras then;
Mark the encounter: if he love her not
And be not from his reason fallen thereon,
Let me be no assistant for a state,
But keep a farm and carters.
    KING.   We will try it.
    QUEEN. But, look, where sadly the poor wretch
        comes reading.
    POLONIUS. Away, I do beseech you, both away:
I'll board him presently.
            (*Exeunt* KING, QUEEN, *and* Attendants.)
            (*Enter* HAMLET, *reading.*)
                O, give me leave: 170
How does my good Lord Hamlet?
    HAMLET. Well, God-a-mercy.
    POLONIUS. Do you know me, my lord?
    HAMLET. Excellent well; you are a fishmonger.
    POLONIUS. Not I, my lord.
    HAMLET. Then I would you were so honest a man.
    POLONIUS. Honest, my lord!
    HAMLET. Ay, sir; to be honest, as this world goes,
is to be one man picked out of ten thousand.
    POLONIUS. That's very true, my lord.   180
    HAMLET. For if the sun breed maggots in a dead

---

105. **Perpend,** consider, attend. 120. **ill . . . numbers,** unskilled in making these verses. 121. **reckon,** number metrically, that is, scan. 124. **machine,** bodily frame. 126. **more above,** moreover. 127. **fell out,** happened, occurred. **means,** opportunity of access. 136. **played . . . table-book,** kept things shut up in my desk or notebook. 137. **given . . . winking,** given my heart a signal to remain silent. 139. **round,** straight, directly. 140. **bespeak,** address. 141. **out of thy star,** above thee in position; thy fortune is not to compete with such a high destiny.

148. **watch,** wakefulness, sleeplessness. 149. **lightness,** light-headedness, giddiness. **declension,** decline, deterioration. 159. **centre,** middle point of the earth. 163. **arras,** tapestry; Arras, in northern France, was famous for its tapestries. 164. **encounter,** style and manner of conversation at the meeting. 170. **board,** accost, address. 174. **fishmonger,** in Elizabethan slang, a bawd, a pimp.

dog, being a god kissing carrion,—Have you a daughter?

POLONIUS. I have, my lord.

HAMLET. Let her not walk i' the sun: conception is a blessing: but not as your daughter may conceive. Friend, look to 't.

POLONIUS (*aside*). How say you by that? Still harping on my daughter; yet he knew me not at first; he said I was a fishmonger: he is far gone, far gone: and truly in my youth I suffered much extremity for love; very near this. I'll speak to him again. What do you read, my lord?

HAMLET. Words, words, words.

POLONIUS. What is the matter, my lord? 195

HAMLET. Between who?

POLONIUS. I mean, the matter that you read, my lord.

HAMLET. Slanders, sir: for the satirical rogue says here that old men have grey beards, that their faces are wrinkled, their eyes purging thick amber and plum-tree gum and that they have a plentiful lack of wit, together with most weak hams: all which, sir, though I most powerfully and potently believe, yet I hold it not honesty to have it thus set down, for yourself, sir, should be old as I am, if like a crab you could go backward.

POLONIUS (*aside*). Though this be madness, yet there is method in 't. Will you walk out of the air, my lord?

HAMLET. Into my grave. 210

POLONIUS. Indeed, that is out o' the air. (*Aside.*) How pregnant sometimes his replies are! a happiness that often madness hits on, which reason and sanity could not so prosperously be delivered of. I will leave him, and suddenly contrive the means of meeting between him and my daughter.—My honorable lord, I will most humbly take my leave of you.

HAMLET. You cannot, sir, take from me any thing that I will more willingly part withal: except my life, except my life, except my life. 220

POLONIUS. Fare you well, my lord.

HAMLET. These tedious old fools!

(*Enter* ROSENCRANTZ *and* GUILDENSTERN.)

POLONIUS. You go to seek the Lord Hamlet; there he is.

ROSENCRANTZ (*to* POLONIUS). God save you, sir!

(*Exit* POLONIUS.)

GUILDENSTERN. My honored lord!

ROSENCRANTZ. My most dear lord!

HAMLET. My excellent good friends! How dost thou, Guildenstern? Ah, Rosencrantz! Good lads, how do ye both? 230

ROSENCRANTZ. As the indifferent children of the earth.

GUILDENSTERN. Happy, in that we are not over-happy;
On fortune's cap we are not the very button.

HAMLET. Nor the soles of her shoe?

ROSENCRANTZ. Neither, my lord.

HAMLET. Then you live about her waist, or in the middle of her favors?

GUILDENSTERN. 'Faith, her privates we.

HAMLET. In the secret parts of fortune? O, most true; she is a strumpet.
What's the news? 240

ROSENCRANTZ. None, my lord, but that the world's grown honest.

HAMLET. Then is Doomsday near: but your news is not true. Let me question more in particular: what have you, my good friends, deserved at the hands of fortune, that she sends you to prison hither?

GUILDENSTERN. Prison, my lord!

HAMLET. Denmark's a prison.

ROSENCRANTZ. Then is the world one. 250

HAMLET. A goodly one, in which there are many confines, wards, and dungeons, Denmark being one o' the worst.

ROSENCRANTZ. We think not so, my lord.

HAMLET. Why, then, 'tis none to you; for there is nothing either good or bad, but thinking makes it so: to me it is a prison.

ROSENCRANTZ. Why then, your ambition makes it one; 'tis too narrow for your mind. 259

HAMLET. O God, I could be bounded in a nut-shell and count myself a king of infinite space, were it not that I have bad dreams.

GUILDENSTERN. Which dreams indeed are ambition, for the very substance of the ambitious is merely the shadow of a dream.

HAMLET. A dream itself is but a shadow.

ROSENCRANTZ. Truly, and I hold ambition of so airy and light a quality that it is but a shadow's shadow. 268

182. **god kissing carrion,** the sun-god shining on a dead body; the phrase, however, has had several readings, emendations, and interpretations and is one of the most difficult cruxes in the text of *Hamlet*. 185. **i' the sun,** suggesting "in the sunshine of princely favors." But the sun was long regarded as a powerful agent in the stimulation of conception. Possibly, too, there is a pun here on the word *sun* to suggest the eventuality of Hamlet, the son, as the impregnator of Ophelia. There is in all likelihood, moreover, a clear play on the two common meanings of *conception*. Hamlet, in his "mad speech," is given to all kinds of double-talk. 188. **by,** concerning, in reference to. 195. **matter,** substance (of what you are reading). 196. **Between who?** Hamlet is deliberately choosing another meaning of *matter*, denoting an issue or dispute. 198 ff. **the satirical rogue,** etc. Resemblance has been pointed out between these lines and the tenth satire of the Roman poet Juvenal, but there were any number of similar descriptions of old age from the Middle Ages to Shakespeare's time, and it is certainly impossible to deduce from these lines what particular book Hamlet was reading. 200. **purging,** discharging, excreting. 204. **honesty,** decency. 213. **happiness,** felicity of expression. 214. **prosperously,** successfully. 220. **withal,** with.

231. **indifferent,** ordinary, average. 264. **very . . . ambitious,** the elusive and hypothetically substantial thing which the ambitious pursue, like "the bubble reputation" in *As You Like It*, Act II, Scene 7, l. 152.

HAMLET. Then are our beggars bodies, and our monarchs and outstretched heroes the beggars' shadows. Shall we to the court? for, by my fay, I cannot reason.

ROSENCRANTZ AND GUILDENSTERN. We'll wait upon you.

HAMLET. No such matter: I will not sort you with the rest of my servants, for, to speak to you like an honest man, I am most dreadfully attended. But, in the beaten way of friendship, what make you at Elsinore?

ROSENCRANTZ. To visit you, my lord; no other occasion. 279

HAMLET. Beggar that I am, I am even poor in thanks; but I thank you: and sure, dear friends, my thanks are too dear a halfpenny. Were you not sent for? Is it your own inclining? Is it a free visitation? Come, deal justly with me: come, come; nay, speak.

GUILDENSTERN. What should we say, my lord?

HAMLET. Why, any thing, but to the purpose. You were sent for; and there is a kind of confession in your looks which your modesties have not craft enough to color: I know the good king and queen have sent for you. 291

ROSENCRANTZ. To what end, my lord?

HAMLET. That you must teach me. But let me conjure you, by the rights of our fellowship, by the consonancy of our youth, by the obligation of our ever-preserved love, and by what more dear a better proposer could charge you withal, be even and direct with me, whether you were sent for, or no?

ROSENCRANTZ (aside to GUILDENSTERN). What say you? 300

HAMLET (aside). Nay, then, I have an eye of you. —If you love me, hold not off.

GUILDENSTERN. My lord, we were sent for.

HAMLET. I will tell you why; so shall my anticipation prevent your discovery, and your secrecy to the king and queen moult no feather. I have of late—but wherefore I know not—lost all my mirth, forgone all custom of exercises; and indeed it goes so heavily with my disposition that this goodly frame, the earth, seems to me a sterile promontory, this most excellent canopy, the air, look you, this brave o'erhanging firmament, this majestical roof fretted with golden fire, why, it appears no other thing to me than a foul and pestilent congregation of vapors. What a piece of work is a man! how noble in reason! how infinite in faculty! in form and moving how express and ad-

mirable! in action how like an angel! in apprehension how like a god! the beauty of the world! the paragon of animals! And yet, to me, what is this quintessence of dust? Man delights not me; no, nor woman neither, though by your smiling you seem to say so. 323

ROSENCRANTZ. My lord, there was no such stuff in my thoughts.

HAMLET. Why did you laugh then, when I said, 'man delights not me'? 327

ROSENCRANTZ. To think, my lord, if you delight not in man, what lenten entertainment the players shall receive from you: we coted them on the way; and hither are they coming, to offer you service. 331

HAMLET. He that plays the king shall be welcome; his majesty shall have tribute of me; the adventurous knight shall use his foil and target; the lover shall not sigh gratis; the humorous man shall end his part in peace; the clown shall make those laugh whose lungs are tickle o' the sere; and the lady shall say her mind freely, or the blank verse shall halt for 't. What players are they? 340

ROSENCRANTZ. Even those you were wont to take delight in, the tragedians of the city.

HAMLET. How chances it they travel? their residence, both in reputation and profit, was better both ways. 345

ROSENCRANTZ. I think their inhibition comes by the means of the late innovation.

HAMLET. Do they hold the same estimation they did when I was in the city? are they so followed? 350

ROSENCRANTZ. No, indeed, are they not.

HAMLET. How comes it? do they grow rusty?

ROSENCRANTZ. Nay, their endeavor keeps in the wonted pace: but there is, sir, an aery of children, little eyases, that cry out on the top of the question, and are most tyranically clapped for 't: these are now the fashion, and so berattle the common stages—so

272. fay, faith. reason, argue. 273. wait upon you, accompany you. 274. sort, class, group (v.). 276. dreadfully attended, poorly or meanly attended (with servants). 277. in the beaten . . . friendship, as a matter of general course among friends. what make you, what are you doing? 282. dear a halfpenny, dear at the cost of a halfpenny. 284. free, voluntary. 294. conjure, adjure, implore. 295. consonancy . . . youth, the fact that our ages are the same. 297. better proposer, one more skillful in finding suggestions. 305. prevent your discovery, forestall your disclosure. 313. fretted, adorned. 318. express, exact, accurate; but the meaning is obscure.

319. apprehension, understanding, comprehension. 321. quintessence, in ancient philosophy this was the fifth essence which transcended the four elements of earth, air, fire, and water, and yet was supposed to be latent in all existing things. 329. lenten, meager, sparse, barren. 330. coted, overtook and passed beyond. 334. foil and target, sword and shield. 338. tickle o' the sere, easy on the trigger. 338–340. lady . . . for 't, the lady (fond of talking) will have the opportunity to talk, blank verse or no blank verse. 344. residence, remaining in one place. 346. inhibition, formal prohibition from acting plays either in the city or at court. 347. innovation. This is probably an allusion to the introduction into Elizabethan plays of satire on persons still living or to the establishing of the Children of the Revels in Blackfriars' Theatre, which took place in January 1603; if the latter, it is a valuable clue to the dating of Hamlet. The children's troupe was so successful that it drove the professional adult actors to the "roads" and provinces for a time. This is, in other words, a direct reference to the so-called "War of the Theatres." 352–379. How comes . . . load too. This is probably the most famous passage in Elizabethan literature dealing with the War of the Theatres, which lasted through the first three or four years of the sixteenth century. 354. aery, nest. 355. eyases, young hawks. 355–356. cry . . . question. This difficult passage has been variously interpreted: "to speak in a high key dominating conversation" and "to shout loudly in controversy." 356. tyranically, outrageously. 358. berattle, fill with noise. common stages, public theaters.

they call them—that many wearing rapiers are afraid of goose-quills and dare scarce come thither. 360

HAMLET. What, are they children? who maintains 'em? how are they escoted? Will they pursue the quality no longer than they can sing? will they not say afterwards, if they should grow themselves to common players—as it is most like, if their means are no better—their writers do them wrong, to make them exclaim against their own succession? 368

ROSENCRANTZ. 'Faith, there has been much to do on both sides; and the nation holds it no sin to tarre them to controversy: there was, for a while, no money bid for argument, unless the poet and the player went to cuffs in the question.

HAMLET. Is 't possible? 374

GUILDENSTERN. O, there has been much throwing about of brains.

HAMLET. Do the boys carry it away?

ROSENCRANTZ. Ay, that they do, my lord; Hercules and his load too. 379

HAMLET. It is not very strange; for mine uncle is king of Denmark, and those that would make mows at him while my father lived, give twenty, forty, fifty, an hundred ducats a-piece for his picture in little. 'Sblood, there is something in this more than natural, if philosophy could find it out. 385

(*Flourish of trumpets within.*)

GUILDENSTERN. There are the players.

HAMLET. Gentlemen, you are welcome to Elsinore. Your hands, come then: the appurtenance of welcome is fashion and ceremony: let me comply with you in this garb, lest my extent to the players, which, I tell you, must show fairly outward, should more appear like entertainment than yours. You are welcome: but my uncle-father and aunt-mother are deceived. 394

GUILDENSTERN. In what, my dear lord?

HAMLET. I am but mad north-north-west: when the wind is southerly I know a hawk from a handsaw.

(*Re-enter* POLONIUS.)

POLONIUS. Well be with you, gentlemen!

HAMLET. Hark you, Guildenstern; and you too: at each ear a hearer: that great baby you see there is not yet out of his swaddling-clouts. 401

ROSENCRANTZ. Happily he's the second time come to them; for they say an old man is twice a child.

HAMLET. I will prophesy he comes to tell me of the players; mark it. You say right, sir: o' Monday morning; 'twas so indeed.

POLONIUS. My lord, I have news to tell you.

HAMLET. My lord, I have news to tell you. When Roscius was an actor in Rome,— 410

POLONIUS. The actors are come hither, my lord.

HAMLET. Buz, buz!

POLONIUS. Upon mine honor,—

HAMLET. Then came each actor on his ass,—

POLONIUS. The best actors in the world, either for tragedy, comedy, history, pastoral, pastoral-comical, historical-pastoral, tragical-historical, tragical-comical-historical-pastoral, scene individable, or poem unlimited: Seneca cannot be too heavy, nor Plautus too light. For the law of writ and the liberty, these are the only men. 421

HAMLET. O Jephthah, judge of Israel, what a treasure hast thou!

POLONIUS. What a treasure had he, my lord?

HAMLET. Why,

'One fair daughter, and no more,
The which he loved passing well.'

POLONIUS (*aside*). Still on my daughter.

HAMLET. Am I not i' the right, old Jephthah?

POLONIUS. If you call me Jephthah, my lord, I have a daughter that I love passing well. 431

HAMLET. Nay, that follows not.

POLONIUS. What follows, then, my lord?

HAMLET. Why,

'As by lot, God wot,'

and then, you know,

359–360. **many . . . goose-quills,** many men of fashion (wearing rapiers) are afraid to patronize the theater lest they be satirized by the playwrights who write for the children's companies. The goose-quill implies satire. 362. **escoted,** maintained, kept. 363–364. **no longer . . . sing,** until their voices change. 365. **common,** regular. 368. **exclaim against,** run down, detract. **succession,** future careers. 371. **tarre,** set on, as dogs are set on a victim. 372. **argument,** the plot of a play. 373. **question,** dispute, controversy. 377. **carry it away,** win the day, succeed in their plan. 378–379. **Hercules . . . load.** The Globe Theater in Elizabethan London had for its sign Hercules bearing the world on his shoulder. 382. **ducats,** coins worth 9 s., 4d. apiece. 383. **in little,** in miniature. 390. **comply,** etc. A good example of the elaborate formality of court manners. **garb,** manner. **extent,** showing of kindness. 396. **I . . . north-north-west,** "I am mad in only one point of the compass," that is, in only one direction. 397. **hawk from a handsaw.** Critics have emended *handsaw,* to *hernshaw,* "young heron," or *hawk* to *hack* ("pickaxe") to bring conformity to the two elements in this statement; but in view of Hamlet's assumed eccentricity of speech, neither emendation seems necessary.

401. **swaddling-clouts,** diapers. 402. **Happily,** fortunately, by chance. 407. **o' Monday morning,** an inconsequential phrase to mislead the officiously listening Polonius. 410. **Roscius,** the most famous Roman actor known to us. 412. **Buz, buz.** This is considered a piece of Oxford slang common in the Elizabethan age to denote stale news. 414. **came . . . ass.** This, as well as several other phrases in Hamlet's speeches in this scene, is probably a quotation from an old play now unidentified. 418. **scene individable,** a play observing the so-called unity of place, with no change of scene permitted. **poem unlimited,** a play disregarding the unities of both time and place. **Seneca,** the famous Roman playwright of the first century after Christ, noted for his tragedies of terror. **Plautus,** a Roman writer of high comedy, who flourished about 200 B.C. Both Seneca and Plautus served as models to the Elizabethan writers of tragedy and comedy, respectively. 420. **law . . . liberty,** generally taken to mean the obligation to be faithful to the text of written plays while at the same time reserving the right to improvise; or it may refer to the distinction between plays written according to rules and those free from such regulation (the classical vs. the romantic manner). 422. **Jephthah,** judge of Israel. There was a popular Elizabethan ballad, *Jephthah's Daughter,* which recounted the affecting story of Jephthah's sacrifice of his daughter to fulfill his vow to God, as told in the Biblical book of Judges. Hamlet quotes from the ballad.

'It came to pass, as most like it was,'—
the first row of the pious chanson will show you
more; for look, where my abridgement comes.   439
(*Enter four or five* Players.)
You are welcome, masters; welcome, all. I am glad
to see thee well. Welcome, good friends. O, my old
friend! thy face is valanced since I saw thee last:
comest thou to beard me in Denmark? What, my
young lady and mistress! By 'r lady, your ladyship is
nearer to Heaven than when I saw you last, but the
altitude of a chopine. Pray God, your voice, like a
piece of uncurrent gold, be not cracked within the
ring. Masters, you are all welcome. We'll e'en to 't
like French falconers, fly at anything we see: we'll
have a speech straight: come, give us a taste of your
quality; come, a passionate speech.   452
FIRST PLAYER. What speech, my lord?
HAMLET. I heard thee speak me a speech once, but
it was never acted; or, if it was, not above once; for
the play, I remember, pleased not the million; 'twas
caviare to the general: but it was—as I received it,
and others, whose judgments in such matters cried in
the top of mine—an excellent play, well digested in
the scenes, set down with as much modesty as   461
cunning. I remember, one said there were no sallets
in the lines to make the matter savory, nor no matter
in the phrase that might indict the author of affectation; but called it an honest method, as wholesome as
sweet, and by very much more handsome than fine.
One speech in it I chiefly loved: 'twas Aeneas's tale
to Dido; and thereabout of it especially, where he
speaks of Priam's slaughter: if it live in your memory,
begin at this line: let me see, let me see—   471
'The rugged Pyrrhus, like the Hyrcanian beast,'—
it is not so:—it begins with Pyrrhus:—
'The rugged Pyrrhus, he whose sable arms,
Black as his purpose, did the night resemble
When he lay couched in the ominous horse,
Hath now this dread and black complexion smeared
With heraldry more dismal; head to foot

Now is he total gules; horridly tricked
With blood of fathers, mothers, daughters, sons,   480
Baked and impasted with the parching streets,
That lend a tyranous and damned light
To their lord's murder: roasted in wrath and fire,
And thus o'er-sized with coagulate gore,
With eyes like carbuncles, the hellish Pyrrhus
Old grandsire Priam seeks.'
So, proceed you.
POLONIUS. 'Fore God, my lord, well spoken, with
good accent and good discretion.
FIRST PLAYER.   'Anon he finds him   490
Striking too short at Greeks; his antique sword,
Rebellious to his arm, lies where it falls,
Repugnant to command: unequal matched,
Pyrrhus at Priam drives; in rage strikes wide;
But with the whiff and wind of his fell sword
The unnerved father falls. Then senseless Ilium,
Seeming to feel this blow, with flaming top
Stoops to his base, and with a hideous crash
Takes prisoner Pyrrhus' ear: for, lo! his sword,
Which was declining on the milky head   500
Of reverend Priam, seemed i' the air to stick:
So, as a painted tyrant, Pyrrhus stood,
And like a neutral to his will and matter,
Did nothing.
But, as we often see, against some storm,
A silence in the heavens, the rack stand still,
The bold winds speechless and the orb below
As hush as death, anon the dreadful thunder
Doth rend the region, so, after Pyrrhus' pause,   509
Aroused vengeance sets him new a-work;
And never did the Cyclops' hammers fall
On Mars's armour forged for proof eterne
With less remorse than Pyrrhus' bleeding sword
Now falls on Priam.
Out, out, thou strumpet, Fortune! All you gods,
In general synod, take away her power;
Break all the spokes and fellies from her wheel,
And bowl the round nave down the hill of Heaven,
As low as to the fiends!'
POLONIUS. This is too long.   520
HAMLET. It shall be to the barber's, with your
beard. Prithee, say on: he's for a jig or a tale of
bawdry, or he sleeps: say on: come to Hecuba.
FIRST PLAYER. 'But who, O, who had seen the
mobled queen—'

438. **row,** stanza. 439. **abridgement comes,** the opportunity comes to
cut short this conversation. 442. **valanced,** fringed with a beard.
447. **chopine,** a shoe raised by great thickness of the heel, much the
fashion in Renaissance Italy, particularly in Venice. 448. **uncurrent,**
not passing currency, not valid. **cracked . . . ring.** In the center of a
Renaissance coin were rings enclosing the head of the sovereign
reigning; if the coin was cracked within these rings, it was unfit for
currency. 451. **straight,** immediately, at once. 457. **caviare . . .
general,** not relished by the common people, like caviar. 459. **cried
. . . mine,** spoke with greater authority than mine. 460. **digested,**
arranged. 461. **modesty,** moderation. **cunning,** skill. 462. **sallets,**
salads; here for spicy improprieties. 464. **indict,** convict. 466–467.
as wholesome . . . fine. Its virtue lay not in its elaborate ornament
or decoration but in its simplicity and order. 468. **Aeneas's tale,**
etc. The lines recited below by Hamlet are an imitation of an older
play by Marlowe and Nashe called *Dido, Queen of Carthage.* The introduction of a play within a play by Shakespeare is most skillfully
handled. 472. **Pyrrhus,** a Greek hero of the Trojan War, the slayer
of King Priam of Troy (l. 469). **Hyrcanian beast,** tiger. 476. **ominous horse,** Trojan horse.

479. **total gules,** entirely red; gules is the term in heraldry for the
color red. **tricked,** spotted, smeared, decorated. 481. **impasted,**
made into a paste. **o'er-sized,** covered over with a size or glue.
493. **Repugnant,** resisting by fighting. 496. **senseless Ilium,** insensible Troy. 502. **painted tyrant,** tyrant in a picture. 503. **matter,** task, business. 505. **against,** before. 506. **rack,** mass of clouds.
509. **region,** the sky. 512. **proof eterne,** eternal resistance to attack.
516. **synod,** assembly. 517. **fellies,** pieces of wood joined together
to make the rim of a wheel. 518. **nave,** hub of a wheel. 522. **jig,**
comic performance given at the end or between the acts of a play,
usually featured by a lively dance—later, the dance itself. 523.
Hecuba, the wife of Priam and Queen of Troy. 525. **mobled,** muffled.

HAMLET. 'The mobled queen?'

POLONIUS. That's good; 'mobled queen' is good.

FIRST PLAYER. 'Run barefoot up and down, threatening the flames

With bisson rheum; a clout upon that head

Where late the diadem stood, and for a robe, 530

About her lank and all o'er-teemed loins,

A blanket, in the alarm of fear caught up;

Who this had seen, with tongue in venom steeped,

'Gainst Fortune's state would treason have pronounced:

But if the gods themselves did see her then

When she saw Pyrrhus make malicious sport

In mincing with his sword her husband's limbs,

The instant burst of clamor that she made,

Unless things mortal move them not at all,

Would have made milch the burning eyes of Heaven,

And passion in the gods.' 541

POLONIUS. Look, whether he has not turned his color and has tears in 's eyes. Pray you, no more.

HAMLET. 'Tis well; I'll have thee speak out the rest soon. Good my lord, will you see the players well bestowed? Do you hear, let them be well used; for they are the abstract and brief chronicles of the time: after your death you were better have a bad epitaph than their ill report while you live. 551

POLONIUS. My lord, I will use them according to their desert.

HAMLET. God's bodykins, man, much better: use every man after his desert, and who should 'scape whipping? Use them after your own honor and dignity: the less they deserve, the more merit is in your bounty. Take them in.

POLONIUS. Come, sirs. 559

HAMLET. Follow him, friends: we'll hear a play tomorrow.

(*Exit* POLONIUS *with all the* Players *but the first.*)
Dost thou hear me, old friend; can you play the Murder of Gonzago?

FIRST PLAYER. Ay, my lord.

HAMLET. We'll ha' tomorrow night. You could, for a need, study a speech of some dozen or sixteen lines, which I would set down and insert in 't, could you not?

FIRST PLAYER. Ay, my lord. 569

HAMLET. Very well. Follow that lord; and look you mock him not. (*Exit first* Player.)

My good friends, I'll leave you till night: you are welcome to Elsinore.

ROSENCRANTZ. Good my lord!

HAMLET. Ay, so, God be wi' ye.

(*Exeunt* ROSENCRANTZ *and* GUILDENSTERN.)
Now I am alone.

O, what a rogue and peasant slave am I! 576

Is it not monstrous that this player here,

But in a fiction, in a dream of passion,

Could force his soul so to his own conceit

That from her working all his visage wanned,

Tears in his eyes, distraction in 's aspect,

A broken voice, and his whole function suiting 582

With forms to his conceit? and all for nothing!

For Hecuba!

What's Hecuba to him, or he to Hecuba,

That he should weep for her? What would he do,

Had he the motive and the cue for passion

That I have? He would drown the stage with tears

And cleave the general ear with horrid speech, 589

Make mad the guilty and appal the free,

Confound the ignorant, and amaze indeed

The very faculties of eyes and ears.

Yet I,

A dull and muddy-mettled rascal, peak,

Like John-a-dreams, unpregnant of my cause,

And can say nothing: no, not for a king,

Upon whose property and most dear life

A damned defeat was made. Am I a coward?

Who calls me villain? breaks my pate across?

Plucks off my beard, and blows it in my face? 600

Tweaks me by the nose? gives me the lie i' the throat,

As deep as to the lungs? who does me this?

Ha!

'Swounds, I should take it: for it cannot be

But I am pigeon-livered and lack gall

To make oppression bitter, or ere this

I should have fatted all the region kites

With this slave's offal: bloody, bawdy villain!

Remorseless, treacherous, lecherous, kindless villain!

O, vengeance! 610

Why, what an ass am I! This is most brave,

That I, the son of a dear father murdered,

Prompted to my revenge by Heaven and Hell,

Must, like a whore, unpack my heart with words,

And fall a-cursing, like a very drab,

A scullion!

529. **bisson rheum**, blinding tears. **clout**, rag. 531. **o'er-teemed**, worn out by child-bearing. 534. **state**, power, majesty. 540. **milch**, moist with tears. 542. **turned**, changed. 548. **abstract**, summarizing account, epitome. 554. **God's bodykins**, by God's little body; the diminutive merely weakens the severity of the oath. 567. **dozen . . . lines**. There have been many guesses as to which were the "dozen or sixteen" lines inserted by Hamlet; the general opinion is that they come in the speech of Lucianus; Act III, Scene 2, ll. 266 ff.

576. **peasant**, base (used here as an adjective). 579. **conceit**, imagination. 580. **wanned**, grew pale and wan. 582–583. **his whole function . . . conceit**, his whole being responding with forms appropriate to his thoughts. 590. **free**, free from guilt, innocent. 594. **muddy-mettled**, dull-spirited, ineffectual. **peak**, mope, pine. 595. **John-a-dreams**, a generic name in Elizabethan English for the visionary and the dreamer. **unpregnant of**, not quickened or made alive by. 597. **property**, proprietorship (of kingship as well as life). 598. **defeat**, destruction. 605. **pigeon-livered**. It was the belief in Elizabethan England that the pigeon had no gall-bladder, and therefore could secrete no gall. Gall in the human system produces bitterness, according to further belief. 607. **region kites**, the predatory birds of the sky. 609. **kindless**, unnatural. 616. **scullion**, kitchen-servant.

Fie upon 't! foh! About, my brain! I have heard
That guilty creatures sitting at a play
Have by the very cunning of the scene
Been struck so to the soul that presently   620
They have proclaimed their malefactions;
For murder, though it have no tongue, will speak
With most miraculous organ. I'll have these players
Play something like the murder of my father
Before mine uncle: I'll observe his looks;
I'll tent him to the quick; if he but blench,
I know my course. The spirit that I have seen
May be the devil: and the devil hath power
To assume a pleasing shape; yea, and perhaps,
Out of my weakness and my melancholy,   630
As he is very potent with such spirits,
Abuses me to damn me: I'll have grounds
More relative than this: the play's the thing
Wherein I'll catch the conscience of the king. (*Exit.*)

ACT III

SCENE 1. *A room in the castle*

(*Enter* KING, QUEEN, POLONIUS, OPHELIA, ROSEN-
CRANTZ, *and* GUILDENSTERN.)

KING. And can you, by no drift of circumstance,
Get from him why he puts on this confusion,
Grating so harshly all his days of quiet
With turbulent and dangerous lunacy?
ROSENCRANTZ. He does confess he feels himself
distracted;
But from what cause he will by no means speak.
GUILDENSTERN. Nor do we find him forward to be
sounded,
But, with a crafty madness, keeps aloof,
When we would bring him on to some confession
Of his true state.
QUEEN.   Did he receive you well?   10
ROSENCRANTZ. Most like a gentleman.
GUILDENSTERN. But with much forcing of his dis-
position.
ROSENCRANTZ. Niggard of question; but, of our
demands,
Most free in his reply.
QUEEN.   Did you assay him
To any pastime?
ROSENCRANTZ. Madam, it so fell out, that certain
players
We o'er-raught on the way: of these we told him;

And there did seem in him a kind of joy
To hear of it: they are about the court.
And, as I think, they have already order   20
This night to play before him.
POLONIUS.   'Tis most true:
And he beseeched me to entreat your majesties
To hear and see the matter.
KING. With all my heart; and it doth much content
me
To hear him so inclined.
Good gentlemen, give him a further edge,
And drive his purpose on to these delights.
ROSENCRANTZ. We shall, my lord.
(*Exeunt* ROSENCRANTZ *and* GUILDENSTERN.)
KING.   Sweet Gertrude, leave us too;
For we have closely sent for Hamlet hither,
That he, as 'twere by accident, may here   30
Affront Ophelia:
Her father and myself, lawful espials,
Will so bestow ourselves that, seeing, unseen,
We may of their encounter frankly judge,
And gather by him, as he is behaved,
If 't be the affliction of his love or no
That thus he suffers for.
QUEEN.   I shall obey you.
And for your part, Ophelia, I do wish
That your good beauties be the happy cause
Of Hamlet's wildness: so shall I hope your virtues   40
Will bring him to his wonted way again,
To both your honors.
OPHELIA.   Madam, I wish it may.
(*Exit* QUEEN.)
POLONIUS. Ophelia, walk you here. Gracious, so
please you,
We will bestow ourselves. (*To* OPHELIA.) Read on
this book;
That show of such an exercise may color
Your loneliness. We are oft to blame in this,—
'Tis too much proved—that with devotion's visage
And pious action we do sugar o'er
The devil himself.
KING (*aside*).   O, 'tis too true!
How smart a lash that speech doth give my con-
science!   50
The harlot's cheek, beautied with plastering art,
Is not more ugly to the thing that helps it
Than is my deed to my most painted word:
O heavy burthen!—

617. **About,** get about your business! 626. **tent,** probe (v.). 628. **May be the devil.** As pointed out in the notes to Act I, Scene 4, l. 71, the habit of the devil of going about as a ghost of some loved one was firmly fixed in the Elizabethan mind. 631. **spirits,** the afore-mentioned humors (l. 630). 632. **Abuses,** deceives. 633. **relative,** closely related, germane.
Act III, Scene 1. 1. **drift of circumstance,** roundabout or devious method. 7. **forward,** willing. 12. **forcing of his disposition,** effort of temper and will. 13. **Niggard of question,** not inclined to conversation. 14. **assay,** challenge, tempt. 17. **o'er-raught,** overtook.

26. **edge,** incitement. 29. **closely,** secretly. 31. **Affront,** confront. 32. **lawful espials,** legitimate spies. 40. **wildness,** madness. 43. **Gracious,** your Grace, gracious one. Polonius is addressing the king. 45. **exercise,** act of devotion. 52. **ugly to,** ugly in comparison to. **thing,** the cosmetic. 54. **O heavy burthen!** This sudden expression of repentance by the king has the practical dramatic purpose of satisfying the audience of King Claudius' guilt. Moreover, the suddenness would not disturb an Elizabethan audience, because it was a current psychological belief that a sudden shift of spirits in the human body could bring about sudden conflicting moods.

POLONIUS. I hear him coming: let's withdraw, my
    lord.   (*Exeunt* KING *and* POLONIUS.)
         (*Enter* HAMLET.)
    HAMLET. To be, or not to be: that is the question,
Whether 'tis nobler in the mind to suffer
The slings and arrows of outrageous fortune,
Or to take arms against a sea of troubles,
And by opposing end them? To die; to sleep;   60
No more; and by a sleep to say we end
The heart-ache and the thousand natural shocks
That flesh is heir to, 'tis a consummation
Devoutly to be wished. To die, to sleep;
To sleep: perchance to dream; ay, there's the rub;
For in that sleep of death what dreams may come
When we have shuffled off this mortal coil,
Must give us pause: there's the respect
That makes calamity of so long life;
For who would bear the whips and scorns of time,   70
The oppressor's wrong, the proud man's contumely,
The pangs of despised love, the law's delay,
The insolence of office and the spurns
That patient merit of the unworthy takes,
When he himself might his quietus make
With a bare bodkin? who would fardels bear,
To grunt and sweat under a weary life,
But that the dread of something after death,
The undiscovered country from whose bourn
No traveller returns, puzzles the will   80
And makes us rather bear those ills we have
Than fly to others that we know not of?
Thus conscience does make cowards of us all;
And thus the native hue of resolution
Is sicklied o'er with the pale cast of thought,
And enterprises of great pitch and moment
With this regard their currents turn awry,
And lose the name of action.—Soft you now!
The fair Ophelia! Nymph, in thy orisons
Be all my sins remembered.
    OPHELIA.   Good my lord,   90
How does your honor for this many a day?
    HAMLET. I humbly thank you; well, well, well.

59. **sea**, etc. The curious mixed metaphor in this line has suggested
the possibility that "sea" should be emended to "siege." 65. **rub**, in
the game of bowls, an obstacle or hazard. 67. **shuffled off**, sloughed
off or cast off. **coil**, turmoil; or the figure here may be that of the body
wrapped around the soul like a coil of rope. Numerous emendations
have been suggested, but the entire line has become so familiar as it
stands that tampering with it would be mere pedantry. 68. **respect**,
consideration. 69. Insert "a" between "long" and "life." 73.
office, either office or office-holders; probably both meanings are
appropriate. 74. **takes**, takes from; the "from" is expressed as "of"
in this same line. 75. **quietus**, a legal term signifying acquittance;
here used metaphorically for death. 76. **fardels**, burdens. 79.
bourn, boundary. 83. **conscience**, both in our modern sense of our
"psychological monitor" against wrongdoing and in the old (medieval) sense of tender feelings, which makes us timid about any kind
of radical action. 85. **sicklied o'er**, given a sickly tinge. **cast**, shade
of color. 86. **pitch**, height; the metaphor is from falconry. **moment**,
importance. 87. **regard**, consideration, respect. **currents**, courses.
89. **orisons**, prayers.

    OPHELIA. My lord, I have remembrances of yours,
That I have longed long to re-deliver;
I pray you, now receive them.
    HAMLET.   No, not I;
I never gave you aught.
    OPHELIA. My honored lord, you know right well
        you did;
And, with them, words of so sweet breath composed
As made the things more rich: their perfume lost,
Take these again; for to the noble mind   100
Rich gifts wax poor when givers prove unkind.
There, my lord.
    HAMLET. Ha, ha! are you honest?
    OPHELIA. My lord!
    HAMLET. Are you fair?
    OPHELIA. What means your lordship?
    HAMLET. That if you be honest and fair, your hon-
esty should admit no discourse to your beauty.
    OPHELIA. Could beauty, my lord, have better com-
merce than with honesty?   110
    HAMLET. Ay, truly; for the power of beauty will
sooner transform honesty from what it is to a bawd
than the force of honesty can translate beauty into
his likeness: this was sometime a paradox, but now
the time gives it proof. I did love you once.
    OPHELIA. Indeed, my lord, you made me believe so.
    HAMLET. You should not have believed me; for
virtue cannot so inoculate our old stock but we shall
relish of it: I loved you not.   120
    OPHELIA. I was the more deceived.
    HAMLET. Get thee to a nunnery; why wouldst thou
be a breeder of sinners? I am myself indifferent honest; but yet I could accuse me of such things that it
were better my mother had not borne me: I am very
proud, revengeful, ambitious, with more offences at
my beck than I have thoughts to put them in, imagination to give them shape, or time to act them in.
What should such fellows as I do crawling between
earth and Heaven? We are arrant knaves, all; believe
none of us. Go thy ways to a nunnery. Where's your
father?   133
    OPHELIA. At home, my lord.
    HAMLET. Let the doors be shut upon him, that he
may play the fool no where but in 's own house. Farewell.
    OPHELIA. O, help him, you sweet heavens!

103. **honest**, sincere, truthful; but also with the idea of chastity in a
woman. 105. **fair**, just, honorable. 107. **honest and fair**, chaste and
beautiful; note the play on words in reference to ll. 103 and 105
above. 108. **honesty**, chastity. **discourse to**, familiar intercourse
with. 110. **commerce**, intercourse. 115. **time**, the (present) time.
119. **inoculate**, graft; the metaphor is from horticulture. 120. **but
we . . . it**, but we still have a taste of the old stock. 128. **beck**,
command. 133. **Where's your father?** At this point it has been a
tradition for Polonius to stick his head out from behind the tapestry
so that Hamlet catches sight of him. Ophelia's lie ("At home, my
lord") therefore convinces Hamlet of her unreliability. It is to be
noticed that from this point in the play Hamlet's feigned madness
assumes a more violent form.

HAMLET. If thou dost marry, I'll give thee this plague for thy dowry: be thou as chaste as ice, as pure as snow, thou shalt not escape calumny. Get thee to a nunnery, go; farewell. Or, if thou wilt needs marry, marry a fool; for wise men know well enough what monsters you make of them. To a nunnery, go, and quickly too. Farewell. 146

OPHELIA. O heavenly powers, restore him!

HAMLET. I have heard of your paintings too, well enough; God has given you one face, and you make yourselves another; you jig, you amble, and you lisp, and nick-name God's creatures, and make your wantonness your ignorance. Go to, I'll no more on 't; it hath made me mad. I say, we will have no more marriages; those that are married already, all but one, shall live; the rest shall keep as they are. To a nunnery, go. (*Exit.*)

OPHELIA. O, what a noble mind is here o'erthrown! 158
The courtier's, soldier's, scholar's, eye, tongue, sword;
The expectancy and rose of the fair state, 160
The glass of fashion and the mould of form,
The observed of all observers, quite, quite down!
And I, of ladies most deject and wretched,
That sucked the honey of his music vows,
Now see that noble and most sovereign reason,
Like sweet bells jangled, out of tune and harsh;
That unmatched form and feature of blown youth
Blasted with ecstasy: O, woe is me,
To have seen what I have seen, see what I see!

(*Re-enter* KING *and* POLONIUS.)

KING. Love! his affections do not that way tend; 170
Nor what he spake, though it lacked form a little,
Was not like madness. There's something in his soul,
O'er which his melancholy sits on brood;
And I do doubt the hatch and the disclose
Will be some danger: which for to prevent,
I have in quick determination
Thus set it down: he shall with speed to England,
For the demand of our neglected tribute:
Haply the seas and countries different
With variable objects shall expel 180
This something-settled matter in his heart,
Whereon his brains still beating puts him thus
From fashion of himself. What think you on't?

POLONIUS. It shall do well: but yet I do believe
The origin and commencement of his grief

Sprung from neglected love. How now, Ophelia!
You need not tell us what Lord Hamlet said;
We heard it all. My lord, do as you please;
But, if you hold it fit, after the play
Let his queen mother all alone entreat him 190
To show his grief: let her be round with him;
And I'll be placed, so please you, in the ear
Of all their conference. If she find him not,
To England send him, or confine him where
Your wisdom best shall think.

KING.   It shall be so:
Madness in great ones must not unwatched go.
(*Exeunt.*)

SCENE 2. *A hall in the castle.*

(*Enter* HAMLET *and* Players.)

HAMLET. Speak the speech, I pray you, as I pronounced it to you, trippingly on the tongue: but if you mouth it, as many of your players do, I had as lief the town-crier spoke my lines. Nor do not saw the air too much with your hand, thus, but use all gently; for in the very torrent, tempest, and, as I may say, the whirlwind of passion, you must acquire and beget a temperance that may give it smoothness. O, it offends me to the soul to hear a robustious 10 periwig-pated fellow tear a passion to tatters, to very rags, to split the ears of the groundlings, who for the most part are capable of nothing but inexplicable dumb-shows and noise: I would have such a fellow whipped for o'erdoing Termagant; it out-Herods Herod: pray you, avoid it.

FIRST PLAYER. I warrant your honor. 17

HAMLET. Be not too tame neither, but let your own discretion be your tutor: suit the action to the word, the word to the action; with this special observance, that you o'erstep not the modesty of nature: for anything so overdone is from the purpose of playing, whose end, both at the first and now, was and is, to hold, as 't were, the mirror up to nature; to show virtue her own feature, scorn her own image, and the very age and body of the time his form and pressure. Now this overdone, or come tardy off, though it 28

145. **monsters,** referring to the horns which grow on the foreheads of all cuckolds. 150. **jig,** move with jerky motions, probably a reference to the dance which takes place in the dramatic trifle known as the jig (see note to Act II, Scene 2, l. 522). 152-153. **make . . . ignorance,** excuse your wantonness on the grounds of your ignorance. 156. **one,** King Claudius. 160. **expectancy,** source of hope for the future. 167. **feature,** whole shape of the body, figure and stature as well. 168. **ecstasy,** madness. 174. **disclose,** that which will be disclosed when the shell is broken; the image seems to be that of an egg. 180. **variable,** various. 183. **puts . . . himself,** keeps him out of his natural manner or condition.

193. **find him,** find him out, discover what is wrong with him. *Act III, Scene 2.* 10. **robustious,** violent, boisterous. 12. **groundlings,** members of the audience who stood in the "yard" (i.e., on the floor) of the theater; they constituted the less discriminating portion of the spectators. 13. **capable of,** susceptible to, comprehending. 16. **Termagant,** a god of the Saracens. He appears in the medieval St. Nicholas play; one of the characters in the play, leaving Termagant in charge of some goods, returns to find them stolen, whereupon he beats the pagan divinity most lustily, and the vociferous howling of the god is received by the audience with the greatest delight. Herod, the king of Judaea who played a part in the early years of the story of Jesus, also appeared in medieval plays, where his part was played with great sound and fury. 17. **warrant,** promise. 26. **age and body,** generation. 27. **pressure,** stamp, impressed character. 28. **come tardy off,** badly timed and inadequately done.

make the unskilful laugh, cannot but make the judicious grieve; the censure of the which one must in your allowance o'erweigh a whole theatre of others. O, there be players that I have seen play, and heard others praise, and that highly, not to speak it profanely, that, neither having the accent of Christians nor the gait of Christian, pagan, nor man, have so strutted and bellowed that I have thought some of nature's journeymen had made men and not made them well, they imitated humanity so abominably. 39

FIRST PLAYER. I hope we have reformed that indifferently with us, sir. 41

HAMLET. O, reform it altogether. And let those that play your clowns speak no more than is set down for them; for there be of them that will themselves laugh, to set on some quantity of barren spectators to laugh too; though, in the meantime, some necessary question of the play be then to be considered: that's villainous, and shows a most pitiful ambition in the fool that uses it. Go, make you ready. 50

(*Exeunt* Players.)

(*Enter* POLONIUS, ROSENCRANTZ, *and* GUILDENSTERN.)

How now, my lord! will the king hear this piece of work?

POLONIUS. And the queen too, and that presently.

HAMLET. Bid the players make haste.

(*Exit* POLONIUS.)

Will you two help to hasten them?

ROSENCRANTZ AND GUILDENSTERN. We will, my lord.

(*Exeunt* ROSENCRANTZ *and* GUILDENSTERN.)

HAMLET. What ho! Horatio!

(*Enter* HORATIO.)

HORATIO. Here, sweet lord, at your service.

HAMLET. Horatio, thou art e'en as just a man
As e'er my conversation coped withal. 60

HORATIO. O, my dear lord,—

HAMLET. Nay, do not think I flatter;
For what advancement may I hope from thee
That no revenue hast but thy good spirits,
To feed and clothe thee? Why should the poor be flattered?
No, let the candied tongue lick absurd pomp,

And crook the pregnant hinges of the knee
Where thrift may follow fawning. Dost thou hear?
Since my dear soul was mistress of her choice
And could of men distinguish, her election
Hath sealed thee for herself; for thou hast been 70
As one, in suffering all, that suffers nothing,
A man that fortune's buffets and rewards
Hast ta'en with equal thanks: and blest are those
Whose blood and judgment are so well commingled,
That they are not a pipe for fortune's finger
To sound what stop she please. Give me that man
That is not passion's slave, and I will wear him
In my heart's core, ay, in my heart of heart,
As I do thee.—Something too much of this.—
There is a play tonight before the king; 80
One scene of it comes near the circumstance
Which I have told thee of my father's death:
I prithee, when thou seest that act afoot,
Even with the very comment of thy soul
Observe mine uncle: if his occulted guilt
Do not itself unkennel in one speech,
It is a damned ghost that we have seen,
And my imaginings are as foul
As Vulcan's stithy. Give him heedful note;
For I mine eyes will rivet to his face, 90
And after we will both our judgments join
In censure of his seeming.

HORATIO. Well, my lord;
If he steal aught the whilst this play is playing,
And 'scape detecting, I will pay the theft.

HAMLET. They are coming to the play; I must be idle:
Get you a place.

(*Danish march. A flourish. Enter* KING, QUEEN, POLONIUS, OPHELIA, ROSENCRANTZ, GUILDENSTERN, *and others.*)

KING. How fare our cousin Hamlet?

HAMLET. Excellent, i' faith; of the chameleon's dish: I eat the air, promise-crammed; you cannot feed capons so. 100

KING. I have nothing with this answer, Hamlet; these words are not mine.

HAMLET. No, nor mine now. (*To* POLONIUS.) My lord, you played once i' the university, you say?

---

31. **the which one,** one of whom (the judicious). 38. **journeymen,** laborers hired by the day—not yet masters of their trade. 41. **indifferently,** fairly well, tolerably. 43. **clowns.** Evidently the parts played by the clowns in the Elizabethan theater were often not written down at all—they were allowed the broadest latitude in ad-libbing —and their jests were often unpremeditated interruptions to serious actions. But during the time of Shakespeare there was more and more of a tendency to fix the parts by writing them down, so as to inhibit the often unlicensed range of the star comedian. 44. **of.** Insert "some" before "of." 46. **barren,** devoid of wit or intelligence or taste. 59. **just,** honest, reliable. 60. **conversation,** intercourse, experience. **coped,** met, encountered. 63. **revenue.** Note that this word is accented on the second syllable.

66. **pregnant,** receptive, inclined to fawn. 67. **thrift,** profit, success. 76. **stop,** the hole in a wind instrument for controlling the sound. 77. **passion's slave,** etc. The whole passage, from lines 59 to 79, has been considered as evidence for Shakespeare's conception of Hamlet as a man in whom reason and emotions were not kept in even balance and who for this reason came to grief in the pinch. Obviously he is far less even-tempered than Horatio; but then Horatio did not have the same provocations. 84. **very comment . . . soul,** inward and wise criticism of the self. 85. **occulted,** hidden. 89. **stithy,** smithy; *stith* is the old word for *anvil.* 91–92. **judgments . . . seeming,** judgments and criticism of his behavior and appearance. 95. **idle,** crazy, unable to attend to anything serious. 98. **chameleon's dish.** Chameleons were popularly supposed to subsist on nothing but air. 101. **have nothing with,** make nothing of. 102. **are not mine,** are of no significance to me.

POLONIUS. That did I, my lord; and was accounted a good actor.

HAMLET. What did you enact?

POLONIUS. I did enact Julius Caesar: I was killed i' the Capitol; Brutus killed me.

HAMLET. It was a brute part of him to kill so capital a calf there. Be the players ready? 111

ROSENCRANTZ. Ay, my lord; they stay upon your patience.

QUEEN. Come hither, my dear Hamlet, sit by me.

HAMLET. No, good mother, here's metal more attractive.

POLONIUS (*to the* KING). O, ho! do you mark that?

HAMLET. Lady, shall I lie in your lap?

(*Lying down at* OPHELIA's *feet.*)

OPHELIA. No, my lord. 120

HAMLET. I mean, my head upon your lap?

OPHELIA. Ay, my lord.

HAMLET. Do you think I meant country matters?

OPHELIA. I think nothing, my lord.

HAMLET. That's a fair thought to lie between maids' legs.

OPHELIA. What is, my lord?

HAMLET. Nothing.

OPHELIA. You are merry, my lord.

HAMLET. Who, I? 130

OPHELIA. Ay, my lord.

HAMLET. O God, your only jig-maker. What should a man do but be merry? for, look you, how cheerfully my mother looks, and my father died within these two hours.

OPHELIA. Nay, 'tis twice two months, my lord. 136

HAMLET. So long? Nay then, let the devil wear black, for I'll have a suit of sables. O heavens! die two months ago, and not forgotten yet? Then there's hope a great man's memory may outlive his life half a year: but, by 'r lady, he must build churches, then; or else shall he suffer not thinking on, with the hobby-horse, whose epitaph is 'For, O, for, O, the hobby-horse is forgot.' 145

Hautboys play. The dumb-show enters.

Enter a King and a Queen very lovingly; the Queen embracing him, and he her. She kneels, and makes show of protestation unto him. He takes her up, and declines his head upon her neck: lays him down upon a bank of flowers: she, seeing him asleep, leaves him. Anon comes in a fellow, takes off his crown, kisses it, and pours poison in the King's ears,

and exit. The Queen returns; finds the King dead, and makes passionate action. The Poisoner, with some two or three Mutes, comes in again, seeming to lament with her. The dead body is carried away. The Poisoner woos the Queen with gifts: she seems loath and unwilling awhile, but in the end accepts his love.

(*Exeunt.*)

OPHELIA. What means this, my lord?

HAMLET. Marry, this is miching mallecho; it means mischief.

OPHELIA. Belike this show imports the argument of the play. 150

(*Enter* Prologue.)

HAMLET. We shall know by this fellow: the players cannot keep counsel; they'll tell all.

OPHELIA. Will he tell us what this show meant?

HAMLET. Ay, or any show that you'll show him: be not you ashamed to show, he'll not shame to tell you what it means.

OPHELIA. You are naught, you are naught; I'll mark the play.

PROLOGUE. For us, and for our tragedy,
Here stooping to your clemency, 160
We beg your hearing patiently. (*Exit.*)

HAMLET. Is this a prologue, or the posy of a ring?

OPHELIA. 'Tis brief, my lord.

HAMLET. As woman's love.

(*Enter two* Players, King *and* Queen.)

PLAYER KING. Full thirty times hath Phoebus' cart
gone round
Neptune's salt wash and Tellus' orbed ground,
And thirty dozen moons with borrowed sheen
About the world have times twelve thirties been,
Since love our hearts and Hymen did our hands
Unite commutual in most sacred bands. 170

PLAYER QUEEN. So many journeys may the sun and
moon
Make us again count o'er ere love be done!
But, woe is me, you are so sick of late,
So far from cheer and from your former state,
That I distrust you. Yet, though I distrust,
Discomfort you, my lord, it nothing must;
For women's fear and love holds quantity;
In neither aught, or in extremity.
Now, what my love is, proof hath made you know;
And as my love is sized, my fear is so: 180
Where love is great, the littlest doubts are fear;
Where little fears grow great, great love grows there.

---

132. **your only,** only your.   138. **suit of sables,** garments trimmed with sable fur, but Hamlet is playing on the other meaning of sable, the heraldic term for black.   144. **hobby-horse . . . 'forgot.'** This is evidently an allusion to a popular song of the time (quoted partially in *Love's Labour's Lost*, Act III, Scene 1, l. 30). The hobby-horse was a character which appeared, in the English folk-plays, in the Morris Dance; it is believed to be a reincarnation of the eight-legged steed ridden by Woden, king of the ancient Germanic gods.   145. ff. *Stage Direction: Hautboys,* wooden double-reed wind-instruments of a high pitch, the ancestor of the modern oboe.

147. **miching mallecho,** sneaking (or mincing) mischief; the latter word is supposed to be derived from the Spanish *malhecho.*   157. **naught,** improper, bad. The entire dialogue between Ophelia and Hamlet in this scene is extremely broad and risqué.   160. **stooping,** bowing.   162. **posy,** motto.   166. **Tellus' orbed ground.** Tellus was in classical mythology an ancient goddess of the earth, which—since the earth had been demonstrated to be round—is referred to here as "orbed ground."   167. **borrowed,** reflected.   169. **Hymen,** god of marriage in classical mythology.   170. **commutual,** intensely mutual.   175. **distrust,** am anxious about, worry about.   177. **holds quantity,** keeps proportion between.

PLAYER KING. 'Faith, I must leave thee, love, and
    shortly too;
My operant powers their functions leave to do:
And thou shalt live in this fair world behind,
Honored, beloved; and haply one as kind
For husband shalt thou—
    PLAYER QUEEN.   O, confound the rest!
Such love must needs be treason in my breast:
In second husband let me be accursed!   189
None wed the second but who killed the first.
    HAMLET (aside). Wormwood, wormwood.
    PLAYER QUEEN. The instances that second marriage
    move
Are base respects of thrift, but none of love:
A second time I kill my husband dead,
When second husband kisses me in bed.
    PLAYER KING. I do believe you think what now you
    speak;
But what we do determine oft we break.
Purpose is but the slave to memory,
Of violent birth, but poor validity;
Which now, like fruit unripe, sticks on the tree;   200
But fall, unshaken, when they mellow be.
Most necessary 'tis that we forget
To pay ourselves what to ourselves is debt:
What to ourselves in passion we propose,
The passion ending, doth the purpose lose.
The violence of either grief or joy
Their own enactures with themselves destroy:
Where joy most revels, grief doth most lament;
Grief joys, joy grieves, on slender accident.
This world is not for aye, nor 'tis not strange   210
That even our loves should with our fortunes change;
For 'tis a question left us yet to prove,
Whether love lead fortune, or else fortune love.
The great man down, you mark his favorite flies;
The poor advanced makes friends of enemies.
And hitherto doth love on fortune tend;
For who not needs shall never lack a friend,
And who in want a hollow friend doth try,
Directly seasons him his enemy.
But, orderly to end where I begun,   220
Our wills and fates do so contrary run
That our devices still are overthrown;
Our thoughts are ours, their ends none of our own;
So think thou wilt no second husband wed;
But die thy thoughts when thy first lord is dead.

PLAYER QUEEN. Nor earth to me give food, nor
    Heaven light!
Sport and repose lock from me day and night!
To desperation turn my trust and hope!
An anchor's cheer in prison be my scope!
Each opposite that blanks the face of joy   230
Meet what I would have well and it destroy!
Both here and hence pursue me lasting strife,
If, once a widow, ever I be wife!
    HAMLET. If she should break it now!
    PLAYER KING. 'Tis deeply sworn. Sweet, leave me
    here awhile;
My spirits grow dull, and fain I would beguile
The tedious day with sleep.   (Sleeps.)
    PLAYER QUEEN.   Sleep rock thy brain;
And never come mischance between us twain!
                            (Exit.)
    HAMLET. Madam, how like you this play?   239
    QUEEN. The lady doth protest too much, methinks.
    HAMLET. O, but she'll keep her word.
    KING. Have you heard the argument? Is there no
offence in 't?
    HAMLET. No, no, they do but jest, poison in jest;
no offence i' the world.
    KING. What do you call the play?   246
    HAMLET. The Mouse-trap. Marry, how? Tropi-
cally. The play is the image of a murder done in
Vienna: Gonzago is the duke's name; his wife,
Baptista: you shall see anon; 'tis a knavish piece of
work: but what o' that? your majesty and we that
have free souls, it touches us not; let the galled jade
wince, our withers are unwrung.
            (Enter LUCIANUS.)
This is one Lucianus, nephew to the king.
    OPHELIA. You are as good as a chorus, my lord.   255
    HAMLET. I could interpret between you and your
love, if I could see the puppets dallying.
    OPHELIA. You are keen, my lord, you are keen.
    HAMLET. It would cost you a groaning to take off
my edge.   260
    OPHELIA. Still better, and worse.
    HAMLET. So you must take your husbands. Begin,
murderer; pox, leave thy damnable faces, and begin.

---

184. **operant,** active, operating. **leave,** cease. 187. **confound,** strike dumb. 191. **Wormwood.** The Old English drink, *wermod*, was a spirituous liquor closely related to absinthe, and noted for its bitter taste. Hence, the relation of this word to bitterness, although it should be remarked that it has no relation to worms—the form *wormwood* is due to a process known as folk etymology. In actual fact, the immediate descendant of this drink is the wine known as vermouth. 192. **instances,** inducements, motives. 193. **respects of thrifts,** considerations of material interest. 207. **enactures,** fulfillments. 219. **seasons,** matures. Insert "as" between "him" and "his."

229. **anchor's,** anchorite's. **cheer,** fare, subsistence. 230. **opposite,** opponent, adversary. **blanks,** causes to grow pale. 248. **tropically,** figuratively, metaphorically; a *trope* is a figure of speech. **image,** dramatic representation. 249. **Gonzago.** There was an actual murder of a Duke Gonzago of Urbano, Italy, in 1538 accomplished by pouring a lethal lotion in his ears. A tragedy was written on the incident some time later in the century. 253. **galled jade,** a broken-down horse whose hide has been irritated to the point of inflammation by saddle or harness (galled). **withers,** the area between a horse's shoulder-blades. **unwrung,** not wrung or twisted or cramped. 255. **chorus.** In many Elizabethan plays—for example, Shakespeare's *Henry V*—the action was explained and commented upon by an actor known as the Chorus. At a puppet-show, on the other hand, the action was explained by a so-called "interpreter," which explains the reference in l. 256. 261. **Still better, and worse,** more shrewd but less proper. 263. **pox,** an imprecation, referring since early times to either the Black Death (bubonic plague) or syphilis.

Come: 'the croaking raven doth bellow for revenge.'

LUCIANUS. Thoughts black, hands apt, drugs fit,
    and time agreeing;
Confederate season, else no creature seeing;
Thou mixture rank, of midnight weeds collected,
With Hecate's ban thrice blasted, thrice infected,
Thy natural magic and dire property,   270
On wholesome life usurp immediately.

    (*Pours the poison into the sleeper's ears.*)

HAMLET. He poisons him i' the garden for 's estate.
His name's Gonzago: the story is extant, and writ in
choice Italian: you shall see anon how the murderer
gets the love of Gonzago's wife.

OPHELIA. The king rises.

HAMLET. What, frighted with false fire?

QUEEN. How fares my lord?

POLONIUS. Give o'er the play.

KING. Give me some light: away!   280

ALL. Lights, lights, lights!

    (*Exeunt all but* HAMLET *and* HORATIO.)

HAMLET. Why, let the stricken deer go weep,
    The hart ungalled play;
    For some must watch, while some must
        sleep:
    So runs the world away.
Would not this, sir, and a forest of feathers—if the
rest of my fortunes turn Turk with me—with two
Provincial roses on my razed shoes, get me a fellowship in a cry of players, sir?

HORATIO. Half a share.   290

HAMLET. A whole one, I.
    For thou dost know, O Damon dear,
      This realm dismantled was
    Of Jove himself; and now reigns here
      A very, very—pajock.

HORATIO. You might have rhymed.

HAMLET. O good Horatio, I'll take the ghost's word
for a thousand pound. Didst perceive?

HORATIO. Very well, my lord.

HAMLET. Upon the talk of the poisoning.

HORATIO. I did very well note him.   301

HAMLET. Ah, ha! Come, some music! come, the
recorders!
    For if the king like not the comedy,
      Why then, belike, he likes it not, perdy.
Come, some music!

    (*Re-enter* ROSENCRANTZ *and* GUILDENSTERN.)

GUILDENSTERN. Good my lord, vouchsaf me a
word with you.

HAMLET. Sir, a whole history.

GUILDENSTERN. The king, sir—   310

HAMLET. Ay, sir, what of him?

GUILDENSTERN. Is in his retirement marvellous distempered.

HAMLET. With drink, sir?

GUILDENSTERN. No, my lord, rather with choler.

HAMLET. Your wisdom should show itself more
richer to signify this to his doctor; for, for me to put
him to his purgation would perhaps plunge him into
far more choler.   319

GUILDENSTERN. Good my lord, put your discourse
into some frame and start not so wildly from my
affair.

HAMLET. I am tame, sir; pronounce.

GUILDENSTERN. The queen, your mother, in most
great affliction of spirit, hath sent me to you.

HAMLET. You are welcome.   325

GUILDENSTERN. Nay, good my lord, this courtesy is
not of the right breed. If it shall please you to make
me a wholesome answer, I will do your mother's
commandment; if not, your pardon and my return
shall be the end of the business.

HAMLET. Sir, I cannot.   331

GUILDENSTERN. What, my lord?

HAMLET. Make you a wholesome answer; my wit's
diseased; but, sir, such answer as I can make, you
shall command; or, rather, as you say, my mother:
therefore no more, but to the matter; my mother, you
say,—

ROSENCRANTZ. Then thus she says; your behavior
hath struck her into amazement and admiration.   339

HAMLET. O wonderful son, that can so astonish a
mother! But is there no sequel at the heels of this
mother's admiration? Impart.

ROSENCRANTZ. She desires to speak with you in her
closet, ere you go to bed.

HAMLET. We shall obey, were she ten times our
mother. Have you any further trade with us?

ROSENCRANTZ. My lord, you once did love me.

HAMLET. So I do still, by these pickers and stealers.

264–265. **'the croaking . . . revenge,'** suggested by the lines of the
older anonymous play, the *True Tragedie of Richard the Third:* "The
screeking raven sits croaking for revenge. Whole herds of beasts come
bellowing for revenge." 267. **Confederate**, conspiring to assist the
murderer. 269. **Hecate**, in classical mythology the goddess of witchcraft and sorcery. **ban**, curse. 277. **false fire**, either "fireworks" or
"blank cartridges." 282–285. **Why, let . . . world away**, probably
a quotation from another popular song of the times, with reference to
the belief that a wounded deer always retires to the woods to die,
weeping before his death. 286. **this**, i.e., the play. **feathers**, referring
to the plumes worn by Elizabethan actors portraying men of distinction. 287. **Turn Turk with**, go back on; the Turk was to Elizabethan England a symbol of cruelty and treachery. 288. **Provincial
roses**, roses either from Provins or Provence in France. **razed**, cut or
slashed for purposes of ornament. 289. **fellowship . . . players**,
partnership in a theatrical company. **cry**, the baying of a pack of
hounds. 290. **Half a share**, a reference to the practice in dramatic
companies of the time of dividing the ownership into a number of
shares among the householders. 292–295. **For thou . . . pajock**,
evidently an excerpt from an old ballad about Damon and Pythias.
293. **dismantled**, stripped, divested. 295. **pajock**, probably a peacock, a bird with a bad reputation.

303. **recorders**, wind-instruments like the flute. 305. **perdy**, a corruption of the French oath, *par dieu!* 315. **choler**, strictly speaking,
a bilious disorder; but the later meaning of anger is also implicit.
321. **frame**, order, shape. 328. **wholesome**, sensible. 337. **matter**,
business in hand. 339. **admiration**, wonder, amazement. 348.
pickers and stealers, hands, from the catechism, "to keep my hands
from picking and stealing."

ROSENCRANTZ. Good my lord, what is your cause of distemper? you do, surely, bar the door upon your own liberty, if you deny your griefs to your friend.

HAMLET. Sir, I lack advancement.

ROSENCRANTZ. How can that be, when you have the voice of the king himself for your succession in Denmark?

HAMLET. Ay, sir, but 'While the grass grows,'—the proverb is something musty.   359

(Re-enter Players with recorders.)

O, the recorders! let me see one. To withdraw with you:—why do you go about to recover the wind of me, as if you would drive me into a toil?

GUILDENSTERN. O, my lord, if my duty be too bold, my love is too unmannerly.   364

HAMLET. I do not well understand that. Will you play upon this pipe?

GUILDENSTERN. My lord, I cannot.

HAMLET. I pray you.

GUILDENSTERN. Believe me, I cannot.

HAMLET. I do beseech you.   370

GUILDENSTERN. I know no touch of it, my lord.

HAMLET. 'Tis as easy as lying: govern these ventages with your fingers and thumb, give it breath with your mouth, and it will discourse most eloquent music. Look you, these are the stops.

GUILDENSTERN. But these cannot I command to any utterance of harmony; I have not the skill.   378

HAMLET. Why, look you now, how unworthy a thing you make of me! You would play upon me; you would seem to know my stops; you would pluck out the heart of my mystery; you would sound me from my lowest note to the top of my compass: and there is much music, excellent voice, in this little organ; yet cannot you make it speak. 'Sblood, do you think I am easier to be played on than a pipe? Call me what instrument you will, though you can fret me, yet you cannot play upon me.

(Enter POLONIUS.)

God bless you, sir!   390

POLONIUS. My lord, the queen would speak with you, and presently.

HAMLET. Do you see yonder cloud that's almost in the shape of a camel?

POLONIUS. By the mass, and 'tis like a camel, in-deed.

HAMLET. Methinks it is like a weasel.

POLONIUS. It is backed like a weasel.

HAMLET. Or like a whale?

POLONIUS. Very like a whale.   399

HAMLET. Then I will come to my mother by and by. They fool me to the top of my bent. I will come by and by.

POLONIUS. I will say so.

HAMLET. By and by is easily said. (Exit POLONIUS.)
Leave me, friends.
(Exeunt all but HAMLET.)
'Tis now the very witching time of night,
When churchyards yawn and Hell itself breathes out
Contagion to this world: now could I drink hot blood,
And do such bitter business as the day
Would quake to look on. Soft! now to my mother.
O heart, lose not thy nature; let not ever   411
The soul of Nero enter this firm bosom:
Let me be cruel, not unnatural:
I will speak daggers to her, but use none;
My tongue and soul in this be hypocrites;
How in my words soever she be shent,
To give them seals never, my soul, consent!   (Exit.)

SCENE. 3. A room in the castle.

(Enter KING, ROSENCRANTZ, and GUILDENSTERN.)

KING. I like him not, nor stands it safe with us
To let his madness range. Therefore prepare you;
I your commission will forthwith dispatch,
And he to England shall along with you:
The terms of our estate may not endure
Hazard so near us as doth hourly grow
Out of his lunacies.

GUILDENSTERN.   We will ourselves provide:
Most holy and religious fear it is
To keep those many many bodies safe
That live and feed upon your majesty.   10

ROSENCRANTZ. The single and peculiar life is
bound,
With all the strength and armor of the mind,
To keep itself from noyance; but much more
That spirit upon whose weal depend and rest
The lives of many. The cease of majesty
Dies not alone; but, like a gulf, doth draw
What's near it with it: it is a massy wheel,
Fixed on the summit of the highest mount,
To whose huge spokes ten thousand lesser things
Are mortised and adjoined; which, when it falls,   20

356. voice, support.   358. 'While the grass grows—' The rest of the proverb goes, 'the silly (empty) horse starves.' Hamlet may be destroyed while waiting to succeed to the throne.   360. withdraw, speak in private.   361. recover the wind, in nautical phraseology, to get back on the windward side.   362. toil, snare, trap.   363-364. if my duty . . . unmannerly, if I am being too bold in my duty, it is because of my love for you.   373. ventages, the stops or finger holes of the recorder.   384. compass, range of voice.   385. organ, any musical instrument; here, the recorder.   388. fret. There is here a play on the meaning of the word as "irritate" and the "piece of wood" which regulates the fingering.

401. top . . . bent, limit of endurance, the extent to which a bow can be bent.   402. by and by, immediately.   406. witching time, the time when spells are cast, from midnight until one o'clock in the morning.   412. soul of Nero. It should be recalled that the Roman emperor Nero had his mother, Agrippina, murdered.   416. shent, rebuked, insulted.   417. give them seals, confirm them by some irrevocable deed.
Act III, Scene 3.   5. estate, state.   8. fear, caution.   11. single and peculiar, individual and private.   13. noyance, harm.   16. gulf, whirlpool.

Each small annexment, petty consequence,
Attends the boisterous ruin. Never alone
Did the king sigh, but with a general groan.
  KING. Arm you, I pray you, to this speedy voyage;
For we will fetters put upon this fear,
Which now goes too free-footed.
  ROSENCRANTZ AND GUILDENSTERN. We will haste us.
    (*Exeunt* ROSENCRANTZ *and* GUILDENSTERN.)
    (*Enter* POLONIUS.)
  POLONIUS. My lord, he's going to his mother's
    closet:
Behind the arras I'll convey myself,
To hear the process; I'll warrant she'll tax him home:
And, as you said, and wisely was it said,   30
'Tis meet that some more audience than a mother,
Since nature makes them partial, should o'erhear
The speech of vantage. Fare you well, my liege:
I'll call upon you ere you go to bed,
And tell you what I know.
  KING.   Thanks, dear my lord.
    (*Exit* POLONIUS.)
O, my offence is rank, it smells to Heaven;
It hath the primal eldest curse upon 't,
A brother's murder. Pray can I not,
Though inclination be as sharp as will:
My stronger guilt defeats my strong intent;   40
And, like a man to double business bound,
I stand in pause where I shall first begin,
And both neglect. What if this cursed hand
Were thicker than itself with brother's blood,
Is there not rain enough in the sweet heavens
To wash it white as snow? Whereto serves mercy
But to confront the visage of offence?
And what's in prayer but this two-fold force,
To be forestalled ere we come to fall,   49
Or pardoned being down? Then I'll look up;
My fault is past. But, O, what form of prayer
Can serve my turn? 'Forgive me my foul murder'?
That cannot be; since I am still possessed
Of those effects for which I did the murder,
My crown, mine own ambition and my queen.
May one be pardoned and retain the off nce?
In the corrupted currents of this world
Offence's gilded hand may shove by justice,
And oft 'tis seen the wicked prize itself
Buys out the law: but 'tis not so above;   60
There is no shuffling, there the action lies
In his true nature; and we ourselves compelled,
Even to the teeth and forehead of our faults,
To give in evidence. What then? what rests?

Try what repentance can: what can it not?
Yet what can it when one can not repent?
O wretched state! O bosom black as death!
O limed soul, that, struggling to be free,
Art more engaged! Help, angels! Make assay!
Bow, stubborn knees; and, heart with strings of
    steel,   70
Be soft as sinews of the new-born babe!
All may be well.   (*Retires and kneels.*)
    (*Enter* HAMLET.)
  HAMLET. Now might I do it pat, now he is praying;
And now I'll do 't. And so he goes to Heaven;
And so am I revenged. That would be scanned:
A villain kills my father; and for that,
I, his sole son, do this same villain send
To Heaven.
O, this is hire and salary, not revenge.
He took my father grossly, full of bread;   80
With all his crimes broad blown, as flush as May;
And how his audit stands who knows save Heaven?
But in our circumstance and course of thought,
'Tis heavy with him: and am I then revenged,
To take him in the purging of his soul,
When he is fit and seasoned for his passage?
No!
Up, sword; and know thou a more horrid hent:
When he is drunk asleep, or in his rage,
Or in the incestuous pleasure of his bed;   90
At gaming, swearing, or about some act
That has no relish of salvation in 't;
Then trip him, that his heels may kick at Heaven,
And that his soul may be as damned and black
As Hell, whereto it goes. My mother stays:
This physic but prolongs thy sickly days.   (*Exit.*)
  KING (*rising*). My words fly up, my thoughts re-
    main below:
Words without thoughts never to Heaven go. (*Exit.*)

SCENE 4. *The Queen's closet.*

    (*Enter* QUEEN *and* POLONIUS.)
  POLONIUS. He will come straight. Look you lay
    home to him:

24. **Arm**, prepare. 28. **convey**, betake, with the suggestion of secrecy or stealth. 29. **process**, interview, business. **tax him home**, reprove him up to the hilt. 33. **of vantage**, from a vantage point. 39. **sharp as will**, though his desire be as strong as his determination. 47. **confront**, oppose directly. 55. **ambition**, the realization of ambition. 56. **offence**, the benefits derived from the offence. 58. **gilded hand**, hand offering gold as a bribe. 61. **shuffling**, escaping by trickery. **lies**, is sustainable.

68. **limed**, caught as with the bird lime. 69. **assay**, trial. 73–95. **Now might I . . . days.** This is generally considered the critical point in the delineation of Hamlet's character. One group of students of the play believes that Hamlet refrains from killing the king through sheer weakness of will and is here merely rationalizing his conduct and finding excuses for not doing his duty. But a more recent group insists that Hamlet is delaying only to make his revenge more complete by not sending the King to Heaven, for it was believed that anyone dying while engaged in prayer—provided the prayer was sincere—would not die in sin and so would certainly be received in Heaven. 75. **would be scanned**, would need to be looked into. 80. **full of bread**, full of physical appetites and life. 81. **broad blown**, in full bloom. **flush**, lusty. 83. **in our circumstance . . . thought**, as we see it in our situation in life. 88. **hent**, seizing. 89. **drunk asleep**, in a drunken sleep. **rage**, sexual passion. 96. **physic**, purging by prayer.
Act III, Scene 4. 1. **lay home**, talk plainly.

Tell him his pranks have been too broad to bear with,
And that your grace hath screened and stood be-
    tween
Much heat and him. I'll sconce me even here.
Pray you, be round with him.
HAMLET (*within*). Mother, mother, mother!
QUEEN.   I'll warrant you,
Fear me not: withdraw, I hear him coming.
                (POLONIUS *hides behind the arras.*)
                (*Enter* HAMLET.)
HAMLET. Now, mother, what's the matter?
QUEEN. Hamlet, thou hast thy father much of-
    fended.
HAMLET. Mother, you have my father much of-
    fended.   10
QUEEN. Come, come, you answer with an idle
    tongue.
HAMLET. Go, go, you question with a wicked
    tongue.
QUEEN. Why, how now, Hamlet?
HAMLET.   What's the matter now?
QUEEN. Have you forgot me?
HAMLET.   No, by the rood, not so:
You are the queen, your husband's brother's wife;
And—would it were not so!—you are my mother.
QUEEN. Nay, then, I'll set those to you that can
    speak.
HAMLET. Come, come, and sit you down; you shall
    not budge;
You go not till I set you up a glass
Where you may see the inmost part of you.   20
QUEEN. What wilt thou do? thou wilt not murder
me? Help, help, ho!
POLONIUS (*behind*). What, ho! help, help, help!
HAMLET (*drawing*). How now! a rat? Dead, for a
    ducat, dead!
             (*Makes a pass through the arras.*)
POLONIUS (*behind*). O, I am slain! (*Falls and dies.*)
QUEEN. O me, what hast thou done?
HAMLET.   Nay, I know not;
Is it the king?
QUEEN. O, what a rash and bloody deed is this!
HAMLET. A bloody deed! almost as bad, good
    mother,
As kill a king, and marry with his brother.
QUEEN. As kill a king!
HAMLET.   Ay, lady, 'twas my word.   30
    (*Lifts up the arras and discovers* POLONIUS.)
Thou wretched, rash, intruding fool, farewell!
I took thee for thy better: take thy fortune;
Thou find'st to be too busy is some danger.
Leave wringing of your hands: peace! sit you down,
And let me wring your heart; for so I shall,

If it be made of penetrable stuff,
If damned custom have not brassed it so
That it be proof and bulwark against sense.
QUEEN. What have I done, that thou darest wag
    thy tongue
In noise so rude against me?
HAMLET.   Such an act   40
That blurs the grace and blush of modesty,
Calls virtue hypocrite, takes off the rose
From the fair forehead of an innocent love
And sets a blister there, makes marriage-vows
As false as dicers' oaths: O, such a deed
As from the body of contraction plucks
The very soul, and sweet religion makes
A rhapsody of words: Heaven's face doth glow;
Yea, this solidity and compound mass,
With tristful visage, as against the doom,   50
Is thought-sick at the act.
QUEEN.   Ay me, what act,
That roars so loud, and thunders in the index?
HAMLET. Look here, upon this picture, and on this.
The counterfeit presentment of two brothers.
See, what a grace was seated on this brow:
Hyperion's curls; the front of Jove himself;
An eye like Mars, to threaten and command;
A station like the herald Mercury
New-lighted on a heaven-kissing hill;
A combination and a form indeed,   60
Where every god did seem to set his seal,
To give the world assurance of a man;
This was your husband. Look you now, what follows:
Here is your husband; like a mildewed ear,
Blasting his wholesome brother. Have you eyes?
Could you on this fair mountain leave to feed,
And batten on this moor? Ha! have you eyes?
You cannot call it love; for at your age
The hey-day in the blood is tame, it's humble,
And waits upon the judgment: and what judgment   70
Would step from this to this? Sense, sure, you have,
Else could you not have motion; but sure, that sense
Is apoplex'd; for madness would not err,
Nor sense to ecstasy was ne'er so thralled
But it reserved some quantity of choice,

2. **broad**, unrestrained. 4. **heat**, the King's anger. **sconce**, ensconce, place, hide. **26. Is it the king?** Hamlet, thinking the man hiding to be the king, nevertheless does not hesitate to strike, which suggests that he is not the weakling often portrayed.

37. **brassed**, brazoned, hardened. 38. **proof**, armor, protection. **sense**, feeling. 44. **sets a blister**, brands as a harlot. 46. **contraction**, pledge, betrothal. 48. **rhapsody**, fantastic expression. 49. **this solidity . . . mass**, the solid earth itself. 50. **tristful**, full of sadness. **the doom**, Judgment Day. 51. **thought-sick**, sick with worry and anxiety. 52. **index**, prelude or preface. 54. **counterfeit presentment**, pictorial representation—the two pictures are thought of by some as miniatures carried about by Hamlet and by others as portraits on the wall. 56. **Hyperion**, the sun god; see Act 1, Scene 2, l. 140 and note. 58. **station**, manner of standing, stance. 64. **mildewed ear.** The figure is suggested by the story of Joseph as told in Genesis, 41:5–7, in which the diseased ears of grain spread their blight to the healthy ears. 67. **batten**, feed, pasture (v.). 71–72. **Sense . . . motion.** Sense and motion are functions of the "middle" or the sensible representation of sense, since the possession of sense is a necessary basis for motion. 73. **apoplex'd**, paralyzed (as a result of apoplexy). Elizabethan medicine classified mental disease into three kinds: apoplexy, ecstasy, and possession by a devil.

To serve in such a difference. What devil was 't
That thus hath cozened you at hoodman-blind?
Eyes without feeling, feeling without sight,
Ears without hands or eyes, smelling sans all,
Or but a sickly part of one true sense   80
Could not so mope.
O shame! where is thy blush? Rebellious Hell,
If thou canst mutine in a matron's bones,
To flaming youth let virtue be as wax,
And melt in her own fire; proclaim no shame
When the compulsive ardor gives the charge,
Since frost itself as actively doth burn
And reason pandars will.
    QUEEN.   O Hamlet, speak no more:
Thou turnest mine eyes into my very soul;
And there I see such black and grained spots
As will not leave their tinct.
    HAMLET.   Nay, but to live   91
In the rank sweat of an enseamed bed,
Stewed in corruption, honeying and making love
Over the nasty sty,—
    QUEEN.   O speak to me no more;
These words, like daggers, enter in mine ears;
No more, sweet Hamlet!
    HAMLET.   A murderer and a villain;
A slave that is not twentieth part the tithe
Of your precedent lord; a vice of kings;
A cutpurse of the empire and the rule,
That from a shelf the precious diadem stole,   100
And put it in his pocket!
    QUEEN.   No more!
HAMLET. A king of shreds and patches,—
          (Enter Ghost.)
Save me, and hover o'er me with your wings,
You heavenly guards! What would your gracious
      figure?
    QUEEN. Alas, he's mad!
    HAMLET. Do you not come your tardy son to chide,
That, lapsed in time and passion, lets go by
The important acting of your dread command?
O, say!
    GHOST. Do not forget: this visitation   110
Is but to whet thy almost blunted purpose.
But, look, amazement on thy mother sits:

O, step between her and her fighting soul:
Conceit in weakest bodies strongest works:
Speak to her, Hamlet.
    HAMLET.   How is it with you, lady?
    QUEEN. Alas, how is 't with you,
That you do bend your eye on vacancy
And with the incorporal air do hold discourse?
Forth at your eyes your spirits wildly peep;
And, as the sleeping soldiers in the alarm,   120
Your bedded hair, like life in excrements,
Start up, and stand on end. O gentle son,
Upon the heat and flame of thy distemper
Sprinkle cool patience. Whereon do you look?
    HAMLET. On him, on him! Look you, how pale he
      glares!
His form and cause conjoined, preaching to stones,
Would make them capable. Do not look upon me;
Lest with this piteous action you convert
My stern effects: then what I have to do   129
Will want true color; tears perchance for blood.
    QUEEN. To whom do you speak this?
    HAMLET.   Do you see
    nothing there?
    QUEEN. Nothing at all; yet all that is I see.
    HAMLET. Nor did you nothing hear?
    QUEEN.   No, nothing but ourselves.
    HAMLET. Why, look you there! look, how it steals
      away!
My father, in his habit as he lived!
Look, where he goes, even now, out at the portal!
          (Exit Ghost.)
    QUEEN. This is the very coinage of your brain:
This bodiless creation ecstasy
Is very cunning in.
    HAMLET.   Ecstasy!
My pulse, as yours, doth temperately keep time,   140
And makes as healthful music: it is not madness
That I have uttered: bring me to the test,
And I the matter will re-word, which madness
Would gambol from. Mother, for love of grace,
Lay not that flattering unction to your soul,
That not your trespass, but my madness speaks:
It will but skin and film the ulcerous place,
Whiles rank corruption, mining all within,
Infects unseen. Confess yourself to Heaven;
Repent what's past; avoid what is to come;   150
And do not spread the compost on the weeds,

77. **cozened**, tricked, deceived. **hoodman-blind**, the old game of blind man's buff. 79. **sans**, without. 83. **mutine**, mutiny, rebellion against convention. 86. **charge**, command. 88. **reason pandars will.** Normally reason is supposed to guide the will in the direction of good; but here reason has been perverted and serves only to cater to the baser instincts and desires of the will. 90. **grained**, dyed in grain. 92. **enseamed**, spotted with grease and dirt. Hamlet's imagination in respect to his mother's marriage-bed is of a distinctly morbid nature. 98. **precedent lord**, Hamlet's father. **vice of kings**, buffoon or clown of kings; in the medieval morality plays a vice was often portrayed as a clown or jester. 102. **shreds and patches**, motley, the variegated costume of the medieval Vice in the morality plays—see note to l. 98. 107. **lapsed . . . passion**, having allowed time to pass and passion to cool. 108. **important**, urgent, demanding. 112. **amazement**, frenzy, distraction, hysteria.

114. **Conceit**, imagination. 118. **incorporal**, immaterial, unsubstantial. 121. **bedded**, laid down in smooth layers—an interesting reference to the kind of hairdress affected by the Elizabethan gentleman. **excrements.** The hair was believed to be an excrement, or voided part, of the human body. 126. **conjoined**, united. 127. **capable**, susceptible. 128–129. **convert . . . effects**, divert me from my serious duty. 130. **want true color**, lack good reason so that I shall shed tears instead of blood. 143. **re-word**, repeat. 145. **unction**, ointment used either medicinally or as a religious sacrament; the implication here is that forgiveness for sin is not so easy to achieve. 148. **mining**, undermining. 150. **what is to come**, the unseen future.

To make them ranker. Forgive me this my virtue;
For in the fatness of these pursy times
Virtue itself of vice most pardon beg,
Yea, curb and woo for leave to do him good.
   QUEEN. O Hamlet, thou hast cleft my heart in
     twain.
   HAMLET. O, throw away the worser part of it,
And live the purer with the other half.
Good night: but go not to mine uncle's bed;
Assume a virtue, if you have it not.   160
That monster, custom, who all sense doth eat,
Of habits devil, is angel yet in this,
That to the use of actions fair and good
He likewise gives a frock or livery,
That aptly is put on. Refrain tonight,
And that shall lend a kind of easiness
To the next abstinence: the next more easy;
For use almost can change the stamp of nature,
And either (master) the devil, or throw him out
With wondrous potency. Once more, good night: 170
And when you are desirous to be blessed,
I'll blessing beg of you. For this same lord,
              (Pointing to POLONIUS)
I do repent: but Heaven hath pleased it so,
To punish me with this and this with me,
That I must be their scourge and minister.
I will bestow him, and will answer well
The death I gave him. So, again, good night.
I must be cruel, only to be kind:
Thus bad begins and worse remains behind.
One word more, good lady.
   QUEEN.   What shall I do?   180
   HAMLET. Not this, by no means, that I bid you do:
Let the bloat king tempt you again to bed:
Pinch wanton on your cheek; call you his mouse;
And let him, for a pair of reechy kisses,
Or paddling in your neck with his damned fingers,
Make you to ravel all this matter out,
That I essentially am not in madness,
But mad in craft. 'Twere good you let him know;
For who, that's but a queen, fair, sober, wise,
Would from a paddock, from a bat, a gib,   190
Such dear concernings hide? who would do so?
No, in despite of sense and secrecy,
Unpeg the basket on the house's top,
Let the birds fly, and, like the famous ape,

To try conclusions, in the basket creep,
And break your own neck down.
   QUEEN. Be thou assured, if words be made of
     breath,
And breath of life, I have no life to breathe
What thou hast said to me.
   HAMLET. I must to England; you know that?
   QUEEN.   Alack,   200
I had forgot: 'tis so concluded on.
   HAMLET. There's letters sealed: and my two
     schoolfellows,
Whom I will trust as I will adders fanged,
They bear the mandate; they must sweep my way,
And marshal me to knavery. Let it work;
For 'tis the sport to have the enginer
Hoist with his own petar: and 't shall go hard
But I will delve one yard below their mines,
And blow them at the moon: O, 'tis most sweet,
When in one line two crafts directly meet.   210
This man shall set me packing:
I'll lug the guts into the neighbor room.
Mother, good night. Indeed this counsellor
Is now most still, most secret and most grave,
Who was in life a foolish prating knave.
Come, sir, to draw toward an end with you.
Good night, mother.
(Exeunt severally; HAMLET dragging in POLONIUS.)

ACT IV

SCENE 1. A room in the castle.

(Enter KING, QUEEN, ROSENCRANTZ, and
GUILDENSTERN.)
   KING. There's matter in these sighs, these profound
     heaves:
You must translate; 'tis fit we understand them.
Where is your son?
   QUEEN. Bestow this place on us a little while.
     (Exeunt ROSENCRANTZ and GUILDENSTERN.)
Ah, mine own lord, what have I seen tonight!
   KING. What, Gertrude? How does Hamlet?
   QUEEN. Mad as the sea and wind, when both con-
     tend
Which is the mightier: in his lawless fit,
Behind the arras hearing something stir,
Whips out his rapier, cries, 'A rat, a rat!'   10
And, in this brainish apprehension, kills

---

153. **fatness**, grossness. **pursy**, short-winded, corpulent. 155. **curb**, bow. 163. **use**, custom. 169. **(master)**. This word has been restored by virtually all editors. 176. **answer**, account for. 184. **reechy**, foul, stinking. 187. **essentially**, in my true nature. 190. **paddock**, toad. **gib**. A gib (short for Gilbert) is a tom (short for Thomas) cat. 191. **dear concernings**, important affairs. 194. **famous ape**. This seems to be an old folk tale, difficult to identify except through passing references. We are indebted to Sir John Suckling, the graceful and attractive Cavalier poet of the seventeenth century for the following details: "It is the story of the jacka-napes and the partridges; thou starest after a beauty till it be lost to thee, then let'st out another, and starest after that till it be gone too."

195. **conclusions**, experiments. 204. **sweep my way**, clear my path. 206. **enginer**, the constructor of military works, or perhaps an artilleryman. 207. **Hoist**, lifted, blown up. **petar**, petard, a small engine of war used to blow up or effect a breach in a fortified wall; perhaps it may mean a case full of explosive materials. At any rate, the expression has become proverbial for "the biter bit!" 210. **two crafts**, two acts of guile; also, in double meaning, "two ships." 211. **set me packing**, set me to making schemes. 216. **draw**, drag; but there is a quibble on the sense of "draw."
Act IV, Scene I. 11. **brainish apprehension**, headstrong, passionate, compulsion.

The unseen good old man.

KING.   O heavy deed!
It had been so with us, had we been there:
His liberty is full of threats to all;
To you yourself, to us, to every one.
Alas, how shall this bloody deed be answered?
It will be laid to us, whose providence
Should have kept short, restrained and out of haunt,
This mad young man: but so much was our love,
We would not understand what was most fit;   20
But, like the owner of a foul disease,
To keep it from divulging, let it feed
Even on the pith of life. Where is he gone?
    QUEEN. To draw apart the body he hath killed:
O'er whom his very madness, like some ore
Among a mineral of metals base,
Shows itself pure; he weeps for what is done.
    KING. O Gertrude, come away!
The sun no sooner shall the mountains touch,
But we will ship him hence: and this vile deed   30
We must, with all our majesty and skill,
Both countenance and excuse. Ho, Guildenstern!
    (Re-enter ROSENCRANTZ and GUILDENSTERN.)
Friends both, go join you with some further aid:
Hamlet in madness hath Polonius slain,
And from his mother's closet hath he dragged him:
Go seek him out; speak fair, and bring the body
Into the chapel. I pray you, haste in this.
    (Exeunt ROSENCRANTZ and GUILDENSTERN.)
Come, Gertrude, we'll call up our wisest friends;
And let them know, both what we mean to do,   39
And what's untimely done, (so viperous slander),
Whose whisper o'er the world's diameter,
As level as the cannon to his blank,
Transports his poisoned shot, may miss our name,
And hit the woundless air. O, come away!
My soul is full of discord and dismay.   (Exeunt.)

SCENE 2. Another room in the castle.

(Enter HAMLET.)

HAMLET. Safely stowed.
    ROSENCRANTZ AND GUILDENSTERN (within). Hamlet! Lord Hamlet!
    HAMLET. But soft, what noise? who calls on Hamlet? O, here they come.
    (Enter ROSENCRANTZ and GUILDENSTERN.)
    ROSENCRANTZ. What have you done, my lord, with the dead body?
    HAMLET. Compounded it with dust, whereto 'tis kin.
    ROSENCRANTZ. Tell us where 'tis, that we may take it thence
And bear it to the chapel.

---

17. providence, foresight, foreknowledge. 18. short; that is, on a short tether. 42. blank, a white spot in the center of a target, the bull's-eye. 44. woundless, invulnerable.

HAMLET. Do not believe it.
    ROSENCRANTZ. Believe what?   10
    HAMLET. That I can keep your counsel and not mine own. Besides, to be demanded of a sponge! what replication should be made by the son of a king?
    ROSENCRANTZ. Take you me for a sponge, my lord?
    HAMLET. Ay, sir, that soaks up the king's countenance, his rewards, his authorities. But such officers do the king best service in the end: he keeps them, like an ape, in the corner of his jaw; first mouthed, to be last swallowed: when he needs what you have gleaned, it is but squeezing you, and, sponge, you shall be dry again.   23
    ROSENCRANTZ. I understand you not, my lord.
    HAMLET. I am glad of it: a knavish speech sleeps in a foolish ear.
    ROSENCRANTZ. My lord, you must tell us where the body is, and go with us to the king.
    HAMLET. The body is with the king, but the king is not with the body. The king is a thing—
    GUILDENSTERN. A thing, my lord!   31
    HAMLET. Of nothing: bring me to him. Hide fox, and all after.   (Exeunt.)

SCENE 3. Another room in the castle.

(Enter KING, attended.)

KING. I have sent to seek him, and to find the body.
How dangerous is it that this man goes loose!
Yet must not we put the strong law on him:
He's loved of the distracted multitude,
Who like not in their judgment, but their eyes;
And where 'tis so, the offender's scourge is weighed,
But never the offence. To bear all smooth and even,
This sudden sending him away must seem
Deliberate pause: diseases desperate grown
By desperate appliance are relieved,   10
Or not at all.
    (Enter ROSENCRANTZ.)
            How now! what hath befallen?
    ROSENCRANTZ. Where the dead body is bestowed,
        my lord,
We cannot get from him.

Act IV, Scene 2. 11. keep your counsel. Hamlet is aware of the treachery of Rosencrantz and Guildenstern, but says nothing about it. 12. demanded of, questioned by. 13. replication, reply. 17. countenance, favor, patronage. authorities, backing, support. 29–30. body . . . body. This ambiguous line has received many interpretations: "The body lies in death with the king, my father; but my father walks disembodied"; "Claudius has the bodily possession of kingship, but kingliness, or justice of inheritance, is not in him"; "The King is still alive in his body, but he is not with the dead body of Polonius." 32–33. Hide . . . after, a signal cry in the old game of hide-and-seek.
Act IV, Scene 3. 4. distracted, without the ability to form correct or logical judgments—a characteristic attitude of both the Middle Ages and the Renaissance toward the democratic spirit. 6. scourge, punishment. 9. Deliberate pause, considered action.

KING. But where is he?

ROSENCRANTZ. Without, my lord; guarded, to know your pleasure.

KING. Bring him before us.

ROSENCRANTZ. Ho, Guildenstern! bring in my lord.

(*Enter* HAMLET *and* GUILDENSTERN.)

KING. Now, Hamlet, where's Polonius?

HAMLET. At supper.

KING. At supper! where? 19

HAMLET. Not where he eats, but where he is eaten: a certain convocation of politic worms are e'en at him. Your worm is your only emperor for diet: we fat all creatures else to fat us, and we fat ourselves for maggots; your fat king and your lean beggar is but variable service, two dishes, but to one table; that's the end. 26

KING. Alas, alas!

HAMLET. A man may fish with the worm that hath eat of a king, and eat of the fish that hath fed of that worm. 30

KING. What dost thou mean by this?

HAMLET. Nothing but to show you how a king may go a progress through the guts of a beggar.

KING. Where is Polonius?

HAMLET. In Heaven; send thither to see: if your messenger find him not there, seek him i' the other place yourself. But indeed, if you find him not within this month, you shall nose him as you go up the stairs into the lobby.

KING. Go seek him there. 40

(*To some* Attendants.)

HAMLET. He will stay till you come.

(*Exeunt* Attendants.)

KING. Hamlet, this deed, for thine especial safety,—

Which we do tender, as we dearly grieve

For that which thou hast done,—must send thee hence

With fiery quickness: therefore prepare thyself;

The bark is ready, and the wind at help,

The associates tend, and everything is bent

For England.

HAMLET. For England!

KING. Ay, Hamlet.

HAMLET. Good.

KING. So is it, if thou knewest our purposes.

HAMLET. I see a cherub that sees them. But, come; for England!

Farewell, dear mother.

KING. Thy loving father, Hamlet. 52

HAMLET. My mother: father and mother is man and wife; man and wife is one flesh; and so, my mother. Come, for England! (*Exit.*)

21. convocation . . . worms, a jesting allusion to the Diet of Worms (1521), from which Luther departed to continue the German Reformation. politic, crafty. 25. variable service, a variety of dishes, a change of diet. 33. progress, a royal journey of state. 43. tender, hold dear, value. 50. cherub, the angel of knowledge.

KING. Follow him at foot; tempt him with speed aboard;

Delay it not; I'll have him hence tonight:

Away! for every thing is sealed and done

That else leans on the affair: pray you, make haste.

(*Exeunt* ROSENCRANTZ *and* GUILDENSTERN.)

And, England, if my love thou holdest at aught— 60

As my great power thereof may give thee sense,

Since yet thy cicatrice looks raw and red

After the Danish sword, and thy free awe

Pays homage to us—thou mayst not coldly set

Our sovereign process; which imports at full,

By letters congruing to that effect,

The present death of Hamlet. Do it, England:

For like the hectic in my blood he rages,

And thou must cure me: till I know 'tis done, 69

Howe'er my haps, my joys were ne'er begun. (*Exit.*)

SCENE 4. *A plain in Denmark.*

(*Enter* FORTINBRAS, a Captain, *and* Soldiers, *marching.*)

FORTINBRAS. Go, captain, from me greet the Danish king;

Tell him that, by his license, Fortinbras

Craves the conveyance of a promised march

Over his kingdom. You know the rendezvous.

If that his majesty would aught with us,

We shall express our duty in his eye;

And let him know so.

CAPTAIN. I will do 't, my lord.

FORTINBRAS. Go softly on.

(*Exeunt* FORTINBRAS *and* Soldiers.)

(*Enter* HAMLET, ROSENCRANTZ, GUILDENSTERN, *and Others.*)

HAMLET. Good sir, whose powers are these?

CAPTAIN. They are of Norway, sir. 10

HAMLET. How purposed, sir, I pray you?

CAPTAIN. Against some part of Poland.

HAMLET. Who commands them, sir?

CAPTAIN. The nephew to old Norway, Fortinbras.

HAMLET. Goes it against the main of Poland, sir, Or for some frontier?

CAPTAIN. Truly to speak, and with no addition,

We go to gain a little patch of ground

That hath in it no profit but the name.

To pay five ducats, five, I would not farm it; 20

Nor will it yield to Norway or the Pole

A ranker rate, should it be sold in fee.

56. at foot, close behind, on his heels. 63. free awe, awe not inspired by threat of force. 65. process, formal command, mandate. 68. hectic, fever. 70. haps, fortunes.
Act IV, Scene 4. 2. license, leave. 3. conveyance, convoy, escort. 6. in his eye, in his presence. 8. softly, slowly. 15. main, the chief part of the country, the country itself. 17. addition, amplification, elaboration. 20. farm it, take a lease of it. 22. ranker, higher, better. in fee, in fee simple, outright.

HAMLET. Why, then the Polack never will defend
  it.
CAPTAIN. Yes, it is already garrisoned.
HAMLET. Two thousand souls and twenty thousand
  ducats
Will not debate the question of this straw:
This is the imposthume of much wealth and peace,
That inward breaks, and shows no cause without
Why the man dies. I humbly thank you, sir.
CAPTAIN. God be wi' you, sir.   (*Exit.*)
ROSENCRANTZ. Will 't please you go, my lord?   30
HAMLET. I'll be with you straight. Go a little be-
  fore.   (*Exeunt all except* HAMLET.)
How all occasions do inform against me,
And spur my dull revenge! What is a man,
If his chief good and market of his time
Be but to sleep and feed? a beast, no more.
Sure, he that made us with such large discourse,
Looking before and after, gave us not
That capability and god-like reason
To fust in us unused. Now, whether it be
Bestial oblivion, or some craven scruple   40
Of thinking too precisely on the event,
A thought which, quartered, hath but one part wis-
  dom
And ever three parts coward, I do not know
Why yet I live to say 'This thing's to do';
Sith I have cause and will and strength and means
To do 't. Examples gross as earth exhort me:
Witness this army of such mass and charge
Led by a delicate and tender prince,
Whose spirit with divine ambition puffed
Makes mouths at the invisible event,   50
Exposing what is mortal and unsure
To all that fortune, death and danger dare,
Even for an egg-shell. Rightly to be great
Is not to stir without great argument,
But greatly to find quarrel in a straw
When honor's at the stake. How stand I then,
That have a father killed, a mother stained,
Excitements of my reason and my blood,
And let all sleep? while, to my shame, I see
The imminent death of twenty thousand men,
That, for a fantasy and trick of fame,   61
Go to their graves like beds, fight for a plot
Whereon the numbers cannot try the cause,
Which is not tomb enough and continent
To hide the slain? O, from this time forth,
My thoughts be bloody, or be nothing worth! (*Exit.*)

---

26. debate . . . straw, settle this trivial matter. 27. imposthume, a purulent abscess or swelling. 32. occasions, happenings, events. inform against, show up, betray; Hamlet is becoming impatient at his own dilatory behavior. 34. chief good . . . time, profit derived from selling (making use) of his time. 36. discourse, power of reasoning. 39. fust, grow moldy, decay. 41. event, outcome. 45. Sith, since. 54. argument, cause, reason. 58. Excitements of, incentives, inspirations to. blood, passion. 61. trick, toy, trifle. 64. continent, containing, holding (adj.)

SCENE 5. *Elsinore. A room in the castle.*

(*Enter* QUEEN, HORATIO, *and* a Gentleman.)
QUEEN. I will not speak with her.
GENTLEMAN. She is importunate, indeed distract:
Her mood will needs be pitied.
QUEEN.   What would she have?
GENTLEMAN. She speaks much of her father; says
  she hears
There's tricks i' the world; and hems, and beats her
  heart;
Spurns enviously at straws; speaks things in doubt,
That carry but half sense: her speech is nothing,
Yet the unshaped use of it doth move
The hearers to collection; they aim at it,   9
And botch the words up fit to their own thoughts;
Which, as her winks, and nods, and gestures yield
  them,
Indeed would make one think there might be
  thought,
Though nothing sure, yet much unhappily.
HORATIO. 'Twere good she were spoken with: for
  she may strew
Dangerous conjectures in ill-breeding minds.
QUEEN. Let her come in.
                      (*Exit* HORATIO.)
To my sick soul, as sin's true nature is,
Each toy seems prologue to some great amiss:
So full of artless jealousy is guilt,
It spills itself in fearing to be spilt.   20
(*Re-enter* HORATIO, *with* OPHELIA.)
OPHELIA. Where is the beauteous majesty of Den-
  mark?
QUEEN. How now, Ophelia!
OPHELIA (*sings*). How should I your true love
          know
          From another one?
          By his cockle hat and staff,
          And his sandal shoon.
QUEEN. Alas, sweet lady, what imports this song?
OPHELIA. Say you? nay, pray you, mark.
          He is dead and gone, lady,
          He is dead and gone;   30
          At his head a grass-green turf,
          At his heels a stone.
QUEEN. Nay, but, Ophelia,—

Act IV, Scene 5. 5. tricks, deceptions, deceits. 6. Spurns enviously, kicks spitefully. 8. unshaped, unformed, artless. 9. collection, inference. aim, guess. 10. botch, patch. 11. yield, bring them forth. 13. nothing, not at all. 18. toy, trifle. great amiss, great disaster, calamity. 19–20. So full . . . spilt. Guilt is so full of suspicion that it unskilfully betrays itself in fearing to be revealed. 25. cockle hat, a hat worn with a cockle-shell attached to it, as a sign that the wearer had been on a pilgrimage to the famous shrine of Saint James (Santiago) of Compostella. In medieval romances the dress of a pilgrim, or palmer, was a conventional disguise for a lover. 26. shoon, the old *n* plural of shoe.

OPHELIA. Pray you, mark

> (*Sings*). White his shroud as the moun-
>   tain snow,—

(*Enter* KING.)

QUEEN. Alas, look here, my lord.

OPHELIA (*sings*). Larded with sweet flowers;
>   Which bewept to the grave did
>   go
>   With true-love showers.

KING. How do you, pretty lady?   40

OPHELIA. Well, God 'ild you! They say the owl was a baker's daughter. Lord, we know what we are, but know not what we may be. God be at your table!

KING. Conceit upon her father.

OPHELIA. Pray you, let's have no words of this; but when they ask you what it means, say you this:

> (*Sings*). Tomorrow is Saint Valentine's
>   day,
>   All in the morning betime,
>   And I a maid at your window,
>   To be your Valentine.   51
>   Then up he rose, and donned
>   his clothes,
>   And dupped the chamber-
>   door;
>   Let in the maid, that out a maid
>   Never departed more.

KING. Pretty Ophelia!

OPHELIA. Indeed, la, without an oath, I'll make an end on 't:

> (*Sings*). By Gis and by Saint Charity,
>   Alack, and fie for shame!   60
>   Young men will do 't, if they
>   come to 't;
>   By cock, they are to blame,
>   Quoth she, 'Before you tumbled
>   me,
>   You promised me to wed.'
>   'So would I ha' done, by yonder
>   sun,
>   An thou hadst not come to
>   my bed.'

KING. How long hath she been thus?

OPHELIA. I hope all will be well. We must be patient; but I cannot choose but weep, to think they should lay him i' the cold ground. My brother shall know of it: and so I thank you for your good counsel.

Come, my coach! Good night, ladies; good night, sweet ladies; good night, good night. (*Exit.*)   74

KING. Follow her close; give her good watch, I pray you.

(*Exit* HORATIO.)

O, this is the poison of deep grief; it springs
All from her father's death. O Gertrude, Gertrude,
When sorrows come, they come not single spies,
But in battalions. First, her father slain:
Next, your son gone; and he most violent author   80
Of his own just remove: the people muddied,
Thick and unwholesome in their thoughts and whis-
   pers,
For good Polonius' death; and we have done but
   greenly,
In hugger-mugger to inter him: poor Ophelia
Divided from herself and her fair judgment,
Without the which we are pictures, or mere beasts:
Last, and as much containing as all these,
Her brother is in secret come from France;
Feeds on his wonder, keeps himself in clouds,
And wants not buzzers to infect his ear   90
With pestilent speeches of his father's death;
Wherein necessity, of matter beggared,
Will nothing stick our person to arraign
In ear and ear. O my dear Gertrude, this,
Like to a murdering-piece, in many places
Gives me superfluous death.

>   (*A noise within.*)

QUEEN.   Alack, what noise is this?

KING. Where are my Switzers? Let them guard the
   door.

(*Enter another* Gentleman.)

What is the matter?

GENTLEMAN.   Save yourself, my lord:
The ocean, overpeering of his list,
Eats not the flats with more impetuous haste
Than young Laertes, in a riotous head,   101
O'erbears your officers. The rabble call him lord;
And, as the world were now but to begin,
Antiquity forgot, custom not known,
The ratifiers and props of every word,
They cry, 'Choose we: Laertes shall be king':
Caps, hands, and tongues, applaud it to the clouds:
'Laertes shall be king, Laertes king!'   108

QUEEN. How cheerfully on the false trail they cry!
O, this is counter, you false Danish dogs!

---

37. **Larded,** decorated, garnished. 41. **God 'ild,** God yield or reward. 42. **owl . . . daughter,** referring to an old medieval legend that a baker's daughter, refusing bread to Christ, was turned into an owl. 45. **Conceit . . . father,** her imagination is directed toward her dead father. 51. **Valentine,** according to the old tradition, the first girl seen by a man on the morning of St. Valentine's Day was his valentine or sweetheart. Ophelia makes the legend work in reverse. 53. **dupped,** opened. 59. **Gis,** a corruption of Jesus. 62. **cock,** a perversion of God used in oaths. 66. **An,** if.

83. **greenly,** foolishly, in immature fashion. 84. **hugger-mugger,** secret and confused haste. 89. **in clouds,** invisible. 90. **buzzers,** gossipers, tattletales. 93. **nothing stick,** not hesitate in any way. 94. **in ear and ear,** in everybody's ear. 95. **murdering-piece,** a small cannon loaded with many small missiles, a kind of cannonized shotgun. 97. **Switzers,** Swiss guards, mercenaries. 99. **overpeering of his list,** overflowing his boundaries. 101. **head,** armed force. 102. **O'erbears,** overcomes, seduces. 105. **word,** title, custom. 110. **counter,** an old hunting term indicating that the trail is being followed in a direction opposite to that taken by the game.

KING. The doors are broke.

(Noise within.)

(Enter LAERTES, armed; Danes following.)

LAERTES. Where is this king? Sirs, stand you all
   without.

DANES. No, let's come in.

LAERTES.   I pray you, give me leave.

DANES. We will, we will.

(They retire without the door.)

LAERTES. I thank you: keep the door. O thou vile
   king,

Give me my father!

KING.   Calmly, good Laertes.

LAERTES. That drop of blood that's calm proclaims
   me bastard,

Cries cuckold to my father, brands the harlot

Even here, between the chaste unsmirched brow

Of my true mother.

KING.   What is the cause, Laertes,

That thy rebellion looks so giant-like?   121

Let him go, Gertrude; do not fear our person:

There's such divinity doth hedge a king,

That treason can but peep to what it would,

Acts little of his will. Tell me, Laertes,

Why thou art thus incensed. Let him go, Gertrude.

Speak, man.

LAERTES. Where is my father?

KING.   Dead.

QUEEN.   But not by him.

KING. Let him demand his fill.

LAERTES. How came he dead? I'll not be juggled
   with: 130

To Hell, allegiance! vows, to the blackest devil!

Conscience and grace, to the profoundest pit!

I dare damnation. To this point I stand,

That both the worlds I give to negligence,

Let come what comes; only I'll be revenged

Most thoroughly for my father.

KING.   Who shall stay you?

LAERTES. My will, not all the world:

And for my means, I'll husband them so well,

They shall go far with little.

KING.   Good Laertes,

If you desire to know the certainty   140

Of your dear father's death, is 't writ in your revenge,

That, swoopstake, you will draw both friend and foe,

Winner and loser?

LAERTES.   None but his enemies.

KING.   Will you know them then?

LAERTES. To his good friends thus wide I'll ope
   my arms;

And like the kind life-rendering pelican,

Repast them with my blood.

KING.   Why, now you speak

Like a good child and a true gentleman.

That I am guiltless of your father's death,

And am most sensibly in grief for it,   150

It shall as level to your judgment pierce

As day does to your eye.

DANES (within).   Let her come in.

LAERTES. How now! what noise is that?

(Re-enter OPHELIA.)

O heat, dry up my brains! tears seven times salt,

Burn out the sense and virtue of mine eye!

By Heaven, thy madness shall be paid with weight,

Till our scale turn the beam. O rose of May!

Dear maid, kind sister, sweet Ophelia!

O heavens! is 't possible, a young maid's wits

Should be as mortal as an old man's life?   160

Nature is fine in love, and where 'tis fine,

It sends some precious instance of itself

After the thing it loves.

OPHELIA (sings). They bore him barefaced on the
            bier;

           Hey non nonny, nonny, hey
           nonny;

           And in his grave rained many
           a tear:—

Fare you well, my dove!

LAERTES. Hadst thou thy wits, and didst persuade
   revenge,

It could not move thus.

OPHELIA (sings). You must sing a-down a-down,
          An you call him a-down-a.   171

O how the wheel becomes it! It is the false steward,

that stole his master's daughter.

LAERTES. This nothing's more than matter.

OPHELIA. There's rosemary, that's for remembrance; pray, love, remember: and there is pansies,
that's for thoughts.

LAERTES. A document in madness, thoughts and
remembrance fitted.   179

OPHELIA. There's fennel for you, and columbines:
there's rue for you; and here's some for me: we may
call it herb-grace o' Sundays: O, you must wear your
rue with a difference. There's a daisy: I would give

---

122. **fear,** have fears for.   132. **grace,** God's favor.   134. **both the worlds . . . negligence,** I have contempt for both the present and the hereafter.   142. **swoopstake,** one who gathers all his winnings at dice in one swoop; hence, any indiscriminate action.

146. **pelican,** an allusion to the old belief that a pelican fed its young with its own blood.   147. **repast,** feed.   150. **sensibly,** feelingly. 154. **heat,** emotion, passion—both of which were supposed to gener- ate heat.   172. **wheel,** possibly a refrain; possibly referring to a spinning-wheel which accompanied the singing of the song. **false steward.** The exact story to which this is an allusion is not precisely known, but the false steward is a stock figure in medieval romances and ballads.   175. **rosemary,** used as a symbol of remembrance both at weddings and at funerals.   177. **pansies,** symbols of love and courtship.   178. **document,** a lesson or piece of instruction.   180. **fennel,** the symbol of flattery. **columbines,** symbols of unchastity and ingratitude.   181. **rue,** the symbol of repentance; when mingled with holy water it was called "herb of grace." But Ophelia is probably playing on the two meanings of the word: "repentant" and "having pity."   183. **difference,** in heraldry, a distinction in the coats of arms for different branches of the family.

you some violets, but they withered all when my father died: they say he made a good end,— 186
(*Sings*): For bonny sweet Robin is all my joy.

LAERTES. Thought and affliction, passion, Hell itself,
She turns to favor and to prettiness. 189

OPHELIA (*sings*).   And will he not come again?
And will he not come again?
No, no, he is dead:
Go to thy death-bed:
He never will come again.

His beard was as white as snow,
All flaxen was his poll;
He is gone, he is gone,
And we cast away moan:
God ha' mercy on his soul!

And of all Christian souls, I pray God. God be wi' ye.
(*Exit.*)

LAERTES. Do you see this, O God? 201

KING. Laertes, I must commune with your grief,
Or you deny me right. Go but apart,
Make choice of whom your wisest friends you will,
And they shall hear and judge 'twixt you and me:
If by direct or by collateral hand
They find us touched, we will our kingdom give,
Our crown, our life, and all that we call ours,
To you in satisfaction; but if not,
Be you content to lend your patience to us, 210
And we shall jointly labor with your soul
To give it due content.

LAERTES.   Let this be so;
His means of death, his obscure funeral—
No trophy, sword, nor hatchment o'er his bones,
No noble rite nor formal ostentation—
Cry to be heard, as 'twere from heaven to earth,
That I must call 't in question.

KING.   So you shall;
And where the offence is let the great axe fall.
I pray you, go with me.   (*Exeunt.*)

SCENE 6. *Another room in the castle.*

(*Enter* HORATIO *and a* Servant.)

HORATIO. What are they that would speak
with me?

SERVANT. Sailors, sir: they say they have letters
for you.

HORATIO. Let them come in.   (*Exit* Servant.)
I do not know from what part of the world
I should be greeted, if not from lord Hamlet.

(*Enters* Sailors.)

FIRST SAILOR. God bless you, sir.

HORATIO. Let him bless thee too.

FIRST SAILOR. He shall, sir, an 't please him.
There's a letter for you, sir; it comes from the ambassador that was bound for England; if your name
be Horatio, as I am let to know it is. 11

HORATIO (*reads*). 'Horatio, when thou shalt have
overlooked this, give these fellows some means to
the king: they have letters for him. Ere we were two
days old at sea, a pirate of very warlike appointment
gave us chase. Finding ourselves too slow of sail, we
put on a compelled valor, and in the grapple I
boarded them: on the instant they got clear of our
ship; so I alone became their prisoner. They have
dealt with me like thieves of mercy: but they knew
what they did; I am to do a good turn for them. Let
the king have the letters I have sent; and repair thou
to me with as much speed as thou wouldst fly death.
I have words to speak in thine ear will make thee
dumb; yet are they much too light for the bore of
the matter. These good fellows will bring thee where
I am. Rosencrantz and Guildenstern hold their course
for England; of them I have much to tell thee. Farewell. 30

'He that thou knowest thine,
HAMLET.'

Come, I will make you way for these your letters;
And do 't the speedier, that you may direct me
To him from whom you brought them. (*Exeunt.*)

SCENE 7. *Another room in the castle.*

(*Enter* KING *and* LAERTES.)

KING. Now must your conscience my acquittance
seal,
And you must put me in your heart for friend,
Sith you have heard, and with a knowing ear,
That he which hath your noble father slain
Pursued my life.

LAERTES.   It well appears: but tell me
Why you proceeded not against these feats,
So crimeful and so capital in nature,
As by your safety, wisdom, all things else,
You mainly were stirred up.

KING.   O, for two special reasons;
Which may to you, perhaps, seem much unsinewed,
But yet to me they are strong. The queen his mother
Lives almost by his looks; and for myself— 12

---

184. **daisy,** symbol of faithlessness and dissembling; **violets,** on the other hand, symbolize constancy and sincerity. 187. **For bonny . . . joy,** probably a line from a Robin Hood ballad. 188. **Thought,** melancholy thoughts. 189. **favor,** attraction, charm. 190–199. **And will . . . soul,** a popular song of the time entitled *The Merry Milkmaids* or, somewhat confusingly, *The Milkmaids' Dumps.* 196. **poll,** head. 203. **right,** my rights. 206. **collateral,** indirect. 207. **touched,** implicated, involved. 214. **hatchment,** in heraldry, a tablet displaying the armorial bearings of a deceased person.

Act IV, Scene 6. 14. **means,** access. 16. **appointment,** equipment and manner. 21. **thieves of mercy.** This is an old rhetorical device, *thieves of mercy* equals *merciful thieves.* 27. **bore,** caliber, scope. *Act IV, Scene 7.* 1. **conscience,** knowledge that a thing is true. 9. **mainly,** greatly, mightily.

My virtue or my plague, be it either which—
She's so conjunctive to my life and soul,
That, as the star moves not but in his sphere,
I could not but by her. The other motive,
Why to a public count I might not go,
Is the great love the general gender bear him;
Who, dipping all his faults in their affection,
Would, like the spring that turneth wood to stone,
Convert his gyves to graces; so that my arrows,   21
Too slightly timbered for so loud a wind,
Would have reverted to my bow again,
And not where I had aimed them.

LAERTES. And so have I a noble father lost;
A sister driven into desperate terms,
Whose worth, if praises may go back again,
Stood challenger on mount of all the age
For her perfections: but my revenge will come.

KING. Break not your sleeps for that: you must not
        think   30
That we are made of stuff so flat and dull
That we can let our beard be shook with danger
And think it pastime. You shortly shall hear more:
I loved your father, and we love ourself;
And that, I hope, will teach you to imagine—

(*Enter a* Messenger.)

How now! what news?

MESSENGER.   Letters, my lord, from Hamlet:
This to your majesty; this to the queen.

KING. From Hamlet! who brought them?

MESSENGER. Sailors, my lord, they say; I saw them
        not: 39
They were given me by Claudio; he received them
Of him that brought them.

KING.   Laertes, you shall hear them.
Leave us.   (*Exit* MESSENGER.)
(*Reads*). 'High and mighty, You shall know I am set
naked on your kingdom. Tomorrow shall I beg leave
to see your kingly eyes: when I shall, first asking your
pardon thereunto, recount the occasion of my sudden
and more strange return.

                                            HAMLET.'

What should this mean? Are all the rest come back?
Or is it some abuse, and no such thing?   51

LAERTES. Know you the hand?

KING.   'Tis Hamlet's character. 'Naked!'
And in a postscript here, he says 'alone.'
Can you advise me?

LAERTES. I'm lost in it, my lord. But let him come;
It warms the very sickness in my heart,

That I shall live and tell him to his teeth,
'Thus didst thou.'

KING.   If it be so, Laertes—
As how should it be so? how otherwise?—
Will you be ruled by me?

LAERTES.   Ay, my lord;   60
So you will not o'errule me to a peace.

KING. To thine own peace. If he be now returned,
As checking at his voyage, and that he means
No more to undertake it, I will work him
To an exploit, now ripe in my device,
Under the which he shall not choose but fall:
And for his death no wind of blame shall breathe,
But even his mother shall uncharge the practice
And call it accident.

LAERTES.   My lord, I will be ruled;
The rather, if you could devise it so   70
That I might be the organ.

KING.   It falls right.
You have been talked of since your travel much,
And that in Hamlet's hearing, for a quality
Wherein, they say, you shine; your sum of parts
Did not together pluck such envy from him
As did that one, and that, in my regard,
Of the unworthiest siege.

LAERTES.   What part is that, my lord?

KING. A very riband in the cap of youth,
Yet needful too; for youth no less becomes
The light and careless livery that it wears   80
Than settled age his sables and his weeds,
Importing health and graveness. Two months since,
Here was a gentleman of Normandy:—
I've seen myself, and served against, the French,
And they can well on horseback: but this gallant
Had witchcraft in 't; he grew upon his seat;
And to such wondrous doing brought his horse,
As had he been incorpsed and demi-natured
With the brave beast: so far he topped my thought,
That I, in forgery of shapes and tricks,   90
Came short of what he did.

LAERTES.   A Norman was 't?

KING. A Norman.

LAERTES. Upon my life, Lamond.

KING.   The very same.

---

14. **conjunctive,** conformable, closely joined.   16. Insert "be" between "but" and "by."   17. **count,** account, reckoning.   18. **general gender,** the common people.   20. **spring,** snare so heavily limed as to cake wood.   26. **terms,** state, condition.   28. **on mount,** set up on high as a model.   37. **to the queen.** The content of Hamlet's letter to his mother is never told; in fact, the missive seems to have slipped completely from Shakespeare's mind.   40. **Claudio.** This character does not appear on the stage at any time in the play.   44. **naked,** without retinue or followers.   51. **abuse,** deception.   53. **character,** handwriting.

59. **how should . . . otherwise?** How can this be true? And yet, with this evidence of the letter, can Hamlet's return be anything but true?   63. **checking at,** in falconry, the term used to denote the action of a bird's leaving the pursuit of the quarry in order to attack a passing bird.   68. **uncharge the practice,** not object to the plan.   71. **organ,** instrument, means, agent.   77. **siege,** rank, seat.   81. **sables . . . weeds,** rich garments and clothing appropriate to old age.   82. **health,** wealth and prosperity, worldly success.   85. **can well,** know well how to perform, are skilled.   88. **incorpsed and demi-natured,** inclosed in one body and nearly of one nature, as a centaur contains the man and the horse in one body and is chiefly horselike.   90. **forgery,** invention.   93. **Lamond.** Pietro Monte, instructor to the Master of Horse at the court of Louis XII, King of France in Shakespeare's day, is very likely disguised here under the name of Lamond.

LAERTES. I know him well: he is the brooch indeed
And gem of all the nation.
KING. He made confession of you,
And gave you such a masterly report
For art and exercise in your defence
And for your rapier most especial.
That he cried out, 'twould be a sight indeed, 100
If one could match you: the scrimers of their nation,
He swore, had neither motion, guard, nor eye,
If you opposed them. Sir, this report of his
Did Hamlet so envenom with his envy
That he could nothing do but wish and beg
Your sudden coming o'er, to play with him.
Now, out of this,—
LAERTES. What out of this, my lord?
KING. Laertes, was your father dear to you?
Or are you like the painting of a sorrow,
A face without a heart?
LAERTES. Why ask you this? 110
KING. Not that I think you did not love your father;
But that I know love is begun by time;
And that I see, in passages of proof,
Time qualifies the spark and fire of it.
There lives within the very flame of love
A kind of wick or snuff that will abate it;
And nothing is at a like goodness still;
For goodness, growing to a plurisy,
Dies in his own too much: that we would do,
We should do when we would; for this 'would'
changes 120
And hath abatements and delays as many
As there are tongues, are hands, are accidents;
And then this 'should' is like a spendthrift sigh,
That hurts by easing. But, to the quick o' the ulcer:—
Hamlet comes back; what would you undertake,
To show yourself your father's son in deed
More than in words?
LAERTES. To cut his throat i' the church.
KING. No place, indeed, should murder sanctuarize;
Revenge should have no bounds. But, good Laertes,
Will you do this, keep close within your chamber. 130
Hamlet returned shall know you are come home:
We'll put on those shall praise your excellence
And set a double varnish on the fame
The Frenchman gave you, bring you in fine together
And wager on your heads: he, being remiss,

Most generous and free from all contriving,
Will not peruse the foils; so that, with ease,
Or with a little shuffling, you may choose
A sword unbated, and in a pass of practice
Requite him for your father.
LAERTES. I will do 't: 140
And, for that purpose, I'll anoint my sword.
I bought an unction of a mountebank,
So mortal that, but dip a knife in it,
Where it draws blood no cataplasm so rare,
Collected from all simples that have virtue
Under the moon, can save the thing from death
That is but scratched withal: I'll touch my point
With this contagion, that, if I gall him slightly
It may be death.
KING. Let's further think of this;
Weigh what convenience both of time and means 150
May fit us to our shape: if this should fail,
And that our drift look through our bad performance,
'Twere better not assayed: therefore this project
Should have a back or second, that might hold,
If this should blast in proof. Soft! let me see:
We'll make a solemn wager on your cunnings:
I ha 't:
When in your motion you are hot and dry—
As make your bouts more violent to that end—
And that he calls for drink, I'll have prepared him 160
A chalice for the nonce, whereon but sipping,
If he by chance escape your venomed stuck,
Our purpose may hold there.
(Enter QUEEN.)
How now, sweet queen!
QUEEN. One woe doth tread upon another's heel,
So fast they follow: your sister's drowned, Laertes.
LAERTES. Drowned! O, where?
QUEEN. There is a willow grows aslant a brook,
That shows his hoar leaves in the glassy stream;
There with fantastic garlands did she make
Of crow-flowers, nettles, daisies, and long purples 170
That liberal shepherds give a grosser name,
But our cold maids do dead men's fingers call them;
There, on the pendent boughs her coronet weeds
Clambering to hang, an envious sliver broke;
When down her weedy trophies and herself
Fell in the weeping brook. Her clothes spread wide;
And, mermaid-like, awhile they bore her up:

96. confession of you, a report of you. 98. art and exercise, skillful exercise. defence, self-defence with sword and rapier. 101. scrimers, fencers. 106. play, fence. 113. passages of proof, proved instances or occasions. 117. still, ever, always. 118. plurisy, excess, plethora. 119. his own too much, its own excess. 121. abatements, diminutions, losses. 122. accidents, events, happenings. 123. spendthrift. There was an old belief that each sigh cost the human heart a drop of blood. 124. quick o' the ulcer, the core of the abscess, the heart of the matter. 128. sanctuarize, protect from punishment. In medieval times, certain religious places were endowed with the privilege of sanctuary; all criminals taking refuge in those places were immune from arrest pending consideration of their cases by church authorities.

139. unbated, not blunted or dulled. pass of practice, an unexpected and treacherous thrust. 144. cataplasm, a plaster used as a poultice. 145. simples, herbs, recipes, prescriptions. 146. Under the moon. To pick an herb by moonlight was to enhance its medicinal effects. 148. gall, scratch, graze. 151. shape, planned action. 152. drift . . . performance, intention be revealed through our bungling. 155. blast in proof, burst or explode in testing, as a cannon. 156. cunnings, skills. 162. stuck, thrust; cf. Italian stoccado. 167. willow, dramatically appropriate, for this tree was a symbol of forsaken love. 170. crow-flowers, buttercups. long purples, the early purple orchis. 171. liberal, free- or broad-spoken. 173. coronet, garlanded; an adjective here. 174. sliver, branch; envious, in the sense of evil, malicious.

Which time she chanted snatches of old tunes;
As one incapable of her own distress,
Or like a creature native and indued   180
Unto that element: but long it could not be
Till that her garments, heavy with their drink,
Pulled the poor wretch from her melodious lay
To muddy death.
   LAERTES.   Alas, then, she is drowned?
   QUEEN. Drowned, drowned.
   LAERTES. Too much of water hast thou, poor
     Ophelia,
And therefore I forbid my tears: but yet
It is our trick; nature her custom holds,
Let shame say what it will: when these are gone,
The woman will be out. Adieu, my lord: 190
I have a speech of fire, that fain would blaze,
But that this folly douts it.   (*Exit.*)
   KING.   Let's follow, Gertrude:
How much I had to do to calm his rage!
Now fear I this will give it start again;
Therefore let's follow.   (*Exeunt.*)

ACT V

SCENE 1. *A churchyard.*

(*Enter two* Clowns, *with spades, etc.*)

   FIRST CLOWN. Is she to be buried in Christian
burial that wilfully seeks her own salvation?
   SECOND CLOWN. I tell thee she is; and therefore
make her grave straight: the crowner hath sat on her,
and finds it Christian burial.   5
   FIRST CLOWN. How can that be, unless she
drowned herself in her own defence?
   SECOND CLOWN. Why, 'tis found so.
   FIRST CLOWN. It must be 'se offendendo'; it cannot
be else. For here lies the point: if I drown myself
wittingly, it argues an act: and an act hath three
branches: it is, to act, to do, and to perform: argal,
she drowned herself wittingly.   14
   SECOND CLOWN. Nay, but hear you, goodman
delver,—

   FIRST CLOWN. Give me leave. Here lies the water;
good; here stands the man: good; if the man go to
this water, and drown himself, it is, will he, nill he,
he goes,—mark you that; but if the water come to
him and drown him, he drowns not himself: argal,
he that is not guilty of his own death shortens not his
own life.
   SECOND CLOWN. But is this law?   23
   FIRST CLOWN. Ay, marry, is 't; crowner's quest law.
   SECOND CLOWN. Will you ha' the truth on 't? If this
had not been a gentlewoman, she should have been
buried out o' Christian burial.   28
   FIRST CLOWN. Why, there thou sayest: and the
more pity that great folk should have countenance
in this world to drown or hang themselves, more than
their even Christian. Come, my spade. There is no
ancient gentleman but gardeners, ditchers, and
grave-makers: they hold up Adam's profession.
   SECOND CLOWN. Was he a gentleman?
   FIRST CLOWN. A' was the first that ever bore arms.
   SECOND CLOWN. Why, he had none.   39
   FIRST CLOWN. What, art a heathen? How dost thou
understand the Scripture? The Scripture says 'Adam
digged': could he dig without arms? I'll put another
question to thee: if thou answerest me not to the
purpose, confess thyself—   44
   SECOND CLOWN. Go to.
   FIRST CLOWN. What is he that builds stronger than
either the mason, the shipwright, or the carpenter?
   SECOND CLOWN. The gallows-maker, for that frame
outlives a thousand tenants.   50
   FIRST CLOWN. I like thy wit well, in good faith: the
gallows does well: but how does it well? it does well
to those who do ill: now thou dost ill to say the gal-
lows is built stronger than the church: argal, the
gallows may do well to thee. To 't again, come.
   SECOND CLOWN. 'Who builds stronger than a mason, a shipwright, or a carpenter?'
   FIRST CLOWN. Ay, tell me that, and unyoke.
   SECOND CLOWN. Marry, now I can tell.   60
   FIRST CLOWN. To 't.
   SECOND CLOWN. Mass, I cannot tell.
   (*Enter* HAMLET *and* HORATIO, *at a distance.*)
   FIRST CLOWN. Cudgel thy brains no more about it,
for your dull ass will not mend his pace with beating;
and, when you are asked the question next, say 'a
grave-maker': the houses that he makes last till
doomsday. Go, get thee to Yaughan: fetch me a stoup
of liquor.   (*Exit second* Clown.)
         (*He digs and sings.*)

---

179. **incapable,** unable to comprehend. 180. **indued,** endowed with qualities enabling her to live in water. 186–187. **Too much of water . . . tears.** Evidently puns and conceits of this sort were not considered inappropriate for even the most solemn occasions in Elizabethan courtly fashion. 188. **trick,** way, the way of the world. 189–190. **when these . . . will be out,** when these tears have been shed, my womanlike feelings will be satisfied. 192. **douts it,** does it out, suppresses or extinguishes it.
Act V, Scene 1. Stage Direction: **Clowns.** The word *clown* was used to denote a peasant as well as a professional humorous character; the gravediggers here are of the rustic type of clown. 4. **straight,** straightway, immediately. **crowner,** coroner. 9. **'se offendendo.'** The grave-digger means '*se defendendo,*' a term used in verdicts of justifiable homicides committed in self-defense. 12. **three branches,** a broad take-off on legal language. 13. **argal,** a corruption of the Latin *ergo,* "therefore." The clown may perhaps be unwittingly committing a pun on "argue."

24. **quest,** inquest. 29. **there thou sayest,** that's right, "you've got something there." 31. **countenance,** privilege, the "face" to do something. 32. **even Christian,** fellow Christian. 44. **confess thyself.** "And be hanged" completes the quotation. 59. **unyoke,** after your effort you may unharness your oxen. 62. **Mass,** by the Mass. 68. **Yaughan,** probably a London tavern-keeper of some sort of note, but the word has been subjected to much scrutiny. **stoup,** a two-quart measure.

In youth, when I did love, did love,
　　Methought it was very sweet, 　　　　　70
To contract, O, the time, for, ah, my behove,
　　O, methought, there was nothing meet.

HAMLET. Has this fellow no feeling of his business, that he sings at grave-making?

HORATIO. Custom hath made it in him a property of easiness.

HAMLET. 'Tis e'en so: the hand of little employment hath the daintier sense.

FIRST CLOWN (*sings*).
　　But age, with his stealing steps,
　　　　Hath clawed me in his clutch, 　　　80
　　And hath shipped me intil the land,
　　　　As if I had never been such.
　　　　　　　　(*Throws up a skull.*)

HAMLET. That skull had a tongue in it, and could sing once; how the knave jowls it to the ground, as if it were Cain's jaw-bone, that did the first murder! It might be the pate of a politician, which this ass now o'erreaches; one that might circumvent God, might it not?

HORATIO. It might, my lord. 　　　　　89

HAMLET. Or of a courtier; which could say 'Good morrow, sweet lord! How dost thou, good lord?' This might be my lord such-a-one, that praised my lord such-a-one's horse, when he meant to beg it; might it not?

HORATIO. Ay, my lord. 　　　　　　95

HAMLET. Why, e'en so: and now my Lady Worm's; chapless, and knocked about the mazzard with a sexton's spade: here's fine revolution, an we had the trick to see 't. Did these bones cost no more the breeding, but to play at loggats with 'em? mine ache to think on 't. 　　　　　　　　101

FIRST CLOWN (*sings*).
　　A pick-axe, and a spade, a spade,
　　　　For and a shrouding sheet:
　　O, a pit of clay for to be made
　　　　For such a guest is meet.
　　　　　　　(*Throws up another skull.*)

HAMLET. There's another: why may not that be the skull of a lawyer? Where be his quiddities now, his quillets, his cases, his tenures, and his tricks? why does he suffer this rude knave to knock him about the sconce with a dirty shovel, and will not tell him of his action of battery? Hum! This fellow might be in's time a great buyer of land, with his statutes, his recognizances, his fines, his double vouchers, his recoveries: is this the fine of his fines, and the recovery of his recoveries, to have his fine pate full of fine dirt? will his vouchers vouch him no more of his purchases, and double ones too, than the length and breadth of a pair of indentures? The very conveyances of his lands will hardly lie in this box; and must the 　121 inheritor himself have no more, ha?

HORATIO. Not a jot more, my lord.

HAMLET. Is not parchment made of sheepskins? 　123

HORATIO. Ay, my lord, and of calf-skins too.

HAMLET. They are sheep and calves which seek out assurance in that. I will speak to this fellow. Whose grave's this, sirrah?

FIRST CLOWN. Mine, sir.
　　(*Sings*). O, a pit of clay for to be made
　　　　　For such a guest is meet. 　　130

HAMLET. I think it be thine, indeed, for thou liest in 't.

FIRST CLOWN. You lie out on 't, sir, and therefore it is not yours: for my part, I do not lie in 't, and yet it is mine.

HAMLET. Thou dost lie in 't, to be in 't and say it is thine; 'tis for the dead, not for the quick; therefore thou liest.

FIRST CLOWN. 'Tis a quick lie, sir; 'twill away again, from me to you. 　　　　　　140

HAMLET. What man dost thou dig it for?

FIRST CLOWN. For no man, sir.

HAMLET. What woman, then?

FIRST CLOWN. For none, neither.

HAMLET. Who is to be buried in 't?

FIRST CLOWN. One that was a woman, sir; but, rest her soul, she's dead. 　　　　　　147

HAMLET. How absolute the knave is! we must speak by the card, or equivocation will undo us. By

---

69 ff. **In youth . . . As if I had never been such.** These two stanzas, plus some nonsensical variations as sung by the clown, are from a popular song of the Tudor period attributed to Lord Vaux and printed in Tottel's famous *Miscellany* of English lyric poetry in 1557. The *O*'s and *ah*'s in ll. 71 and 72 are evidently grunts from the clown as he labors to dig the grave. 71. **behove,** benefit. 76. **property of easiness,** a habit to which he easily conforms. 84. **jowls,** dashes, hurls. 85. **Cain's jaw-bone.** It was a popular confusion that led to the belief that Cain slew his brother Abel (Genesis, 4:8) with the jaw-bone of an ass; actually, the legend is that it was Samson who slew a thousand Philistines with this surprising implement (see Judges, 15:15). 87. **politician,** a schemer or intriguer. **o'erreaches,** a play on the literal meaning of "reaching over" and "circumventing" or "defeating." 97. **chapless,** without a lower jaw. 98. **mazzard,** head. 100. **loggats,** an old English country game based on the principle of horseshoe pitching, in which six sticks are thrown as nearly as possible against a stake in the ground or a block of wood fixed to the floor. 103. **For and,** in addition to.

107. **quiddities,** subtleties, quibbles, quirks. 108. **quillets,** verbal niceties and hair splittings. **tenures,** either the actual holding of a piece of property or an office or else the conditions and terms governing such holding. 110. **sconce,** head. 114. **statutes, recognizances,** legal terms involved in the possession and transfer of land. 115. **fines,** ends, with ensuing obvious puns. 115. **vouchers,** persons called upon to guarantee the title to land. **recoveries,** the process for transfer of an entailed estate. 119. **indentures . . . conveyances,** contracts and deeds of transfer. 124. **calf-skins,** parchments. 132. **liest, etc.** There follows now a series of puns on *lie*. 139. **quick,** live; there is a pun in the next line. 148. **absolute,** literal, positive. 149. **by the card,** by the compass; that is, precisely, accurately. The mariner's card was marked with all the points of the compass. **equivocation,** ambiguity, double-talk.

the Lord, Horatio, these three years I have taken note of it: the age is grown so picked that the toe of the peasant comes so near the heel of the courtier, he galls his kibe. How long hast thou been a grave-maker?

FIRST CLOWN. Of all the days i' the year, I came to 't that day that our last king Hamlet overcame Fortinbras. 157

HAMLET. How long is that since?

FIRST CLOWN. Cannot you tell that? every fool can tell that: it was the very day that young Hamlet was born; he that is mad, and sent into England.

HAMLET. Ay, marry, why was he sent into England?

FIRST CLOWN. Why, because he was mad: he shall recover his wits there; or, if he do not, it's no great matter there.

HAMLET. Why?

FIRST CLOWN. 'Twill not be seen in him there; there the men are as mad as he. 170

HAMLET. How came he mad?

FIRST CLOWN. Very strangely, they say.

HAMLET. How strangely?

FIRST CLOWN. Faith, e'en with losing his wits.

HAMLET. Upon what ground?

FIRST CLOWN. Why, here in Denmark: I have been sexton here, man and boy, thirty years.

HAMLET. How long will a man lie i' the earth ere he rot? 179

FIRST CLOWN. I' faith, if he be not rotten before he die—as we have many pocky corses now-a-days, that will scarce hole the laying in—he will last you some eight year or nine year: a tanner will last you nine year. 184

HAMLET. Why he more than another?

FIRST CLOWN. Why, sir, his hide is so tanned with his trade, that he will keep out water a great while; and your water is a sore decayer of your whoreson dead body. Here's a skull now; this skull has lain in the earth three and twenty years. 191

HAMLET. Whose was it?

FIRST CLOWN. A whoreson mad fellow's it was: whose do you think it was?

HAMLET. Nay, I know not.

FIRST CLOWN. A pestilence on him for a mad rogue! a' poured a flagon of Rhenish on my head once. This same skull, sir, was Yorick's skull, the king's jester.

HAMLET. This? 200

FIRST CLOWN. E'en that.

HAMLET. Let me see. (*Takes the skull.*) Alas, poor Yorick! I knew him, Horatio: a fellow of infinite jest, of most excellent fancy: he hath borne me on his back a thousand times; and now, how abhorred in my imagination it is! my gorge rises at it. Here hung those lips that I have kissed I know not how oft. Where be your gibes now? your gambols? your songs? your flashes of merriment, that were wont to set the table on a roar? Not one now, to mock your own grinning? quite chap-fallen? Now get you to my lady's chamber, and tell her, let her paint an inch thick, to this favor she must come; make her laugh at that. Prithee, Horatio, tell me one thing.

HORATIO. What's that, my lord?

HAMLET. Dost thou think Alexander looked o' this fashion i' the earth?

HORATIO. E'en so. 220

HAMLET. And smelt so? pah!

(*Puts down the skull.*)

HORATIO. E'en so, my lord.

HAMLET. To what base uses we may return, Horatio! Why may not imagination trace the noble dust of Alexander, till he find it stopping a bung-hole? 226

HORATIO. 'Twere to consider too curiously, to consider so.

HAMLET. No, faith, not a jot; but to follow him thither with modesty enough, and likelihood to lead it: as thus: Alexander died, Alexander was buried, Alexander returneth into dust; the dust is earth; of earth we make loam; and why of that loam, whereto he was converted, might they not stop a beer-barrel?

Imperious Caesar, dead and turned to clay,
Might stop a hole to keep the wind away:
O, that that earth, which kept the world in awe, 238
Should patch a wall to expel the winter's flaw!

But soft! but soft! aside; here comes the king.

(*Enter* Priests, *etc., in procession; the corpse of* Ophelia; LAERTES *and* Mourners, *following*: KING, QUEEN; *their trains, etc.*)

The queen, the courtiers: who is this they follow? 241
And with such maimed rites? This doth betoken
The corse they follow did with desperate hand
Fordo it own life: 'twas of some estate.
Couch we awhile, and mark.

(*Retiring with* HORATIO.)

LAERTES. What ceremony else?

HAMLET. That is Laertes,
A very noble youth: mark.

LAERTES. What ceremony else?

---

150. **three years.** Some have seen in this an allusion to the poor laws of 1601 (which would date Hamlet as late as 1604). In any event, such laws were regarded by the nobility as dangerous concessions to the common herd; and it must be remembered that Hamlet, throughout the scene with the gravedigger, is the somewhat condescending young aristocrat. 152. **picked,** finicky, fastidious. 153. **kibe,** chilblain, sore heel. 177. **thirty years.** This is manifestly a confirmation of the fact that Hamlet is thirty years of age at the time of the action of the play. 181. **pocky,** rotten, diseased. 198. **Yorick.** Will Kemp was the great comedian of the Elizabethan stage; Yorick is supposed to be Will Tarleton, Kemp's celebrated predecessor.

215. **favor,** countenance, face, expression. 227. **curiously,** minutely, pedantically. 230. **modesty,** moderation, restraint. 236. **Imperious,** imperial. 239. **flaw,** a gust of wind. 244. **Fordo,** destroy. **it,** its. 245. **Couch,** lie low, hide.

FIRST PRIEST. Her obsequies have been as far en-
    larged
As we have warranty: her death was doubtful;
And, but that great command o'ersways the order, 251
She should in ground unsanctified have lodged
Till the last trumpet; for charitable prayers,
Shards, flints and pebbles should be thrown on her:
Yet here she is allowed her virgin crants,
Her maiden strewments and the bringing home
Of bell and burial.

    LAERTES. Must there no more be done?

    FIRST PRIEST.   No more be done:
We should profane the service of the dead
To sing a requiem and such rest to her   260
As to peace-parted souls.

    LAERTES.   Lay her in the earth:
And from her fair and unpolluted flesh
May violets spring! I tell thee, churlish priest,
A ministering angel shall my sister be,
When thou liest howling.

    HAMLET.   What, the fair Ophelia!

    QUEEN. Sweets to the sweet: farewell!
                        (*Scattering flowers.*)
I hoped thou shouldst have been my Hamlet's wife;
I thought thy bride-bed to have decked, sweet maid,
And not have strewed thy grave.

    LAERTES.   O, treble woe
Fall ten times treble on that cursed head,   270
Whose wicked deed thy most ingenious sense
Deprived thee of! Hold off the earth awhile,
Till I have caught her once more in mine arms:
                    (*Leaps into the grave.*)
Now pile your dust upon the quick and dead,
Till of this flat a mountain you have made,
To o'ertop old Pelion, or the skyish head
Of blue Olympus.

    HAMLET (*advancing*). What is he whose grief
Bears such an emphasis? whose phrase of sorrow
Conjures the wandering stars, and makes them stand
Like wonder-wounded hearers? This is I,   280
Hamlet the Dane.
                (*Leaps into the grave.*)

    LAERTES.   The devil take thy soul!
                   (*Grappling with him.*)

    HAMLET. Thou pray'st not well.
I prithee, take thy fingers from my throat;
For, though I am not splenitive and rash,

Yet have I in me something dangerous,
Which let thy wiseness fear: hold off thy hand.

    KING. Pluck them asunder.

    QUEEN.   Hamlet, Hamlet!

    ALL. Gentlemen,—

    HORATIO.   Good my lord, be quiet.
    (*The* Attendants *part them, and they come out of
the grave.*)

    HAMLET. Why, I will fight with him upon this
       theme
Until my eyelids will no longer wag.   290

    QUEEN. O my son, what theme?

    HAMLET. I loved Ophelia: forty thousand brothers
Could not, with all their quantity of love,
Make up my sum. What wilt thou do for her?

    KING. O, he is mad, Laertes.

    QUEEN. For love of God, forbear him.

    HAMLET. 'Swounds, show me what thou 'lt do:
Woo 't weep? woo 't fight? woo 't fast? woo 't tear thy-
       self?
Woo 't drink up eisel? eat a crocodile?
I'll do 't. Dost thou come here to whine?   300
To outface me with leaping in her grave?
Be buried quick with her, and so will I:
And, if thou prate of mountains, let them throw
Millions of acres on us, till our ground,
Singeing his pate against the burning zone,
Make Ossa like a wart! Nay, an thou 'lt mouth,
I'll rant as well as thou.

    QUEEN.   This is mere madness:
And thus awhile the fit will work on him;
Anon, as patient as the female dove,
When that her golden couplets are disclosed,
His silence will sit drooping.

    HAMLET.   Hear you, sir;   311
What is the reason that you use me thus?
I loved you ever: but it is no matter;
Let Hercules himself do what he may,
The cat will mew and dog will have his day. (*Exit.*)

    KING. I pray you, good Horatio, wait upon him.
                      (*Exit* HORATIO.)
(*To* LAERTES.) Strengthen your patience in our last
       night's speech;
We'll put the matter to the present push.
Good Gertrude, set some watch over your son.
This grave shall have a living monument: 320
An hour of quiet shortly shall we see;
Till then, in patience our proceeding be.   (*Exeunt.*)

249. **enlarged,** extended; a reference to the fact that suicides are not given full burial rites, although it is not at all clear that Ophelia committed suicide. 250. **doubtful,** suspicious. 254. **Shards,** broken bits of pottery or stone. 255. **crants,** garlands hung upon the biers of unmarried women. 256. **strewments,** strewing of flowers. 256–257. **bringing home . . . burial,** the funeral procession to the church. 261. **peace-parted,** a reference to the *Nunc Dimittis;* see Luke 2:29: "Lord, lettest now thy servant depart in peace." 271. **ingenious sense,** reason. 276. **Pelion . . . Olympus,** two famous mountains of northern Greece. 279. **wandering stars,** planets. 284. **splenitive,** quick-tempered, irritable.

290. **wag,** move. The word did not have the somewhat ridiculous sense it now has. 293. **quantity,** possibly used in an ironical sense, implying that a brother's love is, beside a lover's, comparatively small. 296. **forbear,** leave alone. 298. **Woo't,** wilt thou, dost thou wish. 299. **eisel,** vinegar. 310. **golden couplets.** The female pigeon is popularly supposed to lay two eggs, and her young, when newly hatched, are covered with a fine golden-colored down. 317. **in,** by referring to or remembering. 318. **present push,** immediate test. 320. **living,** lasting.

SCENE 2. *A hall in the castle.*

(*Enter* HAMLET *and* HORATIO.)

HAMLET. So much for this, sir: now shall you see
  the other;
You do remember all the circumstance?

HORATIO. Remember it, my lord!

HAMLET. Sir, in my heart there was a kind of
  fighting,
That would not let me sleep: methought I lay
Worse than the mutines in the bilboes. Rashly,
And praised be rashness for it, let us know,
Our indiscretion sometimes serves us well,
When our deep plots do pall: and that should teach
  us
There's a divinity that shapes our ends,   10
Rough-hew them how we will,—

HORATIO.   That is most certain.

HAMLET. Up from my cabin,
My sea-gown scarfed about me, in the dark
Groped I to find out them; had my desire,
Fingered their packet, and in fine withdrew
To mine own room again; making so bold,
My fears forgetting manners, to unseal
Their grand commission; where I found, Horatio,—
O royal knavery!—an exact command,
Larded with many several sorts of reasons   20
Importing Denmark's health and England's too,
With, ho! such bugs and goblins in my life,
That, on the supervise, no leisure bated,
No, not to stay the grinding of the axe,
My head should be struck off.

HORATIO.   Is 't possible?

HAMLET. Here's the commission: read it at more
  leisure.
But wilt thou hear me how I did proceed?

HORATIO. I beseech you.

HAMLET. Being thus be-netted round with vil-
  lanies,—
Ere I could make a prologue to my brains,   30
They had begun the play—I sat me down,
Devised a new commission, wrote it fair:
I once did hold it, as our statists do,
A baseness to write fair and labored much
How to forget that learning, but, sir, now
It did me yeoman's service: wilt thou know
The effect of what I wrote?

HORATIO.   Ay, good my lord.

HAMLET. An earnest conjuration from the king,
As England was his faithful tributary,
As love between them like the palm might flourish,   40
As peace should still her wheaten garland wear
And stand a comma 'tween their amities,
And many such-like 'As'es of great charge,
That, on the view and knowing of these contents,
Without debatement further, more or less,
He should the bearers put to sudden death,
Not shriving-time allowed.

HORATIO.   How was this sealed?

HAMLET. Why, even in that was Heaven ordinant.
I had my father's signet in my purse,
Which was the model of that Danish seal;   50
Folded the writ up in form of the other,
Subscribed it, gave 't the impression, placed it safely,
The changeling never known. Now, the next day,
Was our sea-fight; and what to this was sequent
Thou know'st already.

HORATIO. So Guildenstern and Rosencrantz go to 't.

HAMLET. Why, man, they did make love to this
  employment;
They are not near my conscience; their defeat
Does by their own insinuation grow:
'Tis dangerous when the baser nature comes   60
Between the pass and fell incensed points
Of mighty opposites.

HORATIO.   Why, what a king is this!

HAMLET. Does it not, thinkest thee, stand me now
  upon—
He that hath killed my king and whored my mother,
Popped in between the election and my hopes,
Thrown out his angle for my proper life,
And with such cozenage—is 't not perfect conscience,
To quit him with this arm? and is 't not to be
  damned,
To let this canker of our nature come
In further evil?   70

HORATIO. It must be shortly known to him from
  England
What is the issue of the business there.

HAMLET. It will be short: the interim is mine;
And a man's life's no more than to say 'One.'
But I am very sorry, good Horatio,
That to Laertes I forgot myself;

Act V, Scene 2. 6. **mutines,** mutineers, rebels. **bilboes,** shackles. 9. **pall,** fail. 11. **Rough-hew,** to shape roughly, perhaps to bungle or botch. 13. **sea-gown,** a coarse, high-collared, short-sleeved overgarment, reaching below the knees, much used by Elizabethan seamen. 15. **Fingered,** pilfered, stole. 20. **Larded,** interspersed. 22. **such bugs . . . my life,** such imaginary dangerous qualities in my way of living. 23. **supervise,** perusal. **leisure bated,** delay allowed. 30–31. **prologue . . . play;** that is, before I could begin to think I had already reached a decision. 33. **statists,** statesmen. 34. **fair,** clearly, legibly. 36. **yeoman's service,** loyal, faithful, and energetic service.

41. **wheaten garland,** a symbol of peace. 42. **comma,** the slightest possible break. 43. **'As'es,'** no doubt the "whereases" of a legal document. 48. **ordinant,** directing, guiding. 54. **sequent,** subsequent, following. 58. **defeat,** destruction and death. 59. **insinuation,** interference, meddling. 61. **pass,** thrust; a term of fencing. **fell incensed,** fiercely angered. 63. **stand me . . . upon,** incumbent upon me, my duty. 65. **election.** The Danish throne in early medieval times, like that of the Anglo-Saxons, was hereditary on approval of the earls and nobles—in this sense, there was an election of the king. 66. **angle,** fish-hook. **proper,** own. 67. **cozenage,** trickery. 68. **quit,** pay off, requite. 69. **canker,** a worm which eats buds and leaves; possibly used here in the secondary sense of "ulcer."

For, by the image of my cause, I see
The portraiture of his: I'll court his favors:
But, sure, the bravery of his grief did put me
Into a towering passion.

HORATIO.   Peace! who comes here?   80
          (*Enter* OSRIC.)

OSRIC. Your lordship is right welcome back to Denmark.

HAMLET. I humbly thank you, sir. Dost know this water-fly?

HORATIO. No, my good lord.

HAMLET. Thy state is the more gracious; for 'tis a vice to know him. He hath much land, and fertile: let a beast be lord of beasts, and his crib shall stand at the king's mess: 'tis a chough; but, as I say, spacious in the possession of dirt.   90

OSRIC. Sweet lord, if your lordship were at leisure, I should impart a thing to you from his majesty.

HAMLET. I will receive it, sir, with all diligence of spirit. Put your bonnet to his right use; 'tis for the head.

OSRIC. I thank your lordship, it is very hot.

HAMLET. No, believe me, 'tis very cold; the wind is northerly.

OSRIC. It is indifferent cold, my lord, indeed.   100

HAMLET. But yet methinks it is very sultry and hot for my complexion.

OSRIC. Exceedingly, my lord; it is very sultry,—as 'twere,—I cannot tell how. But, my lord, his majesty bade me signify to you that he has laid a great wager on your head: sir, this is the matter,—

HAMLET. I beseech you, remember—   108
          (HAMLET *moves him to put on his hat.*)

OSRIC. Nay, good my lord; for mine ease, in good faith. Sir, here is newly come to court Laertes; believe me, an absolute gentleman, full of most excellent differences, of very soft society and great showing: indeed, to speak feelingly of him, he is the card or calendar of gentry, for you shall find in him the continent of what part a gentleman would see.   116

HAMLET. Sir, his definement suffers no perdition in you; though, I know, to divide him inventorially would dizzy the arithmetic of memory, and yet but yaw neither, in respect of his quick sail. But, in the verity of extolment, I take him to be a soul of great article; and his infusion of such dearth and rareness, as, to make true diction of him, his semblable in his mirror; and who else would trace him, his umbrage, nothing more.   126

OSRIC. Your lordship speaks most infallibly of him.

HAMLET. The concernancy, sir? why do we wrap the gentleman in our more rawer breath?

OSRIC. Sir?   130

HORATIO. Is 't not possible to understand in another tongue? You will do 't, sir, really.

HAMLET. What imports the nomination of this gentleman?

OSRIC. Of Laertes?

HORATIO. His purse is empty already; all's golden words are spent.

HAMLET. Of him, sir.

OSRIC. I know you are not ignorant—   139

HAMLET. I would you did, sir; yet, in faith, if you did, it would not much approve me. Well, sir?

OSRIC. You are not ignorant of what excellence Laertes is—

HAMLET. I dare not confess that, lest I should compare with him in excellence; but, to know a man well, were to know himself.

OSRIC. I mean, sir, for his weapon; but in the imputation laid on him by them, in his meed he's unfellowed.   150

HAMLET. What's his weapon?

OSRIC. Rapier and dagger.

HAMLET. That's two of his weapons: but, well.

OSRIC. The king, sir, hath wagered with him six Barbary horses; against the which he has imponed, as I take it, six French rapiers and poniards, with their assigns, as girdle, hangers, and so: three of the carriages, in faith, are very dear to fancy, very responsive to the hilts, most delicate carriages, and of very liberal conceit.   160

HAMLET. What call you the carriages?

---

79. **bravery,** bravado, showy swaggering.   84. **water-fly,** idle, vain, buzzing, or chattering person. Osric is a beautiful example of the social climber among courtiers.   89. **crib . . . mess,** his eating-place will be at the king's table. He would be one of a group of persons, usually four in number, assigned to a table at a royal banquet. Hamlet implies that Osric's social climbing will undoubtedly bring him material success. **chough,** jackdaw, a chattering, noisy bird; possibly also a pun on "chuff," a boor or churl.   90. **spacious . . . possession,** amply possessed.   100. **indifferent,** moderately, somewhat.   108. **remember,** remember thy courtesy; a conventional invitation for a subordinate to keep his hat on.   109. **for mine ease,** a conventional reply to the conventional invitation just mentioned. Osric knows all the answers expected of polite society.   112. **differences,** peculiarities. **soft,** gentle, refined.   113. **showing,** distinguished appearance.   114. **feelingly,** with just appreciation of his refinement. **card,** map, model.   115. **continent,** that which contains fully, the sum and substance.   117. **definement,** definition, description. **perdition,** loss, diminution. Hamlet is deliberately talking in extremely artificial language to show his ironic contempt of Osric's character.

118. **divide him inventorially,** to itemize all his good points.   120. **yaw,** in nautical terms, an unsteady movement of a ship. Dowden's note on this difficult metaphor is worth quoting: "To enumerate in detail the perfections of Laertes would bewilder the computations of memory, yet for all that—in spite of their calculations—the enumeration would stagger to and fro (yaw), and so fall behind, in comparison with Laertes's quick sailing."   122. **article,** importance.   123. **infusion,** infused temperament, or character imparted by nature. **dearth,** scarcity, rareness.   126. **umbrage,** shadow.   128. **concernancy,** import.   129. **breath,** speech.   131–132. **Is 't . . . tongue,** "Is it not possible for you to understand your jargon when someone else uses it?"   133. **What imports . . . gentleman?** What is this gentleman's name?   141. **approve,** commend.   146–147. **but, to know . . . himself,** to know a man as excellent would be to know Laertes.   149. **imputation,** reputation.   150. **meed,** merit.   156. **imponed,** wagered, bet.   158. **hangers,** straps on the sword-belt from which the sword hung.   159. **dear to fancy,** expensively fashioned. **responsive,** suited to, corresponding well to.   160. **delicate;** that is, in workmanship.

HORATIO. I knew you must be edified by the margent ere you had done.

OSRIC. The carriages, sir, are the hangers.

HAMLET. The phrase would be more german to the matter, if we could carry cannon by our sides: I would it might be hangers till then. But, on: six Barbary horses against six French swords, their assigns, and three liberal-conceited carriages; that's the French bet against the Danish. Why is this 'imponed', as you call it? 171

OSRIC. The king, sir, hath laid, that in a dozen passes between yourself and him, he shall not exceed you three hits: he hath laid on twelve for nine; and it would come to immediate trial, if your lordship would vouchsafe the answer.

HAMLET. How if I answer 'no'?

OSRIC. I mean, my lord, the opposition of your person in trial. 179

HAMLET. Sir, I will walk here in the hall: if it please his majesty, 'tis the breathing-time of day for me; let the foils be brought, the gentleman willing, and the king hold his purpose, I will win for him an I can; if not, I will gain nothing but my shame and the odd hits. 185

OSRIC. Shall I re-deliver you e'en so?

HAMLET. To this effect, sir; after what flourish your nature will.

OSRIC. I commend my duty to your lordship.

HAMLET. Yours, yours. (*Exit* OSRIC.) He does well to commend it himself; there are no tongues else for 's turn.

HORATIO. This lapwing runs away with the shell on his head. 194

HAMLET. He did comply with his dug, before he sucked it. Thus has he—and many more of the same breed that I know the drossy age dotes on—only got the tune of the time and outward habit of encounter; a kind of yesty collection, which carries them through and through the most fond and winnowed opinions; and do but blow them to their trial, the bubbles are out. 202

(*Enter a* Lord.)

LORD. My lord, his majesty commended him to you by young Osric, who brings back to him, that you attend him in the hall: he sends to know if your pleasure hold to play with Laertes, or that you will take longer time.

HAMLET. I am constant to my purposes; they follow the king's pleasure: if his fitness speaks, mine is ready; now or whensoever, provided I be so able as now. 211

LORD. The king and queen and all are coming down.

HAMLET. In happy time.

LORD. The queen desires you to use some gentle entertainment to Laertes before you fall to play

HAMLET. She well instructs me. (*Exit* Lord.)

HORATIO. You will lose this wager, my lord.

HAMLET. I do not think so; since he went into France, I have been in continual practice; I shall win at the odds. But thou wouldst not think how ill all's here about my heart: but it is no matter.

HORATIO. Nay, good my lord,— 224

HAMLET. It is but foolery; but it is such a kind of gain-giving, as would perhaps trouble a woman.

HORATIO. If your mind dislike any thing, obey it: I will forestall their repair hither, and say you are not fit. 229

HAMLET. Not a whit, we defy augury: there's a special providence in the fall of a sparrow. If it be now, 'tis not to come; if it be not to come, it will be now; if it be not now, yet it will come: the readiness is all: since no man has aught of what he leaves, what is 't to leave betimes? Let be. 235

(*Enter* KING, QUEEN, LAERTES, Lords, OSRIC, *and* Attendants *with foils, etc.*)

KING. Come, Hamlet, come, and take this hand from me.

(*The* KING *puts* LAERTES's *hand into* HAMLET's.)

HAMLET. Give me your pardon, sir: I've done you wrong;
But pardon 't, as you are a gentleman.
This presence knows,
And you must needs have heard, how I am punished 240
With sore distraction. What I have done,
That might your nature, honor and exception
Roughly awake, I here proclaim was madness.
Was 't Hamlet wronged Laertes? Never Hamlet;
If Hamlet from himself be ta'en away,
And when he's not himself does wrong Laertes,
Then Hamlet does it not, Hamlet denies it.
Who does it, then? His madness: if it be so,
Hamlet is of the faction that is wronged;
His madness is poor Hamlet's enemy. 250
Sir, in this audience,
Let my disclaiming from a purposed evil
Free me so far in your most generous thoughts,
That I have shot mine arrow o'er the house,
And hurt my brother.

163. margent, margin, marginal notes. 165. german, germane, related to, appropriate to. 176. answer, encounter. 181. breathing-time, exercise-period. 193. lapwing, or peewit; this bird has the habit of drawing a visitor away from its nest, and, when newly hatched, of running about with some of its shell still on its head. 195. comply . . . dug, he (Osric) no doubt paid compliments to his mother's breast. 197. drossy, cheap, frivolous. 199. yesty, frothy, yeasty. 201. fond and winnowed, both foolish and sensible; they are capable of saying both wise and foolish things. 202. blow them . . . bubbles are out, put them to the test and their ignorance is exposed.

214. In happy time, a conventional courtesy phrase. 226. gain-giving, misgiving. 239. presence, not only the royal presence itself but also the assembling of the entire court. 242. exception, disapproval.

LAERTES.   I am satisfied in nature,
Whose motive, in this case, should stir me most
To my revenge: but in my terms of honor
I stand aloof; and will no reconcilement,
Till by some elder masters, of known honor,
I have a voice and precedent of peace,   260
To keep my name ungored. But till that time,
I do receive your offered love like love,
And will not wrong it.

HAMLET.   I embrace it freely;
And will this brother's wager frankly play.
Give us the foils. Come on.

LAERTES.   Come, one for me.

HAMLET. I'll be your foil, Laertes: in mine igno-
    rance
Your skill shall, like a star i' the darkest night,
Stick fiery off indeed.

LAERTES.   You mock me, sir.

HAMLET. No, by this hand.

KING. Give them the foils, young Osric. Cousin
    Hamlet,   270
You know the wager?

HAMLET.   Very well, my lord;
Your grace hath laid the odds o' the weaker side.

KING. I do not fear it; I have seen you both:
But since he is bettered, we have therefore odds.

LAERTES. This is too heavy, let me see another.

HAMLET. This likes me well. These foils have all
    a length?   (*They prepare to play.*)

OSRIC. Ay, my good lord.

KING. Set me the stoups of wine upon that table.
If Hamlet give the first or second hit,
Or quit in answer of the third exchange,   280
Let all the battlements their ordnance fire;
The king shall drink to Hamlet's better breath;
And in the cup an union shall he throw,
Richer than that which four successive kings
In Denmark's crown have worn. Give me the cups;
And let the kettle to the trumpet speak,
The trumpet to the cannoneer without,
The cannons to the heavens, the heavens to the earth,
'Now the king drinks to Hamlet.' Come, begin:
And you, the judges, bear a wary eye.   290

HAMLET. Come on, sir.

LAERTES.   Come, my lord.
                                    (*They play.*)

HAMLET.   One.

LAERTES.   No.

HAMLET.   Judgment.

OSRIC. A hit, a very palpable hit.

LAERTES.   Well; again.

KING. Stay; give me drink. Hamlet, this pearl is
    thine;
Here's to thy health.
    (*Trumpets sound, and cannon shot off within.*)
                    Give him the cup.

HAMLET. I'll play this bout first; set it by awhile.
Come. (*They play.*) Another hit; what say you?

LAERTES. A touch, a touch, I do confess.

KING. Our son shall win.

QUEEN.   He's fat, and scant of breath.
Here, Hamlet, take my napkin, rub thy brows: 299
The queen carouses to thy fortune, Hamlet.

HAMLET. Good madam!

KING.   Gertrude, do not drink.

QUEEN. I will, my lord; I pray you, pardon me.

KING (*aside*). It is the poisoned cup; it is too late.

HAMLET. I dare not drink yet, madam; by and by.

QUEEN. Come, let me wipe thy face.

LAERTES. My lord, I'll hit him now.

KING.   I do not think 't.

LAERTES (*aside*). And yet 'tis almost 'gainst my
    conscience.

HAMLET. Come, for the third, Laertes: you do but
    dally;
I pray you, pass with your best violence;
I am afeard you make a wanton of me.   310

LAERTES. Say you so? come on.
                                    (*They play.*)

OSRIC. Nothing, neither way.

LAERTES. Have at you now!
(LAERTES *wounds* HAMLET; *then, in scuffling,
they change rapiers, and* HAMLET *wounds* LAERTES.)

KING.   Part them; they are incensed.

HAMLET. Nay, come, again.
                            (*The* QUEEN *falls.*)

OSRIC.   Look to the queen there, ho!

HORATIO. They bleed on both sides. How is it, my
    lord?

OSRIC. How is 't, Laertes?

LAERTES. Why, as a woodcock to mine own
    springe, Osric;
I am justly killed with mine own treachery.

HAMLET. How does the queen?

KING.   She swounds to see them bleed.

QUEEN. No, no, the drink, the drink,—O my dear
    Hamlet,—   320
The drink, the drink! I am poisoned!   (*Dies.*)

HAMLET. O villany! Ho! let the door be locked:
Treachery! Seek it out.

---

255. **nature.** Laertes replies that he is personally satisfied, but he feels nevertheless that his honor must be satisfied by the rules of the "code of honor." 260. **voice,** authority, authoritative statement. 266. **foil.** There is here a quibble on foil in the sense of "contrast" and of "blunted rapier." 268. **Stick fiery off,** shine forth brilliantly. 283. **union,** pearl. 286. **kettle,** kettle-drum.

293. **pearl is thine.** At this point the King puts the poison in Hamlet's cup. 298. **fat.** Richard Burbage, the original Hamlet, was a corpulent man; some editors, however, prefer to think of fat merely as "soft, out of condition," or perhaps "sweating." Some would emend the word to "faint." 300. **carouses,** drinks a toast. 310. **wanton,** spoiled child, sissy. 314. **ho!** probably "stop!" in the sense of "stop the contest!" 317. **woodcock,** a slang expression for a blockhead; the woodcock was considered a particularly stupid, gullible bird. **springe,** snare, trap. 319. **swounds,** swoons, faints.

LAERTES. It is here, Hamlet: Hamlet, thou art
  slain;
No medicine in the world can do thee good;
In thee there is not half an hour of life;
The treacherous instrument is in thy hand,
Unbated and envenomed: the foul practice
Hath turned itself on me; lo, here I lie,   329
Never to rise again: thy mother's poisoned:
I can no more: the king, the king's to blame.
  HAMLET. The point envenomed too! . . .
Then, venom, to thy work!
                    (*Stabs the* KING.)
  ALL. Treason! Treason!
  KING. O, yet defend me, friends; I am but hurt.
  HAMLET. Here, thou incestuous, murderous,
  damned Dane,
Drink off this potion. Is thy union here?
Follow my mother.   (KING *dies.*)
  LAERTES.   He is justly served;
It is a poison tempered by himself.
Exchange forgiveness with me, noble Hamlet:
Mine and my father's death come not upon thee, 341
Nor thine on me!   (*Dies.*)
  HAMLET. Heaven make thee free of it! I follow
  thee.
I am dead, Horatio. Wretched queen, adieu!
You that look pale and tremble at this chance,
That are but mutes or audience to this act,
Had I but time—as this fell sergeant, death,
Is strict in his arrest—O, I could tell you—
But let it be. Horatio, I am dead;
Thou livest; report me and my cause aright
To the unsatisfied.
  HORATIO.   Never believe it: 351
I am more an antique Roman than a Dane:
Here's yet some liquor left.
  HAMLET.   As thou 'rt a man,
Give me the cup; let go; by Heaven, I'll have 't.
O good Horatio, what a wounded name,
Things standing thus unknown, shall live behind me!
If thou didst ever hold me in thy heart,
Absent thee from felicity awhile,
And in this harsh world draw thy breath in pain,
To tell my story.
              (*March afar off, and shot within.*)
              What warlike noise is this?
  OSRIC. Young Fortinbras, with conquest come from
  Poland,   361
To the ambassadors of England gives
This warlike volley.
  HAMLET.   O, I die, Horatio;
The potent poison quite o'ercrows my spirit;

I cannot live to hear the news from England;
But I do prophesy the election lights
On Fortinbras: he has my dying voice;
So tell him, with the occurrents, more and less,
Which have solicited. The rest is silence.   (*Dies.*)
  HORATIO. Now cracks a noble heart. Good night,
    sweet prince;   370
And flights of angels sing thee to thy rest!
Why does the drum come hither?   (*March within.*)
  (*Enter* FORTINBRAS, *the* English Ambassadors, *and
others.*)
  FORTINBRAS. Where is this sight?
  HORATIO.   What is it ye would see?
If aught of woe or wonder, cease your search.
  FORTINBRAS. This quarry cries on havoc. O proud
    death,
What feast is toward in thine eternal cell,
That thou so many princes at a shot
So bloodily hast struck?
  FIRST AMBASSADOR.   The sight is dismal;
And our affairs from England come too late:
The ears are senseless that should give us hearing,
To tell him his commandment is fulfilled,   381
That Rosencrantz and Guildenstern are dead:
Where should we have our thanks?
  HORATIO.   Not from his mouth,
Had it the ability of life to thank you:
He never gave commandment for their death.
But since, so jump upon this bloody question,
You from the Polack wars, and you from England,
Are here arrived, give order that these bodies
High on a stage be placed to the view;   389
And let me speak to the yet unknowing world
How these things came about: so shall you hear
Of carnal, bloody, and unnatural acts,
Of accidental judgments, casual slaughters,
Of deaths put on by cunning and forced cause,
And, in this upshot, purposes mistook
Fallen on the inventors' heads: all this can I
Truly deliver.
  FORTINBRAS.   Let us haste to hear it,
And call the noblest to the audience.
For me, with sorrow I embrace my fortune:
I have some rights of memory in this kingdom,   400
Which now to claim my vantage doth invite me.
  HORATIO. Of that I shall have also cause to speak,
And from his mouth whose voice will draw on more:
But let this same be presently performed,
Even while men's minds are wild; lest more mis-
    chance,
On plots and errors, happen.

328. **Unbated,** with the foil removed. **practice,** plot, stratagem, sharp or treacherous doings. 339. **tempered,** mixed, prepared. 346. **mutes,** actors or players to whom no lines are assigned. 347. **sergeant,** sheriff's officer, officer of the law. 352. **Roman.** It was the Roman custom for a subordinate to follow his master in death. 364. **o'ercrows,** crows over, gloats over, triumphs over.

368. **occurrents,** events, incidents, happenings. 369. **solicited,** moved, caused. 375. **quarry,** heap of dead. **cries on havoc,** calls for slaughter. 376. **toward,** to come. 383. **his mouth;** that is, the King's. 386. **jump,** immediately following. **question,** dispute. 393. **casual,** accidental, chance. 400. **of memory,** traditional. 403. **draw on more,** lead more to speak. 406. **On,** in addition to, on top of; possibly, on account of.

FORTINBRAS.   Let four captains
Bear Hamlet, like a soldier, to the stage;
For he was likely, had he been put on,
To have proved most royally: and, for his passage,
The soldiers' music and the rites of war   410
Speak loudly for him.

409. **passage,** passing, death.

Take up the bodies: such a sight as this
Becomes the field, but here shows much amiss.
Go, bid the soldiers shoot.

(*A dead march. Exeunt, bearing off the dead
bodies; after which a peal of ordnance is shot off.*)

413. **field,** battlefield.

"Four Soldiers," engraving by the German Master M Z, who was active about 1500. From the Art Institute of Chicago.

Nicolaus Copernicus

1473–1543

The greatest of the Humanists, inspired by the literary achievements and ethical teachings of the ancients, had no interest in natural science, which seemed irrelevant to their exploration of human nature. Through the influence of Petrarch and Erasmus, who dismissed it with contempt, science was neglected for generations. But the new intellectual freedom eventually led to a renewal of scientific speculation in the sixteenth century and the discoveries upon which modern science is founded.

Copernicus, the Polish astronomer, was not a scientist in the modern sense but half churchman and half Humanist, who was led to revolutionize our view of the heavens not by a telescope but by developing the suggestion of an ancient philosopher. At Cracow and later Bologna he studied Ptolemaic astronomy along with canon law and medicine and pursued his interest in the stars through a life crowded with administrative duties. Early in his studies he became skeptical of the geocentric astronomy of the Middle Ages because of its complexity and was aroused by finding that some ancient followers of Pythagoras believed the sun to be the center of our universe. With meager instruments he began to observe the heavens and eventually verified this heliocentric view to his own satisfaction. He cautiously announced his refutation of the orthodox theory in a manuscript first circulated in 1530, but not until 1543, the year of his death, did a disciple venture to publish his treatise, *De Revolutionibus Orbium Celestium.*

Although some churchmen were shocked by this reversal of traditional authority, Copernicus protected himself from persecution by announcing his theory as a hypothesis based on mathematical calculation rather than the result of scientific observation. It sprang from his search for a simpler explanation of the motions of the planets than the complicated Ptolemaic system provided. Such reasoning reminds one of Dante, who also demanded that a Christian universe should be neat and simple. The quest of Copernicus for simplicity actually led him into error, for he insisted, like Dante, upon circular orbits for his planets, because God would necessarily give a perfect order to his creation. It remained for Johannes Kepler, his successor, to substitute direct observation for reasoning and to prove that the orbits of the planets are elliptical. Scientific method lagged behind scientific findings, which in the sixteenth century had still the quality of magnificent accidents. But the great discovery of Copernicus was a major step in the long development of modern science.

The Revolutions of the Heavenly Bodies

I CAN well believe, most holy father, that certain people, when they hear of my attributing motion to the earth in these books of mine, will at once declare that such an opinion ought to be rejected. Now, my own theories do not please me so much as not to consider what others may judge of them. Accordingly, when I began to reflect upon what those persons who accept the stability of the earth, as confirmed by the opinion of many centuries, would say when I claimed that the earth moved, I [10] hesitated for a long time as to whether I should publish that which I have written to demonstrate its motion, or whether it would not be better to follow the example of the Pythagoreans, who used to hand down the secrets of philosophy to their relatives and friends only in oral form. As I well considered all this, I was almost impelled to put the finished work wholly aside, through the scorn I had reason to anticipate on account of the newness and apparent contrariness of my theory to reason. [20]

My friends, however, dissuaded me from such a course and admonished me that I ought to publish my book, which had lain concealed in my possession not only nine years, but already into four times the ninth year. Not a few other distinguished and very learned men asked me to do the same thing, and told me that I ought not, on account of my anxiety, to delay any longer in consecrating my work to the general service of mathematicians.

But your holiness will perhaps not so much wonder [30] der that I have dared to bring the results of my night labors to the light of day, after having taken so much care in elaborating them, but is waiting instead to hear how it entered my mind to imagine that the earth moved, contrary to the accepted opinion of mathematicians—nay, almost contrary to ordinary human understanding. Therefore I will not conceal from your holiness that what moved me to consider another way of reckoning the motions of the heavenly bodies was nothing else than the fact [40] that the mathematicians do not agree with one another in their investigations. In the first place, they are so uncertain about the motions of the sun and moon that they cannot find out the length of a full year. In the second place, they apply neither the same laws of cause and effect in determining the

The Revolutions of the Heavenly Bodies. ⁸ Translated by William S. Knickerbocker. Reprinted by permission of Appleton-Century-Crofts, Inc.
14. **Pythagoreans,** followers of the Greek philosopher, **Pythagoras** (sixth century B.C.).

motions of the sun and moon and of the five planets, nor the same proofs. Some employ only concentric circles, others use eccentric and epicyclic ones, with which, however, they do not fully attain the desired end. They could not even discover nor compute the main thing—namely, the form of the universe and the symmetry of its parts. It was with them as if some should, from different places, take hands, feet, head, and other parts of the body, which although very beautiful, were not drawn in their proper relations, and, without making them in any way correspond, should construct a monster instead of a human being.

Accordingly, when I had long reflected on this uncertainty of mathematical tradition, I took the trouble to read again the books of all the philosophers I could get hold of, to see if some one of them had not once believed that there were other motions of the heavenly bodies. First I found in Cicero that Hicetas had believed in the motion of the earth. Afterwards I found in Plutarch, likewise, that some others had held the same opinion. This induced me also to begin to consider the movability of the earth, and, although the theory appeared contrary to reason, I did so because I knew that others before me had been allowed to assume rotary movements at will, in order to explain the phenomena of these celestial bodies. I was of the opinion that I, too, might be permitted to see whether, by presupposing motion in the earth, more reliable conclusions than hitherto reached could not be discovered for the rotary motions of the spheres. And thus, acting on the hypothesis of the motion which, in the following book, I ascribe to the earth, and by long and continued observations, I have finally discovered that if the motion of the other planets be carried over to the relation of the earth and this is made the basis for the rotation of every star, not only will the phenomena of the planets be explained thereby, but also the laws and the size of the stars; all their spheres and the heavens themselves will appear so harmoniously connected that nothing could be changed in any part of them without confusion in the remaining parts and in the whole universe.

That the universe is spherical

First we must remark that the universe is spherical in form, partly because this form being a perfect whole requiring no joints, is the most complete of all, partly because it makes the most capacious form, which is best suited to contain and preserve everything; or again because all the constituent parts of the universe, that is the sun, moon, and the planets appear in this form; or because everything strives to

attain this form, as appears in the case of drops of water and other fluid bodies if they attempt to define themselves. So no one will doubt that this form belongs to the heavenly bodies.

That the earth is also spherical

That the earth is also spherical is therefore beyond question, because it presses from all sides upon its center. Although by reason of the elevations of the mountains and the depressions of the valleys a perfect circle cannot be understood, yet this does not affect the general spherical nature of the earth. This appears in the following manner. To those who journey towards the North the north pole of the daily revolution of the heavenly sphere seems gradually to rise, while the opposite seems to sink. Most of the stars in the region of the Bear seem not to set, while some of the southern stars seem not to rise at all. So Italy does not see Canopes, which is visible to the Egyptians. And Italy sees the outermost star of the Stream, which our region of a colder zone does not know. On the other hand, to those who go towards the South the others seem to rise and those to sink which are high in our region. Moreover, the inclination of the Poles to the diameter of the earth bears always the same relation, which could happen only in the case of a sphere. So it is evident that the earth is included between the two poles, and is therefore spherical in form. Let us add that the inhabitants of the East do not observe the eclipse of the sun or of the moon which occurs in the evening, and the inhabitants of the West those which occur in the morning, while those who dwell between see those later and these earlier. That the water also has the same form can be observed from ships, in that the land which cannot be seen from the deck is visible from the mast-tree. And conversely, if a light be placed at the mast-head it seems to those who remain on the shores gradually to sink and at last still sinking to disappear. It is clear that the water also, according to its nature, continually presses like the earth downward and does not rise above its banks higher than its convexity permits. So the land extends above the ocean as much as the land happens to be higher.

Whether the earth has a circular motion, and concerning the location of the earth

As it has been already shown that the earth has the form of a sphere, we must consider whether a movement also coincides with this form, and what place the earth holds in the universe. Without this there will be no secure results to be obtained in regard to the heavenly phenomena. The great majority of authors, of course, agree that the earth stands still in the center of the universe, and consider it inconceivable and ridiculous to suppose the opposite.

20. **Hicetas**, a Pythagorean philosopher of Syracuse, probably antedating Aristotle, who is mentioned in Cicero's *Academica*, II, 39.

But if the matter is carefully weighed it will be seen that the question is not yet settled and therefore by no means to be regarded lightly. Every change of place which is observed is due to a movement of the observed object or of the observer, or to movements of both, naturally in different directions, for if the observed object and the observer move in the same manner and in the same direction, no movement will be seen. Now it is from the earth that the revolution of the heavens is observed, and it is produced for our eyes. Therefore, if the earth undergoes no movement this movement must take place in everything outside of the earth, but in the opposite direction than if everything on the earth moved, and of this kind is the daily revolution. So this appears to affect the whole universe, that is, everything outside the earth with the single exception of the earth itself. If, however, one should admit that this movement was not peculiar to the heavens, but that the earth revolved from west to east, and if this was carefully considered in regard to the apparent rising and setting of the sun, the moon, and the stars, it would be discovered that this was the real situation. Since the sky, which contains and shelters all things, is the common seat of all things, it is not easy to understand why motion should not be ascribed rather to the thing contained than to the containing, to the located rather than to the location. From this supposition follows another question of no less importance, concerning the place of the earth, although it has been accepted and believed by almost all that the earth occupies the middle of the universe. But if one should suppose that the earth is not at the center of the universe, that, however, the distance between the two is not great enough to be measured on the orbits of the fixed stars, but would be noticeable and perceptible on the orbit of the sun or of the planets: and if one was further of the opinion that the movements of the planets appeared to be irregular, as if they were governed by a center other than the earth, then such a one could perhaps have given the true reasons for the apparently irregular movement. For since the planets appear now nearer and now farther from the earth, this shows necessarily that the center of their revolutions is not the center of the earth: although it does not settle whether the earth increases and decreases the distance from them or they their distance from the earth.

Refutation of the argument of the ancients that the earth remains still in the middle of the universe, as if it were its center

From this and similar reasons it is supposed that the earth rests at the center of the universe and that there is no doubt of the fact. But if one believed that the earth revolved, he would certainly be of the opinion that this movement was natural and not arbitrary. For whatever is in accord with nature produces results which are the opposite of those produced by force. Things upon which force or an outside power has acted must be injured and cannot long endure: what happens by nature, however, preserves itself well and exists in the best condition. So Ptolemy feared without good reason that the earth and all earthly objects subject to the revolution would be destroyed by the act of nature, since this latter is opposed to artificial acts, or to what is produced by the human spirit. But why did not he fear the same, and in a much higher degree, of the universe, whose motion must be as much more rapid as the heavens are greater than the earth? Or has the heaven become so immense because it has been driven outward from the center by the inconceivable power of the revolution; while if it stood still, on the contrary, it would collapse and fall together? But surely if this is the case the extent of the heavens would increase infinitely. For the more it is driven higher by the outward force of the movement, so much the more rapid will the movement become, because of the ever-increasing circle which must be traversed in 24 hours; and, conversely, if the movement grows, the immensity of the heavens grows. So the velocity would increase the size and the size would increase the velocity unendingly. According to the physical law that the endless cannot wear away nor in any way move, the heavens must necessarily stand still.

But it is said that beyond the sky no body, no place, no vacant space, in fact nothing at all exists; then it is strange that something should be enclosed by nothing. But if the heaven is endless and is bounded only by the inner hollow, perhaps this establishes all the more clearly the fact that there is nothing outside the heavens, because everything is within it, but the heaven must then remain unmoved. The highest proof on which one supports the finite character of the universe is its movement. But whether the universe is endless or limited we will leave to the physiologues; this remains sure for us that the earth enclosed between the poles is bounded by a spherical surface. Why therefore should we not take the position of ascribing to a movement conformable to its nature and corresponding to its form, rather than suppose that the whole universe whose limits are not and cannot be known moves? And why will we not recognize that the appearance of a daily revolution belongs to the heavens, but the actuality to the earth; and that the relation is similar to that of which one says: "We run out of the harbor, the lands and cities retreat from us." Because if a ship sails along quietly, everything outside of it appears to those on board as if it moved with the motion of the boat, and the boatman thinks that the boat with all on board is standing still, this

Copernicus, from a biography of the astronomer by Pierre Gassendi published in 1655.

rising and falling in the air is in relation to the universe a double one, being always made up of a rectilinear and a circular movement. Since that which seeks of its own weight to fall is essentially earthy, so there is no doubt that these follow the same natural law as their whole; and it results from the same principle that those things which pertain to fire are forcibly driven on high. Earthly fire is nourished with earthly stuff, and it is said that the flame is only burning smoke. But the peculiarity of the fire consists in this that it expands whatever it seizes upon, and it carries this out so consistently that it can in no way and by no machinery be prevented from breaking its bonds and completing its work. The expanding motion, however, is directed from the center outward; therefore, if any earthly material is ignited it moves upward. So to each single body belongs a single motion, and this is evinced preferably in a circular direction as long as the single body remains in its natural place and its entirety. In this position the movement is the circular movement, which, as far as the body itself is concerned, is as if it did not occur. The rectilinear motion, however, seizes upon those bodies which have wandered or have been driven from their natural position or have been in any way disturbed. Nothing is so much opposed to the order and form of the world as the displacement of one of its parts. Rectilinear motion takes place only when objects are not properly related, and are not complete according to their nature because they have separated from their whole and have lost their unity. Moreover, objects which have been driven outward or away, leaving out of consideration the circular motion, do not obey a single, simple, and regular motion, since they cannot be controlled simply by their lightness or by the force of their weight, and if in falling they have at first a slow movement the rapidity of the motion increases as they fall, while in the case of earthly fire, which is forced upwards—and we have no means of knowing any other kind of fire—we will see that its motion is slow as if its earthly origin thereby showed itself. The circular motion, on the other hand, is always regular, because it is not subject to an intermittent cause. Those other objects, however, would cease to be either light or heavy in respect to their natural movement if they reached their own place, and thus they would fit into that movement. Therefore, if the circular movement is to be ascribed to the universe as a whole and the rectilinear to the parts, we might say that the revolution is to the straight line as the natural state is to sickness. That Aristotle divided motion into three sorts, that from the center out, that inward toward the center, and that around about the center appears to be merely a logical convenience, just as we distinguish point, line, and surface, although one can-

same thing may hold without doubt of the motion of the earth, and it may seem as if the whole universe revolved. What shall we say, however, of the clouds and other things floating, falling or raising in the air—except that not only does the earth move with the watery elements belonging with it, but also a large part of the atmosphere, and whatever else is in any way connected with the earth; whether it is because the air immediately touching the earth has the same nature as the earth, or that the motion has become imparted to the atmosphere. A like astonishment must be felt if that highest region of the air be supposed to follow the heavenly motion, as shown by those suddenly appearing stars which the Greeks call comets or bearded stars, which belong to that region and which rise and set like other stars. We may suppose that part of the atmosphere, because of its great distance from the earth, has become free from the earthly motion. So the atmosphere which lies close to the earth and all things floating in it would appear to remain still, unless driven here and there by the wind or some other outside force, which chance may bring into play; for how is the wind in the air different from the current in the sea? We must admit that the motion of things

not exist without the others, and none of them are found apart from bodies. This fact is also to be considered, that the condition of immovability is held to be nobler and more divine than that of change and inconstancy, which latter therefore should be ascribed rather to the earth than to the universe, and I would add also that it seems inconsistent to attribute motion to the containing and locating element rather than to the contained and located object, which the earth is. Finally since the planets plainly are at one time nearer and at another time farther from the earth, it would follow, on the theory that the universe revolves, that the movement of the one and same body which is known to take place about a center, that is the center of the earth, must also be directed toward the center from without and from the center outward. The movement about the center must therefore be made more general, and it suffices if that single movement be about its own center. So it appears from all these considerations that the movement of the earth is more probable than its fixity, especially in regard to the daily revolution, which is most peculiar to the earth.

Giordano Bruno

c. 1548–1600

Among those who were inspired by Copernicus to further speculation about the universe was an earnest Dominican friar named Giordano Bruno, who produced an exposition of the Copernican theory in 1584. Educated as a churchman at Naples, he had been forced to flee from Italy and renounce his monastic order, because his reason led him to deny the doctrine of transubstantiation, the miracle of the eucharist by which the bread and wine are transformed into the body and blood of Jesus. But so strong was his love of Italy that he could find no spiritual peace in exile and lectured his way discontentedly through Calvinist Switzerland, Anglican England, and Lutheran Germany without sympathy for any of the Protestant sects. At last his homesickness and poverty made him return to Italy as tutor to a Venetian gentleman, who was soon so scandalized by his heresies that he turned him over to the Inquisition. Frightened, Bruno abjectly recanted his blasphemy against the Pope and orthodox dogma and for eight long years languished in prison, until at last he defiantly reaffirmed his faith in a new conception of the universe and was burned at the stake as an arrogant heretic on February 17, 1600.

This great martyr to the new science was not a scientist but a philosopher whose passionate imagination was led by Copernicus to a new idea of the universe that later science was laboriously to confirm. His metaphysical speculations are spread through many treatises, but his major hypothesis is contained in *On the Infinite*

(1584). Copernicus had destroyed the medieval notion that the earth must be the center of the universe because man, the lord of the earth, was the climax of God's creation. But in making the sun the center of things he had still assumed a finite universe operated by simple and rational laws not unlike those accepted by Dante. Bruno, with a sudden poetic vision, jumped from the idea of the earth as center to the idea of no center at all. Because the nearness of man to his own earth had made it seem larger than the sun, which seemed to revolve about it, might not the nearness of our sun to us have misled Copernicus to assume that the more distant stars revolved about our sun? As the imagination of Bruno freed itself from medieval dogma, he announced the heresy that the stars are suns like our sun, which seem smaller and much less bright only because they are farther away from us. Once released from the snug medieval conception of a finite universe, he began to see stars beyond stars and concluded that the universe is infinite and that the stars are all moving in space, fixed only in their relation to each other. Having destroyed the Christian distinction between Earth and Heaven and dotted the universe with an infinity of worlds, he was led to assume that these other worlds might be inhabited by living things as is our own. God is accordingly not the special father of his human creatures on this planet, but the single unifying soul of this infinite universe. "Nature is God in things!"

The poetic soul of Bruno, if it lost the mystical vision of Christianity, found a new excitement in the vision of a still greater God who appears everywhere in every natural force. So Bruno passed from the idea of an infinite universe and an infinite relativity among its parts to a triumphant pantheism. He was still a religious thinker at heart, though his imagination led him to two key principles of modern science.

Of the Infinite Universe and Innumerable Worlds

A PREFATORY DEDICATION

I KNOW myself to be for the most part accounted a sophist, more desirous to appear subtle than to be really solid; an ambitious fellow, that studies rather to set up a new and false sect than to confirm the ancient and true doctrine; a deceiver, that aims at purchasing brightness to his own fame by engaging others in the darkness of error; a restless spirit, that overturns the edifice of sound discipline and makes himself a founder to some hut of perversity. But so may all the holy Deities deliver me from those that unjustly hate me, so may my own God be ever propitious to me, so may the Governors of this our globe show me their favor, so may the stars furnish me with such a seed for the field and with

Of the Infinite Universe and Innumerable Worlds. Translated by John Toland.

such a field for the seed, that the world may reap the useful and glorious fruit of my labor, by awakening the genius and opening the understanding of such as are deprived of light: so may all these things happen, I say, as it is most certain that I neither fain nor pretend. If I err, I am far from thinking that I do so; and whether I speak or write, I dispute not for the mere love of victory (for I look upon all reputation and conquest to be hateful to God, to be most vile and dishonorable, without Truth) but it is for the love of true WISDOM, and by the studious admiration of this mistress, that I fatigue, that I disquiet, that I torment myself.

This will be made evident by the demonstrative arguments I offer, drawn from lively reasons; as these are derived from regulated sense, which is informed by positive Ideas, that like so many ambassadresses are sent abroad from the subjects of nature: being obvious to those that seek for them, clear to those that conceive them, distinct to those that consider them, and certain to those that comprehend them. But it is time that I present you with my Contemplations about *the infinite Universe and innumerable Worlds.*

In this dialogue then you'll find, first, that the inconstancy of our senses shows they are not the principle of certitude, which is only acquired by a kind of comparison, or by conferring one sensible object, or one sense with another; and so it is concluded that the same truth may be in different subjects, as in the sensible object and in the understanding.

Secondly, you come to the beginning of the demonstration for the infinity of the universe, whereof the first argument alleged is, that those who by their imaginations would set walls or bounds to it are not able themselves to assign or fix the extremities of it. . . .

The topic of the sixth argument is that by making the world finite, a vacuum cannot be avoided, if that be void where there is nothing; though we shall evince this void to be impossible. . . .

The eighth argument is that none of the senses excludes infinity, since we cannot deny it, merely because not comprehended by any of our senses; but rather assert it, because by it the senses are comprehended, and reason comes to their help to confirm it: nay, if we further consider, our senses do ever suppose infinity, since we always see one thing terminated by another thing; and that we never perceived anything by internal or external sense that was not terminated by a thing like itself or by some other thing different from itself. . . . Even by what we see, then, we ought rather to infer infinity than otherwise, because nothing occurs in nature that is not terminated by another and no one thing whatsoever is terminated by itself. . . .

[Many other arguments follow.]

Here you'll meet with the reasons why we should not fear that any part of this Universe should fall or fly off, that the least particle should be lost in empty space or be truly annihilated. Here you'll perceive the reason of that vicissitude which may be observed in the constant change of all things, whereby it happens that there is nothing so ill but may befall us or be prevented, nor anything so good but may be lost or obtained by us; since in this infinite field the parts and modes do perpetually vary, though the substance and the whole do eternally persevere the same.

From this contemplation (if we do but rightly consider) it will follow that we ought never to be dispirited by any strange accidents through excess of fear or pain, nor ever be elated by any prosperous event through excess of hope or pleasure; whence we have the way to true Morality, and, by following it, we would become the magnanimous despisers of what men of childish thoughts do fondly esteem, and the wise judges of the history of nature which is written in our minds, and the strict executioners of those divine laws which are engraven in the center of our hearts. We would know that it is no harder thing to fly from hence up to Heaven than to fly from heaven back again to the Earth, that ascending thither and descending hither are all one; that we are no more circumferential to the other Globes than they are to us, nor they more central to us than we are to them, and that none of them is more above the stars than we, as they are no less than we covered over or comprehended by the sky. Behold us therefore free from envying them! behold us delivered from the vain anxiety and foolish care of desiring to enjoy that good afar off which in as great a degree we may possess so near at hand, and even at home! Behold us freed from the terror that they should fall upon us, anymore than we should hope that we might fall upon them; since every one as well as all of those globes are sustained by infinite Ether, in which this our animal freely runs, and keeps to his prescribed course, as the rest of the planets do to theirs.

Did we but consider and comprehend all this, oh! to what much further considerations and comprehensions should we be carried! as we might be sure to obtain that happiness by virtue of this science, which in other sciences is sought after in vain. This is that philosophy which opens the senses, which satisfies the mind, which enlarges the understanding, and which leads man to the only true beatitude whereof he's capable according to his natural state and constitution; for it frees him from the solicitous pursuit of pleasure and from the anxious apprehensions of pain, making him enjoy the good things of the present hour, and not to fear more than he hopes from the future; since that same providence, or fate, or fortune, which causes the vicissitudes of our particular being will not let us know more of the one than we are ignorant of the other. At first sight, indeed, we are apt to be dubious and perplexed: but when we more profoundly consider the essence and accidents of that matter into which we are mutable, we'll find that there is no death attending ours or the substance of any other thing; since nothing is substantially diminished, but only everything changing form by its perpetual motion in this infinite space. And seeing that everything is subject to a good and most perfect efficient cause, we ought neither to believe nor to hope otherwise than that as everything proceeds from what is good, so the whole must needs be good, in a good state, and to a good purpose: the contrary of which appears only to them who consider no more than is just before them, as the beauty of an edifice is not manifest to one that has seen only some small portion of the same, as a stone, the plastering, or part of a wall; but is most charming to him that saw the whole and had leisure to observe the symmetry of the parts.

We fear not therefore that what is accumulated in this world should by the malice of some wandering spirit or by the wrath of some evil genius be shaken and scattered, as it were into smoke or dust, out of this cupola of the sky, and beyond the starry mantle of the firmament; nor that the nature of things can otherwise come to be annihilated in substance, than as it seems to our eyes that the air contained in the concavity of a bubble is become nothing when that bubble is burst; because we know that in the world one thing ever succeeds another, there being no utmost bottom, whence, as by the hand of an artificer, things are irreparably struck into nothing. There are no ends, limits, margins, or walls that keep back or subtract any parcel of the infinite abundance of things. Thence it is that the earth and sea are ever equally fertile, and thence the perpetual brightness of the sun; eternal fuel circulating to those devouring fires, and a supply of waters being eternally furnished to the evaporated seas, from the infinite and ever-renewing magazine of matter. . . .

Look to it now, Gentlemen Astrologers, with your humble servants the Natural Philosophers, and see to what use you can put your Circles that are described by the imaginary nine moveable Spheres, in which you so imprison your brains that you seem to me like so many parrots in their cages, hopping and dancing from one perch to another, yet always turning and winding within the same wires. But be it known unto you that so great an Emperor has not so narrow a palace, so miserable a throne, so low a tribunal, so scanty a court, so little and weak a representative; as that a fancy can bring it forth, a dream overlay it, madness repair it, a chimera shatter it, a disaster lessen it, another accident increase

it, and a thought make it perfect again, being brought together by a blast and made solid by a shake. It is, on the contrary, an immense portraiture, an admirable image, an exalted figure, a most high vestige, an infinite representation of an infinite original, and a spectacle befitting the excellence and eminence of Him that can neither be imagined, nor conceived, nor comprehended.

Thus the excellence of God is magnified, and the grandeur of his Empire made manifest. He's not glorified in one but in numberless Suns, not in one Earth or in one World, but in ten hundred thousand, in infinite Globes: so that this faculty of the intellect is not vain or arbitrary, that ever will and can add space to space, quantity to quantity, unity to unity, number to number. By this science we are loosened from the chains of a most narrow dungeon and set at liberty to rove in a most august empire. We are removed from conceited boundaries and poverty to the innumerable riches of an infinite space, of so worthy a field, and of such beautiful worlds.

Sir Francis Bacon

1561–1626

Francis Bacon had the outstanding intellect of Elizabethan England, and his achievements in a wide variety of fields reflect the ideal versatility of the Renaissance man. His own age knew him as a statesman who rose to political heights as lord chancellor of James I. He is popularly remembered as the author of some pithy and worldly-wise essays on moral subjects. A few enthusiastic but misguided scholars have even credited him with writing the plays of Shakespeare. But he thought of himself as a philosopher and aspired to review and renew all the sciences in the manner of Aristotle. Perhaps his greatest service to Western culture lay in articulating a scientific method and bridging the gap between Renaissance scientists and modern science.

This ambitious thinker was ideally trained for his remarkable career. His distinguished father, Sir Nicholas Bacon, was Lord Keeper of the Seal under Elizabeth and educated his two promising sons, Anthony and Francis, at Cambridge. Anthony's later career in politics was only slightly less distinguished than his younger brother's. Francis left Cambridge at fourteen to study law and interrupted his law preparation a year later to join a diplomatic embassy to France. He was admitted to the bar in 1582 and soon entered Parliament. With the accession of James I in 1603 he rose rapidly to a commanding political position. He was knighted and eventually was created Baron Verulam. Between 1607 and 1618 he rose from solicitor-general through the offices of attorney-general, privy councilor, and Lord Keeper of the Seal to be lord chancellor of England.

Three years later he fell suddenly from this eminence when he was accused of having taken bribes; he confessed to the charge and was deprived of all his offices and even barred from court and Parliament. Deeply impressed by the political philosophy of Machiavelli, he had long preached a pragmatic morality in his essays and had apparently applied it to his own political activities. It was regrettable that the great thinker of this age should have stooped to dishonesty in his public career but it is by no means inconsistent with his completely materialistic philosophy. In the five years remaining to him he pursued his legal and scientific studies and died of a chill contracted in experimenting with snow as a preservative of meat.

At no time in his life was Bacon too busy to study and write. The three editions of his *Essays* belong to the three periods of his career: his political apprenticeship (1597), his rise to power (1612), and his disgrace and retirement (1625). These little epigrammatic studies offer highly practical wisdom on many subjects: marriage and the single life, youth and age, love and friendship, health and riches, ambition, superstition, and the nature of man. Bacon's clear-cut, aphoristic style concentrates a world of common sense in a few memorable sentences.

But the *Essays* were merely relaxation for his energetic mind. His philosophy he committed to Latin in which language he projected a thorough review of existing sciences as well as the discovery of new knowledge by a new organon, or method of approaching the facts of nature. He planned his total scientific compendium as the *Great Instauration,* or renovation, of natural knowledge. The first part, *The Advancement of Learning* (1605), was first published in English and only later formed part of the larger scheme when elaborated as *De Augmentis Scientiarum.* It gave a review of the state of knowledge in Bacon's time and suggested a system of classifying the various branches of learning. The second part, the *Novum Organum* (1620), described the new method of true science in opposition to older methods beclouded by phantoms, or "idols," of the mind. This greatest of all Bacon's works divorced science from superstition, theology, and even philosophy as older ages had known it. Although Bacon was not himself free from a priori reasoning about science and understood the experimental method only imperfectly, he paved the way for the modern science of the seventeenth century. The later parts of his *Magna Instauratio* are only fragments of his projected study of nature by the new method. The most intriguing of all his works is the *New Atlantis* (1624), a utopian sketch that describes an ideal commonwealth of scholars pursuing a scientific analysis of nature for the profit of mankind. Bacon's vision bore fruit in 1662 with the establishment in London of the Royal Society for Improving Natural Knowledge.

As an enthusiastic pioneer, Bacon promised far more than he achieved. Misinterpreting nature as a simple phenomenon, he lived to see that no one man could explore it all. A more serious defect was his disregard of the hypothesis as the starting point of scientific method. He despised mere authority and syllogistic reasoning so much that he placed too great trust in the mere observation of natural things. Demanding certainty rather than probability, he failed to see that the scientist must begin with a probable assumption, or hypothesis, to guide his experiment. He was right in affirming that science reaches its conclusions by induction, finding general truths in particular instances. He was right in condemning the reverse reasoning from generals to particulars, but he slighted the role of scientific imagination in initiating the observation of particulars. Still he cleared the ground of older prejudices, and his magnificent plea for observing facts without preconceptions makes him the most revered spokesman for science in the Renaissance.

Novum Organum

1.

MAN, being the servant and interpreter of Nature, can do and understand so much and so much only as he has observed in fact or in thought of the course of nature: beyond this he neither knows anything nor can do anything.

2. Neither the naked hand nor the understanding left to itself can effect much. It is by instruments and helps that the work is done, which are as much wanted for the understanding as for the hand. And as the instruments of the hand either give motion or guide it, so the instruments of the mind supply either suggestions for the understanding or cautions.   10

3. Human knowledge and human power meet in one; for where the cause is not known the effect cannot be produced. Nature to be commanded must be obeyed; and that which in contemplation is as the cause is in operation as the rule.

4. Towards the effecting of works, all that man can do is to put together or put asunder natural bodies. The rest is done by nature working within. . . .   20

26. The conclusions of human reason as ordinarily applied in matter of nature, I call for the sake of distinction *Anticipations of Nature* (as a thing rash or premature). That reason which is elicited from facts by a just and methodical process, I call *Interpretation of Nature.*

27. Anticipations are a ground sufficiently firm for consent; for even if men went mad all after the same fashion, they might agree one with another well enough.   30

28. For the winning of assent, indeed, anticipations are far more powerful than interpretations; because being collected from a few instances, and those for the most part of familiar occurrence, they straightway touch the understanding and fill the

*Novum Organum.*⁸ Translated by James Spedding.

imagination; whereas interpretations on the other hand, being gathered here and there from very various and widely dispersed facts, cannot suddenly strike the understanding; and therefore they must needs, in respect of the opinions of the time, seem harsh and out of tune; much as the mysteries of faith do.

29. In sciences founded on opinions and dogmas, the use of anticipations and logic is good; for in them the object is to command assent to the proposition, not to master the thing.

30. Though all the wits of all the ages should meet together and combine and transmit their labours, yet will no great progress ever be made in science by means of anticipations; because radical errors in the first concoction of the mind are not to be cured by the excellence of functions and remedies subsequent.

31. It is idle to expect any great advancement in science from the superinducing and engrafting of new things upon old. We must begin anew from the very foundations, unless we would revolve for ever in a circle with mean and contemptible progress.

32. The honour of the ancient authors, and indeed of all, remains untouched; since the comparison I challenge is not of wits or faculties, but of ways and methods, and the part I take upon myself is not that of a judge, but of a guide.

33. This must be plainly avowed: no judgment can be rightly formed either of my method or of the discoveries to which it leads, by means of anticipations (that is to say, of the reasoning which is now in use); since I cannot be called on to abide by the sentence of a tribunal which is itself on its trial. . . .

36. One method of delivery alone remains to us; which is simply this: we must lead men to the particulars themselves, and their series and order; while men on their side must force themselves for awhile to lay their notions by and begin to familiarize themselves with facts.

37. The doctrine of those who have denied that certainty could be attained at all, has some agreement with my way of proceeding at the first setting out; but they end in being infinitely separated and opposed. For the holders of that doctrine assert simply that nothing can be known; I also assert that not much can be known in nature by the way which is now in use. But then they go on to destroy the authority of the senses and understanding; whereas I proceed to devise and supply helps for the same.

38. The idols and false notions which are now in possession of the human understanding, and have taken deep root therein, not only so beset men's minds that truth can hardly find entrance, but even after entrance obtained, they will again in the very instauration of the sciences meet and trouble us, unless men being forewarned of the danger fortify themselves as far as may be against their assaults.

39. There are four classes of Idols which beset men's minds. To these for distinction's sake I have assigned names,—calling the first class *Idols of the Tribe;* the second, *Idols of the Cave;* the third, *Idols of the Market-place;* the fourth, *Idols of the Theatre.* . . .

41. The Idols of the Tribe have their foundation in human nature itself, and in the tribe or race of men. For it is a false assertion that the sense of man is the measure of things. On the contrary, all perceptions as well of the sense as of the mind are according to the measure of the universe. And the human understanding is like a false mirror, which, receiving rays irregularly, distorts and discolours the nature of things by mingling its own nature with it.

42. The Idols of the Cave are the idols of the individual man. For every one (besides the errors common to human nature in general) has a cave or den of his own, which refracts and discolours the light of nature; owing either to his own proper and peculiar nature; or to his education and conversation with others; or to the reading of books, and the authority of those whom he esteems and admires; or to the differences of impressions, accordingly as they take place in a mind preoccupied and predisposed or in a mind indifferent and settled; or the like. So that the spirit of man (according as it is meted out to different individuals) is in fact a thing variable and full of perturbation, and governed as it were by chance. Whence it was well observed by Heraclitus that men look for sciences in their own lesser worlds, and not in the greater or common world.

43. There are also Idols formed by the intercourse and association of men with each other, which I call Idols of the Market-place, on account of the commerce and consort of men there. For it is by discourse that men associate; and words are imposed according to the apprehension of the vulgar. And therefore the ill and unfit choice of words wonderfully obstructs the understanding. Nor do the definitions or explanations wherewith in some things learned men are wont to guard and defend themselves, by any means set the matter right. But words plainly force and overrule the understanding, and throw all into confusion, and lead men away into numberless empty controversies and idle fancies.

44. Lastly, there are Idols which have immigrated into men's minds from the various dogmas of philosophies, and also from wrong laws of demonstration. These I call Idols of the Theatre; because in my judgment all the received systems are but so many stage-plays, representing worlds of their own creation after an unreal and scenic fashion. Nor is it

88. **Heraclitus,** the Greek philosopher of Ephesus (fl. 515 B.C.), who taught that man's narrow experience gives him a false belief in the permanence of external things.

only of the systems now in vogue, or only of the ancient sects and philosophies, that I speak; for many more plays of the same kind may yet be composed and in like artificial manner set forth; seeing that errors the most widely different have nevertheless causes for the most part alike. Neither again do I mean this only of entire systems, but also of many principles and axioms in science, which by tradition, credulity, and negligence have come to be received. But of these several kinds of Idols I must speak more largely and exactly, that the understanding may be duly cautioned.

45. The human understanding is of its own nature prone to suppose the existence of more order and regularity in the world than it finds. And though there be many things in nature which are singular and unmatched, yet it devises for them parallels and conjugates and relatives which do not exist. Hence the fiction that all celestial bodies move in perfect circles; spirals and dragons being (except in name) utterly rejected. Hence too the element of Fire with its orb is brought in, to make up the square with the other three which the sense perceives. Hence also the ratio of density of the so-called elements is arbitrarily fixed at ten to one. And so on of other dreams. And these fancies affect not dogmas only, but simple notions also.

46. The human understanding when it has once adopted an opinion (either as being the received opinion or as being agreeable to itself) draws all things else to support and agree with it. And though there be a greater number and weight of instances to be found on the other side, yet these it either neglects and despises, or else by some distinction sets aside and rejects; in order that by this great and pernicious predetermination the authority of its former conclusions may remain inviolate. And therefore it was a good answer that was made by one who when they showed him hanging in a temple a picture of those who had paid their vows as having escaped shipwreck, and would have him say whether he did not now acknowledge the power of the gods,— "Aye," asked he again, "but where are they painted that were drowned after their vows?" And such is the way of all superstition, whether in astrology, dreams, omens, divine judgments, or the like; wherein men, having a delight in such vanities, mark the events where they are fulfilled, but where they fail, though this happen much oftener, neglect and pass them by. But with far more subtlety does this mischief insinuate itself into philosophy and the sciences; in which the first conclusion colours and brings into conformity with itself all that come after, though far sounder and better. Besides, independently of that delight and vanity which I have described, it is the peculiar and perpetual error of the human intellect to be more moved and excited by affirmatives than by negatives; whereas it ought properly to hold itself indifferently disposed towards both alike. Indeed in the establishment of any true axiom, the negative instance is the more forcible of the two.

47. The human understanding is moved by those things most which strike and enter the mind simultaneously and suddenly, and so fill the imagination; and then it feigns and supposes all other things to be somehow, though it cannot see how, similar to those few things by which it is surrounded. But for that going to and fro to remote and heterogeneous instances, by which axioms are tried as in the fire, the intellect is altogether slow and unfit, unless it be forced thereto by severe laws and overruling authority.

48. The human understanding is unquiet; it cannot stop or rest, and still presses onward, but in vain. Therefore it is that we cannot conceive of any end or limit to the world; but always as of necessity it occurs to us that there is something beyond. Neither again can it be conceived how eternity has flowed down to the present day; for that distinction which is commonly received of infinity in time past and in time to come can by no means hold; for it would thence follow that one infinity is greater than another, and that infinity is wasting away and tending to become finite. The like subtlety arises touching the infinite divisibility of lines, from the same inability of thought to stop. But this inability interferes more mischievously in the discovery of causes: for although the most general principles in nature ought to be held merely positive, as they are discovered, and cannot with truth be referred to a cause; nevertheless the human understanding being unable to rest still seeks something prior in the order of nature. And then it is that in struggling towards that which is further off it falls back upon that which is more nigh at hand; namely, on final causes: which have relation clearly to the nature of man rather than to the nature of the universe; and from this source have strangely defiled philosophy. But he is no less an unskilled and shallow philosopher who seeks causes of that which is most general, than he who in things subordinate and subaltern omits to do so.

49. The human understanding is no dry light, but receives an infusion from the will and affections; whence proceed sciences which may be called "sciences as one would." For what a man had rather were true he more readily believes. Therefore he rejects difficult things from impatience of research; sober things, because they narrow hope; the deeper things of nature, from superstition; the light of experience, from arrogance and pride, lest his mind should seem to be occupied with things mean and transitory; things not commonly believed, out of deference to the opinion of the vulgar. Numberless in

short are the ways, and sometimes imperceptible, in which the affections colour and infect the understanding. . . .

96. We have as yet no natural philosophy that is pure; all is tainted and corrupted; in Aristotle's school by logic; in Plato's by natural theology; in the second school of Platonists, such as Proclus and others, by mathematics, which ought only to give definiteness to natural philosophy, not to generate or give it birth. From a natural philosophy pure and unmixed, better things are to be expected.

97. No one has yet been found so firm of mind and purpose as resolutely to compel himself to sweep away all theories and common notions, and to apply the understanding, thus made fair and even, to a fresh examination of particulars. Thus it happens that human knowledge, as we have it, is a mere medley and ill-digested mass, made up of much credulity and much accident, and also of the childish notions which we at first imbibed. . . .

99. Again, even in the great plenty of mechanical experiments, there is yet a great scarcity of those which are of most use for the information of the understanding. For the mechanic, not troubling himself with the investigation of truth, confines his attention to those things which bear upon his particular work, and will not either raise his mind or stretch out his hand for anything else. But then only will there be good ground of hope for the further advance of knowledge, when there shall be received and gathered together into natural history a variety of experiments, which are of no use in themselves, but simply serve to discover causes and axioms; which I call *"Experimenta lucifera,"* experiments of *light*, to distinguish them from those which I call *"fructifera,"* experiments of *fruit*.

Now experiments of this kind have one admirable property and condition; they never miss or fail. For since they are applied, not for the purpose of producing any particular effect, but only of discovering the natural cause of some effect, they answer the end equally well whichever way they turn out; for they settle the question. . . .

104. The understanding must not however be allowed to jump and fly from particulars to remote axioms and of almost the highest generality (such as the first principles, as they are called, of arts and things), and taking stand upon them as truths that cannot be shaken, proceed to prove and frame the middle axioms by reference to them; which has been the practice hitherto; the understanding being not only carried that way by a natural impulse, but also by the use of syllogistic demonstration trained and inured to it. But then, and then only, may we hope well of the sciences, when in a just scale of ascent, and by successive steps not interrupted or broken, we rise from particulars to lesser axioms; and then to middle axioms, one above the other; and last of all to the most general. For the lowest axioms differ but slightly from bare experience, while the highest and most general (which we now have) are notional and abstract and without solidity. But the middle are the true and solid and living axioms, on which depend the affairs and fortunes of men; and above them again, last of all, those which are indeed the most general; such I mean as are not abstract, but of which those intermediate axioms are really limitations.

The understanding must not therefore be supplied with wings, but rather hung with weights, to keep it from leaping and flying. Now this has never yet been done; when it is done, we may entertain better hopes of the sciences.

Martin Luther

1483–1546

Although preceded by various heretical movements within the Roman Church, the Protestant Reformation is officially dated from the posting of Luther's Ninety-five Theses at the German town of Wittenberg in 1517. Luther's attack on papal indulgences led to the suppressive Diet of Worms, and this in turn led to the protest of nineteen German states against obstructions to the Lutheran movement, which gave rise to the term "protestant." Luther was originally innocent of any intent to secede from the Church, and only a chain of circumstances pushed him to the crucial step of an open break.

The son of pious but humble parents, he had secured a schooling at Magdeburg and Eisenach only with the aid of a benevolent patron, but at the University of Erfurt he distinguished himself as a brilliant Latin scholar. Intended for the law, he turned to divinity and eventually entered the Augustine monastery at Erfurt in 1505 because of a long trial of conscience. Having overcome his fears for his soul through deep repentance of his sins, he was ordained priest and became professor of philosophy at Wittenberg.

A trip to Rome on church business in 1510 aroused the ire of the austere preacher against the worldliness and luxury of church leaders. When in 1514 the Humanistic Pope Leo x, a son of Lorenzo de' Medici, resolved to complete the building of Saint Peter's at Rome, he issued a bull granting papal indulgence to all contributors to the building fund. A Dominican friar, John Tetzel, was authorized to preach the indulgence in northern Germany. His appearance near Wittenberg in October 1517 stirred Luther to a furious attack on the sale of papal indulgences, stated in the Ninety-five Theses that he posted on the door of the castle church. With guarded words he argued that salvation comes through inner repentance rather than from an external act of penance. This distinction assumed a personal and direct relationship between the Christian and his God and led eventually to Luther's denying the need of the Church as intermediary.

Although his propositions were denounced as heretical, Luther refused to recant and ignored a summons to Rome and two papal bulls issued against him, since he was protected by German princes who resented the political and taxational power of Rome in their states. As the controversy spread, he grew bolder and more radical in his attack on the authority of the Pope. His defiant appearance before the Diet of Worms was followed by his establishment of an independent German church with a new service that he completed in 1529. The Lutheran Church assumed its official status in 1530 through the publication of the Augsburg Confession, composed by his friend and great disciple, Philip Melanchthon. Yet for all his insistence on freedom of conscience, Luther refused to unite his movement with the Swiss Protestantism of Ulrich Zwingli because of differences over points of doctrine. Although he denounced the intolerance of Rome, he has been criticized for being no more tolerant of those who disagreed with him.

By 1525, Luther's break with Rome was largely completed, and his remaining years were devoted to shaping his church and to writing. In 1534 he completed his translation of the Bible, which remains the standard Protestant version in German. From time to time he composed hymns for a Protestant hymnal (*Eine feste Burg, Aus tiefer Not*), which reveal his deep love of music. But the most attractive product of his last twenty years was his *Table Talk*, actually his casual conversation as it was taken down by twelve devoted disciples. Married in 1525 to a former nun, he made their home an open house for his followers, who have left a charming impression of the domestic quiet and scholarly ease of Luther's later years. In the varied *Table Talk* we see the humanity of the man, his mellow delight in living, his robust piety, and even his occasional coarseness. Only Boswell's *Johnson* equals the frankness of this personal reporting.

Table Talk

11.

I HAVE grounded my preaching upon the literal word; he that pleases may follow me; he that will not may stay. I call upon St. Peter, St. Paul, Moses, and all the Saints to say whether they ever fundamentally comprehended one single word of God without studying it over and over and over again. The Psalm says: *His understanding is infinite.* The saints, indeed, know God's word, and can discourse of it, but the practice is another matter; therein we shall ever remain scholars.

*Table Talk.*⁸ Translated by William Hazlitt.

The school theologians have a fine similitude hereupon, that it is as with a sphere or globe, which, lying on a table, touches it only with one point, yet it is the whole table which supports the globe. Though I am an old doctor of divinity, to this day I have not got beyond the children's learning—the Ten Commandments, the Belief, and the Lord's Prayer; and these I understand not so well as I should, though I study them daily, praying, with my son John and my daughter Magdalen. If I thoroughly appreciated these first words of the Lord's Prayer, *Our Father, which art in Heaven,* and really believed that God, who made heaven and earth and all creatures, and has all things in his hand, was my Father, then should I certainly conclude with myself that I also am a lord of heaven and earth, that Christ is my brother, Gabriel my servant, Raphael my coachman, and all the angels my attendants at need, given unto me by my heavenly Father to keep me in the path, that unawares I knock not my foot against a stone. But that our faith may be exercised and confirmed, our heavenly Father suffers us to be cast into dungeons or plunged in water. So we may see how finely we understand these words, and how belief shakes, and how great our weakness is, so that we begin to think—Ah, who knows how far that is true which is set forth in the Scriptures?

12. No greater mischief can happen to a Christian people than to have God's word taken from them, or falsified, so that they no longer have it pure and clear. God grant we and our descendants be not witnesses of such a calamity.

20. Oh! how great and glorious a thing it is to have before one the Word of God! With that we may at all times feel joyous and secure; we need never be in want of consolation, for we see before us, in all its brightness, the pure and right way. He who loses sight of the word of God falls into despair; the voice of heaven no longer sustains him; he follows only the disorderly tendency of his heart, and of world vanity, which lead him on to his destruction.

33. In all sciences, the ablest professors are they who have thoroughly mastered the texts. A man, to be a good jurisconsult, should have every text of the law at his fingers' ends; but in our time, the attention is applied rather to glosses and commentaries. When I was young, I read the Bible over and over and over again, and was so perfectly acquainted with it that I could, in an instant, have pointed to any verse that might have been mentioned. I then read the commentators, but I soon threw them aside, for I found therein many things my conscience could not approve, as being contrary to the sacred text. 'Tis always better to see with one's own eyes than with those of other people.

39. I never thought the world had been so

wicked, when the Gospel began, as now I see it is; I rather hoped that every one would have leaped for joy to have found himself freed from the filth of the pope, from his lamentable molestations of poor troubled consciences, and that through Christ they would by faith obtain the celestial treasure they sought after before with such vast cost and labour, though in vain. And especially I thought the bishops and universities would with joy of heart have received the true doctrines, but I have been lamentably deceived. Moses and Jeremiah, too, complained they had been deceived.

58. The ungodly papists prefer the authority of the church far above God's Word; a blasphemy abominable and not to be endured; wherewith, void of all shame and piety, they spit in God's face. Truly, God's patience is exceeding great, in that they be not destroyed; but so it always has been.

63. All the works of God are unsearchable and unspeakable, no human sense can find them out; faith only takes hold of them without human power or aid. No mortal creature can comprehend God in his majesty, and therefore did he come before us in the simplest manner, and was made man, ay, sin, death, and weakness.

In all things, in the least creatures and in their members, God's almighty power and wonderful works clearly shine. For what man, how powerful, wise, and holy soever, can make out of one fig a fig-tree, or another fig? or out of one cherry-stone a cherry or a cherry-tree? or what man can know how God creates and preserves all things and makes them grow?

Neither can we conceive how the eye sees or how intelligible words are spoken plainly when only the tongue moves and stirs in the mouth; all which are natural things, daily seen and acted. How then should we be able to comprehend or understand the secret counsels of God's majesty, or search them out with our human sense, reason, or understanding. Should we then admire our own wisdom? I, for my part, admit myself a fool, and yield myself captive.

67. When one asked where God was before heaven was created, St. Augustin answered: He was in himself. When another asked me the same question, I said: He was building Hell for such idle, presumptuous, fluttering, and inquisitive spirits as you. After he had created all things, he was everywhere, and yet he was nowhere, for I cannot take hold of him without the Word. But he will be found there where he has engaged to be. The Jews found him at Jerusalem by the throne of grace (Exod. xxv.) We find him in the Word and faith, in baptism and the sacraments; but in his majesty, he is nowhere to be found.

91. God, in this world, has scarce the tenth part of the people; the smallest number only will be saved. The world is exceeding ungodly and wicked; who would believe our people should be so unthankful towards the gospel?

100. Our loving Lord God wills that we eat, drink, and be merry, making use of his creatures, for therefore he created them. He will not that we complain, as if he had not given sufficient, or that he could not maintain our poor carcases; he asks only that we acknowledge him for our God, and thank him for his gifts.

123. Dr. Jonas, inviting Luther to dinner, caused a bunch of ripe cherries to be hung over the table where they dined, in remembrance of the creation, and as a suggestion to his guests to praise God for creating such fruits. But Luther said: Why not rather remember this in one's children, that are the fruit of one's body? For these are far more excelling creatures of God than all the fruits of trees. In them we see God's power, wisdom, and art, who made them all out of nothing, gave them life and limbs, exquisitely constructed, and will maintain and preserve them. Yet how little do we regard this. When people have children, all the effect is to make them grasping, raking together all they can to leave behind them. They do not know that before a child comes into the world, it has its lot assigned already, and that it is ordained and determined what and how much it shall have. In the married state we find that the conception of children depends not on our will and pleasure; we never know whether God will give us a son or a daughter. All this goes on without our counsel. My father and mother did not imagine they should have brought a spiritual overseer into the world. 'Tis God's work only, and this we cannot enter into. I believe that, in the life to come, we shall have nothing to do, but to meditate on and marvel at our Creator and his creatures.

171. Idolatry is all manner of seeming holiness and worshipping, let these counterfeit spiritualities shine outwardly as glorious and fair as they may; in a word, all manner of devotion in those that would serve God without Christ the Mediator, his Word and command. In Popedom it was held a work of the greatest sanctity for the monks to sit in their cells and meditate of God and of his wonderful works; to be kindled with zeal, kneeling on their knees, praying, and having their imaginary contemplations of celestial objects with such supposed devotion that they wept for joy. In these their conceits, they banished all desires and thoughts of women, and what else is temporal and evanescent. They seemed to meditate only of God and of his wonderful works. Yet all these seeming holy actions of devotion, which the wit and wisdom of man holds to be angelical sanctity, are nothing else but works of the flesh. All manner of religion, where people serve God without his Word and command, is simply

idolatry, and the more holy and spiritual such a religion seems, the more hurtful and venomous it is; for it leads people away from the faith of Christ, and makes them rely and depend upon their own strength, works, and righteousness.

In like manner, all kinds of orders of monks, fasts, prayers, hairy shirts, the austerities of the Capuchins, who in Popedom are held to be the most holy of all, are mere works of the flesh; for the monks hold they are holy, and shall be saved, not through Christ, whom they view as a severe and angry judge, but through the rules of their order.

No man can make the papists believe that the private mass is the greatest blaspheming of God, and the highest idolatry upon earth, an abomination the like to which has never been in Christendom since the time of the apostles; for they are blinded and hardened therein, so that their understanding and knowledge of God and of all divine matters is perverted and erroneous. They hold that to be the most upright and greatest service of God which, in truth, is the greatest and most abominable idolatry. And again, they hold that for idolatry which, in truth, is the upright and most acceptable service of God, the acknowledging Christ and believing in him. But we that truly believe in Christ and are of his mind, we, God be praised, know and judge all things, but are judged of no human creature.

178. The papists took the invocation of saints from the heathen, who divided God into numberless images and idols, and ordained to each its particular office and work.

These the papists, void of all shame and Christianity, imitated, thereby denying God's almighty power; every man, out of God's Word, spinning to himself a particular opinion, according to his own fancy; as one of their priests, celebrating mass, when about to consecrate many oblations at the altar at once, thought it would not be congruously spoken, or according to grammar rules, to say, "This is my body," so said, "These are my bodies;" and afterwards highly extolled his device, saying: "If I had not been so good a grammarian, I had brought in a heresy and consecrated but one oblation."

Such like fellows does the world produce; grammarians, logicians, rhetoricians, and philosophers, all falsifying the Holy Writ and sophisticating it with their arts, whereas it ought to remain every point in its own place whereto God ordered and appointed it. Divinity should be empress, and philosophy and other arts merely servants, not to govern and master her, as Servetus, Campanus, and other seducers would do. God preserve his church, which by him is carried as a child in the mother's womb, and defend her from such philosophical divinity.

The invocation of saints is a most abominable blindness and heresy; yet the papists will not give up. The Pope's greatest profit arises from the dead; for the calling on dead saints brings him infinite sums of money and riches, far more than he gets from the living. But thus goes the world; superstition, unbelief, false doctrine, idolatry obtain more credit and profit than the upright, true, and pure religion.

250. No sinner can escape his punishment, unless he be sorry for his sins. For though one go scot-free for awhile, yet at last he will be snapped, as the Psalm says: "God indeed is still judge on earth."

Our Lord God suffers the ungodly to be surprised and taken captive in very slight and small things, when they think not of it, when they are most secure and live in delight and pleasure, leaping for joy. In such manner was the Pope surprised by me, about his indulgences and pardons, comparatively a slight matter.

574. The greatest punishment God can inflict on the wicked is when the church, to chastise them, delivers them over to Satan, who, with God's permission, kills them or makes them undergo great calamities. Many devils are in woods, in waters, in wildernesses, and in dark pooly places, ready to hunt and prejudice people; some are also in the thick black clouds which cause hail, lightnings, and thunderings and poison the air, the pastures, and grounds. When these things happen, then the philosophers and physicians say it is natural, ascribing it to the planets and showing I know not what reasons for such misfortunes and plagues as ensue.

581. August 25, 1538, the conversation fell upon witches who spoil milk, eggs, and butter in farmyards. Dr. Luther said: "I should have no compassion on these witches; I would burn all of them. We read in the old law that the priests threw the first stone at such malefactors. 'Tis said this stolen butter turns rancid and falls to the ground when any one goes to eat it. He who attempts to counteract and chastise these witches is himself corporeally plagued and tormented by their master, the devil. Sundry schoolmasters and ministers have often experienced this. Our ordinary sins offend and anger God. What, then, must be his wrath against witchcraft, which we may justly designate high treason against divine majesty, a revolt against the infinite power of God. The jurisconsults who have so learnedly and pertinently treated of rebellion, affirm that the subject who rebels against his sovereign, is worthy of death. Does not witchcraft, then, merit death, which is a revolt of the creature against the Creator, a denial to God of the authority it accords to the demon?"

591. A pastor, near Torgau, came to Luther and complained that the devil tormented him without intermission. The Doctor replied: He plagues and harasses me too, but I resist him with the arms of

faith. I know of one person at Magdeburg who put Satan to the rout by spitting at him; but this example is not to be lightly followed; for the devil is a presumptuous spirit, and not disposed to yield. We run great risk when, with him, we attempt more than we can do. One man, who relied implicitly on his baptism, when the devil presented himself to him, his head furnished with horns, tore off one of the horns; but another man, of less faith, who attempted the same thing, was killed by the devil.

605. I would rather die through the devil than through the Emperor or Pope; for then I should die through a great and mighty prince of the world. But if he eat a bit of me, 'twill be his bane; he shall spew me out again; and, at the day of judgment, I in requital will devour him.

672. Erasmus is very pitiful with his prefaces, though he tries to smooth them over; he appears to see no difference between Jesus Christ our Saviour and the wise pagan legislator Solon. He sneers at St. Paul and St. John; and ventures to say that the Epistle to the Romans, whatever it might have been at a former period, is not applicable to the present state of things. Shame upon thee, accursed wretch! 'Tis a mere Momus, making his mows and mocks at everything and everybody, at God and man, at papist and protestant, but all the while using such shuffling and double-meaning terms, that no one can lay hold of him to any effectual purpose. Whenever I pray, I pray for a curse upon Erasmus.

721. The state of matrimony is the chief in the world after religion; but people shun it because of its inconveniences, like one who, running out of the rain, falls into the river. We ought herein to have more regard to God's command and ordinance, for the sake of the generation and the bringing up of children, than to our untoward humours and cogitations; and further, we should consider that it is a physic against sin and unchastity. None, indeed, should be compelled to marry; the matter should be left to each man's conscience, for bride-love may not be forced. God has said: "It is not good that the man should be alone;" and St. Paul compares the church to a spouse, or bride and a bridegroom. But let us ever take heed that, in marrying, we esteem neither money nor wealth, great descent, nobility, nor lasciviousness.

726. Marrying cannot be without women, nor can the world subsist without them. To marry is physic against incontinence. A woman is, or at least should be, a friendly, courteous, and merry companion in life, whence they are named by the Holy Ghost house-honours, the honour and ornament of the house, and inclined to tenderness, for there-unto are they chiefly created, to bear children and be the pleasure, joy, and solace of their husbands.

25. **Momus,** the Greek god of mockery and censure.

728. On what pretence can man have interdicted marriage, which is a law of nature? 'Tis as though we were forbidden to eat, to drink, to sleep. That which God has ordained and regulated is no longer a matter of the human will, which we may adopt or reject with impunity. 'Tis the most certain sign of God's enmity to Popedom that he has allowed it to assail the conjugal union of the sexes.

732. 'Tis a grand thing for a married pair to live in perfect union, but the devil rarely permits this. When they are apart, they cannot endure the separation, and when they are together, they cannot endure the always seeing one another. 'Tis as the poet says: *Nec tecum vivere possum, nec sine te.* Married people must assiduously pray against these assaults of the devil. I have seen marriages where, at first, husband and wife seemed as though they would eat one another up: in six months they have separated in mutual disgust. 'Tis the devil inspires this evanescent ardour in order to divert the parties from prayer.

739. There was at Frankfort-on-the-Oder, a schoolmaster, a pious and learned man, whose heart was fervently inclined to theology, and who had preached several times with great applause. He was called to the dignity of deacon, but his wife, a violent, fierce woman, would not consent to his accepting the charge, saying she would not be the wife of a minister.

It became a question what was the poor man to do? Which was he to renounce, his preachership or his wife? Luther at first said jocosely: "Oh, if he has married, as you tell me, a widow, he must needs obey her." But, after awhile, he resumed severely: "The wife is bound to follow her husband, not the husband his wife. This must be an ill woman, nay, the devil incarnate, to be ashamed of a charge with which our Lord and his apostles were invested. If she were my wife, I should shortly say to her: 'Wilt thou follow me, aye or no? Reply forthwith,' and if she replied no, I would leave her and take another wife."

752. The reproduction of mankind is a great marvel and mystery. Had God consulted me in the matter, I should have advised him to continue the generation of the species by fashioning them of clay, in the way Adam was fashioned; as I should have conselled him also to let the sun remain always suspended over the earth, like a great lamp, maintaining perpetual light and heat.

840. Music is one of the best arts; the notes give life to the text; it expels melancholy, as we see in king Saul. Kings and princes ought to maintain music, for great potentates and rulers should protect good and liberal arts and laws; though private

70. *Nec tecum . . . sine te,* "I cannot live with you, nor without you." (See Martial, XII, 47.)

people have desire thereunto and love it, yet their ability is not adequate. We read in the Bible, that the good and godly kings maintained and paid singers. Music is the best solace for a sad and sorrowful mind; by it the heart is refreshed and settled again in peace.

John Milton

1608–1674

The separation of the English Church from Rome by Henry VIII was largely a political move; the true Protestant movement in England came with the radical nonconformists of the sixteenth century, who denounced the intermediation of any church, Catholic or Anglican, between man and his Maker. Inspired by Calvin, English Protestants placed a terrifying personal responsibility on man, weighed down with a depraved nature since Adam's original sin. Confronted with a powerful and even angry God, they sought to free themselves from the taint of worldliness and renounced the show of ecclesiastical vestments and fashionable dress alike to signalize the austerity of their reformed way of life. Since they wished to purify the English Church by replacing ritual with direct spiritual contact with God, they were called the Puritans. Aspiring to a theocratic state of their own and faced with persecution, they came to constitute a political party, which precipitated the Civil War of 1642–1649 in England and ruled under Cromwell for a decade (1649–1659).

Despite the sternness of their way of life, the Puritans were not without a feeling for art and beauty. Indeed, John Milton showed that a magnificent epic poem could be built upon the Calvinist doctrine of human depravity and original sin. This great Puritan poet was scarcely typical of his sect, and yet he was all his life a dissenter and nonconformist, who took an active part in the government of Cromwell. An earnest conscience had led him to renounce his Anglican background and embrace the principles of the Puritans. His father, a prosperous and cultured scrivener, educated the sensitive, artistic youth at St. Paul's School and Christ's College, Cambridge, where he considered for a time a career in the Anglican Church. But his disgust with the High Church tyranny at Cambridge led him to retire with an M.A. degree in 1632 to pursue study and writing on his father's estate at Horton, twenty miles from London. To his Horton period (1632–1637) belong the best of his minor poems: the companion pieces L'Allegro and Il Penseroso (1632), the masque Comus (1634), and the pastoral elegy Lycidas (1637) in memory of his college mate Edward King. His Latin poems, though now little read, are among the finest in the Latin revival. His interest in the culture of Renaissance Italy led him to take a leisurely tour through Paris, Genoa, Florence, and Venice, which he cut short in 1639 with the rumor of civil war at home.

The second period of his career (1639–1660) corresponds to the period of civil war and the Puritan Commonwealth in England, and it converted the accomplished young man, half Puritan in his abstemious living, half Cavalier in his elegant tastes, into the mature and ardent spokesman for Cromwell's Puritan theocracy. Serving first as private tutor in London and later as Latin Secretary to the Commission of Foreign Affairs, Milton supported the cause with a series of prose tracts that crowded poetry out of his life for twenty years. These tracts began in 1641 with Of Reformation Touching Church Discipline in England, which pleaded for the complete abolishment of Catholic ritual and the episcopal system from the Church. His unsuccessful marriage in 1643 to Mary Powell, a girl half his age, probably led to his tract, The Doctrine and Discipline of Divorce Restored, to the Good of Both Sexes, in which he argued that incompatibility of temperaments was as just ground for divorce as infidelity. When he was threatened with censorship for his advanced views, he replied with the best of his prose writings, Areopagitica (1644), a memorable plea for freedom of the press. The deep-seated independence of his spirit flared into a fiery radicalism in political and ecclesiastical matters, and he militantly supported the execution of Charles I in his Tenure of Kings and Magistrates (1649). But most of the prose writings of his second period lack general interest today. The death of his first wife in 1652 left him three small daughters to rear; and his second wife, whom he married in 1656, died in childbirth a year later. In addition to this, his eyesight had been failing throughout this period, so that by 1652 he was totally blind and had to perform his duties as Secretary through an assistant.

With restoration of the monarchy under Charles II, Milton lost his power and became for a time a fugitive from the vengeful Cavaliers. But this reversal of fortune returned his interests to poetry and led to his major poems of the last period (1660–1671). Dictating his verses to his three unappreciative daughters or his kindly third wife, he first delivered his masterpiece, Paradise Lost (1667). To this he added by 1671 a shorter epic of the triumph of Christ over Satan, Paradise Regained, and a Biblical tragedy in classical form, Samson Agonistes, in which the blind but still resisting Samson represents the blind Milton, unyielding to the end. Though he lived to see the Puritan cause in eclipse, his later years were sustained by his faith in himself and his poetry. Posterity has justified his faith.

Paradise Lost

Milton chose the most ambitious and forbidding of all literary forms, the epic, to give the Protestant world a noble counterpart of Dante's Divine Comedy. Beginning as a Calvinist, the English poet pushed his rebellion from Catholicism even further and ended as a member of no sect but rather a Protestant extremist of individual nature. *Paradise Lost* rings with the prophetic strain, as he musters his burning religious faith, his classical learning, and masterful poetic skill for an apocalyptic account of what he considered the greatest event in human history, the fall of Adam, which has encumbered man with the taint of sin from that day to this. Few poets have dared to undertake such a cosmic theme. In the vastness of his design and the sublime heights of his vision he makes demands on his reader that put him beyond popular appeal. In the words of Dr. Johnson, *"Paradise Lost* is one of the books which the reader admires and lays down, and forgets to take up again. None ever wished it longer than it is. We read Milton for instruction, retire harassed and overburdened, and look elsewhere for recreation; we desert our master, and seek for companions." The Olympian heights of Aeschylus are not easily scaled; the terrifying depths of Dante's Inferno demand hardy spirits. Milton brought the Olympian nobility of the ancients to the Christian tale of man's first fall. We must rise above everyday thought and feeling if we are to grasp his moral message and lofty poetic dream.

His purpose is simply stated: "to justify the ways of God to men," by proving that evil came not from God but from a counterspirit as evil as God is good and loving and merciful. His plot is the simple story of the tempting of Eve and Adam and of their expulsion from Eden, but he prefixes to this an account of how evil was born with the rebellion of Satan and his cohorts against the power of God in Heaven. Sworn to everlasting war with his Maker, Satan seduces the newly created man and woman in Paradise to sin, but for his arrogance is reduced to the mean estate of serpent. Man, on the other hand, is comforted with the promise of a Saviour in God's own Son.

Milton's first source was the Bible, and his poem is filled with allusions to both the Old and the New Testaments. There is much of Dante too in his description of Hell, and a strongly Calvinist interpretation of original sin and salvation by atonement. But Milton belonged also to the Renaissance and reveals on every page his classical learning and especially his indebtedness to Homer. The epic invocation; the beginning *in medias res* with the actual fall of Satan; the throwback narratives in the discussions of Adam, Eve, and the Angel; the roll call of the leaders; the epic commonplaces and elaborate similes, all remind us of the influence of Homer and Virgil in Renaissance epics. But the poem is a religious epic, not a national one, and is built around no one hero, as are the *Iliad* and the *Odyssey*. Indeed, the arch villain is the best-defined character in the poem, and the heroic treatment of Satan may suggest Milton's unconscious sympathy with a fellow rebel. *Paradise Lost* is a work of Milton's own conception, and he matched his grand intent with a noble style. His blank verse strides across older limitations to form actual paragraphs, by which larger units of narrative and thought can be developed in melodious language. The perfect harmony of thought and expression within this free framework has produced a lofty, if austere, poetic creation.

BOOK I

The Argument

This first Book proposes, first in brief, the whole subject, man's disobedience, and the loss thereupon of Paradise wherein he was placed: then touches the prime cause of his fall, the serpent, or rather Satan in the serpent; who revolting from God, and drawing to his side many legions of angels, was by the command of God driven out of Heaven with all his crew into the great deep. Which action past over, the poem hastes into the midst of things, presenting Satan with his angels now fallen into Hell, described here, not in the centre (for Heaven and Earth may be supposed as yet not made, certainly not yet accursed) but in a place of utter darkness, fitliest called Chaos: here Satan with his angels lying on the burning lake, thunder-struck and astonished, after a certain space recovers, as from confusion, calls up him who next in order and dignity lay by him; they confer of their miserable fall. Satan awakens all his legions, who lay till then in the same manner confounded; they rise, their numbers, array of battle, their chief leaders named, according to the idols known afterwards in Canaan and the countries adjoining. To these Satan directs his speech, comforts them with hope yet of regaining Heaven, but tells them lastly of a new world and new kind of creature to be created, according to an ancient prophecy or report in Heaven; for that angels were long before this visible creation, was the opinion of many ancient fathers. To find out the truth of this prophecy, and what to determine thereon he refers to a full council. What his associates thence attempt. Pandemonium, the palace of Satan, rises, suddenly built out of the deep: the infernal peers there sit in council.

OF man's first disobedience, and the fruit
　　Of that forbidden tree, whose mortal taste
Brought Death into the world, and all our woe,
With loss of Eden, till one greater Man
Restore us, and regain the blissful seat,　　5
Sing, Heavenly Muse! that on the secret top

The Argument. **into the midst of things,** a translation of *in medias res* from Horace's *Ars Poetica,* the critical principle that an epic poem should begin in the midst of an action and later, by an "epic throwback," recount the antecedent action. This is the plan followed by Milton; Books V and VI, as in the *Odyssey,* the *Iliad,* and the *Aeneid,* put the earliest part of the story into the mouth of a narrator who took part in the antecedent action. **Pandemonium,** literally, (the place) of all demons. **1. man's . . . disobedience.** Milton conceived the fall of man as a nobler subject than the wrath of Achilles in the *Iliad,* and the greater man (l. 4)—that is, Christ—a greater figure than Odysseus or Ulysses. **6. Heavenly Muse,** not merely the classical Muse of Greek and Latin poetry, but rather the holy spirit that inspired Moses, David, and the prophets; in fact, Milton implicitly contrasts these with the pagan divinities. In Renaissance tradition, however, the ninth Muse, Urania, was the inspirer of all great men; it is therefore likely that Milton, with his Renaissance leanings, had Urania in mind at this point.

Of Oreb, or of Sinai, didst inspire
That shepherd, who first taught the chosen seed,
In the beginning how the Heavens and Earth
Rose out of Chaos: or if Sion Hill   10
Delight thee more, and Siloa's brook that flowed
Fast by the oracle of God; I thence
Invoke thy aid to my adventurous song,
That with no middle flight intends to soar
Above th' Aonian Mount, while it pursues   .   15
Things unattempted yet in prose or rhyme.
And chiefly Thou, O Spirit, that dost prefer
Before all temples th' upright heart and pure,
Instruct me, for Thou know'st; Thou from the first
Wast present, and with mighty wings outspread   20
Dove-like satst brooding on the vast abyss
And mad'st it pregnant: what in me is dark
Illumine, what is low raise and support,
That to the highth of this great argument
I may assert Eternal Providence,   25
And justify the ways of God to men.
    Say first, for Heaven hides nothing from thy view
Nor the deep tract of Hell, say first what cause
Moved our grand parents in that happy state,
Favoured of Heaven so highly, to fall off   30
From their Creator, and trangress His will
For one restraint, lords of the world besides?
Who first seduced them to that foul revolt?
The infernal serpent; he it was, whose guile,
Stirred up with envy and revenge, deceived   35
The mother of mankind, what time his pride
Had cast him out from Heaven, with all his host
Of rebel angels, by whose aid aspiring
To set himself in glory above his peers,
He trusted to have equalled the most High,   40
If He opposed; and with ambitious aim
Against the throne and monarchy of God
Raised impious war in Heaven and battle proud
With vain attempt. Him the Almighty Power

Hurled headlong flaming from the ethereal sky   45
With hideous ruin and combustion down
To bottomless perdition, there to dwell
In adamantine chains and penal fire,
Who durst defy the Omnipotent to arms.
Nine times the space that measures day and night   50
To mortal men, he with his horrid crew
Lay vanquished, rolling in the fiery gulf
Confounded though immortal; but his doom
Reserved him to more wrath; for now the thought
Both of lost happiness and lasting pain   55
Torments him; round he throws his baleful eyes
That witnessed huge affliction and dismay
Mixed with obdurate pride and steadfast hate:
At once as far as angel's ken he views
The dismal situation waste and wild,   60
A dungeon horrible, on all sides round,
As one great furnace flamed, yet from those flames
No light, but rather darkness visible
Served only to discover sights of woe,
Regions of sorrow, doleful shades, where peace   65
And rest can never dwell, hope never comes
That comes to all; but torture without end
Still urges, and a fiery deluge, fed
With ever-burning sulphur unconsumed:
Such place Eternal Justice had prepared   70
For those rebellious, here their prison ordained
In utter darkness, and their portion set
As far removed from God and light of Heaven
As from the centre thrice to th' utmost pole.
O how unlike the place from whence they fell!   75
There the companions of his fall, o'erwhelmed
With floods and whirlwinds of tempestuous fire,
He soon discerns, and weltering by his side
One next himself in power, and next in crime,
Long after known in Palestine, and named   80

7. **Oreb,** Horeb, the mountain near Mount Sinai on which God spoke to Moses from the burning bush, as told in Exodus, 3. It was atop Mount Sinai that Moses received from God the laws to govern the Hebrews, as told in Exodus, 19.   8. **That shepherd,** Moses, to whom was attributed the authorship of the Book of Genesis, which includes the story of the Creation.   10. **Sion Hill,** the hill on which Jerusalem was built.   11. **Siloa's brook,** a stream which flowed near the hill on which the Temple was built in Jerusalem.   15. **Aonian Mount,** Mount Helicon in Boeotia, Greece, which was sacred to the Muses; but Milton insists that his inspiration is higher than that of the classical poets, whence the preposition "Above."   17. **Spirit,** the Spirit of God which in the Creation moved upon the Face of the Waters (see Genesis, 1, 2); perhaps we may read it here as "The Holy Ghost." 21. **Dove-like;** cf. Luke, 3:22: "And the Holy Ghost descended in a bodily shape like a dove."   26. **justify . . . men.** The purpose of Milton in writing the epic.   32. **For one restraint,** because of one prohibition.   34. **infernal serpent.** It was a common belief in the Renaissance and later Middle Ages that devils became like serpents, dragons, worms, or creeping and crawling things. This reference of course anticipates the later event recounted in Book x, 509–540, when Satan and his entire concourse of devils are reduced to serpent-forms.

45. ff. **Hurled headlong,** etc. Cf. Isaiah, 14:12: "How art thou fallen from Heaven, O Lucifer, son of the morning!" and Jude, 1: 6: "angels which kept not their first estate . . . in everlasting chains, under darkness."   50. **Nine times,** etc. Milton is probably reminded here of the ancient Greek legend, as told by Hesiod, where Zeus, newly established King of the Gods, hurled the vanquished Titans into Tartarus; their fall took nine days and nights. There are many such classical "recalls" in Milton's epic poetry.   63. **darkness visible,** an ancient but always effective poetic paradox.   64. **discover,** reveal, disclose.   66–67. **hope . . . comes,** an obvious reminiscence of Dante's "All hope abandon, ye who enter here!" in the *Inferno,* III, 9. 68. **urges,** pushes, drives.   72. **utter,** outer, remote; not "absolute." 74. **centre . . . pole.** Although Milton knew well enough the new cosmogony based upon the Copernican system, in which the planets revolve about the sun as their center, he adopted for the purposes of his plot in *Paradise Lost* the old Ptolemaic system. In this system the center was the circle of the stellar universe, and at the center of this circle was the Earth; around it, each on its own orbit, revolved the planets, and there was a special sphere for the fixed stars. Above was Heaven; at the opposite extreme was Hell, formed out of Chaos. The radius of the stellar circle was one-third the distance from Heaven to Hell. Throughout *Paradise Lost,* therefore, Milton used the term *centre* to mean the Earth. The utmost pole is a part of Milton's special conception of the created, or stellar, universe as encased in a shell with a lower pole sunk in Chaos and an upper pole pointing toward, but not touching, Heaven.

Beëlzebub. To whom the Arch-Enemy,
And thence in Heaven called Satan, with bold words
Breaking the horrid silence thus began:

'If thou beest he; but O, how fallen! how changed
From him, who in the happy realms of light   85
Clothed with transcendent brightness didst outshine
Myriads though bright: if he whom mutual league,
United thoughts and counsels, equal hope,
And hazard in the glorious enterprise,
Joined with me once, now misery hath joined   90
In equal ruin: into what pit thou seest
From what highth fallen, so much the stronger
      proved
He with His thunder: and till then who knew
The force of those dire arms? yet not for those,
Nor what the potent victor in his rage   95
Can else inflict, do I repent or change,
Though changed in outward lustre: that fixed mind
And high disdain, from sense of injured merit,
That with the mightiest raised me to contend,
And to the fierce contention brought along   100
Innumerable force of spirits armed
That durst dislike His reign, and me preferring,
His utmost power with adverse power opposed
In dubious battle on the plains of Heaven,
And shook His throne. What though the field be
      lost?   105
All is not lost; the unconquerable will,
And study of revenge, immortal hate,
And courage never to submit or yield:
And what is else not to be overcome.
That glory never shall His wrath or might   110
Extort from me. To bow and sue for grace
With suppliant knee, and deify His power
Who from the terror of this arm so late
Doubted His empire, that were low indeed,
That were an ignominy and shame beneath   115
This downfall; since by Fate the strength of gods
And this empyreal substance cannot fail,
Since through experience of this great event
In arms not worse, in foresight much advanced,
We may with more successful hope resolve   120
To wage by force or guile eternal war
Irreconcilable, to our grand Foe,
Who now triumphs, and in th' excess of joy
Sole reigning holds the tyranny of Heaven.'

So spake th' apostate angel, though in pain,   125
Vaunting aloud, but racked with deep despair;
And him thus answered soon his bold compeer:

'O Prince, O Chief of many throned Powers,
That led th' embattled Seraphim to war
Under thy conduct, and in dreadful deeds   130
Fearless, endangered Heaven's perpetual King;
And put to proof His high supremacy,
Whether upheld by strength, or chance, or Fate,
Too well I see and rue the dire event,
That with sad overthrow and foul defeat   135
Hath lost us Heaven, and all this mighty host
In horrible destruction laid thus low,
As far as Gods and Heavenly Essences
Can perish: for the mind and spirit remains
Invincible, and vigor soon returns,   140
Though all our glory extinct, and happy state
Here swallowed up in endless misery.
But what if He our conqueror (whom I now
Of force believe almighty, since no less
Than such could have o'erpowered such force as
      ours),   145
Have left us this our spirit and strength entire
Strongly to suffer and support our pains,
That we may so suffice His vengeful ire,
Or do Him mightier service as His thralls
By right of war, whate'er His business be   150
Here in the heart of Hell to work in fire,
Or do His errands in the gloomy deep;
What can it then avail though yet we feel
Strength undiminished, or eternal being
To undergo eternal punishment?'   155
Whereto with speedy words the arch-fiend replied:

'Fallen cherub, to be weak is miserable,
Doing or suffering; but of this be sure,
To do aught good never will be our task,
But ever to do ill our sole delight,   160
As being the contrary to His high will
Whom we resist. If then His Providence
Out of our evil seek to bring forth good,
Our labour must be to pervert that end,
And out of good still to find means of evil;   165
Which oft-times may succeed, so as perhaps
Shall grieve Him, if I fail not, and disturb
His inmost counsels from their destined aim.
But see, the angry victor hath recalled
His ministers of vengeance and pursuit   170
Back to the gates of Heaven; the sulphurous hail
Shot after us in storm, o'erblown hath laid
The fiery surge, that from the precipice
Of Heaven received us falling, and the thunder,

---

81. **Beelzebub,** considered the captain of the first of the nine orders of Devils, and generally placed second in rank to Satan himself. 92. **so much the stronger proved.** Observe the backward-pointing allusion to the Battle in Heaven, which is described later in the poem (Book VI). 98. **injured merit.** The emphasis in the poem on Satan's abilities and merit gives his character tragic implications. 107. **study,** pursuit of, zeal for. 114. **Doubted,** feared for. 115. **ignominy.** The third syllable of this word was frequently dropped in seventeenth-century English, with a resulting pronunciation of *ignomy.*

128–129. **Powers . . . Seraphim.** Milton follows the celestial hierarchy described by Dante in his *Paradiso,*XXVIII. The order presents (1) Seraphim; (2) Cherubim; (3) Thrones; (4) Dominions; (5) Virtues; (6) Powers; (7) Principalities; (8) Archangels; (9) Angels. 138. **Heavenly Essences,** the supernaturally material bodies of spirits. There is some doubt in the minds of the demons themselves whether or not their essences are perishable; note Book II, lines 99 and 145–154 below. 144. **Of force,** of necessity, necessarily. 148. **so suffice . . . ire.** Milton follows Dante in believing that evil spirits are sometimes permitted to wander and thereby carry out the judgments of God. 158. **Doing or suffering,** that is, whether active or passive.

Winged with red lightning and impetuous rage, 175
Perhaps hath spent his shafts, and ceases now
To bellow through the vast and boundless deep.
Let us not slip the occasion, whether scorn,
Or satiate fury yield it from our Foe.
Seest thou yon dreary plain, forlorn and wild, 180
The seat of desolation, void of light,
Save what the glimmering of these livid flames
Casts pale and dreadful? Thither let us tend
From off the tossing of these fiery waves,
There rest, if any rest can harbour there, 185
And reassembling our afflicted powers,
Consult how we may henceforth most offend
Our Enemy, our own loss how repair,
How overcome this dire calamity,
What reinforcement we may gain from hope, 190
If not what resolution from despair.'
    Thus Satan talking to his nearest mate
With head up-lift above the wave, and eyes
That sparkling blazed, his other parts besides
Prone on the flood, extended long and large 195
Lay floating many a rood, in bulk as huge
As whom the fables name of monstrous size,
Titanian, or Earth-born, that warred on Jove,
Briareos or Typhon, whom the den
By ancient Tarsus held, or that sea-beast 200
Leviathan, which God of all His works
Created hugest that swim the ocean stream:
Him haply slumbering on the Norway foam
The pilot of some small night-foundered skiff,
Deeming some island, oft, as seamen tell, 205
With fixed anchor in his scaly rind
Moors by his side under the lee, while night
Invests the sea, and wishéd morn delays:
So stretched out huge in length the arch-fiend lay
Chained on the burning lake, nor ever thence 210
Had risen or heaved his head, but that the will
And high permission of all-ruling Heaven
Left him at large to his own dark designs,
That with reiterated crimes he might
Heap on himself damnation, while he sought 215
Evil to others, and enraged might see
How all his malice served but to bring forth
Infinite goodness, grace and mercy shown
On man by him seduced, but on himself
Treble confusion, wrath and vengeance poured. 220

Forthwith upright he rears from off the pool
His mighty stature; on each hand the flames
Driven backward slope their pointing spires, and
    rolled
In billows, leave in the midst a horrid vale.
Then with expanded wings he steers his flight 225
Aloft, incumbent on the dusky air
That felt unusual weight, till on dry land
He lights, if it were land that ever burned
With solid, as the lake with liquid fire;
And such appeared in hue, as when the force 230
Of subterranean wind transports a hill
Torn from Pelorus, or the shattered side
Of thundering Aetna, whose combustible
And fuelled entrails thence conceiving fire,
Sublimed with mineral fury, aid the winds, 235
And leave a singéd bottom all involved
With stench and smoke; such resting found the sole
Of unblessed feet. Him followed his next mate,
Both glorying to have scaped the Stygian flood
As gods, and by their own recovered strength, 240
Not by the sufferance of supernal power.
    'Is this the region, this the soil, the clime,'
Said then the lost archangel, 'this the seat
That we must change for Heaven, this mournful
    gloom
For that celestial light? Be it so, since He 245
Who now is Sovereign can dispose and bid
What shall be right: farthest from Him is best;
Whom reason hath equalled, force hath made su-
    preme
Above His equals. Farewell, happy fields!
Where Joy forever dwells. Hail, horrors! hail, 250
Infernal world! and thou profoundest Hell,
Receive thy new possessor: one who brings
A mind not to be changed by place or time.
The mind is its own place, and in itself
Can make a Heaven of Hell, a Hell of Heaven. 255
What matter where, if I be still the same,
And what I should be, all but less than He
Whom thunder hath made greater? Here at least
We shall be free; the Almighty hath not built
Here for His envy, will not drive us hence: 260
Here we may reign secure, and in my choice
To reign is worth ambition, though in Hell:
Better to reign in Hell than serve in Heaven.
But wherefore let we then our faithful friends,
The associates and copartners of our loss 265
Lie thus astonished on the oblivious pool,

---

186. **afflicted,** conquered, cast down. 199. **Briareos or Typhon,** in
Greek myth, two monsters. Briareos had a hundred hands; Typhon a
hundred fire-breathing heads. They attempted to overthrow the
sovereignty of Zeus, king of the gods of Olympus. Typhon lived in
Cilicia, of which the ancient city of Tarsus was capital; the locale is,
of course, Asia Minor. 201. **Leviathan.** There is more than one
Biblical allusion to the monster Leviathan; Milton seems here to be
thinking of that in Isaiah, 27:1: ". . . the piercing serpent, even
Leviathan, that crooked serpent; and he shall slay the dragon that is
in the sea." There is a very ancient tradition of the sea-monster or
sea-serpent so large that he is often mistaken for an island, to the
disaster of mariners; the Middle Ages often used this monster as
symbol of the Devil, as in the Medieval Bestiary. Note l. 204.

232. **Pelorus,** the northeastern cape on the island of Sicily, near the
great volcano Aetna (l. 233). 235. **Sublimed,** purified by incan-
descence—an alchemical term. 239. **Stygian flood,** a lake derived
from the river Styx of the classical Underworld. 242. **clime,** region.
254–255. **mind . . . Heaven,** a favorite idea of thinking men in the
Renaissance, an idea antithetical to current beliefs in the Middle
Ages—perhaps we can call it an unshakable trait in the modern mind,
though analogies can be found in ancient literature. 266. **oblivious,**
bestowing forgetfulness or oblivion.

And call them not to share with us their part
In this unhappy mansion, or once more
With rallied arms to try what may be yet
Regained in Heaven, or what more lost in Hell?'   270
    So Satan spake, and him Beëlzebub
Thus answered: 'Leader of those armies bright,
Which but the Omnipotent none could have foiled,
If once they hear that voice, their liveliest pledge
Of hope in fears and dangers, heard so oft   275
In worst extremes, and on the perilous edge
Of battle when it raged, in all assaults
Their surest signal, they will soon resume
New courage and revive, though now they lie
Groveling and prostrate on yon lake of fire,   280
As we erewhile, astounded and amazed,
No wonder, fallen such a pernicious highth.'
    He scarce had ceased when the superior fiend
Was moving toward the shore; his ponderous shield
Ethereal temper, massy, large and round,   285
Behind him cast; the broad circumference
Hung on his shoulders like the moon, whose orb
Through optic glass the Tuscan artist views
At evening from the top of Fesolè,
Or in Valdarno, to descry new lands,   290
Rivers or mountains in her spotty globe.
His spear, to equal which the tallest pine
Hewn on Norwegian hills, to be the mast
Of some dread Ammiral, were but a wand,
He walked with to support uneasy steps   295
Over the burning marl, not like those steps
On Heaven's azure, and the torrid clime
Smote on him sore besides, vaulted with fire;
Natheless he so endured, till on the beach
Of that inflamed sea, he stood and called   300
His legions, angel forms, who lay entranced
Thick as autumnal leaves that strow the brooks
In Vallombrosa, where the Etrurian shades
High overarched embower; or scattered sedge
Afloat, when with fierce winds Orion armed   305
Hath vexed the Red Sea coast, whose waves o'er-
    threw
Busiris and his Memphian chivalry,
While with perfidious hatred they pursued

The sojourners of Goshen, who beheld
From the safe shore their floating carcasses   310
And broken chariot-wheels, so thick bestrown
Abject and lost lay these, covering the flood,
Under amazement at their hideous change.
He called so loud, that all the hollow deep
Of Hell resounded: 'Princes, Potentates,   315
Warriors, the flower of Heaven, once yours, now lost,
If such astonishment as this can seize
Eternal spirits; or have ye chosen this place
After the toil of battle to repose
Your wearied virtue, for the ease you find   320
To slumber here, as in the vales of Heaven?
Or in this abject posture have ye sworn
To adore the Conqueror? Who now beholds
Cherub and seraph rolling in the flood
With scattered arms and ensigns, till anon   325
His swift pursuers from Heaven's gates discern
Th' advantage, and descending tread us down
Thus drooping, or with linkéd thunderbolts
Transfix us to the bottom of this gulf.
Awake! arise! or be forever fallen!'   330
    They heard, and were abashed, and up they
        sprung
Upon the wing, as when men wont to watch
On duty, sleeping found by whom they dread,
Rouse and bestir themselves ere well awake.
Nor did they not perceive the evil plight   335
In which they were, or the fierce pains not feel;
Yet to their General's voice they soon obeyed
Innumerable. As when the potent rod
Of Amram's son in Egypt's evil day
Waved round the coast, up called a pitchy cloud   340
Of locusts, warping on the eastern wind,
That o'er the realm of impious Pharaoh hung
Like night, and darkened all the land of Nile:
So numberless were those bad angels seen
Hovering on wing under the cope of Hell   345
'Twixt upper, nether, and surrounding fires;
Till, as a signal given, th' uplifted spear
Of their great Sultan waving to direct
Their course, in even balance down they light
On the firm brimstone, and fill all the plain;   350
A multitude, like which the populous north
Poured never from her frozen loins, to pass
Rhene or the Danaw, when her barbarous sons
Came like a deluge on the south, and spread
Beneath Gibraltar to the Lybian sands.   355
Forthwith from every squadron and each band
The heads and leaders thither haste where stood
Their great commander; Godlike shapes and forms

276. **edge**, front-line in battle. 282. **pernicious**, death-dealing. 285. **Ethereal temper**, tempered into a subtle, superearthly texture. 288. **optic glass**, telescope. **Tuscan artist**, the Italian astronomer and physicist Galileo (1564–1642), whom Milton had met at Florence on his travels to Italy; he was an ardent defender of the Copernican theory of astronomy (see note to 74 above). 289. **Fesolè**, Fiesole, a hill near Florence. 290. **Valdarno**, the valley of the Arno River, which flows through Florence. 294. **Ammiral**, admiral, but here applied to the flag-ship rather than to the officer himself. 303. **Vallombrosa**, a valley twenty miles east of Florence. Etruria is an ancient section of Italy comprising present-day Tuscany and a portion of Umbria. 305. **Orion**, in Greek legend a hunter who was transformed into a constellation, one of the most striking and famous in the northern heavens. 307. **Busiris**, a legendary king of England, not, however, the Pharaoh who pursued the people of Israel, as told in Exodus, 14.

309. **sojourners of Goshen.** Before the Exodus from Egypt, the Israelites had inhabited a district of northern Egypt called Goshen. 339. **Amram's son**, Moses. For the account of the plague of locusts (ll. 340–341), see Exodus, 10:12–19. 353. **Rhene . . . Danaw**, the Rhine and Danube; the reference here is, of course, to the migrations of the Germanic barbarians, which extended even into northern Africa.

[handwritten margin note: borrowed names from pagan mythology Egypt, etc.]

Excelling human, princely dignities,
And powers that erst in Heaven sat on thrones;   360
Though of their names in heavenly records now
Be no memorial, blotted out and rased
By their rebellion, from the Books of Life.
Nor had they yet among the sons of Eve   364
Got them new names, till wandering o'er the earth,
Through God's high sufferance for the trial of man,
By falsities and lies the greatest part
Of mankind they corrupted to forsake
God their Creator, and the invisible
Glory of Him, that made them, to transform   370
Oft to the image of a brute, adorned
With gay religions, full of pomp and gold,
And devils to adore for deities:
Then were they known to men by various names,
And various idols through the heathen world.   375
Say, Muse, their names then known, who first, who last,
Roused from the slumber, on that fiery couch,
At their great Emperor's call, as next in worth
Came singly where he stood on the bare strand,
While the promiscuous crowd stood yet aloof?   380
The chief were those who from the pit of Hell
Roaming to seek their prey on earth, durst fix
Their seats long after next the Seat of God,
Their altars by His altar, Gods adored
Among the nations round, and durst abide   385
Jehovah thundering out of Sion, throned
Between the Cherubim; yea, often placed
Within His sanctuary itself their shrines,
Abominations; and with cursèd things
His holy rites, and solemn feasts profaned,   390
And with their darkness durst affront His light.
First *Moloch*, horrid king besmeared with blood
Of human sacrifice, and parents' tears,
Though for the noise of drums and timbrels loud
Their children's cries unheard, that passed through fire   395
To his grim idol. Him the Ammonite
Worshipped in Rabba and her watery plain,
In Argob and in Basan, to the stream
Of utmost Arnon. Nor content with such

[handwritten margin note: Catalogue of fallen angels]

Audacious neighbourhood, the wisest heart   400
Of Solomon he led by fraud to build
His Temple right against the Temple of God
On that opprobrious hill, and made his grove
The pleasant valley of Hinnom, Tophet thence
And black Gehenna called, the type of Hell.   405
Next *Chemos*, th' obscene dread of Moab's sons,
From Aroar to Nebo, and the wild
Of southmost Abarim, in Hesebon
And Hornoaim, Seon's realm, beyond
The flowery dale of Sibma clad with vines,   410
And Eleale to th' Asphaltic Pool.
Peor his other name, when he enticed
Israel in Sittim on their march from Nile
To do him wanton rites, which cost them woe.
Yet thence his lustful orgies he enlarged   415
Even to that hill of scandal, by the grove
Of Moloch homicide, lust hard by hate;
Till good Josiah drove them thence to Hell.
With these came they, who from the bordering flood
Of old Euphrates to the brook that parts   420
Egypt from Syrian ground, had general names
Of Baalim and Ashtaroth, those male,
These feminine. For spirits when they please
Can either sex assume, or both; so soft
And uncompounded is their essence pure,   425
Not tied or manacled with joint or limb,
Nor founded on the brittle strength of bones,
Like cumbrous flesh; but in what shape they choose
Dilated or condensed, bright or obscure,
Can execute their airy purposes,   430
And works of love or enmity fulfill.
For those the race of Israel oft forsook
Their living strength, and unfrequented left
His righteous altar, bowing lowly down
To bestial gods; for which their heads as low   435

401. **Solomon . . . fraud.** King Solomon was persuaded by some of his multitudinous wives to build a temple to Moloch.   403. **that opprobrious hill,** the Mount of Olives, so-called not from its association with the story of Christ but because it was the site of Solomon's temple to Moloch.   404. **valley . . . Tophet.** A place of sacrifice to Moloch was appointed in the valley of Hinnom (called in Greek Gehenna); this place was called Tophet, and it was later the place of incineration for all the city refuse of Jerusalem.   406. **Chemos,** a god of the Moabites, another ancient tribe living east of the River Jordan.   407–411. **Aroar . . . Asphaltic Pool,** the names of towns and mountains in the Jordan River district extending south to the Dead Sea, or Asphaltic Pool, so-called because of the large amount of bitumen found in it.   413–414. **Israel . . . woe.** At Shittim, during the wanderings of the Jewish people, thousands of them were executed for taking Moabitish wives and for worshiping Baal-peor (note l. 412), god of the Moabites; see Numbers, 25. It is clear that every one of the gods and peoples mentioned by Milton in this passage was defeated by the Hebrews' Jehovah.   416. **hill of scandal,** the Mount of Olives; see l. 403 above.   418. **Josiah,** King of Isreal, called "good" because he restored the worship of Jehovah.   420–421. **Euphrates . . . Syrian ground.** In King David's time the Euphrates River bounded Palestine to the east, and Besor Brook, named in I Samuel, 30:10, separated Palestine from Egypt to the south.   422. **Baalim and Ashtaroth,** collective names for manifestations of the sun-god and the moon-goddess.   423–424. **spirits . . . assume.** The power of demons to metamorphose themselves is traceable in both Greek and Hebrew legend from time immemorial.

376. **Say . . . names.** This roll-call of leaders was no doubt suggested to Milton by the naming and numbering of the Greek and Trojan warriors in the second book of the *Iliad.* It was the belief that the rebel Angels lost their original names at the time of the War in Heaven. Milton has named them after famous heathen gods.   383. **next the Seat.** Milton is referring to the numerous occasions in Hebrew history when, as in the reign of Solomon, shrines to foreign gods were erected in or near the Temple of Jehovah. His bitterness toward the desecration of the Temple is indicated by lines 387 ff.   392. **Moloch,** originally a fire-god worshiped by the sacrifice of infants incinerated in the heated arms of his statue. He was a god of the Ammonites, who occupied land to the south and east of Palestine; see I Kings, 11:7.   394–395. **noise . . . unheard.** When the children were sacrificed to Moloch, drums and cymbals were sounded to drown out the victims' cries.   397. **Rabba,** the ancient capital of the Ammonites; other Ammonite place-names are Argob (398), Basan (398), and Arnon (399), all situated east of the River Jordan.

Bowed down in battle, sunk before the spear
Of despicable foes. With these in troop
Came *Astoreth*, whom the Phoenicians called
Astarte, queen of Heaven, with crescent horns;
To whose bright image nightly by the moon   440
Sidonian virgins paid their vows and songs,
In Sion also not unsung, where stood
Her temple on the offensive mountain, built
By that uxorious king, whose heart though large,
Beguiled by fair idolatresses, fell   445
To idols foul. *Thammuz* came next behind,
Whose annual wound in Lebanon allured
The Syrian damsels to lament his fate
In amorous ditties all a summer's day,
While smooth *Adonis* from his native rock   450
Ran purple to the sea, supposed with blood
Of Thammuz yearly wounded: the love-tale
Infected Sion's daughters with like heat,
Whose wanton passions in the sacred porch
Ezekiel saw, when by the vision led   455
His eye surveyed the dark idolatries
Of alienated Judah. Next came one
Who mourned in earnest, when the captive Ark
Maimed his brute image, head and hands lopped off
In his own temple, on the grunsel edge,   460
Where he fell flat, and shamed his worshippers:
Dagon his name, sea monster, upward man
And downward fish: yet had his temple high
Reared in Azotus, dreaded through the coast
Of Palestine, in Gath and Ascalon,   465
And Accaron and Gaza's frontier bounds.
Him followed *Rimmon*, whose delightful seat
Was fair Damascus, on the fertile banks
Of Abbana and Pharphar, lucid streams.
He also against the house of God was bold: 470
A leper once he lost and gained a king,
Ahaz his sottish conqueror, whom he drew
God's altar to disparage and displace
For one of Syrian mode, whereon to burn
His odious offerings, and adore the gods   475

Whom he had vanquished. After these appeared
A crew who, under names of old renown,
Osiris, Isis, Orus and their train
With monstrous shapes and sorceries abused
Fanatic Egypt and her priests, to seek   480
Their wandering gods, disguised in brutish forms
Rather than human. Nor did Israel scape
The infection when their borrowed gold composed
The calf in Oreb: and the rebel king
Doubled that sin in Bethel and in Dan,   485
Likening his Maker to the grazed ox,
Jehovah, who in one night when he passed
From Egypt marching, equalled with one stroke
Both her first-born and all her bleating gods.
Belial came last, than whom a spirit more lewd 490
Fell not from Heaven, or more gross to love
Vice for itself: to him no temple stood
Or altar smoked; yet who more oft than he
In temples and at altars, when the priest
Turns atheist, as did Eli's sons, who filled   495
With lust and violence the house of God.
In courts and palaces he also reigns
And in luxurious cities, where the noise
Of riot ascends above their loftiest towers,
And injury and outrage: and when night   500
Darkens the streets, then wander forth the sons
Of Belial, flown with insolence and wine.
Witness the streets of Sodom, and that night
In Gibeah, when the hospitable door
Exposed a matron to avoid worse rape.   505
These were the prime in order and in might;
The rest were long to tell, though far renowned,
The Ionian gods, of *Javan's* issue held
Gods, yet confessed later than Heaven and earth
Their boasted parents; *Titan*, Heaven's first-born 510
With his enormous brood, and birthright seized

438. Astarte, the Phoenician goddess of beauty and love, comparable to the classical Venus or Aphrodite. **441. Sidonian**, from the Phoenician city of Sidon. **444. that uxorious king**, Solomon. In addition to the temple of Moloch already mentioned (l. 403 above and note), Solomon also erected a temple to Astarte. **446. Thammuz, the** Phoenician equivalent of the Greek Adonis, whose death in classical legend symbolized the coming of Autumn. He was once a river-god whose name was given to a river in Lebanon; this river brings down a quantity of red mud in a freshet, whence the references to Adonis and the annual wound (ll. 447 and 450 ff.). **453. Sion's daughters**, the women of Jerusalem. The passing of Adonis was celebrated by wholesale lamentation on the part of women, for Adonis (Thammuz) symbolized not only the regenerative powers of nature through love and beauty, but also the spring and summer seasons. **455. Ezekiel saw**, see Ezekiel, 8:14. **460. grunsel edge**, threshold; see I Samuel, 5:4. **462. Dagon**, a sea-god of the Philistines, who occupied the coast of ancient Palestine. **464-466. Azotus . . . Gaza,** the five chief cities of the Philistines. **467. Rimmon**, a god of ancient Damascus. **471. A leper**, the Syrian general Naaman, who was cured by bathing in the River Jordan; see II Kings, 16. **472. Ahaz**, King of Judah (see II Kings, 16).

481. brutish forms. The famous Egyptian deities mentioned in l. 478 were in the following animal shapes: Osiris was a bull; Isis, a cow; and Orus, a solar animal. **484. The calf in Oreb**, the heretical worship of this image by the Israelites, during the absence of Moses, is told in Exodus, 32. **the rebel king,** Jereboam, who rebelled with Ten Tribes of Israel against Rehoboam, son of Solomon, and established idolatry with two golden calves as the object of worship in Bethel and Dan, two northern cities. The story is told in I Kings, 12:28-33. **487-488. Jehovah . . . equalled.** By slaying the first-born in the tenth plague (as told in Exodus, 12), Jehovah made equal in death the first-born and the false gods themselves. **490. Belial**, the prince of the third order of demons. **495-496. Eli's sons . . . God.** See I Samuel, ii, 12-17, where the sons of the High Priest Eli are likened to "the sons of Belial [i.e., worthlessness]; they knew not the Lord." **498. luxurious**, lecherous, lustful. **501-502. sons of Belial,** a common nickname among the Puritans for the courtiers and followers of King Charles I; these lines are then a slap at roistering Cavaliers. **502. flown**, flushed. **503. Sodom**, the "wicked city" of the plain, destroyed with its sister-city Gomorrah (see Genesis, 29:1-11). **504-505. Gibeah . . . rape;** see Judges, 19. **508. Ionian**, Greek. **Javan**, son of Japhet, and therefore grandson of Noah (Genesis, 10:2); he was considered in legend the founder of the Greeks. **509-510. confessed . . . parents.** In Greek mythology, Heaven and Earth were the parents of the first gods, the Titans; but Milton shares the belief that all pagan divinities have been human beings deified by man. **510. Titan**, the first son of Uranus (Heaven) and Ge (Earth).

luxury - used to mean
lechery & lustfulness.
REBIRTH AND DISCOVERY Satan belief (City center of vice)

By younger *Saturn*, he from mightier *Jove*,
His own and Rhea's son, like measure found;
So Jove usurping reigned: these first in Crete
And Ida known, thence on the snowy top   515
Of cold Olympus ruled the middle air,
Their highest Heaven; or on the Delphian cliff,
Or in Dodona, and through all the bounds
Of Doric land; or who with Saturn old
Fled over Adria to the Hesperian fields,   520
And o'er the Celtic roamed the utmost isles.
All these and more came flocking; but with looks
Downcast and damp, yet such wherein appeared
Obscure some glimpse of joy, to have found their
      chief
Not in despair, to have found themselves not lost 525
In loss itself; which on his countenance cast
Like doubtful hue: but he his wonted pride
Soon recollecting, with high words, that bore
Semblance of worth, not substance, gently raised
Their fainting courage, and dispelled their fears. 530
Then straight commands that at the warlike sound
Of trumpets loud and clarions be upreared
His mighty standard; that proud honour claimed
Azazel at his right, a Cherub tall:
Who forthwith from the glittering staff unfurled 535
The imperial ensign, which full high advanced
Shone like a meteor streaming to the wind
With gems and golden lustre rich imblazed,
Seraphic arms and trophies: all the while
Sonorous metal blowing martial sounds: 540
At which the universal host upsent
A shout that tore Hell's concave, and beyond
Frighted the reign of Chaos and old Night.
All in a moment through the gloom were seen
Ten thousand banners rise into the air   545
With orient colours waving: with them rose
A forest huge of spears; and thronging helms
Appeared, and serried shields in thick array
Of depth immeasurable: anon they move
In perfect phalanx to the Dorian mood   550
Of flutes and soft recorders; such as raised

To highth of noblest temper heroes old
Arming to battle, and instead of rage
Deliberate valour breathed, firm and unmoved
With dread of death to flight or foul retreat,   555
Nor wanting power to mitigate and 'suage
With solemn touches, troubled thoughts, and chase
Anguish and doubt and fear and sorrow and pain
From mortal or immortal minds. Thus they
Breathing united force with fixed thought   560
Moved on in silence to soft pipes that charmed
Their painful steps o'er the burnt soil; and now
Advanced in view they stand, a horrid front
Of dreadful length and dazzling arms, in guise
Of warriors old with ordered spear and shield,   565
Awaiting what command their mighty chief
Had to impose: he through the armed files
Darts his experienced eye, and soon traverse
The whole battalion views, their order due,
Their visages and stature as of Gods,   570
Their number last he sums. And now his heart
Distends with pride, and hardening in his strength
Glories: for never since created man,
Met such embodied force, as named with these
Could merit more than that small infantry   575
Warred on by cranes: though all the giant brood
Of Phlegra with the heroic race were joined
That fought at Thebes and Ilium, on each side
Mixed with auxiliar gods; and what resounds
In fable or romance of Uther's son   580
Begirt with British and Armoric knights;
And all who since, baptized or infidel
Jousted in Aspramont or Montalban,
Damasco, or Marocco, or Trebisond,
Or whom Biserta sent from Afric shore   585
When Charlemain with all his peerage fell
By Fontarabbia. Thus far these beyond
Compare of mortal prowess, yet observed
Their dread commander; he above the rest
In shape and gesture proudly eminent   590
Stood like a tower; his form had yet not lost
All her original brightness, nor appeared
Less than archangel ruined, and th' excess

---

512. **Saturn,** a younger brother of Titan, who supplanted him and
was in turn supplanted by his son Zeus (Jove or Jupiter).   514 ff.
these first, etc. Milton is here surveying the range of the gods of
Olympus throughout the Greek world from Crete to the north.   515.
Ida. According to Greek legend, Zeus was born on Mount Ida and
established his dwelling on Mount Olympus.   517. **Delphian cliff,**
in northern Greece, famous as the site of the most celebrated oracle
of Apollo.   518. **Dodona,** also in northern Greece, the site of an
oracle of Zeus.   520. **Adria,** the Adriatic Sea. **Hesperian fields,** Italy,
where the older Greek gods were worshiped by the Romans.   521.
Celtic . . . isles, France and Spain, primarily, although Britain
may be included.   534. **Azazel,** a name taken from Leviticus, 16:8;
he is here the lord of demons on Earth, and one of the four standard-
bearers of Satan.   536. **advanced,** raised.   543. **reign of Chaos.** Milton is here anticipating his account in Book II, lines 890–1009.   546.
orient, bright, pertaining to the dawn.   550. **phalanx,** body of troops
in close, serried lines. **Dorian mood,** that ancient scale of music considered appropriate for martial effects.   551. **recorders,** early wind
instruments somewhat like the flute.

563. **horrid,** bristling with spears.   568. **traverse,** across.   573. **since
created man,** since man was created.   575. **small infantry.** In classical
legend the Pigmies of Ethiopia waged continual war with the cranes
that attacked them.   576. **giant brood,** the Titans were defeated by
the Olympian gods at Phlegra, a promontory in Macedonia.   578.
Thebes and Ilium, in Greek heroic legend, the two cities about which
were centered, respectively, the War of the Seven against Thebes
and the Trojan War.   580. **Uther's son,** King Arthur of British
legendry, at one time the hero of a projected epic poem by Milton.
581. **Armoric,** Breton, from Brittany.   583–584. **Aspramont . . .
Trebisond.** Places associated with contests celebrated in the medieval
romances and the chronicles of the Crusades. Aspramont was near
Nice, France; Montalban, or Montauban, is in southern France not
far from Toulouse; Trebisond, or Trebizond, is on the southern shores
of the Black Sea. Morocco and Damascus need no comment.   585.
Biserta, the modern Bizerte, in northern Africa; it was in the Middle
Ages an important center of western Moslem civilization.   587.
Fontarabbia, actually some forty miles from Roncevals, site of the
famous battle on which is based the *Song of Roland.*

Of glory obscured: as when the sun new risen
Looks through the horizontal misty air   595
Shorn of his beams, or from behind the moon
In dim eclipse disastrous twilight sheds
On half the nations, and with fear of change
Perplexes monarchs. Darkened so, yet shone
Above them all the archangel: but his face   600
Deep scars of thunder had entrenched, and care
Sat on his faded cheek, but under brows
Of dauntless courage, and considerate pride
Waiting revenge: cruel his eye, but cast
Signs of remorse and passion to behold   605
The fellows of his crime, the followers rather
(Far other once beheld in bliss) condemned
Forever now to have their lot in pain,
Millions of spirits for his fault amerced
Of Heaven, and from eternal splendors flung   610
For his revolt, yet faithful how they stood,
Their glory withered. As when Heaven's fire
Hath scathed the forest oaks, or mountain pines
With singéd top their stately growth, though bare,
Stands on the blasted heath. He now prepared   615
To speak; whereat their doubled ranks they bend
From wing to wing, and half enclose him round
With all his peers: attention held them mute.
Thrice he essayed, and thrice in spite of scorn,
Tears such as angels weep, burst forth: at last 620
Words interwove with sighs found out their way:
  'O myriads of immortal spirits, O powers
Matchless, but with the Almighty, and that strife
Was not inglorious, though the event was dire,
As this place testifies, and this dire change   625
Hateful to utter: but what power of mind
Foreseeing or presaging, from the depth
Of knowledge past or present, could have feared,
How such united force of gods, how such
As stood like these, could ever know repulse?   630
For who can yet believe, though after loss,
That all these puissant legions, whose exile
Hath emptied Heaven, shall fail to re-ascend
Self-raised, and re-possess their native seat?
For me, be witness all the host of Heaven,   635
If counsels different, or danger shunned
By me, have lost our hopes. But he who reigns
Monarch in Heaven, till then as one secure
Sat on His throne, upheld by old repute,
Consent or custom, and his regal state   640
Put forth at full, but still His strength concealed,
Which tempted our attempt, and wrought our fall.
Henceforth His might we know, and know our own
So as not either to provoke, or dread
New war, provoked; our better part remains   645
To work in close design, by fraud or guile

What force effected not: that He no less
At length from us may find, who overcomes
By force, hath overcome but half his foe.
Space may produce new worlds; whereof so rife   650
There went a fame in Heaven that He ere long
Intended to create, and therein plant
A generation, whom His choice regard
Should favour equal to the sons of Heaven:
Thither, if but to pry, shall be perhaps   655
Our first eruption, thither or elsewhere:
For this infernal pit shall never hold
Celestial spirits in bondage, nor the abyss
Long under darkness cover. But these thoughts
Full counsel must mature: peace is despaired,   660
For who can think submission? War then, War
Open or understood, must be resolved.'
  He spake: and to confirm his words, out flew
Millions of flaming swords, drawn from the thighs
Of mighty Cherubim; the sudden blaze   665
Far round illumined Hell: highly they raged
Against the Highest, and fierce with grasped arms
Clashed on their sounding shields the din of war,
Hurling defiance toward the vault of Heaven.
  There stood a hill not far whose grisly top   670
Belched fire and rolling smoke; the rest entire
Shone with a glossy scurf, undoubted sign
That in his womb was hid metallic ore,
The work of sulphur. Thither winged with speed
A numerous brigad hastened. As when bands   675
Of pioners with spade and pickax armed
Forerun the royal camp, to trench a field,
Or cast a rampart. *Mammon* led them on,
Mammon, the least erected spirit that fell
From Heaven, for even in Heaven his looks and
                                         thoughts 680
Were always downward bent, admiring more
The riches of Heaven's pavement, trodden gold,
Than aught divine or holy else enjoyed
In vision beatific; by him first
Men also, and by his suggestion taught,   685
Ransacked the center, and with impious hands
Rifled the bowels of their mother Earth
For treasures better hid. Soon had his crew
Opened into the hill a spacious wound
And digged out ribs of gold. Let none admire   690
That riches grow in Hell; that soil may best
Deserve the precious bane. And here let those
Who boast in mortal things, and wondering tell

---

603. **considerate,** based on well-founded thought.   609. **amerced,** punished (a legal term).   642. **tempted our attempt.** Note the play on words.   646. **close,** secret.

651. **fame,** rumor, report.   674. **work of sulphur.** It was an old belief of alchemy that all minerals came from a combination of sulphur and mercury.   675. **brigad,** brigade; the accent is on the first syllable.   676. **pioners,** soldiers whose duty it was to dig trenches, lay roads and mines (sappers), or do anything else pertaining to military engineering labor battalions.   678. **Mammon.** The name is derived from an Aramaic word meaning wealth or riches, but was believed in the Middle Ages to be the name of a devil.   690. **admire,** wonder (v.).   692. **bane,** evil, curse; not the old meaning of 'slayer.'

Of Babel, and the works of Memphian kings,
Learn how their greatest monuments of fame,   695
And strength and art are easily outdone
By spirits reprobate, and in an hour
What in an age they with incessant toil
And hands innumerable scarce perform.
Nigh on the plain in many cells prepared,   700
That underneath had veins of liquid fire
Sluiced from the lake, a second multitude
With wondrous art founded the massy ore,
Severing each kind, and scummed the bullion dross:
A third as soon had formed within the ground   705
A various mould, and from the boiling cells
By strange conveyance filled each hollow nook,
As in an organ from one blast of wind
To many a row of pipes the sound-board breathes.
Anon out of the earth a fabric huge   710
Rose like an exhalation, with the sound
Of dulcet symphonies and voices sweet,
Built like a temple, where pilasters round
Were set, and Doric pillars overlaid
With golden architrave; nor did there want   715
Cornice or frieze, with bossy sculptures graven;
The roof was fretted gold. Not Babylon,
Nor great Alcairo such magnificence
Equalled in all their glories, to enshrine
Belus or Serapis their gods, or seat   720
Their kings, when Egypt with Assyria strove
In wealth and luxury. The ascending pile
Stood fixed her stately highth, and straight the doors
Opening their brazen folds discover, wide
Within, her ample spaces, o'er the smooth   725
And level pavement: from the arched roof
Pendant by subtle magic many a row
Of starry lamps and blazing cressets fed
With naphtha and asphaltus yielded light
As from a sky. The hasty multitude   730
Admiring entered, and the work some praise
And some the architect: his hand was known
In Heaven by many a towered structure high,
Where sceptered angels held their residence,
And sat as princes, whom the supreme King   735
Exalted to such power, and gave to rule,
Each in his hierarchy, the Orders bright.
Nor was his name unheard or unadored

In ancient Greece; and in Ausonian land
Men called him *Mulciber*; and how he fell   740
From Heaven, they fabled, thrown by angry Jove
Sheer o'er the crystal battlements: from morn
To noon he fell, from noon to dewy eve,
A summer's day; and with the setting sun
Dropped from the zenith like a falling star,   745
On Lemnos the Aegaean Isle: thus they relate,
Erring; for he with his rebellious rout
Fell long before; nor aught availed him now
To have built in Heaven high towers; nor did he scape
By all his engines, but was headlong sent   750
With his industrious crew to build in Hell.
Meanwhile the winged heralds by command
Of sovereign power, with awful ceremony
And trumpets' sound throughout the host proclaim
A solemn council forthwith to be held   755
At *Pandemonium*, the high capital
Of Satan and his peers: their summons called
From every band and squared regiment
By place or choice the worthiest; they anon
With hundreds and with thousands trooping came
Attended: all access was thronged, the gates   761
And porches wide, but chief the spacious hall
(Though like a covered field, where champions bold
Wont ride in armed, and at the Soldan's chair
Defied the best of Paynim chivalry   765
To mortal combat or career with lance)
Thick swarmed, both on the ground and in the air,
Brushed with the hiss of rustling wings. As bees
In spring time, when the sun with Taurus rides,
Pour forth their populous youth about the hive   770
In clusters; they among fresh dews and flowers
Fly to and fro, or on the smoothed plank,
The suburb of their straw-built citadel,
New rubbed with balm, expatiate and confer
Their state affairs. So thick the airy crowd   775
Swarmed and were straitened; till the signal given,
Behold a wonder! they but now who seemed
In bigness to surpass Earth's giant sons
Now less than smallest dwarfs, in narrow room
Throng numberless, like that pygmean race   780
Beyond the Indian mount, or Faery elves,
Whose midnight revels, by a forest-side
Or fountain some belated peasant sees,

694. **Babel,** the first city built in the kingdom of Nimrod, famous for the unfinished Tower which was to reach to Heaven. 709. **sound-board.** The word is used here with specific reference to the organ; in which the sound-board is the surface which transmits air from the bellows to the pipes of the instrument. 713–716. **pilasters . . . frieze.** The materials described are elements of particular significance to later Renaissance, or baroque, architecture. 718. **Alcairo,** Cairo, Egypt. 720. **Belus or Serapis,** the Assyrian god Bel and the Egyptian deity, respectively. 728. **cressets,** fire-baskets for illumination. 737. **Each . . . hierarchy.** See note to l. 128 above.

739. **Ausonian land,** an ancient name for what is now Italy. 740. **Mulciber,** Vulcan or the Greek Hephaestos. 756. **Pandemonium,** the place of all demons. 764. **wont,** was wont, was accustomed to. **Soldan,** sultan, Saracen potentate. 765. **Paynim chivalry,** etc., an allusion to tournaments or conflicts between Christian and pagan knights, as told in the medieval romances or in medieval chronicles about the Crusades. 769. **Taurus,** the second constellation of the Zodiac. The sun is in this constellation from about April 20 to May 20; in other words, the constellation is a symbol of springtime. 774. **expatiate,** walk abroad. 780. **pygmean race,** etc. See note to l. 575 above.

[handwritten top margin: satan still has qualities of good - beauty, glory etc.]

Or dreams he sees, while overhead the moon
Sits arbitress, and nearer to the Earth   785
Wheels her pale course, they on their mirth and
    dance
Intent, with jocund music charm his ear;
At once with joy and fear his heart rebounds.
Thus incorporeal spirits to smallest forms
Reduced their shapes immense, and were at large,
Though without number still amidst the hall   791
Of that infernal court. But far within
And in their own dimensions like themselves
The great Seraphic Lords and Cherubim
In close recess and secret conclave sat   795
A thousand demi-gods on golden seats,
Frequent and full. After short silence then
And summons read, the great consult began.

BOOK II

[handwritten: council in Hell.]

The Argument

    The consultation begun, Satan debates whether another battle is to be hazarded for the recovery of Heaven: some advise it, others dissuade; a third proposal is preferred, mentioned before by Satan, to search the truth of that prophecy or tradition in Heaven concerning another world, and another kind of creature equal or not much inferior to themselves, about this time to be created: their doubt who shall be sent on this difficult search; Satan their chief undertakes alone the voyage, is honoured and applauded. The council thus ended, the rest betake them several ways and to several employments, as their inclinations lead them, to entertain the time till Satan return. He passes on his journey to Hell Gates, finds them shut, and who sat there to guard them, by whom at length they are opened, and discover to him the great gulf between Hell and Heaven; with what difficulty he passes through, directed by Chaos, the power of that place, to the sight of this new world which he sought.

    High on a throne of royal state, which far
Outshone the wealth of Ormus and of Ind,
Or where the gorgeous East with richest hand
Showers on her kings barbaric pearl and gold,
Satan exalted sat, by merit raised   5
To that bad eminence; and from despair
Thus high uplifted beyond hope, aspires
Beyond thus high, insatiate to pursue
Vain war with Heaven, and by success untaught
His proud imaginations thus displayed: 10
    'Powers and Dominions, Deities of Heaven,
For since no deep within her gulf can hold

[handwritten: satan's speech]

Immortal vigor, though oppressed and fallen,
I give not Heaven for lost. From this descent
Celestial virtues rising, will appear   15
More glorious and more dread than from no fall,
And trust themselves to fear no second fate:
Me though just right, and the fixed laws of Heaven
Did first create your leader, next, free choice,
With what besides, in counsel or in fight,   20
Hath been achieved of merit, yet this loss
Thus far at least recovered, hath much more
Established in a safe unenvied throne
Yielded with full consent. The happier state
In Heaven, which follows dignity, might draw   25
Envy from each inferior; but who here
Will envy whom the highest place exposes
Foremost to stand against the Thunderer's aim
Your bulwark, and condemns to greatest share
Of endless pain? where there is then no good   30
For which to strive, no strife can grow up there
From Faction; for none sure will claim in Hell
Precedence, none, whose portion is so small
Of present pain, that with ambitious mind
Will covet more. With this advantage then   35
To union, and firm faith, and firm accord,
More than can be in Heaven, we now return
To claim our just inheritance of old,
Surer to prosper than prosperity
Could have assured us; and by what best way,   40
Whether of open war or covert guile,
We now debate; who can advise, may speak.'

[handwritten margin right: wouldn't it be better to get back to heaven - would be more glorious if did]

[handwritten: manipulating followers "tough job, but I'll do it!" — end of satan]

    He ceased, and next him Moloch, sceptered king,
Stood up, the strongest and the fiercest spirit
That fought in Heaven; now fiercer by despair: 45
His trust was with th' Eternal to be deemed
Equal in strength, and rather than be less
Cared not to be at all; with that care lost
Went all his fear: of God, or Hell, or worse
He recked not, and these words thereafter spake: 50
    'My sentence is for open war. Of wiles,   51
More unexpert, I boast not: them let those
Contrive who need, or when they need, not now.
For while they sit contriving, shall the rest,
Millions that stand in arms, and longing wait   55
The signal to ascend, sit lingering here
Heaven's fugitives, and for their dwelling place
Accept this dark, opprobrious den of shame,
The prison of His tyranny who reigns
By our delay? no, let us rather choose   60
Armed with Hell-flames and fury all at once
O'er Heaven's high towers to force resistless way,
Turning our tortures into horrid arms

---

795. **close recess,** secret meeting-place. **conclave,** inner chamber. 797. **frequent,** crowded. 798. **consult,** consultation, meeting. 2. **Ormus,** Ormuz, an ancient and very rich trading city on an island in the Persian Gulf. **Ind,** India. 9. **success,** experience, consequence.

15. **virtues,** rank in the hierarchy of Hell. 25. **dignity,** worth, merit. 28. **Thunderer,** an epithet applied particularly to Jove (Jupiter or Zeus), although Thor, in the Germanic Pantheon, was also associated with thunder. Satan is here clearly picturing God as a tyrant like Zeus or Thor. 51. **sentence,** opinion, decision. 52. **unexpert,** inexperienced.

Against the torturer; when to meet the noise
Of His almighty engine He shall hear   65
Infernal thunder, and for lightning see
Black fire and horror shot with equal rage
Among His angels; and His throne itself
Mixed with Tartarean sulphur, and strange fire,
His own invented torments. But perhaps   70
The way seems difficult and steep to scale
With upright wing against a higher foe.
Let such bethink them, if the sleepy drench
Of that forgetful lake benumb not still,
That in our proper motion we ascend   75
Up to our native seat: descent and fall
To us is adverse. Who but felt of late
When the fierce foe hung on our broken rear
Insulting, and pursued us through the deep,
With what compulsion and laborious flight   80
We sunk thus low? The ascent is easy, then;
The event is feared; should we again provoke
Our stronger, some worse way His wrath may find
To our destruction, if there be in Hell
Fear to be worse destroyed; what can be worse   85
Than to dwell here, driven out from bliss, con-
          demned
In this abhorred deep to utter woe,
Where pain of unextinguishable fire
Must exercise us without hope of end,
The vassals of His anger, when the scourge   90
Inexorably, and the torturing hour,
Calls us to penance? More destroyed than thus
We should be quite abolished and expire.
What fear we then? what doubt we to incense
His utmost ire? which to the highth enraged,   95
Will either quite consume us, and reduce
To nothing this essential, happier far
Than miserable to have eternal being:
Or if our substance be indeed divine,
And cannot cease to be, we are at worst   100
On this side nothing; and by proof we feel
Our power sufficient to disturb His Heaven,
And with perpetual inroads to alarm,
Though inaccessible, His fatal throne:
Which if not victory is yet revenge.'   105
          He ended frowning, and his look denounced
Desperate revenge, and battle dangerous
To less than gods. On the other side up rose
Belial, in act more graceful and humane;
A fairer person lost not Heaven; he seemed   110
For dignity composed and high exploit:
But all was false and hollow; though his tongue
Dropped manna, and could make the worse appear
The better reason, to perplex and dash

Maturest counsels: for his thoughts were low;   115
To vice industrious, but to nobler deeds
Timorous and slothful; yet he pleased the ear,
And with persuasive accent thus began:
          'I should be much for open war, O Peers,
As not behind in hate; if what was urged   120
Main reason to persuade immediate war,
Did not dissuade me most, and seem to cast
Ominous conjecture on the whole success:
When he who most excels in fact of arms,
In what he counsels and in what excels   125
Mistrustful, grounds his courage on despair
And utter dissolution, as the scope
Of all his aim, after some dire revenge.
First, what revenge? the towers of Heaven are filled
With armed watch, that render all access   130
Impregnable; oft on the bordering deep
Encamp their legions, or with obscure wing
Scout far and wide into the realm of night,
Scorning surprise. Or could we break our way
By force, and at our heels all Hell should rise   135
With blackest insurrection, to confound
Heaven's purest light, yet our great Enemy
All incorruptible would on His throne
Sit unpolluted, and the ethereal mould
Incapable of stain would soon expel   140
Her mischief, and purge off the baser fire
Victorious. Thus repulsed, our final hope
Is flat despair; we must exasperate
The Almighty Victor to spend all His rage,
And that must end us, that must be our cure,   145
To be no more; sad cure. For who would lose,
Though full of pain, this intellectual being,
Those thoughts that wander through Eternity,
To perish rather, swallowed up and lost
In the wide womb of uncreated night,   150
Devoid of sense and motion? and who knows,
Let this be good, whether our angry Foe
Can give it, or will ever? how He can
Is doubtful; that He never will is sure.
Will He, so wise, let loose at once His ire,   155
Belike through impotence, or unaware,
To give His enemies their wish, and end
Them in His anger, whom His anger saves
To punish endless? wherefore cease we then?
Say they who counsel war, we are decreed,   160
Reserved and destined to eternal woe;
Whatever doing, what can we suffer more,
What can we suffer worse? is this then worst,
Thus sitting, thus consulting, thus in arms?
What when we fled amain, pursued and struck   165
With Heaven's afflicting thunder, and besought
The deep to shelter us? this Hell then seemed
A refuge from those wounds; or when we lay
Chained on the burning lake? that sure was worse.

69. **Tartarean.** Milton in characteristic fashion conceives of Hell as identical with the classical Tartarus. The forgetful lake (74) is another classical reminiscence or recall.   89. **exercise,** agitate, torment.   97. **essential,** being, substance (sb.).   104. **fatal,** established by fate.   106. **denounced,** threatened.

124. **fact,** deed.

What if the breath that kindled those grim fires   170
Awaked should blow them into sevenfold rage
And plunge us in the flames? or from above
Should intermitted vengeance arm again
His red right hand to plague us? what if all
Her stores were opened, and this firmament   175
Of Hell should spout her cataracts of fire,
Impendent horrors, threatening hideous fall
One day upon our heads; while we perhaps
Designing or exhorting glorious war,
Caught in a fiery tempest shall be hurled   180
Each on his rock transfixed, the sport and prey
Of racking whirlwinds, or forever sunk
Under yon boiling ocean, wrapped in chains;
There to converse with everlasting groans,
Unrespited, unpitied, unreprieved,   185
Ages of hopeless end; this would be worse.
War therefore, open or concealed, alike
My voice dissuades; for what can force or guile
With Him, or who deceive His mind, whose eye
Views all things at one view? He from Heaven's
    highth   190
All these our motions vain, sees and derides;
Not more almighty to resist our might
Than wise to frustrate all our plots and wiles.
Shall we then live thus vile, the race of Heaven
Thus trampled, thus expelled to suffer here   195
Chains and these torments? better these than worse,
By my advice; since Fate inevitable
Subdues us, and omnipotent decree,
The Victor's will. To suffer, as to do,
Our strength is equal, nor the law unjust   200
That so ordains: this was at first resolved,
If we were wise, against so great a foe
Contending, and so doubtful what might fall.
I laugh, when those who at the spear are bold
And venturous, if that fail them, shrink and fear   205
What yet they know must follow, to endure
Exile, or ignominy, or bonds, or pain,
The sentence of their Conqueror: this is now
Our doom, which if we can sustain and bear,
Our supreme Foe in time may much remit   210
His anger, and perhaps thus far removed
Not mind us not offending, satisfied
With what is punished; whence these raging fires
Will slacken, if His breath stir not their flames.
Our purer essence then will overcome   215
Their noxious vapour, or inured not feel,
Or changed at length, and to the place conformed
In temper and in nature, will receive
Familiar the fierce heat, and void of pain;
This horror will grow mild, this darkness light,   220
Besides what hope the never-ending flight

181. **Each . . . transfixed;** like Prometheus in Greek legend or Ajax in the story of the Trojan War. 191. **All . . . derides.** Cf. Psalms, 2:4: "He that sitteth in the heavens shall laugh; the Lord shall have them in derision." 216. **inured,** accustomed. 218. **temper,** temperament.

Of future days may bring, what chance, what
    change
Worth waiting, since our present lot appears
For happy though but ill, for ill not worst,   *Belial*
If we procure not to ourselves more woe.'   225
    Thus Belial with words clothed in reason's garb
Counselled ignoble ease, and peaceful sloth,
Not peace; and after him thus Mammon spake:
    'Either to disenthrone the king of Heaven
We war, if war be best, or to regain   230
Our own right lost: him to unthrone we then
May hope, when everlasting Fate shall yield
To fickle chance, and Chaos judge the strife:
The former vain to hope argues as vain
The latter; for what place can be for us   235
Within Heaven's bound, unless Heaven's Lord su-
    preme
We overpower? Suppose He should relent
And publish grace to all, on promise made
Of new subjection; with what eyes could we
Stand in His presence humble, and receive   240
Strict laws imposed, to celebrate His throne
With warbled hymns, and to His Godhead sing
Forced Hallelujahs; while He lordly sits
Our envied Sovereign, and His altar breathes
Ambrosial odours and ambrosial flowers,   245
Our servile offerings? This must be our task
In Heaven, this our delight; how wearisome
Eternity so spent in worship paid
To whom we hate. Let us not then pursue
By force impossible, by leave obtained   250
Unacceptable, though in Heaven, our state
Of splendid vassalage, but rather seek
Our own good from ourselves, and from our own   *not true-*
Live to ourselves, though in this vast recess,   *locked up in hell.*
Free, and to none accountable, preferring   255
Hard liberty before the easy yoke   *"Free from God"-*
Of servile pomp. Our greatness will appear   *not really*
Then most conspicuous, when great things of small,   *servile*
Useful of hurt, prosperous of adverse   *before*
We can create, and in what place soe'er   260   *fall.*
Thrive under evil, and work ease out of pain
Through labour and endurance. This deep world
Of darkness do we dread? How oft amidst
Thick clouds and dark doth Heaven's all-ruling Sire
Choose to reside, His glory unobscured,   265
And with the majesty of darkness round
Covers His throne; from whence deep thunders roar
Mustering their rage, and Heaven resembles Hell?
As He our darkness, cannot we His light
Imitate when we please? This desert soil   270
Wants not her hidden lustre, gems and gold;
Nor want we skill or art, from whence to raise
Magnificence; and what can Heaven show more?

245. **ambrosial,** yielding ambrosia, the food of the gods in Olympus and the perfume of wine poured in libations to them. 249. **pursue.** seek to obtain.

wants to imitate heaven - fix hell up; get visibilia to imitate heaven

Destroy Man

Our torments also may in length of time
Become our elements, these piercing fires   275
As soft as now severe, our temper changed
Into their temper; which must needs remove
The sensible of pain. All things invite
To peaceful counsels, and the settled state
Of order, how in safety best we may   280
Compose our present evils, with regard
Of what we are and where, dismissing quite
All thoughts of war; ye have what I advise.'

    He scarce had finished, when such murmur filled
The assembly, as when hollow rocks retain   285
The sound of blustering winds, which all night long
Had roused the sea, now with hoarse cadence lull
Seafaring men o'erwatched, whose bark by chance
Or pinnace anchors in a craggy bay
After the tempest: such applause was heard   290
As Mammon ended, and his sentence pleased,
Advising peace: for such another field
They dreaded worse than Hell: so much the fear
Of thunder and the sword of Michael
Wrought still within them; and no less desire   295
To found this nether empire, which might rise
By policy, and long process of time,
In emulation opposite to Heaven.
Which when Beëlzebub perceived, than whom,
Satan except, none higher sat, with grave   300
Aspect he rose, and in his rising seemed
A pillar of state; deep on his front engraven
Deliberation sat and public care;
And princely counsel in his face yet shone,
Majestic though in ruin: sage he stood   305
With Atlantean shoulders fit to bear
The weight of mightiest monarchies; his look
Drew audience and attention still as night
Or summer's noon-tide air, while thus he spake:
    'Thrones and Imperial Powers, off-spring of
        Heaven,   310
Ethereal Virtues; or these titles now
Must we renounce, and changing style be called
Princes of Hell? for so the popular vote
Inclines, here to continue, and build up here
A growing empire, doubtless, while we dream,   315
And know not that the King of Heaven hath doomed
This place our dungeon, not our safe retreat
Beyond His potent arm, to live exempt
From Heaven's high jurisdiction, in new league

Banded against His throne, but to remain   320
In strictest bondage, though thus far removed,
Under th' inevitable curb, reserved
His captive multitude; for He, be sure,
In highth or depth, still first and last will reign
Sole king, and of His kingdom lose no part   325
By our revolt, but over Hell extend
His empire, and with iron sceptre rule
Us here, as with his golden those in Heaven.
What sit we then projecting peace and war?
War hath determined us, and foiled with loss   330
Irreparable; terms of peace yet none
Vouchsafed or sought. For what peace will be given
To us enslaved, but custody severe,
And stripes, and arbitrary punishment
Inflicted? and what peace can we return,   335
But to our power hostility and hate,
Untamed reluctance, and revenge though slow,
Yet ever plotting how the Conqueror least
May reap His conquest, and may least rejoice
In doing what we most in suffering feel?   340
Nor will occasion want, nor shall we need
With dangerous expedition to invade
Heaven, whose high walls fear no assault or siege,
Or ambush from the deep. What if we find
Some easier enterprise? There is a place   345
(If ancient and prophetic fame in Heaven
Err not), another world, the happy seat
Of some new race called *Man*, about this time
To be created like to us, though less
In power and excellence, but favored more   350
Of Him who rules above; so was His will
Pronounced among the gods, and by an oath,
That shook Heaven's whole circumference, con-
    firmed.
Thither let us bend all our thoughts, to learn
What creatures there inhabit, of what mould,   355
Or substance, how endued, and what their power,
And where their weakness, how attempted best,
By force or subtlety: though Heaven be shut,
And Heaven's high Arbitrator sit secure
In His own strength, this place may lie exposed,   360
The utmost border of His Kingdom, left
To their defence who hold it; here perhaps
Some advantageous act may be achieved
By sudden onset, either with Hell fire
To waste His whole creation, or possess   365
All as our own, and drive as we were driven,
The puny habitants, or if not drive,
Seduce them to our party, that their God
May prove their foe, and with repenting hand
Abolish His own works. This would surpass   370

275. **Become our elements.** It was the tradition that devils had immediate power over the four terrestrial elements of earth, air, fire, and water—an explanation of the essential hostility of these elements, when unchecked, toward mankind.   288. **o'erwatched,** worn out from watching.   294. **Michael,** the chief warrior in the hosts of Heaven; this archangel's combat with Satan in that battle is described later in Book VI.   297. **policy,** statesmanship.   302. **front,** forehead, brow.   306. **Atlantean,** like Atlas, who in Greek mythology held up the sky on his shoulders.   311. **Virtues,** one of the orders on the celestial hierarchy; see note to Book I, l. 128 above.   312. **style,** the formal term of address to one of royal or noble birth   315. **doubtless.** Note the sarcasm.

324. **first and last.** See Revelation, 1:2, 21:6, and 22:13: "I am Alpha and Omega, the beginning and the end, the first and last."   327. **iron sceptre.** See Psalms, 2:9: "Thou shalt break them with a rod of iron."   336. **to our power,** to the limit of our power.   346. **fame,** report.   356. **endued,** invested or gifted with qualities of mind.

Hurt God indirectly.

Common revenge, and interrupt His joy
In our confusion, and our joy upraise
In His disturbance; when His darling sons
Hurled headlong to partake with us, shall curse
Their frail original, and faded bliss,   375
Faded so soon. Advise if this be worth
Attempting, or to sit in darkness here
Hatching vain empires.' Thus Beëlzebub
Pleaded his devilish counsel, first devised
By Satan, and in part proposed: for whence   380
But from the author of all ill could spring
So deep a malice, to confound the race
Of mankind in one root, and Earth with Hell
To mingle and involve, done all to spite
The great Creator? But their spite still serves   385
His glory to augment. The bold design
Pleased highly those infernal states, and joy
Sparkled in all their eyes; with full assent
They vote; whereat his speech he thus renews:
'Well have ye judged, well ended long debate,
Synod of Gods, and like to what ye are,   391
Great things resolved, which from the lowest deep
Will once more lift us up, in spite of Fate,
Nearer our ancient seat; perhaps in view
Of those bright confines, whence with neighboring
    arms   395
And opportune excursion we may chance
Re-enter Heaven; or else in some mild zone
Dwell not unvisited of Heaven's fair light
Secure, and at the brightening orient beam
Purge off this gloom; the soft delicious air,   400
To heal the scar of these corrosive fires
Shall breathe her balm. But first, whom shall we
    send
In search of this new world, whom shall we find
Sufficient? who shall tempt with wandering feet
The dark unbottomed infinite abyss   405
And through the palpable obscure find out
His uncouth way, or spread his airy flight
Upborne with indefatigable wings
Over the vast abrupt, ere he arrive
The happy isle; what strength, what art can then
Suffice, or what evasion bear him safe   411
Through the strict sentries and stations thick
Of angels watching round? Here he had need
All circumspection, and we now no less
Choice in our suffrage; for on whom we send,   415
The weight of all and our last hope relies.'

This said, he sat; and expectation held
His look suspense, awaiting who appeared
To second, or oppose, or undertake
The perilous attempt; but all sat mute,   420
Pondering the danger with deep thoughts; and each
In other's countenance read his own dismay
Astonished: none among the choice and prime
Of those Heaven-warring champions could be found
So hardy as to proffer or accept   425
Alone the dreadful voyage; till at last
Satan, whom now transcendent glory raised
Above his fellows, with monarchal pride
Conscious of highest worth, unmoved thus spake:
    'O Progeny of Heaven, empyreal Thrones,   430
With reason hath deep silence and demur
Seized us, though undismayed; long is the way
And hard, that out of Hell leads up to light;
Our prison strong, this huge convex of fire,
Outrageous to devour, immures us round   435
Ninefold, and gates of burning adamant
Barred over us prohibit all egress.
These passed, if any pass, the void profound
Of unessential Night receives him next
Wide gaping, and with utter loss of being   440
Threatens him, plunged in that abortive gulf.
If thence he scape into whatever world,
Or unknown region, what remains him less
Than unknown dangers and as hard escape.
But I should ill become this throne, O Peers,   445
And this imperial sovereignty, adorned
With splendor, armed with power, if aught pro-
    posed
And judged of public moment, in the shape
Of difficulty or danger could deter
Me from attempting. Wherefore do I assume   450
These royalties, and not refuse to reign,
Refusing to accept as great a share
Of hazard as of honour, due alike
To him who reigns, and so much to him due
Of hazard more, as he above the rest   455
High honoured sits? Go therefore, mighty Powers,
Terror of Heaven, though fallen; intend at home,
While here shall be our home, what best may ease
The present misery, and render Hell
More tolerable; if there be cure or charm   460
To respite or deceive, or slack the pain
Of this ill mansion: intermit no watch
Against a wakeful foe, while I abroad
Through all the coasts of dark destruction seek
Deliverance for us all: this enterprise   465
None shall partake with me.' Thus saying rose

He set it up this way

375. **original**, "original parent" rather than "original state"—in other
words, Adam. 379. **first devised**; see Book I, ll. 650–654 above.
387. **states**, estates, authorities, as in the modern "three estates."
391. **Synod**, any kind of assembly, as used here. 394. **seat**, established home. 405. **abyss**, the undefined portion of the cosmic space
between Heaven and Hell. 407. **uncouth**, unknown, uncertain. 409.
abrupt, here a noun meaning the space or gulf in Chaos between Hell
and Earth. **arrive**, reach. 410. **isle**. The Earth and its universe is
likened to an island in the great ocean of Chaos. 412. **sentries**. This
word should probably be read in the old form "senteries," inasmuch
as the three syllables are necessary for the meter.

432–433. **long is the way**, etc., an obvious reminiscence of the words
of the Cumaean Sibyl to Aeneas in Virgil's _Aeneid_, in which she warns
him that the descent to Hades is easy but the return long and difficult. 434. **convex**, used here for a sphere entire. 439. **unessential**,
lacking substance, material or essence; formless. 457. **intend**, consider, deliberate. 461. **deceive**, beguile. 462. **mansion**, seat; see
l. 394 above and note.

The monarch, and prevented all reply,
Prudent, lest from his resolution raised
Others among the chief might offer now
(Certain to be refused) what erst they feared;   470
And so refused might in opinion stand
His rivals, winning cheap the high repute
Which he through hazard huge must earn. But they
Dreaded not more the adventure than his voice
Forbidding; and at once with him they rose;   475
Their rising all at once was as the sound
Of thunder heard remote. Towards him they bend
With awful reverence prone; and as a god
Extol him equal to the Highest in Heaven:
Nor failed they to express how much they praised,
That for the general safety he despised   481
His own: for neither do the spirits damned
Lose all their virtue; lest bad men should boast
Their specious deeds on Earth, which glory excites,
Or close ambition varnished o'er with zeal.   485
Thus they their doubtful consultations dark
Ended, rejoicing in their matchless chief:
As when from mountain-tops the dusky clouds
Ascending, while the north wind sleeps, o'erspread
Heaven's cheerful face, the lowering element   490
Scowls o'er the darkened landscape snow, or shower;
If chance the radiant sun with farewell sweet
Extend his evening beam, the fields revive,
The birds their notes renew, and bleating herds
Attest their joy, that hill and valley rings.   495
O shame to men! Devil with devil damned
Firm concord holds, men only disagree
Of creatures rational, though under hope
Of Heavenly Grace; and, God proclaiming peace,
Yet live in hatred, enmity, and strife   500
Among themselves, and levy cruel wars,
Wasting the Earth, each other to destroy:
As if (which might induce us to accord)
Man had not hellish foes enow besides,
That day and night for his destruction wait.   505
    The Stygian council thus dissolved; and forth
In order came the grand Infernal Peers,
Midst came their mighty paramount, and seemed
Alone the antagonist of Heaven, nor less
Than Hell's dread emperor with pomp supreme,   510
And God-like imitated state; him round
A globe of fiery Seraphim enclosed
With bright emblazonry, and horrent arms.
Then of their session ended they bid cry
With trumpet's regal sound the great result: 515
Toward the four winds four speedy Cherubim
Put to their mouths the sounding alchemy
By herald's voice explained: the hollow abyss

Heard far and wide, and all the host of Hell
With deafening shout, returned them loud acclaim.
Thence more at ease their minds and somewhat
            raised   521
By false presumptuous hope, the rangéd powers
Disband, and wandering each his several way
Pursues, as inclination or sad choice
Leads him perplexed, where he may likeliest find
Truce to his restless thoughts, and entertain   526
The irksome hours, till his great chief return.
Part on the plain, or in the air sublime
Upon the wing, or in swift race contend,
As at the Olympian games or Pythian fields;   530
Part curb their fiery steeds, or shun the goal
With rapid wheels, or fronted brigades form.
As when to warn proud cities war appears
Waged in the troubled sky, and armies rush
To battle in the clouds, before each van   535
Prick forth the airy knights, and couch their spears
Till thickest legions close; with feats of arms
From either end of Heaven the welkin burns.
Others with vast Typhaean rage more fell
Rend up both rocks and hills, and ride the air   540
In whirlwind; Hell scarce holds the wild uproar,—
As when Alcides from Oechalia crowned
With conquest, felt the envenomed robe, and tore
Through pain up by the roots Thessalian pines,
And Lichas from the top of Oeta threw   545
Into the Euboic Sea. Others more mild,
Retreated in a silent valley, sing
With notes angelical to many a harp
Their own heroic deeds and hapless fall
By doom of battle; and complain that Fate   550
Free Virtue should enthrall to Force or Chance.
Their song was partial, but the harmony
(What could it less when spirits immortal sing?)
Suspended Hell, and took with ravishment   554
The thronging audience. In discourse more sweet
(For eloquence the soul, song charms the sense),
Others apart sat on a hill retired,
In thoughts more elevate, and reasoned high
Of Providence, Foreknowledge, Will, and Fate,
Fixed Fate, freewill, foreknowledge absolute,   560
And found no end, in wandering mazes lost.
Of good and evil much they argued then,
Of happiness and final misery,

---

468. **raised,** heightened, emboldened. 484. **specious,** showy, os-
tentatious. 507. **Peers.** No doubt Milton has in mind the English
House of Peers or Lords in Parliament. 508. **Midst,** amidst, in the
midst. **paramount,** chief, leader. 512. **globe,** a solid body of soldiers.
513. **horrent,** bristling. 517. **alchemy.** "Alchemy" gold, so-called,
was an alloy much like brass used particularly in wind-instruments.

522. **powers,** armies. 530. **Olympian . . . Pythian,** the famous
athletic meets of ancient Greece. 531. **shun the goal.** The reference
here is to the chariot race, in which the driver wheeled as closely as
possible to the turning-posts in the course without, of course, touching it. 539. **Typhaean**; see Book I, note to l. 199. 543. **Alcides, etc.**
Hercules, son of Alcaeus (Alcides), returning with his bride Deianira
from one of his successful exploits, slew with a poisoned arrow the
centaur Nessus, who had attempted to abduct the bride. Dying,
Nessus told Deianira to give her husband a robe anointed with his
blood. The centaur's blood was itself fatally poisonous. The victim
Hercules, maddened by the pain, threw his servant Lichas (545) into
the sea. 560. **Fate, freewill, foreknowledge,** "predestination."

Passion and apathy, and glory and shame,
Vain wisdom all, and false philosophy: 565
Yet with a pleasing sorcery could charm
Pain for a while or anguish, and excite
Fallacious hope, or arm the obdured breast
With stubborn patience as with triple steel.
Another part in squadrons and gross bands,   570
On bold adventure to discover wide
That dismal world, if any clime perhaps
Might yield them easier habitation, bend
Four ways their flying march, along the banks
Of four infernal rivers that disgorge   575
Into the burning lake their baleful streams—
Abhorred *Styx*, the flood of deadly hate,
Sad *Acheron* of sorrow, black and deep;
Cocytus, named of lamentation loud
Heard on the rueful stream; fierce *Phlegeton*,   580
Whose waves of torrent fire inflame with rage.
Far off from these a slow and silent stream,
Lethe, the river of Oblivion, rolls
Her watery labyrinth, whereof who drinks,
Forthwith his former state and being forgets,   585
Forgets both joy and grief, pleasure and pain.
Beyond this flood a frozen Continent
Lies dark and wild, beat with perpetual storms
Of whirlwind and dire hail, which on firm land
Thaws not, but gathers heap, and ruin seems   590
Of ancient pile; all else deep snow and ice,
A gulf profound as that Serbonian bog
Betwixt Damiata and Mount Casius old,
Where armies whole have sunk: the parching air
Burns frore, and cold performs the effect of fire.   595
Thither by Harpy-footed Furies haled,
At certain revolutions all the damned
Are brought: and feel by turns the bitter change
Of fierce extremes, extremes by change more fierce,
From beds of raging fire to starve in ice   600
Their soft ethereal warmth, and there to pine
Immovable, infixed, and frozen round,
Periods of time, thence hurried back to fire.
They ferry over this Lethean sound
Both to and fro, their sorrow to augment,   605
And wish and struggle, as they pass, to reach
The tempting stream, with one small drop to lose
In sweet forgetfulness all pain and woe,
All in one moment, and so near the brink;
But Fate withstands, and to oppose th' attempt   610

Medusa with Gorgonian terror guards
The ford, and of itself the water flies
All taste of living wight, as once it fled
The lip of Tantalus. Thus roving on
In confused march forlorn, the adventurous bands
With shuddering horror pale and eyes aghast   616
Viewed first their lamentable lot, and found
No rest: through many a dark and dreary vale
They passed, and many a region dolorous,
O'er many a frozen, many a fiery Alp,   620
Rocks, caves, lakes, fens, bogs, dens, and shades of
     death, *summation*
A universe of death, which God by curse
Created evil, for evil only good,
Where all life dies, death lives, and Nature breeds,
Perverse, all monstrous, all prodigious things,   625
Abominable, unutterable, and worse
Than fables yet have feigned, or fear conceived,
Gorgons and Hydras, and Chimeras dire.
satan lives Meanwhile the Adversary of God and Man,   629
Satan, with thoughts inflamed of highest design,
Puts on swift wings, and toward the Gates of Hell
Explores his solitary flight; sometimes
He scours the right hand coast, sometimes the left,
Now shaves with level wing the deep, then soars
Up to the fiery concave towering high.   635
As when far off at sea a fleet descried
Hangs in the clouds, by equinoctial winds
Close sailing from Bengala, or the Isles
Of Ternate and Tidore, whence merchants bring
Their spicy drugs: they on the trading flood   640
Through the wide Ethiopian to the Cape
Ply stemming nightly toward the Pole, so seemed
Far off the flying fiend: at last appear
Hell-bounds high reaching to the horrid roof,
And thrice three-fold the Gates; three folds were
     brass,   645
Three iron, three of adamantine rock,
Impenetrable, impaled with circling fire,
Yet unconsumed. Before the Gates there sat *Death & Sin*
On either side a formidable shape;
The one seemed woman to the waist, and fair,   650
But ended foul in many a scaly fold
Voluminous and vast, a serpent armed

---

564. **apathy,** here, the absence of passion, an ideal of ancient Stoic philosophy.   570. **gross,** large.   575. **four infernal rivers.** These are enumerated below as Styx (577); Acheron (578); Cocytus (579); and Phlegeton (580). These were all, of course, from classical mythology. 592. **Serbonian bog,** Serbonis Lake, which had the deceitful appearance of solid ground but was in reality a dangerous quagmire.   595. **frore,** frozen.   596. **Furies,** the Eumenides of Greek tradition, who avenged unnatural crimes. They are described as monstrous birds with the faces of women and huge claw-like feet, like the Harpies. 600. **starve,** die, kill (when used transitively, as here).

611. **Medusa with Gorgonian terror.** In Greek mythology, Medusa was the monstrous Gorgon, with snaky locks and aspect so terrifying that one glance at it was sufficient to turn the beholder to stone. She was slain by Perseus, who attacked her with the aid of a mirror. 614. **Tantalus.** For offending Hera, or Juno, queen of the gods of Olympus, this legendary king was punished in Hades by the torture of ever unsatisfied hunger and thirst; cf. our *tantalize.*   620. **Alp,** any high mountain.   628. **Gorgons . . . Hydras . . . Chimeras,** generalized names for various monsters of the classical Underworld. 632. **Explores,** pursues uncertainly.   638–639. **Bengala . . . Ternate . . . Tidore.** In order, these are the names of an arm of the Indian ocean (the Bay of Bengal) and two small islands in the Dutch East Indies (in the Molucca group).   641. **Ethiopian,** the Indian Ocean. The allusions in these lines are striking evidence of the newly-discovered trading centers in the Far East.

surrounded by Hell hounds

With mortal sting: about her middle round
A cry of Hell-hounds never ceasing barked   654
With wide Cerberean mouths full loud, and rung
A hideous peal: yet, when they list, would creep,
If aught disturbed their noise, into her womb,
And kennel there, yet there still barked and howled
Within unseen. Far less abhorred than these
Vexed Scylla bathing in the sea that parts   660
Calabria from the hoarse Trinacrian shore:
Nor uglier follow the night-hag, when called
In secret, riding through the air she comes
Lured with the smell of infant blood, to dance
With Lapland witches, while the labouring moon
Eclipses at their charms. The other shape,   666
If shape it might be called that shape had none
Distinguishable in member, joint, or limb,
Or substance might be called that shadow seemed,
For each seemed either: black it stood as night,   670
Fierce as ten Furies, terrible as Hell,
And shook a dreadful dart; what seemed his head
The likeness of a kingly crown had on.
Satan was now at hand, and from his seat
The monster moving onward came as fast,   675
With horrid strides, Hell trembled as he strode.
The undaunted fiend what this might be admired,
Admired, not feared; God and His Son except,
Created thing naught valued he nor shunned;
And with disdainful look thus first began: 680

'Whence and what art thou, execrable shape,
That darest, though grim and terrible, advance
Thy miscreated front athwart my way
To yonder Gates? through them I mean to pass,
That be assured! without leave asked of thee: 685
Retire, or taste thy folly, and learn by proof,
Hell-born, not to contend with spirits of Heaven!'

To whom the goblin, full of wrath, replied:
'Art thou that traitor angel, art thou he,
Who first broke peace in Heaven and faith, till then
Unbroken, and in proud rebellious arms   691
Drew after him the third part of Heaven's sons
Conjured against the Highest, for which both thou
And they, outcast from God, are here condemned
To waste eternal days in woe and pain?   695
And reckonest thou thyself with spirits of Heaven,
Hell-doomed, and breathest defiance here and scorn,
Where I reign king, and to enrage thee more,
Thy king and lord? Back to thy punishment,

False fugitive, and to thy speed add wings,   700
Lest with a whip of scorpions I pursue
Thy lingering, or with one stroke of this dart
Strange horror seize thee, and pangs unfelt before!'
So spake the grisly terror, and in shape,
So speaking and so threatening, grew tenfold   705
More dreadful and deform: on the other side
Incensed with indignation Satan stood
Unterrified, and like a comet burned,
That fires the length of Ophiuchus huge
In the Arctic sky, and from his horrid hair   710
Shakes pestilence and war. Each at the head
Levelled his deadly aim; their fatal hands
No second stroke intend, and such a frown
Each cast at th' other, as when two black clouds,
With Heaven's artillery fraught, come rattling on
Over the Caspian, then stand front to front   716
Hovering a space, till winds the signal blow
To join their dark encounter in mid-air:
So frowned the mighty combatants, that Hell
Grew darker at their frown, so matched they stood;
For never but once more was either like   721
To meet so great a foe: and now great deeds
Had been achieved, whereof all Hell had rung,
Had not the snaky sorceress that sat
Fast by Hell Gate, and kept the fatal key,   725
Risen, and with hideous outcry rushed between.
'O Father, what intends thy hand,' she cried,
'Against thy only son? What fury, O son,
Possesses thee to bend that mortal dart
Against thy father's head? and knowest for whom?
For Him who sits above and laughs the while   731
At thee ordained His drudge, to execute
Whate'er His wrath, which He calls Justice, bids,
His wrath which one day will destroy ye both!'
She spake, and at her words the hellish pest   735
Forbore, then these to her Satan returned:
'So strange thy outcry, and thy words so strange
Thou interposest, that my sudden hand
Prevented spares to tell thee yet by deeds
What it intends; till first I know of thee,   740
What thing thou art, thus double-formed, and why
In this infernal vale first met thou callest
Me father, and that phantasm call'st my son?
I know thee not, nor ever saw till now
Sight more detestable than him and thee.'   745
To whom thus the portress of Hell Gate replied:
'Hast thou forgot me, then, and do I seem
Now in thine eye so foul, once deemed so fair
In Heaven, when at the Assembly, and in sight
Of all the Seraphim with thee combined   750
In bold conspiracy against Heaven's king,

---

655. **Cerberean mouths,** maws like those of Cerberus, the famous three-headed monster and Hell-hound in classical mythology. 660. **Scylla,** a female sea-monster destructive to sea-faring men. 662. **night-hag,** Hecate, a goddess of the classical Underworld; in later European folklore she is queen of the witches, as in Shakespeare's *Macbeth.* 665. **Lapland.** In Milton's time this remote section of the northland was believed to be the abode of witches. 677. **admired,** wondered at. 688. **goblin,** fiend—much more awe-inspiring than the modern "goblin." 692. **third . . . sons,** referring doubtless to the dragon seen by Saint John in the Apocalypse, "whose tail drew the third part of the stars of Heaven, and did cast them to Earth." See Revelation, 12:3–4. 693. **Conjured,** drawn together by an oath.

709. **Ophiuchus,** the constellation of the Serpent in the northern hemisphere, a long and sprawling aggregation of undistinguished stars. 716. **Caspian.** This great inland sea of southeastern Russia has long had the reputation of being stormy. 722. **meet . . . foe.** Both Satan and Death were, of course, still to meet Christ.

All on a sudden miserable pain
Surprised thee, dim thine eyes, and dizzy swum
In darkness, while thy head flames thick and fast
Threw forth, till on the left side opening wide,   755
Likest to thee in shape and countenance bright,
Then shining heavenly fair, a goddess armed
Out of thy head I sprung; amazement seized
All the Host of Heaven; back they recoiled afraid
At first, and called me *Sin,* and for a sign   760
Portentous held me; but familiar grown,
I pleased, and with attractive graces won
The most averse, thee chiefly, who full oft
Thyself in me thy perfect image viewing
Becam'st enamoured, and such joy thou took'st   765
With me in secret, that my womb conceived
A growing burden. Meanwhile War arose,
And fields were fought in Heaven; wherein remained
(For what could else) to our Almighty Foe
Clear victory, to our part loss and rout   770
Through all th' Empyrean: down they fell,
Driven headlong from the pitch of Heaven, down
Into this deep, and in the general fall
I also; at which time this powerful key
Into my hand was given, with charge to keep   775
These Gates forever shut, which none can pass
Without my opening. Pensive here I sat
Alone, but long I sat not, till my womb
Pregnant by thee, and now excessive grown,
Prodigious motion felt and rueful throes.   780
At last this odious offspring whom thou seest,
Thine own begotten, breaking violent way,
Tore through my entrails, that with fear and pain
Distorted, all my nether shape thus grew
Transformed: but he, my inbred enemy,   785
Forth issued, brandishing his fatal dart
Made to destroy: I fled, and cried out *Death;*
Hell trembled at the hideous name, and sighed
From all her caves, and back resounded *Death.*
I fled, but he pursued (though more, it seems,   790
Inflamed with lust than rage) and swifter far,
Me overtook his mother all dismayed,
And in embraces forcible and foul
Engendering with me, of that rape begot
These yelling monsters that with ceaseless cry   795
Surround me, as thou saw'st, hourly conceived
And hourly born, with sorrow infinite
To me, for when they list into the womb
That bred them they return, and howl and gnaw
My bowels, their repast; then bursting forth   800
Afresh with conscious terrors vex me round,
That rest or intermission find I none.

758. **Out of thy head,** etc. Milton has borrowed this idea from the Greek legend according to which Pallas Athene (Minerva) sprang full-fledged from the head of Zeus. 768. **fields,** battles. 781. **odious offspring,** a personification of the old Biblical idea that "the wages of Sin is Death."

"The Temptation of Adam and Eve," by Albrecht Dürer. This engraving was made in 1504.

Before mine eyes in opposition sits
Grim *Death,* my son and foe, who sets them on,
And me his parent would full soon devour   805
For want of other prey, but that he knows
His end with mine involved; and knows that I
Should prove a bitter morsel, and his bane,
Whenever that shall be; so Fate pronounced.
But thou, O father, I forewarn thee, shun   810
His deadly arrow; neither vainly hope
To be invulnerable in those bright arms,
Though tempered heavenly, for that mortal dint,
Save He who reigns above, none can resist.'
    She finished, and the subtle fiend his lore   815
Soon learned, now milder, and thus answered
        smooth:
'Dear daughter, since thou claimest me for thy sire,
And my fair son here show'st me, the dear pledge
Of dalliance had with thee in Heaven, and joys
Then sweet, now sad to mention, through dire
        change   820
Befallen us unforeseen, unthought of, know
I come no enemy, but to set free
From out this dark and dismal house of pain,
Both him and thee, and all the heavenly host
Of spirits that in our just pretenses armed   825
Fell with us from on high: from them I go

825. **pretenses,** legal claims.

This uncouth errand sole, and one for all
Myself expose, with lonely steps to tread
The unfounded deep, and through the void immense
To search with wandering quest a place foretold
Should be, and, by concurring signs, ere now   831
Created vast and round, a place of bliss
In the purlieus of Heaven, and therein placed
A race of upstart creatures, to supply
Perhaps our vacant room, though more removed,
Lest Heaven surcharged with potent multitude   836
Might hap to move new broils: be this or aught
Than this more secret now designed, I haste
To know, and this once known, shall soon return,
And bring ye to the place where thou and Death
Shall dwell at ease, and up and down unseen   841
Wing silently the buxom air, embalmed
With odours; there ye shall be fed and filled
Immeasurably, all things shall be your prey.'
He ceased, for both seemed highly pleased, and
        Death   845
Grinned horrible a ghastly smile, to hear
His famine should be filled, and blessed his maw
Destined to that good hour; no less rejoiced
His mother bad, and thus bespake her sire:
    'The key of this infernal pit by due,   850
And by command of Heaven's all-powerful king
I keep, by Him forbidden to unlock
These adamantine Gates; against all force
Death ready stands to interpose his dart,
Fearless to be o'ermatched by living might.   855
But what owe I to His commands above
Who hates me, and hath hither thrust me down
Into this gloom of Tartarus profound,
To sit in hateful office here confined,
Inhabitant of Heaven, and heavenly-born,   860
Here in perpetual agony and pain,
With terrors and with clamors compassed round
Of mine own brood, that on my bowels feed:
Thou art my father, thou my author, thou
My being gavest me; whom should I obey   865
But thee, whom follow? thou wilt bring me soon
To that new world of light and bliss, among
The gods who live at ease, where I shall reign
At thy right hand voluptuous, as beseems
Thy daughter and thy darling, without end.   870
    Thus saying, from her side the fatal key,
Sad instrument of all our woe, she took;
And towards the Gate rolling her bestial train,
Forthwith the huge portcullis high up drew,
Which but herself not all the Stygian powers   875
Could once have moved; then in the key-hole turns
The intricate wards, and every bolt and bar

827. uncouth, unknown. 829. unfounded, without foundations or
bottom. deep, Chaos. 842. buxom, yielding, unresisting. 869.
right hand voluptuous. Sin is picturing herself as eventually sitting
in her true nature at the right hand of Satan, just as Christ is described in the scriptures as sitting after the Day of Judgment at the
right hand of God.

Of massy iron or solid rock with ease
Unfastens: on a sudden open fly
With impetuous recoil and jarring sound   880
The infernal doors, and on their hinges grate
Harsh thunder, that the lowest bottom shook
Of Erebus. She opened, but to shut
Excelled her power: the Gates wide open stood,
That with extended wings a bannered host   885
Under spread ensigns marching might pass through
With horse and chariots ranked in loose array;
So wide they stood, and like a furnace-mouth
Cast forth redounding smoke and ruddy flame.
Before their eyes in sudden view appear   890
The secrets of the hoary deep, a dark
Illimitable ocean without bound,
Without dimension, where length, breadth, and
        highth,
And time and place are lost; where eldest Night
And Chaos, ancestors of Nature, hold   895
Eternal anarchy, amidst the noise
Of endless wars, and by confusion stand.
For hot, cold, moist, and dry, four champions fierce
Strive here for mastery, and to battle bring
Their embryon atoms; they around the flag   900
Of each his faction, in their several clans,
Light-armed or heavy, sharp, smooth, swift or slow,
Swarm populous, unnumbered as the sands
Of Barca or Cyrene's torrid soil,
Levied to side with warring winds, and poise   905
Their lighter wings. To whom these most adhere,
He rules a moment; Chaos umpire sits,
And by decision more embroils the fray
By which he reigns: next him high arbiter
Chance governs all. Into this wide abyss,   910
The womb of Nature and perhaps her grave,
Of neither sea, nor shore, nor air, nor fire,
But all these in their pregnant causes mixed
Confusedly, and which thus must ever fight,
Unless the almighty Maker them ordain   915
His dark materials to create more worlds,
Into this wild abyss the wary fiend
Stood on the brink of Hell and looked a while,
Pondering his voyage: for no narrow frith
He had to cross. Nor was his ear less pealed   920
With noises loud and ruinous (to compare
Great things with small) than when Bellona storms,
With all her battering engines bent to raze
Some capital city, or less than if this frame
Of Heaven were falling, and these elements   925
In mutiny had from her axle torn
The steadfast Earth. At last his sail-broad vans
He spreads for flight, and in the surging smoke
Uplifted spurns the ground, thence many a league

883. Erebus, darkness. 889. redounding, billowing. 904. Barca, the
Libyan desert between Egypt and Tunis. Cyrene, an ancient city
near the site of the present Tripoli. 920. pealed, struck by noise.
922. Bellona, the Roman goddess of war, partner of Mars.

As in a cloudy chair ascending rides 930
Audacious, but that seat soon failing, meets
A vast vacuity; all unawares
Fluttering his pennons vain plumb down he drops
Ten thousand fathom deep, and to this hour
Down had been falling, had not by ill chance 935
The strong rebuff of some tumultuous cloud
Instinct with fire and nitre hurried him
As many miles aloft: that fury stayed,
Quenched in a boggy Syrtis, neither sea,
Nor good dry land: nigh foundered on he fares, 940
Treading the crude consistence, half on foot,
Half flying; behoves him now both oar and sail.
As when a gryphon through the wilderness
With winged course o'er hill or moory dale,
Pursues the Arimaspian, who by stealth 945
Had from his wakeful custody purloined
The guarded gold: so eagerly the fiend
O'er bog or steep, through strait, rough, dense, or
    rare,
With head, hands, wings, or feet pursues his way,
And swims or sinks, or wades, or creeps, or flies:
At length a universal hubbub wild 951
Of stunning sounds and voices all confused
Borne through the hollow dark assaults his ear
With loudest vehemence: thither he plies,
Undaunted to meet there whatever power 955
Or spirit of the nethermost abyss
Might in that noise reside, of whom to ask
Which way the nearest coast of darkness lies
Bordering on light; when straight behold the throne
Of Chaos, and his dark pavilion spread 960
Wide on the wasteful deep; with him enthroned
Sat sable-vested Night, eldest of things,
The consort of his reign; and by them stood
Orcus and *Ades*, and the dreaded name
Of *Demogorgon;* Rumor next and Chance, 965
And Tumult and Confusion all embroiled,
And Discord with a thousand various mouths.
    To whom Satan turning boldly, thus: 'Ye Powers
And Spirits of this nethermost abyss,
Chaos and ancient Night, I come no spy, 970
With purpose to explore or to disturb
The secrets of your realm, but by constraint
Wandering this darksome desert, as my way
Lies through your spacious empire up to light,
Alone, and without guide, half lost, I seek 975
What readiest path leads where your gloomy bounds

Confine with Heaven; or if some other place
From your dominion won, the ethereal King
Possesses lately, thither to arrive
I travel this profound, direct my course; 980
Directed, no mean recompense it brings
To your behoof, if I that region lost,
All usurpation thence expelled, reduce
To her original darkness and your sway
(Which is my present journey) and once more 985
Erect the standard there of ancient Night;
Yours be the advantage all, mine the revenge.'
    Thus Satan; and him thus the anarch old
With faltering speech and visage incomposed
Answered: 'I know thee, stranger, who thou art,
That mighty leading Angel, who of late 991
Made head against Heaven's King, though over-
    thrown.
I saw and heard, for such a numerous host
Fled not in silence through the frighted deep
With ruin upon ruin, rout on rout, 995
Confusion worse confounded; and Heaven's Gates
Poured out by millions her victorious bands
Pursuing. I upon my frontiers here
Keep residence; if all I can will serve,
That little which is left so to defend 1000
Encroached on still through our intestine broils
Weakening the sceptre of old Night: first Hell
Your dungeon stretching far and wide beneath;
Now lately Heaven and Earth, another world
Hung o'er my realm, linked in a golden chain 1005
To that side Heaven from whence your legions fell:
If that way be your walk, you have not far;
So much the nearer danger; go and speed;
Havoc and spoil and ruin are my gain.'
    He ceased; and Satan stayed not to reply, 1010
But glad that now his sea should find a shore,
With fresh alacrity and force renewed
Springs upward like a pyramid of fire
Into the wild expanse, and through the shock
Of fighting elements, on all sides round 1015
Environed wins his way; harder beset
And more endangered, than when Argo passed
Through Bosphorus betwixt the jostling rocks:
Or when Ulysses on the larboard shunned
Charybdis, and by the other whirlpool steered. 1020
So he with difficulty and labour hard
Moved on, with difficulty and labour he;
But he once past, soon after when Man fell,
Strange alteration! Sin and Death amain
Following his track, such was the will of Heaven,
Paved after him a broad and beaten way 1026

939. **Syrtis,** quicksands off the coast of northern Africa near Tripoli. 943. **gryphon,** or griffin, a fabulous monster with a lion's body and an eagle's head and wings. 945. **Arimaspian,** one-eyed people of Scythia who, according to tradition, fought against the gryphons to obtain the gold treasure which the monsters guarded—another of a long line of tales about unusual creatures keeping watch over hoards of treasure. 964. **Orcus,** a personification in Roman myth of the Underworld. **Ades,** a similar personification of Death. 965. **Demogorgon,** a mysterious infernal deity originating in the early days of the Roman empire who was so powerful as to control the destinies of both gods and men.

977. **Confine,** have borders with. 988. **anarch.** Chaos is the king of misrule. 989. **incomposed,** not "discomposed" but rather "not composed at all." 1005. **golden chain.** According to classical legend, Zeus drew the gods, the Earth, the sea, and the whole universe upon a single golden chain, which integrated all existence. 1017. **Argo,** the ship which the Greek hero Jason used to sail to his adventure of the Golden Fleece. 1020. **Charybdis,** see note to 660 above.

Over the dark abyss, whose boiling gulf
Tamely endured a bridge of wondrous length
From Hell continued reaching the utmost orb
Of this frail world; by which the spirits perverse
With easy intercourse pass to and fro   1031
To tempt or punish mortals, except whom
God and good angels guard by special grace.
But now at last the sacred influence
Of light appears, and from the walls of Heaven
Shoots far into the bosom of dim Night   1036
A glimmering dawn; here Nature first begins
Her farthest verge, and Chaos to retire,
As from her outmost works, a broken foe,
With tumult less and with less hostile din,   1040
That Satan with less toil, and now with ease
Wafts on the calmer wave by dubious light
And like a weather-beaten vessel holds
Gladly the port, though shrouds and tackle torn;
Or in the emptier waste, resembling air,   1045
Weighs his spread wings, at leisure to behold
Far off the empyreal Heaven, extended wide
In circuit, undetermined square or round,
With opal towers and battlements adorned
Of living sapphire, once his native seat;   1050
And fast by hanging in a golden chain
This pendant world, in bigness as a star
Of smallest magnitude close by the moon.
Thither, full fraught with mischievous revenge,
Accursed, and in a curséd hour he hies.   1055

[Since Milton chose to plunge at once into the middle of the action of his epic, the narrative substance of a part of the Books following is necessarily concerned with summing up the earlier stages of the story. These also tell of the temptation of Adam and Eve by Satan and of their repentance for their sin. In the eleventh book God accepts their prayers, "but declares that they must no longer abide in Paradise; sends Michael with a band of Cherubim to dispossess them . . ." Michael descends to Eden, breaks to Adam and Eve the news of their banishment, yet of their ultimate redemption, then, taking Adam upon a high hill, unfolds to him in a vision all that shall happen on earth down to the time of the Flood.]

BOOK XII

The Argument

The Angel Michael continues from the Flood to relate what shall succeed; then, in the mention of *Abraham*, comes by degrees to explain, who that Seed of the woman shall be, which was promised Adam and Eve in the Fall; His Incarnation, Death, Resurrection, and Ascension; the state of the Church till His Second Coming. Adam, greatly satisfied and re-comforted by these relations and promises, descends the hill with Michael; wakens Eve, who all this while had slept, but with gentle

1029. **orb,** the outermost sphere of those which surround the earth, according to the old cosmogony. 1039. **her,** Nature's.

dreams composed to quietness of mind and submission. Michael in either hand leads them out of Paradise, the fiery sword waving behind them, and the Cherubim taking their stations to guard the place.

As one who in his journey bates at noon,
Though bent on speed, so here the Archangel
     paused
Betwixt the world destroyed and world restored,
If Adam aught perhaps might interpose;
Then with transition sweet new speech resumes: 5
'Thus thou hast seen one world begin and end;
And Man as from a second stock proceed.
Much thou hast yet to see, but I perceive
Thy mortal sight to fail; objects divine
Must needs impair and weary human sense: 10
Henceforth what is to come I will relate,
Thou therefore give due audience, and attend.
This second source of men, while yet but few,
And while the dread of Judgment past remains
Fresh in their minds, fearing the Deity,   15
With some regard to what is just and right
Shall lead their lives, and multiply apace,
Labouring the soil, and reaping plenteous crop,
Corn, wine and oil; and from the herd or flock,
Oft sacrificing bullock, lamb, or kid,   20
With large wine-offerings poured, and sacred feast,
Shall spend their days in joy unblamed, and dwell
Long time in peace by families and tribes
Under paternal rule; till one shall rise
Of proud ambitious heart, who not content   25
With fair equality, fraternal state,
Will arrogate Dominion undeserved
Over his brethren, and quite dispossess
Concord and Law of Nature from the Earth;
Hunting (and men, not beasts, shall be his game)
With war and hostile snare such as refuse   31
Subjection to his empire tyrannous:
A mighty hunter thence he shall be styled
Before the Lord, as in despite of Heaven,
Or from Heaven claiming second sovereignty;   35
And from rebellion shall derive his name,
Though of rebellion others he accuse.
He with a crew, whom like ambition joins
With him or under him to tyrannize,
Marching from Eden towards the West, shall find
The plain, wherein a black bituminous gūrge   41
Boils out from under ground, the mouth of Hell;
Of brick, and of that stuff they cast to build
A city and tower, whose top may reach to Heaven;
And get themselves a name, lest far dispersed   45
In foreign lands their memory be lost,
Regardless whether good or evil fame.
But God, who oft descends to visit men

1. **bates,** abates speed, pauses. 5. **transition,** summary, epitome. 18. **Labouring,** working, used here transitively. 24. **one,** Nimrod. The story is told in Genesis, 10:9 ff.

Unseen, and through their habitations walks
To mark their doings, them beholding soon,　　50
Comes down to see their city, ere the tower
Obstruct Heaven Towers, and in derision sets
Upon their tongues a various spirit to rase
Quite out their native language, and instead
To sow a jangling noise of words unknown:　　55
Forthwith a hideous gabble rises loud
Among the builders; each to other calls
Not understood, till hoarse, and all in rage,
As mocked they storm; great laughter was in
　　　Heaven,
And looking down, to see the hubbub strange　60
And hear the din; thus was the building left
Ridiculous, and the work Confusion named.'
　　Whereto thus Adam fatherly displeased:
'O execrable son, so to aspire
Above his brethren, to himself assuming　　65
Authority usurped, from God not given:
He gave us only over beast, fish, fowl
Dominion absolute; that right we hold
By His donation; but Man over men
He made not Lord; such title to Himself　　70
Reserving, human left from human free.
But this usurper his encroachment proud
Stays not on Man; to God his tower intends
Siege and defiance: wretched man! what food
Will he convey up thither to sustain　　75
Himself and his rash army, where thin air
Above the clouds will pine his entrails gross,
And famish him of breath, if not of bread?'
　　To whom thus Michael: 'Justly thou abhorrest
That son, who on the quiet state of men　　80
Such trouble brought, affecting to subdue
Rational Liberty; yet know withal,
Since thy original lapse, true Liberty
Is lost, which always with right Reason dwells
Twinned, and from her hath no dividual being:　85
Reason in Man obscured, or not obeyed,
Immediately inordinate desires
And upstart passions catch the government
From Reason, and to servitude reduce
Man till then free. Therefore since he permits　90
Within himself unworthy powers to reign
Over free Reason, God in judgment just
Subjects him from without to violent lords;
Who oft as undeservedly enthrall
His outward freedom: tyranny must be,　　95
Though to the tyrant thereby no excuse.
Yet sometimes nations will decline so low
From virtue, which is reason, that no wrong,
But Justice, and some fatal curse annexed,

Deprives them of their outward liberty,　　100
Their inward lost: witness the irreverent son
Of him who built the Ark, who for the shame
Done to his father, heard this heavy curse,
Servant of Servants, on his vicious race.
Thus will this latter, as the former world,　　105
Still tend from bad to worse, till God at last,
Wearied with their iniquities, withdraw
His presence from among them, and avert
His holy eyes; resolving from thenceforth
To leave them to their own polluted ways;　　110
And one peculiar nation to select
From all the rest, of whom to be invoked,
A nation from one faithful man to spring:
Him on this side Euphrates yet residing,
Bred up in idol-worship; O that men　　115
(Canst thou believe?) should be so stupid grown,
While yet the Patriarch lived, who scaped the Flood,
As to forsake the living God, and fall
To worship their own work in wood and stone
For gods! yet him God the most High vouchsafes
To call by vision from his Father's house,　　121
His kindred and false gods, into a land
Which He will show him, and from him will raise
A mighty nation, and upon him shower
His benediction so, that in his seed　　125
All nations shall be blessed; he straight obeys,
Not knowing to what land, yet firm believes:
I see him, but thou canst not, with what faith
He leaves his gods, his friends, and native soil,
Ur of Chaldaea, passing now the ford　　130
To Haran, after him a cumbrous train
Of herds and flocks, and numerous servitude;
Not wandering poor, but trusting all his wealth
With God, who called him, in a land unknown.
Canaan he now attains; I see his tents　　135
Pitched about Sechem, and the neighbouring plain
Of Moreh; there by promise he receives
Gift to his progeny of all that land;
From Hamath northward to the desert south
(Things by their name I call, though yet unnamed),
From Hermon east to the great Western Sea,　141
Mount Hermon, yonder Sea, each place behold
In prospect, as I point them; on the shore

101. **irreverent son,** Ham, son of Noah, and father of Canaan. Note Genesis, 9:25: "And Noah said, 'Cursed be Canaan; a servant of servants shall he be unto his brethren.' " Ham became the ancestral progenitor of all the colored peoples of the world. 111. **one peculiar nation,** Israel. 113. **one faithful man,** Abraham. 130–131. **Ur . . . Haran.** The ancient city of Ur has been tentatively located on the western shore of the River Euphrates not far down the river from Babylon. **Haran** was across the river. 132. **servitude,** a collective noun for servants. 136. **Sechem,** or Shechem, the site of Abraham's first encampment in the land of Canaan; it is the present town of Nablus, between Mounts Ebal and Gerizim. 139. **Hamath,** on the River Orontes in eastern Syria; it is named in Numbers, 34:8 as the northern boundary-mark of the ancient land of Canaan. 141. **Hermon,** the highest mountain in Palestine, northeast of the Sea of Galilee. **Western Sea,** the Mediterranean.

53. **various spirit,** a spirit of contention, at variance with order and conformity. 61–62. **building . . . Confusion,** the Tower of Babel, the "confusion of tongues"; see Genesis, 11:2–9. 83–85. **Liberty . . . twinned.** The coupling of Liberty and Reason is virtually a commonplace in Milton's political and social views.

Mount Carmel; here the double-founted stream
Jordan, true limit eastward; but his sons   145
Shall dwell to Senir, that long ridge of hills.
This ponder, that all nations of the Earth
Shall in his seed be blessed; by that seed
Is meant thy great Deliverer, who shall bruise
The Serpent's head; whereof to thee anon   150
Plainlier shall be revealed. This Patriarch blest,
Whom faithful *Abraham* due time shall call,
A son, and of his son a grandchild leaves,
Like him in faith, in wisdom, and renown;
The grandchild with twelve sons increased, departs
From Canaan, to a land hereafter called   156
Egypt, divided by the River Nile;
See where it flows, disgorging at seven mouths
Into the Sea; to sojourn in that land
He comes, invited by a younger son   160
In time of dearth, a son whose worthy deeds
Raise him to be the second in that realm
Of Pharaoh; there he dies, and leaves his race
Growing into a nation, and now grown
Suspected to a sequent king, who seeks   165
To stop their overgrowth, as inmate guests
Too numerous; whence of guests he makes them
          slaves
Inhospitably, and kills their infant males;
Till by two brethren (those two brethren call
Moses and *Aaron*) sent from God to claim   170
His people from enthrallment, they return
With glory and spoil back to their Promised Land.
But first the lawless tyrant, who denies
To know their God, or message to regard,
Must be compelled by signs and judgments dire;
To blood unshed the rivers must be turned,   176
Frogs, lice, and flies must all his palace fill
With loathed intrusion, and fill all the land;
His cattle must of rot and murrain die,
Botches and blains must all his flesh emboss,   180
And all his people; thunder mixed with hail,
Hail mixed with fire must rend the Egyptian sky
And wheel on the Earth, devouring where it rolls;
What it devours not, herb, or fruit, or grain,
A darksome cloud of locusts swarming down   185
Must eat, and on the ground leave nothing green:
Darkness must overshadow all his bounds,
Palpable darkness, and blot out three days;
Last with one midnight stroke all the first-born
Of Egypt must lie dead. Thus with ten wounds   190
The river-dragon, tamed at length, submits
To let his sojourners depart, and oft
Humbles his stubborn heart, but still as ice

144. **Mount Carmel,** a high cape projecting from the shore of Palestine into the Mediterranean. 146. **Senir,** a peak in the Mount Hermon range. 153. **A son,** Isaac. 175 ff. **signs and judgments,** the Ten Plagues; see Exodus, 7:19 ff. 180. **emboss,** cover with swellings and abscesses. 190-191. **Thus . . . the river-dragon;** see Ezekiel, 29:3: "Behold, I am against thee, Pharaoh King of Egypt, the great dragon that lieth in the midst of his rivers."

More hardened after thaw, till in his rage,
Pursuing whom he late dismissed, the Sea   195
Swallows him with his host, but them lets pass
As on dry land between two crystal walls,
Awed by the rod of Moses so to stand
Divided, till his rescued gain their shore:
Such wondrous power God to His saint will lend,
Though present in His Angel, who shall go   201
Before them in a cloud, and pillar of fire,
By day a cloud, by night a pillar of fire,
To guide them in their journey, and remove
Behind them, while the obdurate king pursues: 205
All night he will pursue, but his approach
Darkness defends between till morning-watch;
Then through the fiery pillar and the cloud,
God looking forth will trouble all his host
And craze their chariot-wheels; when by command
Moses once more his potent rod extends   211
Over the Sea; the Sea his rod obeys;
On their embattled ranks the waves return,
And overwhelm their war: the race elect
Safe towards Canaan from the shore advance   215
Through the wild desert, not the readiest way,
Lest entering on the Canaanite alarmed
War terrify them inexpert, and fear
Return them back to Egypt, choosing rather
Inglorious life with servitude; for life   220
To noble and ignoble is more sweet
Untrained in arms, where rashness leads not on.
This also shall they gain by their delay
In the wide wilderness; there they shall found
Their government, and their great senate choose
Through the Twelve Tribes, to rule by laws or-
          dained: 226
God from the Mount of Sinai, whose gray top
Shall tremble, He descending, will Himself
In thunder, lightning, and loud trumpet's sound
Ordain them Laws; part such as appertain   230
To civil justice, part religious rites
Of sacrifice, informing them, by types
And shadows, of that destined seed to bruise
The Serpent, by what means He shall achieve
Mankind's deliverance. But the voice of God   235
To mortal ear is dreadful; they beseech

202-203. **cloud . . . fire.** When the Israelites were on their way out of Egypt to the Promised Land, as told in Exodus, 13:21 ff., God showed them the way by leading them in the form of a cloud by day and a pillar of fire by night. 207. **defends,** prevents, forbids—by interposing Himself between the Israelites and the pursuing Egyptians. 210. **craze,** shatter, destroy. 213-214. **embattled . . . war.** The destruction of the hosts of Pharaoh in the Red Sea is told in Exodus, 14. 218. **War,** armies, military forces. 225. **senate.** According to Exodus, 24:1-9 and Numbers, 11:16-30, there were seventy elders who witnessed some of the more important acts of Moses. No doubt it was from the nature of this group that Milton used the word *senate.* 236. **mortal . . . dreadful.** The beliefs that the voice of God is too mighty for mortal hearing and the sight of God too dazzling for mortal eyes are both too ancient for mere tracing; no doubt Milton is remembering the passage from Exodus, 20:19: "Speak thou with us, and we will hear; but let not God speak with us, lest we die."

That Moses might report to them His will,
And terror cease; He grants what they besought,
Instructed that to God is no access
Without mediator, whose high office now   240
Moses in figure bears, to introduce
One greater, of whose day he shall foretell,
And all the prophets in their age the times
Of great *Messiah* shall sing. Thus laws and rites
Established, such delight hath God in men   245
Obedient to His will, that He vouchsafes
Among them to set up His tabernacle,
The holy One with mortal men to dwell:
By his prescript a sanctuary is framed
Of cedar, overlaid with gold, therein   250
An Ark, and in the Ark His testimony,
The records of His covenant, over these
A mercy-seat of gold between the wings
Of two bright Cherubim, before him burn
Seven lamps, as in a zodiac representing   255
The heavenly fires; over the tent a cloud
Shall rest by day, a fiery gleam by night,
Save when they journey, and at length they come,
Conducted by His Angel to the land
Promised to Abraham and his seed: the rest   260
Were long to tell, how many battles fought,
How many kings destroyed, and kingdoms won,
Or how the Sun shall in mid-Heaven stand still
A day entire, and night's due course adjourn,
Man's voice commanding, Sun in Gibeon stand,   265
And thou, Moon, in the vale of Ajalon,
Till Israel overcome; so call the third
From Abraham, son of Isaac, and from him
His whole descent, who thus shall Canaan win.'
    Here Adam interposed. 'O sent from Heaven,   270
Enlightener of my darkness, gracious things
Thou hast revealed, those chiefly which concern
Just Abraham and his seed: now first I find
Mine eyes true opening, and my heart much eased,
Erewhile perplexed with thoughts what would be-
        come   275
Of me and all Mankind; but now I see
His day, in whom all nations shall be blessed,
Favour unmerited by me, who sought
Forbidden knowledge by forbidden means.
This yet I apprehend not, why to those   280
Among whom God will deign to dwell on Earth
So many and so various laws are given;
So many laws argue so many sins
Among them; how can God with such reside?'
    To whom thus Michael: 'Doubt not but that sin
Will reign among them, as of thee begot;   286
And therefore was Law given them to evince

Their natural pravity, by stirring up
Sin against Law to fight; that when they see
Law can discover Sin, but not remove,   290
Save by those shadowy expiations weak,
The blood of bulls and goats, they may conclude
Some blood more precious must be paid for Man,
Just for unjust, that in such righteousness
To them by Faith imputed, they may find   295
Justification toward God, and peace
Of Conscience, which the law by ceremonies
Cannot appease, nor Man the moral part
Perform, and not performing cannot live.
So Law appears imperfect, and but given   300
With purpose to resign them in full time
Up to a better covenant, disciplined
From shadowy types to Truth, from flesh to spirit,
From imposition of strict laws, to free
Acceptance of large Grace, from servile Fear   305
To filial, works of law to works of faith.
And therefore shall not Moses, though of God
Highly beloved, being but the minister
Of Law, his people into Canaan lead;
But *Joshua*, whom the Gentiles Jesus call,   310
His name and office bearing, who shall quell
The adversary Serpent, and bring back
Through the world's wilderness long wandered Man
Safe to eternal Paradise of rest.
Meanwhile they in their earthly Canaan placed   315
Long time shall dwell and prosper, but when sins
National interrupt their public peace,
Provoking God to raise them enemies:
From whom as oft he saves them penitent
By judges first, then under kings; of whom   320
The second, both for piety renowned
And puissant deeds, a promise shall receive
Irrevocable, that his regal throne
Forever shall endure; the like shall sing
All prophecy, that of the royal stock   325
Of David (so I name this king) shall rise
A Son, the Woman's seed to thee foretold,
Foretold to Abraham, as in whom shall trust
All nations, and to kings foretold, of kings
The last, for of his reign shall be no end.   330
But first a long succession must ensue,
And his next son, for wealth and wisdom famed,
The clouded Ark of God till then in tents
Wandering shall in a glorious temple enshrine.
Such follow him, as shall be registered   335
Part good, part bad, of bad the longer scroll,
Whose foul idolatries, and other faults
Heaped to the popular sum, will so incense
God, as to leave them, and expose their land,

240. mediator. Moses is regarded as the first mediator between God and Man. 249–256. sanctuary . . . fires. The description of God's Tabernacle given in this passage is based on Exodus, 25. 263. Sun . . . stand still. When Joshua was fighting the armies of the Five Kings in Gibeah, the Sun, by God's intervention, stood still until the Israelites had defeated their enemies. See Joshua, 10:12–13.

291. shadowy, symbolic. 298. nor Man the moral part, etc. The meaning is that no mere man can perform all the moral obligations of Moses' law. 321. second, King David. 332. next son, King Solomon. 337. foul idolatries. The defections of Solomon are explained in Book I, ll. 399–403 and notes.

Their city, His temple, and His holy Ark,   340
With all His sacred things, a scorn and prey
To that proud city, whose high walls thou saw'st
Left in confusion, Babylon thence called.
There in captivity He lets them dwell
The space of seventy years, then brings them back,
Remembering mercy, and His covenant sworn   346
To David, established as the days of Heaven.
Returned from Babylon by leave of kings
Their lords, whom God disposed, the house of God
They first re-edify, and for a while   350
In mean estate live moderate, till grown
In wealth and multitude, factious they grow;
But first among the priests dissension springs,
Men who attend the Altar, and should most
Endeavour Peace; their strife pollution brings   355
Upon the Temple itself: at last they seize
The sceptre, and regard not David's sons,
Then lose it to a stranger, that the true
Anointed King *Messiah* might be born
Barred of His right; yet at His birth a star   360
Unseen before in Heaven proclaims Him come,
And guides the eastern sages, who inquire
His place, to offer incense, myrrh, and gold;
His place of birth a solemn angel tells
To simple shepherds, keeping watch by night;   365
They gladly thither haste, and by a choir
Of squadroned angels hear His carol sung.
A virgin is His mother, but His sire
The power of the Most High; He shall ascend
The throne hereditary, and bound His reign   370
With Earth's wide bounds, His glory with the
          Heavens.'
He ceased, discerning Adam with such joy
Surcharged, as had like grief been dewed in tears,
Without the vent of words, which these he breathed:
'O Prophet of glad tidings, finisher   375
Of utmost hope! now clear I understand
What oft my steadiest thoughts have searched in
          vain,
Why our great expectation should be called
The seed of woman: Virgin Mother, hail!
High in the love of Heaven, yet from my loins   380
Thou shalt proceed, and from thy womb the Son

347. **days of Heaven.** The Captivity of the Jews in Babylon (from 606 to 536 B.C.) is construed as fulfilling God's covenant with David to make "his throne as the days of Heaven." See Psalms, 89:29. 348. **kings,** Cyrus the Great, Darius, and Artaxerxes. 353. **dissension springs.** The serious factional disputes between rival claimants for the High Priesthood of Israel are recounted in the apocryphal Book of II Maccabees, 3 and 4. 356. **they,** the Asmonean family, who held control of the High Priesthood from 153 to 35 B.C. 357. **David's sons,** represented by Zerubbabel, who brought back the returning Hebrews to Jerusalem; he was a direct descendant of David. 358. **a stranger,** probably King Antiochus the Great, who held Palestine against Judas Maccabeus and his successors until the time of Christ. 360. **Barred . . . right.** Christ, as the descendant of David, was born King of the Jews, although he was barred from his occupancy of the throne. 364. **solemn,** appropriate to a religious rite or ceremony. 366. **thither,** to the place of the nativity. 374. **which,** of which.

Of God Most High; so God with Man unites.
Needs must the Serpent now his capital bruise
Expect with mortal pain: say where and when
Their fight, what stroke shall bruise the Victor's
          heel.'   385
To whom thus Michael: 'Dream not of their fight,
As of a duel, or the local wounds
Of head or heel: not therefore joins the Son
Manhood to Godhead, with more strength to foil
Thy enemy; nor so is overcome   390
Satan, whose fall from Heaven, a deadlier bruise,
Disabled not to give thee thy death's wound:
Which He, who comes thy Saviour, shall recure,
Not by destroying Satan, but his works
In thee and in thy seed; nor can this be,   395
But by fulfilling that which thou didst want,
Obedience to the Law of God, imposed
On penalty of death, and suffering death,
The penalty to thy transgression due,
And due to theirs which out of thine will grow: 400
So only can high Justice rest appaid.
The Law of God exact He shall fulfill
Both by obedience and by love, though love
Alone fulfill the Law; thy punishment
He shall endure by coming in the flesh   405
To a reproachful life and cursed death,
Proclaiming life to all who shall believe
In His redemption, and that His obedience
Imputed becomes theirs by faith, His merits
To save them, not their own, through legal works.
For this He shall live hated, be blasphemed,   411
Seized on by force, judged, and to death condemned
A shameful and accursed, nailed to the Cross
By His own nation, slain for bringing life;
But to the Cross He nails thy Enemies,   415
The Law that is against thee, and the sins
Of all Mankind, with Him there crucified,
Never to hurt them more who rightly trust
In this His satisfaction; so He dies,
But soon revives, Death over Him no power   420
Shall long usurp; ere the third dawning light
Return, the stars of morn shall see Him rise
Out of His grave, fresh as the dawning light,
Thy ransom paid, which Man from death redeems,
His death for Man, as many as offered life   425
Neglect not, and the benefit embrace
By faith not void of works: this God-like act
Annuls thy doom, the death thou shouldst have died,
In sin forever lost from life; this act
Shall bruise the head of Satan, crush his strength
Defeating Sin and Death, his two main arms,   431
And fix far deeper in his head their stings

383. **capital,** a play on words, referring to the fact that the injury to Satan was not only a chief injury but was sustained in the head (Lat. *caput*). 393. **recure,** heal. 401. **appaid,** satisfied, requited. 409. **His merits.** This should be construed as a direct object of *believes* in line 407. 424. **Thy,** referring not only to Adam but to all Mankind.

Than temporal death shall bruise the Victor's heel,
Or theirs whom He redeems, a death like sleep,
A gentle wafting to immortal life.   435
Nor after resurrection shall He stay
Longer on Earth than certain times to appear
To His disciples, men who in His life
Still followed Him; to them shall leave in charge
To teach all nations what of Him they learned   440
And His salvation, them who shall believe
Baptizing in the profluent stream, the sign
Of washing them from guilt of sin to life
Pure, and in mind prepared, if so befall,
For death, like that which the Redeemer died.   445
All nations they shall teach; for from that day
Not only to the sons of Abraham's loins
Salvation shall be preached, but to the sons
Of Abraham's faith wherever through the world;
So in His seed all nations shall be blest.   450
Then to the Heaven of Heavens He shall ascend
With victory, triumphing through the air
Over His foes and thine; there shall surprise
The Serpent, prince of air, and drag in chains
Through all His realm, and there confounded leave;
Then enter into glory, and resume   456
His seat at God's right hand, exalted high
Above all names in Heaven; and thence shall come,
When this world's dissolution shall be ripe,
With glory and power to judge both quick and dead,
To judge the unfaithful dead, but to reward   461
His faithful, and receive them into bliss,
Whether in Heaven or Earth, for then the Earth
Shall all be Paradise, far happier place
Than this of Eden, and far happier days.'   465
    So spake the Archangel Michael, then paused,
As at the world's great period; and our sire,
Replete with joy and wonder thus replied:
    'O goodness infinite, goodness immense!
That all this good of evil shall produce,   470
And evil turn to good; more wonderful
Than that which by Creation first brought forth
Light out of darkness! full of doubt I stand,
Whether I should repent me now of sin
By me done and occasioned, or rejoice   475
Much more, that much more good thereof shall
        spring,
To God more glory, more goodwill to men
From God, and over wrath grace shall abound.
But say, if our Deliverer up to Heaven
Must re-ascend, what will betide the few   480
His faithful, left among the unfaithful herd,
The enemies of truth; who then shall guide
His people, who defend? Will they not deal

Worse with His followers than with Him they dealt?'
    'Be sure they will,' said the Angel; 'but from
        Heaven   485
He to His own a Comforter will send,
The promise of the Father, who shall dwell
His Spirit within them, and the law of faith
Working through love, upon their hearts shall write,
To guide them in all truth, and also arm   490
With spiritual armor, able to resist
Satan's assaults, and quench his fiery darts,
What Man can do against them, not afraid,
Though to the death, against such cruelties
With inward consolations recompensed,   495
And oft supported so as shall amaze
Their proudest persecutors: for the Spirit
Poured first on His apostles, whom He sends
To evangelize the nations, then on all
Baptized, shall them with wondrous gifts endue   500
To speak all tongues, and do all miracles,
As did their Lord before them. Thus they win
Great numbers of each nation to receive
With joy the tidings brought from Heaven: at length
Their ministry performed, and race well run,   505
Their doctrine and their story written left,
They die; but in their room, as they forewarn,
Wolves shall succeed for teachers, grievous wolves,
Who all the sacred mysteries of Heaven
To their own vile advantages shall turn   510
Of lucre and ambition, and the truth
With superstitions and traditions taint,
Left only in those written records pure,
Though not but by the Spirit understood.
Then shall they seek to avail themselves of names,
Places and titles, and with these to join   516
Secular power, though feigning still to act
By spiritual, to themselves appropriating
The Spirit of God, promised alike and given
To all believers; and from that pretense,   520
Spiritual laws by carnal power shall force
Out every conscience; laws which none shall find
Left them enrolled, or what the Spirit within
Shall on the heart engrave. What will they then
But force the spirit of Grace itself, and bind   525
His consort Liberty; what, but unbuild
His living temples, built by Faith to stand,
Their own faith, not another's: for on Earth
Who against faith and conscience can be heard
Infallible? yet many will presume: 530
Whence heavy persecution shall arise
On all who in the worship persevere
Of Spirit and Truth; the rest, far greater part,
Will deem in outward rites and specious forms
Religion satisfied; Truth shall retire   535

---

442. **profluent,** running; according to Milton the ideal baptism could
be performed only in running water.   446 ff. **All nations,** etc. See
Galatians, 3:8: "And the scripture, foreseeing that God would justify
the heathen through faith, preached before the gospel unto Abraham,
saying, 'In thee shall all nations be blessed.'"

525. **force . . . Grace.** Cf. II Corinthians, 3:17: "Now the Lord is
that Spirit; and where the Spirit of the Lord is, there is Liberty."
527. **living temples.** According to St. Paul (I Corinthians, 6:19), the
human body is a "temple of the Holy Ghost."

Bestuck with slanderous darts, and works of Faith
Rarely be found: so shall the world go on,
To good malignant, to bad men benign,
Under her own weight groaning, till the day
Appear of respiration to the just,   540
And vengeance to the wicked, at return
Of Him so lately promised to thy aid,
The Woman's seed, obscurely then foretold,
Now amplier known thy Saviour and thy Lord,
Last in the clouds from Heaven to be revealed   545
In glory of the Father, to dissolve
Satan with his perverted world, then raise
From the conflagrant mass, purged and refined,
New Heavens, new Earth, ages of endless date
Founded in righteousness and peace and love,   550
To bring forth fruits, joy and eternal bliss.'
    He ended; and thus Adam last replied:
'How soon hath thy prediction, Seer blest,
Measured this transient world, the race of Time,
Till Time stand fixed; beyond is all abyss,   555
Eternity, whose end no eye can reach.
Greatly instructed I shall hence depart,
Greatly in peace of thought, and have my fill
Of knowledge, what this vessel can contain;
Beyond which was my folly to aspire.   560
Henceforth I learn, that to obey is best,
And love with fear the only God, to walk
As in His presence, ever to observe
His Providence, and on Him sole depend,
Merciful over all His works, with good   565
Still overcoming evil, and by small
Accomplishing great things, by things deemed weak
Subverting worldly strong, and worldly wise
By simple meek; that suffering for Truth's sake
Is fortitude to highest victory,   570
And to the faithful, Death the Gate of Life;
Taught this by His example whom I now
Acknowledge my Redeemer ever blest.'
    To whom thus also the Angel last replied:
'This having learned, thou hast attained the sum
Of wisdom; hope no higher, though all the stars   576
Thou knew'st by name, and all the ethereal Powers,
All secrets of the deep, all Nature's works,
Or works of God in Heaven, air, Earth, or sea,
And all the riches of this world enjoy'dst,   580
And all the rule, one empire; only add
Deeds to thy knowledge answerable, add Faith,
Add Virtue, Patience, Temperance; add Love,
By name to come called Charity, the soul
Of all the rest: then wilt thou not be loath   585
To leave this Paradise, but shalt possess
A Paradise within thee, happier far.
Let us descend now therefore from this top
Of speculation; for the hour precise
Exacts our parting hence; and see the guards,   590

540. respiration, refreshment, encouragement. 559. this vessel, Adam's body. 589. speculation, looking out.

By me encamped on yonder hill, expect
Their motion, at whose front a flaming sword,
In signal of remove, waves fiercely round;
We may no longer stay: go, waken Eve;
Her also I with gentle dreams have calmed,   595
Portending good, and all her spirits composed
To meek submission: thou at season fit
Let her with thee partake what thou hast heard,
Chiefly what may concern her faith to know,
The great deliverance by her Seed to come   600
(For by the Woman's Seed) on all Mankind.
That ye may live, which will be many days,
Both in one Faith unanimous though sad,
With cause for evils past, yet much more cheered
With meditation on the happy end.'   605
    He ended, and they both descend the hill;
Descended, Adam to the bower where Eve
Lay sleeping ran before, but found her waked;
And thus with words not sad she him received:
    'Whence thou return'st, and whither went'st, I
        know;   610
For God is also in sleep, and dreams advise,
Which he hath sent propitious, some great good
Presaging, since with sorrow and heart's distress
Wearied I fell asleep: but now lead on;
In me is no delay; with thee to go,   615
Is to stay here; without thee here to stay
Is to go hence unwilling; thou to me
Art all things under Heaven, all places thou,
Who for my wilful crime art banished hence.
This further consolation yet secure   620
I carry hence; though all by me is lost,
Such favor I unworthy am vouchsafed,
By me the promised Seed shall all restore.'
    So spake our mother Eve, and Adam heard
Well pleased, but answered not; for now too nigh
The Archangel stood, and from the other hill   626
To their fixed station, all in bright array
The Cherubim descended; on the ground
Gliding meteorous, as evening mist
Risen from a river o'er the marish glides,   630
And gathers ground fast at the laborer's heel
Homeward returning. High in front advanced,
The brandished sword of God before them blazed
Fierce as a comet; which with torrid heat,
And vapor as the Libyan air adust,   635
Began to parch that temperate clime; whereat
In either hand the hastening Angel caught
Our lingering parents, and to the Eastern Gate
Led them direct, and down the cliff as fast
To the subjected plain; then disappeared.   640

611. God . . . advise. There is a trace of classical paganism in this statement, although it is a belief often found in rabbinical lore. 630. marish, marsh, swampland. 632. advanced, held aloft. 635. adust, burned, scorched. Milton conceives of the sword of God as burning Paradise as a blast from the Libyan desert can scorch the land. Note the choice of brand for sword in l. 643, which conforms etymologically to the idea. 640. subjected, lying below.

They looking back, all the eastern side beheld
Of Paradise, so late their happy seat,
Waved over by that flaming brand, the Gate
With dreadful faces thronged and fiery arms;
Some natural tears they dropped, but wiped them
        soon;   645
The world was all before them, where to choose
Their place of rest, and Providence their guide;
They, hand in hand, with wandering steps and slow,
Through Eden took their solitary way.

Jonathan Edwards

1703–1758

The dominance of the national Anglican Church in English religious and political life from the time of Queen Elizabeth brought restriction and even persecution to other Christian sects, both Catholic and Protestant. As English explorers opened up the New World to colonization, the religious minorities came to seek havens along the stern Atlantic coast of North America, which the national government encouraged with grants of land. Catholics settled Maryland, but the religious migration was essentially Protestant, as Puritans founded Massachusetts and Quakers the friendly colony of Pennsylvania. Since the Puritans still held the conservative view that the civil government could control the consciences of men and punish violations of religious decrees, Massachusetts became a theocratic state which the Quakers and Roger Williams found as intolerant and oppressive as the Anglican government in England.

Many fire-breathing divines arose in Puritan New England to preach the austere Calvinist doctrine which was embodied in the civil legislation of the colonies. John Cotton, Thomas Hooker, Richard Mather, and Increase Mather were seventeenth-century predecessors of Jonathan Edwards, in whom the Puritan tradition found its greatest American spokesman. The son of a distinguished minister of Windsor, Connecticut, he was educated at Yale and prepared himself for the ministry there. Taking over the pastorate of his maternal grandfather at Northampton, Massachusetts, in 1726, Edwards was roused by the moral lethargy of the community to preach a series of terrifying sermons on the damnation awaiting sinners who did not follow stern Puritan rules of conduct. For twenty years he electrified not only his own community but all of New England with his discourses on "the Great Awakening" necessary in the souls of his contemporaries to the evils in man's nature and the hellfire that lay beyond the grave.

The best known of these grim warnings is *Sinners in the Hands of an Angry God*, preached at Enfield, Connecticut, on July 8, 1741. Taking his text from Deuteronomy ("Their foot shall slide in due time"), he develops the idea that "there is nothing that keeps wicked men at any moment out of hell, but the mere pleasure

of God." Moreover, "the God that holds you over the pit of hell, much as one holds a spider, or some loathsome insect over the fire, abhors you, and is dreadfully provoked." This shocking message sent the Enfield congregation into hysteria as the austere minister read it calmly without gesture or modulation of voice. "There was such a breathing of distress, and weeping, that the preacher was obliged to speak to the people and desire silence that he might be heard."

The "Great Awakening" took the form of an avalanche of conversions to the pious life. Northampton was only one community whipped into a fervor of conscience by the Calvinist Savonarola. This emotional approach to salvation was justified by Edwards in his *Treatise concerning Religious Affections* (1746), which argued that knowledge of the gospel was not enough, but that a spiritual awakening to divine love shown in a radical change in living was essential to church membership. When he demanded that sinners, regardless of social position, should be disciplined by the community, his Northampton flock grew wary and awakened from their nightmare of holiness to dismiss Edwards from his pastorate (1750). His *Farewell Sermon* appealed to a Higher Judge above the congregation that had condemned him. Thereafter he served for six years as missionary to the Indians in the frontier town of Stockbridge and was called to the presidency of Princeton only two months before his death in March 1758.

Although Edwards is popularly remembered for his brimstone sermons, he was also a great theologian and Christian philosopher. His treatise on *Freedom of Will* (1754) argued for predestination along orthodox Calvinist lines against the views of the Dutch theologian, Arminius, who favored the free will of man to choose good or evil. Despite his sternness, Edwards was a humanitarian in his approach to his fellow men and was known as a staunch friend as well as an affectionate husband and father. Though he may have smugly lectured his contemporaries on Puritan principles, his own life was a model one.

Sinners in the Hands of an Angry God

DEUT. XXXII. 35

—Their foot shall slide in due time.—

In this verse is threatened the vengeance of God on the wicked unbelieving Israelites, who were God's visible people, and who lived under the means of grace; but who, notwithstanding all God's wonderful works towards them, remained (as ver. 28.) void of counsel, having no understanding in them. Under all the cultivations of heaven, they brought forth bitter and poisonous fruit; as in the two verses

*Sinners in the Hands of an Angry God.*ᴬ Preached at Enfield, Connecticut, July 8, 1741.

next preceding the text.—The expression I have chosen for my text, *Their foot shall slide in due time,* seems to imply the following things, relating to the punishment and destruction to which these wicked Israelites were exposed.

1. That they were always exposed to *destruction;* as one that stands or walks in slippery places is always exposed to fall. This is implied in the manner of their destruction coming upon them, being represented by their foot sliding. The same is expressed, Psalm lxxiii. 18. "Surely thou didst set them in slippery places; thou castedst them down into destruction."

2. It implies, that they were always exposed to sudden unexpected destruction. As he that walks in slippery places is every moment liable to fall, he cannot foresee one moment whether he shall stand or fall the next; and when he does fall, he falls at once without warning: Which is also expressed in Psalm lxxiii. 18, 19. "Surely thou didst set them in slippery places; thou castedst them down into destruction: How are they brought into desolation as in a moment!"

3. Another thing implied is, that they are liable to fall *of themselves,* without being thrown down by the hand of another; as he that stands or walks on slippery ground needs nothing but his own weight to throw him down.

4. That the reason why they are not fallen already, and do not fall now, is only that God's appointed time is not come. For it is said, that when that due time, or appointed time comes, *their foot shall slide.* Then they shall be left to fall, as they are inclined by their own weight. God will not hold them up in these slippery places any longer, but will let them go; and then, at that very instant, they shall fall into destruction; as he that stands on such slippery declining ground, on the edge of a pit, he cannot stand alone, when he is let go he immediately falls and is lost.

The observation from the words that I would now insist upon is this.—"There is nothing that keeps wicked men at any one moment out of hell, but the mere pleasure of God"—By the *mere* pleasure of God, I mean his *sovereign* pleasure, his arbitrary will, restrained by no obligation, hindered by no manner of difficulty, any more than if nothing else but God's mere will had in the least degree, or in any respect whatsoever, any hand in the preservation of wicked men one moment.—The truth of this observation may appear by the following considerations.

1. There is no want of *power* in God to cast wicked men into hell at any moment. Men's hands cannot be strong when God rises up. The strongest have no power to resist him, nor can any deliver out of his hands.—He is not only able to cast wicked

men into hell, but he can most easily do it. Sometimes an earthly prince meets with a great deal of difficulty to subdue a rebel, who has found means to fortify himself, and has made himself strong by the number of his followers. But it is not so with God. There is no fortress that is any defence from the power of God. Though hand join in hand, and vast multitudes of God's enemies combine and associate themselves, they are easily broken in pieces. They are as great heaps of light chaff before the whirlwind; or large quantities of dry stubble before devouring flames. We find it easy to tread on and crush a worm that we see crawling on the earth; so it is easy for us to cut or singe a slender thread that any thing hangs by: thus easy is it for God, when he pleases, to cast his enemies down to hell. What are we, that we should think to stand before him, at whose rebuke the earth trembles, and before whom the rocks are thrown down?

2. They *deserve* to be cast into hell; so that divine justice never stands in the way, it makes no objection against God's using his power at any moment to destroy them. Yea, on the contrary, justice calls aloud for an infinite punishment of their sins. Divine justice says of the tree that brings forth such grapes of Sodom, "Cut it down, why cumbereth it the ground?" Luke xiii. 7. The sword of divine justice is every moment brandished over their heads, and it is nothing but the hand of arbitrary mercy, and God's mere will, that holds it back.

3. They are already under a sentence of *condemnation* to hell. They do not only justly deserve to be cast down thither, but the sentence of the law of God, that eternal and immutable rule of righteousness that God has fixed between him and mankind, is gone out against them, and stands against them; so that they are bound over already to hell. John iii. 18. "He that believeth not is condemned already." So that every unconverted man properly belongs to hell; that is his place; from thence he is, John viii. 23. "Ye are from beneath:" And thither he is bound; it is the place that justice, and God's word, and the sentence of his unchangeable law assign to him.

4. They are now the objects of that very same *anger* and wrath of God, that is expressed in the torments of hell. And the reason why they do not go down to hell at each moment, is not because God, in whose power they are, is not then very angry with them; as he is with many miserable creatures now tormented in hell, who there feel and bear the fierceness of his wrath. Yea, God is a great deal more angry with great numbers that are now on earth: yea, doubtless, with many that are now in this congregation, who it may be are at ease, than he is with many of those who are now in the flames of hell.

So that it is not because God is unmindful of their wickedness, and does not resent it, that he does not let loose his hand and cut them off. God is not altogether such an one as themselves, though they may imagine him to be so. The wrath of God burns against them, their damnation does not slumber; the pit is prepared, the fire is made ready, the furnace is now hot, ready to receive them; the flames do now rage and glow. The glittering sword is whet, and held over them, and the pit hath opened its mouth under them.

5. The *devil* stands ready to fall upon them, and seize them as his own, at what moment God shall permit him. They belong to him; he has their souls in his possession, and under his dominion. The scripture represents them as his goods, Luke xi. 12. The devils watch them; they are ever by them at their right hand; they stand waiting for them, like greedy hungry lions that see their prey, and expect to have it, but are for the present kept back. If God should withdraw his hand, by which they are restrained, they would in one moment fly upon their poor souls. The old serpent is gaping for them; hell opens its mouth wide to receive them; and if God should permit it, they would be hastily swallowed up and lost.

6. There are in the souls of wicked men those hellish *principles* reigning, that would presently kindle and flame out into hell fire, if it were not for God's restraints. There is laid in the very nature of carnal men, a foundation for the torments of hell. There are those corrupt principles, in reigning power in them, and in full possession of them, that are seeds of hell fire. These principles are active and powerful, exceeding violent in their nature, and if it were not for the restraining hand of God upon them, they would soon break out, they would flame out after the same manner as the same corruptions, the same enmity does in the hearts of damned souls, and would beget the same torments as they do in them. The souls of the wicked are in scripture compared to the troubled sea, Isa. lvii. 20. For the present, God restrains their wickedness by his mighty power, as he does the raging waves of the troubled sea, saying, "Hitherto shalt thou come, but no further;" but if God should withdraw that restraining power, it would soon carry all before it. Sin is the ruin and misery of the soul; it is destructive in its nature; and if God should leave it without restraint, there would need nothing else to make the soul perfectly miserable. The corruption of the heart of man is immoderate and boundless in its fury; and while wicked men live here, it is like fire pent up by God's restraints, whereas if it were let loose, it would set on fire the course of nature; and as the heart is now a sink of sin, so if sin was not restrained, it would immediately turn the soul into a fiery oven, or a furnace of fire and brimstone.

7. It is no security to wicked men for one moment, that there are no visible means of death at hand. It is no security to a natural man, that he is now in health, and that he does not see which way he should now immediately go out of the world by any accident, and that there is no visible danger in any respect in his circumstances. The manifold and continual experience of the world in all ages, shows this is no evidence, that a man is not on the very brink of eternity, and that the next step will not be into another world. The unseen, unthought-of ways and means of persons going suddenly out of the world are innumerable and inconceivable. Unconverted men walk over the pit of hell on a rotten covering, and there are innumerable places in this covering so weak that they will not bear their weight, and these places are not seen. The arrows of death fly unseen at noon-day; the sharpest sight cannot discern them. God has so many different unsearchable ways of taking wicked men out of the world and sending them to hell, that there is nothing to make it appear, that God had need to be at the expence of a miracle, or go out of the ordinary course of his providence, to destroy any wicked man, at any moment. All the means that there are of sinners going out of the world, are so in God's hands, and so universally and absolutely subject to his power and determination, that it does not depend at all the less on the mere will of God, whether sinners shall at any moment go to hell, than if means were never made use of, or at all concerned in the case.

8. Natural men's prudence and care to preserve their own lives, or the care of others to preserve them, do not secure them a moment. To this, divine providence and universal experience do also bear testimony. There is this clear evidence that men's own wisdom is no security to them from death; that if it were otherwise we should see some difference between the wise and politic men of the world, and others, with regard to their liableness to early and unexpected death: but how is it in fact? Eccles. ii. 16. "How dieth the wise man? even as the fool."

9. All wicked men's pains and *contrivance* which they use to escape hell, while they continue to reject Christ, and so remain wicked men, do not secure them from hell one moment. Almost every natural man that hears of hell, flatters himself that he shall escape it; he depends upon himself for his own security; he flatters himself in what he has done, in what he is now doing, or what he intends to do. Every one lays out matters in his own mind how he shall avoid damnation, and flatters himself that he contrives well for himself, and that his schemes will not fail. They hear indeed that there are but few

saved, and that the greater part of men that have died heretofore are gone to hell; but each one imagines that he lays out matters better for his own escape than others have done. He does not intend to come to that place of torment; he says within himself, that he intends to take effectual care, and to order matters so for himself as not to fail.

But the foolish children of men miserably delude themselves in their own schemes, and in confidence in their own strength and wisdom; they trust to nothing but a shadow. The greater part of those who heretofore have lived under the same means of grace, and are now dead, are undoubtedly gone to hell; and it was not because they were not as wise as those who are now alive: it was not because they did not lay out matters as well for themselves to secure their own escape. If we could speak with them, and inquire of them, one by one, whether they expected, when alive, and when they used to hear about hell, ever to be the subjects of that misery: we doubtless, should hear one and another reply, "No, I never intended to come here: I had laid out matters otherwise in my mind; I thought I should contrive well for myself: I thought my scheme good. I intended to take effectual care; but it came upon me unexpected; I did not look for it at that time, and in that manner; it came as a thief: Death outwitted me: God's wrath was too quick for me. Oh, my cursed foolishness! I was flattering myself, and pleasing myself with vain dreams of what I would do hereafter; and when I was saying, Peace and safety, then suddenly destruction came upon me."

10. God has laid himself under *no obligation*, by any promise to keep any natural man out of hell one moment. God certainly has made no promises either of eternal life, or of any deliverance or preservation from eternal death, but what are contained in the covenant of grace, the promises that are given in Christ, in whom all the promises are yea and amen. But surely they have no interest in the promises of the covenant of grace who are not the children of the covenant, who do not believe in any of the promises, and have no interest in the Mediator of the covenant.

So that, whatever some have imagined and pretended about promises made to natural men's earnest seeking and knocking, it is plain and manifest, that whatever pains a natural man takes in religion, whatever prayers he makes, till he believes in Christ, God is under no manner of obligation to keep him a moment from eternal destruction.

So that, thus it is that natural men are held in the hand of God, over the pit of hell; they have deserved the fiery pit, and are already sentenced to it; and God is dreadfully provoked, his anger is as great towards them as to those that are actually suffering the executions of the fierceness of his wrath in hell, and they have done nothing in the least to appease or abate that anger, neither is God in the least bound by any promise to hold them up one moment; the devil is waiting for them, hell is gaping for them, the flames gather and flash about them, and would fain lay hold on them, and swallow them up; the fire pent up in their own hearts is struggling to break out: and they have no interest in any Mediator, there are no means within reach that can be any security to them. In short, they have no refuge, nothing to take hold of; all that preserves them every moment is the mere arbitrary will, and uncovenanted, unobliged forbearance of an incensed God.

APPLICATION

The use of this awful subject may be for awakening unconverted persons in this congregation. This that you have heard is the case of every one of you that are out of Christ.—That world of misery, that lake of burning brimstone, is extended abroad under you. There is the dreadful pit of the glowing flames of the wrath of God; there is hell's wide gaping mouth open; and you have nothing to stand upon, nor any thing to take hold of; there is nothing between you and hell but the air; it is only the power and mere pleasure of God that holds you up.

You probably are not sensible of this; you find you are kept out of hell, but do not see the hand of God in it; but look at other things, as the good state of your bodily constitution, your care of your own life, and the means you use for your own preservation. But indeed these things are nothing; if God should withdraw his hand, they would avail no more to keep you from falling, than the thin air to hold up a person that is suspended in it.

Your wickedness makes you as it were heavy as lead, and to tend downwards with great weight and pressure towards hell; and if God should let you go, you would immediately sink and swiftly descend and plunge into the bottomless gulf, and your healthy constitution, and your own care and prudence, and best contrivance, and all your righteousness, would have no more influence to uphold you and keep you out of hell, than a spider's web would have to stop a fallen rock. Were it not for the sovereign pleasure of God, the earth would not bear you one moment; for you are a burden to it; the creation groans with you; the creature is made subject to the bondage of your corruption, not willingly; the sun does not willingly shine upon you to give you light to serve sin and Satan; the earth does not willingly yield her increase to satisfy your lusts; nor is it willingly a stage for your wickedness to be acted upon; the air does not willingly serve you for breath to maintain the flame of life in your vitals, while you spend your life in the service of God's enemies. God's creatures are good, and were made for men to serve God with, and do not willingly subserve to any other purpose, and groan when they are abused to purposes so directly contrary to their nature and end. And the world would spew you out, were it not for the sovereign hand of him who hath subjected it in hope. There are black clouds of God's wrath now hanging directly over your heads, full of the dreadful storm, and big with thunder; and were it not for the restraining hand of God, it would immediately burst forth upon you. The sovereign pleasure of God, for the present, stays his rough wind; otherwise it would come with fury, and your destruction would come like a whirlwind, and you would be like the chaff of the summer threshing floor.

The wrath of God is like great waters that are dammed for the present; they increase more and more, and rise higher and higher, till an outlet is given; and the longer the stream is stopped, the more rapid and mighty is its course, when once it is let loose. It is true, that judgment against your evil works has not been executed hitherto; the floods of God's vengeance have been withheld; but your guilt in the mean time is constantly increasing, and you are every day treasuring up more wrath; the waters are constantly rising, and waxing more and more mighty; and there is nothing but the mere pleasure of God, that holds the waters back, that are unwilling to be stopped, and press hard to go forward. If God should only withdraw his hand from the floodgate, it would immediately fly open, and the fiery floods of the fierceness and wrath of God, would rush forth with inconceivable fury, and would come upon you with omnipotent power; and if your strength were ten thousand times greater than it is, yea, ten thousand times greater than the strength of the stoutest, sturdiest devil in hell, it would be nothing to withstand or endure it.

The bow of God's wrath is bent, and the arrow made ready on the string, and justice bends the arrow at your heart, and strains the bow, and it is nothing but the mere pleasure of God, and that of any angry God, without any promise or obligation at all, that keeps the arrow one moment from being made drunk with your blood. Thus all you that never passed under a great change of heart, by the mighty power of the Spirit of God upon your souls; all you that were never born again, and made new creatures, and raised from being dead in sin, to a state of new, and before altogether unexperienced light and life, are in the hands of an angry God. However you may have reformed your life in many things, and may have had religious affections, and may keep up a form of religion in your families and closets, and in the house of God, it is nothing but his mere pleasure that keeps you from being this moment swallowed up in everlasting destruction. However unconvinced you may now be of the truth of what you hear, by and by you will be fully convinced of it. Those that are gone from being in the like circumstances with you, see that it was so with them; for destruction came suddenly upon most of them; when they expected nothing of it, and while they were saying, Peace and safety: now they see, that those things on which they depended for peace and safety, were nothing but thin air and empty shadows.

The God that holds you over the pit of hell, much as one holds a spider, or some loathsome insect over the fire, abhors you, and is dreadfully provoked: his wrath towards you burns like fire; he looks upon you as worthy of nothing else, but to be cast into the fire; he is of purer eyes than to bear to have you in his sight; you are ten thousand times more abominable in his eyes, than the most hateful venomous serpent is in ours. You have offended him infinitely more than ever a stubborn rebel did his prince; and yet it is nothing but his hand that holds you from falling into the fire every moment. It is to be ascribed to nothing else, that you did not go to hell the last night; that you was suffered to awake again in this world, after you closed your eyes to sleep. And there is no other reason to be given, why you have not dropped into hell since you arose in the morning, but that God's hand has held you up. There is no other reason to be given why you have not gone to hell, since you have sat here in the house of God, provoking his pure eyes by your sinful wicked manner of attending his solemn worship. Yea, there is nothing else that is to be given as a reason why you do not this very moment drop down into hell.

O sinner! Consider the fearful danger you are in: it is a great furnace of wrath, a wide and bottomless pit, full of the fire of wrath, that you are held over in the hand of that God, whose wrath is provoked and incensed as much against you, as against many of the damned in hell. You hang by a slender thread, with the flames of divine wrath flashing about it, and ready every moment to singe it, and burn it asunder; and you have no interest in any Mediator, and nothing to lay hold of to save yourself, nothing to keep off the flames of wrath, nothing of your own, nothing that you ever have done, nothing that you can do, to induce God to spare you one moment. . . .

Therefore, let every one that is out of Christ, now awake and fly from the wrath to come. The wrath of Almighty God is now undoubtedly hanging over a great part of this congregation: Let every one fly out of Sodom: "Haste and escape for your lives, look not behind you, escape to the mountain, lest you be consumed."

Francesco Petrarca

1304–1374

The father of the Renaissance, as Petrarch is often called, is best remembered today, not as the enthusiastic popularizer of the ancient classics, but as the exquisite poet of the sonnets to Laura. This irony reflects the continuous conflict in his own nature between the scholarly recluse and the graceful poet and man of the world. Petrarch's father, a political exile from Florence who settled at Avignon, intended his son for the law and was so angry to find him neglecting his legal studies at Bologna in order to read Roman literature that he summarily burned his precious books, except for a Virgil and a Cicero that Francesco begged him to spare. But he eventually abandoned the youth to his own interests, and Francesco took minor orders in the Church to gain leisure for study and literature. Yet Petrarch lived as well the fashionable life of a dandy at Avignon, which had taken on great luster as the seat of the papacy during the "Babylonian Captivity."

To this aspect of his career belongs his love for Laura, whom he first saw at the Church of St. Clara in Avignon on Good Friday, April 6, 1327. Whether or not she was that Laura de Sade, wife of a gentleman of the city, as later scholars supposed her to be, she soon became the shining center of Petrarch's love life, so that she remained the ideal source of his poetic inspiration long after her death in the plague of 1348. To her he directed the 331 poems of his *Canzoniere* in Italian, 287 of them in the sonnet form that he popularized for later poets of the Renaissance in Italy, France, England, and Spain. Rearranged in the order of their likely composition, these exquisite lyrics trace the whole progress of his passion, from his first sight of Laura to his lingering grief at her death. The various moods of the distracted lover, here frustrated by his beloved's marriage to another, are revealed through a subtle analysis of mental states. The reality and intensity of the poet's emotions are not injured by his care to preserve Laura's anonymity or by her apparent indifference to his earnest attentions.

To his worldly self belongs also his ambition for fame as an epic poet. Infatuated with the stately refinement of Cicero and Virgil, Petrarch turned from Italian to a stiff sort of Latin in his epistles to friends of his own day and Horace's and in his dull Latin epic on Scipio Africanus, entitled *Africa* (1339). In an age newly aware of the treasures of antiquity, this polished imitation of Virgil gained great fame and led to the crowning of Petrarch as supreme poet of the Christian world by the University of Paris and the Roman Senate on the Capitoline Hill on April 8, 1341. This great triumph, which appealed to his abundant vanity, marked the climax of his worldly life. Princes vied with popes for the honor of knowing him and for the favor of his Latin pen.

But even as he was winning his fame, he frequently fled from society to his secluded farm in the valley of Vaucluse, where his best works were written. The death of Laura and many of his closest friends in 1348 brought a real turning point in his career. The characteristics of the retiring scholar which his father had found in the teen-age youth led him to forsake the social and political world for study and meditation in his library. Although he performed minor diplomatic missions for the city of Milan in his later years, we think of the older Petrarch at work in his Venetian palace or on the little farm in the Euganean hills where he died. Appropriately, he was found in his library with his head at rest on an open book. Unlike some Humanists who followed him, Petrarch was not a deep thinker and made little use of the knowledge he absorbed from the ancients. But his romantic enthusiasm for their literary form and pagan ideas made him the first spokesman of their message to modern times.

Vision

When I behold this fickle trustles state
    Of vaine worlds glorie, flitting too and fro,
And mortall men tossed by troublous fate
    In restles seas of wretchedness and woe;
I wish I might this wearie life forgoe,   5
    And shortly turne unto my happie rest,
Where my free spirite might not anie moe
    Be vext with sights, that doe her peace molest,
And ye, faire ladie, in whose bounteous brest
    All heavenly grace and vertue shrinèd is,   10
When ye these rythmes doo read, and vew the rest,
    Loath this base world, and thinke of heavens blis:
And though ye be the fairest of God's creatures,
Yet thinke, that Death shall spoyle your goodly
    features.

Love's Inconsistency

I FIND no peace, and all my war is done;
    I fear and hope, I burn, and freeze like ice;
    I fly aloft, yet can I not arise;
And nought I have, and all the world I seize on,
That locks nor loseth, holdeth me in prison,   5
    And holds me not, yet can I scape no wise:
    Nor letteth me live, nor die, at my devise,
And yet of death it giveth me occasion.
Without eye I see; without tongue I plain:
    I wish to perish, yet I ask for health;   10
    I love another, and I hate myself;
I feed me in sorrow, and laugh in all my pain.
    Lo, thus displeaseth me both death and life,
    And my delight is causer of this strife.

Vision. Translated by Edmund Spenser.
1. fickle, uncertain.
Love's Inconsistency. Translated by Sir Thomas Wyatt.

Signs of Love

IF amorous faith, a heart of guileless ways,
　Soft langours, courteously controlled desire,
　And virtuous will, kindled with noble fire,
And lengthened wanderings in a lightless maze;
If thoughts, which evermore the brow displays,　5
　Or words that faint and brokenly suspire,
　Still checked with fear and shame; if hues no
　　higher
Than the pale violet hath, or love displays;
If holding some one than one's self more dear,
　If sorrowing and sighing evermore,　10
　If chewing grief, and rage, and many a cross,
If burning far away, and freezing near,
　Are signs that Love consumes me to the core,
　Yours, lady, is the fault and mine the loss.

The Beauty
and Virtue of Laura

SAY from what part of heaven 'twas Nature drew,
　From what idea, that so perfect mold
　To form such features, bidding us behold,
In charms below, what she above could do?
What fountain nymph, what dryad maid e'er threw
　Upon the wind such tresses of pure gold?　6
　What heart such numerous virtues can unfold?
Although the chiefest all my fond hopes slew.
He for celestial charms may look in vain
　Who has not seen my fair one's radiant eyes,　10
　And felt their glances pleasingly beguile.
How Love can heal his wounds, then wound again,
　He only knows who knows how sweet her sighs,
　How sweet her converse, and how sweet her
　　smile.

Wherein His Heart,
by Laura Rejected,

MUST OF A CERTAINTY
PERISH UNLESS SHE RELENT

A THOUSAND times, O my sweet warrior,
　Burning to purchase peace of those proud
　　eyes,
Have I held forth the heart your heart denies,
Which your nobility will not bend for.
And if some other lady love it more,　5
Vain is her hope and false: what you despise
I must disdain, since what you do not prize
I spurn, and what you hate cannot adore.
Exiled by me, what then if it shall find
With you no word of mercy now or later,　10
And so, when others call it, stay behind,
Afraid to go, afraid of its dear hater?
Though guilt to both of us must be assigned,
It loves you more, and thus your guilt is greater.

Wherein
He Pursues Solitude,

BUT LOVE SHADOWS
HIM EVERYWHITHER

ALONE, thought-sick, I pace where none has been
　Roaming the desert with dull steps and slow,
And still glance warily about to know
If the herd follows, if the world has seen:
How else the hoofprint of the Philistine　5
Escape, but in some cave with grief to go!
I look distraught and haggard: I must show
No one how keen Love's tooth is, O how keen!
Meseems the very mountains and the shores,
Rivers and woods must guess the secret I　10
So seek to hide from men by desert doors—
O tell me where beneath a savage sky
Is any space the foot of Love ignores,
But with Love's whisper and my soul's rings high!

Wherein
He Tells the Course

OF TRUE LOVE

IF this should not be Love, O God, what shakes
　me?
If Love it is, what strange, what rich delight!
If Love be kind, why has it fangs to bite?
If cruel, why so sweet the barb that rakes me?　4
If Love I crave, why this lament that breaks me?
If not, what tears or sighs can mend my plight?
O Death in Life, dear pain, where lies thy might
If I refuse the doom that overtakes me?
If I consent, without a cause I grieve:
So in a tempest do my fortunes heave,　10
By winds contrary and by waters tost;
So, in a stupor, like a blind man lost
In mischievous error, lured from doubt to doubt,
June freezes, January thaws me out.

Signs of Love. Translated by C. B. Cayley.
The Beauty and Virtue of Laura. Translated by John Nott.
Wherein His Heart, By Laura Rejected. . . . Translated by Joseph Auslander. Reprinted from The Sonnets of Petrarch, published by Longmans, Green and Company, Ltd., copyright 1931.

Wherein He Pursues Solitude . . . ; Wherein He Tells the Course of True Love. Translated by Joseph Auslander. Reprinted from The Sonnets of Petrarch, published by Longmans, Green and Company, Ltd., copyright 1931.

Wherein
He Envies

WHATSOEVER OF LOVELY
IN NATURE
HER PRESENCE MAKES LOVELIER

O RICH and happy flowers forever apart
 On which my pensive Lady puts her heel!
O golden acres privileged to feel
Her phrase, her footprint pressed upon your heart!
Trees silver green with April's earliest art;   5
Pale passionate violets; dark grove that can steal
Only so much of sun as may reveal
Your swarthy steeples in a radiant dart!
O comely landscape! O translucent stream
Mirroring her pure face, her intense eyes   10
And seizing all alive their bluest beam!
I envy you your crystal burglaries!
No rock, however cold, but with my theme
Shall henceforth kindle and consume in sighs!

If It Be Destined

I F it be destined that my Life, from thine
 Divided, yet with thine shall linger on
Till, in the later twilight of Decline,
 I may behold those Eyes, their luster gone;
When the gold tresses that enrich thy brow   5
 Shall all be faded into silver-gray,
From which the wreaths that well bedeck them now
 For many a Summer shall have fallen away;
Then should I dare to whisper in your ears
 The pent-up Passion of so long ago,   10
That Love which hath survived the wreck of years
 Hath little else to pray for, or bestow,
Thou wilt not to the broken heart deny
The boon of one too-late relenting Sigh.

The Death-Bed
of Laura

N o power of darkness, with ill influence, dared
 Within a space so holy to intrude,
Till Death his terrible triumph had declared.
 Then hushed was all lament, all fear subdued;
Each on those beauteous features gazed intent,   5
 And from despair was armed with fortitude.

Wherein He Envies. . . . Translated by Joseph Auslander. Reprinted from *The Sonnets of Petrarch*, published by Longmans, Green
and Company, Ltd., copyright 1931.
If It Be Destined. Translated by Edward Fitzgerald.
The Death-Bed of Laura. Translated by Lady Dacre.

As a pure flame that not by force is spent,
 But faint and fainter softly dies away
Passed gently forth in peace the soul, content;
 And as a light of clear and steady ray.   10
When fails the source from which its brightness
  flows,
 She to the last held on her wonted way.
Pale was she? no; but white as shrouding snows,
 That, when the winds are lulled, fall silently,
She seemed as one o'erwearied to repose.   15
 E'en as in balmy slumbers lapt to lie
(The spirit parted from the form below),
 In her appeared what th'unwise term to die;
And Death sate beauteous on her beauteous brow.

On the Announcement
of the Death of Laura

A LAS! that touching glance, that beauteous face!
 Alas! that dignity with sweetness fraught!
Alas! that speech which tamed the wildest
  thought!
That roused the coward, glory to embrace;
Alas! that smile which in me did encase   5
 The fatal dart, whence here I hope for naught.
Oh! hadst thou earlier our regions sought,
The world had then confessed thy sovereign grace!
In thee I breathed; life's flame was nursed by thee,
 For I was thine; and since of thee bereaved,   10
 Each other woe hath lost its venomed sting:
My soul's blest joy! when last thy voice on me
 In music fell, my heart sweet hope conceived;
 Alas! thy words have sped on zephyrs' wing!

He Thanks Her
that from Time to Time

SHE RETURNS TO CONSOLE HIM
WITH HER PRESENCE

W HEN welcome slumber locks my torpid
  frame,
 I see thy spirit in the midnight dream;
 Thine eyes that still in living lustre beam:
In all but frail mortality the same.
Ah! then, from earth and all its sorrows free,   5
 Methinks I meet thee in each former scene,
 Once the sweet shelter of a heart serene;
Now vocal only while I weep for thee.
For thee!—ah, no! From human ills secure,

On the Announcement of the Death of Laura. Translated by Susan
Wollaston.
He Thanks Her that from Time to Time. . . . Translated by Anne
Bannerman.

Thy hallowed soul exults in endless day;   10
'Tis I who linger on the toilsome way.
No balm relieves the anguish I endure,
Save the fond feeble hope that thou art near
To soothe my sufferings with an angel's tear.

Wherein
Laura Is Forever

A PRESENT APPARITION

IF the lone bird lament or the green leaves
  Shiver beneath the summer's soft caresses,
Or rapid streams flash from dark wildernesses
Churning the rock that with my sorrow grieves,
While Love his slow eternal elegy weaves,   5
Then, then I see her whom this blind earth presses!
Those eyes like wells of stars, those golden tresses,
That voice like tears, that silver breast which heaves:
"Unhappy soul, why weep? Ah why, sad lover,
Thus, thus with anguish and remorse devour   10
Your splendid manhood in its perfect flower?
Yet light and warmth its radiance recover:
Bewail me not: the brightness that seemed over
Has burst into one white perpetual hour!"

Wherein Soaring
in an Ecstasy

OF THOUGHT TO HEAVEN
HE ENCOUNTERS LAURA

AN ecstasy of thought upraised me where
  She wanders, that shall no more walk with
    me:
There!—lovelier, humbler—there, ah there I see—
I see her in the third celestial sphere!
She takes my hand and whispers, "With me here   5
Thou shalt again taste pure felicity:
For I am she that pained thee, even she
That perished in the blossom of her year.
My bliss no mortal hope has ever spanned;
Thee only I await, and that sweet veil   10
Thou didst so love, my body's golden shell."—
Why did she stop? Ah why release my hand?
Alas! Her tones, her touch beyond control
Had swept me heavenward, snatched my ravished
    soul!

The Spring Returns,

BUT NOT TO HIM RETURNS

THE spring returns, the spring wind softly blow-
    ing
Sprinkles the grass with gleam and glitter of showers,
Powdering pearl and diamond, dripping with
    flowers,
Dropping wet flowers, dancing the winter's going;
The swallow twitters, the groves of midnight are
    glowing   5
With nightingale music and madness; the sweet fierce
    powers
Of Love flame up through the earth; the seed-soul
    towers
And trembles; Nature is filled to overflowing . . .
The spring returns, but there is no returning
Of spring for me. O heart with anguish burning!   10
She that unlocked all April in a breath
Returns not . . . And these meadows, blossoms,
    birds,
These lovely gentle girls—words, empty words,
As bitter as the black estates of death!

Wherein
He Makes Confession

AND INTREATS
THE LORD'S GRACE

WEEPING, I still regret the years that went
  In empty sacrifice to mortal things;
No swooping starward, though my soul had wings
Which might have brushed Thy burning element.
O Thou, that know'st so well how I repent,   5
Sovereign of space, immortal King of Kings,
Succour the soul torn with self-torturings—
To Thee it turns: O prove Thou provident!
To my war-shattered life appoint Thou still
Death as the port of peace; and if my course   10
Was idle, let it find a quiet hill!
O for the brief remainder, let remorse
Not darken, let Thy hand the end fulfill!
Thou know'st in Thee alone rests my resource!

Wherein Laura Is Forever a Present Apparition; Wherein Soaring in an Ecstasy. . . . Translated by Joseph Auslander. From *The Sonnets of Petrarch*, published by Longmans, Green and Company, Ltd., copyright 1931.

The Spring Returns . . . ; *Wherein He Makes Confession*. . . . Translated by Joseph Auslander. Reprinted from *The Sonnets of Petrarch*, published by Longmans, Green and Company, Ltd., copyright 1931.

François Villon

1431–c.1461

Although he lived out his brief and disreputable life a full century after Petrarch and Boccaccio, Villon is as much the last voice of the French Middle Ages as he is the harbinger of the Renaissance. He was well educated but in the ecclesiastical curriculum of the conservative University of Paris, whose solemn pedantry Rabelais was to satirize a century later. Born François de Montcorbier, the future poet apparently lost his father early in life and owed his education to a kindly priest, Guillaume de Villon, whose name he took in gratitude. His mother, to whom he refers affectionately in a famous poem, was an unlettered woman who contributed nothing to his intellectual development.

François was a brilliant but reckless student, who took his bachelor's degree at eighteen and his master of arts three years later. But he always preferred the company of rogues and sharpers in the streets and taverns of Paris to the dull scholars of the university. Several of these low characters had fancy criminal records ending with the gibbet, and Villon himself narrowly escaped hanging more than once. Others were simply rollicking students who excelled in drinking, gluttony, and debauchery. Villon tells us of many mistresses of his own who must have inspired his lusty poems in praise of women. Of all these, only one, Catherine de Vaucelles, aroused anything like real love. But her mercenary nature made her indifferent to the indigent poet of the city streets, and she was apparently the cause of his downfall. A brawl with a rival for her affections ended in the death of a priest and the banishment of Villon for six months. When powerful patrons persuaded the French king to relax the sentence, Villon returned to Paris and a life of crime as one leader of a notorious gang. Burglaries committed against churches and even the university treasury led to his arrest and two sentences to death. But he avoided them both with the assistance of the new king, Louis XI, and apparently died of tuberculosis and a general physical collapse brought on by years of dissipation and eventual starvation.

Despite his short and turbulent life, Villon found time to become an exquisite poet, the supreme master of that delicate and complex French form, the ballade. The slender volume of his verses is addressed to the people of Paris in the form of two fanciful wills or *Testaments*, the *Greater* and the *Lesser*. As he makes his imaginary bequests in rhyme, he runs through all classes of the medieval city but shows more love for shifty-eyed criminals and humble chimney sweeps than for scholars and elegant nobles. Villon, the best of the vagabond poets, brings a teeming medieval metropolis to life in his graceful, melodious stanzas.

No, I Am Not As Others Are

No, I am not, as others are,
　Child of the angels, with a wreath
Of planets or of any star.
My father's dead, and lies beneath
The churchyard stone: God rest his breath!　5
I know that my poor old mother
(And she too knows) must come to death,
And that her son must follow her.

I know that rich and poor and all,
Foolish and wise, and priest and lay,　10
Mean folk and noble, great and small,
High and low, fair and foul, and they
That wore rich clothing on the way,
Being of whatever stock or stem,
And are coiffed newly every day,　15
Death shall take every one of them.

Paris and Helen are both dead.
Whoever dies, dies with much pain;
For when his wind and breath are sped
His gall breaks on his heart, and then　20
He sweats, God knows that sweat of men!
Then shall he pray against his doom
Child, brother, sister, all in vain:
None will be surety in his room.

Death makes him tremble and turn pale,　25
His veins stretch and his nose fall in,
His flesh grow moist and his neck swell,
Joints and nerves lengthen and wax thin;
Body of woman, that hath been
Soft, tender, precious, smooth and even,　30
Must thou be spoiled in bone and skin?
Yes, or else go alive to heaven.

His Mother's Service to Our Lady

Lady of Heaven and earth, and therewithal
　Crowned Empress of the nether clefts of
　　Hell,—
I, thy poor Christian, on thy name do call,
　Commending me to thee, with thee to dwell,
　Albeit in nought I be commendable.　5
But all mine undeserving may not mar
Such mercies as thy sovereign mercies are;

No, I Am Not As Others Are. Translated by Arthur Symons.
His Mother's Service To Our Lady. Translated by D. G. Rossetti.

Without the which (as true words testify)
No soul can reach thy Heaven so fair and far.
  Even in this faith I choose to live and die.   10

Unto thy Son say thou that I am His,
  And to me graceless make Him gracious.
Sad Mary of Egypt lacked not of that bliss,
  Nor yet the sorrowful clerk Theophilus,
  Whose bitter sins were set aside even thus   15
Though to the Fiend his bounden service was.
Oh help me, lest in vain for me should pass
  (Sweet Virgin that shalt have no loss thereby!)
The blessed Host and sacring of the Mass.
  Even in this faith I choose to live and die.   20

A pitiful poor woman, shrunk and old,
  I am, and nothing learn'd in letter-lore.
Within my parish-cloister I behold
  A painted Heaven where harps and lutes adore,
  And eke an Hell whose damned folk seethe full
    sore: 25
One bringeth fear, the other joy to me.
That joy, great Goddess, make thou mine to be,—
  Thou of whom all must ask it even as I;
And that which faith desires, that let it see.
  For in this faith I choose to live and die.   30

O excellent Virgin Princess! thou didst bear
King Jesus, the most excellent comforter,
Who even of this our weakness craved a share
  And for our sake stooped to us from on high,
Offering to death His young life sweet and fair.   35
Such as He is, Our Lord, I Him declare,
  And in this faith I choose to live and die.

The Ballade
of Dead Ladies

Tell me now in what hidden way is
  Lady Flora the lovely Roman?
Where's Hipparchia, and where is Thais,
  Neither of them the fairer woman?
  Where is Echo, beheld of no man,   5
Only heard on river and mere,—
  She whose beauty was more than human? . . .
But where are the snows of yester-year?

Where's Heloïse, the learned nun,
  For whose sake Abeillard, I ween,   10

14. **Theophilus,** a legendary churchman who, like Faust, sold his soul to the devil, but later did penance for thirty days and was redeemed upon the intercession of the Virgin. 19. **sacring,** the consecrated elements of the mass.
The Ballade of Dead Ladies. Translated by D. G. Rossetti.

Lost manhood and put priesthood on?
  (From Love he won such dule and teen!)
  And where, I pray you, is the Queen
Who willed that Buridan should steer
  Sewed in a sack's mouth down the Seine? . . .
But where are the snows of yester-year?   16

White Queen Blanche, like a queen of lilies,
  With a voice like any mermaidèn,—
Bertha Broadfoot, Beatrice, Alice,
  And Ermengarde the lady of Maine,—   20
  And that good Joan whom Englishmen
At Rouen doomed and burned her there,—
  Mother of God, where are they then? . . .
But where are the snows of yester-year?

Nay, never ask this week, fair lord,   25
  Where they are gone, nor yet this year,
Save with this much for an overword,—
  But where are the snows of yester-year?

Ballade
of the Women
of Paris

Albeit the Venice girls get praise
  For their sweet speech and tender air,
And though the old women have wise ways
  Of chaffering for amorous ware,
  Yet at my peril dare I swear,   5
Search Rome, where God's grace mainly tarries,
  Florence and Savoy, everywhere,
There's no good girl's lip out of Paris.

The Naples women, as folk prattle,
  Are sweetly spoken and subtle enough;   10
German girls are good at tattle,

28. It is enough to know of these ladies that they were all beautiful or otherwise wonderful, and all dead. But for the curious the following may be added (on the authority of J. U. Nicholson in his *Complete Works of François Villon*): **Flora** was the name of many Roman courtesans, here especially the first of them for whom an annual festival was established. **Hipparchia** may be the mistress of the Greek philosopher Crates. **Thais** was a mistress of Alexander the Great. **Echo** was the Greek nymph changed into an echo. **Heloïse,** daughter of Canon Fulbert, was the beloved of the medieval churchman Abelard. **Queen Marguerite** of Navarre, notorious as an adulteress, was popularly thought to have commanded the death of Jehan Buridan, a rector of the University of Paris and learned doctor. **Queen Blanche** of Castile was supposed to have enjoyed singing the songs that her lover, King Tibalt of Navarre, composed for her. **Bertha Broadfoot** was the mother of Charlemagne. **Beatrice** may be the wife of Charles de France, son of Louis VIII. **Alice** may be Alix de Champagne, wife of Louis VII. **Ermengarde** is probably the daughter of Hélie de la Fléche, Count of Maine. **Joan** is of course Joan of Arc.
Ballade of the Women of Paris. Translated by Algernon Charles Swinburne.

And Prussians make their boast thereof;
  Take Egypt for the next remove,
Or that waste land the Tartar harries,
  Spain or Greece, for the matter of love,   15
There's no good girl's lip out of Paris.

Breton and Swiss know nought of the matter,
  Gascony girls or girls of Toulouse;
Two fisherwomen with a half-hour's chatter
  Would shut them up by threes and twos;   20
  Calais, Lorraine, and all their crews,
(Names enow the mad song marries.)
  England and Picardy, search them and choose,
There's no good girl's lip out of Paris.

Prince, give praise to our French ladies   25
  For the sweet sound their speaking carries;
'Twixt Rome and Cadiz many a maid is,
  But no good girl's lip out of Paris.

The Tree
of Love

I HAVE a tree, a graft of Love,
  That in my heart has taken root;
Sad are the buds and blooms thereof,
  And bitter sorrow is its fruit;
  Yet, since it was a tender shoot,   5
So greatly hath its shadow spread,
That underneath all joy is dead,
  And all my pleasant days are flown,
Nor can I slay it, nor instead
  Plant any tree, save this alone.   10

Ah, yet, for long and long enough
  My tears were rain about its root,
And though the fruit be harsh thereof,
  I scarcely looked for better fruit
  Than this, that carefully I put   15
In garner, for the bitter bread
Whereon my weary life is fed:
  Ah, better were the soil unsown
That bears such growths; but Love instead
  Will plant no tree, but this alone.   20

Ah, would that this new spring, whereof
  The leaves and flowers flush into shoot,
I might have succor and aid of Love,
  To prune these branches at the root,
  That long have borne such bitter fruit,   25
And graft a new bough, comfortèd
With happy blossoms white and red;
  So pleasure should for pain atone,

The Tree of Love. Translated by Andrew Lang. From *The Poetical Works of Andrew Lang.* Reprinted by permission of Longmans, Green and Company, Ltd., and the representatives of the late Andrew Lang.

Nor Love slay this tree, nor instead
  Plant any tree, but this alone.   30

  L'envoy

Princes, by whom my hope is fed,
My heart thee prays in lowlihead
  To prune the ill boughs overgrown,
Nor slay Love's tree, nor plant instead
  Another tree, save this alone.

Ballade
Written
for a Bridegroom

Which Villon gave to a gentleman newly married to send to his wife whom he had won with the sword.

AT daybreak, when the falcon claps his wings,
    No whit for grief, but noble heart and
      high,
With loud glad noise he stirs himself and springs,
  And takes his meat and toward his lure draws
    nigh;
  Such good I wish you! Yea, and heartily   5
I am fired with hope of true love's meed to get;
  Know that Love writes it in his book; for why,
This is the end for which we twain are met.

Mine own heart's lady with no gainsayings
  You shall be always wholly till I die;   10
And in my right against all bitter things
  Sweet laurel with fresh rose its force shall try;
  Seeing reason wills not that I cast love by
(Nor here with reason shall I chide or fret)
  Nor cease to serve, but serve more constantly;   15
This is the end for which we twain are met.

And, which is more, when grief about me clings
  Through Fortune's fit or fume of jealousy,
Your sweet kind eye beats down her threatenings
  As wind doth smoke; such power sits in your eye.
  Thus in your field my seed of harvestry   21
Thrives, for the fruit is like me that I set;
  God bids me tend it with good husbandry;
This is the end for which we twain are met.

Princess, give ear to this my summary;   25
  That heart of mine your heart's love should forget,
Shall never be: like trust in you put I:
  This is the end for which we twain are met.

Ballade Written for a Bridegroom. Translated by Algernon Charles Swinburne. Addressed to Robert d'Estouteville, who won the hand of Ambroise de Lore at a great tournament in 1446. The French original of this poem includes the bride's name as an acrostic in the first two stanzas.

Rondel

GOOD-BY, the tears are in my eyes;
   Farewell, farewell, my prettiest;
Farewell, of women born the best;
Good-bye! the saddest of good-byes.
Farewell! with many vows and sighs   5
   My sad heart leaves you to your rest;
Farewell! the tears are in my eyes;
Farewell! from you my miseries
   Are more than now may be confessed,
   And most by thee have I been blessed,   10
Yea, and for thee have wasted sighs;
Good-bye! the last of my good-byes.

To Death, of His Lady

DEATH, of thee do I make my moan,
   Who hadst my lady away from me,
Nor wilt assuage thine enmity
Till with her life thou hast mine own;
For since that hour my strength has flown.   5
   Lo! what wrong was her life to thee,
      Death?

Two we were, and the heart was one;
   Which now being dead, dead I must be,
   Or seem alive as lifelessly   10
As in the choir the painted stone,
      Death!

Villon's Straight Tip to All Cross Coves

SUPPOSE you screeve? or go cheap-jack?
   Or fake the broads? or fig a nag?
Or thimble-rig? or knap a yack?
   Or pitch a snide? or smash a rag?
Suppose you duff? or nose and lag?   5
Or get the straight, and land your pot?

How do you melt the multy swag?
Booze and the blowens cop the lot.

Fiddle, or fence, or mace, or mack;
   Or moskeneer, or flash the drag;   10
Dead-lurk a crib, or do a crack;
   Pad with a slang, or chuck a fag;
   Bonnet, or tout, or mump and gag;
Rattle the tats, or mark the spot;
   You can not bank a single stag;   15
Booze and the blowens cop the lot.

Suppose you try a different tack,
   And on the square you flash your flag?
At penny-a-lining make your whack,
   Or with the mummers mug and gag?   20
   For nix, for nix the dibbs you bag!
At any graft, no matter what,
   Your merry goblins soon stravag:
Booze and the blowens cop the lot.

The Moral

It's up the spout and Charley Wag   25
With wipes and tickers and what not.
   Until the squeezer nips your scrag,
Booze and the blowens cop the lot.

The Dispute of the Heart and Body of François Villon

WHO is this I hear?—Lo, this is I, thine
      heart,
That holds on merely now by a slender string.
Strength fails me, shape and sense are rent apart,
   The blood in me is turned to a bitter thing,
   Seeing thee skulk here like a dog shivering.—
Yea, and for what?—For that thy sense found
      sweet.—   6
What irks it thee?—I feel the sting of it.—
   Leave me at peace.—Why?—Nay now, leave me
      at peace;
I will repent when I grow ripe in wit.—
   I say no more.—I care not though thou cease.—

What are thou, trow?—A man worth praise, per-
      fay.—   11
   This is thy thirtieth year of wayfaring.—
'Tis a mule's age.—Art thou a boy still?—Nay.—
   Is it hot lust that spurs thee with its sting,

Rondel. Translated by Andrew Lang. From *The Poetical Works of Andrew Lang.* Reprinted by permission of Longmans, Green and Company, Ltd., and the representatives of the late Andrew Lang.
To Death, of His Lady. Translated by D. G. Rossetti.
Villon's Straight Tip to All Cross Coves. Translated by W. E. Henley. Reprinted by permission of Charles Scribner's Sons. Villon's cynical advice to his underworld friends has been amusingly translated by Henley into English thieves' slang of an older day. Some of the expressions—land your pot, melt the swag, booze cops the lot—are still intelligible enough. With the others the *Oxford English Dictionary* will help those who want to know just which skin-games and crimes Villon is reviewing. But regardless of how much "dough" they may bring in, "booze and the blowens cop the lot."

The Dispute of the Heart and Body of François Villon. Translated by Algernon Charles Swinburne. Debate poems of this kind were common in medieval literature and, in the case of such works as the Middle English *Debate of the Body and Soul,* were used as vehicles for sermons on hell and damnation.

Grasping thy throat? Know'st thou not any-
    thing?—   15
Yea, black and white, when milk is specked with
    flies,
I can make out.—No more?—Nay, in no wise.
    Shall I begin again the count of these?—
Thou art undone.—I will make shift to rise.—
    I say no more.—I care not though thou cease.—

I have the sorrow of it, and thou the smart.   21
    Wert thou a poor mad fool or weak of wit,
Then might'st thou plead this pretext with thine
    heart;
    But if thou know not good from evil a whit,
    Either thy head is hard as stone to hit,   25
Or shame, not honor, gives thee most content.
What canst thou answer to this argument?—
    When I am dead I shall be well at ease.—
God! What good hope!—Thou art over eloquent.—
    I say no more.—I care not though thou cease.—

Whence is this ill?—From sorrow and not from sin.
    When Saturn packed my wallet up for me   32
I well believe he put these ills therein.—
    Fool, wilt thou make thy servant lord of thee?
    Hear now the wise king's counsel; thus saith he;
All power upon the stars a wise man hath;   36
There is no planet that shall do him scathe.—
    Nay, as they made me I grow and I decrease.—
What say'st thou?—Truly this is all my faith.—   39
    I say no more.—I care not though thou cease.—

Wouldst thou live still?—God help me that I may!—
Then thou must—What? turn penitent and gray?—
Read always—What?—Grave words and good to say;
    Leave off the ways of fools, lest they displease.—
Good; I will do it.—Wilt thou remember?—Yea.—
Abide not till there come an evil day.   46
    I say no more.—I care not though thou cease.

Epistle
in Form of a Ballade
to His Friends

Have pity, pity, friends, have pity on me,
    Thus much at least, may it please you,
    of your grace!
I lie not under hazel or hawthorn-tree
    Down in this dungeon ditch, mine exile's place
    By leave of God and fortune's foul disgrace.   5

32. **Saturn,** the Roman god honored in the Saturnalia with feasting,
drinking, and general carousal. 35. **wise king's counsel;** a reference
to Solomon.
Epistle in Form of a Ballade to His Friends. Translated by Algernon
Charles Swinburne.

Girls, lovers, glad young folk and newly wed,
Jumpers and jugglers, tumbling heel o'er head,
    Swift as a dart, and sharp as needle-ware,
Throats clear as bells that ring the kine to shed,
    Your poor old friend, what, will you leave him
    there?   10

Singers that sing at pleasure, lawlessly,
    Light, laughing, gay of word and deed, that race
And run like folk light-witted as ye be
    And have in hand nor current coin nor base,
    Ye wait too long, for now he's dying apace.   15
Rhymers of lays and roundels sung and read,
Ye'll brew him broth too late when he lies dead.
    Nor wind nor lightning, sunbeam nor fresh air,
May pierce the thick wall's bound where lies his
    bed;
    Your poor old friend, what, will you leave him
    there?   20

O noble folk, from tithes and taxes free,
    Come and behold him in this piteous case,
Ye that nor king nor emperor holds in fee,
    But only God in heaven; behold his face
    Who needs must fast, Sundays and holidays,   25
Which makes his teeth like rakes; and when he hath
    fed
With never a cake for banquet but dry bread,
    Must drench his bowels with much cold watery
    fare,
With board nor stool, but low on earth instead;
    Your poor old friend, what, will you leave him
    there?   30

Princes afore-named, old and young foresaid,
Get me the king's seal and my pardon sped,
    And hoist me in some basket up with care:
So swine will help each other ill bested,
For where one squeaks they run in heaps ahead,   35
    Your poor old friend, what, will you leave him
    there?

Ballade
of the Gibbet

An epitaph in the form of a ballad that François
Villon wrote of himself and his company, they expecting
shortly to be hanged.

Brothers and men that shall after us be,
    Let not your hearts be hard to us:
For pitying this our misery
    Ye shall find God the more piteous.

Ballade of the Gibbet. Translated by Andrew Lang. From *The Poetical
Works of Andrew Lang.* Reprinted by permission of Longmans, Green
and Company, Ltd., and the representatives of the late Andrew Lang.

Look on us six that are hanging thus, 5
And for the flesh that so much we cherished
  How it is eaten of birds and perished,
    And ashes and dust fill our bones' place,
Mock not at us that so feeble be,
  But pray God pardon us out of His grace. 10

Listen, we pray you, and look not in scorn,
  Though justly, in sooth, we are cast to die;
Ye wot no man so wise is born
  That keeps his wisdom constantly.
    Be ye then merciful, and cry 15
To Mary's Son that is piteous,
  That His mercy take no stain from us,
    Saving us out of the fiery place.
We are but dead, let no soul deny
  To pray God succor us out of His grace. 20

The rain out of heaven has washed us clean,
  The sun has scorched us black and bare,
Ravens and rooks have pecked at our eyne,
  And feathered their nests with our beards and
    hair.
    Round are we tossed, and here and there, 25
This way and that, at the wild wind's will,
  Never a moment my body is still;
    Birds they are busy about my face.
Live not as we, not fare as we fare;
  Pray God pardon us out of His grace. 30

L'envoy

Prince Jesus, Master of all, to thee
We pray Hell gain no mastery,
  That we come never anear that place;
And ye men, make no mockery,
  Pray God pardon us out of His grace.

Pierre de Ronsard

1524–1585

From Villon to Ronsard is a long step out of
the uncouth Middle Ages of France into the
elegant Renaissance. In contrast to the underworld that
Villon knew, Ronsard grew up at the court of Francis I,
where he served as page boy to the Dauphin. In later
life he was the favorite of six French kings and numbered both Elizabeth of England and Mary of Scotland
among his patrons. But deafness cut short his hope for
a diplomatic career, and he turned to scholarship and
poetry. Schooled in Greek as well as in Latin, he turned
against the medieval poetic tradition and was fired by
the urge to establish in modern France a school of poetry
equal to the ancients in genius and refinement. With
other enthusiasts among his friends he formed the circle
of seven scholar-poets called the Pleiades. These earnest
young men developed a common doctrine of art based
on imitation of the classics and slaved at writing correct
verses with almost religious zeal.

Of this group, only Ronsard revealed the genius of
a first-rate poet, and even he was hampered at first by
his subjection to ancient models. Indeed he shows the
best and worst features of the typical Renaissance poet,
who was both inspired and restrained by a worship of
antiquity. His careful but affected copies of Pindar,
Anacreon, and Horace lack personal conviction, and his
attempt in the *Franciade* (1572) to produce a classical
epic on royal demand ended in embarrassing failure.
But during the last ten years of his life Ronsard relaxed
his rigid compliance with the forms of ancients and,
enkindled by his late love for Hélène de Surgères, wrote
a series of exquisite sonnets to her, illuminated by personal feeling and a sure command of poetic language.
Although Petrarch inspired them, these melodious lyrics
express the delicate sentiments of a court poet who has
at last dared to speak for himself. His classical imitations
had a revolutionary effect on the course of French poetry, but his reputation today rests on a few lyrics in
which he told his own love story. Reworked beyond
recognition in the next generation by the ponderous clas-
sicist Malherbe, they were rediscovered in their original
form as recently as 1827 by the great critic Sainte-
Beuve.

Summer's Revel

Oh! but my mind is weary!
  Long I have conned the dreary
    Tomes of Aratus.
Surely 'tis time to play now!
Ho! to the fields away now! 5
Shall we not live to-day now?
  What though dull fools berate us!

What is the use of learning,
When it but brings new yearning
  Problems to tease us? 10
When, or at eve or morning,
Soon, but without a warning,
Pleadings and pity scorning,
  Orcus the dark shall seize us.

Corydon, lead the way, and 15
Find where good wine's to pay, and
  Cool me a flagon!
Then in vine-trellised bowers,
Bedded on thick-strewn flowers,
Hours upon idle hours 20
  Sweetly shall haste or lag on.

Summer's Revel. Translated by Curtis Hidden Page. From *Songs and
Sonnets of Pierre de Ronsard*, by Curtis Hidden Page. Reprinted by
permission of Mrs. Alice T. Loomis.
3. **Aratus** (c. 315–245 B.C.), a minor Greek poet. 14. **Orcus,** the
land of the dead.

Artichokes bring me, mellow
Apricots, melons yellow,
  Creams, and strawberries.
These have the sweetest savor   25
Eaten in forest cave, or
Lying by brooks that rave or
  Streamlet that singing tarries.

Now in my youth's fresh buoyance
Laughter shall wait on joyance,   30
  Wine shall flow fast now;
Lest, when my life grows colder,
Sickness, by age made bolder,
Say, as he taps my shoulder:
  "Come, friend—you've drunk your last now."

Fragment
of a Sonnet

Nature withheld Cassandra in the skies,
 For more adornment, a full thousand years;
She took their cream of Beauty's fairest dyes,
And shaped and tinted her above all Peers:
Meanwhile Love kept her dearly with his wings,   5
And underneath their shadow filled her eyes
With such a richness that the cloudy Kings
Of high Olympus uttered slavish sighs.
When from the Heavens I saw her first descend,
My heart took fire, and only burning pains,   10
They were my pleasures—they my Life's sad end;
Love poured her beauty into my warm veins.

Love's Charming

Maid of fifteen, in childlike beauty dight,
 Fair head with crinkled ringlets golden-
  tressed,
 Rose-petalled forehead, cheeks like amethyst,
Laughter that lifts the soul to Heaven's delight;
And neck like snow, and throat than milk more
  white,   5
 And heart full-blossomed neath a budding breast—
 Beauty divine in human form expressed,
And virtue worthy of that beauty bright—
An eye whose light can change the night to day,
 A gentle hand that smooths away my care,   10
 Yet holds my life caught in its fingers' snare;
Withal a voice that's ever fain to sing,
 Still stopped by smiles, or sweet sighs languish-
  ing—
 These are the spells that charmed my wits away.

Fragment of a Sonnet. Translated by John Keats.
Love's Charming. Translated by Curtis Hidden Page. From *Songs and Sonnets of Pierre de Ronsard*, by Curtis Hidden Page. Reprinted by permission of Mrs. Alice T. Loomis.

To His Young Mistress

Fair flower of fifteen springs, that still
 Art scarcely blossomed from the bud,
Yet hast such store of evil will,
 A heart so full of hardihood,
  Seeking to hide in friendly wise   5
  The mischief of your mocking eyes.

If you have pity, child, give o'er,
 Give back the heart you stole from me,
Pirate, setting so little store
 On this your captive from Love's sea,   10
  Holding his misery for gain,
  And making pleasure of his pain.

Another, not so fair of face,
 But far more pitiful than you,
Would take my heart, if of his grace,   15
 My heart would give her of Love's due;
  And she shall have it, since I find
  That you are cruel and unkind.

Nay, I would rather that I died,
 Within your white hands prisoning,   20
Would rather that it still abide
 In your ungentle comforting,
  Than change its faith, and seek to her
  That is more kind, but not so fair.

Even unto Death

To think one thought a hundred hundred ways,
 'Neath two loved eyes to lay your heart quite
  bare,
 To drink the bitter liquor of despair
And eat forever ashes of lost days—
In spirit and flesh to know youth's bloom decays,   5
 To die of pain, yet swear no pain is there,
 The more you sue, to move the less your fair,
Yet make her wish, the law your life obeys—
Anger that passes, faith that cannot move;
 Far dearer than yourself your foe to love;   10
 To build a thousand vain imaginings,
To long to plead, yet fear to voice a breath,
 In ruin of all hope to hope all things—
 These are the signs of love—love even to death.

To His Young Mistress. Translated by Andrew Lang. From *The Poetical Works of Andrew Lang.* Reprinted by permission of Longmans, Green and Company, Ltd., and the representatives of the late Andrew Lang.
Even unto Death. Translated by Curtis Hidden Page. From *Songs and Sonnets of Pierre de Ronsard,* by Curtis Hidden Page. Reprinted by permission of Mrs. Alice T. Loomis.

Love's Flower

TAKE thou this rose, sweet even as thou art,
  Thou rose of roses rarest, loveliest,
  Thou flower of freshest flowers, whose fragrance
    blest
Enwraps me, ravished from myself apart.
Take thou this rose, and with it take my heart,   5
  My heart that hath no wings, unto thy breast,
  So constant that its faith stands manifest,
Though wounded sore with many a cruel dart.
The rose and I are diverse in one thing:
  Each morning's rose at eve lies perishing,   10
  While countless mornings see my love new-born
But never night shall see its life decay. . . .
  Ah! would that love, new-blossomed in the morn,
  Even as a flower had lasted but a day.

Roses

I SEND you here a wreath of blossoms blown,
  And woven flowers at sunset gatherèd,
  Another dawn had seen them ruined, and shed
Loose leaves upon the grass at random strown.
By this, their sure example, be it known,   5
  That all your beauties, now in perfect flower,
  Shall fade as these, and wither in an hour.
Flower-like, and brief of days, as the flower sown.
Ah, time is flying, lady—time is flying;
  Nay, 'tis not time that flies but we that go,   10
Who in short space shall be in churchyard lying,
  And of our loving parley none shall know,
Nor any man consider what we were;
Be therefore kind, my love, whilst thou art fair.

The Rose

SEE, Mignonne, hath not the Rose,
  That this morning did unclose
Her purple mantle to the light,
Lost before the day be dead,
The glory of her raiment red,   5
  Her color, bright as yours is bright?

Ah, Mignonne, in how few hours
The petals of her purple flowers
  All have faded, fallen, died;

Sad Nature, mother ruinous,   10
That seest thy fair child perish thus
  'Twixt matin song and even-tide.

Hear me, my darling, speaking sooth,
Gather the fleet flower of your youth,
  Take ye your pleasure at the best;   15
Be merry ere your beauty flit,
For length of days will tarnish it
  Like roses that were loveliest.

The Poet's Gift

THAT century to century may tell
  The perfect love Ronsard once bore to you,
How he was reason-reft for love of you
And thought it freedom in your chains to dwell;
That age on age posterity full well   5
  May know my veins were filled with beauty of
    you
  And that my heart's one wish was only you,
I bring for gift to you this immortelle.
Long will it live in freshness of its prime.
  And you shall live, through me, long after death—
  So can the well-skilled lover conquer Time,   11
Who loving you all virtue followeth.
  Like Laura, you shall live the cynosure
  Of earth, so long as pens and books endure.

Of His Lady's Old Age

WHEN you are very old, at evening
  You'll sit and spin beside the fire, and
    say,
Humming my songs, "Ah well, ah well-a-day!
When I was young, of me did Ronsard sing."
None of your maidens that doth hear the thing,   5
  Albeit with her weary task foredone,
  But wakens at my name, and calls you one
Blest, to be held in long remembering.

I shall be low beneath the earth, and laid
On sleep, a phantom in the myrtle shade,   10
  While you beside the fire, a grandame gray;
My love, your pride, remember and regret;
Ah, love me, love! we may be happy yet,
  And gather roses, while 'tis called to-day.

Love's Flower. Translated by Curtis Hidden Page. From *Songs and Sonnets of Pierre de Ronsard*, by Curtis Hidden Page. Reprinted by permission of Mrs. Alice T. Loomis.
Roses; The Rose. Translated by Andrew Lang. From *The Poetical Works of Andrew Lang.* Reprinted by permission of Longmans, Green and Co., Ltd., and the representatives of the late Andrew Lang.

The Poet's Gift. Translated by Curtis Hidden Page. From *Songs and Sonnets of Pierre de Ronsard*, by Curtis Hidden Page. Reprinted by permission of Mrs. Alice T. Loomis.
Of His Lady's Old Age. Translated by Andrew Lang. From *The Poetical Works of Andrew Lang.* Reprinted by permission of Longmans, Green and Company, Ltd., and the representatives of the late Andrew Lang.

To His Valet

I WANT three days to read the Iliad through!
  So, Corydon, close fast my chamber door.
If anything should bother me before
I've done, I swear you'll have somewhat to rue!
No! not the servant, nor your mate, nor you   5
  Shall come to make the bed or clean the floor.
I must have three good quiet days—or four.
Then I'll make merry for a week or two.
Ah! but—if any one should come from HER,
  Admit him quickly! Be no loiterer,   10
  But come and make me brave for his receiving.
But no one else!—not friends or nearest kin!
  Though an Olympian God should seek me, leaving
His Heaven, shut fast the door! Don't let him in!

The Revenge

F AIR rebel to thyself and Time,
    Who laugh'st at all my tears,
When thou has lost thy youthful prime,
    And age his trophy rears,

Weighing thy inconsiderate pride,   5
    Thou shalt in vain accuse it:
"Why beauty am I now denied,
    Or knew not then to use it?"

Then shall I wish, ungentle Fair,
    Thou in like flames may'st burn!   10
Venus, if just, will hear my prayer,
    And I shall laugh my turn.

Deadly Kisses

A H, take these lips away; no more,
    No more such kisses give to me.
My spirit faints for joy; I see
Through mists of death the dreamy shore,
And meadows by the water-side,   5
    Where all about the Hollow Land
Fare the sweet singers that have died,
    With their lost ladies, hand in hand;
Ah, Love, how fireless are their eyes,
    How pale their lips that kiss and smile.   10
So mine must be in little while
If thou wilt kiss me in such wise.

To His Valet. Translated by Curtis Hidden Page. From *Songs and Sonnets of Pierre de Ronsard*, by Curtis Hidden Page. Reprinted by permission of Mrs. Alice T. Loomis.
The Revenge. Translated by Thomas Stanley.
Deadly Kisses. Translated by Andrew Lang. From *The Poetical Works of Andrew Lang*. Reprinted by permission of Longmans, Green and Company, Ltd., and the representatives of the late Andrew Lang.

His Lady's Death

T WAIN that were foes, while Mary lived, are fled;
    One laurel-crowned abides in heaven, and one
Beneath the earth has fared, a fallen sun,
A light of love among the loveless dead.
The first is Chastity, that vanquished   5
    The archer Love, that held joint empery
With the sweet beauty that made war on me,
When laughter of lips with laughing eyes was wed.

Their strife the Fates have closed, with stern control,
The earth holds her fair body, and her soul   10
    An angel with glad angels triumpheth;
Love has no more than he can do; desire
Is buried, and my heart a faded fire,
    And for Death's sake, I am in love with Death.

His Lady's Tomb

A s in the gardens, all through May, the rose,
    Lovely, and young, and fair apparelled,
Makes sunrise jealous of her rosy red,
When dawn upon the dew of dawning glows;
Graces and Loves within her breast repose,   5
    The woods are faint with the sweet odor shed,
    Till rains and heavy suns have smitten dead
The languid flower, and the loose leaves unclose,—

So this, the perfect beauty of our days,
When earth and heaven were vocal of her praise,   10
    The fates have slain, and her sweet soul reposes;
And tears I bring, and sighs, and on her tomb
Pour milk, and scatter buds of many a bloom,
    That dead, as living, she may be with roses.

Transit Mundus

A NOTHER Winter comes. The last comes soon, I
    know.
For six and fifty years have blanched my head with
    snow.
The time is here to say, Farewell, to love and song,
And take my leave of life's best days, for oh! how
    long! . . .   4

His Lady's Death; His Lady's Tomb. Translated by Andrew Lang. From *The Poetical Works of Andrew Lang*. Reprinted by permission of Longmans, Green and Company, Ltd., and the representatives of the late Andrew Lang.
Transit Mundus. Translated by Curtis Hidden Page. From *Songs and Sonnets of Pierre de Ronsard*, by Curtis Hidden Page. Reprinted by permission of Mrs. Alice T. Loomis. *Transit mundus* means the world passes by.

Yet I have lived. So much stands safe beyond recall.
I grudge not life its joys. I have tasted one and all,
Nor e'er refrained my hand from pleasures within
    reach,
Save but as Reason set due measure unto each.
The part assigned me I have played on this life's
    stage
In costume fitted to the times and to my age.   10

I've seen the morning dawn, and evening come
    again.
I've seen the storm, the lightning-flash, the hail, the
    rain.
Peoples I've seen, and kings!—For twenty years now
    past
I've seen each day rise upon France as though her
    last.
Wars I have seen, and strife of words, and terms of
    truce   15
First made and then unmade again, then made by
    ruse
To break and make again! . . . I've seen that neath
    the moon
All was but change and chance, and danced to
    Fortune's tune.
Though man seek Prudence out for guide, it boots
    him naught;
Fate ineluctable doth hold him chained and caught,
Bound hand and foot, in prison; and all he may pro-
    pose   21
Fortune and Fate, wisely mayhap, themselves dis-
    pose.

Full-feasted of the world, even as a wedding-guest
Goes from the banquet-hall, I go to my long rest;
As from a king's great feast, I go not with ill grace
Though after me one come, and take the abandoned
    place.

English Lyricists

The English Renaissance produced a great chorus of lyric voices extending from Wyatt and Surrey at the court of Henry VIII to Herrick and Waller well over a century later. A flood of spontaneous song characterized the writing of this long period, its plays and romances as well as its exquisite sonnet sequences. It overflows into the prose, whether in the ornate diction of Sidney's *Arcadia*, overladen with dainty figures of speech, or the simple music of the King James version of the Bible. At their best, Renaissance lyrics were written to be sung, and the lovely songs in Shakespeare's plays have inspired composers from his day to ours.

The favorite lyric form was the sonnet, introduced from Italy by Sir Thomas Wyatt around 1535; and many a poet's love affair, real or imagined, was embodied in a sonnet cycle after the manner of Petrarch, Boccaccio, and Ronsard. Sidney wrote his to Stella, Spenser to Elizabeth, Samuel Daniel to Delia, Thomas Lodge to Phyllis, Shakespeare to a mysterious youth and an equally mysterious "dark lady." Wyatt had adhered to the Italian sonnet form of Petrarch, with its sharp division between the octave (rhymed *abbaabba*) and the sestet (*cdecde,* or some variation thereof), which came to be called the Italian sonnet in English. Surrey experimented with variations of the fourteen-line stanza closer to the simplicity of English verse and developed a so-called English form (*ababcdcdefefgg*), which was later popularized by Shakespeare.

The early lyrics of the Renaissance were the work of gentleman-amateurs and circulated in manuscript among their friends, often until after the poets' deaths. Many were lost because they eluded publication, while others found their way into later anthologies, such as *Tottel's Miscellany* (1557), *The Paradise of Dainty Devices* (1576), and *England's Helicon* (1600). Even the sonnets of Shakespeare, although they were published as a separate volume in 1609, were written at least ten years before.

These Shakespearean sonnets offer a perennial enigma to literary scholars. Of the 154 in the collection, the first 126 are addressed to a young man of noble birth and great beauty in terms of idealistic affection, while the last twenty-eight are in praise of a dark-haired lady, who apparently scorned the poet's devotion. The nature of Shakespeare's attachment to the well-endowed youth has occasioned as much scholarly argument as has his identity. A cryptic dedication of the poems by the publisher to "Mr. W. H., the onlie begetter of these ensuing sonnets," has inspired attempts to identify the young man with various patrons of the poet—Henry Wriothesley, Earl of Southampton, and William, Lord Herbert, among others—but none of these theories has been generally accepted. The ordinary reader can brush aside such speculations and be happy to find in this uneven cycle some of the noblest and most musical sonnets in the language.

The graceful lyrics of Ben Jonson (1573–1637) were the least characteristic of all his many writings. This blunt, pugnacious commoner began his career as a bricklayer and common soldier in English wars on the Continent, but he improved his early schooling at Westminster by private study, until he became the most scholarly of all Elizabethan playwrights. His natural talent for the stage was obstructed by his classical theories in the heavy, stilted tragedies, *Sejanus* and *Cataline;* but in his classical comedies, such as *Volpone* and *The Alchemist,* it united with his skill in social satire to produce a brilliant and biting comedy of humors. Though the pedantic Jonson admired Shakespeare, he could never quite forgive the lack of ancient learning in his great contemporary.

Jonson outlived Shakespeare by twenty years, and during that period presided over a circle of devoted friends and disciples, who were proud to call themselves "the tribe of Ben." Their favorite haunt was the Devil Tavern, where the flow of wine and wit betrayed their devotion to the Greek Anacreon and Roman Horace. It was a Royalist stronghold on the eve of Puritan revolution, the resort of brilliant young cynics bred on the pagan philosophies of antiquity.

The finest artist in this remarkable tribe was Robert Herrick (1591–1674), the exquisite poet who carries the pagan spirit of Jonson through the seventeenth century. Yet his carefree delight in the physical world was complicated in later life by a career in the church, which actually rounded out his varied experience. Reared in the rustic setting of a charming village near London, which he often remembered in his verses, Herrick was educated at St. John's College, Cambridge, and became attached to Jonson and his classical circle in London. Failure at court led him to take orders in the Anglican Church and accept exile from city society in the provincial parish of Dean Prior. During the Puritan regime his Royalist sympathies lost him his church position, but he returned to it after the Restoration in 1662.

Herrick published only one volume of verses, the *Hesperides* (1648), which immediately followed his ejection from his church post, but contributions to other collections brought his total to about 1300 poems. Of these some are the "noble numbers" inspired by his serious life as a clergyman, but the best loved are the melodious little pastoral lyrics which praise natural, happy living in the sophisticated accents of a rollicking cavalier. Herrick is the poet of spring sunshine and May wine, of youthful love and laughter. He bids us live for today, free from care for the future, which may bring sadness and decay but is sure to bring a heaven above as rich and happy as our heaven on earth. His pagan love songs, brimful of color and spontaneous life, have the perennial charm of youth in their graceful meters.

John Donne (1573–1631) was also a preacher and poet, but his serious side won out, even in the most mundane of his love lyrics. Educated at both Oxford and Cambridge, he at first studied law and served as secretary to the Lord Keeper of the Great Seal. But dismissal from this post for an indiscretion led him to seek security in a church career. Ordained an Anglican priest in 1615, he served as dean of St. Paul's from 1621 until his death and became renowned for the most brilliant sermons of his generation.

Donne's poems belong to his youth, though they were not published until after his death. Written in a time when Petrarchian sonnets and convivial Anacreontics were all the rage, they break sharply with the graceful court fashion in their subtle, cynical reasoning and crabbed, whimsical style. Intellect in Donne has by no means submerged emotion, but it cramps and confines it and sometimes warps it into bizarre or perverse forms. His love poems are full of cutting irony; his satires are sometimes pointed and direct, sometimes complicated by odd bits of learning and excessive intellectual refinement. He deliberately tangles his ideas in obscurities and refuses to give us the melody of which he was abundantly capable. In this fondness for the unusual he predicts the so-called metaphysical poets of the seventeenth century, Herbert, Crashaw, and Vaughan, whose serious and difficult verses match subtle introspection with a taut and crotchety style. Yet Donne's intellect and individual manner have inspired a large school of poets in the twentieth century, and it is now the fashion to praise him.

WILLIAM SHAKESPEARE

from *Love's Labor's Lost*

WHEN icicles hang by the wall,
    And Dick the shepherd blows his nail,
And Tom bears logs into the hall,
    And milk comes frozen home in pail,
When blood is nipped and ways be foul,   5
Then nightly sings the staring owl,
"Tu-whit, tu-who!" A merry note,
While greasy Joan doth keel the pot.

When all aloud the wind doth blow,
    And coughing drowns the parson's saw,   10
And birds sit brooding in the snow,
    And Marian's nose looks red and raw,
When roasted crabs hiss in the bowl,
Then nightly sings the staring owl,
"Tu-whit, tu-who!" A merry note,   15
While greasy Joan doth keel the pot.

from *The Two Gentlemen of Verona*

WHO is Silvia? What is she,
    That all our swains commend her?
Holy, fair, and wise is she;
    The heaven such grace did lend her,
That she might admiréd be.   5

Is she kind as she is fair?
    For beauty lives with kindness.
Love doth to her eyes repair,
    To help him of his blindness;
And, being helped, inhabits there.   10

Then to Silvia let us sing,
    That Silvia is excelling;
She excels each mortal thing
    Upon the dull earth dwelling.
To her let us garlands bring.

Love's Labor's Lost. 2. **blows his nail,** blows on his fingers to warm them. 8. **keel,** cool by stirring to prevent its boiling over. 13. **crabs,** hot crabapples to flavor the ale.

from *The Merchant of Venice*

TELL me where is fancy bred,
 Or in the heart, or in the head?
How begot, how nourishèd?
 Reply, reply.
It is engend'red in the eyes,   5
With gazing fed; and fancy dies
In the cradle where it lies.
Let us all ring fancy's knell;
I'll begin it—Ding, dong, bell.
 Ding, dong, bell.

from *Much Ado about Nothing*

SIGH no more, ladies, sigh no more;
 Men were deceivers ever;
One foot in sea, and one on shore,
 To one thing constant never.
Then sigh not so, but let them go,   5
 And be you blithe and bonny,
Converting all your sounds of woe
 Into "Hey nonny, nonny!"

Sing no more ditties, sing no moe
 Of dumps so dull and heavy;   10
The fraud of men was ever so,
 Since summer first was leavy.
Then sigh not so, but let them go,
 And be you blithe and bonny,
Converting all your sounds of woe   15
 Into "Hey nonny, nonny!"

from *As You Like It*

UNDER the greenwood tree
 Who loves to lie with me,
And turn his merry note
Unto the sweet bird's throat,
Come hither, come hither, come hither!   5
 Here shall he see
 No enemy
But winter and rough weather.

Who doth ambition shun,
 And loves to live i' the sun,   10
Seeking the food he eats,
And pleased with what he gets,
Come hither, come hither, come hither!
 Here shall he see
 No enemy   15
But winter and rough weather.

———

It was a lover and his lass,
 With a hey, and a ho, and a hey nonino,
That o'er the green corn-field did pass
 In the spring time, the only pretty ring time,
 When birds do sing, hey ding a ding, ding!   5
 Sweet lovers love the spring.

Between the acres of the rye,
 With a hey, and a ho, and a hey nonino,
These pretty country folks would lie,
 In spring time, the only pretty ring time,   10
 When birds do sing, hey ding a ding, ding!
 Sweet lovers love the spring.

This carol they began that hour,
 With a hey, and a ho, and a hey nonino,
How that a life was but a flower   15
 In spring time, the only pretty ring time,
 When birds do sing, hey ding a ding, ding!
 Sweet lovers love the spring.

And therefore take the present time,
 With a hey, and a ho, and a hey nonino,   20
For love is crownéd with the prime
 In spring time, the only pretty ring time,
 When birds do sing, hey ding, a ding, ding!
 Sweet lovers love the spring.

———

 Blow, blow, thou winter wind,
 Thou art not so unkind
 As man's ingratitude;
 Thy tooth is not so keen,
 Because thou art not seen,   5
 Although thy breath be rude.
Heigh-ho! sing, heigh-ho! unto the green holly:
Most friendship is feigning, most loving mere folly:
 Then, heigh-ho, the holly!
 This life is most jolly.   10

 Freeze, freeze, thou bitter sky,
 That dost not bite so nigh
 As benefits forgot:
 Though thou the waters warp,
 Thy sting is not so sharp   15
 As friend remember'd not.
Heigh-ho! sing, &c.

from *Twelfth Night*

O MISTRESS mine, where are you roaming?
 O, stay and hear; your true love's coming,
 That can sing both high and low.
Trip no further, pretty sweeting,

Journey's end in lovers meeting, 5
  Every wise man's son doth know.

What is love? 'Tis not hereafter;
Present mirth hath present laughter;
  What's to come is still unsure.
In delay there lies no plenty; 10
Then come kiss me, sweet-and-twenty,
  Youth's a stuff will not endure.

from *Measure for Measure*

TAKE, oh, take those lips away,
  That so sweetly were forsworn;
And those eyes, the break of day,
  Lights that do mislead the morn.
But my kisses bring again, 5
  Bring again;
Seals of love, but sealed in vain,
  Sealed in vain.

from *Cymbeline*

HARK, hark! The lark at heaven's gate sings,
  And Phoebus 'gins arise,
His steeds to water at those springs
  On chaliced flowers that lies;
And winking Mary-buds begin 5
  To ope their golden eyes.
With every thing that pretty is,
  My lady sweet, arise!
  Arise, arise!

Fear no more the heat o' the sun,
  Nor the furious winter's rages;
Thou thy worldly task hast done,
  Home art gone, and ta'en thy wages.
Golden lads and girls all must, 5
As chimney-sweepers, come to dust.

Fear no more the frown o' the great;
  Thou art past the tyrant's stroke;
Care no more to clothe and eat;
  To thee the reed is as the oak.
The scepter, learning, physic, must 10
All follow this, and come to dust.

Fear no more the lightning-flash,
  Nor the all-dreaded thunder-stone;
Fear not slander, censure rash; 15

Cymbeline. 4. **chaliced flowers;** like cups full of dew being dried by the sun.

Thou hast finished joy and moan.
All lovers young, all lovers must
Consign to thee, and come to dust.

No exorciser harm thee!
  Nor no witchcraft charm thee! 20
Ghost unlaid forbear thee!
  Nothing ill come near thee!
Quiet consummation have;
  And renownéd be thy grave!

from *The Winter's Tale*

WHEN daffodils begin to peer,
  With hey! the doxy over the dale,
Why, then comes in the sweet o' the year;
  For the red blood reigns in the winter's pale.

The white sheet bleaching on the hedge, 5
  With hey! the sweet birds, oh, how they sing!
Doth set my pugging tooth on edge;
  For a quart of ale is a dish for a king.

The lark, that tirra-lirra chants,
  With hey! with hey! the thrush and the jay, 10
Are summer songs for me and my aunts,
  While we lie tumbling in the hay.

from *The Tempest*

FULL fathom five thy father lies:
  Of his bones are coral made;
Those are pearls that were his eyes;
  Nothing of him that doth fade,
But doth suffer a sea-change 5
Into something rich and strange.
Sea-nymphs hourly ring his knell:
Hark! now I hear them—Ding, dong, bell!

Sonnets

18

SHALL I compare thee to a summer's day?
  Thou art more lovely and more temperate:
Rough winds do shake the darling buds of May,
And summer's lease hath all too short a date:
Sometime too hot the eye of heaven shines, 5
And often is his gold complexion dimm'd;
And every fair from fair sometime declines,
By chance or nature's changing course untrimm'd;

The Winter's Tale. 2. **doxy,** prostitute. 7. **pugging tooth,** urge to thieving. 11. **aunts,** thieves' slang for prostitutes.
Sonnet 18. 7. **fair,** beautiful person. 8. **untrimm'd,** deprived of beauty.

But thy eternal summer shall not fade
Nor lose possession of that fair thou owest; 10
Nor shall Death brag thou wander'st in his shade,
When in eternal lines to time thou growest:
   So long as men can breathe or eyes can see,
   So long lives this, and this gives life to thee.

29

When, in disgrace with fortune and men's eyes,
I all alone beweep my outcast state
And trouble deaf heaven with my bootless cries
And look upon myself and curse my fate,
Wishing me like to one more rich in hope, 5
Featured like him, like him with friends possess'd,
Desiring this man's art and that man's scope,
With what I most enjoy contented least;
Yet in these thoughts myself almost despising,
Haply I think on thee, and then my state, 10
Like to the lark at break of day arising
From sullen earth, sings hymns at heaven's gate;
   For thy sweet love remember'd such wealth brings
   That then I scorn to change my state with kings.

30

When to the sessions of sweet silent thought
I summon up remembrance of things past,
I sigh the lack of many a thing I sought,
And with old woes new wail my dear time's waste:
Then can I drown an eye, unused to flow, 5
For precious friends hid in death's dateless night,
And weep afresh love's long since cancell'd woe,
And moan the expense of many a vanish'd sight:
Then can I grieve at grievances foregone,
And heavily from woe to woe tell o'er 10
The sad account of fore-bemoanèd moan,
Which I new pay as if not paid before.
   But if the while I think on thee, dear friend,
   All losses are restored and sorrows end.

33

Full many a glorious morning have I seen
Flatter the mountain-tops with sovereign eye,
Kissing with golden face the meadows green,
Gilding pale streams with heavenly alchemy;
Anon permit the basest clouds to ride 5
With ugly rack on his celestial face,
And from the forlorn world his visage hide,
Stealing unseen to west with this disgrace:
Even so my sun one early morn did shine
With all-triumphant splendor on my brow; 10
But out, alack! he was but one hour mine;
The region cloud hath mask'd him from me now.
   Yet him for this my love no whit disdaineth;
   Suns of the world may stain when heaven's sun
    staineth.

Sonnet 18. 14. this, poem.
Sonnet 33. 6. rack, high, broken clouds.

54

O, how much more doth beauty beauteous seem
By that sweet ornament which truth doth give!
The rose looks fair, but fairer we it deem
For that sweet odour which doth in it live.
The canker-blooms have full as deep a dye 5
As the perfumed tincture of the roses,
Hang on such thorns and play as wantonly
When summer's breath their masked buds discloses:
But, for their virtue only is their show,
They live unwoo'd and unrespected fade, 10
Die to themselves. Sweet roses do not so;
Of their sweet deaths are sweetest odours made:
   And so of you, beauteous and lovely youth,
   When that shall fade, my verse distills your truth.

55

Not marble, nor the gilded monuments
Of princes, shall outlive this powerful rhyme;
But you shall shine more bright in these contents
Than unswept stone besmear'd with sluttish time.
When wasteful war shall statues overturn, 5
And broils root out the work of masonry,
Nor Mars his sword nor war's quick fire shall burn
The living record of your memory.
'Gainst death and all-oblivious enmity
Shall you pace forth; your praise shall still find room
Even in the eyes of all posterity 11
That wear this world out to the ending doom.
   So, till the judgement that yourself arise,
   You live in this, and dwell in lovers' eyes.

60

Like as the waves make towards the pebbled shore,
So do our minutes hasten to their end;
Each changing place with that which goes before,
In sequent toil all forwards do contend.
Nativity, once in the main of light, 5
Crawls to maturity, wherewith being crown'd,
Crooked eclipses 'gainst his glory fight,
And Time that gave doth now his gift confound.
Time doth transfix the flourish set on youth
And delves the parallels in beauty's brow, 10
Feeds on the rarities of nature's truth,
And nothing stands but for his scythe to mow:
   And yet to times in hope my verse shall stand,
   Praising thy worth, despite his cruel hand.

64

When I have seen by Time's fell hand defaced
The rich proud cost of outworn buried age;
When sometime lofty towers I see down-razed

Sonnet 54. 5. canker-blooms, the dog rose, with color but no scent.
Sonnet 60. 5. the main of light, the sun. 10. delves the parallels, digs the furrows.

And brass eternal slave to mortal rage;
When I have seen the hungry ocean gain 5
Advantage on the kingdom of the shore,
And the firm soil win of the watery main,
Increasing store with loss and loss with store;
When I have seen such interchange of state,
Or state itself confounded to decay; 10
Ruin hath taught me thus to ruminate,
That Time will come and take my love away.
　　This thought is as a death, which cannot choose
　　But weep to have that which it fears to lose.

66

Tired with all these, for restful death I cry,
As, to behold desert a beggar born,
And needy nothing trimm'd in jollity,
And purest faith unhappily forsworn,
And gilded honour shamefully misplaced, 5
And maiden virtue rudely strumpeted,
And right perfection wrongfully disgraced,
And strength by limping sway disabled,
And art made tongue-tied by authority,
And folly, doctor-like, controlling skill, 10
And simple truth miscall'd simplicity,
And captive good attending captain ill:
　　Tired with all these, from these would I be gone,
　　Save that, to die, I leave my love alone

73

That time of year thou mayst in me behold
When yellow leaves, or none, or few, do hang
Upon those boughs which shake against the cold,
Bare ruin'd choirs, where late the sweet birds sang.
In me thou see'st the twilight of such day 5
As after sunset fadeth in the west,
Which by and by black night doth take away,
Death's second self, that seals up all in rest.
In me thou see'st the glowing of such fire
That on the ashes of his youth doth lie, 10
As the death-bed whereon it must expire,
Consumed with that which it was nourish'd by.
　　This thou perceivest, which makes thy love more
　　　　strong
　　To love that well which thou must leave ere long.

95

How sweet and lovely dost thou make the shame
Which, like a canker in the fragrant rose,
Doth spot the beauty of thy budding name!
O, in what sweets doth thou thy sins enclose!
That tongue that tells the story of thy days, 5
Making lascivious comments on thy sport,
Cannot dispraise but in a kind of praise;
Naming thy name blesses an ill report.
O, what a mansion have those vices got
Which for their habitation chose out thee, 10

Sonnet 66. 1. **these,** injustices that follow.

Where beauty's veil doth cover every blot,
And all things turn to fair that eyes can see!
　　Take heed, dear heart, of this large privilege;
　　The hardest knife ill-used doth lose his edge.

102

My love is strengthen'd, though more weak in seem-
　　ing;
I love not less, though less the show appear:
That love is merchandized whose rich esteeming
The owner's tongue doth publish everywhere.
Our love was new and then but in the spring 5
When I was wont to greet it with my lays,
As Philomel in summer's front doth sing
And stops her pipe in growth of riper days:
Not that the summer is less pleasant now
Than when her mournful hymns did hush the night,
But that wild music burthens every bough 11
And sweets grown common lose their dear delight.
　　Therefore like her I sometime hold my tongue,
　　Because I would not dull you with my song.

104

To me, fair friend, you never can be old,
For as you were when first your eye I eyed.
Such seems your beauty still. Three winters cold
Have from the forests shook three summers' pride,
Three beauteous springs to yellow autumn turn'd 5
In process of the seasons have I seen.
Three April perfumes in three hot Junes burn'd,
Since first I saw you fresh, which yet are green.
Ah! yet doth beauty, like a dial-hand,
Steal from his figure, and no pace perceived; 10
So your sweet hue, which methinks still doth stand,
Hath motion, and mine eye may be deceived:
　　For fear of which, hear this, thou age unbred;
　　Ere you were born was beauty's summer dead.

106

When in the chronicle of wasted time
I see descriptions of the fairest wights,
And beauty making beautiful old rhyme
In praise of ladies dead and lovely knights,
Then, in the blazon of sweet beauty's best, 5
Of hand, of foot, of lip, of eye, of brow,
I see their antique pen would have express'd
Even such a beauty as you master now.
So all their praises are but prophecies
Of this our time, all you prefiguring; 10
And, for they look'd but with divining eyes,
They had not skill enough your worth to sing:
　　For we, which now behold these present days,
　　Have eyes to wonder, but lack tongues to praise.

109

O, never say that I was false of heart,
Though absence seem'd my flame to qualify.

A French fifteenth-century drawing of three ladies.

As easy might I from myself depart
As from my soul, which in thy breast doth lie:
That is my home of love: if I have ranged,   5
Like him that travels, I return again,
Just to the time, not with the time exchanged,
So that myself bring water for my stain.
Never believe, though in my nature reign'd
All frailties that besiege all kinds of blood,   10
That it could so preposterously be stain'd,
To leave for nothing all thy sum of good!
    For nothing this wide universe I call,
    Save thou, my rose; in it thou art my all.

116

Let me not to the marriage of true minds
Admit impediments. Love is not love
Which alters when it alteration finds,
Or bends with the remover to remove:
O, no! it is an ever-fixéd mark   5
That looks on tempests and is never shaken;
It is the star to every wandering bark,
Whose worth's unknown, although his height be
    taken.
Love's not Time's fool, though rosy lips and cheeks
Within his bending sickle's compass come;   10
Love alters not with his brief hours and weeks,
But bears it out even to the edge of doom.
    If this be error and upon me proved,
    I never writ, nor no man ever loved.

121

'Tis better to be vile than vile esteem'd,
When not to be receives reproach of being,
And the just pleasure lost which is so deem'd
Not by our feeling but by others' seeing:
For why should others' false adulterate eyes   5
Give salutation to my sportive blood?
Or on my frailties why are frailer spies,
Which in their wills count bad what I think good?
No, I am that I am, and they that level
At my abuses reckon up their own: 10
I may be straight, though they themselves be bevel;
By their rank thoughts my deeds must not be shown;

Unless this general evil they maintain,
All men are bad, and in their badness reign.

BEN JONSON

To the Memory
of My Beloved,
Master William Shakespeare

To draw no envy, Shakespeare, on thy name,
    Am I thus ample to thy book and fame;
While I confess thy writings to be such
As neither man, nor muse, can praise too much.
'Tis true, and all men's suffrage. But these ways   5
Were not the paths I meant unto thy praise;
For silliest ignorance on these may light,
Which, when it sounds at best, but echoes right;
Or blind affection, which doth ne'er advance
The truth, but gropes, and urgeth all by chance;   10
Or crafty malice might pretend this praise,
And think to ruin, where it seemed to raise.
These are, as some infamous bawd or whore
Should praise a matron. What could hurt her more?
But thou art proof against them, and, indeed,   15
Above the ill fortune of them, or the need.
I therefore will begin. Soul of the age!
The applause, delight, the wonder of our stage!
My Shakespeare, rise! I will not lodge thee by
Chaucer, or Spenser, or bid Beaumont lie   20
A little further, to make thee a room;
Thou art a monument without a tomb,
And art alive still while thy book doth live
And we have wits to read and praise to give.
That I not mix thee so, my brain excuses,   25
I mean with great, but disproportioned Muses;
For if I thought my judgment were of years,
I should commit thee surely with thy peers,
And tell how far thou didst our Lyly outshine,
Or sporting Kyd, or Marlowe's mighty line.   30
And though thou hadst small Latin and less Greek,
From thence to honor thee, I would not seek
For names; but call forth thundering Aeschylus,
Euripides, and Sophocles to us;
Pacuvius, Accius, him of Cordova dead,   35
To life again, to hear thy buskin tread,
And shake a stage; or, when thy socks were on,

To the Memory of My Beloved, Master William Shakespeare. Prefixed to the first complete edition of Shakespeare's plays, 1623. **2. ample**, contributing something additional to. **20. Chaucer, Spenser, Beaumont,** all of whom were buried in Westminster Abbey. **30. Kyd,** Thomas Kyd (1557?–1595?), an early English playwright. **35. Pacuvius, Accius,** Roman tragedians of the second century B.C. **him of Cordova dead.** Seneca, born in Córdoba, Spain, was the classical inspiration of Elizabethan tragedy. **36. buskin.** Buskin and sock were ancient symbols of tragedy and comedy, after the footgear worn by Greek actors.

Leave thee alone for the comparison
Of all that insolent Greece or haughty Rome
Sent forth, or since did from their ashes come.   40
Triumph, my Britain, thou hast one to show
To whom all scenes of Europe homage owe.
He was not of an age, but for all time!
And all the Muses still were in their prime,
When, like Apollo, he came forth to warm   45
Our ears, or like a Mercury to charm!
Nature herself was proud of his designs
And joyed to wear the dressing of his lines!
Which were so richly spun, and woven so fit,
As, since, she will vouchsafe no other wit.   50
The merry Greek, tart Aristophanes,
Neat Terence, witty Plautus, now not please,
But antiquated and deserted lie,
As they were not of Nature's family.
Yet must I not give Nature all; thy art,   55
My gentle Shakespeare, must enjoy a part.
For though the poet's matter nature be,
His art doth give the fashion; and, that he
Who casts to write a living line, must sweat
(Such as thine are) and strike the second heat   60
Upon the Muses' anvil; turn the same
(And himself with it) that he thinks to frame,
Or, for the laurel, he may gain a scorn;
For a good poet's made, as well as born.
And such wert thou! Look how the father's face   65
Lives in his issue; even so the race
Of Shakespeare's mind and manners brightly shines
In his well turnèd, and true filèd lines;
In each of which he seems to shake a lance,
As brandished at the eyes of ignorance.   70
Sweet Swan of Avon! what a sight it were
To see thee in our waters yet appear,
And make those flights upon the banks of Thames,
That so did take Eliza, and our James!
But stay, I see thee in the hemisphere   75
Advanced, and made a constellation there!
Shine forth, thou Star of poets, and with rage
Or influence, chide or cheer the drooping stage,
Which, since thy flight from hence, hath mourned
    like night,
And despairs day, but for thy volume's light.

Song: to Celia

COME, my Celia, let us prove,
  While we may, the sports of love.
Time will not be ours forever;
He, at length, our good will sever;

Spend not then his gifts in vain.   5
Suns that set may rise again;
But if once we lose this light,
'Tis with us perpetual night.
Why should we defer our joys?
Fame and rumor are but toys.   10
Cannot we delude the eyes
Of a few poor household spies?
Or his easier ears beguile,
Thus removèd by our wile?
'Tis no sin love's fruit to steal;   15
But the sweet theft to reveal,
To be taken, to be seen,
These have crimes accounted been.

Song to Celia

DRINK to me only with thine eyes,
  And I will pledge with mine;
Or leave a kiss but in the cup,
  And I'll not look for wine.
The thirst that from the soul doth rise   5
  Doth ask a drink divine;
But might I of Jove's nectar sup,
  I would not change for thine.
I sent thee late a rosy wreath,
  Not so much honoring thee   10
As giving it a hope, that there
  It could not withered be.
But thou thereon didst only breathe,
  And sent'st it back to me;
Since when it grows, and smells, I swear,   15
  Not of itself, but thee.

Simplex Munditiis

STILL to be neat, still to be drest,
  As you were going to a feast;
Still to be powdered, still perfumed;
Lady, it is to be presumed,
Though art's hid causes are not found,   5
All is not sweet, all is not sound.

Give me a look, give me a face
That makes simplicity a grace;
Robes loosely flowing, hair as free.
Such sweet neglect more taketh me   10
Than all the adulteries of art;
They strike mine eyes, but not my heart.

69. shake a lance; pun on "shake spear." 71. Sweet Swan of Avon.
The river Avon flows through Stratford, Shakespeare's birthplace.
74. Eliza, James, Queen Elizabeth and King James I.

Song to Celia. 13. his; a reference to her husband.
Simplex Munditiis. Inspired by Horace's Ode I, 5.

Epitaph
on Elizabeth L. H.

Would'st thou hear what man can say
   In a little? Reader, stay.
Underneath this stone doth lie
As much beauty as could die,
Which in life did harbor give   5
To more virtue than doth live.

If at all she had a fault,
Leave it buried in this vault.
One name was Elizabeth,
The other, let it sleep with death!   10
Fitter, where it died, to tell,
Than that it lived at all. Farewell!

It Is Not Growing
Like a Tree

It is not growing like a tree
   In bulk, doth make men better be;
Or standing long an oak, three hundred year,
To fall a log at last, dry, bald, and sear:
   A lily of a day   5
   Is fairer far in May;
Although it fall and die that night,
It was the plant and flower of light.
In small proportions we just beauties see,
And in short measures life may perfect be.

A Song

Oh, do not wanton with those eyes,
   Lest I be sick with seeing,
Nor cast them down, but let them rise,
   Lest shame destroy their being.
O, be not angry with those fires,   5
   For then their threats will kill me;
Nor look too kind on my desires,
   For then my hopes will spill me.
O, do not steep them in my tears,
   For so will sorrow stay me;   10
Nor spread them as distract with fears—
   Mine own enough betray me.

It Is Not Growing Like a Tree. From *A Pindaric Ode on the Death of H. Morison.*

Song

Go and catch a falling star,
   Get with child a mandrake root,
Tell me where all past years are,
   Or who cleft the devil's foot;
Teach me to hear mermaids singing.   5
Or to keep off envy's stinging,
     And find
     What wind
Serves to advance an honest mind.

If thou be'st born to strange sights,   10
   Things invisible go see,
Ride ten thousand days and nights
   Till Age snow white hairs on thee;
Thou, when thou return'st, wilt tell me
All strange wonders that befell thee,   15
     And swear
     No where
Lives a woman true and fair.

If thou find'st one, let me know;
   Such a pilgrimage were sweet.   20
Yet do not; I would not go,
   Though at next door we might meet.
Though she were true when you met her,
And last till you write your letter,
     Yet she   25
     Will be
False, ere I come, to two or three.

The Ecstasy

Where, like a pillow on a bed,
   A pregnant bank swelled up, to rest
The violet's reclining head,
   Sat we two, one another's best.
Our hands were firmly cemented   5
   With a fast balm, which thence did spring,
Our eye-beams twisted, and did thread
   Our eyes, upon one double string;
So t' intergraft our hands, as yet
   Was all the means to make us one,   10
And pictures in our eyes to get
   Was all our propagation.

Song. 2. **mandrake,** an herb of southern Europe with a forked root resembling a human figure, the object of many superstitions.

As 'twixt two equal armies, fate
  Suspends uncertain victory,
Our souls (which to advance their state,   15
  Were gone out) hung 'twixt her, and me.
And whil'st our souls negotiate there,
  We like sepulchral statues lay;
All day, the same our postures were,
  And we said nothing, all the day.   20
If any, so by love refined
  That he soul's language understood,
And by good love were grown all mind,
  Within convenient distance stood,
He (though he knew not which soul spake,   25
  Because both meant, both spake the same)
Might thence a new concoction take,
  And part far purer than he came.
This Ecstasy doth unperplex
  (We said) and tell us what we love;   30
We see by this, it was not sex,
  We see, we saw not what did move:
But as all several souls contain
  Mixtures of things, they know not what,
Love, these mixed souls, doth mix again,   35
  And makes both one, each this and that.
A single violet transplant,
  The strength, the color, and the size,
(All which before was poor, and scant)
  Redoubles still, and multiplies.   40
When love, with one another so
  Interinanimates two souls,
That abler soul, which thence doth flow,
  Defects of loneliness controls.
We then, who are this new soul, know   45
  Of what we are composed, and made,
For, th' atomies of which we grow,
  Are souls, whom no change can invade.
But O alas, so long, so far
  Our bodies why do we forbear?   50
They are ours, though they are not we; we are
  The intelligences, they the sphere.
We owe them thanks, because they thus,
  Did us, to us, at first convey,
Yielded their forces, sense, to us,   55
  Nor are dross to us, but allay.
On man heaven's influence works not so,
  But that it first imprints the air,
So soul into the soul may flow,
  Though it to body first repair.   60
As our blood labors to beget
  Spirits, as like souls as it can,
Because such fingers need to knit
  That subtle knot, which makes us man:

So must pure lovers' souls descend   65
  T' affections, and to faculties,
Which sense may reach and apprehend,
  Else a great prince in prison lies.
T' our bodies turn we then, that so
  Weak men on love revealed may look;   70
Love's mysteries in souls do grow,
  But yet the body is his book.
And if some lover, such as we,
  Have heard this dialogue of one,
Let him still mark us, he shall see   75
  Small change, when we're to bodies gone.

Love's Infiniteness

IF yet I have not all thy love,
  Dear, I shall never have it all,
I cannot breathe one other sigh, to move,
Nor can intreat one other tear to fall,
And all my treasure, which should purchase thee,   5
Sighs, tears, and oaths, and letters, I have spent.
Yet no more can be due to me,
Than at the bargain made was meant;
If then thy gift of love were partial,
That some to me, some should to others fall,   10
  Dear, I shall never have thee all.

Or if then thou gavest me all,
All was but all, which thou hadst then;
But if in thy heart, since, there be or shall,
New love created be, by other men,   15
Which have their stocks entire, and can in tears,
In sighs, in oaths, and letters outbid me,
This new love may beget new fears,
For, this love was not vowed by thee;
And yet it was, thy gift being general,   20
The ground, thy heart is mine, what ever shall
  Grow there, dear; I should have it all.

Yet I would not have all yet;
He that hath all can have no more,
And since my love doth every day admit   25
New growth, thou shouldst have new rewards in
    store;
Thou canst not every day give me thy heart,
If thou canst give it, then thou never gavest it;
Love's riddles are, that though thy heart depart,
It stays at home, and thou with losing savest it;   30
But we will have a way more liberal,
Then changing hearts, to join them, so we shall
  Be one, and one another's all.

32 **We see . . . did move.** We see now that we did not see then
what moved us to love.   **33. several,** separate.   **56. allay,** alloy.

The Funeral

WHOEVER comes to shroud me, do not harm
    Nor question much
That subtle wreath of hair about mine arm;
The mystery, the sign you must not touch,
    For 'tis my outward soul,   5
Viceroy to that which, unto heav'n being gone,
    Will leave this to control
And keep these limbs, her provinces, from dissolu-
    tion.

For if the sinewy thread my brain lets fall
    Through every part   10
Can tie those parts, and make me one of all;
Those hairs, which upward grew, and strength and
    art
    Have from a better brain,
Can better do 't: except she meant that I
    By this should know my pain,   15
As prisoners then are manacled, when they're
    condemned to die.

Whate'er she meant by 't, bury it with me,
    For since I am
Love's martyr, it might breed idolatry
If into other hands these reliques came   20
    As 't was humility
To afford to it all that a soul can do,
    So 't is some bravery
That, since you would have none of me, I bury
    some of you.

Death

DEATH, be not proud, though some have called
    thee
Mighty and dreadful, for thou art not so;
For those whom thou think'st thou dost overthrow
Die not, poor Death; nor yet canst thou kill me.
From rest and sleep, which but thy picture be,   5
Much pleasure; then from thee much more must
    flow;
And soonest our best men with thee do go—
Rest of their bones and souls' delivery!
Thou'rt slave to fate, chance, kings, and desperate
    men,
And dost with poison, war, and sickness dwell;   10
And poppy or charms can make us sleep as well
And better than thy stroke. Why swell'st thou then?
One short sleep past, we wake eternally,
And Death shall be no more: Death, thou shalt die!

ROBERT HERRICK

The Argument
of His Book

I SING of brooks, of blossoms, birds, and bowers,
    Of April, May, of June and July flowers;
I sing of May-poles, hock-carts, wassails, wakes,
Of bridegrooms, brides, and of their bridal cakes;
I write of youth, of love, and have access   5
By these to sing of cleanly wantonness;
I sing of dews, of rains, and, piece by piece,
Of balm, of oil, of spice and ambergris;
I sing of times trans-shifting, and I write
How roses first came red and lilies white;   10
I write of groves, of twilight, and I sing
The Court of Mab, and of the Fairy King.
I write of hell; I sing (and ever shall)
Of heaven, and hope to have it after all.

An Ode
for Ben Jonson

AH, Ben!
    Say how or when
Shall we, thy guests,
Meet at those lyric feasts,
Made at the Sun,   5
The Dog, the Triple Tun;
Where we such clusters had,
As made us nobly wild, not mad?
And yet each verse of thine
Out-did the meat, out-did the frolic wine.   10

My Ben!
Or come again,
Or send to us
Thy wit's great overplus;
But teach us yet   15
Wisely to husband it,
Lest we that talent spend;
And having once brought to an end
That precious stock, the store
Of such a wit the world should have no more.

The Argument of His Book.   3. **hock-carts,** the last carts loaded at
the harvest home festival. **wakes,** parish festivals.
An Ode for Ben Jonson.   5–6. **the Sun, the Dog, the Triple Tun,**
three London taverns.   7. **clusters;** of grapes; hence, wine.

The Night Piece, to Julia

HER eyes the glow-worm lend thee;
    The shooting stars attend thee;
      And the elves also,
      Whose little eyes glow
Like the sparks of fire, befriend thee.   5

No will-o'-the-wisp mislight thee,
Nor snake or slow-worm bite thee;
    But on, on thy way
    Not making a stay,
Since ghosts there's none to affright thee.   10

Let not the dark thee cumber;
What though the moon does slumber?
    The stars of the night
    Will lend thee their light,
Like tapers clear without number.   15

Then, Julia, let me woo thee,
Thus, thus to come unto me;
    And when I shall meet
    Thy silv'ry feet,
My soul I'll pour into thee.

Delight in Disorder

A SWEET disorder in the dress
    Kindles in clothes a wantonness.
A lawn about the shoulders thrown
Into a fine distraction;
An erring lace, which here and there   5
Enthrals the crimson stomacher;
A cuff neglectful, and thereby
Ribbands to flow confusedly;
A winning wave, deserving note,
In the tempestuous petticoat;   10
A careless shoestring, in whose tie
I see a wild civility;—
Do more bewitch me, than when art
Is too precise in every part.

Upon Julia's Clothes

WHEN AS in silks my Julia goes,
    Then, then, methinks, how sweetly flows
The liquefaction of her clothes.

Next, when I cast mine eyes, and see
That brave vibration, each way free,   5
Oh, how that glittering taketh me!

Cherry-Ripe

CHERRY-RIPE, ripe, ripe, I cry,
    Full and fair ones; come and buy!
If so be you ask me where
They do grow, I answer, there,
Where my Julia's lips do smile;   5
There's the land, or cherry-isle,
Whose plantations fully show
All the year where cherries grow.

Upon Mistress Susanna Southwell Her Feet

HER pretty feet
    Like snails did creep
A little out, and then,
As if they playéd at bo-peep,
Did soon draw in again.   5

To Daffodils

FAIR daffodils, we weep to see
    You haste away so soon;
As yet the early-rising sun
    Has not attained his noon.
      Stay, stay   5
    Until the hasting day
      Has run
    But to the evensong;
And, having prayed together, we
    Will go with you along.   10
We have short time to stay, as you,
    We have as short a spring;
As quick a growth to meet decay,
    As you, or anything.
      We die   15
    As your hours do, and dry
      Away
    Like to the summer's rain;
Or as the pearls of morning's dew,
    Ne'er to be found again.

To the Virgins to Make Much of Time

GATHER ye rosebuds while ye may,
    Old Time is still a-flying;
And this same flower that smiles today,
    Tomorrow will be dying.

Cherry Ripe. 1. Cherry-ripe . . . ; like the cherry-seller in the London streets.

The glorious lamp of heaven, the sun,   5
   The higher he's a-getting,
The sooner will his race be run,
   And nearer he's to setting.

That age is best which is the first,
   When youth and blood are warmer;   10
But being spent, the worse and worst
   Times still succeed the former.

Then be not coy, but use your time,
   And while ye may, go marry;
For, having lost but once your prime,   15
   You may forever tarry.

To Dianeme

SWEET, be not proud of those two eyes,
   Which star-like sparkle in their skies:
Nor be you proud that you can see
All hearts your captives; yours, yet free.
Be you not proud of that rich hair,   5
Which wantons with the Love-sick air:
When as that Ruby, which you wear,
Sunk from the tip of your soft ear,
Will last to be a precious stone,
When all your world of beauty's gone.   10

To Anthea,
Who May Command Him
Anything

BID me to live, and I will live
   Thy protestant to be:
Or bid me love, and I will give
   A loving heart to thee.

A heart as soft, a heart as kind,   5
   A heart as sound and free,
As in the whole world thou canst find,
   That heart I'll give to thee.

Bid that heart stay, and it will stay,
   To honor thy decree: 10
Or bid it languish quite away,
   And 't shall do so for thee.

Bid me to weep, and I will weep,
   While I have eyes to see:
And having none, yet I will keep   15
   A heart to weep for thee.

Bid me despair, and I'll despair,
   Under that cypress tree:

Or bid me die, and I will dare
   E'en Death, to die for thee.   20

Thou art my life, my love, my heart,
   The very eyes of me:
And hast command of every part,
   To live and die for thee.

To Electra

I DARE not ask a kiss;
   I dare not beg a smile;
Lest having that, or this,
   I might grow proud the while.

No, no, the utmost share   5
   Of my desire shall be
Only to kiss that Air
   That lately kissèd thee.

To Primroses
Filled with Morning-dew

WHY do ye weep, sweet babes? can tears
     Speake grief in you,
   Who were but born
   Just as the modest morn
   Teemed her refreshing dew?   5
Alas, you have not known that shower
     That mars a flower;
     Nor felt the unkind
     Breath of a blasting wind;
   Nor are ye worn with years;   10
     Or warped, as we,
     Who think it strange to see,
Such pretty flowers, like to orphans young,
To speak by tears, before ye have a tongue.

Speak, whimpering younglings, and make known
     The reason why   16
     Ye droop and weep;
     Is it for want of sleep?
     Or childish lullaby?
Or that ye have not seen as yet   20
     The violet?
     Or brought a kiss
     From that sweetheart to this?
   No, no, this sorrow shown
     By your tears shed,   25
     Would have this lecture read,
That things of greatest, so of meanest worth,
Conceived with grief are, and with tears brought
   forth.

To Daisies,
Not to Shut So Soon

SHUT not so soon; the dull-eyed night
  Has not as yet begun
To make a seizure on the light,
  Or to seal up the sun.

No marigolds yet closéd are;   5
  No shadows great appear;
Nor doth the early shepherds' star
  Shine like a spangle here.

Stay but till my Julia close
  Her life-begetting eye;   10
And let the whole world then dispose
  Itself to live or die.

The Fairies

IF ye will with Mab find grace,
  Set each platter in his place:
Rake the fire up, and get
Water in, ere sun be set.
Wash your pails, and cleanse your dairies;   5
Sluts are loathsome to the fairies:
Sweep your house: Who doth not so,
Mab will pinch her by the toe.

The Hag

THE hag is astride
  This night for to ride,
The devil and she together;
  Through thick and through thin,
  Now out, and then in,   5
Though ne'er so foul be the weather.

  A thorn or a burr
  She takes for a spur,
With a lash of a bramble she rides now;
  Through brakes and through briars,   10
  O'er ditches and mires,
She follows the spirit that guides now.

  No beast for his food
  Dares now range the wood,
But hushed in his lair he lies lurking: 15
  While mischiefs by these,
  On land and on seas,
At noon of night are a-working.
The Hag. 18. noon of night, midnight.

The storm will arise
And trouble the skies   20
This night; and, more for the wonder,
  The ghost from the tomb
  Affrighted shall come,
Called out by the clap of the thunder.

His Prayer
for Absolution

FOR those my unbaptizéd rimes,
  Writ in my wild, unhallowed times,
For every sentence, clause, and word
That's not inlaid with thee, my Lord,
Forgive me, God, and blot each line   5
Out of my book that is not thine.
But if, 'mongst all, thou find'st here one
Worthy thy benediction,
That one of all the rest shall be
The glory of my work and me.

Litany
to the Holy Spirit

IN the hour of my distress,
  When temptations me oppress,
And when I my sins confess,
  Sweet Spirit, comfort me!

When I lie within my bed,   5
Sick in heart and sick in head,
And with doubts discomfortéd,
  Sweet Spirit, comfort me!

When the house doth sigh and weep,
And the world is drowned in sleep,   10
Yet mine eyes the watch do keep,
  Sweet Spirit, comfort me!

When the artless doctor sees
No one hope, but of his fees,
And his skill runs on the lees,   15
  Sweet Spirit, comfort me!

When his potion and his pill,
His, or none, or little skill,
Meet for nothing but to kill,
  Sweet Spirit, comfort me!   20

When the passing bell doth toll,
And the furies in a shoal
Come to fright a parting soul,
  Sweet Spirit, comfort me!

When the tapers now burn blue,
And the comforters are few,
And that number more than true,
    Sweet Spirit, comfort me!   25

When the priest his last hath prayed,
And I nod to what is said,
'Cause my speech is now decayed,   30
    Sweet Spirit, comfort me!

When, God knows, I'm tossed about
Either with despair or doubt;
Yet before the glass be out,   35
    Sweet Spirit, comfort me!

35. **the glass,** the hour-glass.

When the tempter me pursu'th
With the sins of all my youth,
And half damns me with untruth,
    Sweet Spirit, comfort me!   40

When the flames and hellish cries
Fright mine ears and fright mine eyes,
And all terrors me surprise,
    Sweet Spirit, comfort me!

When the Judgment is revealed,   45
And that opened which was sealed,
When to Thee I have appealed,
    Sweet Spirit, comfort me!

Bibliography

To this edition of *The World in Literature* an extensive bibliography has been appended for the convenience of teachers who may want to assign and students who may want to read beyond the text. The entries cover these major areas: 1) general reference works; 2) political, economic, and social history; 3) cultural history; 4) literature; 5) individual writers. The organization follows that of *The World in Literature*. Whenever possible, readily available, authoritative, and inexpensive works (many in paperback) have been listed, and occasionally outstanding historical fiction has been included.

GENERAL STUDY AIDS

HORNSTEIN, LILLIAN H., *et al.*, eds. *The Reader's Companion to World Literature*. N.Y., Mentor, 1962.

SHIPLEY, J. T., ed. *Dictionary of World Literature: Criticism, Forms, Technique*. N.Y., Philosophical Library, 1943. (Also Paterson, N.J., Littlefield Adams, 1962.)

SMITH, HORATIO, ed. *Columbia Dictionary of Modern European Literature*. N.Y., Columbia Univ. Pr., 1947.

STEINBERG, S. H., ed. *Cassell's Encyclopedia of World Literature*. 2 vols. N.Y., Funk & Wagnalls, 1954.

WELLEK, RENÉ, and AUSTIN WARREN. *Theory of Literature*. N.Y., Harcourt, 1956. (Harvest Books. An advanced study of the methodology of literary study and evaluation; contains extensive bibliographies)

WEISSTEIN, U., ed. *The Yearbook of Comparative and General Literature*. Bloomington, Indiana Univ. Pr. (formerly Univ. N. Car. Pr.), 1952-1965. (Annual volumes contain reviews and current bibliography)

ANDERSON, Q., and J. A. MAZZEO. *The Proper Study: Essays on Western Classics*. N.Y., St. Martin's Pr., 1962. (An anthology of outstanding critical essays on Homer, the Greek dramatists, Plato, Virgil, Dante, Machiavelli, Montaigne, *et al.*)

BARNES, H. E. *An Intellectual and Cultural History of the Western World*. N.Y., Random House, 1937. (Also 3 vols. N.Y., Dover, 1965.)

FLEMING, WILLIAM. *Arts and Ideas*, rev. ed. N.Y., Holt, Rinehart and Winston, 1963. (A copiously illustrated history of art, architecture, music, drama in the context of evolving culture from 5th C. B.C. Athens to 20th C.)

GUÉRARD, ALBERT. *Preface to World Literature*. N.Y., Holt, 1940.

HOPPER, V. D., and B. D. N. GREBANIER. *Bibliography of European Literature*. (Medieval through 19th C.) N.Y., Barron's, 1954.

HORTON, R. W., and V. HOPPER. *Backgrounds of European Literature*. (The Political, Social, and Intellectual Development Behind the Great Books of Western Civilization). N.Y., Appleton-Century-Crofts, 1954. (Con-tains useful bibliographies at end of major sections: Greece, Rome, Hebrews, etc.)

BOOK ONE: THE ANCIENT FOUNDATIONS

CHINA THE REMOTE

GRANET, MARCEL. *Chinese Civilization*. N.Y., Meridian, 1963. (Covers ancient period)

LIN YUTANG, ed. *The Wisdom of China and India*. N.Y., Random House, 1942. (Also Modern Library. Anthology of writings by Laotze, Chuangtse, Mencius, Motse, Confucius; also proverbs, tales, etc.)

SHAO CHANG LEE. "Chinese Literature" in Laird, *The World Through Literature*. N.Y., Appleton-Century-Crofts, 1951, 47-76.

CH'U TZ'U. *Songs of the South*, tr. David Hawkes. Boston, Beacon, 1964. (Famous 2nd C. anthology of Chinese poetry)

LIU, JAMES J. Y. *The Art of Chinese Poetry*. Chicago, Univ. of Chicago Pr., 1964.

Chinese Philosophy in Classical Times. N.Y., Everyman's Library, n.d.

FUNG YU-LAN. *The Spirit of Chinese Philosophy*. Boston, Beacon, 1963.

GRANET, MARCEL. *Festivals and Songs of Ancient China*. N.Y., Dutton, 1932.

WALEY, ARTHUR. *The Book of Songs*. Boston, Houghton, 1937.

LIN YUTANG, ed. and tr. *Translations from the Chinese*. N.Y., Meridian, 1963.

WELCH, HOLMES. *Taoism: The Parting of the Way*. Boston, Beacon, 1966.

CREEL, HERRLEE G. *Confucius and The Chinese Way*. N.Y., Harper, 1960.

CROW, CARL. *Master Kung: The Story of Confucius*. N.Y., Halcyon House, 1940.

HSU, LEONARD S. *The Political Philosophy of Confucianism*. N.Y., Dutton, 1932.

LIU, WU-CHI. *Confucius, His Life and Times*. N.Y., Philosophical Library, 1955.

—————. *A Short History of Confucian Philosophy*. N.Y., Dell, 1964.

NIVISON, DAVID S., ed. *Confucianism in Action*. Stanford, Stanford Univ. Pr., 1959. (A series of papers from 1957-1958 Conference of the Assoc. for Asian Studies)

STARR, FREDERICK. *Confucianism: Ethics, Philosophy, Religion*. N.Y., Covici, 1930.

WANG, KUNG-HSING. *The Chinese Mind*. N.Y., John Day, 1946.

WRIGHT, ARTHUR F., ed. *Confucianism and Chinese Civilization*. N.Y., Atheneum, 1964.

LAO TZU. *The Tao-te Ching* (The Way), tr. and with introd. by Wing-t'sit Chan. Indianapolis, Bobbs Libr. of Liberal Arts, 1966.

WALEY, ARTHUR. *The Poetry and Career of LiPo*. N.Y., Macmillan, 1958.

HUNG, WILLIAM. *TuFu, China's Greatest Poet*. Cambridge, Harvard Univ. Pr., 1952. (Also a supplementary vol. of notes as Vol. 2)

INDIA AND THE WORLD OF THE SPIRIT

BASHAM, A. L. *Wonder That Was India*. N.Y., Evergreen, 1965.

BHARATIYA, ITIHASA SAMITI. *History and Culture of the Indian People*. London, Allen & Unwin, 1951.

RAWLINSON, H. G. *India: A Short Cultural History*. N.Y., Praeger, 1964.

SPEAR, PERCIVAL. *History of India*. 2 vols. N.Y., Penguin, 1965.

BUCK, PHILO. "Indian Literature" in Laird, *The World Through Literature*. N.Y., Appleton-Century-Crofts, 1951, 99-134.

LIN YUTANG. *The Wisdom of China and India*. N.Y., Random House, 1942. (Also Modern Library. Includes selections from Rigveda, Upanishads, the Ramayana, Panchatantra, Buddhist writings, etc.)

BADARAYANA. *The Brahma Sutra: The Philosophy of Spiritual Life*, tr. with an introd. London, Allen & Unwin, 1960.

BARNETT, LIONEL D. *Brahma-knowledge, an outline of the philosophy of the Vedanta as set forth by the Upanishads*. London, Murray, 1920.

BLOOMFIELD, MAURICE. *The Religion of the Veda . . . from Rig-Veda to Upanishads*. N.Y., Putnam, 1908.

DEUSSEN, PAUL. *The Philosophy of the Upanishads*. Edinburgh, T. & T. Clark, 1906.

KEITH, ARTHUR B. *The Religion and Philosophy of the Veda and Upanishads*. Cambridge, Harvard Univ. Pr., 1925.

LEVY, JOHN. *The Nature of Man, According to the Vedanta*. London, Routledge, 1956.

RADHA-KRISHNAN, S. *Indian Philosophy*. 2 vols. N.Y., Macmillan, 1958.

The Ramayana and The Mahabharata, condensed into English verse. N.Y., Everyman's Library, 1911.

MEYER, JOHANN J. *Sexual Life in Ancient India*. N.Y., Dutton, 1930. (Based on Mahabharata and Ramayana)

RADHA-KRISHNAN, S. *Indian Philosophy*, 2nd ed. N.Y., Macmillan, 1929, I:478-509 (on Mahabharata); I:510-580 (on the Gita).

SHARMA, RAM KARAN. *Elements of Poetry in the Mahabharata*. Berkeley, Univ. of Calif. Pr., 1964.

GHOSE, AUROBINDO. *Essays on the Gita*. N.Y., Dutton, 1953.

HARRIS, M. B. *Kalidasa: Poet of Nature*. Boston, Meador Pr., 1936.

RYDER, ARTHUR W., tr. *The Panchatantra*. Chicago, Univ. of Chicago Pr., 1965. (Tales from Sanskrit in the great tradition of the *1001 Nights, Decameron, Canterbury Tales*)

THE HEBREWS AND THEIR GOD

DRIVER, S. R. *An Introduction to the Literature of the Old Testament*. N.Y., Meridian, 1964.

OESTERLEY, W. O. E., and T. H. ROBINSON. *An Introduction to the Books of the Old Testament*. N.Y., Meridian, 1963.

ST. AUGUSTINE. *On the Psalms*. 2 vols. Westminster, Ind., Newman Pr., 1960-1961.

BRIGGS, C. A. *A Critical and Exegetical Commentary on the Book of Psalms*. 2 vols. N.Y., Scribner's, 1917.

JAMES, FLEMING. *Thirty Psalmists, a study in the personalities of the psalter. . .* N.Y., Putnam, 1938. (Bohlen Lecture for 1936)

LEWIS, C. S. *Reflections on the Psalms*. London, G. Bles, 1958.

MOWINCKEL, SIGMUND O. P. *The Psalms in Israel's Worship*. 2 vols. Oxford, Blackwell, 1962.

MERTON, THOMAS. *Bread in the Wilderness*. N.Y., New Directions, 1953.

SCOTT, R. B. Y., tr. *Proverbs (and) Ecclesiastes: introd., transl., and notes*. Garden City, Anchor, 1965.

JONES, EDGAR DEW. *Proverbs and Ecclesiastes: introd. and commentary*. N.Y., Macmillan, 1961.

TOY, CRAWFORD H. *A Critical and Exegetical Commentary on the Book of Proverbs*. N.Y., Scribner's, 1916.

BARTON, GEORGE A. *A Critical and Exegetical Commentary on the Book of Ecclesiastes*. N.Y., Scribner's, 1909.

GORDIS, ROBERT. *The Song of Songs: a study, modern transl., and commentary*. N.Y., Jewish Theological Seminary, 1961.

ORIGENES (ST. ORIGEN). *The Song of Songs: Commentary and homilies, transl. and annotated*. Westminster, Ind., Newman Pr., 1957.

MYERS, JACOB MARTIN. *The Linguistic and Literary Form of the Book of Ruth*. Leiden, E. J. Brill, 1955.

GREECE AND THE BIRTH OF THE WEST

History

BAIKIE, JAMES. *Sea Kings of Crete*, 4th ed. London, Black, 1926.

BOTSFORD, G. W., and C. A. ROBINSON. *Hellenic History*, 4th ed. N.Y., Macmillan, 1956.

BREASTED, J. H. *Ancient Times*, 2nd ed. N.Y., Ginn, 1935. (Extensive bibliography)

BURN, A. R. *Pericles and Athens*. N.Y., Macmillan, 1949.

————. *Persia and the Greeks*. N.Y., St. Martin's Pr., 1962.

BURY, J. B. *The Ancient Greek Historians*. N.Y., Macmillan, 1909.

————. *A History of Greece*. N.Y., Modern Library, 1937.

BURY, J. B., *et al. The Cambridge Ancient History*. Vols. IV-VI. N.Y., Macmillan, 1926-1928.

FORSDYKE, JOHN. *Greece Before Homer*. N.Y., Norton, 1964.

HAMMOND, N. G. L. *A History of Greece to 322 B.C.* N.Y., Oxford Univ. Pr., 1959.

HERODOTUS. *The Persian Wars*. Vol. I of *The Greek Historians*. N.Y., Random House, 1942.

HUTCHINSON, R. W. *Prehistoric Crete*. Baltimore, Penguin, n.d.

JOHNSON, A. C., *et al*. *The Greek Political Experience*. Princeton, Princeton Univ. Pr., 1941.

ROBINSON, C. E. *Hellas: A Short History of Ancient Greece*. Boston, Beacon, n.d.

ROSTOVTZEFF, M. *Greece*. N.Y., Oxford Univ. Pr., 1963.

STARR, CHESTER G. *A History of the Ancient World*. N.Y., Oxford Univ. Pr., 1965. (With extensive bibliographical essays)

STOBART, J. C. *Glory That Was Greece*. N.Y., Everyman's Library, n.d.

THOMSON, GEORGE. *Studies in Ancient Greek Society: The Prehistoric Aegean*. N.Y., Citadel Pr., 1965.

THUCYDIDES. *The Peloponnesian War*. N.Y., Penguin, 1961.

WEBSTER, T. B. L. *From Mycenae to Homer*. N.Y., Norton, 1964.

ZIMMERN, ALFRED E. *The Greek Commonwealth: Politics and Economics in 5th Century Athens*, 5th ed. Oxford, Oxford Univ. Pr., 1931. (Also Galaxy Books)

Culture

AUDEN, W. H., ed. *The Portable Greek Reader*. N.Y., Viking, 1948. (Anthology of the whole spectrum of Greek culture)

BOARDMAN, JOHN. *The Greeks Overseas*. Baltimore, Pelican, 1965. (Artisans, traders, and travelers in the ancient world)

BONNARD, ANDRÉ. *Greek Civilization*. 3 vols. N.Y., Macmillan, 1957-1963.

BOWRA, C. M. *Classical Greece*. N.Y., Time Inc., 1965. (Great Ages of Man Series. Copiously illustrated.)

—————. *The Greek Experience*. N.Y., World, 1957.

—————. *The Greeks*. N.Y., Penguin, 1962.

COULANGES, FUSTEL DE. *The Ancient City. . . the religious and civil institutions of ancient Greece and Rome*. N.Y., Anchor, 1956.

DICKINSON, G. LOWES. *The Greek View of Life*. Ann Arbor, Univ. of Mich. Pr., 1965.

DURANT, WILL. *The Life of Greece*. N.Y., Simon & Schuster, 1939.

GARDINER, E. N. *Athletics of the Ancient World*. N.Y., Oxford Univ. Pr., 1930.

GREENE, W. C. *Moira: Fate, Good, and Evil in Greek Thought*. Cambridge, Harvard Univ. Pr., 1944. (Also Harper Torch)

HALE, W. H., *et al*. *The Horizon Book of Ancient Greece*. N.Y., Amer. Heritage, 1965. (Copiously illustrated chapters on all aspects of Greek life)

HAMILTON, EDITH. *The Greek Way to Western Civilization*. N.Y., Mentor, 1948.

JAEGER, WERNER. *Paideia; The Ideals of Greek Culture*. 3 vols. N.Y., Oxford Univ. Pr., 1939.

JONES, A. H. M. *Athenian Democracy*. Oxford, Clarendon, 1957.

KERENYI, C. *Heroes of the Greeks*. N.Y., Everyman's Library, n.d.

QUENNELL, MARJORIE and C. H. B. *Everyday Things in Ancient Greece*. N.Y., Putnam, 1954.

RENAULT, MARY. *The King Must Die*. N.Y., Pantheon, 1958.

—————. *The Bull from the Sea*. N.Y., Pantheon, 1962. (Superb archaeological novels on the life and times of Theseus in Crete, Athens, etc.)

SAMBURSKY, S. *Physical World of the Greeks*. N.Y. Collier, 1965.

WINDELBAND, W. *History of Philosophy*. Vol. I: Greek, Roman, Medieval. N.Y., Harper Torch, n.d.

BERVE, HELMUT, *et al*. *Greek Temples, Theatres and Shrines*. N.Y., Abrams, 1962.

DINSMOOR, WILLIAM B. *The Architecture of Ancient Greece*. London, Batsford, 1950.

LAWRENCE, A. W. *Greek Architecture*. N.Y., Penguin, 1957.

LULLIES, R., and MAX HIRMER. *Greek Sculpture*. N.Y., Abrams, 1960.

RICHTER, GISELA. *Handbook of Greek Art*. N.Y., Phaidon, 1960.

ROBERTSON, D. S. *A Handbook of Greek and Roman Architecture*. Cambridge, Cambridge Univ. Pr., 1959.

ROBERTSON, MARTIN. *Greek Painting* (Skira). N.Y., World, 1959.

SCHODER, R. V. *Masterpieces of Greek Art*. N.Y., N.Y. Graphic Soc., 1960.

SCRANTON, R. L. *Greek Architecture*. N.Y., Braziller, 1965. (Paperback)

SELTMAN, CHARLES. *Approach to Greek Art*. N.Y., Everyman's Library, n.d. (Over 200 illustrations)

COHEN, M. R., and I. E. DRABKIN. *A Source Book in Greek Science*. Cambridge, Harvard Univ. Pr., 1959.

FARRINGTON, BENJAMIN. *Greek Science*. N.Y., Penguin, 1965.

TAYLOR, H. O. *Greek Biology and Medicine*. N.Y., Cooper Sq. Pub., 1963.

GRANT, MICHAEL. *Myths of the Greeks and Romans*. N.Y., Meridian, 1964.

GRAVES, ROBERT. *The Greek Myths*. 2 vols. Baltimore, Penguin, n.d.

GUTHRIE, W. K. C. *The Greeks and Their Gods*. Boston, Beacon, 1955.

HARRISON, JANE ELLEN. *Prolegomena to the Study of Greek Religion*. N.Y., Meridian, 1964.

—————. *Themis: A study of the social origins of Greek religion*. N.Y., Meridian, 1965.

LAROUSSE *Encyclopedia of Mythology*. N.Y., Putnam, 1959.

NILSSON, M. P. *A History of Greek Religion*, 2nd ed. Oxford, Clarendon, 1949.

—————. *Mycenaean Origins of Greek Mythology*. N.Y., Norton, 1965.

OTTO, WALTER F. *The Homeric Gods*, tr. M. Hadas. Boston, Beacon, n.d. (A masterful study)

ROSE, H. J. *Gods and Heroes of the Greeks*. N.Y., Meridian, 1963.

SEYFFERT, OSKAR. *Dictionary of Classical Antiquities.* N.Y., Meridian, 1956.

ARMSTRONG, A. H. *An Introduction to Ancient Philosophy.* Boston, Beacon, 1964.

BAILEY, CYRIL. *The Greek Atomists and Epicurus.* Oxford, Clarendon, 1928.

BARKER, ERNEST. *Greek Political Theory,* 2nd ed. London, Methuen, 1925.

BURNET, JOHN. *Early Greek Philosophy,* 4th ed. N.Y., Meridian, 1963.

CORNFORD, F. M. *From Religion to Philosophy. A study in the origins of Western speculation.* N.Y., Harper Torch, n.d.

——————. *Principium Sapientiae: a study of the origins of Greek philosophical thought.* N.Y., Harper Torch, n.d.

FREEMAN, K. *The Pre-Socratic Philosophers.* Oxford, Clarendon, 1946.

GUTHRIE, W. K. C. *Greek Philosophers from Thales to Aristotle.* N.Y., Harper Torch, n.d.

NIETZSCHE, F. *Philosophy of the Tragic Age of the Greeks.* Chicago, Regnery (Gateway), n.d.

ROBIN, LEON. *Greek Thought and the Origins of the Scientific Spirit.* N.Y., Knopf, 1928.

SCOON, R. M. *Greek Philosophy Before Plato.* Princeton, Princeton Univ. Pr., 1928.

ZELLER, EDUARD. *Outlines of the History of Greek Philosophy.* N.Y., Meridian, 1955.

Literature

ATKINS, J. W. H. *Literary Criticism in Antiquity.* Cambridge, Cambridge Univ. Pr., 1934.

BOWRA, C. M. *Ancient Greek Literature.* N.Y., Oxford Galaxy, 1960.

——————. *Landmarks in Greek Literature.* N.Y., World, 1965. (Descriptive and critical history with bibliographies)

CROISET, ALFRED and MAURICE. *Histoire de la Littérature Grecque,* 3rd ed. Paris, 1910. (Standard) English tr., N.Y., Macmillan, n.d.

HADAS, MOSES. *A History of Greek Literature.* N.Y., Columbia Univ. Pr., 1950.

HARVEY, PAUL. *The Oxford Companion to Classical Literature.* Oxford, Clarendon, 1937.

HIGHET, GILBERT. *The Classical Tradition: Greek and Roman Influence on Western Literature.* N.Y., Oxford Univ. Pr., 1949.

LUCAS, F. L. *Greek Poetry for Everyman.* N.Y., Macmillan, n.d.

OATES, W. J., and C. F. MURPHY. *Greek Literature in Translation.* N.Y., Longmans, 1945.

REINHOLD, MEYER. *Essentials of Greek and Roman Classics.* Great Neck, N.Y., Barron's, 1949. (Contains critical analyses and extensive bibliographies)

ROSE, H. J. *A Handbook of Greek Literature from Homer to. . .Lucian.* London, Methuen, 1934. (Also Everyman's Library)

SINCLAIR, T. A. *History of Classical Greek Literature: Homer to Aristotle.* N.Y., Collier, 1965.

THOMSON, J. A. K. *The Greek Tradition.* London, Allen & Unwin, 1915.

ANDERSON, M. J., ed. *Classical Drama and Its Influence: A Festschrift . . . to Prof. H. D. F. Kitto.* N.Y., Barnes & Noble, 1965.

BIEBER, MARGARETE. *The History of the Greek and Roman Theatre.* Princeton, Princeton Univ. Pr., 1961.

FLICKINGER, ROY C. *The Greek Theatre and Its Drama.* Chicago, Univ. of Chicago Pr., 1960.

GRENE, DAVID, and RICHMOND LATTIMORE. *The Complete Greek Tragedies.* Chicago, Univ. of Chicago Pr., 1958.

HARSH, P. W. *A Handbook of Classical Drama.* Stanford, Stanford Univ. Pr., 1944.

KITTO, H. D. F. *Greek Tragedy: A Literary Study.* N.Y., Anchor, 1954.

LATTIMORE, RICHMOND. *The Poetry of Greek Tragedy.* Baltimore, Johns Hopkins, 1958.

NORWOOD, GILBERT. *Greek Comedy.* N.Y., Hill & Wang, 1963.

——————. *Greek Tragedy.* N.Y., Hill & Wang, 1960.

OATES, W. J., and EUGENE O'NEILL, JR. *The Complete Greek Drama.* 2 vols. N.Y., Random House, 1938.

PAGE, D. L. *A New Chapter in the History of Greek Tragedy.* Cambridge, Harvard Univ. Pr., 1951.

PICKARD-CAMBRIDGE, A. W. *Dithyramb, Tragedy, and Comedy.* N.Y., Oxford Univ. Pr., 1927.

——————. *The Theatre of Dionysus in Athens.* N.Y., Oxford Univ. Pr., 1946.

WEBSTER, THOMAS B. L. *Greek Theatre Production.* London, Methuen, 1956.

Writers

AUERBACH, ERICH. "Odysseus's Scar" in *The Proper Study: Essays on Western Classics.* N.Y., St. Martin's Pr., 1962, 30-50.

BASSETT, SAMUEL E. *The Poetry of Homer.* Berkeley, Univ. of Calif. Pr., 1938.

BOWRA, C. M. *Tradition and Design in the Iliad.* Oxford, Clarendon, 1930.

CARPENTER, M. RHYS. *Folk Tale, Fiction, and Saga in the Homeric Epics.* Berkeley, Univ. of Calif. Pr., 1946.

FINLEY, J. H., JR. *The World of Odysseus.* N.Y., Viking, 1962.

KIRK, C. *The Homeric Poems as History.* Cambridge, Cambridge Univ. Pr., 1963.

MURRAY, GILBERT. *Rise of the Greek Epic.* N.Y., Oxford Galaxy, 1960.

PAGE, DENYS L. *History of the Homeric Iliad.* Berkeley, Univ. of Calif. Pr., 1964.

ROUSE, W. H. D. *Homer.* London, Nelson, 1939.

SCOTT, JOHN A. *Homer and His Influence.* N.Y., Cooper Sq. Pub., 1964.

——————. *The Unity of Homer.* Berkeley, Univ. of Calif. Pr., 1921.

STEINER and FAGLES, eds. *Homer: a collection of critical essays.* Englewood Cliffs, N.J., Prentice, 1964.

TAYLOR, CHARLES H., ed. *Essays on the Odyssey: selected modern criticism.* Bloomington, Indiana Univ. Pr., 1964. (Midland Books)

VAN DOREN, MARK. *The Noble Voice.* N.Y., Holt, 1946. (Contains two outstanding essays on Homer's *Odyssey* and *Iliad*)

WEIL, SIMONE. "The Iliad or the Poem of Force" in *The Proper Study: Essays on Western Classics.* N.Y., St. Martin's Pr., 1962, 3-29.

WHITMAN, CEDRIC H. *Homer and the Heroic Tradition.* N.Y., Norton, 1965.

FINLEY, J. H., JR. *Pindar and Aeschylus.* Cambridge, Harvard Univ. Pr., 1955.

LATTIMORE, RICHMOND. "Introduction to the Orestia" in *The Complete Greek Tragedies.* Chicago, Univ. of Chicago Pr., 1953. (Also reprinted in Anderson and Mazzeo, *The Proper Study*, 51-77)

MURRAY, GILBERT. *Aeschylus, Creator of Tragedy.* N.Y., Oxford Univ. Pr., 1940.

OWEN, E. T. *The Harmony of Aeschylus.* Toronto, Univ. of Toronto Pr., 1952.

SHEPPARD, J. T. *Aeschylus and Sophocles: their work and influence,* 2nd ed. N.Y., Longmans, 1946. N.Y., Cooper Sq. Pub., 1965.

THOMSON, G. D. *Aeschylus and Athens: a study of the social origins of drama.* London, Lawrence & Wishart, 1941.

ADAMS, S. M. *Sophocles the Playwright.* Toronto, Univ. of Toronto Pr., 1957.

BOWRA, C. M. *Sophoclean Tragedy.* N.Y., Oxford Univ. Pr., 1944.

COOK, ALBERT. *Oedipus Rex: a mirror for Greek drama.* Belmont, Calif., Wadsworth, 1965. (Text, criticism from Aristotle to present, chapters on the Greek theatre, the myth, and the play)

EHRENBERG, V. *Sophocles and Pericles.* Oxford, Clarendon, 1954.

KIRKWOOD, G. M. *A Study of Sophoclean Drama.* Ithaca, Cornell Univ. Pr., 1958.

KNOX, B. M. W. *Oedipus at Thebes.* New Haven, Yale Univ. Pr., 1957.

LUCAS, D. W. *The Greek Tragic Poets.* N.Y., Norton, 1965.

SHEPPARD, J. T. *Aeschylus and Sophocles: their work and influence.* N.Y., Cooper Sq. Pub., 1965.

WHITMAN, C. *Sophocles: a study of heroic humanism.* Cambridge, Harvard Univ. Pr., 1951.

WOODARD, J., ed. *Sophocles: a collection of critical essays.* Englewood Cliffs, N.J., Prentice, 1966.

GREENWOOD, L. H. G. *Aspects of Euripidean Tragedy.* Cambridge, Harvard Univ. Pr., 1953.

GRUBE, G. M. A. *The Drama of Euripides.* London, Methuen, 1941.

KITTO, H. D. F. *Greek Tragedy.* N.Y., Anchor, 1954. (Four chapters on Euripides)

LUCAS, F. L. *Euripides and His Influence.* Boston, Marshall Jones, 1928. N.Y., Cooper Sq. Pub., 1963.

MURRAY, GILBERT. *Euripides and His Age.* N.Y., Holt, 1913. N.Y., Oxford Univ. Pr., n.d.

NORWOOD, G. *Essays on Euripidean Drama.* Cambridge, Harvard Univ. Pr., 1954.

CORNFORD, FRANCIS M. *Origin of Attic Comedy.* N.Y., Anchor, 1963. (Section on Aristophanes)

EHRENBERG, V. *The People of Aristophanes: a sociology of old Attic comedy,* 2nd ed. Oxford, Clarendon, 1951.

LEVER, K. *The Art of Greek Comedy.* London, Methuen, 1956.

LORD, L. E. *Aristophanes: His Plays and His Influence.* Boston, Marshall Jones, 1925. N.Y., Cooper Sq. Pub., 1964.

MURRAY, GILBERT. *Aristophanes.* N.Y., Oxford Univ. Pr., 1933.

NORWOOD, G. *Greek Comedy.* London, Methuen, 1931.

BURY, J. B. *The Ancient Greek Historians.* N.Y., Macmillan, 1909.

COCHRANE, CHARLES N. *Thucydides and the Science of History.* London, Oxford Univ. Pr., 1929.

FINLEY, J. H., JR. *Thucydides.* Cambridge, Harvard Univ. Pr., 1942.

GRENE, MARJORIE. *Greek Political Theory: The Image of Man in Thucydides and Plato.* Chicago, Univ. of Chicago Pr., 1965.

BLUCK, R. S. *Plato's Life and Thought.* London, Chapman Hall, 1949.

CORNFORD, FRANCIS M. *Before and After Socrates.* Cambridge, Harvard Univ. Pr., 1932.

FRIEDLANDER, W. *Plato: An Introduction.* N.Y., Harper, 1965.

GRUBE, G. M. A. *Plato's Thought.* Boston, Beacon, 1964.

GUARDINI, ROMANO. *The Death of Socrates.* N.Y., Meridian, 1964. (Interpretation of the Platonic dialogues)

KENYON, A. R. *The Socratic Problem.* New Haven, Yale Univ. Pr., 1933.

MORE, PAUL E. *The Religion of Plato.* Princeton, Princeton Univ. Pr., 1921.

SHOREY, PAUL. *Platonism, Ancient and Modern.* Berkeley, Univ. of Calif. Pr., 1938.

——————————. *What Plato Said.* Chicago, Univ. of Chicago Pr., 1957.

TAYLOR, A. E. *Plato.* N.Y., Meridian, 1962.

VOEGELIN, ERIC. *Plato and Aristotle.* Baton Rouge, La. St. Univ. Pr., 1957. (Cf. the selection in Anderson and Mazzeo, *The Proper Study*, 160-178)

ALLAN, DONALD JAMES. *The Philosophy of Aristotle.* N.Y., Oxford Univ. Pr., 1952.

BUTCHER, S. H. "The Function of Tragedy" in *Aristotle's Theory of Poetry and Fine Art.* London, Macmillan, 1894. (Reprinted in Anderson and Mazzeo, *The Proper Study*, 180-191)

——————————. *The Poetics of Aristotle,* 4th ed. London, Macmillan, 1911.

COOPER, LANE. *A Bibliography of the Poetics of Aristotle.* New Haven, Yale Univ. Pr., 1928.

——————————. *The Poetics of Aristotle: its meaning and influence.* Boston, Marshall Jones, 1923.

ELSE, GERALD F. *Aristotle's Poetics: the argument.* Cambridge, Harvard Univ. Pr., 1957.

GRANT, SIR ALEXANDER. *The Ethics of Aristotle,* ill. with essays and notes, 4th ed. rev. 2 vols. London, Longmans, 1885.

Grene, Marjorie. *A Portrait of Aristotle*. Chicago, Univ. of Chicago Pr., 1963.

Herrick, Marvin T. *The Poetics of Aristotle in England*. New Haven, Yale Univ. Pr., 1930.

House, Humphrey. *Aristotle's Poetics*. London, R. Hart-Davis, 1956.

Jaeger, Werner. *Aristotle . . . history of his development*. Oxford, Clarendon, 1934. (Also Oxford paperback)

Joachim, H. H. *Aristotle. The Nicomachean Ethics: a commentary*. Oxford, Clarendon, 1951.

Lucas, F. L. *Tragedy in Relation to Aristotle's Poetics*. N.Y., Harcourt, 1928.

Mure, G. R. G. *Aristotle*. N.Y., Oxford Univ. Pr., 1932. (Also Galaxy Books)

Owen, Arthur S. *Aristotle on the Art of Poetry. An analytic commentary and notes*. Oxford, Clarendon, 1931.

Potts, L. J. *Aristotle on the Art of Fiction*. Cambridge, Cambridge Univ. Pr., 1953.

Randall, John H. *Aristotle*. N.Y., Columbia Univ. Pr., 1960.

Veatch, Henry B. *Rational Man: a modern interpretation of Aristotelian ethics*. Bloomington, Indiana Univ. Pr., 1962.

Allinson, Francis G. *Lucian, Satirist and Artist*. Boston, Marshall Jones, 1926.

Chapman, John J. *Lucian, Plato, and Greek Morals*. N.Y., Houghton, 1931.

Bowra, C. M. *Early Greek Elegists*. Cambridge, Harvard Univ. Pr., 1938.

_____. *Greek Lyric Poetry from Alcman to Simonides*. Oxford, Clarendon, 1936.

Robinson, D. M. *Sappho and Her Influence*. Boston, Marshall Jones, 1924.

Symonds, J. A. *Studies of the Greek Poets*, 3rd ed. N.Y., Harper, 1920. (Includes Sappho)

Stark, Freya. *Ionia: A Quest*. N.Y., Harcourt, 1954. (Anacreon)

Edmonds, John Maxwell. *The Greek Bucolic Poets*. London, Heinemann, 1928. N.Y., Macmillan, 1928. (Loeb Classical Library, now Harvard Univ. Pr.)

Gow, A. S. F., ed. and tr. *Theocritus: with translation and commentary*. 2 vols. Cambridge, Cambridge Univ. Pr., 1952.

Trevelyan, Robert C. *The Idylls of Theocritus*. London, The Casanova Soc., 1925.

Lawton, William C. *The Soul of the Anthology*. New Haven, Yale Univ. Pr., 1923. (English transl. of the *Anthologia Graeca*)

Paton, W. R. *The Greek Anthology, with an English translation*. 3 vols. Cambridge, Harvard Univ. Pr., 1916-1918. (Loeb Classical Library)

THE WEST UNDER ROMAN SWAY

History

Adcock, F. E. *The Roman Art of War Under the Republic*. N.Y., Barnes, 1960.

_____. *Roman Political Ideas and Practices*. Ann Arbor, Univ. of Mich. Pr., 1959.

Boak, Arthur E. R. *A History of Rome to 565 A.D.*, 5th ed. N.Y., Macmillan, 1965.

Burn, A. R. *Agricola and Roman Britain*. N.Y., Collier, 1964.

Caesar, Julius. *War Commentaries*, tr. Rex Warner. N.Y., Mentor, 1962.

Cambridge Ancient History. Vols. VII-XII. Cambridge, Cambridge Univ. Pr., 1926.

Carcopino, Jerome. *Daily Life in Ancient Rome*. New Haven, Yale Univ. Pr., 1964.

Cary, M. *History of Rome Down to . . . Constantine*, 2nd ed. N.Y., St. Martin's Pr., 1954.

Dill, Samuel. *Roman Society from Nero to . . . Aurelius*. N.Y., Meridian, 1963.

_____. *Roman Society in the Last Century of the Empire*. N.Y., Meridian, 1962.

Ferrero, G., and C. Barbagallo. *Short History of Rome*. 2 vols. N.Y., Putnam Capricorn, 1964.

Frank, Tenney. *An Economic History of Rome*, 2nd ed. Baltimore, Johns Hopkins, 1927.

_____. *A History of Rome*. N.Y., Holt, 1923.

Gibbon, Edward. *The Portable Gibbon: Decline and Fall of the Roman Empire*. N.Y., Viking, 1952.

Hadas, Moses. *A History of Rome*. London, Bell, 1958.

Haywood, Richard. *The Myth of Rome's Fall*. N.Y., Apollo, 1962.

Holmes, T. R. *The Architect of the Roman Empire*. Oxford, Clarendon. N.Y., Oxford Univ. Pr., 1931. (Augustus)

Livy. *A History of Rome*. N.Y., Modern Library, 1962.

Lucan. *Pharsalis*, tr. Robert Graves. Baltimore, Penguin, 1957.

Mattingly, Harold. *Roman Imperial Civilization*. N.Y., St. Martin's Pr., 1957.

Mommsen, Theodor. *A History of Rome*. 5 vols. N.Y., Free Pr., 1957. N.Y., Meridian, 1963.

Moore, Ralph W. *The Roman Commonwealth*. London, Botsford, 1942.

Scullard, H. H. *A History of the Roman World from 753 to 146 B.C.*, 3rd ed. N.Y., Barnes, 1961. (Vol. IV of Methuen's History of the Greek and Roman World)

Marsh, Frank. *A History of the Roman World from 146–30 B.C.*, 3rd ed. N.Y., Barnes, 1963.

Parker, H. M. D. *A History of the Roman World from 30 B.C.–138 A.D.*, 3rd ed. N.Y., Barnes, 1959.

_____. *A History of the Roman World from 138–337 A.D.*, 2nd ed. N.Y., Barnes, 1958.

Nilsson, Martin P. *Imperial Rome*. N.Y., Schocken, 1962.

Rostovtzeff, M. *History of the Ancient World*. Vol. II. N.Y., Oxford Univ. Pr., 1930.

_____. *Social and Economic History of the Roman Empire*, 2nd ed. 2 vols. N.Y., Oxford Univ. Pr., 1957.

_____. *Rome*. N.Y., Oxford Galaxy, 1963.

Scullard, Howard H. *From the Gracchi to Nero . . . a history of Rome from 133 B.C. to 68 A.D.* N.Y., Barnes, 1965.

Treble, H. A., and K. M. King. *Everyday Life in Rome in the Life of Caesar and Cicero*. N.Y., Oxford Univ. Pr., 1931.

Culture

ALTHEIM, F. *A History of Roman Religion.* N.Y., Dutton, 1938.

APULEIUS. *The Golden Ass,* tr. W. Aldington. N.Y., Modern Library, 1932. (Fictional autobiography and classic social satire)

BAILEY, CYRIL. *The Legacy of Rome.* N.Y., Oxford Univ. Pr., 1924.

——————. *Phases in the Religion of Ancient Rome.* Berkeley, Univ. of Calif. Pr., 1932.

BARROW, R. H. *The Romans.* Baltimore, Penguin, 1962. ("Rome's achievements and . . . contributions to . . . Western Civilization")

BRION, MARCEL. *Pompeii and Herculaneum: The Glory and the Grief.* N.Y., Crown, 1960.

BROWN, FRANK E. *Roman Architecture.* N.Y., Braziller, 1961.

CARY, M., *et al. The Oxford Classical Dictionary.* N.Y., Oxford Univ. Pr., 1953.

DUDLEY, D. R. *The Civilization of Rome.* N.Y., Mentor, n.d. (Cultural and sociological history)

DURANT, WILL. *The Story of Civilization.* Vol. III: *Caesar and Christ.* N.Y., Simon & Schuster, 1944.

FRIEDLANDER, LUDWIG. *Roman Life and Manners Under the Early Empire,* tr. L. A. Magnus. 4 vols. N.Y., Dutton, 1909.

GRANT, MICHAEL. *The Birth of Western Civilization: Greece and Rome.* N.Y., McGraw, 1964.

GREENE, WILLIAM C. *The Achievement of Rome.* Cambridge, Harvard Univ. Pr., 1933.

GRIMAL, PIERRE. *In Search of Ancient Italy.* N.Y., Hill & Wang, 1964.

GWYNN, A. O. *Roman Education from Cicero to Quintilian.* Oxford, Clarendon, 1924.

HADAS, MOSES, *et al. Imperial Rome.* N.Y., Time Inc., 1965. (Great Ages of Man Series. 8 essays, profusely illustrated, on life and culture.)

HAMILTON, EDITH. *The Roman Way to Western Civilization.* N.Y., Mentor, 1961.

HAUFMANN, GEORGE. *Roman Art.* N.Y., N.Y. Graphic Soc., 1964.

HOWE, G., and G. HARRER. *A Handbook of Classical Mythology.* N.Y., Crofts, 1929.

KAHLER, HEINZ. *The Art of Rome and Her Empire.* N.Y., Crown, 1963.

MACKENDRICK, PAUL. *The Mute Stones Speak. The story of archaeology in Italy.* N.Y., St. Martin's Pr., 1960.

——————. *The Roman Mind at Work.* N.Y., Van Nostrand, 1958.

MAIURI, A., and A. SKIRA. *Roman Painting.* N.Y., World, 1953.

MARCUS AURELIUS. *Meditations,* tr. M. Stainforth. Baltimore, Penguin, n.d.

MASSON, GEORGINA. *Italian Gardens.* N.Y., Abrams, 1961.

MATTINGLY, H. *Roman Imperial Civilization.* N.Y., St. Martin's Pr., 1957.

NAPHTALI, LEWIS, and MEYER REINHOLD. *Roman Civilization.* 2 vols. N.Y., Columbia Univ. Pr., 1951, 1959. (Also Harper Torch)

PAYNE, ROBERT, *et al. The Horizon Book of Ancient Rome.* N.Y., Amer. Heritage, 1966. (Copiously illustrated chapters on all aspects of Roman life)

PLUTARCH. *Lives of the Noble Romans.* N.Y., Dell, 1963. (10 classic biographies)

ROBERTSON, DONALD S. *Greek and Roman Architecture,* 2nd ed. Cambridge, Cambridge Univ. Pr., 1943.

ROSE, H. J. *Religion in Greece and Rome.* N.Y., Harper Torch, 1963.

SCHERER, MARGARET R. *Marvels of Ancient Rome.* N.Y., Phaidon, 1955. (Also N.Y. Graphic Soc.)

SELTMAN, C. *Women in Antiquity.* N.Y., St. Martin's Pr., 1955.

SHOWERMAN, GRANT. *Monuments and Men of Ancient Rome.* N.Y., Appleton, 1935.

STARR, C. G. *Civilization and The Caesars: The Intellectual Revolution in the Roman Empire.* Ithaca, Cornell Univ. Pr., 1954.

STEVENSON, G. H. *Roman Provincial Administration.* N.Y., Oxford Univ. Pr., 1939.

STOBART, J. C. *The Grandeur That Was Rome,* 4th ed. N.Y., Hawthorne, 1962.

TOYNBEE, JOCELYN. *Art in Roman Britain.* N.Y., Phaidon, 1962. (Also N.Y. Graphic Soc.)

VOLBACH, W. F. *Early Christian Art.* N.Y., Abrams, 1962.

WENLEY, R. M. *Stoicism and Its Influence.* Boston, Marshall Jones, 1924.

WOLFF, HANS J. *Roman Law.* Norman, Univ. of Okla. Pr., 1951.

WORMSER, RENÉ. *The Story of the Law,* rev. ed. N.Y., Simon & Schuster, 1962.

Literature

CHARLTON, H. B. *The Senecan Tradition in Renaissance Tragedy.* Manchester, Manchester Univ. Pr., 1946.

DUFF, J. W. *A Literary History of Rome.* 2 vols. London, Allen & Unwin, 1927.

——————. *Roman Satire: its outlook on social life.* Berkeley, Univ. of Calif. Pr., 1936.

GRANT, MICHAEL. *Roman Literature.* Baltimore, Penguin, 1964.

HARVEY, PAUL. *The Oxford Companion to Classical Literature,* N.Y., Oxford Univ. Pr., 1937.

HIGHET, GILBERT. *Poets in a Landscape.* N.Y., Knopf, 1957. (Charming essays on the Roman poets and their milieu)

MACKAIL, J. W. *Latin Literature.* N.Y., Scribner's, 1904.

MENDELL, CLARENCE W. *Latin Poetry: The New Poets and the Augustans.* New Haven, Yale Univ. Pr., 1965.

REINHOLD, MEYER. *Essentials of Greek and Roman Classics.* Great Neck, N.Y., Barron's, 1949.

ROSE, H. J. *A Handbook of Latin Literature.* N.Y., Dutton, 1936.

SANDYS, JOHN E. *A Companion to Latin Studies,* 3rd ed. N.Y., Hafner, 1935.

SELLAR, W. Y. *The Roman Poets of the Augustan Age.* Oxford, Clarendon, 1889.

SIKES, E. E. *Roman Poetry.* London, Methuen, 1923.

Collections

DAVENPORT, B., ed. *The Portable Roman Reader.* N.Y., Viking, 1951.

DUCKWORTH, GEORGE E. *The Complete Roman Drama.* 2 vols. N.Y., Random House, 1942.

GODOLPHIN, F. R. B. *The Latin Poets.* N.Y., Modern Library, 1949.

GUINAGH, K., and A. P. DORJAHN. *Latin Literature in Translation.* N.Y., Longmans, 1948. (Extensive anthology of best selections from 28 authors)

HARSH, P. W., ed. *Anthology of Roman Drama.* N.Y., Rinehart, 1960.

HOWE, G., and G. A. HARRER. *Roman Literature in Translation.* N.Y., Harper, 1924.

The Oxford Book of Latin Verse. N.Y., Oxford Univ. Pr., 1912.

PLINY. *The Letters,* tr. B. Radice. Baltimore, Penguin, 1963.

PLUTARCH. *Lives,* ed. P. Turner. Carbondale, Southern Ill. Univ. Pr., 1963.

——————. *Selected Essays: On Love, the Family and the Good Life,* tr. and introd. by M. Hadas. N.Y., Mentor, n.d.

ROBINSON, C. A., JR. *Selections from Greek and Roman Historians.* N.Y., Rinehart, 1951.

SUETONIUS. *Lives of the 12 Caesars,* tr. Robert Graves. Baltimore, Penguin, 1957.

Writers

BOISSIER, G. *Cicero and His Friends. A study of Roman society.* N.Y., Putnam, 1925.

CARCOPINO, J. *Cicero: The Secrets of His Correspondence.* 2 vols. London, Routledge, 1951.

CICERO. *The Basic Works,* ed. with introd. by M. Hadas. N.Y., Modern Library, 1951.

——————. *Letters to Atticus,* ed. D. R. Shackleton Bailey. 2 vols. Cambridge, Cambridge Univ. Pr., 1965. (Latin and English texts)

COWELL, F. R. *Cicero and the Roman Republic.* Baltimore, Penguin, 1965.

DOREY, T. A., ed. *Cicero.* N.Y., Basic Books, 1965. (A group of studies by various writers)

HASKELL, A. J. *This Was Cicero.* N.Y., Knopf, 1942.

PETERSSON, TORSTEN. *Cicero, a Biography.* Berkeley, Univ. of Calif. Pr., 1920.

ROLFE, JOHN C. *Cicero and His Influence.* Boston, Marshall Jones, 1923. (Also N.Y., Cooper Sq. Pub. Our Debt to Greece and Rome Series)

SHOWERMAN, GRANT. *Monuments and Men of Ancient Rome.* N.Y., Appleton, 1935. (Several sections on Cicero)

STRACHAN-DAVIDSON, J. L. *Cicero and the Fall of the Roman Republic.* N.Y., Putnam, 1903.

HADZSITS, G. D. *Lucretius and His Influence.* N.Y., Longmans, 1935.

HERFORD, C. H. *The Poetry of Lucretius.* Manchester, Manchester Univ. Pr., 1918.

MASSON, JOHN. *Lucretius, Epicurean and Poet.* N.Y., Dutton, 1907.

SANTAYANA, GEORGE. *Three Philosophical Poets.* N.Y., Anchor, 1953.

SIKES, E. E. *Lucretius, Poet and Philosopher.* Cambridge, Cambridge Univ. Pr., 1936.

WINSPEAR, ALBAN D. *Lucretius and Scientific Thought.* Montreal, Harvest House, 1963.

BEARE, W. *The Roman Stage,* 2nd ed. London, Methuen, 1955. (Section on Plautus)

DUCKWORTH, G. E. *The Nature of Roman Comedy: a study of popular entertainment.* Princeton, Princeton Univ. Pr., 1952. (Basic for study of Plautus)

NORWOOD, G. *Plautus and Terence.* N.Y., Longmans, 1932.

WRIGHT, FREDERICK A. *Three Roman Poets: Plautus, Catullus, Ovid.* London, Routledge, 1938.

BOWRA, C. M. *From Virgil to Milton.* London, Macmillan, 1945. (Influence on English literature)

BUXTON, C. R. *Prophets of Heaven and Hell.* Cambridge, Cambridge Univ. Pr., 1945.

CRUTTWELL, ROBT. W. *Virgil's Mind at Work . . . the symbolism of the Aeneid.* Oxford, Blackwell, 1946. N.Y., Macmillan, 1947.

FRANK, TENNEY. *Virgil: a biography.* N.Y., Holt, 1922.

GLOVER, T. R. *Virgil,* 6th ed. London, Methuen, 1930.

HIGHET, GILBERT. *The Classical Tradition.* N.Y., Oxford, 1949. (Virgil's influence on English literature)

KNIGHT, W. F. J. *Roman Vergil.* London, Faber, 1944.

LETTERS, F. J. H. *Virgil.* N.Y., Sheed & Ward, 1946.

NITCHIE, ELIZABETH. *Virgil and the English Poets.* N.Y., Columbia Univ. Pr., 1919.

OTIS, BROOKS. *Virgil, a study in civilized poetry.* Oxford, Clarendon, 1964.

PRESCOTT, H. W. *The Development of Virgil's Art.* Chicago, Univ. of Chicago Pr., 1927.

RAND, E. K. *In Quest of Virgil's Birthplace.* Cambridge, Harvard Univ. Pr., 1930.

—————— ——————. *The Magical Art of Virgil.* Cambridge, Harvard Univ. Pr., 1931.

SAUNDERS, CATHERINE. *Virgil's Primitive Italy.* N.Y., Oxford Univ. Pr., 1930.

SPARGO, JOHN WEBSTER. *Virgil the Necromancer.* Cambridge, Harvard Univ. Pr., 1934. (His fame, especially in the Middle Ages)

BRINK, CHARLES O. *Horace on Poetry.* Cambridge, Cambridge Univ. Pr., 1963. (Prolegomena to the literary Epistles)

D'ALTON, JOHN F. *Horace and His Age: a study in historical background.* N.Y., Russell, 1962.

FRAENKEL, EDUARD. *Horace.* Oxford, Clarendon, 1957.

GOAD, CAROLINE. *Horace in the English Literature of the 18th Century.* New Haven, Yale Univ. Pr., 1918.

GLOVER, T. R. *Horace, a Return to Allegiance.* Cambridge, Harvard Univ. Pr., 1932.

HAIGHT, ELIZABETH. *Horace and His Art of Enjoyment.* N.Y., Dutton, 1925.

OATES, W. J. *The Influence of Simonides . . . Upon Horace.* Princeton, Princeton Univ. Pr., 1932.

PERRET, J. M. *Horace.* N.Y., N.Y. Univ. Pr., 1965.

SHOWERMAN, G. *Horace and His Influence.* Boston, Marshall Jones, 1922. (Also N.Y., Cooper Sq. Pub.)

SMILEY, C. N. *Horace, His Poetry and Philosophy.* N.Y., King's Crown, 1945.

WILKINSON, L. P. *Horace and His Lyric Poetry.* Cambridge, Harvard Univ. Pr., 1945.

ELLIS, ROBINSON. *A Commentary on Catullus,* 2nd ed. Oxford, Clarendon, 1889.

GREGORY, HORACE. *The Poems of Catullus.* N.Y., Covici, 1931.

HARRINGTON, K. P. *Catullus and His Influence.* N.Y., Cooper Sq. Pub., 1964.

HAVELOCK, E. A. *The Lyric Genius of Catullus.* Oxford, Clarendon, 1939.

WHEELER, A. L. *Catullus and the Traditions of Ancient Poetry.* Berkeley, Univ. of Calif. Pr., 1934.

BRADFORD, GAMALIEL. "Ovid Among the Goths" in *A Naturalist of Souls.* Boston, Houghton, 1936.

BREWER, WILMON. *Ovid's Metamorphoses in European Culture.* Boston, Cornhill Pub., 1933.

RAND, EDWARD K. *Ovid and His Influence.* N.Y., Longmans, n.d. (Our Debt to Greece and Rome Series)

THIBAULT, JOHN C. *The Mystery of Ovid's Exile.* Berkeley, Univ. of Calif. Pr., 1964.

WILKINSON, J. G. *Ovid Surveyed.* Cambridge, Cambridge Univ. Pr., 1963.

DUFF, J. W. *Roman Satire: Its Outlook on Social Life.* Berkeley, Univ. of Calif. Pr., 1936. (Chapter on Juvenal)

HIGHET, GILBERT. *Juvenal the Satirist.* Oxford, Clarendon, 1954.

JUVENAL. *Satires,* tr. J. Mazzeo, with introd. and notes. Ann Arbor, Univ. of Mich. Pr., 1965.

SCOTT, I. G. *The Grand Style in the Satires of Juvenal.* Northampton, Smith Coll. Class Studies, 1927.

NIXON, PAUL. *Martial.* N.Y., Longmans, 1924. (Our Debt to Greece and Rome Series)

——————. *Martial and the Modern Epigram.* N.Y., Longmans, 1927.

SMITH, KIRBY F. *Martial . . . and Other Essays.* Baltimore, Johns Hopkins, 1920.

BOOK TWO: CENTURIES OF TRANSITION

THE MOHAMMEDAN WORLD

History

BROCKELMANN, CARL. *History of the Islamic Peoples.* N.Y., Putnam Capricorn, 1964.

GIBB, SIR H. A. R. *Mohammedanism: an historical survey.* N.Y., Oxford Galaxy, 1965.

HITTI, PHILIP K. *History of the Arabs,* 4th ed. London, Macmillan, 1948.

HOUTSMA, M. THOMAS, *et al.,* eds. *Encyclopedia of Islam.* London, 1913-1934. *Supplement,* 1938.

VON GRUNEBAUM, GUSTAVE E. *Medieval Islam.* Chicago, Univ. of Chicago Pr., 1946.

Literature

BROWNE, E. G. *A Literary History of Persia.* 4 vols. N.Y., Oxford Univ. Pr., 1902-1924.

CHEW, SAMUEL C. *The Crescent and the Rose.* N.Y., Oxford Univ. Pr., 1937.

JURJI, EDWARD J. "Arabic Literature" in Laird, *The World Through Literature.* N.Y., Appleton-Century-Crofts, 1951, 145-171.

NICHOLSON, R. A. *Literary History of the Arabs.* Cambridge, Cambridge Univ. Pr., 1930.

STOREY, C. A. *Persian Literature: a biobibliographic survey.* 2 vols. London, London Univ. Pr., 1927-1936.

Individual Works

BALLOU, ROBERT O., ed. *The World Bible.* N.Y., Viking, 1944. (Cf. "The Moslem," pp. 437 ff., and selections from "The Koran," pp. 451-469.)

BELL, RICHARD. *Introduction to the Qur'an.* Edinburgh, Univ. of Edinburgh Pr., 1963.

CALVERLEY, EDWIN E. "The Koran" in Laird, *The World Through Literature.* N.Y., Appleton-Century-Crofts, 1951, 135-141.

JEFFERY, ARTHUR. *The Qur'an as Scripture.* N.Y., R.F. Moore, 1952.

BURTON, RICHARD R., tr. *The Arabian Nights' Entertainment . . .* selected by B. A. Cerf. N.Y., Modern Library, 1932.

GERHARDT, MIA. *The Art of Story-telling: a literary study of The Thousand and One Nights.* Leiden, E. J. Brill, 1963.

HMANN, E. L. "Alf Laylah Wa-Laylah" in *Encyclopedia of Islam,* 2nd ed. Vol. I, Fasc. 6, 1956.

Persian Poems: verse translations from 25 Persian poets. N.Y., Dutton, n.d. (Everyman's Library)

OMAR KHAYYAM. *The Romance of the Rubaiyat:* Edw. Fitzgerald's first ed. reprinted with introd. and notes. N.Y., Macmillan, 1959.

LAMB, HAROLD. *Omar Khayyam, a Life.* N.Y., Doubleday, 1936.

SHIRAZI, J. K. M. *Life of Omar Khayyam.* Chicago, McClurg, 1905.

FARZAAD, M. *Haafez and His Poems.* Hertford, Herts, 1949.

THE CHRISTIAN IDEAL

The Bible

BATES, ERNEST S., ed. *The Bible, designed to be read as living literature . . . in the King James Version.* N.Y., Simon & Schuster, 1951.

BETTERSON, H., ed. *Documents of the Christian Church.* London, Oxford Univ. Pr., 1947. (World's Classics)

ROBINSON, HENRY WHEELER. *The Bible in Its Ancient and English Versions.* Oxford, Clarendon, 1940.

SCHONFIELD, H. J., tr. *The Authentic New Testament.* London, Dobson, 1956. N.Y., Mentor, 1958.

STORR, V. F., ed. *The English Bible.* London, Methuen, 1938.

History and Criticism

CARPENTER, SPENCER CECIL. *Christianity.* London, Murray, 1953.

COOK, STANLEY. *An Introduction to the Bible.* London, Penguin, 1945.

DAICHES, DAVID. *The King James Version*. Chicago, Univ. of Chicago Pr., 1941.

DUCHESNE, LOUIS. *Christian Worship: Its Origin and Evolution,* 5th ed. London, Macmillan, 1927.

GILBERT, GEORGE HOLLEY. *Greek Thought in the New Testament*. N.Y., Macmillan, 1928.

JAEGER, WERNER. *Early Christianity and Greek Paideia*. Cambridge, Belknap Pr., 1961.

KENYON, FREDERICK GEORGE. *Our Bible and the Ancient Manuscripts*. N.Y., Harper, 1940.

LABRIOLLE, PIERRE C. DE. *History of Literature of Christianity from Tertullian to Boethius*. Vol. V of *History of Civilization*. N.Y., Knopf, 1925.

LEWIS, CLIVE STAPLES. *The Literary Impact of the Authorized Version*. London, Macmillan, 1950.

LOWES, JOHN LIVINGSTON. "The Noblest Monument of English Prose" in *Essays in Appreciation*. Boston, Houghton, 1936.

MCNEILL, J. T. *Makers of the Christian Tradition*. N.Y., Harper, 1964.

POWICKE, FREDERICK MAURICE. *The Christian Life in the Middle Ages*. N.Y., Oxford Univ. Pr., 1935.

REID, MARY ESSON, ed. *The Bible Read as Literature*. Cleveland, Howard Allen, 1964. (Anthology of essays, both by scholars and general readers with bibliography)

SCHONFIELD, HUGH J. *A History of Biblical Literature*. N.Y., Mentor, 1962.

SYPHERD, WILBUR O. *The Literature of the English Bible*. N.Y., Oxford Univ. Pr., 1938.

WEISS, JOHANNES. *Earliest Christianity: a history of the period* A.D. *30-150*. N.Y., Harper Torch, 1965.

Commentaries

FILSON, FLOYD V. *A Commentary on the Gospel According to St. Matthew*. N.Y., Harper, 1960.

FOX, EMMET. *The Sermon on the Mount, a general introd. . . . [and] key to Matthew V–VII*. N.Y., Harper, 1938.

KILPATRICK, GEORGE DUNBAR. *The Origins of the Gospel According to St. Matthew*. Oxford, Clarendon, 1946.

ROBERTSON, ARCHIBALD. *A Critical and Exegetical Commentary on the First Epistle of St. Paul to the Corinthians*. N.Y., Scribner's, 1911.

DEISSMANN, ADOLF. *Paul: a Study in Social and Religious History*. N.Y., Harper Torch, 1963.

FOAKES-JACKSON, FREDERIC JOHN. *The Life of St. Paul*. N.Y., Boni & Liveright, 1926.

GOODSPEED, EDGAR J. *Paul*. Nashville, Abingdon, 1965.

KLAUSNER, JOSEPH. *From Jesus to Paul*. Boston, Beacon, n.d.

SCHWEITZER, ALBERT. *Paul and His Interpreters*. N.Y., Schocken, 1965.

BETHUNE-BAKER, JAMES F. *Introduction to the Early History of Christian Doctrine,* 9th ed. London, Methuen, 1951. (Nicaean Creed)

HASTINGS, JAMES, ed. *Encyclopedia of Religion and Ethics*. N.Y., Scribner's, 1908-1927.

KELLY, JOHN N. D. *Early Christian Creeds,* 2nd ed. London, Longmans, 1963.

LEITH, JOHN H., ed. *Creeds of the Churches: a reader in Christian doctrine from the Bible to the present*. N.Y., Anchor, 1965.

SCHAFF, PHILIP. *Bibliotheca Symbolica Ecclesiae Universalis: The Creeds of Christendom with a history and critical notes*. 3 vols. N.Y., Harper, 1919.

THOMAS A KEMPIS. *The Imitation of Christ*. N.Y., Washington Sq. Pr., 1965.

DE MONTMORENCY, JAMES E. G. *Thomas à Kempis; his age and book*. London, Methuen, 1907.

WILLIAMS, JAMES. *Thomas of Kempen*. London, K. Paul, *et al.,* 1911.

CAMERON, MARY LOVETT. *Inquiring Pilgrim's Guide to Assisi and the first Life of St. Francis, by Thomas of Celano*. London, Methuen, 1926.

CHESTERTON, G. K., *Life of St. Francis of Assisi*. N.Y., Doubleday, 1931.

ENGLEBERT, OMER. *Life of St. Francis of Assisi*. N.Y., Longmans, 1950.

KAZANTZAKIS, NIKOS. *St. Francis, A Novel*. N.Y., Simon & Schuster, 1962.

THE MIDDLE AGES

History

BARKER, ERNEST. *The Crusades*. London, Oxford Univ. Pr., 1923.

BLOCH, MARC. *Feudal Society*. Chicago, Univ. of Chicago Pr., 1961.

BOISSONADE, P. *Life and Work in Medieval Europe*. N.Y., Knopf, 1927.

CANTOR, NORMAN F. *Medieval History*. N.Y., Macmillan, 1963.

CHENEY, E. P. *The Dawn of Modern Europe*. N.Y., Harper, 1936.

COLLIS, LOUISE. *Memoirs of a Medieval Woman: the life and times of Margery Kempe*. N.Y. Crowell, 1964.

COULTON, G. G. *Medieval Panorama: the English Scene from Conquest to Reformation*. N.Y., Meridian, 1955.

EVANS, JOAN. *Life in Medieval France*. London, Phaidon, 1957.

FROISSART, SIR JOHN. *The Chronicles of England, France and Spain*. N.Y., Dutton, 1930. (Everyman's Library. A classic eyewitness account of life in 14th C. Europe.)

GANSHOF, FRANÇOIS L. *Feudalism*. N.Y., Harper, 1961.

JARRETT, BEDE. *Social Theories of the Middle Ages, 1200-1500*. London, Ernest Benn, 1926.

NEWTON, A. P., ed. *Travel and Travellers in the Middle Ages*. N.Y., Knopf, 1926.

OMAN, C. W. C. *The Dark Ages, 476-918*. London, Rivington, n.d.

PAINTER, SIDNEY. *French Chivalry . . . Ideas and Practices*. Baltimore, Johns Hopkins, 1940.

PIRENNE, HENRI. *Medieval Cities*. Princeton, Princeton Univ. Pr., 1925.

POWER, EILEEN. *Medieval People*. London, Methuen, 1924. N.Y., Barnes & Noble, n.d.

POWICKE, F. M. "Middle Ages" in *Encyclopaedia Britannica*, 14th ed. 1955. XV, 448-450.

RICE, DAVID T., ed. *Dawn of European Civilization: The Dark Ages*. N.Y., McGraw, 1965. (Anthology of essays on the various peoples and regions. Lavishly illustrated.)

RICKERT, EDITH, ed. *Chaucer's World*. N.Y., Columbia Univ. Pr., 1948.

STEPHENSON, CARL. *A Brief Survey of Medieval Europe*. N.Y., Harper, 1941.

—————. *Medieval Feudalism*. Ithaca, Cornell Univ. Pr., 1942.

STRAYER, JOSEPH R. *Western Europe in the Middle Ages: A Short History*. N.Y., Appleton-Century-Crofts, 1955.

THOMPSON, JAMES W. *Economic and Social History of the Middle Ages*. 2 vols. N.Y., Frederick Ungar, 1959.

THOMPSON, JAMES W., and E. N. JOHNSON. *An Introduction to Medieval Europe, 300-1500*. N.Y., Norton, 1937.

VILLEHARDOUIN, G. DE, and J. DEJOINVILLE. *Memoirs of the Crusades*. N.Y., Dutton, 1933. (Everyman's Library)

UNDSET, SIGRID. *Kristin Lavransdatter*. N.Y., Knopf, 1929. (Fiction)

WADDELL, HELEN. *Peter Abelard*. N.Y., Holt, 1933. (Fiction)

—————. *The Wandering Scholars*. London, Constable, 1927.

Culture

AQUINAS, ST. THOMAS. *Selected Writings*. N.Y., Dutton, 1934. (Everyman's Library)

AUGUSTINE, ST. *The Confessions of St. Augustine*. N.Y., Dutton, 1936. (Everyman's Library)

COULTON, G. G. *Medieval Village, Manor, and Monastery*. N.Y., Harper Torch, 1964.

CRUMP, C. G., and E. F. JACOB, eds. *The Legacy of the Middle Ages*. Oxford, Clarendon, 1926.

DAWSON, C. H., *The Making of Europe*. N.Y., Sheed & Ward, 1932. (Masterly interpretation of the early period)

DURANT, WILL. *The Story of Civilization*. Vol. IV: *The Age of Faith*. N.Y., Simon & Schuster, 1950.

FREMANTLE, ANNE, *et al. The Age of Faith*. N.Y., Time Inc., 1965. (Copiously illustrated chapters on all aspects of life in the Middle Ages)

HEARNSHAW, F. J. C., ed. *Medieval Contributions to Modern Civilization*. London, Harrap, 1921.

HUIZINGA, JOHAN. *The Waning of the Middle Ages*. London, Arnold, 1924.

KELLY, AMY. *Eleanor of Aquitaine and the Four Kings*. N.Y., Vintage Books, n.d.

RAND, EDWARD K. *Founders of the Middle Ages*. Cambridge, Harvard Univ. Pr., 1928. (Chapters on Ambrose, Jerome, Boethius, Augustine, Dante)

ROSS, J. B., and N. M. McLAUGHLIN. *The Portable Medieval Reader*. N.Y., Viking, 1950. (Anthology of writings representing virtually all phases of medieval life)

TAYLOR, HENRY O. *The Classical Heritage of the Middle Ages*. N.Y., Macmillan, 1929.

—————. *The Medieval Mind: A History of the Development of Thought and Emotion in the Middle Ages*, 4th ed. 2 vols. N.Y., Macmillan, 1925.

TILLEY, A., ed. *Medieval France*. Cambridge, Cambridge Univ. Pr., 1922. (Variorum anthology)

COULTON, G. G. *Five Centuries of Religion*. 3 vols. Cambridge, Cambridge Univ. Pr., 1923-1936. (Essentially a history of monasticism)

DAWSON, C. H. *Medieval Religion*. N.Y., Sheed & Ward, 1934.

GONTARD, FRIEDRICH. *The Chair of Peter: A History of the Papacy*. N.Y., Holt, 1964.

The Horizon History of Christianity. N.Y., Amer. Heritage, 1964. (Copiously illustrated, especially valuable for its historical treatment of Christian art)

COPLESTON, FREDERICK C. *Medieval Philosophy*. N.Y., Harper Torch, n.d.

GILSON, E. H. *Reason and Revelation in the Middle Ages*. N.Y., Scribner's, 1938.

HASKINS, C. H. *The Renaissance of the 12th Century*. Cambridge, Harvard Univ. Pr., 1927. (Also Meridian)

—————. *The Rise of the Universities*. N.Y., Holt, 1923.

HAWKINS, B. J. *A Sketch of Medieval Philosophy*. London, Sheed & Ward, 1946.

LEFF, GORDON. *Medieval Thought from St. Augustine to Ockham*. N.Y., Penguin, n.d.

McKEON, R. P. *Selections from Medieval Philosophers*. 2 vols. N.Y., Scribner's, 1929.

WULF, MAURICE. *History of Medieval Philosophy*. N.Y., Dover, 1952.

ADAMS, HENRY. *Mont-Saint-Michel and Chartres*. N.Y., Houghton, 1963.

CONANT, KENNETH J. *Carolingian and Romanesque Architecture: 800-1200*. N.Y., Penguin, 1957.

FOCILLON, HENRI. *The Art of the West in the Middle Ages*. Vol. I: *Romanesque Art*. Vol. II: *Gothic Art*. N.Y., Phaidon, 1963.

GIMPEL, JEAN. *The Cathedral Builders*. N.Y., Peter Smith, 1962.

MOREY, C. R. *Christian Art*. N.Y., Longmans, 1935.

—————. *Medieval Art*. N.Y., Norton, 1942.

NORDENFALK, CARL, and ANDRÉ GRABAR. *Early Medieval Painting* (Skira). N.Y., World, 1957.

REESE, GUSTAVE. *Music in the Middle Ages*. N.Y., Norton, 1940. (Contains a useful list of recordings)

SIMSON, OTTO VON. *The Gothic Cathedral*. N.Y., Pantheon, 1962.

Literature

FISCHER, JOHN H., ed. *The Medieval Literature of Western Europe: A Review of Research, Mainly 1930–1960*. N.Y., N.Y. Univ. Pr., 1966.

CHADWICK, H. M. and N. K. *The Growth of Literature*. 3 vols. Vol. I: *The Ancient Literatures of Europe*. N.Y., Macmillan, 1932.

CHAMBERS, E. K. *The Medieval Stage.* 2 vols. Oxford, Oxford Univ. Pr., 1903.

CHAYTOR, HENRY J. *From Script to Print: an Introduction to Medieval Literature.* N.Y., Macmillan; London, Cambridge Univ. Pr., 1945.

CURTIUS, ERNST R. *European Literature and the Latin Middle Ages.* N.Y., Pantheon, 1953.

JACKSON, W. T. H. *Medieval Literature: a History and a Guide.* N.Y., Collier, n.d.

KER, W. P. *The Dark Ages.* N.Y., Mentor, 1958. (History of medieval literature, 5th C.-12th C. First published 1904.)

——————. *Epic and Romance.* London, Macmillan, 1897.

KOHT, H. *The Old Norse Sagas.* N.Y., Norton, 1931.

LEWIS, C. S. *The Allegory of Love.* London, Oxford Univ. Pr., 1938. (Classic study of both allegory and courtly love)

PARIS, GASTON. *Medieval French Literature.* London, J. M. Dent, n.d. (Temple Classics)

RABY, FREDERIC J. E. *A History of Christian Latin Poetry from the Beginnings to the Close of the Middle Ages.* N.Y., Oxford Univ. Pr., 1927.

——————. *A History of Secular Latin Poetry in the Middle Ages.* 2 vols. Oxford, Clarendon, 1934.

SCHOFIELD, W. H. *English Literature from Norman Conquest to Chaucer.* London, Macmillan, 1931.

THOMPSON, STITH. *The Folk Tale.* N.Y., Dryden, 1946.

WADDELL, HELEN, tr. *Medieval Latin Lyrics.* N.Y., Holt, 1938.

YOUNG, KARL. *The Drama of the Medieval Church.* 2 vols. N.Y., Oxford Univ. Pr., 1933.

Collections

JONES, CHARLES WILLIAM, ed. *Medieval Literature in Translation.* N.Y., Longmans, 1950.

HOPPER, V. F., and G. B. LAHEY, eds. *Medieval Mysteries, Moralities, and Interludes.* Brooklyn, Barron's, 1965. (Text of the best English medieval dramas with 67-page introd.)

LOOMIS, R. S., and R. WILLARD, eds. *Medieval English Verse and Prose in Modernized Versions.* N.Y., Appleton-Century-Crofts, 1948.

LOOMIS, R. S. and L. H., eds. *Medieval Romances.* N.Y., Modern Library, 1957. (Contains 8 romances)

SCHLAUCH, MARGARET. *Medieval Narrative: a Book of Translations.* N.Y., Prentice, 1934. (Includes sagas, chansons, legends, saints' lives, fabliaux, miracle tales, etc.)

STURLUSON, SNORRE. *Heims Kringla: The Olaf Sagas.* 2 vols. N.Y., Dutton, n.d. (Everyman's Library)

ZENKOVSKY, S., tr. and ed. *Medieval Russia's Epics, Chronicles and Tales.* N.Y., Dutton, n.d. (Everyman's Library)

Arthur and the Grail

BROWN, ARTHUR C. L. *The Origin of the Grail Legend.* Cambridge, Harvard Univ. Pr., 1943.

CHAMBERS, E. K. *Arthur of Britain.* London, Oxford Univ. Pr., 1927.

(CHRETIEN). *The High History of the Holy Grail,* tr. Sebastian Evans. N.Y. Dutton, 1929. (Everyman's Library. By Chretien and his continuators, especially Mannesier.)

DETROYES, CHRETIEN. *Arthurian Romances.* N.Y. Dutton, 1935. (Everyman's Library)

LOOMIS, R. S. *Arthurian Tradition and Chretien de Troyes.* N.Y., Columbia Univ. Pr., 1949.

——————. *Development of Arthurian Romance.* N.Y., Harper Torch, 1964.

——————. *The Grail: from Celtic Myth to Christian Symbol.* N.Y., Columbia Univ. Pr., 1963.

——————. *Wales and the Arthurian Legend.* Cardiff, Univ. of Wales Pr., 1956.

NEWSTEAD, HELAINE H. *Bran the Blessed in Arthurian Romance.* N.Y., Columbia Univ. Pr., 1939.

RICHEY, MARGARET F. *The Story of Parzifal and the Grail.* N.Y., Peter Smith, 1935.

WESTON, JESSIE L. *From Ritual to Romance.* N.Y., Peter Smith, 1941.

——————. *The Quest of the Holy Grail.* N.Y., Barnes, 1964.

Other Types and Legends

MASON, EUGENE, tr. *Aucassin and Nicolette and Other Medieval Romances.* N.Y., Dutton, 1928. (Everyman's Library. Includes some 15 of the best.)

——————. *French Medieval Romances from the Lays of Marie de France.* N.Y., Dutton, 1932. (Everyman's Library)

DE LORRIS, G., and JEAN DE MEUN. *The Romance of the Rose.* N.Y., Dutton, n.d. (Everyman's Library)

CAWLEY, A. C., ed. *Everyman and Medieval Miracle Plays.* N.Y., Dutton, 1926. (Everyman's Library)

CHADWICK, H. M. *The Heroic Age.* Cambridge, Cambridge Univ. Pr., 1912. (Society, myth, poetry of the Germanic peoples)

CRAIGIE, W. A. *The Icelandic Sagas.* London, Cambridge Univ. Pr., 1913.

GREGORY, LADY I. A. *Cuchulain of Muir Themne.* London, Murray, 1902. (Includes among other Irish sagas and tales "The Fate of the Sons of Usnach")

GUEST, LADY CHARLOTTE, tr. *The Mabinogion: 11 Welsh Tales.* N.Y. Dutton, 1937. (Everyman's Library)

MACLEAN, MAGNUS. *The Literature of the Celts,* new ed. London, Blackie & Son, 1926.

Writers

BOROFF, MARIE. *Sir Gawain and the Green Knight: a Stylistic and Metrical Study.* New Haven, Yale Univ. Pr., 1962. (Contains extensive bibliography)

GARDNER, JOHN C. *The Complete Works of the Gawain-Poet.* Chicago, Univ. of Chicago Pr., 1965. (Modern English version with critical introduction)

KITTREDGE, G. L. *A Study of Gawain and the Green Knight.* Cambridge, Harvard Univ. Pr., 1916.

LOOMIS, R. S. *Wales and the Arthurian Legend.* Cardiff, Univ. of Wales Pr., 1956.

SAVAGE, H. L. *The Gawain-Poet.* Chapel Hill, Univ. of N. Car. Pr., 1956.

WESTON, JESSIE L. *Gawain and the Green Knight* . . . retold in modern prose with introd. and notes. London, D. Nutt, 1907. N.Y., Scribner's, 1909.

AUERBACH, ERICH. "Roland Against Ganelon" in *Mimesis*. N.Y., Anchor, 1957, 85-106.

BACON, LEONARD. *Song of Roland*. New Haven, Yale Univ. Pr., 1919. (Translated into English verse)

JONES, GEORGE F. *The Ethos of the Song of Roland*. Baltimore, Johns Hopkins, 1963.

SHERWOOD, MERRIAM, tr. *Song of Roland*. London, Longmans, 1938.

ARMOUR, MARGARET, tr. *The Fall of the Nibelungs done into English*. London, J. M. Dent, 1908. (Everyman's Library)

MOWATT, D. G. *The Nibelungenlied: The Fall of the Nibelungs*. N.Y. Dutton, n.d. (Everyman's Library)

MUELLER, WERNER A. *The Nibelungenlied Today*. Chapel Hill, Univ. of N. Car. Pr., 1962

SHUMWAY, D. B., tr. *The Nibelungenlied*. Boston, Houghton, 1909.

FRANK, G. *Medieval French Drama*. N.Y., Oxford Univ. Pr., 1954, 237 ff. (Aucassin)

HOLMES, URBAN T. *A History of Old French Literature*. N.Y., Russell & Russell, 1962.

MASON, EUGENE, tr. "Introduction" to *Aucassin and Nicolette and Other Medieval Romances*. N.Y., Dutton, 1928. (Everyman's Library)

PATER, WALTER. "Two Early French Stories" in *The Renaissance*. N.Y., Modern Library, n.d.

ALLEN, P. S. "The Origins of German Minnesong" in *Medieval Latin Lyrics*. Chicago, Univ. of Chicago Pr., 1931.

BRIFFAULT, ROBERT. *The Troubadours*. Bloomington, Indiana Univ. Pr., 1965.

CHAYTOR, H. J. *The Troubadours*. Cambridge, Cambridge Univ. Pr., 1912.

FLEMING, JOHN A. *The Troubadours of Provence*. Glasgow, W. MacLellan, 1952.

HILL, RAYMOND, ed. *Anthology of the Provencal Troubadours*. New Haven, Yale Univ. Pr., 1941.

LINKER, ROBERT W. *Music of the Minnesinger and Early Meistersinger, a Bibliography*. Chapel Hill, Univ. of N. Car. Pr., 1962.

ROBERTSON, J. G. *A History of German Literature*. N.Y., Putnam, 1931, 115-140.

TAYLOR, ARCHIE. *The Literary History of Meistergesang*. London, Oxford Univ. Pr., 1937.

VALENCY, MAURICE. *In Praise of Love: an Introduction to the Love Poetry of the Renaissance*. N.Y., Macmillan, 1958.

AUERBACH, ERICH. *Dante, Poet of the Secular World*. Chicago, Univ. of Chicago Pr., 1961.

BARBI, MICHELE. *Life of Dante*, tr. and ed. P.G. Ruggiers. Berkeley, Univ. of Calif. Pr., 1963.

BERGIN, THOMAS G. *Dante*. N.Y., Orion, 1965. (Contains extensive bibliography)

BRANDEIS, IRMA, ed. *Discussions of the Divine Comedy*. Boston, Heath, 1961.

CROCE, BENEDETTO. *The Poetry of Dante*. N.Y., Holt, 1922.

ELIOT, T. S. "Dante" in *Selected Essays*. N.Y., Harcourt, 1932.

FLETCHER, J. B. *Dante*. Notre Dame, Univ. of Notre Dame Pr., 1964.

—————. *Symbolism of the Divine Comedy*. N.Y., Columbia Univ. Pr., 1921.

FRECCERO, JOHN, ed. *Dante*. N.Y., Prentice, 1965. ("20th Century Views")

KNIGHT, G. WILSON. *The Christian Renaissance with interpretation of Dante, Shakespeare, Goethe and a note on T. S. Eliot*. Toronto, Macmillan, 1932.

LOWELL, JAMES R. "Dante" in *Among My Books*. Boston, Houghton, 1894.

MUSA, MARK, ed. *Essays on Dante*. Bloomington, Indiana Univ. Pr., 1964.

PAGE, THOMAS NELSON. *Dante and His Influence*. N.Y., Scribner's, 1923.

SANTAYANA, GEORGE. "Dante" in *Three Philosophical Poets*. N.Y., Anchor, 1953.

SAYERS, D. *Introductory Papers on Dante*. N.Y., Harper, 1954.

SINGLETON, CHARLES S., *Dante Alighieri: His Life and Works*. N.Y., Harper Torch, n.d.

TAYLOR, H. O. "The Medieval Synthesis: Dante" in *The Medieval Mind*, 2nd ed. N.Y., Macmillan, 1914, II, 555-590.

TOYNBEE, PAGET. *Dante Alighieri: His Life and Works*. N.Y., Harper Torch, 1965.

VOSSLER, KARL. *Medieval Culture: an Introduction to Dante and His Times*. 2 vols. N.Y., Harcourt, 1929.

WILLIAMS, CHARLES. *The Figure of Beatrice: a study in Dante*. N.Y., Noonday Pr., 1961.

ROBINSON, F. N., ed. *The Works of Geoffrey Chaucer*, 2nd ed. Boston, Houghton, 1957. (Cf. bibliography, pp. 641-645)

The Chaucer Review. University Park, Pa. St. Univ. Pr., 1966. (Publishes annual bibliography)

BENNETT, H. S. *Chaucer and the 15th Century*. N.Y., Oxford Univ. Pr., 1947.

CHUTE, MARCHETTE. *Geoffrey Chaucer of England*. N.Y., Dutton, 1946. (Everyman's Library)

COGHILL, NEVILL. *The Poet Chaucer*. London, Oxford Univ. Pr., 1947.

COULTON, G. G. *Chaucer and His England*, 3rd ed. N.Y., Dutton, 1921.

FRENCH, R. D. *A Chaucer Handbook*, 2nd ed. N.Y., Crofts, 1947.

GRIFFITH, D. D. *Bibliography of Chaucer 1908–1953*. Seattle, 1955.

JUSSERAND, J. J. *English Wayfaring Life in the Middle Ages*, rev. ed. N.Y., Putnam, 1925.

LAWRENCE, W. W. *Chaucer and the Canterbury Tales*. N.Y., Columbia Univ. Pr., 1950.

LEWIS, C. S. *The Allegory of Love: a study of medieval tradition*. N.Y., Oxford Univ. Pr., 1936.

LOWES, J. L. *The Art of Geoffrey Chaucer*. London, Oxford Univ. Pr., 1930.

MALONE, KEMP. *Chapters on Chaucer*. Baltimore, Johns Hopkins, 1951.

RICKERT, EDITH. *Chaucer's World,* ed. C. C. Olson and M. M. Crow. N.Y., Columbia Univ. Pr., 1948.

ROOT, R. K. *The Poetry of Chaucer,* rev. ed. Boston, Houghton, 1922.

TATLOCK, J. S. P. *The Mind and Art of Chaucer.* Syracuse, Syracuse Univ. Pr., 1950.

WAGENKNECHT, EDWARD P., ed. *Chaucer: Modern Essays in Criticism.* N.Y., Oxford Univ. Pr., 1959.

BRONSON, BERTRAND H. *The Traditional Tunes of the Child Ballads with Their Texts.* Princeton, Princeton Univ. Pr., 1959.

CHILD, F. J. *English and Scottish Popular Ballads.* Boston, Houghton, 1904.

ENTWISTLE, W. J. *European Balladry.* Oxford, Clarendon, 1939. (History and criticism)

FRIEDMAN, ALBERT B. *The Ballad Revival. Studies in the influence of popular on sophisticated poetry.* Chicago, Univ. of Chicago Pr., 1961.

GUMMERE FRANCIS B. *The Beginnings of Poetry.* N.Y., Macmillan, 1901.

──────. *The Popular Ballad.* Boston, Houghton, 1907.

POUND. LOUISE. *Poetic Origins and the Ballad.* N.Y., Macmillan, 1921. (Critical of Gummere, above)

THE RENAISSANCE

History

BRUCKER, GENE A. *Florentine Politics and Society, 1343–1378.* Princeton, Princeton Univ. Pr., 1962.

The New Cambridge Modern History. Vol. I: *The Renaissance.* Vol. II: *The Reformation.* Cambridge, Cambridge Univ. Pr., 1957 and 1958.

CHEYNEY, E. P. *The Dawn of a New Era: 1250–1453.* N.Y., Harper, 1936.

FERGUSON, WALLACE K. *Europe in Transition, 1300–1520.* Boston, Houghton, 1962.

GREEN, V. H. H. *Renaissance and Reformation, a survey of European History . . . 1450–1660.* London, Arnold, 1952.

HAKLUYT, RICHARD. *Voyages.* 8 vols. N.Y., Dutton, n.d. (Everyman's Library)

HAY, DENIS. *The Italian Renaissance in Its Historical Background.* Cambridge, Cambridge Univ. Pr., 1962.

HAYDN, HIRAM. *The Counter-Renaissance.* New York, Scribner's, 1950.

LUCAS, HENRY S. *The Renaissance and The Reformation.* N.Y., Harper, 1960.

LUCAS-DUBRETON, JEAN. *Daily Life in Florence in the Time of the Medici.* N.Y., Macmillan, 1961.

NEWTON, A. P., ed. *The Great Age of Discovery.* London, Univ. of London Pr., 1932.

PENROSE, BOIES. *Travel and Discovery in the Renaissance, 1420–1620.* Cambridge, Harvard Univ. Pr., 1952.

PLUMB, J. H. *The Italian Renaissance.* N.Y., Harper Torch, 1965.

SCHEVILL, FERDINAND. *Medieval and Renaissance Florence.* 2 vols. N.Y., Harper Torch, 1963.

SMITH, PRESERVED. *The Age of the Reformation.* N.Y., Holt, 1920.

TREVOR-DAVIES, R. *The Golden Century of Spain, 1501–1621.* N.Y., Harper Torch, 1964.

Culture

BAINTON, R. H. *The Reformation of the 16th Century.* Boston, Beacon, 1952.

BAKER, C. H. *The Dignity of Man: Studies in the Persistence of an Idea.* Cambridge, Harvard Univ. Pr., 1947.

BENESCH, OTTO. *The Art of the Renaissance in Northern Europe: Its Relation to Contemporary Spiritual and Intellectual Movements.* Cambridge, Harvard Univ. Pr., 1945.

BERENSON, BERNARD. *Italian Painters of the Renaissance.* London, Phaidon, 1957. (Also Meridian)

BLUNT, ANTHONY. *Artistic Theory in Italy: 1450–1600.* Oxford, Clarendon, 1940.

BRANDES, GEORG. *Michelangelo: His Life . . . Times . . . Era.* N.Y., Frederick Ungar, 1963.

BRION, MARCEL. *Michelangelo.* N.Y., Greystone Pr., 1940.

CLEMENTS, ROBERT J. *Michelangelo's Theory of Art.* N.Y., N.Y. Univ. Pr., 1961.

SALMI, MARIO, ed. *The Complete Work of Michelangelo.* Firenze, 1961. (A magnificent volume: 1040 ills., 32 full color plates, 600 pp. text)

STONE, IRVING. *The Agony and the Ecstasy.* N.Y., Signet, 1964. (A biographical novel of the life and times of Michelangelo)

BUKOFZER, M. F. *Studies in Medieval and Renaissance Music.* N.Y., Norton, 1950.

BURCKHARDT, JACOB. *The Civilization of the Renaissance in Italy.* London, Phaidon, 1960.

BUTTERFIELD, HERBERT. *The Origins of Modern Science, 1300–1800.* London, G. Bell, 1950.

CASSIRER, ERNST, *et al.,* eds. *The Renaissance Philosophy of Man.* Chicago, Univ. of Chicago Pr., 1948.

CELLINI, BENVENUTO. *The Autobiography.* N.Y., Penguin, 1963.

CHASTEL, ANDRÉ. *The Age of Humanism: Europe 1480–1530.* N.Y., McGraw, 1963.

CHEW, S. C. *The Crescent and The Rose. Islam and England during the Renaissance.* N.Y., Oxford Univ. Pr., 1937.

CLARK, SIR KENNETH M. *Leonardo da Vinci . . . His Development as an Artist,* 2nd ed. Cambridge, Cambridge Univ. Pr., 1952.

DAVINCI, LEONARDO. *Selections from the Notebooks.* London, Oxford World's Classics, 1950. (Also Mentor Classics)

HALE, JOHN R. *Leonardo da Vinci.* N.Y., Reynal, 1956.

MEREJKOWSKI, DMITRI. *The Romance of Leonardo da Vinci.* N.Y., Washington Sq. Pr., 1965.

DURANT, WILL. *The Story of Civilization.* Vol. V: *The Renaissance.* N.Y., Simon & Schuster, 1953.

FERGUSON, WALLACE K. *The Renaissance in Historical Thought.* Boston, Houghton, 1948.

FOSDICK, H. E., ed. *Great Voices of the Reformation.* N.Y., Random House, 1952.

GILMORE, MYRON P. *The World of Humanism: 1453–1517.* N.Y., Harper, 1952.

HALE, JOHN R., *et al.*, eds. *Great Ages of Man . . .: Renaissance.* N.Y., Time Inc., 1965. (Excellent chapters on Renaissance culture, copiously illustrated)

HEARNSHAW, F. J. C., ed. *The Social and Political Ideas of Some Great Thinkers of the Renaissance and Reformation.* London, Harrap, 1925.

HEXTER, J. H. *More's Utopia: the Biography of an Idea.* Princeton, Princeton Univ. Pr., 1952.

Horizon Book of the Renaissance (American Heritage). N.Y., Doubleday, 1961. (Copiously illustrated)

HUIZINGA, JOHAN. *The waning of the Middle Ages, a study of . . . life, thought, and art in France and the Netherlands in the 14th and 15th centuries.* London, Arnold, 1937.

HUYGHE, RENÉ, ed. *Larousse Encyclopedia of Renaissance and Baroque Art.* N.Y., Prometheus Pr., 1964.

JANSON, HORST W. *History of Art.* N.Y., Prentice and Abrams, 1963.

KRISTELLER, PAUL O. *Renaissance Thought: The Classic, Scholastic, and Humanist Strains.* N.Y., Harper Torch, n.d.

MCCARTHY, MARY. *The Stones of Venice.* N.Y., Harcourt, 1959.

PANOFSKY, ERWIN. *Albrecht Dürer,* 3rd ed. Princeton, Princeton Univ. Pr., 1948.

PATER, WALTER. *The Renaissance.* N.Y., Modern Library, 1951.

POPE-HENNESSY, JOHN. *Italian Renaissance Sculpture.* London, Phaidon, 1958.

REESE, GUSTAVE. *Music in the Renaissance.* N.Y., Norton, 1959.

ROEDER, RALPH. *The Man of the Renaissance.* N.Y., Meridian, 1960.

ROSS, J. B., and M. N. MCLAUGHLIN, eds. *The Portable Renaissance Reader.* N.Y., Viking, 1950.

SCHEVILL, F. *The First Century of Italian Humanism.* N.Y., Crofts, 1928.

SEEBOHM, FREDERIC. *The Oxford Reformers: . . . Colet, . . . Erasmus, . . . More.* N.Y., Dutton, 1914. (Everyman's Library)

SYMONDS, JOHN A. *The Renaissance in Italy.* 3 vols. N.Y., Peter Smith, 1961. (Also Modern Library Giants)

TAWNEY, R. H. *Religion and the Rise of Capitalism.* N.Y., Pelican, 1938.

TAYLOR, HENRY O. *Thought and Expression in the 16th Century.* N.Y., Macmillan, 1920.

THORNDIKE, LYNN. *A History of Magic and Experimental Science.* 6 vols. N.Y., Columbia Univ. Pr., 1923–1941. (Especially Vols. IV-VI)

VASARI, GIORGIO. *Lives of the Painters, Sculptors, and Architects.* 4 vols. N.Y., Dutton, 1963. (Everyman's Library. Also 1-vol. Modern Library)

VERMEULE, CORNELIUS. *European Art and the Classical Past.* Cambridge, Harvard Univ. Pr., 1964.

WÖLFFLIN, HEINRICH. *Art of the Italian Renaissance.* N.Y., Schocken, 1963.

——————. *Classic Art: an Introduction to the Italian Renaissance.* London, Phaidon, 1952.

Literature

ALDIS, H. G. *The Printed Book,* 3rd ed., rev. Cambridge, Cambridge Univ. Pr., 1951.

BLANCHARD, H. H., ed. *Prose and Poetry of the Continental Renaissance in Translation.* N.Y., Longmans, 1949.

BUSH, DOUGLAS. *The Renaissance and English Humanism.* Toronto, Univ. of Toronto Pr., 1939.

GOLDSCHMIDT, E. P. *The Printed Book of the Renaissance.* Cambridge, Cambridge Univ. Pr., 1950.

TILLEY, A. A. *The Dawn of the French Renaissance.* Cambridge, Cambridge Univ. Pr., 1918.

TILLYARD, E. M. W. *The Elizabethan World Picture.* London, Chatto, 1943.

Writers

SYMONDS, JOHN A. *Wine, Women, and Song: Medieval Latin students' songs . . . translated . . . with an essay.* London, Chatto, 1884.

WADDELL, HELEN. *The Wandering Scholars.* Boston, Houghton, 1927. (Latin text with transl. of Goliardic poets)

WHICHER, GEORGE F., tr. *The Goliard Poets: Medieval Latin songs and satires with verse translations.* Norfolk, Conn., New Directions, 1949.

DULLES, AVERY R. *Princeps Concordiae: Pico della Mirandola and the Scholastic Tradition.* Cambridge, Harvard Univ. Pr., 1941.

EHRMAN, SIDNEY H. *Three Renaissance Silhouettes.* N.Y., Putnam, 1928. (Includes Pico della Mirandola)

MIRANDOLA, GIOVANNI PICO DELLA. "Oratio de dignitate hominis" in F.A. Gragg, ed. *Latin Writings of the Italian Humanists.* N.Y., Scribner's, 1927.

MORE, SIR THOMAS, tr. *Giovanni Pico Della Mirandola: his life by his nephew . . . also three . . . letters* (etc.). London, D. Nutt, 1890. (Also forthcoming in Yale Univ. Pr. ed. of More's complete works)

PATER, WALTER. *Studies in the Renaissance.* N.Y., Modern Library, 1951. (Essay on Pico)

DEAN, LEONARD F., ed. *The Praise of Folly by Desiderius Erasmus . . . a new transl. with introd. and notes.* N.Y., Hendricks House, 1952.

ERASMUS, DESIDERIUS. *Christian Humanism and the Reformation: Selected Writings,* ed. J. C. Olin. N.Y., Harper Torch, 1965.

ADAMS, ROBERT P. *The Better Part of Valor: More, Erasmus, et al.* Seattle, Univ. of Wash. Pr., 1962.

ALLEN, P. S. *The Age of Erasmus.* Oxford, Clarendon, 1914.

——————. *Erasmus, Lectures and Wayfaring Sketches.* Oxford, Clarendon, 1934.

FROUDE, JAMES A. *Life and Letters of Erasmus.* N.Y., Scribner's, 1894.

HUIZINGA, JOHAN. *Erasmus and the Age of Reformation.* N.Y., Scribner's, 1924; N.Y. Harper Torch, 1965.

——————. *Erasmus of Rotterdam.* London, Phaidon, 1952.

HYMA, A. *Erasmus and the Humanists.* N.Y., Crofts, 1930.

SEEBOHM, F. *The Oxford Reformers.* N.Y., Dutton, 1914. (Everyman's Library)

SMITH, PRESERVED. *Erasmus.* N.Y., Harper, 1923.

ZWEIG, STEFAN. *Erasmus of Rotterdam.* N.Y., Viking, 1934. (Also Compass Books, 1963)

KRUTCH, J. W. *Five Masters.* N.Y., Cape & Smith, 1930. (Essay on Boccaccio)

McMANUS, F. *Boccaccio.* N.Y., Sheed & Ward, 1947.

BROWN, H. *Rabelais in English Literature.* Cambridge, Harvard Univ. Pr., 1933.

CHAPPELL, A. F. *The Enigma of Rabelais.* Cambridge, Cambridge Univ. Pr., 1924.

FRANCE, ANATOLE. *François Rabelais.* N.Y., Holt, 1929.

NOCK, A. J., and C. R. WILSON. *François Rabelais: The Man and His Work.* N.Y., Harper, 1929.

PLATTARD, JEAN. *The Life of Rabelais.* London, Routledge, 1930.

PUTNAM, SAMUEL. *François Rabelais, Man of the Renaissance.* N.Y., Cape & Smith, 1929.

MONTAIGNE, M. DE. *The Complete Works of . . . Essays, Journal, Letters,* tr. Donald M. Frame. Stanford, Stanford Univ. Pr., 1957.

BOASE, A. M. *The Fortunes of Montaigne: a History of the Essays in France 1580–1669.* London, Methuen, 1935.

FRAME, DONALD M. *Montaigne in France, 1812–1852.* N.Y., Columbia Univ. Pr., 1940.

GIDE, ANDRÉ. *Montaigne.* N.Y., McGraw, 1964.

LOWENTHAL, M. *The Autobiography of M. de Montaigne.* Boston, Houghton, 1935.

LÜTHY, HERBERT. "Montaigne, or the art of being truthful" in *Encounter,* Nov. 1953. (Also in Anderson and Mazzeo, *The Proper Study,* 318-336.)

MURRY, JOHN MIDDLETON. *Heroes of Thought.* N.Y., Julian Messner, 1938.

BELL, A. F. *Cervantes.* Norman, Univ. of Okla. Pr., 1947.

ENTWISTLE, W. J. *Cervantes.* Oxford, Clarendon, 1940.

FLORES, A., ed. *Cervantes Across the Centuries.* N.Y., Dryden, 1947.

KRUTCH, J. W. *Five Masters.* N.Y., Cape & Smith, 1930.

MADARIAGA, SALVADOR DE. *Don Quixote.* Oxford, Clarendon, 1935.

UNAMUNO, MIGUEL DE. *The Life of Don Quixote and Sancho.* N.Y., Knopf, 1927.

VAN DOREN, MARK. *Don Quixote's Profession.* N.Y., Columbia Univ. Pr., 1958.

ADY, JULIA C. *Baldassare Castiglione, the Perfect Courtier: His Life and Letters.* London, Murray, 1908.

ROEDER, R. *The Man of the Renaissance.* N.Y., Viking, 1933. (Also Meridian)

JONES, H. S. V. *A Spenser Handbook.* N.Y., Crofts, 1930.

JUDSON, ALEXANDER E. *The Life of Spenser* in *Works: a variorum ed.* Baltimore, Johns Hopkins, 1945.

LEWIS, C. S. "The Faerie Queene" in *The Allegory of Love.* N.Y., Oxford Univ. Pr., 1936, 304-346.

BARINCON, EDWARD. *Machiavelli.* N.Y., Evergreen, 1965.

CASSIRER, E. *The Myth of the State.* London, Oxford Univ. Pr., 1961.

GILBERT, A. H. *Machiavelli's Prince and Its Forerunners.* Durham, Duke Univ. Pr., 1938.

HALE, JOHN R. *Machiavelli and Renaissance Italy.* N.Y., Macmillan, 1961.

RIDOLFI, ROBERTO. *The Life of Nicolo Machiavelli.* Chicago, Univ. of Chicago Pr., 1963.

VILLARE, PASQUALE. *The Life and Times of Nicolo Machiavelli.* 2 vols. N.Y., Scribner's, 1929.

DUNNING, WILLIAM A. *A History of Political Theories from Luther to Montesquieu.* London, Macmillan, 1921, 153-191. (Section on Grotius)

KNIGHT, W. M. S. *Life and Works of Hugo Grotius.* London, Sweet & Maxwell, 1925.

LEE, ROBERT WARDEN. *Hugo Grotius.* London, H. Milford, 1931.

VREELAND, HAMILTON. *Hugo Grotius . . . father of . . . international law.* N.Y., Oxford Univ. Pr., 1917.

FITZMAURICE-KELLY, J. *Lope de Vega and the Spanish Drama.* N.Y., R. B. Johnson, 1902.

FLORES, ANGEL. *Lope de Vega, Monster of Nature.* N.Y., Brentano's, 1930.

PERRY, H. T. E. *Masters of Dramatic Comedy and their Social Times.* Cambridge, Harvard Univ. Pr., 1939.

SCHEVILL, R. *The Dramatic Art of Lope de Vega.* Berkeley, Univ. of Calif. Pr., 1918.

BERMAN, RONALD. *Reader's Guide to Shakespeare's Plays: a discursive bibliography.* Glenview, Ill., Scott, 1965.

BRADLEY, A. C. *Shakespearean Tragedy.* Greenwich, Conn., Fawcett, 1965.

CHAMBERS, E. K. *William Shakespeare: a study of facts and problems.* 2 vols. Oxford, Oxford Univ. Pr., 1930.

FERGUSSON, FRANCIS. "Hamlet . . . the analogy of Action" in Anderson and Mazzeo, *The Proper Study,* 337-374. (Also in *The Idea of a Theatre.* N.Y., Anchor, 1953.)

GRANVILLE-BARKER, H. *Prefaces to Shakespeare:* Series III: *Hamlet.* London, Sidgwick, 1937.

KNIGHT, G. WILSON. *The Wheel of Fire: Shakespeare's Sombre Tragedies.* N.Y., Oxford Univ. Pr., 1949.

LEAVENWORTH, RUSSELL E., ed. *Interpreting Hamlet: Materials for Analysis.* San Francisco, Chandler, 1960. (Anthology of discussions and interpretations from Garrick and Goethe to Gielgud and Francis Fergusson)

SPENCER, HAZELTON. *The Art and Life of William Shakespeare.* N.Y., Harcourt, 1940. (Extensive bibliography, pp. 419-475)

SPURGEON, CAROLINE F. E. *Shakespeare's Imagery.* Cambridge, Cambridge Univ. Pr., 1935.

STOLL, ELMER E. *Hamlet: an historical and comparative study.* Minneapolis, Univ. of Minn. Pr., 1919.

WILSON, JOHN D. *What Happens in Hamlet.* London, Cambridge Univ. Pr., 1935.

ARMITAGE, ANGUS. *Copernicus, Founder of Modern Astronomy.* N.Y., T. Yoseloff, 1957.

KESTEN, HERMANN. *Copernicus and His World.* N.Y., Roy Pub., 1945.

KUHN, THOMAS S. *The Copernican Revolution.* Cambridge, Harvard Univ. Pr., 1957.

REICHENBACH, HANS. *From Copernicus to Einstein.* N.Y., Philosophical Library, 1942.

BOULTING, WILLIAM. *Giordano Bruno, his life, thought and martyrdom.* N.Y., Dutton, 1915.

GREENBERG, SIDNEY. *The Infinite in Giordano Bruno,* with a transl. of his dialogue "Concerning the Cause, Principle, and One." N.Y., King's Crown, 1950.

SINGER, DOROTHEA W. *Giordano Bruno, His Life and Thought,* with annotated transl. of . . . "On the Infinite Universe . . ." N.Y., Schuman, 1950.

YATES, FRANCES A. *Giordano Bruno and the Hermetic Tradition.* Chicago, Univ. of Chicago Pr., 1964.

BACON, FRANCIS. *The Complete Essays . . . including New Atlantis and Novum Organum,* ed. with introd. by H. L. Finch. N.Y., Washington Sq. Pr., 1965.

ANDERSON, F. H. *The Philosophy of Bacon.* Chicago, Univ. of Chicago Pr., 1948.

BOWEN, CATHERINE D. *Francis Bacon: the temper of a man.* Boston, Little, Brown, 1963.

FARRINGTON, BENJAMIN. *Francis Bacon.* N.Y., Collier, n.d.

BAINTON, ROLAND H. *Here I Stand, a Life of Martin Luther.* N.Y., Abingdon, 1950.

BOEHMER, HEINRICH. *Martin Luther: Road to Reformation.* N.Y., Meridian, 1964.

ERIKSON, ERIK H. *Young Man Luther, a study in psychoanalysis and history.* N.Y., Norton, 1958.

FIFE, ROBERT HERNDON. *The Revolt of Martin Luther.* N.Y., Columbia Univ. Pr., 1959.

GREEN, VIVIAN H. H. *Luther and the Reformation.* N.Y., Putnam, 1964.

HEADLEY, JOHN M. *Luther's View of Church History.* New Haven, Yale Univ. Pr., 1963.

KOOIMAN, WILLEM J. *By Faith Alone, the Life of Martin Luther.* N.Y., Philosophical Library, 1955.

_____. *Luther and the Bible.* Philadelphia, Muhlenberg Pr., 1961.

RITTER, GERHARD. *Luther, His Life and Work.* N.Y., Harper, 1963.

SMITH, PRESERVED. *The Life and Letters of Martin Luther.* N.Y., Houghton, 1911.

_____. *Luther's Table Talk: a critical study.* N.Y., Columbia Univ. Pr., 1907.

SWIHART, ALTMAN K. *Luther and the Lutheran Church 1483–1960.* N.Y., Philosophical Library, 1960.

ADAMS, ROBERT M. *Ikon: Milton and the Modern Critics.* Ithaca, Cornell Univ. Pr., 1955.

BARKER, ARTHUR E., ed. *Milton: Modern Essays in Criticism.* N.Y., Oxford Univ. Pr., 1965.

BUSH, DOUGLAS. *John Milton, a Sketch of His Life and Writings.* N.Y., Macmillan, 1964.

COPE, JACKSON I. *The Metaphoric Structure of Paradise Lost.* Baltimore, Johns Hopkins, 1964.

HANFORD, JAMES H. *John Milton—Englishman.* N.Y., Crown, 1944.

_____. *A Milton Handbook.* N.Y., Crofts, 1946.

KERMODE, FRANK, ed. *The Living Milton.* London, Routledge, 1960.

LEWIS, C. S. *A Preface to Paradise Lost.* London, Oxford Univ. Pr., 1941.

NICOLSON, MARJORIE. *John Milton: a reader's guide to his poetry.* N.Y., Noonday Pr., 1963. (Extensive bibliography, pp. 374-380)

TILLYARD, E. M. W. *The English Epic and Its Background.* N.Y., Oxford Univ. Pr., 1954.

MILLER, PERRY. *Jonathan Edwards.* N.Y., Meridian, 1965.

FOSCOLO, UGO. *Essays on Petrarch.* London, Murray, 1953.

WHITFIELD, J. H. *Petrarch and the Renascence.* Oxford, Blackwell, 1943.

WILKINS, ERNEST HATCH. *Studies in the Life and Works of Petrarch.* Cambridge, Mass., Mediaeval Academy of Am., 1955.

BELLOC, H. *Avril.* N.Y., Sheed & Ward, 1945. (Villon)

CHANEY, E. F. *François Villon in His Environment.* Oxford, Blackwell, 1946.

BISHOP, MORRIS. *Ronsard, Prince of Poets.* N.Y., Oxford Univ. Pr., 1940.

LEWIS, D. B. WYNDHAM, *Ronsard.* N.Y., Coward-McCann, 1944.

WOLFE, H. *Ronsard and French Romantic Poetry.* Oxford, Clarendon, 1935.

HUBLER, EDWARD. *The Sense of Shakespeare's Sonnets.* Princeton, Princeton Univ. Pr., 1952.

LEISHMAN, J. B. *Theme and Variations in Shakespeare's Sonnets.* N.Y., Harper Torch, 1966.

WILSON, JOHN DOVER. *An Introduction to the Sonnets of Shakespeare.* London, Cambridge Univ. Pr., 1964.

BARISH, JONAS A. *Ben Jonson: a collection of critical essays.* Englewood Cliffs, N.J., Prentice, 1963.

CHUTE, MARCHETTE. *Ben Jonson of Westminster.* N.Y., Dutton, 1953.

HERFORD, C. H., and P. SIMPSON. *Life of [Ben] Jonson,* Vols. I and II of *Works* (11 vols.). Oxford, Oxford Univ. Pr., 1925–1952.

JOHNSTON, GEORGE B. *Ben Jonson, Poet.* N.Y., Columbia Univ. Pr., 1945.

ELIOT, T. S. "The Metaphysical Poets" in *Selected Essays.* N.Y., Harcourt, 1932.

GOSSE, EDMUND. *Life and Letters of John Donne.* 2 vols. N.Y., Dodd, 1899.

KERMODE, FRANK, ed. *Discussions of John Donne.* Boston, Heath, 1962.

LE COMTE, EDWARD S. *Grace to a Witty Sinner: a Life of Donne.* N.Y., Walker, 1965.

MUELLER, WILLIAM R. *John Donne, Preacher.* Princeton, Princeton Univ. Pr., 1962.

STEIN, ARNOLD S. *John Donne's Lyrics.* Minneapolis, Univ. of Minn. Pr., 1962.

TUVE, ROSAMOND. *Elizabethan and Metaphysical Imagery.* Chicago, Univ. of Chicago Pr., 1961.

UNGER, LEONARD. *Donne's Poetry and Modern Criticism.* Chicago, Regnery, 1950.

WHITE, HELEN C. *The Metaphysical Poets.* N.Y., Macmillan, 1936, 70-94.

WILLIAMSON, GEORGE. *The Donne Tradition.* N.Y., Noonday Pr., 1963.

BROOKS, CLEANTH. *The Well-Wrought Urn.* London, Dobson, 1960.

CHUTE, MARCHETTE. *Two Gentle Men: the lives of George Herbert and Robert Herrick.* N.Y., Dutton, 1959.

MOORMAN, FREDERIC W. *Robert Herrick: a biographical and critical study.* London and N.Y., John Lane, 1910.

General Index

The name of an author represented by selections appears in capitals and small capitals (SHAKESPEARE, WILLIAM): the number in boldface after the name is the page on which his biographical sketch begins.

Selections that are reprinted in this book are listed in boldface italic; the number in boldface after the title is the page on which the selection begins; other numbers are pages on which it is mentioned. A few selections without titles are listed according to first lines.

Aage and Else, II:249
Abgesang, II:151
About Myself, I:419
Academy, I:104, I:273; founding of by Plato, I:246
Achaean League, I:108
Achaians. *See* Greeks.
Acharnians, The, I:102, I:216
Achilles, I:94; as Greek hero, I:109–110; in Trojan War, I:109
Actors, of Renaissance, II:279, II:280
Ad Leuconoen, I:412
Ad Xanthiam Phoceum, I:413
Addressed Humorously to Tu Fu, I:25
Advancement of Learning, The, II:506
Aeneas, and founding of Rome, I:306; as Roman hero, I:355, I:356
Aeneid, The, I:306, I:317, I:355, I:356, I:357
Aeolians, I:90; and Greek lyric, I:98
AESCHYLUS, I:93, I:97, I:99, I:101, I:166; criticized by Aristophanes, I:216; and *Prometheus Bound,* I:89
Africa, II:548
After a Quarrel, I:426
Agamemnon, in Trojan war, I:109
Agamemnon, I:168
AGATHIAS, I:298
Age, I:294
Ages of Man, according to Hesiod, I:89
Agni, God of Fire, I:27
Aladdin and His Lamp, II:28
Alba Longa, I:306
Albertus Magnus, II:8, II:15, II:265, II:277
ALBRECHT VON JOHANNSDORF, II:152
Alcaeus, I:98, I:289
Alcestis, I:101, I:201
Alcibiades, I:92
Alcuin, II:8
Alexander the Great, death of, I:106; empire of, I:105; and spread of Greek culture, I:106
Alexandria, Egypt, and Hellenistic culture, I:106
Ali Baba and the Forty Thieves, II:28
All Things Drink, I:293

Allah, in *Koran,* II:25
Allegory, Puritan, II:286
Alone in Her Beauty, I:27
Amadis of Gaul, II:286, II:347
Amores, I:318, I:428–429
Amoretti, II:396
Amphitryon, I:342
Anabasis, I:102
ANACREON, I:98, I:291; influence of on Horace, I:317; influence of on Ovid, I:317
Anacreontic tradition, I:291
Analects, I:6, I:17
Andronicus, Livius, I:311
Anglican Church, origin of, II:276
Anglo-Saxon, epic poetry, II:6–8
Antigone, I:101, I:187
ANTIPATER, I:298
Anti-remonstrants, II:421
Antoninus, Marcus Aurelius, I:314, I:321; and Stoicism, I:310
Antony, Mark, and Cicero, I:321; defeated by Octavian, I:313
Aphrodite, I:88
Apollo, I:88
Apology, I:247
Aquinas, Thomas, II:8, II:15, II:265
Aquino, Maria d', II:301
Arabian Nights, The, II:20, II:28, II:29
Arabian Nights Entertainment, The, II:20
Arabic, use of in *Koran,* II:25
Arabs, scientific knowledge of, II:19, II:277; in Spain, II:269
ARCHIAS OF BYZANTIUM, I:299
Archimedes, I:106
Architecture, of the Greeks, I:97; Roman, I:314
Areopagitica, II:514
ARGENTARIUS, MARCUS, I:301
Argives. *See* Greeks.
Argument of His Book, The, II:571
Arianism, II:65
Ariosto, Ludovico, II:278, II:281
Aristarchus, I:106
Aristocles. *See* Plato.
ARISTOPHANES, I:99, I:102, I:186, I:200, I:215
ARISTOTLE, I:96, I:273; criticism of in Renaissance, II:277; and dramatic unity, I:101; influence of on Christianity, I:319; his opinion of *Oedipus,* I:187, 188; place of in Greek philosophy, I:104; place of in medieval philosophy, I:105; on position of women, I:95
Arius, II:65
Arjuna, I:30
Ark of the Covenant, I:13
Armada, Spanish, II:425
Art, of the Greeks, I:96–97
Art of Love, The, I:318, I:429
Art of Poetry, The, I:318, I:410, I:422

Cassius, and Caesar, I:307–308; defeated by Octavian, I:313

CASTIGLIONE, BALDASSARE, II:272, II:282, **II:388**

Catholic Church, and Arian heresy, II:65; attitude of Erasmus toward, II:293; and Avignonese papacy, II:275; and Ghibellines, II:158; and Great Schism, II:275; and Guelphs, II:158; and Nicaean Creed, II:65; organization of, II:2–3; and origin of drama, II:13; and Reformation, II:275–276; significance of in Middle Ages, II:2; temporal power of in Middle Ages, II:4. *See also* Christian Church, Papacy, Pope.

Cato, I:306

CATULLUS, GAIUS VALERIUS, I:312, **I:425**

Catullus Contrasts Quintia with Lesbia, I:426

Catullus Struggles to Be Free, I:427

Cellini, Benvenuto, II:273, II:278, II:282

Cephalas, Constantine, and *Greek Anthology,* I:298

CERVANTES, MIGUEL DE, II:286–288, **II:346**, II:388

Chansons de geste, II:10; described, II:111

Chante-fable form, II:137

Charlemagne, campaign of in Spain (778), II:110; government of, II:6, II:8; in *The Song of Roland,* II:111

Charles I, king of Spain, II:269

Charles V, Holy Roman Emperor, II:269

Charles VIII, king of France, II:282

CHAUCER, GEOFFREY, **II:201**; compared to Dante, II:23; compared to Spenser, II:395–396

Cheat of Cupid, The, I:291

Cherry-Ripe, **II:572**

Child, Francis J., and collection of ballads, II:246

Ch'in dynasty, I:4

China, cultural characteristics, I:3, I:4; geography of, I:4; history of, I:4–5; poetry of, I:6–7

Ching-Ting Mountain, The, I:23

Chivalry, decline of, II:271; effect of on literature, II:9; in medieval romance, II:10–11; of Minnesingers, II:151; satirized by Cervantes, II:346–347; satirized in *Aucassin and Nicolete,* II:137; in *Sir Gawain and the Green Knight,* II:88; in Spain, II:286

Choephoroe. See Libation-Bearers, The.

Chorus, in Greek drama, I:99; use of by Aeschylus, I:101; use of by Euripides, I:101; use of by Sophocles, I:101

Chou dynasty, I:4

Chrestien de Troyes, II:11

Christian Church, and *Divine Comedy,* II:159; Eastern, II:19; establishment of, II:48

Christianity, Aristotle's influence on, I:319; ideals of in Matthew, II:48; recognized by Constantine, II:65; in Roman Empire, I:314; and Roman tradition, I:319; in *The Song of Roland,* II:111

Chrysostom, John, I:72

CICERO, MARCUS TULLIUS, I:312, **I:321**; murder of, I:313; and Stoicism, I:310

Circus Maximus, I:316

City Life and Country Life, **I:420**

City-states, Italian, II:268

Cleon, and Aristophanes, I:215, I:216

Cleopatra, and Antony, I:313; and Caesar, I:307

Clergy, Catholic, decline of temporal power, II:271; influence of on medieval literature, II:14–15; and writing of romances, II:12

Clio, I:239

Clodia, I:425

Clouds, The, I:102, I:216, **I:217**

Cnossus, destruction of by Greeks, I:87

Code of Justinian, and Roman law, I:320

Colet, John, II:283; and Erasmus, II:293

Colin Clout's Come Home Again, II:396

Columbus, Christopher, II:267

Combat, The, **I:292**

Comedias. See Comedy, Spanish.

Comedy, of Aristophanes, I:216; of Ben Jonson, II:285; in Greece, I:102; Middle, I:102; New, I:216, I:311, I:342; Old Comedy, I:102; I:216; of Plautus, I:311–312, I:342; Spanish, II:288

Commedia. See Divine Comedy, The.

Commerce, of Renaissance Europe, II:266–267

Comus, II:286, **II:514**

Confessions of Golias, The, **II:289**

Confucianism, philosophy of, I:6

CONFUCIUS, I:17; and Lao-Tzŭ, I:5; teachings of, I:6

Consolation of Philosophy, The. See De Philosophiae Consolatione.

Constitution of Athens, The, I:273

Conte del Graal, II:15

Contentment, I:418

Cook, The, I:447

Copernican theory, expounded by Bruno, II:503

COPERNICUS, NICOLAUS, II:277, **II:499**

Corinthians, Paul's Epistles to, II:48. *See First Epistle of Paul to the Corinthians.*

Counter-Reformation, history of, II:276; in Spain, II:269

Courtiers, and English literature, II:283; Italian, II:282; position of in Renaissance, II:271; and Renaissance monarchs, II:272; as seen by Castiglione, II:388–389

Covenant, of the Jews, I:12, I:13

Cradle, The, **II:308**

CRATES, I:300

Crethis, **I:299**

Crito, I:247, **I:258**

Cromwell, Oliver, II:514

Crusader Hymns, II:151

Crusades, II:21

Cup, The, **I:293**

Cyclops, The (Idyll XI), **I:295**

Cymbeline, songs from, **II:564**

Cynewulf, II:8

Cynewulfian cycle, II:10

Daedalus and Icarus, I:436

Danaans. *See* Greeks.

Danaians. *See* Greeks.

DANTE ALIGHIERI, **II:157,** II:265; compared to Chaucer, II:23; influence of on Boccaccio, II:301; influence of on Milton, II:515; love of for Beatrice, II:158; medievalism of, II:10; and Virgil, I:356; and writing of *Divine Comedy,* II:158–159

Darius I, I:91, I:92

David, as author of Psalms, I:13, I:73

De Contemptu Mundi, II:9

De Finibus, I:321

De Monarchia, II:158

De Philosophiae Consolatione, II:8, II:202

De Revolutionibus Orbium Celestium. See Revolutions of the Heavenly Bodies, The.

Deadly Kisses, **II:560**

Death, **II:571**

Death-Bed of Laura, The, **II:550**

Decameron, II:280, II:301

Delian Confederacy, I:92

Delight in Disorder, **II:572**

DELLA MIRANDOLA, PICO, II:273, **II:291**

Democritus, I:330

Denmark, ballads of, II:246–247

Deus ex machina, used by Euripides, I:201

Devotion to the Cross, The, II:288

Dharma, I:9, I:30

Dialogue, use of in medieval teaching, II:18–19

Dialogues of the Dead, I:283, **I:287**

Dialogues of the Gods, I:283

Diaspora, of Jews, I:15–16

DIETMAR VON AIST, II:151

Dietrich Saga, II:125

Dinner Gift, A, I:299

Dion of Tarsus, I:303

Dionysus, I:88; in *The Frogs,* I:216; and origin of Greek drama, I:98; cult of and Christianity, I:319; Theater of, I:99

Discourses on the First Ten Books of Livy, II:415

Dispute of the Heart and the Body of François Villon, The, **II:555**

Dithyramb, in Greek drama, I:98

Divan, The, **II:44**

Divine Comedy, The, **II:160;** interpretation of, II:158–159; numerical symbols in, II:159

Domitian, I:313

Don Federigo's Falcon, **II:303**

Don Quixote de la Mancha, II:286–288, **II:347**

DONNE, JOHN, II:283, **II:562**

Dorians, I:90

Doubt, **I:426**

Down Chung-nan Mountain to the Kind Pillow and Bowl of Hu Ssü, I:23

Drama, development of in Middle Ages, II:13; Elizabethan, II:285; French, II:279; Greek, I:98–102; of Lope de Vega, II:426; and Puritan opposi-

tion, II:286; Renaissance, II:279–280; of the Roman Republic, I:311–312; Sanskrit, I:12; of Shakespeare, II:285, II:447–448; Spanish, II:279–280, II:288, **II:425–426**

Drinking Alone in the Moonlight, **I:22**

Du Bellay, Jean, II:309

Duns Scotus, II:8, II:15, II:265

Dust of Timas, The, **I:291**

Eastern Orthodox Church, II:19

Ecclesiastes, I:13, **I:75**

Ecclesiastical History of the English People, II:8

Eclogue IV (The Messiah), I:317, **I:356**

Eclogues, I:294, I:317, I:355

Ecstasy, The, **II:569**

Eddic Poems. *See Elder Edda* and *Younger Edda.*

Education, effect of Renaissance on, II:275

Edward, **II:249**

Edward III, king of England, II:88; and Chaucer, II:201

EDWARDS, JONATHAN, II:276, **II:543**

Elckerlijk. See Everyman.

Elder Edda, II:125

Electra, I:167

Elements, I:106

Elizabeth, queen of England, II:269, II:283; and drama, II:279; and English Reformation, II:276

Empire, Roman, decline of, I:314–317; described by Tacitus, I:318; at greatest extent, I:314; history of, I:312–317; literature of, I:317–319

Endless Yearning, **I:24**

England, ballads of, II:246–248; colonization by, II:267; history of during Renaissance, II:268–269; and Hundred Years' War, II:267; Reformation in, II:276; Renaissance drama of, II:279; Renaissance literature of, II:283–286

Ennius, I:311

Epic, defined, I:97–98; early medieval, II:6–8, II:10; Germanic, II:125; in Greece, I:98; *The Song of Roland* as, II:111; *The Nibelungenlied* as, II:25

Epic form, as *chanson de geste,* II:111

Epic lays, French, II:110

Epic period, of Greek literature, I:97

Epics, of Ariosto and Tasso, II:281

Epictetus, I:310, I:321

Epicure, The, **I:292**

Epicureanism, in Rome, I:311

Epicurus, and influence of Lucretius, I:330; philosophy of, I:311

Epidaurus, Theater of, I:99; *pictured,* I:100

Epigram, use of by Martial, I:444

Epistle in the Form of a Ballade to His Friends, **II:556**

Epistle to the Corinthians, I, II:48, **II:63**

Epistles, of Horace, I:410

Epitaph on Elizabeth L. H., **II:569**

Epithalamion, II:396

ERASMUS, DESIDERIUS, II:275, **II:293;** as northern Humanist, II:273–274
Eratosthenes, I:106
Eros, I:88
Essay, use by Montaigne, II:278
Essays (of Francis Bacon), II:506
Essays (of Michel de Montaigne), II:325
Etruscans, I:306
Euclid, I:106
Eudemian Ethics, I:274
Eumenides, The, I:93. *See Furies, The.*
Euphues, or the Anatomy of Wit, II:285
Euphuism, II:285
EURIPIDES, I:99, I:101, **I:200;** influence of on Seneca, I:317; satirized by Aristophanes, I:216
Even Unto Death, **II:558**
Everyman, II:13
Excursion, The, I:26
Exempla, II:12
Extremum Tanain, I:415

Fabliau, II:12
Faerie, Queene, The, II:272, II:285, **II:396**
"*Fair and Colder*," I:411
Fairies, The, **II:574**
Faith Renewed, I:413
False Appearances, I:447
Farewell, A, I:302
Farewell to Anactoria, I:290
Fasces, I:308
Fate, in Greek tragedy, I:188
Fear no more the heat o' the sun, **II:564**
Feast of Bricriu, The, II:88
Ferdinand, king of Spain, II:269
Feudalism, decline of, II:266–267; organization of, II:3–4; significance of in Middle Ages, II:2; struggle of with Church, II:4
Fiammetta. *See Aquino, Maria d'.*
Fiammetta, La, II:301
Filocolo, Il, II:301
Filostrato, Il, II:301
Fioretti di San Francesco. See Little Flowers of Saint Francis, The.
Firdousi, II:19, II:20
First Epistle of Paul to the Corinthians, II:63
Fitzgerald, Edward, II:37, II:38
Five Classics, I:17
Florence, II:10; commerce of with east, II:266; Medici, rule of, II:268; plague of, II:301; politics of, II:414–415; and start of Renaissance, II:265
Forgotten, I:290
Fourth Eclogue, I:317. *See Eclogue IV (The Messiah).*
Fragment of a Sonnet, **II:558**
Fragments, I:290
Framework device, use of in *The Arabian Nights*, II:29; used by Boccaccio, II:301; used by Chaucer, II:203

France, Golden Age of, II:269; history of during Renaissance, II:269; and Hundred Years' War, II:267; Renaissance drama of, II:279; Renaissance literature of, II:282–283
Franciscan Friars, founding of, II:74; and Rabelais, II:309
Freedom of Will, II:543
Freemen, in medieval society, II:4
Friar Onion and the Relics of the Angel Gabriel, **II:305**
Friendship, II:325
Frogs, The, I:102, I:187, I:200, I:216
Fuente Ovejuna. See Sheep Well, The.
Full many a glorious morning have I seen, **II:565**
Funeral, The, **II:571**
Funeral Speech of Pericles, I:239, I:240
Furies, in Greek mythology, I:88, I:89
Furies, The, I:167

Galatea, II:347
Galilei, Galileo, II:277
Galla's Hair, **I:447**
Gama, Vasco da, II:267, II:269
Garden of Eden, as visualized by Dante, II:159
Gargantua and Pantagruel, II:274, II:283, **II:310;** analyzed, II:309–310
Garland for Heliodora, A, **I:301**
Gaul, subdued by Caesar, I:307
Gauls, early conquest of Rome by, I:306
Gautama Buddha. *See Buddha.*
Genoa, II:10; commerce of with east, II:266
Georgic, invention of, I:98
Georgics, I:317, I:355
Germanic epic, II:125
Germany, history of during Renaissance, II:268. *See Holy Roman Empire.*
Ghettos, I:16
Girl, A, **I:290**
Gita, The, **I:30**
Gladiators, Roman, I:316
GLAUCUS, I:299
Gold, Age of, I:89
Golden Age, of Athens, I:91; of English literature, II:269; of French art, II:269; of Greek literature, I:97; of Rome, I:317; of Spanish art, II:271
Goliardic verse, II:289
Goliards. *See* WANDERING SCHOLARS.
Golias, Bishop, II:289
Gospel According to Saint Matthew, The, II:47, II:48
GOTTFRIED VON STRASBURG, II:11, II:151
Grapes, **I:302**
Grasshopper, The, **I:293**
Gravitas, as Roman ideal, I:309
Gray Friars. *See Franciscan Friars.*
Great Schism, II:275

Greece, annexed by Rome, 1:306–307; geography of, 1:85–86; Macedonian conquest of, 1:105. *See* Greeks.

Greek Anthology, The, 1:298

Greek literature, in Middle Ages, 11:272; rediscovery of, 11:273–274

Greeks, art of, 1:96–97; and athletics, 1:95; attitude of toward women, 1:94–95; compared to Romans, 1:314–315; drama of, 1:98–102; government of, 1:91–92; and Hellenistic culture, 1:106–108; historians of, 1:102–104; history of, 1:87–93, 1:105–108; influence of on Christianity, 1:319; influence of on Rome, 1:108; language of, 1:88; literary renaissance of, 1:283; and lyric, 1:98; periods of literature, 1:97–98; philosophers of, 1:104–105; point of view of, 1:93–97; and public life, 1:95; religion of, 1:88–89, 1:93, 1:94; and slavery, 1:94

Green Knight, The, 11:88

Grocyn, William, 11:283, 11:293

GROOT, HUIG VAN. *See* GROTIUS, HUGO.

GROTIUS, HUGO, 11:271, **11:421**

Grundtvig, Svend, 11:246

Guilds, 11:9; and production of plays, 11:13

Guillaume de Lorris, 11:15–18

Gulistan, 11:20

Hades, 1:88; Greek concept of, 1:94

Hadrian, and Greek Renaissance, 1:283; as Roman Emperor, 1:314

HAFIZ, 11:19, 11:20, **11:44**

Hag, The, **11:574**

Hamilcar, 1:306

Hamlet, 11:285, **11:449**; analyzed, 11:448

HAMMERKEN, THOMAS. *See* THOMAS À KEMPIS.

Hannibal, assisted by Macedonia, 1:108; in Punic Wars, 1:306

Hard Road, The, **1:24**

Hark, hark! The lark at heaven's gate sings, **11:564**

Haroun al-Raschid, 11:19, 11:20

He Thanks Her That from Time to Time . . . , **11:550**

Heaven, in medieval teaching, 11:5–6; as visualized by Dante, 11:159

Heavyweight, A, **1:300**

Hebrews, agricultural life of, 1:72; cultural characteristics of, 1:3; diaspora of, 1:15–16; effect on Christianity of, 1:3–4; history of, 1:12–16; music of, 1:72; prophets of, 1:13–14; and rabbinical law, 1:16; and settling of Canaan, 1:12; and Zionism, 1:16

Hector, 1:109

Helen, 1:109

Heliand, 11:10

Heliocentric theory, 11:277

Hell, in medieval teaching, 11:5; as visualized by Dante, 11:159; *diagram of,* 11:175

Hellas. *See* Greece.

Hellenes. *See* Greeks.

Hellenica, 1:102

Hellenistic culture, 1:106–108; 1:283

Hellenistic period, of Greek literature, 1:97–98

Henry II, king of England, 11:4

Henry IV, Holy Roman Emperor, 11:4

Henry IV, king of France, 11:269; and Grotius, 11:421

Henry VII, king of England, 11:269

Henry VIII, king of England, 11:276, 11:283, 11:293

Hephaestos, 1:88

Hera, 1:88

Heracles, and Age of Bronze, 1:89

Heraclitus, **1:299**

Herodotus, 1:97, 1:102; compared to Thucydides, 1:239

Heroes, Age of, 1:89

Heroides, **1:429**

HERRICK, ROBERT, 11:283, **11:562**

Hesiod, 1:98; and ages of Man, 1:89; and Greek religion, 1:88; influence of on Virgil, 1:317

Hesperus the Bringer, **1:291**

Hidden lovers' woes, **11:157**

Hildebrandslied, 11:10

Himalayas, influence of on Hindus, 1:9

Hindu caste system, 1:3, 1:9

Hinduism, 1:9–10; influence of on West, 1:7–8

Hinted Wish, A, **1:448**

Hippolytus, 1:201, **1:202**

His Lady's Death, **11:560**

His Lady's Tomb, **11:560**

His Mother's Service to Our Lady, **11:552**

Historians, Greek, 1:102–104; Roman, 1:318

Historiography, contribution of Bede to, 11:8

History, origin of, 1:102

History of Herodotus, 1:97, 1:102

History of the Peloponnesian War, 1:102, 1:239. *See* ***Funeral Speech of Pericles*** and ***Melian Dialogue.***

Holiday, **1:415**

Holy Grail, 11:12

Holy Land. *See* Israel.

Holy Roman Emperor, struggle of with Pope, 11:158

Holy Roman Empire, and German weakness, 11:268; and Italy, 11:268

HOMER, 1:95, **1:109**; and Age of Heroes, 1:89; importance of to Greeks, 1:94; influence of on Virgil, 1:317, 1:355; translated by Boccaccio, 11:301

HORACE (QUINTUS HORATIUS FLACCUS), 1:316, 1:317, 1:318, **1:409**

How sweet and lovely dost thou make the shame, **11:566**

Hrostvitha, 11:13

Huguenots, 11:269; and Massacre of St. Bartholomew's Day, 11:325; origin of, 11:276

Humanism, of Boccaccio, 11:300–301; development of, 11:272–274; of Erasmus, 11:293–294; French, 11:282–283; Italian, 11:280–281; origin of term,

II:273; of Pico della Mirandola, II:291; of Rabelais, II:309; of Wandering Scholars, II:289

Humanists, Italian, II:272–273; Northern, II:273–274; use of Latin by, II:278; versatility of, II:273

Hundred Years' War, II:267, II:269; and French Renaissance, II:282

Huss, John, II:10, II:275

Hymnes in Honor of Love and Beautie, II:396

Idyll, invention of form, I:106

Idylls, of Theocritus, I:294

If It Be Destined, **II:550**

Il Penseroso, II:514

Iliad, The, I:109, **I:111**

Imitatio Christi. See Imitation of Christ, The.

Imitation of Christ, The, **II:66**

Immortality of Verse, The, **I:415**

In the Quiet Night, **I:24**

India, cultural characteristics of, I:3; geography of, I:8–9; literature of, I:9, I:10–12. *See* Hinduism.

Individualism, in Italian city-states, II:10; in Renaissance literature, II:278; of Renaissance man, II:265–266

Induction, use of by Francis Bacon, II:278, II:506

Inquisition, II:503

Inscription by the Sea, An, **I:299**

Internationalism, of Grotius, II:271

Invitation to Youth, The, **II:290**

Ionians, characteristics of, I:90–91

Iphigenia, sacrifice of, I:109, I:167

Iphigenia at Aulis, I:101, I:200

Iron, Age of, I:89

Isabella, queen of Spain, II:269

Islam, compared with Christianity, II:20; compared with medieval Europe, II:19–20; penetration of into Europe, II:21

Israel, as Promised Land, I:12

Israelites. *See* Hebrews.

It Is Not Growing Like a Tree, **II:569**

It was a lover and his lass, **II:563**

Italy, commerce of with east, II:266; geography of, I:305–306; history of during Renaissance, II:268; literature of, II:280–281

James I, king of England, and Francis Bacon, II:505

James II, king of England, II:276

Jason, I:89

Jeremiah, I:13–14

Jerome, I:319

Jerusalem, capture of, I:13; rebuilding of, I:15; siege of by Titus, I:15

Jerusalem Delivered, II:281

Jesuits, founding of, II:276

Jesus, life of in Matthew, II:48; as Messiah of Jews, I:15

Jews. *See* Hebrews.

Joan of Arc, II:269

Johanan ben Zakkai, I:15

John, king of England, II:4, II:8–9

John of Salisbury, II:15

Johnie Armstrong, **II:263**

JONAH, I:73, I:80

JONSON, BEN, II:285, **II:561**

Journey's End, **I:427**

Judah, two tribes of, I:13

Judah Halevi, I:16

Judaism, becomes monotheism, I:15; effect of on Christianity, I:3–4; spread of, I:15

JULIANUS ANTECESSOR, I:299

Juno, I:315

Jupiter, I:315

JUVENAL (DECIMUS JUNIUS JUVENALIS), I:313, I:317, I:318, **I:440**

KALIDASA, I:11, **I:40**

Kemp Owyne, **II:262**

Kena-Upanishad, **I:28**

King, emergence of in England, II:268–269; emergence of in France, II:269; position of in medieval state, II:3; position of in Renaissance, II:267 ff.

Kings, Greek, I:89; and Reformation, II:274–275

Knights, The, I:102, I:216

Knight's Tale, The, II:202

Koran, The, **II:19, II:25**; compared to New Testament, II:20

Krishna, I:30

Kronos, I:88

La Boetie, Etienne de, II:325

Labors of Persiles and Sigismunda, II:347

Lalage, **I:412**

L'Allegro, II:514

Lancelot, II:11, II:12; as French chivalric hero, II:89

Lao-Tzŭ, and founding of Taoism, I:5

Lares, I:315

Last Journey, The, **I:300**

Latin, influence of on languages, I:319–320; origin of, I:306; use of by Humanists, II:278

Latins, I:306

Laura, II:548; death of in Florence, II:301

Law, The, in Hebrew Bible, I:72

Laws, I:247, I:321

Leiche, II:151

Leicester, Earl of, II:396

Leonardo da Vinci, II:273; scientific studies of, II:277

LEONIDAS, of Alexandria, I:299

LEONIDAS, of Tarentum, **I:300**

Lesbos, I:98, I:289

Let me not to the marriage of true minds, **II:567**

Li, and Confucius, I:17

LI PO, **I:22**

Libation-Bearers, The, I:93, I:167

Life a Bane, **I:302**

Life a Boon, **I:302**

Pax Romana, I:313, I:314
Pearl, The, II:88
PEARL POET, THE, II:23, II:88
Peloponnesian War, I:92; described by Thucydides, I:102
Penates, I:309
Percy Manuscript, II:246
Pericles, as leader, I:92; on social position of women, I:96
Peripatetics, I:273
Perseus, I:89
Persia, medieval renaissance of, II:19; Shirazists of, II:20
Persian Fopperies, **I:413**
Persian Peril, The, **I:303**
Persian Wars, I:91–92; described by Herodotus, I:102
Persians, The, I:97, I:101, I:167
PETRARCA, FRANCESCO, II:280, **II:548**; as first Humanist, II:273; friendship of with Boccaccio, II:300–301
Phaedo, I:247, **I:263**
Phaedrus, I:247
Philip of Macedonia, I:105
Philip II, king of Spain, II:269
Philip III, king of Spain, II:347
Philip IV, king of France, II:275
Philosophy, Confucian, I:6; Greek, I:104–105; Hindu, I:9–10; Stoic, I:322–323
Phoenicians, and Greek language, I:88
Phormio, I:312
Piers Plowman, II:247
Piers Plowman Poet, II:23
Pietas, I:309
Pilgrim's Progress, The, II:286
Pindar, I:98
PLATO, I:96, **I:246**; and Aristotle, I:273; place of in Greek philosophy, I:104; poems of, I:302
Platonic Academy, II:280, II:286, II:291; founding of, II:273
Platonic love, I:247
PLAUTUS, I:311, **I:342**
Plebs, I:306
Pleiades, II:282, II:557
Pliny the Younger, I:313
Plutus, I:216
Poetic Edda. See *Elder Edda.*
Poetics, I:104, I:187, I:274, **I:278**
Poetry, Chinese, I:6–7; of French Renaissance, II:282–283; Greek, I:97–98; of Hafiz, II:44; Indian, I:10; of Minnesingers, II:151; of Omar Khayyam, II:37–38; Roman, I:317–318; of Shakespeare, II:448, II:561; of Wandering Scholars, II:289
Poet's Gift, The, **II:559**
Politics, I:104, I:274
Pompey, I:307
Pope, position of in medieval Church, II:2–3; strug-

gle of with Holy Roman Emperor, II:4, II:9, II:158; during Renaissance, II:275–276
Popular Ballads, British and Danish, **II:246**
Portugal, II:269
Portuguese, explorations of, II:267
Poseidon, I:88
Posidippus, **I:302**
Post-Obits and the Poets, **I:445**
Pot of Gold, The, **I:342**
Praise of Folly, The, II:274, II:275, **II:294**
Predestination, defended by Edwards, II:543
Presentation Copies, **I:447**
Pretty Pair, A, **I:448**
Prince, The, II:268, II:282, **II:415**
Prioress's Tale, The, II:202
Procrastination, **I:446**
Productive Estate, A, **I:448**
Prometheus, I:89
Prometheus Bound, I:89, I:101, I:167
Promising Youth, A, **I:447**
Propertius, I:317
Prophets, of the Hebrews, I:13–14
Prose, of Renaissance Italy, II:282
Prose Edda. See *Younger Edda.*
Protestantism, English, II:514; and Erasmus, II:293; Lutheran, II:276. *See also* Reformation, Lutheranism, Calvinism, Puritanism.
Proverbs, I:13, **I:74**
Psalms, I:13, **I:73**
Ptolemaic theory, II:499; challenged by Copernicus, II:277; and medieval Church, II:158
Punic Wars, I:306
Purgatory, in medieval teaching, II:5; as visualized by Dante, II:159; *diagram of,* II:175
Puritanism, in England, II:276, II:514; literature of, II:286; in North America, II:276, II:543
Pyramus and Thisbe, **I:434**

Quixote, Don. See *Don Quixote de la Mancha.*

RABELAIS, FRANÇOIS, II:283, **II:309**; as Humanist thinker, II:274
Rabbis, and Jewish ritual, I:16
Rain Tomorrow, **I:416**
Râmâyana, I:11
Rationalism, of Erasmus, II:293; of Montaigne, II:324–325
Rebirth of learning. See Renaissance.
Reformation, Catholic. *See* Counter-Reformation.
Reformation, connection of with Renaissance, II:275; English, II:276; forerunners of, II:275; French, II:325; German, II:276; history of, II:274–276; influence of on English literature, II:286; and Martin Luther, II:509–510
REINMAR VON HAGENAU, II:152
Religion, Buddhist, I:10–11; Greek, I:88–89, I:93, I:94; Hindu, I:9–10; Roman, I:309–310: *See also*

Catholic Church, Christian Church, Hebrews, Protestantism, Reformation.

Reliques of Ancient English Poetry, II:247

Remonstrants, II:421

Remus, I:306

Renaissance, commercial life of, II:266–267; effect of on Reformation, II:274; English, II:269; English literature of, II:283–286; essay on, II:265–288; general features of, II:265–266; Humanism of, II:272–274; literature of, II:278 ff.; Spanish literature of, II:286

Renaissance, Greek, I:283

Renouncing Love, I:416

Republic, Roman, history of, I:306–308; literature of, I:311–312; organization of, I:306

Republic, I:104, I:246, I:247, **I:267**

Republic, of Cicero, I:321

Resourcefulness, I:302

Respectability, I:447

Return Favors, I:447

Revenge, I:417

Revenge, The, II:560

Revolutions of the Heavenly Bodies, The, II:277, **II:499**

Rhea, I:88

Rhetoric, of Aristotle, I:274

Richard II, king of England, II:202

Riches, I:303

Riddles Wisely Expounded, II:248

Rights of War and Peace, II:271, II:421

Rig-Veda, I:10, **I:27,** I:28

Robin Hood ballads, II:247

Robin Hood's Death and Burial, II:257

Roland, as epic hero, II:111; described by Einhard, II:110

Roman de la Rose, II:12, II:15–18, II:265; influence of on Chaucer, II:202

Romance, Celtic, II:88; chivalric, II:21; German, II:151; medieval, emergence of, II:10–12; Middle English, II:88; moral, II:12, II:21, II:88

Romans, early drama of, I:311–312; economic life of, I:314; and Epicureanism, I:311; family life of, I:309; and Stoicism, I:310; view of life, I:308–311. *See also* Rome.

Rome, architecture of, I:314; Christian writers of, I:319; early history of, I:306; engineering of, I:314; expansion of in Italy, I:306; expansion of outside Italy, I:307; founding of, I:306; growth of Empire, I:312–314; influence of Greeks on, I:108; under Julius Caesar, I:307; law of, I:320; literature of the Empire, I:317–319; public games of, I:314–316; religion of, I:309–310; republic of, I:306–308; republican literature of, I:311–312; and the Western tradition, I:319–320

Romulus, I:306

Rondel, II:555

RONSARD, PIERRE DE, **II:557**

Rope, The, I:342

Rose, The, **II:559**

Roses, **II:559**

Rubaiyat, The, II:37, **II:38**

RUFINUS, I:302

Rustum, II:20

Ruth, I:73, **I:82**

Saadya, I:16

Sabines, I:306

Sacraments, II:2

Sadi, II:19, II:20

Saint Bartholomew's Day, Massacre of, II:325

SAINT FRANCIS OF ASSISI, **II:74,** II:265; stigmata of, II:75

Saint George, and English chivalry, II:88

Sale of the Philosophers, I:283

Samosata, I:283

Samson Agonistes, II:286, II:514

Sanskrit, drama, I:12; language, I:9

Saon of Acanthus, I:299

Sapphic meter, I:289

SAPPHO, I:98, **I:289;** influence of on Catullus, I:425

Saracens, II:21; in Spain, II:110

Satan, fall of according to Dante, II:159

Satire, of Juvenal, I:318; of Martial, I:318–319

Satires, of Horace, I:410, **I:418**

Satyr play, I:167

Saul of Tarsus. *See* Paul.

Savonarola, Girolamo, II:275

Scholasticism, in thirteenth century, II:8–9

Scholastics, II:21; attacked by Roger Bacon, II:277; writings of, II:8–9

Science, Arabic, II:19; and medieval mind, II:5; of Renaissance era, II:276–278

Scientific method, formulated by Francis Bacon, II:278; used by Roger Bacon, II:277

Scop, II:8

Scotland, ballads of, II:246–247

Sculpture, Greek, I:97

Sea Dirge, I:299

Second Nun's Tale, The, II:202

Senate, Roman, I:306

Seneca, I:310; relations of with Nero, I:318

Sent to Li Po as a Gift, **I:25**

Serfdom, II:3–4

Shah Nameh, II:20

SHAKESPEARE, WILLIAM, II:279, II:285, **II:447;** compared to Lope de Vega, II:425, II:426; as lyric poet, II:561

Shakuntala, I:11, **I:41**

Shall I compare thee to a summer's day? **II:564**

She That I Loved, **I:428**

Sheep Well, The, II:288, **II:426;** proletariat in, II:272

SHEMSUDDIN MOHAMMED. *See* HAFIZ.

Shepheardes Calender, The, II:285, II:396

Ship of State, The, **I:412**

Shiraz, ii:44; and Persian literature, ii:20
Sidney, Sir Philip, ii:389, ii:396
Siegfried, as epic hero, ii:125
Sigh no more, ladies, sigh no more, ii:563
Signs of Love, ii:549
Silver, Age of, i:89
Silver Age, of Roman literature, i:318
SIMMIAS OF THEBES, i:302
SIMONIDES, i:298
Simplex Munditiis, ii:568
Sinners in the Hands of an Angry God, ii:276, ii:543
Sir Gawain and the Green Knight, ii:88, ii:89; as moral romance, ii:12
Sir Luno and the Mermaid, ii:261
Sir Patrick Spens, ii:252
Sirmio, i:428
Siva, i:10
Skene, of Greek theater, i:99
Skepticism, of Montaigne, ii:324–325
Slavery, in Greece, i:94; in Rome, i:314
Sock, in Greek comedy, i:99
Socrates, life of, i:104; portrayed by Plato, i:246; portrayed by Xenophon, i:246; satirized by Aristophanes, i:216
Socratic method, i:104
SOLOMON, i:13
Song, ii:569
Song, A, ii:569
Song of Ch'ang-kan, A, i:24
Song of Roland, The, ii:10, ii:110, ii:111
Song of Songs, The, i:13, i:73, i:78
Song of the Open Road, A, ii:289
Song: To Celia, ii:568
Song to Celia, ii:568
Sonnet, use of by English lyricists, ii:561; use of by Petrarch, ii:19
Sonnets, of Petrarch, **ii:548;** of Petrarch and Boccaccio, ii:280; of Shakespeare, **ii:564;** of Spenser, ii:396
Sophists, i:104, i:215, i:216
SOPHOCLES, i:101, **i:186**
Spain, and Columbus, ii:267; history of during Renaissance, ii:269–271; Renaissance drama of, ii:279–280; Renaissance literature of, ii:286–288
Sparta, geographic factors, i:87; and Peloponnesian War, i:92; in Persian War, i:92
SPENSER, EDMUND, ii:285; **ii:395;** and courtly ideals, ii:272
Spinning Woman, The, i:300
Spring, i:300
Spring and Autumn, i:17
Spring Returns, but Not to Him Returns, ii:551
Spruch, ii:151
Stay in Town, i:299
Stoicism, origin of, i:310; of Romans, i:310–311; of Roman Republic, i:321

Stratford-on-Avon, ii:285; ii:448
Sufism, and Hafiz, ii:44; of Persian writers, ii:20
Summer Day, A, i:23
Summer's Revel, **ii:557**
Suppliant Women, The, i:101, i:166, i:167
Suras, ii:25
Surrey, Earl of, ii:283
Switzerland, and Calvinist reforms, ii:276
Symphonia Platonis et Aristotelis, ii:291
Symposium, i:104, i:246, i:247
Syracusan Ladies, The (Idyll xv), i:294, i:297

Table Talk, **ii:510**
Tacitus, i:318
Tagelied, ii:151
Tagore, Rabindranath, i:11–12
Take, oh, take those lips away, ii:564
Talavakâra-Upanishad. See Kena-Upanishad.
Tale of Savitri, The, **i:31**
Talmud, i:16
Tamerlane. *See* Timur.
T'ang dynasty, i:4–5
Tannhäuser. *See Ballad of Sir Tannhäuser, T, e.*
Tao Teh Ching, i:5
Taoism, founding of, i:5; and Li Po, i:17; philosophy of, i:5–6
Tarquin the Proud, i:306
Tasso, Torquato, ii:278, ii:281
Tears of the Muses, The, ii:396
Teatro Olimpico, ii:279
Tell me where is fancy bred, **ii:563**
Tempest, The, song from, **ii:564**
Ten of War and Peace, ii:414–415
Tenure of Kings and Magistrates, **ii:514**
Terence, i:311, i:312
Tertullian, i:319
Terza rima, developed by Dante, ii:159
Teseide, ii:301
Tetzel, John, ii:509
That time of year thou mayest in me behold, **ii:566**
That We Taste Nothing Pure, **ii:341**
Thatched House Unroofed by an Autumn Gale, The, i:25
Theaters, Greek, i:99; in Renaissance Italy, ii:279
Thebes, hegemony of, i:93
Themistocles, i:92
THEOCRITUS, i:97, **i:294;** influence of on Virgil, i:317; and invention of idyll, i:106
There's No Lust Like to Poetry, **ii:291**
Thermopylae, battle of, i:92
Theseus, i:89
Thesmophoriazusae, i:102, i:200
Thespis, i:99, i:166
Third Satire (Juvenal), **i:440**
Thirty Tyrants, i:93, i:239
This Stone, **i:303**
Thomas à Becket, Archbishop, ii:4

Virtus, as Roman ideal, ɪ:310
Vishnu, ɪ:10
Vision, ɪɪ:548
Visit to Fan with Li Po, A, ɪ:25
Vita Nuova, ɪɪ:158
Volsungasaga, ɪɪ:11, ɪɪ:125

Waldensians, ɪɪ:275
Waldo, Peter, ɪɪ:275
WALTHER VON DER VOGELWEIDE, ɪɪ:11, ɪɪ:151, ɪɪ:152, ɪɪ:153
WANDERING SCHOLARS, THE, ɪɪ:289
War of the Roses, ɪɪ:267, ɪɪ:268
Went a maid fair to behold, ɪɪ:153
What Makes a Happy Life, ɪ:448
What sweetness into that old word *woman* grew, ɪɪ:152
Whatever be my faults, one quality, ɪɪ:152
When daffodils begin to peer, ɪɪ:564
When I have seen by Time's fell hand defaced, ɪɪ:565
When icicles hang by the wall, ɪɪ:562
When, in disgrace with fortune and men's eyes, ɪɪ:565
When in the chronicle of wasted time, ɪɪ:566
When to the sessions of sweet silent thought, ɪɪ:565
Wherein He Envies Whatsoever of Lovely . . . , ɪɪ:550
Wherein He Makes Confession . . . , ɪɪ:551
Wherein He Pursues Solitude . . . , ɪɪ:549
Wherein He Tells the Course of True Love, ɪɪ:549

Wherein His Heart, by Laura Rejected . . . , ɪɪ:549
Wherein Laura Is Forever a Present Apparition, ɪɪ:551
Wherein Soaring in an Ecstasy . . . , ɪɪ:551
Who is Sylvia? ɪɪ:562
Who slays the lion, who slays the dragon? ɪɪ:153
Wife of Usher's Well, The, ɪɪ:255
"Will you take this wilding wreath?" ɪɪ:152
William the Conqueror, ɪɪ:111, ɪɪ:268
Winter's Tale, The, song from, ɪɪ:564
Wittenberg Church, ɪɪ:275, ɪɪ:509
WOLFRAM VON ESCHENBACH, ɪɪ:151, ɪɪ:157
Works and Days, ɪ:98
Worms, Diet of, ɪɪ:510
Wounded Cupid, The, ɪ:291
Wyatt, Sir Thomas, ɪɪ:283
Wycliffe, John, ɪɪ:10, ɪɪ:275

Xenophon, ɪ:102, ɪ:246
Xerxes ɪ, ɪ:92

Yahveh, ɪ:12–13
Yiddish, ɪ:16
Young Engel, ɪɪ:258
Younger Edda, ɪɪ:125
Youthful Age, ɪ:294

Zeno, ɪ:310
Zeus, ɪ:88
Zionism, ɪ:16

10 11 12 13 14 15 16 17 18 19 20 –KPK– 82 81 80 79 78 77 76